Ten-Year Summary of Rates and Allowances

The paragraph numbers below correspond to those in CHAPTER 1 ALLOWANCES AND TAX RATES. See those paragraphs for further details. For Scottish income tax rates and rate bands for 2020/21, see 1.3, and for earlier years, see 1.4.

Para No.		2011/12	2012/13	2013/14	2014/15	2015/16
6	Starting rate for savings	10%	10%	10%	10%	0%
6	Starting rate limit	£2,560	£2,710	£2,790	£2,880	£5,000
3, 4	Basic rate	20%	20%	20%	20%	20%
3, 4	Basic rate limit	£35,000	£34,370	£32,010	£31,865	£31,785
3, 4	Higher rate	40%	40%	40%	40%	40%
3, 4	Higher rate limit	£150,000	£150,000	£150,000	£150,000	£150,000
3, 4	Additional rate	50%	50%	45%	45%	45%
7	Personal savings allowance: basic rate taxpayer	—	—	—	—	—
7	Personal savings allowance: higher rate taxpayer	—	—	—	—	—
5	Dividend allowance	—	—	—	—	—
5	Dividend ordinary rate	10%	10%	10%	10%	10%
5	Dividend upper rate	32.5%	32.5%	32.5%	32.5%	32.5%
5	Dividend additional rate	42.5%	42.5%	37.5%	37.5%	37.5%
PERSONAL RELIEFS						
17	Personal allowance	£7,475	£8,105	£9,440	£10,000	£10,600
17	Income limit for personal allowance	£100,000	£100,000	£100,000	£100,000	£100,000
18	Transferable tax allowance	—	—	—	—	£1,060
	Personal allowance (65 or over; for 2013/14 onwards, born after 5.4.1938 but before 6.4.1948)	£9,940	£10,500	£10,500	£10,500	—
	Personal allowance (75 or over; for 2013/14 onwards, born before 6.4.1938)	£10,090	£10,660	£10,660	£10,660	£10,660
19	Married couple's allowance (born before 6.4.1935 and 75 or over)	£7,295	£7,705	£7,915	£8,165	£8,355
19	Income limit for age-related allowances	£24,000	£25,400	£26,100	£27,000	£27,700
19	Basic married couple's allowance	£2,800	£2,960	£3,040	£3,140	£3,220
20	Blind person's allowance	£1,980	£2,100	£2,160	£2,230	£2,290
CLASS 4 NIC						
	Rate	9%	9%	9%	9%	9%
	Band	£7,225–£42,475 plus 2% on excess	£7,605–£42,475 plus 2% on excess	£7,755–£41,450 plus 2% on excess	£7,956–£41,865 plus 2% on excess	£8,060–£42,385 plus 2% on excess
Accumulated or discretionary income						
	Trust rate	50%	50%	45%	45%	45%
	Dividend trust rate	42.5%	42.5%	37.5%	37.5%	37.5%
	Standard rate band	£1,000	£1,000	£1,000	£1,000	£1,000
Pensions annual allowance		£50,000	£50,000	£50,000	£40,000	£40,000
Pensions lifetime allowance		£1.8m	£1.5m	£1.5m	£1.25m	£1.25m

2016/17	2017/18	2018/19	2019/20	**2020/21**		Para No.
0%	0%	0%	0%	**0%**	Starting rate for savings	6
£5,000	£5,000	£5,000	£5,000	**£5,000**	Starting rate limit	6
20%	20%	20%	20%	**20%**	Basic rate	3, 4
£32,000	£33,500	£34,500	£37,500	**£37,500**	Basic rate limit	3, 4
40%	40%	40%	40%	**40%**	Higher rate	3, 4
£150,000	£150,000	£150,000	£150,000	**£150,000**	Higher rate limit	3, 4
45%	45%	45%	45%	**45%**	Additional rate	3, 4
£1,000	£1,000	£1,000	£1,000	**£1,000**	Personal savings allowance: basic rate taxpayer	7
£500	£500	£500	£500	**£500**	Personal savings allowance: higher rate taxpayer	7
£5,000	£5,000	£2,000	£2,000	**£2,000**	Dividend allowance	5
7.5%	7.5%	7.5%	7.5%	**7.5%**	Dividend ordinary rate	5
32.5%	32.5%	32.5%	32.5%	**32.5%**	Dividend upper rate	5
38.1%	38.1%	38.1%	38.1%	**38.1%**	Dividend additional rate	5
					PERSONAL RELIEFS	
£11,000	£11,500	£11,850	£12,500	**£12,500**	Personal allowance	17
£100,000	£100,000	£100,000	£100,000	**£100,000**	Income limit	17
£1,100	£1,150	£1,190	£1,250	**£1,250**	Transferable tax allowance	18
—	—	—	—	—	Personal allowance (65 or over; for 2013/14 onwards, born after 5.4.1938 but before 6.4.1948)	
—	—	—	—	—	Personal allowance (75 or over; for 2013/14 onwards, born before 6.4.1938)	
£8,355	£8,445	£8,695	£8,915	**£9,075**	Married couple's allowance (born before 6.4.1935 and 75 or over)	19
£27,700	£28,000	£28,900	£29,600	**£30,200**	Income limit	19
£3,220	£3,260	£3,360	£3,450	**£3,510**	Basic married couple's allowance	19
£2,290	£2,320	£2,390	£2,450	**£2,500**	Blind person's allowance	20
					CLASS 4 NIC	
9%	9%	9%	9%	**9%**	Rate	
£8,060–£43,000 plus 2% on excess	£8,164–£45,000 plus 2% on excess	£8,424–£46,350 plus 2% on excess	£8,632–£50,000 plus 2% on excess	**£9,500–£50,000 plus 2% on excess**	Band	
					Accumulated or discretionary income	
45%	45%	45%	45%	**45%**	Trust rate	
38.1%	38.1%	38.1%	38.1%	**38.1%**	Dividend trust rate	
£1,000	£1,000	£1,000	£1,000	**£1,000**	Standard rate band	
£40,000	£40,000	£40,000	£40,000	**£40,000**	Pensions Annual allowance	
£1m	£1m	£1.03m	**£1.055m**	**£1.0731m**	Pensions Lifetime allowance	

Tolley's Income Tax

This edition gives the position as at 1 July 2020 for the tax year 2020/21 and covers all legislation, HMRC's published guidance and other relevant sources of information including the provisions of Finance Act 2020.

Tolley's Income Tax 2020/21

105th Edition

by

David Smailes FCA

Tolley®

LexisNexis® UK & Worldwide

United Kingdom — RELX (UK) Limited trading as LexisNexis®, 1–3 Strand, London WC2N 5JR and 9–10 St Andrew Square, Edinburgh EH2 2AF

LNUK Global Partners — LexisNexis® encompasses authoritative legal publishing brands dating back to the 19th century including: Butterworths® in the United Kingdom, Canada and the Asia-Pacific region; Les Editions du Juris Classeur in France; and Matthew Bender® worldwide. Details of LexisNexis® locations worldwide can be found at www.lexisnexis.com

Published by LexisNexis®
This is a Tolley title

A CIP Catalogue record for this book is available from the British Library.

ISBN for this volume: 9780754556794

Printed and bound by CPI Group (UK) Ltd, Croydon, CRO 4YY

Visit LexisNexis UK at www.lexisnexis.co.uk

About This Book

This edition includes coverage of all income tax provisions of Finance Act 2020 and all other relevant material to 1 July 2020, e.g. statutes, statutory instruments, court cases, tribunal decisions, online announcements/guidance, Statements of Practice, concessions, HMRC Manuals, HMRC Briefs, and other publications. The law and practice for the four years prior to 2020/21 are also covered in this edition. Chapter 82 summarises the relevant provisions of Finance Act 2020. The chapters are arranged alphabetically. Numerous worked examples are given.

We are grateful to Andrew Hubbard for contributing the chapter on Making Tax Digital.

We welcome all comments and suggestions for improvement to this work. You can contact us in this respect by e-mailing the Editor, Esther Adetoba at esther.adetoba@lexisnexis.co.uk. Any technical queries will be passed on to the author.

Contributors

Andrew Hubbard BMus, PhD, CTA

Andrew Hubbard is a consultant at RSM and editor in chief of Taxation magazine published by LexisNexis. Andrew initially trained as an inspector of taxes before joining the accountancy profession. He was a partner in BDO Stoy Hayward and then Tenon before joining RSM and LexisNexis. He is also past president of both the ATT and CIOT as well as an accomplished musician.

Contents

Abbreviations and References

Abbreviations

Art	article.
CAA	Capital Allowances Act.
CA	Court of Appeal.
CCA	Court of Criminal Appeal.
CCAB	Consultative Committee of Accountancy Bodies.
CES	Court of Exchequer (Scotland).
CGT	Capital Gains Tax.
CIR	Commissioners of Inland Revenue.
Ch D	Chancery Division.
CJEC	Court of Justice of the European Communities.
CS	Scottish Court of Session.
CTA	Corporation Tax Act.
EC	European Communities.
ECHR	European Court of Human Rights.
EEC	European Economic Community.
ESC	Extra-Statutory Concession.
EU	European Union.
Ex D	Exchequer Division (now absorbed into Chancery Division).
FA	Finance Act.
F(No 2)A	Finance (No 2) Act.
F(No 3)A	Finance (No 3) Act.
FRS	Financial Reporting Standard.
FTT	First-tier Tribunal.
GAAP	Generally Accepted Accounting Practice.
HC	High Court.

HC(I)	High Court of Ireland.
HL	House of Lords.
HMRC	Her Majesty's Revenue & Customs.
ICAEW	Institute of Chartered Accountants in England and Wales.
ICTA	Income and Corporation Taxes Act.
IHT	Inheritance Tax.
IHTA 1984	Inheritance Tax Act 1984.
IR	Inland Revenue.
ITA 2007	Income Tax Act 2007.
ITEPA 2003	Income Tax (Earnings and Pensions) Act 2003.
ITTOIA 2005	Income Tax (Trading and Other Income) Act 2005.
KB	King's Bench Division.
LIFFE	London International Financial Futures Exchange.
NI	Northern Ireland.
NIC	National Insurance Contributions.
oao	on application of.
PC	Privy Council.
PDA	Probate, Divorce and Admiralty Division. (Now Family Division).
Pt	Part.
QB	Queen's Bench Division.
Reg	regulation.
s	section.
SC	Supreme Court.
SC(I)	Irish Supreme Court.
Sch	Schedule.
SI	Statutory Instrument.
SP	Statement of Practice.
Sp C	Special Commissioners.
SR&O	Statutory Rules and Orders.
SSAP	Statement of Standard Accounting Practice.
TC	Tax Chamber (First-tier Tribunal).
TCGA 1992	Taxation of Chargeable Gains Act 1992.

TIOPA 2010	Taxation (International and Other Provisions) Act 2010.
TMA 1970	Taxes Management Act 1970.
TPA 2014	Taxation of Pensions Act 2014.
UT	Upper Tribunal.
VAT	Value Added Tax.
VATA 1994	Value Added Tax Act 1994.

References

AER	All England Law Reports (LexisNexis , Lexis House 30 Farringdon Street London, EC4A 4HH).
All ER (D)	All England Reporter Direct (LexisNexis).
ATC	Annotated Tax Cases (publication discontinued).
ITC	Irish Tax Cases (Government Publications, 1 and 3 G.P.O. Arcade, Dublin 1).
LTR	Law Times Reports.
SC	Special Commissioners.
SFTD	Simon's First-tier Tax Decisions (LexisNexis).
SLR	Scottish Law Reporter.
SLT	Scots Law Times.
SSCD	Simon's Tax Cases Special Commissioners' Decisions (LexisNexis).
STC	Simon's Tax Cases (LexisNexis).
STI	Simon's Weekly Tax Intelligence (LexisNexis).
TC	Official Tax Cases (The Stationery Office — see below).
TLR	Times Law Reports.
TR	Taxation Reports (publication discontinued).

The first number in the citation refers to the volume, and the second to the page, so that [1995] 1 AER 15 means that the report is to be found on page fifteen of the first volume of the All England Law Reports for 1995. Where no volume number is given, only one volume was produced in that year. Some series have continuous volume numbers. Where legal decisions are very recent and in the lower courts, it should be noted that they could be reversed on appeal.

In English cases, Scottish and N. Irish decisions (unless there is a difference of law between the countries) are generally followed but are not binding, and Republic of Ireland decisions are considered (and vice-versa).

Acts of Parliament, Cmnd. Papers, 'Hansard' Parliamentary Reports and Statutory Instruments (SI) formerly Statutory Rules and Orders (SR & O)) are obtainable from The Stationery Office online bookshop www.tsoshop.co.uk. Many items are available free of charge at www.legislation.gov.uk. **Hansard** references are to daily issues and do not always correspond to the columns in the bound editions. **N.B.** Statements in the House, while useful as indicating the intention of enactments, have no legal authority if the Courts subsequently interpret the wording of the Act differently, but see **5.33** APPEALS for circumstances in which evidence of parliamentary intent may be considered by the Courts.

1

Allowances and Tax Rates

Introduction to allowances and tax rates

[1.1] This chapter deals primarily with the computation of income tax liability (**1.10–1.13**), the personal reliefs available to individuals (**1.17–1.20**) and the rates of income tax to be applied (**1.3–1.6**). The Scottish rates of income tax are covered at **1.8** and the Welsh rates at **1.9**. A number of worked examples illustrating the operation of rates and allowances for 2020/21 are included at the end of the chapter (**1.22**). All income tax rates and personal reliefs for the last four years are listed in this chapter.

The tax year

[1.2] The 'tax year' (or 'year of assessment' or 'fiscal year') runs from 6 April in one calendar year to 5 April in the next (e.g. the tax year 2020/21 starts on 6 April 2020 and ends on 5 April 2021). [*ITA 2007, s 4*].

Rates of tax — 2020/21

[1.3] The main rates of UK income tax for 2020/21 are as follows.

	Rate	On Taxable Income	Cumulative tax
Basic Rate	20%	£0–£37,500	£7,500.00
Higher Rate	40%	£37,501–£150,000	£52,500.00
Additional Rate	45%	Over £150,000	

For 2019/20 and earlier years, see **1.4** below.

The figure of £37,500 is known as the basic rate limit. The £0–£37,500 band is known as the basic rate band. The figure of £150,000 is known as the higher rate limit. The higher and additional rates apply only to individuals.

[*ITA 2007, ss 6, 6C, 9A, 10, 11, 11C; Scotland Act 2016, s 14(3)(4)(6)(15); FA 2016, s 6(2)(3)(5)–(9)(24); FA 2019, s 5(1); FA 2020, ss 1–3*].

Scottish taxpayers

The above figures do not apply to 'Scottish taxpayers' (see **1.8** below), to whom rates and thresholds set by the Scottish Parliament apply instead. The main rates for Scottish taxpayers for 2020/21 (as set by the Scottish Parliament on 6 February 2020) are as follows.

	Rate	On Taxable Income
Starter Rate	19%	£0–£2,085
Scottish Basic Rate	20%	£2,085–£12,658
Intermediate Rate	21%	£12,659–£30,930
Higher Rate	41%	£30,931–£150,000
Top Rate	46%	Over £150,000

(See www.gov.scot/publications/scottish-income-tax-2020-2021/.)

Liability of Scottish taxpayers to the dividend ordinary, upper and additional rates and the basic, higher and additional rates on savings income is determined by reference to UK rate thresholds, as is the amount (if any) of the personal savings allowance. This means, for example, that Scottish taxpayers could be higher rate taxpayers for non-savings income but basic rate taxpayers for savings income. See the **example** at **1.22**(ix) below.

Welsh taxpayers

For 2020/21, 'Welsh taxpayers' are chargeable at the main UK rates above. See **1.9** below.

All UK taxpayers

A special rate of **0%** (the **starting rate for savings**) applies to **savings income** (other than dividend income) to the extent that such income does not exceed a 'starting rate limit' (**£5,000**), treating savings income as the highest part of an individual's income other than dividend income. The starting rate for savings applies only to individuals. See **1.6** below. See **1.7** below for the personal savings allowance, which operates in conjunction with the starting rate for savings.

See **1.5** below for the **dividend allowance** and the **rates applicable to dividends** (comprising the dividend ordinary rate, upper rate and additional rate).

See **1.16** below as to indexation of rate bands.

See **70.1**, **70.11** SETTLEMENTS as regards income tax rates applicable to trusts.

See **56.8** PENSION INCOME for special rules on the taxation of State pension lump sums where these were available.

Rates of tax — 2019/20 to 2016/17

[1.4] The main rates of tax for these years are as follows.

Basic, higher and additional rate for 2019/20 [*ITA 2007, ss 6, 6C, 9A, 10, 11, 11C; Scotland Act 2016, s 14(3)(4)(6)(15); FA 2016, s 6(2)(3)(5)–(9)(24); FA 2019, ss 1, 3, 4, 5(1)*]

	Rate	On Taxable Income	Cumulative tax
Basic Rate	20%	£0–£37,500	£7,500.00
Higher Rate	40%	£37,501–£150,000	£52,500.00
Additional Rate	45%	Over £150,000	

The starting rate for savings is 0%, and the starting rate limit is £5,000; see **1.6** below.

The main rates for **Scottish taxpayers** (as set by the Scottish Parliament) are as follows.

	Rate	**On Taxable Income**
Starter Rate	19%	£0–£2,049
Scottish Basic Rate	20%	£2,050–£12,444
Intermediate Rate	21%	£12,445–£30,930
Higher Rate	41%	£30,931–£150,000
Top Rate	46%	Over £150,000

Liability of Scottish taxpayers to the dividend ordinary, upper and additional rates and the basic, higher and additional rates on savings income is determined by reference to UK rate thresholds, as is the amount (if any) of the personal savings allowance. This means, for example, that Scottish taxpayers could be higher rate taxpayers for non-savings income but basic rate taxpayers for savings income.

Welsh taxpayers are chargeable at the main UK rates above. See **1.9** below.

Basic, higher and additional rate for 2018/19 [*ITA 2007, ss 6, 6C, 9A, 10, 11, 11C; Scotland Act 2016, s 14(3)(4)(6)(15); FA 2016, s 6(2)(3)(5)–(9)(24); FA 2018, ss 1, 3, 4; SI 2017 No 1184, Art 2*]

	Rate	On Taxable Income	Cumulative tax
Basic Rate	20%	£0–£34,500	£6,900.00
Higher Rate	40%	£34,501–£150,000	£53,100.00
Additional Rate	45%	Over £150,000	

The starting rate for savings is 0%, and the starting rate limit is £5,000; see **1.6** below.

The main rates for **Scottish taxpayers** (as set by the Scottish Parliament) are as follows.

	Rate	**On Taxable Income**
Starter Rate	19%	£0–£2,000
Scottish Basic Rate	20%	£2,001–£12,150
Intermediate Rate	21%	£12,151–£31,580
Higher Rate	41%	£31,581–£150,000
Top Rate	46%	Over £150,000

Liability of Scottish taxpayers to the dividend ordinary, upper and additional rates and the basic, higher and additional rates on savings income is determined by reference to UK rate thresholds, as is the amount (if any) of the personal savings allowance. This means, for example, that Scottish taxpayers could be higher rate taxpayers for non-savings income but basic rate taxpayers for savings income.

Basic, higher and additional rate for 2017/18 [*ITA 2007, ss 6, 6C, 9A, 10, 11, 11C; FA 2015, s 4; Scotland Act 2016, s 14(3)(4)(6)(15); FA 2016, ss 2, 6(2)(3)(5)–(9)(24); FA 2017, ss 1, 2, 3(1)*]

	Rate	On Taxable Income	Cumulative tax
Basic Rate	20%	£0–£33,500	£6,700.00
Higher Rate	40%	£33,501–£150,000	£53,300.00
Additional Rate	45%	Over £150,000	

The starting rate for savings is 0%, and the starting rate limit is £5,000; see **1.6** below.

The main rates for *Scottish taxpayers* are the same as above *except* that the basic rate limit is £31,500 instead of £33,500. Liability to the dividend ordinary, upper and additional rates and the basic, higher and additional rates on savings income is determined by reference to UK rate thresholds, as is the amount (if any) of the personal savings allowance. This means, for example, that Scottish taxpayers could be higher rate taxpayers for non-savings income but basic rate taxpayers for savings income.

Basic, higher and additional rate for 2016/17 [*ITA 2007, ss 6, 10; FA 2015, s 4; F(No 2)A 2015, s 6; FA 2016, s 1*]

	Rate	On Taxable Income	Cumulative tax
Basic Rate	20%	£0–£32,000	£6,400.00
Higher Rate	40%	£32,001–£150,000	£53,600.00
Additional Rate	45%	Over £150,000	

The starting rate for savings is 0%, and the starting rate limit is £5,000; see **1.6** below.

Taxation of dividend income

[1.5] A dividend paid (or other distribution made) in a tax year is chargeable as income of that tax year (see **65.10** SAVINGS AND INVESTMENT INCOME). Each individual is entitled to a **dividend allowance.**

For 2018/19 onwards, the dividend allowance is **£2,000,** and dividend income in excess of the allowance is taxed at the following rates:

- 7.5% (**dividend ordinary rate**) on dividend income within the basic rate band;
- 32.5% (**dividend upper rate**) on dividend income within the higher rate band; and
- 38.1% (**dividend additional rate**) on dividend income above the higher rate limit.

For 2016/17 and 2017/18, the dividend allowance was £5,000. The dividend ordinary, upper and additional rates were the same as for 2018/19 onwards. See **1.3** and **1.4** above for the basic rate band, higher rate band and higher rate limit. See below for the meaning of 'dividend income'.

There is no distinction between dividends from UK companies and those from overseas companies; all dividend income potentially attracts the dividend allowance.

The dividend allowance is not a deduction in arriving at total income or taxable income. Instead, the first £2,000 (previously £5,000) of dividend income attracts a zero rate of income tax (the '*dividend nil rate*'). See HMRC dividend allowance factsheet at www.gov.uk/government/publications/dividen d-allowance-factsheet.

For the purpose of determining whether dividend income falls within an individual's basic rate band or higher rate band, or exceeds the higher rate limit, it is treated as the highest part of total income. Exceptions are chargeable event gains on life policies etc. (see **44.3** LIFE ASSURANCE POLICIES), provided they do not carry a notional tax credit, and income chargeable under *ITEPA 2003, ss 401–416* (payments and benefits on termination of office or employment — see **18.4** COMPENSATION FOR LOSS OF EMPLOYMENT (AND DAMAGES)).

A Scottish taxpayer pays tax on dividends at UK rates. In determining the rates of tax that apply to dividend income, a Scottish taxpayer is assumed to pay income tax by reference to UK rate thresholds. See **1.8** below.

Remittance basis

The dividend ordinary, upper and additional rates do not apply to income chargeable on the REMITTANCE BASIS (**61**); the normal basic, higher and additional rates at **1.3** above apply instead.

Income taxpayers other than individuals

Dividend income received by income taxpayers other than individuals is generally chargeable at the dividend ordinary rate (unless the remittance basis applies). But see **70.11** SETTLEMENTS as regards income chargeable at the dividend trust rate (generally applicable to, but not restricted to, the income of discretionary trusts and accumulation trusts). See **75.115** TRADING INCOME as regards dealers in securities.

Meaning of 'dividend income'

'*Dividend income*' comprises:

(a) dividends and other distributions from UK resident companies (see **65.10** SAVINGS AND INVESTMENT INCOME);
(b) dividends from non-UK resident companies (see **65.17** SAVINGS AND INVESTMENT INCOME);
(c) stock dividends from UK resident companies (see **65.19** SAVINGS AND INVESTMENT INCOME);
(d) income within **65.21** SAVINGS AND INVESTMENT INCOME (release of loan to participator in a close company); and
(e) income within **49.7** MISCELLANEOUS INCOME (income not otherwise charged) which constitutes a distribution from a non-UK resident company which falls outside the charge under (b) above but which would be chargeable under (a) above if the company were UK resident.

Certain payments (and other items normally treated as distributions) made by a company for the redemption, repayment or purchase of its own shares are not treated as distributions and are not treated as income. See Tolley's Corporation Tax under Purchase by a Company of its own Shares.

[*ITA 2007, ss 8, 13, 13A, 14, 16, 19; Scotland Act 2016, s 14(11)(15); FA 2016, ss 5(3)(5)(10), 6(13)(24); F(No 2)A 2017, s 8*].

See the **examples** at **1.22**(iv) and (v) below.

Taxation of savings income

[1.6] Subject to the personal savings allowance at **1.7** below, 'savings income' is chargeable to income tax at the basic rate to the extent that it falls within an individual's basic rate band. To the extent that savings income exceeds the basic rate limit, it is chargeable at the higher rate. To the extent that savings income exceeds the higher rate limit, it is chargeable at the additional rate. See **1.3** above for the basic rate band, the basic rate limit, the higher rate and the higher rate limit.

A Scottish taxpayer pays tax on savings income at UK rates. In determining the rates of tax that apply to savings income, a Scottish taxpayer is assumed to pay income tax by reference to UK rate thresholds. See **1.8** below.

Starting rate for savings

However, to the extent that an individual's savings income does not exceed the starting rate limit, it is taxed at the **starting rate for savings**, which is **0%**. The starting rate limit is **£5,000**.

The personal savings allowance (see **1.7** below) operates in conjunction with the starting rate for savings.

For the purpose of determining whether savings income exceeds an individual's starting rate limit, it is treated as the highest part of his total income apart from dividend income (as in **1.5** above) and income chargeable under *ITEPA 2003, ss 401–416* (payments and benefits on termination of office or employment — see **18.4** COMPENSATION FOR LOSS OF EMPLOYMENT (AND DAMAGES)). Chargeable event gains on life policies etc. (see **44.3** LIFE ASSURANCE POLICIES) have priority over both dividend income and other savings income. This does not apply to life assurance gains that do not carry a notional tax credit, though such gains do still have equal priority to other types of savings income; examples are certain friendly society policies (see **44.25** LIFE ASSURANCE POLICIES) and offshore policies (see **44.23** LIFE ASSURANCE POLICIES). Note also that the personal allowance is treated as reducing income of different descriptions in the manner which will result in the greatest reduction in tax liability (see Step 3 at **1.10** below).

It follows that wherever the amount of an individual's taxable income, apart from savings income and dividend income, equals or exceeds the starting rate limit, the starting rate for savings cannot apply to any of his income.

See the example at **1.22**(iii) below.

Income taxpayers other than individuals

Savings income received by income taxpayers other than individuals is generally chargeable at the basic rate. But see **70.11** SETTLEMENTS as regards income chargeable at the trust rate or the dividend trust rate (generally applicable to, but not restricted to, the income of discretionary trusts and accumulation trusts).

Meaning of 'savings income'

'*Savings income*' comprises:

(a) any income chargeable under *ITTOIA 2005, ss 369–381* (interest — see **65.2** SAVINGS AND INVESTMENT INCOME), *ITTOIA 2005, ss 422–426* (purchased life annuities — see **65.23** SAVINGS AND INVESTMENT INCOME and **23.11**(c) DEDUCTION OF TAX AT SOURCE) or *ITTOIA 2005, ss 427–460* (deeply discounted securities — see **65.24–65.30** SAVINGS AND INVESTMENT INCOME), except for any income chargeable on the REMITTANCE BASIS (**61**), but otherwise including foreign income, and except for annuities within *ITTOIA 2005, s 718(2)*;

(b) income chargeable under the ACCRUED INCOME SCHEME (**2**); and

(c) chargeable event gains on life policies etc. on which an individual or the personal representatives of a deceased individual are liable to income tax (see **44.3** LIFE ASSURANCE POLICIES).

Deduction of tax at source

Where income tax at the basic rate has been deducted at source from savings income (see **23** DEDUCTION OF TAX AT SOURCE), and that income is chargeable at the starting rate for savings, repayment of the excess tax deducted can be claimed. In some other cases, notional tax is treated as having been paid at source (but is not refundable), e.g. chargeable event gains on life policies. This leaves a higher rate taxpayer to pay the excess of tax at the higher rate over tax at the basic rate. Income from which a deduction of tax at source falls to be made (or is treated as made) at the basic rate in force for a tax year is chargeable as income of that tax year.

Tax is not generally deductible at source from interest paid by banks, building societies or National Savings.

[*ITA 2007, ss 7, 7A, 9A, 11C, 12, 16, 17, 18, 31(2)(4), 946; FA 2014, s 3(1)–(3)(5), s 11(4)(12); Scotland Act 2016, s 14(12)(15); FA 2016, ss 4(3), 6(2)(4)(9)(10)(13)(14)(24), Sch 1 paras 63(3), 73; FA 2017, ss 3(2), 4; FA 2018, ss 4(2), 5; FA 2019, s 4(2), 6; FA 2020, ss 3(2), 4; SI 2015 No 1810, Arts 1, 14(2); SI 2019 No 201, Arts 1, 12*].

Simon's Taxes. See **E1.101E, E1.4.**

Personal savings allowance

[1.7] Depending on level of income, each individual is entitled to a personal savings allowance (PSA). The PSA is **£1,000** for basic rate taxpayers, i.e. individuals who have no income chargeable at the higher or additional rates or the dividend upper and additional rates. For individuals with income chargeable at the higher rate or dividend upper rate but not at the additional rate or dividend additional rate, the PSA is **£500**. Individuals with income chargeable at the additional rate or dividend additional rate are *not* entitled to a PSA. Note that if dividend income is, in fact, chargeable at the dividend nil rate because of the dividend allowance at **1.5** above but would otherwise have been chargeable at the dividend upper or additional rate, it is treated as if it had been chargeable at the dividend upper or additional rate for the purpose of determining the amount (if any) of the PSA. Savings income must itself be taken into account for that purpose. Persons chargeable to income tax who are not individuals are *not* entitled to a PSA: examples are trusts and personal representatives.

The PSA is not a deduction in arriving at total income or taxable income. Instead, the savings income covered by the PSA (whether the available PSA be £500 or £1,000) attracts a zero rate of income tax (the '*savings nil rate*') instead of the basic or higher rate (whichever would otherwise apply).

The PSA operates in conjunction with the starting rate for savings at **1.6** above, where applicable.

For the purpose of applying these rules, savings income is treated as the highest part of an individual's total income apart from dividend income and the other limited exceptions mentioned at **1.6** above. The starting rate for savings takes priority over the PSA; thus if so much of an individual's taxable income (see Step 3 at **1.10** below) as is savings income is all taxable at the starting rate, the savings nil rate is not applicable. See **1.6** for the *meaning* of 'savings income'. Where tax at a rate greater than the savings nil rate has been paid on income on which tax falls to be charged at the savings nil rate, repayment of the excess tax can be claimed.

In determining the amount of the PSA, a Scottish taxpayer (see **1.8** below) is assumed to pay income tax by reference to UK rate thresholds.

[*ITA 2007, ss 7(2), 12A, 12B, 16, 17; Scotland Act 2016, s 14(12)(15); FA 2016, ss 4(3)(5)–(7)(17), 6(11)–(14)(24)*].

See the **examples** at **1.22**(iv) and (v)(b) below

Scottish rates of income tax

[1.8] With effect for 2017/18 onwards, the Scottish Parliament is empowered to set its own income tax rates and thresholds for Scottish taxpayers (as defined below) independently of, and not linked to, UK rates. See **1.3** above for the rates and thresholds set for 2020/21 and **1.4** above for 2019/20, 2018/19 and 2017/18.

There are no restrictions on the rates or thresholds that the Scottish Parliament can set, except that it cannot set different rates for different types of income. These provisions do not apply to dividend and savings income, which remain chargeable at UK rates. Liability to the dividend ordinary, upper and additional rates and the basic, higher and additional rates on savings income is determined by reference to UK rate thresholds, as is the amount (if any) of the personal savings allowance. This means, for example, that Scottish taxpayers could be higher rate taxpayers for non-savings income but basic rate taxpayers for savings income. Other aspects of income tax also remain in the power of the UK Parliament, including the imposition of the annual charge to income tax, the personal allowance, the ability to introduce, repeal and amend tax reliefs and the definition of income. CGT rates (see **11.3** CAPITAL GAINS TAX) are determined as if a Scottish taxpayer paid income tax at UK rates. Income tax throughout the whole of the UK continues to be collected and administered by HMRC.

[*ITA 2007, s 11A; Scotland Act 1998, Pt 4A; Scotland Act 2016, ss 13, 14(8)–(10)(15); FA 2014, Sch 38 paras 5, 12; SI 2016 No 1161*].

See the **example** at **1.22**(ix) below.

For 2016/17 only, the three main UK rates of income tax (basic, higher and additional rate) were each reduced by ten percentage points for Scottish taxpayers. The Scottish Parliament was then able to set a Scottish rate of income tax for those taxpayers, which was added to each of those reduced UK rates. These provisions did not apply to dividend and savings income, which remained chargeable at UK rates. In fact, the Scottish Parliament set the Scottish rate at 10% for 2016/17, with the result that Scottish taxpayers paid income tax for that year at exactly the same rates as other UK taxpayers.

[*ITA 2007, ss 6A, 11A; Scotland Act 1998, Pt 4A; FA 2014, Sch 38 paras 3, 5, 12*].

HMRC published a technical note 'Clarifying the Scope of Scottish Income Tax Powers' (www.gov.uk/government/uploads/system/uploads/attachment_data/file/573519/FSITP_TechNote.pdf).

Scottish taxpayers

A person is a '*Scottish taxpayer*' in any tax year if he is an individual, is UK resident for income tax purposes (see **63** RESIDENCE AND DOMICILE) and meets one of the following conditions:

(a) he has a 'close connection' with Scotland; or
(b) he does not have a 'close connection' with any part of the UK other than Scotland and spends more days of that tax year in Scotland than in any other part of the UK; or
(c) he is a member of Parliament for a Scottish constituency, a member of the Scottish Parliament or a member of the European Parliament for Scotland.

For the purposes of (a) and (b) above, an individual has a '*close connection*' with a particular part of the UK if:

- he has only one place of residence in the UK;
- that place of residence is in that part of the UK; and
- he lives at that place for at least part of the tax year in question.

An individual also has a '*close connection*' with a particular part of the UK if:

- he has two or more places of residence in the UK;
- for at least part of the tax year in question, his main place of residence in the UK is in that part of the UK;
- the times in the year when his main place of residence is in that part of the UK comprise (in aggregate) at least as much of the year as the times when his main place of residence is in any one other part of the UK; and
- for at least part of the year, he lives at a place of residence in that part of the UK.

A 'place' includes a place on board a vessel or other means of transport.

For the purposes of (b) above, an individual is treated as spending a day in a particular part of the UK he is in that part at the end of that day. If an individual arrives in the UK on one day and departs on the next, he is not treated as spending a day in the UK (despite his presence at the end of the day of arrival) if between arrival and departure he does not engage in activities that are to a substantial extent unrelated to his passage through the UK, i.e. he is merely a passenger in transit.

[*Scotland Act 1998, ss 80D–80F; Scotland Act 2012, s 25*].

HMRC have published technical guidance on 'Scottish taxpayer' status. This includes *inter alia* the meaning of 'residence', 'place of residence', and 'main place of residence', examples on 'close connection' and the kind of evidence needed to establish presence at a particular home and whether or not a home existed. See www.gov.uk/government/publications/scottish-taxpayer-technical-guidance.

Simon's Taxes. See **E1.102C, E1.102D.**

Welsh rates of income tax

[1.9] Under *Wales Act 2014*, the Welsh Assembly has power to set Welsh rates of income tax for 'Welsh taxpayers' for 2019/20 onwards. The three main UK rates of income tax (basic, higher and additional rate) are each reduced by ten percentage points, and the Welsh rates of income tax for those taxpayers are added to each of those reduced UK rates. This does not affect dividend and savings income, which remain chargeable at UK rates. The definition of a '*Welsh taxpayer*' is along very similar lines to that of a Scottish taxpayer at **1.8** above (see HMRC Welsh Taxpayer Technical Guidance Manual). [*ITA 2007, ss 6B, 11B; Government of Wales Act 2006, ss 116D–116K; Wales Act 2014, ss 8, 9; SI 2018 No 892*].

The Assembly sets three rates: the Welsh basic rate, the Welsh higher rate and the Welsh additional rate, together referred to as the Welsh rates. For example, if the UK basic, higher and additional rates of income tax are 20%, 40% and 45% respectively and the equivalent Welsh rates were set at 12%, 14% and 16%, the basic, higher and additional rates for Welsh taxpayers would be 22%, 44% and 51% respectively.

For **2020/21**, the Welsh Government set each of the three rates at 10%, which means that for that year income tax is payable by Welsh taxpayers at the same rates as those payable by English and Northern Irish taxpayers (gov.wales/sites/default/files/publications/2019-12/2020-2021-draft-budget-narrative.pdf at para 4.09). The same applied for 2019/20.

HMRC published a technical note 'Clarifying the scope of the Welsh rates of income tax' (www.gov.uk/government/consultations/clarifying-the-scope-of-the-welsh-rates-of-income-tax-technical-note-and-draft-legislation) covering charitable giving, pensions tax relief, trust and estate income and other issues. Generally, the policy positions taken match those already taken in relation to Scottish income tax.

Simon's Taxes. See **E1.102F.**

Calculation of income tax liability

[1.10] The calculation of an individual's income tax liability for a tax year proceeds as follows.

Step 1.

Identify and add together the amounts of income on which the individual is chargeable to income tax. This may include, for example, TRADING INCOME (**75**), EMPLOYMENT INCOME (**28**), PROPERTY INCOME (**60**), SAVINGS AND INVESTMENT INCOME (**65**), PENSION INCOME (**56**), SHARE-RELATED EMPLOYMENT INCOME (**71**), FOREIGN INCOME (**32**), income from PARTNERSHIPS (**52**), income from SETTLEMENTS (**70**), estate income (see **22** DECEASED ESTATES), income from INTELLECTUAL PROPERTY (**41**), income of UNDERWRITERS AT LLOYD'S (**79**), MISCELLANEOUS INCOME (**49**) and income deemed to arise under certain ANTI-AVOIDANCE (4) provisions. Expenses deductible in computing the amount of a particular type of income, e.g. trading expenses and most CAPITAL ALLOWANCES (9 and 10), should be duly deducted before arriving at the income to be included at this Step. An alphabetical list of some of the income exempt from income tax (and thus not to be included) forms the basis of **30** EXEMPT INCOME. Separate exemptions are covered in other chapters where appropriate, e.g. in SHARE-RELATED EMPLOYMENT INCOME AND EXEMPTIONS (71).

The aggregate of all income included at Step 1 is the individual's **total income.**

Certain stand-alone income tax liabilities are not included in this calculation and the related income should therefore not be included. These are mainly liabilities arising from the recovery of excessive tax relief, liabilities arising from specified anti-avoidance provisions, certain charges that can arise in connection with registered pension schemes and certain liabilities that are not directly connected to the individual's own tax position, e.g. tax deducted at source from payments made by him (for which see **23** DEDUCTION OF TAX AT SOURCE). A full list of the liabilities in this category is given at *ITA 2007, s 32.*

Step 2.

Identify and deduct from the income in Step 1 those deductions than can be made from total income (other than personal reliefs, which are deductible in Step 3 or given effect at Step 6 depending on their nature). A full list of the potential deductions at this Step is given at *ITA 2007, s 24.* It includes, for example, various allowable LOSSES (45), allowable INTEREST PAYABLE (42), annual payments (see **1.13** below), specified capital allowances (other than those deductible in arriving at amounts included at Step 1 above), relievable gifts of assets to CHARITIES AND CHARITABLE GIVING (see **14.19**), contributions to registered pension schemes in the limited circumstances where these are deductible from income on the making of a claim (see **57.12** PENSION PROVISION), post-cessation expenditure (see **59.5** POST-CESSATION RECEIPTS AND EXPENDITURE) and post-employment deductions (see **28.65** EMPLOYMENT INCOME).

There is a cap on certain deductions which may be made at Step 2 by individuals. See **1.11** below.

In order, for example, to apply the correct rates of tax at Step 4 below, the deductions at Step 2 must be set against the various components of total income, in other words against income of different descriptions. The general rule is that these deductions are treated as reducing income of different descriptions in such manner as will result in the greatest reduction in income tax liability. However, there are various provisions dictating that a particular deduction must be set against a particular type of income, and these take priority over the general rule; for example, certain reliefs for trading losses can only be set against profits from the same trade. These provisions are covered throughout this work where relevant; a list of them is given at *ITA 2007, s 25(3).*

A deduction from a component of income cannot produce a negative figure; the deduction is restricted to the amount required to reduce the component to nil. In some cases the excess deduction can then be set against other components. If it is one of those deductions that can only be made against a specified type of income, there may be rules enabling the excess to be carried forward or back to other tax years; such rules are covered throughout this work where relevant. Where more than one deduction can be made against a single component, the general rule is again that deductions are made in the manner most beneficial to the taxpayer (even if in such case the benefit arises in a different tax year).

The figure remaining after carrying out Step 2 is the individual's **net income.**

Step 3.

Deduct from the individual's net income his personal allowance (see **1.17** below) and, where applicable, his entitlement to blind person's allowance (see **1.20** below). These deductions must be set against the various components of net income; they are treated as reducing income of different descriptions in such manner as will result in the greatest reduction in income tax liability. See the examples at **1.22**(v)(b) and (c) below.

This gives the individual's **taxable income.**

Step 4.

Apply the appropriate tax rates (see **1.3–1.6** above) to the various components of taxable income.

Step 5.

Add together the amounts of tax calculated at Step 4.

Step 6.

Deduct from the total in Step 5 any tax reductions to which the individual is entitled for the year — see **1.12** below. Subject to Step 7, the resultant figure is the individual's income tax liability for the year.

Step 7.

Where relevant, certain amounts of tax must be added to the figure resulting from Step 6 in order to arrive at the individual's income tax liability for the year. These comprise:

- any tax to which the individual is liable as a donor under the Gift Aid rules, i.e. where there are insufficient tax liabilities to cover the tax treated as deducted at source from the donation — see **14.13** CHARITIES AND CHARITABLE GIVING;
- any tax liability due on a State pension lump sum — see **56.8** PENSION INCOME;
- any tax to which the individual is liable under the lifetime allowance provisions or the annual allowance provisions (see respectively **57.18** and **57.23** PENSION PROVISION);
- any tax to which the individual is liable under **57.26**(a), (b), (d), (e) or (h) PENSION PROVISION;
- any tax to which the individual is liable under the tainted donations rules at **14.21** CHARITIES AND CHARITABLE GIVING;

- the high income child benefit charge at **73.4** SOCIAL SECURITY AND NATIONAL INSURANCE;
- for any year for which the Scottish or Welsh basic rate differs from the UK basic rate, any recovery due under *FA 2004, s 192B* of excess relief for pension contributions (see **57.12** PENSION PROVISION);
- for any year for which the Scottish or Welsh basic rate is less than the UK basic rate, any recovery under *ITA 2007, s 414A* of excessive Gift Aid relief (see **14.13** CHARITIES AND CHARITABLE GIVING); and
- any income tax chargeable under **21.7** CORONAVIRUS **(COVID-19)** (recovery of coronavirus support payments where recipient not entitled).

The above calculation also applies to other persons within the charge to income tax, e.g. trusts and estates, but with the necessary modification allowing for the fact that such persons are not entitled to all the same tax reliefs as individuals.

[*ITA 2007, ss 22–25, 30, 31(5), 32; FA 2016, s 32(3)(4), Sch 5 para 3; SI 2015 No 1810, Arts 1, 5; SI 2019 No 201, Arts 1, 12*].

The amount of income tax (if any) payable directly by the individual to HMRC (or repayable) is subject to, for example, any tax he has paid under PAYE, tax deducted at source from his savings income and tax credits on dividends (except that the latter cannot create a repayment). These and similar items are not deductions from the tax liability as such but a means by which the liability is settled (or partially settled). They do not enter into the above calculation.

Simon's Taxes. See **E1.101B.**

Cap on unlimited tax reliefs

[1.11] The total amount of prescribed income tax reliefs that individuals can claim is capped. The affected reliefs are listed below. The aggregate amount of those reliefs for the tax year cannot exceed the *greater* of £50,000 or 25% of the individual's 'adjusted total income' for the year (see below).

Reliefs affected

The prescribed reliefs are as follows:

(a) relief for trading losses against general income (see **45.2** LOSSES), net of any amount attributable to overlap relief (see **75.14** TRADING INCOME), any business premises renovation allowances (BPRA) (see **9.3** CAPITAL ALLOWANCES) and any part of the loss relieved against profits of the trade to which the loss relates;

(b) relief against general income for losses in the early years of a trade (see **45.7** LOSSES), net of any of the items mentioned in (a) above;

(c) share loss relief (see **45.23** LOSSES), except where the loss arises on EIS shares (see **28** ENTERPRISE INVESTMENT SCHEME), SEIS shares (see **66** SEED ENTERPRISE INVESTMENT SCHEME) or shares to which SOCIAL INVESTMENT TAX RELIEF (72) is attributable;

(d) relief for employment losses against general income (see **45.31** LOSSES);

(e) relief for post-cessation expenditure against income (see **59.5** POST-CESSATION RECEIPTS AND EXPENDITURE and **60.16** PROPERTY INCOME), net of any part of such expenditure relieved against profits of the business to which the expenditure relates;

(f) relief for property business losses against general income (see **60.25** PROPERTY INCOME), net of any BPRA and any part of the loss relieved against profits of the business to which the loss relates;

(g) relief for payments of interest on loans within **42.6–42.11** INTEREST PAYABLE;

(h) post-employment deductions for employee liabilities (see **28.65** EMPLOYMENT INCOME);

(i) relief for losses on listed deeply discounted securities held since before 27 March 2003 (see **65.25** SAVINGS AND INVESTMENT INCOME); and

(j) relief for losses on strips of government securities (see **65.27** SAVINGS AND INVESTMENT INCOME).

Adjusted total income

An individual's '*adjusted total income*' for a tax year is computed as follows.

First, take the individuals total income for the year, i.e. the amount arrived at in Step 1 at **1.10** above.

Secondly, add back any deductions made under the payroll giving scheme (see **14.18** CHARITIES AND CHARITABLE GIVING) in arriving at that total income.

Finally, deduct:

- the gross equivalent of any contribution made to a registered pension scheme on which basic rate relief has been given at source (see **57.12** PENSION PROVISION); and
- any amount deductible under Step 2 at **1.10** above in the limited circumstances in which relief for registered pension scheme contributions is given by deduction in arriving at net income.

Losses carried back beyond 2013/14

The cap applies for 2013/14 onwards. Where a loss is capable of being carried back to an earlier tax year (as is the case with losses within (a)–(d) above), and consequently a loss relating to 2013/14 or a subsequent tax year (a '*later year*') is carried back to a year before 2013/14 (the '*earlier year*'), the cap applies for the earlier year. In applying the cap for the earlier year, there is taken into account only the aggregate amount of reliefs within (a)–(d) and then only to the extent that they relate to a loss sustained in a later year.

[*ITA 2007, s 24A; FA 2013, Sch 3 paras 4, 5*].

For official guidance see www.gov.uk/government/publications/limit-on-income-tax-reliefs-hs204-self-assessment-helpsheet.

Simon's Taxes. See **E1.101D**.

Tax reductions

[1.12] The tax reductions referred to at Step 6 of **1.10** above are set out below. To the extent that they are relevant in his case, the reductions in (1) to (8) below must be deducted from an individual's tax liability in the order in which they are listed.

(1) Venture capital trust investment relief (see **81.3** VENTURE CAPITAL TRUSTS).
(2) Enterprise investment scheme relief (see **29.4** ENTERPRISE INVESTMENT SCHEME).
(3) Seed enterprise investment scheme relief (see **66.3** SEED ENTERPRISE INVESTMENT SCHEME).
(4) Social investment tax relief (see **72** SOCIAL INVESTMENT TAX RELIEF).
(5) Community investment tax relief (see **17.3** COMMUNITY INVESTMENT TAX RELIEF).
(6) Interest relief on pre-9 March 1999 loan to purchase a life annuity (see **42.12** INTEREST PAYABLE).
(7) Relief for qualifying maintenance payments (see **48.9** MARRIED PERSONS AND CIVIL PARTNERS).
(8) Married couple's allowance (see **1.19** below).

The total reductions within (1)–(5) above cannot exceed the individual's tax liability after Step 5 at **1.10** above less any tax deemed to have been deducted by him from Gift Aid donations (see **14.13** CHARITIES AND CHARITABLE GIVING).

The reductions in the following list are made in the order which will result in the greatest reduction in the individual's income tax liability for the tax year. To that end, any of the following may be made before, in between or after those in (1) to (8) above:

- life assurance top slicing relief (see **44.9** LIFE ASSURANCE POLICIES);
- life assurance deficiency relief (see **44.15** LIFE ASSURANCE POLICIES);
- spreading relief in respect of patent royalties received (see **41.4** INTELLECTUAL PROPERTY);
- relief under *ITTOIA 2005, s 401* (distribution repaying shares or security issued in earlier distribution — see **65.14** SAVINGS AND INVESTMENT INCOME);
- relief under *ITTOIA 2005, ss 677, 678* where income is received from a foreign estate that has borne UK income tax (see **22.11** DECEASED ESTATES);
- any part of a personal allowance transferred to the individual by the individual's spouse or civil partner (see **1.18** below);
- for any year in which the Scottish or Welsh basic rate differs from the UK basic rate, any additional relief due under *FA 2004, s 192A* for pension contributions (see **57.12** PENSION PROVISION);
- for any year in which the Scottish or Welsh basic rate is greater than the UK basic rate, any additional Gift Aid relief due under *ITA 2007, s 414A* (see **14.13** CHARITIES AND CHARITABLE GIVING);
- (for 2017/18 onwards) relief for mortgage interest and other finance costs of a residential property business (see **60.12** PROPERTY INCOME); and
- (for 2017/18 onwards) interest relief on loan to invest in a partnership carrying on a residential property business (see **42.10** INTEREST PAYABLE).

Finally, if the individual is entitled to relief for foreign tax (by way of reduction in UK income tax liability), whether under a double tax treaty or unilaterally (see respectively **27.2** and **27.6** DOUBLE TAX RELIEF), that reduction is made after all other reductions have been made.

In all cases, a tax reduction must be restricted to the extent (if any) that it would otherwise exceed the individual's income tax liability before Step 7 at **1.10** above (or his remaining income tax liability after other reductions have been made).

For persons other than individuals, any reductions are made in the order which will result in the greatest reduction in the person's income tax liability for the tax year, except that a reduction in respect of double tax relief is made after all other reductions (apart from any reduction available at **70.19** SETTLEMENTS (trusts with vulnerable beneficiaries), which is made last of all).

[*ITA 2007, ss 26–29; FA 2016, Sch 1 paras 63(2), 73; SI 2015 No 1810, Arts 1, 5; SI 2019 No 201, Arts 1, 12*].

Simon's Taxes. See **E1.102.**

Annual payments

[1.13] Subject to the detailed provisions below, relief for annual payments is given by means of a deduction in computing net income for the tax year in which the payment is made (see Step 2 at **1.10** above). The amount deductible in computing net income is the *gross* amount of the payment, i.e. the amount before deduction of income tax.

The relief is available for payments from which income tax is required to be deducted at source under *ITA 2007, s 900(2)* (qualifying annual payment by an individual for commercial reasons in connection with his trade etc.) or *ITA 2007, s 901(3)* (qualifying annual payment by person other than an individual). For those provisions and for the meaning of 'qualifying annual payment', see **23.7–23.10** DEDUCTION OF TAX AT SOURCE. For the manner in which the payer accounts for the tax he deducts at source, see **23.18**. If a payment is deductible in calculating the payer's income from any source (e.g. his trading income), it cannot be deducted in computing net income. See below for restriction by reference to 'modified net income'. Certain payments made by persons other than individuals are ineligible for relief (see below).

With certain exceptions, annual payments made for non-taxable consideration are payable gross and are not deductible — see **4.42** ANTI-AVOIDANCE.

In *Bingham v CIR* Ch D 1955, 36 TC 254 a deduction was refused for alimony payable under a foreign Court Order as the payer was not empowered to deduct tax at source (cf. *Keiner v Keiner* QB 1952, 34 TC 346). Where an interest in a business is transferred in consideration for periodical payments based on subsequent profits, whether the payments are 'annual payments' rests on the facts. See *Ramsay* CA 1935, 20 TC 79 and *Ledgard* KB 1937, 21 TC 129 in which a deduction was refused and contrast *Hogarth* CS 1940, 23 TC 491.

Restriction by reference to 'modified net income'

The total amount for which relief can be obtained as above for a tax year cannot exceed the amount of the payer's 'modified net income' for that year.

A person's '*modified net income*' is defined (by *ITA 2007, s 1025*) as what would have been his net income if Steps 1 and 2 at **1.10** above applied with the following modifications.

(1) Ignore any relief that may be due for annual payments.
(2) Omit any 'non-qualifying income' (see below) from the person's total income.
(3) Ignore any relief for trading losses incurred (or treated as incurred) in a tax year subsequent to the one under review.
(4) Ignore any carry back of a post-cessation receipt from a tax year subsequent to the one under review (see **59.4** POST-CESSATION RECEIPTS AND EXPENDITURE).
(5) Ignore any relief for post-cessation expenditure (see **59.5** POST-CESSATION RECEIPTS AND EXPENDITURE) incurred (or treated as incurred) in a tax year subsequent to the one under review.
(6) Ignore any adjustment of profits resulting from an averaging claim by a creative artist or by a farmer or market gardener (see respectively **75.60, 75.78** TRADING INCOME) in respect of which the year under review is any year other than the last of the years being averaged.
(7) Ignore the making, amending or revoking of any claim for tax relief if such action would have been out of time had it not been for an averaging claim by a creative artist or by a farmer or market gardener (see respectively **75.60, 75.78** TRADING INCOME).

Non-qualifying income

'*Non-qualifying income*' in (2) above is any of the following:

(a) dividends and other company distributions received by non-UK residents (see **65.11** SAVINGS AND INVESTMENT INCOME);
(b) chargeable event gains arising to individuals or trustees and carrying a notional tax credit (see **44.8** LIFE ASSURANCE POLICIES);
(c) income corresponding to that in (e) above but arising to personal representatives and included in the aggregate income of an estate (see **22.5**(c)–(e) DECEASED ESTATES); and
(d) discretionary income from a settlor-interested trust and carrying a notional tax credit under *ITTOIA 2005, s 685A* (see **70.25** SETTLEMENTS).

Ineligible payments by persons other than individuals

A payment otherwise within the above relief provisions and made by a person other than an individual is ineligible for relief if, or in so far as:

- the payment can lawfully be made only out of capital or out of income that is exempt from income tax; or
- it is charged to capital; or
- it is treated by the payer as made out of income that is exempt from income tax, but only if such treatment makes a difference to the current or future rights or obligations of any person; or
- it is not ultimately borne by the payer, unless the reason it is not ultimately borne is that the payer receives (or benefits from) an amount on which he is liable to income tax.

[*ITA 2007, ss 447–452, 1025, 1026; FA 2016, s 25(9)(12), Sch 1 paras 63(17), 73*].

Simon's Taxes. See **E1.801.**

Claims

[1.14] Allowances unclaimed or not deducted from assessments (and relief for tax suffered by deduction at source) may be claimed within four years after the end of the tax year for which the claim is made. [*TMA 1970, s 43; SI 2009 No 403*]. See **16** CLAIMS.

Allowances depend upon 'the facts as they exist at the time' and cannot afterwards be withdrawn (or fresh assessments made) by reason of facts 'which arose after the year of assessment' (*Dodworth v Dale* KB 1936, 20 TC 285).

See 7 BANKRUPTCY for claims by bankrupts.

Non-residents

[1.15] Non-UK residents generally pay income tax at the normal rates on UK chargeable income, and are not entitled to personal reliefs *except* as stated in **1.17**, **1.19** and **1.20** below and at **50.2** NON-RESIDENTS. See, however, **50.3** NON-RESIDENTS for a limit on the income tax chargeable on the income of a non-resident. Non-residents may also be entitled to reliefs and exemptions under DOUBLE TAX RELIEF (**27**) agreements.

Indexation of personal reliefs and tax thresholds

[1.16] The basic rate limit, the starting rate limit for savings, the personal allowance, the married couple's allowance, the blind person's allowance and the income limit for age-related allowances are increased by the same percentage as the percentage increase (if any) in the consumer prices index (CPI) for the September preceding the tax year over that for the previous September. The resultant figures in the case of the basic rate limit and the income limit for age-related allowances are rounded up to the nearest £100 and in the case of the starting rate limit and the personal reliefs to the nearest £10.

The new figures are specified in a statutory instrument by HM Treasury before the tax year begins, but no change is required in PAY AS YOU EARN (**53**) deductions or repayments before (normally) 18 May in the tax year.

The above automatic increases may be varied by Parliament by means of the annual *Finance Act*.

[*ITA 2007, ss 21, 57; FA 2019, s 5(3)–(5)*].

Simon's Taxes. See **E1.101E, E1.910.**

Personal allowance

[1.17] The personal allowance takes the form of a deduction in arriving at taxable income (see Step 3 at **1.10** above). Strictly it requires a claim to be made but in practice it is nearly always given automatically. It is available to all UK-resident individuals. It is also available to certain other claimants as set out at **50.2** NON-RESIDENTS. The allowance is given for all tax years including that in which death occurs. An individual who claims the remittance basis loses his entitlement to the personal allowance (see **61.8** REMITTANCE BASIS). See below for the reduction of the personal allowance in the case of 'high income' individuals. See **1.18** below for the ability to transfer part of the personal allowance to a spouse or civil partner.

The personal allowance is as follows.

For	**2020/21**	**£12,500**
For	2019/20	£12,500
For	2018/19	£11,850
For	2017/18	£11,500
For	2016/17	£11,000

Reduction in personal allowance

The personal allowance is not available in full to an individual whose 'adjusted net income' (see below) exceeds a limit of £100,000. The basic personal allowance is reduced by one-half of the excess above £100,000. If any allowance remains, it will be rounded up to the nearest pound. It follows that if the excess of adjusted net income over £100,000 is at least twice the amount of the basic personal allowance, the individual will be entitled to no personal allowance at all.

See the example at **1.22**(ii) below.

Adjusted net income

An individual's net income is his total income less amounts (other than personal reliefs) deductible therefrom (see Step 2 at **1.10** above). Grossed up contributions to registered pension schemes are deducted in arriving at '*adjusted net income*' (see **57.12** PENSION PROVISION). The aggregate grossed up amount of any qualifying donations made by the individual under Gift Aid are similarly deductible from net income in arriving at adjusted net income (subject to the tainted donations rules at **14.21** CHARITIES AND CHARITABLE GIVING). Conversely, payments attracting tax relief under *ITA 2007, s 457* or *458* (certain payments to trade unions or police organisations — see **44.2** LIFE ASSURANCE POLICIES) are, for these purposes, not deductible in arriving at adjusted net income, and must therefore be added back to net income. For further guidance and examples, see www.gov.uk/adjusted-net-income.

[*ITA 2007, ss 35–37, 41, 58; FA 2014, ss 1(3), 2(1)(2)(4)(5)(9); FA 2016, ss 3, 6(17)(24); FA 2019, s 5(2); SI 2013 No 3088, Art 3; SI 2015 No 1810, Arts 1, 14(5); SI 2017 No 1184, Art 3; SI 2018 No 459, Arts 1, 6(3)*].

See **1.16** above as regards provision for personal reliefs to be increased each year at least in line with inflation.

Simon's Taxes. See **E1.910**.

Transfer between spouses or civil partners

[1.18] Subject to the conditions below, an individual may transfer part of his or her personal allowance to a spouse or civil partner. The amount transferable (the '*transferable tax allowance*') is equivalent to 10% of the basic personal allowance for the year. If, in any year, the transferable tax allowance would not otherwise be a multiple of £10, it is rounded up to the nearest £10. The transferable tax allowance is thus as follows.

For	**2020/21**	**£1,250**
For	2019/20	£1,250
For	2018/19	£1,190
For	2017/18	£1,150
For	2016/17	£1,100

Relief is given to the transferee spouse/partner by means of a reduction (see Step 6 at **1.10** above) in what would otherwise be the transferee's income tax liability (a '*tax reduction*') equal to tax at the basic rate for the year on the transferred amount. See the example at **1.22**(vi) below. The order in which tax reductions are given against an individual's tax liability is set out at **1.12** above, which also makes clear that a tax reduction must be restricted to the extent (if any) that it would otherwise exceed the individual's remaining income tax liability after making all prior reductions.

The transferable tax allowance is sometimes described by HMRC as the 'marriage allowance'. This appellation is eschewed in this publication to avoid confusion with the married couple's allowance available where at least one spouse or civil partner was born before 6 April 1935 (see **1.19** below).

Regardless of whether an individual is a party to more than one marriage or civil partnership in a tax year, the individual is not entitled to more than one tax reduction under these provisions for the year, or to have more than one election under *ITA 2007, s 55C* in operation for the year. If an individual who is entitled to the above tax reduction for a tax year dies during that year, he or she remains entitled to the tax reduction but the personal allowance of the transferor spouse or civil partner is not reduced.

With effect on and after 29 November 2017, an individual can elect to transfer to a deceased spouse or civil partner, and a deceased individual's personal representatives can make any transferable tax allowance election that the deceased could have made. This applies even if the death occurred before that date. As any such election can be made at any time within the four years after the end of the tax year to which it relates (see below), this change was effectively backdated to 2015/16 when the transferable tax allowance was introduced.

Transferor conditions

The *transferor* spouse or civil partner must make an election under *ITA 2007, s 55C* to reduce his personal allowance by the transferable tax allowance. See below for procedure. This election can be made only if:

(a) the transferor is married to, or in a civil partnership with, the same person when the election is made and for at least part of the tax year in question;

(b) the transferor is entitled to the personal allowance for the year;

(c) on the assumption that the election was successful, the transferor would not for that year be liable to income tax at the higher or additional rate or the dividend upper or additional rate or the Welsh higher or additional rate or any Scottish rate above the intermediate rate; and

(d) in a case of a non-UK resident transferor entitled to personal reliefs by virtue of **50.2** NON-RESIDENTS, the transferor's hypothetical net income for the tax year is less than the amount of his or her personal allowance (before reduction).

For the purposes of (d) above, an individual's '*hypothetical net income*' is the amount that would be that individual's net income (see Step 2 at **1.10** above) if his or her income tax liability were calculated on the basis that the individual:

- was both UK resident and UK domiciled for the year (and the year was not a split year for residence purposes);
- did not fall to be regarded as resident in a country outside the UK for the purposes of a double tax treaty; and
- had made a claim for any available double tax relief.

To the extent that the hypothetical net income needs to be converted into sterling, this is done using the average exchange rate for the twelve months ending on 31 March in the tax year in question.

Transferee conditions

The conditions relating to the *transferee* spouse or civil partner are that:

- the transferee is married to, or in a civil partnership with, a person who has made an election under *ITA 2007, s 55C* (see above) which is in force for the tax year in question;
- the transferee is not liable for that year to income tax at the higher or additional rate or the dividend upper or additional rate or the Welsh higher or additional rate or any Scottish rate above the intermediate rate;
- the transferee is UK resident for the year or, if non-UK resident, is eligible for personal reliefs as in **50.2** NON-RESIDENTS; and
- neither the transferee nor the transferee's spouse or civil partner makes a claim to married couple's allowance (see **1.19** below) for the year.

Election procedure

The transferor's election under *ITA 2007, s 55C* must be made no later than four years after the end of the tax year to which it relates. There is no necessity for it to be made in a tax return. Provided the conditions in (a)–(d) above continue to be met, the election, once made, continues in force for each subsequent tax year unless:

- it is made after the end of the tax year to which it relates or after the death of one of the individuals (in which case it has effect only for the tax year to which it relates); or

- it is withdrawn by notice given by the individual by whom it was made (but an election made by personal representatives cannot be withdrawn); or
- the transferor's spouse or civil partner does not obtain a tax reduction in respect of a tax year for which an election is in force, in which case it ceases to have effect for subsequent tax years (but not so as to prevent the individual from making a fresh election).

The withdrawal of an election does not normally have effect until the tax year *after* the one in which notice of withdrawal is given. However, it has effect for the tax year *in* which the notice is given if the marriage or civil partnership comes to an end in that year (by divorce, dissolution, annulment or judicial separation). Once made, an election cannot otherwise be amended or withdrawn.

[ITA 2007, ss 55A–55E; TMA 1970, s 42(10A); FA 2016, ss 4(8)(17), 5(6)(7)(10), 6(15)(16)(24); FA 2018, s 6; SI 2015 No 1810, Arts 1, 14(3)(4); SI 2019 No 459, Arts 1, 6(2); SI 2019 No 201, Arts 1, 12].

Simon's Taxes. See **E1.910B.**

Married couple's allowance

[1.19] Married couple's allowance is available to any married couple where at least one spouse was born **before 6 April 1935**. Subject to this age requirement, the allowance is available to any UK resident claimant who is, at any time in the tax year, a married man whose wife is 'living with him' (for which see **48.8** MARRIED PERSONS AND CIVIL PARTNERS), but see below as regards marriages on or after 5 December 2005. It is similarly available to certain other claimants as set out at **50.2** NON-RESIDENTS. For polygamous marriages under Muslim law, see *Nabi v Heaton* CA 1983, 57 TC 292, in which, at HMRC's request, the taxpayer's appeal from the Ch D decision against him was allowed by consent.

Entitlement to married couple's allowance is extended to same-sex couples who are **civil partners** under *Civil Partnership Act 2004*, subject to the same requirement that at least one partner was born before 6 April 1935.

An individual who claims the remittance basis loses any entitlement he may have to the married couple's allowance (see **61.8** REMITTANCE BASIS).

Where available, married couple's allowance is not given as a deduction from total income but by means of a reduction in the claimant's income tax liability (see Step 6 at **1.10** above). The reduction is **10%** of the amount of the allowance. The order in which tax reductions are given against an individual's tax liability is set out at **1.12** above, which also makes clear that a tax reduction must be restricted to the extent (if any) that it would otherwise exceed the individual's remaining income tax liability after making all prior reductions.

See **48.3, 48.4** MARRIED PERSONS AND CIVIL PARTNERS as regards the transfer of all or half of the basic married couple's allowance, and the transfer of excess married couple's allowance, between spouses and civil partners.

The basic married couple's allowance is as follows.

For	**2020/21**	**£3,510**
For	2019/20	£3,450
For	2018/19	£3,360
For	2017/18	£3,260
For	2016/17	£3,220

But a higher married couple's allowance is available where the claimant or his wife is at any time in the tax year aged 75 or over, or would have been but for his or her death in that year. Where the claimant's 'adjusted net income' (see below) is at or below the level of the income limit, the maximum higher allowance is available (subject to it being given as a percentage reduction in income tax liability as described above). Where the claimant's adjusted net income exceeds the income limit, the maximum allowance is reduced by one-half of the excess, except that it cannot be reduced to less than the basic married couple's allowance above. See the example at **1.22**(vii) below.

Adjusted net income

An individual's net income is his total income less amounts (other than personal reliefs) deductible therefrom (see Step 2 at **1.10** above). Grossed up contributions to registered pension schemes are deducted in arriving at '*adjusted net income*' (see **57.12** PENSION PROVISION). The aggregate grossed up amount of any qualifying donations made by the individual under Gift Aid are similarly deductible from net income in arriving at adjusted net income (subject to the tainted donations rules at **14.21** CHARITIES AND CHARITABLE GIVING). Conversely, payments attracting tax relief under *ITA 2007, s 457* or *458* (certain payments to trade unions or police organisations — see **44.2** LIFE ASSURANCE POLICIES) are not deductible in arriving at adjusted net income, and must therefore be added back to net income.

The maximum higher married couple's allowance and the income limit are as follows.

		Maximum married couple's allowance	Income limit
For	**2020/21**	**£9,075**	**£30,200**
For	2019/20	£8,915	£29,600
For	2018/19	£8,695	£28,900
For	2017/18	£8,445	£28,000
For	2016/17	£8,355	£27,700

See **1.16** above as regards provision for personal reliefs to be increased each year at least in line with inflation.

For marriages entered into **before 5 December 2005**, married couple's allowance is given to the husband (subject to the right of transfer to the wife at **48.3** MARRIED PERSONS AND CIVIL PARTNERS), and the amount of the allowance is determined by the level of the husband's income (regardless of any election to transfer all or half of the basic allowance to the wife or to transfer excess allowances).

For marriages and civil partnerships entered into **on or after 5 December 2005**, married couple's allowance is given to whichever of the two individuals has the higher net income for the tax year in question, and the amount of the allowance is determined by the level of that individual's income. (If their net incomes are exactly the same, they may make a joint election to determine which of them receives the allowance; such election must be made no later than four years after the tax year in question.) Once the claimant has been thus determined, the right to transfer all or half of the basic allowance to the claimant's spouse or civil partner does, however, remain, as does the right to transfer excess allowances (see **48.3, 48.4** MARRIED PERSONS AND CIVIL PARTNERS). Entitlement to the allowance in the first place is dependent on the couple having lived together for at least part of the tax year whilst being married to, or civil partners of, each other (see also **48.8** MARRIED PERSONS AND CIVIL PARTNERS). The increased level of allowances for the over 75s continues to be available where either of the two individuals is aged 75 or over at some time in the tax year or would have been but for his or her death in that year; this is the case regardless of which of those individuals is the claimant, but the amount of the allowance remains dependent on the income level of the claimant.

A couple who married before 5 December 2005 may make a **joint election** to be brought within the above rules for couples marrying on or after that date. The election must be made before the start of the first tax year for which it is to have effect but then continues to have effect for all succeeding tax years and is irrevocable.

No more than one married couple's allowance may be claimed by any person for any one tax year.

A decree of nullity does not operate retrospectively to disentitle the husband to the married couple's allowance during the years the parties lived together (*Dodworth v Dale KB* 1936, 20 TC 285).

Year of marriage etc.

Where the marriage or civil partnership is entered into during the tax year in question (and the individual concerned had not previously in that year been entitled to the married couple's allowance), the allowance is reduced by one-twelfth for each 'fiscal month' of the tax year ending before the date of the marriage or civil partnership. A '*fiscal month*' is a month ending on 5 May, 5 June, 5 July and so on. The reduction in the allowance is computed *after* applying any necessary restriction by reference to the income limit.

Year of death

Where either the husband or wife, or either civil partner, dies, married couple's allowance is available as if the marriage or civil partnership had continued until the end of the tax year in which death occurs, i.e. there are no reductions similar to those in the year of marriage.

[*ITA 2007, ss 29, 43–46, 54, 55, 58; FA 2014, s 2(6)(7)(9); FA 2016, s 6(17)(24); SI 2015 No 1810, Arts 1, 14(5); SI 2016 No 1175; SI 2017 No 1184, Art 3; SI 2018 No 459, Arts 1, 6(3); SI 2018 No 1150; SI 2020 No 343*].

Simon's Taxes. See E1.920.

Blind person's allowance

[1.20] The blind person's allowance takes the form of a deduction in arriving at taxable income (see Step 3 at **1.10** above). It is available to all UK-resident individuals. It is also theoretically available to certain other claimants as set out at **50.2** NON-RESIDENTS if, exceptionally, they can satisfy the necessary conditions below. The allowance is given in full for all tax years including that in which death occurs. An individual who claims the remittance basis loses any entitlement he may have to the blind person's allowance (see **61.8** REMITTANCE BASIS).

The allowance is as follows.

For	**2020/21**	**£2,500**
For	2019/20	£2,450
For	2018/19	£2,390
For	2017/18	£2,320
For	2016/17	£2,290

The allowance can be claimed if, for at least part of the tax year, the individual:

- is registered as a blind person under the *National Assistance Act 1948, s 29* (which refers to registers kept by local authorities in England and Wales); or
- is ordinarily resident in Scotland or NI and, because of blindness, is unable to do work for which eyesight is essential.

An individual becoming registered as a blind person during a tax year is treated for this purpose as if he became registered in the previous tax year if the evidence on which the registration is based (e.g. the ophthalmologist's certificate) was obtained in that previous year.

[*ITA 2007, ss 38, 41; SI 2016 No 1175; SI 2017 No 1184, Art 3; SI 2018 No 1150; SI 2020 No 343*].

For transfer of allowances between spouses and civil partners, see **48.6** MARRIED PERSONS AND CIVIL PARTNERS.

Simon's Taxes. See E1.917.

Miscellaneous reliefs

[1.21] For relief for interest, see **42** INTEREST PAYABLE. For relief for pension contributions, see **57** PENSION PROVISION. For miscellaneous life assurance-related reliefs, see **44.2** LIFE ASSURANCE POLICIES.

Examples on allowances and tax rates

[1.22] The following examples illustrate the calculation of tax payable for 2020/21. References in brackets are to paragraph numbers above. In all these examples, with the exception of that at (ix) below, which features a Scottish taxpayer, the taxpayer's liability to income tax is at the main UK rates (or the identical Welsh rates).

(i) General

A **single person** receives in 2020/21 employment income of £22,325, building society interest of £1,160 and national savings bank interest of £60.

		£	£
	Employment income		22,325
(1.6)	Building society interest		1,160
	National savings bank interest		60
(1.10)	Total and net income		23,545
(1.17)	*Deduct* Personal allowance		12,500
	Taxable income		£11,045
	Tax liability (non-savings income):		
(1.3)	£9,825 @ 20% (basic rate)		1,965.00
(1.6)	(savings income):		
(1.7)	£1,000 @ 0% (personal savings allowance)	—	
	£220 @ 20% (basic rate)	44.00	44.00
	Tax payable		£2,009.00

(ii) Restriction of personal allowance

A single person has employment income of £121,000 for 2020/21 and makes Gift Aid donations of £4,800.

		£	£
	Employment income		121,000
(1.10)	Total and net income		121,000
(1.17)	*Deduct* Personal allowance	12,500	
	Less reduction for excess adjusted net income over £100,000 (½ × 15,000) (note (a))	7,500	£5,000
	Taxable income		£116,000
(1.3)	Tax liability:		
	£43,500 @ 20% (note (b))		8,700.00
	£72,500 @ 40%		29,000.00
	Tax payable		£37,700.00

Notes

(a) Net income of £121,000 is reduced to adjusted net income of £115,000 by deducting the grossed up amount of the Gift Aid donations (£4,800 × 100/80 = £6,000).

(b) Whilst the Gift Aid donations are deductible in arriving at adjusted net income, they are not deductible in arriving at taxable income. Instead, the basic rate band is extended by the grossed up amount of the donations. See **14.13** CHARITIES AND CHARITABLE GIVING.

(iii) Starting rate for savings

A single person has a tax-adjusted trading profit of £13,730 for the year to 31 March 2021 and receives bank deposit interest of £6,200 in 2020/21. She has no other taxable income.

		£
	Trading income	13,730
(1.6)	Savings income	6,200
(1.10)	Total and net income	19,930
(1.17)	*Deduct* Personal allowance	12,500
	Taxable income	£7,430
	Tax liability (non-savings income):	
(1.3)	£1,230 @ 20% (basic rate)	246.00
	(savings income):	
(1.6)	(£5,000 – £1,230 =) £3,770 @ 0% (starting rate for savings)	—
(1.7)	£1,000 @ 0% (personal savings allowance)	—
	£1,430 @ 20% (basic rate)	£286.00
	Tax payable	£532.00

Note

(1.10) The personal allowance is deducted from the trading income in priority to the savings income as this gives the greatest reduction in tax liability (see also the examples at (v)(b) and (c) below).

(iv) Personal savings allowance (PSA)

A single person has pension income of £43,000, bank deposit interest of £5,500 and dividends of £1,800 for 2020/21.

				£
	Pension income			43,000
(1.6)	Savings income			5,500
(1.5)	Dividend income			1,800
(1.10)	Total and net income			50,300
(1.17)	*Deduct* Personal allowance			12,500
	Taxable income			£37,800
	Taxable as follows:			
	£			
	30,500	@ 20%	(non-dividend/non-savings income net of personal allowance)	6,100.00
(1.7)	500	@ 0%	(savings income covered by PSA)	—
(1.7)	5,000	@ 20%	(savings income taxable at basic rate)	1,000.00
(1.5)	1,500	@ 0%	(dividends covered by dividend allowance)	—
(1.3)	37,500		Basic rate limit	
(1.5)	300	@ 0%	(further dividends covered by dividend allowance)	—
	£37,800			
	Tax payable			£7,100.00

Notes

(a) The taxpayer in this example has income within the higher rate band, but is not an additional rate taxpayer, and is thus entitled to a PSA of £500. No part of his income is actually taxable at the higher rate (due to the availability of the dividend allowance) but this is not a factor in determining the amount of the PSA.

(b) As the taxpayer has taxable non-savings income in excess of the £5,000 starting rate limit, the starting rate for savings (see **1.6** above) does not apply to any of his income. This example reflects the fact that dividend income is generally treated as the highest part of an individual's income, and savings income treated as the next highest.

(c) See (v) below for further examples on the taxation of dividends and savings income.

(v) Dividend taxation

(a) A single person has pension income of £46,000 and dividends of £5,000 for 2020/21.

				£
	Pension income			46,000
(1.5)	Dividend income			5,000
(1.10)	Total and net income			51,000
(1.17)	*Deduct* Personal allowance			12,500
	Taxable income			£38,500
	Taxable as follows:			
	£			
	33,500	@ 20%	(non-dividend income net of personal allowance)	6,700.00
(1.5)	2,000	@ 0%	(dividends covered by dividend allowance)	—
(1.5)	2,000	@ 7.5%	(dividends taxable at the dividend ordinary rate)	150.00
(1.3)	37,500		Basic rate limit	
(1.5)	1,000	@ 32.5%	(dividends taxable at the dividend upper rate)	325.00
	£38,500			
	Tax payable			£7,175.00

Note

(a) The methodology is similar where dividend income straddles the higher rate limit, with dividends above the limit (and in excess of the £2,000 dividend allowance) being taxed at the dividend additional rate of 38.1%.

(b) For 2020/21, a single person has employment income of £10,500, savings income of £7,000 and dividends of £3,500.

		Savings income	Dividend income	Other income	Total income
		£	£	£	£
(1.10)	Total and net income	7,000	3,500	10,500	21,000
(1.17)	*Deduct* Personal allowance	1,000	1,000	10,500	12,500
	Taxable income	£6,000	£2,500	—	£8,500
	Taxable as follows:				
(1.6)	£5,000 @ 0% (starting rate for savings)	—			—
(1.7)	£1,000 @ 0% (personal savings allowance)	—			—
(1.5)	£2,000 @ 0% (dividend allowance)		—		—
(1.5)	£500 @ 7.5% (dividend ordinary rate)		37.50		37.50
	Tax payable	—	£37.50		£37.50

Note

(a) This example illustrates how the personal allowance is best utilised against income so as to minimise the tax liability (see Step 3 at **1.10** above). In this example, what remains of the personal allowance (£2,000) is set firstly against savings income but only to the extent necessary to produce a nil liability on savings income. If the £2,000 were set wholly against savings income there would a total liability of £112.50 (£1,500 @ 7.5%) on the dividend income. If the £2,000 were set wholly against dividend income it would wipe out the liability on dividend income but produce a liability of £200 on savings income (£1,000 @ 20%). See also (c) below.

(c) A single person has pension income of £44,500, bank deposit interest of £2,500 and dividends of £5,000 for 2020/21.

				£
	Pension income			44,500
(1.6)	Savings income			2,500
(1.5)	Dividend income			5,000
(1.10)	Total and net income			52,000
(1.17)	*Deduct* Personal allowance			12,500
	Taxable income			£39,500
	Taxable as follows:			
	£			
	35,000	@ 20%	(non-dividend/non-savings income net of personal allowance)	7,000.00
(1.7)	500	@ 0%	(savings income covered by PSA)	—
(1.7)	2,000	@ 20%	(savings income taxable at basic rate)	400.00
(1.3)	37,500		Basic rate limit	
(1.5)	2,000	@ 0%	(dividends covered by dividend allowance)	—
	£39,500			
	Tax payable			£7,400.00

Notes

(a) In this case, £3,000 of the personal allowance has been set firstly against dividend income leaving £9,500 to be set against pension income. The advantage of doing this is that £2,000 of dividends that would otherwise be chargeable at the dividend upper rate of 32.5% are instead charged at 0%. A more conventional calculation, with all of the personal allowance set against pension income, produces a tax liability of £7,525.00.

(b) See note (a) to (iv) above as to the amount of the personal savings allowance (PSA).

(vi) Transferable tax allowance

A married woman with small children receives income (net of allowable expenses) of £11,460 in 2020/21 from occasional freelance proofreading. She has no other taxable income. She elects under *ITA 2007, s 55C* to transfer part of her personal allowance to her husband. Her husband has employment income of £47,000 but no other taxable income. The couple are not eligible for married couple's allowance.

Husband			£
(1.10)	Net income		47,000
(1.17)	*Deduct* Personal allowance		£12,500
	Taxable income		£34,500
(1.3)	Tax liability: £34,500 @ 20% (basic rate)		6,900.00
(1.18)	*Deduct* Transferable tax allowance £1,250 @ 20%		250.00
			£6,650.00
Wife			
(1.10)	Net income		11,460
(1.17)	*Deduct* Personal allowance	12,500	
(1.18)	*Deduct* transferable tax allowance	1,250	
			11,250
	Taxable income		£210
(1.3)	Tax liability: £210 @ 20% (basic rate)		£42.00

Note

(a) This couple save tax of £208 by electing to use the transferable tax allowance. The husband makes a saving of £250.00 (£1,250 @ 20%) while the wife has to pay tax of £42.00 to which she would not otherwise have been liable. If the transferor's income had been £11,250 (equal to 90% of the personal allowance) or less, the couple would have achieved the maximum saving of £250.00.

(vii) Married couple's allowance

A married man born before 6 April 1935 has a net income of £38,020 for 2020/21 (all of which is non-savings/non-dividend income). He and his wife married many years ago and have not elected to be brought within the rules for couples marrying on or after 5 December 2005.

		£	£
(1.10)	Net income		38,020
(1.17)	*Deduct* Personal allowance		12,500
	Taxable income		£25,520
	Taxable as follows:		
	£25,520 @ 20%		5,104.00
(1.19)	*Deduct* Married couple's allowance £5,165 (see below) @ 10%		516.50
	Tax payable		£4,587.50
	Calculation of married couple's allowance		
(1.19)	Married couple's allowance		9,075
	Less reduction for excess income:		
	Net income	38,020	
	Income limit	30,200	
	Excess	£7,820	
	Allowance reduced for excess (1/2 × 7,820)		3,910
			£5,165

(viii) Transfer of married couple's allowance

A married man born before 6 April 1935 has a net income for 2020/21 of £14,200. His wife, born after that date, has a net income of £18,105. She elects to receive one-half of the basic married couple's allowance. Neither spouse has any savings income or dividend income. The couple married many years ago and have not elected to be brought within the rules for couples marrying on or after 5 December 2005.

Husband		£
(1.10)	Net income	14,200
(1.17)	*Deduct* Personal allowance	12,500
	Taxable income	£1,700
(1.3)	Tax liability: £1,700 @ 20% (basic rate)	340.00
(1.19)	*Deduct* Married couple's allowance (£9,075 – ½ × £3,510) = £7,320 £7,320 @ 10% = £732.00 but restricted to	340.00
	Tax payable	Nil
Wife		
(1.10)	Net income	18,105
(1.17)	*Deduct* Personal allowance	12,500
	Taxable income	£5,605
	£5,605 @ 20%	1,121.00
(1.19)	*Deduct* Married couple's allowance (under election) £1,755 (£3,510 × ½) @ 10%	175.50
	Tax payable (subject to below)	£945.50

Note

(a) The unused balance of the husband's married couple's allowance is (£732 – £340) × 100/10 = £3,920. On a claim, this may be transferred to the wife, who will then be entitled to a further income tax reduction of £392.00 (£3,920 @ 10%), reducing tax payable to £553.50.

(ix) Scottish taxpayer

Duncan is a Scottish taxpayer (within the definition at **1.8** above). For 2020/21, he has earnings of £47,300, bank interest of £1,400 and no other taxable income.

				£
	Employment income			47,300
(**1.6**)	Savings income			1,400
(**1.10**)	Total and net income			48,700
(**1.17**)	*Deduct* Personal allowance			12,500
	Taxable income			£36,200
	Taxable as follows:			
	£			
(**1.3**)	2,085	@ 19%	(Scottish starter rate on non-savings income)	396.15
(**1.3**)	10,573	@ 20%	(Scottish basic rate on non-savings income)	2,114.60
(**1.3**)	18,272	@ 21%	(Scottish intermediate rate on non-savings income)	3,837.12
	30,930		(Scottish intermediate rate limit)	
(**1.3**)	3,870	@ 41%	(Scottish higher rate on non-savings income)	1,586.70
(**1.7**)	1,000	@ 0%	(personal savings allowance)	—
(**1.7**)	400	@ 20%	(savings income taxable at UK basic rate)	80.00
	£36,200			
	Tax payable			£8,014.57

Notes

(a) In this example the personal allowance is set against non-savings income as this gives the best result. This leaves taxable non-savings income of £34,800 which is taxed at the Scottish rates. However, the savings income falls entirely within the UK basic rate band and is thus chargeable at the UK basic rate (to the extent that it exceeds the personal savings allowance).

(b) In determining the amount of the personal savings allowance (PSA), a Scottish taxpayer is assumed to pay income tax by reference to UK rate thresholds. In this example the PSA is £1,000 because taxable income does not exceed the UK basic rate limit of £37,500 and the taxpayer would not be liable above basic rate if he were not a Scottish taxpayer.

2

Accrued Income Scheme

Introduction to accrued income scheme

[2.1] Bondwashing is the practice of converting income into capital gains by disposing of securities at a time when the price obtained reflects a significant element of accrued interest. Under the accrued income scheme (introduced to counter this practice), interest on securities is treated as accruing on a day to day basis, and on transfer of the securities a person is charged to income tax on the interest that accrues during the period of his ownership with appropriate adjustments to the taxable incomes of transferor and transferee.

HMRC guidance is available at www.gov.uk/government/publications/accrued-income-scheme-hs343-self-assessment-helpsheet and at HMRC Savings and Investment Manual SAIM4000–4400.

Simon's Taxes. See D9.4.

Definitions

[2.2] '*Securities*' include any loan stock or similar security of any government, or public or local authority, or any company, or other body, whether or not secured or carrying a right to interest of a fixed amount or at a fixed rate per cent and whether or not in bearer form. *Not included* are shares in a company (other than certain building society shares); national and war savings certificates (including Ulster savings certificates); CERTIFICATES OF DEPOSIT (**12**); uncertificated eligible debt security units as defined in *ITA 2007, s 986* and certain other rights for which a certificate of deposit could be, but has not been, issued (see **12.3** CERTIFICATES OF DEPOSIT); deeply discounted securities within *ITTOIA 2005, ss 430–460* (see **65.24** *et seq.* SAVINGS AND INVESTMENT INCOME), except where the person making the disposal has held the security continuously since before 27 March 2003 and the security was listed at some time before that date; and any security redeemable at a price exceeding its issue price and carrying no other return. [*ITA 2007, s 619(1)–(5)*].

Securities are '*of the same kind*' if so treated by a recognised stock exchange or if they would be so treated if dealt with on such an exchange. [*ITA 2007, s 619(6)*].

'*Transfer*' in relation to securities includes transfer by way of sale, exchange, gift or otherwise; conversions (see **2.13** below); and redemptions of variable rate securities (see **2.15** below). There are separate rules treating an event or transaction as a transfer in relation to strips of gilt-edged securities (see **2.20** below), new issues (see **2.22** below), trading stock appropriations (see **2.12** below), owners becoming entitled as a trustee (see **2.7** below) and securities ceasing to be held on charitable trusts (see **2.17** below). A transfer for these purposes does not include securities vesting in personal representatives on a death after 5 April 1996 or the transfer of deeply discounted securities where the person making the transfer has held the security continuously since before 27 March 2003 and the security was listed at some time before that date. It does not include an exchange or conversion of securities solely as a result of actions to effect a '*euroconversion*', i.e. a change from the currency of a State which has adopted the euro into euros (see *SI 1998 No 3177, Regs 3, 32*). A transfer takes effect when an agreement for transfer is made and the transferee becomes entitled to them at the same time. A person '*acquires*' securities when he becomes entitled to them and '*holds*' them on any day if he is entitled to them at the end of that day. Partners in Scottish partnerships are treated as being entitled to securities held by the firm and as carrying out themselves any partnership dealings. [*ITA 2007, ss 620, 675; SI 2007 No 1820, Reg 4*].

'*Interest*' includes dividends and any other return (however described) except a return consisting of the excess of a security's redemption amount over its issue price. [*ITA 2007, s 671*].

An '*interest payment day*' is a day on which interest is payable or, where payment may be made on more than one day, the first such day. [*ITA 2007, s 672*].

An '*interest period*' is normally the period beginning with the day after one interest payment day (or the day after issue) and ending with the next (or first) such day. If, however, an interest period would otherwise exceed twelve months, it is divided into successive twelve month interest periods with any remaining months forming a separate interest period. The last interest period normally ends with the last interest payment day. For the purpose of determining when an interest period ends, conversions and exchanges of gilt-edged securities for strips are ignored. [*ITA 2007, s 673*].

The '*settlement day*', where securities are transferred through a recognised market such as the Stock Exchange, is the agreed settlement day or, if the transferee may settle on more than one day, the day he settles. If the transfer is not through such a market and the consideration is money alone and there is no interest payment day between the agreement for transfer and the agreed payment day or days, that day (or the latest such day) is the settlement day. If the transfer is not through such a market and either there is no consideration, or it is treated as a transfer by virtue of special provisions in *ITA 2007, ss 620(1)(b)(c), 648(1)(3), 650, 651, 652* (see **2.13, 2.15, 2.20, 2.12, 2.7, 2.17** respectively below), the settlement day is the day of transfer. If the settlement day is not established by one of the above, it is decided by an officer of HMRC, subject to review by the Appeal Tribunal on appeal. [*ITA 2007, s 674*].

Deemed payments

[2.3] When securities are transferred, interest is effectively apportioned between the old and new owners so that the former is charged to income tax on the interest accrued up to the date of transfer while the latter is similarly charged on the interest accruing from that date. This is achieved by a system of deemed payments between transferor and transferee, described below.

The interest actually received is chargeable to tax in the normal way. It may, however, be reduced, or a further charge may arise — see **2.4** below.

Subject to exceptions in **2.5** below, if the transfer is *with accrued interest* (i.e. with the right to receive the next interest due, or 'cum div'), the transferor is treated as receiving a payment from the transferee. The amount of the payment is either the gross interest accruing to the settlement day (see **2.2** above) where this is accounted for separately by the transferee (as happens with short-dated gilts), or the proportion of the interest that has accrued between the last interest payment day (or the beginning of the first interest period of the securities) and the settlement day. This is given by the formula I x A/B, where I is the interest due on the first payment day following the settlement day, A is the number of days in the interest period up to and including the settlement day and B is the number of days in the whole period.

If, on the other hand, the transfer is *without accrued interest* (i.e. 'ex div') the transferor is treated as making a payment to the transferee. The amount of the payment is either the gross interest accruing from the settlement day to the next interest payment day (see **2.2** above) where this is accounted for separately by the transferor, or the proportion of the interest that has accrued during that period. This is given by the formula I x A/B, where I is the interest due on the first payment day following the settlement day, A is the number of days from the day after the settlement day up to and including the payment day and B is the number of days in the whole period.

Where the transfer of securities is a *Pt 5* transfer under *Proceeds of Crime Act 2002* (as in **9.2**(x) CAPITAL ALLOWANCES) and no compensating payment is made to the transferor, these provisions do not apply. [*ITA 2007, ss 623, 624, 632, 633; Proceeds of Crime Act 2002, Sch 10 paras 4, 10*].

Euroconversions

Where, in any interest period, there is both a transfer of securities and a '*euroconversion*' of those securities, i.e. a change from the currency of a State which has adopted the euro into euros, the adjustment to be made under the accrued income provisions is such amount as is just and reasonable. A euroconversion does not generally of itself give rise to a transfer within these provisions (see **2.2** above), but certain capital sums received in connection with euroconversions of securities which, on a just and reasonable view, may be attributable to a reduction or deferral of interest on those securities may give rise to adjustments under these provisions. [*SI 1998 No 3177, Regs 3, 34, 35*].

Determination of accrued income profit/loss

[2.4] The various payments which a person is deemed to have made or received as in **2.3** above and which relate to securities of a particular kind in an interest period (see **2.2** above) are aggregated to give either an accrued income profit or loss. If the overall result is a profit, the full amount is taxed as income received at the end of the interest period. [*ITA 2007, ss 616, 617(1)(2)*]. If, on the other hand, the overall result shows a loss, relief is given by way of an exemption in relation to the actual interest received at the end of the interest period so that only the amount exceeding the loss is charged to tax. If this exemption is not possible because no interest is received at the end of the interest period, the loss is carried forward to be taken into account as a payment in calculating the accrued income profits or losses in the next interest period. [*ITA 2007, ss 637, 679*].

Income on which tax is chargeable under these provisions is charged at the rate of tax applicable to savings income — see **1.6** ALLOWANCES AND TAX RATES.

See **49.11** MISCELLANEOUS INCOME for the set-off of miscellaneous losses against accrued income scheme income.

See **2.9** below for the application of the remittance basis to accrued income profits arising as a result of a transfer of foreign securities.

Excluded transferors/transferees

[2.5] The following are excluded from being transferors or transferees under the accrued income scheme. Payments made by or to such persons are ignored. [*ITA 2007, s 638*].

- Persons who account for such transfers in the computation of their trading profits or losses (e.g. financial traders).

- Individuals, personal representatives and trustees of a disabled person's trusts (as defined in *TCGA 1992, Sch 1C para 3*, previously, before 2019/20, *TCGA 1992, Sch 1 para 1(1)*), provided that the nominal value of securities held in the capacity in question does not exceed £5,000 on any day in the tax year in which the interest period ends or in the preceding tax year. Special rules apply to transfers with unrealised interest and transfers of variable rate securities (see *ITA 2007, ss 639(2)–(4), 640(2)–(4), 641(2)–(4)*).
- Persons who are non-resident in the UK throughout the tax year in which the transfer is made, unless trading in the UK through a branch or agency. However, where such a person does so trade in the UK, the accrued income scheme only applies to securities situated in the UK (within the meaning of *TCGA 1992, s 275*) and acquired for use by, or for, the purposes of the branch or agency.
- Charitable trusts (see **2.17** below).
- Pension scheme trustees (see **2.18** below).
- Makers of manufactured payments (see **2.25** below).

Note that no liability to income tax arises in respect of profits from FOTRA securities (see **65.4** SAVINGS AND INVESTMENT INCOME) where the appropriate conditions are met.

[*ITA 2007, ss 638–647; FA 2019, Sch 1 paras 100, 101, 120*].

Example

[2.6]

The following transactions take place between individuals during the year ended 5 April 2021.

Settlement day	Sale by	Purchase by	Securities
14.8.20	X (cum div)	Y	£4,000 6¼% Treasury Loan 2023
17.9.20	X (ex div)	P	£4,000 8% Treasury Loan 2021
4.4.21	S (cum div)	Y	£2,500 4% Treasury Loan 2022

Interest payment days are as follows.

6¼% Treasury Loan 2023	25 May, 25 November
8% Treasury Loan 2021	27 March, 27 September
4% Treasury Loan 2022	7 March, 7 September

Both X and Y owned chargeable securities with a nominal value in excess of £5,000 at some time in either 2019/20 or 2020/21, and both are resident in the UK. P is non-resident in the UK throughout 2020/21. The maximum value of securities held by S at any time in 2020/21 and 2021/22 is £4,000.

14.8.20 transaction

The transaction occurs in the interest period from 26.5.20 to 25.11.20 (inclusive).

Number of days in interest period	184
Number of days in interest period to 14.8.20	81
Interest payable on 25.11.20	£125

The deemed payment is

$$£125 \times \frac{81}{184} = £55$$

X is treated as receiving a payment of £55 on 25.11.20. Assuming no other transfers in this kind of security in the interest period (see 2.2 above), this will also be the figure of accrued income profit chargeable.

Y is treated as making a payment of £55. Assuming no other transfers in this kind of security in the interest period (see 2.2 above), this will also be the figure of accrued income loss to set against the interest of £125 he receives on 25.11.20 £70 remains taxable.

17.9.20 transaction

The transaction occurs in the interest period from 28.3.20 to 27.9.20 (inclusive).

Number of days in interest period	184
Number of days in interest period from 17.9.20	10
Interest payable on 27.9.20	£160

The deemed payment is:

$$£160 \times \frac{10}{184} = £9$$

X is treated as making a payment of £9. Assuming no other transfers in this kind of security in the interest period (see 2.2 above), this will also be the figure of accrued income loss to set against the interest of £160 he receives on 27.9.20. £151 remains taxable.

P is an excluded transferee as he is non-resident in the UK throughout 2020/21.

4.4.21 transaction

The transaction occurs in the interest period from 8.3.21 to 7.9.21 (inclusive).

Number of days in interest period	184
Number of days in interest period to 4.4.21	28
Interest payable on 7.9.21	£50

The deemed payment is:

$$£50 \times \frac{28}{184} = £7$$

S is an excluded transferor as his holdings do not exceed £5,000 at any time in 2020/21 or 2021/22 (the year in which the interest period ends).

Y is treated as making a payment of £7. Assuming no other transfers in this kind of security in the interest period (see **2.2** above), this will also be the figure of accrued income loss to set against the interest of £50 he receives on 7.9.21 so £43 remains taxable.

Special cases

Nominees and trustees

[2.7] Transfers made by or to a nominee, or by or to a trustee of a person or persons absolutely entitled as against the trustee (including persons who would be so entitled if not an infant or under a disability), are treated for accrued income scheme purposes as being made by or to the person on whose behalf the nominee or trustee acts. [*ITA 2007, s 666*].

A person who becomes entitled to securities as trustee immediately after holding them in another capacity is treated as making a transfer within the new legislation. Such a transfer is 'with accrued interest' (see **2.3** above) if the person was entitled to receive any interest payable on the day of transfer where that is also an interest payment day, or in any other case on the next interest payment day. Where the person is not so entitled, the transfer is 'without accrued interest'. [*ITA 2007, ss 651, 623(1)(4), 624(4), 674(4)(5)*].

Trustees' accrued income (i.e. excluding that deemed to be that of a beneficiary, see above) is chargeable at the trust rate (see **70.12** SETTLEMENTS).

Where the trustees of a settlement are treated as making accrued income profits (see **2.4** above), or where they would have been treated as making, or making a greater amount of, accrued income profits if they had been UK resident or domiciled, the SETTLEMENTS (**70**) provisions apply with the effect that the accrued amount is, broadly, treated as income of the settlor where any actual income would be so treated. [*ITA 2007, s 667*].

Interest payable in foreign currency

[2.8] Provision is made for establishing the rate of exchange to be used in converting into sterling certain figures used in calculating accrued income profits.

Deemed payments (see **2.3** above). Where accrued interest is accounted for separately and the parties specify a sterling equivalent themselves, this figure is used. Otherwise a deemed payment is converted at the rate of exchange (the London closing rate) on the settlement day.

Nominal values are converted at the London closing rate for the day in question.

[*ITA 2007, ss 664, 677*].

Foreign securities — application of the remittance basis

[2.9] If, as a result of a transfer of 'foreign securities', accrued income profits are made by an individual to whom the remittance basis applies (i.e. he is within any of **61.2**(1)–(3) REMITTANCE BASIS for the tax year in which the profits are made), those profits are treated as 'relevant foreign income' (as in **32.2** FOREIGN INCOME), with the consequences in **61.4** REMITTANCE BASIS. For this purpose, securities are '*foreign securities*' if income from them would be relevant foreign income.

See **61** REMITTANCE BASIS for the meaning of 'remitted to the UK' etc. For the purpose of applying the provisions in that chapter to a remittance of accrued income profits:

(a) if the individual is the transferor (but subject to (b) below), treat any consideration for the transfer as deriving from the accrued income profits;
(b) if the individual is the transferor and he does not receive consideration equal to (or exceeding) the market value of the securities, treat the securities as deriving from the accrued income profits; and
(c) if the individual is the transferee, treat the securities as deriving from the accrued income profits.

[*ITA 2007, s 670A*].

Foreign securities — delayed remittances

[2.10] A person (or his personal representatives) may claim to reduce accrued income profits by the amount of any payments deemed to be made to him in respect of transfers of a foreign security where the transfer proceeds are unremittable. If the amount of such payments exceeds accrued income profits, those profits are reduced to nil.

Transfer proceeds are unremittable if the person was unable to bring them to the UK, either because of the laws or government action of the territory in question or because of the impossibility of obtaining transferable foreign currency there.

The claim must be made no later than four years after the tax year in which the profits would have been chargeable.

Such reductions in accrued income profits are brought back into account in the chargeable period in which the transfer proceeds cease to be unremittable.

[*ITA 2007, ss 668–670*].

Death

[2.11] Death is *not* treated as giving rise to a transfer to the personal representatives (see **2.2** above). Where a transfer by the personal representatives to a legatee takes place in the interest period in which the death occurs, the transfer is disregarded for the purposes of the current provisions. [*ITA 2007, s 636*].

Trading stock — appropriations etc

[2.12] A transfer is deemed to be made under these provisions where a person appropriates to trading stock securities previously held as investments, and vice versa. Such a transfer is 'with accrued interest' (see **2.3** above) if the person was entitled to receive any interest payable on the day of transfer where that is also an interest payment day, or in any other case on the next interest payment day. Where the person is not so entitled, the transfer is 'without accrued interest'. [*ITA 2007, ss 650, 623(1)(4), 624(4), 674(4)(5)*].

Conversions

[2.13] On a conversion of securities within *TCGA 1992, s 132*, the person entitled to them immediately before the conversion is treated as transferring them on the day of the conversion (if there is no actual transfer). The transfer is 'with accrued interest' (see **2.3** above) if the person was entitled to receive any interest payable on the day of conversion or on the next interest payment day thereafter. Where the person is not so entitled, the transfer is 'without accrued interest'. The 'interest period' (see **2.2** above) in which the conversion is made is treated as ending on the day on which it would have ended but for the conversion. [*ITA 2007, ss 620(1)(b),(7), 623(3)(4), 624(3)(4), 673(4), 674(4)(5)*].

Transfer of unrealised interest (bearer securities)

[2.14] Provision is made to ensure that accrued interest which has already become payable before the settlement day (e.g. on bearer securities) does not escape the accrued income scheme. The transferor is treated as receiving a payment equal to the unrealised interest. However, the transferee is not deemed to have made any payment and is not taxed when he actually receives the interest. Where, exceptionally, the settlement day falls after the last or only interest period of the securities, the transferor is treated as making accrued income profits equal to the unrealised interest and arising in the tax year which contains the settlement day.

The exceptions at **2.5** above apply to a charge so arising on the transferor and to the relief arising to the transferee. The capital gains tax calculation of the gain on the disposal by the transferor is adjusted to exclude the accrued interest from the consideration received and the transferee's base cost is similarly reduced by the amount of the relief obtained as above. Where necessary, the unrealised interest is converted into sterling at the London closing rate of exchange on the settlement day. Where the transfer of securities is a *Pt 5* transfer under *Proceeds of Crime Act 2002* (as in **9.2**(x) CAPITAL ALLOWANCES) and no compensating payment is made to the transferor, these provisions do not apply. [*ITA 2007, ss 617(3), 625, 630, 631, 634, 664(5), 681; TCGA 1992, s 119(4)(5); Proceeds of Crime Act 2002, Sch 10 paras 4, 10*]. See also **2.16** below where there is a default in interest payments.

Variable rate bonds

[2.15] Special rules apply to the transfer of securities unless either:

(a) they carry interest from issue to redemption at one, and only one, of the following rates:
   (i) a constant fixed rate (see *Cadbury Schweppes plc and another v Williams* CA 2006, [2007] STC 106); or

(ii) a rate fixed in relation to a standard published base rate or the retail prices index (or foreign equivalent), or

(b) they were deep discount securities (prior to their abolition from 6 April 1996) for which the rate of interest for each interest period did not exceed the yield to maturity.

Where an interest rate change may arise solely from provision for actions required to effect a '*euroconversion*' of a security, i.e. a change from the currency of a State which has adopted the euro into euros, this does not of itself bring the security concerned within these provisions (see *SI 1998 No 3177, Regs 3, 33*).

Where securities not within (a) or (b) above are transferred at any time between issue and redemption, then:

(1) there is a deemed payment to the transferor;
(2) the deemed payment is equal to such amount (if any) as is just and reasonable; and
(3) no one is treated as making the payment, so there is no deemed payment in calculating the transferee's accrued income profit/loss (see **2.4** above).

The redemption of variable rate securities is itself a transfer for the purposes of the accrued income scheme if there has been a previous transfer.

Where the settlement day in relation to a transfer falls after the end of the only or last interest period in relation to the securities the transferor is treated as making accrued income profits of a just and reasonable amount. Such profits are treated as made in the tax year in which the settlement day falls.

[*ITA 2007, ss 617(3), 620(1)(c), 627, 630, 631*].

Interest in default

[2.16] Where there has been a failure to pay interest on the securities, deemed payments under the accrued income scheme on transfer are calculated by reference to the value of the right to receive the interest on the interest payment day in question rather than the full amount of the interest payable. The provisions regarding transfers of unrealised interest (see **2.14** above) similarly apply by reference to the value of the right to receive the interest (if less than the amount of the unrealised interest). Any unrealised interest subsequently received by the transferee is exempt in so far as it does not exceed the value of the right to receive the interest at the time of purchase. If he transfers the securities with the unrealised interest, the accrued income profit is restricted to any increase in the value of the right to receive the interest between purchase and re-sale. Special rules apply where unrealised interest is partially repaid and where part of a holding of securities is transferred. [*ITA 2007, ss 659, 660, 661, 681; TCGA 1992, s 119(5)*]. For the application of these provisions in practice, see HMRC Savings and Investment Manual SAIM4290, 4300.

Charities

[2.17] Charities are excluded from the accrued income scheme if any interest actually received would be exempt under **14.5** CHARITIES AND CHARITABLE GIVING, but where securities cease to be subject to charitable trusts the trustees are treated for the purposes of the legislation as making a transfer at that time. Such a transfer is 'with accrued interest' (see **2.3** above) if the trustees were entitled to receive any interest payable on the day of transfer or on the next interest payment day thereafter. Where the trustees were not so entitled, the transfer is 'without accrued interest'. [*ITA 2007, ss 623(3)(4), 624(3)(4), 645, 652*].

Retirement schemes

[2.18] Transfers to or by pension funds are excluded from the accrued income scheme as regards the pension fund if any interest received would be exempt under *FA 2004, s 186*. [*ITA 2007, s 646*].

Sale and repurchase of securities

[2.19] On a sale and repurchase of securities the accrued income scheme provisions are disapplied to both transfers. A sale and repurchase of securities involves an agreement (or agreements entered into under the same arrangement) for securities to be sold and the transferor, or a person connected with him (within **19** CONNECTED PERSONS) to buy them, or similar securities, back. The repurchase may be triggered by an obligation to purchase, or the exercise of an option (put or call) under the agreement or a related agreement. However, if the sale and repurchase rules are themselves disapplied because the agreements are not arm's length or the interim holder assumes the risks and benefits of ownership, then the accrued income scheme provisions will apply.

Securities are 'similar' for this purpose if they entitle the holder to the same rights against the same persons as to capital and interest, and to the same enforcement remedies, and where securities are converted from the currency of a State which has adopted the euro into euros (a '*euroconversion*'), the new securities are treated as 'similar' (see *SI 1998 No 3177, Regs 3, 14*).

[*ITA 2007, ss 654, 655*].

The Treasury has broad powers to make regulations providing for the above provisions to apply with modifications (including exceptions and omissions) in relation to cases involving non-standard arrangements. These include any arrangement for the sale and repurchase of securities where the obligation to repurchase is not performed, or the repurchase option not exercised, or where provision is made by or under any agreement:

(a) for different or additional securities to be treated as, or included with, securities which, for the purposes of the repurchase, are to represent securities transferred in pursuance of the original sale; or
(b) for any securities to be treated as not included with securities which, for repurchase purposes, are to represent securities transferred in pursuance of the original sale; or
(c) for the sale or repurchase price to be determined or varied wholly or partly by reference to fluctuations, in the period from the making of the agreement for the original sale, in the value of securities transferred in pursuance of that sale, or in the value of securities treated as representing those securities; or

(d) for any person to be required, where there are such fluctuations, to make any payment in the course of that period and before the repurchase price becomes due.

Regulations may also make such modifications in relation to cases where corresponding arrangements are made by an agreement, or by related agreements, in relation to securities which are to be redeemed in the period after their sale, those arrangements being such that the vendor (or a person connected with him), instead of being required to repurchase the securities or acquiring an option to do so, is granted rights in respect of the benefits that will accrue from their redemption.

[*ITA 2007, ss 656–658*].

Gilt strips

[2.20] Where a person exchanges a gilt-edged security for strips of that security, that person is deemed to have transferred the security with accrued interest (unless the exchange is after the balance has been struck for a dividend on the security but before the day the dividend becomes payable), without any person being treated as the transferee for the purposes of the deemed payment provisions (see 2.3 above), and without affecting the end of the interest period in which the exchange takes place. Similarly where strips are reconstituted by any person into the security from which they derived, the security is deemed to have been transferred to that person with accrued interest (unless the reconstitution is after the balance has been struck for a dividend on the security but before the day the dividend becomes payable) without any person being treated as the transferor. [*ITA 2007, ss 648, 673(4)(5)*].

Stock lending

[2.21] The accrued income scheme provisions are specifically disapplied in relation to stock lending transactions disregarded for chargeable gains purposes under *TCGA 1992, s 263B(2)*. [*ITA 2007, s 653*].

New issues

[2.22] Where:

(a) securities of a particular kind are issued (being the original issue of securities of that kind),
(b) new securities of the same kind are issued subsequently,
(c) a sum (the 'extra return') is payable by the issuer in respect of the new securities, to reflect the fact that interest is accruing on the old securities and calculated accordingly, and
(d) the issue price of the new securities includes an element (separately identified or not) representing payment for the extra return,

then, for the purposes of the accrued income scheme:

(i) the new securities are treated as transferred *to* the person to whom they are issued, but are not treated as transferred *by* any person; and

(ii) the transfer is treated as being 'with accrued interest' (see **2.3** above) and as made on the actual day of issue of the new securities (the 'new issue day'), that day being treated as the settlement day (notwithstanding *ITA 2007, s 674* — see **2.2** above).

These rules do not apply if the new securities are variable rate securities (see **2.15** above).

If the new securities are issued under an arrangement whereby the 'extra return' (see (c) above) is accounted for separately to the issuer by the person to whom the securities are issued, the deemed payment (see **2.3** above) is equal to the extra return so accounted for. If there is no such separate accounting, the deemed payment by the transferee is a proportion of the interest payable on the new securities on the first 'interest payment day' (see **2.2** above) after the new issue day (subject, however, to the rules on interest in default: see **2.16** above). This is the proportion that the number of days in the period from the last interest payment day prior to the new issue (or, if there is no such day, the day on which the original securities were issued) to the new issue day (the 'relevant period') bears to the number of days from the beginning of the relevant period to the first interest payment day after the new issue day.

For foreign currency securities, the deemed payment is the sterling equivalent calculated by reference to the London closing rate of exchange on the settlement day.

[*ITA 2007, ss 649, 662, 664*].

Interaction with capital gains tax

[2.23] Adjustments are necessary to capital gains tax computations where the accrued income scheme applies. The consideration for the disposal is adjusted to exclude or add the deemed payments as appropriate (see **2.3** above) and the sums allowed as a deduction to the transferee on a future disposal are correspondingly adjusted. [*TCGA 1992, s 119(1)–(3)*]. Where there is a CGT disposal which is not a transfer (see **2.2** above) for accrued income scheme purposes but which would give rise to deemed payments if it were such a transfer, a transfer is deemed to be made on the day of the disposal and the capital gains tax consideration and sums deductible are adjusted accordingly as above. [*TCGA 1992, s 119(6)–(9)*]. Where there is a conversion of securities within *TCGA 1992, s 132* or an exchange not involving a disposal within *TCGA 1992, Pt IV, Ch II* (reorganisations etc.) a capital gains tax adjustment is made to allow for the effect of the accrued income scheme. Any payment which the transferor is treated as receiving (see **2.3** above) is first treated as reducing any consideration receivable on the conversion etc., and then to the extent it exceeds any consideration receivable it is treated as consideration given for the conversion etc., while any deemed payment by the transferor is treated as consideration received for the conversion etc. [*TCGA 1992, s 119(10)(11)*].

Double tax relief

[2.24] Where a person is treated as making accrued income profits (see **2.4** above) and any interest actually received would be liable both to UK tax and to foreign tax, he is allowed unilateral credit (see **27.6** DOUBLE TAX RELIEF) against the UK tax on accrued income profits. The credit is for foreign tax at the rate at which such tax would be payable on interest on the securities.

Where a person is entitled to a credit for foreign tax against UK tax on interest treated as reduced under the accrued income scheme (see **2.4** above), the credit is also reduced. It is reduced to the same proportion that the interest actually taxable bears to the interest which would have been taxable without the reduction. There is a similar reduction where double tax relief is allowed by way of deduction of the foreign tax from the interest received (see **27.10**(a)(iii) DOUBLE TAX RELIEF).

[*TIOPA 2010, ss 10, 39, 112(1)(2)*].

Anti-avoidance

[2.25] Certain anti-avoidance measures are affected by the accrued income scheme legislation.

Transfer of assets abroad

Where a non-UK resident or non-UK domiciled person would have been treated as making accrued income profits (see **2.4** above) if he had been so resident or domiciled, the accrued income profits which he would have been treated as making are treated as income becoming payable to him for the purposes of *ITA 2007, Pt 13 Ch 2* (transfer of assets abroad). A corresponding reduction in interest payable for these purposes is made where an exemption arises under the accrued income scheme (see **2.4** above). See **4.14–4.18** ANTI-AVOIDANCE. [*ITA 2007, s 747*].

Other matters

The provisions relating to manufactured payments (see **4.13** ANTI-AVOIDANCE) take precedence over the accrued income scheme, which does not apply to the extent that the transfer is covered by those provisions. [*ITA 2007, ss 647, 663*]. See HMRC Savings and Investment Manual SAIM4220.

3

Alternative Finance Arrangements

Introduction to alternative finance arrangements

[3.1] The legislation described below provides for the taxation of certain finance arrangements (known as '*alternative finance arrangements*') that do not involve the receipt or payment of interest. It is intended to provide a tax regime for financial products that are economically equivalent to conventional banking products but which, instead of interest, involve arrangements of the kind described in **3.2–3.8** below. The legislation seeks to ensure that such products are taxed no more or less favourably than equivalent products involving interest. Such products are usually aimed at individuals who wish to adhere to Shari'a law, which prohibits the receipt or payment of interest. Prior to 2005, the tax treatment of such products was in some areas uncertain and in others could produce anomalous results. For example, finance arrangements based on asset sale and purchase might have fallen within the CGT rules, but this in turn could have depended on the nature of the asset; and returns from profit-share arrangements could have been treated as distributions.

The legislation is not restricted to Shari'a-compliant products but applies to any finance arrangement that falls within its terms. It does not change the nature of the financial arrangements, nor does it deem interest to arise where there is none. Instead, it brings certain types of finance arrangements, and the returns from those arrangements, within the pre-existing tax regime for receipts and payments of interest.

The Treasury have power by statutory instrument to designate arrangements further to those in **3.2**, **3.4**, **3.7** and **3.8** below as alternative finance arrangements and to amend pre-existing legislation in response to commercial and other developments. Any newly designated arrangements must equate in substance to a loan, deposit or other transaction that does not involve the payment of interest but achieves a similar effect. [*TIOPA 2010, s 366*]. See, for example, **17.28** COMMUNITY INVESTMENT TAX RELIEF.

For an article on alternative finance arrangements, with particular reference to Shari'a law, see *Taxation Magazine*, 6 October 2005, p 10.

The provisions at **3.2–3.8** below are subject to **3.10** below.

Simon's Taxes. See **A1.3**.

Alternative finance return — purchase and re-sale

[3.2] These provisions apply to arrangements entered into between two persons, X and Y (at least one of whom is a 'financial institution' — see **3.3** below), whereby X buys an asset and sells it, either immediately or in circumstances where both the conditions below are met, to Y for a consideration which is greater than the purchase price and at least part of which is deferred, such that the excess of sale price over purchase price (the '*effective return*') equates, in substance, to the return on an investment of money at interest. The conditions are that X is a 'financial institution' and that the asset was purchased by X for the purpose of entering into any such arrangements.

Where the whole of the sale price is paid on one day, the whole of the effective return is treated as '*alternative finance return*' (i.e. the equivalent of interest) included in the sale price. Where the sale price is to be paid by instalments, each instalment is taken to include alternative finance return equal to an amount of interest that would have been included in the instalment if:

(i) the effective return were interest payable on a loan by X to Y of an amount equal to the purchase price of the asset;
(ii) the instalment were a part repayment of the principal with interest; and
(iii) the loan were made on arm's length terms and accounted for under generally accepted accounting practice (see **75.21** TRADING INCOME).

The alternative finance return is treated for income tax purposes in the hands of X as if it were interest and thus within the charge at **65.2** SAVINGS AND INVESTMENT INCOME. The rules relating to relief for interest payable under *ITA 2007, s 383* (see **42.5** INTEREST PAYABLE) apply as regards Y as if the arrangements involved the making of a loan by X to Y and as if the alternative finance return were the interest on that loan. Insofar as a person is a party to alternative finance arrangements for the purposes of a trade, profession or vocation or of a property business (see **60.2** PROPERTY INCOME), alternative finance return paid by that person is to be treated as an expense of the trade etc. Relief under *ITTOIA 2005, s 58* for incidental costs of obtaining finance (see **75.97** TRADING INCOME) applies as if references to a loan included references to alternative finance arrangements and references to interest included references to alternative finance return. The alternative finance return is excluded in determining the consideration given for the purchase or sale of the asset for any other income tax purpose.

Foreign currency

If the alternative finance return is paid in a currency other than sterling by or to a person other than a company and otherwise than for the purposes of a trade, profession, vocation or property business, then, as regards that person, the alternative finance return is to be calculated in that other currency, and each payment of alternative finance return is to be translated into sterling at a spot rate of exchange for the day on which the payment is made.

[*ITA 2007, ss 564C, 564I, 564J, 564M–564O, 564V(1)*].

Simon's Taxes. See **A1.302, A1.304.**

Meaning of 'financial institution'

[3.3] '*Financial institution*' for the purposes of the alternative finance return provisions means:

- a bank (within *ITA 2007, s 991*) or a wholly-owned subsidiary of a bank;
- a building society (within the meaning of *Building Societies Act 1986*) or a wholly-owned subsidiary of a building society;
- a person authorised by a licence under *Consumer Credit Act 1974, Pt 3* to carry on a consumer credit business or a consumer hire business within the meaning of that Act;
- a person authorised in a non-UK jurisdiction to receive deposits or other repayable funds from the public and to grant credits for its own account;
- an insurance company (as defined);
- a person who is authorised in a jurisdiction outside the UK to carry on a business which consists of effecting or carrying out contracts of insurance or substantially similar business but not an insurance special purpose vehicle (as defined); or
- a bond-issuer within **3.5** below, but only in relation to any bond assets which are rights under purchase and re-sale arrangements (**3.2** above), diminishing shared ownership arrangements (**3.4** below) or profit share agency arrangements (**3.8** below).

[*ITA 2007, s 564B*].

Alternative finance return — diminishing shared ownership

[3.4] These provisions apply to arrangements under which a financial institution (X) (see **3.3** above) acquires a beneficial interest in an asset and another person (Y):

(a) also acquires a beneficial interest in the asset;
(b) is to make a series of payments to X amounting in total to the amount paid by X for its beneficial interest;
(c) is to acquire (in stages or otherwise) X's beneficial interest as a result of those payments;
(d) is to make additional payments to X (whether under a lease or otherwise);
(e) has the exclusive right to occupy or otherwise use the asset; and
(f) is exclusively entitled to any income, profit or gain arising from or attributable to the asset, including, in particular, any increase in its value.

It is immaterial whether or not X acquires its beneficial interest from Y (for example, in a case where there is an initial conveyance of real property to Y followed by a sub-sale from Y to X), whether Y (or some person other than X and Y) has an interest in the asset as well as X and whether or not X has a legal interest in the asset.

The condition in (e) above does not preclude Y's granting an interest or right in the asset to someone else, e.g. he may sub-let the asset; but the person to whom the interest or right is granted cannot be X, a person controlled by X, or a person controlled by a person who also controls X, and the grant must not be required by X or by arrangements to which X is a party. The condition in (f) above does not preclude X's having to bear any loss (or a share of any loss) resulting from a decrease in the asset's value (and the total payments in (b) above may be reduced to reflect any such loss).

Payments made by Y under these arrangements are treated as alternative finance return, except insofar as they are the payments within (b) above or they constitute arrangement fees or legal or other expenses.

In the event that X is within the charge to income tax, the alternative finance return is treated for income tax purposes in his hands as if it were interest and thus within the charge at **65.2** SAVINGS AND INVESTMENT INCOME. Generally, other income tax consequences ensue as they do for alternative finance arrangements involving purchase and resale (see **3.2** above), for example the treatment of alternative finance return as an expense of the payer's trade etc. Although arrangement fees and legal costs etc. are not treated as alternative finance return, relief may be available for these items as incidental costs of obtaining finance (see **75.97** TRADING INCOME). The alternative finance return is excluded in determining the consideration given for the purchase or sale of the asset for any other income tax purpose.

Arrangements within these provisions are not to be treated as a partnership for tax purposes.

[*ITA 2007, ss 564D, 564K, 564M–564O, 564V(2), 564W*].

An example of an arrangement that the above is intended to cover is the Shari'a compliant finance product known as diminishing musharaka. 'Musharaka' denotes a partnership or joint venture, and covers a wide spectrum, including arrangements identical to a normal partnership under which the partners share income or profits from a business or other asset. The above conditions are intended to exclude such arrangements (which are taxed in the same way as a conventional partnership — see **52** PARTNERSHIPS) from the scope of these provisions. (Treasury Explanatory Notes to the 2006 Finance Bill).

Capital allowances

HMRC consider that Y is the person entitled to any plant and machinery capital allowances available in respect of the asset in question — in accordance with the rules at **10.58** CAPITAL ALLOWANCES ON PLANT AND MACHINERY (HMRC Brief 26/07, 21 March 2007).

Simon's Taxes. See **A1.302, A1.304.**

Alternative finance return — investment bond arrangements

[3.5] These provisions apply to arrangements which:

- provide for one person ('the bond-holder') to pay a sum of money ('the capital') to another ('the bond-issuer');
- identify assets (or a class of assets) which the bond-issuer will acquire for the purpose of generating a return ('the bond assets');
- specify the period for which the arrangements are to have effect ('the bond term'),

and under which the bond-issuer undertakes to dispose of the bond assets at the end of the bond term, to make a repayment of capital to the bond-holder during or at the end of the bond term (whether or not in instalments) and to make one or more additional payments to the bond-holder either during or at the end of the bond term, with the total additional payments not exceeding what would be a reasonable commercial return on a loan of the capital.

The provisions apply only if the following further conditions are met:

- under the arrangements the bond-issuer undertakes to arrange for the management of the bond assets with a view to generating income sufficient to make the above payments to the bond-holder;
- the bond is transferable;
- the bond is a listed security on a recognised stock exchange (within *ITA 2007, s 1005* but see also below) or, for 2018/19 onwards, is admitted to trading on a multilateral trading facility (as defined) operated by a recognised stock exchange regulated in the UK, the EEA or Gibraltar; and
- under international accounting standards, the bond falls to be accounted for as a financial liability of the bond-issuer (or would so fall if the bond-issuer applied those standards).

Certain additional stock exchanges are designated as recognised stock exchanges for the above purposes only (Order of the Commissioners of HMRC, 20 July 2007).

See also *ITA 2007, s 564G(2)* which allows for a range of possibilities within the above conditions; for example, the bond may (but need not) be convertible into, or exchangeable for, shares or securities at the end of its term.

Where these provisions apply (and subject to what is said below under 'Discount'), the additional payments are treated as alternative finance return. Generally, the income tax consequences are the same as for alternative finance arrangements involving purchase and resale (see **3.2** above), e.g. the treatment of the alternative finance return as interest.

The following additional consequences ensue for tax purposes:

- the arrangements are treated as securities (and, if appropriate conditions are met, may be corporate bonds for CGT purposes);
- the arrangements are not treated as a unit trust scheme or as an offshore fund;

- the bond-holder is not treated as having a legal or beneficial interest in the bond assets and is not entitled to relief for capital expenditure in connection with the assets;
- the bond-issuer is not treated as a trustee of the bond assets;
- profits accruing to the bond-issuer in connection with the bond assets are profits of the bond-issuer and not of the bond-holder (and do not arise to the bond-issuer in a fiduciary or representative capacity);
- the payments made by the bond-issuer to the bond-holder are not made in a fiduciary or representative capacity;
- the alternative finance return is excluded in determining, for any other income tax purpose, the consideration given for any sale of an asset by one party to the arrangements to the other party.

Discount

If part of the additional payments equates in substance to discount, that part is not treated as alternative finance return for income tax purposes but is taxed under the rules applicable to discounts (see **65.2** and **65.24** *et seq.* SAVINGS AND INVESTMENT INCOME). One consequence of this is that there can be no requirement to deduct tax (as in **23.12** DEDUCTION OF TAX AT SOURCE) from the discount element of the payments.

[*ITA 2007, ss 564G, 564L(3)–(6), 564M–564O, 564R–564U, 564V(3), 1005(2A); FA 2018, s 34(2)(4); SI 2019 No 689, Reg 15(7)*].

The main effect of the above provisions are to apply the rules on alternative finance arrangements to a form of Shari'a compliant investment bond known (in the plural) as sukuk that is similar in economic substance to a debt security (Treasury Explanatory Notes to the 2007 Finance Bill).

Stamp duty land tax, CGT and capital allowances

FA 2009, Sch 61 facilitates the issue of alternative finance investment bonds based on real property. It seeks to ensure that disposals and acquisitions of interests in land in connection with such bonds do not incur liabilities to stamp duty land tax or CGT and that entitlements to plant or machinery capital allowances or structures and buildings allowances are preserved. [*FA 2009, Sch 61; SI 2019 No 1087, Reg 8*].

Simon's Taxes. See **A1.302, A1.304.**

Alternative finance return — profit share return

[3.6] Profit share return (for which see **3.7** and **3.8** below) is a type of alternative finance return and is treated for income tax purposes as if it were interest and thus within the charge at **65.2** SAVINGS AND INVESTMENT INCOME. Where a person is a party to alternative finance arrangements for the purposes of a trade, profession or vocation, or of a property business (see **60.2** PROPERTY INCOME), profit share return paid by that person is to be treated as an expense of the trade etc. Relief under *ITTOIA 2005, s 58* for incidental costs of obtaining finance (see **75.97** TRADING INCOME) applies as if references to a loan included references to alternative finance arrangements and references to interest included references to profit share return. [*ITA 2007, ss 564M–564O*].

Simon's Taxes. See A1.303, A1.304.

Profit share return — deposit arrangements

[3.7] These provisions apply to arrangements under which a person deposits money with a financial institution (see **3.3** above), which is used by that institution, together with other money deposited, with a view to profit. Payments out of that profit are then made or credited to the depositor in proportion to the amount deposited, such that the return equates, in substance, to the return on an investment of money at interest.

Amounts paid or credited as above are profit share return, with tax consequences as in **3.6** above.

[*ITA 2007, ss 564E, 564L(1)*].

Simon's Taxes. See A1.303.

Profit share return — agency arrangements

[3.8] These provisions apply to arrangements under which:

- a person ('the principal') appoints an agent;
- one or both of the principal and agent is a financial institution (see **3.3** above);
- the agent uses money provided by the principal with a view to producing profits;
- the principal is entitled to those profits to a specified extent;
- the agent is entitled to any profits in excess of those to which the principal is entitled (and may also be entitled to be paid a fee by the principal); and
- the payment to the principal of his entitlement to profits equates, in substance, to the return on an investment of money at interest.

Amounts paid or credited in satisfaction of the principal's profit entitlement as above are profit share return, with tax consequences as in **3.6** above. For tax purposes, the agent, and not the principal, is treated as entitled to the profits themselves.

[*ITA 2007, ss 564F, 564L(2), 564X*].

An example of an arrangement that the above is intended to cover is the Shari'a compliant finance product known as wakala (Treasury Explanatory Notes to the 2006 Finance Bill).

Simon's Taxes. See A1.303.

Non-residents

[3.9] Where income arising to a non-UK resident consists of alternative finance return within **3.4**, **3.5** or **3.8** above, neither the other party to the alternative finance arrangements nor any person acting for the non-resident in relation to the arrangements is regarded as the UK representative (within **50.7** NON-RESIDENTS) of the non-resident in relation to the income. [*ITA 2007, s 835J*].

Arrangements not at arm's length

[3.10] The arrangements at **3.2**, **3.4**, **3.5**, **3.7** and **3.8** above are not treated as alternative finance arrangements if:

- they are not entered into at arm's length,
- the transfer pricing rules at **4.19** *et seq.* ANTI-AVOIDANCE require the alternative finance return or profit share return (or amount representing it) to be recomputed on an arm's length basis, and
- the party receiving the return is not subject to income tax or corporation tax, or a corresponding tax under a foreign jurisdiction, on the return.

In any such case, the person paying the return is not entitled to any deduction in respect of it in computing profits for income tax purposes or in calculating net income.

[*ITA 2007, ss 564H, 564Y*].

Simon's Taxes. See A1.304.

4

Anti-Avoidance

Cross-references. See **2** ACCRUED INCOME SCHEME; CAPITAL ALLOWANCES at **9.7, 9.13, 9.23, 9.26, 9.28** for sales between connected persons; CAPITAL ALLOWANCES ON PLANT AND MACHINERY at **10.61, 10.62** for sales between connected persons and **10.62–10.64** re certain leasing arrangements; **25** DISCLOSURE OF TAX AVOIDANCE SCHEMES; **27** DOUBLE TAX RELIEF for amounts taxed abroad; **27.5** DOUBLE TAX RELIEF for wide-ranging anti-avoidance provisions concerning relief under double tax agreements; **42.2** INTEREST PAYABLE for certain interest; **45.9–45.18** LOSSES for restrictions relating to the use of losses in a trade, profession or vocation; **51** OFFSHORE FUNDS; **52.13–52.17** PARTNERSHIPS for restrictions on loss reliefs and interest reliefs due to non-active partners; **52.21** PARTNERSHIPS in relation to certain company partnership arrangements; **52.24, 52.26** PARTNERSHIPS for restrictions on loss reliefs due to, respectively, limited partners and members of limited liability partnerships; **60.27** PROPERTY INCOME for certain transactions in leases; **65.13** SAVINGS AND INVESTMENT INCOME for provisions on company distributions in a winding-up; **70.25–70.35** SETTLEMENTS for provisions treating income of settlements as income of the settlor.

Introduction to anti-avoidance

[4.1] For the general approach of the Courts to transactions entered into solely to avoid or reduce tax liability, leading cases are *Duke of Westminster v CIR* HL 1935, 19 TC 490; *W T Ramsay Ltd v CIR, Eilbeck v Rawling* HL 1981, 54 TC 101; *CIR v Burmah Oil Co Ltd* HL 1981, 54 TC 200 and *Furniss v Dawson (and related appeals)* HL 1984, 55 TC 324. See also *Cairns v MacDiarmid* CA 1982, 56 TC 556; *Ingram v CIR* Ch D, [1985] STC 835; *Craven v White and related appeals* HL 1988, 62 TC 1; *Shepherd v Lyntress Ltd* Ch D 1989, 62 TC 495; *Moodie v CIR and Sinnett* HL 1993, 65 TC 610; *Hatton v CIR* Ch D, [1992] STC 140; *Ensign Tankers (Leasing) Ltd v Stokes* HL 1992, 64 TC 617; *Countess Fitzwilliam and Others v CIR and related appeals* HL, [1993] STC 502; *Pigott v Staines Investment Co Ltd* Ch D 1995, 68 TC 342; *CIR v McGuckian* HL 1997, 69 TC 1; *MacNiven v*

Westmoreland Investments Ltd HL 2001, 73 TC 1; *CIR v Scottish Provident Institution* HL 2004, 76 TC 538 and *Barclays Mercantile Business Finance Ltd v Mawson* HL 2004, 76 TC 446.

The classical interpretation of the constraints upon the Courts in deciding cases involving tax avoidance schemes is summed up in Lord Tomlin's statement in the *Duke of Westminster* case that ' . . . every man is entitled if he can to order his affairs so that the tax attaching . . . is less than it otherwise would be.' The case concerned annual payments made under covenant by a taxpayer to his domestic employees, which were in substance, but not in form, remuneration. The judgment was thus concerned with the tax consequences of a single transaction, but in *Ramsay*, and subsequently in *Furniss v Dawson*, the Courts have set bounds to the ambit within which this principle can be applied in relation to modern sophisticated and increasingly artificial arrangements to avoid tax. *Ramsay* concerned a complex 'circular' avoidance scheme at the end of which the financial position of the parties was little changed, but it was claimed that a large CGT loss had been created. It was held that where a preconceived series of transactions is entered into to avoid tax, and with the clear intention to proceed through all stages to completion once set in motion, the *Duke of Westminster* principle does not compel a consideration of the individual transactions and of the fiscal consequences of such transactions taken in isolation.

The HL opinions in *Furniss v Dawson* are of outstanding importance, and establish, inter alia, that the *Ramsay* principle is not confined to 'circular' devices, and that if a series of transactions is 'preordained', a particular transaction within the series, accepted as genuine, may nevertheless be ignored if it was entered into solely for fiscal reasons and without any commercial purpose other than tax avoidance, even if the series of transactions as a whole has a legitimate commercial purpose.

However, in *Craven v White* the House of Lords indicated that for the *Ramsay* principle to apply all the transactions in a series have to be pre-ordained with such a degree of certainty that, at the time of the earlier transactions, there is no practical likelihood that the transactions would not take place. It is not sufficient that the ultimate transaction is simply of a kind that was envisaged at the time of the earlier transactions.

The inheritance tax case *Fitzwilliam v CIR* appears to further restrict the application of the *Ramsay* principle, in that the HL found for the taxpayer in a case in which all their Lordships agreed that, once the scheme was embarked upon, there was no real possibility that the later transactions would not be proceeded with. There is, however, some suggestion that a decisive factor was that the first step in the transactions took place before the rest of the scheme had been formulated. Again, in the case of *MacNiven v Westmoreland Investments Ltd* it was held that the *Ramsay* principle did not apply where a company loaned money to a subsidiary to enable it to pay up outstanding interest and thus crystallise tax losses. The interest had been paid within the meaning of the legislation and the manner in which the payment was funded was irrelevant.

The HL judgments in *MacNiven v Westmoreland Investments Ltd* and, in particular, *Barclays Mercantile Business Finance Ltd v Mawson*, suggest that the essence of the current approach of the Courts to the *Ramsay* principle is 'to give the statutory provision a purposive construction in order to determine the nature of the transaction to which it was intended to apply and then to decide whether the actual transaction (which might involve considering the overall effect of a number of elements intended to operate together) answered to the statutory description'.

Simon's Taxes. See **A2.115–A2.124.**

Anti-avoidance legislation is intended to counteract transactions designed to avoid taxation, but bona fide transactions may sometimes be caught also. The provisions relating to income tax are detailed below and as further indicated in the cross-references above.

4.9–4.12	Transactions in securities. [*ITA 2007, ss 682–713*].
4.13	Manufactured payments. [*ITA 2007, ss 614ZA–614ZD*].
4.14–4.18	Transfer of assets abroad. [*ITA 2007, ss 714–751*].
4.19–4.28	Transfer pricing. [*TIOPA 2010, ss 146–217*].
4.29	Sales of occupation income. [*ITA 2007, ss 773–789*].
4.30	Transactions in land. [*ITA 2007, ss 752–772* now repealed].
4.31	Land sold and leased back — payments connected with transferred land. [*ITA 2007, ss 681A–681AN*].
4.32	Land sold and leased back — new lease of land after assignment or surrender. [*ITA 2007, ss 681B–681BM*].
4.33	Leased trading assets. [*ITA 2007, ss 681C–681CG*].
4.34	Leased assets — capital sums. [*ITA 2007, ss 681D–681DP*].
4.35	Transfers of income streams. [*ITA 2007, ss 809AZA–809AZF*].
4.36	Disposals of income streams through partnerships. [*ITA 2007, ss 809AAZA, 809AAZB*].
4.37	Disposals of assets through partnerships. [*ITA 2007, ss 809DZA, 809DZB*].
4.38	Disguised investment management fees from investment schemes. [*ITA 2007, ss 809EZA–809EZH*].
4.39	Factoring of income receipts etc. [*ITA 2007, ss 809BZA–809BZS*].
4.40	Loan or credit transactions. [*ITA 2007, ss 809CZA–809CZC*].
4.41	Leases of plant and machinery. [*ITA 2007, ss 809ZA–809ZF*].
4.42	Annual payments for non-taxable consideration etc. [*ITA 2007, ss 843, 904*].
4.43	Benefits from pre-owned assets. [*FA 2004, s 84, Sch 15*].

General anti-abuse rule (GAAR)

The GAAR gives HMRC the power to counteract tax advantages arising from tax arrangements that are abusive. See **4.2** below.

Disclosure of tax avoidance schemes

Legislation imposes a disclosure obligation on promoters of certain tax avoidance schemes and in some cases on persons entering into transactions under such schemes. See **25** DISCLOSURE OF TAX AVOIDANCE SCHEMES.

Follower and accelerated payment notices

HMRC have power to require, by way of a 'follower notice', a person using an avoidance scheme which is defeated in the courts in relation to another taxpayer to concede his position to reflect the court's decision. See **4.44–4.48** below. HMRC also have power to issue an 'accelerated payment notice' which requires a user of an avoidance scheme to pay tax upfront before the success or failure of the scheme has been finally determined. See **4.49–4.52** below.

Serial avoiders regime

This is a regime of warnings and escalating sanctions for taxpayers who persistently engage in tax avoidance schemes that are defeated by HMRC. See **4.53–4.60** below.

Simon's Taxes. See **A2.125**.

General anti-abuse rule (GAAR)

[4.2] The GAAR is intended to counteract tax advantages arising from 'tax arrangements' which are 'abusive'. For official guidance and other information, see www.gov.uk/government/publications/tax-avoidance-general-anti-abuse-rules or, for arrangements entered into before 28 March 2018, www.gov.uk/government/publications/tax-avoidance-previous-guidance-on-general-anti-abuse-rule. Before HMRC can take action under the GAAR, they must generally first refer the case to an independent GAAR Advisory Panel (see **4.3** below). With effect on and after 15 September 2016 and before 22 July 2020, HMRC could, however, make a provisional counteraction under the GAAR before referral to the Panel where, for example, assessing time limits were about to expire (see **4.5** below). On and after 22 July 2020, this system is replaced with protective GAAR notices intended to operate in broadly the same way as normal enquiry notices and to enable HMRC to carry out enquiries beyond the 12-month time limit that they had under the previous system. With effect on and after 15 September 2016, a GAAR Advisory Panel opinion allows HMRC to apply the GAAR to equivalent arrangements used by other taxpayers without further referral (see **4.6**, **4.7** below). See **4.8** below for the 60% penalty which applies to arrangements entered into on or after 15 September 2016 which are counteracted by the GAAR. The GAAR Advisory Panel's published opinion notices are available at www.gov.uk/government/collections/tax-avoidance-general-anti-abuse-rule-gaar.

Arrangements are '*tax arrangements*' if, having regard to all the circumstances, it would be reasonable to conclude that the obtaining of a tax advantage was a main purpose of the arrangements. 'Arrangements' include any agreement, understanding, scheme, transaction or series of transactions, whether or not legally enforceable. A 'tax advantage' includes relief or increased relief from tax, repayment or increased repayment of tax, avoidance or reduction of a tax charge or tax assessment, avoidance of a possible tax assessment, deferral of a payment of tax or advancement of a repayment of tax, and avoidance of an obligation to deduct or account for tax.

Tax arrangements are '*abusive*' if entering into them or carrying them out cannot reasonably be regarded as a reasonable course of action in relation to the relevant tax provisions. Regard must be had to all the circumstances including (but not limited to):

- whether the substantive results of the arrangements are consistent with any principles on which those tax provisions are based (whether express or implied) and the policy objectives of those tax provisions;
- whether the means of achieving those results involves one or more contrived or abnormal steps; and
- whether the arrangements are intended to exploit any shortcomings in those tax provisions.

Where the tax arrangements form part of other arrangements, regard must be had also to those other arrangements. However, where those other arrangements were entered into before 17 July 2013, when the GAAR was introduced, they are to be ignored, unless their being taken into account would assist the taxpayer in that the tax arrangements would no longer be abusive.

The legislation provides the following *non-exhaustive* list of things that might indicate that tax arrangements are abusive:

- the arrangements result in an amount of income, profits or gains for tax purposes that is significantly less than the amount for economic purposes,
- the arrangements result in deductions or losses of an amount for tax purposes that is significantly greater than the amount for economic purposes,
- the arrangements result in a claim for the repayment or crediting of tax (including foreign tax) that has not been, and is unlikely to be, paid,

but, in each case, only if it is reasonable to assume that the result was not anticipated when the relevant tax provisions were enacted.

The fact that tax arrangements accord with established practice, and HMRC had, at the time the arrangements were entered into, indicated their acceptance of that practice, might (not does) indicate that the arrangements are not abusive.

Counteraction

If tax arrangements are abusive, the tax advantages that would otherwise arise are to be counteracted under *FA 2013, s 209* by the making of such adjustments as are just and reasonable. In particular, the adjustments may impose as well as increase a liability to tax. The adjustments may be made in respect of the tax in question or any other tax to which the GAAR applies (such taxes being listed by *FA 2013, s 206(3)*). For example, an abusive arrangement may attempt to reduce or eliminate a charge to capital gains tax, but the counteraction may involve an adjustment to income tax. The adjustments required to be made (whether by HMRC or the taxpayer) may be made by way of an assessment, the modification of an assessment, amendment or disallowance of a claim, or otherwise. They have effect for all purposes.

No adjustments could be made before **22 July 2020** by an officer of HMRC under *FA 2013, s 209* unless the procedural requirements at **4.3–4.7** below had been complied with. Adjustments can be made earlier by an officer on or after that date but the effect of the adjustments is suspended until those procedural requirements have been complied with. The power to make such adjustments is subject to any time limits imposed elsewhere in the tax legislation. On and after 22 July 2020, these two rules must be read in conjunction with **4.4** below (protective GAAR notices and substantive notices), and have no effect on any adjustments made otherwise than by virtue of *section 209*.

For arrangements entered into on or after 15 September 2016, where a matter is referred to the GAAR Advisory Panel (see **4.3**(4) or (6) below), the taxpayer cannot make any adjustments to counteract the tax advantage himself in the '*closed period*' beginning with the 31st day after the end of the 45-day period for making representations (see **4.3**(2) below) and ending immediately before the day on which the person is given notice of HMRC's final decision after considering the opinion of the Panel. Similarly a person cannot make any such adjustments in the closed period following the issue of a pooling notice or notice of binding (see **4.6** below). For this purpose, the 'closed period' is as defined at **4.6**.

Proceedings before court or tribunal

In any proceedings before a court or tribunal in connection with the GAAR, HMRC must show both that there are tax arrangements that are abusive and that the adjustments made to counteract the resulting tax advantages are just and reasonable.

In determining any issue in connection with the GAAR, a court or tribunal *must* take into account:

- HMRC's guidance on the GAAR that was approved by the GAAR Advisory Panel (see **4.3** below) at the time the tax arrangements were entered into; and
- any relevant opinion of the GAAR Advisory Panel (see **4.3**(9), **4.6** and **4.7** below).

A court or tribunal *may* take into account:

- guidance, statements or other material (whether of HMRC, a Government minister or anyone else) that was in the public domain at the time the arrangements were entered into; and
- evidence of established practice at that time.

Consequential relieving adjustments

Where the counteraction of a tax advantage is 'final', a person has twelve months, beginning with the day on which the counteraction becomes final, to make a claim for one or more consequential adjustments to be made in respect of any tax to which the GAAR applies. On a claim, an officer of HMRC must make such of the claimed adjustments (if any) as are just and reasonable. Consequential adjustments may be made in respect of any period and may affect any person (whether or not a party to the tax arrangements). However, an officer is not required or permitted to make a consequential adjustment the effect of which is to increase a person's liability to any tax.

Where an officer makes a consequential adjustment, he must give the claimant written notice describing the adjustment. Adjustments may be made by way of an assessment, the modification of an assessment, the amendment of a claim, or otherwise; they can be made notwithstanding any time limit imposed by or under any enactment outside these provisions.

For these purposes, the counteraction of a tax advantage is '*final*' when the adjustments made to effect the counteraction, and any amounts arising as a result of those adjustments, can no longer be varied, on appeal or otherwise.

There is no requirement that a claim for consequential adjustments be included in a tax return. If the claim relates to income tax, *TMA 1970, Sch 1A* applies to it (claims outside returns — see **16.3** CLAIMS).

Miscellaneous

Any 'priority rule' has effect subject to the GAAR (notwithstanding the terms of the priority rule). A '*priority rule*' means a rule (however expressed) to the effect that particular tax provisions have effect to the exclusion of, or otherwise in priority to, anything else.

[*FA 2013, ss 206–212A, 214, 215; TMA 1970, s 42(3ZC); FA 2016, ss 157(4)–(9), 158(4)(15); FA 2020, Sch 14 paras 2, 10, 15*].

Procedural requirements

[4.3] Except where a provisional counteraction notice is issued as in **4.5** below, the following procedure must be followed before HMRC can make an adjustment under the GAAR.

(1) An HMRC officer designated by the Commissioners for HMRC for the purpose of the GAAR must give the taxpayer a written notice specifying:
- the arrangements and the tax advantage;
- why the officer considers that a tax advantage has arisen from abusive tax arrangements;
- the counteraction which the officer considers should be taken;
- the period within which the taxpayer can make representations (see (2) below); and
- the effect of the rules in (3)–(5) below and of the penalty at **4.8** below that may apply if the proposed counteraction takes effect.

The notice may set out steps that the taxpayer may take to avoid the application of the GAAR.

Where the notice is given on or after 22 July 2020, specifies particular adjustments in respect of a particular period or matter and is given within, broadly, the ordinary assessing time limit applicable to those adjustments, the notice has similar effect to a protective GAAR notice (in addition to its primary function). See **4.4** below under Substantive notices.

(2) The taxpayer has 45 days starting with the day on which HMRC's notice is given to send written representations in response to the notice to the designated HMRC officer. The designated officer may extend the period if the taxpayer makes a written request.

(3) For arrangements entered into on or after 15 September 2016, where a person who has been given a notice under (1) above takes 'corrective action' before the beginning of the closed period (see **4.2** above under Counteraction), the matter is not referred to the GAAR Advisory Panel under (4) or (6) below. A person takes '*corrective action*' for this purpose only if he amends a return or claim to counteract the tax advantage or relinquishes the tax advantage by entering into a written agreement with HMRC to determine an appeal. A person can amend a return or claim for this purpose during an enquiry even if the normal time limits have expired. No appeal may then be made against any enquiry closure notice (see **64.8** RETURNS) to the extent that it takes into account an amendment made as corrective action. The person must notify HMRC of the action taken and the additional tax amount which has or will become due. Where a person takes corrective action in this way no penalty can be charged under **4.8** below.

(4) If the taxpayer makes no representations and, where relevant, does not take corrective action, a designated HMRC officer must refer the matter to the GAAR Advisory Panel. This is a panel established by the Commissioners for HMRC for the purposes of the GAAR; its role is to approve HMRC's guidance on the GAAR and to provide opinions on cases to which HMRC considers the GAAR to apply.

The officer must at the same time notify the taxpayer that the matter is being referred. The notice must inform the taxpayer of the period for making representations under (6) below and of the requirement to send any such representations to the officer. The officer must provide the Panel with a copy of the notice given to the taxpayer at step (1) above and the notice informing the taxpayer that the matter has been referred to the Panel.

(5) If the taxpayer does make representations but, where relevant, does not take corrective action, the representations must be considered by a designated HMRC officer.

(6) If the designated HMRC officer in (5) above still considers that the GAAR should apply, he must refer the matter to the GAAR Advisory Panel, together with a copy of the taxpayer's representations and any comments he has on those representations. With effect from 15 September 2016 the officer must notify the taxpayer of his decision on whether or not to refer the matter to the GAAR Advisory Panel as soon as is reasonably practicable.

The same requirements for the officer to notify the taxpayer and to provide information to the Panel apply as at step (4) above. The notice to the taxpayer must, however, also include a copy of any comments on the taxpayer's representations sent by the officer to the Panel.

(7) The taxpayer has 21 days to send written representations to the Panel and the designated HMRC officer about the notice given at step (1) above and any comments made by HMRC on the taxpayer's original representations. The Panel may extend the period for making representations if the taxpayer makes a written request.

(8) If the taxpayer makes representations at step (7) above but did not make representations at step (2) above, the designated HMRC officer may provide the Panel and the taxpayer with comments on the step (7) representations.

(9) A sub-panel of three members of the Panel will consider the matter in question. The sub-panel may invite the taxpayer or the designated HMRC officer to supply further information within a specified period. Information supplied to the sub-panel must also be sent to the other party.

The sub-panel must produce an opinion notice stating its collective opinion as to whether or not the entering into and carrying out of the tax arrangements was a reasonable course of action in relation to the relevant tax provisions, having regard to the circumstances outlined at **4.2** above. An opinion notice may indicate that the sub-panel considers that it is not possible to reach a view on the information available. Alternatively, the sub-panel may produce two or three opinion notices which, taken together, state the opinions of all the members. An opinion notice must include the reasons for the opinion and is given to both the designated HMRC officer and the taxpayer.

The GAAR Advisory Panel's published opinion notices are available at www.gov.uk/government/collections/tax-avoidance-general-anti-abuse-rule-gaar.

(10) The designated HMRC officer must, having considered the sub-panel's opinion or opinions, give the taxpayer a written notice (a '*final counteraction notice*') setting out whether or not the tax advantage under the arrangements is to be counteracted under the GAAR. It should be noted that HMRC are not bound by the decision of the sub-panel and may proceed with the application of the GAAR even if the sub-panel's opinion is that the GAAR ought not to apply.

If the GAAR is to apply, the counteraction notice must specify the adjustments required and any steps that the taxpayer must take to give effect to them.

HMRC are not required to know for certain that a tax advantage has arisen before they embark on this procedure. A designated HMRC officer may carry out the above steps where he considers that a tax advantage might have arisen to the taxpayer. Any notice he gives may be expressed to be given on the assumption that a tax advantage arises.

[*FA 2013, Sch 43; FA 2016, s 157(11)(30), s 158(8)(9)(15)*].

Protective GAAR notices and substantive notices

Protective GAAR notices

[4.4] A protective GAAR notice can be given on or after **22 July 2020**, regardless of when the tax arrangements in question were entered into. However, no such notice may be given in relation to any adjustments under the GAAR if a provisional counteraction notice (see **4.5** below) had given before that date in respect of those adjustments. These notices are intended to operate in broadly the same way as normal enquiry notices and will enable HMRC to carry out enquiries beyond the twelve-month time limit that they had under the previous system of provisional counteraction notices (see **4.5** below and the technical note at www.gov.uk/government/publications/technical-note-for-general-anti-abuse-rule-amendments-announced-at-budget-2018). A protective GAAR notice will have to be given within the normal assessing time limit, but once it has been given there will no longer be a deadline for HMRC to complete their enquiries.

An officer of HMRC can give a written notice (a '*protective GAAR notice*') to a person stating that the officer considers that a tax advantage may have arisen to the person from tax arrangements that are abusive and that, if that is the case, it ought to be counteracted. The notice must specify (i) the tax arrangements and the tax advantage, and (ii) the adjustments that the officer proposes be made.

The notice must normally be given within the ordinary assessing time limit applicable to the proposed adjustments; this means the time limit imposed by any tax legislation (other than on the GAAR) for the making of the adjustments in question. If, however, a 'tax enquiry' is 'in progress' into a return, and the return relates to the tax in respect of which the adjustments are to be made, the notice must instead be given no later than the time the enquiry is completed. References to a '*tax enquiry*' and to its being '*in progress*' have the same meaning as in **4.44** below.

Notice of appeal may be given, not against the protective GAAR notice itself but against the adjustments specified therein (whether or not the adjustments are also made otherwise than by virtue of *FA 2013, s 209*). Any appeal against the specified adjustments (whether or not those adjustments are made by virtue of *section 209*) is automatically stayed (i.e. put on hold) for a period beginning with the day on which the protective GAAR notice is given and ending 12 months afterwards (or, if earlier, on the day a final GAAR counteraction notice is given).

Effect of protective GAAR notice and of adjustments

The adjustments specified in the protective GAAR notice have effect as if they are made by virtue of *FA 2013, s 209* at **4.2** above.

If:

- notice of appeal is not given against the adjustments, or if it is given but the appeal is subsequently withdrawn or determined by agreement; and
- no 'final GAAR counteraction notice' is given,

the protective GAAR notice has effect for all purposes (other than to enable a penalty to be levied as in **4.8** below) as if it had been given as a final GAAR counteraction notice (and, accordingly, as if the 'GAAR procedural requirements' had been complied with).

In any other case, the adjustments in question have no effect (so far as they are made by virtue of *FA 2013, s 209*) unless they (or 'lesser adjustments') are subsequently specified in a final GAAR counteraction notice. By virtue of the protective GAAR notice having been given, that final GAAR counteraction notice is treated as meeting the time limit requirements in *section 209* (see **4.2** above) for the making of the adjustments. '*Lesser adjustments*' means adjustments specified in the final GAAR counteraction notice which assume a smaller tax advantage than was assumed in the protective GAAR notice.

For the above purposes, a '*final GAAR counteraction notice*' has the meaning given in **4.3**(10) above, **4.6** below and **4.7** below. '*GAAR procedural requirements*' means the procedural requirements at **4.3**, **4.6** or **4.7**.

[*FA 2013, ss 209AA, 209AC; FA 2020, Sch 14 paras 3, 5, 11, 15*].

Substantive notices

The provisions described below have effect in relation to 'substantive notices' given on or after **22 July 2020** (whenever the tax arrangements in question were entered into). These provisions are similar to those above in that they impose a system broadly resembling ordinary tax enquiries except that they do not involve the issue of a protective GAAR notice (as the substantive notice should itself sufficiently alert the person that an HMRC officer believes the GAAR to be in point). The other main difference is that an appeal against the specified adjustments is not stayed. The term '*substantive notice*' is used here to refer to a notice of proposed counteraction (as in **4.3**(1) above) or a pooling notice or notice of binding (both as in **4.6** below).

The provisions apply where:

- a person is given a substantive notice that specifies particular adjustments in respect of a particular period or matter;
- the notice is given within the 'relevant time limit' applicable to the adjustments in question; and
- the adjustments in question have not previously been specified in a provisional counteraction notice (as in **4.5** below) or a protective GAAR notice (as above).

The '*relevant time limit*' generally means the ordinary assessing time limit applicable to the adjustments in question; this means the time limit imposed by any tax legislation (other than on the GAAR) for the making of those adjustments. If, however, a 'tax enquiry' is 'in progress' into a return made by the person concerned, and the adjustments relate to that return, the relevant time limit is instead the time the enquiry is completed. References to a '*tax enquiry*' and to its being '*in progress*' have the same meaning as in **4.44** below.

The effect of the provisions is the same as that described above under Effect of protective GAAR notice and of adjustments, substituting a reference to the substantive notice for each reference there to the protective GAAR notice.

[*FA 2013, ss 209AB, 209AC; FA 2020, Sch 14 paras 4, 5, 12, 15*].

Provisional counteraction notices

[4.5] The following provisions took effect on 15 September 2016, regardless of when the tax arrangements in question were entered into. The provisions are **repealed** with effect on and after **22 July 2020**, but not so as to affect their operation in relation to provisional counteraction notices given before that date. The system of provisional counteraction notices is replaced by protective GAAR notices as in **4.4** above.

Prior to the above-mentioned repeal, an HMRC officer could issue a provisional counteraction notice under the GAAR. Such a notice would, for example, be issued to protect against loss of tax where an assessing time limit was about to expire. A notice had to:

- specify adjustments (as in **4.2** above) which the HMRC officer reasonably believes may be required to counteract a tax advantage that would arise to the recipient from tax arrangements;
- detail the arrangements and tax advantage concerned; and
- explain the appeals procedure and the circumstances in which the notice may be cancelled.

Adjustments specified in a provisional counteraction notice which are made by HMRC are treated as effecting a valid counteraction of the tax advantage under the GAAR. The taxpayer may appeal against adjustments, stating the grounds of appeal, within the 30 days beginning with the date he receives the notice. If the taxpayer appeals, the adjustments are treated as cancelled after 12 months from the date on which the provisional counteraction notice is given, unless, before that time (and whether before or after the issue of the provisional counteraction notice), an HMRC officer gives a notice to the taxpayer:

(1) cancelling the adjustments or withdrawing the notice (without cancelling the adjustments);
(2) issuing a notice within **4.3**(1) above in respect of the same arrangements and tax advantage and specifying the same or lesser adjustments as the counteraction which should be taken;
(3) issuing a pooling notice or notice of binding (see **4.6** below) in respect of the same arrangements and tax advantage and specifying the same or lesser adjustments as the counteraction which should be taken; or
(4) issuing a generic referral notice (see **4.7** below) in respect of the same arrangements and tax advantage and specifying the same or lesser adjustments as the counteraction which should be taken.

Where a notice within (2)–(4) above specifies lesser adjustments, the provisional counteraction notice must be amended accordingly (unless it was issued after the notice in (2)–(4) above).

If a notice within (2) above is given and the matter is not referred to the GAAR Advisory Panel or if a notice within (2)–(4) above is given and subsequently the taxpayer is given a notice stating that the tax advantage is not to be counteracted under the GAAR, the adjustments in the provisional counteraction notice are treated as cancelled unless HMRC has the power to make the adjustments under provisions other than the GAAR and they state that the adjustments are therefore not cancelled. If a notice within (4) above is withdrawn, the adjustments in the provisional counteraction notice are likewise treated as cancelled, subject to the same exception.

Where a notice within (2)–(4) above is given and subsequently the taxpayer is given a notice stating that the tax advantage is to be counteracted, the adjustments in the provisional counteraction notice are confirmed so far as specified in the notice as adjustments required to give effect to the counteraction and are otherwise treated as cancelled.

[*FA 2013, ss 209A–209F; FA 2016, s 156; FA 2020, Sch 14 paras 6, 13, 15*].

See HMRC factsheets CC/FS34 and CC/FS36 listed at **37.1** HMRC EXPLANATORY PUBLICATIONS.

Counteraction of equivalent arrangements

[4.6] With effect on and after 15 September 2016, regardless of when the tax arrangements were entered into, there are provisions to enable the counteraction of 'equivalent' arrangements entered into by other taxpayers. The provisions enable HMRC to issue a 'pooling notice'

A designated HMRC officer may issue a '*pooling notice*' to a taxpayer (R), where:

(a) a person has been given a notice under **4.3**(1) above in relation to tax arrangements ('*lead arrangements*');
(b) the 45-day period for representations in **4.3**(2) above has expired but no final counteraction notice under **4.3**(10) above or the generic referral provisions at **4.7** below has been given in respect of the matter;
(c) the officer considers that a tax advantage has arisen, or may have arisen, to R from tax arrangements (other than the lead arrangements) which are abusive;
(d) the officer considers that those arrangements are equivalent to the lead arrangements; and
(e) the officer considers that the advantage should be counteracted.

The notice places R's arrangements in a pool comprising all the arrangements in relation to which pooling notices have been served in respect of the same lead arrangements. Before 5 December 2017, the lead arrangements were themselves in the pool along with the equivalent arrangements. A pooling notice may not be given if R has already been given a notice under **4.3**(1) above.

A designated HMRC officer may issue a '*notice of binding*' to a taxpayer (R), where:

(i) a person has been given a final counteraction notice, under either **4.3**(10) above or the generic referral provisions at **4.7** below, in relation to tax arrangements ('*counteracted arrangements*');

(ii) the officer considers that a tax advantage has arisen, or may have arisen, to R from tax arrangements (other than the counteracted arrangements) which are abusive;
(iii) the officer considers that those arrangements are equivalent to the counteracted arrangements; and
(iv) the officer considers that the advantage should be counteracted.

A notice of binding may not be given if R has already been given a pooling notice or a notice under **4.3**(1) above.

A pooling notice or notice of binding must be given by the officer as soon as is reasonably practicable after the officer becomes aware of the relevant facts. The notice must specify the tax arrangements and tax advantage concerned; explain why the officer considers them to be equivalent to the lead arrangements or the counteracted arrangements and why a tax advantage is considered to have arisen from abusive arrangements; set out the counteraction that the officer considers should be taken; and the effects of the notice. It may, but is not required to, set out steps R could take to avoid the proposed counteraction.

Arrangements are '*equivalent*' if they are substantially the same as one another, having regard to their results, the means of achieving those results, and the characteristics on the basis of which it could reasonably be argued in each case that the arrangements are abusive tax arrangements under which a tax advantage has arisen.

Where a person who has been given a pooling notice or a notice of binding takes 'corrective action' before the beginning of the 'closed period', he is treated as not having been given the notice and the arrangements are accordingly no longer in the pool. A person takes '*corrective action*' for this purpose only if he amends a return or claim to counteract the tax advantage or relinquishes the tax advantage by entering into an agreement with HMRC. A person can amend a return or claim for this purpose during an enquiry even if the normal time limits have expired. No appeal may then be made against any enquiry closure notice (see **64.8** RETURNS) to the extent that it takes into account an amendment made as corrective action. The person must notify HMRC of the action taken and the additional tax amount which has or will become due. The '*closed period*' begins on the thirty-first day after the day on which the pooling notice or notice of binding was given. In the case of a pooling notice, the closed period ends immediately before the day on which the person is given notice of HMRC's final decision after considering the opinion of the GAAR Advisory Panel (see below). In the case of a notice of binding, the period is treated as ending at the same time as it begins. Where a person takes corrective action in this way no penalty can be charged under the provisions at **4.8** below.

Before 5 December 2017, if the person mentioned in (a) above took corrective action within the 75-day period beginning with the day on which the notice under **4.3**(1) above was given, the lead arrangements were treated as ceasing to be in the pool. (On and after that date the lead arrangements are not pooled in any case.)

Where, after a pooling notice has been issued to a person, the GAAR Advisory Panel issues an opinion notice (see **4.3**(9) above) in respect of the lead arrangements or another set of arrangements in the pool (the *'referred arrangements'*), the HMRC officer must give the person a *'pooled arrangements opinion notice'* setting out a report of the opinion and the person's right to make representations. Only one such notice may be given to a person about the same arrangements. The taxpayer has 30 days from the date of the notice to make representations that no tax advantage has arisen to him or that his arrangements are materially different from the referred arrangements.

The HMRC officer must consider any opinion of the GAAR Advisory Panel about the referred arrangements, together with any representations made, and issue a written notice with his decision as to whether the tax arrangements under consideration are to be counteracted under the GAAR. If so, the notice must set out the adjustments required to give effect to the counteraction and any steps that the taxpayer must take to give effect to it.

Where a designated HMRC officer gives a notice of binding, he must at the same time give a *'bound arrangements opinion notice'* setting out a report of any opinion of the GAAR Advisory Panel about the counteracted arrangements and the person's right to make representations. The taxpayer has 30 days from the date of the notice to make representations that no tax advantage has arisen to him or that his arrangements are materially different from the counteracted arrangements.

The HMRC officer must then consider any opinion of the GAAR Advisory Panel about the counteracted arrangements, together with any representations made, and issue a written notice (a *'final counteraction notice'*) with his decision as to whether the tax arrangements under consideration are to counteracted under the GAAR. If so, the notice must set out the adjustments required to give effect to the counteraction and any steps that the taxpayer must take to give effect to it.

On and after 5 December 2017, anything that may or must be done by a given designated HMRC officer under the above provisions may be done instead by any other designated HMRC officer.

[*FA 2013, s 209(9), Sch 43A; FA 2016, ss 157(2)(30), 158(4); FA 2020, Sch 14 para 8; SI 2017 No 1090, Regs 1–10*].

Where a pooling notice or notice of binding is given on or after 22 July 2020, specifies particular adjustments in respect of a particular period or matter and is given within, broadly, the ordinary assessing time limit applicable to those adjustments, the notice has similar effect to a protective GAAR notice (in addition to its primary function). See **4.4** above under Substantive notices.

See HMRC factsheets CC/FS35 and CC/FS37 listed at **37.1** HMRC EXPLANATORY PUBLICATIONS.

Generic referral of equivalent arrangements to GAAR Advisory Panel

[4.7] With effect on and after 15 September 2016, regardless of when the tax arrangements were entered into, there are provisions for HMRC to make a generic referral to the GAAR Advisory Panel of arrangements in a pool.

Where:

- (on or after 5 December 2017) further to pooling notices given as in **4.6** above, two or more sets of arrangements are in a pool relating to any lead arrangements, and the person mentioned in **4.6**(a) took corrective action within the 75-day period beginning with the day on which the notice under **4.3**(1) above was given (or within such longer period as that person and HMRC may have agreed); or
- (before 5 December 2017) pooling notices had placed one or more sets of arrangements in a pool with lead arrangements, and those lead arrangements ceased to be in the pool,

then, provided none of the pooled arrangements have been referred to the GAAR Advisory Panel (see **4.3**(4), (6) above), a designated HMRC officer may give to each of the taxpayers whose arrangements are in the pool a notice of a proposal to make a generic referral to the Panel in respect of the arrangements in the pool. The notices must specify the arrangements and the tax advantage and the period within which the taxpayer can make a proposal (see below).

A person who has been given a notice has 30 days beginning with the day the notice was given to propose to HMRC that it should give him a notice under **4.3**(1) above and should not proceed with the generic referral.

If none of the notified taxpayers makes such a proposal within the 30-day period, the HMRC officer must make a referral (a '*generic referral*') to the GAAR Advisory Panel. If at least one of the recipients makes a proposal within the 30-day period, the officer must, after that period ends, decide whether to give one of the taxpayers a notice under **4.3**(1) above or to make a generic referral. On and after 5 December 2017, the officer must make a generic referral if a taxpayer is duly given a notice under **4.3**(1) above but, because of **4.3**(3) above, the matter is not referred to the GAAR Advisory Panel.

Where HMRC make a generic referral to the GAAR Advisory Panel, the designated HMRC officer must provide the Panel with a general statement of the material characteristics of the arrangements together with a declaration that this is applicable to *all* the arrangements and that nothing material to the panel's consideration has been omitted. The general statement must contain a factual description as well as HMRC's opinion, and a copy must be provided to the taxpayers.

A sub-panel of three members of the Panel will consider the referral. The sub-panel must produce an opinion notice stating its collective opinion as to whether or not the entering into and carrying out of the tax arrangements described in the general statement was a reasonable course of action in relation to the relevant tax provisions. An opinion notice may indicate that the sub-panel considers that it is not possible to reach a view on the information available. Alternatively, the sub-panel may produce two or three opinion notices which, taken together, state the opinions of all the members. An opinion notice must include the reasons for the opinion and is given to the designated HMRC officer.

The HMRC officer must then provide a copy of the opinion notice (or notices) to each taxpayer, any one of whom may then, within 30 days, make representations that:

- no tax advantage has arisen to him;
- he has already been given a bound arrangements opinion notice in relation to the arrangements concerned (see **4.6** above); or
- a matter set out in HMRC's general statement is materially incorrect.

The officer must then, for each taxpayer, consider any opinion of the GAAR Advisory Panel, together with any representations made, and send a written notice (a '*final counteraction notice*') with his decision as to whether the tax arrangements under consideration are to be counteracted under the GAAR. If so, the notice must set out the adjustments required to give effect to the counteraction and the steps that the taxpayer must take to give effect to it.

On and after 5 December 2017, anything that may or must be done by a given designated HMRC officer under the above provisions may be done instead by any other designated HMRC officer.

[*FA 2013, s 214(3), Sch 43B; FA 2016, s 157(3)(10)(30); SI 2017 No 1090, Regs 1, 11–14*].

Penalty

[4.8] A person (P) is liable to a penalty if:

- a tax advantage arising from tax arrangements entered into on or after 15 September 2016 has been counteracted by the making of adjustments under the GAAR following a referral to the GAAR Advisory Panel;
- a tax document has been given to HMRC on the basis that the tax advantage arises to P from the arrangements; and
- the document was given to HMRC by P or another person and P knew, or ought to have known, that the document was given on the basis that the tax advantage arises to P from the arrangements.

For this purpose, a '*tax document*' means a return, claim or other document submitted in compliance (or purported compliance) with any provision of an Act. Giving a document to HMRC includes communicating information in any form and by any method (post, fax, email, telephone or otherwise).

The penalty is 60% of the '*value of the counteracted advantage*', i.e. the additional amount due or payable in respect of tax as a result of the counteraction. This includes any amount previously repaid by HMRC which is now payable, together with any amount which would be repayable by HMRC if the counteraction were not made and any consequential adjustments. If the counteraction affects P's liability to more than one tax, each of the taxes is considered together in determining the value of the counteracted advantage. To the extent that the counteracted advantage has resulted in a loss being wrongly recorded or increased but the counteracted loss has not been wholly used to reduce tax payable, the value of the counteracted advantage is increased by 10% of the part of the counteracted loss not so used. However, the value of a counteracted loss is nil if, due to the nature of the loss or the person's circumstances, there is no reasonable prospect of the loss ever being used to reduce the tax liability of any person. For these purposes, a loss includes a charge, expense, deficit or other amount which may be available for, or relied on to claim, a deduction or relief. To the extent that the counteracted advantage is a deferral of tax, the value of the advantage is 25% of the amount of deferred tax for each year of the deferral, but not so as to exceed 100% of the total amount of deferred tax.

The Commissioners for HMRC have discretion to mitigate a penalty under these provisions, or stay or compound any proceedings for such a penalty. They may also, after judgment, further mitigate or entirely remit the penalty.

Interaction with other penalties

The following applies where (i) more than one penalty arises in respect of the same amount; (ii) one of those penalties is a GAAR penalty; and (iii) one or more of the others is incurred under *FA 2007, Sch 24* (errors in documents — see **55.6–55.8**, PENALTIES), *FA 2008, Sch 41* (failure to notify chargeability — see **55.2–55.4** PENALTIES), *FA 2009, Sch 55* (failure to make return — see **55.5** PENALTIES) or *FA 2016, Sch 18* (serial avoiders — see **4.59** below). The general rule is that the aggregate penalty must not exceed 100% of the amount in question or, if at least one of the penalties is a £300 penalty under *FA 2009, Sch 55*, £300 (if greater). But where the maximum penalty under one of the other provisions is more than 100% because of the rules for offshore matters and offshore transfers, the aggregate penalty must not exceed that higher maximum percentage. See **4.48** below for the maximum aggregate penalties where a GAAR penalty and a penalty under *FA 2014, s 212* (follower notices) is incurred in respect of the same tax.

Assessment

The GAAR penalty is charged by HMRC assessment. The assessment is treated in the same way as, and can be combined with, an assessment to tax and can be enforced accordingly. The penalty must be paid before the end of the period of 30 days beginning with the day on which the notice of assessment is issued. The notice of assessment must state the tax year in respect of which the penalty is assessed. Subject to the time limits below, HMRC can make a supplementary assessment if an existing assessment operates by reference to an underestimate of the value of the counteracted advantage and an assessment may be revised if it overestimates that value. Where, following the making of a penalty assessment, consequential adjustments are made (see **4.2** above), HMRC must make any just and reasonable alterations to the penalty assessment to take account of those adjustments, and may do so regardless of any time limits which would otherwise prevent them.

An assessment to a penalty must be made before the end of the 12 months beginning with the the date (or the latest of the dates) on which the counteraction under the GAAR (see **4.2** above) becomes final. (For this purpose, the counteraction becomes final when the adjustments made, and any amounts resulting from them, can no longer be varied, on appeal or otherwise.) Slightly different rules applied where liability to a penalty arose before 22 July 2020, but it is not certain that these were entirely workable (see the technical note at www.gov.uk/government/publications/technical-note-for-general-anti-abuse-rule-amendments-announced-at-budget-2018).

Appeals

An appeal can be made against the imposition of a GAAR penalty or against the amount of a GAAR penalty. An appeal must be made within the 30-day period beginning with the date on which the notice of the penalty assessment is issued. An appeal against the imposition of a penalty can only be made on the grounds that the arrangements concerned were not abusive or that there was no tax advantage to be counteracted (see **4.2** above). An appeal against the amount of a penalty can only be made on the grounds that the penalty is based on an overestimate of the counteracted advantage.

If the appeal is against the imposition of a penalty and it is heard by the Tribunal, the Tribunal may affirm or cancel HMRC's decision to impose the penalty. If the appeal is against the amount of a penalty and it is heard by the Tribunal, the Tribunal may affirm the amount charged or substitute its own amount (but only an amount that HMRC could have chosen to charge). Subject to this, the general APPEALS (5) provisions apply as they apply to assessments to income tax, but not so as to require payment of the penalty before the appeal is determined.

[*FA 2013, s 212A, Sch 43C; FA 2016, s 158(2)(3)(14)(15); FA 2020, Sch 14 paras 9, 14, 15*].

Transactions in securities

[4.9] There are provisions for counteracting income advantages obtained or obtainable in specified circumstances in respect of a transaction or transactions in securities. [*ITA 2007, Pt 13 Ch 1*].

Subject to the exception below, the provisions apply where, in consequence of one or more 'transaction(s) in securities' combined with any of the circumstances listed below, a person is able to obtain an 'income tax advantage' (see **4.10** below). They apply only if a main purpose of the transaction or, as the case may be, any of the transactions is to obtain an income tax advantage. 'Securities' includes shares and stock, and, in the case of a company not limited by shares, includes an interest of a member of the company in whatever form. HMRC may make adjustments to counteract the tax advantage (see **4.11** below).

[*ITA 2007, ss 684, 685, 713; FA 2016, ss 33(2)–(4)(8)(9), 34(7)–(9)*].

For advance clearance, see **4.12** below.

A '*transaction in securities*' means a transaction, of whatever description, relating to securities, and includes in particular:

(i) the purchase, sale or exchange of securities;
(ii) issuing or securing the issue of new securities;
(iii) applying or subscribing for new securities;

(iv) altering or securing the alteration of the rights attached to securities;
(v) a repayment of share capital or share premium; and
(vi) a distribution in respect of securities in a winding-up.

[*ITA 2007, ss 684(2), 713; FA 2016, s 33(3)(8)(9)*].

See *CIR v Joiner* HL 1975, 50 TC 449 (in which a variation of rights prior to a liquidation was held to be a transaction in securities) and *CIR v Laird Group plc* HL 2003, 75 TC 399 (in which the payment of a dividend representing previously undistributed profits was held not to be).

The circumstances mentioned above, only one of which needs to be met, are those in (A) or (B) below, but see also below under Excluded circumstances.

(A) As a result of the transaction in securities (or any one or more of the transactions in securities) the person in question receives 'relevant consideration' in connection with:
 (i) the distribution, transfer or realisation of assets of a 'close company'; or
 (ii) the application of assets of a close company in discharge of liabilities; or
 (iii) the direct or indirect transfer of assets of one close company to another close company;

 and does not pay or bear income tax on the consideration.

 The expression '*close company*' throughout these provisions has the meaning given in *CTA 2010, Pt 10 Ch 2* (broadly a company under the control of five or fewer participators) but also includes a company that would be a close company if it were UK resident.

(B)
 (i) In connection with the transaction in securities (or any one or more of the transactions in securities) the person in question receives 'relevant consideration';
 (ii) two or more close companies are concerned in the transaction(s); and
 (iii) the person does not pay or bear income tax on the consideration.

For the purposes of (A)(i) and (ii) above, '*relevant consideration*' means consideration which:

(a) is or represents the value of assets available for distribution by way of dividend by the company (or which would have been so available apart from anything done by the company); or
(b) is received in respect of future receipts of the company; or
(c) is or represents the value of trading stock of the company.

The assets mentioned in (a) above do not include any assets that would otherwise be included solely because the law of the country in which the company is incorporated allows assets of that kind to be distributed by way of dividend.

For the purposes of (A)(iii) and (B) above, '*relevant consideration*' means consideration which consists of any share capital or any security issued by a close company and which is or represents the value of assets which:

- are available for distribution by way of dividend by the company (or would have been so available apart from anything done by the company); or
- are trading stock of the company.

In each of the above definitions of 'relevant consideration', the assets available for distribution by way of dividend by the company must be taken to include assets available for distribution to the company by a company under its control.

As regards (A)(iii) and (B) above, in so far as the consideration consists of non-redeemable share capital these provisions are triggered only so far as the share capital is repaid (in a winding-up or otherwise, including any distribution made in respect of any shares in a winding-up or dissolution).

Excluded circumstances

If the circumstances are as in (A) or (B) above, there is nevertheless a let-out if:

- immediately before the transaction in securities (or the first of two or more such transactions) the person in question (P) holds shares (or an interest in shares) in the close company in question, and
- there is a 'fundamental change of ownership' of the close company.

There is a '*fundamental change of ownership*' of the close company if, as a result of the transaction(s), the original shareholder(s), taken together with any associate(s), do not directly or indirectly hold more than 25% of the close company's ordinary share capital or an entitlement to more than 25% of the distributions or more than 25% of the voting rights. Anything held by a person controlled by an original shareholder is attributed to that shareholder for these purposes. An original shareholder means any person who, immediately before the transaction (or the first of the series), held any of the close company's ordinary share capital.

The question of whether persons are associates of each other is determined as in **4.34** below, but with the addition that a trustee of a settlement and an individual are associates if one or more of the beneficiaries are connected or associated with the individual.

[*ITA 2007, ss 685, 686, 713, 989; FA 2016, s 33(4)(5)(7)–(9)*].

Simon's Taxes. See **D9.1**.

Meaning of 'income tax advantage'

[4.10] For the purposes of **4.9** above, a person obtains an '*income tax advantage*' if the amount of income tax (if any) which would be payable by him in respect of the 'relevant consideration' (see **4.9** above) if it constituted a distribution exceeds the amount of capital gains tax payable in respect of it (which may be a nil amount). The amount of the income tax advantage is equal to the amount of that excess. For this purpose only, the relevant consideration is limited (if it would otherwise be greater) to the maximum amount that could in any circumstances have been paid to the person or an associate (see **4.9** above) by way of a distribution when the circumstances in **4.9**(A) or (B) are met.

[*ITA 2007, s 687; FA 2016, s 33(6)(8)(9), Sch 1 paras 63(10), 73*].

For 'tax advantage' see *CIR v Cleary* HL 1967, 44 TC 399 (tax advantage obtained where taxpayers' company purchased shares from them) and contrast *CIR v Kleinwort, Benson Ltd* Ch D 1968, 45 TC 369 (no tax advantage where merchant bank purchased debentures with interest in arrear shortly before redemption). The decision in *Sheppard and another (Trustees of the Woodland Trust) v CIR (No 2)* Ch D 1993, 65 TC 724 that no tax advantage could arise where relief was obtained by virtue of charitable exemption was doubted in *CIR v Universities Superannuation Scheme Ltd* Ch D 1996, 70 TC 193, in which the opposite conclusion was reached. Prior to the hearing of the latter case, the Inland Revenue had, in any event, indicated that they would continue to proceed under the legislation on the footing that tax-exempt bodies obtain a tax advantage whenever they receive abnormal dividends, since they considered that there would have been good grounds for challenging the earlier decision had it not been for a defect in the assessment under appeal. (Revenue Tax Bulletin August 1993 p 90, April 1998 p 537, October 1998 pp 590–592). For the quantum of the tax advantage, see *Bird v CIR* HL 1988, 61 TC 238.

Procedure

[4.11] The following procedure applies if an officer of HMRC believes that the provisions at **4.9** above may apply in a particular case.

(i) The officer may open an enquiry into the transaction(s) in question. The officer must give notice to the taxpayer (or his personal representatives if deceased) of his intention to do so. The notice of enquiry must be given no later than six years after the tax year to which the income tax advantage relates. [*ITA 2007, ss 695, 712; FA 2016, s 34(2)(8)(9)*]. See *Balen v CIR* CA 1978, 52 TC 406.

(ii) Where notice of enquiry is given as in (i) above, an HMRC officer may choose to conclude the enquiry by giving the taxpayer a notice (a '*no-counteraction notice*') stating that no counteraction is required and giving the reasons. At any time while an enquiry remains open the taxpayer may apply to the Appeal Tribunal for a direction requiring HMRC to conclude the enquiry, i.e. by issuing either a counteraction notice as in (iv) below or a no-counteraction notice. The Tribunal must give the direction applied for unless satisfied that there are reasonable grounds for keeping the enquiry open. [*ITA 2007, s 698A; FA 2016, s 34(6)(8)(9)*].

(iii) The following ensues if the HMRC officer determines on enquiry that the provisions at **4.9** above do apply. HMRC will make adjustments to counteract the income tax advantage. The adjustments required to be made, and the basis on which they are to be made, must be specified in a notice (a '*counteraction notice*') served on the taxpayer by an HMRC officer. The adjustments may take the form of an assessment, the cancellation of a tax repayment and/or a recalculation of profits or gains or liability to income tax.
[*ITA 2007, s 698; FA 2016, s 34(4)(5)(8)(9)*].
The date from which interest on late paid tax accrues is 31 January following the tax year in question.

If **4.9**(A)(iii) or (B) above is in point, and is triggered by the repayment of share capital, the assessment must be for the tax year in which that repayment occurs. [*ITA 2007, s 700*].

(iv) A person on whom a counteraction notice has been served may appeal, by giving notice to the Commissioners for HMRC within 30 days of the service of the notice, on the grounds that the provisions do not apply to him in respect of the transaction(s) in question or that the stated adjustments are inappropriate. The Tribunal may then affirm, vary or cancel the counteraction notice or affirm, vary or quash an assessment made in accordance with the notice. [*ITA 2007, ss 705–707*].

(v) The application of these provisions is outside self-assessment, so returns should be made without having regard to a possible charge (although taxpayers may wish to draw HMRC's attention to any correspondence with the Clearance and Counteraction Team (see **4.12** below) in connection with any particular transaction). Enquiries into the possible application of these provisions will accordingly be carried out independently of any enquiry into the self-assessment return (see **64.6** RETURNS). (Revenue Tax Bulletin April 2000 pp 742, 743).

Clearance

[4.12] Where **4.9** above may be in point, the taxpayer may take the initiative by submitting to HMRC particulars of any transaction effected or contemplated; HMRC may, within 30 days of receipt, call for further information (to be supplied within 30 days). Subject to this, they must notify their decision within 30 days of receipt of the particulars or further information, and if they are satisfied that no liability arises the matter is concluded as regards that transaction by itself, provided that all facts and material particulars have been fully and accurately disclosed. [*ITA 2007, ss 701, 702; FA 2016, s 33(10)*].

HMRC are not obliged to give reasons for refusal of clearance but where the applicant has given full reasons for his transactions the main grounds for refusing clearance will be indicated. A refusal to give clearance indicates that counteraction would be taken if the transaction were completed. (HMRC SP 3/80).

Applications for clearance should be directed to the Clearance and Counteraction Team at BAI Clearance, HMRC, BX9 1JL; market-sensitive applications should be marked for the attention of 'The Team Leader'. Applications may also be emailed to reconstructions@hmrc.gsi.gov.uk. Only a single application need be made as above for clearances under any one or more of a number of specified statutory income tax, corporation tax and capital gains tax provisions (including *ITA 2007, s 701*). For the list of the specified provisions and more details on this clearance procedure, see www.gov.uk/guidance/seeking-clearance-or-approval-for-a-transaction under Statutory applications for advance clearance.

Manufactured payments

[4.13] These provisions have effect in relation to any payment representative of a dividend or interest. For income tax purposes a person (P) has a '*manufactured payment relationship*' if the following conditions are met:

(a) under any arrangements, an amount is payable, or any other benefit is given, by or to P;
(b) the arrangements relate to the transfer of 'securities'; and
(c) the amount in (a) or the value of the other benefit in (a) is representative of a dividend or interest on the securities (or will fall to be treated as representative of such a dividend or interest when the amount is paid or the benefit is given).

For the purposes of (a) above, the release of the whole or part of any liability to pay an amount counts as a benefit. The reference in (a) to an amount being payable, or a benefit being given, *by* P includes a reference to an amount being payable, or a benefit being given, by another person on P's behalf.

In (b) above, '*securities*' means shares in a company and loan stock or similar securities (including government loan stock and whether issued in the UK or elsewhere).

Meaning of 'manufactured payment'

In relation to a manufactured payment relationship, a '*manufactured payment*' means an amount, or the value of a benefit, within (a) above.

Treatment of the payer of a manufactured payment

Where P has a manufactured payment relationship under which a manufactured payment is paid by him or on his behalf, no deduction is allowed in respect of the payment in calculating any profits or other income of P for income tax purposes. This does not apply, however, insofar as the manufactured payment is legitimately brought into account in calculating the profits of a trade carried on by P.

Treatment of the recipient of a manufactured payment

Where P has a manufactured payment relationship under which a manufactured payment is payable to him, P is treated for income tax purposes as if the manufactured payment were a dividend or (as the case may require) interest on the securities. This does not apply insofar as the manufactured payment is brought into account in calculating the profits of a trade carried on by P. It has no effect for the purposes of determining any entitlement to DOUBLE TAX RELIEF (**27**) in respect of any dividend or interest.

[*ITA 2007, ss 614ZA–614ZD; FA 2016, Sch 1 paras 63(9), 73*].

Deduction of tax at source

If P pays a manufactured payment representative of interest on UK securities other than shares (';*manufactured interest*'), and P is either UK resident or pays the manufactured interest in the course of a trade carried on in the UK through a branch or agency, P must, on making the payment, deduct basic rate income tax from the gross amount. The gross amount of manufactured interest is equal to the gross amount of the interest of which it is representative. The obligation to deduct tax does not apply in the case of gilt-edged securities or securities which are not gilt-edged but on which the interest is payable gross. [*ITA 2007, ss 919, 921*].

Transfer of assets abroad

Liability of transferor

[4.14] Where, as a result of a transfer of assets, either alone or in conjunction with any associated operations (see below), income becomes payable to non-UK residents, or to persons not domiciled in the UK, then, subject to the exemptions at **4.17** below, the following provisions apply.

(1) If, by virtue of the transfer of assets, or one or more associated operations, or the transfer in conjunction with associated operations (see *Vestey v CIR* HL 1979, 54 TC 503 overruling *Congreve v CIR* HL 1948, 30 TC 163; and also *CIR v Pratt and Others* Ch D 1982, 57 TC 1), the transferor, being an individual resident in the UK, has power to enjoy, forthwith or in the future, any income of a 'person abroad' (see below) which would be taxable if it were the income of the UK resident individual received in the UK, an amount of income is treated as arising to that individual.

'Assets' is given a wide definition by *ITA 2007, s 717*, and see *CIR v Brackett* Ch D 1986, 60 TC 134, 639; *Hoey v HMRC*, FTT (TC 7292), [2019] UKFTT 489 (TC).

For 2016/17 and earlier years, the amount of income treated as arising to the UK resident individual is equal to the amount of the income of the person abroad that would be taxable if it were the income of the UK resident individual received in the UK. For 2017/18 onwards, this continues to be the case if the UK resident individual is domiciled in the UK at any time in the tax year or if that individual is deemed to be UK domiciled as a result of being born in the UK with a UK domicile of origin (see the first of the two conditions at **63.36** RESIDENCE AND DOMICILE). If neither of these is the case, the amount of income treated as arising to the UK resident individual is equal to so much of the income of the person abroad as is *not* 'protected foreign-source income'. Income is '*protected foreign-source income*' for this purpose if:

- (a) the income would be relevant foreign income (see **32.2** FOREIGN INCOME) if it were the individual's;
- (b) the person abroad is the trustees of a settlement;
- (c) the trustees are non-UK resident for the tax year (see **70.5** SETTLEMENTS as to residence of trustees);
- (d) when the settlement was created the individual was not domiciled in the UK and, if it was created on or after 6 April 2017, the individual was not deemed domiciled in the UK under the deemed domicile rule; and
- (e) subject to exceptions (see below), no property or income is provided (directly or indirectly) for the purposes of the settlement by the individual, or by the trustees of any other settlement of which the individual is a beneficiary or settlor, at any time in the period from 6 April 2017 (or from the creation of the settlement if later than that) to the end of the tax year in question

when the individual is domiciled or deemed domiciled in the UK. In this regard, the addition of value to property comprised in the settlement is treated as the direct provision of property for the purposes of the settlement.

Income is also '*protected foreign-source income*' for this purpose if the conditions at (a), (c), (d) and (e) above are met but:

- the person abroad is a company;
- the trustees of a settlement are participators (within *CTA 2010, s 454*) in the company (or are participators in the first in a chain of companies where the last company in the chain is the person abroad and where each chain company except the last) is a participator in the next company in the chain); and
- the individual's power to enjoy the income results from the trustees being such participators.

The exceptions referred to at (e) above are the same (and with the same caveats) as those in **70.27** SETTLEMENTS.

(2) If an individual such as in (1) above receives, or has received in any earlier year, or is entitled to, any capital sum by way of loan etc. (see *Lee* KB 1941, 24 TC 207), or other non-income payment not for full consideration, which is in any way connected with the transfer etc., an amount of income is treated as arising to the resident individual. A sum which a third person receives, or is entitled to receive, at the individual's direction or by assignment of the right to receive it, is treated as such a capital sum. There is no deemed income for a tax year in respect of a loan to the individual which has been wholly repaid before the beginning of that year.

For 2016/17 and earlier years, the amount of income treated as arising to the UK resident individual is equal to the amount of the income which, by virtue of the transfer etc., has become payable to the person abroad. For 2017/18 onwards, this continues to be the case if the UK resident individual is domiciled in the UK at any time in the tax year or if that individual is deemed to be UK domiciled as a result of being born in the UK with a UK domicile of origin. If neither of these is the case, the amount of income treated as arising to the UK resident individual is equal to so much of the income of the person abroad as is not 'protected foreign-source income'. Income is '*protected foreign-source income*' for this purpose if conditions (a)–(e) in (1) above are met. Income is also '*protected foreign-source income*' for this purpose if the conditions at (1)(a), (c), (d) and (e) above are met but:

- the person abroad is a company;
- the trustees of a settlement are participators (within *CTA 2010, s 454*) in the company (or are participators in the first in a chain of companies where the last company in the chain is the person abroad and where each chain company except the last) is a participator in the next company in the chain); and
- the trustees are participators as a result of a transfer of assets or associated operation within these provisions (whether or not it is also met by any other means); and
- the income has become the income of the person abroad as a result of that transfer etc.

The question of whether income has arisen to a person abroad, or of whether an individual has power to enjoy any such income, is determined irrespective of the individual's residence status for the tax year in which the transfer of assets took place and regardless of whether the avoiding of liability to income tax is a purpose for which the transfer was effected.

Where the individual otherwise chargeable is liable for income tax charged on the income of the person abroad by virtue of a charge other than under these provisions *and* all that income tax has been paid, there is no charge under these provisions.

[*ITA 2007, ss 721, 721A, 721B, 728(1)(1A)(2A)(3), 729, 729A; F(No 2)A 2017, Sch 8 paras 28, 29, 31, 32, 39*].

The charge to tax under (1) and (2) above is made under *ITA 2007, s 720* and *ITA 2007, s 727* respectively.

References to an individual include the individual's spouse or civil partner. [*ITA 2007, s 714(4)*].

Power to enjoy income

For the above purposes an individual is deemed to have power to enjoy income of a person abroad if:

- (i) the income is so dealt with by *any* person so as to benefit the individual at some point of time, whether as income or not; or
- (ii) the income increases the value to the individual of assets held by him or for his benefit; or
- (iii) the individual receives, or is entitled to receive, at any time any benefit provided out of the income, or out of money available by the effect of associated operations on that income or assets representing it, directly or indirectly; or
- (iv) the individual may obtain beneficial enjoyment of the income in the event of the exercise of one or more powers, by whomsoever exercisable and whether with or without the consent of any other person; or
- (v) the individual is able to control application of the income,

regard being had to the substantial effect of the transfer and associated operations and bringing into account all resultant benefits to the individual whether or not he has rights in law or equity to those benefits. [*ITA 2007, ss 722, 723*].

Meaning of 'person abroad'

A '*person abroad*' means a person who is resident outside the UK or an individual who is domiciled outside the UK. Persons treated as non-UK resident under the rules relating to settlements (see **70.5** SETTLEMENTS) and personal representatives (see **63.31** RESIDENCE AND DOMICILE) are treated as resident outside the UK for these purposes. The deemed domicile rule at **63.36** RESIDENCE AND DOMICILE applies for these purposes for 2017/18 onwards. [*ITA 2007, s 718, Sch 2 paras 134–137; F(No 2)A 2017, Sch 8 para 13*].

Associated operations

An '*associated operation*' is an operation of any kind effected by any person in relation to any of the assets transferred (or any assets representing those transferred) or to the income from those assets or to any assets representing accumulations of the income from those assets. (See also *Corbett's Exors* CA 1943, 25 TC 305; *Bambridge* HL 1955, 36 TC 313 and *Fynn* CD 1957, 37 TC 629.) It is made clear that:

- associated operations are to be taken into account for the purposes of these provisions whether they are effected before, at the same time as or after the transfer;
- income which arises by virtue of associated operations alone is to be taken into account for the purposes of the charging provisions; and
- income which an individual has power to enjoy includes income which he has power to enjoy by virtue of associated operations alone.

[*ITA 2007, ss 719(2), 721(2), 728(1), Sch 2 para 141*].

Deductions, reliefs and rates of tax

For the purpose of determining any deductions and reliefs available to the individual within the charge to tax under *ITA 2007, s 720* or *721* above, the individual is treated as if he had actually received the amount by reference to which the income treated as arising to him is determined.

Income tax at the basic rate or starting rate for savings (when that rate is more than 0%) is not charged under *ITA 2007, s 720* or *721* above in respect of any income if (and to the corresponding extent that) the income of the person abroad has borne tax at that rate by deduction or otherwise. For 2018/19 onwards, income tax at the Scottish starter rate and basic rate is similarly not charged if and to the extent that the income of the person abroad has borne tax at the basic rate. For 2019/20 onwards, the same applies to income tax at the Welsh basic rate. Otherwise, income of the person abroad that would be dividend income if it were the income of the individual with power to enjoy is charged to tax under these provisions as if it were dividend income (see **1.5** ALLOWANCES AND TAX RATES).

[*ITA 2007, ss 745, 746; FA 2016, s 4(9)(17), Sch 1 paras 63(12), 73; SI 2018 No 459, Arts 1, 6(6); SI 2019 No 201, Arts 1, 12*].

Non-UK domiciled individuals

Special rules apply to non-UK domiciled individuals. They apply where income is deemed to arise to an individual under (1) or (2) above in a tax year and the remittance basis applies to the individual for that year (by virtue of his being within any of **61.2**(1)–(3) REMITTANCE BASIS). 'Foreign deemed income' is treated as 'relevant foreign income' (see **32.2** FOREIGN INCOME) of the individual, with the consequences in **61.4** REMITTANCE BASIS, except that split year treatment does not apply. The income deemed to arise is '*foreign deemed income*' if it would be relevant foreign income if it were the individual's own income. See **61** REMITTANCE BASIS for the meaning of 'remitted to the UK' etc. For the purposes of applying the provisions described in that chapter, treat so much of the deemed income as would be relevant foreign income if it were the individual's as deriving from the foreign deemed income.

Where the tax year in which foreign deemed income arises is any year before 2017/18, the remittance basis does not apply to that income insofar as it is remitted to the UK in 2017/18 or subsequently and is 'transitionally protected income'. '*Transitionally protected income*' means any foreign deemed income where (i) the income of the person abroad arises prior to 2017/18; (ii) the income would have been protected foreign-source income had it arisen in 2017/18 onwards; and (iii) the income was not distributed prior to 6 April 2017 by the trustees of the settlement in question. For this purpose, the definition of protected foreign-source income in (1) or (2) above (whichever is relevant) applies, but with the omission of the condition at (1)(e).

[*ITA 2007, ss 726, 730; F(No 2)A 2017, Sch 8 paras 30, 33, 39*].

HMRC information powers

HMRC have power to require from any person, under penalty, particulars of transactions where he acted for others (even if he considers no liability arises), and of what part he took in them. The request must be reasonable with regard to the purposes of the legislation. [*ITA 2007, s 748*]. These powers are limited in the case of *solicitors* (but not accountants or others), and *bankers* are not obliged to furnish particulars of any *ordinary* banking transactions carried out in the *ordinary* course of a banking business. [*ITA 2007, ss 749, 750*]. 'Bank' for this purpose is defined by *ITA 2007, s 991* (see **8.1** BANKS AND BUILDING SOCIETIES). See *Royal Bank of Canada* Ch D 1971, 47 TC 565, where held particulars required were not ordinary banking transactions and *Clinch v CIR* QB 1973, 49 TC 52 for powers of Revenue.

Case law

See *Philippi v CIR* CA 1971, 47 TC 75 for burden on taxpayer to prove that avoidance was not a purpose.

For general principles, see the cases cited above and *Cottingham's Exors* CA 1938, 22 TC 344; *Beatty cases* KB 1940, 23 TC 574; *Lord Howard de Walden* CA 1941, 25 TC 121; *Aykroyd* KB 1942, 24 TC 515; *Latilla* HL 1943, 25 TC 107; *Sassoon* CA 1943, 25 TC 154; *Vestey's Exors* HL 1949, 31 TC 1; *Ramsden* Ch D 1957, 37 TC 619; *Chetwode v CIR* HL 1977, 51 TC 647; *Vestey (Nos 1 & 2)* HL 1979, 54 TC 503; *CIR v Schroder* Ch D 1983, 57 TC 94; *CIR v Botnar* CA, [1999] STC 711; *Seesurrun v HMRC* FTT (TC 3900), [2014] UKFTT 783 (TC), 2014 STI 3196; *Fisher v HMRC* UT, [2020] STC 1218, [2020] UKUT 62 (TCC); *Davies v HMRC* UT, [2020] STC 649, [2020] UKUT 67 (TCC).

In *CIR v Willoughby* HL 1997, 70 TC 57, the Inland Revenue's refusal of exemption under the predecessor to *ITA 2007, s 739* in relation to 'personal portfolio bonds' (the holder of which has a degree of control of the management of the underlying investments but no proprietary interest therein) was overturned on appeal.

Simon's Taxes. See **E1.1103–E1.1116.**

Liability of others

[4.15] Where, as a result of a transfer of assets or one or more associated operations (see **4.14** above), income becomes payable to a 'person abroad' (see **4.14**) *and* an individual receives a benefit provided out of the assets, then, subject to the exemptions at **4.17** below, the provisions below apply in respect of the benefit. Before 2017/18, these provisions applied only if the individual was not liable as the transferor under **4.14** above, and would not be so liable in the absence of special rules for non-UK domiciled individuals. For 2017/18 onwards, these provisions continue to apply where the individual is not liable as the transferor but this is taken into account only if at some point in the tax year of receipt the individual is UK domiciled or is deemed UK domiciled by virtue of the first condition at **63.36** RESIDENCE AND DOMICILE.

The value of the benefit, up to the amount of 'relevant income' of tax years up to and including the year in which received, is treated as income arising to the recipient individual. '*Relevant income*' of a tax year is any income arising in that year to a person abroad which by virtue of the said transfer or associated operations can be used (directly or indirectly) for providing a benefit for the recipient individual. Firstly, ascertain the total amount or value of benefits received by the individual in all tax years up to and including the current one. Deduct the total amount of income treated as arising to the individual for tax years before the current one. (For 2017/18 onwards, where any of that income is matched deemed income (see below), it is to be deducted only insofar as it is matched deemed income on which tax has been charged under these provisions.) The result is the '*total untaxed benefits*'. Next, ascertain the relevant income of the tax year and earlier tax years in relation to the individual, and deduct from it the same amount that was deducted in arriving at total untaxed benefits. The result is the 'available relevant income'. The amount of the income treated as arising to the individual for the tax year is the total untaxed benefits or the available relevant income, whichever is lower. The process must be repeated each year until there are no remaining untaxed benefits.

For 2016/17, these provisions applied only if the individual receiving the benefit was UK resident for the tax year in which it was received. For 2017/18 onwards, this condition is removed. However, where the individual is non-UK resident for the tax year in which the benefit is received, there is a charge to tax on any 'matched deemed income':

- only so far as that matched deemed income can be matched, under the matching rules in *ITA 2007, s 735A* (which are deemed to apply for this purpose) with an amount of relevant income that is protected income for the purposes of *ITA 2007, s 733A* below; and
- only if the individual is the settlor of the settlement in question or the benefit is received by the individual at a time when the individual is a close member of the family of the settlor of that settlement. For this purpose, a close family member means a spouse or civil partner or a minor child of the settlor or of the spouse or civil partner; cohabiting unmarried couples are treated as if married or civil partners.

'*Matched deemed income*' is income which is treated as arising to the individual under these provisions and can be matched, under the matching rules in *ITA 2007, s 735A* (which are deemed to apply for this purpose), with the benefit. (*ITA 2007, s 735A* is referred to below under Application of remittance basis.)

Before 2018/19, it could have been possible to avoid a charge by routing benefits to individuals outside the scope of the charge who would then gift them onwards. See **4.16** below for rules applicable for 2018/19 onwards that seek to prevent this.

The charge under these provisions takes priority over any charge for 2018/19 onwards under **70.34** and **70.35** SETTLEMENTS.

[*ITA 2007, ss 731–733; F(No 2)A 2017, Sch 8 paras 34, 35, 39; FA 2018, Sch 10 paras 13, 14, 21(1)*].

Where benefits provided as mentioned above are received in a tax year and, in that year or subsequently, chargeable gains under specified provisions of *TCGA 1992* accrue to a person, or income is treated under **70.34** or **70.35** SETTLEMENTS as arising to a person, by reference to the whole or part of any benefits so provided, the total untaxed benefits as above is subsequently reduced by the amount of those gains or of that income. [*ITA 2007, ss 734, 734A; FA 2018, Sch 10 paras 17, 18, 21(1)*].

The HMRC information powers at **4.14** above apply equally here.

Settlor liable for tax in certain cases

Under *ITA 2007, s 733A*, liability for the tax charged under these provisions is transferred in certain circumstances to the settlor of the settlement referred to in the definitions of protected foreign-source income in **4.14**(1) and (2) above. This applies where all of conditions (a)–(f) below are met. In such a case, if the individual is non-UK resident at any time in the tax year, or if the remittance basis applies to the individual for the tax year and none of the amount treated as arising is remitted to the UK in the year, the settlor is liable for the tax charged on that amount as if it were income arising to the settlor in the year (and the individual is not liable in any later year for income tax on that amount). If the remittance basis applies to the individual and part of the amount treated as arising is remitted to the UK in the year, the settlor's liability is restricted to the tax charged on the remainder of that amount. The settlor is entitled to recover the tax from the individual, and for this purpose is entitled to require HMRC to supply a certificate specifying the amount of the income concerned and the amount of tax paid. The conditions are that:

(a) an amount of income is treated as arising to an individual for a tax year under the provisions of *ITA 2007, ss 731–733* above;

(b) under matching rules that amount can be matched:
   - (i) with an amount of relevant income (see above) that is 'protected income'; and
   - (ii) with a benefit received by the individual at a time when he was a 'close member of the family of the settlor' of the settlement concerned (see below);

(c) there is no time in the year when the trustees of the settlement are non-UK resident (see **70.5** RESIDENCE AND DOMICILE as regards residence of trustees);
(d) there is a time in the year when the settlor is UK resident;
(e) there is no time in the year when the settlor is domiciled in the UK; and
(f) there is no time in the year when the settlor is deemed domiciled in the UK by virtue of the first condition of the deemed domicile rule at **63.36** RESIDENCE AND DOMICILE.

The matching rules referred to in (b) above are those in *ITTOIA 2005, s 735A* referred to below under Application of remittance basis. For the purpose of (b)(i) above, an amount of income is protected income only if **4.14**(1) or (2) above applies by reference to protected foreign-source income. The '*protected income*' is the income of the person abroad that is protected foreign-source income. In (b)(ii) above, the reference to the settlement concerned is to the settlement referred to in the definitions of protected foreign-source income.

Close family members

For the purposes of (b)(ii) above and **4.16** below, the following persons are '*close members of the family of the settlor*' at any time (provided the settlor is living at that time):

- the settlor's current spouse or civil partner; and
- any minor child of the settlor (or of the settlor's current spouse or civil partner).

Cohabiting couples are treated for the above purpose as if they were spouses or civil partners.

[*ITA 2007, ss 721(3BA), 728(1B), 733A; F(No 2)A 2017, Sch 8 paras 28, 31, 36, 39; FA 2018, Sch 10 paras 15, 21(1)(5); SI 2019 No 1458, Sch 3 para 29(2)*].

For technical guidance, see www.gov.uk/government/publications/trust-protections-and-capital-gains-tax-changes.

Application of remittance basis

The following rules apply where income is deemed to arise to an individual as above in a tax year and the remittance basis applies to the individual for that year (by virtue of his being within any of **61.2**(1)–(3) REMITTANCE BASIS). 'Foreign deemed income' is treated as 'relevant foreign income' (see **32.2** FOREIGN INCOME) of the individual, with the consequences in **61.4** REMITTANCE BASIS, except that split year treatment does not apply. The income deemed to arise is '*foreign deemed income*' if it would be relevant foreign income if it were the individual's own income. See **61** REMITTANCE BASIS for the meaning of 'remitted to the UK' etc. For the purposes of applying the provisions described in that chapter, treat relevant income, or a benefit, that 'relates to' any part of the foreign deemed income as deriving from that part of the foreign deemed income. Special 'matching' rules in *ITA 2007, s 735A* are used to determine how income '*relates to*' relevant income and to benefits.

Where (i) income is treated as arising to an individual for a tax year, (ii) a settlor is liable for the tax under *ITA 2007, s 733A* above, and (iii) the remittance basis applies to the settlor for that year, the income is treated as relevant foreign income of the settlor. See *ITA 2007, s 735B(3)* as regards the application of the provisions described in **61** REMITTANCE BASIS in relation to the settlor.

[*ITA 2007, ss 735, 735A, 735B; F(No 2)A 2017, Sch 8 paras 37–39*].

Value of certain benefits

With effect in relation to benefits received in 2017/18 onwards, a means is given of determining the value of a benefit provided to a person where the benefit involves a loan or the making available of tangible movable property or land.

The value of the benefit provided to a person (P) by a payment by way of **loan** to P is, for each tax year in which the loan is outstanding, the amount (if any) by which the interest that would have been payable on the loan at the official rate exceeds the interest actually paid by P. The official rate is the rate applied to cheap employee loans — see **28.32** EMPLOYMENT INCOME.

The value of the benefit provided by making **tangible movable property** (other than money) available, without any transfer of the property in it, to P is, for each tax year in which the benefit is provided:

$$\left(\frac{CC \times R \times D}{Y}\right) - T$$

where:

CC	=	the capital cost of the movable property ('*the asset*'), judged at the time it is first made available to P in the tax year, where that capital cost is the consideration given for the asset by the person providing the benefit (or, if greater, its market value when acquired by that person) plus any enhancement expenditure incurred on it by that person to date;
D	=	the number of days in the tax year on which the asset is made available to P (the '*relevant period*');
R	=	the official rate of interest (or the average official rate) for the relevant period;
Y	=	the number of days in the tax year; and
T	=	the total paid by P in the tax year, to the person providing the benefit, in respect of the asset's availability to P, plus any other amounts paid by P for the repair, insurance, maintenance or storage of the asset.

The value of the benefit provided by making **land** available for the use of a P (without transferring the whole of the provider's interest in the land to P) is, for each tax year in which the benefit is provided, the excess of:

- the land's 'rental value' for the period of the tax year during which it is made available to P over;
- the total paid by P in the tax year, to the person providing the benefit, in respect of the land's availability to P, plus any other amounts paid by P for the repair, insurance or maintenance of the land.

The 'rental value' of the land is broadly its letting value in the open market on the assumption that the tenant pays all taxes, rates and charges usually paid by a tenant, and the landlord bears the cost of repairs, maintenance and insurance.

For technical guidance, see www.gov.uk/government/publications/trust-protections-and-capital-gains-tax-changes.

[*ITA 2007, ss 742B–742E; F(No 2)A 2017, Sch 9 paras 2, 3*].

Simon's Taxes. See **E1.1117–E1.1121, E1.1130.**

Onward gifts

[4.16] There are provisions bringing onward gifts within the charge to tax where these are made by individuals in receipt of benefits within **4.15** above that are outside the scope of the charge due to the residence and/or domicile status of the person otherwise chargeable. These have effect in relation to onward payments made on or after **6 April 2018** (including where the onward payment is referable to a benefit received before that date) where the following conditions are met:

(i) an amount of income is treated as arising under the provisions of *ITA 2007, ss 731–733* above to an individual (the '*original beneficiary*') in a tax year (Year Z);

(ii) under matching rules the amount is matched (a) with an amount of relevant income that is 'protected income' and (b) with the whole or part of a benefit received by the original beneficiary;

(iii) at the time the benefit in (ii)(b) above is received by the original beneficiary, there are arrangements, or there is an intention, to pass on the benefit (or part of it) to another person who it is anticipated will be UK resident when the benefit is passed on;

(iv) the original beneficiary makes a gift (the '*onward payment*') to a person (the '*subsequent recipient*') in anticipation of the benefit being received or within the three years after the benefit is provided;

(v) the gift is of, or includes, the whole or part of the benefit or anything deriving from it or the gift is of other property but the benefit is provided with a view to enabling or facilitating, or otherwise in connection with, the making of the gift;

(vi) (except in a case within (vii) below) the original beneficiary is non-UK resident for Year Z, or is chargeable on the remittance basis for that year and none of the amount mentioned in (i) above is remitted before the end of the 'charging year' and in a tax year for which the original beneficiary is UK resident; and

(vii) (in a case where under *ITA 2007, s 733A* a settlor of a settlement is liable for tax on the amount in (i) above — see **4.15** above) that settlor is chargeable on the remittance basis for Year Z and none of the amount mentioned in (i) above is remitted before the end of the 'charging year' and in a tax year for which that settlor is UK resident.

In a case where the original beneficiary or the settlor in (vii) above is chargeable on the remittance basis for Year Z and *part* of the amount in (i) above is remitted as mentioned in (vi) or (vii), the above conditions are judged as if the amount in (i) above is the amount not so remitted.

The matching rules referred to in (ii) above are those in *ITTOIA 2005, s 735A*, referred to in **4.15** above under Application of remittance basis, which are deemed to apply for this purpose. '*Protected income*' has the meaning in **4.15** (under Settlor liable for tax in certain cases). Where (iv) and (v) above are met, it is to be presumed (unless shown to the contrary) that (iii) is also met. If the onward payment is made in anticipation of the benefit being received (see (iv) above), it is treated for the purposes of these provisions as made immediately after, and in the tax year in which, the benefit is received by the original beneficiary. In (vi) and (vii) above, the '*charging year*' is the later of the tax year in which the onward payment is made in (iv) is made and the 'matching year'. The '*matching year*' is the first tax year in which the matching mentioned in (ii) would occur.

The charge

If the above conditions are met and the subsequent recipient is UK resident for the tax year in which the onward payment is made (the '*gift year*'), and also for the matching year if that is later than the gift year, income is treated as arising as in **4.15** above to the subsequent recipient for the charging year. The amount of that income (Amount A) is equal to so much of the amount or value of the onward payment as falls within (v) above. If the subsequent recipient is chargeable on the remittance basis for the charging year, the amount treated as income is equal to so much (if any) of Amount A as is remitted to the UK in that year. In either case the amount treated as income is reduced by any part of it on which the subsequent recipient is liable to income tax otherwise than under this charge. If the amount to be treated as income (after any such reduction) would otherwise exceed the amount mentioned in (i) above, it is restricted to that amount.

If the subsequent recipient is non-UK resident for the gift year, or if the matching year is later than the gift year and the subsequent recipient is UK resident for the gift year but not for the matching year, it will be seen that the above charge cannot have effect. In such a case, the subsequent recipient is treated as if he were an individual within (i) above, with the result that the charge can apply in the event of a further onward payment, but only if it is made no later than three years after the benefit is provided to the original beneficiary. The amount of the income for the purpose of (i) above (Amount B) is so much of the amount or value of the onward payment as falls within (v) above and is not treated as arising to a settlor under the rules below (under Transfer of chargeability to settlor). A similar rule applies if the subsequent recipient is UK resident for both the gift year and the matching year (if later than the gift year) and is chargeable on the remittance basis for the charging year, but there is at least a part of the onward payment that is not remitted to the UK in the charging year. In this case the amount of the income for the purpose of (i) is so much of Amount B as is not remitted. In either case, the amount of the income for the purpose of (i) is not to exceed the amount mentioned in (i) in the case of the original beneficiary. In applying the charge above in the event of a subsequent onward payment, the conditions at (i)–(vii) above have effect with the following modifications: (ii) and (iii) are omitted; the reference in (iv) to the benefit is to the previous onward payment being made; and the reference in (v) to the benefit is a reference to so much of that onward payment as was on that previous occasion within (v).

The original beneficiary is not liable to tax, and the settlor is not is liable under *ITA 2007, s 733A* (see **4.15** above), for any year after the charging year on so much of the amount mentioned in (i) above as is treated as above as arising to the subsequent recipient.

Transfer of chargeability to settlor

Where conditions (i)–(vii) above are met, chargeability is transferred in the circumstances set out below from the subsequent recipient to the settlor of a settlement. The settlement in question is the one referred to in the definitions of protected foreign-source income at **4.14** above that are brought into play by (ii)(a) above. The circumstances are that:

- the subsequent recipient is a close member of the settlor's family when the onward payment is made and either is UK resident for the charging year and chargeable to tax on the remittance basis for that year or is non-UK resident for that year;
- (in a case where the subsequent recipient is UK resident and chargeable on the remittance basis) none, or part only, of the onward payment is remitted to the UK in the charging year;
- there is a time in the charging year when the settlor is UK resident; and
- there is no time in the charging year when the settlor is domiciled in the UK or is deemed domiciled by virtue of the first of the two conditions at **63.36** RESIDENCE AND DOMICILE.

The settlor is treated as an individual to whom income is treated as arising as in **4.15** above for the charging year. The amount of that income (Amount C) is equal to the amount or value of so much of the onward payment as falls within (v) above. In a case where part only of Amount C is remitted to the UK in the charging year, the amount treated as income is equal to so much of Amount C as is not remitted. In either case the amount treated as income is reduced by any part of it on which the settlor is liable to income tax otherwise than under this charge. If the amount to be treated as income (after any such reduction) would otherwise exceed the amount mentioned in (i) above, it is restricted to that amount.

Where chargeability is effectively transferred as above to the settlor from the subsequent recipient, the settlor is entitled to recover from the subsequent recipient the amount of tax paid. For this purpose, the settlor is entitled to require from an officer of HMRC a certificate specifying the amount of income in question and the amount of tax paid.

The original beneficiary is not liable to tax for any year after the charging year on so much of the amount mentioned in (i) above as is treated as above as arising to the settlor.

[*ITA 2007, ss 733B–733E; FA 2018, Sch 10 paras 16, 21(1)(4)*].

Application of remittance basis

Where income is treated as arising to an individual under the above provisions for a tax year, and the individual is chargeable on the remittance basis for that year, the income is treated as relevant foreign income of the individual, with the consequences in **61.4** REMITTANCE BASIS but ignoring the reference there to split year treatment. For the purpose of applying the remittance basis rules, treat the onward payment, or (as the case may be) the part of it whose amount or value is equal to the amount of the income, as deriving from the income. [*ITA 2007, s 735C; FA 2018, Sch 10 paras 19, 21(1)*].

Simon's Taxes. See **E1.1122–E1.1126.**

Exemptions from above liabilities

[4.17] An individual is not liable under the transfer of assets abroad rules at **4.14–4.16** above by reference to the 'relevant transactions' if he satisfies HMRC that:

- it would not be reasonable to draw the conclusion, from all the circumstances of the case, that the purpose of avoiding liability to taxation was the purpose, or one of the purposes, for which the 'relevant transactions' or any of them were effected; or that
- all the 'relevant transactions' were genuine 'commercial transactions' *and* it would not be reasonable to draw the conclusion, from all the circumstances of the case, that any one or more of them was more than incidentally designed for the purpose of avoiding liability to taxation.

In determining the purposes of 'relevant transactions', the intentions and purposes of any person who designs or effects them or provides advice on them must be taken into account.

'*Relevant transactions*' means the transfer and any 'associated operations' (see **4.14** above). Transactions are '*commercial transactions*' only if they are effected in the course of, or with a view to setting up, a trade or business and, in either case, for the purposes of that trade or business. The making and/or managing of investments is not regarded as a trade or business for this purpose unless the person by whom and the person for whom it is done are independent persons (i.e. persons not connected with each other as in **19** CONNECTED PERSONS) dealing at arm's length. Non-arm's length transactions are not commercial transactions. Any associated operation that would not otherwise fall to be taken into account can nevertheless be taken into account if it would cause either of the above tests to be failed.

Any decision taken by HMRC on these tests is subject to review by the Appeal Tribunal on appeal.

[*ITA 2007, ss 737, 738, 751*].

There is provision for apportionment in a case where a transfer and any associated operations met the second of the two exemption tests, but one or more subsequent associated operations result in liability under *ITA 2007, ss 720, 727* as a result of their failing to meet the second of the two tests. The amount otherwise chargeable under *ss 720, 727* is to be reduced to the proportion of it (if any) that is considered by HMRC to be justly and reasonably attributable to the subsequent associated operations. Again, the Tribunal has jurisdiction, on appeal, to review any decision of HMRC on this matter.

[*ITA 2007, ss 741, 742, 751*].

Different exemption rules applied in relation to transactions before 5 December 2005 (see *ITA 2007, s 739*) and in cases where one or more of the relevant transactions was entered into before that date and one or more on or after that date (see *ITA 2007, s 740*).

For successful appeals against HMRC refusal to apply the exemption, see *Beneficiary v CIR* (Sp C 190), [1999] SSCD 134 (in which the grounds were that a transfer involved tax mitigation rather than tax avoidance) and *Carvill v CIR* (Sp C 233), [2000] SSCD 143 (in which the Special Commissioner accepted that the transfer had been for bona fide commercial purposes). In *Rialas v HMRC* FTT (TC 7316), [2019] UKFTT 520 (TC), the interposition of a non-UK resident trust between the individual and the assets had a tax avoidance motive, i.e. a reduction in the individual's exposure to UK inheritance tax, and thus the individual did not meet the above conditions for exemption; it was irrelevant that all other steps taken in the matter were commercial.

Exemption for genuine transactions

Income is to be left out of account under **4.14** or **4.15** above insofar as the individual otherwise chargeable satisfies an officer of HMRC that the income is attributable to a transaction that meets both conditions A and B below.

> Condition A is that if, viewed objectively, the transaction were to be considered to be a genuine transaction having regard to any arrangements under which it is effected and any other relevant circumstances, the individual's liability to tax under **4.14** or **4.15** above would, in contravention of a 'European treaty provision', constitute an unjustified and disproportionate restriction on a freedom protected under that treaty provision. The treaty provisions in question protect freedom of movement of persons, capital, services and goods.
>
> Condition B is that the individual satisfies an officer of HMRC that the transaction should be thus considered.

The Appeal Tribunal has jurisdiction, on appeal, to review any decision of HMRC on these matters. In *Hoey v HMRC*, FTT (TC 7292), [2019] UKFTT 489 (TC), the Tribunal concluded that whilst the transfer of assets abroad legislation did infringe the principle of the free movement of capital, it was a reasonable and proportionate response to achieve the objective of preventing the transfer of income abroad from the UK, and thus the exemption did not apply.

Transactions not at arm's length

A transaction on terms that would not have been made between unconnected persons dealing at arm's length, or that would not have been entered into between such persons so dealing, will not generally be considered to be a genuine transaction. This rule does not apply if 'the relevant transfer' (see below) is made for no consideration by an individual who makes it wholly for personal (and not commercial) reasons and for the personal (and not the commercial) benefit of other individuals. Any assets and income listed in (a)–(d) below in relation to the transfer must be used accordingly.

If the above rule applies to only part of a transaction, and an officer of HMRC is satisfied as to the other part, the exemption can still apply to income attributable to that other part.

Business considerations

Further considerations apply if any of the following assets or income are used for the purposes of, or are received in the course of, activities carried on in a territory outside the UK by a person (P) through a business establishment which P has in that territory:

(a) any of the assets transferred by 'the relevant transfer' (see below);
(b) any assets directly or indirectly representing any of those assets;
(c) any income arising from assets within (a) or (b); or
(d) any assets directly or indirectly representing accumulations of income arising from assets within (a) or (b).

In order for the transaction to be considered a genuine transaction the said activities must consist of the provision by P of goods or services to others on a commercial basis, and must involve:

- the use of staff (i.e. employees, agents or contractors of P) in numbers, and with competence and authority,
- the use of premises and equipment, and
- the addition of economic value by P to those to whom the goods or services are provided,

commensurate with the size and nature of those activities. The question of whether a person has a business establishment in a territory outside the UK is determined in accordance with *CTA 2010, ss 1141, 1142(1), 1143* as if references in those provisions to a company were to a person and references to a permanent establishment were to a business establishment.

Meaning of 'the relevant transfer'

A relevant transfer is a transfer of assets as a result of which, or as a result of operations associated with which, income becomes payable to a person abroad. If the transaction under review is the relevant transfer, the references above to '*the relevant transfer*' are to that transfer; if the transaction under review is an associated operation (see **4.14** above), those references are to the relevant transfer to which it relates.

[*ITA 2007, ss 716, 742A, 751*].

Simon's Taxes. See **E1.1127–E1.1129.**

Miscellaneous

[4.18] The following miscellaneous matters apply.

Exclusion of double charge

No income can be charged more than once under the provisions at **4.14–4.17** above, and, where there is a choice as to persons to be assessed, HMRC may allocate income as appears just and reasonable. Appeal can be made to the Appeal Tribunal against HMRC's decision. Income is treated as having been charged to tax:

- in full, where charged under *ITA 2007, ss 720, 727* as income;
- to the extent of the value of any benefit charged under **4.14**(iii) above; and
- to the amount of relevant income taken into account in charging any benefit under *ITA 2007, s 731*.

If an amount of income is taken into account in charging income tax on an individual under the provisions at **4.14–4.17** above and the individual subsequently receives that income, the income received is treated as not being the individual's income for income tax purposes.

[*ITA 2007, ss 743, 744, 751*].

Trustees and personal representatives

In relation to benefits received on or after 15 June 1989, relevant income for the purposes of *ITA 2007, s 731* (see **4.15** above) includes income arising to trustees or personal representatives before 6 April 1989, notwithstanding that one or more of the trustees or personal representatives was not resident outside the UK, unless they have been charged to tax in respect of that income. [*ITA 2007, Sch 2 para 135*].

Accrued income on certain securities

See **2.25** ACCRUED INCOME SCHEME as regards deemed income arising on transfer of certain securities.

Offshore funds

The transfer of assets abroad rules apply in relation to an offshore income gain arising to a person resident or domiciled outside the UK as if it were foreign income becoming payable to that person (see **51.10** OFFSHORE FUNDS).

Deeply discounted securities

Where a non-UK resident or non-UK domiciled person realises a profit from the discount on a deeply discounted security, it is treated for the purposes of **4.14–4.17** above as income of that person (see **65.30** SAVINGS AND INVESTMENT INCOME).

Controlled foreign companies

See Tolley's Corporation Tax under Controlled Foreign Companies as regards *ITA 2007, s 720* relief in certain cases where a charge is made in respect of profits of such companies. [*ITA 2007, s 725*].

Transfer pricing

[4.19] The transfer pricing legislation at *TIOPA 2010, Pt 4 (ss 146–217)* is to be construed so as best to secure consistency between the effect given to the basic statutory rule (see **4.20** below) and the principles of *Article 9* of the OECD Model Tax Convention and transfer pricing guidelines. [*TIOPA 2010, s 164; FA 2016, s 75(1)(3); SI 2018 No 266*]. The guidelines are published by the OECD (Organisation for Economic Co-operation and Development) as 'Transfer Pricing Guidelines for Multinational Enterprises and Tax Administrations', and are available at www.oecd-ilibrary.org/taxation/oecd-transfer-pricing-guidelines-for-multinational-enterprises-and-tax-administrations-2017_tpg-2017-en. See also HMRC International Manual at INTM421000 *et seq.*

The transfer pricing legislation applies not only to international transactions but to transactions both parties to which are in the UK.

There are exemptions (see **4.22** below) for small and medium-sized businesses.

See HMRC International Manual at INTM410000 *et seq.* for further guidance.

The HMRC International Division, Room 311, Melbourne House, Aldwych, London WC2B 4LL may be approached for pre-transaction guidance on the likely tax treatment in particular cases when financial arrangements are in the process of being put in place. See Revenue Tax Bulletin October 1998 pp 579–582 for guidance on the nature of the risk assessment carried out by HMRC before undertaking a transfer pricing enquiry and a suggested timetabling framework for such enquiries.

With relevance to transfer pricing, HMRC SP 1 (2018) (previously SP 1/11) considers the use of mutual agreement procedure (MAP) under UK double tax agreements and/or the EU Arbitration Convention (see **4.28** below) and also describes the UK's approach to the use of arbitration as part of the MAP process.

See Tolley's Corporation Tax under Transfer Pricing for matters relevant only to companies.

See **Simon's Taxes D2.6.**

The basic rule

[4.20] The transfer pricing legislation applies where:

(a) provision (the '*actual provision*') has been made or imposed as between two persons (the '*affected persons*') by means of a transaction or series of transactions;
(b) the 'participation condition' is met (see **4.21** below); and
(c) the actual provision differs from the provision (the '*arm's length provision*') which would have been made as between independent enterprises.

If the actual provision confers a 'potential advantage' in relation to UK taxation on one (or both) of the affected persons, the profits and losses of the potentially advantaged person (or both of them) are computed for tax purposes as if the arm's length provision had been made or imposed instead of the actual provision. The resulting increase in profits (or decrease in losses) is often referred to as the '*transfer pricing adjustment*'.

The above applies equally if provision is made or imposed as between two persons but no provision would have been made as between independent enterprises. In such a case, the reference to the 'arm's length provision' is a reference to no provision being made.

See **4.22** below for exemptions to the basic rule above. There is also an exemption for certain oil transactions (see *TIOPA 2010, s 147(7)*) and special rules for oil-related ring-fence trades.

The actual provision confers a '*potential advantage*' on a person in relation to UK taxation where its effect, compared to that of the corresponding arm's length provision, would be a reduction in that person's profits or income or an increase in his losses for any chargeable period. Any income of a non-UK resident that is 'disregarded income' (within **50.3** NON-RESIDENTS) is left out of account in determining whether there is any such reduction or increase. 'Losses' for these purposes include relief under *ITTOIA 2005, s 57* for pre-trading expenditure (see **75.106** TRADING INCOME) and relief for interest paid under the trade losses rules (see **64** RETURNS and **45** LOSSES).

A 'transaction' for these purposes includes arrangements, understandings and mutual practices (whether or not legally enforceable). An 'arrangement' means any scheme or arrangement of any kind. A 'series' of transactions includes a number of transactions entered into (whether or not consecutively) in pursuance of, or in relation to, the same arrangement. A series of transactions is not prevented from being regarded as the means by which provision has been made or imposed between two persons by reason only that:

- there is no transaction in the series to which both those persons are parties; or
- the parties to any arrangement in pursuance of which the transactions are entered into do not include one or both of those persons; or
- there is one or more transactions in the series to which neither of those persons is a party.

[*TIOPA 2010, ss 147, 149–151, 155, 156*].

The participation condition

[4.21] The '*participation condition*' in **4.20**(b) above is met if:

(a) one of the affected persons was directly or indirectly participating in the management, control or capital of the other; or
(b) the same person (or persons) was (or were) directly or indirectly participating in the management, control or capital of each of the affected persons.

See below as to what is meant by 'directly or indirectly participating' in (a) and (b) above.

Generally, the participation condition is met only if (a) or (b) above is fulfilled at the time the actual provision is made or imposed. However, if and insofar as the actual provision is provision relating to 'financing arrangements', the participation condition is met if (a) or (b) above is fulfilled at that time or at any time in the next six months; so transfer pricing adjustments may be triggered by events occurring up to six months before the necessary relationship exists between the parties. '*Financing arrangements*' means arrangements made for providing or guaranteeing, or otherwise in connection with, any debt, capital or other form of finance.

Direct participation

For the purposes of (a) and (b) above, a person (B) is directly participating in the management, control or capital of another person (C) at a particular time if and only if, at that time, C is a body corporate or partnership which B controls (within *CTA 2010, s 1124*).

Indirect participation

For the purposes of (a) and (b) above (but subject to the special rules for financing arrangements), a person (P) is indirectly participating in the management, control or capital of another person (A) at a particular time:

(i) if P would be *directly* participating in the management, control or capital of A at that time if certain rights and powers (see *TIOPA 2010, ss 159(3)–(7), 163*) were attributed to him; these include *future* rights and powers; or
(ii) if P is, at that time, one of a number of 'major participants' in A's enterprise.

A person (Q) is a '*major participant*' in the enterprise of another person (B) if B is a body corporate or partnership, and Q is one of two persons who control B (within *CTA 2010, s 1124*), each of whom has at least 40% of the holdings, rights and powers which give them that control. In deciding whether this test is met, certain rights and powers are attributed as in (i) above.

In cases involving 'financing arrangements' (see above), the meaning of indirect participation is extended to include circumstances where a number of parties act together in relation to the financing arrangements of a business and could collectively control the business. So, for the purposes of (a) above, a person (X) is treated as indirectly participating in the management etc. of another person (Y) if:

- the actual provision relates, to any extent, to financing arrangements for Y (where Y is a body corporate or partnership);
- X and other persons acted together in relation to the arrangements; and
- X would be taken to have control of Y if, at a 'relevant time', there were attributed to X the rights and powers of each of those other persons (taking into account any additional rights or powers that would be attributed to any person under (i) above if it were being decided whether that person is indirectly participating).

'*Relevant time*' means any time when X and the other persons were acting together in relation to the financing arrangements or any time in the six months after they ceased to do so.

For the purposes of (b) above, the rule applies where the actual provision relates to financing arrangements for one of the affected persons and X would be taken to have control of each of the affected persons. It is immaterial whether the persons acting together did so at the time the actual provision is made or imposed or did so at some earlier time.

[*TIOPA 2010, ss 148, 157–163, 217(1)*].

Exemptions from the basic rule

[4.22] No transfer pricing adjustment (as in **4.20** above) is made in computing profits or losses of a potentially advantaged person (see **4.20** above) for a tax year for which that person is a 'small enterprise' or a 'medium-sized enterprise'. See below for exceptions to this rule.

For this purpose, a '*small enterprise*' is one defined as such in the Annex to *Commission Recommendation 2003/361/EC* published by the EC on 6 May 2003 (as modified by *TIOPA 2010, s 172(4)–(7)*) and a '*medium-sized enterprise*' is one which falls within the category of micro, small and medium-sized enterprises as defined in that Annex (as modified) but which is not a 'small enterprise'. Broadly, the entity must meet the following criteria (see HMRC guidance at HMRC International Manual INTM412080).

	Maximum number of staff	And less than one of these limits	
		Annual turnover	*Balance sheet total*
Small enterprise	50	10 million euros	10 million euros
Medium-sized enterprise	250	50 million euros	43 million euros

'Balance sheet total' means, broadly, total assets (without netting off liabilities). Associated entities etc. must be taken into account in determining whether the criteria are met. The modifications made to the Annex ensure, in particular, that qualification as small or medium-sized depends on the entity's data for the tax year under review and without reference to past history.

A small or medium-sized enterprise may make an irrevocable election to disapply the exemption for a particular tax year.

HMRC may override the exemption for any tax year (in relation to one or more particular provisions made or imposed) where the potentially advantaged person is a *medium-sized* enterprise. They do so by issuing a '*transfer pricing notice*' to the potentially advantaged person. A transfer pricing notice can be given only after an enquiry has been opened into the person's tax return (and an enquiry can be opened specifically for this purpose) potentially advantaged person can appeal against the notice (within 30 days) but only on the grounds that he is not a medium-sized enterprise. A person in receipt of a transfer pricing notice has 90 days in which to make the necessary amendments to his tax return, beginning on the date of issue of the notice or, where relevant, on the date the appeal against the notice is finally determined or abandoned. Failure to do so results in the return becoming an incorrect return (so that penalties potentially apply — see, for example, **55.6** PENALTIES). The enquiry into the tax return cannot be closed until either the amendment is made or the 90-day period expires (though this does not prevent the issue of a partial closure notice that is unrelated to any matter to which the transfer pricing notice relates). (See **64.6–64.10** RETURNS for enquiries into returns generally.)

The exemption does not apply to either a small or a medium-sized enterprise in relation to an actual provision made or imposed if, at the time the provision is made or imposed, the other affected person or a 'party to a relevant transaction' is a 'resident' of a 'non-qualifying territory' (regardless of whether he is also a resident of a 'qualifying territory'). A person is a '*party to a relevant transaction*' if the actual provision was imposed by means of a series of transactions and he was a party to one or more of them. For these purposes, a person is a '*resident*' of a territory if he is liable to tax there by reason of his domicile, residence or place of management, unless he is so liable only in respect of income from sources in that territory or capital situated there.

'*Qualifying territory*' means the UK or any territory with which the UK has a double tax agreement (see **27.2** DOUBLE TAX RELIEF) containing a standard non-discrimination provision (see HMRC International Manual INTM412090 for a list of countries with which the UK has an appropriate agreement). '*Non-qualifying territory*' is construed accordingly. However, territories may also be designated as 'qualifying' or 'non-qualifying' by Treasury regulations made for the purposes of these provisions.

[*TIOPA 2010, ss 166–173; TMA 1970, s 9A(4); F(No 2)A 2017, Sch 15 paras 40, 44*].

Elimination of double counting

[4.23] Where:

- a potential advantage is conferred (as in **4.20** above) on only one of the affected persons (the '*advantaged person*'); and
- the other person (the '*disadvantaged person*') is within the charge to income tax or corporation tax in respect of profits arising from the activities in relation to which the actual provision was made or imposed,

then the disadvantaged person may claim application of the arm's length provision rather than the actual provision (overriding any applicable time limits for the necessary adjustments).

The above claim can be made only if the arm's length provision has similarly been applied in the case of the advantaged person (in his return or as a result of a determination). The claim must be consistent with the calculation made in the case of the advantaged person. The claim must be made within two years after the making of the return by the advantaged person or the giving of the notice taking account of the determination, as the case may be. A claim based on a return which is subsequently the subject of such a notice may be amended within two years after the giving of the notice.

If notice taking account of a transfer pricing determination is given to the advantaged person, HMRC have a duty to inform a disadvantaged person of the potential for a claim. If there is a breach of this duty, the Commissioners for HMRC have discretion to extend the time allowed for the making or amendment of a claim.

The above claim cannot be made if the advantaged person is a company and the disadvantaged person is a person (other than a company) within the charge to income tax in respect of profits arising from the said activities (see technical note at www.gov.uk/government/publications/compensating-adjustments-technical-discussion-note).

Financing arrangements

Where the conditions at **4.21**(a) and (b) above are satisfied only by virtue of the special rules for financing arrangements, no claim by the disadvantaged person can be made where the actual provision is provision in relation to a security issued by one of the affected persons and the security is guaranteed by a person with whom the issuer of the security has a 'participatory relationship'. Appropriately modified versions of **4.21**(a) and (b) above apply to determine the existence or otherwise of a '*participatory relationship*' (see *TIOPA 2010, s 175(2)*).

Closing stock or work in progress

A claim by the disadvantaged person to apply the arm's length provision does not affect the amount he is required to bring into account as closing trading stock or work in progress for any accounting period of his which ends on or after the last day of the accounting period of the advantaged person in which the actual provision was made or imposed. In the absence of such a rule, the benefit to him of applying the arm's length provision would effectively be delayed until the stock were sold or the work in progress realised.

Double tax reliefs

Where the above claim is made, it is assumed, as respects any foreign tax credit which has been (or may be) given to the disadvantaged person:

- that the foreign tax does not include any tax which would not be (or would not have become) payable if the arm's length provision had also been made or imposed for the purposes of that tax; and
- that the profits from the activities in relation to which the actual provision was made or imposed and in respect of which the tax credit relief arises are reduced to the same extent as they are treated as reduced by virtue of the claim.

Where the application of the arm's length provision in a computation following such a claim involves a reduction in the amount of any income, and that income also falls to be treated as reduced under *TIOPA 2010, s 112(1)* by an amount of foreign tax (where credit relief is not available), the first-mentioned reduction is treated as made before the latter. The deductible foreign tax excludes that paid on so much of the income as is represented by the amount of the first-mentioned reduction.

Any adjustment to double tax reliefs as above may be given effect by set-off against any relief or repayment arising from the claim, and may be made without regard to any time limit on assessments or amendments.

Balancing payments

Where one or more payments (‘*balancing payments*’) are made to the advantaged person by the disadvantaged person to compensate for the transfer pricing adjustment, they are not taken into account in computing either person's taxable profits or allowable losses to the extent that they do not in aggregate exceed the ‘available compensating adjustment’. The ‘*available compensating adjustment*’ is the difference between the profits/losses of the disadvantaged person computed on the basis of the actual provision and those profits/losses computed on the basis that the disadvantaged person makes a claim as above to apply the arm's length provision instead.

[*TIOPA 2010, ss 174, 174A, 175–178, 180, 185, 186, 188–190, 195, 196, 216*].

Determinations requiring HMRC sanction

[4.24] A determination of an amount falling to be brought into account under **4.20** above, other than in certain cases where an agreement has been reached between HMRC and the person concerned (see *TIOPA 2010, s 209*), requires the sanction of the Commissioners for HMRC. Where such a determination is made for the purpose of giving a closure notice, making a discovery assessment or giving a discovery notice amending a partnership return, and the notice or assessment is given to a person:

- without the determination, so far as taken into account in the notice or assessment, having been approved by HMRC; or
- without a copy of the Commissioners' approval having been served on that person at or before the time the notice was given,

the closure or amendment notice or discovery assessment is deemed to have been given or made (and in the case of an assessment notified) as if the determination had not been taken into account. The Commissioners' approval must be given specifically to the case in question and must apply to the amount determined, but may otherwise be given (either before or after the making of the determination) in any such form or manner as the Commissioners may determine. An appeal relating to a determination approved by the Commissioners may not question the Commissioners' approval except to the extent that the grounds for questioning the approval are the same as the grounds for questioning the determination itself.

[*TIOPA 2010, ss 208–211*].

Appeals

[4.25] The following rules apply in so far as the question in dispute on an appeal:

- is or involves a determination of whether the transfer pricing legislation has effect; and
- relates to any provision made or imposed as between two persons each of whom is within the charge to income tax or corporation tax in respect of profits arising from the activities in relation to which the actual provision was made or imposed.

The rules are that:

- each of the persons as between whom the actual provision was made or imposed is entitled to be a party in any proceedings;
- the Appeal Tribunal is to determine the question separately from any other question in the proceedings; and
- the Tribunal's determination on the question has effect as if made in an appeal to which each of those persons was a party

[*TIOPA 2010, ss 212, 216*].

Miscellaneous

Capital allowances

[4.26] The transfer pricing provisions do not generally affect the computation of capital allowances or balancing charges under *CAA 2001*. However, this does *not* apply for the purposes of **4.23** above (elimination of double counting). [*TIOPA 2010, s 213*].

Interest paid

Where a person pays interest under the actual provision and a transfer pricing adjustment falls to be made, such that some or all of the interest paid is disallowed, then, if the recipient makes a claim under **4.23** above (elimination of double counting), the disallowed interest is not chargeable to income tax or corporation tax in his hands and the payer is not required to deduct tax at source.

Where it is not possible to make the claim under **4.23** above because the advantaged person is a company and the disadvantaged person is a person within the charge to income tax, the disallowed interest is treated for income tax purposes as a dividend paid by the company which paid the interest. This does not apply in relation to '*pre-commencement interest*', i.e. an amount of interest to the extent that it is, in accordance with generally accepted accounting practice, referable to a period before 25 October 2013 (see technical note at www.gov.uk/government/publications/compensating-adjustments-technical-discussion-note).

[*TIOPA 2010, ss 187, 187A; FA 2016, Sch 1 paras 68(3), 73*].

Employee share schemes

For an article on the application of the transfer pricing rules to employee share scheme costs, in particular in relation to the decision in *Waterloo plc v CIR* (Sp C 301), [2002] SSCD 95, see Revenue Tax Bulletin February 2003 pp 1002–1007.

Advance pricing agreements (APAs)

[4.27] A person ('the taxpayer') may apply to the Commissioners for HMRC for a written agreement (an advance pricing agreement) determining a method for resolving pricing issues in advance of a return being made. Provided the terms of the agreement are complied with, they provide assurance that the treatment of those pricing issues will be accepted by both HMRC and the enterprise for the period covered by the agreement.

An advance pricing agreement (APA) must contain a declaration that it is an agreement made for the purposes of *TIOPA 2010, s 218*. It may contain provision relating to chargeable periods ending before the agreement is made. If the taxpayer is not a company (and subject to special provision for oil-related ring-fence trades), the APA must relate to one or more of the following.

(a) The attribution of income to a branch or agency through which the taxpayer has been carrying on, or is proposing to carry on, a trade in the UK.
(b) The attribution of income to any permanent establishment of the taxpayer's (wherever situated) through which the taxpayer has been carrying on, or is proposing to carry on, any business.
(c) The extent to which income which has arisen or which may arise to the taxpayer is to be taken for any purpose to be income arising outside the UK.
(d) The treatment for tax purposes of any provision made or imposed (whether before or after the date of the APA) as between the taxpayer and any 'associate' of his.

For the purposes of (d) above, persons are 'associates' for this purpose if (at the time of the making or imposition of the provision).

- one of them is directly or indirectly participating in the management, control or capital of the other; or
- the same person or persons is or are directly or indirectly participating in the management, control or capital of each of the two persons,

with further special provision in relation to sales of oil. For the meaning of direct and indirect participation, see **4.21** above.

Where an APA is in force in relation to a chargeable period, questions relating to the matters in (a)–(d) above are, to the extent provided for in the APA, to be determined in accordance with the APA rather than by reference to the legislative provisions which would otherwise have applied. However, where the relevant matter falls within (d) above and not within (a), (b) or (c) above, the only legislative provisions which can be displaced are those contained in the transfer pricing legislation. Where an APA relating to a chargeable period beginning or ending before the date of the APA provides for the manner in which consequent adjustments are to be made, those adjustments are to be made in the manner provided for in the APA.

An APA does not, however, have effect in relation to the determination of any question which relates to:

- a time after that from which an officer of HMRC has revoked the APA in accordance with its terms; or
- a time after or in relation to which any provision of the APA has not been complied with, where the APA was conditional upon compliance with that provision; or
- any matter as respects which any other essential conditions have not been, or are no longer, met.

The application for the APA must be an application for the clarification by agreement of the effect in the taxpayer's case of provisions by reference to which questions relating to any one or more of the matters in (a)–(d) above are to be, or might be, determined. The application must set out the taxpayer's understanding of what would in his case be the effect, in the absence of any agreement, of the provisions in relation to which clarification is sought, and in what respects clarification is required. It must also propose how the clarification might be effected in a manner consistent with that understanding.

It is for HMRC to ensure that the APA is modified so as to be consistent with any mutual agreement made under, and for the purposes of, a double taxation treaty.

Where the APA makes provision for its modification or revocation by HMRC, this may take effect from such time (including a time before the modification or revocation) as HMRC may determine.

A party to an APA must provide HMRC with all such reports and other information as he may be required to provide under the APA or by virtue of any request made by an officer of HMRC in accordance with the APA.

If, before an APA was made, the taxpayer fraudulently or negligently provided HMRC with false or misleading information in relation to the application for the APA or in connection with its preparation, the APA is deemed never to have been made. HMRC must notify the taxpayer that the APA is nullified by reason of the misrepresentation. A penalty of up to £10,000 may apply for so giving such false or misleading information.

Effect of APA on third parties

Where an APA has effect in relation to any provision between the taxpayer and another person, then in applying the double counting rules in **4.23** above to the other person, the arrangements set out in the APA similarly apply in determining any question as to:

- whether the taxpayer is a person on whom a potential advantage in relation to UK taxation is conferred by the actual provision; or
- what constitutes the arm's length provision in relation to the actual provision.

This is subject to any APA made between HMRC and the other person.

[*TIOPA 2010, ss 218–230*].

For detailed guidance about how HMRC interpret the APA legislation and apply it in practice, see HMRC SP 2/10. The contact address for APA applications and expressions of interest is APA Lead, Business Assets & International, Transfer Pricing Team, 9th Floor, Mail Point 3, 10 South Colonnade, Central Mail Unit, Newcastle, NE98 1ZZ (email: APA.mailbox@hmrc.gov.uk).

Simon's Taxes. See **D2.665, D2.666.**

EU Arbitration Convention

[4.28] The Convention (*90/436/EEC*) on the elimination of double taxation in connection with the adjustment of profits of associated enterprises requires EU member States to adopt certain procedures and to follow the opinion of an advisory commission in certain cases of dispute relating to transfer pricing adjustments. The Convention contains a provision which enables the bilateral application of the Convention between those member States that have ratified it, which include the 15 older member States. For further information, see ec.europa.eu/taxation_customs/taxation/company_tax/transfer_pricing/arbitration_convention/index_en.htm.

There is legislation providing for UK domestic enactments to be overridden where necessary to give effect to a Convention determination. The legislation also provides powers and imposes confidentiality requirements in relation to disclosures of information to an advisory commission. [*TIOPA 2010, ss 126–128*].

The EU Directive on the resolution of double taxation disputes (at **27.2** DOUBLE TAX RELIEF) operates as an additional mechanism to the EU Arbitration Convention, but a claim brought under the Directive has the effect of terminating proceedings brought under the Convention.

HMRC SP 1 (2018) (previously SP 1/11) considers the use of mutual agreement procedure (MAP) under UK double tax agreements and/or the EU Arbitration Convention.

Simon's Taxes. See **D2.668.**

Sales of occupation income

[4.29] Where:

(i) transactions or arrangements are made (having as their *main* object, or one of their main objects, the avoidance or reduction of income tax) which enable some other person to enjoy income or receipts, including copyrights, licences or rights etc., deriving, directly or indirectly, from occupational activities, past or present, which an individual carries on wholly or partly in the UK; and
(ii) in connection therewith, or in consequences thereof, that individual obtains, for himself or for some other person, *a capital amount* (i.e. any amount not otherwise includible in any computation of income for tax purposes),

any such amount is (subject to certain exceptions, as below) to be treated as income arising to that individual when the capital sum is receivable (or, if it consists of property or a right, when it is sold or realised). That income is chargeable to income tax on the full amount so treated as arising in the tax year. [*ITA 2007, s 776(2)*]. Note that apportionment is necessary where a non-resident carries on an occupation partly in the UK (see *ITA 2007, ss 1015, 1016*).

Capital amounts from the disposal of:

(a) shares in a company, so far as their value is attributable to the value of the company's business as a going concern; or
(b) assets (including goodwill) of a profession or vocation, or a share in a professional or vocational partnership, so far as their value is attributable to the value of the profession etc., as a going concern,

are exempted from the above treatment. But these exemptions do not apply to any part of the capital amount which represents any part of the going-concern value of the business, profession etc., as above, materially deriving from prospective income etc., from the individual's activities in the occupation, whether as partner or employee, for which he will not receive full consideration (disregarding all capital amounts).

Where the person charged to tax is not the one for whom the capital amount was obtained (see (ii) above) he may recover from the latter person any part of that tax which he pays (for which purpose HMRC will supply, on request, a certificate of income in respect of which tax has been paid).

[*ITA 2007, ss 773–789*].

Where the person liable is non-UK resident, HMRC may direct that any part of an amount taxable under these provisions on that person be paid under deduction of income tax at the basic rate (for the tax year of payment). [*ITA 2007, s 944; FA 2016, s 79(6)*].

Account may be taken of any method, however indirect, to transfer any property or right, or enhance or diminish its value, e.g. by sales at less, or more, than full consideration, assigning share capital or rights in a company or partnership or an interest in settled property, disposal on the winding-up of any company, partnership or trust etc. Any such transfer or enhancement may be an occasion when tax is charged under the above provisions. [*ITA 2007, s 780*]. Where it is necessary to determine the extent to which the value of any property or right is derived from any other property or right, value may be traced through any number of companies, partnerships and trusts, at each stage attributing property held by the company, partnership or trust to its shareholders etc. in such manner as is appropriate in the circumstances. [*ITA 2007, s 781*].

See **28.13** EMPLOYMENT INCOME for possible treatment as employment income of any excess of the value of goodwill transferred to a company on incorporation of a business over its true value.

Simon's Taxes. See **E1.12.**

Transactions in land

[4.30] Certain gains on disposals of land before **5 July 2016** are treated as income chargeable to income tax where:

(a) the land (or any property deriving its value from the land) is acquired with the sole or main object of realising a gain from disposing of it; or
(b) the land is held as trading stock; or
(c) the land is developed with the sole or main object of realising a gain from disposing of it when developed.

In consequence of the introduction of separate provisions in **78** TRANSACTIONS IN UK LAND, these provisions are **repealed** with effect in relation to disposals on or after 5 July 2016.

The provisions apply if all or any part of the land in question is in the UK and a gain of a capital nature is obtained (for himself or for 'another person') from the disposal of all or part of the land by the person acquiring, holding or developing it or by any connected person (within **19** CONNECTED PERSONS), or a person party to, or concerned in, any arrangement or scheme to realise the gain indirectly or by a series of transactions.

For this purpose, a gain is of a capital nature if it does not (apart from these provisions and the equivalent corporation tax provisions) fall to be included in any computation of income for tax purposes. Any number of transactions may be treated as a single arrangement or scheme if they have, or there is evidence of, a common purpose. '*Another person*' may include a partnership or partners in a partnership, the trustees of settled property and personal representatives and for this purpose these are regarded as persons distinct from the individuals or persons who are for the time being partners, trustees or personal representatives.

'*Land*' is as defined in *Interpretation Act 1978, Sch 1*.

'*Property deriving its value from land*' includes any shareholding in a company, partnership interest, or interest in settled property, deriving its value, directly or indirectly, from land, and any option, consent or embargo affecting the disposition of land. See, however, 'Exemptions' below.

Land is '*disposed of*' for the above purpose if, by any one or more transactions or by any arrangement or scheme (whether concerning the land or any property deriving its value therefrom), the property in, or control over, the land is effectively disposed of. See also under 'General' below.

The gain from the disposal is treated as income arising when the gain is realised and the charge for any tax year is on the full amount of any such income treated as arising in that year. The person liable for the tax is the person whose income it is. Usually this will be the person realising the gain, but, if all or part of any gain is derived from value provided directly or indirectly by another person (as above) or from an opportunity of realising a gain provided directly or indirectly by another person, the income is that other person's.

An amount treated as arising under these provisions to a non-UK resident is treated as being from a source in the UK only to the extent that the land to which the disposal relates is in the UK.

The above provisions apply subject to *ITTOIA 2005, Pt 5 Ch 5* (amounts treated as income of settler — see **70.25** SETTLEMENTS) and to any other provision treating income as belonging to a particular person.

[*ITA 2007, ss 752–759, 763, 772; FA 2016, ss 79(5), 82(1)*].

See *Yuill v Wilson* HL 1980, 52 TC 674 and its sequel *Yuill v Fletcher* CA 1984, 58 TC 145; *Winterton v Edwards* Ch D 1979, 52 TC 655; and *Sugarwhite v Budd* CA 1988, 60 TC 679. *Bona fide* transactions, not entered into with tax avoidance in view, may be caught by the legislation — see *Page v Lowther and Another* CA 1983, 57 TC 199.

For the date of the capital gain where instalments are involved, see *Yuill v Fletcher* CA 1984, 58 TC 145.

Computation of gain

Gains are to be computed 'as is just and reasonable in the circumstances', taking into account the value of what is obtained for disposing of the land and allowing only for expenses attributable to the land disposed of. The following may be taken into account:

(A) if a leasehold interest is disposed of out of a freehold, the treatment under *ITTOIA 2005, Pt 2* (trading income) in computing the profits in such a case of a person dealing in land (see **75.107** TRADING INCOME); and
(B) any adjustments under *ITTOIA 2005, s 158* for tax on lease premiums.

Any necessary apportionments of consideration, expenses etc., are to be made on a just and reasonable basis.

[*ITA 2007, ss 760, 764; FA 2016, ss 79(5), 82(1)*].

Trustees

Income treated as above as arising to trustees of a settlement is treated as being income chargeable at the trust rate. See **70.12** SETTLEMENTS.

Exemptions

(i) An individual's gain made from the *sale etc., of his residence* exempted from capital gains tax under *TCGA 1992, ss 222–226* or which would be so exempt but for *TCGA 1992, s 224(3)* (acquired for purpose of making a gain).
(ii) A gain on the sale of *shares in a company holding land as trading stock* (or a company owning, directly or indirectly, 90% of the ordinary share capital of such a company) *provided that* the company disposes of the land by normal trade and makes all possible profit from it, and the share sale is not part of an arrangement or scheme to realise a land gain indirectly. This does not apply if the person obtaining the gain is only a party to, or concerned in, an arrangement or scheme to realise the gain indirectly or by a series of transactions. See *Chilcott v CIR* Ch D 1981, 55 TC 446.
(iii) (If the liability arises solely under (c) above) any part of the gain fairly attributable to a period *before the intention was made* to develop the land.

[*ITA 2007, ss 765–767; FA 2016, ss 79(5), 82(1)*].

Recovery of tax

Where tax under the above provisions is assessed on, and paid by, a person other than the one who actually realised the gain, the person paying the tax may recover it from the other party (for which purpose HMRC will, on request, supply a certificate of income in respect of which tax has been paid). [*ITA 2007, ss 768, 769; FA 2016, ss 79(5), 82(1)*].

Clearance

The person who made or would make the gain may (if he considers that (a) or (c) above may apply), submit to HMRC particulars of any completed or proposed transactions. If he does so HMRC must, within 30 days of receiving those particulars, notify the taxpayer whether or not they are satisfied that liability under these provisions does not arise. If HMRC are so satisfied the gain is not chargeable to income tax, provided that all material facts and considerations have been fully and accurately disclosed. [*ITA 2007, s 770; FA 2016, ss 79(5), 82(1)*].

General

Provisions similar to *ITA 2007, ss 780, 781* (for which see **4.29** above) apply for the purposes of these provisions. [*ITA 2007, ss 761, 762; FA 2016, ss 79(5), 82(1)*].

Where the person liable is non-UK resident, HMRC may direct that any part of an amount taxable under these provisions on that person be paid under deduction of income tax at the basic rate (for the tax year of payment). [*ITA 2007, s 944; FA 2016, ss 79(6), 82(1)*].

For the above purposes HMRC may require, under penalty, any person to supply them with any particulars thought necessary, including particulars of:

(I) transactions or arrangements in which he acts, or acted, on behalf of others; and
(II) transactions or arrangements which in the opinion of HMRC should be investigated; and
(III) what part, if any, he has taken, or is taking, in specified transactions or arrangements. (A *solicitor* who has merely acted as professional adviser is not treated as having taken part in a transaction or arrangement.)

A solicitor who has merely acted as professional adviser is not compelled to do more than state that he acted and give his client's name and address.

[*ITA 2007, s 771; FA 2016, ss 79(5), 82(1)*].

The transactions of which particulars are required need not be identified transactions (*Essex v CIR* CA 1980, 53 TC 720).

Simon's Taxes. See **B5.235–B5.246.**

Land sold and leased back — payments connected with transferred land

[4.31] The consequences described below ensue where land (or any interest or estate in land) is transferred (by sale, lease, surrender or forfeiture of lease etc.) and, as a result of:

- a lease of the land, or any part of it, granted at the time of transfer or subsequently by the transferee to the transferor; or
- another transaction or transactions affecting the land or interest or estate,

the transferor, or a person associated (see below) with the transferor, becomes liable to make a payment of rent under a lease of the land or part of it (including any premium treated as rent — see **60.29** PROPERTY INCOME), or any other payment connected with the land or part of it (whether it is a payment of rentcharge or under some other transaction), which would be allowable as a deduction:

- in computing the profits of a trade, profession or vocation; or
- in computing the profits of a UK property business; or
- in computing profits or income under any of the provisions listed at *ITA 2007, s 1016* (see **49.8** MISCELLANEOUS INCOME) or in computing losses for which relief is available as in **49.11** MISCELLANEOUS INCOME; or
- from earnings, under *ITEPA 2003, s 336*; or
- in calculating losses in an employment.

A transfer of an estate or interest in land includes:

(a) the granting of a lease or another transaction involving the creation of a new estate or interest in the land;
(b) the transfer of the lessee's interest under a lease by surrender or forfeiture of the lease; and
(c) a transaction or series of transactions affecting land or an estate or interest in land, such that some person is the owner (or one of the owners) before and after the transaction(s) but another person becomes or ceases to be one of the owners.

With regard to (c), a person is to be regarded as a transferor for the purposes of these provisions if the person is an owner before the transaction(s) and is not the sole owner afterwards.

The consequences are that the deduction for tax purposes in respect of the rent or other payment is limited to the 'commercial rent' of the land to which it relates for the period for which the payment is made. In fact, except where the deduction is made against earnings or in computing an employment loss, the position is judged on a cumulative basis. For any 'relevant period', amount E (which may be nil) is the expense or total expenses to be brought, in accordance with generally accepted accounting practice (GAAP), into account in the period in respect of the payments made (excluding any just and reasonable portion which relates to services, tenant's rates, or the use of assets other than land). A '*relevant period*' is generally a period of account, but if no accounts are drawn up it is the basis period for a trade, profession or vocation or otherwise a tax year. Take the amount of E for the current relevant period and for every previous relevant period ending on or after the date of the transfer. Subtract from the aggregate amount the total deductions given for every such previous relevant period. What remains is the cumulative unrelieved expenses for the current period, and it is this figure which is then compared to the commercial rent for the period and restricted if necessary. The cumulative unrelieved expenses cannot, however, be carried forward to a relevant period beginning after the payments have ceased; no deduction is available under these provisions for any such expenses.

Where the deduction is made against earnings or in computing an employment loss, it must not exceed the commercial rent for the period for which the payment is made. There is provision for carrying forward non-deductible amounts but not to a period beyond that for which the final payment is made (see *ITA 2007, s 681AF*). To the extent that a payment is actually made for a period more than twelve months ahead, it is treated as made for the period comprising the next twelve months.

In the case of a lease, '*commercial rent*' means the open-market rent, at the time the actual lease was created, under a lease whose duration and maintenance/repair terms are the same as under the actual lease but stipulating a rent payable at uniform intervals at a uniform rate, or progressively increasing proportionately to any increases provided by the actual lease. For other transactions, it is the open market rent which would be payable under a tenant's repairing lease (as defined by *ITA 2007, s 681AK(3)*) for the period over which payments are to be made (subject to a maximum of 200 years.

In these provisions, 'lease', as well as having its normal meaning, includes (i) an underlease, sublease, tenancy or licence, (ii) an agreement for a lease, underlease, sublease, tenancy or licence, and (iii) in the case of land outside the UK, an interest corresponding to a lease. 'Rent' includes any payment under a lease.

For the purposes of these provisions, the following persons are associated with one another:

(i) the transferor in an 'affected transaction' and the transferor in another affected transaction, if the two persons are acting in concert or if the two transactions are in any way reciprocal;

(ii) any person who is an associate of either of the associated transferors in (i);

(iii) two or more bodies corporate if they participate in, or are incorporated for the purposes of, a scheme for the reconstruction, or amalgamation, of a body corporate or bodies corporate.

In addition, persons are associated with one another if they are associates as defined in *ITA 2007, s 681DL* (see **4.34** below). In (i) above, an 'affected transaction' is a transfer within these provisions or within the corresponding corporation tax provisions.

[*ITA 2007, ss 681A–681AN*].

Simon's Taxes. See **B5.247**.

Land sold and leased back — new lease of land after assignment or surrender

[4.32] In certain circumstances where a lease of land is assigned or surrendered and another lease is granted or assigned, consideration received for the assignment or surrender of the first lease is chargeable to income tax and tax relief is allowed for rent under the other lease. These provisions apply where all of the following conditions are met:

(a) a person (L) is a lessee of land under a lease which has 50 years or less to run ('the original lease') and is entitled to income tax relief on the rent;
(b) L assigns the original lease to another person or surrenders it to the landlord, and the consideration for the assignment or surrender would not be taxable except as capital in L's hands;
(c) another lease ('the new lease') for a term of 15 years or less is granted, or assigned, to L (or to a person linked to L);
(d) the new lease comprises or includes all or part of the land which was the subject of the original lease; and
(e) neither L (nor a person linked to L) had, before 22 June 1971, a right enforceable at law or in equity to the grant of the new lease.

The reference in (a) to income tax relief is to any of the allowable deductions listed in **4.31** above. For the purposes of (c) and (e), a person is linked to L if he is a partner of L, an associate of L or an associate of a partner of L. Persons are associated with one another if they are associates as defined in *ITA 2007, s 681DL* (see **4.34** below).

A proportion of the consideration mentioned in (b) above (the 'appropriate proportion') is taxed as income (and not treated as a capital receipt). If it is received by L in the course of a trade, profession or vocation and the rent payable under the new lease is allowable as a deduction in calculating the profits or losses of a trade, profession or vocation for tax purposes, the appropriate proportion is treated as a receipt of L's trade etc. If not, it is treated as an amount chargeable to income tax. The '*appropriate proportion*' is the proportion of the consideration found by applying to it the formula:

$$\frac{16 - N}{15}$$

where N = the term of the new lease expressed in years (taking part of a year as an appropriate proportion of a year).

If the consideration is paid in instalments, the formula is applied to each instalment. If the term of the new lease is one year or less, the appropriate proportion of the consideration or instalment is the whole of it. If the property which is the subject of the new lease does not include all the property which was the subject of the original lease, the consideration must be reduced as is reasonable before applying the formula.

Provided the rent under the new lease is payable by a person within the charge to income tax, all provisions of *ITTOIA 2005* providing for deductions or allowances by way of income tax relief in respect of payments of rent apply in relation to the rent payable under the new lease.

There are provisions (see *ITA 2007, ss 681BE–681BI*) whereby for the above purposes the term of the new lease is deemed to end (i) on an earlier date if the rent is reduced or (ii) if the lessor or lessee has power to determine the lease or the lessee has power to vary its terms, on the earliest date on which it can be so determined or varied.

If conditions (a)–(d) above are met but condition (e) is not (such that the above provisions do not apply), and the rent under the new lease is payable by a person within the charge to income tax:

- no part of the rent paid under the new lease is to be treated as a payment of capital; and
- all provisions of *ITTOIA 2005* providing for deductions or allowances by way of income tax relief in respect of payments of rent apply accordingly in relation to that rent.

In these provisions, 'lease', as well as having its normal meaning, includes (i) an agreement for a lease, and (ii) any tenancy, but does not include a mortgage. 'Rent' includes a payment by a tenant for work to maintain or repair leased land or premises which the lease does not require the tenant to carry out.

Consequences ensue if all of the following conditions are met:

(A) a person (M) is a lessee of land under a lease which has 50 years or less to run ('the original lease') and is entitled to income tax relief on the rent;
(B) M varies the original lease by agreement with the landlord;
(C) under the variation, M agrees to pay a rent greater than that payable under the original lease and, does so in return for a consideration which would not be taxable except as capital in M's hands; and
(D) under the variation, the period during which the greater rent is to be paid not more than 15 years after the date on which the consideration is paid to M (or, where applicable, the final instalment of the consideration is paid to M).

The consequences are that M is treated as having surrendered the original lease for the consideration mentioned in (C) and as having been granted a new lease for a term of 15 years or less but otherwise on the terms of the original lease varied as mentioned in (B). The provisions described above are then applied accordingly.

[*ITA 2007, ss 681B–681BM*].

Simon's Taxes. See **B5.248**.

Leased trading assets

[4.33] In certain circumstances where a payment is made under a lease of a trading asset, income tax relief for the payment is restricted. The provisions apply where:

- a payment is made by a person under a lease of an asset (other than land or an interest in land) created after 14 April 1964;
- a deduction is allowed for the payment in calculating the profits of a trade, profession or vocation for income tax purposes; and
- at a time before the lease was created the asset was used for the purposes of the trade etc. or for the purposes of another trade etc. carried on by the lessee, and was then owned by the person carrying on the trade etc. in which it was used.

The deduction for the payment is limited to the 'commercial rent' of the asset to which it relates for the period for which the payment is made. In fact, the position is judged on a cumulative basis in similar manner to that described in **4.31** above, taking into account the payments for every previous 'relevant period' ended on or after the date the lease was created. It is the cumulative unrelieved expenses for the current period which is then compared to the commercial rent for the period and restricted if necessary. The cumulative unrelieved expenses cannot, however, be carried forward to a relevant period beginning after the payments have ceased; no deduction is available under these provisions for any such expenses. A '*relevant period*' is generally a period of account, but if no accounts are drawn up it is the basis period for the trade etc. for the tax year.

The '*commercial rent*' is the rent which might at the time the lease is created be expected to be paid under a lease of the asset if the lease were for the rest of the asset's 'expected normal working life' (as defined), the rent were payable at uniform intervals and at a uniform rate, and the rent gave a reasonable return for the asset's market value at that time, taking account of the terms and conditions of the actual lease. If the asset is used at the same time partly for the purposes of the trade etc. and partly for other purposes, the commercial rent is to be determined by reference to what would be paid for such partial use.

For the above purposes, a lease is an agreement or arrangement under which payments are made for the use of, or otherwise in respect of, the asset. It includes an agreement or arrangement under which the payments (or any of them) represent instalments of, or payments towards, a purchase price.

The above provisions do not apply to payments due under a lease which is a long funding finance lease as regards the lessee (see **10.50** CAPITAL ALLOWANCES ON PLANT AND MACHINERY).

[*ITA 2007, ss 681C–681CG*].

Simon's Taxes. See **B5.413**, **B5.410**.

Leased assets — capital sums

[4.34] In certain circumstances where a payment is made under a lease of an asset (other than one created on or before 14 April 1964), and a 'capital sum' is obtained in respect of an interest in the asset, income tax is chargeable. This does not apply if **4.33** above (or corporation tax equivalent) applies to the payment or would do so were it not for the exclusion in **4.33** of payments under long funding finance leases. A lease is defined as in **4.33** above. A '*capital sum*' is any sum of money, or any money's worth, except in so far as it falls to be taken into account as a trading receipt or is chargeable to income tax as miscellaneous income).

The provisions apply where a payment is made under a lease of an asset (other than land or an interest in land), the payment is one for which a tax deduction is available (see below) and any one of the following conditions is met:

- the person making the payment (P) obtains a capital sum in respect of the lessee's interest in the lease; or
- 'an associate' (see below) of P obtains a capital sum by way of consideration in respect of the lessee's interest in the lease; or
- the lessor's interest in the lease, or any other interest in the asset, belongs to an associate of P, and the associate obtains a capital sum in respect of the interest; or
- the lessor's interest in the lease, or any other interest in the asset, belongs to an associate of P, and an associate of that associate obtains a capital sum by way of consideration in respect of the interest.

Conditions (a)–(d) may be met before, at or after the time when the payment is made, but can be met only if the person obtaining the capital sum is within the charge to income tax. The conditions are not met if the lease is a hire-purchase agreement for plant or machinery and the capital sum has to be brought into account as the whole or part of the capital allowances disposal value of the plant or machinery (and provided, in the case of (c) or (d), that the capital sum is obtained in respect of the lessee's interest in the lease).

The reference above to a tax deduction is to a deduction allowable:

- in computing the profits of a trade, profession or vocation for income tax purposes; or
- in computing profits or income under any of the provisions listed at *ITA 2007, s 1016* (see **49.8** MISCELLANEOUS INCOME) or in computing losses for which relief is available as in **49.11** MISCELLANEOUS INCOME; or
- against earnings, under *ITEPA 2003, s 336*; or
- in calculating losses in an employment; or
- in computing trading profits for corporation tax purposes; or
- in computing profits or income under any of the provisions listed at *CTA 2010, s 1173* (miscellaneous income) or in computing losses for which relief is available under *CTA 2010, s 91* (miscellaneous losses); or
- under *CTA 2009, s 1219* (management expenses of a company's investment business); or
- as an adjusted BLAGAB (basic life assurance and general annuity business) management expense of an insurance company for the purposes of *FA 2012, s 73*.

The person obtaining the capital sum is treated as receiving, at the time the sum is obtained, an amount chargeable to income tax. The amount is equal to the amount(s) of the payment for which the above-mentioned tax deduction is made, but is not to exceed the capital sum. Where the lease is a hire-purchase agreement and the capital sum is obtained in respect of the lessee's interest in the lease, the recipient's capital expenditure on the asset is taken as reducing the capital sum for the purpose of applying this rule (see *ITA 2007, s 681DE*).

If a payment or part of a payment is taken into account in deciding the chargeable amount in respect of a capital sum, the payment or part must be left out of account in deciding whether a charge arises under these provisions in respect of another capital sum and, if so, the chargeable amount. This rule is applied in the order in which capital sums are obtained. If the capital sum is received before the payment is made, any necessary adjustment to the recipient's tax position can be made within the period ending with the fifth anniversary of 31 January following the tax year in which payment is made.

If a person disposes of an interest in an asset to a person who is his 'associate' (as below), he is regarded as obtaining the greatest of the actual sum obtained, the open market value and the value of the interest to the person to whom it is transferred.

Reference above to any sum obtained in respect of an interest in an asset includes any insurance money obtained in respect of the interest and any sum representing money or money's worth obtained in respect of the interest by a transaction or series of transactions disposing of it. Reference to any sum obtained in respect of the lessee's interest in a lease of an asset includes any sums representing consideration for a surrender of the interest to the lessor, an assignment of the lease, the creation of a sublease or another interest out of the lease or a transaction or series of transactions under which the lessee's rights are merged in any way with the lessor's rights or with any other rights as respects the asset.

There is provision for payments to be apportioned where made by persons in partnership and for sums to be apportioned where obtained by persons in partnership or by persons jointly entitled to the interest in an asset (see *ITA 2007, ss 681DJ, 681DK*).

Meaning of 'associates'

For the above purposes, the following are associated with each other:

- an individual and the individual's spouse, civil partner or relative (meaning a brother, sister, ancestor or lineal descendant);
- an individual and a spouse or civil partner of a relative of the individual;
- an individual and a relative of the individual's spouse or civil partner;
- an individual and a spouse or civil partner of a relative of the individual's spouse or civil partner;
- a trustee of a settlement and an individual who is the settlor or any person associated with that individual;
- a person and a body of persons (which may be a partnership) of which he has control (within the meaning of *ITA 2007, s 995*);

- a person and a body of persons of which persons associated with the person have control;
- a person and a body of persons of which the person and persons associated with the person have control;
- two or more bodies of persons associated with the same person;
- in relation to a disposal by joint owners, the joint owners and any person associated with any of them.

[*ITA 2007, ss 681D–681DP*].

Simon's Taxes. See **B5.410–B5.412, B5.414.**

Transfers of income streams

[4.35] The legislation described below is designed to prevent the avoidance of tax where a person transfers to another person a right to taxable receipts without transferring any asset from which the right to the receipts arises.

The legislation applies where a person within the charge to income tax transfers to another person a right to 'relevant receipts' without transferring to him an asset from which a right to relevant receipts arises. '*Relevant receipts*' means any income which, but for the transfer, would fall either to be charged to income tax as the transferor's income or to be included in computing his taxable profits. The legislation additionally applies if a person within the charge to income tax transfers to another person a right to relevant receipts in consequence of a transfer to him of all the rights under an agreement for annual payments.

The consideration for the transfer of the right is treated as income of the transferor and is brought into the charge to income tax in the same way and to the same extent as the relevant receipts would have been brought into charge had the transfer not taken place. If the consideration is substantially less than the market value of the right at the time of the transfer, of if the consideration is nil, the market value is brought into charge instead of the consideration.

The income is treated as arising in the tax year in which the transfer takes place. A special rule applies, however, if any of the relevant receipts would have been taken into account in computing the profits of a trade, profession, vocation or property business and, in accordance with generally accepted accounting practice (GAAP), would have been recognised otherwise than wholly in the tax year in which the transfer takes place. If the income is based on the amount of consideration, it is treated as arising in the tax year(s) in which the consideration is recognised under GAAP. If the income is based on market value, it is treated as arising in the tax year(s) in which the consideration would have been recognised under GAAP if it had been equal to market value.

Income is not to be brought into account as above to the extent (if any) that it is otherwise brought into the charge to income tax. Also, these provisions do not apply if the consideration for the transfer is the advance under a structured finance arrangement (see **4.39** below) in relation to either the transferor or a partnership of which he is a member. Also excepted from these provisions are transfers of (i) a right to annual payments under a life annuity, or (ii) a right to annual payments under an annuity which is pension income.

For the purposes of applying this legislation, the grant or surrender of a lease of land is to be regarded as a transfer of the land, and the disposal of an interest in an oil licence is to be regarded as a transfer of the oil licence. However, the transfer of an asset under a sale and repurchase agreement is not regarded for these purposes as a transfer of the asset. A 'transfer' includes a sale, an exchange, a gift, an assignment and any other arrangement which equates in substance to a transfer. A transfer to or by any partnership of which the transferor or transferee is a member counts as a transfer for the purposes of this legislation, as does a transfer to the trustees of any trust of which the transferor is a beneficiary.

Partnerships

If the transferor is a member of a partnership and the transfer of a right to relevant receipts consists of a reduction in his profit share, he is to be regarded as transferring an asset (i.e. the partnership property) from which the right arose. Thus, the transfer will not fall within the above provisions.

See also **4.36** and **4.37** below as regards partnerships.

[*ITA 2007, ss 809AZA–809AZG*].

Simon's Taxes. See **D9.301A, D9.301B, E1.468.**

Disposals of income streams through partnerships

[4.36] An amount of consideration falls to be treated as income of the transferor if directly or indirectly in consequence of, or otherwise in connection with, arrangements (as widely defined) and involving a person within the charge to income tax ('*the transferor*') and another person ('*the transferee*'):

(a) there is (or is in substance) a disposal of a right to 'relevant receipts' by the transferor to the transferee;
(b) the disposal is effected (wholly or partly) by or through a partnership;
(c) at any time (not necessarily at the same time) the transferor is a member of the partnership or of an 'associated partnership' and the transferee is a member of the partnership or of an 'associated partnership'; and
(d) a main purpose of one or more steps taken in effecting the disposal is the obtaining for any person of a tax advantage (as defined by *CTA 2010, s 1139*) in relation to income tax or the charge to corporation tax on income.

However, no amount falls to be treated as income if the transferor and transferee are married, or in a civil partnership, and are living together, or if the transferor is a brother, sister, ancestor or lineal descendant of the transferee. In (a) above, a disposal of a right to relevant receipts includes, but is not limited to, anything constituting a disposal of such a right for capital gains tax purposes. '*Relevant receipts*' means any income which, had it not been for the disposal:

- would be charged to income tax as income of the transferor (whether directly or as a member of a partnership); or
- would be brought into account as income in calculating profits of the transferor (whether directly or as a member of a partnership) for income tax purposes.

The disposal in (b) above might, in particular, be effected by an acquisition or disposal of an interest in the partnership (including a share of profits or assets or an interest in such a share) or an increase or decrease in such an interest. In (c) above, references to the transferor and transferee include persons connected (within **19** CONNECTED PERSONS) with the transferor, as the case may be, the transferee. A partnership is an '*associated partnership*' if it is a member of the partnership in question or it is a member of a partnership which is itself an associated partnership of the partnership in question. Throughout these provisions a 'partnership' includes a limited liability partnership.

The consideration for the disposal of the right is treated as income of the transferor and is brought into the charge to income tax in the same way and to the same extent as the relevant receipts would have been brought into charge had the disposal not taken place. If the consideration is substantially less than the market value of the right at the time of the disposal, or if the consideration is nil, the market value is brought into charge instead of the consideration. The income is treated as arising in the tax year in which the disposal takes place. A special rule applies, however, if any of the relevant receipts would have been taken into account in computing the profits of a trade, profession, vocation or property business and, in accordance with generally accepted accounting practice (GAAP), would have been recognised otherwise than wholly in the tax year in which the disposal takes place. If the income is based on the amount of consideration, it is treated as arising in the tax year(s) in which the consideration is recognised under GAAP. If the income is based on market value, it is treated as arising in the tax year(s) in which the consideration would have been recognised under GAAP if it had been equal to market value.

If both the above provisions and those at **4.37** below would otherwise apply to the disposal, priority is given to the provisions that produce the greater amount of taxable income. If both produce the same amount, the above provisions take priority.

[*ITA 2007, ss 809AAZA, 809AAZB*].

For a Technical Note see www.gov.uk/government/uploads/system/uploads/attachment_data/file/298221/Partnerships_Mixed_membership_partnerships__Alternative_investment_fund_managers__Transfer_of_assets___income_Streams_through_partnerships.pdf.

Simon's Taxes. See **B7.143**.

Disposals of assets through partnerships

[4.37] An amount of consideration falls to be treated as income of the transferor if both conditions A and B below are met.

Condition A is that directly or indirectly in consequence of, or otherwise in connection with, arrangements (as widely defined) and involving a person within the charge to income tax (*'the transferor'*) and another person (*'the transferee'*):

(a) there is (or is in substance) a disposal of an asset by the transferor to the transferee;
(b) the disposal is effected (wholly or partly) by or through a partnership;
(c) at any time (not necessarily at the same time), the transferor is a member of the partnership or of an 'associated partnership' and the transferee is a member of the partnership or of an 'associated partnership'; and
(d) a main purpose of one or more steps taken in effecting the disposal is the obtaining for any person of a tax advantage (as defined by *CTA 2010, s 1139*) in relation to income tax or the charge to corporation tax on income.

However, no amount falls to be treated as income if the transferor and transferee are married, or in a civil partnership, and are living together, or if the transferor is a brother, sister, ancestor or lineal descendant of the transferee.

In (a) above, a disposal of an asset includes, but is not limited to, anything constituting a disposal of an asset for capital gains tax purposes. The disposal in (b) above might, in particular, be effected by an acquisition or disposal of an interest in the partnership (including a share of profits or assets or an interest in such a share) or an increase or decrease in such an interest. In (c) above, references to the transferor and transferee include persons connected (within **19** CONNECTED PERSONS) with the transferor or, as the case may be, the transferee. A partnership is an *'associated partnership'* if it is a member of the partnership in question or it is a member of a partnership which is itself an associated partnership of the partnership in question. Throughout these provisions a 'partnership' includes a limited liability partnership.

Condition B is that it is reasonable to assume that, had the asset instead been disposed of directly by the transferor to the transferee, the taxable amount (or any part of it):

- would have been chargeable to income tax as income of the transferor; or
- would have been brought into account as income in calculating profits of the transferor.

The 'taxable amount' is treated as income of the transferor and is brought into the charge to income tax in the same way and to the same extent as that in which it would have been chargeable had the disposal not taken place. The *'taxable amount'* is the consideration for the disposal. If the actual consideration is substantially less than the market value of the asset at the time of the disposal, or if it is nil, the consideration is deemed to be equal to market value. The income is treated as arising in the tax year in which the disposal takes place. A special rule applies, similar to that in **4.36** above, if any part of the taxable amount would have been taken into account in computing the profits of a trade etc. and, in accordance with GAAP, would have been recognised otherwise than wholly in the tax year in which the disposal takes place.

If both the above provisions and those at **4.36** above would otherwise apply to the disposal, priority is given to the provisions that produce the greater amount of taxable income. If both produce the same amount, the provisions at **4.36** take priority.

[*ITA 2007, ss 809DZA, 809DZB*].

For a Technical Note see www.gov.uk/government/uploads/system/uploads/attachment_data/file/298221/Partnerships_Mixed_membership_partnerships__Alternative_investment_fund_managers__Transfer_of_assets___income_Streams_through_partnerships.pdf.

Simon's Taxes. See **B7.142**.

Disguised investment management fees

[4.38] Where one or more 'disguised fees' arise to an individual in a tax year from one or more 'investment schemes' (whether or not by virtue of the same arrangements), the individual is liable for income tax for the tax year in respect of the disguised fee(s) as if the individual were carrying on a trade the profits of which are the disguised fee(s). The trade is treated as carried on in the UK to the extent that the individual performs the related investment management services in the UK.

An '*investment scheme*' means a collective investment scheme or an investment trust. The term 'collective investment scheme' is widened in this context to include arrangements permitting an investor to participate in investments acquired by the scheme without participating in the scheme itself and arrangements under which sums arise to an individual performing investment management services for the scheme but do not arise from the scheme itself.

A '*disguised fee*' arises to an individual in a tax year from an investment scheme if:

(a) the individual at any time performs (or is to perform) investment management services (as defined) directly or indirectly in respect of the scheme under any arrangements (as widely defined);
(b) the arrangements involve at least one partnership;
(c) under the arrangements a 'management fee' arises (in whatever form) to the individual in the tax year from an investment scheme; and
(d) at least some part of the management fee falls neither to be taxed on the individual as employment income for any year nor taxed as profits of a trade or profession of his. That part is the disguised fee.

Any sum which arises to an individual is a management fee for these purposes, except insofar as it:

- constitutes 'carried interest' other than 'income-based carried interest'; or
- is by way of return or repayment of an investment made by the individual in the scheme; or
- is an arm's length return (as defined) on an investment made by the individual in the scheme.

See below for the meaning of 'carried interest' and 'income-based carried interest'.

Sums are treated as arising to an individual for the above purposes if they arise to a connected person other than a company or if the individual (or any such connected person) has power to enjoy (as defined) the sum or any part of it. Where the sum in question is carried interest, this does not apply if the carried interest arises in connection with the disposal of a partnership asset (or assets) before 22 October 2015.

In determining whether the above charge applies in relation to an individual, no regard is to be had to any arrangements a main purpose of which is to secure that the charge would not apply. There is allowance for the avoidance of double taxation on sums charged as above. This enables the individual to claim a consequential adjustment if at any time income tax or another tax is charged on the individual or another person under any other tax provision in respect of the disguised fee. The consequential adjustment cannot exceed the lesser of the two charges. Where the disguised fee arises to the individual by way of a loan or advance, there is similar allowance for avoidance of double taxation where income tax or another tax is charged on an amount (other than the disguised fee) arising to the individual under the arrangements and some or all of the loan or advance has to be repaid as a result of that sum having arisen.

Special rules apply where a UK resident individual to whom disguised fees consisting of income-based carried interest arise (see below) has previously been non-UK resident for at least five consecutive tax years. The rules apply where the year in question is the first tax year following the non-resident years or where it is the second, third, or fourth tax year and the individual has remained UK resident. To the extent that the income-based carried interest arises by virtue of services (i.e. investment management services) performed in the UK during the non-resident years, the individual is liable for income tax for the year in question as if the income-based carried interest were the profits of a notional trade carried on by him in that year. The same applies in relation to services performed outside the UK but the resulting notional trade is separate and distinct from the aforementioned notional trade (if any).

[*ITA 2007, ss 809EZA, 809EZB, 809EZDA, 809EZDB, 809EZE–809EZH; FA 2016, ss 36, 37(1)(4), 38*].

For official guidance see www.gov.uk/government/uploads/system/uploads/attachment_data/file/417049/Disguised_Investment_Management_Fees_Guidance.pdf.

Carried interest

'*Carried interest*' means a sum which arises to the individual under the arrangements by way of 'profit-related return'. A sum arises by way of '*profit-related return*' if under the arrangements:

- the sum can arise only if there are profits for a period on, or from the disposal of, the scheme investments or on particular scheme investments;
- the amount of the sum is variable, to a substantial extent, by reference to those profits; and

- returns to external investors are also determined by reference to those profits.

Where any part of the sum does not meet these conditions, that part is not to be regarded as arising by way of profit-related return. Where one or more sums arise to the individual under the arrangements by way of profit-related return in a tax year, but there was no significant risk that a sum of at least a certain amount would fail to arise, only the excess (if any) over that amount is carried interest. There are rules for determining how that amount is to be apportioned between the actual sums arising where more than one such sum arises in the tax year (see *ITA 2007, s 809EZC(7)(8)*). There are also rules for assessing the risk (see *ITA 2007, s 809EZC(4)–(6)*).

A sum is regarded as '*carried interest*', notwithstanding the above definition, if all, or substantially all, of the investments in the scheme made by the participants have been repaid to the participants, and each external investor has received a 'preferred return' on all, or substantially all, of his investments in the scheme. This also applies, with appropriate modification, where the scheme profits and preferred return are calculated on the basis of particular investments. '*Preferred return*' is an amount at least equivalent to compound interest on an investment at 6% per annum, with annual rests, for the whole of the period during which the investment was invested in the scheme.

For these purposes, the amount of investment made by a person who holds a share in an investment scheme which is a company limited by shares, but who acquired it from a person other than the scheme, is the consideration given for the acquisition of the share or, if less, its market value at the time of acquisition.

Income-based carried interest

The extent, if any, to which carried interest is '*income-based carried interest*' depends on the average period for which the investment scheme holds investments. The income-based carried interest is a percentage of the carried interest ranging from 0% where the average holding period is at least 40 months to 100% where it is less than 36 months. Carried interest arising from certain direct lending funds is income-based carried interest in its entirety. There are rules which exempt carried interest conditionally from being income-based in the early years of a fund's existence where the fund expects to hold the investments for more than four years. See *ITA 2007, Pt 13, Ch 5F (ss 809FZA–809FZZ)* for the full rules, and in particular *ITA 2007, s 809FZB* for the complete range of percentages and *ITA 2007, s 809FZC* for the calculation of the average holding period. The rules have no application to employment-related securities.

[*ITA 2007, ss 809EZC–809EZE, 809FZA–809FZZ; FA 2016, ss 36, 37(2)(4)*].

Factoring of income receipts etc.

[4.39] The provisions described below are intended to counter the situation in which a person enters into financing arrangements that equate in substance to his taking out a loan but which are structured in such a way as to effectively give him tax relief for repayment of principal as well as for finance charges.

Say, for example, B has the opportunity to take out a loan of £50,000 with L, under which B would repay the loan over five years together with total interest of £5,000. Tax relief might be available for the £5,000 interest but not for the repayment of the £50,000 principal. As an alternative, B transfers to L for £50,000 an asset that is fully expected to produce income of £55,000 over the next five years, at the end of which the asset will be transferred back to B for nothing. L receives £55,000 for an outlay of £50,000. B then claims that the transfer of the asset to L either gives rise only to a chargeable gain (which may be relatively small due to high base cost and available reliefs) or is not taxable at all, and that he is not chargeable on the income of £55,000 which is received not by him but by L. B effectively obtains tax relief on £55,000 (less any CGT payable).

Sometimes, instead of the borrower forgoing income, the arrangements generate a tax deduction for the borrower. Say B grants a long lease of freehold property to L for a premium of £50,000. L then grants a five-year sub-lease back to B at a rent of £11,000 per year. The arrangements will provide for the benefits of ownership to revert to B at the end of the five years. Again, L receives £55,000 for an outlay of £50,000. B obtains tax relief for rent payments of £55,000.

Arrangements involving disposals of assets

The anti-avoidance provisions apply where there is a '*structured finance arrangement*'. Such an arrangement exists where:

(i) under the arrangement a person (the borrower) receives from another person (the lender) any money or other asset (the advance) in any period;

(ii) in accordance with generally accepted accounting practice (GAAP) the accounts of the borrower for that period record a financial liability in respect of the advance;

(iii) the borrower (or a person connected with him) disposes of an asset (the security) under the arrangement to or for the benefit of the lender (or a person connected with him);

(iv) the lender (or a person connected with him) is entitled under the arrangement to payments in respect of the security; and

(v) in accordance with GAAP those payments reduce the amount of the financial liability recorded in the borrower's accounts.

For these purposes, the rules in **19** CONNECTED PERSONS apply to determine whether persons are connected, except that the borrower and lender cannot be regarded as a connected with one another. For the purposes of (iv) above, it does not matter if the entitlement of the lender etc. is subject to any condition. If the borrower is a partnership, references above to accounts are to the accounts of any member of the partnership as well as the partnership itself. 'Arrangement' is widely defined for the purposes of these provisions to include any agreement or understanding (whether or not legally enforceable). 'Payments' is also widely defined to include any obtaining of value or benefit, and encompasses the situation where an asset replaces the original asset within the arrangement. Where it is not the case, these provisions apply as if the accounts in question had been prepared in accordance with GAAP. In determining whether accounts record an amount as a financial liability in respect of an advance, it has to be assumed that the period of account in which the advance is received ended immediately after the receipt of the advance.

If an arrangement is a structured finance arrangement, then:

(a) if, as a result of the arrangement, an amount of otherwise chargeable income would escape tax in the hands of the borrower (or a person connected with him), it does not escape tax;

(b) if, as a result of the arrangement, any amount would otherwise not fall to be taken into account in computing income of the borrower (or a person connected with him) for tax purposes, that amount shall be so brought into account; and

(c) if, as a result of the arrangement, the borrower (or a person connected with him) would otherwise be entitled to a deduction in computing any taxable income, or a deduction against total income, he shall not be so entitled.

If the borrower is a partnership, the above have effect by reference to any member of the partnership.

If a structured finance arrangement would *not* have had the result mentioned in (a), (b) or (c) above, the payments to which the lender (or a person connected with him) is entitled under the arrangement are treated as income of the borrower in respect of the security. This applies whether or not the payments are also the income of another person for tax purposes.

In all the above cases, if the borrower is within the charge to income tax and, in accordance with GAAP, his accounts record a finance charge in respect of the advance, he can treat the finance charge as if it were interest on a loan. The intended effect is to place the borrower in the same position for tax purposes as if he had taken out a loan instead of entering into the structured finance arrangement. (If the borrower is a partnership, it is the partnership itself that is deemed to be paying interest, even if the finance charge appears in the accounts of a member.) The time at which this notional interest is to be treated as having been paid depends on the timing of the payments made to the lender in respect of the security; each such payment is treated as if it were part repayment of principal and part interest.

See also below under Exceptions.

Arrangements involving partnership changes

More complex types of arrangement might be involved where the 'borrower' is a partnership. For example, B might transfer an income-producing asset to a partnership of which he is a member. L then joins the partnership for a capital contribution of £50,000 in return for the right to receive partnership profits of £55,000 over the next 5 years but no profits beyond that period. B claims not to be taxable on the £55,000 of partnership profits diverted to L. In another scenario, an established partnership may already hold an income-producing asset and the above steps then follow without the need for the initial transfer of an asset by B. In this case, the members of the partnership whose profits are thereby reduced claim not to be taxable on the partnership profits diverted to L.

There are similar anti-avoidance provisions to catch these types of arrangement. See *ITA 2007, ss 809BZF–809BZL*. These provisions rely on alternative definitions of 'structured finance arrangement', tailored to the type of arrangement at which they are aimed. If, as a result, an arrangement is a structured finance arrangement in relation to the borrower partnership, the partnership change is treated for tax purposes as if it had not occurred. For this purpose, the 'partnership change' might be the admission of the lender as a partner or a change in profit sharing ratios affecting the lender's share. The provisions are widely drawn so as also to catch changes made indirectly and/or involving a person connected with the lender. Again, as above, there is provision for a finance charge to be treated as if it were interest paid on a loan.

See also below under Exceptions.

Exceptions

The above provisions are disapplied if the whole of the advance under the structured finance arrangement falls to be brought into account in determining the taxable income of a 'relevant person'. This includes a case where the advance falls to be brought into account as a disposal receipt, or in otherwise computing a balancing charge, for capital allowances purposes, but not if any such balancing charge would fall to be restricted under the capital allowances legislation. A '*relevant person*' means the borrower under the arrangements or a person connected with the borrower or, if the borrower is a partnership, a member of the partnership.

There are also exclusions in cases where other statutory provisions specified in *ITA 2007, s 809BZN* do in any case result in the arrangement being properly taxed. These include, for example, certain repo and stock lending arrangements, ALTERNATIVE FINANCE ARRANGEMENTS (**3**) and certain sale and finance leaseback transactions. In relation to periods of account beginning on or after 1 January 2019, there is an additional exclusion where the arrangement is a right-of-use lease (see **10.50**(5) CAPITAL ALLOWANCES ON PLANT AND MACHINERY) and the borrower etc. is a lessee who would not have accounted for the arrangement as a finance lease or loan if required to do so under GAAP. The Treasury have power to specify further exclusions by statutory instrument, and any such exclusions may be given retrospective effect.

Miscellaneous

The lease premium rules at *ITTOIA 2005, ss 277–281* (see **60.26** PROPERTY INCOME) are disapplied where the grant of the lease constitutes the disposal of an asset for the purposes of these provisions.

See *TCGA 2002, s 263E* as regards the CGT consequences of structured finance arrangements.

[*ITA 2007, ss 809BZA–809BZS; FA 2019, Sch 14 paras 3, 6(1)*].

Loan or credit transactions

[4.40] Where, with reference to lending money or giving credit (or varying the terms of a loan or credit), a transaction provides for the payment of an annuity or other annual payment (other than interest), that payment is treated as if it were a payment of yearly interest. Where, with similar reference, any person surrenders, waives or forgoes income on property, that person is chargeable to income tax on a sum equal to the income surrendered, waived etc. This does not apply if the person concerned is chargeable, as a result of **4.39** above, on the income surrendered etc. If credit is given for the purchase price of property and during the subsistence of the debt, the buyer's rights to income from the property are suspended or restricted, he is treated for this purpose as if he had made a surrender of that income. Transactions with CONNECTED PERSONS (**19**) are brought within the ambit of the provisions. [*ITA 2007, ss 809CZA–809CZC; SI 2013 No 2819, Regs 1, 37*].

Simon's Taxes. See **E1.405**.

Leasing of plant and machinery

[4.41] If, under a lease of plant or machinery, there is an unconditional obligation to make a 'relevant capital payment' or if such a payment is made after that date without obligation, the lessor is treated for income tax purposes as receiving income attributable to the lease of an amount equal to the 'capital payment'. The income is treated as income for the period of account in which the obligation first arose or, as the case may be, income for the period of account in which the payment is made. These provisions apply to long funding leases (see **75.98** TRADING INCOME) as well as to other plant or machinery leases. The provisions apply equally if the obligation arises, or the payment is made, under an agreement or arrangement relating to a lease of plant or machinery, whether made before, during or after the currency of the lease itself.

For these purposes, a payment includes the provision of value by whatever means. A '*capital payment*' is any payment other than one which, if made to the lessor, would fall to be included in the lessor's income for tax purposes or which would fall to be included were it not for *ITTOIA 2005, s 148A* (which determines the amount to be brought into account as taxable income from such a lease — see **75.99** TRADING INCOME).

A capital payment is a '*relevant capital payment*' if either:

- it is payable by lessee to lessor in connection with the grant, assignment, novation or termination of the lease or with any provision of the lease or, as the case may be, the agreement or arrangement (including the variation or waiver of any such provision); or
- the lease rentals are less than (or payable later than) they might reasonably be expected to be if there were no obligation to make the capital payment and the capital payment were not made.

However, a capital payment is *not* a '*relevant capital payment*' if, or to the extent that:

- it reduces the lessor's expenditure for the purposes of plant and machinery capital allowances — see the rules on expenditure met by another's contributions at **10.2**(vi) CAPITAL ALLOWANCES ON PLANT AND MACHINERY — or would do so if the circumstances were not such that the contributions rules are disapplied; or

- it represents compensation for damage to, or damage caused by, the plant or machinery in question.

Where a capital payment is an initial payment under a long funding lease (see **10.48** *et seq.* CAPITAL ALLOWANCES ON PLANT AND MACHINERY) whose inception is on or after 13 November 2008 and before 22 April 2009, the commencement of the term of the lease is an event that requires the lessor to bring a disposal value into account, the payment is not a relevant capital payment. If the inception of the lease is on or after 22 April 2009, the payment *is* a relevant capital payment but only to the extent (if any) that it exceeds the disposal value.

'*Lease*' is defined to include a licence and also the letting of a ship or aircraft on charter or any other asset on hire. For these purposes, a lease of plant or machinery includes a lease of plant or machinery together with other property, in which case the payment is apportioned on a just and reasonable basis and only the amount apportioned to the plant or machinery is chargeable under these provisions. It does not, however, include a lease all the lessor's income from which (if any) would be chargeable as PROPERTY INCOME (**59**) or a long funding lease of plant or machinery on which the lessor would have been treated as having incurred qualifying expenditure for the purposes of plant and machinery capital allowances if it were not for *CAA 2001, s 34A* at **10.51** CAPITAL ALLOWANCES ON PLANT AND MACHINERY.

There is bad debt relief if the above provisions have applied by virtue of an unconditional obligation and at any time the lessor reasonably expects that the relevant capital payment will not be paid (or will not be fully paid). The lessor is allowed a deduction for the expected shortfall in computing his profits for the period of account in which that time falls.

Consideration for taking over payment obligations as lessee

Where, under any arrangements (as widely defined), a person (P) becomes entitled to tax deductions (whether in calculating income or profits) as a result of agreeing to take over obligations (by whatever means) of another person (Q) as lessee under a lease of plant or machinery, P is chargeable to income tax on any consideration received for the agreement. The consideration is treated as income received by P in the tax year in which he takes over the obligations. Consideration includes the provision of any benefit, the assumption of any liability and the transfer of money or money's worth, and includes any payment made (directly or indirectly) in connection with the agreement if the agreement would not have been made had the payment not been provided for. The charge applies equally where the person becoming entitled to tax deductions or the person to whom consideration is payable is a person connected with P (within **19** CONNECTED PERSONS). It does not apply to the extent (if any) that the consideration is otherwise taxable as income in the hands of P or a person connected with him.

[*ITA 2007, ss 809ZA–809ZFA; FA 2016, s 68(2)(3)*].

Simon's Taxes. See **B5.415A.**

Annual payments for non-taxable consideration etc.

[4.42] Any payment (whenever the liability to make it was incurred, but subject to exceptions as below) of an annual payment (which includes an annuity but does not include interest) satisfying the conditions below can be neither a qualifying annual payment (see **23.8** DEDUCTION OF TAX AT SOURCE) nor a patent royalty subject to deduction of tax (see **23.14** DEDUCTION OF TAX AT SOURCE). Consequently it is paid without deduction of tax. It is not allowed as a deduction in computing a person's income from any source. The conditions are that the payment:

- is charged to income tax under *ITTOIA 2005, Pt V* (miscellaneous income) (otherwise than as relevant foreign income — see **32.2** FOREIGN INCOME), or is chargeable to corporation tax under specified provisions of *CTA 2009* or as income from an exempt unauthorised unit trust; and
- is made under a liability incurred for consideration in money or money's worth, all or any of which either (a) consists of, or of the right to receive, a dividend, or (b) is not required to be brought into account in calculating for tax purposes the income of the person making it.

Exceptions to the above provisions are any payments:

(i) which fall within **70.29**(i) or (ii) SETTLEMENTS; or
(ii) to an individual for surrendering, assigning or releasing an interest in settled property to a person having a subsequent interest; or
(iii) of any annuity granted in the ordinary course of a business of granting annuities.

For Scotland, reference to settled property refers to property held in trust and references to an individual include a Scottish partnership if at least one partner is an individual. For position prior to these provisions see *CIR v Plummer* HL 1979, 54 TC 1, and *Moodie v CIR and Sinnett* HL 1993, 65 TC 610, in which the decision in *Plummer* on similar facts was reversed on *Ramsay* principles (see **4.1** above).

As regards the recipient, a payment to which these provisions apply is excluded from the exemption of annual payments from tax at **30.3** EXEMPT INCOME.

[*ITA 2007, ss 843, 904; SI 2009 No 23, Regs 1, 5(4); SI 2013 No 2819, Regs 1, 37*].

Simon's Taxes. See **E1.801**.

Benefits from pre-owned assets

[4.43] Subject to certain exemptions, a *de minimis* limit and a transitional right to elect to disapply these provisions (with inheritance tax (IHT) consequences), an income tax charge applies for 2005/06 onwards as described below on the annual benefit of using property previously owned by the user and not disposed of by him at arm's length. The legislation is intended to counter avoidance schemes which bypass the IHT 'gifts with reservation' rules, for which see Tolley's Inheritance Tax, but is not restricted to cases where such schemes have been used. For guidance, see HMRC Inheritance Tax Manual IHTM44000 *et seq*.

The main charge applies where an individual (whether alone or together with others) occupies any land or is in possession of, or has the use of, any chattel and *either* of the following two conditions is met.

The *first condition* is that, at some time after 17 March 1986, the individual owned the land or chattel, or owned other property the proceeds of disposal of which were applied, directly or indirectly, by another person towards the acquisition of the land or chattel, and the individual has disposed of all or part of his interest in the land, chattel or other property other than by way of an 'excluded transaction' (see below).

The *second condition* is that, at some time after 17 March 1986, the individual has provided, directly or indirectly but other than by way of an 'excluded transaction', any of the consideration given by another person for the acquisition of the land or chattel or of any other property the proceeds of disposal of which were applied by another person towards the acquisition of the land or chattel.

The above references to land include an interest in land, ownership of a chattel means sole or joint ownership, and references to the acquisition or disposal of any property generally include acquisitions and disposals of an interest in that property.

A disposition which creates a new interest in land or a chattel out of an existing interest is treated as a part disposal of the existing interest.

Where the above applies to an individual at any time in 2005/06 or any subsequent tax year, then subject to the exemptions from charge detailed below, the chargeable amount computed as below is treated as income of his, chargeable to income tax, for the tax year in question.

Excluded transactions

Any of the following disposals of the land, chattel or other property in question is an '*excluded transaction*' for the purposes of the first condition above:

- a disposal of the individual's entire interest in the property (except for any right expressly reserved by him over the property) by a transaction made at arm's length with a person not connected with him or by a transaction such as might be expected to be made at arm's length between persons not connected with each other;
- a transfer of the property to the individual's spouse or civil partner (or, by court order, to his former spouse or civil partner);
- a gift (or a transfer for the benefit of a former spouse or civil partner made in accordance with a court order) by virtue of which the property became settled property in which the individual's spouse or civil partner or former spouse or civil partner has an interest in possession which either still subsists or has come to an end on the death of the spouse or civil partner or former spouse or civil partner;
- a disposition which is exempt from IHT under *IHTA 1984, s 11* (dispositions for maintenance of family);
- an outright gift to an individual which is covered by the IHT annual exemption or small gifts exemption;

- a disposal, made at arm's length and otherwise than to a connected person, of part of the vendor's interest in the property;
- a disposal before 7 March 2005, by way of a transaction such as might be expected to be made at arm's length between persons not connected with each other, of part of the vendor's interest in the property; and
- a disposal on or after 7 March 2005, by way of a transaction such as might be expected to be made at arm's length between persons not connected with each other, of part of the vendor's interest in the property for a consideration not in the form of money or 'readily convertible assets' (as defined by *ITEPA 2003, s 702* — see **53.4**(a) PAY AS YOU EARN).

For the purposes of these provisions, the rules in **19** CONNECTED PERSONS apply to determine whether or not persons are connected with each other *but* as if a relative also included an uncle, aunt, nephew or niece and as if 'settlement', 'settlor' and 'trustee' had the meaning they have for IHT purposes.

For the purposes of the second condition above, the provision by the individual of consideration for another person's acquisition of property is an '*excluded transaction*' if:

- the other person is the individual's spouse or civil partner (or, where the transfer has been ordered by the court, his former spouse or civil partner); or
- on its acquisition the property became settled property in which the individual's spouse or civil partner or former spouse or civil partner has an interest in possession which either still subsists or has come to an end on the death of the spouse or civil partner or former spouse or civil partner; or
- the provision of the consideration was an outright gift of money made at least seven years before the individual first occupied the land in question or had possession of, or the use of, the chattel in question; or
- the provision of the consideration is a disposition which is exempt from IHT under *IHTA 1984, s 11* (dispositions for maintenance of family); or
- the provision of the consideration is an outright gift to an individual which is covered by the IHT annual exemption or small gifts exemption.

Exemptions from charge

The charge under these provisions does not apply by reference to any property at a time when that property would fall to be treated for IHT purposes as property which, in relation to the individual concerned, is property subject to a reservation (or would fall to be so treated were it not for specified IHT exemptions). See generally Tolley's Inheritance Tax under Gifts with Reservation. This exemption also applies at any time where property deriving its value from the property in question would fall to be so treated; however, if such other property reflects some of, but substantially less than the whole of, the value of the property in question, the exemption does not apply but the chargeable amount is scaled down accordingly.

The charge does not apply by reference to any property at a time when the individual's estate for IHT purposes includes that property or includes other property whose value is derived from it. If such other property reflects some of, but substantially less than the whole of, the value of the original property, the exemption does not apply but the chargeable amount is scaled down accordingly. This exemption (or partial exemption) is subject to anti-avoidance provision where the value of the estate is reduced by certain associated liabilities.

The above exemption is removed in a case where the property (or any derived property) falls into the individual's estate by virtue of it being an interest in possession in settled property created after the property originally left his estate or after he provided consideration for its acquisition. Such property is also not to be treated as property subject to a reservation, so that the first of the above exemptions is also disapplied. This removal of the exemptions is aimed at the situation where the settled property may in due course revert to the settlor (or to the spouse or civil partner or the widow, widower or surviving civil partner of the settlor) in circumstances such that, by virtue of *IHTA 1984, s 53(3)* or *s 53(4)* or *s 54*, no IHT charge arises when the individual's interest in possession comes to an end.

The provisions do not apply to a person for any tax year during which he is not UK-resident. If in any tax year a person is UK-resident but not UK-domiciled (as defined for IHT, not income tax, purposes — see Tolley's Inheritance Tax under Domicile), the provisions apply to him only if the land or chattel is situated in the UK. In applying the provisions to a person previously domiciled outside the UK, no regard is to be had to any property which is 'excluded property' as defined for IHT purposes (see Tolley's Inheritance Tax under Excluded Property).

The Treasury may confer additional exemptions by regulations. See below for *de minimis* limit.

The chargeable amount

In the case of an individual chargeable under these provisions as a result of his occupation of **land**, the amount chargeable to tax in respect of any tax year is the 'appropriate rental value' less any payments made, under a legal obligation, by the individual to the owner for his occupation of the land. The '*appropriate rental value*' is:

$$R \times \frac{DV}{V}$$

where R = the 'rental value' of the land, V = the value of the land, and DV = (depending on the circumstances) (i) the value of the interest in the land that the individual disposed of or (ii) such part of the land's value as can reasonably be attributed to the other property that the individual disposed of, or (iii) (where it is the second condition above that is met) such part of the land's value as can reasonably be attributed to the consideration provided by the individual. So, in the most straightforward case where the individual disposed of the whole of the land he now occupies, the value of DV/V will be one and the tax charge will be on the rental value (subject to any deduction for payments made). Where it is the first condition above that is met and the disposal (whilst not being an excluded transaction as above) was a money sale of the individual's entire interest in the land or other property at less than market value, DV is scaled down proportionately so as to only take account of the gift element.

The '*rental value*' of land is the rent that would have been payable by the individual for the tax year if the land had been let to him at an annual rent equal to that which might reasonably be expected under a standard lease under which the landlord bears the cost of repairs, maintenance and insurance and the tenant pays all taxes, rates and other charges usually paid by a tenant. Regulations prescribe the continuing use of such rental value for five tax years.

In the case of an individual chargeable under these provisions as a result of his use or possession of a **chattel**, the amount chargeable to tax in respect of any tax year is the 'appropriate amount' less any payments made, under a legal obligation, by the individual to the owner for his use or possession of the chattel. The '*appropriate amount*' is:

$$N \times \frac{DV}{V}$$

where N = a notional amount of interest (at a rate prescribed by regulations) on the value of the chattel, and V and DV have similar meanings as in the above formula for land.

Where the individual is within these provisions during part only of a tax year, references above to the tax year, as regards both land and chattels, are to that shorter period within the tax year. The date at which *valuations* are to be made for these purposes is to be prescribed by statutory instrument, which may also prescribe the continuing use of such valuations for subsequent tax years (subject to any prescribed adjustments).

Regulations prescribe 6 April in each tax year as being the date at which valuations are to be made (or, if later and where applicable, the date in the tax year on which the asset first becomes chargeable). Land and chattels are to be valued every five years, with the valuation arrived at for the first year being used for that year and each of the next four years. The prescribed rate of interest for chattels is the same as the official rate (i.e. the rate applied to cheap employee loans — see **28.32** EMPLOYMENT INCOME) as at the valuation date. The official rate is 2.25% for 2020/21, 2.5% for 2017/18, 2018/19 and 2019/20 and 3% for 2016/17.

De minimis limit

A person is not chargeable under these provisions for a particular tax year if, for that year, the aggregate of any amounts given by the above formulae and (where applicable) the chargeable amount for intangible property in a settlement (see below) is **£5,000** or less. Note that in determining whether or not the *de minimis* applies, no deduction is made at this stage for any payments made under legal obligation by the individual for occupation of land or for use or possession of chattels; it is thus possible for a tax charge to arise on an amount equal to or less than the *de minimis*.

Miscellaneous

The **value** of any property for the purposes of these provisions is its open market value, disregarding any potential reduction on the ground that the whole of the property is placed on the market at the same time.

A disposition made in relation to an interest in a deceased person's estate is disregarded for the purposes of these provisions if, by virtue of *IHTA 1984, s 17*, it is not a transfer of value for IHT purposes. This takes into account **instruments of variation, disclaimers etc.** — see Tolley's Inheritance Tax under Deeds Varying Dispositions on Death. So, for example, an individual is not treated as having formerly owned and disposed of any property simply by virtue of a will or intestacy that was subsequently varied.

A person who merely acts as **guarantor** in respect of a loan taken out by another person to acquire a property is not regarded for the purposes of these provisions as having thereby funded the acquisition.

Where for any tax year amounts are chargeable, in respect of a person's occupation of any land or his use or possession of any chattel, both under these provisions and, under *ITEPA 2003*, as **earnings** (including benefits in kind), the charge under *ITEPA 2003* takes priority and the charge under these provisions is limited to the excess (if any) of the amount otherwise chargeable under these provisions over the amount chargeable as earnings.

Election to disapply these provisions

An election may be made, in prescribed form (Form IHT 500), to disapply the above provisions by reference to any particular property, with the consequence described below. (HMRC will not accept an election made other than on Form IHT 500.) Such election has effect for the first tax year for which a charge under these provisions would otherwise arise by reference to enjoyment of the property in question (or any substituted property) and for all subsequent tax years. It must be made on or before **31 January** following that first tax year or such later date as an officer of HMRC may, in a particular case, allow. For circumstances in which HMRC may accept a late election, see HMRC Inheritance Tax Manual IHTM44077. The election can be revoked or varied (but only by the chargeable person and not by his personal representatives) at any time on or before the said 31 January. The consequence of the election is that, for as long as that person continues to enjoy the property (or any substitute property), the property is treated for IHT purposes as property subject to a reservation; it will thus potentially attract an IHT charge if the person dies whilst continuing to enjoy the property or within seven years after ceasing to do so (see Tolley's Inheritance Tax under Gifts with Reservation). There are rules to eliminate a potential double IHT charge that could otherwise arise in certain limited circumstances where the election is made (see *SI 2005 No 724, Reg 6*). If the property falls into the chargeable person's estate by virtue of it being an interest in possession in settled property, the consequence of the election is instead to disapply the exemptions otherwise available under *IHTA 1984, s 53(3)(4)* and *s 54* on the coming to an end of the interest in possession. Where, in the absence of an election, the charge to income tax would arise by reference to only a proportion of the value of the property, only a proportion of the property is brought into the scope of IHT as above. The foregoing references to enjoyment of property are to occupation of the property where it is land and to use or possession of the property where it is a chattel.

If, instead of making the election, a taxpayer chooses to avoid the charge by dismantling pre-owned assets arrangements previously made, there are regulations to eliminate a double IHT charge that could otherwise potentially arise in certain circumstances (*SI 2005 No 3441*). These apply where an individual enters into arrangements under which there are transfers both of property and of a debt owed to him, the debt is then written off and, on the individual's death, both the property and the debt are chargeable to inheritance tax.

Intangible property comprised in a settlement

Also included in these provisions is a charge on certain intangible property comprised in a settlement in which the settlor has an interest. The charge applies where:

(a) the terms of a settlement, as they affect any property comprised in it, are such that any income arising from the property would be treated by virtue of *ITTOIA 2005, s 624* (see **70.29** SETTLEMENTS) as the settlor's income (but *not* where it would be so treated only because the settlor's spouse or civil partner could benefit from the settlement); and

(b) that property includes any intangible property (meaning any property other than chattels or interests in land) which is, or which represents, property which the settlor settled, or added to the settlement, after 17 March 1986.

For the purpose of deciding whether the condition in (a) above is met, the exclusion at **70.27** SETTLEMENTS (exclusion for certain foreign income arising under a settlement for 2017/18 onwards) is to be disregarded.

Where the above applies at any time in a tax year, an amount is treated as income of the settlor for that tax year. That amount is N minus T, where N is a notional amount of interest (at a rate prescribed by regulations) on the value of the intangible property in (b) above and T is the amount of income tax and/or capital gains tax payable (if any) by the settlor under specified enactments including *ITTOIA 2005, s 624*, so far as that tax is attributable to that property. The prescribed rate of interest is the same as the official rate (i.e. the rate applied to cheap employee loans — see **28.32** EMPLOYMENT INCOME) as at the valuation date. The official rate is 2.25% for 2020/21, 2.5% for 2017/18, 2018/19 and 2019/20 and 3% for 2016/17.

The exemptions etc. described above apply equally in relation to this charge. Where for any tax year a person would be chargeable under the above provisions by reason of his enjoyment of any land or chattel and also by reference to intangible property which derives its value (wholly or partly) from that land or chattel, he is chargeable only under whichever provision produces the greater chargeable amount; and only that amount is taken into account for the purposes of applying the *de minimis* limit above.

With appropriate modifications, the above election to disapply is also available, with similar consequences, in relation to the charge on intangible property.

[*FA 2004, s 84, Sch 15; F(No 2)A 2017, Sch 8 paras 19, 39; SI 2005 No 724; SI 2007 No 3000*].

Simon's Taxes. See I3.7.

Follower notices

[4.44] Users of avoidance schemes which have been defeated in a tribunal or court hearing in another taxpayer's case can be required to concede their position to reflect the decision of the tribunal or the court. HMRC can issue a notice (a '*follower notice*') requiring such users for whom there is an open enquiry or appeal to amend their tax return or agree to resolve their appeal in accordance with the decision. The provisions cover a number of taxes but are described below to the extent only that they relate to income tax. For official guidance see www.gov.uk/government/publications/follower-notices-and-accelerated-payments.

Definitions

Arrangements (as widely defined) are '*tax arrangements*' if, having regard to all the circumstances, it would be reasonable to conclude that the obtaining of a tax advantage was a main purpose of them. For this purpose, a tax advantage includes relief or increased relief from tax, repayment or increased repayment of tax, avoidance or reduction of a charge or assessment to tax, deferral of a payment, or advancement of a repayment, of tax and avoidance of an obligation to deduct or account for tax.

An '*enquiry*' means an enquiry under *TMA 1970, s 9A* or *TMA 1970, s 12AC* into a tax return or partnership return (see **64.6, 64.12** RETURNS) or an enquiry under *TMA 1970, Sch 1A para 5* into a claim (see **16.3** CLAIMS). An enquiry is '*in progress*' during the period beginning with the day on which notice of enquiry is given and ending on the day on which the enquiry is completed. An '*appeal*' means an appeal or further appeal against an assessment, an amendment of a self-assessment, a closure notice, an amendment of a partnership return or a counteraction notice under **4.11** above (transactions in securities).

A '*judicial ruling*' means a ruling of a court or tribunal on one or more issues. Such a ruling is relevant to particular tax arrangements if it relates to tax arrangements, it is a 'final ruling' and the principles laid down, or reasoning given, in the ruling would, if applied to the arrangements in question, deny the asserted tax advantage or part of it. HMRC have to be of the opinion that the principles or reasoning in the ruling in question would deny the tax advantage, not merely that they would be more likely than not to do so; a follower notice was quashed for this reason by the CA in *R (oao Haworth) v HMRC* CA, [2019] STC 1063. Notices were quashed in *R (oao Locke) v HMRC* CA, [2019] STC 2543 on the basis that the ruling was not relevant; it was noted that the test is as above and is *not* whether the particular arrangements are identical or similar to the arrangements with which the earlier ruling was concerned. A ruling by the Supreme Court is always a '*final ruling*'. Otherwise, a judicial ruling is a '*final ruling*' if no further appeal can be made (including a case where a time limit for further action by the appellant has expired) or if a further appeal was abandoned or otherwise disposed of before it was determined; the ruling is treated as made at the time when the time limit expired or the appeal was abandoned or disposed of.

[*FA 2014, ss 201–203, 205*].

Simon's Taxes. See **A7.247.**

Giving of follower notices

[4.45] HMRC may give a follower notice to a person if:

(a) an enquiry into a return or claim made by that person is in progress or that person has made an appeal which has not been determined by the tribunal or court to which it is addressed, abandoned or otherwise disposed of;
(b) the return, claim or appeal is made on the basis that a particular tax advantage results from particular 'tax arrangements' (see **4.44** above);
(c) HMRC are of the opinion that there is a 'judicial ruling' (see **4.44** above) which is relevant to those arrangements; and
(d) no previous follower notice has been given to the same person (and not withdrawn) by reference to the same tax advantage, tax arrangements, judicial ruling and tax year.

A follower notice must identify the judicial ruling in (c) above, explain why HMRC consider that the ruling is relevant to the tax arrangements and explain the effects of the notice. A follower notice may not be given after the end of the twelve-month period beginning with the later of the date of the judicial ruling in (c) and the date the return or claim in (a) was received by HMRC or the appeal in (a) was made. Where the judicial ruling was made before 17 July 2014, the notice may not be given after the later of 16 July 2016 and the end of the twelve months beginning with the date the return or claim was received by HMRC or the appeal was made.

The recipient of a follower notice has 90 days beginning with the date the notice is given to send written representations to HMRC objecting to the notice on the grounds that any of (a), (b) or (d) above are not satisfied, that the judicial ruling is not relevant to the arrangements or that the notice was not given within the time limit. Having considered the representations HMRC will confirm the notice (with or without amendments) or withdraw it, and notify the recipient accordingly.

For a judicial review case in which it was contended, ultimately with success, that the issue of a follower notice was wrong in law, and in the course of which a number of aspects of the follower notice regime were examined, see *R (oao Haworth) v HMRC* CA, [2019] STC 1063. See also *R (oao Broomfield) v HMRC* QB, [2018] STC 1790 in this regard.

Partnerships

A follower notice may be given to a partnership in respect of a partnership return (see **64.12** RETURNS) or an appeal relating to such a return. The notice is given to the representative partner (i.e. the partner responsible for dealing with the return) or to the successor of that partner (see **64.12** RETURNS). For the purposes of (b) above, a return or appeal is made on the basis that a particular tax advantage results from particular tax arrangements if the arrangements increase or reduce any of the items required to be included in the partnership statement included in the return and they result in a tax advantage for one or more partners. Where a partnership follower notice is given to a person as representative partner or to the successor of that partner, (d) above does not prevent a follower notice from being given to that person in another capacity. All notices given to the representative partner and any successor, in that capacity, are treated as given to the same person for the purposes of (d) above.

[*FA 2014, ss 204, 206, 207, 217, Sch 31 paras 2, 3*].

Action required after giving of follower notice

[4.46] Where a person is given a follower notice and it is not withdrawn, he (or, in the case of a partnership notice given to a representative partner who is no longer available, his successor) must take the ensuing corrective action before the time specified below. Where an enquiry is in progress, the person must amend the return or claim to counteract the tax advantage denied by principles laid down, or reasoning given, in the judicial ruling. If an appeal is open, the person must take all necessary action to enter into a written agreement with HMRC for the purpose of relinquishing the denied advantage. After carrying out the necessary action the person must, before the specified time, notify HMRC that he has done so, including details of the denied advantage and (except in the case of a partnership follower notice) any additional amount of tax that has or will become due and payable.

If no representations were made following the giving of the notice (see **4.45** above), the specified time is the end of the period of 90 days beginning with the day on which the notice was given. If representations were made and the notice confirmed, the specified time is the later of the end of that 90-day period and the end of the period of 30 days beginning with the day on which the person is notified of HMRC's decision to confirm the notice.

Where the corrective action requires an amendment to a return or claim, such an amendment is not prevented by any time limit. No appeal may be brought against an amendment made by an enquiry closure notice to the extent that it takes into account an amendment to a return or claim resulting from corrective action under the above provision.

Where a person fails to take the necessary corrective action before the specified time, a penalty arises. See **4.48** below.

[*FA 2014, s 208, Sch 31 para 4*].

Late appeal against judicial ruling

[4.47] Where what would otherwise have been a final judicial ruling is reopened because a court or tribunal grants leave to appeal out of time, and a follower notice has been given based on that ruling, the notice is suspended until HMRC notify the taxpayer that the appeal has resulted in a final judicial ruling or has been abandoned or otherwise disposed of. HMRC must notify the taxpayer that the follower notice has been suspended. No new follower notice may be issued in respect of the original ruling unless the new appeal is abandoned or disposed of without being determined by a court or tribunal, but this does not prevent a follower notice from being issued in respect of a new final ruling resulting from the appeal. Where the appeal is abandoned or so disposed of, the period beginning when leave to appeal out of time was granted and ending when the appeal is disposed of does not count towards the twelve-month time limit for issuing follower notices in respect of the original ruling (see **4.45** above).

If a new final ruling results from the appeal and it is not relevant to the tax arrangements in question, a suspended follower notice ceases to have effect. In any other case it continues to have effect after the suspension ends and, if there is a new final ruling, the notice is treated as if it were in respect of that ruling. HMRC's notification to the taxpayer that the suspension has ended must indicate which of these outcomes applies. If there is a new final ruling, the notification must also make any amendments to the follower notice needed to reflect the new ruling.

The period during which a follower notice is suspended does not count in determining the specified time by which corrective action must be taken (see **4.46** above).

[*FA 2014, s 216*].

Penalties for non-compliance

[4.48] Where a person who has been given a follower notice (see **4.44** above) fails to take the necessary corrective action before the specified time (see **4.46** above), that person is liable to a penalty of 50% of the value of the denied tax advantage. If, before the specified time, the person takes the necessary corrective action in respect only of part of the denied tax advantage, the penalty is 50% of the value of the remainder of the advantage.

The value of the denied tax advantage for this purpose is the amount of tax attributable to the advantage. This includes any additional amount payable to HMRC, and any amount no longer repayable by HMRC, due to the advantage being denied.

Where the denied tax advantage resulted in a wrongly recorded loss which has been partly used to reduce the tax due or payable, the value of the denied advantage is increased by 10% of the part of the loss not so used. This rule applies both where the entire loss is attributable to the denied advantage and where only part of the loss is so attributable (but in the latter case, the rule applies only to that part). To the extent that, because of its nature or the taxpayer's circumstances, there is no reasonable prospect of a loss resulting from a denied advantage being used to reduce a tax liability of any person, the value of the denied advantage is nil.

To the extent that the denied advantage is a deferral of tax (other than one resulting from a loss), the value of it is 25% of the amount of deferred tax for each year of deferral and a proportion of 25% for each period of deferral (if any) of less than a year. The value cannot exceed 100% of the deferred tax.

In the case of a partnership follower notice, each person who was a partner during the period for which the return in question was required is liable to the penalty, but the total penalty is 20% rather than 50%. The value of the denied tax advantage for this purpose is the net amount of the amendments made, or required to be made, to the partnership return to counteract the denied advantage. Each partner is liable for a share of the total penalty; the share is based on the profit-sharing arrangements for the period except that, if HMRC do not have sufficient information to apportion the total on that basis, HMRC may determine how it should be apportioned.

HMRC may reduce a penalty to reflect the quality (including the timing, nature and extent) of any co-operation by the taxpayer. It cannot be reduced to less than 10% of the value of the denied advantage, or 4% in the case of a partnership follower notice. A taxpayer co-operates only if he does one or more of the following:

- provides HMRC with reasonable assistance in quantifying the tax advantage;
- counteracts the denied tax advantage;
- provides HMRC with information enabling corrective action to be taken by HMRC;
- provides HMRC with information enabling them to enter an agreement with the taxpayer for the purpose of counteracting the denied advantage; and
- allows HMRC to access tax records to ensure that the denied advantage is fully counteracted.

Interaction with other penalties

Where a taxpayer incurs a penalty under the above provisions and a penalty under *FA 2007, Sch 24* (see **55.6–55.13** PENALTIES), *FA 2008, Sch 41* (see **55.3, 55.4** PENALTIES), *FA 2009, Sch 55* (see **55.5** PENALTIES), *FA 2013, s 212A* (see **4.8** above) or *FA 2016, Sch 18 Pt 5* (see **4.59** below) in respect of the same amount of tax, the aggregate of the penalties is restricted to a maximum of the highest percentage of the amount of tax chargeable under any of the provisions (subject to a minimum of 100%). Where one of the penalties is a £300 penalty under *FA 2009, Sch 55*, the aggregate penalty cannot be less than £300.

Assessment and appeals

The above penalties are charged by HMRC assessment. The assessment is treated in the same way as an assessment to tax and can be enforced accordingly. It may also be combined with a tax assessment. The notice of assessment must state the tax year in respect of which the penalty is assessed. The penalty must be paid within the 30 days beginning with the date of issue of the notice of assessment. Subject to the time limits below, HMRC can make a supplementary assessment if an earlier assessment underestimated the value of the denied tax advantage, and an assessment can be revised if it overestimated that value.

Where the follower notice was given whilst an enquiry was in progress, an assessment of a penalty must be made before the end of the period of 90 days beginning with the day the enquiry is completed. Where the follower notice was given whilst an appeal was open, an assessment of a penalty must be made before the end of the period of 90 days beginning with the earliest of the day on which the taxpayer takes the necessary corrective action, the day on which a final ruling is made on that appeal or any further appeal and the day on which the appeal, or further appeal, is abandoned or otherwise disposed of before being finally determined.

An appeal can be made against the imposition of a penalty or against the amount of a penalty. An appeal on these matters in relation to a partnership follower notice must be made by the representative partner or his successor, but no appeal can be made against the apportionment of a penalty between partners. An appeal must be made within the 30 days beginning with the date of issue of the notice of assessment. If the appeal is against the imposition of a penalty and it goes to the Appeal Tribunal, the Tribunal may affirm or cancel HMRC's decision to impose. If the appeal is against the amount of a penalty and it goes to the Tribunal, the Tribunal may affirm the amount charged or substitute its own amount (but only an amount that HMRC could have chosen to charge). An appeal against imposition may, in particular, be on the grounds that any of **4.45**(a), (b) or (d) above are not satisfied, that the judicial ruling is not relevant to the arrangements or that the notice was not given within the time limit. It may also be on the grounds that it was reasonable in all the circumstances for the taxpayer to continue his dispute rather than take corrective action; in this case any cancellation by the Tribunal of HMRC's decision to impose does not negate the validity of the follower notice, or of any accelerated payment notice or partner payment notice under **4.50** below that is related to the follower notice. Otherwise, the general APPEALS (5) provisions apply as they apply to assessments to income tax.

[*FA 2014, ss 208(2), 209–214, Sch 30, Sch 31 paras 4(2), 5; FA 2016, s 158(11), Sch 18 para 60*].

Accelerated payment notices

[4.49] Users of avoidance schemes may be required to pay tax upfront before the success or failure of the scheme has been finally determined. HMRC may issue a notice (an '*accelerated payment notice*') which overrides any postponement of tax pending an appeal or, where there is no appeal, requires the payment of disputed tax within a specified time. There are special provisions for partnerships. The provisions cover a number of taxes but are described below to the extent only that they relate to income tax. Where relevant, the definitions at **4.44** above apply for the purposes of these provisions. For official guidance see www.gov.uk/government/publications/follower-notices-and-accelerated-payments; and see also HMRC factsheet CC/FS24 listed at **37.1** HMRC EXPLANATORY PUBLICATIONS.

Simon's Taxes. See A7.248–A7.248D.

Giving of accelerated payment notice

[4.50] HMRC may give an accelerated payment notice to a person if:

(a) an enquiry into a return or claim made by that person is in progress or that person has made an appeal which has not been finally determined, abandoned or otherwise disposed of;
(b) the return, claim or appeal is made on the basis that a particular tax advantage results from particular arrangements; and
(c) either:
- HMRC has given a follower notice (see **4.44** above) in relation to the same return, claim or appeal by reason of the same tax advantage and arrangements; or
- the arrangements are 'DOTAS arrangements'; or
- a final counteraction notice under the GAAR (see **4.3**, **4.6** and **4.7** above) has been given for the tax advantage (or part of it) and arrangements in circumstances in which at least two members of the sub-panel of the GAAR Advisory Panel which considered the case concluded that entering into the tax arrangements (or the equivalent arrangements the Panel considered) was not a reasonable course of action (see **4.3**(8), **4.6** and **4.7** above).

In (c) above, '*DOTAS arrangements*' are notifiable arrangements under the provisions for DISCLOSURE OF TAX AVOIDANCE SCHEMES (**25**) to which HMRC has allocated a reference number; or notifiable arrangements implementing a notifiable proposal where HMRC has allocated a reference number to the proposed notifiable arrangements; or arrangements in respect of which the promoter must provide prescribed information by reason of the arrangements being substantially the same as notifiable arrangements. Notifiable arrangements are excluded if HMRC have given notice that promoters need not notify the reference number to clients.

The accelerated payment notice must specify which of the requirements in (c) above applies and must explain the effects of the notice. If the notice is given whilst an enquiry is in progress, it must specify the accelerated payment required; if given while an appeal is open it must specify the 'disputed tax' (see **4.51** below).

The recipient of an accelerated payment notice has 90 days beginning with the date the notice is given to send written representations to HMRC objecting to the notice on the grounds that any of (a)–(c) above are not satisfied or objecting to the amount specified. Having considered the representations HMRC will notify the recipient of whether they have decided to confirm the notice, to withdraw it or to amend the amount specified in it.

[*FA 2014, ss 219, 220(1)(2), 221(1)(2), 222; FA 2016, s 157(18)–(20)*].

An application to the court for interim relief from a notice (in the context of an application for judicial review) was refused in *R (oao Dunne) v HMRC* QB, [2015] EWHC 1204; the court did grant limited relief in the form of an order that, if the claimants established hardship, HMRC would not without first applying to the court take steps to enforce any sum due and payable under the notice, but HMRC had already expressed their willingness to submit to such an order. Judicial review applications challenging notices on various grounds, including breaches of human rights, legitimate expectation, motive and abuse of power by reversing the effect of tax postponement agreements, were dismissed by the courts in *R (oao Rowe) v HMRC* CA, [2018] STC 462; *Walapu v HMRC* QB, [2016] STC 1682; *R (oao Dickinson) v HMRC* CA, [2019] STC 319 and *R (oao Carlton) v HMRC* QB, [2018] STC 589. A taxpayer who sought judicial review before making representations to HMRC, as above, was not entitled to have her costs paid by HMRC (*R (oao Archer) v HMRC* CA, [2019] STC 1353).

Partnerships

Where a partnership return (see **64.12** RETURNS) has been made, no accelerated payment notice may be given to the representative partner (i.e. the partner responsible for dealing with the return) or to the successor of that partner (see **64.12** RETURNS). Instead, a '*partner payment notice*' may be given to each person who was a partner at any time in the period to which the return relates if:

(i) an enquiry is in progress into that return or an appeal has been made against an amendment of that return or, following an enquiry into that return, a conclusion stated in a closure notice;

(ii) the return or appeal is made on the basis that a particular advantage results from particular arrangements; and

(iii) either
- HMRC has given a follower notice (see **4.44** above) to the representative partner or successor in relation to the same return or appeal by reason of the same tax advantage and arrangements; or
- the arrangements are DOTAS arrangements; or
- the partner in question has been given a final counteraction notice under the GAAR (see **4.3**, **4.6** and **4.7** above) for the tax advantage (or part of it) and arrangements in circumstances in which at least two members of the sub-panel of the GAAR Advisory Panel which considered the case concluded that entering into the tax arrangements (or the equivalent arrangements the Panel considered) was not a reasonable course of action (see **4.3**(8), **4.6** and **4.7** above).

For the purposes of (ii) above, a return or appeal is made on the basis that a particular tax advantage results from particular tax arrangements if the arrangements increase or reduce any of the items required to be included in the partnership statement included in the return and they result in a tax advantage for at least one of the partners.

There are provisions as to the contents of a notice, and as to representations by the recipient, which are similar to those applicable to accelerated payment notices above.

[*FA 2014, Sch 32 paras 1–3, 4(1), 5; FA 2016, s 157(26)–(28)*].

The above provisions apply to limited liability partnerships as they do to other partnerships (*Sword Services Ltd v HMRC* QB 2016, [2017] STC 596).

Withdrawal, modification or suspension

HMRC may withdraw a notice at any time and if they do so the notice is treated as never having had effect and any accelerated payments (and penalties) paid must be repaid. If a notice is given as a result of more than one of the requirements in (c) above (or, for partnerships, (iii) above), HMRC may at any time withdraw it to the extent that it is given by one of those requirements (leaving it effective to the extent it was given by virtue of the remaining requirements). HMRC may also reduce the amount of the accelerated payment (or partner payment) required or the disputed tax specified in the notice (and, where an accelerated payment has already been made in excess of the reduced amount, that excess must be repaid). Where a partnership return to which an accelerated payment (or partner payment) notice relates is amended under **64.14** PARTNERSHIPS (amendment following Tribunal determination of referred dispute between partners), HMRC may by notice make consequential amendments to the accelerated payment (or partner payment) notice; if the amount of the payment is thus reduced, any overpayment is repayable; if the amount is increased, the extra tax must be paid within 30 days or, if later, by the end of the payment period in **4.51** below.

An accelerated payment (or partner payment) notice given by virtue of a follower notice must be withdrawn if the follower notice is withdrawn (to the extent that it is given by virtue of the follower notice). If a follower notice is suspended following a late appeal against a judicial ruling (see **4.47** above), the accelerated payment (or partner payment) notice is similarly suspended and the period of suspension does not count towards the 30-day and 90-day periods in **4.51** below. A notice is not so suspended if it was also given (and not withdrawn) by virtue of either of the other requirements in (c) (or (iii)) above. If a follower notice is amended following such a late appeal, HMRC may by notice make consequential amendments to the accelerated payment (or partner payment) notice.

HMRC must withdraw a notice to the extent that it is given by virtue of DOTAS arrangements if they give notice under *FA 2004, s 312(6)* with the result that promoters are no longer required to notify clients of the reference number (see **25.4** DISCLOSURE OF TAX AVOIDANCE SCHEMES).

Where a notice is given by virtue of more than one of the requirements in (c) (or (iii)) above and is withdrawn to the extent that it was given by virtue of one of those requirements and that requirement was the one stated in the notice to apply to determine the accelerated payment required or the 'disputed tax' (see **4.51** below), HMRC must modify the notice to specify one of the remaining requirements as the one which applies for that purpose (and to reduce the specified amount where necessary). This rule also applies where a follower notice by virtue of which the accelerated payment notice was given is suspended, but any modification then applies only during the period of suspension.

[*FA 2014, s 227, Sch 32 para 8; FA 2018, Sch 6 paras 13(4)(5), 14*].

Effects of accelerated payment notice

[4.51] If an accelerated payment notice is given whilst an enquiry is in progress, the recipient of the notice must make the payment specified in it. If no representations were made following the giving of the notice, the payment must be made before the end of the 'payment period'. The '*payment period*' is the 90 days beginning with the day on which the notice was given. If representations were made and the notice confirmed or amended, the payment period is extended where necessary to the end of the 30 days beginning with the day on which the taxpayer is notified of HMRC's decision to confirm the notice.

The amount of the payment required is (subject to any representations) the amount which a designated HMRC officer determines, to the best of his information and belief, as the 'understated tax'. The '*understated tax*' is the additional amount that would be due and payable if:

(a) where the notice is given as a result of a follower notice, the necessary corrective action under the follower notice were taken in respect of what the officer determines as the denied advantage;
(b) where the notice is given because the arrangements are DOTAS arrangements, adjustments were made to counteract what the officer determines as the denied advantage; and
(c) where the notice is given as a result of a GAAR counteraction notice, the adjustments set out in that notice which counteract the denied tax advantage were made.

In determining the understated tax, no account is taken of any dispute between partners which has been referred to an Appeal Tribunal as in **64.14** PARTNERSHIPS and not yet determined.

Where more than one of the requirements in **4.50**(c) above would otherwise apply, the notice must stipulate which of them is to apply, and the required payment must be determined accordingly. The accelerated payment is treated as a payment on account of the understated tax. Where any of the tax included in the required payment has already been paid, the required payment is to that extent treated as having been paid at the time of the earlier payment. HMRC's recovery powers apply to the required payment as they apply to payments of tax (see **54** PAYMENT OF TAX).

If an accelerated payment notice is given (and not withdrawn) whilst an appeal is open, the understated tax or the 'disputed tax' cannot be postponed (see **54.5** PAYMENT OF TAX) pending the outcome of the appeal. If an amount of disputed tax is postponed immediately before the giving of an accelerated payment notice, it ceases to be postponed at that time and becomes due and payable on or before the last day of the 90 days beginning with the day the notice is given. If representations are made against the notice (see **4.50** above), the tax becomes due and payable on or before the later of the end of that 90-day period and the end of the 30 days beginning with the day on which the taxpayer is notified of HMRC's decision to confirm the notice. To the extent that the tax results from an amendment to an accelerated payment notice in consequence of a Tribunal determination under **64.14** PARTNERSHIPS (determination of referred dispute between partners), it becomes due and payable in similar fashion except that the due date cannot be earlier than the end of the 30-day period beginning when the notice of amendment is given.

The '*disputed tax*' is so much of the tax which is the subject of the appeal as a designated HMRC officer determines, to the best of his information and belief, as the amount required to counteract what that officer determines as the denied tax advantage (calculated in the same way as the understated tax above). Where more than one of the requirements in **4.50**(c) above would otherwise apply, the notice must stipulate which of them is to apply, and the denied advantage must be determined accordingly. 'Disputed tax' can include tax arising from a determination under *SI 2003 No 2682, Reg 80* (as in **53.19** PAY AS YOU EARN) (*Sheiling Properties v HMRC* UT, [2020] UKUT 175 (TCC)).

Where an accelerated payment notice is in force in relation to an open appeal and a court or the Appeal Tribunal decides against HMRC who then seek permission to appeal against the decision, HMRC may ask the court or Tribunal from which they are seeking permission to appeal to disapply the normal rule requiring repayment of tax in accordance with the decision (see **5.22** APPEALS). If the court or Tribunal considers it necessary for the protection of public revenue, it may give permission to withhold the affected repayment or to require the provision of adequate security before repayment is made.

The First-tier Tribunal has no jurisdiction to determine whether the amount of the payment required by an accelerated payment notice corresponds to the correct amount of tax due (*Beadle v HMRC* CA, [2020] STC 1058).

Partnerships

The above provisions apply similarly in relation to partner payment notices (see **4.50** above) as they do in relation to accelerated payment notices, except that a partner payment notice will always require an accelerated payment.

[*TMA 1970, ss 55(8B)–(8E), 56(4)–(6); FA 2014, ss 220(3)–(7), 221(3)–(5), 223(1)–(5)(7)–(9), 224(1), 225(1), Sch 32 paras 4(2)–(5), 6; FA 2016, s 157(21); FA 2018, Sch 6 paras 10(8), 13(2)(5), 14*].

Penalties for non-compliance

[4.52] Where a person who has been given an accelerated payment notice whilst an enquiry is in progress (or has been given a partner payment notice) fails to pay any amount of the accelerated payment within the time limit (see **4.51** above) an initial penalty of 5% of the unpaid amount is chargeable. If any amount is still unpaid at the end of a further period of five months, a second penalty of 5% of the unpaid amount is chargeable. A third 5% penalty applies to any amount remaining unpaid at the end of a further six months after the second penalty becomes chargeable.

The provisions at **43.4** LATE PAYMENT INTEREST AND PENALTIES as to reasonable excuse, suspension of penalty where 'time to pay' arrangement in place, reduction in special circumstances, double jeopardy, assessment of penalty and appeals apply, with any necessary modifications, to a penalty in relation to a failure to pay an amount of accelerated payment as they apply to a late payment penalty in relation to a failure to pay an amount of tax.

Where an amendment to an accelerated payment notice (or partner payment notice) is made in consequence of a Tribunal determination under **64.14** PARTNERSHIPS (determination of referred dispute between partners), such that the amount of the payment is increased, the increase is to be ignored when computing and charging penalties.

[*FA 2014, s 226(1)–(5)(7), Sch 32 para 7; FA 2018, Sch 6 paras 13(3)(5), 14*].

HMRC were unable to charge penalties where they had failed to comply with the statutory procedure concerning representations (see **4.50** above) by the recipient of a partner payment notice (*Rai v HMRC* FTT (TC 5930), [2017] UKFTT 467 (TC)). A penalty may be reduced on appeal if HMRC have not estimated the amount of the accelerated payment on which the penalty is based to the best of their information or belief or have made an obvious mistake in its calculation (*Graham v HMRC* FTT (TC 6809), [2018] UKFTT 661 (TC)).

Serial avoiders regime

[4.53] The serial avoiders regime is a regime of warnings and escalating sanctions for taxpayers who persistently engage in tax avoidance schemes that are successfully counteracted ('*defeated*') by HMRC. Following the first defeat of a scheme, HMRC will place the taxpayer on a warning (see **4.54**, **4.55** below). The taxpayer has to annually provide HMRC with information during a five-year warning period (see **4.56**). If the taxpayer uses any such avoidance scheme while under warning, penalties of up to 60% of the understated tax will be charged (see **4.59**). If three avoidance schemes which exploit reliefs are used while under warning and are defeated, the taxpayer is denied further benefit of reliefs until the warning period expires (see **4.57**). If HMRC defeat three avoidance schemes while the taxpayer is on warning, the taxpayer's details can be published (see **4.60**). See **4.58** for the application of the regime to partnerships. For official guidance see www.gov.uk/government/publications/serial-tax-avoidance-regime-guidance. See also HMRC factsheet CC/FS38a listed at **37.1** HMRC EXPLANATORY PUBLICATIONS.

The regime applies to a number of direct and indirect taxes and also national insurance contributions (see *FA 2016, Sch 18 para 4* for the full list). It is described below in terms of its application to income tax, but it should be noted that the regime does not operate independently for each type of tax but embraces all avoidance schemes that a person uses which cover any tax on the list.

In relation to taxes other than VAT, '*tax advantage*' is defined widely by *FA 2016, Sch 18 para 7* for the purposes of these provisions.

Commencement

The serial avoiders regime has effect in relation to 'relevant defeats' (see **4.55** below) incurred after 15 September 2016, except for defeats incurred before 6 April 2017 in relation to arrangements entered into before 15 September 2016. A relevant defeat incurred on or after 6 April 2017 in relation to any such pre-15 September 2016 arrangements is outside the regime if, before 6 April 2017, the person incurring the defeat makes a full disclosure of the arrangements or both gives HMRC notice of a firm intention to do so and makes the disclosure within any time limit HMRC may set.

A warning notice given to any person is to be disregarded for the purposes of **4.57** below (restriction of reliefs) and **4.60** below (publishing taxpayer's details) if the defeat specified in the notice relates to arrangements entered into before 15 September 2016. As regards any such pre-15 September 2016 arrangements, a relevant defeat incurred in relation to the arrangements and any warning notice specifying such a defeat are disregarded for the purposes of the penalty at **4.59** below.

[*FA 2016, Sch 18 paras 63–65*].

Warning notices

[4.54] Where a person has incurred a 'relevant defeat' (see **4.55** below) in relation to any arrangements (as widely defined), HMRC must give that person a written notice (a '*warning notice*') within the 90 days beginning with the day on which the defeat is incurred. The warning notice must specify the defeat in question, state when the 'warning period' begins and ends and explain the statutory consequences of the notice. The '*warning period*' is the five years following the day on which the warning notice is given. If a person incurs a relevant defeat during a warning period, that period is extended to the end of the five years following the day on which the defeat occurs. [*FA 2016, Sch 18 paras 2, 3*].

Associated persons

Where a person (P) incurs a relevant defeat in relation to any arrangements, any person who is 'associated' with P at the time when P is given the warning notice is also treated for the above purposes as having incurred that relevant defeat. However, a warning notice thus given to an associated person is disregarded for the purposes of **4.57** below (restriction of relief notices) and **4.59** below (penalties). For these purposes, two persons are '*associated*' with one another only if one of them is a body corporate which is controlled (as defined) by the other or if they are bodies corporate under common control (as defined). [*FA 2016, Sch 18 paras 47, 48*].

Meaning of 'relevant defeat'

[4.55] For the purposes of taxes other than VAT, a person (P) incurs a '*relevant defeat*' in relation to arrangements if any of conditions A to C below is met in relation to P and the arrangements. The relevant defeat is incurred when the condition in question is first met.

- Condition A is that a tax advantage has arisen to P from the arrangements and this has been counteracted as in **4.2** above (the GAAR), with the counteraction having become final.
- Condition B is that (in a case not falling within Condition A) a follower notice (see **4.44** above) has been given to P by reference to the arrangements (and not withdrawn) and either the necessary corrective action has been taken (see **4.46** above) or the denied tax advantage has been otherwise counteracted), with the counteraction having become final (determined in the same manner as under **4.2** above).
- Condition C is that (in a case not falling within Condition A or B) the arrangements are 'DOTAS arrangements' (see below) on which P has relied, and the arrangements have been counteracted, with the counteraction having become final. The time at which it falls to be determined whether or not the arrangements are DOTAS arrangements is when the counteraction becomes final.

Condition B applies also where the follower notice is a partnership follower notice in connection with a partnership return and is given to a partnership in which P was a partner in the period covered by the return.

For the purposes of Condition C, P relies on the arrangements if he makes a return, claim or election, or a partnership return is made, on the basis that a 'relevant tax advantage' arises, or if P fails to discharge a 'relevant obligation' and there is reason to believe that the failure is connected with the arrangements. A '*relevant tax advantage*' is one which the arrangements might be expected to enable P to obtain. An obligation is a '*relevant obligation*' if the arrangements might be expected to have the result that the obligation does not arise.

Arrangements are counteracted for the purposes of Condition C if P's tax position is adjusted (other than at his own behest), or an HMRC assessment is made on P, or any other action is taken by HMRC, on the basis that the whole or part of the relevant tax advantage does not arise or that the relevant obligation does arise. Contract settlements (see **6.9** ASSESSMENTS) are treated as assessments for this purpose. P's tax position is adjusted at his own behest if he makes the adjustment at a time when he had no reason to believe that an HMRC enquiry was in the offing (regarding the tax in question) or if HMRC make the adjustment as a result of a full and explicit disclosure by P which is made at such a time.

A counteraction is final for the purposes of Condition C when the assessment, adjustments or action in question, and any amounts thereby arising, can no longer be varied on appeal or otherwise.

[*FA 2016, Sch 18 paras 11–14, 54*].

Meaning of 'DOTAS arrangements'

For the purposes of the serial avoiders regime, arrangements are '*DOTAS arrangements*' at any time if they are 'notifiable arrangements' at that time and a person has provided information in relation to them under *FA 2004, s 308(3)* (obligation of promoter in relation to notifiable arrangements), *s 309* (obligation of person dealing with non-UK promoter) or *s 310* (obligation of parties to notifiable arrangements not involving a promoter) or has failed to comply with any of those provisions in relation to the arrangements. They do not include arrangements in respect of which HMRC has given notice that promoters are not under a duty to notify clients of the reference number. However, they do include arrangements which are excepted from the notification requirement for the reason only that they either had been notified as proposed arrangements or are substantially the same as arrangements already notified.

For the meaning of 'notifiable arrangements' and more on the above-mentioned *FA 2004* provisions, see **25.3** DISCLOSURE OF TAX AVOIDANCE SCHEMES. For the above purposes, a person fails to comply with any of those provisions if (and only if) the Appeal Tribunal has determined this to be the case (or has determined against a reasonable excuse), and their determination can no longer be appealed, or the person has made a written admission of such failure to HMRC.

[*FA 2016, Sch 18 paras 8, 10*].

Requirement of annual information notices

[4.56] A person (P) who has been given a warning notice (as in **4.54** above) must give HMRC a written notice (an '*information notice*') in respect of each 'reporting period' within the warning period. The information notice must be given within 30 days after the end of the reporting period to which it relates. The first '*reporting period*' begins with the first day of the warning period and ends with a day specified by HMRC. The remainder of the warning period is divided into further reporting periods of 12 months duration, though the final reporting period ends at the same time as the warning period, even if that results in a reporting period of less than 12 months.

An information notice must state whether, in the reporting period, P:

(a) has made a return, claim or election on the basis that a 'relevant tax advantage' arises (and this includes a return made on that basis since the reporting period ended if the return was due in the reporting period); or
(b) has failed to take action which he would be required to take under, or by virtue of, any tax enactment if it were not for particular DOTAS arrangements (see **4.55** above) or 'disclosable VAT arrangements' (within *FA 2016, Sch 18 para 9*) to which he is a party; or
(c) has become a party to arrangements relating to a supplier's VAT position which might be expected to enable P to obtain a relevant tax advantage in connection with the supplies,

and whether or not P has failed to make any return that he was required to make by a date falling in the reporting period.

A '*relevant tax advantage*' is a tax advantage which particular DOTAS arrangements or disclosable VAT arrangements enable, or might be expected to enable, P to obtain. If (a) above is in point, P must include in the information notice an explanation of how the tax advantage arises and its amount. If (b) is in point, P must similarly explain how the arrangements result in there being no requirement to take the action in question and state the amount of any resulting tax advantage. If (c) is in point, P must state whether it is his view that the relevant tax advantage arises to him and, if so, he must explain how the arrangements enable him to obtain the advantage and state its amount.

If the due date for a return falls within the reporting period and P fails to make the return in that period, HMRC may require from P a supplementary information notice setting out any matters which he would have been required to include in the original information notice if it had not been for that failure. Any such HMRC requirement must be notified in writing and must state the period allowed for compliance.

If P fails to provide a notice (whether an information notice or a supplementary information notice) or provides a notice that is defective, HMRC may by written notice extend the warning period to the end of the five years beginning with the day by which the notice should have been given, or the day on which the defective notice was given. The warning period cannot thus be extended by more than five years from what would otherwise have been its expiry date.

[*FA 2016, Sch 18 para 17*].

Restriction of reliefs

[4.57] HMRC must give a person a written notice (a '*restriction of relief notice*') if:

- the person incurs a relevant defeat (see **4.55** above) in relation to arrangements which he has used whilst in a warning period (see **4.54** above);
- he has been given at least two warning notices in respect of other relevant defeats of arrangements used in that same warning period;
- all the relevant defeats are by virtue of Condition A, B or C in **4.55** (as opposed to conditions relating to VAT that are not reproduced here);
- all the relevant defeats relate to the misuse of a relief; and
- in the case of each of the relevant defeats, either the counteraction was made on the basis that a particular 'avoidance-related rule' applied in relation to a person's affairs or the misused relief in question was a relief for LOSSES (45).

If a person has been given a single warning notice in relation to two or more relevant defeats, he is treated for the above purposes as having been given a separate warning notice in relation to each defeat. The time at which, for the purposes of the serial avoiders regime, a person has 'used' arrangements is determined by *FA 2016, Sch 18 para 55* in terms of the filing date for returns (meaning the earlier of the actual filing date and the due date), the dates on which claims and elections are made and the date of any failure to comply with an obligation (meaning the date on which the person is first in breach of the obligation).

A relevant defeat relates to the misuse of a relief if the tax advantage in question (or part of it), results from a relief (or an increased relief) or it is reasonable to conclude that the making of a particular claim for relief, or the use of a particular relief, is a significant component of the arrangements in question. A relief means any relief from tax (however described) which must be claimed; any relief for losses; or any other relief listed in *ITA 2007, s 24* (reliefs deductible at Step 2 of the calculation of income tax liability at **1.10** ALLOWANCES AND TAX RATES).

'*Avoidance-related rule*' is defined by *FA 2016, Sch 18 para 25*, which also includes an example of such a rule. A statutory rule to the effect that the avoidance of tax must not be a main object or an expected benefit of a transaction or arrangements, or that an action must be carried out for commercial reasons, would be an avoidance-related rule.

The restricted period

A restriction of relief notice must explain its effect (see below) and state when the 'restricted period' begins and ends. The '*restricted period*' is the three years beginning with the day on which the restriction of relief notice is given. If during the restricted period the person to whom a restriction of relief notice has been given incurs a further relevant defeat, HMRC must give him a written notice (a '*restricted period extension notice*'); this extends the restricted period to the end of the three years beginning with the day on which the further defeat occurs. A further defeat is taken into account for this purpose only if it is incurred by virtue of Condition A, B or C in relation to arrangements which the person used in the warning period and relates to the misuse of a relief. If a person to whom a restriction of relief notice has been given incurs a further defeat after the restricted period has ended but during a warning period which at some time ran concurrently with the restricted period, HMRC must give that person a restriction of relief notice.

Effect of restriction of relief notice

A person to whom a restriction of relief notice has been given may not, in the restricted period, make any claim for relief. (For the purposes of the serial avoiders regime, 'claim for relief' includes any election or similar action which is in substance a claim for relief.) Reliefs for charitable giving and contributions to a registered pension scheme are excluded from this restriction, as are claims for relief under a double tax treaty. In calculating the person's net income for a tax year whose first day falls within the restricted period, no deduction can be made for trading or property losses brought forward from previous years. The person is not entitled to relief for annual payments (see **1.13** ALLOWANCES AND TAX RATES) for any payment made in the restricted period.

Mitigation, reasonable excuse and appeals

The Commissioners for HMRC may mitigate, in any way they think appropriate, the effect of a restriction of relief notice insofar as it appears to them that there are exceptional circumstances such that it would otherwise have an unduly serious impact with respect to the tax affairs of the taxpayer concerned or another person.

If a person (P) who has incurred a relevant defeat satisfies HMRC or, on appeal, the Tribunal that he had a reasonable excuse for the matters to which the defeat relates, he is treated for the purposes of the restriction of relief provisions as not having incurred that defeat, and any warning notice given to him in relation to that defeat is treated as not having been given. Reasonable excuse does not include insufficiency of funds (unless attributable to events outside P's control), reliance on another person to do anything (unless P took reasonable care to avoid the failure or inaccuracy in question) or reliance on advice if that advice is addressed to, or was given to, a person other than P or takes no account of P's individual circumstances. A person with a reasonable excuse is treated as having continued to have it if the failure or inaccuracy in question was remedied without unreasonable delay after the excuse ceased.

A person may appeal against a restriction of relief notice or a restricted period extension notice within 30 days beginning with the day on which the notice is given. The appeal is to be treated in the same way as an appeal against an income tax assessment. The Appeal Tribunal, on an appeal brought before it, may cancel or affirm HMRC's decision to issue the notice. It may also mitigate the effect of a notice to the same extent as HMRC (see above) or to a different extent, but in the latter case only if the Tribunal regards HMRC's decision on mitigation as flawed.

[*FA 2016, Sch 18 paras 19–29, 55*].

Partnerships

[4.58] The consequences described below apply in relation to a partnership tax return under *TMA 1970, s 12AA* if:

- the return has been made on the basis that a tax advantage arises to a partner from any arrangements and that partner has incurred, in relation to that tax advantage and those arrangements, a relevant defeat by virtue of Condition A or Condition C in **4.55** above; or
- a person has incurred a relevant defeat by virtue of Condition B in **4.55** above and the follower notice in question is a partnership follower notice.

A partnership return is regarded as made on the basis that a particular tax advantage arises to a partner from particular arrangements if it is made on the basis that an increase or reduction in any of the items at **64.13**(a)–(c) RETURNS (partnership statements) results from those arrangements and that increase or reduction results in that tax advantage for the partner. Limited liability partnerships are within these rules in the same way as other partnerships. For the above purposes a relevant defeat does not include one which an associated person is treated as having incurred (see **4.54** above).

Each 'relevant partner' is treated for the purposes of the serial avoiders regime as having also incurred the relevant defeat in question. A '*relevant partner*' is any person who was a member of the partnership at any time during the period covered by the partnership return.

The appropriate partner (meaning a partner nominated by HMRC for this purpose) must give HMRC a written notice (a '*partnership information notice*') in respect of each sub-period in the 'information period'. The '*information period*' is the five years following the day of the relevant defeat.

If a new information period (relating to another partnership return) begins during an existing information period, those periods are treated as a single period. An information period ends if the partnership ceases. The partnership information notice must be given within 30 days after the end of the sub-period to which it relates. The first sub-period begins with the first day of the information period and ends with a day specified by HMRC. The remainder of the information period is divided into further sub-periods of 12 months duration, though the final sub-period ends at the same time as the information period, even if that results in a sub-period of less than 12 months. A partnership information notice must state (i) whether or not any partnership return which was, or was required to be, delivered in the sub-period has been made on the basis that a 'relevant tax advantage' arises; and (ii) whether or not there has been a failure to deliver a partnership return in the sub-period. A '*relevant tax advantage*' is a tax advantage which particular DOTAS arrangements (see **4.55** above) enable, or might be expected to enable, a member of the partnership to obtain. Where relevant, the information notice must go on to explain how the DOTAS arrangements enable the tax advantage to be obtained and describe any variation in the amounts required to be stated in the partnership statement included in the return. There is similar provision to require supplementary information notices as in **4.56** above, and similar consequences for failure to provide an accurate information notice.

There is provision to the effect that if a partnership return is amended, whether by the partnership itself or by HMRC following an unprompted disclosure, then, for the purpose of applying Condition C in **4.55** above, each affected partner is treated as having simultaneously amended his own return so as to give effect to the amendment of the partnership return.

[*FA 2016, Sch 18 paras 49–53, 58(1)(4)*].

Penalties

[4.59] A person is liable to a penalty if he incurs a relevant defeat (see **4.55** above) in relation to any arrangements which he has used whilst in a warning period (see **4.54** above). The time at which a person has 'used' arrangements is determined by *FA 2016, Sch 18 para 55* (see **4.57**). The standard penalty is 20% of the 'value of the counteracted advantage'. If, before the relevant defeat is incurred, the person has been given (or become liable to be given) 'prior warning notices', the penalty is increased. It is increased to 40% where there has been a single prior warning notice, and to 60% where there has been more than one such notice. A '*prior warning notice*' is a warning notice in relation to the defeat of arrangements which the person has used in the warning period.

If a person incurs simultaneously two or more relevant defeats in relation to different arrangements, then for the purpose of determining the penalty those defeats are placed in order of value, the defeat of greatest value being deemed to be the first incurred; the value of a defeat is the value of the counteracted advantage. If a person has been given a single warning notice in relation to two or more relevant defeats, he is treated for penalty purposes as having been given a separate warning notice in relation to each defeat.

Value of the counteracted advantage

The '*value of the counteracted advantage*' is the additional amount of tax due or payable as a result of the counteraction or corrective action. To the extent that the counteracted advantage has resulted in a loss being wrongly recorded or increased but the counteracted loss has not been wholly used to reduce tax payable, the value of the counteracted advantage is increased by 10% of the part of the counteracted loss not so used. However, the value of a counteracted loss is nil if, due to the nature of the loss or the person's circumstances, there is no reasonable prospect of the loss ever being used to reduce the tax liability of any person. To the extent that the counteracted advantage is a deferral of tax, the value of the advantage is 25% of the amount of deferred tax for each year of the deferral, but not so as to exceed 100% of the total amount of deferred tax.

Assessment, appeals etc.

The above penalty is charged by HMRC assessment. The assessment is treated in the same way as an assessment to tax and can be enforced accordingly. It may also be combined with a tax assessment. The notice of assessment must state the tax year in respect of which the penalty is assessed. The penalty must be paid within the 30 days beginning with the date of issue of the notice of assessment. The assessment itself must be made within the 12 months beginning with the date of the relevant defeat in question. HMRC can make a supplementary assessment if an earlier assessment underestimated the value of the counteracted advantage, and an assessment can be revised if it overestimated that value.

The amount of a penalty is to be reduced by any other penalty incurred by the person if the amount of that other penalty is determined by reference to the same tax liability. Other penalties do not for this purpose include the GAAR penalty at **4.8** above and the penalties at **4.48** and **4.52** above (follower notices and accelerated payments notices).

A person is not liable to a penalty in respect of a relevant defeat if he satisfies HMRC or, on appeal, the Tribunal that he had a reasonable excuse for the failures or inaccuracies in question. In determining the rate of penalty an earlier warning notice is disregarded if it relates to a relevant defeat in respect of which the person had a reasonable excuse. Otherwise, the same comments apply regarding 'reasonable excuse' as in **4.57** above.

An appeal can be made against the imposition of a penalty or against the amount of a penalty. It must be made within the 30 days beginning with the date of issue of the notice of assessment. The appeal is to be treated in the same way as an appeal against an income tax assessment. The Appeal Tribunal, on an appeal brought before it, may affirm HMRC's decision in relation to the penalty or may substitute for HMRC's decision another decision that HMRC has power to make. The Commissioners for HMRC have discretion to mitigate a penalty under these provisions, or stay or compound any proceedings for such a penalty. They may also, after judgment, further mitigate or entirely remit the penalty.

[*FA 2016, Sch 18 paras 30–44*].

Publishing taxpayer's details

[4.60] The Commissioners for HMRC may publish information about a person if he incurs a relevant defeat (see **4.55** above) in relation to arrangements which he has used in a warning period and has been given at least two warning notices (see **4.54** above) in respect of other defeats of arrangements which were used in the same warning period. If a person has been given a single warning notice in relation to two or more relevant defeats, he is treated for these purposes as having been given a separate warning notice in relation to each of those defeats.

The Commissioners can publish the person's name (including trading name, previous name or pseudonym), address, the nature of any business carried on, information about the fiscal effect of relevant defeated arrangements (had they not been defeated), e.g. the amount of tax understated, the amount of any penalty, the periods in which or times when relevant defeated arrangements were used, and any other information which they consider appropriate in order to make the person's identity clear. In the case of a person carrying on a trade or business in partnership, the information which may be published includes any trading name of the partnership and the names and addresses of the partners. Defeated arrangements are relevant if the person used them in the said warning period and has been given a warning notice in respect of them. The information may be published in any manner the Commissioners consider appropriate. It can only be first published in the period of one year beginning with the giving of the most recent of the warning notices in question, and information cannot continue to be published for more than a year. Before publishing the information, the Commissioners must inform the person that they are doing so and provide a reasonable opportunity to make representations about whether it should be published.

[*FA 2016, Sch 18 para 18*].

5

Appeals

Cross-references. See **6.5** ASSESSMENTS as regards querying a 'simple assessment'; **16.3** CLAIMS for appeals in connection with claims and elections made outside returns; **35.8** HMRC — ADMINISTRATION for HMRC's Litigation and Settlement Strategy; **39** HMRC INVESTIGATORY POWERS; **54.5, 54.6** PAYMENT OF TAX for payment of tax in relation to appeals; **55.26, 55.27,** PENALTIES for appeals relating to penalties; **63.39** RESIDENCE AND DOMICILE.

Simon's Taxes. See Part **A5, E1.268.**

Introduction to appeals

[5.1] A taxpayer who disagrees with an assessment or other decision made by HMRC can appeal against it. This is done by giving notice in writing to HMRC, stating the grounds of appeal. The notice must normally be given within 30 days after the date of issue of the assessment or decision, although late appeals can be made in some circumstances (see **5.4** below).

After a taxpayer appeals there are three main options:

- a different HMRC officer can carry out a review of the decision;
- the taxpayer can ask the Tribunal to decide the matter in dispute;
- the appeal can be settled by agreement at any time.

Reviews are not compulsory, and where HMRC carry out a review but the taxpayer still disagrees with the decision, he can ask the Tribunal to decide the issue (or continue negotiations with HMRC in order to settle the appeal by agreement).

For HMRC reviews, see **5.6** below and for settlement by agreement, see **5.9** below.

Where the taxpayer asks the Tribunal to decide the appeal, the case is usually dealt with by the First-tier Tribunal. The appeal is allocated to one of four categories, default paper, basic, standard or complex, and the process differs according to the category. Basic, standard and complex cases are normally decided at a hearing at which the taxpayer (or his representative) and HMRC are able to present their cases.

Default paper cases can also be decided at a hearing where one of the parties requests a hearing. Complex cases may be transferred for hearing by the Upper Tribunal.

For the First-tier Tribunal process, see **5.11–5.23** below.

If either the taxpayer or HMRC disagree with a decision of the First-tier Tribunal, there is a further right of appeal to the Upper Tribunal, but only on a point of law. Permission to appeal must be obtained from the First-tier Tribunal, or where it refuses permission, from the Upper Tribunal.

For the Upper Tribunal process, see **5.24–5.32** below. Where either party disagrees with an Upper Tribunal decision, there is a similar right of appeal to the Court of Appeal. See **5.33** below.

Where there is no right of appeal or a taxpayer is dissatisfied with the exercise by HMRC or the Tribunal of administrative powers, he may in certain circumstances seek a remedy by way of application for judicial review. See **5.34** below.

Costs can be awarded to or against a taxpayer in cases dealt with by either Tribunal or by the courts. See **5.23**, **5.33** and **5.35** below.

See factsheet HMRC1 at www.gov.uk/government/publications/hm-revenue-and-customs-decisions-what-to-do-if-you-disagree.

Alternative dispute resolution

[5.2] Alternative dispute resolution (ADR) is available to individuals and businesses. Under ADR, HMRC arrange for someone who has not been involved in the case to work with the taxpayer and the HMRC officer in charge of the case. This person will be an HMRC mediator who has been trained in mediation skills and techniques. ADR aims to help resolve disputes or reach agreement on which issues need to be taken for a legal ruling. The taxpayer can apply for ADR at any stage of an enquiry and at any stage of Tribunal proceedings. Even when using ADR, the taxpayer should still give notice of appeal so as to preserve his legal rights. For more details see www.gov.uk/guidance/tax-disputes-alternative-dispute-resolution-adr and the factsheet at www.gov.uk/government/publications/compliance-checks-alternative-dispute-resolution-ccfs21.

In June 2020, the First-tier Tribunal issued a statement setting out its practice in appeals against HMRC decisions where the parties wish to engage in ADR after an appeal has been made to the Tribunal (www.judiciary.uk/wp-content/uploads/2020/06/200615-FTT-Tax-Chamber-Practice-Statement-on-ADR-1.pdf).

It is a general rule of law that material arising from an ADR process is 'without prejudice' material and cannot be used in relation to subsequent proceedings before a tribunal. See the discussion in *Ritchie v HMRC* FTT (TC 5258), [2016] UKFTT 509 (TC).

Right of appeal

[5.3] A taxpayer can appeal against:

(a) any assessment other than a self-assessment;
(b) any conclusion stated, or amendment made, by a final or partial closure notice on completion or part completion of an enquiry into a personal, trustees' or partnership tax return (see **64.8** RETURNS);
(c) any HMRC amendment (of a self-assessment) made, during an enquiry, to prevent potential loss of tax (see **64.9** RETURNS);
(d) any amendment of a partnership return where loss of tax is 'discovered' (see **6.6** ASSESSMENTS).

The right of appeal in (a) above includes a right of appeal against a 'simple assessment', but an appeal can be made only after the person assessed has raised a query about the assessment and has been given a final response to that query. See **6.5** ASSESSMENTS.

The right of appeal in (b) above includes a right of appeal by a partnership member against amendments made to his own tax return in consequence of an enquiry into the partnership return (*Philips v HMRC* FTT (TC 276), [2010] SFTD 332).

The hearing of an appeal within (b) above should not be limited to the conclusions stated, or amendments made, by the closure notice. Any such limitation 'might prevent a taxpayer from advancing a legitimate factual or legal argument which had hitherto escaped him or deprive, on the other hand, the public of the tax to which it is entitled'. The only limitation on issues which might be entertained by the First-tier Tribunal is that those issues must arise out of the subject-matter of the enquiry and consequently its conclusion, and they must be subject to the case management powers of the Tribunal. (*HMRC v Tower MCashback LLP 1 and another* SC 2011, 80 TC 641). The Supreme Court did go on to state that this should not be taken as an encouragement to officers of HMRC to draft closure notices in wide and uninformative terms.

An appeal within (c) above while an enquiry is in progress in relation to any matter affected by the amendment cannot be taken forward until a partial closure notice is issued in relation to the matter or, if no such notice is issued, a final closure notice is issued (see **64.8** RETURNS).

[*TMA 1970, s 31(1)(2)(3A); FA 2016, s 167, Sch 23 para 4; F(No 2)A 2017, Sch 15 paras 18, 44*].

A number of enactments give the right of appeal against a decision of the Commissioners for HMRC or an officer of HMRC in specified circumstances or an HMRC notice or determination (see, for example, *SI 2003 No 2682, Reg 18* as regards PAYE codings). Such rights are referred to in the appropriate section of this work. Further, certain matters are dealt with as appeals (see, for example, **75.116** TRADING INCOME as regards disputes as to the transfer price of trading stock on a discontinuance). There is, however, no right of appeal against a determination of liability made by HMRC in the event of non-submission of a self-assessment tax return (see **64.11** RETURNS). For appeals in connection with claims and elections made outside the tax return, see **16.3** CLAIMS.

Unless otherwise stated or required by context, the remainder of this chapter applies to all appeals and all matters treated as appeals, and not only to appeals within (a)–(d) above. [*TMA 1970, s 48*].

Making an appeal

[5.4] An appeal is made by giving notice in writing, to the officer of Revenue and Customs concerned and specifying the grounds of appeal. Notice must normally be given within 30 days after the date of issue of the assessment or determination, the closure notice or the notice of amendment. In the case of a 'simple assessment' (see **6.5** ASSESSMENTS) notice of appeal must be given within 30 days after the date on which the person assessed is given notice by HMRC of their final response to his query about the assessment. [*TMA 1970, s 31A; FA 2016, s 167, Sch 23 para 5*].

Late appeals

If a taxpayer fails to make an appeal within the normal time limit, an appeal can still be made if HMRC agree or, where HMRC do not agree, the Tribunal gives permission.

HMRC must agree to a written request for a late appeal if they are satisfied that there was a reasonable excuse for not making the appeal within the time limit and that the request was made without unreasonable delay after the reasonable excuse ceased.

[*TMA 1970, s 49*].

The legal principles pertinent to applications to the Tribunal for permission to submit a late appeal were helpfully set out in *Martland v HMRC* UT, [2018] UKUT 178 (TCC). In the event of refusal to accept a late appeal, the decision is not subject to further appeal (*R v Special Commrs (ex p. Magill)* QB (NI) 1979, 53 TC 135), but is subject to judicial review (see *R v Hastings and Bexhill General Commrs and CIR (ex p. Goodacre)* QB 1994, 67 TC 126, in which a refusal was quashed and the matter remitted to a different body of Commissioners and *Advocate General for Scotland v General Commrs for Aberdeen City* CS 2005, 77 TC 391 in which HMRC successfully sought to overturn a decision to allow a late appeal). In *R (oao Browallia Cal Ltd) v General Commissioners of Income Tax* QB 2003, [2004] STC 296, it was held that the Appeal Commissioners had a wider discretion than HMRC in considering a late appeal. The court held that the Commissioners in that case had misunderstood their powers and that the lack of any reasonable excuse was 'potentially relevant' but was 'not conclusive'. The decision was followed in *R (oao Cook) v General Commissioners of Income Tax* QB, [2007] STC 499 in which the General Commissioners' refusal of a late appeal application was quashed because they had only considered the lack of a reasonable excuse and did not consider the possible merits of the appeal itself. A similar outcome ensued in *O'Flaherty v HMRC* UT, [2013] UKUT 0161 (TCC), 2013 STI 1771. (When *R (oao Cook)* was remitted to the General Commissioners, they again refused the late appeal, and the court upheld their decision — see *R (oao Cook) v General Commissioners of Income Tax (No. 2)* QB, [2009] STC 1212).

COVID-19 (coronavirus) special measure

Individuals and businesses affected by the 2020 COVID-19 pandemic are given an extra three months to appeal against an assessment or HMRC decision dated February 2020 or later (www.gov.uk/tax-appeals/decision).

Withdrawing an appeal

An appeal once made cannot, strictly, be withdrawn unilaterally (see *R v Special Commissioners (ex p. Elmhirst)* CA 1935, 20 TC 381 and *Beach v Willesden General Commissioners* Ch D 1981, 55 TC 663). If, however, a taxpayer or his agent gives HMRC oral or written notice of his desire not to proceed with an appeal, the appeal is treated as if settled by agreement, so that the provisions at **5.9** below apply (and the appeal is settled without any variation). Agreement is effective from the date of the taxpayer's notification. This does not apply if HMRC give written notice of objection within 30 days of the taxpayer's notice. [*TMA 1970, s 54(4)(5)*].

Payment of tax

For postponement of tax pending appeal and for payment of tax on determination of the appeal, see respectively **54.5** and **54.6** PAYMENT OF TAX.

The appeal process

[5.5] When an appeal to HMRC is made, there are four options for the appeal to proceed:

(a) the appellant can require HMRC to review the matter in question;
(b) HMRC can offer to review the matter in question;
(c) the appellant can notify the appeal to the Tribunal for it to decide the matter in question; or
(d) the appeal can be settled by agreement between HMRC and the appellant.

Where the appellant requires an HMRC review, he can still notify the appeal to the Tribunal if he disagrees with the review's conclusions or HMRC fail to complete a review within the required time. If HMRC offer a review and the appellant does not accept the offer, he can likewise notify the appeal to the Tribunal. Taking any of options (a) to (c) above does not prevent the appeal from being settled by agreement at any time.

[*TMA 1970, s 49A*].

For details of the review process, see **5.6** below; for notifying an appeal to the Tribunal, see **5.8** below; and for settlement of appeals by agreement, see **5.9** below.

Notices

All notices given under the appeal provisions must be made in writing. Notifications by the appellant can be made by a person acting on his behalf, but all HMRC notifications must be made directly to the appellant (although copies can be sent to his agent). [*TMA 1970, s 49I*].

HMRC review

[5.6] Where an appellant notifies HMRC that he requires them to review the matter in question, HMRC must first notify him of their view of the matter. They must do this within the 30 days beginning with the day on which they receive the notification from the appellant, or within such longer period as is reasonable. They must then carry out a review of the matter in question, as described at 5.7 below.

The appellant cannot request a second review of the matter in question and neither can he request a review if he has already notified the appeal to the Tribunal.

If it is HMRC who offer to review the matter in question, they must, when they notify the appellant of the offer, also notify the appellant of their view of the matter. The appellant then has 30 days beginning with the date of the document notifying him of the offer to notify HMRC of acceptance of it. If the appellant does so, HMRC must then carry out a review of the matter in question, as described at 5.7 below. Alternatively, the appellant can, within the same 30-day period, notify the appeal to the Tribunal for it to decide the matter in question.

If the appellant does not either accept the offer of review or notify the appeal to the Tribunal within the 30-day period, then HMRC's view of the matter in question is treated as if it were an contained in a written agreement for the settlement of the appeal, so that the provisions at 5.9 below apply (and the appeal is settled on the basis of HMRC's view). The appellant's normal right to withdraw from such agreements does not apply to the deemed agreement. The Tribunal may, however, give permission for the appellant to notify the appeal to it after the 30-day period has ended.

HMRC cannot make a second offer of a review or make an offer if the appellant has already required a review or has notified the appeal to the Tribunal.

[*TMA 1970, ss 49B, 49C, 49H*].

Conduct of the review

[5.7] The nature and extent of HMRC's review will be determined by them as seems appropriate in the circumstances, but they must take into account the steps taken before the start of the review both by them in deciding the matter in question and by anyone else seeking to resolve the disagreement. They must also take into account representations made by the appellant, provided that these are made at a stage which gives HMRC a reasonable opportunity to consider them.

The review must be completed and HMRC's conclusions notified to the appellant in writing within 45 days beginning with:

- (where the appellant required the review) the day HMRC notified him of their view of the matter in question; or
- (where HMRC offered the review) the day HMRC received notification of the appellant's acceptance of the offer.

HMRC and the appellant can, however, agree any other period for completion of the review.

If HMRC fail to notify the appellant of their conclusions within the required period, the review is treated as if the conclusion was that HMRC's original view of the matter in question were upheld. HMRC must notify the appellant in writing accordingly.

[*TMA 1970, s 49E*].

Effect of conclusions

HMRC's notice stating the conclusions to the review is treated as a written agreement for the settlement of the appeal, so that the provisions at 5.9 below apply (and the appeal is settled on the basis of those conclusions). The appellant's normal right to withdraw from such agreements does not apply to the deemed agreement.

The appellant does, however, have a further opportunity to notify the appeal to the Tribunal for them to determine the matter in question. This must normally be done within the period of 30 days beginning with the date of the document notifying the conclusions of the review. Where, however, HMRC have failed to notify the conclusions within the required period, the time limit is extended to 30 days after the date of the document notifying the appellant that the review is to be treated as if concluded on the basis of HMRC's original opinion. The Tribunal may give permission for an appeal to be notified to them after the time limits have expired.

[*TMA 1970, ss 49F, 49G*].

HMRC practice

Reviews are carried out by HMRC officers who have experience of the subject matter of the appeal but are independent of the decision maker and the decision maker's line management (HMRC Appeals, Reviews and Tribunals Guide, ARTG4310).

The review officer will consider whether the case is one which HMRC would want to defend before the Tribunal, and in particular will consider:

- whether the facts have been established, and whether there is disagreement about the facts;
- the technical and legal merits of the case;
- whether it would be an efficient or desirable use of resources to proceed with an appeal that will cost more than the sum in dispute;
- the likelihood of success; and
- whether the appeal raises unusual questions of law or general policy or may in some other way potentially have an effect on future decisions.

(HMRC Appeals, Reviews and Tribunals Guide, ARTG4080).

Review officers are instructed generally to avoid discussing the case with the caseworker during the review in order to ensure that the review remains independent. If exceptionally it is necessary discuss a case with the caseworker in any depth during the review the review officer will tell the appellant and offer equivalent telephone or face to face contact with him or his agent, so the appellant has an equal opportunity to make representations. (HMRC Appeals, Reviews and Tribunals Guide, ARTG4620).

See further HMRC Appeals, Reviews and Tribunals Guide, ARTG4000–4860.

Appeal to the Tribunal

[5.8] A taxpayer who has appealed to HMRC can notify the appeal to the Tribunal without requesting an HMRC review first. If he does so, HMRC cannot then make an offer of a review. [*TMA 1970, s 49D*].

An appellant can also notify an appeal to the Tribunal if he does not wish to accept an HMRC offer of a review or if he disagrees with the conclusions of a review. In both cases there are short time limits within which notification must be made, although the Tribunal can give permission for notification to be made outside those limits: see **5.6** and **5.7** above. There is no provision for HMRC to notify an appeal to the Tribunal.

Notice of appeal must include the appellant's details, details of the decision etc. appealed against, the result the appellant is seeking and the grounds of appeal. The notice must be accompanied by a copy of any written record of the decision and the reasons for it that the appellant has or can reasonably obtain. If the notice is made late it must also include a request for extension of time and the reason for lateness. [*SI 2009 No 273, Rule 20*].

Notices of Appeal should be sent to HM Courts & Tribunals Service, First-tier Tribunal (Tax Chamber), PO Box 16972, Birmingham, B16 6TZ. A Notice of Appeal form can be obtained at www.gov.uk/government/publications/notice-of-appeal-ask-a-tax-judge-to-examine-a-dispute-form-t240 or by phoning 0300 123 1024.

See **5.10** onwards below for the process by which an appeal notified to the Tribunal is decided.

Settlement by agreement

[5.9] At any time before an appeal is determined by the Tribunal, it may be settled by agreement between HMRC and the appellant or his agent. Where such an agreement is reached, in writing or otherwise, the assessment or decision as upheld, varied, discharged, or cancelled by that agreement, is treated as if it had been determined on appeal. Oral agreements are, however, effective only if confirmed in writing by either side (the date of such confirmation then being the effective date of agreement).

The taxpayer may withdraw from the agreement by giving written notice within 30 days of making it. There is no authority for a taxpayer's resiling from the agreement outside that time limit (*Bull v HMRC* FTT (TC 7135), [2019] SFTD 911, [2019] UKFTT 307 (TC)).

[*TMA 1970, s 54(1)–(3)(5)*].

The agreement must specify the figure for assessment or a precise formula for ascertaining it (*Delbourgo v Field* CA 1978, 52 TC 225).

The agreement only covers the assessments (or decisions) which are the subject of the appeal, and does not bind HMRC for subsequent years, for example where relievable amounts are purported to be carried forward from the year in question (*MacNiven v Westmoreland Investments Ltd* HL 2001, 73 TC 1 and see also *Tod v South Essex Motors (Basildon)* Ltd Ch D 1987, 60 TC 598).

An enquiry (see **64.6** RETURNS) cannot subsequently be opened into the particular matter or point at issue that is the subject of the agreement (*Easinghall Ltd v HMRC* UT, [2016] STC 1476).

The issue of an amended notice of assessment cannot in itself constitute an offer for the purposes of a *section 54* agreement; nor can a lack of response by the taxpayer constitute acceptance of an offer (*Schuldenfrei v Hilton* CA 1999, 72 TC 167). For the general requirements for an agreement, see *Cash & Carry v Inspector* (Sp C 148), [1998] SSCD 46.

An agreement based on a mutual mistake of fact was as a result invalid, so that the taxpayer could proceed with his appeal (*Fox v Rothwell* (Sp C 50), [1995] SSCD 336).

See *Gibson v General Commissioners for Stroud* Ch D 1989, 61 TC 645 for a case where there was held not to have been a determination and *R v Inspector of Taxes, ex p. Bass Holdings Ltd; Richart v Bass Holdings Ltd* QB 1992, 65 TC 495 for one where rectification of an agreement was ordered where a relief had been deducted twice contrary to the intention of Revenue and taxpayer.

See *CIR v West* CA 1991, 64 TC 196 for a case where the taxpayer was unsuccessful in seeking leave to defend a Crown action for payment of tax on the ground that the accountant who had entered into an agreement had no authority to do so given him by the taxpayer.

An appeal that has been settled by the taxpayer's trustee in bankruptcy cannot subsequently be reopened by the taxpayer (*Ahajot (Count Artsrunik) v Waller* (Sp C 395), [1994] SSCD 151).

For the extent to which further assessments or error or mistake relief claims are permissible if an appeal has been determined by agreement, see **6.6** ASSESSMENTS.

The Tribunal

[5.10] Under the unified tribunal system established by the *Tribunals, Courts and Enforcement Act 2007*, there are two Tribunals; the First-tier Tribunal and the Upper Tribunal. The Tribunals are presided over by a Senior President of Tribunals. [*TCEA 2007, s 3*].

The First-tier Tribunal. Tax appeals notified to the Tribunal are in most cases initially heard and decided by the First-tier Tribunal. [*TMA 1970, s 47C*].

The First-tier Tribunal is organised into separate chambers each with responsibility for different areas of the law and with its own Chamber President. With certain exceptions, the Tax Chamber is responsible for all appeals, applications, references or other proceedings in respect of the functions of HMRC. It is also responsible for appeals etc. in respect of the exercise of Revenue functions by the National Crime Agency (formerly by the Serious Organised Crime Agency) (see **35.17** HMRC — ADMINISTRATION) and for appeals relating to certain other non-tax matters. The exceptions relate to certain tax credit and national insurance matters and to matters for which the Upper Tribunal is responsible. [*TCEA 2007, s 7; SI 2010 No 2655, Arts 2, 7*].

The First-tier Tribunal has no jurisdiction in relation to an extra-statutory concession; the correct remedy is an application for judicial review (see **5.34** below) (*Michael Prince and others v HMRC* FTT (TC 1852), [2012] SFTD 786).

The work of the First-tier Tribunal was naturally affected by the 2020 COVID-19 (coronavirus) pandemic. The Tribunal published guidance on 5 June 2020 on the services it was currently providing and the practicalities of litigation in the Tribunal 'at the present time and in the coming months' (www.judiciary.uk/wp-content/uploads/2020/06/200612-COVID-19-FTT-Tax-Chamber-FAQ-1.pdf).

The Upper Tribunal

The Upper Tribunal is a superior court of record, so that its decisions create legally binding precedents. [*2007, s 3(5)*].

It is similarly divided into chambers, including the Tax and Chancery Chamber. In relation to tax matters, the Chamber is responsible for:

(a) further appeals against decisions by the First-tier Tribunal Tax Chamber (see **5.26** below);
(b) applications by HMRC for a tax-related penalty under *FA 2008, Sch 36 para 50* in respect of failure to comply with an information notice or obstruction of an inspection (see **55.15** PENALTIES);
(c) complex appeals, applications or references transferred from the First-tier Tribunal (see **5.28** below);
(d) matters referred to the Upper Tribunal following a decision by the First-tier Tribunal Tax Chamber to set aside its own original decision (see **5.29** below); and
(e) applications for judicial review (see **5.34** below).

[*SI 2010 No 2655, Arts 9, 13*].

Overriding objective

The Tribunal Procedure Rules which govern the operation of the Tribunals include an explicit statement of their overriding objective, which is to deal with cases fairly and justly. The Tribunals are required to deal with each case in ways proportionate to its importance, its complexity and the anticipated costs and resources of the parties to the appeal etc. They must avoid unnecessary formality and delay and seek flexibility in the proceedings. They must ensure that the parties are able to participate fully in the proceedings.

The parties to the appeal etc. are in turn required to help the Tribunal to further the overriding objective and to co-operate with the Tribunal generally.

[*SI 2008 No 2698, Rule 2; SI 2009 No 273, Rule 2*].

In the interests of fairness it is inappropriate for HMRC to cite an *unpublished* decision of the Special Commissioners (the forerunners of the FTT) in tribunal proceedings (*Ardmore Construction Limited v HMRC* FTT (TC 3580), [2014] UKFTT 453 (TC), [2014] SFTD 1077).

Alternative dispute resolution

The Tribunals also have an explicit duty to point out to the parties the availability of any alternative procedure for resolving the dispute and to facilitate the use of the procedure if the parties wish. [*SI 2008 No 2698, Rule 3; SI 2009 No 273, Rule 3*]. In June 2020, the First-tier Tribunal issued a statement setting out its practice in appeals against HMRC decisions where the parties wish to engage in alternative dispute resolution (see **5.2** above) after an appeal has been made to the Tribunal (www.judiciary.uk/wp-content/uploads/2020/06/200615-FTT-Tax-Chamber-Practice-Statement-on-ADR-1.pdf).

Composition of Tribunals

Both the First-tier and Upper Tribunal consist of judges who have particular legal qualifications or experience, and other members who are not legally qualified but meet specified selection criteria. Judges of the Upper Tribunal are appointed by the Crown on the recommendation of the Lord Chancellor. Judges and members of the First-tier Tribunal, and members of the Upper Tribunal, are appointed by the Lord Chancellor. See *TCEA 2007, ss 4, 5, Schs 2, 3*.

First-tier Tribunal procedure

Case management

[5.11] The Tribunal has wide powers to regulate its own procedures and to give directions about the conduct or disposal of cases. In particular it can, by direction:

- consolidate or hear two or more cases together or treat a case as a lead case (see *SI 2009 No 273, Rule 18*);
- permit or require a party to the case or another person to provide documents, information or submissions to the Tribunal or another party;
- hold a hearing to consider any matter, including a case management hearing;
- decide the form of any hearing;
- require a party to produce a bundle of documents for a hearing.

The Tribunal can also substitute a party to a case where necessary or add a person to the case as a respondent. A person who is not a party to the case can apply to the Tribunal to be added as a party.

Either party to a case can apply for the Tribunal to make a direction, either in writing or orally at a hearing, or the Tribunal can make a direction on its own initiative. Applications for a direction must include the reason for making it. Directions can be challenged by applying for a further direction.

Any action required to be done in relation to a case on or by a particular day must be done before 5pm on that day (or, if that day is not a working day, by 5pm on the next working day).

For the duration of the 2020 COVID-19 (coronavirus) pandemic, the Tribunal may make a decision which disposes of proceedings without a hearing if: the matter is urgent; it is not reasonably practicable for there to be a hearing (even if conducted wholly or partly as video or audio proceedings); and it is in the interests of justice to make that decision.

[*SI 2009 No 273, Rules 5, 5A, 6, 9, 12; SI 2020 No 416, Rules 1, 7*].

Administration of cases referred to the Tribunal, including the categorisation of cases (see **5.13** below), is carried out by the Tribunals Service.

Starting proceedings

See **5.9** above for how to notify an appeal to the Tribunal. There are also rules for proceedings to be determined without notice to a respondent (*Rule 19*), and for proceedings started by originating application or reference (*Rule 21*).

Representation

A party to a case can appoint a representative to represent him in the proceedings. The representative does not need to be a lawyer. The party has to notify the Tribunal and the other parties of the appointment of a representative and they will then treat the representative as authorised until notified otherwise.

Where no such person has been appointed, a party can, with the Tribunal's permission, nevertheless be accompanied at a hearing by another person who can act as a representative or assist in presenting the case.

[*SI 2009 No 273, Rule 11*].

Withdrawal from a case

Subject to any legislation relating to withdrawal from or settlement of particular proceedings, a party can notify the Tribunal of the withdrawal of its case, or part of it. This can be done in writing or orally at a hearing. If the case is to be settled without a hearing, written notice must be given before the Tribunal disposes of the case.

A party who has withdrawn its case can, however, apply (in writing) to the Tribunal to reinstate it. The application must be received by the Tribunal within 28 days after it received the withdrawal notice or the date of the hearing.

[*SI 2009 No 273, Rule 17*].

Disclosure of documents

Where a third party applies to the Tribunal for copies of HMRC's statement of case and both parties' skeleton arguments, such disclosure is permitted if the third party has a legitimate interest in the documents (as in this particular case where the documents were relevant to the third party's arguments in a different case) (*Hastings Insurance Services Ltd v HMRC (KPMG LLP, third party)* FTT (TC 6656), [2018] SFTD 1459, [2018] UKFTT 478 (TC)).

Failure to comply with rules

[5.12] An irregularity resulting from any failure to comply with the Tribunal Procedure Rules, a practice direction or a direction by the Tribunal does not in itself make the proceedings void.

Where a party fails to comply with the Rules etc. the Tribunal can take such action as it considers just. This could be to require compliance or waive the requirement, to strike the case out (see below) or, in certain cases, to refer the failure to the Upper Tribunal.

The Tribunal can refer to the Upper Tribunal any failure to:

- attend a hearing, or otherwise be available, to give evidence;
- to swear an oath in connection with giving evidence;
- to give evidence as a witness;
- to produce a document; or

- to facilitate the inspection of a document or other thing (including premises).

The Upper Tribunal then has the same powers as the High Court to deal with the failure (which may include financial penalties).

[*TCEA 2007, s 25; SI 2009 No 273, Rule 7*].

Striking out a case

A case will automatically be struck out if the appellant fails to comply with a direction which states that failure to comply will lead to striking out.

The Tribunal can also strike out a case if the appellant fails to comply with a direction which states that failure to comply may lead to striking out, if the appellant has failed to co-operate with the Tribunal to such an extent that the case cannot be dealt with fairly and justly, or if the Tribunal considers that there is no reasonable prospect of the appellant's case succeeding. In the last two cases, however, the Tribunal must first give the appellant an opportunity to make representations.

If the case is struck out because of the appellant's failure to comply with a direction, the appellant can apply for the case to be reinstated. This must be done in writing within 28 days after the date the Tribunal sent the notification of the striking out.

The above rules also apply to respondents except that, instead of the case being struck out, the respondent is barred from taking any further part in the case.

[*SI 2009 No 273, Rule 8*].

Categorisation of cases

[5.13] When an appeal, application or reference is notified to the Tribunal, the Tribunals Service allocate it to one of four categories of case:

(a) default paper;
(b) basic;
(c) standard; or
(d) complex.

An application under *CAA 2001, s 563* (see **9.2**(ix) CAPITAL ALLOWANCES) must be allocated to (c) or (d). Cases may be re-categorised by the Tribunal at any time either on the application of one of the parties or on the Tribunal's own initiative.

[*SI 2009 No 273, Rules 1(3), 23(1)–(3)*].

The process by which the appeal etc. will be decided varies according to the category to which the case is allocated as described below.

Default paper cases

[5.14] The following types of cases must normally be categorised as default paper cases:

- appeals against fixed penalties of not more than £2,000 for late filing of returns, statements, accounts or documents, and late submission of notices of being chargeable to tax; and
- appeals against penalties of not more than £2,000 for late payment of tax.

Cases can be allocated to a different category if the Tribunal considers it appropriate to do so.

(Tribunals Practice Statement, 29 April 2013).

In a default paper case, the respondent (i.e., in an appeal, HMRC) must provide a statement of case to the Tribunal, the appellant and any other respondents to be received within 42 days after the Tribunal sends it notice of the proceedings (or by such time as the Tribunal directs). The statement must state the legislation under which the decision in question was made and set out the respondent's position. If the statement is late it must also include a request for a time extension and give the reason for lateness.

The statement can also contain a request for the case to be dealt with either at or without a hearing.

Once such a statement has been given to the appellant, he may send a written reply to the Tribunal. The reply must be received within 30 days after the date on which the respondent sent its statement to the appellant and must be sent also to each respondent. The reply may include the appellant's response to the respondent's statement of case, provide any further relevant information and contain a request for the case to be dealt with at a hearing. If the reply is late it must also include a request for a time extension and give the reason for lateness.

The Tribunal must hold a hearing before determining a case if any party has requested one in writing. Otherwise, on receipt of the appellant's reply or the expiry of the time limit for such a reply, the Tribunal will determine the case without a hearing, unless it directs otherwise.

[*SI 2009 No 273, Rules 25, 26*].

Default paper cases are decided by one judge or other member of the First-tier Tribunal. (Tribunals Practice Statement, 10 March 2009).

Basic cases

[5.15] The following types of cases must normally be allocated as basic cases (unless they must be allocated as default paper cases:

(a) appeals against penalties for late filing and late payment;
(b) appeals against penalties for inaccurate returns or documents, except where the penalties are for deliberate action or cases where an appeal is also brought against the assessment of the tax to which the return or document relates;
(c) appeals seeking the mitigation or reduction of penalties, and those in which a reasonable excuse is asserted;

(d) appeals against information notices and penalties for non-compliance with information notices;
(e) appeals against PAYE coding notices;
(f) applications for permission to make or notify a late appeal (see **5.4** above);
(g) applications for the postponement of tax pending an appeal (see **54.5** PAYMENT OF TAX); and
(h) applications for a direction that HMRC close an enquiry into a return (see **64.8** RETURNS).

Appeals against penalties for deliberate action or where an appeal is also brought against the assessment to which the penalty relates are excluded from (b) above (as are indirect tax cases).

Cases can be allocated to a different category if the Tribunal considers it appropriate to do so.

(Tribunals Practice Statement, 29 April 2013).

Basic cases normally proceed directly to a hearing, without the need for the respondent to produce a statement of case. Where, however, the respondent intends to raise grounds at the hearing of which the appellant has not been informed, the appellant must be notified of those grounds as soon as is reasonably practicable. The respondent must include sufficient detail to enable the appellant to respond to the grounds at the hearing. [*SI 2009 No 273, Rule 24*].

A decision in a basic case that disposes of proceedings or determines a preliminary issue made at, or following, a hearing must be made by either one, two or, where the Chamber President so decides, three members. The members can be judges or other members as the Chamber President decides, and he will choose one of them to be the presiding member. Any other decision will be made by one judge or other member. (Tribunals Practice Statement, 10 March 2009).

Standard cases

[5.16] In a standard case, the respondent (i.e., in an appeal, HMRC) must provide a statement of case to the Tribunal, the appellant and any other respondents to be received within 42 days after the Tribunal sends it notice of the proceedings (or by such time as the Tribunal directs). The statement must state the legislation under which the decision in question was made and set out the respondent's position. If the statement is late it must also include a request for a time extension and give the reason for lateness.

The statement can also contain a request for the case to be dealt with either at or without a hearing.

Within 42 days after the date on which the respondent sent the statement of case, each party to the case must send to the Tribunal and each other party a list of documents of which that party has possession (or the right to take possession or make copies) and on which the party intends to rely or to produce in the proceedings. The other parties must then be allowed to inspect or copy those documents, except for any which are privileged.

The case will then normally proceed to a hearing (see **5.18** below).

[*SI 2009 No 273, Rules 25, 27*].

A decision in a standard case that disposes of proceedings or determines a preliminary issue made at, or following, a hearing must be made by one judge or by one judge and one or two members as determined by the Chamber President. The judge will be the presiding member, unless one or more of the other members is also a judge, in which case the Chamber President will choose the presiding member. Any other decision will be made by one judge. (Tribunals Practice Statement, 10 March 2009).

Complex cases

[5.17] A case can be classified as a complex case only if the Tribunal considers that it will require lengthy or complex evidence or a lengthy hearing, involves a complex or important principle or issue, or involves a large financial sum. [*SI 2009 No 273, Rule 23(4)*].

The criteria for categorising a case as complex were considered in *Capital Air Services Ltd v HMRC* UT, [2010] STC 2726 and *Dreams plc v HMRC* FTT (TC 2290), [2013] SFTD 111.

The procedures in a complex case are the same as those described at **5.16** above for standard cases. The same rules regarding the membership of the Tribunal also apply.

Transfer to Upper Tribunal

The Tribunal can, with the consent of the parties, refer a complex case to the Chamber President with a request for transfer to the Upper Tribunal. The Chamber President can then, with the agreement of the President of the Tax and Chancery Chamber of the Upper Tribunal, direct that the case be so transferred. [*SI 2009 No 273, Rule 28*].

Costs

See **5.23** below for the taxpayer's option to request that a complex case be excluded from potential liability for costs.

The hearing

[5.18] Basic, standard and complex cases normally require a hearing before they are decided (and see **5.14** above for hearings in default paper cases).

This does not apply, however, if all of the parties consent to a decision without a hearing and the Tribunal considers that it is able to make a decision without a hearing. Hearings are also not required for the correction, setting aside, review or appeal of a Tribunal decision (see **5.19–5.21** below) or where the Tribunal strikes out a party's case (see **5.12** above).

Each party to the proceedings is normally entitled to attend the hearing and the Tribunal must give reasonable notice of its time and place. Where the hearing is to consider disposal of the proceedings, at least 14 days' notice must be given except in urgent or exceptional circumstances or with the consent of the parties.

Hearings are normally held in public (but see below under Anonymisation). For the duration of the 2020 COVID-19 (coronavirus) pandemic, the Tribunal may direct in appropriate circumstances that the proceedings be conducted wholly or partly as video or audio proceedings.

Anonymisation

The public interest generally requires the precise facts relevant to the decision to be a matter of public record, and not to be veiled by a process of anonymisation or redaction (*HMRC v Banerjee (No 2)* Ch D, 80 TC 625; [2009] STC 1930). The Tribunal may, however, direct that a hearing should be private if it considers that restricting access is justified in the interests of public order or national security, to protect a person's right to respect for their private and family life, to maintain the confidentiality of sensitive information, to avoid serious harm to the public interest or because not to do so would prejudice the interest of justice. The fact that a taxpayer is rich, or in the public eye, is not good reason for a private hearing, nor any basis on which the Tribunal could direct an anonymised or redacted decision (*A v HMRC* FTT (TC 2217), [2012] UKFTT 541 (TC); *Andre v HMRC* FTT (TC 5575), [2016] UKFTT 850 (TC)). It would not be in the public interest to release a decision which, by concealing the appellant's personal characteristics, made it impossible for the reader to reach a full understanding of why the appeal had been determined as it had (*Clunes v HMRC* FTT (TC 5692), [2017] UKFTT 204 (TC)). In cases involving mental disability, there is a difficult line to be drawn between certain non-neuro typical personalities, behaviours disorders and illnesses which do not of themselves justify the protection of anonymity and others which do (*The Appellant v HMRC* FTT (TC 5564), [2017] UKFTT 839 (TC); *JK v HMRC* FTT (TC 7226), [2019] UKFTT 411 (TC)).

[*SI 2009 No 273, Rules 29–32A; SI 2020 No 416, Rules 1, 7; SI 2020 No 651, Rules 1, 7(3)*].

Failure to attend hearing

If a party fails to attend a hearing, the Tribunal can nevertheless proceed with the hearing if it considers that it is in the interests of justice to do so. The Tribunal must be satisfied that the party was notified of the hearing or that reasonable steps were taken to notify the party. [*SI 2009 No 273, Rule 33*].

The following cases were decided under the rather different provisions applicable before 1 April 2009 to failure to attend a hearing of the General Commissioners (the forerunners of the current Appeal Tribunal), but may be relevant to the above provision. Determinations in the absence of the taxpayer or his agent were upheld where notice of the meeting was received by the appellant (*R v Tavistock Commrs (ex p. Adams) (No 1)* QB 1969, 46 TC 154; *R v Special Commr (ex p. Moschi)* CA, [1981] STC 465 and see *Fletcher & Fletcher v Harvey* CA 1990, 63 TC 539), but Commissioners were held to have acted unreasonably in refusing to re-open proceedings when the taxpayer's agent was temporarily absent when the appeal was called (*R & D McKerron Ltd v CIR* CS 1979, 52 TC 28). Where the taxpayer was absent through illness, a determination was quashed because the Commissioners, in refusing an adjournment, had failed to consider whether injustice would thereby arise to the taxpayer (*R v Sevenoaks Commrs (ex p. Thorne)* QB 1989, 62 TC 341 and see *Rose v Humbles* CA 1971, 48 TC 103). See also *R v O'Brien (ex p. Lissner)* QB, [1984] STI 710 where the determination was quashed when the appellant had been informed by the inspector that the hearing was to be adjourned.

Evidence and submissions

The Tribunal has wide powers to make directions as to issues on which it requires evidence or submissions, including the nature of such evidence or submissions, the way in which and time at which it must be provided and the need for expert evidence. It may also limit the number of witnesses whose evidence a party can put forward.

The Tribunal can accept evidence whether or not it would be admissible in a civil trial and can exclude evidence provided late or not in accordance with a direction.

[*SI 2009 No 273, Rule 15(1)(2)*].

The following cases relate to evidence given at hearings of the General Commissioners (the forerunners of the current Appeal Tribunal) before 1 April 2009, but may be relevant to the above provision. A party to the proceedings could not insist on being examined on oath (*R v Special Commrs (in re Fletcher)* CA 1894, 3 TC 289). False evidence under oath would be perjury under criminal law (*R v Hood Barrs CA*, [1943] 1 All ER 665). A taxpayer was held to be bound by an affidavit he had made in other proceedings (*Wicker v Fraser* Ch D 1982, 55 TC 641). A remission to Commissioners to hear evidence directed at the credit of a witness was refused in *Potts v CIR* Ch D 1982, 56 TC 25. Rules of the Supreme Court under which evidence can be obtained from a witness abroad could not be used in proceedings before the Commissioners (*Leiserach v CIR* CA 1963, 42 TC 1). As to hearsay evidence under *Civil Evidence Act 1968*, see *Forth Investments Ltd v CIR* Ch D 1976, 50 TC 617 and *Khan v Edwards* Ch D 1977, 53 TC 597.

The Commissioners were under no obligation to adjourn an appeal for the production of further evidence (*Hamilton v CIR* CS 1930, 16 TC 28; *Noble v Wilkinson* Ch D 1958, 38 TC 135), and were held not to have erred in law in determining assessments in the absence abroad of the taxpayer (*Hawkins v Fuller* Ch D 1982, 56 TC 49).

Witnesses

The Tribunal, on the application of any party to the proceedings or its own initiative, can issue a summons (in Scotland, a citation) requiring any person either to attend the hearing of those proceedings to give evidence or to produce any relevant document in his possession or control. A witness required to attend a hearing must be given 14 days notice or a shorter period if the Tribunal so directs and, if the witness is not a party, the summons or citations must make provision for necessary expenses of attendance and state who is to pay them. If, before the summons or citation was issued, the witness did not have an opportunity to object, he may apply to the Tribunal for the summons to be varied or set aside. The application must be made as soon as reasonably practicable after the summons or citation is received.

A witness cannot be compelled to give evidence or produce documents which he could not be compelled to give or produce in an action in a court of law.

[*SI 2009 No 273, Rule 16*].

As to whether the Tribunal can issue a witness summons to a non-UK resident with no home or place of business in the UK, see *Clavis Liberty Fund LP1 v HMRC* UT, [2015] STC 1645.

The Tribunal's decision

[5.19] In an appeal case, if the Tribunal decides:

(a) that the appellant is overcharged or undercharged by a self-assessment;
(b) that any amounts in a partnership statement (see **64.13** RETURNS) are excessive or insufficient; or
(c) that the appellant is overcharged or undercharged by an assessment other than a self-assessment,

the assessment or amounts are reduced or increased accordingly, but otherwise the assessment or statement stands good. The Tribunal is given the power to vary the extent to which a claim or election included in a tax return is disallowed following an enquiry. (Separate rules apply to claims and elections made outside returns, for which see **16.3** CLAIMS). In a case within (c) above, the Tribunal can normally only reduce or increase the amount assessed, and this determines the appeal; the Tribunal is not obliged to determine the revised tax payable. In a case within (b) above, HMRC must amend the partners' own tax returns to give effect to the reductions or increases made.

The Tribunal's decision is final and conclusive, subject to:

(i) the correction of clerical mistakes etc. (see **5.20** below);
(ii) the setting aside of a decision (see **5.20** below); and
(iii) a further appeal against the decision (see **5.21** below).

[*TMA 1970, s 50(6)–(11)*].

The Tribunal can give its decision orally at a hearing or in writing. In either case it will give each party a decision notice in writing within 28 days after making a decision which finally disposes of all the issues in the case or as soon as practicable. The notice will also inform the party of any further right of appeal.

Unless each party agrees otherwise the notice should also include a summary of the findings of fact and the reason for the decision. If it does not, any party to the case can apply for full written findings and reasons, and must do so before applying for permission to appeal (see **5.21** below). The application must be made in writing so that the Tribunal receives it within 28 days after the date it sent the decision notice.

[*SI 2009 No 273, Rule 35*].

Case law

The following cases relate to decisions of the General Commissioners (the forerunners of the current Appeal Tribunal) before 1 April 2009, but may be relevant to the above provisions.

In reaching their decision, the Commissioners could not take into account matters appropriate for application for judicial review (*Aspin v Estill* CA 1987, 60 TC 549). They did not generally have the power to review on appeal the exercise of a discretion conferred on HMRC by statute (see *Slater v Richardson & Bottoms Ltd* Ch D 1979, 53 TC 155; *Kelsall v Investment Chartwork Ltd* Ch D 1993, 65 TC 750).

Onus of proof

The onus is on the appellant to displace an assessment. See *Brady v Group Lotus Car Companies plc* CA 1987, 60 TC 359 where the onus of proof remained with the taxpayer where the amount of normal time limit assessment indicated contention of fraud. The general principle emerges in appeals against estimated assessments in 'delay cases', which, before self-assessment, made up the bulk of appeals heard by the General Commissioners. For examples of cases in which the Commissioners have confirmed estimated assessments in the absence of evidence that they were excessive, see *T Haythornthwaite & Sons Ltd v Kelly* CA 1927, 11 TC 657; *Stoneleigh Products Ltd v Dodd* CA 1948, 30 TC 1; *Rosette Franks (King St) Ltd v Dick* Ch D 1955, 36 TC 100; *Pierson v Belcher* Ch D 1959, 38 TC 387. In a number of cases, the courts have supported the Commissioners' action in rejecting unsatisfactory accounts (e.g. *Cain v Schofield* Ch D 1953, 34 TC 362; *Moll v CIR* CS 1955, 36 TC 384; *Cutmore v Leach* Ch D 1981, 55 TC 602; *Coy v Kime* Ch D 1986, 59 TC 447) or calling for certified accounts (e.g. *Stephenson v Waller* KB 1927, 13 TC 318; *Hunt & Co v Joly* KB 1928, 14 TC 165; *Wall v Cooper* CA 1929, 14 TC 552). In *Anderson v CIR* CS 1933, 18 TC 320, the case was remitted where there was no evidence to support the figure arrived at by the Commissioners (which was between the accounts figure and the estimated figure assessed), but contrast *Bookey v Edwards* Ch D 1981, 55 TC 486. The Commissioners were entitled to look at each year separately, accepting the appellant's figures for some years but not all (*Donnelly v Platten* CA(NI) 1980, [1981] STC 504). Similarly, the onus is on the taxpayer to substantiate his claims to relief (see *Eke v Knight* CA 1977, 51 TC 121; *Talib v Waterson* Ch D, [1980] STC 563).

For the standard of proof required in evidence, see *Les Croupiers Casino Club v Pattinson* CA 1987, 60 TC 196.

Consent orders. The case can also be settled by the Tribunal making a consent order where the parties have reached agreement. Such an order is made at the request of the parties but only if the Tribunal considers it appropriate to do so. No hearing is necessary if such an order is made. [*SI 2009 No 273, Rule 34*].

Correction of mistakes in a decision

[5.20] The Tribunal can correct any clerical mistake or other accidental slip or omission in a decision at any time by notifying the parties of the amended decision. This rule applies also to directions and any other document produced by the Tribunal. [*SI 2009 No 273, Rule 37*].

Setting aside a decision

The Tribunal can set aside a decision disposing of a case and re-make the decision if it considers that to do is in the interests of justice and one of the following applies:

- a relevant document was not sent to, or was not received at an appropriate time by, a party or his representative;
- a relevant document was not sent to the Tribunal at a relevant time;
- there was some other procedural irregularity; or
- a party or representative was not present at a hearing.

A party to a case can apply for a decision to be set aside. The application must be in writing and must be received by the Tribunal within 28 days after the date on which the Tribunal sent the decision notice.

[*SI 2009 No 273, Rule 38*].

An application for a decision to be set aside was successful in *Wright v HMRC* [2009] SFTD 748.

Appeal against the Tribunal's decision

[5.21] A further appeal to the Upper Tribunal can be made against the First-tier Tribunal's decision. The appeal can be made only on a point of law. No appeal can be made against a decision on whether or not to review a decision (see below), to set aside a decision (see **5.20** above) or to refer a matter to the Upper Tribunal.

A person wishing to appeal must make a written application to the First-tier Tribunal for permission to appeal. Such an application must be received by the Tribunal no later than 56 days after the latest of the dates that the Tribunal sent to that person the decision notice or full reasons for the decision. Where a decision has been amended or corrected following a review (see below) or an application (other than a late application) for a decision to be struck out has been unsuccessful (see **5.20** above), the 56 day limit runs from the date on which the Tribunal sent the notification of amended reasons or correction of the decision or of the failure of the striking out application. The Tribunal can direct that the 56 days within which a party may apply for permission to appeal against a decision that disposes of a preliminary issue shall run from the date of the decision that disposes of all issues in the proceedings.

The application must identify the alleged errors in the decision and state the result sought. Late applications must include a request for extension of time and the reason for lateness.

On receiving an application, the Tribunal will first consider whether to review the decision. It can do so only if satisfied that there was an error in law in the decision. Unless it decides to take no action following the review, the Tribunal will notify the parties of the outcome and must give them an opportunity to make representations before taking any action.

If the Tribunal decides not to review the decision or, following a review, decides to take no action, it will then consider whether to give permission to appeal to the Upper Tribunal. It will send a record of its decision to the parties as soon as practicable together with, where it decides not to give permission, a statements of its reasons for refusal and details of the right to apply directly to the Upper Tribunal for permission to appeal (see **5.26** below). The Tribunal's permission can be in respect of part only of the decision or on limited grounds.

[*TCEA 2007, s 11; SI 2009 No 273, Rules 39–41*].

Payment of tax pending further appeal

[5.22] Tax is payable or repayable in accordance with the decision of the Tribunal even if a party appeals to the Upper Tribunal. If the amount charged in the assessment concerned is subsequently altered by the Upper Tribunal, any amount undercharged is due and payable at the end of the thirty days beginning with the date on which HMRC issue the appellant a notice of the amount payable in accordance with the Upper Tribunal's decision. Any amount overpaid will be refunded along with such interest as may be allowed by the decision. This provision applies equally to any further appeal from a decision of the Upper Tribunal to the Courts. See **4.51** ANTI-AVOIDANCE for applications to the court or Tribunal by HMRC to disapply the requirement to repay tax where an accelerated payment notice is in force. [*TMA 1970, s 56*].

Award of costs

[5.23] The Tribunal can make an order awarding costs (or, in Scotland, expenses):

(a) under *TCEA 2007, s 29(4)* ('wasted costs') and costs incurred in applying for such costs;
(b) where it considers that a party or representative has acted unreasonably in bringing, defending or conducting the case; and
(c) in a complex case (see **5.17** above), where the taxpayer has not sent a written request that the case be excluded from potential liability for costs or expenses.

A request within (c) above must be sent within 28 days of the taxpayer receiving notice that the case has been allocated as a complex case.

'*Wasted costs*' are any costs incurred by a party because of an improper, unreasonable or negligent act or omission by any representative or employee of a representative, which the Tribunal considers it unreasonable for the party to pay.

Before making an order for costs, the Tribunal must give the person who will have to pay them the chance to make representations. If the payer is an individual, it must consider his financial means.

The Tribunal can make an order on its own initiative or on an application from one of the parties. Such an application must be sent both to the Tribunal and to the person from whom costs are sought, together with a schedule of the costs claimed. An application must be made no later than 28 days after the date on which the Tribunal sends a notice recording the decision which finally disposes of all the issues or notice of its receipt of a withdrawal which ends the case.

The amount of costs will be decided either by agreement of the parties, by summary assessment by the Tribunal or, if not agreed, by assessment. Where the amount is to be decided by assessment, either the payer or the person to whom the costs are to be paid can apply to a county court, the High Court or the Costs Office of the Supreme Court for a detailed assessment of the costs on the standard basis or, where the Tribunal's order so specifies, the indemnity basis. Upon making an order for the assessment of costs, the Tribunal may order an amount to be paid on account before the costs are assessed.

[*TCEA 2007, s 29(4); SI 2009 No 273, Rule 10*].

For a failed application for costs arising from a successful application to have a case reallocated as a complex case, see *Capital Air Services Ltd v HMRC* UT, [2011] STC 617. An award of costs should be compensatory, not punitive (*Scofield v HMRC (No 2)* FTT (TC 2344), [2012] UKFTT 673 (TC), 2013 STI 325); in this case the Tribunal decided that HMRC had acted unreasonably in conducting the case but declined to award costs as the unreasonable conduct did not result in any prejudice to the appellant or cause him to incur additional costs. In an appeal against a £300 penalty imposed it is in the interests of justice to do so or failure to comply with an information notice, an award of costs was made against an appellant said to have conducted the appeal unreasonably in allowing it to proceed with no prospect of success to almost the last moment before withdrawing it; costs awarded were £832.20, based on 5.7 hours of HMRC's time at £146 per hour (*R P Baker (Oxford) Ltd v HMRC* FTT (TC 3549), [2014] UKFTT 420 (TC)).

Upper Tribunal procedure

Case management

[5.24] The powers of the Upper Tribunal to regulate its own proceedings are broadly the same as the powers of the First-tier Tribunal. See *SI 2008 No 2698, Rules 5, 5A, 6, 9, 12* and **5.11** above.

Representation

The same rights to representation in a case before the Upper Tribunal apply as in a case before the First-tier Tribunal. See *SI 2008 No 2698, Rule 11* and **5.11** above.

Withdrawal from a case

A party can notify the Upper Tribunal of the withdrawal of its case, or part of it. This can be done in writing or orally at a hearing. The withdrawal only takes effect, however, if the Tribunal consents (but this requirement does not apply to the withdrawal of an application for permission to appeal).

A party who has withdrawn its case can, however, apply (in writing) to the Tribunal to reinstate it. The application must be received by the Tribunal within one month after it received the withdrawal notice or the date of the hearing.

[*SI 2008 No 2698, Rule 17*].

Failure to comply with rules

[5.25] An irregularity resulting from any failure to comply with the Tribunal Procedure Rules, a practice direction or a direction by the Upper Tribunal does not in itself make the proceedings void.

Where a party fails to comply with the Rules etc. the Upper Tribunal can take such action as it considers just. This could be to require compliance or waive the requirement, to strike the case out (see below) or to restrict a party's participation in the case.

The Upper Tribunal has the same powers as the High Court to deal with the failure (which may include financial penalties).

[*TCEA 2007, s 25; SI 2008 No 2698, Rule 7*].

Striking out a case

The Upper Tribunal has similar powers to strike out a case as the First-tier Tribunal. See *SI 2008 No 2698, Rule 8* and **5.12** above. Note, however, that the Upper Tribunal cannot strike out an appeal from the decision of another Tribunal or judicial review proceedings on the grounds that there is no reasonable prospect of the appellant's case succeeding.

Appeal against decisions of the First-tier Tribunal

[5.26] A party to a case who disagrees with a decision of the First-tier Tribunal can apply for permission to appeal against it. Applications must first be made to the First-tier Tribunal (see **5.21** above), but if that Tribunal refuses permission a further application can be made to the Upper Tribunal.

Applications to the Upper Tribunal must be in writing and must be received no later than one month after the date on which the First-tier Tribunal sent the notice refusing permission to appeal. An application must include the grounds for appeal and state whether the appellant wants the application to be dealt with at a hearing. It must be accompanied by copies of any written record of the decision being challenged, any statement of reasons for that decision, and the notice of the First-tier Tribunal's refusal of permission to appeal. Late applications must include a request for extension of time and the reason for lateness.

If the application to the First-tier Tribunal for permission to appeal was refused because it was made out of time, the application to the Upper Tribunal must include the reason for the lateness of the first application. The Upper Tribunal can then admit the application only if it considers that it is in the interests of justice to do so.

If the Tribunal refuses permission to appeal it will notify the appellant of its decision and its reasons. If the refusal is made without a hearing the appellant can apply in writing for the decision to be reconsidered at a hearing. The application must be received by the Tribunal within 14 days after the date that written notice of its decision was sent. This rule applies also where the Tribunal gives permission on limited grounds or subject to conditions without a hearing.

If the Tribunal grants permission, the application for permission is then normally treated as a notice of appeal, and the case will proceed accordingly. If all the parties agree, the appeal can be determined without obtaining any further response.

[*SI 2008 No 2698, Rules 21, 22*].

Notice of appeal

[5.27] If the First-tier Tribunal gives permission to appeal to the Upper Tribunal (or the Upper Tribunal gives permission but directs that the application for permission should not be treated as a notice of appeal) an appellant can appeal to the Upper Tribunal by providing a notice of appeal. This must be received by the Tribunal within one month after the notice giving permission to appeal was sent.

The notice must include the grounds for appeal and state whether the appellant wants the application to be dealt with at a hearing. If the First-tier Tribunal gave permission to appeal, the notice must be accompanied by copies of any written record of the decision being challenged, any statement of reasons for that decision, and the notice of permission to appeal. Late applications must include a request for extension of time and the reason for lateness.

A copy of the notice and the documents provided will then be sent by the Upper Tribunal to the respondents who can provide a written response. The response must be received by the Tribunal not later than one month after the copy of the notice of appeal was sent. (Where an application for permission to appeal stands as the notice of appeal (see **5.26** above), the response must be received not later than one month after the Tribunal sent to the respondent notice that if had granted permission to appeal).

The response must indicate whether the respondent opposes the appeal, and if so, the grounds for opposition (which can include grounds which were unsuccessful before the First-tier Tribunal) and whether the respondent wants the case to be dealt with at a hearing. Late responses must include a request for extension of time and the reason for lateness.

A copy of the response and any documents provided will then be sent by the Tribunal to the appellant and any other parties to the case who can, in turn, provide a written reply. The reply must be received by the Tribunal within one month of the date the Tribunal sent the copy of the respondent's response.

[*SI 2008 No 2698, Rules 23–25*].

Other cases before the Upper Tribunal

[5.28] Where a case has been transferred or referred to the Upper Tribunal from the First-tier Tribunal (see **5.17** above) or where a case is started by direct application to the Upper Tribunal, the Upper Tribunal will determine by direction the procedure for considering and disposing of the case. [*SI 2008 No 2698, Rule 26A; SI 2019 No 925, Rule 2(5)*].

The hearing

[5.29] The Upper Tribunal can make any decision with or without a hearing, but in deciding whether to hold a hearing, it must have regard to any view expressed by any party to the case.

Each party is normally entitled to attend the hearing and the Upper Tribunal must give reasonable notice of its time and place. At least 14 days' notice must normally be given except in urgent or exceptional circumstances or with the consent of the parties. In application for permission to bring judicial review cases, the notice period must normally be at least two days.

Hearings are normally held in public, but the Tribunal can direct that a hearing, or part of it, should be held in private. For the duration of the 2020 COVID-19 (coronavirus) pandemic, the Tribunal may direct in appropriate circumstances that the proceedings be conducted wholly or partly as video or audio proceedings.

[*SI 2008 No 2698, Rules 34–37A; SI 2020 No 416, Rules 1, 5*].

Failure to attend hearing

If a party fails to attend a hearing, the Upper Tribunal can nevertheless proceed with the hearing if it considers that it is in the interests of justice to do so. The Tribunal must be satisfied that the party was notified of the hearing or that reasonable steps were taken to notify the party. [*SI 2008 No 2698, Rule 38*].

Evidence and witnesses

Similar rules apply in relation to evidence, submission and witnesses as apply to the First-tier Tribunal. See *SI 2008 No 2698, Rules 15, 16* and **5.18** above.

The Upper Tribunal's decision

[5.30] If the Upper Tribunal decides that the First-tier Tribunal's decision involved an error on a point of law it can set aside that decision and either remit the case back to the First-tier Tribunal or remake the decision itself.

If it remits the case to the First-tier Tribunal, the Upper Tribunal can direct that the case is reheard by different members.

If it decides to remake the decision itself, the Upper Tribunal is free to make any decision that the First-tier Tribunal could make if it were rehearing the case (see **5.19** above) and can make such findings of fact as it considers appropriate.

[*TCEA 2007, s 12*].

The Upper Tribunal can give its decision orally at a hearing or in writing. In either case it will give each party a decision notice in writing as soon as practicable. The notice will include written reasons for the decision unless the decision was made with the consent of the parties or the parties have consented to the Tribunal not giving written reasons. The notice will also inform the party of any further right of appeal. [*SI 2008 No 2698, Rule 40*].

Consent orders

The case can also be settled by the Upper Tribunal making a consent order where the parties have reached agreement. Such an order is made at the request of the parties but only if the Tribunal considers it appropriate to do so. No hearing is necessary if such an order is made. [*SI 2008 No 2698, Rule 39*].

Correction of mistakes in a decision

Identical provisions to those applicable to decisions by the First-tier Tribunal apply to decisions of the Upper Tribunal. See *SI 2008 No 2698, Rule 42* and 5.20 above. Setting aside a decision. Virtually identical provisions to those applicable to decisions by the First-tier Tribunal apply to decisions of the Upper Tribunal. An application for a decision to be set aside must be received by the Upper Tribunal no later than one month after the date on which the Tribunal sent the decision notice. See *SI 2008 No 2698, Rule 43* and 5.20 above.

Appeal against the Tribunal's decision

[5.31] A further appeal to the Court of Appeal (in Scotland, the Court of Session) can be made against the Upper Tribunal's decision. The appeal can be made only on a point of law and the Tribunal will give permission to appeal only if the appeal would raise some important point of principle or practice or there is some other compelling reason for the Court to hear it.

A person wishing to appeal must make a written application to the Tribunal for permission to appeal. Such an application must be received by the Tribunal within one month after the date the Tribunal sent written reasons for the decision to that person. Where a decision has been amended or corrected following a review (see below) or an application (other than a late application) for a decision to be struck out has been unsuccessful (see 5.25 above), the one month limit runs from the date on which the Tribunal sent the notification of amended reasons or correction of the decision or of the failure of the striking out application.

The application must identify the alleged errors of law in the decision and state the result sought. Late applications must include a request for extension of time and the reason for lateness.

On receiving an application, the Upper Tribunal will first consider whether to review the decision. It can do so only if either it overlooked a legislative provision or binding authority which could have affected the decision or if a court has subsequently made a decision which is binding on the Upper Tribunal and could have affected the decision.

The Tribunal will notify the parties of the outcome of a review. If it decides to take any action following a review without first giving every party an opportunity to make representations, the notice must state that any party not given such an opportunity can apply for the action to be set aside and for the decision to be reviewed again.

If the Tribunal decides not to review the decision or, following a review, decides to take no action, it will then consider whether to give permission to appeal. It will send a record of its decision to the parties as soon as practicable together with, where it decides not to give permission, a statements of its reasons for refusal and details of the right to apply directly to the court for permission to appeal (see 5.33 below). The Tribunal's permission can be in respect of part only of the decision or on limited grounds.

[*TCEA 2007, s 13; SI 2008 No 2698, Rules 44–46; SI 2008 No 2834*].

See **5.22** above for the payment of tax pending an appeal from a decision of the Upper Tribunal.

Award of costs

[5.32] The Upper Tribunal can make an order awarding costs (or, in Scotland, expenses):

(a) in proceedings on appeal from the Tax Chamber of the First-tier Tribunal;
(b) in judicial review cases (see **5.34** below);
(c) in cases transferred from the Tax Chamber of the First-tier Tribunal;
(d) under *TCEA 2007, s 29(4)* (wasted costs — see **5.23** above) and costs incurred in applying for such costs; or
(e) where the Tribunal considers that a party or representative has acted unreasonably in bringing, defending or conducting the case.

Before making an order for costs, the Tribunal must give the person who will have to pay them the chance to make representations. If the payer is an individual, it must consider his financial means.

The Tribunal can make an order on its own initiative or on an application from one of the parties. Such an application must be sent both to the Tribunal and to the person from whom costs are sought, together with a schedule of the costs claimed. An application must be made no later than one month after the date on which the Tribunal sends the notice recording the decision which finally disposes of all the issues in the case or notice that a withdrawal which ends the proceedings has taken effect.

The amount of costs will be decided either by agreement of the parties, by summary assessment by the Tribunal or, if not agreed, by assessment. Where the amount is to be decided by assessment, either the payer or the person to whom the costs are to be paid can apply to a county court, the High Court or the Costs Office of the Supreme Court for a detailed assessment of the costs on the standard basis or, where the Tribunal's order so specifies, the indemnity basis. Upon making an order for the assessment of costs, the Tribunal may order an amount to be paid on account before the costs are assessed.

[*SI 2008 No 2698, Rule 10*].

Appeal to the Court of Appeal

[5.33] As noted at **5.31** above a party who disagrees with a decision of the Upper Tribunal can ask the Tribunal for permission to appeal to the Court of Appeal (in Scotland, the Court of Session). The appeal can be made only on a point of law.

If the Tribunal refuses permission, the party can seek permission to appeal directly from the Court. The Court will give permission only if the appeal would raise some important point of principle or practice or there is some other compelling reason for the Court to hear it.

[*TCEA 2007, s 13; SI 2008 No 2834*].

There are no tax-specific rules governing the making of applications for permission to appeal or for notifying appeals where permission has been given by the Court or Upper Tribunal. The *Civil Procedure Rules 1998, SI 1998 No 3132* therefore apply.

The Court's decision. If the Court finds that the decision of the Upper Tribunal involved an error on a point of law it can set aside the decision. It must then either remake the decision itself or remit the case back to either the Upper Tribunal or the First-tier Tribunal, with directions for its reconsideration. Those directions can include a direction that the case is to be re-heard by different Tribunal members.

Where the case is remitted to the Upper Tribunal, it can itself decide to remit the case to the First-tier Tribunal.

If the Court decides to remake the decision itself, it can make any decision that the Upper Tribunal or first-tier Tribunal could have made, and can make such findings of fact as it considers appropriate.

[*TCEA 2007, s 14*].

Case law

The following cases relate to the pre-1 April 2009 appeal process (which involved initial appeal to the High Court rather than the Court of Appeal) but remain relevant to the new process.

Withdrawal etc.

Once set down for hearing, a case cannot be declared a nullity (*Way v Underdown* CA 1974, 49 TC 215) or struck out under *Order 18, Rule 19 of the Rules of the Supreme Court* (*Petch v Gurney* CA 1994, 66 TC 473), but the appellant may withdraw (*Hood Barrs v CIR (No 3)* CA 1960, 39 TC 209, but see *Bradshaw v Blunden (No 2)* Ch D 1960, 39 TC 73). Where the appellant was the inspector and the taxpayer did not wish to proceed, the Court refused to make an order on terms agreed between the parties (*Slaney v Kean* Ch D 1969, 45 TC 415).

Remission of cases to Tribunal

In *Consolidated Goldfields plc v CIR* Ch D 1990, 63 TC 333, the taxpayer company's request that the High Court remit a case to the Commissioners for further findings of fact was refused. Although the remedy was properly sought, it would only be granted if it could be shown that the desired findings were (a) material to some tenable argument, (b) reasonably open on the evidence adduced, and (c) not inconsistent with the findings already made. However, in *Fitzpatrick v CIR* CS 1990, [1991] STC 34, a case was remitted where the facts found proved or admitted, and the contentions of the parties, were not clearly set out, despite the taxpayer's request for various amendments and insertions to the case, and in *Whittles v Uniholdings Ltd (No 1)* Ch D, [1993] STC 671, remission was appropriate in view of the widely differing interpretations which the parties sought to place on the Commissioners' decision (and the case was remitted a second time (see [1993] STC 767) to resolve misunderstandings as to the nature of a concession made by the Crown at the original hearing and apparent inconsistencies in the Commissioners' findings of fact). If a case is remitted, the taxpayer had the right to attend any further hearing by the Commissioners (*Lack v Doggett* CA 1970, 46 TC 497) but the Commissioners could not, in the absence of special circumstances, admit further evidence (*Archer-Shee v Baker* CA 1928, 15 TC 1; *Watson v Samson Bros* Ch D 1959, 38 TC 346; *Bradshaw v Blunden (No 2)* Ch D 1960, 39 TC 73), but see *Brady v Group Lotus Car Companies plc* CA 1987, 60 TC 359 where the Court directed the Commissioners to admit further evidence where new facts had come to light suggesting the taxpayers had deliberately misled the Commissioners. Errors of fact in the case may be amended by agreement of the parties prior to hearing of the case (*Moore v Austin* Ch D 1985, 59 TC 110). See *Jeffries v Stevens* Ch D 1982, 56 TC 134 as regards delay between statement of case and motion for remission.

Appeal restricted to point of law

Many court decisions turn on whether the Commissioners' decision was one of fact supported by the evidence, and hence final. The courts will not disturb a finding of fact if there was reasonable evidence for it, notwithstanding that the evidence might support a different conclusion of fact. The leading case is *Edwards v Bairstow & Harrison* HL 1955, 36 TC 207, in which the issue was whether there had been an adventure in the nature of trade. The Commissioners' decision was reversed on the ground that the only reasonable conclusion from the evidence was that there had been such an adventure. For a recent discussion of the application of this principle, see *Milnes v J Beam Group Ltd* Ch D 1975, 50 TC 675.

A new question of law may be raised in the courts on giving due notice to the other parties (*Muir v CIR* CA 1966, 43 TC 367) but the courts will neither admit evidence not in the stated case (*Watson v Samson Bros* Ch D 1959, 38 TC 346; *Cannon Industries Ltd v Edwards* Ch D 1965, 42 TC 625; *Frowd v Whalley* Ch D 1965, 42 TC 599, and see *R v Great Yarmouth Commrs (ex p. Amis)* QB 1960, 39 TC 143) nor consider contentions of which evidence in support was not produced before the Commissioners (*Denekamp v Pearce* Ch D 1998, 71 TC 213).

Use of Parliamentary material

Following the decision in *Pepper v Hart* HL 1992, 65 TC 421, the courts are prepared to consider the parliamentary history of legislation, or the official reports of debates in Hansard, where all of the following conditions are met.

- Legislation is ambiguous or obscure, or leads to an absurdity.
- The material relied upon consists of one or more statements by a Minister or other promoter of the Bill together if necessary with such other parliamentary material as is necessary to understand such statements and their effect.
- The statements relied upon are clear.

Any party intending to refer to an extract from Hansard in support of any argument must, unless otherwise directed, serve copies of the extract and a brief summary of the argument intended to be based upon the extract upon all parties and the court not less than five clear working days before the first day of the hearing (Supreme Court Practice Note, 20 December 1994) (1995 STI 98).

Status of decision

A court decision is a binding precedent for itself or an inferior court except that the House of Lords, while treating its former decisions as normally binding, may depart from a previous decision should it appear right to do so. For this see *Fitzleet Estates Ltd v Cherry* HL 1977, 51 TC 708. Scottish decisions are not binding on the High Court but are normally followed. Decisions of the Privy Council and of the Irish Courts turning on comparable legislation are treated with respect. A court decision does not affect other assessments already final and conclusive (see 5.7 assessments) but may be followed, if relevant, in the determination of any open appeals against assessments and in assessments made subsequently irrespective of the years of assessment or taxpayers concerned (*Re Waring decd* Ch D, [1948] 1 All ER 257; *Gwyther v Boslymon Quarries Ltd* KB 1950, 29 ATC 1; *Bolands Ltd v CIR* SC(I) 1925, 4 ATC 526). Further, a court decision does not prevent the Crown from proceeding on a different basis for other years (*Hood Barrs v CIR (No 3)* CA 1960, 39 TC 209).

For joinder of CIR in non-tax disputes, see In *re Vandervell's Trusts* HL 1970, 46 TC 341.

Judicial review

[5.34] A taxpayer who is dissatisfied with the exercise of administrative powers may in certain circumstances (e.g. where HMRC has exceeded or abused its powers or acted contrary to the rules of natural justice, or where the Tribunal has acted unfairly or improperly) seek a remedy in a mandatory or prohibiting order or a quashing order. This is done by way of application for judicial review to the High Court under *Supreme Court Act 1981, s 31* and *Part 54 of the Civil Procedure Rules*. The High Court can in certain cases transfer an application for judicial review or for leave to apply for judicial review to the Upper Tribunal (see *Supreme Court Act 1981, s 31A*).

The issue on an application for leave to apply for judicial review is whether there is an arguable case (*R v CIR (ex p Howmet Corporation and another)* QB, [1994] STC 413). The procedure is generally used where no other, adequate, remedy, such as a right of appeal, is available. See *R v Special Commrs (ex p Stipplechoice Ltd) (No 1)* CA 1985, 59 TC 396, *R v HMIT (ex p Kissane and Another)* QB, [1986] STC 152, *R v Sevenoaks Commrs (ex p Thorne)* QB 1989, 62 TC 341, *R v Hastings and Bexhill General Commrs and CIR (ex p Goodacre)* QB 1994, 67 TC 126 and *R v CIR (ex p Ulster Bank Ltd)* CA 1997, 69 TC 211.

There is a very long line of cases in which the courts have consistently refused applications where a matter should have been pursued through the ordinary channels as described above. See, for example, *R v Special Commrs (ex p*

Morey) CA 1972, 49 TC 71; *R v Special Commrs (ex p Emery)* QB 1980, 53 TC 555; *R v Walton General Commrs (ex p Wilson)* CA, [1983] STC 464; *R v Special Commrs (ex p Esslemont)* CA, 1984 STI 312; *R v Brentford Commrs (ex p Chan)* QB 1985, 57 TC 651; *R v CIR (ex p Caglar)* QB 1995, 67 TC 335. See also, however, *R v HMIT and Others (ex p Lansing Bagnall Ltd)* CA 1986, 61 TC 112 for a successful application where the inspector issued a notice under a discretionary power on the footing that there was a mandatory obligation to do so, and *R v Ward, R v Special Commr (ex p Stipplechoice Ltd) (No 3)* QB 1988, 61 TC 391, where insufficient notice was given of revision of an accounting period prior to appeal hearing.

In *R v CIR (ex p J Rothschild Holdings)* CA 1987, 61 TC 178, the Revenue were required to produce internal documents of a general character relating to their practice in applying a statutory provision, but in *R v CIR (ex p Taylor)* CA 1988, 62 TC 562 discovery of internal Revenue correspondence was refused as there was no material indication that it had any bearing on the question of whether the decision taken by the inspector could be challenged. In *R v CIR (ex p Unilever plc)* CA 1996, 68 TC 205, an application for judicial review for a Revenue decision to refuse a late loss relief claim was successful: the Revenue's refusal was 'so unreasonable as to be, in public law terms, irrational' in view of an administrative procedure established with the company over many years of raising assessments on estimates of net taxable profits, adjusted when the final accounts became available without regard to the loss claim time limit. A different decision was reached in *R (oao Bampton Property Group and others) v King* QB, [2012] STC 1321: where an officer of HMRC was exercising a discretion as to whether to allow a time-barred claim, no mandatory requirement to give reasons for the decision should be implied (though there were cases where fairness might require it).

A confirmation by the local tax office that capital allowances were available in relation to an enterprise zone property trust scheme was not binding where the promoters were aware that clearance applications were required to be made to a specialist department, and failed to disclose that the scheme involved 'artificial provisions' (*R v CIR (ex p Matrix-Securities Ltd)* HL 1994, 66 TC 587). As regards informal advice by the Revenue generally, they were not bound by anything less than a clear, unambiguous and unqualified representation (*R v CIR (ex p MFK Underwriting Agencies Ltd)* QB 1989, 62 TC 607), and in *R v CIR (ex p Bishopp and another)* QB, [1999] STC 531, an application for judicial review of informal advice given by the Revenue in relation to a proposed transaction was refused. See also *R (oao Hely-Hutchinson) v HMRC* CA, [2017] STC 2048 (in which it was held that where a public body has changed its policy after acting under error, the question is whether or not there would be sufficient and conspicuous unfairness to prevent its being able to correct its mistake); *R v CIR (ex p S G Warburg & Co Ltd)* QB 1994, 68 TC 300, where a decision not to apply a published practice was upheld; *R (oao Bamber) v HMRC* QB 2005, [2006] STC 1035, where a Revenue decision to resile from a written agreement was upheld as being in the public interest; *R (oao Huitson) v HMRC* CA, [2011] STC 1860, where the courts rejected the claimant's contention that retrospective tax legislation was in breach of human rights legislation; *R v CIR (ex p Camacq Corporation)* CA 1989, 62 TC 651, where a Revenue decision to revoke its authorisation to pay a dividend gross was upheld. (In the Bamber case a subsequent claim for damages was rejected (*R (oao Bamber) v HMRC (No 2)* QB, [2008] STC 1864)). But see *Cameron and others v HMRC* QB, [2012] STC 1691 in which it was held that a taxpayer is entitled to rely upon a statement made in a formal HMRC publication unless and until the statement is revoked, withdrawn or altered.

The underlying facts in *Carvill v CIR (No 3)* Ch D, [2002] STC 1167 were that in two separate appeals relating to different tax years, income from an identical source had been held liable to tax for some years (the earlier years) but not others. An appeal against the Revenue's refusal to refund tax, and interest on tax, paid for the earlier years was rejected; the assessments for those years were valid assessments which the Special Commissioner in question had had jurisdiction to determine, and the taxpayer the right to challenge, and those assessments had not been set aside. An application for judicial review on the grounds that the Revenue's refusal to repay was unfair was dismissed (*Carvill (R oao) v CIR* QB 2003, 75 TC 477).

The first step is to obtain leave to apply for judicial review from the High Court. Application for leave is made ex parte to a single judge who will usually determine the application without a hearing. The Court will not grant leave unless the applicant has a sufficient interest in the matter to which the application relates. See *CIR v National Federation of Self-employed and Small Businesses Ltd* HL 1981, 55 TC 133 for what is meant by 'sufficient interest' and for discussion of availability of judicial review generally, and cf. *R v A-G (ex p ICI plc)* CA 1986, 60 TC 1.

Time limit

Applications must be made **within three months** of the date when the grounds for application arose. The Court has discretion to extend this time limit where there is good reason, but is generally very reluctant to do so. See e.g. *R v HMIT (ex p Brumfield and Others)* QB 1988, 61 TC 589 and *R v CIR (ex p Allen)* QB 1997, 69 TC 442. Grant of leave to apply for review does not amount to a ruling that application was made in good time (*R v Tavistock Commrs (ex p Worth)* QB 1985, 59 TC 116).

Costs

[5.35] Costs may be awarded by the Courts in the usual way. In suitable cases, e.g. 'test cases', HMRC may undertake to pay the taxpayer's costs. See 5.23 and 5.32 above for the award of costs by the First-tier and Upper Tribunals. Costs awarded by the Courts may include expenses connected with the drafting of the stated case (*Manchester Corporation v Sugden* CA 1903, 4 TC 595). Costs of a discontinued application for judicial review were refused where the Revenue was not informed of the application (*R v CIR ex p Opman International UK* QB 1985, 59 TC 352). Law costs of appeals not allowable for tax purposes (*Allen v Farquharson* KB 1932, 17 TC 59; *Rushden Heel and Smith's Potato cases* HL 1948, 30 TC 298 & 267, and see *Spofforth* KB 1945, 26 TC 310).

6

Assessments

Cross-references. As regards particular assessments, see also **28** EMPLOYMENT INCOME and **53** PAY AS YOU EARN for assessments on employment income; **52** PARTNERSHIPS; **70** SETTLEMENTS for assessment on trust income.

Simon's Taxes. See **A4.3.**

Introduction to assessments

[6.1] All assessments which are not self-assessments (see **67** SELF-ASSESSMENT) must (unless otherwise provided) be made by an officer of HMRC, notice of such assessment to be served on the person assessed stating the date of issue and the time limit for making APPEALS (5). The assessment may not then be altered except as expressly provided under the *Taxes Acts*. All income tax falling to be assessed other than by self-assessment may be included in a single assessment, notwithstanding that the liability may have arisen under more than one Part or Chapter of *ITEPA 2003* or *ITTOIA 2005*. [*TMA 1970, s 30A*].

Normal time limits for assessments

[6.2] The normal time limit for the making of an income tax assessment is four years after the end of the tax year. [*TMA 1970, s 34(1)*].

In relation to employment income, pension income or social security income received in a tax year later than that for which it is chargeable, an assessment can be made at any time within four years after the tax year in which the income is received. [*TMA 1970, s 35*].

An objection to the making of an assessment on the grounds that it is out of time can only be made on an appeal against the assessment. [*TMA 1970, s 34(2)*].

The time limit in *TMA 1970, s 34(1)* above has no application to a self-assessment. This was established by *R (oao Higgs) v HMRC* UT, [2015] STC 1600 and subsequently given statutory effect. [*TMA 1970, s 34(3); FA 2016, s 168(2)*]. However, see the separate time limit in **67.4** SELF-ASSESSMENT.

For extended time limits in certain cases, see **6.3**, **6.4** below.

Simon's Taxes. See **A4.320, A4.321.**

Extended time limits for assessments

[6.3] Extended time limits apply for making assessments (superseding **6.2** above) in the circumstances set out below.

The six-year rule

The time limit for making an assessment on a person in a case involving a loss of income tax brought about 'carelessly' by that person (or by a person acting on his behalf) is no later than six years following the end of the tax year.

For these purposes and those below, a loss of tax is brought about '*carelessly*' by a person if that person fails to take reasonable care to avoid bringing about that loss. See *HMRC v Hicks* UT, [2020] STC 254, [2020] UKUT 12 (TCC) in which carelessness was upheld where a person, having taken on the role of tax adviser, had not met the standard expected of a reasonably competent tax adviser giving advice to a taxpayer on the matter in question.

Where information is provided to HMRC and the person who provided it (or the person on whose behalf it was provided) discovers later that it was inaccurate but then fails to take reasonable steps to inform HMRC, any loss of tax brought about by the inaccuracy is treated as having been brought about carelessly by that person. [*TMA 1970, s 118(5)(6)*].

The 20-year rule

The time limit for making an assessment on a person in a case involving a loss of income tax brought about deliberately by that person (or by a person acting on his behalf) is no later than 20 years following the end of the tax year. This extended time limit does not constitute a taxpayer being 'charged with a criminal offence' for the purpose of invoking Human Rights legislation (*Personal Representative of Wood (Deceased) v HMRC* UT, [2016] UKUT 346 (TCC)).

The 20-year time limit also applies in the case of a loss of tax attributable to:

- failure to notify chargeability as in **55.2** PENALTIES;
- arrangements in respect of which there has been a failure to comply with specified obligations to provide information to HMRC under **25** DISCLOSURE OF TAX AVOIDANCE SCHEMES; or
- arrangements which were expected to result in a tax advantage in respect of which the taxpayer was under an obligation to notify HMRC of a monitored promoter's reference number under the special compliance regime for high-risk promoters (see **25.17** DISCLOSURE OF TAX AVOIDANCE SCHEMES) but failed to do so.

In no case, however, does this apply where the tax year in question is 2008/09 or an earlier year unless the assessment is made for the purpose of making good a loss of tax attributable to the negligent conduct of the person assessed (or of a person acting on his behalf).

[*TMA 1970, s 36(1)(1A)(1B)*].

References to a loss of tax brought about deliberately by a person include a loss of tax arising as a result of a deliberate inaccuracy in a document given to HMRC by or on behalf of that person. [*TMA 1970, s 118(7)*].

Offshore matters and transfers: the 12-year rule

The time limit for making an assessment on a person is extended in a case where a loss of income tax either involves an offshore matter or involves an offshore transfer which makes the lost tax significantly harder to identify. The assessment can be made at any time no later than 12 years following the end of the tax year to which the loss of tax relates. This generally has effect where the tax year in question is 2015/16 or a subsequent year. But where the loss of tax is brought about carelessly by the person concerned (or by a person acting on that person's behalf), it has effect two years earlier, i.e. where the tax year in question is 2013/14 or a subsequent year. The extension is subject to the 20-year rule above, which takes priority.

There are two situations where the 12-year rule does not apply. Firstly, an assessment cannot be made where, as a result of receiving 'relevant overseas information', HMRC could reasonably be expected both to have become aware of the loss of tax and to make the assessment in sufficient time to avoid using the 12-year rule. '*Relevant overseas information*' means information provided to HMRC by an overseas territory under EU tax law or under any agreement to which the UK and the overseas territory are parties. This includes information received under the Common Reporting Standard (see **35.14** HMRC — ADMINISTRATION). Secondly, an assessment cannot be made under the 12-year rule to the extent that the liability to the lost tax arises from a transfer pricing adjustment (see **4.20** ANTI-AVOIDANCE).

For these purposes, a loss of income tax involves an *offshore matter* if it is charged on or by reference to:

- income arising from a source in a territory outside the UK;
- assets situated or held in any such territory;
- income or assets received in any such territory;
- activities carried on wholly or mainly in any such territory; or
- anything having effect as if it were such income, assets or activities.

'Assets' has the same meaning as for capital gains tax purposes (see TCGA 1992, s 21(1)) but also includes sterling.

A loss of income tax involves an *offshore transfer* if it does not involve an offshore matter and some or all of the income on or by reference to which it is charged (or assets derived from or representing that income) is transferred to a territory outside the UK before the 'relevant date'. In a case where a tax return has been delivered for the tax year in question, the '*relevant date*' is the date of delivery; otherwise, the '*relevant date*' is 31 January following the tax year.

Cases in which an offshore transfer makes the lost tax significantly harder to identify include (but are not restricted to) those where, because of the transfer, HMRC were significantly less likely to become aware of the lost tax or were likely to become aware of it at a significantly later time.

[*TMA 1970, s 36A(1)–(10); FA 2019, s 80(2)(5)*].

Supplementary

There is an overriding deadline for making assessments in respect of deceased persons (see **6.4** below).

As part of the balance between HMRC and the taxpayer, in relation to appeals against discovery assessments (see **6.6** below) and extended time limit assessments, HMRC must satisfy the FTT that the relevant conditions for those assessments to have been validly made have been met (*Burgess v HMRC* UT, [2016] STC 579, [2015] UKUT 578 (TCC)).

Where total income is increased as a result of an extended time limit assessment, this does not affect the validity of any excess married couple's allowance or any blind person's allowance transferred between spouses or civil partners. In other words, the transferred allowance is not restored to the transferor. [*TMA 1970, s 37A; FA 2019, s 80(3)(5)*].

Persons in partnership with a person responsible for a loss of tax as above may themselves be subject to extended time limit assessments in respect of additional partnership profits. [*TMA 1970, ss 36(2), 36A(11); FA 2019, s 80(2)(5)*].

If the person assessed so requires, an extended time limit assessment can give effect to reliefs or allowances to which he would have been entitled had he made the necessary claims within the relevant time limits (excluding certain elections for the transfer of the married couple's allowance). The facility to claim late reliefs and allowances is similarly available in relation to an HMRC amendment to a personal or partnership tax return (see **64.8** RETURNS). [*TMA 1970, ss 36(3)(3A), 36A(11); FA 2019, s 80(2)(5)*].

Simon's Taxes. See **A4.325–A4.328.**

Extended time limits for assessments — deceased persons

[6.4] Notwithstanding anything in **6.3** above, the time for assessing the personal representatives of a deceased person cannot extend to more than four years after the end of the tax year in which death occurred. [*TMA 1970, s 40(1); FA 2019, s 80(4)(5)*].

In a case involving a loss of tax brought about carelessly or deliberately by a person who has died (or another person acting on that person's behalf before that person's death), assessments to make good the tax lost can be made for any of the six tax years preceding the tax year in which death occurred. But no such assessment can be made later than four years after the end of that tax year.

[*TMA 1970, s 40(2)*].

Simon's Taxes. See **A4.329**.

Simple assessments

[6.5] HMRC can make a 'simple assessment' of an individual's or trustee's income tax or capital gains tax liability without the taxpayer first being required to complete a self-assessment tax return. The simple assessment will be made on the basis of information already held by HMRC, whether it was received from the taxpayer or a third party. HMRC can withdraw a simple assessment by notice to the taxpayer, and it is then taken as never having had any effect.

The notice of assessment must include particulars of the income and gains, and any relief or allowance, taken into account in the assessment, and must state the amount payable, net of any income tax deducted at source, and the due date for payment (see **54.1** PAYMENT OF TAX). In the case of a trust, the notice of assessment can be given to any one or more of the relevant trustees (see **67.11** SELF-ASSESSMENT). HMRC can make more than one simple assessment on a person for any tax year. A simple assessment cannot be made if the taxpayer has already made a return or if he has been given notice to do so and that notice has not been withdrawn.

[*TMA 1970, ss 28H–28J; FA 2016, s 167, Sch 23 para 3*].

Querying a simple assessment

An appeal can be made against a simple assessment (see **5.3** APPEALS) but only after the person assessed has raised a query about the assessment and has been given a final response to that query. The person may query the simple assessment by notifying HMRC of his belief that the assessment is, or may be, incorrect, and stating the reasons for that belief. He must do so within 60 days after the date the notice of assessment was issued or such longer period as HMRC may allow in a particular case. He can withdraw his query at any time.

HMRC must consider a query and give a final response. If they need more time or information, they can postpone the simple assessment in whole or part (according to how much of it is being queried) and notify the taxpayer accordingly. If the simple assessment is postponed in part, HMRC must state the amount that remains payable. The taxpayer is under no obligation to pay a postponed amount. After considering the query, HMRC's final response must be to confirm, amend or withdraw the assessment, and in each case to notify the taxpayer in writing. An amended simple assessment given as a final response to a query cannot itself be queried.

[*TMA 1970, s 31AA; FA 2016, s 167, Sch 23 para 6*].

Removing taxpayers from self-assessment

HMRC have so far announced that they are removing the following groups of taxpayer from the obligation to complete a self-assessment tax return:

- PAYE taxpayers who have underpaid tax but cannot have the underpayment collected via their tax code;
- new State pensioners whose pension exceeds the personal allowance; and
- (for 2017/18 onwards) pre-existing State pensioners whose pension exceeds the personal allowance.

Taxpayers removed from self-assessment will instead be sent a simple assessment (www.gov.uk/government/publications/issue-briefing-simple-assessment-ending-the-tax-return).

Further assessments on 'discovery'

[6.6] If an officer of HMRC or the Commissioners for HMRC 'discover', as regards any person (the taxpayer) and a tax year, that:

(a) any income or chargeable gains which ought to have been assessed to tax (see **67.3** SELF-ASSESSMENT) have not been assessed, or
(b) an assessment is or has become insufficient, or
(c) any relief given is or has become excessive,

then with the exceptions below, an assessment (a discovery assessment) may be made to make good to the Crown the apparent loss of tax. In limited circumstances, a discovery assessment may be made even though the deadline for opening an enquiry into the return (see **64.6** RETURNS) has not passed (see Revenue Tax Bulletin August 2001 pp 875, 876).

A discovery assessment was quashed in *Wilkes v HMRC* FTT (TC 7740), [2020] UKFTT 0256 (TC) on the grounds that there was no income to be assessed. This was a high income child benefit case (see **73.4** SOCIAL SECURITY AND NATIONAL INSURANCE) but the decision could conceivably be applied to any situation where tax is collectible at Step 7 of the income tax calculation at **1.10** ALLOWANCES AND TAX RATES and no tax return is issued.

No discovery assessment may be made, in respect of a chargeable period, where a return under *TMA 1970, s 8* or *s 8A* (see **64.2** RETURNS) has been delivered:

(1) if it would be attributable to an error or mistake in the return as to the basis on which the liability ought to have been computed and the return was, in fact, made on the basis, or in accordance with the practice, generally prevailing at the time when it was made; or
(2) unless either
    (a) the loss of tax is brought about carelessly or deliberately by the taxpayer or a person acting on his behalf, or
    (b) at the time when an HMRC officer either ceased to be entitled to enquire (see **64.6** RETURNS) into the return or, where an enquiry has been opened, has issued a closure notice, he could not have been reasonably expected, on the basis of the information so far made available to him, to be aware of the loss of tax. On and after 16 November 2017, the reference here to a closure notice is to a final closure notice or to a partial closure notice in respect of a matter to which the discovery relates (see **64.8** RETURNS).

For a useful discussion on the meaning of 'carelessly' in (2)(a) above see *Anderson v HMRC* FTT (TC 5092), [2016] UKFTT 335 (TC), [2017] SFTD 100. Holding a genuine belief that something was the case is not sufficient to establish that there was no carelessness; that belief must also have been reasonably held (*Supaglazing Ltd v HMRC* FTT (TC 6855), [2018] UKFTT 712 (TC)).

For the purposes of (2)(b) above, information is regarded as having been made available to the officer if it has been included in:

- (i) the return (or accompanying accounts, statements or documents) for the chargeable period concerned or for either of the two immediately preceding it, or
- (ii) a partnership return (see **64.12** RETURNS), where applicable, in respect of the chargeable period concerned or either of the two immediately preceding it, or
- (iii) any claim for the chargeable period concerned, or
- (iv) documents etc. produced for the purposes of any enquiries into such a return or claim,

or is information the existence and relevance of which could reasonably be expected to be inferred from the above-mentioned information or are notified in writing by the taxpayer to HMRC. See also below.

An objection to a discovery assessment on the grounds that neither (a) nor (b) in (2) above applies can be made only on an appeal against the assessment. (See **5.3** APPEALS for right of appeal.)

[*TMA 1970, s 29; F(No 2)A 2017, Sch 15 paras 14, 44*].

See **67.8** SELF-ASSESSMENT as regards due date of payment.

A change of opinion by HMRC on information previously made available to them is not grounds for a discovery assessment.

Particularly in large or complex cases, the standard accounts information details and other information included in the tax return (see **64.2** RETURNS) may not provide a means of disclosure adequate to avoid falling within (2)(b) above. The submission of further information, including perhaps accounts, may be considered appropriate but will not necessarily provide protection against a discovery assessment beyond that arising from submission of the return alone. The reasonable expectation test (see (2)(b) above) must be satisfied. Where voluminous information beyond the accounts and computations is sent with the return, HMRC recommend that there should be a brief indication of the relevance of the material. HMRC will accept that for *TMA 1970, s 29* purposes documents submitted within a month of the return 'accompany' it (see (i) above) provided the return indicates that such documents have been or will be submitted. They will consider sympathetically a request that this condition be treated as satisfied where the time lag is longer than a month. (Revenue Press Release 31 May 1996 and Tax Bulletin June 1996 pp 313–315).

The categories in (i)–(iv) above constitute an exhaustive definition of 'information made available to an officer of HMRC' for the purpose of (2)(b) above; an officer is not precluded from making a discovery assessment simply because some other information (not normally part of the officer's immediate checks) might be available (in the instant case a form P11D) that might place doubt on the sufficiency of the self-assessment (*Langham v Veltema* CA 2004, 76 TC 259). Following this important CA decision, HMRC produced a guidance note; this was later reclassified as HMRC SP 1/06. In particular, a taxpayer can protect himself from a discovery assessment by stating (truthfully) in his tax return:

- (in cases involving valuations) that a valuation has been used and that it was carried out by a named independent and suitably qualified valuer on an appropriate basis (but such protection is not available in the circumstances present in *Langham v Veltema*, i.e. where the same transaction is the subject of an agreed valuation in a tax return made by another party to the transaction);
- (in cases involving other judgmental issues, for example where expenditure on property is allocated between non-deductible capital expenditure, e.g. improvements to property, and deductible revenue expenditure, e.g. repairs) that a programme of work has been carried out and the expenditure allocated on a particular basis; and
- (where such is the case) that a view of the law has been taken which differs from a published view taken by HMRC.

In no case does the taxpayer need to supply sufficient information to *quantify* a possible insufficiency in the self-assessment; the object of the exercise is merely to draw HMRC's attention to the possible existence of such insufficiency.

In *Pattullo v HMRC* UT, [2016] STC 2043, an HMRC officer had newly discovered, as a result of expert examination of the taxpayer's return, that the taxpayer was probably a participant in a named tax avoidance scheme and he believed that this might lead there to be an insufficiency. It was held that this was a discovery (a new fact had come to light: the taxpayer's probable membership of the scheme). Although the taxpayer had disclosed certain related transactions in his return, these were held insufficient to alert a hypothetical officer to a possible insufficiency; such an officer, even of the requisite knowledge and expertise, could not be expected to have been aware not only that a tax avoidance scheme was being used but also that it was a tax avoidance scheme which did not work.

In *Anderson and another (personal representatives of Anderson (deceased))* FTT (TC 206), [2009] UKFTT 258 (TC), the fact that HMRC had received the information they needed in the form of a chargeable event certificate did not prevent a discovery assessment being validly made. The certificate was provided to HMRC by an insurance company and not by the appellant or her representatives, and was therefore to be disregarded.

There is no warrant for extending the meaning of (i) above to include trust tax returns in addition to the personal tax return of the taxpayer whose affairs are under review (*Trustees of the Bessie Taube Discretionary Settlement Trust and others v HMRC* FTT (TC 735), [2011] SFTD 153), and see also *Miesegaes v HMRC* FTT (TC 5129), [2016] UKFTT 375 (TC), [2016] SFTD 719.

In *HMRC v Lansdowne Partners Ltd Partnership* CA 2011, 81 TC 318, it was held that the combined effect of a letter which the taxpayer had submitted and the tax knowledge expected of an officer of HMRC was that the officer could have been reasonably expected to be aware that the amount of the profits included in the return was insufficient.

In *Sanderson v HMRC* CA, [2016] STC 638, a case involving a marketed avoidance scheme, it was held that HMRC were entitled to make a discovery assessment notwithstanding an entry in the 'white space' of the tax return. The information contained in the return might have been sufficient to have caused a hypothetical officer to ask further questions but was not enough to have made such an officer aware of an insufficiency of tax. A similar decision was reached in *Smith v HMRC* FTT (TC 2768), [2013] UKFTT 368 (TC). However, in *HMRC v Charlton* UT, [2012] UKUT 770 (TCC) it was held that the information provided with the taxpayer's return was sufficient to show that 'no officer could have missed the point that an artificial tax avoidance scheme had been implemented' and that 'on the basis of the information made available to him before the closure of the enquiry window, an officer would have been reasonably expected to have been aware of the insufficiency of tax such as to justify an assessment'; therefore, no discovery assessment was possible. It was not necessary that a hypothetical officer should have been able to comprehend all the workings of the scheme, or the legal and factual arguments that might arise, or be able to form a reasoned view of those matters. In *Cooke v HMRC* FTT (TC 6239), [2018] SFTD 633, [2017] UKFTT 844 (TC), the First-tier Tribunal, in allowing the taxpayer's appeal, found that a hypothetical officer was expected to have some understanding of double tax relief and the limitations on the relief that can be claimed, and thus could have been reasonably expected to be aware that the double tax relief claims in the appellant's return were excessive.

Where an agreement has been made under *TMA 1970, s 54* to settle an appeal (see **5.9** APPEALS), it is not open to HMRC to make a discovery assessment unless it is founded upon a point other than the particular matter or point at issue that was the subject of the agreement (*Cenlon Finance Co Ltd v Ellwood* HL 1962, 40 TC 176; *Olin Energy Systems Ltd v Scorer* HL 1985, 58 TC 592; *Easinghall Ltd v HMRC* UT, [2016] STC 1476).

A confiscation order made by a court under *Proceeds of Crime Act 2002* does not of itself preclude HMRC from raising a discovery assessment on the unlawful income (*Martin v HMRC* UT, [2015] UKUT 161 (TCC)).

As part of the balance between HMRC and the taxpayer, in relation to appeals against discovery assessments and assessments outside normal time limits, HMRC must satisfy the FTT that the relevant conditions for those assessments to have been validly made have been met (*Burgess v HMRC* UT, [2016] STC 579). There is nothing in *TMA 1970 , 29* which says anything about how soon a discovery assessment must follow the discovery (*Miesegaes v HMRC* FTT (TC 5129), [2016] UKFTT 375 (TC), [2016] SFTD 719), but it is accepted that a discovery may become 'stale' if not acted upon and that no discovery assessment can then be made; in this case, the delay was two-and-a-half years (*Beagles v HMRC* UT, [2019] STC 54, [2018] UKUT 380 (TCC)). See also *Hargreaves v HMRC* FTT (TC 7090), [2019] UKFTT 244 (TC) and *Bashir*

Ahmed Jafari v HMRC FTT (TC 7465), [2019] UKFTT 692 (TC) in which similar conclusions were reached. A discovery assessment may, however, be made on a 'new' discovery relating to the same tax position as an earlier discovery (*Atherton v HMRC* UT, [2019] STC 575, [2019] UKUT 41 (TCC)). Time spent in trying to reach a negotiated settlement with the taxpayer following a discovery does not itself cause that discovery to become stale (*Chaudhary v HMRC* FTT (TC 6982), [2019] UKFTT 99 (TC)).

Whilst ruling against the taxpayer in *Clark v HMRC* CA, [2020] STC 589, the CA did find that the scope of a discovery assessment, and of any appeal from it, has to be defined by the subjective discovery that the assessing officer has made; the scope of the assessment cannot be extended by virtue of the appeal process itself.

Under Human Rights legislation, *TMA 1970 , 29* should be construed as enabling HMRC to issue an assessment (where the conditions are met) which makes good a loss of tax but only after taking into account in the assessment a related overpayment which arises as a result of the circumstances giving rise to the underpayment (*Fessal v HMRC* FTT (TC 5059), [2016] SFTD 585, [2016] UKFTT 285 (TC)).

The HMRC officer has to have newly discovered that an assessment to tax is insufficient; a discovery assessment is not validly triggered just because the officer has found a new reason for contending that an assessment is insufficient, or because he has decided to invoke a different mechanism for addressing an insufficiency in an assessment he already knew was present (*HMRC v Tooth* CA, [2019] STC 1316).

In *Cussens v HMRC* FTT (TC 7337), [2019] UKFTT 543 (TC), the Tribunal concluded that the discovery assessments raised were so 'wild, extravagant and unreasonable' that they were not raised for the purpose of making good to the Crown a loss of tax and so were not authorised by *TMA 1970 , 29*; a proper exercise must be undertaken to arrive at a fair and reasonable assessment, rather than inflated assessments being issued with a view to bringing a taxpayer to heel.

For a useful discussion on what is meant by 'practice generally prevailing' in (1) above, see *Boyer Allan Investment Services Ltd v HMRC* FTT (TC 2235), [2012] UKFTT 558 (TC), [2013] SFTD 73.

See **16.9** CLAIMS for extended time limits for claims where a discovery assessment is made in a case where neither fraudulent nor negligent conduct is involved.

Amendment of partnership return on discovery

Provisions broadly similar to those described above apply as regards an understatement of profits or excessive claim for relief or allowance in a partnership statement (see **64.13** RETURNS), although HMRC's remedy in this case is to amend the partnership return, with consequent amendment of partners' own returns. [*TMA 1970, s 30B; F(No 2)A 2017, Sch 15 paras 17, 44; FA 2018, Sch 6 paras 10(7), 14*]. See **5.3** APPEALS for right of appeal.

Simon's Taxes. See **A4.315–A4.317, A6.701–A6.704, A6.706–A6.709.**

Double assessment

[6.7] The taxing acts 'nowhere authorise the Crown to take income tax twice over in respect of the same source for the same period of time' (Lord Sumner in *English Sewing Cotton Co* HL 1923, 8 TC at 513). An *alternative* income tax assessment may, however, be raised in respect of transactions already the subject of a final CGT assessment (*Bye v Coren* CA 1986, 60 TC 116), and where more than one of a number of alternative assessments become final and conclusive, the Crown may institute collection proceedings in respect of any one (but not more than one) of them (*CIR v Wilkinson* CA 1992, 65 TC 28). For alternative assessments generally, see *Lord Advocate v McKenna CS*, [1989] STC 485.

Where there has been double assessment for the same cause and for the same tax year a claim may be made to HMRC (with a right of appeal against refusal) for the overcharge to be vacated. [*TMA 1970, s 32*]. See **16.7** CLAIMS for recovery of tax.

Finality of assessments

[6.8] An assessment cannot be altered after the notice has been served except in accordance with the express provisions of the *Taxes Acts* (e.g. where the taxpayer appeals — see 5 APPEALS). [*TMA 1970, s 30A(4)*]. Where over-assessment results from a mistake in a return, see **16.7** CLAIMS. An assessment as determined on appeal or not appealed against is final and conclusive.

Contract settlements

[6.9] In cases where penalties are chargeable, the taxpayer may be invited to offer a sum in full settlement of liability for tax, interest and penalties (a 'contract settlement') and such offers are often accepted by HMRC without assessment of all the tax. A binding agreement so made cannot be repudiated afterwards by the taxpayer or his executors.

See *CIR v Nuttall* CA 1989, 63 TC 148 for confirmation of power to enter into such agreements. Amounts due under such an agreement which are unpaid may be pursued by an action for a debt, but the Crown does not rank as a preferential creditor in respect of the sums due (*Nuttall* above; *CIR v Woollen* CA 1992, 65 TC 229).

See **55.23** PENALTIES for mitigation of penalties and certificates of full disclosure. See **39.11** HMRC INVESTIGATORY POWERS for HMRC's contractual disclosure facility.

Simon's Taxes. See **A6.420, A6.421.**

7

Bankruptcy

Simon's Taxes. See **A1.608, C4.240.**

[7.1] Income received by trustee during bankruptcy is not income of bankrupt for purposes of claiming personal allowances, etc. (*Fleming CS* 1928, 14 TC 78). Trustee is assessable on such income including profits of bankrupt's business continued by him notwithstanding requirement to hand over to creditors (*Armitage v Moore* QB 1900, 4 TC 199). And see *Hibbert v Fysh* CA 1962, 40 TC 305 (bankrupt assessable on remuneration retainable by him). The trustee continues generally to act following the death (undischarged) of the bankrupt as if he or she were still alive.

8

Banks and Building Societies

Introduction to banks and building societies

[8.1] In general, the term 'bank' is defined by reference to the carrying on of a *bona fide* banking business, but for certain purposes it is specially defined as:

(a) the Bank of England;
(b) a person who has permission under *Financial Services and Markets Act 2000, Pt 4A* to accept deposits (excluding building and friendly societies, credit unions and insurance companies);
(c) an EEA firm within *Financial Services and Markets Act 2000, Sch 3 para 5(b)* which has permission under *para 15* of that *Schedule* (as a result of qualifying for authorisation under *para 12(1)*) to accept deposits;
(d) the European Investment Bank; or
(e) an international organisation of which the UK is a member and which is designated as a bank for the particular purpose by Treasury order.

See **14.10** CHARITIES AND CHARITABLE GIVING, **23.12** DEDUCTION OF TAX AT SOURCE.

[*ITA 2007, s 991*].

Post-Brexit

With effect on and after Implementation Period completion day, expected to be 31 December 2020, EEA firms at (c) are removed from the above list (a)–(e). This does not, however, apply where the firm qualifies for authorisation by virtue of *Financial Services and Markets Act 2000 (Gibraltar) Order 2001 (SI 2001 No 3084)*.

[*ITA 2007, s 991; SI 2019 No 689, Regs 1, 15(12), 41; European Union (Withdrawal Agreement) Act 2020 Sch 5 para 1(1)*].

Building societies

A building society is one within the meaning of *Building Societies Act 1986*. [*ITA 2007, s 989*].

Interest received by depositors and investors

See **65.2** SAVINGS AND INVESTMENT INCOME for the charge to tax on interest generally, and note that building society *dividends* are generally taxed as interest and not as dividends.

Returns

Banks must make returns of interest paid to depositors. Building societies are required to make returns of dividends and interest paid to investors. See **39.14** HMRC INVESTIGATORY POWERS.

Simon's Taxes. See **A4.429, D7.7, D7.8.**

Building society marketable securities

[8.2] Dividends or interest paid in respect of securities issued by a building society (other than 'qualifying certificates of deposit', a 'qualifying uncertificated eligible debt security unit', or a 'quoted Eurobond' — all as defined) which were listed, or capable of being listed, on a recognised stock exchange when the dividend etc. became payable are subject to deduction of tax under *ITA 2007, s 889*. 'Permanent interest bearing shares' (see Tolley's Corporation Tax under Building Societies) issued by a society are within this provision. Dividends on 'core capital deferred shares', i.e. deferred shares that form part of the core tier one capital of a building society, are outside this provision, and are taxed in the same way as dividends generally. [*SI 2013 No 460*].

In relation to payments made before 12 February 2019, the obligation to deduct tax at source did not apply to payments in respect of '*regulatory capital securities*' as defined by *SI 2013 No 3209, Reg 2*, including Additional Tier 1 instruments and Tier 2 instruments issued in accordance with EU Regulations. For regulatory capital securities issued before 1 January 2019, this exception continues until 31 December 2023. [*SI 2013 No 3209, Regs 1, 2, 6, 8; FA 2019, Sch 20 paras 1, 16*].

Transfer of building society business to a company

[8.3] The acquisition by members of shares on such a transfer is granted certain reliefs from capital gains tax and from treatment as a distribution. [*FA 1988, s 145, Sch 12; TCGA 1992, ss 216, 217; FA 2016, Sch 6 paras 19, 28*]. See Tolley's Corporation Tax under Building Societies.

Declarations as to non-UK residence made or given to building societies which then incorporate are treated as having been made or given to the successor company. [*SI 2008 No 2682, Reg 19*].

Simon's Taxes. See **D7.827–D7.830.**

9

Capital Allowances

Cross-reference. See **10** CAPITAL ALLOWANCES ON PLANT AND MACHINERY.

Simon's Taxes. See Part **B3**.

Other sources. See Tolley's Capital Allowances.

Introduction to capital allowances

[9.1] The law relating to capital allowances was consolidated in *Capital Allowances Act 2001* (*CAA 2001*) as part of the Tax Law Rewrite programme.

Capital allowances (balancing charges) are a deduction from (addition to) the profits etc. of trades and other qualifying activities in arriving at the taxable amount. The amount of depreciation charged in the accounts of a business is not so allowed. They are generally treated as trading expenses (receipts) of the period of account (see **9.2**(i) below) to which they relate. [*CAA 2001, ss 2, 6; SI 2019 No 1087, Reg 3(3)*].

Certain allowances are given only in relation to trades, some only in relation to particular kinds of trade, and some additionally given against particular sources of non-trading income — details are given in the relevant section of the chapter. The allowances described in this chapter are not available for a chargeable period for which the profits of a trade, profession, vocation or property business are calculated on the cash basis (see **76** TRADING INCOME — CASH BASIS FOR SMALLER BUSINESSES and **60.4** PROPERTY INCOME). No disposal proceeds are generally brought into account for any such chargeable period and no balancing charges arise (but see **10.26** CAPITAL ALLOWANCES ON PLANT AND MACHINERY for an exception to this, which applies equally in relation to the allowances in this chapter). [*CAA 2001, ss 1(4), 1A; F(No 2)A 2017, Sch 2 paras 49, 50, 64(1)*].

Capital allowances are available in respect of expenditure on plant and machinery, which is a sufficiently large and important subject to warrant its own chapter — see **10** CAPITAL ALLOWANCES ON PLANT AND MACHINERY. They are also available in respect of certain other types of expenditure as detailed in **9.3–9.35**.

A new structures and buildings allowance has been introduced for expenditure on the construction of commercial buildings and structures. The allowance is available on eligible construction costs incurred on or after 29 October 2018, and is given at an annual rate on a straight-line basis. See **9.30–9.35**.

Capital allowances — matters of general application

[9.2] The following matters are pertinent to more than one type of capital allowance.

(i) **Meaning of 'chargeable period' and 'period of account'.** For capital allowances purposes, a '*chargeable period*' is a 'period of account'. For persons carrying on a trade, profession or vocation, a '*period of account*' means a period for which accounts are drawn up, except that where such a period exceeds 18 months, it is deemed to be split into two or more periods of account, beginning on, or on an anniversary of, the date on which the actual period begins. Exceptionally, where there is an

interval between two periods of account, it is deemed to form part of the first such period, and where two periods of account overlap, the common period is deemed to form part of the first such period only. For non-traders, a period of account is a tax year.
[*CAA 2001, s 6*].
See the examples at **10.36** CAPITAL ALLOWANCES ON PLANT AND MACHINERY.

(ii) **Claims.** Capital allowances are given only if a claim is made. Such a claim can only be made by inclusion in the annual tax return (subject to the very limited exceptions at *CAA 2001, s 3(4)*). A claim for allowances under **9.3** below (business premises renovation) or **9.30** below (structures and buildings allowances) must be separately identified as such in the return. [*CAA 2001, s 3, Sch 2 para 103(2); SI 2019 No 1087, Reg 3(4)*]. See **64.4** RETURNS as regards amendments to income tax returns, and the time allowed for making them.

(iii) **Capital expenditure.** References in the capital allowances legislation to the incurring of capital expenditure and the paying of capital sums exclude any sums allowed as deductions in computing the payer's profits or earnings, any expenditure incurred at a time when profits are calculated on the cash basis, and certain sums payable under deduction of tax. Corresponding rules apply as regards the receipt of such sums. [*CAA 2001, s 4, Sch 3 para 9; F(No 2)A 2017, Sch 2 paras 51, 64(1)*].

(iv) **Time expenditure incurred.** Capital expenditure (other than that constituted by an 'additional VAT liability' — see (viii) below) is generally treated, for capital allowances purposes, as incurred as soon as there is an unconditional obligation to pay it, even if all or part of it is not required to be paid until some later date. However, expenditure is treated as incurred on a later date in the following circumstances.

- Where any part of the expenditure is not required to be paid until a date more than four months after the date determined as above, it is treated as incurred on that later date.
- Where an obligation to pay becomes unconditional earlier than in accordance with normal commercial usage, with the sole or main benefit likely to be the bringing forward of the chargeable period in which the expenditure would otherwise be treated as incurred, it is instead treated as incurred on the date on or before which it is required to be paid.

Where, as a result of an event such as the issuing of a certificate, an obligation to pay becomes unconditional within one month after the end of a chargeable period, but at or before the end of that chargeable period the asset concerned has become the property of, or is otherwise attributed under the contract to, the person having the obligation, the expenditure is treated as incurred immediately before the end of that chargeable period.
The above provisions do not override any specific rule under which expenditure is treated as incurred later than the relevant time given above.
[*CAA 2001, s 5*].
Simon's Taxes. See **B3.104, B3.107.**

(v) **Exclusion of double allowances.** Where an allowance is made to a person under one of the following codes of allowances, he cannot obtain an allowance under another of those codes in respect of that expenditure or the provision of any asset to which that expenditure related:

- allowances for expenditure on business premises renovation (**9.3** below);
- allowances for expenditure on dredging (**9.10** below);
- allowances for expenditure on flat conversion (**9.13** below);
- allowances for mineral extraction (**9.15–9.25** below);
- research and development allowances (**9.28** below);
- structures and buildings allowances (**9.30** below).

Similarly, no allowance under any of the above codes can be made in respect of any expenditure that has been allocated to a plant and machinery pool (see **10.26** CAPITAL ALLOWANCES ON PLANT AND MACHINERY), and on which a plant or machinery allowance (or balancing charge) has consequently been given (or made), or any related asset (as above); and expenditure which has attracted an allowance under any of the above codes (and any related asset) cannot be allocated to a plant and machinery pool.

Additional rules apply under *CAA 2001, s 9* to prevent double allowances in relation to plant or machinery treated as fixtures (as at **10.37** *et seq.* CAPITAL ALLOWANCES ON PLANT AND MACHINERY). These do not prevent a person making a fixtures claim in respect of capital expenditure if the only previous claim was for industrial buildings allowances (now abolished), research and development allowances or business premises renovation allowances, but see **10.46** CAPITAL ALLOWANCES ON PLANT AND MACHINERY for restrictions on the amount of expenditure on which plant and machinery allowances can be claimed.

[*CAA 2001, ss 7–10, Sch 3 para 10; SI 2019 No 1087, Reg 3(6)*].

Where an item of expenditure qualifies for more than one type of capital allowance, it is the taxpayer's choice as to which to claim, but he cannot alter his choice in later years. (HMRC Capital Allowances Manual CA16000, HMRC Brief 12/09, 31 March 2009).

Simon's Taxes. See **B3.114.**

(vi) **Expenditure met by another's contributions.** Subject to the exceptions below, a person is not regarded as incurring expenditure for capital allowances purposes (other than for dredging — see below) to the extent that it is met, or will be met, directly or indirectly by another person or by a '*public body*', i.e. the Crown or any government or public or local authority (whether in the UK or elsewhere). For the scope of 'public authority', see *McKinney v Hagans Caravans (Manufacturing) Ltd* CA(NI) 1997, 69 TC 526. There is an exception where the expenditure is met by a Regional Development Grant or NI equivalent. In practice, applications for Regional Development Grants were no longer accepted after 31 March 1988, but NI equivalents continued to be available until 31 March 2003. Expenditure met by insurance or other compensation money due in respect of a destroyed, demolished or defunct asset is not excluded from allowances.

As regards allowances for dredging (see **9.10** below), the above is replaced by a rule to the effect that a person is not regarded as incurring expenditure for the purposes of his trade or future trade to the extent that it is met, or will be met, directly or indirectly by a public body or by capital sums contributed by another person *for purposes other than those of the fore-mentioned trade.*

The main rule above (but not the rule for dredging) is disapplied, and allowances are thus available, if the contributor is not a public body and can obtain neither a capital allowance on his contribution by virtue of (vii) below nor a deduction against profits of a trade, profession or vocation. This exception to the main rule does not apply to structures and buildings allowances at **9.30** below.

[*CAA 2001, ss 532–536, Sch 2 para 19, Sch 3 paras 106–108; SI 2019 No 1087, Reg 3(9)*].

Simon's Taxes. See **B3.111.**

(vii) **Contribution allowances.** Persons contributing a capital sum towards another person's expenditure may receive allowances ('*contribution allowances*') where the expenditure would otherwise have entitled the other person (assuming him not to be a public body) to mineral extraction allowances or structures and buildings allowances (SBAs). Contribution allowances are not available where the contributor and the other person are CONNECTED PERSONS (**19**).

As regards mineral extraction allowances (see **9.15** below), the contribution must be to expenditure on the provision of an asset, and must be made for the purposes of a trade, profession or vocation carried on (or to be carried on) by the contributor (C). The allowances available to C are such as would have been made if the contribution had been expended on the provision for C's trade etc. of a similar asset and as if the asset were at all material times used for the purposes of C's trade etc. (so that balancing adjustments do not apply to such contributions). On a transfer of C's trade etc., or part thereof, the allowances (or part) are subsequently made to the transferee.

As regards SBAs (see **9.30** below), the contribution must be to expenditure which is qualifying expenditure for SBAs purposes (see **9.15** below), and must be made for the purposes of a qualifying activity (as in **9.30**) carried on (or to be carried on) by a tenant of land in which C has an interest or, if the other person (R) is a public body (whether in the UK or elsewhere), by either C or any such tenant. C is treated for the purposes of SBAs as if:

(a) the contribution were expenditure incurred by C on the construction or acquisition of the building or structure;

(b) the building etc. were brought into qualifying use on the day on which R brought it into qualifying use; and

(c) the day on which the qualifying expenditure is incurred were the day on which C made the contribution.

If R is a public body, the day referred to in (b) above is, if earlier, the day on which R first brought the building etc. into *non-residential* use. This applies in relation to contributions made on or after 11 March 2020.

If, at any time in the period beginning with the making of the contribution and ending with the bringing of the building into non-residential use, C does not have a relevant interest, C is treated for SBAs purposes as having had a relevant interest in the building at the beginning of that period, and is not treated as ceasing to have that interest on any subsequent sale of R's relevant interest in the building. In relation to contributions made before 11 March 2020, C is treated as having had a relevant interest in the building etc. on the day on which R brought it into qualifying use.

In the event of the building being demolished, there is provision under *TCGA 1992, s 24A* (see Tolley's Capital Gains Tax) for C, if he does not have an interest in the building etc., to claim an allowable loss for CGT purposes equal to his unused SBAs.

In determining, for the above purposes, the day on which R first brings a building etc. into non-residential use, any use of it which is insignificant is ignored.

[*CAA 2001, ss 537, 538A, 541, 542; TCGA 1992, s 24A; FA 2020, Sch 5 paras 3, 9; SI 2019 No 1087, Regs 3(10)(11), 4(3)*].

Capital contributions towards expenditure on dredging (see **9.10** below) are treated as expenditure incurred by the contributor on that dredging. [*CAA 2001, s 543*].

Simon's Taxes. See **B3.112.**

(viii) **VAT capital goods scheme.** Under the VAT capital goods scheme, the input tax originally claimed on the acquisition of certain capital assets is subject to amendment within a specified period of adjustment in accordance with any increase or decrease in the extent to which the asset is used in making taxable, as opposed to exempt, supplies for VAT purposes. The items covered by the scheme are limited to land and buildings (or parts of buildings) worth at least £250,000 and computers (and items of computer equipment) worth at least £50,000. See Tolley's Value Added Tax under Capital Goods Scheme for a full description.

Special capital allowances provisions apply where a VAT adjustment is made under the capital goods scheme. These affect allowances for business premises renovation and research and development, and the provisions specific to each are described in the appropriate sections of this chapter. General definitions and provisions are described below.

'*Additional VAT liability*' and '*additional VAT rebate*' mean, respectively:

- an amount which a person becomes liable to pay; or
- an amount which he becomes entitled to deduct,

by way of adjustment under the VAT capital goods scheme in respect of input tax. Generally (but see below), such a liability or rebate is treated as incurred or made on the last day of the period:

- which is one of the periods making up the applicable VAT period of adjustment under the VAT capital goods scheme; and
- in which occurred the increase or decrease in use giving rise to the liability or rebate.

However, for the purpose of determining the chargeable period (see (i) above) in which it accrues, an additional VAT liability or rebate is treated as accruing on whichever is the relevant day below.

- Where the liability or rebate is accounted for in a VAT return, the last day of the period covered by that return.
- If, before the making of a VAT return, HMRC assess the liability or rebate, the day on which the assessment is made.
- If the trade is permanently discontinued before the liability or rebate has been accounted for in a VAT return and before the making of an assessment, the last day of the chargeable period in which the cessation occurs.

Where an allowance or charge falls to be determined by reference to a proportion only of the expenditure incurred or a proportion only of what that allowance or charge would otherwise have been, a related additional VAT liability or rebate is similarly apportioned.
[*CAA 2001, ss 546–551; SI 2019 No 1087, Reg 3(13)*].
Simon's Taxes. See **B3.103, B3.104.**

(ix) **Partnerships and successions.** Following a change in the persons carrying on an activity (i.e. a trade, profession, vocation or property business) in partnership, other than one resulting in the activity being treated as permanently discontinued, subsequent allowances and charges are made as if the new partnership had carried on the activity before the change. Following a change in persons carrying on an activity, such that the activity is treated as permanently discontinued, any asset transferred, without being sold, to the successor for continuing use in the activity is treated as if sold at market value on the date of change. These rules apply for the purposes of all the allowances in this chapter other than research and development allowances. [*CAA 2001, ss 557–559*].

(x) **Composite sales** may be apportioned by the Appeal Tribunal regardless of any separate prices attributed in the sale agreement. [*CAA 2001, ss 562–564*]. See *Fitton v Gilders & Heaton* Ch D 1955, 36 TC 233, and *Wood v Provan* CA 1968, 44 TC 701.
Simon's Taxes. See **B3.110.**

(xi) **Recovery of assets under *Proceeds of Crime Act 2002, Pt 5*.** *Proceeds of Crime Act 2002, Pt 5 Ch 2* provides for the recovery, in civil proceedings before the High Court (or, in Scotland, the Court of Session), of property which is, or represents, property obtained through 'unlawful conduct' (as defined in the Act). If the Court is satisfied that any property is recoverable under the provisions, it will make a '*recovery order*', vesting the property in an appointed trustee for civil recovery. Alternatively, the Court may make an order under *s 276* of the Act staying (or, in Scotland, sisting) proceedings on terms agreed by the parties. The vesting of property in a trustee for civil recovery or any other person, either under a recovery order or in pursuance of a *s 276* order, is known as a *Pt 5* transfer. A '*compensating payment*' may in some cases be made to the person who held the property immediately before the transfer. If the order provides for the creation of any interest in favour of that person, he is treated as receiving (in addition to any other compensating payment) a compensating payment equal to the value of the interest. [*Proceeds of Crime Act 2002, ss 240(1), 266(1)(2), 276, 316(1), 448, Sch 10 para* 2].

Where the property in question is plant or machinery, the relevant interest in a flat (within **9.13** below), or an asset representing qualifying expenditure on research and development (within **9.28** below), there are provisions to ensure that the *Pt 5* transfer has a tax-neutral effect, unless a compensating payment is made to the transferor in which case its amount and/or value must be brought into account as a disposal value or, as the case may be, as proceeds from a balancing event. [*Proceeds of Crime Act 2002, Sch 10 paras 12–29*].

(xii) **Avoidance affecting proceeds of balancing event.** There is an anti-avoidance rule to prevent a balancing allowance being created or increased by means of any tax avoidance scheme that depresses an asset's market value and thus the amount to be brought into account on a balancing event (e.g. a sale) or as a disposal value. The rule denies entitlement to a balancing allowance, though the unrelieved balance of expenditure immediately after the event must be computed as if the allowance had been made. The rule applies to allowances for business premises renovation, flat conversion expenditure and mineral extraction. It applies in relation to any event that would otherwise occasion a balancing allowance, except where it occurs in pursuance of a contract entered into on or before that date and is not consequent upon the exercise after that date of any option or right. [*CAA 2001, s 570A*].

Simon's Taxes. See **B3.108C.**

Business premises renovation allowances (obsolescent)

[9.3] For expenditure incurred before 6 April 2017, 100% capital allowances (known as business premises renovation allowances) are available for qualifying expenditure incurred by individuals and companies (whether as landlords or tenants) on the conversion or renovation of vacant business premises in designated development areas of the UK for the purpose of bringing those premises back into business use. The premises had to have been unused for at least one year before the date the work began. Certain trades are excluded. [*CAA 2001, ss 360A–360Z4; SI 2007 No 945, Reg 2A*].

Business premises renovation allowances are available to the person who incurred the qualifying expenditure and has the 'relevant interest' (see below) in the qualifying building. [*CAA 2001, s 360A(2)*].

See the 2019/20 and earlier editions of this work for the meaning of 'qualifying expenditure' and 'qualifying building'.

Relevant interest

In its simplest form, the '*relevant interest*' is the interest (freehold or leasehold) in the qualifying building to which the person incurring the qualifying expenditure was entitled when it was incurred. If there is more than one such interest, and one was reversionary on all the others, the reversionary interest is the relevant interest. The creation of a subordinate interest (e.g. leasehold out of freehold) does not transfer the relevant interest. An interest arising on, or as a result of completion of, construction is treated as having been held when the expenditure was incurred. If a leasehold relevant interest is extinguished by surrender, or by the person entitled to it acquiring the interest reversionary on it, the interest into which it merges becomes the relevant interest. [*CAA 2001, ss 360E, 360F*].

Leases

'*Lease*' is defined (as are related expressions accordingly), and in particular includes an agreement for a lease whose term has begun and a tenancy. [*CAA 2001, s 360Z4*].

Termination of leases

The following apply if a lease is terminated

- Where a lease ends and the lessee, with the lessor's consent, remains in possession without a new lease being granted, the lease is treated as continuing.
- A new lease granted on the termination of an old lease on exercise of an option available under the old lease is treated as a continuation of the old lease.
- If on termination of a lease the lessor pays any sum to the lessee in respect of a building comprised in the lease, the lease is treated as surrendered in consideration of the payment.
- If, on the termination of a lease, a lessee who is granted a new lease makes a payment to the lessee under the old lease, the two leases are treated as the same lease, the old lessee having assigned it to the new lessee for payment.

[*CAA 2001, s 360Z3*].

Providing of State aid information

A claim for business premises renovation allowances must include any information required by HMRC for the purpose of complying with certain EU State aid obligations. This may include information about the claimant (or his activities), information about the subject matter of the claim and other information relating to the grant of State aid through the provision of the allowances. See **36.5** HMRC — CONFIDENTIALITY OF INFORMATION as regards the publishing by HMRC of State aid information. [*FA 2016, s 180(1)–(4)(10), Sch 24 Pt 1*].

Simon's Taxes. See **B3.11**.

Allowances and charges

[9.4] Allowances and charges under the business premises renovation allowances regime for expenditure incurred before 6 April 2017 arise as follows.

Initial allowance

The initial allowance is 100% of the qualifying expenditure, may be claimed in whole or in part, and is made for the chargeable period (see **9.2**(i) above) in which the expenditure is incurred. The initial allowance is not available if the qualifying building is not qualifying business premises at the 'relevant time'; any initial allowance already made is withdrawn in such circumstances, and is also withdrawn if the person to whom the allowance was made has sold the relevant interest before the 'relevant time'. The '*relevant time*' is the time the premises are first used by the person with the relevant interest or, if not so used, are first suitable for letting for qualifying purposes. [*CAA 2001, ss 360G, 360H*].

Writing-down allowances

Writing-down allowances (WDAs) are available where the expenditure has not been wholly relieved by an initial allowance. The annual WDA is 25% of the qualifying expenditure, on a straight line basis, proportionately reduced or increased if the chargeable period is less or more than a year, and may be claimed in whole or in part. The WDA cannot exceed the residue, i.e. the unrelieved balance, of the qualifying expenditure. The person who incurred the expenditure is entitled to a WDA for a chargeable period if *at the end of that period*:

- he is entitled to the relevant interest (see **9.3** above) in the qualifying building;
- he has not granted, out of the relevant interest, a long lease (exceeding 50 years) of the qualifying building for a capital sum; and
- the qualifying building is qualifying business premises.

[*CAA 2001, ss 360I–360K, 360Q, 360R*].

Balancing allowances and charges

If a 'balancing event' occurs, a balancing adjustment, i.e. a balancing allowance or balancing charge, is made to or on the person who incurred the qualifying expenditure and for the chargeable period in which the event occurs. If more than one balancing event occurs, a balancing adjustment is made only on the first of them. **No balancing adjustment** is made in respect of a balancing event occurring more than five years after the time the premises were first used, or suitable for letting, for qualifying purposes. For expenditure incurred before 6 April 2014, the stipulated period is seven years rather than five. Any of the following is a '*balancing event*':

(i) the sale of the relevant interest (see **9.3** above) in the qualifying building;
(ii) the grant, out of the relevant interest, of a long lease (exceeding 50 years) of the qualifying building for a capital sum;
(iii) (where the relevant interest is a lease) the coming to an end of the lease otherwise than on the person entitled to it acquiring the reversionary interest;
(iv) the death of the person who incurred the qualifying expenditure;
(v) the demolition or destruction of the qualifying building;
(vi) the qualifying building's otherwise ceasing to be qualifying business premises.

The proceeds of a balancing event depend upon the nature of the event and are as follows.

(a) On a sale of the relevant interest, the net sale proceeds receivable by the person who incurred the qualifying expenditure.
(b) On the grant of a long lease, the capital sum involved or, if greater, the premium that would have been paid in an arm's length transaction.
(c) In an event within (iii) above, where the persons entitled to, respectively, the lease and the superior interest are CONNECTED PERSONS (**19**), the market value of the relevant interest in the qualifying building at the time of the event.
(d) On death, the residue (see below) of qualifying expenditure.
(e) On demolition or destruction, the net amount received for the remains by the person who incurred the qualifying expenditure, plus any insurance or capital compensation received by him.
(f) On the qualifying building's otherwise ceasing to be qualifying business premises, the market value of the relevant interest in the qualifying building at the time of the event.

If the residue, i.e. the unrelieved balance, of qualifying expenditure immediately before the event exceeds the proceeds of the event (including nil proceeds), a balancing allowance arises, equal to the excess. (This is subject to the anti-avoidance rule at **9.2**(xii) above.) If the proceeds exceed the residue (including a nil residue), a balancing charge arises, normally equal to the excess but limited to the total initial allowances and WDAs previously given to the person concerned in respect of the expenditure.

[*CAA 2001, ss 360M–360P*].

Note that, by virtue of *CAA 2001, s 572*, a surrender for valuable consideration of a leasehold interest is treated as a sale (for equivalent proceeds), and thus falls within (a) above (if not caught by (c) above).

Any proceeds of sale of the relevant interest or other proceeds of a balancing event are, if attributable to both, apportioned on a just and reasonable basis between assets representing qualifying expenditure and other assets, and only the first part taken into account as above. [*CAA 2001, s 360Z2*].

Demolition costs

Where a qualifying building is demolished, the net cost (after crediting any money received for remains) of demolition borne by the person who incurred the expenditure is added to the residue of qualifying expenditure immediately before the demolition, and is thus taken into account in computing the balancing adjustment; no amount included in gross demolition costs can then be included for any capital allowances purposes as expenditure on replacement property. [*CAA 2001, s 360S*].

Making of allowances and charges

[9.5] If the person entitled to business premises renovation allowances or liable to charges carries on a trade or occupies the qualifying building for the purposes of a trade, profession or vocation, the allowances/charges are treated as expenses/receipts of the trade, profession or vocation.

If the taxpayer's interest in the qualifying building is an asset of a property business (see **60.2** PROPERTY INCOME) carried on by him at any time in the chargeable period (see **9.2**(i) above) in question, allowances/charges under these provisions are treated as expenses/receipts of that business. If the above is not the case but his interest in the building is nevertheless subject to a lease or a licence, he is deemed to be carrying on a property business anyway, and allowances/charges given effect accordingly.

[*CAA 2001, ss 360Z, 360Z1*].

See **60.25** PROPERTY INCOME as regards relief for property business losses.

Example

[9.6]

Mickey is a jeweller who has been in business for many years and makes up accounts to 30 June each year. On 1 July 2016, he purchased the freehold of a building in the Speke ward in Liverpool. The building had been empty since June 2014, having been used before that time as a pawnbrokers. In the year ended 30 June 2017, but before 6 April 2017, Mickey incurred capital expenditure of £40,000 in renovating the building for use as his business premises. Mickey claimed a reduced business premises renovation initial allowance of 40% of the expenditure for the year ended 30 June 2017.

The renovation was completed on 1 August 2017, and Mickey started to use the building for the purposes of his trade on that date. In September 2019, he sells the freehold for £260,000. Of the net sale proceeds, £45,000 can be attributed to assets representing the renovation expenditure.

Mickey's allowances are as follows:

			Residue of expenditure
		£	£
2017/18	Qualifying expenditure		40,000
	Initial allowance (maximum 100%)	16,000	(16,000)
2018/19	Writing-down allowance (25% of £40,000)	10,000	(10,000)
2019/20	Writing-down allowance (25% of £40,000)	10,000	(10,000)
			4,000
2020/21	Writing-down allowance	—	—
	Sale proceeds		(45,000)
	Excess of sale proceeds over residue of expenditure		£41,000
	Balancing charge (restricted to allowances made, £16,000 + £10,000 + £10,000)		£36,000

Note

(a) No writing-down allowance is available for the year ended 30 June 2017 as the building is not in use for the purposes of the trade (and hence is not qualifying business premises) on 30 June 2017. It becomes qualifying business premises on 1 August 2017, so that a writing-down allowance is available for the year ended 30 June 2018. Mickey does not hold the relevant interest in the building on 30 June 2020, having sold it in September 2019, so no writing-down allowance is available for the year ended 30 June 2020.

Connected persons and other anti-avoidance

[9.7] Special provisions apply to sales of property where:

(a) the sale results in no change of control; or
(b) the sole or main benefit which might be expected is the obtaining of a capital allowance.

Paragraph (a) also covers sales between CONNECTED PERSONS (**19**), and (b) includes cases where the anticipated benefit is a reduction in a charge or the increase of an allowance. Where these provisions apply, market value is substituted for purchase price (if different), and this also applies to transfers other than by way of sale. [*CAA 2001, ss 567, 568, 570(1), 573, 575, 575A, 577(4); SI 2019 No 689, Reg 10(7)(8)*].

Effect of grants on entitlement to allowances

[9.8] No initial allowance or WDA is available to the extent that the qualifying expenditure if a 'relevant grant or payment' is made towards the expenditure or any 'related expenditure'. '*Related expenditure*' means any other expenditure incurred by any person in respect of the same qualifying building and on the same 'single investment project' as the qualifying expenditure. Any allowance already made is withdrawn if a relevant grant or payment is subsequently made towards the qualifying expenditure or if within the three years beginning when that expenditure was incurred, a relevant grant or payment is made towards any related expenditure. If a person who has made a return becomes aware that anything in it has become incorrect because of this rule, he must give notice to an officer of HMRC specifying how the return needs to be amended; the notice must be given within three months beginning with the day on which he first becomes aware of the inaccuracy.

A '*relevant grant or payment*' means an EU State aid or any other grant or subsidy nominated by Treasury order for this purpose. 'EU state aid' is not for this purpose limited to State aid required to be notified to and approved by the European Commission. '*Single investment project*' has the same meaning as in Commission Regulation (EU) No 651/2014 (General Block Exemption Regulation).

[*CAA 2001, s 360L*].

Additional VAT liabilities and rebates

[9.9] See 9.2(viii) above as regards these generally. The initial allowance is also available in respect of any additional VAT liability incurred at a time when the qualifying building is, or is about to be, qualifying business premises; the allowance is made for the chargeable period in which the liability accrues. For the purposes of writing down allowances, the residue of qualifying expenditure is treated as increased by the amount of an additional VAT liability at the time it accrues. The making of an additional VAT rebate is a balancing event, but it does not give rise to a balancing allowance and gives rise to a balancing charge only if it exceeds the residue (including a nil residue) of qualifying expenditure at the time the rebate accrues; otherwise the residue is treated as reduced by the amount of the rebate at the time it accrues. [*CAA 2001, ss 360T–360Y*].

Dredging allowances

[9.10] Writing-down and balancing allowances may be claimed for capital expenditure on **dredging** incurred for the purposes of a *qualifying trade* (provided that plant and machinery allowances (see **10** CAPITAL ALLOWANCES ON PLANT AND MACHINERY) are not available in respect of the same expenditure).

'*Dredging*' must be done in the interests of navigation, and either:

(a) the qualifying trade must consist of the maintenance or improvement of navigation of a harbour, estuary or waterway; or
(b) the dredging must be for the benefit of vessels coming to, leaving or using docks or other premises used in the qualifying trade.

It includes removal, by any means, of any part of, or projections from, any sea or inland water bed (whether then above water or not), and the widening of any inland waterway.

A '*qualifying trade*' is:

- a trade within (a) above; or
- a trade consisting of:
  - the manufacture, processing, maintaining or repairing of goods or materials; or
  - the storage of raw materials for manufacture, goods to be processed, goods manufactured or processed but not yet delivered to a purchaser, or (d) goods on arrival in the UK from a place outside the UK; or
  - agricultural contracting; or
  - the catching of fish or shellfish; or
  - the working of a source of mineral deposits; or
- an undertaking that is an electricity, water, hydraulic power, sewerage, transport, highway, tunnel, bridge, inland navigation or dock undertaking.

Expenditure only partly for a qualifying trade is apportioned as may be just and reasonable, and for this purpose, where part only of a trade qualifies, the qualifying and non-qualifying parts are treated as separate trades.

[*CAA 2001, ss 484, 485*].

Writing-down allowances

Writing-down allowances of 4% p.a. (although a lesser amount may be claimed) are given to the person for the time being carrying on the trade during a writing-down period of 25 years beginning with the first day of the chargeable period in which the expenditure was incurred, subject to an overall limit equal to the amount of the expenditure. No allowance is given for a chargeable period in which a balancing allowance arises (see below).

[*CAA 2001, ss 487, 489, Sch 3 para 103*].

Expenditure incurred for a trade before it is carried on attracts allowances as if it were incurred on the first day on which the trade was carried on. Similarly, expenditure incurred in connection with a dock etc. with a view to occupying it for the purposes of a qualifying trade other than one within (a) above attracts allowances as if it were incurred when the dock etc. is first so occupied. [*CAA 2001, s 486*].

Balancing allowances

A balancing allowance is given for the chargeable period of *permanent discontinuance* of the trade, equal to expenditure incurred less writing-down allowances given, to the person last carrying on the trade.

Permanent discontinuance includes sale of the business (unless it is a sale between CONNECTED PERSONS (**19**), or without change of control, or one the sole or main benefit of which appears to be a capital allowance advantage), but not deemed discontinuance under **75.17** TRADING INCOME.

[*CAA 2001, s 488, Sch 3 para 104*].

Contributions to expenditure

See **9.2**(vi)(vii) above.

Simon's Taxes. See B3.8.

Example

[9.11]

D is the proprietor of an estuary maintenance business preparing accounts to 30 June. Expenditure qualifying for dredging allowances is incurred as follows.

	£
Year ended 30.6.19	4,000
Year ended 30.6.20	5,000

On 2 January 2021, D sells the business to an unconnected third party.

The allowances available are:

Date of expenditure	Cost	Residue brought forward	Allowances WDA 4%	Residue carried forward
	£	£	£	£
2019/20 (year ended 30.6.19)				
2019	4,000		160	£3,840
2020/21				
Year ended 30.6.20				
2019	4,000	3,840	160	3,680
2020	5,000		200	4,800
			£360	£8,480
Six months ending 2.1.21				
Balancing allowance			£8,480	
Total allowances 2020/21 (360 + 8,480)			£8,840	

Enterprise zone building allowances

[9.12] Advantageous provisions applied before 6 April 2011 to expenditure on the construction of an 'industrial building', 'qualifying hotel' or 'commercial building', which was incurred (or contracted for) within ten years of the inclusion of the site in a designated enterprise zone. An initial allowance of 100% was available on the expenditure. If any part of the initial allowance was not claimed, then writing-down allowances at 25% p.a. of cost on the straight line basis were given on the unclaimed balance. [*CAA 2001, ss 306(1)(2), 310(1)(a)*]. For full coverage of enterprise zone allowances, see HMRC Capital Allowances Manual CA37000–37760.

Despite the abolition of enterprise zone allowances with effect on and after 6 April 2011, a balancing charge can still arise in a chargeable period (see **9.2**(i) above) beginning on or after that date on the disposal of a building on which enterprise zone allowances had been claimed. This will be the case if an event occurs within seven years after the building is first used, and the event is such that, disregarding the abolition, it would have been a balancing event giving rise to a balancing charge. Similarly, if an initial allowance falls to be withdrawn by virtue of *CAA 2001, s 307*, it will be withdrawn notwithstanding the abolition, but only if the event giving rise to the withdrawal occurs within seven years after the end of the chargeable period for which the initial allowance was made. See further below.

Withdrawal of an initial allowance

An initial allowance which has been made in respect of a building which is to be a qualifying building is withdrawn if, when the building is first used, it is not a qualifying building. An initial allowance which has been made in respect of a building which has not yet been used is withdrawn if the person to whom it was made sells his interest in the building prior to first use. [*CAA 2001, s 307*]. Notwithstanding the abolition of enterprise zone allowances, there will be a withdrawal under these rules if, within seven years after the end of the chargeable period for which the initial allowance was made, an event occurs which, if *CAA 2001, s 307* remained in force, would result in that allowance being withdrawn. [*FA 2008, Sch 27 paras 32, 35*].

Balancing charges

Notwithstanding the abolition of enterprise zone allowances, a balancing charge arises if a balancing event occurs on or after 6 April 2011 and within seven years after the building is first used. [*FA 2008, Sch 27 paras 31, 35*].

The amount of a balancing charge is the excess (if any) of the proceeds of the balancing event over the amount of unrelieved qualifying expenditure on the building immediately before the event. However, the amount of a balancing charge made on any person cannot exceed the aggregate amount of enterprise zone allowances made to that person in respect of the building. A balancing event occurs when a building is sold or is destroyed or is permanently put out of use or when the person's interest in the building is lost on the termination of a lease or foreign concession. The proceeds of a balancing event are the net proceeds of sale or any insurance, salvage or compensation monies received as a result of the event. [*CAA 2001, ss 314–316, 320*].

A balancing event can also occur upon the receipt of capital value attributable to a subordinate interest in the building. This is to prevent taxpayers avoiding a balancing charge by disposing of the commercial substance of their interest in the building while retaining the interest itself. It normally applies only where the payment of capital value is made (or an agreement to make it is made) seven years or less after the making of the agreement under which the qualifying expenditure was incurred (or, if that agreement was conditional, seven years or less after it became unconditional); however, this restriction does not have effect in certain cases involving guaranteed exit arrangements. [*CAA 2001, ss 327–331, Sch 3 para 71*]. For details, see HMRC Capital Allowances Manual CA37700.

For those carrying on trades, professions or vocations, a balancing charge is given effect as a receipt in calculating profits. [*CAA 2001, s 352*]. The timing of the charge is by reference to events occurring in a period of account (see **9.2**(i) above). As regards lessors and licensors, a balancing charge is treated as a receipt of a UK property business (see **60.2** PROPERTY INCOME) or, if the lease or licence is an asset of an overseas property business (see **60.2** PROPERTY INCOME), as a receipt of that business. Where the building is not an asset of any property business, the charge is treated as a receipt of a notional UK property business. [*CAA 2001, s 353*]. The timing of the charge is by reference to events occurring in a tax year.

Simon's Taxes. See **B3.261–B3.265**.

Flat conversion allowances (abolished)

[9.13] Flat conversion allowances were abolished with effect for expenditure incurred on or after 6 April 2013. Writing-down allowances on earlier expenditure also ceased to be available for chargeable periods (as in **9.2**(i) above) beginning on or after 6 April 2013. However, notwithstanding the abolition of flat conversion allowances, balancing adjustments continue to apply for chargeable periods beginning on or after 6 April 2013 in relation to expenditure incurred before that date.

Balancing adjustments

If a 'balancing event' occurs, a balancing adjustment, i.e. a balancing allowance or balancing charge, is made to or on the person who incurred the qualifying expenditure and for the chargeable period in which the event occurs. If more than one balancing event occurs, a balancing adjustment is made only on the first of them. No balancing adjustment is made in respect of a balancing event occurring **more than seven years** after the time the flat was first suitable for letting as a dwelling. Any of the following is a '*balancing event*':

(i) the sale of the 'relevant interest' (see below) in the flat;
(ii) the grant, out of the relevant interest, of a long lease (exceeding 50 years) of the flat for a capital sum;
(iii) (where the relevant interest is a lease) the coming to an end of the lease otherwise than on the person entitled to it acquiring the reversionary interest;
(iv) the death of the person who incurred the qualifying expenditure;
(v) the demolition or destruction of the flat;
(vi) the flat's otherwise ceasing to be a qualifying flat.

The proceeds of a balancing event depend upon the nature of the event and are as follows.

(1) On a sale of the relevant interest, the net sale proceeds receivable by the person who incurred the qualifying expenditure.
(2) On the grant of a long lease, the capital sum involved or, if greater, the premium that would have been paid in an arm's length transaction.
(3) In an event within (iii) above, where the persons entitled to, respectively, the lease and the superior interest are CONNECTED PERSONS (**19**), the market value of the relevant interest in the flat at the time of the event.
(4) On death, the residue (see below) of qualifying expenditure.
(5) On demolition or destruction, the net amount received for the remains by the person who incurred the qualifying expenditure, plus any insurance or capital compensation received by him.
(6) On the flat's otherwise ceasing to be a qualifying flat, the market value of the relevant interest in the flat at the time of the event.

If the residue, i.e. the unrelieved balance, of qualifying expenditure immediately before the event exceeds the proceeds of the event (including nil proceeds), a balancing allowance arises, equal to the excess. (This is subject to the anti-avoidance rule at **9.2**(xii) above.) If the proceeds exceed the residue (including a nil residue), a balancing charge arises, normally equal to the excess but limited to the total initial and writing-down allowances previously given to the person concerned in respect of the expenditure.

[*CAA 2001, ss 393M–393P*].

Note that, by virtue of *CAA 2001, s 572*, a surrender for valuable consideration of a leasehold interest is treated as a sale (for equivalent proceeds), and thus falls within (1) above (if not caught by (3) above).

Any proceeds of sale of the relevant interest or other proceeds of a balancing event are, if attributable to both, apportioned on a just and reasonable basis between assets representing qualifying expenditure and other assets, and only the first part taken into account as above. [*CAA 2001, s 393U*].

The '*relevant interest*' is determined in similar manner, with appropriate modifications, as for business renovation allowances (see **9.3** above). In its simplest form, the relevant interest is the interest in the flat to which the person who incurred the expenditure was entitled when it was incurred. [*CAA 2001, ss 393F, 393G*]. As regards termination of leases, provisions similar to those in **9.3** above apply. [*CAA 2001, s 393V*]. '*Lease*' is defined (as are related expressions accordingly), and in particular includes an agreement for a lease whose term has begun and a tenancy. [*CAA 2001, s 393W*].

Demolition costs

Where a qualifying flat is demolished, the net cost (after crediting any money received for remains) of demolition borne by the person who incurred the expenditure is added to the residue of qualifying expenditure immediately before the demolition, and is thus taken into account in computing the balancing adjustment; no amount included in gross demolition costs can then attract capital allowances of any kind. [*CAA 2001, s 393S*].

Making of allowances and charges

If the taxpayer's interest in the flat is an asset of a UK property business (see **60.2** PROPERTY INCOME) carried on by him at any time in the chargeable period (see **9.2**(i) above) in question, allowances/charges under these provisions are treated as expenses/receipts of that business. If the above is not the case, he is deemed to be carrying on a UK property business anyway, and allowances/charges given effect accordingly. [*CAA 2001, s 393T*]. See **60.25** PROPERTY INCOME as regards relief for property business losses.

Simon's Taxes. See B3.10.

Know-how allowances

[9.14] Expenditure on acquiring 'know-how' (so far as not otherwise deductible for income tax purposes) gives rise to writing-down and balancing allowances (and balancing charges) where the person acquiring it either:

(i) is then carrying on a trade for use in which it is acquired; or
(ii) subsequently commences such a trade (in which case the expenditure is treated as incurred on commencement); or

(iii) acquires it with a trade (or part) in which it was used, and either the parties to the acquisition make the appropriate joint election under *ITTOIA 2005, s 194* (see **75.95** TRADING INCOME), or corporation tax equivalent, or the trade was carried on wholly outside the UK before the acquisition.

The same expenditure may not be taken into account in relation to more than one trade.

Expenditure is, however, *excluded* where the buyer and seller are bodies of persons (which includes partnerships) under common control.

[*CAA 2001, ss 452(1), 454, 455*].

'*Know-how*' means any industrial information and techniques of assistance in (a) manufacturing or processing goods or materials, (b) working, or searching etc. for, mineral deposits, or (c) agricultural, forestry or fishing operations. [*CAA 2001, s 452(2)(3)*]. For expenditure on offshore divers' training courses treated as on know-how, see HMRC Capital Allowances Manual CA74000.

All qualifying expenditure of a trade is pooled, and:

(1) if the 'available qualifying expenditure' exceeds the 'total disposal value', a writing-down allowance is available of **25%** of the excess, proportionately reduced or increased where the period is less or more than one year, or if the trade has been carried on for part only of a chargeable period (and subject to any lesser amount being claimed), *except that* if the chargeable period is that of permanent discontinuance of the trade, a balancing allowance of **100%** of the excess is available;
(2) if the 'total disposal value' exceeds the 'available qualifying expenditure', a balancing charge arises of **100%** of the excess.

'*Available qualifying expenditure*' in a pool for a chargeable period consists of qualifying expenditure allocated to the pool for that period and any unrelieved qualifying expenditure brought forward in the pool from the previous chargeable period (usually referred to as the written-down value brought forward). In allocating qualifying expenditure to the pool, rules identical to those for patent rights at **9.26**(i) and (ii) below must be observed.

The '*total disposal value*' is the aggregate of any disposal values to be brought into account for the period, i.e. the net sale proceeds (being capital sums) from any disposal of know-how on which qualifying expenditure was incurred (but excluding any sale the consideration for which is treated as a payment for goodwill under *ITTOIA 2005, s 194(2)* (see **75.95** TRADING INCOME) or corporation tax equivalent).

The allowances and charges are given effect as deductions or receipts of the relevant trade.

[*CAA 2001, ss 456–461, 462, 463*].

For 2017/18 onwards, the plant and machinery allowances rules for persons entering and leaving the cash basis (see respectively **10.26** and **10.35** CAPITAL ALLOWANCES ON PLANT AND MACHINERY), insofar as they relate to trades, apply also (with appropriate modifications) for the purposes of know-how allowances. [*CAA 2001, ss 461A, 462A; F(No 2)A 2017, Sch 2 paras 56, 57*].

For receipts arising from sales of know-how, see also **75.95** TRADING INCOME.

Simon's Taxes. See **B3.615, B3.616.**

Mineral extraction allowances

[9.15] Mineral extraction allowances are available in respect of qualifying expenditure (see **9.16** below) incurred by a person carrying on a 'mineral extraction trade'.

A '*mineral extraction trade*' is a trade consisting of or including the working of a source of 'mineral deposits'. This applies to the extent only that the profits of the trade are within the charge to UK tax. '*Mineral deposits*' means deposits of a wasting nature, and includes any natural deposits or geothermal energy capable of being lifted or extracted from the earth. A '*source of mineral deposits*' includes a mine, an oil well and a source of geothermal energy.

[*CAA 2001, s 394*].

A *share* in an asset may qualify for mineral extraction allowances. [*CAA 2001, s 435*].

Simon's Taxes. See **B3.4.**

Qualifying expenditure

[9.16] '*Qualifying expenditure*' means capital expenditure, incurred for the purposes of a mineral extraction trade, on:

(a) '*mineral exploration and access*' (i.e. searching for or discovering and testing the mineral deposits of any source, or winning access to any such deposits);
(b) acquisition of a '*mineral asset*' (i.e. any mineral deposits or land comprising mineral deposits, or any interest in or right over such deposits or land) (subject to the limitations in **9.17** below);
(c) construction of works, in connection with the working of a source of mineral deposits, which are likely to become of little or no value when the source ceases to be worked;
(d) construction of works which are likely to become valueless when a foreign concession under which a source of mineral deposits is worked comes to an end;
(e) net expenditure incurred on the restoration of the site of a source of mineral deposits (or land used in connection with working such a source) within three years after the cessation of the trade, unless relieved elsewhere. In this case, the expenditure is treated as incurred on the last day of trading.

Expenditure on the acquisition of, or of rights over, mineral deposits or the site of a source of mineral deposits falls into (b) rather than (a) above. Expenditure (including appeal costs) incurred on or after 17 July 2014 on seeking such planning permission for the undertaking of mineral exploration and access or the working of mineral deposits falls into (a) rather than (b), whether permission is granted or not. Expenditure incurred before that date on seeking such planning permission fell into (a) above only if permission was not granted.

However, the following are *not* qualifying expenditure:

- expenditure on the provision of plant or machinery (except certain pre-trading expenditure — see below), and see **9.24** below;
- expenditure incurred by a person for the purposes of a mineral extraction trade if, at the time the expenditure is incurred, either the person is carrying on the trade but it is not a mineral extraction trade (and see the definition at **9.15** above) or the person is not yet carrying on the trade but when he begins to do so it is not a mineral extraction trade;
- expenditure on acquisition of, or of rights in or over, the *site* of any works in (c) or (d) above;
- expenditure on works constructed wholly or mainly for processing the raw products, unless the process is designed to prepare the raw products for use as such;
- (subject to *CAA 2001, s 415* — see below) expenditure on buildings and structures for occupation by, or welfare of, workers;
- expenditure on a building constructed *entirely* for use as an office; and
- expenditure on the office part of a building or structure constructed *partly* for use as an office, where such expenditure exceeds 10% of the capital expenditure on construction of the whole building.

[*CAA 2001, ss 395–399, 400(1), 403(1)(2)(2A), 414, 416*].

Qualifying expenditure also includes capital contributions, for the purposes of a mineral extraction trade carried on outside the UK, to the cost of accommodation buildings, and certain related utility buildings and welfare works, for employees engaged in working a source, provided that the buildings or works are likely to be of little or no value when the source ceases to be worked, that the expenditure does not result in the acquisition of an asset, and that relief is not due under any other tax provision. [*CAA 2001, s 415*].

Pre-trading expenditure

Pre-trading expenditure for the purposes of a mineral extraction trade is treated as incurred on the first day of trading. This applies equally to pre-trading expenditure on mineral exploration and access, but in determining whether such expenditure is qualifying expenditure within (a) above, the following limitations apply.

(i) In the case of pre-trading expenditure on plant or machinery which is used at a source but is sold, demolished, destroyed or abandoned before commencement of the mineral extraction trade, qualifying expenditure is limited to net expenditure after taking account of sale proceeds, insurance money or capital compensation.

(ii) In the case of pre-trading exploration expenditure other than on plant or machinery, qualifying expenditure is limited to net expenditure after taking into account any reasonably attributable capital sums received before the first day of trading.

In either case, if mineral exploration and access is not continuing at the source on the first day of trading, qualifying expenditure is further limited to net expenditure incurred in the six years ending on that day.

[*CAA 2001, ss 400(2)–(5), 401, 402, 434*].

Simon's Taxes. See **B3.405–B3.410.**

Limitations on qualifying expenditure

[9.17] Qualifying expenditure within **9.16**(b) above (acquisition of mineral asset) is limited in the following circumstances.

If the mineral asset is an interest in land, an amount equal to the 'undeveloped market value' of the interest is excluded. '*Undeveloped market value*' is the market value of the interest at the time of acquisition ignoring the mineral deposits and assuming that development of the land (other than that already lawfully begun or for which planning permission has already been granted) is, and will remain, unlawful. Where the undeveloped market value includes the value of buildings or structures which, at any time after acquisition, permanently cease to be used, their value at acquisition (exclusive of land and after deducting any net capital allowances received in respect of them) is treated as qualifying expenditure incurred at the time of cessation of use. These provisions operate by reference to the actual time of acquisition, regardless of any different time given by the pre-trading expenditure provisions at **9.16** above. They do not apply where an election is made under *CAA 2001, s 569* (election to treat connected persons transactions as made at written-down value). [*CAA 2001, ss 403(3), 404, 405, Sch 3 para 84*].

Where a deduction has been allowed under *ITTOIA 2005, ss 60–67* in respect of a premium under a lease (see **75.108** TRADING INCOME), the qualifying expenditure allowable in respect of the acquisition of the interest in land to which the premium relates is correspondingly reduced. [*CAA 2001, s 406*].

Simon's Taxes. See **B3.410.**

Second-hand assets

[9.18] Where:

(a) an asset is acquired from another person; and
(b) either that person or any previous owner incurred expenditure on it in connection with a mineral extraction trade,

the buyer's qualifying expenditure is restricted to the seller's qualifying expenditure on the asset less net allowances given to him. If an oil licence (or an interest therein) is acquired, the buyer's qualifying expenditure is limited to the amount of the original licence fee paid (or such part of it as it is just and reasonable to attribute to the interest). However, these restrictions do not affect amounts treated under rules below as qualifying expenditure on mineral exploration and access.

Where:

(i) the purchased asset above is a mineral asset; and
(ii) part of its value is properly attributable to expenditure on mineral exploration and access incurred as in (b) above,

so much if any of the buyer's expenditure as it is just and reasonable to attribute to the part of the value in (ii) above (not exceeding the amount of original expenditure to which it is attributable) is treated as qualifying expenditure on mineral exploration and access, with the remainder treated as expenditure on acquisition of a mineral asset. Expenditure deducted by a previous owner in computing taxable profits is excluded for these purposes from the original expenditure.

Where:

- capital expenditure is incurred in acquiring assets for a mineral extraction trade from a person (the seller) who did *not* carry on a mineral extraction trade; and
- the assets represent expenditure on mineral exploration and access incurred by the seller,

the buyer's qualifying expenditure is limited to the amount of the seller's expenditure. Assets include any results obtained from any search, exploration or inquiry on which the expenditure was incurred. This restriction does not apply if the asset is an interest in an oil licence acquired by the buyer; in this case, so much if any of the buyer's expenditure as it is just and reasonable to attribute to the part of the value of the licence attributable to the seller's expenditure (but limited to the amount of that expenditure) is treated as qualifying expenditure on mineral exploration and access, with the cost of the oil licence being reduced by the buyer's expenditure so attributable (without limitation).

[*CAA 2001, ss 407–409, 411, Sch 3 paras 85–87*].

Simon's Taxes. See **B3.411, B3.412.**

Writing-down allowances and balancing adjustments

[9.19] For each item of qualifying expenditure (see **9.16** above), a **writing-down allowance (WDA)** is available for each chargeable period (see **9.2**(i) above) and is equal to a set percentage (as below) of the amount (if any) by which 'unrelieved qualifying expenditure' exceeds the total of any disposal values falling to be brought into account as in **9.20** below. The WDA is proportionately reduced or increased if the chargeable period is less or more than a year, or if the mineral extraction trade has been carried on for part only of the chargeable period.

In the circumstances listed at **9.21** below, a **balancing allowance** is available, instead of a WDA, equal to the excess (if any) of (1) 'unrelieved qualifying expenditure' over (2) total disposal values. (This is subject to the anti-avoidance rule at **9.2**(xii) above.) If, for any chargeable period, (2) exceeds (1), there arises a liability to a **balancing charge**, normally equal to that excess but limited to net allowances previously given. A claim for a WDA *or* a balancing allowance may require it to be reduced to a specified amount.

Rates of WDA are as follows:

Acquisition of a mineral asset (see **9.16**(b) above)	10% p.a.

Other qualifying expenditure	25% p.a.

'*Unrelieved qualifying expenditure*' means qualifying expenditure (other than first-year qualifying expenditure) incurred in the chargeable period and the tax written-down value brought forward (i.e. net of allowances and any disposal values) of qualifying expenditure (including first-year qualifying expenditure) incurred in a previous chargeable period.

[*CAA 2001, ss 417–419*].

The net demolition costs (i.e. the excess, if any, of demolition costs over money received for remains) of an asset representing qualifying expenditure is added to that expenditure in determining the amount of any balancing allowance or charge for the chargeable period of demolition, and is not then treated as expenditure incurred on any replacement asset. [*CAA 2001, s 433*].

There is no provision for pooling expenditure (in contrast to plant and machinery at **10.26** CAPITAL ALLOWANCES ON PLANT AND MACHINERY). In practice, HMRC do not object to the grouping together of assets for computational convenience, provided individual sources are kept separate and assets attracting different rates of WDA are not grouped with each other. However, where a disposal value falls to be brought into account or a balancing allowance arises, it will sometimes be necessary to reconstruct separate computations for individual items of expenditure previously grouped. (HMRC Capital Allowances Manual CA50410).

For 2017/18 onwards, the plant and machinery allowances rules for persons entering and leaving the cash basis (see respectively **10.26** and **10.35** CAPITAL ALLOWANCES ON PLANT AND MACHINERY), insofar as they relate to trades, are also applied (with appropriate modifications) to mineral extraction allowances. This would appear to be of academic interest as mineral extraction trades are currently excluded trades for cash basis purposes (see **76.3** TRADING INCOME — CASH BASIS FOR SMALLER BUSINESSES). [*CAA 2001, ss 419A, 431D; F(No 2)A 2017, Sch 2 paras 54, 55*].

Simon's Taxes. See **B3.419–B3.422.**

Disposal events and values

[9.20] A disposal value must be brought into account (by deduction from unrelieved qualifying expenditure — see **9.19** above), for the chargeable period in which the event occurs, on the occurrence of any of the following events.

(i) An asset representing qualifying expenditure (see **9.16** above) is disposed of or permanently ceases to be used for the purposes of a mineral extraction trade (whether because of cessation of trade or otherwise).

(ii) A mineral asset begins to be used (by the trader or another person) in a way which constitutes development which is neither 'existing permitted development' nor development for the purposes of a mineral extraction trade. Development is '*existing permitted development*' if, at the time of acquisition, it had already lawfully begun or the appropriate planning permission had already been granted.

(iii) In a case not within (i) or (ii) above, a capital sum is received which, in whole or in part, it is reasonable to attribute to qualifying expenditure.

The amount to be brought into account depends upon the nature of the event.

(a) On an event within (i) or (ii) above, it is an amount determined in accordance with the list at **10.27**(a)–(g) CAPITAL ALLOWANCES ON PLANT AND MACHINERY (disregarding (f), the reference to abandonment at (d) and the text immediately following the list). However, if the asset is an interest in land, the amount so ascertained is then restricted by excluding the '*undeveloped market value*', determined as in **9.17** above but by reference to the time of disposal.
(b) On an event within (iii) above, it is so much of the capital sum as is reasonably attributable to the qualifying expenditure.

[*CAA 2001, ss 420–425*].

Simon's Taxes. See **B3.420**.

Balancing allowances

[9.21] A person is entitled to a balancing allowance (instead of a writing-down allowance) for a chargeable period if:

- the chargeable period is that in which the first day of trading falls, and either the qualifying expenditure is pre-trading expenditure on plant or machinery within **9.16**(i) above or it is pre-trading exploration expenditure within **9.16**(ii) above where mineral exploration and access is not continuing at the source on the first day of trading; or
- the qualifying expenditure was on mineral exploration and access, and in that chargeable period he gives up the exploration, search or inquiry to which the expenditure related, without subsequently carrying on a mineral extraction trade consisting of or including the working of related mineral deposits; or
- in that chargeable period he permanently ceases to work particular mineral deposits, and the qualifying expenditure was on mineral exploration and access relating solely to those deposits or on the acquisition of a mineral asset consisting of those deposits or part of them; but where two or more mineral assets are comprised in, or derive from, a single asset, the above applies only when *all* the relevant mineral deposits cease to be worked; or
- the qualifying expenditure falls within *CAA 2001, s 415* (capital contributions to certain buildings or works for benefit of employees abroad — see **9.16** above), and in that chargeable period, the buildings or works permanently cease to be used for the purposes of or in connection with the mineral extraction trade; or
- the qualifying expenditure was on the provision of any assets, and in that chargeable period any of those assets is disposed of or otherwise permanently ceases to be used for purposes of the trade; or
- the qualifying expenditure is represented by assets, and in that chargeable period those assets are permanently lost or cease to exist (due to destruction, dismantling or otherwise) or begin to be used wholly or partly for purposes other than those of the mineral extraction trade; or

- the mineral extraction trade is permanently discontinued in that chargeable period.

[*CAA 2001, ss 426–431*].

Simon's Taxes. See **B3.421**.

Making of allowances and charges

[9.22] Mineral extraction allowances (or balancing charges) are given (or made) as trading expenses (or trading receipts) in calculating the profits of the mineral extraction trade. [*CAA 2001, s 432*].

Simon's Taxes. See **B3.423**.

Connected persons and other anti-avoidance

[9.23] Special provisions apply to sales of property where:

(a) the sale results in no change of control; or
(b) the sole or main benefit which might be expected is the obtaining of a capital allowance.

Paragraph (a) also covers sales between CONNECTED PERSONS (**19**), and (b) includes cases where the anticipated benefit is a reduction in a charge or the increase of an allowance. Normally, where these provisions apply, market value is substituted for purchase price (if different), and this also applies to transfers other than by way of sale. However, provided that (b) above does not apply, for sales within (a) above and other transfers the parties may elect for the substitution of the unrelieved qualifying expenditure (see **9.19** above) immediately before the sale if this is lower than market value, and for any subsequent balancing charge on the buyer to be calculated by reference to allowances etc. of both buyer and seller. Such an election is *not* available if the circumstances are such that an allowance or charge which otherwise would or might fall, in consequence of the sale, to be made to or on *any* of the parties to the sale cannot fall to be made. The election must be made within two years after the sale.

[*CAA 2001, ss 567–570, 573, 575, 575A, 577(4); SI 2019 No 689, Reg 10(7)(8)*].

Plant and machinery allowances

[9.24] Plant and machinery is normally excluded from relief under the current provisions, but certain pre-trading expenditure may qualify (see **9.16** above). The normal plant and machinery rules (see **10** CAPITAL ALLOWANCES ON PLANT AND MACHINERY) apply to plant and machinery provided for mineral exploration and access in connection with a mineral extraction trade. However, expenditure is not treated as incurred by a person for the purposes of a mineral extraction trade if, at the time the expenditure is incurred, either the person is carrying on the trade but it is not a mineral extraction trade (and see the definition at **9.15** above) or the person is not yet carrying on the trade but when he begins to do so it is not a mineral extraction trade. [*CAA 2001, ss 159, 160*].

Where expenditure is incurred prior to the date of commencement of a mineral extraction trade and the plant or machinery is still owned at that date, it is treated as if sold immediately before that date and re-acquired on that date. The capital expenditure on re-acquisition is deemed to be equal to the actual expenditure previously incurred. This does not apply if there was a prior time when the person carried on the trade and it was not at that time a mineral extraction trade (and see the definition at **9.15** above). [*CAA 2001, s 161, Sch 3 para 25*].

Example

[9.25]

X has for some years operated a mining business with two mineral sources, G and S. Accounts are prepared to 30 September. On 31 December 2019, the mineral deposits and mineworks at G are sold at market value to Z for £80,000 and £175,000 respectively. A new source, P, is purchased on 30 April 2020 for £170,000 (including land with an undeveloped market value of £70,000) and the following expenditure incurred before the end of the period of account ended on 30 September 2020.

	£
Plant and machinery	40,000
Construction of administration office	25,000
Construction of mining works which are likely to have little value when mining ceases	50,000
Staff hostel	35,000
Winning access to the deposits	150,000
	£300,000

During the year to 30 September 2020, X also incurred expenditure of £20,000 in seeking planning permission to mine a further plot of land, Source Q. Permission was refused.

Residue of expenditure brought forward (based on accounts to 30 September 2019)		£
Mineral exploration and access	– Source G	170,000
	– Source S	200,000
Mineral assets	– Source G	95,250
	– Source S	72,000

The mineral extraction allowances due for the year ending 30 September 2020 are as follows.

Source G	£	£
Mineral exploration and access		
WDV b/f	170,000	
Proceeds	175,000	
Balancing charge	£5,000	(5,000)

Mineral assets			
WDV b/f		95,250	
Proceeds		80,000	
Balancing allowance		£15,250	15,250
Source S			
Mineral exploration and access			
WDV b/f		200,000	
WDA 25%		(50,000)	50,000
WDV c/f		£150,000	
Mineral assets			
WDV b/f		72,000	
WDA 10%		(7,200)	7,200
WDV c/f		£64,800	
Source P			
Mineral exploration and access			
Expenditure		150,000	
WDA 25%		(37,500)	37,500
WDV c/f		£112,500	
Mineral assets			
Expenditure	note (c)	100,000	
WDA 10%		(10,000)	10,000
WDV c/f		£90,000	
Mining works			
Expenditure		50,000	
WDA 25%		(12,500)	12,500
WDV c/f		£37,500	
Source Q			
Mineral exploration and access			
Expenditure	note (b)	20,000	
WDA 25%		(5,000)	5,000
WDV c/f		£15,000	
Total allowances (net of charges)			£132,450

Notes

(a) Allowances are not due on either the office or staff hostel. The plant and machinery qualify for plant and machinery allowances (see **10** CAPITAL ALLOWANCES ON PLANT AND MACHINERY) rather than for mineral extraction allowances (see **9.24** above).

(b) Abortive expenditure on seeking planning permission is qualifying expenditure as if it were expenditure on mineral exploration and access (see **9.16** above).

(c) The undeveloped market value of land is excluded from qualifying expenditure (see **9.17** above).

Patent right allowances

[9.26] Allowances are available, and balancing charges made, in respect of 'qualifying expenditure' on the purchase of patent rights, i.e. the right to do or authorise the doing of anything which would, but for that right, be a patent infringement. The obtaining of a right to acquire future patent rights and the acquisition of a licence in respect of a patent are each treated for these purposes as a purchase of patent rights. '*Qualifying expenditure*' may be either:

- '*qualifying trade expenditure*', i.e. capital expenditure incurred by a person on purchase of patent rights for the purposes of a trade carried on by him and within the charge to UK tax; or
- '*qualifying non-trade expenditure*', i.e. capital expenditure incurred by a person on purchase of patent rights if the above does not apply but any income receivable by him in respect of the rights would be liable to tax.

Expenditure incurred by a person for the purposes of a trade he is about to carry on is treated as if incurred on the first day of trading, unless all the rights in question have been sold before then. The same expenditure cannot be qualifying trade expenditure in relation to more than one trade.

The grant of a licence in respect of a patent is treated as a sale of part of patent rights. The grant by a person entitled to patent rights of an exclusive licence, i.e. a licence to exercise the rights to the exclusion of the grantor and all others for the remainder of their term, is, however, treated as a sale of the whole of those rights.

[*CAA 2001, ss 464–469*].

Qualifying expenditure is pooled for the purpose of determining entitlement to writing-down allowances and balancing allowances and liability to balancing charges. A separate pool applies for each separate trade and for all qualifying non-trade expenditure.

For each pool of qualifying expenditure, a **writing-down allowance (WDA)** is available for each chargeable period (see **9.2**(i) above) other than the 'final chargeable period' and is equal to a maximum of **25%** of the amount (if any) by which 'available qualifying expenditure' exceeds the total of any disposal values falling to be brought into account. The WDA is proportionately reduced or increased if the chargeable period is less or more than a year, or if (where relevant) the trade has been carried on for part only of the chargeable period. A claim for a WDA may require it to be reduced to a specified amount. For the 'final chargeable period', a **balancing allowance** is available, equal to the excess (if any) of (1) 'available qualifying expenditure' over (2) total disposal values. If, for *any* chargeable period, (2) exceeds (1), there arises a liability to a **balancing charge**, equal to that excess.

The '*final chargeable period*', as regards a pool of qualifying trade expenditure, is the chargeable period in which the trade is permanently discontinued. As regards a pool of non-qualifying trade expenditure, it is the chargeable period in which the last of the patent rights in question either comes to an end (without any such rights being revived) or is wholly disposed of.

'*Available qualifying expenditure*' in a pool for a chargeable period consists of qualifying expenditure allocated to the pool for that period and any unrelieved qualifying expenditure brought forward in the pool from the previous chargeable period (usually referred to as the written-down value brought forward).

In allocating qualifying expenditure to a pool, the following must be observed.

(i) Qualifying expenditure can be allocated to a pool for a chargeable period only to the extent that it has not been included in available qualifying expenditure for an earlier chargeable period. (There is now nothing to prohibit the allocation of *part only* of a particular amount of qualifying expenditure for a particular chargeable period.)
(ii) Qualifying expenditure cannot be allocated to a pool for a chargeable period earlier than that in which it is incurred.
(iii) Qualifying expenditure cannot be allocated to a pool for a chargeable period if in any earlier period the rights in question have come to an end (without any of them being revived) or have been wholly disposed of.

[*CAA 2001, ss 470–475*].

A *disposal value* falls to be brought into account for a chargeable period in which a person sells the whole or part of any patent rights on the purchase of which he has incurred qualifying expenditure. The disposal value is equal to the net sale proceeds (limited to *capital* sums), except that:

(1) it cannot exceed the qualifying expenditure incurred on purchase of the rights in question; and
(2) where the rights were acquired as a result of a transaction between CONNECTED PERSONS (**19**) (or a series of such transactions), (1) above shall have effect as if it referred to the greatest capital expenditure incurred on the purchase of those rights by any of those connected persons.

[*CAA 2001, ss 476, 477*].

Persons entering or leaving the cash basis

For 2017/18 onwards, the plant and machinery allowances rules for persons entering and leaving the cash basis (see respectively **10.26** and **10.35** CAPITAL ALLOWANCES ON PLANT AND MACHINERY), insofar as they relate to trades, apply also (with appropriate modifications) for the purposes of patent right allowances. [*CAA 2001, ss 475A, 477A; F(No 2)A 2017, Sch 2 paras 58, 59*].

Connected persons and other anti-avoidance

Where a person incurs capital expenditure on the purchase of rights either from a connected person (see **19** CONNECTED PERSONS), or so that it appears that the sole or main benefit from the sale and any other transactions would have been the obtaining of an allowance under these provisions, the amount of that expenditure taken into account as qualifying expenditure may not exceed an amount determined as follows:

(a) where a disposal value (see above) falls to be brought into account, an amount equal to that value;

(b) where no disposal value falls to be brought into account, but the seller receives a capital sum chargeable under *ITTOIA 2005, s 587* (see **41.6** INTELLECTUAL PROPERTY), an amount equal to that sum;

(c) in any other case, an amount equal to the smallest of
- market value of the rights;
- the amount of capital expenditure, if any, incurred by the seller on acquiring the rights;
- the amount of capital expenditure, if any, incurred by any person connected with the seller on acquiring the rights.

[*CAA 2001, s 481, Sch 3 para 102*]. Previously, the restriction was by reference to the disposal value only. See also (2) above.

Making of allowances and charges

An allowance (or balancing charge) in respect of qualifying *trade* expenditure is given effect as a trading expense (or trading receipt). [*CAA 2001, s 478*].

An allowance in respect of qualifying *non-trade* expenditure is set against the person's 'income from patents' for the same tax year, with any excess being carried forward without time limit against such income for subsequent tax years. The allowance is given effect by deduction at Step 2 of the calculation of income tax liability (see **1.10** ALLOWANCES AND TAX RATES). A balancing charge is assessed as taxable income. For these purposes, '*income from patents*' embraces royalties and similar sums, balancing charges under these provisions, and receipts from the sale of patent rights taxable under *ITTOIA 2005, s 587, 593* or *594* (see **41.6, 41.7** INTELLECTUAL PROPERTY). [*CAA 2001, ss 479, 480, 483*].

General

See **41** INTELLECTUAL PROPERTY for treatment of patent royalties and capital sums received, and **75.103** TRADING INCOME for trading income and expenses re patents.

Simon's Taxes. See **B3.601–B3.609**.

Example

[9.27]

P, who prepares accounts to 31 December, acquires two new patent rights for trading purposes.

	Date	Term	Cost
Patent 1	19.4.19	15 years	£4,500
Patent 2	5.10.20	5 years	£8,000

On 1.12.20, P sold part of his rights under patent 1 for £2,000.

The allowances for each patent are

	Pool	WDA
Y/e 31.12.19	£	£
Expenditure (patent 1)	4,500	
WDA 25%	(1,125)	£1,125
	3,375	
Y/e 31.12.20		
Expenditure (patent 2)	8,000	
Disposal proceeds (patent 1)	(2,000)	
	9,375	
WDA 25%	(2,344)	£2,344
WDV c/f	£7,031	

Research and development allowances

[9.28] 'Qualifying expenditure' incurred by a trader on 'research and development' (R & D) attracts an allowance equal to **100%** of the expenditure. A claim for an allowance may require it to be reduced to a specified amount (but the part of the allowance thus forgone cannot be claimed for a later chargeable period).

'*Qualifying expenditure*' is capital expenditure incurred by a trader on R & D related to the trade and undertaken directly or on his behalf (i.e. by an agent or other person in a similar contractual relationship, see *Gaspet Ltd v Elliss CA 1987, 60 TC 91*). It includes such expenditure incurred before commencement of the trade (pre-commencement expenditure). Expenditure potentially leading to or facilitating an extension of the trade is related to that trade, as is expenditure of a medical nature specially related to the welfare of workers in the trade. A just and reasonable apportionment may be made of capital expenditure only partly qualifying.

Expenditure on the acquisition of, or of rights in or over, land cannot be qualifying expenditure, except insofar as, on a just and reasonable apportionment, such expenditure is referable to a building or structure already constructed on the land, or to plant or machinery which forms part of such a building or structure, and otherwise qualifies as R & D expenditure.

Expenditure on R & D includes all expenditure incurred for carrying out (or providing facilities for carrying out) R & D. Expenditure on the acquisition of rights in, or arising out of, R & D is, however, excluded. Also excluded is expenditure on provision of a *dwelling*, except where not more than 25% of the expenditure (disregarding any 'additional VAT liability' or 'rebate' — see **9.2**(viii) above) on a building consisting partly of a dwelling and otherwise used for R & D is attributable (on a just and reasonable apportionment) to the dwelling, in which case the dwelling can be ignored and the whole of the building treated as used for R & D.

An 'additional VAT liability' (see **9.2**(viii) above) incurred in respect of qualifying expenditure is itself qualifying expenditure, provided the same person still owns the asset in question and it has not been demolished or destroyed.

Meaning of research and development

'*Research and development*' means activities that fall to be treated as such in accordance with generally accepted accounting practice (see **75.21** above) and includes oil and gas exploration and appraisal (within *ITA 2007, s 1003*). However, this is subject to Treasury regulations which narrow the definition by reference to guidelines issued by the Department of Trade and Industry (DTI). [*CAA 2001, s 437(2)(3)*]. The latest regulations refer to Government guidelines issued on 5 March 2004 and since updated (for which see www.gov.uk/government/publications/guidelines-on-the-meaning-of-research-and-development-for-tax-purposes). [*SI 2004 No 712*].

For special provisions relating to oil licences, see *CAA 2001, ss 552–556, Sch 3 para 91* as amended.

Making of allowances

The allowance is given as a trading expense of the chargeable period (see **9.2**(i) above) in which the expenditure is incurred (or, in the case of pre-commencement expenditure, the chargeable period in which the trade commences). An allowance in respect of an additional VAT liability is similarly given, but by reference to the time the *liability* is incurred.

[*CAA 2001, ss 437(1), 438–441, 447, 450, Sch 3 paras 89, 90*].

Disposal events and balancing charges

If a disposal value (see below) falls to be brought into account for the same chargeable period as that for which the related allowance falls to be given, the allowance is given on the excess (if any) of the expenditure over the disposal value.

If a disposal value falls to be brought into account for the chargeable period after that for which the related allowance is given, liability to a balancing charge arises for that later chargeable period. Effect is given to the charge by treating it as a trading receipt. The charge is equal to disposal value (or, where a reduced allowance was claimed, the excess, if any, of disposal value over unrelieved expenditure), except that it cannot exceed the allowance given (less any earlier balancing charges arising from 'additional VAT rebates' — see below).

A disposal value falls to be brought into account for a chargeable period in which a disposal event occurs, or, if such an event occurs later, for the chargeable period in which the trade is permanently discontinued. If, exceptionally, a disposal event occurs *before* the chargeable period for which the related allowance falls to be given, it is brought into account for the later chargeable period.

Either of the following is a disposal event (unless it gives rise to a balancing charge under the rules for plant and machinery allowances).

(a) The trader ceases to own the asset representing the qualifying expenditure;
(b) An asset representing the qualifying expenditure is demolished or destroyed before the trader ceases to own it.

On the sale of an asset, the seller is treated for these purposes as ceasing to own it at the earlier of the time of completion and the time when possession is given.

The amount of the disposal value depends on the nature of the disposal event, as follows.

- If the event is a sale of the asset at not less than market value, it is the net sale proceeds.
- If the event is the demolition or destruction of the asset, it is the net amount received for the remains, plus any insurance or capital compensation received (but see below as regards demolition costs).
- In any other event, it is the market value of the asset at the time of the event.

An 'additional VAT rebate' (see **9.2**(viii) above) made in respect of qualifying expenditure, before the asset in question ceases to belong to the trader or has been demolished or destroyed, must be brought into account as a disposal value (or as an addition to a disposal value otherwise arising) for the chargeable period in which the rebate accrues or, if later, the chargeable period in which the trade commences.

[*CAA 2001, ss 441(1), 442–444, 448, 449–451*].

Demolition costs

On demolition of an asset (within (b) above), the disposal value is reduced (or extinguished) by any demolition costs incurred by the trader. If the demolition costs exceed the disposal value, then, provided the asset had not begun to be used for non-qualifying purposes, the excess is itself treated as qualifying R & D expenditure, incurred at time of demolition (or, if earlier and where relevant, immediately before cessation of the trade). The demolition costs cannot be treated for any capital allowances purposes as expenditure on any replacement asset.

[*CAA 2001, s 445*].

Connected persons and other anti-avoidance

Connected persons and other anti-avoidance provisions apply to substitute market value for sale consideration on certain 'sole or main benefit' transactions, sales without change of control and sales between connected persons. For most sales, the election referred to at **9.23** above is available, with the result that an asset representing expenditure for which an R & D allowance has been made as above will be treated as transferred for nil consideration. [*CAA 2001, ss 567–570, 575, 575A; SI 2019 No 689, Reg 10(7)*].

General

A tax deferral scheme resulting in the price purportedly paid for scientific research being significantly in excess of its value was successfully challenged by HMRC in *Brain Disorders Research Ltd Partnership v HMRC* CA, [2018] STC 2382.

For R & D expenditure of a revenue nature, see **75.113** TRADING INCOME.

Simon's Taxes. See B3.7.

Example

[9.29]

C is in business manufacturing and selling cosmetics, and he prepares accounts annually to 30 June. For the purposes of this trade, he built a new laboratory adjacent to his existing premises, incurring the following expenditure.

		£
April 2018	Laboratory building	50,000
June 2018	Technical equipment	3,000
March 2019	Technical equipment	4,000
July 2019	Plant	2,500
August 2020	Extension to existing premises comprising 50% further laboratory area and 50% sales offices	30,000

In September 2019, a small fire destroyed an item of equipment originally costing £2,000 in June 2018; insurance recoveries totalled £3,000. In March 2020, the plant costing £2,500 in July 2019 was sold for £1,800.

The allowances due are as follows.

		£
Y/e 30.6.18		
Laboratory building		50,000
Technical equipment		3,000
		£53,000
Y/e 30.6.19		
Technical equipment		4,000
		£4,000
Y/e 30.6.20		
Net allowance on plant sold	(note (a))	£700
Balancing charge on equipment destroyed	(note (b))	(£2,000)
Y/e 30.6.21		
Extension (qualifying R&D expenditure only)		£15,000

Notes

(a) As the plant is sold in the period of account in which the expenditure is incurred, the disposal value of £1,800 is set against the expenditure of £2,500, resulting in a net allowance of £700.

(b) The destruction of the equipment in the year to 30 June 2020 results in a balancing charge limited to the allowance given. The charge accrues in the period of account in which the event occurs.

Structures and buildings allowances

[9.30] A new structures and buildings allowance (SBA) has been introduced for expenditure on the construction of commercial (non-residential) buildings and structures. The relief extends to capital expenditure on the improvement of existing structures and buildings, including converting existing premises to qualifying business use.

SBA is available on eligible construction costs incurred on or after **29 October 2018**, at an annual rate on a straight-line (i.e. not a reducing balance) basis. On and after 6 April 2020, the annual rate is **3%**; it was previously 2%. There is no system of balancing charges or balancing allowances on a subsequent disposal of the asset. Instead, a purchaser continues to claim the allowance at the annual rate on the original cost. The amount eligible for relief is not increased where a structure or building is purchased, or where it has appreciated in value, as this does not represent the cost of construction. Relief is available for UK and overseas structures and buildings, where the business is within the charge to UK tax. The cost of land or rights over land, and the costs of obtaining planning permission, are not eligible for relief. Relief is not available for structures or buildings where a contract for the construction works was entered into before 29 October 2018.

The legislation was introduced by statutory instrument (*SI 2019 No 1087*), which added new *CAA 2001, ss 270AA–270IH* to the statute book and made consequential amendments to pre-existing legislation.

See also HMRC Technical Note, 29 October 2018 at www.gov.uk/government/publications/capital-allowances-for-structures-and-buildings-technical-note, but note that some of its content has been superseded by the legislation. HMRC guidance is available at www.gov.uk/guidance/claiming-capital-allowances-for-structures-and-buildings.

Throughout this commentary, references to a 'building' include a structure, unless the context demands otherwise.

The entitlement conditions

An SBA is potentially available for 'qualifying expenditure' (see **9.31** below) incurred, on or after 29 October 2018 on the construction or acquisition of a building whose construction commenced on or after that date, provided the building is not in 'residential use' (see **9.32** below). A person carrying on a 'qualifying activity' is entitled to an SBA for a chargeable period (see **9.2**(i) above) if, on any day in that period, he has the 'relevant interest' in the building in relation to the expenditure (see **9.33** below) and the building is in 'non-residential use' (see **9.32** below), provided the beginning of that day falls:

- on or after the later of the day on which the building is first brought into 'qualifying use' (see **9.32** below) by the person and the day on which the qualifying expenditure is incurred (in either case, whether the day is in the same or an earlier chargeable period); and
- within the 33⅓ years beginning with the later of the day on which the building is first brought into non-residential use and the day on which the qualifying expenditure is incurred.

A person ceases to be entitled to an SBA if the building is demolished.

[*CAA 2001, s 270AA(1)(2)(4)(6); FA 2020, s 29(2)(6)(7), Sch 5 paras 4, 10; SI 2019 No 1087, Reg 2*].

The construction of a building is treated as having commenced before 29 October 2018 (with the result that no SBA is available) if any contract for works to be carried out in the course of the construction of that particular building (whether or not the contract also relates to the construction of other buildings or structures) was entered into before that date. [*CAA 2001, s 270AB; SI 2019 No 1087, Reg 2*].

A claim for an SBA must be separately identified as such in the tax return in which it is made. [*CAA 2001, s 3(2ZA); SI 2019 No 1087, Reg 3(4)*].

Rate of allowance and length of writing-down period

With effect on and after 6 April 2020, regardless of when the qualifying expenditure was incurred, the SBA for a chargeable period of one year is 3% of the qualifying expenditure, such that the expenditure is fully relieved only over a writing-down period of 33⅓ years. Before 6 April 2020, the rate was 2%, and the writing-down period was 50 years.

The allowance is proportionately increased or reduced for chargeable periods of more or less than one year. It is also proportionately reduced if the above conditions for entitlement to an SBA are met for only part of the chargeable period (including where the writing-down period ends part way through the chargeable period) or if that entitlement ceases due to demolition (see above) at some time during the chargeable period.

For the purpose only of computing the allowance for a chargeable period straddling 6 April 2020, that period is split into two separate notional chargeable periods, the second beginning on that date. So, for example, for a period of account covering the year to 31 December 2020, the allowance for expenditure meeting the entitlement conditions throughout the year will be based on 96 days at 2% and 270 days at 3%.

The reduction from 50 to 33⅓ in the number of years comprised in the writing-down period applies equally to qualifying expenditure which had already attracted an allowance at the old 2% rate before 6 April 2020. This is achieved by enabling the shortfall in allowances to be claimed in the chargeable period in which the writing-down period of 33⅓ years comes to an end. It applies only if the person entitled to the allowance on 5 April 2020 does not dispose of the relevant interest in the building before the time that the writing-down period ends and continues to be entitled to an allowance in respect of the expenditure at that time.

[*CAA 2001, ss 270AA(2)(5)(6), 270EA, 270GD; FA 2020, s 29(2)(3)(5)–(7); SI 2019 No 1087, Reg 2*].

Buildings in multiple use

A person may meet the above entitlement conditions by reference to a building which is put to multiple uses in a chargeable period. A building is put to multiple uses if:

- it is used for the purposes of two or more qualifying activities;
- part of it is in use for the purposes of a qualifying activity and part of it for the purposes of another activity; or
- part of it is used both for the purposes of a qualifying activity and for those of another activity (but the part of the building in question must not be an area within a dwelling-house).

In relation to any particular qualifying activity, the SBA for a chargeable period of one year is 3% (2% before 6 April 2020) of the appropriate proportion of the qualifying expenditure. The appropriate proportion is arrived at by apportioning the qualifying expenditure between all the activities for which the building is used. This apportionment must be carried out on a just and reasonable basis and with particular regard to the extent to which the building is used for each activity in the chargeable period.

[*CAA 2001, s 270EB; FA 2020, s 29(4)(6)(7); SI 2019 No 1087, Reg 2*].

Disposal of the building

It should be noted that the above entitlement conditions do not require the qualifying expenditure to have been incurred by the person who currently has the relevant interest. If the relevant interest in the building is sold at any time after the building is brought into use, the potential entitlement to the SBA passes from seller to purchaser, but only in relation to the historical qualifying expenditure and not to the amount paid for the interest by the purchaser. See also the definition of 'qualifying expenditure' at **9.31** below. The sale does not give rise to any balancing charge or balancing allowance, but the seller ceases to be entitled to the SBA as regards any time falling after the sale.

An adjustment is made for capital gains tax (CGT) purposes where a person disposes of an interest in a building by reference to which he has obtained an SBA. If the expenditure by reference to which the SBA has been made is allowable as a deduction in computing the gain or loss on disposal, the consideration for the disposal is treated as increased by the amount of the SBA given to the seller. [*TCGA 1992, s 37B; SI 2019 No 1087, Reg 4(4)*].

Demolition of the building

As stated above, entitlement to an SBA ceases if the building in question is demolished. Demolition generally counts as a disposal for CGT purposes by virtue of *TCGA 1992, s 24* (see Tolley's Capital Gains Tax). In the computation of a loss accruing to a person making a disposal, there is normally excluded from the sums allowable as a deduction any expenditure to the extent to which a capital allowance has been made in respect of it. [*TCGA 1992, s 41*]. This rule is disapplied in the case of the SBA to enable a person to obtain relief from CGT for so much of the capital expenditure on a building as has failed to attract SBAs as a result of its demolition. [*TCGA 1992, s 41(4A); SI 2019 No 1087, Reg 4(7)*].

Disuse of the building

A building which, immediately before falling into disuse, was in non-residential use is treated, for the purposes of the above entitlement conditions as continuing to be in non-residential use. [*CAA 2001, s 270AA(3); SI 2019 No 1087, Reg 2*]. Thus, allowances remain available in periods of disuse.

Qualifying activities

Each of the following is a '*qualifying activity*' for the purposes of the SBA:

- a trade, profession or vocation;
- a UK property business or overseas property business (see **60.2** PROPERTY INCOME), excluding (in both cases) so much of the business as consists of furnished holiday lettings;
- any of the concerns listed in *ITTOIA 2005, s 12(4)* (mines, quarries and sundry other undertakings); and
- managing the investments of a company with investment business,

but to the extent only that the profits therefrom are within the charge to UK tax (or would be if there were any profits).

If, for the purposes of a qualifying activity, a person incurs expenditure before the date on which he starts to carry on the activity (but on or after 29 October 2018), the expenditure is treated as if it were incurred on the date on which he starts to carry on the activity.

[*CAA 2001, ss 270BN, 270CA, 270CB; SI 2019 No 1087, Reg* 2].

Making of allowances

An SBA is given effect by treating the allowance as a deductible expense in calculating profits or losses of the qualifying activity for the chargeable period. [*CAA 2001, ss 270HA–270HD; SI 2019 No 1087, Reg* 2].

Structures and buildings allowance — qualifying expenditure

[9.31] '*Qualifying expenditure*' for the purposes of the SBA is expenditure which is 'qualifying capital expenditure' on the construction or purchase of a building, and which is not 'excluded expenditure'.

Capital expenditure incurred on construction is '*qualifying capital expenditure*' if the 'relevant interest' in the building (see **9.33** below) has not been sold or has been sold only after the building was brought into 'non-residential use' (see **9.32** below).

As regards capital expenditure on the purchase of a building, the question of whether (and to what extent) the expenditure is qualifying capital expenditure depends firstly on whether or not the building is purchased from a developer. If not, the capital sum paid by the purchaser for the relevant interest in the building is potentially qualifying capital expenditure only if that relevant interest was sold to the purchaser before the building was first used. The portion of the capital sum that is '*qualifying capital expenditure*' cannot be greater than the capital expenditure incurred on the construction. It may be that the building is sold unused on more than one occasion, in which case only the capital sum paid on the last such sale is potentially qualifying capital expenditure.

If the construction expenditure was incurred by a developer (i.e. a person carrying on a trade consisting wholly or partly in the construction of buildings with a view to their sale), and the relevant interest in the building is sold by the developer in the course of the development trade before the building is first used, the following rules apply. If the sale of the relevant interest by the developer was the only sale of the relevant interest before the building is first used, any capital sum paid by the purchaser for that interest is '*qualifying capital expenditure*'. If the sale of the relevant interest by the developer was not the only such sale of the relevant interest before the building is first used, any capital sum paid by the purchaser for that interest on the last such sale is potentially qualifying capital expenditure. The portion of the capital sum that is '*qualifying capital expenditure*' cannot be greater than the sum paid for the relevant interest on the earlier sale by the developer.

In each case, the qualifying expenditure is treated as incurred by the purchaser when the capital sum in question is paid.

The following applies if the construction expenditure is incurred by a developer, and the relevant interest in the building is sold in the course of the development trade after the building is first used. In relation to the person to whom the relevant interest is sold (and any person who subsequently acquires that interest), the expenditure on the construction of the building is treated as if it had been '*qualifying capital expenditure*', with the result that the person concerned can potentially claim the SBA.

Any expenditure whose amount cannot be provably quantified does not count as expenditure on the construction of a building. If an item of expenditure falls to be apportioned between expenditure for which an SBA can be made and other expenditure, the apportionment is to be made on a just and reasonable basis. An apportionment must similarly be made if the sum paid for the sale of the relevant interest in a building is attributable partly to assets representing expenditure for which an SBA can be made and partly to assets representing other expenditure.

Excluded expenditure

For the above purposes, expenditure is '*excluded expenditure*' if it is expenditure:

(a) on the acquisition of land (including fees, stamp duty land tax, land and buildings transaction tax, land transaction tax and other incidental costs);
(b) on the '*alteration of land*', i.e. land reclamation, land remediation (as defined), or landscaping (other than so as to create a structure);
(c) on, or in connection with, the seeking of planning permission (including fees and related costs);
(d) of a capital nature on the provision of plant or machinery (as in **10** CAPITAL ALLOWANCES ON PLANT AND MACHINERY); or
(e) in excess of market value.

The market value rule in (e) above excludes any expenditure in excess of:

- (in a case where the qualifying capital expenditure is the capital sum paid for the relevant interest in the building) the market value of the relevant interest; and

- (in any other case) the '*market value amount*' of the works, services and other matters to which it relates, i.e. the amount of expenditure which it would have been normal and reasonable to incur on the works etc. in the prevailing market conditions on the assumption that the transaction giving rise to that expenditure was on arm's length terms in the open market.

Expenditure treated as expenditure on construction

Expenditure incurred on the renovation or conversion of a part of a building, or on repairs to a part of a building that are incidental to the renovation or conversion of that part, is treated as if it were expenditure on the construction for the first time of that part of the building. Such expenditure is to be treated as capital expenditure if it is not deductible in computing the taxable profits or losses of the qualifying activity.

What this means in practice is that the renovation etc. expenditure is treated as entirely separate from the original construction expenditure for the building. The renovation etc. expenditure has its own writing-down period, which continues after the expiry of the writing-down period for the original expenditure. See also below under Expenditure incurred on different days.

In relation to a building that was brought into use before 29 October 2018 any such renovation or conversion of, or repairs to, a part of the building are treated as if they represented the construction of that part for the first time (so that they are not disbarred from qualifying for SBAs).

If a person incurs capital expenditure, other than alteration expenditure within (b) above, for the purposes of preparing land as a site for the construction of a building, this counts as capital expenditure on the construction of the building.

Expenditure incurred on different days

Capital expenditure may be incurred on the construction of a building after it has been brought into 'non-residential use' (see **9.32** below) and on different days (whether or not in the same chargeable period). This may, for example, apply to expenditure on renovation, conversion and repairs as above. For ease of administration, e.g. to avoid having a separate writing-down period for every such item of expenditure, the expenditure can be treated for SBA purposes as having been incurred:

- on the latest day on which any qualifying capital expenditure on the construction is incurred (Day L); or
- on the first day of the chargeable period following that in which Day L falls; or
- on the first day of the chargeable period following that in which falls the day on which the expenditure in question is actually incurred.

[*CAA 2001, ss 270BA–270BM; FA 2020, Sch 5 paras 5, 6, 10; SI 2019 No 1087, Reg 2*].

Structures and buildings allowance — qualifying use

[9.32] A building or structure is in '*qualifying use*' for the purposes of the SBA if it is in 'non-residential use' (see below) for the purposes of a qualifying activity (see **9.30** above) carried on by the person who has the relevant interest (see **9.33** below) in the building. The extent to which a building is in use for the purposes of a particular activity is to be determined on a just and reasonable basis. A building is treated as not being in use for the purposes of a particular activity if such use is insignificant.

A building is treated as being used for the purposes of a property business during any period if the person with the relevant interest is entitled, under the terms of a lease or otherwise, to rents, or other receipts, of such amounts as may reasonably have been expected to have been payable if the transaction had been between on arm's length terms in the open market.

Residential and non-residential use

A building is in '*residential use*' if it is used as (or for purposes ancillary to use as) a dwelling-house, residential accommodation for school pupils, student accommodation (as defined), residential accommodation for members of the armed forces, a home or other institution providing residential accommodation for children or adults (but not where that accommodation is provided together with personal care for persons in need of it by reason of old age, disability, alcohol or drug dependence or mental disorder), or a prison or similar establishment. Any part of a building that is used as a dwelling house (whether or not it is also used for any other purposes) is not in qualifying use.

A building situated on land that is (or is intended to be) occupied or enjoyed (together with a building in residential use) as a garden or grounds is automatically treated as being in residential use.

A building is in '*non-residential use*' if it is in use which is not residential use.

[*CAA 2001, ss 270CE–270CG; SI 2019 No 1087, Reg 2*].

Structures and buildings allowance — the relevant interest

[9.33] The relevant interest in relation to any 'qualifying expenditure' (as in **9.31** above) is the interest in the building to which the person who incurred the expenditure on its construction was entitled when the expenditure was incurred. If that person was entitled to more than one interest in the building at that time, and one of those interests was reversionary on all the others, the reversionary interest is the relevant interest.

Subject to the rules below on leases granted for 35 years or more, an interest does not cease to be the relevant interest merely because of the creation of a lease or other interest to which that interest is subject. Thus, on the grant of a lease, the relevant interest, and potential entitlement to the SBA, remains with the lessor.

If the relevant interest is a leasehold interest which is extinguished upon the person entitled to it acquiring the interest which is reversionary upon it, the interest into which the leasehold interest merges becomes the relevant interest.

In determining the relevant interest, a person who incurs expenditure on the construction of a building, and is entitled to an interest in it upon completion of construction, is treated as having had that interest when the expenditure was incurred.

On the sale of the relevant interest, the seller (and not the purchaser) is treated for the purposes of the entitlement conditions at **9.30** above as the person who has the relevant interest on the day of transfer.

Leases granted for 35 years or more

The following rule applies if:

- 'qualifying capital expenditure' (as in **9.31** above) has been incurred on the construction or acquisition of a building;
- a lease of the building is granted out of the interest which is the relevant interest in relation to the qualifying expenditure; and
- the effective duration of the lease (see below) is at least 35 years.

If the market value of the retained interest in the building is less than one-third of the capital sum given as consideration for the lease (see below):

- the lessee is treated as acquiring the relevant interest upon the grant of the lease; and
- the lessor is treated as acquiring the relevant interest from the lessee upon the expiry or surrender of the lease.

The relevant interest, and potential entitlement to the SBA, is thus transferred to the lessee.

For this purpose, the capital sum given as consideration for the lease is treated as excluding the amount, in respect of any premium required to be paid under the lease, that is brought into account as a receipt in calculating the lessor's profits (see **60.26** PROPERTY INCOME).

[*CAA 2001, ss 270DA–270DE; SI 2019 No 1087, Reg 2*].

ITTOIA 2005, ss 303, 304 contain rules for ascertaining the effective duration of a lease, which is not necessarily the same as its contractual duration; in particular, any rights the tenant has to extend the lease, or any entitlement of his to a further lease of the same premises, may be taken into account.

Transfers treated as sales

If there is a transfer of the interest in a building which is the relevant interest but the transfer is not a sale, it is treated for the purposes of SBAs as a sale at market value of the relevant interest. [*CAA 2001, s 573; SI 2019 No 1087, Reg 3(14); SI 2019 No 689, Reg 10(8)*].

Structures and buildings allowance — miscellaneous

[9.34] The following miscellaneous provisions apply for the purposes of the SBA.

Requirement for an allowance statement

In determining the amount of an SBA due to a person (P), the amount of the qualifying expenditure is treated as nil unless, before P first makes a claim for an SBA by reference to the building, the 'allowance statement requirement' is met. The '*allowance statement requirement*' is met if:

- in a case where P incurred the qualifying expenditure, P makes an 'allowance statement'; and
- in any other case, P obtains an allowance statement (or a copy of it) from any person previously entitled to a relevant interest in the building.

An '*allowance statement*' is a written statement, identifying the building to which it relates, of:

- the date of the earliest contract (written or oral) for the construction of the building;
- the amount of qualifying expenditure (see **9.31** above) incurred on its construction or purchase; and
- the date on which it is first brought into non-residential use (see **9.32** above).

[*CAA 2001, s 270IA; FA 2020, Sch 5 paras 7, 10; SI 2019 No 1087, Reg 2*].

Buildings qualifying for research and development allowances

There are provisions to deal with cases in which expenditure on a building potentially qualifies for both SBAs and the research and development (R & D) allowance (at **9.28** above).

Sale of relevant interest on or after 11 March 2020

If, on or after 11 March 2020, a person sells the relevant interest in a building to another person (P), the total SBAs available to P are reduced (but not below nil) by the amount of any R & D allowance available to P by reference to the building.

Additionally, if the sale in question, or a sale of the relevant interest at an earlier time, is by a person entitled to an R & D allowance by reference to the building *and* the amount paid on any of those sales is less than the total remaining SBAs available at the time of sale, the total SBAs available to the buyer cannot exceed the 'permitted maximum'. The '*permitted maximum*' is:

- the lowest sum paid for the relevant interest on the sale in question or any of the earlier such sales, less
- the total SBAs arising since the earliest such sale.

In applying these provisions, reference to the total SBAs is to the total to which an entitlement has arisen or would have arisen if the building had been in continuous qualifying use since first brought into non-residential use.

Sale of relevant interest before 11 March 2020

Different provisions applied where the relevant interest was sold before 11 March 2020. If the purchaser (P) was entitled to an R & D allowance in respect of expenditure incurred on the acquisition of the building, the total amount of SBAs available to P by reference to the building was limited to the excess of the qualifying expenditure (as in **9.31** above) over the aggregate of:

- the total SBAs that could have been claimed in respect of it before the sale on the assumption that it had been in continuous qualifying use (see **9.32** above) since it was first brought into non-residential use; and
- the amount of R & D allowance to which P is entitled.

If the seller of the relevant interest was entitled to an R & D allowance in respect of his expenditure on the acquisition of the building, but the purchaser (P) is not entitled to an R & D allowance, the total amount of SBAs available to P by reference to the building is limited to the lower of:

- the excess of the qualifying expenditure over the total SBAs that could have been claimed in respect of it before the sale on the assumption that it had been in continuous qualifying use since first being brought into non-residential use; and
- the capital sum paid by P for the relevant interest.

[*CAA 2001, s 270EC; FA 2020, Sch 5 paras 2, 8; SI 2019 No 1087, Reg 2*].

Anti-avoidance

If, at any time, tax avoidance arrangements exist in relation to a building (whether or not a person with a relevant interest in the building is party to them), and a person would obtain an SBA-related tax advantage as a result, the advantage is to be counteracted by the making of such adjustments as are just and reasonable. Adjustments thus made may affect the tax treatment of persons other than the person in relation to whom the advantage is counteracted. An SBA-related tax advantage includes obtaining an SBA that is in any way more favourable to a person than the one that would otherwise be obtained. [*CAA 2001, s 270IB; SI 2019 No 1087, Reg 2*].

Additional VAT liabilities and rebates

The following applies if a person is entitled to an SBA by reference to qualifying expenditure (as in **9.31** above) that he has incurred, and he incurs an 'additional VAT liability' (see **9.2**(viii) above) in respect of that expenditure. For the purpose of calculating SBAs the qualifying expenditure is increased, at the beginning of the chargeable period (see **9.2**(i) above) in which the additional VAT liability accrues, by the amount of the liability. If, at the end of the writing-down period, the person who is entitled to an SBA by reference to qualifying expenditure is the person who incurred that expenditure, that person is entitled to an additional amount of SBA for the chargeable period in which the writing-down period ends. That amount is equal to the excess of the additional VAT liability over the total amount of SBAs to which the person has been entitled during the writing-down period in respect of that liability. In a case where an additional VAT rebate has also made to that person in respect of the qualifying expenditure, this additional amount is subject to the restriction below on the total amount of SBAs available.

The following applies if a person is entitled to an SBA by reference to qualifying expenditure that he has incurred, and an 'additional VAT rebate' (see **9.2**(viii) above) is made to that person in respect of that expenditure. For the purpose of calculating SBAs, the qualifying expenditure is reduced, at the beginning of the chargeable period in which the additional VAT rebate accrues, by the amount of the rebate. The *total* amount of SBAs available by reference to the qualifying expenditure incurred by that person is restricted to the excess of the qualifying expenditure (including any additional VAT liability as above) over the additional VAT rebate.

[*CAA 2001, ss 270GA–270GC; SI 2019 No 1087, Reg 2*].

Co-ownership authorised contractual schemes (CoACS)

A CoACS (see **80.9** UNIT TRUSTS ETC.) is broadly transparent for tax purposes, i.e. the scheme itself incurs no tax liability. This means that its investors are treated as if they had invested directly in the underlying assets of the scheme and are subject to personal taxation accordingly. Provisions similar to those at **10.70** CAPITAL ALLOWANCES ON PLANT AND MACHINERY apply in relation to the SBA. This includes the making of an election whereby the operator of a CoACS carrying on a qualifying activity can elect to compute SBAs and allocate them to the investors.

If an election under **10.70** (a plant and machinery election) was made before 5 July 2019, a separate election is required in respect of SBAs. A plant and machinery election made on or after that date automatically applies to SBAs as well. Where a plant and machinery election was made before 5 July 2019 and an SBA is available by reference to a building which is subject to the CoACS, the operator can as an alternative withdraw the plant and machinery election (see **10.70**).

[*CAA 2001, ss 262AEA, 270IC–270IF; SI 2019 No 1087, Regs 1, 2, 3(8)*].

Highway undertakings

For the purposes of the SBA, the carrying on of a highway undertaking (as defined) is treated as the carrying on of an undertaking by way of trade; and a person carrying on a highway undertaking is treated as occupying, for the purposes of the undertaking, any road in relation to which it is carried on. *CAA 2001, ss 270FA–270FC; SI 2019 No 1087, Reg 2* deal with aspects of the SBA peculiar to highway undertakings.

Leases

A lease includes an agreement for a lease if the term to be covered by the lease has begun, a tenancy and, in the case of land outside the UK, an interest corresponding to a lease. There are rules that treat a lease as continuing in various circumstances, for example if it is renewed, extended or replaced. There are also rules dealing with certain events that may occur on the termination of a lease. For example if another lease is then granted to a different lessee (B) and, in connection with the transaction, B pays a sum to the previous lessee (A), then the two leases are to be treated as if they were the same lease which had been assigned by A to B in consideration of the payment. [*CAA 2001, ss 270IG, 270IH; SI 2019 No 1087, Reg 2*].

Example

[9.35]

Bedrock Moors is an established partnership of individuals trading as car mechanics and preparing accounts to 5 April each year. In its 12-month period of account to 5 April 2021, the firm incurs qualifying expenditure of £180,000 on the construction of a building on freehold land it holds in the UK, which it intends to use for the purposes of the trade. It begins to use the building for those purposes on 1 June 2021. Bedrock Moors can claim structures and buildings allowances as follows.

2020/21 (y/e 5.4.21)

No allowance is due as the building has not been brought into qualifying use before the end of the period of account.

2021/22 (y/e 5.4.22)

The building is brought into qualifying use on 1 June 2021. The allowance is therefore due for the period 1 June 2021 to 5 April 2022 (309 days).

The allowance (to be deducted as an expense of the trade) is £180,000 × 3% × 309/365 = £4,572.

2022/23 (y/e 5.4.23)

The allowance is £180,000 × 3% = £5,400

If Bedrock Moors continues to own the freehold and to carry on a qualifying activity, and that the building is not demolished or brought into residential use, the partnership will continue to be entitled to an allowance of £5,400 for each period of account up to and including the year ended 5 April 2054 and thus the tax year 2053/54. For 2054/55 (based on the year ended 5 April 2055), only the period up to 30 September 2054 falls within the period of 33⅓ years from first use, so the allowance will be £180,000 × 3% × 178/365 = £2,628. Allowances will then have been given on the full expenditure of £180,000 ((£5,400 x 32 years) + £4,572 + £2,628).

10

Capital Allowances on Plant and Machinery

Cross-references. See **9** CAPITAL ALLOWANCES. See also **75.88** TRADING INCOME for gifts of plant or machinery to charities.

Simon's Taxes. See B3.3.

Other sources. See Tolley's Capital Allowances.

Introduction to capital allowances on plant and machinery

[10.1] The law relating to capital allowances was consolidated in *Capital Allowances Act 2001* (*CAA 2001*) as part of the Tax Law Rewrite programme.

Capital allowances (balancing charges) are a deduction (addition) in computing the profits of trades and other qualifying activities for a 'chargeable period' (as in **10.2**(i) below). In the case of a trade, they are generally treated as trading expenses (receipts) of the period of account (see **10.2**(i) below) to which they relate. [*CAA 2001, ss 2, 6; SI 2019 No 1087, Reg 3(3)*].

Generally, the allowances described in this chapter are not available for a chargeable period for which the profits of a trade, profession, vocation or property business are calculated on the cash basis (see **76** TRADING INCOME — CASH BASIS FOR SMALLER BUSINESSES and **60.4** PROPERTY INCOME). No disposal values are generally brought into account for any such chargeable period and no balancing charges arise (but see also **10.26** below). The foregoing does not, however, apply in respect of expenditure on a car (as defined by *CAA 2001, s 268A* — see **10.15**(ii) below). [*CAA 2001, ss 1(4)(5), 1A(1)–(5)(11)(12); F(No 2)A 2017, Sch 2 paras 49, 50, 64(1)*].

For a full list of qualifying activities in relation to which plant and machinery allowances are available, see **10.4** below.

Capital allowances — matters of general application

[10.2] The following matters are pertinent to capital allowances generally.

(i) **Meaning of 'chargeable period' and 'period of account'.** For capital allowances purposes, a '*chargeable period*' is a 'period of account'. For persons carrying on a trade, profession or vocation, a '*period of account*' means a period for which accounts are drawn up, except that where such a period exceeds 18 months, it is deemed to be split into two or more periods of account, beginning on, or on an anniversary of, the date on which the actual period begins. Exceptionally, where there is an interval between two periods of account, it is deemed to form part of the first such period, and where two periods of account overlap, the common period is deemed to form part of the first such period only. For non-traders, a period of account is a tax year.
[*CAA 2001, s 6*].
See the examples at **10.36** below.

(ii) **Claims.** Capital allowances are given only if a claim is made. Such a claim can only be made by inclusion in the annual tax return (subject to the very limited exceptions at *CAA 2001, s 3(4)*). [*CAA 2001, s 3, Sch 2 para 103(2); SI 2019 No 1087, Reg 3(4)*]. See **64.4** RETURNS as regards amendments to income tax returns, and the time allowed for making them.

(iii) **Capital expenditure and receipts.** References in the capital allowances legislation to the incurring of capital expenditure and the paying of capital sums exclude any sums allowed as deductions in computing the payer's profits or earnings, any expenditure incurred (other than on a car) at a time when profits are calculated on the cash basis, and certain sums payable under deduction of tax. Corresponding rules apply as regards the receipt of such sums. [*CAA 2001, s 4, Sch 3 para 9; F(No 2)A 2017, Sch 2 paras 51, 64(1)*].

(iv) **Time expenditure incurred.** Capital expenditure (other than that constituted by an 'additional VAT liability' — see (viii) below) is generally treated, for capital allowances purposes, as incurred as soon as there is an unconditional obligation to pay it, even if all or part of it is not required to be paid until some later date. However, expenditure is treated as incurred on a later date in the following circumstances.

- Where any part of the expenditure is not required to be paid until a date more than four months after the date determined as above, it is treated as incurred on that later date.
- Where an obligation to pay becomes unconditional earlier than in accordance with normal commercial usage, with the sole or main benefit likely to be the bringing forward of the chargeable period in which the expenditure would otherwise be treated as incurred, it is instead treated as incurred on the date on or before which it is required to be paid.

Where, as a result of an event such as the issuing of a certificate, an obligation to pay becomes unconditional within one month after the end of a chargeable period, but at or before the end of that chargeable period the asset concerned has become the property of, or is otherwise attributed under the contract to, the person having the obligation, the expenditure is treated as incurred immediately before the end of that chargeable period.

The above provisions do not override any specific rule under which expenditure is treated as incurred later than the relevant time given above.

[*CAA 2001, s 5*].

Simon's Taxes. See **B3.104, B3.107.**

(v) **Exclusion of double allowances.** No allowance under any of the codes listed below can be made in respect of any expenditure that has been allocated to a plant and machinery pool (see **10.26** below), and on which a plant or machinery allowance (or balancing charge) has consequently been given (or made), or any related asset (as above); and expenditure which has attracted an allowance under any of those codes (and any asset to which that expenditure related) cannot be allocated to a plant and machinery pool.

- allowances for expenditure on business premises renovation (**9.3** CAPITAL ALLOWANCES);
- allowances for expenditure on dredging (**9.10** CAPITAL ALLOWANCES);
- allowances for expenditure on flat conversion (**9.13** CAPITAL ALLOWANCES);
- allowances for mineral extraction (**9.15–9.25** CAPITAL ALLOWANCES);
- research and development allowances (**9.28** CAPITAL ALLOWANCES);
- structures and buildings allowances (**9.30** CAPITAL ALLOWANCES).

Additional rules apply under *CAA 2001, s 9* to prevent double allowances in relation to plant or machinery treated as fixtures (as at **10.37** *et seq.* below). These do not prevent a person making a fixtures claim in respect of capital expenditure if the only previous claim was for industrial buildings allowances (now abolished), research and development allowances or business premises renovation allowances, but see **10.46** below for restrictions on the amount of expenditure on which plant and machinery allowances can be claimed.

[*CAA 2001, ss 7–10, Sch 3 para 10; SI 2019 No 1087, Reg 3(6)*].

Where an item of expenditure qualifies for more than one type of

capital allowance, it is the taxpayer's choice as to which to claim, but he cannot alter his choice in later years. (HMRC Capital Allowances Manual CA16000, HMRC Brief 12/09, 31 March 2009).
Simon's Taxes. See **B3.114**.

(vi) **Expenditure met by another's contributions.** Subject to the exceptions below, a person is not regarded as incurring expenditure for capital allowances purposes to the extent that it is met, or will be met, directly or indirectly by another person or by a '*public body*', i.e. the Crown or any government or public or local authority (whether in the UK or elsewhere). For the scope of 'public authority', see *McKinney v Hagans Caravans (Manufacturing) Ltd* CA(NI) 1997, 69 TC 526. There is an exception where the expenditure is met by a Regional Development Grant or NI equivalent. In practice, applications for Regional Development Grants were no longer accepted after 31 March 1988, but NI equivalents did continue to be available until 31 March 2003. Expenditure met by insurance or other compensation money due in respect of a destroyed, demolished or defunct asset is not excluded from allowances.
The above rule is disapplied, and allowances are thus available, if the contributor is not a public body and can obtain neither a capital allowance on his contribution by virtue of (vii) below nor a deduction against profits of a trade, profession or vocation or any qualifying activity within **10.4**(iii)–(vi) below.
[*CAA 2001, ss 532–536, Sch 2 para 19, Sch 3 paras 106–108; SI 2019 No 1087, Reg 3(9)*].
Simon's Taxes. See **B3.111**.

(vii) **Contribution allowances.** Contributors towards another person's capital expenditure on plant or machinery may receive allowances ('*contribution allowances*') where the contribution is for the purposes of a trade or 'relevant activity' carried on (or to be carried on) by the contributor, and where the expenditure would otherwise have entitled the other person (assuming him not to be a public body) to plant and machinery allowances. Contribution allowances are not available where the contributor and the other person are CONNECTED PERSONS (**19**). A '*relevant activity*' is a profession or vocation or an activity within **10.4**(iii)–(vi) below.
Contribution allowances are such as would have been made if the contribution had been expended on the provision for the contributor's trade etc. of similar plant or machinery and as if the plant or machinery were at all material times used for the purposes of the contributor's trade etc. (so that balancing adjustments do not apply to such contributions). The contributor's deemed expenditure can only be allocated to a single asset pool (see **10.26** below). On a transfer of the trade etc., or part thereof, the allowances (or part) are subsequently made to the transferee.
[*CAA 2001, ss 537, 538, Sch 3 para 109; SI 2019 No 1087, Reg 3(10)*].
Simon's Taxes. See **B3.112**.

(viii) **VAT capital goods scheme.** Under the VAT capital goods scheme, the input tax originally claimed on the acquisition of certain capital assets is subject to amendment within a specified period of adjustment in accordance with any increase or decrease in the extent to which the asset is used in making taxable, as opposed to exempt, supplies for VAT purposes. The items covered by the scheme are limited to land and buildings (or parts of buildings) worth at least £250,000, computers (and items of computer equipment) worth at least £50,000, and aircraft, ships, boats or other vessels worth at least £50,000. See Tolley's Value Added Tax under Capital Goods Scheme for a full description.

Special capital allowances provisions apply where a VAT adjustment is made under the capital goods scheme.

'*Additional VAT liability*' and '*additional VAT rebate*' mean, respectively:

- an amount which a person becomes liable to pay, or
- an amount which he becomes entitled to deduct,

by way of adjustment under the VAT capital goods scheme in respect of input tax. Generally (but see below), such a liability or rebate is treated as incurred or made on the last day of the period:

- which is one of the periods making up the applicable VAT period of adjustment under the VAT capital goods scheme, and
- in which occurred the increase or decrease in use giving rise to the liability or rebate.

However, for the purpose of determining the chargeable period (see (i) above) in which it accrues, an additional VAT liability or rebate is treated as accruing on whichever is the relevant day below.

- Where the liability or rebate is accounted for in a VAT return, the last day of the period covered by that return.
- If, before the making of a VAT return, HMRC assess the liability or rebate, the day on which the assessment is made.
- If the trade (or other qualifying activity — see **10.4** below) is permanently discontinued before the liability or rebate has been accounted for in a VAT return and before the making of an assessment, the last day of the chargeable period in which the cessation occurs.

Where an allowance or charge falls to be determined by reference to a proportion only of the expenditure incurred or a proportion only of what that allowance or charge would otherwise have been, a related additional VAT liability or rebate is similarly apportioned.

[*CAA 2001, ss 546–551; SI 2019 No 1087, Reg 3(13)*].

Simon's Taxes. See **B3.103, B3.104.**

(ix) **Composite sales** may be apportioned by the Appeal Tribunal regardless of any separate prices attributed in the sale agreement. [*CAA 2001, ss 562–564*]. See *Fitton v Gilders & Heaton* Ch D 1955, 36 TC 233, and *Wood v Provan* CA 1968, 44 TC 701.

Simon's Taxes. See **B3.110.**

(x) **Finance leasing.** See **75.83** TRADING INCOME as regards restrictions on capital allowances where certain finance leasing arrangements are involved. These are disapplied from, broadly, 1 April 2006 in relation to long funding leases. See also **10.48** *et seq.*, **10.58, 10.62, 10.63** below.

(xi) **Recovery of assets under *Proceeds of Crime Act 2002, Pt 5*.** *Proceeds of Crime Act 2002, Pt 5 Ch 2* provides for the recovery, in civil proceedings before the High Court (or, in Scotland, the Court of Session), of property which is, or represents, property obtained through 'unlawful conduct' (as defined in the Act). If the Court is satisfied that any property is recoverable under the provisions, it will make a '*recovery order*', vesting the property in an appointed trustee for civil recovery. Alternatively, the Court may make an order under *s 276* of the *Act* staying (or, in Scotland, sisting) proceedings on terms agreed by the parties. The vesting of property in a trustee for civil recovery or any other person, either under a recovery order or in pursuance of a *s 276* order, is known as a *Pt 5* transfer. A '*compensating payment*' may in some cases be made to the person who held the property immediately before the transfer. If the order provides for the creation of any interest in favour of that person, he is treated as receiving (in addition to any other compensating payment) a compensating payment equal to the value of the interest. [*Proceeds of Crime Act 2002, ss 240(1), 266(1)(2), 276, 316(1), 448, Sch 10 para* 2].

Where the property in question is plant or machinery, the relevant interest in a flat (within **9.13** CAPITAL ALLOWANCES), or an asset representing qualifying expenditure on research and development (within **9.28** CAPITAL ALLOWANCES), there are provisions to ensure that the *Pt 5* transfer has a tax-neutral effect, unless a compensating payment is made to the transferor in which case its amount and/or value must be brought into account as a disposal value or, as the case may be, as proceeds from a balancing event. [*Proceeds of Crime Act 2002, Sch 10 paras 12–29*].

Qualifying expenditure

[10.3] Allowances are available in respect of 'qualifying expenditure' incurred by a person carrying on a trade or other 'qualifying activity' (see **10.4** below). Subject to **10.6–10.12** below and to other specific exclusions, expenditure is '*qualifying expenditure*' if it is 'capital expenditure' (see **10.2**(iii) above) incurred on the provision of plant or machinery wholly or partly for the purposes of the qualifying activity carried on by that person, and as a result of which that person owns the plant or machinery (for which see the paragraph on 'Ownership' in **10.19** below). [*CAA 2001, s 11*]. See **10.32** below as regards partial use for other purposes. Provided these tests are met (but subject to specific restrictions — see, for example, **10.62** below), it is irrelevant whether or not the object of the person incurring the expenditure was, or included, the obtaining of capital allowances (see the CA judgment in *Barclays Mercantile Business Finance Ltd v Mawson* HL 2004, 76 TC 446, a case involving complex 'finance leasing' arrangements).

Expenditure incurred for the purposes of, and prior to the commencement of, a qualifying activity is treated as incurred on the first day on which the activity is carried on. [*CAA 2001, s 12*].

Expenditure incurred on the provision of plant or machinery for long funding leasing is excluded from being qualifying expenditure in the hands of the lessor (see **10.51** below). See **10.37** *et seq.* below as regards fixtures which become part of land or buildings.

Whether plant or machinery is acquired new or second-hand is generally irrelevant (but see **10.62** below as regards certain sales between connected persons etc.). A *share* in plant or machinery can qualify for allowances [*CAA 2001, s 270*].

See also Eligible expenditure at **10.6–10.12** below.

Vehicles for which fixed rate deductions allowed

Capital expenditure incurred on a vehicle in a period of account of a trade, profession or vocation is *not* qualifying expenditure if a fixed rate deduction (see **77.2** TRADING INCOME — FIXED RATE DEDUCTION SCHEME) is allowed for the period in respect of the expenditure. [*CAA 2001, s 38ZA*].

Simon's Taxes. See **B3.305**.

Qualifying activities

[10.4] Any of the following is a '*qualifying activity*':

(i) a trade, profession or vocation (but see the exclusion in **10.1** above for trades etc. in relation to which a cash basis election has effect);
(ii) an employment or office (excluding any duties the earnings for which are taxable on the remittance basis — see generally **28.4–28.8** EMPLOYMENT INCOME);
(iii) a UK property business or overseas property business (see **60.2** PROPERTY INCOME);
(iv) a UK furnished holiday lettings business or overseas furnished holiday lettings business (see **60.20** PROPERTY INCOME);
(v) any of the concerns listed in *ITTOIA 2005, s 12(4)* (mines, quarries and sundry other undertakings);
(vi) managing the investments of a company with investment business;
(vii) special leasing, i.e. the hiring out of plant or machinery otherwise than in the course of another qualifying activity (see **10.55** below),

but (other than for the purposes of **10.60** below) to the extent only that the profits therefrom are within the charge to UK tax (or would be if there *were* any profits).

[*CAA 2001, ss 15–17, 17A, 17B, 18, 19(1), 20*].

As regards (iii) and (vii) above, expenditure in providing plant or machinery for use in a dwelling-house (or flat — see HMRC Capital Allowances Manual CA20020, 20040) is not qualifying expenditure. Expenditure on plant and machinery partly for such use is apportioned as is just and reasonable. [*CAA 2001, s 35*]. See HMRC Brief 45/10, 22 October 2010 as regards the meaning of 'dwelling-house' generally and university halls of residence in particular.

As regards (ii) above, the plant or machinery must be *necessarily* provided for use in performing the duties of the employment etc. and mechanically propelled road vehicles and cycles are excluded. [*CAA 2001, s 36*]. Plant provided by a vicar so as to give visual sermons was held not to comply with this requirement (*White v Higginbottom* Ch D 1982, 57 TC 283). With minor exceptions, expenditure on plant or machinery used for providing business entertainment is excluded [*CAA 2001, s 269, Sch 2 para 51*], as is certain expenditure incurred by members of the House of Commons, the Scottish Parliament or the Wales or Northern Ireland Assemblies in or in connection with the provision or use of residential or overnight accommodation. [*CAA 2001, s 34*].

Simon's Taxes. See **B3.304.**

Making of allowances and charges

[10.5] Where the qualifying activity is within **10.4**(i) or (iii)–(v) above, plant and machinery allowances are treated as expenses of, and balancing charges are treated as receipts of, the trade, profession, vocation, UK property business, overseas property business, furnished holiday lettings business or *ITTOIA 2005, s 12(4)* concern. Where the qualifying activity is an employment or office (as in **10.4**(ii) above), allowances are given as deductions from taxable earnings and balancing charges are themselves treated as earnings. [*CAA 2001, ss 247–250, 250A, 251, 252, 262*].

Allowances and charges are computed for income tax purposes by reference to events in periods of account (see **10.2**(i) above). [*CAA 2001, ss 2(1), 6(1)*].

See **10.55** below as regards a qualifying activity of special leasing (as in **10.4**(vii) above).

See **10.2**(ii) above as regards the *claiming* of capital allowances.

Simon's Taxes. See **B3.380–B3.386.**

Eligible expenditure

[10.6] The capital expenditure eligible for allowances includes that on alteration of existing buildings incidental to the installation of plant or machinery for the purposes of a trade or other qualifying activity [*CAA 2001, s 25*] and on demolition of plant or machinery which it replaces [*CAA 2001, s 26(1)(2)*]. There is, however, a distinction between alterations incidental to the installation of plant or machinery and alterations consequential upon the installation of plant or machinery (*J D Wetherspoon plc v HMRC* UT 2012, 81 TC 588); the Tribunal report includes detailed consideration of the application of *CAA 2001, s 25* in the context of a public house.

Costs of moving plant from one site to another and re-erecting it, so far as not deductible in computing profits, qualify for allowances (HMRC Capital Allowances Manual CA21190). Capital expenditure on animals and other living creatures kept for the purposes of farming or any other trade, or on shares in such animals etc., is excluded. [*CAA 2001, s 38*].

Film expenditure

Film production and acquisition expenditure incurred by a person carrying on a trade is treated for income tax purposes as revenue expenditure. In relation to certified films (broadly, British or European films), an election may be made to disapply this rule (and effectively to treat the expenditure as capital expenditure on plant) where the master version is expected to realise its value over a period of two years or more. See *Ensign Tankers (Leasing) Ltd v Stokes* HL 1992, 64 TC 617 for relief to investor in film production partnership. Otherwise, see **75.80** TRADING INCOME as regards the above matters and film tax reliefs generally.

Depreciation

Where it appears that any sums, not otherwise taxable, are to be payable, directly or indirectly, to the owner of plant or machinery in respect of, or to take account of, the *whole* of the depreciation of that plant or machinery, the expenditure incurred in providing that plant or machinery for the purposes of the qualifying activity is not qualifying expenditure. [*CAA 2001, s 37*]. As regards subsidies towards *partial* depreciation, see **10.71** below.

Simon's Taxes. See **B3.305–B3.312.**

Meaning of plant or machinery — leading cases

[10.7] 'Plant' and 'machinery' are not statutorily defined; instead case law is heavily relied upon. '*Machinery*' is given its ordinary meaning, but '*plant*' has been considered in many cases before the courts and tribunals. It includes apparatus kept for permanent employment in the trade etc., but a line is drawn between that which performs a function in the business operations (which may be plant) and that which provides the place or setting in which these operations are performed (which is not). See *Cole Bros Ltd v Phillips* HL 1982, 55 TC 188 (electric wiring and fittings in department store held not to be plant) and *St. John's School v Ward* CA 1974, 49 TC 524 (prefabricated school buildings held not to be plant) and contrast *CIR v Barclay, Curle & Co Ltd* HL 1969, 45 TC 221 (dry docks, including cost of excavation, held to be plant) and *CIR v Scottish & Newcastle Breweries Ltd HL* 1982, 55 TC 252 (lighting and decor of licensed premises held to be plant). If an item used for carrying on a business does not form part of the premises and is not stock-in-trade, then it is plant (*Wimpy International Ltd v Warland* CA 1988, 61 TC 51).

Permanent employment in the trade

Permanent employment demands some degree of durability, see *Hinton v Maden & Ireland Ltd* HL 1959, 38 TC 391 (shoe manufacturer's knives and lasts, average life three years, held to be plant). In practice, a life of two years or more is sufficient, and this applies equally as regards animals functioning as apparatus with which a trade is carried on (see HMRC Capital Allowances Manual CA21100, 21220).

Held to be plant

Movable office partitions (*Jarrold v John Good & Sons Ltd* CA 1962, 40 TC 681); mezzanine platforms installed in a warehouse (but not ancillary lighting) (*Hunt v Henry Quick Ltd* Ch D 1992, 65 TC 108); swimming pools for use on caravan site (*Cooke v Beach Station Caravans Ltd* Ch D 1974, 49 TC 514); grain silos (*May v HMRC* FTT (TC 6928), [2019] UKFTT 32 (TC); *Schofield v R & H Hall Ltd* CA(NI) 1974, 49 TC 538); barrister's books (*Munby v Furlong* CA 1977, 50 TC 491); Building Society window screens (*Leeds Permanent Building Society v Proctor* Ch D 1982, 56 TC 293); light fittings (*Wimpy International Ltd v Warland* CA 1988, 61 TC 51; *J D Wetherspoon plc v HMRC* UT 2012, 81 TC 588); synthetic grass football pitch (*CIR v Anchor International Ltd* CS 2005, 77 TC 38); wooden gazebo placed in garden of public house to provide shelter (*Andrew v HMRC* FTT (TC 799), [2011] SFTD 145).

Held not to be plant

Stallions (*Earl of Derby v Aylmer* KB 1915, 6 TC 665); wallpaper pattern books (*Rose & Co Ltd v Campbell* Ch D 1967, 44 TC 500); canopy over petrol-filling station (*Dixon v Fitch's Garage Ltd* Ch D 1975, 50 TC 509); ship used as floating restaurant (*Benson v Yard Arm Club Ltd* CA 1979, 53 TC 67); false ceilings (*Hampton v Fortes Autogrill Ltd* Ch D 1979, 53 TC 691); a football stand (*Brown v Burnley Football Co Ltd* Ch D 1980, 53 TC 357); an inflatable tennis court cover (*Thomas v Reynolds* Ch D 1987, 59 TC 502); shop fronts, wall and floor coverings, suspended floors, ceilings and stairs etc. (*Wimpy International Ltd v Warland, Associated Restaurants Ltd v Warland* CA 1988, 61 TC 51); permanent quarantine kennels (allowances having been granted for movable kennels) (*Carr v Sayer* Ch D 1992, 65 TC 15); lighting ancillary to mezzanine platform installation qualifying as plant (*Hunt v Henry Quick Ltd* Ch D 1992, 65 TC 108); a planteria (a form of glasshouse — see also **10.8** below) (*Gray v Seymours Garden Centre (Horticulture)* CA 1995, 67 TC 401); access site and wash hall containing car wash equipment (*Attwood v Anduff Car Wash Ltd* CA 1997, 69 TC 575); housing for underground electricity sub-station (*Bradley v London Electricity plc* Ch D 1996, 70 TC 155); golf putting greens (*Family Golf Centres Ltd v Thorne* (Sp C 150), [1998] SSCD 106); an all-weather horse racing track (*Shove v Lingfield Park 1991 Ltd* CA 2004, 76 TC 363); decorative wood panelling and toilet cubicle walls and doors in a public house (*J D Wetherspoon plc v HMRC* UT 2012, 81 TC 588); a caravan occupied by a warden of a caravan site (*Telfer v HMRC* FTT (TC 5350), [2016] UKFTT 614 (TC)).

In *McVeigh v Arthur Sanderson & Sons Ltd* Ch D 1968, 45 TC 273, it was held that the cost of blocks etc. of a wallpaper manufacturer (admitted to be plant) should include something for the cost of the designs but that the designs, following *Daphne v Shaw* KB 1926, 11 TC 256, were not themselves plant. (*Daphne v Shaw* has since been overruled by *Munby v Furlong* above.)

Borrowings

Interest etc. on money borrowed to finance purchases of plant and charged to capital, held not eligible for capital allowances (*Ben-Odeco Ltd v Powlson* HL 1978, 52 TC 459 and cf *Van Arkadie v Sterling Coated Materials Ltd* Ch D 1982, 56 TC 479). In *HMRC v Tower MCashback LLP 1 and another* SC 2011, 80 TC 641, by virtue of an arrangement involving 75% of the purchase price being funded by the making of non-recourse loans (on extreme terms) to the partners, the price ostensibly paid by an LLP for software was vastly in excess of its true market value. The CA concluded that the terms of the borrowing should be considered in relation to the fundamental question of whether the taxpayer suffered the economic burden of paying the full amount and that on this basis capital allowances were available on the full price. The Supreme Court disagreed, holding that the LLPs were entitled only to 25% of the allowances which they had claimed. Lord Walker held that the composite transactions in this case 'did not, on a realistic appraisal of the facts, meet the test laid down by the Capital Allowances Act, which requires real expenditure for the real purpose of acquiring plant for use in a trade'.

Buildings

[10.8] See **10.11** below for allowances for expenditure after 5 April 2008 on integral features (as defined) of buildings and structures.

See **10.12** below for provisions restricting allowances for certain expenditure on buildings and structures.

Certain expenditure on buildings, as below, is treated for capital allowance purposes as being on plant and machinery (unless tax relief could otherwise be obtained). On any disposal, the disposal value (see **10.27** below) in respect of expenditure within (i) below is taken as nil [*CAA 2001, s 63(5)*].

(i) Expenditure on *thermal insulation of existing building* by a person occupying the building for the purposes of a trade carried on by him or letting the building in the course of a UK property business or overseas property business (other than a furnished holiday lettings business). This measure is subject to the overriding rule, where the building is let, that expenditure incurred in providing plant or machinery for use in a *dwelling-house* cannot be qualifying expenditure (see **10.3** above). Expenditure incurred within this category qualifies for writing-down allowances at the special rate (see **10.28** below). [*CAA 2001, ss 27, 28*].

(ii) *Hotels and restaurants.* HMRC regard as eligible for capital allowances expenditure on *apparatus* to provide electric light or power, hot water, central heating, ventilation or air conditioning, alarm and sprinkler systems. Also on cost of hot water pipes, baths, wash basins etc. (CCAB Statement, 9 August 1977). See now *Cole Bros Ltd v Phillips* HL 1982, 55 TC 188 and *CIR v Scottish & Newcastle Breweries Ltd* HL 1982, 55 TC 252.

Professional fees

Fees such as survey fees, architects' fees, quantity surveyors' fees, structural engineers' fees, service engineers' fees or legal costs, only qualify as expenditure on the provision of plant or machinery if they relate directly to the acquisition, transport and installation of the plant or machinery. Where professional fees are paid in connection with a building project that includes the provision of plant or machinery, only the part, if any, which relates to services that can properly be regarded as on the provision of plant or machinery can be qualifying expenditure for plant or machinery allowances.

Preliminary expenses

The same applies to preliminary expenses, e.g. site management, insurance, general purpose labour, temporary accommodation and security, in connection with a building project. (HMRC Capital Allowances Manual CA20070). Where preliminary expenses are allocable or apportionable to expenditure on alterations to a building incidental to the installation of plant or machinery they can rank as eligible expenditure so long as the cost of the alterations is eligible expenditure (*J D Wetherspoon plc v HMRC* UT 2012, 81 TC 588).

Cable television

The cost of provision and installation of ducting in connection with construction of cable television networks is regarded as expenditure on plant or machinery (Revenue Press Release 15 March 1984).

Glasshouses and polytunnels

Glasshouses are likely to be accepted as plant only where, during construction, sophisticated environmental control systems are permanently installed, incorporating e.g. a computer system controlling heating, temperature and humidity control, automatic ventilation systems and automatic thermal or shade screens (HMRC Capital Allowances Manual CA22090). See, for example, *Gray v Seymours Garden Centre (Horticulture)* CA, 67 TC 401, where a 'planteria' was held to be premises. See also **10.12** below and, as regards whether glasshouses are 'long-life assets', **10.34** below.

As regards polytunnels, used mainly by the farming and horticulture industry, see HMRC Capital Allowances Manual CA22090, and see HMRC Brief 32/12, December 2012.

Pig industry

HMRC have published guidance illustrating the range of assets on which the pig industry might claim plant and machinery capital allowances (HMRC Brief 03/10, February 2010).

Slurry storage systems

Slurry storage systems, used for the temporary storage of slurry, qualify as plant or machinery, but any building or structure which is part of a slurry storage facility does not qualify (HMRC Brief 66/08, 29 December 2008).

See generally HMRC Capital Allowances Manual CA21000 *et seq.*

Simon's Taxes. See **B3.308, B3.310.**

Expenditure on security assets

[10.9] Except where tax relief could otherwise be obtained, expenditure by an individual, or partnership of individuals, carrying on a trade or any other qualifying activity within **10.4**(i), (iii) or (iv) above, in connection with the provision for or use by the individual, or any of them, of a security asset (being an asset which improves personal security), is treated as if it were capital expenditure on plant or machinery. On any disposal the disposal value (see **10.27** below) is taken as nil. They apply only where certain conditions, very similar to those described in **75.114** TRADING INCOME, are satisfied, both as regards the provision or use of the asset and the type of asset that may qualify. An appropriate proportion of the expenditure may qualify in cases where the asset is intended to be used *only partly* to improve personal physical security. [*CAA 2001, ss 27, 33, 63(5)*]. See also **28.75** EMPLOYMENT INCOME.

Computer software

[10.10] Where capital expenditure is incurred on the acquisition of computer software for the purposes of a trade or other qualifying activity, the software, if it would not otherwise be plant, is treated as such for capital allowances purposes. Similarly, where capital expenditure is incurred after that date in acquiring for such purposes a right to use or otherwise deal with computer software, both the right and the software are treated as plant provided for the purposes of the qualifying activity and (so long as entitlement to the right continues) as belonging to the person incurring the expenditure.

Where a right is granted to another person to use or deal with the whole or part of software or rights which are treated as plant, and the consideration for the grant consists of (or would if it were in money consist of) a capital sum, a disposal value (see **10.27** below) has to be brought into account (unless the software or rights have previously begun to be used wholly or partly for purposes other than those of the qualifying activity, or the activity for which they were used has been permanently discontinued). The amount of the disposal value to be brought into account is the net consideration in money received for the grant, plus any insurance moneys or other capital compensation received in respect of the software by reason of any event affecting that consideration. However, market value is substituted where the consideration for the grant was not, or not wholly, in money, or where:

- no consideration, or money consideration less than market value, was given for the grant;
- there is no charge under *ITEPA 2003* (i.e. on employment, pension or social security income); and
- the grantee cannot obtain plant and machinery or research and development allowances for his expenditure or is a dual resident investing company connected with the grantor.

Where a disposal value falls to be calculated in relation to software or rights, then for the purpose of determining whether it is to be limited by reference to the capital expenditure incurred (see **10.27** below), that disposal value is increased by any disposal value previously falling to be brought into account as above in respect of the same person and the same plant.

[*CAA 2001, ss 71–73, Sch 3 para 18*].

See also **75.102** TRADING INCOME.

Simon's Taxes. See **B3.341**.

Integral features of buildings and structures

[10.11] Where a person incurs expenditure after 5 April 2008 on the provision of an 'integral feature' of a building or structure used by him for the purposes of a qualifying activity (see **10.4** above) that he carries on, that expenditure is treated for the purposes of plant and machinery allowances as qualifying expenditure on plant or machinery. Expenditure so treated qualifies for writing-down allowances at the special rate (see **10.28** below). No deduction is then available for the expenditure in calculating income from the activity (whether or not such a deduction would be available under general principles).

For these purposes, an '*integral feature*' is any of the following:

- an electrical system (including a lighting system);
- a cold water system;
- a space or water heating system, a powered system of ventilation, air cooling or air purification, and any floor or ceiling comprised in such a system;
- a lift, escalator or moving walkway; or
- external solar shading.

The above list is not, however, to be taken as including any asset whose principal purpose is to insulate or enclose the interior of a building or to provide an interior floor, wall or ceiling which is intended to remain permanently in place. The Treasury may vary the above list by statutory instrument, but they can add an asset only if it would not otherwise qualify for plant and machinery allowances and can remove an asset only if it would thereby qualify for plant and machinery allowances at a rate other than the special rate.

Expenditure incurred on the *replacement* of an integral feature also qualifies as above. For this purpose, an integral feature is treated as replaced if the amount of the expenditure is more than half the cost of replacing the feature at the time the expenditure is incurred. If a person incurs expenditure which does not meet this test but, within twelve months, incurs further expenditure on the integral feature, the test is again applied but by reference to the aggregate expenditure. If the aggregate amount is more than half the cost of replacing the feature at the time the initial expenditure was incurred, both the initial expenditure and the further expenditure qualifies. It is not a requirement that the further expenditure be incurred in the same chargeable period as the initial expenditure; the tax return covering the earlier chargeable period can be amended if necessary.

[*CAA 2001, ss 33A, 33B*].

Simon's Taxes. See **B3.345**.

Restrictions on eligible expenditure

[10.12] Legislation excludes certain expenditure from the definition of plant and machinery for capital allowances purposes.

General exceptions

Expenditure falling within any of *CAA 2001, ss 28–33, 71* and *ITTOIA 2005, s 143* (relating to thermal insulation, security assets, computer software, and films and sound recordings — see **10.6–10.8** and **10.10** above) is not affected by the legislation described below. The same applies to expenditure within *CAA 2001, s 33A* (integral features of buildings and structures — see **10.11** above). [*CAA 2001, s 23(1)(2)*].

Expenditure on buildings which does not qualify for allowances

Expenditure on the construction or acquisition of a building does not qualify for plant and machinery allowances (subject to the general exceptions above and the specific exceptions listed at (1)–(32) below). For these purposes the expression 'building' includes:

- any assets incorporated in the building;
- any assets which, although not incorporated in the building (because they are movable or for some other reason), are nevertheless of a kind which are normally incorporated into buildings; and
- any of the following:
  - (i) walls, floors, ceilings, doors, gates, shutters, windows and stairs;
  - (ii) mains services, and systems, of water, electricity and gas;
  - (iii) waste disposal systems;
  - (iv) sewerage and drainage systems;
  - (v) shafts or other structures in which lifts, hoists, escalators and moving walkways are installed; and
  - (vi) fire safety systems.

[*CAA 2001, s 21; FA 2019, s 35*].

Expenditure on structures which does not qualify for allowances

'*Structure*' means a fixed structure of any kind, other than a building. A structure is 'any substantial man-made asset' (see Revenue Press Release 17 December 1993).

Expenditure on the construction or acquisition of a structure or any other asset listed immediately below, or on any works involving the alteration of land, does not qualify for plant and machinery allowances (subject to the general exceptions above and the specific exceptions listed at (1)–(32) below).

- A tunnel, bridge, viaduct, aqueduct, embankment or cutting.
- A way, hard standing (such as a pavement), road, railway, tramway, a park for vehicles or containers, or an airstrip or runway.
- An inland navigation, including a canal or basin or a navigable river.
- A dam, reservoir or barrage (including any sluices, gates, generators and other equipment associated with it).
- A dock, harbour, wharf, pier, marina or jetty, or any other structure in or at which vessels may be kept or merchandise or passengers may be shipped or unshipped.
- A dike, sea wall, weir or drainage ditch.
- Any structure not included above, except:

(i) a structure (other than a building) within the definition of an 'industrial building');
(ii) a structure in use for the purposes of a gas undertaking; or
(iii) a structure in use for the purposes of a trade consisting in the provision of telecommunications, television or radio services,

and see *CIR v Anchor International Ltd CS 2005, 77 TC 38*, in which a synthetic football pitch was held not to be within this exclusion.

[*CAA 2001, s 22, Sch 3 para 13; FA 2019, s 35*].

In *HMRC v SSE Generation Ltd* UT, [2020] STC 107, [2019] UKUT 332 (TCC), the UT produced a very useful analysis as to both the function and interpretation of *CAA 2001, s 22*. It held inter alia that if, as a result of any of the exceptions at (i)–(iii) above, the expenditure is not disqualified, then that is the end of the matter and the expenditure qualifies; there is no separate consideration as to whether the construction of the structure or asset involves the alteration of land. The UT also held that the provision of a structure includes all the costs of construction, including the necessary preparatory work in excavating the land, its building in situ and its subsequent covering over.

Specific exceptions

The above exclusions do not affect the question as to whether expenditure on any of the items listed in (1)–(32) below qualifies for plant and machinery allowances. Note that items (1)–(15) do not include any asset whose principal purpose is to insulate or enclose the interior of a building or to provide an interior wall, floor or ceiling which (in each case) is intended to remain permanently in place.

(1) Any machinery (including devices for providing motive power) not within any other item in this list.
(2) Gas and sewerage systems provided mainly to meet the particular requirements of the qualifying activity, or provided mainly to serve particular plant or machinery used for the purposes thereof.
(3) Manufacturing or processing equipment; storage equipment, including cold rooms; display equipment; and counters, checkouts and similar equipment.
(4) Cookers, washing machines, dishwashers, refrigerators and similar equipment; washbasins, sinks, baths, showers, sanitary ware and similar equipment; and furniture and furnishings.
(5) Hoists.
(6) Sound insulation provided mainly to meet the particular requirements of the qualifying activity.
(7) Computer, telecommunication and surveillance systems (including their wiring or other links).
(8) Refrigeration or cooling equipment.
(9) Fire alarm systems; sprinkler and other equipment for extinguishing or containing fires.
(10) Burglar alarm systems.
(11) Strong rooms in bank or building society premises; safes.
(12) Partition walls, where movable and intended to be moved in the course of the qualifying activity.

(13) Decorative assets provided for the enjoyment of the public in hotel, restaurant or similar trades.
(14) Advertising hoardings; signs, displays and similar assets.
(15) Swimming pools (including diving boards, slides and structures on which such boards or slides are mounted).
(16) Any glasshouse constructed so that the required environment (namely, air, heat, light, irrigation and temperature) for the growing of plants is provided automatically by means of devices forming an integral part of its structure; see also below.
(17) Cold stores.
(18) Caravans provided mainly for holiday lettings. (Under *CAA 2001, s 23(5)*, 'caravan' includes, in relation to a holiday caravan site, anything treated as such for the purposes of the *Caravan Sites and Control of Development Act 1960* (or NI equivalent).
(19) Buildings provided for testing aircraft engines run within the building.
(20) Movable buildings intended to be moved in the course of the qualifying activity.
(21) The alteration of land for the purpose only of installing plant or machinery (and see below).
(22) The provision of dry docks.
(23) The provision of any jetty or similar structure provided mainly to carry plant or machinery.
(24) The provision of pipelines, or underground ducts or tunnels with a primary purpose of carrying utility conduits.
(25) The provision of towers provided to support floodlights.
(26) The provision of any reservoir incorporated into a water treatment works or any service reservoir of treated water for supply within any housing estate or other particular locality.
(27) The provision of silos provided for temporary storage (see *May v HMRC* FTT (TC 6928), [2019] UKFTT 32 (TC) in which the temporary nature of storage of grain in a silo was unsuccessfully disputed by HMRC); or storage tanks.
(28) The provision of slurry pits or silage clamps.
(29) The provision of fish tanks or fish ponds.
(30) The provision of rails, sleepers and ballast for a railway or tramway.
(31) The provision of structures and other assets for providing the setting for any ride at an amusement park or exhibition.
(32) The provision of fixed zoo cages.

[*CAA 2001, s 23(3)–(5)*].

However, for capital allowances claims made on or after 29 October 2018, nothing in the above list (1)–(32) enables allowances to be claimed on costs relating to plant or machinery which is itself ineligible under *CAA 2001, s 21* or *s 22* above. [*CAA 2001, ss 21(4), 22(4); FA 2019, s 35*]. In particular, this seeks to ensure that expenditure on the alteration of land (item 21 above) will be eligible for capital allowances only where the alteration is made for the purpose of installing *eligible* plant or machinery. This partly reversed a decision made at First-tier Tribunal stage in *HMRC v SSE Generation Ltd* UT, [2020] STC 107, [2019] UKUT 332 (TCC).

As regards expenditure on *glasshouses* (item 16 above), see **10.8** above for the HMRC approach to allowances for such expenditure, and **10.34** below as regards whether glasshouses are 'long-life assets'.

Interests in land

Expenditure on the provision of plant or machinery does not include expenditure incurred on the acquisition of an interest in land, but this restriction does not apply to any asset which is so installed or otherwise fixed in or to any description of land as to become, in law, part of that land. 'Land' does not include buildings or other structures but is otherwise as defined in *Interpretation Act 1978, Sch 1*. 'Interest in land' for these purposes has the same meaning as in *CAA 2001, s 175* (allowances for fixtures — see **10.37** *et seq.* below). [*CAA 2001, s 24*].

Simon's Taxes. See **B3.308.**

Annual investment allowance

[10.13] A person is entitled to an annual investment allowance (AIA) for a chargeable period (see **10.2**(i) above) in respect of any 'AIA qualifying expenditure' which he incurs in that period on plant or machinery which he owns at some time during that period. Subject to the exclusions in **10.15** below, qualifying expenditure (see **10.3** above) is '*AIA qualifying expenditure*' if it is incurred by an individual or by a partnership consisting entirely of individuals (or by a company, as regards which see Tolley's Corporation Tax under Capital Allowances on Plant and Machinery). In determining whether expenditure is AIA qualifying expenditure, any effect of *CAA 2001, s 12* (pre-commencement expenditure — see **10.3** above) on the time at which it is to be treated as incurred is disregarded. Other entities, such as a trust or a partnership consisting of both companies and individuals, are not entitled to an AIA. As regards ownership of plant or machinery, see **10.19** below under *Ownership*.

See **10.14** below for the maximum amount of the AIA, **10.15** for basic rules and exclusions, **10.16** for a restriction where related qualifying activities are under common control, and **10.17** as regards additional VAT liabilities.

[*CAA 2001, ss 38A, 51A(1)*].

Simon's Taxes. See **B3.329.**

Amount of the AIA

[10.14] The maximum annual investment allowance (AIA) is as follows.

For expenditure incurred on and after 1 January 2021	£200,000
For expenditure incurred on and after 1 January 2019 and before 1 January 2021	**£1,000,000**
For expenditure incurred on and after 1 January 2016 and before 1 January 2019	£200,000

For expenditure incurred on and after 6 April 2014 and before 1 January 2016	£500,000

The amount of the AIA available is either the maximum as above or the actual amount of the AIA qualifying expenditure (see **10.13** above), whichever is the lower. A person may choose to claim less than the full AIA available. The above maximum is proportionately increased, or reduced, if the chargeable period is more than, or less than, twelve months.

Periods straddling 1 January 2021

Where a chargeable period straddles 1 January 2021, the maximum for that period is the sum of:

- the entitlement, based on the previous £1 million maximum, for the portion of the chargeable period ending on 31 December 2020, and
- the entitlement, based on the new £200,000 maximum, for the portion of the chargeable period beginning on 1 January 2021,

as if those portions were separate chargeable periods.

Thus, if exactly half of the chargeable period fell before 1 January 2021, the maximum for the full chargeable period would be £600,000 (half of £1 million plus half of £200,000) or, if lower, the amount of the AIA qualifying expenditure. This is subject to an overriding rule, as regards expenditure incurred in the part of the chargeable period falling after 31 December 2020, that no more than the appropriate proportion of £200,000 can qualify for the AIA. So if the business in this example incurred, say, £550,000 of AIA qualifying expenditure in the chargeable period but all of it was incurred in the second half of that period, the AIA for the chargeable period would be restricted to £100,000 (half of £200,000).

Periods straddling 1 January 2019

Where a chargeable period straddles 1 January 2019, the maximum for that period is the sum of:

- the entitlement, based on the previous £200,000 maximum, for the portion of the chargeable period ending on 31 December 2018, and
- the entitlement, based on the new £1 million maximum, for the portion of the chargeable period beginning on 1 January 2019,

as if those portions were separate chargeable periods.

Thus, if exactly one-quarter of a chargeable period fell before 1 January 2019, the maximum for the full chargeable period would be £800,000 (one-quarter of £200,000 plus three-quarters of £1 million) or, if lower, the amount of the AIA qualifying expenditure. This is subject to an overriding rule that no more than £200,000 of expenditure incurred in the part of the chargeable period falling before 1 January 2019 can qualify for the AIA. So if the business in this example incurred, say, £700,000 of AIA qualifying expenditure in the chargeable period but all of it was incurred in the first quarter of that period, the AIA for the chargeable period would be restricted to £200,000.

Periods straddling 1 January 2016

Where a chargeable period straddles 1 January 2016, the maximum for that period is the sum of:

- the entitlement, based on the previous £500,000 maximum, for the portion of the chargeable period ending on 31 December 2015, and
- the entitlement, based on the new £200,000 maximum, for the portion of the chargeable period beginning on 1 January 2016,

as if those portions were separate chargeable periods.

Thus, if exactly two-fifths of the chargeable period fell before 1 January 2016, the maximum for the full chargeable period would be £320,000 (two-fifths of £500,000 plus three-fifths of £200,000) or, if lower, the amount of the AIA qualifying expenditure. The overriding rule, as regards expenditure incurred in the part of the chargeable period falling after 31 December 2015, is that no more than the appropriate proportion of £200,000 can qualify for the AIA. So if the business in this example incurred, say, £150,000 of AIA qualifying expenditure in the chargeable period but all of it was incurred in the last three-fifths of that period, the AIA for the chargeable period would be restricted to £120,000 (three-fifths of £200,000).

[*CAA 2001, s 51A(3)–(9); FA 2013, s 7, Sch 1 paras 1–4; FA 2014, s 10, Sch 2 para 4; FA 2019, s 32, Sch 13 paras 1, 2*].

HMRC accept that in computing the maximum AIA it is just and reasonable to make any time-apportionments on either a daily or monthly basis where the chargeable period in question consists of whole calendar months. In other cases, they will require an apportionment made on a daily basis. (HMRC Capital Allowances Manual CA23085).

Basic rules and exclusions

[10.15] The annual investment allowance (AIA) is made for the chargeable period in which the AIA qualifying expenditure (see **10.13** above) is incurred. (See **10.2**(iv) above as regards the date on which expenditure is treated as having been incurred.)

The taxpayer is free to decide how to allocate the AIA between different classes of AIA qualifying expenditure; he might, for example, choose to allocate it to expenditure qualifying for writing-down allowances at the special rate (see **10.28** below) in priority to expenditure qualifying at the normal rate.

An AIA and a first-year allowance cannot be claimed in respect of the same expenditure (see **10.18** below).

If expenditure is incurred partly for the purposes of a qualifying activity and partly for other purposes, any resultant AIA must be reduced as is just and reasonable.

See **10.26** below for how the AIA interacts with writing-down allowances.

[*CAA 2001, ss 51A(1)(2), 205*].

For worked examples on the AIA, see **10.36** below.

Exclusions

Expenditure is not AIA qualifying expenditure in any of the following circumstances.

(i) The expenditure is incurred in the chargeable period in which the qualifying activity is permanently discontinued. (A discontinuance of a trade at the end of a chargeable period is a discontinuance of that trade *in* that chargeable period (*Keyl v HMRC* UT, [2016] STC 410, [2015] UKUT 383 (TCC)).

(ii) The expenditure is incurred on the provision of a '*car*', defined for these purposes (by *CAA 2001, s 268A*) as a mechanically propelled road vehicle which is neither (1) of a construction primarily suited for the conveyance of goods or burden of any description nor (2) of a type not commonly used as a private vehicle and unsuitable for such use. Motor cycles do qualify for the AIA. It is confirmed on page 12 of an HMRC Technical Note published in December 2008 ('Modernising tax relief for business expenditure on cars') that the above definition means that black hackney cabs (e.g. London taxis) are not regarded as cars for this purpose. A double cab pick-up may qualify as a car — see HMRC Employment Income Manual EIM23150.
As regards (2), see employee benefits case of *Gurney v Richards* Ch D, [1989] STC 682 (fire brigade car equipped with flashing light held within excluded class), decided on similarly worded legislation (see **28.23** EMPLOYMENT INCOME). See also *Bourne v Auto School of Motoring* Ch D 1964, 42 TC 217 (driving school cars) and *Roberts v Granada TV Rental Ltd* Ch D 1970, 46 TC 295 (mini-vans etc.).

(iii) The provision of the plant or machinery is connected with a change in the nature or conduct of a trade or business carried on by a person other than the person incurring the expenditure on its provision, and the obtaining of an AIA was the main benefit, or one of the main benefits, which could reasonably be expected to arise from the making of the change.

(iv) The provision of the plant or machinery is by way of gift (see **10.65** below).

(v) The plant or machinery was previously used by the owner for purposes other than those of the qualifying activity (see **10.66** below), which includes the purposes of long funding leasing (see **10.51** below).

(vi) The plant or machinery is acquired by means of a transaction with a connected person (within **19** CONNECTED PERSONS), or a sale and lease-back transaction or a transaction the sole or main benefit of which would be the obtaining of a plant and machinery allowance (see *CAA 2001, ss 217, 232*).

In addition, if an arrangement is entered into and a main purpose of it is to enable a person to claim an AIA to which he would not otherwise be entitled, the AIA is not made or, if already made, is withdrawn.

[*CAA 2001, ss 38B, 218A, 268A*].

Restriction where related qualifying activities are under common control

[10.16] Where, in the same tax year, two or more qualifying activities are carried on by one or more persons (other than companies), are controlled by the same person and are 'related' to each other, they do not each attract the maximum annual investment allowance (AIA). For this purpose, a person carries on a qualifying activity in a tax year if he carries it on at the end of the chargeable period for that activity ending in that tax year. If the activities in question are carried on by the same person, he is entitled to a single AIA. If the activities are carried on by more than one person, they are entitled to a single AIA between them. In each case, the amount of the AIA is determined by reference to the aggregate amount of AIA qualifying expenditure (see **10.13** above) incurred in the chargeable periods for the qualifying activities ending in the tax year. The maximum in this case is determined without regard to the length of the chargeable periods. The person or persons involved may allocate the AIA to the qualifying expenditure as he or they think fit; they could, for example, choose to allocate it to expenditure qualifying for special rate writing-down allowances (see **10.28** below) in priority to expenditure qualifying for normal writing-down allowances. The amount allocated to AIA qualifying expenditure cannot exceed the maximum amount that would have been available in respect of that expenditure if the restriction had not applied.

For the above purposes a qualifying activity is controlled by a person in a tax year if it is controlled by that person at the end of the chargeable period for that activity ending in that tax year. A qualifying activity carried on by an individual is treated as controlled by that individual. A qualifying activity carried on by a partnership is treated as controlled by the individual (if any) who controls the partnership (within the meaning of *CAA 2001, s 574(3)*). Where partners who between them control one partnership also between them control another partnership, the qualifying activities carried on by the partnerships are treated as controlled by the same person.

Where a qualifying activity has more than one chargeable period ending in the same tax year, each such period must be considered separately, i.e. as if it were the only chargeable period for that activity ending in the tax year, in determining if the restriction applies.

A qualifying activity (A1) is '*related*' to another qualifying activity (A2) in a tax year if they meet either of the two conditions below (or both of them). If A1 is thereby related to A2, A1 is also related to any qualifying activity to which A2 is related. The conditions are as follows.

(1) The shared premises condition. This condition is met if, at the end of the 'relevant chargeable period' for one or both of the qualifying activities, they are carried on from the same premises.
(2) The related activities condition. This condition is met if, at the end of the 'relevant chargeable period' for one or both of the qualifying activities, they are of the same NACE classification. This means the first level of the common statistical classification of economic activities in the EU established by Regulation (EC) No 1893/2006 of the European Parliament and the Council of 20 December 2006 (as that Regulation

has effect in EU law). NACE is a well-established statutory industry classification system. The first level divides activities into 17 main classifications. A list of these classifications is included at HMRC Capital Allowances Manual CA23090.

The '*relevant chargeable period*' for an activity is the chargeable period for that activity ending in the tax year in question.

If the restriction applies and the relevant chargeable period for one of the qualifying activities (A1) in question is longer than a year, an additional amount of AIA may be available for A1 if there is an amount of unused allowance for an earlier tax year which coincides at least in part with A1's long chargeable period (or for more than one such earlier tax year). Say that X controls two related businesses, A1 and A2. A1 is a new business commenced on 6 October 2016. The maximum AIA for expenditure incurred on and after 1 January 2016 is £200,000. In the tax year 2017/18, accounts for A1 are prepared for the 18 months to 5 April 2018 and accounts for A2 are prepared as usual for the year ended on that date. For 2017/18, A1 and A2 have AIA qualifying expenditure of £240,000 and £80,000 respectively but the restriction means that, in the absence of a special rule, X would be entitled to an AIA of only £200,000. For the year ended 5 April 2017, A2 had AIA qualifying expenditure of £72,000, so, in theory, there is unused AIA qualifying expenditure of £128,000 (£200,000 – £72,000); however, this is capped at £100,000 (£200,000 × ½) as only six months of A1's long period of account falls within 2016/17. The unused amount of £100,000 is added to the 2017/18 amount of £200,000 to give a theoretical AIA of £300,000 for 2017/18; this must still be compared to the maximum available AIA for A2 in 2017/18, which in this case gives the same figure of £300,000 (£200,000 × 18/12). X can allocate this between A1 and A2 as he likes, except that the AIA for each business cannot exceed what would have been the available AIA if the related activity restriction had not applied, i.e. £300,000 for A1 (which will clearly not be exceeded) and £80,000 for A2.

The special rule above also applies if the relevant chargeable period for *two or more* of the qualifying activities in question is longer than a year, but with the modifications in *CAA 2001, s 51N* if those activities were related in an earlier tax year.

Periods straddling 1 January 2016

If any of the chargeable periods straddle 1 January 2016, the general rules in **10.14** above for periods straddling that date apply in determining the maximum AIA to be shared between qualifying activities. There is to be taken into account only chargeable periods of one year or less, and, if there is more than one such period, only that period which gives rise to the greatest maximum allowance; for this purpose only, a chargeable period of more than a year ending in 2015/16, 2016/17 or 2017/18 is to be treated as being a chargeable period of one year ending on the date the actual period ends.

Say there are three related activities, A, B and C, with chargeable periods ending in 2015/16. Say these periods end on, respectively, 31 January 2016, 29 February 2016 and 31 March 2016. The maximum time-apportioned AIAs for A, B and C are computed to be, respectively, £475,000, £450,000 and

£425,000. The maximum total claim is £475,000. If A claims AIA of £475,000, nothing can be claimed by B or C. Alternatively, if, say, A claims nothing and C claims its maximum of £425,000, no more than £50,000 (£475,000 – £425,000) could be claimed by B.

Periods straddling 1 January 2019 or 2021

If any of the chargeable periods straddle either 1 January 2019 or 1 January 2021, the general rules in **10.14** above for periods straddling those dates apply in determining the maximum AIA to be shared between qualifying activities. There is to be taken into account only chargeable periods of one year or less, and, if there is more than one such period, only that period which gives rise to the greatest maximum allowance. If a chargeable period is longer than one year and any part of it is within the period of two years beginning with 1 January 2019, the chargeable period is divided for these purposes only into two separate chargeable periods: period B consisting of the one year ending when the actual chargeable period ends, and period A consisting of the balance of the actual chargeable period.

Say there are three related activities, D, E and F, with 12-month chargeable periods ending on, respectively, 30 June 2019, 30 September 2019 and 31 December 2019. The maximum time-apportioned AIAs for D and E are computed to be, respectively, £600,000 and £800,000, and the maximum AIA for F is £1 million. The maximum total claim is £1 million. If F claims AIA of £1 million, nothing can be claimed by D or E. Alternatively, if, say, F claims nothing and D claims its maximum of £600,000, no more than £400,000 could be claimed by E.

[*CAA 2001, ss 51G(7); 51H–51N; FA 2014, s 10, Sch 2 para 5; FA 2019, Sch 13 para 3; SI 2019 No 689, Reg 10(2)*].

Additional VAT liabilities

[10.17] In general, where expenditure was AIA qualifying expenditure (see **10.13** above), any 'additional VAT liability' (see **10.2**(viii) above), incurred in respect of that expenditure at a time when the plant or machinery in question is provided for the purposes of the qualifying activity, is also AIA qualifying expenditure — for the chargeable period in which the liability accrues. Any additional VAT liability incurred at a time when the plant or machinery is used for overseas leasing other than protected leasing (see *CAA 2001, s 105*) is not AIA qualifying expenditure. [*CAA 2001, ss 236, 237*].

First-year allowances

[10.18] A person is entitled to a first-year allowance (FYA) for a chargeable period (see **10.2**(i) above) in respect of any 'first-year qualifying expenditure' which he incurs in that period on plant or machinery which he owns (see **10.19** below under *Ownership*) at some time during that period. He may claim the allowance in respect of the whole or a part of the first-year qualifying expenditure. In determining for these purposes the time at which expenditure is incurred, *CAA 2001, s 12* (pre-commencement expenditure — see **10.3** above) is disregarded. Otherwise, see **10.2**(iv) above as regards the date on which expenditure is treated as having been incurred. FYAs are available only for expenditure within (a)–(f) below.

An FYA and an annual investment allowance (AIA) (see **10.13** above) cannot be claimed in respect of the same expenditure; where both allowances are possible, the taxpayer can choose which, if any, to claim.

Subject to the exclusions below, qualifying expenditure (as in **10.3** above) is '*first-year qualifying expenditure*' if it is incurred:

(a) **before 6 April 2020** by any person on **'energy-saving plant or machinery'** (see **10.20** below) which is unused and not second-hand, in which case the maximum FYA is **100%**; or

(b) **before 6 April 2020** by any person on **'environmentally beneficial plant or machinery'** (see **10.21** below), unused and not second-hand, in which case the maximum FYA is **100%** (but long-life asset expenditure, see **10.34** below, does not qualify);

(c) **before 1 April 2021** (but see below) by any person on cars first registered after 16 April 2002 which are either **'electrically-propelled'** or have **'low CO_2 emissions'** (see **10.22** below), and which are unused and not second-hand, in which case the maximum FYA is **100%;**

(d) **before 1 April 2021** (but see below) by any person on plant or machinery, unused and not second-hand, installed at a **'gas refuelling station'** (see **10.23** below) for use solely for or in connection with refuelling vehicles with natural gas, biogas or hydrogen fuel, in which case the maximum FYA is **100%;**

(e) **before 6 April 2021** (but see below) by any person on **'zero-emission goods vehicles'**, unused and not second-hand, in which case the maximum FYA is **100%**. This is subject to exclusions and to a monetary limit on the total FYAs of this type that can be claimed by any person. See **10.24** below; or

(f) **on and after 23 November 2016 and before 6 April 2023** by any person on plant or machinery for an **electric vehicle charging point**, unused and not second-hand, installed solely for the purpose of charging electric vehicles, in which case the maximum FYA is **100%**.

Future developments

As regards (c) and (d) above, the period for which 100% FYAs are available for these types of expenditure will be extended from 1 April 2021 to 1 April 2025. As regards (e), the period will be extended from 6 April 2021 to 6 April 2025. See www.gov.uk/government/publications/capital-allowance-carbon-dioxide-emissions-thresholds-for-business-cars-goods-vehicles-and-equipment-for-gas-refuelling-stations-from-april-2021.

Exclusions

FYAs are not available under *any* of (a)–(f) above in the circumstances listed below (and note also the exclusion of long-life assets from (b) above).

(i) The expenditure is incurred in the chargeable period in which the qualifying activity is permanently discontinued.

(ii) The expenditure is incurred on the provision of a '*car*' (defined as in **10.15**(ii) above).
This exclusion does *not* apply as regards (c) above, in relation to which the above-mentioned definition of 'car' applies but with the specific inclusion of any mechanically-propelled road vehicle of a type commonly used as a hackney carriage. Motor cycles have always been excluded from the definition of car for the purposes of (c) above.

(iii) The plant or machinery would be a long-life asset but for the transitional provisions of *CAA 2001, Sch 3 para 20* (see **10.34** below).

(iv) The expenditure is on plant or machinery for leasing (whether or not in the course of a trade). For this purpose, 'leasing' expressly includes the letting of a ship on charter or of any other asset on hire. This exclusion does *not* apply as regards expenditure within (a) or (b) above but only if the plant or machinery is leased under an 'excluded lease of background plant or machinery for a building' (see **10.50**(1)(B) below). Expenditure by a company on plant and machinery to be used by its subsidiary in return for an annual charge fell within the exclusion (*M F Freeman (Plant) Ltd v Jowett* (Sp C 376), [2003] SSCD 423).
Where a business supplies plant or machinery with an operator, and the equipment is to be operated solely by the operator thus provided, HMRC accept that this is the provision of a service and not merely plant hire. FYAs are not excluded. HMRC similarly accept that the provision of building access services by the scaffolding industry (but not simply the supply of scaffolding poles etc. for use by others) is the provision of a service. (HMRC Capital Allowances Manual CA23115).
In a case involving the temporary supply of plant to the construction industry without labour but with a package of other services, the appellant was held to be providing an overall service beyond the leasing of assets and to be entitled to FYAs (*MGF (Trench Construction Systems) Ltd v HMRC* FTT (TC 2399), [2012] UKFTT 739 (TC); [2013] SFTD 281).

(v) The provision of the plant or machinery is connected with a change in the nature or conduct of a trade or business carried on by a person other than the person incurring the expenditure on its provision, and the obtaining of an FYA was the main benefit, or one of the main benefits, which could reasonably be expected to arise from the making of the change.

(vi) The provision of the plant of machinery is by way of gift (see **10.65** below).

(vii) The plant or machinery was previously used by the owner for purposes other than those of the qualifying activity (see **10.66** below), which includes the purposes of long funding leasing (see **10.51** below).

For exclusions from (e) above, see **10.24** below.

[*CAA 2001, ss 39, 45A–45EA, 45H–45J, 46, 50, 51, 52, 52A, 268A–268C, Sch 3 paras 14, 48–50; F(No 2)A 2017, s 38; FA 2019, ss 33(1)(2)(5), 34; SI 2016 No 984, Arts 2–4; SI 2017 No 1304*].

See also the anti-avoidance rules at **10.62** below which restrict a buyer's entitlement to FYAs in certain types of transaction.

Simon's Taxes. See B3.320–B3.325, B3.330.

Miscellaneous matters

[10.19] *Partial use for non-trade etc. purposes* results in FYAs being scaled down as is just and reasonable. [*CAA 2001, s 205*]. See **10.32** below as regards writing-down allowances in such cases.

See **10.71** below for the scaling down of FYAs where it appears that a *partial depreciation subsidy* will be payable.

See **10.69** below for the denial of FYAs on plant and machinery treated as changing hands by virtue of certain partnership changes and other *successions*.

Ownership

Before *CAA 2001* came into effect (see **10.1** above), the question of whether a person *owns* plant and machinery at some time in the chargeable period in which the expenditure is incurred was expressed in terms of whether it *belonged* to him at some time during the chargeable period related to the incurring of the expenditure. [*CAA 1990, s 22(1)*]. 'Belongs' has its ordinary meaning and normally entails a right of disposition over the thing possessed. See also *Bolton v International Drilling Co Ltd* Ch D 1982, 56 TC 449, *Ensign Tankers (Leasing) Ltd v Stokes* HL 1992, 64 TC 617, *Melluish v BMI (No 3) Ltd* HL 1995, 68 TC 1 and *BMBF (No 24) Ltd v CIR* Ch D 2002, 79 TC 352. Following the decision in *Stokes v Costain Property Investments Ltd* CA 1984, 57 TC 688, specific provisions were introduced to determine entitlement to allowances for plant or machinery which are fixtures (see **10.37** *et seq.* below). See **10.58** below as regards plant and machinery acquired on hire-purchase, and **10.72** below as regards certain expenditure incurred by a lessee under the terms of a lease. For ownership of certain assets transferred under oil production sharing contracts to the government or representative of the production territory, see *CAA 2001, s 171*. The change in terminology in *CAA 2001* was not intended to be a change in the law.

Ships (postponement of FYAs)

Where a ship qualifies for an FYA, the person entitled may, by written notice, *postpone* all or part of the allowance. The amount to be postponed must be specified in the notice. Where an FYA is claimed in respect of part only of the qualifying expenditure, the above applies in respect of the FYA claimed. The notice must be given no later than the first anniversary of 31 January following the tax year in which ends the chargeable period for which the allowance is due. Available qualifying expenditure for writing-down allowances (see **10.26** below) is computed as if the postponed FYA had, in fact, been made. Postponed FYAs may be claimed over one or more subsequent chargeable periods. [*CAA 2001, ss 130(1)(3)–(6), 131(1)(2)(4)(7)*]. See **10.31** below for postponement of writing-down allowances and deferment of balancing charges.

Additional VAT liabilities

See **10.25** below.

Energy-saving plant or machinery

[10.20] '*Energy-saving plant or machinery*', for the purposes of **10.18**(a) above, is plant or machinery which, either at the time the expenditure is incurred or at the time the contract for its provision is entered into, is of a description specified by Treasury order *and* meets the energy-saving criteria specified by Treasury order for plant or machinery of that description. See below as regards the impact of receiving feed-in tariffs or renewable heat incentive payments. See generally HMRC Capital Allowances Manual CA23140.

A Treasury order may identify qualifying plant or machinery by reference to lists of technology or products issued by the relevant Secretary of State; the Treasury orders refer, in fact, to the Energy Technology Product List (ETPL). The technology classes included in the ETPL, subject to the appropriate criteria, certification or product approval, are: air-to-air energy recovery equipment; automatic monitoring and targeting equipment; boiler equipment; compressed air equipment; heat pumps; heating, ventilation and air conditioning equipment; high speed hand air dryers; motors and drives; radiant and warm air heaters; refrigeration equipment; solar thermal systems and collectors; and uninterruptible power supplies.

A Treasury order can also provide that, in specified cases, no FYA is to be given under **10.18**(a) above unless a '*relevant certificate of energy efficiency*' is in force, i.e. a certificate issued by the Secretary of State, the Scottish Ministers, the Welsh Assembly or the relevant NI department, or by persons authorised by them, to the effect that a particular item, or an item constructed to a particular design, meets the relevant energy-saving criteria. The case currently specified is plant or machinery falling within the technology class 'Combined Heat and Power' specified in the Energy Technology Criteria List (ETCL). If a certificate is revoked, it is treated as having never been in issue, with the result that FYAs under **10.18**(a) above will not have been available. Subject to penalty under *TMA 1970, s 98* for non-compliance, a person who has consequently made an incorrect tax return must give notice to HMRC, specifying the amendment required to the return, within three months of his becoming aware of the problem.

The ETPL and ETCL can be accessed from www.gov.uk/guidance/energy-technology-list.

If one or more components of an item of plant and machinery qualify under these provisions, but the whole item does not, normal apportionment rules are disapplied, and instead the first-year qualifying expenditure under **10.18**(a) above is limited to the amount (or aggregate amount) specified in the ETPL for that component (or those components); where relevant, each *instalment* of expenditure falls to be apportioned in the same way as the whole.

Feed-in tariffs and renewable heat incentives

Expenditure incurred on plant or machinery is to be treated as never having qualified for FYAs as energy-saving plant or machinery if:

(a) a payment is made, or another incentive is given, under a scheme established by virtue of *Energy Act 2008, s 41* (feed-in tariffs) (or under a corresponding NI scheme) in respect of electricity generated by the plant or machinery; or

(b) a payment is made, or another incentive is given, under a scheme established by regulations under *Energy Act 2008, s 100* (renewable heat incentives) (or *Energy Act 2011, s 113* (renewable heat incentives in NI)) in respect of heat generated, or gas or fuel produced, by the plant or machinery.

FYAs already given will be withdrawn by means of an assessment or amended assessment. If a person who has made a tax return subsequently becomes aware that anything in it has become incorrect as a result of the above, he must give notice to HMRC specifying how the return needs to be amended. The notice must be given within three months of his becoming so aware.

[*CAA 2001, ss 45A, 45AA, 45B, 45C; FA 2019, s 33(1)(4)(5); SI 2018 No 268; SI 2019 No 501*].

Simon's Taxes. See B3.324.

Environmentally beneficial plant or machinery

[10.21] '*Environmentally beneficial plant or machinery*', for the purposes of **10.18**(b) above, is plant or machinery which, either at the time the expenditure is incurred or at the time the contract for its provision is entered into, is of a description specified by Treasury order *and* meets the environmental criteria specified by Treasury order for plant or machinery of that description. A Treasury order may identify qualifying plant or machinery by reference to technology lists or product lists issued by the relevant Secretary of State. The intention is to promote the use of technologies, or products, designed to remedy or prevent damage to the physical environment or natural resources (Revenue Press Release BN 26, 9 April 2003). An order may provide that, in specified cases, no FYA is to be given under **10.18**(b) above unless a '*relevant certificate of environmental benefit*' is in force, i.e. a certificate issued by the Secretary of State, the Scottish Ministers, the Welsh Assembly or the relevant NI department, or by persons authorised by them, to the effect that a particular item, or an item constructed to a particular design, meets the relevant environmental criteria. If a certificate is revoked, it is treated as having never been in issue, with the result that FYAs under **10.18**(b) above will not have been available. Subject to penalty under *TMA 1970, s 98* for non-compliance, a person who has consequently made an incorrect tax return must give notice to HMRC, specifying the amendment required to the return, within three months of his becoming aware of the problem.

Eligible products are detailed on the Water Technology List (WTL) (see www.gov.uk/government/publications/water-efficient-enhanced-capital-allowances). Technologies currently included in the WTL, subject to the appropriate criteria or product approval, are listed below:

- flow controllers;
- leakage detection equipment;

- meters and monitoring equipment;
- efficient taps;
- efficient toilets;
- rainwater harvesting equipment;
- water reuse systems (see also below);
- cleaning in place equipment;
- efficient showers;
- efficient washing machines;
- (before 29 March 2019) small scale slurry and sludge dewatering equipment;
- (before 29 March 2019) vehicle wash waste reclaim units;
- water efficient industrial cleaning equipment;
- water management equipment for mechanical seals; and
- greywater recovery and reuse equipment.

Expenditure on the following items falling within the category of 'water reuse systems' will qualify only if a relevant certificate of environmental benefit (see above) is in force:

- efficient membrane filtration systems for the treatment of wastewater for recovery and reuse; and
- efficient wastewater recovery and reuse systems.

If one or more components of an item of plant and machinery qualify under these provisions, but the whole item does not, normal apportionment rules are disapplied, and instead the first-year qualifying expenditure under **10.18**(b) above is limited to the amount (or aggregate amount) specified in the WTL for that component (or those components); where relevant, each *instalment* of expenditure falls to be apportioned in the same way as the whole.

[*CAA 2001, ss 45H–45J; FA 2019, s 33(1)(3)(5); SI 2003 No 2076; SI 2016 No 952; SI 2019 No 499*].

See generally HMRC Capital Allowances Manual CA23135.

Simon's Taxes. See **B3.324D.**

Energy-efficient cars

[10.22] For the purposes of **10.18**(c) above, a car has 'low CO_2 emissions' if it is first registered on the basis of a qualifying emissions certificate (see *CAA 2001, s 268C*) and has CO_2 emissions (see *CAA 2001, s 268C*) of 50g/km or less (previously, for expenditure incurred before 1 April 2018, 75g/km or less). A car is '*electrically-propelled*' if it is propelled solely by electrical power derived from an external source or from a storage battery not connected to any source of power when the car is in motion. See also HMRC Capital Allowances Manual CA23153. [*CAA 2001, s 45D; SI 2016 No 984, Arts 2–4*].

As stated at **10.18**(c), the car must be 'unused and not second-hand'. A car is considered to be '*unused and not second-hand*' even if it has been driven a limited number of miles for the purposes of testing, delivery, test driving by a potential purchaser, or use as a demonstration car (HMRC Capital Allowances Manual CA23153).

Future development

For expenditure incurred on and after 1 April 2021, the above emissions threshold is to be reduced from 50g/km to 0g/km. See www.gov.uk/government/publications/capital-allowance-carbon-dioxide-emissions-thresholds-for-business-cars-goods-vehicles-and-equipment-for-gas-refuelling-stations-from-april-2021.

Simon's Taxes. See B3.324A.

Gas refuelling stations

[10.23] For the purposes of **10.18**(d) above, a '*gas refuelling station*' is any premises (or part) where mechanically-propelled road vehicles are refuelled with natural gas, biogas or hydrogen fuel. Plant or machinery installed for use solely for or in connection with such refuelling includes any storage tank for such fuels, any compressor, pump, control or meter used in the refuelling and any equipment for dispensing such fuels to vehicles' fuel tanks. [*CAA 2001, s 45E*].

Simon's Taxes. See B3.324B.

Zero-emissions goods vehicles

[10.24] A '*zero-emissions goods vehicle*', for the purposes of **10.18**(e) above, is a 'goods vehicle' which cannot in any circumstances emit CO_2 by being driven. A '*goods vehicle*' is a mechanically propelled road vehicle which is of a design primarily suited for the conveyance of goods or burden of any description. The vehicle must be registered but it does not matter whether it is first registered before or after the expenditure is incurred. [*CAA 2001, s 45DA*].

As stated at **10.18**(e), the vehicle must be 'unused and not second-hand'. A vehicle is considered to be '*unused and not second-hand*' even if it has been driven a limited number of miles for the purposes of testing, delivery, test driving by a potential purchaser or use as a demonstration vehicle (HMRC Capital Allowances Manual CA23145).

Exclusions

Expenditure does not qualify if, at the time the claim for the FYA is made, the person who incurred the expenditure is, or forms part of, an undertaking that is:

- an undertaking in difficulty for the purposes of Commission Regulation (EU) No 651/2014 (General Block Exemption Regulation); or
- subject to an outstanding recovery order made by virtue of *Art 108(2)* of the Treaty on the Functioning of the European Union (Commission Decision declaring aid illegal and incompatible with the common market).

Also excluded is expenditure:

(a) incurred for the purposes of a qualifying activity in the fishery or aquaculture sector or relating to the management of waste of other undertakings; or

(b) taken into account for the purposes of a 'relevant grant or payment' made towards it.

For the purposes of (b) above, a grant or payment is a '*relevant grant or payment*' if it is a State aid (whether or not notified to and approved by the EC) or if it is declared by Treasury Order to be relevant.

If a relevant grant or payment is made *after* the making of an FYA on a zero-emission goods vehicle, the allowance is to be withdrawn. An assessment or tax adjustment to withdraw the FYA can be made at any time no later than three years after the end of the chargeable period in which the grant or payment was made.

[*CAA 2001, s 45DB*].

Cap on first-year allowances

No one person can claim FYAs of more than 85 million euros on zero-emission goods vehicles. This is not an annual limit but an aggregate limit over the five-year period during which these FYAs are available. If expenditure on a vehicle exceeds the limit or takes the aggregate spending on such vehicles over the limit, the excess does not qualify for these FYAs. For this purpose, expenditure incurred in sterling or any other currency is to be converted into euros using the spot rate of exchange for the day on which the expenditure is incurred.

The 85 million euro limit applies to expenditure per 'undertaking'. An '*undertaking*' means an 'autonomous enterprise' or an 'enterprise' together with its 'partner enterprises' (if any) and its 'linked enterprises' (if any). All these expressions have the meaning given by Annex 1 to Commission Regulation (EU) No 651/2014 (General Block Exemption Regulation).

There are rules to take account of the fact that an individual enterprise could be an autonomous, linked or partner enterprise at different times during the five-year period for which these FYAs are available. For the purpose of applying the cap, the historic expenditure incurred by a person whilst an undertaking in his/her/its own right, or part of a larger linked or partner enterprise, is added to the historic expenditure incurred by any other undertaking of which that person becomes part. The rules also ensure that the original undertaking (assuming it still exists) is still required to take into account the historic expenditure incurred by a person who was, but is no longer, part of that undertaking.

Scenario 1

X is an autonomous enterprise and has claimed FYAs of 20 million euros on zero-emission goods vehicles. X then becomes part of a linked enterprise (Y) which has already claimed FYAs of 50 million euros on zero-emission goods vehicles. For the purpose of applying the cap going forward, Y is now deemed to have claimed FYAs of 70 million euros on zero-emission goods vehicles.

Scenario 2

W was part of a linked enterprise Z but subsequently becomes autonomous. At that time, Z had already claimed FYAs of 25 million euros on zero-emission goods vehicles. For the purpose of applying the cap going forward, both W and Z are now deemed to have claimed FYAs of 25 million euros on zero-emission goods vehicles.

[*CAA 2001, s 212T*].

See generally HMRC Capital Allowances Manual CA23145–23149.

Providing of State aid information

A claim made on or after 1 July 2016 for FYAs on zero-emissions goods vehicles must include any information required by HMRC for the purpose of complying with certain EU State aid obligations. This may include information about the claimant (or his activities), information about the subject-matter of the claim and other information relating to the grant of State aid through the provision of the FYAs. See **36.5** HMRC — CONFIDENTIALITY OF INFORMATION as regards the publishing by HMRC of State aid information. [*FA 2016, s 180(1)–(4)(10), Sch 24 Pt 1*].

Simon's Taxes. See B3.324F.

Additional VAT liabilities

[10.25] In general, where expenditure has qualified for an FYA, any 'additional VAT liability' (see **10.2**(viii) above), incurred in respect of that expenditure at a time when the plant or machinery in question is provided for the purposes of the qualifying activity, also qualifies — at the same rate and for the chargeable period in which the liability accrues. An additional VAT liability incurred at a time when the plant or machinery is used for overseas leasing other than protected leasing (see *CAA 2001, s 105*) does not qualify for an FYA. However, there is nothing to prevent an FYA in respect of an additional VAT liability from being available in the chargeable period in which the qualifying activity is permanently discontinued, notwithstanding exclusion **10.18**(i) above, where the liability (but not the original expenditure) is incurred in that period. [*CAA 2001, ss 236, 237, Sch 3 paras 46–50*].

Simon's Taxes. See B3.375.

Pooling, writing-down allowances and balancing adjustments

[10.26] Qualifying expenditure (as in **10.3** above) is *pooled* for the purpose of determining entitlement to writing-down allowances and balancing allowances and liability to balancing charges. In addition to the *main pool* for each qualifying activity, there may be a *single asset pool* and/or a *class pool*, and qualifying expenditure falling to be allocated to either of the latter (see **10.29–10.34, 10.71** below) cannot be allocated to the main pool.

For each pool of qualifying expenditure, a **writing-down allowance (WDA)** is available for each chargeable period (see **10.2**(i) above) other than the 'final chargeable period' and is equal to a maximum of **18%** of the amount (if any) by which 'available qualifying expenditure' exceeds the total of any disposal values (see **10.27** below) falling to be brought into account. See **10.28** below (special rate expenditure) for an exception to the normal rate. The WDA is proportionately reduced or increased if the chargeable period is less or more than a year, or if the qualifying activity has been carried on for part only of the chargeable period. A claim for a WDA may require it to be reduced to a specified amount. For the 'final chargeable period', a **balancing allowance** is available, equal to the excess (if any) of (1) 'available qualifying expenditure' over (2) total disposal values. If, for *any* chargeable period, (2) exceeds (1), there arises a liability to a **balancing charge**, equal to that excess.

The maximum rate of WDA in a main pool or a special rate pool is increased to 100% if the balance of the pool (i.e. 'available qualifying expenditure' less total disposal values) is £1,000 or less (proportionately reduced or increased if the chargeable period is less or more than a year, or if the qualifying activity has been carried on for part only of the chargeable period).

The '*final chargeable period*', as regards the main pool, is the chargeable period in which the trade or other qualifying activity is permanently discontinued. As regards a single asset pool, it is normally the first chargeable period in which a disposal event (see **10.27** below) occurs. As regards class pools, see **10.28** (special rate expenditure) below.

Available qualifying expenditure

'*Available qualifying expenditure*' in a pool for a chargeable period consists of qualifying expenditure allocated to the pool for that period and any unrelieved qualifying expenditure brought forward in the pool from the previous chargeable period (usually referred to as the written-down value brought forward). There are rules requiring an allocation to a pool in specific circumstances, for example where an item falls to be transferred from one type of pool to another, and prohibiting the allocation of certain excluded expenditure. These are listed in *CAA 2001, s 57(2)(3)*, and are covered elsewhere in this chapter where appropriate. See **10.60** below as regards restrictions under connected persons and other anti-avoidance provisions.

In allocating qualifying expenditure to the appropriate pool, the following rules must be observed (and see below for interaction with first-year allowances).

(a) Qualifying expenditure can be allocated to a pool for a chargeable period only to the extent that it has not been included in available qualifying expenditure for an earlier chargeable period. (There is nothing to prohibit the allocation of *part only* of a particular amount of qualifying expenditure for a particular chargeable period.)
(b) Qualifying expenditure cannot be allocated to a pool for a chargeable period earlier than that in which it is incurred.
(c) Qualifying expenditure can be allocated to a pool for a chargeable period only if the person concerned *owns* the plant or machinery at some time in that period. (Before *CAA 2001* came into effect, see **10.1**

above, this was expressed in terms of the item *belonging* to that person, but no change in the law is intended; see **10.19** above and **10.38** below for meaning of 'belongs'. See **10.72** below as regards certain expenditure by a lessee.)

Where an 'additional VAT liability' (see **10.2**(viii) above) is incurred in respect of qualifying expenditure, at a time when the plant or machinery in question is provided for the purposes of the qualifying activity, it is itself expenditure on that plant or machinery and may be taken into account in determining available qualifying expenditure for the chargeable period in which it accrues.

The net cost of demolition of plant and machinery demolished during a chargeable period, and not replaced, is allocated to the appropriate pool for that chargeable period.

Interaction with annual investment allowance

If an annual investment allowance (AIA) (see **10.13** above) is made in respect of an amount of AIA qualifying expenditure, the expenditure is nevertheless added to the appropriate pool (or pools). Such allocation is necessary to enable a disposal value to be properly brought into account when a disposal event occurs in relation to the item in question. Following the allocation, the available qualifying expenditure in the pool (or in each pool) is reduced by the amount of the AIA on the expenditure allocated. It follows that any excess of the AIA qualifying expenditure over the AIA made will qualify for WDAs beginning with the chargeable period in which the expenditure is incurred.

Interaction with first-year allowances

If a first-year allowance (FYA) (see **10.18** above) is made in respect of an amount of first-year qualifying expenditure, none of that amount can be allocated to a pool for the chargeable period in which the expenditure is incurred, and only the balance (after deducting the FYA) can be allocated to a pool for a subsequent chargeable period.

However, expenditure which qualifies for an FYA for a chargeable period is not excluded from being allocated to a pool for that period if either (1) the FYA is not claimed or (2) it is claimed in respect of part only of the expenditure (in which case the remaining part can be so allocated).

If an FYA is made in respect of an amount of qualifying expenditure, at least some of the balance (after deducting the FYA) must be allocated to a pool for a chargeable period no later than that in which a disposal event (see **10.27** below) occurs in relation to the item in question. It will usually be beneficial to choose to allocate the whole balance. A nil balance (following a 100% FYA) is deemed to be so allocated. Such allocation is necessary to enable a disposal value to be properly brought into account.

Businesses entering the cash basis

A person carrying on a trade, profession or vocation enters the cash basis for a tax year if a cash basis election is in force for that tax year but no such election was in force for the preceding tax year. A person carrying on a property business enters the cash basis for a tax year if profits are calculated on the cash basis for that tax year but were calculated in accordance with generally accepted accounting practice (GAAP) for the preceding tax year.

Generally, if a person enters the cash basis for a tax year, no 'cash basis deductible amount' can be carried forward as unrelieved qualifying expenditure from the chargeable period ending with the basis period for the previous tax year (or, in the case of a property business, from the previous tax year). A '*cash basis deductible amount*' is any amount that would have been deductible on the cash basis if it had been paid in the tax year for which the person enters the cash basis. Prior to 2017/18, no unrelieved qualifying expenditure could be carried forward unless it was on a car (as defined by *CAA 2001, s 268A* — see **10.15**(ii) above). Except where unrelieved qualifying expenditure is in a single asset pool, the amounts that can and cannot be carried forward are to be determined on a just and reasonable basis. Any unrelieved qualifying expenditure that cannot be carried forward will normally be relieved as a deduction in calculating profits on the cash basis unless the asset is not fully paid for (see **76.8** TRADING INCOME — CASH BASIS FOR SMALLER BUSINESSES and **60.7** PROPERTY INCOME).

The general rule in **10.1** above that no balancing charge can arise, and no disposal value is brought into account, in a chargeable period for which profits are calculated on the cash basis, does not apply for 2017/18 onwards in relation to qualifying expenditure where:

- the qualifying expenditure was incurred at a time when profits were not calculated on the cash basis;
- the person carrying on the qualifying activity entered the cash basis for a tax year; and
- the expenditure would not have been deductible on the cash basis if it had been paid in that tax year.

As regards persons *leaving* the cash basis, see **10.35** below.

Vehicles for which fixed rate deductions allowed

Where, in the case of a trade, profession or vocation:

- an amount of unrelieved qualifying expenditure is carried forward from one chargeable period (period A) to the next (period B) in respect of a vehicle,
- in the tax year for which period B is the basis period a fixed rate deduction is allowed in relation to the vehicle (see **77.2** TRADING INCOME — FIXED RATE DEDUCTION SCHEME), and
- (in relation to 2017/18 or an earlier year) the trader etc. does not enter the cash basis for that tax year (see **76.8** TRADING INCOME — CASH BASIS FOR SMALLER BUSINESSES),

the unrelieved qualifying expenditure cannot be brought forward to period B. Where the tax year is 2018/19 or a subsequent year, the bringing forward of unrelieved qualifying expenditure is prohibited regardless of whether or not the trader enters the cash basis. Where the unrelieved qualifying expenditure is not in a single asset pool, the amount of unrelieved qualifying expenditure in respect of the vehicle is to be determined on a just and reasonable basis. For 2017/18 onwards, a similar prohibition applies in the case of a property business.

See also **10.3** above.

[*CAA 2001, ss 1A(6)–(12), 26(3)–(5), 53–56, 56A, 57–59, 65, 235; F(No 2)A 2017, Sch 2 paras 49, 50, 52, 64(1); FA 2018, s 36(6)–(8)*].

See the examples at **10.36** below.

Simon's Taxes. See **B3.331–B3.333, B3.375.**

Disposal events and values

[10.27] Where a person has incurred qualifying expenditure (see **10.3** above) on plant or machinery, a **disposal value** must be brought into account for a chargeable period (see **10.2**(i) above) in which any one of the following **disposal events** occurs (but normally only in relation to the first such event to occur in respect of that plant or machinery).

- (i) The person ceases to own the plant or machinery.
- (ii) He loses possession of it, and it is reasonable to assume the loss is permanent.
- (iii) It has been in use for 'mineral exploration and access' (see **9.16**(a) CAPITAL ALLOWANCES) and the person abandons it at the site where it was so in use.
- (iv) It ceases to exist as such (by reason of its destruction, dismantling or otherwise).
- (v) It begins to be used wholly or partly for purposes other than those of the qualifying activity.
- (vi) It begins to be leased under a long funding lease (see **10.51** below).
- (vii) The qualifying activity is permanently discontinued.

The amount to be brought into account depends upon the nature of the event.

- (a) On a sale (other than one within (b) below), it is the net sale proceeds plus any insurance or capital compensation received (by the person concerned) by reason of any event affecting the sale price obtainable.
- (b) On a sale at less than market value, it is market value, unless:
  - (i) the buyer (not being a dual resident investing company connected with the seller) can claim plant or machinery or research and development allowances for his expenditure; or
  - (ii) the sale gives rise to a charge to tax under *ITEPA 2003* (i.e. on employment, pension or social security income),

  in which case (a) above applies.
- (c) On demolition or destruction, it is the net amount received for the remains, plus any insurance or capital compensation received.
- (d) On permanent loss (otherwise than within (c) above), or on abandonment as in (iii) above, it is any insurance or capital compensation received.

(e) On commencement of a long funding lease, it is as stated in **10.51** below.
(f) On permanent discontinuance of the qualifying activity preceding an event in (a)–(e) above, it is whatever value would otherwise have applied on the occurrence of that event.
(g) On a gift giving rise to a charge to tax on the recipient under *ITEPA 2003* (i.e. on employment, pension or social security income), it is nil. See also HMRC Capital Allowances Manual CA23250.
(h) On any other event, it is market value at the time of the event.

However, the disposal value is in all cases limited to the qualifying expenditure incurred on the plant or machinery by the person in question. In addition, there is no requirement to bring a disposal value into account if none of the qualifying expenditure in question has been taken into account in determining the person's available qualifying expenditure (see **10.26** above) for any chargeable period up to and including that in which the disposal occurs. As regards both these rules, see also **10.61** below as regards certain transactions between connected persons.

See **10.49** below for a further disposal event in the case of long funding leasing, and for the appropriate disposal value.

Additional VAT rebates

Where an 'additional VAT rebate' (see **10.2**(viii) above) is made in respect of an item of qualifying expenditure, a disposal value of an equivalent amount must be brought into account (on its own or as an addition to any other disposal value brought into account for that item) for the chargeable period in which the rebate accrues. Any disposal value brought into account for a subsequent chargeable period is limited to the original qualifying expenditure less all additional VAT rebates accrued in all chargeable periods up to (but not including) that chargeable period. If the disposal value is itself the result of an additional VAT rebate, it is limited to the original qualifying expenditure less *any* disposal values brought into account as a result of earlier events.

[*CAA 2001, ss 60, 61, 62(1), 63(1), 64(1)(5), 238, 239*].

Anti-avoidance

In response to identified avoidance schemes, the disposal value is restricted on an event within (a), (b) or (h) above where:

- the plant or machinery is subject to a lease, and
- arrangements have been entered into that have the effect of reducing the disposal value in so far as it is attributable to rentals payable under the lease.

The disposal value is to be determined as if the arrangements had not been entered into. This does not apply where the arrangements take the form of a transfer of relevant receipts as in **4.35** ANTI-AVOIDANCE such that an amount has been treated as taxable income.

[*CAA 2001, s 64A*].

See **10.61** below for other anti-avoidance rules.

Simon's Taxes. See B3.331, B3.334, B3.335, B3.375.

Special rate expenditure

[10.28] Certain expenditure qualifies for writing-down allowances (WDAs) at a special rate of **6%** of the amount (if any) by which available qualifying expenditure (see **10.26** above) exceeds the total of any disposal values (see **10.27** above) falling to be brought into account. This is known as '*special rate expenditure*'. The special rate was 8% before 6 April 2019 (see also below under Hybrid rate for periods straddling 6 April 2019) and 10% before 6 April 2012. Special rate expenditure comprises the following:

(i) expenditure on thermal insulation within **10.8**(i) above;
(ii) expenditure on integral features of buildings and structures (see **10.11** above);
(iii) long-life asset expenditure within **10.34** below;
(iv) expenditure on most cars (see below);
(v) expenditure on the provision of cushion gas, i.e. gas that functions, or is intended to function, as plant in a particular gas storage facility; and
(vi) expenditure on the provision of solar panels.

In addition, long-life asset expenditure is also special rate expenditure.

Cars

A car is within (iv) above if it is not one of the following:

- a car with 'low CO_2 emissions';
- an electrically-propelled car (as defined by *CAA 2001, s 268B*); or
- a car first registered before 1 March 2001.

A car has '*low CO_2 emissions*' if, when first registered, it was registered on the basis of a qualifying emissions certificate (as defined by *CAA 2001, s 268C*) and its CO_2 emissions (see *CAA 2001, s 268C*) do not exceed 110g/km (130g/km for expenditure incurred before 1 April 2018). '*Car*' is as defined by *CAA 2001, s 268A* (see **10.15**(ii) above) and excludes a motor cycle.

See **10.3, 10.26** above for where a fixed rate deduction (see **77.2** TRADING INCOME — FIXED RATE DEDUCTION SCHEME) is allowed in relation to a car (or other vehicle).

Future development

For expenditure incurred on and after 1 April 2021, the above emissions threshold is to be reduced from 110g/km to 50g/km. See www.gov.uk/government/publications/capital-allowance-carbon-dioxide-emissions-thresholds-for-business-cars-goods-vehicles-and-equipment-for-gas-refuelling-stations-from-april-2021.

Hybrid rate for periods straddling 6 April 2019

Where a period of account (see **10.2**(i) above) begins before and ends on or after 6 April 2019, the special rate is a hybrid rate computed as follows and rounded up, if necessary, to two decimal places:

$$R = \left(8 \times \frac{BD}{PA}\right) + \left(6 \times \frac{AD}{PA}\right)$$

where:

R = the hybrid special rate;
BD = the number of days in the period of account falling before 6 April 2019;
AD = the number of days in the period of account falling on or after 6 April 2019; and
PA = the number of days in the period of account.

Supplementary

If only a part of the expenditure on any item is special rate expenditure, the part which is and the part which is not are treated as if they were separate items of plant or machinery; any necessary apportionments must be made on a just and reasonable basis.

If special rate expenditure is incurred wholly and exclusively for the purposes of the qualifying activity, and does not fall to be allocated to a single asset pool, it is allocated to a class pool known as the '*special rate pool*'. Even if allocated to a single asset pool, the special rate of WDAs still applies. As regards the special rate pool, see **10.26** above for the 100% rate of WDAs where the balance of the pool is no more than £1,000. The special rate WDA is proportionately reduced or increased if the chargeable period is less or more than a year, or if the qualifying activity has been carried on for part only of the chargeable period. A claim for a WDA can require it to be reduced to a specified amount. The final chargeable period (see **10.26** above) of a special rate pool is that in which the qualifying activity is permanently discontinued.

[*CAA 2001, ss 65(1), 104A, 104AA, 104B–104D, 104G; FA 2019, s 31; SI 2016 No 984, Arts 2, 3, 5*].

Long-life asset expenditure — transitional

At the end of the chargeable period straddling 6 April 2008 (the '*straddling period*'), the balance of the long-life asset pool (representing expenditure incurred before 6 April 2008) is transferred to the special rate pool. If a chargeable period ends on 5 April 2008, such that there is no straddling period, the balance of the long-life asset pool at the end of that day is transferred to a special rate pool. In either case, the balance transferred is generally treated subsequently as if it had always been special rate expenditure. Long-life asset expenditure in a single asset pool remains in that pool but is treated subsequently as special rate expenditure in a single asset pool. [*FA 2008, s 83*]. See also **10.34** below.

Connected persons transactions — transitional

If, after 5 April 2008, there is a sale between CONNECTED PERSONS (**19**) of an integral feature (see **10.11** above) on which expenditure was incurred on or before that date and the buyer's expenditure would otherwise be special rate expenditure, the buyer's expenditure is qualifying expenditure only if the original expenditure was qualifying expenditure or if the buyer's expenditure would have been qualifying expenditure if incurred at the time the original expenditure was incurred. If expenditure is thereby prevented from being qualifying expenditure, this rule is again applied if there is a further sale between connected persons, but reference to the original expenditure is always to the pre-6 April 2008 expenditure. [*FA 2008, Sch 26 para 15*]. This rule is designed to prevent allowances being claimed after 5 April 2008 on an integral feature if allowances would not have been available for that feature on or before that date (Treasury Explanatory Notes to the 2008 Finance Bill).

Other anti-avoidance

Where a disposal value less than the 'notional written-down value' would otherwise fall to be brought into account in respect of special rate expenditure which has attracted restricted allowances as above, an adjustment may be required. Where the event giving rise to the disposal value is part of a scheme or arrangement a main object of which is the obtaining of a tax advantage under the plant and machinery allowances provisions, the 'notional written-down value' is substituted for the disposal value. The '*notional written-down value*' is qualifying expenditure on the item in question less maximum allowances to date, computed on the assumptions that the item was the only item of plant or machinery, that the expenditure (if on a long-life asset) was not excluded from being long-life asset expenditure by the operation of a monetary limit and that all allowances have been made in full. [*CAA 2001, s 104E*].

Simon's Taxes. See B3.331.

Exclusions from the main pool

[10.29] The majority of items excluded from the main pool of qualifying expenditure are set out in **10.30–10.34** below. In addition to those, the following items are excluded:

- special rate expenditure (see **10.28** above); and
- plant and machinery in respect of which a partial depreciation subsidy is received (see **10.71** below).

Cars

[10.30] Expenditure on cars used exclusively for the purposes of the qualifying activity goes into the main pool unless the expenditure is special rate expenditure. Cars with an element of non-business use are not pooled but attract only the special rate of writing-down allowances if the expenditure is special rate expenditure. See **10.28** above for details of those cars the expenditure on which is special rate expenditure. A 'car' excludes a motor cycle, which means that a motor cycle is treated like any other item of plant or machinery.

See **75.50** TRADING INCOME as regards expenditure on *hiring* a car.

See **10.3**, **10.26** above for where a fixed rate deduction (see **77.2** TRADING INCOME — FIXED RATE DEDUCTION SCHEME) is allowed in relation to a car (or other vehicle).

Simon's Taxes. See B3.342.

Ships

[10.31] Qualifying expenditure (see **10.3** above) on the provision of a ship for the purposes of a trade or other qualifying activity can only be allocated to a *single asset pool* (see **10.26** above), known as a *single ship pool.* This does not apply if:

- an election is made to exclude such treatment (see below); or
- the qualifying activity is one of special leasing (see **10.55** below); or
- the ship is otherwise provided for leasing (which expressly includes letting on charter), *unless* it is not used for 'overseas leasing' (other than 'protected leasing') at any time in the 'designated period' *and* it appears that it will be used only for a 'qualifying purpose' in that period. Plant or machinery is used for overseas leasing if it is used for the purpose of being leased to a person who is not resident in the UK and does not use the plant or machinery exclusively for earning profits chargeable to UK tax. See *CAA 2001 Pt 2 Ch 11* for the meaning of the other expressions used here.

When a disposal event occurs in relation to a single ship pool, the available qualifying expenditure (see **10.26** above) in that pool for the chargeable period in question is transferred to the '*appropriate non-ship pool*' (i.e. the pool to which the expenditure would originally have been allocated in the absence of the single ship pool rules), and the single ship pool is brought to an end with no balancing allowance or charge. The disposal value is brought into account in the pool now containing the qualifying expenditure. In addition to the circumstances at **10.27** above, a disposal event occurs if a ship is provided for leasing or letting on charter and begins to be used otherwise than for a qualifying purpose at some time in the first four years of the designated period.

If the ship ceases to be used by the person who incurred the qualifying expenditure, without his having brought it into use for the purposes of the qualifying activity, then, in addition to any adjustments required as above, any writing-down allowances (WDAs) previously made (or postponed — see below) are withdrawn, and the amount withdrawn is allocated to the 'appropriate non-ship pool' (see above) for the chargeable period in question.

A person who has incurred qualifying expenditure on a ship may elect, for any chargeable period, to disapply the single ship pool provisions in respect of:

- all or part of any qualifying expenditure that would otherwise be allocated to a single ship pool in that period; or
- all or part of the available qualifying expenditure (see **10.26** above) already in a single ship pool,

with the result that the amount in question is allocated to the 'appropriate non-ship pool' (see above). The election must be made no later than the first anniversary of 31 January following the tax year in which ends the chargeable period in question.

Postponement of WDAs

A person entitled to a WDA for a chargeable period in respect of a single ship pool may, by written notice, postpone all or part of it to a later period. The amount to be postponed must be specified in the notice. Where a reduced WDA is claimed, all or part of the reduced amount may be postponed. The time limits for giving notice are the same as for the election referred to immediately above. Available qualifying expenditure (see **10.26** above) is computed as if the postponed WDA had, in fact, been made. Postponed WDAs may be claimed over one or more subsequent chargeable periods. See **10.19** above for postponement of first-year allowances.

[*CAA 2001, ss 105(1)(2), 127–129, 130(2)(7), 131(1)(3)–(7), 132, 133, 157(1)*].

Deferment of balancing charges on qualifying ships

Balancing charges on ships may be deferred and set against subsequent expenditure on ships for a maximum of six years from the date of disposal. A claim for deferment of the whole or part of a balancing charge may be made by the shipowner where a disposal event within **10.27**(i)–(iv) above occurs in relation to a 'qualifying ship' (the old ship). A '*qualifying ship*' is, broadly, a ship of a sea-going kind of 100 gross registered tons or more, excluding offshore installations (as defined by *ITA 2007, s 1001*) and ships of a kind used or chartered primarily for sport or recreation (but passenger ships and cruise liners are not so excluded). The provisions also apply to ships of less than 100 tons in cases where the old ship is totally lost or is damaged beyond worthwhile repair. A ship brought into use in the trade must within three months of first use (unless disposed of during those three months) be registered in the UK, the Channel Islands, Isle of Man, a colony (as to which see Revenue Tax Bulletins April 1995 p 208, June 1998 p 553), a European Union State or a European Economic Area State and must continue to be so until at least three years from first use or, if earlier, until disposed of to an unconnected person. It is a further condition that no amount in respect of the old ship has been allocated to a 'partial use' single asset pool (see **10.32** below), a 'partial depreciation subsidy' single asset pool (see **10.71** below) or a pool for a qualifying activity consisting of special leasing (see **10.55** below).

The balancing charge on the old ship is in effect calculated as if allowances had been granted, and the charge arises, in a single ship pool, with appropriate assumptions where that is not, in fact, the case (see *CAA 2001, s 139*).

Deferment is achieved by allocating the amount deferred to the 'appropriate non-ship pool' (see above) for the chargeable period in question, so that it is effectively set against the disposal value brought into account in that pool (see above) as a result of the disposal event concerned. The *maximum deferment* is the *lowest* of (i) the amount treated as brought into account in respect of the old ship under *CAA 2001, s 139* (see above), (ii) the amount to be expended on new shipping (see below), so far as not already set against an earlier balancing charge, in the six years starting with the date of disposal of the old ship, (iii) the amount which, in the absence of a deferment claim, would have been the total balancing charge for the chargeable period in question in the appropriate non-ship pool, and (iv) the amount needed to reduce the profit of the trade or other qualifying activity to nil (disregarding losses brought forward), no deferment being possible if no such profit has been made. If the amount actually expended within (ii) above turns out to be less than the amount deferred, the amount of the deficiency is reinstated as a balancing charge for the chargeable period to which the claim relates.

Where an amount is expended on new shipping within the six-year period allowed and is attributed by the shipowner, by notice to HMRC, to any part of an amount deferred, an amount equal to the amount so matched is brought into account as a disposal value, for the chargeable period in which the expenditure is incurred, in the single ship pool to which the expenditure is allocated, thus reducing the amount on which allowances may be claimed on the new ship. No amount of expenditure can be attributed to a deferment if there is earlier expenditure on new shipping within the said six-year period which has not been attributed to that or earlier deferments. An attribution may be varied by the trader by notice to the inspector within a specified time (see *CAA 2001, s 142*).

For the purposes of these provisions, an amount is expended on new shipping if it is qualifying expenditure, incurred by the claimant wholly and exclusively for the purposes of a qualifying activity, on a ship (the new ship) which will be a qualifying ship (see above) for at least three years from first use or, if earlier, until disposed of to an unconnected person. Expenditure is treated as incurred by the claimant if it is incurred by a successor following a partnership change (see **52.7** PARTNERSHIPS) or company reconstruction (see Tolley's Corporation Tax) in consequence of which the qualifying activity was not treated as discontinued. Expenditure incurred on a ship which has belonged to either the shipowner or a connected person within the previous six years or which is incurred mainly for tax avoidance reasons does not qualify. The expenditure must be allocated to a single ship pool. If an election is made to disapply the single ship pool provisions, the expenditure is deemed never to have been expenditure on new shipping (but must nevertheless be treated as such in matching expenditure with deferments, so that the election prevents further matching of amounts already deferred).

For income tax purposes, the claim for deferment must be made within twelve months after 31 January following the tax year in which ends the chargeable period of deferment. Before the current year basis of assessment applied, the claim had to be made within two years after the end of that chargeable period. Where a claim for deferment is found to be erroneous as a result of subsequent circumstances, the shipowner must, within three months after the end of the chargeable period in which those circumstances first arise, notify HMRC accordingly (failure to do so incurring a penalty under *TMA 1970, s 98*); consequential assessments may be made within twelve months after notice is given, notwithstanding normal time limits.

[*CAA 2001, ss 134–158, Sch 3 para 24; SI 1996 No 1323; SI 1997 No 133*].

Simon's Taxes. See **B3.350–B3.353.**

Plant and machinery partly used for non-trade etc. purposes

[10.32] Qualifying expenditure (see **10.3** above) incurred partly for the purposes of the trade or other qualifying activity and partly for other purposes can only be allocated to a *single asset pool* (see **10.26** above). (See **10.19** above as regards first-year allowances.) Where in other cases plant or machinery *begins to be used* partly for other purposes, such that a disposal value falls to be brought into account (see **10.27**(v) above) in a pool, an amount equal to the disposal value is allocated to a single asset pool for the chargeable period in question. In respect of a single asset pool under these provisions, writing-down allowances and balancing allowances and charges are reduced to such amount as is just and reasonable (though the full amount is deducted in arriving at any unrelieved qualifying expenditure carried forward).

Where, circumstances change such that the proportion of use for purposes other than those of the qualifying activity increases during a chargeable period, and the market value of the plant or machinery at the end of the period exceeds the available qualifying expenditure (see **10.26** above) in the pool for that period by more than £1 million, then if no disposal value would otherwise fall to be brought into account for the period, a disposal value must be brought into account (equal to market value — see **10.27**(g) above) and, in the next or a subsequent chargeable period, an equivalent amount may be allocated to a new single asset pool as if it were qualifying expenditure newly incurred.

[*CAA 2001, ss 206–208, Sch 3 para 42*].

See also *Kempster v McKenzie* Ch D 1952, 33 TC 193 and *G H Chambers (Northiam Farms) Ltd v Watmough* Ch D 1956, 36 TC 711 and HMRC Capital Allowances Manual CA 23530, 27100 as regards further adjustment for any element of personal choice.

Simon's Taxes. See **B3.359.**

Short-life assets

[10.33] A person who has incurred qualifying expenditure (see **10.3** above) on an item of plant or machinery may elect for it to be treated as a short-life asset, provided it is not an excluded item (see list below). There is no requirement as to the expected useful life of the item, but short-life asset treatment will be of no practical benefit where the item remains in use for more than eight years (or, for expenditure incurred before 6 April 2011, for more than four years). The election is irrevocable and must be made no later than the first anniversary of 31 January following the tax year in which ends the chargeable period in which the expenditure (or earliest expenditure) is incurred.

Identification

In general, HMRC will require sufficient information in support of an election to minimise the possibility of any difference of view at a later date (e.g. on a disposal) about what was and was not covered by the election, and to ensure that it does not incorporate any excluded items (see list below). Where separate identification of short-life assets acquired in a chargeable period is either impossible or impracticable, e.g. similar small or relatively inexpensive items held in very large numbers, perhaps in different locations, then the information required in support of the election may be provided by reference to batches of acquisitions. (HMRC SP 1/86).

Exclusions

Each of the following items of plant or machinery is excluded from being a short-life asset.

(i) A car, defined as at **10.15**(ii) above with the exception of cars hired out to disabled persons in receipt of certain disability allowances, independence payments or mobility supplements.

(ii) A ship.

(iii) An item which is the subject of special leasing (see **10.55** below).

(iv) An item acquired partly for the purposes of a trade or other qualifying activity and partly for other purposes.

(v) An item which is the subject of a partial depreciation subsidy (see **10.71** below).

(vi) An item received by way of gift or whose previous use by the person concerned did not attract capital allowances (see **10.65**, **10.66** below and, as regards long funding leasing, **10.51** below).

(vii) An item the expenditure on which is long-life asset expenditure (see **10.34** below).

(viii) An item the expenditure on which is special rate expenditure (see **10.28** above) unless it is a car hired out to persons receiving certain disability allowances, independence payments or mobility supplements.

(ix) An item provided for leasing, unless it will be used within the 'designated period' (see *CAA 2001, s 106*) for a 'qualifying purpose' (see *CAA 2001, ss 122–125*), and with the exception in any case of cars hired out to persons receiving certain disability allowances, independence payments or mobility supplements.

Treatment of short-life assets

Qualifying expenditure in respect of a short-life asset can only be allocated to a *single asset pool* (see **10.26** above), known as a *short-life asset pool*. If no disposal event within **10.27**(i)–(vi) above occurs in any of the chargeable periods ending on or before the 'relevant anniversary' (referred to below as the '*cut-off date*'), the short-life asset pool is brought to an end on the cut-off date but with no balancing allowance or charge and no denial of a writing-down allowance for the final period. The item ceases to be a short-life asset and the available qualifying expenditure in the pool is allocated to the main pool for the first chargeable period ending *after* the cut-off date. (If the item is a car the expenditure on which was special rate expenditure (see **10.28** above), it is allocated to the special rate pool rather than the main pool.)

The '*relevant anniversary*' (and thus the cut-off date) is the eighth anniversary (or, where any of the expenditure on the asset was incurred before 6 April 2011, the fourth anniversary) of the end of the chargeable period in which the expenditure was incurred (or the first such period in which any of it was incurred).

The following applies where short-life asset treatment has been claimed on the basis that the item has been provided for leasing, but will be used within the designated period for a qualifying purpose (so is not excluded by (ix) above). If, at any time in a chargeable period ending on or before the cut-off date (as above), the item begins to be used otherwise than for such a purpose, and that time falls within the first eight years of the 'designated period' (or, where any of the expenditure on the asset was incurred before 6 April 2011, the first four years), the short-life asset pool is brought to an end at that time but with no balancing allowance or charge and no denial of a writing-down allowance for the final period. The item ceases to be a short-life asset and the available qualifying expenditure in the pool is allocated, for the chargeable period in which that time falls, to the main pool.

If at any time before the cut-off date (as above), a short-life asset is disposed of to a connected person (within **19** CONNECTED PERSONS), short-life asset treatment continues in the connected person's hands (though the original cut-off date remains unchanged). If both parties so elect (within two years after the end of the chargeable period in which the disposal occurs), the disposal is treated as being at a price equal to the available qualifying expenditure (see **10.26** above) then in the short-life asset pool, and certain anti-avoidance provisions on transactions between connected persons are disapplied. If no election is made, the anti-avoidance provisions at **10.60** below apply in full, and the exception at **10.27**(b)(i) above is disapplied (so that market value can be substituted for a lesser sale price even where the buyer is entitled to capital allowances).

If a disposal event occurs in respect of a short-life asset pool such that the pool ends and a balancing *allowance* arises (see **10.26** above), and an 'additional VAT liability' (see **10.2**(viii) above) is subsequently incurred in respect of the item concerned, a further balancing allowance of that amount is given for the chargeable period in which the additional VAT liability accrues.

HMRC accept that it may not be practicable for individual pools to be maintained for every short-life asset, especially where they are held in very large numbers. Statement of Practice SP 1/86 sets out examples of acceptable bases of computation where the inspector is satisfied that the actual life in the business of a distinct class of assets with broadly similar average lives, before being sold or scrapped, is likely to be less than five years.

[*CAA 2001, ss 83–89, 240, 268D*].

When deciding whether or not to elect for short-life asset treatment, it should be borne in mind that this is only beneficial if the asset is both disposed of within the period of eight years, and for less than the current written-down value, which in relation to cost (and assuming the rate of writing-down allowance to be 18%) would be:

Period of account after date of acquisition	**% of cost**
1st	100
2nd	82
3rd	67
4th	55

Period of account after date of acquisition	% of cost
5th	45
6th	37
7th	30
8th	25

See example (A) at **10.36** below.

Simon's Taxes. See B3.343.

Long-life assets

[10.34] There are special provisions relating to certain '*long-life asset expenditure*', i.e. qualifying expenditure (as in **10.3** above) incurred on the provision of a 'long-life asset' for the purposes of a qualifying activity (but see below for exclusions by reference to a monetary limit).

Subject to below, a '*long-life asset*' is plant or machinery which it is reasonable to expect will have a useful economic life of at least 25 years (or where such was a reasonable expectation when the plant or machinery was new, i.e. unused and not second-hand). For these purposes, the useful economic life of plant or machinery is the period from first use (by any person) until it ceases to be, or to be likely to be, used by anyone as a fixed asset of a business. As an introduction to a detailed discussion of what constitutes a long-life asset (including twelve examples), HMRC have stated that they 'will generally accept the accounting treatment as determining whether an asset is long-life provided it is not clearly unreasonable' (Revenue Tax Bulletin August 1997 pp 445–450). For whether glasshouses (for which see generally **10.8** and **10.12**(17) above) are long-life assets, see Revenue Tax Bulletin June 1998 p 552. For aircraft, see Revenue Tax Bulletin June 1999 pp 671, 672, April 2000 pp 739, 740 and December 2003 pp 1074, 1075.

The following *cannot* be long-life assets.

(i) Fixtures (see **10.37** below) in, or plant or machinery provided for use in, a building used wholly or mainly as a dwelling-house, showroom, hotel, office or retail shop or similar retail premises, or for purposes ancillary to such use.
(ii) Cars, as defined at **10.15**(ii) above.
(iii) Motor cycles.

Long-life asset expenditure which is incurred wholly and exclusively for the purposes of a qualifying activity, and which does not require allocation under other rules to a single asset pool, can only be allocated to a *class pool* (see **10.26** above). If the expenditure was incurred on or before 5 April 2008, it was allocated to a class pool known as the *long-life asset pool*. The final chargeable period (see **10.26** above) of a long-life asset pool is that in which the qualifying activity is permanently discontinued. If the expenditure is incurred after 5 April 2008, it is allocated to the special rate pool in **10.28** above.

Writing-down allowances for a chargeable period in respect of long-life asset expenditure (whether in a class pool or a single asset pool) are restricted to:

- 6% for chargeable periods ending before 6 April 2008;
- the special rate of WDAs for chargeable periods beginning after 5 April 2008 (as in **10.28** above);
- a hybrid rate for chargeable periods straddling 6 April 2008, based on how much of the period fell before that date, how much of it falls on or after that date and whether the expenditure was incurred before or on or after that date,

proportionately reduced or increased if the chargeable period is less or more than a year, or if the qualifying activity has been carried on for part only of the chargeable period. A claim for a writing-down allowance may require it to be reduced to a specified amount. Where plant and machinery allowances have been claimed for long-life asset expenditure, any earlier or later expenditure on the same asset for which allowances are subsequently claimed, unless excluded by (i)–(iii) above, is treated as also being long-life asset expenditure if it would not otherwise be so. This over-rides the exclusion of expenditure within the monetary limit referred to below. The hybrid rate applies only to expenditure incurred before 6 April 2008; expenditure incurred after that date qualifies at the rate in **10.28** above.

At the end of the chargeable period ending on or straddling 5 April 2008, the balance of the long-life asset pool (representing expenditure incurred before 6 April 2008) was transferred to the special rate pool. The balance transferred is generally treated subsequently as if it had always been special rate expenditure. Long-life asset expenditure in a single asset pool remains in that pool but is treated subsequently as special rate expenditure in a single asset pool. Expenditure incurred on or before 5 April 2008 is treated in the same way as post-5 April 2008 expenditure if it is not allocated to a pool until a chargeable period beginning after that date.

Where a disposal value less than the 'notional written-down value' would otherwise fall to be brought into account in respect of pre-6 April 2008 long-life asset expenditure which has attracted restricted allowances as above, an adjustment may be required. Where the event giving rise to the disposal value is part of a scheme or arrangement a main object of which is the obtaining of a tax advantage under these provisions, the 'notional written-down value' is substituted for the disposal value. The '*notional written-down value*' is qualifying expenditure on the item in question less maximum allowances to date, computed on the assumptions that the expenditure was not excluded from being long-life asset expenditure by the operation of the monetary limit below and that all allowances have been made in full. For expenditure incurred after 5 April 2008, this rule is subsumed by an identical rule for special rate expenditure in **10.28** above.

Monetary limit

Expenditure is not long-life asset expenditure if it is expenditure to which the monetary limit (see below) applies and it is incurred in a chargeable period for which that limit is not exceeded. The limit applies to expenditure incurred by an individual who devotes substantially the whole of his time in that chargeable period to the carrying on of the qualifying activity for the purposes of which the expenditure was incurred. In the case of a partnership of individuals, at least half the partners must satisfy the requirement as to devotion of time, but a company falls outside that requirement. In any case, the monetary limit does not apply to the following types of expenditure:

- expenditure on a share in plant or machinery; or
- a contribution treated as plant or machinery expenditure under *CAA 2001, s 538* (see **10.2**(vii) above); or
- expenditure on plant or machinery for leasing (whether or not in the course of a trade).

The monetary limit is £100,000, proportionately reduced or increased for chargeable periods of less or more than a year and, as regards companies, divided by one plus the number of associated companies (as under *CTA 2010, ss 25–30*). For the purpose of applying the monetary limit, all expenditure under a contract is treated as incurred in the first chargeable period in which any expenditure under the contract is incurred.

Transitional rule for second-hand assets

A second-hand asset is excluded from the long-life asset provisions if:

- the previous owner properly claimed plant and machinery allowances for expenditure on its provision;
- his expenditure did not fall to be treated as long-life asset expenditure; and
- his expenditure would have fallen to be so treated if the long-life asset rules (apart from this transitional rule) had always been law.

A provisional claim to normal writing-down allowances may be made by a purchaser on this basis, before the vendor has made the appropriate return, provided that reasonable steps have been taken to establish that entitlement will arise, and that the appropriate revisions will be made, and assessments accepted, if entitlement does not in the event arise (Revenue Tax Bulletin August 1997 p 450).

[*CAA 2001, ss 56(5), 65(1), 90–104, 268A, Sch 3 para 20*].

For an article explaining how HMRC interpret and operate these provisions, see Revenue Tax Bulletin August 1997 pp 445–450. For their application to modern equipment used in the printing industry, see Revenue Tax Bulletin February 2002 pp 916, 917.

See example (B) at **10.36** below.

Simon's Taxes. See **B3.344.**

Persons leaving the cash basis

[10.35] Provision is made for the case where a person leaving the cash basis has incurred expenditure that would have been qualifying expenditure on plant or machinery if the cash basis had not been in use when the expenditure was incurred. It is a condition that some or all of the expenditure was relieved on the cash basis, but to the extent (if any) that it was not, the expenditure qualifies for plant and machinery capital allowances. This provides relief where plant or machinery has been acquired but has not been fully paid for, such as under a hire-purchase agreement (HMRC Technical Note, 28 March 2013, Chapter 4 para 11) but also ensures that a disposal value must be brought into account on a subsequent disposal event (see **10.27** above). For the cash basis, see **76** TRADING INCOME — CASH BASIS FOR SMALLER BUSINESSES.

For these purposes, a person carrying on a trade, profession or vocation leaves the cash basis in a chargeable period if a cash basis election was in force immediately before the beginning of that chargeable period but no such election is in force for the chargeable period itself. A person carrying on a property business leaves the cash basis in a chargeable period (in this case a tax year) if profits are calculated in accordance with GAAP for that tax year but were calculated on the cash basis for the preceding tax year. The '*relieved portion*' of any expenditure on plant or machinery is the higher of the amount of that expenditure for which a deduction was allowed in calculating profits on the cash basis and the amount of that expenditure for which a deduction would have been allowed if the expenditure had been incurred wholly and exclusively for business purposes. Any remaining balance of expenditure is the '*unrelieved portion*'.

For the purposes of determining any entitlement to an annual investment allowance (see **10.13** above) or a first-year allowance (see **10.18** above), a person is treated as incurring the unrelieved portion of any expenditure in the chargeable period in which he leaves the cash basis. For the purposes of determining a person's available qualifying expenditure in a pool (see **10.26** above) for the chargeable period in which he leaves the cash basis:

- the whole of the expenditure must first be allocated to the appropriate pool (or pools) in that chargeable period; and
- the available qualifying expenditure in a pool to which any of the expenditure is allocated is then reduced by the relieved portion of the expenditure so allocated.

Once the expenditure is brought into account for capital allowances, the provisions at **10.27** above apply in the case of any subsequent disposal event relating to the plant or machinery in question.

[*CAA 2001, s 66A; F(No 2)A 2017, Sch 2 paras 53, 64(1)*].

Capital allowances on plant and machinery — examples

[10.36] The following examples illustrate a number of matters detailed above.

(A) Short-life assets

A prepares trading accounts to 30 September each year, and buys and sells machines, for use in the trade, as follows.

	Cost	Date of acquisition	Disposal proceeds	Date of disposal
Machine X	£40,000	30.4.12	£13,000	1.12.13
Machine Y	£25,000	1.9.12	£1,500	1.12.20

A elects under *CAA 2001, s 83* for these machines to be treated as short-life assets. It is assumed for the purposes of the example that no annual investment allowance is claimed for any of the expenditure. His main pool of qualifying expenditure brought forward at the beginning of period of account 1.10.11–30.9.12 is £80,000.

A's capital allowances are as follows.

	£	£	£	£
	Main Pool	Short-life asset pools		Total Allow-ances
		Machine X	Machine Y	
Period of account 1.10.11–30.9.12				
WDV b/f	80,000			
Additions		40,000	25,000	
WDA 19.03% – note (b)	(15,224)	(7,612)	(4,758)	£27,594
	64,776	32,388	20,242	
Period of account 1.10.12–30.9.13				
WDA 18%	(11,660)	(5,830)	(3,644	£21,134
	53,116	26,558	16,598	
Period of account 1.10.13–30.9.14				
Disposal		(13,000)		
Balancing allowance		£13,558		13,558
WDA 18%	(9,561)		(2,988)	12,549
				£25,107
	43,555		13,610	
Six periods of account 1.10.14–30.9.20				
WDA for 6 years	(30,314)		(9,472)	£39,786
	13,241		4,138	

Period of account 1.10.20–30.9.21			
Transfer to pool	4,138	(4,138)	
	17,379	—	
Disposal	1,500		
	15,879		
WDA 18%	(2,858)		£2,858
	£13,021		

Notes

(a) The eighth anniversary of the end of the chargeable period in which the expenditure on Machine Y is incurred is 30.9.20 (the cut-off date). The balance of expenditure on Machine Y is thus transferred to the main pool in the period of account 1.10.20–30.9.21, this being the first chargeable period ending after the cut-off date.

(b) The hybrid rate of WDA for the year to 30 September 2012 is 19.03%, computed as follows (where 188 is the number of days from 1 October 2011 to 5 April 2012, 178 is the number of days from 6 April 2012 to 30 September 2012 and 366 is the total days in the period of account).

$$R = \left(20 \times \frac{188}{366}\right) + \left(18 \times \frac{178}{366}\right) = 19.03$$

(c) For convenience the WDAs for the six periods of account from 1 October 2014 to 30 September 2020, calculated at 18% p.a. on the reducing balance, have been combined in this example.

(B) Long-life assets and special rate pool

B prepares trading accounts to 31 December. In the year to 31 December 2007, he had new factory premises built for use in his trade, which included a building mainly in use as offices (on which 20% of the cost of the premises was expended). The main plant and machinery pool written-down value at 1 January 2007 was £800,000, and the disposal value to be brought into account in respect of plant and machinery in B's previous premises was £720,000. Machines installed in the new factory cost £920,000. No first-year allowances were available.

B also claimed, for the year to 31 December 2007, plant and machinery allowances for expenditure of £520,000 incurred on fixtures integral to the new premises, which were agreed to have an expected life in excess of 25 years. Of this expenditure, it was agreed £120,000 should be apportioned to the offices.

On 1 May 2008, B incurred additional expenditure on upgrading the fixtures of £19,000, none of it relating to office fixtures.

On 1 May 2019, B moves to new premises, disposing of the old premises for a consideration including £425,000 relating to the integral fixtures (of which £95,000 relates to the office fixtures) and £510,000 relating to other plant and machinery.

Plant and machinery in the new premises costs £1,460,000, of which £180,000 is agreed to be long-life asset expenditure and £620,000 relates to integral features as defined in **10.11** above. The full £1,460,000 is AIA qualifying expenditure. The AIA available for expenditure incurred in the two years beginning 1 January 2019 is £1 million but B chooses to claim an AIA of only £500,000.

The plant and machinery allowances computations for relevant periods are as follows.

	Main Pool	Long-life asset pool	Special rate pool	Total allow-ances
	£	£	£	
Year ending 31.12.07				
WDV b/f	800,000	—		
Additions (see note (a))	1,040,000	400,000		
Disposals	(720,000)	—		
	1,120,000	400,000		
WDA 25%/6%	280,000	24,000		£304,000
WDV c/f	840,000	376,000		
Year ending 31.12.08				
Additions (see note (b))	—	19,000		
	840,000	395,000		
WDA (see note (e))	179,004	35,353		£214,357
WDV c/f	660,996	359,647		
Transfer to special rate pool (see note (c))		(359,647)	359,647	
WDV c/f		—	359,647	
Year ending 31.12.09				
WDA @ 20%/10%	132,199		35,965	£168,164
WDV c/f	528,797		323,682	
2010 to 2018 inclusive				
WDA	444,977		178,251	£623,228
WDV c/f at 31.12.18	83,820		145,431	
Year ending 31.12.19				
Additions	660,000		800,000	
	743,820		945,431	
AIA 100% (see note (d))			500,000	500,000
			445,431	
Disposals	(605,000)		(330,000)	
	138,820		115,431	
WDA @ 18%/6.52% (see note (f))	24,988		7,526	32,514
				£532,514
WDV c/f at 31.12.19	113,822		107,905	
Year ending 31.12.20				
WDA @ 18%/6%	20,488		6,474	£26,962
WDV c/f at 31.12.20	£93,334		£101,431	

Notes

(a) Expenditure on fixtures provided for use in offices is excluded from being long-life asset expenditure. (Such expenditure is nevertheless special rate expenditure if it relates to integral features as defined in **10.11** above.)

(b) Additional expenditure on existing long-life assets is within the provisions even if within the annual monetary limit.

(c) The balance of the long-life asset pool at the end of the period of account straddling 5 April 2008 is transferred to the special rate pool, and the long-life asset pool ceases to exist.

(d) The AIA claimed of £500,000 has been allocated to special rate expenditure as this maximises the writing-down allowances available in subsequent years.

(e) The WDAs in the main pool and long-life asset pool are at a hybrid rate for periods of account straddling 5 April 2008, calculated as follows.

Main pool (where 96 is the number of days from 1 January 2008 to 5 April 2008, 270 is the number of days from 6 April 2008 to 31 December 2008 and 366 is the total days in the period of account):

$$R = \left(25 \times \frac{96}{366}\right) + \left(20 \times \frac{270}{366}\right) = 21.31\%$$

Long-life asset pool:

$$R = \left(6 \times \frac{96}{366}\right) + \left(10 \times \frac{270}{366}\right) = 8.95\%$$

(f) The WDAs in the special rate pool are at a hybrid rate for periods of account straddling 5 April 2019, calculated as follows (where 95 is the number of days from 1 January 2019 to 5 April 2019, 270 is the number of days from 6 April 2019 to 31 December 2019 and 365 is the total days in the period of account):

$$R = \left(8 \times \frac{95}{365}\right) + \left(6 \times \frac{270}{365}\right) = 6.52\%$$

(C) Pooling, annual investment allowance, writing-down allowances, cars, partial non-business use, acquisitions from connected persons and balancing adjustments

A is in business as a builder and demolition contractor. He makes up his accounts to 31 December. The accounts for the year to 31 December 2020 reveal the following additions and disposals.

Additions		£
Plant		
Wagon		30,000
Concrete mixer		45,000
Excavator 1		32,000
Excavator 2		50,000
Dumper Truck		5,000
Bulldozer		20,000
Fittings		
Office furniture and equipment		52,000
Motor Vehicles		
Van		7,000
Car 2		21,000
Car 3		2,000
Disposals	Cost	Proceeds
	£	£
Excavator 1	32,000	30,000
Digger loader	15,000	4,000
Car 1	14,200	3,600
Fittings	3,500	500

The dumper truck was bought second-hand from Q, brother of A, but had not been used in a trade or other qualifying activity. The truck had originally cost Q £6,000, but its market value at sale was only £2,000.

Excavator 1 was sold without having been brought into use.

The bulldozer and Car 3 were both purchased from P, father of A and had originally cost P £25,000 and £3,500 respectively. Both assets had been used for the purposes of a qualifying activity. In both cases, the price paid by A was less than the market value.

Car 1 sold and the new Car 2 are both used for private motoring by A. Private use has always been 30%. Car 2 has CO_2 emissions of over 110g/km. Car 3 is occasionally borrowed by A's daughter, and the private use proportion is 20%. Car 3 has CO_2 emissions of less than 110g/km.

The written-down values at 1 January 2020 of the main plant and machinery pool and Car 1 are £80,500 and £3,225 respectively.

The plant and machinery allowances for the 12-month period of account ending on 31 December 2020 are:

	£ Expenditure qualifying for AIA	£ Main pool	£ Car 1 partial use pool	£ Car 2 partial use pool	£ Car 3 partial use pool	£ Total allowances
WDV b/f		80,500	3,225			

	£	£	£	£	£	£
Additions						
Wagon	30,000	30,000				
Concrete mixer	45,000	45,000				
Excavator 1 (note (a))	32,000	32,000				
Excavator 2	50,000	50,000				
Dumper truck (notes (b)(c))		2,000				
Bulldozer (notes (b)(d))		20,000				
Furniture etc.	52,000	52,000				
Van	7,000	7,000				
Cars				21,000	2,000	
	£216,000					
AIA (100% on £216,000)		(216,000)				216,000
Disposals						
Excavator		(30,000)				
Digger		(4,000)				
Fittings		(500)				
Audi			(3,600)			
		68,000	(£375)	21,000	2,000	
WDA (18%)		(12,240)			(360)	12,600
WDA (6%)				(1,260)		1,260
Private use restriction:						
Car 2 — £1,260 @ 30%						(378)
Car 3 — £360 @ 20%						(72)
WDV c/f		£55,760		£19,740	£1,640	
Total allowances						£229,410
Balancing charge (Car 1) £375 less 30% private use						£262

Notes

(a) The AIA (**10.13** above) and writing-down allowances (**10.26** above) are available even though an item of plant or machinery is disposed of without being brought into use, always provided that the expenditure is, respectively, AIA qualifying expenditure (see **10.13** above) and general qualifying expenditure (see **10.3** above). See **10.26** above as regards the requirement, where an AIA has been given, to allocate the expenditure to a pool.

(b) No AIA is available in respect of an item of plant or machinery purchased from a connected person. See **10.15**(vi) above.

(c) Qualifying expenditure (and AIA qualifying expenditure) on the dumper truck is restricted to the lowest of:
  (i) market value;
  (ii) capital expenditure incurred by the vendor (or, if lower, by a person connected with him);
  (iii) capital expenditure incurred by the purchaser.

  See **10.62** below.

(d) Qualifying expenditure on the bulldozer is the lesser of A's actual expenditure and the disposal value brought into account in the vendor's computations (see **10.62** below). (The vendor's disposal value would have been market value but for the fact that the purchaser is himself entitled to claim capital allowances on the acquisition (see **10.27**(b)(i) above).) A's qualifying expenditure is thus equal to his actual expenditure. The same applies to the purchase of Car 3.

(e) Cars 2 and 3 are allocated to separate single asset pools by virtue of their being used partly for non-business purposes (see **10.30** above), and the same applied to Car 1. Car 2 qualifies for writing-down allowances (WDAs) at the special rate of 6% because of its CO_2 emissions level (see **10.28** above). See note (d) above as regards the amount of qualifying expenditure to be brought into account in respect of Car 3.

(D) Period of account not exceeding 18 months

James commences business on 1 October 2017 preparing accounts initially to 30 September. He changes his accounting date in 2019, preparing accounts for the 15 months to 31 December 2019. The following capital expenditure is incurred.

	Plant	Car
	£	£
1 October 2017 to 30 September 2018	74,400	4,000 (no private use)
1 October 2018 to 31 December 2019	7,500	
Year ended 31 December 2020	4,000	

An item of plant was sold for £500 (original cost £1,000) on 25 September 2019. All of the expenditure on plant additions is AIA qualifying expenditure. The expenditure on the car is not special rate expenditure (see **10.28**, **10.30** above). James chooses to claim a reduced AIA of £60,000 for the year ended 30 September 2018.

Profits *before* capital allowances but otherwise as adjusted for tax purposes are as follows:

	£
Year ended 30 September 2018	96,000
Period ended 31 December 2019	81,000
Year ended 31 December 2020	100,000

The capital allowances are:

	AIA qualifying expenditure	Main pool	Allow-ances
	£	£	£
Year ended 30.9.18			
Qualifying expenditure	74,400	4,000	
AIA 100% (note (b))	60,000		60,000
Transfer to main pool	(14,400)	14,400	
		18,400	
WDA 18%		(3,312)	3,312
WDV at 30.9.18		15,088	
Total allowances			£63,312
15 months ended 31.12.19			
Additions	7,500	7,500	
AIA 100% (note (b))		(7,500)	7,500
Disposals		(500)	
		14,588	
WDA 18% × 15/12 (note (c))		(3,281)	3,281
WDV at 31.12.19		11,307	
Total allowances			£10,781
Year ended 31.12.20			
Additions	4,000	4,000	
AIA 100% (maximum £1 million)		(4,000)	4,000
		11,307	
WDA 18%		(2,035)	2,035
WDV at 31.12.20		£9,272	
Total allowances			£6,035

Taxable profits for the accounting periods concerned are:

	Before CAs	CAs	After CAs
	£	£	£
Year ended 30 September 2018	96,000	63,312	32,688
Period ended 31 December 2019	81,000	10,781	70,219
Year ended 31 December 2020	100,000	6,035	93,965

Taxable profits for the first four tax years of the business are:

	£	£
2017/18 (1.10.17–5.4.18) (£32,688 × $^{6}/_{12}$)		16,344
2018/19 (y/e 30.9.18)		32,688
2019/20 (1.10.18–31.12.19)	70,219	
Deduct Overlap relief £16,344 × $^{3}/_{6}$	8,172	62,047

2020/21 (y/e 31.12.20)	93,965

Notes

(a) Capital allowances are calculated by reference to periods of account and are treated as trading expenses (see **10.1**, **10.2**(i), **10.5** above).

(b) The maximum AIA for the twelve-month period of account to 30 September 2018 is £200,000 as in **10.14** above. All of James's qualifying expenditure of £74,400 would attract AIAs but he has chosen to claim only £60,000.

The maximum AIA for the 15-month period of account to 31 December 2019 is £1,040,000 (£1 million + (£200,000 × 3/15)), subject to an overriding rule that no more than £200,000 of expenditure incurred in the part of the chargeable period falling before 1 January 2019 can qualify for the AIA.

(c) Where a period of account exceeds 12 months as is the case with the 15-month period to 31 December 2019 in this example, WDAs are proportionately increased (see **10.26** above).

(E) Period of account exceeding 18 months

Anastasia commenced business on 1 October 2017 preparing accounts initially to 30 June. She changes her accounting date in 2019/20, preparing accounts for the 21 months to 31 March 2020. The following capital expenditure is incurred:

	Plant	Car
	£	£
9 months to 30 June 2018	60,000	20,000 (no private use)
21 months to 31 March 2020	10,600	
Year ended 31 March 2021	8,000	

Of the £10,600 of expenditure incurred in the 21-month accounting period to 31 March 2020, £3,600 was incurred in January 2019 and £7,000 in the nine months to 31 March 2020. Apart from the car, all expenditure is AIA qualifying expenditure. The expenditure on the car is special rate expenditure (see **10.28** above). Anastasia chooses to claim a reduced AIA of £48,000 for the nine-month period ended 30 June 2018.

An item of plant is sold for £512 (original cost £1,100) on 3 November 2019.

Profits *before* capital allowances but otherwise as adjusted for tax purposes are as follows:

	£
Period ended 30 June 2018	64,000
Period ended 31 March 2020	112,000
Year ended 31 March 2021	85,000

The capital allowances are:

	AIA qualifying expenditure	Main pool	Car	Total allow-ances
	£	£	£	£
9 months ended 30.6.18				
Qualifying expenditure	60,000		20,000	
AIA (note (d))	(48,000)			48,000
	12,000			
Transfer to main pool	(12,000)	12,000		
WDA 18% x $^9/_{12}$ (note (e))		1,620		1,620
WDA 8% x $^9/_{12}$ (note (e))			(1,200)	1,200
WDV at 30.6.18		10,380	18,800	
Total allowances				£50,820
12 months ended 30.6.19				
Additions	3,600			
AIA 100% (note (d))	(3,600)			3,600
WDA 18%		(1,868)		1,868
WDA 7.53% (note (f))			(1,416)	1,416
WDV at 30.6.19		8,512	17,384	
Total allowances				£6,884
9 months ended 31.3.20				
Additions	7,000			
AIA 100% (note (d))	(7,000)			7,000
Disposals		(512)		
		8,000		
WDA 18% × $^9/_{12}$ (note (e))		(1,080)		1,080
WDA 6% × $^9/_{12}$ (note (e))			(782)	782
WDV at 31.3.20		6,920	16,602	
Total allowances				£8,862
Year ended 31.3.21				
Additions	8,000			
AIA 100% (note (d))	(8,000)			8,000
WDA 18%		(1,246)		1,246
WDA 6%			(996)	996
WDV at 31.3.21		£5,674	£15,606	
Total allowances				£10,242

Taxable profits for the periods of account concerned are:

	Before CAs	CAs	After CAs
	£	£	£
Period ended 30 June 2018	64,000	50,820	13,180
Period ended 31 March 2020	112,000	(6,884 + 8,862)	96,254
Year ended 31 March 2021	85,000	10,242	74,758

Taxable profits for the first four tax years of the business are:

	£	£
2017/18 (1.10.17 – 5.4.18) (£13,180 × 6/9)		8,786
2018/19 (1.10.17 – 30.9.18):		
1.10.17 – 30.6.18	13,180	
1.7.18 – 30.9.18 (£96,254 × 3/21)	13,750	26,930
2019/20 (1.10.18 – 31.3.20) (£96,254 × 18/21)	82,504	
Deduct Overlap relief	(8,786)	73,718
2020/21 (1.4.20 – 31.3.21)		74,758

Notes

(a) Where a period of account for capital allowances purposes would otherwise exceed 18 months, it is broken down into shorter periods, the first beginning on the first day of the actual period and each subsequent period beginning on an anniversary of the first day of the actual period. No period can therefore exceed 12 months. See **10.2**(i) above.

(b) The capital allowances computed for the notional periods of account referred to in (a) above are deductible in aggregate in arriving at the adjusted profit for the actual period of account.

(c) A period of account exceeding 18 months cannot normally result in an immediate change of basis period. However, the conditions at **75.10** TRADING INCOME do not have to be satisfied if the change of accounting date occurs in the second or third tax year of a new business, as in this example.

(d) The maximum AIA (as in **10.14** above) for the nine-month period of account to 30 June 2018 is £150,000 (£200,000 × 9/12). All of Anastasia's qualifying expenditure of £60,000 would attract AIAs but she has chosen to claim only £48,000.

The maximum AIA for the notional 12-month period of account ended 30 June 2019 is £600,000 ((£200,000 × 6/12) + (£1,000,000 × 6/12)), subject to an overriding rule that no more than £200,000 of expenditure incurred in the part of the chargeable period falling before 1 January 2019 can qualify for the AIA.

The maximum AIA for the notional nine-month period of account ended 31 March 2020 is £750,000 ((£1,000,000 × 9/12)).

The maximum AIA for the notional 12-month period of account ended 31 March 2021 is £800,000 ((£1,000,000 × 9/12) + (£200,000 × 3/12)), subject to an overriding rule, as regards expenditure incurred in the part of the chargeable period falling after 31 December 2020, that no more than the appropriate proportion (in this case 3/12) of £200,000 can qualify for the AIA.

(e) Where the period of account is less than twelve months, WDAs are proportionately reduced (see **10.26** above).

(f) The WDAs in the special rate pool (comprising only the car) are at a hybrid rate for periods of account straddling 5 April 2019, calculated in this case as follows (where 279 is the number of days from 1 July 2018 to 5 April 2019, 86 is the number of days from 6 April 2019 to 30 June 2019 and 365 is the total days in the period of account):

$$R = \left(8 \times \frac{279}{365}\right) + \left(6 \times \frac{86}{365}\right) = 7.53\%$$

Fixtures

[10.37] There are special provisions to determine entitlement to allowances on fixtures, i.e. plant or machinery which, by law, becomes part of the building or land on which it is installed or otherwise fixed, including any boiler or water-filled radiator installed as part of a space or water heating system. A dispute may arise as to whether fixtures have, in law, become part of a building or land. Where two or more persons' tax liabilities are affected by the outcome of such a dispute, the question is determined for tax purposes by the Appeal Tribunal, and each of the parties concerned is entitled to be a party to the proceedings. [*CAA 2001, ss 172(1)(2), 173, 204(1)–(3)*].

In *J C Decaux (UK) Ltd v Francis* (Sp C 84), [1996] SSCD 281, automatic public conveniences and other street furniture such as bus shelters were held to be fixtures forming part of the land (and see **10.38** below).

These provisions determine ownership for capital allowances purposes of plant or machinery that is (or becomes) a fixture and determine entitlement to allowances in each of the various circumstances described at **10.38–10.43** below. See **10.52** below for the disapplication of these provisions in cases involving long funding leases of plant or machinery that is (or becomes) a fixture. The provisions do not affect the entitlement of a contributor towards capital expenditure (see **10.2**(vii) above). [*CAA 2001, s 172(1)(2)(5)*]. The availability of capital allowances to the purchaser is conditional upon (a) previous business expenditure on fixtures being pooled by the seller before their transfer to the purchaser, and (b) the seller and purchaser, within two years of the transfer, fixing their agreement on the value of the fixtures transferred. See **10.47** below for details. See, respectively, **10.44, 10.45** and **10.46** below for provisions determining cessation of ownership (and consequent disposal values), acquisition of ownership in certain cases and restrictions of qualifying expenditure where allowances previously claimed.

Although the rules apply strictly on an asset-by-asset basis, HMRC accept that in practice they may be applied to groups of assets provided that this does not distort the tax computation (Revenue Tax Bulletin June 1998 p 552).

For the purposes of the fixtures provisions, an '*interest in land*' means:

(i) the fee simple estate in the land;
(ii) in Scotland, in the case of feudal property prior to abolition of feudal tenure, the estate or interest of the proprietor of the *dominium utile*, and in any other case, the interest of the owner;

(iii) a lease (defined for these provisions in relation to land as any leasehold estate in (or, in Scotland, lease of) the land (whether a head-lease, sub-lease or under-lease) or any agreement to acquire such an estate (or lease));
(iv) an easement or servitude;
(v) a licence to occupy land,

and any agreement to acquire an interest as in (i)–(iv) above. Where an interest is conveyed or assigned by way of security subject to a right of redemption, the interest is treated as continuing to belong to the person having the redemption right. [*CAA 2001, ss 174(4), 175, Sch 3 para 29*]. As regards (v) above, for the HMRC view of when a licence to occupy land exists for these purposes, see Revenue Tax Bulletin June 2000 p 761.

See generally HMRC Capital Allowances Manual CA26000 *et seq.*

Finance leasing

See **75.83** TRADING INCOME as regards restrictions on capital allowances where certain finance leasing arrangements are involved. See also **10.48, 10.58, 10.62, 10.63** below.

Simon's Taxes. See **B3.355–B3.358.**

Expenditure incurred by holder of interest in land

[10.38] Where a person having an interest in land incurs capital expenditure on plant or machinery which becomes a fixture in relation to that land, for the purposes of a trade or other qualifying activity, then, subject to the election in **10.39** or **10.43** below, the fixture is treated as belonging to that person. If there are two or more such persons, with different interests, the only interest to be taken into account for this purpose is:

(i) an easement or servitude, or any agreement to acquire same;
(ii) if (i) does not apply to any of those interests, a licence to occupy the land;
(iii) if neither (i) nor (ii) applies to any of those interests, that interest which is not directly or indirectly in reversion on any other of those interests in the land (in Scotland, that of whichever of those persons has, or last had, the right of use of the land).

[*CAA 2001, s 176*].

In *J C Decaux (UK) Ltd v Francis* (Sp C 84), [1996] SSCD 281, suppliers to local authorities of automatic public conveniences and other street furniture such as bus shelters, which were held to be fixtures forming part of the land, were held not to have an interest in the land.

Simon's Taxes. See **B3.356.**

Expenditure incurred by equipment lessor

[10.39] An 'equipment lease' exists where:

- a person incurs capital expenditure on an item of plant or machinery for leasing;
- an agreement is entered into for the lease, directly or indirectly from that person (the '*equipment lessor*'), of the item to another person (the '*equipment lessee*');
- the item becomes a fixture; and
- the item is not leased as part of the land in relation to which it is a fixture.

Such an agreement, or a lease entered into under such an agreement, is an '*equipment lease*'. Provided that:

(i) under the equipment lease, the plant or machinery is leased for the purposes of a trade or other qualifying activity carried on (or to be carried on in future) by the equipment lessee;
(ii) it is not for use in a dwelling-house;
(iii) the equipment lessor and equipment lessee are not CONNECTED PERSONS (**19**);
(iv) if the expenditure on the fixture had been incurred by the equipment lessee, he would have been entitled to allowances under **10.38** above,

the equipment lessor and equipment lessee may jointly elect for the fixture to be treated, from the time the expenditure is incurred by the equipment lessor (or, if later, from the commencement of the lessee's qualifying activity), as owned by the lessor and not the lessee.

Where the following conditions are met, (i) and (iv) above do not have to be satisfied (and the potentially later start date of the election is not relevant):

(1) the plant or machinery becomes a fixture by being fixed to land which is neither a building nor part of a building;
(2) the lessee has an interest in that land when he takes possession of the plant or machinery under the equipment lease;
(3) under the terms of the equipment lease the lessor is entitled, at the end of the lease period, to sever the plant or machinery from the land to which it is then fixed, whereupon it will be owned by the lessor;
(4) the nature of the plant or machinery and the way it is fixed to the land are such that its use does not, to any material extent, prevent its being used, after severance, for the same purposes on different premises; and
(5) the equipment lease is such as falls under generally accepted accounting practice (see **75.21** TRADING INCOME) to be treated in the accounts of the equipment lessor as an operating lease.

The election must be made no later than the first anniversary of 31 January following the tax year in which ends the equipment lessor's chargeable period in which the expenditure is incurred.

[*CAA 2001, ss 174(1)–(3), 177–180, 203, Sch 3 paras 30–33*].

See **10.43** below as regards expenditure incurred by an energy services provider.

Simon's Taxes. See **B3.356.**

Expenditure included in consideration for acquisition of existing interest in land

[10.40] Where a person acquires a pre-existing interest in land to which a fixture is attached, for a consideration in part treated for capital allowance purposes as being expenditure on provision of the fixture, the fixture is treated as belonging to the person acquiring the interest. This applies equally where the fixture in question was previously let under an 'equipment lease' (see**10.39** above) and, in connection with the acquisition, the purchaser pays a capital sum to discharge the equipment lessee's obligations under that lease. It also applies where the fixture was provided under an energy services agreement (see **10.43** below) and, in connection with the acquisition, the purchaser pays a capital sum to discharge the client's obligations under that agreement.

[*CAA 2001, ss 181(1)(4), 182(1), 182A(1), Sch 3 paras 34, 35*].

Where the above provisions would otherwise apply, they are treated as not applying (and as never having applied) where the following conditions are met:

(i) a person is treated as the owner of the fixture (other than under *CAA 2001, s 538* (contributions to expenditure — see **10.2**(vii) above)) immediately before the time of the above acquisition, in consequence of his having incurred expenditure on its provision; and
(ii) that person is entitled to, and claims, an allowance in respect of that expenditure.

Where any person becomes aware that a return of his has become incorrect because of the operation of this provision, the necessary amendments to the return must be notified to HMRC within three months of his becoming so aware, subject to penalties for failure.

[*CAA 2001, ss 181(2)(3), 182(2)(3), 182A(2)(3), 203*].

Simon's Taxes. See **B3.356.**

Expenditure incurred by incoming lessee — election to transfer lessor's entitlement to allowances

[10.41] Where a person with an interest in land to which a fixture is attached grants a lease and he would (or if chargeable to tax would) be entitled, for the chargeable period in which the lease is granted, to capital allowances in respect of the fixture, and the consideration given by the lessee falls, in whole or in part, to be treated for plant and machinery allowances purposes as expenditure on the provision of the fixture, an election is available to the lessor and lessee. They may jointly elect (by notice to HMRC within two years after the date on which the lease takes effect) that, from the grant of the lease, the fixture is treated as belonging to the lessee and not to the lessor. No such election is available if lessor and lessee are CONNECTED PERSONS (**19**. These provisions apply to the entering into of an agreement for a lease as they apply to a grant of a lease. [*CAA 2001, ss 174(4), 183, Sch 3 para 36*].

Simon's Taxes. See **B3.356.**

Expenditure incurred by incoming lessee — lessor not entitled to allowances

[10.42] Where:

- a person with an interest in land to which a fixture is attached grants a lease;
- the provisions at **10.41** above do not apply, because the lessor is not entitled to capital allowances in respect of the fixture;
- before the lease is granted, the fixture has not been used for the purposes of a trade or other qualifying activity by the lessor or a person connected with him (see **19** CONNECTED PERSONS); and
- the consideration given by the lessee includes a capital sum falling, in whole or in part, to be treated for plant and machinery allowances purposes as expenditure on the provision of the fixture,

the fixture is treated as belonging to the lessee from the time the lease is granted.

Rules similar to those of *CAA 2001, s 181(2)(3), s 182(2)(3), s 182A(2)(3), s 203* at **10.40** above apply (by reference to the time of grant).

[*CAA 2001, s 184, Sch 3 para 37*].

Simon's Taxes. See **B3.356.**

Expenditure incurred by energy services provider

[10.43] An '*energy services agreement*' is an agreement entered into by an 'energy services provider' and his client that provides, with a view to the saving or more efficient use of energy, for:

- the design of plant or machinery or of systems incorporating it;
- the obtaining and installation of the plant or machinery; and
- its operation and maintenance,

and under which any payment by the client in respect of the operation of the plant or machinery is wholly or partly linked to the energy savings or increased energy efficiency. An '*energy services provider*' is a person carrying on a qualifying activity consisting wholly or mainly in providing energy management services. [*CAA 2001, s 175A*].

Where:

- an energy services agreement is entered into;
- the energy services provider incurs capital expenditure under the agreement on an item of plant or machinery;
- the item becomes a fixture;
- at the time the item becomes a fixture, the client has an interest in the land in relation to which it is a fixture but the provider does not;
- the item is neither leased nor used in a dwelling-house;
- the operation of the item is carried out wholly or substantially by the provider or a person connected with him; and
- provider and client are not CONNECTED PERSONS (**19**),

the energy services provider and the client may jointly elect for the fixture to be treated, from the time the expenditure is incurred, as owned by the former and not the latter. This opens the way for the energy services provider to claim 100% first-year allowances where his expenditure is within **10.18**(a) above. The election must be made no later than the first anniversary of 31 January following the tax year in which ends the income tax period of account in which the expenditure is incurred. If the client would not have been entitled to allowances under **10.38** above if he had incurred the expenditure himself, the election is available only if the item belongs to the technology class 'Combined Heat and Power' in the Energy Technology Criteria List (see **10.20** above). The intention is that, in such specified cases, allowances to the provider are not to be denied only because the client is a non-taxpayer. [*CAA 2001, s 180A*]. See also HMRC Capital Allowances Manual CA23150.

Simon's Taxes. See **B3.356.**

Cessation of ownership

[10.44] The following points apply.

(A) If a person is treated as owning a fixture under *CAA 2001, s 176* (see **10.38** above) *s 181, 182* or *182A* (see **10.40** above), *s 183* (see **10.41** above) or *s 184* (see **10.42** above), he is treated as ceasing to be the owner if and when he ceases to have the 'qualifying interest'. The '*qualifying interest*' is the interest in the land in question, except that where **10.41** or **10.42** apply it is the lease there referred to. There are rules (see *CAA 2001, s 189*) for identifying the qualifying interest in special cases.

(B) Where, under **10.41** above, the lessee begins to be treated as owning the fixture, the lessor is treated as ceasing to own it at that time.

(C) Where a fixture is permanently severed from the building or land, such that it is no longer owned by the person treated as owning it, he is treated as ceasing to own it at the time of severance.

(D) Where an equipment lessor is treated as owning a fixture (see **10.39**) above) and either he assigns his rights under the equipment lease or the financial obligations of the equipment lessee (or his assignee etc.) are discharged, the equipment lessor is treated as ceasing to own the fixture at that time (or the earliest of those times).

(E) Where an energy services provider is treated as owning a fixture (see **10.39** above) and either he assigns his rights under the energy services agreement or the financial obligations of the client (or his assignee etc.) are discharged, the energy services provider is treated as ceasing to own the fixture at that time (or the earliest of those times).

[*CAA 2001, ss 188–192A*].

The *disposal value* to be brought into account in relation to a fixture depends upon the nature of the event.

(1) On cessation of ownership under (A) above due to a sale of the qualifying interest (other than where (2) below applies), and subject to the election below, it is that part of the sale price that falls (or would,

if there were an entitlement, fall) to be treated for plant and machinery allowances purposes as expenditure by the purchaser on the provision of the fixture.

(2) On cessation of ownership under (A) above due to a sale of the qualifying interest at less than market value (unless the buyer (not being a dual resident investing company connected with the seller) can claim plant or machinery or research and development allowances for his expenditure, in which case (1) above applies), it is the amount that, if that interest were sold at market value (determined without regard to the disposal event itself) at that time, would be treated for plant and machinery allowances purposes as expenditure by the purchaser on provision of the fixture.

(3) On cessation of ownership under (A) above where neither (1) or (2) above applies but the qualifying interest continues (or would do so but for being merged with another interest), it is an amount determined as in (2) above.

(4) On cessation of ownership under (A) above due to the expiry of the qualifying interest, it is any capital sum received by reference to the fixture, or otherwise nil.

(5) On cessation of ownership under (B) above, and subject to the election below, it is that part of the capital sum given by the lessee for the lease as qualifies for plant and machinery allowances as the lessee's expenditure on the fixture.

(6) On cessation of ownership under (C) above, it is market value at time of severance.

(7) On cessation of ownership under (D) above, it is the consideration for the assignment or, as the case may be, the capital sum, if any, paid to discharge the equipment lessee's financial obligations.

(8) On cessation of ownership under (E) above, it is the consideration for the assignment or, as the case may be, the capital sum, if any, paid to discharge the client's financial obligations.

(9) On permanent discontinuance of the trade or other qualifying activity followed by the sale of the qualifying interest, it is an amount determined as in (1) above.

(10) On permanent discontinuance of the qualifying activity followed by demolition or destruction of the fixture, it is the net amount received for the remains, plus any insurance or capital compensation received.

(11) On permanent discontinuance of the qualifying activity followed by permanent loss (other than as in (10) above) of the fixture, it is any insurance or capital compensation received.

(12) On the fixture's beginning to be used wholly or partly for purposes other than those of the qualifying activity, it is that part of the sale price that would fall to be treated for plant and machinery allowances purposes as expenditure by the purchaser on the provision of the fixture if the qualifying interest were sold at market value.

[*CAA 2001, s 196, Sch 3 para 41*].

Fixtures are treated as disposed of at their 'notional written-down value' (if greater than would otherwise be the case) where the disposal event is part of a scheme or arrangement having tax avoidance (whether by increased allowances or reduced charges) as a main object. The '*notional written-down value*' is qualifying expenditure on the item in question less maximum allowances to date, computed on the assumption that all allowances have been made in full. [*CAA 2001, s 197*].

A special election is available where the disposal value of fixtures falls to be determined under (1), (5) or (9) above. Subject as below and to *CAA 2001, ss 186, 186A, 187* (see **10.46** below) *and s* 197 (above), the seller and purchaser (or, where (5) above applies, the lessor and lessee under **10.41** above) may jointly elect under *CAA 2001, s 198* to fix the amount so determined. Where (5) above applies, the lessor and lessee under **10.41** above may make a similar election under *CAA 2001, s 199.*The election fixes the amount at a figure not exceeding either the capital expenditure treated as incurred on the fixtures by the seller (or lessor) or the actual sale price (or capital sum). The remainder (if any) of the sale price (or capital sum) is attributed to the other property included in the sale.

The notice of election must (subject to below) be given within two years after the interest is acquired (or the lease granted), and is irrevocable. A copy must also accompany the return of the persons making the election. The notice must contain prescribed information and must quantify the amount fixed by the election, although if subsequent circumstances reduce the maximum below that fixed, the election is treated as being for that reduced maximum amount. There are provisions for the determination of questions relating to such elections by the Appeal Tribunal. Where any person becomes aware that a return of his has become incorrect because of such an election (or because of subsequent circumstances affecting the election), the necessary amendments to the return must be notified to HMRC within three months of his becoming so aware, subject to penalties for failure.

If **10.47**(A) below applies, and the application to the Tribunal is not determined before the end of the two-year period for making the above election, that period is extended until such time as the application is determined or withdrawn.

[*CAA 2001, ss 198–201, 203, 204(4)–(6)*].

In practice, HMRC normally accept an election covering a group of fixtures, or all the fixtures in a single property, but not one covering fixtures in different properties (e.g. where a portfolio of properties is sold) (Revenue Tax Bulletin June 1998 p 552).

Simon's Taxes. See **B3.357**, **B3.358**.

Acquisition of ownership in certain cases

[10.45] If, on the termination of a lease, the outgoing lessee is treated under **10.44**(A) above as ceasing to own a fixture, the lessor is thereafter treated as the owner. This applies in relation to a licence as it does in relation to a lease. [*CAA 2001, s 193*].

The following apply where an election is made under **10.39** above (election to treat fixture as owned by equipment lessor), and either:

- the equipment lessor assigns his rights under the equipment lease; or
- the equipment lessee's financial obligations under the lease (or those of his assignee etc.) are discharged (on the payment of a capital sum).

If the former applies, then, from the time of the assignment, the fixture is treated as belonging to the assignee for capital allowance purposes, and the consideration for the assignment treated as consideration given by him on provision of the fixture. If the assignee makes any further assignment, he is treated under this provision as if he were the original lessor.

If the latter applies, the capital sum is treated as consideration for the fixture, and the fixture is treated from the time of the payment as belonging to the equipment lessee (or to any other person in whom his obligations under the lease have become vested).

[*CAA 2001, ss 194, 195*].

The same applies, with appropriate modifications, where the election in question was under **10.43** above (election to treat fixture as owned by energy services provider). [*CAA 2001, ss 195A, 195B*].

Simon's Taxes. See B3.357.

Restriction of qualifying expenditure where allowance previously claimed

[10.46] Where:

(i) a fixture is treated under these provisions as belonging to any person (the current owner) in consequence of his incurring capital expenditure on its provision; and

(ii) the plant or machinery is treated (other than under *CAA 2001, s 538* — contributions to expenditure, see **10.2**(vii) above) as having belonged at a 'relevant earlier time' to a person (who may be the same as the person within (i) above) in consequence of his incurring expenditure other than that within (i) above; and that person, having claimed a plant and machinery allowance for that expenditure, must bring a disposal value into account,

so much (if any) of the expenditure referred to in (i) above as exceeds the 'maximum allowable amount' is left out of account in determining the current owner's qualifying expenditure or, as the case may be, is taken to be expenditure which should never have been so taken into account.

A '*relevant earlier time*' is any time before the earliest time when the plant or machinery is treated as belonging to the current owner in consequence of the expenditure referred to in (i) above. The relevant earlier time does not, however, include any time before an earlier sale of the plant or machinery other than as a fixture and other than between CONNECTED PERSONS (**19**).

The '*maximum allowable amount*' is the sum of the disposal value referred to in (ii) above and so much (if any) of the expenditure referred to in (i) above as is deemed under *CAA 2001, s 25* (installation costs, see **10.6** above) to be on provision of the plant or machinery. Where (ii) above is satisfied in relation to more than one disposal event, only the most recent event is taken into account for this purpose.

Where any person becomes aware that a return of his has become incorrect because of the operation of this provision, the necessary amendments to the return must be notified to HMRC within three months of his becoming so aware, subject to penalties for failure.

[*CAA 2001, ss 185, 203, Sch 3 para 38*].

Previous claim for industrial buildings allowances

Where:

(a) a person has claimed industrial buildings allowances (now abolished) for expenditure partly on the provision of plant or machinery, and transfers the relevant interest in the building concerned; and
(b) the transferee, or any other person to whom the plant or machinery is subsequently treated under these provisions as belonging, claims plant and machinery allowances for expenditure incurred thereon when it is a fixture in the building,

the claim in (b) above may not exceed the '*maximum allowable amount*', i.e. an amount equal to the proportion of the 'notional residue' that the part of the consideration for the transfer attributable to the fixture bears to the total consideration.

The '*notional residue*' is the residue of qualifying expenditure which would have been attributable to the relevant interest immediately after the transfer (calculated on the assumption that the transfer was a sale) if the transfer had occurred immediately before the abolition of industrial buildings allowances on 6 April 2011. If, however, the consideration for the transfer does not exceed that notional residue, the '*maximum allowable amount*' is restricted to the part of the consideration that is attributable to the fixture.

[*CAA 2001, s 186, Sch 3 para 39*].

Previous claim for research and development allowances

Where:

- a person ('*the past owner*') has claimed research and development allowances (see **9.28** CAPITAL ALLOWANCES) on expenditure ('*the original expenditure*');
- an asset representing the whole or part of that expenditure has ceased to be owned by that person;
- the asset was, or included, plant or machinery; and
- the new owner (i.e. the person who acquired the asset, or any other person who is subsequently treated as the owner of the plant or machinery) claims plant and machinery allowances for expenditure incurred thereon when it is a fixture,

the new owner's qualifying expenditure cannot exceed the 'maximum allowable amount'. The '*maximum allowable amount*' is:

$$\frac{F}{T} \times A$$

where:

F = the part of the consideration for the past owner's disposal of the asset that is attributable to the fixture;
T = the total consideration for that disposal; and
A = the smaller of (i) the disposal value of the asset when the past owner ceased to own it and (ii) so much of the original expenditure as related to the asset.

[*CAA 2001, s 187, Sch 3 para 40*].

Previous claim for business premises renovation allowances

Where:

- a person ('*the past owner*') has claimed business premises renovation allowances (see **9.3** CAPITAL ALLOWANCES) on expenditure ('*the original expenditure*');
- there has been a balancing event as a result of which an asset representing the whole or part of the original expenditure ceased to be owned by the past owner;
- the asset was, or included, plant or machinery; and
- the new owner (i.e. the person who acquired the asset, or any other person who is subsequently treated as the owner of the plant or machinery) claims plant and machinery allowances for expenditure incurred thereon when it is a fixture,

the new owner's qualifying expenditure cannot exceed the 'maximum allowable amount'. If the proceeds from the balancing event exceed R (see below), the '*maximum allowable amount*' is:

$$\frac{F}{T} \times R$$

where:

F = so much of the proceeds from the balancing event as are attributable to the fixture;
T = the total proceeds from the balancing event; and
R = the qualifying expenditure incurred by the past owner on the asset less the net business premises renovation allowances (i.e. total allowances less any balancing charges) in respect of that asset.

If the proceeds from the balancing event do not exceed R, the '*maximum allowable amount*' is so much of the proceeds from the balancing event as are attributable to the fixture.

[*CAA 2001, s 186A*].

Simon's Taxes. See B3.358.

Effect of changes in ownership of a fixture

[10.47] The availability of capital allowances to a purchaser of fixtures is conditional upon previous business expenditure on fixtures being pooled by the seller before their transfer to the purchaser, and the seller and purchaser, within two years of the transfer, fixing their agreement on the value of the fixtures transferred. These provisions apply where:

(a) a fixture is treated under these provisions as belonging to any person (*'the current owner'*) in consequence of his incurring capital expenditure (*'new expenditure'*) on its provision;
(b) the plant or machinery is treated (other than under *CAA 2001, s 538* — contributions to expenditure, see **10.2**(vii) above) as having belonged at a 'relevant earlier time' to any person (who may be the same as the person within (a) above) in consequence of his incurring expenditure other than that within (a) above (*'historic expenditure'*); and
(c) a person within (b) above was entitled to claim plant and machinery allowances on his expenditure.

Where (c) above is satisfied in relation to more than one amount of historic expenditure, only the most recently incurred expenditure is taken into account for these purposes. A *'relevant earlier time'* in (b) above is any time before the earliest time when the plant or machinery is treated as belonging to the current owner in consequence of his incurring the new expenditure. A relevant earlier time does not, however, include any time before an earlier sale of the plant or machinery other than as a fixture and other than between CONNECTED PERSONS (**19**). Where the past owner's period of ownership was entirely before 6 April 2012, that period of ownership is treated as not occurring at a relevant earlier time, so that these provisions do not apply in relation to such ownership.

In determining the current owner's qualifying expenditure where these provisions apply, the new expenditure is treated as nil (and thus no allowances are due) in the following circumstances:

- the 'pooling requirement' is not met in relation to the past owner (i.e. the person within (c) above); or
- the 'fixed value requirement' applies in relation to the past owner but is not met; or
- the 'disposal value statement requirement' applies in relation to the past owner but is not met.

None of the above affects the disposal value (if any) which falls to be brought into account by the past owner as a result of his having claimed allowances on the historic expenditure. It is up to the current owner to show whether either of the fixed value or disposal value statement requirements applies and, if so, whether the requirement is met. For this purpose, he must provide an officer of HMRC, on request, with a copy of any Tribunal decision, election or statement by reason of which the requirement in question is met.

The pooling requirement

The '*pooling requirement*' is that the historic expenditure must have been allocated to a pool in a chargeable period beginning on or before the day on which the past owner ceases to be treated as the owner of the fixture. The pooling requirement is also treated as met if a first-year allowance was claimed on the historic expenditure or any part of it.

The fixed value requirement

The fixed value requirement *applies* if the past owner is or has been required (as a result of having claimed allowances on the historic expenditure) to bring the disposal value of the plant or machinery into account in accordance with **10.44**(1), (5) or (9) above.

In a case falling within **10.44**(1) or (9) above, the '*fixed value requirement*' is that either:

(i) a 'relevant apportionment' of the sale price has been made; or
(ii) the case is one where the person who purchased the fixture from the past owner was not entitled to claim a plant and machinery allowance, and the current owner has obtained both:
- a written statement made by that person that (i) above has not been satisfied and is no longer capable of being satisfied; and
- a written statement made by the past owner of the amount of disposal value that he brought into account.

For the purposes of (i) above, a '*relevant apportionment*' of the sale price is made if:

(A) the Appeal Tribunal determines the part of the sale price that constitutes the disposal value, on an application made by either the past owner or the person who purchased the fixture from him, before the end of the two years beginning with the date when the purchaser acquires the qualifying interest (see **10.44** above); or
(B) an election in respect of the sale price is made under *CAA 2001, s 198* (see **10.44** above), jointly by the two persons mentioned in (A) above. For this purpose, the election must be made either before the end of the two years beginning with the date when the purchaser acquires the qualifying interest or, if an application is made as mentioned in (A) above and not determined or withdrawn by the end of that two-year period, before the application is determined or withdrawn.

In a case falling within **10.44**(5) above (incoming lessee paying a capital sum for the lease), the '*fixed value requirement*' is as above except that: references to the sale price are to the capital sum given by the lessee for the lease; references to the person who purchased the fixture from the past owner are to the lessee; references to the two years beginning with the date when the purchaser acquires the qualifying interest are to the two years beginning with the date when the lessee is granted the lease; and the reference to an election under *CAA 2001, s 198* is to an election under *CAA 2001, s 199*.

The disposal value statement requirement

The disposal value statement requirement *applies* if the past owner is or has been required (as a result of having claimed allowances on the historic expenditure) to bring the disposal value of the plant or machinery into account in accordance with **10.44**(2) or (3) above or **10.27**(h) above. This is designed to cater for a small subset of disposal events that may occur other than by virtue of an immediate sale of, or grant of a lease of, the fixtures. Say, for example, a past owner had previously ceased his qualifying activity and had brought the market value of the fixtures into account in accordance with **10.27**(h). If, some years later, he sells his former business premises with its fixtures, the disposal value statement requirement will apply on that sale.

The '*disposal value statement requirement*' is that the past owner has, no later than two years after he ceased to own the plant or machinery, made a written statement of the amount of disposal value that he was required to bring into account. The current owner must obtain that statement, directly or indirectly, from the past owner.

Miscellaneous

Amounts specified in a statement by the past owner of the amount of disposal value that he brought into account have effect in place of any apportionment that could have been made under *CAA 2001, ss 562–564* (see **10.2**(ix) above).

[*CAA 2001, ss 187A, 187B*].

Long funding leasing

[10.48] The rules on leasing of plant and machinery were reformed as set out at **10.49–10.53** below with effect from, broadly, 1 April 2006 (and see **10.54** below for commencement and transitional provisions). For 'long funding leases', the current regime grants entitlement to capital allowances to the lessee rather than to the lessor as previously. There were corresponding changes to the tax treatment of lease rentals, to ensure that the lessor is not taxed on, and the lessee does not obtain a deduction for, the capital element of rentals (see **75.98** TRADING INCOME). The regime applies only to leases which are essentially financing transactions, known as '*funding leases*', comprising mainly finance leases but also some operating leases. Leases of no more than five years' duration are excluded from the regime, as are pre-1 April 2006 leases (subject to transitional rules). There are transitional rules to enable leases finalised on or after 1 April 2006 to remain within the pre-existing regime in appropriate circumstances. The coverage below is divided into sections on lessees (**10.49**), relevant definitions (**10.50**), lessors (**10.51**), fixtures (**10.52**), miscellaneous (**10.53**) and commencement/ transitional provisions (**10.54**).

For an HMRC Technical Note published on 1 August 2006 on the long funding leasing rules, see webarchive.nationalarchives.gov.uk/20140109143644/http://www.hmrc.gov.uk/leasing/tech-note.pdf. See also HMRC Business Leasing Manual BLM20000 *et seq.* (defining long funding leases), HMRC Business Leasing Manual BLM40000 *et seq.* (taxation of income and expenditure under long funding leases) and HMRC Capital Allowances Manual CA23800 *et seq.* (capital allowances aspects of long funding leases).

Simon's Taxes. See B3.340Y–B3.340ZC.

Lessees

[10.49] Where a person carrying on a qualifying activity (see **10.4** above) incurs expenditure (whether or not capital expenditure) on the provision of plant or machinery for the purposes of that activity under a 'long funding lease' (see **10.50**(1) below), the plant or machinery is treated as owned by him at all times whilst he is the lessee. He is then treated as having incurred *capital expenditure* on the provision of the plant or machinery, of an amount determined as below depending on whether the lease is a 'long funding operating lease' (see **10.50**(3) below) or a 'long funding finance lease' (see **10.50**(4) below), at the 'commencement' (see *CAA 2001, s 70YI(1)*) of the term of the lease. The combined effect is to treat that capital expenditure as qualifying expenditure (as in **10.3** above) of the lessee for the purposes of plant and machinery capital allowances and, where appropriate, as first-year qualifying expenditure (as in **10.18** above) for the purposes of first-year allowances.

If the lease is a 'long funding operating lease' (see **10.50**(3) below), the capital expenditure is equal to the market value of the plant or machinery as at the commencement of the term of the lease or, if later, the date on which the plant or machinery is first brought into use for the purposes of the qualifying activity.

If the lease is a 'long funding finance lease' (see **10.50**(4) below), then, subject to the possible addition and restriction described below, the capital expenditure is equal to the present value, as at the commencement of the term of the lease or, if later, the date on which the plant or machinery is first brought into use for the purposes of the qualifying activity, of the 'minimum lease payments' (see **10.50**(6) below). Present value is computed as it would be if accounts were prepared in accordance with generally accepted accounting practice (GAAP) on the date on which that value is first recognised in the lessee's books or other financial records. The present value of any 'relievable amount' included in the minimum lease payments must be excluded. An amount (amount X) is a '*relievable amount*' if:

- an arrangement is in place which was entered into on or after 9 March 2011 and under which all or part of any residual amount (see **10.50**(6) below) is guaranteed by the lessee or a person connected with him;
- amount X is within the minimum lease payments because of that arrangement; and
- it is reasonable to assume that, were amount X to be incurred under the arrangement, relief would be available as a result (other than relief which would in any case be available due to amount X being within the minimum lease payments). In deciding whether relief would be available as a result, no account is taken of any part of the arrangement other than the part providing the guarantee or any other arrangement connected with the arrangement or forming part of a set of arrangements that includes the arrangement.

If the lessee paid rentals under the lease before its term commenced, the capital expenditure also includes the amount of any such rentals for which tax relief is otherwise unavailable (and would still have been unavailable even if the plant or machinery had been used pre-commencement). If a main purpose of entering into the lease (or arrangements that include the lease) was to obtain capital allowances on an amount materially greater than the market value of the leased asset at the commencement of the term of the lease, the capital expenditure is restricted to that market value.

As regards long funding finance leases, the same principles apply whether the lease is accounted for as a lease or as a loan.

[*CAA 2001, ss 70A–70C*].

An attempt to use these rules to generate allowances was defeated in *Cape Industrial Services Ltd v HMRC* FTT (TC 7648), [2020] UKFTT 162 (TC) but only because the FTT took a purposive approach to what was a composite transaction without any enduring commercial consequences.

If the *lessor* under the long funding finance lease subsequently incurs additional expenditure such that the lease rentals increase (disregarding any increase attributable to a 'relievable amount' as above), the *lessee* is treated as incurring further capital expenditure on the plant or machinery. The further expenditure is equal to the increase (if any) in the present value of the minimum lease payments and is treated as incurred on the date it is first recognised in the lessee's books or other financial records.

[*CAA 2001, s 70D*].

Transfer and long funding leasebacks

Consequences ensue where plant or machinery is the subject of a 'transfer and long funding leaseback'. A '*transfer and long funding leaseback*' occurs if:

(a) a person (S) transfers (see *CAA 2001, s 70Y(3)*) plant or machinery to another person (B); and
(b) at any time after the date of the transfer, the plant or machinery is available to be used by S, or by a person (other than B) who is connected (within **19** CONNECTED PERSONS) with S (CS), under a long funding plant or machinery lease.

The consequences are that no annual investment allowance (see **10.13** above) or first-year allowance (see **10.18** above) is available in respect of the expenditure of S or CS under the lease. Also, in determining the qualifying expenditure of S or CS, there is disregarded any excess of his expenditure over the disposal value to be brought into account by S. Where no such disposal value falls to be brought into account, the qualifying expenditure of S or CS (if otherwise greater) is normally restricted to the lesser of the market value of the plant or machinery, the capital expenditure (if any) incurred on it by S before the transfer and any capital expenditure incurred on it before the transfer by any person connected with S. The qualifying expenditure of S or CS is restricted to nil if:

- S is not required to bring a disposal value into account on the transfer in (a) above; and

- at any time before that transfer, S or a 'linked person' became owner of the plant or machinery without incurring either capital expenditure or 'qualifying revenue expenditure' on its provision.

A '*linked person*' is a person (LP) who owned the plant or machinery at any time before the transfer in (a) above and who was connected with S at any time during LP's ownership and before the said transfer. Expenditure is '*qualifying revenue expenditure*' if it is expenditure of a revenue nature that was incurred at no less than an arm's length price or that was incurred by a manufacturer and represented no less than the normal cost of manufacturing the plant or machinery.

[*CAA 2001, s 70DA*].

Disposal events and values

Any of the following events is a disposal event, and a disposal value (see **10.27** above) must be brought into account by the lessee for the chargeable period in which that event occurs:

- the termination of the lease;
- the plant or machinery beginning to be used wholly or partly for purposes other than those of the qualifying activity; and
- the permanent discontinuance of the qualifying activity.

The disposal value is (QE – QA) + R where:

> QE is the person's qualifying expenditure on the provision of the plant or machinery;
> QA is the 'qualifying amount' (see below); and
> R is any 'relevant rebate' (see below) plus any other 'relevant lease-related payment' (see below).

If the event in question would also give rise to a disposal event within **10.27** above in the case of the lessee, that disposal event is ignored.

Meaning of 'qualifying amount'

If the lease is a 'long funding operating lease', the '*qualifying amount*' is the aggregate amount of the reductions made under *ITTOIA 2005, s 148I* (see **75.100** TRADING INCOME under Lessees) (and its corporation tax equivalent) for periods of account in which the person concerned was the lessee.

If the lease is a 'long funding finance lease', the '*qualifying amount*' is the aggregate of the payments made to the lessor by the lessee (including any initial payment and any payment under a guarantee of any 'residual amount' (see **10.50**(6) below)) other than any 'relievable payment' (see below). It excludes so much of any payment as, in accordance with GAAP, falls (or would fall) to be shown in the lessee's accounts as finance charges, or interest expenses, in respect of the lease. Any payment representing charges for services or representing 'taxes' (as in **10.50**(6) below) to be paid by the lessor is also excluded. If the long funding finance lease is not an arm's length transaction, the qualifying amount is reduced to so much of the aggregate payments (net of exclusions) as would reasonably be expected to have been made if the lease had been an arm's length transaction.

Meaning of 'relevant rebate'

If the disposal event is the termination of the long funding operating or finance lease, '*relevant rebate*' means any amount payable to the lessee (or a person connected with him) that is calculated by reference to 'termination value' (as defined by *CAA 2001, s 70YH*), e.g. lease rental refunds. In any other case, '*relevant rebate*' means any such amount that would have been so payable if, when the relevant event occurred, the lease had terminated and the plant or machinery had been sold for its then market value. In all cases, if the lease is not an arm's length transaction, 'relevant rebate' includes any amount that would reasonably be expected to have been so payable if the lease had been such a transaction.

Meaning of 'relievable payment'

A payment (payment X) is a '*relievable payment*' if:

- an arrangement is in place under which all or part of any residual amount (see **10.50**(6) below) is guaranteed by the lessee or a person connected with him;
- payment X is within the 'minimum lease payments' (see **10.50**(6) below) because of that arrangement; and
- it is reasonable to assume that relief would be available as a result of making payment X (other than relief which would in any case be available due to payment X being within the minimum lease payments). In deciding whether relief would be available as a result, no account is taken of any part of the arrangement other than the part providing the guarantee or any other arrangement connected with the arrangement or forming part of a set of arrangements that includes the arrangement.

Meaning of 'relevant lease-related payment'

'*Relevant lease-related payment*' means any payment which:

- is payable at any time for the benefit (directly or indirectly) of the lessee or a person connected with him;
- is connected with the long funding lease, or with any arrangement connected with that lease; and
- is not within the exclusions provided for by *CAA 2001, s 70E(2FA)(c)*,

if, and to the extent that, the payment is not otherwise brought into account for tax purposes as income or a disposal receipt by the person for whom the benefit is payable (or would not be if that person were within the charge to tax). 'Payment' includes the provision of any benefit, the assumption of any liability and any other transfer of money's worth. If the lease is not an arm's length transaction, 'relevant lease-related payment' includes any amount that would reasonably be expected to have been so payable if the lease had been such a transaction.

[*CAA 2001, s 70E; FA 2019, Sch 14 paras 1(3), 6(1)*].

Definitions

[10.50] The following definitions apply for these purposes.

(1) A '*long funding lease*' is a 'funding lease' (as in (2) below) that is not a 'short lease' (see (A) below), is not an 'excluded lease of background plant or machinery for a building' (see (B) below) and is not excluded under the *de minimis* provision at (C) below for plant or machinery leased with land. Where, at the 'commencement' (see *CAA 2001, s 70YI(1)*) of the term of a plant or machinery lease (as widely defined by *CAA 2001, s 70K*), the plant or machinery is not being used for the purposes of a qualifying activity, but subsequently is so used, the lease is a long funding lease if it would otherwise have been a long funding lease at its 'inception' (see *CAA 2001, s 70YI(1)*); this covers, for example, the situation where either the lessor or the lessee is originally non-UK resident and subsequently becomes UK resident. However, the treatment of a lease as a long funding lease as regards the *lessee* is always subject to the following two conditions.

- The lessee must treat the lease as a long funding lease in his first tax return (and thus his first accounts) the profits declared by which are affected by the question of whether or not the lease is a long funding lease. Once a lease has or has not been so treated in a return, tax cannot be recovered on a claim within **16.7** CLAIMS due to the return having made on that basis.

  A lessee cannot use the above to turn what would otherwise be a long funding lease into a non-long funding lease if:

  (i) (in relation to leases entered into after 12 December 2007), at any time in the 'relevant period', he the lessee himself is a sub-lessor of any of the same plant or machinery under a long funding lease. The 'relevant period' is the period from inception of the first-mentioned lease to (i) the making of the said tax return or (ii) where relevant, the making of the final amendment to that tax return; or

  (ii) (in relation to leases commenced on or after 13 November 2008) the lease is the leaseback in a 'transfer and long funding leaseback' (see above).

- A lease is not a long funding lease as regards the lessee if either the lessor or any superior lessor under a chain of leases (as defined) is entitled, at the commencement of the term of the lease, to any capital allowance (not necessarily a plant or machinery allowance) in respect of the leased plant or machinery. This also applies if such entitlement would have arisen but for *CAA 2001, s 70V* (see **10.53** below under Tax avoidance involving international leasing). It also applies if the entitlement arose at an earlier time but no requirement has yet arisen to bring into account a disposal value as described in **10.51** below. These conditions are applied on the assumption that the lessor in question is within the charge to UK tax, even if that is not, in fact, the case. However, where the inception of the lease is before 28 June 2006 and the lessor remains entitled to capital allowances by virtue only of the exception under (2)(iii) below the lease is still regarded as a long funding lease as regards the lessee.

[*CAA 2001, ss 70G, 70H, 70Q*].

The above-mentioned exclusions from long funding lease treatment are defined in (A)–(C) below.

(A) A '*short lease*' is defined as a lease whose term is seven years or less (five years or less for leases entered into before 1 January 2019). The 'term' of a lease is defined by *CAA 2001, s 70YF* (as amended by *FA 2019, Sch 14 paras 8(2), 10*). There is an anti-avoidance rule at *section 70I(9)* aimed at preventing arrangements between CONNECTED PERSONS (**19**) being used to create artificially short leases.

A lease entered into before 1 January 2019 whose term is more than five years but no more than seven is nevertheless a short lease if three conditions are met. The first two conditions are that (i) the lease falls to be treated under GAAP as a finance lease, and (ii) the residual value of the plant or machinery implied in the terms of the lease is not more than 5% of its market value at commencement of the lease term. The third condition compares the lease rentals due in each year of the lease term (ignoring any variations resulting from changes in published interest rates); the total rentals due in Year 1 must not be more than 10% less than those due in Year 2, and the total rentals due in any of Years 3 to 7 must not be more than 10% greater than those due in Year 2.

The finance lease in a sale and finance leaseback caught by *CAA 2001, s 221* (see **10.62** below) is excluded from being a 'short lease' (if it otherwise would be) where the sale etc. part of the arrangement occurs after 8 October 2007. Where the sale etc. occurs after 11 March 2008, this treatment extends to *any* finance lease that is part of the leaseback arrangement. However, if certain conditions are satisfied, a joint (irrevocable) election may be made by the seller (or assignor) and the lessor (within two years of the sale etc.) to disapply the exclusion. The conditions are the same as those relating to the similar election in *CAA 2001, s 227* (see **10.62** below), in particular that the sale etc. takes place not more than four months after the plant or machinery is first brought into use; the effect of the election is also the same as that of the *CAA 2001, s 227* election.

The finance lease in a lease and finance leaseback caught by *CAA 2001, s 228A* (see **10.63** below) is excluded from being a 'short lease' (if it otherwise would be) where the original lease is granted after 11 March 2008. This treatment extends to any other finance lease that is part of the lease and finance leaseback arrangements except for the original lease.

[*CAA 2001, s 70I; FA 2019, Sch 14 paras 8(1), 10*].

(B) An '*excluded lease of background plant or machinery for a building*' occurs where 'background plant or machinery' is affixed to (or otherwise installed in or on) land that consists of (or includes) a building and is leased with that land under a 'mixed lease' (as defined by *CAA 2001, s 70L* — broadly a lease of plant or machinery plus other assets — see also **10.53** below under Mixed leases). '*Background plant or machinery*' is plant or machinery of such description as might reasonably be expected to be installed in various buildings and whose sole or main purpose is to contribute to the functioning of the building or its site as an environment in which activities can be carried on. There is provision for the Treasury to supplement this definition by statutory instrument and to similarly designate particular types of plant or machinery as being, or as not being, background plant or machinery — see now *SI 2007 No 303*. There are anti-avoidance provisions to prevent this exclusion from applying if a main purpose of the mixed lease (or of transactions of which it is part) is to entitle the lessor to capital allowances on the background plant or machinery or if the rentals vary according to the value of allowances available to the lessor. [*CAA 2001, ss 70R–70T; SI 2007 No 303*].

(C) The *de minimis* provision referred to above applies in a case in which relatively small amounts of plant and machinery are leased with land and the exclusion at (B) above would have applied but for the plant or machinery not being 'background plant or machinery'. The lease is excluded from long funding lease treatment if, at commencement of its term, the aggregate market value of all such plant or machinery does not exceed 10% of the aggregate market value of any 'background plant or machinery' leased with the land *and* does not exceed 5% of the market value of the land (including buildings and fixtures and assuming an absolute interest). [*CAA 2001, s 70U*].

See also HMRC Business Leasing Manual BLM20000 *et seq.*

(2) A '*funding lease*' is a plant or machinery lease (as widely defined by *CAA 2001, s 70K*) which meets the 'finance lease test', the 'lease payments test' or the 'useful economic life test' (see bullet points below) (or meets more than one of these tests) and does not fall within either of the exceptions below. A plant or machinery lease whose inception is on or after 1 April 2010 is automatically a funding lease if the plant or machinery is cushion gas, i.e. gas that functions, or is intended to function, as plant in a particular gas storage facility.

- A lease meets the '*finance lease test*' as regards any person if it is one that, under GAAP, falls (or would fall) to be treated in that person's accounts as either a finance lease or a loan. A lease also meets the finance lease test as regards *the lessor* if is one that, under GAAP, falls (or would fall) to be so treated in the accounts of a person connected with him (within **19** CONNECTED PERSONS). The Treasury has power to vary the finance lease test by statutory instrument.
- A lease meets the '*lease payments test*' if the present value of the 'minimum lease payments' (see (6) below) is not less than 80% of the 'fair value' of the leased plant or machinery. Present value is calculated using the interest rate implicit in the lease. The latter is arrived at by applying normal commercial criteria including GAAP. If it cannot be so arrived at, it is taken to be 1% above LIBOR (as defined by *CAA 2001, s 70O(5)*; for leases

entered into before 1 January 2019, it is the temporal discount rate for the purposes of *FA 2005, s 70*. '*Fair value*' means market value less any grants receivable towards the purchase or use of the plant or machinery.

- A lease meets the '*useful economic life test*' if the term of the lease exceeds 65% of the remaining useful economic life (see *CAA 2001, s 70YI(1)*) of the leased plant or machinery. The 'term' of a lease is defined by *CAA 2001, s 70YF* (as amended by *FA 2019, Sch 14 paras 8(2), 10*).

Exceptions.

(i) A contract within **10.58** below (hire-purchase contracts etc.) is not a funding lease.

(ii) A lease is not a funding lease if, before the 'commencement' (see *CAA 2001, s 70YI(1)*) of its term, the lessor has leased the same plant or machinery under one or more other plant or machinery leases, none of which were funding leases, and the aggregate term of those other leases exceeds 65% of the remaining useful economic life of the plant or machinery at the commencement of the earliest lease; for this purpose only, any person who was a lessor under a pre-1 April 2006 lease is treated as the same person as the lessor under the first post-1 April 2006 lease.

(iii) A lease is not a funding lease as regards the lessor if, before 1 April 2006, the plant or machinery had, for a period or periods totalling at least ten years, been the subject of one or more leases and the lessor was also the lessor of the plant or machinery on the last day before 1 April 2006 on which it was leased.

[*CAA 2001, ss 70J, 70N–70P, 70YJ; FA 2019, Sch 14 paras 9, 10*].

(3) A '*long funding operating lease*' is any long funding lease that is not a long funding finance lease within (4) below. [*CAA 2001, s 70YI(1)*].

(4) A '*long funding finance lease*' is a long funding lease that meets the *finance lease test* at (2) above (disregarding the connected persons rule). In relation to periods of account beginning on or after 1 January 2019, and in relation only to a lessee, a '*long funding finance lease*' is additionally defined as a right-of-use lease (see (5) below) which is a long funding lease that meets the lease payments test or useful economic life test in (2) above but which was not previously classified as a long funding operating lease. This means that there is no change in the tax treatment of a long funding operating lease following a lessee's adoption of IFRS 16 (see **75.82** TRADING INCOME). [*CAA 2001, s 70YI(1); FA 2019, Sch 14 paras 1(5), 6(1)*].

(5) A '*right-of-use lease*', in relation to a lessee, is a lease in respect of which, under GAAP, a right-of-use asset falls (or would fall) at the commencement date of the lease to be recognised in the lessee's accounts (which will be the case if the lessee has adopted IFRS 16 — see **75.82** TRADING INCOME), or a right-of-use asset would fall to be so recognised but for the lessee's sub-leasing the asset. In determining whether a lease meets this definition at any time in an accounting period, it is to be assumed that the accounting policy applied for the period also applied at the commencement date of the lease. [*CAA 2001, s 70YI(1); FA 2019, Sch 14 paras 1(5), 6(1)*].

(6) The '*minimum lease payments*' are the minimum payments under the lease over the term of the lease (including any initial payment). In the case of the lessee, they also include so much of any 'residual amount' as is guaranteed by him or a person connected with him. In the case of the lessor, they also include so much of any 'residual amount' as is guaranteed by the lessee or a person who is not connected with the lessor. Any payment representing charges for services or representing 'taxes' to be paid by the lessor must be excluded from 'minimum payments' for the purposes of this definition. ('*Taxes*' means UK or foreign taxes or duties, but not income tax, corporation tax or foreign equivalents.) '*Residual amount*' means so much of the 'fair value' (see the 'lease payments test' in (2) above) of the plant or machinery subject to the lease as cannot reasonably be expected to be recovered by the lessor from the payments under the lease. [*CAA 2001, s 70YE*]. This definition of 'minimum lease payments' is based on GAAP (Treasury Explanatory Notes to Finance Bill 2006).

(7) For the purposes of these provisions, the *market value* of any plant or machinery at any time is to be determined on the assumption of a disposal by an absolute owner free from all leases and other encumbrances. [*CAA 2001, s 70YI(2)*].

Lessors

[10.51] Expenditure incurred on the provision of plant or machinery for leasing under a long funding lease is not qualifying expenditure for the purposes of plant and machinery capital allowances. [*CAA 2001, s 34A*].

Where expenditure on plant or machinery is already included in qualifying expenditure and the plant or machinery begins to be leased under a long funding lease, a disposal event then occurs and a disposal value must be brought into account as follows.

- If the lease is a 'long funding operating lease' (see **10.50**(3) above), the disposal value is the market value of the plant or machinery at commencement of the lease.
- If the lease is a 'long funding finance lease' (see **10.50**(4) above), the disposal value depends on the date of the 'inception' (see *CAA 2001, s 70YI(1)*) of the lease.

  Where the inception of the lease is on or after 13 November 2008, the disposal value is the greater of the market value of the plant or machinery at commencement of the lease and the 'qualifying lease payments'. The '*qualifying lease payments*' means the minimum payments under the lease, including any initial payment but excluding so much of any payment as falls (or would fall) under GAAP to be treated as the gross return on investment, i.e. the interest element. Any payment representing charges for services or representing 'taxes' (as in **10.50**(6) above) to be paid by the lessor must also be excluded.

  Where the inception of the lease was before 13 November 2008, the disposal value was the amount that would have fallen to be recognised as the lessor's net investment in the lease if accounts had been prepared in accordance with GAAP on the date (the '*relevant date*') on which the lessor's net investment in the lease was first recognised in his books or other financial records. In relation to leases granted after 12 December 2007, any rentals made (or due) under the lease on or before the relevant date were treated for these purposes as made (and due) on the day after the relevant date. In relation to leases granted after 11 March 2008, the lessor's net investment in the lease was calculated for these purposes as if he had no liabilities of any kind at any time on the relevant date, but only if the effect of doing so was to increase the disposal value.

[*CAA 2001, s 61(1)(ee), (2), (6)–(9)*]. (See **10.27** above as regards disposal events and disposal values generally.)

Where the owner of plant or machinery has been leasing it under a long funding lease and ceases to do so but continues to use it for the purposes of a qualifying activity (see **10.4** above), writing-down allowances are available to him as if he had, on the day after the cessation, incurred capital expenditure on the acquisition of that plant or machinery and as if he owned it as a result of that notional capital expenditure. The plant or machinery is thereafter treated as if it were not the same plant or machinery that existed previously. The amount of the notional capital expenditure is equal to the 'termination amount' in relation to the long funding lease under which the plant or machinery was last leased. [*CAA 2001, s 13A*]. However, neither an annual investment allowance (see **10.13** above) nor a first-year allowance (see **10.18** above) is available on the notional capital expenditure, and nor can it qualify for short-life asset treatment as in **10.33** above. The *termination amount*' is determined as follows.

- If that lease terminated as a result of a disposal event or if a disposal event is triggered by the termination, the termination amount is the disposal value that would have fallen to be brought into account by the lessor on the fictional assumptions that he had been entitled to capital allowances on the plant or machinery and had claimed his full entitlement. 'Disposal event' is itself to be construed in accordance with those assumptions. See generally **10.27** above as regards disposal events and disposal values.
- If the above does not apply and the lease is a 'long funding operating lease' (see **10.50**(3) above), the termination amount is the market value of the plant or machinery immediately after the termination.
- If the above does not apply and the lease is a 'long funding finance lease' (see **10.50**(4) above), the termination amount is the value at which, immediately after the termination, the plant or machinery is recognised in the lessor's books or other financial records.

[*CAA 2001, s 70YG*].

Note that where plant or machinery either begins or ceases to be leased under a long funding lease, there is also, by virtue of *TCGA 1992, s 25A*, as amended, a deemed disposal and reacquisition, at similar values as above, for CGT purposes. See Tolley's Capital Gains Tax.

Election available to lessors

The Treasury has made regulations enabling a lessor to elect for his plant and machinery leases to be treated as long funding leases if they would not otherwise be so treated; the election cannot be made on an individual lease by lease basis. For guidance, see the HMRC Technical Note referred to in **10.48** above and see also HMRC Business Leasing Manual BLM24005–24300. The election (a 'long funding lease election') applies to all the lessor's 'eligible leases' (as defined by *SI 2007 No 304, Reg 3*) and 'qualifying incidental leases' that are finalised on or after the effective date, but does not affect the lessees' position. The election must be made during the period beginning with the end of the tax year to which it relates and ending on the first anniversary of 31 January following that tax year; it must be made in a tax return or an amended tax return. It can be revoked, by means of an amended return, within the permitted time for making it but is thereafter irrevocable. The election must specify the effective date, which cannot precede the period of account or (as the case may be) the tax year to which it relates. Leases of less than 12 months' duration (except as below) and leases finalised before 1 April 2006 are excluded from being eligible leases for these purposes, as are certain other leases. A '*qualifying incidental lease*' is a plant or machinery lease that is wholly incidental to an eligible lease and which would itself have been an eligible lease if its term were 12 months or more. [*FA 2006, Sch 8 para 16; SI 2007 No 304*].

Fixtures

[10.52] The fixtures rules at **10.37** *et seq.* above do not apply, to determine either ownership or entitlement to allowances of either the lessee or the lessor, where plant or machinery that is (or becomes) a fixture is the subject of a long funding lease. If the lessee under the long funding lease himself leases out all or any of the plant or machinery under a lease that is not a long funding lease, the provisions at **10.37** *et seq.* are similarly disapplied as regards both the lessor and the lessee under that sub-lease. [*CAA 2001, ss 172(2A), 172A*]. Thus, the allowances (for expenditure on fixtures) available to any such lessors and lessees are to be determined under the rules applicable to long funding leases, rather than the rules applicable to fixtures.

Miscellaneous

[10.53] The following matters are relevant.

Mixed leases

There is provision for a situation where plant or machinery is leased with other types of asset (whether plant or machinery or not). In such case, different leases are deemed to exist so that the above rules (and those at **75.98–75.100** TRADING INCOME) can be applied to each such notional lease (known as a '*derived lease*' — see, for example, **10.50**(1)(B) above). [*CAA 2001, ss 70L, 70M*].

Transfers, assignments etc.

Where a *lessor* of plant or machinery transfers it to a new lessor (other than by granting him a lease), it is treated for the purposes of these provisions (as regards lessors) as the termination of the existing lease and the creation of a new lease commencing at the date of transfer (which may or may not be the case in reality). Provided there is effectively no change to the term of the original lease or to the payments due under it, then, as regards the new lessor, the new lease retains the classification of the original lease (i.e. as a long funding lease or as a lease other than a long funding lease, as the case may be) and, as regards the lessee, the old and new leases are treated as a single continuing lease. [*CAA 2001, s 70W*].

The above also applies, with the appropriate modifications, where a *lessee* of plant or machinery transfers it to a new lessee. [*CAA 2001, s 70X*].

Extension of the term of a lease

Where the term of a *long funding operating lease* (see **10.50**(3) above) is extended as a result of one or more specified events (involving variations to the provisions of the lease, the granting or exercise of options etc.), a new lease is deemed to begin. [*CAA 2001, s 70YB*].

Where the term of a lease that is *not* a long funding lease is extended as a result of one or more specified events (as above), it is necessary to consider whether or not it thereby becomes a long funding lease. If, were it to be assumed that the lease has then terminated and a new lease commenced, the new lease would be a long funding lease, or at least that assumption is made, and the 'new' lease is a long funding lease as regards the lessor. If not, the term of the lease is taken to be the term as extended. [*CAA 2001, s 70YC*].

Tax avoidance involving international leasing

There are anti-avoidance rules aimed at arrangements made to lease plant and machinery into the UK, and then lease it back out again (other than under a long funding lease) in order to obtain the benefit of UK capital allowances. The rules deem the leasing by the UK resident to be long funding leasing, so that capital allowances are not available to him. They apply where the provision of the asset by the non-UK resident is itself long funding leasing as regards the UK resident or is under a contract within **10.58** below (hire-purchase contracts etc.), such that the UK resident would otherwise be entitled to capital allowances. They are not aimed at normal commercial arrangements (see also Treasury Explanatory Notes to Finance Bill 2006). [*CAA 2001, s 70V*].

Sale and leaseback/lease and leaseback arrangements

Where an existing long funding lessor transfers (e.g. by selling or leasing) the plant or machinery that is the subject of the existing lease to another person and leases the plant or machinery back from him, the leaseback is a long funding lease as regards both of them. Similar treatment is applied where the leaseback is via a series of leases. [*CAA 2001, s 70Y*].

Change in the accountancy classification of a long funding lease

There are rules to cater for changes in generally accepted accounting practice (GAAP) such that an operating lease falls to be reclassified as a finance lease for accounting purposes or *vice versa*. In relation to periods of account beginning on or after 1 January 2019, these rules are disapplied where a long funding lease is thus reclassified upon the adoption of a different accounting standard or a change to an accounting standard, but at the same time are extended to cover the case where a right-of-use lease (see **10.50**(5) above) which is a 'long funding finance lease' (see **10.50**(4) above begins to be accounted for as an operating lease. [*CAA 2001, s 70YA; FA 2019, Sch 14 paras 1(4), 6(1)*].

Increase in proportion of residual amount guaranteed

The following applies as regards the lessor if, in the case of a lease other than a long funding lease and as a result of arrangements, there is an increase in the proportion of the residual amount that is guaranteed by the lessee (or by a person not connected with the lessor) (as to which see **10.50**(6) above) and the lease would have been a long funding lease if those arrangements had been made before its 'inception' (see *CAA 2001, s 70YI(1)*). The lease is treated as terminated, and a new lease treated as commenced, as at the time of the arrangement (or the latest arrangement if more than one). [*CAA 2001, s 70YD*].

Commencement/transitional provisions

[10.54] The long funding leasing rules above (and those at **75.98–75.100** TRADING INCOME) apply in respect of a lease where one of the conditions at (a) and (b) below is met. However, regardless of these conditions, a lease 'finalised' (see below) before 21 July 2005 cannot be a long funding lease (but this let-out is itself disapplied if the lessor does not come within the charge to UK tax until after 17 May 2006).

(a) Condition 1 is that the lease is not an 'excepted lease' and that it is 'finalised' on or after 1 April 2006 or the 'commencement' (see *CAA 2001, s 70YI(1)*) of its term is on or after that date.
(b) Condition 2 applies if the commencement of the term of the lease was before 1 April 2006 but the plant or machinery is not brought into use by the person concerned for the purposes of a qualifying activity (see **10.4** above) until on or after that date. (This covers, for example, the situation where the person concerned becomes UK resident on or after that date, such that his activity becomes a qualifying activity.) The person concerned may be the lessor or the lessee depending on from whose point of view one is applying the provisions.

There are regulations enabling a *lessor* to elect for a lease to be treated, as regards him only, as a long funding lease if it would not otherwise be such a lease, but the election cannot be made on an individual lease by lease basis. See **10.51** above.

For these purposes, a lease is '*finalised*' when there is a written contract for it between lessor and lessee, the contract is unconditional (or any conditions have already been met) and there are no terms still to be agreed.

For the purposes of (a) above, a lease is an '*excepted lease*' if it meets *all* the following conditions.

(i) Condition 1 is that before 21 July 2005 there was written evidence of an agreement or common understanding (the '*pre-existing heads of agreement*') between (or effectively between) lessor and lessee as to the 'principal terms of the lease' (as defined).
(ii) Condition 2 is that the leased plant or machinery was 'under construction' (as defined) before 1 April 2006.
(iii) Condition 3 is that the lease is 'finalised' (see above) before 1 April 2007 (but see below).
(iv) Condition 4 is that the commencement of the term of the lease is before 1 April 2007 (but see below).
(v) Condition 5 is that the lessee is the person(s) identified as such in the 'pre-existing heads of agreement' (within (i) above).
(vi) Condition 6 is that the principal terms of the lease are not materially different from those in the 'pre-existing heads of agreement' (within (i) above).

The date in (iii) and (iv) above is deferred to 1 April 2009 if construction of the asset proceeds continuously from 1 April 2006 (and at the normal pace for an asset of its type) and the lease commences as soon as is practicable after construction is substantially complete. There is provision to treat this condition as satisfied if it is failed only by reason of unforeseen events beyond the control of the parties (including the main constructor).

There are rules (see *FA 2006, Sch 8 paras 20, 25*) as to how these transitional provisions are to be applied in a case where the 'pre-existing heads of agreement' (see (i) above) relates to two or more assets.

If a person incurs expenditure before 19 July 2006 for leasing under a long funding lease which does not meet all the conditions in (i)–(vi) above, but in respect of which there was a 'pre-existing heads of agreement' before 21 July 2005 (as in (i) above), such expenditure (the '*old expenditure*') is treated as separate from any expenditure incurred on or after date (the '*new expenditure*'). *FA 2006, Sch 8 para 22* provides rules, for this purpose only, as to the time at which an amount of expenditure is treated as being incurred. The old and new expenditure are treated as if incurred on separate assets leased under separate leases; the notional lease relating to the old expenditure is then deemed to be an excepted lease. The lease rentals are apportioned between the two notional leases in a just and reasonable manner. These splitting provisions apply in determining the income tax or corporation tax liability of anyone who is at any time the lessor or the lessee under the actual lease.

Mixed leases

Where a lease is a mixed lease (see **10.53** above), it is first necessary to consider whether the mixed lease is itself an 'excepted lease' for the purposes of these transitional provisions. If it is not, one can then consider separately, in the case of each derived lease, whether that lease is an 'excepted lease'.

Transfers

There is provision to ensure that a lease that is outside the long funding leasing regime (by virtue of the commencement/transitional provisions) remains outside that regime if it is transferred from one lessor to another or from one lessee to another. For this to have effect, there must be no effective change to the term of the lease or to the payments due under it, and the lessor or lessee (as the case may be) must be within the charge to UK tax immediately before the transfer.

[*FA 2006, Sch 8 paras 15–27*].

Special leasing

[10.55] '*Special leasing*' is the hiring out of plant or machinery otherwise than in the course of a trade or other qualifying activity. It is itself a qualifying activity for the purpose of claiming plant and machinery allowances. However, plant or machinery provided for use in a dwelling-house or flat is excluded from being qualifying expenditure. See **10.3** above. See HMRC Brief 45/10, 22 October 2010 as regards the meaning of 'dwelling-house'.

Where a person hires out more than one item of plant and machinery, he has a *separate qualifying activity* in relation to each item. A qualifying activity of special leasing begins when the plant or machinery is first hired out. It is permanently discontinued if the lessor permanently ceases to hire it out. [*CAA 2001, s 19(2)–(4)*].

Manner of making allowances and charges for special leasing

For income tax purposes, a plant and machinery allowance is given effect by deduction from the person's income for the tax year in question from qualifying activities of special leasing. If, however, the plant or machinery was not used for the whole (or for a part) of the tax year for the purposes of a qualifying activity carried on by the *lessee*, the allowance (or a proportionate part) can only be set against the lessor's income from that particular qualifying activity of special leasing. In all cases the deduction is given effect at Step 2 of the calculation of income tax liability (see **1.10** ALLOWANCES AND TAX RATES). A claim for an allowance may be made outside a tax return. Any excess of allowances over the income for a tax year against which they may be set is carried forward without time limit against future such income. A balancing charge is taxed as income and is included in the income against which an allowance may be set as above.

[*CAA 2001, ss 3(4), 258*].

Simon's Taxes. See B3.385.

Overseas leasing (obsolescent)

[10.56] Special rules apply to qualifying expenditure incurred on the provision of plant or machinery used for overseas leasing (as defined). These include the reduction of allowances and, in some cases, the prohibition of allowances. They are, however, in the course of being phased out; in determining for the purposes of these rules whether plant or machinery is used for overseas leasing, no account is to be taken of any lease finalised on or after 1 April 2006. [*CAA 2001, s 105(2A)*]. See the 2015/16 and earlier editions of this work for these provisions.

Simon's Taxes. See B3.340T–B3.340X.

Capital allowances on plant and machinery — miscellaneous

[10.57] The additional matters discussed at **10.58–10.72** below apply for the purposes of capital allowances on plant and machinery.

Hire-purchase and similar contracts

[10.58] The following applies where a person incurs capital expenditure, on the provision of plant or machinery for the purposes of a trade or other qualifying activity, under a contract providing that he will (or may) become the owner of it on performance of the contract. One example of such a contract is a hire-purchase agreement. That person is treated for the purposes of plant and machinery allowances as the sole owner of the plant or machinery for as long as he is entitled to the benefit of the contract. When the plant or machinery is brought into use for the purposes of the qualifying activity, the full outstanding capital cost (i.e. excluding the hire or interest element) attracts capital allowances immediately. Any such capital payments made before it is brought into use attract allowances as they fall due.

As regards any such contract that, in accordance with generally accepted accounting practice (GAAP), falls to be treated as a lease (or would so fall if the person prepared accounts), the person mentioned above is treated as owning the plant or machinery only if the contract falls (or would fall) under GAAP to be treated by that person as a *finance lease*. In relation to periods of account beginning on or after 1 January 2019, this rule also has effect if the person is a lessee under a right-of-use lease (see **10.50**(5) above) and the contract would fall to be treated in his accounts as a finance lease *if* he were required under GAAP to determine whether it falls to be so treated; this applies to a lessee who has adopted IFRS 16 (see **75.82** TRADING INCOME) and is thus not required in his accounts to distinguish between finance leases and operating leases. At any time at which, by virtue only of the preceding rule, the lessee is *not* treated as owning the plant or machinery, no-one else is treated as owning it either; so, in these circumstances, neither lessee nor lessor are entitled to capital allowances.

These provisions are extended so as to apply where the plant or machinery is used for the purposes of any overseas activity that would be a qualifying activity within **10.4** above if the person carrying it on were UK resident. Any two or more agreements (or undertakings) are treated for the purposes of these provisions as a single contract if, when taken together, they have the effect that the person concerned will (or may) become the owner of the plant or machinery on performance of the 'contract'.

If the person mentioned above is treated as owning the plant or machinery but the contract is not completed, so that he does not, in fact, become the owner of the plant or machinery, he is treated as ceasing to own it when he ceases to be entitled to the benefit of the contract. The resulting disposal value (see **10.27** above) depends on whether the plant or machinery has been brought into use for the purposes of the qualifying activity. If it has, the disposal value is

(i) the total of any capital sums received by way of consideration, compensation, damages or insurance in respect of the person's rights under the contract or the plant or machinery itself, plus

(ii) the capital element of all instalments treated as paid (see above) but not, in fact, paid.

This is subject to the overriding rule that the disposal value cannot exceed the qualifying expenditure brought into account (see **10.27** above).

If the plant or machinery has not been so brought into use, the disposal value is the total in (i) above (but see below as regards assignments).

[*CAA 2001, ss 67, 68, Sch 3 para 15; FA 2019, Sch 14 paras 1(2), 6(1)*].

Disapplication of above rules

The above rules do not apply to expenditure incurred on 'fixtures' within *CAA 2001, ss 172–204* (see **10.37** *et seq*. above), and if plant or machinery which has been treated under the above rules as owned by a person becomes such a fixture, he is treated as ceasing to own it at that time (unless it is treated as belonging to him under *sections 172–204*). [*CAA 2001, s 69, Sch 3 para 16*].

The above rules similarly do not apply (except in relation to deemed ownership of the asset concerned) if the person mentioned above acquires the plant or machinery for leasing under a 'finance lease' (as defined in **10.62** below, and note the exclusion of long funding leases from that definition). [*CAA 2001, s 229(3), Sch 3 para 44*]. See also **10.62, 10.63** below and **75.83** TRADING INCOME as regards finance lease allowance restrictions. See **10.48** above as regards long funding leasing.

Assignment of contract

If the person entitled to the benefit of a hire-purchase or similar contract assigns that benefit before the plant or machinery is brought into use, and the assignee's allowances fall to be restricted under the anti-avoidance provisions at **10.62** below, both the disposal value and the expenditure against which it is set are increased by the capital expenditure he would have incurred if he had wholly performed the contract. The same applies in finance lease cases. This is to protect the assignee against an undue repression of qualifying expenditure by reference to the assignor's disposal value (see **10.62** below). [*CAA 2001, s 229*].

Transfer followed by hire-purchase etc.

Consequences ensue where:

(a) a person (S) transfers (see *CAA 2001, s 70Y(3)*) plant or machinery to another person (B);

(b) at any time after the date of the transfer, the plant or machinery is available to be used by S or by a person (other than B) who is connected (within **19** CONNECTED PERSONS) with S (CS);

(c) it is available to be so used under a contract entered into on or after 13 November 2008 which provides that S or CS will (or may) become the owner of the plant or machinery on the performance of the contract (e.g. a hire-purchase agreement); and

(d) S or CS incurs capital expenditure on the provision of the plant or machinery under that contract.

The consequences are that no annual investment allowance (see **10.13** above) or first-year allowance (see **10.18** above) is available in respect of the expenditure of S or CS under the contract. Also, in determining the qualifying expenditure of S or CS, there is disregarded any excess of his expenditure over the disposal value to be brought into account by S. Where no such disposal value falls to be brought into account, the qualifying expenditure of S or CS (if otherwise greater) is normally restricted to the lesser of the market value of the plant or machinery, the capital expenditure (if any) incurred on it by S before the transfer and any capital expenditure incurred on it before the transfer by any person connected with S. *CAA 2001, ss 214, 215* (see **10.62** below) do not then apply in relation to the contract. The qualifying expenditure of S or CS is restricted to nil if:

- S is not required to bring a disposal value into account on the transfer in (a) above; and
- at any time before that transfer, S or a 'linked person' became owner of the plant or machinery without incurring either capital expenditure or 'qualifying revenue expenditure' on its provision.

A '*linked person*' is a person (LP) who owned the plant or machinery at any time before the transfer in (a) above and who was connected with S at any time during LP's ownership and before the said transfer. Expenditure is '*qualifying revenue expenditure*' if it is expenditure of a revenue nature that was incurred at no less than an arm's length price or that was incurred by a manufacturer and represented no less than the normal cost of manufacturing the plant or machinery.

[*CAA 2001, s 229A*].

For a further anti-avoidance rule, see **10.53** above under Tax avoidance involving international leasing.

Simon's Taxes. See **B3.340A, B3.340G.**

Abortive expenditure

[10.59] The rules at **10.58** above for hire-purchase and similar contracts can equally be applied to expenditure under other contracts which proves to be abortive. A disposal value falls to be brought into account as in **10.58** above when the contract fails to be completed. Thus, for example, plant and machinery allowances can be obtained in respect of a non-refundable deposit paid on an item of plant or machinery which is never actually supplied, notwithstanding the fact that the item is never owned by the person incurring the expenditure.

Connected persons, leasebacks and other anti-avoidance measures

[10.60] Anti-avoidance measures are described in **10.61–10.64** below. See **19** CONNECTED PERSONS for the definition of that term for these purposes.

See also **10.58** above and **75.83** TRADING INCOME as regards finance lease allowance restrictions. See **10.48** above as regards long funding leasing.

See **10.69** below as regards succession to a trade or other qualifying activity carried on by a connected person.

Simon's Taxes. See **B3.311A, B3.334, B3.340H–340S, B3.342, B3.365, B3.366, B3.377.**

Restrictions on disposal values

[10.61] For disposals of plant or machinery acquired as a result of transaction(s) between connected persons, the limit on the disposal value (see **10.27** above) is to the greatest amount of qualifying expenditure incurred on it by any of the participants in the transaction(s) (after deducting any 'additional VAT rebates' made — see **10.2**(viii) above).

The normal absence of any requirement to bring a disposal value into account if none of the qualifying expenditure in question has been taken into account in determining available qualifying expenditure (see **10.27** above) does not apply if the person concerned acquired the plant or machinery as a result of such transaction(s) as are mentioned above *and* any earlier participant was required to bring a disposal value into account. Instead, the current participant's qualifying expenditure is deemed to be allocated (if this is not actually the case), for the chargeable period in which the current disposal event occurs, to whichever pool is appropriate, thus requiring the bringing into account of a disposal value (which is then subject to the above-mentioned limit).

[*CAA 2001, ss 62(2)–(4), 64(2)–(5), 239(5)(6)*].

Restrictions on allowances

[10.62] Where plant or machinery is purchased:

(i) in a transaction with a connected person, or
(ii) in a 'sale and leaseback transaction',

no annual investment allowance (AIA) or first-year allowances (FYAs) (where otherwise relevant) are available (see **10.15, 10.18** above). Also, in determining the buyer's qualifying expenditure, there is disregarded any excess of his expenditure (including any 'additional VAT liability' incurred in respect thereof — see **10.2**(viii) above) over the disposal value to be brought into account by the seller. Where no such disposal value is to be brought into account (e.g. where the seller is non-UK resident), the buyer's qualifying expenditure (if otherwise greater) is normally restricted to the lesser of:

(a) market value at time of the transaction; and
(b) the capital expenditure, if any, incurred by the seller or any person connected with him,

with modifications to allow for 'additional VAT liabilities' and 'rebates' — see **10.2**(viii) above. The buyer's qualifying expenditure is restricted to nil if:

- no disposal value is required to be brought into account by the seller; and

- at any time before the transaction, the seller or a 'linked person' became owner of the plant or machinery without incurring either capital expenditure or 'qualifying revenue expenditure' on its provision.

A '*linked person*' is a person (LP) who owned the plant or machinery at any time before the said transaction and who was connected with the seller at any time during LP's ownership and before the said transaction. Expenditure is '*qualifying revenue expenditure*' if it is expenditure of a revenue nature that was incurred at no less than an arm's length price or that was incurred by a manufacturer and represented no less than the normal cost of manufacturing the plant or machinery.

These provisions apply to contracts for future delivery, hire-purchase etc. contracts, and assignments of hire-purchase etc. contracts as they do to direct sales.

See also below under Transactions to obtain tax advantages.

For the above purposes, a sale is a '*sale and leaseback transaction*' if the plant or machinery:

- continues to be used for the purposes of a 'qualifying activity' carried on by the seller or by a connected person other than the buyer); or
- is used at some time after the sale for the purposes of a 'qualifying activity' carried on by the seller (or by a connected person other than the buyer) without having been used in the meantime for the purposes of any other 'qualifying activity' except that of leasing the plant or machinery.

For the purposes of these provisions, a '*qualifying activity*' is any activity within **10.4**(i)–(vii) above regardless of whether or not profits therefrom are within the charge to UK tax.

The 'sole or main benefit' restrictions referred to above do not generally apply to straightforward finance leasing transactions (*Barclays Mercantile Industrial Finance Ltd v Melluish* Ch D 1990, 63 TC 95).

Supply in the ordinary course of business

Neither the restriction to the buyer's qualifying expenditure nor the denial of AIA and FYAs normally has effect in relation to the sale (or the supply for future delivery or on hire-purchase) of unused plant or machinery in the ordinary course of the seller's business. However, both the restriction and the denial do apply in these circumstances if the transaction in question falls within the provisions described below under Transactions to obtain tax advantages

Election available in sale and leasebacks

In the case of sale and leaseback transactions, a joint (irrevocable) election under *CAA 2001, s 228* may be made by the seller (or assignor) and the lessor (within two years of the sale etc.) provided that:

- the seller (or assignor) incurred capital expenditure on acquiring the plant or machinery unused (and not second-hand) and not under a transaction itself within the above provisions;

- the sale etc. takes place not more than four months after the plant or machinery is first brought into use for any purpose; and
- the seller (or assignor) has not claimed capital allowances for the expenditure or included it in a pool of qualifying expenditure.

The effect of the election is that no allowances are made to the seller (or assignor) in respect of the expenditure, and that allowances which are accordingly available to the lessor are given by reference to the smaller of his expenditure and the amount in (b) above, i.e. disregarding the current market value at the time of the sale etc.

[*CAA 2001, ss 213(1)(2), 214–218, 227, 228, 230–233, 241, 242, 244, 245, 268E*].

Transactions to obtain tax advantages

Capital allowances are restricted if plant or machinery is purchased in a transaction that has an 'avoidance purpose' or is part of, or occurs as a result of, a scheme or arrangement that has an 'avoidance purpose'. This applies whether the scheme or arrangement was made before or after the transaction was entered into and whether or not the scheme or arrangement is legally enforceable. The provisions apply to contracts for future delivery, hire-purchase etc. contracts, and assignments of hire-purchase etc. contracts as they do to direct sales, and the references below to the buyer should be read accordingly.

A transaction, scheme or arrangement has an '*avoidance purpose*' if a main purpose of a party in entering into it is to enable any person to obtain a tax advantage under the plant and machinery allowances code that would not otherwise be obtained. This includes *inter alia*:

- the obtaining of an allowance that is in any way more favourable than the one that would otherwise be obtained; and
- avoiding liability for the whole or part of a balancing charge to which liability would otherwise arise.

The consequences depend on the nature of the tax advantage, as set out in (1), (2) and (3) below. If a transaction, scheme or arrangement involves more than one kind of tax advantage, the rules below operate separately in relation to each.

(1) If the nature of the tax advantage is:
    - that an allowance to which the buyer is entitled for a chargeable period is calculated using a percentage rate that is higher than the one that would otherwise be used; or
    - that the buyer is entitled to an allowance sooner than he would otherwise be entitled to it,

    the consequences are as follows. Firstly, no AIA or FYAs are available to the buyer. Secondly (under *CAA 2001, s 218ZA*), the tax advantage is negated, i.e. the percentage rate of any allowance or (as the case may be) the timing of the buyer's entitlement to any allowance is presumed to be what it would be if no tax advantage had been obtained.

The above applies whether or not the buyer's qualifying expenditure falls to be restricted as a result of (i) or (ii) above or as a result of an election under *CAA 2001, s 228* (sale and leasebacks — see above) or as a result of the election mentioned in **10.50**(1)(A) above (long funding leasing).

(2) If the nature of the tax advantage is something other than the above, and the tax advantage is not within (3) below, the consequences are as follows. Firstly, no AIA or FYAs are available to the buyer. Secondly (under *CAA 2001, s 218ZA*), all or part of the buyer's capital expenditure on the plant or machinery is to be left out of account in determining his available qualifying expenditure. Subject to below, the amount of expenditure to be left out of account is such amount as would, or would in effect, cancel out the tax advantage (whether that advantage is obtained by the buyer or by another person and whether it relates to the transaction in question or to something else). If that amount would exceed the whole of the buyer's expenditure under the transaction, the whole of that expenditure is left out of account.

If the buyer's qualifying expenditure also falls to be restricted as a result of (i) or (ii) above or as a result of an election under *CAA 2001, s 228* (sale and leasebacks — see above) or as a result of the election mentioned in **10.50**(1)(A) above (long funding leasing), the amount of expenditure to be left out of account is the greater of the two restrictions.

(3) The following consequence ensues (under *CAA 2001, s 218ZB*) where:

- the tax advantage relates to the disposal value of the plant or machinery under the transaction (whether the advantage is the obtaining of a more favourable allowance or the avoidance of all or part of a balancing charge); and
- a 'payment' is made (or is to be made) to any person under the transaction, scheme or arrangement, some or all of which would not be taken into account in determining the disposal value of the plant or machinery.

The disposal value is to be adjusted in a just and reasonable manner so as to include an amount representing so much of the payment as would cancel out the tax advantage. 'Payment' extends here to the providing of any benefit, the assuming of any liability and any other transfer of money or money's worth.

[*CAA 2001, ss 213, 215, 217, 218ZA, 218ZB, 268E; FA 2016, s 70*].

Sale and finance leasebacks

The above restrictions (other than those under *CAA 2001, s 218ZA*) on the buyer's qualifying expenditure and on his entitlement to AIA and FYAs do not apply if plant or machinery is the subject of a 'sale and finance leaseback'. However, where the finance lessor in a sale and finance leaseback has substantially divested himself of any risk that the lessee will default, the lessor's expenditure does not qualify for plant and machinery allowances at all (and this applies regardless of the election generally available in sale and leasebacks — see above).

A '*sale and finance leaseback*' is a transaction:

- in which the plant or machinery continues to be used for the purposes of an activity carried on by the seller or by a connected person other than the buyer; or
- in which the plant or machinery is used at some time after the sale for the purposes of a qualifying activity carried on by the seller (or by a connected person other than the buyer) without having been used in the meantime for the purposes of any other qualifying activity except that of leasing the plant or machinery; or
- in which the plant or machinery is used at some time after the sale etc. for the purposes of a non-qualifying activity carried on by the seller (or by a connected person other than the buyer) without having been used in the meantime for the purposes of a qualifying activity except that of leasing the plant or machinery,

where the availability of the plant or machinery for the use in question is a direct or indirect consequence of its having been leased under a 'finance lease'.

'*Finance lease*' means any arrangements for plant or machinery to be leased or made available such that the arrangements (or arrangements in which they are comprised) would fall, in accordance with generally accepted accounting practice (see **75.21** TRADING INCOME), to be treated in the accounts of one or more of those companies as a finance lease or as a loan.

[*CAA 2001, ss 219, 221, 225, 230, Sch 3 para 45*].

Sale and finance leasebacks are generally excluded from 'short lease' treatment and are thus within the scope of the long funding leasing rules at **10.48** above (see **10.50**(1)(A) above).

Plant or machinery subject to further operating lease

The following rules apply where plant or machinery, whilst continuing to be the subject of a sale and finance leaseback, is leased to the original owner, or a person connected with him, under an operating lease. In computing the income/profits of the lessee (i.e. the lessee under the operating lease), the deduction for operating lease rentals is restricted to the 'relevant amount'. In computing the income/profits of the lessor (i.e. the lessor under the operating lease), amounts receivable by him under the operating lease are included as income without netting off any amounts due by the lessor to the lessee. However, amounts receivable are not included as income to the extent that they exceed the 'relevant amount'. In each case, the '*relevant amount*' is the maximum amount of finance lease rentals deductible in computing the finance lessee's income/profits (see above). In applying these rules, such apportionments are to be made as are just and reasonable where only some of the plant or machinery subject to the sale and finance leaseback is also subject to the operating lease. For the above purposes, an operating lease is a lease that does not fall under GAAP to be treated in the lessee's accounts as a finance lease or, for periods of account beginning on or after 1 January 2019 in the case of a lessee using IFRS 16 (see **75.82** TRADING INCOME, would not fall to be so treated if the accounts were required to distinguish between finance leases and operating leases).

[*CAA 2001, s 228J; FA 2019, Sch 14 paras 1(6), 6(1)*].

Cars

A special rule applies where a disposal value is required to be brought into account on a sale (or on the performance of a contract) within any of the provisions above, and the asset is a car the expenditure on which is allocated to a single asset pool due to non-business use. If allowances fall to be restricted as above, the disposal value is equal to the lesser of market value at the time of the disposal event and the capital expenditure incurred (or treated as incurred) on the car by the person disposing of it. The new owner is treated as having incurred capital expenditure on the car of the same amount. [*CAA 2001, s 208A*].

Lease and finance leasebacks

[10.63] A '*lease and finance leaseback*' occurs if a person ('L') leases plant or machinery to another ('F') in circumstances such that, had it been a sale, the transaction would have been a sale and finance leaseback as defined in **10.62** above (except that the availability of the plant or machinery for the use in question must in this case be a *direct* consequence of its having been leased under a finance lease). For this purpose, a person is regarded as leasing an item of plant or machinery to another person only if he grants him rights over the item for consideration and is not required to bring all of that consideration into account under the plant and machinery capital allowances code.

In calculating L's income or profits for a period of account, the amount deductible in respect of finance lease rentals cannot exceed the 'permitted maximum'. Normally, the '*permitted maximum*' is the amount of the finance charges shown in the accounts, but relation to a period of account during which the leaseback terminates it also includes a proportion of the net book value of the item immediately before the termination, such proportion to be computed in accordance with a formula in *CAA 2001, s 228B(4)*.

If the use of the plant or machinery under the leaseback includes use by a person other than L or F, but who is connected with L, the above applies in relation to that person as it does in relation to L.

In the period of account in which the leaseback terminates, L's income/profits from the qualifying activity for the purposes of which the leased item was used immediately before the termination are increased by a proportion of the original consideration for the lease, such proportion to be computed in accordance with a formula in *CAA 2001, s 228C(3)*. The above restriction on deductible finance lease rentals does not apply to any refund of finance lease rentals on the termination of a leaseback.

The above rules do not apply to a person who becomes the finance lessee by means of an assignment of the lease.

For the above purposes, a '*termination*' of a leaseback includes an assignment of L's interest, the making of any other arrangements under which a person other than L becomes liable to make payments under the leaseback and any variation as a result of which the leaseback ceases to be a finance lease.

Special provision is made for cases in which accounts are not drawn up in accordance with generally accepted accounting practice (GAAP). Additionally, the above rules are adapted in a case where the leaseback does not fall under

GAAP to be treated in L's accounts as a finance lease but does fall to be so treated in the accounts of a person connected with L. If the leaseback falls to be so treated in the accounts of neither L nor a person connected with him, those rules are disapplied. In that case, however, L's income/profits for the period of account during which the term of the leaseback begins are increased by the consideration payable to L for the grant of the original lease.

For the above purposes, the consideration given for the lease do not include rentals payable under that grant. Nor does it include any 'relevant capital payment' within **4.41** ANTI-AVOIDANCE; if some but not all of the consideration is a relevant capital payment, the above provisions have effect subject to such modifications as are just and reasonable.

[*CAA 2001, ss 228A–228C, 228G–228H*].

Finance leases in lease and finance leasebacks are generally excluded from 'short lease' treatment and are thus within the scope of the long funding leasing rules at **10.48** above (see **10.50**(1)(A) above).

Plant or machinery subject to further operating lease

CAA 2001, s 228J (see **10.62** above) applies equally where plant or machinery is the subject of a lease and finance leaseback.

Transitional provisions

In relation to any leasebacks whose term commenced before 17 March 2004, transitional rules seek to preserve the pre-existing treatment of lease rentals payable before that date or in respect of any period ending before that date and a time proportion of lease rentals payable for periods straddling that date. For the effect on L's lease rental deductions, see *FA 2004, Sch 23 paras 2, 3*.

The increase in L's income/profits for the period of account in which the leaseback terminates is capped, in accordance with a formula in *FA 2004, Sch 23 para 5*, if a pre-17 March 2004 leaseback terminates early, i.e. other than by expiry of its term.

The increase in L's income/profits for the period of account in which the leaseback terminates is abated if a pre-17 March 2004 leaseback terminates early, L reacquires ownership of the plant or machinery and L's capital expenditure on reacquisition is itself restricted under **10.62** above. If the restriction equals or exceeds the increase in profits/income, the increase is cancelled; in other cases, the increase is reduced by the restriction. However, the increase is reinstated in modified form if a disposal event (see **10.27** above) occurs in relation to the whole or part of the plant or machinery within six years after the leaseback terminates. See *FA 2004, Sch 23 para 6*.

Where a pre-17 March 2004 lease and finance leaseback terminates and L then disposes of the plant or machinery, there is provision for his chargeable gain to be reduced for capital gains tax purposes. See *FA 2004, Sch 23 para 10*.

Leasing — restriction of lessor's qualifying expenditure

[10.64] A lessor's qualifying expenditure for the purposes of plant and machinery allowances may fall to be restricted to the 'value of the asset to the lessor'. The restriction applies if, at the time the lessor incurs the capital expenditure on the asset (i.e. the plant or machinery):

- the asset is leased or arrangements exist under which it is to be leased; and
- arrangements have been entered into in relation to payments under the lease that reduce the value of the asset to the lessor.

The '*value of the asset to the lessor*' is the sum of (i) the present value of the lessor's anticipated taxable income from the lease of the asset and (ii) the present value of the residual value of the asset (reduced by the amount of any rental rebate).

In calculating the lessor's anticipated taxable income from the lease, one excludes any amount brought into account as a disposal value as in **10.27** above and any amounts that represent charges for services or 'taxes' to be paid by the lessor. ('*Taxes*' means UK or foreign taxes or duties, but not income tax, corporation tax or foreign equivalents.) Present value is calculated by using the 'interest rate implicit in the lease' (see *CAA 2001, s 228MB*). A rental rebate means any sum payable to the lessee that is calculated by reference to the value of the plant or machinery at or about the time when the lease terminates (see *CAA 2001, s 228MC*).

Where the lessor has previously incurred capital expenditure on the same asset, the qualifying expenditure falling to be restricted is his total qualifying expenditure on that asset. This covers the possibility that the lessor may incur the capital expenditure in instalments.

For the above purposes, a 'lease' includes any arrangements which provide for plant or machinery to be leased or otherwise made available by one person to another.

[*CAA 2001, ss 228MA–228MC*].

The above legislation was a response to identified avoidance schemes. There should be no need to consider whether it applies in the case of a normal commercial lease as the value of the asset to the lessor would not normally be less than the capital expenditure incurred by him.

Simon's Taxes. See **B3.311A.**

Plant or machinery received by way of gift

[10.65] Where plant or machinery received by way of gift is brought into use for the purposes of a trade or other qualifying activity carried on by the donee, the donee is entitled to writing-down allowances as if he had purchased it from the donor at the time it is brought into use and at its market value at that time. The deemed expenditure cannot qualify for first-year allowances (see **10.18** above) or for the annual investment allowance (see **10.13** above). [*CAA 2001, ss 14, 213(3), Sch 3 paras 12, 43*]. **Simon's Taxes.** See **B3.303.**

Previous use outside the business

[10.66] Where a person brings into use, for the purposes of a trade or other qualifying activity carried on by him, plant or machinery which he previously owned for purposes not entitling him to plant and machinery allowances in respect of that activity, writing-down allowances are calculated as if the trader etc. had, at the time of bringing it into use, incurred expenditure on its acquisition equal to its market value at that time. If, however, actual cost is less than market value, the actual cost is used instead. The actual cost for this purpose is reduced to the extent that it would have been reduced under the anti-avoidance provisions of *CAA 2001, s 218* or (prior to its repeal) *CAA 2001, s 224* (see **10.62** above) had it been expenditure on plant or machinery for use in the qualifying activity.

The deemed expenditure cannot qualify for first-year allowances (see **10.18** above) or for the annual investment allowance (see **10.13** above).

[*CAA 2001, s 13, Sch 3 para 11*].

Simon's Taxes. See **B3.303.**

See also **10.51** above as regards an asset ceasing to be used for long funding leasing but being retained by the lessor for use in a qualifying activity.

Plant or machinery moving between property businesses

[10.67] There is a rule to cover the situation where a person carrying on any of the four types of property business uses an item of plant or machinery in rotation between the different types whilst retaining ownership throughout. The four types are: an ordinary UK property business, an ordinary overseas property business, a UK furnished holiday lettings business or an EEA furnished holiday lettings business. See **60.20** PROPERTY INCOME for furnished holiday lettings. The rule recognises that a single letting may move in and out of furnished holiday lettings status from one tax year to another depending on whether or not all the conditions for that status are met for a particular year.

The rule applies where the person acquired the item for the purposes of one business (Business A) and has begun to use it for the purposes of a second business (Business B). If he then ceases to use the item for the purposes of Business B and recommences to use it for the purposes of Business A, he is treated as having incurred capital expenditure on the day following the cessation on the provision of the item of plant or machinery for the purposes of Business A. The amount of that notional capital expenditure is the lower of the market value of the item on the date of cessation and the original expenditure on the item. The item is then regarded as an item of plant or machinery distinct from the original item.

It would appear that on the initial movement of the item from Business A to Business B, a full disposal value (see **10.27** above) is required to be brought into account. The above rule operates only where the item reverts to being used in Business A.

[*CAA 2001, s 13B*].

Partnerships

[10.68] Partnerships are entitled to allowances in respect of an item of plant or machinery used for the trade or other qualifying activity carried on by the partnership, and owned by one or more partners without being partnership property. Any transfer of the item between partners, whilst it continues to be so used, does not require a disposal value to be brought into account. These provisions do not apply if such an item is *let* by one or more partners to the partnership or otherwise made available to it in consideration of a tax-deductible payment. [*CAA 2001, s 264*].

Following a change in the persons carrying on a trade or other qualifying activity, other than one resulting in the activity being treated as permanently discontinued, allowances are subsequently given and balancing charges subsequently made as if the new partnership etc. had carried on the activity before the change. For this purpose, a '*qualifying activity*' does not include an office or employment but otherwise includes any of the activities at **10.4**(i)–(vii) above regardless of whether or not the profits therefrom are within the charge to UK tax. [*CAA 2001, s 263*]. See **10.69** below as regards partnerships treated as discontinued and successions to trades generally.

Simon's Taxes. See **B3.390.**

Successions

[10.69] Following a change in the persons carrying on a trade or other qualifying activity, such that the activity is treated as permanently discontinued, any plant or machinery transferred, without being sold, to the new owner for continuing use in the qualifying activity is treated as sold at market value on the date of change, although no annual investment allowance or first-year allowance (where otherwise applicable) is available to the new owner. For this purpose, a '*qualifying activity*' does not include an office or employment but otherwise includes any of the activities at **10.4**(i)–(vii) above regardless of whether or not the profits therefrom are within the charge to UK tax. These provisions apply equally to plant or machinery not in use but provided and available for use for the purposes of the qualifying activity. [*CAA 2001, s 265*].

If a beneficiary succeeds to a 'qualifying activity' (as above) under a deceased proprietor's will or intestacy, he may elect for written-down value to be substituted (if less) for market value. [*CAA 2001, s 268, Sch 3 para 53*].

Where a person succeeds to a trade or other qualifying activity carried on by a person 'connected' with him, each is within the charge to UK tax on the profits, and the successor is not a dual resident investing company, they may jointly elect, within two years after the date of change, for plant or machinery to be treated as transferred at a price giving rise to neither a balancing allowance nor a balancing charge. This applies to plant or machinery which immediately before and after the succession is owned by the person concerned and either in use, or provided and available for use, for the purposes of the qualifying activity, and regardless of any actual sale by the predecessor to the successor. Allowances and charges are subsequently made as if everything done to or by the predecessor had been done to or by the successor. Where *CAA 2001* has effect, it is expressly provided that the deemed sale takes place when the succession takes place.

For this purpose, persons are '*connected*' if:

(a) they are CONNECTED PERSONS (**19**); or

(b) one of them is a partnership in which the other has the right to a share of assets or income, or both are partnerships in both of which some other person has the right to such a share; or
(c) one of them is a body corporate over which the other has control (within *CAA 2001, s 574*), or both are bodies corporate, or one a body corporate and one a partnership, over both of which some other person has control.

The above election precludes the application of *CAA 2001, s 104E* (disposal value in connection with special rate expenditure in avoidance cases — see **10.28** above), *CAA 2001, s 104* (disposal value of long-life assets in avoidance cases — see **10.34** above), *CAA 2001, s 265* (see above). An annual investment allowance or first-year allowance would appear to be precluded by **10.62** above.

[*CAA 2001, ss 266, 267, Sch 3 para 52; SI 2019 No 689, Reg 10(3)*].

Simon's Taxes See **B3.390**.

Co-ownership authorised contractual schemes (CoACS)

[10.70] A CoACS (see **80.9** UNIT TRUSTS ETC.) is broadly transparent for tax purposes, i.e. the scheme itself incurs no tax liability. This means that its investors are treated as if they had invested directly in the underlying assets of the scheme and are subject to personal taxation accordingly. Where the participants in a CoACS together carry on a qualifying activity, then on and after 16 November 2017 each participant in the scheme is regarded as carrying on the qualifying activity to the extent that the profits arising to the participant from the activity are, or (if there were any) would be, chargeable to tax.

Available election

For scheme accounting periods beginning on or after 1 April 2017, the operator of a CoACS carrying on a qualifying activity can elect to compute plant and machinery capital allowances and allocate them to the investors. The election is made by notice to an HMRC officer and must specify an accounting period of the scheme as the first such period for which the election has effect. That first accounting period must not exceed 12 months. The election then has effect for that first accounting period and all subsequent accounting periods of the scheme. The election is normally irrevocable but see below under Interaction with structures and buildings allowances.

Effect of the election

Where an election has effect for a scheme accounting period, the operator of the scheme must calculate the capital allowances that would be available to the scheme on the basis of various assumptions, e.g. that the scheme is a person, that the accounting period is a chargeable period and that the qualifying activity carried on by the participants is carried on by the scheme. It is assumed that property which was subject to the scheme at the beginning of the first accounting period for which the election has effect was acquired by the scheme at that time at its tax written-down value. Property which ceases to be subject to the scheme at any time is treated as if it ceased to be owned by the scheme, and a disposal value at tax written-down value must be brought into account. There is no entitlement to annual investment allowances or first-year allowances on any expenditure. The operator must allocate to each participant a proportion (which may be zero) of the capital allowances calculated. The allocation is to be on the basis of what is 'just and reasonable'. If there is more than one qualifying activity, the calculation and allocation of allowances are to be made separately for each activity.

In determining what is '*just and reasonable*' for the purposes of these provisions, regard may be had in particular to the relative size of each participant's holding of scheme units, but no regard is to be had to circumstances relating to a participant's tax liability.

A participant cannot claim capital allowances other than those allocated to him by the operator. A participant is treated as ceasing to own his interest in the property subject to the scheme at the beginning of the first scheme accounting period for which the election has effect, and must bring in a disposal value (see **10.27** above) equal to tax written-down value.

Where property consisting of a fixture ceases to be subject to the scheme at any time when an election has effect and a person (the '*current owner*') is subsequently treated as the owner of the fixture as a result of incurring capital expenditure on its provision (the '*new expenditure*'):

(a) the new expenditure is treated as nil if the 'disposal value statement requirement' is not met; and
(b) in any other case the new expenditure is treated as equal to the disposal value that the operator brought into account as above on the fixture's ceasing to be subject to the scheme.

The '*disposal value statement requirement*' is that the operator has, within two years after the fixture's ceasing to be property subject to the scheme, made a written statement of the disposal value in (b) above, and that the current owner has obtained that statement or a copy of it. The provisions at **10.46** and **10.47** above are disapplied in relation to the new expenditure.

Interaction with structures and buildings allowances

Provisions similar to those above apply in relation to structures and buildings allowances (SBAs) (see **9.30** CAPITAL ALLOWANCES). This includes the making of an election whereby the operator of a CoACS carrying on a qualifying activity can elect to compute SBAs and allocate them to the investors. An election made on or after 5 July 2019 under the above provisions (a plant and machinery election) automatically has effect for SBAs as well.

As stated above, a plant and machinery election is normally irrevocable. An election made before 5 July 2019 can, however, be withdrawn, by notice to an HMRC officer, if an SBA is available by reference to a building or structure which is subject to the scheme. The notice of withdrawal may not be given more than 12 months after the end of the accounting period in which the building or structure is first brought into qualifying use for the purposes of the SBA. The election ceases to have effect for the accounting period in which notice of withdrawal is given and all subsequent accounting periods of the scheme. Upon withdrawal, the property which was subject to the scheme at the beginning of that accounting period is treated as ceasing to be owned by the scheme at that time and as being acquired by the participants at that time in such proportions as are 'just and reasonable' (see above). The disposal value to be brought into account in relation to the cessation of ownership is the tax written-down value of the plant and machinery.

See also **9.34** CAPITAL ALLOWANCES.

[*CAA 2001, ss 262AA–262AE, 262AEA, 262AF; F(No 2)A 2017, s 40; SI 2019 No 1087, Regs 1, 3(7)(8)*].

See the HMRC technical note at www.gov.uk/government/publications/technical-note-co-ownership-authorised-contractual-schemes.

Partial depreciation subsidies

[10.71] Partial depreciation subsidies, i.e. sums, not otherwise taxable on the recipient, are payable to him, directly or indirectly, by any other person in respect of, or to take account of, *part* of the depreciation of plant or machinery resulting from its use in the recipient's trade or other qualifying activity.

Where it appears that a partial depreciation subsidy will be payable, an annual investment allowance or first-year allowance (where available — see **10.13**, **10.18** above) can nevertheless be given, but must be scaled down as is just and reasonable (though the full amount is deducted in arriving at the balance of expenditure available for writing-down allowances).

Qualifying expenditure (see **10.3** above) which has been the subject of a partial depreciation subsidy can only be allocated to a *single asset pool* (see **10.26** above). Where qualifying expenditure has otherwise been allocated to a pool and a partial depreciation subsidy is received for the first time in respect of it, it must be transferred to a single asset pool. This is achieved by bringing in a disposal value (equal to market value — see **10.27**(g) above) in the original pool for the chargeable period in which the subsidy is paid and allocating an equivalent amount to the single asset pool. Writing-down allowances and balancing allowances and charges in respect of the single asset pool are reduced to such amounts as are just and reasonable (though the full amount is deducted in arriving at any unrelieved qualifying expenditure carried forward).

[*CAA 2001, ss 209–212*].

See **10.6** above as regards subsidies towards the whole of such depreciation. See **10.2**(vi)(vii) above as regards contributions by others towards *expenditure* qualifying for plant and machinery and other capital allowances.

Simon's Taxes. See **B3.360**.

Lessee required to provide plant or machinery

[10.72] A lessee required to provide plant or machinery under the terms of the lease (including any tenancy), and using it for the purposes of a trade or other qualifying activity, is treated as if he owned it (for as long as it is used for those purposes), but is not required to bring in a disposal value (see **10.27** above) on termination of the lease. If:

- the plant or machinery continues to be so used until termination of the lease;
- the lessor holds the lease in the course of a qualifying activity; and
- on or after termination, a disposal event occurs at a time when the lessor owns the plant or machinery,

the *lessor* is required to bring in a disposal value, for the chargeable period in which the disposal event occurs, in the pool to which the expenditure would have been allocated if incurred by the lessor. These rules do not, however, apply where the plant or machinery becomes, by law, part of the building in which it is installed or attached (see **10.37** above) under a lease. [*CAA 2001, s 70, Sch 3 para 17*].

Simon's Taxes. See **B3.340B.**

11

Capital Gains Tax

For full details of CGT provisions, see Tolley's Capital Gains Tax. For date due, see **54.1** PAYMENT OF TAX.

Capital gains tax (CGT)

[11.1] The legislation applying to individuals and companies was consolidated by the *Taxation of Chargeable Gains Act 1992* (*TCGA 1992*) and references to that Act are given throughout this book where appropriate. For full details see Tolley's Capital Gains Tax.

Exclusion of amounts otherwise taxed

[11.2] Gains for CGT purposes are calculated exclusive of receipts chargeable to income tax (except items giving rise to balancing charges or disposal values for capital allowances purposes). However, the capitalised value of a rentcharge, ground annual, feu duty or other series of income receipts can be taken into account for CGT purposes. [*TCGA 1992, s 37; CAA 2001, Sch 2 para 77; FA 2016, ss 79(8), 82(1); F(No 2)A 2017, Sch 2 paras 44, 64(1)*].

Rates of CGT

[11.3] Subject to any available business asset disposal relief (previously called entrepreneurs' relief) or investors' relief, the rate of CGT applicable to an individual is 10% or, where the individual is liable at the higher rate or dividend upper rate on any part of his taxable income, 20%. Where there is no higher rate or dividend upper rate income tax liability, but the amount chargeable to CGT exceeds the unused part of the basic rate band, the CGT rate on the excess is 20%.

The above rates do not apply to '*upper rate gains*', i.e. gains accruing on the disposal of interests in non-exempt residential properties and gains arising in respect of carried interest (as defined); these gains are taxable at 18% (as opposed to 10%) or 28% (as opposed to 20%).

See **1.3**, **1.4** ALLOWANCES AND TAX RATES for the higher rate and the basic rate limit, and **1.5** ALLOWANCES AND TAX RATES as regards the dividend upper rate. See **1.10** ALLOWANCES AND TAX RATES (Step 3) as regards taxable income.

In determining for the above purposes the unused part of an individual's basic rate band and whether any income is liable at the higher rate or the dividend upper rate, account is taken of certain special provisions, such as top slicing relief on life assurance gains and life assurance deficiency relief. See *TCGA 1992, s 1J* (previously, before 2019/20, *TCGA 1992, s 4A*). In determining, for the above purposes only, whether an individual is liable at the higher rate or dividend upper rate or whether an individual has any unused part of the basic rate band, a Scottish taxpayer (see **1.8** ALLOWANCES AND TAX RATES) is assumed to pay income tax at UK rates rather than Scottish rates.

The rate of CGT applicable to gains accruing to the trustees of a settlement or the personal representatives of a deceased person is 20%. Again, this does not apply to upper rate gains, which are charged at 28%.

If the gains accruing to a person in a tax year are chargeable to CGT at different rates, allowable capital losses may be deducted from those gains, and the CGT annual exempt amount may be used against those gains, in the way that is most beneficial to that person. Also, if an individual's gains straddle the basic rate limit and some of those gains are upper rate gains, the individual may choose which gains should utilise the unused part of the basic rate band so that this is used in the most beneficial way.

For business asset disposal relief (entrepreneurs' relief) and investors' relief, see Tolley's Capital Gains Tax.

[*TCGA 1992, ss 1F, 1H–1J; FA 2019, Sch 1 paras 2, 120* (previously, before 2019/20, *TCGA 1992, ss 4, 4A, 4B, 4BA; Scotland Act 2016, s 15(3)–(5)(7); FA 2016, ss 6(23)(24), 82(1)–(13)(16)–(18)*)].

Simon's Taxes. See **C1.107.**

Set-off of income tax reliefs against capital gains

[11.4] See **45.5** LOSSES for set-off of trading losses against capital gains. See **59.5** POST-CESSATION RECEIPTS AND EXPENDITURE for relief for certain post-cessation expenditure, and **28.65** EMPLOYMENT INCOME for relief for certain post-employment expenditure.

12

Certificates of Deposit

Simon's Taxes. See **E1.459–E1.461**.

Definition of certificate of deposit

[12.1] A certificate of deposit is a document:

- relating to the deposit of money in any currency;
- recognising an obligation to pay a stated principal amount to bearer or to order, with or without interest; and
- by the delivery of which, with or without endorsement, the right to receive that stated amount, with or without interest, is transferable.

[*ITTOIA 2005, s 552(2); ITA 2007, s 1019*].

Charge to tax

[12.2] Profits or gains on certificates of deposit are chargeable to income tax under *ITTOIA 2005, ss 551–554* (if not taxable as a trading receipt). These provisions do not apply to exempt pension funds. [*ITTOIA 2005, s 551*]. See **14.9** CHARITIES AND CHARITABLE GIVING for the exemption applicable to charitable trusts.

Relief for a loss on a certificate of deposit can be claimed against interest chargeable in respect of that certificate. [*ITA 2007, s 154; FA 2015, s 22(4)(8)*].

Uncertificated deposit rights

[12.3] Where, in a transaction in which no certificate of deposit or security (as defined by *TCGA 1992, s 132*) is issued, but an amount becomes payable with interest (by a bank, similar institution or person regularly engaging in similar transactions), then if the right to receive the amount or interest is disposed of or exercised, any profit (or loss) will be treated as in **12.2** above. [*ITTOIA 2005, s 552(1)*]. Where a right to receive an amount (with or without interest) in pursuance of a deposit of money comes into existence without a certificate of deposit, but the person entitled to the right could call for the issue of such a certificate, a profit (or loss) on disposal of the right before the issue of such a certificate is similarly treated as in **12.2** above. A disposal of the right to receive the interest is outside these provisions, but see the more general provisions on transfers of income streams at **4.35** ANTI-AVOIDANCE. [*ITTOIA 2005, s 552(1)(2)*].

Trustees

[12.4] Profits within **12.2** or **12.3** above arising to trustees of a settlement are chargeable at the trust rate. See **70.12** SETTLEMENTS.

Proceeds of crime

[12.5] Neither **12.2** nor **12.3** above applies to a transfer of a right that is a *Pt 5* transfer under *Proceeds of Crime Act 2002* (as in **9.2**(x) CAPITAL ALLOWANCES) where no compensating payment is made to the transferor. [*Proceeds of Crime Act 2002, Sch 10 paras 6, 10*].

13

Certificates of Tax Deposit

Simon's Taxes. See **A4.635**.

[13.1] Before **23 November 2017**, taxpayers could make deposits, evidenced by Certificates of Tax Deposit (CTDs), with HMRC for the subsequent payment of their own tax and Class 4 NIC liabilities generally (other than PAYE and tax deducted from payments to construction sub-contractors and corporation tax — see further below). If a deposit is tendered in respect of any liability, that liability will be treated as paid on the later of the certificate date and the normal due date for that liability (see **54** PAYMENT OF TAX). On and after that date, the CTD scheme is closed for new purchases, and existing certificates cannot be topped up, but pre-existing certificates will continue to be honoured until **23 November 2023**. Any certificates remaining after this date should be promptly submitted to HMRC for a refund. Thereafter, HMRC will seek to repay the balance of any certificate which remains unpaid and unclaimed. However, if they are unable to do so (for example, if they fail in reasonable efforts to contact the certificate holder) they will regard the balance as forfeited (Autumn Budget 2017 at www.gov.uk/government/publications/autumn-budget-2017-overview-of-tax-legislation-and-rates-ootlar/autumn-budget-2017-overview-of-tax-legislation-and-rates-ootlar, para 2.71).

Deposits made in a partnership name are not accepted in settlement of an individual partner's tax liability.

Interest, which is payable gross but taxable, will accrue for up to six years from the date of deposit to the date of payment of tax or, if earlier, the 'deemed due date' for payment of the liability against which the deposit (plus accrued interest) is set. The '*deemed due date*' is generally the normal due date for payment of the tax under the relevant legislation, and does not change if for any reason an assessment is made late or the liability is not payable until later (e.g. following settlement of an appeal). A deposit may be withdrawn for cash at any time (and note above that any remaining deposits on 23 November 2023 *must* then be cashed) but will then receive a reduced rate of interest. Where a certificate is used in settlement of a tax liability, interest at the higher rate up to the normal due date may be less than interest at the encashment rate up to the reckonable date. In such circumstances the taxpayer may instruct HMRC to calculate interest on the latter basis. (ICAEW Technical Release TAX 13/93, 30 June 1993). The rates of interest, published by the Treasury, and calculated by reference to the rate on comparable investment with the Government, vary with the size and period of the deposit, and the rate payable on a deposit is adjusted to the current rate on each anniversary of the deposit.

Deposits are not transferable except to personal representatives of a deceased person.

Rates of interest are given at **13.2** below. For full details of the CTD scheme, including current interest rates, see www.gov.uk/guidance/certificate-of-tax-deposit-scheme.

[13.2] The rates of interest on date of deposit or anniversary on Series 6 and Series 7 Certificates for deposits of under £100,000, whether used to pay tax or withdrawn for cash, have been nil since 5 December 2008. From 6 March 2009 onwards, the rates of interest on date of deposit or anniversary on Series 6 or Series 7 Certificates for deposits of £100,000 or more are as follows:

	Period of deposit in months				
	Under 1	**1 but under 3**	**3 but under 6**	**6 but under 9**	**9 but under 12**
Used to meet a scheduled liability	Nil	0.75%	0.75%	0.75%	0.75%
Withdrawn for cash	Nil	0.25%	0.25%	0.25%	0.25%

14

Charities and Charitable Giving

- For detailed guidance, see www.gov.uk/government/publications/charities-detailed-guidance-notes and www.gov.uk/charities-and-tax.
- See also specialist HMRC guidance 'Giving to charity: individuals' at www.gov.uk/donating-to-charity, and 'Fund raising events: exemption for charities and other qualifying bodies' at www.gov.uk/government/publications/charity-fundraising-events-exemptions.

Cross-reference. 75.74 TRADING INCOME for employees seconded to charities.

Simon's Taxes. See **C5.1**.

Other sources. See Tolley's Charities Manual.

Introduction to charities and charitable giving

[14.1] This chapter considers the income tax position of charitable trusts and also of persons within the charge to income tax who give to charity. In **14.2** below, the meaning for tax purposes of 'charity' and 'charitable trust' is set out, and **14.3–14.10** then deal with the income tax position of a charitable trust, the exemptions available to it and the circumstances in which those exemptions are restricted. The remainder of the chapter covers donations to charity, with particular reference to the income tax position of the donor. Tax-efficient methods of giving to charity comprise Gift Aid (**14.13–14.16**), payroll giving by employees (**14.18**) and qualifying gifts of shares, securities or real property (**14.19**). Individuals can donate pre-eminent objects to the nation in return for a reduction in their UK tax liability (**14.20**). There are anti-avoidance rules (the 'tainted donations rules') that deny tax reliefs to the donor where he enters into arrangements to obtain a financial advantage in return for his donation (**14.21**).

Definition of charity for tax purposes

[14.2] For tax purposes, a '*charity*' is a body of persons or trust that:

- is established for 'charitable purposes' only (see below), and
- meets the jurisdiction, registration and management conditions below.

A '*charitable trust*' is a charity (within the above definition) that is a trust. A '*charitable company*' is a charity (within the above definition) that is a body of persons.

Charitable purposes

A '*charitable purpose*' is one which is for the public benefit and which is within one of the following categories:

(a) the prevention or relief of poverty;
(b) the advancement of education;
(c) the advancement of religion;
(d) the advancement of health or the saving of lives;
(e) the advancement of citizenship or community development;
(f) the advancement of the arts, culture, heritage or science;
(g) the advancement of amateur sport;
(h) the advancement of human rights, conflict resolution or reconciliation or the promotion of religious or racial harmony or equality and diversity;
(i) the advancement of environmental protection or improvement;
(j) the relief of those in need by reason of youth, age, ill-health, disability, financial hardship or other disadvantage;
(k) the advancement of animal welfare;
(l) the promotion of the efficiency of the armed forces of the Crown, or of the efficiency of the police, fire and rescue services or ambulance services;
(m) any purposes not within (a) to (l) above but recognised as charitable purposes under *Charities Act 2011, s 5*;
(n) any purposes that may reasonably be regarded as analogous to, or within the spirit of, any purposes falling within (a) to (m) above; and
(o) any purposes that may reasonably be regarded as analogous to, or within the spirit of, any purposes which have been recognised under charity law as falling within (n) above or this category.

Jurisdiction condition

A body of persons or trust meets the jurisdiction condition if it falls to be subject to the control of:

- a UK court (the High Court, Court of Session or the High Court in NI) in the exercise of its jurisdiction with respect to charities; or
- any other court in the exercise of a corresponding jurisdiction under the law of an EU member State or a territory specified by statutory instrument. Norway, Iceland and Liechtenstein are specified territories by virtue of *SI 2010 No 1904* and *SI 2014 No 1807*.

Registration condition

In the case of a body of persons or trust that is a charity within the meaning of *Charities Act 2011, s 10*, the registration condition is met if the body or trust has complied with any requirement to be registered in the register of charities kept under *s 3* of that Act. In any other case, the registration condition is met if the body of persons or trust has complied with any corresponding requirement under the law of a territory outside England and Wales.

Management condition

A body of persons or trust meets the management condition if its managers are fit and proper persons to be managers of the body or trust. For this purpose, the 'managers' are the persons having the general control and management of the administration of the body or trust.

In relation to any period for which the management condition is not met, it is nevertheless treated as met if the Commissioners for HMRC consider that:

- the failure to meet the condition has not prejudiced the charitable purposes of the body or trust; or
- it is just and reasonable in all the circumstances for the condition to be treated as met throughout the period in question.

For HMRC guidance on the 'fit and proper persons' test and how it is applied in practice, see www.gov.uk/government/publications/charities-fit-and-proper-persons-test. HMRC assumes that all people appointed by charities are fit and proper persons unless they have information to suggest otherwise. Provided charities take appropriate steps on appointing personnel they may assume that they meet the test at all times unless, exceptionally, they are challenged by HMRC.

[*FA 2010, Sch 6 paras 1–5, 7; SI 2019 No 689, Reg 19*].

General matters

HMRC may publish the name and address of any body of persons or trust that appears to them to meet, or at any time to have met, the above definition of a charity. [*FA 2010, Sch 6 para 6*].

Charitable status is granted for tax purposes to the Commonwealth War Graves Commission and its separate Endowment Fund. [*FA 2015, s 123*].

Charities are regulated in England and Wales by the Charity Commission and in Scotland by the Office of the Scottish Charities Regulator. Under *Charities Act 2011, ss 54–59*, HMRC may disclose information regarding charities to the Charity Commission. The Charity Commission publishes advice for charity trustees in 'Charities and Fund-raising' (CC20), available at their website (www.charity-commission.gov.uk).

A donation by one charity to another has been applied for charitable purposes even though merely added to the funds of the other charity (*Helen Slater Charitable Trust Ltd* CA 1981, 55 TC 230). The application of income to the making of loans at interest to the subsidiaries from whom the income was derived was held to be for charitable purposes in *Nightingale Ltd v Price* (Sp C 66), [1996] SSCD 116.

As regards the time at which charitable purposes arise, see *Guild and Others (as Trustees of the William Muir (Bond 9) Ltd Employees' Share Scheme) v CIR* CS 1993, 66 TC 1 (trustees of share scheme required to repay loans out of proceeds of distribution and to apply balance to charitable purposes; it was held that they did not apply to proceeds of distribution for charitable purposes).

Simon's Taxes. See **C5.105–C5.114**.

Charities — specific exemptions and reliefs

[14.3] Apart from the exemptions at **14.4–14.9** below, charities are subject to tax on investment and rental income and gains and on profits from trades carried on in order to raise funds.

The exemptions, as they relate to income tax, were rewritten in *ITA 2007*, and are applied to 'charitable trusts' (see **14.2** above). The corresponding corporation tax exemptions apply to 'charitable companies' (see **14.2** above). The commentary at **14.4, 14.5, 14.6–14.10** below deals with the income tax position only. For convenience, the expression 'charitable trust' is used throughout. See Tolley's Corporation Tax for the provisions applying to charitable companies.

The exemptions are subject to the restrictions at **14.10** below.

Claims must be made for the exemptions (other than those at **14.9** below) to apply, generally within the time limit at **16.4** CLAIMS, to HMRC Charities, St John's House, Merton Road, Bootle, Merseyside L69 9BB or, in Scotland, HMRC Charities, Meldrum House, 15 Drumsheugh Gardens, Edinburgh EH3 7UL. [*ITA 2007, s 538(1)(2)*].

Simon's Taxes. See **C5.117A** *et seq.*

Property income

[14.4] The following income is exempt from income tax to the extent that it is applied to charitable purposes only.

- Income otherwise chargeable to income tax under *ITTOIA 2005, Pt 3* (property income) which arises from an estate, interest or right in or over any land vested in any person in trust for a charitable trust or for charitable purposes.
- Income otherwise chargeable to income tax under *ITTOIA 2005, Pt 2* (trading income) by virtue of *ITTOIA 2005, s 261* (provisions to be given priority over *Pt 3* — see **60.1** PROPERTY INCOME) which arises from rents or other receipts from an estate, interest or right in or over any land vested in any person in trust for a charitable trust or for charitable purposes.
- Distributions out of tax-exempt profits of a UK Real Estate Investment Trust (as in **60.24** PROPERTY INCOME).

[*ITA 2007, s 531*].

Where the letting of premises amounts to a trade otherwise than under *ITTOIA 2005, s 261* (because of the provision of other services), this exemption will not be available (see *Rotunda Hospital, Dublin v Coman HL 1920, 7 TC 517*). The trade may, however, qualify for the exemption at **14.7** below.

Simon's Taxes. See **C5.117I.**

Savings and investment income

[14.5] Income of a charitable trust, or applicable for charitable purposes only under an Act, charter, court judgment, trust deed or will, is exempt so far as applied to charitable purposes only and consisting of:

(a) income within *ITTOIA 2005, Pt 4 Ch 2* (interest), *Ch 7* (purchased life annuity payments) or *Ch 8* (profits from deeply discounted securities); or
(b) dividends or other distributions from UK resident companies; or
(c) distributions from non-UK resident companies; or
(d) non-trading royalties etc. from intellectual property within *ITTOIA 2005, s 579*; or
(e) non-trading income from telecommunications rights within *ITTOIA 2005, Pt 5 Ch 4*;
(f) annual payments charged to tax under *ITTOIA 2005, Pt 5 Ch 7*; or
(g) income treated as received by a unit holder from an exempt unauthorised unit trust (see **80.8** UNIT TRUSTS ETC.).

Income within (a)–(c) above must be income which would otherwise fall within and be dealt with under *ITTOIA 2005, Pt 4* (see *ITTOIA 2005, s 366* for provisions given priority over *Pt 4*).

[*ITA 2007, ss 532, 536*].

Where under a will, a business was bequeathed to trustees to carry it on and pay the net profits to a charity, the amounts so paid were held to be annual payments (*R v Special Commrs (ex p Shaftesbury Homes)* CA 1922, 8 TC 367). For annual payments generally, see **23.10** DEDUCTION OF TAX AT SOURCE.

Public revenue dividends (as defined) on securities in the name of trustees are exempt so far as they are applicable and applied only towards repairs of any cathedral, college, church, chapel etc.

[*ITA 2007, s 533*].

Simon's Taxes. See C5.117J.

Estate income

[14.6] Estate income (see **22.4** *et seq.* DECEASED ESTATES) of a trustee of a charitable trust is exempt so far as it is applied for the purposes of the charitable trust only. [*ITA 2007, s 537*]. This provision enables the trustee to recover any income tax suffered by the personal representatives on the income (see **22.3** DECEASED ESTATES).

Simon's Taxes. See C5.117O.

Trading profits

[14.7] Profits of a trade carried on by, and applied solely for the purposes of, a charitable trust, are exempt if the profits are profits of a tax year in relation to which the trade is a 'charitable trade'.

The exemption is extended to include adjustment income (see **75.24** TRADING INCOME) from such a trade arising in a tax year in which the trade is a charitable trade and POST-CESSATION RECEIPTS (**59**) from a trade which was a charitable trade in the tax year of cessation. As with trading profits, the adjustment income or post-cessation receipt must be applied to the purposes of the trust only.

For this purpose, a trade is a '*charitable trade*' in relation to a tax year if throughout the basis period (see **75.6** TRADING INCOME) for the year:

(a) the trade is exercised in the course of carrying out a primary purpose of the charitable trust; or
(b) the work is mainly carried out by its beneficiaries.

A trade exercised partly as in (a) above and partly otherwise is treated as two separate trades for this purpose, receipts and expenditure being apportioned between them on a just and reasonable basis. Similarly, where the work is carried out partly, but not mainly, by beneficiaries (see (b) above), the part in connection with which work is carried out by beneficiaries and the other part are treated as separate trades.

[*ITA 2007, ss 524, 525*].

For trades held to fall within the exemption, see *Glasgow Musical Festival Assn* CS 1926, 11 TC 154; *Royal Choral Society v CIR* CA 1943, 25 TC 263 and *Dean Leigh Temperance Canteen Trustees v CIR* Ch D 1958, 38 TC 315. For regular trading, see *British Legion, Peterhead Branch v CIR* CS 1953, 35 TC 509. (In practice, HMRC may in such cases allow a reasonable deduction for services etc. provided free.)

In practice, HMRC extend the exemptions above to related 'ancillary activities' such as the provision of a bar to theatre patrons and a coffee shop for patrons of a museum or similar concern. Guidance on ancillary activities is at para 7 at www.gov.uk/government/publications/charities-detailed-guidance-notes/annex-iv-trading-and-business-activities-basic-principles#12.

There are also three specific exemptions as follows.

Exemption for small trades and miscellaneous income and gains

Profits of a trade not otherwise exempt from income tax which is carried on by, and applied solely for the purposes of, a charitable trust, are exempt for a tax year provided that the resources condition described below is met in relation to that year.

The exemption is extended to include adjustment income (see **75.24** TRADING INCOME) and POST-CESSATION RECEIPTS (**59**) from a trade carried on by a charitable trust which are applied to the purposes of the trust only. Any adjustment income must arise in, and any post-cessation receipt must be received in, a tax year for which the resources condition below is met.

The exemption also applies for a tax year to income or gains of a charitable trust which is chargeable to income tax under any of the provisions listed in *ITA 2007, s 1016* (see **49.8** MISCELLANEOUS INCOME) and is not otherwise exempted from income tax, provided that the income or gains are applied solely for the purposes of the trust and that the resources condition below is met in relation to that year.

The resources condition is that:

(i) the sum of the trust's trading and miscellaneous incoming resources (broadly, the gross income potentially within this exemption and before deducting expenses) for the tax year does not exceed the 'requisite limit'; or
(ii) the trustees had, at the beginning of the tax year, a reasonable expectation that its trading and miscellaneous incoming resources (as above) would not exceed that limit.

For 2019/20 onwards, the '*requisite limit*' is 25% of the charitable trust's total incoming resources, subject to a minimum requisite limit of £8,000 and a maximum of £80,000. For 2018/19 and earlier years, these figures were £5,000 and £50,000 respectively.

The extension of the exemption to miscellaneous income is intended to cover miscellaneous fund-raising activities not counted as trading. Certain specified tax charges listed in *ITA 2007, s 1016* are excluded from the exemption (see *ITA 2007, s 527(2)*).

[*ITA 2007, ss 526–528; FA 2016, ss 79(4), 82(1); FA 2019, s 41(1)(2)*].

HMRC will consider any evidence to satisfy the reasonable expectation test in (b) above. Such evidence may include minutes of meetings at which the expectations were discussed, cash-flow forecasts, business plans and previous years' accounts (see HMRC guidance on trading by charities in para 16 at www.gov.uk/government/publications/charities-detailed-guidance-notes/annex-iv-trading-and-business-activities-basic-principles#direct-tax-what-if-the-charity-provides-goods-or-services-to-the-sponsor).

Fund-raising events

The profits of a trade carried on by a charitable trust are exempt so far as they arise from a VAT-exempt event and are either applied for charitable purposes or transferred to another charity. An event is VAT-exempt for this purpose if the supply of goods and services by the trust in connection with the event would be exempt from value added tax under Group 12 of *VATA 1994, Sch 9* (fund-raising events by charities and other qualifying bodies). [*ITA 2007, s 529*].

There is guidance on this exemption and the corresponding VAT exemption at www.gov.uk/government/publications/charity-fundraising-events-exemptions.

Lotteries

Lottery profits applied solely to the charitable trust's purposes are exempt, provided that the lottery is an exempt lottery within the meaning of *Gambling Act 2005* by virtue of *Pt 1* or *Pt 4* of *Sch 11* of that Act or is promoted in accordance with a lottery operating licence within the meaning of *Pt 5* of that Act or is promoted and conducted in accordance with relevant NI legislation [*ITA 2007, s 530*].

Simon's Taxes. See C5.117D, C5.117E, C5.117G, C5.117H.

Capital gains

[14.8] Charitable trusts are exempt from capital gains tax on gains applicable, and applied, for charitable purposes. [*TCGA 1992, s 256(1)*]. But this exemption does not apply to gains arising where property which ceases to be subject to charitable trusts is then deemed to have been sold, and immediately re-acquired, at market value. Any CGT on such gains may be assessed within three years after the year of assessment in which the cessation occurs. [*TCGA 1992, s 256(2)*]. The exemption applies to liability under *TCGA 1992, s 87* in respect of capital payments received from offshore trusts. (Revenue Tax Bulletin August 1998 pp 573, 574).

Simon's Taxes. See C5.124.

Miscellaneous

[14.9] The following miscellaneous items are relevant.

Offshore income gains

Offshore income gains (see **51.3** OFFSHORE FUNDS) of a charitable trust are exempt if applicable and applied to charitable purposes. No claim is needed for the exemption to apply. [*ITA 2007, ss 535, 538(2); SI 2009 No 3001, Reg 129(4)*].

Where property representing directly or indirectly an offshore income gain ceases to be subject to charitable trusts, the trustees are treated as if they had disposed of and immediately re-acquired the property at market value. Any offshore income gain accruing does not attract the above exemption. [*SI 2009 No 3001, Reg 31(3)–(6)*].

Transactions in deposits

Profits or gains arising to a charitable trust from the disposal, or (except so far as the right is a right to receive interest) the exercise, of 'exempt deposit rights' are exempt so far as applied solely for charitable purposes. For this purpose, '*exempt deposit rights*' are:

- a right to receive, with or without interest, a principal amount stated in, or determined in accordance with, the current terms of issue of an 'eligible debt security' (as defined), where in accordance with those terms the issue of 'uncertificated units' (as defined) of the security corresponds to the issue of a certificate of deposit (see **12** CERTIFICATES OF DEPOSIT);
- a right to receive the principal amount stated in a certificate of deposit with or without interest; and
- an 'uncertificated right' (i.e. a right in respect of which no certificate of deposit has been issued, although the person entitled to it is entitled to call for the issue of such a certificate) to receive a principal amount, with or without interest, as a result of a deposit of money.

No claim is needed for the exemption to apply.

[*ITA 2007, ss 534, 538(1)*].

Simon's Taxes. See **C5.117L, C5.117M.**

Restrictions on exemptions

[14.10] A restriction of the exemptions referred to in **14.3–14.9** above applies for any tax year in which a charitable trust incurs (or is treated as incurring) 'non-charitable expenditure' (see below).

Exemption is denied in respect of so much of any income or gains which are attributed to the 'non-exempt amount' for the year. For this purpose, the '*non-exempt amount*' for a tax year is equal to the non-charitable expenditure for the year or, if less, the '*attributable income and gains*' for the year (i.e. the total of the otherwise exempt income and gains for the year).

Attributable income and/or attributable gains are to be attributed to the non-exempt amount until the whole of that amount is used up. The charitable trust may itself specify by notice to HMRC which particular items of income and gains are to be so attributed; but if HMRC require a charitable trust to give such notice and the trust fails to comply within 30 days of the requirement being imposed, HMRC may then determine which amounts are to be treated as attributed.

[*ITA 2007, ss 539–542; TCGA 1992, ss 256(3), (4)–(6), 256A, 256B*].

If the non-charitable expenditure exceeds the charity's 'available income and gains' for the tax year, the excess is carried back and treated as non-charitable expenditure of earlier tax years ending not more than six years before the end of the year in which the expenditure was actually incurred, taking later years in priority to earlier years. The amount of the excess to be attributed to an earlier year cannot be greater than the amount, if any, by which the available income and gains for that earlier year exceed the non-charitable expenditure for that year (including any excess expenditure attributed to the year as a result of a previous operation of these provisions).

For the above purpose, a charitable trust's '*available income and gains*' is the aggregate of its otherwise exempt income and gains, its chargeable income and gains and its other non-chargeable receipts such as donations and legacies.

[*ITA 2007, ss 562–564, Sch 2 para 107*].

A charitable trust's '*non-charitable expenditure*' for a tax year is:

(a) any loss made in the year (i.e. any loss made in the basis period for the year) in a trade other than a trade within one of the exemptions at **14.7** above;
(b) any payment made in the year in connection with a trade where post-cessation expenditure relief is available (see **59.5** POST-CESSATION RECEIPTS AND EXPENDITURE) unless the trade was within one of the exemptions at **14.7** above at cessation;
(c) any loss made in the year in a trade, UK or overseas property business where the loss relates to land and any profits generated from the land for the year would not have been within the exemption at **14.4** above;
(d) any payment made in the year in connection with a trade or UK or overseas property business where post-cessation expenditure relief is available (see **59.5** POST-CESSATION RECEIPTS AND EXPENDITURE) where the payment relates to land and any profits generated from the land immediately before cessation would not be within the exemption at **14.4** above;
(e) any loss made in the year in a 'miscellaneous transaction' entered into otherwise than in the course of carrying on a charitable purpose;
(f) any 'expenditure' incurred in the tax year not within (b) or (d) above which is not incurred solely for charitable purposes and is not required to be taken into account in calculating the profits or losses of any trade or property business or miscellaneous transaction;
(g) the amount of any funds invested in the year in any investment which is not an 'approved charitable investment'; and
(h) any amount lent in the year by the trust, if the loan is neither an investment nor an 'approved charitable loan'.

Any amount falling within more than one of the above categories is treated as non-charitable expenditure only once.

For the purposes of (e) and (f) above, a '*miscellaneous transaction*' is a transaction any income or gains from which would have been chargeable to income tax under any of the provisions listed in *ITA 2007, s 1016* (see **49.8** MISCELLANEOUS INCOME) but for the miscellaneous income and gains exemption at **14.7** above, where the trustees of the charitable trust would have been liable for the tax.

For the purposes of (f) above, '*expenditure*' includes capital expenditure but does not include the investment of any of the charitable trust's funds, the making of a loan by the trust or the repayment by the trust of the whole or part of a loan. Expenditure which is referable to commitments (contractual or otherwise) entered into before or during a particular tax year is treated as incurred in that year if, had accounts been drawn up in accordance with UK generally accepted accounting practice for the year, it would have had to be taken into account in preparing those accounts. A payment made (or to be made) to a body situated outside the UK is non-charitable expenditure within (f) above unless the charitable trust has taken all reasonable steps to ensure that the payment will be applied for charitable purposes. Any claim that such a payment is charitable expenditure must be supported by evidence sufficient to satisfy the Commissioners for HMRC that such reasonable steps were taken.

If, in any tax year, a charitable trust (wholly or partly) realises an investment made in that year which is not an approved charitable investment or is repaid a loan made in that year which is neither an investment nor an approved charitable loan, any further investment or lending in that year of the amount realised or repaid (to the extent that it does not exceed the amount originally invested or lent) cannot be treated for a second time as non-charitable expenditure.

[*ITA 2007, ss 543–548, Sch 2 para 105*].

The following are '*approved charitable investments*'.

(i) An investment in securities (including shares, stocks and debentures (as defined)):
   - issued or guaranteed by the UK Government, or the government of an EU member state, or the government or a governmental body of any territory or part of a territory;
   - issued by an international entity listed in the Annex to Council Directive 2003/48/EC;
   - issued by an entity meeting the four criteria set out at the end of that Annex;
   - issued by a building society;
   - issued by a credit institution operating on mutual principles which is authorised by an appropriate governmental body in the territory of issue;
   - issued by an open-ended investment company (within *CTA 2010, ss 613, 615*);
   - issued by a company and listed on a recognised stock exchange (within *ITA 2007, s 1005*); or
   - issued by a company and not listed on a recognised stock exchange.

   Further conditions (see *ITA 2007, s 560*) must be met in the case of certain of the above securities.

(ii) An investment in a common investment fund established under *Charities Act 1960, s 22* (or NI equivalent), *Charities Act 1993, s 24* or *Charities Act 2011, s 96*.

(iii) An investment in a common deposit fund established under *Charities Act 1960, s 22A*, *Charities Act 1993, s 25* or *Charities Act 2011, s 100*.

(iv) An investment in a fund which is similar to those in (ii) or (iii) above which is established for the exclusive benefit of charities by or under legislation relating to any particular charities or class of charities.

(v) An interest in land other than an interest held as security for a debt.

(vi) Any bills, certificates of tax deposit, savings certificates or tax reserve certificates issued in the UK by the Government.

(vii) Northern Ireland Treasury bills.

(viii) Units in a unit trust scheme within *Financial Services and Markets Act 2000, s 237(1)* or in a recognised scheme within *Financial Services and Markets Act 2000, s 237(3)*.

(ix) A deposit with a bank (within *ITA 2007, s 991*) in respect of which interest is payable at a commercial rate, but excluding a deposit made as part of an arrangement under which the bank makes a loan to a third party.

(x) A deposit with the National Savings Bank, a building society or a credit institution operating on mutual principles which is authorised by an appropriate governmental body in the territory in which the deposit is taken.

(xi) CERTIFICATES OF DEPOSIT (**12**) within *ITTOIA 2005, s 552(2)*, including uncertificated eligible debt security units as defined in *ITA 2007, s 986(3)*.

(xii) Any loan or other investment as to which HMRC are satisfied, on a claim, that it is made for the benefit of the charitable trust and not for the avoidance of tax (whether by the trust or any other person). Loans secured by mortgage etc. over land are within this heading.

[*ITA 2007, ss 558–560; SI 2019 No 689, Reg 15(6)*].

As regards swap contracts, e.g. interest rate or currency swaps, see Revenue Tax Bulletin August 2003 p 1056.

The following are '*approved charitable loans*' if they are not made by way of investment.

- A loan made to another charity for charitable purposes only.
- A loan to a beneficiary of the charitable trust which is made in the course of carrying out the purposes of the trust.
- Money placed on a current account with a bank (within *ITA 2007, s 991*), but excluding a loan made as part of an arrangement under which the bank makes a loan to a third party.
- Any other loan as to which HMRC are satisfied, on a claim, that the loan is made for the benefit of the charitable trust and not for the avoidance of tax (whether by the trust or by some other person).

[*ITA 2007, s 561*].

See the detailed guidance on all aspects of these provisions at www.gov.uk/government/publications/charities-detailed-guidance-notes/annex-ii-non-charitable-expenditure. For HMRC guidance on approved charitable investments and loans, see www.gov.uk/government/publications/charities-detailed-guidance-notes/annex-iii-approved-charitable-investments-and-loans.

Simon's Taxes. See **C5.127**.

Gifts to charitable trusts

[14.11] The receipt by a charitable trust of a '*qualifying donation*' under the Gift Aid scheme (see **14.15** below) is treated as the receipt, under deduction of basic rate income tax for the tax year in which the gift is made, of a gift equal to the 'grossed up amount of the gift' (i.e. the amount of the gift grossed up by reference to the basic rate for the tax year in which the gift is made). The income tax so treated as deducted is treated as income tax paid by the trustees, so that they can normally reclaim the tax from HMRC (a '*gift aid exemption claim*'). So far as a gift is not applied to charitable purposes only, however, the grossed up amount of the gift is charged to income tax. The charge is on the amounts arising in the tax year and the trustees are liable for any tax so charged. [*ITA 2007, ss 520, 521*].

In the case of other gifts under the Gift Aid Scheme, a claim by the charity for exemption from tax can be made either within or outside a tax return. Claims made outside the return are known as free-standing claims, and may be made during the tax year in which the income is received ('in-year claims'). HMRC have the power to make regulations limiting the number of free-standing claims that can be made in a tax year. Charities can also make free-standing in-year claims for repayment of tax treated as deducted at source from Gift Aid payments and tax actually deducted at source from other income as specified in *ITA 2007, s 538A(A1)(b)*. They can also make free-standing claims for exemption from tax on income so specified. [*TMA 1970, s 42(3ZA)(3ZB); ITA 2007, s 538A*].

Where a charity receives a payment on which it bears income tax by deduction as above, the tax does not have to be set off against any income tax due before it can be repaid, thus facilitating in-year repayment claims. [*TMA 1970, s 59B(7)*].

The receipt by a charitable trust of a donation made under the payroll giving scheme (see **14.18** below) is chargeable to tax to the extent that it is not applied to charitable purposes only. The charge is on the full amounts arising in the tax year and the trustees are liable for any tax so charged. [*ITA 2007, s 521A*].

Gifts of money from companies (other than companies which are charities — see **14.12** below) are also charged to income tax except so far as applied to charitable purposes only. The charge is on the full amount of such gifts arising in the tax year and the trustees are liable for any tax so charged. [*ITA 2007, s 522*].

See also **14.17** below (small cash donations).

Simon's Taxes. See **C5.117A.**

Payments from other charities

[14.12] Any payments received by a charitable trust from other charities, other than in return for full consideration, which would otherwise not be chargeable to income tax (and which are not of a description which on a claim would be exempt from income tax under any of the relieving provisions at **14.4–14.7, 14.9** above), are chargeable to income tax. The charge is on the full amount of the payments arising in the tax year and the trustees of the charitable trust are liable for the tax charged. The amount charged is subject, where relevant, to the provisions at **70.11** SETTLEMENTS regarding discretionary payments by trustees.

The above provision does not apply to payments arising from a source outside the UK or to payments so far as applied solely for charitable purposes.

[*ITA 2007, s 523*].

Simon's Taxes. See C5.117A.

Gift aid donations by individuals

[14.13] Gifts of money made by individuals to charities which are 'qualifying donations' (see **14.15** below) attract tax relief under the Gift Aid scheme described below.

For the purposes of these provisions, '*charity*' has the meaning in **14.2** above but also includes the Trustees of the National Heritage Memorial Fund, the Historic Buildings and Monuments Commission for England, and registered community amateur sports clubs under *CTA 2010, ss 658–671* (but club membership fees are not gifts for the purposes of these provisions). [*ITA 2007, s 430*].

See **14.11** above for the treatment of charitable trusts receiving qualifying donations. See Tolley's Corporation Tax for the application of the relief to gifts to community amateur sports clubs and for the treatment of charitable companies.

A detailed guide to Gift Aid is available at www.gov.uk/government/publications/charities-detailed-guidance-notes/chapter-3-gift-aid.

The Gift Aid scheme

Where a 'qualifying donation' to charity is made by an individual ('*the donor*') in a tax year, then, for that year, he is treated for the purposes of income tax (and capital gains tax) as if:

(a) the gift had been made after deduction of income tax at the UK basic rate; and
(b) the basic rate limit and higher rate limit (see **1.3** ALLOWANCES AND TAX RATES) were increased by an amount equal to the 'grossed up amount of the gift', i.e. the amount which, after deducting income tax at the basic rate for the tax year in which the gift is made, leaves the amount of the gift.

The donor obtains higher rate relief, where applicable, by virtue of (b) above. For this purpose, higher rate relief generally means relief for the excess of tax at the higher rate over tax at the basic rate for which relief is effectively given at source by virtue of (a) above (but see the second example at **14.14** below for the situation where there is dividend income). (The increase in the basic rate limit does not apply for the purposes of computing top slicing relief as in **44.9** LIFE ASSURANCE POLICIES.) Individuals liable at the additional rate obtain relief at that rate in the same way. For Scottish taxpayers the basic rate, intermediate rate and higher rate thresholds are similarly increased.

To the extent, if any, necessary to ensure that the amount of income tax and capital gains tax to which the donor is charged for a tax year in which one or more gifts is made is an amount at least equal to the tax treated under (a) above as deducted from the gift or gifts, the donor is *not* entitled to the following reliefs for that year:

- the personal allowance;
- the blind person's allowance;
- the married couple's allowance; and
- the miscellaneous life assurance-related reliefs at **44.2** LIFE ASSURANCE POLICIES.

The restriction does not adversely affect the donor's ability to transfer unused married couple's allowance to a spouse or civil partner as in **48.4** MARRIED PERSONS AND CIVIL PARTNERS.

Where the tax treated as deducted exceeds the amount of income tax and capital gains tax to which the donor is charged for the year after taking into account the above restriction of reliefs, the donor is liable to an income tax charge for the year, the tax chargeable being equal to the excess.

The amount of income tax to which the donor is charged for a tax year for these purposes is calculated according to the steps at **1.10** ALLOWANCES AND TAX RATES, but with the following modifications.

(i) At Step 6 (tax reductions), the following tax reductions are ignored:
   - relief for qualifying maintenance payments (see **48.9** MARRIED PERSONS AND CIVIL PARTNERS); and
   - any DOUBLE TAX RELIEF (**27**) (whether given under a double tax agreement or unilaterally).

(ii) Step 7 is ignored.

(iii) The following amounts are deducted:
   - any notional tax treated as having been paid under *ITTOIA 2005, s 399* (dividends etc. received by non-UK residents — see **65.11** SAVINGS AND INVESTMENT INCOME), *ITTOIA 2005, s 530* (life assurance gains — see **44.8** LIFE ASSURANCE POLICIES), or *ITTOIA 2005, s 685A* (payments from settlor-interested settlements — see **70.25** SETTLEMENTS); and
   - any tax treated as deducted from estate income to the extent that it is treated as paid out of life assurance gains.

The amount of capital gains tax to which the donor is charged for a tax year for these purposes is similarly calculated without regard for any double tax relief due, whether under a double tax agreement or unilaterally.

The legislation recognises that there may in future be a time when the UK basic rate differs from the Scottish or Welsh basic rate. If the UK basic rate is less than the Scottish or Welsh basic rate, a Scottish or Welsh taxpayer (see **1.8** and **1.9** ALLOWANCES AND TAX RATES) will receive additional Gift Aid relief by way of a tax reduction at Step 6 of the calculation of tax liability. The relief is calculated by applying the rate difference to the grossed up amount of the gift or, if less, the amount of income liable to the Scottish or Welsh basic rate. If the UK basic rate is greater than the Scottish or Welsh basic rate, a Scottish or Welsh taxpayer will have an additional tax charge to recover the excess Gift Aid relief. The charge is calculated in the same way as a reduction except that it cannot exceed the amount of tax the individual has saved by virtue of (b) above.

Gift Aid relief is subject to the tainted donations rules at **14.21** below.

See **1.17**, **1.19** ALLOWANCES AND TAX RATES for the deduction of the aggregate grossed up amount of a donor's qualifying donations for a tax year in calculating adjusted net income for the purpose of applying the income limits for the personal allowance and the married couple's allowance.

[*ITA 2007, ss 413, 414, 414A, 415, 423–425; FA 2016, s 6(18)(19)(24), Sch 1 paras 63(4), 73; SI 2015 No 1810, Arts 1, 14(6)(7); SI 2017 No 468, Regs 1, 10; SI 2018 No 459, Arts 1, 6(4)(5); SI 2019 No 201, Arts 1, 12*].

See the examples at **14.14** below.

Carry-back of relief

The donor may elect for a qualifying donation to be treated for the purposes of the relief as having been made in the previous tax year, provided that the condition below is satisfied.

The condition is that the donor's 'charged amount' for that previous tax year must be at least equal to the 'increased total of gifts'. For this purpose, the donor's '*charged amount*' for a tax year is the sum of his 'modified net income' and the amount on which he is chargeable to capital gains tax for the year. The definition of '*modified net income*' at **1.13** ALLOWANCES AND TAX RATES applies for this purpose as if the first modification listed there were omitted. The '*increased total of gifts*' is the aggregate of the sum of the grossed up amounts of all the gifts made in the current year which are to be, or have already been (by an earlier election) carried back to the previous year and the sum of the grossed up amounts of any qualifying donations actually made in the previous year (and not themselves carried back). All the grossed up amounts are calculated for this purpose as if the gifts were made in the previous year.

The election must be made in writing to HMRC by the date of delivery of the self-assessment return for the previous year, and not later than 31 January following the end of that year. The election affects only the tax position of the donor. As regards the recipient charity, the donation continues to be treated as made in the tax year in which it is in fact made. The 'date of delivery of the self-assessment return' means the date of delivery of the original return and not an amended return (*Cameron v HMRC* FTT (TC 415), [2010] SFTD 664).

[*ITA 2007, ss 426, 427*].

Simon's Taxes. See **E1.810, E1.811.**

Examples

[14.14]

Higher rate taxpayer (1). Peter has total income of £51,425 for 2020/21 which consists entirely of employment income. During that year, he makes a number of payments to charity, all of them qualifying donations, amounting in total to £600. Peter's liability to income tax is at the main UK rates.

	£
Total and net income	51,425
Less Personal Allowance	12,500

Taxable Income			£38,925
Tax Liability			
	38,250	@ 20%	7,650.00
	675	@ 40%	270.00
	£38,925		
			£7,920.00

Note

The basic rate limit of £37,500 is increased by the grossed up amount of the qualifying donations (£600 × 100/80 = £750) and becomes £38,250. Peter thereby saves tax of £150 (£750 × 20% (40% – 20%)). The charities will reclaim basic rate tax of £150 (£750 × 20%) and will thus receive £750 in all. The net cost to Peter is £450 (£600 – £150), a saving of 40%.

Higher rate taxpayer (2).The tax relief can, in fact, exceed 40% where the effect of extending the basic rate limit is that an additional amount of dividend income falls within the basic rate band and is taxed at 7.5% instead of at 32.5%. Imagine the facts are as above but that £10,000 of Peter's income is dividend income with the remaining £41,425 being employment income.

			£
Taxable Income as in (1) above			£38,925
Tax Liability			
	28,925	@ 20%	5,785.00
	2,000	@ 0% (dividend nil rate)	—
	7,325	@ 7.5% (dividend ordinary rate)	549.37
	38,250		
	675	@ 32.5% (dividend upper rate)	219.37
	£38,925		
			£6,553.74

Note

Peter now saves tax of £187.50 (£750 × 25% (32.5% – 7.5%)). The charities will still reclaim basic rate tax of £150 (£750 × 20%) and will receive £750 in all. The net cost to Peter is £412.50 (£600 – £187.50), a saving of 45%.

Additional rate taxpayer. Catherine has total income of £175,000 for 2020/21, none of which is dividend income. During that year, she makes qualifying donations to charity of £2,400. Catherine's liability to income tax is at the main UK rates.

			£
Total and net income			175,000
Less Personal Allowance			Nil
Taxable Income			£175,000
Tax Liability			
	40,500	@ 20%	8,100.00
	112,500	@ 40%	45,000.00

22,000	@ 45%	9,900.00
£175,000		
		£63,000.00

Note

Both the basic rate limit of £37,500 and the higher rate limit of £150,000 are increased by the grossed up amount of the qualifying donations (£2,400 × 100/80 = £3,000) and become £40,500 and £153,000 respectively. Catherine thereby saves tax of £750 (£3,000 × 25% (45% – 20%)). The charities will reclaim basic rate tax of £600 (£3,000 × 20%) and will thus receive £3,000 in all. The net cost to Catherine is £1,650 (£2,400 – £750), a saving of 45%. (No personal allowance is available in this example as income is too high — see **1.17** ALLOWANCES AND TAX RATES.)

Low income taxpayer. For 2020/21, Ivan has pension income of £11,650 and dividends of £1,200. He makes a qualifying donation of £400 to charity. Ivan's liability to income tax is at the main UK rates.

			£
Pension income			11,650
Dividends			1,200
Total and net income			12,850
Less	Personal Allowance	12,500	
	Restricted by (note (a))	1,350	11,150
Taxable Income			£1,700
Tax Liability			
£500	@ 20% (basic rate)		100.00
£1,200	@ 0% (dividend nil rate)		–
	Total liability		£100.00

Note

(a) The personal allowance is restricted by such amount as is necessary to leave tax of £100.00 in charge, this being the amount of basic rate tax deemed to have been deducted at source from the qualifying donation (£400 × 20/80 = £100).

Qualifying donations

[14.15] A '*qualifying donation*' is a gift to a charity by an individual which meets the following conditions:

(a) it takes the form of a payment of a sum of money;
(b) it is not subject to a condition as to repayment;
(c) it is not deductible under the payroll deduction scheme — see **14.18** below;
(d) it is not deductible in calculating the donor's income from any source;
(e) it is not conditional on, or associated with, or part of an arrangement involving, the acquisition of property by the charity, otherwise than by way of gift, from the donor or a person connected with him;

(f) neither the donor nor any person connected with him (see **19** CONNECTED PERSONS) receives any benefit, in consequence of making it, in excess of specified limits (see **14.16** below); and

(g) the individual (or, after 5 April 2017, an intermediary representing the individual) gives the charity (or, after 5 April 2017, an intermediary representing the charity) a 'gift aid declaration' in relation to the gift.

A gift to charity is not a qualifying donation if the payment is by way of, or amounts in substance to, a waiver by the individual of entitlement to sums (whether principal or interest) due to him from the charity in respect of an amount advanced to the charity on which social investment income tax relief has been obtained (see **72** SOCIAL INVESTMENT TAX RELIEF).

A '*gift aid declaration*' for the purposes of (g) above is a declaration which is given in the manner prescribed by regulations. It may be made in writing, by SMS text, online (including via social media) or orally (e.g. by telephone). It must contain the donor's name and address, the name of the charity, a description of the gift(s) to which it relates, and a statement that the gift(s) is (are) to be qualifying donations for these purposes. In order for the declaration to have effect, it must have been explained to the donor that he must pay sufficient income tax or capital gains tax to cover the tax deemed to be deducted at source from the donation. A donor can give a single declaration (an enduring declaration) to a charity that, in addition to covering the current gift, also covers future gifts that the donor makes to the charity. A charity must maintain a satisfactory auditable (by HMRC) record of gift aid declarations given to it. A donor may cancel a gift aid declaration by giving oral or written notice to the charity. Similar rules apply after 5 April 2017 in relation to donations by intermediaries. An intermediary cannot give an enduring declaration to a charity but an individual may authorise an intermediary to create gift aid declarations on his behalf for all subsequent donations made in the tax year in question.

For the purpose of (g) above, an '*intermediary*' is a person authorised by an individual to give a gift aid declaration to a charity on his behalf, or a person authorised by a charity to receive a gift aid declaration on its behalf, or a person authorised to perform both those roles. Gifts made by individuals through intermediaries will often be made via digital channels. HMRC have the power to impose penalties of up to £3,000 per tax year if a donor intermediary fails to comply with certain requirements imposed by regulations (see *SI 2016 No 1195, Regs 12–17*). For requirements as to record-keeping by donor intermediaries and the providing of an annual statement by donor intermediaries to donors, see *SI 2016 No 1195, Regs 7, 8*.

[*ITA 2007, ss 416, 417, 422, 428; FA 2015, s 20; FA 2016, s 173; SI 2000 No 2074; SI 2005 No 2790; SI 2016 Nos 1010, 1195*].

As regards (f) above, the benefit does not have to be received from the charity to be taken into account (see *St Dunstan's v Major* (Sp C 127), [1997] SSCD 212, in which the saving of inheritance tax by personal representatives as a result of the variation of a will to provide for a donation which would otherwise qualify under these provisions constituted a benefit).

The release of a loan not for consideration and not under seal cannot amount to a gift of money (see *Battle Baptist Church v CIR and Woodham* (Sp C 23), [1995] SSCD 176).

Limits on donor benefits

[14.16] Where the donor or a person connected with him (see **19** CONNECTED PERSONS) receives a benefit or benefits in consequence of making the gift, the gift will not be a qualifying donation if:

(a) the aggregate value of the benefits received exceeds:
- where the gift is £100 or less, 25% of the amount of the gift;
- where the gift exceeds £100, £25 plus 5% of the excess; or

(b) the aggregate of the value of the benefits received in relation to the gift and the value of any benefits received in relation to any qualifying donations previously made to the charity by the donor in the same tax year exceeds £2,500.

For gifts made before 6 April 2019, the thresholds in (a) above were:

- where the gift was £100 or less, 25% of the amount of the gift;
- where the gift exceeded £100 but was no more than £1,000, £25; and
- where the gift exceeded £1,000, 5% of the amount of the gift.

The operation of (a) above is modified where a benefit:

(1) consists of the right to receive benefits at intervals over a period of less than 12 months;
(2) relates to a period of less than 12 months;
(3) is one of a series of benefits received at intervals in consequence of making a series of gifts at intervals of less than 12 months; or
(4) is not one of a series of benefits but the gift is one of a series of gifts made at intervals of less than 12 months.

Where (1), (2) or (3) above apply, the value of the benefit and the amount of the gift are 'annualised' for the purposes of (a) above. Where (4) above applies, the amount of the gift (but not the value of the benefit) is likewise annualised. For these purposes a gift or benefit is '*annualised*' by multiplying the amount or value by 365 and dividing the result by the number of days in the period of less than 12 months or the average number of days in the intervals of less than 12 months as appropriate.

In determining whether a gift is a qualifying donation, the benefit of any 'right of admission' received in consequence of the gift is disregarded for the purpose of applying the above limits if all the following conditions are satisfied.

- The opportunity to make a gift and to receive an admission right as a consequence must be available to the public.
- The admission right must be a right granted by the charity to view property preserved, maintained, kept or created by a charity for its charitable purposes, including, in particular, buildings, grounds or other land, plants, animals, works of art (but not performances), artefacts and property of a scientific nature.

- Either:
  (i) the admission right must be valid for a least a year and, during its period of validity, must include all times at which the public can gain admission; or
  (ii) a member of the public could purchase the same admission right, and the amount of the gift is greater by at least 10% than the purchase price.

For these purposes, a '*right of admission*' is a right granted to the donor, or to the donor and members of his family, to be admitted to premises or property for which a public admission fee applies and to be so admitted for no admission fee or for a reduced admission fee. An admission right is within (i) above even if it does not apply on certain days specified by the charity as an '*event day*' (i.e. a day on which an event is take place on the premises concerned), so long as no more than five such days are specified for the period of validity (if the period is one year) or for each calendar year of which the period of validity forms all or part (if the period is more than one year).

[*ITA 2007, ss 417–421, Sch 2 para 99; FA 2019, s 40(1)(2)*].

See www.gov.uk/government/publications/charities-detailed-guidance-notes/chapter-3-gift-aid for guidance on the rules above.

Acknowledgement of a donor in the charity's literature does not amount to a benefit *provided that* it does not take the form of an advertisement for the donor's business (see para 3.27 of the HMRC guide referred to at **14.13** above).

Small cash donations

[14.17] A charity in receipt of a cash donation of £30 or less (for 2019/20 onwards, previously £20 or less) in the UK from an individual (a '*small donation*') can apply for a Gift Aid style payment in respect of the donation without the need to obtain a Gift Aid declaration. There is no tax relief for the individual. For 2017/18 onwards, this treatment is extended to contactless payments made in the UK and not just to cash donations; it continues not to apply to donations made via SMS text or other mobile donation services or by card donations made online, by telephone or using chip and PIN.

A charity can claim this payment (a '*top-up payment*') from HMRC on small donations made to it in the tax year if:

- the charity is an 'eligible charity' for a tax year; and
- it has made a successful gift aid exemption claim (see **14.11** above) in respect of gifts made to it in the tax year.

The amount of the top-up payment is the amount representing basic rate tax on the grossed-up amount of the small donations to which the claim relates. However, a charity is not entitled to top-up payments in respect of small donations made to it in a tax year in excess of the 'maximum donations limit' for the charity for the tax year. The '*maximum donations limit*' is an amount equal to the *lesser* of ten times the 'gift aid donations amount' for the charity for the tax year and £8,000. The '*gift aid donations amount*' is the amount of the gifts made to the charity in the tax year and in respect of which it has made successful gift aid exemption claims.

The £8,000 maximum quoted above is subject to special rules for charities connected with each other (as defined) and charities running charitable activities in community buildings (as defined).

Eligible donations

A small donation cannot include a membership fee, nor must it be conditional upon, or in connection with, the acquisition of property (other than by way of gift) by the charity from the donor or a person connected with the donor (within **19** CONNECTED PERSONS). There must be no benefits associated with the gift, other than benefits of negligible value (e.g. a lapel sticker designed to acknowledge the making of a gift). The gift must not be subject to any condition as to repayment nor be deductible in calculating the individual's income from any source for income tax purposes; it must be one in relation to which no gift aid declaration is given to the charity and must not be made under an approved payroll giving scheme. If a small donation (or any part of it) made to a charity is applied to purposes other than charitable purposes, the donation (or part) is to be treated as if it were not a small donation; this does not apply to the Trustees of the National Heritage Memorial Fund, the Historic Buildings and Monuments Commission for England, the Trustees of the British Museum or the Trustees of the Natural History Museum.

Eligible charities

A charity is an '*eligible charity*' for a tax year if it is not an 'excluded charity' for that year. A charity is an *excluded charity*' if a penalty (other than a suspended penalty or one overturned on appeal) has been imposed on it in connection with either a gift aid exemption claim or a claim under these provisions. The charity is then an excluded charity both for the tax year in which the claim was made and for the following tax year.

For 2016/17 and earlier years, an additional rule applied whereby a charity was an '*eligible charity*' for a tax year only if:

(a) the charity's 'start-up period' expired before that year; and
(b) it had made a successful gift aid exemption claim in at least two of the previous four tax years.

A charity's '*start-up period*' is the first period of two consecutive tax years during which it is at all times a charity. If a charity did not make any successful gift aid exemption claims for two consecutive tax years, any claim made in an earlier tax year is to be disregarded for the purposes of (b).

[*Small Charitable Donations Act 2012; Small Charitable Donations and Childcare Payments Act 2017, ss 1–4; SI 2019 No 337*].

SI 2013 No 938 provides for the administration of top-up payment claims. It applies and incorporates, for the purposes of such administration, those provisions of the *Tax Acts* and *TMA 1970* which apply for the purposes of gift aid relief.

See guidance at www.gov.uk/guidance/claiming-a-top-up-payment-on-small-charitable-donations.

Simon's Taxes. See **C5.141.**

Payroll giving schemes

[14.18] Under an 'approved payroll giving scheme', an individual may make charitable donations, without limit, by deduction from earnings (or pension income or taxable social security income) subject to PAYE (**53**). At the individual's request, the employer (or other payer) withholds sums from gross pay as 'donations'. The amount of the donations is allowed as a deduction from gross pay for PAYE purposes and in calculating the individual's taxable income. The deduction is made from the particular type of income (e.g. employment income) in respect of which the donations are made. The deduction is made for the tax year in which the donation is withheld or, as regards pension and social security income only, for the tax year in which the income out of which the deduction is made is chargeable to tax. A donation made under a payroll giving scheme is not a qualifying donation for Gift Aid purposes (see **14.15** above).

'*Donations*' are sums withheld by the payer under a scheme which at that time is an 'approved payroll giving scheme' and which constitute gifts by the individual to one or more charities specified by him and satisfy any conditions set out in the scheme. An '*approved payroll giving scheme*' is a scheme approved by (or of a kind approved by) HMRC under which the payer is required to pay to an 'approved agent' the sums withheld and the agent is required to pass them on to the specified charities. An '*approved agent*' is a body approved by HMRC for the purpose of paying donations to one or more charities; if the agent is itself a charity specified by the individual, it may retain any sum due to itself.

For these purposes, '*charity*' includes the bodies listed in *CTA 2010, s 468*.

Administrative regulations are made by statutory instrument (*SI 1986 No 2211*) regarding such matters as:

(i) the grant or withdrawal of approval by HMRC of schemes and agents, and appeals against HMRC's decision;
(ii) the requirements of kinds of schemes and qualifications of agents;
(iii) production of other information to HMRC.

Penalties apply for failure to comply with (iii) above under *TMA 1970, s 98*.

The tax relief is subject to the tainted donations rules at **14.21** below.

[*ITEPA 2003, ss 713–715, Sch 8; SI 1986 No 2211; SI 2009 No 3054, Arts 2, 3, Sch*].

For HMRC guidance on payroll giving, see www.gov.uk/government/publications/charities-detailed-guidance-notes/chapter-4-payroll-giving and www.gov.uk/government/publications/charities-detailed-guidance-notes.

Administrative costs

Voluntary contributions made by an employer to assist an approved agent with its costs in managing a payroll giving scheme on the employer's behalf are deductible in computing the profits of a trade, profession or vocation. [*ITTOIA 2005, s 72*].

Simon's Taxes. See **E4.1114.**

Gifts of shares, securities and real property to charities

[14.19] Income tax relief is available on a non-arm's length disposal, by an individual to a 'charity', of the whole of the beneficial interest in a 'qualifying investment'. This is in addition to the pre-existing capital gains tax relief for assets generally, for which see the corresponding chapter of Tolley's Capital Gains Tax. For this purpose, '*charity*' includes the Trustees of the National Heritage Memorial Fund and the Historic Buildings and Monuments Commission for England. A '*qualifying investment*' is any of the following:

(a) shares or securities listed on a recognised stock exchange (within *ITA 2007, s 1005*) or dealt in on any market in the UK that is designated for this purpose by HMRC Order;
(b) units in an authorised unit trust (within *CTA 2010, ss 616, 619*);
(c) shares in an open-ended investment company (within *CTA 2010, ss 613, 615*);
(d) holdings in certain foreign collective investment schemes, generally schemes set up outside the UK that are similar to authorised unit trusts and open-ended investment companies (www.gov.uk/government/publications/charities-detailed-guidance-notes at Chapter 5.3); and
(e) a 'qualifying interest in land'.

On a claim to that effect (within the time allowed at **16.4** CLAIMS), the 'relievable amount' (see below) is deductible in computing the donor's net income for the tax year of disposal. See below as regards adjustments for incidental costs and consequential benefits. The deduction is disregarded for the purposes of computing top slicing relief in respect of gains on life assurance gains (see **44.9** LIFE ASSURANCE POLICIES). Where the claim is made, no relief is available under **75.88** TRADING INCOME or any other provision in respect of the same disposal.

The '*relievable amount*' is, subject to the adjustments below, the value of the 'net benefit to the charity' either at the time the disposal is made or immediately after that time (whichever gives the lower value), or the excess (if any) of that value over any consideration given for the disposal.

The '*net benefit to the charity*' is normally the market value of the investment. Where, however, the charity is, or becomes, subject to a 'disposal-related obligation' to *any* person (whether or not the donor or a connected person), it is the market value of the investment reduced by the aggregate '*disposal-related liabilities*' of the charity. An obligation is a '*disposal-related obligation*' if it is reasonable to suppose, taking into account all the circumstances, that the disposal would not have been made in its absence or if it relates to, or is framed by reference to, or is conditional upon the charity receiving, the investment in question or a disposal-related investment (as widely defined); 'obligation' is itself widely defined so as to include any scheme, arrangement or understanding (whether or not legally enforceable) and any series of obligations. A charity's '*disposal-related liabilities*' are its liabilities under the disposal-related obligation (or under each of them). Contingent obligations are taken into account if the contingency actually occurs.

The market value of the investment is determined as for capital gains tax purposes, but the market value of an interest in an offshore fund for which separate buying and selling prices are published is the buying price published on the date of the disposal or, if none were published on that date, the most recent published buying price.

In computing the relievable amount, any consideration for the disposal is brought into account without any discount for postponement of the right to receive any of it and without regard to any risk of part of it being irrecoverable or to the right to receive any part of it being contingent. Where any part of the consideration subsequently proves irrecoverable, the donor can make a claim for the relievable amount to be adjusted accordingly.

Adjustments are made to the relievable amount as follows. The amount is increased by any 'incidental costs of disposal' incurred by the person making it. Where consideration is received for the disposal, this increase is limited to the excess, if any, of the deemed consideration for capital gains tax purposes (disposal deemed to be at no gain/no loss) over the actual consideration.

The relievable amount is reduced by the value of any benefits received, in consequence of the disposal, by the person making it or a person connected with him (within **19** CONNECTED PERSONS).

The '*incidental costs of disposal*' are:

- fees, commission or remuneration paid for the professional services of a surveyor, valuer, auctioneer, accountant, agent or legal adviser incurred by the person making the disposal wholly and exclusively for the purposes of the disposal;
- costs of transfer or conveyance wholly and exclusively incurred by that person for the purposes of the disposal;
- costs of advertising to find a buyer; and
- costs reasonably incurred in making any valuation or apportionment for the purposes of these provisions.

An anti-avoidance rule applies if:

- the qualifying investment, or anything from which it derives or which it represents, was acquired by the individual making the disposal within the period of four years ending with the day on which the disposal is made;
- the acquisition was made as part of a scheme (as widely defined); and
- a main purpose of the individual in entering into the scheme was to obtain relief, or an increased amount of relief, under the above provisions.

Where the rule applies, the 'net benefit to the charity' is the 'acquisition value' of the qualifying investment if lower than its market value. The relievable amount is reduced accordingly. The '*acquisition value*' is the consideration given for the qualifying investment by the individual less any amount received in connection with the acquisition, by the individual or a person connected with him, as part of the scheme in question. In the case where the thing acquired was something from which the qualifying investment derives or which it represents, the acquisition value is first computed by reference to the thing acquired and is then reduced to such proportion of that value as it is just and reasonable to attribute to the qualifying investment.

A '*qualifying interest in land*' is a freehold interest (or a leasehold interest which is a term of years absolute) in UK land (but not an agreement to acquire freehold land or for a lease). The following two circumstances are additionally brought within the relief.

- Where there is a disposal of the beneficial interest in a qualifying interest in land, and there is also a disposal to the charity of any easement, servitude, right or privilege so far as benefiting that land, relief is also available for the latter disposal.
- Where a person with a freehold or leasehold interest in UK land grants to a charity a lease, for (except in Scotland) a term of years absolute, of the whole or part of that land, this is regarded as a disposal for which the relief is available.

In the application of the above in Scotland:

- references to a freehold interest in land are to the interest of the owner;
- references to a leasehold interest in land which is a term of years absolute are to a tenant's right over or interest in a property subject to a lease; and
- references to an agreement for a lease do not include missives of let that constitute an actual lease.

The following supplementary provisions apply to disposals of qualifying interests in land.

- Where two or more persons are entitled jointly or in common to a qualifying interest in land, the relief applies only if each person disposes of the whole of his beneficial interest in the land to the charity. Relief is then allowed to any of those persons who qualify (including companies qualifying under the equivalent corporation tax provisions), being apportioned between or amongst them as they may agree. See *ITA 2007, s 443* for the calculation of the relievable amount in these circumstances.
- The relief is dependent on the receipt by the person disposing of the interest of a certificate given by or on behalf of the charity specifying the description of the interest concerned and the date of the disposal, and stating that the charity has acquired the interest.
- If a 'disqualifying event' occurs at any time in the period from the date of the disposal to the fifth anniversary of 31 January following the tax year of the disposal, the person (or each of the persons) making the disposal is treated as never having been entitled to the relief in respect

of the disposal (and HMRC has the necessary assessment etc. powers). A '*disqualifying event*' occurs if the person (or any one of the persons) who made the disposal, or any connected person (within **19** CONNECTED PERSONS), either becomes entitled to an interest or right in relation to all or part of the land to which the disposal relates, or becomes party to an arrangement under which he enjoys some right in relation to all or part of that land, otherwise than for full consideration in money or money's worth. This does *not* apply if the person became entitled to such an interest or right as a result of a disposition of property on death, whether by will, by intestacy or otherwise.

The tax relief is subject to the tainted donations rules at **14.21** below.

[*ITA 2007, ss 431–438, 438A, 439–446, 1005*].

The cost of the asset to the charity for capital gains tax purposes is reduced by the relievable amount as above, or, if it is less than that amount, is reduced to nil. [*TCGA 1992, s 257(2A)–(2C)*].

Relief was disallowed in *Ferguson v HMRC* FTT (TC 3562), [2014] UKFTT 433 (TC), [2014] SFTD 934 on the grounds that the series of transactions in question had to be seen as a single composite transaction the overall effect of which was that there was no gift to the charity.

Simon's Taxes. See **E1.813**.

Cultural gifts scheme

[14.20] Individuals can make 'qualifying gifts' to the nation in return for a reduction in their UK tax liability. (The scheme is also available to corporate donors — see the corresponding chapter of Tolley's Corporation Tax.) For these purposes, a person makes a '*qualifying gift*' if:

- he offers to give 'pre-eminent property' to be held for the benefit of the public or the nation;
- he is legally and beneficially entitled to the property and does not own it jointly (or in common) with others;
- the offer is made in accordance with the scheme set up for these purposes by the Department for Culture, Media and Sport (DCMS);
- the offer is registered in accordance with the scheme;
- the offer, or a part of it, is accepted: and
- the gift is made pursuant to the offer, or the part of the offer, accepted.

[*FA 2012, Sch 14 paras 1, 36*].

A gain is not a chargeable gain if it accrues on a disposal that is a qualifying gift. [*TCGA 1992, s 258(1A); FA 2012, Sch 14 para 34*].

The details of how the application and acceptance process operates is set out in guidance issued by the DCMS (see www.artscouncil.org.uk/document/cgs-guidance-and-application-27-january-2015. Applicants are required to provide information concerning the object's estimated value. A panel of experts will consider the offer and, if it considers the property is pre-eminent and should be accepted, the panel will agree the value of the property with the donor. The total reduction in tax liabilities each year under this scheme and the pre-existing IHT Acceptance in Lieu scheme (see Tolley's Inheritance Tax under National Heritage) must fall within a limit of £30 million. This annual limit is administered by the expert panel, who will take into account the amount available for total tax reductions when deciding whether to accept an offer. The Secretary of State for Culture, Media and Sport has overall accountability for ensuring that the annual limit is not exceeded.

The tax relief

If an individual makes a qualifying gift as above, a portion of his personal income tax liability (calculated as in **1.10** ALLOWANCES AND TAX RATES) and capital gains tax (CGT) liability for each 'relevant tax year' is treated as satisfied, as if he had paid that portion when it became due. If the portion became due before the offer registration date (being the date when the offer was registered in accordance with the scheme), it is deemed to have been paid on that date instead. The relief cannot satisfy any tax liability arising to the individual as a trustee or personal representative.

The '*relevant tax years*' must be identified in the agreed terms (being the recorded terms on which acceptance of the offer was agreed). Any number of years from one to five may be chosen by the individual as relevant tax years but the choice of years is restricted to the tax year in which the offer registration date falls and the next four years. The total tax reduction figure is 30% of the value set out in the agreed terms as the agreed value of the property forming the subject of the qualifying gift. This figure must be allocated in advance between the relevant tax years, and the allocation must be set out in the agreed terms. A specific amount must be allocated to each relevant year; it is not possible, for example, to allocate X amount to Year 1 with the remainder to be split between years 2 to 5 in a manner to be agreed at a later date. For each relevant tax year, the portion of the individual's combined income tax and CGT liability that is treated as satisfied is an amount equal to the smaller of:

(a) the tax reduction figure allocated to that tax year; and
(b) the individual's total combined liability for that year less any portion of that amount that is treated as satisfied in consequence of any previous qualifying gift made by the individual.

If (a) is smaller than (b), the default position is that the reduction be applied to income tax in priority to CGT. However, this may be overridden in the agreed terms. If the amount of the individual's tax liability for a relevant tax year is later revised, the portion of the liability that is treated as satisfied must be recalculated. The agreed terms cannot themselves be revised, even if it is subsequently found that the individual does not have enough tax liability in a relevant tax year to fully utilise the tax reduction allocated to that year. In such a case the unutilised part of the tax reduction will be lost.

Effect on interest and penalties

Any liability to pay:

- late payment interest (as in **43.2** LATE PAYMENT INTEREST AND PENALTIES) accrued on the 'relevant portion' during the 'negotiation period'; and

- a late payment penalty (as in **43.4** LATE PAYMENT INTEREST AND PENALTIES) to which the donor became liable in the negotiation period for failing to pay the relevant portion (together with any interest on such a penalty),

is treated as having ceased when the qualifying gift is made, as if the liability had never arisen. The '*relevant portion*' is the portion of the donor's tax liability that is treated as satisfied as above. The '*negotiation period*' is the period beginning with the offer registration date and ending with the day on which the qualifying gift is made. In determining whether or to what extent late payment interest or a late payment penalty for a relevant tax year is attributable to the relevant portion, any attribution or apportionment is to be done in the way that is most beneficial to the taxpayer. (For these purposes, 'late payment interest' also includes old regime interest on overdue tax as in **43.3** LATE PAYMENT INTEREST AND PENALTIES.)

Suspension of tax payment pending negotiations

If an offer of a qualifying gift has been made and registered and is under negotiation, the donor may request that an obligation of his to make a tax payment for a relevant year be suspended until the negotiations conclude. The negotiations must be expected to be still ongoing on the due date for the payment. For this purpose, negotiations conclude when either a qualifying gift is made, the offer is withdrawn or the offer is rejected. The running total of amounts for which suspension may be requested in respect of the same offer and the same relevant tax year must not exceed the proposed tax reduction figure for that tax year. A suspension request must be made in writing to HMRC at least 45 days before the due date, and must be accompanied by a copy of the donor proposal of what should be in the agreed terms of the offer and such other information as an officer of HMRC may reasonably require. In considering whether or to what extent to agree to a request, HMRC must have regard to all the circumstances of the case (including, for example, the donor's creditworthiness). They may impose conditions with respect to the suspension.

Suspension of payment with HMRC's agreement stops the donor from becoming liable to late payment penalties but does not stop late payment interest from accruing.

HMRC may by notice in writing to the donor withdraw their agreement to the suspension with effect from such date, before conclusion of the negotiations, as is specified in the notice. The donor must then pay the suspended amount, together with any accrued late payment interest, within 30 days of the specified date. The last day of that 30-day period is treated for the purposes of late payment penalties as the date on or before which the tax must be paid.

If suspension is not withdrawn and the negotiations conclude without a qualifying gift being made, the individual must then pay the suspended amount, together with any accrued late payment interest, within the 30 days beginning with the day on which the negotiations concluded. The last day of that 30-day period is treated for the purposes of late payment penalties as the date on or before which the tax must be paid. If the negotiations conclude because a qualifying gift is made pursuant to the offer or a part of the offer, the donor need only pay so much (if any) as is not treated as satisfied as a result of the gift, plus any interest on that amount. If only part of an offer is accepted, HMRC will apply these rules as far as it is reasonably practicable to do so. They may allow suspension of payment to continue to some extent pending negotiations on the remaining parts of the offer.

Gifts set aside etc.

If a qualifying gift is set aside or declared void, for example by order of a court, the portion of the donor's tax liability for each relevant tax year that was treated as satisfied ceases to be so treated, and any effect on interest and penalties is negated. The individual is required to pay the portion due for each relevant tax year, together with any late payment interest and late payment penalties in respect of it, either within 30 days of the gift being set aside or declared void or, if later, on the dates when such amounts would have become due and payable in any case.

[*FA 2012, Sch 14 paras 2–11, 24*].

Pre-eminent property

'*Pre-eminent property*' means:

- any picture, print, book, manuscript, work of art, scientific object or other thing that the relevant Minister is satisfied is pre-eminent for its national, scientific, historic or artistic interest;
- any collection or group of pictures, prints, books, manuscripts, works of art, scientific objects or other things if the relevant Minister is satisfied that the collection or group, taken as a whole, is pre-eminent for its national, scientific, historic or artistic interest; and
- any object that is or has been kept in a significant building (i.e. a building falling within *IHTA 1984, s 230(3)(a)–(d)* (acceptance of property in lieu of tax)) if it appears to the relevant Minister desirable for the object to remain associated with the building.

'National interest' includes interest within any part of the UK. In determining whether an object, collection or group is pre-eminent, regard is to be had to any significant association of the object, collection or group with a particular place. The relevant Minister is by default the Secretary of State for Culture, Media and Sport, but if the item has a Scottish, Welsh or Northern Irish interest it will be a member or department of the appropriate devolved administration.

[*FA 2012, Sch 14 paras 22, 23*].

Simon's Taxes. See **C3.1904.**

Tainted donations

[14.21] The anti-avoidance rules described below (the 'tainted donations rules') have effect in relation to 'relievable charity donations'. The intention is to deny the usual tax reliefs to the donor, and in some cases charge him to income tax, where he enters into arrangements to obtain a financial advantage in return for his donation.

A '*relievable charity donation*' is a gift or other disposal made by a person to a charity and eligible for tax relief, i.e. tax relief would be available to the donor under a statutory provision in respect of the donation and/or the donation entitles the charity to a tax repayment. The statutory provisions under which relief might be available are listed at *ITA 2007, s 809ZI(4)*. They include, for example, the Gift Aid rules at **14.13–14.16** above, payroll giving at **14.18** above and gifts of shares, securities and real property at **14.19** above. They also include corporation tax and capital gains tax provisions. An amount of income which arises under a UK settlement (within *ITTOIA 2005, s 628* — see **70.26** SETTLEMENTS) and to which a charity is entitled under the terms of the settlement is to be regarded as an amount gifted to the charity by the trustees of the settlement so that it is within the scope of these rules. For the purposes of the tainted donation rules, a charity includes a registered community amateur sports club under *CTA 2010, ss 658–671*.

Meaning of 'tainted donation'

The rules come into play where a relievable charity donation is a 'tainted donation'. A donation is a '*tainted donation*' if *all* of Conditions A, B and C below are met in relation to it.

Condition A is that:

- the donor or a person connected with the donor (see below) enters into arrangements (whether before or after the donation is made); and
- it is reasonable to assume that the donation and the arrangements would not have been made or entered into independently of one another.

'Arrangements' is defined widely and includes any that are not legally enforceable. They may involve a single transaction or two or more transactions.

Condition B is that a main purpose of the person in entering into the arrangements is to obtain a financial advantage directly or indirectly from the donee charity (or a 'connected charity' — see below) for the donor or a person connected with the donor (other than a charity). The persons for whom the advantage may be obtained are known collectively as '*potentially advantaged persons*'. Certain financial advantages are disregarded (see below).

Condition C is that the donor is neither a qualifying charity-owned company (as defined) nor a relevant housing provider (as defined) linked with the charity to which the donation is made.

For the purpose of Condition B, the legislation sets out a particular scenario in which a person is deemed to obtain a financial advantage. It is important to note that this is not an exhaustive definition of a financial advantage and does not in any way limit the circumstances in which a person may be regarded as obtaining such an advantage. The scenario is that the donor or a person connected with him enters into arrangements which involve a transaction to which he or any other connected person (Person X) and another person (Person Y) are parties. Y could be the charity itself or any other person. X obtains a financial advantage from the charity to which the donation is made or a connected charity if:

- the terms of the transaction are less beneficial to Y or more beneficial to X (or both) than those which might reasonably be expected in an arm's length transaction; or
- the transaction is unlikely to have happened at all if a person dealing at arm's length were a party to it instead of Y.

Certain financial advantages disregarded

For the purposes of Condition B above, a financial advantage is ignored if any of the following apply:

- the person who obtained the financial advantage applies it for charitable purposes only;
- the financial advantage is a benefit associated with a gift which is a qualifying donation under the Gift Aid rules, in which case it is dealt with under the rules at **14.16** above rather than under the tainted donation rules;
- the donation is a disposal under **14.19** above (gifts of shares, securities and real property to charities) and the financial advantage is a benefit the value of which would be taken into account in determining the relievable amount on that disposal; or
- the donation is a gift in respect of which tax relief would be available under *ITTOIA 2005, s 108* (gifts of trading stock to charities etc. — see **75.88** TRADING INCOME) and the financial advantage is a benefit attributable to the making of the gift which thus falls to be brought into account as a trading receipt or post-cessation receipt.

Whether persons are connected

The question of whether the donor and another person are connected is determined as in *ITA 2007, s 993* (see **19** CONNECTED PERSONS) as modified for these purposes (see below), but the connection is taken into account only if it subsists at some time during the period beginning with the earliest, and ending with the latest, of the following times: the time the arrangements are entered into, the time the donation is made and the time the arrangements are first materially implemented.

The modifications to *ITA 2007, s 993* are as follows.

- Cohabiting couples are treated as if they were spouses or civil partners.
- A beneficiary of a settlement is connected with any trustee and with the settlor.
- A 'close company' includes any company that would be a close company if it were UK resident.

A '*connected charity*' in relation to another charity is a charity which is connected with that other charity in a matter relating to the structure, administration or control of either charity.

Denial of reliefs

Where income tax relief would otherwise be available to the donor in respect of the tainted donation, that relief is denied. Where income tax relief would otherwise be available in respect of an 'associated donation', that relief is also denied.

An '*associated donation*' is a relievable charity donation (see above) which is made in accordance with the arrangements mentioned in Condition A above in relation to the tainted donation and by a person other than a qualifying charity-owned company (as defined) or a relevant housing provider (as defined) linked with the charity to which the donation is made.

Where relief is denied in respect of a donation made under Gift Aid or the payroll giving scheme, the tax treatment of the donation in the hands of the charity (see **14.11** above) is unaffected. In the case of a Gift Aid donation, the donation is not deductible in arriving at the donor's adjusted net income (as in **1.17, 1.19** ALLOWANCES AND TAX RATES.

Charge to income tax

Where relief falls to be denied in relation to a Gift Aid donation and the charity to which it is made is entitled to claim a repayment of tax in respect of the donation (as in **14.11** above), income tax is chargeable. The tax charge is equal to the value of the Gift Aid repayment that the charity can claim in respect of the donation, whether the charity makes such a claim or not. Each of the following is jointly and severally liable for the tax charged:

- the donor;
- if different, the donor in respect of the tainted donation (i.e. if the donation in question is an associated donation);
- each potentially advantaged person (see Condition B above) under the arrangements relating to the tainted donation; and
- (subject to below) any charity to which the donation in question (or, if different, the tainted donation) is made and any connected charity.

A charity can only be liable for the tax if it was a party to the arrangements and the charity knew, at the time it entered into those arrangements, that they were arrangements for the donor (or a person connected with him) to obtain a financial advantage directly or indirectly from the charity. The tax charge does not apply at all to the extent (if any) that the tax repayment is made to the charity but is itself repaid to HMRC under any other tax provision.

Trust donations

A similar charge to income tax arises where relief falls to be denied in relation to a donation, the charity to which it is made is entitled to claim a repayment of tax in respect of the donation, and the donation is a payment by the trustees of a settlement of income arising under the settlement. In this case, the persons jointly and severally liable for the tax charged are as follows:

- the trustees of the settlement who made the trust donation;
- if different, the donor in respect of the tainted donation (i.e. if the trust donation is an associated donation);
- where the settlor retains an interest in the settlement, such that income is excluded by **70.26** SETTLEMENTS when given to charity, the settlor;
- each potentially advantaged person (see Condition B above) under the arrangements relating to the tainted donation;
- any beneficiary of the settlement who is party to the arrangements; and

- (subject to the same let-out as above) any charity to which the trust donation (or, if different, the tainted donation) is made and any connected charity.

[*ITA 2007, ss 809ZH–809ZR; SI 2019 No 1458, Sch 3 para 29(3)*].

For official guidance see www.gov.uk/government/publications/charities-detailed-guidance-notes/annex-viii-tainted-charity-donations.

Simon's Taxes. See **E1.813A.**

15

Children

Cross-references. See **28.58** EMPLOYMENT INCOME for employer-provided child-care; **30.12** EXEMPT INCOME for Child Trust Funds; **30.31** EXEMPT INCOME for Junior ISAs; **73.4** SOCIAL SECURITY AND NATIONAL INSURANCE for the clawback of child benefit; **73.6** SOCIAL SECURITY AND NATIONAL INSURANCE for child tax credit.

[15.1] All of a child's taxable income is chargeable on the child (subject to below) and he has full entitlement to personal allowances and reliefs. In most cases only the personal allowance (see **1.17** ALLOWANCES AND TAX RATES) will be available.

[15.2] The rights and obligations of a child with taxable income rest with the child; his or her representatives are able to act on the child's behalf under general law. In *R v Newmarket Commrs (ex p Huxley)* CA 1916, 7 TC 49, it was held that assessments can be raised on a minor, without the interposition of a guardian or trustee.

[15.3] If a parent makes a settlement in favour of his child, then the income arising thereon is treated (subject to certain exceptions) as that of the parent and not of the child for tax purposes. The definition of 'settlement' for this purpose is wide enough to cover gifts e.g. of money, or shares. See **70.30** SETTLEMENTS. See also the other provisions in **70.25–70.36** SETTLEMENTS whereby income of a settlement can be treated as that of the settlor for tax purposes.

[15.4] Under general law throughout the UK, an **adopted child** is treated as if born as the child of the adopter(s). Thus, no specific provision to that effect is required or provided in tax law.

15

Children

16

Claims

Cross-references. See ALLOWANCES AND TAX RATES at **1.14** onwards for claims to personal allowances and reliefs; **9.2**(ii) CAPITAL ALLOWANCES, **10.2**(ii) CAPITAL ALLOWANCES ON PLANT AND MACHINERY for capital allowances claims; **27** DOUBLE TAX RELIEF for claims under DTR agreements etc.; **42** INTEREST PAYABLE for relief for interest paid; **50.2** NON-RESIDENTS for reliefs claimable by non-residents; **70** SETTLEMENTS for claims by beneficiaries and contingent trust claims.

Introduction to claims

[16.1] Claims and elections may be made to an officer of HMRC (or to the Commissioners for HMRC in certain specified cases) whenever the *Taxes Acts* provide for relief to be given or other thing to be done.

A formal procedure applies as regards the making of claims and elections. A claim for a relief, allowance or tax repayment (other than one to be given effect by a PAYE coding adjustment — see also **16.3** below) must be for an amount quantified at the time of the claim.

Where notice has been given by HMRC requiring the delivery of a return (see **64.2**, **64.12** RETURNS), a claim etc. (other than one to be given effect by a PAYE coding adjustment) can only be made at any time by inclusion in such a return (or by virtue of an amendment to a return) *unless it could not be so included* either at that time or subsequently. See the following for exceptions to this: **14.11** CHARITIES AND CHARITABLE GIVING as regards certain free-standing claims by charitable trusts; **4.2** ANTI-AVOIDANCE as regards claims for consequential relieving adjustments after counteraction of a tax advantage under the GAAR; and **1.18** ALLOWANCES AND TAX RATES as regards the transfer of part of the personal allowance between spouses or civil partners.

In the case of a partnership business, a claim or election under any of numerous provisions specified in *TMA 1970, s 42(7)* must be made by a partner nominated by the partnership if it cannot be included in a partnership return (or amendment thereto). See **16.3** below for provisions applying where a claim etc. is made otherwise than by inclusion in a return.

Where a claimant discovers an error or mistake has been made in a claim (whether or not made in a return), he may make a supplementary claim within the time allowed for making the original claim.

[*TMA 1970, s 42; F(No 2)A 2017, Sch 2 paras 42, 64(1)*].

Claims are personal matters and can be made only by the person entitled to the relief (cf. *Fulford v Hyslop* Ch D 1929, 8 ATC 588). For claims to personal allowances etc. by persons receiving tax-free annuities, see **23.16** DEDUCTION OF TAX AT SOURCE. See **64.2** RETURNS for signing of claims by attorney.

Where an official form is provided for use in making a claim or election not included in a return, it is permissible to fill out a photocopy of the blank form, provided that, where double sided copying is not available, all the pages (including any notes) are present and attached in the correct order. Although such copying is in strictness a breach of HMSO copyright, this will only be pursued if forms are copied on a large scale for commercial gain. (HMRC SP 5/87). See also **64.2** RETURNS.

See **16.5** below as regards the making of income tax claims by telephone or other method not in writing.

Simon's Taxes. See **A4.202, A4.211** and **A4.219–A4.221.**

Claims for relief involving two or more years

[16.2] The provisions described below are designed to facilitate the administration under self-assessment of claims, elections etc. which affect more than one tax year. They generally deem the claim to be that of the later year, with consequent effect on the dates from which interest on unpaid and overpaid tax will run.

Relief for losses and other payments

A claim, under whatever provision, for a loss incurred or payment made (for example, a personal pension contribution) in one year of assessment to be carried back to an earlier year need not be made in a return, is treated as a claim for the year of loss or payment (the later year), must be for an amount equal to what would otherwise have been the tax saving for the earlier year (after taking into account any associated claims, see below, to which effect has already been given) and is given effect *in relation to the later year* by repayment, set-off etc. or by treating the said amount for the purposes of **67.7** SELF-ASSESSMENT as a tax payment made on account. See Revenue Tax Bulletin April 1996 p 299 for the practical effect.

HMRC have confirmed that under these provisions a carry-back claim (whether in the return for the year of loss or payment or not) will be given immediate effect provided that the tax return for the earlier year has been made and the tax calculated. Relief is given in terms of tax by set-off or repayment, and, provided that the claim (and, where appropriate, the payment) is made before 31 January in the year of loss or payment, may be by set-off against outstanding liabilities for the earlier year. Relief will be given by repayment where there are no outstanding liabilities. (Revenue Tax Bulletin

December 1996 pp 361–365, June 1997 p 443; Revenue 'Working Together' Bulletin No 12, March 2003). See *Norton v Thompson* (Sp C 399), [2004] SSCD 163 for an illustration, and confirmation, of the principles involved.

Where a claim to carry back trading losses is made, the taxpayer must make a claim in his tax return in respect of the later year, and HMRC may therefore open an enquiry under *TMA 1970, s 9A* (see **64.6** RETURNS) into the claim included in that later year return (*R (oao De Silva) v HMRC* SC, [2017] STC 2483; *Knibbs v HMRC; R (oao Astley) v HMRC* CA, [2019] STC 2262).

These provisions do *not* apply to share loss relief (see **45.23** LOSSES (*R (oao Derry) v HMRC* SC, [2019] STC 926) where the loss is carried back to the preceding year).

Averaging of farming or market gardening profits

Where a farmer or market gardener makes a claim to average the profits of two or five consecutive years of assessment (see **75.78** TRADING INCOME), the claim is treated as a claim for the last of the two or five years (the '*later year*'). To the extent that the claim would otherwise have affected the profits of an earlier year, it must be for an amount equal to the tax that would consequently have become payable or repayable for that earlier year (after taking into account any associated claims, see below, to which effect has already been given) and is given effect *in relation to the later year* by increasing the tax payable or treating the amount in question for the purposes of **67.7** SELF-ASSESSMENT as a tax payment made on account, whichever is appropriate. Where the later year is included in a subsequent averaging claim, i.e. it is then averaged with one or more subsequent years, the application of these provisions to the first claim is ignored in computing the effect of the subsequent claim.

Where, having made an averaging claim, a person then makes, amends or revokes any other claim for relief for any of the two or five years involved, which would be out of time but for the provisions of *ITTOIA 2005, s 224(4)*, the claim, amendment or revocation is treated as relating to the last of the two or five years (the '*later year*'). To the extent that it relates to income for an earlier year, the amount claimed (or, as appropriate, the increase or reduction therein) must be equal to the tax that would consequently have become payable or repayable for that earlier year (after taking into account any associated claims, see below, to which effect has already been given) and is given effect *in relation to the later year* by increasing the tax payable or treating the amount in question for the purposes of **67.7** SELF-ASSESSMENT as a tax payment made on account, whichever is appropriate.

For articles on these rules and on the completion of the relevant tax returns, see Revenue Tax Bulletin February 1997 pp 392–394 and August 1998 p 575.

Election for post-cessation receipts to be treated as if received on date of discontinuance

Where a person elects under *ITTOIA 2005, s 257* (see **59.4** POST-CESSATION RECEIPTS AND EXPENDITURE) for a post-cessation receipt to be treated as if received on the date of cessation of trade rather than in the year of receipt (the later year), the election is treated as a claim for the later year, must be for an amount equal to what would otherwise have been the additional tax payable for the year of assessment (the earlier year) in which the sum is treated as received (after taking into account any associated claims, see below, to which effect has already been given) and is given effect *in relation to the later year* by increasing the tax payable for that year.

Averaging of profits of creative artists

Where a creative artist, i.e. an author, designer, composer etc., makes a claim to average the profits of two consecutive years of assessment (see **75.60** TRADING INCOME), the claim is given effect in the same way as a claim to average the profits of a farmer or market gardener over two years (see above). The consequent making, amending or revoking of any other claim, where this would otherwise be out of time, is also given effect in the same way as for farmers.

Associated claims

For the purposes of all the above provisions, two or more claims, elections etc. (including, where appropriate, amendments and revocations) made by the same person and within these provisions are '*associated*' if the same tax year is the earlier year in relation to each of them.

[*TMA 1970, s 42(11A), Sch 1B; FA 2016, s 25(10)–(12)*].

See Revenue Tax Bulletin August 2000 pp 774, 775 for an article concerning the admission of earlier year claims, including those affecting the liability of another taxpayer, consequential on carry-back claims as above. See also **62.2** REPAYMENT INTEREST.

Simon's Taxes. See A4.202.

Claims etc. not included in returns

[16.3] Subject to any specific provision requiring a claim or election to be made to the Commissioners for HMRC, a claim or election made otherwise than in a return (see **16.1** above) must be made to an officer of HMRC. The claim etc. must include a declaration by the claimant that all particulars are correctly stated to the best of his information or belief. No claim requiring a tax repayment can be made unless the claimant has documentary proof that the tax has been paid or deducted. The claim must be made in a form determined by HMRC and may require, *inter alia*, a statement of the amount of tax to be discharged or repaid and (except as below) supporting information and documentation. In the case of a claim by or on behalf of a person who is not resident (or who claims to be not resident or not domiciled) in the UK, HMRC may require a statement or declaration in support of the claim to be made by affidavit.

A person who may wish to make a claim must keep all such records as may be requisite for the purpose and must preserve them until such time as HMRC may no longer enquire into the claim (see below) or any such enquiry is completed. There is a maximum penalty of £3,000 for non-compliance in relation to any claim *actually made*. Similar provisions and exceptions apply as in **64.5** RETURNS as to the preservation of copies of documents instead of originals and the exception from penalty for non-compliance in relation to dividend vouchers, interest certificates etc.

Provisions similar to those in **64.4** RETURNS (amendments of self-assessments) apply to enable a claimant (within twelve months of the claim) or officer of HMRC (within nine months of the claim) to amend a claim etc. HMRC have power of enquiry into a claim etc. (or amendment thereof) similar to that in **64.6, 64.7** RETURNS (enquiries into returns). Notice of intention to enquire must be given by the first anniversary of 31 January following the year of assessment (or where the claim relates to a period other than a year of assessment the first anniversary of the end of that period) or, if later, the quarter day (meaning 31 January, 30 April etc.) next following the first anniversary of the date of claim etc. Where an enquiry is in progress, the effect of the claim etc. (or amendment thereof) is suspended, but an officer of HMRC may give provisional effect to it to such extent as he thinks fit. Provisions similar to those in **64.8, 64.9** RETURNS apply as regards completion of enquiries and amendments of claims upon completion (except that there is no provision for issuing *partial* closure notices). HMRC must give effect (by assessment, discharge or repayment) to an amendment arising out of an enquiry within 30 days after the date of issue of the closure notice. An appeal may be made against any conclusion stated, or amendment made, by a closure notice by giving written notice to the relevant officer within 30 days after the date of issue of the closure notice, extended to three months where certain specified issues concerning residence are involved. If an amendment is varied on appeal, HMRC must give effect to the variation within 30 days. Where a claim etc. does not give rise to a discharge or repayment of tax (for example, a claim to carry forward trading losses), there are provisions for disallowance of the claim on completion of enquiry, with appeal procedures similar to those above.

[*TMA 1970, s 42(11), Sch 1A; SI 2009 No 56, Sch 1 paras 53–58; SI 2009 No 402; SI 2009 No 404, Arts 2, 5*].

See **16.5** below as regards the making of income tax claims by telephone or other method not in writing and also the use of photocopied blank claim forms.

Claims affecting more than one year

Where a claim affects more than one tax year, the above enquiry procedure applies to the return for the earlier year if the taxpayer has accounted for the claim in his self-assessment of the tax due for that earlier year. Otherwise, the correct procedure is an enquiry under *TMA 1970, Sch 1A* (as in **16.3** CLAIMS). See *HMRC v Cotter* SC, [2013] STC 2480; *R (oao Derry) v HMRC* SC, [2019] STC 926; *R (oao Rouse) v HMRC* UT 2013, [2014] STC 230.

In the above cases, the claims were for loss reliefs to be carried back (see **16.2** CLAIMS) from one year (Year 2) to another year (Year 1). In broadly similar cases the courts made the important distinction that the year being enquired into was Year 2 and not, as in the above cases, Year 1 (*R (oao De Silva) v HMRC* SC, [2017] STC 2483; and see *Spring Salmon & Seafood Ltd v HMRC*

UT, [2017] UKUT 205 (TCC)). For a useful discussion of the *De Silva* decision and its ramifications, see *Knibbs v HMRC; R (oao Astley) v HMRC* CA, [2019] STC 2262, in which the CA followed *De Silva*.

Claims given effect by PAYE coding adjustment

Claims for a tax year may be made during that year, and thus before a tax return is issued, and given effect by adjustment to a PAYE code (see **53.13** PAY AS YOU EARN), for example a claim to married couple's allowance. Such in-year claims may subsequently be reflected in a tax return. Where no such return is issued, the claim will become final under the above provisions by the first anniversary of 31 January following the tax year, i.e. the final date for HMRC to give notice of intention to enquire. Except in cases of 'discovery' (see **6.6** ASSESSMENTS), HMRC will in practice apply the same deadline to claims rolled forward from one year to the next and automatically included in code numbers and to those included on the basis of preliminary information given by the taxpayer before the start of the tax year. (Revenue Tax Bulletin October 1996 pp 350, 351).

Simon's Taxes. See **A4.202.**

Time limits for claims

[16.4] *Unless otherwise prescribed*, a claim with respect to income tax must be made within four years after the end of the tax year to which it relates. [*TMA 1970, s 43(1)*].

There is nothing in the reasonable excuse provisions of *TMA 1970, s 118(2)* (see **55.38** PENALTIES) that gives a person the right to appeal against an HMRC refusal to allow a late claim (*HMRC v Raftopoulou* CA, [2018] STC 988; *Ames v HMRC* FTT (TC 4523), [2015] UKFTT 337 (TC)).

See **16.9** below for claims following late assessments, and see generally **74** TIME LIMITS.

Simon's Taxes. See **A4.211.**

Telephone claims and other services

[16.5] HMRC have powers to accept income tax claims by telephone (or by any other method not in writing), where a written claim would otherwise be required, for which purpose they must publish general directions as regards the circumstances in which, and conditions subject to which, such claims will be accepted. The time for making the claim and the contents may not be altered by the directions. No directions may be given in relation to claims by an individual as trustee, partner or personal representative, to capital allowances claims or to claims under *TMA 1970, Sch 1B* (see **16.2** above). Directions may similarly be given as regards the making of elections, the giving of notice, the amendment or withdrawal of claims, elections and notices and the amendment of returns. [*TMA 1970, ss 43E, 43F; FA 1998, s 118*].

All tax offices offer certain telephone services, as set out in HMRC SP 2/03 and, for tax offices served by a Contact Centre, HMRC SP 1/10, with which are published the appropriate directions. These include acceptance of telephone claims for personal allowances, pension contributions, Gift Aid donations and certain employment expenses. They also enable taxpayers to notify items of income and changes in their personal details. Certain types of notification are accepted only if within specified monetary limits. Content Centres will additionally accept telephone amendments to self-assessment tax returns. These services are available to individuals and, subject to identity and authorisation checks, to agents acting for individuals.

Tax repayment claims

[16.6] A self-assessment tax return (see **64.2** RETURNS) may give rise to a tax repayment. Otherwise, a tax repayment claim can be made on form R40. The form and related Guidance Notes are available on the HMRC website or from tax offices. There is no requirement to send vouchers, certificates or other supporting documents with the claim (though these *can* be sent if the taxpayer so wishes) but they must be retained under the record-keeping requirements at **64.5** RETURNS as applied by **16.3** above. A tax repayment claim is also subject to the enquiry provisions at **16.3** above.

See **16.4** above for the time limit for making a claim. Where an overpayment of tax has arisen because of official error, and there is no doubt or dispute as to the facts, claims to repayment of tax are accepted outside the statutory time limit (HMRC ESC B41).

A tax repayment claim can be made *before* the end of the tax year to which it relates, though HMRC do not normally make in-year repayments of less than £50. If further income is expected between the making of the claim and the end of the tax year, i.e. the claim is an interim claim, a full-year estimate should be given for each such item of income as well as details of the actual income to date.

See **54.7** PAYMENT OF TAX for the situation where the right to receive a tax repayment is transferred from one person to another.

HMRC may withhold repayments to the extent that the claims that produce them constitute (in their opinion) tax avoidance, and where they are challenging or considering challenging those claims by enquiry. In so doing, they are looking to prevent people obtaining temporary cash-flow benefits from engaging in avoidance. (HMRC Brief 28/13, 17 September 2013).

Overpayment relief

[16.7] Where a person has paid an amount of income tax (or capital gains tax) and believes that the tax is not due, he can make a claim to HMRC for repayment of the tax. Where a person has been assessed to pay an amount of tax, or there has been a determination or direction to that effect, he can likewise make a claim for the amount to be discharged if he believes that the tax is not due. For these purposes, tax paid by one person on behalf of another is treated as paid by the other person.

HMRC will not give effect to such a claim if:

(a) the amount is excessive because of a mistake in an election, claim or notice or a mistake consisting of making or giving, or failing to make or give, an election, claim or notice; or
(b) the amount is excessive because of a mistake in allocating (or not allocating) expenditure to a pool for capital allowances purposes; or
(c) the amount is excessive because of a mistake in bringing into account (or not bringing into account) a disposal value for capital allowances purposes; or
(d) the claimant can seek relief by taking other steps under tax legislation; or
(e) the claimant could have sought relief by taking such other steps within a period which has expired by the time the claim is made, if he knew, or ought reasonably to have known, before the end of that period that such relief was available; or
(f) the claim is made on grounds that have been put to a court or tribunal in the course of an appeal relating to the amount or on grounds that have been put to HMRC in the course of such an appeal settled by agreement (as in **5.9** APPEALS); or
(g) the claimant knew, or ought reasonably to have known, of the grounds for the claim before the latest of the date an appeal relating to the amount was determined by a court or tribunal, the date on which such an appeal was withdrawn by the claimant, and the end of the period in which the claimant could have appealed; or
(h) the amount was due as a result of proceedings by HMRC against the claimant; or
(i) the amount was due under an agreement between the claimant and HMRC in settlement of proceedings by HMRC against the claimant; or
(j) the amount is excessive because of a mistake in calculating the claimant's liability where the liability was calculated in accordance with the practice generally prevailing at the time; or
(k) the amount is excessive because of a mistake in a PAYE assessment or PAYE calculation where the assessment or calculation was made in accordance with the practice generally prevailing at the end of the period of twelve months following the tax year for which the assessment or calculation was made.

Items (j) and (k) above do not apply where the amount paid, or liable to be paid, is tax which has been charged contrary to EU law. For this purpose, tax is charged contrary to EU law if, in the circumstances in question, the charge to tax is contrary to the provisions relating to free movement of goods, persons, services and capital in Titles II and IV of Part 3 of the Treaty on the Functioning of the European Union (or any replacement provisions made by a subsequent treaty).

[*TMA 1970, s 33, Sch 1AB paras 1, 2*].

In relation to claims for recovery of tax overcharged contrary to EU law, the above legislation does not exclude a right of action at common law (*Test Claimants in the FII Group Litigation v HMRC* SC, [2012] STC 1362).

Making a claim

For income tax (and capital gains tax) purposes, a claim must be made within four years after the end of the tax year concerned. Where the claim relates to tax overpaid, that year is the year in respect of which the payment was made or, where the amount paid is excessive due to a mistake in a tax return or returns, the year to which the return (or, if more than one, the first return) relates. Where the claim relates to a liability under an assessment, determination or direction, and the person believes that the tax is not due, the year concerned is:

(i) where the liability is excessive by reason of a mistake in a tax return, the tax year to which the return (or, if more than one, the first return) relates; and
(ii) in any other case, the tax year to which the assessment, determination or direction relates.

A claim cannot be made in a tax return.

[*TMA 1970, Sch 1AB para 3*].

Where, under PAYE, the construction industry scheme or other tax legislation, one person (P) is accountable to HMRC for tax payable by another person or for any other amount that has been or is to be set off against another person's liability, a claim in respect of the amount can only be made by that other person. If, however, P has paid such an amount but was not in fact accountable to HMRC for it, P, and only P, can make a claim in respect of that amount. Effect will not be given to such a claim by P to the extent that the amount has been repaid to, or set against amounts payable by, the other person. [*TMA 1970, Sch 1AB para 4*].

Partnerships

A claim in respect of an amount paid or due by one or more partners in accordance with a self-assessment which is excessive because of a mistake in a partnership return must be made by a nominated partner (or his personal representative). The partner must have been a partner at some time in the period for which the return was made. [*TMA 1970, Sch 1AB para 5*].

Discovery assessment etc. following claim

Where the grounds for a claim also provide grounds for HMRC to make a discovery assessment or determination (see **6.6** ASSESSMENTS) for any period and such an assessment or determination could not otherwise be made as a result of one of the restrictions noted below, those restrictions are disregarded and an assessment or determination is not out of time if made before the final determination of the claim (i.e. before the time at which the claim can no longer be varied). The restrictions concerned are those at **6.6**(2) ASSESSMENTS and the expiry of a time limit for making a discovery assessment or determination (see **6.2**, **6.3** ASSESSMENTS).

Similar provisions apply in relation to amendments of partnership returns following discovery. [*TMA 1970, Sch 1AB paras 6, 7*]

Contract settlements

The above provisions apply also to amounts paid under a contract settlement (see **6.9** ASSESSMENTS). If the person who paid the amounts due under the settlement (the '*payer*') was not the person from whom the tax was due (the '*taxpayer*'), then the provisions are modified accordingly. If an amount is repayable to the payer as a result of a claim, HMRC can set the amount repayable against any amount payable by the taxpayer under any discovery assessment or determination made as a result of the claim.

[*TMA 1970, Sch 1AB para 8*].

Simon's Taxes. See **A4.219, A4.220.**

Special relief

[16.8] Where, in the absence of a return, HMRC has determined a taxpayer's income tax (or capital gains tax) liability, the taxpayer has until three years after the statutory filing date, or, if later, one year after the determination, to displace the determination with his own self-assessment (see **64.11** RETURNS). A special rule applies where:

(i) HMRC have made such a determination, but the taxpayer believes the tax is not due (or, if it has been paid, was not due);
(ii) relief would have been available under **16.7** above if it were not for **16.7**(e) or (h) or if it were not for the fact that the four-year time limit for claims has expired; and
(iii) if **16.7**(h) applies, the taxpayer was neither present nor legally represented during the proceedings in question.

Notwithstanding (ii) above, a claim may be made under **16.7** above for repayment or discharge of the amount in question, provided *all* of the following conditions are met:

(a) in the opinion of the Commissioners for HMRC it would be unconscionable for them to seek to recover the amount (or to withhold repayment of it);
(b) the taxpayer's tax affairs are otherwise up to date or satisfactory arrangements have been put in place to bring them up to date so far as possible; and
(c) the taxpayer has not relied on this special rule on any previous occasion (whether in respect of the same or a different determination or tax).

The fact that the condition at (c) above is not met may be disregarded if warranted by exceptional circumstances. A person is taken to have relied on the special rule on a previous occasion if he has made a claim (or a composite set of claims involving one or more determinations, taxes and tax years) in reliance on the special rule on a previous occasion. It does not matter whether that claim (or set of claims) actually succeeded.

A claim made in reliance on this special rule must include (in addition to anything required by *TMA 1970, Sch 1AB* at **16.7** above) such information and documentation as is reasonably required for the purpose of determining whether the conditions at (a), (b) and (c) above are met.

[*TMA 1970, Sch 1AB para 3A*].

The Appeal Tribunal concluded in *Currie v HMRC* FTT (TC 3997), [2014] UKFTT 882 (TC), [2015] SFTD 51 that 'unconscionable' in (a) above means 'completely unreasonable' or 'unreasonably excessive'. See also the guidance at HMRC Self-Assessment Claims Manual SACM12220–12260. The same Tribunal concluded that its jurisdiction was limited to considering whether an HMRC officer deciding to refuse a special relief claim acted unreasonably. In *Clark v HMRC* FTT (TC 4509), [2015] UKFTT 324 (TC), the FTT considered it unconscionable for HMRC to pursue recovery of tax charged by determinations in the absence of tax returns; the appellant had learning difficulties and was also dyslexic but HMRC had neither recognised nor made any concession to his vulnerability. In *Scott v HMRC* FTT (TC 4597), [2015] UKFTT 420 (TC), it was unconscionable for HMRC to fail to take account of a material factor, the striking disparity between tax due on the determinations made and tax due according to (late) returns, and to take account of an immaterial factor, the appellant's tax compliance history.

Simon's Taxes. See **A4.221**.

Claims following further assessments

[16.9] A claim (including a supplementary claim) which could not have been allowed but for the making of an assessment to income tax or capital gains tax after the tax year to which it relates may be made before the end of the tax year following that in which the assessment was made. [*TMA 1970, s 43(2)*].

In the case of a discovery leading to an assessment under *TMA 1970, s 29* (see **6.6** ASSESSMENTS) which is made other than for the purpose of making good a loss of tax brought about carelessly or deliberately (see **6.3** ASSESSMENTS), the following rules apply:

(a) any 'relevant' claim, election, application or notice which could have been made or given within the normal time limits may be made or given within one year after the end of the tax year in which the assessment is made; and
(b) any 'relevant' claim etc. previously made or given, except an irrevocable one, can, with the consent of the person(s) by whom it was made or given (or their personal representatives), be revoked or varied in the manner in which it was made or given.

Elections for the transfer of the basic married couple's allowance or any part of the personal allowance between spouses or civil partners are excluded from this treatment.

A claim under **16.7** above (recovery of tax overpaid) is '*relevant*' to an assessment for a tax year if it relates to that tax year. Any other claim etc. is '*relevant*' to an assessment for a tax year if:

(i) it relates to, or to an event occurring in, the tax year; and
(ii) it, or its revocation or variation, reduces, or could reduce:
    - the increased tax liability resulting from the assessment; or

- any other liability of the person for that tax year or a later one ending not more than one year after the end of the tax year in which the assessment is made.

The normal APPEALS (5) provisions apply, with any necessary modifications.

If the making etc. of a claim etc. (as above) would alter another person's tax liability, the consent of that person (or his personal representatives) is needed. If such alteration is an increase, the other person cannot make etc. a claim etc. under the foregoing provisions.

If the reduction, whether resulting from one or more than one claim etc., would exceed the additional tax assessed, relief is not available for the excess. If the reduction, so limited, involves more than one period, or more than one person, the inspector will specify by notice in writing how it is to be apportioned; but within 30 days of the notice (or last notice if more than one person is involved) being given, the person, or persons jointly, can specify the apportionment by notice in writing to the inspector.

[*TMA 1970, ss 43A, 43B*].

The provisions of *TMA 1970, ss 43(2), 43A, 43B* above have similar effect in relation to an HMRC amendment to a self-assessment personal or partnership tax return as they would have in relation to a further assessment (see **64.8** RETURNS). Also, any late assessment required to give effect to a claim etc. as above, or as a result of allowing such a claim etc., can be made within a year after the claim etc. becomes final (i.e. becomes no longer capable of being varied, on appeal or otherwise); this applies to claims etc. made as a consequence of either an assessment as above or an amendment to a return. [*TMA 1970, s 43C*].

See also **6.3** ASSESSMENTS.

Simon's Taxes. See **A6.424.**

17

Community Investment Tax Relief

Simon's Taxes. See E3.6.

Introduction to community investment tax relief

[17.1] The Community Investment Tax Credit scheme provides tax relief to individuals and companies investing in Community Development Finance Institutions ('CDFIs') which have been accredited by the Government under the rules of the scheme. The intention is that CDFIs use investors' funds to finance small businesses and social enterprises in disadvantaged communities.

The relief takes the form of a reduction in the investor's income tax or corporation tax liability. The quantum of the relief is a maximum of 25% of the 'invested amount' (as defined — see **17.4** below), spread over five years. [*ITA 2007, ss 333–382*].

This chapter covers the relief due to investors who are individuals. For coverage of the relief due to corporate investors, see the corresponding chapter of Tolley's Corporation Tax.

No exemption is provided for chargeable gains on disposals of investments in CDFIs.

References in this chapter to the '*investment date*' are to the day on which the investment in the CDFI is made, and references to the '*five-year investment period*' are to the five years beginning with that day. [*ITA 2007, s 338*]. The investment term need not, however, be limited to five years.

Guidance on the relief is available in HMRC Community Investment Tax Relief Manual.

Eligibility for relief

[17.2] An individual who makes an investment in a body is eligible for community investment tax relief in respect of that investment if:

(a) the body is accredited as a CDFI (see **17.24** below) at the time the investment is made;
(b) the investment is a 'qualifying investment' (see **17.7** below); and
(c) the general conditions at **17.11** below are satisfied.

[*ITA 2007, s 334*].

For these purposes, an individual makes an investment in a body when:

(i) he makes a loan (whether secured or unsecured) to the body (otherwise than by providing overdraft facilities or acquiring securities); or
(ii) an 'issue of securities or shares' (as defined) of or in the body, for which he has subscribed, is made to him.

Where a loan agreement authorises the body to draw down amounts of the loan over a period of time, the loan is treated for the purposes of (i) above as made when the first amount is drawn down.

[*ITA 2007, ss 336, 378*].

Form of relief

[17.3] Where an individual who is eligible for relief (see **17.2** above) makes a claim for relief for any 'relevant tax year', he is entitled to a reduction in his tax liability equal to 5% of the 'invested amount' (see **17.4** below) in respect of the investment in question.

The tax year in which the investment date falls and each of the four subsequent tax years (but no others) are '*relevant tax years*' for this purpose.

The order in which tax reductions are given against an individual's tax liability is set out at **1.12** ALLOWANCES AND TAX RATES, which also makes clear that a tax reduction must be restricted to the extent (if any) that it would otherwise exceed the individual's remaining income tax liability after making all prior reductions (but see below for carry-forward of unused relief).

Carry-forward of unused relief

Any tax reduction available as above for a relevant tax year is carried forward to the extent (if any) that it is not fully deducted for that year at Step 6 of the calculation of income tax liability at **1.10** ALLOWANCES AND TAX RATES. For each subsequent relevant tax year for which the investor is entitled to a tax reduction for the same investment, he can claim to have the reduction increased by the amount of any of the relief brought forward that remains unused. Relief cannot be carried forward beyond the five-year investment period.

Claims

The investor is entitled to make a claim for relief for a 'relevant tax year' (see above) if he considers that the conditions for the relief are for the time being satisfied. He *must* also have received a tax relief certificate (see also **17.24** below) from the CDFI. No claim can be made before the end of the tax year to which it relates. Otherwise, by default, the general time limit for making claims applies (see **16.4** CLAIMS). See **17.6** below for specific circumstances in which no claim for relief can be made.

No application can be made to postpone tax (see **54.5** PAYMENT OF TAX), pending appeal, on the grounds that the appellant is entitled to community investment tax relief, unless a claim for the relief has been made.

[*ITA 2007, ss 335, 335A, 376*].

Meaning of the 'invested amount'

[17.4] For the purposes of **17.3**, in respect of a **loan**, the '*invested amount*' is as follows.

(a) In the tax year in which the investment date falls, it is the 'average capital balance' (see below) for the first year of the five-year investment period (see **17.1** above).

(b) In each subsequent tax year (subject to (c) below), it is the average capital balance for the one year beginning with the anniversary of the investment date falling in that tax year.

(c) For the third, fourth and fifth tax years for which relief may be claimed, it is initially determined as in (b) above but is restricted to, if less, the average capital balance for the six-month period beginning eighteen months after the investment date. (This is a consequence of the eighteen-month rule for drawdown facilities referred to at **17.8** below. (Treasury Explanatory Notes to Finance Bill 2002).)

For the purposes of (a)–(c) above, the '*average capital balance*' of a loan for any period of time is the mean of the daily balances of capital outstanding during that period.

In respect of **securities or shares**, the '*invested amount*' for any tax year is the amount subscribed for them (not necessarily in that tax year).

[*ITA 2007, s 337*].

See **17.18, 17.19** below for restriction of the invested amount in certain circumstances where value is received.

Examples

[17.5]

(A) Loans

Faith makes a £50,000 loan to a CDFI on 1 September 2016 on terms that it be repaid in annual £10,000 instalments beginning on 1 September 2018. She agrees to increase the loan outstanding by £40,000 on 1 September 2020 (repayable on 1 September 2022). The 'invested amount', and the 5% maximum income tax reduction available, for the five tax years for which relief may be claimed, are as follows.

	Invested amount	Tax reduction
	£	£
2016/17	50,000	2,500
2017/18	50,000	2,500
2018/19	40,000	2,000
2019/20	30,000	1,500
2020/21	50,000*	2,500

* Initially determined at £60,000 (£20,000 + the £40,000 increase) but restricted to £50,000, being the average capital balance for the six-month period 1 March 2018 to 31 August 2018 inclusive (see **17.4** (c) above).

(B) Securities or shares

Bill subscribes £50,000 for shares in a CDFI on 1 September 2016 and holds them for at least five years. The 'invested amount', and the 5% maximum income tax reduction available for each of the tax years 2016/17–2020/21 inclusive, the five years for which relief may be claimed, are £50,000 and £2,500 respectively.

Circumstances in which no claim for relief can be made

[17.6] In the circumstances listed below, no claim for community investment tax relief can be made.

Loans — disposals and excessive repayments/receipts of value

No claim can be made for a tax year in respect of a loan if:

(a) the investor disposes of all or any part of the loan (disregarding any repayment of the loan) before the 'qualifying date' relating to that tax year; or

(b) at any time after the investment is made but before that 'qualifying date', the amount of the capital outstanding on the loan is reduced to nil; or

(c) before that 'qualifying date', cumulative loan repayments (or receipts of value treated as repayments — see **17.18** below) bring into play the withdrawal of relief provisions at **17.17** below.

The '*qualifying date*' relating to a tax year is the next anniversary of the investment date to occur after the end of that tax year.

[*ITA 2007, s 354*].

Thus, if, for example, a loan made on 1 October 2017 is repaid in full by the CDFI on 1 July 2021 (i.e. before 1 October 2021, the qualifying date for 2020/21), no claim for relief can be made for 2020/21, even though the loan remained outstanding throughout that tax year. No claim can be made for 2021/22 either.

Securities or shares — disposals and excessive receipts of value

No claim can be made for a tax year in respect of any securities or shares other than those held by the investor (as sole beneficial owner) continuously (see **17.25** below) throughout the period beginning when the investment is made and ending immediately before the 'qualifying date' (as in (a) above) relating to that tax year. In addition, no claim can be made for a tax year if, before the 'qualifying date' (as in (a) above) relating to that tax year, cumulative receipts of value bring into play the withdrawal of relief provisions at **17.19** below. [*ITA 2007, s 355*].

Loss of accreditation by the CDFI

Where the CDFI ceases to be accredited as such during the first year of the five-year investment period, no claim for relief can be made. Where accreditation is lost at any later time within the five-year investment period, no claim can be made for the tax year in which falls the most recent anniversary of the investment date preceding (or coinciding with) the date the accreditation is lost, or for any subsequent tax year. (There is no withdrawal of relief for any earlier tax year.) [*ITA 2007, s 356*].

Qualifying investments

[17.7] An investment is a '*qualifying investment*' in a CDFI (and thus meets condition (b) at **17.2** above) if:

- the investment consists of a loan, securities or shares satisfying the conditions at **17.8** or, as the case may be, **17.9** below;
- the investor receives from the CDFI a valid tax relief certificate (see also **17.24** below); and
- the conditions at **17.10** below (no pre-arranged protection against risks) are met.

[*ITA 2007, s 344*].

Conditions to be satisfied in relation to loans

[17.8] There are three such conditions. The first is that either the CDFI receives from the investor, on the investment date, the full amount of the loan or, in the case of a loan made under a drawdown facility, the loan agreement provides for the CDFI to receive the full amount of the loan within 18 months after the investment date. The second condition is that the loan must not carry any present or future right to be converted into, or exchanged for, a loan, securities, shares or other rights, any of which are redeemable within the five-year investment period. The third is that the loan must not be made on terms that allow any person to require:

(a) repayment within years 1 and 2 (of the five-year investment period) of any of the loan capital advanced during those two years; or
(b) repayment within year 3 of more than 25% of the balance of loan capital outstanding at the end of year 2; or
(c) repayment before the end of year 4 of more than 50% of the balance of loan capital outstanding at the end of year 2; or
(d) repayment before the end of year 5 of more than 75% of that balance.

Any of the above percentages may be altered by Treasury order, but only in relation to loans made on or after a date specified in the order. For the above purposes, there is disregarded any requirement to repay that may arise as a consequence of certain standard commercial default provisions in the loan agreement.

[*ITA 2007, s 345*].

Conditions to be satisfied in relation to securities or shares

[17.9] There are two such conditions. The first is that the securities or shares must be subscribed for wholly in cash and fully paid for as at the investment date. The second is that they must not carry:

- any present or future right to be redeemed within the five-year investment period; or
- any present or future right to be converted into, or exchanged for, a loan, securities, shares or other rights, any of which are redeemable within the five-year investment period.

[*ITA 2007, ss 346, 347*].

No pre-arranged protection against risks

[17.10] Any arrangements (as very broadly defined) under which the investment in the CDFI is made (or arrangements preceding the investment but relating to it) must not include arrangements a main purpose of which is to provide (by means of any insurance, indemnity, guarantee or otherwise) complete or partial protection for the investor against the normal risks attaching to the investment. Arrangements are, however, allowed if they do no more than provide the kind of commercial protection, e.g. the use of property as security for a loan, that might be expected if the investment were made by a bank. [*ITA 2007, s 349*].

General conditions for eligibility

[17.11] The following conditions apply.

No control of CDFI by investor

The investor must not control the CDFI at any time in the five-year investment period. 'Control' is construed in accordance with *ITA 2007, s 995* where the CDFI is a body corporate, with similar rules applying in other cases, with any potential future rights and powers of the investor, and any rights and powers held or exercisable by another on his behalf, taken into account. References to 'the investor' include any person connected with him (within **19** CONNECTED PERSONS).

Beneficial ownership

The investor must be the sole beneficial owner of the investment when it is made (which in the case of a loan means sole beneficial entitlement to repayment).

No acquisition of share in partnership

Where the CDFI is a partnership, the investment must not consist of or include any capital contributed by the investor on becoming a member of the partnership. This includes the provision of loan capital treated as partners' capital in the partnership accounts.

No tax avoidance purpose

The investment must not be made as part of a scheme or arrangement a main purpose of which is the avoidance of tax.

[*ITA 2007, ss 350–353, 1021*].

Withdrawal or reduction of relief

[17.12] Community investment tax relief may fall to be withdrawn or reduced on a disposal of the investment (see **17.15** below), on repayment of an investment consisting of a loan (see **17.17** below), or if value is received in respect of the investment (see **17.18–17.21** below).

Where relief given falls to be withdrawn or reduced, and also where it is found not to have been due in the first place, the withdrawal etc. is achieved by means of an income tax assessment for the tax year *for which the relief was obtained.* The assessment must be made no later than six years after the tax year for which the relief was obtained. This restriction is without prejudice to the extension of time limits in cases of loss of income tax brought about deliberately (see **6.3** ASSESSMENTS). No such assessment can be made by reason of any event occurring after the investor's death. [*ITA 2007, ss 371, 372; SI 2009 No 403*].

Information

[17.13] Certain events giving rise to withdrawal or reduction of investment relief must be notified to HMRC by the investor. An individual investor must give such notice no later than 31 January following the tax year in which the event occurs. If the requirement arises from the receipt of value by a connected person, the above deadline is extended to, if later, the end of the period of 60 days beginning when the investor comes to know of the event. The penalty provisions of *TMA 1970, s 98* apply in the event of non-compliance. [*ITA 2007, s 373*].

Attribution of relief

[17.14] Community investment tax relief is said to be 'attributable' to any investment in respect of a tax year if relief as in **17.3** above has been obtained in respect of that investment and has not been withdrawn (as opposed to reduced). Where for any tax year relief has been obtained by reason of a single investment (i.e. one loan, or securities or shares comprised in one issue), the relief attributable to it is the reduction made in the investor's tax liability. Where the relief has been obtained by reason of two or more investments, it is attributed to those investments in proportion to the invested amounts (see **17.4** above) for the year in which relief is due (not, in the case of carried forward relief, the year in which it is given). Relief attributable to any one issue of securities or shares is attributed *pro rata* to each security or share in that issue, and any reduction of relief is similarly apportioned between the securities or shares in question. For these purposes, any bonus shares, issued in respect of the original shares and being shares in the same company, of the same class and carrying the same rights, are treated as if comprised in the original issue, and relief is apportioned to them accordingly. This applies only if the original shares have been continuously held (see **17.25** below) by the investor (as sole beneficial owner) since their issue, and, where it does apply, the bonus shares are themselves treated as having been continuously held since the time of the original issue. [*ITA 2007, ss 357, 358, 382(1)(2)*].

Disposals

[17.15] For the purposes below, an investment is regarded as being disposed of if it is so regarded for the purposes of tax on chargeable gains, and see also **17.23** below (certain company reconstructions treated as disposals). [*ITA 2007, s 379*].

Loans

Where the investment consists of a loan, and the investor disposes of the whole of it within the five-year investment period (see **17.1** above), otherwise than by way of a 'permitted disposal', or disposes of part of it during that period, any relief attributable to the investment (see **17.14** above), for any tax year, is withdrawn. See **17.12** above for consequences of withdrawal. Repayment of the loan does not count as a disposal. A disposal is a '*permitted disposal*' if it is:

- by way of a distribution in the course of dissolving or winding up the CDFI; or
- a disposal within *TCGA 1992, s 24(1)* (entire loss, destruction etc. of asset — see Tolley's Capital Gains Tax under Disposal); or

- a deemed disposal under *TCGA 1992, s 24(2)* (assets of negligible value — see Tolley's Capital Gains Tax under Losses); or
- made after the CDFI has ceased to be accredited as such.

[*ITA 2007, s 360*].

Securities or shares

Where the investment consists of securities or shares, and the investor disposes of the whole or any part of the investment within the five-year investment period, any relief attributable to the investment (see **17.14** above), in respect of any tax year, is withdrawn or reduced as set out below. This does not apply if the CDFI has ceased to be accredited before the disposal or if the disposal arises from the repayment, redemption or repurchase by the CDFI of any of the securities or shares. See **17.12** above for consequences of withdrawal etc.

In the case of a 'permitted disposal' (defined as for *Loans* above) or a disposal by way of a bargain made at arm's length, the relief attributable to the investment in respect of any tax year (including any carried forward to a subsequent year) is withdrawn, or is reduced by 5% of the disposal consideration (if such reduction would not amount to full withdrawal). Where relief has been carried forward, relief given in a later tax year is reduced in priority to relief given in an earlier year. If the relief initially obtained for any tax year (plus any obtained by carry-forward) is less than 5% of the invested amount (see **17.4** above), i.e. because the investor's tax liability is insufficient to fully absorb the available relief, the reduction is correspondingly restricted.

In the case of any other disposal, the relief for all tax years is withdrawn.

[*ITA 2007, s 361*].

Identification rules on disposal of securities or shares

[17.16] The rules below apply, for the purpose of identifying shares disposed of, where the investor makes a part disposal of a holding of shares of the same class in the same company, and the holding includes shares to which community investment tax relief is attributable (see **17.14** above) and which have been held continuously (see **17.25** below) since the time of issue. The rules apply for the purposes of **17.15** above and this chapter generally and for the purposes of taxing chargeable gains; as regards the latter, the normal identification rules are disapplied. The rules below apply to securities as they apply to shares.

Where shares comprised in the holding have been acquired on different days, a disposal is identified with acquisitions on a first in/first out basis. In matching the shares disposed of with shares acquired on a particular day, shares to which relief is attributable, and which have been held continuously since issue, are treated as being disposed of *after* any other shares included in the holding and acquired on that day. If, on a reorganisation of share capital (e.g. a scrip issue), a new holding falls, by virtue of *TCGA 1992, s 127* (or any other chargeable gains enactment which applies that *section* — see Tolley's Capital Gains Tax under Shares and Securities, and see also **17.22** below), to be equated with the original shares, shares comprised in the new holding are deemed for these purposes to have been acquired when the original shares were acquired.

[*ITA 2007, ss 377, 382(2); TCGA 1992, s 151BA*].

Excessive repayments of loan capital

[17.17] Where the investment consists of a loan, and the 'average capital balance' for the third, fourth or final year of the five-year investment period (see **17.1** above) is less than the 'permitted balance' for the year in question (other than by an amount of 'insignificant value'), any relief attributable to the investment (see **17.14** above), for any tax year, is withdrawn. See **17.12** above for consequences of withdrawal.

For these purposes, the '*average capital balance*' of the loan for any period of time is the mean of the daily balances of capital outstanding during that period, disregarding any 'non-standard repayments' made in that period or at any earlier time. The '*permitted balance*' of the loan is as follows:

- for the third year of the five-year investment period, 75% of the average capital balance for the six months beginning eighteen months after the investment date;
- for the fourth year, 50% of that balance; and
- for the final year, 25% of that balance.

For these purposes, an amount is of '*insignificant value*' if it does not exceed £1,000 or if it is insignificant in relation to the average capital balance for whichever year of the five-year investment period is under consideration.

'Non-standard repayments' are repayments made:

- at the choice or discretion of the CDFI and not under any obligation under the loan agreement; or
- as a consequence of certain standard commercial default provisions in the loan agreement.

[*ITA 2007, s 362*].

Value received by investor — loans

[17.18] Where the investment consists of a loan, and the investor 'receives value' (see **17.20** below), other than an amount of 'insignificant value', from the CDFI during the 'six-year period', the investor is treated as having received a repayment equal to the amount of value received. This may have consequences for **17.4** above (determination of invested amount) and **17.17** above (withdrawal of relief where excessive repayments made). Where the value is received in the first or second year of the 'six-year period', the repayment is treated as made at the beginning of that second year. Where the value is received in a later year, the repayment is treated as made at the beginning of the year in question. The repayment is not treated as a 'non-standard repayment' for the purposes of **17.17** above.

For these purposes, an amount is of '*insignificant value*' if it does not exceed £1,000 or if it is insignificant in relation to the 'average capital balance' for the year of the 'six-year period' in which the value is received (treating any value received in the first year as received at the beginning of the second). There are provisions to aggregate a receipt of value, whether insignificant or not, with amounts of insignificant value received previously, and treating that aggregate, if it is not itself an amount of insignificant value, as an amount of value received at the time of the latest actual receipt. The '*average capital balance*' of the loan for any year is the mean of the daily balances of capital outstanding during that year, disregarding the receipt of value in question.

[*ITA 2007, ss 363, 365*].

The '*six-year period*' is the period of six years beginning one year before the investment date. [*ITA 2007, s 359(3)*].

These provisions apply equally to receipts of value by and from persons connected (within **19** CONNECTED PERSONS), at any time in the period of restriction, with the investor or, as the case may be, the CDFI. [*ITA 2007, s 370*]. See **17.20** below for the meaning of 'value received' and the determination of the *amount* of value received.

Value received by investor — securities or shares

[17.19] Where the investment consists of securities or shares, and the following circumstances are present, any relief attributable (see **17.14** above) to the 'continuing investment' (see (b) below), for any tax year, is withdrawn. See **17.12** above for consequences of withdrawal. The circumstances are that:

(a) the investor 'receives value' (see **17.20** below), other than an amount of 'insignificant value', from the CDFI during the 'six-year period' (defined as in **17.18** above);
(b) the investment or a part of it has been continuously held (and see **17.25** below) by the investor (as sole beneficial owner) since the investment was made (the '*continuing investment*'); and
(c) the receipt wholly or partly exceeds the permitted level of receipts (see below) in respect of the continuing investment (other than by an amount of 'insignificant value').

The permitted level of receipts is exceeded where:

(i) any value is received by the investor (disregarding any amounts of 'insignificant value') in the first three years of the 'six-year period'; or
(ii) the aggregate value received by the investor (disregarding any amounts of 'insignificant value') exceeds,
   - before the beginning of the fifth year of the 'six-year period', 25% of the amount subscribed for the securities or shares comprising the continuing investment;
   - before the beginning of the final year of that period, 50% of that amount;
   - before the end of that period, 75% of that amount.

Where a receipt of value in (a) above is not an amount of 'insignificant value' but is nevertheless insufficient to trigger any withdrawal of relief under the above rules, any tax relief subsequently due is computed as if the amount subscribed for the securities or shares comprising the continuing investment (and thus the invested amount at **17.4** above) were reduced by the amount of value received. This restriction applies for tax years ending on or after the anniversary of the investment date falling immediately before (or coinciding with) the receipt of value.

For the above purposes, an amount is of '*insignificant value*' if it does not exceed £1,000 or if it is insignificant in relation to the amount subscribed by the investor for the securities or shares comprising the continuing investment. There are provisions to aggregate a receipt of value, whether insignificant or not, with amounts of insignificant value received previously, and treating that aggregate, if it is not itself an amount of insignificant value, as an amount of value received at the time of the latest actual receipt.

[*ITA 2007, ss 364, 365, 369*].

These provisions apply equally to receipts of value by and from persons connected (within **19** CONNECTED PERSONS), at any time in the 'six-year period', with the investor or, as the case may be, the CDFI. [*ITA 2007, s 370*]. See **17.20** below for the meaning of 'value received' and the determination of the *amount* of value received.

Meaning of, and amount of, value received

[17.20] For the purposes of **17.18** and **17.19** above, the investor '*receives value*' from the CDFI at any time when the CDFI (and see **17.18**, **17.19** above *re* connected persons):

(a) repays, redeems or repurchases any securities or shares included in the investment;
(b) releases or waives any liability of the investor to the CDFI (which it is deemed to have done if discharge of the liability is twelve months or more overdue) or discharges (or agrees to discharge) any liability of the investor to a third party;
(c) makes a loan or advance to the investor which has not been repaid in full before the investment is made; for this purpose a loan includes any debt incurred, other than an ordinary trade debt (as defined), and any debt due to a third party which is assigned to the CDFI;
(d) provides a benefit or facility for the investor, or for any associates (as defined) of the investor — except in circumstances such that, if a *payment* had been made of equal value, it would have been a 'qualifying payment';
(e) disposes of an asset to the investor for no consideration or for consideration less than market value (as defined), or acquires an asset from the investor for consideration exceeding market value; or
(f) makes a payment to the investor other than a 'qualifying payment'.

References above to a debt or liability do not include one which would be discharged by making a 'qualifying payment'. References to a payment or disposal include one made indirectly to, or to the order of, or for the benefit of, the person in question.

Each of the following is a '*qualifying payment*':

- a reasonable (in relation to their market value) payment for any goods, services or facilities provided by the investor in the course of trade or otherwise;
- the payment of interest at no more than a reasonable commercial rate on money lent;
- the payment of a dividend or other distribution which represents no more than a normal return on investment;
- a payment to acquire an asset at no more than its market value;
- a payment not exceeding a reasonable and commercial rent for property occupied;
- a payment discharging an 'ordinary trade debt' (as defined).

The amount of value received is:

- in a case within (a) above, the amount received;
- in a case within (b) above, the amount of the liability;
- in a case within (c) above, the amount of the loan etc. less any amount repaid before the making of the investment;
- in a case within (d) above, the cost to the CDFI (net of any consideration given for it by the investor or his associate) of providing the benefit etc.;
- in a case within (e) above, the difference between market value and the consideration received (if any); and
- in a case within (f) above, the amount of the payment.

[*ITA 2007, ss 366, 367, 381, 382(3)*].

Value received where more than one investment

[17.21] Where the investor makes more than one investment in the CDFI for which he is eligible for, and claims, relief, any value received (other than value within **17.20**(a) above) is apportioned between the investments by reference to the average capital balances of loans and the amounts subscribed for securities or shares. [*ITA 2007, s 368*].

Company restructuring

Reorganisations of share capital

[17.22] The following apply where the CDFI is a company and the investment consists of shares or, in the case of **17.23** below, shares or securities.

Rights issues etc.

Where:

- a reorganisation (within *TCGA 1992, s 126*) involves an allotment of shares or debentures in respect of, and in proportion to, an existing holding of shares of the same class in the CDFI held by the investor in a single capacity;
- community investment tax relief is attributable (see **17.14** above) to the shares in the existing holding or to the allotted shares; and

- if the relief is attributable to the shares in the existing holding, those shares have been held continuously (and see **17.25** below) by the investor since they were issued,

the share reorganisation rules of *TCGA 1992, ss 127–130* are disapplied. The effect is that the allotted shares are treated as a separate holding acquired at the time of the reorganisation. This does not, however, apply in the case of bonus shares where these are issued in respect of shares comprised in the existing holding and are of the same class and carry the same rights as those shares. (For *TCGA 1992, ss 126–130*, see Tolley's Capital Gains Tax under Shares and Securities.)

Reorganisation involving issue of QCB

If, in a case otherwise within *TCGA 1992, s 116(10)* (see Tolley's Capital Gains Tax under Qualifying Corporate Bonds):

- the old asset consists of shares to which community investment tax relief is attributable (see **17.14** above) and which have been held continuously (see **17.25** below) by the investor since they were issued; and
- the new asset consists of a qualifying corporate bond,

the usual treatment is disapplied. The effect is that the investor is deemed to have disposed of the shares at the time of the reorganisation, and the resulting chargeable gain or allowable loss crystallises *at that time*.

[*TCGA 1992, s 151BB*].

Company reconstructions

[17.23] *TCGA 1992, s 135* (exchange of securities for those in another company) and *s 136* (schemes of reconstruction involving issue of securities), which normally equate the new holding with the original shares, are disapplied in the following circumstances:

- an investor holds shares in or debentures of a company (company A);
- community investment tax relief is attributable (see **17.14** above) to those shares;
- those shares have been held continuously (see **17.25** below) by the investor since they were issued; and
- there is a reconstruction whereby another company issues shares or debentures in exchange for, or in respect of, company A shares or debentures.

The result is that the transaction is treated, both for the purposes of this chapter and for the purposes of taxing chargeable gains, as a disposal of the original securities or shares (and an acquisition of a new holding). (For *TCGA 1992, ss 135, 136*, see Tolley's Capital Gains Tax under Shares and Securities.)

[*TCGA 1992, s 151BC*].

Accreditation and tax relief certificates

Accreditation

[17.24] A body may apply to the Department for Business, Energy and Industrial Strategy for accreditation as a CDFI. The body's principal objective must be to provide (directly or indirectly) finance, or finance and access to business advice, for enterprises for disadvantaged communities. The latter term includes enterprises located in disadvantaged areas and enterprises owned or operated by, or designed to serve, members of disadvantaged groups. The body must also satisfy such other criteria asare specified in Treasury regulations. Any such regulations may distinguish between 'wholesale' CDFIs, i.e. those whose objective is to finance other, generally smaller, CDFIs, and 'retail' CDFIs, i.e. those whose objective is to invest directly in enterprises. The terms and conditions of accreditation are also set by regulations; these may include a right of appeal against a refusal to accredit, and provision for the withdrawal of an accreditation, and the possible imposition of penalties, in consequence of any breach of terms and conditions. An accreditation normally has effect for three years. A new accreditation may, if the CDFI so claims, displace an existing accreditation. [*ITA 2007, ss 340–343; SI 2003 No 96*].

Tax relief certificates

Before an investment in a CDFI can qualify for tax relief, the CDFI must issue to the investor a tax relief certificate (see **17.3**, **17.7**(b) above) in a specified form. In relation to an accreditation period, a CDFI may issue tax relief certificates in respect of investments made in it within that period of an aggregate value of up to £20 million in the case of a wholesale CDFI (see above) or £10 million in the case of a retail CDFI. The Treasury may substitute other figures by order but not so as to reduce them for periods beginning before the order takes effect. Any tax relief certificate issued in contravention of these limits is invalid (and thus the investment in question does not satisfy **17.7**(b) above and does not attract tax relief). A CDFI is liable to a penalty of up to £3,000 for the issue of a tax relief certificate made fraudulently or negligently. [*ITA 2007, s 348*].

Community investment tax relief — miscellaneous

Circumstances in which investment not held 'continuously'

[17.25] An investor is not treated for the purposes of this chapter as having held an investment (or a part of an investment) continuously throughout a period if:

- under any provision of *TCGA 1992*, the investment (or part) has been deemed to be disposed of and immediately reacquired by the investor at any time in that period; or
- there has been at any time in that period a transaction treated, by virtue of **17.23** above (company reconstructions etc.), as a disposal by the investor.

[*ITA 2007, s 380*].

Nominees and bare trustees

[17.26] For the purposes of this chapter, actions of a person's nominee or bare trustee in relation to loans, shares or securities are treated as actions of that person. [*ITA 2007, s 375*].

Disclosure of information

[17.27] There are provisions for the exchange of information between the Secretary of State and HMRC in so far as this is necessary to enable them both to discharge their functions appertaining to community investment tax relief. Information thus obtained cannot be further disclosed except for the purposes of legal proceedings arising out of those functions. [*ITA 2007, s 374*].

Alternative finance arrangements

[17.28] The provisions described in this chapter apply as if references to a loan included references to arrangements falling within **3.2** (alternative finance return — purchase and re-sale), **3.7** (profit share return — deposit) or **3.8** (profit share return — agency) ALTERNATIVE FINANCE ARRANGEMENTS and as if references to interest included references to alternative finance return or profit share return as appropriate. [*ITA 2007, ss 372A–372D*]. *ITA 2007, ss 372B–372D* set out the mechanics of how the provisions have effect in relation to each of those types of arrangement.

18

Compensation for Loss of Employment (and Damages)

Cross-references. See **75.56** TRADING INCOME ('Compensation, Damages etc. — Receipts') and **75.55** ('Compensation, Damages etc. — Payments') for treatment in relation to trading profits and **75.69** for allowability of payments to employees; **28.71** EMPLOYMENT INCOME for Redundancy Payments, **28.73** for Restrictive Covenants, **28.82** for certain payments to MPs etc. and **28.95** for payments in lieu of notice.

Simon's Taxes. See **E4.8.**

Introduction to compensation for loss of employment

[18.1] The following paragraphs apply to lump sums paid on termination of an office or employment and, at **18.11** below, to the reduction of an award for damages by reference to the tax liability. The statutory exemption for the first £30,000 of a termination payment is covered at **18.3–18.10** below.

In determining the correct treatment for tax purposes of a sum receivable by a director or employee on termination of his office or employment, it is first necessary to see whether it is taxable as employment income under the rules for taxing general earnings (see **28.1** EMPLOYMENT INCOME). See **18.2** below for an outline of the principles to be applied. If it is within the general rules, it is taxable in full under PAYE (**53**) at the time of the payment.

If it is not within the general earnings rules, such a sum will generally be taxable as employment income by virtue of, and in accordance with, the special provisions in *ITEPA 2003, ss 401–416*. See **18.3–18.9** below for the application of these provisions, and **18.10** below for exemptions.

The income tax treatment of termination payments is amended with effect for 2018/19 onwards. There are also changes to the national insurance treatment of termination payments. Whether or not they are entitled to a contractual payment in lieu of notice, employees pay tax and Class 1 NICs on the amount of basic pay that they would have received if they had worked their notice in ful (see **18.6** below). For 2020/21 onwards, employers will pay Class 1A NICs on the excess of a termination payment over the £30,000 exemption threshold (see **18.4** below).

Compensation for termination of office or employment — general tax law

[18.2] The following principles apply in determining whether a sum received in compensation for termination of office or employment is taxable under the general earnings rules in **28 EMPLOYMENT INCOME**. See **18.3** *et seq.* below as regards such payments not within these rules.

A payment made to a director or employee by way of reward for services, past, present or future, is within the general earnings rules. It was considered by the Revenue that this could include any termination payment received under the terms of a contract of service, or where there was an expectation of receiving such a payment firm enough to allow the payment to be viewed as part of the reward for services. In *Mairs v Haughey* HL 1993, 66 TC 273, however, it was held that a non-statutory redundancy payment would not be within the general earnings charge, being compensation for the employee's not being able to receive emoluments from the employment rather than emoluments from the employment itself. (The case concerned a payment for the waiver of a contingent right to such a payment, which was to be accorded the same tax treatment.) Following the decision in *Mairs v Haughey*, the Revenue published Statement of Practice SP 1/94. This acknowledges that lump sum payments under a non-statutory redundancy scheme are liable to income tax only under what are now *ITEPA 2003, ss 401–416*), provided that they are genuinely made solely on account of redundancy as defined in *Employment Rights Act 1996, s 139*, whether the scheme is a standing scheme forming part of the conditions of service or an *ad hoc* scheme devised to meet a particular situation. SP 1/94 indicates, however, that the Revenue is concerned to distinguish payments which are in reality terminal bonuses or other reward for services, which are fully taxable under the general earnings rules, and that in view of the often complex arrangements for redundancy, and the need to consider each scheme on its own facts, employers may submit proposed schemes (together with any explanatory letter to be sent to employees) to the inspector for advance clearance. (HMRC SP 1/94).

The following decided cases reflect the different approaches the courts have adopted in relation to such compensation. Proper compensation for loss of office is usually exempt from the charge on earnings (see *Clayton v Lavender* Ch D 1965, 42 TC 607) except where payable under service agreement (see *Dale v De Soissons* CA 1950, 32 TC 118) or under rights conferred by company's articles (*Henry v Foster* CA 1932, 16 TC 605). But an agreed sum payable for waiving such rights was held not chargeable (*Hunter v Dewhurst*

HL 1932, 16 TC 605), as also a payment in lieu of agreed pension (*Wales v Tilley* HL 1943, 25 TC 136). Payment in settlement of claim re breach of service contract also exempt from charge (*Du Cros v Ryall* KB 1935, 19 TC 444), but cf. *Carter v Wadman* CA 1946, 28 TC 41 and *Richardson v Delaney* Ch D 2001, 74 TC 167. Voluntary payments on retirement held to be personal testimonials and not taxable (*Cowan v Seymour* CA 1919, 7 TC 372; *Mulvey v Coffey* HC(I) 2 ITC 239). But voluntary payments of £30,000 each made to the former directors of a family company the day after their resignation and retirement and minuted as being 'in appreciation of [their] services to the company over many years' were held by a Special Commissioner to be for services rendered and chargeable to tax as general earnings (*Allum v Marsh* (Sp C 446), [2005] SSCD 191).

An ex gratia payment of £150,000 to compensate a director for the benefits she was giving up as a result of her resignation for the good of the company were held not to be chargeable as general earnings (*Resolute Management Services Ltd v HMRC; Haderlein v HMRC* (Sp C 710), [2008] SSCD 1202). A transfer fee paid by his old club to a professional footballer held to be assessable under general earnings rules and not as a termination payment (*Shilton v Wilmshurst* HL 1991, 64 TC 78). A payment of £600,000 paid to an employee on leaving was held to be in respect of a threatened claim for race discrimination and not taxable either under general earnings rules or as a termination payment; the FTT focused on the reason for the payment and not how it was made up (*Mr A v HMRC* FTT (TC 4381), [2015] SFTD 678).

Sums paid on cessation of office in lieu of future income were held not to be chargeable as general earnings in *Duff v Barlow* KB 1941, 23 TC 633; *Carter v Wadman* CA 1946, 28 TC 41; and *Clayton v Lavender* Ch D 1965, 42 TC 607 (in which a decision against the taxpayer in *Hofman v Wadman* KB 1946, 27 TC 192 was not followed). Consideration for the abandonment of contracted rights was held not to be taxable remuneration in *Henley v Murray* CA 1950, 31 TC 351. In *Tottenham Hotspur v HMRC* UT 2017, [2018] STC 81; [2017] UKUT 453 (TCC), sums paid by mutual agreement on termination of contract (where there was no breach of contract) were similarly held not to be chargeable as earnings; the UT distinguished between cases where the entire contract of employment is abrogated in exchange for the termination payment (as in this case and *Henley* above) and those where the payment is made in pursuance of a pre-existing obligation to make such a payment arising under a contract of employment.

The following items paid during continuance of office were held to be chargeable: agreed sum paid to director to remain in office (*Prendergast v Cameron* HL 1940, 23 TC 122); for surrender of rights to fees or commission (*Leeland v Boarland* KB 1945, 27 TC 71; *Wilson v Daniels* KB 1943, 25 TC 473; *Bolam v Muller* KB 1947, 28 TC 471 and *McGregor v Randall* Ch D 1984, 58 TC 110); and for accepting lower fees (*Wales v Tilley* HL 1943, 25 TC 136). See also *Williams v Simmonds* Ch D 1981, 55 TC 17.

Statutory redundancy payments under *Employment Rights Act 1996* (or NI equivalent) are otherwise exempt from tax (see *ITEPA 2003, s 309*) but must be taken into account for the purposes of the special legislation in *ITEPA 2003, ss 401–416*. A proposed supplementary redundancy payment which, following a change in circumstances, was made to all employees whether or not made redundant, was held to be assessable under the general earnings rules where made to employees not made redundant (*Allan v CIR; Cullen v CIR* CS 1994, 66 TC 681). However, in *Mimtec Ltd v CIR* (Sp C 277), [2001] SSCD 101 a Special Commissioner held that certain payments made following redundancy negotiations 'in recognition of any entitlements under the consultation process including pay in lieu of notice etc.' were not taxable as earnings.

See **28.95** EMPLOYMENT INCOME for the Revenue view of payments in lieu of notice.

Sum paid as compensation for loss of benefit under an abandoned refuse salvage scheme held assessable (*Holland v Geoghegan* Ch D 1972, 48 TC 482).

See **4.29** ANTI-AVOIDANCE regarding capital sums received in lieu of earnings.

See generally HMRC Employment Income Manual EIM12800 *et seq*.

Termination payments and benefits — special provisions

[18.3] The general position in **18.2** above is subject to the special provisions in *ITEPA 2003, ss 401–416* (see **18.4–18.10** below). See generally HMRC Employment Income Manual EIM13000 *et seq*.

For the interaction of these provisions and *Gourley* principles (see **18.11** below) see *Stewart v Glentaggart Ltd* CS 1963, 42 ATC 318; *Bold v Brough* QB, [1963] 3 AER 849 and *Parsons v BNM Laboratories Ltd* CA, [1963] 2 AER 658.

Simon's Taxes. See **E4.802F, F4.802BA, E4.802BB, E4.802BB, E4.841C, E4.824.**

Termination payments and benefits — the charge to tax

[18.4] Payments and other 'benefits' within the special provisions referred to at **18.3** above are chargeable to tax as employment income if *and to the extent that* they amount in aggregate to more than £30,000. See **18.5–18.9** below as to whether payments are within the special provisions. The charge is for the tax year in which the payment or benefit is received. For these purposes, a cash benefit is treated as received when payment is made (including any payment on account) or when the recipient becomes entitled to require such payment. A non-cash benefit is treated as received when it is used or enjoyed. See **18.10** below for exemptions from charge.

The charge is on the employee or, in the event of his death, on his personal representatives. The amount chargeable is treated as the highest part of the employee's total income for the year (apart from life assurance gains subject to top-slicing relief). The legislation does not allow the chargeable amount to be reduced by reference to share options forfeited on termination of employment (*Sjumarken v HMRC* UT, [2017] STC 239).

A payment or benefit within the special provisions is 'taxable specific income', which means that the charge is not dependent on the employee's residence or domicile status. See **28.1** EMPLOYMENT INCOME and also *Nichols v Gibson* CA 1996, 68 TC 611.

Meaning of 'benefit'

A '*benefit*' includes anything which would be taxable earnings from the office or employment (or would be charged to tax as such) if received for performance of the duties thereof. However, a right to receive payments or benefits is not itself regarded as a benefit. A benefit also includes anything which would be taxable earnings, if received for the performance of duties, but for the availability of an 'earnings-only exemption'. However, the following earnings-only exemptions can be disregarded:

- any benefit received in connection with a change in duties or earnings to the extent that, were it received for the performance of duties, it would fall within the exemption at **28.72** EMPLOYMENT INCOME (exempt removal benefits and expenses on relocation); and
- certain benefits received in connection with the termination of an office or employment which, were they received for the performance of duties, would fall within certain specified exemptions (see *ITEPA 2003, s 402(2)*).

An '*earnings-only exemption*' is defined in *ITEPA 2003, s 227*, but, unhelpfully, such exemptions are not listed; broadly, it is an exemption that removes a charge to tax as general earnings as opposed to a wider exemption that removes any charge to tax as employment income; this was explained in greater detail in the Explanatory Notes (on clause 227) to the Income Tax (Earnings and Pensions) Bill. See **28.63, 28.83** EMPLOYMENT INCOME for the termination-related exemptions of *ITEPA 2003, ss 310, 311* (counselling and retraining); these, for example, are not earnings-only exemptions and thus can be disregarded entirely for the purposes of these provisions.

Value of non-cash benefits

The amount of a non-cash benefit is normally its cash equivalent as determined under the benefits code (see **28.54** EMPLOYMENT INCOME) as applied, with the necessary modifications (including a modified version of the rules for valuing the benefit of living accommodation) by *ITEPA 2003, s 415*. If, however, a greater figure would thus result, the benefit is the amount of earnings it would give rise to if received by an employee for duties of the employment (money's worth), thus bringing into charge any appreciation in the value of an asset since its acquisition by the person providing it. Where the cash equivalent of a beneficial loan (see **28.32** EMPLOYMENT INCOME) is charged under these provisions for any tax year, the taxpayer is treated as having paid interest for that year of an amount equal to that brought into charge (but not to the extent that the amount otherwise chargeable is covered by the £30,000 threshold); general principles then apply to determine whether such notional interest is allowable for tax purposes (see **42** INTEREST PAYABLE).

Application of £30,000 threshold

The £30,000 threshold is utilised against payments and benefits received in earlier tax years before those of later years. In any one tax year, the threshold (or so much of it as remains unutilised in earlier years) is set firstly against any cash benefits as they are received and any balance is set against the aggregate of non-cash benefits for the year. The threshold applies to the aggregate of payments and benefits provided in respect of the same person in respect of the same employment or of different employments with the same employer or 'associated' employers (as defined in *ITEPA 2003, s 404*) or successors.

[*ITEPA 2003, ss 402, 402A, 403, 404, 404A, 404B, 415, 416; F(No 2)A 2017, s 5(3)–(6)(10)*].

National insurance contributions

Before 6 April 2020, an amount of payments and benefits within the charge to income tax under the special provisions (disregarding the availability of the £30,000 threshold) was subject to neither employer nor employee national insurance contributions (NICs). For 2020/21 onwards, any excess over the £30,000 threshold is liable to employer Class 1A NICs, but the pre-existing exemptions for employer NICs on the first £30,000 and employee NICs on the full amount remain in place. The change in the rules does not apply to termination awards received on or after 6 April 2020 in respect of employment terminated before that date. In the case of awards received in instalments, the change does not apply to instalments received on or after 6 April 2020 if the first instalment was received before that date. [*Social Security Contributions and Benefits Act 1992, s 10(1A)–(1C)(3A)(4A); Social Security Contributions and Benefits (Northern Ireland) Act 1992, s 10(1A)–(1C)(3A)(4A); National Insurance Contributions (Termination Awards and Sporting Testimonials) Act 2019, ss 1, 2, 5; SI 2020 No 285, Reg 2*].

The above Class 1A charge on termination awards must be reported and paid to HMRC through PAYE in real time. See **53.22** PAY AS YOU EARN as regards Real Time Information (RTI) generally. There is an exception where the award consists of the benefit of the use of an asset without any transfer of ownership; in this case the Class 1A charge is payable after the year end in line with other types of Class 1A liability. [*SI 2001 No 1004, Reg 40C; SI 2020 No 300, Regs 1, 7*].

See also Tolley's National Insurance Contributions.

Miscellaneous

See **28.65** EMPLOYMENT INCOME for exemption from these provisions for payment made or benefit provided to reimburse the employee for cost of indemnity insurance or certain liabilities relating to the employment.

For MPs, see *ITEPA 2003, s 291*, and for European MPs, **28.82** EMPLOYMENT INCOME. As to whether *compensation to auditor* and others falls within these provisions, see **28.66** EMPLOYMENT INCOME.

Payments within special provisions before 2018/19

[18.5] These provisions apply to payments and other benefits which are received directly or indirectly in consideration or in consequence of, or otherwise in connection with:

(a) the termination of a person's employment;
(b) a change in the duties of a person's employment; or
(c) a change in the earnings from a person's employment.

The payment or benefit may be received by the person, or the person's spouse, civil partner, blood relative, dependant or personal representatives, or provided on the employee's behalf or to his order. A payment taxable under any other tax legislation is not within these provisions.

[*ITEPA 2003, s 401*].

Payments within special provisions for 2018/19 onwards

[18.6] For 2018/19 onwards, the special provisions referred to in **18.3** above apply to the payments and benefits described in **18.5** above, subject to additional rules, as set out below, which apply the charge to tax on general earnings to certain payments and benefits within **18.5**(a). The intended effect is that, whether or not they are entitled to a contractual payment in lieu of notice, employees will pay tax on the amount of basic pay that they would have received if they had worked their notice in full.

For the purposes of the additional rules, a '*termination award*' is a payment or other benefit to which the special provisions apply (or would apply apart from these rules) because of **18.5**(a) above. However, for the purposes of the additional rules only, a termination award does not include a statutory redundancy payment (within *ITEPA 2003, s 309* — see **18.2** above). Nor does it include so much of an approved contractual payment (as also defined by *ITEPA 2003, s 309*) as is no greater than what would have been due if a statutory redundancy payment had been made.

If the 'post-employment notice pay' (see **18.7** below) is greater than or equal to the total amount of the termination awards made in respect of the termination in question, all of those termination awards are treated as taken out of the special provisions and into the charge to tax on general earnings. This means that the exemption for the first £30,000 is lost. If the post-employment notice pay is less than the total amount of the termination awards, the amount of the post-employment notice pay is treated as taken out of the special provisions and into the charge on general earnings. The balance of the termination awards remains subject to the £30,000 exemption.

[*ITEPA 2003, ss 402A–402C; F(No 2)A 2017, s 5(3)(10)*].

See HMRC Employment Income Manual EIM13874 *et seq*.

National insurance contributions

Any amount of post-employment notice pay treated as taken out of the special provisions and into the charge on general earnings will also become subject to employer and employee Class 1 NICs.

Post-employment notice pay

[18.7] For the purposes of 18.6 above, the '*post-employment notice pay*' is given by:

$$\left(\frac{BP \times D}{P}\right) - T$$

where:

BP	=	the employee's 'basic pay' from the employment in respect of the last 'pay period' to end before the 'trigger date';
P	=	the number of days in that pay period;
D	=	the number of days in the 'post-employment notice period'; and
T	=	the total amount of any payments or benefits received in connection with the termination which are already taxable as earnings apart from these provisions, but not including any bonus payable for the termination or any pay in respect of holiday entitlement for a period before the employment ends. The purpose of deducting T in the formula is to avoid any double charge.

If the formula gives a negative amount, the post-employment notice pay is nil. 'Pay period' is not defined by statute but, in relation to a payment of earnings is taken to mean the period in respect of which the payment is made. If there is no pay period of the employee which ends before the trigger date, BP is the employee's basic pay for the period starting with the first day of the employment and ending with the trigger date, and P is the number of days in that period. Where the last pay period to end before the trigger date is a month and both the contractual 'minimum notice' and the post-employment notice period are expressed in whole months, then for simplification purposes the formula is applied by reference to months, so that P = 1, and D = the length of the post-employment notice period expressed in months.

Where the last pay period is a month and the employee's salary is paid by 12 equal monthly instalments, but the post-employment notice period is not a whole number of months (e.g. it may be expressed as a number of days or weeks), then on and after 16 October 2019 a figure of 30.42 (being 365/12) can be substituted as the value of P in the calculation where this is to the employee's advantage (HMRC Employment Income Manual EIM13886).

Where any arrangements (as widely defined) have as their purpose the avoidance of tax by causing post-employment notice pay to be less than it would otherwise be, post-employment notice pay is taken to be what it would have been without the arrangements.

Definitions

'*Basic pay*' means the employment income from the employment excluding:

- any amount received in connection with the termination of the employment;
- any amount received by way of overtime, bonus, commission, gratuity or allowance;
- any amount treated as earnings under the benefits code (see **28.21** EMPLOYMENT INCOME) (or which would be so treated were it not chargeable as general earnings — see **28.20** EMPLOYMENT INCOME);
- any amount treated as earnings under any of *ITEPA 2003, ss 221–226E* (see **28.73, 28.77, 28.79, 28.81** EMPLOYMENT INCOME, **53.14** PAY AS YOU EARN and **71.78** SHARE-RELATED EMPLOYMENT INCOME AND EXEMPTIONS);
- SHARE-RELATED EMPLOYMENT INCOME (**71**); and
- any employment-related shares (or securities) (see **71.4** SHARE-RELATED EMPLOYMENT INCOME AND EXEMPTIONS) that constitute earnings under *ITEPA 2003, s 62* (see **28.13, 28.76** EMPLOYMENT INCOME).

Any amount which the employee has given up the right to receive, but which would otherwise have fallen within the above definition, is also brought within the definition of basic pay.

if the termination is a 'notice case', the '*trigger date*' is the day on which notice is given. Otherwise it is the last day of the employment. The termination is a '*notice case*' if the employer or employee gives notice to the other to terminate the employment. It is of no consequence whether the notice is equal to the 'minimum notice' or if the employment ends before the notice expires.

The '*post-employment notice period*' is the period beginning at the end of the last day of the employment, and ending with the 'earliest lawful termination date'. (If the earliest lawful termination date is no later than the last day of the employment, the number of days in the post-employment notice period is nil.) The '*earliest lawful termination date*' is the last day of the period which is equal in length to the 'minimum notice' and begins at the end of the trigger date. A modification of this rule is applied by *ITEPA 2003, s 402E(8)–(10)* where the employment contract is a limited-term contract (as defined by *Employment Rights Act 1996, s 235(2A)*) and does not include provision for termination by notice by the employer.

'*Minimum notice*' is the minimum notice required to be given by the employer in accordance with the law and the terms of the employment contract. Where the termination is a notice case (see above) it is judged by reference to the law and contractual terms effective immediately before notice is given. In other cases, it is judged by reference to the law and contractual terms effective immediately before the employment ends or, where the employment ends by agreement entered into during the course of the employment, immediately before that agreement is entered into.

[*ITEPA 2003, ss 402D, 402E; F(No 2)A 2017, s 5(3)(10)*].

See HMRC Employment Income Manual EIM13874–13898.

Simon's Taxes. See E4.802C.

Example

[18.8]

Yujin is a monthly-paid employee on a salary of £65,000 per annum (£5,416.67 per month). On 10 April 2020, her employment is terminated. She is given three months notice as required by her employment contract, and it is agreed that she will receive £35,000 compensation. On 1 May 2020, the employer asks her to leave immediately and pays her a PILON of £12,200, which was not required under the terms of her contract. It is assumed for the purposes of the example that Yujin is not entitled to a statutory redundancy payment.

In the formula at **18.7** above:

BP	=	£5,416 (Yujin's basic pay for the last monthly pay period ended before 10 April 2020 (the trigger date)
P	=	31 (the number of days in that pay period)
D	=	69 (the number of days in the post-employment notice period, which runs from 2 May to 9 July 2020 inclusive)
T	=	Nil

		£
Post-employment notice pay	$\left(\frac{5,416 \times 69}{31}\right) - 0$	£12,055

The post-employment notice pay of £12,055 is less than the total termination awards of £47,200. Therefore, £12,055 is treated as taken out of the special provisions and into the charge on general earnings. The balance of the termination awards is £35,145, and this is taxable under the special provisions and subject to the £30,000 exemption. Therefore, £12,055 is taxable as earnings and £5,145 under the special provisions.

For NICs purposes, £12,055 is liable to employer and employee Class 1 NICs. Under the rules at **18.4** above, £5,145 is liable to employer Class 1A NICs.

Whether payments are within special provisions — case law

[18.9] Where an individual suffered constructive dismissal on grounds of discrimination, the Sp C found that the amount awarded by a tribunal was within the charge under the special provisions referred to in **18.3** above to the extent that it related to loss of income but not to the extent that it covered injury to feelings (*Walker v Adams* (Sp C 344), [2003] SSCD 269). However, in *Moorthy v HMRC* CA, [2018] STC 1028, it was decided that there was nothing in these provisions to exclude from charge non-pecuniary awards such as damages for injury to feelings. The only question was whether the payment was directly or indirectly in consideration of, in consequence of, or otherwise in connection with, the termination of a person's employment.

In another constructive dismissal case, HMRC allocated only £10,000 of a £250,000 award to 'injury to feelings', and this was upheld by the Sp C (*'A' v HMRC* (Sp C 734), [2009] SSCD 269). In *Crompton v HMRC* FTT (TC 12),

[2009] SSCD 504, the Tribunal found that on the proper interpretation of 'in connection with' in the statute, there had to be some sort of link, joint or bond between two things. In this case there was no such link between a payment of compensation and the termination of the appellant's employment, and the compensation was not taxable. For the reporting requirements in relation to taxable termination payments, see **53.21** PAY AS YOU EARN.

In *Oti-Obihara v HMRC* FTT (TC 819), [2011] SFTD 202, the Tribunal applied *Walker v Adams* above, and then apportioned a £500,000 out-of-court compensation settlement as to £165,000 for loss of office (taxable subject to the £30,000 threshold) and £335,000 for injury to feelings for discrimination (non-taxable), notwithstanding HMRC's contention, based on employment law, that compensation awards for injury feelings for discrimination should not normally exceed £25,000, even in the most serious cases. However, in *Moorthy v HMRC* above the CA held that the FTT in *Oti-Obihara* was wrong to conclude that amounts paid in connection with the termination of employment fall within the scope of the special provisions only to the extent that they represent compensation for financial losses (the £165,000 in this case).

A statutory redundancy payment under *Employment Rights Act 1996* (or NI equivalent) is specifically brought within these provisions. [*ITEPA 2003, s 309(3)*]. For the position as regards a payment under a non-statutory redundancy scheme, see **18.2** above. Payments representing 'interim relief' under *Employment Rights Act 1996, s 128* have the character of compensation payments and are subject to the £30,000 threshold (*Turullols v HMRC* FTT (TC 3795), [2014] UKFTT 672 (TC), [2014] SFTD 1099).

Compensation for unfair dismissal, in a case in which the employment tribunal also made a reinstatement order, was held to be within these provisions (and thus subject to the £30,000 threshold) notwithstanding that the effect of the reinstatement order was to treat the taxpayer as if he had never been dismissed (*Wilson v Clayton* CA 2004, 77 TC 1). In *Clinton v HMRC* FTT (TC 278), 2010 STI 487 a lump sum payment equivalent to three months' salary was held to be have been made either on an ex gratia basis or to settle the appellant's common law claim for constructive dismissal and was not a payment in lieu of notice; it was thus subject to the £30,000 threshold.

An award from a stock bonus plan, granted whilst in employment but subsequently included in a termination agreement and vesting two years after date of redundancy, was held to be within these provisions and not general earnings (*Porter v HMRC* (Sp C 501), [2005] SSCD 803).

Expenses incurred by the taxpayer in obtaining an award for unfair dismissal or securing fresh employment were held to be non-deductible (*Warnett v Jones* Ch D 1979, 53 TC 283).

A lump sum payment made as compensation for a change in contractual redundancy entitlement was held to be within these provisions in *HMRC v Colquhoun* UT, [2011] STC 394. An actual redundancy payment made some years later in respect of the same employment was within these provisions but fully taxable as the £30,000 threshold had been utilised against the earlier compensation payment.

A gratuitous payment of £150,000 held to be within these provisions was nevertheless held not to be within the term 'salaries, wages and other similar remuneration' for the purposes of the UK/USA double tax agreement, with the result that the whole payment escaped UK tax (*Resolute Management Services Ltd v HMRC; Haderlein v HMRC* (Sp C 710), [2008] SSCD 1202).

A Spanish citizen began working in 1991 for a Spanish company which was a member of an international group. In 2000 he was transferred to a UK company in the group. In 2003 his employment was terminated and he received compensation. HMRC's contention that the compensation was a contractual entitlement under the 1991 contract of employment was rejected. On the facts, the 1991 contract had terminated in 2000 and did not revive thereafter. (*Alfredo Gomez Rubio v HMRC* FTT (TC 2047), [2012] UKFTT 361 (TC), 2012 STI 2468).

Exemptions from charge

[18.10] The following are exempted from the charge under **18.4** above on termination payments and benefits (or, in the case of (vi) below, may be subject to reduction). In each case the exception (or reduction) applies equally to payments and benefits falling to be treated as general earnings by virtue of **18.6** above. See generally HMRC Employment Income Manual EIM13600 *et seq*.

(i) Payments and other benefits where termination arises from death, injury or disability of the employee or office holder. For 2017/18 onwards, it is clarified that 'injury' includes psychiatric injury but, for 2018/19 onwards, it does not include injured feelings. [*ITEPA 2003, s 406; F(No 2)A 2017, s 5(7)(10)*].
'Disability' covers not only a condition resulting from a sudden affliction but also continuing incapacity to perform the duties of an office or employment arising out of the culmination of a process of deterioration of physical or mental health caused by chronic illness. (HMRC SP 10/81). In applying this exception from charge the issue is the subjective motive for the payment by the person making it. See *Horner v Hasted* Ch D, [1995] STC 766 and *Flutter v HMRC* FTT (TC 4443), [2015] UKFTT 249 (TC) (relief refused in both cases). The CA in *Moorthy v HMRC* CA, [2018] STC 1028 decided that 'injury' included injury to feelings (but this is now overturned by statute as above).

(ii) Benefits provided before 1 December 1993, or on or after that date under retirement benefit schemes entered into before that date and not varied on or after that date, for the provision of which the employee has been charged under *ICTA 1970, s 220* or *ICTA 1988, s 595* (subsequently re-enacted as *ITEPA 2003, s 386*). [*ICTA 1988, s 188(1)(c)*].

(iii) Any payment or other benefit provided under a tax-exempt pension scheme (as defined) by way of compensation for loss of office or employment or for loss or diminution of earnings, in either case because of ill-health, or properly regarded as earned by past service. [*ITEPA 2003, s 407*].

(iv) Certain payments and other benefits (including redundancy payments/benefits and commutation of annual sums) provided to members of the armed forces. [*ITEPA 2003, s 411*].

(v) A benefit provided under a pension scheme administered by a Commonwealth government or a payment of compensation, for loss of career, interruption of service etc. in connection with constitutional change in a Commonwealth country, to a person employed in the public service of that country. [*ITEPA 2003, s 412*].

(vi) Payments and other benefits where the office or employment in question included foreign service (as defined). See below under Foreign service and note the change in the law where the date of termination is on or after 6 April 2018.

(vii) A contribution to a registered pension scheme or an employer-financed retirement benefit scheme (see respectively **57.4**, **57.34** PENSION PROVISION) to provide benefits in accordance with the scheme as part of an arrangement relating to the termination of an office or employment. [*ITEPA 2003, s 408*].

(viii) Legal costs. Where an employee takes action to recover compensation for termination of office or employment, any legal costs recovered from the employer are, subject to conditions, outside the charge at **18.4** above. The effect is that such costs are not taken into account in determining whether aggregate termination payments exceed the £30,000 tax-free limit. The rule only effectively comes into play where the aggregate of compensation plus legal costs exceeds this limit, and allows the legal costs to be treated as non-taxable. The conditions are that:

- the payment by the employer meets the whole or part of legal costs incurred by the employee exclusively in connection with the termination of his employment; and
- the payment is made pursuant to an order of a court or tribunal or, under a settlement agreement, directly to the employee's lawyer.

'Legal costs' are restricted for this purpose to fees payable for the services and disbursements of a lawyer.
[*ITEPA 2003, s 413A*].

(ix)

- Any payment received in connection with a change in duties or earnings to the extent that, were it received for the performance of duties, it would fall within the exemption at **28.72** EMPLOYMENT INCOME (exempt removal benefits and expenses on relocation); and
- any contribution made, in connection with the termination of an office or employment, to the employee's approved personal pension scheme.
- [*ITEPA 2003, s 405*].

(x) A payment or other benefit provided in the form of a lump sum under a superannuation fund to which *ICTA 1988, s 615(3)* applies (see **57.40** PENSION PROVISION). [*ITEPA 2003, s 414A*].

Foreign service

Depending on length of foreign service (as defined) in relation to total service, payments and benefits may be wholly exempted, or the amount otherwise chargeable may be proportionately reduced. This no longer applies to payments etc. on termination of employment where the date of termination is on or after **6 April 2018** and the payment etc. is received after 13 September 2017, *unless* the employee is non-UK resident for the tax year in which the employment terminates. The exemption/reduction continues to apply, regardless of UK residence status, to payments etc. within **18.5**(b) and (c) above, i.e. those in connection with a change in the duties of, or the earnings from, a person's employment. There continues to be an exemption/reduction for seafarers (as defined by *ITEPA 2003, s 384* — see **28.10** EMPLOYMENT INCOME). [*ITEPA 2003, ss 413, 414, 414B, 414C; F(No 2)A 2017, s 5(8)(10); FA 2018, s 10*].

Simon's Taxes. See **E4.802DA, E4.802F, E4.827.**

Damages — reduction for tax

[18.11] Tax liability is taken into account in fixing *damages* for injury, see *British Transport Commission v Gourley* HL 1955, 34 ATC 305. For application of *Gourley* principle see *West Suffolk CC v W Rought Ltd* HL 1956, 35 ATC 315 and contrast *Stoke-on-Trent City Council v Wood Mitchell & Co Ltd* CA 1978, [1979] STC 197 (compulsory purchase of land); *Lyndale Fashion Mfrs v Rich* CA 1972, [1973] STC 32 (tax on damages calculated as if top slice of income after expenses deducted); *In re Houghton Main Colliery* Ch D 1956, 23 ATC 320 (lump sum payable re pensions); *Stewart v Glentaggart* CS 1963, 42 ATC 318; *Parsons v BNM Labs* CA 1963, 42 ATC 200 (damages for wrongful dismissal); *McGhie & Sons v BTC* QB 1962, 41 ATC 144 (prohibition from mining under railway — cf. **75.56**(c) TRADING INCOME); and *John v James* Ch D, [1986] STC 352 (no deduction for tax paid by defendant on sums wrongfully retained or for tax plaintiff would have been liable for on these sums or on compound interest award). But cf. *Spencer v Macmillan's Trustees* CS 1958, 37 ATC 388 (breach of contract). A PAYE refund was deducted in *Hartley v Sandholme* QB, [1974] STC 434. In a case involving taxable damages paid to a large group of Lloyd's Names, it was held that the fact that certain of the Names would receive a tax benefit, due to the differential tax rates applicable to the damages and the corresponding loss reliefs, did not require a departure from the general principle that no account is to be taken of taxation where both damages and lost profits are taxable (*Deeny and others v Gooda Walker Ltd* HL 1996, 68 TC 458).

As regards whether interest on awarded damages should take account of the extent to which the damages are taxable, see *Deeny and others v Gooda Walker Ltd (in liquidation) and others (No 4)* QB, [1995] STC 696.

Simon's Taxes. See **E4.831–E4.836.**

19

Connected Persons

[*ITA 2007, ss 993, 994; CAA 2001, ss 575, 575A*]

Simon's Taxes. See **A1.156.**

[19.1] For many tax purposes, certain persons are treated as being so closely involved with each other that they must either be viewed as the same person or that transactions between them must be treated differently from transactions 'at arm's length'. These 'connected persons' are generally defined for tax purposes as below. It should, however, be noted that a modified definition may be applied in relation to any specific legislation, to which reference is made as appropriate in the text describing that legislation.

[19.2] An individual ('A') is connected with another individual ('B') if:

- A is B's spouse or civil partner;
- A is a relative of B;
- A is the spouse or civil partner of a relative of B;
- A is a relative of B's spouse or civil partner; or
- A is the spouse or civil partner of a relative of B's spouse or civil partner.

See definition of 'relative' in **19.8** below. A widow or widower is no longer a spouse (*Vestey's Exors and Vestey v CIR* HL 1949, 31 TC 1). Spouses divorced by decree nisi remain connected persons until the decree is made absolute (*Aspden v Hildesley* Ch D 1981, 55 TC 609).

[19.3] A trustee of a settlement, in his capacity as such, is connected with:

(a) any individual who is a settlor in relation to the settlement;
(b) any person connected with such an individual;
(c) any close company (see *CTA 2010, s 439* and Tolley's Corporation Tax under Close Companies) whose participators include the trustees of the settlement;
(d) any non-UK resident company which, if it were UK resident, would be a close company whose participators include the trustees of the settlement;
(e) any body corporate controlled (within *ITA 2007, s 995*) by a company within (c) or (d) above;
(f) (if the settlement is the principal settlement in relation to one or more sub-fund settlements — see **70.6** SETTLEMENTS), any trustee (in his capacity as such) of the sub-fund settlement(s); and
(g) (if the settlement is itself a sub-fund settlement), any trustee (in his capacity as such) of any other sub-fund settlements in relation to the same principal settlement.

See **19.8** below for relevant definitions.

[19.4] A partner in a partnership is connected with:

- any partner in the partnership;
- the spouse or civil partner of any individual who is a partner in the partnership; and

- a relative of any individual who is a partner in the partnership.

But none of the above applies in relation to acquisitions and disposals of partnership assets made pursuant to genuine commercial arrangements.

See **19.8** below for relevant definitions.

[19.5] A company is connected with another company if:

- the same person controls both; or
- a person has control of one company and persons connected with that person have control of the other company;
- a person ('A') has control of one company and A together with persons connected with A have control of the other company;
- the same group of persons controls both; or
- the companies are controlled by separate groups which could be regarded as the same group if (in one or more cases) a member of either group were replaced by a person with whom the member is connected.

See **19.8** below for relevant definitions.

[19.6] A company is connected with another person ('A') if:

- A has control of the company; or
- A together with persons connected with A have control of the company.

See **19.8** below for relevant definitions.

[19.7] Persons acting together to secure or exercise control of a company are treated in relation to that company as connected with each other and with any other person acting on the direction of any of them to secure or exercise such control. For the meaning of 'acting together to secure or exercise control', see *Steele v EVC International NV (formerly European Vinyls Corp (Holdings) BV)* CA 1996, 69 TC 88. Control may be 'exercised' passively. See *Floor v Davis* HL 1979, 52 TC 609.

[19.8] The following **definitions** apply for the above purposes.

'*Company*' includes any body corporate, unincorporated association or unit trust scheme (within *ITA 2007, s 1007*). It does not include a partnership.

'*Control*' is as defined by *CTA 2010, ss 450, 451* (see Tolley's Corporation Tax under Close Companies) except in **19.3**(e) above.

'*Relative*' means brother, sister, ancestor or lineal descendant.

'*Settlement*' is given its wider definition so as to include any disposition, trust, covenant, agreement, arrangement or transfer of assets, wherever made. See **70.28** SETTLEMENTS.

'*Settlor*' is as defined in **70.3** SETTLEMENTS.

In relation to a settlement that would otherwise have no trustees, it is expressly provided that '*trustee*' means any person in whom the settled property or its management is for the time being vested.

20

Construction Industry Scheme (CIS)

Simon's Taxes. See E5.5.

Introduction to CIS

[20.1] The framework of the construction industry scheme is provided for in *FA 2004*, but much of the detail is contained in regulations (see *FA 2004, ss 73, 75, 77(8)* for the principal regulation-making powers given to HMRC and the Treasury); see *SI 2005 No 2045*.

For HMRC guidance see Explanatory Booklet CIS340 Construction Industry Scheme — Guide for contractors and subcontractors. For links to other HMRC guidance on the scheme, see www.gov.uk/topic/business-tax/construc tion-industry-scheme.

Outline of the CIS

Where a contractor makes a contract payment to a sub-contractor under a construction contract, and that sub-contractor is either registered for payment under deduction (as opposed to being registered for gross payment), or is not registered at all, the contractor must make a deduction from the payment (see **20.6** below). The deduction is at 20% if the sub-contractor is registered for payment under deduction and 30% if he is unregistered. The terms 'contractor', 'contract payment', 'sub-contractor' and 'construction contract' are all defined by the legislation (see **20.2–20.6** below). The topic of registration is dealt with at **20.7–20.10** below.

It is up to the contractor to verify with HMRC the registration status of a sub-contractor (see **20.11** below). The contractor must then make periodic returns to HMRC concerning contract payments, as well as providing information about such payments to the sub-contractor (see **20.11** below).

HMRC can require in certain circumstances a security from contractors for payment of amounts due from them under the CIS — see **20.11** below.

Future development

Legislation is to be introduced in *FA 2021* to allow HMRC to reduce or deny the CIS credit claimed on sub-contractor employer returns where the sub-contractor cannot evidence the deductions and does not correct their return when asked. The legislation will also simplify the rules covering deemed contractors, clarify the rules on allowable deductions for expenditure on materials, and expand the scope of the penalty for supplying false information when registering for CIS. (Para 2.49 of overview at www.gov.uk/government/publications/budget-2020-overview-of-tax-legislation-and-rates-ootlar; see also the consultation at www.gov.uk/government/consultations/tackling-construction-industry-scheme-abuse).

Simon's Taxes. See E5.540–E5.565.

Payments from which tax must be deducted

[20.2] The scheme is concerned with payments (see **20.6** below) under a 'construction contract'. A contract of employment is specifically excluded from the definition of a construction contract, and it follows that the first question to be addressed before making any payment is whether the recipient is an employee. If so, the CIS is not in point (and the contractor will have to declare, in periodic returns to HMRC, that none of the contracts to which the return relates is a contract of employment — see **20.11** below). For the indicators of employment status, see **58.38** PERSONAL SERVICE COMPANIES ETC. and **28.66** EMPLOYMENT INCOME.

A '*construction contract*' must relate to 'construction operations' (see **20.3** below) and involve a 'sub-contractor' (see **20.4** below) and a 'contractor' (see **20.5** below).

[*FA 2004, s 57*].

Simon's Taxes. See E5.545.

Construction operations

[20.3] '*Construction operations*' include:

- construction, alteration, repair, extension, demolition or dismantling of buildings or structures, including offshore installations and temporary structures;
- construction, alteration, repair, extension or demolition of works forming part of the land, and this specifically includes walls, road-works, power-lines, electronic communications apparatus, aircraft run-ways, docks and harbours, railways, inland waterways, pipe-lines, reservoirs, water-mains, wells, sewers, industrial plant and installations for purposes of land drainage, coast protection or defence;
- installation of heating, lighting, air-conditioning, ventilation, power supply, drainage, sanitation, water supply or fire protection;

- internal cleaning if carried out during construction, alteration, repair, extension or restoration; and
- painting or decorating (internal and external).

Operations which are an integral part of, or are preparatory to, the operations in the above list are also included, for instance: site clearance, earth-moving, excavation, tunnelling and boring, laying of foundations, erection of scaffolding, site restoration, landscaping and the provision of roadways and other access works.

Specifically excluded from the definition of construction operations are:

- operations outside the UK;
- drilling for, or extraction of, oil or natural gas, and extraction of minerals;
- manufacture of building or engineering components or equipment, and delivery of these to site;
- manufacture of components for heating, ventilation etc. systems and delivery to site;
- the work of architects, surveyors and consultants;
- making, installing or repairing artistic works;
- signwriting, and erecting, installing or repairing signboards and advertisements;
- installation of seating, blinds and shutters; and
- installation of security systems and public address systems.

The Treasury may, by order, amend either of the above lists.

[*FA 2004, s 74*].

Carpet fitting is treated as outside the scope of the CIS (HMRC SP 12/81).

Simon's Taxes. See **E5.541.**

Sub-contractors

[20.4] A person is a '*sub-contactor*' if the contract imposes on him a duty to:

- carry out construction operations; or
- furnish his own labour or the labour of others in carrying out construction operations; or
- arrange for the labour of others to be furnished in carrying out construction operations.

Alternatively, a person may be a sub-contractor if, under the construction contract, he is answerable to the contractor for construction operations carried out by others (whether under a contract or other arrangements).

[*FA 2004, s 58*].

Simon's Taxes. See **E5.543.**

Contractors

[20.5] The term '*contractor*' in relation to a construction contract includes someone who is at the same time a party to that contract and a sub-contractor in another construction contract relating to any or all of the same construction operations. [*FA 2004, s 57(2)(b)*]. This would include, for instance, a gang-leader.

Other than that, the definition of a '*contractor*' may be divided into three categories.

(i) Persons who are automatically classed as contractors. These are:
   (a) any person carrying on a business which includes construction operations; and
   (b) the Secretary of State if the contract is made by him under *Housing Associations Act 1985, s 89*.

(ii) Persons carrying on a business which exceeds a set level of expenditure on construction operations. That level is:
   - £1 million per year on average over the period of three years ending at the same time as the last period of account; or
   - where the business was not being carried on at the beginning of that three-year period, £3 million over the whole of the truncated period.

   Once defined as a contractor under this category, the person is deemed to continue to be a contractor until HMRC are satisfied that expenditure on construction operations has been less than £1 million for each of three successive years beginning in or after the period of account in which contractor status was acquired. For the purposes of all these limits, where a trade is transferred from one company to another and *CTA 2010, Pt 22 Ch 1* (no change of ownership) applies, the transferor's expenditure will be treated as the transferee's, with apportionment by HMRC (subject to appeal) when only part of the trade is transferred.

(iii) Specified bodies or persons specified, provided their average annual expenditure on construction operations in any three-year period exceeds £1 million. Contractor status ceases to apply if, subsequently, there are three successive years in which expenditure on construction operations is less than £1 million. The bodies or persons specified are:
   - any public office or department of the Crown (including any NI department and any part of the Scottish Administration);
   - the Corporate Officer of the House of Lords, the Corporate Officer of the House of Commons, and the Scottish Parliamentary Corporate Body;
   - any local authority;
   - any development corporation or new town commission;
   - the Commission for the New Towns;
   - the Housing Corporation, a housing association, a housing trust, Scottish Homes, and the Northern Ireland Housing Executive;
   - any NHS trust;
   - any Health and Social Services trust.

HMRC may add to this list by means of regulations.

Under *FA 2004, s 73A* (see **24.1** DIPLOMATIC ETC. IMMUNITY), the Treasury may designate any international organisation of which the UK is a member as being outside the above definition of a contractor.

[*FA 2004, s 59*].

Simon's Taxes. See **E5.542.**

Deductions from contract payments

[20.6] Deductions on account of tax must be made from '*contract payments*'. These are defined as payments under a construction contract by the contractor to:

- a sub-contractor; or
- a nominee of the sub-contractor or the contractor; or
- a nominee of a person who is a sub-contractor under another construction contract relating to the construction operations.

Where the contractor makes a payment to a third party which discharges his obligation to pay a person within the above list, that payment is deemed to have been made directly to that person.

There are four exceptions to this definition of a contract payment:

(a) payments to agency workers treated, by virtue of *ITEPA 2003, Pt 2 Ch 7* as earnings from employment (see **28.96** EMPLOYMENT INCOME);

(b) (in relation to payments made under a construction contract on or after 6 April 2021) payments that can reasonably be taken to be for the services of an individual where the provision of those services gives rise to an engagement within the rules at **58.23–58.36** PERSONAL SERVICE COMPANIES ETC. (workers' services provided through intermediaries to public sector or to medium/large clients), but this is subject to the qualification below;

(c) payments where the recipient is registered for gross payment (see **20.7** below) when the payment is made (although this is subject to certain qualifications in the case of nominees and partnerships — see below); and

(d) payments excepted by regulations; these comprise:
   - small payments, i.e. payments made by contractors within **20.5**(i)(b), (ii) or (iii) above and approved for this purpose, in a case where the total payments under the construction contract (excluding direct cost of materials) do not, or are not likely to, exceed £1,000;
   - payments made by a contractor within **20.5**(i)(a) above, and approved for this purpose, to a body or person for work carried out on land owned by that body or person or on agricultural property (as defined) of which that body or person is a tenant, in a case where the total payments under the construction contract (excluding direct cost of materials) do not, or are not likely to, exceed £1,000;

- reverse premiums (within the meaning of *ITTOIA 2005, s 99* — see **75.109** TRADING INCOME — as modified for this purpose);
- payments by local authority maintained schools under devolved budgets;
- payments made by contractors within **20.5**(ii) above in respect of construction operations relating to property used (as defined) in their own or in another group company's business;
- payments made by public bodies within **20.5**(i)(b) or (iii) above under a private finance transaction (as defined); and
- payments made by any body of persons or trust established for charitable purposes only.

The qualification mentioned in (b) above is that the exception does not apply if, in the case of the engagement referred to, the client (see **58.25**(a) PERSONAL SERVICE COMPANIES ETC.) is not a public authority (see **58.23**) and, for the tax year in which the payment is made, either qualifies as small (see **58.16**) or does not have a UK connection (see **58.22**).

The qualifications mentioned in (c) above (where the recipient is registered for gross payment) are as follows.

- Where the recipient is a nominee, then the nominee, the person who nominated him and the person for whose labour (or the company for whose employees' labour) the payment is made must all be registered for gross payment when the payment is made.
- Where the recipient is registered for gross payment as a partner in a firm, the exception only applies to payments in respect of the firm's business (i.e. under contracts where the firm is a sub-contractor or, where the firm has been nominated to receive payments, the person who nominated the firm is a sub-contractor and is himself registered for gross payment).
- Where a person registered for gross payment other than as a partner in a firm becomes a partner in a firm, the exception does not apply to payments in respect of the firm's business (i.e. under contracts where the firm is a sub-contractor, or, where the firm has been nominated to receive payments, the person who nominated the firm is a sub-contractor).

[*FA 2004, s 60; FA 2020, Sch 1 paras 20, 27; SI 2005 No 2045, Regs 18–24*].

Upon making a contract payment, the contractor must make a deduction on account of tax. The deductible amount is calculated by first excluding the cost of materials and any VAT charged and then applying the 'relevant percentage', which is set by Treasury order. The *maximum* relevant percentage varies in accordance with the registration status of the person for whose labour (or, in the case of companies, for whose employees' labour) the payment is made, as follows.

- If registered for payment under deduction (see **20.7** below), the relevant percentage may not exceed the basic rate of tax for the tax year in which the payment is made;
- If unregistered, the relevant percentage may not exceed the higher rate of tax for that year.

The actual relevant percentages are **20%** if the sub-contractor is registered for payment under deduction and **30%** if he is not.

The contractor must pay the amount deducted to HMRC. For the purposes of computing the contractor's taxable profits, the full amount of the contract payment (i.e. the amount paid to the sub-contractor plus the amount paid to HMRC) is allowed as a deduction (assuming the payment itself is allowable under general principles).

Where the sub-contractor is not a company, the amounts deducted from contract payments are treated as income tax paid in respect of the profits of the trade. Any excess of those amounts over the income tax liability on those profits is treated as discharging any Class 4 National Insurance contributions payable in respect of those profits.

Where the sub-contractor is a company, the treatment of the amounts deducted is to be governed by regulations. The order of set-off is firstly against payments due to HMRC, for the tax year in which the deduction is made, under the contractor's obligations as an employer or contractor (e.g. PAYE, Class 1 National Insurance contributions, deductions under the CIS) and secondly against corporation tax. Any excess is repayable to the sub-contractor.

[*FA 2004, ss 61, 62; SI 2007 No 46*].

Simon's Taxes. See **E5.545–E5.547.**

A company making contract payments to an Isle of Man company for onward payment to UK construction workers should have deducted and accounted for tax (*Island Contract Management (UK) Ltd v HMRC* UT, [2015] UKUT 472 (TCC)).

Where the recipient is a managed service company (see **47** MANAGED SERVICE COMPANIES) acting as an intermediary for the worker, the contractor must ensure that he correctly establishes the contractual relationships involved and the true nature of the services provided. The intermediary may not be a sub-contractor within **20.4** above, but a nominee of the worker, in which case it will not be sufficient that the intermediary is registered for gross payment. In order for payment to be made gross, the worker must be registered also — see the first qualification above. (HMRC Statement, 3 December 2008 at webarchive.nationalarchives.gov.uk/+/http://www.hmrc.gov.uk/news/cis-msc.htm). See also webarchive.nationalarchives.gov.uk/+/http://www.hmrc.gov.uk/news/cis-msc-faqs.htm (employment agencies or businesses placing workers in the construction sector).

Registration as a sub-contractor

[20.7] In order to be registered, an applicant must provide sufficient documents, records and information to establish, to the satisfaction of HMRC, his identity and address. If the required documents etc. have been provided, HMRC must register the applicant. If, in addition, the requirements for gross payment are met (see below) then the applicant must be registered for gross payment. There is provision for an appeal against HMRC's refusal to register for gross payment (see below). Otherwise, the applicant must be registered for payment under deduction. Once again, there is provision for an appeal against a refusal by HMRC to register.

There is a penalty of up to £3,000 for knowingly or recklessly making a statement, or supplying a document, which is false in a material particular (i.e. which contains a falsehood that is relevant to the decision regarding registration). See HMRC factsheet CC/FS41 at www.gov.uk/government/publications/compliance-checks-construction-industry-scheme-penalties-for-false-registration-ccfs41.

[*FA 2004, ss 63, 72*].

The requirements for registration for gross payment vary, depending upon whether the applicant is:

- an individual (see **20.8** below);
- a company (see **20.10** below); or
- an individual or company applying as a partner in a firm (see **20.9** below).

Details in respect of the documents, records and information to be provided to HMRC in support of an application for registration (for gross payment or for payment under deduction) are set out in regulations. [*SI 2005 No 2045, Reg 25*]. The Treasury is specifically empowered to alter, by means of an order, the conditions relating to registration for gross payment. [*FA 2004, Sch 11 para 13*].

Cancellation of registration

Failure to comply with the requirements of the CIS may result in the cancellation of a person's registration.

In the case of registration for gross payment, the conditions relating to cancellation may be divided into two by reference to the gravity of the offence. Lesser offences are if:

- at the time in question, HMRC would refuse a hypothetical application for gross payment registration;
- the person has made an incorrect return or provided incorrect information (whether as a contractor or a sub-contractor); or
- there is any failure to comply with the provisions of the CIS (whether as a contractor or a sub-contractor).

If it appears to HMRC that any of these apply, a determination may be made cancelling a person's registration with effect from 90 days after the date of notice of cancellation (see below). However, the effective date of cancellation may be delayed by an appeal (see below) to the latest of:

- the abandonment of the appeal;
- determination by the First-tier Tribunal; or
- determination by the Upper Tribunal or a court.

If gross payment registration is cancelled because of the above type of offence, the person must then be registered for payment under deduction.

More serious offences are:

- becoming registered for gross payment on the basis of false information;
- making a fraudulently incorrect return, or fraudulently providing incorrect information; or
- knowingly failing to comply with the provisions of the CIS.

HMRC must have reasonable grounds to suspect such an offence, and if so they may make a determination cancelling registration with immediate effect. HMRC then have discretion whether to register the person for payment under deduction.

On any cancellation, HMRC must, without delay, give a notice stating the reasons for the cancellation. The person whose registration is cancelled may not re-apply for gross payment registration for at least a year.

HMRC's power to make the above determinations is discretionary rather than obligatory. They are required to exercise that discretion in deciding whether to make a determination and cannot make a determination without exercising that discretion (*Scofield v HMRC* FTT (TC 1068), [2011] SFTD 560). The financial consequences of cancellation of gross payment registration are not a relevant factor to be taken into account by HMRC when deciding how to exercise their discretion (*JP Whitter (Water Well Engineers) Ltd v HMRC* SC, [2018] STC 1394).

[*FA 2004, ss 66, 67(5); SI 2005 No 2045, Reg 26*].

In the case of registration for payment under deduction, the conditions relating to cancellation (and appeal against such a decision) are governed by regulations. [*FA 2004, s 68; SI 2005 No 2045, Reg 25*].

Entering into a 'time to pay' arrangement (see **54.12** PAYMENT OF TAX) will not result in cancellation of the taxpayer's gross payment registration (www.gov.uk/what-you-must-do-as-a-cis-subcontractor/annual-review).

Appeals

An appeal may be made against the cancellation or refusal of a registration for gross payment by giving notice to HMRC within 30 days of the decision. The notice must state the reasons why the decision is believed to be unjustified. On appeal to the Appeal Tribunal, the Tribunal may review any relevant decision made in relation to registration. [*FA 2004, s 67*]. In the case of registration for payment under deduction, the conditions relating to refusal (and appeal against such a decision) are governed by regulations. [*SI 2005 No 2045, Reg 25*].

Simon's Taxes. See E5.547L, E5.550–E5.554.

Registration for gross payment — individuals

[20.8] The conditions to be satisfied by individuals comprise three tests: a business test, a turnover test, and a compliance test.

The business test

The business carried on by the individual must be carried on in the UK. It must include either carrying out 'construction operations' (see **20.3** above), or furnishing labour for construction operations, or arranging for the furnishing of labour. Finally, it must, to a substantial extent, be carried on using an account with a bank; the phrase 'to a substantial extent' is not further defined in the legislation. The evidence required to prove the satisfaction of these conditions (prescribed by *SI 2005 No 2045, Reg 27*) includes the business address, invoices, contracts or purchase orders and payment details for the construction work, the business's books and accounts and details of the business bank account, including bank statements.

The turnover test

The applicant must satisfy HMRC that the likely receipt of 'relevant payments' in the year following the application is not less than £30,000. '*Relevant payments*' means payments under contracts relating to 'construction operations' (see **20.3** above), or contracts relating to the work of individuals in the carrying out of construction operations. Payments representing the cost of materials are excluded.

The evidence required to satisfy the turnover test (prescribed by *SI 2005 No 2045, Reg 29*) comprises:

- evidence of turnover during the twelve months prior to the application (the '*qualifying period*');
- evidence of relevant payments, which may include bank statements and paid cheques;
- evidence that total relevant payments received in the qualifying period equalled or exceeded £30,000;
- documentary evidence that construction operations were carried out during the qualifying period.

An individual who does not meet the turnover test can be treated as if he did if:

- the business does not consist mainly of construction operations;
- total turnover in the year prior to making the application exceeded £30,000; and
- in the year following making the application the individual is likely to receive relevant payments in relation to construction operations which are incidental to the main business.

This is designed to cover the situation where overall turnover exceeds the threshold but relevant payments derive from an ancillary part of the business and are less than the threshold.

The compliance test

In the twelve months prior to the application (the '*qualifying period*') the individual must have complied with specified tax compliance obligations concerning payment of tax and submission of returns. Over the same period, the applicant must have supplied any requested information and accounts concerning any business of his (i.e. not just the business relating to the application). These requirements also apply to a company controlled by the applicant. Compliance must be within any required time limits or at the required time. That is to say, late compliance is no compliance at all for the purposes of this test.

The above compliance requirements are relaxed in two respects, as follows.

- There is a 'reasonable excuse' defence. This is accompanied by the usual requirement to have remedied any failure without unreasonable delay once the excuse ceased.
- There are disregards of specified compliance failures set out in regulations which are intended to make loss of gross payment status attach to quite serious combinations of defaults (see *SI 2005 No 2045, Reg 32, Table 3*). Late or non-payment of an amount due to HMRC is disregarded if the amount is less than £100. Non-submission of Real Time Information returns and other PAYE returns (other than P11D and P9D) is not regarded as a compliance failure for these purposes.

The applicant may state that he was not subject to compliance obligations, e.g. because of absence abroad, or unemployment, or being in full-time education, but must provide evidence prescribed by *SI 2005 No 2045, Regs 33, 35, 36*. In the case of absence abroad, the applicant must also provide prescribed evidence of compliance with comparable obligations under the tax laws of the country in which he was living (see *SI 2005 No 2045, Reg 34*).

The applicant must have paid any national insurance contributions as they fell due. This is not subject to the 'reasonable excuse' defence.

Finally, there must be reason to expect that the applicant will continue to comply with compliance obligations and requests for documents etc., and continue to pay his National Insurance contributions, after the qualifying period.

[*FA 2004, s 64(2), Sch 11 paras 1–4, 13–16; SI 2005 No 2045, Regs 27–29, 31–37*].

Unusually, in *Mutch v HMRC*, FTT (TC 232), [2009] UKFTT 288 (TC), the Tribunal accepted insufficiency of funds as a reasonable excuse for compliance failures. Difficulty balancing childcare with full-time work during school holidays was accepted as a reasonable excuse in *Cormac Construction Ltd v HMRC* FTT (TC 315), [2009] UKFTT 380 (TC). A tribunal has no discretion to take the impact of a loss of gross payment status into account as it cannot consider proportionality, having regard to the decision in *Barnes v Hilton Main Construction* Ch D, [2005] STC 1532. The 'exceptional and extraordinary trading conditions' a company faced in a recession, coupled with the 'unhelpful banking environment' which prevailed during the period under review, were together accepted as a reasonable excuse for compliance failures, though the Tribunal emphasised that the decision should not be seen as providing a 'blanket excuse' for sub-contractors generally (*Prior Roofing Ltd v HMRC*, FTT (TC 246), [2009] UKFTT 302 (TC). Cash flow difficulties at a time of unprecedented national financial crisis were accepted as a reasonable excuse in *Connaught Contracts v HMRC* FTT (TC 798), [2010] UKFTT 545 (TC).

Simon's Taxes. See E5.551.

Registration for gross payment — partners

[20.9] An individual applying for gross payment as a partner in a firm must first meet the compliance test for individuals (see **20.8** above). A company applying for gross payment as a partner in a firm must first meet all the tests applicable to companies (see **20.10** below). In addition, the firm itself must meet the following business, turnover and compliance tests.

The business test

The test for a firm's business is the same as that for a business carried on by an individual (see **20.8** above).

The turnover test

The partners must satisfy HMRC that the likely receipt of 'relevant payments' (see **20.8** above) in the year following the application is not less than a threshold figure. The threshold is the smaller of:

- £100,000; and
- the 'multiple turnover threshold'.

The '*multiple turnover threshold*' is obtained by adding together:

(i) an amount found by multiplying the number of individuals in the partnership by the £30,000 turnover threshold for individuals (see **20.8** above); and
(ii) in respect of each company (if any) in the partnership, the threshold that would obtain were the company to be applying in its own behalf (see **20.10** below).

In calculating the figure in (ii) above, there is disregarded any company whose only shareholders are other companies that are limited by shares and registered for gross payment.

The evidence required to satisfy the turnover test (prescribed by *SI 2005 No 2045, Reg 29*) is similar to the evidence prescribed for individuals as in **20.8** above but by reference to the above turnover threshold. Where the number of partners has fluctuated over the course of the qualifying period, the threshold is computed by reference to the greatest number of partners at any one time during that period. In a case where this evidence cannot be supplied because the business is new, the following evidence may be given instead, but only in relation to one application for registration for gross payment:

- evidence of relevant payments, which may include bank statements and paid cheques;

- evidence of turnover of partners during the qualifying period; and
- evidence of construction contracts entered into by the firm including payment schedules where the aggregate value of these contracts exceeds £100,000 and payments have been made of at least £30,000.

In similar circumstances as for individuals (see **20.8** above), a firm that does not meet the turnover test may be treated as if it did.

The compliance test

Each of the partners at the time of the application must, during the qualifying period (i.e. the twelve months prior to the application), have complied with tax compliance obligations (as in **20.8** above) in relation to any income tax or corporation tax charge which was computed by reference to the firm's business. Over the same period, each partner must have supplied all requested information and accounts concerning the firm's business or his share of the profits of that business. Compliance must be within any required time limits or at the required time.

There are similar 'reasonable excuse' and regulatory relaxations as for individuals (see **20.8** above). There must be reason to expect that, following the qualifying period, each of the persons who are from time to time partners in the firm will continue the record of compliance.

The compliance test does not need to be met if one or more of the partners are already registered for gross payment, as an individual or as a partner in another firm, and that partner (or those partners together) have a right to at least half the assets or half the income of the applicant firm.

[*FA 2004, s 64(3), Sch 11 paras 5–8, 8A, 13–16; SI 2005 No 2045, Regs 27–37*].

Simon's Taxes. See **E5.551.**

Registration for gross payment — companies

[20.10] In order to register for gross payment, a company must pass the business, turnover and compliance tests described below.

In addition to those tests, HMRC may make a direction applying the conditions relating to individuals (see **20.8** above) to the directors of the company. If the company is a close company, this is extended to include the beneficial owners of shares. Rather than apply all the conditions to all of the directors or shareholders, the direction may specify which conditions are to apply, and to which directors or shareholders. In particular, HMRC may make such a direction where there has been a change in control of a company that either is, or is applying to be, registered for gross payment. HMRC are empowered to make regulations requiring the submission of information concerning changes in control of such companies. [*FA 2004, ss 64(5), 65*].

The business test

The test for a company's business is the same as that for a business carried on by an individual (see **20.8** above).

The turnover test

A company may pass this test in either of two ways:

- satisfying HMRC that its only shareholders are companies limited by shares and registered for gross payment; or
- providing HMRC with evidence that 'relevant payments' (see **20.8** above) received in the year following the application are likely to equal or exceed a set threshold.

The set threshold is the smaller of:

(i) an amount found by multiplying the number of 'relevant persons' in relation to the company by the £30,000 turnover threshold for individuals (see **20.8** above); and
(ii) £100,000.

For a close company, a '*relevant person*' for the purposes of (i) above is a director or a beneficial owner of shares; for other companies, the definition is limited to a director. 'Director' is defined by reference to *ITEPA 2003, s 67*.

The evidence required to satisfy the turnover test (prescribed by *SI 2005 No 2045, Reg 29*) is similar to the evidence prescribed for individuals as in **20.8** above but by reference to the above set threshold. Where the number of relevant persons has fluctuated over the course of the qualifying period, the threshold is computed by reference to the greatest number of relevant persons at any one time during that period. In a case where this evidence cannot be supplied because the business is new, the following evidence may be given instead, but only in relation to one application for registration for gross payment:

- evidence of relevant payments, which may include bank statements and paid cheques;
- evidence of turnover of relevant persons during the qualifying period;
- evidence of construction contracts entered into by the company including payment schedules where the aggregate value of these contracts exceeds £100,000 and payments have been made of at least £30,000; and
- where the business was transferred from another person, firm or company, similar evidence in relation to the transferor as would otherwise be required from the applicant in relation to the business, together with evidence that the transferor would have passed the compliance test at the date of transfer.

In similar circumstances as for individuals (see **20.8** above), a company that does not meet the turnover test may be treated as if it did.

The compliance test

The provisions relating to companies mirror those relating to individuals (see **20.8** above). However, in addition to this a company must have complied with specified *Companies Acts* obligations during the qualifying period. Where a member of a joint venture company is already registered for gross payment, the company does not need to satisfy the compliance test if the member owns at least 50% of its share capital or voting power.

[*FA 2004, s 64(4), Sch 11 paras 9–12, 12A, 13–16; SI 2005 No 2045, Regs 27–37*].

Simon's Taxes. See E5.551.

CIS procedures and administration

[20.11] Detailed procedures and administrative arrangements for the operation of the scheme are contained in *SI 2005 No 2045*. There are detailed provisions governing verification by contractors of sub-contractors' registration status, monthly returns by contractors, payments and recovery of tax deducted, electronic communications and methods of payment, and HMRC powers to inspect records. See **20.12** below for the late filing penalty for returns.

Multiple contractors

A contractor may elect to be treated as different contractors in relation to different groups of sub-contractors. The election must be made (or revoked) by notice to an officer of HMRC before the beginning of the tax year for which it is to have effect. There are special provisions which apply where a contractor acquires the business of another contractor. [*SI 2005 No 2045, Reg 3*].

Verification of status of sub-contractors

Anyone making contract payments must verify with HMRC the registration status of the recipient, which, for 2017/18 onwards with minor exceptions, must be done electronically. HMRC will confirm whether the payment should be made gross or under deduction. Verification is not necessary if the recipient has been included in the contractor's returns (see below) in the current or previous two tax years. Where the contractor is a company, the return could be one made by another company in the same group and, where a multiple contractors election has been made (see above), the return could be one made in relation to a different group of sub-contractors. If the contractor acquired the contract under which the payment is to be made in a transfer of a business as a going concern and the transferor satisfied these conditions, the contractor does not need to verify if he has notified HMRC of the transfer. HMRC must notify a contractor if a person registered for gross payment becomes registered for payment under deduction, or vice versa, or if a registered person has ceased to be registered. Once a person has been verified or notified as being registered (whether for gross payment or payment under deduction) the contractor is entitled to assume that the person has not subsequently ceased to be so registered. [*FA 2004, s 69; SI 2005 No 2045, Reg 6; SI 2016 No 348*].

HMRC automatically notify affected contractors when a sub-contractor changes status.

Monthly returns by contractors

There are detailed provisions for monthly returns by contractors of payments made to sub-contractors. A contractor must make monthly returns to HMRC within 14 days after the end of every tax month and written information must also be provided to sub-contractors who are registered for payment under deduction or who are not registered. There is no statutory obligation to make a nil return where applicable, but HMRC encourage contractors to make voluntary nil returns. Contractors' monthly returns are subject to the late filing penalty at **20.12** below. Subject to minor exceptions, returns must be made electronically. [*FA 2004, ss 70, 76, Sch 12 paras 7, 8; SI 2005 No 2045, Reg 4*].

Scheme representative

A contractor company may appoint another company in the same group ('a scheme representative') to act on its behalf in relation to the requirement to make a return or other such requirements under the regulations. [*SI 2005 No 2045, Reg 5*].

Collection and recovery of sums deducted

The arrangements for accounting for tax deductions, late payment and repayment interest and penalties for late in-year payments broadly follow those for PAYE (see **53.24, 53.24** PAY AS YOU EARN and HMRC Explanatory Booklet CIS340 referred to at **20.1** above). However, Real Time Information (see **53.24** PAY AS YOU EARN) does not apply to the CIS. There are detailed provisions governing methods of payment, including electronic payment. [*FA 2004, s 71; FA 2009, Sch 56; SI 2005 No 2045, Regs 7, 7A, 8–17, 44–49, 58, 59; SI 2020 No 240, Reg 4*].

In an appeal against determinations made by HMRC under *SI 2005/2045, Reg 13*, in relation to amounts which should have been deducted from payments made to sub-contractors, it was held that amounts could not be excluded from the determinations on the grounds that the sub-contractors had included them in their self-assessment tax returns (*Ormandi v HMRC* FTT (TC 7442), [2019] UKFTT 667 (TC)).

Security for payments to HMRC

With effect on and after **6 April 2019**, HMRC can require in certain circumstances a security from contractors for amounts due from them under the CIS. Failure to provide a security by the required date is a criminal offence punishable in England and Wales by a fine, and in Scotland and NI by a fine not exceeding level 5 on the standard scale (i.e. £5,000 under *Criminal Justice Act 1982, s 37*). The requirement to provide a security is restricted to circumstances where an HMRC officer considers it necessary for the protection of the revenue. *SI 2005 No 2045, Reg 17C* lists the persons from whom security may be required (which includes, for example, the contractor, the directors of the contractor if it is a company and the members of the contractor if it is a partnership), and provides that liability to give security is joint and several in cases where it is required from more than one person. The date by which security is required is delayed if, before the security is due to be provided, the contractor makes a request to HMRC to enter into a 'time to pay' arrangement. The detailed provisions are similar to those at **53.20** PAY AS YOU EARN (security for payment of PAYE). In line with those provisions, it is likely that HMRC will accept security only in the form of an electronic payment to a specified HMRC bank account, a cheque or banker's draft or a guarantee in the form of a performance bond authorised and approved by a financial institution. [*FA 2004, s 70A; FA 2019, s 82; SI 2005 No 2045, Regs 17A–17K; SI 2019 No 384*].

Simon's Taxes. See **E5.542A–E5.542D, E5.546A–E5.547K, E5.555–E5.565.**

Late filing penalty

[20.12] The late filing penalty relates to the monthly returns to be made by contractors of payments made to sub-contractors (see **20.11** above). An initial penalty of £100 is payable for failure to make a return on or before the filing date. A further penalty of £200 is payable where the contractor's failure to make the return continues after the end of two months beginning with the day on which the initial penalty is triggered; this is the day after the filing date and is known as the '*penalty date*'.

If the failure continues after the end of a six-month period beginning with the penalty date, the contractor is liable to a penalty equal to the *greater* of £300 and 5% of any liability to make tax payments which would have been shown in the return in question.

A second tax-geared penalty is payable if the failure continues after the end of a twelve-month period beginning with the penalty date. The amount of this second penalty depends on whether or not, by failing to make the return, the contractor is deliberately withholding information that would enable or assist HMRC to assess the tax due, as shown below.

	Penalty is the *greater* of		
	Fixed amount	and	% of liability
Deliberate and concealed withholding of information	£3,000		100%
Deliberate but not concealed withholding of information	£1,500		70%
In any other case	£300		5%

If the failure continues after the end of a twelve-month period beginning with the penalty date and the information required in the return relates only to persons registered for gross payment, the two higher penalties in the table above apply (by reference to the fixed amounts only) if, by failing to make the return, the contractor is deliberately withholding information which relates to such persons.

For the first return that a contractor makes (together with any return with an earlier filing date than that return), the total fixed penalties (£100 and £200) cannot exceed an upper limit of £3,000. Also, where a tax-geared penalty arises that would otherwise be the greater of £300 and 5% of the payments due, it is instead 5% of the payments due.

For the above purposes, the withholding of information by a contractor is concealed if the contractor makes arrangements to conceal that it has been withheld.

The same rules apply as under **55.5** PENALTIES as regards reasonable excuse, reduction for disclosure, reduction in special circumstances, reduction for other penalties and double jeopardy. The same rules apply as regards assessment of penalties and appeals against penalty assessments as for other penalties under *FA 2009, Sch 55* — see respectively **55.25** and **55.26** PENALTIES.

[*FA 2009, Sch 55 paras 1, 7–13, 27*].

Late payment interest (see **43.2** LATE PAYMENT INTEREST AND PENALTIES) is chargeable on late paid penalties, and REPAYMENT INTEREST (**62**) arises on overpaid penalties

Simon's Taxes. See **E5.547L.**

21

Coronavirus (COVID-19)

Introduction to Coronavirus (COVID-19)

[21.1] '*Coronavirus*' is statutorily defined as severe acute respiratory syndrome coronavirus 2 (SARS-CoV-2), and '*coronavirus disease*' as COVID-19 (the official designation of the disease caused by coronavirus). [*Coronavirus Act 2020, s 1; FA 2020, s 106(5)*]. As is common, this publication uses the term 'COVID-19' to embrace both coronavirus and coronavirus disease.

In response to the COVID-19 pandemic, the UK Government began to impose lockdown and social distancing measures on 16 March 2020. This meant that a great many businesses were unable to continue operating. Over the succeeding weeks and months, a number of coronavirus support schemes were introduced to relieve the impact of the pandemic. These included, in particular, the Coronavirus Job Retention Scheme (CJRS) under which employers can furlough employees and apply for Government funding to cover a proportion of their pay (see www.gov.uk/guidance/claim-for-wage-costs-through-the-coronavirus-job-retention-scheme), and the Self-Employment Income Support Scheme (SEISS) under which the self-employed can claim a Government grant based on a percentage of average monthly trading profits (see www.gov.uk/guidance/claim-a-grant-through-the-coronavirus-covid-19-self-employment-income-support-scheme). There are also various coronavirus business support grant schemes, a non-exclusive list of which is given at **21.2**.

Although full lockdown was lifted on 4 July 2020, a number of businesses were still unable to operate, and those that were able could operate only with the imposition of restrictions based on a continuing need for social distancing and hygiene measures.

FA 2020, s 106, Sch 16 confirms that coronavirus support payments made to businesses/employers are within the scope of tax as income, and sets out the rules for applying this (see **21.2–21.6**). It also imposes a charge to income tax (see **21.7–21.10**) on a recipient of certain coronavirus support payments who was not entitled to the payment in accordance with the scheme under which it was made, which includes the case where a payment under the CJRS is not used for the purposes for which it was made.

A number of tax measures have also been taken, by primary or secondary legislation or by concession, to relieve the impact of the COVID-19 pandemic. To the extent that these relate to income tax, they are covered throughout this publication wherever appropriate, and a signpost to that coverage is provided at **21.11**.

Taxation of coronavirus support payments

[21.2] For the purposes of the provisions on taxation of coronavirus support payments in *FA 2020, s 106, Sch 16*, a '*coronavirus support payment*' means a payment made (whether before or after Royal Assent to *FA 2020*) under any of the following schemes:

(a) the coronavirus job retention scheme (CJRS);
(b) the self-employment income support scheme (SEISS);
(c) any other scheme that is the subject of a Treasury direction given under *Coronavirus Act 2020, s 76* (HMRC functions in relation to COVID-19);
(d) the coronavirus statutory sick pay rebate scheme;
(e) a coronavirus business support grant scheme (see below);
(f) any other scheme that may be specified or described in Treasury regulations under these provisions.

Items (a) and (d) are referred to collectively as '*employment-related schemes*'.

The Treasury can make regulations further providing about the application of the taxation of coronavirus support payments provisions to a scheme within (c)–(f) above; any such provision may have retrospective effect.

A coronavirus business support grant scheme in (e) above is any scheme (whenever announced), other than a scheme within (a) to (d), under which a public authority makes grants to businesses with the object of providing support to those businesses in connection with any effect or anticipated effect (direct or indirect) of COVID-19. Examples of such schemes (as at 24 June 2020) include:

- the small business grant fund (SBGF) (www.gov.uk/guidance/check-if-youre-eligible-for-the-coronavirus-small-business-grant-fund);
- the retail, hospitality and leisure grant fund (RHLGF) (www.gov.uk/guidance/check-if-youre-eligible-for-the-coronavirus-retail-hospitality-and-leisure-grant-fund);
- the local authority discretionary grants fund (www.gov.uk/guidance/apply-for-the-coronavirus-local-authority-discretionary-grants-fund;
- any scheme corresponding to any of those above in Scotland, Wales and Northern Ireland.

[*FA 2020, s 106*].

For the purposes of the taxation of coronavirus support payments provisions, a business means a trade, profession or vocation, a UK or overseas property business or a business consisting wholly or partly of the making of investments. [*FA 2020, Sch 16 para 1(6)*].

Taxation of support payments referable to a business

[21.3] The following applies if a person carrying on a business (see **21.2** above), either alone or in partnership, receives a coronavirus support payment (see **21.2**) that is referable to the business. So much of the support payment as is referable to the business is a receipt of a revenue nature for income tax or corporation tax purposes and is to be brought into account in calculating the profits of that business for tax purposes. If an amount of the support payment is referable to more than one business or business activity, the amount is to be allocated between those businesses or activities on a just and reasonable basis.

If the recipient of a coronavirus support payment is a person who used to carry on a business, so much (if any) of the payment as is referable to the business but which is not referable to activities of the business undertaken while it was being carried on by the recipient is to be treated for income tax purposes as follows instead of as above:

- an amount referable to a trade, profession or vocation is to be treated as a post-cessation receipt (see **59.1** POST-CESSATION RECEIPTS AND EXPENDITURE); and
- an amount referable to a UK property business or an overseas property business is to be treated (in either case) as a post-cessation receipt from a UK property business (see **60.16** PROPERTY INCOME, which applies the post-cessation receipts rules for trades to UK property businesses).

In any case not within the above, the recipient of the support payment is to be treated as if carrying on, at the time of receipt of the amount, the business to which the amount is referable. That amount is to be treated as if it were referable to activities undertaken by the business at that time, and is thus brought into account under the main rule above. Where the recipient incurred expenses that are referable to that payment and would be deductible in calculating the profits of the business if it were being carried on at the time of receipt of that payment, those expenses are deductible from that payment; but this does not apply to expenses arising directly or indirectly from the person's ceasing to carry on business.

The Treasury may by regulations modify the application of any tax legislation that affects (or would otherwise affect) the treatment of receipts brought into account under the main rule above or as post-cessation receipts.

[*FA 2020, Sch 16 paras 1, 2, 7*].

Payments under employment-related schemes

An amount of a coronavirus support payment made under an employment-related scheme (see **21.2** above) is referable to the business of the person entitled to the payment as an employer (even if the person is not for other purposes the employer of the employees to whom the payment relates). For the CJRS, this will be the PAYE employer. It is not referable to any other business. No deduction for the employment costs which are the subject of the support payment is allowed in calculating the profits of any other business or in calculating the liability of any other person to tax on post-cessation receipts. [*FA 2020, Sch 16 para 3(1)*].

Payments under the SEISS

An amount of a coronavirus support payment made under the SEISS is referable to the business of the individual to whom the payment relates. The whole of the amount brought into account in calculating the profits of that business is treated as a revenue receipt of the tax year 2020/21 (irrespective of the date of receipt and in which period of account it falls); this does not apply to an SEISS payment made in respect of a partner of a firm if the amount is distributed amongst the partners, rather than being retained by the partner.

Where an SEISS payment is made in respect of a partner of a firm and is retained by the partner, rather than being distributed amongst the partners, it is not to be treated as a receipt of the partnership. Accordingly, the receipt is not to be included in the calculation of partnership profits for the purposes of determining each partner's share of profits or losses, but is instead to be added to the profit share of the partner who retained it.

[*FA 2020, Sch 16 para 3(2)–(6)*].

Charge where no business carried on

[21.4] Income Tax is charged on a coronavirus support payment, other than a payment made under an employment-related scheme (see **21.2** above) or the SEISS, if:

- the payment is neither brought into account, as in **21.3** above, in calculating profits nor treated as a post-cessation receipt; and
- at the time the support payment was received, the recipient did not carry on a business whose profits are charged to income tax or corporation tax and to which the payment could be referable.

The person liable for the tax is the recipient of the support payment. For the purposes of applying the exemption for trading and miscellaneous income of charities in **14.7** CHARITIES AND CHARITABLE GIVING, the amount chargeable is treated as if it were chargeable to income tax under a provision listed in *ITA 2007, s 1016*.

The Treasury may by regulations modify the application of any tax legislation that affects (or would otherwise affect) the treatment of amounts charged under the above rule.

[*FA 2020, Sch 16 paras 6, 7*].

Charge where employment costs deductible by another

[21.5] Income tax is charged on a coronavirus support payment made under an employment-related scheme (see **21.2** above) if:

- the support payment is neither brought into account, as in **21.3** above, in calculating the profits of a business carried on by the person (P) entitled to the payment as an employer nor treated as a post-cessation receipt arising from the carrying on of such a business; and
- expenses incurred by another person (Q) in respect of the employment costs which are the subject of the support payment and to which the payment relates are deductible in calculating, for income tax or corporation tax purposes, the profits of a business carried on by Q or in calculating post-cessation receipts of Q.

The person liable for the tax charged is P.

The Treasury may by regulations modify the application of any tax legislation that affects (or would otherwise affect) the treatment of amounts charged under the above rule.

[*FA 2020, Sch 16 paras 5, 7*].

Interaction with other income tax provisions

[21.6] Some rules are required on how the tax treatment receipt of a coronavirus support payment interacts with some pre-existing income tax rules. These are set out below.

Trading allowance

The trading allowance (see **75.3** TRADING INCOME) is not available to an individual in respect of a coronavirus support payment made under the SEISS and brought into account as trading profits. However, the support payment does not count towards 'relevant income' for the purposes of that allowance. [*FA 2020, Sch 16 para 4(4)(5)*].

Pre-trading expenditure

No relief is given for pre-trading expenditure (see **75.106** TRADING INCOME) consisting of employment costs where a coronavirus support payment made under an employment-related scheme (see **21.2** above) relates to those costs. This applies equally when applying the pre-trading expenditure provisions to property businesses (see **60.5**, **60.10** PROPERTY INCOME). [*FA 2020, Sch 16 para 4(6)*].

Mutual trading

A coronavirus support payment that relates only to mutual activities of a business that carries on a mutual trade (see **75.38** TRADING INCOME) is to be treated as if it were income arising from those activities, and accordingly the payment is not taxable. [*FA 2020, Sch 16 para 4(1)*].

Charities

A coronavirus support payment is to be ignored when applying the resources condition at **14.7** CHARITIES AND CHARITABLE GIVING (exemption for small trades and miscellaneous income and gains). [*FA 2020, Sch 16 para 4(2)*].

Recovery of coronavirus support payments

[21.7] A recipient of a coronavirus support payment is liable to income tax if the recipient is not entitled to the payment in accordance with the scheme under which it was made. This does not apply to payment made under a coronavirus business support grant scheme or the coronavirus statutory sick pay rebate scheme. The reference to a person not being entitled to the payment includes, in the case of a payment made under the CJRS, a case where the person ceases to be entitled to retain the amount after it was received, either because of a change of circumstances or because the person has not, within a reasonable period, used the amount to pay the costs which it was intended to reimburse. Note that the charge is to income tax even if the recipient is a company.

The amount of income tax chargeable is equal to so much of the support payment as the recipient is not entitled to and has not been repaid.

The time at which tax becomes chargeable is generally the time the coronavirus support payment is received. In the case where a person was entitled to the a payment under the CJRS but subsequently ceases to be entitled to retain it, the time at which tax becomes chargeable is the time the person ceases to be entitled to retain the payment.

In applying the above charge, a partnership is not regarded as receiving a coronavirus support payment made under the SEISS in respect of a partner if the payment is retained by the partner, as opposed to its being distributed amongst the partners.

Where income tax chargeable as above is the subject of an assessment, the rules at **21.3–21.6** above do not apply to the amount of the coronavirus support payment that gives rise to the assessment. The amount on which the tax is charged does not count as the taxpayer's income for tax purposes, and is thus excluded from Step 1 of the calculation of income tax liability at **1.10** ALLOWANCES AND TAX RATES. For a person within the charge to income tax, the tax chargeable is added at Step 7 of the calculation of liability. No loss, deficit, expense or allowance may be taken into account in calculating, or may be deducted from or set off against, any amount of income tax charged as above.

[*FA 2020, Sch 16 paras 8, 10(1)*].

Assessment of income tax

[21.8] If an HMRC officer considers (whether or not on the basis of information or documents obtained by virtue of the exercise of **HMRC** INVESTIGATORY POWERS (**39**) under *FA 2008, Sch 36*) that a person has received a coronavirus support payment to which the person is not entitled, the officer may make an assessment of the income tax which ought in the officer's opinion to be charged under **21.7** above. The normal and extended time limits at **6.2** and **6.3** assessments apply to the making of such assessments. The provisions of *TMA 1970* as to assessments, appeals, payment of tax and recovery of tax unpaid apply to such assessments. Payment is thus due within 30 days after the date on which the notice of assessment is made (by virtue of *TMA 1970, s 59B(6)* — see **54.1** PAYMENT OF TAX).

Where income tax is chargeable under **21.7** above in relation to a coronavirus support payment received by a partnership:

- an assessment may be made on any of the partners in respect of the total amount of tax thus chargeable on the partnership;
- each of the partners is jointly and severally liable for the tax assessed; and
- if the total amount of tax chargeable is included in a self-assessment tax return made by one of the partners, the other partners are not required to include the tax in their own tax return.

[*FA 2020, Sch 16 para 9*].

Notification of chargeability

[21.9] The provisions of *TMA 1970, s 7* for notifying chargeability to income tax (see **55.2** PENALTIES) apply in relation to income tax chargeable under **21.7** above with the following modifications:

- the fact that a person may have received a notice to file a self-assessment tax return does not relieve them of the requirement to notify chargeability; and
- the period in which notification must be given (the '*notification period*') is the period of 90 days commencing on the day on which the income tax became chargeable (see **21.7** above), except that the period cannot end any earlier than 20 October 2020 (the 90th day after the date of Royal Assent to *FA 2020*).

In relation to income tax chargeable under **21.7** above in relation to a coronavirus support payment received by a partnership, the duty to notify chargeability is taken to have been complied with by each of the partners if complied with by one of the partners.

Where the time limit for raising an assessment would otherwise be extended to 20 years, due specifically to a failure to notify chargeability (see **6.3** ASSESSMENTS), this applies to income tax chargeable under **21.7** above only if the person knew at the time the tax first became chargeable that they were not entitled to the coronavirus support payment (and see also below under Penalty for failure to notify).

[*FA 2020, Sch 16 para 12*].

Penalty for failure to notify

The penalty provisions of *FA 2008, Sch 41* for failure to notify chargeability to income tax (see **55.3** PENALTIES) apply in relation to income tax chargeable under **21.7** above. In determining potential lost revenue for this purpose, the tax year for which the income tax is payable is that in which the income tax became chargeable. [*FA 2020, Sch 16 para 10(2)*].

Where a recipient of a coronavirus support payment knew at the time the tax became chargeable (see **21.7**) that they were not entitled to the payment, the failure is to be treated as deliberate and concealed, so that the penalty is 100%

of the potential lost revenue. The potential lost revenue is treated in such a case as being the amount of income tax which would have been assessable on the person concerned at the end of the last day of the 'notification period' (see above). [*FA 2020, Sch 16 para 13*].

Partnerships

Where the failure to notify chargeability is by a member of a partnership that received the coronavirus support payment in question, each partner is taken to know anything that any of the other partners knows. Where a partner would otherwise be liable to a penalty under *FA 2008, Sch 41*, the partner is instead jointly and severally liable with the other partners to a single penalty under those provisions for the failures by each of them to notify. In a case outside *FA 2020, Sch 16 para 13* above, if the failure of at least one of the partners was deliberate and concealed, the single penalty is treated as a penalty for a deliberate and concealed failure. If the failure of at least one of the partners was deliberate but not concealed, the single penalty is treated as a penalty for a deliberate but not concealed failure. The potential lost revenue is treated as being the amount of income tax which would have been assessable on any one of the partners:

- in a case within *FA 2020, Sch 16 para 13*, at the end of the last day of the notification period; and
- in a case not within *FA 2020, Sch 16 para 13*, at the end of 31 January following the tax year in which the coronavirus support payment was received by the partnership.

The normal rule whereby a member of a limited liability partnership can be held liable to pay a portion of the failure to notify penalty (see **55.3** PENALTIES) does not apply in this case.

[*FA 2020, Sch 16 para 14*].

Liability of officers of insolvent companies

[21.10] There is provision for an individual to be held jointly and severally liable for a liability of a company to income tax charged under **21.7** above. This applies where the company is subject to an insolvency procedure or there is a serious possibility of the company becoming subject to such a procedure. There must be also be a serious possibility that some or all of the income tax liability will not be paid by the company. There is a further condition that the individual was responsible for the management of the company at the time the income tax became chargeable and that the individual knew at that time that the company was not entitled to the coronavirus support payment in relation to which the income tax is chargeable. An individual is responsible for the management of a company if the individual is a director or shadow director or is concerned (directly or indirectly) in, or takes part in, the management of the company. Where the conditions are met, an officer of HMRC can give notice of liability to the individual. Among other things, the notice must offer the individual a review of the decision to give the notice and inform the individual of their right of appeal to the First-tier Tribunal. An individual who is given such a notice is jointly and severally liable with the company (and with any other individual who is given such a notice) to the amount of the income tax liability specified in the notice. [*FA 2020, Sch 16 para 15*].

Signpost to COVID-19 income tax coverage

[21.11] A number of tax measures have been taken, by primary or secondary legislation or by concession, to relieve the impact of the 2020 COVID-19 (coronavirus) pandemic. To the extent that these relate to income tax, they are covered throughout this publication wherever appropriate, and a signpost to that coverage is provided below. The measures are listed here in the order in which they appear in this work.

Paragraph	*Brief description of measure*
5.4	**Appeals.** An extra three months is given to appeal against an assessment or HMRC decision.
5.10	**Appeal hearings.** The First-tier Tribunal published guidance on 5 June 2020 on the services it was currently providing and the practicalities of litigation in the Tribunal 'at the present time and in the coming months'.
5.11	**Appeal hearings.** For the duration of the pandemic, the First-tier Tribunal may in some circumstances make a decision which disposes of proceedings without a hearing.
5.18	**Appeal hearings.** For the duration of the pandemic, the First-tier Tribunal may direct that proceedings be conducted wholly or partly as video or audio proceedings.
5.29	**Appeal hearings.** For the duration of the pandemic, the Upper Tribunal may direct that proceedings be conducted wholly or partly as video or audio proceedings.
26.10	**Disguised remuneration.** If an employee car ownership scheme loan has to be extended in circumstances arising from the pandemic, but not beyond a term of four years, HMRC accept that this does not give rise to a tax charge under the disguised remuneration rules.
28.14	**Salary sacrifice arrangements.** An arrangement is not regarded as being varied if the variation is directly in connection with COVID-19 and no more than that.

28.15	**Homeworkers.** Where employers have required their employees to work from home for a limited period of time as a result of a temporary closure of the business premises during the pandemic, HMRC accept that for the duration of that period the definition of 'homeworker employee' would be met and the related tax exemption is available. HMRC have published guidance as to which expenses are taxable if an employee works from home due to the pandemic.
28.15	**Home office equipment expenses.** There is no charge to tax for an amount reimbursed to an employee on or after 16 March 2020 and before 6 April 2021 in respect of home office equipment expenses (as defined).
28.17	**Qualifying travelling expenses: living accommodation.** Tax relief is available for employees who are provided with living accommodation by their employer when working at a temporary workplace because of the pandemic.
28.17	**Qualifying travelling expenses: ordinary commuting and private travel.** Where, due to the pandemic, an employee became furloughed or required to work from home at a time when they were travelling to a temporary workplace, the period of furlough or working from home is part of the period of continuous work
28.24	**Company cars.** A link is provided to HMRC guidance on company car availability and unavailability where an employee is furloughed or working from home due to the pandemic.
28.26	**Company car fuel benefit charge.** HMRC have advised that where the cost of fuel for volunteer mileage related to the pandemic is funded by the employer, this should not be taken into account for the purposes of the car fuel benefit charge.
28.50	**Miscellaneous employment-related benefits: PPE.** Where an employer provides personal protective equipment (PPE) to employees working in a situation where the risk of COVID-19 transmission is very high, and the employer's risk assessment shows that PPE is required, its provision is non-taxable. The same applies if the employer reimburses the expenses of employees who purchase the PPE themselves.
28.50	**Miscellaneous employment-related benefits: COVID-19 tests.** The Chancellor has stated that the Government is to introduce an income tax exemption for COVID-19 antigen tests provided by employers, which would otherwise have resulted in a taxable benefit on the employee.

30.27 **Lifetime ISAs.** The 5% penalty charge does not apply to withdrawals made during the period 6 March 2020 to 5 April 2021 inclusive. The total charge is thus reduced from 25% to 20% of the withdrawn amount.

35.16 **EU disclosure rules for cross-border tax arrangements (DAC 6).** The first UK reporting deadlines are deferred by six months.

43.5 **Waiver of late payment interest.** Subject to the making of a Treasury order after Royal Assent to *FA 2020*, HMRC's powers to waive interest in cases of national disaster or emergency are extended. For example, no interest will arise from the deferral of the second self-assessment payment on account for 2019/20 (see below at **67.5**).

53.25 **PAYE settlement agreements (PSAs).** Expenses and benefits related to COVID-19 can be reported on a PSA.

53.49 **PAYE: short-term business visitors.** Due to the pandemic, HMRC extended the deadline for 2019/20 returns and payment under the special PAYE arrangement for short-term business visitors to 31 July 2020.

55.26 **Appeals.** An extra three months is given to appeal against a penalty.

55.38 **Reasonable excuse.** HMRC will consider COVID-19 as a reasonable excuse for missing some tax obligations (such as payments or filing dates).

57.1 **Protected pension age.** After becoming entitled to their pension benefits, individuals can be re-employed by their former employer (or a connected employer) without losing the benefit of their protected pension age. The re-employment must commence during the period 1 March 2020 to 1 November 2020 inclusive, and the sole or main reason for it must be to help the employer to respond to the public health, social, economic or other effects of COVID-19.

57.35 **Employer-financed retirement benefits schemes.** NHS England and NHS Wales are paying a lump sum in respect of the deaths of NHS and social care staff which are caused by COVID-19. Any such lump sum does not count as a relevant benefit and is thus not taxable on the recipient.

63.4	**Statutory residence test.** The statutory residence test is amended by *FA 2020* with the effect that days between 1 March 2020 and 1 June 2020 inclusive spent by individuals in the UK for specified reasons connected with the detection, treatment or prevention of COVID-19 will not count towards the relevant tests.
63.8	**Statutory residence test.** A day at the end of which an individual is present in the UK due only to exceptional circumstances beyond their control that prevent their leaving the UK does not count as a day spent by the individual in the UK. A reference is provided to HMRC guidance on circumstances resulting from the impact of COVID-19 that are accepted by HMRC as being exceptional.
67.5	**Self-assessment payments on account.** Self-assessment taxpayers can choose to delay making their second payment on account for 2019/20 otherwise due on 31 July 2020. Those opting to delay will have until 31 January 2021 to make the payment.
71.28	**Share incentive plans (SIPs).** HMRC have confirmed that CJRS (Coronavirus Job Retention Scheme) payments to employees furloughed during the pandemic can constitute a salary and that SIP contributions can be deducted from CJRS payments.
71.42	**Enterprise management incentives: valuations.** Provided that there has been no change that may affect an appropriate value, enterprise management incentive valuations will remain valid for 120 days instead of the usual 90.
71.43	**Enterprise management incentives: disqualifying events.** Legislation introduced by *FA 2020* seeks to ensure that a disqualifying event does not occur purely as a result of an individual taking leave, being furloughed or working reduced hours because of the pandemic.
71.57	**SAYE option schemes.** For participants who find themselves unable to make monthly contributions from their salary, due to having to take unpaid leave during the pandemic, HMRC will permit payments to be made via standing order.
71.57	**SAYE option schemes: contributions holidays.** Where participants are unable to contribute because they are furloughed or on unpaid leave during the pandemic, HMRC will extend the normal contributions holiday terms, so that monthly contributions can be postponed in excess of 12 months where the additional months are due to COVID-19.

22

Deceased Estates

Cross-references. See **42.11** INTEREST PAYABLE and **43.7** LATE PAYMENT INTEREST AND PENALTIES.

Simon's Taxes. See **A1.431–A1.436, C4.1.**

Introduction to deceased estates

[22.1] The first part of this chapter (22.2 and 22.3) considers the liability to tax of the personal representatives of a deceased person (being either executors appointed under the will or administrators if there was no will). The next part of the chapter (22.4–22.14) examines entitlement of beneficiaries to income from deceased estates during administration: how it is computed (by reference to tax years) and how it is taxed in a beneficiary's hands. This will depend upon the type of interest a beneficiary has (an absolute interest, a limited interest or a discretionary interest) and whether the estate is a UK or foreign estate. See also the full contents list above.

The '*administration period*', in relation to the estate of a deceased person, means the period beginning with death and ending with the completion of the administration of the estate. [*ITTOIA 2005, s 653(1)*].

Liability of personal representatives

[22.2] Personal representatives of a deceased person are liable for all tax due from the deceased to the date of his death. [*TMA 1970, s 74*]. Personal allowances may be claimed in full for the year of death.

Income may be assessed and charged on (and in the name of) any one or more of the persons who, in the tax year in which the income arises, are personal representatives of the deceased person or on any subsequent personal representatives. [*TMA 1970, s 30AA*].

See **75.12, 75.17** TRADING INCOME for cessation of a business on death and **75.34** TRADING INCOME for trading (or not) by the executors. See **6.4** ASSESSMENTS for time limits for assessments. See Tolley's Capital Gains Tax for capital gains tax position on death.

Liability on estate income

[22.3] Personal representatives are also liable to income tax at the basic rate and dividend ordinary rate on estate income which they receive subsequent to the death. Dividends falling due after death are treated as the income of the estate, and not of the deceased, for all tax purposes, including exemption claims, although they accrued before the death (*Reid's Trustees v CIR* CS 1929, 14 TC 512; *CIR v Henderson's Exors* CS 1931, 16 TC 282), and the same principle applies in respect of interest payments, including bank and building society interest, falling due after the date of death. The accrued annuity to the date of death of an annuitant is income of his estate and not his income (*Bryan v Cassin* KB 1942, 24 TC 468) and similarly as to the accrued income of which he was life-tenant (*Wood v Owen* KB 1940, 23 TC 541; *Stewart's Exors v CIR* Ch D 1952, 33 TC 184).

Strictly, the personal representatives should notify HMRC that they are liable to tax on estate income no later than six months after the tax year in which they become liable (in accordance with **55.2** PENALTIES) and should file self-assessment tax returns and pay any tax due on normal self-assessment payment dates (see **67.5–67.8** SELF-ASSESSMENT). However, HMRC operate informal procedures. They will accept a single computation and one-off payment of an estate's income tax and capital gains tax liability if: (i) the total liability over the whole of the administration period is no more than £10,000; (ii) probate value is no more than £2.5 million; (iii) the proceeds of assets sold in any one tax year are no more than £500,000; and (iv) the estate is not regarded as complex, such that it can be dealt with without the personal representatives having to complete a return. (HMRC Trusts, Settlements and Estates Manual TSEM7410; HMRC Trusts and Estates Newsletter, August 2018 at www.gov.uk/government/publications/hm-revenue-and-customs-trust s-and-estates-newsletters).

Income from deceased estates during administration (estate income)

[22.4] Beneficiaries of deceased estates in administration are chargeable to tax in respect of income treated as arising from their interest in the residue of the estate (referred to in *ITTOIA 2005* as '*estate income*'). For this purpose, where different parts of an estate are subject to different residuary dispositions, those parts are treated as if they were separate estates. [*ITTOIA 2005, s 649*]. Liability under these provisions depends on the type of interest that the beneficiary has (an 'absolute interest', a 'limited interest' or a 'discretionary interest') and whether the estate is a 'UK estate' or a 'foreign estate'. See **22.5** below for definitions.

Tax certificates

A personal representative has a duty to supply a beneficiary on request with a statement of income and tax borne for a tax year. [*ITTOIA 2005, s 682A*].

Definitions

[22.5] The following definitions apply for the purposes of the provisions.

A person has an '*absolute interest*' in the whole or part of the residue of an estate if the capital of the residue (or part) is properly payable to him or would be so payable if the residue had been ascertained. A person has a '*limited interest*' in the whole or part of the residue of an estate during any period if he does not have an absolute interest and the income from the residue (or part) would be properly payable to him if it had been ascertained at the beginning of the period. A person has a '*discretionary interest*' in the whole or part of an estate if a discretion may be exercised in his favour so that any income of the residue during the whole or part of the administration period would be properly payable to him if the residue had been ascertained at the beginning of that period. For this purpose, an amount is only treated as properly payable to a person if it is properly payable to that person, or to another in his right, for his benefit (whether directly or through a trustee or other person). The personal representatives of a deceased person are treated as having an absolute or limited interest in the whole or part of the estate of another deceased person (A) if they have a right in their capacity as personal representatives and, were the right vested in them for their own benefit, they would have that interest in A's estate. [*ITTOIA 2005, s 650*].

An estate is a '*UK estate*' for a tax year if:

(i) either of the following apply:
- all of the income of the estate (disregarding any 'excepted income' — see below) has either borne UK income tax by deduction or is income in respect of which the personal representatives are directly assessable to income tax for the year; and
- none of the income of the estate (disregarding any excepted income) is income for which the personal representatives are not liable to income tax for the year by virtue of being not UK resident; or

(ii) the income of the estate for the year consists only of excepted income.

For the purposes of (i) and (ii) above, '*excepted income*' means life assurance gains and income within (c) and (d) below.

If an estate is not a UK estate for a tax year it is a '*foreign estate*' for that year.

[*ITTOIA 2005, s 651; FA 2016, Sch 1 paras 20, 73*].

The '*aggregate income*' of an estate for a tax year is the total of:

(a) income of the personal representatives in that capacity which is charged to income tax for the year, less any allowable deductions;
(b) income of the personal representatives in that capacity which would have been chargeable to income tax if it were income from a UK source of a person resident in the UK, less any deduction which would have been allowable;
(c) any stock dividends that would be chargeable on the personal representatives if such income were so chargeable (see **65.19** SAVINGS AND INVESTMENT INCOME);
(d) any amount that would be chargeable on the personal representatives on release of a loan to a participator in a close company if such amounts were so chargeable (see **65.21** SAVINGS AND INVESTMENT INCOME); and
(e) any gain from a life insurance contract that would have been treated as income of the personal representatives in that capacity if the condition for such gains to be so treated were met (see **44.3** LIFE ASSURANCE POLICIES).

Income from property devolving on the personal representatives otherwise than as assets for payment of the deceased's debts and income to which any person is or may become entitled under a specific disposition (as defined) is, however, excluded.

[*ITTOIA 2005, s 664*].

The '*residuary income*' of an estate for a tax year is the aggregate income of the estate for the year less deductions for:

- all interest paid in the year by the personal representatives in that capacity (other than interest on unpaid inheritance tax under *IHTA 1984, s 233*);
- all annual payments for the year which are properly payable out of residue;
- all expenses of management of the estate paid in the year (but only where, ignoring any specific direction in a will, properly chargeable to income); and
- any excess of allowable deductions for the previous year over the aggregate income of the estate for that year.

No deduction is allowed for any amount allowable in calculating the aggregate income of the estate.

[*ITTOIA 2005, s 666*].

For the reduction of residuary income of an estate in respect of income which accrued before the death of the deceased and which is taken into account in calculating for inheritance tax purposes the value of the estate on death, see **22.16** below.

A transfer of assets or the appropriation of assets by personal representatives to themselves is treated for the purposes of these provisions as the payment of an amount equal to the assets' value at the date of the transfer or appropriation. The set off or release of a debt is treated as the payment of amount equal to it. If at the end of the administration period there is an obligation to transfer assets to any person or the personal representatives are entitled to appropriate assets to themselves, an amount equal to the assets' value at that time is treated as payable then. If at that time there is an obligation to release or set off a debt owed by any person or the personal representatives are entitled to release or set off a debt in their own favour, a sum equal to the debt is treated as payable then. [*ITTOIA 2005, s 681*].

Grossing-up of estate income

[22.6] In the case of a UK estate, in arriving at the amount of estate income, the basic amounts treated as income of the beneficiary are 'grossed up' by the basic rate of tax or the dividend ordinary rate, depending on the type of income and the tax year in which it arose. The estate income is then treated as having borne income tax at that rate or rates. In determining the rate applicable it is assumed first that amounts are paid to beneficiaries out of the different parts of the aggregate income of the estate in such proportions as are just and reasonable for their different interests, and then that payments are made from those parts bearing tax at the basic rate before they are made from those parts bearing tax at the dividend ordinary rate.

If any of the aggregate income of the estate consists of life assurance gains, it is assumed that an amount is paid from other income in priority to that income. The above assumptions are then made separately in relation to payments out of life assurance gains and payments out of other income.

Insofar as the aggregate income of the estate consists of income within **22.5**(c) and (d) above, it is treated for grossing-up purposes as having borne income tax at 0%.

Where income consisting of life assurance gains is grossed up, no repayment of the notional tax can be made to a beneficiary. With regard to payments out of a foreign estate, grossing-up is applicable only to income in these categories.

[*ITTOIA 2005, ss 656, 657, 663, 679, 680, Sch 2 para 137; FA 2016, Sch 1 paras 21, 22, 24, 73*].

Income bearing tax at the dividend ordinary rate (see **1.5** ALLOWANCES AND TAX RATES) or at the above-mentioned 0% rate is treated in the hands of the recipient as dividend income. Where the income relates to a discretionary interest paid indirectly through a trustee and is taxable under *ITTOIA 2005, s 662* on the ultimate recipient (see **22.10** below), it is treated as dividend income of the trustee. [*ITTOIA 2005, s 680A; FA 2016, Sch 1 paras 25, 73*].

HMRC have clarified that where dividends were received by the estate before 6 April 2016 but are not paid over to the beneficiary until after that date, the beneficiary is deemed to have paid tax at 7.5% (the dividend ordinary rate for 2016/17 onwards) on the grossed-up amount of the dividend. This tax credit will be set against the beneficiary's tax liability on estate income but is a notional tax credit and thus not repayable. As regards dividends received by the estate on or after 6 April 2016 the personal representatives will pay tax on them at 7.5%, and beneficiaries will be entitled to credit for the tax paid. See HMRC Trusts Estates newsletter, December 2016 at www.gov.uk/government/publications/hm-revenue-and-customs-trusts-and-estates-newsletters.

Absolute interests

[22.7] A beneficiary with an absolute interest is chargeable to income tax on income treated as arising in a tax year from the interest if he has an 'assumed income entitlement' for the year and a payment is made in respect of the interest in the year and before the end of the administration period. For the year in which the administration period ends (the '*final tax year*'), income is treated as arising if the beneficiary has an assumed income entitlement for the year (whether or not any payments are made).

Subject to the grossing-up provisions at **22.6** above, the amount so treated as income for a tax year is the lower of the total amount of all sums paid in the year in respect of the interest and the person's assumed income entitlement for the year. For the final tax year, the amount is the person's assumed income entitlement for the year. Where, however, the residuary income of the estate for the final tax year is nil as a result of the allowable deductions exceeding the aggregate income of the estate, the amount for the year is reduced by the excess (or, where the interest is in part of the residue only, a just and reasonable part of that excess).

A person's '*assumed income entitlement*' for a tax year is the excess of the total of the person's share of the residuary income of the estate (less, in the case of a UK estate, income tax on that amount at the appropriate rate) for the year and for each previous tax year for which he held the interest over the total of the amounts (before grossing-up) relating to the interest in respect of which he was liable to tax for all previous years (or would have been liable had he been within the charge to income tax). In the case of income within **22.5**(c) and (d) above, the appropriate rate is 0%.

If the total of all sums paid during or payable at the end of the administration period in respect of the interest (grossed-up, in the case of a UK estate, at the basic rate for the tax year of payment or the final tax year) are less than the total of the beneficiary's shares of the residuary income for all years, the deficiency is applied to reduce his share of the residuary income, firstly for the final tax year, then for the previous year and so on.

[*ITTOIA 2005, ss 652, 653, 659(1), 660, 665, 667, 668, 670, Sch 2 para 136(1)(2); FA 2016, Sch 1 paras 23, 73*].

Example

[22.8]

C died on 5 July 2018 leaving his estate of £400,000 divisible equally between his three children. The income arising and administration expenses paid in the administration period which ends on 25 January 2021 are as follows.

	Period to 5.4.19		Year to 5.4.20		Period to 25.1.21	
	£	£	£	£	£	£
UK dividends		18,760		9,900		3,720
Dividend ordinary tax thereon payable by personal representatives		(1,407)		(743)		(279)
		17,353		9,157		3,441
Administration expenses chargeable to income		(1,479)		(750)		(366)
		15,874		8,407		3,075
Other income (gross)	10,000		3,200		975	
Basic rate tax thereon payable by personal representatives	(2,000)		(640)		(195)	
		8,000		2,560		780
Net income distributed		£23,874		£10,967		£3,855
Each child's share		£7,958		£3,656		£1,285

Dates and amounts of payments to *each* child are as follows.

	Payment
	£
30.4.19	5,000
16.10.19	3,500
21.6.20	2,500
22.1.21	1,000
30.7.21	899

Each child's assumed income entitlement is as follows.

	2018/19	2019/20	2020/21
	£	£	£
Cumulative income entitlement (net)	7,958	11,614	12,899
Deduct net equivalents of amounts taxed in previous years	Nil	Nil	8,500
Assumed income entitlement	£7,958	£11,614	£4,399

For all years other than the final tax year (i.e. the year in which the administration period ends), compare the assumed income entitlement with the payments made.

	2018/19	2019/20
Assumed income entitlement	£7,958	£11,614
Payments made	Nil	£8,500
Lower amount is the taxable amount (subject to grossing up)	Nil	£8,500

For the final tax year (2020/21), the taxable amount (subject to grossing up) is the amount of the assumed income entitlement (£4,399).

The children's income from the estate for tax purposes is as follows.

	2018/19	2019/20	2020/21
Each child's share of income (net)	Nil	£8,500	£4,399
		£	£
Each child's share of basic rate income	Nil	3,520*	260
Basic rate tax (20/80)	Nil	880	65
Grossed-up basic rate income	Nil	£4,400	£325

* £(8,000 + 2,560) × 1/3 = £3,520

Each child's share of dividend income	Nil	4,980	4,139
Dividend ordinary rate tax (7.5/92.5)	Nil	404	335
Grossed-up dividend income	Nil	£5,384	£4,474

Notes

(a) Each beneficiary would receive tax certificates (Forms R185 (Estate Income)) showing the gross amount of his entitlement and the tax paid by the personal representatives. Where the estate has dividend income bearing tax at the dividend ordinary rate, the tax certificate shows such income separately from income which has borne tax at the basic rate. The dividend ordinary rate is 7.5% for each of the three years illustrated.

(b) Estate income which has borne tax at the dividend ordinary rate is treated as dividend income in the hands of a beneficiary. For example, such income will attract the dividend allowance. See **22.6** above as to the notional tax credit available to beneficiaries where dividends were received by an estate before 6 April 2016 but are not paid over to a beneficiary until after that date.

(c) Payments to a beneficiary of an estate are deemed to be made out of his share of income bearing tax at the basic rate in priority to his share of income bearing tax at the dividend ordinary rate. This means that administration expenses chargeable to income are effectively relieved primarily against dividend income.

Limited interests

[22.9] Subject to the grossing up provisions at **22.6** above, sums paid (including assets transferred, debts released etc.) to a beneficiary with a limited interest *during administration* are treated as his income for the tax year of payment and are chargeable to tax accordingly. Any amount which remains payable in respect of the limited interest *on completion of administration* is treated as income of the beneficiary for the tax year in which the administration period ends. If the interest ceases earlier, any amount then remaining payable is treated as income for the tax year in which the interest ceased. [*ITTOIA 2005, ss 654, 659(1), 661*].

Discretionary interests

[22.10] The person in whose favour the discretion is exercised is charged to income tax on the total payments made in a tax year in exercise of the discretion, grossed up, where appropriate, as indicated at **22.6** above. [*ITTOIA 2005, ss 655, 659(2), 662*].

This applies whether the payments are out of income as it arises, or out of income arising to the personal representatives in earlier years and retained pending exercise of the discretion. See HMRC SP 4/93.

Foreign estates

[22.11] Where estate income arises from a foreign estate it is deemed to arise from a source outside the UK and is 'relevant foreign income' (see **32.2** FOREIGN INCOME). [*ITTOIA 2005, s 658*]. See **60** for the REMITTANCE BASIS, **32.4** FOREIGN INCOME for amounts deductible from income and **32.5** FOREIGN INCOME for relief for unremittable income.

Where income tax is charged for a tax year on estate income from a foreign estate and income tax has already been borne by part of the aggregate income of the estate for the year, the taxpayer may make a claim for the income tax charged to be reduced in accordance with the formulae in *ITTOIA 2005, ss 677, 678*. The relief is given by way of a tax reduction at Step 6 of the calculation of income tax liability at **1.10** ALLOWANCES AND TAX RATES.

Successive interests

[22.12] Special rules apply to the calculation of estate income where there are two or more successive absolute or limited interests during the period of administration. [*ITTOIA 2005, ss 671–676, Sch 2 para 136(3)–(7)*].

Adjustments, assessments etc. after the administration period

[22.13] If, after the administration period ends, it is clear that a person's liability under **22.7–22.12** above for a tax year is greater or less than previously appeared, all necessary assessments, adjustments etc. can be made. Assessments may be made or adjusted and relief may be claimed within three years after 31 January following the tax year in which administration was completed. [*ITTOIA 2005, s 682*].

Non-UK resident beneficiaries

[22.14] By concession, a beneficiary, who is not resident or not ordinarily resident in the UK, may claim to have his tax liability on income from an absolute or limited interest in a UK estate adjusted to what it would be if such income had arisen to him directly from the respective sources of residuary income. The relief or exemption must be claimed within five years and ten months of the end of the tax year in which the beneficiary is deemed to have received the income. It is dependent upon the personal representatives having made all required estate returns, paid all tax and any interest, surcharge and penalties, and keeping available for inspection any relevant tax certificates and copies of the estate accounts for all years of the administration period showing details of all sources of estate income and payments to beneficiaries. No tax will be repayable in respect of income treated as bearing income tax within *ITTOIA 2005, s 680*. (HMRC ESC A14; Revenue Press Release 1 April 1999).

However, where the beneficiary is resident in a country with which the UK has a double taxation agreement, and the 'Other Income' Article in that agreement gives sole taxing rights in respect of such income to that country, the above concession does not apply. The tax paid by the personal representatives will be repaid to the beneficiary, subject to the conditions in the Article being met. (HMRC SP 3/86).

Residence of personal representatives

[22.15] See 63.31 RESIDENCE AND DOMICILE for special provisions where personal representatives are partly UK resident and partly non-UK resident.

Relief for inheritance tax attributable to income accrued at death

[22.16] Where, on a death, income accrued at the death is treated both as capital of the estate for inheritance tax purposes and as residuary income of the estate in the hands of a beneficiary having an absolute interest in the residue, in arriving at the 'excess liability' of the beneficiary the residuary income is reduced by the grossed-up amount of the inheritance tax attributable to the excess of the accrued income over any liabilities taken into account in both valuing the estate and arriving at the residuary income. '*Excess liability*' means the excess of income tax at the higher rate, additional rate, dividend upper rate, dividend additional rate, any Scottish rate above basic rate (other than the Scottish intermediate rate) or the Welsh higher or additional rate over income tax at the basic rate or dividend ordinary rate. [*ITTOIA 2005, s 669; FA 2016, s 4(13)(18); SI 2015 No 1810, Arts 1, 10; SI 2017 No 468, Regs 1, 8; SI 2018 No 459, Arts 1, 4; SI 2019 No 201, Arts 1, 10*].

Deceased estates — miscellaneous

[22.17] Otherwise the tax position in respect of deceased estates is similar to that of settlements (or trusts as they are often called) and reference should be made to the following items under 70 SETTLEMENTS which contain details of tax cases relating to both deceased estates and settlements.

70.8	Assessments on trust income
70.17	Personal position of trustee
70.18	Income of beneficiaries
70.22	Annuities etc. out of capital
70.23	Foreign trust income

23

Deduction of Tax at Source

Cross-references. See **4.42** ANTI-AVOIDANCE re annual payments for non-taxable consideration; **20** CONSTRUCTION INDUSTRY SCHEME; **27.12** DOUBLE TAX RELIEF for reduced rate of deduction on payments abroad; **28.73** EMPLOYMENT INCOME for payments for restrictive covenants; **42** INTEREST PAYABLE; **50.11** NON-RESIDENTS for non-resident entertainers and sportsmen; **53** PAY AS YOU EARN; **57.12** PENSION PROVISION for contributions to a registered pension scheme; **60.31** PROPERTY INCOME for non-resident landlords; **65.23** SAVINGS AND INVESTMENT INCOME as regards the income element of purchased life annuities; **70.11** SETTLEMENTS for distributions from discretionary and accumulation trusts.

Simon's Taxes. See A4.4.

Introduction to deduction of tax at source

[23.1] The approach of the legislation is to set out which payments must be made under deduction of tax at source whilst providing for certain exceptions [*ITA 2007, Pt 15*]. Deduction is at the basic rate of tax in force for the year in which the payment is made (see **1.3**, **1.4** ALLOWANCES AND TAX RATES; for over-deductions and under-deductions, see **23.4** below). Collection of the tax involved is via the payer's self-assessment return or by direct assessment [*ITA 2007, ss 963, 964*]: it is identified separately from the payer's own liability to tax (see **23.18** below).

The duty to deduct income tax from a payment may be disapplied by regulations relating to double tax relief (see **27** DOUBLE TAX RELIEF). Where income is exempt from income tax it is disregarded for the purposes of deduction of tax at source. [*ITA 2007, s 849(1)(3)(5)*].

Deduction of tax at source

[23.2] A duty to deduct a sum representing income tax is imposed in relation to the following types of payment.

(a) Certain payments of yearly interest (see **23.12** below).
(b) Certain payments of UK public revenue dividends (see **23.12** below and **65.4** SAVINGS AND INVESTMENT INCOME).
(c) Certain annual payments (see **23.7–23.10** below).
(d) Certain royalty payments (see **23.14** below).
(e) Certain manufactured payments (see **4.13** ANTI-AVOIDANCE).
(f) Certain issues of funding bonds (see **65.7** SAVINGS AND INVESTMENT INCOME).
(g) Certain payments to non-residents taxable under anti-avoidance provisions relating to transactions in land and sales of occupation income where HMRC direct that a deduction should be made (see **23.9** below).

The amount deducted is treated as income tax paid by the recipient, and as such taken into account in determining the tax payable by, or repayable to, the recipient (although this rule does not apply to income tax deducted under the rules relating to visiting performers (see **50.11** NON-RESIDENTS) or non-resident landlords (see **60.31** PROPERTY INCOME)). [*ITA 2007, s 848; ITTOIA 2005, ss 602, 618, 686*].

A payment made under deduction of tax is income (equal to the grossed-up equivalent) of the tax year by reference to which the rate of tax deducted from the payment was determined, without regard to the period over which the income accrued (and see *CIR v Crawley* Ch D 1986, 59 TC 728). [*ITA 2007, s 31(2)(4); SI 2015 No 1810, Arts 1, 14(2); SI 2019 No 201, Arts 1, 12*].

There are other regimes that involve the deduction of tax at source: see especially:

(i) PAYE (see **53** PAY AS YOU EARN);
(ii) CIS (see **20** CONSTRUCTION INDUSTRY SCHEME);
(iii) visiting performers (see **50.11** NON-RESIDENTS);
(iv) non-resident landlords (see **60.31** PROPERTY INCOME);
(v) Real Estate Investment Trusts (see **60.24** PROPERTY INCOME).

Annuities from former retirement annuity contracts are within PAYE, and other deduction of tax at source rules do not apply — see **53.27** PAY AS YOU EARN. The same applies to annuities within *ITEPA 2003, s 610* (annuities under an occupational pension scheme that is not a registered pension scheme) — see **56.2**(e) PENSION INCOME.

With effect on and after 5 November 2019, it is confirmed that there is no duty to deduct tax at source from a payment charged to income tax under *ITTOIA 2005, Pt 5 Ch 2A* (offshore receipts in respect of intangible property — see Tolley's Corporation Tax under Intangible assets). [*ITA 2007, s 981A; SI 2019 No 1452, Regs 1, 15*].

Rate of tax deductible

[23.3] The rate of tax deductible is the basic rate for the year in which payment is made.

Alterations in tax rate

[23.4] Where deductions are made by reference to a tax rate greater or less than the rate subsequently fixed for the tax year:

(a) **under-deductions** in respect of any half-yearly or quarterly payments of interest, dividends or other annual payments, other than company dividends and other distributions, are charged under *ITTOIA 2005, Pt 4 Ch 2*. [*ITA 2007, s 849(2)*];

(b) **under-deductions** in respect of any rent, interest, annuity or other annual payment, any copyright royalties, public lending right payments or design royalties paid to non-residents and patent royalties may be deducted from future payments or, if none, recovered from the payee. [*ITA 2007, s 849(2)*]. See *Nesta v Wyatt* KB 1940, 19 ATC 541;

(c) **over-deductions** of tax under the deduction at source rules can generally be recovered from HMRC provided that the tax has been accounted for and no adjustment made between the parties. See *Provisional Collection of Taxes Act 1968, s 2*; and

(d) **over-deductions** of tax by a 'body corporate' on interest (not being a distribution) on its securities may be adjusted in the next payment but any repayments must be made no later than a year from the passing of the Act imposing the tax, and enure to the benefit of the person entitled at date of adjustment or repayment. [*ITA 2007, s 849(2)*].

Statement of tax deducted

[23.5] Where a person makes a payment from which a sum representing income tax must be deducted (see items (a)–(h) in **23.2** above) and if the recipient so requests, that person must provide a written statement showing the gross amount of the payment, the amount deducted and the actual amount paid. [*ITA 2007, s 975*].

A similar rule applies where a payment representing interest has been made by the Financial Services Compensation Scheme ('FSCS') and is made net of an amount equivalent to income tax (see **65.2** SAVINGS AND INVESTMENT INCOME). [*ITA 2007, s 979A(5)(6)*].

ITA 2007, s 975 above does not apply where interest is paid in kind (as in **65.3** SAVINGS AND INVESTMENT INCOME) or in the form of funding bonds where the issuer is under a duty to retain bonds (see **65.7** SAVINGS AND INVESTMENT INCOME).

In these cases the person making the payment *must* provide the recipient with a written statement showing the amount of the interest paid in kind or as a funding bond, the amount of tax deducted (if any), the net amount paid, and the date of payment. The statement must be provided on the date the payment is made (or, in the case of funding bonds, treated as made). The duty to comply is enforceable by the recipient. [*ITA 2007, s 975A*].

Omission to deduct tax

[23.6] The following should be noted.

(a) The provisions governing the collection of tax (see **23.18** below) operate on payments where there is a requirement to deduct a sum representing income tax. That requirement is not removed simply because the sum has not in fact been deducted.

(b) Tax not deducted at the time of payment cannot generally be recovered afterwards. For this see *Shrewsbury v Shrewsbury* CA 1907, 23 TLR 224; *Re Hatch* Ch D 1919, 1 Ch 351; *Ord v Ord* KB 1923, 39 TLR 437; *Taylor v Taylor* CA 1937, 16 ATC 218; *Brine v Brine* KB 1943, 22 ATC 177; *Hemsworth v Hemsworth* KB 1946, 25 ATC 466; *Tenbry Investments Ltd v Peugeot Talbot Motor Co Ltd* Ch D, [1992] STC 791. But where trustees omitted to deduct tax from annuities through an honest error of fact, not an error of law, they were authorised to recoup the tax from future payments (*Re Musgrave, Machell v Parry* Ch D, [1916] 2 Ch 417). See also *Turvey v Dentons* (1923) Ltd QB 1952, 31 ATC 470. Only net amount of alimony available to satisfy contra account (*Butler v Butler* CA 1961, 40 ATC 19). See also *Fletcher v Young* CS 1936, 15 ATC 531; *Hollis v Wingfield* CA 1940, 19 ATC 98.

(c) The Courts may rectify documents shown not to embody the intentions of the parties. For cases where rectification sought in relation to deduction of tax see *Burroughes v Abbott* Ch D 1921, 38 TLR 167; *Jervis v Howle & Talke Colliery Co Ltd* Ch D 1936, 15 ATC 529; *Fredensen v Rothschild* Ch D 1941, 20 ATC 1; *Van der Linde v Van der Linde* Ch D 1947, 26 ATC 348; *Whiteside v Whiteside* CA 1949, 28 ATC 479.

(d) A penalty of £50 is incurred by refusal to allow the deduction of tax, and any 'agreement' not to deduct is void to that extent. [*TMA 1970, s 106*]. See **23.16** below for 'free of tax' payments.

Annual payments

[23.7] There is a duty to deduct a sum representing income tax from certain 'qualifying annual payments'. [*ITA 2007, ss 900, 901*]. See **23.8** below for the meaning of 'qualifying annual payments', **23.9** below for the duty to deduct and **23.10** below for the meaning of 'annual payment'.

Simon's Taxes. See **A4.432–A4.434.**

Qualifying annual payments

[23.8] A '*qualifying annual payment*' is an annual payment (see **23.10** below) arising in the UK that is charged to income tax under:

(a) *ITTOIA 2005, Pt 4 Ch 7* (purchased life annuity payments);
(b) *ITTOIA 2005, s 579* (royalties etc. from intellectual property);
(c) *ITTOIA 2005, Pt 5 Ch 4* (certain telecommunication rights: non-trading income);
(d) *ITTOIA 2005, Pt 5 Ch 7* (annual payments not otherwise charged);
(e) *ITEPA 2003, s 609* (annuities for the benefit of dependants); or
(f) *ITEPA 2003, s 611* (annuities in recognition of another's services).

Where the recipient is a company, the annual payment must be charged to income tax as in (a)–(d) above, under legislation on unauthorised unit trusts or under specified provisions of *CTA 2009*.

However, the annual payment must *not* be a payment of interest, a qualifying donation for gift aid purposes (see **14.15** CHARITIES AND CHARITABLE GIVING), a payment where income tax is treated as paid by a beneficiary or settlor in relation to a discretionary trust (or would do so but for the trustees being non-UK resident) (see **70.11** SETTLEMENTS), or an annual payment for non-taxable consideration (see **4.42** ANTI-AVOIDANCE).

[*ITA 2007, s 899*].

Duty to deduct

[23.9] Where the payer is an individual, a sum representing income tax must be deducted from qualifying annual payments (see **23.8** above) that are made for genuine commercial reasons in connection with that individual's trade, profession or vocation. [*ITA 2007, s 900*]. The amount of the deduction is the basic rate of tax in force for the year of payment. The tax is collected through the individual's self-assessment return (see **23.18** COLLECTION OF TAX).

Personal representatives fulfilling a liability incurred by the deceased need not make a deduction from a qualifying annual payment unless the payment would have been made for genuine commercial reasons in connection with the deceased's trade, profession or vocation. [*ITA 2007, s 901(2)*].

For amounts taxable under *ITA 2007, Pt 13 Ch 4* (tax avoidance: sales of occupation income — see **4.29** ANTI-AVOIDANCE) and, for disposals before 5 July 2016, *ITA 2007, Pt 13 Ch 3*, (tax avoidance: transactions in land — see **4.30** ANTI-AVOIDANCE), if the person liable is non-UK resident HMRC may direct that they be subjected to deduction of tax at the basic rate in force for the year in which the payment is made. [*ITA 2007, s 944; FA 2016, ss 79(6), 82(1)*]. Such a direction may, however, only be made once there is entitlement to the consideration, i.e. on execution of a contract (*Pardoe v Entergy Power Development Corp* Ch D 2000, 72 TC 617).

The duty to deduct does not apply on and after 28 February 2018 to payments made by or on behalf of a securitisation company. [*SI 2006 No 3296, Reg 14A; SI 2018 No 143, Regs 1, 8*].

For annual payments under certain life assurance policies (i.e. guaranteed income bonds) not treated as such for tax purposes, see **44.17** LIFE ASSURANCE POLICIES.

For an exemption from the duty to deduct in relation to superannuation funds for overseas employees, see **57.40** PENSION PROVISION.

See also 4.42 ANTI-AVOIDANCE where certain annual payments are made for non-taxable consideration.

Definition of 'annual payment'

[23.10] The leading case law authorities establish that an annual payment is a payment which has four characteristics, as follows:

- it must be payable under a legal obligation;
- it must recur or be capable of recurrence (although the obligation to pay may be contingent);
- it must constitute income and not capital in the hands of the recipient; and
- it must represent 'pure income profit' to the recipient.

'*Pure income profit*' is essentially income that is received without the recipient having to do or expend anything in return. The question as to whether a payment amounts to pure income profit in the hands of the recipient should be determined by establishing in the light of the facts whether it is a taxable receipt in the hands of the recipient without any deduction for expenses or the like.

Leading cases on defining an annual payment are *Earl Howe v CIR* CA 1919, 7 TC 289 (insurance premiums under covenant not annual payments) and *CIR v Epping Forest Conservators* HL 1953, 34 TC 293 (yearly contributions to meet the deficiencies of a charity held to be annual payments). Payments for the use of chattels not annual payments (*In re Hanbury, decd* CA 1939, 38 TC 588). See also *CIR v Whitworth Park Coal Co Ltd* HL 1959, 38 TC 531. Payments to a County Council under deed of covenant in consideration of the Council's paying special school fees of the covenantor's handicapped child held not annual payments (*Essex County Council v Ellam* CA 1989, 61 TC 615). The profits of a business bequeathed to a charity were held to be annual payments (*R v Special Commrs (ex p Shaftesbury Homes)* CA 1922, 8 TC 367). For covenanted subscriptions see *CIR v National Book League* CA 1957, 37 TC 455 and *Taw & Torridge Festival Society Ltd v CIR* Ch D 1959, 38 TC 603. Covenanted payments to a charity as part of arrangements under which it acquired the business of the payer not annual payments (*Campbell v CIR* HL 1968, 45 TC 427). Payments by a film company of a share of certain receipts as part of arrangements for cancellation of a contract were annual payments (*Asher v London Film Productions Ltd* CA 1943, 22 ATC 432) as were payments under a guarantee of the dividends of a company (*Aeolian Co Ltd v CIR* KB 1936, 20 TC 547; *Moss Empires Ltd v CIR* HL 1937, 21 TC 264). But not payments by the principal subscribers to a newsfilm service to make good its operating deficit (*British Commonwealth International Newsfilm Agency Ltd v Mahany* HL 1962, 40 TC 550).

Instalments of the purchase price of a mine held not annual payments (*Foley v Fletcher* 1858, 7 WR 141) nor instalment repayments of a debt (*Dott v Brown* CA 1936, 15 ATC 147). Where the Secretary of State for India acquired a railway in consideration of annuities for 48 years, tax held to be deductible only from the interest element actuarially ascertained (*Scoble v Secretary of State for India* HL 1903, 4 TC 478, 618 and cf. the two *East India Railway* cases at 21 TLR 606 and 40 TLR 241). Similarly where shares were sold for payments over 125 years, the actuarially ascertained interest element in the payments was held to be income in the hands of the recipient for surtax (*Vestey v CIR* Ch D 1961, 40 TC 112). See also *Goole Corporation v Aire etc. Trustees* KB 1942, 21 ATC 156 (tax held deductible from interest element in yearly payments to local authority to meet street repairs). In *CIR v Church Commissioners* HL 1976, 50 TC 516 rent charges paid as the consideration for property were held wholly income and not (as contended for Crown) partly income and partly capital. The HL judgments are an important review of the possibility of dissecting periodical payments in return for valuable consideration between income and capital and *Vestey v CIR* above, although not overruled, was called 'the high water of dissection cases' (Lord Wilberforce) and some of the reasoning in it was not approved. See also *Chadwick v Pearl Life Insce* KB 1905, 21 TLR 456. For reimbursement of expenditure calculated by reference to an interest factor, see *Re Euro Hotel (Belgravia) Ltd* Ch D 1975, 51 TC 293 and *Chevron Petroleum (UK) Ltd v BP Petroleum Development Ltd* Ch D 1981, 57 TC 137.

Payments in satisfaction of the transfer of a business etc., and based on profits held not to be annual payments in *CIR v Ramsay* CA 1935, 20 TC 79 and *CIR v Ledgard* KB 1937, 21 TC 129 but contrast *CIR v Hogarth* CS 1940, 23 TC 491. Payments of a percentage of receipts over 40 years for the use of a secret process held to be annual payments (*Delage v Nugget Polish Co Ltd* KB 1905, 21 TLR 454) as were quarterly payments for the use of a firm's name etc. (*Mackintosh v CIR* KB 1928, 14 TC 15). See also *CIR v 36/49 Holdings Ltd* CA 1943, 25 TC 173. Where a business was bequeathed for life and the trustees were directed to carry a percentage of the profits to reserve, the amounts set aside were held to be annual payments (*Stocker v CIR* KB 1919, 7 TC 304).

In *Watkins v CIR* KB 1939, 22 TC 696, payments by a husband for the maintenance of his wife (of unsound mind) were held not to be annual payments. Payments to trustees as 'remuneration' are annual payments (*Baxendale v Murphy* KB 1924, 9 TC 76; *Hearn v Morgan* KB 1945, 26 TC 478) but not *Sch E* remuneration (*Jaworski v Institution of Polish Engineers* CA 1950, 29 ATC 385). On an analysis of the terms of the contractual arrangements, Loyalty Bonus payments paid by a platform service provider were pure income profit (notwithstanding that they were dependent on the investor paying management charges) and were capable of recurrence; they were thus annual payments (*HMRC v Hargreaves Lansdown Asset Management Ltd* UT, [2019] STC 1745).

See also HMRC Brief 04/13, 25 March 2013 at **49.5** MISCELLANEOUS INCOME (rebates of investment annual management charges etc.).

Annuities

[23.11] The following matters are relevant.

(a) **General.** In order for an annuity to be subject to deduction of tax at source, it would have to fall within the definition of a qualifying annual payment (see **23.8** above). This will, in fact, generally be the case.

Normally, an annuity cannot be dissected between the capital, if any, in consideration of the annuity and an 'interest element', but see **65.23** SAVINGS AND INVESTMENT INCOME as regards purchased life annuities. For a full discussion of this, see the HL opinions in *CIR v Church Commissioners* HL 1976, 50 TC 516. See also **23.7–23.10** above. For tax-free annuities see **23.16** below.

Statutory exceptions to this general rule are below.

(b) **Annuities for non-taxable consideration.** See **4.42** ANTI-AVOIDANCE.

(c) **Purchased life annuities.** See **65.23** SAVINGS AND INVESTMENT INCOME.

(d) **Annuities** charged under *ITEPA 2003* as **pension income** (see **56.2** PENSION INCOME), other than those arising from retirement annuity contracts and certain employment-related annuities from UK sources. From 6 April 2007, annuities from former retirement annuity contracts are brought within PAYE, and thus are within this exception — see **53.27** PAY AS YOU EARN. The same applies to annuities within *ITEPA 2003, s 610* (annuities under an occupational pension scheme that is not a registered pension scheme) — see **56.2**(e) PENSION INCOME.

(e) **'Capital and income'** policies are those where in the event of death within a selected period, a lump sum and an annuity for the rest of the period is paid. The annuity may (conditionally) be treated as instalments of capital, not subject to tax deduction. Some companies arrange for return of part of *capital* over a number of years, followed by an ordinary annuity subject to tax deduction. But if assigned or settled for benefit of a third party see **70.22** SETTLEMENTS.

(f) For **children's education policies** see *Perrin v Dickson* CA 1929, 14 TC 608 in which the yearly payments were held to be a return of the premiums with interest, only the interest being taxable. The decision was questioned in *Sothern-Smith v Clancy* CA 1940, 24 TC 1. Purchased life annuities are now regulated, see (c) above.

(g) For **guaranteed income bonds**, see **44.17** LIFE ASSURANCE POLICIES.

Yearly interest

[23.12] A sum representing income tax at the basic rate in force for the year of payment must be deducted from payments of 'yearly interest' arising in the UK if made by a company (other than in a fiduciary or representative capacity), a local authority (other than in a fiduciary or representative capacity), or a partnership which includes a company; or if made to a person whose usual place of abode is outside the UK. The meaning of '*yearly interest*' is derived from case law and refers, broadly, to interest on a debt where the debtor and creditor intend that the debt should exist for more than a year, or where it is mutually accepted that the interest may be paid from year to year. Payments of yearly interest specifically include interest paid by a registered industrial and provident society in respect of any mortgage, loan, loan stock or deposit; or any interest, dividend or bonus in respect of a holding in its share capital.

A payment of interest which is payable to an individual in respect of *compensation* is to be treated as a payment of yearly interest (irrespective of the period in respect of which the interest is paid). An example of interest paid in respect of compensation is that paid by financial institutions in cases of financial mis-selling. The Commissioners for HMRC may make regulations which disapply this in prescribed circumstances.

In determining for the above purposes whether a payment of interest arises in the UK, no account is to be taken of the location of any deed under which the interest is paid.

[*ITA 2007, s 874(1)(2)(5)(5A)(5B)(6)(6A)*].

As regards local authorities, see HMRC Brief 22/08, 9 April 2008. As regards interest paid by a company that falls to be treated as a distribution, see HMRC Brief 47/08, 26 September 2008. For interest paid to a person outside the UK, see HMRC Savings and Investment Manual SAIM9200–9260. As to whether interest arises in the UK, see HMRC Savings and Investment Manual SAIM9090, but see also *Ardmore Construction Ltd v HMRC* CA, [2018] STC 1487.

Statutory interest paid to creditors in a company administration is yearly interest if paid in respect of a period exceeding one year (*HMRC v Joint Administrators of Lehman Brothers International* SC, [2019] STC 661, [2019] UKSC 12).

For the particular treatment of distributions by authorised investment funds, see **80.2** UNIT TRUSTS ETC. [*ITA 2007, s 874(4)*].

Generally, these provisions apply to alternative finance return and profit share return (for which see **3.2–3.8** ALTERNATIVE FINANCE ARRANGEMENTS) as they do to interest. [*ITA 2007, s 564Q; FA 2016, Sch 6 paras 20, 28*]. For an exception from the duty to deduct tax from certain payments between companies, see **23.19** below.

For the collection of tax deducted at source, see **23.18** below.

Exceptions

The obligation to deduct tax on payments of yearly interest is subject to numerous exceptions, as listed below:

(a) payments of interest made by a building society; but the obligation to deduct tax does apply if the interest is payable to an individual in respect of compensation (see above);
(b) payments of interest by a 'deposit-taker' where the investment is a 'relevant investment' (see **23.13** below for meaning of deposit-taker and relevant investment);
(c) payments of interest that are public revenue dividends (see below);
(d) payments of interest by a bank if made in the ordinary course of its business; but the obligation to deduct tax does apply if the interest is payable to an individual in respect of compensation (see above);
(e) payments of interest on advances from banks or building societies or from the European Investment Bank (providing, in the case of a bank, that the person beneficially entitled to the interest is within the charge to corporation tax);
(f) payments of interest on deposits with the National Savings Bank;

(g) dividends from investment trust companies which are designated as interest distributions (see **65.6** SAVINGS AND INVESTMENT INCOME);
(h) interest distributions by authorised unit trusts (see **80.2** UNIT TRUSTS ETC.);
(i) interest distributions by open-ended investment companies (see **80.3** UNIT TRUSTS ETC.);
(j) payments of interest on peer-to-peer loans (see below);
(k) payments of interest on a 'quoted Eurobond', i.e. any interest-bearing security that is issued by a company and listed on a recognised stock exchange or, in relation to payments of interest made on or after 1 April 2018, admitted to trading on a multilateral trading facility (as defined) operated by a recognised stock exchange regulated in the UK, EEA or Gibraltar (see HMRC Company Taxation Manual CTM35218);
(l) payments of interest on loans to buy a life annuity: such loans are already subject to deduction of tax, see **42.12** INTEREST PAYABLE;
(m) payments of interest which are chargeable as relevant foreign income (as defined — see **32.2** FOREIGN INCOME);
(n) payments of interest by a person authorised under *Financial Services and Markets Act 2000* whose business consists wholly or mainly of dealing as principal in financial instruments (as defined) and who pays the interest in the ordinary course of that business;
(o) payments of interest by a recognised clearing house or recognised investment exchange (both as defined) which are made in the ordinary course of carrying on the business of providing a central counterparty clearing service (as defined);
(p) payments of yearly interest by a registered industrial and provident society (as defined) in respect of any mortgage, loan, loan stock or deposit, or any interest, dividend or bonus in respect of a holding in its share capital, if made to a person whose usual place of abode is in the UK. The society must make returns of such payments to HMRC;
(q) payments of interest under the *Late Payment of Commercial Debts (Interest) Act 1998* ('statutory interest');
(r) (before 12 February 2019) payments in respect of '*regulatory capital securities*' as defined by *SI 2013 No 3209, Reg 2*, including Additional Tier 1 instruments and Tier 2 instruments issued in accordance with EU Regulations; for regulatory capital securities issued before 1 January 2019, this exception continues until 31 December 2023;
(s) payments of interest on 'qualifying private placements'; a '*qualifying private placement*' is a form of unlisted debt instrument, issued by a company, in relation to which the conditions set out in *SI 2015 No 2002* are met; and
(t) (on and after 15 December 2017) payments of interest made to investors in relation to insurance risk transformation investments (as defined), subject to provisions in *SI 2017 No 1271, Regs 6–8* which remove the exception in specified circumstances.

[*ITA 2007, ss 874(3), 875–888, 888A–888D, 987; FA 2016, Sch 6 paras 2, 26, 28; FA 2017, Sch 5 paras 1, 4, 5; FA 2018, s 34(1)(3); FA 2019, Sch 20 paras 1, 16; SI 2013 No 3209, Regs 1, 2, 6, 8, 9; SI 2015 No 2002; SI 2017 No 1271, Regs 1, 5; SI 2019 No 689, Reg 15(11)*].

UK public revenue dividends

A '*UK public revenue dividend*' (see (c) above) is any income from securities which is paid out of the public revenue of the UK or NI, excluding interest on local authority stock. Interest on gilt-edged securities (as defined), securities issued by the National Savings Bank and securities which are the subject of a Treasury direction are payable gross (unless the holder of the security has made a deduction at source application). Otherwise, the person by or through whom the payment is made must deduct tax at the basic rate in force for the year of payment. HMRC have wide powers to make regulations governing the accounting arrangements and modifying the provisions governing the collection of tax deducted at source (see **23.18** below) in their application to UK public revenue dividends. [*ITA 2007, ss 890–895; FA 2016, Sch 6 paras 27, 28*].

See also **65.4** SAVINGS AND INVESTMENT INCOME.

Local authority and company stock

Tax is deductible under *ITA 2007, s 874* (see above) except in the circumstances set out in **50.13** NON-RESIDENTS. [*ITA 2007, s 981*]. See (k) above as regards the exception for interest on quoted Eurobonds.

Peer-to-peer loans

As stated at (j) above, tax is not deductible at source from payments of interest made on or after 6 April 2017 on peer-to-peer (P2P) loans. [*ITA 2007, s 888E; FA 2017, Sch 5 paras 3, 5*]. See **65.9** SAVINGS AND INVESTMENT INCOME as to the nature of P2P lending.

For 2016/17 and earlier years, the question of whether the law required tax to be deducted from interest paid on a P2P loan depended on the identity of both lender and borrower. The many-to-many lending model used by the P2P industry meant that the application of the yearly interest rule was complex for loans made through P2P platforms and could lead to inconsistent tax treatment. In practice, interest on P2P loans could be paid *without* deduction of tax. This applied to interest payments made by (i) a UK borrower to a UK P2P platform; (ii) a UK P2P platform to anyone; and (iii) any intermediary to or from a UK P2P platform. In all cases the P2P platform must be authorised by the Financial Conduct Authority (including interim authorisation). (HMRC Brief 2 (2016), 8 January 2016).

Simon's Taxes. See A4.421–A4.427.

Meaning of deposit-taker and relevant investment

[23.13] For the purposes of 23.12(b) above, a '*deposit-taker*' means the Bank of England, persons authorised under the *Financial Services and Markets Act 2000* (but excluding building societies, friendly societies, credit unions and insurance companies), the Post Office (until its dissolution), a local authority, a company in respect of which a local authority has passed an appropriate resolution, and any other deposit-taker prescribed by Treasury order. Any authorised person (i.e. under Financial Services and Markets Act 2000) whose business consists wholly or mainly of dealing as principal in 'financial instruments' (as defined) is included.

An 'investment' means a deposit, which is in turn defined as a sum of money paid on terms which mean it will be repaid, with or without interest, either on demand or at an agreed time or in agreed circumstances. A deposit-taker must treat all investments as relevant investments unless satisfied to the contrary, but if so satisfied can treat an investment as not being a relevant investment until it comes into possession of information reasonably indicative that the investment is, or may be, a relevant investment.

A '*relevant investment*' (subject to the exclusions below) is an investment where either:

(a) the person beneficially entitled to any interest is an individual (or the persons so entitled are all individuals), or is a Scottish partnership all the partners of which are individuals; or
(b) the person entitled to the interest receives it as the personal representative of a deceased individual; or
(c) the interest arises to the trustees of a discretionary or accumulation settlement (as defined in *ITA 2007, s 873*).

Excluded are:

(i) deposits in respect of which a CERTIFICATE OF DEPOSIT (**12**) has been issued for £50,000 or more (or foreign equivalent at the time the deposit is made) and which are repayable within five years (a 'qualifying certificate of deposit');
(ii) non-transferable deposits of at least £50,000 made before 6 April 2012 where neither partial withdrawals nor additions may be made and which are repayable at the end of a specified period of not more than five years ('*qualifying time deposits*');
(iii) a deposit in respect of which a deposit-taker has issued a qualifying uncertificated eligible debt security unit (as defined);
(iv) debentures (as defined in *Companies Act 2006, s 738*) issued by the deposit-taker;
(v) loans made *by* a deposit-taker in the ordinary course of its business;
(vi) debts on securities listed on a recognised stock exchange;
(vii) deposits in a '*general client account deposit*', i.e. a client account, other than an account for specific clients, if the depositor is required by law to make payments representing interest to any of the clients whose money it contains;
(viii) Lloyd's UNDERWRITERS (**79**) premiums trust funds;
(ix) investments held at non-UK branches of UK resident deposit-takers;
(x) investments with non-UK resident deposit-taker held other than in UK branches;

[*ITA 2007, ss 853–857, 863–868, 870; FA 2016, Sch 6 paras 7–11, 14, 15, 28; SI 2019 No 689, Reg 15(10)*].

Royalties

[23.14] The provisions below have effect in connection with the deduction of tax at source from payments of royalties.

Intellectual property royalties

Royalties (or other payments) for the use of, or the right to use, intellectual property are subject to deduction of tax at source where within the charge to income tax or corporation tax and paid to owners or assignors of intellectual property whose usual place of abode is outside the UK. Deduction is at the basic rate in force for the year in which the payment is made and, where paid through a UK-resident agent, is applied net of commission (unless the entitlement or amount of commission is unknown). There is an exemption in relation to copies of works or articles which have been exported from the UK for distribution outside the UK. Where both apply, these rules take precedence over those relating to annual payments and patent royalties.

The definition of intellectual property for the above purposes is broadened with effect in respect of payments made on or after 28 June 2016. There are anti-forestalling rules which disregard any arrangements (whenever entered into) of which a main purpose is to avoid the effect of the wider definition; in particular the accelerating of payments to earlier than 28 June 2016 is ignored in determining when a payment is made for the purposes of the deduction at source rules. The original definition referred to copyrights, design rights and public lending rights in respect of a book. The new definition refers to (i) copyright of literary, artistic or scientific works; (ii) patents, trade marks, designs, models, plans and secret formulas or processes; (iii) information concerning industrial, commercial or scientific experience; and (iv) public lending rights as before. The copyright in a cinematographic film or video recording and the sound track of any such film or video (except insofar as it is separately exploited) are excluded under both the old and new definitions.

[*ITA 2007, ss 906, 907, 908; FA 2016, s 40*].

Copyright royalties payable to an author/originator of a literary, dramatic, musical or artistic work that has been created in the course of his profession are fees for professional services and do not fall within the rules above (HMRC International Manual INTM342590).

Collection is by HMRC assessment (see **23.18** below). The payer is assessable, even if he has not deducted the tax (*Rye & Eyre v CIR* HL 1935, 19 TC 164).

A payment is treated as made when it is made by the first person who makes it. The duty to make a deduction applies also to payment on account of royalties. If the rules requiring a deduction apply, any agreement to pay without deduction is void. [*ITA 2007, s 909*].

A payment to foreign author, for right to sell translation, has been held to be within the above provisions (*Longmans, Green* KB 1932, 17 TC 272). Solicitors remitting royalties to overseas residents on behalf of the payer must deduct and account for tax (*Rye & Eyre v CIR* HL 1935, 19 TC 164).

Where a person makes an intellectual property royalty payment (defined in accordance with *ITA 2007, s 907* above) to a 'connected' person under 'DTA tax avoidance arrangements', the duty to deduct tax applies without regard to the provisions of any double tax treaty. Payer and payee are '*connected*' for this purpose if the participation condition (as at **4.21** ANTI-AVOIDANCE but suitably modified) is met as between them. '*DTA tax avoidance arrangements*' are arrangements (as widely defined) having as a main purpose the obtaining a 'tax advantage' (as in **4.2** ANTI-AVOIDANCE) by virtue of a double tax treaty where this is contrary to the object and purpose of the treaty. There are provisions whereby arrangements made before 28 June 2016 are regarded as DTA tax avoidance arrangements in relation to payments made on or after that date where a main purpose is to obtain a tax advantage by virtue of a double tax treaty not involving the UK. [*ITA 2007, s 917A; FA 2016, ss 41, 42(7)(8)*].

For more detail on the above changes effective from 28 June 2016, see the technical note at www.gov.uk/government/publications/income-tax-royalty-withholding-tax.

Patent royalties

A deduction must be made from a patent royalty if:

- it is *not* a qualifying annual payment (see **23.8** above) nor an annual payment for non-taxable consideration under *ITA 2007, s 904* (see **4.42** ANTI-AVOIDANCE);
- it arises in the UK;
- it is chargeable to income tax or corporation tax.

Any deduction is to be made at the basic rate in force for the year in which the payment is made. Collection is via the self-assessment return or, if the payer is not an individual and has no modified net income (see **1.13** ALLOWANCES AND TAX RATES), by HMRC assessment (although there is a separate collection mechanism for companies) (see **23.18** below).

[*ITA 2007, s 903*].

The sale by a non-UK resident of patent rights is subject to deduction at source provided the seller is chargeable to tax on profits of the sale under the provisions at **41.6** INTELLECTUAL PROPERTY. The deduction is applied to the net proceeds, i.e. the proceeds less any incidental expenses of the sale which are deducted before payment. The rate is the basic rate in force for the year of payment. See **23.19** below for an exception for certain payments between companies. Collection is by HMRC assessment (although there is a separate collection mechanism for companies) (see **23.18** below). [*ITA 2007, s 910*].

Instalments of fixed amount for five-year use of patent were held to be capital (*Desoutter Bros Ltd* KB 1936, 15 ATC 49). A lump sum payment on signing a ten-year agreement held capital but ten fixed yearly payments royalties (*CIR v British Salmson Aero Engines Ltd* CA 1938, 22 TC 29). Awards by a Royal Commission for use of inventions and patents in 1914–1918 war held patent royalties (*Constantinesco v Rex* HL 1927, 11 TC 730; *Mills v Jones* HL 1929, 14 TC 769). See also *Jones v CIR* KB 1919, 7 TC 310; *Wild v Ionides* KB 1925, 9 TC 392; *International Combustion Ltd v CIR* KB 1932, 16 TC 532 and cf. *Rank Xerox Ltd v Lane* HL 1979, 53 TC 185.

Special provision in relation to royalties

Companies may exercise a discretion to pay royalties under deduction at a treaty rate where there is a reasonable belief that the payee is entitled to relief under a double tax treaty. If the payee was not so entitled, the company must account for the tax as if the above rule had never applied, and HMRC have powers to direct the company that it is not to apply to a particular payment or payments. [*ITA 2007, ss 911–913*]. For details, see Tolley's Corporation Tax under Income Tax in relation to a Company.

Simon's Taxes. See **A4.435, A4.441, A4.442, A4.445, A4.454, B5.317.**

Tax-free arrangements

[23.15] An agreement which provides for an annual payment without deduction of tax is void [*TMA 1970, s 106(2)*] but a provision to pay interest at a stated rate after deduction of tax is treated as requiring payment at the gross rate. [*ITA 2007, s 976(4)–(6)*]. An agreement to make payments 'free of tax' is not avoided by *TMA 1970, s 106(2)* (*CIR v Ferguson* HL 1969, 46 TC 1). See **23.16** below for tax-free annuities.

Tax-free annuities etc.

[23.16] The following matters are relevant.

(a) **General.** A direction under a will or settlement for an annuity to be paid 'free of tax' (or similar wording) is a direction to pay an annuity of such an amount which after deduction of the tax will produce the specified figure (cf. *CIR v Ferguson* HL 1969, 46 TC 1). This is a matter, however, in which it is important the wording used should express clearly and unambiguously what is intended. The large number of court cases referred to below have arisen mostly because of the imprecision of the relevant wording.
The wording was held *not* to confer freedom from tax in *Abadam v Abadam* 1864, 10 LT 53 ('payable without any deduction whatsoever'); *Shrewsbury v Shrewsbury* Ch D 1906, 22 TLR 598 ('clear of all deductions'); *In re Loveless* Ch D 1918, 34 TLR 356 ('clear'); *In re Well's Will Trusts* Ch D 1940, 19 ATC 158 ('clear of all deductions'); *In re Best's Marriage Settlement* Ch D 1941, 20 ATC 235 ('such a sum as shall after deductions'); *CIR v Watson* CS 1942, 25 TC 25 (annuity payable out of 'whole free residue' of income); *In re Hooper* Ch D 1944, 1 AER 227 ('free of all duty . . . and . . . free of all deductions whatsoever'); *In re Wright* Ch D 1952, 31 ATC 433 ('net'). The wording was held to confer freedom from tax in *In re Buckle* 1894, 1 Ch 286 ('free of legacy duty and every other deduction' under a codicil to a will in which originally 'clear of all deductions whatsoever, except income tax'); *In re Shrewsbury Estate Acts* CA 1923, 40 TLR 16 ('clear of all deductions whatsoever for taxes or otherwise'). *In re Hooper* above was not followed in *In re Cowlishaw* Ch D 1939, 18 ATC 377 where the wording was similar, but in a later case (*In re Best's Marriage Settlement* above) *Cowlishaw* was described as special to its context.

(b) **Excess liability.** All the decisions below relate to super-tax or surtax but it would seem that, suitably adapted, they are equally applicable to excess liability, i.e. the excess of income tax liability over what it would be if all taxable income were charged at the basic rate, starting rate for savings or dividend ordinary rate to the exclusion of the higher rate or dividend upper rate. Here it is relevant that an annuity is investment income.

An annuity of a sum such 'as after deduction of the income tax' would give the prescribed amount was held not to be free of super-tax (*In re Bates* Ch D 1924, 4 ATC 518). However an annuity 'free of income tax' was held to be free of surtax on the ground that surtax was an additional income tax and there was no indication in the will to restrict the wording to 'income tax as known for many years'. The previous decision was distinguished as there the wording referred to 'deduction' and surtax was not deductible at source (*In re Reckitt* CA 1932, 11 ATC 429; followed in *Prentice's Trustees* CS 1934, 13 ATC 612). A direction to pay an annuity free of super-tax was held to cover surtax (*In re Hulton* Ch D 1930, 9 ATC 570).

The surtax is normally taken as the part of the annuitant's total surtax proportionate to the ratio of the annuity grossed at the standard rate to the annuitant's total income (*In re Bowring* 1918, 34 TLR 575; followed in *In re Doxat* 1920, 125 LT 60 and other cases). In *Baird's Trustees* CS 1933, 12 ATC 407 the surtax was calculated on the basis that the annuity was the annuitant's only income, but this decision was distinguished in *Richmond's Trustees 1935* CS, 14 ATC 489 and *In re Bowring* was followed. See also *In re Horlick's Settlement* CA 1938, 17 ATC 549.

The surtax/excess liability borne on behalf of the annuitant by the trust fund is itself, grossed-up, income in his hands (*Meeking v CIR* KB 1920, 7 TC 603; *Lord Michelham's Trustees v CIR* CA 1930, 15 TC 737. See also *Shrewsbury & Talbot v CIR* KB 1936, 20 TC 538 and compare *CIR v Duncanson* KB 1949, 31 TC 257). The practice is to treat the liability so borne for year 1 as an addition for grossing-up purposes to the annuity for year 2.

(c) **Tax repayments of annuitants.** In a tax-free annuity the question arises whether the benefit conferred on the annuitant should be limited to the tax actually suffered by him after taking into account his allowances etc.

Where the annuity under a will was 'free of income tax' it was held that the annuitant must hand to the trustees a part of the tax repaid to her on account of her reliefs, in proportion to the ratio of the net annuity to her net income after tax (*In re Pettit, Le Fevre v Pettit* Ch D 1922, 38 TLR 787). But where the annuity was expressed to be of such an amount as after deduction of the tax at the current rate would give the prescribed sum it was held, distinguishing *In re Pettit*, that the annuitant was entitled to retain any tax repaid to him (*In re Jones* Ch D 1933, 12 ATC 595). For cases in which these two decisions were considered and applied as appropriate to the precise wording of the provision of the annuity, see *Richmond's Trustees* CS 1935, 14 ATC 489; *In re Maclennan* CA 1939, 18 ATC 121; *In re Eves* Ch D 1939, 18 ATC 401; *Rowan's Trustees* CS 1939, 18 ATC 378; *In re Jubb* Ch D 1941, 20 ATC 297; *In re Tatham* Ch D 1944, 23 ATC 283; *In re Williams* Ch D 1945, 24 ATC 199; *In re Bates's Will Trusts* Ch D 1945,

24 ATC 300; *In re Arno* CA 1946, 25 ATC 412. *Tatham* and *Arno* give useful reviews of the subject as does *CIR v Cook* HL 1945, 26 TC 489 (in which it was held that the Inland Revenue must repay the tax on the grossed-up amount of a tax-free annuity notwithstanding that the annuitant would not be liable to tax if the annuity was not grossed-up and that the whole of the repayment would be handed over to the trustees). The annuitant must, if required by the trustees, exercise his right to repayment (*In re Kingcombe* Ch D 1936, 15 ATC 37). If the annuitant is a married woman *In re Pettit* applies to tax repayable to the husband but, if necessary, she must apply for separate assessment (*In re Batley* CA 1952, 31 ATC 410). It applies to loss relief (*In re Lyons* CA 1951, 30 ATC 377). For the effect of an *In re Pettit* refund on the annuitant's total income for surtax see *CIR v Duncanson* KB 1949, 31 TC 257.

(d) **Tax-free alimony etc. payments.** The *In re Pettit* rule (see (c) above) does not apply to tax-free Court Orders and in *CIR v Ferguson* HL 1969, 46 TC 1, Lord Diplock explicitly refrained from deciding whether it applied to a separation agreement. Whether a free of tax Court Order would confer freedom from surtax/ excess liability does not seem to have arisen. Subject to the foregoing, (a), (b) and (c) above apply, where appropriate, to tax-free alimony payments etc.
For tax-free alimony payments by non-residents, see *Ferguson* above and *Stokes v Bennett* Ch D 1953, 34 TC 337.

(e) For **overseas taxes** under tax-free annuities, see *Re Frazer* Ch D 1941, 20 ATC 73 and compare *Havelock v Grant* KB 1946, 27 TC 363.

Deduction of tax under foreign agreements or by non-residents

[23.17] UK tax legislation cannot alter rights not within the jurisdiction of UK courts. See *Keiner v Keiner* QB 1952, 34 TC 346 (tax not deductible from alimony under American agreement paid by UK resident ex-husband to non-resident ex-wife); *Bingham v CIR* Ch D 1955, 36 TC 254 (maintenance payments under foreign Court Order not deductible in arriving at total income as tax not deductible); *Westminster Bank v National Bank of Greece* HL 1970, 46 TC 472 (interest on foreign bonds paid in London by guarantor held within *Sch D, Case IV* and tax not deductible). But where under a UK contract a non-UK resident paid interest to another non-UK resident and the payer died, held his executors (resident in UK) must deduct tax from interest they paid (*CIR v Broome's Exors* KB 1935, 19 TC 667). And where 'free of tax' alimony was payable under UK agreements etc., payments by the ex-husband no longer resident in the UK were held to have been paid subject to deduction of tax, the onus being on the Crown to collect the tax (*Stokes v Bennett* Ch D 1953, 34 TC 337). See also *CIR v Ferguson* HL 1969, 46 TC 1.

Collection of tax

[23.18] There are three mechanisms to collect the income tax relating to payments made under deduction at source.

(a) UK resident companies, deposit-takers and building societies are subject to a system of regular returns and payments during an accounting period. [*ITA 2007, Pt 15 Ch 15*]. For details, see Tolley's Corporation Tax under Income Tax in relation to a Company.
(b) Tax on certain payments (listed at *ITA 2007, s 963(1)*) is collected by HMRC assessment. There is an accompanying requirement for the payer to deliver to HMRC an account of the payment 'without delay' and subject to a penalty under *TMA 1970, s 98*. [*ITA 2007, s 963*].
(c) Tax in relation to certain annual payments and certain patent royalty payments is collected through the payer's self-assessment return. The tax is treated for the purposes of *TMA 1970* as if it were charged on the payer. It is taken into account in addition to (but separately from) the normal calculation of liability. [*ITA 2007, s 964*].

As regards (b) above, the Commissioners for HMRC have power to make regulations via statutory instrument to amend the time and manner in which the payer must account for and pay the sum withheld to HMRC. The power will enable the collection procedures relating to individuals and other non-corporate persons to be updated as and when necessary, for example by introducing new forms or online arrangements. [*ITA 2007, s 963A*].

Exception for payments between companies etc.

[23.19] For payments made by one company to another, there is no requirement to deduct tax from interest, royalties, annuities or other annual payments where the recipient company is within the charge to corporation tax in respect of that income. There are detailed rules requiring the paying company to satisfy itself that the recipient company is eligible to receive the payment gross. Gross payment may also be made by companies to a wide range of tax-exempt bodies (and to their nominees), and the provisions are extended to apply to payments by local authorities subject to similar conditions. [*ITA 2007, Pt 15 Ch 11; SI 2002 No 2931*]. For details, see Tolley's Corporation Tax under Income Tax in relation to a Company. See also Revenue Tax Bulletin August 2001 pp 867, 868 for an article outlining the original provisions.

Simon's Taxes. See **A4.460.**

24

Diplomatic Immunity etc.

Simon's Taxes. See **E1.575, E5.401, E5.401C, E6.464.**

Diplomatic Agents etc.

[24.1] Diplomatic agents (i.e. heads of mission or members of diplomatic staff) of foreign states (recognised by HM Government, see *Caglar v Billingham* (Sp C 70), [1996] SSCD 150) are exempt from tax except on income or capital gains arising from *private* investments or immovable property in the UK under *Diplomatic Privileges Act 1964*. Similar exemption is given to *Agents-General* and their staffs and to certain official agents of Commonwealth countries [*ITA 2007, s 841*] (and see *SI 1997 No 1334* as regards certain Hong Kong officials). *Consuls* and *official agents* of foreign States in the UK (not British subjects or citizens of Eire and not trading) are exempt on income from their official employment [*ITEPA 2003, ss 300, 301*].

Subject to any Order in Council, consular officers and employees, provided they are foreign nationals and not British (or overseas British) citizens, are exempt from tax on employment income. Provided they are either permanent employees or were non-UK resident for each of the two tax years preceding the tax year in which the employment commenced, and are not otherwise engaged in any UK trade, profession, vocation or employment, they are also exempt from tax on relevant foreign income (see **32.2** FOREIGN INCOME) and foreign social security benefits.

[*ITTOIA 2005, ss 771, 772; ITEPA 2003, ss 302, 646A, 681A*]. See also *Consular Relations Act 1968*.

In *Jimenez v CIR* (Sp C 419), [2004] SSCD 371, a person employed as a cook by the Namibian High Commission in London was denied income tax exemption on her earnings, otherwise available under *Diplomatic Privileges Act 1964* and *article 37(3)* of the *Vienna Convention on Diplomatic Relations* (which provides exemption for 'members of the service staff' of a diplomatic mission who are not 'permanently resident in the receiving State'), because she had not been notified to the UK authorities as a member of a diplomatic mission in the UK.

International organisations

[24.2] International organisations (e.g. the United Nations (*SI 1974 No 1261*)), their representatives, officers, members of committees, persons or missions etc. may be specified by Order in Council as exempt from certain taxes under *International Organisations Act 1968*. Also other bodies under the *European Communities Act 1972* (e.g. the North Atlantic Salmon Conservation Organisation (*SI 1985 No 1773*)) and certain financial bodies under the *Bretton Woods Agreements Act 1945* (e.g. the International Monetary Fund (*SI 1946 No 36*)).

Exemption from income tax is given to the remuneration of the Commissioners of the European Communities and their staffs under *Art. 13 of Chap. V of the Protocol on the Privileges and Immunities of the European Communities*. See *Hurd v Jones* CJEC, [1986] STC 127 as regards exemption of certain payments out of Community funds, although see now *SI 1990 No 237*. See also *Tither v CIR* CJEC, [1990] STC 416, where exclusion of EU official from MIRAS scheme upheld. Experts seconded to the European Commission under the detached national experts scheme are exempt from income tax on their daily subsistence allowances [*ITEPA 2003, s 304*], and certain education allowances under the Overseas Services Aid Scheme are similarly exempt (see HMRC ESC A44). The Treasury may also designate any of the international organisations of which the UK is a member for the purpose of exemption from various requirements for the deduction of tax from payments made in the UK (see e.g. *SI 1997 No 168*).

[*ITA 2007, s 979*].

25

Disclosure of Tax Avoidance Schemes

Introduction to DOTAS

[25.1] Promoters of certain tax avoidance schemes, and in some cases persons entering into transactions under such schemes, are obliged to disclose those schemes to HMRC under the Disclosure of Tax Avoidance Schemes (DOTAS) regime. See **25.2–25.11** below. HMRC publish detailed guidance notes on the disclosure rules (see www.gov.uk/government/publications/disclosure-of-tax-avoidance-schemes-guidance). The legislation is policed by HMRC's Counter Avoidance Directorate at HM Revenue & Customs, Counter-Avoidance DOTAS Enforcement team, PO Box 194, Bootle, L69 9AA. See www.gov.uk/dealing-with-hmrc/tax-avoidance, which includes links to the legislation and the official guidance plus various forms to be used for making disclosures.

See also **55.20** penalties as regards a prospective new penalty for 'enablers' of tax avoidance.

Special compliance regime for high-risk promoters

A special compliance regime applies to promoters of tax avoidance schemes who satisfy one or more 'threshold conditions' relating to previous behaviour. The regime provides for the issuing of a 'conduct notice' requiring the person to whom it is given to comply with specified conditions. Promoters who fail to comply with a conduct notice may be issued with a monitoring notice. Names of promoters subject to such a notice may be published by HMRC, including details of how the conduct notice was breached, and promoters are required to notify their monitored status to clients. Information powers and penalties apply to promoters subject to a conduct notice and to promoters subject to a monitoring notice and their clients and intermediaries. See **25.13–25.23** below.

Simon's Taxes. See **A7.2.**

Arrangements covered by DOTAS

[25.2] The DOTAS regime applies potentially to any kind of direct tax avoidance scheme, but a scheme need only be disclosed if it falls within any one or more of the following descriptions (referred to by HMRC as '*hallmarks*').

- **Confidentiality in cases involving a promoter.** A scheme falls within this description if the promoter would wish to keep confidential from other promoters the way in which any element of the scheme (including the way the scheme is structured) secures the expected tax advantage or if (in order to facilitate its continued or repeated use in the future) he would wish such a matter to be kept confidential from HMRC. In a case involving a non-UK promoter or a case in which duty to disclose is transferred from promoter to client due to legal professional privilege (see **25.7** below), the second part of the test instead considers whether the scheme user wishes to keep the matter confidential from HMRC.
- **Confidentiality where no promoter involved.** A scheme falls within this description if there is no promoter (e.g. it is an in-house scheme), the intended user is a business which is *not* a 'small or medium-sized enterprise', and the user wishes to keep confidential from HMRC (in order to facilitate its continued or repeated use in the future or to avoid an HMRC enquiry or the possible withholding of a tax repayment) the way in which any element of the scheme (including the way the scheme is structured), secures the expected tax advantage. A scheme also falls within this description if, had there been a promoter, the promoter would have wished to keep such matters confidential from HMRC in order to facilitate continued or repeated use.
- **Premium fee.** A scheme falls within this description if it might reasonably be expected that a promoter (or a person connected with a promoter) of arrangements that are the same as, or substantially similar to, the arrangements in question would be able to obtain for them a 'premium fee' (as above) from a person experienced in receiving services of the type being provided, e.g. tax advice. However, a scheme does not fall within this description if there is no promoter *and* the tax advantage is intended to be obtained by an individual or a business which is a 'small or medium-sized enterprise'.

- **Standardised tax products.** A scheme falls within this description if it is a standardised tax product, i.e. it has standardised documentation the substance of which does not need to be materially tailored to enable a person to implement it, requires a person implementing it to enter into a specific transaction or series of transactions that are standardised in form and it is made available by a promoter to more than one person. There are specific exclusions (see *SI 2006 No 1543, Reg 11*). This hallmark is aimed at what are often referred to as 'mass-marketed schemes'.
- **Loss schemes.** A scheme falls within this description if the promoter expects more than one individual to implement substantially the same arrangements and it is such that an informed observer could reasonably conclude that its main benefit is to generate losses for the purpose of reducing liability to income tax or capital gains tax. This is aimed at schemes that generate tax losses greater than the amount the individual has, in economic substance, contributed.
- **Leasing arrangements.** This hallmark applies only to certain high value plant and machinery leases. See *SI 2006 No 1543, Regs 13–17*. A scheme does not fall within this description if there is no promoter *and* the tax advantage is intended to be obtained by an individual or a business which is a 'small or medium-sized enterprise'.
- **Employment income provided through third parties.** A scheme falls within this description if its main benefit is that an amount that would otherwise count as employment income under the rules on DISGUISED REMUNERATION (**26**) is reduced or eliminated. This includes (but is not limited to) the situation where one or more of the exclusions at **26.10** is in point and the scheme involves one or more contrived or abnormal steps being taken or a step being treated as taking place.
- **Financial products.** The purpose of this hallmark is to catch schemes using financial products where there is a direct link between the product and the gaining of the tax advantage, i.e. where the inclusion of the financial product is not merely incidental to the tax advantage. A scheme falls within this description if it includes at least one of the financial products specified in *SI 2006 No 1543, Reg 20*, a main benefit of including such a product is to produce a tax advantage, and either:
  - any such financial product contains at least one term which is unlikely to have been entered into by the persons concerned were it not for the tax advantage; or
  - the scheme involves one or more contrived or abnormal steps without which the tax advantage could not be obtained.

  Certain circumstances are specified whereby one or both of these latter conditions will be treated as not having been met (see *SI 2006 No 1543, Reg 19(6)–(9)*).

For detail as to how HMRC interpret these hallmarks, see the HMRC guidance notes referred to in **25.1** above. For the purposes of the hallmarks, the definition of '*small or medium-sized enterprise*' is based on *Commission Recommendation 2003/361/EC* published by the EC on 6 May 2003 (as modified for these purposes by *SI 2006 No 1543, Reg 4*); it operates by reference to specified maxima for turnover, assets and staff, similar to those quoted for transfer pricing purposes at **4.22** ANTI-AVOIDANCE.

[*SI 2004 Nos 1863, 2429; SI 2006 No 1543; SI 2007 No 2484, Reg 4; SI 2017 No 1171, Regs 1, 3, 4*].

Obligations to disclose

[25.3] The *Tax Avoidance Schemes (Information) Regulations 2012 (SI 2012 No 1836)* set out the procedural rules for DOTAS, dealing with the manner and timing of disclosure and the information to be provided.

Information to be provided under any of the provisions in *FA 2004, s 316* must be provided in the prescribed form and manner or the provision will not be regarded as complied with.

Obligations of promoters

A person who is a 'promoter in relation to a notifiable proposal' (see below) must provide HMRC (on form AAG1) with specified information on the proposal within five business days after the 'relevant date'. The '*relevant date*' is the earliest of the following:

- the date he first makes a 'firm approach' (see below) to another person;
- the date on which he makes the proposal available for implementation by any person; and
- the date he first becomes aware of any transaction forming part of arrangements implementing the proposal.

A '*notifiable proposal*' is a proposal for arrangements which, if entered into, would be '*notifiable arrangements*', i.e. arrangements falling within any description prescribed by regulations (see **25.2** above) which enable (or might be expected to enable) any person to obtain a tax advantage (as widely defined) and are such that the main benefit, or one of the main benefits, that might be expected from them is the obtaining of that advantage.

There is a separate requirement for a person who is a 'promoter in relation to notifiable arrangements' (see below) to provide HMRC (on form AAG1) with specified information relating to the arrangements and to do so within five business days after the date on which he first becomes aware of any transaction forming part of those arrangements; but this does not apply if the arrangements implement a proposal which has been notified as above.

If a promoter has discharged his obligations in relation to a proposal or arrangements, he is not required to notify proposals or arrangements which are substantially the same as those already notified (whether or not they relate to the same parties).

Broadly, where any two persons are promoters in relation to substantially the same proposal or arrangements, notification by one promoter discharges the obligations of the other. The promoter who makes the notification must give HMRC the other promoter's identity and address unless the other promoter has the reference number allocated to the arrangements (see **25.4** below), and the other promoter must have details of the information provided to HMRC by the first promoter in discharge of his obligation.

Meaning of promoter

A person is a '*promoter in relation to a notifiable proposal*' if, in the course of a 'relevant business':

(i) he is to any extent responsible for the design of the proposed arrangements; or
(ii) he makes a 'firm approach' to another person with a view to making the proposal available for implementation by that person or any other person; or
(iii) he makes the notifiable proposal available for implementation by another person.

Regulations exclude from the definition of 'promoter' (i) a company providing taxation services to another company in the same 51% group and (ii) an employee of the promoter or of a person entering into the proposed arrangements. The exclusion of employees is disapplied in cases where a non-UK resident promoter fails to disclose. Regulations also prescribe various circumstances in which a person to some extent responsible for the design of proposed arrangements is not to be regarded as a promoter by virtue of that fact alone.

A person is a '*promoter in relation to notifiable arrangements*' if:

- he is a promoter by virtue of (ii) or (iii) above in relation to a notifiable proposal which is implemented by the arrangements;
- in the course of a 'relevant business', he is to any extent responsible for the design or the organisation or management of the arrangements; or
- he is to any extent responsible for the organisation or management of the arrangements.

A '*relevant business*' is any trade, profession or business which involves the provision to other persons of taxation services or is carried on by a bank or a securities house. Where companies form a 51% group, anything done by one group company for the purposes of another company's relevant business is brought within the above disclosure requirements.

For these purposes, a person makes a '*firm approach*' to another person if he makes a 'marketing contact' with that person when the proposed arrangements have been 'substantially designed'. A promoter makes a '*marketing contact*' with another person if he communicates information about the proposal, including an explanation of the tax advantage to be obtained, with a view to that person or any other person entering into transactions forming part of the proposed arrangements. Arrangements have been '*substantially designed*' at such time when the nature of the transactions to form part of them has been sufficiently developed for it to be reasonable to believe that a person wishing to obtain the tax advantage might enter into such transactions (or transactions which are not substantially different).

Obligation of person dealing with non-UK promoter

A person who enters into any transaction forming part of notifiable arrangements in relation to which there is a non-UK resident promoter (and no UK resident promoter) must himself provide HMRC (on form AAG2) with specified information relating to those arrangements. He must do so within five business days after entering into the transaction. This obligation is discharged if a promoter makes disclosure of the notifiable proposal for the arrangements in question.

Obligation of parties to notifiable arrangements not involving a promoter

A person who enters into any transaction forming part of notifiable arrangements in respect of which neither he nor any other person in the UK has an obligation as above must himself provide HMRC (on form AAG3) with specified information relating to those arrangements. He must make the disclosure within 30 days after the first transaction forming part of the notifiable arrangements.

Duty to provide additional information

Where:

- a person has provided the required information about notifiable proposals or arrangements in accordance with any of the obligations under the three main sub-headings above, or
- a person has provided information in purported compliance with the second or third of those sub-headings but HMRC believe that not all the required information has been provided,

HMRC may require the person to provide further specified information about the proposals or arrangements (in addition to that required under the above obligations) and to provide documents relating to the proposals or arrangements. The information or documents must be provided within the ten working days (as defined) beginning with the day on which HMRC imposed the requirement or within such longer period as HMRC may direct in a particular case.

Duty to provide updated information

Where, in compliance with the main obligations above, information has been provided to HMRC about notifiable arrangements, or proposed notifiable arrangements, and a reference number has been allocated to the arrangements (see **25.4** below), the promoter must inform HMRC of:

(a) any change in the name by which the notifiable arrangements are known; and
(b) any change in the name or address of any person who is a promoter in relation to the notifiable arrangements or the notifiable proposal.

The promoter must give HMRC the updated information in writing within 30 days after the change occurs. If there is more than one promoter, the obligation to inform HMRC of a change within (b) above falls on the promoter whose details have changed. Once a promoter has informed HMRC of a change within (a) or (b), the duty of any other promoter to inform HMRC of that change is discharged.

[*FA 2004, ss 306, 307, 308, 309, 310, 310A, 310C, 316, 318(1), 319; SI 2004 No 1865; SI 2012 No 1836; SI 2017 No 1171, Regs 1, 6–8*].

Reference numbers allocated to arrangements

[25.4] Where a person has made a disclosure as in **25.3** above, HMRC may within 90 days allocate a reference number to the arrangements in question and must notify the number to that person and, where relevant, to any other person whose obligation is discharged by the first person's disclosure.

A person who is a promoter in relation to notifiable arrangements and who is providing (or has provided) services to a client in connection with those arrangements must pass on to the client (on form AAG6) the reference number for those arrangements or for arrangements which are substantially the same as those arrangements. He must do so within 30 days after the later of the date he first becomes aware of any transaction which forms part of the arrangements and the date on which the reference number is notified to him (by HMRC or any other person). However, if the promoter is also a promoter in relation to a notifiable proposal which is substantially the same as the notifiable arrangements and he provides services to the client in connection with both the arrangements and the proposal, his above duty is discharged if he has provided the client with the reference number for the proposed arrangements. HMRC may give notice that, in relation to notifiable arrangements specified in that notice, promoters do not have to pass on reference numbers after the date specified in the notice.

The client is required to provide to the promoter, within a prescribed time limit, information consisting primarily of his unique tax reference number and national insurance number (or confirmation that he has no such number(s)), the purpose being to enable HMRC to identify the client. The prescribed time limit is ten business days from the later of the date the client receives the reference number and the date he first enters into a transaction which forms part of the notifiable arrangements.

Where the client receives a reference number he must pass it on (on form AAG6) to any other person:

- who he might reasonably be expected to know is, or is likely to be, a party to the notifiable arrangements or proposed arrangements; and
- who might reasonably be expected to gain a tax advantage covered by the DOTAS regime by reason of the arrangements or proposed arrangements.

The period during which the client must comply with the above is the 30 days beginning with the later of the date the client becomes aware of any transaction forming part of the arrangements and the date the reference number is notified to the client. Regulations may exempt a client from complying with this duty in prescribed circumstances.

Where client is an employer

Where the client is an employer and receives, or might reasonably be expected to receive, by reason of the notifiable arrangements, a tax advantage covered by the DOTAS regime in relation to the employment of any of the client's employees, the client must, within 30 days, provide (on form AAG7) the reference number to each of the employees in question. For this purpose, 'employee' includes an office holder and a former employee. Regulations may exempt a client from complying with this duty in prescribed circumstances.

HMRC may give notice that, in relation to notifiable arrangements or a notifiable proposal specified in that notice, clients do not have to pass on reference numbers after the date specified in the notice.

Duty to report number to HMRC

A party to any notifiable arrangements giving rise to an income tax or capital gains tax advantage must quote the allocated reference number in his personal tax return for the year in which the person first enters into a transaction forming part of the arrangements and in all subsequent returns until the advantage ceases to apply to him. He must also quote the tax year in which, or the date on which, the advantage is expected to arise. Comparable provisions apply for corporation tax. Persons not required to file a tax return must instead provide HMRC (on form AAG4) with specified information no later than what would have been the filing date for such a return. If the notifiable arrangements give rise to a claim (made outside a tax return) to relieve a trading loss, the claimant must provide HMRC (on form AAG4) with specified information at the time the claim is made. These duties are disapplied for employees in cases where an employer has a duty under **25.6** below to provide HMRC with information relating to those employees.

HMRC may give notice that, in relation to notifiable arrangements specified in that notice, the above obligation does not apply after the date specified in the notice. To this end, a list of withdrawn scheme reference numbers is now published at www.gov.uk/dealing-with-hmrc/tax-avoidance. Clients and other parties who have received any of these reference numbers no longer have a duty to notify them to HMRC on their tax returns or on form AAG4 from the date shown on the list.

Duty to provide additional information

Where, as above, a promoter is required to pass on to the client the reference number for arrangements, or a client is required to pass on the reference number to other parties, HMRC may specify additional information which must be simultaneously passed on in each case. This is confined to information supplied by HMRC relating to notifiable proposals or notifiable arrangements in general. HMRC may specify the form and manner in which such additional information is to be provided.

[*FA 2004, ss 311, 312, 312A, 312B, 313, 316, 316A, 319; SI 2012 No 1836, Regs 2, 6–8, 8A, 8B, 9–12; SI 2017 No 1171, Regs 1, 6–8*].

Duty of promoter to provide client details

[25.5] The following applies if a promoter of notifiable arrangements provides services to any client in connection with the arrangements and either:

(a) the promoter is subject to the requirement to provide the client with specified information relating to the reference number of the arrangements (see **25.4** above); or

(b) he would be subject to that requirement if he had not failed to make the necessary disclosure of the proposal or arrangements.

The promoter must provide HMRC with specified information about the client within 30 days after the end of the calendar quarter during which the promoter becomes subject to the requirement in (a) above. (This does not apply if HMRC have cancelled the obligation to notify the reference number to the client — see **25.4** above.) Calendar quarters end on 31 March, 30 June etc. In certain circumstances, the 30-day limit is extended to 60 days to the extent that the specified information consists of the client's unique tax reference number and national insurance number.

Where a promoter has provided HMRC with the above information and HMRC suspect that a person other than the client is or is likely to be a party to the arrangements, they may by written notice require the promoter to provide specified information in relation to any such other person who the promoter might reasonably be expected to know is or is likely to be a party to the arrangements (but only if such person is likely to sell the arrangements or achieve a tax advantage by implementing them). The promoter is obliged only to disclose such information as is in his possession at the time of receipt of the written notice. He must comply within ten business days of receipt of the written notice or such longer period as HMRC may in a particular case direct.

The information to be provided as above must be provided in the prescribed form and manner or the duty will not be regarded as complied with.

[*FA 2004, s 313ZA, 313ZB, 316; SI 2012 No 1836, Regs 2, 13, 13A*].

For further details and examples of how this requirement operates, and how to provide the information, see www.gov.uk/government/publications/disclosure-of-tax-avoidance-schemes-guidance at Chapter 16.

Duty of client to provide employee details

[25.6] The following applies if a promoter of notifiable arrangements, or a notifiable proposal, provides services to any client in connection with the arrangements or proposal and the following conditions are met:

(a) the client receives from the promoter the reference number allocated to the arrangements (or proposed arrangements) as in **25.4** above; and
(b) the client is an employer, and, as a result of the notifiable arrangement (or proposed arrangement):
    (i) one or more of the client's employees receive, or might reasonably be expected to receive, in relation to their employment, an advantage in relation to any tax covered by the DOTAS regime; or
    (ii) the client receives, or might reasonably be expected to receive, any such advantage in relation to the employment of one or more of the client's employees.

Where an employee is within sub-s (b)(i) above, or is an employee within (b)(ii), the client must provide HMRC with prescribed information relating to the employee within 14 days after the end of the final PAYE tax month or quarter of the tax year in which any person first enters into a transaction forming part of the notifiable arrangements and on the same date in each subsequent year until an advantage ceases to apply to either employee or employer. For this purpose, 'employee' includes an office holder and a former employee. Regulations may exempt a client from complying with this duty in prescribed circumstances.

The information to be provided as above must be provided in the prescribed form and manner or the duty will not be regarded as complied with. If, as in 25.4 above, HMRC have given notice, in relation to specified notifiable arrangements, that promoters no longer have to pass on reference numbers, or that parties do not have to report such numbers to HMRC, the client is discharged from the above obligation in relation to those arrangements.

[*FA 2004, ss 313ZC, 316; SI 2012 No 1836, Reg 13B*].

For further details and examples of how this requirement operates, and how to provide the information, see www.gov.uk/government/publications/disclosure-of-tax-avoidance-schemes-guidance at Chapter 17.

Legal professional privilege

[25.7] The DOTAS regime does not require the disclosure of privileged information, i.e. information with respect to which a claim to legal professional privilege (or Scottish equivalent) could be maintained in legal proceedings. *However*, the obligation to disclose is simply transferred from the promoter to the client; this is achieved by treating a case in which the promoter claims the protection of legal professional privilege as a case involving notifiable arrangements not involving a promoter (for which see 25.3 above). In these circumstances, the client must make disclosure (on form AAG3) within the period of five business days after entering into the transaction. Alternatively the client has the option of informing the promoter that he does not wish to maintain a claim to legal privilege, in which case the obligation is passed back to the promoter. [*FA 2004, ss 314, 319*].

See www.gov.uk/government/publications/disclosure-of-tax-avoidance-schemes-guidance at para 3.10.

HMRC powers in cases of non-compliance

[25.8] HMRC have powers as listed below in relation to cases in which they suspect non-compliance with the obligations at 25.3 above. These powers may be exercised on or after that date in relation to, or by virtue of, matters arising at any time, even if they arose wholly or partly before that date.

(a) Where HMRC suspect that a person is the promoter of a proposal or arrangements that may be notifiable, they may by written notice require him to state his opinion as to whether or not the specified proposal or arrangements are notifiable by him as in 25.3 above and, if not, to state the reasons why. Any reasons given must be based on the legislation and cannot merely point to the fact that professional advice has been received; if the assertion is that the scheme does not fall within any of the hallmarks at **25.2** above, sufficient information must be provided to enable HMRC to confirm that this is so. The person must comply with the notice within ten business days or such longer period as HMRC may direct.

The above applies equally where HMRC suspect that a person is an 'introducer' (as in (f) below) of a proposal.

(b) Where HMRC have received a statement of reasons (whether or not under (a) above) as to why a proposal or arrangements are not notifiable by a particular person, they may apply to the Appeal Tribunal for an order requiring that person to supply specified information or documents in support of those reasons. The person must comply within 14 business days after the date of the order or such longer period as HMRC may direct.

(c) HMRC may apply to the Appeal Tribunal for an order that a specified proposal or arrangements be treated as notifiable. The application must specify the promoter. The Tribunal can grant the application only if satisfied that HMRC have taken all reasonable steps to establish whether the proposal or arrangements are notifiable and have reasonable grounds (see, for example, *FA 2004, s 306A(5)*) for suspecting that they may be. Where such an order is made, the promoter must comply within ten business days after the date of the order.

(d) HMRC may apply to the Appeal Tribunal for an order that a specified proposal or arrangements is notifiable. This is a separate power to that in (c) above. The application must specify the promoter. The Tribunal can grant the application only if satisfied that the arrangements in question fall within the statutory definition of 'notifiable arrangements' (see **25.3** above under 'Obligations of promoters'). For an example of such a hearing see *HMRC v EDF Tax Ltd (in creditor's voluntary liquidation)* FTT (TC 7381), [2020] SFTD 161, [2019] UKFTT 598 (TC).

(e) If a promoter has supplied information in purported compliance with his normal obligations under these provisions (see **25.3** above) but HMRC believe that he has not provided all the necessary information, they may apply to the Appeal Tribunal for an order requiring the promoter to provide specified information or documents. The Tribunal can grant the application only if satisfied that HMRC have reasonable grounds for suspecting that the information or documents form part of the information required under the promoter's normal obligations or will support or explain it. Where such an order is made, the promoter must comply within ten business days after the date of the order or such longer period as HMRC may direct. The requirement imposed by the order is treated as part of the promoter's normal disclosure obligations.

(f) Where HMRC suspect that a person (P) is an 'introducer' in relation to a proposal and that the proposal is notifiable, they may by written notice require P to provide them with specified information in relation to each person who has provided P with information relating to the proposal. HMRC may also, or alternatively, require P to provide them with similar information in relation to each person with whom P has made a 'marketing contact' (see **25.3** above) in relation to the proposal. P must comply within ten business days (or such longer period as

HMRC may direct in a particular case). A person is an '*introducer*' in relation to a proposal if he makes a marketing contact with another person in relation to the proposal. Regulations may in future prescribe circumstances in which a person is not to be regarded as an introducer. HMRC have the power to issue a person with more than one such notice per notifiable proposal (*HMRC v Connaught Corporate Solutions Ltd* FTT (TC 6797), [2019] SFTD 369, [2018] UKFTT 649 (TC)).

(g) Where HMRC believe that a person has failed to provide further information or documents as required in **25.3** above under the sub-heading 'Duty to provide additional information', they may apply to the Appeal Tribunal for an order requiring the information or documents to be provided. The Tribunal may make such an order only if satisfied that HMRC have reasonable grounds for suspecting that the information or documents will assist them in considering the notifiable proposals or arrangements. If the Tribunal make an order, the information or documents must be provided within the ten working days (as defined) beginning with the day on which the order is made or within such longer period as HMRC may direct in a particular case.

[*FA 2004, ss 306A, 307(1A)(5)(6), 308A, 310B, 313A, 313B, 313C, 314A, 317A, 318(1); SI 2012 No 1836, Regs 14, 15*].

Penalties

[25.9] Penalties are chargeable for failures to comply with the following duties under the DOTAS regime:

(a) duty of promoter to notify HMRC of notifiable proposals or arrangements (*FA 2004, s 308(1)(3)*) (**25.3** above);
(b) duty of taxpayer to notify where the promoter is not UK-resident (*FA 2004, s 309(1)*) (**25.3** above);
(c) duty of parties to arrangements to notify where there is no promoter (*FA 2004, s 310*) (**25.3** above);
(d) duty of person within (a)–(c) above to provide HMRC with further information or documents where required to do so (*FA 2004, s 310A*) (**25.3** above);
(e) duty of promoter to provide updated information (*FA 2004, s 310C*) (**25.3** above);
(f) duty of promoter to notify parties of the scheme reference number (*FA 2004, s 312(2)*) (**25.4** above);
(g) duty of client to notify parties of the reference number (*FA 2004, s 312A(2)*) (**25.4** above);
(h) duty of client who is an employee to notify relevant employees of the reference number (*FA 2004, s 312A(2A)*) (**25.4** above);
(i) duty of client to provide information about himself to promoter (*FA 2004, s 312B*) (**25.4** above);
(j) duty to provide additional information (*FA 2004, s 316A*) (**25.4** above);
(k) duty of promoter to provide details of clients (*FA 2004, s 313ZA*) (**25.5** above);
(l) duty of promoter to provide details of persons other than clients (*FA 2004, s 313ZB*) (**25.5** above);

(m) duty of client who is an employer to provide details of employees (*FA 2004, s 313ZC*) (**25.6** above);
(n) duty of promoter to respond to inquiry (*FA 2004, ss 313A, 313B*) (**25.8**(a)(b) above); and
(o) duty of introducer to give details of persons who have provided information or have been provided with information (*FA 2004, s 313C*) (**25.8**(f) above).

There is an initial penalty of up to £5,000 for any failure to comply with any one of the above duties. However, where the failure relates to (a), (b), (c) or (d) above, the initial penalty is up to £600 for each day during the 'initial period'. The '*initial period*' begins with the day after that on which the time limit for complying with the requirement expires and ends with the earlier of the day on which the penalty is determined and the last day before the failure ceases. The actual amount of the daily penalty should be arrived at after taking account of all relevant considerations, including the desirability of providing a deterrent and the amount of fees likely to be received by a promoter or the tax saving sought by the taxpayer. If, after taking account of those considerations, the maximum daily penalty seems inappropriately low, it can be increased to any amount up to £1 million.

Penalties are determined by the First-tier Tribunal — see **55.27** PENALTIES. Where HMRC consider that a daily penalty has been determined to run from a date later than it should, they can commence proceedings for a redetermination of the penalty.

A further penalty or penalties of up to £600 applies for each day on which the failure continues after the initial penalty is imposed.

Wherever daily penalties apply, the maximum is increased to £5,000 per day where, in relation to the proposal or arrangements in question, an order has been made by the Tribunal under **25.8**(c) or (d) above. Where the order is made under **25.8**(d), the increased maximum only applies to days falling after the period of ten business days beginning with the date of the order. This also applies where the order is made under **25.8**(c).

Where an order is made by the Tribunal under **25.8**(c) or (d) above, doubt as to notifiability is not a reasonable excuse for the purposes of *TMA 1970, s 118(2)* (see **55.38** PENALTIES) after the expiry of ten business days beginning with the date of the order.

Where a person fails to comply with a duty within (b) above and the promoter is a 'monitored promoter' for the purposes of the special compliance regime for high-risk promoters at **25.12–25.23** below or with a duty within (c) above where the arrangements concerned are arrangements of a monitored promoter, then legal advice which the person took into account is disregarded in determining whether he has a reasonable excuse if the advice was given or procured by that monitored promoter. In determining whether a monitored promoter has a reasonable excuse for a failure to comply with any duty of his falling within (a)–(o) above, reliance on legal advice is taken automatically not to be a reasonable excuse if either the advice was not based on a full and accurate description of the facts or the conclusions in the advice were unreasonable.

Failure to notify reference number to HMRC

A party to notifiable arrangements who fails to notify HMRC of the reference number (for example, by including it in his tax return) as required by **25.4** above is liable to a penalty of up to £5,000 for each scheme (i.e. each set of notifiable arrangements) to which the failure relates. A second such failure within a period of 36 months gives rise to a penalty of up to £7,500 per scheme (including any scheme to which the first failure relates). A third or subsequent failure within 36 months gives rise to a penalty of up to £10,000 per scheme (including any scheme to which any of the previous failures relates). The normal penalty regime for incorrect tax returns does not, however, apply in relation to any such failure.

Interest on penalties

Interest is chargeable on the above penalties if paid later than the due date. On and after 1 June 2019, the charge to interest is under the harmonised regime at **43.2** LATE PAYMENT INTEREST AND PENALTIES. Previously it was under the old regime at **43.3** LATE PAYMENT INTEREST AND PENALTIES.

On and after 1 June 2019, interest is payable by HMRC on the above penalties if they fall to be repaid. The interest is payable under the harmonised regime at **62.2** REPAYMENT INTEREST.

[*TMA 1970, s 98C; FA 2004, ss 315, 319; SI 2007 No 3104; SI 2012 No 1836, Reg 16; SI 2019 No 918*].

Voluntary disclosure of information to HMRC

[25.10] No duty of confidentiality or other restriction on disclosure (however imposed) prevents the voluntary disclosure by any person to HMRC of information or documents which the person has reasonable grounds for suspecting will assist HMRC in determining whether there has been a breach of any requirement imposed as above under the DOTAS regime. [*FA 2004, s 316B*].

Publication of information by HMRC

[25.11] HMRC may publish specified information about notifiable arrangements (or proposed notifiable arrangements) to which a reference number is allocated (see **25.4** above) and any person who is a promoter in relation to them. This can include information identifying a person as a promoter, but in this case HMRC must first inform him that they are considering publishing that information and give him reasonable opportunity to make representations about whether it should be published. No information can be published that identifies a person who enters into a transaction forming part of the notifiable arrangements (unless he is identified as a promoter).

Once any such information has been published about notifiable arrangements, HMRC must also publish information about any ruling of a court or tribunal that is made in relation to arrangements intended to secure a tax advantage if, in HMRC's opinion, the ruling is relevant to the notifiable arrangements in question. A ruling is relevant to the notifiable arrangements if it is final and if the principles laid down, or reasoning given, in the ruling would, if applied to the notifiable arrangements, allow the purported tax advantage arising from those arrangements.

[*FA 2004, ss 316C, 316D*].

Special compliance regime for high-risk promoters

[25.12] A special compliance regime applies to promoters of tax avoidance schemes who satisfy one or more 'threshold conditions' (see **25.15** below) relating to previous behaviour or, with effect on and after 15 September 2016, who regularly promote avoidance schemes which are defeated. The regime provides for the issuing of a 'conduct notice' (see **25.16** below) requiring the person to whom it is given to comply with specified conditions. Promoters who fail to comply with a conduct notice may be issued with a monitoring notice (see **25.17** below). Names of promoters subject to a monitoring notice may be published by HMRC, including details of how the conduct notice was breached, and promoters are required to notify their monitored status to clients. Information powers and penalties apply to promoters subject to a conduct notice and to promoters subject to a monitoring notice and their clients and intermediaries. Clients who fail to comply with their duty to provide HMRC with a monitored promoter's reference number are subject to extended time limits for assessment (see **6.3** ASSESSMENTS). Special rules apply to partnerships — see **25.22** below.

A number of taxes are covered by the special compliance regime. The coverage at **25.13–25.23** below is concerned primarily with its application to income tax. For HMRC guidance, see www.gov.uk/government/uploads/system/uploads/attachment_data/file/403423/Promoters_of_Tax_Avoidance_Schemes_Guidance.pdf.

Arrangements (as widely defined) are subject to the provisions if they enable, or might be expected to enable, any person to obtain a tax advantage and a main benefit that might be expected to arise from the arrangements is the obtaining of that advantage. A proposal is subject to the provisions if it is a proposal for arrangements which, if entered into, would themselves be subject to the provisions (whether the proposal relates to a particular person or to any person who may seek to use it). A tax advantage includes relief or increased relief from tax, repayment or increased repayment of tax, avoidance or reduction of a charge or assessment to tax, avoidance of a possible assessment to tax, deferral of a payment of tax, advancement of a repayment of tax, and avoidance of an obligation to deduct or account for tax.

Definitions

A person carrying on a business in the course of which he is, or has been, a promoter in relation to a proposal or arrangements carries on that business 'as a promoter'. A person is a '*promoter*' in relation to a proposal if:

(a) he is to any extent responsible for the design of the proposed arrangements; or

(b) he makes a 'firm approach' to another person with a view to making the proposal available for implementation by that, or any other, person; or
(c) he makes the proposal available for implementation by other persons.

A person is a '*promoter*' in relation to arrangements if:

- he is a promoter by virtue of (b) or (c) above in relation to a proposal which is implemented by the arrangements; or
- he is to any extent responsible for the design, organisation or management of the arrangements.

A person is not, however, a promoter by reason of anything done in such circumstances as may be prescribed by regulations. *SI 2015 No 130* excludes the following from the definition of 'promoter':

- a company providing in-house taxation services to companies in the same group and not marketing avoidance schemes to the public; and
- a professional who provides advice on a discrete point of law or accountancy but does not advise on tax matters or is not aware that there is a tax avoidance scheme.

Where a promoter (a '*monitored promoter*') of a proposal is subject to a monitoring notice (see **25.16** below), the proposal is a '*monitored proposal*' if the promoter, on or after the date the notice takes effect:

- first makes a firm approach to another person about the proposal;
- first makes the proposal available for implementation by another person; or
- first becomes aware of any transaction forming part of the proposed arrangements being entered into by any person.

Where a promoter of arrangements is a monitored promoter, the arrangements are '*monitored arrangements*' if:

- the promoter is, by virtue of (b) or (c) above, a promoter of a proposal implemented by the arrangements and, on or after the date the notice takes effect:
  - he first makes a firm approach to another person about the proposal;
  - he first makes the proposal available for implementation by another person;
  - he first becomes aware of any transaction forming part of the proposed arrangements being entered into by any person;
- the date on which the promoter first takes part in designing, organising or managing the arrangements is on or after the date on which the notice takes effect; or
- the arrangements enable, or are likely to enable, the person entering into the transactions forming them to obtain the tax advantage on or after the date the notice takes effect.

A person makes a '*firm approach*' to another person if he provides information about the proposal, including an explanation of the expected tax advantage, at a time when the proposed arrangements have been 'substantially designed', with a view to that, or any other, person entering into transactions forming part of the proposed arrangements. Arrangements have been '*substantially designed*' when it would be reasonable to believe that a person wishing to obtain the tax advantage might use the scheme or a scheme which is not substantially different.

A person is an '*intermediary*' in relation to a proposal if he is not a promoter of it but he communicates information about it to another person in the course of a business with a view to that, or any other, person entering into transactions forming part of the proposed arrangements.

'*Prescribed*' means prescribed, or of a description prescribed, in regulations made by HMRC by statutory instrument.

A person (P) is a '*controlling member*' of a partnership (see **25.22** below) at any time when P has a right to a share of more than half the assets or income of the partnership. Any interests or rights of any individual who is connected with P (if P is an individual) and of any body corporate controlled by P are attributed to P for this purpose. The following are connected with P: P's spouse or civil partner; P's relatives (i.e. a brother, sister, ancestor or lineal descendant); the spouse or civil partner of P's relatives; relatives of P's spouse or civil partner; and the spouse or civil partner of a relative of P's spouse or civil partner. P controls a body corporate if P has power to secure that its affairs are conducted in accordance with P's wishes either by means of holding shares or voting power in a body corporate (whether or not the body corporate in question) or as a result of powers under the articles of association or other document regulating a body corporate.

A '*managing partner*' of a partnership is a member of the partnership who directs, or is on a day to day level in control of, the management of the partnership's business.

An '*authorised HMRC officer*' is an HMRC officer who is, or is a member of a class of officers who are, authorised by the Commissioners for HMRC for the purposes of the special compliance regime.

[*FA 2014, ss 234–236, 254, 282, 283, Sch 36 paras 19–21; FA 2016, s 160(8)(9); SI 2015 No 130*].

Simon's Taxes. See **A7.250–A7.259.**

Threshold conditions

[25.13] A person meets a threshold condition if:

(a) HMRC publish information about the person under the deliberate tax defaulter provisions in *FA 2009, s 94* (see **55.35** PENALTIES);
(b) the person has been given a conduct notice under the dishonest conduct of tax agents provisions at **39.10** HMRC INVESTIGATORY POWERS and either the time limit for making an appeal against the notice has expired or an appeal has been made and rejected by the Appeal Tribunal;
(c) the person fails to comply with requirements under *FA 2004, ss 308–310* (obligations to disclose — see **25.3** above) or *FA 2004, s 313ZA* (duty of promoter to provide client details — see **25.5** above), including where the person had a reasonable excuse for non-compliance (see also below);

(d) the person is charged with a specified criminal offence (see below); but such a charge is disregarded for this purpose if it has been dismissed, if the proceedings have been discontinued or following final acquittal;

(e) arrangements of which the person is a promoter have been referred to the GAAR Advisory Panel (see **4.3** ANTI-AVOIDANCE and **55.20** PENALTIES) or are in a pool (see **4.6** ANTI-AVOIDANCE) in respect of which a referral has been made; the referral has been subject to one or more opinion notices of the sub-panel considering the case that the arrangements are not reasonable; and those notices, taken together, state the opinion of at least two of the members of the sub-panel;

(f) the person carries on a trade or profession that is regulated by a specified professional body, is found guilty of misconduct of a type prescribed for this purpose, has prescribed action taken against him, and has a prescribed penalty imposed on him (see below);

(g) the Financial Conduct Authority, Financial Services Authority or another prescribed regulatory body imposes a sanction for prescribed misconduct (see *SI 2015 No 131, Reg 6*);

(h) the person fails to comply with an information notice under *FA 2008, Sch 36 paras 1, 2, 5* or *5A* (see **39.3** HMRC INVESTIGATORY POWERS);

(i) the person (P) enters into an agreement with another person (C) which relates to a proposal or arrangements of which P is the promoter on terms which impose certain contractual obligations on C (see further below); or

(j) the person has been given a 'stop notice' (see below) and, after the end of the period of 30 days beginning on the day the notice is given, makes a 'firm approach' (see **25.12** above) to another person with a view to making an '*affected proposal*' (i.e. a proposal which is in substance the same as the proposal specified in the stop notice) available for implementation by that person or another or makes an affected proposal available for implementation by other persons.

As regards (c) above, it is clarified that a failure to comply with a said requirement occurs only at the time (if any) that:

- the 'appeal period' ends following a determination by the Appeal Tribunal that such a failure occurred, or that it would have occurred but for the person's having a reasonable excuse, and it has ended without the determination being overturned; or
- the person admits in writing to HMRC that he has failed to comply with the requirement in question.

The '*appeal period*' is the period during which an appeal could have been made or, where an appeal has been made, the period during which it has not yet been finally determined, withdrawn or otherwise disposed of.

For the purposes of (d) above, the following offences are specified:

- a common law offence of cheating the public revenue;
- in Scotland, an offence of fraud or uttering;
- an offence under *Theft Act 1968, s 17* (false accounting) or NI equivalent;
- an offence under *TMA 1970, s 106A* (fraudulent evasion of income tax);

- an offence under *TMA 1970, s 107* (false statements: Scotland);
- an offence under *Customs and Excise Management Act 1979, s 50(2)* (improper importation of goods with intent to defraud or evade duty), *s 167* (untrue declarations etc.), *s 168* (counterfeiting documents etc.), *s 170* (fraudulent evasion of duty) or *s 170B* (taking steps for the fraudulent evasion of duty);
- an offence under *VATA 1994, s 72(1)* (being knowingly concerned in the evasion of VAT), *s 72(3)* (false statement etc.), or *s 72(8)* (conduct involving commission of other offence);
- an offence under *Fraud Act 2006, s 1*;
- an offence under *CRCA 2005, s 30* (impersonating a Commissioner or officer of HMRC), *s 31* (obstruction of HMRC officer etc.) or *s 32* (assault of HMRC officer);
- an offence under *SI 2007 No 2157, Reg 45(1)* (money laundering); and
- an offence under *Criminal Justice and Licensing (Scotland) Act 2010, s 49(1)* (possession of articles for use in fraud).

For the purposes of (f) above, the type of misconduct prescribed is conduct by a person which a professional body describes as misconduct or which is a breach of a rule or condition imposed by such a body and which is relevant to the provision of tax advice or tax-related services. Prescribed action means any action by a professional body which results in any claim of misconduct being referred to a disciplinary process or a conciliation, arbitration or similar settlement process. A prescribed penalty means a fine or financial penalty greater than £5,000 and/or a condition or restriction attached to, or the suspension, withdrawal or non-renewal of, a practising certificate, or suspension, expulsion or exclusion from membership of the professional body, whether it be temporary or permanent. In (f) above, the specified professional bodies are the Institutes of Chartered Accountants in England and Wales and of Scotland, the General Council of the Bar, the Faculty of Advocates, the General Council of the Bar in Northern Ireland, the Law Society, the Law Societies of Scotland and Northern Ireland, the Association of Accounting Technicians, the Association of Chartered Certified Accountants, the Association of Taxation Technicians, the Chartered Institute of Taxation and Chartered Accountants Ireland. The threshold condition is not confined to decisions and actions taken by the professional body itself and may thus take account of decisions and actions by independent bodies in matters of relevant forms of professional misconduct.

Note that, where the threshold condition in question is within (h) above, it is treated as met when the time limit for compliance with the information notice expires without the promoter complying with it.

The threshold condition in (i) above is met if the contractual obligation prevents or restricts the disclosure by C to HMRC of information about the proposals or arrangements, whether or not by referring to a wider class of persons, or if the obligation requires C to impose a similar contractual obligation on any tax adviser to whom C discloses information. The condition is also met if contractual obligations require C:

- to meet the whole or part of the costs of, or contribute to a fund to meet the costs of, any 'proceedings' relating to arrangements promoted by C (whether or not implemented by C) or, where C implements the arrangements, to take out an insurance policy to insure against the risk of having to meet such costs; and
- to obtain P's consent before making any agreement with HMRC regarding arrangements promoted by P or withdrawing or discontinuing any appeal against a decision about such arrangements.

'*Proceedings*' for this purpose include any sort of proceedings for resolving disputes (i.e. not just court proceedings) which are commenced or contemplated.

Stop notices

An authorised HMRC officer may give a person (P) a '*stop notice*' (see (j) above) if:

- a person has been given a follower notice (see **4.44** ANTI-AVOIDANCE) relating to particular arrangements;
- P is a promoter of a proposal implemented by those arrangements; and
- 90 days have passed since the follower notice was given, the notice has not been withdrawn and, if representations objecting to the notice were made, HMRC have confirmed the notice.

A stop notice must specify the arrangements which are the subject of the follower notice, specify the court or tribunal ruling identified in that notice, specify the proposal implemented by those arrangements and explain the effect of the stop notice. An authorised HMRC officer may notify P in writing that a stop notice is to cease to have effect from a specified date (which may be before the notice is given).

[*FA 2014, Sch 34 paras 1–12, 14; FA 2016, s 157(29); F(No 2)A 2017, Sch 16 paras 61, 62; SI 2015 No 131*].

Relevant defeat

[25.14] For the purposes of the special compliance regime, and subject to the commencement rules below, a '*defeat*' of arrangements occurs in any of the following circumstances.

(A) A tax advantage arising from the arrangements is counteracted (wholly or partly) by HMRC under the GAAR (see **4.2** ANTI-AVOIDANCE) and the counteraction is 'final'.

(B) A follower notice (see **4.44** ANTI-AVOIDANCE) has been given by reference to the arrangements (and not withdrawn) and either the taxpayer takes corrective action or the denied tax advantage is counteracted (wholly or partly) and the counteraction is final.

(C) A tax advantage arising from 'DOTAS arrangements' is counteracted and the counteraction is final. '*DOTAS arrangements*' are arrangements which a person has disclosed to HMRC under *FA 2004, s 308, s 309* or *310* (see **25.3** above) or in respect of which a person has 'failed to comply' (as defined) with a requirement to do so. Arrangements which a person would be so required to disclose but for certain specified exceptions are treated for this purpose as having been disclosed. A tax advantage is counteracted if 'adjustments' are made to the taxpayer's position on the basis that the whole or part of the advantage does not arise. Arrangements in respect of which HMRC have given notice that the reference number need no longer be notified to clients (see **25.4** above) are excluded.

(D) A tax advantage arising from 'disclosable VAT arrangements' (as defined) is counteracted and the counteraction is final.

(E) A final judicial ruling holds that a particular 'avoidance-related rule' applies to counteract the whole or part of a tax advantage arising from the arrangements. '*Avoidance-related rule*' is defined by *FA 2014, Sch 34A para 18*, which also includes an example of such a rule. A statutory rule to the effect that the avoidance of tax must not be a main object or an expected benefit of a transaction or arrangements, or that an action must be carried out for commercial reasons, would be an avoidance-related rule.

A counteraction is '*final*' for these purposes when the assessment or adjustments made to effect it, and any amounts arising as a result, can no longer be varied on appeal or otherwise. A judicial ruling is '*final*' if it is a Supreme Court ruling or a ruling of any other tribunal or court against which no further appeal can be made. '*Adjustments*' means any adjustments, by assessment, modification of an assessment or return, amendment or disallowance of a claim, entering into a contract settlement or otherwise.

A defeat of arrangements entered into by any person which are 'promoted arrangements' of a promoter is a '*relevant defeat*' in relation to that promoter if either:

(i) the arrangements are not 'related' to any other promoted arrangements of the promoter; or

(ii) they are related to other promoted arrangements of the promoter and any of cases 1–3 below applies (in which case there is a relevant defeat of the arrangements in question and of each of the related arrangements).

If there has been a relevant defeat in relation to promoted arrangements of a promoter there can be no further relevant defeat of those arrangements or of any related arrangements.

For the purpose of (ii) above, case 1 applies if any of (A)–(D) above are met in relation to any of the arrangements and the decision to make the counteraction in question has been upheld by a judicial ruling which is final. Case 2 applies if (E) above is met in relation to any of the arrangements. Case 3 applies if at least 75% of the 'tested arrangements' have been defeated and no final judicial ruling has upheld a corresponding tax advantage under any of the arrangements. The '*tested arrangements*' are any of the arrangements in respect of which: there has been an enquiry or investigation by HMRC into a return, claim or election; HMRC has assessed a taxpayer on the basis that the tax advantage (or part of it) does not arise; a final counteraction notice under the

GAAR (see **4.3–4.6** ANTI-AVOIDANCE) has been given in relation to the tax advantage (or part of it); or HMRC have taken any other action on the basis that a tax advantage does not arise under the arrangements.

Arrangements are '*promoted arrangements*' in relation to a promoter if they are arrangements to which the special compliance regime applies or would apply if that regime applied generally to VAT. Separate arrangements are '*related*' to each other if they are substantially the same. For this purpose, arrangements which have been allocated the same reference number under **25.4** above or the equivalent VAT provisions are treated as substantially the same (if they would not otherwise be so treated). Arrangements which are subject to follower notices by reference to the same judicial ruling are likewise treated as substantially the same. Where a notice of binding under the GAAR has been given (see **4.6** ANTI-AVOIDANCE, the bound arrangements are treated as being substantially the same as the lead arrangements and any other arrangements otherwise treated as substantially the same as the lead arrangements.

Attribution of relevant defeat

A relevant defeat in relation to a person (Q) is treated as a relevant defeat in relation to another person (P), whether or not it is also treated as a relevant defeat of Q, if:

(1) where P is not an individual:
- at a time when the defeated arrangements were promoted arrangements in relation to Q either P was a body corporate or partnership controlled by Q or Q was a body corporate or partnership controlled by P; and
- at the time of the relevant defeat, P was a body corporate or partnership controlled by Q, Q was a body corporate or partnership controlled by P or both were bodies corporate or partnerships controlled by a third person; or

(2) where P and Q are both bodies corporate or partnerships, at a time when the defeated arrangements were promoted arrangements in relation to Q, a third person (C) controlled Q and C controls P at the time of the relevant defeat.

This rule applies even if Q has ceased to exist or if P did not exist at any time when the defeated arrangements were promoted arrangements in relation to Q. For the purposes of the rule, in determining whether arrangements are promoted arrangements in relation to Q, the definition of 'promoter' in **25.12** above applies as if the word 'design' were omitted.

A person controls a body corporate if he has power to secure that the affairs of the body corporate are conducted in accordance with his wishes, whether by means of the holding of shares, the possession of voting power or the articles of association or other document or by means of his controlling a partnership. A person controls a partnership if he is a 'controlling member' or 'managing partner' of the partnership (see **25.12** above).

[*FA 2014, s 237D(6), Sch 34A paras 1–17, 19, 24–31; FA 2016, s 160(2)(5)*].

Defeat notices

Subject to the commencement rules below, an authorised HMRC officer may give a person carrying on a business as a promoter a '*defeat notice*' if:

(a) he becomes aware of one (and only one) relevant defeat in relation to the promoter in the previous three years (in which case the notice is a '*single defeat notice*'); or

(b) he becomes aware of two (but not more than two) relevant defeats in relation to the promoter in the previous three years (a '*double defeat notice*').

If, after a single defeat notice has ceased to have effect because of a judicial ruling (see below), the officer becomes aware of a further relevant defeat in relation to the promoter which occurred whilst the notice was in effect, he may issue a further single defeat notice (even if the further defeat did not occur in the three years preceding the issuing of the notice).

A defeat notice must be given before the end of the 90 days beginning with the date on which the defeat in question came to HMRC's attention. The notice must state the 'look-forward period' and explain the effect of the notice (see **25.15** below). A notice given to a partnership must state that it is a partnership defeat notice. A defeat notice has effect throughout the look-forward period unless it ceases to have effect because the relevant defeat is 'overturned'. The '*look-forward period*' is the five years beginning the day after the notice is given or, in the case of a further single defeat notice, the period beginning the day after the notice is given and ending five years from the day on which the further relevant defeat occurred.

A single defeat notice ceases to have effect if, and on and after the day that, the relevant defeat is overturned. If one (and only one) of the relevant defeats on which a double defeat notice is based is overturned, the notice is treated as if it had always been a single defeat notice based on the other relevant defeat. If both the relevant defeats on which a double defeat notice is based are overturned on the same date, the notice ceases to have effect on that date. HMRC must notify the promoter accordingly.

Only a relevant defeat to which case 3 above applies can be overturned. Such a defeat is '*overturned*' if, before the notice was given, less than 100% of the tested arrangements had been defeated and, at a time when the notice has effect, a court or tribunal upholds a tax advantage arising under any of the arrangements taken into account in determining the case 3 relevant defeat. The relevant defeat is overturned on the day on which the judicial ruling becomes final. For this purpose, a court or tribunal upholds a tax advantage if it makes a ruling that no part of the advantage is to be counteracted and that ruling is final.

Deemed defeat notices

Provision is made for a defeat notice to be deemed to have been given to a person (P) who is carrying on a business as a promoter when certain conditions are met in respect of 'third party defeats'. This applies where an authorised officer becomes aware at any time (the '*relevant time*') that a relevant defeat has occurred in relation to P and in the preceding three years there have been one or two third party defeats. A '*third party defeat*' is a relevant defeat which has occurred in relation to a person other than P.

Where there has been one such third party defeat, then if

- a conduct notice or single or double defeat notice has been given to the other person in respect of the third party defeat; at the time of that defeat, HMRC would have been able to give a defeat notice to P under the rules for attributing relevant defeats above if they had been aware that the defeat was also a relevant defeat in relation to P; and so far as the HMRC officer is aware, the conditions for giving P a defeat notice in respect of the defeat have never otherwise been met; and
- had a defeat notice in respect of the third party defeat been given to P at the time of that defeat, the defeat notice would still have effect at the relevant time,

the special compliance regime applies as if the officer had, with due authority, given P a single defeat notice at the time of the third party defeat.

Where there have been two third party defeats, then if:

- a conduct notice or single or double defeat notice has been given to the other person in respect of each, or both, of the third party defeats; at the time of the second defeat, HMRC would have been able to give a double defeat notice to P under the rules for attributing relevant defeats above if they had been aware that either of the defeats was also a relevant defeat in relation to P; and so far as the HMRC officer is aware, the conditions for giving P a defeat notice in respect of either or both of the defeats have never otherwise been met; and
- had a defeat notice in respect of the two third party defeats been given to P at the time of the second defeat, the defeat notice would still have effect at the relevant time,

the special compliance regime applies as if the officer had, with due authority, given P a single defeat notice at the time of the third party defeat.

Commencement

The above provisions, and those at **25.15** below under the headings 'Defeat of promoted arrangements' and 'Related companies and partnerships — defeat of promoted arrangements' apply with effect on and after 15 September 2016.

A defeat of arrangements is treated for the purposes of those provisions as not having occurred if there was a final judicial ruling before 15 September 2016 as a result of which the counteraction in (A)–(D) above is final or, where (E) above applies, if the judicial ruling in question became final on or before that date. This does not apply, however, if at any time on or after 17 July 2014 a promoter takes action as a result of which he or an associated person becomes a promoter in relation to the arrangements or related arrangements or would have become a promoter in relation to those arrangements had he not already been a promoter in relation to them. For this purpose two persons (P and Q) are associated if P is a body corporate or partnership and is controlled by Q, Q is a body corporate, P is not an individual and Q is controlled by P or if P and Q are bodies corporate or partnerships and a third person controls both of them. Control is defined as above.

A defeat of arrangements is also treated for the purposes of the provisions as not having occurred if it would otherwise occur on or before 15 September 2017 by virtue of (A)–(D) above otherwise than as a result of a final judicial ruling.

[*FA 2014, ss 241A, 241B, Sch 34A para 18, Sch 36 para 4A; FA 2016, s 160(3)(5)(11)(20)–(25)*].

Conduct notices

[25.15] A '*conduct notice*' is a notice requiring the person to whom it is given to comply with specified conditions. HMRC must issue such a notice in any of the four situations described below.

A conduct notice has effect from the date specified in it and may be amended at any time by an authorised HMRC officer. A notice ceases to have effect after two years or on an earlier date specified in the notice. It also ceases to have effect if a monitoring notice (see **25.16** below) takes effect. A notice may also be withdrawn by an authorised HMRC officer. A provisional notice may cease to have effect as a result of a judicial decision (see further below).

Threshold condition satisfied

An 'authorised HMRC officer' (see **25.12** above) must issue a conduct notice if he becomes aware at any time that a person carrying on a business as a promoter has, in the previous three years and at a time when he was carrying on such a business, met one or more of the threshold conditions (see **25.13** above) and the officer determines that the meeting of the condition(s) should be regarded as significant in view of the purposes of the special compliance regime. For this purpose, meeting any of the threshold conditions in **25.13**(a), (b), (d) or (e) is automatically treated as significant. No conduct notice need be issued if the officer determines that it is inappropriate to do so, having regard to the extent of the impact that the promoter's activities are likely to have on the collection of tax. A conduct notice cannot be issued if the promoter is already subject to such a notice or to a monitoring notice (see **25.16** below). A conduct notice given to a partnership must state that it is a partnership conduct notice.

Related companies and partnerships — threshold conditions

An authorised HMRC officer must also issue a conduct notice if he becomes aware at any time (the '*relevant time*') that:

(i) a person (P1) has, in the previous three years, met one or more of the threshold conditions;
(ii) at the relevant time another person (P2) is treated as meeting one or more of the threshold conditions by virtue of the 'control rules' described below; and

(iii) P2 is, at the relevant time, carrying on a business as a promoter,

and the officer determines that the meeting of the condition(s) by both P1 and P2 should be regarded as significant in view of the purposes of the special compliance regime.

The officer must issue the conduct notice to P2, unless he determines that it is inappropriate to do so, having regard to the extent of the impact that P2's activities are likely to have on the collection of tax. The giving of a conduct notice to P2 does not prevent the giving of such a notice to P1 in his own right.

The '*control rules*' referred to in (ii) above treat persons under another's control, persons in control of others and persons under common control as meeting a threshold condition at the relevant time as set out below. From 8 March 2017, persons with 'significant influence' over a body corporate or partnership fall within the control rules in the same way as if they controlled the body corporate or partnership.

For these purposes a person controls a body corporate if he has power to secure that its affairs are conducted in accordance with his wishes, whether by means of the holding of shares, the possession of voting power or the articles of association or other document or by means of his controlling a partnership. From 8 March 2017, two or more persons together control a body corporate if together they have the power to secure by any of those means that its affairs are conducted in accordance with their wishes.

From 8 March 2017, a person controls a partnership if he is a member of the partnership and either has the right to a share of more than half its assets or income or directs, or (on a day-to-day level) is in control of, the management of its business. Two or more persons together control a partnership if they are members of the partnership and together meet one of those conditions. For these purposes, the interests or rights of any individual who is connected with a person (if the person is an individual) and of any body corporate controlled by the person are attributed to the person; see **25.12** above (under the definition of 'controlling member') for more details. Before 8 March 2017, a person controls a partnership if he is a 'controlling member' or 'managing partner' of the partnership (see **25.12** above).

A person has '*significant influence*' over a body corporate or partnership if, whilst not controlling it, he exercises, or is able to exercise, significant influence over it (whether or not as the result of a legal entitlement). Two or more persons together have significant influence over a body corporate or partnership if together they meet that condition.

The changes described here as applying from 8 March 2017 have effect for the purposes of determining whether a person meets a threshold condition in a period of three years ending on or after that date.

Persons under another's control

P2 is treated as meeting a threshold condition at the relevant time if it is controlled by P1 at that time and P1 met the threshold condition at a time when either P1 was carrying on a business as a promoter or P2 was carrying on a business as a promoter and P1 controlled P2. However, where P1 is an individual, this treatment applies only where the threshold condition in question is one within **25.13**(a) or (b) or any of (d)–(h) above. From 8 March 2017, the provisions are amended to allow for the possibility of a body corporate or partnership being controlled by two or more persons.

Persons in control of others

Where P2 is a person other than an individual, P2 is treated as meeting a threshold condition at the relevant time if P1 is a body corporate or partnership and met the threshold condition at a time (the 'earlier time') when it was carrying on a business as a promoter and was controlled by P2. This applies additionally if at the earlier time it was another body corporate or partnership controlled by P2 that was carrying on a business as a promoter. Before 8 March 2017, neither of these rules applied if P2 was an individual.

Persons under common control

Where P2 is a body corporate or partnership, P2 is treated as meeting a threshold condition at the relevant time if:

- P2 or another body corporate or partnership met the threshold condition at a time (the 'earlier time') when it was controlled by P1;
- at the earlier time there was a body corporate or partnership controlled by P1 which carried on a business as a promoter; and
- P2 is controlled by P1 at the relevant time.

From 8 March 2017, the provisions are amended to allow for the possibility of a body corporate or partnership being controlled by two or more persons.

Defeat of promoted arrangements

The following applies subject to the commencement rules in **25.14** above. An authorised HMRC officer must issue a conduct notice if he becomes aware at any time (the '*relevant time*') that a person who is carrying on a business as a promoter meets any of the following conditions and the officer determines that the meeting of the condition(s) should be regarded as significant in view of the purposes of the special compliance regime. The conditions are that:

(I) in the previous three years, at least three 'relevant defeats' have occurred in relation to the promoter; or

(II) at least two relevant defeats have occurred in relation to the promoter at times when he was subject to a single defeat notice (see **25.14** above); or

(III) at least one relevant defeat has occurred in relation to the promoter at a time when he was subject to a double defeat notice (see **25.14** above).

A determination that either of the conditions at (II) or (III) above is met can only be made while the relevant defeat notice is still in effect or on or before the 90th day after that on which it ceased to have effect. No conduct notice need be issued if the officer determines that it is inappropriate to do so, having regard to the extent of the impact that the promoter's activities are likely to have on the collection of tax.

A conduct notice cannot be issued in these circumstances if the promoter is already subject to a conduct notice or a monitoring notice. If an HMRC officer is considering at the same time whether or not a conduct notice must be given because of a threshold condition, the meeting of a condition in (I)–(III) above is treated as meeting a threshold condition and any conduct notice must be given on that basis.

An authorised HMRC officer must give a further conduct notice to a promoter if:

(1) a conduct notice has ceased to have effect otherwise than because of a judicial ruling or because it is withdrawn or a monitoring notice is given, and the notice was 'provisional';
(2) the officer determines that the promoter had failed to comply with one or more conditions in the conduct notice;
(3) the conduct notice relied on a case 3 relevant defeat (see **25.14** above) but less than 100% of the tested arrangements had been defeated before the notice was given;
(4) after the conduct notice ceased to have effect, one or more case 1 or 2 relevant defeats has occurred in relation to the promoter and any arrangements to which the case 3 relevant defeat also relates; and
(5) had that defeat or defeats occurred before the conduct notice ceased to have effect, HMRC would have had to notify the promoter that it was no longer provisional.

A further conduct notice cannot be issued in these circumstances if the promoter is already subject to a conduct notice or a monitoring notice and need not be issued if the HMRC officer determines that it is inappropriate to do so, having regard to the extent of the impact that the promoter's activities are likely to have on the collection of tax.

A conduct notice is '*provisional*' if (3) above applies to it, unless an authorised HMRC officer notifies the promoter that it is no longer provisional. A notice ceases to be provisional if:

(A) (i) two, or all three, of the relevant defeats by reference to which the notice is given would not have been relevant defeats if case 3 in **25.14** above had required 100% of the tested arrangements to have been defeated, and (ii) the same number of 'full relevant defeats' occur in relation to the promoter; or
(B) where (A)(i) above does not apply, a full relevant defeat occurs in relation to the promoter.

A '*full relevant defeat*' is either a relevant defeat other than one under case 3 or a case 3 relevant defeat where all of the tested arrangements are defeated. For this purpose, the rule that there can be only one relevant defeat of particular arrangements and any related arrangements (see **25.14** above) does not prevent a full relevant defeat from occurring in respect of arrangements in relation to which a relevant defeat under case 3 has previously occurred.

A provisional conduct notice ceases to have effect if a court or tribunal upholds a tax advantage arising under any of the arrangements taken into account in determining the case 3 relevant defeat. For this purpose, a court or tribunal upholds a tax advantage if it makes a ruling that no part of the advantage is to be counteracted and that ruling is final. HMRC must notify the promoter accordingly.

Related companies and partnerships — defeat of promoted arrangements

The following applies subject to the commencement rules in **25.14** above. An authorised HMRC officer must also issue a conduct notice if he becomes aware at any time (the '*relevant time*') that:

(a) a person (P1) meets any of conditions (I)–(III) above;
(b) at the relevant time another person (P2) meets that condition by virtue of the 'control rules' described below; and
(c) P2 is, at the relevant time, carrying on a business as a promoter,

and the officer determines that the meeting of these conditions by both P1 and P2 should be regarded as significant in view of the purposes of the special compliance regime.

The officer must issue the conduct notice to P2, unless he determines that it is inappropriate to do so, having regard to the extent of the impact that P2's activities are likely to have on the collection of tax. The giving of a conduct notice to P2 does not prevent the giving of such a notice to P1 in his own right.

A conduct notice cannot be issued in these circumstances if P2 is already subject to a conduct notice or a monitoring notice. If an HMRC officer is considering at the same time whether or not a conduct notice must be given because of a threshold condition, P2's meeting of the condition in (b) above is treated as P2 meeting a threshold condition and any conduct notice must be given on that basis.

The '*control rules*' referred to in (b) above treat persons under another's control, persons in control of others and persons under common control as meeting a condition within (I)–(III) above at the relevant time as set out below. From 8 March 2017, persons with significant influence over a body corporate or partnership fall within the control rules in the same way as if they controlled the body corporate or partnership. See above under Related companies and partnerships — threshold conditions for as to when a person controls, or has significant influence over, a body corporate or partnership.

The changes described here as applying from 8 March 2017 have effect for the purposes of determining whether a person meets a condition in (I)–(III) above in a period of three years ending on or after that date.

Persons under another's control

Where P2 is a body corporate or partnership, P2 is treated as meeting a condition at the relevant time if it is controlled by P1 at that time and P1 met the condition at a time when either P1 was carrying on a business as a promoter or P2 was carrying on a business as a promoter and P1 controlled P2. However, this rule does not apply where P1 is an individual. From 8 March 2017, the provisions are amended to allow for the possibility of a body corporate or partnership being controlled by two or more persons.

Persons in control of others

P2 is treated as meeting a condition at the relevant time if P1 is a body corporate or partnership and met the condition at a time (the 'earlier time') when it was carrying on a business as a promoter and was controlled by P2. This applies additionally if at the earlier time it was another body corporate or partnership controlled by P2 that was carrying on a business as a promoter. Before 8 March 2017, neither of these rules applied if P2 was an individual.

Persons under common control

Where P2 is a body corporate or partnership, P2 is treated as meeting a condition at the relevant time if:

- another body corporate or partnership met the condition at a time (the 'earlier time') when it was controlled by P1;
- at the earlier time there was a body corporate or partnership controlled by P1 which carried on a business as a promoter; and
- P2 is controlled by P1 at the relevant time.

From 8 March 2017, the provisions are amended to allow for the possibility of a body corporate or partnership being controlled by two or more persons.

Terms of a conduct notice

The terms of a conduct notice are determined by the officer giving it, but are limited to conditions that it is reasonable to impose to ensure that the promoter:

(a) provides adequate information (as defined, and including an assessment of the risk that the expected tax advantage will not be achieved) to clients (as defined) about proposals and arrangements of which he is a promoter;
(b) provides adequate information to intermediaries about proposals of which he is a promoter;
(c) does not fail to comply with any specified duties under the disclosure of tax avoidance schemes provisions (see **25.3** above) or under *FA 2008, Sch 36 paras 1–9* (see **39.3** HMRC INVESTIGATORY POWERS);
(d) does not discourage others from complying with any specified disclosure obligation;
(e) does not enter into an agreement which imposes on another person contractual obligations within **25.13**(i) above;
(f) does not promote proposals or arrangements which rely on, or involve a proposal to rely on, one or more contrived or abnormal steps to produce a tax advantage; and
(g) does not fail to comply with any stop notice (see **25.13** above).

In the case of a partnership conduct notice, conditions may be imposed relating to the persons who are partners when the notice is given and to persons who subsequently become partners.

Before deciding on the terms of a notice, the officer must provide an opportunity for the promoter to comment on the proposed terms.

[*FA 2014, ss 237, 237A–237D, 238–241, Sch 34, paras 13, 13A–13D, 14, Sch 34A paras 19–23, Sch 36, paras 4, 5, 20, 21; FA 2016, s 160(2)(5)(6); FA 2017, s 24*].

Information

HMRC may (as often as is necessary) by notice in writing require a person subject to a conduct notice to provide information or produce a document which is reasonably required for the purpose of monitoring compliance with the notice. [*FA 2014, s 262*].

Monitoring notices

[25.16] If an 'authorised HMRC officer' (see **25.12** above) determines that a promoter has failed to comply with one or more conditions in a conduct notice, he must apply to the Appeal Tribunal for approval to give the promoter a notice (a '*monitoring notice*'), unless the conditions in question were imposed under any of **25.15**(a)–(c) above and the officer considers the failure to comply to be such a minor matter that it should be disregarded. An application for approval must include a draft notice and the officer must also notify the promoter of the application. The notice to the promoter must state which conditions have not been complied with and the officer's reasons for determining that there has been a failure to comply.

No application can be made to the Tribunal in respect of a conduct notice which is provisional. Any failure to comply with a condition in such a notice can, however, be taken into account in determining whether to make an application if the notice ceases to be provisional.

The Appeal Tribunal may approve the giving of a monitoring notice only if it is satisfied that the officer would be justified in giving it and that the promoter has been given a reasonable opportunity to make representations to the Tribunal. If the promoter's representations include a statement that it was not reasonable to include a particular condition in the conduct notice and the Tribunal is satisfied that it was not so reasonable, the Tribunal must assume that there was no failure to comply with the condition (and must refuse HMRC's application if this applies to all the conditions which HMRC consider have not been complied with). If the Tribunal gives approval it may amend the draft notice. A promoter may appeal against the decision of the Tribunal in the usual way (see 5 APPEALS).

A monitoring notice must explain its effect and specify the date from which it takes effect (which cannot be earlier than the date the notice is given). It must also inform the recipient of the right to request its withdrawal (see further below). The notice must state the conditions of the conduct notice which HMRC have determined that the promoter has failed to comply with and the reasons for that determination. A notice given to a partnership must state that it is a partnership monitoring notice. If the notice is a replacement notice given to a former partner of a partnership itself subject to a monitoring notice (see **25.22** below) it must also state the date of that notice and the name of the partnership.

Withdrawal of a monitoring notice

An authorised HMRC officer may withdraw a notice if he thinks it is no longer necessary, taking into account matters including the promoter's behaviour and compliance whilst the notice has had effect and likely future behaviour.

A person subject to a monitoring notice (a '*monitored promoter*') may make a request in writing to an authorised HMRC officer that the notice should cease to apply. Such a request can be made at any time after the twelve months beginning with the end of the period in which an appeal against the Appeal Tribunal's decision to approve the giving of the notice could have been made or, where such an appeal was made, the twelve months beginning with the date on which the appeal was finally determined, withdrawn or otherwise disposed of. If the notice is a replacement notice, the twelve-month period applies by reference to appeals against the Tribunal's decision about the original notice. HMRC must determine whether or not the notice should cease to apply within the 30 days beginning with the date on which the request is received and must notify the promoter of their determination specifying the date from which the notice is to cease to apply (and whether or not a follow-on conduct notice is to be given — see below) or their reasons for refusal of the request.

A monitored promoter can appeal against a refusal by HMRC by notice in writing within 30 days beginning with the date on which the refusal notice was given, stating the grounds of appeal.

If HMRC decide to withdraw a notice or, following a request from the promoter, decide that a notice should cease to apply, they may issue a follow-on conduct notice to take effect immediately after the monitoring notice ceases to have effect.

[*FA 2014, ss 242–247, Sch 36 para 6; FA 2016, s 160(4)*].

Effects of a monitoring notice

[25.17] A monitoring notice has the effects set out below (and see also **25.18–25.20** below).

Publication by HMRC

HMRC may publish the name (including business name and any previous name or pseudonym) of a monitored promoter together with the business address or registered office, the nature of the business carried on, a statement of the conditions in a conduct notice with which the promoter has failed to comply and any other information which they consider appropriate to publish to make clear the promoter's identity. Where the monitored promoter is a partnership, it is the details of the partnership which may be published (and not those of particular partners). Publication may not take place before the end of the period in which an appeal against the Appeal Tribunal's decision to approve the giving of the notice can be made or, where such an appeal is made, before the appeal is finally determined, withdrawn or otherwise disposed of. If the notice is a replacement notice (see **25.22** below), the restriction applies by reference to appeals against the Tribunal's decision about the original notice. If HMRC publish details of a monitored promoter they must publish the fact of a withdrawal of the notice in the same way. [*FA 2014, s 248, Sch 36 para 14*].

Publication by monitored promoter

The monitored promoter must give a notice stating that he is a monitored promoter and which conduct notice conditions have not been complied with to anyone who is a client (as defined) at the time the monitoring notice takes effect and to anyone who becomes a client whilst the notice has effect. The notice must also identify the original monitoring notice if the monitoring notice in question is a replacement notice (see **25.22** below). The requirement to give such notices does not apply until ten days after the end of the period in which an appeal against the Appeal Tribunal's decision to approve the giving of the notice can be made or, where such an appeal is made, ten days after the appeal is finally determined, withdrawn or otherwise disposed of. If the notice is a replacement notice, the requirement applies by reference to appeals against the Tribunal's decision about the original notice. In the case of someone becoming a client whilst the monitoring notice has effect, the promoter must give them the required notice within ten days of their first becoming a client.

HMRC may, by regulations, require such information to be published online, together with the promoter's reference number (see below). Regulations may also prescribe publications or correspondence in which the information and reference number must be included and the form and manner in which notices are to be given and information published (see now *SI 2015 No 549, Regs 2, 3*).

[*FA 2014, s 249; SI 2015 No 549, Regs 1–3*].

Reference number

Once all rights to appeal against the decision of the Appeal Tribunal to approve the giving of the monitoring notice (or original notice) are exhausted, HMRC will allocate a reference number to the monitored promoter. HMRC then notify the number to the promoter or, if the promoter is non-UK resident, to any person who HMRC know is an 'intermediary' (see **25.12** above) in relation to a proposal of the promoter. A promoter so notified must in turn notify the number to anyone who becomes a client while the monitoring notice has effect or who is an intermediary whilst the notice has effect. Unless the monitoring notice is a replacement notice, he must also notify the number to any person he can reasonably be expected to know has entered into arrangements, in the period in which the conduct notice preceding the monitoring notice had effect, which are likely to enable that person to obtain a tax advantage whilst the monitoring notice has effect if the monitored promoter is a promoter of those arrangements or of a proposal implemented by those arrangements. Notification must be given within 30 days of HMRC's notification of the number or later event triggering the requirement to notify.

An intermediary who is notified by HMRC of a reference number or a person so notified by a promoter must, within 30 days of being so notified, provide the number to any other person they might reasonably be expected to know has become, or is likely to have become, a client of the monitored promoter whilst the monitoring notice has had effect. An intermediary must also, within 30 days, provide the number to any person to whom he has communicated, in the course of a business and since the monitoring notice took effect, information about a proposal of the monitored promoter and to any person who he might reasonably be expected to know has, since the notice took effect, entered into, or is likely to enter into, transactions forming part of arrangements of which the monitored promoter is a promoter. An intermediary or other person notified of a reference number by the promoter does not have to provide the number to a person if he reasonably believes that the person has already been provided with the number.

A person who has been notified of a reference number under any of the above provisions must report it to HMRC if he expects to obtain a tax advantage from arrangements of which the promoter to whom the number relates is a promoter. The report must normally be made in each tax return for any period which includes a period for which the tax advantage is obtained (irrespective of whether the return relates to the tax affected). If no tax return has to be made for such periods or if a tax return is not submitted by the filing date, a separate report must be made in accordance with *SI 2015 No 549, Regs 4(1), 5, 6*. In a case where the tax return is not submitted by the filing date, the report must be made by the end of the fifth working day following the filing date. In a case where no return has to be made, the report must be made by 31 January following the tax year within which the tax advantage arises. If the arrangements give rise to a claim under *TCGA 1992, s 261B* (set-off of trading losses against capital gains — see **45.5** LOSSES) and that claim is made outside of a tax return, the claim must include the reference number.

[*FA 2014, ss 250–253; SI 2015 No 549, Regs 1, 4–6, Schs 1, 2*].

Information powers where monitoring notice in effect

[25.18] HMRC may by notice in writing require a monitored promoter or a person who is an 'intermediary' (see **25.12** above) in relation to a 'monitored proposal' (see **25.12** above) to provide information or produce a document which is reasonably required by HMRC for:

- considering the possible consequences of implementing a monitored proposal for the tax positions of those implementing it;
- checking the tax position of any person that HMRC believe has implemented a monitored proposal;
- checking the tax position of any person that HMRC believe has entered into transactions forming monitored arrangements.

A notice can be given to an intermediary only after he has been notified of the promoter's reference number. A notice given for the purpose of checking the tax position of a person cannot be given more than four years after that person's death. '*Checking*' and '*tax position*' are defined as for HMRC's general information powers (see **39.2** HMRC INVESTIGATORY POWERS) but a person's tax position also includes his position as regards deductions or repayments of tax, or sums representing tax, that he is required to make under PAYE regulations or other provisions and the withholding by him of another person's PAYE income (within *ITEPA 2003, s 683* — see **53.2** PAY AS YOU EARN).

Information or a document required under a notice must be provided or produced within ten days beginning with the day the notice is given or within such longer period as HMRC direct.

The giving of a notice under the above provisions must be approved by the Appeal Tribunal if it requires a promoter or intermediary to provide information or produce a document relating (wholly or partly) to a person who is not that promoter or intermediary and not an 'undertaking' of which the promoter or intermediary is the 'parent undertaking'. The promoter or intermediary must normally have been told that the information or documents are required and have been given a reasonable opportunity to make representations to HMRC, but is not entitled to be present at the hearing. The Tribunal must be given a summary of any representations made. Where the Tribunal is satisfied that informing the promoter or intermediary would prejudice the assessment or collection of tax, it can approve the giving of the notice without the taxpayer having been informed. There is no right of appeal against a decision of the Tribunal. '*Undertaking*' and '*parent undertaking*' are defined as in *Companies Act 2006, ss 1161, 1162, Sch 7.*

[*FA 2014, ss 255, 256*].

Ongoing duty to provide information

HMRC may give a notice to a monitored promoter requiring him to provide the information, and produce the documents, prescribed by *SI 2015 No 549, Reg 7* relating to all monitored proposals and monitored arrangements of which he is a promoter at the time of the notice or of which he becomes a promoter after that time but before the monitoring notice ceases to have effect. A notice must specify the time within which information must be provided or a document produced. [*FA 2014, s 257; SI 2015 No 549, Regs 1, 7*].

Person dealing with non-resident monitored promoter

Where a non-UK resident monitored promoter fails to comply with a duty to provide information under either of the above powers, HMRC may issue a notice requiring the information from:

(1) a person who is an 'intermediary' (see **25.12** above) in relation to the monitored proposal concerned;
(2) a person to whom the promoter has made a 'firm approach' (see **25.12** above) with a view to making the proposal available for implementation by a third person;
(3) where HMRC are not aware of any person within (1) or (2) above to whom a notice could be given, a person who has implemented the proposal in question; or
(4) where the duty in question relates to monitored arrangements, a person who has entered into any transaction forming part of those arrangements.

The HMRC officer giving the notice must reasonably believe that the person to whom the notice is given is able to provide the information. Information required under a notice must be provided within ten days beginning with the day the notice is given or within such longer period as HMRC direct.

[*FA 2014, s 258*].

Duty to provide information about clients

HMRC may give notice to a monitored promoter under which the promoter must give HMRC, for each 'relevant period', the name, address and the information prescribed by *SI 2015 No 549, Reg 8* for each client (as defined) for whom such information has not been given for a previous relevant period. Each of the following is a 'relevant period':

(a) the 'calendar quarter' in which the notice is given (but excluding any time before the monitoring notice takes effect);
(b) any period from the time the monitoring notice takes effect until the start of the period in (a) above; and
(c) each subsequent calendar quarter (excluding any time after the monitoring notice ceases to have effect).

A '*calendar quarter*' is a period of three months beginning on 1 January, 1 April, 1 July or 1 October.

Information must be provided within the 30 days beginning with the end of each relevant period or, for a relevant period within (b) above, within the 30 days beginning with the day on which the notice is given, if later.

A similar notice may be given to a person who is an intermediary in relation to a monitored proposal.

Where a promoter or intermediary has provided information under the above provisions in connection with a particular proposal or particular arrangements but an 'authorised HMRC officer' (see **25.12** above) suspects that a person for whom such information has not been provided has been, or is likely to be, a party to transactions implementing the proposal or is a party to a transaction forming the whole or part of the arrangements, the officer may by notice in writing require the promoter or intermediary to provide the information prescribed by *SI 2015 No 549, Reg 10* about any such person. Information required under a notice must be provided within ten days beginning with the day the notice is given or within such longer period as HMRC direct. A notice does not require information to be provided if it has already been provided under the above provisions.

[*FA 2014, ss 259–261, 283(1); SI 2015 No 549, Regs 1, 8–10*].

Duty to notify HMRC of address

A monitored promoter must inform HMRC of its address within 30 days of the end of any calendar quarter at the end of which the monitoring notice applies. [*FA 2014, s 263*].

Duty of client or intermediary to provide information to promoter

An intermediary or client who is informed of a monitored promoter's reference number must within ten days notify the promoter of his national insurance number and unique taxpayer reference number. If he has neither of those numbers he must inform the promoter of that fact within ten days. There is no need to provide the information if the client or intermediary has previously provided it to the promoter. [*FA 2014, s 265*].

Confidentiality

No duty of confidentiality or other restriction on disclosure (however imposed) prevents the voluntary disclosure to HMRC of information or documents about a monitored promoter of monitored proposals or arrangements by a client or intermediary. [*FA 2014, s 273*].

Information powers: further provisions

[25.19] Where a person has provided information or produced a document in purported compliance with any of the information powers at **25.15** or **25.18** above (other than those under *FA 2014, s 263* or *s 265*), HMRC may apply to the Appeal Tribunal for an order for the person to provide further specified information or produce further specified documents which they have reasonable grounds for suspecting are required by the information power in question or will support or explain information required by the power.

If the Appeal Tribunal grants such an order the information or documents must be provided or produced within ten days or such later date as HMRC direct. The duty to provide information or produce a document under such a notice is treated as part of the duty under the original information power (for the purposes of penalties etc.).

[*FA 2014, s 264*].

Appeals

A person given a notice under any of the information powers at **25.15** or **25.18** above (other than those under *FA 2014, s 263* or *s 265*) may appeal against the notice as a whole or against any particular requirement in the notice. There is, however, no right of appeal where the information or documents form part of the person's 'statutory records' or where the Appeal Tribunal has approved the giving of the notice (see **25.18** above).

Notice of appeal must be given in writing to the HMRC officer who gave the notice within the period of 30 days beginning with the date on which the notice was given and must state the grounds of appeal. A decision by the Appeal Tribunal in this respect is final (so that there is no further right of appeal to the Upper Tribunal or Court of Appeal). Where the Tribunal confirms or varies the notice or a requirement in it, the person to whom the notice was given must comply with the notice or requirement within the period specified by the Tribunal. If the Tribunal does not specify such a period, compliance must be within such period as an HMRC officer reasonably specifies in writing.

Subject to the above, the appeal provisions of *TMA 1970, Pt 5* (see **5** APPEALS) apply to an appeal against a notice.

For this purpose, '*statutory records*' are information and documents which a taxpayer is required to keep and preserve under any tax enactment (see **64.5** RETURNS). Information and documents cease to be statutory records when the statutory period for which they must be kept and preserved ends.

[*FA 2014, s 266*].

Compliance with a notice

HMRC may specify the form and manner in which information must be provided or documents produced. Documents must be produced for inspection either at a place agreed to by the recipient of the notice and an HMRC officer or at a place (other than one used solely as a dwelling) that an HMRC officer reasonably specifies. Subject to any conditions or exceptions set out in regulations made by HMRC (and see now *SI 2015 No 549, Reg 11*), copies of documents can be produced unless the notice requires the production of the original document or an HMRC officer in writing subsequently requests the original document. Where an officer makes such a request, the document must be produced within the period and at the time and by the means reasonably requested by the officer.

The production of a document under these provisions does not break any lien (i.e. any right) claimed on it.

[*FA 2014, ss 261, 268; SI 2015 No 549, Regs 1, 11*].

Restrictions on information powers

[25.20] The recipient of a notice under any of the information powers at **25.16** or **25.18** above is not required to:

(a) produce a document if it is not in his possession or power;
(b) provide or produce information that relates to the conduct of a pending tax appeal or any part of a document containing such information;
(c) provide journalistic material (within *Police and Criminal Evidence Act 1984, s 13*) or information contained in such material;
(d) subject to the exceptions below, provide or produce 'personal records' (within *Police and Criminal Evidence Act 1984, s 12*); or
(e) produce a document the whole of which originates more than six years before the giving of the notice.

With regard to (d) above, a notice may require a person to produce documents that are personal records, omitting any personal information (i.e. information the inclusion of which in the documents makes them personal records) and to provide any information in personal records that is not personal information.

[*FA 2014, ss 269, 270*].

Legal professional privilege

A notice cannot require a person to provide information in respect of which a claim to legal professional privilege (or, in Scotland, a claim to confidentiality of communications) could be maintained in legal proceedings. [*FA 2014, s 271*].

Tax advisers

A notice under **25.18**(3) or (4) above does not require a 'tax adviser' to provide information about, or to produce documents which are his property and which consist of, communications between him and a person in relation to whose tax affairs he has been appointed or between him and any other tax adviser of such a person, the purpose of which is the giving or obtaining of advice about any of those tax affairs. For this purpose, a '*tax adviser*' is a person appointed (directly or by another tax adviser) to give advice about the tax affairs of another person.

This restriction does not apply to any information, or any document containing information, which explains any information or document which the tax adviser has, as tax accountant, assisted any client in preparing for, or delivering to, HMRC. The restriction does, however, apply if the information concerned, or a document containing the information, has already been provided or produced to an HMRC officer. [*FA 2014, s 272*].

Concealing, destroying or disposing of documents

[25.21] A person must not conceal, destroy or otherwise dispose of, or arrange for the concealment, destruction or disposal of, a document that is subject to a requirement under the information powers in *FA 2014, s 262* (see **25.16** above) or *FA 2014, ss 255, 257* (see **25.18** above). This does not apply if:

(a) the person does so after the document has been produced to HMRC in accordance with the notice, unless an HMRC officer has notified him in writing that the document must continue to be available for inspection (and has not withdrawn the notification); or
(b) a copy of the document was produced in compliance with the notice and the destruction etc. takes place after the end of the six months beginning with the day on which the copy was produced unless within that period, an HMRC officer makes a request for the original document.

Similarly, where a person has been informed that a document is, or is likely to be, the subject of such a notice addressed to him, he must not conceal, destroy or otherwise dispose of, or arrange for the concealment, destruction or disposal of, the document. This does not apply if he acts more than six months after he was so informed (or was last so informed).

A person who conceals, destroys or otherwise disposes of, or arranges for the concealment, destruction or disposal of, a document in breach of the above provisions is treated as having failed to comply with the duty to produce the document under the provision in question. If more than one provision is in question the person is treated as only having failed to comply with the duty under *FA 2014, s 255* or, if that section is not in question, with the duty under *FA 2014, s 257*.

[*FA 2014, Sch 35 paras 6, 7*].

Criminal offences

Subject to the same let-outs as in (a) and (b) above, it is a criminal offence for a person required to produce a document by a notice under *FA 2014, s 255* (see **25.18** above) which has been approved by the Appeal Tribunal to conceal, destroy or otherwise dispose of the document or to arrange for its concealment, destruction or disposal. It is also a criminal offence for a person to conceal, destroy or otherwise dispose of a document, or to arrange for its concealment, destruction or disposal, after an HMRC officer has informed him in writing that the document is, or is likely to be, the subject of such a notice and approval for giving the notice is to be obtained from the Appeal Tribunal. This does not apply if the person so acts more than six months after he was so informed (or was last so informed). On summary conviction of either of these offences the offender is liable to a fine. On conviction on indictment the punishment is imprisonment for a maximum of two years and/or a fine. [*FA 2014, ss 278–280*].

For civil penalties under the special compliance regime, see **25.23** below.

Partnerships

[25.22] Persons carrying on a business in partnership (within the meaning of *Partnership Act 1890*) are treated as a person for the purposes of the special compliance regime. A partnership is treated as continuing to be the same partnership (and the same person) regardless of a change in membership, provided that a person who was a member before the change remains a member after the change. Accordingly, a partnership is taken to have done any act which bound the members (restricted, in the case of a limited partnership, to the general partners) and to have failed to comply with any obligation of the firm (within the meaning of *Partnership Act 1890*) which the members failed to comply with. Where, however, a member has done, or failed to do, an act at any time, the partnership is not treated at any later time as having done or failed to do that act if at that later time neither that member nor any other person who was a member at the earlier time is still a member.

A 'partnership' does not include, for the purposes of the special compliance regime, a body of persons forming a legal person that is distinct from themselves.

Responsibility of partners

A notice under the special compliance regime given to a partnership has effect at any time in relation to the persons who are members of the partnership at that time (the '*responsible partners*'). This does not, however, affect any liability of a member who has left the partnership for anything that the responsible partners did or failed to do before he left. Anything which must be done by the responsible partners must be done by all of them (but see below regarding 'nominated partners'). References in the provisions to a right of a person (such as a right of appeal) must be interpreted accordingly.

The responsible partners are jointly and severally liable to any penalty under **25.23** below and to any interest on such a penalty, but no amounts can be recovered from a person who did not become a responsible partner until after the act or omission which led to the penalty occurred or, in the case of a daily penalty or interest accruing for a particular day, until after the beginning of that day.

Anything which must be done by the responsible partners can instead be done by a '*nominated partner*', i.e. a partner nominated by the majority of the partners to act as the partnership's representatives for the purposes of the special compliance regime. The partnership must notify HMRC of a nomination or its revocation.

A notice given to a partnership by HMRC must be served either on all of the current partners or on a 'representative partner'. For this purpose a '*representative partner*' means a nominated partner or, if there is no nominated partner, a partner designated by an 'authorised HMRC officer' (see **25.12** above) as a representative partner and notified to the partnership as such.

Partnership changes

Where the business of a partnership subject to a defeat notice, conduct notice or monitoring notice starts to be carried on by one of the partners but not in partnership (i.e. where the other partners leave the partnership), the notice continues to apply to the continuing partner.

Where a 'controlling member' (see **25.12** above) of a partnership subject to a defeat notice leaves the partnership and carries on a business as a promoter, an authorised HMRC officer may give that person a replacement defeat notice. If the business is conducted by a partnership of which that person is a controlling member the replacement notice may be given to the partnership, but the notice will cease to have effect if that person leaves the partnership. Similar provisions apply to allow the giving of replacement conduct notices and monitoring notices.

Where a partner in a partnership which is subject to a defeat notice, conduct notice or monitoring notice ceases to carry on the partnership's business but continues to carry on a part (but not the whole) of the business, an authorised HMRC officer may give that partner a replacement notice. If the departing partner carries on the part of the business in partnership, a replacement notice may be given to that partnership, but the notice will cease to have effect if the partner leaves the partnership. These rules apply whether it is one, some or all of the partners in the original partnership who carry on a part of the business.

A replacement conduct notice ceases to have effect on the date on which the original notice would have ceased to have effect and must state that date as its expiry date. Such a notice may not be given after the expiry of the original notice. The look-forward period in **25.14** above for a replacement defeat notice begins on the day after that on which the notice is given and ends at the end of the look-forward period of the original notice. Such a notice cannot be given after the end of the look-forward period of the original notice. A replacement conduct notice or monitoring notice may not be given to a person if a conduct notice or monitoring notice previously given to that person still has effect.

[*FA 2014, Sch 36 paras 1–3, 7–13, 15–18; FA 2016, s 160(12)–(16)*].

Penalties for non-compliance

[25.23] Penalties are chargeable for failure to comply with any duty imposed under the special compliance regime at **25.12–25.22** above. The maximum penalty for failure to comply with each duty is set out in the table below.

	Provision	Maximum penalty
(1)	Duty to notify clients of monitoring notice (*FA 2014, s 249(1)*)	£5,000
(2)	Duty to publicise monitoring notice (*FA 2014, s 249(3)*)	£1,000,000
(3)	Duty to include information in correspondence etc. (*FA 2014, s 249(10)*)	£1,000,000
(4)	Duty of promoter to notify client of reference number (*FA 2014, s 251*)	£5,000
(5)	Duty of others to notify clients and intermediaries of reference number (*FA 2014, s 252*)	£5,000
(6)	Duty to notify HMRC of reference number (*FA 2014, s 253*)	(a) £5,000 unless (b) or (c) apply;
		(b) £7,500 where the person has previously failed to comply with the duty once during the 36 months before the current failure;
		(c) £10,000 where the person has previously failed to comply with the duty two or more times during the 36 months before the current failure.
(7)	Duty to provide information or produce document (*FA 2014, s 255*)	£1,000,000
(8)	Ongoing duty to provide information or produce document (*FA 2014, s 257*)	£1,000,000
(9)	Duty of person dealing with non-resident promoter (*FA 2014, s 258*)	£1,000,000
(10)	Duty of monitored promoter to provide information about clients (*FA 2014, s 259*)	£5,000
(11)	Duty of intermediary to provide information about clients (*FA 2014, s 260*)	£5,000
(12)	Duty to provide information about clients following enquiry (*FA 2014, s 261*)	£10,000
(13)	Duty to provide information required to monitor conduct notice (*FA 2014, s 262*)	£5,000
(14)	Duty to provide information about address (*FA 2014, s 263*)	£5,000
(15)	Duty to provide information to promoter (*FA 2014, s 265*)	£5,000

For failures within (1), (4), (5), (10) or (11) above, the maximum penalty specified is a maximum which may be imposed on each person to whom the failure relates.

The amount of the penalty actually imposed must be arrived at after taking account of all relevant considerations, including the desirability of setting it at a level which appears appropriate for deterring the person on whom it is imposed, or other persons, from similar future failures. In particular, regard must be had, for penalties within (7) and (8) above, to the amount of fees received and, for penalties within (9) above imposed for a failure to comply with a duty within **25.18**(3) or (4) above, the tax advantage gained or sought.

If the failure to comply with a duty within (7)–(14) above continues after a penalty has been imposed, a further daily penalty not exceeding £600 or, where the initial maximum penalty was £1,000,000, £10,000 may be imposed for each day on which the failure continues after the day on which the initial penalty was imposed.

A failure to do anything required to be done within a limited time period does not give rise to a penalty under these provisions if the duty is complied with within such further time as HMRC or the Appeal Tribunal have allowed.

Reasonable excuse

No penalty arises under the above provisions if there is a reasonable excuse for the failure. Insufficiency of funds is not a reasonable excuse for this purpose unless attributable to events outside the control of the person who failed to comply with the duty, and neither is that person's reliance on another person to do anything, unless the first person took reasonable care to avoid the failure. If the person had a reasonable excuse, he is treated as continuing to have a reasonable excuse after the excuse has ceased if the failure is remedied without unreasonable delay. Reliance by a monitored promoter on legal advice is automatically taken not to constitute a reasonable excuse if either it was not based on a full and accurate description of the facts or the conclusions in the advice that the promoter relied on were unreasonable. Reliance on legal advice is also automatically taken not to constitute a reasonable excuse for failure to comply with a duty within (9) above if the advice was given or procured by the monitored promoter.

Inaccurate information and documents

Where a person provides inaccurate information or produces a document which contains an inaccuracy in complying with a duty within (7)–(14) above, the person is liable to a penalty if:

(a) the inaccuracy is careless or deliberate; or
(b) the person knows of the inaccuracy at the time of providing the information or producing the document but does not inform HMRC at that time; or
(c) the person subsequently discovers the inaccuracy and fails to take reasonable steps to inform HMRC.

In (a) above, an inaccuracy is careless if it is due to a failure by the person to take reasonable care. In determining whether or not a monitored promoter took reasonable care, reliance on legal advice is disregarded if either it was not based on a full and accurate description of the facts or the conclusions in the advice that the promoter relied on were unreasonable. Reliance on legal advice is disregarded in determining whether or not a person complying with a duty within (9) above took reasonable care if the advice was given or procured by the monitored promoter.

The maximum penalty is the same as the maximum penalty for failure to comply with the duty in question. If the information or document contains more than one inaccuracy, only one penalty is payable.

Interaction with other penalties etc.

A person is not liable to a penalty under these provisions for anything in respect of which he has been convicted of an offence. A person is not liable to a penalty under the provisions at **25.9** above and **55.6** PENALTIES (errors in documents), or under any other provision prescribed by statutory instrument, by reason of any failure to include in any return or account a reference number required by *FA 2014, s 253* (see (6) above).

Procedure

Penalties under the above provisions are imposed by the Appeal Tribunal, using the procedure in **55.27** PENALTIES. This does not apply, however, to daily penalties for continuing failure to comply with a duty where the maximum penalty is £600; such penalties are instead imposed by HMRC using the procedure at **55.25** PENALTIES.

[*FA 2014, Sch 35 paras 1–5, 8–10, 12, 13*].

Interest on penalties

On and after 1 June 2019, interest is chargeable on these penalties if paid later than the due date; the charge to interest is under the harmonised regime at **43.2** LATE PAYMENT INTEREST AND PENALTIES. Similarly, interest is payable by HMRC if, and to the extent that, the penalty falls to be repaid; the interest is payable under the harmonised regime at **62.2** REPAYMENT INTEREST. [*FA 2014, Sch 35 para 11; FA 2019, s 88(3); SI 2019 No 921*].

26

Disguised Remuneration

Cross-references. See **28** EMPLOYMENT INCOME; **57** PENSION PROVISION for employer-financed retirement benefit schemes; **75.39**, **75.40** TRADING INCOME for the charge to income tax on trading profits disguised as other receipts.

Simon's Taxes. See **E4.135–E4.145**, **E4.1116.**

Introduction to disguised remuneration

[26.1] Anti-avoidance legislation is introduced by *FA 2011, Sch 2* and aimed at employers, directors and employees who use third-party arrangements, commonly involving trusts and other vehicles, to avoid, reduce, or defer liabilities to income tax on rewards of an employment or to avoid restrictions on pensions tax relief. Where third parties, e.g. trusts or other intermediate vehicles, are used in arrangements aimed at providing value to an individual for what is in substance a reward or recognition in connection with his employment, or a loan in connection with his employment, the legislation provides for an employment income charge to be made. This is known as the charge to tax on employment income provided through third parties or alternatively the charge to tax on disguised remuneration. It has effect for, broadly, **2011/12** onwards. However, there are also anti-forestalling provisions effective on and after 9 December 2010 (see **26.13** below).

It is worth noting that some of the types of transaction which are chargeable under this legislation (for example the earmarking of funds held in a discretionary trust) are not accepted by HMRC as being effective in avoiding tax under pre-existing law and may be challenged in litigation or otherwise. In a case involving payments to employee benefit trusts, the SC decided that the payments were a component of the employees' remuneration for services rendered, regardless of the fact that they were made, with the agreement or acquiescence of the employees, to a third party or that the employees had no right to receive the payments themselves; the payments were accordingly earnings subject to tax (*RFC 2012 plc (in liquidation) (formerly The Rangers Football Club plc) v Advocate General for Scotland* SC, [2017] STC 1556).

For official guidance see HMRC Employment Income Manual EIM45000 *et seq*.

See **26.8** below for the 'loan charge', which applies to loans outstanding on 5 April 2019.

The Government announced at Autumn Statement 2015 that it may legislate in future Finance Bills to stop schemes designed to avoid tax on earned income and may backdate any such measure to 25 November 2015 (see www.gov.uk/government/uploads/system/uploads/attachment_data/file/479749/52229_Blue_Book_PU1865_Web_Accessible.pdf).

Disguised remuneration — the basic conditions

[26.2] The charge to tax at **26.4** below is made if:

(a) a person (A) is a present, former or prospective employee of another person (B);
(b) there is an arrangement ('*the relevant arrangement*') to which A is a party or which otherwise (wholly or partly) covers A or relates to A;
(c) it is reasonable to suppose that the relevant arrangement (or so much of it as relates to A) is (wholly or partly) a means of providing rewards or recognition or loans in connection with A's employment (current, former or prospective) with B (or is otherwise concerned (wholly or partly) with the provision of such rewards etc.);
(d) a 'relevant step' is taken by a third party (see below); and
(e) it is reasonable to suppose that:
  - the relevant step is taken (wholly or partly) in pursuance of the relevant arrangement; or
  - there is some other connection (direct or indirect) between the relevant step and the relevant arrangement.

See **26.3** below (close companies' gateway) for an additional set of circumstances in which the charge to tax at **26.4** below applies in relation to relevant steps taken on or after 6 April 2018.

The reference to A in (b) above and the first reference to A in (c) above include any person 'linked with A' (see below). The legislation applies where the relevant step in (d) above is taken on or after 6 April 2011 but see also the anti-forestalling provisions at **26.13** below. See **26.7** below for what counts as a 'relevant step' and **26.10** below for exclusions.

Where a payment (payment X) made to a person other than A (or to A as a trustee) is of earnings, taxable (wholly or partly) as such but other than under the disguised remuneration rules, from A's employment with B, this does not prevent a 'redirected-earnings arrangement' from falling within (b) above. It also does not prevent rewards or recognition or loans being in connection with A's employment with B for the purposes of (c) above if payment X is used to provide at least part of the rewards etc. An arrangement is a '*redirected-earnings arrangement*' if it (wholly or partly) covers, or relates to, payment X. References here to payment X include any sum or other property which represents or derives from that payment. This applies in relation to relevant steps taken on or after 22 November 2017, but does so regardless of when payment X was made (even if it was made before 6 April 2011).

'Arrangement' in (b) above includes any agreement, scheme, settlement, transaction, trust or understanding (whether or not it is legally enforceable). For the purposes of (c) it does not matter whether or not the relevant arrangement includes the full details of the steps which will or may be taken to achieve the desired outcome. In (d) above, the expression 'third party' covers a genuine third party but may also be either A or B acting as a trustee. It may also be a member of the same group of companies as B (if B is a company) and a wholly-owned subsidiary of B if B is a limited liability partnership, but this does not apply in cases where there is a connection between the relevant step and a tax avoidance arrangement (for which see *ITEPA 2003, s 554Z(16)*). The relationship of a company to B is judged at the time the relevant step is taken. For the purposes of the second leg of (e) above, there is a connection between the relevant step and the relevant arrangement if, for example, the relevant step is taken in pursuance of an arrangement at one end of a series of arrangements with the relevant arrangement being at the other end, and it does not matter that the person taking the relevant step may be unaware of the relevant arrangement.

Persons 'linked with A'

For the purposes of these provisions any of the following are '*linked with A*':

- a person who is, or has been, connected with A (within **19** CONNECTED PERSONS but treating cohabiting couples as if they were married or in a civil partnership);
- a close company (or a company that would be a close company if it were UK resident) in which A or any other person within this list is, or has been, a participator (see Tolley's Corporation Tax for the meaning of these terms); and
- a company which is a 51% subsidiary of any such company.

[*ITEPA 2003, ss 554A, 554Z(3), 554Z1; FA 2018, Sch 1 paras 1, 13; SI 2019 No 1458, Sch 3 para 25(4)*].

Close companies' gateway

[26.3] With effect in relation to relevant steps taken on or after **6 April 2018** the charge to tax at **26.4** below is also made if:

(a) there is an arrangement ('*the relevant arrangement*') to which an individual (A) is a party or which otherwise (wholly or partly) covers A or relates to A;

(b) it is reasonable to suppose that the relevant arrangement (or so much of it as relates to A) is (wholly or partly) a means of providing payments, benefits or loans 'linked to A' (see below) or is otherwise concerned (wholly or partly) with the provision of such payments etc.;

(c) a close company (B) enters into a 'relevant transaction' (see below);

(d) it is reasonable to suppose that:
- the relevant transaction is entered into (wholly or partly) in pursuance of the relevant arrangement; or
- there is some other connection (direct or indirect) between the relevant transaction and the relevant arrangement;

(e) at the time B enters into the relevant transaction, or at any time in the three years ending with it, A is a 'director' or employee of B or has a 'material interest' in B (or both);

(f) a relevant step is taken by a 'third party' (see **26.7** below for what counts as a relevant step and **26.10** below for exclusions);

(g) it is reasonable to suppose that the sum of money or asset which is the subject of the relevant step represents, or has arisen or derives from, the sum of money or asset which is the subject of the relevant transaction, or vice versa; and

(h) there is a time in the 'relevant period' when a main purpose of operating, implementing, maintaining or terminating the relevant arrangement (or so much of it as is in question) is the avoidance of income tax, national insurance contributions, corporation tax or a charge to tax under *CTA 2010, s 455* (charge to tax on loans to close company participators). The '*relevant period*' is the period between the time of the relevant transaction and that of the relevant step but also includes any time around each of those two times.

The above set of circumstances is known as the close companies' gateway. For further information see the technical notes of 13 September 2017 at www.gov.uk/government/publications/draft-legislation-tackling-disguised-remuneration-avoidance-schemes/tackling-disguised-remuneration-technical-note and www.gov.uk/government/publications/disguised-remuneration-transfer-of-liability-technical-note/tackling-disguised-remuneration. A close company is broadly a company under the control of five or fewer participators (see *CTA 2010, s 439* and Tolley's Corporation Tax); but for the purposes of these provisions, a close company includes any company that would be a close company if it were UK resident.

The reference to A in (a) above, and the first such reference in (b) above, include any person linked with A (as in **26.2** above). Broadly similar rules to those in **26.2** above apply where a payment made to a person other than A (or to A as a trustee) is of earnings, taxable as such but other than under the disguised remuneration rules, from A's employment with B or, in this case, A's office as director of B. In addition to those rules, any such payment is not preventing from being the entering into of a relevant transaction.

'Arrangement' in (a) above includes any agreement, scheme, settlement, transaction, trust or understanding (whether or not it is legally enforceable). For the purposes of (b) it does not matter whether or not the relevant arrangement includes the full details of the steps which will or may be taken to achieve the desired outcome. '*Director*' has an extended meaning in (e) above so as to embrace any person in accordance with whose directions or instructions the directors of the company are accustomed to act (so-called shadow directors), but does not thereby include someone giving advice purely in a professional capacity. For the purposes of (e) above, a person has a '*material interest*' in a company if, broadly, his and/or his associates' interests in the company do not exceed 5%; a person carrying on business as a promoter in relation to the relevant arrangement is treated as an associate of A, as is any associated company of the promoter (if a company). In (f) above, the expression 'third party' covers a genuine third party but may also be either A or B acting as a trustee.

Payments etc. linked to A

For the purposes of (b) above, a payment, benefit or loan is '*linked to A*' if:

- it is being provided to A, or a person chosen by A or within a class of persons chosen by A;
- it is being provided to a person on A's behalf, or at A's direction or request; or
- it is being provided to a person linked with A and it is reasonable to suppose that the main reason, or one of the main reasons, for it being provided is that the person is linked with A (as in **26.2** above).

Relevant transaction

For the above purposes, B enters into a '*relevant transaction*' (see (c) above) if B does any of the following (unless it is an 'excluded transaction' — see below):

- pays a sum of money to a third party;
- transfers an asset to a third party;
- acquires a right to payment of a sum of money or transfer of assets where there is a connection between the acquisition of the right and a payment (by way of loan or otherwise), or a transfer of assets, to a third party;
- releases or writes off (in whole or part) a loan made to a third party or an acquired right of the kind mentioned immediately above;
- takes a step by virtue of which a third party acquires an asset consisting of securities, interests in securities or securities options;
- makes available a sum of money or asset for use, or makes it available under an arrangement which permits its use, as security for a loan to a third party or as security for the meeting of any liability, or the performance of any undertaking, which a third party may have; or
- grants to a third party a lease of any premises the effective duration of which is likely to exceed 21 years (and *ITEPA 2003, s 554AB(7)(8)* contain rules concerning the likely effective duration of a lease).

References above to a loan include any form of credit and any payment purported to be by way of loan.

Any of the following is an '*excluded transaction*':

- a distribution made by B;
- a transaction entered into by B in the ordinary course of its business on arm's length terms; and

- a transaction entered into to facilitate the disposal, on arm's length terms, of shares in B.

For these purposes a distribution includes any distribution made in the winding-up of the company. A distribution or transaction cannot, however be an excluded transaction if a main purpose of it is the avoidance of tax.

[*ITEPA 2003, ss 554AA–554AF, 554Z(3); FA 2018, Sch 1 paras 2, 14*].

Disguised remuneration — the charge to tax

[26.4] Where these provisions apply, the value (see below) of the relevant step in question counts as employment income of A in respect of his employment with B (where A and B are the persons referred to in **26.2** or **26.3** above) and is charged to income tax accordingly. This employment income is normally treated as arising in the tax year in which the relevant step is taken. The exception is that if the relevant step is taken before A begins his employment with B, this employment income is treated as arising in the tax year in which the employment begins. With effect on and after 15 September 2016, where the value of a relevant step would count as employment income of more than one person it is apportioned between them on a just and reasonable basis.

If the relevant step gives rise to an amount which would otherwise be taxable as a benefit-in-kind, the charge under these provisions takes priority. In particular, in a case in which the relevant step is the making of an employment-related loan, the loan is not to be treated for any tax year as a cheap loan taxable under **28.32** EMPLOYMENT INCOME. Similarly, if the relevant step gives rise to an amount which would otherwise be taxable as a UK dividend, the charge under these provisions takes priority.

Where these provisions apply in the case of a relevant step within **26.7** below taken on or after 6 April 2018 by reason only of **26.3** above (close companies' gateway), and the relevant step gives rise to a tax charge under *ITTOIA 2005, s 415* (release of loan to close company participator — see **65.21** SAVINGS AND INVESTMENT INCOME), that charge takes priority over the charge under these provisions. The same applies if the relevant step gives rise to a tax charge under *CTA 2010, s 455* (loans to close company participators) but in this case only if either (i) the *CTA 2010, s 455* charge is paid in full by the due date; or (ii) the liability to that charge is reported in a company tax return made by B and HMRC agree not to apply the disguised remuneration rules.

See **26.7** below as to what constitutes a relevant step. See **26.5** for the application of the remittance basis where applicable, and see **26.6** below for other supplementary provisions concerning the charge to tax.

Application of PAYE

The employment income arising as above is also PAYE income, which means that PAYE must be accounted for by B when the income arises to A. See **53.3**(h), **53.5** PAY AS YOU EARN.

Effect of temporary non-UK residence

Where the 'year of departure' is 2013/14 or any subsequent year, certain relevant steps taken when A is 'temporarily non-UK resident' are treated for the purposes of the charge to tax as if they were taken in the 'period of return'. For what is meant by '*temporarily non-UK resident*', the '*year of departure*' and the '*period of return*', see **63.29** RESIDENCE AND DOMICILE.

A relevant step is treated in this way if:

- it is the payment of a lump sum to a 'relevant person' (as defined in **26.7** below under Payment of sum, transfer of asset etc.);
- the lump sum is a 'relevant benefit' (see **57.35** PENSION PROVISION) provided under an employer-financed retirement benefits scheme (within **57.34** PENSION PROVISION) or a superannuation fund to which *ICTA 1988, s 615(3)* applies (see **57.40** PENSION PROVISION);
- the step is taken in the 'temporary period of non-UK residence' (see **63.29**(d) RESIDENCE AND DOMICILE); and
- the step does not otherwise give rise to a charge to tax but would have done if it were not for a double tax treaty. This includes a case where a charge to tax could be prevented by the making of a claim to double tax relief but no claim has yet been made.

Nothing in any double tax treaty is to be read as preventing the individual from being chargeable to income tax in respect of any relevant step treated as taken in the period of return.

[*ITEPA 2003, s 554Z4A*].

Employment income thereby *treated as* chargeable for the year of return is not subject to PAYE. [*ITEPA 2003, s 683(3ZA)*].

The value of the relevant step

If the relevant step involves a sum of money, its value is the amount of that sum. In any other case, the value of the relevant step is the *greater* of:

- the market value when the relevant step is taken of the asset which is the subject of the step; and
- the cost of the relevant step, i.e. the expense incurred in connection with the relevant step (including a proper proportion of any expense relating only partly to the relevant step) by the person(s) at whose cost the relevant step is taken.

In the following circumstances, the cost of the relevant step is disregarded, and market value thus automatically applies:

- where Rule 4 below applies; and
- where the relevant step is within **26.7**(iii) below (acquisition of shares etc.) and, by virtue of the acquisition, any of **71.4–71.14** or **71.80** SHARE-RELATED EMPLOYMENT INCOME AND EXEMPTIONS apply.

If an asset is within **71.8** or **71.80** SHARE-RELATED EMPLOYMENT INCOME AND EXEMPTIONS (convertible shares and research institution spin-out companies), its market value for the above purposes is subject to adjustment in the same way as described in those paragraphs.

The value of a relevant step may be reduced in accordance with Rules 1 to 5 below, which, insofar as they are applicable, must be applied in numerical order (but note that Rule 2A contains provision that effectively overrides this in that particular case).

Rule 1 — residence issues

Once the value of a relevant step has been determined, the tax year or years that the value is 'for' must be established, using the same rules as for general earnings (see **28.3** EMPLOYMENT INCOME). (This does not change the tax year for which the value of the relevant step counts as employment income, which has already been established above.)

If it is thereby found that the value of the relevant step, or a part of it, is 'for' a tax year in which A in **26.2** above is non-UK resident, there must be deducted from it so much as is derived (as determined on a just and reasonable basis) from duties performed outside the UK. If it is found that the value of the relevant step, or a part of it, is 'for' a tax year that is a split year (see **63.19** RESIDENCE AND DOMICILE) as regards A, there must be deducted from it so much as is both attributable (on a just and reasonable basis) to the overseas part of the split year and derived (as determined on a just and reasonable basis) from duties performed outside the UK.

Where the relevant step is the payment of a lump sum which is a relevant benefit (see **57.35** PENSION PROVISION) under an employer-financed retirement benefits scheme (within **57.34** PENSION PROVISION), and the recipient is UK resident in the tax year of receipt, neither of the above deductions apply if the lump sum is wholly in respect of rights accruing on or after 6 April 2017. If the lump sum is wholly in respect of rights accrued before that date, the appropriate deduction applies in full; if it is only partly in respect of such rights, the deduction is proportionately restricted (see *ITEPA 2003, s 554Z4(9)* for the calculation).

Rule 2 — overlap with earlier relevant step

This rule has effect only in relation to relevant steps taken before 6 April 2017. (For relevant steps taken on or after that date, see Rule 2A below instead.) The value of a relevant step is to be reduced by the value of any earlier relevant step relating to the same employment (and within the charge to tax under these provisions) if there is an overlap between the sum of money or asset which is the subject of the relevant steps. There is such an overlap if:

- the sum of money or asset which is the subject of the relevant steps is the same sum of money or asset; or
- the sum of money or asset which is the subject of the later relevant step (sum or asset T) essentially replaces the sum of money or asset which is the subject of the earlier relevant step (sum or asset S).

Furthermore, if any reductions were made under this Rule to the value of the earlier relevant step, sum or asset T is treated as overlapping with any other sum of money or asset insofar as that other sum of money or asset was treated as overlapping with sum or asset S.

If the overlap covers the whole of sum or asset S, the value of the later relevant step is reduced by that of the earlier relevant step. If the overlap covers only part of sum or asset S, the value of the later relevant step is reduced by that part of the value of the earlier relevant step which corresponds to the part of sum or asset S covered by the overlap (as determined on a just and reasonable basis). For these purposes, the value of the earlier relevant step is its value as reduced (if applicable) under Rule 1 above, under this Rule or under Rule 4 below but before any reductions under Rules 3 and 5 below.

Rule 2A — overlap with money or asset subject to earlier tax liability

This rule has effect in relation to relevant steps taken on or after 6 April 2017, and seeks to ensure that where there are two income tax charges relating to the same underlying money or asset, the later charge is reduced to nil if the earlier charge has been paid in full or is not yet due and payable. For relevant steps taken before 6 April 2017, see Rule 2 above instead. Rule 2A applies if there is an overlap (see below) between:

- the sum of money or asset (sum or asset P) which is the subject of the relevant step; and
- a sum of money or asset (sum or asset Q) by reference to which, on an occasion preceding the taking of the relevant step, A became subject to an income tax liability (the '*earlier tax liability*').

Where either the payment condition or liability condition below is met, the value of the relevant step is reduced by an amount equal to so much of the sum of money, or (as the case may be) the value of so much of the asset, as is within the overlap. For this purpose, the value of the earlier relevant step is its value as reduced (if applicable) under Rule 1 above, under this Rule or under Rule 4 below but before any reductions under Rules 3 and 5 below.

The payment condition is that, at the time the relevant step is taken, the earlier tax liability has become due and payable and either it has been paid in full or terms have been agreed with HMRC for its discharge. The fact that payments may have been made on account, or pending determination of an appeal, does not mean for this purpose that tax has been paid. The liability condition is that, at the time the relevant step is taken, the earlier tax liability is not yet due and payable.

For these purposes, there is an overlap between sum or asset P and sum or asset Q insofar as it is just and reasonable to conclude either that they are the same sum of money or asset or that sum or asset P represents (directly or indirectly) sum or asset Q. Furthermore, if the earlier tax liability arose by virtue of the disguised remuneration provisions applying by reason of an earlier relevant step and any reductions were made under this Rule to the value of that step, sum or asset P is treated as overlapping with any other sum of money or asset insofar as that other sum of money or asset was treated as overlapping with sum or asset Q.

References in this Rule to A include any person linked with A (see **26.2** above). References to an earlier tax liability do not include any liability arising under **28.32** EMPLOYMENT INCOME (benefit of taxable cheap loan treated as earnings). This Rule does not apply if the earlier tax liability arose by reason of a pre-6 April 2011 step falling under Earmarking etc. of money and assets in **26.7** below and the value of the relevant step is subject to reduction under *FA 2011, Sch 2 para 59* (see **26.13** below under Pre-6 April 2011 steps where tax settled by agreement etc.).

See the draft official guidance at www.gov.uk/government/publications/tackling-disguised-remuneration-draft-guidance-for-changes-to-part-7a for examples of how this Rule works. See also **26.6** below under Avoidance of double tax charge: earlier income tax liability; this deals with the possibility of a double tax charge where the circumstances are as above except that, when the relevant step is taken, the earlier tax liability has become due and payable but all or part of it remains unpaid.

Rule 3 — overlap with certain earnings

If the relevant step gives rise to 'relevant earnings' of A from A's employment with B and those earnings are either:

(i) 'for' a tax year in which A is UK resident (see also Rule 1 above), or
(ii) 'for' a tax year in which A is non-UK resident (see also Rule 1 above) but which are in respect of duties performed in the UK,

the value of the relevant step is reduced by the amount of the relevant earnings.

If earnings otherwise within (i) above are 'for' a tax year that is a split year (see **63.19** RESIDENCE AND DOMICILE) as regards A, they are not within (i) above if they are 'excluded' earnings. For this purpose, earnings are '*excluded*' if they are attributable to the overseas part of the split year and are not general earnings in respect of duties performed in the UK.

For the purpose of this Rule, any of the following are 'relevant earnings':

- earnings as defined in **28.13** EMPLOYMENT INCOME, or
- payments treated as earnings by any of *ITEPA 2003, ss 221, 222, 223* or *225*, or
- a deemed employment payment (see **58.6** PERSONAL SERVICE COMPANIES ETC.) or part of such a payment,

but anything which is exempt income, or which is taxable as UK dividends, is not relevant earnings.

Rule 4 — exercise price of share options

A deduction is to be made from the value of the relevant step in certain circumstances where an amount has to be paid to exercise a share option. The conditions are that:

(a) the relevant step is the earmarking of assets (see **26.7** below);
(b) B in **26.2** or **26.3** above is a company;
(c) B has an employee share scheme under which a right (the share option) may be granted to A to acquire 'relevant shares' or to receive a sum of money the amount of which is to be determined by reference to the market value of relevant shares;
(d) in order to exercise the share option, A would be required under its terms to pay a sum of money the amount of which can be determined at the time of the grant of the option;

(e) the subject of the relevant step is relevant shares which are earmarked, or otherwise start being held, solely with a view to providing shares, or paying a sum of money, pursuant to such a share option granted to A;
(f) the number of relevant shares of any type which are earmarked does not exceed the maximum number of relevant shares of that type which might reasonably be expected to be needed for providing shares, or paying a sum of money, pursuant to the share option which is granted or expected to be granted; and
(g) there is no connection between the relevant step and a tax avoidance arrangement (for which see *ITEPA 2003, s 554Z(16)*).

'*Relevant shares*' are broadly shares in, or securities of, B (see *ITEPA 2003, s 554I(4)* for a full definition). The value of the relevant step is reduced by the amount of the sum of money which A would have to pay as mentioned in (d) above. If the value of the relevant step has already been reduced under Rule 1 above, the amount of the reduction under this Rule is X% of that sum of money, where X% is the proportion of the value of the relevant step remaining after the deduction made under Rule 1.

A special rule applies if the relevant step is taken in relation to the expected grant of a share option, the grant is not made before the end of the date (the final grant date) which falls three months after the date on which the relevant step is taken, and at the final grant date any of the earmarked shares continue to be held. The same rule applies if, at any time after the taking of the relevant step, any of the earmarked shares cease to be held on the basis set out in (e) above but continue to be held on the basis set out in **26.7**(a) or (b) below. The special rule is that a relevant step within **26.7**(a) or (b) below is deemed to be taken at the end of the final grant date or when the shares cease to be held on the basis set out in (e) above.

This Rule (but not the special rule above) also applies if the relevant step is a step treated as being taken by *ITEPA 2003, s 554L(9)* or *s 554M(8)*.

Rule 5 — cases where consideration given for relevant step

A deduction is to be made from the value of the relevant step in two sets of circumstances where consideration is given by A for the relevant step. The conditions for the first set of circumstances are that:

- the relevant step is within **26.7**(i), (ii) or (iii) or **26.7**(I) or (II) below;
- the relevant step is for consideration given by A in the form of the transfer of an asset by A to the person taking the relevant step;
- the transfer of the asset by A is made before, or at or about, the time the relevant step is taken and is not by way of loan; and
- there is no connection between the transfer of the asset by A and a tax avoidance arrangement. *ITEPA 2003, s 554Z8(3)(4)* set out particular circumstances in which it is to be assumed that the transfer is connected with a tax avoidance arrangement, but these are by no means exhaustive.

The value of the relevant step is reduced by the market value of the asset transferred by A as at the time of its transfer. If the value of the relevant step has already been reduced under Rule 1 above, the amount of the reduction under this Rule is X% of that market value, where X% is the proportion of the value of the relevant step remaining after the deduction made under Rule 1.

The conditions for the second set of circumstances are that:

- the relevant step is within **26.7**(ii), (iii) or (v) below, or **26.7**(A) or (B) below, and does not also involve a sum of money;
- the relevant step is for consideration given by A in the form of the payment of a sum of money by A to the person taking the relevant step;
- the payment by A is made before, or at or about, the time the relevant step is taken; and
- there is no connection (direct or indirect) between the payment by A and a tax avoidance arrangement.

The value of the relevant step is reduced by the amount of the consideration given. If the value of the relevant step has already been reduced under Rule 1 above, the amount of the reduction under this Rule is X% of that amount, where X% is the proportion of the value of the relevant step remaining after the deduction made under Rule 1.

References in this Rule to A include any person linked with A (see **26.2** above).

[*ITEPA 2003, ss 554Z(10), 554Z2, 554Z2A, 554Z3–554Z8; FA 2016, s 18(2)(3)(9); FA 2017, Sch 3 para 7, Sch 6 paras 6, 10, 13; F(No 2)A 2017, Sch 11 paras 38, 46(5); FA 2018, Sch 1 paras 3, 14; FA 2020, Sch 2 para 25*].

The remittance basis

[26.5] The application of the REMITTANCE BASIS (**61**) to these provisions depends on whether A in **26.2** above does or does not meet the section 26A test in **28.7** EMPLOYMENT INCOME.

Where A does not meet the section 26A test

If

(a) the value of the relevant step (or a part of it) is 'for' a tax year, established as under Rule 1 in **26.4** above,

(b) the remittance basis applies to A for that tax year (see **61.2** REMITTANCE BASIS),

(c) A does not meet the section 26A test for that tax year,

(d) A's employment with B in that tax year is employment with a 'foreign employer' (see **28.6** EMPLOYMENT INCOME), and

(e) the duties of A's employment with B in that tax year are performed wholly outside the UK,

then subject to what is said below under Dual contract arrangements, the employment income arising to A under these provisions (or the part of it in question) is taxable specific income (see **28.1** EMPLOYMENT INCOME) in a tax year insofar as it is remitted to the UK in that year. If the relevant step is within **26.8** below (the loan charge), the employment income arising to A is taxable specific income in the tax year in which the relevant step is treated as being taken insofar as the income is remitted to the UK in that year or in any previous tax year. For these purposes, any income which is remitted before A begins his employment with B is treated as being remitted in the tax year in which the employment begins.

If, in the tax year referred to in (a) to (e) above, A has 'associated employments' the duties of which are *not* performed wholly outside the UK, the amount of employment income to which the above applies is limited to such amount as is just and reasonable having regard to all relevant circumstances but in particular the factors listed in *ITEPA 2003, s 554Z9(5)*. '*Associated employments*' are employments with B or with employers associated with B.

Supplementary

Where (a) above applies to only a part of the value of the relevant step, any reductions in that value under Rules 2 to 5 in **26.4** above are applied proportionately to that part.

See **61** REMITTANCE BASIS for the meaning of 'remitted to the UK'. For the purposes of applying the provisions described in that chapter, the sum of money or asset which is the subject of the relevant step is treated as deriving from the employment income arising to A (or the part of it in question) that is classified as taxable specific income as above; a special rule in *ITEPA 2003, s 554Z11(7)(8)* applies where there is an overlap with a later relevant step (within the meaning of Rule 2 in **26.4** above).

Where A meets the section 26A test

If

(i) the value of the relevant step (or a part of it) is 'for' a tax year, established as under Rule 1 in **26.4** above,
(ii) the remittance basis applies to A for that tax year (see **61.2** REMITTANCE BASIS), and
(iii) A meets the section 26A test for that tax year.

the 'overseas portion' of the employment income arising to A under these provisions (or the part of it in question) is taxable specific income (see **28.1** EMPLOYMENT INCOME) in a tax year insofar as it is remitted to the UK in that year. If the relevant step is within **26.8** below (the loan charge), the overseas portion of the employment income arising to A is taxable specific income in the tax year in which the relevant step is treated as being taken insofar as the overseas portion is remitted to the UK in that year or in any previous tax year. The '*overseas portion*' is so much of the income in question as is not in respect of duties performed in the UK (determined on a just and reasonable basis).

For these purposes, any income which is remitted before A begins his employment with B is treated as being remitted in the tax year in which the employment begins.

Similar supplementary provisions apply as where A does not meet the section 26A test (see above).

Dual contract arrangements

There is legislation aimed at preventing non-UK domiciled individuals from avoiding tax by dividing the duties of a single employment into a UK and an overseas contract. See **28.6** EMPLOYMENT INCOME for details. This legislation applies equally to prevent employment income arising under the disguised remuneration provisions from qualifying for the remittance basis where A does not meet the section 26A test.

[*ITEPA 2003, ss 24A, 24B, 554Z9–554Z11; F(No 2)A 2017, Sch 11 paras 40–42*].

Effect of temporary non-UK residence

Where the 'year of departure' is 2013/14 or any subsequent year, certain amounts remitted to the UK when A is 'temporarily non-UK resident' are treated for the above purposes as if they were remitted in the 'period of return'. For what is meant by '*temporarily non-UK resident*', the '*year of departure*' and the '*period of return*', see **63.29** RESIDENCE AND DOMICILE.

An amount is treated in this way if:

- it is all or part of a 'relevant benefit' (see **57.35** PENSION PROVISION) provided to a 'relevant person' (as defined in **26.7** below under Payment of sum, transfer of asset etc.) under an employer-financed retirement benefits scheme (within **57.34** PENSION PROVISION) or a superannuation fund to which *ICTA 1988, s 615(3)* applies (see **57.40** PENSION PROVISION);
- it is provided in the form of a lump sum;
- it is remitted to the UK in the 'temporary period of non-UK residence' (see **63.29**(d) RESIDENCE AND DOMICILE); and
- the remittance does not otherwise give rise to a charge to tax under the above provisions but would have done so if it were not for a double tax treaty. This includes a case where a charge could be prevented by the making of a claim to double tax relief but no claim has yet been made.

Nothing in any double tax treaty is to be read as preventing the individual from being chargeable to income tax in respect of any income treated as remitted to the UK in the period of return.

[*ITEPA 2003, s 554Z11A; F(No 2)A 2017, Sch 11 para 43*].

Other provisions concerning the charge to tax

[26.6] *ITEPA 2003, s 554Z12* deals with who is chargeable to tax or liable for the tax under these provisions if:

- the relevant step is taken on or after the death of A in **26.2** above; or
- the remittance basis applies and any of the employment income arising to A under these provisions is remitted to the UK on or after A's death.

There is no such liability if A died without commencing employment with B, and the above is of no relevance where the relevant step is the earmarking of money or assets as in **26.7**(a) or (b) below or if it is within **26.7**(I) or (II) below.

Avoidance of double tax charge: earlier income tax liability

ITEPA 2003, ss 554Z11B–554Z11G deal with the possibility of a double tax charge where the circumstances are as in Rule 2A at **26.4** above except that, when the relevant step is taken, the earlier tax liability has become due and payable but all or part of it remains unpaid (and not otherwise accounted for) and the person liable has not agreed any terms with HMRC for its discharge. These sections have effect in relation to relevant steps taken on or after 6 April 2011. They also have effect in relation to a relevant step taken between 9 December 2010 and 5 April 2011 inclusive if the disguised remuneration provisions would have applied by reason of that step had it been taken between 6 April 2011 and 5 April 2017 inclusive.

Where, after the relevant step is taken, an amount (Amount X) is paid in respect of all or part of the 'earlier charge' (or any late payment interest on that charge), an amount equal to Amount X is treated as a payment on account of the 'overlap charge' (or if that charge has been paid in full, any late payment interest payable on that charge). The '*earlier charge*' is so much of the earlier tax liability as relates to the overlap between sum or asset P and sum or asset Q. The '*overlap charge*' is so much of the 'current tax liability' as relates to that overlap. The '*current tax liability*' is the income tax liability arising under the disguised remuneration provisions by reason of the relevant step. The amount of a tax liability that relates to the overlap is to be determined on a just and reasonable basis.

Where an amount (Amount Y) is paid in respect of all or part of the overlap charge (or any late payment interest thereon), an amount equal to Amount Y is treated as a payment on account of the earlier charge (or if that charge has been paid in full, any late payment interest payable thereon).

The intention behind the above is to provide a flexible approach to giving relief where more than one charge exists in respect of the same money or asset. The approach recognises that a payment can be made against one liability or the other, and gives relief by treating a payment of one liability as also being a payment on account of the other. See the draft official guidance at www.gov.uk/government/publications/tackling-disguised-remuneration-draft-guidance-for-changes-to-part-7a for more details and for examples of where overlaps may occur.

There may be more than two liabilities arising at different times all of which relate to the overlap between sum or asset P and sum or asset Q. In this case, an amount equal to Amount Z is allocated to the earlier charges in such proportions as are just and reasonable in all the circumstances. Amount Z is the amount paid in respect of all or part of two or more overlap charges (or late payment interest in respect of any of them). For more details, see the draft official guidance referenced above.

Where a notional payment of PAYE income is treated as having been made to an employee (see **53.14** PAY AS YOU EARN), by reason of the value of the relevant step counting as employment income, the notional payment is reduced by so much of sum or asset P as is within the overlap and in relation to which a payment on account of either the earlier charge or the overlap charge is treated as made as above.

Provisional payments of tax

In determining for the above purposes whether an amount of tax has been paid, a person is not regarded as having paid (or otherwise accounted for) any tax by reason only of making a 'provisional payment of tax', except in accordance with a successful application to that effect (see below). A '*provisional payment of tax*' is a payment on account (but not something treated as a payment on account as above), a payment treated as a payment on account under the accelerated payments rules (see **4.51** ANTI-AVOIDANCE) or a payment pending determination of an appeal.

Application may be made to HMRC for a provisional payment of tax to attract the above treatment as if it were not provisional. The application must be made in such form and manner, and contain such information, as may be specified by the Commissioners for HMRC. An HMRC officer must notify the applicant of the decision on the application, and where the application is granted the provisional payment of tax cannot be repaid.

If a provisional payment of tax is made in respect of an earlier charge in relation to an overlap, it is treated as also being made in respect of the overlap charge in relation to the overlap, and vice versa. The effect of this is to prevent late payment interest accruing on both liabilities. It can also be allocated to earlier charges where there is more than one. If a provisional payment of tax is repaid, and late payment interest on the earlier charge or the overlap charge would have accrued during the 'relevant period' if the provisional payment had not been made, the interest is treated as having accrued anyway. The '*relevant period*' is the period beginning on the day on which the provisional payment of tax is made and ending with the day on which the repayment is made.

Avoidance of double tax charge: subsequent income tax liability

ITEPA 2003, s 554Z13 deals with the possibility of a double tax charge where:

- an event takes place after a relevant step; and
- this later event would give rise to an income tax liability (other than under these provisions or any of **71.4 –71.16** and **71.80** SHARE-RELATED EMPLOYMENT INCOME AND EXEMPTIONS or on PENSION INCOME (**56**)).

Insofar as it is just and reasonable in order to avoid a double charge to income tax in respect of the sum of money or asset which is the subject of the relevant step, there is to be no liability to income tax by virtue of the later event.

Earmarking not followed by further relevant step

ITEPA 2003, s 554Z14 provides for relief to be given where earmarking of money or assets as in **26.7**(a) or (b) below is not followed by a further relevant step. An application for relief may be made by A (or by his personal representatives following his death) to an officer of HMRC if:

(a) these provisions have applied by reason of a relevant step within **26.7**(a) or (b) below taken by a person (P);
(b) there occurs a subsequent event which is not a relevant step in relation to the sum of money or asset which is (or derives from) the subject of the relevant step in (a) above;

(c) by reason of the subsequent event no further relevant step is or will be taken by P or any other person in relation to the sum of money or asset in (b) above; and
(d) there is no connection between the subsequent event and a tax avoidance arrangement.

The application for relief must be made within four years from the time when the subsequent event occurs. If satisfied that the requirements are met, HMRC must give such relief (if any) as the officer considers just and reasonable in respect of income tax paid on any previously charged amount. The relief is to be given by repayment or otherwise as appropriate.

Location of employment duties

ITEPA 2003, s 554Z15 brings into play, with appropriate modifications, the rules in **28.3**(i)–(iii), (v) EMPLOYMENT INCOME, which are relevant to the location of employment duties.

[*ITEPA 2003, ss 554Z11B–554Z11G, 554Z12–554Z15; FA 2017, Sch 6 paras 7, 11, 15*].

Disguised remuneration — relevant steps

[26.7] Subject to the exclusions at **26.10** below and the additional rules at **26.8** below for loans etc. outstanding on 5 April 2019 (the loan charge), three types of action as described below are designated as '*relevant steps*' for the purposes of **26.2**(d) above and the provisions in general. With effect for steps taken on or after 6 April 2017, it is specified that a step can be a relevant step even if it constitutes, or contributes to, a breach of trust, and even if the step is wholly or partly void as a result of breach of trust.

Earmarking etc. of money and assets

A person (P) takes a relevant step if:

(a) a sum of money or asset held by or on behalf of P is earmarked (however informally) by P with a view to a later relevant step being taken by P or any other person in relation to that sum or asset (or any sum or asset derived from it); or
(b) a sum of money or asset otherwise starts being held by or on behalf of P, specifically with a view, so far as P is concerned, to a later relevant step being taken by P or any other person in relation to that sum or asset (or any sum or asset derived from it).

It does not matter if:

- details of the later relevant step have not been worked out; or
- the later relevant step will be taken only upon the meeting of a condition; or
- any condition which needs to be met before the later relevant step is taken might never be met; or
- A (the person referred to in **26.2** or **26.3** above), or any person linked with A (see **26.2**), has no legal right to have a relevant step taken in relation to any such sum of money or asset.

For the purposes of (b) above, it does not matter whether or not the sum of money or asset in question has previously been held by or on behalf of P on a different basis.

The charge to tax in **26.4** above does not apply by reason of a relevant step of the above kind taken on or after A's death.

Payment of sum, transfer of asset etc.

A person (P) takes a relevant step if he:

(i) pays a sum of money to a 'relevant person'; or
(ii) transfers an asset to a relevant person; or
(iii) takes a step by virtue of which a relevant person acquires shares, an interest in shares or share options (see below); or
(iv) makes available a sum of money or asset for use (or makes it available under an arrangement which permits its use) as security for a loan made or to be made to a relevant person, or otherwise to secure the meeting of any liability or the performance of any undertaking of a relevant person; or
(v) grants to a relevant person a lease of premises the effective duration of which is likely to be more than 21 years.

'*Relevant person*' means A (the person referred to in **26.2** or **26.3** above) or a person chosen by A or within a class of person chosen by A, but also includes, if P is taking a step on A's behalf or otherwise at A's direction or request, any other person. References to A include any person linked with A (see **26.2**).

In (i) above, the payment of a sum of money includes a payment by way of loan. For the purposes of (iii) above, 'shares' and 'share options' have the extended meaning given by **71.3** SHARE-RELATED EMPLOYMENT INCOME AND EXEMPTIONS and shares are deemed to be acquired when the beneficial entitlement to them is acquired and not, if different, at the time of conveyance or transfer. For the purposes of (iv) above, it does not matter if the money or asset is made available in an informal way or if the relevant person has a legal right to use the money or asset as security or actually does use it for such purpose. For the purposes of (v) above, there are provisions in *ITEPA 2003, s 554C(7)–(10)* for determining the effective duration of a lease, which may be longer than its actual duration.

On and after 6 April 2017, a person (P) also takes a relevant step if he:

(I) acquires a right to payment of a sum of money, or to a transfer of assets, where there is a connection (direct or indirect) between the acquisition of the right and a payment made (by way of a loan or otherwise) to a 'relevant person' (as defined above) or a transfer of assets to a relevant person; or
(II) releases or writes off the whole or a part of a loan made to a relevant person or an acquired right of the kind in (I) above.

For these purposes, a loan includes any form of credit and any payment purported to be made by way of a loan. If one person (T) acquires from another (L) (whether or not for consideration):

- a right to payment (or part payment) of a loan which T himself is liable to repay; or
- a right to payment of a sum of money or to a transfer of assets, where T himself is the person liable to pay the sum or transfer the assets,

L is treated for the purposes of (II) above as releasing the loan or right (in whole or in part as the case may be).

The charge to tax in **26.4** above does not apply by reason of a relevant step within (II) above if the step is taken on or after A's death.

Making an asset available

A person (P) takes a relevant step if, without actually transferring the asset to the relevant person,

(A) he at any time makes an asset available for a 'relevant person' (see above) to benefit from in a way which is substantially similar to the way in which that person would have been able to benefit from the asset had it been transferred to him at that time; or
(B) he at or after the end of the 'relevant period' makes an asset available for a relevant person to benefit from.

The '*relevant period*' is the period of two years starting with the day on which A's employment with B ceases (where A and B are the persons referred to in **26.2** or **26.3** above). Where P makes an asset available (for a relevant person to benefit from) before the end of the relevant period and continues to make it so available after the end of that period, P is treated as taking a step at the end of that period, i.e. it falls within (B) above.

The following factors (among others) may be taken into account in determining whether a step is taken by virtue of (A) above:

- any limitations on the way in which the relevant person may benefit from the asset;
- the period over which the asset is being made available and (if relevant) the extent to which that period covers the expected remaining useful life of the asset;
- the extent to which the relevant person has (or is to have) a say over the disposal of the asset; and
- the extent to which the relevant person may benefit from any proceeds arising from disposal or otherwise have a say in how the proceeds are used.

[*ITEPA 2003, ss 554A(2)(4), 554AF(2), 554B–554D, 554Z(7); FA 2017, Sch 6 paras 2–4, 13; F(No 2)A 2017, Sch 11 para 46(2); FA 2018, Sch 1 paras 2, 13*].

Loans and quasi-loans outstanding on 5 April 2019 (the 'loan charge')

[26.8] A person (P) is treated as taking a relevant step for the purposes of the disguised remuneration provisions if P has made a loan or quasi-loan to a 'relevant person' on or after 9 December 2010 and any part of it remains outstanding immediately before the end of 5 April 2019. This is subject to the exclusions at **26.9** below.

The loan charge was originally to apply to loans made on or after 6 April 1999. Loans made before 9 December 2010 were removed from charge by *FA 2020, s 15*. See www.gov.uk/guidance/find-out-how-the-changes-to-the-loan-charge-affect-you.

For those who earned less than £50,000 in the tax year 2017/18 and have no other source of wealth, HMRC will agree a payment plan spread over a minimum of five years. For those who earned less than £30,000, they will agree a payment plan of at least seven years. Other payment plans might be agreed based on individual circumstances. See www.gov.uk/guidance/find-out-how-the-changes-to-the-loan-charge-affect-you. Interest will be charged from 1 October 2020 (see below under Relief from late paid interest).

See also www.gov.uk/guidance/report-and-account-for-your-disguised-remuneration-loan-charge.

Relevant step and relevant person

'*Relevant person*' is defined in **26.7** above under Payment of sum, transfer of asset etc. The relevant step is treated as being taken immediately before the end of 5 April 2019. In ascertaining whether the condition at **26.2**(e) or **26.3**(g) is met, the relevant step is taken to be the making of the loan or quasi-loan. In determining the value of the relevant step (see **26.4** above), the step is treated as involving a sum of money equal to the amount of the loan or quasi-loan outstanding at the time the step is treated as being taken; the value of the relevant step is equal to that sum.

Election to spread charge over three years

Where P is treated as taking a relevant step by reason of making a loan or quasi-loan, an irrevocable election (under *F(No 2)A 2017, Sch 11 para 1A*) can be made by A in **26.2** or **26.3** above (usually the employee) to effectively spread the charge over the three tax years 2018/19 to 2020/21. Any election should be made via HMRC's loan charge reporting form (see www.gov.uk/guidance/find-out-how-the-changes-to-the-loan-charge-affect-you).

The effect of the election is to treat the chargeable amount as split into three equal parts. This is achieved by treating P as having taken three relevant steps. The first of these notional steps is treated as taken at the time P is treated as taking the actual relevant step (see above). The second and third notional steps are treated as taken on the second and third anniversaries of that time. Each notional step is treated as involving a sum of money equal to one-third of the amount of the loan or quasi-loan outstanding at the time P is treated as taking the actual relevant step. In the event of A's death after the time of the first notional step but before the time of the second or third, the charge to tax still arises by reference to the value of all three notional steps.

The election must be made before 1 October 2020, unless an HMRC officer allows a later election in a particular case. The Commissioners for HMRC may by regulations apply a later time limit to any class of persons specified in the regulations. Any person who has made the similar election at **75.40** TRADING INCOME is treated as having made this election also (and vice versa). The election cannot be made until the duty to provide information to HMRC (see below), or where applicable the equivalent duty under the rules at **75.40**, has been complied with.

Loans and quasi-loans

A 'loan' includes any form of credit and any payment purported to be made by way of a loan. A '*quasi-loan*' is made by P to a relevant person if (and when) P acquires a right to a payment or a transfer of assets and a connection exists between the acquisition of the right and a payment made (by way of a loan or otherwise) to the relevant person or a transfer of assets to the relevant person. Where loans or quasi-loans are replaced by other loans or quasi-loans, the replacement loans or quasi-loans are within the scope of these provisions.

Loans and quasi-loans: amounts outstanding

The question of whether and to what extent a loan or quasi-loan is outstanding at a particular time is determined in accordance with the following, and does not depend on the loan or quasi-loan subsisting at that time.

An amount of a loan is outstanding if the principal lent exceeds the amount repaid. The principal lent is exclusive of any capitalised interest. The amount repaid for this purpose is the amount of principal that was repaid on or before 16 March 2016 plus payments in money made by the relevant person after that date by way of repayment of principal. However, no such post-16 March 2016 payment can be included in the amount repaid if: (i) there is any connection between the payment and an arrangement which has a tax avoidance purpose (other than the arrangement under which the loan was made); or (ii) the payment (or a sum or asset representing it) is the subject of a relevant step (within **26.7** above) taken after the payment is made but before the end of 5 April 2019, and any resultant tax liability remains unpaid. (If a payment falls within (ii), *F(No 2)A 2017, Sch 11 para 4(6)* imposes a restriction on the operation of Rule 2A (overlap with money or asset subject to earlier tax liability) at **26.4** above.)

If P has made a loan on or after 9 December 2010 to a relevant person, and before the end of 5 April 2019 A or B acquires (whether or not for consideration) a right to payment of any amount of the loan, that amount is treated for the purposes of these provisions as an amount, of the loan made by P to the relevant person, that is outstanding immediately before the end of 5 April 2019. In determining the value of the relevant step, that amount is also treated as outstanding at the time P is treated as taking the relevant step. A and B are the persons referred to in **26.2** or **26.3** above.

An amount of a quasi-loan is outstanding if the 'initial debt amount' exceeds the amount repaid. The '*initial debt amount*' is the value of the right acquired by P (at the time it was acquired) plus the value of any additional debt that occurs on the acquisition of further rights by P (to a payment or a transfer of assets) in connection with the original payment or transfer of assets made to the relevant person. Where the right is to a payment, its value is the amount payable. However, where a further right acquired is a right to a payment, and the additional debt accrues to P by means of the capitalisation of interest, the value of that further right is nil. Where the right is to a transfer of assets, its value is the market value of the assets at the time the right is acquired (or, if the assets are non-fungible and not then in existence, the value of the right at that time) or, if higher, the cost of the assets at that time.

The amount repaid in the case of a quasi-loan is the amount (if any) by which the initial debt amount has been reduced (by way of repayment) on or before 16 March 2016 plus any payments in money made by the relevant person after that date by way of repayment of the initial debt amount. If the debt is a right to a transfer of assets, and the assets have been transferred, an amount equal to the market value of the assets at the time of transfer also constitutes an amount repaid. A similar rule applies as for loans so that no post-16 March 2016 payment, and no transfer of assets at any time, can be included in the amount repaid if certain conditions are met, e.g. connection with a tax avoidance arrangement (see *F(No 2)A 2017, Sch 11 para 12*).

If P has made a quasi-loan on or after 9 December 2010 to a relevant person, and before the end of 5 April 2019 A or B acquires (whether or not for consideration) a right to the payment or transfer of assets to which P acquired the right on making the quasi-loan, an amount equal to the value of the right acquired by A or B is treated for the purposes of these provisions as an amount, of the quasi-loan made by P to the relevant person, that is outstanding immediately before the end of 5 April 2019. In determining the value of the relevant step, that amount is also treated as outstanding at the time P is treated as taking the relevant step. Where the right acquired by A or B is to a payment, its value is the amount payable. Where the right is to a transfer of assets, its value is the market value of the assets at the time the right is acquired (or, if the assets are non-fungible and not then in existence, the value of the right at that time) or, if higher, the cost of the assets at that time.

There are special rules to determine whether and to what extent a loan or quasi-loan is outstanding at a particular time where the loan or quasi-loan is made in a currency other than sterling or is repayable in a currency other than that in which it was made or is made in a currency expected to depreciate against sterling. For these rules, see *F(No 2)A 2017, Sch 11 paras 6–10, 14–18*.

Reduction of loan charge where reasonable disclosure made

Where a person is treated as taking a relevant step by reason of making a loan or quasi-loan, the chargeable amount will be reduced where:

- a reasonable case could have been made that, for any tax year earlier than 2016/17, A was chargeable to income tax on an amount referable to the loan or quasi-loan;

- at a time when HMRC still had power to recover (from A or any other person) income tax for the year in question in respect of that amount, a 'qualifying tax return' (or two or more qualifying tax returns of the same type taken together) contained a reasonable disclosure of the loan or quasi-loan; and
- as at 6 April 2019 HMRC had not taken steps to recover that tax.

The reduction does not apply if a reasonable case could be made that A was chargeable to income tax on all or part of the loan amount identified above (or an amount representing that loan amount) in an alternative tax year, and either the alternative year is a later year than 2015/16 or HMRC took steps before 6 April 2019 to recover the tax for the alternative year. Where the reduction does apply, the amount of the loan or quasi-loan that is outstanding immediately before the end of 5 April 2019 is reduced by the amount identified above.

For this purpose there are two types of '*qualifying tax return*': a self-assessment tax return made by A or B for 2015/16 or any earlier year, and any accompanying accounts, statements or documents, and a company tax return made by B for an accounting period beginning before 6 April 2016. In order to have contained a reasonable disclosure of the loan or quasi-loan, the qualifying tax return(s) must have identified the loan or quasi-loan, identified the person to whom it was made (if other than A), identified the arrangements in pursuance of which, or in connection with which, it was made, and provided such other information sufficient for it to be apparent that a reasonable case could be made that for the year in question A was chargeable to income tax on an amount referable to the loan or quasi-loan.

References above to A being chargeable to income tax are to A being chargeable other than by virtue of a cheap loan treated as a benefit-in-kind (as in **28.32** EMPLOYMENT INCOME.

See also www.gov.uk/guidance/find-out-how-the-changes-to-the-loan-charge-affect-you.

Repayment or waiver of voluntary restitution

The Government has agreed that HMRC should repay voluntary restitution that has been paid by individuals and employers under settlement agreements, entered into since the loan charge was announced in March 2016 in cases where the loan charge would have applied but for the removal from charge of loans made before 9 December 2010 (see above) and cases involving loans made on or after date where reasonable disclosure was made.

The Commissioners for HMRC are thus legally obliged to establish a scheme under which they may, on an application made to them before 1 October 2021, repay an amount paid (or treated as paid) to them under a 'qualifying agreement' or waive the payment of certain amounts payable to them under such an agreement. Amounts can be repaid or waived in whole or in part. A '*qualifying agreement*' is an agreement made with the Commissioners for HMRC on or after 16 March 2016 and before 11 March 2020 which imposes an obligation on any party thereto to pay an amount of income tax that is referable to any such loan or quasi-loan.

The scheme applies to any amount referable (directly or indirectly) to a loan or quasi-loan made on or after 6 April 1999 and before 6 April 2016, provided the amount is one that HMRC had no power to recover at the time the agreement was made. An amount referable to a loan or quasi-loan made on or after 9 December 2010 is within the scope of the scheme only if, at a time when HMRC had power to recover the amount, a tax return (or two or more tax returns of the same type taken together), contained a reasonable disclosure of the loan or quasi-loan. What constitutes reasonable disclosure is defined similarly as above under Reduction of loan charge where reasonable disclosure made. For this purpose there are two types of tax return: a self-assessment tax return, and any accompanying accounts, statements or documents, and a company tax return.

An amount paid, treated as paid or due to be paid under a qualifying agreement is also within the scope of the scheme if it is interest on another amount paid, treated as paid or due to be paid under that agreement and within the scope of the scheme.

HMRC have published a draft scheme at www.gov.uk/government/publications/implementation-of-changes-to-the-loan-charge.

Relief from late paid interest

Where a person is chargeable to income tax on any amount by reason of the loan charge, relief from late payment interest (see **43.2** LATE PAYMENT INTEREST AND PENALTIES) has effect provided that:

- the person files a self-assessment return for 2018/19 before 1 October 2020;
- at the beginning of 1 October 2020 the self-assessment included in that return is complete and accurate.

The relief applies equally to cases where income tax would be chargeable but for the removal from charge of loans made before 9 December 2010 or the reduction of the loan charge where reasonable disclosure was made (see above in each case).

The relief takes the following form. If before 1 October 2020 the person discharges their liability to income tax and CGT for 2018/19:

(a) any amount paid in discharging that liability (other than a self-assessment payment on account) is to be taken as not carrying interest;
(b) any self-assessment payment on account made for 2019/20 is to be taken as not carrying interest.

The reliefs in (a) and (b) above also apply if before 1 October 2020 the person enters into an agreement with HMRC as to the discharge of their liability to income tax and capital gains tax for 2018/19. In this case, the relief in (a) applies only to amounts paid before 1 October 2020 (other than a self-assessment payment on account). In addition, the late payment interest start date, in respect of any amount *subsequently* paid under the agreement, is deferred to 1 October 2020.

The relief in (b) above does not apply if by the end of January 2021 the person has neither discharged their liability to income tax and CGT for 2019/20 nor entered into an agreement with HMRC as to its discharge.

The Commissioners for HMRC may by regulations provide that the above applies to any class of persons specified in those regulations as if the references to 1 October 2020 were to a later date.

Interaction with accelerated payments rules

A special rule applies where an accelerated payment notice (or partner payment notice) has been given by HMRC in relation to a charge to tax (and/or NICs) arising by reason of the relevant step, and an accelerated payment is made by the relevant person on or before 5 April 2019 in respect of the understated or disputed tax (and/or NICs) to which the notice relates. The special rule applies only if the amount of the accelerated payment is at least equal to the outstanding amount of the loan or quasi-loan at the end of 5 April 2019. It is suitably modified where more than one notice has been given by HMRC in relation to the same charge. See **4.50** ANTI-AVOIDANCE as regards the giving of an accelerated payment notice (or partner payment notice).

The relevant person could make an application to the Commissioners for HMRC to be treated as taking the relevant step only if any part of the accelerated payment is repaid, whether on withdrawal of the notice or the determination of an appeal. If HMRC grant the application, and a repayment is subsequently made, the relevant step is treated as being taken immediately before the end of the 30 days beginning with the date of repayment or, if later, immediately before the end of 5 April 2019. The application had to be made in 2018, unless an HMRC officer considered it reasonable for it to be made at a later date in any particular case. The grant of an application can be revoked, and treated as never having been made, if the application is found to have contained deliberately inaccurate information.

[*ITEPA 2003, s 554A(2)(4); F(No 2)A 2017, Sch 11 paras 1, 1A, 1B, 2–18, 23, 24, 35ZA, 44, 45; FA 2018, Sch 1 para 8; FA 2020, ss 15(1), 16(1)–(3), 17(1), 18, 19(3), 20, 21, Sch 2 paras 1–12, 24, 26–38*].

Duty to provide loan charge information to HMRC

Certain information must be provided to the Commissioners for HMRC in any of the following circumstances.

(i) A person (P) is treated as taking a relevant step immediately before the end of 5 April 2019 as above, and the charge to tax under the disguised remuneration provisions applies as a result.

(ii)

- A loan or quasi-loan is made by a person (S) to a relevant person, and an application is made by that person in response to an accelerated payment notice (see above) and in relation to the relevant step in question;
- a favourable decision is made on the application before 6 April 2019 (and is not revoked before that date);
- circumstance (i) above does not apply; and
- A is still living immediately before the end of 30 September 2019 or, if earlier, the time the relevant step would be treated as taken.

(iii) None of the first two circumstances applies but a person (T) would have been treated as taking a relevant step immediately before the end of 16 March 2016, to which the charge to tax under the disguised remuneration provisions applies, if the legislation related to loans etc. outstanding at that date rather than 5 April 2019. This circumstance applies only if A is still living immediately before the end of 5 April 2019.

The information is to be provided to HMRC by A (i.e. the employee) (or A's personal representatives) after 5 April 2019 and before 1 October 2020, and must be provided in such form and manner as may be specified by HMRC. HMRC have specified that their loan charge reporting form should be used (see www.gov.uk/guidance/find-out-how-the-changes-to-the-loan-charge-affect-you). If an appropriate third party (i.e. as the case may be, P, S or T) receives a request from A (or A's personal representatives) for information reasonably required to comply with the obligation thus imposed, the third party is legally bound to meet that request; or at least to supply a statement confirming that any of the information not supplied is information that is not available to the third party. The information, and any such statement, must be supplied promptly and, in any event, before the end of 30 days beginning with date of receipt of the request.

The information to be provided to HMRC (the '*loan charge information*') is listed in *F(No 2)A 2017, Sch 11 para 35D* and includes information about A and, if different, the person(s) providing the information; the name of B in **26.2** or **26.3** above; the name of the recipient of the loan or quasi-loan if someone other than A; specified information on the loan or quasi-loan itself; the name of the relevant arrangement referred to in **26.2**(b) or **26.3**(a) and any reference number allocated to it by HMRC; any other reference number allocated by HMRC in connection with the relevant step; and information identifying any terms agreed with HMRC for partial discharge of liability for income tax arising.

The requirement to provide information to HMRC does not apply if, before 1 October 2019, terms were agreed with HMRC for the discharge of all liability for income tax arising on the relevant step in question, whether taken by P, S or T in (i)–(iii) above, or result in there being no such liability.

Penalties

Failure to comply with the duty to provide information results in a fixed penalty of £300, plus a penalty of up to £60 for each day, up to a maximum of 90, on which the failure continues after the fixed penalty is imposed. Liability to these penalties is cancelled if the person satisfies HMRC, or the Tribunal on appeal, that there is a reasonable excuse for the failure. Reasonable excuse does not include insufficiency of funds (unless attributable to events outside the person's control) or reliance on another person (unless the first person took reasonable care to avoid the failure). A reasonable excuse is treated as continuing if the failure is remedied without unreasonable delay after the excuse ceased.

If a person provides *inaccurate* information, that person is liable to a penalty of up to £3,000 if:

- the inaccuracy is either careless (i.e. due to a failure to take reasonable care) or deliberate; or
- the person knows of the inaccuracy at the time the information is provided but does not inform HMRC at that time; or
- the person discovers the inaccuracy some time later but fails to take reasonable steps to inform HMRC.

Where the information contains more than one inaccuracy, there is a separate penalty for each one.

All of the above penalties are chargeable by HMRC assessment. Neither a fixed nor a daily penalty can be assessed any later than 30 September 2021. No penalty for inaccuracy can be assessed after 30 September 2023. There is a right of appeal against the imposition or the amount of any of these penalties, the appeal to be made in writing to HMRC, stating grounds of appeal, within 30 days of the issue of the notice of assessment. On an appeal against imposition of the penalty that is notified to the Appeal Tribunal, the Tribunal may confirm or cancel the imposition. If the appeal is against the amount of the penalty, the Tribunal may confirm the amount assessed or substitute any different amount that HMRC had the power to assess.

A penalty must be paid within 30 days of its being assessed, and may be enforced as if it were income tax charged in an assessment and due and payable. If appealed against, the penalty is instead payable within 30 days of the appeal being determined or withdrawn.

[*F(No 2)A 2017, Sch 11 paras 35A–35K; FA 2018, Sch 1 para 10; FA 2020, s 19(2), Sch 2 paras 13–15*].

Duty to provide loan charge information to employer

Where P made a loan (or quasi-loan) on or after 9 December 2019 to a relevant person, and the loan is outstanding on or after 17 March 2016, and before the end of 5 April 2019, each of A and P had to ensure that the 'loan charge information' (see above) was provided to B before 15 April 2019. A and B are the persons referred to in **26.2** or **26.3** above. [*F(No 2)A 2017, Sch 11 paras 36, 45; FA 2018, Sch 1 para 11; FA 2020, s 19(3), Sch 2 para 16*].

Miscellaneous

The charge to tax in **26.4** above does not apply by reason of a relevant step of the above kind which is treated as being taken on or after A's death (where A is the person referred to in **26.2** above). [*ITEPA 2003, s 554A(4); F(No 2)A 2017, Sch 11 para 46(3)*].

Where P is treated as taking a relevant step by reason of making an employment-related loan, the loan is not to be regarded, for the tax year in which the relevant step is treated as being taken and any subsequent tax year, as a cheap loan taxable under **28.32** EMPLOYMENT INCOME. [*F(No 2)A 2017, Sch 11 para 37*].

Where P would otherwise be treated as taking a relevant step of the above kind, and the loan in question gives rise to a tax charge under *CTA 2010, s 455* (loans to close company participators), P is not treated as taking that relevant step if either (i) the *CTA 2010, s 455* charge is paid in full by the 'key date'; or (ii) the liability to that charge is reported in a company tax return made by B and HMRC agree not to apply these rules. The '*key date*' is the later of 5 April 2019 and the due date of the tax under *CTA 2010, s 455*. If neither condition is met, P is treated as taking the relevant step immediately before the end of the key date. [*F(No 2)A 2017, Sch 11 para 36A; FA 2018, Sch 1 para 4*].

Loans and quasi-loans — exclusions

[26.9] There are certain situations and circumstances, of which the following is a summary, in which the charge to tax under the disguised remuneration provisions does not apply notwithstanding that a relevant step within **26.8** above is treated as having been taken. In most of these cases, the exclusion is expressly denied if there is a connection between the relevant step and a tax avoidance arrangement (for which see *ITEPA 2003, s 554Z(13)–(16)*).

Commercial transactions

This exclusion applies where P is treated as taking the relevant step by reason of the payment of a sum of money by way of a loan, and the loan is (at the time it is made) a loan on ordinary commercial terms (defined as in **28.32** EMPLOYMENT INCOME, but disregarding **28.32**(b) and (c)). [*F(No 2)A 2017, Sch 11 paras 25, 44*].

Transfers of employment-related loans

This exclusion applies where P is treated as taking the relevant step by reason of making a quasi-loan by acquiring a right to payment of an amount equal to the whole or part of a payment made by way of a loan to a relevant person. It closely follows the equivalent exclusion at **26.10** below. [*F(No 2)A 2017, Sch 11 para 27*].

Transactions under employee benefit packages

This exclusion applies where P is treated as taking the relevant step by reason of the payment of a sum of money by way of a loan, and is similar to the equivalent exclusion at **26.10** below. [*F(No 2)A 2017, Sch 11 para 29*].

Cases involving employment-related securities

This exclusion applies where P is treated as taking the relevant step by reason of the payment of a sum of money by way of a loan. The charge to tax does not apply if the loan is made and used solely for the purpose of enabling the exercise of an employment-related share option and the exercise of the option gives rise to employment income. [*F(No 2)A 2017, Sch 11 para 31*].

Employee car ownership schemes

The charge to tax does not apply where P is treated as taking the relevant step by reason of the making of a car loan under an employee car ownership scheme (for which see the equivalent exclusion at **26.10** below) provided the employee car ownership scheme is not a tax avoidance arrangement. [*F(No 2)A 2017, Sch 11 para 33*].

Acquisition of unlisted employer shares

This exclusion applies where:

- the loan or quasi-loan in question was made before 9 December 2010;
- if P is treated as taking the relevant step by reason of the payment of a sum of money by way of loan, the sum is used by A solely to acquire 'employer shares';
- if P is treated as taking the relevant step by reason of making a quasi-loan, the transfer of assets to the relevant person is the transfer of employer shares to A;
- the employer shares are acquired, or transferred, no later than one year after the loan or quasi-loan was made; and
- the employer shares are not listed on a recognised stock exchange at any time during the period from the making of the loan or quasi-loan to the day on which A ceases to hold the shares or the day the loan or quasi-loan is repaid, whichever is earlier.

'*Employer shares*' are shares that form part of the ordinary share capital of B or of any company which is a member of the same group as B at the time the shares are acquired. A and B are the persons referred to in **26.2** or **26.3** above.

If the above exclusion has been applied but any amount of the loan or quasi-loan is outstanding 12 months after A ceases to hold the shares, a relevant step within **26.8** above is treated as being taken at that time by reason of the making of a loan or quasi-loan equal to the amount then outstanding.

[*F(No 2)A 2017, Sch 11 para 35*].

Disguised remuneration — exclusions

[26.10] There is a large number of situations and circumstances, of which the following is a summary, in which the charge to tax under these provisions does not apply notwithstanding that a relevant step within **26.7** above has been taken. Further exclusions may be added, possibly with retrospective effect, by HMRC via regulations made by statutory instrument. [*ITEPA 2003, s 554Y*]. The items below are listed in the order in which they appear in *ITEPA 2003*. In some of these cases, the exclusion is expressly denied if there is a connection between the relevant step and a tax avoidance arrangement (for which see *ITEPA 2003, s 554Z(13)–(16)*).

Steps under certain schemes etc.

The charge to tax does not apply by reason of a relevant step taken under: tax-advantaged employee share schemes (within **71.25**, **71.41**, **71.53** or **71.66** SHARE-RELATED EMPLOYMENT INCOME AND EXEMPTIONS); registered pension schemes; pension schemes of overseas governments for the benefit of their employees; arrangements for the provision of excluded benefits (within **57.35** PENSION PROVISION); or certain holiday pay schemes.

There is no exclusion if the step is taken for the purpose of acquiring, holding or providing shares under a tax-advantaged employee share scheme and the number of shares held immediately before or after the taking of the step exceeds the number that might reasonably be expected to be required. Also, if money or assets have been earmarked for such a purpose, and the exclusion applied to the relevant step represented by such earmarking, a further (non-excluded) relevant step is deemed to be taken at any time when the money or assets cease to be held for that purpose whilst still being held on the basis mentioned in **26.7**(a) or (b) above.

The charge to tax does not apply by reason of a relevant step taken by the Independent Parliamentary Standards Authority in relation to a member of the House of Commons.

[*ITEPA 2003, s 554E*].

Commercial transactions

The charge to tax does not apply by reason of a relevant step consisting of the payment of a sum of money by way of loan if the loan is on ordinary commercial terms (defined as in **28.32** EMPLOYMENT INCOME, but disregarding **28.32**(b) and (c)).

The charge to tax does not apply by reason of any other relevant step taken by a person (P) if the step is taken for the sole purpose of a transaction which P has with A (the person referred to in **26.2** or **26.3** above) or a person linked with A (as in **26.2**) and which P entered into in the ordinary course of his business. It is a condition that a substantial proportion of P's business involves similar transactions with members of the public on terms similar to those on which he has entered into the transaction in question. [*ITEPA 2003, s 554F; F(No 2)A 2017, Sch 11 para 26*].

Transactions under employee benefit packages

The charge to tax does not apply by reason of a relevant step taken by a person (P) if:

- the step is taken for the sole purpose of a transaction which P has with A (the person referred to in **26.2** or **26.3** above) or a person linked with A (as in **26.2**) and which P entered into in the ordinary course of his business;
- the step is neither the payment of a sum of money by way of loan nor taken under a pension scheme; and
- the transaction is part of a package of benefits available to a substantial proportion of B's UK employees (B being the person referred to in **26.2** or **26.3**) or to a substantial proportion of those UK employees of B whose status as employees is comparable with that of A.

There are further conditions to do mainly with ensuring that A is not being treated favourably in comparison to other employees to whom the benefit package is available.

If the first two of the above conditions are met except that the relevant step is the payment of a sum of money by way of loan, the third condition is instead that a substantial proportion of P's business involves making similar loans to members of the public and the transaction is part of a package of benefits available to a substantial proportion of B's employees. It is then a further condition that the package will not be wholly or mainly conferred on directors, senior employees, any other employees in receipt of the highest levels of remuneration and (where B is a company and part of a group) senior employees, or those receiving the highest levels of remuneration, in the group.

[*ITEPA 2003, s 554G; F(No 2)A 2017, Sch 11 para 30*].

Earmarking of deferred remuneration

This exclusion applies if:

- on a date (the '*award date*') A is awarded remuneration (the '*deferred remuneration*') in respect of his employment with B, where A and B are the persons referred to in **26.2** or **26.3** above;
- the main purpose of the award is not the provision of relevant benefits (which has the meaning given in **57.35** PENSION PROVISION except that the term does in this case include benefits charged to tax as PENSION INCOME (**56**));
- the deferred remuneration is awarded on terms the main purpose of which is to defer the provision to A of the deferred remuneration to a specified date (the '*vesting date*'), while providing that the award is revoked if specified conditions are not met on or before the vesting date;
- the vesting date is not more than five years after the award date;
- as at the award date, there is a reasonable chance that the award will be revoked because of conditions not being met by the vesting date;
- if the deferred remuneration were to be provided to A by any person on the award date, that action would be a payment of PAYE income;
- before the end of the vesting date, a person ('P') takes a relevant step within **26.7**(a) or (b) above (earmarking etc.) by reason of which the charge to tax under these provisions would apply if it were not for this exclusion; and
- the sum of money or asset which is the subject of the relevant step represents the deferred remuneration or any part of it (and nothing else).

The charge to tax does not apply by reason of the relevant step. If at any time any sum of money or asset held by or on behalf of P on the basis mentioned in **26.7**(a) or (b) ceases to represent the earmarked deferred remuneration whilst continuing to be held by or on behalf of P on that basis, a further (non-excluded) relevant step is deemed to be taken at that time. If by the end of the vesting date the earmarked deferred remuneration (or any part of it) has neither been paid to A as PAYE income nor revoked, a further (non-excluded) relevant step is deemed to be taken at the end of the vesting date.

[*ITEPA 2003, s 554H*].

Earmarking for employee share schemes

See **26.11** below.

Other cases involving employment-related shares etc.

The charge to tax does not apply by reason of a relevant step the subject of which is employment-related shares if, by virtue of the step, the shares are acquired by a person and the tax exemption in **71.4** SHARE-RELATED EMPLOYMENT INCOME AND EXEMPTIONS applies (tax exemption on acquisition of restricted shares).

The charge to tax does not apply by reason of a relevant step the subject of which is an employment-related share option if, by virtue of the step, the option is acquired by a person and, as in **71.15** SHARE-RELATED EMPLOYMENT INCOME AND EXEMPTIONS, no liability to income tax arises in respect of the acquisition.

The charge to tax does not apply by reason of certain events within **71** SHARE-RELATED EMPLOYMENT INCOME AND EXEMPTIONS (as listed in *ITEPA 2003, s 554N(5)*) by virtue of which an amount counts as employment income (or would have done had it not been for certain exclusions and elections (as listed in *ITEPA 2003, s 554N(6)*) available under those provisions).

The charge to tax does not apply by reason of a relevant step within **26.7**(i) above if the step is the payment of a sum of money by way of loan, the loan is made and used solely for the purpose of enabling the exercise of an employment-related share option and the exercise of the option gives rise to employment income. If the loan is not fully repaid by the end of a period of 40 days starting with the date of the relevant step, a further (non-excluded) relevant step is deemed to have been taken at the end of that period; the subject of that relevant step is the amount of loan outstanding.

There is a further exclusion where an acquisition of shares (or an interest in shares) gives rise to earnings at least equal to market value, or where market value has been paid by A (the person referred to in **26.2** or **26.3** above) on acquisition. The exclusion also applies if shares (or an interest in shares) are acquired on the exercise of an employment-related share option and the acquisition is a chargeable event. In both cases, the charge to tax does not apply by reason of a relevant step taken after the acquisition if the subject of the relevant step is the shares (or interest).

For the above purposes, 'shares' and 'share option' have the extended meaning given by **71.3** SHARE-RELATED EMPLOYMENT INCOME AND EXEMPTIONS.

[*ITEPA 2003, s 554N; F(No 2)A 2017, Sch 11 para 32*].

Employee car ownership schemes

For this purpose an '*employee car ownership scheme*' is an arrangement which:

- provides for A (the person referred to in **26.2** or **26.3** above) to purchase a new car from another person (S) by means of a loan (the '*car loan*') to be made to A by a licensed lender;
- specifies the date (the '*repayment date*') by which the car loan must be fully repaid, which must be no later than four years after the date on which it is made; and

- permits A, in order to obtain funds to repay the car loan, to sell the car back to S on a specified date at a specified price based on an estimate (made at the time the arrangement is made) of the likely outstanding amount of the car loan on the specified date.

The charge to tax does not apply by reason of a relevant step taken for the sole purpose of the purchase of the car or its sale-back or the making of the car loan, provided the arrangement is not a tax avoidance arrangement. If the charge to tax under these provisions would otherwise have applied by reason of the making of the car loan, and the car loan is not fully repaid by the end of the repayment date, a further (non-excluded) relevant step is deemed to have been taken at the end of the repayment date. This relevant step constitutes the payment of a sum of money within **26.7**(i) above.

If the loan has to be extended in circumstances arising from the 2020 COVID-19 (coronavirus) pandemic, but *not* beyond a term of four years, HMRC accept that this does not give rise to the tax charge (www.gov.uk/guidance/how-to-treat-certain-expenses-and-benefits-provided-to-employees-during-coronavirus-covid-19).

[*ITEPA 2003, s 554O; F(No 2)A 2017, Sch 11 para 34*].

Transfers of employment-related loans

Subject to conditions, the charge to tax does not apply by reason of a relevant step taken on or after 6 April 2017 by a person (P) if the step is the acquisition of a right to repayment of a loan to a relevant person (as defined in **26.7** above under Payment of sum, transfer of asset etc.). The conditions are that:

- the loan, at the time it was made, was an employment-related loan (as defined at **28.32** EMPLOYMENT INCOME);
- at all times in the tax year in which the relevant step is taken, the amount outstanding on the loan does not exceed the cheap loans de minimis exemption (currently £10,000 — see **28.32** EMPLOYMENT INCOME);
- at the time the relevant step is taken, the borrower is an employee, or a prospective employee, of P; and
- there is no connection between the relevant step and a tax avoidance arrangement (see *ITEPA 2003, s 554Z(13)–(16)*).

The following rules apply where two or more employment-related loans are made by the same employer in relation to the same employee:

- the *aggregate* outstanding amount on the loans must not exceed the de minimis exemption; and
- if, during the tax year in which the relevant step is taken, a person acquires a right to payment of an amount equal to the whole or part of the payment made by way of any of those loans, that amount is nevertheless treated as an amount outstanding for the purpose of applying the de minimis exemption.

[*ITEPA 2003, s 554OA; FA 2017, Sch 6 paras 5, 13; F(No 2)A 2017, Sch 11 para 28*].

Employment income exemptions

The charge to tax does not apply by reason of a relevant step if an employment income exemption (within *ITEPA 2003, Pt 4 (ss 227–326)*) applies to the subject of the relevant step. If the employment income exemption applies to the subject of the relevant step in part only, the relevant step is treated for these purposes as two separate relevant steps, one to which the exemption applies and one to which it does not. The sum of money or asset which is the subject of the relevant step is apportioned between the two notional relevant steps on a just and reasonable basis. *ITEPA 2003, s 271* (limited exemption of removal benefits and expenses — see **28.72** EMPLOYMENT INCOME) counts as an employment income exemption for these purposes even though it is strictly speaking an earnings-only exemption (see *ITEPA 2003, s 227* for the difference). [*ITEPA 2003, s 554P*].

Income arising from earmarked sum or asset

This exclusion applies if a sum of money or asset was the subject of a relevant step within **26.7**(a) or (b) above (earmarking etc.) taken by a person (P) and the charge to tax under these provisions applied by the reason of the relevant step (or would have applied but for other specified exclusions). If income arises from that sum or asset whilst it is held by or on behalf of P and still earmarked etc., and the income is itself the subject of a relevant step within **26.7**(a) or (b) taken by P, the charge to tax does not apply by reason of the last-mentioned relevant step. The exclusion does not apply if the income represents a return from the sum or asset in excess of the return which might be expected if all relevant connected persons acted at arm's length of each other. [*ITEPA 2003, s 554Q*].

Acquisitions out of sums or assets

This exclusion applies if the facts are similar to those immediately above except that, instead of income arising from the sum of money or asset held by or on behalf of P, a new sum of money or asset is acquired by or on behalf of P wholly out of the earmarked sum or asset. This particularly includes the situation where the new sum or asset represents the proceeds of the disposal of the original sum or asset. If, on its acquisition, the new sum or asset is itself the subject of a relevant step within **26.7**(a) or (b) above taken by P, the charge to tax does not apply by reason of that relevant step. The exclusion does not apply if the new sum or asset is acquired (directly or indirectly) from A (the person referred to in **26.2** or **26.3** above) or a person linked with A (as in **26.2**). It also does not apply if, at the time of its acquisition, the value of the new sum or asset is greater or less than the comparative value of the old, and the difference (or any part of it) might not have been expected if all relevant connected persons had acted at arm's length of each other.

There is a supplementary exclusion which prevents the charge to tax from applying by reason of a relevant step within **26.7**(i), (ii) or (iii) above, or **26.7**(I) or (II) above, which is taken (in relation to the new sum or asset or the old sum or asset) solely for the purpose of the acquisition of the new sum or asset.

[*ITEPA 2003, s 554R*].

Repayments of loans

This exclusion applies if a right to repayment of principal under a loan made on or after 6 April 1999 is held by or on behalf of a person (P) and, at any time on or after 9 December 2010, a sum of money is acquired by or on behalf of P by way of repayment of principal under the loan. If:

- on its acquisition, the sum of money in question (the '*repayment sum*') is the subject of a relevant step taken by P on or after 9 December 2010 which falls under the heading 'Earmarking etc. of money and assets' at **26.7** above; or
- for the sole purpose of the acquisition, the making of the payment of the repayment sum is a relevant step within section **26.7**(i) above (payment of sum of money),

the charge to tax does not apply by reason of the relevant step if, on its acquisition, the repayment sum is held by or on behalf of P on the same basis as that on which the right to repayment was held by or on behalf of P immediately before the acquisition. This exclusion does not apply where there is any connection (direct or indirect) between the acquisition of the repayment sum and a tax avoidance arrangement (other than the arrangement under which the loan was made). [*ITEPA 2003, s 554RA; FA 2017, Sch 6 paras 8, 14*].

Taxable pension income

The charge to tax does not apply by reason of a relevant step within any of **26.7**(i)–(v) above or within **26.7**(I) or (II), or **26.7**(A) or (B), if the step is the provision of pension income which is chargeable to income tax under, or is exempt under, PENSION INCOME (55). [*ITEPA 2003, s 554S(1)*].

Employee pension contributions

This exclusion and the next four exclusions are to be applied, insofar as they are applicable, in the order in which they are listed.

The charge to tax does not apply by reason of a relevant step within **26.7**(a) or (b) above (earmarking etc.) if the sum of money or asset which is the subject of the step arises or derives (directly or indirectly) from an 'excluded pension contribution' paid by A (the person referred to in **26.2** or **26.3** above) on or after 6 April 2011. The charge also does not apply by reason of a relevant step within any of **26.7**(i)–(v) above, or within **26.7**(I) or (II), or **26.7**(A) or (B), if the sum of money or asset which is the subject of the step represents 'relevant benefits' and arises or derives (directly or indirectly) from an 'excluded pension contribution' paid by A.

An '*excluded pension contribution*' is a contribution:

- which is made to an arrangement by A by way of a payment of a sum of money;
- by virtue of which A acquires rights to receive 'relevant benefits' under the arrangement (and nothing else);
- which is neither a relievable pension contribution (i.e. a contribution within **57.12** PENSION PROVISION) nor a tax-relieved contribution (i.e. a contribution within **57.28**(a) (overseas pension schemes)); and

- which has nothing to do with any loan or with a sum of money or asset which has been the subject of a relevant step within **26.7**(iv) above.

'*Relevant benefits*' has the meaning given in **57.35** PENSION PROVISION except that the term does in this case include benefits charged to tax as PENSION INCOME (**56**).

If the sum of money or asset arises or derives only partly from the excluded pension contribution, the relevant step is treated for these purposes as two separate relevant steps, one which arises or derives as stated and one which does not. The sum or asset is apportioned between the two notional relevant steps on a just and reasonable basis.
[*ITEPA 2003, ss 554S(2), 554T*].

Pre-2006/07 contributions to employer-financed retirement benefit schemes

This exclusion applies if B (the person referred to in **26.2** or **26.3** above) paid a sum of money before 6 April 2006 to an employer-financed retirement benefits scheme (see **57.34** PENSION PROVISION) with a view to the provision of benefits under the scheme and A (the person referred to in **26.2** or **26.3**) has been taxed in respect of this sum. The charge to tax does not apply by reason of a relevant step if the subject of the step is a sum of money or asset which has arisen or derived (directly or indirectly) from the contribution made by B to the scheme. If the sum of money or asset has arisen or derived only partly from the contribution made to the scheme, the relevant step is treated for these purposes as two separate relevant steps, one which has arisen or derived as stated and one which has not. The sum or asset is apportioned between the two notional relevant steps on a just and reasonable basis. If B is a company which is a member of a group of companies, the exclusion applies equally in relation to contributions made by other group companies to the scheme. [*ITEPA 2003, s 554U*].

Purchases of annuities out of pension scheme rights

This exclusion applies if an annuity contract is purchased from an insurance company wholly out of pre-6 April 2011 rights which A (the person referred to in **26.2** or **26.3** above) has under a pension scheme. The charge to tax does not apply by reason of certain relevant steps taken by the purchaser or the insurance company in this connection. There is provision for treating a relevant step as two notional relevant steps where appropriate. [*ITEPA 2003, s 554V*].

Certain retirement benefits etc.

This exclusion applies if a relevant benefit (within **57.35** PENSION PROVISION) is provided under a 'relevant scheme' by way of a payment of a lump sum wholly out of pre-6 April 2011 rights which A (the person referred to in **26.2** or **26.3** above) has under the scheme. If the payment of the lump sum is a relevant step within any of **26.7**(i)–(v) above, or **26.7**(I) or (II), the charge to tax does not apply by reason of that step. There is provision for treating the relevant step as two notional relevant steps if the rights out of which the lump sum is paid are only partly pre-6 April 2011 rights; the lump sum is apportioned between the two notional relevant steps on a just and reasonable basis. A '*relevant scheme*' means an employer-financed retirement benefits scheme (within **57.34** PENSION PROVISION) or a superannuation fund to which *ICTA 1988, s 615(3)* applies (see **57.40** PENSION PROVISION). [*ITEPA 2003, s 554W*].

Transfers between certain overseas pension schemes

This exclusion ensures that, in certain specified circumstances, if tax relief has been given in relation to an overseas pension scheme, the charge to tax does not apply to a transfer from that scheme to another overseas pension scheme. The exclusion is concerned only with rights under schemes in relation to which claims were accepted under *ITEPA 2003, s 390*. *Section 390* provided an exception, for non-UK domiciled employees with foreign employers, from the charge then imposed by *ITEPA 2003, s 386* on payments to non-approved retirement benefits schemes. *Sections 386* and *390* were repealed by *FA 2004* for 2006/07 onwards. [*ITEPA 2003, s 554X*].

Other relevant steps in connection with UK tax-relieved pension schemes

An exclusion applies if the subject of the relevant step is a sum of money or asset which represents a UK tax-relieved fund or transfer fund under a non-UK pension scheme within **57.28**(a)–(c) PENSION PROVISION, or which has arisen or derived from any such sum or assets. This exclusion effectively mirror the exclusion under *ITEPA 2003, s 554E* above for relevant steps taken by registered pension schemes.

An exclusion also applies if the subject of the relevant step is a sum of money or asset which has arisen or derived from a payment made by a registered pension scheme where the payment was subject to the unauthorised payments charge (see **57.26**(d) PENSION PROVISION).

In both cases there is provision for treating the relevant step as two notional relevant steps if the condition is only partly met; the sum of money or asset is apportioned between the two notional relevant steps on a just and reasonable basis.

[*SI 2011 No 2696*].

Payments in respect of a tax liability

The charge to tax does not apply by reason of a relevant step taken on or after 6 April 2017 consisting of the payment of a sum of money if that payment is made to HMRC in respect of a 'relevant liability' for inheritance tax or corporation tax. (For relevant steps taken between 6 April and 20 July 2017 inclusive, this applied also to a relevant liability for income tax or NICs.) This does not apply to a provisional payment of tax (as in **26.6** above). A liability is a '*relevant liability*' if, whether under the terms of an agreement for its discharge or by way of a decision on an application to HMRC for this purpose, an HMRC officer agrees that the liability is to be treated as arising in respect of the relevant arrangement (as in **26.2** or **26.3** above) in question. The said application must be made in such form and manner, and contain such information, as may be specified by the Commissioners for HMRC; an officer must notify the applicant of HMRC's decision on the application.

Where the relevant step consists of the payment of a sum of money to someone else so that the recipient can make a payment to HMRC in respect of a relevant liability for one of those taxes, this exclusion still applies provided the recipient makes that payment within 60 days in an amount equal to the amount paid to him.

[*ITEPA 2003, s 554XA; FA 2017, Sch 6 paras 9, 13; F(No 2)A 2017, s 34(1)(2)*].

Earmarking for employee share schemes

[26.11] These exclusions apply only if B (the person referred to in **26.2** or **26.3** above) is a company, and are concerned with:

- steps within **26.7**(a) or (b) above (earmarking etc.) taken in relation to awards of certain shares or securities or awards of sums of money determined by reference to the market value of certain shares or securities (see *ITEPA 2003, ss 554J, 554K*); and
- steps within **26.7**(a) or (b) taken in relation to grants of rights to acquire certain shares or securities or to receive sums of money determined by reference to the market value of certain shares or securities (see *ITEPA 2003, ss 554L, 554M*).

Exclusion 1

The conditions for this exclusion to apply are that:

(a) there is an arrangement ('*B's employee share scheme*') under which, in respect of his employment with B, an award may be made to A (the person referred to in **26.2** or **26.3** above) of '*relevant shares*' (meaning, broadly, shares in, or securities of, B or, where applicable, any other company in the same group as B) or a sum of money the amount of which is to be determined by reference to the market value of any relevant shares at the time the sum is to be paid;
(b) the main purpose of the award would not be the provision of relevant benefits (which has the meaning given in **57.35** PENSION PROVISION except that the term does in this case include benefits charged to tax as PENSION INCOME (**56**));
(c) the award would be on terms the main purpose of which is to defer the receipt of the shares by A, or the payment of the sum of money to A, to a specified date (the '*vesting date*'), while providing that the award is revoked if specified conditions are not met on or before the vesting date;
(d) the vesting date would not be more than ten years after the date ('*award date*') on which the award is made; and
(e) as at the award date, there would be a reasonable chance that the award will be revoked because of conditions not being met by the vesting date.

The charge to tax under these provisions does not apply by reason of a relevant step within **26.7**(a) or (b) above (earmarking etc.) taken by a person (P) if:

(i) the subject of the relevant step is relevant shares ('*earmarked shares*') which are earmarked, or otherwise start being held, solely with a view to the meeting of the award referred to in (a) above; and

(ii) the number of earmarked shares does not exceed the maximum number which might reasonably be expected to be needed for meeting the award.

If the award is not made on or before the date falling three months after the date of the relevant step, and any of the earmarked shares then continue to be held by or on behalf of P solely on the basis mentioned in (i) above, a further (non-excluded) relevant step within **26.7**(a) or (b) above is deemed to have been taken at the end of that later date.

If, at any time, any of the earmarked shares cease to be held by or on behalf of P solely on the basis mentioned in (i) above but continue to be held by or on behalf of P on the basis mentioned in **26.7**(a) or (b) above, a further (non-excluded) relevant step within **26.7**(a) or (b) is deemed to have been taken at that time.

If the award in (i) above is duly made, a further (non-excluded) relevant step within **26.7**(a) or (b) above is deemed to have been taken at the end of the vesting date unless:

- A has received the awarded shares or sum of money and the receipt has given rise to employment income, or
- the award has been revoked in accordance with its terms,

and, in either case, no shares continue to be held by any person in relation to the award.

Exclusion 2

The conditions for this exclusion to apply are that:

(A) there is an arrangement identical to that in (a) above;
(B) the main purpose of the award would not be the provision of relevant benefits (as in (b) above);
(C) the relevant shares would be shares in, or securities of, a trading company or a company which controls a trading company;
(D) the award would be on terms the main purpose of which is to ensure that the shares are received by A, or the sum of money is paid to him, only if a specified 'exit event', or an exit event within a specified description, occurs; and
(E) at the time the award is made, there would be a reasonable chance that the specified exit event, or an exit event within the specified description, will occur.

The charge to tax under these provisions does not apply by reason of a relevant step within **26.7**(a) or (b) above (earmarking etc.) taken by a person (P) if:

(I) the subject of the relevant step is relevant shares ('*earmarked shares*') which are earmarked, or otherwise start being held, solely with a view to the meeting of the award within (A) above; and
(II) the number of earmarked shares does not exceed the maximum number which might reasonably be expected to be needed for meeting the award.

An '*exit event*' (as in (D) above) occurs if:

- shares in the '*relevant company*' (i.e. the company whose shares or securities are the subject of the award) are admitted to trading on a stock exchange; or
- all the shares in the relevant company, or a substantial proportion of them, are disposed of to persons none of whom is connected with any of the persons making any disposal; or
- if the relevant company is a trading company, the company's trade, or a substantial part of it, is transferred to a person who is not a 'relevant connected person'; or
- the relevant company's assets, or a substantial proportion of them, are disposed of to a person who is not a relevant connected person; or
- the winding-up of the relevant company begins; or
- a person who controls the relevant company ceases to control it, so long as no person connected with him then starts to control it.

A '*relevant connected person*' is a person who is connected with the relevant company or who is a shareholder (or is connected with a shareholder) in the relevant company. **19** CONNECTED PERSONS applies to determine whether persons are connected.

Under Exclusion 1 above, there are three sets of circumstances under which further (non-excluded) relevant steps are deemed to have been taken. The first two of these apply equally to Exclusion 2. In addition, if the award in (I) above is duly made and the specified exit event, or an exit event within the specified description, occurs, a further (non-excluded) relevant step within **26.7**(a) or (b) above is deemed to have been taken at the end of the 'exit period' unless:

- A has received the awarded shares or sum of money before the end of the exit period and the receipt has given rise to employment income; and
- no shares continue to be held by any person in relation to the award.

The '*exit period*' is the period of six months starting with the date on which the exit event occurs.

Exclusion 3

This operates in a similar manner to Exclusion 1 above except that it is to do with an arrangement under which, in respect of his employment with B, a right may be granted to A to acquire relevant shares or to receive a sum of money the amount of which is to be determined by reference to the market value of any relevant shares at the time the sum is to be paid. In certain circumstances, Rule 4 in **26.4** above applies to reduce the value of a further (non-excluded) relevant step.

Exclusion 4

This operates in a similar manner to Exclusion 2 above except that it is to do with an arrangement under which, in respect of his employment with B, a right may be granted to A to acquire relevant shares or to receive a sum of money the amount of which is to be determined by reference to the market value of any relevant shares at the time the sum is to be paid. In certain circumstances,

Rule 4 in **26.4** above applies to reduce the value of a further (non-excluded) relevant step. If the exit event is that shares in the relevant company are admitted to trading on a stock exchange, the '*exit period*' is extended from six months to five years.

[*ITEPA 2003, ss 554I–554M*].

Undertakings by employers etc. in relation to retirement benefits etc.

[26.12] A charge to tax also arises under these provisions where an employer gives an undertaking to pay a contribution to an unregistered pension scheme (e.g. an employer-financed retirement benefits scheme as in **57.34** PENSION PROVISION) and subsequently assures that the contribution will be paid by either earmarking property for the purpose or otherwise providing security.

The provisions potentially apply where:

- there is an undertaking (the '*relevant undertaking*'), whether or not conditional or legally enforceable, that a contribution be paid to an arrangement which is not a registered pension scheme;
- in connection with that arrangement, relevant benefits (see **57.35** PENSION PROVISION) are to be provided out of the contribution by a third party (see **26.2** or **26.3** above);
- the provision of the relevant benefits would be a relevant step; and
- the contribution is neither tax-relieved nor tax-exempt as in **57.28**(a) and (b) PENSION PROVISION (certain overseas pension schemes).

Provided the above conditions are met, if B (the person in **26.2** or **26.3** above) takes either Step 1 or Step 2 described below, the rules at **26.2–26.10** have effect with specified modifications in relation to the step:

- as if B were a third party as in **26.2**(d); and
- as if the step were a relevant step within **26.7** (if this would not otherwise be the case).

As a result, the value of the step counts as employment income. The modifications to **26.2–26.10** above are set out in *ITEPA 2003, s 554Z17(2)–(5)* and their main effect is to disapply certain rules which it is felt are not appropriate in these circumstances. The references to B in these particular provisions do not include B acting as a trustee but do include members of the same group of companies as B (if B is a company) and any wholly-owned subsidiary of B if B is a limited liability partnership.

Step 1 — earmarking etc.

B takes Step 1 if:

(a) a sum of money or asset held by or on behalf of B is earmarked (however informally) by B with a view to the 'relevant undertaking' (see above) being performed at a later time (wholly or partly) out of that sum of money or asset (or any sum or asset derived from it); or

(b) a sum of money or asset otherwise starts being held by or on behalf of B, specifically with a view, so far as B is concerned, to the relevant undertaking being performed at a later time (wholly or partly) out of that sum of money or asset (or any sum or asset derived from it).

For the purposes of (b) above, it does not matter whether or not the sum of money or asset in question has previously been held by or on behalf of B on a different basis.

Step 2 — provision of security

B takes Step 2 if he provides security (however informally) for the performance of the 'relevant undertaking' (see above). If, when the step is taken, the security covers other undertakings as well as the relevant undertaking, the sums of money and/or assets which are the subject of the security should be apportioned between undertakings on a just and reasonable basis.

The value of the relevant step

If **26.2–26.10** above apply as a result of B taking Step 1 above, the value of the relevant step is determined under **26.4**. If **26.2–26.10** apply as a result of B taking Step 2, the value of the relevant step is instead the lower of:

(i) the amount to be paid as a contribution under the relevant undertaking determined, as at the time the step is taken, on a just and reasonable basis assuming that any condition to be met before any payment is made will be met; and
(ii) the value of the security.

In (ii) above, the value of the security comprises the total amount of any sums of money and the total market value of any assets which are the subject of the security. This is, however, subject to a just and reasonable reduction to take account of any term of the security which limits the total amount which may be made available under it for the performance of the relevant undertaking to an amount which is lower than the amount otherwise determined.

If at the end of an anniversary of the taking of Step 2 B continues to provide the security for the performance of the relevant undertaking, his so doing constitutes the taking of a new Step 2 at that time. If the total amount of sums of money which are the subject of the security varies from time to time, a special rule applies in determining the sums of money which are the subject of the security for the purposes of the new Step 2. Instead of judging the matter at the time the step is taken, the matter is judged at the time during the preceding year at which the total amount of the sums of money is at its highest. For the purpose of valuing the relevant step treated as taken by virtue of the new Step 2, the market value of any asset may be determined as at any time during the preceding year, provided the asset was the subject of the security, or one of the assets which was the subject of the security, at that time.

Relief if Step 1 or 2 not followed by contribution etc.

In **26.6** above, it is explained that *ITEPA 2003, s 554Z14* provides for relief to be given where earmarking of money or assets as in **26.7**(a) or (b) above is not followed by a further relevant step. This also applies, but with the following modifications, where the charge to tax has arisen by virtue of the taking of Step 1 or Step 2 above. there occurs a subsequent event which is neither the payment of the relevant contribution (or any part of it) nor the provision of any relevant benefit. Instead of the condition at **26.6**(c), the condition is that by reason of the subsequent event the relevant contribution (or any part of it) will not be paid or a relevant benefit will not be provided. For these purposes, the relevant contribution is the contribution to be paid under the relevant undertaking, and relevant benefit means a relevant benefit to be provided out of the relevant contribution.

[*ITEPA 2003, ss 554Z16–554Z21*].

Disguised remuneration — anti-forestalling provisions

[26.13] Anti-forestalling provisions apply to the payment of sums, and the provision of readily convertible assets for the purposes of securing the payment of sums (including loans), where the sum is paid, or the asset is provided before 6 April 2011 and, if paid or provided on or after 6 April 2011, it would have been caught by **26.2–26.12** above. These are described in more detail below.

Early step involving payment of money

If:

- a step (the '*early step*') is taken on or after 9 December 2010 but before 6 April 2011;
- the step is a payment of a sum of money;
- the step would have been a relevant step within **26.7**(i) above had it been taken on or after 6 April 2011; and
- the early step is not chargeable to income tax by virtue of *FA 2004, Sch 34* (overseas pension schemes — see **57.28** PENSION PROVISION),

then **26.2–26.12** above apply by reason of the early step. Generally this chapter has effect by reference to the actual date on which the early step was taken, but for the purposes listed below the step is treated as having been taken on **6 April 2012**:

(a) for determining the tax year for which the value of the relevant step counts as employment income (see **26.4** above);
(b) for determining the time at which a payment of PAYE income is treated as being made (see **53.5** PAY AS YOU EARN); and
(c) for determining the time at which a qualifying benefit is provided as in **75.65** TRADING INCOME.

The amount which would otherwise count as employment income of A is to be reduced by an amount to reflect so much (if any) of the sum paid as has been repaid to P (the person mentioned in **26.7** above) before 6 April 2012 by the person to whom the payment was made. The amount of any such reduction is to be determined on a just and reasonable basis. In relation to the amount repaid, this chapter is treated as never having applied by reason of the early step.

Rule 2 in **26.4** above (overlap with earlier relevant step) does not apply in relation to the early step; and insofar as that Rule applies in relation to any other relevant step (whenever taken), the early step is to be ignored. *ITEPA 2003, s 554Z12* (referred to in **26.6** above) does not apply in relation to the early step.

[*FA 2011, Sch 2 para 53*].

Early step involving readily convertible asset

If:

- a step (the '*early step*') is taken on or after 9 December 2010 but before 6 April 2011;
- the step does not involve a sum of money;
- the step would have been a relevant step within **26.7**(iv) above had it been taken on or after 6 April 2011 (but for this purpose **26.7**(iv) is to be read as if the words in parentheses were omitted);
- the asset which is the subject of the step is a readily convertible asset (within *ITEPA 2003, s 702(1)(a)–(c)*, broadly an asset easily turned into money) which P makes available to secure the payment of a sum of money; and
- the early step is not chargeable to income tax by virtue of *FA 2004, Sch 34* (overseas pension schemes — see **57.28** PENSION PROVISION),

then **26.2–26.12** above apply by reason of the early step. Generally this chapter has effect by reference to the actual date on which the early step was taken, but for the purposes listed in (a) to (c) above the step is treated as having been taken on **6 April 2012**.

The amount which would otherwise count as employment income of A is to be reduced to nil if the readily convertible asset is returned to P (the person mentioned in **26.7** above) before 6 April 2012 and is not being used at that date to secure the payment of the sum of money (or any part of it). This chapter is then treated as never having applied by reason of the early step.

Rule 2 in **26.4** above (overlap with earlier relevant step) does not apply in relation to the early step; and insofar as that Rule applies in relation to any other relevant step (whenever taken), the early step is to be ignored. Rule 5 (cases where consideration given for relevant step) is modified in relation to the early step. *ITEPA 2003, s 554Z12* (referred to in **26.6** above) does not apply in relation to the early step.

[*FA 2011, Sch 2 para 54*].

Exclusions modified or extended

In both of the above cases, the exclusions in *ITEPA 2003, ss 554G, 554N* and *554O* (see **26.10** above) are modified in relation to the early step. The exclusions in *ITEPA 2003, ss 554Q* and *554R* (see **26.10** above) are extended to cover income arising from sums of money and assets earmarked before 6 April 2011. [*FA 2011, Sch 2 paras 55–57*].

Undertakings in relation to retirement benefits etc.

If in **26.12** above:

- B takes Step 2 by providing security for the performance of an undertaking, but does so before 6 April 2011,
- on or after 6 April 2011 at a time when B is still providing the security, there is a change in the terms of the undertaking which does not amount to the giving of a new undertaking, and
- as a result of the change, the amount to be paid as a contribution (the '*early contribution*') under the undertaking increases,

then **26.12** has effect:

- as if the change were a new undertaking to pay a contribution to cover the increase in the amount of the early contribution (determined on a just and reasonable basis); and
- as if B, in continuing to provide the security, provides security for the performance of the new undertaking at the time of the change.

[*FA 2011, Sch 2 para 58*].

Pre-6 April 2011 steps where tax settled by agreement etc.

Relief is allowed in cases where sums of money or assets earmarked before 6 April 2011 gave rise to taxable earnings on which the tax has been settled. The conditions are that:

(i) a relevant step (the '*chargeable step*') is taken and gives rise to a charge to tax within this chapter;

(ii) the chargeable step is within:
  - any of **26.7**(i)–(v) above (payment of sum, transfer of asset etc.); or
  - **26.7**(I) or (II) (payment of sum, transfer of asset etc.); or
  - **26.7**(A) or (B) (making an asset available); or
  - **26.8** (making of a loan or quasi-loan which is outstanding on 5 April 2019 — the loan charge);

(iii) in a tax year before 2011/12 a step was taken under the heading 'earmarking etc. of money and assets' in **26.7**;

(iv) an agreement was made between HMRC and either A or B in **26.2** (or both of them) to the effect that (or A's tax liability was otherwise decided on the basis that) the pre-6 April 2011 step was to be treated as giving rise to taxable earnings for the tax year in which the step was taken;

(v) any tax payable as a consequence was paid before the chargeable step was taken; and

(vi) the value of the chargeable step is representative of those taxable earnings or any return on those earnings since the taking of the pre-6 April 2011 step.

Where the conditions are met, the value of the chargeable step (as already reduced where appropriate under Rules 1 to 5 in **26.4** above) is to be reduced by an amount reflecting the extent to which the value of the chargeable step is representative of the taxable earnings or (as the case may be) the return on those earnings (such extent to be determined on a just and reasonable basis). If the reduction is to reflect the extent to which the value of the chargeable step is representative of the *return* on the taxable earnings, either the agreement in

(iv) above had to be made before 1 April 2017 and the tax in (v) above had to be paid in accordance with that agreement or, where applicable, the decision in (iv) above had to be made before 1 April 2017 and the tax had to be paid before that date. The references here to the return on earnings do not include any return over and above what might have been expected if all relevant connected persons were acting at arm's length of each other.

In relation to chargeable steps taken on or after 16 March 2016, the condition in (v) above (that tax be paid) is not met by making a payment on account, a payment treated as a payment on account under the accelerated payments rules (see **4.51** ANTI-AVOIDANCE) or a payment pending the determination of an appeal.

[*FA 2011, Sch 2 para 59; FA 2016, s 18(5)–(7)(10); FA 2017, Sch 6 paras 12, 16; F(No 2)A 2017, Sch 11 para 47*].

27

Double Tax Relief

Cross-references. See generally **50** NON-RESIDENTS. See also HMRC's Digest of Double Taxation Treaties at www.gov.uk/government/publications/double-taxation-treaties-territory-residents-with-uk-income.

Simon's Taxes. See **E6.4.**

Introduction to double tax relief

[27.1] Where the same income is liable to be taxed in both the UK and another country, relief may be available:

(a) under the specific terms of a double tax agreement between the UK and that other country — see **27.2** below [*TIOPA 2010, s 2*];
(b) under special arrangements with Ireland — see **27.4** below; or
(c) under the unilateral double tax relief provisions contained in UK tax legislation — see **27.6** below. [*TIOPA 2010, s 8*].

See **35.12–35.16** HMRC — ADMINISTRATION as regards arrangements for exchange of information between the UK and other countries.

Double tax agreements

[27.2] A list is given below of the bilateral double tax agreements (also known as double tax treaties or double tax conventions) made by the UK. For texts of agreements, see **Simon's Taxes F1.6.** Representations on points interested parties would like to see addressed in negotiating particular treaties, or on other matters relating to the treaty negotiation programme or the treaty network, should be addressed to HMRC, CT, International and Stamps, Tax Treaty Team, Room 3C/03, 100 Parliament Street, London, SW1A 2BQ (email taxtreaty.team@hmrc.gov.uk).

Under these agreements certain classes of income derived from those countries by UK residents are given complete exemption from income taxes in the country from which they arise and reciprocal exemption from UK income tax is given to similar income derived from the UK by residents of those countries. Exemption may also be granted in respect of taxes on capital gains.

[*TIOPA 2010, ss 2–7; FA 2016, Sch 1 paras 68(2), 73; FA 2018, s 32*].

Other classes of income derived from those countries are not exempted, or only partially exempted, by the double tax agreements and in these cases relief from UK income tax is generally given in the agreement in the form of a credit, calculated by reference to the foreign tax suffered, which is set against and reduces the UK tax chargeable on the doubly taxed income. The relief is given as a tax reduction at Step 6 of the calculation of income tax liability (see **1.10, 1.12** ALLOWANCES AND TAX RATES). [*TIOPA 2010, s 18*]. See the Example at **27.7** below.

Relief by way of credit is not available against any UK tax for any tax year unless the person on whose income the UK tax is chargeable is resident in the UK for that year. [*TIOPA 2010, s 26(1)*].

Where relief by credit is available by double tax agreement, no deduction for foreign tax is generally allowed in taxing foreign income. [*TIOPA 2010, s 31(2)*]. However, if a taxpayer chooses not to take relief by credit (whether by double tax agreement or unilaterally — see **27.6** below), any tax paid on the foreign income in the place where it arises is *deductible* from the income for the purposes of charging it to UK tax — see **27.10**(a)(iii) below.

See the **general anti-avoidance rule** at **27.5** below.

HMRC International Manual INTM153000 *et seq.* provides a brief description of the contents of each Article normally found in a double tax agreement to which the UK is party.

Mutual agreement procedures

Double tax agreements normally contain a mutual agreement procedure (MAP) enabling a taxpayer who considers that the action of a tax authority has resulted, or will result, in taxation not in accordance with the agreement to present his case to the competent authority in his state of residence. For the presentation of such cases, and for giving effect to solutions and agreements reached under such procedures, see *TIOPA 2010, ss 124, 125*. HMRC Statement of Practice 1 (2018) considers the use of MAP under UK double tax agreements and/or the EU Arbitration Convention and describes the UK's approach to the use of arbitration as part of the MAP process.

Resolution of double taxation disputes

The European Council adopted Council Directive (EU) 2017/1852 on 10 October 2017 regarding tax dispute resolution mechanisms in the EU. The Directive seeks to establish an effective regime for the resolution of tax disputes, and to minimise the risk of double taxation for businesses operating across borders. This followed a review concluding that the mechanisms provided for in bilateral tax treaties and in the EU Arbitration Convention might not result in double taxation disputes being resolved in a timely manner. The Directive operates as an additional mechanism to the EU Arbitration Convention (see **4.28** ANTI-AVOIDANCE), but a claim brought under the Directive has the effect of terminating proceedings brought under the Convention. The Directive has been implemented in the UK by regulations taking effect on 14 February 2020 in relation to any income earned, or capital gained, in respect of a tax period commencing on or after 1st January 2018. [*TIOPA 2010, ss 128A–128C; FA 2019, s 83; SI 2020 No 51*].

BEPS and MLI

SI 2018 No 630 gives effect in the UK to the Multilateral Convention to Implement Tax Treaty Related Measures to Prevent Base Erosion and Profit Shifting (BEPS). The Convention (also known as the Multilateral Instrument or MLI) entered into force in the UK on 1 October 2018 but the dates from which UK tax treaties are modified by the MLI depend on each individual treaty. BEPS refers to tax planning strategies that exploit gaps and mismatches in tax rules to artificially shift profits to low or no-tax locations where there is little or no economic activity, resulting in little or no corporate tax being paid. The Convention modifies the application of double tax agreements already given effect by *TIOPA 2010, s 2*, but only where both the UK Government and the other party to the agreement give notice that they wish them to be. Agreements thus modified will be known as 'Covered Tax Agreements'. For more details see the explanatory memorandum to *SI 2018 No 630* at www.legislation.gov.uk/uksi/2018/630/memorandum/contents.

See **27.3** below for further points on double tax relief by agreement.

List of bilateral agreements

The following bilateral agreements (*SI* numbers in round brackets) supersede the provisions of *TIOPA 2010, ss 8–17* (unilateral relief) to the extent, and as from the operative dates, specified therein. Where more than one agreement is listed for a particular country or territory, readers should generally refer to the most recent, which may contain provision to the effect that the agreement wholly supersedes the preceding agreement(s) listed or does so to a specified extent.

Albania (2013/3145), **Algeria** (2015/1888 (applies from 6 April 2017 (UK), but from 1 January 2017 as regards taxes withheld at source, and 1 January 2017 (Algeria))), **Antigua and Barbuda** (1947/2865; 1968/1096), **Argentina** (1997/1777), **Armenia** (2011/2722), **Australia** (1968/305; 1980/707; 2003/3199 (modified by the MLI with effect from 6 April 2020 (UK) and 1 July 2019 (Australia) for taxable periods beginning on or after that date, but from 1 January 2019 in both territories as regards taxes withheld at source on amounts paid or credited to non-residents)), **Austria** (1970/1947; 1979/117; 1994/768; 2010/2688; 2019/255 (applies from 6 April 2019 (UK) and 1 January 2020 (Austria))), **Azerbaijan** (1995/762),

Bahrain (2012/3075), **Bangladesh** (1980/708), **Barbados** (1970/952; 1973/2096; 2012/3076), **Belarus** (2018/778 (applies from 6 April 2019 (UK) and 1 January 2019 (Belarus) but from 1 October 2018 in both territories as regards taxes withheld at source)), **Belgium** (1987/2053 (modified by the MLI with effect from 6 April 2020 (UK) and 1 April 2020 (Belgium) for taxable periods beginning on or after that date, but from 1 January 2020 in both territories as regards taxes withheld at source on amounts paid or credited to non-residents); 2010/2979; 2014/1875 (2014 protocol not yet in force)), **Belize** (1947/2866; 1968/573; 1973/2097), **Bolivia** (1995/2707), **Bosnia-Herzegovina** (see note below under Yugoslavia), **Botswana** (1978/183; 2006/1925), **Brazil** (2011/2723 (aircraft crew only) (applies from 6 April 2018 (UK) and 1 January 2018 (Brazil))), **British Honduras** (see Belize), **Brunei Darussalam** (1950/1977; 1968/306; 1973/2098; 2013/3146), **Bulgaria** (1987/2054; 2015/1890),

Canada (1980/709 (modified by the MLI with effect from 6 April 2021 (UK) and 1 June 2020 (Canada) for taxable periods beginning on or after that date, but from 1 January 2020 in both territories as regards taxes withheld at source on amounts paid or credited to non-residents); 1980/780; 1980/1528; 1985/1996; 1987/2071; 1996/1782; 2000/3330; 2003/2619; 2014/3274); 2015/2011 (2015 exchange of notes applies from 21 December 2016 in both territories)), **Cayman Islands** (2010/2973), **Chile** (2003/3200), **China** (1981/1119; 1984/1826 (and see note below); 1996/3164; 2011/2724; 2013/3142), **Colombia** (2018/377 (applies from 6 April 2020 (UK), but from 1 January 2020 as regards taxes withheld at source, and 1 January 2020 (Colombia))), **Croatia** (2015/1889) and see note below under Yugoslavia), **Cyprus** (1975/425; 1980/1529; 2018/839 (applies from 6 April 2019 (UK), but from 1 January 2019 as regards taxes withheld at source, and 1 January 2019 (Cyprus)); 2019/1113 (protocol applies from 6 April 2019 (UK), but from 1 January 2019 as regards taxes withheld at source, and 1 January 2019 (Cyprus))), **Czech Republic** (see note below),

Denmark (1980/1960; 1991/2877; 1996/3165),

Egypt (1980/1091), **Estonia** (1994/3207), **Ethiopia** (2011/2725),

Falkland Islands (1997/2985), **Faroes** (2007/3469), **Fiji** (1976/1342), **Finland** (1970/153 (modified by the MLI with effect from 6 April 2020 (UK) and 1 January 2020 (Finland) for taxable periods beginning on or after that date, but from 1 January 2020 in both territories as regards taxes withheld at source on amounts paid or credited to non-residents); 1980/710; 1985/1997; 1991/2878; 1996/3166), **France** (1968/1869; 1973/1328; 1987/466; 1987/2055; 2009/226 (modified by the MLI with effect from 6 April 2020 (UK) and 1 July 2019 (France) for taxable periods beginning on or after that date, but from 1 January 2019 in both territories as regards taxes withheld at source on amounts paid or credited to non-residents)),

Gambia (1980/1963), **Georgia** (2004/3325 (modified by the MLI with effect from 6 April 2020 (UK) and 1 January 2020 (Georgia) for taxable periods beginning on or after that date, but from 1 January 2020 in both territories as regards taxes withheld at source on amounts paid or credited to non-residents); 2010/2972), **Germany** (1967/25; 1971/874; 2010/2975); 2014/1874), **Ghana** (1993/1800), **Gibraltar** (2020/275 (applies from 6 April 2020 (UK) and 1 July 2020 (Gibraltar) but from 1 May 2020 in both territories as regards taxes withheld at source)), **Greece** (1954/142), **Grenada**

(1949/361; 1968/1867), **Guernsey** (1952/1215; 1994/3209; 2009/3011; 2015/2008 (applies from 6 April 2016 (UK) and 1 January 2017 (Guernsey)); 2016/750; 2018/1345 (applies from 6 April 2019 (UK) and 1 January 2020 (Guernsey) but from 1 March 2019 in both territories as regards taxes withheld at source)), **Guyana** (1992/3207),

Hong Kong (2010/2974), **Hungary** (1978/1056; 2011/2726),

Iceland (1991/2879; 2014/1879), **India** (1981/1120; 1993/1801 (modified by the MLI with effect from 6 April 2020 (UK) and 1 April 2020 (India) for taxable periods beginning on or after that date, but from 1 January 2020 (UK) and 1 April 2020 (India) as regards taxes withheld at source on amounts paid or credited to non-residents); 2013/3147), **Indonesia** (1994/769), **Ireland** (see **27.4** below), **Isle of Man** (1955/1205; 1991/2880; 1994/3208; 2009/228; 2013/3148; 2016/749; 2018/1347 (applies from 6 April 2019 in both territories but from 1 February 2019 as regards taxes withheld at source)), **Israel** (1963/616; 1971/391; 2019/1111 (protocol applies from 6 April 2020 (UK), but from 1 January 2020 as regards taxes withheld at source, and 1 January 2020 (Israel))), **Italy** (1990/2590), **Ivory Coast** (1987/169),

Jamaica (1973/1329), **Japan** (1970/1948; 1980/1530; 2006/1924 (modified by the MLI with effect from 6 April 2020 (UK) and 1 July 2019 (Japan) for taxable periods beginning on or after that date, but from 1 January 2019 in both territories as regards taxes withheld at source on amounts paid or credited to non-residents); 2014/1881), **Jersey** (1952/1216; 1994/3210; 2009/3012; 2015/2009 (applies from 6 April 2016 (UK) and 1 January 2017 (Jersey)); 2016/752; 2018/1348 (applies from 6 April 2019 (UK) and 1 January 2019 (Jersey) but from 1 February 2019 in both territories as regards taxes withheld at source)), **Jordan** (2001/3924),

Kazakhstan (1994/3211; 1998/2567), **Kenya** (1977/1299), **Kiribati and Tuvalu** (1950/750; 1968/309; 1974/1271), **Korea (South)** (1996/3168), **Kosovo** (2015/2007 and see note below under Yugoslavia), **Kuwait** (1999/2036), **Kyrgyzstan** (2018/525 (not yet in force)),

Latvia (1996/3167), **Lesotho** (1997/2986; 2018/376 (applies from 6 April 2019 (UK) and 1 January 2019 (Lesotho), but from 1 November 2018 in both territories as regards taxes withheld at source)), **Libya** (2010/243), **Liechtenstein** (2012/3077), **Lithuania** (2001/3925 (modified by the MLI with effect from 6 April 2020 (UK) and 1 July 2019 (Lithuania) for taxable periods beginning on or after that date, but from 1 January 2019 in both territories as regards taxes withheld at source on amounts paid or credited to non-residents), 2002/2847), **Luxembourg** (1968/1100 (modified by the MLI with effect from 6 April 2020 (UK) and 1 February 2020 (Luxembourg) for taxable periods beginning on or after that date, but from 1 January 2020 in both territories as regards taxes withheld at source on amounts paid or credited to non-residents); 1980/567; 1984/364; 2010/237),

Malawi (1956/619; 1964/1401; 1968/1101; 1979/302), **Malaysia** (1973/1330; 1987/2056; 1997/2987; 2010/2971, **Malta** (1995/763 (modified by the MLI with effect from 6 April 2020 (UK) and 1 January 2020 (Malta) for taxable periods beginning on or after that date, but from 1 January 2020 in both territories as regards taxes withheld at source on amounts paid or credited to non-residents)), **Mauritius** (1981/1121; 1987/467; 2003/2620; 2011/2442; 2018/840 (2018 protocol applies from 28 February 2018 in both territories)), **Mexico** (1994/3212; 2010/2686), **Moldova** (2008/1795), **Mongolia** (1996/2598), **Montenegro** (see note below under Yugoslavia), **Montserrat** (1947/2869; 1968/576; 2011/1083), **Morocco** (1991/2881), **Myanmar** (1952/751),

Namibia (1962/2352; 1967/1490), **Netherlands** (1967/1063; 1980/1961; 1983/1902; 1990/2152; 2000/3330; 2009/227 (modified by the MLI with effect from 6 April 2020 (UK) and 1 January 2020 (Netherlands) for taxable periods beginning on or after that date, but from 1 January 2020 in both territories as regards taxes withheld at source on amounts paid or credited to non-residents); 2013/3143), **New Zealand** (1984/365; 2004/1274; 2008/1793 (modified by the MLI with effect from 6 April 2019 (UK) and 1 April 2019 (New Zealand) for taxable periods beginning on or after that date, but from 1 January 2019 in both territories as regards taxes withheld at source)), **Nigeria** (1987/2057), **North Macedonia** (2007/2127), **Norway** (1985/1998; 2000/3247; 2013/3144),

Oman (1998/2568; 2010/2687),

Pakistan (1987/2058), **Panama** (2013/3149), **Papua New Guinea** (1991/2882), **Philippines** (1978/184), **Poland** (1978/282; 2006/3323 (modified by the MLI with effect from 6 April 2019 (UK) and 1 April 2019 (Poland) for taxable periods beginning on or after that date, but from 1 January 2019 in both territories as regards taxes withheld at source)), **Portugal** (1969/599),

Qatar (2010/241); 2011/1684,

Romania (1977/57), **Russia** (1994/3213),

St. Christopher (St. Kitts) and Nevis (1947/2872), **Saudi Arabia** (2008/1770), **Senegal** (2015/1892 (applies from 6 April 2016 (UK) and 1 January 2017 (Senegal) but from 30 March 2016 in both territories as regards exchange of information)), **Serbia** (see note below under Yugoslavia), **Sierra Leone** (1947/2873; 1968/1104), **Singapore** (1997/2988 (modified by the MLI with effect from 6 April 2020 (UK) and 1 October 2019 (Singapore) for taxable periods beginning on or after that date, but from 1 January 2020 in both territories as regards taxes withheld at source on amounts paid or credited to non-residents); 2010/2685; 2012/3078), **Slovak Republic** (see note below), **Slovenia** (2008/1796 (modified by the MLI with effect from 6 April 2019 (UK), but from 1 January 2019 as regards taxes withheld at source, and 1 April 2019 (Slovenia) for taxable periods beginning on or after that date)), **Solomon Islands** (1950/748; 1968/574; 1974/1270), **South Africa** (1969/864; 2002/3138; 2011/2441), **South West Africa** (see Namibia), **Spain** (1976/1919; 1995/765; 2013/3152), **Sri Lanka** (1980/713), **Sudan** (1977/1719), **Swaziland** (1969/380), **Sweden** (1961/619; 1984/366; 2000/3330; 2015/1891), **Switzerland** (1978/1408; 1982/714; 1994/3215; 2007/3465; 2010/2689; 2012/3079; 2018/627 (applies from 6 April 2020 (UK), but from 1 January 2020 as regards taxes withheld at source, and 1 January 2020 (Switzerland))) (see also **27.11** below),

Taiwan (2002/3137), **Tajikistan** (2014/3275), **Thailand** (1981/1546), **Trinidad and Tobago** (1983/1903), **Tunisia** (1984/133), **Turkey** (1988/932), **Turkmenistan** (2016/1217 (applies from 6 April 2017 (UK), but from 1 January 2017 as regards taxes withheld at source, and 1 January 2017 (Turkmenistan) but from 19 December 2016 in both territories as regards exchange of information)),

Uganda (1993/1802), **Ukraine** (1993/1803; 2018/779 (applies from 6 April 2020 (UK), but from 1 January 2020 as regards taxes withheld at source, and 1 January 2020 (Ukraine))), **United Arab Emirates** (2016/754 (applies from 1 January 2017 in both territories; modified by the MLI with effect from 6 April 2020 (UK) and 1 March 2020 (UAE) for taxable periods beginning on or after that date, but from 1 January 2020 in both territories as regards taxes withheld at source on amounts paid or credited to non-residents)), **Uruguay** (2016/753 (applies from 1 January 2017 in both territories)), **USA** (1980/568; 2002/2848), **USSR** (see note below), **Uzbekistan** (1994/770; 2018/628 (applies from 6 April 2019 (UK) and 1 January 2019 (Uzbekistan) but, in both territories, from 1 August 2018 as regards taxes withheld at source and 1 June 2018 as regards exchange of information etc.)),

Venezuela (1996/2599), **Vietnam** (1994/3216), **Virgin Islands** (2009/3013),

Yugoslavia (see note below),

Zambia (1972/1721; 1981/1816; 2014/1876), **Zimbabwe** (1982/1842).

Shipping & Air Transport only — Algeria (Air Transport only) (1984/362), Brazil (1968/572), Cameroon (Air Transport only) (1982/1841), China (Air Transport only) (1981/1119), Ethiopia (Air Transport only) (1977/1297), Hong Kong (Air Transport only) (1998/2566), Hong Kong (Shipping only) (2000/3248), Iran (Air Transport only) (1960/2419), Jordan (1979/300), Kuwait (Air Transport only) (1984/1825), Lebanon (1964/278), Saudi Arabia (Air Transport only) (1994/767), Zaire (1977/1298).

Exchange of Information only (see **35.12** HMRC — ADMINISTATION and see notes below) — **Anguilla** (2010/2677; 2014/1357 (not yet in force)), **Antigua and Barbuda** (2011/1075), **Aruba** (2011/2435), **Bahamas** (2010/2684), **Belize** (2011/1685), **Bermuda** (2018/518 (applies on and after 24 April 2018), superseding 2008/1789 from that date), **Brazil** (2015/1887 (not yet in force)), **Dominica** (2011/1686), **Gibraltar** (2010/2680; 2014/1356), **Grenada** (2011/1687), **Guernsey** (2009/3011; 2013/3154 (2013 protocol applies on and after 29 July 2014)), **Jersey** (2009/3012; 2013/3151 (2013 protocol applies on and after 28 July 2014)), **Liberia** (2011/2434), **Liechtenstein** (2010/2678), **Macao** (2015/801), **Marshall Islands** (2013/3153 (not yet in force)), **Monaco** (2015/804), **Netherlands Antilles** (2011/2433), **Saint Christopher (Saint Kitts) and Nevis** (2011/1077), **Saint Lucia** (2011/1076), **Saint Vincent and the Grenadines** (2011/1078), **San Marino** (2011/1688), **Turks and Caicos Islands** (2010/2679; 2014/1360 (not yet in force)), **Uruguay** (2014/1358 (applies on and after 20 October 2016 in both countries regarding criminal matters, and otherwise for taxable periods commencing, or charges to tax arising, on or after 20 October 2016)), **Virgin Islands** (2009/3013; 2014/1359 (2013 exchange of letters not yet in force)).

Notes on double tax agreements

Copies of double tax agreements and other statutory instruments are available at www.legislation.gov.uk/uksi.

China

The Agreement published as *SI 1984 No 1826* does not apply to the Hong Kong or Macao Special Administrative Regions which came into existence on 1 July 1997. (Revenue Tax Bulletin October 1996 p 357).

Czechoslovakia

The Agreement published as *SI 1991 No 2876* between the UK and Czechoslovakia is treated as remaining in force between the UK and, respectively, the Czech Republic and the Slovak Republic. (HMRC SP 5/93). In its application to the Slovak Republic, it is modified by the MLI with effect from 6 April 2020 (UK) and 1 July 2019 (Slovak Republic) for taxable periods beginning on or after that date, but from 1 January 2019 in both territories as regards taxes withheld at source on amounts paid or credited to non-residents.

USA

For HMRC's understanding of how certain provisions of the latest Agreement published as *SI 2002 No 2848* will be interpreted and applied, see Revenue Tax Bulletin Special Edition 6, April 2003.

USSR

The Agreement published as *SI 1986 No 224* between the UK and the former Soviet Union was to be applied by the UK as if it were still in force between the UK and the former Soviet Republics until such time as new agreements took effect with particular countries. It later came to light that Armenia, Georgia, Kyrgyzstan, Lithuania and Moldova did not consider themselves bound by the UK/USSR convention and were not operating it in relation to UK residents. Accordingly, the UK ceased to apply it to residents of those countries from 6 April 2002 for income tax and capital gains tax. (The Agreement published as *SI 2001 No 3925* between the UK and Lithuania has effect from those dates, and note the new Agreements between the UK and, respectively, Armenia, Georgia, Kyrgyzstan and Moldova.) It subsequently emerged that Tajikistan did not consider itself bound by the UK/USSR convention either, and accordingly HMRC did not apply it for income and gains arising on or after 6 April 2014, and note the new Agreement published as *SI 2014 No 3275* between the UK and Tajikistan. (HMRC SP 4/01; HMRC Notice, 20 February 2014.) Agreements have now been made with all the former Soviet Republics.

Yugoslavia

The Agreement published as *SI 1981 No 1815* between the UK and Yugoslavia is regarded as remaining in force between the UK and, respectively, Bosnia-Herzegovina, Montenegro and Serbia. (HMRC Statement of Practice SP 03/07). That Agreement ceased to be so regarded with respect to Croatia, Kosovo, Slovenia and North Macedonia when new treaties between the UK and those territories came into force. As regards Serbia, the 1981 Agreement between the UK and Yugoslavia is modified by the MLI (see above under BEPS) with effect from 6 April 2019 in the UK (1 January 2019 for taxes withheld at source) and 1 April 2019 for taxes levied by Serbia for taxable periods beginning on or after that date.

Notes on exchange agreements

The UK and all the crown dependencies and overseas territories have adopted the Common Reporting Standard (CRS) (see **35.14** HMRC — ADMINISTRATION) for sharing financial account information. The CRS has fully superseded these earlier automatic tax information exchange agreements. Of the countries listed above under Exchange of Information only, this covers Anguilla, Bermuda, Gibraltar, Guernsey, Jersey, Turks and Caicos Islands and Virgin Islands. It also covers Cayman Islands, Isle of Man and Montserrat. (www.gov.uk/government/publications/automatic-exchange-of-information-agreements-other-uk-agreements/automatic-exchange-of-information-agreements-other-uk-agreements).

See also **27.11** below as regards the special agreement with **Switzerland** (now terminated) to tackle offshore tax evasion. See **35.13** HMRC — ADMINISTRATION as regards the FATCA agreement with the **USA** and **35.15** for similar agreements (now superseded by the CRS) with Guernsey, Jersey, the Isle of Man and Gibraltar. See **35.16** for EU disclosure rules for cross-border tax arrangements (DAC 6).

See the general anti-avoidance rule at 27.5 below.

Double tax treaty relief — further points

[27.3] As regards the concept of 'permanent establishment' on which taxation rights are based under most treaties, HMRC take the view that a website, or a server on which e-commerce is conducted through a website, is not of itself a permanent establishment (Revenue Press Release 11 April 2000).

Certificate of residence

In order to grant relief or exemption (from foreign tax) for non-UK income and/or gains received by a UK resident individual, some territories require a document from HMRC, known as a '*certificate of residence*', confirming that the individual was resident in the UK for a particular period. See www.gov.uk/guidance/get-a-certificate-of-residence and HMRC International Manual INTM162000 *et seq.*

Distributions

See *Memec plc v CIR* CA 1998, 71 TC 77 in which receipts under a silent partnership agreement were held not to attract relief. In this connection, see HMRC International Manual INTM180000 *et seq.* as regards the classification of foreign entities for UK tax purposes and for a list of such classifications.

On the basis of the principles set out in *Memec* above, it is HMRC's general practice in relation to US Limited Liability Companies (LLCs) to tax a UK resident member only if and when the LLC distributes profits to its members, with no double tax relief due against income tax. In *HMRC v Anson* SC, [2015] STC 1777, it was held by the FTT, and confirmed by the Supreme Court, that the profits of a particular US LLC belonged to the individual members as they arose and that the UK member was entitled to double taxation relief for US tax paid on his share of the LLC's profits. HMRC has since dismissed *Anson* as specific to the facts of that case; its default policy remains to treat US LLCs as companies, and individuals claiming double tax relief and relying on *Anson* will be considered on a case-by-case basis (HMRC Brief 15 (2015), 25 September 2015). For an analysis see *Tax Journal*, 16 October 2015, p 9.

Employees working in the UK

Under many double tax agreements, employees working in the UK, who are resident in the overseas territory but not resident in the UK, and who are not physically present in the UK for more than 183 days in the tax year, are exempt from UK tax on earnings paid by or on behalf of a non-UK resident employer. For this purpose, fractions of days are counted. (CCAB Memorandum TR 508, 9 June 1983). This exemption does not usually apply to public entertainers (and see now **50.11** NON-RESIDENTS), nor, under certain agreements, does it extend to employees working on the UK continental shelf (Revenue Press Release 3 March 1989).

When counting up the 183 days, any part of a day counts as a full day. Any days during which the taxpayer is UK resident should not be included in the calculation. (HMRC Double Taxation Relief Manual DT1921).

For employees commencing a work assignment in the UK, claims will be refused where the cost of an employee's remuneration is borne by a UK resident company acting as the 'economic employer'. This would apply where, for example, the employee is seconded to the UK company, which obtains the benefit and bears the risks in relation to work undertaken by the employee, and to which the non-resident employer recharges the remuneration costs. It would also apply where the non-resident employer carries on a business of hiring out staff to other companies. (Revenue Tax Bulletin June 1995 p 220). In the absence of a formal contract of employment, HMRC would not consider a UK company to be the employer of a short-term business visitor who is in the UK for less than 60 days in a tax year (the '*60-day rule*'), provided that that period does not form part of a more substantial period (for example, a period spanning two tax years) when the taxpayer is in the UK (Revenue Tax Bulletins October 1996 p 358, December 2003 pp 1069–1071).

UK partnerships

A UK partnership cannot be classed as UK resident for the purposes of claiming reliefs under a double tax agreement (as the partnership is not itself an entity chargeable to UK tax). For the purpose of enabling UK resident partners to claim such reliefs, HMRC will, if requested, confirm that those partners are UK resident and entitled to benefit from those reliefs. The information required by HMRC before they will issue a certificate of residence in respect of those partners is listed in HMRC Tax Bulletin August 2006 pp 1308, 1309. HMRC will not confirm partners' UK residence if they are of the opinion that to do so would not be in accordance with the relevant double tax agreement.

Special relationships — interest

Double tax agreements making provision in relation to interest may also contain a rule (a '*special relationship rule*') dealing with cases where, owing to a special relationship, the amount of interest paid exceeds the amount which would have been paid in the absence of that relationship, and requiring the interest provision to be applied only to that lower amount. Any such special relationship rule has to be construed:

- as requiring account to be taken of all factors, including whether, in the absence of the relationship, the loan would have been made at all, or would have been in a different amount, or a different rate of interest and other terms would have been agreed; this does not apply, however, where the special relationship rule expressly requires regard to be had to the debt on which the interest is paid in determining the excess interest (and accordingly expressly limits the factors to be taken into account); and
- as requiring the taxpayer either to show that no special relationship exists or to show the amount of interest which would have been paid in the absence of that relationship.

[*TIOPA 2010, s 131*].

Simon's Taxes. See **E1.570, F1.5.**

Special relationships — royalties

Double tax agreements may contain a special relationship rule in relation to royalties. Such a rule operates similarly to a special relationship rule in relation to interest (see above). The special relationship rule may expressly require regard to be had to the use, right or information for which the royalties are paid in determining the excess royalties (and accordingly expressly limits the factors to be taken into account). The special relationship rule is to be read as requiring the taxpayer to show either that no special relationship exists or the amount of royalties which would have been payable in the absence of the relationship.

If the asset in respect of which the royalties are paid, or any asset which it represents or from which it is derived, has previously been in the beneficial ownership of:

(a) the person (P) who is liable to pay the royalties;
(b) person who is, or has at any time been, an associate (as specially defined) of P;
(c) a person who has at any time carried on a business which, at the time when the liability to pay the royalties arises, is being carried on wholly or in partly by P; or
(d) a person who is, or has at any time been, an associate (as specially defined) of a person within (c) above.

the special relationship rule is to be read as requiring account to be taken of the following factors:

(i) amounts paid under the transaction(s) which resulted in the asset falling into its present beneficial ownership;
(ii) the amounts which would have been so paid in the absence of the special relationship; and
(iii) the question as to whether the transaction(s) would have taken place at all in the absence of that relationship.

The special relationship rule is to be read as requiring the taxpayer to either show that (a)–(d) above are not applicable or show that the transaction(s) mentioned in (i)–(iii) above would have taken place in the absence of a special relationship and the amounts which would then have been paid under those transaction(s).

[*TIOPA 2010, ss 132, 133*].

Simon's Taxes. See **E1.570, F1.522.**

Double tax relief — Ireland

[27.4] [*SI 1976 Nos 2151, 2152; SI 1995 No 764; SI 1998 No 3151*].

A Convention and Protocol 1976 (as subsequently amended) replaced previous provisions between UK and Ireland. It is modified by the MLI (see **27.2** above) with effect from 6 April 2020 (UK) and 1 November 2019 (Ireland) for taxable periods beginning on or after that date, but from 1 January 2020 in both territories as regards taxes withheld at source on amounts paid or credited to non-residents). Shipping and air transport profits, certain trading profits not arising through a permanent establishment, interest, royalties, pensions (other than Government pensions and salaries which are normally taxed by the paying Government only) are taxed in the country of residence. Salaries, wages and other similar remuneration derived by a resident of one country (country A) in respect of an employment are taxable only in country A unless the employment is exercised in the other country (country B). Remuneration derived by a resident of country A in respect of an employment exercised in country B is taxable only in country A if: (a) the recipient is present in country B for not more than 183 days in the fiscal year; (b) the remuneration is paid by, or on behalf of, an employer who is not a resident of country B; and (c) the remuneration is not borne by a permanent establishment or a fixed base which the employer has in country B.

Where income is taxable in both countries, relief is given in the country of residence for the tax payable in the country of origin.

The recipient of a dividend from a company resident in the other country is entitled to any related tax credit (except where the recipient is a company which controls, alone or with associates, 10% or more of the voting power of the paying company). Income tax up to 15% of aggregate of dividend and tax credit may be charged in country of source (but not on charity or superannuation scheme exempt in other country). Dividend tax credits were abolished in the UK for 2016/17 onwards.

Anti-avoidance — relief by credit under double tax agreement

[27.5] Where relief by way of credit against UK tax is available under a double tax agreement for foreign tax suffered on any income or chargeable gain of a person and:

- there is a scheme or arrangement the main purpose of which is to provide for an amount of foreign tax to be taken into account;
- the scheme or arrangement is a 'prescribed scheme or arrangement'; and
- the aggregate amount of credit relief which can be or has been claimed for that tax year by that person, and by any persons connected with him (within **19** CONNECTED PERSONS), is at least £100,000 (see HMRC International Manual INTM170120),

the effects of the scheme or arrangement are to be nullified by the making of such adjustments as are necessary. Those adjustments are to be made by way of an assessment, the modification of an assessment, the amendment or disallowance of a claim, or otherwise. It is for the taxpayer to consider as part of his self-assessment whether adjustments are required, but they can also be made by HMRC. This applies in relation to tax returns with a filing date of 1 April 2018 or later. Previously, if HMRC had reasonable grounds to believe that the above circumstances applied, they were required to issue a counter-action notice to the person concerned requiring that he make adjustments to (or amend) his tax return for the year in question to nullify the effects of the scheme or arrangement.

According to HMRC International Manual INTM170120, the above provisions do not apply in the simple case of an individual holding foreign shareholdings within an investment portfolio where the dividends are taxed as investment income (with credit for foreign tax deducted), but this let-out will not apply if income is received by a person for the purpose of benefiting from the let-out, for example where income is deliberately diverted from one person to another for that purpose.

There is no formal clearance procedure but HMRC will be prepared to give advice concerning actual or proposed transactions and, where appropriate, will confirm that the provisions do not apply in respect of the disclosed transactions (see HMRC International Manual INTM170110).

A scheme or arrangement is a '*prescribed scheme or arrangement*' if any one or more of the following applies to it.

(i) The scheme enables foreign tax that is properly attributable to one source of income or gain to be paid in respect of a different source of income or gain.

(ii) It enables any scheme participant to claim credit for a payment of foreign tax that increases the total amount of foreign tax paid by all the scheme participants by less than the amount which that person can claim (for example, because the payment made by the claimant is matched by a tax saving for another scheme participant).

(iii) Under the scheme, there is an amount of notional foreign tax and either:

- when the claimant entered into the scheme, it could reasonably be expected that, under the scheme, no *real* foreign tax would be paid or payable by a participant; or
- when the claimant entered into the scheme, it could reasonably be expected that, under the scheme, some real foreign tax would be paid or payable by a participant but it increases the total amount of foreign tax paid by all the scheme participants by less than the amount which the claimant can claim in respect of the notional foreign tax.

(iv) It involves a scheme participant making a claim or election etc. or omitting to make a claim or election etc. which in either case has the effect of increasing the credit for foreign tax available to any scheme participant. References here to claims and elections or suchlike are to claims etc. made under the law of any territory or under the terms of a double tax agreement. A step taken or not taken by a scheme participant can be a step taken or omitted before a scheme comes into existence, and the reason for taking or not taking a step does not matter provided the effect is to increase the credit for foreign tax available to a scheme participant.

(v) It has the effect of reducing a scheme participant's total UK tax liability on income and chargeable gains to less than it would have been in the absence of the transactions made under the scheme. This will be the case, for example, where the credit for foreign tax on the scheme income covers not only the UK tax on that income but at least some of the UK tax on other income, thereby reducing total liability. In relation to any credit for foreign tax which relates to a payment of foreign tax on or after 22 November 2017, it is provided that the tax liabilities of connected persons (within *CTA 2010, s 1122*) must be taken into account also.

(vi) Under the scheme, a tax deductible payment is made by a person, in return for which that person, or a person connected with him (within **19** CONNECTED PERSONS), receives consideration which is taxable in a foreign territory (and thus on which credit relief can be obtained in respect of the foreign tax).

[*TIOPA 2010, ss 81–85, 85A, 86–88; FA 2018, s 31(2)(3)(6)(7)*].

Counteraction notices

The following provisions applied only where HMRC were required to issue a counteraction notice (see above).

Where a tax return was made within 90 days after the issue of a counteraction notice, the notice could be disregarded when making the return, as long as the return was then amended in accordance with the notice before the end of that 90-day period. Once a tax return had been made, HMRC could only issue a counteraction notice if a notice of enquiry had been issued in respect of the return, but an enquiry could be opened for just that purpose. If a counteraction notice was then issued, the taxpayer had to amend the return accordingly within the 90 days beginning with the date of issue of the notice.

Failure to make or amend a return in accordance with a counteraction notice resulted in the return becoming an incorrect return (so that penalties potentially applied — see, for example, **55.6** PENALTIES). An enquiry could not be closed until either the amendment was made or the 90-day period for making it expired (though this did not prevent the issue of a partial closure notice that was unrelated to any matter to which the counteraction notice related). Disputes between HMRC and taxpayer were settled under the normal self-assessment enquiry procedures and with the normal rights of appeal (see HMRC International Manual INTM170080). (See **64.6–64.10** RETURNS for enquiries into returns generally.)

Where an enquiry into a return had been completed, a counteraction notice could only be issued where HMRC could not have been reasonably expected to realise that a notice was required on the basis of the information supplied before the enquiry was completed, or, had requests for information by HMRC in the course of the enquiry been complied with, it was reasonable to suppose that they would have issued a notice at that time. Where an enquiry was only partly completed, the reference here to an enquiry and a counteraction notice is to an enquiry and a counteraction notice relating to the matters covered by the partial closure notice. Once a counteraction notice was issued in such circumstances, a related 'discovery' assessment could not be made until either the necessary amendment was made to the tax return or the 90-day period for making it expired. The conditions at **6.6**(2) ASSESSMENTS for making a discovery assessment are disapplied (being replaced by the above conditions for issuing the notice).

[*TIOPA 2010, ss 89–95; TMA 1970, s 29(7A); F(No 2)A 2017, Sch 15 paras 38, 39, 44; FA 2018, s 31(4)(6)*].

See generally HMRC International Manual INTM170000–170140.

Simon's Taxes. See **E6.437–E6.437B.**

Unilateral relief by UK

[27.6] The following applies where no credit is available for foreign tax under the bilateral double tax agreements in **27.2** above. Where:

- tax is paid under the law of a territory outside the UK;
- the tax is calculated by reference to income arising in that territory; and
- the tax is charged on income and corresponds to UK income tax or is charged on income or gains and corresponds to UK corporation tax (see further below).

Credit for the foreign tax is allowed against any UK income tax calculated by reference to that income.

Profits from personal or professional services performed in a territory are to be treated as income arising in that territory. The same applies to remuneration for such services.

[*TIOPA 2010, s 9(1)(3)(4)*].

See the Example at **27.7** below.

Corresponding taxes

Tax may correspond to income tax, corporation tax or capital gains tax even if it is payable under the law of a province, state or other part of a country or it is levied by or on behalf of a municipality or other local body. [*TIOPA 2010, s 9(6)*]. In *Yates v GCA International Ltd and cross-appeal* Ch D 1991, 64 TC 37, a tax imposed on gross receipts less a fixed 10% deduction was held to correspond to UK income tax or corporation tax. Following that decision, HMRC amended their practice (HMRC SP 7/91). Foreign taxes will be examined to determine whether, in their own legislative context, they serve the same function as UK income tax and corporation tax in relation to business profits, and are thus eligible for unilateral relief. As regards those foreign taxes which HMRC considers admissible (or inadmissible) for relief, these are listed by country in HMRC Double Taxation Relief Manual at DT2100 *et seq*. See also HMRC Business Income Manual BIM45900. Inadmissible foreign taxes may nevertheless be an allowable expense in computing income taxable in the UK under normal trading income rules. (HMRC International Manual INTM161080).

Residence requirement

The general rule is that relief by way of credit is not available against any UK tax for any tax year unless the person on whose income the UK tax is chargeable is resident in the UK for that year. [*TIOPA 2010, s 26(1)*]. This is subject to the following exceptions as regards unilateral relief.

(a) **Channel Islands and Isle of Man.** Credit is allowed for tax paid under the law of the Isle of Man or any of the Channel Islands, if the claimant is resident either in the UK or in the Isle of Man or any of the Channel Islands, as the case may be. [*TIOPA 2010, s 28*].

(b) **Employment income.** Credit for overseas tax on income from an office or employment, the duties of which are wholly or mainly performed in the overseas territory is given, against income tax on employment income computed by reference to that income, if the claimant is resident either in the UK or in the overseas territory. [*TIOPA 2010, s 29*].

(c) **UK branch or agency.** Credit is available for foreign tax paid on the income of the UK branch or agency of a non-UK resident person provided the overseas territory in question is not one in which the person is liable to tax by reason of domicile, residence or place of management. However, the relief may not exceed the relief that would have been available if the branch or agency were a UK resident person. [*TIOPA 2010, s 30*].

Apportionment of income

Where appropriate an apportionment must be made to determine what part of income may be regarded as 'arising in' the overseas territory, and in making that apportionment it is the principles of UK tax law which are to be applied (see *Yates v GCA International Ltd and cross-appeal* Ch D 1991, 64 TC 37 and HMRC SP 7/91).

Circumstances where no unilateral relief permitted

Unilateral relief will not be allowed where credit could be claimed under a double tax agreement under **27.2** above, or in cases or circumstances in which a double tax agreement specifically prohibits relief. [*TIOPA 2010, s 11*].

Channel Islands and Isle of Man

The restriction to tax on income arising *in the territory* does not apply in the case of the Channel Islands or Isle of Man. See also (a) above. [*TIOPA 2010, s 9(7)*].

Community tax

Unilateral relief is available for Community tax deducted from the salaries, transitional allowances and pensions of members of the European Parliament (MEPs) under the Statute for Members of the European Parliament (2005/684/EC, Euratom). The enabling legislation treats such tax as if it were payable under the law of a territory outside the UK. [*FA 2009, s 56(1)(3)*].

Simon's Taxes. See **E6.414**.

Example of relief by credit

[27.7]

Talleyrand, a UK resident, has for 2020/21 UK earnings of £23,955 and foreign income from property of £2,000 on which foreign tax of £300 has been paid.

(a) *Tax on total income*	£	
Earnings	23,955	
Income from property	2,000	(foreign tax £300)
	25,955	
Personal allowance	12,500	
Taxable income	£13,455	
Tax on £13,455 @ 20%	£2,691.00	

(b) *Tax on total income less foreign income*	£
Earnings	23,955
Personal allowance	12,500
Taxable income	£11,455
Tax on £11,455 @ 20%	£2,291.00

The difference in tax between (a) and (b) is £400. The foreign tax is less than this and full credit of £300 is available against the UK tax payable. If the foreign tax was £600, the credit would be limited to £400 and the balance of £200 would be unrelieved.

Limits on relief

[27.8] Where income is chargeable to UK income tax, credit for foreign tax suffered on that income reduces the income tax chargeable in respect of the doubly taxed income. The reduction is made at Step 6 of the calculation of income tax liability — see **1.10, 1.12** ALLOWANCES AND TAX RATES. This applies whether the credit is given under a double tax agreement or unilaterally. [*TIOPA 2010, ss 9(1)–(3), 18*].

But the reduction is limited to the difference between the income tax to which the claimant would be liable (before double tax relief but after any other income tax reduction other than the reduction at **70.19** SETTLEMENTS available to trusts with vulnerable beneficiaries):

(i) if he were charged on his total income; and
(ii) if he were charged on his total income *excluding* the income in respect of which the credit is to be allowed.

In all cases, the tax reduction is restricted to the extent (if any) that it would otherwise exceed the income tax liability after other reductions have been made — see **1.12** ALLOWANCES AND TAX RATES and before making any additions at Step 7 at **1.10** ALLOWANCES AND TAX RATES. For this purpose and for the purposes of the corresponding capital gains relief, a person's combined income tax and capital gains tax liability is reduced by any tax deemed to have been deducted by him from Gift Aid donations (see **14.13** CHARITIES AND CHARITABLE GIVING).

If credit for foreign tax is available in respect of income from more than one source, the comparison at (i) and (ii) above is made successively in relation to the income from each source, taking the sources in the order which will result in the greatest reduction in the person's income tax liability for the tax year. Each time a comparison is made after the first, all the income for which a comparison has previously been made is excluded from total income in (i) and (ii) above.

[*TIOPA 2010, ss 36, 41*].

It is in addition provided that relief is limited to that which would be allowed if all reasonable steps had been taken, including all relevant claims, elections etc., under the law of the territory concerned or under a double tax agreement with that territory, to minimise the foreign tax payable. [*TIOPA 2010, s 33*].

As regards what HMRC consider that taxpayers can and cannot reasonably be expected to do to minimise foreign tax payable, the former is likely to include appeals against excessive assessments, claims for reliefs generally known to be available, and selection of any option which produces a lower tax liability, and the latter is likely to include claims to reliefs whose availability is uncertain, and where disproportionate expenditure would be required to pursue a claim, substituting carry-forward claims for carry-back claims and *vice versa*, and attempting to exercise influence the taxpayer does not have. See HMRC International Manual INTM164140. The taking of reasonable steps should not, however, be interpreted as meaning that the taxpayer should have entered into a completely different, albeit economically similar, transaction to the one actually entered into (*Hill Samuel Investments Ltd v HMRC* (Sp C 738), [2009] SSCD 315).

Trade income

The following additional restriction applies if the tax against which the credit is to be allowed is income tax on 'trade income'. For this purpose, '*trade income*' comprises profits of a trade, profession or vocation (see **75** TRADING INCOME) or of a property business (see **60.2** PROPERTY INCOME), post-cessation receipts from any of these (see **59** POST-CESSATION RECEIPTS AND EXPENDITURE and **60.16** PROPERTY INCOME) and overseas property income (see **60.3** PROPERTY INCOME).

The comparison at (i) and (ii) above is to be undertaken on the basis of net income (after any allowable deductions) rather than, as before, gross income, i.e. the foreign tax credit is restricted by reference to profit rather than income. As well as deducting expenses etc. that are directly attributable to the income, one must also allocate and deduct a just and reasonable proportion of expenses etc. that are only partly attributable, e.g. overheads. In making the said comparison, royalties from different non-UK jurisdictions in respect of the same asset, and foreign tax credits in respect of such income, are to be aggregated.

It is specified that the trade income to be taken into account as above is the trade income arising out of the transaction, arrangement or asset in connection with which the credit for foreign tax arises. The intention is that relief should not be given against UK tax due on income that is unrelated to the payment of the foreign tax.

[*TIOPA 2010, ss 37, 38*].

See HMRC International Manual INTM168010–168065.

Relief for disallowed credit

Where an amount of credit for foreign tax is disallowed because of the application of *TIOPA 2010, s 36* above, the taxpayer's income is treated as reduced by the amount of disallowed credit. This has effect in relation to a credit for foreign tax in connection with either with a payment of foreign tax or with income received in respect of which foreign tax has deducted at source, and has effect notwithstanding the general rule at **27.10**(a)(ii) below. The amount of the reduction is the lower of the disallowed credit and the amount of any loss, *after* deducting the foreign tax, that arises from the transaction that gives rise to the foreign tax payment; if there is no such loss, no reduction is available. [*TIOPA 2010, s 35*].

Simon's Taxes. See **E6.433–E6.433C**.

Claims for relief

[27.9] Claims made for credit relief, whether under a double tax agreement or unilaterally, must be made on or before the later of:

- the fourth anniversary of the end of the tax year in which the income falls to be charged to tax; and
- 31 January following the tax year in which the foreign tax is paid.

[*TIOPA 2010, s 19(2)*].

Written notice must be given to HMRC where any credit allowed for foreign tax has become excessive by reason of an adjustment of the amount of any foreign tax payable (except in the case of UNDERWRITERS AT LLOYD'S (78) where the consequences of such an adjustment are dealt with under regulations). The notice must be given within one year after the making of the adjustment. The maximum penalty for failure to comply is the amount by which the credit was rendered excessive by the adjustment. The time limit for assessments etc. to be revised following such an adjustment is extended to six years after the adjustment is finalised. See HMRC International Manual INTM162120.

[*TIOPA 2010, ss 79, 80*].

For appeals, see **63.39** RESIDENCE AND DOMICILE. Pending final agreement, a provisional allowance can usually be obtained on application to HMRC.

Double tax relief — miscellaneous

[27.10] The following miscellaneous items are relevant.

(i) **Amounts chargeable in UK on the** REMITTANCE BASIS (**61**). Where double tax credit for foreign tax is allowable in respect of it, any income which is chargeable on the remittance basis is treated, for UK tax purposes, as increased by the foreign tax on that income (but ignoring any notional foreign tax under (d) below). [*TIOPA 2010, s 32(1)(2)(5)(6)*].

(ii) **Amounts chargeable in UK on the arising basis.** Where income is chargeable to income tax on the basis of the full amount arising (i.e. not on the remittance basis as in (i) above), and double tax credit relief is allowable given by credit in respect of foreign tax suffered on it, no deduction may can be made for any foreign tax in computing the amount of the income for UK tax purposes. [*TIOPA 2010, s 31(1)(2)*].

(iii) **If the taxpayer does not take any credit** by way of either bilateral or unilateral relief, or if no UK double tax credit is otherwise allowable in respect of foreign income, any tax paid on that income in the place where it arises is generally deductible from the income for the purposes of charging it to UK tax, unless the charge to UK tax is on the remittance basis. Where foreign tax for which such a deduction has been given is subsequently adjusted, similar provisions to those which apply by virtue of *TIOPA 2010, s 80* in the case of foreign tax credits (see **27.9** above) apply as regards the requirement to notify HMRC of the adjustment and extended time limit for assessments etc. [*TIOPA 2010, ss 112–115*].

(b) **Exchange rate.** Foreign tax is normally converted into sterling at the rate of exchange obtaining on the date it became payable. (HMRC International Manual INTM162160). Where part of foreign tax repaid and sterling was devalued in the period between payment and repayment, held relief due on net tax in foreign currency at the old rate (*Greig v Ashton* Ch D 1956, 36 TC 581).

(c) **Lloyd's underwriters.** For special arrangements for double tax relief for Lloyd's underwriters, see *SI 1997 No 405*.

(d) **Notional foreign tax.** It may be provided in a double tax agreement that any tax which would have been payable in a foreign country but for a relief under the law of that territory given with a view to promoting industrial, commercial, scientific, educational or other development therein is nevertheless treated for purposes of credit against UK tax as if it had been paid. [*TIOPA 2010, ss 4, 20*].

(e) **Overlap profits.** Credit for foreign tax paid in respect of 'overlap profits' (see **75.14** TRADING INCOME) arising in taxing a trade etc. is allowed against UK income tax chargeable for any year in respect of that income, notwithstanding that credit for that foreign tax has already been allowed in an earlier year. There are overriding provisions limiting the credit allowable for any year by reference to the total of credit due for all the relevant years as above, and for cases where the number of UK tax years exceeds the number of foreign periods of assessment. The relief requires a claim to be made on or before the fifth anniversary of 31 January following the tax year for which relief is claimed or, if there is more than one, following the later of those tax years.

Recovery of excess credit applies where, and to the extent that, relief is given for overlap profits either on cessation of the trade or on a change of accounting date resulting in a basis period of longer than twelve months. Recovery is achieved by reducing the credit otherwise available for the year of relief and, if there is still an excess, by charging an amount of income tax for that year.

[*TIOPA 2010, ss 22–24; F(No 2)A 2017, Sch 3 paras 12, 13*].

(f) **Partnerships.** It was held in the case of *Padmore v CIR* CA 1989, 62 TC 352 that, where profits of a non-UK resident partnership were exempt under the relevant double tax treaty, the profit share of a UK resident partner was thereby also exempt. This decision was, however, reversed by subsequent legislation with retrospective effect, see **52.22** PARTNERSHIPS.

(g) **Prevention of double relief.** Credit will not be given for foreign tax for which relief is available in the territory in which it would otherwise be payable, either under a double tax agreement or under the law of that territory in consequence of any double tax agreement or in cases or circumstances in which such an agreement specifically prohibits relief. [*TIOPA 2010, s 25*].

(h) **Royalties and 'know-how' payments.** Notwithstanding that credit for overseas tax is ordinarily given only against income which arises (or is deemed to arise) in the overseas territory concerned, HMRC's treatment as regards this class of income is as follows.

Income payments made by an overseas resident to a UK trader for the use, in that overseas territory, of any *copyright, patent, design, secret process or formula, trade mark etc.*, may be treated, for credit purposes (whether under double tax agreements or by way of unilateral relief) as income arising outside the UK — *except* so far as they represent consideration for services (other than merely incidental) rendered in the UK by the recipient to the payer (HMRC ESC B8).

For the treatment of sales of 'know-how' etc., see **75.95** TRADING INCOME.

(i) **UK residents and foreign enterprises.** Where a double tax agreement contains the following provision (however expressed), it is not to be taken as preventing income of a *UK resident* person being chargeable to income tax. For these purposes, a person is UK resident if he is UK resident for the purposes of the double tax agreement. The provision is that the profits of an enterprise which is resident outside the UK, or carries on a trade, profession or business the control or management of which is situated outside the UK, are not to be subject to UK tax except in so far as they are attributable to a permanent establishment of the enterprise in the UK. [*TIOPA 2010, s 130*].

(j) **Payments by reference to foreign tax.** Where a person (P) is entitled under a double tax agreement to a credit for foreign tax paid and a payment is made by a tax authority to P by reference to that foreign tax, the amount of the credit is reduced by the amount of the payment. The same applies if the payment is made to a person connected with P (within **19** CONNECTED PERSONS) or if it is made to some other person in consequence of a scheme (as widely defined) that has been entered into. [*TIOPA 2010, s 34*]. If relief for the foreign tax is given by way of deduction as opposed to credit (see (a)(iii) above), P's income is increased by the amount of the payment made. [*TIOPA 2010, s 112(3)(7)(8)*].

Where any credit allowed for foreign tax has become excessive by reason of a reduction as above, *TIOPA 2010, s 80* (see **27.9** above) applies as regards the requirement to notify HMRC of the reduction and as regards the extended time limit for assessments and claims. A similar requirement and extension applies under *TIOPA 2010, ss 114, 115* where the amount of P's income falls to be increased as above.

(k) **Taxation of pensions etc.** Where a double tax agreement contains the provision below (however expressed), it is not to be taken as preventing income of a *UK resident* being chargeable to income tax if certain conditions are met. The intention is to prevent double tax agreements being used to avoid taxation of foreign pensions where pension savings have been transferred to a non-UK pension scheme.

The said provision is that pensions and other similar remuneration (e.g. pension scheme lump sums) which arise outside the UK and are paid to UK residents are not to be subject to UK tax.

The conditions are that:

- the pension or other similar remuneration is paid out of sums or assets that were the subject of a 'relevant transfer' (or out of related sums or assets); and
- a main purpose of the relevant transfer or any transaction forming part of that transfer was to secure a tax advantage under one of the UK's double tax agreements.

However, there is nothing to stop double tax relief being given by way of credit against an amount taxable in the UK as a result of the above. A '*relevant transfer*' is broadly a transfer of sums or assets out of a UK pension scheme into an overseas scheme.

[*TIOPA 2010, s 130A*].

Special agreement with Switzerland (terminated)

[27.11] In 2011, the UK Government entered into an agreement with Switzerland to tackle offshore tax evasion. The agreement came into force on 1 January 2013. It covers not only ordinary bank accounts held by individual UK taxpayers in Switzerland but any form of bankable assets booked or deposited with a Swiss paying agent, including cash, precious metals, stocks, options and structured financial products. Safe deposit boxes, real property and chattels are, however, excluded. The agreement also gives HMRC powers to discover whether an individual UK taxpayer has an account in Switzerland. The agreement was given legal effect in the UK by *FA 2012, s 218, Sch 36*, which also set out the effect of the agreement on UK tax liabilities.

The agreement was **terminated** by mutual agreement with effect on and after **1 January 2017**. The UK and Switzerland will instead share information under the Common Reporting Standard (see **35.14** HMRC — ADMINISTRATION).

See www.gov.uk/government/publications/uk-swiss-confederation-taxation-co-operation-agreement.

One-off tax deduction

Under the agreement, Swiss bank accounts etc. were subject to a one-off tax deduction on 31 May 2013, provided the account was open on 31 December 2010 and still open on 31 May 2013. The deduction was a percentage of capital based on a complex formula dependent on such matters as how long ago the account was opened and when the funds were deposited; the percentage was between 21% and 41%. The Swiss accounted to HMRC for the tax deducted. The deduction was not to be applied if the account holder instructed the Swiss bank to disclose details of the account to HMRC, in which case HMRC would pursue any unpaid taxes together with interest and penalties where appropriate.

The effect is, in most cases, that amounts which have suffered the deduction and on which the taxpayer should have paid tax, but which are untaxed, cease to be liable to UK tax. In certain cases, however, the deduction is instead treated as a credit against UK tax, interest and penalties in respect of the untaxed amount. Where the UK liability is removed, there are provisions to ensure that the taxpayer's liability to tax on other income or gains is what it would be if the amounts no longer liable to UK tax had remained so liable. See *FA 2012, Sch 36 paras 2–12*.

There is no legal requirement for HMRC to make a refund to an individual where the one-off deduction, correctly levied, exceeds the individual's UK tax liability after full disclosure. For a discussion of the very limited circumstances in which HMRC may choose to make a refund at their discretion, see *Vrang v HMRC* QB, [2017] STC 1192.

Withholding tax

In addition, from 1 January 2013, income and gains arising on the said investments are subject to a regular withholding tax of 48% on interest, 40% on dividends and 27% on gains. Again, the withholding tax does not apply if the account holder authorises disclosure of both income and gains to HMRC and pays any associated taxes. The effect is that the taxpayer ceases to be liable to income tax or capital gains tax on the income or gain to which withholding tax is applied. However, the taxpayer can elect that the withholding tax is not treated as settling liability if all affected amounts relating to the underlying account are included in a tax return or amended return. This gives him the option to calculate tax liability on the normal basis with the withholding tax allowed as a credit against that liability. An election must be made in the return in which the affected amounts are included. See *FA 2012, Sch 36 paras 13–19.*

The withholding tax does not apply where a retention is made under the terms of the 2004 Agreement between the EU and Switzerland on the taxation of savings income ('the EUSA'), but instead a tax finality payment is made so that the overall outcome is equivalent to that achieved by the withholding tax. If a claim is made for credit to be given for the withholding tax retained under the EUSA, the taxpayer is treated as making the above-mentioned election.

The withholding tax came to an end on 31 December 2016 in line with the termination of the agreement.

Non-domiciles

Non-UK domiciled individuals are also subject to both the one-off deduction and the withholding tax to the extent that amounts would be chargeable to UK tax if the accounts were disclosed to HMRC.

Remittance basis

Where the REMITTANCE BASIS (**61**) applies to a taxpayer, foreign income and gains are treated as not remitted to the UK when money is brought to the UK pursuant to a transfer to HMRC in accordance with the agreement. This does not apply to money brought to the UK if, or to the extent that, it is set off against other tax liabilities, repaid or refunded by HMRC. Where the charge levied under the agreement is withholding tax on foreign income or gains remitted to the UK, the exemption applies only if the charge is levied within 45 days beginning with the date on which the amount derived from the income or gain in question was remitted. Where the transfer to which the exemption applies is made from a mixed fund, it is treated as an 'offshore transfer' for the purposes of determining the composition of the fund (as in **61.17** REMITTANCE BASIS). [*FA 2012, Sch 36 paras 26A, 26B*].

Simon's Taxes. See **A6.1216.**

Payments abroad by UK residents

[27.12] Under *SI 1970 No 488*, if a UK resident pays income to a resident of a country with which the UK has a double tax agreement income, and under that agreement the income is wholly or partially relieved, the payer may be required, by notice from the Commissioners for HMRC, to make such payments without deducting UK income tax, or under deduction of tax at, or not exceeding, a specified rate. Applications for such relief from deduction should be sent to IR International — Centre for Non-Residents, Fitz Roy

House, PO Box 46, Nottingham NG2 1BD. Where a notice is given, the payer, if otherwise chargeable with, or liable to account for, tax on such payments (23 DEDUCTION OF TAX AT SOURCE) is exempted from that liability if the notice requires him to pay the income gross, and in other cases need account for tax only at the rate specified.

For HMRC practice in relation to claims for payment of interest to non-residents without deduction of tax, and in particular where payments are made in full in advance of the issue (or refusal) of a gross payment notice, see Revenue Tax Bulletin August 1994 p 153.

For review of applications for relief from deduction where loans are re-denominated from one currency to another (e.g. to or from the euro), see Revenue Tax Bulletin February 1999 pp 631, 632.

Double Taxation Treaty Passport Scheme

This is an administrative scheme designed to assist foreign lenders in accessing reduced withholding tax rates on interest that are available within the UK's double tax treaties with other territories. For loans entered into on or after 6 April 2017, the scheme is available to all UK borrowers, including UK partnerships, individuals and charities, who are obliged to deduct withholding tax from interest payments to overseas lenders. Previously, it was restricted to overseas corporate lenders and UK corporate borrowers. Eligible lenders must make an application to HMRC to be awarded passport holder status. For current guidance, including eligibility, terms and conditions and details of the application process, see www.gov.uk/government/consultations/double-taxation-treaty-passport-scheme-review.

Double tax relief for companies

[27.13] Companies enjoy the benefit of the foregoing double tax reliefs and they can in certain circumstances claim relief for 'underlying tax' in respect of overseas dividends receivable by them. 'Underlying tax' refers to the overseas taxes borne by the paying company on its profits). See the corresponding chapter of Tolley's Corporation Tax.

28

Employment Income

Cross-references. See **18** COMPENSATION FOR LOSS OF EMPLOYMENT; **26** DISGUISED REMUNERATION; **27** DOUBLE TAX RELIEF; **45** LOSSES; **47** MANAGED SERVICE COMPANIES; **63**

RESIDENCE AND DOMICILE for definitions of those terms; 53 PAY AS YOU EARN; 54 PAYMENT OF TAX; 56 PENSION INCOME; 57 PENSION PROVISION; 58 PERSONAL SERVICE COMPANIES ETC.; 71 SHARE-RELATED EMPLOYMENT INCOME AND EXEMPTIONS; 73 SOCIAL SECURITY AND NATIONAL INSURANCE for taxation of State benefits.

Simon's Taxes. See PART E4.

Introduction to employment income

[28.1] This chapter is concerned with the taxation of income from employment. 'Employment' is not exhaustively defined, but includes any employment under a contract of service or apprenticeship or in the service of the Crown. [*ITEPA 2003, s 4*]. Except as otherwise provided, the provisions apply equally to any 'office', which in particular includes any position which has an existence independent of the person holding it and may be filled by successive holders (and see HMRC Employment Status Manual ESM2502 *et seq.*). [*ITEPA 2003, s 5*].

The charge to tax on employment income is divided into a charge on 'general earnings' (see **28.13** below) and a charge on '*specific employment income*', i.e. amounts which count as employment income (in particular payments to and benefits from pension schemes, see **56** PENSION PROVISION; payments and benefits on termination of employments etc., see **18** COMPENSATION FOR LOSS OF EMPLOYMENT; share-related income, see **71** SHARE-RELATED EMPLOYMENT INCOME AND EXEMPTIONS; and DISGUISED REMUNERATION (**26**)). The provisions described in **28.3–28.9** below relate only to the charge on general earnings. [*ITEPA 2003, ss 6, 7; FA 2017, Sch 1 paras 10, 15; F(No 2)A 2017, s 5(2)(10); SI 2018 No 282, Arts 1, 4*].

The amount of *general earnings* chargeable for a particular year from an employment is the net taxable earnings for the year from the employment. The taxable earnings are determined as described in **28.3–28.9** below.

Subject to the possible application of the remittance basis to share-related income (see **71.22–71.24** SHARE-RELATED EMPLOYMENT INCOME AND EXEMPTIONS and DISGUISED REMUNERATION (**26.5**) the amount of *specific employment income* chargeable for a particular year from an employment is the net taxable specific income from the employment. The taxable specific income is the full amount which counts as employment income for that year under the relevant provision.

The deductions allowed in arriving at *net taxable earnings* or *net taxable specific income* from an employment are as described in **28.16–28.19** below, but such deductions may not reduce the taxable amount from any source below nil. If there is more than one kind of specific employment income from an employment in a year, a separate calculation is required for each. If, exceptionally, taxable earnings or net taxable earnings are negative, loss relief against general income may be available as in **45.31** LOSSES.

[*ITEPA 2003, ss 9–12*].

Legislation provides for an employment income charge to be made where third parties, e.g. trusts or other intermediate vehicles, are used in arrangements aimed at providing value to an individual for what is in substance a reward, recognition or loan in connection with his employment. This is known as the charge to tax on employment income provided through third parties or alternatively the charge to tax on disguised remuneration. See **26** DISGUISED REMUNERATION.

For the tax treatment of particular occupations, see HMRC Employment Income Manual EIM50000 *et seq.*

Person liable for tax

[28.2] On *general earnings*, the person liable to tax thereon is the person to whose employment the earnings relate. If the tax is on such earnings received, or remitted to the UK, after the death of that person, the liability falls on the personal representatives, and is payable out of the estate. On *specific employment income*, the person liable to tax thereon is the person in relation to whom the income is to count as employment income under the provision in question.

If the tax is on share-related income (see **71** SHARE-RELATED EMPLOYMENT INCOME AND EXEMPTIONS) received, or remitted to the UK, after the death of the person liable as above, the liability falls on the personal representatives, and is payable out of the estate.

In relation to the charge to tax on DISGUISED REMUNERATION (**26**), if the relevant step in **26.7** is taken, or (where the remittance basis applies) the income is remitted to the UK, after the death of the employee, the employee's personal representatives are liable and the tax is payable out of the estate. This is subject to more detailed rules on liability in *Income Tax (Earnings and Pensions) Act 2003 (ITEPA 2003), s 554Z12* referred to at **26.6**.

[*ITEPA 2003, s 13*].

General earnings — basis of assessment

[28.3] The basis on which taxable general earnings for a tax year are determined depend on whether the employee is, in that year, (a) UK resident (see **63** RESIDENCE AND DOMICILE), (b) a person to whom the remittance basis applies (see **61.2** REMITTANCE BASIS) or (c) non-UK resident. See **28.4–28.8** below.

Subject to any specific provision requiring earnings to be treated as 'for' a particular tax year, general earnings are earned 'for' a period if they are earned in, or in respect of, the period. If the period is or is within a tax year, they are earned for that year: if the period extends over two or more tax years, they are apportioned between those years on a just and reasonable basis. Earnings (other than benefits-in-kind, see **28.50** below) which would accordingly be treated as for a tax year in which the employee does not hold the employment are instead treated as for the first year in which the employment is held (if later) or the last such year (if earlier).

[*ITEPA 2003, ss 14, 16, 17, 20, 29, 30*].

The following **general matters** apply.

(i) **Leave periods etc.** If a person ordinarily performs the whole or part of the duties of an employment in the UK, general earnings for periods of absence from the employment are treated as for duties performed in the UK except insofar as, but for that absence, they would have been for duties performed outside the UK. [*ITEPA 2003, s 38*]. An airline pilot, the great majority of whose work was performed outside the UK, could not rely on this provision to treat his days of absence from work as days of absence from the UK in the same proportion as his working days (*Leonard v Blanchard* CA 1993, 65 TC 589).

(ii) **Incidental duties in the UK.** If an employment is substantially one where the duties for a year fall to be performed outside the UK, any duties incidental thereto performed in the UK are treated as if performed abroad. [*ITEPA 2003, s 39*]. As to whether duties 'incidental' to foreign duties see *Robson v Dixon* Ch D 1972, 48 TC 527 (airline pilot employed abroad but occasionally landing in UK where family home maintained, held UK duties more than incidental). HMRC will normally disregard a single take-off and landing on *de minimis* grounds. (HMRC SP A10). See also Leaflet HMRC6, para 10.6 at https://assets.publishing.service.gov.uk/government/uploads/system/uploads/attachment_data/file/430830/hmrc6.pdf and www.gov.uk/government/uploads/system/uploads/attachment_data/file/365889/dual-contracts.pdf and HMRC Employment Income Manual EIM40203, 40204. Different rules apply in relation to the 100% foreign earnings deduction available to seafarers (see **28.10** below).

(iii) **Duties deemed to be performed in the UK.** As regards certain overseas *employments under the Crown*, see **28.7** below.
Duties of *seafarers and aircraft crew* are treated as performed in the UK if (i) the voyage does not extend to a port outside the UK or (ii) the person concerned is UK-resident and either (a) the voyage or flight begins or ends in the UK or (b) it is a part, beginning or ending in the UK, of a voyage or flight which does not begin or end in the UK. As regards seafarers' duties on board ship, this does *not* apply for the purpose of determining whether the duties of an 'associated employment' are performed wholly outside the UK (for which see **28.6** below); for this purpose, duties performed on a ship during a voyage beginning or ending outside the UK (other than any part of it beginning and ending there), or on a part beginning or ending outside the UK of any other voyage, are treated as performed outside the UK. The UK includes areas designated under *Continental Shelf Act 1964, s 1(7)* for this purpose. A 'ship' does not include an offshore installation (within *ITA 2007, s 1001*). [*ITEPA 2003, s 40*]. See **28.10** below for the meaning of 'seafarer'.

(iv) **Duties performed in the UK: apportionment of earnings.** The extent to which general earnings are in respect of duties performed in the UK is to be determined on a just and reasonable basis. [*ITEPA 2003, s 41ZA*]. HMRC are likely to accept apportionment based on the split between UK and non-UK workdays calculated at the end of the year, except where this would be clearly inappropriate. The amount thus apportioned to non-UK duties is known as 'overseas workday relief'.

(v) **United Kingdom** for these purposes includes the UK sector of the continental shelf (under *Continental Shelf Act 1964, s 1(7)* as regards duties performed there in connection with exploration or exploitation activities. [*ITEPA 2003, s 41*].

'Exploration or exploitation activities' includes decommissioning (*Dunne v HMRC* FTT (TC 6979), [2019] UKFTT 96 (TC)).

(vi) **Directors' fees received by other companies.** Where a company (C) makes a payment to a director which would otherwise be employment income, and the director was appointed by another company (D), the payment is treated for tax purposes as a receipt of a trade carried on by D, provided:

- D's profits are within the charge to UK tax;
- under an agreement with D, the director is required to account to D for the payment;
- either (a) D had the right to appoint the director by virtue of its shareholding in, or an agreement with, C, or (b) D is not a company over which the director, or any person connected with the director, or the director together with connected persons, has control. For this purpose, 'control' has the meaning given by *ITA 2007, s 995*, and the following persons are connected with the director: the director's spouse, civil partner, parent, child, son-in-law and daughter-in-law.

[*ITTOIA 2005, s 16B; CTA 2009, s 40A; SI 2018 No 282, Arts 1, 5, 6*].

These statutory rules apply for 2018/19 onwards but applied previously by concession (see HMRC ESC A37). For directors' fees and other earnings received by professional practitioners, see **28.66** below.

(vii) **Changes in practice.** Where income dealt with under PAY AS YOU EARN (**53**) was received more than 12 months before the beginning of the year *in* which the assessment on the income is made, that assessment, if made after the period of 12 months following the year *for* which it is made, is to accord with the practice generally prevailing at the end of that period. [*ITEPA 2003, s 709*]. This cannot, however, displace an unqualified statutory exemption relating to the income in question (*Walters v Tickner* CA 1993, 66 TC 174).

(viii) **Divers.** See **75.29** TRADING INCOME for treatment of earnings of certain divers etc. as trading income.

Simon's Taxes. See **E4.101–E4.132, E4.403.**

Employee resident in the UK

[28.4] Subject to **28.5** below, where general earnings are for a tax year in which the employee is resident in the UK, the full amount of such earnings 'received' in a tax year (see **28.9** below) is taxable earnings in that year, whether or not the employment is held when the earnings are received. Where the tax year is a split year (see **63.19** RESIDENCE AND DOMICILE), the above does not apply to any part of general earnings that is 'excluded'. General earnings are '*excluded*' if they are attributable (on a just and reasonable basis) to the overseas part of the split year and are neither in respect of duties performed in the UK nor 'from overseas Crown employment subject to UK tax' (see **28.7** below).

[*ITEPA 2003, s 15*].

See **28.5** below for the various circumstances in which the earnings of an employee to whom the remittance basis applies fall within the above paragraph.

Employee to whom the remittance basis applies

[28.5] For the question of whether the remittance basis applies to an individual for a tax year, see **61.2** REMITTANCE BASIS) and note in particular that the remittance basis can only apply to an individual if he is resident but not domiciled in the UK, but that it does not automatically apply to such an individual.

Allowable deductions under the remittance basis

Expenses which would be allowable (see **28.16–28.19** below) against earnings taxed on the receipts basis are generally allowable against earnings taxed on the remittance basis. No deduction is, however, allowable for an amount paid in respect of the duties of an employment to which earnings taxed other than on the remittance basis relate. Capital allowances are not available for expenditure on plant or machinery (see **10.4**(ii) CAPITAL ALLOWANCES ON PLANT AND MACHINERY). [*ITEPA 2003, ss 353, 354*].

Employee not meeting section 26A test

[28.6] To the extent that they are 'chargeable overseas earnings' for a tax year, the full amount of general earnings remitted to the UK in any tax year (not necessarily the year in which they arose) is taxable earnings in that year, whether or not the employment is held when the earnings are remitted. See **61** REMITTANCE BASIS for the meaning of 'remitted to the UK' etc.

General earnings are overseas earnings for a tax year if the employee does not meet the 'section 26A test', the remittance basis applies to him, the employment is with a 'foreign employer' and the duties of the employment are performed wholly outside the UK. Generally, '*chargeable overseas earnings*' are the full amount of overseas earnings reduced by any deductions which would be allowable if they were taxable earnings (but see below under Dual contract arrangements). The '*section 26A test*' is explained in **28.7** below but in broad terms can be met only where the employee has a recent history of non-UK residence for three consecutive tax years.

'*Foreign employer*' means an individual, partnership or body of persons (including a company) resident outside, and not resident in, the UK.

Associated employments

Where the duties of any 'associated' employment are not performed wholly outside the UK, the chargeable overseas earnings are then limited to a reasonable proportion of the aggregate earnings (after allowable deductions) from all the employments, having regard to the nature of and the time devoted to duties performed outside and in the UK and to all other relevant considerations. Employments are '*associated*' if they are with the same employer, or the employers are under common control or one controls the other, control being as in *CTA 2010, ss 450, 451* (for companies) and *ITA 2007, s 995* (for individuals and partnerships). The amount by which chargeable overseas earnings are thus restricted falls back into charge under **28.4** above.

Split year treatment

Where the tax year is a split year (see **63.19** RESIDENCE AND DOMICILE), only so much of the full amount of overseas earnings as is attributable (on a just and reasonable basis) to the UK part of the split year is taken into account in computing chargeable overseas earnings. Where chargeable overseas earnings fall to be restricted due to the associated employments rule, only so much of the full amount of the aggregate earnings as is so attributable is taken into account.

Application to earnings for years before 2008/09

The above applies equally to general earnings for 2007/08 and earlier years where those earnings are remitted to the UK in 2008/09 or a later year, but only if in the year the earnings arose the employee was UK resident and either not domiciled in the UK or not ordinarily resident in the UK (see **63.34** RESIDENCE AND DOMICILE).

Dual contract arrangements

There is legislation aimed at preventing non-UK domiciled individuals from avoiding tax by dividing the duties of a single employment into a UK and an overseas contract. It operates by excluding general earnings for a tax year from being chargeable overseas earnings where all of conditions (a)–(d) below are met. The result is that those earnings become taxable as they arise and not on the remittance basis. The legislation can apply only where the employee does not meet the 'section 26A test'. The conditions are that:

(a) the employee holds a UK employment at a time in the tax year in question when he also holds the employment from which the overseas earnings arise (the '*relevant employment*');

(b) the UK employer is the same as the employer in respect of the relevant employment (the '*relevant employer*') or is 'associated' with the relevant employer (see above under Associated employments);

(c) the UK employment and the relevant employment are related to one another (see below); and

(d) the foreign tax rate that applies to the overseas earnings is less than 65% of the UK additional rate of tax (see **1.3** ALLOWANCES AND TAX RATES). Thus, with an additional rate of 45%, this condition is met if the foreign tax rate is less than 29.25% (i.e. 45 × 65%). The foreign tax rate is calculated in accordance with *ITEPA 2003, s 24B* by reference to the amount of foreign tax credit relief (see **27.2** DOUBLE TAX RELIEF) available against the overseas earnings, on the assumptions that claims are made on time and that all reasonable steps are taken to minimise tax payable.

If the tax year in question is a split year (see **63.19** RESIDENCE AND DOMICILE), (a) above applies by reference to any time in the UK part of the split year. As regards (c) above, *ITEPA 2003, s 24A(9)* gives a list of separate circumstances in which the two employments are to be assumed to be related to one another, though this is without prejudice to the generality of the condition. The list includes the circumstance where the employee is a director (as widely defined) or senior employee of either the UK or the relevant employer or is one of the higher paid employees of either employer. A director is excluded if he has no material interest (i.e. broadly if his and/or his associates' interests in the company do not exceed 5%) in either employer (but may still fall to be included as a senior or higher paid employee). For the purpose of this circumstance, 'UK employer' and 'relevant employer' include any person with which the UK employer or the relevant employer (as the case may be) is associated; if either employer is a company, the employer and all companies with which the employer is associated are considered as if they were one company.

There is a let-out from the legislation where:

- the duties of the relevant employment, if they were duties of the UK employment instead, could not lawfully be performed in the territory in which they *are* performed, by virtue of any regulatory requirements imposed by that territory; and
- the duties of the UK employment, if they were duties of the relevant employment instead, could not lawfully be performed in the part of the UK in which they *are* performed, by virtue of any regulatory requirements imposed by that part of the UK.

Where the legislation applies, foreign tax credit relief is available against any UK tax charge in the usual way. Earnings from each relevant employment (where more than one) are considered independently; i.e. the income and foreign tax credit relief available for all relevant employments are not aggregated for the purposes of the test in (d) above. Income taxable only as a result of this legislation is not within PAYE.

[*ITEPA 2003, ss 22–24, 24A, 24B, 721(1); FA 2008, Sch 7 para 82; FA 2013, Sch 46 para 26*].

For official guidance see www.gov.uk/government/publications/remittance-basis-of-taxation-dual-contracts-restrictions-for-foreign-domiciled-employees and HMRC Employment Income Manual EIM40109. For HMRC's long-standing approach to dual contract arrangements prior to the above legislation, see HMRC Employment Income Manual EIM77030. See also www.gov.uk/government/uploads/system/uploads/attachment_data/file/365889/dual-contracts.pdf. A non-UK domiciled employee may, for example, be offered two employment contracts, one with a UK employer and the other with an associated 'foreign employer', the intended effect being to create or maximise 'chargeable overseas earnings'. HMRC take the view that a dual contract arrangement based solely or mainly on a geographical split of employment duties without commercial underpinning is vulnerable to challenge on the grounds that there is in reality a single employment with duties in and outside the UK. In such cases, HMRC offices will fully investigate the facts and circumstances including the commercial rationale and context and assess an employee to tax where the evidence shows that there is in fact a single employment. Their view is that a dual contract arrangement is unlikely to work unless there are two distinguishable jobs.

Employee meeting section 26A test

[28.7] If they are 'foreign earnings' for a tax year, the full amount of general earnings remitted to the UK in any tax year (not necessarily the year in which they arose) is taxable earnings in that year, whether or not the employment is held when the earnings are remitted. See **61** REMITTANCE BASIS for the meaning of 'remitted to the UK' etc.

General earnings are '*foreign earnings*' for a tax year if the employee meets the 'section 26A test', the remittance basis applies to him and the earnings are neither in respect of duties performed in the UK nor 'from overseas Crown employment subject to UK tax'.

The section 26A test

An employee meets the '*section 26A test*' for a tax year (year 6) if he was:

- non-UK resident for years 3, 4 and 5; or
- UK resident for year 5 but non-UK resident for years 2, 3 and 4; or
- UK resident for years 4 and 5 but non-UK resident for years 1, 2 and 3; or
- non-UK resident for year 5, UK resident for year 4 and non-UK resident for years 1, 2 and 3.

The residence status of the employee prior to the three years of non-UK residence is of no relevance.

Split year treatment

Where the tax year is a split year (see **63.19** RESIDENCE AND DOMICILE), only so much of general earnings as is attributable (on a just and reasonable basis) to the UK part of the split year is taken into account in computing foreign earnings.

Overseas Crown employment subject to UK tax

General earnings are '*from overseas Crown employment subject to UK tax*' if they are from employment of a public nature under the Crown in respect of duties performed outside the UK, and are payable out of UK or NI public revenue. (This includes civil servants (*Graham v White* Ch D 1971, 48 TC 163 and *Caldicott v Varty* Ch D 1976, 51 TC 403) and HM Forces.) Earnings are excluded from this definition if they are so excluded by an order made by the Commissioners for HMRC. See HMRC Employment Income Manual EIM40209 for the text of the Commissioners' Order as amended. See also **28.69** below and **30.8**, **30.9** and **30.20** EXEMPT INCOME.

Application to earnings for years before 2008/09

The above applies equally to general earnings for 2007/08 and earlier years where those earnings are remitted to the UK in 2008/09 or a later year, but only if in the year the earnings arose the employee was UK resident and either not domiciled in the UK or not ordinarily resident in the UK (see **63.19** RESIDENCE AND DOMICILE).

[*ITEPA 2003, ss 26, 26A, 28; FA 2008, Sch 7 para 82; FA 2013, Sch 46 para 26*].

Employee non-resident in the UK

[28.8] If the earnings are either in respect of duties performed in the UK or 'from overseas Crown employment subject to UK tax' (see **28.7** above), the full amount of the general earnings 'received' (see **28.9** below) in a tax year is taxable earnings in that year, whether or not the employment is held when the earnings are received.

[*ITEPA 2003, s 27*].

Where duties are performed partly in the UK and partly overseas, time apportionment is generally used to calculate the amount of the general earnings attributable to duties performed in the UK (see HMRC Employment Income Manual EIM40110).

Receipts basis

[28.9] General earnings consisting of money (including money payments chargeable under the benefits code — see **28.21** below) are '*received*' at the earliest of the following times:

(i) the time when payment is actually made of, or on account of, the earnings;
(ii) the time when a person becomes entitled to such payment; and
(iii) where the person concerned is a 'director' of a company at any point in the tax year in which the time falls and the earnings are from employment with that company (whether or not as director), the earliest of:
  - the time when sums on account of earnings are credited in the company's accounts or records (regardless of any restriction on the right to draw those sums);
  - the time when a period of account ends and the amount of earnings for that period has already been determined; and
  - the time when the amount of earnings for a period of account is determined and that period has already ended.

A '*director*' is defined as being any of the following:

(a) a member of a board of directors, or similar body, which manages the company;
(b) a single director, or similar person, who manages the company;

(c) a member of the company, in cases where the company is managed by its members;

(d) any person in accordance with whose directions or instructions, given other than in a professional capacity, the directors, as defined in (a)–(c) above, are accustomed to act.

Non-money general earnings (e.g. benefits-in-kind) are generally treated as received in the tax year for which they are treated as earnings.

[*ITEPA 2003, ss 18, 19, 31, 32; FA 2017, Sch 2 paras 50, 62(2)(5)*].

Murphy v HMRC FTT (TC 7224), [2019] UKFTT 409 (TC) considered the treatment of a one-off retention payment and whether it was taxable over a period of more than one tax year or as a lump sum when received; the Tribunal found that the payment did not accrue over a period but was a reward for continuing in active employment until the date of payment. Applying the above provisions it was taxable in the year of receipt.

Foreign earnings deduction for seafarers

[28.10] Where the duties of a 'seafarer' are performed wholly or partly outside the UK and in the course of an 'eligible period' of 365 days or more, a deduction is made of 100% of the earnings for the duties attributable to that period (i.e. they are completely relieved from tax). Earnings for this purpose means earnings as reduced by capital allowances and all allowable deductions (including mileage allowance relief — see **28.91** below — and contributions to registered pension schemes). The type of earnings on which the 100% deduction is based and against which the deduction is set depends on the tax year — see the relevant headings below.

'Seafarers'

Employment as a '*seafarer*' for this purpose means an employment (other than certain Crown employment) consisting of the performance of duties on a ship (disregarding incidental duties elsewhere). For this purpose, a 'ship' does not include an offshore installation (within *ITA 2007, s 1001*). The distinction between a ship and an offshore installation was considered in *Torr v HMRC and related appeals* (Sp C 679), [2008] SSCD 679 and *Spowage v HMRC and related appeals* FTT (TC 142), [2009] SFTD 393. As a result of those appeals, HMRC revised their interpretation of the distinction — see HMRC Employment Income Manual EIM33105, 33106. The distinction was further considered in *Gouldson v HMRC* UT, [2011] STC 1902 and *Graham Paterson Limited and another v HMRC* FTT (TC 2127), [2012] UKFTT 446 (TC), 2012 STI 2990. Employment in the Royal Fleet Auxiliary Service is not Crown employment for these purposes, and employees are thus not prohibited from claiming the deduction; this applies by statute on and after 15 March 2018 but was previously applied on a concessionary basis (www.gov.uk/government/publications/income-tax-extending-seafarers-earnings-deduction-to-the-royal-fleet-auxiliary).

Duties performed on a ship during a voyage beginning or ending outside the UK (other than any part of it beginning and ending there), or on a part beginning or ending outside the UK of any other voyage, are treated as performed outside the UK for these purposes. Overseas duties merely incidental to a UK employment are treated as performed in the UK, as are duties on a voyage not extending to a port outside the UK.

Eligible period

An '*eligible period*' consists either (i) entirely of consecutive days of absence from the UK or (ii) of days of absence from the UK *plus* any earlier eligible period *plus* an intervening period in the UK not exceeding 183 days, provided that the total number of days in the UK in the intervening period and in the earlier eligible period is not more than one-half of the total number of days in the new eligible period. Successive intervening periods and periods of absence may continue to be eligible as long as these conditions are met in relation to each new period of absence.

A day of absence from the UK requires absence from the UK at the end of the day. For this purpose, the casting off from a UK berth (if allied to passage to an overseas port) is taken as the time of departure from the UK and the time of berthing as the time of arrival in the UK. If the voyage is between UK ports, the matter is determined by the ship's position at midnight (HMRC Employment Income Manual EIM33007).

A period spent in the UK during a contract of employment but not followed by a period abroad may not be included in the eligible period (*Robins v Durkin* Ch D 1988, 60 TC 700).

Leave periods

Earnings for duties attributable to an eligible period include earnings from that employment for a period of leave immediately following that period (and so qualify for the 100% deduction) to the extent that they are earnings for the tax year in which the eligible period ends.

Duties not performed outside UK

Where the duties of the employment or any 'associated employment' (see **28.6** above) are not performed wholly outside the UK, the earnings relievable as above may not exceed a reasonable proportion of the total earnings from all such employments, having regard to the nature of, and time devoted to, duties performed outside and in the UK and to all other relevant considerations.

The deduction

The deduction is given in respect of 'relevant general earnings'. '*Relevant general earnings*' means:

- taxable earnings under any of **28.4–28.7** above; and
- general earnings within **28.8** above (non-UK resident employees) which are for a period in which the employee is liable to tax in a European Economic Area (EEA) State (other than the UK) by reason of domicile or residence.

The EEA consists of: Austria, Belgium, Bulgaria, Cyprus, Czech Republic, Denmark, Estonia, Finland, France, Germany, Gibraltar, Greece, Hungary, Iceland, Ireland, Italy, Latvia, Liechtenstein, Lithuania, Luxembourg, Malta, Netherlands, Norway, Poland, Portugal, Romania, Slovakia, Slovenia, Spain, Sweden, Switzerland and the UK.

[*ITEPA 2003, ss 378–385; FA 2018, s 7*].

Overseas duties — travel etc. expenses

[28.11] For travelling expenses generally, see **28.84** *et seq.* below. For certain EU travel expenses of MPs etc., see **30.33** EXEMPT INCOME.

Where duties of an employment by an employee resident in the UK are performed abroad, the following deductions may be made from taxable earnings. In each case, apportionment applies where expenses are only partly attributable to the purpose in question. If the employer is a foreign employer (see **28.6** above), there is a condition that the employee be domiciled in the UK.

Where duties performed wholly outside the UK

(a) Travelling expenses incurred by the employee from any place in the UK to take up the overseas employment and to return on its termination.
(b) Board and lodging expenses outside the UK provided or reimbursed by the employer to enable the employee to perform the duties of the overseas employment.

Incidental duties performed in the UK are for these purposes treated as performed outside the UK. The deemed domicile rule at **63.35** RESIDENCE AND DOMICILE applies for 2017/18 onwards in determining if the employee is UK domiciled for the purposes of applying (b) above.

[*ITEPA 2003, ss 341, 376; F(No 2)A 2017, Sch 8 para 10(5)(6)*].

Where duties are performed partly outside the UK

Travel facilities, provided or reimbursed to the employee (so far as included in the taxable earnings), between any place in the UK and the place of performance outside the UK of any of the duties of an employment, either:

(i) for the employee, provided that the duties concerned can only be performed outside the UK, and that either the outward and return journeys are wholly exclusively for the purpose of performing those duties or returning after performing them, or the absence from the UK is wholly and exclusively for the purpose of performing those duties and the journeys are from the place of employment of the duties to the UK and return; or
(ii) where there is absence from the UK for a continuous period of 60 days or more, for his spouse (or civil partner) and any children of his under 18 (at beginning of outward journey) accompanying the employee at the beginning of the period of absence or visiting him during that period, including the return journey, but with a limit of two outward and return journeys per person in any tax year.

For these purposes, duties performed on a ship on a voyage extending to a port outside the UK are not treated under *ITEPA 2003, s 40(2)* (see **28.3**(iii) above) as performed in the UK, and the requirements as to place of performance of duties are correspondingly modified.

[*ITEPA 2003, s 370–372*].

More than one employment

Where two or more employments are held and at least one of them is performed wholly or partly outside the UK, and travelling expenses are incurred by the employee in travelling from one place where duties of one employment were performed to another place to perform duties of another, and either or both places are outside the UK, the expenses are deductible from the taxable earnings from the second employment.

[*ITEPA 2003, s 342*].

For travel on leave by HM Forces, see **28.69** below.

Simon's Taxes. See **E4.703G, E4.703H.**

Non-UK domiciled employees — travel costs and expenses

[28.12] A deduction may be allowed from taxable earnings for duties performed in the UK for the cost of travel facilities provided or reimbursed to a non-UK domiciled employee (so far as included in taxable earnings) for journeys ending on the date of arrival in the UK to perform the duties of the employment, or within five years after that date, and for expenses incurred by the employee on any such journey and reimbursed. The deduction applies to travel facilities provided, and expenses reimbursed:

(a) for any journey between the employee's usual place of abode (i.e. the country outside the UK where he normally lives) and any place in the UK in order to perform, or after performing, any duties of the employment; and
(b) where the employee is in the UK for the purpose of performing the duties of any such employment for a continuous period of 60 days or more, for any outward and return journey by his spouse (or civil partner) or child (under 18 at the beginning of the journey to the UK) between his usual place of abode and the place where any of those duties are performed in the UK, either to accompany him at the beginning of the period or to visit him during it (but limited to two outward and return journeys by any person in a tax year).

No deduction is, however, available unless, on a date on which he arrives in the UK to perform the duties, either:

(i) he was not resident in the UK in either of the two tax years immediately preceding that in which that date falls; or
(ii) he was not in the UK for any purpose at any time in the two years ending immediately before that date,

and if condition (i) is satisfied on more than one date in a tax year, relief is given by reference to the first such date only.

The deemed domicile rule at **63.35** RESIDENCE AND DOMICILE applies for the above purposes for 2017/18 onwards.

As regards the 60-day requirement under (b) above, HMRC accept that the 60-day requirement is satisfied where at least two-thirds of working days are spent in the UK over a period of 60 days or more, at both the start and end of which the employee is in the UK for the purpose of performing the duties of the employment. (Revenue Tax Bulletin December 2001 pp 900, 901 and HMRC Employment Income Manual EIM35050, 35055).

[*ITEPA 2003, ss 373–375, Sch 7 para 40; F(No 2)A 2017, Sch 8 para 10(3)(4)(6)*].

Foreign employer

Certain payments made by a non-UK domiciliary out of earnings from an employment with a 'foreign employer' (see **28.6** above) which do not reduce the employee's liability to UK income tax, but which are made 'in circumstances corresponding to those in which it would do so', may be allowed as a deduction from those earnings. The deemed domicile rule at **63.35** RESIDENCE AND DOMICILE applies for this purpose for 2017/18 onwards. [*ITEPA 2003, s 355; F(No 2)A 2017, Sch 8 para 10(2)(6)*]. See HMRC Employment Income Manual EIM32661 *et seq*.

Simon's Taxes. See **E4.701C, E4.703H.**

General earnings

[28.13] The income taxable as '*general earnings*' from employment (see **28.1**, **28.3** above) consists of '*earnings*', i.e. any salary, wages or fee, any gratuity or other incidental benefit of any kind obtained by an employee consisting of money or money's worth, and anything else constituting an emolument of the employment, together with anything treated under any statutory provision as earnings (e.g. benefits, see **28.20** below). '*Money's worth*' means something of direct monetary value to the employee or capable of being converted into money or something of such value. [*ITEPA 2003, ss 7(3)(5), 62; FA 2017, Sch 1 paras 10, 15*].

The general earnings taxable are those arising from the office or employment, regardless of by whom they are provided (see e.g. *Shilton v Wilmshurst* HL 1991, 64 TC 78).

It is well-established that the purpose of an employer in granting a benefit to an employee is an important factor in determining whether it is properly to be regarded as a reward or return for the employee's services (and thus within the charge to tax on general earnings) or whether it is bestowed on him for some other reason (*Tyrer v Smart* HL 1978, 52 TC 533; *Macleod and Mitchell Contractors Ltd v HMRC* UT, [2019] STC 993, [2019] UKUT 46 (TCC)).

Where an employee was granted a share option, the general earnings were the granting of the option (any subsequent increase in value not being general earnings) (*Abbott v Philbin* HL 1960, 39 TC 82). See, however, *Bootle v Bye; Wilson v Bye* (Sp C 61), [1996] SSCD 58, where payments under an agreement with a third party, and not the rights under the agreement, were held to be general earnings.

Where a payment is made for more than one reason, the payment is taxable if any one of the reasons is employment (*Kuehne + Nagel Drinks Logistics Ltd v HMRC* CA, [2012] STC 840). However, payments made up of different components paid for different reasons can be apportioned (*Reid v HMRC* FTT (TC 4872), [2016] SFTD 312, [2016] UKFTT 79 (TC)).

For an early and important statement of the concept of 'money's worth', see *Tennant v Smith* HL 1892, 3 TC 158. Whether money's worth received by an employee comes to him as an emolument may be a difficult question of fact. For modern examples see *Hochstrasser v Mayes* HL 1959, 38 TC 673 (compensation for loss on sale of house on transfer, held not taxable); *Wilcock v Eve* Ch D 1995, 67 TC 223 (payment for loss of rights under share option scheme, held not taxable), and contrast *Hamblett v Godfrey* CA 1986, 59 TC 694 (payment for loss of trade union etc. rights, held taxable); *Laidler v Perry* HL 1965, 42 TC 351; *Brumby v Milner* HL 1976, 51 TC 583; *Tyrer v Smart* HL 1978, 52 TC 533.

Cryptoassets (also known as cryptocurrency), e.g. bitcoin, received as employment income count as 'money's worth' and are subject to income tax on the value of the asset. See HMRC policy paper 'Cryptoassets: tax for individuals', 20 December 2019 at www.gov.uk/government/publications/tax-on-cryptoassets. The cryptoassets may also be readily convertible assets, meaning that PAYE must be applied (see **53.4** PAY AS YOU EARN).

Compensation from the employer for a change in the terms of the employment contract constitutes earnings (*Hill v HMRC* FTT (TC 4480), [2015] UKFTT 295 (TC)).

The meeting by the employer of a *pecuniary liability* of the employee constitutes money's worth, see e.g. *Hartland v Diggines* HL 1926, 10 TC 247 (tax liability), *Nicoll v Austin* KB 1935, 19 TC 531 (rates etc. of employee's residence), and *Glynn v CIR* PC 1990, 63 TC 162 (payment direct to school of child's school fees); this applies to payment of the employee's council tax (Revenue Press Release 16 March 1993), and may apply to payment of employees' parking fines. In the latter case, the tax treatment depends on whether the vehicle is owned by employer or by employee and whether the fixed penalty notice is affixed to the car or handed to the driver (see HMRC Employment Income Manual EIM21686 for a full summary). Congestion charges paid by an employer in connection with an employee-owned vehicle are taxable (see HMRC Employment Income Manual EIM21680). For specific items and legislation modifying the general rule, see **28.20** onwards below.

Hence, subject to any special legislation, board, lodging, uniforms etc. provided by the employer and not convertible into money are not taxable, but cash allowances *in lieu* are generally taxable, e.g. a clothing allowance to a 'plain-clothes' policeman (*Fergusson v Noble* CS 1919, 7 TC 176); a meals allowance when working abnormal hours (*Sanderson v Durbridge* Ch D 1955, 36 TC 239); lodging allowances to army personnel (*Nagley v Spilsbury* Ch D 1957, 37 TC 178); an allowance to meet extra cost of living abroad (*Robinson v Corry* CA 1933, 18 TC 411). Allowances in lieu of uniform to uniformed staff are, however, not treated as emoluments (see HMRC Employment Income Manual EIM10400). See **30.33** EXEMPT INCOME as regards accommodation allowances for Members of Parliament and **28.35–28.45** below as regards living accommodation generally. Where deductions were made from salary for board etc., held gross amount taxable (*Cordy v Gordon* KB 1925, 9 TC 304; *Machon v McLoughlin* CA 1926, 11 TC 83). Where a higher salary may be taken in lieu of the provision of free board and lodging, the value of the provision is taxable.

Where an employee used his car in the course of his duties, a lump sum and mileage allowances were held to be emoluments (*Perrons v Spackman* Ch D 1981, 55 TC 403). See **28.91** below as regards mileage allowances and travelling and subsistence allowances generally. 'Garage allowances' to salesmen with company cars were held to be taxable in *Beecham Group Ltd v Fair* Ch D 1983, 57 TC 733, but no liability arises in respect of workplace parking (see *ITEPA 2003, s 237*).

See **30.51** EXEMPT INCOME for an income tax exemption for payments made by a public body to a person holding a voluntary office with it, or performing services for it (e.g. jury service) for no financial benefit, where the payment is made solely to compensate the person for resulting loss of income from an employment elsewhere. See **30.4** EXEMPT INCOME for an exemption for bursaries paid to young people leaving local authority care to take up apprenticeships.

For the exemption of cash allowances paid to miners in lieu of free coal, see **28.52**(xi) below.

Employer's gift of clothing taxable on *second-hand* value (*Wilkins v Rogerson* CA 1960, 39 TC 344), but gift voucher available for use only in specified shop taxable on face value (*Laidler v Perry* HL 1965, 42 TC 351) but see **28.46** below for legislation now applicable although the case remains an important authority on what constitutes an emolument. Also see *Heaton v Bell* HL 1969, 46 TC 211 (assessment on free use of car connected with reduction in wages, but see company car legislation at **28.23** *et seq*. below).

Interest on money loaned interest-free, subject to conditions and repayable on demand, by the employer to a trust for the benefit of an employee held to be taxable emoluments (*O'Leary v McKinlay* Ch D 1990, 63 TC 729).

Endowment premiums paid by employers are taxable (*Richardson v Lyon* KB 1943, 25 TC 497). But trustees' payments out of fund set up by employers for assisting education of employees' children held not taxable on parent (*Barclays Bank v Naylor* Ch D 1960, 39 TC 256) but see now educational scholarships under **28.74** below. In *Ball v Johnson* Ch D 1971, 47 TC 155, a discretionary payment to employee for passing an examination was held not taxable (but see HMRC Employment Income Manual EIM01100, and see also **28.50** below for treatment of such awards as benefits-in-kind). Commission applied in taking up shares held taxable (*Parker v Chapman* CA 1927, 13 TC 677). In *Clayton v Gothorp* Ch D 1971, 47 TC 168, a loan to a former employee for improving qualifications, which became non-repayable when the employee returned to employer's service after qualification, was held taxable for year in which it became non-repayable. Where wages paid in gold sovereigns, held their market value to be taken as the measure of the emoluments (*Jenkins v Horn* Ch D 1979, 52 TC 591).

There is no liability on payments to an employee (or the employee's spouse or civil partner) under an insurance policy covering health or employment risks taken out by the employer, provided the conditions relating to such policies in *ITTOIA 2005, s 735* are met, and the employee has made contributions in respect of the premiums (see **30.29** EXEMPT INCOME). [*ITEPA 2003, s 325A*].

Whether lump sum payments etc. on taking up an employment are emoluments of the employment or non-taxable inducements is a question of fact. Signing-on fees to an amateur footballer on joining a Rugby League club were held to be taxable in *Riley v Coglan* Ch D 1967, 44 TC 481, distinguishing *Jarrold v Boustead* CA 1964, 41 TC 701. In *Shilton v Wilmshurst* HL 1991, 64 TC 78, a transfer fee paid by his old club to a professional footballer was taxable as an emolument of his new employment. A similar decision was reached in *HMRC v Smith & Williamson Corporate Services Ltd* UT 2015, [2016] STC 1393 (payment to an employee for delivering his existing client relationships to his new employer).

High-profile individuals, such as professional sportsmen, are often offered payments from those who want to use their name, image or other personal characteristic for commercial purposes. These characteristics are often referred to as image rights. If there is an agreement between an employer and an image rights company (IRC) under which the IRC contracts to supply to the employer certain promotional services of the player in return for fees paid by the employer to the IRC, there needs to be commercial justification for differentiating between payment for performance of the duties of the employment and payment for the image rights. See the guidance at www.gov.uk/guidance/tax-on-payments-for-use-of-image-rights and HMRC Employment Income Manual EIM00731. In *Sports Club plc v Inspector of Taxes* (Sp C 253), [2000] SSCD 443, payments by a sports club via third-party companies under separate promotional contracts relating to employees' services were held not to be chargeable as employment income. This case did not progress to the courts, so is seen as informative rather than creating a precedent (HMRC Employment Income Manual EIM00733). In *Hull City AFC (Tigers) Ltd v HMRC* FTT (TC 7074), [2019] SFTD 754, [2019] UKFTT 227 (TC), payments to an offshore company in respect of a footballer's overseas image rights were held to be earnings; the Tribunal found that the club did not have any clearly defined intention or plan to commercially exploit the player's overseas image rights and did not in fact do so, and that the rights had no commercial value.

The value of shares allotted to an accountant on becoming managing director of a company was held not to be taxable in *Pritchard v Arundale* Ch D 1971, 47 TC 680, but an opposite conclusion was reached on the facts in *Glantre Engineering Ltd v Goodhand* Ch D 1982, 56 TC 165. A lump sum payment for giving up rights to trade union representation was taxable (*Hamblett v Godfrey* CA 1986, 59 TC 694).

In *McLoughlin v HMRC* (Sp C 542), [2006] SSCD 467, an agreement entitling a new employee to a percentage of the proceeds of the employer partnership in the event of its being dissolved or sold during his term of employment was held to have not given rise to an emolument at the time of the agreement; instead, an emolument arose when the contingency occurred and was equal to the amount realised by the employee from the entitlement.

The reimbursement by an employer of an employee's bank charges, where these arise solely because of the employer's failure to make a salary payment on time, does not give rise to a tax charge (Revenue Tax Bulletin June 2003 p 1039).

Goodwill transferred to a company on incorporation of a business, if deliberately overvalued as an inducement for the individual concerned to take up employment with the company or in return for future services to be provided by the individual to the company, may (to the extent of the overvalue) be taxed as general earnings or, exceptionally, as a benefit (Revenue Tax Bulletin April 2005 p 1200).

For HMRC's view of the taxation implications of guaranteed selling price (or similar) schemes for houses as part of employee relocation packages, see Revenue Tax Bulletin May 1994 p 122 and April 1995 p 211.

Simon's Taxes. See **E4.4**.

Salary sacrifice arrangements

[28.14] For **2017/18** onwards (subject to transitional rules — see below), where benefits-in-kind are provided via 'salary sacrifice arrangements' (described in the legislation as optional remuneration arrangements), the tax charge is generally on the 'amount forgone' (see below) if greater than the amount that would normally be charged by reference to the cash equivalent of the benefit. For the precise charging provisions, see: **28.24** below for company cars; **28.26** for company car fuel; **28.27** for company vans and fuel; **28.32** for cheap loans; **28.37** and **28.41** for living accommodation; **28.77** for sick pay; **28.47** for non-cash vouchers; **28.48** for cash vouchers; **28.49** for credit tokens; and **28.54** below for other benefits. Low-emission company cars, i.e. those with a CO_2 emissions figure not exceeding 75g/km, are outside the scope of this rule.

For this purpose, a benefit provided for an employee is provided under '*salary sacrifice arrangements*' in so far as it is provided under:

(a) arrangements under which, in return for the benefit, the employee gives up the right (or a future right) to receive an amount of earnings;
(b) arrangements (other than of the kind in (a) above) under which the employee agrees to be provided with the benefit rather than an amount of earnings.

It does not matter whether the arrangements are made before or after the person's employment begins. References to a benefit provided for an employee include a benefit provided for a member of an employee's family or household. A 'benefit' includes any benefit or facility, regardless of its form and the manner of providing it. A benefit is to be regarded as provided under salary sacrifice arrangements in so far as it is just and reasonable to attribute the provision of the benefit to the arrangements in question. Where a benefit is provided partly under salary sacrifice arrangements and partly otherwise than under such arrangements, it is apportioned on a just and reasonable basis for the purpose of charging tax. The mere fact that under the arrangements the employee makes good, or is required to make good, any part of the cost of provision of a benefit does not mean that the benefit is (to any extent) provided otherwise than under salary sacrifice arrangements.

The amount forgone

The '*amount forgone*' is the amount of earnings in (a) or (b) above, whichever is relevant. Where, in order to determine the amount forgone with respect to a particular benefit, it is necessary to apportion an amount of earnings to the benefit, the apportionment is to be made on a just and reasonable basis.

[*ITEPA 2003, ss 69A, 69B; FA 2017, Sch 2 paras 1, 62(1)*].

Transitional

As stated, the above has effect for 2017/18 onwards. However, where the benefit is provided pursuant to pre-6 April 2017 arrangements, the above has effect for **2018/19** onwards instead as regards most benefits. The exception is where the benefit under the pre-6 April 2017 arrangements consists in a company car or van, or fuel for a company car or van, or living accommodation, or school fees. In these cases, the above has effect for **2021/22** onwards.

If any terms of a pre-6 April 2017 arrangement are *varied* on or after 6 April 2017, the benefit in question is treated, from the day the variation takes effect, as *not* being provided pursuant to pre-6 April 2017 arrangements. However, this does not apply to a variation which is required in connection with accidental damage to the benefit or otherwise for reasons beyond the control of the parties to the arrangements. It also does not apply to a variation which occurs in connection with a person's entitlement to statutory sick pay, statutory maternity pay etc. An arrangement is not regarded as being varied if the variation is directly in connection with COVID-19 (coronavirus) and no more than that (www.gov.uk/guidance/how-to-treat-certain-expenses-and-benefits-provided-to-employees-during-coronavirus-covid-19).

If pre-6 April 2017 arrangements are renewed on or after 6 April 2017, the renewed arrangements are treated as new arrangements, such that they are no longer protected by these transitional rules. This includes a renewal which takes effect automatically, as well as any other kind of renewal.

The above provisions regarding variation and renewal do not apply as regards school fees, for which see **28.54** below.

[*FA 2017, Sch 2 para 62(1)–(9)*].

Exclusion from exemptions

In addition to the above, a statutory exemption does not apply (whether to prevent or reduce liability to tax) in respect of a benefit or facility in so far as it is provided pursuant to salary sacrifice arrangements (as defined above). This has effect for 2017/18 onwards or, in the case of pre-6 April 2017 arrangements, 2018/19 onwards. However, it does *not* apply at all to exemptions under:

- *ITEPA 2003, ss 308, 308A* (employer contributions to registered pension schemes and certain overseas schemes — see **57.14** and **57.27** PENSION PROVISION);

- *ITEPA 2003, s 323A* (trivial benefits — see **28.51**(xxiii) below);
- *ITEPA 2003, s 307* in so far as it relates to the provision of retirement benefits as opposed to death benefits (see **28.52**(iii) below);
- *ITEPA 2003, s 317* (free or subsidised meals — see **28.52**(iv) below);
- *ITEPA 2003, s 244* (cycles and cyclists' safety equipment — see **28.52**(xxiii) below);
- *ITEPA 2003, s 266(2)(c)* (non-cash vouchers for use of cycles and cyclists' safety equipment — see **28.52**(xxiii) below);
- *ITEPA 2003, s 320C* (recommended medical treatment — see **28.52**(xxviii) below);
- *ITEPA 2003, s 308B* (independent pensions advice in respect of conversions and transfers of benefits — see **28.52**(xxx) below);
- *ITEPA 2003, s 308C* (employer-provided pensions advice — see **28.52**(xxix) below);
- *ITEPA 2003, ss 289A, 289D* (exemption for otherwise deductible items — see **28.53** below);
- *ITEPA 2003, s 239* (payments and benefits connected with taxable cars and vans and exempt heavy goods vehicles — see **28.23**, **28.30** below);
- *ITEPA 2003, ss 318, 318A* (workplace nurseries and other employer-contracted childcare — see **28.59**, **28.60** below);
- *ITEPA 2003, s 270A* (childcare vouchers — see **28.61** below);
- *ITEPA 2003, s 312A* (bonuses from indirectly employee-owned companies — see **28.56** below);
- *ITEPA 2003, s 310* (counselling services — see **28.63** below);
- *ITEPA 2003, s 309* (redundancy payments — see **28.71** below); and
- *ITEPA 2003, s 311* (retraining courses — see **28.83** below).

[*ITEPA 2003, s 228A; FA 2017, Sch 2 paras 49, 62(2)(3)*].

General

For guidance on the above provisions, see HMRC Employment Income Manual EIM44000. For guidance on salary sacrifice arrangements generally, see www.gov.uk/guidance/salary-sacrifice-and-the-effects-on-paye and HMRC Employment Income Manual EIM42750–42790.

Homeworkers

[28.15] Payments made by an employer to a 'homeworker employee' in respect of reasonable additional 'household expenses' incurred by him after that date in carrying out the duties of his employment at home are exempt from income tax. For these purposes, a '*homeworker employee*' is one who, by arrangement with the employer, regularly performs all or some of those duties at home, and '*household expenses*' are expenses connected with the day-to-day running of his home. [*ITEPA 2003, s 316A*].

Up to £6 per week or £26 per month can be paid without the need to justify the amount paid or to provide supporting evidence of the expenses incurred; for larger payments, the employer must be able to provide supporting evidence that the payment falls wholly within the exemption. These figures apply for 2020/21 onwards; previously the figures were £4 per week and £18 per month. See HMRC Employment Income Manual EIM01472–01478.

COVID-19 (coronavirus)

Employers may have required their employees to work from home for a limited period of time as a result of a temporary closure of the business premises during the 2020 pandemic. HMRC accept that for the duration of that period the above definition of 'homeworker employee' would be met. There is nothing in *ITEPA 2003 s 316A* above that requires the homeworking arrangement to be in place permanently or for a minimum period. If not already working from home before the pandemic, employees should be covered by the exemption.

HMRC have published guidance as to which expenses are taxable if an employee works from home due to the 2020 pandemic (see www.gov.uk/guidance/check-which-expenses-are-taxable-if-your-employee-works-from-home-due-to-coronavirus-covid-19). The Chartered Institute of Taxation (CIOT) also published a detailed guidance note on the various types of expenses relating to working from home (seewww.tax.org.uk/policy-technical/technical-news/ciot-guide-tax-implications-working-home).

See also the COVID-19 special measure below regarding home office equipment.

Unreimbursed homeworking expenses

HMRC provide guidance on the circumstances in which employees working at home can claim a deduction for a proportion of their household expenses. Any element of personal choice as to whether the employee works at home will fail the 'necessarily' test above and will thus preclude a deduction. HMRC will accept that a deduction is available where:

- the duties performed at home are substantive duties of the employment;
- those duties cannot be performed without the use of appropriate facilities;
- either no such facilities are available to the employee on the employer's premises or the nature of the job requires the employee to live too far away from the employer's premises for daily commuting to be a reasonable option; and
- at no time (either before or after the contract is drawn up) is the employee able to choose between working at the employer's premises or elsewhere.

If one or more of these conditions are not satisfied, HMRC will disallow any deduction, subject to the employee's normal right of appeal.

The expenses qualifying for relief under the guidance are limited to the additional unit costs of gas and electricity consumed while a room is being used for work, the metered cost of any water used in the performance of the duties and the unit costs of business telephone calls, including dial-up internet access. For simplicity, a deduction of £6 per week or £26 per month (exclusive of business telephone calls) will be allowed by HMRC without the need for supporting evidence of the actual costs incurred; employees claiming more than that will need to be able to justify it. These figures apply for 2020/21 onwards; previously the figures were £4 per week and £18 per month. No proportion of the following expenses is allowed: council tax, rent, unmetered water rates, mortgage costs and household insurance.

(HMRC Employment Income Manual EIM32760 *et seq.*).

Rental of a *second* telephone line at employee's home is allowed where used exclusively for business calls and there is a genuine business need for the line (but rental of first line or single line is not allowed) (HMRC Employment Income Manual EIM32940).

No deduction is permitted for broadband internet access where the employee is able to use the internet for non-business purposes (HMRC Employment Income Manual EIM32940).

COVID-19 special measure

There is no charge to tax for an amount reimbursed to an employee on or after 11 June 2020 and before 6 April 2021 in respect of 'home office equipment expenses'. HMRC will exercise their discretionary collection and management powers to forgo the collection of tax due on any reimbursed payments made on or after 16 March 2020 and before 11 June 2020, provided the statutory conditions would have been met if reimbursement had been made on or after 11 June 2020. '*Home office equipment expenses*' are expenses incurred by the employee in respect of equipment obtained for the sole purpose of enabling the employee to work from home during the 2020 COVID-19 (coronavirus) pandemic. It is a further condition that the provision of the equipment would have been exempt from income tax under *ITEPA 2003, s 316* (see **28.52**(i) below) if it had been provided directly to the employee by or on behalf of the employer; in particular, there must be no significant private use.

As required by *ITEPA 2003, s 210* (see **28.50** below) the exemption is conditional on the benefit of any reimbursement in respect of home-office equipment expenses being made available to all of the employer's employees generally on similar terms.

[*SI 2020 No 524*].

Unless the employer requires ownership to be transferred to it, the equipment is owned by the employee. There is also no benefit charge if the employee is permitted to keep the equipment if it is something they already own (see www.gov.uk/guidance/check-which-expenses-are-taxable-if-your-employee-works-from-home-due-to-coronavirus-covid-19 under Taxable benefit charge – returning office equipment).

Simon's Taxes. See E4.750, E4.774.

Allowable deductions

[28.16] A deduction is generally allowed from earnings from employment charged on the receipts basis (see generally **28.4–28.8** above) for expenses the holder of an office or employment is obliged to incur and pay which are either qualifying travelling expenses (see **28.17** below) or other amounts incurred wholly, exclusively and necessarily (*ITEPA 2003, s 336*) in the performance of the duties of the employment. See **28.19** below. A deduction is similarly allowed for amounts paid on behalf of, or reimbursed to, the employee and included in the earnings from the employment. The deductions allowable against earnings cannot exceed those earnings. There is a general prohibition on obtaining more than one deduction for any cost or expense.

Where the tax year is a split year (see **63.19** RESIDENCE AND DOMICILE), if the earnings from which a deduction is allowed include earnings that are 'excluded' (as in **28.4** above), the allowable deduction is reduced to a proportion of what it would be if the year were not a split year. That proportion is equal to the proportion that the non-excluded earnings bear to the total earnings. The deductions allowable against earnings cannot exceed the non-excluded earnings.

[*ITEPA 2003, ss 328(1), 329(1)(1A)(2)(3), 330, 333(1)(2), 334(1)(2), 335(1)(2), 336*].

- For deductions from earnings charged on the remittance basis, see **28.5** above.
- For travelling, subsistence and incidental overnight expenses etc. generally, see **28.84–28.93** below, and for other specific deductions, see below at **28.67** (flat rate deductions), **28.80** (subscriptions and professional fees) and **28.83** (training etc.).
- For provision of security assets and services for employees, see **28.75** below.
- For capital allowances where plant or machinery is provided for the purposes of an employment, see **10.4** CAPITAL ALLOWANCES ON PLANT AND MACHINERY.
- For expenditure by Members of Parliament on accommodation, see **28.45** below.
- For charitable donation payroll deduction scheme, see **14.18** CHARITIES AND CHARITABLE GIVING.
- For deduction of agents' fees by artistes, see **28.66** below.
- For indemnity insurance premiums, discharge of employee liabilities, and legal and other costs in relation to the employment, see **28.64** below.
- For deductions from earnings charged on the remittance basis, see **28.5** above.

For HMRC's view on specific employments and expenses, see HMRC Employment Income Manual EIM31622 *et seq*.

Simon's Taxes. See **E4.770–E4.797**.

Qualifying travelling expenses

[28.17] '*Qualifying travelling expenses*' (as referred to in **28.16** above) are amounts necessarily expended on travelling in the performance of the duties of the office or employment, or other travel expenses which:

(i) are attributable to necessary attendance at any place of the holder of the office or employment in the performance of those duties; and
(ii) are not expenses of either 'ordinary commuting' or 'private travel'.

Travel expenses include the actual costs of travel and also the **subsistence** expenditure and other associated costs (e.g. **overnight accommodation**) that are incurred as part of the cost of making the journey (HMRC Employment Income Manual EIM31815, 31820). Tax relief is therefore available for employees who are provided with living accommodation when working at a temporary workplace because of the 2020 COVID-19 (coronavirus) pandemic (www.gov.uk/guidance/how-to-treat-certain-expenses-and-benefits-provided-to-employees-during-coronavirus-covid-19).

Expenses of travel between two places at which duties are performed or different offices or employments under or with companies in the same group are treated as necessarily expended in the performance of the duties to be performed at the destination. Companies are members of the same group for this purpose if one is a 51% subsidiary (by reference to ordinary share capital) of the other or both are 51% subsidiaries of a third company. UK travelling expenses are deductible from earnings if the travel is between employments with two different companies (X and Y), at least one of those employments is as a director, and the individual was appointed a director of company X because company Y, or a company in the same group as company Y, has a shareholding or other financial interest in company X.

Where a vehicle other than a company vehicle is used for business travel, and either mileage allowance payments are received or mileage allowance relief is available in respect of that use (see **28.91** below), no deduction is available for qualifying travelling expenses incurred in connection with that use. However, this does *not* prevent relief for costs incurred other than 'in connection with' the use of the vehicle', e.g. subsistence and accommodation costs (HMRC Employment Income Manual EIM31815, 31820).

Ordinary commuting and private travel

'*Ordinary commuting*' means travel between home (or a place other than a 'workplace' in relation to the office or employment) and a place which is a 'permanent workplace' in relation to the office or employment. The fact that an employee may have a fully-equipped office at home does not prevent it from being her home (*Lewis v HMRC* (Sp C 690), [2008] SSCD 895) but see *Kirkwood v Evans* Ch D 2002, 74 TC 481 for a case in which weekly home to office travel by a homeworker was held to be ordinary commuting.) '*Private travel*' means travel between home and a place that is not a 'workplace', or between two places neither of which is a 'workplace'. Travel which for practical purposes is substantially ordinary commuting or private travel is treated as such. As regards emergency call-outs, see **28.84** below.

A '*workplace*' in relation to an employment is a place at which attendance is necessary in the performance of the duties of the office or employment. It is a '*permanent workplace*' if it is not a 'temporary workplace' and attendance there in the performance of those duties is regular. Except as below, it is a '*temporary workplace*' if the purpose of attendance there is to perform a task of limited duration or some other temporary purpose.

A workplace is *not* a temporary workplace if attendance there is in the course of a 'period of continuous work' at that place lasting more than 24 months or comprising all (or almost all) of the period for which the office or employment is likely to be held, or if it is reasonable to assume that it will be in the course of such a period. See *Phillips v Hamilton; Macken v Hamilton* (Sp C 366), [2003] SSCD 286. A '*period of continuous work*' at a place is a period over which the duties of the employment fall to be performed to a significant extent at that place (i.e. 40% or more of working time is spent there, see HMRC Booklet 490 para 3.13). Actual or contemplated modifications of the place at which the duties are performed which do not have any substantial effect on the journey or on the travelling expenses are disregarded. Where, due to the COVID-19 (coronavirus) pandemic, an employee became furloughed or required to work from home at a time when they were travelling to a temporary workplace, the period of furlough or working from home is part of the period of continuous work (www.gov.uk/guidance/how-to-treat-certain-expenses-and-benefits-provided-to-employees-during-coronavirus-covid-19).

A place regularly attended in the performance of the duties of the office or employment which forms the base from which those duties are performed, or which is the place at which the tasks to be carried out in the performance of those duties are allocated, is treated as a permanent workplace. Similarly where the duties are defined by reference to an area (whether or not requiring attendance outside the area), and attendance is required at different places in the area (none of them a permanent workplace) in the performance of the duties, then that area is treated as a permanent workplace if it would be so treated (as above) were it a place.

In *Reed Employment plc v HMRC* CA, [2015] STC 2516, a case in which the taxpayer's business was to provide temporary employees to its client businesses, it was decided that each temporary assignment represented a separate contract of employment and each location at which an employee worked was a permanent workplace; travel allowances paid by the taxpayer were thus ordinary commuting expenses and not deductible by the employees. It was further held that the company had made single global payments to employees in which the payment for travel expenses was simply part of the their overall wages and thus their earnings for tax purposes.

In *Amara Akhtar v HMRC* FTT (TC 7646), [2020] UKFTT 160 (TC), the FTT rejected HMRC's view that a mobile care worker's travel from home to first client of the day, and from last client of the day to home, was ordinary commuting.

[*ITEPA 2003, ss 337–339, 340, 340A, 359*].

See **28.18** below as regards travelling expenses where services are provided through an employment intermediary, and see **28.94** below as regards local councillors.

For leading articles explaining the above rules, with numerous examples, see Revenue Tax Bulletin December 1997 pp 477–485, February 1998 pp 497–505 and April 1998 pp 524–527. See HMRC Employment Income Manual EIM77010 for HMRC's approach to benefits and expenses paid to employees sent on secondments not exceeding 24 months, in particular those sent by an overseas employer to work in the UK. HMRC Booklet 490 'Employee Travel: A Tax and NICs Guide for Employees' also provides comprehensive general guidance, and see generally HMRC Employment Income Manual EIM32005 *et seq*.

Simon's Taxes. See **E4.780**.

Travelling expenses where services provided through intermediary

[28.18] Relief is denied for home-to-work travel expenditure where an individual (*'the worker'*):

- personally provides services (other than 'excluded services') to another person (*'the client'*);
- those services are provided under arrangements (as widely defined) involving an 'employment intermediary', and not under a contract made directly between the worker and the client (or a person connected with the client).

However, the denial of relief does *not* apply if it is shown that the manner in which the worker provides the services is not subject to (or to the right of) supervision, direction or control by any person.

'Excluded services' are services provided wholly in the client's home.

Where the denial of relief applies, it is achieved by treating each such provision of services (*'engagement'*) as a separate employment for the purpose of the qualifying travelling expenses rules at **28.17** above, so that each workplace will be a permanent workplace. Thus, home-to-work travel will be ordinary commuting and will not qualify for relief.

For these purposes, an *'employment intermediary'* is a person or body, other than the worker or the client, who carries on a business of supplying labour. It is of no consequence whether or not this business is carried on with a view to profit and whether or not it is carried on in conjunction with any other business. The intermediary might be, for example, an agency, a recruitment or employment business, an umbrella company, a managed service company (MSC) or (but see below) a personal service company (PSC).

In determining whether the denial of relief applies, no regard is to be had to any arrangements of which a main purpose is to secure that it does not apply (or does not to some extent apply).

For draft official guidance on these provisions see www.gov.uk/government/publications/employment-intermediaries-travel-expense-guidance.

Personal service companies

If the engagement is made via a PSC such that any of the conditions at **58.4** PERSONAL SERVICE COMPANIES ETC. is met (but see below), the 'supervision, direction or control' let-out above does not have effect.

If the PSC rules are not applicable to an engagement because the condition at **58.2**(d) PERSONAL SERVICE COMPANIES ETC. is not met, but one of the conditions at **58.4** would otherwise have been met (but see below), the engagement is removed from the ambit of these provisions.

Similarly, for 2017/18 onwards, if the PSC rules are not applicable to an engagement because the condition at **58.25**(d) PERSONAL SERVICE COMPANIES ETC. is not met, but one of the conditions at **58.26** would otherwise have been met, the engagement does not come within these provisions.

However, none of the three rules above is of any application if the employment intermediary is an MSC. For this purpose only, an MSC is a company which is a MSC for the purposes of the rules in **47** MANAGED SERVICE COMPANIES or which would have been such an MSC if the criterion at **47.2**(c) did not exist.

Where the employment intermediary is a company, and it is necessary to determine whether the applicable conditions at **58.4** PERSONAL SERVICE COMPANIES ETC. either are met or would have been met, **58.4**(b) is ignored for this purpose.

Anti-avoidance

The following applies if the client or a 'relevant person' provides the employment intermediary (whether before or after the worker begins to provide the services) with a fraudulent document which is intended to constitute evidence that, by virtue of the 'supervision, direction or control' let-out above, the denial of relief does not apply in relation to the services. It has effect only if PAYE deducted and accounted for is understated by the employment intermediary as a result. A '*relevant person*' is a person (other than the client, the worker or a person connected with the employment intermediary) who:

- is resident in the UK or has a place of business there; and
- is party to a contract with the employment intermediary (or a person connected with it) under which the services are provided or payments in respect of the services are made.

For the purpose of recovering the understated amount (the '*unpaid tax*'), the worker is to be treated as having an employment with the client or relevant person who provided the fraudulent document. The duties of that employment consist of the services provided by the worker. The client or relevant person must then account for the unpaid tax under PAYE as if it arose in respect of earnings from that employment.

[*ITEPA 2003, s 339A; FA 2016, s 14(1)(6); FA 2017, Sch 1 paras 12, 15*].

In determining for all the above purposes whether persons are connected, the rules in **19** CONNECTED PERSONS) apply.

Transfer of PAYE debt

Where the employment intermediary is a company, HMRC can recover from a director of the company any debt owed as a result of the denial of relief rules not being operated correctly. See **53.11** PAY AS YOU EARN.

Restrictions on deductions

[28.19] The requirements that expenditure be incurred 'necessarily' and (other than in the case of qualifying travelling expenses within **28.17** above) 'in the performance of the duties' impose additional restrictions on the allowability of deductions from earnings compared with those generally deductible under the rules for computing trading income. 'Necessarily' has been held to require that every holder of the office or employment would have to incur the expenditure, regardless of personal circumstances (see *Ricketts v Colquhoun*

HL 1925, 10 TC 118, *Lewis v HMRC* (Sp C 690), [2008] SSCD 895). As regards 'in the performance of the duties', it follows that expenses incurred prior to entering upon duties or merely in preparation for them or to better qualify the employee for performing them are not allowed (see, for example, *Ansell v Brown* Ch D 2001, 73 TC 338, *Emms v HMRC* (Sp C 668), [2008] SSCD 618 and, in relation to training costs, *Snowdon v Charnock* (Sp C 282), [2001] SSCD 152, *HMRC v Decadt* Ch D 2007, 79 TC 220 and *Perrin v HMRC* (Sp C 671), [2008] SSCD 672). See *Nolder v Walters* KB 1930, 15 TC 380, air pilot allowed hotel expenses because incurred *in course of duty*, but not car and telephone *merely in preparation for it*, and *Bhadra v Ellam* Ch D 1987, 60 TC 466 where a doctor's travelling and secretarial expenses in relation to locum posts obtained through medical agencies were not allowed, as his duties commenced only on arrival at the hospital concerned. But contrast *Pook v Owen* HL 1969, 45 TC 571 where a GP with a part-time hospital appointment was allowed his expenses of travelling to the hospital from his home (where his surgery was), not covered by his mileage allowance, because, on the facts, his home as well as the hospital was a place where he carried out the duties of his appointment. See also *Gilbert v Hemsley* Ch D 1981, 55 TC 419 and **28.84** below generally. Airline pilots who are obliged upon leaving their employment to repay costs of training cannot deduct the amount repaid (*Hinsley v HMRC; Milsom v HMRC* (Sp C 569), [2007] SSCD 63).

Employees' costs of provision, upkeep, replacement or repair of protective clothing or of uniforms (recognisable as such) are allowable where their duties require them to be worn (HMRC Employment Income Manual EIM32465 *et seq.*). See, in particular, the flat rate deductions for laundry costs at **28.67** below.

Expenses of a part-time appointment not allowable against employment income may not be deducted in computing the trading income of an associated business (*Mitchell & Edon v Ross* HL 1961, 40 TC 11).

Entertaining expenses are not allowed, but see **75.76** TRADING INCOME for exceptions. However where an employer is not allowed a deduction for expenditure on business entertainment paid by him, directly or indirectly, to a member of staff, and that sum is also taxable earnings of the employee, the employee is allowed an equivalent deduction from taxable earnings for expenses defrayed out of that sum. [*ITEPA 2003, ss 356–358; SI 2004 No 2310, Sch para 68*].

Expenses not allowed include: employment agency fees (*Shortt v McIlgorm* KB 1945, 26 TC 262); meal expenses paid out of meal allowances (*Sanderson v Durbridge* Ch D 1955, 36 TC 239); living expenses paid out of living allowances when working away from home (*Elderkin v Hindmarsh* Ch D 1988, 60 TC 651); headmaster's course to improve background knowledge (*Humbles v Brooks* Ch D 1962, 40 TC 500); qualified psychiatrist's costs of continuing professional development (*Consultant Psychiatrist v HMRC* (Sp C 557), [2006] SSCD 653); articled clerk's examination fees (*Lupton v Potts* Ch D 1969, 45 TC 643); cost of ordinary clothing (*Hillyer v Leeke* Ch D 1976, 51 TC 90; *Woodcock v CIR* Ch D 1977, 51 TC 698; *Ward v Dunn* Ch D 1978, 52 TC 517; *Williams v HMRC* FTT (TC 397), [2010] UKFTT 86 (TC)); rental of telephone installed at employer's behest, but not used *wholly* and *exclu-*

sively in performance of duties (*Lucas v Cattell* Ch D 1972, 48 TC 353); telephone and other expenses of consultant anaesthetist (*Hamerton v Overy* Ch D 1954, 35 TC 73); journalists' expenditure on newspapers and periodicals (*Fitzpatrick and Others v CIR, Smith v Shuttleworth and Others* HL 1994, 66 TC 407); rugby player's expenditure on dietary supplements (*Ansell v Brown* Ch D 2001, 73 TC 338; *Emms v HMRC* (Sp C 668), [2008] SSCD 618); and payment by a director under a personal guarantee of the company's indebtedness (*Guarantor v HMRC* (Sp C 703), [2008] SSCD 1154).

Expenses not allowed also include: any excess cost of living in place where required by work *Bola v Barlow* KB 1949, 31 TC 136; *Collis v Hore (No 1)* KB 1949, 31 TC 173; *Robinson v Corry* CA 1933, 18 TC 411); cost of domestic assistance where wife employed (*Bowers v Harding* QB 1891, 3 TC 22); cost of looking after widower's children (*Halstead v Condon* Ch D 1970, 46 TC 289).

Where an employer grants a salary increase to an employee to cover expenses, that informal method of reimbursement cannot of itself make the expenses allowable if they would not be so on general principles (*Ling v HMRC* FTT (TC 1629), [2011] UKFTT 793 (TC); 2012 STI 145).

Benefits-in-kind

[28.20] Generally, if an employee receives money or money's worth from his employment he is chargeable to tax on that amount (see **28.13** above). However, he or his family may receive benefits by reason of his employment where special legislation is required if taxation is to apply. That legislation (the 'benefits code' — see **28.21** below) is contained in *ITEPA 2003, Pt 3 Chs 3–7, 10*. A benefit provided by a third party (e.g. a car provided by a car dealer to a football player for promotional purposes) is potentially within the benefits charging provisions where it is provided by reason of the employment.

Where the provision charging a particular benefit does not specify the year of charge, the earnings are treated as received at the time the benefit is provided. [*ITEPA 2003, ss 19(4), 32(4)*].

See **56.1** PENSION INCOME as regards the provision of benefits to retired employees.

Many of the exceptions listed at **28.52** below from the special charge on benefits apply also to amounts in respect of which a charge might also arise under the general charge on employment income. As a general rule there is a relief from all income tax liability in respect of such amounts. Where an amount is taxable both as general earnings and under the benefits code, only the amount (if any) by which the charge under the benefits code exceeds that as general earnings is brought in under the benefits code. This does not apply to the provision of living accommodation (see **28.35** below) or in relation to certain employee shareholdings taxed under the benefits code (see **71.12** SHARE-RELATED EMPLOYMENT INCOME AND EXEMPTIONS). [*ITEPA 2003, s 64*]. See also HMRC Employment Income Manual EIM21640.

See also **53.25** PAY AS YOU EARN as regards PAYE settlement agreements whereby the employer accounts for tax on minor benefits, which do not then count as employees' income.

For HMRC guidance on how to treat certain expenses and benefits provided to employees during the 2020 COVID-19 (coronavirus) pandemic, see www.gov.uk/guidance/how-to-treat-certain-expenses-and-benefits-provided-to-employees-during-coronavirus-covid-19.

The benefits code

[28.21] The benefits code covers expenses payments (see **28.22** below) and benefits-in-kind in respect of the following:

(a) cars, vans and related benefits — see **28.23**;
(b) cheap loans — see **28.32**;
(c) living accommodation — see **28.35**;
(d) vouchers and credit tokens — see **28.46**; and
(e) employment-related benefits not within (a)–(d) above — see **28.50**.

All provisions of the benefits code apply in full to all employees (including directors), subject to special rules for ministers of religion (see **28.62** below) and an exemption for home care workers (see **28.52**(xxxi) below). [*ITEPA 2003, s 63*].

Expenses payments

[28.22] All payments to an employee by reason of the employment in respect of expenses, including sums put at employee's disposal and paid away by him, are taxable. All payments by the employer are 'by reason of the employment' unless the employer is an individual and the payment is made in the normal course of his domestic, family or personal relationships. Deductions may be made as under **28.5** (remittances), **28.11** (under *ITEPA 2003, s 341* or *s 342* (travelling expenses on commencement or termination of employment or between employments)), **28.16** (general allowable deductions), **28.17** (under *ITEPA 2003, s 340* or *s 340A* (travel between group or linked employments), **28.62** (clergymen etc.), **28.64** (employee liabilities and expenses) and **28.80** (subscriptions and professional fees). [*ITEPA 2003, ss 70–72*].

Exemptions are available for expenses payments to employees where the employee would have been eligible for a deduction had he incurred and paid the expenses himself – see **28.53** below.

See **53.25** PAY AS YOU EARN as regards PAYE settlement agreements whereby employer accounts for tax on minor payments of expenses within the agreement, which do not then count as employees' income.

For HMRC guidance on how to treat certain expenses and benefits provided to employees during the 2020 COVID-19 (coronavirus) pandemic, see www.gov.uk/guidance/how-to-treat-certain-expenses-and-benefits-provided-to-employees-during-coronavirus-covid-19.

Motor vehicles provided for private use

[28.23] The provision by an employer to an employee, by reason of the employment, of a car or van partly or wholly for his 'private use', without the transfer of any property in it, is the subject of a special basis of charge. '*Private use*' means any use other than for travel the expenses of which would, if incurred and paid by the employee, have been deductible from his earnings, and a car or van is deemed to be available for private use unless the terms on which it is made available prohibit such use *and* it is not so used. The charge applies equally where the car or van is similarly provided to a member of the employee's family or household, and references below to 'employee' should be read with this in mind.

A car or van provided by an employer is provided 'by reason of the employment' unless:

- the employer is an individual and the provision is made in the normal course of his domestic, family or personal relationships; or
- the vehicle is hired to the employee in the normal course of a business carried on by the employer consisting of the hiring of similar vehicles to the public, and in hiring that vehicle the employee is acting as an ordinary member of the public.

It is stipulated that, where these provisions apply to a car or van, the car or van is a benefit even if it is made available to the employee etc. on terms which constitute a 'fair bargain'. '*Fair bargain*' refers to a situation in which the employee receives something from his employer at the same cost, and subject to the same terms and conditions, as a member of the public or other independent third party dealing with the employer on an arms-length basis.

[*ITEPA 2003, ss 114, 116, 117, 118, 120, 120A, 154, 154A, 171(1); FA 2016, s 7(4)–(7)(9); FA 2017, Sch 2 paras 19, 21, 22, 36, 37, 62(2)(4)*].

See **28.24** below as regards cars and **28.27** below as regards vans.

See **28.84** below as regards business use where more than one place of work. See also *Gilbert v Hemsley* Ch D 1981, 55 TC 419. As regards special arrangements for employees in the motor industry, see HMRC Employment Income Manual EIM23800, 23885. See **28.31** below for an exemption for emergency vehicles.

The special basis of charge continues to apply where the car is in the *co-ownership* of the employer and employee (*Christensen v Vasili* Ch D 2004, 76 TC 116; *GR Solutions Ltd v HMRC* UT, [2013] UKUT 278 (TCC), 2013 STI 2471) and where the car is *leased* by the employer to the employee (*Whitby and another v HMRC* FTT (TC 255), 2010 STI 296).

A car provided by a third party (e.g. by a car dealer to a football player for promotional purposes) is within these provisions where it is provided by reason of the employment (HMRC Employment Income Manual EIM23260). In *Cooper and others v HMRC* FTT (TC 2120), [2012] UKFTT 439 (TC), 2012 STI 2988, cars owned by a partnership whose only business was providing services to a company of which the partners were directors were held to have been provided by reason of the directors' employment with the company.

Where the special basis of charge applies, no other charge arises in respect of any expenses or reimbursements etc. in relation to the vehicle or in respect of vouchers for their provision (e.g. insurance, road tax, congestion charges). It appears that this does not apply to the payment of fines by the employer (although parking fines may escape liability in certain circumstances — see HMRC Employment Income Manual EIM21686). The provision of a driver is a separate benefit under **28.50** below (subject to an expense claim for business use). [*ITEPA 2003, ss 239, 269; FA 2017, Sch 2 paras 53, 62(2)(4); FA 2019, s 7(6)(7)*]. See **28.52**(xx) below for the general exemption of the provision of a mobile phone. The provision of a personalised registration number does not enter into the computation under the special basis of charge under **28.24** below, and is normally excluded from charge as above. (Revenue Tax Bulletin December 1994 p 177). The provision of a benefit which could equally be enjoyed by the employee when using a car of his own (e.g. a season ticket for a toll bridge) is not excluded from charge (HMRC Employment Income Manual EIM23035).

In the case of a low emission car (one whose CO_2 emissions figure does not exceed 75g/km), the mere fact that an employee is offered an alternative (for example, a cash alternative) to the car does not make the benefit chargeable under the general earnings rules as opposed to the special company car provisions. Before 2017/18, this rule applied for all cars and also for vans; it continues to so apply for all years before 2021/22 as regards cars and vans provided pursuant to pre-6 April 2017 salary sacrifice arrangements (see **28.14** above). [*ITEPA 2003, s 119; FA 2017, Sch 2 paras 20, 62(2)(4)*].

Compensation to an employee from whom a company car was withdrawn following a change of policy by the employer was held to be a taxable emolument in *Bird v Martland; Bird v Allen* Ch D 1982, 56 TC 89.

Where the special basis of charge applies to provision of a car or van, a separate charge also arises in respect of provision of any fuel for private use (see **28.26** and **28.27** below for car and van fuel respectively).

As regards mileage allowances for the provision by employees of fuel for business travel in company cars, see **28.91** below.

Definition of car

A car is any mechanically propelled road vehicle *except* (i) a vehicle constructed primarily for carrying goods, (ii) a vehicle of a type unsuitable and not commonly used as a private vehicle, (iii) a motor cycle and (iv) an invalid carriage. [*ITEPA 2003, s 115*]. A car owned by the fire brigade and equipped with a flashing light and other emergency equipment was held to be within (ii) (*Gurney v Richards* Ch D 1989, 62 TC 287). A motor home was adjudged to be a car in *Morris v HMRC; County Pharmacy Ltd v HMRC* Ch D, [2006] STC 1593. In *Jones v HMRC* FTT (TC 1958), [2012] UKFTT 265 (TC); 2012 STI 2246, a Land Rover Discovery might have become primarily suited for the conveyance of goods but this was the result of modifications to the vehicle and not because it was *constructed* for such a purpose.

Definition of van

A van is a mechanically propelled road vehicle, other than a motor cycle, of a construction primarily suited for the conveyance of goods or burden and designed (or adapted) not to exceed a laden weight of 3,500 kgs. in normal use. [*ITEPA 2003, s 115*]. There was apparent confusion initially about the status of 'double cab pick-ups', and HMRC now follow the definitions used for VAT purposes. This means that a double cab pick-up that has a payload of 1 tonne (1,000 kg) or more is regarded as a van. Payload means gross vehicle weight (or design weight) less unoccupied kerb weight; for more details see HMRC Employment Income Manual EIM23150.

Disabled employees

There is a limited exemption for '*disabled employees*', i.e. those with a physical or mental impairment which has a substantial and long-term adverse effect on their ability to carry out normal day-to-day activities. Where a car is made available to such an employee, without any transfer of the property in it, no benefits charge arises on provision of the car, provided that:

(a) the car has been adapted for the employee's special needs (or has an automatic transmission (see **28.24** below) because the employee can only drive such a car); and

(b) the terms of its provision prohibit private use except for home-to-work travel or travel in connection with certain training course, and those terms are complied with.

The provision of, or payment or reimbursement of the cost of, fuel for the car does not give rise to an income tax liability where the conditions in (b) above are met. See also **28.84** below.

Parking facilities

The provision of car and van parking facilities for an employee at or near his place of work (including such provision in relation to a privately-owned vehicle) constitutes neither earnings nor a benefit. [*ITEPA 2003, ss 237, 247*].

Members of same family or household

Where two members of the same family or household are each supplied with a car for their private use by the same employer, each is charged separately according to his/her own usage but is not chargeable in respect of the car supplied to the other. If one of them (M) is in lower-paid employment as a minister of religion (see **28.62** below), the other is not chargeable in respect of the car supplied to M. The above applies equally to any car fuel scale charge, and applies to vans as it does to cars. [*ITEPA 2003, ss 169, 169A*].

Simon's Taxes. See **E4.625**, **E4.630**.

Cars for private use

[28.24] The cash equivalent of the benefit (see **28.54** below) of a company car is a percentage of the 'price of the car' dependent on CO_2 emissions and certain related factors. The cash equivalent is reduced *pro rata* if the car was 'unavailable' for part of the tax year (see below). It is reduced finally by any payment made by the employee for private use (see below). The '*price of the car*' is its 'list price' or, if it has no list price, its 'notional price' (see below) plus in each case the price of any accessories that fall to be taken into account (see below).

In certain circumstances for 2017/18 onwards (or, in some cases, 2021/22 onwards), the taxable benefit of a car provided pursuant to salary sacrifice arrangements is not based on the cash equivalent but computed under separate rules. See below under Salary sacrifice arrangements.

Appropriate percentage

The percentage of the price of the car which determines the cash equivalent of the benefit (the '*appropriate percentage*') depends on the 'applicable CO_2 emissions figure' for the car, expressed in grams per kilometre (g/km).

For 2020/21 onwards, for cars first registered on or after 6 April 2020, the CO_2 emissions figure for the purposes of company car tax is based on the Worldwide Harmonised Light Vehicle Test Procedures (WLTP) (see below under The applicable CO_2 emissions figure). To help support the introduction of WLTP, appropriate percentages for cars measured under WLTP are generally two percentage points fewer for 2020/21 than those for other cars.

Current year

For **2020/21**, for cars *registered before 6 April 2020* and thus not subject to WLTP, the appropriate percentage (AP) for cars with zero CO_2 emissions is 0%. The AP for cars in the 1–50g/km band ranges from 2% to 14% depending on the electric range of the car (i.e. the distance it can be driven in electric mode without recharging); it is 2% for an electric range of 130 miles or more, 5% for 75 to 129 miles, 8% for 40 to 69, 12% for 30 to 39, and 14% for a range of less than 30 miles. A rate of 15% applies if the emissions figure is between 51g/km and 54g/km inclusive. A 16% rate applies if the emissions figure is between 55g/km and 59g/km inclusive. A 17% rate applies if the emissions figure is between 60g/km and 64g/km inclusive. A rate of 18% applies if the emissions figure is between 65g/km and 69g/km inclusive. A 19% rate applies if the emissions figure is between 70g/km and 74g/km inclusive. A rate of 20% applies at an emissions level of 75g/km, and this increases by one percentage point for each additional 5g/km, up to a maximum rate of 37% which applies at 160g/km and above.

If a CO_2 emissions figure of less than 75g/km is not a whole number it is rounded down to the nearest whole number. If a CO_2 emissions figure of 75g/km or more is not a multiple of 5 it is rounded down to the nearest multiple of 5. If an electric range figure is not a whole number it is rounded *up* to the nearest whole number.

For **2020/21**, for cars *registered on or after 6 April 2020* and thus subject to WLTP, the AP for cars with zero emissions is 0%. The AP for cars in the 1–50g/km band ranges from 0% to 12% depending on the electric range of the car; it is 0% for an electric range of 130 miles or more, 3% for 75 to 129 miles, 6% for 40 to 69, 10% for 30 to 39, and 12% for a range of less than 30 miles.

The AP is 13% for the 51–54g/km band, 14% for the 55–59g/km band, 15% for the 60–64g/km band, 16% for the 65–69g/km band and 17% for the 70–74g/km band. A rate of 18% applies at an emissions level of 75g/km, and this increases by one percentage point for each additional 5g/km, up to a maximum rate of 37% which applies at 170g/km and above. The rules for rounding up or down are the same as those above for cars registered before 6 April 2020.

Future years

For **2021/22**, for cars registered *before April 2020*, the appropriate percentages (APs) will stay the same as for 2020/21 except that the AP for cars with zero emissions will increase from 0% to 1%.

For **2021/22**, for cars registered *on or after 6 April 2020*, the APs will all increase by one percentage point from 2020/21, subject still to a maximum of 37% which will thus apply at 165g/km and above.

For **2022/23** onwards, for cars registered before 6 April 2020, the APs will be the same as they were for 2021/22 except that the AP for cars with zero emissions will increase from 1% to 2%. The APs for cars registered on or after 6 April 2020 will be the same for 2022/23 onwards as for cars registered before that date; the maximum rate of 37% will thus apply at 160g/km and above.

Earlier years

For **2019/20**, the AP ranged from 16% to 37%. The 16% rate applied if the applicable CO_2 emissions figure did not exceed 50g/km. A rate of 19% applied if the emissions figure was more than 50g/km but no more than 75g/km. A 22% rate applied for cars emitting more than 75g/km but less than 95g/km. A rate of 23% applied at an emissions level of 95g/km, and this increased by one percentage point for each additional 5g/km, up to a maximum rate of 37% which applied at 165g/km and above. For the purpose of computing the AP at the 23% level upwards, the car's emissions figure was rounded down to the nearest multiple of 5.

For **2018/19**, the AP ranged from 13% to 37%. The 13% rate applied if the applicable CO_2 emissions figure did not exceed 50g/km. A rate of 16% applied if the emissions figure was more than 50g/km but no more than 75g/km. A 19% rate applied for cars emitting more than 75g/km but less than 95g/km. A rate of 20% applied at an emissions level of 95g/km, and this increased by one percentage point for each additional 5g/km, up to a maximum rate of 37% which applied at 180g/km and above. For the purpose of computing the AP at the 20% level upwards, the car's emissions figure was rounded down to the nearest multiple of 5.

For **2017/18**, the AP ranged from 9% to 37%. The 9% rate applied if the applicable CO_2 emissions figure did not exceed 50g/km. A rate of 13% applied if the emissions figure was more than 50g/km but no more than 75g/km. A 17% rate applied for cars emitting more than 75g/km but less than 95g/km. A rate of 18% applied at an emissions level of 95g/km, and this increased by one percentage point for each additional 5g/km, up to a maximum rate of 37% which applied at 190g/km and above. For the purpose of computing the AP at the 18% level upwards, the car's emissions figure was rounded down to the nearest multiple of 5.

For **2016/17**, the AP ranged from 7% to 37%. The 7% rate applied if the applicable CO_2 emissions figure did not exceed 50g/km. A rate of 11% applied if the emissions figure was more than 50g/km but no more than 75g/km. A 15% rate applied for cars emitting more than 75g/km but less than 95g/km. A rate of 16% applied at an emissions level of 95g/km, and this increased by one percentage point for each additional 5g/km, up to a maximum rate of 37% which applied at 200g/km and above. For the purpose of computing the AP at the 16% level upwards, the car's emissions figure was rounded down to the nearest multiple of 5.

The applicable CO_2 emissions figure

The '*applicable CO_2 emissions figure*' is determined as follows.

(a) If the car was first registered after 31 December 1997 but before 1 October 1999 and conformed to a vehicle type with an 'EC type-approval certificate' (as defined), or had a 'UK approval certificate' (as defined), specifying a CO_2 emissions figure in terms of g/km driven, it is that figure.

(b) If the car is first registered after 30 September 1999 on the basis of an 'EC certificate of conformity' (as defined) or UK approval certificate specifying a CO_2 emissions figure in terms of g/km driven, it is that figure or, if more than one figure is quoted, the CO_2 emissions (combined) figure.
For cars first registered before 6 April 2020, any WLTP (worldwide harmonised light vehicles test procedures) values specified in the EC certificate of conformity or UK approval certificate are to be ignored. For 2020/21 onwards, but only for cars first registered on or after that date, any values specified in the EC certificate of conformity or UK approval certificate that are *not* WLTP values are ignored.

(c) If a bi-fuel car is first registered after 31 December 1999 on the basis of an EC certificate of conformity or UK approval certificate specifying separate CO_2 emissions figures in terms of g/km driven for the different fuels, it is the lowest figure specified or, if more than one figure is specified in relation to each fuel, the lowest CO_2 emissions (combined) figure. As regards the use of WLTP values, rules identical to those in (b) above apply.

In determining the electric range figure for a car first registered before 6 April 2020, any WLTP values specified in an EC certificate of conformity, an EC type-approval certificate or a UK approval certificate are to be ignored. For 2020/21 onwards, but only for cars first registered on or after that date, any values specified in any such certificate that are *not* WLTP values are ignored.

The official CO_2 emissions figures referred to in (a)–(c) above are recorded on the vehicle registration document from November 2000. For earlier registrations, an online CO_2 emissions enquiry service has been set up by the Society of Motor Manufacturers and Traders under an agreement with HMRC.

Cars with no CO_2 emissions figure

If a car is first registered after 31 December 1997 but (a)–(c) above do not apply, then if the car has an internal combustion engine with reciprocating piston(s), the appropriate percentage for 2020/21 onwards is 24% if the cylinder capacity is 1,400 cc or less, 35% if it is 1,401–2,000 cc inclusive and 37% if it is more than 2,000 cc. For 2019/20, the first two rates were 23% and 34%. For 2018/19, those two rates were 20% and 31%, for 2017/18, they were 18% and 29%, and for 2016/17, they were 16% and 27%. The highest rate is 37% for each of the years mentioned.

If a car which does not have such an engine cannot in any circumstances emit CO_2 by being driven, the appropriate percentage for 2020/21 is 0%. In any other case it is 37%. For 2019/20 the lower of those two rates was 16%, for 2018/19 it was 13%, for 2017/18 it was 9%, and for 2016/17 it was 7%. For 2021/22 the lower of the two rates will be 1%. For 2022/23 onwards it will be 2%. The higher of the two rates is 37% for each year.

Automatic cars for disabled drivers

Where an employee holding a disabled person's badge can only drive a car with automatic transmission, and an automatic car to which (a) or (b) above applies is made available to him (and not merely deemed to be made available to him or her because it is made available to a member of his family or household), then if the applicable CO_2 emissions figure for the car is higher than that for the 'equivalent manual car', the manual figure is substituted. The '*equivalent manual car*' is the closest non-automatic variant available of the same make and model of car first registered at or about the same time. A car has automatic transmission for these purposes if the gear ratio cannot be varied by the driver independently of the accelerator and brakes, or if the driver can independently vary the gear ratio but not by means of a manually-operated clutch pedal or lever.

If an employee holding a disabled person's badge can only drive a car with automatic transmission, and such a car is made available to him as above, the list price of the equivalent manual car, if lower, is substituted for that of the automatic car in calculating the benefit.

Diesel car supplement

For 2018/19 onwards, a supplement applies to diesel cars (i.e. those propelled solely by diesel) where either:

- the car was first registered on or after 1 January 1998 and before 1 September 2017; or
- the car was first registered on or after 1 September 2017 and does not meet the 'Euro 6d emissions standard'.

Where the supplement applies, the appropriate percentage, determined as above, is increased by 4%, subject to a maximum of 37%. No supplement applies to a diesel car registered on or after 1 September 2017 that meets the emissions standard. A vehicle meets the '*Euro 6d emissions standard*' only if it is first registered on the basis of an EC certificate of conformity which indicates that the exhaust emission level is Euro 6d (but not if it is Euro 6d-TEMP).

For 2017/18 and earlier years, where a diesel car was first registered on or after 1 January 1998, the appropriate percentage was increased by 3%, subject to a maximum of 37%.

Cars registered before 1 January 1998

If the car has an internal combustion engine with reciprocating piston(s), the appropriate percentage for 2019/20 is 23% if the cylinder capacity is 1,400 cc or less, 34% if it is 1,401–2,000 cc inclusive and 37% if it is more than 2,000 cc. In any other case the appropriate percentage is 37%. For 2020/21, the first two rates will be increased to 24% and 35% respectively. For 2018/19, those two rates were 20% and 31%, for 2017/18 they were 18% and 29%, and for 2016/17 they were 16% and 27%. The highest rate and the default rate are 37% for each of the years 2016/17 to 2020/21.

Unavailability

A deduction is made from the cash equivalent of the benefit if the car was 'unavailable' on any day of the tax year. A car is '*unavailable*' on any day if it is a day falling before the first day on which it is made available to the employee (or a member of his family or household) or after the last day on which it is made so available, or on a day falling within a period of 30 or more consecutive days throughout which it is not so available. The deduction is given by the formula U/Y × C where U is the number of days for which the car was unavailable, Y is the total number of days in the tax year, and C is the cash equivalent of the benefit before taking account of any payment made by the employee for private use (see below).

If the car is unavailable for a period of less than 30 days and the employee is provided with a replacement car during that period, the replacement car is effectively ignored, provided that either it is not materially better than the normal car or it is not provided as part of an arrangement to supply a materially better car.

For notes on company car availability and unavailability where an employee is furloughed or working from home due to the 2020 COVID-19 (coronavirus) pandemic, see www.gov.uk/guidance/how-to-treat-certain-expenses-and-benef its-provided-to-employees-during-coronavirus-covid-19).

Payment by employee for private use

Where the employee is required, as a condition of the car being available for private use, to pay for that use and does so, the cash equivalent of the benefit for the tax year in question is reduced (or extinguished) by the amount so paid in respect of that year. This is the final part of the calculation. As regards the charge to tax for 2017/18 onwards, the payment for private use must be made on or before 6 July following the tax year for which the charge arises. For 2016/17, it had to be made *in* the tax year in question. No reduction is allowed for a payment made to the employer to obtain a better car (*Brown v Ware* (Sp C 29), [1995] SSCD 155) or for a payment made for the insurance of the car for both private and business use (*CIR v Quigley* CS, [1995] STC 931).

Price of the car

The '*list price*' of a car is the price published by the manufacturer, importer or distributor (as the case may be) as the inclusive price (including delivery charges and any car tax, value added tax, customs or excise duty or similar duty) appropriate for a car of that kind sold in the UK singly in an open market retail sale on the day before the date of its first registration. The price advertised by a car dealer cannot be used instead of that published by the manufacturer etc. (Revenue Tax Bulletin December 1994 p 177).

In the case of a car that is manufactured so as to be capable of running on road fuel gas and is not a bi-fuel car as within (c) above, the price of the car is reduced by so much of it as is reasonably attributable to the car's being manufactured to be so capable rather than only being capable of running on petrol.

The '*notional price*' of a car is that which might reasonably be expected to have been its list price (as above) had such a price been published.

Accessories

The price of the following 'accessories' must be added to the list price or notional price to find the price of the car:

(A) in the case of a car with a list price, any 'qualifying accessory' that is not a 'standard accessory', is available with the car when it is first made available to the employee and either has a price published by the manufacturer, importer or distributor of the car or is available with the car in the tax year for which the benefit is being computed; and

(B) in the case of *any* car, any 'qualifying accessory' that is available with the car in the tax year in question, was not so available when the car was first made available to the employee, was not made available with the car before 1 August 1993 and has a price of at least £100.

'*Accessory*' means any kind of equipment other than equipment necessarily provided for use in the performance of the duties of the employment, equipment by means of which a car is capable of running on road fuel gas, or 'equipment to enable a disabled person to use a car' (as defined by *ITEPA 2003, s 172*). A mobile phone is specifically excluded from being an accessory. A '*qualifying accessory*' is an accessory that is made available for use with the car without any transfer of the property in the accessory, is made available by reason of the employment, and is attached to the car (whether permanently or not). A '*standard accessory*' is a type of accessory assumed to be available with cars of the same kind as the car in question in arriving at the list price of the car.

Certain security features made available for use with a car are excluded from being accessories if they are provided in order to meet a threat to the employee's personal physical security which arises wholly or mainly because of the nature of his employment. The security features in question are armour, bullet-resistant glass, protective modifications to the fuel tank and any modification made to the car in consequence of any of these.

The price of an accessory is its 'list price' or, if it has no list price, its 'notional price'. The '*list price*' of an accessory within (A) above is the price published by the manufacturer, importer or distributor of the car or, if there is no such price, the price published by the manufacturer, importer or distributor of the accessory. The '*list price*' of an accessory within (B) above is the price published by the manufacturer, importer or distributor of the accessory. The price published by the manufacturer, importer or distributor of the accessory means the inclusive price (including delivery charges, the price for permanently attaching it to the car where relevant, and any relevant taxes or duties) appropriate for an accessory of that kind sold in the UK singly in an open market retail sale at the time immediately before it is first made available for use with the car. The '*notional price*' of an accessory is that which might reasonably be expected to have been its list price (as above) had such a price been published.

Where an accessory within (B) above is available with the car in the tax year for which the benefit is being computed and that accessory replaced a qualifying accessory of the same kind in that year or in an earlier year, the new accessory is treated as a continuation of the old. If, however, the new accessory is superior to the one it replaced, and the old accessory was not a standard accessory, the cash equivalent of the benefit is to be computed ignoring the old accessory. A new accessory is superior to the old if its price exceeds the greater of the price of the old accessory and the price of an accessory equivalent to the old accessory at the time immediately before the new accessory is first made available for use with the car.

Capital contribution by employee

Where the employee makes a capital contribution to the cost of the car or of any qualifying accessories taken into account as above, the price of the car for the purposes of the charge on the employee for the tax year in which the contribution is made and subsequent years is reduced by the lesser of the amount of the contribution (or the sum of such contributions) and £5,000. An agreement for the employee to receive a proportionate return of his capital contribution on disposal of the car will not prejudice relief in respect of the contribution, and will not give rise to any employment income charge on the amount repaid. An agreement to refund the contribution in full will result in the contribution being disregarded. (Revenue Tax Bulletin December 1994 p 177).

Classic cars

There are special provisions substituting market value for the price determined as above where the market value is at least £15,000 and exceeds that price, and the car is 15 years or more old at the end of the tax year concerned. Capital contributions are taken into account on a similar basis to that described above. Market value is judged as at the last day of the tax year or, if earlier, the last day in the tax year in which the car was available to the employee.

Shared cars

Where two or more persons are chargeable in respect of their shared use of the same car, the charge applicable to each of them is reduced on a just and reasonable basis (and a similar reduction is made in any fuel scale charge). The reduction is made before deducting any payment by the employee for private use as above. For pooled vehicles, see **28.29** below.

Salary sacrifice arrangements

For **2017/18** onwards, where a car with a CO_2 emissions figure exceeding 75g/km is made available pursuant to salary sacrifice arrangements, the tax charge is on an amount determined as follows. If the 'modified cash equivalent' of the benefit is greater than or equal to the amount forgone with respect to the benefit of the car for the tax year, the taxable amount is the cash equivalent of the benefit as computed above. Otherwise, the taxable amount is the amount forgone less (i) an amount (see below) representing capital contributions made by the employee to the cost of the car or accessories and (ii) any payments made by the employee for the private use of the car. Where the car is made available pursuant to pre-6 April 2017 arrangements, the introduction of these rules is delayed by four years, and they have effect for **2021/22** onwards instead.

The '*modified cash equivalent*' is calculated in the same way as the cash equivalent above, except that no deductions are made at this stage for capital contributions and payments for private use (though capital contributions *are* taken into account in deciding whether to substitute market value for price in the case of a classic car). When deducting, from the amount forgone, an amount representing any capital contributions made by the employee, the capital contributions are firstly restricted to £5,000 as above and then (for this purpose only) multiplied by the appropriate percentage (as above).

In any case in which the benefit of the car would be exempt from income tax were it not provided under salary sacrifice arrangements (see **28.14** above), the modified cash equivalent of the benefit is treated as zero. See **28.14** as to 'salary sacrifice arrangements', 'the amount forgone' and the effect of pre-6 April 2017 arrangements being varied or renewed on or after that date.

FA 2019, s 7 corrects two anomalies in the calculation of the amount forgone. The corrections have effect for 2019/20 onwards (though not so as to bring the optional remuneration rules into play any sooner than would otherwise be the case as regards pre-6 April 2017 arrangements).

[*ITEPA 2003, ss 120, 120A, 121, 121A, 121B, 122–124, 124A, 125, 125A–132, 132A, 133–139, 139A, 140–147, 147A, 148, 153, 170(1)–(4), 171, 172, Sch 7 paras 22, 23; FA 2015, ss 7, 8; FA 2016, ss 8–10; FA 2017, Sch 2 paras 21–33, 41, 62(2)(4); F(No 2)A 2017, s 1(7)(14), s 2; FA 2018, ss 9, 48(9)–(12); FA 2019, s 7(2)–(4)(7); FA 2020, ss 8–10; SI 1994 Nos 777, 778*].

See **26.10** DISGUISED REMUNERATION as regards employee car ownership schemes (as defined).

See HMRC guidance at www.gov.uk/tax-company-benefits/tax-on-company-cars and see also **53.29** PAY AS YOU EARN. HMRC also provide a company car and car fuel benefit calculator at www.gov.uk/calculate-tax-on-company-cars.

Simon's Taxes. See E4.626A–E4.627A.

Example

[28.25]

A, B and C are employees of D Ltd. Each is provided with a company car throughout 2020/21. The company also bears at least part of the cost of petrol for private motoring (see 28.26 below).

A is provided with a 1,800 cc car first registered in January 2017 with a list price (including VAT, car tax (but not road tax), delivery charges and standard accessories) of £19,000. The car was made available to A in April 2017. It has a diesel engine and an emissions figure of 150g/km. An immobiliser was fitted in September 2017 at a cost of £200. A is required to pay the company £250 per year as a condition of using the car for private motoring, and duly pays this amount by the 6 July 2021 deadline.

B is provided with a 1,400 cc car first registered in March 2016 with a list price of £9,000. It has an emissions figure of 85g/km. B was required to make a capital contribution of £1,000 on provision of the car in January 2017. B leaves the company in March 2021 and returns the car to D Ltd on 16 March. B was required to pay the company £50 per year as a condition of using the car for private motoring, and duly pays this amount by 6 July 2021.

C is provided with a luxury car first registered in February 2019 with a list price of £88,000 (which includes the list price of non-standard accessories). It has an emissions figure of 280g/km. C made a capital contribution of £3,000 in 2018/19.

Car and fuel benefits for 2020/21 are as follows.

		A	B	C
		£	£	£
List price		19,000	9,000	88,000
Later accessories (within 28.24(B) above)		200	—	—
		19,200	9,000	88,000
Capital contributions		—	(1,000)	(3,000)
Price of car		£19,200	£8,000	£85,000
Cash equivalent	£19,200 @ 37% (maximum — see below)	7,104		
	£8,000 @ 22%		1,760	
	£85,000 @ 37%			31,450
Deduction for unavailability (£1,760 × 20/365)			(97)	
			1,663	
Contribution for private use		(250)	(50)	—
Car benefit		6,854	1,613	31,450
Fuel benefit	(£24,500 @ 37%)	9,065		
	(£24,500 @ 22%)		5,390	
	(£24,500 @ 37%)			9,065
Deduction for unavailability (£5,390 × 20/365)			(296)	
Total car and fuel benefits		£15,919	£6,707	£40,515

In A's case, the appropriate percentage excluding diesel supplement is 35%. The diesel supplement would normally be 4% but the appropriate percentage cannot exceed 37% overall.

Car fuel for private use

[28.26] Tax is chargeable on the cash equivalent of the benefit of provision of free fuel for private motoring in a company car, i.e. a vehicle which attracts, or could attract, a charge within **28.24** above. The cash equivalent is obtained by applying the 'appropriate percentage' (see **28.24** above) used in determining the benefit of use of the car to an amount variable by Treasury order. This amount is as follows.

For	**2020/21**	**£24,500**
For	2019/20	£24,100
For	2018/19	£23,400
For	2017/18	£22,600
For	2016/17	£22,200

'Fuel' for these purposes does *not* include electrical energy or energy for a car which cannot in any circumstances emit CO_2 by being driven (previously electrical energy for an electrically propelled vehicle).

This charge does not apply to fuel provided for vans but there is a separate charge for van fuel for which see **28.27** below.

If the employee is required to make good to his employer the cost of *all* company fuel used for private purposes, and in fact does so, the charge is reduced to nil. As regards the charge to tax for 2017/18 onwards, the payment for private use must be made on or before 6 July following the tax year for which the charge arises. Previously it had to be made *in* the tax year in question (or without unreasonable delay thereafter — see HMRC Employment Income Manual EIM25660). Travel between home and work is private for these purposes. In a case in which the cost was made good more than a year retrospectively, neither HMRC nor the Sp C accepted that the charge was so reduced (*Impact Foiling Ltd and others v HMRC* (Sp C 562), [2006] SSCD 764).

Where, in relation to any part of the tax year, either:

- fuel is not provided for the car at all; or
- it is made available only for business travel; or
- the requirements for the 'making good' exemption referred to above are met,

and there is no subsequent time in the year when none of these three conditions is met, the cash equivalent of the fuel benefit is reduced in the proportion that the number of days on which at least one of these conditions is met bears to the number of days in the year. (For example, if for part of a year an employee makes good the cost of all fuel for private use but then ceases to do so later in the same tax year, without one of the other conditions being met, no reduction can be made to the cash equivalent of the benefit for that year.)

HMRC have advised that where the cost of fuel for volunteer mileage related to the 2020 COVID-19 (coronavirus) pandemic is funded by the employer, this should not be taken into account for the purposes of the car fuel benefit charge (www.gov.uk/guidance/how-to-treat-certain-expenses-and-benefits-provided-to-employees-during-coronavirus-covid-19).

The cash equivalent of the fuel benefit is also proportionately reduced if the car is 'unavailable' (see **28.24** above) at any time in the tax year.

Where there is a charge under these provisions, there is no charge under other provisions in respect of the supply of fuel (e.g. on expense allowances or use of credit cards or vouchers which enable the employee to obtain private fuel). The *method* by which private fuel is obtained does not affect the employee's liability.

These provisions do not apply to fuel provided for private use in individuals' own cars, hire cars etc., where the general charging rules continue to apply (i.e. the employer will notify HMRC on form P11D of the actual cost of fuel provided by him). For fuel provided *by the employee* for business use in a car *other than* a company car, see **28.91** below.

See **28.23** above for relief from the fuel scale charge in the cases of certain cars supplied to disabled employees or to members of the same family where there is relief from the charge on provision of the car. See **28.24** above for similar relief in the case of shared cars.

Salary sacrifice arrangements

For **2017/18** onwards, fuel is provided for private motoring in a company car, and its provision is pursuant to salary sacrifice arrangements, the charge is on the greater of the cash equivalent (as above) and the amount forgone. Where the fuel is made available pursuant to pre-6 April 2017 arrangements, the introduction of this rule is delayed by four years, and it has effect for **2021/22** onwards instead. In any case in which the benefit of the fuel would be exempt from income tax were it not provided under salary sacrifice arrangements (see **28.14** above), the cash equivalent of the benefit is treated as zero for this purpose. See **28.14** as to 'salary sacrifice arrangements', 'the amount forgone' and the effect of pre-6 April 2017 arrangements being varied or renewed on or after that date.

[*ITEPA 2003, ss 149, 149A, 150–152, 170(5)(6); FA 2017, Sch 2 paras 34, 35, 62(2)(4); F(No 2)A 2017, s 1(8)(9)(14); SI 2015 No 1979, Arts 1, 2; SI 2016 No 1174, Arts 1, 2; SI 2017 No 1176, Arts 1, 2; SI 2018 No 1176, Arts 1, 2; SI 2020 No 199, Arts 1, 2*].

Advisory fuel rates

HMRC will accept that there is no fuel charge where the employer uses the appropriate rate per mile from the table below to work out the cost of fuel used for private travel that the employee must make good (provided all the miles of private travel are correctly recorded) or to reimburse the employee for business travel in his company car. These advisory rates are not binding where the employer can demonstrate that employees cover the full cost of private fuel by making good at a lower rate per mile. The employer can reimburse business mileage at rates higher than the advisory rates if he can demonstrate that the fuel cost per mile is higher. If the employer cannot demonstrate that fact, there is no fuel benefit charge if the payments are solely for business mileage, but the excess will not be an allowable deduction in computing the employer's profits.

Engine size	*Petrol*	*Diesel*	*LPG**	*Electricity*
1.9.19–30.11.19				
1400 cc or less	12p		8p	
1600 cc or less		10p		
1401 cc to 2000 cc	14p		10p	
1601 cc to 2000 cc		11p		
Over 2000 cc	21p	14p	14p	
Fully electric cars				4p
1.12.19–29.2.20				
1400 cc or less	12p		8p	
1600 cc or less		9p		
1401 cc to 2000 cc	14p		9p	
1601 cc to 2000 cc		11p		
Over 2000 cc	21p	14p	14p	
Fully electric cars				4p
1.3.20–31.5.20				
1400 cc or less	12p		8p	
1600 cc or less		9p		
1401 cc to 2000 cc	14p		10p	
1601 cc to 2000 cc		11p		
Over 2000 cc	20p	13p	14p	
Fully electric cars				4p
1.6.20–31.8.20				
1400 cc or less	10p		6p	
1600 cc or less		8p		
1401 cc to 2000 cc	12p		8p	
1601 cc to 2000 cc		9p		
Over 2000 cc	17p	12p	11p	
Fully electric cars				4p

* LPG = Liquid Petroleum Gas.

The previous rates can be used for up to one month from the date that new rates apply. The rates for diesel cars below 2001 cc are quoted by reference to different engine sizes from petrol cars. Hybrid cars are treated as either petrol or diesel cars for this purpose. As regards the advisory rate quoted for fully electric cars, it should be noted that electricity is not a fuel for car fuel benefit purposes (see also HMRC Employer Bulletin Issue 73, August 2018, page 4 at https://assets.publishing.service.gov.uk/government/uploads/system/uploads/attachment_data/file/734650/Employer_bulletin_August_2018.pdf).

See www.gov.uk/government/publications/advisory-fuel-rates, which also includes a link to earlier rates.

Simon's Taxes. See **E4.629.**

Vans for private use

[28.27] The cash equivalent of the benefit of a 'van' (as defined in **28.23** above) depends on the degree to which private use is permitted or does, in fact, occur.

If the van is made available to the employee mainly for business travel and the terms on which it is made available prohibit its private use otherwise than for the purposes of 'ordinary commuting' (for which see **28.17** above), the cash equivalent of the benefit is nil. For this purpose, the term 'ordinary commuting' is extended to include travel between two places that is for practical purposes substantially ordinary commuting. It is a further condition that neither the employee nor any member of his family or household does, in fact, make private use of the van outside these terms. These requirements must be met throughout the tax year (or throughout that part of the tax year during which the van is available to the employee), but insignificant private use is disregarded. For some examples of what HMRC do and do not consider to be 'insignificant' in this context, see HMRC Employment Income Manual EIM22745, 22880.

If the restricted private use requirements above are not met, the cash equivalent of the benefit for 2020/21 is **£3,490** (£3,430 for 2019/20, £3,350 for 2018/19, £3,230 for 2017/18, £3,170 for 2016/17). See below as regards zero-emission vans.

The cash equivalent is subject to reductions as outlined below for periods when the van is unavailable or if the van is shared or if the employee makes payments for private use. There is a separate fuel benefit charge (see below).

If the van is 'unavailable' on any one or more days during the tax year, the cash equivalent as above is reduced proportionately. For these purposes, a van is '*unavailable*' on any day in the tax year if that day falls before the first day on which it is available to the employee or after the last day on which it is so available or within a period of 30 days or more throughout which it is not so available.

If a van is shared, i.e. if it is made available to two or more employees concurrently by the same employer and is available concurrently for each of those employees' private use (or for private use by any member of their family or household), the cash equivalent as above to each such employee (reduced in each case for any periods of unavailability) is reduced on a just and reasonable basis.

If, as a condition for private use of a van, an employee is required to pay an amount of money (whether by deduction from earnings or otherwise) and makes such payment, the cash equivalent (after applying any reductions as above) is reduced by the amount paid (or by so much of that amount as is required to reduce the cash equivalent to nil). As regards the charge to tax for 2017/18 onwards, the payment for private use must be made on or before 6 July following the tax year for which the charge arises. For 2016/17, it had to be made *in* the tax year in question.

If the van normally available to the employee is not available to him for a period of less than 30 days and is replaced for all or part of that period by another van, the above provisions generally apply as if the replacement van were the normal van.

For heavy goods vehicles, see **28.30** below.

Zero-emission vans

For 2018/19, the cash equivalent of a 'zero-emission van' was 40% of the cash equivalent for conventionally fuelled vans. This was increased to 60% for 2019/20 and is increased to **80%** for **2020/21**. For example, the cash equivalent for 2020/21 is £2,792 (£3,490 @ 80%). For this purpose, a '*zero-emission van*' is a van that cannot in any circumstances emit CO_2 by being driven. Reductions apply as above for periods when the van is unavailable or shared or where the employee makes payments for private use. For 2016/17 and 2017/18, the cash equivalent of a zero-emission van was 20% of the cash equivalent for conventionally fuelled vans.

Future development

The cash equivalent of a zero-emission van was to have been further increased to 90% for 2021/22 and 100% thereafter. However, it was announced at Spring Budget 2020 that the Government will legislate in a future Finance Bill to reduce the van benefit charge to zero for 2021/22 onwards for vans that produce zero carbon emissions (see overview, para 2.2 at www.gov.uk/government/publications/budget-2020-overview-of-tax-legislation-and-rates-ootlar).

Fuel charge for vans

If fuel is provided for a van by reason of the employment and the cash equivalent of the benefit of the van itself falls to be computed on the basis that the restricted private use requirements above are not met, then (subject to the exceptions below) there is a tax charge on fuel as well as on the van itself. Fuel is treated as provided if *inter alia* a liability for such fuel is discharged, a non-cash voucher or credit-token is used to obtain fuel or to obtain money to buy fuel or if any sum is paid for expenses incurred in providing fuel. The fuel benefit charge does not apply for any year up to and including 2021/22 if there is no van benefit, or a reduced van benefit, for the year because the van is a zero-emission van.

The cash equivalent of the benefit of fuel for 2020/21 is **£666** (£655 for 2019/20, £633 for 2018/19, £610 for 2017/18, £598 for 2016/17). However, no charge applies for a tax year if either:

- the fuel is made available for business travel only; or
- the employee is required to make good the full cost of fuel provided for private use and does, in fact, do so. As regards the charge to tax for 2017/18 onwards, the payment for private use must be made on or before 6 July following the tax year for which the charge arises. Previously it had to be made *in* the tax year in question (or without unreasonable delay thereafter — see HMRC Employment Income Manual EIM22945).

Where, in relation to any part of the tax year, either:

(a) fuel is not provided for the van at all; or
(b) it is made available only for business travel; or
(c) the requirements for the 'making good' exemption referred to above are met,

and there is no subsequent time in the year when none of these three conditions is met, the cash equivalent of the fuel benefit is reduced in the proportion that the number of days on which at least one of these conditions is met bears to the number of days in the year. (For example, if for part of a year an employee makes good the cost of all fuel for private use but then ceases to do so later in the same tax year, without one of the other conditions being met, no reduction can be made to the cash equivalent of the benefit for that year.)

The cash equivalent of the fuel benefit is also proportionately reduced if the van is 'unavailable' (see above) at any time in the tax year. As above, a replacement van generally counts as the normal van.

If the cash equivalent of the benefit of the van itself falls to be reduced because the van is shared (see above), a corresponding reduction is made in the cash equivalent of the fuel benefit.

Salary sacrifice arrangements

For **2017/18** onwards, where a van is provided pursuant to salary sacrifice arrangements, the amount chargeable is determined as follows. If the 'modified cash equivalent' of the benefit is greater than or equal to the amount forgone with respect to the benefit of the van, the charge is on is the cash equivalent of the benefit as above. Otherwise, the charge is on the amount forgone less any payments made by the employee, on or before 6 July following the tax year, for private use. Where the van is made available pursuant to pre-6 April 2017 arrangements, the introduction of these rules is delayed by four years, and they have effect for **2021/22** onwards instead.

The '*modified cash equivalent*' is the cash equivalent before any deduction for payments made by the employee for private use. In any case in which the benefit of the van would be exempt from income tax were it not provided under salary sacrifice arrangements (see **28.14** above), the modified cash equivalent is treated as zero for this purpose.

Again for 2017/18 onwards (or 2021/22 onwards in the case of pre-6 April 2017 arrangements), where fuel for a van is provided pursuant to salary sacrifice arrangements, whether or not the van itself is so provided, the amount chargeable in respect of fuel benefit is the amount forgone with respect to the benefit of the fuel if this is greater than the cash equivalent of the benefit (calculated as above under Fuel charge for vans). In any case in which the benefit of the van would be exempt from income tax were it not provided under salary sacrifice arrangements, the cash equivalent is treated as zero for this purpose.

See **28.14** as to 'salary sacrifice arrangements', 'the amount forgone' and the effect of pre-6 April 2017 arrangements being varied or renewed on or after that date.

FA 2019, s 7 corrects an anomaly in the calculation of the amount forgone. The correction has effect for 2019/20 onwards (though not so as to bring the optional remuneration rules into play any sooner than would otherwise be the case as regards pre-6 April 2017 arrangements).

[*ITEPA 2003, ss 154, 154A, 155–158, 158A, 159, 160A, 161–164, 170(1A)(2)(5); FA 2016, s 11; FA 2017, Sch 2 paras 36–40, 62(2)(4); F(No 2)A 2017, s 1(10)–(12)(14); FA 2019, s 7(5)(7); SI 2015 No 1979, Arts 1, 3, 4; SI 2016 No 1174, Arts 1, 3, 4; SI 2017 No 1176, Arts 1, 3, 4; SI 2018 No 1176, Arts 1, 3, 4; SI 2020 No 199, Arts 1, 3, 4*].

Simon's Taxes. See **E4.630B, E4.630C.**

Example

[28.28]

From 1 October 2020 to 5 April 2021, W, an employee of C Ltd, is provided by his employer with exclusive use of a one-year old company van (Van A) on terms such that the restricted private use requirements are not met and which provide for a deduction of £4 per month to be made from his net salary at the end of each month in consideration for private use. Van A was off the road and incapable of use for a three-week period in January 2021; no replacement was provided.

X, Y and Z are also employees of C Ltd, each earning £32,500 per annum. Throughout 2020/21, a single two-year old company van (Van B) is made available to the three of them. The terms are such that the restricted private use requirements are met in relation to X but not in relation to Y and Z. No payment for private use was required from any of them. Van B was damaged and incapable of use for 40 consecutive days in February/March 2021; no replacement was provided. The facts show that a just and reasonable allocation of the benefit for 2020/21 is 0% to X (whose private use was insignificant), 60% to Y and 40% to Z.

Both vans have a normal laden weight not exceeding 3,500 kilograms.

It is not the policy of C Ltd to provide fuel for private travel in its vans. All employees are required to make good the full cost of any fuel used for private purposes and have done so by the 6 July 2021 deadline.

The taxable benefits to W, X, Y and Z for 2020/21 of company vans are calculated as follows.

		£
W		
Cash equivalent of benefit before adjustment		3,490
Exclude	Period of unavailability (see note below):	
	$£3{,}490 \times \frac{178}{365}$ (6.4.20 – 30.9.20)	1,702
		1,788
Deduct	Payment for private use (6 × £4 per month)	24
Cash equivalent of benefit		£1,764
X		
Cash equivalent of benefit		Nil

Y

Cash equivalent of benefit before adjustment		3,490
Exclude	Period of unavailability:	
	$£3{,}490 \times \frac{40}{365}$	383
		3,107
Exclude	Reduction for sharing (40%)	1,243
Cash equivalent of benefit		£1,864

Z

Cash equivalent of benefit before adjustment		3,490
Exclude	Period of unavailability (same as for Y)	383
		3,107
Exclude	Reduction for sharing (60%)	1,864
Cash equivalent of benefit		£1,243

In W's case, the period of unavailability in January 2021 does not count towards the reduction as it is a period of less than 30 consecutive days.

Pooled vehicles

[28.29] Cars or vans provided as *pooled cars* or *pooled vans* will not be treated as being available for private use by any employee.

Conditions are:

(a) the vehicle must have been included for the year in a car or van pool for use of employees of one or more employers and actually used by more than one of those employees by reason of their employment and not ordinarily used by one of them to the exclusion of the others, and

(b) any private use of the vehicle in the year by an employee was merely incidental to his other use of it, and

(c) the vehicle was not normally kept overnight at or near any of the residences of the employees concerned (except on the employer's premises).

[*ITEPA 2003, ss 167, 168*].

As regards (b) above, HMRC interpret the requirement that private use is 'merely incidental to' other use as a qualitative test requiring consideration, in the case of each employee using the vehicle during the year, of whether the private use is independent of the employee's business use (so that it is not 'merely incidental' to it) or follows from the business use (so that it is). Thus if a business journey requiring an early start cannot reasonably be undertaken starting from the normal place of work, the journey from work to home the previous day (although private) is merely incidental to the business use. Similarly minor private use (e.g. to visit a restaurant) while away from home on a business trip is merely incidental to the business use. On the other hand use for an annual holiday would not be merely incidental to business use, no matter how small in comparison to business travel in the year. As regards cars with drivers, carrying and working on confidential papers, whilst a factor in determining whether a journey is business or private (and if private whether merely incidental to business use), is not determinative of the issue. The need to deliver papers to a client, or to have them available for a meeting at the employee's home, may be additional relevant factors. Where a chauffeur is obliged to take the car home for the night, in order to collect or deliver passengers, this does not disqualify the car from treatment as a pooled vehicle. (HMRC SP 2/96).

HMRC accept that condition (c) above is satisfied if the occasions on which the vehicle is taken home by employees do not amount to more than 60% of the year. However, where a vehicle is garaged at employees' homes on a large number of occasions (although less than 60% of the year), they consider it 'unlikely' that all home-to-work journeys would satisfy the 'merely incidental' test in (b) above. Such use by a chauffeur employed to drive a car does not prevent its being a pooled car. (HMRC Employment Income Manual EIM23465, 23480).

Although it is best practice to have written records to show that the above conditions were met, written records are not part of the statutory requirements; in a small office with just a few employees, control of the pooled cars could be achieved without formal written rules (*Industrial Doors (Scotland) Limited v HMRC* FTT (TC 571), 2010 STI 2516; *Isocom Ltd and another v HMRC* FTT (TC 3696), [2014] UKFTT 571 (TC)).

Simon's Taxes. See **E4.630F.**

Heavy goods vehicles

[28.30] No liability to income tax arises where a 'heavy goods vehicle' is made available to an employee provided there is no transfer of the property in the vehicle and that the employee's use of it in the tax year is not wholly or mainly private use. Where this exemption has effect, no liability to income tax arises in respect of the discharge of any liability of an employee in connection with the vehicle or a payment to an employee in respect of expenses incurred in connection with the vehicle, and no liability arises in respect of a benefit connected with the vehicle (though this exemption does not apply to the provision of a driver). A '*heavy goods vehicle*' is defined in the same terms as a van under **28.27** above, but with a design laden weight exceeding 3,500 kgs in normal use. [*ITEPA 2003, ss 238, 239, 269; FA 2017, Sch 2 paras 53, 62(2)(4); FA 2019, s 7(6)(7)*].

Simon's Taxes. See **E4.630D.**

Emergency vehicles

[28.31] For 2017/18 onwards, no benefit arises where an emergency vehicle (as defined but normally with flashing lights) is made available to a person employed in an 'emergency service' if the terms on which it is made available prohibit its private use otherwise than when the person is 'on call' or 'commuting' and the person does not, in fact, make private use of the vehicle outside these terms. For this purpose, a person is '*on call*' when liable, as part of normal duties, to be called upon to use the vehicle to respond to emergencies. A person is '*commuting*' when he is using the vehicle for ordinary commuting (see **28.17** above) or for travel between two places that is for practical purposes substantially ordinary commuting. '*Emergency services*' are police, fire, fire and rescue, ambulance or paramedic services.

There was a similar exemption for 2016/17 and earlier years. For a vehicle to be within that exemption, the terms on which it was made available had to prohibit its private use otherwise than when the person was 'on call' (as above) or 'engaged in on-call commuting'. Again it was necessary that the person did not breach those terms. A person was '*engaged in on-call commuting*' when he was using the vehicle for ordinary commuting (or substantially ordinary commuting as above) *and* was required to do so in order that the vehicle was available for use in responding to emergencies.

[*ITEPA 2003, s 248A; FA 2019, s 9(2)(3)(5)*].

The law was changed from 2017/18 so that employees would be less likely to face an increased tax charge for having their emergency vehicle available for private use; this would have occurred in some cases as a result of changes to the 'use of assets' rules of *ITEPA 2003, s 205* at **28.54** below.

Where, despite the changes from 2017/18, the above exemption conditions are not met, transitional provisions apply for the three years 2017/18 to 2019/20 inclusive. These provide for the cost of the benefit under those 'use of assets' rules to be restricted to the private use proportion, i.e. the proportion of the total annual mileage that is private mileage. They also provide for simplification of the 'unavailability for private use' rules within the 'use of assets' rules. [*FA 2019, s 9(6)–(9)*].

Also for 2017/18 onwards (and with effect beyond 2019/20), fuel provided for an emergency vehicle is not treated as an additional expense under *ITEPA 2003, s 205* at **28.54** below, provided the employer does not incur the cost of any fuel provided for private use in the tax year or any such cost is made good in full by the employee on or before 6 July following the tax year. [*ITEPA 2003, s 205(5)(6); FA 2019, s 9(4)(5)*].

Simon's Taxes. See **E4.630E.**

Cheap loans

[28.32] Where an employee obtains an 'employment-related loan', and the loan is a 'taxable cheap loan' in relation to that year, the cash equivalent of the benefit of the loan is treated as earnings from the employment for that year, subject to the exceptions referred to below. See in particular the de minimis exemption below.

An '*employment-related loan*' is a loan (including any form of credit) made to an employee (or a 'relative' of an employee) by the employer, by a company or partnership under the employer's control, by a company or partnership controlling the employer (being a company or partnership), or by a company or partnership under common control with the employer (being a company or partnership). It also includes a loan by a person having a 'material interest' (broadly *5%* — see *ITEPA 2003, s 68*) in a close company which was the employer or had control of or was controlled by the employer, or in a company or partnership controlling that close company. It does not include a loan made by an individual in the normal course of his domestic, family or personal relationships, or one made to a 'relative' of the employee from which the employee derives no benefit. Loans by a prospective employer are included, and 'making a loan' includes arranging, guaranteeing or in any way facilitating a loan or the continuation of an existing loan, and the assumption of the rights and liabilities of the person who originally made the loan. '*Relative*' means spouse or civil partner of the employee, or parent, ancestor, lineal descendant, brother or sister (or those persons' spouses or civil partners) of the employee or spouse/civil partner.

It is expressly provided that, where these provisions apply to a loan, the loan is a benefit, and the charge under these provisions applies, even if the terms of the loan constitute a 'fair bargain'. '*Fair bargain*' refers to a situation in which an individual receives something from an employer at the same cost, and subject to the same terms and conditions, as a member of the public or other independent third party dealing with the employer on an arms-length basis.

A '*taxable cheap loan*' is an employment-related loan for a tax year if it is outstanding at any time during that year when the employment is held and the interest (if any) paid on the loan for that year is less than would have been payable at the 'official rate'. A loan ceases to be outstanding on the death of the employee.

The **cash equivalent of the benefit** of a loan (which applies to each loan separately) is:

- the interest that would have been payable on the loan for the tax year at the official rate, less
- the interest (if any) actually paid.

It is not necessary for the application of these provisions that there be any benefit from the loan in terms of something of an advantage to the employee (*Williams v Todd* Ch D 1988, 60 TC 727). A loan secured by a charge on a house purchased by a relocated employee, with an agreement that when the charge was called in the employing company would receive the same proportion of the sale price or valuation as the loan bore to the purchase price, was within these provisions (*Harvey v Williams* (Sp C 49), [1995] SSCD 329; (Sp C 168), [1998] SSCD 215). The payment of the expenses of an estate agency by a service company of which one of the partners in the agency was a director was within the provisions from the time the services were provided for so long as the payments were not reimbursed (with agreed mark-up) to the company (*Grant v Watton and cross-appeal* Ch D 1999, 71 TC 333).

The 'official rate' is set in advance for the whole year, although it may be decreased during the year should there be a sharp fall in typical mortgage rates (but will *not* be increased during the year). (Revenue Press Release 25 January 2000). The prescribed rates (for 2016/17 through 2020/21) are as follows.

2.25% p.a. from 6 April 2020
2.50% p.a. from 6 April 2017 to 5 April 2020
3.00% p.a. from 6 April 2016 to 5 April 2017

[*SI 1989 No 1297; SI 2017 No 305; SI 2020 No 194*].

Regulations may provide for a different official rate of interest in relation to a loan in the currency of a country or territory outside the UK, the benefit of which is obtained by reason of the employment of a person who normally lives in that country or territory and who has lived there at some time in the year in question or the preceding five years. In this context, 'lives' and 'has lived' are considered to connote a degree of continuance if not permanence, i.e. more than a return for a short holiday. (Revenue Tax Bulletin October 1994 p 162). The following different rates are applicable.

Japan	3.9% p.a.
Switzerland	5.5% p.a.

[*SI 1994 Nos 1307, 1567*]. For the circumstances in which loans taken out prior to an employee coming to work in the UK are within the beneficial loan provisions, see Revenue Tax Bulletin October 1994 p 161.

The amount taxable in respect of the loan for a tax year is treated as interest paid by the employee on the loan in that year of that amount (other than for the purpose of this or any other benefit charge). It is not treated as income of the lender, but it is treated as accruing during, and paid at the end of, the year (or, if different, the period during the year when the employee was in the employment and the loan was outstanding).

Where the lender is a close company (see Tolley's Corporation Tax under Close Companies) and the borrower a director, the lender may elect, by notice to HMRC on or before 6 July following the tax year, to treat as a single loan all loans with that borrower which are in the same currency, are not 'qualifying loans (see below), were obtained by reason of employment, and the rate of interest on which has been below the official rate throughout the year. This rule does not apply for the purpose of calculating the modified cash equivalent of the benefit under Salary sacrifice arrangements below.

A claim may be made for late payments of interest to be related to the year to which they apply, and for assessments to be adjusted accordingly.

The above provisions do not apply where a loan made for a fixed and unvariable period and at a fixed and unvariable rate of interest (originally not less than the official rate) becomes a taxable cheap loan only by reason of an increase in the official rate.

Salary sacrifice arrangements

For **2017/18** onwards, where a loan is provided pursuant to salary sacrifice arrangements, the amount chargeable is determined as follows. If the 'modified cash equivalent' of the benefit is greater than or equal to the amount forgone with respect to the benefit of the loan, the charge is on is the cash equivalent of the benefit as above. Otherwise, the charge is on the amount forgone less the interest (if any) actually paid on the loan for the tax year. Where the loan is made available pursuant to pre-6 April 2017 arrangements, these rules are delayed by one year and have effect for **2018/19** onwards instead.

The '*modified cash equivalent*' is the cash equivalent before any deduction for interest actually paid. In any case in which the benefit of the loan would be exempt from income tax were it not provided under salary sacrifice arrangements (see **28.14** above), the modified cash equivalent is treated as zero for this purpose.

See **28.14** as to 'salary sacrifice arrangements', 'the amount forgone' and the effect of pre-6 April 2017 arrangements being varied or renewed on or after that date.

[*ITEPA 2003, ss 173–175, 175A, 177, 181, 184, 187, 190(2), 191(2); FA 2016, s 7(8)(9); FA 2017, Sch 2 paras 42–44, 62(2)(5)*].

'Qualifying loans' — interest qualifying for relief

The above provisions do not apply to a loan in any tax year in which, if interest were paid on the loan (whether or not it is in fact so paid), the whole of the interest paid on it would either be eligible for relief under *ITA 2007, s 383* (see **42.5** INTEREST PAYABLE) or would be an allowable deduction to the payer in computing the taxable profits of a trade, profession or vocation carried on wholly or partly in the UK or of a UK property business (see **75.93** TRADING INCOME, **60.10** PROPERTY INCOME). [*ITEPA 2003, s 178*]. Where the interest would only partly so qualify for relief, the above provisions do apply but relief is given where appropriate for the amount chargeable as if it were an amount of interest paid. [*ITEPA 2003, s 184; FA 2017, Sch 2 paras 46, 62(2)(5)*].

De minimis exemption

No amount is treated as earnings (or as interest paid) in respect of a loan within the above provisions if the loan (or aggregate taxable loans) at no time in the year exceeds £10,000. Additionally, if the aggregate taxable loans do exceed £10,000 but the aggregate loans that are not 'qualifying loans' (as above) do not exceed that figure, the above provisions do not apply to those non-qualifying loans.

[*ITEPA 2003, s 180; FA 2017, Sch 2 paras 45, 62(2)(5)*].

Ordinary commercial loans

The above provisions do not apply to a loan on '*ordinary commercial terms*', i.e. a loan made in the ordinary course of business by a lender whose business includes either the lending of money or the supply of goods or services on credit, and in relation to which one of the following conditions is satisfied.

(a) When the loan was made, loans for the same or similar purposes and on the same terms and conditions were available to all those who might be expected to avail themselves of the services provided by the lender in the course of business, and a substantial proportion (broadly 50% or more, see HMRC Employment Income Manual EIM26160) of such loans (including the loan in question) made at or about that time were made to members of the public (i.e. those with whom the lender deals at arm's length). All such loans so made to members of the public at or about that time must be held on the same terms as the loan in question, and any change in those terms since that time must have been imposed in the ordinary course of the lender's business. As regards loans made before 1 June 1994, terms and conditions are considered for this purpose disregarding any fees, commission or other incidental expenses incurred by the borrower to obtain the loan.

(b) If the loan was varied before 6 April 2000, a substantial proportion (as in (a) above) of the loan in question, any existing loans varied at or about the same time so as to be held on the same post-variation terms and any new loans made by the same lender at or about the time of the variation must have been made to members of the public. All such loans so made to members of the public at or about the time of the variation must be held on the same terms as the loan in question, and any change in those terms since that time must have been imposed in the ordinary course of the lender's business. Terms and conditions are considered for these purposes disregarding any fees, commission or other incidental expenses incurred by the borrower to obtain the loan and any penalties, interest or similar amounts incurred by the borrower as a result of varying the loan.

(c) If the loan is varied on or after 6 April 2000, a substantial proportion (as in (a) above) of the loan in question, of any existing loans varied at or about the same time so as to be held on the same post-variation terms and of any new loans made by the same lender at or about the time of the variation must have been made to members of the public. At the time of the variation, members of the public who had loans from the lender for similar purposes must have had a right to vary their loans on the same terms and conditions as applied in relation to the variation of the loan in question, and the post-variation terms on which any existing loans so varied and the loan in question are held must be the same. Any change in those terms since that time must have been imposed in the ordinary course of the lender's business. Terms and conditions are considered for these purposes disregarding any fees, commission or other incidental expenses incurred by the borrower to obtain the loan and any penalties, interest or similar amounts incurred by the borrower as a result of varying the loan.

[*ITEPA 2003, s 176*].

In *Amri v HMRC* FTT (TC 3451), [2014] UKFTT 317 (TC), a bank employee had two loans in a single mortgage account, one a cheap loan and the other at a rate available to the general public: HMRC's contention that this represented a single loan to which the ordinary commercial loan exemption did not apply was rejected by the FTT.

Bridging loans

By concession, reimbursement by an employer of the net interest on a bridging loan is not charged to tax, nor is the benefit of a bridging loan advanced by an employer in excess of the relief limit. See **28.72** below.

Expense advances

There is also no charge on advances for an employee's incidental overnight expenses (see **28.86** below) or other expenses necessarily incurred in performance of the duties of the employment, provided that:

- the maximum amount outstanding at any one time in the tax year does not exceed £1,000 (or such higher figure as may be set by Treasury order);
- the advances are spent within six months; and
- the employee accounts to his employer at regular intervals for the expenditure of the sum advanced.

Where there are good reasons for exceeding either the monetary limit or the time limit, the employer may apply for an increased limit. Where the conditions are met, no entry is required on form P11D for taxable loans but details of expense payments are still necessary.

[*ITEPA 2003, s 179*].

Alternative finance arrangements

A 'loan' for these purposes includes arrangements entered into after 21 March 2006 which are alternative finance arrangements within **3.2** or **3.4** ALTERNATIVE FINANCE ARRANGEMENTS or which would be such arrangements if one of the parties thereto were a financial institution. In relation to such arrangements, all references in these provisions to interest are to be taken as references to alternative finance return. For an arrangement within **3.2** ALTERNATIVE FINANCE ARRANGEMENTS, the amount of the 'loan' treated as outstanding at any time is the excess of the purchase price of the asset therein referred to over such part of the aggregate payments to date as does not represent alternative finance return. For an arrangement within **3.4** ALTERNATIVE FINANCE ARRANGEMENTS, the amount treated as outstanding at any time is the excess of the amount of X's original beneficial interest in the asset therein referred to over such part of the aggregate payments to date as does not represent alternative finance return. [*ITEPA 2003, s 173A*].

Calculation of interest at the official rate

The normal method for any tax year ('the relevant year') is as follows.

- Take the average of the maximum amounts of the loan outstanding on 5 April immediately preceding the relevant year and 5 April in the relevant year (or at the date the loan was made or discharged (or the employee died) if falling within that year).
- Multiply that figure by the number of whole months (a month begins on sixth day of each calendar month) during which the loan was outstanding in that year and divide by twelve.

- Multiply the result by the official rate of interest in force, or if the rate changed, the average rate (on a daily basis), for the period during which the loan was outstanding during the year.

[*ITEPA 2003, ss 182, 190(1)*].

A replacement loan is treated for averaging purposes as being the same loan as the original if it is a 'further employment-related loan' which replaces (i) the original loan or (ii) a non-employment related loan which itself replaced the original, the second replacement occurring in the same tax year, or within 40 days thereafter, as the first. A '*further employment-related loan*' is a loan the benefit of which is obtained by reason of the same employment or other employment with the same employer or a person connected with him (within **19** CONNECTED PERSONS). These rules do not apply for the purpose of calculating the modified cash equivalent of the benefit under Salary sacrifice arrangements above. [*ITEPA 2003, s 186*].

There is an alternative method which may be imposed by HMRC or for which the employee may elect. Notice of imposition or election must be given within twelve months after 31 January following the relevant tax year. This alternative method is to calculate the figures by reference to the daily amounts of the loan and official rates of interest. [*ITEPA 2003, s 183, Sch 7 para 26*].

See the example at **28.33** below.

General

Where two or more employees are chargeable under the above provisions in respect of the same loan, the cash equivalent is apportioned between them in a fair and reasonable manner, the portion allocated to each being treated as the cash equivalent as far as that employee is concerned. Any election for the alternative method of calculation in such a case must be made by all the employees concerned. [*ITEPA 2003, ss 183(4), 185*].

Interest on money loaned interest-free, subject to conditions and repayable on demand, by the employer to a trust for the benefit of an employee was held to be taxable earnings (*O'Leary v McKinlay* Ch D 1990, 63 TC 729).

A 'discount' payment containing no element other than a LIBOR based return, which was differentiated from interest only because it was paid at the end, rather than during the term, of the loan, could not properly be said to be anything other than a payment of interest for these purposes (*Leeds Design Innovation Centre Ltd and others v HMRC* FTT (TC 3051), [2014] SFTD 681).

Simon's Taxes. See **E4.631–E4.637.**

Example

[28.33]

D, who is an employee of A Ltd earning £25,000 per annum, obtained a loan of £10,000 from the company on 10 October 2007 for the purpose of buying a car. Interest at a nominal rate is charged on the outstanding balance while the principal is repayable by instalments of £1,000 on 31 December and 30 June commencing 31 December 2007. The interest paid by D amounted to £50 in 2007/08 and to £250 in 2008/09. The official rate of interest is 6.25% until 28 February 2009 and 4.75% thereafter; the average rate for 2008/09 is 6.1%.

D is assessed for 2007/08 as follows.

	£
Normal method (averaging)	
Average balance for period $\frac{£10,000 + £9,000}{2}$	£9,500
£9,500 × $^5/_{12}$	£3,958
£3,958 × 6.25%	247
Deduct Interest paid in year	50
Cash equivalent of loan benefit	£197

Alternative method

Period	Balance of loan in period	Interest at official rate on balance	
	£		£
10.10.07 – 31.12.07	10,000	£10,000 × 6.25% × $^{83}/_{365}$	142
1.1.08 – 5.4.08	9,000	£9,000 × 6.25% × $^{95}/_{365}$	146
			288
Deduct Interest paid in year			50
Cash equivalent of loan benefit			£238
Amount chargeable to tax note (b)			£238

D is assessed for 2008/09 as follows.

	£
Normal method (averaging)	
Average balance for period $\frac{£9,000 + £7,000}{2}$	
	£8,000
£8,000 × 6.1%	488
Deduct	250
Cash equivalent of loan benefit	£238

Alternative method

Period	Balance of loan in period	Interest at official rate on balance	
	£		£
6.4.08 – 30.6.08	9,000	£9,000 × 6.25% × 86/365	132
1.7.08 – 31.12.08	8,000	£8,000 × 6.25% × 184/365	252
1.1.09 – 28.2.09	7,000	£7,000 × 6.25% × 59/365	71
1.3.09 – 5.4.09	7,000	£7,000 × 4.75% × 36/365	33
			488
Deduct Interest paid in year			250
Cash equivalent of loan benefit			£238
Amount chargeable to tax note (b)			£238

Notes

(a) The period 10 October 2007 to 5 April 2008 is, for the purpose of calculating the average balance, five complete months (months begin on the sixth day of each calendar month). However, in applying the interest rate change, the actual number of days during which the loan was outstanding is taken into account.

(b) HMRC will probably require the alternative method to be applied for 2007/08. For 2008/09, both methods happen to give the same result.

(c) This example illustrates the year 2008/09 as that was the latest year in which the official rate was changed in-year. The principles illustrated here continue to apply for subsequent years.

Loans written off

[28.34] Any amount released from, or written off, an 'employment-related loan' (see **28.32** above) will be charged as taxable earnings, unless otherwise taxable as income. Where, however, it would be taxable under *ITEPA 2003, s 403* (see **18.4** COMPENSATION FOR LOSS OF EMPLOYMENT) it will instead be taxable under this provision, and where the loan is one which is a capital sum within *ITTOIA 2005, s 633* (see **70.32** SETTLEMENTS) the charge will be on the excess of the amount released over sums previously treated as the employee's income under *s 633*. These provisions continue to apply after employment has terminated become lower-paid employment (see **28.62** below), and to a loan replacing the original loan, but they cease on death of the employee. If the loan is wholly or partly repaid after a charge has arisen under this provision, a claim may be made for the appropriate relief. [*ITEPA 2003, ss 188–190, 191(3), Sch 7 paras 25, 27*].

Where the lender is a close company in which the employee is a participator and an amount is released or written off, a charge arises on the participator under the provisions at **65.21** SAVINGS AND INVESTMENT INCOME). The charge under those provisions takes priority over the charge described above, so that the same amount will not give rise to a charge under both provisions (HMRC Employment Income Manual EIM21746).

Simon's Taxes. See E4.638.

Living accommodation

[28.35] Provision of living accommodation for an employee may be taxable earnings under general principles (see **28.13** above). In *Nicoll v Austin* KB 1935, 19 TC 531, a company maintained a large house owned and occupied by its managing director and controlling shareholder, paying the rates, fuel bills and other outgoings. The expenditure was held to be taxable on him as emoluments of his office.

There may, however, be liability under special legislation as described at **28.36–28.41** below. This takes priority over any charge under general principles, the latter applying only if, and to the extent that, the charge would exceed that under the special legislation or if the charge under the special legislation is nil. [*ITEPA 2003, s 109; FA 2016, s 7(3)(9); FA 2017, Sch 2 paras 18, 62(2)(4)*].

'Living accommodation' for these purposes includes all kinds of residential accommodation – e.g. mansions, houses, flats, houseboats, holiday homes or apartments – but not overnight or hotel accommodation or board and lodging (HMRC Employment Income Manual EIM11321). Whether such accommodation is provided for an employee is a question of fact — see HMRC Employment Income Manual EIM11405, 11406.

For expenses related to living accommodation, see **28.43** below.

Simon's Taxes. See **E4.607–E4.608A.**

The basic charge

[28.36] For any employee, the 'cash equivalent' of any living accommodation provided to him, or to members of his family or household, by his employer for any period during or comprising a tax year is treated as earnings for that year unless:

- the accommodation is provided in the normal course of domestic, family and personal relationships; or
- any of the exemptions at **28.39** and **28.40** below apply.

For 2017/18 onwards (or, in some cases, 2021/22 onwards), special rules apply instead of the above where the accommodation is provided pursuant to salary sacrifice arrangements. See **28.37** below.

A deduction is allowed for any amounts which would have been allowed had the employee paid for the accommodation out of earnings.

A charge similarly arises where the accommodation is provided by someone other than the employer but 'by reason of' the employment, i.e. where the accommodation would not have been provided but for the employment. In practice HMRC normally assume that a benefit which is provided by someone other than the employer but which is plainly connected with the employment has been provided by reason of the employment. (HMRC Employment Income Manual EIM11408, 20503).

The '*cash equivalent*' of the provision of accommodation for a period is the 'rental value' of the accommodation for that period less any sum made good by the employee to the person at whose cost the accommodation is provided and attributable to that provision. The '*rental value*' is normally an amount equal to rent for the period at an annual rent equal to the annual value ascertained under *ITEPA 2003, s 110*, which for UK property is equivalent to the gross rateable value. In Scotland, where the 1985 rating revaluation produced annual values out of line with those in the rest of the UK, a figure lower than the gross rateable value is, by concession, used as annual value. The 1985 valuation figure is scaled back by the average increase in Scottish rateable values between 1978 and 1985 (170%), e.g. a 1985 value of £270 becomes £100 for this purpose. (HMRC ESC A56). For new properties which do not appear on the domestic rating lists, and for those where there has been a material change since the lists ceased to be maintained, estimates will be agreed of what the gross annual value would have been had domestic rates been continued. In the case of Scotland these will then be scaled back to 1978 values. (Revenue Press Release 19 April 1990).

For determination of the annual value of property situated outside the UK, see HMRC Employment Income Manual EIM11440, 11441. Disputes as to annual value may be referred to the Appeal Tribunal.

Alternatively, if the person at whose cost the accommodation is provided pays actual rent for the whole or part of the period at an annual rate greater than the annual value (as above), then that actual rent is the rental value for the period (or part). See **28.38** below for property acquired on a short lease at a premium.

As regards the charge to tax for 2017/18 onwards, any making good, if it is to be deductible, must be done on or before 6 July following the tax year for which the charge arises; previously no deadline was specified.

It is stipulated that where living accommodation is provided to an individual on terms which constitute a 'fair bargain', the living accommodation is a benefit, and the charge under these provisions applies, regardless. '*Fair bargain*' refers to a situation in which an individual receives something from an employer at the same cost, and subject to the same terms and conditions, as a member of the public or other independent third party dealing with the employer on an arms-length basis.

[*ITEPA 2003, ss 97, 102, 103, 105, 110, 111, 364; FA 2016, s 7(2)(9); FA 2017, Sch 2 paras 7, 13, 14, 62(2)(4); F(No 2)A 2017, s 1(5)(14)*].

See also the additional charge at **28.41** below.

Salary sacrifice arrangements

[28.37] For **2017/18** onwards (subject to the transitional provision below), if the benefit of the living accommodation is provided pursuant to salary sacrifice arrangements (see **28.14** above), the amount to be treated as earnings for the tax year is calculated as set out below. The exemption at **28.36** above for accommodation provided in the normal course of domestic, family and personal relationships applies in such a case, but the exemptions at **28.39** and **28.40** below do not.

To find the amount to be treated as earnings, first determine which (if any) is the greater of (a) the 'modified cash equivalent' of the benefit of the accommodation and (b) the amount forgone. The '*modified cash equivalent*' is equal to the rental value (as in **28.36**) of the accommodation. See **28.14** as to 'the amount forgone'. If (a) is greater than or equal to (b), the taxable amount is the cash equivalent of the benefit (as in **28.36**). Otherwise, the taxable amount is the amount forgone less any sum made good, on or before 6 July following the tax year, by the employee that is properly attributable to the provision of the accommodation. In any case in which the benefit of the accommodation would be exempt from income tax were it not provided under such arrangements (see **28.14**), the modified cash equivalent is treated as zero for these purposes.

Transitional provision

Where the accommodation is provided pursuant to pre-6 April 2017 arrangements, the introduction of the above rules is delayed by four years, and they have effect for **2021/22** onwards instead. See **28.14** as to the effect of pre-6 April 2017 arrangements being varied or renewed on or after that date.

[*ITEPA 2003, ss 102(1B), 103A(1)–(7)(10), 105(2A); FA 2017, Sch 2 paras 13, 15, 16, 62(2)(4)*].

Premium treated as rent

[28.38] In this paragraph the person at whose cost the accommodation is provided is known as P. Where the accommodation is leased by P under a lease entered into on or after 22 April 2009 of ten years or less and P pays a premium, the 'net premium' is treated for the purposes of **28.36** above as if it were a payment of rent (or additional rent). In determining the amount to be so treated for any tax year (or part of a tax year) the net premium is regarded as accruing evenly throughout the term of the lease. The '*net premium*' means the total amount paid or payable by P by way of premium, less any part of that amount that has been repaid or is (or will become) repayable. These rules come into play only if the premises are mainly used by P for providing employee living accommodation. They apply if the accommodation represents all or part of the premises leased. A pre-22 April 2009 lease is brought within the rules if it is extended on or after that date, but only by reference to the additional term of the lease and ignoring any premium payable in respect of the unextended term. A premium includes a premium under the lease or otherwise under the terms on which the lease is granted; in Scotland, a premium includes a grassum.

Special rules apply if a lease contains one or more 'break clauses' if the right to terminate the lease that any such clause confers is capable of being exercised in such a way that the term of the lease is then ten years or less. A '*break clause*' is a provision of a lease that gives a person a right to terminate the lease so that its term is shorter than it otherwise would be. In applying the above provisions, both the term of the lease and the net premium are to be determined on the assumption that any such break clause is exercised in such a way that the term of the lease is as short as possible. If, in fact, the break clause is not exercised, so that the lease continues, the parties to the lease are treated as if they had entered into a further lease. The above provisions are then applied to this notional lease, taking the net premium to be a time-apportioned amount of so much of the premium payable under the actual lease as has not already been treated as a payment of rent. Appropriate modifications apply if there is a further break clause in that part of the term of the actual lease that coincides with the notional lease.

[*ITEPA 2003, ss 105A, 105B*].

This legislation was enacted in response to an apparently widely used scheme involving the use of lease premium arrangements by employers to provide living accommodation to employees with the intention of minimising the tax and national insurance charge on the benefit of the accommodation. The accommodation was often provided via an employee benefit trust or similar entity. HMRC always considered that such arrangements were ineffective and the aim of the legislation was to put this beyond doubt.

Exemptions

[28.39] There is an exemption from the charge at **28.36** above (but not from the charge at **28.37** above) where:

(a) the employer is a local authority, and the accommodation is provided on terms no more favourable than for non-employees; or
(b) it is necessary for the proper performance of his duties for the employee to reside in the accommodation; or
(c) the employment is such that it is customary for employees to be provided with accommodation for the better performance of their duties; or
(d) there is a special threat to the employee's personal security, and he resides in the accommodation as part of special security arrangements in force; or
(e) the accommodation is in Chevening House or certain related premises and the employee is a person nominated in accordance with the Chevening Estate trusts.

[*ITEPA 2003, ss 98, 99(1)(2), 100, 101; FA 2017, Sch 2 paras 8–10, 12, 62(2)(4)*].

See also **28.40** below (overseas holiday homes etc.).

See *Vertigan v Brady* Ch D 1988, 60 TC 624 as regards the scope of (b) and (c) above.

As regards (c) above, it is accepted that the following employees are within the exemption: police officers; MOD police; prison governors, officers and chaplains; clergymen and ministers of religion (unless engaged on purely administrative duties); members of HM forces; members of the Diplomatic Service; managers of newsagent shops with paper rounds; live-in managers of public houses; managers of off-licences with opening hours broadly equivalent to those of public houses; boarding school head teachers and certain other staff provided with accommodation on or near the school premises; stable staff of racehorse trainers who live on the premises and certain key workers who live close to the stables. Veterinary surgeons assisting in veterinary practices and managers of camping and caravan sites living on or adjacent to the site will be accepted as meeting the test that provision of accommodation is 'customary', but must individually satisfy the test that the provision is for the 'better performance' of their duties. (HMRC Employment Income Manual EIM11351, 11352).

Employees who were treated as representative occupiers at 5 April 1977 are treated by concession as exempt from charge, provided circumstances remain unchanged. This also applies to employees who succeed to a particular post regarded as carrying representative status. This concession is withdrawn with effect on and after 6 April 2021. See HMRC Employment Income Manual EIM11336–11339.

Council tax and rates

Where (b), (c) or (d) above applies, there is also no liability if the water or sewerage charges or rates or council tax are paid or reimbursed by the employer. [*ITEPA 2003, s 314*].

Directors

Neither (b) nor (c) above applies to accommodation provided by a company, or associated company, to its director unless for each such directorship he has no material interest in the company (i.e. broadly if his and/or his associates' interests in the company do not exceed 5%) *and either* he is a full-time working director *or* the company is non-profit-making (i.e. it does not carry on a trade nor is its main function the holding of investments or other property) *or* the company is a charitable company. [*ITEPA 2003, ss 68, 99(3)–(5)*].

Overseas holiday homes etc.

[28.40] There is a further exemption from the charge at **28.36** above (but not from the charge at **28.37** above) which is intended mainly for UK resident individuals who set up or acquire an overseas company for the purpose of owning an overseas property, generally for use as a holiday home. It applies where a property outside the UK is owned by a company that is itself wholly owned (with or without other individuals) by the director or other officer on whom a taxable living accommodation benefit would otherwise arise. The company must be the '*holding company of the property*', i.e.

- it must own a '*relevant interest*' in the property, being an interest that confers (or would but for any inferior interest confer) a right to exclusive possession;
- its interest in the property must be its sole or main asset; and
- it must undertake no activities other than those incidental to its ownership of that interest.

A company can also be the '*holding company of the property*' if the property is owned by a wholly owned subsidiary of the company. The subsidiary must meet the three conditions above and the company itself must meet the second and third conditions by reference to its interest in the subsidiary.

The company must also have been the holding company of the property at all times since the 'relevant time'. The '*relevant time*' is normally the time the company first owned a relevant interest in the property. If, however, the director or officer acquired his interest in the company after that time, and otherwise than from a connected person (see **19** CONNECTED PERSONS), the '*relevant time*' is the time the director or officer acquired that interest.

The exemption does *not* apply in any of the following circumstances:

- if the company's interest in the property was acquired from a 'connected company' at an undervalue (as defined) or derives from an interest that was so acquired;
- if, at any time after the relevant time (as above), expenditure in respect of the property has been incurred by a 'connected company' or any borrowing of the company from a 'connected company' has been outstanding (disregarding any borrowing at a commercial rate or which results in a charge under **28.32** above (cheap loan arrangements) on the director or officer concerned); or
- if the living accommodation is provided in pursuance of an arrangement (as widely defined) a main purpose of which is the avoidance of tax or National Insurance contributions.

For the purposes of the above, a '*connected company*' is a company connected with the director or officer concerned (or with a member of his family or with his employer) or a company connected with such a company. Reference to the company's acquiring an interest include an interest being granted to it.

[*ITEPA 2003, ss 100A, 100B; FA 2017, Sch 2 paras 11, 62(2)(4)*].

Additional charge on properties costing over £75,000

[28.41] For all employees, if there is a liability to tax on living accommodation under the basic charge in **28.36** above (or there would be a liability if the employee's contributions towards the cost were disregarded) and the cost of providing the accommodation exceeds £75,000, the employee will, in addition to any basic charge, be taxable on the 'additional value' to him of the accommodation. Where, however, the basic charge is based on the full open market rent the property might fetch, HMRC will, by concession, not seek to impose an additional charge (HMRC ESC A91).

The '*additional value*' is the rent which would have been payable for the period if the annual rent was the 'appropriate percentage' of the amount by which the cost of providing the accommodation exceeds £75,000. The '*appropriate percentage*' is the 'official rate' in force, for the purposes of taxing cheap loan arrangements under *ITEPA 2003, s 181* (see **28.32** above), at the beginning of the tax year (e.g. 2.25% for 2020/21; 2.5% for 2017/18, 2018/19 and 2019/20; 3% for 2016/17). Any rent paid by the employee which exceeds the value of the accommodation as determined for the purposes of the basic charge is deducted from the additional value. As regards the charge to tax for 2017/18 onwards, any such rent, if it is to be deductible, must be paid on or before 6 July following the tax year for which the charge arises; previously no deadline was specified.

The cost of providing the accommodation is the aggregate of expenditure incurred by any 'relevant person' in acquiring the property together with any improvement expenditure incurred before the tax year in question *less* any payments by the employee to any relevant person as reimbursement of such expenditure or as consideration for the grant of a tenancy, or subtenancy, to him. Where the employee first occupies the property on a date after 30 March 1983 and an estate or interest in the property was held by a relevant person throughout the period of six years ending with the date of first occupation, then the cost of providing the accommodation, for the purposes of calculating the additional value (but not for determining whether the additional charge applies), is calculated as follows. Take the market value of the property at the date of first occupation and add any improvement expenditure incurred after that date and before the start of the tax year. Deduct from the total any payments made by the employee to any relevant person as reimbursement of any part of the cost of acquiring the estate or interest held when the employee first occupied the property (up to the market value on that date) or of the improvement expenditure, or as consideration for the grant of a tenancy, or subtenancy, to him. A '*relevant person*' is the person providing the accommodation, or, if different, the employee's employer, and any person, other than the employee, connected with such persons (within **19** CONNECTED PERSONS). '*Market value*' is open market value assuming vacant possession and disregarding any options on the property held by the employee, a person connected with him or any relevant person as defined above.

Where an employee is provided with more than one property, the £75,000 limit is applied separately to each property (Revenue Press Release 22 November 1990). Where a property is provided as living accommodation to more than one employee or director in the same period, the total of the basic and additional charges cannot exceed the amount which would have been chargeable if the property had been provided to a single employee in that period.

Salary sacrifice arrangements

The additional charge also applies where the basic charge is under **28.37** above (living accommodation provided pursuant to salary sacrifice arrangements) for 2017/18 onwards (or 2021/22 onwards where the transitional rule in **28.37** applies). To find the total amount to be treated as earnings, first determine which (if any) is the greater of (a) the 'modified cash equivalent' of the benefit of the accommodation and (b) the amount forgone. The '*modified cash equivalent*' is equal to the rental value (as in **28.36** above) of the accommodation plus the 'additional value' (calculated as above). See **28.14** above as to 'the amount forgone'. If (a) is greater than or equal to (b), the taxable amount is what would have been the taxable amount if the accommodation was not provided pursuant to salary sacrifice arrangements. Otherwise, the taxable amount is the amount forgone less (i) so much of the total of any sums made good, on or before 6 July following the tax year, by the employee that is properly attributable to the provision of the accommodation, as does not exceed the rental value of the accommodation, and (ii) any rent paid by the employee, on or before 6 July following the tax year, which exceeds the rental value of the accommodation. In any case in which the benefit of the accommodation would be exempt from income tax were it not provided under such arrangements (see **28.14**), the modified cash equivalent is treated as zero for these purposes.

[*ITEPA 2003, ss 103A(8), (9), 104, 106–108, 112, Sch 7 para 21; FA 2017, Sch 2 paras 15, 17, 62(2)(4); F(No 2)A 2017, s 1(6)(14)*].

Example

[28.42]

S, the founder and managing director of S Ltd, a successful transport company, has since April 2015 occupied a mansion house owned by S Ltd. The house was acquired by S Ltd in August 2009 for £150,000 and, since acquisition, but before 6 April 2019, £80,000 has been spent by S Ltd on alterations and improvements to the house. The gross annual value of the house for rating purposes before 1 April 1990 (when the community charge replaced general rates) was £1,663. S pays annual rental of £2,000 to the company for 2020/21 only. He pays all expenses relating to the property.

S will have taxable benefits in respect of his occupation of the house for 2019/20 and 2020/21 as follows.

	£	£
2019/20		
Gross annual value		1,663
Additional charge		
Acquisition cost of house	150,000	
Cost of improvements	80,000	
	230,000	
Deduct	75,000	
Additional value	£155,000	
Additional value at 2.5%		3,875
		£5,538
2020/21		
Gross annual value		Nil*
Additional charge		
Acquisition cost of house	150,000	
Cost of improvements	80,000	
	230,000	
Deduct	75,000	
Additional value	£155,000	
Additional value at 2.25%		3,487
		3,487
Rental payable by S	2,000	
Deduct Gross annual value	1,663	
		337*
		£3,150

* No taxable gross annual value arises in 2020/21 because the rental of £2,000 payable by S exceeds the gross annual value of £1,663. The excess is deductible from the amount of the benefit arising under the additional charge.

Expenses connected with living accommodation

[28.43] Certain expenses connected with the provision of living accommodation which are met on behalf of, or reimbursed to, the employee may give rise to liability either as benefits-in-kind for directors and certain employees or directly as earnings for all employees. The following reliefs apply.

(i) *Alterations and repairs* to accommodation provided for employees will not be treated as benefits if:
- the alterations or additions are of a structural nature; or
- the repairs would be the obligation of the lessor if the premises were leased and *Landlord and Tenant Act 1985, s 11* applied.

[*ITEPA 2003, s 313*].

(ii) Where one of the exemptions in **28.39**(b), (c) or (d) above applies, any amount to be treated as earnings in respect of expenditure on *heating, lighting, cleaning, repairs, maintenance, decoration, provision of furniture etc.* normal for domestic occupation is limited to 10% of the net earnings from the employment for the period concerned less any sum made good by the employee. Earnings include any from an associated company (i.e. where one company has control of the other or both are under control of the same person). Net earnings are after deducting capital allowances, allowable expenses, mileage allowance relief, and contributions to registered pension schemes and disregarding the benefit in question. [*ITEPA 2003, s 315*]. The earnings to be taken into account are those for the year under review, regardless of the year in which they are chargeable (HMRC Employment Income Manual EIM21723).

Example

[28.44]

N is employed by the G Property Co Ltd, earning £14,500 p.a. He occupies, rent-free, the basement flat of a block of flats for which he is employed as caretaker/security officer. The annual value of the flat is determined at £250. In 2020/21, G Ltd incurred the following expenditure on the flat.

	£
Heat and light	700
Decoration	380
Repairs	230
Cleaning	190
	1,500
Conversion of large bedroom into two smaller bedrooms	3,000

In addition, the company pays N's council tax which amounts to £500.

N pays a personal pension premium of £160 net of tax (equivalent to £200 gross) into a registered scheme on 31 October 2020, but apart from his personal allowance, he has no other reliefs. N's liability to income tax is at the main UK rates.

N's taxable income for 2020/21 is

	£
Salary	14,500
Annual value of flat	—
Heat and light, decoration, repairs, cleaning £1,500 restricted to	1,430
	15,930
Deduct	
Personal allowance	12,500
Taxable	£3,430

Notes

(a) N is not chargeable on the annual value of the flat as long as he can show that it is necessary for the proper performance of his duties for him to reside in the accommodation.

(b) The structural alterations costing £3,000 will not be regarded as a benefit.

(c) The earnings treated as having arisen in respect of the heat and light, decoration, repairs and cleaning costs will be restricted to the lesser of:
   (i) the expenses incurred £1,500;
   (ii) 10% × £14,300 (net earnings) £1,430.
   The contribution to a registered pension scheme is deductible in arriving at net earnings for this purpose. (The contribution is not shown above as a deduction from taxable income as basic rate relief has been given at source and higher and additional rate relief are not applicable.)

Living accommodation — miscellaneous

[28.45] The following cases, decided under earlier legislation, may be relevant to a charge under the benefits code in respect of expenses related to living accommodation. *Butter v Bennett* CA 1962, 40 TC 402 ('representative occupier' held to be taxable on provisions for fuel and gardening); *Doyle v Davison* QB(NI) 1961, 40 TC 140 (repairs paid for by employer held to be benefits); *McKie v Warner* Ch D 1961, 40 TC 65 (flat provided at reduced rent held to be benefit); *Luke* HL 1963, 40 TC 630 (certain expenses held not to be benefits — house owned by employer); *Westcott v Bryan* CA 1969, 45 TC 476 (apportionment approved where company house provided to accommodate company guests).

As regards board and lodging allowances, see **28.13** above and for subsistence allowances, see **28.84** below. For deductibility of the cost of living accommodation etc., see **28.19** above.

Compulsory transfers

Guarantee payments making good loss on sale of employee's house when compulsorily transferred were held not taxable in *Hochstrasser v Mayes, Jennings v Kinder* HL 1959, 38 TC 673.

Members of Parliaments and Assemblies

Members of the House of Commons, the Scottish Parliament or the Wales or Northern Ireland Assemblies are not allowed a deduction for expenses incurred on residential or overnight accommodation to enable duties to be performed where the body of which they are a member sits or in the area which they represent. In relation to a member of the House of Commons, overnight stays in hotels that are excluded from the exemption in **30.33** EXEMPT INCOME are also excluded from this disallowance. [*ITEPA 2003, s 360*].

Vouchers and credit tokens

[28.46] The items at **28.47–28.49** below, when provided for an employee (or a member of his family, i.e. his spouse, civil partner, parent, child or spouse/civil partner of his child or any dependant of the employee) by reason of the employment, are taxable earnings of the employment. [*ITEPA 2003, ss 74, 81, 83, 87, 91, 94*]. Their supply by the employer is regarded as 'by reason of the employment' unless the employer is an individual and the supply is made in the normal course of his domestic, family or personal relationships. [*ITEPA 2003, ss 73(2), 82(2), 90(2)*]. The provisions do not apply to vouchers etc. of a kind made available to the public generally and provided to the employee (or family) on no more favourable terms than to the public generally. [*ITEPA 2003, ss 78, 85, 93*]. Where they do apply, no liability arises in respect of the money goods or services obtained for the voucher. [*ITEPA 2003, s 95; FA 2017, Sch 2 paras 51, 62(2)(5)*].

For a summary of the amounts chargeable and the tax year in which liability arises, see HMRC Employment Income Manual EIM16140.

For the exemption from income tax liability of the provision of vouchers or credit-tokens which can be used to obtain specified benefits the direct provision of which would be exempt, see *ITEPA 2003, ss 266, 267*. The Treasury are now empowered to specify further exempt benefits by means of statutory instrument. [*ITEPA 2003, s 96A*].

For the application of PAYE, see **53.3** PAY AS YOU EARN.

Non-cash vouchers

[28.47] 'Non-cash vouchers' are within the charge at **28.46** above. '*Non-cash vouchers*' means vouchers, stamps or similar documents or tokens capable of being exchanged, either singly or together, immediately or later, for money, goods or services or any combination of these but not cash vouchers — see also HMRC Employment Income Manual EIM16040). The tax charge is on the cost of provision less any amount made good by the employee. The cost of provision is the expense incurred by the person at whose cost the voucher, and the money, goods or services for which it is capable of being exchanged, are provided, and in or in connection with that provision (with just and reasonable apportionment in the case of schemes relating to groups of employees). As regards the charge to tax for 2017/18 onwards, any making good, if it is to be deductible, must be done on or before 6 July following the tax year for which the charge arises; previously no deadline was specified. The charge is reduced to the extent that general deductions would have been allowable if the costs had been incurred by the employee. The tax year in which the earnings are treated as received is the year in which the voucher is received by the employee. The voucher is treated as received by the employee in the tax year in which the cost of its provision is incurred by the employer, if this is earlier than the year in which the voucher is actually received by, or appropriated to, the employee. Cheque vouchers, however, are treated as received in the year in which the voucher is handed over in exchange for money, goods or services. [*ITEPA 2003, ss 82, 83, 84(1)(2), 87, 88, 362; FA 2017, Sch 2 paras 5, 54, 62(2)(5); F(No 2)A 2017, s 1(2)(3)(14)*].

Expense incurred by the employer in providing vouchers or any other incentive awards includes expenses beyond the direct cost of buying the goods or services provided where the expenses contribute more or less directly to the advantage enjoyed by the employee, e.g. costs of selecting and testing goods or services, or of after-sales service, or of storage and distribution. More remote expenses, e.g. costs of planning or administering a scheme or of promotional literature etc., are excluded. See HMRC SP 6/85.

A voucher used by an employee to obtain the use of a *car parking space* (or a cycle, motor cycle or van parking space) at or near his place of work is excluded from these provisions. A voucher provided neither by the employer nor by a person connected with the employer (within **19** CONNECTED PERSONS) and used to obtain *entertainment* for the employee (or a relation) is similarly excluded, subject to the same conditions as are specified in **28.52**(xiv) below. [*ITEPA 2003, s 266(1)*]. See also **28.78** below for the exclusion of vouchers relating to certain sports and recreational facilities.

For a limited exemption in respect of *childcare vouchers*, see **28.61** below.

Salary sacrifice arrangements

For 2017/18 onwards, where a non-cash voucher is provided pursuant to salary sacrifice arrangements, the cost of provision (as above) is compared with the amount forgone. If the latter is greater, the charge is on the amount forgone less any part of the cost of provision made good by the employee on or before 6 July following the tax year in which the voucher is received (or treated as received) by the employee. In any case in which the benefit of the voucher would be exempt from income tax were it not provided under such arrangements (see **28.14** above), the cost of provision is for these purposes treated as zero. Where the voucher is provided pursuant to pre-6 April 2017 arrangements, these rules are delayed by one year and have effect for 2018/19 onwards instead. See **28.14** as to 'salary sacrifice arrangements', 'the amount forgone' and the effect of pre-6 April 2017 arrangements being varied or renewed on or after that date.

If a non-cash voucher is provided under pre-6 April 2017 arrangements and is used to obtain anything (whether money, goods or services) that is provided on or after 6 April 2018 (‘*delayed benefits*’), so much of the benefit of the voucher as it is reasonable to regard as being applied to obtain the delayed benefits is to be treated as *not* having been provided pursuant to pre-6 April 2017 arrangements.

[*ITEPA 2003, s 87A; FA 2017, Sch 2 paras 4, 62(2)(5)(13)*].

Transport vouchers

‘Transport vouchers’ are specifically included in the above provisions but *not included* is a voucher provided for an employee of a passenger transport undertaking under arrangements in operation on 25 March 1982 to enable that employee (including spouse or family, as in **28.46** above) to obtain passenger transport services from his employer or his employer’s subsidiary or parent company or another passenger transport undertaking. ‘*Transport voucher*’ means any ticket, pass or other document or token intended to enable a person to obtain passenger transport services (whether or not in exchange for it). [*ITEPA 2003, ss 84(3), 86, 87(4)*]. See also **28.52**(xxii)(xxiii) below.

Cheque vouchers

‘Cheque vouchers’ are also included in the above provisions. ‘*Cheque voucher*’ means a cheque provided for an employee and intended for his use wholly or mainly for payment for particular goods or services or for goods or services of one or more particular classes. [*ITEPA 2003, s 84(4)*].

Incidental overnight expenses

There is excluded from these provisions a voucher used to obtain goods or services (or to obtain money to buy goods or services) incidental to the employee’s being away from home on business during a ‘qualifying absence’ in relation to which the authorised maximum (£5 per night spent in the UK and £10 per night spent abroad) is not exceeded, where the cost of such goods or services is not otherwise deductible from earnings. [*ITEPA 2003, s 268, Sch 7 paras 33, 34*]. See also **28.86** below.

Simon’s Taxes. See **E4.605, E4.720.**

Cash vouchers

[28.48] ‘Cash vouchers’ are within the charge at **28.46** above. ‘*Cash voucher*’ means any voucher, stamp or similar document capable of being exchanged, either singly or together, immediately or later, for a sum of money not substantially less than the cost to the person at whose cost it is provided, but excluding any document for a sum which would not have been employment income if paid to the employee directly and excluding any savings certificate on which accumulated interest is exempt from tax. Where the sum of money is substantially less than the cost, any part of the difference representing benefits in connection with sickness, personal injury or death will be disregarded in deciding if the voucher is a cash voucher.

The charge is on the cash equivalent of the benefit, i.e. the amount for which the voucher is capable of being exchanged. This is treated as earnings for the tax year in which the voucher is received by the employee.

Where, as in some holiday pay schemes, a cash voucher is provided for an employee for redemption for cash which will be an emolument, tax is to be charged on the redemption amount when the voucher is received by, or appropriated to, the employee, with 'just and reasonable' apportionment in the case of schemes relating to groups of employees, *unless* the voucher is issued under a scheme which is approved by the Commissioners for HMRC as being practicable for PAYE to be applied at the time the vouchers are exchanged for cash.

Salary sacrifice arrangements

For 2017/18 onwards, where a cash voucher is provided pursuant to salary sacrifice arrangements, the charge is on the greater of the cash equivalent (as above) and the amount forgone. In any case in which the benefit of the voucher would be exempt from income tax were it not provided under such arrangements (see **28.14** above), the charge is on the amount forgone. Where the voucher is provided pursuant to pre-6 April 2017 arrangements, these rules are delayed by one year and have effect for 2018/19 onwards instead. See **28.14** as to 'salary sacrifice arrangements', 'the amount forgone' and the effect of pre-6 April 2017 arrangements being varied or renewed on or after that date.

[*ITEPA 2003, ss 73, 75–77, 79–81; FA 2017, Sch 2 paras 3, 62(2)(5)*].

Simon's Taxes. See **E4.604**.

Credit tokens

[28.49] 'Credit tokens' are within the charge at **28.46** above. Tax is charged when the employee (or a relative — see **28.46**) uses a credit token to obtain money, goods or services. The tax charge is on the cost of provision less any amount made good by the employee. The cost of provision is the expense incurred by the person at whose cost the token, and the money, goods or services for which it is capable of being exchanged, are provided, and in or in connection with that provision (with just and reasonable apportionment in the case of schemes relating to groups of employees). See **28.47** above as regards valuation of expenses incurred. As regards use of a token in 2017/18 onwards, any making good, if it is to be deductible, must be done on or before 6 July following the tax year in question; previously no deadline was specified. The chargeable amount is reduced by any deductions which would have been allowable if the costs had been incurred by the employee. [*ITEPA 2003, ss 90, 94, 363; FA 2017, Sch 2 paras 56, 62(2)(5); F(No 2)A 2017, s 1(4)(14)*].

'*Credit-token*' means a card, token or other thing given to a person by another person who undertakes that (a) on the production of it (whether or not some other action is also required) he will supply money, goods or services on credit or (b) on *similar* production to a third party, he will pay that third party for the money etc. supplied (whether or not taking any discount or commission). '*Production*' includes the use of an object provided to operate a machine. Not included is a non-cash voucher within **28.47** above or a cash voucher within **28.48** above. [*ITEPA 2003, s 92*].

A token used by an employee to obtain the use of a *car parking space* (or a cycle, motor cycle or van parking space) at or near his place of work is excluded from these provisions. A token provided neither by the employer nor by a person connected with the employer (within **19** CONNECTED PERSONS) and used to obtain *entertainment* for the employee (or a relation) is similarly excluded, subject to the same conditions as are specified in **28.52**(xiv) below. [*ITEPA 2003, s 267(2)*].

Salary sacrifice arrangements

For 2017/18 onwards, where a credit token is used pursuant to salary sacrifice arrangements, the aggregate cost of provision is compared with so much of the amount forgone as is attributable on a just and reasonable basis to such use of the token. If the latter is greater, the charge is on the attributed part of the amount forgone less any part of the aggregate cost of provision made good by the employee on or before 6 July following the tax year which contains the occasion of use of the token to which the making good relates. The aggregate cost of provision is found by adding together the cost of provision (as above) for each occasion of use of the token by the employee in the tax year pursuant to the salary sacrifice arrangements. In any case in which the use of the token in the tax year would be exempt from income tax were it not used pursuant to such arrangements (see **28.14** above), the aggregate cost of provision is for these purposes treated as zero. Where the token is used pursuant to pre-6 April 2017 arrangements, these rules are delayed by one year and have effect for 2018/19 onwards instead. See **28.14** as to 'salary sacrifice arrangements', 'the amount forgone' and the effect of pre-6 April 2017 arrangements being varied or renewed on or after that date. [*ITEPA 2003, s 94A; FA 2017, Sch 2 paras 6, 62(2)(5)*].

The amount taxed under PAYE when a credit token is used pursuant to salary sacrifice arrangements is what would have been the taxable amount had it not been so provided (see **53.3**(c) PAY AS YOU EARN).

Incidental overnight expenses

There is excluded from these provisions a token used to obtain goods or services (or to obtain money to buy goods or services) incidental to the employee's being away from home on business during a 'qualifying absence' in relation to which the authorised maximum (£5 per night spent in the UK and £10 per night spent abroad) is not exceeded, where the cost of such goods or services is not otherwise deductible from earnings. [*ITEPA 2003, s 268, Sch 7 paras 33, 34*]. See also **28.86** below.

Simon's Taxes. See **E4.606, E4.720.**

Other employment-related benefits

[28.50] All benefits or facilities of any kind (other than those within the special charging provisions at **28.23–28.49** above) provided for an employee (or for an employee's family or household) by reason of the employment are taxable on the cash equivalent of the benefit (see **28.54** below). Benefits are 'provided' by those at whose cost they are provided, and benefits provided by someone other than the employer may be included. All benefits provided by the employer are 'by reason of the employment' unless the employer is an individual and the provision is made in the normal course of his domestic, family or personal relationships. [*ITEPA 2003, ss 201, 202, 209*].

Whether a person is a member of another's family or household is determined by *ITEPA 2003, s 721(4)(5)*. In *Baylis v HMRC* FTT (TC 5454), [2016] UKFTT 725 (TC), [2017] SFTD 217 it was held that HMRC has no discretion in allocating tax charges to family members (in this case to a father or daughter) and that *section 721(4)* itself provides a hierarchy with 'spouse' coming before 'parent'.

In a case in which, by virtue of an earlier change in control agreement, the appellant had disposed of shares in his employer company *to* that company for more than their market value, the excess was held to be a benefit provided to the appellant by reason of his employment and thus chargeable to tax as a benefit (*Smith v HMRC* FTT (TC 163), [2009] SFTD 731).

The Treasury does, however, have powers to exempt minor benefits by order, such exemption being conditional on the benefit(s) in question being made available to the employer's employees generally on similar terms. Provision of a voucher evidencing entitlement to such an exempt minor benefit is also exempt from charge under *ITEPA 2003, s 87* (non-cash vouchers — see **28.47** above). The following minor benefits have been the subject of such regulatory exemption.

(a) Welfare counselling (excluding advice on finance (other than debt problems), tax, leisure or recreation and legal advice). HMRC has agreed with the UK Employee Assistance Professionals Association (EAPA) that legal information provided within the context of welfare counselling will not prevent the exemption from applying as long as it remains within agreed guidelines, for which see www.gov.uk/expenses-and-benefits-counselling. Medical treatment used to be specifically excluded from the exemption but this exclusion is removed for 2020/21 onwards. Thus, medical treatment such as cognitive behavioural therapy that is provided to the employee as part of the employer's welfare counselling services is brought within the exemption.

(b) Provision of buses for journeys of ten miles or less from the workplace to shops etc. on a working day.

(c) Certain benefits provided to disabled employees (e.g. hearing aids or wheelchairs) to enable them to perform the duties of the employment.

(d) (For 2016/17 and earlier years) pensions information and advice given to an employee on the employer's behalf where the cash equivalent of the benefit (see **28.54** below) does not in total exceed £150 for the tax year. If there is an excess over £150, the full amount is taxable and not just the excess. This exemption is replaced for 2017/18 onwards by the exemption at **28.52**(xxix) below.

(e) For amounts reimbursed during the period 11 June 2020 to 5 April 2021, but also by concession from 16 March 2020 to 10 June 2020, reimbursed expenses incurred by an employee in respect of equipment obtained by the employee for the sole purpose of enabling the employee to work from home as a result of the 2020 COVID-19 (coronavirus) pandemic. See **28.15** above.

[*ITEPA 2003, ss 210, 266(4); F(No 2)A 2017, s 3(3)–(5); SI 2000 No 2080; SI 2002 Nos 205, 1596; SI 2003 No 1434; SI 2004 No 3087; SI 2007 No 2090; SI 2012 No 1808; SI 2020 No 291; SI 2020 No 524*].

Exemptions are available for benefits provided to employees where the employee would have been eligible for a deduction had he incurred and paid the equivalent expense himself — see **28.53** below. See **28.51** below as regards an exemption for trivial benefits.

In relation to the timing of a benefit, 'provided' refers to the receipt by the employee of the benefit, rather than to steps taken or costs incurred by the employer (*Templeton v Jacobs* Ch D 1996, 68 TC 735).

See **56.1** PENSION INCOME as regards benefits provided to retired employees.

Where an asset (other than a car or van) is placed at the disposal of an employee for his use, whilst remaining in the employer's ownership, a taxable benefit can arise irrespective of whether it is used and whether any such use is private or in furtherance of the employer's business (subject to any deduction available under *ITEPA 2003, s 365* at **28.54** below) (*Rockall and another v HMRC* FTT (TC 3767), [2014] UKFTT 643 (TC)).

Following the decision in *Wicks v Firth* HL 1982, 56 TC 318, payments of cash are potentially within the benefits legislation, so that, for example, examination awards which would otherwise not be taxable following *Ball v Johnson* (see **28.13** above) fall within the benefits charge (ICAEW Technical Memorandum TR 786, 15 March 1990).

Legal expenses incurred by a company in defending a dangerous driving charge against a director were held to be a benefit (*Rendell v Went* HL 1964, 41 TC 641). Parking etc. fines met by employer would generally constitute a benefit (see **28.13** above). Legal costs incurred by a company in proceedings to which the managing director lent his name and from which he personally benefited were held to be a taxable benefit; the fact that the company also benefited was irrelevant, except that the benefit should be restricted to that proportion of total costs which is attributed to the employee on a fair basis (*XI Software Ltd v Laing* (Sp C 450), [2005] SSCD 249).

Allocations of moneys by trustees of an *employee benefit trust* to sub-funds for individual employees were not taxable as benefits-in-kind (*Macdonald v Dextra Accessories Ltd and Others* Ch D 2003, 77 TC 146). A director with no personal interest in horses or horseracing did not receive any taxable benefit from having company-owned racehorses registered in his name (*Chepstow Plant International Ltd and another v HMRC* FTT (TC 1035), [2011] UKFTT 166 (TC); 2011 STI 1703).

See **28.75** below as regards provision of security assets and services for employees.

See **53.25** PAY AS YOU EARN as regards PAYE settlement agreements whereby employer accounts for tax on minor benefits within the agreement, which do not then count as employees' income.

PPE and COVID-19 tests

Where an employer provides personal protective equipment (PPE) to employees working in a situation where the risk of COVID-19 transmission is very high, and the employer's risk assessment shows that PPE is required, its provision is non-taxable. If an employee requires PPE to carry out their role and the employer is unable to provide this, the employer must reimburse the expenses of employees who purchase PPE themselves. This is non-taxable, but neither can employees claim tax relief on the expense if not reimbursed (www.gov.uk/guidance/how-to-treat-certain-expenses-and-benefits-provided-to-employees-during-coronavirus-covid-19#coronavirus-covid-19-tests).

The Chancellor has stated that the Government is to introduce an income tax exemption for 2020/21 onwards for COVID-19 antigen tests provided by employers, which would otherwise have resulted in a taxable benefit on the employee (https://twitter.com/CommonsTreasury/status/1280796126292123648?s=20, 8 July 2020).

Trivial benefits

[28.51] A statutory exemption has effect which enables employers to identify and treat certain low value benefits as 'trivial'. These benefits are then exempt from income tax and do not need to be reported to HMRC.

A benefit is '*trivial*' if:

- it is not cash or a cash voucher (see **28.48** above);
- the cost of providing the benefit does not exceed £50;
- it is not provided pursuant to salary sacrifice arrangements or any other contractual obligation; and
- it is not provided in recognition of particular services performed by the employee or in anticipation of such services.

If a benefit is provided to more than one person and it is impractical to calculate the cost of providing it to each person, the cost of providing the benefit is taken for these purposes to be the average cost per person of providing it.

If the employer (E) is a close company (broadly a company controlled by five or fewer participators — see Tolley's Corporation Tax) and the employee is a director of E, there is an annual cap of £300 on the amount of benefits that can be regarded as trivial. A benefit that would take the employee over the £300 limit is not to any extent a trivial benefit. Benefits received by a member of the family of any such director, where the family member is not an employee of E at the time, count towards the cap. The amount to be thus counted is found by taking the cost of providing the benefit and dividing it by the number of persons who are members of the director's family and are also any of the following: (i) directors of E; (ii) employees of E who are family members of a director within (i); (iii) former employees of E who have been directors at any time when E was a close company; or (iv) former employees of E who are family members of a person within (iii). All references above to directors also include office-holders, and references to members of a person's family include members of his household.

Where a member of the family or household of a close company director is also an employee of the company, that individual is subject to a £300 cap in his own right.

[*ITEPA 2003, ss 323A–323C; FA 2016, s 13*].

For official guidance, including examples, see HMRC Employment Income Manual EIM21864–21872. This includes guidance, at EIM21871, that where a benefit is covered both by the trivial benefits exemption and by another exemption, the outcome that is most favourable to the employee should be applied.

Other exceptions from charge

[28.52] Exceptions from the charge on benefits-in-kind are listed below, with those introduced in recent years towards the end of the list. See also the minor exemptions listed in **28.50** above, and see **28.51** above as regards trivial benefits.

(i) **Provision of accommodation, supplies or services** used by the employee in performing the duties of the employment, provided that either:
   (a) if the benefit is provided on premises occupied by the employer or other person providing it, any private use (i.e. use other than in performing those duties) by the employee (or by the employee's family or household) is not significant; or
   (b) in any other case, the sole purpose of providing the benefit is to enable the employee to perform those duties, any private use (as in (a)) is 'not significant', and the benefit is not an 'excluded benefit'.

   Whether private use under (b) above meets the 'not significant' test will depend on all the circumstances of any given case, but provided that:
   - the employer's policy is clearly stated to employees, setting out the circumstances in which occasional private use may be made; and
   - any decision of the employer not to recover the costs of private use is a commercial decision, for example based on the impractical nature of doing so, rather than a desire to reward the employee,

   HMRC will usually accept that the 'not significant' test is met. Employers are not expected to keep detailed records of private use. The 'not significant' condition should not be decided purely on the absolute time spent on different uses of the asset or service provided; instead, it should be considered in the context of the employee's duties and the necessity for the employee to have the asset or service in order to carry out those duties. (HMRC Employment Income Manual EIM21613).
   Subject to Treasury regulations (which may provide that a benefit is an 'excluded benefit' only if prescribed conditions are met as to the terms on which, and persons to whom, it is provided), '*excluded benefit*' consists of the provision of a motor vehicle, boat or aircraft, or of a benefit which involves the extension, conversion or alteration of any

living accommodation or the construction, extension, conversion or alteration of a building or other structure on land adjacent to and enjoyed with living accommodation.
[*ITEPA 2003, s 316*].
The exemption can extend to the provision of a telephone line and/or broadband internet access in the employee's home (HMRC Employment Income Manual EIM21615–21617). See generally EIM21610–21614.

(ii) **Provision of living accommodation and connected expenses** in certain circumstances, see **28.39**, **28.43** above. [*ITEPA 2003, ss 313–315*].

(iii) **Provision of retirement and death benefits.** The exemption covers the provision by the employer of a pension, annuity, lump sum, gratuity or other like benefit to be paid or given to the employee, his dependants or any other members of his family or household on the employee's retirement or death. This exemption applies to (but is not restricted to) provision made under a registered pension scheme (as in **57.4** PENSION PROVISION). It does not extend to any amount paid to insure against the risk that a retirement or death benefit under an employer-financed retirement benefits scheme (see **57.34** PENSION PROVISION) cannot be paid due to the employer's insolvency. For **2019/20** onwards, the scope of the exemption is widened to allow the employee to nominate any individual (whether or not a dependant etc.) or a registered charity as the beneficiary of his retirement or death benefits. [*ITEPA 2003, s 307; FA 2019, s 11*].

(iv) **Provision by the employer of free or subsidised meals** in a canteen or on the employer's business premises where, in either case, the meals are provided on a reasonable scale and all of the employer's employees (or all of them at a particular location) may obtain such a meal or a voucher, ticket, pass etc. to enable them to obtain such a meal. Light refreshments are regarded as meals for these purposes. If the meals are provided in the restaurant or dining-room of a hotel or a catering etc. business at a time when meals are served to the public, the exemption applies only if the staff meals are taken in a part designated for staff use only. In a case where tea, coffee or cooled water is outside the exemption due to its not being available to all employees, the trivial benefit rules at **28.51** above should provide an exemption.
The exemption is not available where the employee's entitlement to free or subsidised meals arises in conjunction with salary sacrifice arrangements or 'flexible remuneration arrangements'. For example, the employee might agree to accept a reduced salary in return for being provided with food and drink (or the means of obtaining it) of a value that is commensurate with the amount of income given up. It matters not whether the arrangements are made before or after the employment commences. For this purpose, '*flexible remuneration arrangements*' are arrangements under which employer and employee agree that the employee is to be provided with free or subsidised meals rather than receive some other description of employment income.
[*ITEPA 2003, ss 266(3)(e), 317*].

Where the provision of subsidised meals to employees is exempt as above, the provision of those meals to others who are working at the employer's premises but are not employees of that employer is also exempt. [*SI 2002 No 205, Reg 6*].

(v) **Provision of travel, accommodation and subsistence** during public transport disruption caused by industrial action. [*ITEPA 2003, s 245*]. See also **28.84** below.

(vi) **Provision of means of transport between home and place of employment (or training) for disabled employees.** [*ITEPA 2003, ss 246, 247*]. See also **28.23, 28.84** below.

(vii) **Provision of transport for occasional late night journeys from work to home**, or following a failure of car-sharing arrangements, subject to certain conditions. [*ITEPA 2003, s 248*]. See **28.85** below.

(viii) **Provision of transport between mainland and offshore rig etc.**, and necessary overnight accommodation on the mainland, for offshore oil and gas workers. [*ITEPA 2003, s 305*].

(ix) **Travelling expenses** of:

  (a) an unremunerated director of a not-for-profit company; or
  (b) a director who holds that position as part of a trade, profession or vocation (including one carried on in partnership), provided no claim is made to a deduction in computing trading etc. profits.

  [*ITEPA 2003, ss 241A, 241B*].

(x) **Removal expenses.** For the statutory relief from charge as employment income of certain payments and benefits received in connection with job-related residential moves, see **28.72** below.

  For HMRC's view of the taxation implications of guaranteed sale price (or similar) schemes for houses as part of employee relocation packages, particularly in relation to the application of the exemption at (xviii) below, see HMRC Employment Income Manual EIM03134–03137.

(xi) **Miners' free coal and allowances in lieu thereof.**

(xii) **Medical insurance** for treatment and medical services where the need for treatment arises **while abroad** in performance of duties. [*ITEPA 2003, s 325*].

(xiii) **Vehicle parking facilities.** No benefit arises from the provision for the employee of a car, a cycle, a motor cycle or a van parking space at or near his place of work, and where such a benefit is convertible into cash, e.g. under a salary sacrifice arrangement, no charge to tax on general earnings arises. [*ITEPA 2003, s 237(1)(3)*]. See also **28.13** and **28.46** above.

(xiv) **Entertainment by third parties.** No income tax liability arises from the provision of hospitality of any kind for the employee (or for his family or household), unless it is provided either:

  - in recognition or anticipation of particular services by the employee in the course of the employment; or
  - directly or indirectly by or on behalf of the employer or by any person connected with the employer (within **19** CONNECTED PERSONS).

  [*ITEPA 2003, s 265*].

'Hospitality' covers dinners, parties, hospitality tents at sporting events etc., and events such as theatrical performances or sporting events where a host invites someone to accompany him as a guest. It includes associated costs, such as transport or overnight accommodation. (HMRC Employment Income Manual EIM21836).
See also **28.46** above and, as regards concessionary relief in respect of gifts from third parties, **28.68** below.

(xv) **Christmas parties etc.** No benefit arises from expenditure on an annual Christmas party or similar annual function open to the staff generally, or to staff at a particular location, of up to £150 per head per annum, including VAT and any transport or accommodation costs, or of non-cash vouchers for obtaining such provision (see **28.47** above). Where expenditure exceeds this amount the full amount will be taxable. The total cost is for this purpose divided by the total number of people attending the function to determine whether the limit is exceeded. The expenditure may be split between more than one annual event, and where the total expenditure for the year exceeds the £150 limit, a function or functions whose cost or the sum of whose costs is within the limit will not be taxed, the cost of the remaining functions being taxed in full (unless they are covered by the trivial benefit exemption at **28.51** above). Casual hospitality is not regarded as constituting an annual function for these purposes. No P11D return (see **53.21** PAY AS YOU EARN) is required in respect of expenditure not exceeding the limit. [*ITEPA 2003, s 264*].

(xvi) **Certain training and counselling expenses**, see **28.63, 28.83** below.

(xvii) **Medical check-ups and health-screenings.** The provision by an employer of one health-screening assessment and/or one medical check-up per employee per tax year does not confer a chargeable benefit. The provision of a voucher or credit-token (see generally **28.46** above) to obtain such screenings and/or check-ups is similarly exempt. Where the employee has more than one employer at the same time, the exemption applies only to one medical check-up and one health-screening per tax year provided by any of them. There is no requirement that these benefits be available to all employees of a particular employer. [*ITEPA 2003, ss 266(3), 267(2), 320B*].

(xviii) **Asset acquisition costs.** Normal purchaser's costs in relation to the sale or transfer of an asset by the employee to the employer (or to some other person by reason of the employment) are disregarded in calculating any benefit arising to the employee. [*ITEPA 2003, s 326*]. See HMRC Employment Income Manual EIM03134–03137 as regards the application of this exemption in relation to guaranteed sale price (or similar) schemes for houses as part of employee relocation packages (and see (x) above).

(xix) **Incidental overnight expenses.** A benefit is exempt from tax where its provision is incidental to the employee's being away from home on business during a 'qualifying absence' in relation to which the authorised maximum (£5 per night spent in the UK and £10 per night spent abroad) is not exceeded, being a benefit the cost of which is not otherwise deductible from earnings. [*ITEPA 2003, ss 240, 241, Sch 7 paras 33, 34*]. See also **28.86** below.

(xx) **Mobile phones.** No benefit arises from the making available (without any transfer of property) of a single mobile phone to an employee (but *not* to any member of his family or household). The exemption covers line rental for, and calls from, a single mobile phone number. Where the benefit of the phone is convertible into cash, e.g. under a salary sacrifice arrangement, no charge to tax on general earnings arises. The provision of a voucher or credit-token (see generally **28.46** above) to obtain use of a mobile phone is exempt if direct provision of the phone would have been exempt. '*Mobile phone*' is defined so as to exclude a cordless extension to a land-line, but not so as to exclude a telephone provided in connection with a vehicle. HMRC accept that smartphones fall within the definition (HMRC Brief 02/12, 20 February 2012). [*ITEPA 2003, ss 266(2), 267(2), 319*].

(xxi) **Computer equipment.** For 2005/06 and earlier years, the making available (without any transfer of property) of certain computer equipment gave rise to a benefits charge only to the extent that the aggregate cash equivalent of the benefit exceeded £500 for a tax year. This partial exemption was abolished for 2006/07 onwards. However, where computer equipment was first provided to an employee (or to a member of his family or household) before 6 April 2006, the partial exemption continues to have effect for 2006/07 onwards as regards that particular equipment. In most cases, there needs to have been a binding agreement in place before 6 April 2006 for loan of the equipment to the employee. [*ITEPA 2003, s 320; FA 2006, s 61*]. For points on the transition, see HMRC Employment Income Manual EIM21699.

In any case, where employers provide computer equipment to employees solely to enable them to carry out the duties of the employment at home, HMRC take the view that in many cases private use is likely to be 'not significant' (see (i) above), when compared with the primary business purpose of providing the equipment, in which case no taxable benefit should arise (HMRC Internet Statement 12 June 2006). For HMRC guidance (with examples) on how the term 'not significant' should be interpreted in this respect, see HMRC Employment Income Manual EIM21613.

(xxii) **Bus services.** Two exemptions apply in relation to bus services for employees.

(a) No benefit arises from the provision for employees of a '*works transport service*', i.e. a service provided by means of a 'bus' or a 'minibus' for conveying employees of one or more employers on 'qualifying journeys'. For this purpose a '*bus*' is a road passenger vehicle with a seating capacity of 12 or more, and a '*minibus*' is a vehicle constructed or adapted for the carriage of 9, 10 or 11 passengers (no account being taken in the case of a minibus of seats which do not meet the relevant 'construction and use requirements' under *Road Traffic Act 1988, Pt II* or NI equivalent). Seating capacity is determined as under *Vehicle Excise and Registration Act 1994, Sch 1 Pt III*. A '*qualifying journey*' for an employee is a journey (or part of a journey) between home and workplace (i.e. a place at which the employee's attendance is necessary in performance of the duties of the employment) or thereabouts (see Hansard Standing Committee B, 25 May 1999), or between workplaces, in connection with the performance of those duties. The service must be available generally to employees of the employer(s) concerned, and the main use must be for qualifying journeys by those employees. The service must also substantially be used only by those employees or their children aged under 18 (including step- and illegitimate children). Provision of a voucher for use of such a service is similarly exempt from charge under *ITEPA 2003, s 87* (non-cash vouchers – see **28.47** above), and it is made clear that the company car provisions (see **28.24** above) cannot apply to a works bus service.

(b) No income tax liability arises in respect of financial or other support for a public passenger transport service provided by means of a road vehicle and used by employees of one or more employers for 'qualifying journeys'. A '*qualifying journey*' is as under (a) above. The service must be available generally to employees of the employer(s) concerned. The terms on which it is available must not be more favourable than those available to other passengers, although this condition does not apply in the case of a 'local bus service' within *Transport Act 1985, s 2* and provision of a voucher for use of the service is similarly exempt from charge under *ITEPA 2003, s 87* (non-cash vouchers – see **28.47** above).

[*ITEPA 2003, ss 242, 243, 249, 266(2)*].

See **28.50** above as regards exemption of minor benefits of provision of transport to shops etc.

(xxiii) **Cycles and cyclists' safety equipment.** No benefit arises from the provision (without any transfer of property) for an employee of a cycle or cyclist's safety equipment, provided that:

(a) the facility is available generally to employees of the employer concerned; and

(b) the employee uses the cycle or equipment mainly for 'qualifying journeys' (as under (xxii)(a) above). Employers are not, however, expected to monitor employees' other cycling journeys (see Hansard Standing Committee B, 25 May 1999).

Where such a benefit is convertible into cash, e.g. under a salary sacrifice arrangement, no charge to tax on general earnings arises.

Provision of a voucher for use of a cycle or safety equipment is similarly exempt from charge under *ITEPA 2003, s 87* (non-cash vouchers, see **28.47** above).

See also (xiii) above, **28.13** above and **28.47**, **28.49** above as regards cycle parking facilities at work places.

[*ITEPA 2003, ss 244, 249, 266(2)*].

See also **28.50** above as regards exemption of minor benefit of cyclists' breakfasts.

If ownership of a cycle is transferred to an employee after a period of use during which the above exemption applied, the employee will be taxable on the difference between its market value at the date of transfer and the amount paid by him (if any) in consideration for the transfer. HMRC offer an optional simplified approach to valuing cycles in these circumstances. (HMRC Employment Income Manual EIM21667, 21668).

(xxiv) **Emergency vehicles.** See **28.31** above.

(xxv) **Eye tests and corrective glasses.** If health and safety legislation requires an employer to provide eye tests and eyesight tests for employees, particularly in relation to employees' use of Visual Display Units (VDUs), the provision of the tests themselves, and of any corrective glasses shown by the tests to be necessary, is exempt. The provision of a voucher or credit-token (see generally **28.46** above) to obtain such tests and/or glasses is similarly exempt. It is a condition that the benefit be made available to all employees for whom it is meant to be provided under the health and safety rules. [*ITEPA 2003, ss 266(3), 267(2), 320A*].

(xxvi) **Fees relating to monitoring schemes relating to vulnerable persons.** In Scotland, it is an offence for an employer to hire a person who is barred from working with children or vulnerable adults to undertake certain kinds of regulated work. As a result, prospective and current employees in this field are required to be registered under the Protection of Vulnerable Groups Scheme (PVGS) launched on 28 February 2011. Where an employer pays or reimburses the employee's PVGS registration fee, the benefit is exempt from income tax.

Employees in England and Wales who work with vulnerable groups and are subject to checks under the criminal records regime may apply to join the update service provided by Disclosure and Barring Service (DBS). No income tax liability arises by virtue of the payment or reimbursement by the employer of fees for subscribing to the DBS update service or fees for criminal records certificates applied for when a subscription to the update service is active.

[*ITEPA 2003, s 326A*].

(xxvii) **Advice relating to proposed employee shareholder agreements.** Under *Growth and Infrastructure Act 2013, s 31*, an employee shareholder agreement (see **71.78** SHARE-RELATED EMPLOYMENT INCOME AND EXEMPTIONS) is ineffective unless the employee first receives independent advice as to the terms and effect of the proposed agreement. Reasonable costs incurred by the employee in obtaining the advice (whether or not he does become an employee shareholder) must be met by the company. No liability to income tax arises by virtue of the provision of such advice or the payment or reimbursement of any reasonable costs incurred by the employee in obtaining such advice. This may include tax advice to the extent that it consists only of an explanation of the tax effects of employee shareholder agreements generally. [*ITEPA 2003, s 326B*].

The above exemption continues notwithstanding the abolition of tax reliefs in connection with shares acquired under employee shareholder agreements (for which see **71.78** SHARE-RELATED EMPLOYMENT INCOME AND EXEMPTIONS).

(xxviii) **Recommended medical treatment.** The provision of 'recommended' medical treatment to an employee, or the payment or reimbursement by the employer of the costs of such treatment, is exempt from income tax. The exemption does not apply to the extent that the earnings exempted would otherwise exceed £500 per employee per tax year. Medical treatment is '*recommended*' if it is provided in accordance with a recommendation which:

- is made to the employee as part of occupational health services either provided under *Employment and Training Act 1973, s 2* or by (or in accordance with arrangements made by) the employer;
- is made for the purpose of assisting the employee to return to work after a period of absence due to injury or ill-health; and
- meets any other requirements specified in Treasury regulations (see below).

The exemption is not available where the provision, payment or reimbursement is pursuant to salary sacrifice arrangements or 'flexible remuneration arrangements' (defined in similar terms as in (iv) above). The regulations specify that a recommendation can only be given after the employee has been assessed by a health care professional (as defined) as unfit for work for at least 28 consecutive days or is absent from work due to injury or ill-health for at least that amount of time. A recommendation must be made in writing by a health care professional, must be provided to both employee and employer and must specify the medical treatment being recommended.

[*ITEPA 2003, s 320C*].

See HMRC Employment Income Manual EIM21774–21777.

(xxix) **Pensions advice: general.** For **2017/18** onwards, no liability to income tax arises on the first **£500** worth of 'pensions advice' provided, paid for or reimbursed by an employer for the benefit of an employee (or a former or prospective employee) in a tax year. This replaces the more limited exemption at **28.50**(d) above. It applies separately to each employment where a person has more than one. '*Pensions advice*' means information or advice in connection with the employee's pension arrangements or the use of his pension funds. The exemption applies only if the advice, payment or reimbursement is provided under a scheme that is open to employees generally or to employees generally at a particular location. That condition is not, however, breached by reason of the benefit being available only to those employees who are within five years of minimum pension age (which is normally 55) or who cannot continue working due to ill-heath. [*ITEPA 2003, s 308C; F(No 2)A 2017, s 3(1)(5)*].

(xxx) **Independent pensions advice in respect of conversions and transfers of benefits.** Under *Pension Schemes Act 2015*, trustees or managers of defined benefit pension schemes are required to ensure that a member or a survivor of a member has obtained appropriate independent advice before converting benefits or making a transfer payment to another pension scheme. No liability to income tax arises where the employer pays for such advice to be provided to an employee or former employee or pays for or reimburses the cost of such advice. The exemption is not available where the provision, payment or reimbursement is pursuant to salary sacrifice arrangements. [*ITEPA 2003, s 308B; Pension Schemes Act 2015, s 54*].

(xxxi) **Carers' board and lodging.** No liability to income tax arises on the benefit of board or lodging (or both) provided to an individual employed as a 'home care worker' if it is provided at the recipient's home, on a reasonable scale and by reason of the individual's employment. For these purposes, an individual is employed as a '*home care worker*' if the duties of the employment consist wholly or mainly of the provision of personal care to another individual at the recipient's home in a case where the recipient is in need of personal care because of old age, mental or physical disability, past or present illness or mental disorder or past or present alcohol or drug dependence. [*ITEPA 2003, s 306A*].

(xxxii) **Battery charging facilities for vehicles.** With backdated effect for **2018/19** onwards, no liability to income tax arises on the providing of facilities (including electricity) for charging a battery of a vehicle used by an employee. This is intended to encourage employers to provide charging facilities for all-electric and plug-in hybrid vehicles. The charging facilities must be provided at or near the employee's workplace, and must be available generally to all the employer's employees at that workplace. The exemption applies equally if the vehicle using the facilities is used by the employee as a passenger. It does not apply to the provision of workplace parking.

Taxable cars and vans, i.e. company cars and vans within the charge to tax as a benefit-in-kind, are excluded from this exemption, but this is only because the provision of charging facilities was already exempt for these vehicles by virtue of *ITEPA 2003, s 239(4)*.

[*ITEPA 2003, s 237A; FA 2019, s 8*

Exemptions for otherwise deductible items

[28.53] The three exemptions described below apply to expenses payments and benefits provided to employees where the employee would have been eligible for a deduction had he incurred and paid the equivalent expense himself.

Firstly, no liability to income tax arises by virtue of any provision of the benefits code in respect of an amount treated as earnings of an employee as a result of the provision of a benefit if an equal amount would otherwise be allowable as a deduction from the employee's earnings.

Secondly, no liability to income tax arises in respect of an amount of expenses paid or reimbursed by a person to an employee (whether or not that person's employee) if:

(a) an amount at least equal to the amount paid or reimbursed would otherwise be allowable as a deduction from the employee's earnings; or

(b) the amount has been calculated and paid or reimbursed in an approved way (commonly known as 'scale rate or flat rate payments') and the two conditions set out below are met.

The first of the conditions referred to in (b) above is that the employer, or a third party, must have a system in place to check that the employee is actually incurring expenses of the kind in question and that they would be allowable deductions. The second condition is that neither the payer nor any other person operating the system knows or suspects (or could reasonably be expected to know or suspect) that the employee has not incurred the expense or that it would not be an allowable deduction. A sum is calculated and paid or reimbursed in an approved way if it is calculated etc. in accordance with regulations to be made by the Commissioners for HMRC or in accordance with an approval given by HMRC to pay expenses at a flat rate (see below).

The third exemption applies for 2019/20 onwards. It is that no liability to income tax arises in respect of an amount paid or reimbursed by a person to an employee (whether or not that person's employee) for expenses in the course of 'qualifying travel' if:

- the amount has been calculated and paid or reimbursed in accordance with regulations made by the Commissioners for HMRC;
- a system is in operation for checking that the employee has undertaken the qualifying travel in question; and
- neither the payer nor any other person operating the system knows or suspects (or could reasonably be expected to) that the travel was not undertaken.

The conditions for the third exemption mean that expenses paid or reimbursed using statutory rates should have the effect of not requiring employers to operate a system for checking receipts or other forms of documentary evidence of employees' expenditure in order to make the payments free of tax. Instead, employers are required only to ensure that employees are undertaking qualifying travel. '*Qualifying travel*' is travel within **28.11** or **28.17** above, the expenses of which are deductible from earnings. See HMRC Employment Income Manual EIM30220.

The first published regulations (*SI 2015 No 1948*) deal with meal allowances (see **28.87** below). The third exemption is brought within the ambit of these regulations for 2019/20 onwards. Also for 2019/20 onwards, the regulations now cover expenses in the course of overseas travel (see **28.90** below under Benchmark scale rates).

None of the above exemptions apply if the payment, reimbursement or benefit is provided pursuant to salary sacrifice arrangements. See also below under Anti-avoidance.

Approval to pay expenses at a flat rate

A person may apply to HMRC for approval to pay or reimburse expenses of the applicant's employees, or employees of another person, at a rate set out in the application. The application must be in such form and manner, and contain such information, as is specified by HMRC. An officer of HMRC may give the approval if satisfied that the proposed rate, or such other rate as is agreed between the applicant and the officer, will be a reasonable estimate of the amount of expenses actually incurred. Approval is given in the form of an approval notice, which must state the type of expenses to which it relates, the agreed flat rate, the date the approval takes effect (which cannot be retrospective) and the date it ceases to have effect. The approval cannot have a currency of more than five years. The approval notice may state that the approval is subject to conditions specified or described therein.

An officer of HMRC may, if in his opinion there is reason to do so, revoke an approval by giving a further notice (a 'revocation notice') to either the applicant or the person who is paying or reimbursing expenses in accordance with the approval or to both those persons. A revocation notice may revoke the approval from the day on which the approval took effect or from a later date specified in the notice. The revocation may be in relation to all expenses or expenses of a description specified in the revocation notice. Any liability to tax that would have arisen in respect of the payment or reimbursement of expenses had it not been for the revocation is to be treated as having arisen. In the event of revocation, any person who has made, and any employee who has received, a payment or reimbursement of expenses calculated in accordance with the approval must make all returns which they would have had to make if it were not for the approval, other than for any period during which the approval did have effect.

Anti-avoidance

Where certain conditions are met, the above exemptions do not apply to an amount paid or reimbursed to an employee in respect of expenses or an amount treated as earnings of an employee as a result of the provision of a benefit. The conditions are that:

- the amount is paid or reimbursed, or the benefit is provided, pursuant to arrangements (as widely defined);
- the amount of the expenses or benefit would have been exempt from income tax were it not for this anti-avoidance rule;
- in the absence of the arrangements, the employee would have received a greater amount of general earnings or specific employment income (see **28.1** above) in respect of which tax would have been chargeable or national insurance contributions would have been payable (whether by the employee or another person); and
- a main purpose of the arrangements is the avoidance of tax or national insurance contributions.

[*ITEPA 2003, ss 289A–289E; FA 2019, s 10*].

See HMRC Employment Income Manual EIM30210 *et seq.*

Cash equivalent of a benefit

[28.54] The cash equivalent of a benefit is the cost of the benefit (including a proper proportion of any expense relating partly to the benefit and partly otherwise) less any part made good (see below) by the employee to those providing the benefit. [*ITEPA 2003, ss 203, 204; F(No 2)A 2017, s 1(13)(14)*].

VAT is included whether or not recoverable by the employer (HMRC SP A6).

In-house benefits

The cost of 'in-house' benefits (i.e. those consisting of services or facilities enjoyed by the employee which it is part of the employer's business to provide to members of the public) is the additional or marginal cost of their provision to the employee, rather than a proportionate part of total costs incurred in their provision both to employees and to the public. See *Pepper v Hart* HL 1992, 65 TC 421, in which only the marginal cost of providing school places for the children of masters at the school was taxable, regardless of whether or not the children occupied places which would otherwise have been provided to members of the public. (*Note*. This decision was based on consideration of statements by the Financial Secretary to the Treasury in Standing Committee debates on the enacting legislation. See **5.33** APPEALS as regards the circumstances in which this is permissible.)

Following this decision, HMRC set out their view of how the marginal cost rule should apply in practice. In particular, nil or negligible cost arises in the case of:

- rail or bus travel by employees (provided fare-payers are not displaced);
- goods sold to employees for not less than the wholesale price; and
- provision of professional services not requiring additional staffing (excluding disbursements).

It is accepted that no additional benefit arises where teachers pay 15% or more of normal school fees.

The decision also affects the calculation of the benefit of the provision of assets for part business, part private use. Fixed costs need not be taken into account where the private use is incidental to the business use. The cash equivalent is the proper proportion of the 'annual value' of the asset (see below) together with any *additional* running expenses.

(Revenue Press Release 21 January 1993).

See **28.47** above as regards valuation of incentive awards.

Use of assets rules

Where the benefit is the *use (without transfer) of an asset* other than a car or van (as to which see **28.24, 28.27** above), the cost of the benefit is the annual value (or if higher, the rent or hire charge paid by those providing the benefit) plus any additional expense related to the asset's provision (excluding the cost of acquiring or producing it and any rent or hire charge payable for the asset by those providing the benefit). This applies only if the asset is made available for private use, but this is treated as being the case unless private use of the asset is specifically prohibited and no private use is, in fact, made of it. For special rules concerning emergency vehicles, see **28.31** above.

Annual value of the use of an asset is:

- *for land*, its 'annual rental value' under *ITEPA 2003, s 207*;
- *in any other case*, **20%** of market value at time asset was first provided as a benefit.

[*ITEPA 2003, ss 205, 207, 208*].

For 2017/18 onwards, where the benefit consists in the use (without transfer) of an asset other than a car or van, the cost of the benefit (computed as above) is time-apportioned by reference to the number of days in the tax year on which the asset is available for private use. An asset is *unavailable* for private use on any day if:

- that day falls before the day on which the asset is first available to the employee (i.e. for private use, by reason of the employment and without any transfer of property) or after the day on which it is last available; or
- for more than 12 hours during that day, the asset: is not in fit condition; is undergoing repair or maintenance; cannot lawfully be used; is in the possession of an independent party who has a lien over it; or is used in a way that is neither use by, nor at the direction of, the employee or a member of his family or household; or
- on that day the employee uses the asset in the performance of the duties of the employment and does not otherwise use it at all.

Also for 2017/18 onwards, if for the whole or part of the tax year the same asset is available for more than one employee's private use *at the same time*, the cost of the benefit for each employee (apportioned as above if necessary) is reduced on a just and reasonable basis, with the proviso that the aggregate for all such employees cannot exceed the total cost of the benefit (before any apportionment as above).

[*ITEPA 2003, ss 205(1B)–(1D), 205A, 205B; FA 2017, s 8(1)–(3)(5)*].

See HMRC Employment Income Manual EIM21873–21895. See **28.31** above for special rules for 2017/18 to 2019/20 inclusive concerning emergency vehicles.

Before 2017/18, where an asset was not available for the whole of a tax year or was available to more than one employee, only a corresponding proportion of the cost of the benefit was brought into charge, but this had effect purely on a non-statutory basis. See HMRC Employment Income Manual EIM21200, 21637 and *Kerr v Brown; Boyd v Brown* (Sp C 333, 333A), [2002] SSCD 434, [2003] SSCD 266.

Transfer of used or depreciated asset

Where the benefit is the *transfer of an asset after it has been used or depreciated* since the transferor acquired it, the cost of the benefit is the market value at the time of the transfer. However, a special basis applies if the asset (not a car or van) was first applied for the provision of any benefit for a person or for members of his family or household by reason of his employment after 5 April 1980 and a person (whether or not the present transferee) has been chargeable to tax on its use. The cost of the benefit (unless a higher benefit is obtained by taking market value at the time of transfer) is its market value when the asset was first so applied less the total cost of the benefit of the *use* of the asset (see above) in the years up to and including the year of transfer.

The special basis is not available for computer equipment within **28.52**(xxi) above or cycles within **28.52**(xxiii) above, with the result that the charge is always on market value at time of transfer.

[*ITEPA 2003, ss 206, 208*].

Making good

'*Making good*' means giving something (often a cash payment), to the person providing a benefit-in-kind, in return for that benefit. With effect for all benefits provided in **2017/18** or subsequent years, a general deadline is introduced by which employees need to make good any part of the cost of the benefit if a deduction is to be allowed for the amount made good. The deadline is 6 July following the tax year in which the benefit is provided. This replaces pre-existing deadlines relating to cars, vans and fuel. It does not apply to voluntarily payrolled benefits (see **53.28** PAY AS YOU EARN), which have their own deadlines for making good.

Deductions

Deductions may be claimed from the cash equivalent calculated as above for allowable payments falling within **28.11, 28.12, 28.16–28.19** above or **28.62** (clergymen etc.), **28.64** (employee liabilities and expenses), **28.66** (artiste's percentage deduction), **28.75** (personal security provision) or **28.80** (subscriptions and professional fees) below. A deduction may be available on this basis where there is mixed use (i.e. partly for private purposes and partly for work) of the asset in question. See HMRC Employment Income Manual EIM21636.

For 2017/18 onwards, deductions on this basis are not available where the benefit is the use (without transfer) of an asset, but see the 'use of assets' rules above.

[*ITEPA 2003, s 365; FA 2017, s 8(4)(5)*].

Salary sacrifice arrangements

For **2017/18** onwards, where a benefit is provided pursuant to salary sacrifice arrangements, the amount chargeable is the cash equivalent as above if the cost of the benefit is greater than or equal to the amount forgone with respect to the benefit. Otherwise the amount chargeable is the amount forgone less any part of the cost of the benefit made good by the employee on or before 6 July following the tax year in which the benefit is provided. In any case in which the benefit would be exempt from income tax were it not provided under salary sacrifice arrangements, the cost of the benefit is treated as zero for this purpose. See HMRC Employment Income Manual EIM44120–44130.

Where the benefit is provided pursuant to pre-6 April 2017 arrangements, the above rules are delayed by one year and have effect for **2018/19** onwards instead, *but* see below as regards school fees. See **28.14** above as to 'salary sacrifice arrangements', 'the amount forgone' and the effect of pre-6 April 2017 arrangements being varied or renewed on or after that date.

School fees

As regards pre-6 April 2017 'school fee arrangements', the introduction of the above rules is delayed by four years, and they have effect for **2021/22** onwards instead. Arrangements are '*school fee arrangements*' if the benefit provided under salary sacrifice arrangements consists in the payment or reimbursement (in whole or in part) of school fees or if it consists in a waiver or reduction of school fees. What is said at **28.14** above as to the effect of pre-6 April 2017 arrangements being varied or renewed on or after that date does not apply for this purpose. Provided they relate to the same employment, the same school and the same child, school fee arrangements to which an employee is a party are treated as the same as any such arrangements to which the employee was previously a party.

[*ITEPA 2003, s 203A; FA 2017, Sch 2 paras 48, 62(2)(5)(10)–(12)(14)*].

Simon's Taxes. See **E4.611–E4.616, E4.7.**

Example

[28.55]

During 2020/21, P Ltd transferred to R a television set which it had previously leased to him for a nominal rent of £4 per month. The company also leased a suit to R under similar arrangements but at a rent of £2 per month.

Television

First leased to R on 6 April 2019 (when its market value was £860); transferred to R on 1 March 2021 for £100, the market value at that time being £375.

R's benefits are		£
2019/20		
Cost of benefit 20% × £860		172
Deduct Rent paid by R		48
Cash equivalent of benefit		£124
2020/21		
Cost of benefit 20% × £860 × $^{330}/_{365}$ note (a)		155
Deduct Rent paid by R (11 months)		44
Cash equivalent of benefit		111
	£	
Greater of		
(i) Market value at transfer	375	
Deduct Price paid by R	100	
	£275	
And		
(ii) Original market value	860	
Deduct Cost of benefits note (b)	327	
	533	
Deduct Price paid by R	100	
	£433	
		433
Total		£544

Suit

First leased to R on 31 July 2020 (when its market value was £580).

R's benefit for 2020/21 is

Cost of benefit 20% × £580 × $^{249}/_{365}$ note (a)	79
Deduct Rent paid by R (8 months)	16
Cash equivalent of benefit	£63

Notes

(a) Where the benefit consists in the use (without transfer) of an asset, the cost of the benefit is time-apportioned by reference to the number of days in the tax year on which the asset is available for private use (see **28.54** above).

(b) On the transfer of the television set, the cost of the benefits to date (£172 + 155), not the cash equivalents, is deducted from the original market value.

(c) It is assumed that the television set and suit have been bought by P Ltd and are not goods provided from within its own business. If the latter was the case, R would be taxed on the marginal cost to P Ltd in providing the benefit (in accordance with *Pepper v Hart* — see **28.54** above).

Bonuses from indirectly employee-owned companies

[28.56] The first £3,600 of 'qualifying bonus payments' (see below) received by a person from an indirectly employee-owned company in a tax year is exempt from income tax. The recipient must be an employee or former employee of the company. An indirectly employee-owned company is broadly a trading company or member of a trading group in which an employee ownership trust has a controlling interest. If the same person receives qualifying bonus payments from two or more companies in a tax year, the exemption applies separately to the payments from each, and may thus exceed £3,600 in total. However, if the companies are members of the same group at the time each of them first makes a qualifying bonus payment to that person in the tax year, only a single exemption applies to the total payments; for this purpose a company that makes a payment when it is a member of a group is treated as remaining a member of that group for the remainder of the tax year even if this is not, in fact, the case. Where the exemption applies, the exempt amount of £3,600 is set against payments in the order in which they are made. If two or more payments are made on the same day, which together take the total payments for the tax year over the exempt amount, the balance of the exempt amount at the start of that day is split proportionately between those payments.

References to a payment to an employee or former employee include a payment made to the personal representatives of a deceased employee or former employee, provided the payment is made within the twelve months beginning with the date of death.

In these provisions (including **28.57** below), a group of companies means broadly a company (the principal company), its 75% subsidiaries, their 75% subsidiaries and so on.

[*ITEPA 2003, ss 312A, 312I*].

Qualifying bonus payments

A payment made by an employer company (E) to an employee or former employee is a '*qualifying bonus payment*' if:

(a) it does not consist of regular salary or wages;
(b) it is awarded under a scheme which meets the requirements as to participation and equality;
(c) E meets the 'trading requirement' and the 'indirect employee-ownership requirement' throughout the 'qualifying period';
(d) E meets the 'office-holder requirement' when the payment is made and on at least the 'requisite number of days' (not necessarily consecutive) in the 'qualifying period';
(e) E is not a 'service company' (see below);
(f) the payment is not an 'excluded payment' (see below); and
(g) in the case of a payment to a former employee, the payment is made in the twelve-month period beginning with the day the employment ceased.

See **28.57** below as regards the requirements referred to in (b), (c) and (d) above. The '*qualifying period*' in (c) and (d) above is the twelve months ending with the day on which the payment is made. However, this is subject to the proviso that the qualifying period cannot include any time before both the controlling interest requirement and the all-employee benefit requirement (see in both cases **28.57** below) were first met. The '*requisite number of days*' in (d) above means, if the qualifying period is twelve months, the number of days in that period reduced by 90 and, if the qualifying period is less than twelve months, the number of days in that period reduced by a corresponding fraction of 90.

[*ITEPA 2003, s 312B*].

Excluded payments

For the purpose of (f) above, a payment is an '*excluded payment*' if the recipient is a party to arrangements (whether made before or after his employment commences) under which he forgoes an amount of general earnings or specific employment income in return for the payment, or the recipient and the employer agree that the recipient is to receive the payment rather than some other description of employment income. [*ITEPA 2003, s 312H*].

Meaning of 'service company'

For the purposes of (e) above, a '*service company*' means a managed service company within **47.2** MANAGED SERVICE COMPANIES or a company (C) in respect of which the following two conditions are met. The first condition is that C's business consists substantially of the provision of the services of persons employed by it. The second condition is that the majority of those services are provided to persons within any of (i)–(iii) below who are not members of the same group as the company making the bonus payment:

(i) a person who controls or has controlled (or two or more persons who together control or have controlled) C or any company of which C is a 51% subsidiary at the time the bonus payment is made;

(ii) a person who (or two or more persons who together) at any time before the bonus payment is made employed all or a majority of the employees of C or of the employees of C and companies in the same group as C;

(iii) any company which is a 51% subsidiary of, controlled by or connected or associated with, any person within (i) or (ii).

The following provisions apply to define concepts in (i)–(iii) above: *CTA 2010, s 449* (associated companies); *ITA 2007, s 995* (meaning of 'control'); and *TCGA 1992, s 286* (connected persons). For the purposes of (i)–(iii), a partnership is treated as a single person; where a partner (alone or with others) has control of a company, the partnership is similarly treated as having control of that company.

[*ITEPA 2003, s 312G*].

The requirements

[28.57] The requirements referred to in **28.56**(b), (c) and (d) above are described below. References to E are to the company making the bonus payment.

The participation and equality requirements

The participation requirement is that all persons in 'relevant employment' when the award in **28.56**(b) is determined must be eligible to participate in that and any other award under the scheme. The equality requirement is that every employee who participates in an award under the scheme must do so on the same terms. A person is in *'relevant employment'* if that person is employed by E or by any company in the same group as E.

The participation requirement is not infringed in any of the following circumstances:

- by reason of a person being excluded from participating because, when the award is determined, he has less than a minimum period of continuous service stipulated by E; but the period stipulated must not exceed twelve months;
- by reason of a person being excluded from participating due to a finding of gross misconduct against him in the twelve months immediately before the award is determined;
- (in a case where a person is at the time of the award subject to disciplinary proceedings) by reason of his eligibility to participate being conditional upon those proceedings being concluded and no finding of gross misconduct being made against him; or
- by a person being treated as never having been eligible to participate where, between the making of the award and the payment, he is summarily dismissed from the employment or a finding of gross misconduct is made against him in disciplinary proceedings taken after the award was made.

The equality requirement is infringed if the amount of an award to an employee under the scheme is determined by reference to factors other than remuneration, length of service or hours worked. The equality requirement is also infringed if an award is made on terms such that some of the participating employees receive nothing. If the amount of an award is determined by reference to more than one of the aforementioned factors, each factor must give rise to a separate entitlement based on level of remuneration, length of service or (as the case may be) hours worked, and the total entitlement must be the sum of those separate entitlements. Subject to the foregoing, the equality requirement is infringed if any feature of the scheme has (or is likely to have) the effect of conferring benefits wholly or mainly on directors (or former directors), higher-paid employees, persons employed in a particular part of the business carried on by E or by a company in the same group as E, or employees carrying on particular kinds of activities.

[*ITEPA 2003, s 312C*].

The trading requirement

A company meets the '*trading requirement*' if it is a 'trading company' or a member of a 'trading group'. '*Trading company*' means a company carrying on 'trading activities' whose activities do not include to a substantial extent activities other than trading activities. '*Trading group*' means a group:

- one or more of whose members carry on 'trading group activities', and
- the activities of whose members, taken together, do not include to a substantial extent activities other than trading group activities.

'*Trading activities*' means activities carried on by the company in the course of, or for the purposes of, a trade being carried on by it; and '*trading group activities*' means activities carried on by a member of the group in the course of, or for the purposes of, a trade being carried on by any member. For the purposes of determining whether a company is a trading company or a member of a trading group, the activities of members of a group are treated as one business (so that intra-group activities are disregarded), and a business carried on by a company in partnership with one or more persons is treated as *not* being a trading activity. In all cases, a trade counts only if conducted on a commercial basis and with a view to the realisation of profits.

[*ITEPA 2003, ss 312D, 312I(1)*].

The indirect employee-ownership requirement

A company meets the '*indirect employee-ownership requirement*' if:

(a) a settlement meets the 'controlling interest requirement' in respect of the company; and
(b) the settlement meets the 'all-employee benefit requirement'.

If the company in question is a member of a trading group but not the principal company, then in (a) above the principal company is substituted for the company in question.

The controlling interest requirement

A settlement meets the '*controlling interest requirement*' in respect of a company if:

(i) the trustees hold more than 50% of the ordinary share capital of the company and have voting powers in the company which would yield a majority of the total available votes;

(ii) the trustees are entitled to more than 50% of the profits available for distribution to the company's equity holders;

(iii) the trustees would be entitled, on a winding-up of the company, to more than 50% of the assets available for distribution to equity holders; and

(iv) there are no provisions in any agreement or instrument affecting the company's constitution or management or its shares or securities under which any of the conditions in (i)–(iii) could cease to be satisfied without the trustees' consent.

The provisions of *CTA 2010, Pt 5 Ch 6* (group relief: equity holders and profits available for distribution) apply for the purposes of (i)–(iv) above. For the purposes of (ii), trustees are treated as entitled to dividends on shares even if they are required or permitted by the trusts to waive their entitlement. In determining whether (iv) applies, there is to be disregarded any provision of a mortgage or charge granted by the trustees to a 'third party' to secure any debt, or any agreement in respect of a loan made to the trustees by a third party, which confers an entitlement on the third party in the event of a default by the trustees. '*Third party*' for this purpose means a person other than the company, a member of a group of which the company is the principal, a person who is, or has at any time in the preceding twelve months been, a participator in the company or is a member of such a group, or a person connected (within *TCGA 1992, s 286*) with such a person.

The all-employee benefit requirement

A settlement meets the '*all-employee benefit requirement*' if the trusts of the settlement do not permit at any time:

- any settled property or income arising from it to be applied otherwise than for the benefit of all the 'eligible employees' on the same terms (the '*equality requirement*');
- the trustees to apply any settled property or income arising from it by creating a trust or transferring property to the trustees of another settlement other than by an authorised transfer (as defined by *TCGA 1992, s 236J(7)*);
- the trustees to make loans to beneficiaries; and
- the trustees or any other person to amend the trusts so that they would not comply with any of the above.

'*Eligible employees*' means employees and office-holders of the company or a member of its group, but certain participators are excluded (see *TCGA 1992, s 236J(5)(6)*). See *TCGA 1992, s 236K* for particular circumstances in which the equality requirement is or is not infringed by the trusts.

If a settlement would not otherwise meet the all-employee benefit requirement at any time during the qualifying period, *TCGA 1992, s 236L* (applied with appropriate modifications) treats the requirement as met in certain circumstances with regard to settlements created before 10 December 2013, unless the requirement has otherwise already been met at some time on or after that date.

[*ITEPA 2003, s 312E; TCGA 1992, ss 236J, 236K, 236M, 236R*].

The office-holder requirement

A company meets the '*office-holder requirement*' if the number of directors and other office-holders does not exceed two-fifths of the total number of employees (including directors and other office-holders). Any employee connected (within **19** CONNECTED PERSONS) with a director or other office-holder is counted as an office-holder for this purpose.

[*ITEPA 2003, s 312F*].

Childcare provision

[28.58] The tax position differs according to whether the childcare is provided by the employer (see **28.59** below), otherwise contracted for by the employer (see **28.60** below) or provided by means of vouchers (see **28.61** below).

See also HMRC's general guidance at www.gov.uk/browse/benefits/tax-credits.

Employer-provided childcare — workplace nurseries

[28.59] No liability to income tax arises in respect of the provision for an employee of 'care' for a 'child' where *all* of the following conditions are met:

- the child is the employee's child or stepchild and is maintained (wholly or partly) at his expense *or* is resident with the employee *or* is a person for whom the employee has parental responsibility (as defined);
- the premises on which the care is provided are not used wholly or mainly as a private dwelling, and any applicable registration requirement (under *Childcare Act 2006, Pt 3* or predecessor legislation or Scottish, Welsh or NI equivalents) is met;
- those premises are made available by the employer operating the childcare scheme (the scheme employer) or, where the care is provided under arrangements made by the scheme employer and other persons, those premises are made available by one or more of those persons with the scheme employer being wholly or partly responsible for financing and managing the care provision; and
- the childcare scheme is open to all the scheme employer's employees or to all those at a particular location and the employee in question is either an employee of the scheme employer or works at the same location as employees of the scheme employer to whom the scheme is open.

If the conditions are met in respect of part only of the childcare provision (for example if the arrangements change partway through the tax year), the exemption applies to that part.

For the above purposes:

- '*care*' means any form of care or supervised activity not provided in the course of the child's compulsory education; and

- a person is regarded as a '*child*' until 1 September following his 15th birthday (or 16th birthday if he is disabled, as defined) and on until the end of the week in which that date falls.

Where the benefit of childcare is convertible into cash, e.g. under a salary sacrifice arrangement, no charge to tax on general earnings arises.

[*ITEPA 2003, ss 318, 318B*].

Simon's Taxes. See E4.754.

Other employer-contracted childcare

[28.60] In cases where the exemption at **28.59** above does not apply, no liability to income tax arises in respect of the provision for an employee of 'care' for a 'child' *except* to the extent that the amount otherwise chargeable in respect of the benefit (see **28.54** above) exceeds £55 per week. (In practice, HMRC take £243 to be the monthly equivalent of the £55 weekly limit.) See below for conditions.

Under *Childcare Payments Act 2014*, the Government make a top-up contribution towards an eligible person's childcare costs. In consequence, the tax exemption for employer-contracted childcare will be unavailable to new entrants on and after 4 October 2018 into an employer-contracted childcare scheme. Where employers closed schemes to new entrants with effect from 6 April 2018, they are nevertheless permitted to operate them for pre-existing members until 3 October 2018 despite condition (c) below no longer being met (HMRC Employer Bulletin Issue 72, June 2018). An employee may voluntarily give up the tax exemption, by giving the employer a 'childcare account notice', in order to qualify for the Government top-up scheme or enable their partner to do so. The notice must be given in writing (which includes email) within 90 days after joining the top-up scheme. For more on the Government scheme see www.gov.uk/help-with-childcare-costs/tax-free-childcare.

Restriction to basic rate

For employees joining an employer's childcare scheme on or after 6 April 2011, the exemption is restricted to the basic rate of tax. This is effectively achieved by restricting the £55 per week limit in cases where the employee's earnings and taxable benefits for the tax year, *as estimated by the employer*, exceed the basic rate limit. The employer is required at the beginning of each tax year (or, if later, when the employee joins the scheme) to estimate the earnings and benefits-in-kind that the employee is likely to receive from him during that year. This fixes the employee's weekly limit for the entire tax year. Where the estimate does not exceed the higher rate limit, the £55 per week limit is reduced to £28. Where the estimate does exceed the higher rate limit, the £55 per week limit is reduced to £25. There is no question of any adjustment being made after the end of the tax year when the employee's actual taxable income from all sources is known. It is thus a rough and ready approach.

In estimating earnings and benefits, the employer should make certain deductions. These are specified by *SI 2011 No 1798, Reg 4* and include, for example, anticipated employee contributions to a registered pension scheme, charitable donations under the payroll giving scheme, expenses deductible in arriving at PAYE income and any personal reliefs due of a kind which are deductible from net income. If the employee begins the employment during the tax year, the estimate must be time-apportioned upwards to its annual equivalent. Earnings includes salary, wages and fees plus various other items listed in *SI 2011 No 1798, Reg 3*.

The restriction applies to any employee unless:

- he joined the employer's scheme before 6 April 2011;
- he has been in continuous employment with the employer since that date; and
- there has not since that date been a continuous period of 52 weeks throughout which care was not being provided for the employee under the scheme.

For these purposes, the employee is taken to have joined the scheme at the time the employer agreed that care would be provided to him under the scheme or, if later, when there is a child within (a) below.

The exemption

The weekly exemption is applied to a tax year by multiplying it by the number of 'qualifying weeks' in the tax year to give an annual exempt amount. Income tax is chargeable on the excess, if any, of the amount otherwise chargeable in respect of the benefit over that exempt amount. For this purpose, a week begins on the first day of the tax year and on every 7th day after that, with the last day of the tax year (or two days if the tax year ends in a leap year) being treated as a week in itself. Any week in which care is provided in compliance with the above conditions counts as a '*qualifying week*'. An employee is entitled to only one exempt amount regardless of the number of children for whom care is provided, but two or more people can be entitled to an exempt amount in respect of the same child. If an employee would otherwise be entitled to an exemption both under these provisions and under the childcare vouchers provisions described at **28.61** below, he is entitled to only one such exemption for any one week.

Where the benefit of childcare is convertible into cash, e.g. under a salary sacrifice arrangement, no charge to tax on general earnings arises.

Conditions

For the exemption to apply, *all* of the following conditions must be met:

(a) the child must be the employee's child or stepchild and must be maintained (wholly or partly) at his expense *or* must be both resident with the employee and a person for whom the employee has parental responsibility (as defined);
(b) the care must be 'qualifying childcare' (see below); and
(c) the care scheme is open to all the employer's employees or to all those at a particular location.

Where the employer's care scheme is delivered through salary sacrifice or flexible remuneration arrangements, the condition at (c) above is not prevented from being met by reason only that the scheme is not open to 'relevant low-paid employees'. '*Relevant low-paid employees*' are employees who are remunerated at such a rate that, if the salary sacrifice or flexible remuneration arrangements applied to them, the rate at which they would then be remunerated would be likely to be lower than the national minimum wage.

If the conditions are met in respect of part only of the childcare provision, the exemption applies to that part. '*Care*' and '*child*' have the same meanings as for employer-provided childcare at **28.59** above.

Qualifying childcare

'*Qualifying childcare*' means 'registered or approved care'. This is defined by one of *subsections (2)–(6)* of *ITEPA 2003, s 318C* depending on whether the care is being provided for a child in England, Wales, Scotland, NI or outside the UK. Care provided by the employee's domestic partner is excluded in all cases from being qualifying childcare, as is care provided by a relative (as defined) of the child wholly or mainly in the child's home or, if different, the home of a person having parental responsibility for the child, and care provided by a foster parent in respect of a child whom that foster parent is fostering.

[*ITEPA 2003, ss 318A, 318AZA, 318AA, 318B–318D; Childcare Payments Act 2014, s 64; FA 2017, Sch 2 paras 55, 62(2)(5); SI 2011 No 1798; SI 2018 Nos 308, 462; SI 2019 No 902*].

Simon's Taxes. See E4.755.

Childcare vouchers

[28.61] No liability to income tax arises in respect of the provision for an employee of 'qualifying childcare vouchers' *except* to the extent that the cash equivalent of the benefit (see **28.54** above) exceeds £55 per week 'plus the voucher administration costs'. (In practice, HMRC take £243 to be the monthly equivalent of the £55 weekly limit.)

Under *Childcare Payments Act 2014*, the Government make a top-up contribution towards an eligible person's childcare costs. In consequence, the tax exemption for childcare vouchers will be unavailable to new entrants on or after 4 October 2018 into an employer childcare voucher scheme. Where employers closed schemes to new entrants with effect from 6 April 2018, they are nevertheless permitted to operate them for pre-existing members until 3 October 2018 despite condition (c) below no longer being met (HMRC Employer Bulletin Issue 72, June 2018). An employee may voluntarily give up the tax exemption, by giving the employer a 'childcare account notice', in order to qualify for the Government top-up scheme or enable their partner to do so. The notice must be given in writing (which includes email) within 90 days after joining the top-up scheme. For more on the Government scheme see www.gov.uk/help-with-childcare-costs/tax-free-childcare.

Restriction to basic rate

For employees joining an employer's childcare scheme on or after 6 April 2011, the exemption is restricted to the basic rate of tax. This is effectively achieved by restricting the £55 per week limit in cases where the employee's earnings and taxable benefits for the tax year, *as estimated by the employer*, exceed the basic rate limit. The employer is required at the beginning of each tax year (or, if later, when the employee joins the scheme) to estimate the earnings and benefits-in-kind that the employee is likely to receive from him during that year. This fixes the employee's weekly limit for the entire tax year. Where the estimate does not exceed the higher rate limit, the £55 per week limit is reduced to £28. Where the estimate does exceed the higher rate limit, the £55 per week limit is reduced to £25. There is no question of any adjustment being made after the end of the tax year when the employee's actual taxable income from all sources is known. It is thus a rough and ready approach.

In estimating earnings and benefits, the employer should make certain deductions. These are specified by *SI 2011 No 1798, Reg 4* and include, for example, anticipated employee contributions to a registered pension scheme, charitable donations under the payroll giving scheme, expenses deductible in arriving at PAYE income and any personal reliefs due of a kind which are deductible from net income. If the employee begins the employment during the tax year, the estimate must be time-apportioned upwards to its annual equivalent. Earnings includes salary, wages and fees plus various other items listed in *SI 2011 No 1798, Reg 3*.

The restriction applies to any employee unless:

- he joined the employer's scheme before 6 April 2011;
- he has been in continuous employment with the employer since that date; and
- there has not since that date been a continuous period of 52 weeks throughout which vouchers were not being provided for the employee under the scheme.

For these purposes, the employee is taken to have joined the scheme at the time the employer agreed that vouchers would be provided to him under the scheme or, if later, when there is a child within (a) below.

The exemption

The exemption is applied to a tax year by multiplying the weekly limit by the number of 'qualifying weeks' in the tax year and then adding the voucher administration costs for the year to give an annual exempt amount. Income tax is chargeable on the excess, if any, of the cash equivalent of the benefit for the year over that exempt amount. For this purpose, a week begins on the first day of the tax year and on every 7th day after that, with the last day of the tax year (or two days if the tax year ends in a leap year) being treated as a week in itself. Any week in respect of which a qualifying childcare voucher is received counts as a '*qualifying week*'. An employee is entitled to only one exempt amount regardless of the number of children for whom care is provided, but two or more people can be entitled to an exempt amount in respect of the same child. If an employee would otherwise be entitled to an exemption both under these provisions and those for employer-contracted childcare at **28.60** above, he is entitled to only one such exemption for any one week. The Treasury has power to alter the amount of the weekly exemption by statutory instrument.

Qualifying childcare vouchers

A '*qualifying childcare voucher*' is a non-cash 'childcare voucher' in relation to which *all* of the following conditions are met:

(a) the voucher is provided to enable the employee to obtain 'care' for a 'child' who is the employee's child or stepchild and is maintained (wholly or partly) at his expense *or* who is both resident with the employee and a person for whom the employee has parental responsibility (as defined);
(b) the voucher can be used only to obtain 'qualifying childcare'; and
(c) the voucher is provided under a scheme that is open to all the employer's employees or to all those at a particular location.

Where the employer's care scheme is delivered through salary sacrifice or flexible remuneration arrangements, the condition at (c) above is not prevented from being met by reason only that the scheme is not open to 'relevant low-paid employees'. '*Relevant low-paid employees*' are employees who are remunerated at such a rate that, if the salary sacrifice or flexible remuneration arrangements applied to them, the rate at which they would then be remunerated would be likely to be lower than the national minimum wage.

'*Care*', '*child*' and '*qualifying childcare*' have the same meanings as in **28.59**, **28.60** above. The '*voucher administration costs*' are the difference between the face value of the vouchers provided and the cost of providing them; administration fees charged to the employer (or whoever provides the vouchers to the employee) are thus included within the exemption.

See **28.46–28.49** above as regards tax liability on vouchers, including non-cash vouchers, generally. A '*childcare voucher*' is a voucher, stamp or similar document intended to enable a person to obtain childcare (whether or not in exchange for the voucher).

[*ITEPA 2003, ss 84(2A), 270A, 270AA, 270B; Childcare Payments Act 2014, s 63; SI 2006 No 882; SI 2011 No 1798; SI 2018 No 462*].

Simon's Taxes. See E4.756.

Clergymen etc.

[28.62] A clergyman or other minister of a religious denomination in full-time employment as such is not taxable on any sums paid for or reimbursed to him in respect of any statutory amount payable, or statutory deduction made, under any Act in connection with the residence made available to him by a charity or ecclesiastical corporation for carrying out his duties (except in so far as they relate to any part of the premises which he lets) and, provided he is in 'lower-paid employment', no account is taken of the value of any expenses relating to his own living accommodation so provided. '*Lower-paid employment*' is defined below under Provisions of benefits code not applicable to lower-paid ministers of religion.

[*ITEPA 2003, s 290*].

No liability arises in respect of payment or reimbursement of a minister's heating, lighting, cleaning or gardening expenses, provided his employment is 'lower-paid employment' (see above). Where an allowance is paid to the minister to meet such costs it will not be taxed except to the extent that it exceeds the costs actually incurred. [*ITEPA 2003, ss 290A, 290B*]. For the purpose of determining whether a minister is in lower-paid employment, these payments, reimbursements or allowances are included in the aggregate at (a) below. [*ITEPA 2003, s 218(1)*].

Expenses wholly, exclusively and necessarily incurred in performance of duties (e.g. postage, stationery, telephone, car etc.) may be deducted from earnings from any employment as a minister (although where a vehicle other than a company vehicle is used for business travel, and either mileage allowance payments are received or mileage allowance relief is available in respect of that use (see **28.91** below), no deduction is available for qualifying travelling expenses (see **28.17** above) incurred in connection with that use). If he pays rent in respect of a dwelling-house any part of which is used mainly or substantially for his duties, up to one-quarter thereof may be deducted from earnings, and in addition he may claim in total one-quarter of the aggregate of any expenses of maintenance, repair, insurance or management of the premises borne by him. [*ITEPA 2003, ss 328(2), 351*]. Relief may also be available for the cost of *locum tenens* for illness or holidays and lighting, heating, cleaning and rates of study (see HMRC Employment Income Manual EIM60046, 60048).

See generally HMRC Employment Income Manual EIM60001–60055.

The expenses of a minister in visiting his congregation were allowed (*Charlton v CIR* CS 1890, 27 SLR 647) but not expenses of a curate in moving from one curacy to another (*Friedson v Glyn-Thomas* KB 1922, 8 TC 302). In *Mitchell v Child* KB 1942, 24 TC 511, cost of opposing a Bill which would have dispossessed rector of parsonage was allowed.

Gifts to a clergyman including voluntary subscriptions and collections (*In re Strong* C/E/S 1878, 1 TC 207; *Slaney v Starkey* KB 1931, 16 TC 45), Easter offerings (*Cooper v Blakiston* HL 1908, 5 TC 347) and grants (*Herbert v McQuade* CA 1902, 4 TC 489; *Poynting v Faulkner* CA 1905, 5 TC 145) are taxable but not where in recognition of past service (*Turner v Cuxson* QB 1888, 2 TC 422). The cost of maintenance of a priest living in communal presbytery held not taxable as not convertible into money (*Daly v CIR* CS 1934, 18 TC 641).

An unbeneficed clergyman was held to be within the charge on employment income (*Slaney v Starkey* above) as was a professed nun employed as a teacher (*Dolan v K* Supreme Court (IFS), 2 ITC 280) but not the headmaster of a school established by a congregation of secular priests (*Reade v Brearley* KB 1933, 17 TC 687).

For *self-employed* clergymen, see **75.53** TRADING INCOME.

Provisions of benefits code not applicable to lower-paid ministers of religion

The provisions of the benefits code mentioned at **28.21** above, *other than* living accommodation and vouchers and credit tokens, do not apply to employees in 'lower-paid employment'. An employment is '*lower-paid employment*' for a tax year if the employment is direct employment as a minister of a religious denomination and the 'earnings rate' for the employment for that year is less than £8,500. An employment is not direct employment for these purposes if it is a deemed employment as in **58** PERSONAL SERVICE COMPANIES ETC. or **47** MANAGED SERVICE COMPANIES or if an amount counts as employment income in respect of it by virtue of **26.4** DISGUISED REMUNERATION.

The '*earnings rate*' for an employment for a tax year is calculated as follows.

(a) Determine the aggregate of:
   - (i) the earnings (see **28.13** above) from the employment for that year; and
   - (ii) the total of any amounts treated as earnings from the employment for that year. This includes all amounts which would be so treated under the benefits code, disregarding the fact that part of that code is excluded where an employment is found to be lower-paid employment.

   Any exempt income is normally disregarded but this does not apply to income exempted by *ITEPA 2003, ss 290A, 290B* above. As regards (ii) above, in the case of provision of living accommodation, the additional charge at **28.41** above where cost exceeds £75,000 does not apply for this purpose, the basic charge being applied regardless of the cost.

(b) Where an alternative is offered to a company car such that, if it had been taxable as earnings rather than under the benefits code, the taxable amount would have exceeded the car and fuel benefits charge computed as in **28.24, 28.26** above, the excess is added to the amount determined under (a) above.

(c) From the amount resulting from (a) and (b) above, subtract any '*authorised deductions*', i.e. any of the deductions listed at *ITEPA 2003, s 290E(4)*.

(d) The earnings rate is the figure resulting from (a)–(c) above, proportionately increased if the employment is held for less than the full number of days in the tax year concerned.

Earnings rates from different but 'related' employments during a year must be aggregated. None of the employments is lower-paid employment if the aggregate is £8,500 or more or if any of them is not lower-paid employment. Employments are '*related*' for this purpose if either they are with the same employer or one is with a body or partnership (A) and the other either with an individual, partnership or body (B) that controls A or with another partnership or body controlled by B.

[*ITEPA 2003, ss 290C–290G*].

Simon's Taxes. See **E4.731, E4.788.**

Counselling services

[28.63] No income tax liability arises in respect of qualifying counselling services and certain necessary related travelling expenses provided for, or paid or reimbursed on behalf of, an employer in connection with the termination of his employment. This applies whether or not the services or expenses are provided or paid by the employer.

The counselling services which qualify are those consisting wholly of giving advice and guidance, imparting or improving skills, and/or providing or making available the use of office equipment or similar facilities to enable an employee to adjust to his job loss and/or find other employment. The employee must have been in the employment throughout the period of two years to the date the services are provided or, if earlier, the time he ceases to be employed. The opportunity to receive the services must be generally available to employees or a particular class of employees. Part-time employees are within the exemption.

[*ITEPA 2003, s 310*].

For relief to the employer, see **75.70** TRADING INCOME.

Simon's Taxes. See **E4.828**.

Employee liabilities and expenses

[28.64] There may be deducted from earnings from a continuing employment:

(a) any amount paid in or towards the discharge of a 'qualifying liability' of the employee;
(b) costs or expenses incurred in connection with any claim that the employee is subject to a 'qualifying liability' or with any related proceedings;
(c) so much of any premium (or similar payment) paid under a 'qualifying contract' of insurance as relates to the indemnification of the employee against a 'qualifying liability' or to the payment of costs or expenses within (b) above or, for 2017/18 onwards, within (d) or (e) below;
(d) (for 2017/18 onwards) costs or expenses incurred in connection with the employee giving evidence about employment-related matters in, or for the purposes of, a proceeding or other process (whether or not involving the employee) or an investigation (whether or not likely to lead to any proceeding or other process involving the employee); and
(e) (for 2017/18 onwards) costs or expenses incurred in connection with a proceeding or other process, or an investigation, in which employment-related acts of the employee or any other employment-related matters are being, or are likely to be, considered.

The purpose of (d) and (e) is to enable deductions to be available for costs and expenses in relation to proceedings where no allegation has been made against the employee. For example, an employee may be asked to give evidence before a public hearing, and legal advice and support may be required. In (d) and (e):

'giving evidence' includes making a formal or informal statement or answering questions; 'proceeding or other process' includes any civil, criminal or arbitration proceedings, any disciplinary or regulatory proceedings of any kind and any process operated for resolving disputes or adjudicating on complaints; and 'acts of the employee' include failures to act and are employment-related if the employee was acting in his capacity as such or in any other capacity in which he was acting in the performance of the duties of the employment.

Where any amount in (a)–(e) above is met by the employer or a third party, there may be made a deduction to offset a resultant taxable benefit. However, no deduction may be made for any such liability, costs or expenses if it would have been unlawful for the employer to insure against them (for example, fines and penalties).

A liability is a '*qualifying liability*' of the employee if it is imposed either:

- in respect of any acts or omissions of the employee in his capacity as such or in any other capacity in which he acts in the performance of his duties; or
- in connection with any proceedings relating to or arising from claims in respect of such acts or omissions.

A '*qualifying contract*' of insurance is one:

(A) which, as regards the risks insured against, relates exclusively to one or more of the following:
  (i) indemnification of any employee against any qualifying liability;
  (ii) indemnification of any person against any vicarious liability in respect of acts or omissions giving rise to a qualifying liability of another;
  (iii) payment of costs and expenses in connection with any claim that a person is subject to a liability to which the insurance relates or with related proceedings;
  (iv) (for 2017/18 onwards) payment of costs and expenses in connection with the employee giving evidence as in (d) above or with a proceeding, other process or investigation as in (e) above; and
  (v) indemnification of any employer against any loss from the payment by him to an employee of his of any amount in respect of either a qualifying liability or costs and expenses as in (iii) above or, for 2017/18 onwards, (iv) above;

(B) which is not 'connected' with any other contract (see below);

(C) a significant part of the premium for which does not relate to rights to payments or benefits other than cover for the risks insured against and any right of renewal; and

(D) the period of insurance under which is not more than two years (disregarding renewals) and which the insured is not required to renew.

Two contracts are '*connected*' (see (B) above) if either was entered into by reference to the other or to enable the other to be, or to facilitate the other being, entered into on particular terms *and* the terms of either contract would have been significantly different if it had not been for the other. Connected contracts, each of which satisfy (A), (C) and (D), are qualifying contracts despite (B) above, where the only significant difference in terms consists in certain premium reductions.

Where applicable, for the purposes of these provisions, an insurance premium may be reasonably apportioned as between the different risks, persons or employments to which the contract relates.

See HMRC Employment Income Manual EIM30501–30523. See **28.65** below as regards payments made after the employment has ceased.

Anti-avoidance

Legislation denies a deduction under these provisions where the payment in respect of which the deduction would otherwise be due has been made in pursuance of arrangements a main purpose of which is the avoidance of tax.

[*ITEPA 2003, ss 346–350; F(No 2)A 2017, s 4(2)(3)(8)*].

Simon's Taxes. See E4.787.

Post-employment deductions

[28.65] Relief may be claimed for payments made by a former employee or office-holder which are made after the day the employment ceases and no later than six years after the end of the tax year in which it ceased and that are of a kind that would have been deductible under **28.64** above if the employment had continued. Relief is given as a deduction in calculating net income for the year in which the payment is made (see Step 2 in the calculation of income tax liability at **1.10** ALLOWANCES AND TAX RATES). Unused relief cannot be carried forward, but it can be set against capital gains of the same year — see below.

Payments made by the former employer, by a successor to the former employer's business or to his liabilities, or by a person connected with any of them (see **19** CONNECTED PERSONS), is not deductible in calculating net income of the former employee *except* insofar as the payment falls to be treated either as general earnings received after the cessation of the employment by the former employee or as a taxable benefit received by the former employee under an employer-financed retirement benefits scheme (see **57.34** PENSION PROVISION). Similarly where a payment made by the former employee is borne wholly or partly by the former employer or other persons mentioned above, so much of the payment as is such taxable earnings or taxable benefit of the former employee is deductible in calculating net income.

There is a cap on the total amount of prescribed income tax reliefs that individuals can claim. See **1.11** ALLOWANCES AND TAX RATES. Post-employment deductions against income are among the prescribed reliefs.

Relief against capital gains

Where a claim is made as above and the claimant's income for the year is insufficient to fully utilise the relief, he may claim to have the excess relief treated as an allowable loss for that year for capital gains tax purposes. The allowable loss may not exceed the amount of the claimant's gains for the year *before* deducting any losses brought forward, the capital gains tax annual exemption, any relief available under **45.5** LOSSES (trading losses set against capital gains) or any relief available to a former trader etc. for post-cessation expenditure (see **59.5** POST-CESSATION ETC. RECEIPTS AND EXPENDITURE); any excess over that amount is *not* available to carry forward against gains of a later year.

Anti-avoidance

Legislation denies a deduction under these provisions where the payment in question is made in pursuance of arrangements a main purpose of which is the avoidance of tax.

[*ITEPA 2003, ss 555, 556, 556A, 557–564; TCGA 1992, s 263ZA; F(No 2)A 2017, s 4(6)–(8)*].

Employee subject to a termination settlement

No tax is charged under *ITEPA 2003, s 403* (see **18.4** COMPENSATION FOR LOSS OF EMPLOYMENT) in respect of any amount paid, or benefit provided, to reimburse the former employee for a payment that, had it not been reimbursed, would have attracted relief under the above provisions. The same applies in the case of a deceased employee as regards amounts paid etc. to his personal representatives. For 2017/18 onwards, this exemption is extended so as also to apply where the payment that would have attracted relief under the above provisions is made by the employer (or former employer) on the former employee's behalf (or on behalf of his personal representatives). [*ITEPA 2003, ss 409, 410; F(No 2)A 2017, s 4(4)(5)(8)*].

Simon's Taxes. See **E4.798**.

Employment or self-employment?

[28.66] Whether a person holds an office or employment or carries on a trade, profession or vocation depends on the facts including the relevant contract(s). A distinction is drawn between a contract *of service* (employment) and a contract *for services* (profession or vocation). A vision mixer engaged under a series of short-term contracts was self-employed (*Hall v Lorimer* CA 1993, 66 TC 349), as was an artiste who entered into a series of engagements (*Davies v Braithwaite* KB 1933, 18 TC 198), but contrast *Fall v Hitchen* Ch D 1972, 49 TC 433 in which a ballet dancer engaged by a theatrical management under a standard form of contract, but able to work elsewhere when not required by the management, was held to be in employment. Entertainers on board cruise ships were held to be self-employed notwithstanding the degree of control exercised by the cruise line (*Matthews v HMRC* UT, [2012] UKUT 229 (TCC), [2014] STC 297). See also below as regards artistes.

A barristers' clerk was not the holder of an office (*McMenamin v Diggles* Ch D 1991, 64 TC 286), but in *Horner v Hasted* Ch D, [1995] STC 766 an unqualified accountant contributing capital to, and sharing profits of, a firm of accountants was held not to be a partner. The provision of catering services under contract at a golf club was held to be a trade (*McManus v Griffiths* Ch

D 1997, 70 TC 218). See *Andrews v King* Ch D 1991, 64 TC 332 as regards agricultural gangmasters. The relationship between a supplier of scaffolding services and the workers he recruited to provide the services was held on the facts to be an informal and undocumented verbal contract for services (*Lewis (t/a MAL Scaffolding) and others v HMRC, Armstrong and others, third parties* (Sp C 527), [2006] SSCD 253). The intention of a private consultant cardiac surgeon and a registrar hired to assist in operations that the latter be regarded as self-employed proved conclusive in a 'borderline case' in which 'none of the tests set forth in the authorities provides a compelling answer' (*Mitchell v HMRC (Bhumagunta, third party)* FTT (TC 1041), [2011] UKFTT 172 (TC); 2011 STI 1703).

See also *Barnett v Brabyn* Ch D 1996, 69 TC 133 for a case in which the taxpayer unsuccessfully appealed against additional assessments on trading income on the grounds that he was employed, where the original assessments had been agreed on the basis of his contention that he was self-employed.

Problems may arise in relation to part-time activities. A part-time medical appointment of a doctor in private practice was held to be an employment (*Mitchell & Edon v Ross* HL 1961, 40 TC 11) as were the lecture fees of a full-time employed consultant (*Lindsay v CIR* CS 1964, 41 TC 661 and see also *Cawdron v HMRC* FTT (TC 7295), [2019] UKFTT 492 (TC)) and a non-practising barrister (*Sidey v Phillips* Ch D 1986, 59 TC 458), the evening class fees of a teacher (*Fuge v McClelland* Ch D 1956, 36 TC 571) and the remuneration as lecturer of a professional singer (*Walls v Sinnett* Ch D 1986, 60 TC 150), but *ad hoc* Crown appointments were held not to be employment (*Edwards v Clinch* HL 1981, 56 TC 367).

Salaries of sub-postmasters carrying on a retail trade from the same premises as the sub-post office used to be treated in practice as part of their trading income. This treatment does not extend to COMPENSATION FOR LOSS OF EMPLOYMENT (**18**), which retains its nature as employment income (subject to the usual exemption of the first £30,000) (*Uppal v HMRC* FTT (TC 516), 2010 STI 2382; *Cude v HMRC* FTT (TC 693), 2010 STI 2924). Where a company operates sub-post offices in its shops with its directors as nominee sub-postmasters, and the directors are required to, and do, hand over their salaries as sub-postmasters to the company, the salaries could similarly be brought into the company's trading income computation and not assessed on the directors as employment income. (HMRC Employment Status Manual ESM4400 and Business Income Manual BIM66301). This concession was withdrawn with effect on and after 6 April 2017, but those already using it can continue to do until 5 April 2019. Following the withdrawal of the concession, remuneration of a sub-postmaster from the Post Office is taxable as employment income (www.gov.uk/government/publications/withdrawal-and-grandfathering-of-extra-statutory-concession-bim-66301-sub-postmasters). As regards sub-postmasters generally, see *Dhendsa v Richardson* (Sp C 134), [1997] SSCD 265.

See generally HMRC Employment Status Manual ESM0500 *et seq*. and, for HMRC's approach to case law in this area, ESM7000 *et seq*. See also HMRC factsheet ES/FS1 at www.gov.uk/government/publications/employment-status-factsheet-esfs1.

See also **58.3**, **58.38** PERSONAL SERVICE COMPANIES ETC. which are concerned with the question of whether an individual providing his services through an intermediary would be an employee if engaged directly by a client, but which are also of wider application. See Tolley's Tax Cases under Employment Income for summaries of relevant Appeal Tribunal and Court decisions, each of which turns on its own facts.

An **apprenticeship** is an employment (see HMRC Employment Status Manual ESM2610).

A **dentist** employed by a Panamanian company, which contracted with a UK practice to supply his services in return for a proportion of the NHS fees and a management charge, was held to be employed, although the legality of the arrangements was in question (*Cooke v Blacklaws* Ch D 1984, 58 TC 255). See generally HMRC Employment Status Manual ESM4030.

Divers etc. employed in the UK area of the Continental Shelf are taxable under the trading income rules (see **75.29** TRADING INCOME). See also HMRC Employment Status Manual ESM4050.

Football referees of the kind who undertake refereeing in their spare time, typically alongside other full-time employment (as opposed to those employed as referees under full-time written employment contracts), are not employees with regard to their match fees and expenses; there is insufficient mutuality of obligation and control in the individual refereeing engagements to amount to employment (*HMRC v Professional Game Match Officials Ltd* UT, [2020] STC 1077, [2020] UKUT 147 (TCC)).

Professional practitioners

Where a company makes a payment to a director which would otherwise be employment income, and the director is a member of a partnership, the payment is treated for income tax purposes as a trading or professional receipt of the partnership, provided:

- the director carries on a profession;
- being a director of a company is a normal incident of that profession and of membership of the partnership;
- the director is required under the partnership agreement to account to the partnership for the payment; and
- the payment is insubstantial compared with the partnership's total trading or professional receipts.

Similarly, where a payment is made to an individual (A) who carries on a profession (whether alone or in partnership), and the payment is made to A as an employee or office-holder (but not as a director) and would otherwise be employment income, then provided the conditions below are met, the payment is treated for income tax purposes as a professional receipt of A or, where A carries on the profession in partnership, of the partnership. The conditions are that:

- the time spent by A in performing the duties of the office or employment is insubstantial compared with the time spent by A in carrying on the profession;

- the office or employment is related to A's profession;
- the payment is insubstantial compared with A's total professional receipts or, in a case where A is in partnership, so much of the partnership's total professional receipts as is attributable to A; and
- (in a case where A is in partnership) A is required under the partnership agreement to account to the partnership for the payment and does so.

[*ITTOIA 2005, ss 16B, 16C; SI 2018 No 282, Arts 1, 5*].

The above covers, for example, appointments such as auditorships and registrarships held by practising accountants or solicitors. These statutory rules apply for 2018/19 onwards but applied previously by concession (see HMRC ESC A37 and HMRC Employment Income Manual EIM03002).

Any compensation payments on the termination of such employment are, however, dealt with under *ITEPA 2003, ss 401–416* — see **18.3** COMPENSATION FOR LOSS OF EMPLOYMENT, and see *Brander & Cruickshank* HL 1970, 46 TC 574 and the cases referred to therein.

For directors' fees received by companies, see **28.3**(vi) above.

Artistes

HMRC accept that the earnings of most artistes (i.e. actors, singers, musicians, dancers and theatrical artists) should be assessed as trading income. Circumstances in which such earnings are employment income subject to PAY AS YOU EARN (**53**) would e.g. be where the artiste is engaged for a regular salary to perform in a series of different productions at the direction of the engager, and with a period of notice stipulated before termination of the contract. This might apply e.g. to permanent members of an opera, ballet or theatre company or an orchestra. (*Taxation Magazine, 8 September 1994, p 553*). See HMRC Business Income Manual BIM50151 for a general discussion of this distinction. In such cases, a deduction of up to 17.5% of earnings may be claimed in respect of percentage fees (and VAT thereon) paid out of those earnings to a licensed employment agency within *Employment Agencies Act 1973* or to a *bona fide* non-profit-making co-operative society acting as agent for the artiste. [*ITEPA 2003, s 352*]. Two well-known television presenters/interviewers were held to be 'theatrical artists' for the purpose of the above deduction for agency fees, i.e. the term is not restricted to those who actually perform in the theatre (*Madeley and another v HMRC* (Sp C 547), [2006] SSCD 513); none of the agency fees in this case could be said to have been incurred in the performance of the duties of the employment and thus the fees did not alternatively qualify for a deduction under **28.16** above.

See generally HMRC Employment Status Manual ESM4121 *et seq*.

Film and television industry

For guidance on the employment status of various occupations within this industry see HMRC Employment Status Manual ESM4100 *et seq*. A vision mixer was held to be self-employed in *Hall v Lorimer* CA 1993, 66 TC 349.

Employment Status Indicator tool

HMRC have produced an interactive tool which can be used as a guide in working out the employment status of individuals or groups of workers. It must be borne in mind that this can do no more than provide a general indication of employment status and that it has no legal authority. See www.gov.uk/guidance/employment-status-indicator.

Simon's Taxes. See **E4.205–E4.224.**

Flat rate deductions

[28.67] For a number of occupations, flat rate deductions are allowed for tools and special clothing necessarily provided by an employee at his own expense. Where the employer reimburses, or would reimburse, part of the expense, the deduction is reduced accordingly. [*ITEPA 2003, ss 330(2), 367*]. See also *Ward v Dunn* Ch D 1978, 52 TC 517.

A list of the flat rate deductions available is provided in HMRC Employment Income Manual at EIM32712. The flat rate amounts are intended to represent the average annual expense incurred by particular classes of employee on the repair, maintenance and replacement of loose tools and special clothing. Special clothing means protective clothing necessary for the job or a uniform or part of a uniform (HMRC Employment Income Manual EIM32465, 32475). An employee who is entitled to a flat rate expense deduction may instead make a claim under the general deduction provisions (see **28.16** above) for the actual expense incurred in any tax year. If an employee deducts an actual expense in one year he is not precluded from deducting the flat rate expense in other years (HMRC Employment Income Manual EIM32715). An advantage of a flat rate deduction is that the employee need not then retain evidence to demonstrate the amount of expenditure actually incurred.

As regards commercial airline pilots (including co-pilots, helicopter pilots, and other uniformed flight deck crew but not cabin crew), see HMRC Employment Income Manual EIM50050. For nurses' clothing allowance, see EIM67200.

Laundry costs

For employees *not* covered by one of the above deductions but who are required to wear protective clothing or uniforms, a flat rate deduction of £60 p.a. is allowed to cover the cost of laundering. If the expense is met partly by the employer the amount of the deduction should be restricted. Larger deductions will not be allowed without adequate evidence of the expenditure incurred. (HMRC Employment Income Manual EIM32485). For nurses (including midwives, auxiliaries, students, nursing assistants and healthcare assistants or workers) the agreed deduction is £100 p.a. (HMRC Employment Income Manual EIM67210, 67240).

HMRC and the Ministry of Defence have agreed an annual flat rate deduction for the laundering of uniforms by qualifying Armed Forces personnel. The rates are £80 for ratings in the Royal Navy and £100 for 'other ranks' in the

Army, RAF and Royal Marines. Relief is given under a net pay arrangement operated by the Ministry of Defence, so individual claims are not required. (HMRC Employment Income Manual EIM50125).

Gifts, awards etc. received

[28.68] Gifts etc. are taxable when they arise out of the employment but not if they are given to the recipient in a personal capacity. The line between the two may be fine. Although payments may be voluntary and irregular, they are taxable. Also all commissions, Christmas presents, 'cost of living', cash and other bonuses. For 'tax-free' payments and awards, see **28.81** below. For payments to clergymen, see **28.62** above.

Bonus to a director described as a gift held taxable (*Radcliffe v Holt* KB 1927, 11 TC 621), and *ex gratia* payments to the retiring chairman of an action group for the successful outcome of litigation similarly held taxable (*McBride v Blackburn* (Sp C 356), [2003] SSCD 139). Proceeds of a *public benefit match* for a cricketer held to be a gift and not chargeable (*Reed v Seymour* HL 1927, 11 TC 625), but see now **28.79** below, and see *Moorhouse v Dooland* CA 1954, 36 TC 1 re collections. In *Davis v Harrison* KB 1927, 11 TC 707, *Corbett v Duff and other cases* KB 1941, 23 TC 763, payments to professional football players *in lieu of benefit* or on *transference to another club*, held taxable. World Cup bonus to professional footballer not taxable (*Moore v Griffiths* Ch D 1972, 48 TC 338). Present to *successful jockey* by owner of racehorse taxable (*Wing v O'Connell* Supreme Court (Ireland) 1926, 1 ITC 170) also *taxi driver's tips* (*Calvert v Wainwright* KB 1947, 27 TC 475) and gifts to Hunt servant (*Wright v Boyce* CA 1958, 38 TC 160). Betting winnings on own games by professional golfer not taxable (*Down v Compston* KB 1937, 21 TC 60).

Gift to employee by company to which his services were lent by employer held not taxable, *Morris* CS 1967, 44 TC 685 as was gift to employee by previous owner of employer company (*Collins v HMRC* FTT (TC 2088), [2012] UKFTT 411 (TC); 2012 STI 2736). But amount to company secretary, agreed by directors for negotiating sale of works and paid by liquidator, held taxable (*Shipway v Skidmore* KB 1932, 16 TC 748) as were payments to a director for negotiating sale of a branch (*Mudd v Collins* KB 1925, 9 TC 297) and to a director for special services abroad (*Barson v Airey* CA 1925, 10 TC 609). Commission for work outside ordinary duties taxable (*Mudd v Collins* KB 1925, 9 TC 297). Sums paid as compensation for loss of benefit under an abandoned salvage scheme held taxable (*Holland v Geoghegan* Ch D 1972, 48 TC 482), also assets distributed to employees on termination of profit-sharing trust fund before termination of employment (*Brumby v Milner* HL 1976, 51 TC 583). See, however, *Bray v Best* HL 1989, 61 TC 705 as regards such a distribution after termination of employment.

In *Shanks v Unilever plc* SC, [2019] UKSC 45, an employee successfully claimed compensation under *Patents Act 1977, s 40* on the basis that the patents for an invention he made in 1982 had been of outstanding benefit to his employer and that he was entitled to a fair share of that benefit. The SC decided that in valuing the benefit to the employer, no account should be taken of corporation tax paid on the profit attributable to it; it was not disputed that the compensation was taxable in the employee's hands.

See **28.76** below regarding gifts of shares.

Pensions (voluntary or otherwise) to retired employees are taxable (see **56.2** PENSION INCOME) as are certain payments in consideration of, in consequence of, or in connection with the termination, or change, of employment (see **18** COMPENSATION FOR LOSS OF EMPLOYMENT).

Suggestion scheme awards

Suggestion scheme awards are not liable to income tax provided that there is a formally constituted scheme open to all employees (or to a particular description of them) on equal terms, and that:

(a) the suggestion relates to the employer's activities;
(b) it could not reasonably have been expected to be made by the employee in the course of the duties of the employment in the light of the employee's experience; and
(c) it is not made at a meeting held for that purpose.

Awards under the scheme must either be 'encouragement' awards of £25 or less, for suggestions with intrinsic merit or showing special effort, or 'financial benefit' awards for suggestions relating to improvements in efficiency or effectiveness which the employer has decided to adopt with a reasonable expectation of financial benefit. The amount of a financial benefit award must not exceed 50% of the first year's expected net benefit, or 10% of the expected benefit over a period of up to five years, with an overall limit of £5,000. Any excess over £5,000 is not covered by the exemption. Where a suggestion is put forward by more than one employee, the award is limited *pro rata*, and any subsequent award(s) for the same suggestion must not exceed the residue of the maximum award. [*ITEPA 2003, ss 321, 322, Sch 7 para 38*].

Long service awards

Long service awards to employees, including directors, for service of 20 years or more, are not liable to income tax to the extent that the cost to the employer does not exceed £50 for each year of service and provided that no similar award has been made to the recipient within the previous ten years. Service may include that with predecessor employers. The award must consist of tangible articles, of shares in the employing company (or in another group company), or of other benefits provided that they are not payments (or cash vouchers or credit-tokens) or other shares or securities (or interests in or rights over them). [*ITEPA 2003, s 323; SI 2003 No 1361, Reg 3*]. Cash awards are taxable (*Weston v Hearn* KB 1943, 25 TC 425).

Gifts from third parties

Gifts received by an employee (or a member of the employee's family or household) from a person other than the employer (or person connected with the employer, see **19** CONNECTED PERSONS), and not directly or indirectly procured by the employer or a connected person, are not liable to income tax, provided that:

(a) they are not made in recognition or anticipation of particular services by the employee in the course of the employment;
(b) they are of goods (i.e. not of cash, securities or the use of a service), or of non-cash vouchers or credit-tokens only capable of being used to obtain goods; and
(c) the total cost to the donor of all such gifts relating to an employee in a tax year is not more than £250 (inclusive of any VAT).

[*ITEPA 2003, ss 270, 324; SI 2003 No 1361, Regs 1, 4*].

Simon's Taxes. See **E4.461–E4.471, E4.764–E4.766.**

HM Forces

[28.69] Mess and ration allowances and certain bounties and gratuities are exempt. [*ITEPA 2003, s 297*]. No tax allowance may be claimed for lodging expenses paid out of taxable lodging allowance (*Evans v Richardson, Nagley v Spilsbury* Ch D 1957, 37 TC 178), nor for mess expenses (*Lomax v Newton* Ch D 1953, 34 TC 558).

See **30.5–30.9** EXEMPT INCOME for various income tax exemptions affecting members of the UK armed forces. Certain payments and other benefits (including redundancy payments/benefits and commutation of annual sums) are exempt from any charge under *ITEPA 2003, s 403* (see **18.10**(iv) COMPENSATION FOR LOSS OF EMPLOYMENT). See also **30.20** EXEMPT INCOME and **56.4** PENSION INCOME. Travel facilities (including allowances, vouchers and warrants) for going on, or returning from, leave are exempt from tax. [*ITEPA 2003, ss 266(3), 296*]. Territorial Army pay is chargeable but not annual bounty and training expenses. [*ITEPA 2003, s 298*].

Uniform allowances

Serving officers generally receive an annual tax-free allowance which, taking one year with another, covers the costs they are obliged to incur in maintaining their uniforms. The allowance is automatically included in their earnings, with a corresponding deduction being made in arriving at taxable earnings. [*ITEPA 2003, ss 328(3), 368*]. No further action is thus generally required.

Legal costs

[28.70] In *Eagles v Levy* KB 1934, 19 TC 23 it was held that (a) costs of action to recover remuneration were not an allowable deduction, and (b) a lump sum amount in settlement of action for balance remuneration was taxable in full.

Where company had special need of director's services and paid more than necessary in legal costs of defence on motoring charge, it was held that no apportionment was to be made between benefits to company and employee and that all the costs were taxable (*Rendell v Went* HL 1964, 41 TC 641).

Simon's Taxes. See **E4.778A.**

Redundancy payments

[28.71] Amounts received under *Employment Rights Act 1996*, or NI equivalent, may be taken into account for purposes of *ITEPA 2003, s 403* — see **18.4** COMPENSATION FOR LOSS OF EMPLOYMENT, but are otherwise exempt earnings. [*ITEPA 2003, s 309*]. Other redundancy payments may be taxable earnings, see **18.4** *et seq.* COMPENSATION FOR LOSS OF EMPLOYMENT.

Relocation packages

[28.72] Certain payments and benefits received in connection with job-related residential moves are exempted from charge as taxable earnings. The exemption applies equally to the charge to tax on DISGUISED REMUNERATION (**26**) but does not apply where the remittance basis applies.

The statutory exemption applies to:

- any sums paid to the employee, or to another person on behalf of the employee, in respect of 'qualifying removal expenses'; and
- any 'qualifying removal benefit' provided for the employee or for members of his family or household (including sons- and daughters-in-law, servants, dependants and guests),

to the extent that they do not exceed a 'qualifying limit' (currently £8,000).

'*Qualifying removal expenses*' are 'eligible removal expenses' reasonably incurred by the employee, and '*qualifying removal benefits*' are 'eligible removal benefits' reasonably provided, on or before the 'limitation day' in connection with a change of the employee's sole or main residence. The change of residence does not require the disposal of the former residence, but the new residence must, on the facts of the particular case, become the main residence of the employee (see Revenue Press Release 14 April 1993).

The change of residence must result from the employee commencing employment with the employer, or from an alteration of his duties in the employment, or from an alteration of the place where those duties are normally to be performed. The change must be made wholly or mainly to bring the employee's residence within a reasonable daily travelling distance of the place he normally performs, or is to perform, those duties. What is a 'reasonable daily travelling distance' is not defined, but is a matter for common sense, taking account of local conditions. It may depend on either or both travelling time or distance (see Revenue Tax Bulletin November 1993 p 94).

The '*limitation day*' is the last day of the tax year following that in which the commencement or change of duties etc. took place, unless the Commissioners for HMRC grant an extension in a particular case to the end of a later tax year.

Eligible removal expenses

'*Eligible removal expenses*' fall into seven different categories.

(i) **Expenses of disposal**, i.e. legal expenses, loan redemption penalties, estate agents' or auctioneers' fees, advertising costs, disconnection charges, and rent and maintenance etc. costs during an unoccupied period, relating to the disposal of his interest (or of the interest of a member of his family or household) in the employee's former residence. Expenses of a sale which falls through are eligible provided that the residence is in fact still changed.

(ii) **Expenses of acquisition**, i.e. legal expenses, loan procurement fees, insurance costs, survey fees, Registry fees, stamp duty and connection charges, relating to the acquisition by the employee (and/or by a member of his family or household) of an interest in his new residence.

(iii) **Expenses of abortive acquisition**, i.e. expenses which would have been within (ii) above but for the interest not being acquired, for reasons beyond the control of the person seeking to acquire it or because that person reasonably declined to proceed with it.

(iv) **Expenses of transporting belongings**, i.e. expenses, including insurance, temporary storage and disconnection and reconnection of appliances, connected with transporting domestic belongings of the employee and of members of his family or household from the former to the new residence.

(v) **Travelling and subsistence expenses** (subsistence meaning food, drink and temporary accommodation). These are restricted to:

- (a) such costs of the employee and members of his family or household on temporary visits to the new area in connection with the change;
- (b) the employee's travel costs between his former residence and new place of work;
- (c) (other than in the case of a new employment) the employee's travel costs, before the change in the employment, between his new residence and old place of work or temporary living accommodation;
- (d) the employee's subsistence costs (not within (a));
- (e) the employee's travel costs between his old residence and any temporary living accommodation;
- (f) the travel costs of the employee and members of his family or household between the former and new residences;
- (g) certain costs incurred to secure continuity of education for a member of the employee's family or household who is under 19 at the beginning of the tax year in which the commencement or change of duties etc. takes place.

Expenses for which a deduction is allowable under *ITEPA 2003, ss 341, 342, 369–375* (certain foreign travel expenses, see **28.11, 28.12** above) are excluded, so that these are in effect allowed in addition to expenses up to the 'qualifying limit' referred to below (HMRC Employment Income Manual EIM03116).

(vi) **Bridging loan expenses**, i.e. interest payable by the employee (or by a member of his family or household) on a loan raised at least partly because there is a gap between the incurring of expenditure in acquiring the new residence and the receipt of the proceeds of disposal of the former residence. Interest on so much of the loan as either:

- exceeds the market value of his interest (or the interest of a member of his family or household) in the former residence (at the time the new residence is acquired); or

- is not used for the purpose of either redeeming a loan raised by the employee (or by a member of his family or household) on his former residence or acquiring his interest (or the interest of a member of his family or household) in the new residence,

is excluded.

(vii) **Duplicate expenses**, i.e. expenses incurred as a result of the change on the replacement of domestic goods used at the former residence but unsuitable for use at the new residence.

The Treasury may by regulation amend these categories so as to add any expenses from a day to be specified in the regulations, with effect for commencements or changes of duties etc. taking place on or after that day.

Eligible removal benefits

'*Eligible removal benefits*' fall into six different categories, consisting of the benefit of services corresponding, as applicable, to the expenses specified under (i)–(v) and (vii) above in relation to eligible removal expenses (but, under (v), excluding the provision of a company car or van also available for general private use (see **28.24**, **28.27** above) in the same tax year in which it is provided for the move). They may include administration fees of a relocation management company charged to the employer. The Treasury has similar powers to those applicable in the case of eligible removal expenses.

Qualifying limit

The '*qualifying limit*' as regards any change of residence applies to the aggregate of qualifying removal expenses paid and the value of qualifying removal benefits received in respect of the change. The value attributed to such benefits is their cash equivalent under the general benefits legislation (**28.54** above) or, as appropriate, the amount of the living accommodation charge under **28.35** *et seq.* above (net of any attributable contribution by the employee and certain allowable deductions).

The amount of the '*qualifying limit*' is **£8,000.**

Bridging loan finance

Bridging loan finance obtained before the 'limitation day' (as above) by reason of the employment within the cheap loan provisions of *ITEPA 2003, s 173* (see **28.32** above) on a move meeting the above conditions may attract a measure of relief where the expenses and benefits for which relief is obtained in respect of the move are in total less than the £8,000 (or increased) limit. Relief is obtained by delaying the implementation of the cheap loan provisions for a number of days after the making of the loan such that the interest (at the official rate at the time the loan was made, see **28.32** above) on the maximum sum borrowed for those days would equate to the amount by which the £8,000 (or increased) limit exceeds the amount of expenses and benefits otherwise relieved. If the loan is discharged before those days have expired, no liability arises. Otherwise, the cheap loan provisions apply as if the loan had been made on the day after the last of the days for which the exemption applies. The tax payable by virtue of those provisions for a tax year ending before the limitation day may be decided on the basis that the maximum relief would be utilised against qualifying removal expenses and benefits, and subsequently adjusted if that is not in fact the case.

[*ITEPA 2003, ss 191(4), 271–289, Sch 7 paras 35, 36*].

General

PAYE should not be applied to payments made under a relocation package, even if the qualifying limit is exceeded. Flat rate allowances may be paid gross, provided that the inspector is satisfied that they do no more than reimburse employees' eligible expenses. Any taxable payments are to be included in the annual return of benefits (see **53.21** PAY AS YOU EARN). See Revenue Press Release 14 April 1993.

For the application of these provisions to relocation company management fees, and in particular to guaranteed sale price schemes, see HMRC Employment Income Manual EIM03127–03137. See generally EIM03100 *et seq.* and guidance at www.gov.uk/expenses-and-benefits-relocation/whats-exempt.

Simon's Taxes. See **E4.723–E4.728.**

Restrictive covenants

[28.73] Where the present, past or future holder of an office or employment, the earnings from which are taxable on the receipts basis (as opposed to the remittance basis — see generally **28.4–28.8** above), gives, in connection therewith, an undertaking (whether qualified or legally valid or not) restricting his conduct or activities, any sum paid to any person in respect of the giving or fulfilment (in whole or part) of the undertaking is, if it would not otherwise be so, treated as earnings from the office or employment for the tax year of payment. If such a payment is made after the death of the individual concerned, it is treated as having been paid immediately before his death. Where valuable consideration rather than money is given, a sum equal to the value of that consideration is treated as having been paid. [*ITEPA 2003, ss 225, 226*].

In *Kent Foods Ltd v HMRC* (Sp C 643), [2008] SSCD 307, the Sp C considered that the statutory phrase 'in connection with' used in the legislation was wide in scope and did not mean exclusively or solely in connection with.

Termination settlements

Financial settlements relating to the termination of an employment may require the employee to undertake that the agreement is in 'full and final settlement' of his claims relating to the employment, and/or not to commence, or to discontinue, legal proceedings in respect of those claims. They may also reaffirm undertakings about the employee's conduct or activity after termination which formed part of the employment terms. HMRC accept that such undertakings do not give rise to a charge under the above provisions, without prejudice to the treatment of other restrictive undertakings, whether or not contained in the settlement. (HMRC SP 3/96).

Where a compromise agreement made at termination of employment includes a repayment clause (typically a clause requiring full or partial repayment by the employee of the sum settled if he subsequently initiates litigation in respect of the employment or its termination), the attribution of any of the sum settled to the undertaking not to litigate would be outside SP 3/96 and thus within the above charging provisions. Other than in exceptional cases, e.g. where the sum settled is clearly excessive in the circumstances, HMRC will not seek to make such an attribution and a charge under the above provisions will not arise. It should be noted that if, exceptionally, a charge *does* arise, there can be no subsequent adjustment to the charge if a repayment is, in fact, made under the clause. (Revenue Tax Bulletin October 2003 p 1063).

Scholarships

[28.74] Where payments are made under scholarship awards, *ITTOIA 2005, s 776* (see **30.46** EXEMPT INCOME) is not to be construed as conferring exemption from tax on any person other than the holder of the scholarship. If a scholarship (including an exhibition, bursary or other similar educational endowment) is provided to a member of the family or household of an employee by reason of the latter's employment the payments are chargeable on the employee under the benefits code. A scholarship is taken to have been provided by reason of a person's employment if provided, directly or indirectly, under arrangements entered into by, or by a person connected with, the employer, unless the employer is an individual and the arrangements are made in the normal course of his domestic, personal or family relationships.

However, the benefits code will not bring into charge a payment under a scholarship awarded out of a trust fund, or under a scheme, to a person receiving full-time instruction at an educational establishment, where 25% or less of the payments made out of the fund etc. in any tax year are scholarship payments provided, or treated as provided, by reason of a person's employment (regardless of whether or not the employment lower-paid employment or in the UK).

Payments which are *in fact* provided by reason of a person's employment are taxable even if the fund meets the 25% test.

[*ITEPA 2003, ss 211–215, Sch 7 para 32(3)*].

For administrative procedures in relation to educational trust scholarships, see HMRC Employment Income Manual EIM30006–30008.

See also **30.44** EXEMPT INCOME for payments to employees to attend sandwich courses and other full-time educational courses.

Simon's Taxes. See **E4.618.**

Security of employees

[28.75] Where an asset or service which improves personal security is provided for an employee by reason of his employment, or is used by the employee, and the cost was (wholly or partly) borne by (or on behalf of) a person other than the employee, then a deduction is allowed to the extent that the provision gives rise to taxable earnings of the employee. The asset or service must be provided or used to meet a special threat to the employee's personal physical security arising wholly or mainly by virtue of the employment, and the sole object of the provider must be the meeting of that threat. In the case of an asset, relief is available only to the extent that the provider intends the asset to be used solely to improve personal physical security (ignoring any other incidental use), and in the case of a service, the benefit to the employee must consist wholly or mainly in such an improvement. Any improvement in the personal physical security of the employee's family resulting from the asset or service provided is disregarded for these purposes.

Excluded from relief is provision of a car, ship or aircraft, or of a dwelling (or grounds appurtenant thereto); but relief may be obtained in respect of equipment or a structure (such as a wall), and it is immaterial whether or not an asset becomes affixed to land and whether or not the employee acquires the property in the asset or (in the case of a fixture) an estate or interest in the land.

Similar relief applies where the employee incurs the expenditure out of his earnings and is reimbursed by some other person, and to office holders.

[*ITEPA 2003, ss 369(1), 377*].

In *Lord Hanson v Mansworth* (Sp C 410), [2004] SSCD 288 (involving the meeting of a potential terrorist threat to the high profile executive chairman of a prominent public company), the above deduction was allowed on appeal.

See also **10.9** CAPITAL ALLOWANCES ON PLANT AND MACHINERY, **75.114** TRADING INCOME.

Simon's Taxes. See **E4.793**.

Shares etc.

[28.76] The value of a gift or transfer of shares to a director or employee, if regarded as a reward for services or part of his earnings, is taxable on him. It was held that liability did not arise in *Bridges v Bearsley* CA 1957, 37 TC 289 (because gift of shares in default of legacy held to be testimonial not remuneration). A similar decision was reached in *Rogers v HMRC* FTT (TC 1036), [2011] SFTD 788 in which the father of the employer company's late owner gratuitously transferred the shares to the employee. Where shares were issued to employees at par value which was less than market value, the difference was held taxable (*Weight v Salmon* HL 1935, 19 TC 174; *Ede v Wilson* KB 1945, 26 TC 381; *Patrick v Burrows* Ch D 1954, 35 TC 138; *Bentley v Evans* Ch D 1959, 39 TC 132; *Tyrer v Smart* HL 1978, 52 TC 533).

A payment received from the parent company of a group after the employing company left the group, in consideration of loss of rights under the parent company's SAYE option scheme (see **71.53** SHARE-RELATED EMPLOYMENT INCOME AND EXEMPTIONS), was not taxable (*Wilcock v Eve* Ch D 1995, 67 TC 223).

For capital gains tax, such gifts are treated as an acquisition for nil consideration where there is no corresponding disposal of the shares, i.e. where the shares are issued by the company concerned. [*TCGA 1992, s 17*].

For the circumstances in which HMRC will accept that shares or share options were acquired by a director or employee in a different capacity and not by reason of the office or employment, see HMRC Share Schemes Manual SSM 4.4.

For priority allocations of shares for employees etc., see **71.79** SHARE-RELATED EMPLOYMENT INCOME AND EXEMPTIONS.

See generally **71** SHARE-RELATED EMPLOYMENT INCOME AND EXEMPTIONS.

Phantom share schemes

Some employers may set up incentive schemes involving 'phantom' or hypothetical shares; the employee is 'allocated' a number of shares in the employer company and potentially receives a future cash bonus linked to the value of those shares. No tax is chargeable at the time of the award (as no value passes), the bonus being chargeable as general earnings for, usually but not invariably, the tax year of receipt. (HMRC Employment Income Manual EIM01600). See also **71.3** SHARE-RELATED EMPLOYMENT INCOME AND EXEMPTIONS.

Sick pay and health insurance

[28.77] Continuing pay from an employer during sickness or other absence from work is taxable as earnings from employment. Any payments of statutory sick pay under *Social Security Contributions and Benefits Act 1992, s 151* are similarly taxable. [*ITEPA 2003, s 660*].

Any sum paid to, or to the order or for the benefit of, an employee in respect of absence from work through sickness or disability (or to his spouse, a son or daughter or spouse, or a parent or dependant) is taxable earnings of the employee for the period of absence (unless otherwise taxable) where it is paid as a result of any arrangements entered into by the employer. There is no liability to the extent that the contributions funding the arrangements are paid by the employee. [*ITEPA 2003, s 221*].

There is no charge under the benefits code (see **28.21** above) on the right to receive any such sums chargeable under *ITEPA 2003, s 221*. However, for 2017/18 onwards, a benefit does not fall within this exemption in so far as it is provided under salary sacrifice arrangements. Where the benefit is provided pursuant to pre-6 April 2017 arrangements, the latter rule is delayed by one year and has effect for 2018/19 onwards instead. See **28.14** above as to 'salary sacrifice arrangements' and the effect of pre-6 April 2017 arrangements being varied or renewed on or after that date. [*ITEPA 2003, s 202; FA 2017, Sch 2 paras 47, 62(2)(5)*].

A lump sum received under a life, accident or sickness or insurance policy is not normally taxable.

See **30.29** EXEMPT INCOME for provisions exempting annual payments falling to be made under certain insurance policies.

See generally HMRC Employment Income Manual EIM01550, 06400 *et seq*.

See also **75.92** TRADING INCOME.

Sporting and recreational facilities

[28.78] The provision to an employee (or to a member of his family or household) of:

- any benefit consisting in, or in a right or opportunity to make use of, any sporting or other recreational facilities made available generally to, or for use by, the employees of the employer in question; or
- any non-cash voucher (see **28.47** above) capable of being exchanged only for such a benefit,

is exempted from any charge to income tax.

Excluded from the relief is any benefit consisting in:

(i) an interest in, or the use of, any mechanically propelled vehicle (including ships, boats, aircraft and hovercraft);
(ii) an interest in, or the use of, any holiday or other overnight accommodation or associated facilities;
(iii) a facility provided on domestic premises (i.e. premises used wholly or mainly as a private dwelling, or belonging to or enjoyed with such premises);
(iv) a facility available to, or for use by, the general public;
(v) a facility not used wholly or mainly by persons whose right or opportunity to use it derives from employment; or
(vi) a right or opportunity to make use of any facility within (i)–(v) above.

As regards (iv) above, where employers group together to provide facilities for members of all their staffs, this does not of itself mean that they are available to members of the general public. In practice, the opening of facilities to a restricted section of the public (e.g. those living in the immediate vicinity) as well as to employees will similarly not result in loss of the relief. (HMRC Employment Income Manual EIM22860, 22862).

As regards (v) above, a right or opportunity derives from employment only if it derives from the person's being (or having been) an employee of a particular employer (or a member of such a person's family or household) and the facility is available generally to employees of that employer.

The Treasury may by regulation prescribe exceptions from, and conditional inclusions in, this relief.

[*ITEPA 2003, ss 261–263*].

Where the provision of recreational facilities to employees is exempt as above, the provision of those facilities to others who are working at the employer's premises but are not employees of that employer is also exempt. [*SI 2002 No 205, Reg 6; SI 2004 No 3087*].

Simon's Taxes. See **E4.716.**

Sporting testimonials

[28.79] Professional sportspersons (referred to below as players) are sometimes granted benefits or testimonials which can consist of a benefit match or a series of events throughout a benefit period. Where the right to a benefit match or benefit period is written into a player's contract, or where the player's club always grants the benefit match or period after a set qualifying period of service, the proceeds are chargeable as earnings under *ITEPA 2003, s 62*. Where this is *not* the case, HMRC's practice has been to treat the proceeds as exempt from income tax. This practice relied on principles established in *Reed v Seymour* HL 1927, 11 TC 625. (HMRC Employment Income Manual EIM64120).

In relation to sporting testimonial events and activities held on or after 6 April 2017 (except where the testimonial was awarded (i.e. made public) before 25 November 2015), income arising from a non-contractual or non-customary sporting testimonial or benefit for an employed player is liable to income tax as employment income. This is achieved by treating a 'sporting testimonial payment' as earnings of the player from the employment or former employment to which the testimonial is most closely linked. It is subject to an exemption for the first **£100,000** (see below).

A '*sporting testimonial payment*' is a payment made by the 'controller' of a sporting testimonial out of money raised for or for the benefit of the player, where the payment is made to the player, a member of his family or household, to any person prescribed by regulations, to the player's order, or otherwise for his benefit. A payment is not a sporting testimonial payment if it otherwise constitutes earnings; this excludes payments from benefits or testimonials that are contractual or customary in nature and thus chargeable as earnings in any case. A '*controller*' is someone who controls the disbursement of money raised for the player from an event or activity. 'Money' includes money's worth, and 'payment' includes the transfer of money's worth or the provision of any benefit.

For the above purposes, anything done for the benefit of the player's estate following his death is to be regarded as done for him, and a payment made to his personal representatives is treated as a payment to him. A payment from a testimonial arranged for the benefit of a deceased person's family would not be brought within the charge on non-contractual payments provided it is not made to the person's estate or to his personal representatives.

For these purposes a sporting testimonial can refer to a series of relevant events or activities which each have the same controller or to a single relevant event or activity not forming part of any such series. An event is a relevant event or activity if its purpose (or one of its purposes) is to raise money for the player, where the only or main reason for doing so is to recognise his service as an employed professional player. An activity consisting solely of inviting and collecting donations is part of a sporting testimonial if it is one of a series of events with the same controller. It is excluded from being a single relevant event or activity if:

- none of the following is responsible for collecting donations or is the controller of the activity (or a member of a committee which is that controller): (i) the player; (ii) the controller of any other relevant event or activity for that player; (iii) any person connected with either of them (within **19 CONNECTED PERSONS**); and (iv) a person acting on behalf of a person within (i), (ii) or (iii); and
- the donations collected do not include any sums paid out of money raised by any other relevant event or activity.

The intention is to exclude from the charge on non-contractual payments any fund-raising activities forming one-off donations that are not part of a sporting testimonial.

For the avoidance of double taxation, the DISGUISED REMUNERATION (26) rules do not apply to a sporting testimonial payment that is within the charge under these provisions (or would be but for the exemption below).

[*ITEPA 2003, s 226E; FA 2016, Sch 2 paras 1, 4; SI 2016 No 1250*].

The pre-existing practice above continues where the testimonial or benefit was awarded before 25 November 2015, regardless of when it is held.

The exemption

There is no liability to income tax on the first £100,000 of sporting testimonial payments made out of money raised by a sporting testimonial which would otherwise be treated under *ITEPA 2003, s 226E* above as a person's earnings. The player can benefit from this exemption in respect of one sporting testimonial only, whether it consists of one event or a series of events. The exemption applies only to amounts paid out of money raised from relevant activities or events taking place within the 12 months beginning with the day on which the first such event or activity took place. If this is before 6 April 2017, the 12 months beginning on that date are substituted instead. If the payments themselves are made over two or more tax years, any part of the exempt amount unused at the end of one year is carried forward to the next. But where payments are made to a deceased player's personal representatives, the exemption applies only to payments made within the 24 months beginning with the date of death.

The controller of a relevant event or activity (or of all the relevant events or activities in a series) constituting the sporting testimonial must be an '*independent person*' if the exemption is to apply. This means a person who is not (or where the controller is a committee, a committee none of whose members are): (i) the player himself or a person connected with him; (ii) an employer or former employer or a person connected with such an employer; or (iii) a person acting on behalf of a person within (i) or (ii).

[*ITEPA 2003, s 306B; FA 2016, Sch 2 paras 2, 4*].

Simon's Taxes. See **E4.469**.

Subscriptions and professional fees

[28.80] There may be deducted from taxable earnings any professional fees paid which are listed in the *Table* in *ITEPA 2003, s 343(2)*. These include fees payable by health (or animal health) professionals, legal professionals, architects, teachers, patent and trade mark agents, driving instructors, aircraft maintenance engineers, air traffic controllers, aircraft flight crew, flight information service officers, HGV drivers and seafarers (including certain related technical and medical examination fees). The Commissioners for HMRC periodically add to the list by means of a statutory instrument amending the Table. In order for fees to be deductible, the duties of the employment must involve the practice of the profession to which the fee relates, and the registration, certification, licensing or other matter in respect of which the fee is payable must be a condition of that profession being practised. [*ITEPA 2003, s 343*].

Subscriptions

There may be deducted from taxable earnings annual subscriptions, or parts thereof, paid to bodies approved by the Commissioners for HMRC whose activities are directed, otherwise than for profit, to advancing or spreading knowledge, maintaining or improving professional conduct and competence, or indemnifying or protecting professional persons against claims incurred in exercising their profession, and are relevant to the office or employment. The body must not be of a mainly local character. [*ITEPA 2003, ss 344, 345*]. A list of bodies approved by HMRC for this purpose is available at www.gov.uk/government/publications/professional-bodies-approved-for-tax-relief-list-3/approved-professional-organisations-and-learned-societies. Applications for approval should be made in writing to HMRC, Personal Tax Division 5, Sapphire House, 550 Streetsbrook Road, Solihull, West Midlands B91 1QU. The PGA lost an appeal against denial of approval on the grounds that its activities, whilst carried on otherwise than for profit, were not wholly or mainly directed to the objects mentioned above (*Professional Golfers' Association Ltd v HMRC* FTT (TC 2992), [2013] UKFTT 605 (TC)).

Bank manager's club subscriptions reimbursed by bank have been disallowed (*Brown v Bullock* CA 1961, 40 TC 1) but subscriptions to clubs to obtain cheaper accommodation on visits to London have been allowed (*Elwood v Utitz* CA (NI) 1965, 42 TC 482).

'Tax-free payments'

[28.81] If an employer pays an employee's tax, this constitutes the payment of a pecuniary liability of the employee as in **28.13** above. If, however, it is agreed between them that the employer will pay the employee such amount as leaves the employee with a stated sum after PAY AS YOU EARN (**53**) deductions, it follows that the employer must account for those deductions to HMRC under the PAYE system and that the employee's taxable earnings are equal to the gross amount before PAYE and not the net amount he actually receives. See *North British Rly v Scott* HL 1922, 8 TC 332; *Hartland v Diggines* HL 1926, 10 TC 247; *Jaworski v Institution of Polish Engineers* CA 1950, 29 ATC 385). See also HMRC Pamphlet P7 (Employer's Guide to PAYE).

Special forms and tax tables are available to assist employers who pay employees on a 'net of tax' basis to calculate how much tax is due (Revenue Press Release 2 March 1984).

Where an employer paying earnings of a director fails, in whole or in part, to deduct and account for PAYE tax at the proper time, and that tax is subsequently accounted for by someone other than the director, such tax paid, less so much as is made good by the director, will be treated as taxable earnings unless the director has no material interest in the company and either he is a full-time working director or the company is non-profit-making or charitable. Any amounts accounted for after cessation of employment are treated as having arisen in the tax year in which the employment ended but no amounts accounted for after the death of the director will be chargeable. [*ITEPA 2003, s 223*].

An agreement to reimburse tax as 'expenses' was held not to be enforceable as the contract was illegal (*Miller v Karlinski* CA 1945, 24 ATC 483, and see also *Napier v National Business Agency* CA 1951, 30 ATC 180).

Interim payments of tax under self-assessment made by an employer on an employee's behalf, as part of *tax equalisation* arrangements where full in-year gross up is used, should not figure in the employment pages of the employee's self-assessment tax return (see Revenue Tax Bulletin June 1998 p 551). See **53.51** PAY AS YOU EARN as regards modified PAYE procedures for tax equalised employees.

Simon's Taxes. See **E4.451, E4.483.**

Taxed award schemes

Employers may, if they wish, enter into arrangements with HMRC to meet the liability of employees on the grossed-up value of non-cash incentive prizes and awards. The arrangements involve a legally binding contract for payment of the related tax together with simplified reporting arrangements. The arrangements may involve payment of tax at the basic rate or at the higher rate or both, although separate contracts are required in relation to basic rate and higher rate schemes. Where only basic rate liabilities are met, higher rate liabilities continue to be collected from employees in the usual way. Valuation of an award will depend on details of the scheme. Details of the arrangements may be obtained from HMRC, Incentive Award Unit, Manchester Blackfriars TDO, Trinity Bridge House, 2 Dearmans Place, Salford M3 5BH (tel. 0161–261 3269), which also deals with national insurance aspects. (Revenue Press Releases 2 November 1984, 18 January 1990; Revenue Tax Bulletin April 2000 p 747).

See generally HMRC Employment Income Manual EIM11235 *et seq.*

For the valuation of incentive awards generally, see **28.47** above and HMRC SP 6/85.

Termination payments

[28.82] See **18.2** COMPENSATION FOR LOSS OF EMPLOYMENT for the assessment of such payments under general principles (see **28.13** above). See also **28.71** above for statutory redundancy payments and **28.95** below for wages in lieu of notice.

Certain payments to persons ceasing to be members of the House of Commons, the European Parliament, the Scottish Parliament, the Assembly for Wales, or the Northern Ireland Assembly or the Greater London Assembly, or to persons ceasing to hold a ministerial (or equivalent) office, including the office of Mayor of London, are exempted from the general charge on earnings. They are, however, liable in the normal way under *ITEPA 2003, s 403* (see **18.4** COMPENSATION FOR LOSS OF EMPLOYMENT). [*ITEPA 2003, s 291*].

Training costs

[28.83] No income tax liability arises in respect of expenditure incurred by the employer in paying or reimbursing retraining course expenses of an employee (or past employee). The employee must begin the course during, or within one year of leaving, the employment, must have left that employment by two years after the end of the course, and must not be re-employed by the employer within two years of leaving. If, after the relief has been given, any of these conditions fail to be met, an assessment may be raised to withdraw the relief within six years of the end of the tax year in which the failure occurred. The employer must notify such failure to the inspector within 60 days of coming to know of it, and the inspector may require information from the employer in relation to any such failure where he has reason to believe that the employer has failed to give such notice. Penalties apply under *TMA 1970, s 98* for failure to give such notice or furnish such information.

The retraining course must:

- be designed to impart or improve skills or knowledge relevant to, and intended to be used in the course of, gainful employment (or self-employment) of any description; and
- be devoted entirely to the teaching and/or practical application of such skills or knowledge; and
- not last more than two years; and
- be available on similar terms to all, or to a particular class or classes of, past or present employees,

and the employee must be employed in the employment throughout the two years prior to starting the course (or prior to his earlier leaving that employment — see above). Part-time employees are within the exemption.

The qualifying expenses are:

- course attendance and examination fees; and
- costs of essential course books; and
- travelling expenses where, if attendance at the course was a duty of the employment and the employee was in that employment when the expenses were incurred and paid them himself, either they would have been deductible under *ITEPA 2003, Pt 5* (see **28.16** above) or mileage allowance relief would have been available if no mileage allowance had been paid (see **28.91** below).

[*ITEPA 2003, ss 311, 312, Sch 7 para 37*].

For relief to the employer, see **75.73** TRADING INCOME.

Work-related training

Subject to the exceptions below, where an employer pays or reimburses the cost of providing 'work-related training' to employees, no income tax liability arises in respect of such expenditure or of any benefit. Similar relief applies to any incidental costs incurred as a result of the employee's undertaking the training, any expenses in connection with an assessment of what the employee has gained from the training, and the costs of obtaining for the employee any consequent qualification, registration or award.

'*Work-related training*' means any training course or other activity designed to impart, instil, improve or reinforce any knowledge, skills or personal qualities likely to prove useful to the employee in performing the duties of the employment or a 'related employment', or which will qualify (or better qualify) the employee to perform such duties or to participate in any charitable or voluntary activities available to be performed in association with any such employment. Participation in a genuine Employee Development Scheme which seeks to improve the employee's attitude towards training by commencing with an enjoyable course, as an introduction to more concentrated job-related training, will qualify, as will participation in activities such as Outward Bound, Raleigh International or Prince's Trust where leadership skills are appropriate to the employee. (HMRC Employment Income Manual EIM01220). A '*related employment*' is an employment, with the same employer or a person connected with him (within **19** CONNECTED PERSONS), which the employee is to hold, has a serious opportunity of holding or can realistically expect to have a serious opportunity of holding in due course.

Exceptions

The above exemption does not apply to the extent that facilities or other benefits are provided or made available for any of the following purposes:

- to enable the employee to enjoy them for entertainment or recreational purposes, or in the course of any leisure activity, unconnected with the promotion of knowledge, skills or personal qualities (as above);
- to reward the employee for the performance of the duties of his employment or for the manner of their performance; or
- to provide the employee with an inducement, unconnected with the promotion of knowledge, skills or personal qualities (as above), to remain in or accept an employment with the employer or a connected person.

The cost of provision of any asset, or of the use of any asset, to the employee is excluded except where:

- the asset is not for use other than in the course of the training or in the performance of the duties of the employment;
- it consists of training materials, e.g. stationery, books, tapes, disks etc.; or
- it consists in something made by the employee during the training, or incorporated into something so made.

Travelling and subsistence expenses are not excluded provided that, if the training had been undertaken in the performance of the duties of the employment and the expenses incurred and paid by the employee, either they would have been allowable under the general deductions provisions or mileage allowance relief would have been available if no mileage allowance had been paid (see **28.91** below).

[*ITEPA 2003, ss 250–254*].

An MBA course costing £18,000 and reimbursed by way of a 'signing bonus' was held on the facts to be for the purpose of qualifying the taxpayer to undertake the employment as opposed to inducing her to accept the employment and was within the exemption; it did not matter that the training took place outside the currency of the employment (*Silva v Charnock* (Sp C 332), [2002] SSCD 426). However, HMRC do not see this case as supporting a general exemption for reimbursements of training costs incurred by individuals before the employment commences, though they will not pursue arrears of tax where such reimbursements have been made tax-free in accordance with specific advice given by tax offices (some of which may have given conflicting advice). HMRC do allow exemption for reimbursement of pre-commencement training costs where there is a strong and demonstrable link between the training and the employment, for example where an individual undergoes training for a job he has already accepted and which he is due to start in the near future. (Revenue Tax Bulletin April 2003 pp 1022, 1023).

See generally HMRC Employment Income Manual EIM01200 *et seq.*

Training costs borne by employees

Training costs borne by employees may attract tax relief under *ITEPA 2003, s 336* (see **28.16** above) but only if they fully satisfy the stringent conditions for such relief. Relief was refused in *Snowdon v Charnock* (Sp C 282), [2001] SSCD 152, *Consultant Psychiatrist v HMRC* (Sp C 557), [2006] SSCD 653, *HMRC v Decadt* Ch D 2007, 79 TC 220 and *Perrin v HMRC* (Sp C 671), [2008] SSCD 672. Relief was allowed in *HMRC v Banerjee (No 1)* CA 2010, 80 TC 205 in which the courses and training that the employee, an NHS trust specialist registrar, attended were compulsory and a pre-requisite of her maintaining her post and employment.

Simon's Taxes. See **E4.711, E4.745.**

Travelling and subsistence

[28.84] See generally HMRC Booklet 490 'Employee Travel — A Tax and NICs Guide for Employers' and HMRC Employment Income Manual EIM31800 *et seq.*

The normal statutory relief for expenses in employment is extended to include certain additional travelling and associated expenses, broadly those of travelling to temporary workplaces (excluding ordinary commuting and private travel). See **28.17** above. The following commentary applies to all travelling and associated expenses which are not the subject of specific statutory relief (or exclusion).

See also:

- **28.85** below — Late night journeys home;
- **28.86** below — Incidental overnight expenses;
- **28.87** below — Meal allowances during business travel;
- **28.88** below — Working Rule Agreements;

28.89 below — Lorry drivers;
28.90 below — Employment abroad;
28.91 below — Private vehicle used for employment;
28.92 below — Mileage allowances for business travel in company car;
28.93 below — Parking facilities;
28.94 below — Members of local authorities.

The general relief for deductions from employment income is for expenses necessarily incurred in the performance of the duties of the office or employment (see **28.16** above). Subject to the special reliefs mentioned above and below relating to temporary workplaces, this excludes expenses of travelling to the place of employment from home or from a place at which a business or another employment is carried on. A leading case here is *Ricketts v Colquhoun* HL 1925, 10 TC 118 in which a barrister practising in London was refused his expenses of travelling to Portsmouth where he was employed as Recorder. See also *Cook v Knott* QB 1887, 2 TC 246; *Revell v Directors of Elworthy Bros & Co Ltd* QB 1890, 3 TC 12; *Nolder v Walters* KB 1930, 15 TC 380; *Burton v Rednall* Ch D 1954, 35 TC 435; *Bhadra v Ellam* Ch D 1987, [1988] STC 239 (see **28.19** above); *Parikh v Sleeman* CA 1990, 63 TC 75; *Smith v Fox* Ch D 1989, 63 TC 304; *Miners v Atkinson* Ch D 1995, 68 TC 629; *Warner v Prior* (Sp C 353), [2003] SSCD 109 and contrast *Pook v Owen*(see below and **28.19** above) and *Taylor v Provan* HL 1974, 49 TC 579 in both of which *Ricketts v Colquhoun* was distinguished. The deduction is refused notwithstanding that the taxpayer is unable to live nearer his place of employment (*Andrews v Astley* KB 1924, 8 TC 589; *Phillips v Keane* HC(IFS), 1 ITC 69). No allowance to an assistant required to attend classes (*Blackwell v Mills* KB 1945, 26 TC 468).

If an emergency call-out requires an employee to travel from home to the normal place of employment, reimbursed travel expenses will be taxable earnings unless the conditions underlying the decision in *Pook v Owen* HL 1969, 45 TC 571 (for which see also **28.19** above) are met, i.e. (i) advice on handling the emergency is given on receipt of the telephone call; (ii) responsibility for those aspects appropriate to the employee's duties is accepted at that time; and (iii) the employee has a continuing responsibility for the emergency whilst travelling to the normal place of employment. A claim for a deduction for expenses not reimbursed will be allowed on the same basis. Where an emergency call-out requires travel from home to a place other than the normal place of employment, reimbursed expenses are not chargeable emoluments, and a claim for expenses not reimbursed should be allowed. (HMRC Employment Income Manual EIM10040, 10050).

Reasonable reimbursement of expenses of home to work travel (or the provision of vouchers etc. for such travel, see **28.46** above) is not taxed where the expenses are incurred either (a) as a result of public transport disruption owing to industrial action, or (b) by disabled employees. [*ITEPA 2003, ss 245, 246*]. See also **28.52**(v)(vi) above.

A claim for a deduction corresponding to living allowances paid while working away from home was refused where an engineer without a permanent work base was required to undertake assignments necessitating his living away from home for long periods (*Elderkin v Hindmarsh* Ch D 1988, 60 TC 651).

In addition, reasonable reimbursement of expenditure on subsistence etc. is, by concession, not taxed where (a) an employee occupies overnight accommodation near his normal place of work as a result of public transport disruption owing to industrial action, or (b) it is necessary for an offshore oil or gas worker to take overnight accommodation near the point of his departure from the mainland for the offshore rig etc. [*ITEPA 2003, ss 245, 305*]. See also **28.52**(v)(vi) above.

See **28.52**(x) as regards certain removal expenses. See **30.19** EXEMPT INCOME as regards subsistence allowances paid to persons seconded to certain EU bodies.

See **49.7** MISCELLANEOUS INCOME as regards **volunteer drivers,** e.g. hospital car service drivers.

Simon's Taxes. See E4.703.

Late night journeys home

[28.85] The provision by an employer of private transport, e.g. taxis, hired cars etc., for the journey home of employees required to work late (or of vouchers etc. for such travel — see **28.46** above) will not result in a charge to income tax on the employee, provided that:

- the employee is required to work later than usual and until at least 9 pm,
- such occasions occur irregularly, and
- either public transport between the employee's place of work and his home has ceased for the day or it would not be reasonable to expect the employee to use it, for example if the journey would take significantly longer than usual due to the lateness of the hour.

This exemption is extended to cover the payment for or provision of transport home by the employer where regular home to work car-sharing arrangements with other employees fail on a particular occasion due to unforeseen or exceptional circumstances. The exemption applies to a maximum of 60 journeys in a tax year, and this applies to the aggregate of journeys under both legs of the exemption (i.e. late night journeys and car-share breakdowns). [*ITEPA 2003, s 248*].

See also HMRC Employment Income Manual 21831–21834 with particular reference to the three conditions above, the 60-journey rule and the standard of record-keeping required.

Incidental overnight expenses

[28.86] Payments made to or on behalf of an employee in respect of his overnight personal incidental expenses (e.g. laundry, newspapers, telephone calls home) while away from home on business are exempt from income tax provided that they do not exceed certain limits. Payments exceeding the limits are taxable in full. The exemption covers expenses incidental to the employee's being away from home during a 'qualifying absence' other than one in relation to which the overall exemption limit is exceeded, being expenses which would not otherwise be deductible. A '*qualifying absence*' is a continuous period throughout which the employee is obliged to stay away from home and which includes at least one overnight stay but does not include any such stay at a place the expenses of travelling to which would not be either deductible under normal rules or exempt under *ITEPA 2003, s 250* (work-related training costs, see **28.83** above) or exempt under *ITEPA 2003, s 255* (individual learning account training). The overall exemption limit, in relation to a qualifying absence, is £5 for each night spent in the UK and £10 for each night any part of which is spent outside the UK. In determining whether the authorised maximum is exceeded, payments by non-cash voucher or credit token and the providing of benefits are taken into account as well as cash payments. [*ITEPA 2003, ss 240, 241, Sch 7 paras 33, 34*].

HMRC guidance notes for employers on the practical application of these provisions (see HMRC Booklet 480 and the Employer's Guide to PAYE (P7)) are available.

Simon's Taxes. See **E4.706.**

Meal allowances during business travel

[28.87] By virtue of regulations made under **28.53** above, an amount (a 'meal allowance') paid or reimbursed to an employee in respect of meals in the course of 'qualifying travel' is exempt provided that the amount does not exceed:

- £5 where the duration of the qualifying travel in that day is at least five hours;
- £10 where it is at least ten hours; and
- £25 where it is at least 15 hours and the qualifying travel is ongoing at 8 pm.

An additional meal allowance not exceeding £10 per day is exempt where a meal allowance within either of the first two categories is paid and the qualifying travel is ongoing at 8 pm. These rates are sometimes referred to by HMRC as benchmark scale rates.

For 2019/20 onwards, employers are not required to operate a system for checking receipts or other forms of documentary evidence of employees' expenditure in order to make the payments free of tax. Instead, they are required only to ensure that employees are undertaking qualifying travel. '*Qualifying travel*' is travel within **28.11** or **28.17** above, the expenses of which are deductible from earnings. See HMRC Employment Income Manual EIM30220.

[*ITEPA 2003, s 289A(2A); SI 2015 No 1948, Reg 2*].

Working rule agreements

[28.88] Working rule agreements are drawn up by employers and trade unions to govern, on a national basis, rates of pay and conditions of work of hourly-paid manual workers in the construction and allied industries. They apply to site-based workers, i.e. those who do not normally work at their employer's base or depot but at a succession of different sites. The agreements include provision for payment of daily travel and lodging allowances. In recognition of the mobility required of construction industry workers, HMRC have agreed specific taxation procedures to be applied to payments of travel and lodging allowances made under working rule agreements. These procedures can operate only where the employer makes payments in strict accordance with the terms and conditions of the agreement. (HMRC Employment Income Manual EIM71300–71340). Details of those working rule agreements for which procedures have been agreed are provided at EIM71320.

Lodging allowances may generally be paid tax-free to employees engaged under the terms of a working rule agreement, provided that, whilst incurring extra expenses on lodging away, they are also responsible for maintaining dependants at their permanent home. This treatment is extended to single and married employees without dependants who certify to their employer that, whilst incurring extra expenses on lodging away, they have continuing liability for the expenses of maintenance of their permanent home in the UK. (HMRC Employment Income Manual EIM71308, 71310).

Lorry drivers

[28.89] Long distance lorry drivers normally receive a payment in respect of each rest period spent away from the home base. The payment includes a subsistence element and, sometimes, an additional round sum payment. Any additional round sum payment is taxable. As regards the subsistence element, HMRC accept £34.90 per night as being no more than fair reimbursement of the costs of accommodation and subsistence in the UK. This figure is reduced by 25% where a sleeper cab is available. Greater amounts may, however, be paid without charge to tax if certain conditions are met. (See HMRC Employment Income Manual EIM66100–66195, which also cover lunch allowances).

Employment abroad

[28.90] Tax will not be charged on the reimbursement to an employee, whose duties are carried on wholly abroad and who retains an abode in the UK, of expenses, including reasonable hotel expenses necessarily incurred, in travelling (whether alone or with his wife and family) to the country where his duties are performed and returning to the UK. Similar relief applies for persons of non-UK domicile travelling between the UK and their abode in the home country. See **28.11, 28.12** above. For allowances for travelling etc. expenses to members of the European Parliament, see *Lord Bruce of Donington v Aspden* CJEC, [1981] STC 761.

For overseas trips generally, see *Newlin v Woods* CA 1966, 42 TC 649 (cost of journey for health reasons disallowed); *Maclean v Trembath* Ch D 1956, 36 TC 653 (business trip accompanied by wife; expenses attributable to wife disallowed); *Thomson v White* Ch D 1966, 43 TC 256 (expenses of farmers and wives on organised trip partly for sightseeing and partly to see farms overseas disallowed); *Owen v Burden* CA 1971, 47 TC 476 (expenses of county surveyor voluntarily to attend overseas road conference disallowed). See **30.33** EXEMPT INCOME as regards certain overseas travel costs of MPs.

Benchmark scale rates

HMRC publish tables of country-by-country benchmark scale rates that employers can use to pay accommodation and subsistence expenses to employees whose duties require them to travel abroad. See www.gov.uk/government/publications/scale-rate-expenses-payments-employee-travelling-outside-the-uk. Accommodation and subsistence payments made at or below the published rates are not liable for income tax, employers need not include them on forms P11D and employees do not have to produce receipts. If an employer pays less than the published rates the employees are not entitled to tax relief for the shortfall; they can obtain relief only for their actual, vouched expenses less any amounts borne by the employer. The scale rates can be paid in addition to the tax-free amounts for incidental overnight expenses referred to at **28.86** above. Employers are not obliged to use the published rates; they may reimburse actual vouched expenses or negotiate a scale rate amount which they believe more accurately reflects their employees' spending. (HMRC Employment Income Manual EIM05250–05280).

For 2019/20 onwards, the above-mentioned tables are given statutory effect under the provisions at **28.53** above. Employers are not required to operate a system for checking receipts or other forms of documentary evidence of employees' expenditure in order to make the payments free of tax. Instead, they are required only to ensure that employees are undertaking 'qualifying travel'. '*Qualifying travel*' is travel within **28.11** or **28.17** above, the expenses of which are deductible from earnings. [*ITEPA 2003, s 289A(2A); SI 2015 No 1948, Reg 3; SI 2019 No 358*].

Private vehicle used for employment

[28.91] There are statutorily exempt mileage allowances for employees (which includes office holders). These allowances are exempt from income tax when paid by the employer, and may also form the basis of a claim by the employee where no (or smaller) mileage allowances are payable.

The statutory exemption applies to:

- 'approved mileage allowance payments' for a 'qualifying vehicle', *provided that* the employee is not a passenger in the vehicle and the vehicle is not a 'company vehicle' (as broadly defined, see *ITEPA 2003, s 236(2)*); and
- 'approved passenger payments' made to an employee for a car or van, *provided that* 'mileage allowance payments' are made to the employee for the vehicle and, if it is made available to the employee by reason of the employment, the employee is chargeable in respect of it as a benefit-in-kind under **28.24** or **28.27** above.

Mileage allowance payments

'*Mileage allowance payments*' are payments (other than 'passenger payments') paid to an employee in respect of expenses in connection with the use by the employee of a 'qualifying vehicle' for 'business travel'. They are '*approved*' if and to the extent that, for a tax year, the total payments made to the employee for the kind of vehicle in question do not exceed the 'approved amount' for mileage allowance payments applicable to that kind of vehicle.

A '*qualifying vehicle*' is a car, van, motor cycle or cycle (each as defined in *ITEPA 2003, s 235*), and '*business travel*' is travel the expenses of which would be deductible under the general provisions (see **28.17** above) if incurred and paid by the employee (but see **28.94** below as regards local councillors). The '*approved amount*' for this purpose is obtained from the formula:

$$M \times R$$

where M is the number of business miles travelled by the employee (other than as a passenger) using the kind of vehicle in question, in the tax year; and

R is the rate applicable for that kind of vehicle. The rates are as follows.

	Per each of the first 10,000 miles	*Per each mile over 10,000*
Cars and vans	45p	25p
Motor cycles	24p	24p
Cycles	20p	20p

The 10,000 mile limit is applied by reference to business travel by car or van in all 'associated employments' (as defined — broadly where the employments are under the same employer or the employers are under common control). All these rates may be altered by the Treasury by regulation.

Passenger payments

'*Passenger payments*' are payments made to an employee because, while using a car or van for business travel, he carries one or more '*qualifying passengers*', i.e. fellow employee(s) for whom the travel is also business travel. They are '*approved*' if and to the extent that, for a tax year, the total passenger payments made to the employee do not exceed the 'approved amount' for passenger payments. The '*approved amount*' for this purpose is:

$$M \times R$$

where M is the number of business miles travelled by the employee by car or van carrying any qualifying passenger in the tax year and in respect of which passenger payments are made. If more than one qualifying passenger is carried, a separate addition is made to the amount in respect of each passenger; and

R is 5p per mile (alterable by the Treasury by regulation).

[*ITEPA 2003, ss 229, 230, 233–236; FA 2017, Sch 2 paras 52, 62(1)(2)(4)(5)*].

Mileage allowance relief

An employee (or office holder) who uses a qualifying vehicle for business travel is entitled to '*mileage allowance relief*' for a tax year if the approved amount for mileage allowance payments (as above) applicable to the kind of vehicle in question exceeds the total amount of mileage allowance payments (if any) made to the employee for the tax year for that kind of vehicle. As above, the relief is not available where the employee is a passenger in a vehicle or the vehicle is a company vehicle. The amount of the relief is the excess of the approved amount over any mileage allowance payments. Where available, the relief is allowed as a deduction from earnings taxable on the receipts basis (see generally **28.4–28.8** above). Any amount of relief which cannot be so given may be deducted from earnings taxable on the remittance basis (see **28.5** above), the deduction for any tax year being of amounts of relief available and otherwise unrelieved for that tax year and for any earlier tax year in which the employee was UK resident, and which would have been deductible from earnings for each such year if the receipts basis had applied.

Where the tax year is a split year (see **63.19** RESIDENCE AND DOMICILE), if the earnings from which a deduction is allowed include earnings that are 'excluded' (as in **28.4** above), the allowable deduction is reduced to a proportion of what it would be if the year were not a split year. That proportion is equal to the proportion that the non-excluded earnings bear to the total earnings.

[*ITEPA 2003, ss 231, 232*].

Simon's Taxes. See E4.704.

Mileage allowances for business travel in company car

[28.92] If employers pay a rate per mile for business travel in a company car that is no higher than the advisory fuel rate (see **28.26** above), HMRC will accept that there is nothing taxable on the employee. It is open to an employer to make a case for paying higher rates in particular circumstances. For one month from the date of change, employers may use either the previous or new current rates, as they choose. (www.gov.uk/advisory-fuel-rates-when-you-can-use-them).

Parking facilities

[28.93] No income tax liability arises in respect of expenditure on the provision of car parking facilities for an employee at or near his place of work, whether the car etc. is company-owned or private. This exemption extends to parking facilities for cycles, motor cycles and vans. Where the benefit is convertible into cash, e.g. under a salary sacrifice arrangement, no charge to tax on general earnings arises. [*ITEPA 2003, s 237*].

Members of local authorities

[28.94] Travel expenses paid to members of local authorities ('*councillors*') are generally subject to the same rules as travel expenses of other employees and office holders. However, a 'qualifying journey' made by a councillor is treated as business travel with regard to 'qualifying payments' paid by the local authority to the councillor for expenses related to his use for the journey of a car, van, motorcycle or cycle. The treatment applies for the purposes of mileage allowance payments (as in **28.91** above) at no more than the approved amount. A qualifying journey does not count as business travel for the purposes of mileage allowance relief (see **28.91**); thus, where the authority pays mileage allowance at less than the approved amount, or pays no mileage allowance, no additional relief is available for the journey. For these purposes the term 'local authority' embraces all the bodies listed at *SI 2016 No 350, Reg 2*.

A journey is a '*qualifying journey*' for these purposes if:

(a) it is a journey between the councillor's home and 'permanent workplace' (see **28.17** above); and
(b) the councillor's home is situated in the area of the local authority or no more than 20 miles outside the boundary of that area.

'*Qualifying payments*' are payments that fall within specified local government regulations and which are made to a councillor by the local authority in connection with activities he undertakes as a member of that authority.

Similar treatment applies to passenger payments (as in **28.91** above) made by the local authority at no more than the approved amount where the journey is a qualifying journey by car or van and both driver and passenger are members of the authority.

In addition, no liability to income tax arises in respect of a qualifying payment (as above) made to a councillor for travel expenses unrelated to his use of a car, van, motorcycle or cycle unless the journey in question is a journey within (a) above and the councillor's home is situated more than 20 miles outside the boundary of the local authority area.

[*ITEPA 2003, ss 235A, 295A; SI 2016 No 350*].

Wages in lieu of notice

[28.95] The taxation treatment of payments in lieu of notice ('PILONs') is governed by the general principles applying to payments on termination of employment, for which see **18.2–18.10** COMPENSATION FOR LOSS OF EMPLOYMENT. Where the payment is *not* within the charge to tax on general earnings, it will generally fall within *ITEPA 2003, s 403*, subject to the exemptions from charge under that those provisions and, in particular, the exemption of the first £30,000. However, for **2018/19** onwards, the rules for taxing termination payments are extended with the intention that, whether or not they are entitled to a contractual payment in lieu of notice, employees will pay tax on the amount of basic pay that they would have received if they had worked their notice in full, and will not be entitled to the £30,000 exemption in respect of such pay. See **18.6, 18.7** COMPENSATION FOR LOSS OF EMPLOYMENT for this extension to the rules. The text below remains relevant for 2017/18 and earlier years.

HMRC have set out their approach to the application of the general employment income charge to PILONs, as follows.

(a) Where contractual arrangements provide for a PILON, the contract is terminated in accordance with its terms on a summary dismissal. The compensation is a contractual entitlement rather than liquidated damages and is chargeable as income from the employment under general principles.
(b) Where the employer and employee agree at the time of termination that the employment is to be terminated without proper notice but on the making of a PILON, and there was no existing understanding in this respect which could be construed as a contractual provision or amendment, the source of the payment lies only in the agreement to terminate the employment. The payment is therefore not income from the employment.
(c) In establishing whether contractual arrangements provide for a PILON, all relevant factors, e.g. rules in staff handbooks or wage agreements, or oral agreements, have to be considered. Even in the absence of any direct contractual arrangements, there may be an implied contractual term of service where an employer has established a practice of making PILONs instead of giving due notice (but see below for a change in HMRC's view on this aspect).
(d) Where neither (a) nor (b) above applies, failure to give due notice is a breach of contract, and a payment made for such a breach represents liquidated damages and is not an emolument from the employment.
(e) The existence of a reserved right or discretion of the employer to make a PILON where due notice is not given is not a determining factor where the right or discretion is not exercised. Where it is exercised, (a) above applies.

HMRC reject the view that a contractual PILON is properly analysed as a payment of damages for breach of contract (in particular by analysis of the true effect of (what is now) *Employment Rights Act 1996, s 86*). They also reject the view that a PILON is a redundancy payment. If a person entitled to a contractual PILON accepts less, in settlement of his claim to enforce the contractual entitlement, it does not alter the nature of the payment so as to bring it within *ITEPA 2003, s 403* (*Goldman v HMRC* FTT (TC 1999), [2012] SFTD 1048).

Payments for a period where notice is given but not in fact worked ('garden leave') are income from the employment. (See *Redundant Employee v McNally* Ch D, 2005 STI 652).

(Revenue Tax Bulletin August 1996 pp 325–327).

A further article in Revenue Tax Bulletin February 2003 pp 999–1001 updates the above in a number of respects.

(i) In the employment law case *Cerberus Software Ltd v Rowley* [2001] ICR 376, the Court of Appeal held that a contractual clause providing that an employer 'may' make a PILON meant that the employer was free to give neither notice nor a PILON, but instead to breach the contract and pay damages for that breach. Such damages would fall within *ITEPA 2003, s 403* (see **18.4** COMPENSATION FOR LOSS OF EMPLOY-

MENT rather than the normal employment income charging provisions. Whether such discretion has been thus exercised in any particular case is a question of fact, but HMRC sets out its views of indicative factors.

(ii) HMRC do not consider that *Cerberus* overrules the *EMI* case referred to below, since the general employment income charge is not expressed in contractual terms, so that many taxable payments are not dependent on any contractual obligation. What is required is that the source of the payment is the employer/employee relationship.

(iii) As regards (c) above, although HMRC now accept that it is unlikely that an implied contractual term in relation to PILONs can exist, they nevertheless consider that where, for example, a PILON is paid as an automatic response to a termination, the payment may be an 'integral part of the employer/employee relationship for the workplace', and as such be taxable under the normal employment income rules.

An article in *Taxation Magazine, 29 September 2005, p 714* confirms that, as suggested in (iii) above, HMRC are increasingly seeking to tax 'auto-PILONs' as general employment income. An '*auto-PILON*' is therein described as a payment made for unworked notice as an automatic response to the termination of a contract of employment in the same way as 'night follows day'. HMRC distinguish this from a payment made following a genuine critical assessment, on an individual by individual basis, to establish the true level of damages, which would fall within *ITEPA 2003, s 403*. Such a payment should reflect the likelihood of the employee's finding alternative employment within the notice period and should be made net of the tax and National Insurance contributions that would have been deductible from a payment made for notice actually worked (the *Gourley* principle).

A further article in *Taxation Magazine, 6 July 2006, p 379* considers HMRC's practice above in the light of the decision in *SCA Packaging Ltd v HMRC* Ch D, [2007] STC 1640 and concludes that, contrary to HMRC's view, the habitual or routine nature of the payment of PILONS does not in itself prevent such a payment being compensation for breach of contract and thus within *ITEPA 2003, s 403*.

In *EMI Group Electronics Ltd v Coldicott* CA 1999, 71 TC 455, it was held that payments following exercise by the employer of a reserved right as under (e) above were chargeable earnings. However, in *Mimtec Ltd v CIR* (Sp C 277), [2001] SSCD 101 a Special Commissioner held that certain payments made following redundancy negotiations 'in recognition of any entitlements under the consultation process including pay in lieu of notice etc.' were not taxable earnings.

Simon's Taxes. See E4.822.

Workers supplied by agencies

[28.96] The treatment described below (the '*section 44 treatment*') has effect where:

- an individual ('*the worker*') personally provides services (other than 'excluded services') to another person ('*the client*'),

- there is a contract between:
  - the client (or a person connected with the client under **19** CONNECTED PERSONS); and
  - a person (‘*the agency*’) other than the worker, the client or a person connected with the client, and
- under or in consequence of the contract, the services are provided, or the client (or any person connected with the client) gives consideration for the services,

but does not apply if:

(a) it is shown that the manner in which the worker provides the services is not subject to (or to the right of) supervision, direction or control by any person (see HMRC Employment Status Manual ESM2055); or

(b) remuneration receivable by the worker for providing the services would in any case constitute employment income of his.

The worker is treated as holding an employment with the agency. The duties of the employment consist of the services the worker provides to the client. All ‘remuneration’ receivable by the worker (from any person) for providing the services is then treated for income tax purposes as earnings from that employment.

‘*Remuneration*’ includes every form of payment, gratuity, profit and benefit, but not anything which would not otherwise be employment income if receivable in connection with an office or employment. ‘*Excluded services*’ means services as an entertainer or model or services provided wholly in the worker’s own home or at other premises which are not under the control or management of the client or at which the services are not required by their nature to be provided.

The section 44 treatment extends to the situation where the worker personally provides the services in question as a partner in a firm or a member of an unincorporated body; remuneration receivable for the providing by the worker of the services is treated as income of the worker and not as income of the firm or body. The section 44 treatment also applies if the agency is an unincorporated body of which the worker is a member.

There is a further rule aimed at remuneration paid by an agency to a worker on their books in respect of a period when the worker is not assigned to a particular client. Thus, if:

- an individual, with a view to personally providing services (other than excluded services) to another person, enters into arrangements with a third person, and
- the arrangements are such that the services (if and when they are provided) will be accorded the above treatment,

any remuneration receivable under or in consequence of the arrangements is treated as earnings from the employment held by the worker with the agency as above.

Anti-avoidance

The section 44 treatment is cancelled in certain cases involving fraudulent documentation. Instead, the worker is treated as holding an employment with the client or (as the case may be) with the 'relevant person', the duties of which consist of the services the worker provides. All remuneration receivable by the worker (from any person) for providing the services is treated for income tax purposes as earnings from that employment. This applies where:

- the client provides the agency with a fraudulent document intended as evidence that, by virtue of (a) above, the section 44 treatment does not apply; or
- a 'relevant person' provides the agency with a fraudulent document intended as evidence that, by virtue of (b) above, the section 44 treatment does not apply.

A '*relevant person*' is any person (other than the client, the worker or a person connected with the client or agency) who is resident, or has a place of business, in the UK and is party to a contract with the agency (or a person connected with it) under or in consequence of which either the services are provided or the agency (or a connected person) makes payments in respect of them.

Subject to the let-outs provided by (a) and (b) above, the section 44 treatment applies in the following set of circumstances if it would not otherwise apply:

- an individual (W) personally provides services (other than excluded services as above) to another person (C); and
- a third person (A) enters into arrangements (as widely defined) a main purpose of which is to secure that the services are not treated as duties of an employment held by W with A.

In applying the section 44 treatment in these circumstances, W is the worker, C is the client, A is the agency, and the above provisions involving fraudulent documentation do not apply.

[*ITEPA 2003, ss 44–46, 46A, 47*].

Where a company incurs an obligation to account under PAYE for a liability arising from the application of either of the above anti-avoidance provisions, HMRC may require payment from any director of the company — see **53.10** PAY AS YOU EARN.

Information powers

HMRC have the power to make regulations imposing record-keeping requirements on 'employment intermediaries' of a specified description and requiring such intermediaries to provide HMRC with specified information, records or documents within a specified period or at specified times. For this purpose, an '*employment intermediary*' is a person who makes arrangements under which an individual works, or is to work, for a third person or an individual is, or is to be, remunerated for work done for a third person. an individual works for a person if he performs any duties of an employment for that person (whether or not he is employed by that person) or provides, or is involved in the provision of, a service to that person. [*ITEPA 2003, s 716B*]. Failure to furnish information or produce records or documents as required by such regulations may incur a penalty of up to £3,000 plus daily penalties of up to £600. [*TMA 1970, s 98(1)(4F)*].

General

For official guidance see HMRC Employment Status Manual ESM2029 *et seq*. These provisions are independent of, and are not affected by, the rules at **47** MANAGED SERVICE COMPANIES and **58** PERSONAL SERVICE COMPANIES ETC.

For the existence of a contract, see *Brady v Hart* Ch D 1985, 58 TC 518. See *Bhadra v Ellam* Ch D 1987, 60 TC 466, where a doctor obtaining locum posts through medical agencies was held to be within the legislation as then enacted. A case in which security guards were provided for building sites was held to be outside the rules because neither the client nor the provider had control or the right of control over how the work was done (*Oziegbe v HMRC* FTT (TC 3733), [2014] UKFTT 608 (TC)).

See **53.10** PAY AS YOU EARN as regards application of PAYE.

Simon's Taxes. See **E4.225**.

29

Enterprise Investment Scheme

Introduction to Enterprise Investment Scheme

[29.1] The Enterprise Investment Scheme (EIS) is a scheme whereby, subject to numerous conditions being met, individuals may obtain income tax relief and capital gains tax reliefs on an investment in newly-issued shares in an unquoted company. An investor is eligible for EIS income tax relief in respect of an amount invested by him on his own behalf for an issue of shares in a company if:

- (with effect for shares issued on or after 15 March 2018) the risk-to-capital condition is met (see **29.26** below);
- the shares are issued to the investor;
- the general requirements at **29.27** below are met in respect of the shares;
- the investor is a 'qualifying investor' (see **29.41** below) in relation to the shares; and
- the company issuing the shares is a 'qualifying company' (see **29.46** below) in relation to the shares.

The EIS applies to shares issued before 6 April 2025 but this date may be amended by the Treasury via statutory instrument.

[*ITA 2007, s 157(1)(1A); FA 2018, s 14(1)(4)(5); SI 2018 No 931, Reg 2*].

This chapter concentrates on the income tax relief but a brief summary of the CGT reliefs is included at **29.23, 29.24** below. For the form of the income tax relief see **29.4** *et seq.* below and for the restriction or withdrawal of relief in certain circumstances see **29.10** *et seq.* below.

See generally HMRC guidance at www.gov.uk/government/publications/the-enterprise-investment-scheme-introduction/enterprise-investment-scheme and HMRC Venture Capital Schemes Manual VCM10000 *et seq.*

Simon's Taxes. See E3.1.

Advance assurance

A company may apply to HMRC for assurance, in advance of a share issue, that it will meet the qualifying conditions of the EIS. Application should be made using form EIS/SEIS(AA) available at www.gov.uk/government/publications/enterprise-investment-scheme-advance-assurance-application-eisseisaa. On and after 4 December 2017, HMRC will not provide advance assurances for investments that, taking into account all the facts that HMRC have available, will fail, or appear likely to fail, the risk-to-capital condition at **29.26** below (HMRC Venture Capital Schemes Manual VCM8550).

Seed Enterprise Investment Scheme (SEIS)

This is a tax-advantaged venture capital scheme, similar to the EIS, but focused on smaller, early stage companies carrying on, or preparing to carry on, a new business. See **66** SEED ENTERPRISE INVESTMENT SCHEME.

Nominees, approved funds and approved knowledge-intensive funds

[29.2] EIS relief is also available where shares are subscribed for by a nominee for the individual claiming relief. [*ITA 2007, s 250(1)*].

Approved knowledge-intensive funds

With effect on and after 6 April 2020, in relation to funds which, on or after that date, are closed for the acceptance of further investments, the 'managers of an approved knowledge-intensive fund' may be nominees for an individual in this regard. Subject to the conditions below, the rules at **29.4**, **29.6** below (dealing with the form and attribution of relief) apply as if any reference to the tax year or other period in which the shares are issued were a reference to the tax year or other period in which the fund closes and as if any reference to the time of the issue or the subscription of the shares were a reference to the time of the closing of the fund. For the purpose of applying the rule on carry-back of EIS income tax relief at **29.4** below, the year in which the fund closes is treated as the year in which the shares are issued, and 'the preceding tax year' is construed accordingly.

The above is on condition that, at the time the individual claims EIS relief:

(a) the shares in question have been issued to the managers as the individual's nominee;
(b) the fund has closed for the acceptance of further investments;
(c) the amounts which the managers have subscribed on the individual's behalf for shares issued within 12 months after the closing of the fund represent at least 50% of the individual's investment in the fund;
(d) the amounts so subscribed for shares issued within 24 months after the closing of the fund represent at least 90% of the individual's investment in the fund;
(e) within the 24-month period in (d) above, at least 80% of the individual's investment in the fund is represented by shares in companies which are knowledge-intensive companies (see **29.32** below) at the time the shares are issued; and

(f) the managers have met such conditions with respect to the provision of information to the Commissioners for HMRC as the Commissioners consider appropriate for these purposes.

The '*managers of an approved knowledge-intensive fund*' means the person(s) having the management of an investment fund:

- which is, in the opinion of the Commissioners, a fund established for the purpose of investing wholly, or substantially wholly, in shares in companies which are knowledge-intensive companies at the time the shares are issued; and
- which is approved by the Commissioners for these purposes, having met such conditions as the Commissioners consider appropriate.

[*ITA 2007, s 251(1)(1A)(2)(2A)(8); FA 2020, s 36(1)–(5), (10)–(12)*].

HMRC have published draft guidelines for the approval of knowledge-intensive funds at www.gov.uk/government/publications/enterprise-investment-scheme-draft-guidelines-for-the-approval-of-knowledge-intensive-funds.

Approved funds before 6 April 2020

Similar rules applied before 6 April 2020 as regards approved funds generally. The fund had to be approved by HMRC but there was no requirement for it to be a knowledge-intensive fund. Instead of conditions (c)–(e) above, there was a single condition that the amounts which the managers had subscribed on the individual's behalf for shares issued within 12 months after the closing of the fund represented at least 90% of the individual's investment in the fund. [*ITA 2007, s 251(1)(2) as previously enacted*].

Bare trustees and nominees

[29.3] EIS relief is available where shares which satisfy the requirement at **29.28**(a) below are held on a bare trust for two or more beneficiaries as if each beneficiary had subscribed as an individual for all of those shares, and as if the amount subscribed by each was the total subscribed divided by the number of beneficiaries. [*ITA 2007, s 250(2)(3)*].

EIS income tax relief

[29.4] Relief is (except as below) given for the tax year in which the shares were issued, by a reduction in what would otherwise be the individual's income tax liability (a '*tax reduction*') equal to tax at the EIS rate for the year on the amount (or aggregate amounts) subscribed for shares in respect of which he is eligible for and claims EIS relief (subject to the minimum and maximum limits at **29.5** below). The EIS rate is 30%.

The order in which tax reductions are given against an individual's tax liability is set out at **1.12** ALLOWANCES AND TAX RATES, which also makes clear that a tax reduction must be restricted to the extent (if any) that it would otherwise exceed the individual's remaining income tax liability after making all prior reductions.

Investors may restrict a claim to EIS relief in respect of a single issue of shares so that relief is given only in respect of some of the shares.

Carry-back

Where shares in respect of which the individual is eligible for relief are issued at any time in a tax year, he may claim relief as if any number of shares up to the full number of shares issued to him had been issued in the preceding tax year. The carry-back is subject to the overriding rule that the total amount of investment on which relief can be obtained for any one year cannot exceed the annual maximum for that year at **29.5** below.

See **16.2** CLAIMS for general provisions regarding claims for payments made in one tax year to be carried back to an earlier year.

[*ITA 2007, s 158(1)(2A)(3)(4); FA 2018, Sch 4 paras 1(5), 10; SI 2018 No 931, Reg 3*].

Simon's Taxes. See **E3.156, E3.159.**

Annual maximum

[29.5] There is an upper limit on the amount in respect of which an individual may obtain relief for a tax year (regardless of whether the shares were issued in that year or in the following year — see **29.4** above). With effect for shares issued on or after 6 April 2018, the limit operates as follows:

(i) if the shares do not include any 'KIC shares', the limit is £1 million;
(ii) if the total amount subscribed for KIC shares is £1 million or more, the limit is £2 million; and
(iii) in any other case, the limit is £1 million plus total amount subscribed for KIC shares.

'*KIC shares*' are shares in any company which is a knowledge-intensive company at the time the shares are issued. See **29.32** below for meaning of knowledge-intensive company, and note the special rule there for companies that have traded for less than three years before issuing the EIS shares.

Prior to 2018/19, the upper limit was £1 million in all cases.

[*ITA 2007, s 158(2)(2ZA)(2ZB); FA 2018, Sch 4 paras 1(2)–(4), 10; SI 2018 No 931, Reg 3*].

Attribution of relief to shares

[29.6] Subject to any reduction or withdrawal of relief (see **29.10** *et seq.* below), where an individual's income tax liability is reduced for a tax year as in **29.4** above by reason of an issue or issues of shares made (or treated as made) in that year, the tax reduction is attributed to that issue or those issues (being apportioned in the latter case according to the amounts claimed for each issue). Issues of shares of the same class by a company to an individual on the same day are treated as a single issue for this purpose. A proportionate amount of the reduction attributed to an issue is attributed to each share in the issue in respect of which the claim was made and is adjusted correspondingly for any subsequent bonus issue of shares of the same class and carrying the same rights.

An issue to an individual part of which is treated as having been made in the preceding tax year (as in **29.4** above) is treated as two separate issues, one made on a day in the previous year.

Where relief attributable to an issue of shares falls to be withdrawn or reduced, the relief attributable to each of the shares in question is reduced to nil (if relief is withdrawn) or proportionately reduced (where relief is reduced).

[*ITA 2007, ss 201, 255*].

Simon's Taxes. See **E3.160.**

Claims for relief

[29.7] A claim for relief must be made not earlier than the end of the four-month minimum period at **29.37** below, and not later than the fifth anniversary of 31 January following the tax year in which the shares are issued.

The claimant must have received a compliance certificate from the issuing company before making the claim. The certificate must state that the requirements for relief, except in so far as they fall to be satisfied by the investor, are for the time being satisfied in relation to the shares in question. A certificate may not be issued without the authority of an HMRC officer. Where a notice under *ITA 2007, s 241* (see **29.25** below), or a notice of certain chargeable events under the EIS capital gains deferral provisions mentioned at **29.24** below, has been given to HMRC, a compliance certificate must not be issued unless the authority is given or renewed after receipt of the notice. For appeal purposes, the inspector's refusal to authorise a certificate is treated as a decision disallowing a claim by the company.

Before issuing such a certificate, the company must supply to HMRC a compliance statement (Form EIS1) that those requirements are fulfilled for the time being and have been fulfilled at all times since the shares were issued. The statement must contain such information as HMRC may reasonably require, and a declaration that it is correct to the best of the company's knowledge and belief. The statement must be provided to HMRC within two years after the end of the tax year in which the shares in question were issued (or, if the four-month minimum period at **29.37** below ends in the following year, within two years after the end of that four-month period). The statement cannot be provided to HMRC before the four-month minimum period expires.

References above to requirements being fulfilled for the time being are, in the case of requirements that cannot be fulfilled until a future date, references to nothing having occurred to prevent their being fulfilled.

If a certificate or statement is made fraudulently or negligently, or a certificate was issued despite being prohibited (as above), the company is liable to a fine of up to £3,000.

No application for postponement of tax pending appeal can be made on the ground that relief is due under these provisions unless a claim has been duly submitted. No regard is to be had to EIS relief for the purposes of PAY AS YOU EARN (**53**) unless a claim for relief has been made.

[*ITA 2007, ss 202–207, 257(8), 989*].

Relief for a year can only be claimed after the end of the year, and any in-year claims for relief by repayment through self-assessment will be rejected. This does not affect the right to claim a reduction in payments on account (see **67.5** SELF-ASSESSMENT), and relief may still be given through a PAYE coding. (Revenue Tax Bulletin April 2002 p 924).

In a case where a company inserted an incorrect issue date when completing Form EIS1, HMRC withdrew a claimant's EIS relief on the grounds that there was no valid compliance certificate; the claimant's assertion on appeal that substance should prevail over form was rejected by the Sp C (*Ashley v HMRC* (Sp C 633), [2008] SSCD 219).

Modified provisions apply to the issue of certificates (Forms EIS5) where shares are held through an approved fund or, after 5 April 2020, an approved knowledge-intensive fund (see **29.2** above). [*ITA 2007, s 251(4)–(8); FA 2020, s 36(6)–(12)*].

Simon's Taxes. See **E3.158, E3.159.**

Relief for loss on disposal

[29.8] See **45.23** LOSSES for income tax relief ('share loss relief') for certain losses on disposals of shares in unlisted trading companies, including shares to which EIS income tax relief is attributable.

Example

[29.9]

Wigram is a UK resident with a salary of £185,000 for 2019/20 and no other income. His liability to income tax is at the main UK rates. For 2019/20, he is entitled to full income tax relief on an investment of £198,000 in a venture capital trust.

In 2019/20, he subscribes for ordinary shares in two unquoted companies issuing shares under the enterprise investment scheme (EIS).

A Ltd was formed by some people in Wigram's neighbourhood to publish a local newspaper. In August 2019, 200,000 ordinary £1 shares were issued at par and the company started trading in September 2019. Wigram subscribed for 15,000 of the shares. Wigram becomes a director of A Ltd in September 2019, and receives director's fees of £3,000 in 2019/20, a level of remuneration which is considered reasonable for services rendered by him to the company in his capacity as a director.

B Ltd, which is controlled by an old friend of Wigram, has acquired the rights to manufacture in the UK a new type of industrial cleaning solvent and requires additional finance. Wigram subscribed for 8,000 ordinary £1 shares at a premium of £1.50 per share in October 2019. The issue increases the company's issued share capital to 25,000 ordinary £1 shares.

Wigram will obtain tax relief in 2019/20 as follows.

Amount eligible for relief

	£
A Ltd note (a)	16,000
B Ltd note (b)	Nil
Total (being less than the maximum of £1,000,000)	£16,000

	£
Salary	185,000
Director's remuneration (A Ltd)	3,000
Total income	188,000
Personal allowance (restricted due to level of income)	Nil
Taxable income	£188,000

	£
Tax payable:	
37,500 @ 20%	7,500.00
112,500 @ 40%	45,000.00
38,000 @ 45%	17,100.00
	69,600.00
Deduct VCT relief £198,000 @ 30%	59,400.00
	10,200.00
Deduct EIS relief £15,000 @ 30%	4,500.00
Net tax liability 2019/20	£5,700.00

Notes

(a) Wigram is entitled to relief on the full amount of his investment in A Ltd. The fact that Wigram becomes a paid director of A Ltd *after* an issue to him of eligible shares does not prevent his qualifying for relief in respect of those shares providing his remuneration as a director is reasonable and he is not otherwise connected with the company (see **29.42** below).

(b) Wigram is not entitled to relief against his income for his investment of £20,000 in B Ltd. As a result of the share issue he owns more than 30% of the issued ordinary share capital (8,000 out of 25,000 shares) and is therefore regarded as connected with the company and denied relief. See **29.42** below.

(c) The VCT investment relief must be deducted before the EIS investment relief.

In 2020/21, Wigram subscribes for shares in three more unquoted UK companies issuing shares under the EIS.

C Ltd is a local company engaged in the manufacture of car components. It issues a further 540,000 ordinary £1 shares at £2 per share in June 2020 and Wigram subscribes for 14,800 shares costing £29,600, increasing his stake in the company to 10%. He had originally held 24,300 shares, acquired by purchase at arm's length in May 2018 for £32,400.

D Ltd has been trading as a restaurant for several years and requires an injection of capital to finance a new restaurant. Wigram and three other unconnected individuals each subscribe for 75,000 ordinary £1 shares at par in November 2020. The balance of 480,000 shares are held by Wigram's sister and niece. D Ltd has the equivalent of 80 full-time employees in November 2020 when the new shares are issued.

E Ltd is an electronics company, with 60 employees, controlled by two cousins of Wigram. The company has not issued any shares in the previous twelve months but is now seeking £5 million extra capital for expansion, and raises it via the EIS. Wigram subscribes for 950,000 ordinary £1 shares at par in December 2020.

Wigram's salary is increased by bonus to £277,000 for 2020/21. His director's fees from A Ltd amount to £7,100, which again is considered reasonable for services rendered. He makes a claim to treat 9,500 of his C Ltd shares (costing £19,000) to be regarded as issued in 2019/20, thereby eliminating his tax liability for that year.

Wigram will obtain tax relief as follows:

2019/20	
C Ltd (note (a)) £19,000 @ 30% =	£5,700
2020/21	
Amount eligible for relief	
	£
C Ltd (£29,600 – £19,000 carried back)	10,600
D Ltd	75,000
E Ltd	950,000
Total	£1,035,600
But amount eligible for relief restricted to subscriptions of	£1,000,000
Relief given	
	£
Salary	277,000
Director's remuneration	7,100
Total income	284,100
Personal allowance (restricted due to level of income)	Nil
Taxable income	£284,100
Tax payable:	
37,500 @ 20%	7,500.00
112,500 @ 40%	45,000.00
134,100 @ 45%	60,345.00
	112,845.00
Deduct EIS relief:	
£1,000,000 @ 30% = £300,000, but restricted to	112,845.00
Net tax liability 2020/21	Nil

Attribution of relief to shares (note (b))

	£
CLtd shares $\dfrac{10,600}{1,035,600} \times £112,845$	1,155
DLtd shares $\dfrac{75,000}{1,035,600} \times £112,845$	8,172

ELtd shares $\frac{950,000}{1,035,600} \times £112,845$	103,518
	£112,845

Notes

(a) The investor may claim relief as if any number of the shares had been issued to him in the preceding tax year. The only restriction (not relevant in this example) is that relief in any one tax year may not be given on subscriptions of more than the annual maximum for that year. The relief will be given in addition to that previously claimed for 2019/20 (see above). See **29.4**, **29.5** above.

(b) Relief is restricted by (i) the £1,000,000 maximum (see **29.5** above), (ii) the available EIS rate (see **29.4** above) and (ii) an insufficiency in Wigram's tax liability. The relief attributable to each issue of shares (which will be relevant in the event of a disposal of the shares or withdrawal of relief — see **29.10** *et seq.* below) is found by apportioning the income tax reduction by reference to the amounts subscribed for each issue. (For this purpose, 9,500 of the C Ltd shares are regarded as having been separately issued in the previous year.) The relief so attributed to each issue is then apportioned equally between all the shares comprised in that issue. See **29.6** above.

Restriction or withdrawal of relief

[29.10] The following provisions apply to restrict or withdraw relief in certain circumstances. References to a reduction of relief include its reduction to nil, and references to the withdrawal of relief in respect of any shares are to the withdrawal of the relief attributable to those shares (see **29.6** above). Where no relief has yet been given, a reduction applies to reduce the amount which apart from the provision in question would be the relief, and a withdrawal means ceasing to be eligible for relief in respect of the shares in question. [*ITA 2007, s 257(4)*].

Disposal of shares

[29.11] Where the investor disposes of shares (or an interest or right in or over shares) to which relief is attributable (see **29.6** above) or grants an option the exercise of which would bind him to sell the shares before the end of 'period A' (see below):

(a) if the disposal is at arm's length, relief attributable to those shares (see **29.6** above) is withdrawn or, if that relief exceeds an amount equal to tax at the 'EIS original rate' on the disposal consideration, reduced by that amount;

(b) otherwise, the relief is withdrawn.

The '*EIS original rate*' is the EIS rate (as in **29.4** above) for the tax year for which the relief was obtained.

Where the relief attributable to the shares was less than tax at the EIS original rate on the amount subscribed for the issue, the amount referred to in (a) above is correspondingly reduced. Where the relief attributable to the shares has been reduced (otherwise than as a result of an issue of bonus shares (see **29.6** above)) before the relief was obtained, in calculating the amount referred to in (a) above, the gross relief attributable to the shares before that reduction is used.

A share exchange is treated as a disposal for these purposes unless it is within **29.22** below.

Relief is also withdrawn where, during the relevant period, an option is granted to the investor, the exercise of which would bind the grantor to purchase shares. There are provisions for identifying the shares to which an option relates, where these form part of a larger holding.

These provisions do not apply to a disposal of shares occurring as a result of the investor's death. See **29.21** below for transfers of shares between spouses or civil partners.

Period A

'*Period A*' is the period beginning with the incorporation of the company or, if later, two years before the date of issue of the shares and ending immediately before the third anniversary of the issue date or, if later and where relevant, the third anniversary of the date of commencement of the intended trade referred to in **29.58**(a) below.

Identification rules

For the above purposes, disposals are identified with shares of the same class issued earlier before shares issued later (i.e. first in/first out (FIFO)). Where shares within two or more of the categories listed below were acquired on the same day, any of those shares disposed of (applying the FIFO basis) are treated as disposed of in the order in which they are listed, as follows:

(i) shares to which no EIS income tax relief, EIS capital gains deferral relief (see **29.24** below) or SEIS relief (see **66** SEED ENTERPRISE INVESTMENT SCHEME) is attributable;
(ii) shares to which SEIS income tax relief is attributable;
(iii) shares to which EIS deferral relief, but not EIS income tax relief, is attributable;
(iv) shares to which EIS income tax relief, but not EIS deferral relief, is attributable;
(v) shares to which both EIS income tax relief and EIS deferral relief are attributable.

Any shares within (iv) or (v) above which are treated as issued on an earlier day by virtue of the carry-back provisions at **29.4** above are to be treated as disposed of before any other shares within the same category. Shares transferred between spouses or civil partners living together are treated as if they were acquired by the transferee spouse or partner on the day they were issued (see also **29.21** below). Shares comprised in a 'new holding' following a reorganisation to which *TCGA 1992, s 127* applies (see Tolley's Capital Gains Tax under Shares and Securities) are treated as having been acquired when the original shares were acquired.

[*ITA 2007, ss 209–212, 246, 254, 256A*].

Simon's Taxes. See E3.167.

Value received by investor

[29.12] Where an investor subscribes for shares in a company, and during 'period C' that investor 'receives value' (other than 'insignificant value') from the company, any relief attributable to those shares (see **29.6** above) and not previously reduced in respect of the 'value received' is withdrawn or, if that relief exceeds an amount equal to tax at the EIS original rate (as in **29.11** above) on the 'value received', reduced by that amount. See also **29.13** below for further computational provisions.

'*Period C*' is the period beginning one year before the issue of the shares and ending immediately before the third anniversary of the issue date or, if later and where relevant, the third anniversary of the date of commencement of the intended trade referred to in **29.58**(a) below. (In determining for these purposes the time at which a qualifying trade begins to be carried on by any 'qualifying 90% subsidiary' (see **29.57** below) of a company, any carrying on of the trade by it before it became such a subsidiary is disregarded.)

The provisions apply equally to value received from a person who is connected (within **19** CONNECTED PERSONS) with the issuing company at any time in period A (as in **29.11** above), whether or not at the time value is received.

An investor '*receives value*' from the issuing company if it:

(a) repays, redeems or repurchases any part of his holding of its share capital or securities, or makes any payment to him for giving up rights on its cancellation or extinguishment; or
(b) repays, in pursuance of any arrangements for or in connection with the acquisition of the shares in respect of which the relief is claimed, any debt owed to him other than one incurred by the company on or after the date of issue of those shares and otherwise than in consideration of the extinguishment of a debt incurred before that date; or
(c) pays him for the cancellation of any debt owed to him other than an '*ordinary trade debt*' (i.e. one incurred for normal trade supply of goods or services on normal trade credit terms (not in any event exceeding six months)) or one in respect of a payment falling within **29.42**(A) or (F) below; or
(d) releases or waives any liability of his to the company (which it is deemed to have done if discharge of the liability is twelve months or more overdue) or discharges or undertakes to discharge any liability of his to a third person; or
(e) makes a loan or advance to him (defined as including any debt either to the company (other than an 'ordinary trade debt' (as above)) or to a third person but assigned to the company) which has not been repaid in full before the issue of the shares; or

(f) provides a benefit or facility for him; or
(g) transfers an asset to him for no consideration or for consideration less than market value, or acquires an asset from him for consideration exceeding market value; or
(h) makes any other payment to him except one either falling within **29.42**(A)–(F) below or in discharge of an 'ordinary trade debt' (as above); or
(i) is wound up or dissolved in circumstances such that the company does not thereby cease to be a 'qualifying company' (see **29.46** below), and he thereby receives any payment or asset in respect of ordinary shares held by him.

However, an individual does *not* receive value from a company by reason only of the payment to him (or to an 'associate' — see **29.42** below) of reasonable remuneration (including any benefit or facility) for services as a company director, and for this purpose, if the individual is also an employee of the company, references to him in his capacity as a director include him in his capacity as an employee.

If an individual to whom shares in a company have been issued entered into a convertible loan agreement with the company under the Future Fund on or after 20 May 2020, and subsequently receives value from the company under the terms of that agreement, the value received is ignored in relation to any EIS relief attributable to shares issued before the individual entered into the agreement. This is to ensure that investors in a company who also support the company using a Future Fund convertible loan note will not lose relief on any previous EIS investments when that loan is redeemed or converted into shares. The Future Fund was set up as part of Government support to companies impacted by the 2020 COVID-19 (coronavirus) pandemic (see www.gov.uk/guidance/future-fund).

Where value is received, the amount of that value is the amount paid to or received by the individual from the company; or the amount of the individual's liability extinguished or discharged; or the difference between the market value of the asset and the consideration (if any) given for it; or the net cost to the company of providing the benefit. In the case of value received within (a), (b) or (c) above, the market value of the shares, securities or debt in question is substituted if greater than the amount receivable.

Additionally, the investor '*receives value*' from the company if any person connected with the company (within **29.42** below) purchases any shares or securities of the company from him, or pays him for giving up any right in relation to such shares or securities. The value received is the amount received or, if greater, the market value of the shares etc.

All payments or transfers, direct or indirect, to, or to the order of, or for the benefit of, the investor or associate are brought within these provisions.

Where relief is withdrawn or reduced by reason of a disposal (see **29.11** above), the investor is not treated as receiving value in respect of the disposal.

An individual who acquired shares by means of a transfer from a spouse or civil partner within **29.21** below is treated for these purposes as the investor.

[*ITA 2007, ss 159(4), 213, 214(1), 216, 217, 221, 256; FA 2020, s 110(1)(2)(5)*].

Insignificant value

An amount of '*insignificant value*' is an amount of value which:

- does not exceed £1,000; or
- in any other case is insignificant in relation to the amount subscribed by the investor for the shares.

If, at any time in the period beginning one year before the date of issue of the shares and ending with the date of issue, there are in existence arrangements (as broadly defined) providing for the investor (or an 'associate', within **29.42** below) to receive, or become entitled to receive, any value from the issuing company (or a 'connected person', within **19** CONNECTED PERSONS) at any time in 'period C' (as above), no amount of value received by the individual is treated as an amount of insignificant value. References to an associate or person connected with the company include anyone who has such status at *any* time in period C.

There are provisions to aggregate a receipt of value, whether insignificant or not, with amounts of insignificant value received previously, and treating that aggregate, if it is not itself an amount of insignificant value, as an amount of value received at the time of the latest actual receipt.

[*ITA 2007, ss 214(2)(3), 215, 257(1)*].

Simon's Taxes. See E3.169.

Reduction in relief — further computational provisions

[29.13] Adjustments are made in the amount by which relief is to be reduced in the following circumstances. Where more than one circumstance is relevant, the adjustments are made in the order in which they are set out below.

(a) Where two or more issues of shares have been made by the same company to the same investor, in relation to each of which income tax relief is claimed, and value is received during the applicable period C for more than one such issue, the value received is apportioned between them by reference to the amounts of relief obtained for each of those issues.

(b) Where any of the shares are treated as issued in the previous tax year by virtue of the carry-back provisions at **29.4** above, the value received is apportioned between the shares allocated to each year on the basis of the amount on which relief was obtained for each year. The normal provisions for reducing relief are then applied to each of the apportioned amounts as if there were separate issues of shares (taking (c) below into account where appropriate, but not (a) above) and the resulting amounts are added together.

(c) Where maximum relief is not obtained, the amount of value received is treated as reduced by multiplying that amount by the relief attributable to the shares divided by tax at the EIS original rate on the amount on which the investor claims relief in respect of the shares. For this purpose, where the relief attributable to the shares has been reduced (otherwise than as a result of an issue of bonus shares — see **29.6** above) before the relief was obtained, the gross relief attributable to the shares before that reduction is used in calculating the reduction in the value received.

[*ITA 2007, ss 218–220*].

Replacement value

[29.14] The 'value received' provisions in **29.12** above (other than **29.12**(i)) are disapplied if the person from whom the value was received (the '*original supplier*') receives, by way of a 'qualifying receipt', and whether before or after the original receipt of value, at least equivalent replacement value from the original recipient. A receipt is a '*qualifying receipt*' if it arises by reason of:

(a) any one, or any combination of, the following:
  (i) a payment by the original recipient to the original supplier other than a payment within (1) to (6) below or a payment covered by (c) below;
  (ii) the acquisition of an asset by the original recipient from the original supplier for consideration exceeding market value;
  (iii) the disposal of an asset by the original recipient to the original supplier for no consideration or for consideration less than market value; or
(b) (where the original receipt of value falls within **29.12**(d) above) an event having the effect of reversing the original event; or
(c) (where the original receipt of value arose from the purchase from the individual by a person connected with the company of shares or securities of the company, including for this purpose a payment for giving up any right in relation to them) the repurchase by the original recipient of the shares or securities in question, or reacquisition of the right in question, for consideration not less than the original value.

The amount of replacement value is:

- in a case within (a) above, the amount of any such payment plus the difference between the market value of any such asset and the consideration received;
- in a case within (b) above, the same as the amount of the original value; and
- in a case within (c) above, the consideration received by the original supplier.

The receipt of replacement value is disregarded if:

- it occurs before the start of period C relating to the shares in question; or
- there was an unreasonable delay in its occurrence; or
- it occurs more than 60 days after the relief falling to be withdrawn (or reduced) has been determined on appeal.

A receipt of replacement value is also disregarded if it has previously been set against a receipt of value to prevent any reduction or withdrawal of relief.

The following payments are excluded from (a)(i) above:

(1) a reasonable (in relation to their market value) payment for any goods, services or facilities provided (in the course of trade or otherwise) by the original supplier;
(2) a payment of interest at no more than a reasonable commercial rate on money lent to the original recipient;
(3) a payment not exceeding a reasonable and commercial rent for property occupied by the original recipient;
(4) a payment not exceeding market value for the acquisition of an asset;
(5) a payment in discharge of an 'ordinary trade debt' (as in **29.12**(c) above);
(6) a payment for any shares or securities in any company in circumstances not within (a)(ii) above.

Each reference in (1)–(3) above to the original supplier or recipient includes a reference to any person who at any time in period C is an 'associate' (as in **29.42** below) of his or, in the case of the supplier, is 'connected' with him (within **19** CONNECTED PERSONS).

Where:

- the receipt of replacement value is a qualifying receipt (as above); and
- the event giving rise to the receipt is (or includes) a subscription for shares by the individual or by a person who is an 'associate' (as in **29.42** below) of his at any time in period C,

the subscriber is not eligible for EIS income tax relief or EIS capital gains deferral relief (see **29.24** below) in relation to those shares or any other shares in the same issue.

For the above purposes, any apportionment made of value received where there are two or more share issues (see **29.13** above) is disregarded in determining the amount of the original receipt of value; and payments to a person include any made indirectly or to his order or for his benefit.

[*ITA 2007, ss 222, 223*].

Simon's Taxes. See **E3.170**.

Value received other than by investor

[29.15] Relief is also restricted or withdrawn where an individual has obtained relief attributable (see **29.6** above) to shares in a company, and at any time during 'period C', the company or any '51% subsidiary' of the company repays, redeems or repurchases any of its share capital belonging to a member other than:

(i) the individual; or
(ii) another individual whose relief is thereby withdrawn or reduced (as above) or who thereby suffers a qualifying chargeable event under the capital gains deferral provisions mentioned at **29.24** below; or
(iii) another individual whose relief under the SEED ENTERPRISE INVESTMENT SCHEME (**66**) is thereby withdrawn or reduced,

or makes any payment to any such member for giving up rights on the cancellation or extinguishment of any of the share capital of the company or subsidiary. See below for the exception for insignificant repayments etc.

The absence of any withdrawal or reduction of the kind referred to in (ii) and (iii) above is disregarded if it is due only to the amount received being of insignificant value.

A '*51% subsidiary*' of a company is one of which the company owns more than 50% of the ordinary share capital at any time in period A (as in **29.11** above), whether or not at the time of the repayment etc.

'*Period C*' is the period beginning one year before the issue of eligible shares and ending immediately before the third anniversary of the issue date or, if later and where relevant, the third anniversary of the date of commencement of the intended trade referred to in **29.58**(a) below. (In determining for these purposes the time at which a qualifying trade begins to be carried on by any 'qualifying 90% subsidiary' (see **29.57** below) of a company, any carrying on of the trade by it before it became such a subsidiary is disregarded.)

This restriction of relief does not apply to the redemption, within twelve months of issue, of any share capital of nominal value equal to the authorised minimum issued to comply with *Companies Act 2006, s 761* (or earlier equivalent).

A repayment etc. is ignored for the above purpose to the extent that relief attributable to any shares has already been withdrawn or reduced on its account.

[*ITA 2007, ss 159(4), 224(1)(3)–(7), 230*].

Computation

The relief is withdrawn or, if it exceeds an amount equal to tax at the EIS original rate on the sum received by the member, reduced by that amount.

Adjustments are made in the amount by which relief is to be reduced in the following circumstances. Where more than one circumstance is relevant, the adjustments are made in the order in which they are set out below.

(1) Where, in relation to the same repayment etc., relief attributable to two or more issues of shares falls to be reduced, the amount received by the member is apportioned between the issues by reference to the amounts of relief obtained for each of those issues.

(2) Where, in relation to the same repayment etc., relief attributable to shares held by two or more individuals falls to be reduced, the amount received by the member is apportioned between the individuals by reference to the amounts of relief obtained by each individual.

(3) Where any of the shares are treated as issued in the previous tax year by virtue of the carry-back provisions at **29.4** above, the amount received by the member is apportioned between the shares allocated to each year on the basis of the amount on which relief was obtained for each year. The normal provisions for reducing relief are then applied to each of the apportioned amounts as if there were separate issues of shares (taking (4) below into account where appropriate, but not (1) or (2) above) and the resulting amounts are added together.

(4) Where maximum relief is not obtained, the amount received by the member is treated as reduced by multiplying that amount by the relief attributable to the shares divided by tax at the EIS original rate on the amount on which the investor claims relief in respect of the shares. For this purpose, where the relief attributable to the shares has been reduced (otherwise than as a result of an issue of bonus shares — see **29.6** above) before the relief was obtained, the gross relief attributable to the shares before that reduction is used in calculating the reduction in the amount received by the member.

[*ITA 2007, ss 224(2), 226–229*].

Insignificant repayments etc.

A repayment etc. is disregarded if both the amount received by the member in question and the market value immediately before the event of the shares to which the event relates is insignificant in relation to the market value immediately after the event of the remaining issued share capital of the company or, as the case may be, 51% subsidiary. The assumption is made that the shares in question are cancelled at the time of the event. This let-out does not apply if, at any time in the period beginning one year before the date of issue of the shares and ending with the date of issue, there are in existence arrangements (as broadly defined) providing for a payment within these provisions to be made, or entitlement to such a payment to come into being, at any time in period C. [*ITA 2007, ss 225, 257(1)*].

Simon's Taxes. See E3.171.

Acquisition of a trade or trading assets

[29.16] Relief attributable (see **29.6** above) to any shares in a company held by an individual is withdrawn if, at any time in period A (as in **29.11** above), the company or any qualifying subsidiary (see **29.56** below), begins to carry on as its trade, business or profession (or part), a trade etc. (or part) previously carried on at any time in that period otherwise than by the company or a qualifying subsidiary, or acquires the whole or the greater part of the assets used for a trade etc. previously so carried on, and the individual is a person who, or one of a group of persons who together, either:

(a) owned more than a half share in the trade etc. previously carried on at any time in period A, and also own or owned at any such time such a share in the trade etc. carried on by the company, or
(b) control (within *CTA 2010, ss 450, 451*), or at any time in period A have controlled, the company, and also, at any such time, controlled another company which previously carried on the trade etc.

In determining, for the purposes of (a) above, the ownership of a trade and, if appropriate, the shares owned by multiple owners, *CTA 2010, s 941(6)* and *s 942* apply.

For the above purposes, interests etc. of 'associates' (see **29.42** below) are taken into account. There are special rules relating to shares held by certain directors of, or of a partner of, the issuing company or any subsidiary.

[*ITA 2007, ss 232, 257(3)*].

Simon's Taxes. See **E3.172.**

Acquisition of share capital

[29.17] Relief attributable (see **29.6** above) to any shares in a company held by an individual is withdrawn if:

- the company, at any time in period A (as in **29.11** above), comes to acquire all the issued share capital of another company; and
- the individual is a person, or one of a group of persons, who control (within *CTA 2010, ss 450, 451*) or has, at any time in period A, controlled the company and who also, at any such time, controlled the other company.

There are special rules relating to shares held by certain directors of, or of a partner of, the issuing company or any subsidiary.

[*ITA 2007, ss 233, 257(3)*].

Simon's Taxes. See **E3.172.**

Relief subsequently found not to have been due

[29.18] Relief is withdrawn if it is subsequently found not to have been due. Relief can be withdrawn on the ground that the issuing company is not a qualifying company (see **29.46** below) or that the purpose of the issue or use of money raised requirements at **29.35**, **29.35** are not met only if:

- the issuing company has given notice under the provisions at **29.25** below (or the equivalent capital gains deferral provisions); or
- an HMRC officer has given notice to the issuing company of his opinion that the whole or part of the relief was not due because of the ground in question.

The issuing company may appeal against an HMRC notice as though it were refusal of a claim by the company. The determination of an appeal against an HMRC notice under the equivalent capital gains deferral provisions (see **29.24** below) is conclusive for the purposes of any income tax relief appeal.

[*ITA 2007, ss 234, 236*].

Simon's Taxes. See **E3.173.**

Procedure for withdrawing or reducing relief

[29.19] An assessment to income tax withdrawing or reducing EIS relief is made for the tax year for which the relief was given.

Such an assessment may not be made, and any notice by an HMRC officer under the provisions at **29.18** above may not be given, more than six years after the end of the tax year in which the time limit for the use of money raised requirement at **29.35** below expires or, if later, the event giving rise to withdrawal or reduction occurs. This restriction is without prejudice to the extension of time limits in cases of loss of income tax brought about deliberately (see **6.3** ASSESSMENTS) or fraudulent or negligent conduct. No assessment may be made by reason of any event occurring after the death of the person to whom the shares were issued.

Where a person has made an arm's length disposal or disposals of all the shares issued to him by a company in respect of which either relief is attributable or period A (as in **29.11** above) has not come to an end, no assessment may be made in respect of those shares by reason of any subsequent event unless he is at the time of that event 'connected with' the company (as in **29.42** below).

The date from which interest accrues (as in **43.3** LATE PAYMENT INTEREST AND PENALTIES) is 31 January following the tax year for which the assessment is made.

[*ITA 2007, ss 235, 237–239*].

Simon's Taxes. See E3.174, E3.175.

Example

[29.20]

In June 2021, Wigram, the investor in **29.9** above, sells 38,100 ordinary £1 shares in C Ltd (see **29.9** above), in an arm's length transaction, for £90,000, leaving him with 1,000 shares.

The position is as follows.

Income tax

2019/20 £

Relief attributable to 9,500 shares treated as issued in 2019/20:

9,500 shares at £2 per share = £19,000 @ 30% 5,700

Consideration received $\left(\frac{9,500}{38,100} \times £90,000\right) = £22,441$ @ 30% 6,732

Excess of tax at the EIS original rate on consideration over relief £1,032

Relief withdrawn by assessment for 2019/20 £5,700

2020/21 £

Relief attributable to 4,300 shares

4,300/5,300 × £1,155 937

Consideration received

$\left(\frac{4,300}{38,100} \times £90,000\right) = £10,157 \times 937/(8,600 @ 30\%) = £3,689$ @ 30% 1,107

Excess of tax at the EIS original rate on adjusted consideration over relief £170

Relief withdrawn by assessment for 2020/21 £937

Capital gains tax

2021/22		£	£
Disposal proceeds (38,100 shares)			90,000
Cost:	24,300 shares acquired May 2018	32,400	
	13,800 shares acquired June 2020	27,600	60,000
Chargeable gain			£30,000

Notes

(a) For both income tax and capital gains tax purposes, a disposal is matched with acquisitions on a first in/first out basis (see **29.11** above and Tolley's Capital Gains Tax). Thus, the 38,100 shares sold in June 2021 are matched with 24,300 shares purchased in May 2018 and with 13,800 of the 14,800 EIS shares subscribed for in June 2020. For these purposes, 9,500 of the EIS shares are treated as having been issued in 2019/20 (by virtue of Wigram's carry-back claim — see **29.9** above). Therefore, those shares are treated as disposed of in priority to those on which relief was given in 2020/21.

Following the disposal, Wigram is left with 1,000 shares in C Ltd acquired in June 2020 for £2,000, to which the EIS relief attributable is £218 (1,155 – 937).

(b) EIS relief is withdrawn if shares are disposed of before the end of the requisite three-year period. In this example, relief attributable to the shares sold is fully withdrawn as consideration received, reduced as illustrated, exceeds the relief attributable. See below for where the reverse applies. The consideration is reduced where the relief attributable (A) is less than tax at the EIS original rate on the amount subscribed (B), and is so reduced by applying the fraction A/B. See **29.11** above.

(c) Relief is withdrawn by means of an assessment for the year(s) in which relief was given (see **29.19** above).

(d) The capital gain on the disposal is fully chargeable as the EIS shares are not held for the requisite three-year period (see Tolley's Capital Gains Tax).

In December 2021, Wigram disposes of his 75,000 ordinary £1 shares in D Ltd (see **29.9** above), in an arm's length transaction, for £60,000.

The position is as follows.

Income tax

2020/21	£
Relief attributable to shares sold	8,172
Consideration received:	
$£60{,}000 \times \dfrac{8{,}172}{£75{,}000 \times 30\%} = £21{,}792$ @ 30%	6,538
Excess of relief over tax at the EIS original rate on adjusted consideration	£1,634

Income tax

Relief withdrawn by assessment for 2020/21		£6,538

Capital gains tax

2021/22	£	£
Disposal proceeds (December 2021)		60,000
Cost (November 2020)	75,000	
Less Relief attributable to shares		
£8,172 – £6,538	1,634	73,366
Allowable loss		£13,366

Notes

(a) The EIS relief withdrawn is limited to tax at the EIS original rate on the consideration received, reduced as illustrated. If the disposal had been made otherwise than by way of a bargain made at arm's length, the full relief would have been withdrawn. See **29.11** above.

(b) An allowable loss may arise for capital gains tax purposes on a disposal of EIS shares, whether or not the disposal occurs within the requisite three-year period. In computing such a loss, the allowable cost is reduced by EIS relief attributable to the shares (and not withdrawn). See Tolley's Capital Gains Tax.

(c) A loss, as computed for capital gains tax purposes, may be relieved against income on a share loss relief claim (see **45.23** LOSSES).

Married persons and civil partners

[29.21] The provisions for withdrawal of relief on the disposal of shares in respect of which relief has been given (see **29.11** above) do not apply to transfers between spouses or civil partners living together. On any subsequent disposal or other event, the spouse or partner to whom the shares were so transferred is treated as if:

- he or she were the person who subscribed for the shares;
- the amount he or she subscribed for the shares were the same amount as subscribed by the transferor spouse or partner;
- his or her liability to income tax had been reduced in respect of the shares by the same amount, and for the same tax year, as applied on the subscription by the transferor spouse or partner; and
- that amount of EIS income tax relief had continued to be attributable to the shares despite the transfer.

Where the amount of EIS relief attributable to the shares had been reduced before the relief was obtained by the transferor spouse or partner, the transferee is treated as if his or her relief had been correspondingly reduced before it was obtained (but this does not prevent the gross relief before reduction being used for the purposes of the calculations at **29.11**, **29.13**(c) and **29.15**(4) above).

Any assessment for reducing or withdrawing relief is made on the transferee spouse or partner. The identification rules for disposals at **29.11** above apply to determine the extent (if any) to which shares to which relief is attributable are comprised in the transfer.

[*ITA 2007, ss 209(4), 245, 246(1)*].

Issuing company acquired by new company

[29.22] Where a company (Company A) has issued shares under the enterprise investment scheme (a certificate having been issued on Form EIS 3 — see **29.7** above) and subsequently, by means of an exchange of shares, all of its shares (the old shares) are acquired by a company (Company B) in which the only previously issued shares are subscriber shares, then, subject to the further conditions below being satisfied:

- the exchange is not regarded as involving a disposal of the old shares (and a consequent withdrawal of relief) and an acquisition of the Company B shares (the new shares); and
- EIS relief attributable to the old shares is regarded as attributable instead to the new shares for which they are exchanged. For EIS purposes generally, the new shares stand in the shoes of the old shares, e.g. as if they had been subscribed for and issued at the time the old shares were subscribed for and issued and as if anything done by or in relation to Company A had been done by or in relation to Company B.

The further conditions are as follows.

(a) The consideration for the old shares must consist entirely of the issue of the new shares.

(b) The consideration for old shares of each description must consist entirely of new shares of the 'corresponding description'.

(c) New shares of each description must be issued to holders of old shares of the 'corresponding description' in respect of and in proportion to their holdings.

(d) Before the issue of the new shares, on the written application (for which see **4.12** ANTI-AVOIDANCE) of either Company A or Company B, HMRC must have notified to that company their satisfaction that the exchange:
   - is for genuine commercial reasons; and
   - does not form part of a scheme or arrangements designed to avoid liability to corporation tax or capital gains tax.

   HMRC may, within 30 days of an application, request further particulars, which must then be supplied within 30 days of the request (or such longer period as they may allow in any particular case).

For the purposes of (b) and (c) above, old and new shares are of a '*corresponding description*' if, assuming they were shares in the same company, they would be of the same class and carry the same rights.

References above to 'shares' (other than those to 'shares issued under the enterprise investment scheme' or 'subscriber shares') include references to securities.

An exchange within these provisions does not breach the control and independence requirement at **29.52** below.

[*ITA 2007, ss 247–249; TCGA 1992, s 138(2)*].

'Subscriber shares' are the shares that are to be issued to those who subscribe to the Memorandum of Association of a company on its initial formation (*Finn and others v HMRC* FTT (TC 3555), [2014] UKFTT 426 (TC)).

Simon's Taxes. See E3.168.

Capital gains tax

[29.23] In determining the gain or loss on a disposal of shares to which any income tax relief is attributable (see **29.6** above):

(a) if a loss would otherwise arise, the consideration the individual is treated as having given for the shares is treated as reduced by the amount of the relief;

(b) if the disposal is after the end of period A (as in **29.11** above) and a gain would otherwise arise, the gain is not a chargeable gain (although this does not prevent a loss arising in these circumstances from being an allowable loss). Where the reduction in liability in respect of the issue of the shares was less than the amount corresponding to income tax at the EIS rate on the amount subscribed for the shares (other than because there is insufficient income tax liability to make full use of the relief), there is a corresponding reduction in the amount of the gain which is not chargeable.

Where a gain (or part of a gain) on a disposal is not a chargeable gain under (b) above, but the income tax relief on the shares disposed of is reduced on account of value received from the company by the claimant or by other persons (see **29.12–29.15**) before the disposal, then a corresponding proportion of the gain is brought back into charge.

The identification rules at **29.11** above apply for the above purposes.

For the exemption in (b) above to apply, it is essential for a claim for income tax relief to have been made and given effect, even in a case where such a claim would have been of little or no value in itself due to insufficient taxable income (*Ames v HMRC* UT, [2018] STC 1704).

See further *TCGA 1992, ss 150A, 150B*. For full coverage, see the corresponding chapter of Tolley's Capital Gains Tax.

Simon's Taxes. See E3.185, E3.190–E3.193.

Capital gains deferral relief

[29.24] A chargeable gain can be deferred to the extent that it could be matched with an investment in EIS shares to which income tax relief was attributable (see **29.6** above).

It is not a requirement that the EIS shares qualify for income tax relief nor that the individual be unconnected with the company. However, the company itself must be a qualifying company (as in **29.46** below) and certain other EIS income tax relief conditions are adopted. The provisions are also extended to trustees. There is no limit on the amount of the gain that can be deferred, but the gross assets requirement at **29.53** below does limit the amount that may be invested in any one EIS company (or group).

Deferral relief applies where:

- a chargeable gain would otherwise accrue to an individual on the disposal by him of any asset;
- the individual makes a 'qualifying investment'; and
- the individual is UK resident both when the chargeable gain accrues to him and when he makes the qualifying investment, and is not, at the time he makes the investment, regarded as resident outside the UK for the purposes of any double taxation arrangements the effect of which would be that he would not be liable to tax on a gain arising on a disposal, immediately after their acquisition, of the shares comprising the qualifying investment, disregarding any exemption available under *TCGA 1992, s 150A* (see **29.23** above).

Subject to the further conditions referred to above, a '*qualifying investment*' is a subscription for shares within **29.28**(a) below (broadly, ordinary, non-preferential, shares) in a qualifying EIS company which are issued within the one year immediately preceding or the three years immediately following the time the chargeable gain in question accrues. These time limits may be extended by HMRC in individual cases. If the shares are issued *before* the gain accrues, they must still be held at the time it accrues. The deferred gain is brought back into charge on the occurrence of (and at the time of) any one of a number of specified chargeable events, in particular the disposal (at any time) of the shares in question.

[*TCGA 1992, s 150C, Sch 5B; FA 2020, s 110(1)(4)(5)*].

The above is intended as a brief summary only. For full coverage, see the corresponding chapter of Tolley's Capital Gains Tax.

Simon's Taxes. See **E3.195, E3.1100–E3.1116.**

Notification requirements and information powers

[29.25] Certain events leading to withdrawal or reduction of income tax relief must be notified to HMRC, generally within 60 days, by either the individual who received the relief, the issuing company, or any person connected with the issuing company having knowledge of the matter. An HMRC officer may require such a notice and other relevant information where he has reason to believe it should have been made.

It should be noted that:

- the notification requirement extends to cases where income tax relief would have fallen to be withdrawn or reduced were it not for the 'replacement value' rules at **29.14** above; and in all cases a notice under these provisions should include details of any such replacement value received (or expected to be received) where this is within the knowledge of the person giving the notice; and

- HMRC's powers extend to cases where notice would have been required were it not for 'value received', or a repayment, redemption etc. of share capital, being of an insignificant amount (see **29.12**, **29.15** above), and they may require notice and other information from persons giving or receiving such value or making or receiving such a repayment etc.

The penalty provisions of *TMA 1970, s 98* apply for failure to comply with the notification requirements.

HMRC also have broad powers to require information in other cases where relief may be withdrawn, restricted or not due. The obligations of secrecy do not prevent HMRC disclosing to a company that relief has been given or claimed on certain of its shares.

[*ITA 2007, ss 240–244*].

Providing of State aid information

On and after 15 September 2016, where EIS income tax relief has been given (whether before, on or after that date) or may in future be given, HMRC may give the EIS company a notice requiring it to supply HMRC with specified information for the purpose of compliance with certain EU State aid obligations. This may include information about the company, its activities and/or its investors, information about the EIS relief and information relating to the grant of State aid through the provision of the relief. See **36.5** HMRC — CONFIDENTIALITY OF INFORMATION as regards the publishing by HMRC of State aid information. [*FA 2016, s 180(5)–(9)(11), Sch 24 Pt 2*].

Simon's Taxes. See **E3.181**.

The risk-to-capital condition

[29.26] The risk-to-capital condition mentioned at **29.1** above is an overarching condition which is met if, having regard to all existing circumstances at the time of issue of the EIS shares, it would be reasonable to conclude that:

- the issuing company has objectives to grow and develop its trade in the longterm; and
- there is a significant risk of loss of capital of an amount greater than the net investment return, i.e. the net return to investors (whether by way of income or capital growth) taking into account the value of EIS relief. The risk and the return is to be determined with reference to the investors in general, and a loss of capital means a loss of at least part of the amounts subscribed for the shares by the investors.

[*ITA 2007, s 157A; FA 2018, s 14(1); SI 2018 No 931, Reg 2*].

As stated at **29.1**, the risk-to-capital condition has effect for shares issued on or after 15 March 2018. The intention is to prevent tax-relieved investment in companies whose activities are geared towards preservation of investors' capital rather than the company's long-term growth and development. *ITA 2007, s 157A(3)* provides an illustrative, non-exhaustive list of the types of circumstance that may be taken into account in reaching any conclusion. For guidance on the condition, with examples, see HMRC Venture Capital Schemes Manual VCM8500–8560.

Enterprise Investment Scheme — general requirements

[29.27] The general requirements mentioned at **29.1** above are described at **29.28–29.40** below.

Simon's Taxes. See **E3.116–E3.124.**

The shares requirement

[29.28] The shares must:

(a) be ordinary shares which do not, at any time during 'period B', carry (subject to below) any present or future preferential right to dividends or to assets on a winding-up or any present or future right to be redeemed; and

(b) (unless they are 'bonus shares') be subscribed for wholly in cash and be fully paid up at the time of issue.

Preferential rights cannot be disregarded for the purposes of (a) above just because they are small or insignificant (*Flix Innovations Ltd v HMRC* UT, [2016] STC 2206). Shares *are* permitted to carry a preferential right to *dividends* provided the amount and timing of the dividends do not depend on a decision of the company (*Foojit Ltd v HMRC* FTT (TC 7467), [2020] SFTD 306, [2019] UKFTT 694 (TC)), the shareholder or any other person and provided the dividends are not cumulative.

For the purposes of (a) above, '*period B*' is the three years beginning with the date of issue. If the company satisfied the purpose of the issue requirement at **29.34** below by virtue of **29.58**(a) below and the trade had not yet commenced on the issue date, period B is the period from date of issue to immediately before the third anniversary of commencement. (In determining for this purpose the time at which a qualifying trade begins to be carried on by any 'qualifying 90% subsidiary' (see **29.57** below) of a company, any carrying on of the trade etc. by it before it became such a subsidiary is disregarded.)

For the purposes of (b) above, '*bonus shares*' are shares issued otherwise than for payment (whether in cash or otherwise). Shares are not fully paid up if there is any undertaking to pay cash to any person at a later date in respect of the acquisition.

[*ITA 2007, ss 159(3), 173, 256, 257(1)*].

For the date on which shares are issued, see *National Westminster Bank plc v CIR; Barclays Bank plc v CIR* HL 1994, 67 TC 1.

The 'maximum amount raised annually through risk finance investments' requirement

[29.29] With effect for shares issued on or after 6 April 2018, the total amount of 'relevant investments' (see **29.30** below) made in the issuing company in the 12 months ending with the date of issue must not exceed:

(i) if the company is a knowledge-intensive company at that date, £10 million; and
(ii) in any other case, £5 million.

See **29.32** below for meaning of knowledge-intensive company, and note the special rule there for companies that have traded for less than three years before issuing the EIS shares.

Prior to the above taking effect the limit is £5 million in all cases.

The following also count towards the above limit:

(a) any relevant investment in a 51% subsidiary (within *CTA 2010, Pt 24 Ch 3*) of the issuing company (including any made before it became a 51% subsidiary but not any made after it last ceased to be one);
(b) any relevant investment made in any company to the extent that the money raised by the investment has been employed for the purposes of a trade (as widely defined) carried on by another company that has at any time in the said 12-month period been a 51% subsidiary of the issuing company (disregarding any money so employed after it last ceased to be such a subsidiary); and
(c) any other relevant investment made in any company to the extent that the money raised has been employed for the purposes of a trade (as widely defined), and within that 12-month period, but after the investment was made, the trade (or a part of it) was transferred to the issuing company, a 51% subsidiary or a partnership of which the issuing company or a 51% subsidiary is a member (but disregarding trades transferred after a 51% subsidiary in question last ceased to be such a subsidiary).

[*ITA 2007, s 173A(1)–(2B)(6)(7); FA 2018, Sch 4 paras 2(2), 10; SI 2018 No 931, Reg 3*].

Relevant investments

[29.30] For the purposes of the EIS requirements, '*relevant investments*' comprise:

(a) investments (of any kind) made by a VENTURE CAPITAL TRUST (VCT) (**81**);
(b) money subscribed for shares issued under the EIS or the SEED ENTERPRISE INVESTMENT SCHEME (SEIS) (**66**);
(c) investments made under the SOCIAL INVESTMENT TAX RELIEF (**72**) scheme; and
(d) any other investment made which is aid received by the company pursuant to a measure approved by the EC as compatible with Article 107 of the Treaty on the Functioning of the European Union in accordance with the principles laid down in the European Commis-

sion's Guidelines on State aid to promote risk finance investment (previously the Community Guidelines on Risk Capital Investments in Small and Medium-sized Enterprises).

As regards (b) above, shares are treated as having been issued under the EIS or SEIS if at any time the investee company provides an EIS compliance statement (see **29.7** above) or SEIS equivalent (see **66.5** SEED ENTERPRISE INVESTMENT SCHEME) in respect of those shares; an investment is regarded as made when the shares are issued. As regards (c) above, an investment is treated as made under the social investment relief scheme if at any time the investee company provides a compliance statement as in **72.6** SOCIAL INVESTMENT TAX RELIEF; *ITA 2007, s 257KB* (see **72.1** SOCIAL INVESTMENT TAX RELIEF) applies in determining when such an investment is made.

[*ITA 2007, s 173A(3)–(5)*].

For the purposes of determining entitlement to EIS income tax relief in respect of shares issued on or after 1 December 2017, investments are not prevented from constituting relevant investments by virtue only of their having been made before certain historical dates. Previously, under earlier transitional provisions, certain investments made before 6 April 2012 did not count as relevant investments. [*FA 2018, s 15*].

The 'maximum risk finance investments at the issue date' requirement

[29.31] The total amount of 'relevant investments' (see **29.30** above) made in the issuing company on or before the date the EIS shares are issued must not exceed £12 million or, if the company is a 'knowledge-intensive company' (see **29.32** below) at the time the shares are issued, £20 million. Relevant investments of the kind in **29.29**(a)–(c) above also count towards these limits, but disregarding references there to a 12-month period and instead taking into account all times before the issue date. [*ITA 2007, s 173AA*].

Knowledge-intensive companies

[29.32] A '*knowledge-intensive company*' is broadly a company whose costs of research and development or innovation are at least 15% of its operating costs in at least one of the years comprising the 'relevant three-year period' or at least 10% of its operating costs in each of those years, and which meets at least one of the two conditions below. The '*relevant three-year period*' is normally the three years ending immediately before the beginning of the last accounts filing period. However, if the last accounts filing period ends more than 12 months before the issue date of the EIS shares in question, the relevant three-year period is the three years ending 12 months before the issue date. A company's operating costs are defined by reference to the items recognised as expenses in its profit and loss account. The conditions to be met are that:

- the company has created, is creating or is intending to create, intellectual property (the '*innovation condition*'); or
- the company's full-time employees with a relevant Masters or higher degree who are engaged in research and development or innovation comprise at least 20% of the total of its full-time employees (the '*skilled*

employee condition'). The skilled employee condition must continue to be met throughout period B (as in **29.28** above) (subject to a let-out for companies entering administration or receivership).

In order to meet the innovation condition, the issuing company must be engaged in intellectual property creation at the time the EIS shares are issued, and it must be reasonable to assume that, within ten years after the issue, the exploitation of its intellectual property, or business which results from new or improved products, processes or services utilising its intellectual property, will form the greater part of its business. A company is engaged in intellectual property creation if intellectual property is being created by the company, or has been created by it within the previous three years; or the company is taking (or preparing to take) steps in order that intellectual property will be created by it; or the company demonstrates via an independent expert's report that it is reasonable to assume it will create intellectual property in the foreseeable future. Intellectual property is taken into account only if the whole or greater part (in terms of value) of it is created by the company and it is created in circumstances in which the right to exploit it vests in the company (whether alone or jointly with others).

If the issuing company is a parent company, the above rules are appropriately modified to also take account of its 'qualifying subsidiaries' (see **29.56** below).

[*ITA 2007, s 252A; FA 2016, s 29(2)(6), s 30*].

Companies that have traded for less than three years

If the issuing company commenced trading less than three years before the date the EIS shares are issued, the above definition is modified for the purposes of **29.5**(i)–(iii) above (annual maximum on which an individual may obtain relief) and **29.29**(i) and (ii) above ('maximum amount raised annually through risk finance investments' requirement). The '*relevant three-year period*' is for those purposes the three years *beginning* on the date of issue of the shares. If the issuing company is a parent company, operating costs of a qualifying subsidiary (at time of issue) are not taken into account for any of those three years during any part of which it is not a qualifying subsidiary. [*ITA 2007, ss 158(6)(7), 173A(5A); FA 2018, Sch 4 paras 1(6), 2(3), 10; SI 2018 No 931, Reg 3*].

The 'maximum risk finance investments during period B' requirement

[29.33] This requirement is tested only during period B (as in **29.28** above) and only if the issuing company effectively acquires a company or trade after it receives the EIS investment in question. The requirement is that at any time in period B the total of the relevant investments (see **29.30** above) so far made must not exceed £12 million or, if the company is a 'knowledge-intensive company' (see **29.32** above) at the time the EIS shares are issued, £20 million. Without this requirement, the investment limits in **29.31** above could be sidestepped where the acquired company or trade had already benefited from earlier relevant investments. Relevant investments of the kind in **29.29**(a)–(c) above also count towards these limits, but disregarding references there to a 12-month period and instead taking into account all times before the time in period B when the requirement is being tested. The requirement applies where:

- a company becomes a 51% subsidiary of the issuing company at a time during period B (other than as a result of an exchange of shares within **29.22** above);
- all or part of the money raised by the issue of the EIS shares in question is employed for the purposes of a qualifying business activity (see **29.58** below) consisting (wholly or partly) of a trade (as widely defined) carried on by that company; and
- the trade (or a part of it) was carried on by that company before that time.

The requirement also applies where all or part of the money raised by the issue of the EIS shares is employed for the purposes of a qualifying business activity consisting (wholly or partly) of a trade (as widely defined) which, during period B, is transferred as in **29.29**(c) above.

[*ITA 2007, ss 173AB, 247(3A)*].

The 'purpose of the issue' requirement

[29.34] The shares, other than any bonus shares, must be issued to raise money (i.e. cash, see *Thompson v Hart* Ch D 2000, 72 TC 543) for the purpose of a 'qualifying business activity' (see **29.58** below). It is made explicit, for EU State aid purposes, that the issuing company must use the money for this purpose so as to promote the growth and development of the company or, where the company is a parent company, the group. [*ITA 2007, s 174*].

The 'purpose of the issue' requirement was held to be satisfied where the money raised was loaned to overseas subsidiaries for the purpose of enabling them to supply information and analysis for the purposes of the issuing company's business (*4Cast Ltd v Mitchell* (Sp C 455), [2005] SSCD 287).

The requirement is *not* satisfied if the money raised by the issue is used partly to pay dividends to investors (*Forthright (Wales) Ltd v A L Davies* Ch D 2004, 76 TC 138). The requirement was not satisfied where a company issued convertible loan notes which it subsequently converted into shares; the issue of the shares was not then for the purpose of raising money (*Optos plc v HMRC* (Sp C 560), [2006] SSCD 687). It *was* satisfied where the money raised was loaned to another company, subsequently repaid and a qualifying trade then acquired; the loan was a means of 'parking' the money until it was needed and was no different to placing it on deposit with a bank (*G C Trading Ltd v HMRC* (Sp C 630), [2008] SSCD 178). Money raised to increase the appellant's interest in a trading partnership was not raised for the purpose of a qualifying business activity (*Harvey's Jersey Cream Ltd v HMRC* FTT (TC 3045), [2014] SFTD 599).

The 'use of money raised' requirement

[29.35] All of the 'money raised' must be employed wholly (disregarding insignificant amounts) for the purpose of the qualifying business activity for which it was raised by the end of the two years following the issue. If the only qualifying business activity falls within **29.58**(a) below, the deadline is extended until the end of the two years starting when the company (or, where applicable, a subsidiary) begins to carry on the qualifying trade.

For these purposes, the '*money raised*' means the money raised by the issue of the shares in question (other than any of them which are bonus shares) and any other shares in the company of the same class (as defined) which are within **29.28**(a) above and which are issued on the same day. In determining the time at which a qualifying trade begins to be carried on by a 'qualifying 90% subsidiary' of a company, any carrying on of the trade etc. by it before it became such a subsidiary is disregarded.

Employing money on the acquisition of shares in a company does not of itself amount to employing it for the purposes of a qualifying business activity. Additionally, employing money on the acquisition of any of the following does not amount to employing it for the purposes of a qualifying business activity: an interest in another company such that a company becomes a 51% subsidiary of the issuing company; a further interest in a 51% subsidiary of the issuing company; a trade (as widely defined); and goodwill or other intangible assets employed for the purposes of a trade.

[*ITA 2007, ss 175, 257(5)*].

Money used to meet the expenses of issuing the shares should be regarded as employed in the same way as the remainder of the money raised. Where the company obtains a listing, for example on the Alternative Investment Market, at the same time as it issues the shares, the use of money to meet the expenses of flotation is normally acceptable. (HMRC Venture Capital Schemes Manual VCM12060).

This requirement is *not* satisfied if the money raised by the issue is used partly to pay dividends to investors (*Forthright (Wales) Ltd v A L Davies* Ch D 2004, 76 TC 138). It is not necessary for money to be spent in order for it to be 'employed', but it must at least be earmarked for some specific purpose and kept in reserve for that purpose (*Richards and another v HMRC* UT 2011, [2012] STC 174).

The 'permitted maximum age' requirement

[29.36] If the EIS shares in question are issued after the 'initial investing period', one of three conditions must be met. These are that:

(a) a 'relevant investment' (see **29.30** above) was made in the issuing company before the end of the initial investing period, and some or all of the money raised by that investment was employed for the purposes of the same qualifying business activity (see **29.58** below) as that for which the money raised by the current issue is employed; or

(b) the total amount of relevant investments made in the issuing company in a period of 30 consecutive days which includes the date of issue of the shares is at least 50% of the annual turnover of the company averaged over five years (see *ITA 2007, s 175A(7)–(8)*), and the money raised by those investments is employed for the purpose of 'entering a new product or geographical market' (as defined in the General Block Exemption Regulation (Commission Regulation (EU) No 651/2014); or

(c) the condition in (b) or the equivalent condition for VCT approval (see **81.12** VENTURE CAPITAL TRUSTS) was previously met in relation to one or more relevant investments in the issuing company, and some or all of the money raised by those investments was employed for the purposes of the same qualifying business activity as that for which the money raised by the current issue is employed.

The '*initial investing period*' is the seven years beginning with the 'relevant first commercial sale' (ten years where the issuing company is a 'knowledge-intensive company' (see **29.32** above) when the EIS shares are issued). '*First commercial sale*' has the same meaning as in the EC's Guidelines on State aid to promote risk finance investments. The '*relevant first commercial sale*' is defined in *ITA 2007, s 175A(6)* by reference to the earliest date of any commercial sale made by (broadly) the company or a 51% subsidiary or any other person who has carried on any trade which is carried on by the company or a subsidiary.

With effect for shares issued on or after 6 April 2018, an issuing company which is a knowledge-intensive company may elect to alter its initial investing period by substituting, for the date of the relevant first commercial sale, the date by reference to which it is treated as reaching an annual turnover of £200,000. That date is normally the last day of the accounting period in which annual turnover first reaches £200,000 or more (with modifications for accounting periods exceeding 12 months). Turnover of other companies in the group (where relevant) must also be taken into account. Any necessary apportionments must be made on a time basis, i.e. in the case of short or long accounting periods or companies joining or leaving the group part way through an accounting period.

[*ITA 2007, ss 175A, 247(3A), 252B; FA 2016, s 29(1)(6), s 30; FA 2018, Sch 4 paras 5, 6, 10; SI 2018 No 931, Reg 3*].

The 'minimum period' requirement

[29.37] The trade or the research and development must have been carried on for a period of at least four months ending at or after the time of the share issue. The trade etc. must have carried on for those months by no person other than the qualifying company or a 'qualifying 90% subsidiary' (see **29.57** below) of that company.

A period shorter than four months is permitted if this is by reason only of the winding-up or dissolution of any company or anything done as a consequence of a company being in administration or receivership, provided the winding-up etc. is for genuine commercial reasons and not part of a tax avoidance scheme or arrangements.

[*ITA 2007, s 176*].

The 'no pre-arranged exits' requirement

[29.38] The arrangements (as broadly defined) under which the shares are issued to the investor (or arrangements preceding the issue but in relation or in connection to it) must not:

(a) provide for the eventual disposal by the investor of the shares in question or other shares or securities of the company; or
(b) provide for the eventual cessation of a trade of the company or of a person connected with it; or
(c) provide for the eventual disposal of all, or a substantial amount (in terms of value) of, the assets of the company or of a person connected with it; or
(d) provide (by means of any insurance, indemnity, guarantee or otherwise) complete or partial protection for investors against the normal risks attaching to EIS investment (but excluding arrangements which merely protect the company and/or its subsidiaries against normal business risks).

Arrangements with a view to the company becoming a wholly-owned subsidiary of a new holding company within the terms of *ITA 2007, s 247(1)* (see **29.22** above) are not caught by (a) above. In relation to shares issued on or after 5 December 2016, arrangements with a view to any shares in the company being exchanged for, or converted into, shares in that company of a different class are also not caught by (a) above. Arrangements applicable only on an unanticipated winding-up of the company for genuine commercial reasons are excluded from (b) and (c) above.

[*ITA 2007, ss 177, 257(1); F(No 2)A 2017, s 11(2)(4)*].

The 'no tax avoidance' requirement

[29.39] The shares must be issued for genuine commercial reasons and not as part of a scheme or arrangement a main purpose of which is the avoidance of tax. [*ITA 2007, s 178*].

The 'no disqualifying arrangements' requirement

[29.40] The shares must not be issued, nor any money raised by the issue spent, in consequence or anticipation of, or otherwise in connection with, 'disqualifying arrangements'. Arrangements (as broadly defined) are '*disqualifying arrangements*' if a main purpose of them is to ensure that any of the 'relevant tax reliefs' are available in respect of the issuing company's business and either or both of conditions A and B below are met. It is immaterial whether the issuing company is a party to the arrangements.

Condition A is that, as a result of the money raised by the issue of the shares being employed as required by **29.35** above, an amount representing the whole or most of the amount raised is, in the course of the arrangements, paid to (or for the benefit of) one or more 'relevant persons'. Condition B is that, in the absence of the arrangements, it would have been reasonable to expect that the whole or greater part of the component activities (as defined) of the qualifying business activity for which the issue of the shares raised money would have been carried on as part of another business by one or more 'relevant persons'.

A '*relevant person*' is a person who is a party to the arrangements or a person connected with such a party (within **19** CONNECTED PERSONS).

The '*relevant tax reliefs*' comprise:

- EIS income tax and CGT reliefs (as in **29.4**, **29.23** and **29.24** above);
- SEIS income tax and CGT reliefs (see **66.3**, **66.17** and **66.18** SEED ENTERPRISE INVESTMENT SCHEME);
- qualification as an investee company for VCT purposes (see **81.17** VENTURE CAPITAL TRUSTS);
- share loss relief (see **45.23** LOSSES); and
- (in relation to shares issued on or after 6 April 2017 but not so as to apply to arrangements involving transactions entered into before that date) SOCIAL INVESTMENT TAX RELIEF (**72**).

[*ITA 2007, ss 178A, 257(1); F(No 2)A 2017, Sch 1 paras 11(2), 16*].

Qualifying investor

[29.41] An individual is a '*qualifying investor*' in relation to shares if the requirements at **29.42–29.45** are met.

Simon's Taxes. See E3.106–E3.115.

The 'no connection with the issuing company' requirement

[29.42] The investor must not (except as below) be at any time in the period specified below 'connected with' the issuing company (whether before or after its incorporation) (i.e. there must be no such connection at any time in that period, see *Wild v Cannavan* CA 1997, 70 TC 554). The specified period is the period beginning two years before the issue of the shares and ending immediately before the third anniversary of the issue date or, if later and where relevant, the third anniversary of the date of commencement of the intended trade referred to in **29.58**(a) below.

In determining the time at which a qualifying trade begins to be carried on by any 'qualifying 90% subsidiary' (see **29.57** below) of a company, any carrying on of the trade by it before it became such a subsidiary is disregarded.

[*ITA 2007, ss 163, 256*].

An investor is '*connected with*' the issuing company if he, or an 'associate' of his, is either:

(a) an employee, partner, or director of, or an employee or director of a partner of, the issuing company or any 'subsidiary'; or
(b) an individual who directly or indirectly possesses or is entitled to acquire (whether he is so entitled at a future date or will at a future date be so entitled):
    (i) more than 30% of the voting power, the ordinary share capital or the issued share capital of the issuing company or any 'subsidiary'; or
    (ii) such rights as would entitle him to more than 30% of the assets of the issuing company or any 'subsidiary' available for distribution to the company's equity holders (as under *CTA 2010, Pt 5 Ch 6* — see Tolley's Corporation Tax under Groups of Companies); or

(c) an individual who has control (as defined by *ITA 2007, s 995*) of the issuing company or any 'subsidiary'; or
(d) an individual who subscribes for shares in the issuing company as part of an arrangement providing for another person to subscribe for shares in another company with which, were that other company an issuing company, the individual (or any other individual party to the arrangement) would be connected as above.

Rights or powers of associates are taken into account as regards (b) and (c) above (see *Cook v Billings* CA, [2001] STC 16 on the similar wording under the earlier BES provisions). An '*associate*' of any person is any 'relative' (i.e. spouse, civil partner, ancestor or linear descendant) of that person, the trustee(s) of any settlement in relation to which that person or any relative (living or dead) is or was a settlor and, where that person has an interest in any shares of obligations of a company which are subject to any trust or are part of a deceased estate, the trustee(s) of the settlement or the personal representatives of the deceased. For this purpose, 'settlor' is defined as in **70.3** SETTLEMENTS.

As regards (b)(i) above, an individual is not connected with the company by virtue only of the fact that he or an associate is a shareholder if at that time the company has issued no shares other than subscriber shares and has neither commenced business nor made preparations for doing so.

A '*subsidiary*' for these purposes is a company more than 50% of whose ordinary share capital is at any time in period A (as in **29.11** above) owned by the issuing company, regardless of whether or not that condition is fulfilled while the individual falls within (a)–(d) above in respect of it.

(In determining for this purpose the time at which a qualifying trade begins to be carried on by any 'qualifying 90% subsidiary' (see **29.57** below) of a company, any carrying on of the trade by it before it became such a subsidiary is disregarded.)

[*ITA 2007, ss 159(2), 166, 167(1)(2), 170, 171, 253, 256*].

As regards (a) above, directorships are taken into account only where the individual or an associate (or a partnership of which either of them is a member) receives or is entitled to receive, during the specified period above, a payment (whether directly or indirectly or to his order or for his benefit) from the issuing company or a 'related person' other than by way of:

(A) payment or reimbursement of allowable expenditure against employment income;
(B) interest at no more than a commercial rate on money lent;
(C) dividends etc. representing no more than a normal return on investment;
(D) payment for supply of goods at no more than market value;
(E) rent at no more than a reasonable and commercial rent for property occupied; or
(F) any reasonable and necessary remuneration for services rendered (other than secretarial or managerial services, or those rendered by the payer) which is taken into account in computing the recipient's trading profits.

A *'related person'* is any company of which the individual or an associate is a director and which is a subsidiary or partner of the issuing company, or a partner of the issuing company or a subsidiary, or any person connected (within *ITA 2007, s 993* — see **19** CONNECTED PERSONS) with such a company; 'subsidiary' for this purpose requiring ownership of more than 50% of ordinary share capital at some time in the specified period.

For these purposes (and those below), in the case of a person who is both a director and an employee of a company, references to him in his capacity as a director include him in his capacity as an employee, but otherwise he is not treated as an employee.

An individual who is connected with the issuing company may nevertheless qualify for relief if he is so connected only by reason of his (or his associate's) being a director of (or of a partner of) the issuing company or any subsidiary receiving, or entitled to receive, remuneration (including any benefit or facility) as such, provided that:

(I) the remuneration (leaving out any within (F) above) is reasonable remuneration for services rendered to the company as a director;

(II) he subscribed for shares in the company meeting the general requirements at **29.27** *et seq.* above at a time when he had never been either:
- (i) connected with the issuing company; or
- (ii) involved (as sole trader, employee, partner or director) in carrying on its (or its subsidiary's) trade, business or profession (or any part thereof).

Where these conditions are satisfied in relation to an issue of shares, subsequent issues are treated as fulfilling (II) where they would not otherwise do so, provided that they are made within three years of the date of the last issue which did fulfil (II). Where relevant, the said three-year period is replaced by a longer period beginning with the date of the last such issue and ending with the date of commencement of the intended trade referred to in **29.58**(a) below. (In determining for these purposes the time at which a qualifying trade begins to be carried on by any 'qualifying 90% subsidiary' (see **29.57** below) of a company, any carrying on of the trade by it before it became such a subsidiary is disregarded.)

[*ITA 2007, ss 167(3), 168, 169, 256*].

The 'no linked loans' requirement

[29.43] No loan may be made to the investor or to an associate (see **29.42** above) at any time in period A (as in **29.11** above) if it would not have been made, or would not have been made on the same terms, if the investor had not subscribed, or had not been proposing to subscribe, for the shares. The giving of credit to, or the assignment of a debt due from, the investor or associate is counted as a loan for these purposes. [*ITA 2007, s 164*].

The test under this requirement is whether the lender makes the loan on terms which are connected with the fact that the borrower (or an associate) is subscribing for the shares. The prime concern is why the lender made the loan rather than why the borrower applied for it. The requirement would be met, for example, in the case of a bank loan if the bank would have made a loan on the same terms to a similar borrower for a different purpose. But if, for example, a loan is made specifically on a security consisting of or including the shares (other than as part of a broad range of assets to which the lender has recourse), the requirement would not be met. Relevant features of the loan terms would be the qualifying conditions to be satisfied by the borrower, any incentives or benefits offered to the borrower, the time allowed for repayment, the amount of repayments and interest charged, the timing of interest payments, and the nature of the security. (HMRC SP 6/98).

The 'existing shareholdings' requirement

[29.44] Shares subscribed for by an individual in a company in which he already holds shares are not eligible for EIS relief unless those other shares are a 'risk-finance investment'. The same applies if the pre-existing shareholding is in a qualifying subsidiary of the company (see **29.56** below). There is a let-out in certain cases where the pre-existing shares are subscriber shares. Shares are a '*risk-finance investment*' if they were issued by the company to the individual under the EIS, SEED ENTERPRISE INVESTMENT SCHEME (**66**) or SOCIAL INVESTMENT TAX RELIEF (**72**) scheme. [*ITA 2007, s 164A*].

The 'no tax avoidance' requirement

[29.45] The shares must be subscribed for by the investor for genuine commercial reasons and not as part of a scheme or arrangement a main purpose of which is the avoidance of tax. [*ITA 2007, s 165*].

Qualifying company

[29.46] The issuing company is a '*qualifying company*' in relation to the shares if the requirements at **29.47–29.55** below are met. The company may be resident in the UK or elsewhere.

'*Period B*' for these purposes is the period beginning with the date of issue of the shares and ending either three years after that date or, where **29.58**(a) below applies and the company (or subsidiary) was not carrying on the qualifying trade on that date, three years after the date on which it begins to carry on the trade. In determining for these purposes the time at which a qualifying trade begins to be carried on by any 'qualifying 90% subsidiary' (see **29.57** below) of a company, any carrying on of the trade by it before it became such a subsidiary is disregarded. [*ITA 2007, s 159(3)*].

Simon's Taxes. See E3.126–E3.137.

The UK permanent establishment requirement

[29.47] The requirement is that the issuing company has a 'permanent establishment' in the UK. The company must meet this requirement throughout period B (as in **29.46** above).

For the above purpose, a company has a '*permanent establishment*' in the UK if (and only if):

- it has a fixed place of business in the UK through which the business of the company is wholly or partly carried on; or
- an agent acting on behalf of the company has the authority to enter into contracts on behalf of the company and habitually exercises that authority in the UK.

The activities carried on at the fixed place of business or carried on in the UK by the agent must, in relation to the company's business as a whole, be more than simply activities of a preparatory or auxiliary character. Examples of such preparatory/auxiliary activities are given at *ITA 2007, s 191A(6)* and include storage.

A company is not regarded as having a permanent establishment in the UK simply because:

- it carries on business in the UK through an independent agent (including a broker or a general commission agent) acting in the ordinary course of his business; or
- it controls a UK resident company or a company carrying on business in the UK (whether or not through a permanent establishment).

[*ITA 2007, ss 180A, 191A, 257(1)*].

The financial health requirement

[29.48] This requirement must be met at the beginning of period B (as in **29.46** above). The requirement is that the issuing company is not 'in difficulty'. A company is '*in difficulty*' if it is reasonable to assume that it would be regarded as a firm in difficulty for the purposes of the *EU Guidelines on State Aid for Rescuing and Restructuring Firms in Difficulty (2004/C 244/02)*. [*ITA 2007, ss 180B, 257(1)*].

The trading requirement

[29.49] The company must, throughout period B (as in **29.46** above), either:

(a) exist wholly for the purpose of carrying on one or more 'qualifying trades' (see **29.59** below) (disregarding purposes having no significant effect on the extent of its activities); or

(b) be a '*parent company*' (i.e. a company that has one or more 'qualifying subsidiaries' (see **29.56** below)) and the business of the '*group*' (i.e. the company and its qualifying subsidiaries) must not consist wholly or as to a substantial part (i.e. generally more than 20% — see HMRC Venture Capital Schemes Manual VCM3010) in the carrying on of 'non-qualifying activities'.

Where the company intends that one or more other companies should become its qualifying subsidiaries with a view to their carrying on one or more qualifying trades, then, until any time after which the intention is abandoned, the company is treated as a parent company and those other companies are included in the group for the purposes of (b) above.

For the purpose of (b) above, the business of the group means what would be the business of the group if the activities of the group companies taken together were regarded as one business. Activities are for this purpose disregarded to the extent that they consist in:

(i) holding shares in or securities of any of the company's subsidiaries;
(ii) making loans to another group company;
(iii) holding and managing property used by a group company for the purposes of a qualifying trade or trades carried on by any group company; or
(iv) holding and managing property used by a group company for the purposes of research and development from which it is intended either that a qualifying trade to be carried on by a group company will be derived or that a qualifying trade carried on or to be carried on by a group company will benefit.

References in (iv) above to a group company include references to any existing or future company which will be a group company at any future time.

Activities are similarly disregarded to the extent that they consist, in the case of a subsidiary whose main purpose is the carrying on of qualifying trade(s) and whose other purposes have no significant effect on the extent of its activities (other than in relation to incidental matters), in activities not in pursuance of its main purpose.

For the ascertainment of the purposes for which a company exists, see HMRC Venture Capital Schemes Manual VCM13050.

Non-qualifying activities

'*Non-qualifying activities*' are:

- excluded activities within **29.59**; and
- non-trading activities (not including research and development — see **29.58** below).

[*ITA 2007, ss 181, 257(1)*].

In *East Allenheads Estate Ltd v HMRC* FTT (TC 4513), [2015] UKFTT 328 (TC), [2015] SFTD 908, the company failed the trading requirement because it was held to exist for the purpose of conferring a personal benefit on its sole investor in the form of lavish improvements to real estate.

Winding-up etc.

Although a winding-up or dissolution in period B generally prevents a company meeting the above conditions, they are deemed met if the winding-up or dissolution is for genuine commercial reasons and not part of a scheme a main purpose of which is tax avoidance. A company does not cease to meet the above conditions by reason of anything done as a consequence of its being in administration or receivership (both as defined by *ITA 2007, s 252*), provided everything so done and the making of the relevant order are for genuine commercial (and not tax avoidance) reasons. These provisions are extended to refer also to the winding-up, dissolution, administration or receivership of any of the company's subsidiaries. [*ITA 2007, s 182*].

The 'issuing company to carry on the qualifying business activity' requirement

[29.50] At no time in period B (as in **29.46** above) must any of the following be carried on by a person other than the issuing company' or a 'qualifying 90% subsidiary' (see **29.57** below) of that company:

- the '*relevant qualifying trade*', i.e. the 'qualifying trade' which is the subject of the 'qualifying business activity' referred to in **29.34** above;
- '*relevant preparation work*', i.e. preparations to carry on a 'qualifying trade' where such preparations are the subject of that qualifying business activity (see **29.58**(a) below);
- research and development which is the subject of that qualifying business activity (see **29.58**(b) below); and
- any other preparations for the carrying on of the qualifying trade.

Where relevant preparation work is carried on by the issuing company or a qualifying 90% subsidiary, the carrying on of the relevant 'qualifying trade' by a company other than the issuing company or one of its subsidiaries is disregarded for these purposes if it occurs before the issuing company or a qualifying 90% subsidiary carries on that trade.

The requirement is not regarded as failing to be met if, by reason only of a company being wound up or dissolved or being in administration or receivership (both as defined by *ITA 2007, s 252*), the relevant qualifying trade ceases to be carried on in period B by the issuing company or any qualifying 90% subsidiary and is subsequently carried on by a person who is not connected (within **19** CONNECTED PERSONS) with the company at any time in 'period C'. This let-out applies only if the winding-up, dissolution or entry into administration or receivership (and everything done as a consequence of the company being in administration or receivership) is for genuine commercial reasons and not part of a tax avoidance scheme or arrangements.

'*Period C*' is the period beginning one year before the issue of eligible shares and ending immediately before the third anniversary of the issue date or, if later and where relevant, the third anniversary of the date of commencement of the intended trade referred to in **29.58**(a) below. In determining for these purposes the time at which a qualifying trade begins to be carried on by any qualifying 90% subsidiary (see **29.57** below) of a company, any carrying on of the trade by it before it became such a subsidiary is disregarded.

[*ITA 2007, ss 159(4), 183*].

Partnerships

HMRC consider that the above requirement is not met where the relevant qualifying trade, preparation work or research and development is carried on by the company in partnership or by a limited liability partnership (LLP) of which the company is a member. This is because where any of these activities are carried on in partnership or by an LLP, there are persons other than the issuing company or a qualifying 90% subsidiary carrying on the activity. (HMRC Brief 77/09, 16 December 2009).

Film and television co-productions

HMRC are of the view that co-productions in film and television will fail to meet the above requirement as the film or programme will have been produced by the activities of more than one party (HMRC Notice, 13 March 2014).

The 'unquoted status' requirement

[29.51] The issuing company must be 'unquoted' when the shares are issued and no arrangements must then exist for it to cease to be unquoted. If, at the time of issue, arrangements exist for the company to become a wholly-owned subsidiary of a new holding company by means of a share exchange within **29.22** above, no arrangements must exist for the new company to cease to be unquoted. A company is '*unquoted*' if none of its shares etc. are listed on a recognised stock exchange or on a foreign exchange designated for the purpose, or dealt in outside the UK by such means as may be designated for the purpose. The Alternative Investment Market (AIM) and the PLUS Markets (with the exception of PLUS-listed) are not considered to be recognised exchanges for this purpose (www.gov.uk/government/publications/the-enterprise-investment-scheme-introduction/enterprise-investment-scheme).

[*ITA 2007, ss 184, 989, 1005*].

The control and independence requirement

[29.52] The issuing company must not at any time in period B (as in **29.46** above) either:

(a) (subject to **29.22** above) control another company other than a qualifying subsidiary (see **29.56** below), 'control' being construed in accordance with *CTA 2010, ss 450, 451* and being considered with or without CONNECTED PERSONS (**19**); or

(b) (subject to **29.22** above) be a 51% subsidiary of another company or otherwise under the control of another company, 'control' being construed in accordance with *ITA 2007, s 995* and again being considered with or without connected persons; or

(c) be capable of falling within (a) or (b) by virtue of any arrangements (as broadly defined).

[*ITA 2007, ss 185, 257(1)(3)*].

The gross assets requirement

[29.53] The value of the issuing company's gross assets must not exceed £15 million immediately before the issue of EIS shares and must not exceed £16 million immediately afterwards. If the issuing company is a parent company, the gross assets test applies by reference to the aggregate gross assets of the company and all its qualifying subsidiaries (disregarding certain assets held by any such company which correspond to liabilities of another). [*ITA 2007, s 186, Sch 2 para 58*].

The general approach of HMRC to the gross assets requirement is that the value of a company's gross assets is the sum of the value of all of the balance sheet assets. Where accounts are actually drawn up to a date immediately before or after the issue, the balance sheet values are taken provided that they reflect usual accounting standards and the company's normal accounting practice, consistently applied. Where accounts are not drawn up to such a date, such values will be taken from the most recent balance sheet, updated as precisely as practicable on the basis of all the relevant information available to the company. Values so arrived at may need to be reviewed in the light of information contained in the accounts for the period in which the issue was made, and, if they were not available at the time of the issue, those for the preceding period, when they become available. The company's assets immediately before the issue do not include any advance payment received in respect of the issue. Where shares are issued partly paid, the right to the balance is an asset, and, notwithstanding the above, will be taken into account in valuing the assets immediately after the issue regardless of whether it is shown in the balance sheet. (HMRC SP 2/06).

The 'number of employees' requirement

[29.54] The issuing company must have fewer than the equivalent of 250 full-time employees when the EIS shares are issued. The limit is doubled to 500 if the issuing company is a 'knowledge-intensive company' (see **29.32** above) at the time the shares are issued. If the company is a parent company (see **29.49**(b) above), the 'number of employees' requirement applies by reference to the aggregate number of full-time employees of the company and its qualifying subsidiaries (see **29.56** below). To ascertain the equivalent number of full-time employees of a company, take the actual number of full-time employees and add to it a just and reasonable fraction for each employee who is not full-time. For this purpose, an 'employee' includes a director but does not include anyone on maternity, paternity, shared parental or parental bereavement leave or a student on vocational training. [*ITA 2007, s 186A; Parental Bereavement (Leave and Pay) Act 2018, Sch para 51; SI 2020 No 45, Reg 2*].

The subsidiaries requirements

[29.55] At all times in period B (as in **29.46** above) any subsidiary of the issuing company must be a 'qualifying subsidiary' (see **29.56** below). [*ITA 2007, s 187*].

The company must not at any time in period B have a 'property managing subsidiary' which is not a 'qualifying 90% subsidiary' (see **29.57** below) of the company. A '*property managing subsidiary*' is a subsidiary whose business consists wholly or mainly in the holding or managing of land or any 'property deriving its value from land'. For this purpose, '*property deriving its value from land*' includes any shareholding in a company, and any partnership interest or interest in settled property, which derives its value directly or indirectly from land and any option, consent or embargo affecting the disposition of land. [*ITA 2007, s 188*].

Qualifying subsidiaries

[29.56] In order to be a '*qualifying subsidiary*' a subsidiary must be a '51% subsidiary' (within *CTA 2010, Pt 24 Ch 3*) of the qualifying company and no person other than the qualifying company or another of its subsidiaries may have control (within *ITA 2007, s 995*) of the subsidiary. Furthermore, no arrangements (as broadly defined) may exist by virtue of which either of these conditions would cease to be satisfied.

However, the above conditions are not regarded as ceasing to be satisfied by reason only of the subsidiary or any other company being wound up or dissolved or by reason only of anything done as a consequence of any such company being in administration or receivership (both as defined by *ITA 2007, s 252*), provided the winding-up, dissolution, entry into administration or receivership or anything done as a consequence of its being in administration or receivership is for genuine commercial reasons and is not part of a tax avoidance scheme or arrangements. Also, the above conditions are not regarded as ceasing to be satisfied by reason only of arrangements being in existence for the disposal of the interest in the subsidiary held by the qualifying company (or, as the case may be, by another of its subsidiaries) if the disposal is to be for genuine commercial reasons and is not to be part of a tax avoidance scheme or arrangements.

[*ITA 2007, ss 191, 257(1), 989*].

A company limited by guarantee, and thus with no share capital, cannot be a qualifying subsidiary (*Hunters Property plc v HMRC* FTT (TC 6354), [2018] UKFTT 96 (TC), [2018] SFTD 910).

Simon's Taxes. See E3.135.

Qualifying 90% subsidiaries

[29.57] A company (the subsidiary) is a '*qualifying 90% subsidiary*' of another company (the relevant company) if:

- the relevant company possesses at least 90% of both the issued share capital of, and the voting power in, the subsidiary;
- the relevant company would be beneficially entitled to at least 90% of the assets of the subsidiary available for distribution to equity holders on a winding-up or in any other circumstances;
- the relevant company is beneficially entitled to at least 90% of any profits of the subsidiary available for distribution to equity holders;
- no person other than the relevant company has control (within *ITA 2007, s 995*) of the subsidiary; and
- no arrangements (as broadly defined) exist by virtue of which any of the above conditions would cease to be met.

For the above purposes, *CTA 2010, Pt 5 Ch 6* applies, with appropriate modifications, to determine the persons who are equity holders and the percentage of assets available to them.

The above conditions are not regarded as ceasing to be satisfied by reason only of the subsidiary or any other company being wound up or dissolved or by reason only of anything done as a consequence of any such company being in administration or receivership (both as defined by *ITA 2007, s 252*), provided the winding-up, dissolution, entry into administration or receivership or anything done as a consequence of its being in administration or receivership is for genuine commercial reasons and is not part of a tax avoidance scheme or arrangements. Also, the above conditions are not regarded as ceasing to be satisfied by reason only of arrangements being in existence for the disposal of the relevant company's interest in the subsidiary if the disposal is to be for genuine commercial reasons and is not to be part of a tax avoidance scheme or arrangements.

A company ('company A') which is a subsidiary of company B is a qualifying 90% subsidiary of company C if:

- company A is a qualifying 90% subsidiary of company B, and company B is a 'qualifying 100% subsidiary' of company C; or
- company A is a 'qualifying 100% subsidiary' of company B, and company B is a qualifying 90% subsidiary of company C.

For this purpose, no account is to be taken of any control company C may have of company A, and '*qualifying 100% subsidiary*' is defined similarly to 'qualifying 90% subsidiary' above but substituting '100%' for '90%'.

[*ITA 2007, ss 190, 257(1)*].

Simon's Taxes. See **E3.136.**

Qualifying business activity

[29.58] Either of the following is a '*qualifying business activity*' in relation to the issuing company.

(a) The issuing company or any 'qualifying 90% subsidiary' (see **29.57** above) (i) carrying on a 'qualifying trade' which, on the date of issue of the shares, the company or any such subsidiary is carrying on or (ii) preparing to carry on such a trade which, on the date of issue of the shares, is intended to be carried on by the company or any such subsidiary and which is begun to be carried on within two years after that date or (iii) actually carrying on the trade mentioned in (ii) above.

(b) The issuing company or any 'qualifying 90% subsidiary' (see **29.57** above) carrying on 'research and development' which, on the date of issue of the shares, the company or any such subsidiary is carrying on or which company or any such subsidiary begins to carry on immediately afterwards, and from which it is intended on that date that a 'qualifying trade' which the company or any such subsidiary will carry on will benefit.

In determining for the purposes of (a) and (b) above the time at which a qualifying trade or research and development begins to be carried on by a qualifying 90% subsidiary of the issuing company, any carrying on of the trade etc. by it before it became such a subsidiary is disregarded. References in (a) and (b) above to a qualifying 90% subsidiary include, in cases where the qualifying trade is not carried on at the time of issue of the shares, references to any existing or future company which will be such a subsidiary at any future time.

'*Research and development*' in (b) above has the meaning given by *ITA 2007, s 1006* (see **75.113** TRADING INCOME).

[*ITA 2007, ss 179, 257(1)*].

In the particular case of a ship chartering trade, the test is satisfied if all charters are entered into in the UK and the provision of crews and management of the ships while under charter take place mainly in the UK. If these conditions are not met, the test may still be satisfied depending on all the relevant facts and circumstances. (HMRC SP 3/00).

For the manner in which the scheme operates where a company wishes to raise money by a single issue of shares either partly for preparing to carry on a trade and partly for the subsequent carrying on of that trade, or for more than one qualifying business activity (e.g. for a trade carried on by one subsidiary and for research and development carried on by another), see Revenue Tax Bulletin April 1996 pp 305, 306.

Simon's Taxes. See **E3.141, E3.143.**

Qualifying trade

[29.59] A trade is a '*qualifying trade*' if it is conducted on a commercial basis with a view to the realisation of profits and it does not, at any time in period B (as in **29.46** above), consist to a substantial extent in the carrying on of 'excluded activities'. For these purposes, 'trade' (except in relation to the trade mentioned in (q) below) does not include a venture in the nature of trade. '*Excluded activities*' are:

(a) dealing in land, commodities or futures, or in shares, securities or other financial instruments;
(b) dealing in goods otherwise than in an ordinary trade of wholesale or retail distribution (see below);
(c) banking, insurance or any other financial activities;
(d) leasing or letting or receiving royalties or licence fees;
(e) providing legal or accountancy services;
(f) 'property development';
(g) farming or market gardening;
(h) holding, managing or occupying woodlands, any other forestry activities or timber production;
(i) shipbuilding (defined by reference to relevant EU State aid rules);
(j) producing coal or steel (both defined by reference to relevant EU State aid rules and including the extraction of coal);
(k) operating or managing hotels or comparable establishments (i.e. guest houses, hostels and other establishments whose main purpose is to offer overnight accommodation with or without catering) or property used as such;
(l) operating or managing nursing homes or residential care homes (both as defined) or property used as such;
(m) generating or exporting electricity or making electricity generating capacity available;
(n) generating heat;

(o) generating any form of energy not within (m) or (n);
(p) producing gas or fuel;
(q) providing services or facilities for any business consisting of activities within any of (a) to (p) and carried on by another person (other than a parent company), where one person has a 'controlling interest' in both that business and the business carried on by the provider.

HMRC regard as 'substantial' for the above purposes a part of a trade which consists of 20% or more of total activities, judged by any reasonable measure (normally turnover or capital employed) (HMRC Venture Capital Schemes Manual VCM3010). As regards (a) above, dealing in land includes cases where steps are taken, before selling the land, to make it more attractive to a purchaser; such steps might include the refurbishment of existing buildings (HMRC Venture Capital Schemes Manual VCM3020).

As regards (b) above, a trade of wholesale distribution is a trade consisting of the offer of goods for sale either to persons for resale (or processing and resale) (which resale must be to members of the general public for their use or consumption) by them. A trade of retail distribution is a trade in which goods are offered or exposed for sale and sold to members of the general public for their use or consumption. A trade is not an ordinary wholesale or retail trade if it consists to a substantial extent of dealing in goods collected or held as an investment (or of that and any other activity within (a)–(o) above), and a substantial proportion of such goods is held for a significantly longer period than would reasonably be expected for a vendor trying to dispose of them at market value. Whether such trades are 'ordinary' is to be judged having regard to the following features, those under (A) supporting the categorisation as 'ordinary', those under (B) being indicative to the contrary.

(i) The breaking of bulk.
(ii) The purchase and sale of goods in different markets.
(iii) The employment of staff and incurring of trade expenses other than the cost of goods or of remuneration of persons connected (within **19** CONNECTED PERSONS) with a company carrying on such a trade.
(i) The purchase or sale of goods from or to persons connected (within **19** CONNECTED PERSONS) with the trader.
(ii) The matching of purchases with sales.
(iii) The holding of goods for longer than would normally be expected.
(iv) The carrying on of the trade at a place not commonly used for wholesale or retail trading.
(v) The absence of physical possession of the goods by the trader.

As regards the application of (d) above, a trade is not excluded from being a qualifying trade solely because at some time in period B it consists to a substantial extent in the receiving of royalties or licence fees substantially attributable (in terms of value) to the exploitation of 'relevant intangible assets'. An intangible asset is an asset falling to be treated as such under generally accepted accounting practice (see **75.21** TRADING INCOME), including all intellectual property and also industrial information and techniques (see HMRC Venture Capital Schemes Manual VCM3060). A '*relevant intangible* *asset*' is an intangible asset the whole or greater part of which (in terms of value) has been created by the issuing company or by a company which was a 'qualifying subsidiary' (within **29.56** above) of the issuing company throughout the period during which it created the whole or greater part of the asset. The definition also includes an intangible asset the whole or greater part of which was created by a company when it was not a qualifying subsidiary of the issuing company, provided it subsequently became a qualifying subsidiary under a particular type of company reconstruction. Where the asset is 'intellectual property', it is treated as created by a company only if the right to exploit it vests in that company (alone or with others). The term '*intellectual property*' incorporates patents, trade marks, copyrights, design rights, etc. and foreign equivalents.

Also as regards (d) above, a trade will not be excluded by reason only of its consisting of letting ships, other than offshore installations (previously oil rigs) or pleasure craft (as defined), on charter, provided that:

(i) the company beneficially owns all the ships it so lets;
(ii) every ship beneficially owned by the company is UK-registered;
(iii) throughout period B, the company is solely responsible for arranging the marketing of the services of its ships; and
(iv) in relation to every letting on charter, certain conditions as to length and terms of charter, and the arm's length character of the transaction, are fulfilled,

and if any of (i)–(iv) above is not fulfilled in relation to certain lettings, the trade is not thereby excluded if those lettings and any other excluded activities taken together do not amount to a substantial part of the trade.

In relation to (d) above, in the Revenue Tax Bulletin August 2001 pp 877, 878, the Inland Revenue set out their views on the scope of the exclusions. The *leasing and letting* exclusion covers all cases where (subject to reasonable conditions imposed by the trader) the customer is free to use the property for the purpose for which it is intended, e.g. television rental, video hire and the provision of self-storage warehousing facilities. In the case of car hire, a distinction has to be drawn between the provision of a *transportation service* and that of a *transportation facility*, only the latter falling within the exclusion. A taxi service would usually fall within the former category, a chauffeured car hire within the latter. *Royalties and licence fees* are received where property rights are exploited by the granting of permission to others to make use of the property. There will, however, be cases (e.g. the retailing of CDs) where, although the sales are made under licence, the receipts are nevertheless consideration for the supply of goods. In the case of *licence fees*, the grant of the right to use the property is often incidental to the supply of services (e.g. a cinema ticket), and the exclusion does not apply in such cases. The principle can be illustrated in relation to sports and leisure facilities provision. Simply making sports facilities available to the general public, with no service provision, would involve the receipt of licence fees. In the more commonly encountered activity of a health club providing a high level of services, including active supervision and advice from qualified staff, the licence to enter the premises and use the equipment would be merely incidental. Similarly where, although there is no direct provision of services, continuous work is required to keep the property in a fit state for use, the question to be considered is the extent to which the fees relate to the cost of such work.

In *Optos plc v HMRC* (Sp C 560), [2006] SSCD 687, the Sp C, in finding for the appellant company on this point, took the view that for these purposes the term 'leasing' should be construed to connote essentially a passive activity where consideration was charged for the use of an asset as opposed to the provision of services.

As regards (e) above, the provision of the services of accountancy personnel is the provision of accountancy services (*Castleton Management Services Ltd v Kirkwood* (Sp C 276), [2001] SSCD 95).

'*Property development*' in (f) above means the development of land by a company, which has (or has had at any time) an 'interest in the land' (as defined), with the sole or main object of realising a gain from the disposal of an interest in the developed land.

The exclusion for farming in (g) above applies to both UK and overseas farming.

Exclusions (k) and (l) above apply only if the person carrying on the activity in question has an estate or interest (e.g. a lease) in the property concerned or occupies that property.

As regards (q) above, a person has a '*controlling interest*' in a business carried on by a company if he controls (within *CTA 2010, ss 450, 451*) the company; or if the company is a close company and he or an 'associate' is a director of the company and the owner of, or able to control, more than 30% of its ordinary share capital; or if at least half of its ordinary share capital is directly or indirectly owned by him. In any other case it is obtained by his being entitled to at least half of the assets used for, or income arising from, the business. In either case, the rights and powers of a person's 'associates' are attributed to him. An '*associate*' of any person is any 'relative' (i.e. spouse, civil partner, ancestor or linear descendant) of that person, the trustee(s) of any settlement in relation to which that person or any relative (living or dead) is or was a settlor and, where that person has an interest in any shares or obligations of a company which are subject to any trust or are part of a deceased estate, the trustee(s) of the settlement or the personal representatives of the deceased and, if that person is a company, any other company which has an interest in those shares or obligations. For this purpose, 'settlor' is defined as in **70.3** SETTLEMENTS.

[*ITA 2007, ss 189, 192–196, 196A–196C, 197, 198, 198A, 198B, 199, 253, 257(3), 996(7); FA 2016, s 28(1)(3)(5)*].

Simon's Taxes. See **E3.142, E3.145–E3.149.**

30

Exempt Income

Cross-references. See **16.6** CLAIMS for repayment of tax suffered; **28.56** EMPLOYMENT INCOME for bonuses from indirectly employee-owned companies; **31** EXEMPT ORGANISATIONS; **33** FOSTER CARE ETC; **56.4**, **56.5** PENSION INCOME; **60.22** PROPERTY INCOME for rent-a-room relief; **65.23** SAVINGS AND INVESTMENT INCOME for exemption of capital portion of purchased life annuities; **70.36** SETTLEMENTS — re heritage maintenance settlements.

Introduction to exempt income

[30.1] The following income is exempt from income tax (to the extent and in the circumstances stated, where appropriate) and any tax suffered may be reclaimed. The paragraphs are arranged in alphabetical order.

Adopters and qualifying guardians, financial support to

[30.2] Financial support paid by local authorities and adoption agencies to adopters or potential adopters, to assist towards the extra costs faced when adopting, or seeking to adopt, a child, is exempted from income tax. The legislation lists the specific types of payment and reward within the exemption, by reference to *Adoption Act 1976* (and Scottish and NI equivalents) and *Adoption and Children Act 2002* (and to regulations under those Acts), and these extend to payment of legal and medical expenses in certain cases. The Treasury is given power to amend the list by order to take account of any future changes in the description of financial support payments. Adoption allowances paid under the *Adoption Allowance Regulations 1991* (and Scottish equivalent) are included in this exemption. The exemption is extended to 'qualifying payments' to 'qualifying guardians'.

'*Qualifying guardians*' are individuals who care for one or more children placed with them under:

- a special guardianship order; or
- a residence order where the individual is not the child's parent or step-parent.

'*Qualifying payments*' are payments by the child's parents or by, or on behalf of, a local authority which are made in relation to a special guardianship order or a residence order.

[*ITTOIA 2005, ss 744–747*].

Simon's Taxes. See E1.555.

Annual payments made by individuals

[30.3] An annual payment arising in the UK, made by an individual (or an individual's personal representatives) or by a Scottish partnership in which at least one partner is an individual, does not form part of the taxable income of the person to whom it is made or of any other person. This rule also applies to payments treated as income of the payer under *ITTOIA 2005, ss 624–628* or *ss 629–632* (see **70.25–70.30** SETTLEMENTS). Excluded from this rule are payments made for commercial reasons in connection with the payer's trade, profession or vocation and, subject to certain exceptions, payments for non-taxable consideration (see **4.42** ANTI-AVOIDANCE). Interest is also effectively excluded, as it is taxable as in **65.2** SAVINGS AND INVESTMENT INCOME.

As a result of the above, maintenance payments do not form part of the recipient's income for tax purposes; see also **48.9** MARRIED PERSONS AND CIVIL PARTNERS. A maintenance payment (as defined) arising outside the UK is similarly exempt if it would have been exempt had it arisen in the UK.

[*ITTOIA 2005, ss 727–730, Sch 2 para 146*].

Simon's Taxes. See **E1.510.**

Apprenticeship bursaries paid to care leavers

[30.4] For 2020/21 onwards, no liability to income tax arises in respect of a 'care leaver's apprenticeship bursary payment'. Subject to any conditions that may be imposed by the Treasury in regulations, a '*care leaver's apprenticeship bursary payment*' is a payment made out of public revenue to a 'care leaver' in connection with that person's employment as an 'apprentice'. The meaning of '*apprentice*' is to be prescribed by Treasury regulations. A '*care leaver*' is a person who is, or was previously, a child looked after by a 'local authority' (within the meaning given by specified primary legislation applicable to the different parts of the UK). [*ITEPA 2003, s 254A; FA 2020, s 11*].

These are one-off £1,000 bursaries paid since 2018 by the Education and Skills Funding Agency (ESFA) to care leavers aged between 16 and 24 who enter an apprenticeship. In the absence of an exemption, such a payment would fall within the general charge to tax on employment income as it derives from employment. For payments already made by ESFA to care leavers before the statutory exemption takes effect, HMRC will use their discretionary collection and management powers to forgo the collection of tax on those payments (www.gov.uk/government/publications/income-tax-and-national-insurance-exemptions-for-bursary-payments-to-care-leavers).

In prescribing additional conditions relating to the definition of a care leaver's apprenticeship bursary payment, the Treasury intend to make reference to the ESFA's funding rules guidance document (letter from the Financial Secretary to the Treasury to the Public Bill Committee, regarding the 2020

Finance Bill clauses that introduce the power to make secondary legislation, at www.gov.uk/government/publications/finance-bill-2020-public-bill-committe e).

Armed forces — accommodation allowances

[30.5] No liability to income tax arises in respect of payments of accommodation allowances to (or in respect of) members of UK armed forces. An accommodation allowance is for these purposes an allowance payable out of public revenue for, or towards, costs of accommodation. The exemption applies only to allowances in respect of which conditions specified in Treasury regulations are met. The exemption has effect in relation to payments made on or after 23 July 2019. The conditions specified are that the allowance is payable by the Ministry of Defence in accordance with the JSP, and is a payment to compensate a member of the armed forces in respect of the cost of rent, mortgage repayments or council tax (to the extent that the cost of council tax is above the national average) or costs incurred in connection with sourcing and signing a tenancy agreement. The JSP is a document (Joint Service Publication 464) published by the Ministry on 31 May 2019. [*ITEPA 2003, s 297D; FA 2018, s 8; SI 2019 Nos 1007, 1160*]. The intention is to allow members of the armed forces to give up their pre-existing entitlement to accommodation in exchange for an allowance to be used to rent or maintain accommodation in the private sector.

Armed forces — Continuity of Education Allowance

[30.6] No liability to income tax arises in respect of payments of the Continuity of Education Allowance (CEA) to, or in respect of, serving and deceased members of the UK armed forces. Previously, CEA was liable to tax as employment income when paid to recipients based in the UK but the tax was paid by the Ministry of Defence on their behalf. The CEA is paid to service personnel to provide a continuity of education for their children that would not otherwise be possible if the children accompanied their parents on frequent assignments at home and overseas. [*ITEPA 2003, s 297C*].

Armed forces — Council Tax Relief payments

[30.7] No liability to income tax arises in respect of payments of Council Tax Relief to members of the UK armed forces. [*ITEPA 2003, s 297B*].

Armed forces — Operational Allowance

[30.8] No liability to income tax arises in respect of payments of the Operational Allowance to members of the UK armed forces. The Operational Allowance is paid to members of the armed forces serving in designated combat zones. [*ITEPA 2003, s 297A*].

Armed forces — training allowances etc.

[30.9] Training allowances and bounties for reserve and auxiliary forces are generally exempt, as are armed forces' **food, drink and mess allowances.** [*ITEPA 2003, ss 297, 298*]. Civil Defence Corps bounties are not exempt because these are paid by local authorities and therefore not 'out of the public revenue' (*Lush v Coles* Ch D 1967, 44 TC 169).

Asbestos compensation settlements

[30.10] The trustees of an 'asbestos compensation settlement' are not liable to income tax in respect of the trust income. An '*asbestos compensation settlement*' is a trust set up before 24 March 2010 as part of an arrangement made by a company with its creditors, specifically to pay compensation to, or in respect of, individuals with asbestos-related conditions, e.g. asbestosis. [*ITA 2007, s 838A*].

Bravery awards

[30.11] Pensions and annuities are exempt if paid to holders of certain awards for bravery in respect of the award (see **56.4**(e) PENSION INCOME).

Child Trust Funds

[30.12] Contributions to Child Trust Funds (CTFs) of up to **£9,000** per year (£4,368 before 6 April 2020, £4,260 before 6 April 2019, £4,128 before 6 April 2018, £4,080 before 6 April 2017) are permitted. Broadly (see below for more details), there is no tax on the income or gains of a CTF. Similarly, there are no tax charges when the fund matures on the child's 18th birthday. Contributions to CTFs used to be made by the Government also, but this ceased in 2010/11. No CTFs can be opened for children born after 2 January 2011. All the savings in a CTF can be transferred to a junior ISA (see **30.31** below) for the child in question, with the CTF then being closed.

At any time, only one 'responsible person' (broadly a person with parental responsibility) is able to instruct the account provider as to the management of the CTF account. This person is designated the '*registered contact*'. The child itself can apply to be the registered contact if aged 16 or over. There is provision for the Government to appoint someone (from 1 October 2017, the Share Foundation) to manage the CTF accounts of looked after children (broadly children under the care or supervision of a local authority).

Accounts may be of two types: stakeholder accounts and non-stakeholder accounts. Stakeholder accounts are subject to stringent rules about the charges that may be deducted from them, and have a more restricted range of permissible investments and investment strategies (see below).

Contributions to the account

Anyone (including the child) may make payments into the CTF. However, there is a limit of £9,000 (£4,368 before 6 April 2020, £4,260 before 6 April 2019, £4,128 before 6 April 2018, £4,080 before 6 April 2017) for such contributions in any one year (the 'subscription year'). A '*subscription year*' is the period from the opening of the account to the child's next birthday, and each succeeding period of twelve months. Thus, for example, a child whose birthday is 1 October has a subscription year that runs to 30 September in each year.

Withdrawals from the account

Withdrawals from the account are not permitted before the child reaches the age of 18. There are three exceptions to this. The first is that the account provider is allowed to make deductions in respect of management charges and incidental expenses. The second is where the child is terminally ill, and the third is where the child dies before reaching 18.

All the savings in a CTF can be transferred to a junior ISA for the child in question, with the CTF then being closed. The transfer must be free of expenses, except for incidentals. Savings thus transferred do not count towards the junior ISA subscription limit.

The investments under a CTF are inalienable — any charge over them, or assignment of them is void. If the child is made bankrupt, creditors may not gain access to the account.

Qualifying investments

Qualifying investments for CTFs are as follows.

(a) Shares issued by a company (other than an investment trust, but see (e) below) wherever incorporated. The shares must be officially listed on a recognised stock exchange or admitted to trading on a recognised stock exchange in the EEA. There are rules to allow the official listing (or admission to trading) condition to be treated as satisfied in the case of shares issued under a public offer and due to be listed (or admitted); however, shares do not qualify if they have been acquired on favourable terms because of a connection with the allocation or allotment of other shares, securities or rights thereto. The EEA (European Economic Area) comprises the EU plus Norway, Iceland and Liechtenstein.

(b) Securities (i.e. secured or unsecured loan stock and similar) issued by a company wherever incorporated. Either the securities must be officially listed on a recognised stock exchange (or alternatively admitted to trading on a recognised stock exchange in the EEA) or the shares in the issuing company or its 75% holding company must be so listed (or admitted to trading).

(c) Gilt-edged securities.

(d) Securities issued by or on behalf of a government of any EEA State, and strips of such securities.

(e) Shares in an investment trust.

(f) Units in, or shares of, a securities scheme, warrant scheme or fund of funds scheme.

(g) Units in, or shares of, a money-market scheme.

(h) Units in, or shares of, a UCITS (Undertaking for Collective Investment in Transferable Securities).

(i) A depositary interest.

(j) Cash deposited in a share or deposit account with a building society or a deposit account with a bank (as defined). However, a deposit or share account is not a qualifying investment if it is 'connected' with any other investment. For this purpose, an account is '*connected*' with another investment if either was opened or acquired with reference to the other, or with a view to enabling the other to be opened or acquired on particular terms, or with a view to facilitating the opening or acquisition of the other on particular terms *and* the terms on which the account was opened would have been significantly less favourable to the holder if the investment had not been acquired. The other investment is disregarded for this purpose if it is held in an ISA, a junior ISA or another child trust fund account.

(k) Designated national savings products.

(l) Life insurance policies satisfying specified conditions (see below).

(m) ALTERNATIVE FINANCE ARRANGEMENTS (3) (e.g. Shari'a products).

(n) 'Qualifying' units in, or shares of, a non-UCITS retail scheme (a category introduced by the New Collective Investment Schemes Sourcebook from March 2004 and covering all types of retail collective investment schemes authorised by the Financial Conduct Authority for sale in Great Britain other than UCITS schemes). Units or shares are '*qualifying*' units or shares for this purpose if they do not restrict savers' ability to access their funds by more than two weeks.

(o) Core capital deferred shares (see **8.2** BANKS AND BUILDING SOCIETIES) officially listed on a recognised stock exchange.

The term '*company*' does not for the above purposes include an OEIC or a UCITS.

A life insurance policy, in order to qualify, must insure the life of the child only. Its terms and conditions must provide:

- that the policy may only be owned or held as a qualifying investment for a CTF account;
- that the policy will terminate if it comes to the notice of the account provider that there has been a breach of the CTF regulations relating to insurance policies, and the breach cannot be remedied as a repair to an invalid account (see below under Administration);
- for the express prohibition of payments resulting from termination or partial surrender to the child before age 18;
- that the policy etc. cannot be assigned other than by transfer of title between approved account providers or by its vesting in the child's personal representatives.

The contract of insurance must either fall within the *Financial Services and Markets Act 2000 (Regulated Activities) Order 2001, Sch 1 Pt 2* (contract of long-term insurance), *para 1* (life insurance) or *para 3* (life insurance where benefits linked to value of property), or be capable of falling within either of those paragraphs were the insurer to be a company with permission under *Financial Services and Markets Act 2000* to effect insurance contracts.

The policy must constitute life insurance and must not be a contract to pay a life annuity, a personal portfolio bond (see **44.20** LIFE ASSURANCE POLICIES) or a contract constituting pension business (as defined). There must be no contractual obligation to pay any premium other than the first (so regular premium policies are excluded). The making of loans by, or by arrangement with, the insurer to, or at the direction of, the child or registered contact is prohibited.

Stakeholder accounts

There are further restrictions on investment, and investment strategy, for stakeholder accounts. Broadly, they must not invest directly in shares, investment trusts or certain types of insurance contract. Investment in securities, authorised unit trusts and open-ended investment companies is subject to specific conditions. Interest must accrue at a specified minimum rate (linked to base rate) in respect of cash held in deposit or share accounts (except where temporarily deposited while dealing in investments). As regards investment strategy, there is a requirement for the account to be exposed to equities. The account provider must have regard to the need for diversification, and must consider investment options in the light of the purpose of the account.

Tax treatment

No tax is chargeable in respect of interest, dividends, distributions or gains on account investments. (For capital gains tax purposes, assets in the fund are treated as sold and immediately re-acquired at market value just prior to the child's 18th birthday.) Capital losses on account investments are not allowable. Any income from account investments is not to be regarded as income for any income tax purposes — this exemption specifically embraces the children's settlements provisions at **70.30** SETTLEMENTS. The exemption on income extends to returns under ALTERNATIVE FINANCE ARRANGEMENTS (3) (e.g. Shari'a products).

There are, in addition, disapplications of provisions taxing profits or gains under the ACCRUED INCOME SCHEME (2), offshore income gains (see **51** OFFSHORE FUNDS), and profits on deeply discounted securities (see **65.24** SAVINGS AND INVESTMENT INCOME). Life assurance gains (see **44.3** LIFE ASSURANCE POLICIES) are not taxable (and a deficiency on termination is not deductible from the child's total income) provided regulatory conditions are not breached (see below). Companies and local authorities may pay interest etc. gross.

It is up to the account provider to make tax claims, conduct appeals, and agree liabilities and reliefs on behalf of the child or registered contact. It is unlikely then that the child or registered contact will have to deal with any tax matters arising from the account. However, there is power for HMRC to make an assessment on the registered contact as an alternative to the account provider in order to withdraw relief or recover tax. This is subject to the right of appeal.

Where a life assurance policy becomes invalid because of a breach of the regulations (see above under Qualifying investments) a chargeable event then occurs. That event, and any prior chargeable event becomes taxable under the normal provisions relating to life assurance gains (see **44.3** *et seq.* LIFE ASSURANCE POLICIES). Basic rate tax is payable by the account provider (with HMRC having the power to tax the registered contact). Any higher rate tax due is payable by the registered contact by assessment within five years after 31 January following the year in which the chargeable event or termination occurred.

Matured child trust fund accounts

CTF accounts started to mature in September 2020 when the first children for whom accounts were opened reached the age of 18. On maturity, the account holder can instruct the account provider to transfer the investments in specie, or to realise them and transfer the proceeds, or to transfer any cash balance. The transfer may be made to an ISA (see further at **30.27** below).

On the 18th birthday of the account holder, if no transfer instructions have been given as above, the account provider must transfer all the account investments into a protected account held with the provider. The protected account may be, at the option of the account provider, either a matured CTF account or a stocks and shares ISA or cash ISA. See **30.27** below as regards protected accounts that are ISAs. No subscriptions can be made to a matured CTF account. Amounts in respect of account investments are to be credited to it. The funds in a matured CTF account retain their tax advantaged status. The account holder can close the account by giving transfer instructions as above.

Administration

Administration of the account largely rests with the account provider. Regulations cover: qualification as an account manager; HMRC approval and withdrawal thereof (and appeals against these decisions); appointment of UK tax representatives of non-UK account managers; account managers ceasing to act or qualify; transfer of accounts to other account providers; annual returns of information; annual and interim tax repayment claims; record-keeping; and information to be provided to the named child (including account statements).

The account provider and the registered contact are required to take any necessary steps to remedy any breach of the regulations surrounding the CTF account. Provided this is done the account remains valid during the period of the breach, although penalties may still be in point. No repair is possible where more than one account is held for the same child.

HMRC have wide powers to require information and to inspect records in relation to CTF accounts. This is subject to a penalty regime analogous to that for special returns in *TMA 1970, s 98* (see **55.22** PENALTIES).

There is a penalty of up to £300 for fraudulently opening, or making a withdrawal from, a CTF account.

[*Child Trust Funds Act 2004; SI 2004 No 1450; SI 2017 Nos 185, 748; SI 2018 No 358; SI 2019 No 381; SI 2020 Nos 29, 269*].

For practical guidance, see www.gov.uk/child-trust-funds/overview.

Simon's Taxes. See E3.5.

Childcare payments top-up scheme

[30.13] Under *Childcare Payments Act 2014*, the Government make a top-up contribution towards an eligible person's childcare costs (see www.gov.uk/help-with-childcare-costs/tax-free-childcare). A Government top-up payment is not taxable income of the recipient. Tax due from a person cannot be collected by set-off under *FA 2008, s 130* (see **54.7** PAYMENT OF TAX) against any top-up payments due to that person. [*Childcare Payments Act 2014, ss 66, 67; SI 2017 No 578, Reg 3*].

Compensation for loss of employment etc. up to £30,000

[30.14] See **18.3–18.10** COMPENSATION FOR LOSS OF EMPLOYMENT for details of exemptions and reliefs for these and other termination payments at the end of an employment.

Compensation for mis-sold pensions products (and interest thereon)

Personal pensions etc.

[30.15] Exemption from both income tax and capital gains tax is conferred on the receipt at any time of a capital sum (which may include a sum otherwise chargeable to income tax) by way of compensation for loss, or likely loss, caused by certain 'bad investment advice' concerning personal pensions etc. '*Bad investment advice*' is investment advice (as defined) in respect of which an action has been or may be brought against the adviser for negligence, breach of contract or fiduciary obligation or by reason of a contravention actionable under certain financial services legislation. The exemption applies where a person (whether or not the person suffering loss), acting on such advice at least some of which was given after 28 April 1988 and before 1 July 1994 (at which date new regulatory safeguards came into force), either:

(a) joined a personal pension scheme or took out a retirement annuity contract whilst eligible, or reasonably likely to become eligible, to join an occupational pension scheme (i.e. an approved retirement benefits scheme, relevant statutory scheme or pre-6 April 1980 approved superannuation scheme); or
(b) left, or ceased to pay into, an occupational pension scheme and instead joined a personal pension scheme or took out a retirement annuity contract; or
(c) transferred to a personal pension scheme his accrued rights under an occupational pension scheme; or
(d) left an occupational pension scheme and instead entered into arrangements for securing relevant benefits by means of an annuity contract with an insurance company.

Interest on the whole or part of a capital sum within the above exemption is itself exempt from income tax to the extent that it covers a period ending on or before the earliest date on which the amount of the capital sum is first determined, whether by agreement or by a court, tribunal, commissioner, arbitrator or appointee.

[*FA 1996, s 148*].

As regards interest on compensation for the mis-selling of other financial products, such as mortgage endowment policies, see **65.2** SAVINGS AND INVESTMENT INCOME.

Freestanding additional voluntary contribution schemes ('FSAVCSs')

By concession, where liability would otherwise arise, the following payments will not be chargeable to income tax (although this will not apply to annuities or other annual payments arising from the compensation), and their receipt will not be treated as the disposal of an asset for capital gains tax purposes.

(i) The payment of a capital sum by way of compensation determined in accordance with the Financial Services Authority guidance for the performance of the review required by the Authority of specified categories of FSAVCSs sold between 28 April 1988 and 15 August 1999 inclusive, and made as a result of the review.

(ii) The payment of interest on the whole or part of the sum within (i) for a period ending on or before the earliest date on which the capital sum was determined.

(HMRC ESC A99).

Damages and compensation for personal injury — periodical payments

[30.16] An income tax exemption is available where an agreement is made settling a claim or action for damages for personal injury (as widely defined) under which the damages are to consist wholly or partly of periodical payments, or where a court order incorporates such terms. (This applies equally in relation to interim court order payments and voluntary payments on account.) The payments are not regarded as income for income tax purposes, and are paid without deduction of tax under *ITA 2007, Pt 15 Ch 6*. This applies as regards the person ('A') entitled to the damages under the agreement or order, and also:

(a) any person receiving the payments on behalf of A; and
(b) any trustee receiving the payments on trust for A's benefit under a trust under which A is (during his lifetime) the sole beneficiary,

and sums paid on to (or for the benefit of) A by a person within (b) above are not regarded as A's income for income tax purposes.

Any or all of the periodical payments may (if the agreement etc., or a subsequent agreement, so provides) be under one or more annuities purchased or provided for (or for the benefit of) A by the person otherwise liable for the payments.

The above provisions apply equally to annuity payments under a compensation award under the Criminal Injuries Compensation Scheme. The Treasury may also apply them (with any necessary modifications) to any other scheme or arrangement making similar provision. The provisions are thus applied to recipients of payments from the Thalidomide Children's Trust. They are also applied to a specified arrangement whereby payments funded by the Department of Health are made to persons infected with HIV through contaminated blood or blood products used by the NHS. They are similarly applied to payments from the Skipton Fund to persons infected with hepatitis C through treatment in the UK with infected blood or blood products, and to payments by the Scottish Infected Blood Support Scheme in relation to both HIV and hepatitis C. On and after 23 October 2017, the above provisions are additionally applied to newly established consolidated schemes making payments to, and providing support for, individuals infected with hepatitis C and/or HIV through contaminated blood or blood products used by the NHS.

[*ITTOIA 2005, ss 731–734; SI 2004 No 1819; SI 2010 No 673; SI 2011 No 1157; SI 2017 Nos 446, 904*].

Simon's Taxes. See **E1.510, E1.553, E4.326.**

Electricity microgeneration for home use

[30.17] No income tax liability arises in respect of income arising to an individual from the sale of electricity generated by a microgeneration system (as defined) installed at or near domestic premises which he occupies, provided the intention is that the amount of electricity generated will not significantly exceed the amount consumed in those premises. [*ITTOIA 2005, s 782A*]. The exemption covers, for example, the sale of surplus power to an energy company.

Subject to the same criteria as above, no income tax liability arises in respect of the receipt by an individual of a renewables obligation certificate (as defined) in connection with the generation of electricity by a microgeneration system. [*ITTOIA 2005, s 782B*]. There is a corresponding exemption from CGT on a gain from the disposal of a renewables obligation certificate (see *TCGA 1992, s 263AZA*).

Equitable Life

[30.18] No liability to income tax arises in respect of payments made to any person which are authorised by the Treasury under *Equitable Life (Payments) Act 2010, s 1* (payments to those adversely affected by maladministration in the regulation before December 2001 of the Equitable Life Assurance Society). [*Equitable Life (Payments) Act 2010, s 1; SI 2011 No 1502, Arts 1, 4*].

Experts seconded to EU bodies

[30.19] No liability to income tax arises in respect of any subsistence allowance paid by a 'relevant EU body' to a person who, on account of his expertise in matters relating to the functions of the EU body, has been seconded to the body by his employer. A '*relevant EU body*' is any of the following:

- the European Medicines Agency;

- the European Police College;
- the European Banking Authority; and
- any other body established by EU instrument and designated for these purposes by Treasury Order made by statutory instrument.

[*ITEPA 2003, s 304A*].

Foreign service allowance

[30.20] Such allowance is exempt where paid to a person in the service of the Crown representing compensation for the extra cost of living abroad. [*ITEPA 2003, s 299*].

German and Austrian annuities and pensions for victims of Nazi persecution

[30.21] Such annuities and pensions payable under German or Austrian law are not treated as income for any income tax purpose. [*ITEPA 2003, s 642*].

Guaranteed income bonds

[30.22] See 44.17 LIFE ASSURANCE POLICIES as regards annuities and annual payments under certain life insurance policies which are excluded from treatment as such.

Help-to-Save scheme

[30.23] No liability to income tax arises on a Government bonus paid to a Help-to-Save account. [*ITTOIA 2005, s 775A; Savings (Government Contributions) Act 2017, s 3*].

Help-to-Save is a Government savings scheme introduced in 2018 to help working people on low incomes to build their savings. Over four years, regular savers can deposit up to £50 a month and receive up to £1,200 from the Government in the form of bonuses paid into the account. Help-to-Save accounts are available to open from 12 September 2018 until September 2023. See www.gov.uk/government/publications/help-to-save-what-it-is-and-who-its-for/the-help-to-save-scheme and www.gov.uk/government/news/savers-to-earn-50p-for-every-1-saved-thanks-to-help-to-save.

Housing grants

[30.24] Except where the expense recouped is deductible from profits, amounts received, under any relevant Act, towards expenses incurred, by the recipient or another, in providing, maintaining or improving residential accommodation are not assessable. [*ITTOIA 2005, ss 769, 879(4), 880(2)*].

Immediate needs annuities

[30.25] An annual payment made under an '**immediate needs annuity**' is exempt from income tax to the extent that it is made to a care provider (as defined) or local authority in respect of the provision of care (as defined) for the person for whose benefit the annuity was made. For this purpose, an '*immediate needs annuity*' is a life annuity contract:

- the purpose of which, or one of the purposes of which, is to protect a person against the consequences of his being unable, at the time the contract is made, to live independently without assistance, due to permanent mental or physical impairment, injury, sickness or other infirmity; and
- under which benefits are payable in respect of the provision of care for that person.

The above definition, and the definition of care provider, may be amended by Treasury Order.

[*ITTOIA 2005, s 725*].

Incentives for electronic communications

[30.26] No liability to income tax arises in respect of anything received by way of incentive under any regulations made in accordance with primary legislation. See **35.11** HMRC — ADMINISTRATION.

See **64.2** RETURNS for initial incentives for making certain returns over the internet and see **53.21** PAY AS YOU EARN as regards incentives for e-filing of PAYE returns where not mandatory.

Individual Savings Accounts (ISAs)

[30.27] Individuals aged 18 or over (16 or over in the case of cash accounts (as below)) who are resident in the UK are able to subscribe up to a fixed amount each tax year to an Individual Savings Account (an ISA) set up in accordance with regulations. There is exemption from income tax and capital gains tax on the investments. An ISA may be a stocks and shares account or a cash account. Shares acquired under tax-advantaged SAYE option schemes or share incentive plans (see **71.53**, **71.25** SHARE-RELATED EMPLOYMENT INCOME AND EXEMPTIONS) may be transferred into a stocks and shares account at market value (with no capital gains tax liability) within the annual subscription limit, but public offer and demutualisation issues may not be transferred in. There is no minimum subscription, no lifetime limit and no loss of relief on withdrawals. See **30.31** below. See towards the end of this coverage for Help to Buy ISAs, Innovative Finance ISAs and Lifetime ISAs.

Annual subscription limits are as follows.

For	**2017/18 onwards**	**£20,000**
For	2016/17	£15,240

The necessary regulation-making powers are provided in general by *ITTOIA 2005, ss 694–701*. *The Individual Savings Account Regulations 1998* (*SI 1998 No 1870*) provide for the setting up by HMRC-approved accounts managers of plans (ISAs) under which individuals may make certain investments, for the conditions under which they may invest and under which the accounts are to operate, for relief from tax in respect of account investments, and for general administration.

General

An application to subscribe to an ISA may be made by an individual who is 18 or over (16 or over in the case of cash accounts) and who is resident in the UK (or who is non-UK resident but has general earnings 'from overseas Crown employment subject to UK tax' — see **28.5** EMPLOYMENT INCOME — or who is a non-UK resident spouse (or civil partner) of an individual with such earnings). Joint accounts are not permitted. An investor who subsequently fails to meet the residence requirement may retain the account and the right to tax exemptions thereunder but can make no further subscriptions to the account until he again comes to meet that requirement. An application made on behalf of an individual suffering from mental disorder, by a parent, guardian, spouse, civil partner, son or daughter of his, is treated as if made by that individual.

Types of account

An ISA may be stocks and shares account, a cash account or an Innovative Finance ISA (for which see below).

A *stocks and shares account* is made up of a single stocks and shares component. An investor can subscribe to only one stocks and shares account in a tax year. Stocks and shares accounts are not available to 16- and 17-year olds.

A *cash account* is made up of a single cash component. Cash accounts are available to any individual of 16 or over who satisfies the general conditions above. An investor can subscribe to only one cash account in a tax year.

There is an overall annual subscription limit, which can be divided between a stocks and shares account and a cash account as the investor sees fit, or subscribed entirely to one type of account or the other. So an individual who subscribes, say, £14,000 to a stocks and shares account in 2019/20 can also subscribe £6,000 to a cash account in that tax year, and vice versa.

An investor is permitted to transfer some or all of the amount saved in ISAs in previous tax years to a stocks and shares account. Such transfers do not count towards the annual subscription limits. An investor is also permitted to transfer the amount saved in the current tax year in a cash account to a stocks and shares account. In this case the transfer must consist of the whole of the amount saved in that tax year in that cash account; for the purpose of applying the annual subscription limits, the cash transferred is treated as if it had been invested directly into a stocks and shares account in that tax year.

Dormant Bank and Building Society Accounts Act 2008 provides the framework for a scheme under which balances in dormant bank and building society accounts can be transferred to a reclaim fund to be used for social or environmental purposes. If, on a claim by the investor for repayment of the balance of a dormant cash account, the account is reinstated as a cash account or the money is paid into a new cash account in the same name and with the same account manager, the amount reinstated or paid does not count towards the subscription limits.

Personal equity plans (PEPs) were abolished for 2008/09 onwards and all then existing PEPs automatically became stocks and shares ISAs on 6 April 2008.

Flexible ISAs

If the account terms and conditions allow it, an ISA investor can withdraw cash from an ISA and pay it back in again (a '*replacement subscription*') during the same tax year without the replacement subscription counting towards the ISA subscription limit for that year. ISAs whose terms allow this are known as '*flexible ISAs*'. Any cash withdrawal in a year is deemed to be made first out of a current year's subscription. Any replacement subscription is deemed to be a replacement first of any cash withdrawal made in the year out of an earlier year's subscription. A replacement subscription to a stocks and shares account may be in the form of the type of employee share scheme shares referred to below under Subscriptions to an ISA.

Subscriptions to an ISA

Subscriptions to an ISA must be made in cash (and must be allocated irrevocably to the agreed component) *except that* shares acquired by the investor under a tax-advantaged SAYE option scheme (see **71.53** SHARE-RELATED EMPLOYMENT INCOME AND EXEMPTIONS) or a tax-advantaged share incentive plan (see **71.25** SHARE-RELATED EMPLOYMENT INCOME AND EXEMPTIONS) may be transferred to a stocks and shares account. Such transfers count towards the annual subscription limits, by reference to the market value of the shares at the date of transfer. No chargeable gain or allowable loss arises on the transfer. A transfer of SAYE scheme shares must be made within 90 days after the exercise of the option, and a transfer of share incentive plan shares must be made within 90 days of the shares ceasing to be subject to the plan. 'Shares' in these cases includes a reference to those held in the form of depositary interests (see (k) below).

It is possible for the investor to sell investments and subscribe the proceeds to an ISA and for the ISA manager to then use those proceeds to acquire investments (often the same investments) within the ISA. This is sometimes known as 'Bed and ISAing'. Provided the funds generated by the disposal are available to meet the purchase on settlement day, the subscription date for the ISA can be the date of disposal, the settlement date for the purchase or any date in between that the investor chooses. (HMRC ISA Bulletin 15, August 2009).

Compensation paid into ISAs for loss of income or capital growth due to failures or delays on the part of ISA managers will not count towards the subscription limit. This does not apply to compensation paid in respect of a delay in opening an ISA, or in accepting a subscription to an ISA. See HMRC Guidance Notes for ISA Managers and PEP and ISA Bulletin 4, 13 December 2001.

Defaulted subscriptions

Either a 'defaulted cash account subscription' or a 'defaulted investment subscription' is disregarded for the purposes of the annual subscription limits above. Where a cash account manager is declared in default by the regulatory authorities, an investor can make a single reinvestment to a cash account (a '*defaulted cash account subscription*') up to the balance of his cash account at the time of default. Where an investor receives compensation in respect of an investment held in a stocks and shares account or an innovative finance account (see below), he may make a single reinvestment to an account (a '*defaulted investment subscription*') up to the value of the compensation received. The reinvestment must be made within 180 days after the default occurs or the compensation is paid.

See guidance at www.gov.uk/government/uploads/system/uploads/attachment_data/file/375684/isa-reinstatement.pdf.

Other matters

ISA investments cannot be purchased otherwise than out of cash held by the account manager under an account, and cannot be purchased from the investor or the investor's spouse or civil partner.

The title to ISA investments (other than cash deposits, national savings products and certain insurance policies) is vested in the account manager (or his nominee) either alone or jointly with the investor, though all ISA investments are in the beneficial ownership of the investor. The investor may elect to receive annual reports and accounts etc. in respect of ISA investments and/or to attend and vote at shareholders' etc. meetings.

The statements and declarations to be made when applying to subscribe to an ISA are specified. The maximum penalty for an incorrect statement or declaration is the amount (if any) of income tax and/or capital gains tax underpaid as a result. Assessments to withdraw tax relief or otherwise recover tax underpaid may be made on the account manager or investor. HMRC have power to require information from, and to inspect records of, account managers and investors.

The terms and conditions of an ISA cannot prevent the investor from withdrawing funds or from transferring his account (or a part of it) to another HMRC-approved account manager (subject to the conditions governing such transfers). The account manager is allowed a reasonable business period (usually not exceeding 30 days) to comply with the investor's instructions in this regard.

Tax exemptions

Except as stated below, no income tax or capital gains tax is chargeable on the account manager or the investor in respect of interest, dividends, distributions or gains on ISA investments. Capital losses are not allowable. The exemption on income extends to returns under ALTERNATIVE FINANCE ARRANGEMENTS (3) (e.g. Shari'a products). Annual building society bonuses are brought within the exemptions on both income and gains from 1 January 2007.

Income arising from a sum paid by a parent into a cash ISA held by his or her 16- or 17-year old child is taxable as the parent's income under the settlements legislation at **70.30** SETTLEMENTS (subject to the £100 limit per parent per child). This is in contrast to the position for junior ISAs at **30.31** below.

Life assurance gains on policies held within an ISA are not subject to income tax (and a deficiency on termination is not deductible from the investor's total income). If it comes to the account manager's notice that such a policy is invalid, i.e. its terms and conditions do not provide (or no longer provide) that it be held only as an ISA investment, a chargeable event then occurs, with any gain taxable. If the policy has already terminated, the chargeable event is deemed to have occurred at the end of the final insurance year (see **44.13** LIFE ASSURANCE POLICIES). Any previous chargeable event which actually occurred in relation to the policy is similarly taxed, by reference to the time it occurred. Basic rate income tax is payable by the account manager (with HMRC also having power to assess the investor). Any higher or additional rate tax due is payable by the investor by assessment no more than four years after end of the tax year in which the chargeable event occurred or was deemed to occur. Top slicing relief (see **44.9** LIFE ASSURANCE POLICIES) is available in the same way as for non-ISA-related chargeable events.

Exempt income and gains do not have to be reported in the investor's personal tax return.

Further capital gains matters

A transfer of ISA investments by an account manager to an investor is deemed to be made at market value, with no capital gain or allowable loss arising. An investor is treated as holding shares or securities in an ISA in a capacity other than that in which he holds any other shares etc. of the same class in the same company, so that share identification rules (see Tolley's Capital Gains Tax under Shares and Securities — Identification Rules) are applied separately to ISA investments (and separately as between different ISAs held by the same investor). The normal share reorganisation rules are disapplied in respect of ISA investments in the event of a reorganisation of share capital involving an allotment for payment, e.g. a rights issue. Shares transferred to an ISA in the limited circumstances described above are deemed for these purposes to have been ISA investments from, in the case of SAYE option scheme shares, their acquisition by the investor and, in the case of share incentive plan shares, their ceasing to be subject to the plan. Where the investor held shares eligible for transfer to an ISA and other shares of the same class but not so eligible, disposals are generally identified primarily with the latter, thus preserving to the greatest possible extent the eligibility of the remaining shares.

Qualifying investments

Qualifying investments are as set out below.

Stocks and shares account

Qualifying investments for a stocks and shares account are as follows.

(a) Shares issued by a company (other than an investment trust, but see (f) below) wherever incorporated. The shares must be officially listed on a recognised stock exchange or admitted to trading on a recognised stock exchange in UK or EEA. There are rules to allow the official listing (or admission to trading) condition to be treated as satisfied in the case of shares issued under a public offer and due to be listed (or admitted); however, shares do not qualify if they have been acquired on favourable terms because of a connection with the allocation or allotment of other shares, securities or rights thereto. The EEA (European Economic Area) comprises the EU plus Norway, Iceland and Liechtenstein.

(b) Securities (i.e. secured or unsecured loan stock and similar) issued by a company wherever incorporated. Either the securities must be officially listed on a recognised stock exchange (or alternatively admitted to trading on a recognised stock exchange in the UK or EEA) or the shares in the issuing company or its 75% holding company must be so listed (or admitted to trading).

(c) Gilt-edged securities and gilt strips.

(d) Securities issued by or on behalf of the UK Government or a government of any EEA State, and strips of such securities.

(e) Securities issued by multilateral institutions as defined by the Organisation for Economic Co-operation and Development (i.e. institutions contributions to which may be reported as official development assistance by governments and other official agencies). The securities must be officially listed on a recognised stock exchange.

(f) Shares in an investment trust.

(g) Units in, or shares of, a 'UK UCITS'. A '*UK UCITS*' is a authorised collective investment scheme which complies with the requirements to be a UCITS scheme (an Undertaking for Collective Investment in Transferable Securities) for the purposes of the Collective Investment Schemes Sourcebook made by the Financial Conduct Authority (see fshandbook.info/FS/html/handbook/COLL), or part of such a scheme equivalent to a sub-fund of an umbrella scheme.

(h) Units in, or shares of, a 'recognised UCITS'. A '*recognised UCITS*' is the broad equivalent of a UK UCITS in (g) above but constituted in another EEA Member State. A change is made to the definition with effect on and after the Brexit implementation period (IP) completion day, expected to be 31 December 2020; a recognised UCITS will be defined by reference to *Financial Services and Markets Act 2000, Pt 17* but will also include an undertaking established in Gibraltar which is a UCITS under the law of that territory. Investments continuing to held before and after IP completion day remain qualifying investments.

(i) 'Qualifying' units in, or shares of, a non-UCITS retail scheme (a scheme to which COLL 5.1, 5.4 and 5.6 of the Collective Investment Schemes Sourcebook apply (see fshandbook.info/FS/html/handbook/COLL) and which comprises all types of retail collective investment schemes authorised by the Financial Conduct Authority for sale in Great Britain other than UCITS schemes). Units or shares are '*qualifying*' units or shares for this purpose if they do not restrict savers' ability to access their funds by more than two weeks.

(j) Shares acquired by the investor under a tax-advantaged SAYE share option scheme or tax-advantaged share incentive plan which are transferred into the ISA as mentioned under '*General*' above.

(k) A 'depositary interest' in or in relation to an investment which is itself a qualifying investment other than cash. A '*depositary interest*' means the rights of any person to investments held by another, effectively as his nominee.

(l) Units in a relevant collective investment scheme specified as a stakeholder product by *SI 2004 No 2738, Reg 5* (the *Financial Services and Markets Act 2000 (Stakeholder Products) Regulations 2004*).

(m) Life insurance policies issued on or after 6 April 2005 which satisfy the conditions summarised below under Life insurance policies.

(n) Life insurance policies previously held in an insurance component and transferred to a stocks and shares account under transitional provisions following abolition of the insurance component of an ISA for 2005/06 onwards.

(o) Cash held on deposit.

(p) In the case of a stocks and shares account which immediately before 6 April 2008 was a PEP, qualifying investments held in the PEP immediately before 6 April 2001 and retained in the plan throughout the intervening period even though they no longer strictly qualified.

(q) Core capital deferred shares (see **8.2** BANKS AND BUILDING SOCIETIES) officially listed on a recognised stock exchange.

The term '*company*' does not for the above purposes include an OEIC, a UK UCITS, recognised UCITS or non-UCITS retail scheme.

Cash account

Qualifying investments for a cash account are as follows.

(i) Cash deposited in a deposit account with a building society, a credit union or a person within *ITA 2007, s 991(2)(b)* or *s 991(2)(c)* (see **8.1**(b)(c) BANKS AND BUILDING SOCIETIES).

(ii) Cash deposited in a building society share account.

(iii) Designated national savings products.

(iv) A deposit account specified as a stakeholder product by *SI 2004 No 2738, Reg 4* (the *Financial Services and Markets Act 2000 (Stakeholder Products) Regulations 2004*).

(v) Depositary interests (see (k) above) in or in relation to an investment which is itself a qualifying investment for a cash account.

(vi) A short-term money market fund which meets the conditions in section COLL 5.9.3.R of the Collective Investment Schemes Sourcebook made by the Financial Conduct Authority (see fshandbook.info/FS/html/handbook/COLL).

(vii) A money market fund which meets the conditions in section COLL 5.9.5R of the Collective Investment Schemes Sourcebook made by the Financial Conduct Authority (see fshandbook.info/FS/html/handbook/COLL).

(viii) Life insurance policies previously held in an insurance component and transferred to a cash account under transitional provisions following abolition of the insurance component of an ISA for 2005/06 onwards.

(ix) ALTERNATIVE FINANCE ARRANGEMENTS (3) (e.g. Shari'a products).

A deposit or share account within (i) or (ii) above is not a qualifying investment if is 'connected' with any other account held within those categories (whether or not by the investor). For this purpose, accounts are '*connected*' if either was opened with reference to the other or with a view to enabling the other to be opened, or facilitating the opening of the other, on particular terms *and* the terms on which the cash account was opened would have been significantly less favourable to the investor if the other had not been opened. The other account is disregarded for this purpose if it is an ISA, junior ISA, child trust fund (CTF) account or CTF matured account. Also, HMRC will accept that an account is not a connected account if it is a 'feeder' account opened to enable investors to fund future deposits into an ISA, provided that the interest on the feeder account is in line with the interest paid on the account manager's other savings accounts (see HMRC Guidance Notes for ISA Managers).

Life insurance policies

Life insurance policies must meet certain conditions to qualify as ISA investments. The insurance must be on the life of the ISA investor only and its terms and conditions must provide:

- that the policy can only be owned or held as a qualifying investment for an ISA;
- that, if found to be in breach of the above condition, it will automatically terminate (and see also above under 'Tax exemptions');
- for an express prohibition of any transfer to the investor of the policy or the rights conferred thereby or any share or interest therein (other than cash proceeds on termination or partial surrender); and
- that the policy etc. cannot be assigned other than by transfer of title between approved ISA managers or by its vesting in the investor's personal representatives.

The policy must constitute life insurance and cannot be a contract to pay a life annuity, a personal portfolio bond (see **44.20** LIFE ASSURANCE POLICIES) or a contract constituting pension business (as defined). There must be no contractual obligation to pay any premium other than the first (so regular premium policies are excluded). 'Connected' policies are excluded in much the same way as connected accounts are excluded from a cash account (see above). The making of loans by, or by arrangement with, the insurer to, or at the direction of, the ISA investor is prohibited.

For these purposes, a '*policy*' includes rights under a linked long-term contract specified as a stakeholder product by *SI 2004 No 2738, Reg 6* (the *Financial Services and Markets Act 2000 (Stakeholder Products) Regulations 2004*).

Repairing of invalid accounts

An account is 'eligible for repair' if either the overall subscription limit is breached or it is the second stocks and shares account or cash account subscribed to by the same investor in the tax year. Where HMRC give notice that an account is '*eligible for repair*', it qualifies for tax relief from the date of the notice. If an investor closes a cash account and opens another cash account, the new account (i.e. the first cash account to be opened after the said closure and in the same tax year) is treated as valid (and thus qualifying for tax relief) from the date it is opened. Repairing of accounts is subject to normal subscription limits, and where necessary HMRC will apportion (i.e. between valid accounts and any one or more accounts eligible for repair) the total amount subscribed in the tax year.

HMRC will seek to void invalid subscriptions only where the investor has either subscribed to a disallowed combination of accounts for more than one year or has significantly exceeded the subscription limits. In all other cases, they will simply issue a letter, drawing the investor's attention to the ISA rules and advising him that they will take no action unless he subscribes to a disallowed combination of ISAs in a later tax year. If he then does so, they will take corrective action for both years. (HMRC PEP and ISA Bulletins No 31, 29 September 2006 and No 33, 10 November 2006).

Closure and death

Subject to the ISA terms and conditions, an investor may close an ISA at any time without affecting tax exemptions up to the date of closure.

Where an investor dies, income and gains in respect of ISA investments which arise after the date of death but before the date of closure are not exempt from tax for 2017/18 and earlier years. With effect on and after 6 April 2018, ISA investments do retain their tax-exempt status for a limited period following the death of the account holder. This operates by exempting the income and gains from ISA investments received by the personal representatives of a deceased account holder, or by a legatee, during the administration of the deceased's estate. The exemption has effect for a maximum of three years after the account holder's death and applies only to investments retained in the ISA. No new subscriptions can be made to the ISA account, and it cannot normally be transferred between ISA providers. Whilst the exemption has effect, the account is designated a '*continuing account of a deceased investor*'. When an investment is transferred from the personal representatives to a legatee whilst the account is so designated, the legatee is treated for CGT purposes as having acquired it at the date of transfer at its then market value. If the transfer occurs after the exemption ceases to have effect, the legatee is treated as having acquired the investment at the date of transfer but at its market value at the time the account ceased to be a continuing account of a deceased investor.

Bereaved investors are permitted to make an additional ISA subscription outside the normal subscription limits following the death of a spouse. This is to enable the surviving spouse to inherit the deceased's ISA tax advantages. The one-off subscription cannot exceed the total value held in the deceased's ISA(s) (disregarding junior ISAs) at the date of death or, if greater and the subscription has not then already been made, upon the account's ceasing to be a continuing account of a deceased investor (see above). The deceased and the surviving spouse must have been 'living together' (within **48.8** MARRIED PERSONS) at date of death. In the case of non-cash assets held in the deceased's ISAs the one-off subscription must be made in the period of 180 days beginning with the distribution of those assets by the deceased's estate to the surviving spouse. The value of a subscription comprising non-cash assets is the value of the assets at the date of the subscription. In any other case the subscription must be made within three years after the date of death or, if later, within 180 days after the administration of the estate is completed. As far as the surviving spouse is concerned, the normal rule that an investor can subscribe to only one cash account or one stocks and shares account in a tax year is ignored for these purposes, and the normal requirements as to UK residence status are disregarded with regard to the one-off subscription. 'Spouse' should be read throughout as including a civil partner.

Account managers

The regulations cover qualification as an account manager, HMRC approval and withdrawal thereof, appointment of UK tax representatives of non-UK account managers, transferring an ISA from one account manager to another, account managers ceasing to act or to qualify, claims for tax relief and agreement of liabilities, returns of income, tax repayment claims, record-keeping, and information to be provided to investors.

Help to Buy ISAs (now closed to new accounts)

The Help to Buy ISA closed to new accounts on 30 November 2019. Existing account holders can continue saving into their account until 30 November 2029, at which time accounts will close to additional contributions. Bonuses must be claimed by 1 December 2030. (www.helptobuy.gov.uk/help-to-buy-isa/faq)

This scheme for first-time home buyers provides a tax-free bonus to each person who has saved via a Help to Buy ISA. The bonus will be paid at the time the savings are used to purchase a home. For every £200 saved, the Government will provide a £50 bonus, up to a maximum of £3,000 on £12,000 of savings. Savers are able to make an initial deposit of £1,000 and a monthly saving of up to £200. It is not possible to subscribe to a Help to Buy ISA and an ordinary cash ISA in the same tax year. The bonus is available on home purchases of up to £450,000 in London and £250,000 elsewhere in the UK. See www.helptobuy.gov.uk, the scheme outline at www.gov.uk/government/publications/help-to-buy-isa and the factsheet at www.gov.uk/government/publications/help-to-buy-isa-factsheet.

A Help to Buy ISA investor who closes his account, only for the intended home purchase not to proceed, may pay into a cash ISA any amount not exceeding that which he withdrew from his Help to Buy ISA on closure. This will not then count towards the ISA subscription limit for the year of subscription. The investor must provide to the account manager evidence of failure to complete purchase, must make the subscription no later than 12 months after the closure of the Help to Buy ISA, and can make only one such subscription even if this is less than the full amount which could have been subscribed.

Any amount held in a Help to Buy ISA on 5 April 2017 could be transferred to a Lifetime ISA (see below) during 2017/18 without this counting towards the £4,000 Lifetime ISA subscription limit (www.gov.uk/government/publications/individual-savings-accounts-lifetime-isa/individual-savings-accounts-lifetime-isa).

Innovative Finance ISAs

Under this type of account, interest and gains from peer-to-peer (P2P) loans can benefit from ISA tax advantages. See **65.9** SAVINGS AND INVESTMENT INCOME as to the nature of P2P lending. Individuals aged 18 or over are able to subscribe in cash to an innovative finance account, which are offered by P2P lending platforms with the appropriate regulatory permissions. Subscriptions to an innovative finance account count towards the overall annual ISA subscription limit, and only one such account can be subscribed to in a tax year. Certain company and charity debentures (including debt securities and bonds made available through crowdfunding offers) are eligible for inclusion in an Innovative Finance ISA.

Lifetime ISAs

Lifetime ISAs were made available by account providers on and after 6 April 2017 for individuals aged 18 to 39 inclusive. The individual must be UK resident, except that Crown servants, and their spouses/civil partners, qualify in the same way as for general ISAs. Eligible investors can contribute up to £4,000 per year to a Lifetime ISA, and will receive a tax-free Government bonus equal to 25% of their contributions. Whilst an account cannot be opened at age 40 or over, contributions can continue to be made to an existing account until the investor reaches the age of 50. Contributions count towards the overall annual ISA subscription limit.

Funds in a Lifetime ISA, including the bonus, can be used to buy a first home (costing up to £450,000) at any time from 12 months after the account is opened, and can be withdrawn from the age of 60. Investors can withdraw their funds at other times, but (except in certain cases of terminal illness) the bonus element (including any interest or growth on that element) must then be returned to the Government, and an additional 5% charge will be applied, making a total charge of 25% of the withdrawn amount (but see below for a COVID-19 special measure). This will be collected and paid to HMRC by the account manager. For example, an investor taking out £750 in cash will see their account balance reduce by £1,000 ('*the amount withdrawn*'); the difference of £250 comprises £200 worth of bonus (20% of the amount withdrawn) and a £50 penalty (5%). No charge will be made in the event of an account holder's death. Any type of investment which qualifies to be held in a cash ISA or stocks and shares ISA also qualifies to be held in a Lifetime ISA. Any amount held in a Help to Buy ISA (see above) at 5 April 2017 could be transferred to a Lifetime ISA during 2017/18 without its counting towards the £4,000 Lifetime ISA contribution limit.

See www.gov.uk/government/publications/individual-savings-accounts-lifetime-isa/individual-savings-accounts-lifetime-isa.

COVID-19 (coronavirus) special measure

As a temporary COVID-19 relieving measure, the 5% penalty charge does not apply to withdrawals made during the period 6 March 2020 to 5 April 2021 inclusive. The total charge is instead 20% of the amount withdrawn, which thus recovers the bonus element of the amount withdrawn without imposing any penalty for the withdrawal. The investor taking out £750 in cash in the above example will see their account balance reduce by only £937.50. See www.gov.uk/guidance/lifetime-isa-withdrawal-charge-reduced-to-20.

Matured child trust fund accounts

On and after 6 April 2020, the investments held in a matured child trust fund (CTF) account (see **30.12** above) can be transferred to an ISA. The transfer neither counts towards the overall annual ISA subscription limit nor prevents the opening of another ISA of the same type in the same tax year, and the account holder does not have to meet UK residence conditions. If, however, the transfer is to a Lifetime ISA it does count towards the annual subscription limit for that type of account. CTF accounts started to mature in September 2020 when the first children for whom accounts were opened reached the age of 18.

Where, on the maturity of a CTF account, the account provider is required to place investments in a protected account pending instructions from the account holder (see **30.12** above), the protected account, if not a matured CTF account, will be a stocks and shares ISA or cash ISA. The transfer to the protected account is disregarded for the purposes of the overall ISA subscription limit. No further subscriptions can be made to the protected account unless and until the account holder has completed an application to open an ISA. Amounts in respect of account investments are to be credited to the account. The funds in a protected account retain their tax advantaged status.

[*SI 1998 No 1870; SI 2016 No 977; SI 2017 Nos 186, 466, 1089; SI 2018 No 359; SI 2019 No 382; SI 2019 No 689, Regs 1, 24; SI 2020 Nos 30, 506; ITTOIA 2005, ss 694A, 775A; FA 2016, s 27; Savings (Government Contributions) Act 2017; European Union (Withdrawal Agreement) Act 2020 Sch 5 para 1(1)*].

Supplementary

See www.gov.uk/individual-savings-accounts. For guidance notes for ISA Managers, see www.gov.uk/government/publications/guidance-notes-for-isa-managers. ISA Bulletins are published at www.gov.uk/government/collection s/bulletins-for-isa-managers.

Simon's Taxes. See E3.3.

International organisations, income from

[30.28] Income from **international organisations** may be exempt under specific provisions, see **24** DIPLOMATIC IMMUNITY.

Insurance policies, annual payments under

[30.29] Annual payments falling to be made under certain **insurance policies** are exempt from income tax. The exemption, described below, will most commonly apply to mortgage payment protection insurance, permanent health insurance, creditor insurance (to meet existing commitments, possibly including domestic utility bills, in event of accident, sickness, disability or unemployment) and certain kinds of long-term care insurance (but only where the policy is taken out before the need for care becomes apparent). (Revenue Press Release REV 6, 28 November 1995).

The exemption applies to policies insuring against a health or employment risk, provided that certain conditions are met and that no part of any premium is deductible in calculating the income of the insured. The exemption therefore does not apply if any premiums under the policy have to any extent qualified for tax relief, either as a deduction from total income or in computing income from any source (e.g. business profits). However, where an employer takes out a group policy to meet the cost of employees' sick pay and the policy would otherwise qualify under these provisions, the proportion of any payment attributable (on just and reasonable apportionment) to employees' contributions to premiums is not treated as employment or pension income despite the deduction available to the employer.

For an annual payment to qualify for the exemption:

(a) it must be made under a policy (or part of a policy) providing insurance against a 'health or employment risk';
(b) the provisions of the policy which insure against that risk must not be significantly affected by other benefits payable under the policy (see below);
(c) the policy must make no provision for payments relating to that risk other than for specified periods (see below); and
(d) the provisions of the policy relating to that risk must always have been such that the insurer runs a genuine risk of loss (i.e. proceeds payable must be capable of exceeding premiums received plus an investment return on those premiums).

A '*health or employment risk*' is either a risk of physical or mental illness, disability, infirmity or defect (including a risk of an existing condition deteriorating) or a risk of loss of employment (including loss of self-employment and loss of office). The persons at risk may include the insured, his spouse (or civil partner), any child under 21 of the insured or his spouse (or civil partner), and, for policies connected with the meeting of liabilities under an identified transaction, a person jointly liable with the insured or his spouse (or civil partner).

The specified periods for which payment may be made are: for as long as the illness etc. or unemployment continues (including in the case of illness etc. any related period of convalescence or rehabilitation) or for as long as the income of the insured etc. (apart from benefits under the policy) is less, in circumstances so insured against, than it otherwise would be. If any such period ends as a result of the death of the insured etc., it is extended to any period immediately following (so that benefits paid to the deceased's spouse or estate are brought within the exemption).

The requirement for the relevant provisions of the policy not to be affected by other benefits is an anti-avoidance measure. The provisions of a policy covering different kinds of benefits must ensure that the terms of the policy relating to the health or employment risk (possibly including the fixing of the amount of premiums), or the way in which they are given effect, would not have been significantly different if the policy insured only against the health or employment risk (where the only difference is that certain benefits are applied for reducing other benefits under the policy this is ignored). A broadly similar rule applies where there are multiple policies. In each case, regard must be had to all the persons for whose benefit insurance is provided against the qualifying risk.

There are provisions enabling benefits relating to illness etc. to qualify for the exemption if paid under an individual policy derived from and superseding an employer's group policy where an employee has left the employment as a consequence of the occurrence insured against.

[*ITTOIA 2005, ss 735–743*].

Where an insurance policy is taken out by a third party, no liability to income tax in respect of employment income arises on a payment, and no liability to income tax arises on a pension or annuity payment, provided the exemption criteria under *ITTOIA 2005, s 735* (see above) are met and two further conditions are satisfied:

- that payments are made: to a person who made payments or contributions in respect of premiums in respect of the insurance policy taken out by a third party wholly or partly for that person's benefit; or to that person's spouse (or civil partner); and
- that the payments are attributable (on a just and reasonable basis) to the contributions in respect of premiums.

[*ITEPA 2003, ss 324A, 644A*].

Benefits which are wholly exempt are paid without deduction of tax. Where they are partially exempt (e.g. in the case of a company policy to which the employee contributes) or the policy holder's income, including the maximum benefits payable, is below taxable income limits, the insurer may pay benefits gross on receipt of an appropriate declaration from the recipient (on form R91). (Revenue Tax Bulletin December 1996 p 377).

Simon's Taxes. See **E1.510, E1.554.**

Interest received

[30.30] The receipt of interest is exempt from income tax where the interest is paid on:

(i) damages for personal injuries or death including similar interest awarded by a foreign court if also exempt from tax in that country. [*ITTOIA 2005, s 751*];

(ii) certain UK government stocks held by non-UK residents (see **65.4** SAVINGS AND INVESTMENT INCOME) and certain borrowings in foreign currency by local authorities and certain statutory bodies (see **23.12** DEDUCTION OF TAX AT SOURCE);

(iii) **Government Savings Certificates;**

(iv) **Save As You Earn** savings arrangements (bonuses under such arrangements also being exempt), provided that they are linked to tax-advantaged SAYE option schemes (see **71.57** SHARE-RELATED EMPLOYMENT INCOME AND EXEMPTIONS). Share option linked savings arrangements may be offered by a wide range of providers. Authorisation by HMRC (previously by the Treasury) is required for the operation of such schemes. [*ITTOIA 2005, ss 702–708*];

(v) overpaid inheritance tax. [*IHTA 1984, ss 233(3), 235(2); SI 2019 No 689, Reg 13(5)*];

(vi) repayments of tax etc., see **62** REPAYMENT INTEREST;

(vii) refunds of amounts over-repaid by borrowers in respect of student loans made under specified statutory provisions. [*ITTOIA 2005, s 753*];

(viii) late paid pension contributions. The Pensions Regulator may, at its discretion, require an employer to pay interest to compensate an employee for late payment of pension contributions by the employer; the interest is paid directly to the employee's pension account to which he has no immediate access. The interest is exempt only if paid in accordance with a compliance notice or unpaid contributions notice issued by the Regulator. [*ITTOIA 2005, s 753A*].

See also **30.34** below (payments to victims of Nazi persecution).

Junior ISAs

[30.31] Tax-free children's savings accounts, known as junior ISAs, have the following key features:

- all UK resident children (under 18) who do not have a Child Trust Fund (CTF) account (see **30.12** above) are eligible for junior ISAs;
- all income and gains are tax-free;
- income arising from a sum paid by a parent into his or her child's junior ISA is not taxed as the parent's income;
- investments can be held either in cash or stocks and shares;
- there is a limit of £9,000 on annual contributions (£4,368 before 6 April 2020, £4,260 before 6 April 2019, £4,128 before 6 April 2018, £4,080 before 6 April 2017);
- all the savings in a CTF account can be transferred to a new junior ISA; and
- funds placed in the account are owned by the child and are locked in until the child reaches the age of 18 at which point the account will automatically become an adult ISA (as in **30.27** above).

General

An application to open a junior ISA with an account manager may only be made if the account will be held in the name of an 'eligible child'. An '*eligible child*' is broadly a child aged under 18 and born either before 1 September 2002 or on or after 3 January 2011 (and thus not eligible for a CTF account at **30.12** above). The child must normally be resident in the UK. A non-UK resident child does qualify if it has general earnings 'from overseas Crown employment subject to UK tax' — see **28.5** EMPLOYMENT INCOME — or it is a dependant of, married to, or in a civil partnership with, an individual with such earnings. The application can be made only by a person aged 16 or over, which could be the child itself or a person with parental responsibility for the child. See also below under Looked after children. The child is the beneficial owner of the account investments.

As soon as the child reaches the age of 18, it follows that the account is no longer held in the name of a child and is therefore no longer a junior ISA. It then falls within the rules for adult ISAs at **30.27** above.

Looked after children

In November 2011 the Government announced their intention to make a payment of £200 into a Junior ISA for each eligible looked after child (broadly a child under the care or supervision of a local authority). The Share Foundation was appointed to manage these arrangements. In this connection, the Share Foundation have authority to open, manage, or assume responsibility of a junior ISA on behalf of a looked after child. The consent of the Foundation is required in circumstances where another person wishes to assume management of the junior ISA (other than where the child reaches 16 or where a court so orders).

Subscriptions, withdrawals and types of account

An eligible child can have only one cash account and only one stocks and shares account at any one time (though for this purpose any account with a balance of less than one penny is disregarded).

Any person may subscribe to a junior ISA but the total amount subscribed by all persons for any tax year to accounts held for any one child must not exceed **£9,000** (£4,368 before 6 April 2020, £4,260 before 6 April 2019, £4,128 before 6 April 2018, £4,080 before 6 April 2017). Only cash subscriptions are allowed. For any child, subscriptions up to the overall maximum can be made either to a cash account or to a stocks and shares account or can be split in any proportion between the two types of account. (If there is a cash account with a balance of less than one penny and a new cash account has been opened for the child, no further subscriptions can be made to the first account; the same applies to stocks and shares accounts.)

Withdrawals cannot normally be made from a junior ISA. This does not prevent withdrawals being made by the account manager to settle any management charges and other incidental expenses which might be due under the management agreement for the account. Withdrawals may be made where the account manager is satisfied that the named child who held the account has died and can also be made where the child is terminally ill.

It is an overriding requirement that any necessary steps be taken to remedy any breach of the junior ISA regulations. Where a breach is remedied (*'repaired'*), the account shall, to the extent of that breach, be treated as having been a valid account at all times.

With regards to defaulted subscriptions, the same rules apply as for adult ISAs at **30.27** above, except that a defaulted investment subscription can also be made to a cash account without counting towards the annual subscription limit.

All the savings in a CTF account can be transferred to a new junior ISA for the child in question, with the CTF account then being closed. Savings thus transferred do not count towards the junior ISA subscription limit.

Tax exemptions

No income tax or capital gains tax is chargeable on the account manager or the child in respect of interest, dividends, distributions or gains on junior ISA investments. Capital losses are not allowable. The detailed rules are the same as for adult ISAs at **30.27** above, except that income arising from a sum paid by a parent into his or her child's junior ISA is *not* taxable as the parent's income under the settlements legislation at **70.30** SETTLEMENTS.

Qualifying investments

Qualifying investments for both a cash account and a stocks and shares account are similar to those for adult ISAs at **30.27** above. The one difference is that, in the case of a stocks and shares account, **30.27**(j) (shares acquired by the investor under a tax-advantaged employee share scheme) is of no relevance to junior ISAs.

Account managers

The regulations cover qualification as an account manager, HMRC approval and withdrawal thereof, appointment of UK tax representatives of non-UK account managers, transferring an ISA from one account manager to another, account managers ceasing to act or to qualify, claims for tax relief and agreement of liabilities, annual returns of income, annual and interim tax repayment claims, record-keeping, and information to be provided to investors.

[*SI 1998 No 1870; SI 2017 No 186; SI 2018 No 359, Regs 1, 4; SI 2019 No 382; SI 2020 No 261*].

Long service awards

[30.32] Such awards to employees are exempt within the limits set out in **28.68** EMPLOYMENT INCOME.

Members of Parliaments or Assemblies

[30.33] The following exemptions apply.

MPs' overnight accommodation expenses

No liability to income tax arises in respect of a payment made for 'accommodation expenses' to a member of the House of Commons under *Parliamentary Standards Act 2009, s 5(1)*. This applies equally to a payment related to, or in consequence of, a payment for accommodation expenses. '*Accommodation expenses*' are expenses necessarily incurred on overnight accommodation that is required for the performance of the member's parliamentary duties in or about the Palace of Westminster or the member's constituency. They do not include the cost of an overnight stay in a hotel that is required only because the House is sitting late, unless the House is sitting beyond 1 am. The exemption also applies to payments for accommodation expenses made at the direction of an MP to a person other than the MP (e.g. to a landlord). The exemption does not cover loans made to MPs for a deposit on a rented property.

The main exemption above has effect in relation to payments made on or after 7 May 2010, unless they are made in accordance with a Commons resolution passed before that date in which case the old rules apply. The old rules were not dissimilar but predated the introduction, by the Independent Parliamentary Standards Authority (IPSA), of a new scheme for paying MPs' expenses. The rules applied to an overnight expenses allowance paid to an MP in accordance with a Commons resolution; the above exclusions did not apply.

[*ITEPA 2003, s 292*].

See also **28.45** EMPLOYMENT INCOME.

Overnight expenses of other elected representatives

Payments to members of the Scottish Parliament or the Wales or Northern Ireland Assemblies for necessary overnight expenses are also exempt from income tax. These are additional expenses necessarily incurred for the purpose of performing duties as a member in staying away from home overnight either where the body of which he is a member sits or in the area he represents. [*ITEPA 2003, s 293*].

MPs' UK travel and subsistence expenses

No liability to income tax arises in respect of a payment made for 'relevant UK travel expenses' or 'relevant subsistence expenses' to a member of the House of Commons under *Parliamentary Standards Act 2009, s 5(1)*. '*Relevant UK travel expenses*' are expenses necessarily incurred on journeys made by the member within the UK that are necessary for the performance of his parliamentary duties. If the member shares caring responsibilities with a spouse or partner, the cost of journeys made by the spouse or partner between the member's London Area residence and the member's constituency residence are also within the exemption. 'Caring responsibilities' and 'London Area residence' have the same meaning as they have in the MPs' expenses scheme for the time being in effect under *Parliamentary Standards Act 2009, s 5*. '*Relevant subsistence expenses*' are expenses necessarily incurred on an evening meal (excluding alcoholic drinks) eaten on the Parliamentary Estate in cases where the member is required to be at the Commons because the House is sitting beyond 7.30 pm.

[*ITEPA 2003, s 293A*].

Other representatives' UK travel expenses

No liability to income tax arises in respect of a statutory payment made for 'relevant UK travel expenses' to a member of the Scottish Parliament, Welsh Assembly or Northern Ireland Assembly. '*Relevant UK travel expenses*' are expenses necessarily incurred on 'allowable journeys' made by the member within the UK that are necessary for the performance of his duties as a member. '*Allowable journeys*' are those between the constituency or region and the Parliament or Assembly to which the member belongs, between the constituency or region and the member's parliamentary home, or within the constituency or region but not a home-to-work journey. If the member shares caring responsibilities with a spouse or partner, the cost of journeys made by the spouse or partner between the constituency or region and the member's parliamentary home are also within the exemption. *ITEPA 2003, s 293B(6)* and *(7)* provide a number of definitions for the purposes of the exemption. The exemption replaces and formalises long-standing extra-statutory exemptions. [*ITEPA 2003, s 293B*].

European travel expenses of MPs and other representatives

No liability to income tax arises in respect of a sum that is paid in respect of 'European travel expenses' to a member of the House of Commons under *Parliamentary Standards Act 2009, s 5(1)*. '*European travel expenses*' means the cost of, and any additional expenses incurred in, travelling between the UK and 'a relevant European location'. A '*relevant European location*' is an EU institution or agency or the national parliament of another member State, of a candidate or applicant country or of any other country that is a member of the Council of Europe. Payments to members of the Scottish Parliament or the Wales or Northern Ireland Assemblies in respect of European travel expenses are similarly exempt.

[*ITEPA 2003, s 294*].

Transport and subsistence for Government ministers etc.

Ministers and certain other office-holders in the UK Government, the Scottish Parliament or the Wales or Northern Ireland Assemblies are exempt from income tax in respect of the provision of transport or subsistence to them or their families or households by or on behalf of the Crown, or the reimbursement of expenditure on such provision. 'Transport' for this purpose includes any car (with or without a driver) and any other benefit in connection with such a car (including fuel). 'Subsistence' includes food, drink and temporary accommodation. [*ITEPA 2003, s 295*].

Simon's Taxes. See E4.732.

Nazi persecution, interest paid to victims of

[30.34] Interest paid to, or in respect of, a victim of Nazi persecution is exempt from income tax if it is paid under a 'qualifying compensation scheme', for a 'qualifying purpose' and in respect of a 'qualifying deposit' of the victim.

A '*qualifying compensation scheme*' is a scheme constituted (whether under UK or foreign law) by written instrument and the purpose (or a purpose) of which is to make payments of interest of the kind contemplated by this exemption. Interest is paid for a 'qualifying purpose' if it either meets a liability to pay such interest on the deposit or is paid to compensate for the effects of inflation on the deposit. A '*qualifying deposit*' is a deposit made by, or on behalf of, the victim and on or before 5 June 1945. [*ITTOIA 2005, s 756A*].

Netherlands Benefit Act for Victims of Persecution 1940–1945

[30.35] No liability to income tax arises on a pension, annuity, allowance or other payment provided in accordance with the provisions of the scheme established under Netherlands law known as Wet uitkeringen vervolgingsslachtoffers 1940–1945. [*ITEPA 2003, s 642A; FA 2016, s 23*]. The Netherlands Government makes payments through this scheme to individuals with a Dutch connection who were victims of persecution in Europe or Asia during the Second World War.

Non-UK domiciliaries

[30.36] Where certain conditions are met, an exemption is available for the foreign income and gains (see **61.6** REMITTANCE BASIS) of low-income non-UK domiciled employees working in the UK. According to HMRC, such individuals will typically be migrant workers employed in seasonal work in the agricultural or service sectors in UK and in other countries in the same tax year and whose overseas income is subject to tax where it is earned (Treasury Explanatory Notes to the 2009 Finance Bill). The exemption removes in most cases the requirement for a self-assessment tax return to be filed.

The conditions (all of which must be met for the tax year in question) are that:

- the individual is UK resident but not domiciled in the UK (see **63.35** RESIDENCE AND DOMICILE, and note that the deemed domicile rule at **63.36** RESIDENCE AND DOMICILE does *not* apply for this purpose);
- the individual has not made a claim to be taxed on the remittance basis (see **61.2**(1) REMITTANCE BASIS);
- the individual has income from an employment the duties of which are performed wholly or partly in the UK;
- the individual's 'relevant foreign earnings' (if any) (see **61.6** REMITTANCE BASIS) do not exceed £10,000 and are all subject to a foreign tax;
- the individual's income consisting of foreign interest (if any) does not exceed £100 and is all subject to a foreign tax;
- the individual has no other foreign income and gains other than 'relevant foreign earnings' or interest;
- the individual would not be liable to UK income tax at a rate other than the basic rate, the Scottish starter, intermediate or basic rate, the savings nil rate or the starting rate for savings if this exemption did not apply; and
- the individual does not file a tax return.

The exemption operates by calculating the individual's income tax liability (L1) without regard to the exemption and then reducing it by so much of that liability (L2) as relates to his foreign income and gains. In computing L2, the foreign income and gains must be reduced by personal reliefs to the extent that these were set against them in the calculation of L1. If any double tax relief is due in respect of the foreign income and gains, this must be deducted in arriving at L2.

[*ITA 2007, ss 828A–828D; FA 2016, ss 4(10)(17), 6(20)(24); SI 2018 No 459, Arts 1, 6(7)*].

Non-UK residents

[30.37] Non-UK residents are exempt from tax on income and capital gains from: certain government stocks (see **65.4** SAVINGS AND INVESTMENT INCOME); securities of the Inter-American Development Bank [*ITTOIA 2005, s 773*]; securities of the OECD Support Fund [*OECD Support Fund Act 1975, s 4*] and certain other international organisations designated by statutory instrument [*ITTOIA 2005, s 774*], including the Asian Development Bank (*SI 1984 No 1215*), the African Development Bank (*SI 1984 No 1634*), the European Bank for Reconstruction and Development (*SI 1991 No 1202*) and any of the European Communities or the European Investment Bank (*SI 1985 No 1172*); and from certain pensions, see **56.5** PENSION INCOME. See also **27.2** DOUBLE TAX RELIEF.

Overseas income

[30.38] Certain overseas income is exempt from UK tax under specific DOUBLE TAX RELIEF (**27**) agreements. If not so exempt, double tax relief may nevertheless be claimable. In some circumstances, overseas income is chargeable on the REMITTANCE BASIS (**61**). See also **50** NON-RESIDENTS.

Pensions

[30.39] Certain pensions are exempt — see **56.4, 56.5** PENSION INCOME.

Premium savings bonds

[30.40] Prizes are free of both income tax and capital gains tax.

Redundancy payments

[30.41] Redundancy payments under *Employment Rights Act 1996* (or NI equivalent) are exempt. [*ITEPA 2003, s 309*]. See also **28.71** EMPLOYMENT INCOME.

Repayment interest

[30.42] Repayment interest (i.e. interest on overpaid tax) in respect of income tax or capital gains tax repayments (see 62 REPAYMENT INTEREST) is disregarded for income tax purposes. The same applies to VAT repayment supplement under *VATA 1994, s 79*, but interest payable on certain VAT repayments under *VATA 1994, s 80* is *not* exempt. [*ITTOIA 2005, ss 749, 777*].

Retirement, lump sums on

[30.43] Certain lump sums under PENSION PROVISION (57) are exempt. See 56.4(a) PENSION INCOME.

Sandwich courses etc.

[30.44] Where an employee is released by employer to take a full-time educational course at a university, technical college or similar institution open to the public at large, payments made by employer to employee for periods of attendance are exempt from income tax subject to the following conditions: (i) that the course lasts at least one academic year, with an average of at least 20 weeks per year of full-time attendance, and (ii) that the total payments, including lodging, subsistence and travel allowances but excluding any tuition fees paid by the employer to the university etc., do not exceed £15,480.

Payments become taxable in full where the rate exceeds the annual limit. However, an increase in the rate of payment over the limit, partway through a course, does not prevent the exemption applying to any payments for the earlier part of the course.

(HMRC SP 4/86; HMRC Internet Statements 12 June 2006, 15 August 2007).

Savings certificates

[30.45] All income arising from savings certificates (as defined) (and including index-linked) and tax reserve certificates is exempt from tax except that arising from:

(i) savings certificates purchased by or on behalf of a person in excess of the amount authorised under the regulations of the particular issue; or
(ii) Ulster savings certificates, unless the holder is resident and ordinarily resident in NI when the certificates are repaid or he was so resident and ordinarily resident when he purchased them. Where repayment is made after the death of the holder, who was resident and ordinarily resident in NI when he purchased them, the exemption is allowed.

[*ITTOIA 2005, ss 692, 693*].

Scholarship income and bursaries

[30.46] Such income is exempt where arising from a scholarship held by a full-time student at an educational establishment. [*ITTOIA 2005, s 776*]. In *Clayton v Gothorp* Ch D 1971, 47 TC 168, discharge of loan made by employer for training course held not scholarship income but was emoluments. See **28.74** EMPLOYMENT INCOME for where scholarship awarded by employer of parent etc. Covenanted 'parental contributions' under *Education Act 1962* not an educational endowment (*Gibbs v Randall* Ch D 1980, 53 TC 513).

Social security benefits etc

[30.47] Exemption applies to certain social security benefits (see **73** SOCIAL SECURITY AND NATIONAL INSURANCE) and corresponding foreign benefits (HMRC ESC A24) and payments under Jobmatch programme (HMRC ESC A97). Disabled Person's Vehicle Maintenance Grants under *National Health Service Act 1977, Sch 2 para 2* or corresponding Scottish or NI Act. [*ITTOIA 2005, s 780*].

Sporting events

[30.48] The following exemptions apply in relation to recent major 'one-off' sporting events held in the UK.

UEFA Champions League final 2017

The final of the UEFA Champions League was held in Cardiff in 2017. There are provisions conferring exemption from income tax to non-UK resident employees and contractors of competing overseas teams in relation to employment income or trading income arising from duties or services performed in the UK from 1 June to 5 June 2017 inclusive in connection with the final. Non-UK resident employees, contractors, officials and delegates of UEFA are also within the exemption, as are employees and officials of national football associations which are members of UEFA. If an individual is UK resident for 2017/18 but the year is a split year (see **63.19** RESIDENCE AND DOMICILE) as regards that individual, he is treated as a non-UK resident for this purpose if the final takes place during the overseas part of the year. The exemption does not apply to income from contracts entered into or amended after the final commences. Where the exemption applies, the deduction at source rules normally applicable to non-UK resident sports persons (see **50.11** NON-RESIDENTS) are accordingly disapplied. [*SI 2017 No 614*].

World Athletics Championships 2017

Accredited competitors in the World Athletics Championship and World Para Athletics Championship held in London in 2017 who meet the 'non-residence condition' were exempt from UK tax on any employment income or trading profits arising from 'Championship activities'. '*Championship activities*' are defined as either competing at the Championships or performing any activity during the 'championships period' the main purpose of which is to support or promote the Championships. The '*championships period*' is the period beginning with 12 July 2017 and ending with 15 August 2017.

The '*non-residence condition*' is that either:

- the accredited competitor is non-UK resident for 2017/18; or

- the accredited competitor is UK resident for 2017/18 but the year is a split year (see **63.19** RESIDENCE AND DOMICILE) as regards the competitor, and the activity is performed in the overseas part of the year.

Where the exemption applies, the deduction at source rules normally applicable to non-UK resident sports persons (see **50.11** NON-RESIDENTS) are accordingly disapplied.

[*SI 2016 No 771, Regs 1, 2, 7–10*].

Troubles Permanent Disablement Payment Scheme

[30.49] No liability to income tax arises in respect of a payment made at any time under the Troubles Permanent Disablement Payment Scheme. Such a payment is to be ignored for all income tax purposes. [*FA 2020, Sch 15 paras 2(4), 3(1)(2)(4)*]. This scheme was introduced by the UK Government on 29 May 2020 to make payments to those permanently disabled as a consequence of injury caused by a '*Troubles-related incident*', i.e. an incident involving an act of violence or force carried out in Ireland, the UK or elsewhere in Europe for a reason related to the constitutional status of Northern Ireland or to political or sectarian hostility between people there. [*Northern Ireland (Executive Formation etc) Act 2019, s 10; SI 2020 No 103*].

Visiting forces etc.

[30.50] No liability to income tax arises on earnings if:

(a) they are paid by the government of a designated country to a member of a visiting force of that country or of a civilian component of such a force; and
(b) that person is not a British citizen, a British overseas territories citizen, a British National (Overseas) or a British Overseas citizen.

Also, no liability to income tax arises on earnings if they are paid by a designated allied headquarters (as defined) to an employee of a category for the time being agreed between the UK Government and the other members of the North Atlantic Council. However, if the employee is in any of the categories listed in (b) above, this exemption applies only if it is necessary for it to do so to give effect to an agreement between parties to the North Atlantic Treaty.

The above exemptions are extended to members of EU military forces and EU civilian staff (working alongside military forces) serving in the UK or attached to international military headquarters in the UK.

[*ITEPA 2003, s 303; SI 2012 Nos 3070, 3071*].

See also **63.38** RESIDENCE AND DOMICILE.

Voluntary office-holders and volunteers

[30.51] The exemptions detailed below have effect.

Financial loss allowances

No liability to income tax arises in respect of a payment (sometimes called a financial loss allowance) made by a 'relevant authority' to a person (P) holding a voluntary office with the authority where P carries out duties of that office in a period in which P is also employed and the payment is made solely to compensate P for lost employment income (and does not exceed the amount of that income). Lost employment income is computed net of tax and national insurance contributions for this purpose. '*Relevant authority*' includes a government (or devolved government) department, a local government body, a trade union, a local medical committee and a body (other than a company) established for the purpose of carrying out functions conferred on it by statute. It also includes a company whose activities consist solely of carrying out some or all of the functions of a relevant authority, otherwise than for profit.

For the above purpose P holds a voluntary office if, when the said payment is made, P is not entitled to, has not received, and does not expect to receive, any payment or benefit in connection with carrying out the duties of the office. Any payment, whether an advance payment or a reimbursement, in respect of reasonable expenses incurred in carrying out those duties is disregarded, as is any payment falling to be taxed as trading income (see **75.56**(f) TRADING INCOME).

[*ITEPA 2003, s 299A; FA 2020, s 14(2)(3); SI 2018 No 282, Arts 1, 2*].

There is no such exemption where P is self-employed and a payment is made to compensate for lost profits. See **75.56**(f) TRADING INCOME.

An identical exemption applies where P does not hold an office with the relevant authority but performs services for it for no financial benefit in a period in which P is also employed. 'Services' include jury service. P performs services for no financial benefit if, when the said payment is made, P is not entitled to, has not received, and does not expect to receive, any payment or benefit (other than compensation for lost employment income) in connection with performing the services. Any payment in respect of reasonable expenses incurred in performing the services is disregarded, as is any payment compensating the person for loss of social security income arising as a result of performing the services. [*ITTOIA 2005, s 782C; SI 2018 No 282, Arts 1, 3(4)*].

The above statutory exemptions apply for 2018/19 onwards but similar exemptions previously applied by concession (see HMRC Employment Income Manual EIM01120, EIM01125).

Payments for expenses

For 2020/21 onwards, no liability to income tax arises on a payment to a person holding a voluntary office if the payment is in respect of reasonable expenses incurred in carrying out the duties of that office. The exemption applies regardless of whether the payment is an advance payment or a reimbursement and whether the person making the payment is the person with whom the office is held. The question of whether a person holds a voluntary office is determined as under *ITEPA 2003, s 299A* above. [*ITEPA 2003, s 299B; FA 2020, s 14(1)(3)*].

The above gives statutory footing to a long-standing HMRC practice to the effect that no tax charge arises on expenses provided to voluntary unpaid office-holders so long as any payments or reimbursements do no more than meet the expenses incurred.

Windrush Compensation Scheme

[30.52] No liability to income tax arises in respect of a payment made at any time under the Windrush Compensation Scheme. Such a payment is to be ignored for all income tax purposes. A payment is also within the exemption if it is not itself made under the Scheme but is made by or on behalf of the Government, or a devolved government, or a local or other public authority, to or in respect of an eligible claimant under the Scheme and in connection with the same circumstances as gave rise to the claimant's eligibility. [*FA 2020, Sch 15 paras 2(2)(3), 3(1)–(3)*]. This scheme was launched by the Home Office on 3 April 2019 and is intended to compensate individuals who have suffered loss in connection with being unable to demonstrate their lawful status in the UK.

Woodlands

[30.53] Profits (and losses) from the commercial occupation of woodlands in the UK are ignored for income tax purposes. For this purpose, the occupation of woodlands is commercial if the woodlands are managed on a commercial basis and with a view to the realisation of profits. Land on which short rotation coppice (i.e. a perennial crop of tree species planted at high density, the stems of which are harvested above ground level at intervals of less than ten years) is cultivated is not woodlands. [*ITA 2007, s 996(4)(6); ITTOIA 2005, ss 11, 267, 768, 876(4)(6)*].

In *Jaggers (trading as Shide Trees) v Ellis* Ch D 1997, 71 TC 164, land on which trees were planted and cultivated in a manner normally associated with Christmas tree production was held not to be woodland.

See 75.77(o) TRADING INCOME for the tax treatment of certain Government grants.

For the purpose of computing the profits of a trade of dealing in land, there is disregarded any part of the cost of purchasing UK woodlands in the course of the trade that is attributable to trees or saleable underwood growing on the land. If the woodlands are subsequently sold in the course of the trade and any of the trees and underwood are still growing, the amount disregarded on purchase is excluded from the sale proceeds. These rules do not apply if the purchase was under a pre-1 May 1963 contract. [*ITTOIA 2005, s 156, Sch 2 para 42*].

31

Exempt Organisations

Introduction to exempt organisations

[31.1] Exemption is given to the organisations etc. below to the extent indicated.

Non-resident central banks

[31.2] Non-UK resident central banks as specified by Order in Council are exempt from tax on certain classes of income. [*ITA 2007, s 840*]. The issue departments of the Reserve Bank of India and the State Bank of Pakistan are exempt from all taxes. [*ITA 2007, s 839; TCGA 1992, s 271(8)*].

Charities

[31.3] Charities are generally exempt but see full details at **14** CHARITIES AND CHARITABLE GIVING.

Local authorities etc.

[31.4] Local authorities and local authority associations, as defined by *ITA 2007, s 999* and *s 1000* respectively, are exempt from income tax. [*ITA 2007, s 838*].

Registered pension schemes

[31.5] Registered pension schemes are exempt from income tax on income derived from investments (including futures contracts and option contracts) or deposits held for the purposes of the scheme. See **57.11** PENSION PROVISION. See, however, **57.30–57.33** PENSION PROVISION as regards the charge to tax where income is derived from certain property held by self-directed registered pension schemes.

32

Foreign Income

Cross-references. See **24.1** DIPLOMATIC ETC. IMMUNITY — INDIVIDUALS AND ORGANISATIONS for exemption from tax on foreign income of consular officers and employees in UK; **27.4** DOUBLE TAX RELIEF regarding Ireland; **28.5**, **28.12** EMPLOYMENT INCOME for foreign employment; **61** REMITTANCE BASIS; and **63** RESIDENCE AND DOMICILE.

Introduction to foreign income

[32.1] Each type of foreign (i.e. non-UK) income is charged to tax under the provisions charging the equivalent type of UK income (except for dividends from non-UK companies, which have their own charging provision). A number of special rules continue to apply to foreign income, however, and these are described in this chapter). *ITTOIA 2005* employs the expression 'relevant foreign income' to indicate the types of income to which many of those rules apply (see **32.2** below).

Relevant foreign income

[32.2] '*Relevant foreign income*' (see **32.1** above) means chargeable income which arises from a source outside the United Kingdom (see **32.3** below) and which falls within any of the following categories:

(a) trade profits (see **75.1** TRADING INCOME);
(b) a partner's share of the profits of a trade arising outside the UK for a tax year if:
- the control and management of the trade is outside the UK; and
- the partner is a UK resident individual who is not domiciled in the UK (see **63.35** RESIDENCE AND DOMICILE) and the REMITTANCE BASIS (**61**) applies to him for the tax year;

(c) adjustment income on change of basis in computing trade profits (see **75.24** TRADING INCOME);
(d) profits of a property business (which may be a UK property business or an overseas property business — see **60.2** PROPERTY INCOME);
(e) interest (see **65.2** SAVINGS AND INVESTMENT INCOME);

(f) dividends from non-UK resident companies (see **65.17** SAVINGS AND INVESTMENT INCOME);
(g) purchased life annuity payments (see **65.23** SAVINGS AND INVESTMENT INCOME);
(h) profits from the disposal of deeply discounted securities (see **65.24** SAVINGS AND INVESTMENT INCOME) which are outside the UK;
(i) royalties and other income from intellectual property within *ITTOIA 2005, s 579* (see **41.1** INTELLECTUAL PROPERTY);
(j) films and sound recordings (non-trade businesses) (see **49.3** MISCELLANEOUS INCOME);
(k) non-trading income from telecommunication rights within **49.4** MISCELLANEOUS INCOME;
(l) estate income within *ITTOIA 2005, s 649* where the estate is not a UK estate (see **22.4** DECEASED ESTATES);
(m) annual payments not otherwise charged within *ITTOIA 2005, ss 683–686* (see **49.5** MISCELLANEOUS INCOME);
(n) income not otherwise charged within *ITTOIA 2005, ss 687–689* (see **49.7** MISCELLANEOUS INCOME);
(o) distributions by the Commonwealth Development Corporation;
(p) foreign pension income within **56.2**(b) PENSION INCOME;
(q) employment-related annuities within **56.2**(e) PENSION INCOME;
(r) pre-1973 pensions paid under the *Overseas Pensions Act 1973* within **56.2**(h) PENSION INCOME;
(s) annual payments within **56.2**(i) PENSION INCOME;
(t) social security income from foreign benefits (see **73.2** SOCIAL SECURITY AND NATIONAL INSURANCE);
(u) accrued income profits (see **2.9** ACCRUED INCOME SCHEME); and
(v) foreign deemed income under the 'transfer of assets' abroad rules (see **4.14, 4.15** ANTI-AVOIDANCE).

In a case where the REMITTANCE BASIS (**61**) applies, the reference above to chargeable income includes income that would be chargeable if the remittance basis did not apply.

See also **51.8** OFFSHORE FUNDS (offshore income gains treated as relevant foreign income in certain circumstances).

Income chargeable:

- as a result of the withdrawal of relief for unremittable income under *ITTOIA 2005, s 844* (see **32.5** below); or
- under **78.3** or **78.4** TRANSACTIONS IN UK LAND,

is not relevant foreign income.

[*ITTOIA 2005, ss 830, 857(1)(3); ITEPA 2003, ss 575(3), 613(4), 631(3), 635(4), 679(2); FA 2016, ss 79(11), 82(1); FA 2017, Sch 3 para 2(4)(6)*].

Simon's Taxes. See **E1.602.**

United Kingdom

[32.3] The United Kingdom for tax purposes comprises England, Scotland, Wales and Northern Ireland. The Channel Islands and the Isle of Man are not included. [*Interpretation Act 1978, Sch 1*]. Great Britain comprises England, Scotland and Wales only.

Territorial extension of tax area

The territorial sea of the UK is regarded as part of the UK for tax purposes. Earnings, profits and gains from exploration or exploitation activities in a designated area (under *Continental Shelf Act 1964, s 1(7)*), are treated as arising in the UK. A licence-holder under *Petroleum Act 1998, Pt I* may be held accountable for the liability of a non-UK resident if the tax in question is related to the licence.

[*ITA 2007, s 1013; ITTOIA 2005, s 874; ITEPA 2003, s 41; TMA 1970, ss 77B–77H, 77J, 77K; TCGA 1992, s 276*].

As regards liability of non-UK resident lessors of mobile drilling rigs, vessels or equipment used in conjunction with exploration or exploitation activities, see HMRC SP 6/84. See **27.3** DOUBLE TAX RELIEF as regards certain UK exemptions *not* extended to continental shelf workers.

Deductions and reliefs

Collection or payment expenses

[32.4] Where relevant foreign income (see **32.2** above) is not chargeable on the REMITTANCE BASIS (**61**), a deduction is allowable for expenses incurred outside the UK that are attributable to the collection or payment of the income. [*ITTOIA 2005, s 838*].

Annual payments

Where relevant foreign income (see **32.2** above) is not received in the UK and is not chargeable on the remittance basis, a deduction is allowable for an annual payment (other than interest) payable out of the income to a non-UK resident.

The deduction is not permitted unless, had the payment arisen in the UK, it would have been chargeable to income tax as:

- income treated as received by a unit holder from an exempt unauthorised unit trust (see **80.8** UNIT TRUSTS ETC.);
- a royalty or other income from intellectual property within *ITTOIA 2005, s 579* (see **41.1** INTELLECTUAL PROPERTY);
- non-trading income from telecommunication rights within **49.4** MISCELLANEOUS INCOME; or
- an annual payment not otherwise charged within *ITTOIA 2005, ss 683–686* (see **49.5** MISCELLANEOUS INCOME);

or would have been chargeable to corporation tax under specified provisions of *CTA 2009*.

[*ITTOIA 2005, s 839; ITEPA 2003, ss 613(5), 635(5); FA 2017, Sch 3 para 2(5)(6)*].

Relief for backdated pensions

There are provisions which treat foreign income from pensions or annuities within **56.2**(b)(e)(i) PENSION INCOME, or an increase in such a pension or annuity, which are granted retrospectively, as arising in the tax year in respect of which the pension, annuity or increase is paid, if that is earlier than the year in which it is paid. A claim to apply these provisions must be made no later than four years after the end of the later tax year. [*ITTOIA 2005, ss 840, 840A, Sch 2 para 152*].

Foreign tax

See **27.10**(a)(ii)(iii) DOUBLE TAX RELIEF.

Unremittable foreign income

[32.5] Relief is available in respect of income arising in a territory outside the UK, not taxable on the remittance basis, which is unremittable (see below). Note that the relief is not restricted to relevant foreign income (see **32.2** above). For this purpose, income is unremittable if:

- it cannot be transferred to the UK because of the laws, or the executive action of the government, of the territory concerned or because of the impossibility of obtaining currency there that could be transferred to the UK; and
- the person chargeable has not realised it outside that territory for an amount in sterling or other currency which can be transferred to the UK.

Where a claim for relief is made, unremittable income is not taken into account for income tax purposes. Claims must be made within twelve months after 31 January following the tax year in which the income would otherwise be chargeable. A claim may not be made if a payment has been made in respect of the income under certain export credit guarantee arrangements (see *ITTOIA 2005, s 842(4)*).

Relief under the above provisions is withdrawn if the income ceases to be unremittable or if a payment under export credit guarantee arrangements is made. In such an event, the income is treated as arising at the time it so ceases to be unremittable or the payment is made, and it is valued for tax purposes as at that time (together with any foreign tax). If the source has ceased at that time then the income is treated as a post-cessation receipt (see **59.1** POST-CESSATION RECEIPTS AND EXPENDITURE) if the source was a trade, profession or vocation or a property business, or in the case of income from another source, the income is taxed as if the source was continuing. Where appropriate, these provisions apply to the personal representative of the taxpayer as they would have to the taxpayer.

Relief under these provisions is not available in respect of profits which a person is treated as making under the accrued income scheme, but a similar relief is provided for in *ITA 2007, ss 668, 669* — see **2.10** ACCRUED INCOME SCHEME.

Where no claim is made under the above provisions in respect of unremittable income, the amount chargeable to tax is determined by reference to the generally recognised market value in the UK of the currency in which the income is denominated or, if there is no such value, according to the official exchange rate of the territory where the income arises.

[*ITTOIA 2005, ss 841–845, Sch 2 para 153*].

See **75.127** TRADING INCOME for relief for certain unremittable income forming part of the profits of trades.

Simon's Taxes. See **E1.607–E1.609.**

33

Foster Care etc.

See also HMRC Helpsheet 236 at www.gov.uk/government/publications/qualifying-care-relief-foster-carers-adult-placement-carers-kinship-carers-and-staying-put-carers-hs236-self-assessment-helpsheet.

Simon's Taxes. See E1.7.

Introduction to foster care etc.

[33.1] Qualifying care receipts are exempt if they do not exceed a limit computed by reference to the individual recipient, and, if the recipient so elects, are subject to an alternative method of computation if they do exceed that limit. The relief (whether it be the exemption or alternative method) is known as qualifying care relief.

Meaning of qualifying care relief

[33.2] An individual qualifies for qualifying care relief for a tax year if he has 'qualifying care receipts' for that year and derives no taxable income, other than qualifying care receipts, from any trade or other arrangement from which he derives qualifying care receipts. An individual has '*qualifying care receipts*' for a tax year if receipts in respect of the 'provision of qualifying care' accrue to him during the 'income period' for those receipts and they would otherwise fall to be brought into account in computing the profits of a trade or to be taxed as miscellaneous income. The '*provision of qualifying care*' means the 'provision of foster care', the 'provision of shared lives care' or the provision of both. Qualifying care may be provided by an individual alone or in partnership with others. The '*income period*' is the basis period for the tax year if the receipts would otherwise be brought into account in computing the profits of a trade; otherwise it is the tax year itself.

Where a cash basis election is in force (see **76** TRADING INCOME — CASH BASIS FOR SMALLER BUSINESSES), the reference above to receipts accruing to an individual during a period should be read as receipts being received by him in that period. Any amounts brought into account under *ITTOIA 2005, s 96A* (capital receipts — see **76.9** TRADING INCOME — CASH BASIS FOR SMALLER BUSINESSES) as a receipt in calculating the profits of a qualifying care trade are treated as receipts in respect of the provision of qualifying care.

Provision of foster care

For these purposes, the '*provision of foster care*' means the provision of accommodation and maintenance for a child by an individual, other than an 'excluded individual', with whom the child has been placed under specified statutory provisions governing foster care in the UK. Receipts from *private* foster care arrangements do not qualify for the exemption. Anyone who is a parent of the child, or has parental responsibility in relation to the child, is an '*excluded individual*' for this purpose, as is (where relevant) anyone in whose favour a residence order (or, in Scotland, a contact order) has been made and was in force immediately prior to the child's being placed in care.

Provision of shared lives care

The '*provision of shared lives care*' means the provision of accommodation and 'care' for an adult or child ('X') by an individual, other than an excluded individual, with whom X has been placed under a social care scheme of a kind specified or described in *SI 2011 No 712*. The accommodation must be in the individual's only or main 'residence', and the accommodation and care must be provided on the basis that X will share the individual's home and daily family life during the placement. The same individuals are excluded as for foster care relief (regardless of the age of X), and care does not count as shared lives care if it is, in fact, foster care. '*Care*' means personal care, including assistance and support. '*Residence*' means a building, or part of a building, occupied or intended to be occupied as a separate residence or a caravan or houseboat. If a building, or part of a building, designed for permanent use as a single residence is temporarily divided into two or more separate residences, it is still regarded as a single residence.

The social care schemes brought within these provisions are, subject to conditions, any scheme, service or arrangement that provides adult placement care, kinship care or staying put care. *SI 2011 No 712* sets out the conditions that apply in each case.

Shared lives care — further condition for relief

An individual does not qualify for qualifying care relief in respect of shared lives care if the placement cap is exceeded for the residence (or any of the residences) used by him to provide the care. The placement cap is exceeded for a residence if, at any given time during the 'relevant period', shared lives care is being provided there (whether by the individual or anyone else) for more than three people in total. The '*relevant period*', in relation to a residence, is the period for which the residence is the individual's only or main residence during the income period for the qualifying care receipts (see above). In determining the number of people for whom shared lives care is being provided at any given time, brothers and sisters (including half-brothers and half-sisters) count as one person. If the placement cap is exceeded but the individual also has qualifying care receipts for the tax year in respect of the provision of foster care, he can still qualify for foster care relief.

[*ITTOIA 2005, ss 804, 804A, 805, 805A, 806, 806A, 806B; F(No 2)A 2017, Sch 2 paras 11, 64; SI 2011 No 712; SI 2018 No 317*].

The exemption

[33.3] The exemption applies where the individual's total qualifying care receipts for the tax year or (as the case may be) the period of account, taking no account of any deduction for expenses etc., do not exceed the individual's limit. This limit is based on a fixed amount of £10,000 per residence plus an amount per adult or child per individual based on the number of weeks (or part weeks) during the income period (i.e. the basis period or, for non-trading arrangements, the tax year) in which the individual provides qualifying care for the adult or child. The amount per adult is £250 per week (or part week). The amount per child is £200 per week (or part week) for a child under 11 and £250 per week (or part week) for a child of 11 or over; a week in which the child reaches the age of 11 qualifies for the higher figure. A week, for these purposes, comprises the seven days beginning with a Monday. A week in which an income period ends is counted as belonging to that income period. Both the fixed and weekly amounts are subject to any amendment made by future Treasury order. If, *in the tax year*, the residence used to provide the qualifying care is also used for provision of qualifying care by one or more other individuals who also have qualifying care receipts for the year, the £10,000 fixed amount is divided equally between them. If an individual's income period is a period other than a year, the fixed amount or, where relevant, his share of it is adjusted proportionately.

Where the exemption applies, the individual is treated, for the tax year in question, as making nil profit and nil loss from the trade or (as the case may be) from each non-trading qualifying care arrangement from which the qualifying care receipts arise. If, in the case of a trade, the individual would otherwise be entitled to relief for an overlap profit (see **75.14** TRADING INCOME), he is given the relief anyway.

In computing the individual's limit in a case where the qualifying care receipts are those of a period of account (other than one ending on 5 April), the fixed amount is that prescribed for the tax year in which the period of account ends, e.g. £10,000 for a period ending in 2019/20. If, in future, the prescribed amounts per adult or child alter, so that different rates apply for two tax years in which the period of account falls, the rates for the first of those tax years apply in respect of adults or children cared for during that part of the period of account preceding 6 April and the new rates will apply in respect of adults or children cared for during that part of the period of account falling after 5 April.

[*ITTOIA 2005, ss 807–814, 821, 822, 828*].

The alternative method of computation

[33.4] If, for the tax year or (as the case may be) the period of account, the individual's total qualifying care receipts would be within the exemption at 33.3 above were it not for the fact that they exceed his limit, he may make an election to be charged to income tax as if his profit were equal to the excess. The election for this alternative method of calculating profit must specify the tax year for which it is made, must be made no later than the first anniversary of 31 January following that tax year (or such later date as HMRC may, in a particular case, allow) and has effect for that tax year only. In the absence of an election, the normal rules for computing profits and losses apply. If no election is made before the deadline but his taxable qualifying care profits are adjusted after the deadline has passed, the individual is given additional time in which to make an election, the revised deadline being the first anniversary of 31 January following the tax year in which the adjustment is made (or, again, such later date as HMRC may, in a particular case, allow). Once made, an election can be withdrawn within the time limits specified for making it. [*ITTOIA 2005, ss 815–821, 823, 828; F(No 2)A 2017, Sch 3 paras 10, 13*].

Example

[33.5]

Dave and Holly, a couple living together, provide foster care by way of trade. Each prepares accounts to 31 December. During their respective periods of account covering the year ending 31 December 2020, they provide care to a twelve-year old (child 1) for the full 52 weeks and to a nine-year old (child 2) for 15 weeks. *Each* of their individual limits is computed as follows.

		£
Fixed amount for 2020/21: £10,000 ÷ 2		5,000
Amounts per child:	child 1 (52 × £250)	13,000
	child 2 (15 × £200)	3,000
		£21,000

Note

(a) Some HMRC offices are believed to have taken the view that, in a case such as this, the amounts per child must be divided between the couple instead of being available separately to each individual. In this example, this would have the effect of reducing each individual's limit by £8,000. In the author's opinion, the legislation does not support such a view; if, however, a couple are trading in partnership (clearly not the case in this example) it becomes arguable that the partnership should take the place of an individual for the purpose of computing the limits, in which case only one amount per child would be available to the partnership.

Capital allowances on plant and machinery

[33.6] As regards capital allowances on plant and machinery used to provide qualifying care, there are special rules to allow for the fact that a carer's profits can be determined using a different method from one year to the next. A carer can claim capital allowances only if his profits are computed under the normal rules for business income and expenditure. It follows that a carer may be able to claim capital allowances for one year but not the next and so on.

Immediately after the beginning of any 'qualifying care relief period' that was not immediately preceded by a qualifying care relief period and for which there is a 'care business pool', a disposal event (see **10.27** CAPITAL ALLOWANCES ON PLANT AND MACHINERY) is treated as occurring. The disposal value to be brought into account is equal to the unrelieved qualifying expenditure brought forward in the pool from the preceding chargeable period. For this purpose, any previous qualifying expenditure not yet allocated to the pool is treated as if it were now allocated and is thus added to the expenditure brought forward. The disposal value thus ensures that there is no remaining unrelieved qualifying expenditure.

A '*qualifying care relief period*' is a chargeable period (see **10.2**(i) CAPITAL ALLOWANCES ON PLANT AND MACHINERY) that corresponds to an income period for a tax year for which either the exemption applies or an election is made to apply the alternative method of calculating profits; it is thus a chargeable period for which the carer cannot claim capital allowances. A '*care business pool*' is a pool of qualifying expenditure incurred wholly or partly for the care business.

If on the first day of the first subsequent chargeable period which is not a qualifying care relief period, the carer still owns any of the plant or machinery which had been in a care business pool and is still using any of it for the purposes of the care business, the carer is deemed to have incurred notional capital expenditure on the provision of that plant or machinery (the '*retained plant or machinery*') at that time; he is then entitled to claim capital allowances on that expenditure. The notional expenditure is equal to the smaller of the market value of the retained plant or machinery and the disposal value last brought into account as above.

Also for the first subsequent chargeable period that is not a qualifying care relief period, the carer can bring into account under *CAA 2001, s 13* any qualifying expenditure on plant or machinery that he has incurred for the purposes of the care business in intervening qualifying care relief periods and which he still owns. He is treated as if he brought the plant or machinery into use on the first day of that chargeable period. The plant or machinery will normally fall to be brought into account at its then market value — see **10.66** CAPITAL ALLOWANCES ON PLANT AND MACHINERY.

It may be that, following a disposal event as above, the carer brings into use some of the plant or machinery in question for the purposes of a qualifying activity other than the care business. *CAA 2001, s 13* (see **10.66**) has effect as if the notional qualifying expenditure incurred on that plant or machinery were equal to the smaller of its market value at the time it is brought into use and the disposal value last brought into account as above.

There are rules (at *ITTOIA 2005, ss 825B(6)–(8)* and *825C(4)(5)*) to further restrict the notional expenditure (and thus prevent double allowances) where either:

- both the retained plant and machinery rule and the rule immediately above apply in relation to different items of plant and machinery for which a notional disposal value has been brought into account; or

- the rule immediately above applies on more than one occasion in relation to different items of plant and machinery for which a notional disposal value has been brought into account.

If at any time there is an actual disposal of plant and machinery, a disposal value must be brought into account under the normal rules at **10.27** notwithstanding that there may already have been a deemed disposal of that plant and machinery under the above rules. The disposal value is not limited by the amount of any notional expenditure on that plant and machinery but only by the amount of qualifying expenditure originally incurred by the individual on the plant and machinery.

[*ITTOIA 2005, ss 824, 825, 825A–825D, 826, 827*].

34

Herd Basis

See generally HMRC Business Income Manual BIM55501–55640.

Simon's Taxes. See **B5.150–B5.154**.

Introduction to herd basis

[34.1] Animals and other living creatures kept for the purposes of farming or similar trades (e.g. animal or fish breeding) are generally treated as trading stock (see **75.116** TRADING INCOME) unless:

- they are part of a herd in relation to which an election is made under *ITTOIA 2005, ss 111–129* for the 'herd basis' (see **34.2** *et seq*. below) to apply;
- the animals etc. are kept wholly or mainly for the work they do in connection with the trade or for public exhibition or racing or other competitive purposes; or
- a cash basis election is in force (see **76** TRADING INCOME — CASH BASIS FOR SMALLER BUSINESSES).

[*ITTOIA 2005, ss 25A(4), 30, 111, 112(1)*].

Animals etc. are exempt from capital gains tax as wasting assets within *TCGA 1992, s 45*.

The herd basis is not available when profits are calculated on the cash basis (see **76** TRADING INCOME — CASH BASIS FOR SMALLER BUSINESSES). [*ITTOIA 2005, s 111A*].

Herd basis — definitions

[34.2] For the purposes of the herd basis rules covered in the remainder of this chapter, an '*animal*' means any living creature, a '*herd*' includes a flock and any other collection of animals, and a '*production herd*' means a herd of animals of the same species, irrespective of breed, kept by a farmer or other trader wholly or mainly for the saleable produce obtainable from the living animal, which includes the young of the animal and any other product obtainable from it without slaughtering it. The herd basis provisions apply equally to animals kept singly and to shares in animals.

Immature animals kept in a production herd are generally not regarded as part of the herd for these purposes, but if:

- the nature of the land on which the herd is kept is such that replacement animals have to be bred and reared on that land (e.g. acclimatised hill sheep);
- the immature animals in question are bred and maintained in the herd for the purpose of replacing animals in the herd;
- it is necessary to maintain the immature animals for that purpose,

the immature animals are regarded as part of the herd insofar as they are required to prevent a fall in numbers.

An immature animal which is not regarded as part of the herd is regarded as added to the herd when it reaches maturity. Female animals are treated as becoming mature when they produce their first young or, in the case of laying birds, when they first lay.

[*ITTOIA 2005, ss 112, 113(5)*].

Herd basis elections

[34.3] An election for the herd basis to have effect must specify the class of production herd to which it relates and must be made on or before the first anniversary of 31 January following the tax year in which the 'first relevant period of account' ends. If, however, that tax year is the one in which the person commences the trade, and that person is not a partnership, the deadline is deferred to the second anniversary of that 31 January. The '*first relevant period of account*' is the first period of account in which the person making the election keeps a production herd of the class specified.

The election is irrevocable, and has effect in relation to all the production herds of the class to which it relates, including any which the trader has ceased to keep before making the election or starts to keep after making the election. The election cannot relate to more than one class of production herd, but separate elections can be made for different classes. Two or more production herds are of the same class if the animals kept in those herds are of the same species (irrespective of breed) and the saleable produce for which the herds are wholly or mainly kept is of the same kind. An election has effect for every period of account in which the trader carries on the trade and keeps a production herd of the relevant class.

Where there is a change in the persons carrying on a trade in partnership (see 52.7 PARTNERSHIPS), whether or not the trade is treated as continuing, a further election is required if the herd basis is to continue to apply. In this case, the 'first relevant period of account' (see above) is that in which the 'new' firm keeps a production herd of the class to which the election relates.

[*ITTOIA 2005, ss 113(2), 124*].

See **34.7** below as regards a further opportunity to make an election in a case of compulsory slaughter.

Further assessments may be made for any year as necessary, and repayments may be made (on a claim), to give effect to a herd basis election. [*ITTOIA 2005, s 129*].

Five-year gap between keeping herds

If a trader has kept a production herd of a particular class, ceases to keep herds of that class for at least five years and then does so once more:

- any herd basis election previously made in relation to herds of that class ceases to have effect; but
- the trader may make a further election by reference to the first period of account in which he again keeps a production herd of that class.

[*ITTOIA 2005, s 125*].

Consequences of herd basis election

[34.4] Where a herd basis election is in force, the animals in the herd are in effect treated as capital assets instead of as trading stock. The initial cost of the herd is not deductible in computing trading profits, and its value is not brought into account. No deduction is allowed for additions to the herd (as opposed to replacement animals — see **34.5** below). If the additional animal was previously part of trading stock, a receipt must be brought into account equal to the cost of breeding it, or acquiring it, and rearing it to maturity. If it is not possible to ascertain actual costs of breeding and rearing, an alternative deemed cost method may be used (HMRC Business Income Manual BIM55410, 55530).

[*ITTOIA 2005, ss 114, 115*].

Replacement animals

[34.5] The replacement of an animal dying or ceasing to be a member of a herd gives rise to a trading receipt equal to the disposal proceeds (if any)of the animal replaced, and a trading deduction equal to the cost of the replacement animal (so far as not otherwise allowable) but limited to the cost of an animal of similar quality to that replaced (for which see Revenue Tax Bulletin October 2001 pp 890, 891). See **34.6** below for meaning of disposal proceeds. Where the animal replaced was slaughtered under a disease control order (as defined), and the replacement animal is of inferior quality, the trading receipt is restricted to the amount allowable as a deduction in respect of the new animal. [*ITTOIA 2005, ss 113(3), 116, 117*].

Whether a particular animal brought into the herd replaces an animal disposed of is a question of fact, requiring a direct connection between the disposal and the later addition rather than a simple restoration of numbers. As a practical matter, inspectors will accept that replacement treatment is appropriate where animals are brought into the herd within twelve months of the corresponding disposal. Where disposal and replacement are in different accounting periods, the overall profit or loss may either be brought in in the first period and any necessary adjustment made in the second, or the profit or loss arising in the first period may be held over to the second period. Where the interval is more than twelve months, there is unlikely to be sufficient evidence to support the necessary connection where the new animal is bought in. Where animals are home bred, however, a longer interval may be reasonable where e.g. there is insufficient young stock to replace unexpected disposals. (Revenue Tax Bulletin October 1994 p 169, February 1997 p 396).

Disposal of animals from the herd

[34.6] Where an animal is disposed of from the herd, any profit is brought into account as a trading receipt and any loss is deductible as an expense. This does not apply if the animal is replaced (for which see **34.5** above) or on a disposal of the whole or a substantial part of the herd within a 12-month period (for which see below). The profit or loss is computed by reference to disposal proceeds and the cost of breeding the animal, or acquiring it, and rearing it to maturity. Market value is substituted for acquisition cost if the animal was acquired other than for valuable consideration. [*ITTOIA 2005, s 118*]. For HMRC's interpretation of this provision, including a change of view on how the profit on such disposals is to be computed, see Revenue Tax Bulletin April 2003 pp 1024, 1025.

For the purposes of the herd basis rules, the disposal of an animal includes its death or destruction as well as its sale, and disposal proceeds include sale proceeds and, in the case of death or destruction, insurance or compensation money received and proceeds of carcass sales. [*ITTOIA 2005, s 113(3)(4)*].

On the disposal of the whole or a substantial part of the herd, either all at once or over a period of 12 months or less, any profit is not brought into account as a receipt and any loss is not deductible as an expense. (20% or more of the herd is regarded as a 'substantial' part of it (but this does not prevent a smaller percentage from being regarded as 'substantial' in any particular case). If, however, the disposal is of *the whole herd* and the trader acquires, or starts to acquire, a new production herd of the same class within 5 years of the disposal, the following rules apply.

(i) The replacement rules at **34.5** above apply as if a number of animals, equal to the smaller of the number in the old herd and the number in the new, had been disposed of in the old herd and replaced in that herd. Disposal proceeds of any animal are brought into account when the 'replacement' animal is acquired.
(ii) If the number of animals in the new herd is smaller than that in the old by an insubstantial margin (i.e. normally less than 20% — see above), the difference is subject to the normal disposal rules in *ITTOIA 2005, s 118* above.
(iii) If the number of animals in the new herd is smaller than that in the old by a substantial margin (i.e. normally 20% or more — see above), the difference is treated as a disposal of a substantial part of the herd.

(iv) If the number of animals in the new herd is greater than that in the old, the difference is treated as additions (within **34.4** above) to the herd.

If the disposal is of *a substantial part of the herd* and the trader acquires, or starts to acquire, a new production herd of the same class within 5 years of the disposal, the following rules apply.

(1) The replacement rules at **34.5** above apply insofar as the animals included in the part disposed of are replaced. Disposal proceeds of an animal included in the part sold are brought into account when the replacement animal is acquired.
(2) If some of the animals included in the part disposed of are not replaced, any profit on their disposal is not brought into account as a receipt and any loss is not deductible as an expense.

Where the disposal of all or a substantial part of a herd is for reasons wholly outside the trader's control and a 'replacement' animal is of inferior quality to the old, the replacement rules at **34.5** above (as applied by either (i) or (1) above) apply as they do when animals are slaughtered under a disease control order (whether or not that is indeed the case).

[*ITTOIA 2005, ss 113(6), 119–123*].

Elections following compulsory slaughter

[34.7] Where compensation is receivable in respect of the whole, or a substantial part (normally 20% or more), of a production herd slaughtered under a disease control order (as defined), the trader may, notwithstanding the time limits in **34.3** above, elect for the herd basis to apply. The time limit for making the election in these circumstances follows the rules in **34.3** above, except that the period of account in which the compensation falls (or would otherwise fall) to be brought into account in computing profits is treated as if it were the first period of account in which the trader kept a production herd of the class in question. The election has effect for that period of account and each subsequent period of account in which the trader carries on the trade and keeps a production herd of that class.

[*ITTOIA 2005, s 126*].

Compensation paid under the BSE Suspects Scheme and the BSE Selective Cull (where the animal was born after 14 October 1990) is for compulsory slaughter, and for these purposes includes Selective Cull 'top-up' payments. Payments under the Calf Processing Scheme, the Over Thirty Month Scheme and the BSE Selective Cull where the animal was born before 15 October 1990 are *not* for compulsory slaughter. See Revenue Tax Bulletin February 1997 pp 396, 397 for this and for the application of these provisions to BSE compensation generally. For compulsory slaughter in cases where the herd basis does not and could not apply, see 75.77(b) TRADING INCOME.

Anti-avoidance

[34.8] There are provisions for the prevention of avoidance of tax in the case of a non-arm's length transfer of all or part of a production herd where either transferor and transferee are bodies of persons under common control or the sole or main benefit of the transfer relates to its effect on a herd basis election. [*ITTOIA 2005, s 127*].

Example on herd basis

[34.9]

A farmer acquires a dairy herd and elects for the herd basis to apply. The movements in the herd and the tax treatment are as follows.

Year 1		*No*	*Value*
			£
Mature			
Bought @ £150		70	10,500
Bought in calf @ £180			
(Market value of calf £35)		5	900
Immature			
Bought @ £75		15	1,125
Herd Account			£
	70 Friesians		10,500
	5 Friesians in calf (5 × £(180 – 35))		725
75	Closing balance		£11,225
Trading Account			£
5 Calves (5 × £35)			175
15 Immature Friesians			1,125
Debit to profit and loss account			£1,300

Year 2		*No*	*Value*
			£
Mature			
Bought @ £185		15	2,775
Sold @ £200		10	2,000
Died		3	—
Immature			
Born		52	—
Matured @ 60% of market value of £200 note (a)		12	1,440
Herd Account		£	£
75	Opening balance		11,225
	Increase in herd		

	15	Purchases	2,775	
	12	Transferred from trading stock	1,440	
	—			
	27		4,215	
—	(13)	Replacement cost £4,215 × 13/27	2,029	
14		Non-replacement animals cost		2,186
89		Closing balance		£13,411

Trading Account	£
Sale of 10 mature cows replaced	(2,000)
Transfer to herd—14 animals	(1,440)
Cost of 13 mature cows purchased to replace those sold/deceased (13/15 × £2,775)	2,405
Net credit to profit and loss account note (b)	£1,035

Year 3	*No*	*Value* £
Mature		
Jerseys bought @ £250	70	17,500
Friesians slaughtered @ £175 (market value £185)	52	9,100
Immature		
Friesians born	20	—
Matured		
Friesians @ 60% of market value of £190 note (a)	15	1,710

	Herd Account	£	£
89	Opening balance		13,411
	Increase in herd		
18	Jerseys		4,500
	52 Improvement Jerseys @	250	
	less Market value of Friesians	185	
	52 @	65	3,380
	Transfer from trading stock		
15	Friesians		1,710
122	Closing balance		£23,001

Trading Account	£
Compensation	(9,100)
Transfer to herd	(1,710)
Purchase of replacements note (c) (52 × £185)	9,620
Net credit to profit and loss account	£(1,190)

Year 4

The farmer ceases dairy farming and sells his whole herd.

	No	Value
		£
Mature		
Jerseys sold @ £320	70	22,400
Friesians sold @ £200	52	10,400
Immature		
Friesians sold @ £100	65	6,500

Herd Account		£
Opening balance		23,001
52	Friesians	
70	Jerseys	
(122)	Sales	(32,800)
	Profit on sale note (d)	£(9,799)

Trading Account	£
Sale of 65 immature Friesians	(6,500)
Credit to profit and loss account	£(6,500)

Notes

(a) The use of 60% of market value was originally by agreement between the National Farmers' Union and the Inland Revenue (see now HMRC Business Income Manual BIM55410). Alternatively, the actual cost of breeding or purchase and rearing could be used.

(b) As the cost of rearing the twelve cows to maturity will already have been debited to the profit and loss account, no additional entry is required to reflect that cost. Due to the fact that the animals were in opening stock at valuation and will not be in closing stock, the trading account will in effect be debited with that valuation.

(c) The cost of the replacements is restricted to the cost of replacing like with like.

(d) Provided these animals are not replaced by a herd of the same class within five years the proceeds will be tax-free (see **34.6** above).

35

HMRC — Administration

Introduction to HMRC administration

[35.1] From 18 April 2005, the collection and management of income tax is administered by the **Commissioners for Her Majesty's Revenue and Customs (HMRC)**. [*TMA 1970, s 1; Commissioners for Revenue and Customs Act 2005, Sch 4 para 12*]. Previously, this tax was administered by the Commissioners of Inland Revenue (normally referred to as 'the Board'). All the functions vested in the Board before that date (with the exception of prosecutions for tax offences — see below) are now vested in the Commissioners for HMRC. [*Commissioners for Revenue and Customs Act 2005, s 5; SI 2005 No 1126*].

Under the Commissioners for HMRC are officers of Revenue and Customs who are civil servants. In relation to income tax, officers of Revenue and Customs have broadly taken over the functions previously vested in officers of the Board of Inland Revenue, inspectors of taxes and collectors of taxes. [*Commissioners for Revenue and Customs Act 2005, ss 6, 7, Sch 1*]. As such they are responsible for processing returns, making assessments, dealing with claims, allowances and appeals, carrying out enquiries and collection and recovery of tax.

Criminal prosecutions of tax offences in England and Wales are conducted by an independent Revenue and Customs Prosecutions Office (RCPO), whose director is appointed by the Attorney General. [*Commissioners for Revenue and Customs Act 2005, ss 34–42, Sch 3*]. The RCPO is part of the Crown Prosecution Service. See **39.11** HMRC INVESTIGATORY POWERS for HMRC's practice in relation to prosecutions.

HMRC Charter

[35.2] The HMRC Charter sets out what persons dealing with HMRC can expect from HMRC, and what HMRC expect from such persons. Under the Charter, HMRC commit to:

- respect their customers and treat them as honest;
- provide a helpful, efficient and effective service;
- be professional and act with integrity;
- protect customers' information and respect their privacy;
- accept that someone else can represent their customers;
- deal with complaints quickly and fairly; and
- tackle those who bend or break the rules.

HMRC expect their customers to:

- be honest and respect their staff;
- work with HMRC to get things right;
- find out what they need to do and keep HMRC informed;
- keep accurate records and protect their information;
- know what their representative does on their behalf;
- respond in good time; and
- take reasonable care to avoid mistakes.

The Charter, with more information on each of the above points, is available at www.gov.uk/government/publications/your-charter/your-charter.

Appeal Tribunals

[35.3] See 5 APPEALS.

'Care and management' powers

[35.4] As noted at **35.1** above, the Commissioners for HMRC have responsibility for the 'collection and management' of taxes, including income tax. Before 18 April 2005, the Board of Inland Revenue had responsibility for the 'care and management' of direct taxes. The extent and limits of these care and management powers were considered before the courts on a number of occasions.

For the validity of amnesties by the Board, see *CIR v National Federation of Self-Employed and Small Businesses Ltd* HL 1981, 55 TC 133. HMRC EXTRA-STATUTORY CONCESSIONS (38) have been the subject of frequent judicial criticism (see Lord Edward Davies' opinion in *Vestey v CIR (No 1)* HL 1979, 54 TC 503 for a review of this) but their validity has never been directly challenged in the Courts. In *R v HMIT (ex p Fulford-Dobson)* QB 1987, 60 TC 168, a claim that the Revenue had acted unfairly in refusing a concession where tax avoidance was involved was rejected, but the taxpayer's right to seek judicial review of a Revenue decision to refuse the benefit of a concession was confirmed in *R v HMIT (ex p Brumfield and Others)* QB 1988, 61 TC 589. A decision by the Revenue to revoke its authorisation to pay a dividend gross was upheld in *R v CIR (ex p Camacq Corporation)* CA 1989, 62 TC 651. For a general discussion of the Board's care and management powers and an example of a ruling by the Court that the Board had exercised a discretionary power reasonably, see *R v CIR (ex p Preston)* HL 1985, 59 TC 1. Where a discretionary power is given to the Revenue, it is an error in law to proceed on the footing that the power is mandatory (*R v HMIT and Others (ex p Lansing Bagnall Ltd)* CA 1986, 61 TC 112). See also *R v CIR (ex p J Rothschild Holdings)* CA 1987, 61 TC 178, where the Revenue were required to produce internal documents of a general character relating to their practice in applying a statutory provision.

The Inland Revenue policy of selective prosecution for criminal offences in connection with tax evasion did not render a decision in a particular case unlawful or *ultra vires*, provided that the case was considered on its merits fairly and dispassionately to see whether the criteria for prosecution were satisfied, and that the decision to prosecute was then taken in good faith for the purpose of collecting taxes and not for some ulterior, extraneous or improper purpose (*R v CIR (ex p Mead and Cook)* QB 1992, 65 TC 1). See *R v CIR (ex p Allen)* QB 1997, 69 TC 442 for an unsuccessful application for judicial review of a Revenue decision to take criminal proceedings.

The making of a 'forward tax agreement', by which the Inland Revenue renounced their right and duty to investigate the true financial and other circumstances of the other party during the period of the agreement in return for payments of money, was not a proper exercise of the Inland Revenue's care and management powers, and was accordingly *ultra vires* and illegal (*Fayed and others v Advocate General for Scotland* CS 2004, 77 TC 273).

The social security authorities are authorised to disclose information held by them to the Commissioners for HMRC, or persons providing certain services to the Commissioners, for investigative purposes or in relation to national insurance contributions. [*FA 1997, s 110; Social Security Administration Act 1992, s 121F*].

Simon's Taxes. See **A3.101A.**

HMRC non-statutory clearances

[35.5] HMRC's non-statutory clearance regime is covered at www.gov.uk/guidance/non-statutory-clearance-service-guidance and www.gov.uk/seeking-clearance-or-approval-for-a-transaction. HMRC will provide clarification on guidance or legislation in relation to a specific transaction. Before using HMRC's clearance service the taxpayer or agent should have first checked that the transaction is not covered by a more appropriate clearance or approval route. The taxpayer/agent can seek clearance only if he has fully considered the relevant HMRC guidance and/or contacted the relevant helpline and has either not been able to find the information needed or remains uncertain about HMRC's interpretation of recent tax legislation. HMRC will then set out their advice in writing within 28 days (or longer if difficult or complicated issues are involved). Further details can be found on the web page, including checklists to help decide what information needs to be provided and details of where to send the clearance application. HMRC will not give clearance on matters of fact, such as if certain activities constitute a business; clearances or advice in respect of the application of the settlements legislation at **70.25** SETTLEMENTS or the tax consequences of executing non-charitable trust deeds or settlements; or clearances relating to the venture capital schemes.

Certain types of transaction have statutory clearance procedures. These are covered throughout this work where appropriate; see, for example, **4.12** ANTI-AVOIDANCE as regards transactions in securities etc.

HMRC automated processes

[35.6] Following judicial challenges to HMRC's ability to automate certain functions, *FA 2020, s 103* puts beyond doubt that functions given to an officer may be carried out by HMRC using automated processes or other means. It affirms what HMRC regard as long-standing and widely accepted operational practice. This legislation is treated as always having been in force, except that it does not apply if, before 11 March 2020, a court or tribunal had ruled against HMRC on the grounds that an action taken by HMRC (e.g. the issuing of a notice to file a tax return) was not taken by an officer (or a particular kind of officer) of HMRC, and the ruling had not been set aside or overturned on appeal.

The legislation provides that anything capable of being done by an officer (or a particular kind of officer) of HMRC by virtue of a function conferred by statute may be done by HMRC, whether by means involving the use of a computer or otherwise. Anything thus done by HMRC has the same effect as it would have if done by an officer. Such functions include, but are not limited to, the giving of notice to file a personal, trustee or partnership tax return, the amendment of a return, the making of an assessment other than a self-assessment, and the making of a determination under *TMA 1970, s 100* (see **55.25** PENALTIES).

[*FA 2020, s 103*].

HMRC error

[35.7] HMRC guidance 'Complain about HMRC' (available at www.gov.uk/complain-about-hmrc) outlines the complaints procedures, and states that HMRC may consider refunding reasonable costs directly caused by HMRC's mistakes or delays. Such costs might include postage, telephone charges and professional fees.

In *Neil Martin Ltd v HMRC* CA 2007, 79 TC 60, an unsuccessful action for damages against HMRC, it was held that HMRC did not have a direct duty of care to process an application for a sub-contractors' tax certificate (under the old construction industry tax deduction scheme) with reasonable expedition, and that an officer of HMRC does not generally owe a common law duty of care for which his employers would be vicariously liable.

HMRC Litigation and Settlement Strategy

[35.8] HMRC's Litigation and Settlement Strategy (LSS) is a framework within which HMRC seeks to resolve tax disputes through civil procedures consistent with the law, whether by agreement with the taxpayer or through litigation. The strategy sets out principles for bringing tax disputes to a conclusion, and the relevant factors for HMRC to consider in deciding whether to agree a settlement with the taxpayer or to proceed to litigation, i.e. statutory appeal to an independent body, including the tribunals or the courts. For the text of the LSS, and commentary, see www.gov.uk/government/publications/litigation-and-settlement-strategy-lss. See also HMRC's 'Code of governance for resolving tax disputes' at www.gov.uk/government/publications/resolving-tax-disputes and HMRC Compliance Handbook CH40000 *et seq.*

Adjudicator's Office

[35.9] A taxpayer who is not satisfied with HMRC's response to a complaint has the option of putting the case to an independent Adjudicator. The Adjudicator's Office considers complaints about HMRC's handling of a taxpayer's affairs, e.g. mistakes, delays, misleading advice, staff behaviour or the exercise of HMRC discretion. Its services are free of charge. Matters subject to existing rights of appeal are excluded. The Adjudicator publishes an annual report.

The address is The Adjudicator's Office, PO Box 10280, Nottingham, NG2 9PF (tel. 0300 057 1111, website www.adjudicatorsoffice.gov.uk). The Adjudicator's Office can also be contacted via an online form (see www.gov.uk/guidance/contact-the-adjudicators-office-online). Complaints normally go to the Adjudicator only after they have been considered by the local HMRC department and the taxpayer is not satisfied with the response. The Adjudicator reviews all the facts, considers whether the complaint is justified, and, if so, settles the complaint by mediation or makes recommendations as to what should be done. HMRC normally accept the recommendations. Following the Adjudicator's review, the complainant, if still unhappy, can ask his MP to refer the complaint to the Parliamentary Ombudsman.

Leave to apply for judicial review of the rejection by the Adjudicator of a complaint concerning the use of information from unidentified informants was refused in *R v Revenue Adjudicator's Office (ex p Drummond)* QB 1996, 70 TC 235.

Office of Tax Simplification

[35.10] The Office of Tax Simplification (OTS) is an independent Office of the Treasury with statutory functions. It is led by a Board of tax experts whose responsibilities are to identify areas where complexities in the tax system for both businesses and individual taxpayers can be reduced and to publish their findings for the Chancellor of the Exchequer to consider. [*FA 2016, ss 184–189, Sch 25; SI 2016 No 1133*].

The OTS can be accessed at www.gov.uk/government/organisations/office-of-tax-simplification.

Use of electronic communications

[35.11] The Commissioners for HMRC have broad powers to make regulations by statutory instrument to facilitate electronic communication in the delivery of information, e.g. tax returns, and the making of tax payments. Such regulations have effect notwithstanding any pre-existing legislation requiring delivery or payment in a manner which would otherwise preclude the use of electronic communications. [*FA 1999, ss 132, 133*]

See *The Income and Corporation Taxes (Electronic Communications) Regulations 2003* (*SI 2003 No 282*) and directions thereunder by the Commissioners, which make provision for electronic communications in relation to delivery of tax returns and other information under various statutory provisions and payments or repayments in connection with the operation of those provisions. Regulations (*SI 2003 No 3143*) provide for electronic delivery of dividend vouchers, interest vouchers and other tax deduction certificates by prior agreement between sender and recipient.

HMRC also have wide powers to make regulations *requiring* the use of electronic communications for delivery of information. [*FA 2002, ss 135, 136*]. See **53.21** PAY AS YOU EARN as regards mandatory electronic filing of PAYE returns.

Regulations may also be made by the Commissioners for the provision of *incentives* to use electronic communications. [*FA 2000, s 143(1), Sch 38*]. Anything received by way of incentive is not regarded as income for tax purposes. [*ITTOIA 2005, s 778*].

International co-operation

[35.12] *FA 2006, ss 173–175* provide for international agreements on mutual assistance in tax enforcement, covering exchange of information foreseeably relevant to the administration, enforcement or recovery of any UK or foreign tax; the recovery of debts relating to any UK or foreign tax; and the service of documents relating to any UK or foreign tax. See, for example, *SI 2007 No 2126*, which brought into effect arrangements relating to international tax enforcement contained in the joint Council of Europe/OECD Convention on mutual administrative assistance in tax matters which was signed on behalf of the UK on 24 May 2007. See also *SI 2007 No 3507*, which provides the necessary machinery for recovering foreign taxes on behalf of a non-EU country with which an appropriate international agreement on mutual assistance is in force. See generally HMRC International Exchange of Information Manual.

Co-operation between tax authorities of EU member States

Council Directive 2011/16/EU on administrative co-operation in the field of taxation provides for the exchange of information between tax authorities of EU member States to enable them to correctly assess tax liabilities. This is transposed into UK domestic law by *SI 2012 No 3062*.

FA 2019, s 84 gave the Treasury the power to make regulations to require disclosure of information about certain cross-border tax arrangements to HMRC to give effect to international rules. This was in response to EU Directive 2018/822/EU (amending Directive 2011/16/EU), known as DAC 6. See now **35.16** below.

See also **35.14** below.

Recovery of taxes etc. due in other EU member States

Provision is made for the recovery in the UK of amounts in respect of which a request for enforcement has been made in accordance with the Mutual Assistance Recovery Directive (*Directive 2010/24/EU*) by an authority in another EU member State. Disclosure of information by a UK tax authority (e.g. the Commissioners for HMRC) for these purposes (or for the purposes of a request for enforcement by the UK) is not generally precluded by any obligation of secrecy.

Broadly, the UK tax authority has the same powers it would have for a corresponding claim in the UK, in particular in relation to penalties and interest. Treasury regulations may make provision for procedural and supplementary matters (see *SI 2011 No 2931*). Regulations may also be made by the UK tax authority for the application, non-application or adaptation of the law applicable to corresponding UK claims.

No proceedings may be taken against a person under these provisions if he shows that proceedings relevant to the liability in question are pending (i.e. still open to appeal), or about to be instituted, before a competent body in the member State in question. This does not apply to any steps which could be taken in similar circumstances in the case of a corresponding UK claim or if the foreign proceedings are not prosecuted or instituted with reasonable expedition. If a final decision on the foreign claim (i.e. one against which no further appeal lies or would be in time), or a part of it, has been given in favour of the taxpayer by a competent body in the member State in question, no proceeding may be taken under these provisions in relation to the claim (or part).

[*FA 2011, s 87, Sch 25*].

Simon's Taxes. See **A4.602, A6.1204, E6.455.**

FATCA agreement with USA

[35.13] In 2010 the USA introduced legislation to combat tax evasion by US persons. These provisions, known as the Foreign Accounts Tax Compliance Act (FATCA), require financial institutions outside the USA to pass information about the accounts of US persons to the US Internal Revenue Service (IRS). Any financial institution that fails to comply is subject to a 30% withholding tax on US source income.

On 12 September 2012, the UK and USA entered into an Intergovernmental Agreement (IGA). Under the IGA, if UK financial institutions comply with legislation that meets the terms negotiated between the two countries, and the UK shares this information with the US, those institutions will be deemed to have complied with FATCA and will not be subject to the withholding tax. The financial institutions must register with the IRS but will provide the required information to HMRC, who will in turn provide it to the IRS.

FA 2013, s 222 gave the Treasury power to make regulations giving effect to the IGA, any agreement modifying or supplementing the IGA and any subsequent agreement or arrangements for the exchange of tax information between the UK and another territory which make provision corresponding, or substantially similar, to the IGA (see the Common Reporting Standard at **35.14** below). The regulations implementing the IGA (*SI 2015 No 878*) define the key terms, such as 'reportable account', included in the IGA and set out the required due diligence and reporting requirements of UK financial institutions. They also contain provision for penalties for non-compliance, and an appeals process. As part of the IGA, the US has agreed to provide the UK with reciprocal data on the US accounts of UK persons.

For official guidance, see www.gov.uk/government/publications/uk-us-automatic-exchange-of-information-agreement/uk-us-automatic-exchange-of-information-agreement.

Simon's Taxes. See **A6.1205A.**

Common Reporting Standard

[35.14] On 9 April 2013 the governments of the UK, France, Germany, Italy and Spain announced an agreement to develop and pilot multilateral tax information exchange based on the Model Intergovernmental Agreement to Improve International Tax Compliance and to Implement FATCA developed between these countries and the USA (see **35.13** above). Other countries subsequently committed to join this pilot. (Treasury Press Release, 9 April 2013; HMRC Press Release, 28 November 2013). On 6 May 2014, the Organisation for Economic Co-operation and Development (OECD) Declaration on Automatic Exchange of Information in Tax Matters was endorsed by its member countries and by several non-member countries. On 21 July 2014, the OECD released the full version of a Common Reporting Standard (CRS) (formally known as the Standard for Automatic Exchange of Financial Account Information in Tax Matters). The CRS calls on governments to obtain detailed account information from their financial institutions and exchange that information automatically with other jurisdictions on an annual basis. For a list of countries that have adopted the CRS see HMRC International Exchange of Information Manual IEIM402340. See generally the OECD website at www.oecd.org/tax/exchange-of-tax-information/automaticexchange.htm for more details. For country-by-country status see www.oecd.org/tax/automatic-exchange/crs-implementation-and-assistance/crs-by-jurisdiction and www.oecd.org/tax/transparency/AEOI-commitments.pdf. For HMRC guidance for UK account holders in financial institutions see www.gov.uk/government/uploads/system/uploads/attachment_data/file/386413/Automatic_exchange_of_information_-_account_holders.pdf.

The regulations implementing the CRS in the UK (*SI 2015 No 878*) define key terms, such as 'reportable account', and set out the required due diligence and reporting requirements of financial institutions. They also contain provision for penalties for non-compliance, and an appeals process.

Under an agreement between the EU and Switzerland, both sides automatically exchange information on the financial accounts of each other's residents from 2018. Member States will receive annually the names and addresses etc. of their residents with accounts in Switzerland, as well as other financial and account balance information. The EU has signed similar agreements with Andorra, Liechtenstein, Monaco and San Marino (see http://ec.europa.eu/taxation_customs/individuals/personal-taxation/taxation-savings-income/international-developments_en)

Exchange agreements with Crown dependencies and Gibraltar (obsolete)

[35.15] In 2013, the UK entered into reciprocal agreements with Guernsey, Jersey, the Isle of Man and Gibraltar. Under these agreements, each government commits to an annual automatic exchange of information relating to financial accounts maintained by financial institutions in their territory which belong to the other party's tax residents ('*Crown Dependencies and Overseas Territories (CDOT) reporting*'). The Agreements are consistent with the FATCA agreement between the UK and USA (see **35.13** above). The regulations define the key terms, such as financial institution and reportable account, included in the Agreements and also set out the required due diligence and reporting requirements of UK financial institutions. (www.gov.uk/government/uploads/system/uploads/attachment_data/file/292466/Int_compliance.pdf). [*SI 2014 No 520*].

For reporting in respect of 2017 and subsequent years, CDOT reporting is fully **superseded** by the CRS at **35.14** above.

EU disclosure rules for cross-border tax arrangements (DAC 6)

[35.16] *FA 2019, s 84* gave the Treasury the power to make regulations (see now *SI 2020 No 25*) to require disclosure to HMRC of information about certain cross-border tax arrangements to give effect to international rules. This is in response to the EU's sixth Directive on Administrative Co-operation in the field of taxation (EU Directive 2018/822/EU (amending Directive 2011/16/EU)) (DAC 6). DAC 6 requires member States to enact rules obliging 'intermediaries' and in some cases taxpayers, to report information to tax authorities about cross-border arrangements that contain certain hallmarks. '*Cross-border*' means concerning more than one member State, or a member State and a third (non-EU) country.

The regulations were originally to have had effect in relation to:

(a) a reportable cross-border arrangement which is, or continues to be, made available for implementation or ready for implementation on or after 1 July 2020;

(b) a reportable cross-border arrangement in respect of which, on or after 1 July 2020, an intermediary provided aid, assistance or advice with respect to designing, marketing, organising, making available for implementation or managing the implementation of the reportable cross-border arrangement; and
(c) a reportable cross-border arrangement the first step in the implementation of which was made on or after 25 June 2018.

Six-month deferral due to COVID-19

However, due to the impact of the 2020 COVID-19 (coronavirus) pandemic, the EU gave member States the option to delay implementation. The Government is accordingly deferring the first reporting deadlines by six months (HMRC International Exchange of Information Manual IEIM800010). Revised dates are as follows:

- For arrangements which were made available for implementation, or which were ready for implementation, or where the first step in the implementation took place between 1 July 2020 and 31 December 2020, reports must now be made within the 30 days beginning on 1 January 2021. Under the original rules, such arrangements would have had to be reported within 30 days of the reporting trigger point being reached.
- For arrangements in respect of which a UK intermediary provided aid, assistance or advice between 1 July 2020 and 31 December 2020, reports must be made within 30 days beginning on 1 January 2021. Again, under the original rules, such arrangements would have had to be reported within 30 days of the aid etc. being provided.
- In a case within (c) above in which the first step is taken before 1 July 2020, the report must be made on or before 28 February 2021 (instead of 31 August 2020 as originally intended).
- Where three-monthly reports are required in relation to marketable arrangements (see below), the first such report must be made by 30 April 2021.

Brexit

The UK is due to leave the EU on Implementation Period completion day, expected to be 31 December 2020. The Government published a report on 8 January 2020 that included a statement that once the UK has left the EU the Government may amend or revoke the regulations (see www.gov.uk/government/publications/international-tax-enforcement-disclosable-arrangements--2). However, given what is said above regarding deferral of the first reporting deadlines, the regulations must be expected to be in operation as at 1 January 2021 and beyond.

Reporting requirements

The reporting obligation applies primarily to intermediaries; however, a secondary one also applies to the taxpayer. An '*intermediary*' is defined as someone with an EU connection who designs, markets, organises or makes available for implementation or manages the implementation of a reportable cross-border arrangement. Such intermediaries are likely to include professional advisers such as lawyers, accountants and tax advisers, as well as banks, financial advisers and, more generally, parties involved in transactions who could be considered to fall under any of the categories above. In addition, intermediary also refers to any person who undertakes to provide aid, assistance or advice in respect of a reportable cross-border arrangement, or any person who could reasonably be expected to know that such aid, assistance or advice relates to a reportable cross-border arrangement.

There is no obligation on a UK intermediary to report if to do so would breach legal professional privilege (LPP). In this case the intermediary must notify another intermediary, or the 'relevant taxpayer', that they are obliged to make a report instead. That report must then be made within 30 days of receiving the notification.

If there is no intermediary, or due to LLP there is no intermediary that can make a report, the obligation to report falls instead on the relevant taxpayer. The '*relevant taxpayer*' is any person to whom a reportable cross-border arrangement is made available for implementation or who is ready to implement a reportable cross-border arrangement, or who has implemented the first step of such an arrangement.

The report must set out the reportable information in relation to the reportable cross-border arrangement that is within the UK intermediary's knowledge, possession or control.

Information on reportable cross-border arrangements must be filed by the UK intermediary with the HMRC within 30 days beginning on the day after the reportable cross-border arrangement is made available for implementation, is ready for implementation, or the first step has been implemented, whichever occurs first. If the intermediary is within these rules because it has provided aid, assistance or advice, it must report within 30 days after giving that aid etc. If the reporting obligation relates to a marketable arrangement, meaning an arrangement that is designed, marketed, ready for implementation or made available for implementation without a need to be substantially customised, the intermediary must make an updated report every three months.

If the reporting obligation falls on a relevant taxpayer (see above), that person must make a report within 30 days of the first of the following: (i) the day after the arrangement is made available for implementation to that taxpayer; (ii) the day after the arrangement is ready for implementation by that taxpayer; and (iii) the first step in implementing the arrangement is made in relation to that taxpayer.

Where a UK relevant taxpayer participates in a reportable cross-border arrangement, that person must make a return for each of the company accounting periods or tax years or for which they obtain a tax advantage from the arrangement. The due date for the return coincides with that for the company tax return or self-assessment tax return.

In order to determine whether or not the reporting requirements have been complied with, an HMRC officer may require a person, who the officer reasonably suspects is a UK intermediary or UK relevant taxpayer, to provide such information or documents as the officer reasonably requires as specified by written notice. The information or documents must be provided within such period, being not less than 30 days, and by such means and in such form, as is reasonably required by the officer.

Reportable arrangements

An arrangement will be reportable if it meets at least one of five hallmarks. The hallmarks are listed in Annex IV to DAC 6 (see https://eur-lex.europa.eu/legal-content/EN/TXT/PDF/?uri=CELEX:32018L0822&from=EN) and are described as presenting an indication of a potential risk of tax avoidance, although there is no requirement for a tax avoidance motive. All of the generic hallmarks, and some of the specific hallmarks, are taken into account for the purposes of DAC 6 only if they fulfil the main benefit test. The main benefit test is fulfilled if a main benefit which, having regard to all relevant facts and circumstances, that a person may reasonably expect to derive from an arrangement is the obtaining of a tax advantage.

The hallmarks are as follows:

(A) Generic hallmarks linked to the main benefit test: arrangements that give rise to performance fees or which involve mass-marketed schemes.

(B) Specific hallmarks linked to the main benefit test: this includes certain tax planning features, such as buying a loss-making company to exploit its losses in order to reduce tax liability. Another example would involve arrangements aimed at converting income into capital in order to obtain a tax benefit.

(C) Specific hallmarks related to cross-border transactions; some of these hallmarks are subject to the main benefit test: for example, deductible cross-border payments between associated enterprises where the recipient is essentially subject to no tax, zero or almost zero tax. Another hallmark is about deductions for the same depreciation on an asset claimed in more than one jurisdiction.

(D) Specific hallmarks concerning the automatic exchange of information and beneficial ownership: an arrangement is reportable if it has the effect of undermining the rules on anti-money laundering, transparency of beneficial ownership or the automatic exchange of financial account information.

(E) Specific hallmarks concerning transfer pricing: these include the use of unilateral safe harbours; the transfer of hard-to-value intangible assets when no reliable comparables exist and the projection of future cash flows or income are highly uncertain.

The generic hallmarks in (A) are concerned with the conditions under which the arrangements are entered into, whilst the specific hallmarks describe attributes of the arrangements themselves. DAC 6 provides that a cross-border arrangement is reportable if it satisfies the main benefit test and one of the following applies:

- confidentiality: the relevant taxpayer or another participant in the arrangement agrees to a confidentiality condition relating to not disclosing to other intermediaries or the tax authorities how the arrangement may secure a tax advantage;

- fee linked to tax advantage: the intermediary is entitled to a fee or other amount by reference to the amount of the tax advantage, or the fee is dependent on the tax advantage being obtained;
- standardised documentation: the arrangement has a substantially standardised set of documentation or structure, and is available to more than one relevant taxpayer without a need to be substantially customised.

Employees

A person (P) is not to be treated as an intermediary in relation to a reportable cross-border arrangement where P is an employee of another person (E) and E is an intermediary or a relevant taxpayer in relation to the arrangement. Where E is connected to another person (F), P is to be treated as an employee of F as well as being an employee of E. For this purpose, E is connected with F where E is closely bound to F by financial, economic or organisational links.

[*SI 2020 No 25, Regs 1–13; SI 2020 No 713*].

Penalties

A fixed penalty of up to £5,000 may be levied for failure to comply with the UK reporting requirements. Daily penalties of £600 may also be charged in some cases during the 'initial period' if the fixed penalty appears to an HMRC officer to be inappropriately low after taking into account all relevant considerations (for which see *SI 2020 No 25, Reg 14(3)*). The '*initial period*' is the period beginning when the default occurs and ending with the earlier of the day the daily penalty is determined and the last day before the failure ceases. HMRC must commence proceedings before the First-tier Tribunal if they are to charge this daily penalty. Amongst other options, the Tribunal may increase the maximum penalty to an amount of up to £1 million.

If the failure continues, further penalties of £600 per day may be levied.

In the case of the obligation on a UK relevant taxpayer to make annual returns, there is a fixed penalty £5,000 in respect of each reportable cross-border arrangement to which the failure relates. This is increased to £7,500 if it is the second such failure during the 36 months ending with the date on which the current failure began. The penalty is increased to £10,000 if there have already been two or more such failures during that 36-month period.

SI 2020 No 25, Reg 18 sets out the time limits for charging the above penalties. A penalty is to be treated for all purposes as if it were tax charged in an assessment. A penalty is due and payable at the end of the 30 days beginning with the issue of the notice of determination by HMRC or (as the case may be) the date of the determination of the penalty by the First-tier Tribunal.

UK intermediaries and relevant taxpayers can appeal against penalties. If an HMRC officer thinks it right because of special circumstances, the officer may reduce a penalty. Penalties may be cancelled if a reasonable excuse exists (see *SI 2020 No 25, Reg 21*). HMRC had said that COVID-19 would be a reasonable excuse for a delay in reporting (HMRC International Exchange of Information Manual IEIM800000), but this may have been largely superseded by the subsequent announcement of a six-month deferral of the first reporting deadlines (see above).

[*SI 2020 No 25, Regs 14–21*].

Simon's Taxes. See **A6.1204A.**

HMRC functions carried out by National Crime Agency

[35.17] Under the *Proceeds of Crime Act 2002, Pt 6*, the National Crime Agency (NCA) is empowered to carry out the functions vested in HMRC and its officers. The NCA must have reasonable grounds to suspect that:

(a) income arising or a gain accruing to a person in respect of a chargeable period is chargeable to income tax or is a chargeable gain and arises or accrues as a result (whether wholly or partly, directly or indirectly) of the 'criminal conduct' of that person or another; or
(b) a company is chargeable to corporation tax on its profits arising in a chargeable period and the profits arise as a result (whether wholly or partly, directly or indirectly) of the criminal conduct of the company or another person,

and must serve a notice on HMRC specifying the person or company, the period or periods concerned, and the functions which he intends to carry out. The periods involved may include periods beginning before the *Act* was passed.

For the purpose of the exercise by the NCA of any function so vested in them, it is immaterial that they cannot identify a source for any income. An assessment made by the NCA under *TMA 1970, s 29* (discovery assessment — see **6.6** ASSESSMENTS) in respect of income charged to tax under *ITTOIA 2005, Pt 5 Ch 8* (income not otherwise charged — see **49.7** MISCELLANEOUS INCOME) cannot be reduced or quashed only because it does not specify (to any extent) the source of the income.

The NCA may cease carrying out the functions specified in the notice at any time (by notifying HMRC), but *must* so cease where the conditions allowing the notice to be made are no longer satisfied. Any assessment made by them under *TMA 1970, s 29* is subsequently invalid to the extent that it does not specify a source for income.

For the above purposes, '*criminal conduct*' is conduct which constitutes an offence anywhere in the UK or which would do so if it occurred there, but does not include conduct constituting an offence relating to a matter under the care and management of HMRC.

It should be noted that the vesting of a function in the NCA under these provisions does not divest HMRC or its officers of the function (so that, for example, HMRC can continue to carry out routine work). Certain functions, as listed in *Proceeds of Crime Act 2002, s 323(3)*, cannot be carried out by the NCA. If the NCA serve notice in relation to a company and in respect of a chargeable period or periods, the general HMRC functions vested in the NCA do not include functions relating to any requirement which is imposed on the company in its capacity as an employer and relates to a tax year which does not fall wholly within the chargeable period(s).

[*Proceeds of Crime Act 2002, ss 317, 318(1)(2), 319, 320(1)–(3), 323(1)(3), 326(1)(2); Serious Crime Act 2007, s 74, Sch 8 paras 92–96; SI 2003 No 120; SI 2007 No 3166, Reg 3; SI 2008 No 755*].

An assessment made by the NCA in carrying out their HMRC functions does not constitute a criminal charge within the ambit of *Article* 6 of the *European Convention on Human Rights* (*Khan v Director of the Assets Recovery Agency* (Sp C 523), [2006] SSCD 154).

Simon's Taxes. See **A6.1113.**

36

HMRC — Confidentiality of Information

Cross-reference. See **55.35** PENALTIES (publishing details of deliberate tax defaulters).

Introduction to confidentiality of information

[36.1] Subject to certain specified exceptions relating to the functions of HMRC (and those at **36.3** below), officials of HMRC may not disclose information held by HMRC. All Commissioners and officers of HMRC must make a declaration acknowledging their duty of confidentiality as soon as reasonably practicable following their appointment. [*Commissioners for Revenue and Customs Act 2005, ss 3, 18*].

One of the exceptions to the confidentiality rule above is that it does not apply to a disclosure made for the purposes of a function of HMRC. [*Commissioners for Revenue and Customs Act 2005, s 18(2)(a)(i)*]. In *R (oao Ingenious Media Holdings plc) v HMRC* SC, [2016] STC 2306, it was held by the SC that the disclosure in question was not justified by this exception; a desire to foster good relations with the media or to publicise HMRC's views about tax avoidance schemes could not possibly justify an official of HMRC discussing the affairs of individual taxpayers with journalists.

Confidentiality of information — general

[36.2] Information acquired by HMRC in connection with one of their functions may be used by them in connection with any other of their functions. [*Commissioners for Revenue and Customs Act 2005, s 17(1)*].

The confidentiality rule does not apply to a disclosure made in pursuance of an order of a court. [*Commissioners for Revenue and Customs Act 2005, s 18(2)(e)*]. This includes an order of the First-tier Tribunal (*Hastings Insurance Services Ltd v HMRC and KPMG LLP* FTT (TC 6656), [2018] UKFTT 478 (TC)).

As to production in Court proceedings of documents in HMRC's possession, see *Brown's Trustees v Hay* CS 1897, 3 TC 598; *In re Joseph Hargreaves Ltd* CA 1900, 4 TC 173; *Shaw v Kay* CS 1904, 5 TC 74; *Soul v Irving* CA 1963,

41 TC 517; *H v H* HC 1980, 52 TC 454. For the overriding of confidentiality by the public interest in the administration of justice, see *Lonrho plc v Fayed and Others (No 4)* CA 1993, 66 TC 220.

Confidentiality of information — specifics

[36.3] HMRC are authorised to disclose information to the following.

(a) **Charity Commission for England and Wales.** There are wide powers under which information may be exchanged between the Charity Commission and HMRC and also between principal regulators of certain charities and HMRC. [*Charities Act 2011, ss 54–59; Charities Act 1993, ss 10–10C*].

(b) **Business Statistics Office of the Department of Industry** or to the **Department of Employment.** HMRC are authorised to disclose, for the purposes of statistical surveys, the names and addresses of employers and employees and the number of persons employed by individual concerns. [*FA 1969, s 58*].

(c) **Tax authorities of other countries.** HMRC are authorised to disclose information where it is necessary to do so for the operation of double taxation agreements. [*TIOPA 2010, s 129; TCGA 1992, s 277(4); IHTA 1984, s 158(5)*]. Disclosure can also be made for the purpose of giving effect, or enabling effect to be given, to EU Council Directive 2011/16/EU on administrative co-operation in the field of taxation (see **35.12** HMRC — ADMINISTRATION). This applies in particular, to any disclosure (to persons in the UK or elsewhere) in connection with a request or proposed request by or on behalf of an applicant authority of any Member State for assistance in accordance with the Directive. [*SI 2012 No 3062*].

   FA 2006, ss 173–175 provide for international agreements on mutual assistance in tax enforcement, covering the exchange of information foreseeably relevant to the administration, enforcement or recovery of any UK or foreign tax; the recovery of debts relating to any UK or foreign tax; and the service of documents relating to any UK or foreign tax (see **35.12** HMRC — ADMINISTRATION). Where such agreements have effect, no obligation of secrecy, whether statutory or otherwise, prevents the disclosure of any information that is authorised to be disclosed under the agreement. However, such information cannot be disclosed by HMRC to a foreign tax authority unless HMRC are satisfied that the foreign tax authority is bound by, or has undertaken to observe, rules of confidentiality at least as strict as those applying in the UK. Post-Brexit technical changes are due to be made to these disclosure rules by *SI 2019 No 689, Reg 14* with effect on and after Implementation Period completion day, expected to be 31 December 2020.

(d) **The Pensions Regulator.** HMRC are authorised to disclose information about pension schemes. [*Pensions Act 2004, s 88(1)(2)*].

(e) **Social Security Departments.** Information held by HMRC may be supplied to the social security authorities for use in relation to social security, employment or training, tax credits, child support, war pensions or prescribed evaluation or statistical studies. Social security authorities are in turn permitted to supply information to HMRC. [*Social Security Administration Act 1992, s 121E; FA 1997, s 110; Tax Credits Act 2002, Sch 5 para 4; Welfare Reform Act 2012, s 127; SI 2002 No 3036*].

(f) **Assistance to police investigation into suspected murder or treason.** [*Royal Commission on Standards of Conduct in Public Life 1976, para 93*].

(g) **Non-UK resident entertainers and sportsmen.** In connection with the deduction of tax from certain payments to such persons, HMRC may disclose relevant matters to any person who appears to HMRC to have an interest. [*ITA 2007, s 970(2)(3)*].

(h) **Land Registry.** Particulars of land and charges. [*Land Registration Act 1925, s 129*].

(i) **Parliamentary Commissioner for Administration.** Information required for the purposes of his investigations. [*Parliamentary Commissioner Act 1967, s 8*].

(j) **National Audit Office.** Information required for the purposes of the Office's examinations. [*National Audit Act 1983, s 8*].

(k) **Data Protection.** Any information necessary for the discharge of the Registrar's or Tribunal's functions. [*Data Protection Act 1984, s 17*].

(l) An **advisory commission** set up under the Convention (*90/463/EEC*) on the elimination of double taxation in connection with the adjustment of profits of associated enterprises (see **4.28** ANTI-AVOIDANCE). [*TIOPA 2010, s 128*].

(m) As regards information held for the purposes of tax credit functions (see **73.6** SOCIAL SECURITY AND NATIONAL INSURANCE) and functions relating to child benefit or guardian's allowance, a **local authority** (or authorised delegate) for use in the administration of housing benefit or council tax benefit. Information must also be provided in the opposite direction if the Commissioners of HMRC so require but only for use for purposes relating to tax credits etc. [*Tax Credits Act 2002, Sch 5 paras 7, 8*].

Also as regards information held for the above-mentioned purposes, **Health Departments** for use for purposes of prescribed functions relating to health, relevant Government Departments for purposes of prescribed functions relating to **employment** or **training** (with provision also for certain information to pass in the opposite direction) and (as regards information held for child benefit and guardian's allowance functions only) any civil servant or other person for purposes of prescribed functions relating to provision of specified services concerning participation by young persons in **education and training.** [*Tax Credits Act 2002, Sch 5 paras 5, 6, 9, 10*].

(n) The **Health and Safety Executive**, the **Government Actuary's Department**, the **Office for National Statistics** or the **Occupational Pensions Regulatory Authority** in relation to National Insurance contributions, statutory sick pay or statutory maternity pay. [*Social Security Administration Act 1992, s 122AA*].

(o) **Financial Conduct Authority** and **Prudential Regulation Authority**. No obligation as to secrecy imposed by statute or otherwise prevents the disclosure of information to these regulators for the purpose of assisting or enabling them to discharge their functions. The same applies if the disclosure is made to the relevant Secretary of State for certain investigatory purposes under *Financial Services and Markets Act 2000, s 168*. A disclosure may be made only by, or under the authority of, the Commissioners for HMRC. [*Financial Services and Markets Act 2000, s 350*]. Note that HMRC may only disclose information in this way if it was obtained or is held in the exercise of a function previously vested in the Inland Revenue. [*Commissioners for Revenue and Customs Act 2005, Sch 2 para 18*].

(p) Under the ***Anti-terrorism, Crime and Security Act 2001, ss 19, 20***, the Revenue and Customs & Excise (now collectively HMRC) are authorised to disclose certain information required for the purposes of that Act. A Code of Practice on this was published jointly by those departments.

(q) **Director of Public Prosecutions and Director of the Serious Fraud Office.** HMRC may disclose information to either Director for the purpose of the exercise of his functions under *Proceeds of Crime Act 2002, Pt 5* or *Pt 8*. [*Proceeds of Crime Act 2002, s 436*]. HMRC may also disclose information to the Lord Advocate and the Scottish Ministers in connection with the exercise of their functions in Scotland under *Proceeds of Crime Act 2002, Pt 3* and *Pt 5* respectively. [*Proceeds of Crime Act 2002, s 439*].

(r) **The Financial Reporting Review Panel.** HMRC may disclose certain information to this Panel for the purposes of facilitating their taking steps to discover whether there are grounds for an application to the courts for a declaration that the annual accounts of a company do not comply with *Companies Acts* requirements (or NI equivalents) or determining whether or not to make such an application (Memorandum of Understanding between HMRC and The Financial Reporting Review Panel, 24 June 2005). For detail and background, see HMRC Tax Bulletin October 2005 pp 1243–1245.

(s) HMRC may disclose information to specified persons in relation to the **Criminal Assets Bureau** in Ireland for the purpose of the exercise of its functions in identifying and recovering proceeds of crime, or for a similar purpose to any public authority (in the UK or elsewhere) that may be specified by Treasury Order. [*Serious Crime Act 2007, s 85; SI 2008 No 403*].

Prosecutions Office

[36.4] HMRC are permitted to disclose information to the Revenue and Customs Prosecutions Office for the purpose of enabling the Office to consider whether to institute criminal proceedings in respect of a matter considered in the course of an investigation by HMRC or to give advice in connection with a criminal investigation. In relation to Scotland, HMRC are similarly authorised to disclose information to the Lord Advocate or a procurator fiscal. In Northern Ireland disclosures to the Director of Public Prosecutions for Northern Ireland are likewise permitted. [*Commissioners for Revenue and Customs Act 2005, s 21*].

Power to publish State aid information

[36.5] The Commissioners for HMRC may publish 'State aid information' to comply with certain EU State aid obligations requiring such publication. They may also disclose State aid information to another person for the purpose of having it published. '*State aid information*' is information relating to the grant of State aid through the providing of a tax advantage. [*FA , ss 181, 182*].

The explanatory notes to the 2016 Finance Bill state that such information will be published via the European Commission's database but only for those beneficiaries in receipt of aid exceeding 500,000 euros. Information will be published in ranges; the specific amount of a tax advantage will not be published.

'Tax functions'

[36.6] It is a criminal offence for a person to disclose information held by him in the exercise of 'tax functions' about any matter relevant to tax in the case of an 'identifiable person' (as defined). '*Tax functions*' include functions relating to the First-tier Tribunal and Upper Tribunal, HMRC and its officers. This applies equally as regards HMRC's tax credit functions and social security functions. It does not apply if (or if he believes) he has lawful authority or the information has lawfully been made available to the public, or if the person to whom the matter relates has consented. [*FA 1989, s 182*]. Similar provisions apply to members of an advisory commission set up under the Convention on transfer pricing arbitration (see **4.28** ANTI-AVOIDANCE). [*FA 1989, s 182A*].

37

HMRC Explanatory Publications

HMRC explanatory leaflets and factsheets

[37.1] HMRC explanatory leaflets and factsheets relating to income tax are listed below. These are available on the gov.uk website (see **37.6** below).

IR 8	Winding-Up Petitions.
IR 115	Paying for Childcare — Getting Help from your Employer (available at www.gov.uk/government/publications/paying-for-childcare-getting-help-from-your-employer-leaflet-ir115).
480	Expenses and Benefits — A Tax Guide (available at www.gov.uk/government/publications/480-expenses-and-benefits-a-tax-guide).
490	Employee Travel — A Tax and NICs Guide (available at www.gov.uk/government/publications/490-employee-travel-a-tax-and-nics-guide).
CWG2	Employer Further Guide to PAYE and NICs (available at www.gov.uk/government/publications/cwg2-further-guide-to-paye-and-national-insurance-contributions).
CC/FS1a	Compliance Checks — General Information about Compliance Checks. See www.gov.uk/government/publications/general-information-about-compliance-checks-ccfs1a.
CC/FS1b	Compliance Checks — General Information about Checks by Compliance Centres. See www.gov.uk/government/publications/general-information-about-checks-by-compliance-centres-ccfs1b.
CC/FS1c	Compliance Checks — General Information about Compliance Checks into Large and Complex Businesses. See www.gov.uk/government/publications/compliance-checks-large-and-complex-businesses-ccfs1c.

CC/FS1f	Compliance Checks — General Information about Compliance Checks into Tax-advantaged Share Schemes. See www.gov.uk/government/publications/compliance-checks-tax-advantaged-shares-schemes-ccfs1f.
CC/FS2	Compliance Checks — Information Notices. See www.gov.uk/government/publications/compliance-checks-checking-a-customers-tax-position-ccfs2.
CC/FS3	Compliance Checks — Visits by Agreement or with Advance Notice. See www.gov.uk/government/publications/compliance-checks-visits-by-agreement-or-advance-notice-ccfs3.
CC/FS4	Compliance Checks — Unannounced Visits for Inspections. See www.gov.uk/government/publications/compliance-checks-unannounced-visits-for-inspections-ccfs4.
CC/FS5	Compliance Checks — Unannounced Visits for Inspections approved by the Tribunal. See www.gov.uk/government/publications/compliance-checks-unannounced-visits-for-inspections-approved-by-the-tribunal-ccfs5.
CC/FS7a	Compliance Checks — Penalties for Inaccuracies in Returns or Documents. See www.gov.uk/government/publications/compliance-checks-penalties-for-inaccuracies-in-returns-or-documents-ccfs7a.
CC/FS7b	Compliance Checks — Penalties for not telling HMRC about an Under-assessment. See www.gov.uk/government/publications/compliance-checks-penalties-for-not-telling-hmrc-about-an-under-assessment-ccfs7b.
CC/FS7c	Compliance Checks — Penalties for Careless Inaccuracies relating to Tax Avoidance. See www.gov.uk/government/publications/compliance-checks-penalties-for-careless-inaccuracies-relating-to-tax-avoidance-ccfs7c.
CC/FS9	Compliance Checks — The Human Rights Act and Penalties. See www.gov.uk/government/publications/compliance-checks-the-human-rights-act-and-penalties-ccfs9.
CC/FS10	Compliance Checks — Suspending Penalties for Careless Inaccuracies in Returns or Documents. See www.gov.uk/government/publications/compliance-checks-suspending-penalties-for-careless-inaccuracies-in-returns-or-documents-ccfs10.
CC/FS11	Compliance Checks — Penalties for Failure to Notify. See www.gov.uk/government/publications/compliance-checks-penalties-for-failure-to-notify-ccfs11.
CC/FS13	Compliance Checks — Publishing Details of Deliberate Defaulters. See www.gov.uk/government/publications/compliance-checks-publishing-details-of-deliberate-defaulters-ccfs13.
CC/FS14	Managing Serious Defaulters. See www.gov.uk/government/publications/compliance-checks-managing-serious-defaulters-ccfs14.
CC/FS15	Self-Assessment and 'Old' Penalty Rules. See www.gov.uk/government/publications/compliance-checks-self-assessment-and-old-penalty-rules-ccfs15.

CC/FS17 Higher Penalties for Offshore Matters. See www.gov.uk/government/publications/compliance-checks-penalties-for-income-tax-and-capital-gains-tax-for-offshore-matters-ccfs17.

CC/FS17a Penalties for Enablers of Offshore Tax Evasion or Non-compliance. See www.gov.uk/government/publications/compliance-checks-penalties-for-enablers-of-offshore-tax-evasion-or-non-compliance-ccfs17a.

CC/FS18a Penalties for Failure to File Annual and Occasional Returns and Documents on time (including Self-Assessment Tax Returns for Income Tax). See www.gov.uk/government/publications/compliance-checks-penalties-if-you-dont-file-income-tax-capital-gains-tax-and-annual-tax-on-enveloped-dwellings-returns-on-time-ccfs18a.

CC/FS18b Penalties for Failure to File Returns on time — the Construction Industry Scheme (CIS). See www.gov.uk/government/publications/compliance-checks-penalties-if-you-dont-file-construction-industry-scheme-returns-on-time-ccfs18b.

CC/FS19 Employer and Contractor returns and 'Old' Penalty Rules. See www.gov.uk/government/uploads/system/uploads/attachment_data/file/367402/cc-fs19_1_.pdf.

CC/FS21 Alternative Dispute Resolution. See www.gov.uk/government/publications/compliance-checks-alternative-dispute-resolution-ccfs21.

CC/FS22 Sending us Electronic Records. See www.gov.uk/government/publications/compliance-checks-sending-hm-revenue-and-customs-electronic-records-ccfs22.

CC/FS23 Third Party Information Notices. See www.gov.uk/government/uploads/system/uploads/attachment_data/file/425253/CC-FS23_05_15.pdf.

CC/FS24 Tax Avoidance Schemes — Accelerated Payments. See www.gov.uk/government/publications/compliance-checks-tax-avoidance-schemes-accelerated-payments-ccfs24.

CC/FS25a Tax Avoidance Schemes — Follower Notices and Accelerated Payments (except Partnerships). See www.gov.uk/government/publications/compliance-checks-tax-avoidance-schemes-follower-notices-except-partnerships-ccfs25a.

CC/FS25b Tax Avoidance Schemes — Partnership Follower Notices and Accelerated Partner Payments. See www.gov.uk/government/publications/compliance-checks-tax-avoidance-schemes-partnership-follower-notices-ccfs25b.

CC/FS26 Tax Avoidance Schemes — Accelerated Payments for Income Tax and National Insurance Contributions through PAYE. See www.gov.uk/government/publications/compliance-checks-tax-avoidance-schemes-accelerated-payments-ccfs26.

CC/FS27	Tax Avoidance Schemes — Follower Notices and Accelerated Payments for Income Tax and National Insurance Contributions through PAYE. See www.gov.uk/government/publications/compliance-checks-tax-avoidance-schemes-follower-notices-and-accelerated-payments-for-income-tax-and-nics-through-paye-ccfs27.
CC/FS30a	Tax Avoidance Schemes — Penalties for Follower Notices. See www.gov.uk/government/publications/compliance-checks-penalties-for-tax-avoidance-schemes-ccfs30a.
CC/FS30b	Tax Avoidance Schemes — Penalties for Partnership Follower Notices. See www.gov.uk/government/publications/compliance-checks-tax-avoidance-schemes-penalties-for-partnership-follower-notices-ccfs30b.
CC/FS32	Employee Tax-advantaged Share Schemes — Penalty for Material Inaccuracy. See www.gov.uk/government/publications/compliance-checks-employee-tax-advantaged-share-schemes-penalty-for-material-inaccuracy-ccfs32.
CC/FS33	Employee Tax-advantaged Share Schemes — Penalties for not meeting the requirements for Tax-advantaged status. See www.gov.uk/government/publications/compliance-checks-employee-tax-advantaged-share-schemes-penalties-for-not-meeting-the-requirements-for-tax-advantaged-status-ccfs33.
CC/FS34	General Anti-Abuse Rule and Provisional Counteraction Notices. See www.gov.uk/government/publications/compliance-checks-general-anti-abuse-rule-and-provisional-counteraction-notices-ccfs34.
CC/FS34a	Information about the General Anti-Abuse Rule. See www.gov.uk/government/publications/compliance-checks-information-about-the-general-anti-abuse-rule-ccfs34a.
CC/FS35	General Anti-Abuse Rule and Pooling Notices. See www.gov.uk/government/publications/general-anti-abuse-rule-and-pooling-notices-ccfs35.
CC/FS36	Provisional Counteraction Notices given under the General Anti-Abuse Rule. See www.gov.uk/government/publications/compliance-checks-provisional-counteraction-notices-given-under-the-gaar-ccfs36.
CC/FS37	General Anti-Abuse Rule and Notices of Binding. See www.gov.uk/government/publications/compliance-checks-general-anti-abuse-rule-and-notices-of-binding-ccfs37.
CC/FS38a	Serial Tax Avoidance Regime — General Information. See www.gov.uk/government/publications/compliance-checks-serial-tax-avoidance-regime-ccfs38a.
CC/FS41	Construction Industry Scheme — Penalties for False Registration. See www.gov.uk/government/publications/compliance-checks-construction-industry-scheme-penalties-for-false-registration-ccfs41.

CC/FS43	Penalties for Enablers of Defeated Tax Avoidance. See www.gov.uk/government/publications/compliance-checks-penalties-for-enablers-of-defeated-tax-avoidance-ccfs43.
CC/FS45	The Human Rights Act and Penalties for Enablers of Defeated Tax Avoidance. See www.gov.uk/government/publications/compliance-checks-the-human-rights-act-and-penalties-for-enablers-of-defeated-tax-avoidance-ccfs45.
C/FS	Complaints. See www.gov.uk/government/publications/putting-things-right-how-to-complain-factsheet-cfs.
CIS340	Construction Industry Scheme — Guide for Contractors and Subcontractors. See www.gov.uk/government/publications/construction-industry-scheme-cis-340.
COP 8	HMRC Fraud Investigation Service. See www.gov.uk/government/publications/specialist-investigations-for-fraud-and-bespoke-avoidance-cop-8.
COP 9	HMRC Investigations where we suspect Tax Fraud. See www.gov.uk/government/publications/code-of-practice-9-where-hm-revenue-and-customs-suspect-fraud-cop-9-2012.
COP-AT	Anti-Terrorism, Crime and Security Act 2001: Code of Practice on the Disclosure of Information. See www.gov.uk/government/publications/anti-terrorism-crime-and-security-act-2001-code-of-practice-on-the-disclosure-of-information.
E24	Tips, Gratuities, Service Charges and Troncs (2015) (available at www.gov.uk/government/uploads/system/uploads/attachment_data/file/430329/E24_2015_v1_0.pdf).
ES/FS1	Employed or Self-employed for Tax and National Insurance Contributions. See www.gov.uk/government/publications/employment-status-factsheet-esfs1
FEU 50	A Guide to Paying Foreign Entertainers (available at www.gov.uk/guidance/pay-tax-on-payments-to-foreign-performers).
HMRC1	HMRC decisions — What to do if You Disagree. See www.gov.uk/government/publications/hm-revenue-and-customs-decisions-what-to-do-if-you-disagree.
Pride1	Taxes and Benefits — Information for our Lesbian, Gay, Bisexual and Transgender customers.
RDR1	Guidance Note: Residence, Domicile and the Remittance Basis. See www.gov.uk/government/publications/residence-domicile-and-remittance-basis-rules-uk-tax-liability.
SS/FS1	Securities in respect of PAYE and National Insurance contributions (available at www.gov.uk/government/publications/securities-in-respect-of-paye-and-national-insurance-contributions).
—	Giving your Business the Best Start with Tax. See www.gov.uk/government/publications/giving-your-business-the-best-start-with-tax-se2.
—	Digest of Double Taxation Treaties. See www.gov.uk/government/publications/double-taxation-treaties-territory-residents-with-uk-income.

- The Swiss/UK Tax Co-operation Agreement and HMRC (factsheet). See www.gov.uk/government/publications/uk-swiss-confederation-taxation-co-operation-agreement.
- List of bodies approved by HMRC under *ITEPA 2003, ss 343, 344* (subscriptions to professional bodies). See www.gov.uk/government/publications/professional-bodies-approved-for-tax-relief-list-3.
- Tempted by Tax Avoidance?. See www.gov.uk/government/publications/tempted-by-tax-avoidance.

HMRC also publish Concessions and Statements of Practice, brief descriptions of which are included in chapters **38** and **40** with appropriate cross-references to the main coverage.

HMRC guidance manuals

[37.2] The HMRC Guidance Manuals provide guidance to HMRC staff on the operation and application of tax law and the tax system and are available online at www.gov.uk/government/collections/hmrc-manuals. Among the more important of the Manuals, as far as income tax is concerned, are the Business Income Manual, the Employment Income Manual and the Capital Allowances Manual. References to HMRC Manuals are made throughout this work where appropriate.

Some material may be withheld from the online versions of the manuals under exemptions contained in the Government's 'Code of Practice on Access to Government Information'.

Whilst going on to find against the taxpayer in *R (oao Aozora GMAC Investment Ltd) v HMRC* CA, [2019] STC 2486, the CA rejected HMRC's contention that because 'the ordinarily sophisticated taxpayer knows that HMRC apply the law but do not make the law', HMRC guidance cannot give rise to a legitimate expectation. It is 'inherent in the nature of guidance that it only fulfils the function of assisting in the management of the collection of taxes if taxpayers can rely on it'.

HMRC Tax Bulletin and HMRC Briefs

[37.3] HMRC used to publish a bi-monthly Tax Bulletin aimed at tax practitioners and giving the views of HMRC technical specialists on various issues. The December 2006 Tax Bulletin was the last published. It was replaced in 2007 by HMRC Briefs, a service covering both direct and indirect taxes which is published online only (see www.gov.uk/government/collections/revenue-and-customs-briefs). These are issued as and when necessary.

HMRC Helpsheets

[37.4] HMRC produce a number of helpsheets designed to explain different aspects of the tax system and to assist in the completion of self-assessment tax returns. Those currently available can be accessed at www.gov.uk/self-assessment-forms-and-helpsheets.

HMRC toolkits

[37.5] HMRC have developed a series of toolkits aimed at helping and supporting taxpayers' agents but which may be helpful to anyone completing a self-assessment tax return. The toolkits highlight common errors in returns and the steps that can be taken to avoid them. They can also be used to help demonstrate that 'reasonable care' has been taken, so as to avoid the penalty at 55.6 PENALTIES. The toolkits typically consist of a checklist, explanatory notes and links to further guidance. Use of the toolkits is entirely voluntary. The toolkits currently available and relevant to income tax are listed below. See www.gov.uk/government/collections/tax-agents-toolkits.

Business Profits
Capital Allowances for Plant and Machinery
Capital v Revenue Expenditure
Expenses and Benefits from Employment
Income Tax Losses
Private and Personal Expenditure
Property Rental
Trusts and Estates

Gov.uk website

[37.6] The websites of all Government departments and many other agencies and public bodies have been merged into the gov.uk website. The HMRC home page on gov.uk is at www.gov.uk/government/organisations/hm-revenue-customs.

38

HMRC Extra-Statutory Concessions

Introduction to extra-statutory concessions

[38.1] The following is a summary of the concessions published online by HMRC at www.gov.uk/government/publications/extra-statutory-concessions-ex-inland-revenue at 6 April 2018, insofar as they relate to subjects dealt with in this work. It should be borne in mind that in a particular case there may be special circumstances which will require to be taken into account in considering the application of a concession. A concession will not be given in any case where an attempt is made to use it for tax avoidance (and see *R v HMIT (ex p Fulford-Dobson)* QB 1987, 60 TC 168). See also **35.4** HMRC — ADMINISTRATION.

The Treasury have power to give statutory effect to any existing HMRC concession. 'Concession' is given a wide interpretation and is not restricted to the HMRC or Inland Revenue statements originally described as extra-statutory concessions and listed in this chapter. The Treasury's power is exercisable by statutory instrument. [*FA 2008, s 160*]. Where a concession listed in this chapter has been withdrawn or superseded by legislation, this is indicated in the listing.

The First-tier Tribunal has no jurisdiction in relation to an extra-statutory concession; the correct remedy is an application for judicial review (see **5.34** below) (*Michael Prince and others v HMRC* FTT (TC 1852), [2012] SFTD 786).

A. APPLICABLE TO INDIVIDUALS

A14 **Deceased person's estate: residuary income received during the administration period.** A legatee resident abroad may have his tax liability on estate income adjusted as if the income had arisen to him directly. See **22.14** DECEASED ESTATES.

A17 **Death of taxpayer before due date for payment of tax.** Interest on tax overdue may not begin to run until after probate or letters of administration are obtained. Superseded by legislation as regards late payment interest. See **43.7** LATE PAYMENT INTEREST AND PENALTIES.

A19 **Arrears of tax arising through official error.** Relief is given. See **54.14** PAYMENT OF TAX for current details.

A32 **Tax relief for life assurance premiums: position of certain pension schemes which are unapproved after 5 April 1980.** Relief is continued. See **44.31**(ii) LIFE ASSURANCE POLICIES.

A37 **Tax treatment of directors' fees received by partnerships and other companies.** Superseded by statute for 2018/19 onwards. Under certain conditions, such fees may be included in computing the partnership profits — see **28.66** EMPLOYMENT INCOME, or in the corporation tax assessment of the other company — see **28.3**(vi) EMPLOYMENT INCOME.

A41 **Qualifying life assurance policies: statutory conditions** may be relaxed in certain circumstances. See **44.35**(h) LIFE ASSURANCE POLICIES.

A44 **Education allowances under Overseas Service Aid Scheme**, payable to officers in the public service of certain overseas territories, which the UK government has undertaken to exempt from income tax, are so exempted. See **24.1** DIPLOMATIC IMMUNITY.

A56 **Benefits in kind: tax treatment of accommodation provided by employers.** The rules are modified in relation to Scotland. See **28.36** EMPLOYMENT INCOME.

A91 **Living accommodation provided by reason of employment.** A charge will not be raised under the special provisions for accommodation costing £75,000 or more where the basic charge was based on the full market rent. See **28.41** EMPLOYMENT INCOME.

A93 **Payments from offshore trusts to minor unmarried child of settlor: claim by settlor for credit of tax paid by trustees** against his liability to tax on income distributed to or for the benefit of the child will be allowed. See **70.15** SETTLEMENTS.

A94 **Profits and losses of theatre backers (angels)** could in certain cases be treated as within *ITTOIA 2005, s 687*, and the requirement for deduction of tax from certain payments was waived. Concession withdrawn from 31 March 2017. See **49.6** MISCELLANEOUS INCOME.

A97 **Jobmatch programme.** Income tax is not charged on payments under the Jobmatch programme or in respect of training vouchers received under its terms. See **30.47** EXEMPT INCOME.

A99 **Tax treatment of compensation for mis-sold freestanding additional voluntary contribution schemes.** Certain compensation payments are exempted from tax. See **30.15** EXEMPT INCOME.

A103 **Tax-advantaged employee share schemes: armed forces reservists.** Armed Forces Reservists called up to active service are enabled to maintain their participation in their civilian employers' tax-advantaged share schemes during the period they are away on service. See **71.2** SHARE-RELATED EMPLOYMENT INCOME AND EXEMPTIONS.

B. CONCESSIONS APPLICABLE TO INDIVIDUALS AND COMPANIES

B8 **Double tax relief: income consisting of royalties and 'know-how' payments** arising to a UK resident from abroad. See **27.10**(h) DOUBLE TAX RELIEF.

B18 **Payments out of discretionary trusts.** Beneficiaries may claim certain reliefs as if they had received the income out of which the payment was made directly. See **70.15** SETTLEMENTS.

B40 **UK investment managers acting for non-resident clients.** The exemptions of *TMA 1970, ss 78(2), 82* are extended in certain cases. See **50.3**, **50.8** NON-RESIDENTS.

B41 **Claims to repayment of tax.** Where an overpayment of tax has arisen because of official error, and there is no doubt or dispute as to the facts, claims to repayment of tax are accepted outside the statutory time limit. See **16.6** CLAIMS.

C. CONCESSIONS APPLICABLE TO COMPANIES ETC.

C32 **Interest relief — companies with tax and NICs liabilities under the personal service rules where the payments for relevant contracts have been received after deduction of tax by virtue of the construction industry scheme provisions.** Corporation tax repayments due may be set against certain liabilities in respect of deemed employment payments for the purposes of interest on overdue tax and NICs on such payments. See **58.11** PERSONAL SERVICE COMPANIES ETC.

39

HMRC Investigatory Powers

Cross-references. See **35.8** HMRC — ADMINISTRATION for HMRC's Litigation and Settlement Strategy; **55** PENALTIES; **64** RETURNS.

See HMRC Compliance Handbook, in particular CH20000 *et seq.* (technical guidance: information and inspection powers) and CH200000 *et seq.* (operational guidance: how to do a compliance check).

See the series of factsheets CC/FS1 to CC/FS9 listed in **37.1** HMRC EXPLANATORY PUBLICATIONS.

Introduction to investigatory powers

[39.1] HMRC have wide powers to enforce compliance with tax legislation. In most cases, the powers used are those for enquiries into self-assessment returns, for which see **64.6–64.10** RETURNS. Those powers do, however, operate in tandem with further powers to obtain evidence both directly from the taxpayer and from third parties, which are described in this chapter.

FA 2008, Sch 36 introduced a common set of information and inspection powers for HMRC covering income tax, capital gains tax and other direct and indirect taxes and levies. [*SI 2009 Nos 404, 3054*]. See **39.2–39.9** below.

In addition to the above powers, HMRC can obtain specialist and bulk information from specified 'data holders' — see **39.14** below.

HMRC have the power to obtain working papers from tax agents engaging in dishonest conduct — see **39.10** below.

HMRC are able to exercise certain powers under the *Police and Criminal Evidence Act 1984* when conducting direct tax criminal investigations — see **39.12** below. They also have power to seek judicial authority to require the delivery of documents (see **39.13** below) but this is restricted to circumstances where the equivalent police power cannot be used.

There are special provisions relating to computer records (see **39.15** below).

HMRC Brief 36/10, 31 August 2010, lists and explains the factsheets HMRC issue to customers during a compliance check.

Information and inspection powers under *FA 2008, Sch 36*

[39.2] *FA 2008, Sch 36* introduced a common set of information and inspection powers for HMRC covering income tax, capital gains tax and other direct and indirect taxes and levies. The powers are covered at **39.3–39.9** below to the extent that they apply for the purposes of income tax. [*SI 2009 No 404, Arts 2, 3; SI 2009 No 3054, Art 2*].

See also **55.19** PENALTIES for the application of these powers, with modifications, for the purposes of the penalty for enablers of offshore evasion.

Territoriality

There is nothing to prevent notices under *FA 2008, Sch 36* being issued to a UK taxpayer or potential UK taxpayer living in an overseas territory (*R (oao Jimenez) v First Tier Tribunal (Tax Chamber) and HMRC* CA, [2019] STC 746). However, before a non-UK resident can be served with a third party notice within **39.3**(b) below, HMRC must show a sufficient connection between the intended recipient and the information sought to be obtained (*Ex parte PQ* FTT (TC 7199), [2019] UKFTT 371 (TC)).

Definitions

For the purposes of the provisions at **39.3–39.9** below, the following definitions apply.

'*Checking*' includes carrying out an investigation or enquiry of any kind. '*Document*' includes a part of a document (unless the context requires otherwise).

An '*authorised HMRC officer*' is an HMRC officer who is, or who is a member of a class of officers, authorised by the Commissioners for HMRC for the particular purpose.

The carrying on of a business includes the letting of property and the activities of a charity, a government department, a local authority (within *ITA 2007, s 999*), a local authority association (within *ITA 2007, s 1000*) or any other public authority. HMRC can make regulations specifying activities as businesses.

'*Tax*' means any or all of income tax, capital gains tax, corporation tax, VAT and the other taxes listed at *FA 2008, Sch 36 para 63(1)*. It also includes taxes of EU member states in respect of which information can be disclosed and taxes of territories to which a tax enforcement agreement applies (see **36.3**(c) HMRC — CONFIDENTIALITY OF INFORMATION).

A person's '*tax position*' is his position at any time and in relation to any period as regards any tax, including his position as to past, present and future liability to any tax, penalties and other amounts which have been paid or are, or may be, payable by or to him in connection with any tax, and any claims, elections, applications and notices that have or may be made or given in connection with the person's liability to pay any tax. A person's tax position also includes matters relating to the withholding by the person of another person's PAYE income (as defined in **53.2** PAY AS YOU EARN). References to a person's tax position also include the tax position of a company that has ceased to exist and an individual who has died.

In relation to income tax, references in this chapter to an '*involved third party*' are to any of the following:

(a) an approved agent under the rules for payroll giving (see **14.18** CHARITIES AND CHARITABLE GIVING);
(b) an ISA account manager (see **30.27** EXEMPT INCOME);
(c) an account provider in relation to a Child Trust Fund (see **30.12** EXEMPT INCOME); or
(d) a person registered as a managing agent at Lloyd's in relation to a syndicate of underwriting members (see **79** UNDERWRITERS AT LLOYD'S).

In relation to an involved third party, references to '*relevant information and relevant documents*' are to information and documents relating to:

(i) (in a case within (a) above) the donations;
(ii) (in a case within (b) above) the account and investments that have been held in the account;
(iii) (in a case within (c) above) the fund and investments that have been held under the fund; and
(iv) (in a case within (d) above) the syndicate and its activities.

[*FA 2008, Sch 36 paras 58–60, 61A, 63, 64*].

Responsibility of company officers

Everything to be done by a company under the provisions at **39.3–39.9** below must be done by it through the '*proper officer*' (i.e. the secretary of a corporate body, except where a liquidator or administrator has been appointed when the latter is the proper officer, or the treasurer of a non-corporate body) or, except where a liquidator has been appointed, any authorised officer. The service of a notice on a company may be effected by serving it on the proper officer. [*TMA 1970, s 108; FA 2008, Sch 36 para 56*].

Simon's Taxes. See **A6.301A, A6.316, A6.610–A6.624**.

Information and documents

[39.3] An HMRC officer may by notice in writing require a person to provide information or to produce a document if it is reasonably required by him:

(a) for the purpose of checking that person's tax position; or
(b) for the purpose of checking the tax position of another person whose identity is known to the officer; or
(c) for the purpose of checking the tax position of a person whose identity is not known to the officer or of a class of persons whose individual identities are not known to the officer; or
(d) for the purpose of checking the tax position of another person, or class of persons, whose identity or identities are not known to the officer but can be ascertained from information (e.g. a bank branch and account number) held by the officer.

Such a notice (an '*information notice*') may require either specified information or documents or information or documents described in the notice (so that a notice is not restricted to information or documents which HMRC can specifically identify). Where it is given with the approval of the Appeal Tribunal (see further below), the notice must say so.

For a discussion of what may be 'reasonably required', see *Holmes v HMRC* FTT (TC 6824), [2019] SFTD 397, [2018] UKFTT 678 (TC). Where HMRC are enquiring into the tax affairs of a sole shareholder and their company, information as to the nature, size and timing of payments made between the company and the individual is 'reasonably required' by HMRC (*Matharu Delivery Service Ltd v HMRC* UT, [2019] UKFTT 553 (TC)).

The information or documents must be provided or produced within the time period and at the time, by the means and in the form (if any) reasonably specified in the notice. Documents must be produced for inspection either at a place agreed to by the recipient of the notice and an HMRC officer or at a place (other than one used solely as a dwelling) that an HMRC officer reasonably specifies. Subject to any conditions or exceptions set out in regulations made by HMRC, copies of documents can be produced unless the notice requires the production of the original document or an HMRC officer in writing subsequently requests the original document. Where an officer makes such a request, the document must be produced within the period and at the time and by the means reasonably requested by the officer.

An HMRC officer may take copies of, or make extracts from, a document (or copy) produced to him, and if it appears necessary to him, he may remove the document at a reasonable time and retain it for a reasonable period. The officer must, without charge, provide a receipt for a document which is removed where this is requested and must also provide, again without charge, a copy of the document if the person producing it reasonably requires it for any purpose. Where a document which has been removed is lost or damaged, HMRC are liable to compensate the owner for expenses reasonably incurred in replacing or repairing it.

The production or removal of a document under these provisions does not break any lien (i.e. any right) claimed on it.

Taxpayer notice

An information notice under (a) above can be given without the approval of the Tribunal, but where such approval is obtained the taxpayer has no right of appeal against the decision of the Tribunal to grant approval or against the notice or a requirement in it.

Where approval is sought from the Tribunal, the application for approval must be made by, or with the agreement of, an authorised HMRC officer. The taxpayer must normally have been told that the information or documents are required and have been given a reasonable opportunity to make representations to HMRC, and the Tribunal must be given a summary of any such representations. Where, however, the Tribunal is satisfied that informing the taxpayer would prejudice the assessment or collection of tax, it can approve the giving of the notice without the taxpayer having been informed.

Third party notice

A notice within (b) above cannot be given without either the agreement of the taxpayer (i.e. the person whose tax position is to be checked) or the approval of the Tribunal and must normally name the taxpayer. Where approval is obtained from the Tribunal, there is no right of appeal against the decision of the Tribunal to grant approval or against the notice or a requirement in it. In *R (oao Derrin Brother Properties Ltd) v HMRC* CA, [2016] All ER (D) 124 (Jan), 2016 STI 209, an application for judicial review was dismissed on the facts.

Where approval is sought from the Tribunal, the application for approval must be made by, or with the agreement of, an authorised HMRC officer. The taxpayer must normally have been given a summary of the reasons why an officer requires the information or documents. The person to whom the notice is to be given must normally have been told that the information or documents are required and have been given a reasonable opportunity to make representations to HMRC and the Tribunal must be given a summary of any such representations. These requirements can, however, be disapplied where the Tribunal is satisfied that informing the recipient of the notice or giving a summary of reasons to the taxpayer would prejudice the assessment or collection of tax.

The Appeal Tribunal can also disapply the requirement to name the taxpayer in the notice if it is satisfied that the officer has reasonable grounds for believing that naming him might seriously prejudice the assessment or collection of tax.

A copy of the notice must normally be given to the taxpayer. The Tribunal can, however, disapply this requirement if an application for approval is made by, or with the agreement of, an authorised HMRC officer and the Tribunal is satisfied that the officer has reasonable grounds for believing that giving a copy of the notice to the taxpayer might prejudice the assessment or collection of tax.

If a third party notice refers only to information or documents that relate to a pensions matter (as defined in *FA 2008, Sch 36 para 34B*), neither the agreement of the taxpayer nor the approval of the Tribunal is required and a copy of the notice need not be given to the taxpayer. However, the HMRC officer must normally give a copy of the notice to certain persons — see also *SI 2010 No 650*).

Where a third party notice is given for the purpose of checking the tax position of more than one of the partners in a business carried on in partnership, in their capacity as such, the above provisions apply as if the taxpayer were at least one of the partners. The requirement for the notice to name the taxpayer is satisfied by stating in the notice that its purpose is checking the tax position of more than one of the partners and giving a name in which the partnership is registered for any purpose. Where a third party notice is given to one of the partners for the purpose of checking the tax position of any of the other partners, neither the agreement of any of the partners nor the approval of the Tribunal is required and a copy does not have to be given to any other partners.

Notice about persons whose identity is not known

The giving of a notice under (c) above requires the approval of the Tribunal. The Tribunal can approve the giving of the notice only if it is satisfied that:

- there are reasonable grounds for believing that the person or class of persons to whom the notice relates may have failed, or may fail, to comply with any provision of the law relating to tax (including the law of a territory outside the UK);
- any such failure is likely to have led, or to lead, to serious prejudice to the assessment or collection of tax; and
- the information or document is not readily available from another source.

There is no right of appeal against a decision of the Tribunal to grant approval.

The approval of the Tribunal is permitted but not required for a notice to be given to a partner in a business carried on in partnership for the purpose of checking the tax position of partners whose identities are not known to the officer giving the notice. Approval is likewise permitted but not required if a notice refers only to information or documents that relate to a pensions matter (as defined in *FA 2008, Sch 36 para 34B*, which also provides that the HMRC officer must give a copy of the notice to certain persons — see also *SI 2010 No 650*).

Notice about person whose identity can be ascertained

A notice within (d) above must be given by an authorised HMRC officer and can require the recipient to provide the name, last known address and/or date of birth of the taxpayer(s) concerned but no more than that. The officer must have reason to believe that the recipient of the notice will be able to ascertain the taxpayer's identity (or taxpayers' identities) from the information held by the officer and that the recipient obtained the information required in the course of carrying on a business. A notice cannot be given if the taxpayer's identity (or taxpayers' identities) can be readily ascertained by other means from the information held by the officer.

[*FA 2008, Sch 36 paras 1–5, 5A, 6–9, 15, 16, 34B, 34C, 37; SI 2009 No 404; SI 2009 No 3054, Art 2; SI 2010 No 650*].

Approval was duly granted by the Tribunal in *Re an Application by HMRC for approval to serve notice on Financial Institution* FTT (TC 148), [2009] UKFTT 195 (TC); *Re an Application by HMRC for approval to serve notice on Financial Institution* FTT (TC 149), [2009] UKFTT 196 (TC); and *Re Applications by HMRC for approval to serve notices on Financial Institutions* FTT (TC 174), [2009] SFTD 780.

For further restrictions on the above powers, see **39.4** below. For appeals against information notices, see **39.5** below.

Restrictions on information notice powers

[39.4] An information notice does not require a person to:

(i) produce a document if it is not in his possession or power;
(ii) provide or produce information that relates to the conduct of a pending tax appeal or any part of a document containing such information;
(iii) provide journalistic material (within *Police and Criminal Evidence Act 1984, s 13*) or information contained in such material;
(iv) subject to the exceptions below, provide or produce 'personal records' (within *Police and Criminal Evidence Act 1984, s 12*); or
(v) produce a document the whole of which originates more than six years before the giving of the notice, unless the notice is given by, or with the agreement of, an authorised officer (ten years in a case where the notice refers only to information or documents relating to a qualifying recognised overseas pension scheme or a scheme that has at any time been such a scheme).

With regard to (iv) above, an information notice may require a person to produce documents (or copies) that are personal records, omitting any personal information (i.e. information whose inclusion in the documents makes them personal records) and to provide any information in personal records that is not personal information.

[*FA 2008, Sch 36 paras 18–20, 34B(4A); Savings (Government Contributions) Act 2017, s 5(3)*].

As regards (i) above, a document which did not exist when the information notice was issued (e.g. a hard copy bank statement), but which could be created by the taxpayer or by another at their instigation, is neither in the possession of that person nor in their power (*Brantjes v HMRC* FTT (TC 7664), [2020] UKFTT 177 (TC)).

Notice where tax return made

Where a person has made a tax return under *TMA 1970, s 8, s 8A* or *s 12AA* (see **64.2, 64.12** RETURNS) in respect of a tax year, a taxpayer notice (see **39.3**(a) above) can be given for the purpose of checking his income tax or capital gains tax position for that year only if:

(a) an enquiry notice under *TMA 1970, s 9A* or *s 12AC* (see **64.6**, **64.12** RETURNS) has been given in respect of either the return or a claim or election for the year to which the return relates and the enquiry has not been completed (or, on and after 16 November 2017, the enquiry has not been completed so far as relating to the matters to which the taxpayer notice relates);

(b) an HMRC officer has reason to suspect, in relation to that person, that an amount that ought to have been assessed to tax may not have been assessed, that an assessment for the period may be or have become insufficient or relief from tax for the period may be or have become excessive;

(c) the notice is given for the purpose of obtaining information or a document that is also required to check the taxpayer's position as regards any tax other than income tax, capital gains tax or corporation tax; or

(d) the notice is given for the purpose of obtaining information or a document that is required to check the taxpayer's position as regards his obligation to make deductions or repayments under PAYE, the Construction Industry Scheme or any other provision.

Where a business is carried in partnership and a partnership return (see **64.12** RETURNS) or a partnership claim or election (see **16.1** CLAIMS) has been made by one of the partners, the above provisions apply as if the return, claim or election had been made by each of the partners.

Conditions (a)–(d) above do not have to be met if:

- the person is carrying on a trade to which the HERD BASIS (**34**) applies, and the taxpayer notice refers only to information or documents that relate to the animals kept for the purposes of the trade or their products; or
- it appears to an officer of HMRC that *ITA 2007, s 684* (see **4.9** ANTI-AVOIDANCE) may apply to the person by reason of one or more transactions, and the taxpayer notice refers only to information or documents relating to the transaction (or to any of the transactions).

[*FA 2008, Sch 36 paras 21, 37(1)(2), 37A, 37B; F(No 2)A 2017, Sch 15 paras 36, 44; SI 2009 No 3054, Art 2*].

Deceased persons

An information notice for the purpose of checking the tax position of a deceased person cannot be given more than four years after death. [*FA 2008, Sch 36 para 22*].

Legal professional privilege (LPP)

An information notice cannot require a person to provide information, or to produce any part of a document, in respect of which a claim to LPP (or, in Scotland, a claim to confidentiality of communications) could be maintained in legal proceedings.

HMRC can make regulations providing a means of resolving disputes over whether a document is privileged. See now *SI 2009 No 1916*, which sets out different procedures depending upon whether the information notice is given in the course of correspondence or in the course of an inspection of premises; both procedures involve recourse to the Appeal Tribunal. See HMRC Brief 54/09, 18 August 2009.

[*FA 2008, Sch 36 para 23*].

LPP does not apply in relation to any professional other than a member of the legal profession, acting as such; thus it does not apply in relation to accountants and non-legally qualified tax advisers (*R (oao Prudential plc and another) v Special Commr of Income Tax and another* SC 2013, 82 TC 64). LPP extends not only to the content of legal advice but to the fact that a person sought legal advice on a particular matter; a client engagement letter is subject to LPP to the extent that it sets out the nature of the legal advice for which a solicitor has been retained (*Behague v HMRC* FTT (TC 2983), [2013] UKFTT 596 (TC), 2013 STI 3577). If tax advisers model their own advice to clients on advice previously given by counsel, this does not bring that advice within the protection of LPP (*R (oao Emblin) v HMRC* QB, [2018] STC 934).

Auditors

An information notice does not require an auditor (i.e. a person appointed as an auditor for the purpose of an enactment) to provide information held in connection with the performance of his functions under that enactment or to produce documents which are his property and which were created by him, or on his behalf, for or in connection with the performance of those functions.

This exclusion does not apply to any information, or any document containing information, which explains any information or document which an auditor has, as tax accountant, assisted any client in preparing for, or delivering to, HMRC. Where the notice is given under **39.3**(c) above, the exclusion also does not apply to information giving the identity or address of a person to whom the notice relates or of a person who has acted on behalf of such a person or to a document containing such information. Where the exclusion is so disapplied, only that part (or parts) of a document which contains the relevant information has to be produced. The exclusion is not disapplied if the information concerned, or a document containing the information, has already been provided or produced to an HMRC officer.

[*FA 2008, Sch 36 paras 24, 26, 27*].

HMRC cannot use the fact that a company's auditor is also its agent for tax purposes to obtain documents clearly related to the statutory audit (*Re an Application by HMRC to give an information notice under Para 3 of Sch 36 to the Finance Act 2008* FTT (TC 6710), [2019] SFTD 117, [2018] UKFTT 541 (TC)).

Tax advisers

An information notice does not require a 'tax adviser' to provide information about, or to produce documents which are his property and which consist of, communications between him and a person in relation to whose tax affairs he has been appointed or between him and any other tax advisor of such a person, the purpose of which is the giving or obtaining of advice about any of those tax affairs. For this purpose, a '*tax adviser*' is a person appointed (directly or by another tax adviser) to give advice about the tax affairs of another person.

This restriction is disapplied in the same circumstances as the restriction applying to auditors is disapplied.

[*FA 2008, Sch 36 paras 25–27*].

In *Qubic Taxassethound Ltd v HMRC* FTT (TC 7701), [2020] UKFTT 215 (TC), the FTT found that these restrictions do not apply to a document which is about fees charged to a client for the provision of tax advice and which did not disclose the content of the tax advice given.

Appeals against information notices

[39.5] A taxpayer can appeal against a taxpayer notice (see **39.3**(a) above) or any requirement in such a notice unless the notice was given with the approval of the Appeal Tribunal. No appeal can be made against a requirement to provide information or to produce a document which forms part of his 'statutory records' (as defined below, and see *Joshy Mathew v HMRC* FTT (TC 4342), [2015] UKFTT 139 (TC)).

A person given a third party notice (see **39.3**(b) above) can appeal against the notice or any requirement in it on the ground that compliance would be unduly onerous. No appeal can be made, however, where the notice was given with the approval of the Tribunal or against a requirement to provide information or produce a document forming part of the taxpayer's statutory records.

Where a third party notice is given for the purpose of checking the tax position of more than one of the partners in a business carried on in partnership, no appeal can be made against a requirement to provide information or produce a document forming part of the statutory records of any of the partners. No appeal can be made against a requirement, in a notice given to a partner for the purpose of checking the tax position of other partners, to produce a document forming part of the statutory records of the partner receiving the notice.

A person given a notice about persons whose identity is not known (see **39.3**(c) above) or a notice about persons whose identity can be ascertained (see **39.3**(d) above) can appeal against the notice or any requirement in it on the ground that compliance would be unduly onerous. No appeal can be made against a requirement, in a notice given to a parent undertaking for the purpose of checking the tax position of one or more subsidiary undertakings, to produce a document forming part of the statutory records of the parent undertaking or any of its subsidiary undertakings. Likewise, no appeal can be made against a requirement, in a notice given to a partner in a business carried on in partnership for the purpose of checking the tax position of other partners, to produce a document forming part of the statutory records of the partner receiving the notice.

For this purpose, '*statutory records*' are information and documents which a taxpayer is required to keep and preserve for tax purposes (see **16.3** CLAIMS, **64.5** RETURNS), for VAT purposes and for the purposes of the other taxes listed at *FA 2008, Sch 36 para 63(1)*. To the extent that information or documents do not relate to the carrying on of a business and are not required to be kept or preserved for the purposes of VAT and other taxes, they form part of a taxpayer's statutory documents only to the extent that the tax year to which they relate has ended. Information and documents cease to be statutory records when the period for which they are required to be preserved ends. Private bank statements can be statutory records if used for making payments of business expenses (*Beckwith v HMRC* FTT (TC 1876), [2012] UKFTT 181 (TC), 2012 STI 1842).

Procedure

Notice of appeal under the above provisions must be given in writing to the HMRC officer who gave the information notice within the period of 30 days beginning with the date on which the information notice was given. A decision on an appeal by the Tribunal is final. Where the Tribunal confirms the notice or a requirement in it, the person to whom the notice was given must comply with the notice or requirement within the period specified by the Tribunal. If the Tribunal does not specify such a period, compliance must be within such period as an HMRC officer reasonably specifies in writing.

Subject to the above, the appeal provisions of *TMA 1970, Pt 5* (see **5** APPEALS) apply to an appeal against an information notice as they apply to an appeal against an income tax assessment.

[*FA 2008, Sch 36 paras 29–33, 37, 62; SI 2009 No 3054, Art 2*].

Concealing, destroying or disposing of documents

[39.6] A person to whom an information notice is addressed must not conceal, destroy or otherwise dispose of, or arrange for the concealment, destruction or disposal of, a document that is the subject of the notice. This does not apply if he does so after the document has been produced to HMRC in accordance with the notice, unless an HMRC officer has notified him in writing that the document must continue to be available for inspection (and has not withdrawn the notification). It also does not apply if a copy of the document was produced in compliance with the notice and the destruction, etc. takes place after the end of the period of six months beginning with the day on which the copy was produced unless within that period, an HMRC officer makes a request for the original document.

Similarly, where a person has been informed that a document is, or is likely, to be the subject of an information notice addressed to him, he must not conceal, destroy or otherwise dispose of, or arrange for the concealment, destruction or disposal of, the document. This does not apply if he acts more than six months after he was so informed (or was last so informed).

[*FA 2008, Sch 36 paras 42, 43*].

Failure to comply with the above provisions may be a criminal offence or result in penalties. See **39.9** below.

Inspection of business premises

[39.7] An HMRC officer may enter a person's 'business premises' and inspect the premises and any 'business assets' and 'business documents' that are on the premises if the inspection is reasonably required for the purpose of checking that person's tax position. The officer may not enter or inspect any part of the premises used solely as a dwelling.

An HMRC officer may also enter business premises of an involved third party (see **39.2** above) and inspect the premises and any business assets and relevant documents that are on the premises if the inspection is reasonably required for the purpose of checking the tax position of any person or class of persons. It is not necessary that the officer know the identity of the person or persons. The officer may not enter or inspect any part of the premises used solely as a dwelling.

The officer may mark business assets and anything containing business assets to indicate that they have been inspected and may obtain and record information (electronically or otherwise) relating to the premises, assets and documents inspected. He may take copies of, or make extracts from, a document (or copy) which he inspects, and if it appears necessary to him, he may remove the document at a reasonable time and retain it for a reasonable period. He must, without charge, provide a receipt for a document which is removed where this is requested and must also provide, again without charge, a copy of the document, if the person producing it reasonably requires it for any purpose. Where a document which has been removed is lost or damaged, HMRC are liable to compensate the owner for expenses reasonably incurred in replacing or repairing it.

An inspection must normally be carried out at a time agreed to by the occupier of the premises. It can, however, be carried out at any reasonable time if:

(i) the occupier has been given at least seven days' notice (in writing or otherwise) of the time of the inspection; or
(ii) the inspection is carried out by, or with the agreement of, an authorised HMRC officer.

Where (ii) above applies, the officer carrying out the inspection must provide a notice in writing stating the possible consequences of obstructing the officer in the exercise of the power. If the occupier is present when the inspection begins, the notice must be given to him. If he is not present, the notice must be given to the person who appears to be the officer in charge of the premises, but if no such person is present, the notice must be left in a prominent place on the premises. The giving of such a notice does not require the approval of the Appeal Tribunal, but such approval can be applied for by, or with the agreement of, an authorised HMRC officer. A penalty for deliberate obstruction of an officer in the course of an inspection can only be charged where such approval has been obtained (see **39.9** below). A decision of the Tribunal to approve an inspection is final and there is no right of appeal.

An officer may not inspect a document if or to the extent that an information notice (see **39.3** above) given at the time of the inspection to the occupier of the premises could not require him to produce the document (see **39.4** above).

For the above purposes, '*business premises*' are premises (including any land, building or structure or means of transport), or a part of premises, that an HMRC officer has reason to believe are used in connection with the carrying on of a business by or on behalf of the taxpayer concerned. '*Business assets*' are assets, other than documents that are neither trading stock nor plant, that an HMRC officer has reason to believe are owned, leased or used in connection with the carrying on of any business. '*Business documents*' are documents, or copies of documents, relating to the carrying on of any business that form part of any person's statutory records.

[*FA 2008, Sch 36 paras 10, 10A, 12–17, 28, 58; SI 2009 No 404; SI 2009 No 3054, Art 2*].

Inspection of premises for valuation purposes

[39.8] An HMRC officer can enter and inspect any premises for the purpose of valuing them. The valuation must be reasonably required for the purpose of checking any person's position as regards income tax or corporation tax. The officer can be accompanied by a valuation expert.

The inspection must normally be carried out at a time agreed to by the occupier of the premises and he must be given notice in writing of the agreed time. If the occupier cannot be identified, agreement can be obtained from, and notice given to, a person who controls the premises. Where, however, the inspection has been approved by the Appeal Tribunal (see below), the only requirement is that the occupier or person controlling the premises be given at least seven days' notice in writing of the time of the inspection. Where such notice is given it must state that the inspection has been approved by the tribunal and indicate the possible consequences of obstructing the inspection (see below).

The giving of a notice does not require the approval of the Tribunal, but such approval can be applied for by, or with the agreement of, an authorised HMRC officer. A penalty for deliberate obstruction of an officer in the course of an inspection can only be charged where such approval has been obtained (see **39.9** below). A decision of the Tribunal to approve an inspection is final and there is no right of appeal. Both the person whose tax position is in question and the occupier of the premises (unless he cannot be identified) must be given a reasonable opportunity to make representations to the HMRC officer and a summary of any representations must be given to the Tribunal.

An officer carrying out an inspection under these powers must produce evidence of his authority to do so if asked by the occupier or any other person who appears to be in charge of the premises or property. He may obtain and record information (electronically or otherwise) relating to the premises and property inspected.

[*FA 2008, Sch 36 paras 12A, 12B, 13, 14, 17; SI 2009 No 3054, Art 2*].

Offences and penalties under *FA 2008, Sch 36*

[39.9] For penalties for failure to comply with an information notice within 39.3 above or deliberately obstructing an HMRC officer in the course of an inspection of premises under the power at 39.7 or 39.8 above that has been approved by the Appeal Tribunal, see 55.15 PENALTIES.

It is an offence for a person required to produce a document by an information notice within 39.3 above which has been approved by the Appeal Tribunal to conceal, destroy or otherwise dispose of the document or to arrange for its concealment, destruction or disposal. This does not apply if he does so after the document has been produced to HMRC in accordance with the notice, unless an HMRC officer has notified him in writing that the document must continue to be available for inspection (and has not withdrawn the notification). It also does not apply if a copy of the document was produced in compliance with the notice and the destruction, etc. takes place after the end of the period of six months beginning with the day on which the copy was produced unless within that period, an HMRC officer makes a request for the original document.

It is also an offence for a person to conceal, destroy or otherwise dispose of, or to arrange for the concealment, destruction or disposal of, a document after an HMRC officer has informed him in writing that the document is, or is likely to be, the subject of an information notice approval for which is to be obtained from the Appeal Tribunal. This does not apply if the person so acts more than six months after he was so informed (or was last so informed).

On summary conviction of either of the above offences the offender is liable to a fine not exceeding the statutory maximum. On conviction on indictment the punishment is imprisonment for a maximum of two years and/or a fine.

[*FA 2008, Sch 36 paras 53–55*].

Power to obtain files of tax agent

[39.10] HMRC have a power to obtain 'working papers' from 'tax agents' who engage in 'dishonest conduct' (and to charge penalties on such agents — see 55.18 PENALTIES). The power applies across most of the taxes administered by HMRC, including income tax. See also 55.37 PENALTIES for HMRC's power to publish details of tax agents who engage in dishonest conduct. [*FA 2012, s 223, Sch 38*].

Nothing in these provisions limits any liability a person may have under any other enactment in relation to conduct in respect of which a person is liable to a penalty under these provisions, or limits any power a person may have under any other enactment to obtain documents. [*FA 2012, Sch 38 para 43*].

See guidance at www.gov.uk/guidance/dishonest-conduct-by-tax-agents.

Meaning of 'tax agent'

A '*tax agent*' is an individual who, in the course of business, assists other persons ('*clients*') with their tax affairs. Individuals who work for or are partners in, or members of, an organisation, person or firm are included, even if it is the organisation that is appointed or engaged to give assistance. Individuals can be tax agents even if they, or the organisations for which they work, are appointed or engaged indirectly or at the request of someone other than the client. For this purpose, assistance with a client's tax affairs includes advising a client in relation to tax, acting or purporting to act as agent on behalf of a client in relation to tax and assistance with any document likely to be relied on by HMRC to determine a client's tax position. Assistance given for non-tax purposes counts as assistance with a client's tax affairs if given in the knowledge that it is likely to be used by a client in connection with his tax affairs. '*Tax*' means any of the taxes listed at *FA 2012, Sch 38 para 37(1)* and includes income tax. [*FA 2012, s 223, Sch 38 paras 2, 37–39, 41*].

Dishonest conduct

An individual engages in '*dishonest conduct*' if, in the course of acting as a tax agent, he does something dishonest with a view to bringing about a loss of tax revenue. It does not matter whether or not an actual tax loss arises nor whether or not the agent is acting on clients' instructions. For this purpose, a loss of tax revenue would be brought about if clients were to account for less tax, or account for tax later, than required by law or if clients were to obtain more 'tax relief', or obtain tax relief earlier, than they were entitled to by law. '*Tax relief*' includes any exemption from, or deduction or credit against or in respect of, tax and any repayment of tax. Doing something dishonest includes dishonestly omitting to do something and advising or assisting a client to do something that the agent knows to be dishonest. A loss of tax revenue is taken to be (or to be capable of being) brought about by dishonest conduct despite the fact that it can be recovered or properly accounted for (following discovery of the conduct or otherwise). [*FA 2012, Sch 38 paras 3, 40*].

Conduct notice

Where HMRC determine that a tax agent has engaged in dishonest conduct they may notify the agent of their determination, stating the grounds on which it was made. The consequences of such a notice are that HMRC may then assess a penalty for dishonest conduct on the tax agent (see **55.18** PENALTIES) and seek to issue a file access notice to obtain the agent's working papers (see below).

The tax agent can appeal against a conduct notice by giving notice in writing within 30 days beginning with the date on which the conduct notice was given. The notice of appeal must state the grounds of appeal. The appeal provisions of *TMA 1970, Pt 5* (see **5** APPEALS) apply to an appeal against a conduct notice as they apply to an appeal against an income tax assessment. Where the appeal is notified to the Appeal Tribunal, the Tribunal may confirm or set aside the determination made in the conduct notice, but setting aside a determination does not prevent a further conduct notice being given for the same conduct if further evidence emerges.

Once a conduct notice has been given to a tax agent, or HMRC have informed a tax agent that a notice will be, or is likely to be, given to him, it is an offence for any person to conceal, destroy or otherwise dispose of (or to arrange for the concealment etc. of) a document that could be sought under a file access notice given to the agent as a result of the conduct notice. The penalty for such an offence is, on summary conviction, a fine not exceeding the statutory maximum or, on conviction on indictment, imprisonment for a term not exceeding two years or a fine, or both. If the concealment etc. takes place after the giving of the conduct notice, no offence is committed if the determination in the notice has been set aside, if more than four years have passed since the giving of the notice, or if the person in question is acting without knowledge of the making of the conduct notice. If the concealment etc. takes place before the giving of the notice but after HMRC have informed the agent that such a notice will be, or is likely to be, given, no offence is committed if the person in question is acting without knowledge of HMRC's having so informed the tax agent or if more than two years have passed after the tax agent was, or was last, so informed. For this purpose, a person is deemed to be acting without knowledge of an event if he is not the tax agent subject to the notice given, or likely to be, given and does not know, and could not reasonably be expected to know, that the event has occurred.

[*FA 2012, Sch 38 paras 4–6*].

File access notice

Subject to the following, an HMRC officer may, by notice in writing (a '*file access notice*') require a tax agent or any other person that the officer believes may hold 'relevant documents' (a '*document-holder*') to provide such documents. It is not necessary for the tax agent still to be a tax agent when the notice is issued. A notice may require the provision of specified relevant documents or all such documents in the document-holder's possession or power. The notice does not need to identify the clients of the tax agent, but if it is addressed to anyone other than the tax agent, it must name him. The notice may require documents to be provided within such period, by such means and in such form, and to such person and at such place as are reasonably specified either in the notice or a document referred to in the notice. Unless otherwise specified in the notice, only copies of the relevant documents need be provided. A document-holder cannot be required to provide documents not in his possession or power.

'*Relevant documents*' means the tax agent's working papers (whenever acting as a tax agent) and any other documents received, created, prepared or used by him for the purposes, or in the course of, assisting clients (including former clients) with their tax affairs. It does not matter who owns the papers or documents concerned. The papers or documents which may be required by a notice are not restricted to those relating to clients with respect to whom the tax agent has engaged in dishonest conduct. 'Document' for this purpose includes a copy of a document.

HMRC can issue a file access notice only with the approval of the Appeal Tribunal and only if:

(a) a conduct notice has been given to the tax agent concerned and either the time allowed for appeal has expired without an appeal being made or, where an appeal has been made, it has been withdrawn or the determination in the conduct notice has been confirmed; or

(b) the tax agent has been convicted of an offence relating to tax that involves fraud or dishonesty; the offence was committed after he became a tax agent (whether or not he was still a tax agent when it was committed and regardless of the capacity in which it was committed); either the time allowed for appeal against the conviction has expired without an appeal being made or, where an appeal has been made, it has been withdrawn or the conviction upheld; and no more than twelve months have passed since the date on which the appeal time limit passed or the appeal was withdrawn or conviction upheld.

For this purpose, a determination or conviction that has been appealed is not considered to be confirmed or upheld until the time allowed for any further appeal has expired or, if a further appeal is brought within that time, that further appeal has been withdrawn or determined.

The Tribunal cannot approve the giving of a file access notice unless:

- the application is made by or with the agreement of an HMRC officer authorised for this purpose;
- the Tribunal is satisfied that the case falls within (a) or (b) above and that, in the circumstances, HMRC are justified in giving the notice;
- the document-holder and, if different, the tax agent, have been told that relevant documents are to be required and given a reasonable opportunity to make representations to HMRC; and
- the Tribunal has been given a summary of any such representations.

Any decision by the Tribunal to approve or refuse the giving of a notice is final. It is not necessary for the Tribunal to determine whether an individual has engaged in dishonest conduct.

An HMRC officer may take copies of, or make extracts from, a document (or copy) provided to him, and if he thinks it necessary, he may retain it for a reasonable period. The officer must, without charge, supply a copy of the document if the document-holder reasonably requires it for any purpose. Where a document which has been retained is lost or damaged, HMRC are liable to compensate the owner for expenses reasonably incurred in replacing or repairing it. The retention of a document under these provisions does not break any lien claimed on it.

Restrictions on powers

A file access notice does not require the document-holder to provide:

(i) parts of a document containing information relating to the conduct of a pending tax appeal;

(ii) journalistic material (within *Police and Criminal Evidence Act 1984, s 13*);

(iii) subject to the exceptions below, personal records (within *Police and Criminal Evidence Act 1984, s 12*);

(iv) a document the whole of which originated more than 20 years before the giving of the notice, provided that no part of the document has a bearing on tax years or other chargeable periods ending within the last 20 years; or

(v) any part of a document in respect of which a claim to legal professional privilege (LPP) (or, in Scotland, a claim to confidentiality of communications) could be maintained in legal proceedings. LPP does not apply in relation to any professional other than a member of the legal profession, acting as such (see **39.4** above).

With regard to (iii) above, a file access notice may require a person to produce documents that are personal records, omitting any information the inclusion of which (whether alone or with other information) makes the original documents personal records. With regard to (v) above, the procedure for resolving disputes as to whether information is privileged is the same as that used in relation to information notices in **39.4** above.

Appeals against file access notices

If the document-holder is not the tax agent, he may appeal against a file access notice or any requirement in it, on the grounds that it would be unduly onerous to comply. Notice of appeal must be given in writing to the HMRC officer who gave the notice within the 30 days beginning with the day the notice was given and must state the grounds of appeal. If the appeal is notified to the Appeal Tribunal, the Tribunal may confirm, vary or set aside the notice or a requirement in it. If the Tribunal confirms or varies the notice or a requirement, the document-holder must comply with the notice or requirement within the period specified by the Tribunal or, if no such period is specified, within a period reasonably specified by HMRC. A decision by the Tribunal is final, but otherwise the appeal provisions of *TMA 1970, Pt 5* (see **5** APPEALS) apply to an appeal against a file access notice as they apply to an appeal against an income tax assessment.

Offences and penalties

For penalties for failure to comply with a file access notice see **55.18** PENALTIES.

It is an offence for any person to conceal, destroy or otherwise dispose of (or to arrange for the concealment etc. of) a document that he is required to provide by a file access notice if either the notice has not been complied with or, if it has been complied with, he has been notified in writing by HMRC that he must continue to preserve the document (and the notification has not been withdrawn). It is similarly an offence for any person to conceal, destroy or otherwise dispose of (or to arrange for the concealment etc. of) a document if, at the time he acts, HMRC have informed him that he will, or is likely to, be required to provide the document by a file access notice and no more than six months have passed since he was, or was last, so informed. The penalty for such an offence is, on summary conviction, a fine not exceeding the statutory maximum or, on conviction on indictment, imprisonment for a term not exceeding two years or a fine, or both.

[*FA 2012, Sch 38 paras 7–21, 38, 42*].

Responsibility of company officers

Everything to be done by a company under the above provisions must be done by it through the '*proper officer*' (i.e. the secretary of a corporate body, except where a liquidator or administrator has been appointed when the latter is the proper officer, or the treasurer of a non-corporate body) or, except where a liquidator has been appointed, any authorised officer. The service of a notice on a company may be effected by serving it on the proper officer. [*TMA 1970, s 108; FA 2012, Sch 38 para 36*].

Simon's Taxes. See **A6.321–A6.323**.

HMRC's practice in tax fraud cases

[39.11] The policy of the Commissioners for HMRC in cases of suspected tax fraud, as set out in Code of Practice COP 9, is as follows:

- The Commissioners reserve complete discretion to pursue a criminal investigation with a view to prosecution where they consider it necessary and appropriate.
- Where a criminal investigation is not commenced the Commissioners may decide to investigate using the COP 9 procedure.
- The recipient of COP 9 will be given the opportunity to make a complete and accurate disclosure of all his deliberate and non-deliberate conduct that has led to irregularities in his tax affairs.
- Where HMRC suspect that the recipient has failed to make a full disclosure of all irregularities, the Commissioners reserve the right to commence a criminal investigation with a view to prosecution.
- The term 'deliberate conduct' means that the recipient knew that an entry or entries included in a tax return and/or accounts were wrong but submitted it/them anyway, or that the recipient knew that a tax liability existed but chose not to tell HMRC at the right time.
- In the course of the COP 9 investigation, if the recipient makes materially false or misleading statements, or provides materially false documents, the Commissioners reserve the right to commence a criminal investigation into that conduct as a separate criminal offence.

If the Commissioners decide to investigate using the COP 9 procedure the taxpayer will be given a copy of the above statement by an authorised officer. The First-tier Tribunal has no jurisdiction to close a COP 9 investigation; the only means of challenge is by judicial review (*Gold Nuts Ltd v HMRC* FTT (TC 4875), [2016] SFTD 371, [2016] UKFTT 82 (TC)).

Under its published Criminal Investigation Policy (see www.gov.uk/government/publications/criminal-investigation), HMRC reserve complete discretion to conduct a criminal investigation in any case, with a view to prosecution by the Revenue and Customs Prosecutions Office (RCPO) in England and Wales or the appropriate prosecuting authority in Scotland and Northern Ireland. Examples of the kind of circumstances in which HMRC will generally consider commencing a criminal, rather than civil, investigation are, inter alia, cases involving organised or systematic fraud including conspiracy; cases where an individual holds a position of trust or responsibility; cases where materially false statements are made or materially false documents are provided in the course of a civil investigation; cases where deliberate concealment, deception, conspiracy or corruption is suspected; cases involving the use of false or forged documents; cases involving money laundering; cases where there is a link to suspected wider criminality; and repeated offences.

See *R v CIR (ex p Mead and Cook)* QB 1992, 65 TC 1 as regards HMRC discretion to seek monetary settlements or institute criminal proceedings. See *R v CIR (ex p Allen)* QB 1997, 69 TC 442 for an unsuccessful application for judicial review of a Revenue decision to take criminal proceedings. HMRC have an unrestricted power to conduct a prosecution in the Crown Court, there being no requirement for the consent of the Attorney-General (*R (oao Hunt) v Criminal Cases Review Commission* DC, [2000] STC 1110). See also **35.4** HMRC — ADMINISTRATION.

The Crown Prosecution Service ('CPS') is not precluded from instituting criminal proceedings in circumstances where the Revenue has accepted a monetary settlement. (*R v W and another* CA, [1998] STC 550). The Attorney-General made it clear, however, in a Parliamentary Written Answer, that proceedings brought by the CPS will ordinarily encompass charges relating to tax evasion only in circumstances where that is incidental to allegations of non-fiscal criminal conduct. A 'Convention between Prosecuting Authorities to provide arrangements for ensuring effective co-ordination of decision making and handling in related cases which are the responsibility of different authorities' was established on 11 February 1998 (for which see the Attorney-General's Press Release of that date). See Hansard Vol 310, No 155 at Cols 230, 231 and Revenue Tax Bulletin June 1998 pp 544, 545.

Statements made or documents produced by or on behalf of a taxpayer are admissible as evidence in proceedings against him notwithstanding that reliance on HMRC's practice above or on their policy for mitigating penalties (see **55.23** PENALTIES) may have induced him to make or produce them. [*TMA 1970, s 105*].

See generally HMRC Fraud Civil Investigation Manual.

Contractual disclosure facility

The contractual disclosure facility (CDF) is an opportunity offered to taxpayers to tell HMRC about any tax fraud in which they have been involved. See www.gov.uk/guidance/admitting-tax-fraud-the-contractual-disclosure-facility-cdf. HMRC will write to taxpayers whom they suspect have committed a tax fraud; their letter will offer a CDF contract and will be accompanied by a copy of COP 9 (see above). Taxpayers have 60 days from date of receipt to either accept or formally reject the offer of a contract. If they accept, they must produce an Outline Disclosure within the same 60-day period; this should consist of an admission and brief description of the deliberate conduct (see above) that brought about a loss of tax. If the Outline Disclosure is accepted, the taxpayer will be required to make progress towards a Formal Disclosure, a certified statement that a full, complete and accurate disclosure has been made of all tax irregularities together with certified statements of assets and liabilities and of all bank accounts and credit cards operated.

Under the terms of the CDF contract the taxpayer will not be criminally investigated, with a view to prosecution, for matters covered by the Outline Disclosure. The customer's co-operation will have the potential to maximise reductions in penalties. If the taxpayer rejects the offer of a contract or makes no response, HMRC have the option of starting a criminal investigation, though in most cases they will pursue a civil investigation.

See also HMRC Fraud Civil Investigation Manual FCIM200000.

If a taxpayer wishes to own up to a fraud without waiting to be contacted by HMRC, he may complete form CDF1 (www.gov.uk/guidance/admitting-tax-fraud-the-contractual-disclosure-facility-cdf#6); HMRC will then consider the taxpayer for a CDF contract.

Simon's Taxes. See **A6.1007–A6.1014.**

HMRC use of police powers

[39.12] Certain police powers under *Police and Criminal Evidence Act 1984* (and similar powers in Scotland and NI) are available to HMRC for the purposes of conducting direct tax criminal investigations. Only HMRC officers authorised by the Commissioners for HMRC are able to exercise the powers. They include powers to require production of information, to apply for search warrants, to make arrests and to search suspects and premises following arrest. They do not include power to take fingerprints or to charge and bail suspects, all of which can only be carried out by the police. Some of the powers in *Police and Criminal Evidence Act 1984* are modified for the purposes of their use by HMRC. [*Police and Criminal Evidence Act 1984, s 114; FA 2007, ss 82–87, Schs 22, 23; SI 2015 No 1783*]. A list of the powers made available in England and Wales can be found in *SI 2015 No 1783, Sch 1*. See generally www.gov.uk/government/publications/criminal-investigation.

See *R (Newcastle United Football Club Ltd) v HMRC* QB, [2017] All ER (D) 17 (Oct) for an unsuccessful judicial review into whether search and seizure warrants had been lawfully applied for and issued.

Simon's Taxes. See **A4.151.**

Order for delivery of documents in serious tax fraud cases

[39.13] Under *TMA 1970, s 20BA, Sch 1AA*, the Commissioners for HMRC may apply to the appropriate judicial authority (a circuit judge in England and Wales, a sheriff in Scotland or a county court judge in NI) for an order requiring any person who appears to have in his possession or power documents specified or described in the order to deliver them to an officer of HMRC within ten working days after the day of service of the notice, or such longer or shorter period as may be specified in the order. The judicial authority must be satisfied, on information on oath given by an authorised officer of HMRC, that there is reasonable ground for suspecting that an offence involving serious tax fraud has been or is about to be committed, and that the documents may be required as evidence in proceedings in respect of the offence. In Scotland, a single sheriff may make orders in respect of persons anywhere in Scotland as long as one of the orders relates to a person residing or having a place of business at an address in the sheriff's own sheriffdom. Orders may not be made in relation to items subject to legal privilege (as defined) unless they are held with the intention of furthering a criminal purpose. Failure to comply with an order is treated as contempt of court, and there are severe penalties for falsification of documents.

These provisions are restricted to circumstances where the equivalent power under the *Police and Criminal Evidence Act 1984* cannot be used because the material concerned cannot be obtained using those powers. [*Police and Criminal Evidence Act 1984, ss 14B, 114; SI 2007 No 3166, Reg 2*]. Similar rules apply for NI.

Schedule 1AA lays down detailed requirements in relation to applications under the main provisions, and these may be supplemented by regulations. In particular, a person is entitled to notice of intention to apply for such an order, and to appear and be heard at the application, unless the judicial authority is satisfied that this would seriously prejudice investigation of the offence. Until the application has been dismissed or abandoned, or an order made and complied with, any person given such notice must not conceal, destroy, alter or dispose of any document to which the order sought relates, or disclose information etc. likely to prejudice the investigation, except with the leave of the judicial authority or the written permission of HMRC. Professional legal advisers may, however, disclose such information etc. in giving legal advice to a client or in connection with legal proceedings, provided that it is not disclosed with a view to furthering a criminal purpose. Failure to comply with these requirements is treated as failure to comply with an order under these provisions. For other procedural requirements, see *SI 2000 No 2875*.

Simon's Taxes. See **A6.315**.

Data-gathering powers

[39.14] HMRC have a single cross-tax power to require by notice the provision of 'relevant data' from a data-holder falling within one of a list of specified categories. The power applies to all UK taxes and also to foreign taxes covered by the EU Directive on administrative co-operation in the field of taxation (Directive 2011/16/EU) or by a tax information exchange agreement (see **36.3**(c) HMRC — CONFIDENTIALITY OF INFORMATION). The power can be used both for the purposes of risk assessment and for obtaining third-party data in connection with specific tax checks. It may be used to obtain personal data such as names and addresses of individuals. It cannot, however, generally be used to check the tax position of the data-holder to whom the notice is sent. '*Relevant data*' is data of a kind specified for each type of data-holder by Treasury regulations made by statutory instrument. A data-holder notice under these provisions must specify the data to be provided. The notice can specify only data that HMRC have reason to believe may be relevant to a chargeable or other period ending within the four years ending with the date of the notice.

A notice under these provisions can be given without the approval of the Appeal Tribunal, but where such approval is obtained by HMRC the data-holder has no right of appeal against the notice or any requirement in it. If approval is not sought by HMRC the data-holder can appeal against the notice or a requirement in it on the grounds that it would be unduly onerous to comply, that the data-holder is not within the list of specified data-holders or that the data specified in the notice is not relevant data. Appeal cannot be made on the first of those grounds against a requirement to provide data forming part of the data-holder's statutory records (i.e. records required to be kept and preserved under any tax enactment). Data ceases to form part of a data-holder's statutory records when the period for which it is required to be preserved has expired. The procedures for appeals are the same as those for appeals against information notices under *FA 2008, Sch 36* (see **39.5** above).

Where approval is sought from the Tribunal, the application for approval must be made by, or with the agreement of, an authorised HMRC officer. The data-holder must normally have been told that the data is required and have been given a reasonable opportunity to make representations to HMRC. The Tribunal must be given a summary of any representations made. Where the Tribunal is satisfied that informing the data-holder would prejudice any purpose for which the data is required, it can approve the giving of the notice without the data-holder having been informed.

The data required by a notice must be provided by such means and in such form as is reasonably specified in the notice. If the notice requires the data to be sent somewhere, it must be sent to such address and within such period as is reasonably specified in the notice. If documents are to be made available for inspection, they must be so made available either at a place (other than one used solely as a dwelling) and time reasonably specified in the notice or at a place and time agreed between an HMRC officer and the data-holder. A notice requiring the provision of specified documents requires their provision only if they are in the data-holder's possession or power. An HMRC officer may take copies of, or make extracts from, documents provided and, if he thinks it reasonable to do so, may retain documents for a reasonable period. If a document is retained, the data-holder may request a copy of it if he reasonably requires it for any purpose. The retention of a document is not regarded as breaking any lien claimed on the document, and HMRC must compensate the owner if a document is lost or damaged.

[*FA 2011, Sch 23 paras 1–7, 28, 29, 45, 46, 65; FA 2017, s 61, Sch 11 para 6(3); SI 2019 No 689, Reg 20(3)*].

Responsibility of company officers

Everything to be done by a company under the above provisions must be done by it through the '*proper officer*' (i.e. the secretary of a corporate body, except where a liquidator or administrator has been appointed when the latter is the proper officer, or the treasurer of a non-corporate body) or, except where a liquidator has been appointed, any authorised officer. The service of a notice on a company may be effected by serving it on the proper officer. [*TMA 1970, s 108; FA 2011, Sch 23 para 43*].

Data-holders

The following is a list of the categories of data-holder who is subject to the above provisions. The provisions also apply to persons who previously fell within a category, but no longer do so.

(1) An employer.
(2) A third party making payments to or in respect of another person's employees.

(3) An approved payroll giving agent (see **14.18** CHARITIES AND CHARITABLE GIVING).

(4) A person carrying on a business (or any other activity carried on by a body of persons) in connection with which certain payments relating to services provided by persons other than employees or in respect of intellectual property rights are made or are likely to be made. For this purpose the making of payments includes the provision of benefits and the giving of any other valuable consideration. There are special rules for services provided under agency contracts (see *FA 2011, Sch 23 para 10*) and certain persons performing in the UK duties of an employment with a non-UK resident employer (see *FA 2011, Sch 23 para 11*).

(5) A person by or through whom interest, building society share dividends, foreign dividends, an amount payable on redemption of a deeply discounted security or an alternative finance return are paid or credited.

(6) A person who is in receipt of money or value of, or belonging to, another.

(7) A person who is the registered or inscribed holder of securities. This category and those at (8)–(10) below apply where HMRC is trying to establish who is the beneficial owner of some shares or securities or beneficially entitled to a particular payment. The limited scope of the information that may be required is set out in *FA 2011, Sch 23 para 14(3)*.

(8) A person who receives a payment derived from securities or would be entitled to do so if a payment were made (and see (7) above).

(9) A person who receives a payment for the purchase by an unquoted company of its own shares (within *CTA 2010, s 1033*) (and see (7) above).

(10) A person who receives a chargeable payment within *CTA 2010, Pt 23 Ch 5* (company distributions: demergers) (and see (7) above).

(11) A person who makes a payment derived from securities that has been received from, or is paid on behalf of, another.

(12) A person by whom a payment out of public funds is made by way of grant or subsidy.

(13) A person by whom licences or approvals are issued or a (local authority or statutory) register is maintained.

(14) A lessee, an occupier of land, a person having the use of land and a person who, as agent, manages land or receives rent or other payments from land. The reference to a person who manages land includes a person who markets property to potential tenants, searches for tenants or provides similar services.

(15) A person who effects, or is a party to, securities transactions (as defined) wholly or partly on behalf of others (whether as agent or principal).

(16) A person who, in the course of business, acts as registrar or administrator in respect of securities transactions.

(17) A person who makes a payment derived from securities to anyone other than the registered or inscribed holder.

(18) A person who makes a payment derived from bearer securities.

(19) An accountable person (within *SI 1986 No 1711*) for the purposes of stamp duty reserve tax.

(20) The committee or other person or body managing a clearing house for any terminal market in commodities.
(21) An auctioneer.
(22) A person carrying on a business of dealing in, or of acting as an intermediary in dealings in, tangible movable property.
(23) A Lloyd's syndicate managing agent.
(24) An ISA plan manager or Child Trust Fund account provider.
(25) A licence holder under *Petroleum Act 1998*.
(26) The responsible person (within *Oil Taxation Act 1975, Pt 1*) for an oil field.
(27) A person involved in an insurance business.
(28) A person who makes arrangements for persons to enter into insurance contracts.
(29) A person concerned in a business which is not an insurance business but who has been involved in the entering into of an insurance contract providing cover for any matter associated with the business.
(30) A person involved in subjecting aggregate to exploitation in the UK or connected activities, making or receiving supplies of commodities subject to climate change levy or landfill disposal.
(31) A person who makes a settlement (within *ITTOIA 2005, s 620*), the trustees of a settlement, a beneficiary under a settlement and any other person to whom income is payable under a settlement.
(32) A charity.
(33) A person (generally known as a merchant acquirer) who has a contractual obligation to make payments to retailers in settlement of credit card, charge card and debit card transactions.
(34) (From 15 September 2016 but in relation to relevant data with a bearing on any period whether before, on or after that date) a person who provides services by which monetary value is stored electronically for the purpose of payments being made in respect of transactions to which the provider of the services is not a party (often known as a digital wallet).
(35) (From 15 September 2016 but in relation to relevant data with a bearing on any period whether before, on or after that date) a person (a 'business intermediary') who provides services to enable or facilitate transactions between suppliers and customers (other than services solely enabling payments to be made) and receives information about such transactions in doing so.
(36) (From 16 November 2017 but in relation to relevant data with a bearing on any period whether before, on or after that date) a money service business, i.e. a business providing money transfer, cheque cashing and currency exchange services (other than a credit institution such as a bank or building society).
(37) (From a date to be appointed) a person involved in producing, packaging or selling soft drinks within the scope of the soft drinks industry levy.

[*FA 2011, Sch 23 paras 8–27, 49; FA 2016, s 176; FA 2017, s 61, Sch 11 para 6(2); F(No 2)A 2017, s 69; SI 2012 No 847; SI 2017 No 1175; SI 2019 No 689, Reg 20(3)*].

In *Qubic Taxassethound Ltd v HMRC* FTT (TC 7701), [2020] UKFTT 215 (TC), the FTT rejected the data-holder company's argument that complying with two notices issued under these provisions would be unduly onerous because they were too vague and difficult to understand.

Penalties

For penalties for failure to comply with a data-holder notice and for the provision of inaccurate information or documents, see **55.16** PENALTIES.

Simon's Taxes. See **A6.330–A6.339**.

Computer records etc.

[39.15] The following applies to any tax provisions requiring a person to produce a document or cause a document to be produced, furnished or delivered, or requiring a person to permit HMRC to inspect a document, to make copies of or extracts from, or remove, a document (i.e. including the provisions at **39.3**, **39.9** and **39.13** above).

For the purposes of such provisions, a reference to a document is a reference to anything in which information of any description is recorded, and a reference to a copy of a document is to anything onto which information recorded in the document has been copied, by whatever means and whether directly or indirectly.

Where a document has been, or may be, required to be produced, inspected etc. under any such provisions, a person authorised by the Commissioners for HMRC can obtain access to any computer and associated apparatus or material used in connection with the document at any reasonable time in order to inspect it and check its operation. Reasonable assistance can be required from the person by whom or on whose behalf the computer has been so used or any person in charge of the computer etc. or otherwise concerned with its operation.

A penalty of £300 applies for obstruction of such access or refusal to provide assistance.

[*FA 2008, s 114*].

40

HMRC Statements of Practice

Introduction to Statements of Practice

[40.1] The following is a summary of those Statements of Practice published online at www.gov.uk/government/collections/statements-of-practice, which are referred to in this work.

Statements are divided into those originally published before 18 July 1978 (which are given a reference letter (according to the subject matter) and consecutive number, e.g. A16) and subsequent Statements (which are numbered consecutively in each year, e.g. SP 1/10 or SP 1 (2018)).

Certain Statements marked by HMRC as obsolete continue to be referred to in the text if they have been relevant at any time within the tax years referred to in that particular text.

A6	**Employment income — VAT.** Expenses and other benefits chargeable on an employee must include VAT, if any. See **53.21** PAY AS YOU EARN, **28.54** EMPLOYMENT INCOME. For PAYE purposes, VAT is excluded from payments for services supplied by a person holding an office in the course of carrying on a trade, profession or vocation. See **53.55** PAY AS YOU EARN.
A10	**Airline pilots.** HMRC practice re duties deemed to be performed in the UK. See **28.3**(ii) EMPLOYMENT INCOME.
A13	**Completion of return forms by attorneys.** In cases of illness, infirmity or old age of the taxpayer, HMRC will accept the signature of an attorney who has full knowledge of the taxpayer's affairs. See **64.2** RETURNS.
A16	**Living expenses abroad: trades, professions and vocations.** A UK resident living abroad for the purposes of his trade etc. will have his personal living expenses allowed as a deduction. See **75.125** TRADING INCOME.
A32	**Goods taken by traders for personal consumption.** HMRC's practice in applying *Sharkey v Wernher* is stated. See **75.118** TRADING INCOME.
B1	**Treatment of VAT.** Guidance on the general principles applied in dealing with VAT in tax computations. See **75.129** TRADING INCOME.

B6 **Goods sold subject to reservation of title.** Such goods should normally be treated as purchases in the buyer's accounts and sales in the supplier's accounts provided that both parties agree. See **75.116** TRADING INCOME.

C1 **Lotteries and football pools.** Where part of the cost of a ticket is to be donated to a club etc., that part is, in certain circumstances, not treated as a trading receipt. See **75.28** TRADING INCOME.

SP 3/78 **Close companies: income tax relief for interest on loans applied in acquiring an interest in a close company.** Relief continues after company ceases to be close. See **42.7** INTEREST PAYABLE.

SP 8/79 **Compensation for acquisition of property under compulsory powers.** Reimbursement of revenue costs are trading receipts. See **75.56**(d) TRADING INCOME.

SP 3/80 **Cancellation of tax advantages from certain transactions in securities: procedure for clearance in advance.** The procedure is explained. See **4.12** ANTI-AVOIDANCE.

SP 5/81 **Expenditure on farm drainage.** The net cost of restoring drainage is allowable as revenue expenditure. See **75.77**(c) TRADING INCOME.

SP 10/81 **Payments on account of disability resulting in cessation of employment.** The interpretation of 'disability' in *ITEPA 2003, s 406* is extended. See **18.10**(i) COMPENSATION FOR LOSS OF EMPLOYMENT.

SP 12/81 **Construction industry scheme (CIS): carpet fitting** is considered to be outside the scope of the scheme. See **20.3** CONSTRUCTION INDUSTRY SCHEME.

SP 1/82 **Interaction of income tax and inheritance tax on assets put into settlement.** Income of a settlement will not be treated as income of the settlor solely because the trustees have power to pay, or do pay, inheritance tax on assets put into the settlement by the settlor. See **70.28**(e) SETTLEMENTS.

SP 6/84 **Non-UK resident lessors: *FA 1973, s 38* (now *TMA 1970, ss 77B–77K*).** The conditions under which profits of non-UK resident lessors of mobile drilling rigs etc. are exempt from tax are outlined. See **32.3** FOREIGN INCOME.

SP 6/85 **Incentive awards.** The basis on which expenses are included is outlined. See **28.81, 28.47** EMPLOYMENT INCOME.

SP 1/86 **Capital allowances: short-life assets.** Guidance is given on some practical aspects of the short-life asset provisions. See **10.33** CAPITAL ALLOWANCES ON PLANT AND MACHINERY.

SP 3/86 **Payments to a non-resident from UK discretionary trusts or UK estates during the administration period: double taxation relief.** A change of practice replaces extra-statutory concessions A14 and B18 in certain cases. See **22.14** DECEASED ESTATES, **70.15** SETTLEMENTS.

SP 4/86 **Scholarship and apprenticeship schemes for employees.** Certain payments to employees attending full-time educational courses are exempt from income tax. See **30.44** EXEMPT INCOME.

SP 9/86 **Partnership mergers and demergers.** The application of the succession rules is explained. See **52.9** PARTNERSHIPS.

SP 5/87 **Tax returns: the use of substitute forms.** The conditions for acceptance of facsimile and photocopied returns and other forms are set out. See **16.1** CLAIMS, **64.2** RETURNS.

SP 3/91 **Finance lease rental payments.** The practice in relation to deduction of rental payments is explained. See **75.82** TRADING INCOME.

SP 7/91 **Double taxation: business profits: unilateral relief.** The practice as regards admission of foreign taxes for unilateral relief is revised. See **27.6** DOUBLE TAX RELIEF.

SP 16/91 **Accountancy expenses arising out of accounts investigations.** HMRC's practice on the allowance of such expenses is explained. See **75.96** TRADING INCOME.

SP 6/92 **Accident insurance policies: chargeable events and gains on policies of life insurance.** Certain accident insurance policies will no longer be considered policies of life insurance for these purposes. See **44.6** LIFE ASSURANCE POLICIES.

SP 4/93 **Deceased persons' estates: discretionary interests in residue.** Payments out of income of the residue are treated as income of the recipient for the year of payment, whether out of income as it arises or out of income arising in earlier years. See **22.10** DECEASED ESTATES.

SP 5/93 **UK/Czechoslovakia double taxation Convention.** The Convention is regarded as applying to the Czech and Slovak Republics. See **27.2** DOUBLE TAX RELIEF.

SP 15/93 **Business tax computations rounded to nearest £1,000** will be accepted from certain large businesses. See **75.20** TRADING INCOME.

SP 1/94 **Non-statutory redundancy payments.** HMRC's practice following the decision in *Mairs v Haughey* is explained. See **18.2** COMPENSATION FOR LOSS OF EMPLOYMENT.

SP 4/94 **Enhanced stock dividends received by trustees of interest in possession trusts.** HMRC's view on the tax treatment of such dividends is explained. See **65.20** SAVINGS AND INVESTMENT INCOME.

SP 6/95 **Legal entitlement and administrative practice** in relation to repayments of tax is revised. See **54.15** PAYMENT OF TAX.

SP 8/95 **Venture capital trusts — default terms in loan agreements.** Certain event of default clauses will not disqualify a loan from being a security for the purposes of approval. See **81.12** VENTURE CAPITAL TRUSTS.

SP 1/96 **Notification of chargeability to income tax.** Employees are relieved in certain circumstances of the obligation to notify chargeability in respect of benefits etc. See **55.2** PENALTIES.

SP 2/96 **Pooled cars: incidental private use.** HMRC's interpretation of the requirement that private use of pooled vehicles be 'merely incidental' to business use is explained. See **28.29** EMPLOYMENT INCOME.

SP 3/96 ***ITEPA 2003, ss 225, 226* — termination payments made in settlement of employment claims.** The circumstances in which a charge will not arise are clarified. See **28.73** EMPLOYMENT INCOME.

SP 4/96 **Income tax — interest paid in the ordinary course of a bank's business.** HMRC's interpretation of this requirement is explained.

SP 5/96 **PAYE settlement agreements.** The detailed operation of the scheme is explained. See generally **53.25** PAY AS YOU EARN.

SP 4/97 **Taxation of commission, cashbacks and discounts.** HMRC's views are outlined. See **75.54** TRADING INCOME.

SP 6/98 **Enterprise investment scheme, venture capital trusts, capital gains tax reinvestment relief and business expansion scheme — loans to investors.** The no linked loan requirement is explained. See **29.43** ENTERPRISE INVESTMENT SCHEME, **81.3** VENTURE CAPITAL TRUSTS.

SP 1/99 **Self-assessment enquiries — *TMA 1970, ss 9A, 12AC.*** Where an enquiry remains open for agreement of a capital gains tax valuation, HMRC will not take advantage of this fact to raise further enquiries which could otherwise not be made. See **64.7** RETURNS.

SP 3/00 **Enterprise management incentives — location of activity.** The requirement that trade(s) be carried on 'wholly or mainly in the UK' is clarified. See **71.45** SHARE-RELATED EMPLOYMENT INCOME AND EXEMPTIONS.

SP 1/01 **Treatment of investment managers and their overseas clients.** Guidance is given on the application of the rules introduced by *FA 1995*. See **50.8** NON-RESIDENTS.

SP 4/01 **Double taxation relief — status of the UK's double taxation conventions with the former USSR and with the now independent states.** The current position is clarified. See **27.2** DOUBLE TAX RELIEF.

SP 2/02 **Exchange rate fluctuations.** HMRC set out their practice in relation to the tax treatment of exchange rate fluctuations in the tax computations of non-corporate traders. See **75.85** TRADING INCOME.

SP 3/02 **Financial futures and options.** HMRC set out their views on the circumstances in which transactions in financial futures and options would be regarded as trading rather than taxed under the chargeable gains rules. See **75.30** TRADING INCOME.

SP 2/03 **Business by telephone — non-Contact Centre taxpayers.** Details are given of the services available by telephone from tax offices not served by a Contact Centre. See **16.5** CLAIMS.

SP 1/06 **Self-assessment: finality and discovery.** HMRC clarify how a taxpayer may protect himself from a later 'discovery' assessment by providing sufficient information in his self-assessment tax return. See **6.6** ASSESSMENTS.

SP 2/06 **Venture capital trusts, the enterprise investment scheme and enterprise management incentives — value of 'gross assets'.** HMRC's general approach to the valuation of gross assets is explained. See **29.53** ENTERPRISE INVESTMENT SCHEME, **71.44** SHARE-RELATED EMPLOYMENT INCOME AND EXEMPTIONS, **81.37** VENTURE CAPITAL TRUSTS.

SP 3/07 **Double tax relief — Yugoslavia.** Details are given as to the application of the UK/Yugoslavia double tax agreement to the countries formerly known as Yugoslavia. See **27.2** DOUBLE TAX RELIEF.

SP 1/10 **Business by telephone — HMRC Taxes Contact Centres.** Details are given of expanded services available by telephone from Taxes Contact Centres dealing with the tax affairs of individuals. See **16.5** CLAIMS, **64.4** RETURNS.

SP 2/10 **Advance pricing agreements (APAs).** Provides guidance about how HMRC interpret the APA legislation and apply it in practice. See **4.27** ANTI-AVOIDANCE.

SP 1 (2018) **Mutual agreement procedure (MAP).** This describes the UK's practice in relation to methods for reducing or preventing double taxation. It considers the use of MAP under UK double tax agreements and/or the EU Arbitration Convention and describes the UK's approach to the use of arbitration as part of the MAP process. Supersedes SP 1/11.

41

Intellectual Property

Cross-references. See **9.14** and **9.26** CAPITAL ALLOWANCES for allowances on capital expenditure in acquiring know-how and patent rights; **23.14** DEDUCTION OF TAX AT SOURCE for patent royalties and for intellectual property royalties paid to overseas residents; **27.10**(h) DOUBLE TAX RELIEF for DTR treatment of royalties from abroad; **49.2** MISCELLANEOUS INCOME for the territorial scope of the charge to tax on receipts from intellectual property; **71.80** SHARE-RELATED EMPLOYMENT INCOME AND EXEMPTIONS as regards research institution spin-out companies; **75.59**, **75.95** and **75.103** TRADING INCOME for trading receipts and expenses re intellectual property.

Simon's Taxes. See B5.3.

Introduction to intellectual property

[41.1] This chapter deals with the charge to tax on royalties and other income from 'intellectual property', income from disposals of know-how and income from sales of patent rights.

'*Intellectual property*' means:

- any patent, trade mark, registered design, copyright, design right or performer's or plant breeder's right;
- any rights under the law of any part of the UK which are similar to such rights;
- any rights under the law of any territory outside the UK which correspond or are similar to such rights; and
- any idea, information or technique not protected by a right within any of the above.

[*ITTOIA 2005, s 579(2)*].

Royalties and other income

[41.2] Subject to the priority provisions at **49.2** MISCELLANEOUS INCOME (which, for example, exclude income from a trade etc.), royalties and other income from 'intellectual property' (as in **41.1** above) are chargeable to income tax.

The full amount of such income arising in the tax year is chargeable (but see below), the person liable for the tax being the person receiving or entitled to the income. Income from intellectual property which also falls within the charge at **49.4** MISCELLANEOUS INCOME (films and sound recordings) is excluded.

See **49.2** MISCELLANEOUS INCOME for the territorial scope of the charge. Where income within the charge arises from a source outside the UK it is 'relevant foreign income' (see **32.2** FOREIGN INCOME). See **32.4** FOREIGN INCOME for amounts deductible from income, **32.5** FOREIGN INCOME for relief for unremittable income and **61** for the REMITTANCE BASIS.

See also **41.4** below for the spreading of patent royalties etc. over several tax years.

[*ITTOIA 2005, ss 576(2), 579(1), 580, 581; FA 2019, Sch 3 paras 3, 7*].

Patent royalties are subject to deduction of tax at source as are intellectual property royalties paid to overseas residents. See **23.14** DEDUCTION OF TAX AT SOURCE.

See **49.8** and **49.11** MISCELLANEOUS INCOME for apportionment rules and for relief for losses.

Expenses

[41.3] Expenses incurred wholly and exclusively for the purpose of generating income within **41.2** above are deductible in calculating the amount chargeable to tax, provided that, if they had been incurred for the purposes of a trade, they would have been deductible in calculating its profits. Where an expense is incurred for more than one purpose, if any identifiable part or proportion of the expense is incurred for the purpose of generating the income, a deduction is allowed for that part or proportion. Expenses for which any kind of relief is given under any other provision are not deductible.

No deductions can be made where the income consists of annual payments (see **23.10** DEDUCTION OF TAX AT SOURCE). In determining whether income consist of annual payments, the frequency with which payments are made is ignored. Deductions are also not permitted where the income is assessable on the REMITTANCE BASIS (**61**).

[*ITTOIA 2005, s 582*].

See also **41.4** below for relief for certain expenditure in relation to patents.

Patent income

[41.4] '*Patent income*' of an individual is any royalties or other sums paid in respect of the use of a patent charged to tax under **41.2** above, amounts on which tax is payable under **41.6** below, and any balancing charges under the capital allowances code for patent rights (see **9.26** CAPITAL ALLOWANCES).

Inventor's expenses etc.

Relief can be claimed for expenses:

- incurred by an individual on devising an invention for which a patent has been granted; and
- incurred by a person, otherwise than for the purposes of a trade, in connection with the grant, maintenance or extension of the term of a patent or in connection with a rejected or abandoned patent application, provided that, if the expenses had been incurred for the purposes of a trade, they would have been allowable in calculating the profits of that trade.

The relief is not available for any expenses for which relief is given under **41.3** above or any other provision. Expenses are also disregarded to the extent that they are met by a '*public body*' (i.e. the Crown or any government, local authority or other public authority in the UK or elsewhere) or by any other person. Where, however, the contributor is not a public body, expenses are not so disregarded if, on the assumption that he is within the charge to tax, the contributor can obtain neither a capital allowance for the contributions (see **9.2**(vii) CAPITAL ALLOWANCES) nor a deduction in calculating the profits of a trade, profession or vocation.

Where a claim is made, the expenses are deducted or set off against the person's 'patent income' for the tax year in which they are incurred with any unallowed balance being carried forward indefinitely against patent income without further claim. Any CAPITAL ALLOWANCES (**9.26**) must be deducted before relief is given for the expenses.

[*ITTOIA 2005, ss 600, 601, 603, 604, Sch 2 para 129*].

Spreading of patent royalties

A relief can be claimed by a person who receives a payment of a royalty or other sum, under deduction of tax at source, for use of a patent that has extended over a period of two years or more. The relief is the excess (if any) of:

(a) the recipient's income tax liability on the payment for the tax year of receipt, over
(b) what would have been the recipient's income tax liability on the payment if the latter had been spread over a number of years.

For the purpose of (b), the payment is deemed to have been made in a number of equal instalments at yearly intervals, with the final instalment made on the date the actual payment was made. The number of instalments is equal to the number of complete years over which the use of the patent extended, subject to a maximum of six years. Once the amount of the relief is established, it is given by means of a tax reduction (see Step 6 at **1.10** ALLOWANCES AND TAX RATES). The order in which tax reductions are given against an individual's tax liability is set out at **1.12** ALLOWANCES AND TAX RATES. [*ITA 2007, s 461*].

Disposal of know-how

[41.5] Subject to the priority and territorial scope provisions at **49.2** MISCELLANEOUS INCOME, profits arising where consideration is received for the disposal of 'know-how' are chargeable to income tax. Tax is chargeable on the full amount of the profits arising in the tax year, the person liable for the tax being the person receiving the consideration. Also included within the charge are profits arising where consideration is received for giving, or wholly or partly fulfilling, an undertaking (whether or not legally enforceable) which is given in connection with a disposal of know-how and which restricts or is designed to restrict any person's activities in any way.

The profits chargeable to tax are the amount of the consideration less any expenditure incurred by the recipient wholly and exclusively in the acquisition or disposal of the know-how. Where know-how is acquired or disposed of together with other property, the acquisition costs or proceeds, as appropriate, must be apportioned on a just and reasonable basis. Expenditure can only be taken into account for tax purposes once (whether under this provision or otherwise).

Expenditure is disregarded in calculating the taxable profits to the extent that it is met by a public body (see **41.3** above) or by any other person. Where, however, the contributor is not a public body, the expenditure is not so disregarded if, on the assumption that he is within the charge to tax, the contributor can obtain neither a capital allowance for the contribution (see **9.2**(vii) CAPITAL ALLOWANCES) nor a deduction in calculating the profits of a trade, profession or vocation.

The charge does not apply if:

- the consideration is brought into account under **41.2** above;
- the consideration is brought into account as a disposal value under the capital allowances know-how code (see **9.14** CAPITAL ALLOWANCES);
- the consideration is treated as a trading receipt (see **75.95** TRADING INCOME);
- the consideration is received as part of the disposal of all or part of a trade and is treated as a capital receipt for goodwill under *ITTOIA 2005, s 194(2)* (see **75.95** TRADING INCOME); or
- the disposal is by way of a sale and the buyer is a body of persons (including a firm) over which the seller or buyer has control or the buyer and seller are both bodies of persons and another person has control over them both.

For the above purposes, '*know-how*' means any industrial information or techniques likely to assist in manufacturing or processing goods or materials, in working, or searching for etc., mineral deposits (as defined), or in carrying out any agricultural, forestry or fishing operations. References above to a sale or disposal of know-how include an exchange of know-how.

[*ITTOIA 2005, ss 583–586, 603–607, Sch 2 para 129*].

See **49.8** and **49.11** MISCELLANEOUS INCOME for apportionment rules and for relief for losses.

Sales of patent rights

[41.6] Subject to the priority provisions at **49.2** MISCELLANEOUS INCOME, profits from sales of the whole or part of any 'patent rights' (including receipts for rights for which a patent has not yet been granted) are chargeable to tax. The seller is charged to tax if a UK resident or, if not UK resident, where the patent is a UK patent. '*Patent rights*' for this purpose means the right to do or authorise the doing of anything which would, but for the right, be an infringement of a patent.

See also **23.14** DEDUCTION OF TAX AT SOURCE for deduction of income tax by the purchaser in the case of a sale by a non-UK resident.

The profits chargeable are any capital sum (defined as for capital allowances purposes, see **9.2**(iii) CAPITAL ALLOWANCES) comprised in the proceeds less the 'capital cost' of the rights sold and any incidental costs incurred in connection with the sale.

For this purpose, the '*capital cost*' of patent rights means any capital sum included in any price paid by the seller to purchase the rights (or the rights out of which they were granted), less any capital sum received for a previous sale of part of the purchased rights. Expenditure is disregarded in calculating the capital cost to the extent that it is met by a public body (see **41.4** above) or by any other person. Where, however, the contributor is not a public body, the expenditure is not so disregarded if, on the assumption that he is within the charge to tax, the contributor can obtain neither a capital allowance for the contribution (see **9.2**(vii) CAPITAL ALLOWANCES) nor a deduction in calculating the profits of a trade, profession or vocation.

The deduction of the capital cost for this purpose does not affect the amount of income tax to be deducted by the purchaser in the case of a sale by a non-UK resident (see **23.14** DEDUCTION OF TAX AT SOURCE), and any adjustment required to give effect to such a deduction is made by repayment of tax.

References above to the sale of patent rights include the exchange of patent rights, and in the case of such an exchange, references above and in **41.7** below to the proceeds of sale and the price include the consideration for the exchange, and references to capital sums included in the proceeds include references to so much of the consideration for the exchange as would have been a capital sum if it had been a money payment. Where patent rights are acquired or disposed of together with other property, the acquisition costs or proceeds, as appropriate, must be apportioned on a just and reasonable basis.

Licences

The acquisition of a licence in respect of a patent is treated for the purposes of the above provisions as a purchase of patent rights, and the grant of a licence is treated as a sale of part of such rights. Where, however, the licence is a licence to exercise the rights to the exclusion of all other persons (including the grantor) for the whole of the period until the rights come to an end, the grant is treated as a sale of the whole of the rights. The use in certain circumstances of an invention, which is the subject of a patent, by the Crown or a foreign government is treated as use under a licence.

[*ITTOIA 2005, ss 587–589, 595(1)(2), 596–599, 603–608, Sch 2 para 129*].

See **49.8** and **49.11** MISCELLANEOUS INCOME for apportionment rules and for relief for losses.

Spreading provisions

[41.7] In the case of a UK-resident seller, the profits from the sale of patent rights are chargeable spread equally over a period of six tax years, starting with the tax year in which the proceeds are received. If the proceeds are received in instalments, each instalment is likewise spread over six tax years. The seller may elect, by notice to an officer of HMRC, to disapply spreading, so that the profits (or instalments) are taxed in the year of receipt. If the seller is not UK-resident, an election is required for spreading to apply; in the absence of an election the profits (or instalments) are taxed in the year of receipt. The elections must be made within twelve months after 31 January following the tax year in which the profits or instalment were received.

Where the seller is a partnership and the sale is in the course of a trade carried on by the partnership, each amount chargeable under the above spreading provisions is chargeable on the partners for the time being carrying on the trade, unless there is a partnership change such that no partner who carried on the trade before the change continues to do so afterwards (i.e. there is a cessation of the partnership trade).

In the latter event, any amounts which would have been chargeable in later tax years are charged instead in the tax year of cessation. Any partner accordingly chargeable to an additional amount of tax in the year of cessation may elect for the amount to be reduced to what would have been chargeable had the amounts that would have been charged in subsequent years been charged in equal instalments in each of the tax years beginning with the year of receipt and ending with the year of cessation. The election must be made within twelve months after 31 January following the tax year of cessation.

Similar provisions apply where a seller dies during the period over which the charge is spread. The personal representatives of a deceased seller may make an election the effect of which is the same as that available to partners above. The same time limit applies.

The making of an election for spreading does not affect the amount of income tax to be deducted by the purchaser in the case of a sale by a non-UK resident (see **23.14** DEDUCTION OF TAX AT SOURCE), and any adjustment required as a result of such an election is made by repayment of tax on a year by year basis.

[*ITTOIA 2005, ss 590–594, 595(1)(3), 596, 861, 862*].

42

Interest Payable

Cross-references. See 3 ALTERNATIVE FINANCE ARRANGEMENTS; 4.40 ANTI-AVOIDANCE; 8 BANKS AND BUILDING SOCIETIES; 23 DEDUCTION OF TAX AT SOURCE; 43 LATE PAYMENT INTEREST AND PENALTIES; 65.7 SAVINGS AND INVESTMENT INCOME for interest paid by issue of funding bonds.

Simon's Taxes. See E1.820–E1.831.

Introduction to interest payable

[42.1] This chapter is concerned with the extent to which interest payable is deductible in computing taxable income for income tax purposes. The first part of the chapter (42.2–42.4) covers interest payable for the purposes of a business. The next part of the chapter (42.5–42.12) covers interest on particular categories of loan which, subject to conditions, is deductible by virtue of specific tax legislation. Provisions to prevent double tax relief are examined in 42.13, and 42.14 details a general anti-avoidance rule.

Business interest payable

[42.2] For the purpose of computing the taxable profits of a trade, profession or vocation, interest payable is revenue expenditure, as opposed to capital, whatever the nature of the loan. [*ITTOIA 2005, s 29*]. Whether or not it is deductible in computing those profits depends on general principles, in particular the 'wholly and exclusively' rule at 75.44 TRADING INCOME. Interest incurred wholly and exclusively for the purposes of a property business is similarly an allowable deduction from the profits of that business (see **60.10** PROPERTY INCOME), but see also **60.12** for 2017/18 onwards. For disallowance of interest where the proprietor's capital account was overdrawn, see *Silk v Fletcher* (Sp C 201), [1999] SSCD 220 and *(No 2)* (Sp C 262), [2000] SSCD 565 and see HMRC Business Income Manual BIM45705–45730.

No relief is given if the interest is within the anti-avoidance provisions of *ITA 2007, s 809ZG* — see **42.14** below.

The conditions in **42.5** *et seq.* below do not apply to interest deductible in computing business profits, but if interest so deductible is also allowable within those conditions, relief may instead be claimed under *ITA 2007, s 383*. See **42.13** below for the exclusion of double relief. Where interest wholly and exclusively for business purposes is dealt with under *ITA 2007, s 383* or its predecessor but not wholly relieved because of insufficiency of income, the unrelieved interest can be treated as a trading loss for certain purposes (see **45.22** LOSSES).

See generally HMRC Business Income Manual BIM45650–45770.

Cash basis

Where a cash basis election is in force (see **76** TRADING INCOME — CASH BASIS FOR SMALLER BUSINESSES), special rules apply instead of the above as regards the deductibility of loan interest paid. See **76.10**. [*ITTOIA 2005, s 51A*].

Interest on loan for property bought by partner for partnership use

[42.3] The following applies where interest is paid by a partnership, and charged as an expense in its accounts, on a loan taken out by a partner to purchase land occupied rent-free by the partnership and used for business purposes. Relief as a trading expense for interest payable by the partnership on the individual's behalf should be available in the normal way. The individual's property income computation would include as a receipt the interest payments made by the partnership on his behalf, but these would be offset by a deduction for interest payable by the individual (which would be allowable regardless of the interest payments actually having been met by the partnership). The taxable property income would therefore generally be nil. (Revenue Tax Bulletin June 1997 pp 437, 438).

Interest on loan for property bought by controlling director for company use

[42.4] The following applies where interest is paid by a company, and charged as an expense in its accounts, on a loan taken out by a controlling director to purchase land occupied rent-free by the company and used for business purposes. Relief as a trading expense for interest payable by the company on the director's behalf should be available in the normal way as a deduction from the company's profits for tax purposes, and the payments would not normally constitute either emoluments or a benefit of the director.

The director's property income computation would include as a receipt the interest payments made by the company on his behalf, but these would be offset by a deduction for interest payable by the director (which would be allowable regardless of the interest payments actually having been met by the company). The taxable property income would therefore generally be nil. (Revenue Tax Bulletin June 1997 pp 437, 438).

Other relief for interest paid

[42.5] Relief for interest on the categories of loan described in **42.6–42.12** below is given for income tax purposes for the tax year in which paid. [*ITA 2007, s 383(1)(2)*].

Relief is not, however, available for interest on overdrafts, credit cards or similar arrangements. Nor will relief be given to the extent that the interest exceeds a reasonable commercial rate. In response to a notified avoidance scheme, a further rule was introduced by *FA 2008* to effectively prevent relief for interest that relates to a tax year later than that in which it is paid. [*ITA 2007, s 384*].

In response to notified tax avoidance schemes, relief for interest is denied if the loan is made as part of arrangements that are certain (ignoring insignificant risk) to enable the borrower to exit the arrangements with a profit by virtue of the interest being eligible for relief. Whilst the legislation is sufficiently wide-ranging to catch most likely variations to these schemes, it is not intended to catch genuine commercial investments in business where there is uncertainty as to the return that will be produced from the investment. [*ITA 2007, s 384A*].

Relief for interest is not granted unless the loan proceeds are so applied within a reasonable time, nor if the loan proceeds are used for some other purpose first (but these conditions do not apply to loans used to purchase plant or machinery as in **42.6** below). The giving of credit can be treated as a loan. [*ITA 2007, s 385(2)–(4)*].

If a loan is a mixed loan, such that part of it qualifies under any of **42.6–42.12** below and part does not qualify at all, a corresponding proportion of the interest qualifies for relief. If the mixed loan is partly repaid, the repayment is applied rateably between the qualifying and non-qualifying parts, so the percentage of interest eligible for relief remains the same. [*ITA 2007, s 386*].

No relief is given if the interest is within the anti-avoidance provisions of *ITA 2007, s 809ZG* — see **42.14** below.

There is a cap on the total amount of prescribed income tax reliefs that individuals can claim. See **1.11** ALLOWANCES AND TAX RATES. Relief for interest on loans within **42.6–42.11** below is one of the prescribed reliefs.

For interest paid to persons other than building societies or local authorities, the person to whom relief is due is entitled to require from the lender by written request a statement in writing showing the date and amount of the debt, the name and address of the debtor and the interest paid in the tax year. [*ITA 2007, s 412*]. See generally Revenue Tax Bulletin April 1995 p 210.

Where the interest is business interest (see **42.2** above), see **42.13** below for the exclusion of double relief and **45.22** LOSSES for the treatment of unrelieved interest as a trading loss.

Method of giving relief

Interest on loans within **42.6–42.11** below is relieved by way of a deduction in arriving at net income for the tax year in question (see Step 2 at **1.10** ALLOWANCES AND TAX RATES), and thus attracts relief at marginal rates. If the deduction exceeds net income, no relief is available for the excess except as in **42.11** below (loans to pay inheritance tax).

Relief for interest on a loan within **42.12** below (pre-9 March 1999 loans for purchasing a life annuity) is restricted to 23% of the eligible interest; the relief is normally given by deduction of tax at source but is otherwise given by way of an income tax reduction (see **1.12** ALLOWANCES AND TAX RATES), and does not save tax at the higher rate (see **42.12** below for more details).

Where, for any tax year, an amount of interest is eligible for relief partly as a deduction in arriving at net income and partly as a tax reduction (for example, because the loan is a mixed loan), it is apportioned by reference to the proportions of the amount borrowed (not the amount still outstanding) applied for different purposes.

[*ITA 2007, s 383(3)(4)*].

Replacement loans

Where, under any of **42.7–42.11** below and subject to the conditions therein, interest is specifically eligible for relief if it is paid on a loan that is used to repay another (eligible) loan, the current loan and the loan it replaced are generally treated for these purposes as if they were one and the same loan. [*ITA 2007, s 408*].

Hire purchase charges

Hire purchase charges (the excess of the hire purchase payments over the cash price) are not interest and therefore not within this relief. (Some hire purchase agreements may specify that the whole balance of the rental after the initial payment is payable within seven days but will leave the hirer the option of paying that balance over a defined period on interest terms. At the date the option is exercised a loan is created and the interest on that loan is true interest under *ITA 2007, s 383* or its predecessor and will qualify for relief if all other relevant conditions are satisfied.)

Loans for purchasing plant or machinery

[42.6] Relief is given under **42.5** above for interest paid by an individual on a loan for the purchase of plant or machinery:

(a) for use for the purposes of a trade, profession or UK property business carried on by a partnership of which the payer is a member and which is entitled to a capital allowance, or liable to a balancing charge, on that item under *CAA 2001, s 264* (see **10.68** CAPITAL ALLOWANCES ON PLANT AND MACHINERY) for the period of account in which the interest is paid; or

(b) for the purposes of an office or employment he holds, and in respect of which he is entitled to plant or machinery capital allowances, or liable to a balancing charge, under *CAA 2001, Pt 2* (or would be so entitled but for a contribution made by his employer).

Relief is given only for interest payable no later than three years after the end of the period of account (where (a) above is relevant), or the tax year (where (b) above is relevant), in which the loan was made. If the plant or machinery is only partly in use for the purposes stated in (a) or (b) above and partly for other purposes, a proportionate part of the interest, determined on a just and reasonable basis, is eligible for the relief.

For the above purposes, a partnership or an individual remains entitled to a capital allowance on an item for so long as no disposal value (see **10.27** CAPITAL ALLOWANCES ON PLANT AND MACHINERY) has been brought into account in respect of that item.

Relief is not available for a tax year by virtue of (a) above if a cash basis election is in force by the partnership to which the loan relates (see **76** TRADING INCOME — CASH BASIS FOR SMALLER BUSINESSES) or, for 2017/18 onwards, if the profits of a UK or overseas property business carried on by the partnership are calculated on the cash basis for the tax year.

[*ITA 2007, ss 384B, 388–391; CAA 2001, Sch 2 para 27; F(No 2)A 2017, Sch 2 paras 63, 64(1)*].

Loans for interests in close companies

[42.7] Subject to the conditions below, relief is given under **42.5** above for interest paid by an individual on a loan used:

(i) for acquiring ordinary shares in a close company (see Tolley's Corporation Tax); and/or
(ii) for lending money to such a company; and/or
(iii) to repay a loan used for any one or more of these purposes.

'Close company' includes for these purposes any company resident in an EEA state (other than the UK) which would be a close company if it were UK resident. The EEA (European Economic Area) comprises the EU plus Norway, Iceland and Liechtenstein. In all cases, the company must not be a close investment-holding company (see below), whether at the time the loan proceeds are applied or the time the interest is paid.

If the loan is within (i) above, relief is denied in relation to shares in respect of which a claim is made to income tax relief under the EIS (see **29** ENTERPRISE INVESTMENT SCHEME) or for deferral of a chargeable gain on reinvestment in an EIS investment, by the person acquiring them or their spouse or civil partner. If the loan is within any of (i)–(iii) above, relief is similarly denied in relation to shares and debentures of a social enterprise where a claim has been made for income tax relief or capital gains deferral relief (see **72** SOCIAL INVESTMENT TAX RELIEF).

If the loan is within (ii) above, the money must be used wholly and exclusively for the purposes of the business of the company or of an associated company (within *CTA 2010, s 449*); any such associated company must also be a close company and not a close investment-holding company.

In a case decided in favour of the taxpayer, reference to the purposes of the 'business', as opposed to the 'trade', was held to be a deliberately unrestricted terminology. The intention behind the legislation must be to allow a flexible and wide approach; it is, however, necessary to consider the facts of each case in order to assess whether, in fact, any 'business' in the wider context is carried out by the close company or whether its business activities are restricted to its principal trade. (*Torkington v HMRC* FTT (TC 706), [2010] UKFTT 441 (TC)).

For an interest payment to qualify for the relief, the individual must not have recovered any capital from the company in the period from the use of the loan to the payment of the interest, except as taken into account in treating the loan as repaid or partly repaid (see below under Capital recovery). In addition, *either* of the following conditions must be met.

(a) **The material interest test.** The individual must have a 'material interest' in the company when the interest is paid. In addition, if the company exists wholly or mainly to hold investments or other property, no property of the company must be used by the individual as a residence, unless, in the period from the use of the loan to the payment of the interest, he has worked for the greater part of his time in the actual management or conduct of the company or an associated company (for which see (b) below). An individual has a '*material interest*' for this purpose if he (either alone or with 'associates') or an 'associate' of his (with or without other 'associates' of his) owns (or can control) more than 5% of the company's ordinary share capital or would be entitled to more than 5% of the assets available for distribution among the participators on a winding-up or in other circumstances. 'Control' is as defined in *CTA 2010, ss 450, 451* and 'participator' is as defined in *CTA 2010, s 454*.

(b) **The full-time working condition test.** The individual must have a holding of ordinary share capital of the company when the interest is paid and, in the period from the use of the loan to the payment of the interest, he must have worked for the greater part of his time in the actual management or conduct of the company or an associated company. The facts of each particular case must be considered, but individuals will normally be regarded as meeting the latter requirement if they are directors or have significant managerial or technical responsibilities. They must, however, be involved in the overall running and policy-making of the company as a whole — responsibility for just a particular area is not sufficient. (Revenue Tax Bulletin November 1993 p 102).

'*Associate*' is defined for the purposes of (a) above by *ITA 2007, s 395*. An individual's associates include his relatives (as defined), his business partners, the trustees of a settlement of which he or a relative is the settlor, the trustees of any settlement by virtue of which he has an interest in the company's shares or obligations and the personal representatives of a deceased person whose estate includes any of the company's shares or obligations in which the individual has an interest. But, in relation to loans made after 26 July 1989, an individual's associates do not generally include the trustees of an employee benefit trust (as defined), as a beneficiary of which the individual has an interest in shares or obligations of the company, unless the 5% ordinary share capital test would be satisfied without their inclusion (for which purpose certain payments received from the trust are treated as giving rise to beneficial ownership of ordinary share capital).

A slightly different definition of 'associate' applies to loans made before 14 November 1986 (see now *ITA 2007, Sch 2 para 93).*

[*ITA 2007, ss 392, 393, 394, 395, Sch 2 paras 91–94; SI 2019 No 689, Reg 15(3)*].

The interest will continue to be allowed if the company ceases to be close after the application of the loan monies (HMRC SP 3/78). Conversely, it is understood that relief will be given where a loan is used to purchase shares in an 'open' company which by that acquisition becomes a close company (Tolley's Practical Tax Newsletter 1981 p 99).

Interest paid by the guarantor of a bank loan to a close company is not within the relief (*Hendy v Hadley* Ch D 1980, 53 TC 353).

Where shares were subscribed for in a 'shell' company to enable it to acquire a business, but the business had not been acquired at the time of the subscription, it could fairly be said that the company existed for the purpose of carrying on that business, so that interest on a loan for the purchase of the shares qualified for relief under these provisions (*Lord v Tustain* Ch D 1993, 65 TC 761).

Interest on a loan applied to the purchase of a close company's convertible loan stock can qualify for relief under these provisions. Relief will, however, cease from the date on which the loan stock is converted to ordinary share capital, since this constitutes a capital recovery (see below). (Revenue Tax Bulletin February 1992 p 13).

Capital recovery

If, at any time after the loan is used as above, the borrower recovers an amount of capital from the company, the loan is treated as repaid at that time to the extent of that amount. This applies regardless of whether or not such repayment is actually made. Relief for subsequent interest payments is restricted accordingly. An individual recovers capital from the company if he sells, exchanges or assigns ordinary shares of the company, obtains a repayment of ordinary share capital, is repaid a loan or advance he has made to the company or assigns a debt due to him from the company. A sale or assignment is treated for this purpose as having been made at market value if it was not a bargain at arm's length. If a loan is used to repay another loan, so that it is within (iii) above, any capital recovery restrictions that were already affecting the original loan similarly affect the new loan. [*ITA 2007, ss 406–408*].

Business successions and reorganisations

Relief on a loan qualifying as above does not cease where shares in the close company are exchanged for, or replaced by, shares in another close company, or by shares in a co-operative (see **42.8** below), or by shares in an employee-controlled company (see **42.9** below), provided that relief would have been available if the loan had been a new loan taken out to invest in the new entity. [*ITA 2007, s 410*].

Woodlands

Interest is ineligible for the above relief to the extent that the business carried on by the close company consists of the occupation of commercial woodlands, i.e. UK woodlands managed on a commercial basis with a view to realisation of profits. See **30.53** EXEMPT INCOME for the general exemption of such woodlands. [*ITA 2007, s 411*].

Meaning of 'close investment-holding company'

A close company is a '*close investment-holding company*' in an accounting period unless throughout the period it exists wholly or mainly for one or more of the following purposes:

(A) the carrying on of trade(s) on a commercial basis;
(B) the making of investments in land, or estates or interests in land, let, or intended to be let, other than to CONNECTED PERSONS (**19**) of the company or to certain individuals related to such connected persons;
(C) the holding of shares in and securities of, or making loans to, a company or companies which, or each of which, is either:
  - a 'qualifying company'; or
  - a company under its control, or under the control of the same company as it, which itself exists wholly or mainly for the purpose of holding shares in or securities of, or making loans to, one or more qualifying companies;

(D) the co-ordination of the administration of two or more qualifying companies;
(E) the purposes of trade(s) carried on on a commercial basis by one or more qualifying companies, or by a company which has control of the company in question; and
(F) the making, by one or more qualifying companies or by a parent company, of investments within (B) above.

'Close company' includes for these purposes any company resident in an EEA state (other than the UK) which would be a close company if it were UK resident. A '*qualifying company*' in relation to the company in question is a company which is under its control, or under the control of the same company as it, and which exists wholly or mainly for either or both of the purposes in (A) or (B) above.

'*Control*' for all these purposes is as under *CTA 2010, s 450*. A company is not treated as a close investment-holding company in the accounting period beginning at the commencement of its winding-up if it was not such a company in the immediately preceding period.

[*ITA 2007, s 393A; CTA 2010, s 34; SI 2019 No 689, Reg 15(4)*].

Loans for investing in co-operatives

[42.8] Subject to the conditions below, relief is given under **42.5** above for interest paid by an individual on a loan used (i) for acquiring shares in a 'co-operative', and/or (ii) for lending money to a co-operative, and/or (iii) to repay a loan used for any one or more of these purposes. If the loan is within (ii) above, the money must be used wholly and exclusively for the purposes of the business of the co-operative or of a 'subsidiary' of the co-operative.

The conditions (all of which must be met) are that:

- the co-operative is still a co-operative when the interest is paid;
- in the period from the use of the loan to the payment of the interest, the individual must have worked for the greater part of his time as an employee of the co-operative or of a subsidiary of the co-operative; and
- in that period the individual must not have recovered any capital from the co-operative, except as taken into account in treating the loan as repaid or partly repaid under the capital recovery provisions referred to below.

'*Co-operative*' (and 'subsidiary') means a common ownership enterprise or a co-operative enterprise as defined in the *Industrial Common Ownership Act 1976, s 2*.

[*ITA 2007, ss 401, 402, Sch 2 para 97*].

The capital recovery provisions at **42.7** above apply equally here (with the appropriate modifications), as does the rule for business successions and reorganisations.

Loans for investing in employee-controlled companies

[42.9] Subject to the conditions below, relief is given under **42.5** above for interest paid by an individual on a loan used:

(i) to acquire ordinary shares in an 'employee-controlled company'; or
(ii) to repay a loan used for the purpose in (i) above.

The individual must acquire the shares before, or not later than twelve months after, the company first becomes an employee-controlled company.

For this purpose, a company is an '*employee-controlled company*' if more than 50% of both the issued ordinary share capital and the voting power is beneficially owned by full-time employees (as defined in (c) below) of the company. But if any one individual's ownership exceeds 10% of either issued ordinary share capital or voting power, the excess is treated as owned otherwise than by a full-time employee.

The conditions (all of which must be met) are that:

(a) throughout the period from the acquisition of the shares to the payment of the interest, the company must be unquoted, resident in the UK or an EEA state and not resident outside the EEA, and either a trading company (i.e. its business consists wholly or mainly of the carrying on of trade(s)) or the holding company of a trading group (i.e. a group, being a company and one or more 75% subsidiaries, the business of whose members, taken together, consists wholly or mainly of carrying on trade(s));

(b) the company must be an employee-controlled company throughout a period of at least nine months in the tax year in which the interest is paid, unless it is the year in which it first becomes an employee-controlled company;

(c) throughout the period from the use of the loan to the payment of the interest, the individual is a full-time employee of the company (i.e. works for the greater part of his time as an employee or director of the company or of a 51% subsidiary); if such employment ceased before, but not more than 12 months before, the payment of the interest, the condition can instead be satisfied by reference to the period from the use of the loan to the date of ceasing full-time employment; and

(d) in the period from the use of the loan to the payment of the interest, the individual must not have recovered any capital from the company, except as taken into account in treating the loan as repaid or partly repaid under the capital recovery provisions referred to below.

In (a) above, the EEA (European Economic Area) comprises the EU plus Norway, Iceland and Liechtenstein.

If the loan qualified before 6 April 1990, the reference in the definition of 'employee-controlled company' to full-time employees is a reference to such employees or their spouses. Ownership of husband and wife is then taken together in applying the 10% condition, unless they are *both* full-time employees. The condition at (c) above can be satisfied by the individual's spouse. Interest on a loan made on or after that date to repay a loan made before that date can be eligible (by virtue of (ii) above) only if interest on the original loan would have been eligible if the original loan had been used on or after that date.

[*ITA 2007, ss 396, 397, 989, 1005, Sch 2 para 95; SI 2019 No 689, Reg 15(5)*].

The capital recovery provisions at **42.7** above apply equally here (with the appropriate modifications), as does the rule for business successions and reorganisations and the exclusion of businesses consisting of the occupation of commercial woodlands.

Loans for investing in partnerships

[42.10] Subject to the conditions and restrictions below, relief is given under **42.5** above for interest paid by an individual on a loan used (i) for purchasing a share in a partnership, and/or (ii) contributing money to the partnership (by way of capital or premium), and/or (iii) advancing money to a partnership, and/or (iv) to repay a loan used for any one or more of these purposes.

If the loan is within (ii) or (iii) above, the money must be used wholly for the purposes of the trade or profession carried on by the partnership. In *Eclipse Film Partners No 35 LLP v HMRC* CA, [2015] STC 1429, it was held that an LLP was carrying on a non-trade business involving the exploitation of films (as in **49.3** MISCELLANEOUS INCOME), and the members' claims for interest relief failed accordingly.

The conditions for the relief (both of which must be met) are that:

- throughout the period from the use of the loan to the payment of the interest, the individual has been a member of the partnership otherwise than as a limited partner in a limited partnership registered under *Limited Partnerships Act 1907* or as a member of an 'investment limited liability partnership' (see **52.24, 52.28** PARTNERSHIPS); and
- in that period the individual must not have recovered any capital from the partnership, except as taken into account in treating the loan as repaid or partly repaid under the capital recovery provisions referred to below.

In the case of a partnership carrying on a profession, certain individuals who are not members of the partnership, for example salaried partners, are treated for these purposes as if they were members. This applies to any individual who is employed by the partnership in a senior capacity, is allowed to act independently in dealing with clients and is allowed to act generally in such a way as to be indistinguishable from the partners in relations with those clients.

The above relief is not available for a tax year if a cash basis election is in force by the partnership to which the loan relates (see **75** TRADING INCOME — CASH BASIS FOR SMALLER BUSINESSES) and the loan was not used for purchasing a share in the partnership.

[*ITA 2007, ss 398, 399; Limited Liability Partnerships Act 2000, s 10(2)*].

For a case in which relief was denied where 'the true net result of the circular transaction [involving a series of payments between spouses] was that no money was contributed or advanced to the partnership which it did not already have', see *Lancaster v CIR* (Sp C 232), [2000] SSCD 138.

The capital recovery provisions at **42.7** above apply equally here (with the appropriate modifications and by reference to the individual's interest in the partnership); the return of capital by the partnership to the individual is one occasion of recovery. The exclusion at **42.7** above of businesses consisting of the occupation of commercial woodlands also applies equally here.

Business successions and reorganisations

Relief on a loan qualifying as above does not cease where the partnership is incorporated into a close company (see **42.7** above), a co-operative (see **42.8** above) or an employee-controlled company (see **42.9** above), provided that relief would have been available if the loan had been a new loan taken out to invest in the new entity. Also, relief does not cease where the partnership is dissolved and a new partnership (of which the individual is, or falls to be treated as, a member) succeeds to the whole or part of its undertaking; in this case the old and new partnerships are treated as the same partnership for the purposes of the relief. [*ITA 2007, ss 409, 410*].

Partnerships carrying on a residential property business

For 2017/18 onwards, a restriction on the above relief is introduced where the partnership carries on a UK or overseas residential property business. The restriction is similar to that on deductions for finance costs in computing residential property income (see **60.12** PROPERTY INCOME). It applies where the partnership property business (or part of it) is carried on for the purpose of generating income from land consisting of a dwelling-house or part of a dwelling-house (or from an estate, interest or right in or over such land). Constructing a dwelling-house, or adapting a property for use as a dwelling-house, from which income is to be generated is treated as being done for this purpose. A property business (or part of a property business) that consists of the commercial letting of furnished holiday accommodation (within **60.20** PROPERTY INCOME) is not within the restriction. A dwelling-house includes for these purposes any land occupied or enjoyed with it as garden or grounds.

The restriction affects so much of the interest as is referable (on a just and reasonable apportionment) to the property business (or the relevant part of it). Only a percentage of that interest attracts the above relief in full, i.e. by deduction in calculating the payer's net income. The balance attracts relief at the basic rate only; the basic rate relief is given as a tax reduction at Step 6 of the calculation of income tax liability at **1.10** ALLOWANCES AND TAX RATES. For 2020/21 onwards, all such interest is relieved at basic rate only. In the meantime, the percentage attracting relief by deduction is as follows.

2017/18	75%
2018/19	50%
2019/20	25%

[*ITA 2007, ss 399A, 399B*].

The order in which tax reductions are given against an individual's tax liability is set out at **1.12** ALLOWANCES AND TAX RATES, which also makes clear that a tax reduction must be restricted to the extent (if any) that it would otherwise exceed the individual's remaining income tax liability after making all prior reductions.

Anti-avoidance measures on changeover to current year basis of assessment

Anti-avoidance provisions applied where a claim for interest relief under the above provisions was made by a partner for 1997/98 in respect of a loan made after 31 March 1994 and there was a transitional overlap profit (see **75.15** TRADING INCOME) on the changeover to the current year basis. Subject to a *de minimis* limit of £7,500 for application of these provisions, that partner's transitional overlap profit (as reduced where applicable by the anti-avoidance provisions at **75.15**) was reduced by the amount of interest paid in respect of the transitional overlap period on any part of the loan proceeds which was contributed or advanced by him to the partnership otherwise than wholly or mainly for *bona fide* commercial reasons or wholly or mainly for a purpose other than the reduction of partnership borrowings for a period falling wholly or partly within the transitional overlap period. [*FA 1995, Sch 22 paras 5, 12*].

Anti-avoidance measure involving film partnerships

In response to an identified avoidance scheme, there is legislation restricting interest relief in the circumstances set out below. For any tax year for which these circumstances apply, relief for the interest on the loan is restricted to 40% of the amount that would otherwise be eligible for relief. The circumstances are that:

- a loan is used by an individual ('the borrower') to buy into (or advance money to) a '*film partnership*', i.e. a partnership carrying on a trade in which the film tax reliefs at **75.80** TRADING INCOME have been used in computing profits or losses;
- the borrower is, or has been, a member of another partnership (the '*investment partnership*');
- the loan used to buy into (or to contribute or advance money to) the film partnership is secured (as widely defined) on an asset or activity of the investment partnership; and
- at any time in the tax year, the proportion of the taxable profits of the investment partnership to which the borrower is entitled is less than the proportion of the partnership's capital contributed by him at that time.

For this purpose, the investment partnership's capital comprises: (i) anything that is (or in accordance with generally accepted accounting practice, would be) accounted for as partners' capital or partners' equity; and (ii) amounts lent to the partnership by partners or persons connected with partners (within **19.2** CONNECTED PERSONS). The proportion of the investment partnership's capital contributed by the borrower at any time includes, in particular:

- any amount paid by the borrower to acquire an interest in the investment partnership (insofar as he still has that interest at that time);
- any amount made available by the borrower (directly or indirectly) to another person who acquires an interest in the investment partnership (in so far as the other person still has that interest at that time);
- any amount lent by the borrower to the investment partnership and not repaid at that time;
- any amount made available by the borrower (directly or indirectly) to another person in so far as any amount lent by that person to the investment partnership has not been repaid at that time; and
- any amount made available in any other manner that may be prescribed by HMRC regulations made by statutory instrument (which may have retrospective effect).

All references above to the borrower include references to anyone connected with him (within **19.2** CONNECTED PERSONS, i.e. spouses, civil partners and relatives).

In a case where both apply, this restriction is applied before applying the percentage restriction for any of the years 2017/18 to 2019/20 for partnerships carrying on a residential property business (see above).

[*ITA 2007, ss 399(4), 399A(7), 400, Sch 2 para 96*].

Loans to pay inheritance tax

[42.11] Relief is given under **42.5** above for interest on a loan to the personal representatives of a deceased person that is used (i) to pay inheritance tax that they are obliged to pay under *IHTA 1984, s 226(2)* (obligation of personal representatives to pay tax on delivery of their account in order to obtain a grant of representation or confirmation), or (ii) to pay interest on such inheritance tax, or (iii) to repay a loan used for any of these purposes. In order to attract relief, the loan interest paid must have been in respect of a period ending within one year from the making of the loan.

If the interest cannot be relieved in the tax year due to insufficiency of income, it is carried back to preceding tax years, latest year first, until it is fully relieved. If the interest cannot be relieved by carry-back, it may instead be carried forward to tax years following the year of payment, earliest year first, until it is fully relieved.

[*ITA 2007, ss 403–405*].

Pre-9 March 1999 loans for purchasing a life annuity

[42.12] Relief is given under **42.5** above for interest on a loan for the purchase of a life annuity by a borrower aged 65 or over under a scheme in which 90% or more of the proceeds of the loan are applied to the purchase by the borrower of an annuity ending with his death (or the last death of two or more annuitants aged 65 or over which include the borrower). The loan must be secured on land in the UK or Eire in which the borrower or one of the annuitants owns an estate or interest. Interest is not eligible unless payable by the borrower or one of the annuitants. The rate of tax relief on interest allowable under these provisions is fixed at **23%** of the amount of the allowable interest.

The loan must have been made before 9 March 1999, or in pursuance of an offer made by the lender before that date (and either written or evidenced by a note or memorandum made by the lender before that date). However, replacement loans made on or after 27 July 1999 qualify for relief if the old loan did so, and this applies where only part of the new loan is applied in paying off the old loan, provided that at least 90% of the balance of the new loan not applied in paying off the old loan is applied to the purchase of an annuity ending with the life of the person to whom the loan is made (or of the survivor of two or more persons including that person).

As regards loans made from 27 March 1974 onwards: (a) the borrower or each of the annuitants must use the land as his only or main residence when the interest is paid or have so used it immediately before 9 March 1999; and (b) relief is granted on loans up to £30,000 only, with apportionment where payable by two or more annuitants. The condition at (a) is treated as satisfied where it ceased to be satisfied at a time falling within the twelve months ending with 8 March 1999 and it was then intended to take steps to dispose of the land within the following twelve months.

As stated at **42.5** above, relief is normally given by deduction of tax at source but is otherwise given by way of an income tax reduction as opposed to a deduction from total income. The reduction is 23% of the amount of interest eligible for relief. The order in which tax reductions are given against an individual's tax liability is set out at **1.12** ALLOWANCES AND TAX RATES, which also makes clear that a tax reduction must be restricted to the extent (if any) that it would otherwise exceed the individual's remaining income tax liability after making all prior reductions.

Relief at source is given via the MIRAS (Mortgage Interest Relief At Source) system which generally applied to tax relief on mortgage interest prior to such relief being abolished with effect from 6 April 2000. Once relief is given under MIRAS, no further tax relief is available but nor is tax relief clawed back if the borrower has insufficient tax liability to cover it.

[*ICTA 1988, ss 353(1A)(1AA)(1AB)(1F)–(1H), 357(1), 365*].

Exclusion of double relief

[42.13] There are provisions to prevent double relief by different methods. The general rule is that any interest relieved under *ITA 2007, s 383* (see **42.5** above) is not deductible for any other purpose. If a payment of interest on a debt has been allowed under **42.2** above in computing the profits of a trade, profession, vocation or property business for a period of account, no relief can be given under *ITA 2007, s 383* for that payment and for any other interest on the same debt in any tax year for which that period is the basis period (see **75.6** TRADING INCOME onwards). Conversely, if a payment of interest has been relieved under *section 383*, that payment cannot be deducted in computing profits for any tax year and any payment of interest on the same debt cannot be deducted in computing profits for any tax year for which the interest relieved under *section 383* could otherwise have been relieved as a trading etc. deduction. For these purposes, all business overdrafts are treated as one debt. Interest is treated as having been relieved under *section 383* when it has been deducted in an assessment that can no longer be varied (whether on appeal or otherwise). [*ITA 2007, s 387; ITTOIA 2005, s 52*].

Anti-avoidance

[42.14] Relief is not available under *any* part of this chapter to a person for a payment of interest if a 'tax relief scheme' has been effected, or 'tax relief arrangements' have been made, in relation to the transaction under which the interest is paid. It matters not whether the scheme is effected, or the arrangements are made, before or after the transaction. The restriction applies whether the relief would otherwise have been given as a deduction in calculating profits or as a deduction or set-off against income. A scheme is a '*tax relief scheme*' in relation to a transaction if it is such that the sole or main benefit that might be expected to accrue to the person from the transaction is the obtaining of a reduction in tax liability by means of interest relief. '*Tax relief arrangements*' are similarly defined.

[*ITA 2007, s 809ZG*].

The above restriction has effect in relation to returns under ALTERNATIVE FINANCE ARRANGEMENTS (**3**) in the same way as it has effect in relation to interest. [*ITA 2007, s 564P*].

See also *Cairns v MacDiarmid* CA 1982, 56 TC 556 and *Lancaster v CIR* (Sp C 232), [2000] SSCD 138.

Deduction of tax from interest payments

[42.15] In general, tax is not deductible at source from interest paid by individuals (except as in **42.12** above).

43

Late Payment Interest and Penalties

Cross-references. See also **53.23, 53.24** PAY AS YOU EARN; **62** REPAYMENT INTEREST.

Simon's Taxes. See **A4.540, A4.543–A4.566, A4.620, A4.621, A6.601.**

Introduction to late payment interest and penalties

[43.1] A harmonised regime for interest applies to all of the taxes and duties administered by HMRC. In relation to interest on late payment of income tax, the regime is described at **43.2** below. For the purposes of income tax self-assessment, it came into force on 31 October 2011. To the extent that the harmonised regime is in force, it replaces the old regime referred to at **43.3** below. To the extent that it applies to late payments of PAYE, it is covered at **53.23** PAY AS YOU EARN; it applies similarly to late in-year payments under the CONSTRUCTION INDUSTRY SCHEME (**20**).

A unified penalty regime for late payment similarly applies across a range of taxes including income tax. In its application to income tax generally, the late payment penalty is described at **43.4** below. To the extent that it applies to late in-year payments of PAYE, it is covered at **53.24** PAY AS YOU EARN; it applies similarly to late in-year payments under the CONSTRUCTION INDUSTRY SCHEME (**20**).

See **43.5** below as regards special arrangements in relation to national disasters or emergencies.

Late payment interest

[43.2] A harmonised regime for interest applies to all of the taxes and duties administered by HMRC. To the extent that this regime is in force in relation to interest on income tax payable, it replaces the rules referred to at **43.3** below.

For the purposes of any 'self-assessment amount' payable by any person to HMRC, the regime came into force on 31 October 2011. A '*self-assessment amount*' means:

- any tax or other amount in relation to which, for any tax year, a personal, trustees' or partnership tax return falls to be made or a discovery assessment is made; and
- any penalties assessed in relation to that tax or amount.

Interest payable on a self-assessment amount is known as '*late payment interest*'. Where interest was already accruing immediately prior to 31 October 2011 on a self-assessment amount, it accrues on and after that date under the harmonised regime.

For the purposes of interest on penalties assessed under *FA 2012, Sch 38* (dishonest conduct by tax agents — see **55.18** PENALTIES), the regime came into force on 1 April 2013. For the purposes of interest on late payments of PAYE (see **53.23** PAY AS YOU EARN) and amounts due under the CONSTRUCTION INDUSTRY SCHEME (**20**), the regime came into force on 6 May 2014.

Late payment interest is payable without deduction of tax at source and is recoverable (as if it were tax) as a Crown debt. Interest is refundable to the extent that the tax concerned is subsequently discharged (and a tax repayment may be treated as a discharge for this purpose).

The rate of late payment interest is set by reference to the official bank rate set by the Bank of England Monetary Policy Committee; for details, see *SI 2011 No 2446, Reg 3*. Changes to the rate are announced by HMRC.

Rates of interest

2.6% p.a.	**from 7 April 2020**
2.75% p.a.	from 30 March 2020 to 6 April 2020
3.25% p.a.	from 21 August 2018 to 29 March 2020
3% p.a.	from 21 November 2017 to 20 August 2018
2.75% p.a.	from 23 August 2016 to 20 November 2017
3% p.a.	from 31 October 2011 to 22 August 2016

Period for which interest accrues

A payment of tax within these provisions carries interest at the late payment interest rate from the 'late payment interest start date' until the date on which payment is made. The '*late payment interest start date*' in respect of any amount is the date on which that amount becomes due and payable. (It matters not that it might be a non-business day.) However, see also below under Assessments and amendments to self-assessments.

A payment to HMRC may take the form of a set-off against an amount payable by HMRC, in which case the date on which the payment is made is the date from which the set-off takes effect. In general, for the date on which an amount is treated as paid to HMRC, see **54.2** PAYMENT OF TAX.

Interim payments and balancing payment

There are provisions to remit interest charged on interim payments to the extent that the interim payments turn out to exceed the income tax liability, such that an overpayment has been made. Late payment interest is payable only on the amount by which each of the payments on account exceeds half of the overpayment.

There are also provisions covering the situation where a taxpayer makes a claim to dispense with or reduce his interim payments (see **67.5** SELF-ASSESSMENT) and the total income tax liability for the year is found to be such that interim payments should have been made or should have been greater. Interest is chargeable as if each interim payment due had been equal to half the current year's liability or half the previous year's liability, whichever is less.

Assessments and amendments to self-assessments

A special rule applies to determine the late payment interest start date if:

(a) there is an amendment or correction to an assessment or self-assessment; or
(b) HMRC make an assessment in place of, or in addition to, an assessment made by a taxpayer; or
(c) HMRC make an assessment in place of an assessment that *ought to have been made* by a taxpayer.

In relation to any amount due and payable as a result of any of the above, the late payment interest start date is what it would have been if:

- the original assessment or self-assessment had been complete and accurate and had been made on the date (if any) by which it was required to be made; and
- accordingly, the amount had been due and payable as a result of that original assessment or self-assessment.

The above rule applies to any assessment or determination (however described) of any amount due and payable to HMRC. A case in which the taxpayer failed to give notice of chargeability to tax when required by law to do so (see **55.2** PENALTIES) falls within (c) above. Where the requirement to give notice of chargeability arises after a notice to make a return was withdrawn (see **64.2** RETURNS), (c) above applies by reference to the assessment which the taxpayer would have been required to make had there been no withdrawal.

Tax postponed

If an amount of tax is postponed pending determination of an appeal against an income tax assessment (see **54.5** PAYMENT OF TAX), this does not have the effect of deferring the late payment interest start date, which is the same as it would have been had there been no appeal.

Tax over-repaid

Where an assessment is raised to collect an amount of income tax previously over-repaid (see **54.16** PAYMENT OF TAX), the late payment interest start date in relation to that amount is 31 January following the tax year for which the assessment is made.

[*FA 2009, ss 101, 103, 104, Sch 53 paras 1, 2, 3–5, 15, 16; TMA 1970, s 69; SI 2011 No 2446*].

Miscellaneous

Interest is similarly charged on late payment of Class 4 national insurance contributions (see **73.7** SOCIAL SECURITY AND NATIONAL INSURANCE).

See 43.5 below as regards special arrangements in relation to national disasters or emergencies.

Interest on overdue tax (the old regime)

[43.3] For the purposes of income tax self-assessment, the old rules were superseded by those at 43.2 above on and after 31 October 2011. Where interest was already accruing immediately prior to 31 October 2011 on a 'self-assessment amount' (as defined in 43.2), it accrues on and after that date under the regime at 43.2.

Late payment penalty

[43.4] A unified penalty regime for late payment applies across a range of taxes including income tax. In its application to income tax generally, the late payment penalty is described below. To the extent that it applies to late in-year payments of PAYE, it is covered at 53.24 PAY AS YOU EARN; it applies similarly to late in-year payments under the CONSTRUCTION INDUSTRY SCHEME (20).

The late payment penalty has effect in relation to:

(a) a balancing payment of income tax (and/or capital gains tax) due under self-assessment (see 67.7 SELF-ASSESSMENT);
(b) an amount of tax becoming due as a result of an HMRC determination (see 64.11 RETURNS) made in the absence of a personal or trustees' tax return filed by the requisite filing date;
(c) an amount of tax becoming due as a result of an HMRC determination being superseded by a self-assessment (see 64.11 RETURNS);
(d) an amount of tax becoming due following an application for postponement of tax pending determination of an appeal, including amounts postponed, amounts not postponed and additional tax becoming payable on determination of the appeal (see 54.5, 54.6 PAYMENT OF TAX);
(e) an amount of tax becoming due as a result of the amendment or correction of a personal or trustees' tax return by the taxpayer or by HMRC (see 64.4, 64.8, 64.9 RETURNS) or the amendment of a partner's tax return to give effect to the amendment or correction of the partnership return (see 64.12 RETURNS);
(f) (on and after a date to be appointed by statutory instrument) an amount of tax payable by virtue of a 'simple assessment' (see 6.5 ASSESSMENTS); and
(g) an amount of tax payable by virtue of an assessment other than a self-assessment (see 67.8 SELF-ASSESSMENT) or a simple assessment.

Subject to the reasonable excuse provisions and right of appeal set out below, an initial penalty is incurred where any part of the tax remains unpaid after the date indicated in the Table below.

Penalty within	*The date immediately after which an initial penalty is incurred*
(a) above	The date falling 30 days after the due date. The due date is normally 31 January following the tax year in question but is deferred in certain cases where tax return is issued late by HMRC (see **67.7** SELF-ASSESSMENT).
(b) above	The date falling 30 days after the date by which the amount would have been required to be paid if it had been shown in the return in question, i.e. the same date as for (a) above.
(c) above	The date falling 30 days after the date on which the amount would have been payable had it fallen within (a) above.
(d) above	The date falling 30 days after the date the amount becomes due and payable, for which see **54.5** PAYMENT OF TAX as regards tax not postponed and **54.6** PAYMENT OF TAX as regards tax becoming payable on determination of the appeal (whether it be tax previously postponed or additional tax).
(e) above	The date falling 30 days after the date the amount becomes due and payable, for which see **67.8** SELF-ASSESSMENT.
(f) above	The date falling 30 days after the date the amount becomes due and payable, for which see **54.1** PAYMENT OF TAX.
(g) above	The date falling 30 days after the due and payable date, which itself is 30 days after the date of the assessment.

The legislation gives two further instances of when the penalty will apply as regards income tax. These appear to be catch-all provisions and it is not clear in exactly what circumstances they would apply. The first envisages amounts becoming due as a result of an amendment or correction of a return but not within *TMA 1970, s 59B(5)* and thus not within (e) above. The second envisages amounts becoming due as a result of an assessment or determination not covered by (b), (f) or (g) above. In these cases, the initial penalty is incurred where any part of the tax remains unpaid after the date falling 30 days after the *later* of the date by which the amount must be paid and the date on which the amendment or correction, or (as the case may be) the assessment or determination, is made.

Amount of the penalties

The initial penalty is 5% of the amount of tax unpaid.

If any amount of the tax remains unpaid after the end of the period of five months beginning with the date the initial penalty is incurred (the '*penalty date*') as given above, there is a further penalty of 5% of that amount.

If any amount of the tax remains unpaid after the end of the period of eleven months beginning with the penalty date, there is a further penalty of 5% of that amount.

Reasonable excuse

If the taxpayer satisfies HMRC or, on appeal, the Tribunal that there is a reasonable excuse for a failure to make a payment, he is not liable to a late payment penalty in relation to that failure. Insufficiency of funds is not a reasonable excuse for this purpose and neither is the taxpayer's reliance on another person to do anything unless the taxpayer took reasonable care to avoid the failure. If the taxpayer had a reasonable excuse, he is treated as continuing to have a reasonable excuse after the excuse has ceased if the failure is remedied without unreasonable delay.

Suspension of penalty where 'time to pay' arrangement in place

Special rules apply where a 'time to pay' arrangement is in place (see **54.12** PAYMENT OF TAX). They apply where:

- a taxpayer ('P') fails to pay an amount of tax when it becomes due and payable;
- P makes a request to HMRC that payment of the amount be deferred; and
- HMRC agree that payment of that amount may be deferred for a period (*'the deferral period'*).

If, between the date on which he makes the request and the end of the deferral period, P would otherwise become liable to a late payment penalty for failing to pay that amount, P is not liable to that penalty. If, however, P breaks the agreement, HMRC may then, by notice served on P, impose any penalty to which P would have been liable had it not been for the agreement. P then becomes liable to the penalty as at the date of the notice. For this purpose, P breaks the agreement if he fails to pay the tax when the deferral period ends or he fails to comply with a condition on which the deferral depends, which may be a condition that he pays part of the tax within the deferral period.

Reduction in special circumstances

HMRC may reduce or stay a penalty or agree a compromise in relation to proceedings for a penalty if they think it right to do so because of special circumstances. Ability to pay and the fact that a potential loss of revenue from one taxpayer is balanced by a potential overpayment by another are not special circumstances for this purpose.

Double jeopardy

A taxpayer is not liable to a late payment penalty in respect of a failure or action in respect of which he has been convicted of an offence.

Assessment of penalty

Where a late payment penalty is incurred, HMRC will raise an assessment to collect it. The notice of assessment must state the period in respect of which the penalty is assessed. The penalty is then payable within 30 days beginning with the date of the assessment.

As assessment of a late payment penalty is to be treated for procedural purposes in the same way as an assessment to tax, may be enforced as if it were an assessment to tax and may be combined with an assessment to tax. There is provision for a supplementary assessment to be raised if the earlier assessment was made by reference to an underestimate of the tax due.

Similarly, an amended assessment may be raised if the earlier assessment was made by reference to an overestimate of the tax due. An amendment to an assessment does not affect when the penalty must be paid.

The assessment of the late payment penalty must be made on or before the later of:

- the last day of the period of 2 years beginning with the last date on which payment of the tax could have been made without incurring a late payment penalty; and
- the last day of the period of 12 months beginning with:
  - the end of the 'appeal period' for the assessment of the amount of tax in question; or
  - if there is no such assessment, the date on which that amount of tax is ascertained.

The '*appeal period*' is the period during which an appeal could be brought or during which an appeal that has been brought is awaiting determination.

A late payment penalty is recoverable (as if it were tax) as a Crown debt.

Appeals

An appeal may be brought against the imposition of a late payment penalty or against its amount. An appeal is to be treated in the same way as an appeal against an assessment to income tax (see **5** APPEALS), but not so as to require the taxpayer to pay the penalty before the appeal against its assessment is determined. Thus, notice of appeal must normally be given within 30 days after the date of issue of the penalty assessment (see **5.4** APPEALS).

If the appeal is against the imposition of a penalty and it goes to the Tribunal, the Tribunal may affirm or cancel HMRC's decision to impose.

If the appeal is against the amount of a penalty and it goes to the Tribunal, the Tribunal may affirm the amount charged or substitute its own amount (but only an amount that HMRC could have chosen to charge). The Tribunal has power, similar but more limited, to that of HMRC to make a 'reduction in special circumstances' (see above). It may rely on the power to reduce to the same extent as HMRC, which may mean applying the same percentage reduction as HMRC but to a different starting point. It may also rely on the power to a different extent to HMRC, but only if it thinks that HMRC's application of the power was 'flawed'. '*Flawed*' means flawed when considered in the light of the principles applicable in proceedings for judicial review.

[*FA 2009, s 107, Sch 56 paras 1, 2, 3, 9, 9A–17; TMA 1970, s 69; FA 2016, s 167, Sch 23 para 9; SI 2011 Nos 702, 703*].

Future development

The current late payment penalty is to be replaced by a two-tiered penalty structure from a date which is still to be determined but will be later than 1 April 2020. This will work as follows:

- No penalty will be due if the tax is paid in full before the end of the 15-day period beginning on the day after the payment due date.

- If the tax due is paid in full after the end of the 15-day period but before the end of the 30-day period beginning on the same date, a penalty will be payable at the end of the 30-day period, and will be based on a set percentage, as yet unspecified, of the tax unpaid after 15 days.
- If tax is still outstanding at the end of the 30-day period, the penalty will instead be a percentage of the tax unpaid after 15 days plus a percentage of the tax still unpaid after 30 days.
- For tax remaining unpaid at the end of the 30-day period, a second penalty will subsequently become payable, and will be calculated, again at a percentage yet to be specified, on amounts outstanding from day 31 until the balance is paid in full.

Both the first and second penalty will be charged by notice of assessment, and must be paid, or appealed, within 30 days of the date of that notice. A reasonable excuse defence will be available. Penalties will not be charged where 'time to pay' arrangements are in place.

(Legislation Day 2018 at www.gov.uk/government/publications/interest-harmonisation-and-sanctions-for-late-payment).

It was announced in July 2019 that the Government remains committed to the above reform and that the timing and details of implementation will be announced at a future fiscal event (www.parliament.uk/business/publications/written-questions-answers-statements/written-statement/Commons/2019-07-11/HCWS1713).

National disasters or emergencies

[43.5] The Treasury are granted power by *FA 2008* to specify by order made by statutory instrument any disaster or emergency which they consider to be of national significance. This will then allow late payment interest to be waived where the late payment is attributable to that disaster or emergency. The regulation-making power envisages the making of agreements for deferred payment of tax between HMRC and individual taxpayers but the waiver will also apply in any case in which HMRC are satisfied that, although no agreement for deferred payment was made, such an agreement could have been made. The power is amended with effect on and after 20 March 2020 so as to enable a Treasury order to specify particular liabilities, thus enabling HMRC to waive interest which would otherwise arise in relation to the specified deferrals. An example of the use of this amended power is the non-charging of interest on the deferral of the second self-assessment payment on account for 2019/20 otherwise due on 31 July 2020 (see **67.5** SELF-ASSESSMENT).

In all cases, no interest on the amount deferred is chargeable in respect of the 'relief period'. The relief period, in relation to a deferred amount, is the period:

- beginning with a date specified in the Treasury order or, if the Commissioners for HMRC so direct, a later date from which the agreement for deferred payment has effect; and
- ending with the date on which the agreement for deferred payment ceases to have effect or, if earlier, the date on which the order is revoked or amended so that it ceases to have effect in relation to the deferred amount.

The agreement for deferred payment ceases to have effect at the end of the period of deferment specified in the agreement or, if the Commissioners for HMRC agree to extend (or further extend) that period by reason of circumstances arising as a result of the disaster or emergency, with the end of that extended (or further extended) period.

[*FA 2008, s 135; FA 2020, s 105*].

HMRC error

[43.6] HMRC publish a Code of Practice (No 1) setting out the circumstances in which they will consider waiving a charge to interest on overdue tax where there has been undue delay on their part. See **35.7** HMRC — ADMINISTRATION.

Death of taxpayer

[43.7] A special rule applies if a person chargeable to an amount of tax dies before the amount becomes due and payable and the executor or administrator is unable to pay the amount until he obtains probate or letters of administration (or, in Scotland, the executor is unable to pay the amount before he obtains confirmation). In relation to that amount, the late payment interest start date in **43.2** above is the *later* of:

- the date which would have been the late payment interest start date apart from this special rule; and
- the date falling 30 days after the date of grant of probate etc.

[*FA 2009, s 101, Sch 53 para 12; SI 2011 No 701*].

44

Life Assurance Policies

(See also HMRC Insurance Policyholder Taxation Manual.)

Introduction to life assurance policies

[44.1] Income tax is charged on gains treated as arising from many life assurance policies, contracts for life annuities and capital redemption policies. A gain (a '*chargeable event gain*') arises when a chargeable event occurs in relation to the policy or contract. Chargeable events include *inter alia* death, maturity, total or partial surrender and total or partial assignment — see **44.6**. See **44.3–44.19** for the main coverage. There is a general exemption for qualifying policies (see **44.6**). The question of whether or not a policy is a qualifying policy is considered at **44.27–44.35**. There is a premium limit for qualifying policies (see **44.36–44.40**).

This chapter also covers personal portfolio bonds (**44.20**), offshore policies (**44.21–44.23**) and friendly society policies (**44.24–44.26**).

Apart from the relatively minor reliefs at **44.2** below, no income tax relief is available on premiums payable by an individual on a life assurance policy. See **75.92** TRADING INCOME as regards premiums paid by employers insuring against death or critical illness of key employees. See **57.12** PENSION PROVISIONS for relief, now obsolescent, for life assurance premium contributions made to a registered pension scheme.

Miscellaneous life assurance-related reliefs

[44.2] The relatively minor reliefs listed below are available to all UK resident individuals; they are also available to certain other claimants as set out at **50.2** NON-RESIDENTS. An individual who claims the remittance basis loses any entitlement he may have to these reliefs (see **61.8** REMITTANCE BASIS).

Payments to trade unions

Relief is available (on a claim) for any part of a payment by an individual to a trade union (as defined) as is attributable to the provision of superannuation, life insurance or funeral benefits. The relief is given as a deduction in calculating net income (see Step 2 at **1.10** ALLOWANCES AND TAX RATES). The deduction is restricted to one-half of the aggregate part of any such payments in the tax year as is so attributable, and the maximum amount deductible for any tax year is £100. [*ITA 2007, s 457*].

Payments to police organisations

Relief is available (on a claim) for any part of a payment by an individual to a police organisation (as defined) as is attributable to the provision of superannuation, life insurance or funeral benefits. The relief is available only if the sum of the parts so attributable in any tax year is at least £20. Otherwise, the relief works in the same way (and the deduction is subject to an identical maximum) as the relief under *ITA 2007, s 457* above. [*ITA 2007, s 458*].

Life assurance gains

[44.3] Income tax is charged on gains treated as arising from those policies and contracts set out in **44.5** below. A gain from a policy or contract (a '*chargeable event gain*') arises when a chargeable event occurs in relation to the policy or contract — see **44.6** below. Tax is charged on the amount of the gains arising in the tax year. See **44.13** below as to the time at which a gain arises on a *partial* surrender or partial assignment.

An individual is liable for income tax on a chargeable event gain if he is UK resident for the tax year in which the gain arises and one of the following conditions is met:

(a) the individual beneficially owns the rights under the policy or contract in question;
(b) those rights are held on non-charitable trusts which the individual created; or
(c) those rights are held as security for a debt of the individual.

Where the tax year is a split year (see **63.19** RESIDENCE AND DOMICILE) as regards an individual, he is not liable for tax in respect of gains treated as arising from policies and contracts in the overseas part of the split year.

[*ITTOIA 2005, ss 461–465*].

Personal representatives of a deceased individual are liable to income tax on a chargeable event gain arising to them (see *ITTOIA 2005, s 466*). As regards liability of trustees, see **44.12** below.

For the determination of liability where two or more persons have an interest in a policy or contract, see *ITTOIA 2005, ss 469–472.*

See **44.7** below as regards computation of the gain and **44.8** below as regards the charge to tax. Top slicing relief (see **44.9** below) may be available to reduce the tax chargeable.

Simon's Taxes. See **E1.440** *et seq.*

Temporary non-UK residence

[44.4] Where the 'year of departure' is 2013/14 or any subsequent year, a 'temporarily non-UK resident' individual is chargeable to income tax under **44.3** above for the tax year that consists of or includes the 'period of return' in respect of any chargeable event gain that meets all the conditions set out below. This does not apply in certain circumstances where the policy or contract in question subsequently terminates (by death, maturity, total surrender etc.) such that a tax charge then arises — see further below.

For what is meant by '*temporarily non-UK resident*', the '*year of departure*' and the '*period of return*', see **63.29** RESIDENCE AND DOMICILE.

The conditions are that:

(a) the gain arises in the 'temporary period of non-UK residence' (see **63.29**(d) RESIDENCE AND DOMICILE);

(b) it arises from a policy issued, or contract made, before the start of that period;
(c) the chargeable event is neither a death nor an annual chargeable event treated as occurring in respect of a personal portfolio bond (see **44.20** below);
(d) neither a body of personal representatives nor a body of trustees are liable to tax on the gain;
(e) no-one is liable as a result of the gain by virtue of *ITTOIA 2005, s 468* (liability of non-resident trustees and foreign institutions — see **44.12** below) for either the tax year that consists of or includes the 'period of return' or any earlier tax year; and
(f) the individual would have been liable under **44.3** above on the assumptions that he were UK resident for the tax year in which the gain arose and that the year was not a split year (see **63.19** RESIDENCE AND DOMICILE).

If the gain thereby chargeable for a tax year later than that in which it arises falls to be proportionately reduced by reference to the policy holder's having been non-UK resident for part of the policy period (see **44.11**, **44.23** below), the reduction is computed without regard to the assumptions mentioned in (f) above.

Where connected policies or contracts fall to be treated as a single policy or contract under **44.5** below, the date of the policy or contract for the purposes of (b) above is the date on which the first such policy was issued or first contract made.

Nothing in any double tax treaty is to be read as preventing the individual from being chargeable to income tax by virtue of the above provisions.

The above provisions do not apply to a gain if:

- in relation to the same policy or contract, a 'terminal event' occurs in the temporary period of non-UK residence or in the period of return;
- the chargeable event giving rise to the gain occurred before the terminal event;
- the chargeable event gain arises on a partial surrender as in **44.13** below;
- the chargeable event is not an event *treated as* a partial surrender as in **44.16** below; and
- a person (whether or not the individual in question) is liable for tax in respect of any gain resulting from the terminal event.

A '*terminal event*' is an event that terminates the policy or contract (e.g. death, maturity, total surrender) and brings to an end the insurance year in which it occurs (see **44.13** below).

[*ITTOIA 2005, s 465B*].

Policies and contracts within the charge

[44.5] The chargeable event gain rules apply to life assurance policies, contracts for life annuities and capital redemption policies. However, see **44.6** below for the exclusion of certain qualifying policies. The rules do not apply to a policy or contract made before 20 March 1968, unless it is a life insurance policy which has been varied after that date to extend the term or increase the benefits; this does not include a policy where the only variation is in the amount of the premium. Certain special types of policy are also excluded from the rules, namely certain mortgage protection policies, certain policies connected with pension schemes, certain group life policies (as defined) providing protection for loans made to individuals by credit unions and other group life policies meeting specified conditions.

Policies or contracts which are connected with each other are treated as a single policy or contract for the purposes of the charge. This applies in relation to policies issued, and contracts made, on or after 21 March 2012. It also applies to a pre-21 March 2012 policy or contract if, on or after that date, it (i) is varied so as to increase the benefits from it or from a connected policy or contract (an exercise of rights conferred by the policy being treated for this purpose as a variation); (ii) is assigned (in whole or in part); or (iii) becomes held as security for a debt. For these purposes, policies are connected where a policy is issued by reference to another policy (a related policy) and the terms of either policy are significantly more or less favourable than would reasonably be expected if the other were ignored or if other related policies were ignored. If there is a policy or contract with which two or more other policies or contracts are connected but the other policies or contracts are not connected with each other, all the policies or contracts are treated as connected with each other.

[*ITTOIA 2005, ss 473, 473A, 478–483, Sch 2 paras 86, 96, 116*].

Chargeable events

[44.6] Subject to the exclusions and disregards below, there is a chargeable event in relation to any kind of policy or contract within **44.5** above where:

- all rights under it are *surrendered* or *assigned* for money or money's worth;
- a sum is payable under a right to participate in profits, if there are no remaining rights;
- the calculation on a *partial* surrender or *partial* assignment shows a gain (see **44.13** below);
- a transaction-based calculation shows a gain (see **44.13** below); or
- a personal portfolio bond calculation shows a gain (see **44.20** below).

There is also a chargeable event:

- in the case of a life insurance policy, on a *death* giving rise to benefits;
- on the *maturity* of a life insurance or capital redemption policy;
- on a payment on death under a life annuity contract, provided the contract was made after 9 December 1974;
- on the payment of a capital sum under a life annuity contract as a complete alternative to annuity payments or to any further annuity payments.

[*ITTOIA 2005, s 484, Sch 2 para 99*].

Exclusion of certain qualifying policies

In the case of a *qualifying policy* (see **44.27** below), any of the events in (i)–(v) below is a chargeable event only:

(a) if the policy has been converted into a paid-up policy within ten years of its issue or, if sooner, three-quarters of the term for which it has to run; or
(b) if a company has an interest in the rights in the policy at the time of the event and the policy was issued after 13 March 1989.

If the policy has been varied to increase the premiums payable, (a) above applies by reference to the date of variation. As regards (b) above, a company has an interest in the rights if a company beneficially owns them, if they are held on trusts created by a company or if they are held as security for a company's debt. A policy is *treated* as issued after 13 March 1989 if it was varied after that date to extend the term or to increase the benefits.

The said events are:

(i) death or maturity;
(ii) the surrender or assignment of all rights;
(iii) a final participation in profits;
(iv) a partial surrender or assignment where the calculation shows a gain; and
(v) where a transaction-based calculation in respect of a qualifying policy shows a gain; this applies only in relation to (a) above.

[*ITTOIA 2005, s 485(1)–(6)(8), Sch 2 para 107*].

See also **44.36–44.40** below (premium limit for qualifying policies).

Replacement of qualifying policies

Where a qualifying policy is replaced by another qualifying policy as a result of a change in the life or lives insured, the two policies are treated as a single policy issued at the time of the old policy, provided that:

- the amount due on surrender of the old policy is retained by the insurer and applied in satisfaction of premiums due under the new policy;
- no other consideration is received by any person on the replacement of the old policy by the new policy;
- the replacement policy was issued after 24 March 1982.

[*ITTOIA 2005, s 542, Sch 2 para 101*].

Disregard of certain assignments

An assignment of rights under a policy or contract or a share in such rights is ignored if it is:

- by way of security for a debt;
- on the discharge of a debt secured by the rights or share; or
- between spouses or civil partners living together.

[*ITTOIA 2005, s 487*].

Pre-26 June 1982 assignments

Where the rights in a policy or contract were assigned before 26 June 1982 for money or money's worth, a subsequent event in respect of that policy or contract is a chargeable event only if, on a date after 23 August 1982:

- the rights have reverted to the original owner; or
- there is a further assignment for money or money's worth (other than between spouses or civil partners or as security for a debt or on the discharge of a debt so secured); or
- there is a payment under the policy or contract by way of premium; or
- loans are taken against security of the policy or contract (but see below).

The last of the above points does not apply if:

- the policy or contract was made before 27 March 1974; or
- the policy is a qualifying policy (see **44.27** below), and either a commercial rate of interest is payable on the loan or it is made to a full-time employee of the insurer to assist in the purchase or improvement of the employee's only or main residence.

[*ITTOIA 2005, Sch 2 para 102*].

Cessation of premium collection on old policies

Where an insurer decides to cease collecting premiums on certain types of policy held for a specified period, and any change to the benefits is limited to a deduction of no more than the premiums forgone, a chargeable event is only treated as occurring in relation to the policy if one would have been treated as occurring had the alteration not occurred. This is dependent upon the policy being at least 20 years old at the time of the change and there being no option under the policy (whether or not previously exercised) for reduction of the premiums to a nominal amount in connection with a right to make partial surrenders after the date of the reduction. [*ITTOIA 2005, ss 488, 489*].

Exclusion of certain accident insurance policies

See HMRC SP 6/92 as regards certain accident insurance policies providing cover against dying as a result of an accident, which are not regarded as life insurance policies for these purposes and therefore cannot give rise to chargeable events. The Statement of Practice applies mainly to group policies, under which a gain might otherwise arise on payment of a death benefit as a result of earlier payments under the policy.

Divorce settlements

The transfer under a Court Order (between spouses as part of a divorce settlement) of the rights conferred by a life policy etc. is not regarded as being for money or money's worth, and thus no chargeable event can arise (Revenue Tax Bulletin December 2003 pp 1071–1073).

Computation of chargeable event gain

[44.7] Subject to the disregards below, the amount of the chargeable event gain is given by the formula TB – (TD + PG) where:

TB is the 'total benefit value' of the policy or contract;
TD is the total allowable deductions; in broad terms, the premiums paid; and
PG is the total amount of gains treated as arising on previous chargeable events (if any) in relation to the policy (including any 'related policy') or contract but only in so far as those gains have been, or fall to be, charged to tax on any person under these provisions or taken into account under the transfer of assets abroad rules at **4.14–4.18** ANTI-AVOIDANCE in calculating a person's total income. The caveat applies only in relation to policies issued, and contracts made, on or after 21 March 2012. However, it does also apply in relation to a pre-21 March 2012 policy or contract if, on or after that date, the policy or contract (i) is varied so as to increase the benefits from it or from a connected policy or contract (an exercise of rights conferred by the policy being treated for this purpose as a variation); (ii) is assigned (in whole or in part); or (iii) becomes held as security for a debt.

A '*related policy*' is one which has been replaced by a new policy by way of an option conferred by the old policy.

The '*total benefit value*' of the policy or contract is the aggregate of:

(a) the value of the policy or contract;
(b) any capital sum paid under the policy or contract before the event;
(c) the value of any other capital benefit conferred by the policy before the event;
(d) any loan made before the event which was treated as a surrender of part of the rights;
(e) in the case of guaranteed income bonds (see **44.17** below), any amount paid before the event which was treated as a surrender of part of the rights; and
(f) in the case of an assignment, the amount or value of any share in the rights assigned before the event.

For the purposes of (b)–(f) above, any 'related policy' (as above) must be taken into account.

The value of a policy or contract

The value of a policy or contract (see (a) above) is determined as follows.

- In the case of a life insurance policy, the value on a death is the surrender value immediately before death.
- In the case of an assignment of all the rights under a policy, the value of the policy is the amount or value of the consideration received. But if the assignment is between CONNECTED PERSONS (**19**), the value is the market value of the policy or contract.
- In the case of a final surrender payment under a guaranteed income bond (see **44.17** below), the value is the amount of the surrender payment.
- In any other case, the value is the total of:
  (i) any sum payable because of the event; and

(ii) in the case of a life insurance policy or capital redemption policy, the amount or value of any other benefits arising because of the event including the capital value of any periodic payments arising because of the event.

[*ITTOIA 2005, ss 491–494*].

Disregards in computing gain

A non-monetary benefit not exceeding £30 in value provided by an insurance company as an inducement to take out a policy or contract is ignored for the purposes of calculating any chargeable event gain.

In computing total benefit value, any sum paid or benefit conferred under a policy is ignored for the purposes of (b) and (c) above if it is attributable to a person's disability. For the purposes of (f) above, where a share in the rights under the policy or contract was assigned by way of gift in an 'insurance year' (see **44.13** below) beginning before 6 April 2001, the value of the share assigned is ignored.

Where a qualifying policy has been replaced, such that *ITTOIA 2005, s 542* applies (see **44.6** above) the premium paid by the insurer on the replacement is ignored in calculating both the total benefit value and the total allowable deductions.

[*ITTOIA 2005, ss 495, 497*].

Whilst not strictly a disregard, any receipt which is taken into account in calculating an amount chargeable to income tax under some other statutory tax provision or chargeable to corporation tax is deductible from the amount of the chargeable event gain. [*ITTOIA 2005, s 527*].

Deductions reduced by commission

For policies taken out on or after 21 March 2007, the amount of premiums deductible in computing most types of chargeable event gain (but not one arising from a death) is reduced by the amount of any commission attributable to those premiums that has effectively been returned to the policy holder or reinvested for his benefit; the intention is to restrict the deduction to the true cost of the policy to the policy holder. This only applies if the premiums paid exceed £100,000 in the tax year in which the chargeable event occurs or in any of the three preceding tax years. There is, however, a rule to prevent this condition being circumvented by the taking out of multiple policies. These rules also apply to a pre-21 March 2007 policy if its terms are varied or a right is exercised, so as to increase benefits, on or after that date. [*ITTOIA 2005, ss 541A, 541B*].

Rebates of annual management charges etc.

See HMRC Brief 04/13, 25 March 2013 at **49.5** MISCELLANEOUS INCOME.

The charge to tax

[44.8] Income tax is charged on the amount of the chargeable event gains arising in the tax year. See **44.13** below as to the time at which a gain arises on a *partial* surrender or partial assignment.

A chargeable event gain is designated as savings income (see **1.6** ALLOWANCES AND TAX RATES). The gain forms part of an individual's total income. If an individual falls to be treated as having paid tax at the basic rate on the amount charged (see below), the amount charged is treated as the highest part of his total income.

[*ITTOIA 2005, ss 465(5), 465A*].

Notional tax credit

Subject to the exceptions below, individuals and trustees are treated as having paid income tax at the basic rate on a chargeable event gain. The tax treated as paid is usually referred to as the '*notional tax credit*'. The notional tax credit is not in any circumstances repayable. If the chargeable event gain is reduced by any deductions at Step 2 or 3 of the calculation of income tax liability at **1.10** ALLOWANCES AND TAX RATES, the notional tax credit is computed by reference to the reduced amount.

[*ITTOIA 2005, s 530*].

If the taxpayer is not liable to income tax on his total income at any rate above the basic rate, he will thus pay no tax on the chargeable event gain. If the gain falls to be charged at the higher rate (or additional rate), then, subject to possible top slicing relief at **44.9** below, he will be liable on the gain at the excess of the higher rate (or additional rate) over the basic rate.

Exceptions

A gain arising on the following types of policy or contract does not carry a notional tax credit:

(i) a foreign policy of life insurance issued by a non-UK resident company (see **44.23** below and note the exceptions therein);
(ii) a foreign capital redemption policy (see **44.23** below);
(iii) a life insurance policy or contract for a life annuity issued by a friendly society in the course of its exempt basic life assurance and general annuity business or eligible permanent health insurance business;
(iv) a contract the effecting or carrying out of which constitutes protection business within the meaning of *FA 2012, s 62*;
(v) a contract not within (iv) but which is treated as made by *FA 2012, s 62(4)*;
(vi) a contract for a life annuity which has at any time not formed part of any insurance company's or friendly society's basic life assurance and general annuity business the income and gains of which are subject to corporation tax, unless:
   - the contract was made before 27 March 1974; or
   - it was made in an accounting period of the insurer beginning before 1 January 1992; or
   - it was an immediate needs annuity contract made before 1 January 2005.

For the sole purpose of calculating top slicing relief at **44.9** below, such gains are, however, treated as if they carried a notional tax credit.

[*ITTOIA 2005, s 531, Sch 2 paras 98, 109, 118*].

Top slicing relief

[44.9] Top slicing relief is a means by which the tax on a chargeable event gain may be reduced in the case of an individual. No claim is necessary for the relief to be given. Whilst the legislation does not restrict the availability of the relief, it is most likely to be of benefit where the gain straddles the basic rate limit, such that it is partly chargeable at the higher rate, or straddles the higher rate limit, such that it is partly chargeable at the additional rate. It could also be beneficial if a personal savings allowance is available (see **1.7** ALLOWANCES AND TAX RATES) and is not fully utilised by other savings income. The relief is given as a tax reduction (at Step 6 of the calculation of income tax liability at **1.10** ALLOWANCES AND TAX RATES) or as a tax repayment.

Top slicing relief is computed as follows.

(a) Find the '*annual equivalent*' of the chargeable event gain by dividing the amount of the gain by (normally but see below) the number of *complete* years for which the policy or contract has run before the chargeable event.

(b) Compute the tax payable on the annual equivalent on the assumptions that the chargeable event gain is limited to that amount and that it forms the highest part of the individual's total income for the tax year. Deduct from it tax at the basic rate on the annual equivalent.

(c) Multiply the amount given by (b) above by the number of years in (a) above.

(d) Compute the individual's tax liability on the chargeable event gain as if no top slicing relief applied and on the assumption that the gain forms the highest part of the individual's total income for the tax year. This liability will be net of tax at the basic rate on the gain.

(e) If the amount given by (d) above exceeds the amount given by (c) above, the difference is the amount of top slicing relief due. If there is no such excess, no top slicing relief is due.

In computing the tax liability in (b) and (d) above, ignore any lease premiums (as in **60.26** PROPERTY INCOME) and any termination payments or benefits taxable as in **18.4** COMPENSATION FOR LOSS OF EMPLOYMENT. See also **14.13** and **14.19** CHARITIES AND CHARITABLE GIVING (relief under Gift Aid and relief for gifts of property to charities to be ignored when computing top slicing relief).

If there is more than one chargeable event gain for the tax year, the above calculation is modified. The computation in (b) above is made by reference to the total of the annual equivalents in (a) above. Instead of applying (c) above, multiply the amount given by (b) by the total chargeable event gains and divide the result by the total of the annual equivalents. Then proceed with (d) and (e) as above.

Computing the annual equivalent

As stated in (a) above, the annual equivalent of the chargeable event gain is normally found by dividing the amount of the gain by the number of complete years for which the policy or contract has run before the chargeable event. If, however, there has been a previous chargeable event in respect of the policy or contract, the amount of the gain is instead divided by the number of complete years since the previous event. (For this purpose, a partial surrender or partial assignment is deemed to take place at the end of the 'insurance year' (see **44.13** below) in question.) If this is not the case but the current policy is a life insurance policy which has replaced an earlier related one, the amount of the gain is divided by the number of complete years since the date the original policy was first replaced. This does not apply in cases where the gain is reduced under *ITTOIA 2005, s 528* to take account of an individual's periods of non-UK residence (see **44.11** and **44.23** below).

Interaction with allowances and reliefs

The interaction of top slicing relief and the reduction of the personal allowance for incomes over £100,000 (see **1.17** ALLOWANCES AND TAX RATES) was discussed, and the calculations set out, in *Silver v HMRC* FTT (TC 7103), [2019] UKFTT 263 (TC) in which the taxpayer's appeal substantially succeeded. With effect for gains arising in 2019/20 onwards, the amount of the personal allowance to be included in the computation in (b) above is determined as if the chargeable event gain is limited to the annual equivalent. This means, for example, that the personal allowance is available in full in that computation if adjusted net income including the annual equivalent is less than £100,000; it gives statutory effect to the FTT decision in *Silver*. This applies only to the personal allowance and not to the amount of any other relief or allowance. The reference to 'any other relief or allowance' includes, for example, loan interest (as in **42.5** INTEREST PAYABLE).

The legislation provides for the above to have effect in relation only to chargeable event gains occurring on or after 11 March 2020, but in practice and by concession HMRC will apply the new rule to all gains arising in 2019/20 onwards (HMRC Insurance Policyholder Taxation Manual IPTM3820).

With effect in relation to chargeable event gains occurring on or after 11 March 2020, the legislation stipulates that, in each of the computations at (b) and (d) above, deductible reliefs and allowances can be set against the chargeable event gain or the annual equivalent only to the extent (if any) that they cannot be set against other income. The general rule that deductions are treated as reducing income of different descriptions in such manner as will result in the greatest reduction in income tax liability (see Steps 2 and 3 in the calculation of income tax liability at **1.10** ALLOWANCES AND TAX RATES) is disapplied for the purposes of these computations.

[*ITTOIA 2005, ss 535–537; FA 2020, s 37*].

Simon's Taxes. See **E1.455B**.

Example

[44.10]

A single policy holder realises, in 2020/21, a gain of £2,600 on a non-qualifying policy which she surrenders after 2½ years. Her other income for 2020/21 comprises employment income of £44,810, bank interest of £2,200 and dividends of £1,910.

The tax chargeable on the gain is calculated as follows.

	Normal basis	With top slicing relief
	£	£
Policy gain	2,600	1,300
Earnings	44,810	44,810
Savings income	2,200	2,200
Dividends	1,910	1,910
	51,520	50,220
Personal allowance	12,500	12,500
	£39,020	£37,720

Tax applicable to policy gain			
Higher rate			
	£		£
£1,520 at 40%	608.00		—
£220 at 40%			88.00
	608.00		88.00
Deduct			
Basic rate			
£1,520 at 20%	304.00		—
£220 at 20%			44.00
			£44.00
Appropriate multiple 2 × £44.00			£88.00
Tax chargeable lower of	£304.00	&	£88.00
top slicing relief (£304.00 – £88.00) = £216.00			
Tax payable is therefore as follows.			£

32,310	@ 20% (basic rate)	6,462.00
500	@ 0% (personal savings allowance)	—
1,700	@ 20% (basic rate on savings income)	340.00
1,910	@ 0% (dividend nil rate)	—
1,080	@ 20% (policy gain at basic rate)	216.00
37,500		
1,520	@ 40% (policy gain at higher rate)	608.00
£39,020		
		7,626.00

	Deduct: Top slicing relief (as above)	216.00
		7,410.00
Deduct:	Basic rate of tax on policy gain (£2,600 @ 20%)	520.00
	Tax liability (subject to PAYE deductions)	£6,890.00

Reduction for periods of non-UK residence

[44.11] As regards life insurance policies issued in respect of insurances made on or after 6 April 2013 and capital redemption policies made on or after that date, a chargeable event gain is reduced to take account of any periods during which the policy holder was not resident in the UK. Where connected policies or contracts fall to be treated as a single policy or contract under **44.5** above, the date of the policy or contract for these purposes is the date on which the first such policy was issued or first contract made. The reduction also applies in relation to an insurance or contract made *before* 6 April 2013 if, on or after that date, the policy or contract is varied so as to increase the benefits (an exercise of rights conferred by the policy or contract being treated for this purpose as a variation), is assigned (in whole or in part) or becomes held as security for a debt.

A similar reduction has long been available for earlier policies but only if they are foreign policies (i.e. they are issued by non-UK resident companies); see **44.23** below for details.

Main rule

The reduction applies where:

- an individual is liable for tax on a chargeable event gain on a life insurance policy or capital redemption policy; and
- there were one or more days in the 'material interest period' on which the individual was not UK resident. It does not matter whether such days fell before or on or after 6 April 2013.

The gain on which tax is chargeable is reduced by a fraction of which the denominator is the total number of days in the material interest period and the numerator is the number of those days when the individual was not UK resident. In a case where a reduction also falls to be made under **44.18** below (restricted relief qualifying policies) or **44.40** below (transitional provision), the above reduction for non-UK residence is made by reference to the gain as so reduced.

To the extent that the material interest period falls on or after 6 April 2013, the number of days when the individual was not UK resident means the number of days falling within any tax year for which the individual was not UK resident and which also fall within the material interest period. The numerator of the fraction must also include any days falling within the overseas part of any tax year that is a split year (see **63.19** RESIDENCE AND DOMICILE) as regards the individual and which also fall within the material interest period.

The '*material interest period*' means so much of the policy period (i.e. the period for which the policy, and any preceding related policy, has run before the chargeable event occurs) during which the individual meets any of the conditions in **44.3**(a)–(c) above in relation to the policy (reading the references in those conditions to rights under the policy as including a share of those rights).

If, before the chargeable event in question, there has been an assignment of rights under the policy or contract (or of a share in such rights) between spouses or civil partners living together, and the individual is the assignee, the material interest period is increased by any part of the policy period falling before the assignment during which the assignor met the said conditions and which is not already included in the material interest period. In relation to any such added period, the fraction above is determined by reference to the number of days when the *assignor* was not UK resident.

[*ITTOIA 2005, s 528; FA 2013, Sch 8 para 7*].

Reduction where the individual is deceased

A reduction similar to the one above is made if:

- personal representatives of a deceased individual are liable to income tax on a chargeable event gain on a life insurance policy or capital redemption policy and there were one or more days in the material interest period on which the deceased was not UK resident; or
- trustees are liable to income tax on a chargeable event gain on such a policy and:
  - the condition at **44.12**(b) below is met (and none of conditions **44.12**(a), (c) or (d) is met);
  - the absent settlor condition which is met is that the person who created the trusts is deceased;
  - there were one or more days in the material interest period on which the deceased was not UK resident; and
  - the death occurred either in a tax year for which the deceased was UK resident (but not one that was a split year) or in the UK part of a split year.

In this case the material interest period does not include any period falling after the date of death. To the extent that the material interest period falls on or after 6 April 2013, the same modifications apply as above.

[*ITTOIA 2005, s 528A; FA 2013, Sch 8 para 7*].

Interaction with top slicing relief

The provisions at **44.9** above regarding the operation of top slicing relief when there has been a previous chargeable event do not apply when a reduction has been made under *ITTOIA 2005, s 528* above in the case of an individual. Also, where such a reduction has been made, the figure for the number of years in the top slicing relief calculation at **44.9** is reduced by the number of complete years consisting wholly of days of non-UK residence. For 2013/14 onwards, instead of deducting complete years, the deduction is computed by taking the number of days during the material interest period on which the person concerned was not UK resident or which fall within the overseas part of a split year, dividing that number by 365 and rounding down the result to the nearest whole number. [*ITTOIA 2005, s 536(6)–(8); FA 2013, Sch 8 para 7*].

Gains arising to trustees

[44.12] Trustees are liable for tax on chargeable event gains if, immediately before the chargeable event occurs, they are UK resident and any of the conditions below are met. Where the trustees are liable, the gain is treated for income tax purposes as their income. The conditions are that the rights under the policy or contract:

(a) are held by the trustees on charitable trusts;
(b) are held by the trustees on non-charitable trusts and one or more of the absent settlor conditions (see below) is met;
(c) are held by the trustees on non-charitable trusts, none of the absent settlor conditions (see below) is met and no individual or personal representatives are chargeable; or
(d) are held as security for a debt owed by the trustees.

The third condition does not apply if the policy was effected before 9 April 2003, it was not varied on or after that date so as to increase benefits or extend the term and none of the rights were assigned to non-charitable trusts on or after that date.

The absent settlor conditions are that the person who created the trusts:

- is non-UK resident; or
- is UK resident but the gain arises in the overseas part of a tax year that is, as regards the person who created the trusts, a split year (see **63.19** RESIDENCE AND DOMICILE); or
- has died; or
- in the case of a company or foreign institution (as defined in *ITTOIA 2005, s 468* below), has been dissolved or wound up or has otherwise come to an end.

If a chargeable event gain arises to a non-charitable trust and none of the absent settlor conditions is met, a UK resident individual settlor may be liable to income tax on the gain as if it had arisen to him (see **44.3** above).

Rates at which tax charged

For charitable trusts, chargeable event gains are charged at the basic rate of tax. Due to the availability of the notional tax credit at **44.8** above, no further tax is payable. (The charge does not apply, however, if the trusts were created before 17 March 1998, the policy was issued before that date (and not varied on or after that date so as to increase benefits or extend the term) and at least one settlor died before that date.)

For non-charitable trusts, gains are chargeable at the trust rate — see **70.12** SETTLEMENTS, but the notional tax credit remains available.

[*ITTOIA 2005, s 467, Sch 2 paras 112, 114*].

Recovery of tax paid from trustees

Where an individual is charged to tax on a chargeable event gain realised by a non-charitable trust (see **44.3** above), he is entitled to recover the amount of the tax charged (as reduced by top slicing relief) from the trustees. The amount recoverable cannot exceed the amount of any sums or benefits received by the trustees from the event giving rise to the gain. The individual may require an officer of HMRC to certify the amount recoverable; such a certificate is conclusive evidence of the amount. Where an individual has recovered an amount as above at any time, and the gain is recalculated under *ITTOIA 2005, s 507A* or *s 512A* (see **44.13** below under Wholly disproportionate gains), the individual must account to the trustees for tax over-recovered. [*ITTOIA 2005, s 538; F(No 2)A 2017, s 9(4)(5)*].

Bare trusts for minors

If a gain arises to a bare trust for a minor, HMRC regard the minor himself as the person chargeable. Where, however, either or both of the child's parents are the settlors of the bare trust (see **70.7** SETTLEMENTS), the children's settlements rules at **70.30** SETTLEMENTS apply in these circumstances so that the parent is potentially the person chargeable. (HMRC Brief 51/08, 8 October 2008).

Non-resident trustees and foreign institutions

A chargeable event gain is taken into account under the 'transfer of asset abroad' rules at **4.14–4.18** ANTI-AVOIDANCE (as modified for this purpose) if:

- it arises to trustees who are not resident in the UK but would be liable if they were so resident; or
- immediately before the chargeable event, a share in the rights is owned by a foreign institution (i.e. a company or other institution resident or domiciled outside the UK) or the rights are held for the purposes of a foreign institution or a share in the rights is held as security for a debt of a foreign institution.

This does not apply if someone is liable under **44.4** above in respect of the gain.

[*ITTOIA 2005, s 468*].

Partial surrenders and partial assignments

[44.13] The following rules apply if a part of, or a share in, the rights under a policy or contract within the charging rules is surrendered or is assigned for money or money's worth. A calculation must be made as at the end of the 'insurance year' in which the surrender or assignment occurs, in order to determine whether a gain has arisen and, if so, the amount of the gain. Any such gain is generally treated as arising at the end of the insurance year and is thus chargeable to income for the tax year in which the insurance year ends (but see below under Transaction-based calculations). No chargeable event occurs as a result of a gain arising under the above calculation if the insurance year is the final insurance year (which may actually consist of a period shorter or greater than one year — see below), but receipts from a partial surrender will fall to be taken into account under **44.7** above in computing a gain on the termination chargeable event that brings the final insurance year to an end.

See below for relief from these rules where they would otherwise produce a wholly disproportionate gain. See **44.6**(iv) above for the exclusion of certain qualifying policies from these rules. Partial surrenders or assignments are sometimes treated as occurring where they would not otherwise do so — see **44.16** below.

Insurance year

An '*insurance year*' is any period of twelve months beginning on the commencement date of the policy or contract or an anniversary of that date. The termination of a policy or contract (by death, maturity or total surrender etc.) brings the then current insurance year to an end. If two insurance years consequently end in a single tax year, they are aggregated and treated as one insurance year.

Computation

The chargeable event gain on a partial surrender or partial assignment is equal to the excess (if any) of the 'net total value of rights surrendered or assigned' over the 'net total allowable payments'. See also the example at **44.14** below.

The '*net total value of rights surrendered or assigned*' is the total value of all surrenders and assignments of the policy since its commencement, less the total of such values which have been brought into account on earlier chargeable events. Surrenders or assignments are left out of this total if they occurred in an insurance year prior to the first such year falling wholly after 13 March 1975. Assignments are generally included only if made for money or money's worth, but assignments made otherwise than for money or money's worth are included if made in an insurance year beginning before 6 April 2001. The value of a partial surrender is normally the amount or value of the sum payable or other benefits arising because of the surrender. If, however, the surrender is a loan (see **44.16** below), the value is the amount of the loan. The value of a partial assignment is the surrender value of the part or share assigned as at the time of the assignment.

The '*net total allowable payments*' is the total of annual fractions of one-twentieth of the premiums paid since the policy commenced, less the total of such fractions which have been brought into account on earlier chargeable events. Annual fractions are left out of this total if they occurred in an insurance year prior to the first such year falling wholly after 13 March 1975. The total number of twentieths included in the total cannot exceed 20.

Transaction-based calculations

Special rules apply if the above computation produces a gain but during the insurance year there has been:

- a part assignment for value; or
- a part surrender followed by an assignment not for value.

In these cases, special calculations ('*transaction-based calculations*') have to be made separately for each such event during the insurance year in accordance with *ITTOIA 2005, ss 510–512*. The normal computation above takes into account the net change in a policyholder's rights under the policy from the beginning to the end of the insurance year. Transaction-based calculations look instead at each separate event within the year. The intention is to ensure that gains are attributed to the right person for tax purposes in situations where this might not otherwise be the case.

The general rule that the gain is treated as arising on the occurrence of a chargeable event at the end of the insurance year does not apply. If the transaction-based calculations show that a transaction resulted in a gain, the transaction is treated as a chargeable event. That chargeable event gain is deemed to arise at the date of the transaction, but is brought into charge for the tax year in which the insurance year ends. If the transaction occurs in the final insurance year, the chargeable event is treated as occurring before the chargeable event that ends that insurance year; there are also rules in *ITTOIA 2005, s 513* to limit the chargeable event gain. See **44.6**(v) above for the exclusion of certain qualifying policies from these rules.

For more on transaction-based calculations see HMRC Insurance Policyholder Taxation Manual IPTM3500, 3580–3595.

[*ITTOIA 2005, ss 498, 499, 507–514, Sch 2 paras 88, 100, 105*].

Wholly disproportionate gains

Legislation having effect on and after 16 November 2017 assists persons who part surrender or part assign their policies or contracts and trigger chargeable event gains far in excess of the underlying economic gain. Such persons can apply to HMRC to have the gain recalculated by HMRC on a just and reasonable basis if HMRC agree that the gain is wholly disproportionate. This applies whether the gain would otherwise be computed under the normal rules or the special rules for transaction-based calculations. The application must be received by an officer of HMRC within the four tax years following that in which the gain arose, or such longer period as the officer may agree. HMRC expect this to affect fewer than ten policy holders per year. [*ITTOIA 2005, ss 507A, 512A; F(No 2)A 2017, s 9(2)(3)*].

Example

[44.14]

Sheridan took out a policy on 4 February 2013 for a single premium of £15,000. The contract permits periodical withdrawals.

(i) Sheridan draws £750 p.a. on 4 February in each subsequent year.

There is no taxable gain because at the end of each insurance year the total value of rights surrendered (VRS) does not exceed the total allowable payments (TAP).

	£	
At 3.2.17 withdrawals have been	2,250	(VRS)
Deduct 4 × 1/20 of the sums paid in	3,000	(TAP)
	No gain	

(ii) On 20.7.17, Sheridan withdrew an additional £3,500.

	£	
At 3.2.18 withdrawals have been	6,500	(VRS)
Deduct 5 × 1/20 of the sums paid in	3,750	(TAP)
Chargeable 2017/18	£2,750	

(iii) Sheridan made no annual withdrawal on 4.2.18 but on 4.2.19 made a withdrawal of £1,000.
In the year 2019/20, the position is:

	£	£	
At 3.2.20 withdrawals have been		7,500	
Deduct Withdrawals at last charge		6,500	
		1,000	(VRS)
Deduct 7 × 1/20 of the sums paid in	5,250		
less amount deducted at last charge	3,750		
		1,500	(TAP)
		No gain	

(iv) Sheridan surrendered the policy on 1.7.20 for £13,250, having made a further £1,000 withdrawal on 4.2.20.
In the year 2020/21, the position is:

		£	£
Proceeds on surrender			13,250
Previous withdrawals			8,500
			21,750
Deduct:	Premium paid	15,000	
	Gains previously charged	2,750	
			17,750
Chargeable 2020/21			£4,000

Notes

(a) The gain on final surrender of the policy is calculated under *ITTOIA 2005, s 491* (see **44.7** above).

(b) The gains in (ii) and (iv) above are subject to any available top slicing relief (see **44.9** above).

Deficiency relief

[44.15] Relief is given (on a claim) to higher rate taxpayers for a deficiency arising on termination of a policy or contract (by death, maturity, total surrender or assignment etc.). The relief is known as '*deficiency relief*'. Deficiency relief is limited to the excess of higher rate tax or dividend upper rate tax over basic rate tax or dividend ordinary rate tax on the amount of the deficiency. The computation is illustrated by means of a series of Steps at *ITTOIA 2005, s 539(5)*, and see also HMRC Tax Bulletin April 2006 pp 1286–1288. The relief is given by means of a tax reduction at Step 6 of the calculation of income tax liability at **1.10** ALLOWANCES AND TAX RATES. (Different rules apply to deficiencies on life annuity contracts made in an accounting period of the insurance company etc. beginning before 1 January 1992 — see *ITTOIA 2005, Sch 2 para 109(4)*.)

With the introduction of the additional rate of tax and the dividend additional rate for 2010/11 onwards (see **1.3** ALLOWANCES AND TAX RATES), it should be noted that deficiency relief remains limited to the excess mentioned above. There are no plans to extend the relief to the additional rates of tax (Budget Report, 22 June 2010 p 51).

A deficiency is treated as arising from a policy or contract on a chargeable event if the termination chargeable event was preceded by one or more chargeable events on which gains accrued and no gain accrues on the termination chargeable event. If, in the calculation in **44.7** above for the termination event, the total allowable deductions equal or exceed the total benefit value, the amount of the deficiency is equal to the total previous gains. If the total benefit value exceeds the total allowable deductions, the amount of the deficiency is equal to the total previous gains less that excess.

For policies effected after 2 March 2004, the deficiency cannot exceed the aggregate amount of earlier gains on the policy that formed part of the same individual's total income for tax purposes for previous tax years; this applies equally where a policy was effected on or before 2 March 2004 but after that date is varied so as to increase the benefits (an exercise of rights conferred by the policy being treated for this purpose as a variation), assigned (in whole or in part) or becomes held as security for a debt.

[*ITTOIA 2005, ss 539–541, Sch 2 para 117; SI 2015 No 1810, Arts 1, 9; SI 2019 No 201, Arts 1, 10*].

In *Scott v HMRC* CA, [2020] STC 353, the courts rejected the taxpayer's claim that his capital gains should be charged at the lower rate of CGT as a result of a claim for deficiency relief, finding no reason to conclude that a relief from income tax should also operate as a corresponding relief from CGT.

Simon's Taxes. See **E1.455D.**

Events treated as partial surrenders or assignments

[44.16] The following events are treated as partial surrenders for the purposes of **44.13** above:

(a) the falling due of a sum payable as a result of a right under a policy or contract to participate in profits where further rights remain under it;

(b) in the case of a contract for a life annuity which provides for a capital sum to be taken as an alternative in part to the annuity payments, taking the capital sum;
(c) the making of a loan as outlined below;
(d) the making of certain payments under guaranteed income bonds (see **44.17** below).

Loans

Subject to the exclusions below, (c) above applies to a loan made by the insurer under a policy or contract to an individual or trustees who would be liable to tax if a chargeable event gain were to arise on that policy or contract. A loan is treated as made by an insurer if it is made by arrangement with the insurer, and a loan is treated as made to a person if it is made at that person's direction. Policies or contracts made before 27 March 1974 are excluded. For policies or contracts made before 9 April 2003, loans to trustees are excluded.

These provisions do not apply to a loan made under a contract for a life annuity if all the interest on the loan is eligible for tax relief as in **42.12** INTEREST PAYABLE. If part of the interest is eligible for tax relief, these provisions apply only to the part of the loan carrying interest which is not eligible.

These provisions do not apply if the policy is a qualifying policy (see **44.27** below) and:

- interest is payable on the loan at a commercial rate; and/or
- the loan was made before 6 April 2000 to a full-time employee of the body issuing the policy to assist the employee in purchasing or improving a dwelling to be used as his only or main residence.

Partial assignments on co-ownership transactions

Where, as a result of any transaction:

- the whole or part of (or a share in) the rights conferred by a policy or contract (the '*ownership interest*') becomes beneficially owned by one person or by two or more persons jointly or in common (the '*new ownership*');
- immediately before that transaction the ownership interest was in the beneficial ownership of one person or two or more persons jointly (the '*old ownership*'); and
- at least one person is common to both the old and the new ownership;

the transaction is treated as having been the assignment by each of the old owners of so much (if any) of his old share as exceeds his new share (if any). The old and new shares in cases of joint ownership are treated as having been equal shares. These provisions generally do not apply in relation to transactions that took place in an insurance year beginning before 6 April 2001.

[*ITTOIA 2005, ss 500–503, 505, 506, Sch 2 paras 87, 97, 115*].

Guaranteed income bonds

[44.17] A guaranteed income bond is a life assurance contract within *Financial Services and Markets Act 2000 (Regulated Activities) Order 2001 (SI 2001 No 544), Sch 1 Pt II para 1 or 3* which is neither an annuity contract nor a contract effected in the course of a company's pension business. Such a bond is designed to provide an income each year with a lump sum on maturity. A payment under a guaranteed income bond which would otherwise be treated as interest or an annual payment is not so treated but is instead treated as a partial surrender as in **44.13** above. However, this treatment does *not* apply to a payment if:

- it is a payment under provisions in the policy which, if taken alone, would constitute a different kind of policy, e.g. a permanent health policy; or
- it is interest on a late payment under the policy.

If a payment under the bond comprises the whole of the final benefit due under the policy (disregarding any interest on late payments) and would otherwise be treated as interest or an annual payment, it is not so treated but is instead treated as a surrender of all the rights under the contract.

[*ITTOIA 2005, ss 490, 500(d), 504*].

Restricted relief qualifying policies

[44.18] *ITTOIA 2005, s 485* (exclusion of certain qualifying policies — see **44.6** above) does not apply in relation to a policy which is a 'restricted relief qualifying policy' (for which see **44.37** below). If, as a result, an individual is liable for tax on a chargeable event gain, the amount of the gain on which the tax is charged is reduced by the amount produced by the fraction:

$$G \times \frac{TAP}{TP}$$

where:

G	=	the chargeable event gain before the reduction;
TAP	=	the total premiums payable during the period for which the policy has run before the chargeable event occurs insofar as they are 'allowable premiums' (see below); and
TP	=	the total premiums payable during the period for which the policy has run before the chargeable event occurs.

If the policy is a 'new policy' in relation to another policy, it is treated as having run from the issue of the other policy or, if the other policy was also a new policy in relation to an earlier policy, from the issue of the earlier policy, and so on. References to premiums payable are to be read as including references to premiums payable under any earlier policy so taken into account. A '*new policy*' is one issued in substitution for, or on the maturity of and in consequence of an option conferred by, another policy (see *ICTA 1988, Sch 15 para 17*).

In determining the premiums payable under a policy, any provision for the waiver of premiums by reason of a person's disability is to be ignored.

So much of a premium payable under a policy as is charged on the grounds of exceptional risk of death or disability is to be left out of account in determining the premiums payable. So much of the first premium payable under a policy the liability for the payment of which is discharged from the proceeds of another policy is also to be left out of account in determining the premiums payable; the maximum that can be left out of account under this rule is £3,600 x N, where N is the number of complete years for which ran the other policy involved (or, if there is more than one other policy involved, the policy which ran for the most number of complete years).

[*ITTOIA 2005, s 463A*].

Allowable premiums

The following apply for the purpose of determining '*allowable premiums*' in applying the above fraction.

A premium under a policy is allowable if it is paid before the '*restricted relief date*', i.e. the date on which the policy became a restricted relief qualifying policy or, if earlier, 6 April 2013.

Premiums payable under a policy in a 'relevant premium period' are allowable insofar as they do not exceed in total the 'premium limit' for the period. (This does not apply if, at the time the policy became a restricted relief qualifying policy, any 'related policy' was itself a restricted relief qualifying policy.) A '*relevant premium period*' is any period of one year that begins with a 'relevant date' and ends during the period for which the policy runs before the chargeable event occurs (the '*policy period*'). A relevant premium period also begins with the last relevant date to fall within the policy period and ends at the time of the chargeable event. '*Relevant date*' means the restricted relief date or any anniversary of the restricted relief date. The '*premium limit*' for a relevant premium period is determined by looking at the total premiums payable in the relevant premium period under 'related policies'. If that total is £3,600 or more, the premium limit is nil (and, accordingly, no premiums payable under the policy in question in the relevant premium period are allowable). If that total is less than £3,600, the premium limit is the difference between that total and £3,600.

For the above purposes, a policy is a '*related policy*' as regards the policy in question if it met the following requirements at the time the policy in question became a restricted relief qualifying policy:

(a) the policy is a qualifying policy under which the individual is a beneficiary (for which see **44.36** below); and
(b) it is neither a protected policy (see **44.38** below) nor a pure protection policy (see **44.36** below).

A policy which is a 'new policy' (see above) in relation to a related policy is also a related policy if it meets the said requirements. A policy ceases to be a related policy if it ceases to meet those requirements.

If:

- a premium ('premium A') is payable under a policy on a day ('day A') which is on or after 21 March 2012 but before 6 April 2013, and

- the next premium payable under the policy is payable on a day ('day B') which is both on or after 6 April 2013 and more than one month after day A,

premium A is treated for the above purposes as if, instead of being one premium payable on day A, it were a series of premiums payable at monthly intervals with the first premium in the series being payable on day A. The number of premiums in the series is equal to the number of complete months in the period beginning with day A and ending with day B. The amount of each premium is the amount of premium A divided by the number of premiums in the series.

[*ITTOIA 2005, s 463B*].

Personal representatives and trusts with deceased settlors

Provisions similar to those above apply where:

- personal representatives would be liable for any tax charged by reason of a chargeable event (see **44.3** above); or
- trustees would be liable for any such tax (see **44.12** above) in a case where the condition at **44.12**(b) is met and the person who created the trusts has died.

For these purposes, (a) above is modified to read: the policy is a qualifying policy under which the deceased was a beneficiary. A policy which would otherwise have ceased to be a related policy on the deceased's death, but continues to run after the death, is treated as a related policy after the death. A policy which is a 'new policy' (see above) in relation to a policy thus treated as a related policy is also a related policy if, apart from the death, it would meet the requirements of (a) and (b) above on its issue. A policy ceases to be treated as a related policy if, apart from the death, it would cease to meet those requirements.

[*ITTOIA 2005, s 463C*].

Assignments and subsequent events

Where:

- **44.36**(A)–(C) below apply in consequence of an event relating to the policy (the '*relevant event*'), and
- the policy is not a qualifying policy after the relevant event because of the provisions at **44.36**,

then, in relation to an event occurring after the relevant event, the reduction in *ITTOIA 2005, s 463A* above applies to a chargeable event gain if such a reduction would have applied but for the provisions at **44.36**. In ascertaining the 'relevant premium period' under *ITTOIA 2005, s 463B* above, the 'policy period' is limited to the part of that period falling before the relevant event. [*ITTOIA 2005, s 463D*].

Simon's Taxes. See **E1.452CA**.

Information requirements

[44.19] To assist policy holders in completing their self-assessment tax returns, insurers must issue them with a certificate in relation to a chargeable event gain. In certain circumstances insurers must send a similar certificate to HMRC. In each case the certificate must normally show *inter alia* the amount of the gain, the number of years for computing top slicing relief and the notional tax credit (where available). [*ICTA 1988, ss 552, 552ZA*].

For the requirement for most overseas insurers (as widely defined) to nominate a UK tax representative responsible for providing such information, see *ICTA 1988, ss 552A, 552B* and regulations thereunder.

Qualifying policies

Under regulations made by the Commissioners for HMRC, individuals who are beneficiaries under qualifying policies are obliged to provide information to the issuer of the policy on the occurrence of certain events — see **44.39** below. Also under those regulations, issuers must pass on this information to HMRC and provide information as to premiums payable. The information must be provided to HMRC within three months after the end of the tax year in which it is received. Information as to premiums must also be provided in relation to any policy which ceased, terminated, matured, or in relation to which the premiums payable have reduced, in that tax year. These requirements do not apply to qualifying policies issued before 6 April 2013 or to 'pure protection policies' (as defined in **44.36** below). [*ICTA 1988, ss 552ZB, 552B(2); SI 2013 No 1820, Reg 5*].

Personal portfolio bonds

[44.20] A 'personal portfolio bond' generally enables the holder to nominate a portfolio of investments on which the interest and capital gains are deferred until the bond matures. The legislation counters this deferral by imposing an annual income tax charge in addition to any other charge under the life assurance gains provisions.

A '*personal portfolio bond*' is a life assurance policy, life annuity contract or capital redemption policy which meets both the following conditions.

(a) Under the terms of the policy or contract, some or all of the benefits are determined by reference to:
   - fluctuations in, or in an index of, the value of property of any description; or
   - the value of, or the income from, property of any description.

   It does not matter whether or not the index or property is specified in the policy or contract.
(b) The terms of the policy or contract permit the policy holder to select the index or some or all of the property. This condition is extended to also include persons connected with the policy holder, persons acting on his behalf etc.

There are, however, exclusions where the only property or index which may be selected is of a description contained in *ITTOIA 2005, ss 517–521*.

The annual charge operates by applying, at the end of each 'insurance year' (as defined in **44.13** above) other than the final insurance year, the formula (PP + TPE – TSG) × 15%, where:

PP is the total amount of premiums paid up to the end of the insurance year in relation to that year;
TPE is the total amount of personal portfolio bond excesses (see below); and
TSG is the total amount of partial surrender gains (see below).

TPE is found by applying the same formula as above for each previous insurance year for which the policy has been in existence, starting with the first year, and aggregating the results. Any years when the policy was not a personal portfolio bond are nevertheless included in the calculation. If there is no previous insurance year, TPE is zero.

TSG is the aggregate of all previous chargeable event gains (if any) computed as in **44.13** above but ignoring any partial assignments.

If the policy is a personal portfolio bond at the end of an insurance year, the amount arrived at by applying the above formula is a chargeable event gain deemed to arise at the end of that insurance year. It will this be chargeable to income tax in the tax year in which that insurance year ends. No top slicing relief is available.

[*ITTOIA 2005, ss 515–526, 535(6); F(No 2)A 2017, s 10; SI 2017 No 1182*].

See HMRC Insurance Policyholder Taxation Manual IPTM7700 *et seq.*

Simon's Taxes. See **E1.454** *et seq.*

Offshore policies

[44.21] A policy issued in respect of an insurance made after 17 November 1983 by a company resident outside the UK (a '*new non-resident policy*') will not be a qualifying policy under *ICTA 1988, Sch 15 Pt II* (see **44.27** below) until the premiums are payable to, and are business receipts of, a UK branch/permanent establishment of the issuing company, and the company is lawfully carrying on life assurance business in the UK.

[*ICTA 1988, Sch 15 para 24; FA 1995, s 55(5)(9)*].

If at any time a previously qualifying new non-resident policy ceases to fulfil the conditions of either (a) or (b) above, it is brought within the chargeable events legislation from that time onwards.

If, immediately before the happening of a chargeable event, an otherwise qualifying policy forms part of the overseas life assurance business of an insurance company or friendly society, it is not treated as a qualifying policy in relation to that event. The gain is chargeable to income tax as in **44.23** below, without the benefit of a notional tax credit.

[*ITTOIA 2005, ss 474(4)(5), 476(3), 531(3)(b)*].

Similar treatment applies to foreign capital redemption policies with a non-UK policy holder (i.e. a capital redemption policy which forms part of the overseas life assurance business of an insurance company). [*ITTOIA 2005, ss 476(3), 531(3)(d)*].

Simon's Taxes. See **E1.441**, **E1.443**, **E1.1340** *et seq.*

Substitution of policies

[44.22] Where one policy is substituted for another and the old policy was a new non-resident policy (as in **44.21** above) but the new policy is not, the rules in *ICTA 1988, Sch 15 paras 17–20* (see **44.35**(d) below) are modified as follows.

(a) If the old policy and any related policy (any preceding policy in a chain of substituted policies) would have been (or, where certification was required, would have been capable of being) a qualifying policy were it not for the new non-resident policy rules, then it is assumed to have been a qualifying policy for the purposes of *ICTA 1988, Sch 15 para 17(2)*. In determining whether a policy would have been (or would have been capable of being) a qualifying policy, *ICTA 1988, Sch 15 para A1* (see **44.36** below) and *paras B1–B3* (see **44.33**, **44.34** and **44.39** below) are to be ignored, but this does not affect the application of any of those paragraphs to the new policy.

(b) If the new policy would otherwise be (or, where certification is required, be capable of being) a qualifying policy, it will nevertheless not qualify unless the circumstances are those specified in *ICTA 1988, Sch 15 para 17(3)* (regarding residence, benefits, the issuing company etc.).

(c) The company issuing the new policy must certify that the old policy for which it is substituted was issued by a company outside the UK with whom they have arrangements for issuing substitute policies to persons coming to the UK.

The modification in (c) above also applied where the old policy was a qualifying policy issued on or before 17 November 1983 which would have been a non-qualifying new non-resident policy if issued after that date while the new policy is issued after that date and is not a new non-resident policy.

If the new policy confers an option to have another policy substituted for it or to have any of its terms changed and thereby falls within *ICTA 1988, Sch 15 para 19(3)* it is to be treated for the purposes of that sub-paragraph as having been issued in respect of an insurance made on the same day as the old policy. [*ICTA 1988, Sch 15 paras 25, 26*].

Tax on chargeable events

[44.23] Gains from foreign policies of life insurance issued by a non-UK resident company are fully chargeable to income tax without the benefit of a notional tax credit. This denial of notional tax credit does not apply if the conditions in (a) or (b) in **44.21** above are fulfilled at all times between the date of issue and the date of the gain, or to gains on certain policies issued by non-UK resident companies within the charge to tax in a territory within the European Economic Area. Similarly, no notional tax credit is available on gains from foreign capital redemption policies, i.e. capital redemption policies issued by non-UK resident companies. [*ITTOIA 2005, ss 474(4), 476(3), 531, 532, Sch 2 paras 103, 104, 111, 113*].

Reduction of chargeable event gain

For policies issued, and contracts made, before 6 April 2013, there is special provision in respect of foreign policies of life insurance or capital redemption to take account of periods when the policy holder is non-UK resident (see **44.21** above with regard to notional tax credit in relation to these policies). Except as below, the gain which would be chargeable is reduced. The amount of the reduction is found by multiplying the gain by the fraction of which the denominator is the number of days in the policy period (i.e. the period for which the policy, and any preceding related policy, has run before the chargeable event) and the numerator is the number of those days when the policy holder was not UK resident. To the extent (if any) that the policy period falls on or after 6 April 2013, the number of days when the policy holder was not UK resident means the number of days falling within any tax year for which the policy holder was not UK resident and which also fall within the policy period. The numerator must also include any days falling within the overseas part of any tax year that is a split year (see **63.19** RESIDENCE AND DOMICILE) as regards the policy holder and which also fall within the policy period.

No reduction is, however, made where, at any time during the life of the policy, it was held either:

(a) by a trustee resident outside the UK, or by two or more trustees any of whom was so resident, *unless* the policy was issued in respect of an insurance made on or before 19 March 1985 *and* it was on that date held by a trustee resident outside the UK or by two or more trustees any of whom was so resident, or

(b) by a '*foreign institution*' (i.e. a company or other institution of non-UK residence or domicile) *unless* the policy was issued in respect of an insurance made on or before 16 March 1998 *and* it was on that date held by a foreign institution.

The gain thus reduced is chargeable to tax in full (see above) but any top slicing relief due (see **44.9** above) is computed as if the notional tax credit were available.

[*ITTOIA 2005, ss 528, 529, 531(1), Sch 2 para 106, 110*].

The figure for the number of years in the top slicing relief calculation at **44.9** above is reduced by the number of days during the policy period on which the policy holder was not UK resident or which fall within the overseas part of a split year, dividing that number by 365 and rounding down the result to the nearest whole number. [*ITTOIA 2005, s 536(7)(8)*]. The provisions at **44.9** above regarding the operation of top slicing relief when there has been a previous chargeable event do not apply to foreign life assurance or capital redemption policies. [*ITTOIA 2005, s 536(6)*].

For policies issued, and contracts made, on or after 6 April 2013, provision for reducing the chargeable event gain to take account of periods when the policy holder was not UK resident is extended to all life insurance policies and capital redemption policies, and not just foreign policies. See **44.11** above for these rules.

Substitution of policies

Where there is a substitution of policies in circumstances where the old policy was a new non-resident policy (as in **44.21** above) and the new policy is not, but the new policy is a qualifying policy, there is no chargeable event on the surrender of rights under the old policy. The new policy is treated as having been issued in respect of an insurance made on the same day as the old policy. [*ITTOIA 2005, ss 485(7), 543*].

Friendly Society policies

Qualifying policies

[44.24] The proceeds from a qualifying policy with a friendly society are generally free of any income tax charge.

Except as below, any policy issued by a friendly society before 19 March 1985 in the course of its exempt basic life assurance and general annuity business or eligible permanent health insurance business is a qualifying policy. [*ICTA 1988, Sch 15 paras 6(1), 6A*]. A policy issued *or varied* after 18 March 1985 in the course of such business is a qualifying policy only if it satisfies the conditions set out in *ICTA 1988, Sch 15 paras 3, 4*.

Certain policies issued under contracts made before 20 March 1991, and expressed at the outset not to be made in the course of tax-exempt life or endowment business, were subsequently determined to have been within the statutory definition of that business. A similar situation arose in relation to certain contracts for qualifying policies assumed, at the outset of the contract, not to be made in the course of tax-exempt life or endowment business (without being expressed either to be or not to be so). By concession, the policy holder is taxed in accordance with the original assumption he will have been given that no charge to tax would arise on the surrender or maturity of the policy. (Revenue Press Release 12 June 1991).

Non-qualifying policies

[44.25] A gain on a chargeable event in respect of a policy which is not a qualifying policy (see **44.24** above), or in respect of certain life annuity contracts, may give rise to a charge to income tax (see **44.5** above). If such a gain arises on a policy issued in the course of a society's exempt basic life assurance and general annuity business or eligible permanent health insurance business, it is fully chargeable to income tax, with no notional tax credit but with the availability of top slicing relief (see **44.9** above). [*ITTOIA 2005, s 531(1), (3)(a)*].

Individual limit

[44.26] The total amount of business which a person may have outstanding with registered or incorporated friendly societies is limited as set out below. If a person obtains a policy which causes his contracts to exceed these limits, the policy will not be a qualifying policy (as in **44.24** above), but earlier policies are not thereby disqualified. [*ICTA 1988, Sch 15 para 6(2)*].

Such business is limited to:

- an annuity or annuities totalling not more than £156 p.a. (£416 p.a. where all the contracts were made before 14 March 1984); and
- a gross sum assured under a contract or contracts under which the total premiums payable in any twelve-month period do not exceed any of the following limits:

for all contracts	£270
for contracts made after 24 July 1991 and before 1 May 1995	£200
for contracts made after 31 August 1990 and before 25 July 1991	£150
for contracts made before 1 September 1990	£100

unless all the contracts were made before 1 September 1987. For these purposes, a premium under an annuity contract made before 1 June 1984 by a friendly society other than an 'old society' is brought into account as if the contract were for the assurance of a gross sum. For contracts made before 1 September 1987, a limit was imposed by reference to the gross sum(s) assured, the limit being £750 (£2,000 if all the contracts were made before 14 March 1984). Where the premium under a contract made after 31 August 1987 and before 1 May 1995 is increased by a variation after 24 July 1991 and before 1 August 1992 or after 30 April 1995 and before 1 April 1996, the contract is to be treated for these purposes as having been made at the time of the variation.

No account is, however, taken of:

- so much of any premium as relates to exceptional death risk;
- 10% of premiums payable more frequently than annually; and
- £10 of the premiums payable in a twelve-month period under any contract made before 1 September 1987 by an 'old society'.

The restrictions on both gross sum and annuity contracts are applied without taking into account any bonus or addition declared upon an assurance or accruing thereon by reference to an increase in the value of any investments. An annuity contract made before 1 June 1984 by a friendly society other than an 'old society' is for these purposes treated as providing both the annual sum assured and a gross sum equal to 75% of the premiums which would be payable if the annuity ran its full term or the person died at age 75.

In relation to contracts made after 18 July 2007, any friendly society policy transferred to an insurance company counts towards the above limits. This includes policies which have become insurance company policies because the friendly society converted to a company.

An '*old society*' is either (i) a registered friendly society which was registered before 4 February 1966, society which either was registered after 3 May 1966; (ii) a registered friendly society which was registered between 4 February 1966 and 3 May 1966 inclusive and which on or before the latter date carried on any life or endowment business; or (iii) an incorporated friendly society which, before its incorporation, was a registered friendly society within (i) or (ii).

[*FA 2012, ss 160, 161; ICTA 1988, ss 464, 466(2)*].

Qualifying policies

[44.27] A policy is a '*qualifying policy*' if it fulfils the conditions at **44.28–44.30** below, subject to the exemptions at **44.31** below and the disqualifications at **44.32–44.34** below. [*ICTA 1988, Sch 15 para 21*].

See **44.21** above for conditions relating to 'new non-resident policies' issued in respect of an insurance made by a company not resident in the UK.

See also **44.36–44.40** below (premium limit for qualifying policies).

Simon's Taxes. See **E1.1311, E1.1320–E1.1324.**

Policies payable only on death (or earlier disability) within a specified period (term assurance)

[44.28] The following apply if a policy is to be a qualifying policy.

(a) If the period *does not exceed ten years*, any surrender value must not exceed the return of premiums paid. [*ICTA 1988, Sch 15 para 1(4)*].

(b) If the specified term *exceeds ten years*, premiums must be payable at yearly, or shorter intervals, during at least ten years or three-quarters of the term, whichever is less, or until the assured's earlier death (or disability), and those payable in any one year, excluding any loading for exceptional mortality risk, must not exceed:
   (i) twice the amount of the premiums payable in any other year; nor
   (ii) one-eighth of the total premiums which would be payable if the policy ran for the full term (or, if appropriate, the sooner of ten years or three-quarters of the term). [*ICTA 1988, Sch 15 para 1(3)(8)*].

(c) For policies issued on or after 1 April 1976, if the specified term ends after the age of 75 years and the policy provides for any payment on the whole or partial surrender of the policy, the capital sum payable on death must not be less than 75% of the total premiums payable if death occurred at 75 years of age. In the case of a policy payable on one of two lives, the age of the older is taken if the sum is payable on the death of the first, and the age of the younger is taken if payment arises on the death of the survivor. If limited to death after 16 (or some lower age) the benefit on earlier death must not exceed the return of premiums paid. [*ICTA 1988, Sch 15 para 1(5)*].
   In calculating total premiums, there will be ignored any weighting due to premiums being payable at lesser than annual intervals (generally taken to be 10% if the reduction is not specified) and in calculating the capital sum, the smallest amount is used if more than one is payable. [*ICTA 1988, Sch 15 para 1(6)(9)*].

Short-term assurances

A policy will not be a qualifying policy under **44.27** above if the capital sum is payable only if death or disability occurs less than one year after making the insurance. [*ICTA 1988, Sch 15 para 10*].

Endowment policies

[44.29] The following apply if a policy is to be a qualifying policy. The term must be for at least ten years, or until the assured's earlier death (or disability). The policy must not provide for any capital benefit to be paid (other than on whole or part surrender of the policy or bonus additions to it or on disability) during its continuance, but it must guarantee on death (or death after 16 or some lower specified age) a sum at least equal to 75% of the total premiums (less any weighting due to premiums being paid at lesser than annual intervals, generally taken to be 10% if the reduction is not specified) which would be payable if the policy ran full term. For a policy effected on or after 1 April 1976 by a person over 55 years of age, the 75% requirement is reduced by 2% for each year the age exceeds 55. If limited to death after 16 (or some lower age) the benefit on earlier death must not exceed the return of premiums paid.

Premiums must be payable annually, or at shorter intervals, for a period of not less than ten years or until death etc. Limitations (i) and (ii) under **44.28**(b) above apply, but with exclusion of wording in brackets at end of (ii). For a policy payable on one of two lives, the rules under **44.28**(c) above apply. [*ICTA 1988, Sch 15 para 2*].

Whole-life policies

[44.30] If a policy is to be a qualifying policy, premiums must be payable annually, or at shorter intervals, until the assured's death (or his earlier disability, if so provided) or for a specified period of at least ten years should he live longer than that period. Premium limitations (i) and (ii) under **44.28**(b) above apply except that the total premiums under (ii) are those for the first ten years or for the specified period, as above, if longer. The provisions under **44.28**(c) above also apply. [*ICTA 1988, Sch 15 para 1(2)*].

Exemptions

[44.31] The above restrictions do not apply to the following.

(i) Policies solely for the payment on an individual's death (or disability) of a sum substantially equal to the then balance of a mortgage (repayable by annual, or shorter, instalments) on his residence or business premises. [*ICTA 1988, s 266(10)(a)*].

(ii) Policies under a sponsored superannuation scheme (as defined by *ICTA 1988, s 624*), if at least half the cost of the scheme is borne by the employer. This provision was repealed on 6 April 1980, but is continued, for policies issued before that date, by extra-statutory concession (HMRC ESC A32).

(iii) Policies issued in connection with a pre-6 April 2006 approved occupational pension scheme under *ICTA 1988, s 590 et seq*. [*ICTA 1988, s 266(10)(b)*].

Although the above policies are not qualifying policies, they are not subject to the charge on life assurance gains (see **44.3** *et seq*. above).

Certain policies issued by a friendly society are qualifying policies. See **44.24** above.

Disqualification of certain connected policies

[44.32] A policy (issued in the UK or elsewhere) evidencing a contract of long-term insurance (within *SI 2001 No 544, Sch 1 Pt II*) is not a qualifying policy if it is 'connected with' another policy the terms of which provide benefits greater than would reasonably be expected if any policy 'connected with' it were disregarded.

A policy is '*connected with*' another policy if:

(a) they are at any time simultaneously in force; and
(b) either of them is issued with reference to the other, or with a view to enabling or facilitating the other to be issued on particular terms. (See Revenue Press Release 16 June 1980 for guidelines.)

This applies to policies issued in respect of insurances made after 25 March 1980 and to an insurance made on or before that date which is connected with one made after it, but not in relation to premiums paid before that date on the earlier policy.

In relation to policies issued in respect of insurances made after 22 August 1983, the above restriction applies where either of the policies concerned provides such excessive benefits as are mentioned above. With respect to payments made after 22 August 1983, this extension of the restriction also applies to insurances made before that date if further premiums exceeding £5 p.a. are made after that date.

[*ICTA 1988, Sch 15 para 14*].

Rights to be beneficially owned by individuals

[44.33] A policy issued in respect of an insurance made on or after 6 April 2013 can be a qualifying policy only if, when it is issued, all the rights under it are beneficially owned by an individual or by two or more individuals taken together. This does not apply if the policy is 'protected'. For this purpose a policy is '*protected*' if it is a 'new policy' in relation to a policy issued in respect of an insurance made before 21 March 2012 or in relation to a policy which is itself protected by this rule. A '*new policy*' is one issued in substitution for, or on the maturity of and in consequence of an option conferred by, another policy (see *ICTA 1988, Sch 15 para 17*). [*ICTA 1988, Sch 15 para B1*].

Effect of assignments

[44.34] If any rights under a qualifying policy are (or any share in any such rights is) assigned on or after 6 April 2013, the policy is *not* a qualifying policy after the assignment. However, this rule is disapplied if the assignment:

(a) is from an individual by way of security for a debt of his; or
(b) is to an individual on the discharge of a debt of his secured by the rights (or share); or
(c) is from an individual to the individual's spouse or civil partner; or
(d) is to an individual in pursuance of a court order; or

(e) is to an individual in pursuance of a legally enforceable obligation relating to a divorce or dissolution of a civil partnership; or
(f) is from an individual where, as a result of the assignment, the rights assigned are (or the share assigned is) held on trusts created by the individual; or
(g) is to an individual where, as a result of the assignment, the rights assigned are (or the share assigned is) no longer held on trusts; or
(h) is to the personal representatives of a deceased individual; or
(i) is to an individual where, as a result of the assignment, a 'deceased beneficiary event' (see **44.36** below) occurs; or
(j) meets conditions prescribed by any regulations that the Commissioners for HMRC may make for this purpose.

[*ICTA 1988, Sch 15 para B2*].

Simon's Taxes. See E1.1334.

General notes on qualifying policies

[44.35] The following should be taken into account.

(a) '*Capital sum*' includes a series of capital sums, or a sum varying with the circumstances. Bonus additions, an option to take an annuity, a payment on whole or part surrender, or a waiver of premiums in the event of disability *do not constitute 'benefits'*. [*ICTA 1988, Sch 15 para 1(7)(9)*].
(b) For *industrial assurance* policies and *family income* and *mortgage protection* policies, see *ICTA 1988, Sch 15 paras 7–9*. After 1 April 1976, industrial assurance policies are generally regarded as qualifying policies even if not meeting all the appropriate conditions. Industrial assurance ceased to be a distinct form of business for tax purposes for accounting periods beginning after 31 December 1995. However, the special treatment afforded to industrial assurance policies continues to be given to policies issued by any company on or after 1 December 2001, provided that the company had previously issued qualifying policies in the course of industrial assurance business and was, on 28 November 1995, offering such policies of the same type as those offered on or after 1 December 2001. [*ICTA 1988, Sch 15 paras 8, 8A; SI 2001 No 3643*].
(c) A variation after 19 March 1968 to a policy taken out before that date so as to increase benefits or extend term ranks as a new policy. [*ICTA 1988, Sch 14 para 8(1)(2)*]. See also **44.6** above as regards cessation of premium collection on certain old policies which is not regarded as a variation.
(d) Where, after 24 March 1982, a qualifying policy is replaced by another qualifying policy as a result of a variation in the life or lives assured (e.g. on marriage or divorce), both policies are treated for the following purposes as a single qualifying policy made at the time of the earlier policy provided that (a) any sum becoming payable in connection with the earlier policy is retained by the insurer and applied towards any premium on the later policy and (b) no consideration (apart from the

benefits under the new policy) is received by any person in connection with the ending of the earlier policy. Any sum applied as in (a) is not treated as a premium for the purposes of life assurance gain computations (see **44.3** *et seq*. above). [*ICTA 1988, Sch 14 para 8(6), Sch 15 para 20*].

Where a premium increases or decreases in connection with an exceptional risk of disability or death, this is not considered for tax purposes as a variation in the terms of the policy and, consequently, there is no need to consider whether or not a qualifying policy retains its status as such. A similar disregard applies to any amendment made to the policy by the insertion, variation or removal of a provision under which, on the grounds of such exceptional risk, a sum may become chargeable as a debt against the capital sum guaranteed. [*ICTA 1988, Sch 15 para 18(4)*].

The transfer under a Court Order (between spouses as part of a divorce settlement) of the rights conferred by a policy is regarded as being for no consideration, and thus the policy may continue to attract life assurance premium relief.

For the effect of other substitutions for, and variations to, policies generally, see *ICTA 1988, Sch 15 paras 17–20.*

(e) Any option to vary a policy issued before 1 April 1976 is disregarded until it is exercised and the policy is then subject to the new qualifying conditions. A policy issued after 1 April 1976 with an option to vary the terms or to have another policy issued in substitution for it is only a qualifying policy if all the specified conditions would continue to be satisfied after the exercise of the option. [*ICTA 1988, Sch 15 para 19*].

(f) As a result of legal advice received, HMRC have not, since 24 February 1988, certified as a qualifying policy any new life assurance policy which may be converted or fundamentally restructured in such a way as to constitute, under contract law, a rescission of the original contract and the creation of a new one, e.g. the conversion of a whole life policy to an endowment policy or vice versa. Such conversions etc. may arise by means of an agreement between the policy holder and the insurer or by the exercising of an option contained in the terms of the policy. Previously, such alterations were regarded as variations of the existing contract which did not, therefore, prejudice the qualifying status of the policy. Policies certified and sold before 25 February 1988 will not lose their qualifying status even if subsequently converted or restructured. (Revenue Press Release 22 January 1988).

(g) HMRC may, by concession, disregard certain minor infringements of the conditions for recognition as a qualifying policy relating to:

   (i) policies back-dated by not more than three months, which may for certain purposes be treated as if the assurance was made on the earlier date;
   (ii) reductions in first year premiums which do not result in any value being credited to the policy holder;
   (iii) trivial non-recurring infringements of arithmetical tests; and
   (iv) policies which could have been certified as qualifying but which were not so certified when the assurance was made.

   (HMRC ESC A41).

(h) In determining whether any policy is a qualifying policy, there is to be disregarded so much of any premium as is charged on the grounds of exceptional risk of death or disability and any provision under which, on those grounds, a sum may become chargeable as a debt against the capital sum guaranteed on death or disability. [*ICTA 1988, Sch 15 para 12*].

(i) If a qualifying policy has either lapsed or been converted to a paid-up policy because of a failure to pay the premiums, it can be reinstated as a qualifying policy on the same terms provided:
- the reinstatement occurs within 13 months after the due date of the first unpaid premium; and
- the policy holder pays all the unpaid premiums before reinstatement.

The policy will be treated for tax purposes as if it has continued without interruption. A similar rule applies if, instead of being reinstated, the policy is replaced by another policy in the same terms. [*ICTA 1988, Sch 15 para 20ZA*].

Premium limit for qualifying policies

[44.36] If a 'post-5 April 2013 relevant event' (see below) occurs, the policy to which the event relates is *not* a qualifying policy after the event if an individual who is a beneficiary under the policy (see below) is in breach of the premium limit for qualifying policies. An individual is in breach of this limit if the total premiums payable under 'relevant policies' in any 'relevant period' exceeds **£3,600**. See HMRC Insurance Policyholder Taxation Manual IPTM2073.

'*Relevant policies*' comprise the policy to which the event relates and any other qualifying policy (see **44.27** above), apart from a 'protected policy' (see **44.38** below) or a 'pure protection policy', under which the individual is a beneficiary. A '*pure protection policy*' is a policy which has no surrender value and is not capable of acquiring one, or a policy under which the benefits payable cannot exceed the premiums paid except on death or disability. A '*relevant period*' is any twelve-month period beginning at or after the time when the event occurs.

The premium limit is also breached if the premiums payable *could* exceed £3,600 as a result of the exercise of any one or more 'relevant options' conferred by one or more relevant policies or the application of one or more terms of one or more relevant policies relating to increases in premiums. A '*relevant option*' is an option conferred by a policy on the person to whom it is issued to have another policy substituted for it or to have any of its terms changed.

In determining the premiums payable under a relevant policy, any provision for the waiver of premiums by reason of a person's disability is to be ignored. So much of a premium payable under a relevant policy as is charged on the grounds of exceptional risk of death or disability is to be left out of account in determining the premiums payable under the policy.

So much of the first premium payable under a relevant policy the liability for the payment of which is discharged from the proceeds of another policy is to be left out of account in determining the premiums payable under the policy. The maximum that can be left out of account under this rule is £3,600 × N, where N is the number of complete years for which ran the other policy involved (or, if there is more than one other policy involved, the policy which ran for the most number of complete years).

The following applies where the application of the premium limit is a consequence of two or more events occurring at the same time (including where one or more such events is a post-5 April 2013 relevant event and one or more is a restricted relief event — see **44.37** below). All the policies to which the events, taken together, relate are relevant policies. If, however, all the policies in question are issued by the same issuer and each of them has a unique identifier in a series of unique identifiers which the issuer gives to its policies, an event relating to a policy (policy A) is treated as occurring before an event relating to another policy (policy B) if policy A's unique identifier comes before that of policy B.

Relevant events

Subject to the exclusions below, each of the following is a '*post-5 April 2013 relevant event*':

(a) the issue of a policy in respect of an insurance made on or after 6 April 2013;
(b) the variation (within *ICTA 1988, Sch 15 para 18*) of a policy on or after 6 April 2013 such as to increase (or potentially increase) the period over which premiums are payable or the total premiums payable in any twelve-month period beginning at or after the time of the variation (or to increase both of these);
(c) the assignment on or after 6 April 2013 of any rights (or any share in any rights) under a policy where the assignment falls within **44.34**(c)–(g) or (j) above;
(d) a 'deceased beneficiary event' on or after 6 April 2013; and
(e) the fulfilment for the first time of the conditions in **44.21** above in respect of a new non-resident policy where this occurs on or after 6 April 2013 and the policy would not otherwise be a qualifying policy.

A variation is ignored for the purposes of (b) above if its effect is nullified before the end of the three-month period beginning after the day on which the variation occurs. For the purposes of (d) above and these provisions generally, a '*deceased beneficiary event*' occurs if, in connection with the death of an individual who was a beneficiary under a policy, another individual becomes a beneficiary under the policy by reference to any rights by reference to which the deceased was a beneficiary. It does not matter if the new beneficiary is already a beneficiary under the policy.

Exclusions

An event falling within (a)–(e) above is *not* a post-5 April 2013 relevant event if:

(i) the policy to which the event relates is:
  - (a) a 'protected policy' (see **44.38** below);
  - (b) a 'restricted relief qualifying policy' (see **44.37** below); or
  - (c) a 'pure protection policy' (see above); or

(ii) the event is the issue of a new policy in substitution for an earlier policy (and not on its maturity) where the only difference is that the life assured under the new policy is different to the life assured under the earlier policy; or

(iii) the event is the reinstatement or replacement of a policy as mentioned in **44.35**(i) above (policy reinstated or replaced after failure to pay premiums); or

(iv) the event is an assignment falling within **44.34**(e) above which is a 'mortgage endowment assignment' (as defined by *ICTA 1988, Sch 15 para A6(3)*).

The exclusion at (i)(a) above has no effect in the case of a relevant event within (e) above. The exclusion at (i)(b) above has no effect in the case of:

(A) an event within (c) or (d) above occurring in relation to a restricted relief qualifying policy (the '*assigned policy*');

(B) any subsequent event relating to the assigned policy; and

(C) any event relating to a later policy which is a 'new policy' in relation to the assigned policy (or in relation to a policy which is itself a new policy in relation to the assigned policy and so on). A '*new policy*' is one issued in substitution for, or on the maturity of and in consequence of an option conferred by, another policy (see *ICTA 1988, Sch 15 para 17*).

In the case of an event within (b) above, the exclusion at (i)(c) above has effect only if the policy is a pure protection policy both before and after the variation.

[*ICTA 1988, Sch 15 paras A1, A3, A6*].

Whether an individual a beneficiary under a policy

For these purposes, an individual is a beneficiary under a policy in any of the following circumstances:

- if he beneficially owns any rights under the policy (or any share in any such rights);
- if any rights under the policy are (or any share in any such rights is) held on non-charitable trusts created by the individual, and those rights are (or that share is) not beneficially owned by any individual;
- if any rights under the policy are (or any share in any such rights is) held as security for a debt of the individual, and those rights are (or that share is) not beneficially owned by any individual.

[*ICTA 1988, Sch 15 para A5*].

Simon's Taxes. See **E1.1332.**

Restricted relief qualifying policies

[44.37] If (i) a 'restricted relief event' occurs; (ii) the policy to which the event relates is a qualifying policy after the event; and (iii) an individual who is a beneficiary under the policy (see **44.36** above) is in breach of the premium limit (as in **44.36** above) for qualifying policies, the policy is a '*restricted relief qualifying policy*' after the event. The consequences of this are explained in **44.18** above.

Restricted relief events

Subject to the exclusions below, each of the following is a '*restricted relief event*':

(a) a 'premium limit event' (see below) in relation to a 'protected policy' (see **44.38** below) on or after 21 March 2012;
(b) the issue of a policy as in **44.38**(b) below if, assuming that the substitution of the protected policy were instead a variation of that policy, there would be a premium limit event in relation to that policy;
(c) the assignment on or after 6 April 2013 of any rights (or any share in any rights) under a protected policy where the assignment falls within **44.34**(c)–(g) or (j) above;
(d) a 'deceased beneficiary event' (see **44.36** above) on or after 6 April 2013 where the policy in question is a protected policy;
(e) the issue of a policy in respect of an insurance made on or after 21 March 2012 but before 6 April 2013 otherwise than as in **44.38**(b) below;
(f) the variation of a policy, other than a protected policy, on or after 21 March 2012 but before 6 April 2013 such as to increase (or potentially increase) the period over which premiums are payable or the total premiums payable in any twelve-month period beginning at or after the time of the variation (or to increase both of these); and
(g) the fulfilment for the first time of the conditions in **44.21** above in respect of a new non-resident policy where this occurs on or after 21 March 2012 but before 6 April 2013 and the policy would not otherwise be a qualifying policy.

A premium limit event or a variation was ignored for the purposes of (a) or (f) above if its effect was nullified before 6 July 2013. A premium limit event which occurs on or after 6 April 2013 is ignored for the purposes of (a) above if its effect is nullified before the end of the three-month period beginning after the day on which the event occurs.

A qualifying policy which is a 'new policy' in relation to an earlier policy is a restricted relief qualifying policy if the earlier policy is a restricted relief qualifying policy. A '*new policy*' is one issued in substitution for, or on the maturity of and in consequence of an option conferred by, another policy (see *ICTA 1988, Sch 15 para 17*). A policy which is a restricted relief qualifying policy remains a restricted relief qualifying policy so long as it is a qualifying policy. For both these purposes, the question of whether a policy is a qualifying policy is determined without reference to **44.36** above (subject to the application of the exclusion at **44.36**(i)(b) above).

Premium limit events

With regard to (a) above, a '*premium limit event*' occurs in relation to a protected policy if:

- the policy is varied or a 'relevant option' is exercised so as to change the terms of the policy; and
- the result (or one result) is to increase (or potentially increase) the period over which premiums are payable or the total premiums payable in any twelve-month period beginning at or after the time of the variation or exercise of the option (or to increase both of these).

A '*relevant option*' is an option conferred by a policy on the person to whom it is issued to have another policy substituted for it or to have any of its terms changed.

A '*premium limit event*' also occurs in relation to a protected policy if on or after 6 April 2013:

- the policy is varied or a relevant option is exercised so as to change the terms of the policy; and
- a result (or one result) is to reduce (or potentially reduce) the period over which premiums are payable or the total premiums payable in any twelve-month period beginning at or after the time of the variation or exercise of the option (or to reduce both of these).

The variation of, or exercise of a relevant option under, a protected policy is not, however, a premium limit event if:

- the policy secures a capital sum payable either on survival for a specified term or on earlier death or on earlier death or disability;
- the policy is issued and maintained for the sole purpose of ensuring that the borrower under an interest-only mortgage will have sufficient funds to repay the principal; and
- the policy is varied, or the relevant option is exercised, for that sole purpose.

Exclusions

An event falling within (a)–(g) above is *not* a restricted relief event if it is a 'pure protection policy' (see **44.36** above) or if any of **44.36**(ii)–(v) applies to the event. In the case of an event within (a) or (f) above, the first exclusion has effect only if the policy is a pure protection policy both before and after the premium limit event or variation.

[*ICTA 1988, Sch 15 paras A2, A6*].

Protected policies

[44.38] For the purposes of these provisions, a policy is 'protected' if:

(a) it is issued in respect of an insurance made before 21 March 2012; or
(b) it is issued in respect of an insurance made on or after 21 March 2012 but is issued in substitution for (though not on the maturity of) an earlier policy which is itself a protected policy.

A policy ceases to be protected if it becomes a 'restricted relief qualifying policy' (see **44.37** above). A policy issued as mentioned in (b) above is not protected if its issue is a restricted relief event (see **44.37**) such that the policy is a restricted relief qualifying policy after that event.

[*ICTA 1988, Sch 15 para A4*].

Information requirements

[44.39] On the occurrence of any of the events listed below, each individual who is a beneficiary under the policy (for which see **44.36** above) must, before the end of the 'statement period', make to the issuer of the policy a statement dealing with matters prescribed by regulations made by the Commissioners for HMRC (see *SI 2013 No 1820*). If an individual does not comply, the policy is *not* a qualifying policy after the event, notwithstanding anything else in this chapter. The events are:

- an event within any of **44.36**(a)–(e) above;
- a premium limit event in relation to a protected policy on or after 6 April 2013 (see **44.37** above); and
- an event on or after 6 April 2013 which would be a premium limit event in relation to a protected policy but for the exclusion for policies linked to interest-only mortgages (see **44.37** under Premium limit events).

Certain exclusions apply to 'pure protection policies' (see **44.36**). These are similar to the exclusions mentioned in **44.36** and **44.37** in relation to such policies. There is a similar exclusion to that in **44.36**(v) for mortgage endowment assignments.

The '*statement period*' is the three-month period beginning after the day on which the event occurs. If, however, the event occurs before the day on which the first regulations come into force, the statement period is the three-month period beginning after that day. An officer may allow an extension to the statement period in any case upon written request by the individual concerned, but only if he is satisfied that there is a reasonable excuse for the required statement not having been on time and that the request was made without unreasonable delay after the excuse ceased.

If there has been a transfer of the whole or part of a business previously carried on by the issuer of a policy, such that the issuer's obligations under the policy are now the obligations of the transferee, the required statement must be made to the transferee.

[*ICTA 1988, Sch 15 para B3; SI 2013 No 1820, Regs 1–4*].

The above requirements are accompanied by obligations on the issuers of policies to themselves provide information to HMRC. See **44.19** above under Qualifying policies.

Simon's Taxes. See **E1.1334**.

Transitional provision

[44.40] Transitional protection applies in certain circumstances to policies issued in respect of insurances made on or after 21 March 2012 but before 6 April 2013. The circumstances are that:

- the issue of the policy is a restricted relief event by virtue of **44.37**(e) above;
- after its issue, the policy is a qualifying policy and not a restricted relief qualifying policy;
- the policy is varied on or after 6 April 2013 and the variation is a post-5 April 2013 relevant event within **44.36** above;
- after the variation, and by virtue of **44.36**, the policy is not a qualifying policy;
- in relation to an event occurring after the variation, an individual is liable for tax on a chargeable event gain on the policy; and
- were it not for **44.36**, the individual would not have been so liable (see **44.6** above under Exclusion of certain qualifying policies).

The chargeable event gain is reduced by the amount produced by the fraction:

$$G \times \frac{TPV}{TP}$$

where:

G	=	the chargeable event gain before the reduction;
TPV	=	the total premiums payable before the variation; and
TP	=	the total premiums payable before the chargeable event.

There is provision similar to that in *ITTOIA 2005, s 463A* in **44.18** above for amounts to be left out of account in certain circumstances in determining the premiums payable. Also in determining the premiums payable, any provision for the waiver of premiums by reason of a person's disability is to be ignored.

[*ITTOIA 2005, s 463E*].

Simon's Taxes. See **E1.452CB.**

45

Losses

Cross-references. See **16.2** claims for claims involving more than one tax year; **49.11** MISCELLANEOUS INCOME; **52.10–52.17, 52.24, 52.26** PARTNERSHIPS; **60.25** PROPERTY INCOME for property losses; **75.16** TRADING INCOME as regards trades carried on wholly outside the UK.

Simon's Taxes. See **B8.2, E3.7.**

Other sources. See also HMRC Business Income Manual BIM85000–85770.

Introduction to losses

[45.1] Unless otherwise stated or the context suggests otherwise, references in this chapter to trading losses are to losses sustained in the carrying on of a trade, profession or vocation.

Trading losses are generally computed according to the same rules as apply in computing profits. [*ITTOIA 2005, s 26*]. Relief may be obtained for trading losses:

- by **set-off** against general income of the same tax year or preceding year — see **45.2** below;
- by **set-off** against **capital gains** of the same tax year or preceding tax year if and to the extent that the loss remains unrelieved after applying (a) above — see **45.5** below.
- by **carry-back** of **losses in early years of a trade** — see **45.7** below;
- by **carry-forward** against subsequent profits of the same trade — see **45.19** below;
- by carry-back of a **terminal loss** — see **45.20** below;

The first three reliefs are sometimes referred to as 'sideways relief'. See **45.9–45.18** below for restrictions.

It is not possible to anticipate a loss by claiming it before the end of the period of account in which the loss arises (and similarly where the results of more than one period are required to determine the loss for a tax year, claims may not precede the end of the last such period). See *Jones v O'Brien* Ch D 1988, 60 TC 706 and Revenue Tax Bulletin August 2001 pp 878, 879.

Where a loss can be relieved under more than one head and it is sufficiently large, the taxpayer can select the order in which the different heads are to be applied, but the whole of the income or profits available for relief under one head must be relieved before passing to the next (*Butt v Haxby* Ch D 1982, 56 TC 547).

Relief against income ('share loss relief') may be obtained for losses on shares in unlisted trading companies. See **45.23** below.

See **16.2** CLAIMS for further provisions regarding claims for a loss incurred in one tax year to be carried back to an earlier tax year.

Set-off of trading losses against general income

[45.2] Where in any tax year a person sustains a loss in a trade, profession or vocation, carried on solely or in partnership, he may make a claim on or before the first anniversary of 31 January following that tax year for relief against general income of:

(i) the tax year in which the loss is incurred;
(ii) the tax year preceding that in which the loss is incurred; or
(iii) both those tax years.

See **45.3** below as regards *late* claims.

A person sustains a trading loss in a tax year if he sustains a loss in the basis period for that tax year (see **75.6–75.14** TRADING INCOME for basis period rules). A claim within (i) above is made under *ITA 2007, s 64(2)(a)*. A claim within (ii) above is made under *ITA 2007, s 64(2)(b)*. A claim within (iii) above is made under *ITA 2007, s 64(2)(c)*. If a claim is made within (i) above and the loss is not wholly exhausted, a subsequent claim can be made (within the time limit) within (ii) above, and *vice versa*.

A claim is given effect by deducting the loss in arriving at net income for the tax year in question (see Step 2 at **1.10** ALLOWANCES AND TAX RATES).

There is a cap on the total amount of prescribed income tax reliefs that individuals can claim. See **1.11** ALLOWANCES AND TAX RATES. Relief for trading losses against general income is one of the prescribed reliefs.

Where a claim is made for a loss to be set against income of both the same tax year and the preceding tax year, there is no statutory order of priority; the claimant must specify the tax year for which the deduction from income should be made first.

Where, against income of the same year, claims are made both under (i) above in respect of that year's loss and under (ii) above in respect of the following year's loss, (i) takes precedence.

[*ITA 2007, ss 61(2), 64, 65*].

For restrictions on relief, see **45.9–45.18** below. In particular, no relief is available where a cash basis election is in force (**45.10** below). See **16.2** CLAIMS for further provisions regarding claims for a loss incurred in one tax year to be carried back to an earlier tax year.

Points to consider

The income against which a loss is set is income *before* deduction of the personal allowance or, where applicable, blind person's allowance (see **1.10** ALLOWANCES AND TAX RATES), which will thus be wasted if the income of a particular tax year is fully covered by a loss claim. A loss claim may also result in wasted dividend allowance (see **1.5** ALLOWANCES AND TAX RATES) and/or personal savings allowance (see **1.7** ALLOWANCES AND TAX RATES). The effect on allowances and rates of tax (including, where available, the starting rate for savings) needs to be carefully considered.

Partial claims against one year's income are not permitted; if a loss is set against income of a particular tax year, it must be fully set against that income until either the loss or the available income is exhausted. However, for any particular tax year, loss relief can be deducted from income in such way as will result in the greatest reduction in the taxpayer's liability to income tax (see Steps 2 and 3 in **1.10** ALLOWANCES AND TAX RATES), which may offer a way of avoiding wasted dividend allowance and/or personal savings allowance (see the first example at **45.4** below).

A claim for a loss for a tax year (Year 2) to be set against income of the preceding year (Year 1) cannot be validly made in the tax return for Year 1 (*Reid and Emblin v HMRC* FTT (TC 6469), [2018] UKFTT 236 (TC)).

Simon's Taxes. See B8.202.

Late claims

[45.3] Although there is no provision for the acceptance of late claims under the provisions at **45.2** above (or under those at **45.7** below), such relief may be granted as would have been due if a timeous claim had been made where the taxpayer or agent either:

(a) was misled by some relevant and uncorrected HMRC error;
(b) made an informal claim within the time limit which he or she reasonably believed to be an acceptable claim, and the need to formalise the claim was not pointed out by HMRC within the time limit; or
(c) was effectively prevented from making a timeous claim for reasons beyond his or her control,

and provided that the late claim is made within a reasonable period (not normally more than three months) after the expiry of the excuse. As regards (c) above, acceptable reasons do *not* normally include: delays in preparing the accounts (unless for reasons beyond the taxpayer's or agent's control); delays in HMRC's agreeing the accounts (although valid claims may be made before the accounts are either submitted or agreed, provided that the loss is clearly identified); misunderstandings and failures to communicate between taxpayer and agent; oversight or neglect by current or previous agents; ignorance of the statutory time limits; or deliberate delays because it was unclear at the expiry of the time limit whether the claim was advantageous. (Revenue Tax Bulletin December 1994 p 183.)

Examples

General

[45.4]

L, a single woman, commences to trade on 1 July 2016, preparing accounts to 30 June, and has the following results (as adjusted for tax purposes) for the first four years.

	Profit/(loss)
	£
Year ended 30 June 2017	27,000
Year ended 30 June 2018	9,000
Year ended 30 June 2019	(3,000)
Year ended 30 June 2020	(25,000)

L has other income of £19,500 for 2019/20 and £22,500 for 2020/21, having had no other income in the earlier years. The 2020/21 income includes dividend income of £1,800.

The taxable profits for the first five tax years of the business are as follows.

	£
2016/17 (1.7.16–5.4.17) (£27,000 × 9/12)	20,250*
2017/18 (y/e 30.6.17)	27,000
2018/19 (y/e 30.6.18)	9,000
2019/20 (y/e 30.6.19)	Nil
2020/21 (y/e 30.6.20)	Nil

* Overlap relief accruing – £20,250.

L claims relief under *ITA 2007, s 64(2)(a)* (set-off against income of the same year) for the 2019/20 loss (£3,000). She also claims relief under *ITA 2007, s 64(2)(b)* (set-off against income of the preceding year) for the 2020/21 loss (£25,000), with a further claim being made under *ITA 2007, s 64(2)(a)* for the balance of that loss.

The tax position for 2019/20 and 2020/21 is as follows.

	£
2019/20	
Total income before loss relief	19,500
Deduct Claim under *ITA 2007, s 64(2)(a)* note (a)	3,000
	16,500
Deduct Claim under *ITA 2007, s 64(2)(b)*	16,500
Net income	Nil
2020/21	
Total income before loss relief	22,500
Deduct Claim under *ITA 2007, s 64(2)(a)* (balance)	8,500
Net income	14,000
Deduct Personal allowance	12,500
Taxable income	£1,500
Tax payable £1,500 @ 0% (dividend nil rate) note (c)	—

Loss utilisation

	£
2019/20	
Loss available under *ITA 2007, s 64(2)(a)*	3,000
Deduct Utilised in 2019/20	3,000
Loss available under *ITA 2007, s 64(2)(b)*	25,000
Deduct Utilised in 2019/20	16,500
Loss available for relief in 2020/21 under *ITA 2007, s 64(2)(a)*	£8,500
2020/21	
Balance of loss available under *ITA 2007, s 64(2)(a)*	8,500
Deduct Utilised in 2020/21	8,500

Notes

(a) Where losses of two different years are set against the income of one tax year, then, regardless of the order of claims, relief for the current year's loss is given in priority to that for the following year's loss (see **45.2** above). This is beneficial to the taxpayer in this example as it leaves £8,500 of the 2020/21 loss to be relieved in that year.

(b) By making the claim under *ITA 2007, s 64(2)(b)* (set-off against income of the preceding year), L has avoided a tax liability for 2019/20 but has also wasted her personal allowance. This claim might not have been made in practice.

(c) Both the personal allowance and loss relief can be deducted in such way as will result in the greatest reduction in the taxpayer's liability to income tax (see Steps 2 and 3 in **1.10** ALLOWANCES AND TAX RATES and see **45.2** above). It is assumed that for 2020/21, L will deduct these firstly from income other than dividend income. This leaves dividend income in charge which will attract the dividend allowance (see **1.5** ALLOWANCES AND TAX RATES).

Losses in early years

Q commenced trading on 1 February 2020 and prepared accounts to 31 December. He made a trading loss of £20,900 in the 11 months to 31 December 2020 and profits of £18,000 and £16,000 in the years to 31 December 2021 and 2022 respectively. Q has substantial other income for 2019/20 and 2020/21 and makes a claim under *ITA 2007, s 64* for both years.

Taxable profits/(allowable losses) are as follows.

	£	£
2019/20(1.2.20–5.4.20) (£20,900) × $^{2}/_{11}$		(3,800)
2020/21(1.2.20–31.1.21)		
1.2.20–31.12.20	(20,900)	
Less already allocated to 2019/20	3,800	
	(17,100)	
1.1.21–31.1.21 £18,000 × $^{1}/_{12}$	1,500	
		(15,600)
2021/22(y/e 31.12.21)		18,000
(Overlap relief accruing — £1,500)		
2022/23(y/e 31.12.22)		16,000

Notes

(a) Losses available for relief for 2019/20 and 2020/21 are £3,800 and £15,600 respectively. If both years' losses are carried forward under *ITA 2007, s 83* instead of being set against other income (under either *ITA 2007, s 64* or *s 72*), the aggregate loss of £19,400 will extinguish the 2021/22 profit and reduce the 2022/23 profit by £1,400. Note that although the actual loss was £20,900, there is no further amount available for carry-forward; the difference of £1,500 has been used in aggregation in 2020/21.

(b) The net profit for the first three accounting periods is £13,100 (£18,000 + £16,000 – £20,900). The net taxable profit for the first four tax years is £14,600 (£18,000 + £16,000 – £3,800 – £15,600). The difference of

> £1,500 represents the overlap relief accrued (see **75.14** TRADING INCOME). Note that the overlap profit of £1,500 is by reference to an overlap period of *three* months, i.e. 1.2.20–5.4.20 (two months — overlap profit nil) and 1.1.21–31.1.21 (one month — overlap profit £1,500).

Set-off of trading losses against capital gains

[45.5] Where relief is available under *ITA 2007, s 64* as in **45.2** above for a tax year and either a claim is made under that section or the person's total income for the year is either nil or does not include any income from which the loss can be deducted, a claim may also be made under *TCGA 1992, s 261B* for the determination of the '*relevant amount*', which is so much of the trading loss as:

(a) is not deducted in calculating the claimant's net income for the year of claim; and
(b) has not already been relieved for any other year.

The claim is not deemed to be determined until the relevant amount for the year can no longer be varied, whether by the Tribunal on appeal or on the order of any court.

The relevant amount, as finally determined, is to be treated for the purposes of capital gains tax as an allowable loss accruing to the claimant in the tax year, except that it cannot exceed the 'maximum amount'. Any such excess remains an income tax loss.

The '*maximum amount*' for this purpose is the amount on which the claimant would be chargeable to capital gains tax for that year, disregarding the effect of this provision and of the capital gains tax annual exemption.

In computing the maximum amount, no account is taken of any event occurring after the determination of the relevant amount and in consequence of which the amount chargeable to capital gains tax is reduced by virtue of any capital gains tax legislation. Thus if, as a result of a subsequent reduction in the chargeable gains against which the maximum amount is set, the maximum amount exceeds those chargeable gains, the excess is carried forward as an allowable capital loss.

No amount treated as an allowable loss under this provision may be deducted from chargeable gains accruing in a tax year which begins after the claimant has ceased to carry on the trade in which the loss was sustained.

A claim must be made on or before the first anniversary of the normal self-assessment filing date for the tax year in which the loss was made.

The above provisions apply also to employment losses relievable under *ITA 2007, s 128* (see **45.31** below).

[*ITA 2007, ss 71, 130; TCGA 1992, ss 261B, 261C*].

No relief is available where a cash basis election is in force (see **45.10** below).

Simon's Taxes. See B8.202.

Example

[45.6]

M has carried on a trade for some years, preparing accounts to 30 June each year. For the year ended 30 June 2020, he makes a trading loss of £17,000. His assessable profit for 2019/20 is £5,000, and his other income for both 2019/20 and 2020/21 amounts to £2,000. He makes a capital gain of £16,400 and a capital loss of £1,000 for 2020/21 and has capital losses brought forward of £12,100. M makes claims for loss relief, against income of 2019/20 and income and gains of 2020/21, under *ITA 2007, ss 64(2)(b), 64(2)(a)* and *TCGA 1992, s 261B*.

Calculation of 'relevant amount'

	£
Trading loss—year ended 30.6.20	17,000
Relieved against other income for 2020/21 (*ITA 2007, s 64(2)(a)*)	(2,000)
Relieved against income for 2019/20 (*ITA 2007, s 64(2)(b)*)	(7,000)
Relevant amount	£8,000

Calculation of 'maximum amount'

		£
Gains for 2020/21		16,400
Deduct	Losses for 2020/21	(1,000)
	Unrelieved losses brought forward	(12,100)
Maximum amount		£3,300

Relief under *TCGA 1992, s 261B*

	£	£
Gains for the year		16,400
Losses for the year	1,000	
Relief under *TCGA 1992, s 261B*	3,300	
		4,300
Gain (covered by annual exemption)		£12,100
Capital losses brought forward and carried forward		£12,100

Loss memorandum

	£
Trading loss	17,000
Claimed under *ITA 2007, s 64(2)(a)*	(2,000)
Claimed under *ITA 2007, s 64(2)(b)*	(7,000)
Claimed under *TCGA 1992, s 261B*	(3,300)
Unutilised loss	£4,700

Note

In this example, £200 of the capital gains tax annual exemption of £12,300 is wasted, but the brought forward capital losses are preserved for carry-forward against gains of future years. If M had *not* made the claim under *TCGA 1992, s 261B*, his net gains for the year of £15,400 would have been reduced to the annual exempt amount by deducting £3,100 of the losses brought forward. Only

> £9,000 of capital losses would remain available for carry-forward against future gains and a further £3,300 of trading losses would have been available for carry-forward against future trading profits. So the effect of the claim is to preserve capital losses at the expense of trading losses.

Losses in early years of a trade

[45.7] If an individual sustains a loss in a trade, profession or vocation in any of the first four tax years in which the trade etc., is first carried on by him, he may claim relief for that loss against his other income of the *three* tax years preceding the year of loss. Income of earlier years is relieved in priority to that of later years. The trade (or if part of a larger undertaking, the whole undertaking) must have been carried on during the 'period of loss' on a commercial basis with a reasonable expectation of profits during that period or within a reasonable time afterwards (an objective test — see *Walls v Livesey* (Sp C 4), [1995] SSCD 12 — and see generally *Walsh v Taylor* (Sp C 386) 2003, [2004] SSCD 48). The '*period of loss*' is the basis period in which the loss is sustained.

The relief is available to an individual trading etc. in partnership by reference to the first four tax years in which he is a partner. However, relief is not available to a married individual where the trade was being carried on by his or her spouse at a time earlier than the three tax years preceding the year of loss (which, for example, precludes relief to that extent where an individual takes his spouse into partnership); this applies to civil partners as it does to married couples. See **52.13–52.17** PARTNERSHIPS for other restrictions on relief available to certain partners.

No relief is available where a cash basis election is in force (see **45.10** below).

There is a cap on the total amount of prescribed income tax reliefs that individuals can claim. See **1.11** ALLOWANCES AND TAX RATES. Relief for early year trading losses against other income is one of the prescribed reliefs.

Claims

A claim is made under *ITA 2007, s 72*. The claim is given effect by deducting the loss in arriving at net income for the earliest of the three years preceding the year of loss (see Step 2 at **1.10** ALLOWANCES AND TAX RATES), then (assuming there is any unrelieved balance) the year after that and finally the latest of the three years. Any amount still unrelieved is potentially available for relief under any of the other trading loss reliefs described in this chapter.

Claims must be made on or before the first anniversary of 31 January following the tax year in which the loss is sustained. For late claims, see **45.3** above.

See **16.2** CLAIMS for further provisions regarding claims for a loss incurred in one tax year to be carried back to an earlier tax year.

Capital allowances

Capital allowances are subject to the restrictions in **45.13**, **45.14** below. See also the anti-avoidance legislation at **45.15–45.17** below.

General

The income against which a loss is set is income *before* deduction of the personal allowance or, where applicable, blind person's allowance (see **1.10** ALLOWANCES AND TAX RATES), which will thus be wasted if the income of a particular tax year is fully covered by a loss claim. The effect on personal allowances, rates of tax etc. needs to be carefully considered. Partial claims are not permitted; if a loss is set against income of a particular tax year, it must be fully set against that income until either the loss or the available income is exhausted. Furthermore, it is not possible to claim to carry back a loss under these provisions against the income of one or two specified years as opposed to all of the three years in question.

[*ITA 2007, ss 61(2), 72–74*].

See also **75.106** TRADING INCOME as regards **pre-trading expenditure.**

Simon's Taxes. See **B8.206**.

Example

[45.8]

F, a single person, commenced to trade on 1 December 2017, preparing accounts to 30 November. The first four years of trading produce tax-adjusted losses of £12,000, £9,000, £2,000 and £1,000 respectively. For each of the four tax years 2014/15 to 2017/18, F had other income of £8,000.

The losses for tax purposes are as follows.

	£	£
2017/18 (1.12.17–5.4.18) (£12,000 × 4/12)		4,000
2018/19 (y/e 30.11.18)	12,000	
Less already allocated to 2017/18	4,000	
		8,000
2019/20 (y/e 30.11.19)		9,000
2020/21 (y/e 30.11.20)		2,000
2021/22 (y/e 30.11.21) note (b)		1,000

Loss relief under *ITA 2007, s 72* is available as follows.

	2017/18	2018/19	2019/20	2020/21
	£	£	£	£
Losses available	4,000	8,000	9,000	2,000
Set against total income				
2014/15	4,000	—	—	—
2015/16	—	8,000	—	—
2016/17	—	—	8,000	—
2017/18	—	—	1,000	2,000
	£4,000	£8,000	£9,000	£2,000

Revised total income is thus £4,000 for 2014/15, nil for 2015/16 and 2016/17, and £5,000 for 2017/18.

Notes
(a) Losses are computed by reference to the same basis periods as profits. Where any part of a loss would otherwise fall to be included in the computations for two successive tax years (as is the case for 2017/18 and 2018/19 in this example), that part is excluded from the computation for the second of those years.
(b) The loss for the year ended 30 November 2021 in this example is not available for relief under *ITA 2007, s 72* as it does not fall into the first four *tax years* of the business (even though it is incurred in the first four years of trading). It is, of course, available for relief under *ITA 2007, s 64* (depending on other income for 2020/21 and 2021/22) or for carry-forward under *ITA 2007, s 83*.

Restrictions on above reliefs

[45.9] A number of restrictions apply to the above loss reliefs; these are set out in **45.10–45.18** below.

Losses on the cash basis

[45.10] Where a person makes a loss in any trade, profession or vocation in a tax year and a cash basis election is in force for that year (see **76** TRADING INCOME — CASH BASIS FOR SMALLER BUSINESSES), relief is not available for the loss under *ITA 2007, s 64* against general income (see **45.2** above), *TCGA 1992, s 261B* against chargeable gains (see **45.5** above) or *ITA 2007, s 72* (losses in early years of trade) against general income (see **45.7** above). [*ITA 2007, s 74E*].

There is nothing to prevent the loss from being carried forward against profits of the same trade, profession or vocation as in **45.19** below.

Non-commercial trades

[45.11] Relief under *ITA 2007, s 64* (see **45.2** above) will not be given for a trade loss unless, throughout the basis period for the tax year in which the loss is sustained, the trade, profession or vocation was carried on:

- on a commercial basis; and
- with a view to the realisation of profits in that trade etc., or in any larger undertaking of which it forms part.

The test is a subjective one — see *Walls v Livesey* (Sp C 4), [1995] SSCD 12 on the similar test under earlier legislation. In *Wannell v Rothwell* Ch D 1996, 68 TC 719 an individual's speculative dealing in stocks, shares and futures was held to be trading but not on a commercial basis, but in *Ali v HMRC* FTT (TC 4816), [2016] UKFTT 8 (TC) similar dealing by an individual was held to be a trade meeting both the above conditions notwithstanding that it had consistently made losses. In *Cliff v HMRC* FTT (TC 7358), [2019] UKFTT 564 (TC) the buying of shares in racing partnerships was considered, if it were a trade at all, not to be a trade meeting the above conditions. A trade which is virtually certain to lead to a loss cannot realistically be described as commercial (*Seven Individuals v HMRC* UT, [2017] STC 874).

See also *Brown v Richardson* (Sp C 129), [1997] SSCD 233; *Delian Enterprises v Ellis* (Sp C 186), [1999] SSCD 103; *Murray v HMRC* FTT (TC 3474), [2014] UKFTT 338 (TC); *Patel v HMRC* FTT (TC 4225), [2015] UKFTT 13 (TC); *Gray v HMRC* FTT (TC 5151), [2016] UKFTT 397 (TC); *Mills v HMRC* FTT (TC 5844), [2017] SFTD 872, [2017] UKFTT 378 (TC); *Beacon v HMRC* FTT (TC 6362), [2018] SFTD 846, [2018] UKFTT 104 (TC); *Roulette V2 Charters LLP v HMRC* FTT (TC 7331), [2019] UKFTT 0537 (TC) and *Sherrington v HMRC* FTT (TC 7629), [2020] UKFTT 128 (TC).

A trade is treated as complying with the second of the above requirements at any time at which it was being carried on so as to afford a reasonable expectation of profit. If there was a change during the basis period in the way in which the trade etc., is carried on, it is treated as having been carried on throughout in the way in which it was being carried on at the end of the basis period.

For the HMRC approach generally, see HMRC Business Income Manual BIM85705–85720.

(The above restrictions do not apply to losses incurred in the exercise of functions conferred by or under an Act (for which see *ITA 2007, s 1018*).)

[*ITA 2007, s 66*].

Simon's Taxes. See **B8.202**.

Farming and market gardening

[45.12] Except as below, relief will not be given under *ITA 2007, s 64* (see 45.2 above) for any loss incurred in a trade of farming or market gardening if losses from that trade were also incurred in each of the five years preceding the tax year in which the loss is sustained. In ascertaining for the purposes of these provisions whether losses have been incurred in preceding tax years, capital allowances and balancing charges are disregarded and losses are computed by reference to actual tax years (apportioning where necessary) as opposed to basis periods.

Similarly, if such a trade is carried on by a company, a loss incurred in any accounting period may not be set off against total profits if there would still be a loss if capital allowances were ignored and there was a loss (similarly computed) in each of the accounting periods wholly or partly comprised in the five years preceding that accounting period (see Tolley's Corporation Tax for details).

There is no disallowance under *ITA 2007, s 64* if the trade commenced during the preceding five tax years but if the trade was transferred during that time from one spouse to the other (or from one civil partner to the other) it is treated for this purpose as not having thereby ceased and a new trade commenced. The same applies if the trade was transferred between an individual and a company which he controls or which his spouse (or civil partner) controls or which they together control.

Relief is not disallowed by virtue of these provisions if:

(a) the trade is part of, and ancillary to, a larger trading undertaking; or
(b) the farming or market gardening activities in the year are carried on in a way which might reasonably be expected to produce profits in the future, and the activities in the preceding five years could not reasonably have been expected at the beginning of the 'prior period of loss' to become profitable until after the year under review.

The expectations included in (b) above are to be considered on the assumption that the activities are carried on by a competent person, and the activities must be regarded as a whole. See *HMRC v Naghshineh* UT, [2020] STC 480, [2020] UKUT 30 (TCC) and *Silvester v HMRC* FTT (TC 4682), [2015] UKFTT 532 (TC). In the event of a change in the nature of the activities, the second leg of (b) must be judged by reference to the nature of the activities as they are carried on in the current tax year and not as they were carried on at the start of the prior period of loss (*Scambler v HMRC* UT, [2017] STC 2108). The '*prior period of loss*' comprises the five preceding tax years plus, if losses were made in successive tax years before those five years, those successive tax years.

[*ITA 2007, ss 67–70*].

By concession, HMRC extend the five-year time limits above to 11 years from commencement in the case of stud farming, i.e. the breeding of thoroughbred horses, provided that the business is potentially profitable (HMRC Business Income Manual BIM55725).

Simon's Taxes. See **B5.175**.

Leasing by individuals

[45.13] Where an individual (alone or in partnership) incurs expenditure on plant or machinery for leasing in the course of a trade, any plant or machinery capital allowances on that expenditure are not to be included in computing a loss for the purposes of *ITA 2007, s 64* (see **45.2** above) or *ITA 2007, s 72* (see **45.7** above) unless:

- the individual carries on the trade for a continuous period of at least six months beginning or ending in the 'period of loss'; and
- he devotes substantially the whole of his time (see HMRC Business Income Manual BIM85730) to the trade throughout the 'period of loss' or, if the trade begins or ceases (or both) in that year, for a continuous period of at least six months beginning or ending in that year.

The '*period of loss*' means the basis period for the tax year in which the loss is sustained.

The same restriction applies if the asset is not leased but payments in the nature of royalties or licence fees are to arise from rights granted by the individual in connection with the asset.

Any relief erroneously given will be withdrawn by assessment. The foregoing provisions are without prejudice to (d) and (e) below.

[*ITA 2007, ss 75, 79*].

A loss derived from capital allowances on a yacht chartered through bareboat leasing, i.e. it did not come with a skipper, was held to be caught by the above restriction (*Johnson v HMRC* FTT (TC 2094), [2012] UKFTT 399 (TC), 2012 STI 2737).

Simon's Taxes. See B5.417.

Capital allowances

[45.14] There are two separate restrictions involving capital allowances, as follows.

(a) **Leasing partnerships.** Where expenditure is incurred on plant or machinery for leasing in the course of a trade (or other qualifying activity — see **10.4** CAPITAL ALLOWANCES ON PLANT AND MACHINERY) carried on, or to be carried on, by a partnership including a company and an individual (with or without other partners), any first-year allowance (see **10.18** CAPITAL ALLOWANCES ON PLANT AND MACHINERY) on that expenditure is not to be included in computing a loss for the purposes of *ITA 2007, s 64* (see **45.2** above) or *ITA 2007, s 72* (see **45.7** above).

(b) **Arrangements.** Where an individual incurs expenditure on an asset, any plant and machinery annual investment allowance (see **10.13** CAPITAL ALLOWANCES ON PLANT AND MACHINERY) or first-year allowance (see **10.18** CAPITAL ALLOWANCES ON PLANT AND MACHINERY) on that expenditure is not to be included in computing a loss for the purposes of *ITA 2007, s 64* (see **45.2** above) or *ITA 2007, s 72* (see **45.7** above) if, under an arrangement or scheme, such loss relief was expected as the sole or main benefit to the individual of incurring the expenditure and (i) he was in partnership then or later, or (ii) he transferred the trade etc. or the relevant asset to a CONNECTED PERSON (**19**), or (iii) he transferred the asset to any person at lower than its market value.

Any relief already given will be withdrawn under (a) or (b) above by assessment.

[*ITA 2007, ss 76–79*].

Simon's Taxes. See B5.417.

Losses derived from film tax reliefs

[45.15] There is a potential exit charge as described below where:

(i) an individual has claimed relief under *ITA 2007, s 64* (see **45.2** above), *TCGA 2002, s 261B* (see **45.5** above) or *ITA 2007, s 72* (see **45.7** above) in respect of a 'film-related loss' sustained by him in a trade (whether carried on solely or in partnership);

(ii) there is a 'disposal' of a right of the individual to profits arising from the trade (a '*relevant disposal*'); and

(iii) an 'exit event' occurs.

A loss is a '*film-related loss*' if the computation of profits or losses that it results from is made in accordance with any of *ITTOIA 2005, ss 130–144*, which give relief, as revenue expenditure, for production and acquisition expenditure on films and sound recordings (see **75.80** TRADING INCOME).

A '*disposal*' is very widely (but not exhaustively) defined (by *ITA 2007, s 799*) for the purposes of (ii) above to include, for example, the disposal, surrender or loss of a right to income, a default in the payment of income, certain changes in profit- or loss-sharing ratios and the individual's leaving a partnership (including a case where the partnership is dissolved). The disposal may be part of a larger disposal.

An '*exit event*' occurs when:

- the individual receives any consideration for the relevant disposal (whether or not as part of a larger sum) which is not otherwise chargeable to income tax;
- the 'losses claimed' become greater than the individual's 'capital contribution' (whether because of a claim for losses or a decrease in that capital contribution); or
- there is an increase in the amount by which the losses claimed exceed the capital contribution.

A **chargeable event** occurs at the time the last of the conditions at (i)–(iii) above is satisfied (regardless of whether or not the individual is still carrying on the trade). The individual is treated as receiving at that time an amount of income equal to the total consideration received for relevant disposals and not otherwise chargeable to income tax plus the excess (if any) of 'losses claimed' over 'capital contribution' (such amounts being judged as at the time immediately after the chargeable event). That income does not form part of the trading profits but is separately chargeable to income tax for the tax year in which the chargeable event occurs. There is provision to avoid double counting where there are successive chargeable events. Consideration from which a deduction has been made in consideration of any person's agreeing to or facilitating a relevant disposal or exit event (e.g. an exit fee) is treated as received free of that deduction.

References above to '*losses claimed*' are to any film-related losses sustained in the trade in any tax year for which the individual has claimed relief under *ITA 2007, s 64, TCGA 2002, s 261B* or *ITA 2007, s 72*. But for members of partnerships, 'losses claimed' are treated as decreased for these purposes by the lesser of any amount clawed back under the recovery provisions at **52.13** PARTNERSHIPS and the amount of *film-related* losses that could potentially have been clawed back under those provisions.

An individual's '*capital contribution*' is the amount he has contributed to the trade as capital, less so much of that amount as:

- he has, directly or indirectly, drawn out or received back;
- he is entitled so to draw out or receive back;
- he has had, directly or indirectly, reimbursed to him by any person; or
- he is entitled to require any person so to reimburse to him,

but not including any such amount drawn out or received back as is chargeable to income tax as profits of a trade. Anything brought into account on a chargeable event as consideration for a relevant disposal is not deducted in arriving at his capital contribution. If the trade is carried on by the individual in partnership, his capital contribution is the amount he has contributed to the firm (as opposed to the trade) but is otherwise determined in like manner; a share of profits (as computed for accounting, rather than tax, purposes) is an amount contributed in so far as that share has been added to the firm's capital. In consequence, the general rules apply with some modification in a case where a partnership carries on more than one trade.

The Commissioners for HMRC are empowered to make regulations (see now *SI 2005 No 2017*), with retrospective effect, excluding from an individual's capital contribution for these purposes any amounts of a description specified in the regulations. These will apply *only* where the individual carries on the trade *in partnership*. Under *SI 2005 No 2017*, such exclusions are made in the following circumstances.

(A) Where an individual takes out a loan in connection with his financing of all or part of his contribution to the trade and either:
   (i) there is, at any time, an agreement or arrangement under which another person will, or may, bear any of the financial cost of repaying the loan;
   (ii) any such financial cost is at any time borne by another person otherwise than under an agreement or arrangement caught by (i) above;
   (iii) the liability to repay the loan is at any time assumed (or released) by any other person; or
   (iv) the financial cost to the individual of repaying the loan over a specified period is substantially less than it would have been on arm's length terms.

   The period specified in (iv) above is the earliest period of five years beginning on or after 2 December 2004 (or, if later, the date the loan was taken out) for which condition (iv) is satisfied. Where conditions (i), (ii) or (iii) are satisfied, the amount in question is excluded from the individual's capital contribution after the time in question. Where condition (iv) is satisfied, the exclusion applies after the end of the five-year period and is equal to the amount of the loan outstanding at the end of that period. References to loans include replacement loans.

(B) Where, at any time, there is an agreement or arrangement under which any of the financial cost of making the capital contribution will be, or may be, reimbursed (directly or indirectly) to the individual by any other person, or where such cost is at any time reimbursed otherwise than under such an agreement or arrangement. The amount in question is excluded from the individual's capital contribution after the time in question.

Neither (A) nor (B) above applies in relation to any financial cost borne or reimbursed by another individual in the normal course of his domestic, family or personal relationships or to any loan repayments not made by the partner due to his financial inability to pay (arising from events outside his control and occurring after the taking out of the loan) or to any amount on which the partner is chargeable to income tax as profits of the trade.

The above provisions are further extended by *SI 2006 No 1639*. They apply where:

- the individual is a limited partner, a member of a limited liability partnership or a non-active partner in a partnership (see, respectively, **52.24, 52.26, 52.13** PARTNERSHIPS);
- he disposes of his right to profits arising from the trade, such that his share of any profits is reduced or extinguished or his share of any losses is increased;
- another person becomes a partner; and
- the new partner contributes (or agrees to contribute) capital to the partnership.

The amount of the new partner's contribution must be apportioned between the partners in accordance with profit sharing arrangements in force immediately before the new partner becomes a partner. The amount thus apportioned to the individual in question is deducted from his capital contribution for the purposes of determining: (i) whether a chargeable event (as above) occurs; and (ii) the amount to be brought into account as income as a result of that event.

[*ITA 2007, ss 790, 796–803, Sch 2 paras 144–149; SI 2005 No 2017; SI 2006 No 1639*].

See **52.17** PARTNERSHIPS for other anti-avoidance provisions concerning losses derived from exploiting films.

Simon's Taxes. See **B5.508**.

Non-active traders

[45.16] Where a trade loss is sustained by an individual for any subsequent year (otherwise than as a partner) and during that tax year he carries on the trade in a 'non-active capacity', the quantum of relief that he can claim for that loss under:

- *ITA 2007, s 64* against general income (and, consequently, *TCGA 1992, s 261B* against chargeable gains) (see **45.2, 45.5** above); or
- *ITA 2007, s 72* (losses in early years of trade) against general income (see **45.7** above),

is restricted to **£25,000.** If the individual sustains more than one such loss in a tax year, the £25,000 cap applies to the aggregate of all such losses. The cap applies to the balance of a trade loss after applying all other restrictions. If the individual is also a member of a partnership, the amount of the cap is reduced by any relief given under the above provisions for his share of any partnership loss which is sustained in the same tax year and to which the similar cap at **52.15** PARTNERSHIPS applies in his case. The amount of the cap may be varied in future by the Treasury via statutory instrument. The cap does *not* apply:

- to so much of any loss as derives from 'qualifying film expenditure' (see below);
- to prevent relief for the loss against profits of the same trade; or
- to UNDERWRITERS AT LLOYD'S (**76**) in connection with their underwriting business.

For these purposes, an individual carries on a trade in a '*non-active capacity*' during a tax year if he carries it on at any time in that tax year and, in the 'relevant period' for that tax year, he does not devote a 'significant amount of time' to it. An individual devotes a '*significant amount of time*' to a trade in the 'relevant period' for a tax year if, in that period, he spends an average of at least ten hours a week personally engaged in activities of the trade. Those activities must be carried on on a commercial basis and with a view to profit. Any relief erroneously given on the assumption that this requirement will be met will be withdrawn by means of an income tax assessment. The '*relevant period*' for a tax year is normally the basis period for that tax year. If, however, the basis period is less than six months because the tax year is the one in which the individual commenced or ceased the trade, the requirement must instead be met by reference to the six months beginning with the commencement date or ending with the cessation date, as the case may be.

Qualifying film expenditure

Expenditure is '*qualifying film expenditure*' if it is:

- expenditure which is deducted, in computing the trade loss, under the statutory relief provisions for certified films, i.e. under any of *ITTOIA 2005, ss 137–142* (see **75.80** TRADING INCOME); or
- incidental expenditure (i.e. expenditure on management, administration or obtaining finance) that, whilst deductible other than under the statutory relief provisions for certified films, was incurred in connection with the production or the acquisition (as defined) of a film in relation to which expenditure was deducted under the said provisions.

It was made clear by the Treasury in relation to the identical definition for the purposes of **52.17** PARTNERSHIPS that qualifying film expenditure does not include expenditure on distribution of a film or 'print and advertising' or production of a film as trading stock (Treasury Explanatory Notes to the Finance Bill 2004).

The extent to which a loss derives from qualifying film expenditure and the extent to which expenditure qualifies as incidental expenditure are to be determined on a just and reasonable basis.

[*ITA 2007, ss 74A, 74C, 74D*].

Tax-generated losses

In addition to the above restriction, if an individual carries on a trade (otherwise than as a partner) in a 'non-active capacity' (as defined above) and makes a trade loss arising (directly or indirectly) in consequence of, or otherwise in connection with, 'tax avoidance arrangements', no relief is available for that loss under:

- *ITA 2007, s 64* against general income (and, consequently, *TCGA 1992, s 261B* against chargeable gains) (see **45.2**, **45.5** above); or
- *ITA 2007, s 72* (losses in early years of trade) against general income (see **45.7** above).

This restriction is superseded by the broader legislation outlined in **45.17** below and does not apply to a loss to which **45.17** potentially applies.

'*Tax avoidance arrangements*' means arrangements (as widely defined) made by the individual a main purpose of which is to obtain a reduction in tax liability by means of one or more of the above-mentioned reliefs. This restriction does not apply to any loss that derives wholly from 'qualifying film expenditure' (see above).

[*ITA 2007, ss 74B–74D*].

Simon's Taxes. See **B8.210.**

Tax-generated losses

[45.17] The following reliefs are denied in the case of a 'tax-generated loss':

- relief under *ITA 2007, s 64* against general income (and, consequently, *TCGA 1992, s 261B* against chargeable gains) (see **45.2, 45.5** above); and
- relief under *ITA 2007, s 72* (losses in early years of trade) against general income (see **45.7** above).

A '*tax-generated loss*' is a loss sustained by a person in carrying on a trade, profession or vocation (whether alone or in partnership) which arises in consequence of, or in connection with, 'relevant tax avoidance arrangements'. '*Relevant tax avoidance arrangements*' are arrangements (as widely defined) to which the person is a party and a main purpose of which is the obtaining of a reduction in tax liability by means of one or more of the above-mentioned reliefs. This denial of relief does not apply in relation to a loss that derives wholly from 'qualifying film expenditure' (as in **45.16** above).

[*ITA 2007, s 74ZA*].

For guidance, including examples, see HMRC Business Income Manual BIM85762.

To decide whether a main purpose of arrangements is to obtain a reduction in tax liability by way of one of the above-mentioned loss reliefs, it is necessary to look at all the circumstances in which the arrangements were entered into, including the participant's overall economic objective. If the loss arises in connection with a marketed tax avoidance scheme, it is almost certain that this will indeed be the case; but the legislation is by no means restricted to such instances.

Simon's Taxes. See **B8.210.**

Miscellaneous

[45.18] See **52.13–52.17** PARTNERSHIPS for restrictions on loss reliefs available to non-active members of partnerships. Special restrictions on the use of losses apply in relation to certain company partnership arrangements [*CTA 2010, ss 958–962*] — see **52.21** PARTNERSHIPS. See **52.24, 52.26** PARTNERSHIPS for restrictions on loss reliefs available to, respectively, limited partners and members of limited liability partnerships.

Loss reliefs are denied if the loss is sustained in a partnership and arrangements are in place to secure that losses are allocated to an individual, rather than to a non-individual. This applies to the reliefs at **45.19** and **45.20** below as well as to sideways relief. See **52.19** PARTNERSHIPS.

Relief under *ITA 2007, s 64* or *s 72* cannot be given against income from oil extraction activities or oil rights except to the extent (if any) that the loss arises from oil extraction activities or oil rights. [*ITA 2007, s 80; ITTOIA 2005, ss 225A, 225B*].

Trading losses carried forward

[45.19] On a claim under *ITA 2007, s 83*, any trading loss not used as above (or any unused balance) may be carried forward to subsequent years without time limit. A claim is given effect by deducting the loss in arriving at net income for subsequent tax years (see Step 2 at **1.10** ALLOWANCES AND TAX RATES). However, it can only be deducted from profits of the same trade, profession or vocation carried on by the same individual. The deduction must be made from the first available profits (and then, if those profits are insufficient, from the next available, and so on until the loss is exhausted). The deduction is made in priority to any other deductions from available profits. The loss must be deducted from available profits even if those profits might otherwise have been covered by personal reliefs; partial deductions are not permitted. [*ITA 2007, ss 61(2), 83, 84*].

See the second example at **45.4** above as regards losses used in aggregation (for which see *CIR v Scott Adamson* CS 1932, 17 TC 379). See *Bispham v Eardiston Farming Co* Ch D 1962, 40 TC 322 as to effect of what is now *ITTOIA 2005, s 9(2)* (all farming by a person treated as one trade — see **75.77** TRADING INCOME) on the carry-forward of farming losses. See **75.18** TRADING INCOME for case law as to whether a trade is the same trade as that carried on previously.

Time limit for claims

By virtue of *TMA 1970, s 43(1)* (see **16.4** CLAIMS), a claim to carry forward a loss must be made within four years after the end of the tax year in which the loss arose. The loss is relieved automatically against subsequent profits with no further claim being necessary.

For a case turning on the failure to establish the year(s) in which losses from an abortive business venture arose, see *Richardson v Jenkins* Ch D 1995, 67 TC 246.

Relief against trade-related interest and dividends

Where full relief for a carried-forward loss cannot be given for any particular year because of an insufficiency of trading profits, any interest or dividends for that year that 'relate to the trade' are treated for this purpose as profits of the trade. Interest or dividends for a tax year *'relate to the trade'* if they arise in the tax year and, were it not for the fact that they have been subjected to tax under other provisions, they would be brought into account in calculating the trading profits. [*ITA 2007, s 85*]. See also **75.94** TRADING INCOME.

Carry-forward on incorporation

If a trade or business carried on by an individual (or by individuals in partnership) is transferred to a company for consideration consisting wholly or mainly of the allotment (to the individual or his nominee) of shares in the company, any unrelieved pre-incorporation trading losses brought forward under the above provisions are deductible from income derived by the individual from the company, which may take the form of dividends on the shares or may be, for example, director's fees.

The brought-forward loss is deductible against such derived income for a particular tax year only if throughout that tax year the individual retains beneficial ownership of the allotted shares *and* the company continues to carry on the trade. In the tax year of incorporation, these conditions must be satisfied throughout the period from the transfer of the business to the following 5 April. In practice, relief should not be refused for any year throughout which shares representing at least 80% of the consideration received for the business are retained (HMRC Business Income Manual BIM85060).

[*ITA 2007, s 86*].

Change of residence

Where, on a sole trader becoming or ceasing to be UK resident, the trade is deemed to be permanently discontinued and a new one commenced, losses of the 'old' trade may be carried forward under the above provisions and set against profits of the 'new' trade. See **75.19** TRADING INCOME (and see **52.22** PARTNERSHIPS for a similar rule as regards an individual trading in partnership).

Miscellaneous

For the treatment in certain circumstances of interest as a loss carried forward, see **45.22**.

For the purpose of relieving a carried-forward loss from **oil-related activities**, profits from other activities may be treated as being from the same trade if that would have been the case apart from the rule at **75.1** TRADING INCOME requiring oil-related activities to be treated as a separate trade. [*ITA 2007, s 87*].

Simon's Taxes. See **B8.204**.

Terminal loss relief

[45.20] If a person ceases to carry on a trade or profession in a tax year and makes 'terminal losses', he may make a claim under *ITA 2007, s 89* to set off the total amount of terminal losses against the profits of the trade etc. for the tax year in which the cessation occurs and the three preceding tax years. The claim is given effect by deducting this amount in arriving at net income for those tax years (see Step 2 at **1.10** ALLOWANCES AND TAX RATES), with the deduction for each year being restricted to the profits available. The deduction must be made firstly for the latest tax year for which there are available profits and then, if those profits are insufficient, for the previous year, and so on until either the total amount of the terminal losses or the maximum three-year carry-back period is exhausted. Any amount still unrelieved is potentially available for relief under any of the other trading loss reliefs described in this chapter (subject to the conditions and time limits for claiming those reliefs).

Subject to the maximum three-year carry-back period, terminal losses must be deducted from available profits even if those profits might otherwise have been covered by personal reliefs; partial deductions are not permitted.

Each of the following is a '*terminal loss*':

(a) the loss (if any) sustained in the final tax year (i.e. the period from 6 April to cessation); and
(b) the loss (if any) sustained in that part of the penultimate tax year that falls within the twelve months immediately preceding cessation,

insofar as such losses have not otherwise been relieved. A terminal relief claim must cover both the loss (if any) at (a) and the loss (if any) at (b); it is not possible to include one and not the other. If there is a profit at (a) but a loss at (b), or *vice versa*, the profit is not netted off against the loss but is simply disregarded — see also the example and note at **45.21** below. If periods of account do not coincide with tax years, time apportionment is used to arrive at the figures at (a) and (b) (unless, exceptionally, a more accurate method is available).

For the inclusion in certain circumstances of interest in a terminal loss, see **45.22**.

Time limit for claims

By virtue of *TMA 1970, s 43(1)* (see **16.4** CLAIMS), a claim for relief must be made within four years after the end of the tax year in which cessation occurs.

See **16.2** CLAIMS for further provisions regarding claims for a loss incurred in one tax year to be carried back to an earlier tax year.

Overlap relief (see **75.14** TRADING INCOME) is a deduction in computing the profit or loss of the final tax year (not the final period of account) and thus falls to be included in full in a terminal loss claim (and may itself create a terminal loss).

Partnerships

Terminal loss relief is available to an outgoing member of a partnership in respect of losses sustained in his notional trade. All partners may claim terminal loss relief on cessation of the actual partnership trade. See **52** PARTNERSHIPS.

Relief against trade-related interest and dividends

Where full relief for terminal losses cannot be given for any particular tax year because of an insufficiency of trading profits, any interest or dividends for that year that 'relate to the trade' are treated for this purpose as profits of the trade. Interest or dividends for a tax year '*relate to the trade*' if they arise in the tax year and, were it not for the fact that they have been subjected to tax under other provisions, they would be brought into account in calculating the trading profits. See also **75.94** TRADING INCOME.

[*ITA 2007, ss 63, 89–93*].

Simon's Taxes. See B8.206.

Example

[45.21]

B, a trader with a 30 September year end, ceases to trade on 30 June 2020. Tax-adjusted results for his last two periods of account are as follows.

	Trading profit/ (loss)
Year ended 30 September 2019	£28,000
Nine months to 30 June 2020	(£9,000)

At cessation, there is unused overlap relief (see **75.14** TRADING INCOME) of £2,000. The terminal loss relief available is as follows.

	£	£
2020/21(6.4.20–30.6.20)		
£9,000 × 3/9		3,000
plus unused overlap relief		2,000
Terminal loss		5,000
2019/20(1.7.19–5.4.20)		
1.10.19–5.4.20 £9,000 × 6/9	6,000	
1.7.19–30.9.19 (£28,000) × 3/12	(7,000)	
	(1,000)	
Terminal loss		Nil
Terminal loss relief		£5,000

Note

In determining the terminal loss arising in a part of the final twelve months (a terminal loss period) that falls into any one tax year, a profit made in that period must be netted off against a loss sustained in that period. In this example, no net loss is incurred in the terminal loss period falling within 2019/20. However, the two different tax years are considered entirely separately, so that the 'net profit' of £1,000 falling within 2019/20 does not have to be netted off against the 2020/21 loss and is instead disregarded. The losses which do not form part of the terminal loss claim may be relieved under *ITA 2007, s 64* (see **45.2** above), and in practice, where other income is sufficient, the whole of the losses would in many cases be claimed under *s 64*.

Treatment of interest as a trade loss

[45.22] Where relief is claimed under *ITA 2007, s 383* (see **42.5** INTEREST PAYABLE) in respect of interest paid wholly and exclusively for the purposes of a trade, profession or vocation carried on wholly or partly in the UK and full effect cannot be given to such relief due to an insufficiency of income, the amount unrelieved may be carried forward as a trading loss under *ITA 2007,* *s 83* (see **45.19** above) or treated as a trading loss for the purposes of computing a terminal loss under *ITA 2007, s 89* (see **45.20** above). The treatment is effectively restricted to interest within **42.6**(a) or **42.10** INTEREST PAYABLE (loans to purchase plant or machinery for, or to invest in, a partnership). [*ITA 2007, ss 88, 94*].

Share loss relief

[45.23] See generally HMRC Venture Capital Schemes Manual VCM70000 *et seq*.

An individual may claim relief from income tax, instead of from capital gains tax, for an allowable loss (as computed for capital gains tax purposes) on a disposal of 'qualifying shares'. The claim is under *ITA 2007, s 132*. The relief is known as 'share loss relief' (or, alternatively, relief for losses on shares in unlisted trading companies).

Share loss relief is available only if:

- the disposal is at arm's length;
- it is by way of a distribution on a winding up;
- the value of the shares has become negligible and a claim to that effect made under *TCGA 1992, s 24(2)* (see Tolley's Capital Gains Tax under Losses); or
- a deemed disposal occurs under *TCGA 1992, s 24(1)* (which deems the entire loss, destruction, dissipation or extinction of an asset to be a disposal — see Tolley's Capital Gains Tax under Disposal).

Relief is not available where the shares are the subject of an exchange or arrangement within *TCGA 1992, ss 135* or *136* and, because of *TCGA 1992, s 137*, that exchange or arrangement involves a disposal of the shares.

'*Qualifying shares*' are ordinary shares or stock:

- in a 'qualifying trading company' for which the individual 'subscribed'; or
- to which EIS income tax relief is attributable (see **29** ENTERPRISE INVESTMENT SCHEME).

For this purpose, an individual '*subscribes*' for shares if they are issued to him by the company in consideration of money or money's worth, or were transferred to him *inter vivos* by his spouse or civil partner who had similarly subscribed for them. The spouses or civil partners concerned must be living together at the time of the transfer, and the shares are treated as issued to the transferee at the time they were issued to the transferor. Where an individual has subscribed for shares, he is treated as having subscribed for any bonus shares subsequently issued to him in respect of those shares provided that the bonus shares are in the same company, of the same class and carry the same rights as the original shares. The bonus shares are treated as issued at the time the original shares were issued.

The definition of 'qualifying trading company' differs according to whether the shares are issued after 5 April 1998 (see **45.26** below) or were issued on or before that date (see **45.28** below).

HMRC accept that share loss relief is available on shares which were subscribed for either in joint names or through a nominee and to which no EIS income tax relief was attributable. In the case of joint ownership, the proportion of the capital loss to be attributed to each owner must be determined as a question of fact, typically based on each owner's contribution to the cost of the shares. (HMRC Brief 41/10, 11 October 2010).

Where, for shares subscribed for before 10 March 1981, the consideration was deemed equal to the market value under *CGTA 1979, s 19(3)*, the loss allowable on disposal cannot exceed what the loss would have been without applying that subsection. (For shares subscribed for after 9 March 1981, market value is not substituted where the consideration is less than market value.)

[*ITA 2007, ss 131, 135, 150, 151(1)(2); FA 2020, s 38(2)(3)*].

For two more or less concurrent cases involving whether or not shares had been subscribed for and producing different results, see *Murray-Hession v HMRC* FTT (TC 5348), [2017] SFTD 299, [2016] UKFTT 612 (TC) (taxpayer's appeal allowed) and *Alberg v HMRC* FTT (TC 5357), [2017] SFTD 406, [2016] UKFTT 621 (TC) (taxpayer's appeal dismissed).

Simon's Taxes. See E3.7.

Operation of (and claims for) relief

[45.24] A loss within **45.23** above may be claimed against income:

- of the tax year in which the loss is incurred; and/or
- of the tax year preceding that in which the loss is incurred.

If a claim is made in relation to both tax years, it must specify the year for which relief is to be given first. The loss is deducted in calculating net income for the specified tax year, and, if the claim relates to both tax years, any remaining part of the loss is then deducted in calculating net income for the other year.

Where, against income of the same year, claims are made both in respect of that year's loss and in respect of the following year's loss, the claim for the current year's loss takes precedence.

There is a cap on the total amount of prescribed income tax reliefs that individuals can claim. See **1.11** ALLOWANCES AND TAX RATES. Share loss relief is one of the prescribed reliefs.

A claim for relief must be made in writing on or before the first anniversary of 31 January following the tax year *in which the loss is incurred*. There is no reason why a claim cannot be made by personal representatives for losses incurred during the deceased's lifetime (*Drown and another v HMRC* FTT (TC 4007), [2014] UKFTT 892 (TC)).

Share loss relief is given in priority to relief under *ITA 2007, s 64* (see **45.2** above) and *ITA 2007, s 72* (see **45.7** above) for the same tax year.

To the extent that share loss relief is obtained in respect of a loss, the loss is not an allowable loss for capital gains tax purposes. Any part of the loss for which income tax relief is not given does, however, remain an allowable loss for capital gains tax purposes.

[*ITA 2007, ss 132, 133; TCGA 1992, s 125A(1)*].

The provisions at **16.2** CLAIMS for relief involving two or more years do not apply where a loss within **45.23** above is claimed against income of the preceding year (*R (oao Derry) v HMRC* SC, [2019] STC 926). The claim will usually be included in the self-assessment for the preceding year, which means that HMRC can enquire into the claim only by means of a notice of enquiry under *TMA 1970, s 9A* (see **64.6** CLAIMS) into the preceding year's return.

Limits on relief

Where an individual claims share loss relief in respect of a loss on the disposal of qualifying shares which form part of a 'section 104 holding' or a '1982 holding' (i.e. holdings of shares which are pooled for capital gains tax purposes) either at the time of disposal or at an earlier time, the relief is restricted to the sums that would have been allowable as deductions in computing the loss if the qualifying shares had not formed part of the holding.

Where the qualifying shares were acquired on the same day as other shares that are not capable of being qualifying shares (see below), such that, by virtue of *TCGA 1992, s 105(1)(a)*, all the shares are treated as acquired by a single transaction, the amount of relief is restricted to the sums that would have been allowable as deductions in computing the loss if the qualifying shares were treated as acquired by a single transaction and the other shares were not so treated.

Where the qualifying shares, taken as a single asset, and other shares or debentures in the same company which are not capable of being qualifying shares, also taken as a single asset, are treated for capital gains tax purposes as the same asset under *TCGA 1992, s 127*, the amount of relief is restricted to the sums that would have been allowable as deductions in computing the loss if the qualifying shares and the other shares were not to be treated as the same asset.

For the above purposes, shares to which EIS income tax relief is not attributable are not capable of being qualifying shares at any time if they were acquired otherwise than by subscription, if the condition at **45.26**(c) below was not met in relation to the issue of the shares or (in relation to disposals made before 24 January 2019) the condition at **45.26**(d) below would not be met if the shares were disposed of at that time. Additionally, for the purposes only of the 'same asset' restriction above, shares to which EIS income tax relief is not attributable are not capable of being qualifying shares at any time if they are shares of a different class from the qualifying shares concerned.

[*ITA 2007, s 147; FA 2020, s 38(2)(3)*].

See HMRC Venture Capital Schemes Manual VCM75400 *et seq.* as to the computation of share loss relief where a holding does not entirely consist of qualifying shares.

Share identification rules

[45.25] The following provisions apply to identify whether a disposal of shares forming part of a mixed holding (i.e. a 'holding' of shares including shares that are not capable of being qualifying shares and other shares) is a disposal of qualifying shares and, if so, to which of any qualifying shares acquired at different times the disposal relates. Except as noted below, the normal capital gains tax identification rules apply and where shares are thereby identified with the whole or any part of a *s 104* holding or a 1982 holding, they are further identified with acquisitions on a last in/first out (LIFO) basis.

The above rules do not apply where the holding includes *any* of the following:

- shares in respect of which the long defunct Business Expansion Scheme relief was given and was not withdrawn;
- shares to which Enterprise Investment Scheme (EIS) income tax relief is attributable (see **29** ENTERPRISE INVESTMENT SCHEME);
- shares to which EIS capital gains deferral relief is attributable (see **29.24** ENTERPRISE INVESTMENT SCHEME);
- shares to which Seed Enterprise Investment Scheme (SEIS) income tax relief is attributable (see **65** SEED ENTERPRISE INVESTMENT SCHEME).

Instead, disposals are identified in accordance with the identification rules generally applicable to BES, EIS and SEIS shares (broadly, first in/first out (FIFO) — see, for example, **29.11** ENTERPRISE INVESTMENT SCHEME). As regards EIS shares, special rules apply where an election under *TCGA 1992, s 105A* (election for alternative treatment: tax-advantaged-scheme shares) is made.

Where the above rules cannot identify the shares disposed of, the identification is to be made on a just and reasonable basis.

A '*holding*' of shares for the above purposes is any number of shares of the same class held by one individual in the same capacity, growing or diminishing as shares of that class are acquired or disposed of. Shares comprised in a 'new holding' following a reorganisation to which *TCGA 1992, s 127* applies are treated as having been acquired when the original shares were acquired. Any shares held or disposed of by a nominee or bare trustees for an individual are treated as held or disposed of by that individual.

[*ITA 2007, ss 148, 149*].

Qualifying trading company — shares issued after 5 April 1998

[45.26] As regards shares issued after 5 April 1998, a '*qualifying trading company*', for the purposes of **45.23** above, is a company which:

(a) either
  (i) on the date of disposal meets the trading requirement, control and independence requirement, qualifying subsidiaries requirement and (for shares issued on or after 17 March 2004) the property managing subsidiaries requirement; or
  (ii) has ceased to meet any of those requirements within three years before the date of disposal and has not since that cessation been an 'excluded company', an investment company (as defined) or a trading company; *and*

(b) either
  (i) has met each of the requirements in (a)(i) above for a continuous period of at least six years prior to the disposal (or prior to the cessation in (a)(ii) above, as the case may be); or
  (ii) has met each of those requirements for a shorter continuous period ending with the disposal or cessation and has not previously been an excluded company, an investment company or a trading company; *and*

(c) met the gross assets requirement both immediately before and immediately after the issue of the shares and (for shares issued after 6 March 2001) met the unquoted status requirement at the 'relevant time'; *and*

(d) (in relation to disposals made before 24 January 2019) has carried on its business wholly or mainly in the UK throughout the period ending with the date of disposal of the shares and beginning with the incorporation of the company, or, if later, one year before the date on which the shares were issued.

See **45.27** below as regards the six requirements mentioned in (a)–(c) above. The requirement in (d) was abolished in relation to disposals made on or after 24 January 2019.

For shares issued before 7 March 2001, it was also a condition that the company be an 'unquoted' company (as defined for the purposes of the unquoted status requirement) throughout that part of the period mentioned in (d) above that falls before 7 March 2001.

An '*excluded company*' is a company which has a trade consisting mainly of dealing in land, in commodities or futures or in shares, securities or other financial instruments or which is not carried on on a commercial basis with a reasonable expectation of profit, or a company which is the holding company of a group other than a 'trading group', or which is a building society (see **8.1** BANKS AND BUILDING SOCIETIES) or a registered industrial and provident society (as defined).

A '*trading group*' is a group (i.e. a company and its 51% subsidiaries) the business of the members of which, taken together, consists wholly or mainly in the carrying on of a trade or trades (disregarding any trade carried on by a subsidiary which is an excluded company.

[*ITA 2007, ss 134, 151(1)(7), Sch 2 paras 38, 50; FA 2020, s 38(1)(3); SI 2007 No 940*].

The six requirements

[45.27] The six requirements referred to at **45.26**(a) to (c) above are as follows.

The trading requirement

The company must either:

(i) exist wholly for the purpose of carrying on one or more 'qualifying trades' (see **29.59** ENTERPRISE INVESTMENT SCHEME) (disregarding purposes having no significant effect on the extent of its activities); or

(ii) be a '*parent company*' (i.e. a company that has one or more 'qualifying subsidiaries' (see **29.56** ENTERPRISE INVESTMENT SCHEME)) and the business of the '*group*' (i.e. the company and its qualifying subsidiaries) must not consist wholly or as to a substantial part in the carrying on of 'non-qualifying activities'.

Where the company intends that one or more other companies should become its qualifying subsidiaries with a view to their carrying on one or more qualifying trades, then, until any time after which the intention is abandoned, the company is treated as a parent company and those other companies are included in the group for the purposes of (ii) above.

For the purpose of (ii) above, the business of the group means what would be the business of the group if the activities of the group companies taken together were regarded as one business. Activities are for this purpose disregarded to the extent that they consist in:

- holding shares in or securities of any of the company's subsidiaries;
- making loans to another group company;
- holding and managing property used by a group company for the purposes of a qualifying trade or trades carried on by any group company; or
- holding and managing property used by a group company for the purposes of research and development from which it is intended either that a qualifying trade to be carried on by a 'group company' will be derived or, for shares issued after 5 April 2007, a qualifying trade carried on or to be carried on by a group company will benefit. '*Group company*' includes, for this purpose, any existing or future company which will be a group company at any future time.

Activities are similarly disregarded to the extent that they consist, in the case of a subsidiary whose main purpose is the carrying on of qualifying trade(s) and whose other purposes have no significant effect on the extent of its activities (other than in relation to incidental matters), in activities not in pursuance of its main purpose.

'*Non-qualifying activities*' are:

- excluded activities within **29.59** ENTERPRISE INVESTMENT SCHEME; and
- non-trading activities (other than research and development (as defined)).

References in the definition of 'qualifying trade' and 'excluded activities' at **29.59** ENTERPRISE INVESTMENT SCHEME to 'period B' are to be taken for the above purposes to refer to the continuous period mentioned in **45.26**(b) above.

A company ceases to meet the trading requirement if before the time that is relevant for the purposes of **45.26**(a) above a resolution is passed or an order is made for the winding up of the company or if the company is dissolved without winding up. This does not, however, apply if the winding-up is for genuine commercial reasons and not part of a scheme a main purpose of which is tax avoidance and the company continues, during the winding up, to be a trading company. (Note that the continuation of trading condition now applies in relation to shares issued after 5 April 2001 but did originally apply up to and including 20 March 2000, after which a drafting error inadvertently altered the law.) For shares issued after 20 March 2000, a company does not cease to meet the trading requirement by reason of anything done as a consequence of its being in administration or receivership (both as defined by *ITA 2007, s 252*), provided everything so done and the entry into administration or receivership are for genuine commercial (and not tax avoidance) reasons. For shares issued after 16 March 2004, these provisions are extended to refer also to the winding up, dissolution, administration or receivership of any of the company's subsidiaries.

The control and independence requirement

Subject to, the share exchange provisions at **45.23** above, the issuing company must not:

(I) control another company other than a qualifying subsidiary (see **29.56** ENTERPRISE INVESTMENT SCHEME) or, for shares issued before 21 March 2000, have a 51% subsidiary other than a qualifying subsidiary, 'control' being construed in accordance with *CTA 2010, ss 450, 451* and being considered with or without connected persons within *ITA 2007, s 993*;

(II) be a 51% subsidiary of another company or otherwise under the control of another company, 'control' being construed in accordance with *ITA 2007, s 995* and again being considered with or without connected persons; or

(III) be capable of falling within (I) or (II) by virtue of any arrangements (as very broadly defined).

The qualifying subsidiaries requirement

The company must not have any subsidiaries other than qualifying subsidiaries (see **29.56** ENTERPRISE INVESTMENT SCHEME).

The property managing subsidiaries requirement

For shares issued on or after 17 March 2004, any 'property managing subsidiary' (see **29.55** ENTERPRISE INVESTMENT SCHEME) that the company has must be a 'qualifying 90% subsidiary' (see **29.57** ENTERPRISE INVESTMENT SCHEME).

The gross assets requirement

The value of the company's gross assets must not exceed £7 million immediately before the issue of the shares in respect of which relief is claimed and must not exceed £8 million immediately afterwards. In relation to shares issued before 6 April 2006, these limits were £15 million and £16 million respectively; the higher limits continue to apply in relation to shares issued after 5 April 2006 to a person who subscribed for them before 22 March 2006. If the issuing company is a parent company, the gross assets test applies by reference to the aggregate gross assets of the company and all its qualifying subsidiaries (disregarding certain assets held by any such company which correspond to liabilities of another).

The general approach of HMRC to the gross assets requirement is that the value of a company's gross assets is the sum of the value of all of the balance sheet assets. Where accounts are actually drawn up to a date immediately before or after the issue, the balance sheet values are taken provided that they reflect usual accounting standards and the company's normal accounting practice, consistently applied. Where accounts are not drawn up to such a date, such values will be taken from the most recent balance sheet, updated as precisely as practicable on the basis of all the relevant information available to the company. Values so arrived at may need to be reviewed in the light of information contained in the accounts for the period in which the issue was made, and, if they were not available at the time of the issue, those for the preceding period, when they become available. The company's assets immediately before the issue do not include any advance payment received in respect of the issue. Where shares are issued partly paid, the right to the balance is an asset, and, notwithstanding the above, will be taken into account in valuing the assets immediately after the issue regardless of whether it is shown in the balance sheet. (HMRC SP 2/00).

The unquoted status requirement

For shares issued on or after 7 March 2001, the company must be 'unquoted' at the time (the '*relevant time*') at which the shares are issued and no arrangements must then exist for it to cease to be unquoted. If, at the time of issue, arrangements exist for the company to become a wholly-owned subsidiary of a new holding company by means of a share exchange within the provisions at **45.29** below, no arrangements must exist for the new company to cease to be unquoted. A company is '*unquoted*' if none of its shares etc., are listed on a recognised stock exchange or on a foreign exchange designated for the purpose, or dealt in outside the UK by such means as may be designated for the purpose. Securities on the Alternative Investment Market ('AIM') are treated as unquoted for these purposes (Revenue Press Release 20 February 1995).

[*ITA 2007, ss 137–144, Sch 2 paras 40–47, 51–57*].

Qualifying trading company — shares issued before 6 April 1998

[45.28] As regards shares issued before 6 April 1998, a '*qualifying trading company*', for the purposes of **45.23** above, is a company none of whose shares have been listed on a recognised stock exchange at any time in the period ending with the date of disposal of the shares and beginning with the incorporation of the company, or, if later, one year before the date on which the shares were subscribed for, and which:

(a) either
  (i) is a trading company (i.e. a company, other than an excluded company, whose business consists wholly or mainly of the carrying on of a trade or trades, or which is the holding company of a 'trading group') on the date of the disposal; or
  (ii) has ceased to be a trading company within the previous three years and has not since that time been an investment company or an 'excluded company'; and

(b) either
  (i) has been a trading company for a continuous period of six years ending on the date of disposal of the shares or the time it ceased to be a trading company; or
  (ii) if shorter, a continuous period ending on that date or that time and had not before the beginning of that period been an excluded company or an investment company; and

(c) (in relation to disposals made before 24 January 2019) has been resident in the UK since incorporation until the date of disposal.

Securities on the Alternative Investment Market ('AIM') are generally treated as unquoted for these purposes (Revenue Press Release 20 February 1995.

A '*trading group*' is a group (i.e. a company and its 51% subsidiaries) the business of the members of which, taken together, consists wholly or mainly in the carrying on of a trade or trades (disregarding any trade carried on by a subsidiary which is an excluded company or which is non-UK resident).

An '*excluded company*' is a company which has a trade consisting mainly of dealing in shares, securities, land, trades or commodity futures or which is not carried on on a commercial basis with a reasonable expectation of profit, or a company which is the holding company of a group other than a trading group, or which is a building society (see **8.1** BANKS AND BUILDING SOCIETIES) or a registered industrial and provident society (as defined).

[*ITA 2007, s 134, Sch 2 para 38; FA 2020, s 38(2)(3)*].

Miscellaneous

[45.29] The following matters are relevant.

Anti-avoidance

Any claim to relief under **45.23** above will bring in the provisions of *TCGA 1992, s 30* (value-shifting to give a tax-free benefit) so that the relief may be adjusted for any benefit conferred whether tax-free or not. [*TCGA 1992, s 125A(2)*].

Company reorganisations etc.

The following applies only to shares to which EIS income tax relief is not attributable. It does not apply where the share exchange provisions below apply. Where shares are disposed of and represent a new holding identifiable under *TCGA 1992, s 127* with 'old shares' after a reorganisation or reduction of share capital, relief under **45.23** above is not available unless it could have been given if an allowable loss had arisen on the disposal of the old shares at arm's length at the reorganisation etc., had this legislation been in force. Where the reorganisation did not so qualify, but new consideration was given for the new shares, relief is limited to such of that new consideration as is an allowable deduction. '*New consideration*' is money or money's worth but excluding any surrender or alteration to the original shares or rights attached thereto, and the application of assets of the company or distribution declared but not made out of the assets.

[*ITA 2007, s 136, Sch 2 para 39*].

See HMRC Venture Capital Schemes Manual VCM75390.

Share exchanges

The following provisions apply in relation to shares to which EIS income tax relief is not attributable. Where, by means of an exchange of shares, all of the shares (the old shares) of a company (the old company) are acquired by a company (the new company) in which the only previously issued shares are subscriber shares, then, subject to the further conditions below being satisfied, the exchange is not regarded as involving a disposal of the old shares and an acquisition of the new company shares (the new shares). Where old shares held by an individual were subscribed for by him and EIS relief was not attributable to them, the new shares stand in the shoes of the old shares, e.g. as if they had been subscribed for and issued at the time the old shares were subscribed for and issued and as if any requirements under the above provisions met at any time before the exchange by the old company had been met at that time by the new company.

The further conditions are as follows.

(a) The consideration for the old shares must consist entirely of the issue of the new shares.
(b) The consideration for old shares of each description must consist entirely of new shares of the 'corresponding description'.
(c) New shares of each description must be issued to holders of old shares of the 'corresponding description' in respect of and in proportion to their holdings.
(d) The exchange of shares must not be treated for capital gains tax purposes as involving a disposal of the old shares or an acquisition of the new shares by virtue of *TCGA 1992, s 127*.

For these purposes, old and new shares are of a '*corresponding description*' if, assuming they were shares in the same company, they would be of the same class and carry the same rights.

References above to 'shares' (other than those to 'shares to which EIS income tax relief is not attributable' or 'subscriber shares') include references to 'securities'.

An exchange within these provisions, or arrangements for such an exchange, do not breach the control and independence requirement at **45.27** above.

[*ITA 2007, ss 145, 146, Sch 2 paras 48, 49*].

Example

[45.30]

Xanthe subscribed for 3,500 £1 ordinary shares at par in ABC Ltd in May 2011. She purchased a further 1,750 such shares on the stock market in September 2016, by which time their market price had risen to £2.50 per share. By 2020, the company's stock market value had slumped. Xanthe feels that it may recover but nonetheless sells 2,625 shares on the market in October 2020 at 40p per share (total proceeds £1,050) and makes a claim for share loss relief. It is accepted that the shares she subscribed for in May 2011 are qualifying shares for share loss relief purposes. At no time have any shares in ABC Ltd qualified for any tax relief under the enterprise investment scheme or seed enterprise investment scheme.

The CGT pool is as follows:

		Shares	*Cost*
			£
May 2011	Subscription	3,500	3,500
Sept 2016	Purchase	1,750	4,375
		5,250	7,875
Oct 2020	Sale	(2,625)	(3,938)
C/fwd		2,625	£3,937

Allowable loss for CGT purposes for 2020/21 (proceeds £1,050 – cost £3,938) = £2,888.

For share loss relief purposes, 1,750 of the shares sold are matched on a LIFO basis with the 1,750 shares purchased in September 2016. These are not qualifying shares as they were not subscribed for.

875 of the shares sold are matched with part of the 3,500 qualifying shares subscribed for in May 2011.

So one-third (875/2,625) of the shares sold relate to qualifying shares. Therefore, the proportion of the allowable loss attributable to the qualifying shares sold is one-third of £2,888 = £963.

However, the actual cost of the qualifying shares sold is only £875 (£3,500 × 875/3,500). The loss qualifying for share loss relief is restricted to this amount.

Share loss relief available to Xanthe for 2020/21 and/or 2019/20 = £875

Allowable loss remaining available for CGT purposes = £2,013 (£2,888 – £875)

Note

(a) Xanthe would consider making the share loss relief claim if she has sufficient taxable income in 2020/21 and/or 2019/20 to set off the loss without wasting allowances and if her net chargeable gains for 2020/21 are within the annual exempt amount such that capital losses for the year are wasted. Even if chargeable gains were in excess of the annual exempt amount it might still be worth making the share loss relief claim so as to obtain relief at income tax rates in preference to CGT rates.

Employment losses

[45.31] Rules very similar to those at **45.2** above apply to enable a loss sustained in an employment or office (an '*employment loss*') in a tax year to be set against general income (i) of the tax year in which the loss is incurred, or (ii) of the tax year preceding that in which the loss is incurred, or (iii) of both those tax years. A claim must be made on or before the first anniversary of 31 January following the tax year in which the loss is made and is given effect by deducting the loss in arriving at net income for the tax year in question (see Step 2 at **1.10** ALLOWANCES AND TAX RATES).

There is a cap on the total amount of prescribed income tax reliefs that individuals can claim. See **1.11** ALLOWANCES AND TAX RATES. Relief for employment losses against general income is one of the prescribed reliefs.

Examples of situations in which an employment loss might arise include managers etc. who are entitled to a share of profits but also have to bear a share of any losses and sales persons who are required to bear the cost of bad debts arising from orders they have obtained. In *Martin v HMRC* UT, [2015] STC 478, the appellant was contractually obliged to repay part of a taxable signing bonus received from his employer in an earlier tax year; the repayable amount was held to constitute negative taxable earnings and eligible for relief under these provisions. Relief is denied for a loss if, and to the extent that, it is sustained as a result of anything done in pursuance of arrangements a main purpose of which is the avoidance of tax. For HMRC's guidance on negative taxable earnings, including examples and reference to *Martin v HMRC*, see HMRC Employment Income Manual EIM00800–00845.

A claim within (i) above is made under *ITA 2007, s 128(2)(a)*. A claim within (ii) above is made under *ITA 2007, s 128(2)(b)*. A claim within (iii) above is made under *ITA 2007, s 128(2)(c)*. If a claim is made within (i) above and the loss is not wholly exhausted, a subsequent claim can be made (within the time limit) within (ii) above, and *vice versa*.

Where a claim is made for a loss to be set against income of both the same tax year and the preceding tax year, there is no statutory order of priority; the claimant must specify the tax year for which the deduction from income should be made first.

Where, against income of the same year, claims are made both under (i) in respect of that year's loss and under (ii) in respect of the following year's loss or under **45.2** above in respect of a trading loss made in that following year, (i) takes precedence.

The facility at **45.5** above to set off surplus trading losses against capital gains is also available in relation to an employment loss. The restrictions at **45.9–45.18** above on set-off of trading losses do not apply in relation to employment losses.

[*ITA 2007, ss 128–130*].

See **16.2** CLAIMS for further provisions regarding claims for a loss incurred in one tax year to be carried back to an earlier tax year.

Simon's Taxes. See **E4.789A.**

46

Making Tax Digital (MTD)

Introduction to making tax digital

[46.1] In his March 2015 Budget speech the Chancellor of the Exchequer George Osborne made a dramatic announcement:

> '*12 million people and small businesses are forced to complete a self-assessment tax return every year. It is complex, costly and time-consuming. So, today I am announcing this. We will abolish the annual tax return altogether. Millions of individuals will have the information the Revenue needs automatically uploaded into new digital tax accounts. A minority with the most complex tax affairs will be able to manage their account online. Businesses will feel like they are paying a simple, single business tax — and again, for most, the information needed will be automatically received. A revolutionary simplification of tax collection. Starting next year. Because we believe people should be working for themselves, not working for the tax man. Tax really doesn't have to be taxing, and this spells the death of the annual tax return.*'

Following the Budget HMRC published a briefing paper *Making Tax Easier*, which set out further details of this vision. The intention was that by 2020, every individual and small business would be able to manage their tax affairs through a digital tax account, removing the need to submit annual tax returns. Businesses were told that 'by 2020 they would be able to manage all of their taxes together' and that 'accounting software would be able to feed data into their digital tax account'.

HMRC's stated ambition was to transform themselves into one of the most digitally advanced tax administrations in the world (November 2015 spending review).

That bold ambition still remains, but in the five years since the Chancellor's original statement, there have been many setbacks on the road to implementation and at the time of writing the picture looks very different to the one which was originally set out. A limited version of Making Tax Digital (MTD) for VAT is in operation and some progress has been made, particularly with digital tax accounts, but in 2020 almost nothing of the original plans for transforming the system for businesses is yet in place. It is still far from clear when businesses will start to see major changes in the way that they manage their tax compliance. The COVID-19 (coronavirus) crisis has further diverted HMRC resources away from MTD developments and there is little sign of an early return to MTD being made a priority.

Stop Press

Shortly before the 2020/21 edition of this book went to print, HMRC announced a resumption of the MTD programme. See www.gov.uk/government/publications/tax-administration-strategy/building-a-trusted-modern-tax-administration-system. The key features are as follows.

- From April 2022, MTD will apply to all VAT-registered businesses: at the moment businesses who have registered for VAT on a voluntary basis do not have to operate MTD for VAT.
- From April 2023, MTD for Income Tax will come into operation. Businesses and landlords with business turnover over £10,000 p.a. will be required to keep digital records and to update HMRC on a quarterly basis using MTD-compliant software.
- A consultation will be launched later in 2020 on the design of MTD for companies.

The Government will be looking at the rules for payment of income tax and will be consulting on proposals to move towards a real-time system for payments of income tax. No details are available and it is likely that any new system will take some time to evolve. The Government recognises that any change will need a transition period to help taxpayers manage the potential effect on cashflow. It also acknowledges that any system will have to work both ways — in other words that where there is a down turn in business, tax repayments can also be made in real time. Finally, the Government has formally recognised that the current legislation underlying the tax administration system is not compatible with a 21st century tax regime and is in need of reform. The process of reform, which is likely to take some considerable time, will start with a call for evidence later in 2020 which will allow interested parties to identify areas which will need to be considered.

Full details of these proposals, and any subsequent developments, will be covered in full in future editions of this work.

A brief history of MTD developments to date

[46.2] In order to assist readers in understanding the current position it is useful briefly to set out the main stages in the development of what has become known as Making Tax Digital (MTD). This is not intended as a full analysis of everything which has happened. For more detailed information, see the House of Commons Library briefing paper no 7949 published on 28 February 2018 (https://researchbriefings.parliament.uk/ResearchBriefing/Summary/CBP-7949).

The first details of how MTD would work for business were published with the Autumn Statement and Spending Review in November 2015. The key features were:

- Businesses and landlords would be required to keep digital records.
- They would be required to update HMRC at least quarterly via their digital tax accounts.
- MTD would be compulsory for all businesses and landlords except for individuals in employment and pensioners unless their secondary incomes from self-employment or property were in excess of £10,000 per year.
- The Government would consult on options to simplify the payment date for taxes, bringing them closer to the date on which profits were earned.
- MTD would be introduced for income tax for unincorporated businesses in 2018, for VAT in 2019 and for companies in 2020.

The proposals to require businesses to update HMRC at least four times a year were controversial and attracted a great deal of criticism. A petition calling on the Government to scrap the plan achieved over 100,000 signatures (something very rare for online petitions), thus triggering a debate in parliament. The minister gave assurances that individuals would not have to complete four tax returns a year. All that was required were updates and these would automatically be generated from the software itself. 'The agony', he said 'of the annual tax return would be a thing of the past'.

There was a significant delay, partly due to the EU Referendum, before any further information emerged. But in August 2016, HMRC published six consultation documents which explained in detail how various aspects of MTD would work. These included a number of cases studies illustrating the proposed flow of information, from a trader scanning an invoice into an app in real time through to software generating the information for the quarterly update to HMRC. The only policy change was an announcement that *all* businesses with turnovers under £10,000 would be exempt and a commitment that businesses with turnovers over £10,000 but below an unspecified limit would be given an extra year before MTD would be made compulsory. It also became clear that the Government had decided not to make any changes to the date on which tax would become due, although there was further consultation on a method of voluntary pay as you go.

The Treasury Committee examined the MTD proposals in 2016 and published its findings in January 2017. It expressed significant concerns about the proposed timetable and recommended a delay until at least 2019/20. It also heavily criticised HMRC's figures for the costs and benefits of the MTD project to business and suggested that the total cost of the programme might exceed any savings which it produced.

In January, 2017 HMRC responded to some of these concerns. They announced that businesses would be able to continue to use spreadsheets to record income and expenditure and that free software would be available to small businesses to enable them to comply with their MTD obligations. They also said that for the first 12 months of MTD no late submission penalties would be imposed on businesses while they got used to the transition to the new way of reporting. They confirmed that HMRC would be piloting the digital systems with 'hundreds of thousands of businesses' before MTD was rolled out on a mandatory basis.

In the 2017 Budget, HMRC expanded on its earlier announcement that there would be a one-year deferral of MTD for smaller businesses, defined as those with a turnover below the VAT registration threshold. The first tranche of MTD legislation, dealing with record-keeping and updating was also announced.

Further pressure was put on HMRC following reports by the House of Lords Economic Affairs Committee and the Treasury Committee in early 2017. These again criticised the timetable and the economic modelling.

The Government responded in July 2017 by announcing a major change to the timetable. MTD for VAT would still be introduced from 2019 but businesses would not be required to keep digital records for income tax or to update HMRC quarterly until at least 2020.

Further cost estimates were published with the Autumn 2017 Budget. These showed that, under the revised timetable, there was likely to be an ongoing net cost to business rather than the savings which were originally projected.

In May 2018, HMRC announced a pause in some of its major transformation projects in the light of the priority needed to be given to Brexit. There would be a delay in work on parts of MTD for individuals, including progress on simple assessment and real time tax code changes, and there would be a slowing of the pace in the creation of the single account for business customers. It was again confirmed that there would be no further mandation of MTD for businesses until 2020 at the earliest.

Finally, in the Spring Statement delivered on 13 March 2019, the Chancellor made the following announcement:

> '*Making Tax Digital (MTD) – Mandatory digital record keeping for VAT for businesses over the VAT threshold (with turnover over £85,000) comes into force from 1 April. This is an important first step in this modernisation of the tax system to which the Government remains committed. The Government can confirm a light touch approach to penalties in the first year of implementation. Where businesses are doing their best to comply, no filing or record keeping penalties will be issued. The focus will be on supporting businesses to transition and the Government will therefore not be mandating MTD for any new taxes or businesses in 2020.*'

This statement did not say when MTD would be mandated for new taxes or businesses, only that it would not be in 2020. At the time of writing, there has been no further clarification from HMRC as to the future of the MTD programme. The commitment to MTD remains (see for example the updated briefing paper issue at Budget 2020 'Making Tax Digital: An evaluation of the VAT service and update on the Income Tax Service' at www.gov.uk/government/publications/making-tax-digital-review, but clearly, the original ambition of the programme has now been scaled back considerably and the bold vision of the death of the tax return by 2020 will no longer be achieved. Given

HMRC's success with the delivery of the IT systems to deliver the various coronavirus support schemes it may be that the experience of those major projects will reanimate the MTD project, but that is something which is unlikely to be seen in the near future.

The remainder of this chapter will concentrate on MTD for business but will first discuss the non-business aspects of MTD for individuals. The VAT aspects of MTD are dealt with in Tolley's Value Added Tax.

Making tax digital — personal tax accounts

[46.3] There is no doubt that considerable progress has been made in the non-business aspects of MTD. The latest figures show that at least 20 million people have personal tax accounts. In correspondence with the Public Accounts committee in 2018 HMRC revealed that 685,000 taxpayers who accessed their digital tax accounts between August 2016 and March 2017 had their returns pre-populated with employment income and taxable benefits information. The reported accuracy rate was in excess of 80%. In the same correspondence HMRC said that, contrary to expectation, pre-population of tax returns did not lead to an increase in the amount of tax collected. HMRC had assumed that where taxpayers made mistakes in completing tax returns the effect would more often be to understate liabilities — by overclaiming expenses or understating income. However, random sampling showed that the reverse was true. The majority of mistakes made by individuals who did not have the benefit of pre-populated returns led them to underclaiming expenses or overstating income.

One of the key drivers for digital tax accounts was that taxpayers would interact digitally with HMRC rather than by telephone or letter. While there has been some reduction in non-digital interaction, it has not been as great as was anticipated. As a result, HMRC have announced that additional services will only be added to the digital tax account 'where they reduce phone or post contact or deliver significant savings'.

The key announcement was that a decision had been made to delay plans to introduce further digital services for individuals. This means halting work on simple assessment and real time code changes. Those were at the heart of the plans for transforming the administration of personal tax and allowing the death of the tax return. HMRC had planned to use real time information to adjust tax codes in year in order to ensure that the right amount of tax on non-employment income was paid via PAYE and so obviate the need for individuals to complete a tax return. This 'dynamic coding' model would have taken considerable IT resource to implement and it is not surprising that work on it has been stopped.

Simple assessment (see **6.5** ASSESSMENTS) has already been implemented in limited form. HMRC issued the first simple assessments in 2017 (see www.gov.uk/government/publications/issue-briefing-simple-assessment-ending-the-tax-return/simple-assessment-ending-the-tax-return) and it is reported that 400,000 such assessments will be issued. These simple assessment deal only with new State pensions with income exceeding the personal allowance and

PAYE taxpayers who cannot have their tax coded out. Most of the taxpayers involved would not have been in self-assessment anyhow so in itself this will not significantly reduce the number of taxpayers who have to complete a tax return. HMRC had planned to develop the simple assessment programme so that further types of income were brought within it but in 2018, as a result of the pressure on resources caused by Brexit, work was halted on the programme and there is no indication that it will be resumed. Thus many taxpayers will remainin self-assessment and all the indications are that they will continue to have to self-assess for at least the next few years. The tax return certainly did not die by 2020 and it is likely to be with us for some time to come.

Making tax digital for business — general overview

[46.4] The long-term aim of MTD for business is that all of a business's tax compliance will be undertaken end-to-end via digital means. A business will keep records electronically, use an app to store those records and produce reports on a regular basis to HMRC. It will have a single digital account which holds all of its tax information and which it can use to monitor its tax position in real time. That still remains the intention, but at explained in **46.2** above the timetable for this has been considerably extended and it will be after 2020 before MTD becomes mandatory for income tax or corporation tax purposes. It may well be some considerable time after that date that the single tax account for business becomes a reality.

MTD does, however, remain in place for VAT. Businesses with turnover above the VAT registration threshold (currently £85,000) will be required to keep digital records for VAT purposes and report VAT information quarterly for each quarterly return period commencing after 31 March 2019. More details of the MTD regime for VAT can be found in Tolley's Value Added Tax.

Making tax digital for business — record-keeping

[46.5] The starting point for MTD for business is electronic record-keeping. Much of the early controversy about MTD was over the requirement for quarterly reporting of information to HMRC and the record-keeping aspect received comparatively little attention. It may however turn out that in practice, this requirement is the most controversial aspect of the entire MTD programme. Hitherto, while the tax legislation has imposed record-keeping requirements for businesses it has not set out prescriptive rules for how those records are to be kept. MTD changes this by setting out detailed rules about the records which need to be maintained.

The legislation requiring digital record-keeping for income tax purposes has already been enacted (though it will not come into force until a date to be appointed). *F(No 2)A 2017* introduces a new *TMA 1970, Sch A1. Sch A1 para 1* sets out the scope of the requirement as follows.

> *(1)* *This Schedule applies to a person within the charge to income tax who, otherwise than in partnership, carries on (or has carried on)—*
>
> > *(a)* *a trade, profession or vocation the profits of which are chargeable to income tax under Part 2 of ITTOIA 2005;*

(b) *a property business the profits of which are chargeable to income tax under Part 3 of ITTOIA 2005; or*
(c) *any other activity which may give rise to profits or other income chargeable to income tax under Part 2 or 3 of ITTOIA 2005.*

The requirements of *Sch A1* do not apply to the trustees of a charitable trust, or the trustees of an exempt unauthorised unit trust (within 80.9 unit trusts etc.).

They also do not apply to certain excluded activities:

- the underwriting business of a member of Lloyd's (within the meaning of *FA 1993, s 184*);
- holding shares in respect of which a distribution may be made which is chargeable to income tax under *ITTOIA 2005, Pt 3* by virtue of *CTA 2010, s 548(6)* (distributions to shareholders in real estate investment trusts — see 59.24 property income); and
- participating in an open-ended investment company which may make distributions chargeable to income tax under *ITTOIA 2005, Pt 3* by virtue of *SI 2006 No 964, Reg 69Z18* (property income distributions — see 80.4 unit trusts).

[*TMA 1970, Sch A1 paras 1, 2; F(No 2)A 2017, s 60(3)*].

Note that a person who is carrying on a business which includes both excluded and non-excluded activities will still be within MTD in respect of its non-excluded activities.

It will, however, be possible for a taxpayer to elect to bring himself within the scope of *Sch A1* if he wishes.

Sch A1 also applies to a partnership if one or more of the partners is within the charge to income tax, again with similar exceptions to the above. A partner must be nominated, either by the partnership or by HMRC, to carry out the obligations under the Schedule on behalf of the partnership. [*TMA 1970, Sch A1 paras 3, 4; F(No 2)A 2017, s 60(3)*].

For the avoidance of doubt nothing in *Sch A1* applies to companies: no legislation or regulations relating to companies has yet been published.

TMA 1970, Sch A1 does not itself set out any specific record-keeping requirements. Instead, it gives HMRC the vires to introduce regulations which specify which records are to be kept.

(1) *The Commissioners may by regulations require a person or partnership to whom this Schedule applies to—*

  (a) *keep specified records relating to the business in electronic form; and*
  (b) *preserve those records in electronic form for a specified period.*

(2) *The records which may be specified are any records the Commissioners consider relevant to ascertaining information required to be provided by regulations under this Part of this Schedule.*
(3) *A requirement imposed by regulations under this paragraph is in addition to, and not in place of, any other requirement that the person or partnership keep and preserve records (or keep and preserve records in a particular form).*

[*TMA 1970, Sch A1 para 11; F(No 2)A 2017, s 60(3)*].

The Act also imposes on HMRC an obligation to make regulations for the digitally excluded. In the case of a partnership each partner must be digitally excluded in order for the partnership to come within the exclusion. A person is digitally excluded if he is a practising member of a religious society or order whose beliefs are incompatible with using electronic communications or keeping electronic records, or if for any reason (including age, disability or location) it is not reasonably practicable for the person or partner to use electronic communications or to keep electronic records. [*TMA 1970, Sch A1 para 14; F(No 2)A 2017, s 60(3)*].

A penalty of up to £3,000 can be imposed for failure to keep digital records. [*TMA 1970, Sch A1 para 12; F(No 2)A 2017, s 60(3)*].

Draft regulations under these provisions were published in January 2017 (https://assets.publishing.service.gov.uk/government/uploads/system/uploads/attachment_data/file/644163/Making_Tax_Digital_Regulations_YYYY__030817_.pdf). They remain in draft and what follows should be read with the knowledge that the final regulations could be significantly different.

Under *para 3* of the draft regulations a person within MTD must use 'functional compatible software' to record and retain digital records for all transactions made in the course of business. These records must include:

- the amounts of the transactions;
- the dates of the transactions, according to the basis used by the relevant entity for recording transactions for the purposes of income tax; and
- the categories of transactions into which the transactions fall, to the extent those categories are specified.

'*Functional compatible software*' means a software program or set of compatible software programs the functions of which include:

- recording and preserving digital records in a digital form;
- providing to HMRC quarterly updates and as applicable, end of period statements or *Sch A1* partnership returns in a digital form and by using the API platform; and
- receiving information from HMRC using the API platform in relation to a relevant entity's compliance with obligations under these regulations

This leaves open two key questions. What exactly is meant by functional compatible software and when do digital records actually have to be recorded? As originally envisaged MTD would have required businesses to take a digital record of every invoice with an app. HMRC now accept that records can be kept on a spreadsheet provided that that spreadsheet can 'talk' to HMRC via a suitable app. Businesses will not however be able to submit the spreadsheet to HMRC with their tax return. The updates and final report will have to be submitted via the app.

As far as the date on which digital records have to be made the draft regulations say that the record must be made *by the date on which the quarterly update is due* (or if earlier the date on which the quarterly update is actually made). Thus, there is no requirement that digital records have to kept in real time. It is understood that although this would clearly be HMRC's preference it is accepted that a business which keeps records in paper form and then puts those details into a spreadsheet at a later date – even after the expiry of the relevant quarter – will be in compliance with the regulations.

There is a recognition that the requirement to make a digital record of each transaction would be too onerous for retailers, and therefore under *para 17* of the draft regulations retailers are given, subject to certain conditions, the right to elect to agree with HMRC an alternative basis of complying with the record-keeping requirement. The details of this are not discussed here.

Making tax digital for business — quarterly updates

[46.6] The next part of the process is that regular updates of information must be given to HMRC. *TMA 1970, Sch A1 para 7* creates the vires for quarterly reporting.

The Commissioners may by regulations require a person or partnership to whom this Schedule applies to provide to HMRC, by electronic communications, specified information about the business of the person or partnership.

The information which may be specified includes any information ('financial information') relevant to calculating profits, losses or income of the business, including information about receipts and expenses.

The regulations may require information to be provided at or for specified intervals, times or periods.

The regulations may not require financial information about the business to be provided more often than once every three months.

[*TMA 1970, Sch A1 para 7; F(No 2)A 2017, s 60(3)*].

Apart from restricting the number of times which information can be required to four times a year the legislation does not set out any detail of what information is required. This is however set out in the draft regulations at *para 7* onwards. Businesses will be required to submit what is described as '*update information*' for each quarter no later than one month after the end of that quarter. Update information includes (but is not restricted to) the following:

- providing designatory information;
- identifying the commencement date and end date of the quarterly period in respect of which a quarterly update is provided;
- providing totals of the amounts falling within specified categories of transactions, being amounts derived from the relevant entity's digital records;
- where more than one information period falls within a quarterly period, identifying how much of those totals is attributable to each information period; and
- identifying the properties which form part of a property business.

Further information is given in a draft Income Tax (Digital Requirements) notice published in September 2017 (*Income Tax Notice XX: Retail Sales, Update Information, End of Period Information and Partnership Information notice*). It is proposed that certain parts of this notice (including the specification of the information which is required) will have the force of law. This is an unusual approach for direct taxes in UK law and is more characteristic of VAT, where certain notices have always had the force of law.

Designatory data, which only has to be provided the first time a business enters MTD, is the following.

Personal Designatory Data

- Name
- Address
- Date of Birth
- Telephone Number
- National Insurance Number

Business Designatory Data

- Business Name
- Unique Tax Reference
- Description of Business
- Business Address – including postcode
- Date business started – DD/MM/YYYY
- Date business ceased – DD/MM/YYYY
- Does the business draw up accounts?
- If so, Accounting Period Start – DD/MM/YYYY
- And Accounting Period End – DD/MM/YYYY
- Basis Period Start – DD/MM/YYYY
- Basis Period End – DD/MM/YYYY
- Does the business account for income tax using the cash basis? – Yes/No
- Has the business made an election under Part 5 of the regulations (retail sales)? – Yes/No
- Trade Type and Classification – Selected from a standardised list

Additional data will be required for partnership and property businesses. This is not listed in this chapter but can be found in the draft notice (https://assets.publishing.service.gov.uk/government/uploads/system/uploads/attachment_data/file/644228/Income_Tax_Digital_Requirements_Regulations.pdf).

The information which is required quarterly will be as follows.

- Update Period Start Date
- Update Period End Date

Business Income

- Turnover – takings, fees, sales or money earned
- Other business income

Business Expenses

- Cost of goods bought for resale or goods used
- Construction Industry – payments to subcontractors
- Wages, salaries and other staff costs

- Car, van and travel expenses
- Rent, rates and insurance costs
- Repairs and maintenance of property and equipment
- Phone, fax, stationery and other office costs
- Advertising
- Business entertainment costs
- Interest on bank and other loans
- Bank, credit card and other financial charges
- Accountancy, legal and other professional fees
- Goods and services for own use
- Total Construction Industry Scheme deductions
- Other business expenses

Business with turnover below the VAT registration threshold (currently £85,000) may if they wish provide only summary information. This is defined as follows.

Income

- Turnover – takings, fees, sales or money earned
- Other business income

Expenses

- Total allowable expenses

Essentially this is the equivalent of the current three-line account format which can be used for small business tax returns (see **75.20** trading income and **60.18** property income).

Again the draft notice gives more detail of what information will be required quarterly for property businesses and partnerships, but this is not repeated here.

A business may if it wishes provide updates to HMRC on a more frequent basis, but is not required to do so.

HMRC are given no powers to enquire into quarterly updates and have been at pains to stress that the information in updates will not itself be used as a reason to open enquiries into tax returns. However, they will be able to take account of such information in any enquiries which are made. But information which is included in a quarterly update will be treated as information available to HMRC for the purpose of determining whether a discovery assessment can or cannot be issued.

Making tax digital for business — annual summary

[46.7] When MTD was first proposed the working assumption was that the four quarterly updates would be sufficient, at least in straightforward cases, to provide all the necessary information to complete a tax filing and that all that would be required would be a declaration that those filings were correct. Tax adjustments could be made with each quarter's update.

It was, however, envisaged that most businesses would need to make a final filing in order to process any errors made during the year or to make any necessary tax adjustments. HMRC originally proposed that the deadline for doing this would be nine months after the end of the period to which the accounts were drawn up. In the consultation response of February 2017 HMRC announced a change of mind and said that the deadline would be 'the earlier of 10 months after the end of the period of account or 31 January in the year of account in which the profits are charged to tax'. However this revised deadline itself created further problems and there was a further change. The legislation as enacted specifies the deadline as the actual date of delivery of the tax return for the year in question (which will be redundant if the tax return is abolished) but no later than 31 January after the end of that year. [*TMA 1970, Sch A1 para 8; F(No 2)A 2017, s 60(3)*]. This effectively preserves the existing self-assessment filing date.

The working assumption (although this is nowhere set out in statute) is that many businesses may be prepared to submit quarterly updates themselves but instruct their accountants to prepare the final update. HMRC have consistently said that agents will be able to operate MTD on behalf of their clients but at the time of writing the precise mechanism under which this will happen is not clear.

Most of the *TMA 1970* provisions relating to tax returns, including such matters as enquiries and assessment will apply to final updates as they currently apply to returns.

Making tax digital for business — start date

[46.8] The start date for MTD has not yet been announced — all that is known at the moment is that it will not be until after 2020. But once the overall start date has been announced there will be rules to determine when each business has to start making quarterly updates. The basic proposition is that businesses will be required to make their first update starting on their first accounts date after the introduction of MTD. There are more detailed rules for business which are, or include, a property business, or where accounts are drawn up for a period which is not 12 months. These are not discussed here.

Making tax digital for business — miscellaneous points

[46.9] The draft regulations include more details about such matters as digital exclusion, partnership, large retailers, error corrections and sundry other issues. In the interests of space these are not covered here.

Although HMRC have repeatedly said that free software will be available to allow business to comply with their MTD obligations they have also stressed that they will not be providing that software and are looking to the commercial market to do so. Some commercial software is now available, at least in beta form. A small-scale pilot of MTD for Income Tax began in April 2017 involving a small number of businesses, agents, and software providers. This was designed to show that the end-to-end MTD Income Tax service could operate successfully in real time. At Budget 2020, HMRC reported that the first businesses in the service had met their income tax obligations entirely through MTD. They were therefore not required to submit an income tax return in the normal way. HMRC has indicated that some 1 million sole traders and landlords are eligible to take part in the pilot. More information about participating in the pilot can be found here www.gov.uk/guidance/follow-the-rules-for-making-tax-digital-for-income-tax.

HMRC have consulted on the interest and penalty aspects of MTD and is considering its response to the issues which were raised. Nothing has yet been enacted, however, and therefore the proposals are not discussed here. Links to the relevant consultations can be found at www.gov.uk/government/consultations/making-tax-digital-interest-harmonisation-and-sanctions-for-late-payment.

Making tax digital for business — the future

[46.10] Given the fundamental changes which have occurred since MTD was first mooted it is difficult to be certain about what direction it will take following the latest announcement of deferral of some of the key projects. Some form of MTD will undoubtedly evolve but what finally comes in may well look very different to the regime which was originally envisaged. It is assumed that the fundamental building blocks of digital record-keeping and quarterly updating will be retained but even this is not certain. Whether or not the regulations discussed in this chapter will be subject to significant change is also an open question. Perhaps the feedback of running the pilot, together with the experience of the early years of MTD for VAT (which has similar, though not identical, record-keeping requirements) will feed through into revised regulations, but that is all for the future. In the Budget 2020 report, HMRC indicated that they would indeed learn from the experience of the MTD for VAT in developing its approach for MTD for income tax. Interestingly, HMRC suggest that they will look at the way that MTD can be the catalyst for a business to consider its wider approach to technology and how it can harness it to drive profits and growth. This appears to be an acknowledgment that MTD cannot operate in a vacuum, but that if it really can be integrated into the way that businesses operate it has a greater chance of being accepted as a positive move rather than as the imposition of obligations with no apparent business benefit.

MTD for companies is still apparently part of the Government's plans but there is as yet no legislation or regulations to give any indication as to how it will operate. A consultation document on this was expected to be published in the spring or summer of 2018 but at the time of writing this still had not been issued.

Practitioners have tended to put MTD for income tax to the back of their minds following the announcement of the deferral until after 2020. This is entirely understandable, and with dealing with COVID-19 now being the priority it is going to be even harder for agents to devote time to thinking about MTD. There is not the urgency that there was, and MTD is now far less likely to result in the wholescale changes to the way that accounting and tax firms manage the compliance process which were once predicted. But it remains an important topic which should be raised with clients, particularly those whose record-keeping is currently unsatisfactory.

HMRC's digital ambition remains in place but the sheer complexity of what is required, as well as the enormity of the Brexit challenge has meant that revolution has been replaced by gradual evolution. As Mark Twain almost said 'reports of the death of the tax return have been greatly exaggerated'.

47

Managed Service Companies

Cross-reference. See 58 PERSONAL SERVICE COMPANIES.

Simon's Taxes. See E4.9.

Introduction to managed service companies

[47.1] Managed service companies (MSCs) (which for this purpose include composite service companies) are intermediaries through which individual workers provide their services to clients. They differ from personal service companies in that the worker, though often a shareholder, is not in business on his own account, is not usually a director of the MSC and does not exercise control over the MSC. Instead, the MSC is controlled by a scheme provider who promotes the use of the MSC and makes its structure available to workers for a fee. The underlying nature of the contracts in which the worker is involved is said to be almost invariably one of employment.

It had always been HMRC's view that the personal service company legislation can be applied equally to MSCs where the conditions at **58.4** PERSONAL SERVICE COMPANIES were satisfied (see Revenue Tax Bulletins August 2002 pp 956, 957 and December 2004 pp 1165–1168). But apparently they found it difficult in practice to enforce the legislation against MSCs. Furthermore, even where a tax debt to HMRC has been established it was difficult to collect the debt as the MSC has no assets and can simply be wound up (with the workers transferring to a new MSC set up for that purpose).

As a result, the provisions described in this chapter take MSCs out of the ambit of the personal service company rules and apply a separate set of rules instead for 2007/08 onwards. Personal service companies remain within the rules described at 58 PERSONAL SERVICE COMPANIES.

For official guidance etc., see HMRC Employment Status Manual ESM3500.

The operation of *ITEPA 2003, ss 44–47* (workers supplied by agencies — see **28.48** EMPLOYMENT INCOME) is not affected by the provisions in this chapter. Nothing in these provisions applies to a payment or transfer subject to deduction of tax under *ITA 2007, s 966(3)* or *(4)* (payments to non-resident entertainers and sportsmen — see **50.11** NON-RESIDENTS). [*ITEPA 2003, s 61A(2)*].

See also **20.6** CONSTRUCTION INDUSTRY SCHEME (CIS) (payments to MSCs in the construction industry) and http://webarchive.nationalarchives.gov.uk/+/http://www.hmrc.gov.uk/news/cis-msc-faqs.htm (employment agencies or businesses placing workers in the construction sector).

Meaning of 'managed service company'

[47.2] For the purposes of these provisions, the meaning of '*company*' is extended to include a partnership (which would include a Limited Liability Partnership) as well as a body corporate. The term 'managed service company' must be read accordingly.

A company is a '*managed service company*' for these purposes if it meets all of the following criteria:

(a) its business consists wholly or mainly of providing (directly or indirectly) the services of an individual to other persons;
(b) payments are made (directly or indirectly) to the individual (or to 'associates' of his) of an amount equal to the amount the company is paid for those services or to the greater part of that amount;
(c) the way in which the payments are made results in the individual (or associates) receiving a greater net amount (after tax and National Insurance) than would have been received if all the payments in respect of the individual's services had been taxable as employment income; and
(d) a person who carries on a business of promoting or facilitating the use of companies to provide the services of individuals ('*an MSC provider*') is 'involved with the company'.

An MSC provider is '*involved with the company*' if he (or an 'associate' of his):

(i) benefits financially on an ongoing basis from the provision of the individual's services; or
(ii) influences or controls the provision of those services; or
(iii) influences or controls the way in which the above-mentioned payments are made; or
(iv) influences or controls the company's finances or any of its activities (other than by merely providing legal or accountancy services in a professional capacity); or
(v) undertakes to indemnify the individual against a tax loss (see *ITEPA 2003, s 61C(5)(6)* for details) or promotes such an undertaking.

A person is not within (d) above merely by virtue of his providing legal or accountancy services in a professional capacity. Also, a person is not within (d) above if he merely carries on a business as an employment agency, i.e. placing individuals with persons who wish to obtain their services, unless he (or an 'associate' of his) does anything within (iii)–(v) above. The Treasury has power to exclude (by statutory instrument) further categories of person from being within (d) above.

See HMRC Employment Status Manual ESM3520. For a discussion on whether an MSC provider was 'involved with the company', see *Christianuyi Ltd v HMRC* CA, [2019] STC 681.

The question of whether a person is an '*associate*' of another person for the purposes of these provisions is determined by *ITEPA 2003, s 61I* (and note that this treats a cohabiting couple as if they were spouses or civil partners). For the purposes of (a)–(d) and of (i)–(v) above, an 'associate' of a person ('P') also includes any person who, in order to secure that the individual's services are provided by a company, acts in concert with P (or with P and others); this is particularly relevant in terms of an associate of the MSC provider.

[*ITEPA 2003, ss 61B, 61C, 61I; SI 2019 No 1458, Sch 3 para 25(3)*].

The 'deemed employment payment'

[47.3] If:

(a) the services of an individual ('the worker') are provided (directly or indirectly) by a managed service company (MSC);
(b) the worker, or an associate of his (within *ITEPA 2003, s 61I*), receives (from any person) a payment or benefit that can reasonably be taken to be in respect of those services; and
(c) the payment or benefit is not earnings received by the worker directly from the MSC,

the MSC is treated as making to the worker, and the worker is treated as receiving, a payment which is to be treated as earnings from an employment ('the deemed employment payment'). The deemed employment payment is treated as made at the time the payment or benefit in (b) above is received.

The reference to a 'payment or benefit' in (b) above means anything that, if received by an employee for performing the duties of an employment, would be general earnings from the employment (for which see **28.13** EMPLOYMENT INCOME). A payment or a cash benefit is treated as received when payment is made. A non-cash benefit is treated as received when it would have been treated as received (see *ITEPA 2003, s 19* or *s 32*) if the worker were an employee and the benefit were provided by reason of the employment.

The above provisions are disapplied, in a case where the payment or benefit mentioned in (b) above is received on or after 6 April 2021, where the provision of the services in (a) above gives rise (directly or indirectly) to an engagement within the rules at **58.23–58.36** PERSONAL SERVICE COMPANIES ETC. (workers' services provided through intermediaries to public sector or to medium/large clients) and either:

- the client (see **58.25**(a) PERSONAL SERVICE COMPANIES ETC.) is a public authority (see **58.23**); or

- for the tax year in which the payment or benefit is received, the client does not qualify as small (see **58.16**) and has a UK connection (see **58.22**).

Previously, the above provisions were similarly disapplied (for 2017/18 onwards), but the disapplication rule has been expanded to take account of the extension of the rules at **58.23–58.36** PERSONAL SERVICE COMPANIES ETC. to private sector engagements.

[*ITEPA 2003, ss 61D, 61F(2)(5); FA 2017, Sch 1 paras 7, 15; FA 2020, Sch 1 paras 18, 26*].

Computation of deemed employment payment

[47.4] The deemed employment payment in **47.3** above is computed as follows.

(1) Take the amount of the payment or benefit referred to at **47.3**(b) above. The amount of a payment or a cash benefit is the amount received. The amount of a non-cash benefit is equivalent to the cash equivalent of the benefit; the latter is determined under the benefits code rules (see **28.51–28.60, 28.69** EMPLOYMENT INCOME), modified in the case of living accommodation. If a payment or benefit relates only partly to the provision of the worker's services and partly to other matters, it is to be apportioned on a just and reasonable basis.

(2) Deduct any expenses met by the worker that would have been deductible under normal rules (see **28.16** EMPLOYMENT INCOME) if the worker had been employed by the person to whom the worker's services are provided ('the client') and those expenses had been met from his earnings. See further below.

If the result is a negative amount, or is nil, there is no deemed employment payment. In any other case, the deemed employment payment is the amount which, together with employer's NICs thereon, is equal to the result of applying steps (1) and (2) above. In other words, allowance is made at this point for the fact that employer's NICs are chargeable on the deemed payment itself (see Tolley's National Insurance Contributions).

Note that step (2) effectively applies the rules on qualifying travelling expenses at **28.16**(a) EMPLOYMENT INCOME as if each engagement with a client were a separate employment at a permanent workplace (thus disallowing relief for travel between the worker's home and that workplace).

If the MSC is a partnership of which the worker is a member, expenses met by the worker on behalf of the partnership can be brought into account at step (2).

If a vehicle is provided by the MSC for the worker or, where the MSC is a partnership of which the worker is a member, a vehicle is provided by the worker for the purposes of the partnership business, mileage allowance relief (see **28.82** EMPLOYMENT INCOME) can also be included in the expenses deductible at step (2) to the extent that it would have been deductible from earnings on the assumption that the worker was employed by the client and that the vehicle was not provided by the client.

[*ITEPA 2003, ss 61E, 61F(3)(4)*].

Tax treatment of deemed employment payment

[47.5] The deemed employment payment is taxed (and PAY AS YOU EARN (53) must be applied) as it would be if the worker were employed by the MSC and the deemed payment were a payment by the MSC of earnings from that employment. However, no deductions can be made from the deemed payment in respect of expenses etc., or mileage allowance relief (such matters having been taken into account as appropriate in the computation of the deemed payment itself — see **47.4** above).

If the worker is UK resident and the services in question are provided in the UK, the MSC is treated as having a place of business in the UK (and is thus obliged to operate PAYE for example — see **53.43** PAY AS YOU EARN) even if this is not, in fact, the case.

To the extent that, by reason of any combination of:

- the worker being resident or domiciled outside the UK or meeting the *section 26A* test in **28.7** EMPLOYMENT INCOME;
- the client being resident outside the UK; and
- the services in question being provided outside the UK,

the worker would not be chargeable if employed directly by the client, he is not chargeable to tax in respect of the deemed employment payment. (See **28.5**, **28.8** EMPLOYMENT INCOME for the relevant charging provisions.)

If the MSC is a partnership of which the worker is a member, the deemed employment payment is treated as received by the worker in his personal capacity and not as income of the partnership.

[*ITEPA 2003, s 61G*].

The total amount of deemed employment payments for a tax year is taken into account in determining whether the worker is a higher- or lower-paid employee for the purpose of applying the benefits code (see **28.21** EMPLOYMENT INCOME). [*ITEPA 2003, s 218(1)(e)*].

Recovery of tax from persons other than the MSC

[47.6] Regulations apply to enable a PAYE debt of an MSC to be recovered from other persons. This covers any amount that an officer of HMRC believes should have been deducted by an MSC from a payment of PAYE income (see **53.2** PAY AS YOU EARN) to an individual; it is not restricted to PAYE becoming due by virtue of the above provisions. The persons from whom such recovery may be made are as follows:

(a) a director or other office-holder, or an associate (within *ITEPA 2003, s 61I*), of the MSC;
(b) an MSC provider who is involved with the MSC (see **47.2** above);
(c) a person who (directly or indirectly) has encouraged, facilitated or otherwise been actively involved in the provision by the MSC of the individual's services; and

(d) a director or other office-holder, or an associate (within *ITEPA 2003, s 61I* but see also below), of a person who is not an individual but is within (b) or (c) above.

A person is not within (c) above merely by virtue of his providing legal or accountancy services in a professional capacity. For the purposes of (d) above, an 'associate' of a person ('P') also includes any person who, in order to secure that the individual's services are provided by a company, acts in concert with P (or with P and others).

The regulations set out the conditions under which a PAYE debt may be transferred to another person, the procedure and time limits for making such a transfer and an appeals procedure. Generally the transferee is required to settle the debt within 30 days of the transfer notice.

[*ITEPA 2003, s 688A; SI 2003 No 2682, regs 97A–97L; FA 2016, s 14(2); SI 2017 No 414, Regs 1, 2*].

Relief where dividends etc. paid by MSC

[47.7] A relief from double taxation is available where a **company** MSC is treated as making a deemed employment payment in any tax year and also pays a dividend (or otherwise makes a distribution) in that or a subsequent tax year. The provisions are similar to those for intermediaries at **58.13** PERSONAL SERVICE COMPANIES.

[*ITEPA 2003, s 61H; FA 2016, Sch 1 paras 61, 73*].

Computation of MSC's business profits

[47.8] In computing for income tax purposes the profits of a trade, profession or vocation carried on by an MSC, a deduction may be made for any deemed employment payment (and related employer's NICs) treated as made in connection with the trade etc. The deduction is made for the period of account in which the deemed employment payment is treated as made. The deduction can reduce the profits to nil for tax purposes but it cannot create a loss.

[*ITTOIA 2005, s 164A*].

The above does not apply in calculating profits on the cash basis (see **76.14** TRADING INCOME — CASH BASIS FOR SMALLER BUSINESSES).

48

Married Persons and Civil Partners

Cross-references. See **1.17**, **1.18**, **1.19** ALLOWANCES AND TAX RATES; **29.21** ENTERPRISE INVESTMENT SCHEME; **52.20** PARTNERSHIPS; **70.28**(a), **70.29** SETTLEMENTS as regards settlements not involving use of trusts.

Simon's Taxes. See E5.1.

Civil partnerships

[48.1] Civil partnerships first became possible in the UK on 5 December 2005 as a result of *Civil Partnership Act 2004*.

Civil partnerships before 31 December 2019

Before 31 December 2019, the effect of *Civil Partnership Act 2004* was to enable same-sex couples to obtain legal recognition of their relationship by forming a civil partnership broadly parallel to marriage. Tax parity between married couples and civil partnerships was achieved by numerous amendments to pre-existing tax legislation made by *SI 2005 No 3229* and *SI 2005 No 3230*. In as far as these amendments relate to income tax, they are reflected throughout this work where appropriate. In some respects, the amendments went beyond their principal purpose by also removing certain perceived inequalities of treatment based on gender and, in the case of a parent, marital status. In certain limited circumstances, income tax law treats a cohabiting unmarried couple in the same way as a married couple, and the amendments reflects this by giving equal treatment, in those same limited circumstances, to all cohabiting same-sex couples whether or not they are civil partners.

It was announced that on and after 5 December 2005 all pre-existing HMRC extra statutory concessions and statements of practice were to be regarded as extended, wherever relevant, so as to apply to civil partners as they do to married couples.

Civil partnerships on and after 31 December 2019

Civil Partnership Act 2004 is amended so as to enable *all* eligible couples in England and Wales, same-sex or otherwise, to enter into a civil partnership on or after 31 December 2019 if they wish. [*Civil Partnership Act 2004; Civil Partnerships, Marriages and Deaths (Registration etc) Act 2019, s 2; SI 2019 No 1458*].

A similar change will be made in Scotland by *Civil Partnership (Scotland) Act 2020* with effect from a date to be appointed, and has been made in Northern Ireland by *SI 2019 No 1514* with effect on and after 11 February 2020.

See www.gov.uk/government/publications/marriage-and-civil-partnership-in-england-and-wales for a table setting out the similarities and differences between civil partnership and marriage in England and Wales.

Transfers of certain personal reliefs

[48.2] See **48.3–48.6** below for transfers of relief between spouses and civil partners, but note that married couple's allowance is available only where at least one individual was born before 6 April 1935. See **1.19** ALLOWANCES AND TAX RATES for full details as to entitlement to, and the amount of, the married couple's allowance.

Spouses and civil partners are able to transfer *part* of their *personal allowance* from one individual to the other, provided that neither is a higher rate taxpayer and neither claims married couple's allowance — see **1.18** ALLOWANCES AND TAX RATES.

Transfer of basic married couple's allowance

[48.3] An individual can elect to be entitled to claim one-half of the *basic* married couple's allowance (see **1.19** ALLOWANCES AND TAX RATES) otherwise due to his or her spouse or civil partner for any tax year. Alternatively, a couple may jointly elect for the full amount of the *basic* allowance to be transferred between them, although the spouse or civil partner initially entitled can subsequently elect to be able to transfer back one-half of the basic allowance. In either case, the transferee must be UK resident or entitled to personal reliefs by virtue of **50.2** NON-RESIDENTS and must make a claim for the transferred amount.

An election under these provisions has to be made in prescribed form (i.e. form 18) before the first tax year for which it is to have effect (or within the first 30 days of that year if prior notification of intention to elect has been given to HMRC before the beginning of that year), and has effect until withdrawn or until a different election is made. If an election is to have effect for the tax year in which the marriage or civil partnership is entered into, it may be made during that year, but will only apply for that year to the fraction of the basic married couple's allowance available (see **1.19** ALLOWANCES AND TAX RATES). An election may be withdrawn with effect from the year following that in which notice of withdrawal is given.

[*ITA 2007, ss 47–50*].

Simon's Taxes. See **E1.923**.

Transfer of excess married couple's allowance

[48.4] Where either spouse's or civil partner's entitlement to an income tax reduction in respect of married couple's allowance exceeds his or her 'comparable tax liability', that individual may give notice to HMRC to transfer the excess, i.e. the unused amount of the reduction to his spouse or civil partner (in addition to any reduction to which his spouse or civil partner is already entitled). The notice must be given in prescribed form, it has effect for that tax year only and cannot be withdrawn. It must be given within four years after the end of the tax year to which it relates.

An individual's '*comparable tax liability*' is his income tax liability immediately after carrying out *Step 6* (subtraction of tax reductions) in the calculation at **1.10** ALLOWANCES AND TAX RATES, except that (for this purpose only):

- any reduction attributable to double tax relief under *TIOPA 2010, ss 2, 6* (double tax agreements) or *TIOPA 2010, s 18(1)(b), (2)* (unilateral relief) must be disregarded; and
- any necessary restriction to the individual's married couple's allowance to leave sufficient tax in charge to cover the tax deemed to be deducted at source from a gift aid donation (see **14.13** CHARITIES AND CHARITABLE GIVING) must be deducted; this leaves a greater amount of excess married couple's allowance available for transfer.

Although the legislation does not make it explicit, it would appear that the reduction attributable to the married couple's allowance itself must also be disregarded for the purpose of arriving at 'comparable tax liability' (see the example at **48.5** below).

[*ITA 2007, ss 51–53*].

Simon's Taxes. See **E1.923**, **E1.925**.

Example

[48.5]

Transfer of excess married couple's allowance

Mr Grey, who was born on 19 July 1933, has pension income of £12,320 and building society interest of £3,900 for 2020/21 and his wife, who was born in 1954, has a salary of £22,465 and building society interest of £2,500. Mr and Mrs Grey also receive interest of £2,800 in 2020/21 from a bank deposit account in their joint names. Each spouse's liability to income tax is at the main UK rates.

The couple have not made the joint election at **1.19** ALLOWANCES AND TAX RATES to be treated in the same way as couples marrying on or after 5 December 2005 for the purposes of the married couple's allowance. Neither have they made the election at **48.3** above to transfer the basic married couple's allowance between them. However, Mr Grey gives notice under *ITA 2007, s 51(4)* to transfer the unused balance of his married couple's allowance for 2020/21 to his wife.

The couple's tax position for 2020/21 is as follows.

		Mr Grey	Mrs Grey
		£	£
Employment income		—	22,465
Pension income		12,320	—
Building society interest		3,900	2,500
Bank deposit interest		1,400	1,400
Total and net income		17,620	26,365
Deduct Personal allowance		12,500	12,500
Taxable income		£5,120	£13,865
Tax payable:			
5,000 @ 0% (starting rate for savings)		—	
120 @ 0% (personal savings allowance)		—	
9,965 @ 20% (basic rate)			1,993.00
1,000 @ 0% (personal savings allowance)			—
2,900 @ 20% (basic rate on savings income)			580.00
		—	2,573.00
Deduct	Married couple's allowance £9,075 @ 10% = £907.50, but restricted to nil	—	
Deduct	Excess married couple's allowance		907.50
Total tax liabilities (subject to PAYE deductions)		Nil	£1,665.50

Transfer of blind person's allowance

[48.6] Any excess of the blind person's allowance (see **1.20** ALLOWANCES AND TAX RATES) over the 'remaining relievable income' of the individual entitled to it can be transferred from one spouse or civil partner to the other. For this purpose, an individual's '*remaining relievable income*' is his net income (i.e. his total income net of amounts, other than personal reliefs, deductible therefrom — see **1.10** ALLOWANCES AND TAX RATES) less his personal allowance. It is a condition of the transfer that the couple be living together, whilst married to, or in a civil partnership with, each other for at least part of the tax year. The transferee must be UK resident or entitled to personal reliefs by virtue of **50.2** NON-RESIDENTS and must make a claim for the transferred amount. The transferor must make an election to transfer the amount; the election must be made within four years after the end of the tax year to which it relates. The election has effect for that tax year only, cannot be withdrawn and also has effect as a notice to transfer excess married couple's allowance as in **48.4** above.

[*ITA 2007, ss 39, 40*].

Simon's Taxes. See **E1.917**.

Jointly-held property

[48.7] Special rules apply for the apportionment between spouses living together (see **48.8** below) of income arising from property held in their joint names. The rules extend to members of a civil partnership who are living together. Provided that at least one of them is beneficially entitled to that income, the spouses (or civil partners) are treated as beneficially entitled to it in equal shares, except in the following circumstances.

(i) Where the income is partnership income falling within **52** PARTNERSHIPS.
(ii) Where the income is from furnished holiday lettings (see **60.20** PROPERTY INCOME).
(iii) To the extent that the income is by any other provision of the *Income Tax Acts* treated as the income either of the spouse (or civil partner) who is not beneficially entitled to the income, or of a third party.
(iv) Where the income consists of a distribution in respect of shares in, or securities of, a close company (broadly a company controlled by five or fewer participators — see Tolley's Corporation Tax) to which the spouses (or civil partners) are beneficially entitled (whether in equal or unequal shares) or to which one of them is beneficially entitled. (The intention behind this is to prevent the normal 50:50 rule being used to circumvent the application of the settlements legislation (see **70.28**(a) SETTLEMENTS) where income is diverted to a spouse (or civil partner) via the payment of dividends.)
(v) Where the spouses (or civil partners) are not beneficially entitled to the income in equal shares, and they make a declaration of their beneficial interests in the income to which the declaration relates and the property from which that income arises, provided that the beneficial interests of the spouses (or civil partners) in the property correspond to their beneficial interests in the income.

A declaration under (v) above has effect in relation to income arising on and after the date of the declaration, and continues to have effect unless and until the beneficial interests of the spouses (or civil partners) in either the income or the property cease to accord with the declaration. Notice of a declaration must be given to HMRC, in a prescribed form (i.e. form 17) and manner, within 60 days of the date of the declaration. HMRC expect evidence of actual beneficial ownership to be submitted with form 17.

[*ITA 2007, ss 836, 837*].

See also HMRC Trusts, Settlements and Estates Manual TSEM9000 *et seq.*

Simon's Taxes. See **E5.103A.**

'Living together'

[48.8] Individuals who are married to, or are civil partners of, each other are treated for income tax purposes as '*living together*' unless they are:

- separated under a Court Order or deed of separation; or
- in fact separated in circumstances in which the separation is likely to be permanent.

[*ITA 2007, s 1011*].

A husband and wife may be separated even though living under the same roof if they have become two households (*Holmes v Mitchell* Ch D 1990, 63 TC 718).

Alimony, maintenance, separation allowances etc.

[48.9] By virtue of *ITTOIA 2005, s 727* (and its predecessor), see **30.3** EXEMPT INCOME, payments of alimony and maintenance do not form part of the taxable income of the person to whom they are made or of any other person. Where any such payments are 'qualifying maintenance payments', the *payer* obtains a limited relief as below. Relief is restricted to cases where at least one party was **born before 6 April 1935**. The relief available is **10%** of the lesser of:

- the total amount of 'qualifying maintenance payments' made by the payer which fall due in the tax year; and
- the amount of the *basic* married couple's allowance for that year (see **1.19** ALLOWANCES AND TAX RATES).

Relief is given by means of a tax reduction (see Step 6 at **1.10** ALLOWANCES AND TAX RATES). The order in which tax reductions are given against an individual's tax liability is set out at **1.12** ALLOWANCES AND TAX RATES, which also makes clear that a tax reduction must be restricted to the extent (if any) that it would otherwise exceed the individual's remaining income tax liability after making all prior reductions.

A '*qualifying maintenance payment*' is a periodical payment (other than an instalment of a lump sum) which:

(A) is made under a Court Order originating in the UK, another European Union (EU) member state or a European Economic Area (EEA) member state, or under a written agreement the law applicable to which is the law of a part of the EU or EEA, or under a maintenance assessment or maintenance calculation made under the *Child Support Act 1991* (or NI equivalent);

(B) is made *either*:
  - (i) by one party to a marriage or civil partnership (or former marriage or civil partnership) to or for the benefit of, and for the maintenance of, the other party; *or*
  - (ii) by one parent of a child to the other parent for the child's maintenance or by one person to another for the maintenance of a 'child of the family';

(C) is due at a time when:
  - (i) (in a case within (B)(i) above) the two parties are not a married couple, or civil partners, living together and the party to whom or for whose benefit the payment is made has not subsequently married or entered into a civil partnership; or
  - (ii) (in a case within (B)(ii) above) the payer and the payee are not living together; and

(D) does not otherwise attract tax relief for the person making the payment (i.e. apart from the relief under these provisions).

As regards (B) above, there is the additional requirement referred to above that at least one of the parties to the marriage (or former marriage) or civil partnership (or former civil partnership) or, in a case within (B)(ii) above, either the payer or the payee (or both), was born before 6 April 1935.

In (B) above, a child means a person under 21, and a '*child of the family*' is a child who is either the child of both parties or has been treated by them both as a child of their family (but not a child who has been boarded out with them by a public authority or voluntary organisation).

As regards (C) above, the fact that the subsequent marriage may itself have been dissolved does not alter the fact that the party to whom or for whose benefit the payment is made has remarried (*Norris v Edgson* Ch D 2000, 72 TC 553).

The above conditions were not satisfied by a payment made by the taxpayer to a former spouse for the maintenance of their child where the agreement required the payment to be made to the child (*Billingham v John* Ch D 1998, 70 TC 380), nor by payments made by one party to a marriage to pay off the joint mortgage on a house continuing to be occupied by the other (*Otter v Andrews* (Sp C 181), [1999] SSCD 67).

Paragraph (B) above is treated as satisfied in relation to periodical payments made to or retained by the Secretary of State (or equivalent NI Department) under a maintenance assessment or maintenance calculation under the *Child Support Act 1991* (or NI equivalent) by any person where another person is, for the purposes of that *Act*, a parent of the child(ren) to whom the assessment or calculation relates. Assessments or calculations under *section 7* of that *Act* (right of child in Scotland to apply for maintenance assessment or calculation) are excluded from this treatment.

Paragraph (B) above is also treated as satisfied in relation to periodical payments made to the Secretary of State (or equivalent NI Department) made by any person under a recovery of benefit order under *Social Security Administration Act 1992, s 106* or *Jobseekers Act 1995, s 23* (or NI equivalent of either) in respect of income support or income-based jobseeker's allowance claimed by another person.

[*ITA 2007, ss 453–456, Sch 2 para 101, Sch 3 Pt 1*].

A maintenance payment (as defined for this purpose) arising outside the UK is exempt from tax on receipt if it would have been exempt as above had it arisen in the UK. [*ITTOIA 2005, s 730*].

General matters

Court Orders for alimony generally take into account the income and the tax liabilities of both parties.

In strict law, the retrospective variation of a Court Order is not effective for tax purposes (*Morley-Clarke v Jones* CA 1985, 59 TC 567). For Orders made or varied after 30 June 1988 which provide for retrospective payments, only payments made on or after the date of the Order count towards the limit on which tax relief is available in any year. Payments made under a legally binding written agreement before the Court Order may of course qualify in their own right. (Revenue Press Release 15 March 1988). Payments made under an agreement voluntarily entered into by a father in favour of his children, for their maintenance following separation, and later confirmed by a Court Order, were not made under that Order and were thus ineffective for tax purposes (*CIR v Craw* CS 1985, 59 TC 56).

Simon's Taxes. See E1.801, E5.104–E5.113.

Example

[48.10]

Green, who was born on 7 October 1933, separated from his wife in June 2005 and, under a Court Order dated 15 July 2006, pays maintenance of £300 per month to his ex-wife and £100 per month to his daughter, payments being due on the first of each calendar month commencing 1 August 2006. Green has pension income of £21,470 and dividends of £2,200 for 2020/21. He re-marries on 6 October 2020. Green's liability to income tax is at the main UK rates.

		£
2020/21		
Pension income		21,470
Dividends		2,200
Total and net income		23,670
Deduct	Personal allowance	12,500
Taxable income		£11,170
Tax payable:		
8,970 @ 20% (basic rate)		1,794.00
2,000 @ 0% (dividend nil rate)		—
200 @ 7.5% (dividend ordinary rate)		15.00
		1,809.00
Deduct	Maintenance relief — wife: £3,600 paid, but restricted to £3,510 @ 10%	351.00
		1,458.00
Deduct	Married couple's allowance £9,075 × $^6/_{12}$ = £4,538 @ 10%	453.80
Tax liability (subject to PAYE deductions)		£1,004.20

49

Miscellaneous Income

Introduction to miscellaneous income

[49.1] *ITTOIA 2005, Pt 5* contains provisions relating to miscellaneous income, not chargeable under any other provisions (see **41.3** below), within the following categories:

(i) income from INTELLECTUAL PROPERTY (**41**);
(ii) films and sound recordings (see **49.3** below);
(iii) telecommunications rights (see **49.4** below);
(iv) amounts treated as income of settlors of SETTLEMENTS (**70.25**);
(v) income of beneficiaries from DECEASED ESTATES (**22.4**);
(vi) annual payments not otherwise charged to tax (see **49.5** below);
(vii) offshore receipts in respect of intangible property (relevant to non-UK resident companies and outside the scope of this work); and
(viii) income not otherwise charged to tax (see **49.7** below).

[*ITTOIA 2005, s 574(1); FA 2019, Sch 3 paras 2, 7*].

Before *ITTOIA 2005*, there was no direct equivalent of *Pt 5*. Income now falling within (viii) above was within *Sch D, Case VI* (see **49.9** below). (If from a non-UK source such income fell within *Sch D, Case V*.) But *Case VI* also applied specifically to various types of income (whether or not from a UK source) which are not now within *Pt 5*, but are the subject of their own specific charge to income tax. Income within (ii) above and certain types of income within (i) and (iii) above were not subject to a specific charge and thus fell within *Case VI* (or *Case V* if from a non-UK source) on general principles. Income within (vi) and the remaining income within (i) and (iii) above fell within *Case III* (or *Case V* if from a non-UK source).

Apportionment rules for miscellaneous income, including those types of income formerly within *Case VI* but not within *Pt 5*, are covered at **49.8** below and loss relief for such income is covered at **49.11** below.

Scope of *ITTOIA 2005, Pt 5*

[49.2] The provisions charging to tax income within the categories listed below take priority over *ITTOIA 2005, Pt 5*. Any income otherwise within *Part 5* which also falls within one of the categories is not taxed under *Part 5*. Instead the provisions appropriate to the relevant category apply. The categories are:

- receipts of a trade, profession or vocation (see **75** TRADING INCOME);
- receipts of a UK property business (see **60.2** PROPERTY INCOME);
- interest and other income taxed as interest (see **65.2** SAVINGS AND INVESTMENT INCOME);
- dividends and other distributions from a UK resident company; or
- EMPLOYMENT INCOME (**28**), PENSION INCOME (**56**) or social security income (see **73** SOCIAL SECURITY AND NATIONAL INSURANCE).

[*ITTOIA 2005, s 575*].

Territorial scope

Income within *ITTOIA 2005, Pt 5* arising to a UK resident is chargeable to tax whether or not from a source in the UK. Income arising to a non-UK resident is chargeable to tax only if from a source in the UK. If income does not have a source, it is treated as having a UK source if it has a comparable connection to the UK. Where the tax year is a split year (see **63.19** RESIDENCE AND DOMICILE), income arising to a UK resident individual in the overseas part of the split year is treated for these purposes as arising to a non-UK resident. [*ITTOIA 2005, s 577; FA 2016, s 42(1)*].

The same applies to the provisions listed at **49.8** below (other than those of *ITTOIA 2005* itself). [*ITA 2007, s 1015*]. See also **41.6** INTELLECTUAL PROPERTY for the charge on sale of patent rights, which has its own territoriality rules.

Where, on or after 28 June 2016, a royalty or other sum is paid in respect of intellectual property by a non-UK resident and the payment is made in connection with a trade carried on by that person through a permanent establishment in the UK, the income arising from the payment is treated for the purposes of *ITTOIA 2005, s 577* above as being from a source in the UK. No regard is to be had to any arrangements (as widely defined and whenever entered into) of which a main purpose is to avoid the effect of this rule; in particular the accelerating of payments to earlier than 28 June 2016 is ignored in determining when a payment is made for these purposes. Where the trade in question is carried on by the non-resident only partly through a UK permanent establishment, it is apportioned on a just and reasonable basis. 'Intellectual property' is as defined at **41.1** INTELLECTUAL PROPERTY. 'Permanent establishment' is defined in accordance with *CTA 2010, Pt 24 Ch 2* (regardless of whether or not the person carrying on the trade is a company). [*ITTOIA 2005, s 577A; FA 2016, s 42(2)–(6)*]. For more detail, see the technical note at www.gov.uk/government/publications/income-tax-royalty-withholding-tax.

Simon's Taxes. See E1.501–E1.503.

Films and sound recordings

[49.3] Subject to the provisions at **49.2** above, income from a business (a '*non-trade business*') involving the exploitation of films or sound recordings where the activities carried on do not amount to a trade is chargeable to income tax. The full amount of such income arising in the tax year is chargeable (but see below), the person liable for the tax being the person receiving or entitled to the income.

Expenses incurred wholly and exclusively for the purpose of generating the income are deductible in calculating the amount chargeable to tax, provided that, if they had been incurred for the purposes of a trade, they would have been deductible in calculating its profits. Where an expense is incurred for more than one purpose, if any identifiable part or proportion of the expense is incurred for the purpose of generating the income, a deduction is allowed for that part or proportion. Expenses for which any kind of relief is given under any other provision are not deductible. Relief is additionally available for expenditure incurred by a non-trade business on the production or acquisition of the original master version of a film or sound recording and preliminary expenditure in relation to a film under the rules at **75.80** TRADING INCOME. In applying those rules to non-trade businesses, the basis period is taken to be the tax year and references to anything not constituting trading stock of a trade are treated as omitted.

The charge to tax under these provisions takes priority over the charge to tax on income from INTELLECTUAL PROPERTY (**41.2**).

Where income within the charge arises from a source outside the UK it is 'relevant foreign income' (see **32.2** FOREIGN INCOME). See **32.4** FOREIGN INCOME for amounts deductible from income, **32.5** FOREIGN INCOME for relief for unremittable income and **61** for the REMITTANCE BASIS.

[*ITTOIA 2005, ss 609–613*].

HMRC's view is that the charge is on income actually received in the tax year. The expenses that are deductible in any year are those allowable expenses that are attributable to the generation of the income received. Accordingly, for an expense to be deductible there needs to be a correlation between the expense and the income received in the year. As the activities do not amount to a trade, there is no requirement to calculate chargeable income in accordance with generally accepted accounting practice. (HMRC Notice, 28 March 2014).

In *Good & Ryan v HMRC* FTT (TC 7531), [2020] UKFTT 25 (TC), the appellants were held to have been carrying on a non-trade business under these provisions. Loan interest was held non-deductible in this case because of the 'wholly and exclusively' rule, and it was not considered possible to identify any part or proportion of the expense that was incurred for the purpose of generating the income. The FTT also found that, if it were wrong about the income being chargeable under these provisions, it would have been chargeable (and the interest still not deductible) under **49.7** below (charge on income not otherwise charged).

See **49.8** below for apportionment rules and **49.11** below for relief for losses.

Telecommunications rights

[49.4] Subject to the provisions at **49.2** above, income from a 'relevant telecommunications right' that is not held or used for the purposes of a trade, profession or vocation is chargeable to income tax. The full amount of such income arising in the tax year is chargeable (but see below), the person liable for the tax being the person receiving or entitled to the income.

Unless the income consists of annual payments (see **23.10** DEDUCTION OF TAX AT SOURCE), expenses incurred wholly and exclusively for the purpose of generating the income are deductible in calculating the amount chargeable to tax, provided that, if they had been incurred for the purposes of a trade, they would have been deductible in calculating its profits. Where an expense is incurred for more than one purpose, if any identifiable part or proportion of the expense is incurred for the purpose of generating the income, a deduction is allowed for that part or proportion. The provisions at **75.122** TRADING INCOME as to the treatment of acquisition costs, disposal proceeds and amounts in respect of revaluation as revenue items apply as they apply for the purpose of calculating the profits of a trade etc.

No deductions can be made where the income consists of annual payments and, for this purpose, in determining whether income consists of annual payments, the frequency with which payments are made is ignored. Deductions are also not permitted where the income is chargeable on the REMITTANCE BASIS (**61**).

Where income within the charge arises from a source outside the UK it is 'relevant foreign income' (see **32.2** FOREIGN INCOME). See **32.4** FOREIGN INCOME for amounts deductible from income, **32.5** FOREIGN INCOME for relief for unremittable income and **61** for the REMITTANCE BASIS.

For the purpose of these provisions '*relevant telecommunications rights*' are the licences and rights covered at **75.122** TRADING INCOME.

Where the income consists of annual payments it may be subject to DEDUCTION OF TAX AT SOURCE (**23.7–23.10**). Any tax so deducted is treated as income tax paid by the recipient.

[*ITTOIA 2005, ss 614–618, Sch 2 paras 130, 131*].

See **49.8** below for apportionment rules and **49.11** below for relief for losses.

Annual payments not otherwise charged

[49.5] There is a residual charge to income tax in respect of annual payments (see **23.10** DEDUCTION OF TAX AT SOURCE) not charged to income tax under any other provision (other than any such payments not so charged only because of an exemption). In determining whether income consists of annual payments, the frequency with which payments are made is ignored.

Income tax is chargeable on the full amount of the annual payments arising in the tax year (unless the remittance basis applies — see below), the person liable for the tax being the person receiving or entitled to the income. Certain payments made by trustees in the exercise of a discretion are, however, subject to grossing up under the provisions at **70.15** SETTLEMENTS.

Where annual payments within the charge arises from a source outside the UK they are 'relevant foreign income' (see **32.2** FOREIGN INCOME). See **32.4** FOREIGN INCOME for amounts deductible from income, **32.5** FOREIGN INCOME for relief for unremittable income and **61** for the REMITTANCE BASIS.

[*ITTOIA 2005, ss 683–685*].

See **70.25** SETTLEMENTS for relief available to avoid double taxation where a discretionary annual payment is received from a trust and a settlor is chargeable on the underlying income from which it is made.

For an exemption for certain annual payments made by individuals, see **30.3** EXEMPT INCOME.

See also **23** DEDUCTION OF TAX AT SOURCE.

Rebates of investment annual management charges etc.

It is HMRC's view that payments of trail commission etc. made to investors in a collective investment scheme, insurance policy or other investment product, by fund managers, fund platforms, advisers, or any other person acting as an intermediary between the fund and the investor are annual payments within the above charge. Basic rate tax should be deducted in accordance with **23.7–23.10** DEDUCTION OF TAX AT SOURCE. In particular, this covers cases where all or part of any trail commission paid by the fund manager to other intermediaries is then paid to (or used to meet the liabilities of or provide a benefit to) the investor. This typically happens as a result of an agreement between the investor and the fund platform, although it could be as a result of an agreement between the investor and his adviser or the fund manager. Such payments are usually characterised as rebates of the annual management charge. (HMRC Brief 04/13, 25 March 2013.)

In *HMRC v Hargreaves Lansdown Asset Management Ltd* UT, [2019] STC 1745, Loyalty Bonus payments paid by a platform service provider were held to be annual payments. HMRC had considered the payments to be trail commission, and thus within the ambit of HMRC Brief 04/13 above, and won on appeal to the Upper Tribunal.

Offshore funds

Offshore funds are not required to withhold tax from rebates of the annual management charge where these payments are made to non-UK resident investors. The payment must be made in respect of the participant's interest in the fund; the payment and its amount must be referable to, and must not be more than, any management fees paid to the manager of the fund in respect of the participant's interest; and any management fee must be no more than a reasonable commercial amount in all the circumstances. [*SI 2009 No 3001, Regs 124A, 124B*].

Authorised investment funds

Authorised investment funds are also relieved, subject to conditions similar to those above for offshore funds, of the duty to withhold tax from rebates of the annual management charge where such payments are made to non-UK resident investors. [*SI 2006 No 964, Regs 46A, 46B*].

Simon's Taxes. See **E1.510.**

Theatrical angels

[49.6] Before 1 April 2017, UK-resident backers of theatrical productions ('angels'), although strictly chargeable under *ITTOIA 2005, s 683* in **49.5** above on any return over and above their original investment (with the capital gains tax rules applicable to any losses), were able by concession treat a profit or loss arising on any particular transaction as being within *ITTOIA 2005, s 687* at **49.7** below, so that the loss relief provisions at **49.11** below apply. Losses thus utilised against income could not also qualify as capital losses. In cases where it would normally be required, HMRC did not insist on deduction of tax at source being applied to payments to angels whose usual place of abode was in the UK. (Non-UK resident angels could apply for authority for tax not to be deducted — see **27.12** DOUBLE TAX RELIEF.) (HMRC ESC A94).

This concession was withdrawn from 31 March 2017. Alongside the concession, a practice had become established whereby profits due to angels were treated as a deductible expense of the production rather than a distribution of profits. This practice was also withdrawn for all new productions from 1 April 2017. Productions using the practice before that date could continue to use it until 31 March 2019. Affected productions were asked to notify HMRC by 31 December 2016 of their intention to take advantage of this (www.gov.uk/government/publications/withdrawal-of-extra-statutory-concession-esc-a94-theatre-angels).

Income not otherwise charged

[49.7] There is a residual charge to income tax in respect of income not charged to income tax under any other provision (other than income not so charged only because of an exemption). Income tax is chargeable on the amount of the income arising in the tax year (but see below), the person liable for the tax being the person receiving or entitled to the income. See **75.3** TRADING INCOME for the relief introduced for 2017/18 onwards for small amounts of income otherwise within this charge.

If the income arises from a source outside the UK, it is 'relevant foreign income' (see **32.2** FOREIGN INCOME). See **32.4** FOREIGN INCOME for amounts deductible from income, **32.5** FOREIGN INCOME for relief for unremittable income and **61** for the REMITTANCE BASIS.

[*ITTOIA 2005, ss 687–689; F(No 2)A 2017, Sch 3 paras 9, 13*].

There is no express provision for deductions in calculating taxable income under the above provisions. Before *ITTOIA 2005* came into effect, HMRC accepted that the rules of *Case I* should be followed where applicable in calculating *Case VI* income (see *Curtis Brown Ltd v Jarvis* KB 1929, 14 TC 744 and HMRC Business Income Manual BIM100155), and this should continue to apply to income under the above provisions (see *ITTOIA 2005, Sch 2 para 159*).

HMRC cannot use these provisions to tax an apparent shortfall of income that cannot be attributed to express sources (*Ashraf v HMRC* FTT (TC 6355), [2018] UKFTT 97 (TC), [2018] SFTD 901).

See **49.10** below for case law on income within *Case VI*, which continues to be relevant in determining whether income falls within the above provisions. See **49.8** below for apportionment rules and **49.11** below for relief for losses.

See also **33** FOSTER CARE ETC and **60.22** PROPERTY INCOME (rent-a-room relief).

Temporary non-UK residence

Subject to conditions, and where the 'year of departure' is 2013/14 or any subsequent year, distributions by a close company (or a company that would be a close company if it were UK resident) otherwise chargeable to income tax under *ITTOIA 2005, ss 687–689* above but receivable by an individual who is 'temporarily non-UK resident' are chargeable for the tax year that consists of or includes the 'period of return'. The conditions are similar to those at **65.18** SAVINGS AND INVESTMENT INCOME, except that there is no let-out for dividends paid in respect of post-departure trade profits. [*ITTOIA 2005, s 689A*].

For what is meant by '*temporarily non-UK resident*', the '*year of departure*' and the '*period of return*', see **63.29** RESIDENCE AND DOMICILE.

Volunteer drivers

Volunteer drivers (e.g. hospital car service drivers) are taxable on the profit element in any mileage allowances. They may use the statutory tax-free mileage rates applicable to employees (see **28.91** EMPLOYMENT INCOME) in determining any profit element, although they have the option of claiming their actual motoring expenses instead. See HMRC guidance at www.gov.uk/guidance/check-if-you-need-to-pay-tax-on-mileage-payments-as-a-volunteer-driver.

Simon's Taxes. See E1.587.

Apportionment of miscellaneous income

[49.8] Where income is chargeable to income tax under any of the provisions listed below and any period for which accounts are drawn up (a '*period of account*') does not coincide with a tax year, the profits or losses for the tax year may, if necessary, be arrived at by apportioning the profits and losses of the relevant periods of account between tax years on a time basis, by reference to the number of days in the respective periods. The taxpayer may use a different method of determining the length of the relevant periods if it is reasonable to do so and that method is used consistently.

The provisions (listed in chronological order) are:

- *ICTA 1988, s 571(1)* (schemes for rationalising industry: cancellation of certificates);
- *ICTA 1988, s 774* (now repealed) (transactions between dealing company and associated company — see Tolley's Corporation Tax);
- *FA 1989, s 68(2)* (chargeable event in relation to trustees of qualifying employee share ownership trusts);
- *FA 1989, s 71(4)* (qualifying employee share ownership trusts: borrowing);
- *CAA 2001, s 258(4)* (special leasing of plant or machinery: balancing charge — see **10.55** CAPITAL ALLOWANCES ON PLANT AND MACHINERY);
- *CAA 2001, s 479(4)* (allowances for patent rights of non-trader: balancing charge — see **9.26** CAPITAL ALLOWANCES);
- *ITEPA 2003, s 394(2)* (charge on administrators of non-approved retirement schemes for employees before 2006/07);
- *ITEPA 2003, s 476(5)* (unapproved share options: charge on occurrence of chargeable event as a result of operation of law— see **71.16** SHARE-RELATED EMPLOYMENT INCOME AND EXEMPTIONS);
- *ITTOIA 2005, s 242* (post-cessation receipts from trades, professions and vocations — see **59.1** POST-CESSATION RECEIPTS AND EXPENDITURE);
- *ITTOIA 2005, s 335* (rent receivable in connection with a UK concern within *ITTOIA 2005, s 12(4)* (mines, quarries etc.) — see **60.34** PROPERTY INCOME);
- *ITTOIA 2005, s 344* (rent receivable for UK electric-line wayleaves — see **60.33** PROPERTY INCOME);
- *ITTOIA 2005, s 349* (post-cessation receipts from UK property businesses — see **60.16** PROPERTY INCOME);
- *ITTOIA 2005, Pt 4 Ch 2* as it relates to interest on funding bonds where the issue is treated as a payment of interest and the person by or through whom they are issued is required to retain bonds but it is impracticable for the person to do so (see **65.7** SAVINGS AND INVESTMENT INCOME);
- *ITTOIA 2005, Pt 4 Ch 9* so far as relating to gains from a policy or contract specified in *ITTOIA 2005, s 531(3)* which do not fall within *ITTOIA 2005, s 532* (see **44.23** LIFE ASSURANCE POLICIES) or *s 534*;
- *ITTOIA 2005, s 551* (disposal of deposit rights — see **12** CERTIFICATES OF DEPOSIT);
- *ITTOIA 2005, s 579* royalties and other income from INTELLECTUAL PROPERTY (**41.2**), but not so far as relating to annual payments;
- *ITTOIA 2005, s 583* (income from disposals of know-how — see **41.5** INTELLECTUAL PROPERTY);
- *ITTOIA 2005, s 587* (income from sales of patent rights — see **41.6** INTELLECTUAL PROPERTY);
- *ITTOIA 2005, s 609* (films and sound recordings: non-trade businesses — see **49.3** above);
- *ITTOIA 2005, s 614* (telecommunication rights: non-trading income), but not so far as relating to annual payments — see **49.4** above);
- *ITTOIA 2005, s 619* (amounts treated as income of settlor — see **70.25** SETTLEMENTS) but not so far as relating to 'distribution income';
- *ITTOIA 2005, s 682(4)* (adjustments after the administration period — see **22.13** DECEASED ESTATES);

- *ITTOIA 2005, s 687* (income not otherwise charged — see **49.7** above);
- *ITTOIA 2005, s 844(4)* (withdrawal of relief for unremittable foreign income after source ceases — see **32.5** FOREIGN INCOME);
- *ITA 2007, Pt 12 Ch 2* (accrued income profits — see **2** ACCRUED INCOME SCHEME);
- *ITA 2007, s 681BB(8)(9)* (sale and lease-back: new lease of land after assignment or surrender — see **4.32** ANTI-AVOIDANCE);
- *ITA 2007, s 681DD* (leased assets: capital sums — see **4.34** ANTI-AVOIDANCE);
- *ITA 2007, s 720, s 727* or s *731* (transfer of assets abroad — see **4.15**, **4.15** ANTI-AVOIDANCE) but, in the case of *s 720* or *s 727*, not so far as relating to dividend income;
- (for disposals before 5 July 2016) *ITA 2007, Pt 13 Ch 3* (transactions in land (now repealed) — see **4.30** ANTI-AVOIDANCE);
- *ITA 2007, s 776* (sales of occupation income — see **4.29** ANTI-AVOIDANCE);
- *ITA 2007, s 796* (losses derived from film reliefs: chargeable event — see **45.15** LOSSES);
- *ITA 2007, s 804* (claw-back of losses derived from exploiting licence: non-active partners — see **52.16** PARTNERSHIPS);
- *ITA 2007, s 809CZC(2)* (loan or credit transactions — see **4.40**(ii) ANTI-AVOIDANCE);
- *CTA 2010, s 1086(2)* (chargeable payments connected with exempt distributions — see Tolley's Corporation Tax); and
- *SI 2009 No 3001, Reg 17* (charge to tax on offshore income gains — see **51.3** OFFSHORE FUNDS).

[*ITA 2007, s 1016; ITTOIA 2005, s 871; FA 2016, ss 79(7), 82(1)*].

Schedule D, Case VI (pre-2005/06)

[49.9] Before *ITTOIA 2005*, tax was charged under Schedule D, Case VI in respect of any annual profits or gains not falling under any other case of Schedule D and not charged by virtue of any other Schedule. See also **49.1** above. Although otherwise of historical interest only, the scope of Case VI does continue to have some relevance in determining whether income now falls within the residual charge at **49.7** above.

Case VI was also specifically applied to various kinds of income including, for example, amounts chargeable under the ACCRUED INCOME SCHEME (**2**); various charges under ANTI-AVOIDANCE (**4**); withdrawal of relief under **29.19** ENTERPRISE INVESTMENT SCHEME; sale of patent rights; CERTIFICATES OF DEPOSIT (**12**); certain easements; certain under-deductions where tax rate changed — see **23** DEDUCTION OF TAX AT SOURCE; interest paid by issue of bonds; gains on certain offshore life insurance policies — see **44.21–44.23** LIFE ASSURANCE POLICIES; formerly unremittable overseas income where source has ceased — see **32.5** FOREIGN INCOME; offshore income gains, see **51** OFFSHORE FUNDS; recovery of tax over-repaid — see **54.16** PAYMENT OF TAX; certain POST-CESSATION ETC. RECEIPTS (**59**); lease premiums and assignments at under-value etc. — see **60.26** *et seq.*

PROPERTY INCOME; certain settlement income — see **70.25** SETTLEMENTS; charges on trustees of qualifying employee share ownership trusts; and recovery of various excess reliefs for double taxation, losses, capital allowances etc.

See the case law at **49.10** below and also the list at **49.8** above which includes the types of income formerly within Case VI in respect of which a loss could arise or against which losses could be set.

Case law

[49.10] Following held to be income within Schedule D, Case VI: commission for guaranteeing overdrafts (*Ryall v Hoare* KB 1925, 8 TC 521 and *Sherwin v Barnes KB* 1931, 16 TC 278); underwriting commission (*Lyons v Cowcher* KB 1926, 10 TC 438); commission for negotiating a sale of shares (*Grey v Tiley* CA 1932, 16 TC 414); commission from an insurance company (*Hugh v Rogers* Ch D 1958, 38 TC 270 and see *Way v Underdown* CA 1974, 49 TC 648); 'earn-out payments' in respect of the transfer of hedge fund management business (*Manduca v HMRC* UT, [2015] STC 2002); shipping dues (the two *Forth Conservancy Board cases* HL 1928, 14 TC 709, HL 1931, 16 TC 103); share of prize monies for letting racehorses (*Norman v Evans* Ch D 1964, 42 TC 188).

Held to be capital were shares allotted to members of a mining finance development scheme (*Whyte v Clancy* KB 1936, 20 TC 679) and shares allotted for a guarantee of dividends (*National United Laundries v Bennet* KB 1933, 17 TC 420).

A payment to an architect for his services relating to a property deal was held income within Case VI in *Brocklesby v Merricks* KB 1934, 18 TC 576, but payments for services in deals are not income if made gratuitously in such circumstances that the recipient has no enforceable right to them. For cases in which such payments held *not* income see *Bradbury v Arnold* Ch D 1957, 37 TC 665; *Bloom v Kinder* Ch D 1958, 38 TC 77; *Dickinson v Abel* Ch D 1968, 45 TC 353. See also *Scott v Ricketts* CA 1967, 44 TC 303 in which a payment to an estate agent linked with a development scheme was held not to be income even though embodied in a contract.

Receipts of the use of copyright material were held income within Case VI in *Hobbs v Hussey* KB 1942, 24 TC 153 (sale of rights in life story to newspaper) and *Housden v Marshall* Ch D 1958, 38 TC 233 and *Alloway v Phillips* CA 1980, 53 TC 372 (receipt for material for newspaper articles by 'ghost writer') but held capital in *Earl Haig Trustees v CIR* CS 1939, 22 TC 725 (payment to trustees for permission to use diaries of deceased); *Beare v Carter* KB 1940, 23 TC 353 (payment for permission to re-print book); *Nethersole v Withers* HL 1948, 28 TC 501 (sale of film rights in work by deceased author).

For other copyright sales see **75.47** and **75.59** TRADING INCOME. For the line between Cases I and VI as regards surpluses on the sales of assets see **75.33** TRADING INCOME.

Losses

[49.11] A loss on a transaction which, if profitable, would have been chargeable to income tax under a provision listed at **49.8** above can be set off against income from transactions chargeable to tax under the same provision (*'relevant miscellaneous income'*) for the same tax year or carried forward against the next available income chargeable under that provision.

For these purposes, the list at **49.8** above is treated as if the following were omitted:

(a) *SI 2009 No 3001, Reg 17* (charge to tax on offshore income gains — see **51.3** OFFSHORE FUNDS); and
(b) *ITTOIA 2005, Pt 4 Ch 9* (life assurance gains — see **44.3** LIFE ASSURANCE POLICIES).

Relief is given effect by deducting the loss in arriving at net income for the tax year for which the relief is given (see Step 2 at **1.10** ALLOWANCES AND TAX RATES). The deduction must be made from relevant miscellaneous income (if any) of the year of loss (and then, if such income is insufficient, from relevant miscellaneous income (if any) of the following tax year, and so on until the loss is exhausted). The deduction is made in priority to deductions of any other reliefs from the available income.

Subject to any express provision to the contrary, the same rules apply in calculating losses as apply in calculating the corresponding income. Loss relief cannot be claimed where any profits or gains from the transaction would have been relevant foreign income (see **32.2** FOREIGN INCOME).

Claims relating to the amount of losses must be made no later than four years after the end of the tax year in which they arose. A further claim for relief for losses brought forward must be made no later than four years after the end of the tax year for which relief is claimed.

Anti-avoidance

Where the loss arises as a result of 'relevant tax avoidance arrangements', the above relief is not available. In addition, no relief is available for a loss, whenever incurred, against miscellaneous income arising as a result of any such arrangements. '*Relevant tax avoidance arrangements*' are arrangements to which the taxpayer is a party and a main purpose of which is to obtain a reduction in tax liability by means of the above relief.

Transitional

Before *ITTOIA 2005*, the above loss relief applied to most losses on transactions which, if profitable, would have been assessable under the now defunct Schedule D, Case VI; such losses could be set off against any profit or gains charged under Case VI. Any Case VI losses which were unrelieved when *ITTOIA 2005* came into effect in 2005/06 are carried forward as losses under the revised provisions above.

[*ITA 2007, ss 152, 153, 154A, 155; ITTOIA 2005, s 872; FA 2009, s 69; F(No 2)A 2017, Sch 2 paras 40, 64(1); SI 2009 No 3001, Reg 129(2)*].

Simon's Taxes. See E1.588.

50

Non-Residents

Cross-references. See **62** RESIDENCE AND DOMICILE for the meaning of those terms. See also **4.14–4.18** ANTI-AVOIDANCE regarding income payable to person abroad assessable on UK resident in certain circumstances; **4.19** for trading transactions with a non-resident under common control; **23** DEDUCTION OF TAX AT SOURCE for certain payments to non-residents; **24** DIPLOMATIC IMMUNITY, including international organisations etc.; **26** DOUBLE TAX RELIEF; **28.1–28.12** EMPLOYMENT INCOME for earnings from work done abroad and expenses; **32** FOREIGN INCOME; **44.23** LIFE ASSURANCE POLICIES; **52** PARTNERSHIPS; **56** PENSION INCOME; **65.4** SAVINGS AND INVESTMENT INCOME for exemption on certain stocks held by non-residents; **78** TRANSACTIONS IN UK LAND for provisions charging tax on the full amount of profits from dealing in or developing land in the UK regardless of residence.

Introduction to non-residents

[50.1] This chapter examines miscellaneous topics concerned with the income taxation of persons non-resident in the UK. **50.2** details the extent to which non-UK resident individuals are entitled to UK personal reliefs. The income tax chargeable on the total income of a non-resident cannot exceed a certain limit, and this is examined in **50.3**. The next part of the chapter (**50.4–50.10**) considers the position of non-residents trading in the UK via a branch or agency. There are special rules concerning payments made to, and the taxation of, performers, i.e. entertainers and sports persons, who are not resident in the UK but perform there from time to time; these are considered in **50.11**. See also the contents list above. See **63.4**, **63.32** RESIDENCE AND DOMICILE as to a person's residence for tax purposes.

Personal reliefs for non-residents

[50.2] As mentioned under **63.3** RESIDENCE AND DOMICILE, a non-UK resident individual is liable to UK tax without any deduction for personal reliefs (i.e. the personal allowance, married couple's allowance and blind person's allowance — see **1.17–1.20** ALLOWANCES AND TAX RATES) except under specific double tax treaties or in cases where the individual concerned is eligible for relief as below. (Foreigners resident here have the same rights to reliefs as British subjects, and where tax is chargeable on the grounds of '*residence*' in the UK, the taxpayer is entitled to the full personal reliefs. This does not apply to tax chargeable because a person is temporarily employed in the UK, but not technically 'resident'.)

The non-resident individuals eligible for personal reliefs are as follows:

(i) all nationals of the UK;
(ii) all nationals of States within the European Economic Area (EEA) (which comprises the EU plus Norway, Iceland and Liechtenstein);
(iii) persons who are or who have been employed in the service of the Crown;
(iv) persons employed in the service of a missionary society;
(v) persons employed in the service of any territory under British protection;
(vi) residents in the Isle of Man or Channel Islands;
(vii) persons abroad for health reasons (including the health of family members living with the person concerned) following residence in the UK; and
(viii) widows or widowers (or surviving civil partners) of Crown Servants.

Personal reliefs are not available (other than by virtue of specific double tax treaties) to non-UK resident Commonwealth citizens.

[*ITA 2007, ss 56, 460, Sch 2 paras 14–17; SI 2020 No 332, Reg 3*].

Claims should be made on Form R43. A right of appeal, within three months of the notice of HMRC's decision, is given by *TMA 1970, Sch 1A para 9(2)*.

Simon's Taxes. See **E6.2**.

Non-residents — limit on liability to income tax

[50.3] The income tax chargeable on the total income of a non-UK resident is not to exceed the aggregate of:

(i) the tax which would otherwise be chargeable if 'disregarded income' and any personal reliefs due (see **50.2** above) were both left out of account; and
(ii) the tax deducted from so much of the 'disregarded income' as is subject to deduction of income tax at source (including tax *treated* as deducted at source).

The above is of no application to income arising to a UK resident in the overseas part of a split year (as in **63.19** RESIDENCE AND DOMICILE).

Income is '*disregarded income*' if it falls into one of the categories below and is not income in relation to which the non-resident has a UK representative for the purposes of the provisions at **50.6** to **50.10** below (i.e. income from or connected with a trade etc. carried on in the UK through a branch or agency, subject to the exclusions at **50.8** below). The categories are:

(a) income chargeable under *ITTOIA 2005, Pt 4 Ch 2* (interest), *Pt 4 Ch 7* (purchased life annuity payments), *Pt 4 Ch 8* profits from deeply discounted securities), *Pt 4 Ch 11* (transactions in deposits), *s 579* (royalties etc. from intellectual property) so far as it relates to annual payments, *Pt 5 Ch 4* (non-trading income from certain telecommunications rights) so far as it relates to annual payments, or *Pt 5 Ch 7* (annual payments not otherwise charged), or income treated as received by a unit holder from an exempt unauthorised unit trust (see **80.8** UNIT TRUSTS ETC.), but not (in any of these cases) income which is relevant foreign income (see **32.2** FOREIGN INCOME);

(b) income chargeable under *ITTOIA 2005, Pt 4 Ch 3* (dividends and other distributions from UK resident companies) and *Ch 5* (stock dividends from UK resident companies);

(c) certain social security benefits (including state pensions);

(d) retirement annuities under contracts that became registered pension schemes on 6 April 2006 (see **57.8** PENSION PROVISION) and UK-sourced employment-related annuities within **56.2**(e) PENSION INCOME;

(e) 'disregarded transaction income', being income which arises as mentioned in **50.8**(2)(3) below (certain income from trading in the UK through a broker or investment manager) and not being Lloyd's underwriting profits; and

(f) any income designated for these purposes by Treasury regulations.

These provisions do not apply to limit the income tax chargeable on a settlement if any actual or potential income beneficiary, whether his interest is absolute or discretionary, is a UK resident individual or a UK resident company.

[*ITA 2007, ss 810–828; FA 2016, Sch 1 paras 63(14)(15), 73*].

Simon's Taxes. See **E6.107–E6.109, D4.122.**

Example

[50.4]

Hugh and Elizabeth are non-UK resident throughout 2020/21. They are each entitled to a UK personal allowance under the provisions in **50.2** above. Their tax liabilities on total UK income for 2020/21, disregarding the limit under **50.3** above, are as follows.

	Hugh	Elizabeth
	£	£
Net rental income (received gross)	2,150	7,200
Bank interest	20,750	8,230
Dividends	1,600	—
Total UK income	24,500	15,430
Deduct Personal allowance	12,500	12,500
Taxable UK income	£12,000	£2,930

Tax on total UK income:

	Hugh	Elizabeth
	£	£
£5,000/2,930 @ 0% (starting rate for savings)	—	—
£1,000 @ 0% (personal savings allowance)	—	
£4,400 @ 20% (basic rate on interest)	880.00	
£1,600 @ 0% (dividend nil rate)	—	
	£880.00	—

But tax is limited under 50.3 above as follows.

	£	£
Property income	2,150	7,200

(Bank interest and dividends are 'disregarded income' — see 50.3 above.)

	£	£
£2,150/£7,200 @ 20% (basic rate)	£430.00	£1,440.00

Hugh's UK income tax liability is therefore restricted to £430.00. Elizabeth's liability remains at zero as in the normal computation.

Temporary non-UK residence

[50.5] The following applies where an individual is 'temporarily non-UK resident', the 'year of departure' is 2013/14 or any subsequent year and the individual has income in the form of close company distributions. For what is meant by '*temporarily non-UK resident*', the '*year of departure*' and the '*period of return*', see **63.29** RESIDENCE AND DOMICILE.

Where an individual's liability to income tax for a tax year (the '*non-resident year*') is limited under **50.3** above and:

- he is 'temporarily non-UK resident',
- the non-resident year falls within the 'temporary period of non-UK residence' (**63.29**(d) RESIDENCE AND DOMICILE), and
- the individual's income for the non-resident year includes 'relevant investment income',

the individual's total income for income tax purposes for the tax year that consists of or includes the 'period of return' is increased by an amount equal to the amount of the relevant investment income. The 'notional UK tax' on that relevant investment income is allowed as a credit against the individual's liability to income tax for that year; the credit is given in the form of a reduction under Step 6 of the calculation of income tax liability at **1.10** ALLOWANCES AND TAX RATES.

Income is '*relevant investment income*' if:

(a) it is chargeable under **65.10** or **65.19** SAVINGS AND INVESTMENT INCOME (dealing respectively with dividends and other distributions from UK resident companies and stock dividends from UK resident companies);
(b) the distributing company is a close company (see Tolley's Corporation Tax under Close Companies); and
(c) the income arises to the individual because he was a 'material participator' (or an associate of a material participator) in the company at any time in the period consisting of the year of departure (or the UK part of the year of departure if it is a split year) and the three preceding tax years.

In (c) above, a '*material participator*' is a participator who has a 'material interest' in the company (within *CTA 2010, s 457*). '*Participator*' and '*associate*' are as defined in *CTA 2010, Pt 10* (see Tolley's Corporation Tax under Close Companies).

However, income in the form of a cash or stock dividend is not relevant investment income to the extent (if any) that the dividend is paid, or the share capital is issued, in respect of 'post-departure trade profits' as defined in **65.16** SAVINGS AND INVESTMENT INCOME. The extent to which a dividend is paid, or share capital is issued, in respect of such profits is to be determined on a just and reasonable basis.

The '*notional UK tax*' on relevant investment income is the total of any tax in respect of that income that was included within **50.3**(ii) above in determining the limit on liability to income tax under **50.3** for the non-resident year. (The extent to which tax is in respect of that income is to be determined on a just and reasonable basis.) That total must, however, be reduced by any credit for foreign tax paid in respect of that income that was allowed by way of DOUBLE TAX RELIEF (**27**) against the individual's liability to income tax for the non-resident year.

Nothing in any double tax treaty is to be read as preventing the individual from being chargeable to income tax under these provisions.

[*ITA 2007, s 812A*].

Non-residents trading via UK branch or agency

[50.6] The provisions described below apply where a non-UK resident carries on a trade, profession or vocation in the UK through a branch or agency. The legislation provides for the branch or agency to be treated as the UK representative of the non-resident in relation to certain amounts chargeable to income tax. It sets out the tax obligations and liabilities of the UK representative. See also **67.11** SELF-ASSESSMENT.

For whether activities of a non-resident person constitute trading *in the UK*, see HMRC International Manual INTM263000 (www.gov.uk/hmrc-internal-manuals/international-manual/intm263000).

Where a non-resident carries on a trade partly in and partly outside the UK, the charge to UK tax is limited to the profits from the part of the trade carried on in the UK, whether or not through a branch or agency (see **75.1** TRADING INCOME). HMRC have reaffirmed that the profits from a part of a trade carried on in the UK are to be measured on the arm's length principle set out in the OECD model tax convention and explained in OECD publications, irrespective of whether a double tax agreement applies (Revenue Tax Bulletin August 1995 pp 237–239).

Simon's Taxes. See **B1.210, B1.211.**

Meaning of 'UK representative'

[50.7] For the purposes of 50.10 below and subject to 50.8 below (persons not treated as UK representatives), a branch or agency in the UK (which for this purpose means any factorship, agency, receivership, branch or management) through which a non-UK resident carries on (alone or in partnership) a trade, profession or vocation is his '*UK representative*' in relation to the following:

- such income from the trade etc. as arises, directly or indirectly, through or from the branch or agency, and
- any income from property or rights used by, or held by or for, the branch or agency.

Where the non-resident ceases to carry on the trade etc. through the branch or agency, it continues to be his UK representative for tax purposes in relation to amounts arising during the period of the agency. A UK representative is a legal entity distinct from the non-resident. Where the branch or agency is carried on in partnership, the partnership is the non-resident's UK representative.

If a partnership carries on a trade or profession in the UK through a branch or agency, the branch or agency is treated as the UK representative of any non-resident partner in relation to that partner's share of the UK profits. If a trade etc. is carried on in the UK by a non-resident in partnership with at least one UK resident partner, the partnership itself is the UK representative in relation to that partner's share of the UK profits, notwithstanding that there may also be a branch or agency which is the non-resident partner's UK representative in respect of those profits. All the partners are therefore jointly liable for tax on the non-resident partner's share of the UK profits.

[*ITA 2007, ss 835C–835F, 835S; TMA 1970, s 118(1)*].

Persons not treated as UK representatives

[50.8] The following are *not* treated as UK representatives for the purposes of these provisions.

(1) **Agents.** An agent is not treated as a non-UK resident's UK representative in relation to income arising from so much of the non-resident's business as relates to transactions carried out through the agent otherwise than in the course of carrying on a regular agency for the non-resident. This extends to income from property or rights which, as a result of any such transactions, are used by, or held by or for, the agent on the non-resident's behalf.

(2) **Brokers.** A broker is not treated as a non-UK resident's UK representative in relation to income arising from so much of the non-resident's business as relates to transactions carried out through the broker and meeting all the conditions below. This extends to income from property or rights which, as a result of any such transactions, are used by, or held by or for, the broker on the non-resident's behalf. The conditions are that:
   - (i) the broker was carrying on the business of broker at the time of the transaction;
   - (ii) the transaction was carried out in the ordinary course of that business;
   - (iii) the broker's remuneration for the transaction was at a rate not less than is customary for that class of business; and
   - (iv) the broker is not the non-resident's UK representative in relation to income chargeable to tax for the same tax year which is not within this let-out.

(3) **Investment managers.** An investment manager is not treated as a non-UK resident's UK representative in relation to income etc. arising from so much of the non-resident's business as relates to investment transactions (as defined) carried out through the investment manager and meeting all the conditions below. This extends to income from property or rights which, as a result of any such transactions, are used by, or held by or for, the investment manager on the non-resident's behalf. The conditions are that:
   - (i) the investment manager was carrying on the business of providing investment management services at the time of the transaction;
   - (ii) the transaction was carried out in the ordinary course of that business;
   - (iii) the manager, when acting on the non-resident's behalf in that transaction, did so in an independent capacity (see below);
   - (iv) the '20% rule' is met in relation to the transaction (see below); and
   - (v) the remuneration for the investment management services in question was at a rate not less than is customary for that class of business.

   See also **50.9** below.

(4) **Lloyd's agents.** Neither a Lloyd's members' agent nor a syndicate managing agent istreated as a non-UK resident Lloyd's underwriter's UK representative in relation to income arising from his underwriting business. See **79** UNDERWRITERS AT LLOYD'S generally.

(5) **Persons acting under alternative finance arrangements.** See **3.9** ALTERNATIVE FINANCE ARRANGEMENTS.

General

Where a person acts as broker or investment manager as part only of a business, that part is deemed to be a separate business for the purposes of (2) and (3) above. A person carries out a transaction on behalf of another where he either undertakes it himself or instructs a third party to do so.

[*ITA 2007, ss 835G–835M, 835R, 835S; SI 2003 No 2172; SI 2007 No 963*].

Further rules on investment managers

[50.9] As regards 50.8(3)(iii) above, a person is not regarded as acting in an independent capacity on behalf of the non-UK resident unless, having regard to its legal, financial and commercial characteristics, their relationship is on an arm's length basis as between independent businesses. HMRC SP 1/01 clarifies the 'independent capacity' requirement. The test will be regarded as met where any of the following applies (although this list is not exhaustive). (A subsidiary may be considered independently of its parent for these purposes.)

- The provision of services to the non-resident (and persons connected with the non-resident) is not a substantial part (i.e. it must be no more than 70%) of the investment management business (or that condition is satisfied within 18 months from the start of a new investment management business).
- An intention to satisfy the above condition was not met for reasons outside the manager's control, despite reasonable steps being taken to fulfil that intention.
- The non-resident person is a widely held collective fund or is being actively marketed so as to become one or is being wound up or dissolved. (This will apply mostly to non-transparent overseas funds, and will be regarded as satisfied if either no majority interest in the fund was held by five or fewer persons (and persons connected with them), or no interest of more than 20% was held by a single person (and persons connected with that person).)

The '*20% rule*' (see **50.8**(3)(iv) above) is that there is a 'qualifying period' in relation to which the investment manager (and persons connected with him) must intend that any interest that they may have in the non-resident's 'relevant disregarded income' will not exceed 20% of that income. If that intention is not fulfilled, the 20% rule will nevertheless be met if the only reason why the intention is not fulfilled is because of matters outside the control of the investment manager (or connected persons) despite his having taken reasonable steps to mitigate the effect of those matters. The non-resident's '*relevant disregarded income*' is the total of his income for the tax years comprised in the qualifying period which derives from investment transactions carried out by the investment manager on his behalf and meeting the conditions for the let-out (disregarding the 20% rule itself). A '*qualifying period*', in relation to a transaction, may be any period consisting in or including the tax year for which the transaction income is chargeable to tax, being, in a case where it is not that tax year, a period of not more than five years comprising two or more tax years including that one.

If a transaction meets the conditions at **50.8**(3)(i) to (v) above except for the 20% rule, it is regarded as meeting the 20% rule to the extent of so much (if any) of the transaction income to which the investment manager (or a person connected with him) has no beneficial entitlement.

HMRC SP 1/01 clarifies the 20% rule and certain other aspects of the conditions for exclusion; in particular the definition of 'investment transactions', the customary rate test at **50.8**(3)(v) above and the interaction between the 'independent capacity test' and the '20% rule'.

Persons are connected for the above purposes if they are connected within *ITA 2007, s 993* (see **19** CONNECTED PERSONS).

Special rules apply (see *ITA 2007, s 835Q*) if amounts arise or accrue to the non- resident as a participant in a collective investment scheme. They apply for the purposes of determining whether the 20% rule is met in relation to a transaction carried out for the purposes of the scheme.

[*ITA 2007, ss 835N–835Q, 835S*].

Obligations etc. imposed on UK representatives

[50.10] As regards the taxation of any amounts in relation to which a non-UK resident has a UK representative (see **50.7–50.9** above), legislation making provision for (or in connection with) the assessment, collection and recovery of income tax (and interest on tax) has effect as if the obligations and liabilities of the non-resident were *also* obligations and liabilities of the UK representative. The discharge of an obligation or liability by either the non-resident or the UK representative is treated as discharging the corresponding obligation or liability of the other. The non-resident is bound by any acts or omissions of his UK representative. Where an obligation or liability depends on the serving of a notice or other document or the making of a request or demand, it is not treated as having been imposed on the UK representative unless the notice etc. was served on or copied to him or he was notified of the request or demand.

A person cannot, by virtue of the above, face criminal proceedings for an offence except where he committed the offence himself or consented to or connived in its commission.

Independent agents

An '*independent agent*', in relation to a non-UK resident (N), is any person who is N's UK representative in respect of any agency in which he is acting on behalf of N in an independent capacity (see **50.9** above). The provisions above apply equally to independent agents as to other UK representatives, with the following applying in addition.

As regards his obligations to furnish information (including anything contained in a return, self-assessment, account, statement or report provided to HMRC), the independent agent is not required to do anything beyond what is practicable by acting to the best of his knowledge and belief after having taken all reasonable steps to obtain the information. In such a case, the non-UK resident is not discharged from his own obligation to furnish the information. But the non-resident is also not bound by any mistakes in the information so furnished by the agent unless the mistakeresults from the non-resident's own act or omission or is one to which he consented or in which he connived.

An independent agent is entitled to be indemnified in respect of any liability discharged by him on the non-resident's behalf under these provisions and to retain, out of monies due by him to the non-resident, amounts sufficient to cover any such liability, whether or not he has already discharged it.

An independent agent is not liable to any civil penalty or surcharge in respect of any act or omission which is neither his own nor one to which he consented or in which he connived, providing he can show that he could not recover the penalty etc. out of monies due to the non-resident after being indemnified for his other liabilities.

[*ITA 2007, ss 835T–835Y*].

Non-resident performers

[50.11] Any person making a payment or transfer (including by way of loan) for, in respect of, or which in any way derives either directly or indirectly from, the performance of a 'relevant activity' performed in the UK by a performer, i.e. an entertainer (as broadly defined), sportsman or sportswoman who is not resident in the UK in the tax year in which that activity is performed, is required to deduct and account to HMRC for an amount representing income tax, at a rate which may not exceed the basic rate of income tax for the tax year (see further below). In the case of a transfer, the actual worth of what is transferred is treated as being a net amount corresponding to a gross amount from which income tax at the basic rate has been deducted. That gross amount is treated as the value of the transfer and the net value is the cost to the transferor less any contribution made by the performer.

A '*relevant activity*' is an activity performed in the UK by a performer in his character as such on or in connection with (including promotion of) a commercial occasion or event (including participation in live or recorded transmissions of any kind) for which he is entitled to receive a payment or transfer or which is designed to promote commercial sales or activity by any means. See *Set, Deuce and Ball v Robinson* (Sp C 373), [2003] SSCD 382 which analysed this definition in relation to non-resident tennis players performing at Wimbledon; on appeal to the HL, it was held that payments made by a foreign company with no UK tax presence are within these provisions (*Agassi v Robinson* HL 2006, 77 TC 68).

Payments or transfers from which tax need not be withheld under these provisions are as follows:

- a payment subject to deduction of tax under some provision of the *Taxes Acts* other than *ITA 2007, s 966* and the *Income Tax (Entertainers and Sportsmen) Regulations 1987* (*SI 1987 No 530*);
- an arm's length payment made to a person resident in the UK, who is not connected or associated with the payee, for services ancillary to the performance of a relevant activity;
- payments representing royalties from the sale of sound recordings;
- any total amount paid in a tax year by a payer, together with persons connected or associated with him, to a non-UK resident performer, together with persons connected or associated with him, which does not exceed the amount of the basic personal allowance for that year (see **1.17** ALLOWANCES AND TAX RATES).

The *Regulations* provide for arrangements to be made in writing between the payer, the performer, or other recipient of the payment, and the Commissioners of HMRC for a reduced tax payment representing, as nearly as may be, the actual liability of the performer, to apply. Such application must be made not later than 30 days before the payment (or transfer) falls to be made and the full basic rate deduction must be made from any payment or transfer made before approval is given by HMRC. There are provisions to prevent any payment suffering withholding tax more than once where it passes through an intermediary, and for reductions to apply where there is a double taxation agreement in force. Similarly, there are anti-avoidance provisions to prevent payments or transfers being routed through third parties such as controlled companies and similar entities.

The sum accounted for to HMRC is treated as paid on account of the income or corporation tax liability of a person other than the person so accounting for it, whether a liability under the *Regulations*, under the main charging provisions below or under any other provision of the *Taxes Acts*. The charge under *ITA 2007, s 966* applies in place of any charge on employment income (any amount charged on which is to be treated as an expense of the separate trade referred to below), under the settlements legislation (see **70.25** *et seq.* SETTLEMENTS) or on company profits (where the connected payment is a receipt falling to be included in the computation of profits of a company which provides the services of the performer). A recipient is entitled to claim in writing that a tax payment deducted is excessive and *TMA 1970, s 42* (see **16.1**, **16.3** CLAIMS) applies to such claims.

Payment of tax is due, whether or not it has been withheld from the connected payment or transfer, before, or at the time when, a quarterly return (see below) is made, whether or not an assessment has been made.

Liability of the performer

Where a payment or other transfer connected with the relevant activity is made, then (regardless of whether or not there is a duty to deduct tax at source) the relevant activity is treated as performed in the course of a trade, profession or vocation carried on in the UK (insofar as it would not otherwise be so treated, for example because the performer already has a UK trade), unless it is performed in the course of an office or employment. Payments and transfers made to a prescribed (by the *Regulations*) person other than the performer himself (typically to a company controlled by the performer), and connected with the relevant activity, are treated, other than in prescribed circumstances, as if made to the performer himself in the course of that trade etc.

Income tax is charged on profits arising from payments and transfers within these provisions as if they were received in the course of a *separate* trade, profession or vocation (distinct from any other trade etc. carried on by the performer, e.g. his world-wide trade). However, for the purposes of loss relief under *ITA 2007, s 72* and *ITA 2007, s 83*, the separate trade and world-wide trade are treated as the same trade, although losses in early years will be relieved only by reference to the date of commencement of the world-wide trade. Terminal loss relief under *ITA 2007, s 89* will only be given in respect of the separate trade if the world-wide trade ceases in the same period.

All other provisions of the *Taxes Acts* as to the time within which an assessment may be made apply to such an assessment as do the provisions for out of time assessments. Tax charged by an assessment is payable within 14 days of the issue of the notice, or by the due date of payment of the tax (see above) if this is earlier. The collection and recovery procedures and the provisions relating to interest on overdue tax in *TMA 1970* apply to such assessments.

Returns (including returns of payments for which a nil deduction rate applied) must be made quarterly in respect of the periods to 30 June, 30 September, 31 December and 5 April within 14 days of the end of each period. HMRC may require, in writing, within a specified time, certain information regarding payments, payees and relevant activities. The penalty provisions of *TMA 1970, s 98* apply to failure to submit returns (see **55.22** PENALTIES).

[*ITA 2007, ss 965–970; ITTOIA 2005, ss 13, 14; SI 1987 No 530*].

The provisions are administered by the Foreign Entertainers Unit (FEU), a specialist unit within HMRC (see www.gov.uk/topic/personal-tax/foreign-entertainer-rules).

See also HMRC booklet FEU50 and HMRC Help sheet IR303.

Specific sporting events

There are provisions conferring exemption from income tax to non-UK resident employees and contractors of competing overseas teams in relation to certain income arising in connection with the 2017 UEFA Champions League final in Cardiff. The exemption extends to certain non-UK resident employees, contractors, officials and delegates of UEFA and its member associations. Non-UK resident competitors in the London Anniversary Games and the 2017 World Athletics Championships are exempt from income tax on any employment income or trading profits arising from Games or Championships activities. See **30.48** EXEMPT INCOME.

Simon's Taxes. See E5.8.

Non-resident dealers in securities etc. trading in the UK

[50.12] If in any tax year:

(a) a person who is not resident in the UK carries on a trade in the UK consisting wholly or partly of dealing in securities or of banking or insurance; and
(b) in calculating the profits of the trade any amount is disregarded as a result of *ITTOIA 2005, s 714* (exemption of profits from FOTRA securities — see **65.4** SAVINGS AND INVESTMENT INCOME) because of a condition subject to which any 3½% War Loan 1952 Or After was issued,

interest on money borrowed for the purposes of the trade is deductible in calculating the profits for that tax year only insofar as it exceeds the total cost of the 3½% War Loan.

[*ITTOIA 2005, s 154A*].

The above does not apply in calculating profits on the cash basis (see **76.14** TRADING INCOME — CASH BASIS FOR SMALLER BUSINESSES).

Interest on foreign currency securities etc.

[50.13] Where foreign currency securities are issued by a local authority or a 'statutory corporation' *and the Treasury so direct*, the interest on the securities is exempt from income tax if their beneficial owner is a non-UK resident. The same applies to interest on a foreign currency loan made to a statutory corporation if the Treasury so direct and the person for the time being entitled to repayment or eventual repayment of the loan is a non-UK resident. In both cases, the exemption does not apply if the interest falls to be treated by tax law as another person's income.

A '*statutory corporation*' is a corporation (other than a company) incorporated by a statute or any other corporation on which functions connected with carrying on an undertaking are conferred by a statute or by an order made under or confirmed by a statute.

A security or loan is a foreign currency one if under its terms the currency to be used for repayment is not sterling. In the case of a security issued or loan made before 6 April 1982, the security or loan is a foreign currency one if under its terms the currency to be used for repayment is not that of a country specified in *Exchange Control Act 1947, Sch 1* at the time the security was issued or the loan was made. If there is an option as to the currency to be used for repayment, the security or loan is only to be treated as a foreign currency one if the option is exercisable only by the holder of the security or the person for the time being entitled to repayment or eventual repayment of the loan.

[*ITTOIA 2005, ss 755, 756, 879(3), 880(1)*].

Where interest is exempt as above, the payer is not required to deduct tax at source — see **23.12** DEDUCTION OF TAX AT SOURCE.

Payment of royalties

[50.14] See 23.14 DEDUCTION OF TAX AT SOURCE as regards the requirement to deduct tax at source from royalties (or other payments) for the use of intellectual property where paid to owners or assignors of such property whose usual place of abode is outside the UK.

51

Offshore Funds

Cross-reference. See **65.5** SAVINGS AND INVESTMENT INCOME (certain distributions of offshore funds treated as interest).

Introduction to offshore funds

[51.1] Gains arising on disposals of certain investments in offshore funds are chargeable to income tax rather than capital gains tax. Broadly, this applies to investments that accumulate income rather than distribute it. Without special rules the accumulated income would be reflected in the value on disposal and would be converted into a chargeable gain. The original statutory regime was replaced by legislation now in *TIOPA 2010* and by *SI 2009 No 3001* (*The Offshore Funds (Tax) Regulations 2009*) with effect in relation to distributions and disposals made on or after 1 December 2009 (subject to transitional rules — see **51.19**).

For official guidance, see HMRC Investment Funds Manual IFM12000, IFM13000.

Simon's Taxes. See B5.7.

See also HMRC Brief 04/13, 25 March 2013 at **49.5** MISCELLANEOUS INCOME (rebates of annual management charges etc.).

Definition of offshore fund

[51.2] A new definition of 'offshore fund' was introduced for the purposes of the current regime with effect in relation to distributions and disposals made on or after 1 December 2009 (subject to transitional rules — see **51.19** below).

An '*offshore fund*' means:

(a) a 'mutual fund' constituted by a non-UK resident body corporate (other than a limited liability partnership);
(b) a 'mutual fund' under which property is held on trust for the participants where the trustees are non-UK resident; or
(c) a 'mutual fund' constituted by other arrangements that create rights in the nature of co-ownership where the arrangements take effect by virtue of the law of a territory outside the UK, but not including a mutual fund constituted by two or more persons carrying on a trade or business in partnership.

'*Mutual fund*' means arrangements with respect to property of any description (including money) that meet all of the conditions set out below, subject to the exceptions in *TIOPA 2010, s 357* and any other exceptions that may be specified by the Treasury in regulations made by statutory instrument. The conditions are that:

- the purpose or effect of the arrangements is to enable the participants to participate in the acquisition, holding, management or disposal of the property or to receive profits or income arising from the acquisition, holding, management or disposal of the property or to receive amounts paid out of such profits or income;
- the participants do not have day-to-day control of the management of the property; and
- under the terms of the arrangements, a reasonable investor participating in the arrangements would expect to be able to realise all or part of his investment on a basis calculated entirely (or almost entirely) by reference to net asset value or to an index of some description.

In the case of 'umbrella arrangements', each part of the arrangements is to be treated as separate arrangements. '*Umbrella arrangements*' means arrangements which provide for separate pooling of the contributions of the participants and the profits or income out of which payments are made to them. Where there is more than one class of interest in arrangements (the '*main arrangements*'), the arrangements relating to each class of interest are to be treated as separate arrangements.

The UCITS Directive (Directive 2009/65/EC of the European Parliament and of the Council) provides that an investment fund authorised under Article 5 of the Directive may have a management company which is not resident in the same State as that in which the fund is established and regulated. Where such a fund is a body corporate treated as tax resident in the EU member State in which it is authorised, it will be treated as not resident in the UK notwithstanding that it may have a UK resident management company.

[*TIOPA 2010, ss 354–363, 363A; FA 2008, ss 40A–40G, 41, 42, 42A; SI 2017 No 1204, Regs 1, 14*].

Charge to tax on participants in non-reporting funds

[51.3] Any fund that is not a reporting fund (for which see **51.13** below) is a '*non-reporting fund*'. [*SI 2009 No 3001, Reg 4*].

Subject to the exceptions at **51.4** below, there is a charge to income tax if a person disposes of an interest (i.e. an investment) in a non-reporting fund and an offshore income gain (see **51.5** below) arises on the disposal. The offshore income gain is treated for tax purposes as miscellaneous income which arises at the time of the disposal to the person making the disposal, and the tax is charged on that person. [*SI 2009 No 3001, Regs 17, 18*].

The charge to income tax may also arise if the interest disposed of is an interest in a reporting fund which has been a non-reporting fund at some time since the interest was acquired — see **51.18** below for details.

A person is within the above charge if the offshore income gain arises in a tax year during any part of which he meets the UK residence conditions for capital gains tax (see *TCGA 1992, s 1A*, previously, before 2019/20, *TCGA 1992, s 2(1)*). [*SI 2009 No 3001, Reg 22(1)(a)*]. See also **51.11** below.

Any offshore income gains arising to trustees of a settlement are charged at the trust rate of income tax (see **70.11** SETTLEMENTS).

A disposal may well give rise to both an offshore income gain chargeable as above and a chargeable gain for capital gains tax (CGT) purposes. See **51.7** below as regards relief from CGT. See **51.6** below as to what constitutes a disposal.

See **51.8** below as regards investors chargeable to tax on the remittance basis.

Special rules apply to authorised investment funds (either unit trusts or open-ended investment companies) which invest in non-reporting offshore funds. See **80.7** UNIT TRUSTS ETC.

Exceptions from charge

[51.4] No charge arises under **51.3** above if:

- the interest in the non-reporting fund is held as trading stock; or
- the disposal of the interest is taken into account in computing the profits of a trade; or
- the interest consists of 'excluded indexed securities' (as defined by *ITTOIA 2005, s 433* — see **65.26** SAVINGS AND INVESTMENT INCOME); or
- the interest is a right arising under a policy of insurance; or
- the interest is a loan (but not if it is a loan where the amount payable on redemption exceeds the issue price by an amount wholly or partly determined by reference to the income of the non-reporting fund); or
- the interest is in an offshore fund falling within **51.2**(b) or (c) above and the fund is a 'transparent fund' (see below for definition and qualifications); or
- the exemption in **14.9** CHARITIES AND CHARITABLE GIVING applies; or
- the transitional protection in **51.19** below applies.

A fund is a '*transparent fund*':

(a) if, in the case of investors who are UK resident individuals, any sums which form part of the income of the fund are of such a nature that they fall within any of **32.2**(a), (c)–(n) FOREIGN INCOME (insofar as the sums are referable to those investors' interests); or
(b) if (a) would apply were it not for the fact that the income is derived from assets within the UK.

If a fund is transparent, such as would be the case for certain unit trusts and contractual funds, then any income arising to the fund is treated as arising to an investor in proportion to his rights. This means that income is charged to tax as it arises, hence the exemption.

The exemption for disposals of interests in transparent funds does not apply if:

(i) during a period beginning with the date the interest (or any part of it) was acquired and ending with the date of disposal, the offshore fund has at any time held interests in other non-reporting funds which amounted in total to more than 5% by value of the offshore fund's assets; or
(ii) the fund is a non-reporting fund and it fails to make sufficient information available to its participants in to enable them to meet their UK tax obligations with respect to their shares of income.

If, on the disposal by an offshore fund of an interest in another non-reporting fund, no liability would arise by virtue of the exemption for disposals of interests in transparent funds, that interest is not taken into account for the purposes of (i) above.

Unlisted trading company exception

For disposals on or after 27 May 2011, no charge arises under **51.3** above if the sole or main purpose of the offshore fund is to invest in unlisted trading companies or unlisted holding companies of trading groups. Throughout a period starting with the date on which the interest was acquired by the investor and ending twelve months before the date of the disposal, the fund must have met an investment condition, which is broadly that at least 90% of the value of the assets of the fund consists of direct or indirect holdings in such companies. If one offshore fund's business consists solely of holding an interest in another offshore fund, a disposal of an interest in the holding fund is exempt from the charge if the investee fund is within the unlisted trading company exception.

[*SI 2009 No 3001, Regs 11, 12, 25(5)(6), 26, 28–31, 31A–31C; SI 2019 No 689, Reg 30(2)*].

Computation of offshore income gain

[51.5] An offshore income gain is computed in the same way as a chargeable gain would be computed under CGT legislation. If such a computation would produce a loss, the offshore income gain is taken to be nil. If the disposal gives rise to a claim for CGT purposes under *TCGA 1992, s 162* (rollover relief on transfer of a business to a company) or *TCGA 1992, s 165* or *260* (gifts holdover relief), these claims have no effect in computing the offshore income gain. In other words, an offshore income gain cannot be deferred for income tax purposes by such a claim.

If a participant's rights in an offshore fund attract the transitional protection in **51.19** below, those rights cannot be pooled for CGT purposes with any rights in the same fund that he acquires on or after 1 December 2009 and which do not attract the transitional protection. Instead, any disposal is treated as being a disposal of the protected rights to the extent that those rights are not yet exhausted. As this affects the computation of the chargeable gain on any such disposal, it similarly affects the amount of the offshore income gain.

[*SI 2009 No 3001, Regs 38, 39, 41–43*].

What constitutes a disposal?

[51.6] Generally there is a disposal for these purposes whenever there would a disposal for CGT purposes. This is subject to the special rules outlined below.

Death is not an occasion of charge for CGT purposes. However, for the purposes of the offshore funds rules, the deceased is deemed to have disposed on the date of death of any interest of his in a non-reporting fund at its market value at its market value at that date. Thus, an offshore income gain, and an income tax charge, may arise.

In specified circumstances, by virtue of *TCGA 1992, s 135*, an *exchange of securities* in one company for securities in another is not treated as a disposal for CGT purposes. Whilst that rule can apply for the purposes of the offshore funds rules, it does not apply where an interest in a non-reporting fund is exchanged for an interest in an entity that is not a non-reporting fund. Instead, the participant is deemed to have made a disposal at market value at the time of the exchange.

Also in specified circumstances, by virtue of *TCGA 1992, s 136*, a *scheme of reconstruction* involving the issue of securities is not treated as a disposal for CGT purposes but as an exchange with similar consequences as above. Again, that rule can apply for the purposes of the offshore funds rules, but does not apply where an interest in a non-reporting fund is deemed to be exchanged for an interest in an entity that is not a non-reporting fund. Instead, the participant is deemed to have made a disposal at market value at the time of the deemed exchange.

[*SI 2009 No 3001, Regs 33–36*].

By virtue of *TCGA 1992, s 127*, a *reorganisation* of a company's share capital is not normally treated for CGT purposes as involving a disposal by the investor. Instead, the new holding of shares or securities stands in the shoes of the old and inherits its CGT acquisition cost. This rule can also apply for the purposes of the offshore funds rules but does not do so if:

- the offshore fund is constituted by a class of interest ('Class A') in 'main arrangements' (see **51.2** above);
- a participant exchanges an interest of Class A for an interest in another offshore fund constituted by a different class of interest (Class B) in those main arrangements;
- the interest of Class A is a non-reporting fund and the interest of Class B is an interest in an entity that is not a non-reporting fund.

Instead, the participant is deemed to have made a disposal at market value at the time of the exchange.

[*SI 2009 No 3001, Reg 37*].

Relief from capital gains tax

[51.7] A single disposal may well give rise to both an offshore income gain (chargeable to income tax as in **51.3** above) and a chargeable gain for CGT purposes. To avoid a double charge, a sum equal to the offshore income gain is deducted from the sum which would otherwise constitute the amount or value of the consideration for the disposal for CGT purposes. Special rules apply if the disposal is a *part* disposal for CGT purposes or is a disposal to which *TCGA 1992, s 162* applies (rollover relief on transfer of a business to a company); for these rules, see Tolley's Capital Gains Tax under Overseas Matters.

A special rule also applies if, on an exchange of securities, a scheme of reconstruction or a reorganisation, there is a disposal for the purposes of the offshore fund rules by virtue of **51.6** above. An amount equal to the offshore income gain on that disposal is treated as having been given by the person making the exchange as consideration for the new holding (so that *TCGA 1992, s 128* applies — see Tolley's Capital Gains Tax under Shares and Securities).

[*SI 2009 No 3001, Regs 44–47*].

Remittance basis

[51.8] If an offshore income gain arises to a non-UK domiciled individual who is chargeable (whether or not as a result of a claim) on the remittance basis) for the tax year in question, it is treated as 'relevant foreign income' (as in **32.2** FOREIGN INCOME) with the consequences in **61.4** REMITTANCE BASIS.

See **61** REMITTANCE BASIS for the meaning of 'remitted to the UK' etc. For the purpose of applying the provisions in that chapter to a remittance of an offshore income gain:

- treat any consideration for the disposal of the interest in the fund as deriving from the offshore income gain; and
- if the consideration is less than the market value of the interest, treat the interest as deriving from the offshore income gain.

[*SI 2009 No 3001, Reg 19*].

Offshore income gains arising to non-UK resident settlements

[51.9] If an offshore income gain arises to a settlement the trustees of which are not resident in the UK in the tax year in question, the gain is not regarded as income for the purposes of applying the provisions at **70.25** SETTLEMENTS (amounts treated as income of settlor). If offshore income gains arise to the trustees of such a settlement, the attribution rules of *TCGA 1992, ss 87, 87A* are applied (with appropriate modifications) to attribute the gain to beneficiaries, who may then be chargeable to income tax depending on their residence/domicile status. See Tolley's Capital Gains Tax under Offshore Settlements for those attribution rules. See also HMRC Investment Funds Manual IFM13420–13432. [*SI 2009 No 3001, Reg 20*].

'Transfer of assets abroad' rules

[51.10] The 'transfer of assets abroad' rules at **4.14–4.18** ANTI-AVOIDANCE apply in relation to an offshore income gain arising to a person resident or domiciled outside the UK as if the offshore income gain were foreign income becoming payable to that person. This does not apply to an offshore income gain that arises to an offshore company and, as a result of the relevant rule in **51.11** below, is treated as arising to a person resident in the UK. It also does not apply that arises to an offshore income gain that arises to the trustees of a non-UK resident settlement and which is consequently treated under **51.9** above as arising to an individual resident in the UK. For more on the interaction between these rules and those at **51.9** above, see HMRC Investment Funds Manual IFM13440. [*SI 2009 No 3001, Reg 21*].

Adoption of certain CGT rules

[51.11] *Market value* for the purposes of the offshore funds rules is generally determined in accordance with CGT rules. However, in the case of an interest in an offshore fund for which there are separate published buying and selling prices, *TCGA 1992, s 272(5)* (market value in relation to rights in unit trust schemes) applies with the necessary modifications to determine market value. [*SI 2009 No 3001, Reg 10*].

UK branch or agency

A person carrying on a trade, profession or vocation in the UK through a branch or agency is chargeable to tax on offshore income gains arising on the disposal of a holding in an offshore fund if the interest was held for the purposes of the UK branch or agency. [*SI 2009 No 3001, Reg 22*].

Temporary non-UK residence

An individual who is 'temporarily non-UK resident' is chargeable to income tax in the 'period of return' on offshore income gains arising during the period of temporary non-residence. For what is meant by 'temporarily non-UK resident' and 'period of return', see **63.29** RESIDENCE AND DOMICILE. [*SI 2009 No 3001, Regs 23, 23A*].

Attribution of gains to members of non-UK resident companies

TCGA 1992, s 13 applied to offshore income gains (with appropriate modifications) in the same way as it applies to chargeable gains. Broadly, *TCGA 1992, s 13* applied to gains arising to non-UK resident companies which would be close companies if they were UK resident, and apportions those gains between any participators in the company who are UK resident. Note that *TCGA 1992, s 13* is effectively repealed by *FA 2019, Sch 1 para 2* for 2019/20 onwards; the equivalent provisions are now in *TCGA 1992, s 3*. See Tolley's Capital Gains Tax. [*SI 2009 No 3001, Reg 24*].

Treatment of certain amounts as distributions

[51.12] If a non-reporting fund which is a transparent fund (see **51.4** above) has an interest in a reporting fund, any such excess as is mentioned in **51.14**(b) below is treated as if it were additional income of the participants in the non-reporting fund in proportion to their rights. Such income is treated as arising on the same date as the excess is treated as made to the non-reporting fund (see **51.15** below) and is chargeable to income tax as 'relevant foreign income' (see **32.2** FOREIGN INCOME). [*SI 2009 No 3001, Reg 16*].

Reporting funds

[51.13] As far as 'reporting funds' are concerned, the post-1 December 2009 offshore funds regime moves away from the previous requirement that an offshore fund distribute a minimum proportion of its income if its UK investors are to benefit from CGT treatment of gains on disposal as opposed to those gains being chargeable to income tax. Instead, the CGT treatment will apply if an offshore fund's income is reported to its UK investors in such a way that they are charged to income tax on their share of the reported income of the fund, regardless of whether that income is distributed to them or accumulated in the fund. See **51.15** below for the tax treatment of participants in reported funds. For non-reporting funds, the charge to income tax on disposals continues (see **51.3** above).

A '*reporting fund*' is an 'eligible offshore fund' that has applied for and been approved by HMRC as a reporting fund. (An '*eligible offshore fund*' is an offshore fund that is not a guaranteed return fund as defined by *SI 2009 No 3001, Reg 9*.) Funds that have applied and been approved are said to be in the reporting funds regime. An existing offshore fund may apply to HMRC for reporting fund status, as may a fund that has yet to be established. A fund cannot apply to be a reporting fund if it has previously been excluded from being a reporting fund as a result of an HMRC notice due to serious breaches of duties or if it has previously left the reporting fund regime voluntarily for any reason other than its ceasing to have any UK-resident participants. Regulations set out the required contents of an application (including undertakings that must be given) and make provision for the timing, amendment and withdrawal of applications, the manner in which HMRC must respond to applications and appeals against refusal of applications. [*SI 2009 No 3001, Regs 51–56, 56A, 56B*].

A reporting fund must comply with various duties as to the preparation of accounts, the computation of its reportable income, the provision of reports to participants (see **51.14** below) and the provision of information to HMRC. [*SI 2009 No 3001, Regs 57–72, 72A–72C, 73–89, 89A–89E, 90–92, 92A–92D, 93, 106, 107; SI 2017 No 240; SI 2019 No 689, Reg 30(3)*].

Regulations set out various potential breaches of duties and their consequences. In the event of certain breaches specified as serious, the consequence (subject to appeal) is exclusion from the reporting fund regime. [*SI 2009 No 3001, Regs 108–115*].

A fund may voluntarily leave the reporting fund regime by giving notice to HMRC. [*SI 2009 No 3001, Regs 116, 117*].

See **51.17** below as regards constant NAV funds, broadly reporting funds whose net asset value remains fairly constant as a result of the nature of their assets, and the frequency with which they distribute their income.

Reports to participants in reporting funds

[51.14] A reporting fund must make a report available to each of its participants for each 'reporting period', and must do so within the six months immediately following the end of the reporting period. The purpose is to provide participants with the information they need to enter on their self-assessment tax returns. A fund's '*reporting period*' is normally its period of account. If, however, a fund has a period of account exceeding 12 months, this is split into two reporting periods; the first reporting period is the first 12 months of the period of account and the second reporting period is the balance of the period of account. The report need not be sent to non-UK resident participants.

The report must show:

(a) the amount distributed to participants per unit of interest in the fund in respect of the reporting period;
(b) the excess of the reportable income per unit for the reporting period over the amount in (a); this may be nil but cannot be a negative amount;
(c) the dates on which distributions were made;
(d) the 'fund distribution date' (see below); this is normally the date on which the report is issued, but if the fund issues the report after the six-month period referred to above, the fund distribution date is the last day of the reporting period;
(e) a statement of whether or not the fund remains a reporting fund at the date it makes the report available; and
(f) certain additional information if the fund operates full equalisation arrangements (as defined in *SI 2009 No 3001, Reg 50A*).

In the case of reporting funds which are 'transparent funds', (a) to (d) and (f) above do not apply, but the report must contain sufficient information to enable the participants to meet their UK tax obligations with respect to their interests in the fund. It must still include the statement at (e) above. For the meaning of '*transparent fund*', see **51.4** above. In (d) above, the '*fund distribution date*' is the last day of the six months immediately following the end of the reporting period.

[*SI 2009 No 3001, Regs 90–92, 92A–92D, 93, 94(4)*].

Income tax treatment of participants in reporting funds

[51.15] Participants within the charge to income tax are taxed on actual distributions from the fund plus their share of any excess of reportable income over distributed income, i.e. the amount at **51.14**(b) above. The precise rules, as described below, depend on whether or not the reporting fund is a 'transparent fund' and also on whether or not it is a corporate fund. For the meaning of '*transparent fund*', see **51.4** above.

If the reporting fund is not a transparent fund, any such excess as is referred to above is treated as additional distributions made to the participants in the fund in proportion to their rights. Where the trustees of a charitable trust are participants in a reporting fund, they are not chargeable to tax on these additional distributions.

If the fund is a transparent fund, any excess of reportable income over the income of the fund (which may occur if the fund holds investments in other reporting funds) is treated as additional income of the participants in the fund in proportion to their rights.

In both cases, the excess is treated as made, on the fund distribution date (see **51.14** above), to participants holding an interest in the fund at the end of the reporting period (see **51.14** above). On and after 27 May 2011, if the reported income in respect of the reporting period is recognised in accounts of the participant on a date earlier than the fund distribution date, the excess is instead treated as made on that earlier date. Also on and after 27 May 2011, in determining whether an interest in the fund is held at the end of the reporting period, a disposal within the reporting period is ignored if CGT matching rules require it to be matched with an interest acquired in the next reporting period.

To the extent that the participant's rights in the fund are rights to which *SI 2009 No 3001, Reg 30* (rights in certain pre-existing holdings — see **51.19** below) applies, the excess is reduced proportionately. Before 27 May 2011, this applied only if the fund was a transparent fund.

If a participant has acquired by way of initial purchase an interest in a reporting fund which operates full equalisation arrangements (see *SI 2009 No 3001, Reg 50A*), the amount of any excess treated as additional distributions made to the participant is reduced by the equalisation amount, and the amount of any actual distributions to the participant is treated as reduced by the amount (if any) by which the equalisation amount exceeds the excess. Alternatively, but only in relation to interests in offshore funds acquired in a reporting period beginning on or after 28 June 2013, the amount of any actual distributions to the participant is reduced by the equalisation amount, and the amount of any excess treated as additional distributions made to the participant is reduced by the amount (if any) by which the equalisation amount exceeds the amount of any actual distributions to the participant.

If the fund is a corporate fund, i.e. it falls within **51.2**(a) above, any actual distribution plus any amount treated as an additional distribution as above is taxed as dividends from a non-UK resident company or, where the conditions at **65.5** SAVINGS AND INVESTMENT INCOME are met, is taxed as interest.

If the fund is a non-transparent fund and it falls within **51.2**(b) or (c) above, i.e. it is not a corporate fund, any actual distribution plus any amount treated as an additional distribution as above is taxed as miscellaneous income or, where the conditions at **65.5** SAVINGS AND INVESTMENT INCOME are met, as interest.

If the fund is a transparent fund, UK investors will be charged to tax on their proportionate share of income from underlying investments of the fund as it arises (less a deduction for trustees' expenses) as if they had made those investments directly. For example, where the fund holds interest-producing investments, investors will be chargeable to tax on income arising to the fund from those investments as if they had received interest. If any amount falls to be treated as additional income of the participants as above, it is chargeable to income tax as 'relevant foreign income' (see **32.2** FOREIGN INCOME).

[*SI 2009 No 3001, Regs 94, 94A, 95–97, 101*].

Special rules apply in calculating the income from interests held by 'financial traders' in diversely owned reporting funds. '*Financial traders*' include banks, insurance businesses (but not life assurance businesses) and businesses dealing in certain financial products such that profits arising from the holding of investments in reporting funds would form part of their trading profits. [*SI 2009 No 3001, Regs 102–105*]. See HMRC Offshore Funds Manual OFM27900.

CGT treatment of disposals by participants in reporting funds

[51.16] A disposal by a participant of his interest in a reporting fund is a disposal of an asset for CGT purposes. Any amount charged to income tax under **51.15** above as an additional distribution made to the participant or as additional income of the participant is treated as part of the CGT acquisition cost of the asset. For disposals on or after 27 May 2011 where the fund operates full equalisation arrangements (see *SI 2009 No 3001, Reg 50A*), any equalisation amount that has resulted in a reduction in actual distributions (see **51.15**) must be deducted in arriving at CGT acquisition cost. Different rules apply on and after 1 January 2018 in the case of 'transparent funds' (within **51.4** above). [*SI 2009 No 3001, Reg 99; SI 2017 No 1204, Regs 1, 14*].

If an offshore fund ceases to be a reporting fund and becomes a non-reporting fund, a participant may make an election to be treated for CGT purposes:

- as disposing of an interest in the reporting fund at the end of that fund's final period of account, and
- as acquiring an interest in the non-reporting fund at the beginning of that fund's first period of account.

The deemed disposal and acquisition are treated as made for a consideration equal to the net asset value of the participant's interest in the fund at the end of the period of account for which the final reported income is reported to him. The election must be made by being included in a tax return for the year which includes the final day of the reporting fund's final period of account, but cannot be made if a report has not been made available to the participant under **51.14** above for that period of account. The normal purpose of an election would be to crystallise the gain accrued to date as a chargeable gain within the charge to CGT; any subsequent gain on actual disposal would be an offshore income gain chargeable to income tax as in **51.3** above.

[*SI 2009 No 3001, Reg 100*].

See Tolley's Capital Gains Tax under Overseas Matters for more details of both rules above.

Constant NAV funds

[51.17] A '*constant NAV fund*' is an offshore fund whose net asset value (expressed in the currency in which units are issued) does not fluctuate by more than an insignificant amount throughout the fund's existence, as a result of the nature of the fund's assets, and the frequency with which it distributes its income. The reporting fund rules at **51.13** above are modified for constant NAV funds. Neither the reporting requirements at **51.14** above nor the tax treatment at **51.15** and **51.16** above apply. If, however, the value of the fund's assets (expressed in the currency in which units are issued) increases by more than an insignificant amount and the fund has not notified HMRC that it has ceased to be a constant NAV fund, a participant who subsequently disposes of his interest in the fund and who makes a chargeable gain on the disposal is treated as making an offshore income gain (chargeable to income tax as in **51.3** above). [*SI 2009 No 3001, Regs 118–124*].

Conversion of a non-reporting fund into a reporting fund

[51.18] If an offshore fund ceases to be a non-reporting fund and becomes a reporting fund as in **51.13** above, a participant may make an election to be treated for tax purposes:

- as disposing of an interest in the non-reporting fund at the end of that fund's final period of account, and
- as acquiring an interest in the reporting fund at the beginning of that fund's first period of account.

The deemed disposal and acquisition are treated as made at market value as at the deemed date of disposal. The election must be made by being included in a tax return for the year which includes the deemed date of disposal. The election can be made only if the deemed disposal would trigger an offshore income gain (chargeable to income tax as in **51.3** above). The election cannot be made in certain circumstances involving AIFM partnerships (as in **52.29** PARTNERSHIPS).

The normal purpose of an election would be to crystallise the gain accrued to date as an offshore income gain, leaving any subsequent gain on actual disposal to be taxed within the CGT regime.

[*SI 2009 No 3001, Reg 48*].

If the above election is *not* made, any subsequent disposal of the interest in the fund will be within the income tax charge at **51.3** above, provided:

- a deemed disposal as above would have triggered an offshore income gain; and
- the interest was an interest in a non-reporting fund during some or all of the 'material period'.

The '*material period*' is the period beginning with the day on which consideration was given for the acquisition of the interest (or on 1 January 1984 if later) and ending with the day on which the fund became a reporting fund. The legislation ensures that the income tax charge cannot be avoided by a merger or reorganisation of the fund in which the interest is held.

[*SI 2009 No 3001, Reg 17(1)(3)(3A)(4)*].

Transition to post-1 December 2009 regime

[51.19] The following applies if a person holds an interest in an offshore fund on 1 December 2009 that fell within the pre-1 December 2009 definition of offshore fund and also falls within the current definition at **51.2** above. If the fund is a non-reporting fund and the person subsequently disposes of his interest, any gain on the disposal will be taxed under **51.3** above in respect of the entire period that the investor held the interest in the fund. [*SI 2009 No 3001, Sch 1 para* 2].

If:

- a person acquired rights in an offshore fund before 1 December 2009,
- the fund is an offshore fund within the current definition at **51.2** above, and
- on the date the rights were acquired, the fund was not an offshore fund within the pre-1 December 2009 regime,

those rights do not come within the current regime. This rule applies equally if the person acquired the rights on or after 1 December 2009 but was obliged to acquire them by virtue of a legally enforceable written agreement made before 30 April 2009, provided any conditions attached to the agreement were satisfied before that date and that the agreement is not varied on or after that date.

[*TIOPA 2010, Sch 9 paras 33, 34*].

If a person disposes of rights in an offshore fund which he acquired before 1 December 2009 (or on or after that date in the circumstances mentioned above), no income tax charge under **51.3** above can arise on the disposal if, when he acquired them, the rights did not constitute a 'material interest in an offshore fund' (within *ICTA 1988, s 759(2)–(4)*). [*SI 2009 No 3001, Reg 30*].

52

Partnerships

Cross-reference. See also **4.36, 4.37** ANTI-AVOIDANCE (for disposals of income streams and assets through partnerships); **58** PERSONAL SERVICE COMPANIES ETC.; **64.12–64.14** RETURNS (for partnership tax returns).

Simon's Taxes. See Part **B7**.

Introduction to partnerships

[52.1] An English partnership is not a legal entity in the same way as a company, but a collection of separate persons. In Scotland though, a firm is a legal person, see *Partnership Act 1890, s 4(2)*.

Under UK tax law, a partnership is *not* generally treated for tax purposes as an entity which is separate and distinct from its members. The taxable profits of a trade, profession or other business carried on in partnership are apportioned between the partners, each of whom is then taxed individually on his own share (see **52.4** below).

See the corresponding chapter of Tolley's Capital Gains Tax as regards the chargeable gains of partnerships and individual partners.

See **64.8, 64.12–64.14** RETURNS for self-assessment provisions regarding partnership returns and general compliance.

For official guidance, see HMRC Partnership Manual at PM100000 *et seq.* This was restructured in summer 2019 and now incorporates material previously found in other HMRC manuals such as the Business Income Manual.

Nature of partnership

[52.2] Whether a partnership exists and, if so, from what date is a question of fact (*Williamson* CS 1928, 14 TC 335; *Calder v Allanson* KB 1935, 19 TC 293; *Ashton v HMRC* FTT (TC 5456), [2016] UKFTT 727 (TC)). The existence of a formal partnership agreement is not conclusive of the existence of a partnership (*Hawker v Compton* KB 1922, 8 TC 306; *Dickenson v Gross* KB 1927, 11 TC 614). Equally, whether a partnership can ante-date the date of the agreement is a question of fact (*Ayrshire Pullman Services v CIR* CS 1929, 14 TC 754; *Waddington v O'Callaghan* KB 1931, 16 TC 187; *Taylor v Chalklin* KB 1945, 26 TC 463; *Alexander Bulloch & Co v CIR* CS 1976, 51 TC 563; *Saywell v Pope* Ch D 1979, 53 TC 40).

Joint transactions may amount to a partnership or joint trading for tax purposes — see *Morden Rigg & Eskrigge v Monks* CA 1923, 8 TC 450 (joint cotton transactions); *Gardner & Bowring Hardy v CIR* CS 1930, 15 TC 602 (temporary joint coal merchanting); *Lindsay Woodward & Hiscox v CIR* CS 1932, 18 TC 43 (joint transactions in whisky in violation of USA law); *George Hall & Son v Platt* Ch D 1954, 35 TC 440 (joint crop growing). See also *Fenston v Johnstone* KB 1940, 23 TC 29.

Where a partnership terminated with open forward contracts, subsequently completed, it was held to continue trading notwithstanding that some of the partners had formed a new partnership to carry on a similar business (*Hillerns & Fowler v Murray* CA 1932, 17 TC 77). A doctor who sold his practice, helping the purchaser for a short time on a profit-sharing basis, was held not to be a partner (*Pratt v Strick* KB 1932, 17 TC 459).

A partnership set up for tax avoidance purposes may nevertheless be a true partnership (*Newstead v Frost* HL 1980, 53 TC 525).

A Rotary Club is not a partnership (*Blackpool Marton Rotary Club v Martin* Ch D 1988, 62 TC 686).

The question of whether an operation conducted with an overseas entity is akin to an English partnership or to a silent partnership (which is not within the rules in this chapter) may arise for the purposes of DOUBLE TAX RELIEF (**27**). See *Memec plc v CIR* CA 1998, 71 TC 77 and *Training Consultant v HMRC* (Sp C 584), [2007] SSCD 231. But see also **27.3** DOUBLE TAX RELIEF under Distributions.

See **60.2** PROPERTY INCOME as regards joint ownership and exploitation of property.

See HMRC Partnership Manual at PM131200 (types of partnership), PM132050 (partners), PM133000 (does a partnership exist?) and PM134000 (when does a partnership commence?).

See **52.24** below as regards limited partnerships and **52.25–52.28** below as regards limited liability partnerships (LLPs).

Simon's Taxes. See B7.102.

Taxation of partnership income

[52.3] See **52.4** below as regards trading profits and losses and **52.5** below as regards non-trading income.

The assignment by a partner of part of his share in the partnership was ineffective for the purpose of displacing his liability to income tax on that part of his share of partnership profits (*Hadlee and Another v Commissioner of Inland Revenue (NZ)* PC, [1993] STC 294).

Company as partner

If a company is a partner, see **52.21** below.

Indirect partners

For **2018/19** onwards, rules are introduced to determine how 'indirect partners' are taxed in a case where a partnership is itself a partner in another partnership. If a partnership (DEF) is a partner in another partnership (ABC), then the partners of DEF are '*indirect partners*' in ABC. If another partnership (GHJ) is a partner in DEF, then GHJ is an indirect partner in ABC. The partners of GHJ are indirect partners in both DEF and ABC. This continues through however many intermediate partnerships. See **52.4, 52.5** below for these rules. [*ITTOIA 2005, s 847(4); FA 2018, Sch 6 para 5(2)(5)*].

Bare trusts

For 2018/19 onwards, where a partner is acting as bare trustee for a beneficiary who is absolutely entitled to that partner's share of the partnership profits, and the beneficiary is chargeable to tax on those profits, the beneficiary is treated for income tax purposes as if he were a partner and is subject to the same rules for calculating profits as actual partners. [*ITTOIA 2005, s 848A; FA 2018, Sch 6 paras 1, 4(1)*].

Capital gains

Capital gains which arise from the disposal of partnership assets are charged on the partners individually. [*TCGA 1992, s 59*]. See Tolley's Capital Gains Tax.

Simon's Taxes. See **B7.401, B7.501.**

Trading/professional profits and losses

[52.4] For any period of account (see **75.1** TRADING INCOME) for which there is at least one partner who is a UK resident individual chargeable to income tax, the profits or losses of the partnership trade or profession are computed for income tax purposes in like manner as if the partnership were a UK resident individual. The taxable profits or allowable losses of the partnership for a period of account (as adjusted for income tax purposes) are apportioned in accordance with the partnership's profit-sharing arrangements during that period of account (but see also **52.11** below as regards losses, and see **64.14** RETURNS (partnership return conclusive as to partnership shares)). In computing profits for any period of account, no account is taken of any losses for any other period of account. The above rules, but not those below, apply equally where a partnership carries on a business other than a trade or profession.

If the tax year is a split year (see **63.19** RESIDENCE AND DOMICILE) as regards a partner, the above has effect as if the partner were non-UK resident in the overseas part of the split year.

Each individual's share of the profit or loss of a partnership trade or profession (as adjusted for income tax purposes) is taxed or relieved as if it derived from a trade or profession (the notional trade) carried on by him alone. The notional trade is treated as commencing at the time the individual becomes a partner (or, if later, when the partnership starts to carry on the actual trade or profession), or, if the actual trade or profession was previously carried on by the individual alone, at the time the actual trade commenced. Similar rules apply as regards cessations.

The notional trade is taxed in accordance with the normal basis period rules including the overlap relief rules (see **75.6–75.14** TRADING INCOME). A change of accounting date of the actual partnership trade that would result in a change of basis period if it were a sole trade changes the basis periods for each partner's notional trade. Where no such change of basis period would result (because the necessary conditions are not satisfied), the basis periods for partners' notional trades are determined by reference to the partnership's old accounting date. Notice of a change of accounting date must be given in a partnership tax return by nominated partner nominated by the partnership for that purpose, and any appeal against a refusal by HMRC to accept the change must similarly be made by a nominated partner. The rule whereby the necessary conditions do not have to be satisfied if the change occurs in the second or third tax year of the business applies only by reference to the second or third tax year of the actual partnership trade and not to the second or third tax year of a partner's notional trade. See **75.10** TRADING INCOME for the detailed rules on changes of accounting date, and **64.12–64.14** RETURNS for partnership tax returns.

Where the partnership trade or profession commenced before 6 April 1994, transitional overlap relief (see **75.15** TRADING INCOME) applies to individual partners' notional trades as it does to sole trades, providing they were partners in 1997/98.

Indirect partners

The notional trade rules above are varied for 2018/19 onwards where:

- a person (T) is a partner in a partnership (PQR);
- PQR is a partner or indirect partner (see **52.3** above) in another partnership (MNO);
- MNO carries on a trade or profession (the '*underlying trade*') in which PQR has a share of the profits or losses; and
- those profits or losses do not themselves arise by virtue of MNO being a member of a partnership.

If T carries on PQR's actual trade (whether alone or in partnership) before MNO commences the underlying trade, T's notional trade commences when T starts to carry on the actual trade. Otherwise, T's notional trade commences when T becomes an indirect partner in MNO or when MNO commences the underlying trade, whichever is the later. If T carries on the actual trade (whether alone or in partnership) after MNO permanently ceases to carry on the underlying trade, T ceases to carry on the notional trade when T ceases to carry on the actual trade. Otherwise, T ceases to carry on the notional trade when T ceases to be an indirect partner in MNO or when MNO ceases to carry on the underlying trade, whichever is the earlier. No special rules existed for these circumstances prior to 2018/19.

[*ITTOIA 2005, ss 846–848, 849(1)(2)(3A), 850(1), 852(1)–(5), 852A, 853(1)–(3); FA 2018, Sch 6 paras 5(3)(5), 11, 14*].

Notes on computation of partnership profits

(i) The notional trade rules above are designed for the purposes of the basis period rules only. For the purpose of computing taxable profits, the trade must still be regarded as carried on in common by all the partners and not by any one individual (*Vaines v HMRC* CA, [2018] STC 297).

(ii) Legal costs and stamps re partnership deeds are not normally permissible deductions.

(iii) Partners' salaries, domestic and personal expenses, interest credited on capital and any benefit of financial value given to a partner are not permissible deductions for tax purposes, being regarded as part of the taxable profits. See e.g. *PDC Copyprint (South) v George* (Sp C 141), [1997] SSCD 326 as regards partners' salaries (and see the example at 52.8 below). But this does not necessarily apply to payments to a partner for goods or services 'altogether disconnected with the partnership business as such' and where the firm's premises are owned by a partner, *bona fide* rent paid to him under legal agreement is a proper deduction for tax purposes (*Heastie v Veitch* CA 1933, 18 TC 305). Contributions towards partners' removal expenses, where partner moved in the interests of the firm, are not deductible (*MacKinlay v Arthur Young McClelland Moores & Co* HL 1989, 62 TC 704).

See *MacKinlay v Arthur Young McClelland Moores & Co* HL 1989, 62 TC 704 as to prohibition on deduction of certain payments made to partners in connection with partnership business.

In *HMRC v Lansdowne Partners Ltd Partnership* CA 2011,81 TC 318, a limited partnership carried on business as a fund manager and claimed a deduction for certain rebated fees, which included fees it had reimbursed to its own partners as well as to external investors. Applying the decision in *MacKinlay v Arthur Young McClelland Moores & Co* above, the reimbursements to partners were not allowable deductions.

Excessive payments to the service company of a professional firm were held not to be deductible (*Stephenson v Payne, Stone Fraser & Co* Ch D 1967, 44 TC 507).

See also **75** TRADING INCOME for adjustments to profits generally and **28.66** EMPLOYMENT INCOME for director's fees received by a professional partnership.

Non-trading income

[52.5] In the case of a trading or professional partnership to which non-trading income (or a relievable non-trading loss) accrues, each individual partner is taxed on his share, computed by reference to the profit sharing arrangements for the period of account of the trade or profession. In the case of 'untaxed income' from one or more sources, the normal basis period rules for *trading* income (see **75.6–75.14** TRADING INCOME) apply as if each individual's share of the income (or loss) were profits (or losses) of a notional business carried on by him alone. For this purpose, '*untaxed income*' means income from which income tax has not been deducted and is not *treated* as having been deducted, but it specifically excludes (i) dividends and other distributions from UK resident companies; (ii) stock dividends; and (iii) income arising on the release or write-off of loans to participators in close companies (see **65.21** SAVINGS AND INVESTMENT INCOME).

The notional business is treated as commencing at the time the individual becomes a partner (or, if later, when the partnership commences a trade or profession) and ceasing when he ceases to be a partner, with each separate source of income treated as continuing until he ceases to be a partner. The same comments apply as in **52.4** above as regards changes of partnership accounting date. Where overlap relief (see **75.14**) in respect of untaxed income falls to be deducted in a tax year (because of a change of accounting date or a permanent cessation of the notional business) and the deduction exceeds the partner's share of untaxed income for that year, the excess is deductible in computing his taxable income for that year.

These special rules for non-trading untaxed income apply only where the associated trade or profession is carried on *in partnership*, so that, for example, if one partner is left to carry on the partnership business as a sole trader, his notional trade ceases at that time and his untaxed income is subsequently taxed on a fiscal year basis. Similarly, if an individual initially carries on the trade as a sole trader, the notional business does not commence until the partnership is set up.

Indirect partners

The notional business rules above are varied for 2018/19 onwards where:

- a person (T) is a partner in a partnership (PQR);
- PQR is a partner or indirect partner (see **52.3** above) in another partnership (MNO);
- MNO carries on a trade or profession (the '*underlying trade*');
- PQR's untaxed income (or relievable loss), as defined above, arises by virtue of untaxed income (or a loss) arising to members of MNO from sources other than the carrying on of a trade or profession; and
- that untaxed income is non-trading income (or that loss is a non-trading loss), and the income (or loss) does not itself arise by virtue of MNO being a member of a partnership.

T's notional business commences when T becomes an indirect partner in MNO or when MNO commences the underlying trade, whichever is the later. T's notional business ceases when T ceases to be an indirect partner in MNO or when MNO ceases to carry on the underlying trade, whichever is the earlier. If T carries on PQR's actual trade (whether alone or in partnership) before PQR starts to carry it on, T's notional business commences when PQR starts to carry on the actual trade. If T carries on the actual trade (whether alone or in partnership) after PQR ceases to carry it on, T's notional business ceases when PQR ceases to carry on the actual trade. No special rules existed for these circumstances prior to 2018/19.

[*ITTOIA 2005, ss 851, 854(1)–(4)(6), 855, 855A, 856; FA 2016, Sch 1 paras 26, 73; FA 2018, Sch 6 para 5(2)(4)(5)*].

Following the abolition of deduction of tax at source from bank and building society interest, new sources of untaxed income may have arisen simply because of this change in the law. The abolition affects interest paid or credited on or after 6 April 2016. Where a firm prepares accounts to, say, 31 July 2016 and has received interest taxed at source on 31 March 2016 and untaxed interest on 30 June 2016, the March interest is taxable for 2015/16 on a fiscal year basis and the June interest is taxable for 2016/17 on an accounts year basis (as far as continuing partners are concerned); the March interest is not taxable on an accounts year basis for 2016/17 (which would give rise to double taxation) as it did not arise from a source of untaxed income.

Example

[52.6]

X and Y began to trade in partnership on 1 July 2016, preparing first accounts to 30 September 2017 and sharing profits equally. Z joins the firm as an equal partner on 1 October 2018. Y leaves the firm on 31 March 2020. Accounts are prepared to that date to ascertain Y's entitlement, but the accounting date then reverts to 30 September and the partnership does not give notice to HMRC of a change of accounting date, so that there is no change of basis period. In addition to trading profits, the partnership had a source of lettings income which ceased in September 2019, and is in receipt of bank interest (received without deduction of tax) from a source commencing in October 2017. Revised figures as adjusted for income tax purposes are as follows.

	Trading income	Property income	Savings income (untaxed interest)
	£	£	£
15 months to 30.9.17	30,000	4,500	—
Year to 30.9.18	24,000	5,000	1,000
Year to 30.9.19	39,000	3,000	900
6 months to 31.3.20	19,500	—	225
6 months to 30.9.20	14,000	—	140

The partners' shares of taxable income from the partnership for the years 2016/17 to 2020/21 inclusive are as follows. (See 52.7 below as regards changes in the membership of a partnership.)

	X	Y	Z
	£	£	£
Trading income			
2016/17			
1.7.16–5.4.17 (£30,000 × 9/15)	9,000	9,000	
2017/18			
1.10.16–30.9.17 (£30,000 × 12/15)	12,000*	12,000*	
* Overlap relief accrued:			
1.10.16–5.4.17 (£30,000 × 6/15)	6,000	6,000	
2018/19			
Y/e 30.9.18	12,000	12,000	
1.10.18–5.4.19 (£39,000 × 6/12 × 1/3)			6,500
2019/20			
Y/e 30.9.19	13,000	13,000	13,000*
1.10.19–31.3.20		6,500	
		19,500	
Less overlap relief		(6,000)	
		13,500	
* Overlap relief accrued			

	X	Y	Z
	£	£	£
1.10.18–5.4.19 (as above)			6,500
2020/21			
Y/e 30.9.20			
1.10.19–31.3.20	6,500		6,500
1.4.20–30.9.20	7,000		7,000
	13,500		13,500
Property income			
2016/17			
1.7.16–5.4.17 (£4,500 × 9/15)	1,350	1,350	
2017/18			
1.10.16–30.9.17 (£4,500 × 12/15)	1,800*	1,800*	
* Overlap relief accrued			
1.10.16–5.4.17 (£4,500 × 6/15)	900	900	
2018/19			
Y/e 30.9.18	2,500	2,500	
1.10.18–5.4.19 (£3,000 × 6/12 × 1/3)			500
2019/20			
Y/e 30.9.19	1,000	1,000	1,000*
1.10.19–31.3.20		—	
		1,000	
Less overlap relief		(900)	
		100	
* Overlap relief accrued			
1.10.18–5.4.19 (as above)			500
Savings income (untaxed interest)			
2018/19			
Y/e 30.9.18	500	500	
1.10.18–5.4.19 (£900 × 6/12 × 1/3)			150
2019/20			
Y/e 30.9.19	300	300	300*
1.10.19–31.3.20		75	
		375	
* Overlap relief accrued			
1.10.18–5.4.19 (as above)			150
2020/21			
Y/e 30.9.20			
1.10.19–31.3.20	75		75
1.4.20–30.9.20	70		70
	145		145

Changes in members of a partnership

[52.7] A partnership trade or profession is *not* treated as having ceased and recommenced when a partner joins or leaves the firm providing there is at least one continuing partner (which also embraces the situation where a sole trader begins to carry on the trade or profession in partnership or a former partner begins to carry it on as a sole trader). Where, exceptionally, the trade or profession continues to be carried on but without any such continuing partner, it is notionally treated as having ceased at that point, with a new trade or profession treated as having commenced.

New partners are taxed on their profit share under the opening years provisions at **75.7** TRADING INCOME and outgoing partners are taxed on their share under the closing year provisions at **75.12** TRADING INCOME (see also **52.3–52.5** above).

Example

[52.8]

P, Q and R have carried on a profession in partnership for a number of years (since before 6 April 1994) sharing profits in the ratio 2:2:1. Accounts are made up to 30 June. P leaves the partnership on 30 June 2015 and Q and R share profits 3:2 for the year to 30 June 2016 and equally thereafter. On 30 June 2018, Q leaves the partnership and on 1 July 2018, S becomes a partner. Profits are then shared between R and S in the ratio 2:1 until 30 September 2020 when the practice comes to an end, neither partner continuing to carry it on as a sole practitioner thereafter. P, Q and R have transitional overlap relief of £18,400, £18,400 and £9,200 respectively by reference to an overlap period of nine months.

Results for the seven periods of account up to 30 September 2020 are as follows.

Period ended	Partners' salaries				*Adjusted Profit*
	P	Q	R	S	
	£	£	£	£	£
30.6.14	4,000	4,000	2,000	—	75,000
30.6.15	18,000	13,000	13,500	—	60,000
30.6.16	—	12,500	12,500	—	80,000
30.6.17	—	12,000	17,000	—	85,000
30.6.18	—	4,000	11,000	—	95,000
30.6.19	—	—	5,000	—	101,000
30.9.20	—	—	3,000	—	58,000

The adjusted profit figures above are after adding back partners' salaries (see **52.4**(iii) above).

The taxable profits for the years 2014/15 to 2020/21 are as follows.

Taxable profits of P, Q & R individually for 2014/15 and 2015/16

	P	Q	R
	£	£	£
2014/15			
Y/e 30.6.14			
Profits £75,000 – £(4,000 + 4,000 + 2,000)	26,000	26,000	13,000
Salaries	4,000	4,000	2,000
Taxable profits	£30,000	£30,000	£15,000

	P	Q	R
	£	£	£
2015/16			
Y/e 30.6.15			
Profits £60,000 – £(18,000 + 13,000 + 13,500)	6,200	6,200	3,100
Salaries	18,000	13,000	13,500
	24,200	19,200	16,600
Less transitional overlap relief	18,400	—	
Taxable profits	£5,800	£19,200	£16,600

Taxable profits of Q, R & S individually from 2016/17 to 2020/21

	Q	R	S
	£	£	£
2016/17			
Y/e 30.6.16			
Profits £80,000 – £(12,500 + 12,500)	33,000	22,000	
Salaries	12,500	12,500	
Taxable profits	£45,500	£34,500	
2017/18			
Y/e 30.6.17			
Profits £85,000 – £(12,000 + 17,000)	28,000	28,000	
Salaries	12,000	17,000	
Taxable profits	£40,000	£45,000	
2018/19			
Y/e 30.6.18			
Profits £95,000 – £(4,000 + 11,000)	40,000	40,000	
Salaries	4,000	11,000	
Taxable profits	44,000	51,000	
Less transitional overlap relief	18,400	—	
Taxable profits	£25,600	£51,000	
Y/e 30.6.19			
Profits £101,000 – £5,000 × 1/3 = £32,000			
Taxable profit 1.7.18–5.4.19			
£32,000 × 9/12			£24,000

	R	S
	£	£
2019/20		
Y/e 30.6.19		
Profits £101,000 – £5,000	64,000	32,000
Salary	5,000	—
Taxable profits	£69,000	£32,000*
*Overlap relief accrued		
1.7.18–5.4.19 as above		£24,000
2020/21		
15 months to 30.9.20		

Profits £58,000 – £3,000	33,000	22,000
Salary	3,000	—
	36,000	22,000
Less overlap relief	9,200	24,000
Taxable profit/(allowable loss)	£26,800	(£2,000)

Note

See **52.6** above for a further example of partners joining and leaving a firm, which also illustrates the position where there is non-trading as well as trading income.

Partnership mergers and demergers

[52.9] Where two businesses carried on in partnership merge, it is a question of fact whether the new partnership has succeeded to the businesses of the old partnerships, or whether the old businesses have ceased and a new business resulted from the merger which is different in nature from either of the two old businesses. Disparity of size between the old partnerships will not of itself be a significant matter. Clearly the former is more likely to be the case where the two old businesses carried on the same sort of activities, and the latter where they were themselves different in nature. Where the former applies, both businesses are treated as continuing. Where the new partnership does not succeed to the old businesses, the trades are treated as having ceased and the closing year rule (see **75.12** TRADING INCOME) will apply to the notional trades of the partners in both old partnerships; the opening year rules (see **75.7** TRADING INCOME) will then apply to the notional trades of the partners in the new partnership.

Similar considerations apply where a partnership is divided up and two or more partnerships are formed, in determining whether any of the separate partnerships has succeeded to the business of the original partnership.

Similar principles apply where sole traders merge into partnership or a partnership business is demerged and carried on by sole traders.

(HMRC SP 9/86).

See *C Connelly & Co v Wilbey* Ch D 1992, 65 TC 208 for a case in which it was held that neither part of a demerged partnership succeeded to the former partnership trade (and in which legal costs relating to the dissolution were disallowed).

The amalgamation of two sole traders into partnership in *Humphries v Cook* KB 1934, 19 TC 121 was held to result in the commencement of a new business and the cessation of both the old businesses, but this is applied sparingly by HMRC, mainly where the new partnership business is of a different nature from those previously carried on.

Simon's Taxes. See **B7.525, B7.530.**

Losses

[52.10] Subject to 52.11 below, partnership losses, as computed for tax purposes, are apportioned between the individual partners in the same way as are profits. The loss of each partner may be:

- set off against his other income (under *ITA 2007, s 64*, or, where applicable, *ITA 2007, s 72*); or
- carried forward against his share of subsequent profits of the partnership (under *ITA 2007, s 83*), including in certain circumstances where a partnership business is converted into a company (*ITA 2007, s 86*); or
- used in a terminal loss claim (under *ITA 2007, s 89*) where either the partnership trade or profession ceases or the individual leaves the partnership.

For full details of these loss claims, see **45** LOSSES. It is for each partner to choose how to utilise his own losses and to make his own claim.

Similarly, losses made by a partner in other businesses may be set-off against his share of partnership profits under *ITA 2007, s 64*.

For restrictions on, and claw-back of, loss reliefs in the case of non-active partners, see **52.13–52.17** below. For restrictions in the case of limited partners and members of limited liability partnerships, see, respectively, **52.24** and **52.26** below.

Simon's Taxes. See **B7.504, B7.522.**

Unusual allocations

[52.11] *Where the firm as a whole makes a profit* (as adjusted for tax purposes) but, after the allocation of prior shares (e.g. salaries and interest on capital) the result is that *an individual partner makes a loss*, the loss-making partner cannot claim tax relief for his loss. Instead, he is treated as making neither profit nor loss, and his 'loss' is reallocated to the profit-making partners in proportion to the profits already allocated to them, thus reducing those profits for tax purposes. Similarly, *where there is an overall partnership loss*, the aggregate losses allocated to loss-making partners cannot exceed the overall loss and no partner can be taxed on a share of profit. Instead, a profit-making partner is treated as making neither profit nor loss, and his 'profit' is reallocated to the loss-making partners in proportion to the losses already allocated to them, thus reducing those losses.

[*ITTOIA 2005, s 850(2)–(6), 850A, 850B*].

Simon's Taxes. See **B7.501, B7.502, B7.503.**

Example

[52.12]

Janet, John and James are full equity partners, sharing profits and losses equally and preparing accounts to 31 May. The partnership agreement also makes provision for partners' salaries. For the year to 31 May 2020, Janet and John are entitled to salaries of £19,000 and £8,000 respectively. However, the firm has an unexpectedly bad year and makes a loss of £21,000. This is the tax adjusted figure after adding back the non-deductible partners' salaries of £27,000.

The initial allocation between the partners is as follows.

	Total	Janet	John	James
	£	£	£	£
Adjusted loss	(21,000)			
Salaries	27,000	19,000	8,000	
Loss after salaries	£48,000	(16,000)	(16,000)	(16,000)
Allocation	(£21,000)	£3,000	(£8,000)	(£16,000)

As the partnership has made a tax loss, no partner can make a taxable profit. A reallocation must be made to reduce Janet's allocated profit of £3,000 to nil. John's allocated loss is reduced by £1,000 (£3,000 × 8,000/(16,000 + 8,000)) and James's by £2,000 (£3,000 × 16,000/(16,000 + 8,000)). The final allocation is as follows.

	Total	Janet	John	James
Tax loss	(£21,000)	Nil	(£7,000)	(£14,000)

Non-active partners — restriction of loss reliefs

[52.13] Trade loss relief under:

(1) *ITA 2007, s 64* (and, consequently, *TCGA 1992, s 261B* against chargeable gains) (see **45.2, 45.5** LOSSES); or

(2) *ITA 2007, s 72* (see **45.7** LOSSES),

is restricted in the case of an individual who is a '*non-active*' partner, i.e. who does not devote 'a significant amount of time' to the trade. The relief available, otherwise than against profits of the trade, is restricted to the amount of the partner's 'contribution to the firm' (see **52.14** below) as at the end of the basis period for the tax year in which the loss is sustained. The restriction applies to losses sustained in the tax year in which the partner first carries on the trade and in any of the next three tax years.

See **52.15** below for a cap on the amount of relief that can be given under any of the provisions at (1) and (2) above for a loss sustained by a non-active partner. The operation of the cap is not limited to the first four years of trading.

The restrictions potentially apply to a loss sustained in any tax year:

- at any time during which the individual carried on the trade as a partner (other than a limited partner within **52.24** below) or as a member of a limited liability partnership (LLP) within **52.25** below and at no time during which he carried it on as a limited partner;
- which is the first, second, third or fourth tax year in which the individual carried on the trade; and
- in the 'relevant period' for which he did not devote 'a significant amount of time' to the trade.

Where relief under any of the provisions at (1) and (2) above has previously been given for losses sustained in tax years which meet the above conditions, such reliefs must be aggregated. The relief that can then be given, otherwise than against profits of the trade, for the current loss is limited to the excess (if any) of the amount of the partner's 'contribution to the firm' at the end of the basis period for the current tax year over the aggregate amount. This aggregate must also include any relief given for losses sustained in any tax year at any time during which the partner carried on the trade as a limited partner or member of an LLP; the aggregate is decreased by the amount of any claw-back under the recovery provisions described at **52.14** below.

These rules do not prevent or restrict a loss from being carried forward under *ITA 2007, s 83* (see **45.19** LOSSES) against subsequent profits of the trade. They do not apply at all to UNDERWRITERS AT LLOYD'S (**79**) in connection with their underwriting business.

'Significant amount of time'

A partner devotes a '*significant amount of time*' to the trade in the 'relevant period' for a tax year if, for the whole of that period, he spends an average of at least 10 hours a week personally engaged in activities of the trade. It is further stipulated that those activities must be carried on on a commercial basis and with a view to profit. Any relief erroneously given on the assumption that this requirement will be met will be withdrawn by means of an income tax assessment. The '*relevant period*' for a tax year is normally the basis period for that tax year. However, if the basis period is less than six months because the tax year is the one in which the individual joined or left the partnership, the requirement must instead be met by reference to the six months beginning with his commencement date or ending with his cessation date. The legislation is silent as to what is meant by personal engagement in the activities of the trade. The Explanatory Notes to the 2004 Finance Bill suggest that this may include, for example, a management or service role such as personnel, accountancy or purchasing, but does not include time spent deciding whether or not to invest, and/or how much to invest, in the partnership or its trade.

Carry-forward

Where a partner's loss relief has been restricted as above, the total amount thereby unrelieved is carried forward to subsequent tax years in which he continues to carry on the trade in partnership. For any such subsequent tax year, that total amount, or so much of it as still remains unrelieved, is treated for the purposes of the provisions in (1) and (2) above as a loss sustained in that year (or as an increase to any loss actually sustained in that year). In ascertaining how much remains unrelieved, any relief given under general rules (e.g. carry-forward and set-off of losses under *ITA 2007, s 83*) is taken into account as is any relief given (or which could have been given had a claim been made) by virtue of this carry-forward rule. For the purpose only of determining whether an amount can be relieved in a subsequent year by virtue of this rule, that year is treated as a year to which these restrictions potentially apply even it is not actually so. Thus, this carry-forward rule does enable restricted relief to be obtained in a subsequent year but only to the extent that capital contributions have increased sufficiently. Any amount remaining unrelieved after applying this rule is again carried forward and the rule once more applied in the following year. An unrelieved amount can also be carried forward to a year in which the partner no longer carries on the trade but makes a contribution to the assets of the partnership on a winding-up; in this case certain conditions that otherwise apply to the loss reliefs in (1) and (2) above (in particular the condition that the trade be carried on commercially with a view to profit) are relaxed in relation to the carried-forward amount.

[*ITA 2007, ss 103, 103B, 110, 112, 113, 790–795, Sch 2 paras 30, 32, 33*].

Simon's Taxes. See **B7.522.**

Partner's contribution to the firm

[52.14] A partner's '*contribution to the firm*' for the purposes of **52.13** above is the sum of the amount he has contributed as capital (net of withdrawals) and any profits of the trade to which he is entitled but has not received in money or money's worth. To the extent that profits have been added to the firm's capital, they should be included as part of capital contributions but not as part of profit entitlement. In determining the profits to which the partner is entitled, any losses are disregarded, and references to profits are to accounting profits, calculated in accordance with generally accepted accounting practice, and not to taxable profits (if different). Profits of any other trade carried on by the partnership are taken into account also.

Exclusions

The Commissioners for HMRC are empowered to make regulations (see *SI 2005 No 2017*) excluding from a partner's 'contribution to the firm' for these purposes any amounts of a description specified in the regulations. Under *SI 2005 No 2017*, such exclusions are made in the following circumstances.

(a) Where an individual takes out a loan in connection with his financing of all or part of his contribution to the firm and either:
   (i) there is, at any time, an agreement or arrangement under which another person will, or may, bear any of the financial cost of repaying the loan; or
   (ii) any such financial cost is at any time borne by another person otherwise than under an agreement or arrangement caught by (i) above; or
   (iii) the liability to repay the loan is at any time assumed (or released) by any other person; or

(iv) the financial cost to the individual of repaying the loan over a specified period is substantially less than it would have been on arm's length terms.

The period specified in (iv) above is the earliest period of five years beginning on or after 2 December 2004 (or, if later, the date the loan was taken out) for which condition (iv) is satisfied. Where conditions (i), (ii) or (iii) are satisfied, the amount in question is excluded from the individual's contribution to the firm after the time in question. Where condition (iv) is satisfied, the exclusion applies after the end of the five-year period and is equal to the amount of the loan outstanding at the end of that period. References to loans include replacement loans.

(b) Where, at any time, there is an agreement or arrangement under which any of the financial cost of making the contribution to the firm will be, or may be, reimbursed (directly or indirectly) to the individual by any other person, or where such cost is at any time reimbursed otherwise than under such an agreement or arrangement. The amount in question is excluded from the individual's contribution to the firm after the time in question.

Neither (a) nor (b) above applies in relation to any financial cost borne or reimbursed by another individual in the normal course of his domestic, family or personal relationships or to any loan repayments not made by the partner due to his financial inability to pay (arising from events outside his control and occurring after the taking out of the loan) or to any amount on which the partner is chargeable to income tax as profits of the trade.

Recovery provisions

There are recovery provisions to claw back any relief given for a loss against other income or gains where the partner's contribution to the firm is *subsequently* reduced by any application of the HMRC regulations referred to above, such that the relief given becomes excessive. The recovery provisions apply equally in relation to losses sustained by a limited partner (see **52.24** below) or by a member of an LLP (see **52.26** below). The partner is treated as receiving, at the time of that subsequent reduction, income chargeable to tax, other than as part of the trading profits, for the tax year in which the reduction occurs. The amount of that chargeable income is the smallest of the following:

(i) the said reduction in the partner's contribution to the firm;
(ii) the partner's post-1 December 2004 losses (decreased by any amount previously clawed back under these recovery provisions); and
(iii) the excess (decreased by any amount previously clawed back under these recovery provisions) of the total losses claimed by the partner under the provisions at **52.13**(1) and (2) above over the partner's contribution to the firm.

The amounts at (ii) and (iii) are to be computed as at the time immediately following the event giving rise to the reduction. The reference in (iii) to total losses are to losses claimed for any tax year to which restrictions of loss reliefs apply (whether under these non-active partner provisions or under **52.24** or **52.26** below). In a case where the partnership carries on more than one trade, these recovery provisions are modified accordingly.

The purpose test

An amount contributed as capital does not count towards a partner's 'contribution to the firm' for these purposes if the main purpose, or one of the main purposes, of making the contribution is the obtaining of a reduction in tax liability by means of any of the provisions at **52.13**(1) and (2) above. However, this does not apply to restrict any loss that derives wholly from 'qualifying film expenditure' (as defined in **52.15** below). In determining whether this purpose test applies, a capital contribution is regarded as made only when the money is paid to the partnership or, in the case of a contribution consisting of a right or other asset, when the right or asset is transferred to the partnership.

[*ITA 2007, ss 111, 113A(1)(3)(4), 114, 790–795, Sch 2 paras 31, 33–35, 142, 143; SI 2005 No 2017*].

Simon's Taxes. See **B7.522**.

Losses cap

[52.15] Where a trade loss is sustained by an individual as a partner in a firm (which includes a member of an LLP — see **52.25** below) and at any time in that tax year he is a 'non-active' partner (as in **52.13** above) or a 'limited partner' (as in **52.24** below), the quantum of relief that he can claim for that loss under:

- *ITA 2007, s 64* (and, consequently, *TCGA 1992, s 261B* against chargeable gains) (see **45.2**, **45.5** LOSSES); or
- *ITA 2007, s 72* (see **45.7** LOSSES),

is restricted to **£25,000**. If the individual sustains more than one such loss in a tax year, the £25,000 cap applies to the aggregate of all such losses. The cap applies to the balance of a trade loss after applying (as appropriate) the restrictions at **52.13** above and **52.17**, **52.24** and **52.26** below. The cap does *not* apply:

- to so much of any loss as derives from 'qualifying film expenditure' (see below);
- to prevent relief for the loss against profits of the same trade; or
- to UNDERWRITERS AT LLOYD'S (**79**) in connection with their underwriting business.

[*ITA 2007, ss 103, 103C; ITTOIA 2005, s 863(2)*].

Qualifying film expenditure

Expenditure is '*qualifying film expenditure*' if it is:

- expenditure which is deducted, in computing the partnership loss, under the statutory relief provisions for certified films, i.e. under any of *ITTOIA 2005, ss 137–142* (now repealed); or
- incidental expenditure (i.e. expenditure on management, administration or obtaining finance) that, whilst deductible other than under the statutory relief provisions for certified films, was incurred in connection with the production or the acquisition (as defined) of a film in relation to which expenditure was deducted under the said provisions.

It was made clear by the Treasury in relation to the identical definition for the purposes of **52.17** below that qualifying film expenditure does not include expenditure on distribution of a film or 'print and advertising' or production of a film as trading stock (Treasury Explanatory Notes to the 2004 Finance Bill).

The extent to which a loss derives from qualifying film expenditure and the extent to which expenditure qualifies as incidental expenditure are to be determined on a just and reasonable basis.

[*ITA 2007, s 103D*].

Simon's Taxes. See B7.522.

Non-active partners — claw-back of losses derived from exploiting a licence

[52.16] There is a potential exit charge as described below where:

(a) an individual carries on a trade in partnership or has done so previously;
(b) he has claimed relief under *ITA 2007, s 64*, *TCGA 1992, s 261B* or *ITA 2007, s 72* (see, respectively, **45.2**, **45.5**, **45.7** LOSSES), against his general income or chargeable gains, for a 'licence-related loss' sustained in the first, second, third or fourth tax year in which he carried on the trade;
(c) the tax year in which the loss was sustained was one in which he did not devote a '*significant amount of time*' (as defined in **52.13** above) to the trade;
(d) there is a 'disposal' of any licence acquired in carrying on the trade or any right to income under any agreement 'related' to, or which contains, such a licence; and
(e) the individual receives any consideration for that disposal (whether or not as part of a larger sum) which is not otherwise chargeable to income tax.

In (b) above, a '*licence-related loss*' means a loss derived to any extent from expenditure incurred in the partnership trade in exploiting the licence referred to in (d) above.

For the purposes of (d) above, an agreement is '*related*' to a licence if they are entered into (in whatever order) under the same arrangement. An agreement which imposes an obligation to do something (as opposed to conferring a right to do it) may itself be a licence for the purposes of these provisions; and fulfilling such obligations may therefore count as exploiting the licence.

A '*disposal*' is very widely (but not exhaustively) defined (by *ITA 2007, s 808*) for the purposes of (d) above to include, for example, a revocation of the licence, the disposal, surrender or loss of rights or income, certain changes in profit- or loss-sharing ratios and the individual's leaving the partnership (including a case where the partnership is dissolved). The disposal may be part of a larger disposal.

Consideration is not within (e) above if its receipt is an exit event under **45.15** LOSSES in relation to film-related losses.

A **chargeable event** occurs at the time the claim in (b) above is made or at the time the consideration in (e) above is received, whichever is the later. For a tax year in which one or more chargeable events occur, so much of the 'total consideration' as does not exceed the 'chargeable amount' is treated as taxable income of the individual. The '*total consideration*' is the aggregate of all the otherwise non-chargeable consideration received in that tax year *and* in previous tax years in relation to the licence in question. The '*chargeable amount*' is found by taking so much of the total consideration as does not exceed the 'net licence-related loss' and reducing that amount by so much (if any) of the consideration as has been taxed in previous years under these provisions. The '*net licence-related loss*' is the amount, computed as at the end of the tax year concerned and in relation to the licence in question, by which the individual's 'claimed licence-related losses' exceed the total of his 'licence-related profits' for all tax years. An individual's '*claimed licence-related losses*' are so much of the losses claimed by the individual under the legislation mentioned in (b) above and potentially subject to claw-back under these provisions as derive from expenditure incurred in the partnership trade in exploiting the licence. An individual's '*licence-related profits*' are so much of his profits as derive from income arising from any agreement that is related to or contains the licence. The extent to which a loss or profit is derived from any particular expenditure or income is determined on a just and reasonable basis.

[*ITA 2007, ss 790, 804–809; Sch 2 paras 150–153*].

Simon's Taxes. See **B5.646B**.

Non-active partners: restriction of loss reliefs derived from exploiting films

[52.17] Relief under:

(1) *ITA 2007, s 64* (and, consequently, *TCGA 1992, s 261B* against chargeable gains) (see **45.2**, **45.5** LOSSES); or
(2) *ITA 2007, s 72* (see **45.7** LOSSES),

is restricted in the circumstances outlined below. Such relief can be given only against income consisting of profits (if any) arising from the trade in question and not against other income or against chargeable gains. This measure is aimed at avoidance schemes which apparently use generally accepted accounting practice to generate large initial losses followed by a guaranteed income stream over several years, thus producing a tax deferral. The rules do not prevent a loss from being carried forward under *ITA 2007, s 83* (see **45.19** LOSSES) against subsequent profits of the trade.

The restriction potentially applies to a loss sustained by an individual, in a trade consisting of or including the exploitation of films, in any tax year:

- in which he carried on the trade in partnership;
- which is the first, second, third or fourth tax year in which he carried on the trade;
- in the 'relevant period' for which he did not devote '*a significant amount of time*' to the trade (see the definitions in **52.13** above); and

- at any time during which there existed a 'relevant agreement' guaranteeing him an amount of income.

For these purposes, a '*relevant agreement*' is an agreement made with a view to the individual's carrying on the trade or in the course of his carrying it on (including any agreement under which he is, or may be, required to contribute an amount to the trade). The definition is extended to include an agreement relating to such an agreement. An agreement guarantees an amount of income if it, or any part of it, is designed to secure the receipt by the individual of that amount (or at least that amount); it is irrelevant as to *when* the income would be received.

The restriction does not apply to the extent (if any) that the loss derives from 'qualifying film expenditure' (as in **52.15** above),

[*ITA 2007, ss 115, 116*].

See **45.15** LOSSES for other anti-avoidance provisions concerning losses derived by individuals (whether trading in partnership or not) from the exploitation of film tax reliefs. For restriction of relief for interest on a loan used to buy into a film partnership in certain circumstances, see **42.10** INTEREST PAYABLE.

Simon's Taxes. See B7.505.

Partnerships with mixed membership

[52.18] A mixed membership partnership is a partnership the members of which include both individuals and non-individuals; the non-individual partners will most often be companies. In relation to mixed membership partnerships (including any that are limited liability partnerships), there are reallocated to an individual any excess profits allocated to a non-individual partner in cases where certain conditions are met. There are separate provisions to deny loss reliefs, for which see **52.19** below. For a Technical Note and guidance see www.gov.uk/government/uploads/system/uploads/attachment_data/file/298221/Partnerships_Mixed_membership_partnerships__Alternative_investment_fund_managers__Transfer_of_assets___income_Streams_through_partnerships.pdf.

Main rules

The above-mentioned conditions are that:

(a) for a period of account, an individual (A) and a non-individual (B) each have a share of the partnership taxable profit;
(b) A's share is a profit or is neither a profit or a loss, and B's share is a profit; and
(c) either:
    (i) amounts representing A's 'deferred profit' are included in B's profit share, with the result that both A's profit share and the 'relevant tax amount' are lower than they would otherwise have been; or
    - B's profit share exceeds the 'appropriate notional profit',
    - A has the 'power to enjoy' B's profit share, and

- B's profit share is attributable (wholly or partly) to A's power to enjoy, and both A's profit share and the 'relevant tax amount' are lower than they would have been in the absence of A's power to enjoy.

Where the conditions are met, A's profit share is increased by so much of B's profit share as is attributable to (1) A's deferred profit, or (2) A's power to enjoy, to be determined on a just and reasonable basis. Any increase by virtue of (2) is not to exceed the excess in (c)(ii) above (after deducting from that excess any increase by virtue of (1)). If B is chargeable to income tax, such adjustments are to be made to B's profit share as are just and reasonable to take account of the increase in A's profit share.

For analysis by the FTT in a case in which HMRC successfully applied these provisions, see *Walewski v HMRC* FTT (TC 7554), [2020] SFTD 521, [2020] UKFTT 58 (TC).

Definitions

In (c)(i) above, A's '*deferred profit*' is any remuneration (or other benefits or returns) the provision of which to A has been deferred (whether conditionally or otherwise). It includes A's share (as determined on a just and reasonable basis) of any remuneration etc. the provision of which to A and one or more other persons (taken together) has been deferred.

The '*relevant tax amount*' in (c)(i) and (ii) above is the total amount of tax which, were it not for these provisions, would be chargeable in respect of A and B's income as partners.

In (c)(ii) above, the '*appropriate notional profit*' is the sum of the 'appropriate notional return on capital' and the 'appropriate notional consideration for services'. The '*appropriate notional return on capital*' is the return that B would receive for the period of account in respect of capital contributed if the return were to be calculated by reference to the time value of money. This figure is found by applying a commercial rate of interest to capital contributed. From the result there must be deducted any return actually received for the period of account in respect of capital contributed which is not included in B's profit share. The capital contributed by B is determined as in **52.26**(a) below but reading references there to the LLP as references to the partnership, ignoring the reference to withdrawals of capital in the five years beginning with the relevant time, and including in capital withdrawn anything withdrawn in circumstances such that it becomes chargeable to income tax as trading profits. The '*appropriate notional consideration for services*' is the amount that B would receive in consideration for any services provided by him to the firm during the period of account were the consideration to be calculated on the basis that B is not a partner and is acting at arm's length. From this amount there must be deducted any amount actually received in consideration for any such services which is not included in B's profit share. Any services, the provision of which involves any partner in the firm in addition to B, are to be ignored.

A has the '*power to enjoy*' B's profit share (see (c)(ii) above) if:

- A is connected with B (as in **19** CONNECTED PERSONS but ignoring **19.4**); or

- A is a party to arrangements (as widely defined) a main purpose of which is to secure that an amount included in B's profit share falls within the UK corporation tax, rather than the income tax, regime; or
- any one or more of a number of 'enjoyment conditions' (see *ITTOIA 2005, s 850C(20)(21)*) is met in relation to B's profit share or any part of it.

AIFM partnerships

A special rule applies in the case of an AIFM partnership (see **52.29** below) if any part of the increase in A's share is allocated by A to the firm itself — see *ITTOIA 2005, s 850C(22)(23)*.

Cases involving individuals who are not partners

There is also provision to reallocate excess profits to an individual who is *not* a partner if it is reasonable to suppose that the individual would have been a partner but for the above rules. The conditions are that:

(i) at a time during a period of account of the partnership, an individual (A) personally performs services for the partnership;
(ii) if A had been a partner throughout the period of account, the computation under **52.4** above in relation to A would have produced a profit;
(iii) a non-individual partner (B) has a share of that profit;
(iv) it is reasonable to suppose that A would have been a partner at a time during the period of account or any earlier period but for the main rules above; and
(v) either condition X or Y below is met.

Condition X is that amounts representing A's 'deferred profit' (defined as above) are included in B's profit share. Condition Y is that:

- B's profit share exceeds the 'appropriate notional profit' (defined as above);
- A has the 'power to enjoy' B's profit share (defined as above); and
- the whole or any part of B's profit share is attributable to A's power to enjoy.

Where conditions (i)–(v) above are met, A is treated as if he were a partner in the firm throughout the period of account. His share of profit is so much of the amount of B's profit share as is attributable on a just and reasonable basis to (1) A's deferred profit or (2) A's power to enjoy. Where (2) applies, A's profit share is to be no greater than the amount by which B's profit share exceeds the appropriate notional profit (after deducting from that excess any increase by virtue of (1)). A's share of profit is chargeable to income tax for the tax year in which the period of account ends. If B is chargeable to income tax, such adjustments are to be made to B's profit share as are just and reasonable to take account of the share of profit attributed to A.

The condition at (iv) above is to be assumed to be met if, at a time during the period of account, A is a member of a partnership or limited liability partnership (FGH) which is 'associated' with the partnership in question

(CDE). FGH is '*associated*' with CDE if it is a member of CDE or it is a member of another partnership or limited liability partnership which is itself associated with CDE.

Payments by B out of B's excess profit share

Where either of the above provisions has effect, such that A's profit share falls to be increased or A falls to be treated as a partner, the following applies if:

- there is an agreement in place in relation to the 'excess part of B's profit share';
- under the agreement, B makes a payment to another person out of that excess part; and
- the payment is not made under any arrangements (as widely defined) a main purpose of which is the obtaining of a tax advantage (as defined by *CTA 2010, s 1139*) for any person.

For income tax purposes, the payment is not treated as income of the recipient and is not to be taken into account in calculating any profits or losses of B or otherwise deducted from any income of B. It is also not to be regarded as a distribution. The '*excess part of B's profit share*' means so much of the amount of B's profit share as is represented by the amount by which A's profit share falls to be increased or, as the case may be, by the amount of the profit share attributed to A upon his falling to be treated as a partner.

[*ITTOIA 2005, ss 850C–850E*].

Simon's Taxes. See **B7.504.**

Losses in mixed membership partnerships etc.

[52.19] If, in a tax year, an individual (A) makes a loss in a trade or profession as a partner and that loss arises in consequence of, or otherwise in connection with, 'relevant tax avoidance arrangements', he is not entitled to any of the following trade loss reliefs: relief against general income; relief against capital gains; relief by carry-back in early years of trade; relief by carry-forward; and terminal relief (see respectively **45.2**, **45.5**, **45.7**, **45.19** and **45.20** LOSSES).

'*Relevant tax avoidance arrangements*' are arrangements (as widely defined) a main purpose of which is to secure that losses of a trade or profession are allocated, or otherwise arise, in whole or in part to A (or to A and other individuals), rather than to a person (B) who is not an individual, with a view to any of the above-mentioned loss reliefs being obtained. It does not matter whether B is or is not a partner or that B may be unknown or may not even exist.

The same rules apply, with appropriate modifications, if A's loss is a loss as a partner in a UK property business or overseas property business (see **60.2** PROPERTY INCOME). In this case the loss reliefs in question are: relief by carry-forward; and limited set-off against general income (see, in both cases, **60.25** PROPERTY INCOME).

[*ITA 2007, ss 116A, 127C*].

Spouse as partner

[52.20] Where a spouse is taken into partnership, perhaps to maximise the benefit of personal reliefs and rate bands, HMRC cannot challenge the apportionment of profits as they could the payment of a salary to a spouse. There is no requirement for the spouse to contribute capital or to participate in management or even to take an active part in the business. Note, however, the possible application of the settlements legislation at *ITTOIA 2005, s 624* where one spouse takes the other into partnership with a share of profits but with no requirement, or insufficient requirement, to contribute capital and/or personal time and effort (see **70.31** SETTLEMENTS). See also HMRC Partnership Manual PM132400, which, as well as discussing the above, also covers the less frequent event of minor children being taken into partnership. 'Spouse' must be taken to include a civil partner.

Simon's Taxes. See **B7.101**.

Corporate partners

[52.21] For any accounting period (see below) of a partnership carrying on a trade or business for which there is at least one partner who is a UK resident company, the profits or losses are computed for corporation tax purposes in like manner as if the partnership were a UK resident company. Similarly, for any accounting period for which there is at least one partner who is a non-UK resident company, the profits or losses are computed in like manner as if the partnership were a non-UK resident company. Thus, two separate computations of profits/losses are needed if the partnership includes both resident and non-resident companies (and a third computation is needed as in **52.4** above if it also includes one or more individuals). See HMRC Company Taxation Manual CTM36510, 36520. As regards non-resident companies, the computation will cover only those profits in respect of which the company is within the charge to UK corporation tax, generally those arising from a permanent establishment within the UK.

No account is taken of any losses for any other accounting period, e.g. losses brought forward. Any interest paid or other distribution made by the partnership is not regarded as a distribution, and is thus not precluded from being deductible in computing profits. The taxable profits or allowable losses of the partnership for the accounting period (as adjusted for corporation tax purposes) are apportioned in accordance with the partnership's profit-sharing arrangements during that accounting period (subject to the corporation tax equivalent of the rules at **52.11** above). If the partnership makes qualifying charitable donations, these are similarly apportioned by reference to the accounting period in which they are paid.

The above references to an accounting period of a partnership are to a period that would be an accounting period if the partnership were a company. If the accounting period of the partnership does not coincide with the company partner's own accounting period, the company's share of profit or loss must be apportioned between those of the company's accounting periods with which the partnership accounting period partially coincides.

Changes of partners are disregarded for corporation tax purposes so long as a company that carried on the trade or business in partnership before the change continues to carry it on in partnership after the change.

For further information, see the corresponding chapter of Tolley's Corporation Tax.

[*CTA 2009, ss 1256–1262, 1265; FA 2018, Sch 6 paras 2, 4(2), 12, 14*].

Where a payment of yearly interest arising in the UK is made by, or on behalf of, a partnership of which a company is a member and is chargeable to tax under *ITTOIA 2005* or *CTA 2009*, it must be paid under deduction of income tax at the basic rate in force for the tax year in which the payment is made. [*ITA 2007, s 874(1)(2)*].

A partnership that includes a company cannot use the cash basis (see **76.3** TRADING INCOME — CASH BASIS FOR SMALLER BUSINESSES).

Anti-avoidance

There are restrictions that apply in certain circumstances (where there are arrangements for transferring relief for losses etc.) on the use (a) by a partner company's losses in a partnership against its other income and (b) of a partner company's losses outside the partnership against its partnership profits. [*CTA 2010, ss 958–962*]. See Tolley's Corporation Tax under Losses. There are provisions aimed at schemes which allocate profit shares disproportionate to the shares of capital contributed so as to enable a company to realise profits as capital rather than as taxable income. [*FA 2004, ss 131–133*]. See Tolley's Corporation Tax under Partnerships.

See also **52.18**, **52.19** above (partnerships with mixed membership).

Simon's Taxes. See **B7.510**, **D7.1**.

Non-resident partners and partnerships controlled abroad

[52.22] There are a number of considerations as set out below.

Partner non-UK resident

The general charging rules in **52.3–52.5** above are applied to a non-UK resident member of a trading etc. partnership in such a way as to ensure that he is taxed only on his share of profits earned in the UK (whereas UK resident partners are taxed on their share of worldwide profits). (A similar rule applies to a non-UK resident company partner.) If the tax year is a split year (see **63.19** RESIDENCE AND DOMICILE) as regards a partner, the partner is regarded for these purposes as non-UK resident in the overseas part of the split year.

Individual partner's change of residence

Where an individual partner becomes or ceases to be UK resident, he is treated for income tax purposes as ceasing to be a partner at that time and becoming a partner again immediately afterwards. This does not prevent his share of any loss sustained before the change from being carried forward under *ITA 2007, s 83* and set against his share of profits after the change.

The above also applies where a tax year is a split year (see **63.19** RESIDENCE AND DOMICILE) as regards the partner. In this case the change of residence is treated as occurring at the start of whichever of the UK part or the overseas part of the split year is the later part.

Individual partner resident but not domiciled etc. in the UK

Where a partnership trade etc. is carried on wholly or partly outside the UK and controlled and managed outside the UK, and the REMITTANCE BASIS (**61**) applies for the tax year to an individual partner who is UK resident but either not domiciled in the UK or not ordinarily resident, his share of trading etc. profits arising outside the UK is treated as 'relevant foreign income' (see **32.2** FOREIGN INCOME), so that the remittance basis may apply to it.

[*ITTOIA 2005, ss 849(3)(3A)(4), 852(6)–(8), 854(5)(5A), 857*].

For a relevant case in which the appellant partnership successfully argued that it was controlled and managed in the Isle of Man, which was where the high level decisions were taken, and thus wholly outside the UK, see *Mark Higgins Rallying (a firm) v HMRC* FTT (TC 1200), [2011] SFTD 936.

Subject to the exception above, UK-resident partners are within the charge to tax on both UK and foreign profits, regardless of where the partnership is controlled.

Double tax arrangements

In the case of *Padmore v CIR* CA 1989, 62 TC 352, it was held that, where profits of a non-UK resident partnership were exempt under the relevant double tax treaty, the profit share of a UK resident partner was thereby also exempt. This decision was, however, reversed by legislation now in *ITTOIA 2005, s 858*, to the effect that arrangements under a double tax treaty relieving partnership income from UK tax are not to affect any UK tax liability in respect of a UK resident partner's share of such income. Similar provisions apply to capital gains. Where a partnership includes a company, similar provisions apply for corporation tax purposes. The provisions apply where the partnership either resides outside the UK or carries on any trade etc. the control and management of which is outside the UK. For the purposes of all these provisions, the members of a partnership are deemed to include any person who is entitled to a share of the income or capital gains of the partnership. [*ITTOIA 2005, s 858; FA 2016, Sch 1 paras 27, 73*]. These changes were deemed always to have had effect. [*F(No 2)A 1987, s 62(2)*]. An appeal based on a claim that the said legislation was ineffective in bringing about the changes described above was dismissed in *Padmore v CIR (No 2)* Ch D 2001, 73 TC 470.

Simon's Taxes. See **B7.515, E6.135.**

Loans for purchasing interest etc. in a partnership

[52.23] See **42.10** INTEREST PAYABLE as regards relief for interest on a loan to an individual for purchasing a share of or making an advance to a partnership.

Limited partnerships

[52.24] The *Limited Partnership Act 1907* allows the formation of limited partnerships, in which the liability of one or more (but not all) of the partners for the firm's debts is limited to a specified amount.

Restriction on loss reliefs

In *Reed v Young* HL 1986, 59 TC 196, it was held that the share of the loss of a limited partner for the purposes of what is now *ITA 2007, s 64* (see **45.2** LOSSES) was not restricted to the amount of her contribution to the partnership capital. The decision was, however, reversed by legislation. Where a 'limited partner' in a partnership sustains a loss in a partnership trade, relief is restricted as below.

For these purposes, a '*limited partner*' is a partner who is an individual carrying on a trade:

- as a limited partner in a limited partnership registered under *Limited Partnerships Act 1907*; or
- as a general partner in a partnership, but who is not entitled to take part in the management of the trade, and who is entitled to have any liabilities (or those beyond a certain limit) for debts or obligations incurred for the purposes of the trade met or reimbursed by some other person; or
- who carries on the trade jointly with others but, under the law of a territory outside the UK, is not entitled to take part in the management of the trade, and is not liable beyond a certain limit for debts or obligations incurred for the purposes of the trade.

The restriction applies to any excess of the loss sustained by a limited partner in respect of a trade as above for a tax year over his contribution to the firm' at the end of the basis period for that tax year. That excess may not be relieved under:

(i) *ITA 2007, s 64* (and, consequently, *TCGA 1992, s 261B* against chargeable gains) (see **45.2**, **45.5** LOSSES); or
(ii) *ITA 2007, s 72* (see **45.7** LOSSES),

other than against profits arising from the same trade.

If relief has previously been given under any of the provisions at (i) and (ii) above to the individual for a loss in the partnership trade in any tax year at any time during which the individual carried on the trade as a limited partner (or to which the restrictions at **52.13** above potentially apply), relief for the loss for the tax year in question is restricted by the excess of the sum of the loss for that tax year and earlier amounts so relieved, over his 'contribution to the firm'. For this purpose, the amount previously relieved is decreased by the amount of any claw-back under the recovery provisions at **52.14** above.

Partner's contribution to the firm

The individual's '*contribution to the firm*' at any time is the aggregate of:

(a) capital contributed and not withdrawn (excluding any capital contributed that the partner is or may be entitled to withdraw at any time he carries on the trade as a limited partner, or which he is or may be entitled to require another person to reimburse to him); and
(b) his total share of profits from the trade (or from all trades carried on by the firm) except in so far as that share has been added to the firm's capital or the individual has received it in money or money's worth.

The amount in (a) above should include the individual's share of any profits of the firm in so far as that share has been added to the firm's capital. References to capital being withdrawn include drawing it out or receiving it back, whether directly or indirectly in either case, but do not include anything withdrawn in circumstances such that it becomes chargeable to income tax as profits of a trade. In determining total share of profits in (b) above, any losses are disregarded. All references to profits are to accounting profits, calculated in accordance with generally accepted accounting practice, and not to taxable profits (if different).

The exclusions referred to in **52.14**(a) and (b) above of amounts from a partner's contribution (i.e. where the costs of providing those amounts is or could be borne by another person) apply equally to a limited partner's contribution to the firm for the above purposes. See also the recovery provisions at **52.14**.

The purpose test at **52.14** above applies in relation to contributions by limited partners as it does to contributions by non-active partners.

[*ITA 2007, ss 103–106, 113A(1)(3)(4), 114, Sch 2 para 27; SI 2005 No 2017*].

See **52.15** above for a cap on the amount of relief that can be given under any of the provisions at (i) and (ii) above for a loss sustained by a limited partner.

See HMRC Partnership Manual PM131310–131320.

Simon's Taxes. See **B7.106, B7.522.**

Limited liability partnerships (LLPs)

[52.25] Where a trade, profession or other business is carried on by an LLP (within *Limited Liability Partnerships Act 2000, s 1*) with a view to profit, all the activities of the LLP (i.e. anything it does) are treated as carried on in partnership by its members and not by the LLP as such. Anything done by, to or in relation to the LLP for the purposes of, or in connection with, any such activities is treated as done by, to or in relation to the members as partners, and property of the LLP is treated as held by the members as partnership property. In the *Tax Acts*, references to a firm or partnership or to members of a firm or partnership include an LLP to which the above applies and members of such an LLP, and references to a company or to members of a company do not include an LLP or members of an LLP.

Where an LLP no longer carries on any trade, profession or other business with a view to profit, the above provisions continue to apply if the cessation is only temporary or during a winding up following a permanent cessation (provided, in the latter case, that the winding up is not for reasons connected in whole or part with tax avoidance and is not unreasonably prolonged). They cease to apply on the appointment of a liquidator or (if earlier) on the making of a winding-up order by the court, or on the occurrence of any corresponding event under the law of a country or territory outside the UK.

[*ITTOIA 2005, s 863; Limited Liability Partnerships Act 2000, s 10(1)*].

Similar provisions apply for capital gains tax purposes (see *TCGA 1992, s 59A*, *TCGA 1992, s 156A* and *TCGA 1992, s 169A*). See Tolley's Capital Gains Tax under Partnerships and Hold-Over Reliefs. An LLP cannot use the cash basis (see **76.3** TRADING INCOME — CASH BASIS FOR SMALLER BUSINESSES). See *Ingenious Games LLP v HMRC* UT, [2019] UKUT 226 (TCC) (TC) for an analysis of the 'with a view to profit' test in the case of an LLP.

See **64.12** RETURNS for an anti-avoidance measure where an LLP has delivered a tax return on the basis of operating with a view to profit but has, in fact, been operating without a view to profit.

See HMRC Partnership Manual PM131410–131570.

Where certain conditions are met, the treatment of a salaried member of an LLP is changed from that of a partner to that of an employee for tax purposes — see **52.27** below.

Simon's Taxes. See **B7.107, B7.513, B7.528.**

Restrictions on LLP loss reliefs

[52.26] Where an individual sustains a loss in any tax year in a trade which he carries on as a member of an LLP, relief is restricted. The restriction applies to any excess of the loss over the member's 'contribution to the LLP' at the end of the basis period for that tax year. That excess may not be relieved under:

(i) *ITA 2007, s 64* (and, consequently, *TCGA 1992, s 261B* against chargeable gains) (see **45.2, 45.5** LOSSES); or
(ii) *ITA 2007, s 72* (see **45.7** LOSSES),

other than against profits arising from the same trade.

If relief has previously been given under any of the provisions at (i) and (ii) above to the individual for a loss in the LLP trade in any tax year at any time during which the individual carried on the trade as a member of an LLP (or to which the restrictions at **52.13** above potentially apply), relief for the loss for the tax year in question is restricted by the excess of the sum of the loss for that tax year and earlier amounts so relieved, over his 'contribution to the LLP'. For this purpose, the amount previously relieved is decreased by the amount of any claw-back under the recovery provisions at **52.14** above.

Individual's contribution to the LLP

The individual's '*contribution to the LLP*' at any time (the 'relevant time') is the aggregate of:

(a) capital contributed (excluding any capital contributed that the partner is or may be entitled to withdraw at any time he is a member of the LLP, or which he is or may be entitled to require another person to reimburse to him) less so much of it (if any) as:

- he has previously withdrawn; or
- he withdraws during the five years beginning with the relevant time; and

(b) his liability on a winding-up of the LLP in so far as that amount is not included in (a). The amount of the liability of a member on a winding up is the amount which he is liable to contribute to the assets of the LLP in the event of its being wound up, and which he remains liable so to contribute for at least the period of five years beginning with the relevant time (or until the LLP is wound up if that happens before the end of that period).

The amount in (a) above should include the individual's share of any profits of the LLP in so far as that share has been added to the LLP's capital. The reference to profits is to accounting profits, calculated in accordance with generally accepted accounting practice, and not to taxable profits (if different). References to capital being withdrawn include drawing it out or receiving it back, whether directly or indirectly in either case, but do not include anything withdrawn in circumstances such that it becomes chargeable to income tax as profits of a trade.

The exclusions referred to in **52.14**(a) and (b) above of amounts from a partner's contribution (i.e. where the costs of providing those amounts is or could be borne by another person) apply equally to a member's contribution to the LLP for the above purposes. See also the recovery provisions at **52.14**.

For a discussion on the meaning of 'contributed' and 'liable to contribute to the assets' see *Hamilton & Kinneil (Archerfield) Ltd v HMRC* UT, [2015] STC 1852.

Purpose test

An amount contributed as capital does not count towards a individual's 'contribution to the LLP' for these purposes if:

- in the basis period for the tax year in which he makes the contribution he is a 'non-active' partner (as defined in **52.13** above); and
- the main purpose, or one of the main purposes, of making the contribution is the obtaining of a reduction in tax liability by means of any of the provisions at (i) and (ii) above.

However, this does not apply to restrict any loss that derives wholly from 'qualifying film expenditure' (as defined in **52.15** above). For the purpose of applying this restriction, a capital contribution is made only when the money is paid to the partnership or, in the case of a contribution consisting of a right or other asset, when the right or asset is transferred to the partnership.

Unrelieved losses

Previous years' losses which, as a result of the above restrictions, have not been relieved are referred to as the member's '*total unrelieved loss*'. In each subsequent tax year in which the member continues to carry on the trade and any of the total unrelieved loss remains outstanding, the balance of the total unrelieved loss is treated for the purposes of the loss reliefs at (i) and (ii) above, and also for the purposes of applying the above restrictions, as having been made in that subsequent tax year. The amount of the total unrelieved loss remaining outstanding in a tax year is the total amount less any part of it for which relief has been given in that or any earlier tax year *other than* by virtue of this provision and any part for which relief has been given for an earlier tax year *under* this provision (or would have been so given had a claim been made).

General

The restrictions at **52.13** above also apply to members of LLPs, and do so in priority to the above restrictions where both sets of restrictions would otherwise apply to the same loss.

[*ITA 2007, ss 107–109, 113A(2)–(4), 114, Sch 2 paras 28, 29; Limited Liability Partnerships Act 2000, s 10; SI 2005 No 2017*].

See **52.15** above for a cap on the amount of relief that can be given under any of the provisions at (i) and (ii) above for a loss sustained by an individual who is a 'non-active' member of an LLP.

See HMRC Partnership Manual PM131520.

Salaried members

[52.27] Where certain conditions are met, the treatment of a salaried member of an LLP is changed from that of a partner to that of an employee for tax purposes. The new rules (the '*salaried member rules*') apply at any time when an individual (M) is a member of an LLP and all of conditions A, B and C below are met. For a Technical Note and guidance see www.gov.uk/government/uploads/system/uploads/attachment_data/file/298222/Partnerships_Salaried_member_rules.pdf.

Condition A

Condition A is that, at the time the question of whether the condition is met is to be determined, it is reasonable to expect that at least 80% of the total amount payable by the LLP in respect of M's performance during the 'relevant period' of services for the LLP in his capacity as a member will be 'disguised salary'. If 'arrangements' were in place at the beginning of 2014/15, the question had to be determined at that time or, if later, at the time M becomes a member of the LLP. It must also be determined at any subsequent time that arrangements are put in place or are modified. If condition A is found to be met, or not to be met, at a particular time, it is to be treated as met, or as not met, at all subsequent times until the question is required to be determined again. The '*relevant period*' is the period from the time the question was determined to the time when it is reasonable to expect that the arrangements will end or be modified. If at the end of the relevant period the arrangements have not ended or been modified, the question of whether condition A is met is to be determined again.

'*Arrangements*' means arrangements (as widely defined) under which amounts are to be, or may be, payable by the LLP in respect of M's performance of services for the LLP in his capacity as a member. An amount is '*disguised salary*' if:

- it is fixed; or
- if it is variable, it is varied without reference to the overall amount of the profits or losses of the LLP; or
- it is not, in practice, affected by the overall amount of those profits or losses.

Condition B

Condition B is that the mutual rights and duties of the members, and of the LLP and its members, do not give M significant influence over the affairs of the LLP.

Condition C

Condition C is that, at the time the question of whether the condition is met is to be determined, M's 'contribution to the LLP' is less than 25% of the disguised salary (see condition A above) which it is reasonable to expect will be payable by the LLP for M's performance during the 'relevant tax year' of services for the LLP in his capacity as a member. The '*relevant tax year*' is the tax year in which falls the time that the aforementioned question is to be determined. That time is the beginning of 2014/15, or (if later) the time M becomes a member of the LLP, and then at the beginning of every tax year. If in any tax year there is a change in M's contribution to the LLP or any other change of circumstances which might affect the question of whether condition C is met, the question must be determined again at the time of the change. If at any time there is an increase in M's contribution to the LLP which would otherwise cause condition C not to be met at that time, the condition is nevertheless treated as met at that time unless it is reasonable to expect that it will not, in fact, be met for the remainder of the tax year. Generally, if, at a particular time, condition C is found to be met, or not to be met, it is to be treated as met, or as not met, at all subsequent times until the question is required to be determined again.

If there are any 'excluded days' in the relevant tax year, M's contribution to the LLP is treated for the above purposes as reduced in the proportion that the number of non-excluded days bears to the total number of days in the year. The following rules apply to determine which days are '*excluded days*', and in these rules the '*determination day*' means the day on which falls the time at which the question of whether condition C is met is being determined.

- Any day in the relevant tax year which is before the 'determination day', and on which M is not a member of the LLP, is an excluded day.
- If, at the time of determination, it is reasonable to expect that M will not be a member of the LLP for the remainder of the relevant tax year, any day in the tax year which is after the determination day, and on which it is expected that M will not be a member, is an excluded day.
- If the time of determination coincides with an increase in M's contribution to the LLP, any day in the relevant tax year which is before the determination day, and on which condition C was met, is an excluded day.

M's contribution to the LLP

For these purposes, M's '*contribution to the LLP*' at a particular time is the total amount which he has contributed to the LLP as capital less so much of that amount (if any) as:

- he has previously drawn out or received back; or
- he is, or may be, entitled to draw out or receive back whilst he is a member of the LLP; or
- he is, or may be, entitled to require another person to reimburse to him.

M's share of any 'profits' of the LLP is to be included in the amount which he has contributed to the LLP as capital insofar as that share has been added to the LLP's capital. '*Profits*' means profits calculated in accordance with generally accepted accounting practice and before any adjustment is made to arrive at taxable profits.

A special rule applies if:

(a) at the beginning of 2014/15 or (if later) the time he becomes a member of the LLP, M has given an undertaking (whether or not legally enforceable) to make a contribution to the LLP's capital but has not yet made the contribution;
(b) the undertaking requires him to make the contribution within the three months ending on 5 July 2014 (period X) or (if it ends later) within the two months beginning when he becomes a member (period Y); and
(c) once made, the contribution will fall to be included in his 'contribution to the LLP'.

For the purpose of determining whether condition C is met at the time mentioned in (a) above or at any subsequent time during period X or Y (whichever is applicable), then (insofar as he has not yet actually made the contribution) M is to be treated as having made the contribution at the time mentioned in (a). If M actually makes the contribution (in whole or in part) during period X or Y (whichever is applicable), the question of whether condition C is met is not to be determined again just because of the making of that contribution. There is provision for the determination already made to be adjusted if it turns out that M does not, within the applicable period in (b) above, make the whole of the contribution he undertook to make.

Anti-avoidance

In determining whether the salaried member rules apply, any arrangements with a main purpose of circumventing the rules are disregarded. The salaried member rules apply equally in the case of an individual who is not a member of an LLP if that individual performs services for the LLP under arrangements involving a non-individual member of the LLP and those arrangements have a main purpose of securing that the salaried member rules would not otherwise apply to the individual. The salaried member rules do not apply to an individual if the reason they would otherwise apply is a consequence of arrangements with a main purpose of circumventing the mixed membership rules at **52.18** above.

[*ITTOIA 2005, ss 863A–863G*].

Deductions in computing profits

Where the salaried member rules apply, any expenses paid by the LLP in respect of the member's deemed employment is deductible in computing profits if they would be so deductible under general principles. [*ITTOIA 2005, s 94AA*].

Simon's Taxes. See **B7.514**.

Investment LLPs and property investment LLPs

[52.28] Certain tax exemptions for income and gains are disapplied where they are received by a member of a 'property investment LLP' as such, and interest relief under **42.10** INTEREST PAYABLE (loan to individual to invest in a partnership) is denied where the partnership is an 'investment LLP'. An '*investment LLP*' is an LLP (see **52.25** above) whose business consists wholly or mainly in the making of investments and the principal part of whose income is derived therefrom, and a '*property investment LLP*' is similarly defined by reference to investments in land. The status of an LLP in this respect is determined for each period for which partnership accounts are drawn up.

In the case of a property investment LLP, the exemptions disapplied include those for pension funds under *ICTA 1988, ss 613(4), 614(3)–(5)* (see **57.40** PENSION PROVISION). Corresponding exemption from the trust rate and dividend trust rate of income tax under *ITA 2007, s 479* (accumulated or discretionary income — see **70.11** SETTLEMENTS) is also disapplied.

[*ITA 2007, ss 399(2)(b)(6), 1004*].

See HMRC Partnership Manual PM131560.

Simon's Taxes. See **B7.107**.

Alternative investment fund managers

[52.29] There is a mechanism for members of 'AIFM partnerships' to allocate certain restricted profits to the partnership. These are profits that those members cannot immediately access because of requirements under the Alternative Investment Fund Managers Directive (AIFMD) (2011/61/EU). This requires AIFM firms to subject part of the remuneration of key individuals to performance conditions and to defer when they can access that remuneration. An '*AIFM partnership*' is a partnership or limited liability partnership that manages alternative investment funds. The AIFM partnership must make an election if these rules are to have effect; the election must be made within six months after the end of the first period of account for which it is to have effect. An officer of HMRC may by notice require a partnership which has made the election to provide information.

Where the election is made, the AIFM partnership is liable to income tax at the additional rate (see **1.3** ALLOWANCES AND TAX RATES) on the allocated profit; no reliefs or allowances can be used to reduce the charge.

Where the restricted profit ultimately 'vests' with the partner who initially allocated it to the partnership, it is treated as taxable income of the partner for the tax year in which the vesting occurs. Credit is given for the tax initially paid by the partnership on the restricted profit, and any overpayment of tax is repayable. For pension contribution purposes, the income is 'relevant UK earnings' (for which see 57.12 PENSION PROVISION). Under European Securities and Markets Authority Guidelines, an amount of remuneration '*vests*' with a person when he receives payment and becomes the legal owner of the remuneration. If the restricted profit never vests, for example because performance targets are not met, no further income tax is payable beyond that already paid by the AIFM partnership, but the tax already paid is not repayable to either the firm or the partner.

[*ITTOIA 2005, ss 863H–863L; TMA 1970, s 12ADA; FA 2004, s 189(2B)*].

For a Technical Note see www.gov.uk/government/uploads/system/uploads/attachment_data/file/298221/Partnerships_Mixed_membership_partnerships__Alternative_investment_fund_managers__Transfer_of_assets___income_Streams_through_partnerships.pdf.

Simon's Taxes. See B7.505.

European Economic Interest Groupings (EEIGs)

[52.30] A European Economic Interest Grouping (EEIG) within *EEC Directive No. 2137/85* (which applies to all EEIGs established within the European Economic Area), wherever it is registered, is regarded as acting as the agent of its members. Its activities are regarded as those of its members acting jointly, each member being regarded as having a share of EEIG property, rights and liabilities, and a person is regarded as acquiring or disposing of a share of the EEIG assets not only where there is an acquisition or disposal by the EEIG while he is a member but also where he becomes or ceases to be a member or there is a change in his share of EEIG property.

A member's share in EEIG property, rights or liabilities is that determined under the contract establishing the EEIG or, if there is no provision determining such shares, it will correspond to the profit share to which he is entitled under the provisions of the contract. If the contract makes no such provision, members are regarded as having equal shares.

Where the EEIG carries on a trade or profession, the members are regarded for income tax purposes as carrying on that trade or profession in partnership.

[*ITA 2007, s 842*].

For the purposes of securing that members of EEIGs are assessed to income tax, corporation tax or capital gains tax, an inspector may, in the case of an EEIG which is registered, or has an establishment registered, in Great Britain or Northern Ireland, by notice require the EEIG to make a return containing such information as the notice may require, accompanied by such accounts and statements as the notice may require, within a specified time. In any other case, he may issue a similar notice to any UK resident member(s) of the EEIG (or if none is so resident, to any member(s)). Notices may differ from one period to another and by reference to the person on whom they are served or the description of EEIG to which they refer. Where a notice is given to an EEIG registered in Great Britain or Northern Ireland (or having an establishment registered there), the EEIG must act through a manager, except that if there is no manager who is an individual, the EEIG must act through an individual designated as a representative of the manager under the *Directive*. The return must in all cases include a declaration that, to the best of the maker's knowledge, it is correct and complete, and where the contract establishing the EEIG requires two or more managers to act jointly for the EEIG to be validly bound, the declaration must be given by the appropriate number of managers. [*TMA 1970, s 12A*]. See **64.1** RETURNS as regards the form and content of returns.

A penalty not exceeding £300 (and £60 per day for continued failure) may be imposed in the case of failure to comply with a notice under the above provisions. No penalty may be imposed after the failure has been remedied, and if it is proved that there was no income or chargeable gain to be included in the return, the maximum penalty is £100. Fraudulent or negligent delivery of an incorrect return etc. or of an incorrect declaration may result in a penalty not exceeding £3,000 for each member of the EEIG at the time of delivery. The £300 and £60 penalties are multiplied by the number of members of the EEIG (but subject to the overall £100 maximum in the circumstances described above); the daily penalty may only be imposed by the Appeal Tribunal (on an application to them by HMRC) and has effect from the day following notification of imposition. [*TMA 1970, s 98B*].

The provisions of *TMA 1970, ss 36, 40* for extended time limits for assessments in cases of loss of income tax brought about deliberately (see **6.3** ASSESSMENTS) or fraudulent or negligent conduct, ASSESSMENTS) are amended so that any act or omission on the part of the EEIG or a member thereof is deemed to be the act or omission of each member of the EEIG. [*TMA 1970, ss 36(4), 40(3)*].

Post-Brexit

With effect on and after Implementation Period completion day, expected to be 31 December 2020, the legislation on EEIGs is updated so as also to refer to UK Economic Interest Groupings (UKEIGs). The term EEIG is then restricted to a grouping registered in a continuing EU member State. [*TMA 1970, ss 12A, 98B; ITA 2007, s 842; SI 2019 No 689, Regs 1, 2, 15(9); European Union (Withdrawal Agreement) Act 2020 Sch 5 para 1(1)*].

Simon's Taxes. See **D4.5**.

53

Pay As You Earn

Cross-references. See also **58.11** PERSONAL SERVICE COMPANIES ETC., **67.12** SELF-ASSESSMENT.

Simon's Taxes. See E4.11.

Introduction to PAYE

[53.1] Pay As You Earn (PAYE) is a system of collection of tax from salaries, wages, pensions etc. See under **28** EMPLOYMENT INCOME for provisions regarding amount chargeable, allowable deductions etc. and see **73.1** SOCIAL SECURITY AND NATIONAL INSURANCE for taxable State benefits.

PAYE is subject to regulations (the 'PAYE regulations'), which were last consolidated in the *Income Tax (Pay As You Earn) Regulations 2003* (*SI 2003 No 2682*). The main regulation-making powers are in *ITEPA 2003, s 684* and enable provision to be made for, *inter alia*, requiring persons making a payment of, or on account of, PAYE income (see **53.2** below) to deduct, at the time of payment, an amount of income tax computed in accordance with HMRC tax tables (see **53.15** below). Specific regulation-making powers enable provision to be made for acceptance by HMRC of the use of electronic means of transmission by employers (see, for example, *SI 2003 No 2682, Pt 10*). [*ITEPA 2003, s 684(2), Sch 7 para 89*].

HMRC can require in certain circumstances a security from employers for payment of amounts due from them under PAYE — see **53.20** below.

It does not matter for the purposes of PAYE if income is wholly or partly income for a tax year other than that in which payment is made. [*ITEPA 2003, s 684(6)*].

This chapter is intended as an outline of the PAYE system. Note that the coverage at **53.26** onwards is arranged in alphabetical order by subject matter. See www.gov.uk/topic/business-tax/paye for index to detailed HMRC guidance. See also HMRC PAYE Manual.

For the vast majority of employers, Real Time Information (RTI) is compulsory. Under RTI, information about tax and other deductions under the PAYE system is transmitted electronically to HMRC by the employer every time an employee is paid. See **53.22** below, and **53.24** below for penalties.

Employee's right to make a tax return

A person within PAYE for a tax year will not necessarily be required to file a self-assessment tax return but may, by written notice, require HMRC to send him such a return for completion and filing. Notice must be given no later than the third anniversary of 31 October following the tax year. [*ITEPA 2003, s 711*].

Scope of PAYE

[53.2] PAYE income (i.e. income potentially within the scope of PAYE) embraces taxable earnings from an employment (see **28** EMPLOYMENT INCOME), 'taxable specific income' from an employment, most taxable pension income and taxable social security income. [*ITEPA 2003, s 683*]. '*Taxable specific income*' includes, in accordance with *ITEPA 2003, s 10(3)*, payments and benefits on termination of office or employment within the special provisions at **18.3–18.10** COMPENSATION FOR LOSS OF EMPLOYMENT, and, subject to the specific inclusions and exclusions in **53.3**(a) and **53.3**(e)–(g) below, amounts falling to be taxed as employment income under **71** SHARE-RELATED EMPLOYMENT INCOME AND EXEMPTIONS.

Not all PAYE income is subject to deduction of tax under PAYE but all *payments* of such income are subject to such deduction. See **53.3** below for items not normally regarded as payments but brought specifically within the scope of PAYE deductions.

See **56.8** PENSION INCOME as regards the application of PAYE to State pension lump sums.

Payments only part of which are PAYE income have been held to be outside the scope entirely (*CIR v Herd* HL 1993, 66 TC 29). It was held in *Paul Dunstall Organisation Ltd v Hedges* (Sp C 179), [1999] SSCD 26 that 'payment', for PAYE purposes, need not be payment in money (but see Taxation Vol 142, No 3692 p 429, 4 February 1999 for an article doubting the correctness of this decision). In *Black and others v Inspector of Taxes* (Sp C 260), [2000] SSCD 540 it was held that, where units in unit trusts were provided in satisfaction of a pre-existing legal entitlement to a payment in money or money's worth, tax should have been deducted and the units provided out of the net sum. In *Sloane Robinson Investment Services Ltd v HMRC* FTT (TC 2132), [2012] UKFTT 451 (TC), [2012] SFTD 1181, involving remuneration to be paid by means of an award of shares made to four employees who were also directors and principal shareholders of the employer company, it was held on the facts that a contractual entitlement to the remuneration arose when the employees agreed a precise division of profits between them, and it was then up to each employee to decide to direct his entitlement to ascertained sums of money to whatever destination he chose; PAYE income arose as soon as the employees became entitled to the monetary sums allocated to them, and it was irrelevant that payment was, in fact, made via an issue of shares.

In *Spectrum Computer Supplies Ltd v HMRC; Kirkstall Timber Ltd v HMRC* (Sp C 559), [2006] SSCD 668, the assignment of trade debts to an employee was held to be a 'payment' to which PAYE should have been applied. In

Sempra Metals Ltd v HMRC (Sp C 698), [2008] SSCD 1062, neither payments to an employee benefit trust nor payments to a trust the beneficiaries of which were members of employees' families were held to be subject to deduction under PAYE, no transfer of cash or its equivalent having been placed unreservedly at the disposal of the employees at that point. It should be noted that the SC in the *Rangers Football Club* case below considered *Sempra Metals* to have been wrongly decided. In *Oco Ltd v HMRC* FTT (TC 6031), [2017] UKFTT 589 (TC), in which benefits were provided to employees mainly by the advancing of interest-free loans to them from sub-trusts of an employee benefit trust, it was held that PAYE should have been applied on the appointment of funds to the sub-trusts; the employees then 'had practical control over them and could use them as they liked'. See also *RFC 2012 plc (formerly Rangers Football Club plc) v Advocate General for Scotland* SC, [2017] STC 1556 at **26.1** DISGUISED REMUNERATION. The Supreme Court decision in that case was followed in *Landid Property Ltd v HMRC* FTT (TC 6111), [2017] UKFTT 692 (TC).

In *Root 2 Tax Ltd v HMRC* FTT (TC 7502), [2019] UKFTT 744 (TC), the FTT held that payments made under spread-betting contracts and associated hedging options gave rise to earnings from employment within PAYE. Although the commercial risk of the bets not producing the intended result was greater than in previous similar cases, the FTT found that the reality of the arrangements was that of the employer company providing its directors with earnings.

For arrangements for relief where both foreign tax and tax under PAYE have to be deducted from the earnings of employees sent to work abroad, see Revenue Tax Bulletin February 2003 p 999.

For the application of the *Ramsay* principle (see **4.1** ANTI-AVOIDANCE) to a PAYE avoidance scheme, see *DTE Financial Services Ltd v Wilson* CA 2001, 74 TC 14.

Extension of scope

[53.3] The following items, not otherwise regarded as *payments* of income, are specifically brought within the scope of PAYE deductions.

(a) Readily convertible assets — see **53.4** below.

(b) 'Non-cash vouchers' (see **28.47** EMPLOYMENT INCOME), where the voucher is capable of being exchanged for anything which, if provided at the time the voucher is provided, would be a readily convertible asset (see **53.4** below) or the voucher would itself be such an asset but for the exclusion of non-cash vouchers from **53.4**. For PAYE purposes, the payment is deemed to be made at the later of the time its cost of provision is incurred and the time of receipt by the employee. If, however, the voucher is a 'cheque voucher' (see **28.47** EMPLOYMENT INCOME), the payment is deemed to be made when the voucher is exchanged for money, goods or services.

(c) 'Credit tokens' (see **28.49** EMPLOYMENT INCOME), not used to meet expenses, on each occasion they are used to obtain money or anything which, if provided at that time, would be a readily convertible asset (see

53.4 below). For 2017/18 onwards, where the token is used pursuant to salary sacrifice arrangements, the taxable amount *for PAYE purposes only* is what would have been the taxable amount had it not been so provided.

(d) 'Cash vouchers' (see **28.48** EMPLOYMENT INCOME), not used to meet expenses, when received by the employee.

(e) A gain on the exercise of a share option where the gain is chargeable as in **71.16** SHARE-RELATED EMPLOYMENT INCOME AND EXEMPTIONS and the shares acquired are readily convertible assets (as in **53.4** below). For PAYE purposes, the payment is deemed to be made at the time the option is exercised and in respect of the employment by reason of which the chargeable person was granted the option. The amount subject to PAYE is the best estimate of the amount chargeable to tax. Account is taken of any deduction likely to be available for employer national insurance contributions borne by the employee.

(f) A gain on the assignment or release of a share option where the gain is chargeable as in **71.16** SHARE-RELATED EMPLOYMENT INCOME AND EXEMPTIONS and regardless of whether or not the shares subject to the option are readily convertible assets. PAYE applies, at the time of the chargeable event, where the consideration for the assignment or release takes the form of a payment or the provision of a readily convertible asset (as in **53.4** below), and the amount subject to PAYE is as in (e) above. The application of PAYE extends to a chargeable event within **71.16**(d) (receipt of benefit in connection with the option) where the benefit takes the form of a payment or the provision of a readily convertible asset.

(g) Any amount taxable as employment income, in relation to 'employment-related shares', by virtue of a chargeable event under **71.5** or **71.9** SHARE-RELATED EMPLOYMENT INCOME AND EXEMPTIONS, the charge on acquisition under **71.10** SHARE-RELATED EMPLOYMENT INCOME AND EXEMPTIONS, the charge under **71.11** SHARE-RELATED EMPLOYMENT INCOME AND EXEMPTIONS, the charge on discharge of a notional loan under **71.12** SHARE-RELATED EMPLOYMENT INCOME AND EXEMPTIONS, the charge on acquisition in avoidance cases under **71.12** SHARE-RELATED EMPLOYMENT INCOME AND EXEMPTIONS, or the charge under **71.13** or **71.14** SHARE-RELATED EMPLOYMENT INCOME AND EXEMPTIONS.

PAYE applies as if the employee were provided with PAYE income in the form of the employment-related shares by the employer on the date of the event in question (or, in the case of **71.11**, on the valuation date in question). (See **71.4** for the meaning of '*employment-related shares*' and **71.3** SHARE-RELATED EMPLOYMENT INCOME AND EXEMPTIONS for the extended meaning of '*shares*' in this connection.) The amount subject to PAYE is the best estimate of the amount chargeable to tax. Where the employment-related shares are not themselves readily convertible assets (as in **53.4** below) but the event is one involving the receipt of consideration or a benefit (whether in the form of a payment or the provision of an asset), PAYE applies to the payment or, if it is a readily convertible asset, to the provision of the asset.

(h) Any amount that counts as employment income under **26.4** DISGUISED REMUNERATION — see **53.5** below.

If, in a case within (e), (f) or (g) above, all or part of the amount chargeable is (or is likely to be) 'foreign securities income' (within **71.22–71.24** SHARE-RELATED EMPLOYMENT INCOME AND EXEMPTIONS), the amount of the payment treated as made for PAYE purposes is limited to the best estimate that can reasonably be made of the difference between the amount that is likely to count as employment income and the amount that is likely to be foreign securities income. This applies where the shares, or as the case may be, the share option is acquired on or after 6 April 2008 (but not where shares are acquired on or after that date under an option acquired before that date). See also HMRC Employment-Related Securities Manual ERSM161000.

[*ITEPA 2003, ss 693–696, 698, 700, 700A, 712; FA 2017, Sch 2 paras 57–59, 62(2)(5)*].

See **53.14** below as regards accounting for tax in respect of items within (a)–(h) above. See Revenue Tax Bulletins May 1994 p 212, February 1997 p 385 and April 2000 pp 734, 735 for practical considerations in operating PAYE in these circumstances.

For voluntary payrolling of specific benefits-in-kind, see **53.28** below.

Readily convertible assets

[53.4] As stated at **53.3**(a) above, 'readily convertible assets' are brought within the scope of PAYE. The amount subject to PAYE is computed on the basis of the best estimate that can reasonably be made of the amount likely to be chargeable to tax.

A '*readily convertible asset*' is an asset (defined as below) capable of being sold on a recognised investment exchange or other specified market, an asset for which 'trading arrangements' exist or are likely to come into existence, an asset consisting of rights in respect of a money debt, property subject to a warehousing regime (as defined) (or rights in respect of such property), or anything likely (without any action by the employee) to give rise to, or become, a right enabling a person to obtain (by any means at all, including the use of the asset as security for a loan) an amount of money similar to or greater than the amount expended in providing the asset (see *ITEPA 2003, s 702*).

For this purpose, 'asset' is widely defined to include any property but specifically *excludes*:

- non-cash vouchers, credit tokens and cash vouchers (but see the separate provisions at **53.3**(b)–(d) above); and
- shares acquired under a tax-advantaged SAYE option scheme or CSOP scheme. In each case, the reference to shares is to ordinary shares in (i) the employer company, or (ii) a company that controls it, or (iii) a member of a consortium (as defined) that owns a company within (i) or (ii), or (iv) a company that controls a consortium member within (iii), and 'share' includes stock. In relation to shares acquired under a tax-advantaged CSOP scheme, the exclusion does not apply (and PAYE therefore does apply) if the shares are acquired by exercise of an option within three years after it was granted (other than in permissible circumstances — see **71.67** SHARE-RELATED EMPLOYMENT INCOME AND EXEMPTIONS) or more than ten years after it was granted.

The exclusions for shares apply only at the instant of their acquisition and therefore do not exclude post-acquisition events from the scope of PAYE.

For this purpose, '*trading arrangements*' are arrangements which enable the recipient of the asset (or a member of his family or household) to obtain (by any means at all, including the use of the asset as security for a loan) an amount of money similar to or greater than the amount expended in providing the asset (see *ITEPA 2003, s 702(2)–(5)*).

These provisions extend to anything *enhancing* the value of an asset in which the employee (or a member of his family or household) has an interest, where the asset, with its value enhanced, would be a readily convertible asset if provided at the time of enhancement.

An asset consisting in securities within **71.3** SHARE-RELATED EMPLOYMENT INCOME AND EXEMPTIONS is treated as a readily convertible asset in all cases unless the securities are shares (or interests therein) that are 'corporation tax deductible'. Shares (and interests) are '*corporation tax deductible*' if they are acquired by reason of employment, or pursuant to an option granted by reason of employment, and the employer company is entitled to corporation tax relief under *CTA 2009, ss 1001–1038B* (see Tolley's Corporation Tax). See *ITEPA 2003, s 702(5A)–(5D)*.

Exchange tokens like bitcoin can be exchanged on one or more token exchanges in order to obtain an amount of money. On that basis, HMRC consider that trading arrangements exist at the point that such tokens are received as employment income, and that the tokens are readily convertible assets. Employers do not have to operate PAYE on payments of earnings that are *not* readily convertible assets; employees must declare the payments in their tax return and account for the tax in their self-assessment. See HMRC policy paper 'Cryptoassets: tax for individuals', 20 December 2019 at www.gov.uk/government/publications/tax-on-cryptoassets.

In *Aberdeen Asset Management plc v HMRC* CS 2013, [2014] STC 438, shares in an Isle of Man company set up for the employee and funded by the employer via an employee benefits trust were held to be a readily convertible asset.

See HMRC Employment Income Manual EIM11900 for further notes on the meaning of 'readily convertible assets'. See Revenue Tax Bulletin August 1998 pp 563–573 for a detailed HMRC view of the application of PAYE to such assets. For notes on the status of shares as readily convertible assets where there is either a long stop provision or a prohibition on employees selling shares, see Revenue Tax Bulletin April 2000 pp 735, 736.

[*ITEPA 2003, ss 696, 697, 701, 702, 712*].

Simon's Taxes. See **E4.1124**.

Disguised remuneration

[53.5] If the value of a relevant step (see **26.7** DISGUISED REMUNERATION) counts as employment income under **26.4** and the relevant step is the payment of a sum of money, B is treated as making a payment of PAYE income of A of an amount which, on the basis of the best estimate which can reasonably be made, is the amount of the employment income. A and B are the persons mentioned in **26.2** or, as the case may be, **26.3**.

Where the facts are as above except that the relevant step is not the payment of a sum of money, B is treated as making a payment of PAYE income of A of an amount which, on the basis of the best estimate which can reasonably be made, is the amount of the employment income *less* so much of that amount (if any) as would fall to be taxed on the remittance basis in accordance with **26.5** DISGUISED REMUNERATION.

In either case, the payment is treated as made on the latest of the following days:

- the day on which the relevant step is taken; and
- the day on which A's employment with B begins.

If, however, the person who takes the relevant step deducts income tax from the payment (if the payment is of a sum of money) and accounts for it under PAYE (whether or not the payment is of a sum of money), B is not treated as making any payment of PAYE income.

[*ITEPA 2003, ss 687A, 695A*].

On and after 13 February 2019, the value of anything treated to date in the employment as a payment of PAYE income as above must be reported by the employer in the RTI return (see **53.22** below). [*SI 2003 No 2682, Sch A1 para 16A; SI 2019 No 83, Regs 1, 4*].

Where it is clear that the employer is unable to settle the PAYE liability, and other options have been exhausted, HMRC practice is to issue a determination under *SI 2003 No 2682, Reg 80* (see **53.19** below) in respect of the unpaid tax. Once this determination has been unpaid for 30 days HMRC will use *SI 2003 No 2682, Reg 81* (see **53.17** below) to transfer the liability to the employee. See the technical note at www.gov.uk/government/publications/disguised-remuneration-transfer-of-liability-technical-note.

Simon's Taxes. See **E4.1116**.

Deduction of tax under PAYE

[53.6] All persons making payments of PAYE income are required to deduct the appropriate amount of tax from each payment (or repay over-deductions) by reference to PAYE Tax Tables, which are so constructed that, as near as may be, tax deducted from payments to date from previous 5 April corresponds with the correct time proportion to date of the net total tax liability (after allowances and reliefs) of the recipient on that income for the year. See *Andrews v King* Ch D 1991, 64 TC 332 as regards extended definition of 'employer' and *Booth v Mirror Group Newspapers plc* QB, [1992] STC 615 as regards application of the PAYE regulations where emoluments are paid by a third party. The 'total tax' may include adjustments for any previous year and it 'may be assumed' that payments to date bear the same proportion to the total emoluments as that part of the year bears to the whole. There is a statutory overriding limit in that the amount of tax to be deducted from a payment of PAYE income cannot exceed 50% of the amount of the payment. [*ITEPA 2003, s 685; SI 2003 No 2682, Regs 2, 21–33; SI 2018 No 267, Regs 1, 6*]. Employers are also required to deduct national insurance contributions at the same time as PAYE tax is deducted.

There are provisions to determine the time at which a payment of income is treated as being made for PAYE purposes. These equate to the rules in **28.9** EMPLOYMENT INCOME for determining when money earnings are to be treated as being received. [*ITEPA 2003, s 686*].

Employers may elect to operate separate PAYE schemes for different groups of employees. [*SI 2003 No 2682, Regs 98, 99*].

An employer cannot shift liability to account for PAYE to enterprises that are in substance no more than payroll agents (*R (oao Oriel Support Ltd) v HMRC* CA, [2009] STC 1397).

Payments by intermediaries

[53.7] Where a payment of, or on account of, PAYE income is made by an 'intermediary' of the employer (i.e. a person acting on behalf, and at the expense, of the employer or a person 'connected' (within **19** CONNECTED PERSONS) with the employer, or trustees holding property for persons including the employee), then unless the intermediary deducts and accounts for tax under PAYE (whether or not the PAYE regulations apply to him), the employer is to be treated for PAYE purposes as having made the payment (grossed up where the recipient is entitled to the amount after deduction of any income tax). [*ITEPA 2003, ss 687, 712, 718*]. See **53.14** below as regards the method of accounting for tax in respect of such notional payments. See also the agency worker rules at **53.10** below and guidance at www.gov.uk/guidance/employment-status-employment-intermediaries.

Simon's Taxes. See **E4.1121.**

Non-UK employer

[53.8] Where, during any period, an employee works for a person (the '*relevant person*') other than his employer, and any payment of his PAYE income for work done in that period is made by the employer (or by an intermediary (see above) of the employer or of the relevant person) outside the scope of PAYE, the relevant person is treated for PAYE purposes as having made the payment (grossed up where the employee is entitled to the payment after deduction of any income tax).

If the employee worked for the relevant person during the period as a result of arrangements made between the relevant person and a third person, and the third person did not make the payment of PAYE income (but PAYE would have applied if he had), the third person is treated for PAYE purposes as having made the payment (again grossed up where appropriate). This takes precedence over the rule above. In practice, the third person will often be a UK agency.

The above rules apply also to items brought within the scope of PAYE by **53.3**(a)–(h) above. They do not apply to PAYE income arising, as a result of the application of **53.5** above, from the charge at **26.8** DISGUISED REMUNERATION on loans and quasi-loans outstanding on 5 April 2019.

The rules do not apply where the rules at **53.9** below apply or where those rules would have applied had it not been for the issue of a certificate by HMRC.

[*ITEPA 2003, s 689; FA 2018, Sch 1 para 12*].

Simon's Taxes. See **E4.1122**.

Oil and gas workers on the continental shelf

[53.9] If a payment of PAYE income of a 'continental shelf worker' is made by the employer (or an intermediary of the employer or of the relevant person) outside the scope of PAYE, the 'relevant person' is treated for PAYE purposes as having made the payment (grossed up where the employee is entitled to the payment after deduction of any income tax). This applies also to items brought within the scope of PAYE by **53.3**(a)–(h) above. A '*continental shelf worker*' is a person in an employment some or all of the duties of which are performed in the UK sector of the continental shelf (as defined in *ITEPA 2003, s 41* — see **28.3**(v) EMPLOYMENT INCOME) and in connection with exploration or exploitation activities (as so defined). The '*relevant person*' is:

- if the employer has an associated company (within *CTA 2010, s 449*) with a place of business or registered office in the UK, the associated company, or
- in any other case, the licence holder under *Petroleum Act 1998, Pt 1* in respect of the area of the UK sector of the continental shelf where the duties of the employment are performed.

There may be more than one relevant person in relation to a continental shelf worker, such that in consequence of the same payment each of them would be treated as making a payment of PAYE income. If one such relevant person accounts for tax under the notional payment rules at **53.14** below, the other relevant persons are relieved of their obligations.

PAYE regulations make provision for the issue of a certificate (a '*UKCS oil field licensee certificate*') by HMRC to a licence holder in respect of one or more continental shelf workers. The certificate will confirm that income tax for the PAYE income of specified continental shelf workers is being duly deducted and accounted for by the employer or intermediary making the payments. As long as the certificate remains in force, the licence holder is relieved of the above obligation to operate PAYE in relation to the specified workers.

[*ITEPA 2003, s 689A; SI 2003 No 2682, Regs 84A–84D*].

Simon's Taxes. See E4.1128.

Agency workers

[53.10] Where an individual's remuneration falls to be treated under the agency worker rules at **28.96** EMPLOYMENT INCOME as earnings from an employment, *ITEPA 2003, ss 687* (**53.7** above), *689* (**53.8** above) and *689A* (**53.9** above), *ss 693–702* (**53.3, 53.4** above) and *s 710* (**53.14** below) have effect as if the individual held the employment with the deemed employer, i.e. the person with whom the individual is treated under **28.96** EMPLOYMENT INCOME as having an employment the duties of which consist of his services. If a person other than the deemed employer (or an intermediary of the deemed employer) makes a payment of PAYE income of the individual, and the payment is not within the rule described below, the person is to be treated for the purposes of *ss 687, 689* and *689A* as making the payment as an intermediary of the deemed employer.

If, however, a payment of PAYE income of the individual is made on behalf of, and at the expense of, 'the client' (see **28.96** EMPLOYMENT INCOME) or a person connected with the client (within **19** CONNECTED PERSONS), and the case is not one in which the client is the deemed employer, *s 687* and *s 710* have effect as if the client, and not the deemed employer, were the employer.

[*ITEPA 2003, ss 688, 718*].

Information powers

For purposes connected with PAYE, HMRC are given the same power, subject to the same penalties as in **28.96** EMPLOYMENT INCOME, to impose record-keeping requirements on employment intermediaries and require them to provide HMRC with information, records and documents. [*ITEPA 2003, s 716B; TMA 1970, s 98(1)(4F)*]. This power has been exercised as follows. Where more than one individual provides services to a client under, or in consequence of, a contract between the agency and one or more clients, other than services provided exclusively on the UK continental shelf (i.e. the area designated under *Continental Shelf Act 1964, s 1(7)*), and the agency makes one or more payments in respect of the services provided, the agency must make a return of specified information to HMRC every tax quarter. The agency must also keep, for at least three years after the tax year to which they relate, records which evidence the specified information. [*SI 2003 No 2682, Regs 84E–84H*].

For guidance see www.gov.uk/government/publications/employment-intermediaries-reporting-requirements.

Lack of clarity in HMRC guidance meant that the appellant had a reasonable excuse for not realising the need to file nil quarterly returns (*Tarrant Howl Ltd v HMRC* FTT (TC 6788), [2019] SFTD 346, [2018] UKFTT 640 (TC)).

Liability of directors

In a case where an amount of 'relevant PAYE debt' of a company is not deducted, accounted for or paid to HMRC by the company, HMRC may serve a notice (a '*personal liability notice*') on any person who on the 'relevant date' was a director of the company. The notice will specify the amount involved and require payment by the director of that amount plus interest calculated at the normal rate for overdue tax and running from the date the notice is served. The director must pay within 30 days beginning with the day the notice is served. If HMRC serve personal liability notices on more than one director of the company in respect of the same amount of relevant PAYE debt, those directors are jointly and severally liable. For these purposes, 'company' includes a limited liability partnership, and 'director' has the meaning given by *ITEPA 2003, s 67*.

For this purpose, a '*relevant PAYE debt*' is any amount that the company is required to deduct or account for by virtue of either of the anti-avoidance provisions at **28.96** EMPLOYMENT INCOME relating to agency workers. It also includes any interest or penalty, in respect of such an amount, for which the company is liable. In a case involving fraudulent documentation, the '*relevant date*' is the date on which the fraudulent document was provided. In a case involving arrangements entered into by a third person, the '*relevant date*' is the date on which the arrangements were entered into.

A person served with a personal liability notice has a right of appeal on the grounds either that all or part of the amount specified in that notice does not represent an amount of relevant PAYE debt of the company or that the person was not a director of the company on the relevant date. Notice of appeal must be given within 30 days. On an appeal that is notified to the Appeal Tribunal, the Tribunal must uphold or quash the personal liability notice. It may also reduce or increase the specified amount so that it does represent an amount of relevant PAYE debt.

An officer of HMRC may withdraw a personal liability notice if the officer considers it appropriate to do so. If one or more personal liability notices are served in respect of an amount of relevant PAYE debt of a company and the amounts paid to HMRC (whether by directors or by the company) exceed the aggregate amount due (inclusive of interest), HMRC must repay the excess on a just and equitable basis and without unreasonable delay. They must pay interest running from the date the amounts paid come to exceed the aggregate due.

[*ITEPA 2003, s 688(2A); SI 2003 No 2682, Regs 97ZA–97ZF*].

See also HMRC Employment Status Manual ESM2046.

Simon's Taxes. See **E4.1188**.

Travel expenses where services provided through intermediary

[53.11] The following should be read in conjunction with **28.18** EMPLOYMENT INCOME, which denies relief for home-to-work travel expenditure in certain circumstances in which a worker is engaged via an employment intermediary.

In a case where an amount of 'relevant PAYE debt' of a company is not deducted by the company, HMRC may serve a notice (a '*personal liability notice*') on any person who on the 'relevant date' was a director of the company. The notice will specify the amount involved and require payment by the director of that amount plus interest calculated at the normal rate for overdue tax and running from the date the notice is served. The director must pay within 30 days beginning with the day the notice is served. If HMRC serve personal liability notices on more than one director of the company in respect of the same amount of relevant PAYE debt, those directors are jointly and severally liable. For these purposes, 'company' includes a limited liability partnership, and 'director' has the meaning given by *ITEPA 2003, s 67*. In relation to a relevant PAYE debt the '*relevant date*' is the date on which the first payment is due on which PAYE is not accounted for. As regards appeals, withdrawal of personal liability notices and repayment by HMRC of tax overpaid, similar rules apply as in **53.10** above under Liability of directors.

For this purpose, a '*relevant PAYE debt*' is any of the following:

- an amount that the company has to account for in accordance with the PAYE regulations by virtue of the anti-avoidance provisions at **28.18** (persons providing fraudulent documents);
- an amount that the company has to deduct and pay in accordance with the PAYE regulations in circumstances where the company is an employment intermediary, has concluded that the 'supervision, direction or control' let-out at **28.18** applies to an engagement but has received no evidence from which it would be reasonable to come to that conclusion (and the mere assertion by a person that the manner in which the worker provided the services was not subject to (or to the right of) supervision, direction or control by any person does not count as such evidence);
- an amount that the company has to deduct and pay in accordance with the PAYE regulations in any case where the 'supervision, direction or control' let-out at **28.18** does not have effect; and
- any interest or penalty in respect of any of the above amounts.

[*ITEPA 2003, s 688B; FA 2016, s 14(3)–(5)(7); SI 2003 No 2682, Regs 97ZG–97ZM*].

For official guidance, see www.gov.uk/government/publications/employment-intermediaries-travel-expense-guidance.

Mobile UK workforce

[53.12] Where a person (the 'relevant person') has entered, or is likely to enter, into an agreement that employees of another person (the 'contractor') will work for him, but not as his employees, for a period, and it is likely that PAYE will not be deducted or accounted for in accordance with the regulations on payments made by (or on behalf of) the contractor of, or on account of, PAYE income of those employees for that period, HMRC may by notice to the relevant person direct that he apply PAYE to any payments made by him in respect of work done in that period by such employees of the contractor. So much of the payment as is attributable to the work done by each such employee is treated for this purpose as a payment of PAYE income of that employee. The notice must specify the relevant person and the contractor to whom it relates, and may similarly be withdrawn by further notice, and notices must, where reasonably practicable, be copied to the contractor. [*ITEPA 2003, s 691*].

PAYE codes

[53.13] The tax deductions to be made are those appropriate to the employee's 'PAYE code' (calculated by HMRC, and notified to both employer and employee, to take account of personal allowances and reliefs due, certain higher and additional rate liabilities and reliefs, underpayments from earlier years, and items within the benefits code (see **28.21** EMPLOYMENT INCOME) from which deductions cannot be made). An 'S code' denotes a Scottish taxpayer, and a 'C code' a Welsh taxpayer. The PAYE code generally represents the total allowances due omitting the final digit. Notice of objection to a code or revised code may be made to HMRC, with the employee having a right of appeal. See **79.4** UNDERWRITERS AT LLOYD'S for a case concerning a request to include an anticipated underwriting loss in a PAYE code.

HMRC often include amounts of non-PAYE income in PAYE codes as a matter of administrative convenience. However, if a taxpayer informs them that he does not want such income to be included in his code, it will be removed (see www.gov.uk/tax-codes). This does not apply to items such as benefits-in-kind, which do constitute PAYE income.

See, respectively, **64.3** RETURNS and **16.3** CLAIMS as regards the coding out of self-assessment liabilities and as regards claims for reliefs etc. given effect by adjustments to codes. See **53.31** below as regards the collection by means of coding adjustment of debts due to HMRC.

Tax offices notify an employer only if there is a change in an employee's code. Until such notification an employer continues to use the same code from year to year.

HMRC can code out a tax credit debt to the extent that the taxpayer does not object. The maximum amounts that can be coded out in this way are the same as those set out in the table in **53.31** below; those limits are all-inclusive and do not apply separately to different types of debt.

[*SI 2003 No 2682, Regs 7, 13, 14, 14A–14C, 15–20; SI 2017 No 414, Regs 1, 2; SI 2018 No 267, Regs 1, 4, 5; SI 2018 No 1327, Regs 1, 4*].

Simon's Taxes. See **E4.1130–E4.1137**.

Notional payments — accounting for tax

[53.14] A '*notional payment*' of PAYE income is a payment treated as made by virtue of any of **53.3**(a)–(h) above or, with the exception of grossed up payments, under the 'payment by intermediary' rules (**53.7** above), 'non-UK employer' rules (**53.8** above) or continental shelf worker rules (**53.9** above). Where a notional payment of PAYE income is made, the income tax thereon is to be deducted from any *actual* payment(s) of PAYE income to the employee made simultaneously or made subsequently but in the same PAYE month or quarter. Where, due to an insufficiency of actual payments, all or part of the tax cannot be so deducted, the employer (or person treated as making the payment) must account to HMRC, within 14 days after the end of the PAYE month or quarter, for any tax he is required, but unable, to deduct. The amount so deducted or accounted for is treated as an amount paid by the employee in respect of his own liability to income tax. It is so treated at the time the notional payment is made.

As regards any amount the employer (or person treated as making the payment of PAYE income) has accounted for (being unable to deduct it from any payments made to the employee), if the employee does not make good the amount to the employer within 90 days after the end of the tax year in which falls the date on which the employer etc. is treated as making the notional payment, the employee is treated as receiving earnings of that amount on that date.

There may be occasions when, as a result of new legislation, items fall to be treated as PAYE income with retrospective effect. If the employer is treated by virtue of any Act as making a notional payment before the date of Royal Assent to that Act:

- the employer must deduct the tax from any actual payment(s) of PAYE income to the employee made simultaneously or made subsequently but before the end of the PAYE month or quarter following that in which the Royal Assent date falls;
- the employer must account to HMRC, within 14 days after the end of the PAYE month or quarter following that in which the Royal Assent date falls, for any tax he is required, but unable, to deduct; and
- the employee has 90 days from the end of the tax year in which falls the Royal Assent date to make good the amount accounted for by the employer. Otherwise, the employee is treated as receiving earnings of that amount on that date.

[*ITEPA 2003, ss 222, 710; SI 2003 No 2682, Reg 62*].

On and after 13 February 2019, a determination under *SI 2003 No 2682, Reg 80* can include tax for which the employer is liable on a notional payment but which he was unable to deduct from an actual payment to the employee. [*SI 2003 No 2682, Reg 80(1A); SI 2019 No 83, Regs 1, 3*].

The PAYE regulations allow for payments which are retrospectively re-characterised as PAYE income. These deal with the recording, reporting and payment to HMRC of PAYE, both where the payments were received in a tax year which has not yet ended (an open year) and in a closed year. They provide a statutory return to enable employers to report payments made to employees in a closed tax year; remove the requirement for electronic reporting and payment in respect of PAYE due on payments made in closed tax years and treated retrospectively as PAYE income; and provide for employers to notify affected employees of their additional taxable income and tax paid on that income.

For notes on the application of the above provisions to share-related benefits, see Revenue Tax Bulletin April 2000 pp 734, 735. For a case in which directors were held to have made good an amount of tax despite the amount in question having erroneously been held in their loan account beyond the 30-day time limit, see *Ferguson and others v CIR* (Sp C 266), [2001] SSCD 1.

Simon's Taxes. See **E4.1120, E4.1145**.

Tax Tables

[53.15] Tax Tables show, in relation to each 'code', the cumulative 'free pay' for each weekly (or monthly) period, which is subtracted from the total gross pay down to that period leaving 'taxable pay' on which is calculated the tax due from (or refundable to) the employee.

Simon's Taxes. See **E4.1138, E4.11109**.

Deductions working sheets

[53.16] Deductions working sheets (Form P11) must be kept in each fiscal year by every employer in respect of each employee for recording the employee's pay, tax and related national insurance contributions. [*SI 2003 No 2682, Reg 66*].

Under-deductions

[53.17] For end-of-year PAYE reconciliations (in cases where tax has been correctly deducted), see **53.46** below.

As to recovery from employee of tax under-deducted see *SI 2003 No 2682, Reg 72*. Recovery from employee is subject to the condition that either:

(i) the employer made an error in good faith having taken reasonable care; or
(ii) with the employee's acquiescence, the employer wilfully failed to deduct the correct tax.

Where (i) above applies, the employer may request HMRC to make a direction to the effect that the employer is not liable. If HMRC agree, they will issue a direction notice, subject to right of appeal by the employee within 30 days. If not, they will issue a refusal notice, subject to similar right of appeal by the employer. Where (ii) above applies, HMRC will issue a direction notice, to the effect that the employer is not liable, to the employee, who again has 30 days in which to appeal. [*SI 2003 No 2682, Regs 72, 72A–72D*]. See also Revenue Tax Bulletin April 2004 pp 1108–1110.

Likewise, HMRC may direct that the employer be relieved of tax determined under *SI 2003 No 2682, Reg 80* (see **53.19** below), with similar right of appeal available to the employee. [*SI 2003 No 2682, Regs 81, 81A*]. See also Revenue Tax Bulletin April 2004 pp 1108–1110.

In *Hoey v HMRC*, FTT (TC 7292), [2019] UKFTT 489 (TC), the Tribunal found that the very wide ranging discretion given to HMRC officers by *ITEPA 2003, s 684(7A)* effectively renders otiose *SI 2003 No 2682, Regs 72, 81,* which permit HMRC to collect the tax due from the employee rather than the employer but only in specified circumstances. *ITEPA 2003, s 684(7A)* provides inter alia that nothing in the PAYE regulations can be read as requiring the employer to comply with the regulations in circumstances in which an HMRC officer is satisfied that it is unnecessary or not appropriate for the employer to do so.

The following applies where an employee has received a payment on which the employer should have accounted for tax under PAYE, the employer has under-accounted for the tax, and it appears to HMRC that the tax is likely to have been self-assessed by the employee or has been accounted for as a self-assessment payment on account by the employee (see **67.5** SELF-ASSESSMENT) or as tax deducted from payments to him under the CIS and treated as paid by him (see **20.6** CONSTRUCTION INDUSTRY SCHEME). If any one of a number of trigger events occurs, HMRC may direct that the liability be transferred from employer to employee. This is of particular relevance where an individual has self-assessed on the grounds that he is self-employed but is subsequently classified as an employee. The employee has a right of appeal (on limited grounds only) but the employer does not. The trigger events are:

- issue of a notice of determination by HMRC under *SI 2003 No 2682, Reg 80* (see **53.19** below) that includes the tax in question;
- receipt by HMRC of a tax return, amended tax return or error or mistake claim from the employee in which the tax is treated as having been deducted under PAYE; and
- receipt by HMRC of a letter of offer from the employer to agree an amount in settlement of his liability that includes the tax in question.

[*SI 2003 No 2682, Regs 72E–72G*].

See also *Bernard & Shaw Ltd v Shaw* KB 1951, 30 ATC 187, and for wilful failure by employer to deduct correct tax, *R v CIR (ex p Chisholm)* QB 1981, 54 TC 722, *R v CIR (ex p Sims)* QB 1987, 60 TC 398 and *R v CIR (ex p Cook)* QB 1987, 60 TC 405. In *R v CIR (ex p McVeigh)* QB 1996, 68 TC 121, accounting entries purporting to deduct tax, where tax not paid over to HMRC, were held not to constitute deduction of tax for these purposes; this decision was followed in *HMRC v West* UT, [2018] STC 1004. In *Blanche v HMRC* FTT (TC 1697), [2011] UKFTT 863 (TC), the employer was held not to have taken reasonable care; therefore the under-deducted tax was not recoverable from the employee.

For tax accounted for by employer in respect of certain notional payments, see **53.14** above.

Form P60

[53.18] Employers must give each employee annually a certificate (form P60) showing his total taxable earnings for the year and total tax deducted therefrom, his appropriate code, national insurance number, and the employer's name and address etc. The form P60 must be provided to the employee no later than 31 May following the tax year to which it relates. [*SI 2003 No 2682, Reg 67*]. See **67.12** SELF-ASSESSMENT for other information to be supplied by employers to employees.

Payment to HMRC

[53.19] The net tax deducted by the employer must be paid to HMRC within 14 days after the end of each tax month (17 days for electronic payments), except in certain cases where payment may be made quarterly. Quarterly payment applies either where the simplified PAYE deduction scheme is in use (see **53.15** above) or where the employer has reasonable grounds for believing that the 'average monthly amount' otherwise payable to HMRC will be less than £1,500 and chooses to pay quarterly instead of monthly. The '*average monthly amount*' is the average, for tax months falling within the current tax year, of:

(a) amounts deducted under PAYE and the CONSTRUCTION INDUSTRY SCHEME (**20**) (disregarding any adjustment thereto in respect of working tax credit);
(b) national insurance contributions (again disregarding working tax credit adjustments and also disregarding any contributions for which liability has been transferred to the employee); and
(c) student loan repayments,

less any payments of:

(i) statutory adoption pay, statutory maternity pay, statutory paternity pay, statutory sick pay, statutory shared parental pay and statutory parental bereavement pay; and
(ii) (in the case of company employers only) amounts suffered by deduction under the construction industry scheme.

Where quarterly payment applies, payment to HMRC must be made within 14 days (or 17 days) after the end of the tax quarter. A tax month ends on the 5th of each month; a tax quarter ends on 5 July, 5 October, 5 January and 5 April.

[*SI 2003 No 2682, Regs 2, 68–71; SI 2020 No 240, Regs 1, 3*].

Similar rules apply under RTI (see **53.22** below) except that the amount of tax to be paid over to HMRC is taken from the relevant figures shown in the RTI returns made under *SI 2003 No 2682, Reg 67B* or *Reg 67D*.

If no tax has been paid within 17 days after the end of a tax month or quarter, or HMRC are not satisfied that any payment made satisfies the employer's liability, HMRC, if they are not aware of the amount the employer is liable to pay, can give notice requiring a return within 14 days showing the amount of that liability; this does not apply under RTI. HMRC may also estimate the amount due and serve notice on the employer requiring payment of that amount within seven days after the issue of the notice; this applies equally under RTI. [*SI 2003 No 2682, Regs 75A, 75B, 77, 78*]. HMRC have the power to determine to the best of their judgement the amount of tax payable for a tax year where it appears to them that tax may have been payable under these regulations but has not been paid; the determination applies as if it were an assessment to tax. [*SI 2003 No 2682, Reg 80*]. See **53.17** above as regards recovery of tax from employee in certain cases.

An employer is not entitled to charge HMRC with costs of PAYE collection (*Meredith v Hazell* QB 1964, 42 TC 435). Where money is stolen, the employer is liable (*A-G v Antoine* KB 1949, 31 TC 213).

Late payment and repayment interest

See **53.23** below.

Penalty for late in-year payments of PAYE

See **53.24** below.

Funding from HMRC

Normally, if an employer needs to make a tax refund to one or more employees, it reduces his monthly or quarterly payment to HMRC of amounts within (a) to (c) above. If the refunds exceed the payment due to HMRC, the excess can be used to reduce subsequent monthly or quarterly payments or the employer can apply to HMRC for funding to cover it. The rules that apply to funding, and the steps involved in claiming it, are explained at www.gov.uk/running-payroll/paying-hmrc.

Mandatory electronic payment for 'large employers'

Employers who at the 'specified date' are 'large employers' (i.e. they were paying PAYE income to at least 250 recipients) are required to use an approved method of electronic payment of PAYE liabilities. The specified date for any particular tax year is 31 October in the preceding tax year.

[*FA 2003, ss 204, 205; SI 2003 No 2682, Regs 190, 191, 198A, 199–204*].

Security for payment of PAYE

[53.20] HMRC can require in certain circumstances a security from employers for amounts due from them under PAYE. Failure to provide a security by the required date is a criminal offence punishable in England and Wales by a fine, and in Scotland and NI by a fine not exceeding level 5 on the standard scale (i.e. £5,000 under *Criminal Justice Act 1982, s 37*). [*ITEPA 2003, s 684(2)(4A); FA 2019, s 82(3); SI 2003 No 2682, Reg 97X*].

The stated intention is that the requirement will be restricted to cases of serious non-compliance where it is considered that payment of amounts due to HMRC under PAYE is severely at risk. HMRC will accept security only in the form of an electronic payment to a specified HMRC bank account, a cheque or banker's draft or a guarantee in the form of a performance bond authorised and approved by a financial institution. See factsheet SS/FS1 at www.gov.uk/government/publications/securities-in-respect-of-paye-and-national-insurance-contributions.

The requirement does not apply to employers authorised to use the simplified PAYE scheme for personal employees (see **53.15** above), care and support employers (see **53.21** above) or employers in 'time to pay' arrangements. *SI 2003 No 2682, Reg 97P* lists the persons from whom security may be required (which includes, for example, the employer itself and the directors of the employer if it is a company), and provides that liability to give security is joint and several in cases where it is required from more than one person. The HMRC notice that security is required must specify the value of security to be given, the manner in which it is to be given, the date on or before which it is to be given (which cannot be earlier than 30 days after the date of the notice) and the period of time for which it is required. The date by which security is required is delayed if, before the security is due to be provided, the employer makes a request to HMRC to enter into a 'time to pay' arrangement. Once security has been given, there is provision for the person who gave it to apply to HMRC in certain circumstances for a reduction in the value of security that they hold. There is provision for an appeal to be made against a notice requiring security or a refusal of an application to reduce the value of security held; the extent of the Appeal Tribunal's jurisdiction on appeal was set out in *D-Media Communications Limited v HMRC* FTT (TC 5183), [2016] UKFTT 430 (TC), [2017] SFTD 1. [*SI 2003 No 2682, Regs 97M–97W*].

Simon's Taxes. See **E4.11140–E4.11144.**

PAYE returns

[53.21] After the end of each tax year the employer must, in respect of each employee for whom he was required to maintain a deductions working sheet, send the following to HMRC.

(a) Not later than 19 May, *except where the employer is an RTI employer* (see **53.22** below):
  - (i) an End of Year Return P14;
  - (ii) a declaration on form P35 (including a nil return where appropriate).

  [*SI 2003 No 2682, Regs 72H, 73*].

(b) Not later than 6 July, form P11D. Particulars (including, where applicable, amounts) of the following are required for all employees:
  - earnings received otherwise than in money, whether from the employer or a 'related third party';
  - payments made on the employee's behalf (and not repaid), whether by the employer or a 'related third party';
  - non-cash vouchers and credit tokens falling to be treated as earnings (see **28.47**, **28.49** EMPLOYMENT INCOME), whether provided by the employer or a 'related third party';
  - any tax on 'notional payments' of PAYE income which has not been made good by the employee (see **53.14** above);
  - living accommodation provided for the employee or his family (see **28.35** *et seq.* EMPLOYMENT INCOME), whether by the employer or a 'related third party';
  - any removal benefits or removal expenses in excess of the qualifying limit (see **28.72** EMPLOYMENT INCOME); and

- whether any earnings relating to business entertainment will be disallowed in computing the employer's profits (see **75.76** TRADING INCOME, **28.19** EMPLOYMENT INCOME).

Particulars of the following are additionally required for all employees whose employment is subject to the benefits code:

- mileage allowance payments other than approved mileage allowance payments and passenger payments other than approved passenger payments (see **28.91** EMPLOYMENT INCOME);
- sums put at the employee's disposal, whether by the employer or a 'related third party', and paid away by the employee; and
- details (including amounts) of taxable benefits-in-kind provided (see *et seq.* EMPLOYMENT INCOME), whether by the employer or a 'related third party'.

An employment is subject to the benefits code (see **28.21** EMPLOYMENT INCOME) if the earnings from the employment for the tax year are (or would be if there were any) general earnings within the charge to UK tax.

Where employers opt into voluntary payrolling of benefits (see **53.28** below), they do not have to make a return on form P11D for the benefits payrolled.

For the above purposes, a '*related third party*' is any person who makes payments or provides benefits to an employee by arrangement with the employer, which includes the employer's guaranteeing or in any way facilitating the payments etc.

For the use of substitute forms P11D, see Revenue Tax Bulletin August 1996 p 334.

[*SI 2003 No 2682, Regs 85–89; SI 2016 No 747; SI 2016 No 1137, Regs 1, 10; SI 2017 No 1263, Regs 1, 14, 15*].

Supplementary returns (form P38A) must be submitted with form P35 for all employees for whom a deductions working sheet is not required. [*SI 2003 No 2682, Regs 72H, 74*].

HMRC failed in an attempt to charge inaccuracy penalties under *FA 2007, Sch 24* (see **55.6** PENALTIES in respect of an end-of-year PAYE return because the statutory requirement (*SI 2003 No 2682, Reg 73* above) was to submit a return setting out the amounts that had been deducted from employees' earnings and not the amounts that *ought* to have been deducted (*Fab Cleaning Management Ltd v HMRC* FTT (TC 4824), [2016] UKFTT 31 (TC)).

A return by the employer is also required not later than 6 July following the end of the tax year in respect of any employee (or former employee) awarded termination payments and other benefits within *ITEPA 2003, ss 401–416* (see **18.4** COMPENSATION FOR LOSS OF EMPLOYMENT) totalling more than £30,000 in the tax year. [*SI 2003 No 2682, Regs 91–93, 96*].

As regards information to be supplied by employers to employees, see **67.12** SELF-ASSESSMENT.

Value added tax paid, if any (and whether or not recoverable), must be included in amounts of expenses and benefits. (HMRC SP A6). See also **53.55** below.

Returns are also required under 53.29 below (cars provided for private use).

Real Time Information

See 53.22 below.

Mandatory e-filing

The Commissioners for HMRC have wide powers to make regulations requiring the use of electronic communications for the delivery of information required or authorised to be delivered under tax legislation. [*FA 2002, ss 135, 136*]. Following a phased introduction based upon size of employer, all employers were required to file electronically for 2009/10 onwards, subject to the limited exceptions below. Penalties for failure to comply range from £100 to £3,000 depending upon the number of employees required to be included in the returns, the maximum penalty applying where there are 1,000 or more. Appeals may be made against penalty determinations on specified grounds including reasonable excuse throughout the default period.

The following employers are exempted from mandatory e-filing:

- practising members of religious societies or orders whose beliefs are incompatible with electronic communication;
- care and support employers, i.e. individuals employing a person to provide domestic or personal services at or from the employer's home where the recipient of the services, being the employer or a member of his family, is elderly, disabled or infirm; and
- those (if any) to whom a direction has been given by HMRC specifying that they are not required to make returns electronically.

[*SI 2003 No 2682, Regs 190, 191, 205–210D*].

Although in-year PAYE returns can be filed online, HMRC do not insist on electronic filing where the returns cover the part of the tax year ending with the date of an insolvency event (e.g. liquidation, receivership, administration or bankruptcy); no online filing penalty will be charged in these circumstances provided a late filing penalty (see 55.22 PENALTIES) does not fall to be charged (Revenue Tax Bulletin October 2004 p 1158).

See 53.33 below as regards 'PAYE in-year online'.

Simon's Taxes. See **E4.11120–E4.11124.**

Real Time Information (RTI)

[53.22] Under RTI, information about tax and other deductions under the PAYE system is transmitted to HMRC by the employer each time an employee is paid. The information to be transmitted is produced automatically from computerised payroll systems. 'RTI employers' are not required to provide information to HMRC using forms P14 and P35 after the end of the tax year (see 53.21 above), or send form P45 or P46 to HMRC when employees start or leave the employment (see 53.34, 53.34 below). (RTI employers do continue to provide form P45 to departing employees but the form does not need to be submitted to HMRC.)

Real Time Information employers etc.

An '*RTI employer*' is any employer other than certain users of special PAYE schemes, e.g. for examination fees and electoral payments, care and support employers, employers with religious objections to electronic communications and those (if any) to whom a direction has been given by HMRC specifying that they are not required to make returns electronically. See also below under Care and support employers etc. [*SI 2003 No 2682, Reg 2A*]. A '*Real Time Information pension payer*' is defined in similar terms. [*SI 2003 No 2682, Reg 2B*].

Becoming an RTI employer

On becoming an RTI employer, an employer must provide to HMRC the information specified in *SI 2012 No 822, Reg 53*. If on the day the employer becomes an RTI employer, he employs 250 or more people, this information must be provided before he makes any RTI returns. Any other employer may provide the information as part of the first return. Within one month after making his first RTI return, an employer must provide to HMRC the information specified in *SI 2012 No 822, Reg 54*. All information must normally be provided electronically. HMRC may notify an employer that his first RTI return must not be submitted until such date as they notify. If in such a case a further return falls to be made before the notified date, it is also to be submitted on that date. [*SI 2012 No 822, Regs 53–57*].

Real time returns of information (RTI returns)

On or before making a 'relevant payment' to an employee, an RTI employer must normally deliver to HMRC by means of a return (an '*RTI return*') the information specified in *SI 2003 No 2682, Sch A1*. The information required includes specified information about the employer, the employee, payments to the employee, commencement of employment (if the return is the first return for that employee) and cessation of the employment (if the return will be the last return for that employee). The return must be made electronically. If payments are made to more than one employee at the same time, the return must include the specified information in respect of each employee to whom a relevant payment is made at that time. If payments are made to more than one employee at the same time and the employer operates more than one payroll, the employer must make a return for each payroll. [*SI 2003 No 2682, Reg 67B*]. The return is known as a Full Payment Submission (FPS).

A '*relevant payment*' is broadly a payment of PAYE income. See *SI 2003 No 2682, Reg 4*.

There are circumstances where employers will not be able to fulfil the requirement to submit a return on or before making a payment to an employee, for example where someone works for a day or does piecework and the employer cannot know the amount actually due until the shift is completed. In such limited circumstances, employers are allowed to submit the return no later than the end of the seven-day period starting with the day after the day on which payment is made. [*SI 2003 No 2682, Regs 67BA–67BC*].

If, in the case of a notional payment (see **53.14** above), the employer is unable to fulfil the requirement on or before making the relevant payment, the employer must instead deliver the information as soon as reasonably practicable after the payment is made and in any event no later than 14 days after the end of the tax month in which the payment is made. [*SI 2003 No 2682, Reg 67C*].

Care and support employers etc.

In the case of care and support employers and employers with religious objections to electronic communications, the employer must deliver to HMRC by means of a return (an '*RTI return*') the information specified in *SI 2003 No 2682, Sch A1* (see above) in respect of each employee to whom relevant payments are made in a tax month. The return must cover all the relevant payments made to each employee in the tax month. It must be made within 14 days after the end of the tax quarter to which it relates and does not have to be made electronically. Where the Commissioners for HMRC are satisfied that it is not reasonably practicable for an employer outside these categories to make a return electronically, they may direct that such an employer be included within these categories. [*SI 2003 No 2682, Reg 67D*].

Errors in returns

There is provision for notifying HMRC of inaccuracies in a return under *Reg 67B* or *Reg 67D* above where this results in total payments to date and total net tax deducted to date being incorrectly stated as regards any employee. The employer must provide the correct information in the first return made after the discovery of the inaccuracy. If the information has not been corrected before 20 April following the end of the tax year in question, then for 2019/20 and earlier years the employer had to make a special return known as an Earlier Year Update (EYU). For the 2020/21 tax year onwards, the EYU is abolished, and *all* corrections must be made via an FPS (see above). This change was first mooted in www.gov.uk/government/publications/employer-bulletin-april-2019 but its implementation was delayed by one year. [*SI 2003 No 2682, Reg 67E*].

Failure to make returns

Where an employer fails to make an RTI return as required by *Reg 67B* or *Reg 67D* above, he must provide the information in the next RTI return made for the tax year in question. If the information has not been provided before 20 April following the end of that tax year, he must make an EYU (see above) (for 2019/20 and earlier years) or an FPS (for 2020/21 onwards). [*SI 2003 No 2682, Reg 67EA*].

Payment to HMRC

Under RTI, payment to HMRC must still be made monthly or quarterly in accordance with **53.19** above. The due dates for payment remain the same. The only difference is that the amount of tax to be paid over to HMRC is taken from the relevant figures shown in the returns under *Reg 67B* or *Reg 67D* above. The due date for payment to HMRC of any amount the employer was liable to deduct from employees during a tax period remains the same for interest purposes regardless of whether or not the amount was actually included in a return. If, because a return includes a correction for an earlier period (period Y), there is an overpayment for a tax period (period Z), the tax which it represents is treated for interest purposes as having been paid to HMRC on the due date for period Z. [*SI 2003 No 2682, Regs 67G, 69*].

Employers paying electronically via the Bacs payment system have to include a reference in their return under *Reg 67B*. The employers' banks must provide to HMRC information relevant to the creation of that reference. [*SI 2003 No 2682, Reg 67CA*].

If during a tax period (i.e. a tax month or quarter) an employer submits an EYU or FPS under *Reg 67E* above, other than where the error arises because of a retrospective tax provision, the tax payable for the final tax period of the tax year covered by the EYU or FPS is adjusted accordingly. If the adjustment results in an amount due to be paid to HMRC, it is treated as payable for that final tax period. If the adjustment results in a repayment due from HMRC, it is treated as repayable for that final tax period; it can either be repaid or be set off against the amount the employer is liable to pay for the tax period in which the EYU or FPS is made. The tax which it represents is treated as having been paid to HMRC on the due date for that final tax period. [*SI 2003 No 2682, Reg 67H*].

Penalties

See **53.24** below.

Late payment and repayment interest

See **53.23** below.

Simon's Taxes. See **E4.1104, E4.11114–E4.11119.**

Late payment and repayment interest

[53.23] In relation to any PAYE amount which is due and payable for any tax period (i.e. a tax month or quarter), interest is chargeable under the provisions at **43.2** LATE PAYMENT INTEREST AND PENALTIES on any late payment to HMRC. With similar effect, in relation to any PAYE amount which was paid to HMRC, repayment interest is payable by HMRC under the provisions at **62.2** REPAYMENT INTEREST on overpayments to HMRC which are either repaid or reallocated to a later charge. In either case, interest is paid without deduction of tax at source and is not taken into account in computing income for tax purposes. [*ITEPA 2003, s 684(2); FA 2009, ss 101, 102*]. See www.gov.uk/guidance/interest-on-late-payment-of-paye-and-cis-employer-guide.

Penalties

[53.24] See also 55.6, 55.22 PENALTIES and *TMA 1970, ss 98, 98A*.

Late filing penalties

If a person (P) fails during a tax month to make a return on or before the '*filing date*' (i.e. the date by which it is required to be made), P is liable to a penalty (a '*normal penalty*') for that month. However, P is not liable to a normal penalty:

(a) for a tax month as a result of any failure to make a return on or before the filing date which occurs during the 'initial period'; or
(b) for a tax month in any tax year if the month is the first month in that year during which P fails to make a return on or before the filing date (disregarding any failure occurring during the 'initial period').

The '*initial period*' is the period of 30 days beginning with the day in year X on which P is first required to make a return. Year X is the first tax year in which P is required to make returns. The let-out in (b) above does not apply for any tax year for which an employer operates an annual PAYE Scheme.

The amount of a normal penalty depends on the number of employees in the tax period to which the return relates, and is £100 where there are 9 employees or fewer; £200 where there are at least 10 but no more than 49; £300 where there are at least 50 but no more than 249; and £400 where there are 250 or more. P cannot be liable to more than one normal penalty for any one tax month.

In addition to the normal penalty, P is separately liable to one or more penalties ('*penalties for extended failures*') if HMRC so decide. An extended failure occurs if the failure to make a return on time continues after the end of a three-month period beginning with the day after the filing date. HMRC must give notice to P specifying the date from which the penalty, or each penalty, is payable. That date may be earlier than the date on which the notice is given, but cannot be earlier than the end of the three-month period in relation to the extended failure in respect of which the penalty is payable (or, if the penalty is payable in respect of more than one extended failure, the one with the latest filing date).

HMRC may decide that a separate penalty for extended failure should be payable in respect of each unpenalised extended failure in the tax year to date; the amount of any such penalty is 5% of any liability to pay tax which would have been shown in the return in question. Alternatively, they may decide that a single penalty should be payable in respect of all unpenalised extended failures in the tax year to date; the amount of the penalty is 5% of the sum of the liabilities to pay tax which would have been shown in the returns in question.

Interest is chargeable on these penalties if paid late; the charge to interest is under the harmonised regime at **43.2** LATE PAYMENT INTEREST AND PENALTIES.

[*FA 2009, Sch 55 paras 1, 6B–6D, 27; FA 2019, s 88(6); SI 2003 No 2682, Regs 67I–67K*].

For HMRC guidance, see www.gov.uk/what-happens-if-you-dont-report-payroll-information-on-time. For assessment of penalties and appeals against penalties see **55.26** PENALTIES.

HMRC do not charge these late filing penalties for delays of three days or less, except in cases of persistent lateness; this currently applies until 5 April 2020 (see the above-mentioned guidance and www.gov.uk/government/publication s/employer-bulletin-august-2019).

Late payment penalties

The following penalty provisions apply. These penalties are automated and are charged in-year, rather than after the end of the tax year.

A person (P) is liable to a penalty each time that he makes a default in relation to a tax year. He makes a default in relation to a tax year when he fails to fully pay an amount of tax due under the PAYE regulations in relation to that year on or before the date on which it becomes due and payable (see **53.19** above). However, the first failure in relation to a tax year does not count as a default, though the Commissioners for HMRC may in regulations specify circumstances in which this is not to apply.

The amount of the penalty for a default made in relation to a tax year is determined by reference to the amount of the tax comprised in the default and the number of previous defaults that P has made in relation to that same tax year. If the default is P's first, second or third default in relation to the tax year, P is liable, at the time of the default, to a penalty of 1% of the amount of tax comprised in the default. In the case of the fourth, fifth or sixth default, the penalty is 2%. In the case of the seventh, eighth or ninth default, it is 3%. In the case of the tenth or subsequent default, it is 4%. The amount of tax comprised in a default is the amount of tax comprised in the payment which P fails to make. A previous default still counts as a default even if it is remedied before the time of the current default.

If any tax remains unpaid six months after a penalty date (i.e. the day following the due date) in relation to that tax, P is liable to a penalty of 5% of the unpaid amount. If any of that tax is still unpaid after a further six months, P is liable to a further penalty of 5% of the unpaid amount.

Where the payments made to HMRC for a tax period are short of the amount due, but the shortfall is £100 or less, it is assumed for the above purposes only that the full amount has been paid. The £100 tolerance applies to the total amount paid to HMRC, i.e. including national insurance, student loan repayments etc. The tolerance does not apply if the payment relates to a return which is made after 19 April following the tax year and is correcting an earlier return.

[*FA 2009, s 107, Sch 56 paras 1(4), 2A, 5–8; SI 2003 No 2682, Reg 69A*].

The above penalty must be paid within 30 days beginning with the day on which the notice of assessment of the penalty is issued. Interest is chargeable if the penalty is paid late; the charge to interest is under the harmonised regime at **43.2** LATE PAYMENT INTEREST AND PENALTIES. There are provisions for HMRC to reduce the penalty in special circumstances, to suspend the penalty during the currency of a 'Time to Pay' agreement (see **54.12** PAYMENT OF TAX) and to assess the penalty, and for P to appeal against the imposition or amount of the penalty. These provisions are similar to those at **43.4** LATE PAYMENT INTEREST AND

PENALTIES. No penalty is due if P shows he had a reasonable excuse for late payment, and any such failure does not count as a default; an insufficiency of funds is not a reasonable excuse unless attributable to events outside P's control. P is not liable to a penalty in relation to any failure or action in respect of which he has been convicted of a criminal offence. [*FA 2009, Sch 56 paras 9, 9A–17; FA 2019, s 88(6)*].

For HMRC guidance, see www.gov.uk/what-happens-if-you-dont-pay-paye-and-national-insurance-on-time.

In a case in which HMRC did not appear to have considered the possibility of special circumstances, their decision was held to have been flawed; however, the Tribunal held that there were no special circumstances and did not reduce the penalty; the correct test is to determine whether the circumstances were out of the ordinary, something uncommon (*Algarve Granite Ltd v HMRC* FTT (TC 2142), [2012] UKFTT 463 (TC); [2012] SFTD 1354). In *Bluu Solutions Ltd v HMRC* FTT (TC 4300), [2015] UKFTT 95 (TC), the FTT partly disagreed with the decision in *Algarve* by concluding that HMRC can exercise their discretion to reduce a penalty in special circumstances at any point up to the conclusion of an appeal hearing, and are not obliged to do so before assessing the penalty.

PAYE settlement agreements

[53.25] HMRC and an employer used to be able to make a non-statutory agreement, known as an annual voluntary settlement, whereby the employer settled by way of lump sum an amount approximating to the tax otherwise payable by his employees on items covered by the settlement, which would be minor, incidental benefits and expenses payments, e.g. reimbursement of telephone expenses, late night taxis home and benefits shared between a number of employees. The employer was then relieved of including such benefits and expenses in his returns and the employees did not have to declare them or include them in their total income.

A statutory framework for such arrangements, known as PAYE settlement agreements (PSAs), was established by regulations provided for by *ITEPA 2003, ss 703–707* and *F(No 2)A 2017, s 6*. See *SI 2003 No 2682, Regs 105–117; SI 2018 No 267, Regs 1, 7–16*. See HMRC PAYE Settlements Agreements Manual and HMRC Statement of Practice SP 5/96 for the detailed rules governing PSAs and the scope of benefits and payments covered. Separate legislation enables national insurance contributions to be comprised in PSAs.

For 2018/19 onwards, the duration of PSAs is extended by removal of the need for annual renewal. Instead, a PSA now continues to have effect for each subsequent tax year until varied or cancelled by either the employer or HMRC. Further changes for 2018/19 onwards allow PSA applications to be processed electronically once digital processes are introduced.

See www.gov.uk/paye-settlement-agreements/how-to-get-a-psa.

COVID-19 special measure

Expenses and benefits related to COVID-19 (coronavirus) can be reported on a PSA (www.gov.uk/guidance/check-which-expenses-are-taxable-if-your-employee-works-from-home-due-to-coronavirus-covid-19).

Simon's Taxes. See **E4.11110.**

Annual payments

[53.26] Tax on certain periodic redundancy and other similar payments by a former employer which are strictly chargeable to tax as annual payments, and payable under deduction of basic rate tax, may, where it is convenient and with the agreement of the parties and the inspector, be dealt with instead under PAYE (Revenue Tax Bulletin February 1995 p 196).

Annuities

[53.27] Pensions and annuities from registered pension schemes are within PAYE. Annuities under an occupational pension scheme that is not a registered pension scheme are also within PAYE (see **56.2**(e) PENSION INCOME). [*ITEPA 2003, ss 590–592, 594, 683(3); FA 2004, Sch 36 para 43*].

Benefits-in-kind

[53.28] Benefits-in-kind constitute PAYE income (see **53.2** above) but are not payments and are not, therefore, directly subject to PAYE deductions (but see below under Voluntary payrolling). They are usually dealt with by set-off against allowances in arriving at an employee's PAYE code (see **53.13** above and *R v Walton Commrs (ex p Wilson)* CA, [1983] STC 464). However, see **53.3**(a)–(h) above for items not normally regarded as payments but brought within the scope of PAYE deductions.

Voluntary payrolling

The PAYE regulations were amended under powers conferred by *FA 2015, s 17* (and extended by *FA 2016, s 15*) to provide for voluntary payrolling of benefits-in-kind. Where authorised to do so by HMRC, employers are able to opt to payroll benefits such as cars, car fuel, medical insurance and gym membership (but not living accommodation or cheap loans). For 2017/18 onwards, non-cash vouchers and credit tokens are added to the list of benefits that may be payrolled. Where employers payroll benefits, they do not have to make a return on form P11D (see **53.21** above) for these benefits. Instead, they report the value of the benefits through Real Time Information (see **53.22** above), and the value counts as PAYE income liable to PAYE deductions. The employer can choose which benefits to include.

The amount chargeable to tax in respect of the benefit is computed under the rules in **28** EMPLOYMENT INCOME and is then divided by the number of PAYE payments to be made to the employee in the tax year. The resulting amount is the amount of the benefit on which PAYE must be operated. The employer must add that amount to each payment when made. There is provision for in-year adjustment, for example on a change to the benefit provided. Where an employer requires an employee to make good within the tax year any amount of a benefit, the employer can take that into account when calculating the taxable benefit subject to PAYE deductions, but any failure to make good must also be accounted for; in the case of car and van fuel, and credit tokens for 2017/18 onwards, the deadline for making good is extended to 1 June following the tax year. Before 1 June following a tax year, an employer must provide a statement to each affected employee detailing the benefits that were payrolled in the tax year and the amounts treated as PAYE income. [*SI 2003 No 2682, Regs 61A–61M; SI 2016 No 1137, Regs 1–9; SI 2017 No 1263, Regs 1–13*].

For official guidance on voluntary payrolling, including the registration and deregistration process referred to below, see www.gov.uk/guidance/payrolling-tax-employees-benefits-and-expenses-through-your-payroll.

Registration

Employers wishing to payroll benefits for the first time have to register online with HMRC before the start of the tax year for which they wish to begin. Registration then continues unless the employer chooses to stop payrolling those benefits, in which case he must deregister online before the start of the tax year for which it is to have effect; it is not possible for a continuing business to cease payrolling benefits during a tax year.

Cars provided for private use

[53.29] See **28.24** EMPLOYMENT INCOME for computation of the charge. A return on form P46 (Car) is required no later than 28 days after a tax quarter (see **53.19** above) if, during that quarter, a company car on which a benefits charge will arise is newly provided to an employee or ceases to be provided to an employee (without being replaced), or an employee to whom a car is provided becomes a P11D employee (see **53.21**(b) above). The form asks for specified particulars required to compute the benefits charge. A return is not required if the car benefit is voluntarily payrolled as in **53.28** above, but see below. [*SI 2003 No 2682, Reg 90; SI 2017 No 1263, Regs 1, 16*].

For 2018/19 onwards, where the benefit of a company car is payrolled as in **53.28** above, the employer must include specified details of the car in the first Real Time Information (RTI) return (see **53.22** above) in which the benefit is payrolled. If the car ceases to be available, or if fuel has been provided for the car and ceases to be provided, this must be reported in the next RTI return following the cessation. Any inaccuracies in information provided must be corrected in the RTI return next made after the employer becomes aware of the inaccuracy. [*SI 2003 No 2682, Sch A1 para 22B; SI 2017 No 1263, Regs 1, 17*].

Charitable donations

[53.30] Such donations are an allowable deduction for PAYE purposes where made under an approved payroll giving scheme. See **14.18** CHARITIES AND CHARITABLE GIVING.

Collection of tax debts via PAYE

[53.31] HMRC have the power to collect tax debts through the PAYE system, thus allowing their debtors to spread their payments. HMRC's general aim is to secure immediate payment of debts in full or, where this is not possible, to set up a 'Time to Pay' agreement (see **54.12** PAYMENT OF TAX). If neither of these options is feasible, and subject to the monetary limits below, they will consider collecting debts through PAYE, i.e. by coding adjustment, as one of a number of remedies available to them as a creditor. If the debtor does not want to pay in this way, HMRC will expect him to make other arrangements for payment. If no such arrangements were forthcoming, HMRC will be able to collect debts in this way at their own option. For interest purposes, the debt will be deemed to have been paid on the first day of the tax year for which the adjustment to the PAYE coding is made.

For employees whose expected amount of PAYE income in the tax year for which the code is determined is less than £30,000, no more than £3,000 can be collected in this way in any tax year without the taxpayer's consent. The limit is increased in accordance with the following table for employees whose expected amount of PAYE income in that tax year is £30,000 or more. There is, however, an overriding limit in that the amount of tax to be deducted from a payment of PAYE income cannot exceed 50% of the amount of the payment.

Expected amount of PAYE income	*Maximum recoverable debt*
Less than £30,000	£3,000
£30,000 or more but less than £40,000	£5,000
£40,000 or more but less than £50,000	£7,000
£50,000 or more but less than £60,000	£9,000
£60,000 or more but less than £70,000	£11,000
£70,000 or more but less than £80,000	£13,000
£80,000 or more but less than £90,000	£15,000
£90,000 or more	£17,000

The right to object to collecting underpayments of income tax and capital gains tax under self-assessment where the due date has not already passed is not disturbed, and neither is the taxpayer's right to appeal against his tax code.

[*ITEPA 2003, s 684(2)(3A)(3B)(7AA)(7AB); SI 2003 No 2682, Regs 2, 14A, 14D, 23(5), 28(5)*].

It should be noted that the above increased limits do not affect the coding out of self-assessment balancing payments, for which the limit is £3,000 regardless of income (see **67.4** SELF-ASSESSMENT). See also www.gov.uk/government/uploads/system/uploads/attachment_data/file/336817/coding-out-tiin.pdf.

Director's remuneration

[53.32] Credit of remuneration voted to a director to an account with the company constitutes 'payment' for PAYE purposes. See generally ICAEW Technical Release TAX 11/93, 9 July 1993, as regards tax implications of payments to directors. [*ITEPA 2003, s 686(1)*]. See also **28.9** EMPLOYMENT INCOME.

Employee arriving

[53.33] A new employee should produce a form P45 and the employer should start a Deductions Working Sheet from the particulars on that form and send Part 3 to the tax office. Other than where RTI applies (see **53.22** above), if a form P45 (or other code authorisation) is not produced, the employer should complete form P46, ask the employee to sign the appropriate certificate, and send to the tax office on making the first payment exceeding the lower earnings limit for Class 1 NIC purposes. A Deductions Working Sheet must be prepared and tax deducted in accordance with the emergency code or 0T code as appropriate. Under RTI, a new employee must also provide information to enable the employer to complete the new employee fields in the first Full Payment Submission (FPS) which covers that employee; the employer must verify the information. If the FPS is sent to HMRC without the new employee fields being completed, the employer must deduct tax in accordance with the the emergency code or 0T code. [*SI 2003 No 2682, Regs 40, 40A, 41–45, 45A, 46–49, 49A–49E, 50, 50A, 51–53*].

Forms P45 and P46 must be submitted to HMRC online (known as 'PAYE in-year online'). Penalties for failure to comply range from £100 to £3,000 depending upon the number of items in each quarter of the tax year to which the failure relates, the maximum penalty applying where the number is 1,000 or more. Appeals may be made against penalty determinations on specified grounds including reasonable excuse throughout the default period. The following employers are exempted from mandatory PAYE in-year online:

- practising members of religious societies or orders whose beliefs are incompatible with electronic communication;
- care and support employers, i.e. individuals employing a person to provide domestic or personal services at or from the employer's home where the recipient of the services, being the employer or a member of his family, is elderly, disabled or infirm; and
- those (if any) to whom a direction has been given by HMRC specifying that they are not required to make returns electronically.

[*SI 2003 No 2682, Regs 205–207, 210, 210B, 210BA, 210C*].

See also **53.22** above (Real Time Information).

Employee leaving

[53.34] Employee leaving must be given certificate (form P45) by former employer showing code, pay and tax deducted to date of leaving (split if more than one employment). Under RTI (see **53.22** above), an employer need not provide form P45 to HMRC, but must instead include the information in a Full Payment Submission). The employer must still give a form P45 to the employee. [*SI 2003 No 2682, Reg 36*].

Payments to employees who have left and which are not included in P45 must have tax deducted using the 0T code, which deducts tax at the basic, higher and additional rates without giving allowances. [*SI 2003 No 2682, Reg 37*].

Employee retiring

At retirement on pension of an employee, no P45 need be completed and tax must be deducted from the pension on a non-cumulative basis. The employer/pension payer must then complete a 'retirement statement' (P46(Pen)) containing specified details and send it to HMRC with a copy to the pensioner. [*SI 2003 No 2682, Regs 36(2A)(3), 55*].

Form P46(Pen) must be submitted to HMRC online (known as 'PAYE in-year online' — see **53.33** above as regards penalties and exemptions).

Employee dying

On the death of an employee, except where RTI applies (see **53.22** above), the employer must send all parts of completed form P45 to HMRC. [*SI 2003 No 2682, Regs 38, 39*].

Real Time Information

See **53.22** above.

Employment and support allowance

[53.35] Contributory employment and support allowance (see **73.1** SOCIAL SECURITY AND NATIONAL INSURANCE) is within PAYE. The Department for Work and Pensions (or in NI, the Department for Social Development) maintain a record of the claimant's cumulative pay and tax in the tax year and of any payments of taxable allowance made to him. At the end of the claimant's period of claim (or at the end of the tax year, if earlier) the Department calculate his tax position, make any repayments of tax due to him and notify the details to him and to HMRC. [*SI 2003 No 2682, Regs 184A–184S; SI 2017 No 414, Regs 1, 5*].

Exemption from PAYE

[53.36] Where a new employee has no other employment and rate of payment is less than a weekly or monthly rate equal to $^1/_{52}$nd or $^1/_{12}$th respectively of the personal allowance (the 'PAYE threshold'), no tax is deductible. [*SI 2003 No 2682, Reg 9*].

Expense payments etc.

[53.37] Such payments must (except as regards pure reimbursement to subordinate employees of specific outlay incurred) be included with pay and taxed with it.

Free of tax payments, awards etc.

[53.38] For remuneration payable free of tax, taxed incentive awards etc., see 28.77 EMPLOYMENT INCOME.

Holiday pay funds

[53.39] Holiday pay paid by a holiday pay fund is taxed at the basic rate at the time of payment. [*SI 2003 No 2682, Regs 134, 136*].

Incapacity benefit

[53.40] Such benefit, where taxable (see **73.1** SOCIAL SECURITY AND NATIONAL INSURANCE), is brought within PAYE by *SI 2003 No 2682, Regs 173–180.*

Jobseekers allowance

[53.41] Jobseekers allowance (so far as taxable, see **73.1** SOCIAL SECURITY AND NATIONAL INSURANCE) is brought within PAYE by *SI 2003 No 2682, Regs 148–172*. The Department for Work and Pensions (or in NI, the Department for Social Development) maintain a record of the claimant's previous cumulative pay and tax in the tax year and of any taxable benefit paid to him. At the end of the claimant's period of benefit claim (or at the end of the tax year, if earlier) the Department calculate his tax position, make any repayments of tax due to him and notify the details to him and to his tax office. See also **53.52** below.

Local councillors' attendance allowances

[53.42] The councillor may opt for deduction of basic rate tax from such allowances (net of an appropriate amount in respect of allowable expenditure) rather than deduction by reference to the appropriate code. [*SI 2003 No 2682, Regs 118–121*].

Overseas matters

[53.43] The following applies where a non-UK resident employee, or an employee who is UK resident but meets the *section 26A* test in **28.7** EMPLOYMENT INCOME, works (or is likely to work) both inside and out of the UK in a tax year. It also applies if it appears to HMRC that a tax year is likely to be a split year as regards an employee who works (or is likely to work) both inside and out of the UK in that year.

If it appears to HMRC that some of the income paid to the employee is PAYE income and some may not be, HMRC may, on application by the employer or a person designated by the employer, by notice give a direction (a '*Section 690 direction*') that only a proportion of any payment made in the year is to be dealt with under PAYE. If no direction is made, the whole of any payment must be so dealt with. The direction may similarly be withdrawn (with at least 30 days' notice) by a further notice. These provisions apply only to payments made by the employer and to payments by a person acting on the employer's behalf and at the expense of the employer or a person connected with him (within **19** CONNECTED PERSONS). They are without prejudice to any income assessment on the employee and to any rights to repayment, or obligations to repay, income tax over- or underpaid. The provisions enable direction to be given, where both these provisions and those of *ITEPA 2003, s 689* or *s 689A* apply, on application made by whoever is the 'relevant person' for the purposes of *s 689* or, as the case may be, *s 689A*. For *s 689* and *s 689A*, see, respectively, **53.8** above (non-UK employer) and **53.9** above (oil and gas workers on the continental shelf).

In a case where the employee is UK resident for a tax year but not domiciled in the UK in that tax year, HMRC may for the above purposes treat the employee as being within **61.2**(1) REMITTANCE BASIS even if no claim for remittance basis has been made, thus allowing the *section 690* directions procedure to remain available in such cases.

[*ITEPA 2003, ss 690, 718*].

For special PAYE arrangements for short-term business visitors see **53.49** below.

See *SI 2003 No 2682, Reg 57* as regards pensions.

A non-UK resident employer must operate PAYE in respect of any taxable earnings of his employees if he has a tax presence in the UK (*Clark v Oceanic Contractors Incorporated* HL 1982, 56 TC 183; *Fryett v HMRC* FTT (TC 3360), [2014] UKFTT 220 (TC), [2014] SFTD 979). See also *Bootle v Bye; Wilson v Bye* (Sp C 61), [1996] SSCD 58, *Telfer v Sakellarios* QB 2013, [2013] All ER (D) 175 (Jun) and HMRC PAYE Manual PAYE81610. See also **53.7** above (payments by intermediaries) and **53.8** above (non-UK employer).

See **Simon's Taxes E4.1182**.

PAYE threshold

[53.44] See 53.36 above.

Pension contributions (the 'net pay arrangement')

[53.45] Employees' allowable pension contributions deducted from salary (see *SI 2003 No 2682, Reg 3*) are also allowable for the purposes of computing PAYE deductions (though not for the purposes of computing national insurance contributions).

Reconciliations (P800 Tax Calculations)

[53.46] Each year HMRC undertakes an end-of-year reconciliation whereby the tax correctly deducted under PAYE for each individual is compared with the actual income tax liability for the year. If this shows an overpayment or underpayment, a P800 Tax Calculation is sent to the individual. Any overpayment is then repaid, and any underpayment is collected from the taxpayer subject to a tolerance level for relatively small amounts (up to £50 per annum). Underpayments may be collected via PAYE. There is no right of appeal against a P800: the correct remedy is an appeal against the coding notice which gives effect to the calculation (*Michael Prince and others v HMRC* FTT (TC 1852), [2012] SFTD 786).

Records

[53.47] Wages sheets, deductions working sheets, certificates, documents relating to P11D information, and other records required to be maintained under the PAYE regulations (and not required to be sent to HMRC), must be kept and preserved by the employer for at least three years after the end of the year to which they relate. [*SI 2003 No 2682, Reg 97*].

Seamen

[53.48] Seamen are subject to standard PAYE procedures on wages from employment. Travelling expenses and subsistence allowances paid to seafarers making regular journeys to the same UK port are subject to PAYE. (Hansard 26 February 1981 Vol 999 Col 442).

Short-term business visitors

[53.49] The following special PAYE arrangements for short-term business visitors (STBV) are available.

STBV Appendix 8

A new special PAYE arrangement for short-term business visitors was introduced with effect on and after 6 April 2020. The arrangement is known as 'Appendix 8' and replaced a previous arrangement. These arrangements are made under *SI 2003 No 2682, Reg 141*, which allows HMRC to arrange for the collection of tax in respect of PAYE income if the normal operation of PAYE is considered impracticable. Each arrangement is a contractual agreement between the employer and HMRC.

Appendix 8 is aimed at UK-based employers who operate internationally. They may have non-UK resident employees who will work in the UK for a short period of time. To ease the employer burden in monitoring employee movements and keeping all records required to report PAYE information in real time, the arrangement allows the employer to return the information, and pay any tax due, no later than 31 May following the tax year. The arrangement can be used only for STBVs whose UK workdays in the tax year amount to 60 days or less, disregarding any days on which only incidental duties are performed (determined as under *ITEPA 2003, s 39* — see **28.3**(ii) EMPLOYMENT INCOME). For full details of Appendix 8 from 6 April 2020, see HMRC PAYE Manual PAYE81950.

The previous arrangement was similar, but the UK workday limit was 30 days rather than 60 and the return had to be delivered by 19 April, and the tax paid by 22 April, following the tax year. However, due to the 2020 COVID-19 (coronavirus) pandemic, HMRC extended the deadline for 2019/20 returns and payment to 31 July 2020 (HMRC Employer Bulletin Issue 84, June 2020, page 8). For details of the previous arrangement, see HMRC PAYE Manual PAYE81949. Employers who were within this arrangement for 2019/20 were given a deadline of 13 July 2020 to notify HMRC of their decision to either use the new Appendix 8 arrangement or cease operating under STBV special arrangements (HMRC Employer Bulletin Issue 84 as above).

EP Appendix 4

For a further arrangement known as 'EP Appendix 4' see HMRC PAYE manual PAYE82000. This applies only where the following conditions are met with regard to an individual (A):

- A is not UK resident under the UK domestic legislation (which means that A is also non-UK resident for the purposes of the relevant double tax agreement);
- A is resident in a country with which the UK has a double tax agreement with an Article that exempts earnings, and that Article is likely to apply;
- A either:
  - is legally employed by a foreign employer (which is not the overseas branch of a UK employer); or
  - has a UK legal employer and A is economically employed by a separate non-resident entity (i.e. not by a foreign branch of the UK employer); and
- A is expected to be in the UK for 183 days or less in any twelve-month period.

Where the Appendix 4 conditions are met, that arrangement should be used in priority to Appendix 8 above.

[*SI 2003 No 2682, Reg 141; SI 2020 No 88*].

See **Simon's Taxes E4.1330, E4.1330A.**

Statutory pay

[53.50] Statutory adoption pay, statutory maternity pay, statutory paternity pay, statutory sick pay, statutory shared parental pay and statutory parental bereavement pay constitute taxable social security income. [*ITEPA 2003, ss 658, 660; Parental Bereavement (Leave and Pay) Act 2018, Sch para 47; SI 2020 No 45, Reg 2*].

Tax equalised employees

[53.51] There are modified PAYE procedures (the 'Appendix 6 arrangement') for tax equalised employees, i.e. employees who come from abroad to work in the UK and are guaranteed a specified level of earnings after tax. The procedures are set out in HMRC PAYE Manual PAYE82002.

See **Simon's Taxes E4.1190.**

Tax refunds arising during unemployment

[53.52] Such refunds are made directly by HMRC, but refunds are withheld from the unemployed who claim jobseeker's allowance and from strikers until the end of the strike. [*ITEPA 2003, s 708*; *SI 2003 No 2682, Regs 64, 65*].

Termination payments

[53.53] For the reporting requirements in relation to taxable termination payments, see **53.21** above.

Tips, organised arrangements for sharing

[53.54] Gratuities and service charge shares under such arrangements (sometimes known as a 'tronc') are within PAYE and the 'tronc-master' (i.e. the person running the arrangements, being a person other than the employer) is regarded as responsible for the tax deductions. The employer, on becoming aware of their existence, must notify HMRC and give the name of the person running them, if known. [*ITEPA 2003, s 692; SI 2003 No 2682, Reg 100*]. For a case in which informal arrangements, under which directors of the employing company collected gratuities and divided them between themselves and the employees, were held not to constitute organised arrangements, see *Figael Ltd v Fox* CA 1991, 64 TC 441.

The above rules apply where the troncmaster acts independently of the employer. If the employer himself acts as troncmaster, or appoints an employee to make distributions in accordance with the employer's own formula or is otherwise involved in the distribution of monies from the tronc, payments made under the arrangements must be dealt with through the employer's own PAYE system. (Revenue Tax Bulletin February 2004 p 1081).

See generally HMRC helpsheet E24 'Tips, Gratuities, Service Charges and Troncs' (available at www.gov.uk/government/publications/e24-tips-gratuities-service-charges-and-troncs) and HMRC PAYE Manual PAYE20160, 20161.

See **Simon's Taxes E4.1112.**

Value added tax

[53.55] Earnings paid to a person holding an office in the course of carrying on a trade, profession or vocation and subject to VAT on services supplied by him should exclude the VAT element for PAYE purposes (HMRC SP A6). See also **53.21** above.

54

Payment of Tax

Cross-references. See **43** LATE PAYMENT INTEREST AND PENALTIES; **53** PAY AS YOU EARN and **62** REPAYMENT INTEREST.

Simon's Taxes. See **A4.6, E1.250–E1.258.**

Introduction and due dates for payment of tax

[54.1] A final payment is due for a tax year if a person's combined income tax and capital gains tax liabilities contained in his self-assessment (see **64.3** RETURNS) exceed the aggregate of any payments on account (whether under *TMA 1970, s 59A* at **67.5** SELF-ASSESSMENT or otherwise) and any income tax deducted at source. If the second total exceeds the first, a repayment will be made. Tax deducted at source has the same meaning as in **67.5**(b) SELF-ASSESSMENT.

Subject to the further provisions referred to below, the normal due date for payment (or repayment) is 31 January following the tax year. Where, however, the person gave notice of chargeability under *TMA 1970, s 7* (see **55.2** PENALTIES) within six months after the end of the tax year, but was not given notice under *TMA 1970, s 8* or *s 8A* (see **64.2** RETURNS) until after 31 October following the tax year, the due date is the last day of the three months beginning with the date of the said notice.

[*TMA 1970, s 59B(1)–(4)(7)(8)*].

See **67.8** SELF-ASSESSMENT for deferral of the due date for payment (or repayment) of an amount of tax as a result of an amendment or correction to a self-assessment or a consequential amendment arising from an amendment or correction to a partnership return or partnership statement (see **64.12** RETURNS).

Where an officer of HMRC enquires into a return (see **64.6** RETURNS) and a repayment is otherwise due, the repayment is not required to be made until the enquiry is fully completed (see **64.8** RETURNS), although the officer may make a provisional repayment at his discretion. [*TMA 1970, s 59B(4A); F(No 2)A 2017, Sch 15 paras 20, 44*]. Tax repayments arising from a partial closure notice (see **64.8**) will not automatically be repaid, e.g. where tax is due in respect of other issues not covered by the partial closure notice (www.gov.uk/government/publications/tax-enquiries-closure-rules).

Simple assessments

In general, the due date for payment of the tax charged by a 'simple assessment' (see **6.5** ASSESSMENTS), net of any payments on account and income tax deducted at source, is 31 January following the tax year to which the assessment relates. However, where a person is given notice of the simple assessment after 31 October following the tax year to which it relates, the due date is deferred until the last day of the period of three months following the day on which the notice was given. [*TMA 1970, s 59BA; FA 2016, s 167, Sch 23 para 8*].

Other assessments

Subject to the appeal and postponement provisions in **5.3** APPEALS and **54.5** below, the due date for payment of tax charged by assessment *otherwise* than by self-assessment or simple assessment is 30 days after the date on which the notice of assessment is made. An example of such an assessment would be a discovery assessment under *TMA 1970, s 29* (see **6.6** ASSESSMENTS).

[*TMA 1970, s 59B(6); FA 2016, s 167, Sch 23 para 7*].

Recovery of debts from taxpayer bank accounts etc.

HMRC may now recover tax and tax credit debts of £1,000 or more directly from taxpayer bank and building society accounts. See **54.8–54.11** below.

Effective dates of payment of tax

[54.2] HMRC take the date of payment in respect of each of the following payment methods to be as follows.

(1) *Cheques, cash, and postal orders* handed in at the HMRC office or received by post — the day of receipt by HMRC *unless* received by post following a day on which the office was closed for whatever reason, in which case it is the day on which the office was first closed.

(2) *Electronic funds transfer* — payment by BACS (transfer over two days) or CHAPS (same day transfer) — one day prior to receipt by HMRC (not applicable to payments by employers under PAY AS YOU EARN (**53**) and by contractors under the CONSTRUCTION INDUSTRY SCHEME (**20**)).

(3) *Bank giro or Girobank* — the date on which payment was made at the bank or post office.

(Revenue 'Working Together' Bulletin July 2000 p 3).

HMRC are able to accept payments made using the Faster Payments Service, thus enabling electronic payments, typically via online or telephone banking, to reach them on the day of payment or the next day.

For the purposes of *TMA 1970* and *FA 2009, s 102* (see **62.2** REPAYMENT INTEREST), where any payment to an officer of HMRC or the Commissioners for HMRC is received by cheque and the cheque is paid on its first presentation to the bank on which it is drawn, the payment is treated as made on the date of receipt of the cheque by the officer or the Commissioners. However, this is subject to any regulations that HMRC may make under *FA 2007, s 95* to the effect that, either generally or in particular circumstances, payment be treated as made only when the cheque clears. [*TMA 1970, s 70A*].

Mandatory electronic payment of tax

[54.3] The Commissioners for HMRC have power to make regulations requiring a person to use electronic means in making specified payments under legislation relating to any tax or duty for which they are responsible. Regulations under *FA 2007, s 95* (see **54.2** above) may, in particular, provide for a payment which is made by cheque in contravention of a requirement to pay electronically to be treated as made only when the cheque clears. [*FA 2003, ss 204, 205*]. See, for example, **53.19** PAY AS YOU EARN as regards mandatory electronic payment for 'large employers'.

Tax paid by credit/debit card

[54.4] HMRC accept certain types of payment by credit card and may make regulations for passing on the associated transaction fees to the taxpayer. Before 1 November 2020, the fees applied to the amount of the payment range from 0.374% to 0.606% for various types of personal credit card (but see below for the position from 13 January 2018) and from 1.7% to 2.8% for business credit cards. The legislation allows HMRC to make similar regulations for other methods of payment, but only where they expect to be charged a fee in connection with payments using that method.

On and after 1 November 2020, fees are extended to the use of business debit cards. For both business credit cards and business debit cards, the fee will no longer be a fixed percentage and will instead be determined according to a formula contained in *SI 2020 No 657, Reg 3*.

[*FA 2008, s 136; SI 2016 No 333 (revoked); SI 2017 No 1262 (revoked); SI 2020 No 657*].

Personal debit cards may also be used in payment, with no transaction fees attached (either before or on or after 1 November 2020).

On and after 13 January 2018, due to an EU Directive, HMRC no longer accept payments made by *personal credit card*. They continue to accept business credit cards, personal debit cards and business debit cards. (Agent update: Issue 62 at www.gov.uk/government/publications/agent-update-issue-62 at page 10).

Payment and postponement of tax pending appeal

[54.5] The provisions described below apply in the case of appeals against:

(i) a conclusion stated or amendment made by a final or partial closure notice on completion or part completion of an enquiry (see **64.8** RETURNS);
(ii) an HMRC amendment to a self-assessment during an enquiry to prevent potential loss of tax (see **64.9** RETURNS); and
(iii) an assessment other than a self-assessment.

In the absence of any application for postponement of tax as below, tax is due and payable as if there had been no appeal.

If the taxpayer has grounds for believing that he is overcharged to tax by the amendment or assessment or as a result of the conclusion stated, as the case may be, he (or his agent) may, by notice in writing stating those grounds, apply to HMRC within 30 days after the 'relevant date' for postponement of a specified amount of tax pending determination of the appeal. In the event that the matter cannot be agreed, the taxpayer may refer the application to the Appeal Tribunal within 30 days after the date of the document notifying HMRC's decision. The '*relevant date*' is the date of issue of the notice of amendment or assessment or, in the case of an appeal within (i) above, the date of issue of the closure notice. A postponement application to the Tribunal is heard in the same way as an appeal. By virtue of *TMA 1970, s 55(6A)*, the Tribunal's decision on the amount to be postponed is final and conclusive and cannot therefore be further appealed; however, a Tribunal has held that *s 55(6A)* is unlawful (*Dong v National Crime Agency (No 2)* FTT (TC 3502), [2014] UKFTT 369 (TC)).

If the taxpayer and HMRC come to an agreement as to the amount of tax (if any) to be postponed, it is not effective unless it is in writing. An agreement not in writing is nevertheless treated as such provided that its existence and terms are confirmed in writing by notice given by either party to the other. (In *Sparrow Ltd v Inspector* (Sp C 289), [2001] SSCD 206, an obvious error by the Inland Revenue, notifying a full rather than the nil postponement previously notified, was held not to constitute such an agreement.)

The amount of tax to be postponed pending determination of the appeal is the amount (if any) in which it appears that there are reasonable grounds for believing that the appellant is overcharged to tax. For a case in which no such 'reasonable grounds' were found, see *Sparrow Ltd* (above).

On the determination of (or agreement as to) the amount of tax to be postponed, the balance of tax *not postponed* (if any) becomes due and payable as if it had been charged by an amendment or assessment issued on the date of that determination or agreement (or on the date of notice of confirmation of the latter) and in respect of which there had been no appeal.

Application for postponement may be made outside the normal 30-day time limit if the appeal was itself made late or if there is a change in the circumstances of the case giving grounds for belief that the appellant is overcharged. In HMRC's view, this requires a change in the circumstances in which the original decision not to apply for postponement was made, not just a change of mind, e.g. further accounts work indicating a substantially excessive assessment, or further reliefs becoming due (see CCAB Statement TR 477, 22 June 1982). A late application does not defer the due date of any balance of tax not postponed.

If, after the determination of an amount of tax to be postponed and as a result of a change in the circumstances of the case, either party has grounds for believing that the amount postponed has become either excessive or insufficient, then unless the parties can agree the matter themselves, the said party may, at any time before the determination of the substantive appeal, apply to the Tribunal for a revised determination of the amount to be postponed. If, on a consequent revised determination, an amount of tax ceases to be postponed, that amount is treated as charged by an assessment issued on the date of the revised determination and in respect of which there had been no appeal. If, on the other hand, an amount of tax has been overpaid, it is repaid.

Tax which is subject to an accelerated payment notice cannot be postponed. Tax which is postponed and subsequently becomes subject to such a notice becomes due and payable. See **4.51** ANTI-AVOIDANCE.

[*TMA 1970, s 55*].

As regards the charging of interest on tax paid late, see **43.2**, **43.3** LATE PAYMENT INTEREST AND PENALTIES.

Payment of tax on determination of appeal

[54.6] Tax payable in accordance with the determination of an appeal within **54.5**(i)–(iii) above, being either postponed or additional tax, becomes due and payable as if it were charged by an amendment or assessment issued on the date on which HMRC issued to the taxpayer a notice of the total amount payable in accordance with the determination, and in respect of which no appeal was made. Any tax found to be overpaid becomes repayable. [*TMA 1970, s 55(9)*].

Collection of tax etc.

[54.7] HMRC's previous power of distraint in *TMA 1970, s 61* has been replaced in England and Wales by the procedure in *Tribunals, Courts and Enforcement Act 2007, Pt 3* (enforcement by taking control of goods), but applies still in NI. [*FA 2008, ss 127, 129, Sch 43 Pt 1*]. See also *Herbert Berry Associates Ltd v CIR* HL 1977, 52 TC 113. See *TMA 1970, s 64* and *FA 2008, s 128* as regards Scotland.

Where an amount of income tax due is less than £2,000, HMRC may within one year after the due date take summary magistrates' court proceedings. They may also recover tax by proceedings in the county court. [*TMA 1970, ss 65,*

66]. For limitations in Scotland and NI, see *TMA 1970, ss 65(4), 66(3)(4), 67*, and for time limits for proceedings see *Mann v Cleaver* KB 1930, 15 TC 367 and *Lord Advocate v Butt* CS 1992, 64 TC 471.

Unpaid tax (and arrears) may also be recovered (with full costs) as a Crown debt in the High Court. [*TMA 1970, s 68*]. The amount of an assessment which has become final cannot be re-opened in proceedings to collect the tax (*Pearlberg* CA 1953, 34 TC 57; *CIR v Soul* CA 1976, 51 TC 86), and it is not open to the taxpayer to raise the defence that HMRC acted *ultra vires* in raising the assessment (*CIR v Aken* CA 1990, 63 TC 395).

FA 2008 gives HMRC formal power to set off an amount owed to a taxpayer against an amount due from that taxpayer. This cannot be used to set off an amount becoming due by HMRC after the taxpayer's insolvency against an amount due by the taxpayer before insolvency. Before 15 September 2016, this power did not apply in Scotland but it is now extended to the whole of the UK. [*FA 2008, ss 130, 131; FA 2016, s 178*].

As regards allocation of payments made to different liabilities, the Tribunal in *AJM Mansell Ltd v HMRC* FTT (TC 2279), [2012] UKFTT 602 (TC) noted the principle, derived from 19th century common law, that where a debtor makes a payment to a creditor the debtor may appropriate the money as they please; however, if the debtor does not make any appropriation, the right of allocation devolves on the creditor. Thus, HMRC can allocate the payments made as they see fit, although their public law duties preclude their making an unreasonable allocation (*Kritikos v HMRC* FTT (TC 7452), [2019] UKFTT 677 (TC)).

Where the right to receive a tax repayment is transferred from one person ('the original creditor') to another ('the new creditor'), the new creditor cannot receive any more from HMRC than if the original creditor had made the repayment claim. Any tax liability of the original creditor that would have been set against the repayment if the original creditor had made the claim will be set against any repayment made to the new creditor. [*FA 2008, s 133*].

For whether unpaid tax is a business liability for commercial etc. purposes, see *Conway v Wingate* CA 1952, 31 ATC 148; *Stevens v Britten* CA 1954, 33 ATC 399; *R v Vaccari* CCA 1958, 37 ATC 104; *In re Hollebone's Agreement* CA 1959, 38 ATC 142.

Direct recovery of unpaid tax from taxpayer accounts

[54.8] HMRC have the power in England, Wales and NI to enforce debts by direct recovery from the debtor's bank or building society accounts (which may include an Individual Savings Account). The power can be used only to recover debts of more than £1,000, and HMRC can recover only so much as to leave a minimum of £5,000 in total in a debtor's accounts after the recovery.

HMRC may issue a hold notice (see **54.10** below) to 'deposit-takers' effectively freezing the funds needed to pay the debt and giving the taxpayer and certain other interested parties an opportunity to object to HMRC against the issuing of the notice. If HMRC dismiss any objections there is a right of appeal to the county court. If there is no objection or appeal or if these are unsuccessful, HMRC may issue a deduction notice (see **54.11** below) requiring the deposit-taker to deduct specified amounts from the taxpayer's accounts and pay them over to HMRC. Before issuing a hold notice HMRC may issue an information notice (see **54.9** below) to ascertain which accounts are held by the taxpayer with a particular deposit-taker. All notices must be given in writing.

The power can be used to collect sums which are due and payable by a person to HMRC under or by virtue of an enactment or under a contract settlement (see **6.9** ASSESSMENTS) where the following conditions are met:

- the sum is at least £1,000;
- the sum is either an 'established debt' or is due under (or is the disputed tax specified in) an accelerated payment notice or partner payment notice (see **4.49** ANTI-AVOIDANCE); and
- HMRC are satisfied that the taxpayer is aware that the sum is due and payable to them.

A sum is an '*established debt*' if there is no possibility that it, or any part of it, will cease to be due and payable to HMRC. This will be the case where there is no right of appeal, where the period for making an appeal has expired without an appeal having been made or where an appeal has been finally determined or withdrawn. Powers to grant permission to make a late appeal are disregarded for this purpose.

Before issuing an information notice or hold notice HMRC must consider whether, to the best of their knowledge, there are any matters as a result of which the taxpayer is, or may be, at a particular disadvantage in dealing with HMRC in relation to the unpaid sum. Any such matters must be taken into account in deciding whether or not to issue a notice. HMRC have published guidance on the factors which they consider to be relevant to deciding whether a person is at a particular disadvantage. The guidance sets out four indicators which HMRC will consider: a disability or long-term health condition; a temporary illness, physical or mental health condition; personal issues (such as redundancy, bereavement or trauma) and lower levels of literacy, numeracy and/or education. See www.gov.uk/government/publications/direct-recovery-of-debts-and-vulnerable-customers/direct-recovery-of-debts-vulnerable-customers.

A '*deposit-taker*' is, broadly, a person who may lawfully accept deposits in the UK in the course of a business. A deposit-taker is not liable for damages for anything done in good faith to comply with these provisions. References in these provisions to an account held by a person include a joint account held by that person together with others.

Both the Treasury and HMRC have wide powers to vary these provisions via regulations.

[*F(No 2)A 2015, s 51, Sch 8 paras 2, 5, 18–24*].

Tax charged by a determination

Where HMRC are taking action under these provisions in respect of tax charged by a determination within **64.11** RETURNS and the determination is superseded by a self-assessment, the action may be continued as if it were an action to recover so much of the tax charged by the self-assessment as is due and payable, has not been paid and does not exceed the amount charged in the determination. [*TMA 1970, s 28C(4A); F(No 2)A 2015, Sch 8 para 25*].

Penalties

A deposit-taker is liable to a fixed penalty of £300 for a failure to comply with a notice or an obligation under these provisions. If the failure continues after the day on which notice of a penalty is given, the deposit-taker is liable to a further penalty or penalties of up to £60 for each day on which the failure continues. If, after receiving an information or hold notice, a deposit-taker makes a disclosure of information (other than the required notice) to the taxpayer or any other person which is likely to prejudice HMRC's ability to use their powers to deduct the unpaid tax, the deposit-taker is again liable to a penalty of £300. [*F(No 2)A 2015, Sch 8 paras 14–17*].

Information notice

[54.9] If it appears to HMRC that a person has failed to pay a sum meeting the conditions in **54.8** above and that the person holds one or more accounts with a deposit-taker, they may give the deposit-taker an information notice:

(a) the taxpayer's name and address, national insurance number, email addresses and phone numbers and, in respect of any joint accounts, the proportion of the balance to which the taxpayer is entitled; and

(b) for each account held by the taxpayer, any account number, roll number and sort code, the type of account (including whether it is a joint account), the account balance (in the currency in which it is held), whether, and what rate of, interest is payable, any minimum balance required to keep the account open, any contractual terms under which the taxpayer or any '*interested third parties*' (i.e. persons with a beneficial interest in an amount in the account) may suffer economic loss as a result of a hold notice or deduction notice, and, for each joint account holder, interested third party or person with power of attorney in respect of the account, the information specified in (a) above.

Information must be provided only if it is in the possession of, or immediately available to, the deposit-taker at the time the notice is given.

A notice must explain the time limit for complying with it and the penalties for non-compliance. HMRC may issue a notice only for the purpose of determining whether to give the deposit-taker a hold notice (see below) in respect of the taxpayer concerned. The recipient of a notice must comply with it within ten working days beginning with the day on which it was given.

[*F(No 2)A 2015, Sch 8 para 3; SI 2015 No 1986, Regs 2–4*].

Hold notice

[54.10] If it appears to HMRC that a person has failed to pay a sum meeting the conditions in **54.8** above and that the person holds one or more accounts with a deposit-taker, they may give the deposit-taker a hold notice. The notice must:

- specify the taxpayer's name and last known address;
- specify an amount;
- specify a 'safeguarded amount';
- set out any rules which are to decide the priority order to be used to determine the held amount for each account (see Step 3 under Held amounts below);
- explain the effects of the notice, the penalties for non-compliance and any regulatory provisions excluding certain types of account and amounts from inclusion in a hold notice; and
- contain a statement about HMRC's compliance with the requirement to consider whether a taxpayer is at a particular disadvantage in dealing with HMRC (see **54.8** above).

The notice may also specify any additional information which HMRC consider might assist the deposit-taker in identifying accounts. It may also exclude an account, a type of account or a specified amount from the notice.

The amount specified in the hold notice must not exceed what is left of the 'notified sum' (see (iii) below) after deducting the specified amounts in any other hold notices which relate to the same debts and which were either given on the same day to other deposit-takers or given on an earlier day to either the same or another deposit-taker. The specified amount of an earlier hold notice is not deducted if HMRC have received a notification from the deposit-taker that there are no affected accounts as a result of that notice (see further below). For this purpose, two hold notices relate to the same debts if at least one of the unpaid sums in respect of which they are issued is the same.

The '*safeguarded amount*' must be at least £5,000, except that HMRC may specify a smaller amount (including a nil amount) if they consider it appropriate to do so having regard to the sterling value of any amounts in a non-sterling account which would be a 'relevant account' (see under Effect of a hold notice below) in relation to the notice if it were denominated in sterling. The safeguarded amount *must* be nil if HMRC have previously given a hold notice relating to the same debts and, within the 30 days ending with the date the current hold notice is given, HMRC have been notified that there is a held amount as a result of the earlier notice.

HMRC may not give more than one hold notice relating to the same debts to a single deposit-taker on the same day.

Effect of a hold notice

A deposit-taker to whom a hold notice is given must, for each 'relevant account' determine whether or not there is a 'held amount' (greater than nil) for that account and if so must either:

(a) put in place arrangements to ensure that it does not do anything, or permit anything to be done, which would reduce the amount in the account below the held amount; or
(b) transfer an amount equal to the held amount into a specially-created 'suspense account' and put in place arrangements to ensure that it does not do anything, or permit anything to be done, which would reduce the amount in the suspense account below the held amount.

The deposit-taker must comply with these requirements as soon as reasonably practicable and, in any event, within five working days beginning with the day on which the notice is given and must maintain any arrangements made under (a) or (b) above until the notice ceases to be in force.

All accounts held by the taxpayer with the deposit-taker are '*relevant accounts*' unless they are not denominated in sterling or are suspense accounts or they have been excluded from the hold notice by HMRC or excluded from such notices generally by regulations. A relevant account is an '*affected account*' if as a result of the notice there is a held amount in relation to it.

A hold notice ceases to be in force when either HMRC cancel it or a deduction notice (see **54.11** below) is given.

If the deposit-taker determines that there are one or more affected accounts it must give HMRC a notice setting out the information prescribed by *SI 2015 No 1986, Reg 5* about each account (and, in the case of a joint account, about the other account holders) and the held amount for each account. Information must be provided only if it is the possession of, or immediately available to, the deposit-taker at the time the hold notice is given. The notice must be given within five working days beginning with the day on which the deposit-taker complies with the hold notice. HMRC must then, as soon as reasonably practicable, give a copy of the hold notice to the taxpayer together with a notice which:

(i) specifies and states the amounts of the unpaid sums to which the hold notice relates;
(ii) states the total of the unpaid amounts to which the notice relates; and
(iii) states the '*notified sum*' for the hold notice, i.e. the total in (ii) above.

HMRC must also give a notice to any joint account holders other than the taxpayer and to any '*interested third parties*' (i.e. persons with a beneficial interest in an amount in the account concerned) in respect of whom information has been provided in the deposit-taker's notice. The notice must explain that a hold notice has been given in respect of the account concerned and explaining the effects of the notice and the objection and appeal provisions below.

Once it has complied with the hold notice, the deposit-taker may (but is not required to) notify the taxpayer, any joint account holders and any interested third parties stating that a hold notice has been received and the effect of the notice on the account concerned.

If the deposit-taker determines that there are no affected accounts as a result of the hold notice it must notify HMRC accordingly within five working days, including in the notice any information which it has taken into account to determine that there are no affected accounts.

Held amounts

If there is only one relevant account, the '*held amount*' for that account is, if the 'available amount' exceeds the safeguarded amount, the excess up to the specified amount. If the available amount is equal to or less than the safeguarded amount then the held amount is nil. If there is more than one relevant account, the held amount for each such account is found using the following steps.

Step 1. Determine the available amount for each relevant account.

Step 2. Add the available amounts together to determine the total of those amounts for all such accounts. If the total is no more than the safeguarded amount then the held amount for all of the accounts is nil.

Step 3. If the total in Step 2 is more than the safeguarded amount, the safeguarded amount is matched against the available amounts in the relevant accounts, taking the accounts in *reverse* priority order. The priority order is determined by the deposit-taker, but joint accounts must have a lower priority than other accounts and any rules included in the hold notice must be followed.

Step 4. Match the specified amount against what remains of the available amounts by taking each account in priority order. The held amount for each account is then so much of the account balance as is so matched; if no part of an account balance is so matched, the held amount for that account is nil. Balances which are excluded from the effect of the hold notice by regulations are not matched.

The '*available amount*' is the amount standing to the credit of the account at the time the deposit-taker complies with the hold notice. In the case of a joint account, the available amount is restricted to the appropriate fraction of that amount, according to the number of account holders.

Cancellation or variation

HMRC may cancel or vary a hold notice by notifying the deposit-taker. Variation may take the form of cancelling the effect of the notice in relation to one or more accounts or in relation to part of the held amount for an account or accounts. HMRC must give a copy of the notice of cancellation or variation to the taxpayer and any other person HMRC consider is affected by it and who is a joint account holder or an interested third party. On receipt of a notice of cancellation or variation the deposit-taker must within five working days cancel or adjust the arrangements accordingly.

Objections and appeals

The taxpayer, an interested third party or a joint account holder may notify HMRC of an objection to a hold notice on the grounds that:

(i) the debts have been wholly or partly paid;
(ii) at the time the hold notice was given there was no unpaid sum or the taxpayer did not hold an account with the deposit-taker;
(iii) the notice is causing or will cause exceptional hardship to the person making the objection or another person; or
(iv) there is an interested third party in relation to one or more of the affected accounts.

The objection notice must state the grounds of objection and must normally be made within 30 days beginning with the day on which a copy of the hold notice was given to the taxpayer. A joint account holder or independent third party who has received a notice from HMRC explaining that a hold notice has been issued may make an objection within 30 days beginning with the day on which that notice was given. HMRC may, however, agree to the making of a late objection and must do so if they are satisfied that there was reasonable excuse for not making the objection in time and that the person making the objection had sent a written request for agreement to the making of a late objection without unreasonable delay after the reasonable excuse ceased.

HMRC must consider any objections within 30 days of being given the objection notice. They must then decide whether to cancel or vary the hold notice (as above) or to dismiss the objection and must notify their decision to the taxpayer, any other person who objected and any other joint account holder or interested third party who HMRC consider to be affected. HMRC must also notify the deposit-taker if they have decided to cancel or vary the hold notice. A copy of HMRC's notice to the deposit-taker must be given to each of the persons to whom HMRC notified their decision.

The taxpayer, any joint account holder or any interested third party may appeal against HMRC's decision, but only on grounds within (i)–(iv) above. The appeal must state the grounds and must normally be made within 30 days beginning with the day on which the appellant was given notice of HMRC's decision. A joint account holder or independent third party who has not received a notice of HMRC's decision may appeal within 30 days beginning with the day on which the taxpayer was given notice of HMRC's decision. The appeal is to the county court which may cancel or vary the notice or dismiss the appeal.

Where an appeal is on the grounds of exceptional hardship (see (iii) above), the appellant may apply to the court to suspend the effect of the hold notice in full or in relation to a particular account or amount while the appeal is pending. Adequate security must be provided.

If the deposit-taker is served with a court order to cancel or vary the hold notice, it must within five working days make any necessary resulting arrangements.

The normal provisions governing APPEALS (5) do not apply to objections or appeals under these provisions.

[*F(No 2)A 2015, Sch 8 paras 4, 6–12; SI 2015 No 1986, Regs 3, 5, 6*].

Deduction notice

[54.11] If it appears to HMRC that a person in respect of whom a hold notice given to a deposit-taker is in force has failed to pay a sum meeting the conditions in **54.8** above and that the person holds one or more accounts with the deposit-taker in respect of which there is a held amount relating to the unpaid sum, they may give the deposit-taker a deduction notice. The notice will specify one or more affected accounts (see **54.10** above) and require the deposit-taker to deduct and pay a 'qualifying amount' from each account to HMRC by the day specified in the notice. If a held amount for a particular account has been transferred to a suspense account (see **54.10**), the deduction must be made from the suspense account. HMRC may amend or cancel the notice by notifying the deposit-taker. Deposit-takers can charge account holders for any reasonably incurred administrative costs up to a maximum of £55 per account holder provided there is an agreement between deposit-taker and account holder that fees may be charged in such circumstances.

A '*qualifying amount*' in an affected account is an amount not exceeding the held amount for that account. The total qualifying amounts specified in a deduction notice must not exceed the unpaid sum. The deposit-taker must not, while a deduction notice is in force, do anything or permit anything to be done that would reduce the amount in a specified account (or a suspense account) to fall below the amount required to make the deduction. A deduction notice must explain this provision and the penalties for non-compliance. A deduction notice comes into force when it is given to the deposit-taker and ceases to be in force when the deposit-taker is given a notice cancelling it or when the final required payment is made.

A deduction notice cannot be given in respect of an account unless the period for making an objection has passed and either no objections were made or any objections have been decided or withdrawn and, if objections were made and decided, unless the period for making an appeal has passed and any appeal or further appeal has been finally determined.

HMRC must give a copy of a deduction notice to the taxpayer and, for each account, must give a notice explaining that a notice has been given and its effect to any joint account holders other than the taxpayer and to any interested third parties about whom HMRC have sufficient information to do so. Similar copies and notices must be given where HMRC cancel or amend a deduction notice.

[*F(No 2)A 2015, Sch 8 para 13; SI 2016 No 44*].

'Time to Pay' arrangements

[54.12] Under a 'time to pay' arrangement, a taxpayer (T) facing financial hardship or in personal difficulty may enter into an agreement with HMRC which takes account of T's specific financial circumstances (e.g. illness, unemployment, unforeseen short-term business difficulties), with T thereby committing to settle T's tax liabilities by monthly instalments. HMRC usually require all instalment payments agreed under 'time to pay' arrangements to be made by direct debit.

HMRC will establish T's ability to pay, using an income and expenditure assessment, looking at income, disposable assets and expenditure so as to arrive at disposable income. HMRC typically expects a taxpayer to pay instalments of no more than 50% of disposable income, though a larger percentage may be required in cases of high disposable income. There is no upper limit on the amount of time that a person can be given to pay. Late payment interest is chargeable in the normal way on the full amount unpaid at the due date and not just on overdue instalments.

A time to pay arrangement can cover all outstanding amounts overdue including penalties and interest. It is intended to be flexible and is not a fixed, formal contract. It can be amended over time, enabling it to be shortened or lengthened if circumstances change.

See www.gov.uk/guidance/find-out-how-to-pay-a-debt-to-hmrc-with-a-time-to-pay-arrangement and www.gov.uk/difficulties-paying-hmrc.

If the taxpayer is a sub-contractor in the construction industry and is registered for gross payment (see **20.7** CONSTRUCTION INDUSTRY SCHEME (CIS), entering into a 'time to pay' arrangement before payment is due will not affect the sub-contractor's gross payment status (www.gov.uk/what-you-must-do-as-a-cis-subcontractor/annual-review).

Simon's Taxes. See **A4.610**.

Managed payment plans (prospective)

[54.13] The legislation provides that, under a managed payment plan, a taxpayer may agree with HMRC to pay income tax or capital gains tax by instalments which are 'balanced' equally before and after the normal due date. If the taxpayer then pays all of the instalments in accordance with the plan, he is treated as having paid the total amount on the due date, so that no interest, late payment surcharge or penalty will arise. However, the then Government decided to defer the implementation of managed payment plans; no commencement date has yet been given (Budget Report 22 June 2010 p 46). Given the passage of time, it must be doubtful now that this legislation will ever be implemented.

Under the proposed plan, where the taxpayer pays one or more of the instalments in accordance with the plan but then fails to pay one or more later instalments, the total of the instalments paid before the failure are treated as paid on the due date. Where the failure takes place before the due date, the taxpayer is, nevertheless, entitled to be paid any interest on the early payments made if he would have been so entitled but for the plan. Where, following a failure, the taxpayer makes payments after the due date, HMRC can notify him that any or all of those payments will not be liable to a late payment surcharge or penalty.

Instalments to be paid before the due date are '*balanced*' with instalments to be paid after it if the aggregate time value of each set of instalments is equal or approximately equal. HMRC can make regulations to determine when, for this purpose, two amounts are approximately equal. The time value of an instalment is calculated by multiplying it by the number of days between the payment date for the instalment and the due date for the tax.

[*TMA 1970, ss 59G, 59H*].

Remission or repayment of tax in cases of official error

[54.14] Arrears of income tax or capital gains tax may be waived if they result from HMRC's failure to make proper and timely use of information supplied by:

(a) a taxpayer about his or her own income, gains or personal circumstances;
(b) an employer, where the information affects a taxpayer's coding; or

(c) the Department for Work and Pensions about a taxpayer's retirement, disability or widow's State pension.

The waiver will normally apply only where the taxpayer could reasonably have believed that his or her tax affairs were in order, and either:

(i) was notified of the arrears more than twelve months after the end of the tax year in which HMRC received the information indicating that more tax was due; or
(ii) was notified of an over-repayment after the end of the tax year following the year in which the repayment was made.

Exceptionally, arrears notified less than twelve months after the end of the relevant tax year may be waived if HMRC either failed more than once to make proper use of the facts they had been given about one source of income, or allowed the arrears to build up over two whole tax years in succession by failing to make proper and timely use of information they had been given.

(HMRC ESC A19).

See also **53.46** PAY AS YOU EARN as regards end-of-year PAYE reconciliations.

Where an **overpayment** of tax has arisen because of official error, and there is no doubt or dispute as to the facts, claims to repayment of tax are accepted outside the statutory time limits (HMRC ESC B41).

Overpayment of tax

[54.15] HMRC's administrative practice relating to repayments of tax is as below.

(i) Where an assessment has been made and this shows a repayment due to the taxpayer, repayment is invariably made of the full amount.
(ii) Under SELF-ASSESSMENT (**67**), any amount repayable will be repaid on request.
(iii) Where the end-of-year check applied to PAYE taxpayers who have not had a tax return for the year in question shows an overpayment of £10 or less, the repayment is not made automatically.
(iv) Where tax assessed has been paid to the Collector in excess of the amount due, and the discrepancy is not noted before the payment has been processed, the excess is not repaid routinely by the computer system unless it is £1 or more, or where clerical intervention is required unless it is £10 or more.

The above tolerances are to minimise work which is highly cost ineffective, they cannot operate to deny a repayment to a taxpayer who has claimed it. (HMRC SP 6/95). Provisional repayments will not be made during the tax year to which a claim or claims relate if the tax involved does not exceed £50 in total. (Revenue Press Release 29 March 1989).

See **54.14** above as regards claims in cases of official error. See also **16.6** CLAIMS as regards repayment procedures.

Allocation of overpayments against underpayments

Where there are underpayments of tax, overpayments will automatically be reallocated against any other tax or Class 4 NICs (or interest thereon) outstanding in respect of the amended assessment unless the amendment is processed before 1 June following the end of the tax year and either the amount to be reallocated to the second instalment is £1,000 or more or the tax is not yet due and the taxpayer requests that no reallocation should be made. (HMRC Assessed Taxes Manual AT 8.701 *et seq.*). For an article on HMRC practice re allocations of overpayments under SELF-ASSESSMENT (**67**), see Revenue Tax Bulletin June 1999 pp 673, 674.

Over-repayments of tax

[54.16] Tax over-repaid (by actual payment or set-off) and not assessable under *TMA 1970, s 29* (see **6.6** ASSESSMENTS) may be recovered by an income tax assessment as if it were unpaid tax. However, this rule is subject to the same exceptions (modified as appropriate) as apply to discovery assessments (see **6.6** ASSESSMENTS). Any excess repayment interest may be included in the assessment or assessed separately as if it were unpaid tax. The normal time limit for such an assessment is extended, if necessary, to the later of the end of the chargeable period following that in which the repayment was made and, where relevant, the day on which an HMRC enquiry into a return delivered by the person concerned is fully completed (see **64.8** RETURNS), but this time limit is without prejudice to the extended time limits which apply in cases of loss of income tax brought about deliberately (see **6.3** ASSESSMENTS) or fraudulent or negligent conduct. [*TMA 1970, s 30; F(No 2)A 2017, Sch 15 paras 16, 44*].

The exercise by HMRC of their discretion to raise an assessment under *TMA 1970, s 30* can be challenged only by way of judicial review (see **5.34** APPEALS) and not by appeal (*Guthrie v Twickenham Film Studios Ltd* Ch D 2002, 74 TC 733).

As regards late payment interest on amounts assessed as above, see **43.2** LATE PAYMENT INTEREST AND PENALTIES.

Recovery of tax paid under mistake of law

[54.17] It was held in *R v CIR (ex p. Woolwich Equitable Building Society)* HL 1990, 63 TC 589 that at common law taxes extracted *ultra vires* are recoverable as of right and without need to invoke mistake of law by the taxpayer (and see **62.4** REPAYMENT INTEREST).

It was further held, *inter alia*, in *Deutsche Morgan Grenfell Group plc v CIR and A-G* Ch D, [2003] STC 1017 that the common law remedy of restitution of payment made under a mistake of law applies to payments of tax as it does to other payments. By virtue of *Limitation Act 1980, s 32(1)(c)*, the six-year period of limitation in such a case does not begin to run until the plaintiff discovers the mistake (or could with reasonable diligence have discovered it). However, under legislation in *FA 2004* (reversing the effect of *Deutsche Morgan Grenfell*), *Limitation Act 1980, s 32(1)(c)* (and Scottish equivalent) does *not* apply in relation to a mistake of law relating to taxes administered by HMRC where the action for restitution is brought after 7 September 2003. The effect is that court actions for restitution based on mistake of law must generally be brought within six years (or five years under Scottish law) of the tax having been paid. If a pre-existing action is amended to include additional years, the amendment is not treated as backdated to the date of the original action. [*FA 2004, ss 320, 321*].

The Ch D decision in *Deutsche Morgan Grenfell* was eventually confirmed by the HL (*Deutsche Morgan Grenfell Group plc v CIR and another* HL 2006, 78 TC 120). The Government subsequently announced that it would legislate to ensure that (for those cases not already caught by the *FA 2004* legislation above) the limitation period for the recovery of direct tax paid by mistake of law is six years from the date of payment (and not from the date of discovery of the mistake). The legislation would have retrospective effect, but not so as to disturb the entitlement of those who have secured what amounts to a final judgment in their favour prior to 6 December 2006. The legislation was duly enacted as *FA 2007, s 107*. The Supreme Court has since ruled that the retrospective nature of *FA 2007, s 107* infringes the EU principle of protection of legitimate expectations and is thus unlawful (*Test Claimants in the FII Group Litigation v HMRC* SC, [2012] STC 1362). Consequently, *FA 2007, s 107* was amended by *FA 2014, s 299* with fully retrospective effect to exclude from its ambit any actions relating to tax charged contrary to EU law. It should be noted that this does not affect actions brought after 7 September 2003, for which see *FA 2004, ss 320, 321* above.

HMRC powers to obtain contact details for debtors

[54.18] An HMRC officer may by notice in writing require a third party to provide contact details (i.e. an address and any other information about how the person may be contacted) for a person in debt to HMRC. The third party must provide the details within such period, and at such time, by such means and in such form (if any), as is reasonably specified or described in the notice, subject to a £300 penalty for non-compliance. The third party may appeal against the notice, or any requirement in it, on the grounds that it would be unduly onerous to comply. In order for these provisions to apply:

- a sum must be payable by a person (the debtor) to HMRC under an enactment or a contract settlement (as in **6.9** ASSESSMENTS);
- the officer must reasonably require contact details for the debtor for the purpose of collection and have reasonable grounds to believe that the third party has such details; and
- either the third party is a company, local authority or local authority association (within *ITA 2007, s 1000*) or the officer has reasonable grounds to believe that the third party obtained the details in the course of carrying on a business (which term includes a profession or a property business).

The above does not apply if the third party is a charity and obtained the details in the course of providing services free of charge or is not a charity but obtained the details in the course of providing free services on behalf of a charity.

[*FA 2009, s 97, Sch 49*].

55

Penalties

Cross-references. See **16.3** CLAIMS, **43** LATE PAYMENT INTEREST AND PENALTIES and **64.5** RETURNS as regards failure to keep records.

See HMRC Compliance Handbook CH80000 *et seq.* (penalties for inaccuracies).

Introduction to penalties

[55.1] This chapter considers HMRC's powers to charge penalties in the event of various tax compliance failures.

Notification of chargeability

[55.2] A person chargeable to income tax or capital gains tax for a particular tax year who has not been required by a notice under *TMA 1970, s 8* (see **64.2** RETURNS) to deliver a return for that year must, within six months after the end of that year, notify an officer of HMRC that he is so chargeable. Where a person chargeable to income tax or capital gains tax has received such a notice, but the notice has subsequently been withdrawn (see **64.2** RETURNS), he must notify HMRC that he is chargeable by the later of the end of the aforementioned six-month period and the end of a period of 30 days beginning immediately after the date on which the notice was withdrawn. For penalties for non-compliance, see **55.3**, **55.4** below.

A person is not required to give notice under these provisions if his total income for the year consists of income from the sources below, he has no chargeable gains and he is not liable to the high income child benefit charge at **73.4** SOCIAL SECURITY AND NATIONAL INSURANCE. The said sources are those in respect of which:

(a) all payments etc. are dealt with under PAYE; or
(b) all income has been or will be taken into account either in determining the chargeable person's liability to tax or under PAYE; or
(c) the income is income from which tax has been, or is treated as having been, deducted, provided that the chargeable person is not liable for that year at a rate other than the basic rate, the Scottish basic rate, the Scottish starter rate, the Scottish intermediate rate, the dividend nil rate, the dividend ordinary rate, the savings nil rate or the starting rate for savings; or
(d) all the income is dividend income (see **1.5** ALLOWANCES AND TAX RATES, provided that the chargeable person is UK resident and for that year is neither liable at the dividend ordinary rate, upper rate or additional rate nor charged to tax on the REMITTANCE BASIS (**60**) on any dividend income; or
(e) all income for that year is income on which the chargeable person could not become liable to tax under a self-assessment under *TMA 1970, s 9* (see **64.3** RETURNS) in respect of that year.

Where a 'simple assessment' is made for a tax year (see **6.5** ASSESSMENTS), the requirement to notify chargeability does not then apply for that year unless the person is chargeable on any income or gain that is not included in the simple assessment.

These provisions also apply with the appropriate modifications to 'relevant trustees' (as defined in **67.11** SELF-ASSESSMENT) of settlements.

[*TMA 1970, s 7(1)–(7), (9); FA 2016, ss 4(15)(17), 5(9)(10), 167, Sch 23 para 2; SI 2018 No 459, Arts 1, 2*].

As regards items within (b) above, HMRC will normally accept that employees in receipt of copy form P11D (or equivalent particulars) from their employer (see **67.12** SELF-ASSESSMENT) can assume that any items on it not already taken into account for PAYE will be so taken into account, so there is no need to notify chargeability in respect of such items. Notice of chargeability is, however, necessary to the extent that the P11D is incorrect or incomplete or if the employee knows that the actual form has not been submitted to HMRC. Employees are not relieved of any obligation to notify chargeability if they have not received a copy P11D or in respect of non-P11D items which ought to have been reported by the employer to HMRC on other returns. (HMRC SP 1/96).

Pension schemes

The trustees of approved occupational pension schemes with income or capital gains are within these provisions. See Pension Schemes Office Update No 49, 24 August 1998 and, for the detailed administrative arrangements, Revenue Tax Bulletin February 1999 pp 628, 629.

Simon's Taxes. See **E1.202**.

Penalty for failure to notify chargeability

[55.3] Penalties for non-compliance with the requirement at **55.2** above come within a unified penalty code for failures relating to a range of taxes including income tax.

A person is not liable to a penalty for a failure in respect of which he has been convicted of an offence.

Amount of penalty

The amount of the penalty depends on whether or not the failure is deliberate and is subject to reduction as detailed below.

The amount of the penalty depends also on whether the inaccuracy involves a domestic matter or an offshore matter. The following summary assumes the inaccuracy involves a domestic matter; see **55.4** below as regards offshore matters.

For a deliberate and concealed failure (i.e. where the failure was deliberate and the taxpayer made arrangements to conceal the situation giving rise to the obligation), the penalty is 100% of the 'potential lost revenue' (see below).

For deliberate but not concealed failure (i.e. where the failure was deliberate but the taxpayer did not make arrangements to conceal the situation giving rise to the obligation), the penalty is 70% of the potential lost revenue.

For any other case, the penalty is 30% of the potential lost revenue.

The '*potential lost revenue*' is in most cases equal to the amount of tax payable for the year that, by reason of the failure, remains unpaid on 31 January following that year. It is based on the amount of tax to which the taxpayer is liable and not, if different, the amount assessed (*HMRC v Robertson* UT, [2019] STC 1602. Where an obligation to notify chargeability arises following the withdrawal of a notice to make a return (see **64.2** RETURNS), the *'potential lost revenue'* is the amount of tax that, by reason of the failure to comply with the obligation, is:

- where the period for notification is extended to 30 days after the date of the withdrawal notification and that period ends after the 'relevant date', unpaid at the end of that period; or
- in any other case, unpaid on the relevant date.

The *'relevant date'* for this purpose is 31 January following the tax year or, if after that date HMRC repay to the taxpayer a payment he has made on account for the year, the day after the refund is issued.

The fact that potential lost revenue may be balanced by a potential overpayment by another person is ignored, except to the extent that the other person's tax liability is required or permitted to be adjusted by reference to the taxpayer's.

No penalty is due in relation to a failure that is not deliberate if the taxpayer satisfies HMRC or, on appeal, the Appeal Tribunal, that there is a reasonable excuse for the failure. Insufficiency of funds is not a reasonable excuse for this purpose, unless attributable to events outside the taxpayer's control, and neither is the taxpayer's reliance on another person to do anything, unless he took reasonable care (see **55.6** below) to avoid the failure. For more on what is or is not a reasonable excuse, see HMRC Compliance Handbook CH71500. If the taxpayer had a reasonable excuse, he is treated as continuing to have a reasonable excuse after the excuse has ceased if the failure is remedied without unreasonable delay.

Reduction for disclosure

A reduction in a penalty will be given where the taxpayer discloses a failure to notify. The penalty will be reduced to a percentage which reflects the quality of the disclosure (see HMRC Compliance Handbook CH73220) and the amount of the reduction will depend on whether the disclosure is 'prompted' or 'unprompted'. A disclosure is *'unprompted'* if made when the taxpayer has no reason to believe HMRC have discovered or are about to discover the failure. In all other cases, disclosures are *'prompted'*.

A person is treated as making a disclosure for these purposes only if he tells HMRC about the failure, he gives them reasonable help in quantifying the tax unpaid and allows them access to records for the purpose of checking how much tax is unpaid.

The penalty cannot be reduced below a minimum percentage as shown in the table below. Where alternate percentages are shown, the higher percentage applies where HMRC do not become aware of the failure until 12 months or more after the time tax first becomes unpaid by reason of the failure, and the lower percentage applies in all other cases. Where a person has taken a significant period (such as three years or more) to correct or disclose his non-compliance, HMRC will usually restrict the maximum reduction for the quality of disclosure to 10 percentage points above the minimum of the penalty range (www.gov.uk/government/publications/compliance-checks-penalties-for-failure-to-notify-ccfs11).

Standard percentage	Minimum percentage for prompted disclosure	Minimum percentage for unprompted disclosure
30%	10% or 20%	0% or 10%
70%	35%	20%
100%	50%	30%

Reduction in special circumstances

HMRC can also reduce or stay a penalty or agree a compromise in relation to proceedings for a penalty if they think it right to do so because of special circumstances. Ability to pay and the fact that a potential loss of revenue from one taxpayer is balanced by a potential overpayment by another are not special circumstances for this purpose.

Reduction for other penalty or surcharge

The amount of a penalty in respect of a failure is reduced by the amount of any other penalty or late payment surcharge, the amount of which is determined by reference to the same tax liability. No reduction is made for a tax-related penalty within **55.15** below, a late payment penalty under **43.2** LATE PAYMENT INTEREST AND PENALTIES, a penalty within **4.48** ANTI-AVOIDANCE (follower notices) or **4.52** ANTI-AVOIDANCE (accelerated payment notices) or a penalty under **55.11** below (asset-based penalty for offshore inaccuracies and failures).

Agents

A person is liable to a penalty under the above provisions where the failure is by a person acting on his behalf. He is not, however, liable to a penalty in respect of anything done or omitted by his agent if he satisfies HMRC or, on appeal, the Appeal Tribunal, that he took reasonable care (see **55.6** below) to avoid the failure.

LLPs

Where a penalty is payable by a limited liability partnership (LLP) for a deliberate act or failure which was attributable to a member of the LLP, the member can be held liable to pay such portion of the penalty (which may be 100%) as HMRC may specify by written notice to the member (but not so as to enable HMRC to obtain more than 100% of the penalty overall). The specified portion is treated as a penalty for the purpose of these provisions, and is payable by the member within the 30 days beginning with the day on which the notice is given.

[*FA 2008, s 123, Sch 41 paras 1, 5, 6, 6A, 6D, 7, 11–13, 14, 15, 20–24; FA 2009, Sch 56 para 9A; FA 2016, Sch 22 para 20(4)*].

See 55.10 below as regards a possible further penalty where assets are moved between overseas territories in order to prevent or delay the discovery of a potential loss of revenue giving rise to the above penalty.

Simon's Taxes. See A4.510–A4.515.

Penalty for failure to notify — offshore matters and transfers

[55.4] The amount of the penalty in 55.3 above depends not only on whether or not the failure is deliberate but also on whether the failure involves (i) a domestic matter or (ii) an offshore matter or offshore transfer.

For these purposes, a failure involves an *offshore matter* if it results in a potential loss of revenue (see 55.3 above) that is charged on or by reference to:

- income arising from a source in a territory outside the UK; or
- assets situated or held in a territory outside the UK; or
- activities carried on wholly or mainly in a territory outside the UK; or
- anything having effect as if it were income, assets or activities of the kind above.

A failure involves an *offshore transfer* if:

- it does not involve an offshore matter;
- it is deliberate (whether or not concealed) and results in a potential loss of revenue; and
- the income on (or by reference to which) the tax is charged (or any part of that income):
  - is received in a territory outside the UK; or
  - is transferred to a territory outside the UK before the date by reference to which the potential lost revenue is to be calculated. The reference to the transfer of income is to be read as including a reference to the transfer of any assets derived from or representing that income.

Where more than one category of territory is involved in an offshore transfer, the level of penalty is to be determined by reference to the highest category of territory involved.

If the failure does not involve an offshore matter or an offshore transfer it involves a domestic matter. Provision made by the Treasury under 55.8 below, as to where a source of income is located, where an asset is situated etc., has effect for the above purposes also. '*Assets*' has the same meaning as for capital gains tax purposes (see *TCGA 1992, s 21(1)*) but also includes sterling.

Category 0

Not yet in operation — see below under Future development.

Category 1

If the failure involves an offshore matter or offshore transfer and the territory in question is a 'category 1 territory', the amounts of the penalties are currently the same as for domestic matters, i.e. the amounts in 55.3 above, but see below under Future development. A '*category 1 territory*' is a territory designated as such by order made by the Treasury.

Category 2

If the inaccuracy involves an offshore matter or offshore transfer and the territory in question is a 'category 2 territory', the amounts of the penalties are as follows.

For a deliberate and concealed failure, the penalty is **150%** of the 'potential lost revenue' (see 55.3 above).

For a deliberate but not concealed failure, the penalty is **105%** of the potential lost revenue.

For any other case, the penalty is **45%** of the potential lost revenue.

A '*category 2 territory*' is a territory that is neither a category 1 territory nor a category 3 territory.

Category 3

If the inaccuracy involves an offshore matter or offshore transfer and the territory in question is a 'category 3 territory', the amounts of the penalties are as follows.

For a deliberate and concealed failure, the penalty is **200%** of the 'potential lost revenue' (see 55.3 above).

For a deliberate but not concealed failure, the penalty is **140%** of the potential lost revenue.

For any other case, the penalty is **60%** of the potential lost revenue.

A '*category 3 territory*' is a territory designated as such by order made by the Treasury.

Failure in more than one category

If a single failure is in more than one category it is treated for these purposes as if it were separate failures, one in each relevant category according to the matters that it involves. The potential lost revenue for each separate failure is such share of the potential lost revenue in respect of the single failure as is just and reasonable.

Categorisation of territories

The classification by the Treasury of territories for the purposes of 55.8 below has effect for these purposes also. The above penalty provisions do not apply to obligations that are to be complied with before the date on which the relevant categorisation order comes into force. *SI 2011 No 976* designates various territories as category 1 or 3.

Reduction for disclosure

A reduction in a penalty will be given where the taxpayer discloses a failure to notify. The penalty will be reduced to a percentage which reflects the quality of the disclosure (see HMRC Compliance Handbook CH73220) and the amount of the reduction will depend on whether the disclosure is 'prompted' or 'unprompted'. A disclosure is '*unprompted*' if made when the taxpayer has no reason to believe HMRC have discovered or are about to discover the failure. In all other cases, disclosures are '*prompted*'.

In the case of a *non-deliberate* failure involving an offshore matter, a person is treated as making a disclosure for these purposes only if he tells HMRC about the failure, gives them reasonable help in quantifying the tax unpaid and allows them access to records for the purpose of checking how much tax is unpaid.

In the case of a *deliberate* failure (whether or not concealed) involving an *offshore matter* or any failure involving an *offshore transfer*, a person (P) will be treated as making a disclosure only if P tells HMRC about the failure, gives them reasonable help in quantifying the tax unpaid, and allows them access to records for the purpose of checking how much tax is unpaid. With effect on and after 1 April 2017, P must also tell HMRC if there is:

- any person who encouraged, assisted or otherwise facilitated the failure; and
- any asset situated or held outside the UK that is held on P's behalf by another person,

and must provide further specified details if either is the case.

For a failure involving an offshore matter or offshore transfer the penalty cannot be reduced below a minimum percentage as shown in the table below. Where alternate percentages are shown, the higher percentage applies where HMRC do not become aware of the failure until 12 months or more after the time tax first becomes unpaid by reason of the failure, and the lower percentage applies in all other cases. Where a person has taken a significant period (such as three years or more) to correct or disclose his non-compliance, HMRC will usually restrict the maximum reduction for the quality of disclosure to 10 percentage points above the minimum of the penalty range (www.gov.uk/government/publications/compliance-checks-penalties-for-failure-to-notify-ccfs11).

Standard percentage	Minimum percentage for prompted disclosure	Minimum percentage for unprompted disclosure
30%	10% or 20%	0% or 10%
45%	15% or 30%	0% or 15%
60%	20% or 40%	0% or 20%
70%	45%	30%
100%	60%	40%
105%	62.5%	40%
140%	80%	50%
150%	85%	55%
200%	110%	70%

Reduction in special circumstances

See **55.3** above.

Reduction for other penalty or surcharge

See **55.3** above.

Future development

With effect on and after a day to be appointed by the Treasury, a new category (category 0) is to be introduced alongside categories 1 to 3 above. A category 0 territory will be a territory designated as such by Treasury order. The intention is that only territories that adopt automatic exchange of information under the Common Reporting Standard (see **35.14** HMRC — ADMINISTRATION) will be given category 0 status.

Category 0 will have the same penalty levels as the current category 1 (and all penalties for domestic matters will be moved to category 0). The current penalty levels for category 1 will be increased from 100%, 70% and 30% to 125%, 87.5% and 37.5% respectively. There will continue to be reductions for prompted and unprompted disclosures. The penalty levels for categories 2 and 3 will remain the same.

[*FA 2008, s 123, Sch 41 paras 6, 6A, 6AA, 6AB, 12, 13, 13A, 14; FA 2016, s 163, Sch 21 paras 5–8; SI 2011 No 976; SI 2017 Nos 259, 345*].

Simon's Taxes. See **A4.575–A4.576.**

Late filing penalty

[55.5] A unified penalty code for failure to make a return on time (the '*late filing penalty*') applies across a range of taxes including income tax. In its application to income tax self-assessment returns, the late filing penalty is described below. For late filing penalties for PAYE Real Time Information returns, see **53.24** PAY AS YOU EARN. For late filing penalties for returns under the construction industry scheme, see **20.12** CONSTRUCTION INDUSTRY SCHEME.

Where a return is required under any of the provisions listed below, and subject to the 'reasonable excuse' let-out below, a late filing penalty is payable if the taxpayer fails to make or deliver the return to HMRC on or before the filing date. For this purpose a requirement to make a return includes the requirement to deliver any accounts, statement or document which must be delivered with the return. The provisions are:

- *TMA 1970, s 8* (personal tax return);
- *TMA 1970, s 8A* (trustees' tax return); and
- *TMA 1970, s 12AA* (partnership tax return).

For the filing dates for personal and trustees' returns, see **64.2** RETURNS. For the filing date for partnership returns, see **64.12** RETURNS. In all cases, the filing date differs according to whether the return is filed manually or online.

Before *FA 2019*, penalties could not be charged for late filing of an unsolicited (voluntary) return, i.e. in a case where notice to file a return had not been given or had been given but not properly served (but see now **64.2** RETURNS under unsolicited returns) (*Wood v HMRC* FTT (TC 6339), [2018] UKFTT 74 (TC)).

If a failure to make a return falls within the terms of more than one of the following penalties, the taxpayer is liable to each of those penalties (subject to the maximum tax-geared penalty below).

Initial penalty

An initial penalty of £100 is payable for failure to make a return on or before the filing date. In contrast to the position for years prior to 2010/11, the penalty is not capped at the amount of the income tax liability as at the filing date.

Daily penalty

HMRC will impose a daily penalty where the taxpayer's failure to make the return continues after the end of three months beginning with the day on which the initial penalty is triggered; this is the day after the filing date and is known as the '*penalty date*'.

The amount of the penalty is £10 for each day that the failure continues during the period of 90 days starting with a date specified by HMRC. HMRC must give notice to the taxpayer specifying the date from which the penalty is payable. The starting date cannot be earlier than the end of the three-month period beginning with the penalty date, but can precede the date of the notice.

In *HMRC v Donaldson*, CA, [2016] STC 2511, the FTT had allowed an appeal against daily penalties on the grounds that HMRC failed to give notice to the taxpayer specifying the date from which the penalty was payable; they considered HMRC's 'notice' on form SA326D to be insufficient to meet this statutory requirement. However, the FTT decision was overturned on appeal.

First tax-geared penalty

If the failure continues after the end of a six-month period beginning with the penalty date, the taxpayer is liable to a penalty equal to the *greater* of £300 and 5% of any tax liability which would have been shown in the return in question.

For this purpose (and that of the second tax-geared penalty below), the tax liability which would have been shown in the return is the amount of income tax which, had a correct and complete return been delivered on the filing date, would have been shown to be due and payable for the period covered by the return. If a penalty is assessed before the return is made, then, for this purpose only, HMRC must determine that tax liability to the best of their information and belief. Then, when the return is subsequently made, the penalty must be re-assessed by reference to the amount of tax shown in the return to be due and payable (subject to any amendments or corrections to the return).

In *HMRC v Duncan Hansard* UT, [2020] STC 336, [2019] UKUT 391 (TCC), the UT found there was nothing to prevent HMRC issuing a minimum penalty of £300 in cases where a return was outstanding at the six-month point, with the option of issuing a supplementary penalty assessment at a later date if necessary. In *Marano v HMRC* FTT (TC 7685), [2020] UKFTT 199 (TC), it was held that, given that the tax-geared penalty is based on the tax liability which would have been shown in the return, payments of tax on account cannot be taken into consideration so as to reduce the quantum of the penalty.

Second tax-geared penalty

A second tax-geared penalty is payable if the failure continues after the end of a twelve-month period beginning with the penalty date. The amount of the penalty depends on whether or not, by failing to make the return, the taxpayer is deliberately withholding information that would enable or assist HMRC to assess the tax liability.

If there is deliberate withholding of information, the amount of the penalty further depends on whether or not the withholding is concealed and in which of three categories the information falls within. The categories are as follows.

- **Category 0.** This category is not yet in operation — see below under Future development.
- **Category 1.** Information involving a 'domestic matter' or involving an 'offshore matter' or 'offshore transfer' where the territory concerned is a 'category 1 territory' or the tax involved is neither income tax nor capital gains tax. A '*category 1 territory*' is a territory designated as such by order made by the Treasury.
- **Category 2.** Information involving an offshore matter or offshore transfer where the territory involved is a 'category 2 territory' and the tax is income tax or capital gains tax. A '*category 2 territory*' is a territory that is neither a category 1 territory nor a category 3 territory.
- **Category 3.** Information involving an offshore matter or offshore transfer where the territory involved is a 'category 3 territory' and the tax is income tax or capital gains tax. A '*category 3 territory*' is a territory designated as such by order made by the Treasury.

If the information withheld is in more than one category, the failure is treated as if it were separate failures, one in each of the categories concerned and the tax liability which would have been shown in the return is apportioned on a just and reasonable basis.

If information does not involve an offshore matter or an offshore transfer it involves a '*domestic matter*'.

Information involves an '*offshore matter*' if the liability which would have been shown in the return includes a liability to tax charged on or by reference to:

- income arising from a source in a territory outside the UK; or
- assets situated or held in such a territory; or
- activities carried on wholly or mainly in such a territory; or
- anything having effect as if it were such income, assets or activities.

Information involves an '*offshore transfer*' if:

- it does not involve an offshore matter;

- it is information which would enable or assist HMRC to assess the taxpayer's liability to income tax;
- by failing to make the return, the taxpayer deliberately withholds the information (whether or not the withholding of the information is also concealed); and
- the income on (or by reference to which) the tax is charged (or any part of that income):
  - is received in a territory outside the UK; or
  - is transferred to a territory outside the UK before the date on which the taxpayer becomes liable to the second tax-geared penalty. The reference to the transfer of income is to be read as including a reference to the transfer of any assets derived from or representing that income.

Where more than one category of territory is involved in an offshore transfer, the level of penalty is to be determined by reference to the highest category of territory involved.

The Treasury may make provision by statutory instrument for determining for the above purposes where a source of income is located, where an asset is situated or held, where activities are carried on, where income is received or transferred and where assets are transferred. '*Assets*' has the same meaning as for capital gains tax purposes (see *TCGA 1992, s 21(1)*) but also includes sterling.

Amount of penalty

The amount of the penalty is the *greater* of £300 and a percentage of the tax liability which would have been shown in the return. That percentage is found using the table below.

	Percentage of tax liability		
	Category 1	*Category 2*	*Category 3*
Deliberate and concealed withholding of information	100%	150%	200%
Deliberate but not concealed withholding of information	70%	105%	140%
In any other case	5%	5%	5%

For this purpose, the withholding of information by a taxpayer is concealed if the taxpayer makes arrangements to conceal that it has been withheld.

See **55.10** below as regards a possible further penalty where the second tax-geared penalty is chargeable and assets are moved between overseas territories in order to prevent or delay the discovery by HMRC of the loss of tax revenue.

Reduction for disclosure

A reduction in the second tax-geared penalty will be given where the taxpayer discloses information that he was withholding by virtue of his failure to make a return. The penalty will be reduced to a percentage which reflects the quality of the disclosure (see HMRC Compliance Handbook CH63220); the amount of the reduction will depend on whether the disclosure is 'prompted' or 'unprompted', but cannot be reduced below a minimum percentage as shown in the tables below. The penalty cannot in any case be reduced below £300. Where a person has taken a significant period (such as three years or more) to disclose the information, HMRC will usually restrict the maximum reduction for the quality of disclosure to 10 percentage points above the minimum of the penalty range (www.gov.uk/government/publications/compliance-checks-penalties-if-you-dont-file-income-tax-capital-gains-tax-and-annual-tax-on-enveloped-dwellings-returns-on-time-ccfs18a).

Information involving a domestic matter

Standard percentage	**Minimum percentage for prompted disclosure**	**Minimum percentage for unprompted disclosure**
70%	35%	20%
100%	50%	30%

Information involving an offshore matter or offshore transfer

Standard percentage	**Minimum percentage for prompted disclosure**	**Minimum percentage for unprompted disclosure**
70%	45%	30%
100%	60%	40%
105%	62.5%	40%
140%	80%	50%
150%	85%	55%
200%	110%	70%

A person (P) is treated as making a disclosure for these purposes only if P tells HMRC about the information, gives them reasonable help in quantifying the tax unpaid by reason of the information having been withheld and allows them access to records for the purpose of quantifying how much tax is unpaid. Where the information disclosed involves an offshore matter or an offshore transfer, then with effect on and after 1 April 2017, P must also tell HMRC if there is:

- any person who encouraged, assisted or otherwise facilitated the withholding of the information; and
- any asset situated or held outside the UK that is held on P's behalf by another person,

and must provide further specified details if either is the case.

A disclosure is '*unprompted*' if made when the taxpayer has no reason to believe HMRC have discovered, or are about to discover, the information. In all other cases, disclosures are '*prompted*'.

Categorisation of offshore territories

In considering how to classify a territory for the purpose of the second tax-geared penalty, the Treasury must have regard to:

- the existence or otherwise of arrangements for the exchange of information between the UK and that territory;
- the quality of any such arrangements (in particular, whether they provide for information to be exchanged automatically or on request);
- the benefit that the UK would be likely to obtain from receiving information from that territory, were such arrangements to exist;
- the existence of any other arrangements between the UK and that territory for co-operation in the area of taxation; and
- the quality of any such other arrangements (in particular, the extent to which the said co-operation will assist in protecting UK tax revenue).

Categorisation orders are to be made by statutory instrument. No penalty is chargeable by reference to a categorisation order if the filing date falls before the date on which that order comes into force. *SI 2011 No 976* designates various territories as category 1 or 3.

Maximum tax-geared penalty

Where both the first and second tax-geared penalties are due in relation to the same tax liability, and are determined by reference to a liability to tax, the total of those penalties cannot exceed the 100%, 150% or 200% limit as appropriate. It was decided in *Jagger v HMRC* FTT (TC 6774), [2018] UKFTT 623 (TC) that even if the penalties had been fixed £300 penalties, they were nevertheless 'determined by reference to a liability to tax' and that this limitation therefore applied; this could produce absurd results and was clearly not the intention of the legislation, but it appears, pending any HMRC appeal of this decision, that the drafting of the legislation has failed to implement its intention.

Partnerships

In the case of a partnership return, where the partner required to make the return or his successor (see **64.12** RETURNS) fails to make the return on or before the filing date, the appropriate late filing penalty is payable by every person who was a partner at any time in the period for which the return is required.

Withdrawal of notice to make a return

Where a person or member of a partnership is liable to any penalty under these provisions and HMRC withdraw the notice to make the return (see **64.2**, **64.12** RETURNS), the notification of withdrawal may include provision cancelling liability to the penalty from the date of withdrawal.

Reasonable excuse

None of the above penalties are due in respect of a failure to make a return if the taxpayer satisfies HMRC or, on appeal, the Tribunal, that there is a reasonable excuse for the failure. Insufficiency of funds is not a reasonable excuse for this purpose and neither is the taxpayer's reliance on another person to do anything, unless the taxpayer took reasonable care to avoid the failure. If the taxpayer had a reasonable excuse, he is treated as continuing to have a reasonable excuse after the excuse has ceased if the failure is remedied without unreasonable delay. For HMRC's approach to reasonable excuse for late filing of a return, see **55.38** below, HMRC Compliance Handbook CH61500 and www.gov.uk/tax-appeals/reasonable-excuses.

Reduction in special circumstances

HMRC can also reduce, stay or agree a compromise in relation to proceedings for a penalty if they think it right to do so because of special circumstances. Ability to pay and the fact that a potential loss of revenue from one taxpayer is balanced by a potential overpayment by another are not special circumstances for this purpose.

Reduction for other penalties

The amount of a tax-geared penalty is reduced by the amount of any other penalty the amount of which is determined by reference to the same tax liability. No such reduction is made for another penalty under the above provisions (but see above for the maximum tax-geared penalty under these provisions), a late payment penalty within **43.4** LATE PAYMENT INTEREST AND PENALTIES, a penalty within **4.48** ANTI-AVOIDANCE (follower notices) or **4.52** ANTI-AVOIDANCE (accelerated payment notices) or a penalty under **55.11** below (asset-based penalty for offshore inaccuracies and failures).

Double jeopardy

A taxpayer is not liable to a penalty for a failure or action in respect of which he has been convicted of an offence.

[*FA 2009, s 106, Sch 55 paras 1–6, 6A, 6AA, 6AB,14, 15, 15A, 16, 17, 17A, 17B, 23–27; FA 2016, ss 163, 169(6)(7), Sch 21 paras 9–12, Sch 22 para 20(5); SI 2011 No 976; SI 2017 Nos 259, 345*].

General

In *Crawford v HMRC* FTT (TC 6594), [2018] UKFTT 392 (TC), the FTT found that an assessment 'fixes or settles a person with liability to the tax as calculated', and that a notice to file a self-assessment tax return can be validly issued simply to assess a known liability to tax; the effect of the decision was that late filing penalties were validly imposed. The UT in *HMRC v Goldsmith* UT, [2019] STC 2512, [2019] UKUT 325 (TCC) followed the decision in *Crawford*, reversing an earlier finding that HMRC had been wrong to issue a notice to file in circumstances where they already knew the tax due. A taxpayer cannot simply ignore a notice to file because no tax is due; penalties can legitimately be charged (*Edwards v HMRC* UT, [2019] STC 1620).

Political objections do not justify failure to make returns (*Turton v Birdforth Commrs* Ch D 1970, 49 ATC 346), nor do objections to the system of taxation (*Walsh v Croydon Commrs* Ch D 1987, 60 TC 442). The submission of a return marked 'to be advised' or some similar phrase does not satisfy the requirements and penalties may be incurred (*Cox v Poole General Commrs* Ch D 1987, 60 TC 445).

Future developments

With effect on and after a day to be appointed by the Treasury, a new category (category 0) is to be introduced for the second tax-geared penalty alongside categories 1 to 3 above. A category 0 territory will be a territory designated as such by Treasury order. The intention is that only territories that adopt automatic exchange of information under the Common Reporting Standard (see **35.14 HMRC** — ADMINISTRATION) will be given category 0 status.

Category 0 will have the same penalty levels as the current category 1 (and all penalties for domestic matters will be moved to category 0). The higher current penalty levels for category 1 will be increased from 100% and 70% to 125% and 87.5% respectively, with the 5% level staying unchanged. Where both the first and second tax-geared penalties are due in relation to the same tax liability, the total of those penalties will not be able to exceed the new 125% limit. There will continue to be reductions for prompted and unprompted disclosures. The penalty levels for categories 2 and 3 will remain the same.

The current system of penalties for late submission of returns is to be replaced by a points-based system from a date which is still to be determined but will be later than 1 April 2020. Each late return will incur one penalty point. No penalties will be charged until a taxpayer reaches two penalty points. A fixed penalty will then be charged each time there is a late return, starting with the return giving rise to the second penalty point. The amount of the penalty has not yet been determined. It is likely to be set at a higher rate than current penalties, but unlike the current penalty regime there will be no escalation to daily or, generally, tax-geared penalties. There will, however, continue to be a tax-geared penalty where, by failing to make the return, the taxpayer is deliberately withholding information that would enable or assist HMRC to assess the tax liability. This will operate in similar fashion to the second tax-geared penalty under the current system above as it applies in cases of deliberate withholding of information. There will be provision for penalty points to expire so as not to expose a taxpayer to penalties in perpetuity. In the simplest case, a penalty point for a one-off failure to file a self-assessment return will expire after two years. An appeal may be made against the award of a penalty point or the imposition of a penalty. A reasonable excuse defence will be available in either case. (Legislation Day 2018 at www.gov.uk/government/publications/late-submission-penalties). HMRC published a Technical Note on these proposed late submission penalties on 6 July 2018. It was announced in July 2019 that the Government remains committed to this reform and that the timing and details of implementation will be announced at a future fiscal event (www.parliament.uk/business/publications/written-questions-answers-statements/written-statement/Commons/2019-07-11/HCWS1713).

Simon's Taxes. See **A4.550–A4.557, A4.562.**

Careless or deliberate errors in documents

[55.6] These provisions apply to a wide range of documents relating to direct and indirect taxes, duties and levies which may be given by a taxpayer to HMRC, including the following which are relevant for the purposes of income tax:

- a tax return under *TMA 1970, s 8* or *s 8A* (personal or trustees' return — see **64.2** RETURNS);
- a return, statement or declaration in connection with a claim for an allowance, deduction or relief;
- accounts in connection with ascertaining liability to tax;
- a partnership return (see **64.12** RETURNS);
- a statement or declaration in connection with a partnership return;
- accounts in connection with a partnership return;
- a quarterly return under *FA 2004, s 254* by the scheme administrator of a registered pension scheme (see **57.9** PENSION PROVISION);
- a PAYE return (see **53.21** PAY AS YOU EARN);
- a CIS return (see **20.11** CONSTRUCTION INDUSTRY SCHEME); and
- any other document (other than one in respect of which a penalty is payable under *TMA 1970, s 98* — see **55.22** below) likely to be relied on by HMRC to determine, without further inquiry, a question about the taxpayer's liability to tax, his payments by way of or in connection with tax, other payments (such as penalties) by the taxpayer or repayments or any other kind of payment or credit to him.

A penalty is payable by a person (P) who gives HMRC such a document if it contains a careless or deliberate inaccuracy on his part which amounts to, or leads to, an understatement of a tax liability or a false or inflated statement of a 'loss' or claim to 'repayment of tax'. If there is more than one inaccuracy in the document a penalty is payable for each inaccuracy.

A penalty is also payable by a person (T) if another person (P) gives HMRC such a document, the document contains an inaccuracy amounting to, or leading to, an understatement of a tax liability or a false or inflated statement of a 'loss' or claim to 'repayment of tax' and the inaccuracy is due to T deliberately supplying false information to P, or deliberately withholding information from P, with the intention of the document containing the inaccuracy. This penalty applies regardless of whether or not P is liable to the main penalty above in respect of the same inaccuracy.

For these purposes, giving HMRC a document includes making a statement or declaration in a document and giving HMRC information in any form and by any method (including post, fax, email or telephone). A '*loss*' includes a charge, expense, deficit or any other amount which may be available for, or relied upon to claim, a deduction or relief. '*Repayment of tax*' includes allowing a credit against tax.

A person is not liable to either of the above penalties for an inaccuracy in respect of which he has been convicted of an offence.

For guidance, see HMRC Briefs 19/08, 1 April 2008 and 29/08, 12 June 2008, and HMRC Compliance Handbook CH80000.

See **55.10** below as regards a possible further penalty where assets are moved between overseas territories in order to prevent or delay the discovery of a potential loss of revenue (as in **55.7** below) giving rise to the above penalty.

HMRC failed in an attempt to charge penalties in respect of an end-of-year PAYE return because the relevant statutory requirement was to submit a return setting out the amounts that had been deducted from employees' earnings and not the amounts that *ought* to have been deducted (*Fab Cleaning Management Ltd v HMRC* FTT (TC 4824), [2016] UKFTT 31 (TC)).

Amount of penalties

See **55.7**, **55.8** below.

Suspension of penalty

HMRC can suspend all or part of a penalty for a careless inaccuracy. A notice in writing must be given to the taxpayer setting out what part of the penalty is to be suspended, the period of suspension (maximum two years) and the conditions of suspension with which the taxpayer must comply. The conditions can specify an action to be taken and a period within which it must be taken. A penalty can be suspended only if compliance with a condition of suspension will help the taxpayer to avoid further penalties under these provisions.

A suspended penalty will become payable:

- at the end of the suspension period, if the taxpayer does not satisfy HMRC that the conditions have been complied with; and
- if, during the suspension period, the taxpayer incurs another penalty under these provisions.

Otherwise, the penalty is cancelled at the end of the suspension period.

In *Testa v HMRC* FTT (TC 2549), [2013] SFTD 723, the appellant had suggested to HMRC the imposition of a suspensive condition to the effect that his tax returns for the next two years be submitted by an appropriate professional adviser. HMRC refused to suspend the penalty on the grounds that their policy was not to suspend penalties in one-off situations. The Tribunal considered this to be flawed, and ordered the penalty to be suspended.

Agents

P is liable to a penalty under the above provisions where a document containing a *careless* inaccuracy is given to HMRC on his behalf. He is not, however, liable to a penalty in respect of anything done or omitted by his agent, if he satisfies HMRC that he took reasonable care (see below) to avoid the inaccuracy. It cannot be said that a person is careless if the negligence is that, and only that, of a professional adviser if the adviser is not acting as a mere agent, administrator or functionary but in a truly professional capacity (*Mariner v HMRC* FTT (TC 3039), [2014] SFTD 504).

Partnerships

Where a partner is liable to a penalty arising from an inaccuracy in, or in connection with, a partnership return, and the inaccuracy affects the amount of tax payable by another partner, that other partner is also liable to a penalty. The potential lost revenue is calculated separately for each partner by reference to the proportions of any tax liability that would be borne by each of them. The suspension provisions above are, however, applied jointly to the partners' penalties.

Company officers

Where a company (as widely defined) is liable to a penalty under the above provisions for a deliberate inaccuracy and the inaccuracy was attributable to a company 'officer', the officer is liable to pay such portion of the penalty (which may be 100%) as HMRC specify by written notice. Various provisions of *FA 2007, Sch 24* (e.g. right of appeal) then apply as if the specified portion were itself a penalty incurred by the officer. In relation to a body corporate, a director, shadow director, manager or secretary of the company is an '*officer*'. In relation to an LLP, a member of the LLP is an '*officer*'. In any other case, a director, manager, secretary or any other person managing or purporting to manage any of the company's affairs is an '*officer*'.

[*FA 2007, s 97, Sch 24 paras 1, 1A, 3, 14, 18–23A, 24–28; F(No 2)A 2017, s 64(3)(5)(6)*].

Reasonable care

An inaccuracy is '*careless*' if the inaccuracy is due to failure by P to take reasonable care. [*FA 2007, s 97, Sch 24 para 3*]. What is 'reasonable care' is viewed in the light of a person's own abilities and circumstances. HMRC do expect each person to make and preserve sufficient records to enable a correct and complete return to be made, and expect a higher degree of care to be taken over large and complex matters than simpler straightforward ones. They consider it is reasonable to expect a person who encounters a transaction or other event with which he is not familiar to take care to ascertain the correct tax treatment or to seek appropriate advice. If after that the person is still unsure, he should draw attention to the entry and the uncertainty when delivering his return or other document. (HMRC Compliance Handbook CH81120).

Presumption of carelessness

With effect in relation to documents given to HMRC on or after 16 November 2017 and relating to a tax period beginning on or after 6 April 2017 and ending on or after 16 November 2017, there is a presumption of carelessness where a document contains a non-deliberate inaccuracy as a result of its being submitted on the basis that particular 'avoidance arrangements' had an effect which in fact they did not have. The presumption is disapplied if P satisfies HMRC or an Appeal Tribunal that he took reasonable care to avoid inaccuracy, but neither HMRC nor the Tribunal can take any account of any evidence of any reliance by P on 'disqualified advice'.

Arrangements (as widely defined) are '*avoidance arrangements*' for this purpose if it would be reasonable to conclude that the obtaining of a tax advantage (also widely defined) was a main purpose of them. There is a let-out for arrangements which accord with established practice accepted by HMRC. Where arrangements are caught by specified anti-avoidance or anti-abuse legislation, they are automatically avoidance arrangements for this purpose, and the let-out does not apply.

'*Disqualified advice*' is defined in broadly similar terms as in **55.12** below. There is a limited exemption for certain advice received in connection with 'avoidance-related rules' (as in **4.57** ANTI-AVOIDANCE). The question of whether P has taken reasonable steps to find out whether or not advice is disqualified, and believes it not to be so, is judged as at the time when the document containing the inaccuracy is given to HMRC. Where a document is given to HMRC by the personal representative of a deceased person, the disqualified advice rules are applied by reference both to the deceased and the personal representative.

[*FA 2007, s 97, Sch 24 paras 3A, 3B; F(No 2)A 2017, s 64(2)(3)(5)(6)*].

Prior to the above rules coming into effect, reliance on legal advice was disregarded in determining whether or not an inaccuracy was careless if the advice was given or procured by a monitored promoter (see **25.12–25.23** DISCLOSURE OF TAX AVOIDANCE SCHEMES) and related to arrangements of which the monitored promoter was a promoter. [*FA 2014, s 276; F(No 2)A 2017, s 64(4)*].

Simon's Taxes. See **A4.5**.

Amount of penalties

[55.7] The amount of the penalty payable by P in **55.6** above depends on whether the inaccuracy is careless or deliberate, and is subject to reduction as detailed below. For this purpose, an inaccuracy in a document which was neither careless nor deliberate is treated as careless if P or a person acting on his behalf discovered the inaccuracy after giving HMRC the document but did not take reasonable steps to inform them.

The amount of the penalty also depends on whether the inaccuracy involves a domestic matter or an offshore matter. The remainder of this paragraph assumes the inaccuracy involves a domestic matter; see **55.8** below as regards offshore matters.

For careless action or omission (i.e. where P or a person acting on his behalf failed to take reasonable care — see **55.6** above), the penalty is **30%** of the 'potential lost revenue' (see below).

For deliberate but not concealed action or omission (i.e. where the inaccuracy was deliberate but P did not make arrangements to conceal it), the penalty is **70%** of the potential lost revenue.

For deliberate and concealed action or omission (i.e. where the inaccuracy was deliberate and P made arrangements to conceal it, for example by submitting false evidence in support of an inaccurate figure), the penalty is **100%** of the potential lost revenue.

The amount of the penalty payable by T in **55.6** above is **100%** of the potential lost revenue. (This is the case regardless of whether the inaccuracy involves a domestic matter or an offshore matter.)

Reduction for disclosure

A reduction in a penalty will be given where a person discloses an inaccuracy in a document or, in relation to the penalty payable by T, a supply of false information or a withholding of information. The penalty will be reduced to a percentage which reflects the quality of the disclosure (see HMRC Compliance Handbook CH82430), and the amount of the reduction will depend on whether the disclosure is 'prompted' or 'unprompted'.

The penalty cannot be reduced below a minimum percentage as shown in the table below.

Standard percentage	Minimum percentage for prompted disclosure	Minimum percentage for unprompted disclosure
30%	15%	0%
70%	35%	20%
100%	50%	30%

A person is treated as making a disclosure for these purposes only if he tells HMRC about the inaccuracy etc., gives HMRC reasonable help in quantifying the inaccuracy etc. and allows them access to records for the purpose of ensuring that the inaccuracy etc. is fully corrected. A disclosure is '*unprompted*' if made when the taxpayer has no reason to believe HMRC have discovered, or are about to discover, the inaccuracy etc. In all other cases, disclosures are '*prompted*'. Where a person has taken a significant period (such as three years or more) to correct or disclose the inaccuracy, HMRC will usually restrict the maximum reduction for the quality of disclosure to 10 percentage points above the minimum of the penalty range (www.gov.uk/government/publications/compliance-checks-penalties-for-inaccuracies-in-returns-or-documents-ccfs7a).

Reduction in special circumstances

HMRC can also reduce, stay, or agree a compromise in relation to proceedings for, either of the penalties in **55.6** above if they think it right to do so because of special circumstances. Ability to pay and the fact that a potential loss of revenue from one taxpayer is balanced by a potential overpayment by another are not special circumstances for this purpose.

Reduction for other penalty or surcharge

The amount of a penalty payable by P in **55.6** above in respect of a document relating to a particular tax year is reduced by the amount of any other penalty, or surcharge for late payment of tax, the amount of which is determined by reference to P's tax liability for the year. No reduction is made for a tax-related penalty within **55.15** below, a late payment penalty under **43.2** LATE PAYMENT

INTEREST AND PENALTIES, a penalty within **4.48** ANTI-AVOIDANCE (follower notices) or **4.52** ANTI-AVOIDANCE (accelerated payment notices) or a penalty under **55.11** below (asset-based penalty for offshore inaccuracies and failures).

Where penalties are imposed on P and T in **55.6** above in respect of the same inaccuracy, the aggregate penalty cannot exceed 100% of the potential lost revenue.

Potential lost revenue

The '*potential lost revenue*' is the additional tax (including NIC) due or payable as a result of correcting the inaccuracy in the document. This includes any amount payable to HMRC having been previously repaid in error and any amount which would have been repaid in error had the inaccuracy not been corrected. The fact that potential lost revenue may be balanced by a potential overpayment by another person is also ignored.

Where the amount of potential lost revenue (in relation to the penalty payable by P) depends on the order in which inaccuracies are corrected, careless inaccuracies are taken to be corrected before deliberate inaccuracies, and deliberate but not concealed inaccuracies are taken to be corrected before deliberate and concealed inaccuracies. Where there are inaccuracies in one or more documents relating to a particular tax year (in relation to the penalty payable by P) and those inaccuracies include both understatements and overstatements, the overstatements are taken into account in calculating the potential lost revenue and are set off against understatements in the order which reduces the level of penalties the least (i.e. against understatements not liable to a penalty first, then against careless understatements, and so on).

Special rules apply where an inaccuracy leads to there being a wrongly recorded loss which has not been wholly used to reduce a tax liability. The potential lost revenue in respect of that part of the loss which has not been so used is restricted to 10% of the unused part. Where, however, there is no reasonable prospect of a loss being used to support a claim to reduce a tax liability (of any person) because of the taxpayer's circumstances or the nature of the loss, the potential lost revenue is nil.

Where an inaccuracy results in an amount of tax being declared later that it would have been (otherwise than because of a wrongly recorded loss), the potential lost revenue is 5% of the delayed tax for each year of delay (applied pro rata for periods of less than a year).

[*FA 2007, s 97, Sch 24 paras 4, 4A, 4B, 4D, 5–10, 11, 12, 24, 28; FA 2009, Sch 56 para 9A; FA 2016, Sch 22 para 20(3)*].

Amount of penalties — offshore matters and transfers

[55.8] The amount of the penalty payable by P in **55.6** above depends not only on whether the inaccuracy is careless or deliberate (see **55.7** above) but also on whether the inaccuracy involves (i) a domestic matter or (ii) an offshore matter or offshore transfer.

For these purposes, an inaccuracy involves an *offshore matter* if it results in a potential loss of revenue (see **55.7** above) that is charged on or by reference to:

- income arising from a source in a territory outside the UK; or
- 'assets' situated or held in a territory outside the UK; or
- activities carried on wholly or mainly in a territory outside the UK; or
- anything having effect as if it were income, assets or activities of the kind above.

An inaccuracy involves an *offshore transfer* if:

- it does not involve an offshore matter;
- it is deliberate (whether or not concealed) and results in a potential loss of revenue; and
- the income on (or by reference to which) the tax is charged (or any part of that income):
  - is received in a territory outside the UK; or
  - is transferred to a territory outside the UK before the date when the document containing the inaccuracy is given to HMRC. The reference to the transfer of income is to be read as including a reference to the transfer of any assets derived from or representing that income.

Where more than one category of territory is involved in an offshore transfer, the level of penalty is to be determined by reference to the highest category of territory involved.

If the inaccuracy does not involve an offshore matter or an offshore transfer it involves a domestic matter. The Treasury may make provision by statutory instrument for determining for the above purposes where a source of income is located, where an asset is situated or held, where activities are carried on, where income is received or transferred and where assets are transferred. Different provision may be made for different cases and for income tax and capital gains tax. '*Assets*' has the same meaning as for capital gains tax purposes (see *TCGA 1992, s 21(1)*) but also includes sterling.

Category 0

Not yet in operation — see below under Future development.

Category 1

If the inaccuracy involves an offshore matter or offshore transfer and the territory in question is a 'category 1 territory', the amounts of the penalties are currently the same as for domestic matters, i.e. the amounts in **55.7** above, but see below under Future development. A '*category 1 territory*' is a territory designated as such by order made by the Treasury.

Category 2

If the inaccuracy involves an offshore matter or offshore transfer and the territory in question is a 'category 2 territory', the amounts of the penalties are as follows.

For careless action or omission (i.e. where P or a person acting on his behalf failed to take reasonable care — see **55.6** above), the penalty is **45%** of the 'potential lost revenue' (see **55.7** above).

For deliberate but not concealed action or omission (i.e. where the inaccuracy was deliberate but P did not make arrangements to conceal it), the penalty is **105%** of the potential lost revenue.

For deliberate and concealed action or omission (i.e. where the inaccuracy was deliberate and P made arrangements to conceal it, for example by submitting false evidence in support of an inaccurate figure), the penalty is **150%** of the potential lost revenue.

A '*category 2 territory*' is a territory that is neither a category 1 territory nor a category 3 territory.

Category 3

If the inaccuracy involves an offshore matter or offshore transfer and the territory in question is a 'category 3 territory', the amounts of the penalties are as follows.

For careless action or omission, the penalty is **60%** of the potential lost revenue.

For deliberate but not concealed action or omission, the penalty is **140%** of the potential lost revenue.

For deliberate and concealed action or omission, the penalty is **200%** of the potential lost revenue.

A '*category 3 territory*' is a territory designated as such by order made by the Treasury.

Inaccuracy in more than one category

If a single inaccuracy is in more than one category it is treated for these purposes as if it were separate inaccuracies, one in each relevant category according to the matters that it involves. The potential lost revenue is to be calculated separately in respect of each separate inaccuracy.

Categorisation of territories

In considering how to classify a territory for these purposes, the Treasury must have regard to:

- the existence or otherwise of arrangements for the exchange of information between the UK and that territory;
- the quality of any such arrangements (in particular, whether they provide for information to be exchanged automatically or on request);
- the benefit that the UK would be likely to obtain from receiving information from that territory, were such arrangements to exist;
- the existence of any other arrangements between the UK and that territory for co-operation in the area of taxation; and
- the quality of any such other arrangements (in particular, the extent to which the said co-operation will assist in protecting UK tax revenue).

Categorisation orders are to be made by statutory instrument. The above penalty provisions do not apply to inaccuracies in a document given to HMRC (or, where appropriate, to inaccuracies discovered by P — see 55.7 above) before the date on which the relevant categorisation order comes into force. *SI 2011 No 976* designates various territories as category 1 or 3.

Reduction for disclosure

A reduction in a penalty will be given where a person discloses an inaccuracy in a document or, in relation to the penalty payable by T in 55.6 above, a supply of false information or a withholding of information. The penalty will be reduced to a percentage which reflects the quality of the disclosure (see HMRC Compliance Handbook CH82430) and the amount of the reduction will depend on whether the disclosure is 'prompted' or 'unprompted'.

A person (X) is treated as making a disclosure for these purposes only if X tells HMRC about the inaccuracy etc., gives HMRC reasonable help in quantifying the inaccuracy etc. and allows them access to records for the purpose of ensuring that the inaccuracy etc. is fully corrected. With effect on and after 1 April 2017, X must also tell HMRC if there is:

- any person who encouraged, assisted or otherwise facilitated the inaccuracy etc.; and
- any asset situated or held outside the UK that is held on X's behalf by another person,

and must provide further specified details if either is the case.

A disclosure is '*unprompted*' if made when the taxpayer has no reason to believe HMRC have discovered, or are about to discover, the inaccuracy etc. In all other cases, disclosures are '*prompted*'.

For an inaccuracy involving an offshore matter or offshore transfer the penalty cannot be reduced below a minimum percentage as shown in the table below.

Standard percentage	Minimum percentage for prompted disclosure	Minimum percentage for unprompted disclosure
30%	15%	0%
45%	22.5%	0%
60%	30%	0%
70%	45%	30%
100%	60%	40%
105%	62.5%	40%
140%	80%	50%
150%	85%	55%
200%	110%	70%

Where a person has taken a significant period (such as three years or more) to correct or disclose the inaccuracy, HMRC will usually restrict the maximum reduction for the quality of disclosure to 10 percentage points above the minimum of the penalty range (www.gov.uk/government/publications/compli ance-checks-penalties-for-inaccuracies-in-returns-or-documents-ccfs7a).

Reduction in special circumstances

See 55.7 above.

Reduction for other penalty or surcharge

Where penalties are imposed on P and T (in **55.6** above) in respect of the same inaccuracy, the aggregate penalty cannot exceed:

- 100% of the potential lost revenue for an inaccuracy in category 1, i.e. the same as in **55.7** above;
- 150% of the potential lost revenue for an inaccuracy in category 2; or
- 200% of the potential lost revenue for an inaccuracy in category 3.

See also **55.7** above.

Future development

With effect on and after a day to be appointed by the Treasury, a new category (category 0) is to be introduced alongside categories 1 to 3 above. A category 0 territory will be a territory designated as such by Treasury order. The intention is that only territories that adopt automatic exchange of information under the Common Reporting Standard (see **35.14** HMRC — ADMINISTRATION) will be given category 0 status.

Category 0 will have the same penalty levels as the current category 1 (and all penalties for domestic matters will be moved to category 0). The current penalty levels for category 1 will be increased from 30%, 70% and 100% to 37.5%, 87.5% and 125% respectively. There will continue to be reductions for prompted and unprompted disclosures. The penalty levels for categories 2 and 3 will remain the same.

Where penalties are imposed on P and T (in **55.6** above) in respect of the same inaccuracy, the aggregate penalty will not be able to exceed 100% of the potential lost revenue for an inaccuracy in new category 0 or 125% of the potential lost revenue for an inaccuracy in amended category 1.

[*FA 2007, Sch 24 paras 4, 4A, 4AA, 10A, 12(4)(5), 21A, 21B, 23B; FA 2016, s 163, Sch 21 paras 1–4; SI 2011 No 976; SI 2017 Nos 259, 345*].

Simon's Taxes. See **A4.575–A4.576.**

Offshore evasion

[55.9] See the enhanced penalties at **55.4** (notification of chargeability), **55.5** (late filing) and **55.8** (inaccuracies in documents) above where the non-compliance involves an offshore matter or an offshore transfer. See also **55.10** below as regards offshore asset moves.

Numerous additional measures have been introduced to deter offshore tax evasion:

- increased minimum penalties following any reduction for disclosure (see **55.4**, **55.5** and **55.8** above);
- an asset-based penalty for offshore inaccuracies and failures (see **55.11** below);
- a penalty for failure to correct past (i.e. pre-6 April 2017) offshore tax non-compliance by 30 September 2018 (see **55.12** below);

- civil sanctions for *enablers* of offshore evasion (see **55.19** below);
- a criminal offence for offshore evasion (see **55.34** below); and
- an extended time limit for raising assessments (see **6.3** ASSESSMENTS).

Client notification requirement

On and after 30 September 2016, persons who provide professional advice or services in respect of taxation or finance involving overseas income or assets were required to notify their clients about matters including the Common Reporting Standard (see **35.14** HMRC — ADMINISTRATION), the penalties for offshore tax evasion and the opportunities to disclose previous offshore evasion to HMRC. The regulations required a standard notification letter, headed 'If you have money or other assets abroad, you could owe tax in the UK', to be sent to affected clients no later than 31 August 2017. Affected clients are those to whom the adviser has provided advice or services about income or assets outside the UK, or who the adviser has referred overseas for such advice or services, but disregarding clients for whom the adviser has completed and submitted a personal tax return reflecting such advice or services. The penalty for non-compliance is £3,000. A similar obligation fell upon financial intermediaries. See www.gov.uk/government/publications/client-notification-income-or-assets-abroad for more information, including the text of the standard letter. [*FA 2013, s 222; SI 2015 No 878, Regs 12A–12F, 13, Sch 3; SI 2016 No 899*].

Penalty for offshore asset moves

[55.10] The '*offshore asset moves penalty*' applies where assets are moved between overseas territories and a main purpose of that movement is to prevent or delay the discovery by HMRC of a potential loss of revenue that itself gives rise to one of the penalties listed below.

The offshore asset moves penalty applies where the person concerned (P) becomes liable to another penalty (the '*original penalty*') and this is either

- the penalty for failure to notify chargeability in **55.3** above;
- the second tax-geared late filing penalty in **55.5** above;
- the penalty for careless or deliberate errors in documents in **55.6** above; or
- the penalty for failure to correct offshore tax non-compliance in **55.12** below.

However, the offshore asset moves penalty applies only where the original penalty is for a deliberate failure or action (regardless of whether or not it was concealed) and where the tax involved is income tax, capital gains tax or inheritance tax (or, for a penalty under **55.3**, income tax or capital gains tax). In the case of a penalty for failure to correct, the failure is deliberate if P was aware at any time during the RTC period (see **55.12**) that at the end of 2016/17 he had offshore tax non-compliance to correct.

The amount of the offshore asset moves penalty is 50% of the amount of the original penalty payable by P. Even though the original penalty may be determined by reference to a liability to tax, the offshore asset moves penalty is not.

For the offshore asset moves penalty to apply, there has to be a 'relevant offshore asset move' which occurs after the 'relevant time'. There is a '*relevant offshore asset move*' if, at a time when P is the beneficial owner of an 'asset' and without his ceasing entirely to be the beneficial owner of it:

- the asset ceases to be situated or held in a 'specified territory' and becomes situated or held in a non-specified territory; or
- the person who holds the asset ceases to be resident in a specified territory and becomes resident in a non-specified territory; or
- there is a change in the arrangements for the ownership of the asset.

Where P disposes of an asset and reinvests all or part of the proceeds in another, the original and new asset are to be treated as the same asset for the purposes of determining whether there is a relevant offshore asset move. '*Asset*' has the same meaning as for capital gains tax purposes (see *TCGA 1992, s 21(1)*) but also includes sterling. The question of whether or not a territory is a specified territory is to be determined as at the time one of these events occurs. A '*specified territory*' is a territory designated as such by the Treasury by means of statutory instrument. A territory will be so designated if it has committed to exchanging information under the Common Reporting Standard.

The '*relevant time*' for income tax purposes is determined according to the nature of the original penalty as follows.

- Where the original penalty is a penalty for failure to notify chargeability, the relevant time is the beginning of the tax year to which the obligation to notify relates.
- Where the original penalty is a second tax-geared late filing penalty, the relevant time is the beginning of the tax year to which the return or document relates.
- Where the original penalty is a penalty for careless or deliberate errors in documents, the relevant time is the beginning of the tax year to which the document containing the inaccuracy relates.
- Where the original penalty is a penalty for failure to correct offshore tax non-compliance, the relevant time is 16 November 2017.

[*FA 2015, Sch 21 paras 1–6, 9; F(No 2)A 2017, Sch 18 para 27; SI 2015 No 866; SI 2017 No 989*].

Asset-based penalty for offshore inaccuracies and failures

[55.11] An asset-based penalty is payable by a person where:

(a) one or more 'offshore tax penalties' have been imposed on a person in relation to a tax year; and
(b) the potential lost revenue threshold is met in relation to that year.

Where the above conditions are met in relation to more than one tax year falling within the same 'investigation period', only one asset-based penalty is payable in that investigation period in relation to any given asset. This penalty is charged by reference to the tax year within the investigation period that has the highest 'offshore PLR' (see below under Potential lost revenue threshold). In relation to a person (P), the first '*investigation period*' begins on the day on which the asset-based penalty regime comes into force and ends on 5 April in the last tax year before P is notified of an asset-based penalty in respect of an asset. Subsequent investigation periods begin on the day following the end of the previous investigation period and end on 5 April in the last tax year before P is notified of a subsequent asset-based penalty in respect of the asset. Different investigation periods may apply in relation to different assets. The investigation period rules do not apply where the offshore tax penalty is a penalty under *F(No 2)A 2017, Sch 18* (failure to correct offshore tax non-compliance). Where such a penalty is imposed, and (b) above is met, only one asset-based penalty is payable in relation to any given asset.

Meaning of 'offshore tax penalty'

For the purposes of (a) above and these provisions generally, an '*offshore tax penalty*' is any of the following:

- a penalty under *FA 2007, Sch 24 para 1* (errors in documents) imposed for deliberate action (whether or not concealed) where the inaccuracy for which the penalty is imposed involves an offshore matter or an offshore transfer (see **55.8** above);
- a penalty under *FA 2008, Sch 41 para 1* (failure to notify chargeability) imposed for deliberate failure (whether or not concealed) where the failure involves an offshore matter or an offshore transfer (see **55.4** above);
- a penalty under *FA 2009, Sch 55 para 6* (the second tax-geared late filing penalty) imposed for deliberate withholding of information (whether or not concealed) where the withholding of information involves an offshore matter or an offshore transfer (see **55.5** above); or
- a penalty under *F(No 2)A 2017, Sch 18* (failure to correct offshore tax non-compliance) where the person was aware at any time during the RTC period that at the end of 2016/17 he had offshore tax non-compliance to correct (see **55.12** below),

but only if the tax at stake is (or includes) a tax within the asset-based penalty regime, i.e. 'asset-based income tax', capital gains tax and, where applicable, inheritance tax. Where the tax at stake includes any taxes other than those, the offshore tax penalty is the part of the penalty which relates to those taxes. '*Asset-based income tax*' is income tax that is charged under any of a significant number of charging provisions listed at *FA 2016, Sch 22 para 13(2)(2A)*; see also below under Identification and valuation of assets. Where the inaccuracy etc. for which a penalty is imposed also involves a domestic matter, the offshore tax penalty is only that part of the penalty that involves the offshore matter or offshore transfer; this is not relevant to a penalty for failure to correct.

For the purposes of (a) above, as regards income tax, the tax year to which an offshore tax penalty relates is the tax year to which the document containing the inaccuracy, the obligation to notify chargeability, the late return or the offshore tax non-compliance relates.

Potential lost revenue threshold

For the purposes of (b) above, the potential lost revenue threshold is reached where the 'offshore PLR' in relation to a tax year exceeds £25,000. The '*offshore PLR*', in relation to a tax year, is the total of:

- the potential lost revenue (as in **55.3** and **55.7** above and **55.12** below); and
- the liability to tax (as in **55.5** above),

by reference to which all of the offshore tax penalties imposed in relation to the tax year are assessed. Where a penalty assessed relates to an offshore tax penalty and one or more other penalties (a '*combined penalty*'), only the potential lost revenue or liability to tax relating to the offshore tax penalty is taken into account in calculating the offshore PLR. Where necessary for the purposes of calculating the offshore PLR in such a case, income and gains relating to domestic matters are taken to have been taxed before income and gains relating to offshore matters and offshore transfers, and income and gains relating to taxes within the asset-based penalty regime are taken to have been taxed before income and gains relating to taxes outside the regime. Where it cannot otherwise be determined, the potential lost revenue or liability to tax relating to the offshore tax penalty is taken to be such share of the total potential lost revenue or liability to tax by reference to which the combined penalty was calculated as is just and reasonable. Where an offshore tax penalty or combined penalty relates to two or more taxes, including asset-based income tax and capital gains tax, then where necessary for the purposes of calculating the offshore PLR, income and gains relating to asset-based income tax are taken to have been taxed before income and gains relating to capital gains tax.

Amount of penalty

The penalty is the lower of (i) 10% of the value of the asset (see below) and (ii) the offshore PLR (see above) x 10.

HMRC must reduce the penalty where the taxpayer makes a disclosure of the inaccuracy or failure relating to the offshore tax penalty, provides HMRC with a reasonable valuation of the asset and provides HMRC with information or access to records that HMRC require for the purposes of valuing the asset. The reduction must reflect the quality of the disclosure, valuation and information provided (and for these purposes 'quality' includes timing, nature and extent). The maximum amount by which a penalty can be reduced is 50% of the standard amount in a case involving only unprompted disclosures and 20% of the standard amount in a case involving prompted disclosures. A case involves only unprompted disclosures if all the offshore tax penalties to which the asset-based penalty relates were reduced on the basis of unprompted disclosures. A case involves prompted disclosures if any of the offshore tax penalties to which the asset-based penalty relates was reduced on the basis of a prompted disclosure. Where a person has taken a significant period (such as three years or more) to correct or disclose the inaccuracy or failure, HMRC will usually restrict the maximum reduction for the quality of disclosure to 10 percentage points above the minimum of the penalty range (www.gov.uk/government/publications/compliance-checks-penalties-for-income-tax-and-capital-gains-tax-for-offshore-matters-ccfs17).

HMRC may also reduce, stay, or agree a compromise in relation to proceedings for, an asset-based penalty because of special circumstances if they think it right to do so. Ability to pay and the fact that a potential loss of revenue from one taxpayer is balanced by a potential overpayment by another are not special circumstances for this purpose.

Identification and valuation of assets

Where the 'principal tax at stake' is asset-based income tax, the above-mentioned list at *FA 2016, Sch 22 para 13(2)(2A)* identifies the assets on which the various income tax charges are based. For example, for the charge on property income the asset is the land that generates the income; for the charge on dividends the asset is the shares on which it is paid; for the charge on interest it is the asset that generates the interest; for the charge to income tax on amounts treated as income of settlor, the asset is the settlement itself; and so on. The '*principal tax at stake*' is the tax to which the offshore tax penalty relates. If the offshore tax penalty relates to more than one tax, it is the tax which gives rise to the highest offshore PLR value, i.e. the potential lost revenue or liability to tax by reference to which the part of the penalty relating to each tax was assessed. An asset-based penalty may relate to more than one asset.

The following applies to value an asset identified as above. Where the charge to income tax was triggered by a disposal of the asset, the value of the asset is taken as its market value on the date of disposal; in the case of a part disposal the value of the asset is to be taken as its full market value immediately before the part disposal took place. In any other case the value of the asset is determined as follows:

- where the taxpayer owns the asset on the last day of the tax year to which the offshore tax penalty relates, the value is its market value on that day;
- where the taxpayer disposed of the asset during that tax year, the value is its market value on the date of disposal; and
- where the taxpayer disposed of part of the asset during that tax year, the value is the sum of the market value of the part disposed of on the date(s) of disposal and the market value of the part still owned on the last day of the tax year.

For the above purpose a person owns an asset if he is liable to asset-based income tax in relation to it, and market value is determined in accordance with *TCGA 1992, s 272*.

If, however, the value of the asset, determined as above, does not appear to HMRC to be a fair and reasonable value, HMRC may value the asset for the purposes of the asset-based penalty in any other way which appears to them to be fair and reasonable.

Where an asset-based penalty is chargeable in relation to an asset that is jointly held by the taxpayer (P) and another person (A), the value of the asset is the value of P's share of it. If P and A are living together in a marriage or civil partnership, the asset is taken to be jointly owned by them in equal shares, unless it appears to HMRC that this is not the case.

[*FA 2016, s 165, Sch 22 paras 1–10, 13, 14, 19; F(No 2)A 2017, Sch 18 para 28; SI 2017 Nos 277, 334*].

Failure to correct offshore tax non-compliance

[55.12] A penalty is payable by a person who has 'offshore tax non-compliance' to correct at the end of 2016/17 and fails to correct it within the period 6 April 2017 to 30 September 2018 inclusive (known as the '*RTC period*'). [*F(No 2)A 2017, Sch 18 para 1*]. The penalty applies to income tax, capital gains tax and inheritance tax non-compliance; the coverage below focuses on its application to income tax. For guidance see www.gov.uk/guidance/requirement-to-correct-tax-due-on-offshore-assets.

Meaning of offshore tax non-compliance

For this purpose, '*offshore tax non-compliance*' means 'tax non-compliance' which involves an 'offshore matter'; or an 'offshore transfer', whether or not it also involves an onshore matter. Tax non-compliance involves an onshore matter to the extent (if any) that it does not involve an offshore matter or an offshore transfer. Any of the following is '*tax non-compliance*' for this purpose:

(a) failure to notify chargeability to income tax by the required date (see **55.2** above);
(b) failure to deliver a tax return or other document (as listed in *F(No 2)A 2017, Sch 18 para 8(3)*) by the required date (see **55.5** above); and
(c) delivery of a return or other document (as listed in *F(No 2)A 2017, Sch 18 para 8(3)(4)*) containing an inaccuracy (whether or not careless or deliberate) amounting to, or leading to, an understatement of a tax liability or a false or inflated statement of a loss or claim to repayment of tax.

The question of whether tax non-compliance involves an '*offshore matter*' is determined in the same way as for other penalties to which this is relevant. See **55.4**, **55.5** and **55.8** above. The determination is made by reference, in a case within (a) above, to the potential loss of revenue; in a case within (b) above, to the tax liability (if any) that would have been shown in the return etc.; and, in a case within (c) above, to the information that should have been given in the document.

Tax non-compliance involves an '*offshore transfer*' if it does not involve an offshore matter and:

- in a case within (a) or (b) above, the income on (or by reference to which) tax is charged (or any part of that income) was received in a territory outside the UK or was transferred before 6 April 2017 to a territory outside the UK; and

- in a case within (c) above (where the tax at stake is income tax), the income on or by reference to which the tax is charged, or any part of the income, was received in a territory outside the UK or was transferred before 6 April 2017 to a territory outside the UK.

In any of these cases, the reference to the transfer of income is to be read as including a reference to the transfer of any assets derived from or representing that income. '*Assets*' has the same meaning as for capital gains tax purposes (see *TCGA 1992, s 21(1)*) but also includes sterling.

It is an overriding condition that tax non-compliance can involve an offshore matter or offshore transfer only, in a case within (b) above, where a complete and accurate return etc. would have included information enabling or assisting HMRC to assess the person's tax liability; and, in a case within (c) above, if the inaccuracy relates to information that would have enabled or assisted HMRC to assess the person's tax liability.

[*F(No 2)A 2017, Sch 18 paras 7–12*].

When the rules apply

A person has offshore tax non-compliance to correct at the end of 2016/17 if:

- Conditions A and B below are met in respect of any offshore tax non-compliance committed before 6 April 2017 (the '*original offshore tax non-compliance*'); and
- Condition C below is met.

Condition A is that the original offshore tax non-compliance has not been fully corrected before the end of 2016/17. Condition B is that the original offshore tax non-compliance involved a potential loss of revenue when it was committed and that, in the case of partial correction before the end of 2016/17, the uncorrected part at that time involved a potential loss of revenue.

Condition C is that on 6 April 2017 HMRC would in law have been able to assess the taxpayer to the tax liability arising from the non-compliance if they had been aware at that time of the information missing as a result of the failure to correct. What is said below under Extension of period for assessment of offshore tax is disregarded for the purpose of applying Condition C.

[*F(No 2)A 2017, Sch 18 paras 3–6*].

Correcting offshore tax non-compliance

Offshore tax non-compliance can be corrected by giving HMRC the 'relevant information' by:

- in a case within (a) above, delivering a tax return;
- in a case within (b) above, delivering the requisite return or document;
- in a case within (c) above, amending the document or delivering a new document;
- using the digital disclosure service (see below) or any other service provided by HMRC as a means of correcting tax non-compliance;
- communicating it to an HMRC officer in the course of an enquiry; or

- using any other method agreed with an HMRC officer.

The '*relevant information*' is the information relating to offshore tax that, were it not for the non-compliance, would have enabled or assisted HMRC to calculate the offshore tax due.

[*F(No 2)A 2017, Sch 18 para 13*].

It is anticipated that in most cases the requirement to correct will be met via HMRC's Worldwide Disclosure Facility at www.gov.uk/guidance/worldwide-disclosure-facility-make-a-disclosure. The Facility is available to anyone disclosing a UK tax liability that relates wholly or partly to an offshore issue. See www.gov.uk/guidance/offshore-disclosure-facilities.

Amount of penalty

The penalty is **200%** of the 'offshore PLR' attributable to the offshore tax non-compliance remaining uncorrected when the RTC period ends. The '*offshore PLR*' is the potential loss of revenue (PLR) attributable to the offshore tax non-compliance in question, and is determined as follows.

- In a case within (a) above, it is calculated in similar manner as in **55.3** above and is thus usually the amount of tax payable that, by reason of the non-compliance, remains unpaid on 31 January following the tax year in question.
- In a case within (b) above, it is the tax liability that would have been shown as due or payable in a complete and accurate return delivered on the due date.
- In a case within (c) above, it is calculated in similar manner as in **55.7** above and is thus usually the additional tax due or payable as a result of correcting the inaccuracy in the document. *F(No 2)A 2017, Sch 18 para 15(3)* modifies the rules in **55.7** for this purpose; the principal modification is that where the amount of PLR depends on the order in which inaccuracies are corrected, the PLR attributable to any offshore tax non-compliance constituted by any one of those inaccuracies is taken to be such amount as is just and reasonable.

Any 'combined tax non-compliance' is treated for these purposes as if it were two separate acts of tax non-compliance. '*Combined tax non-compliance*' is tax non-compliance that involves an offshore matter or an offshore transfer but also involves an onshore matter. The PLR attributable to the offshore tax non-compliance is to taken to be such share of the total PLR as is just and reasonable.

Reductions

HMRC must reduce the penalty if the person liable discloses any of the following matters that is relevant to the non-compliance or its correction or to the assessment or enforcement of the offshore tax attributable to it: chargeability to tax (where the tax non-compliance is a failure to notify chargeability); a missing tax return; an inaccuracy in a document; a supply of false information or a withholding of information; or a failure to disclose an under-assessment. The reduction must reflect the quality of the disclosure (and for these purposes 'quality' includes timing, nature and extent) but the penalty cannot be reduced below 100% of the offshore PLR. A person discloses a matter for these purposes only by: telling HMRC about it; giving HMRC reasonable help in relation to it (for example by quantifying an inaccuracy in a document); informing HMRC of any person who acted as an enabler of the offshore tax non-compliance or the failure to correct it; and allowing HMRC access to records for any reasonable purpose connected with resolving the matter and to ensure that HMRC can identify all persons who may have acted as enablers. A person acts as an enabler of offshore tax non-compliance by another if he encourages, assists or otherwise facilitates the conduct constituting the non-compliance.

HMRC may also reduce, stay, or agree a compromise in relation to proceedings for, the penalty because of special circumstances if they think it right to do so. Ability to pay and the fact that a potential loss of revenue from one taxpayer is balanced by a potential overpayment by another are not special circumstances for this purpose.

Reasonable excuse

Liability to the above penalty does not arise in relation to a particular failure to correct any offshore tax non-compliance within the RTC period if the taxpayer (T) satisfies HMRC or, on appeal, the Appeal Tribunal, that there is a reasonable excuse for the failure. Insufficiency of funds is not a reasonable excuse for this purpose, unless attributable to events outside T's control, and nor is reliance on another person to do anything (unless T took reasonable care to avoid the failure) or reliance on 'disqualified' advice. A person with a reasonable excuse is treated as having continued to have it if the failure in question was remedied without unreasonable delay after the excuse ceased.

Advice is '*disqualified*' if it (i) was given to T by an interested person; or (ii) was given to T as a result of arrangements between an 'interested person' and the person who gave the advice; or (iii) was given by a person without the appropriate expertise; or (iv) did not take account of all T's individual circumstances (so far as relevant); or (v) was addressed to, or given to, a person other than T. However, the advice is not disqualified if, at the end of the RTC period, T has taken reasonable steps to find out whether or not the advice falls within any of (i)–(iv) and reasonably believes that it does not. An '*interested person*' is one who participated in 'relevant avoidance arrangements' or any transaction forming part of them, or one who, for consideration, facilitated T's entering into such avoidance arrangements. Avoidance arrangements are arrangements (as widely defined) in respect of which it would be reasonable to conclude that a main purpose is the obtaining of a tax advantage (also as widely defined); but arrangements are excluded from being avoidance arrangements if they accord with established practice accepted by HMRC. Where any offshore tax non-compliance arose originally because information was submitted to HMRC on the basis that particular avoidance arrangements had an effect which they did not have, those avoidance arrangements are '*relevant avoidance arrangements*' in relation to that non-compliance.

Double jeopardy

A person is not liable to the above penalty in respect of any conduct (or any failure to act) for which he has been convicted of an offence or for which he is liable to, and has been assessed to, a penalty under other provisions (provided the assessment has neither been successfully appealed against nor withdrawn). The reference here to a penalty under other provisions includes the second tax-geared late filing penalty but does not include any of the other late filing penalties in **55.5** above. Where a person is thus liable to both the above penalty and the *first* tax-geared late filing penalty in **55.5**, and the amount of the latter has been determined by reference to a liability to tax, the aggregate penalty must not exceed 200% of that liability to tax.

[*F(No 2)A 2017, Sch 18 paras 14–17, 23, 24*].

Extension of period for assessment of offshore tax

Where:

- at the end of 2016/17 a person has offshore tax non-compliance to correct; and
- the last day on which it would otherwise be lawful for HMRC to assess the person to any 'offshore tax' falls within the period 6 April 2017 to 4 April 2021 inclusive,

the period in which it is lawful for HMRC to assess the person to the offshore tax is extended so as to end with 5 April 2021. This enables offshore tax for any year up to and including 2016/17 to be assessed at any time on or before 5 April 2021, provided the offshore tax could have been assessed later than 5 April 2017 under the time limit otherwise applicable (see **6.2**, **6.3** ASSESSMENTS). '*Offshore tax*' is tax corresponding to the offshore PLR in respect of the offshore tax non-compliance in question.

[*F(No 2)A 2017, Sch 18 para 26*].

Power to publish details

The Commissioners for HMRC may in some circumstances publish information about an individual who incurs penalties under the above provisions — see **55.36** below.

Failure to notify HMRC of error in assessment

[55.13] A penalty is payable by a person if an assessment issued to him by HMRC understates his liability to income tax and he or a person acting on his behalf has failed to take reasonable steps to notify HMRC, within the 30 days beginning with the date of the assessment, of the under-assessment. The penalty is 30% of the potential lost revenue (defined as at **55.7** above, with the necessary modifications), subject to the same reductions that apply under the provisions at **55.7** for disclosure or special circumstances. HMRC must consider whether the taxpayer or a person acting on his behalf knew, or should have known, about the under-assessment and what steps would have been reasonable to take to notify HMRC.

For the above purposes, 'assessment' includes a determination.

A person is not liable to a penalty under this provision in respect of anything done or omitted by his agent, if he satisfies HMRC that he took reasonable care (see **55.6** above) to avoid failure to notify HMRC as above.

The amount of a penalty under this provision in respect of a document relating to a particular tax year is reduced by the amount of any other penalty the amount of which is determined by reference to the person's tax liability for the period (but see **55.7** above for exceptions to this rule).

A person is not liable to a penalty for a failure in respect of which he has been convicted of an offence.

[*FA 2007, s 97, Sch 24 paras 2, 4, 4C, 5–12, 18, 20, 21, 28; FA 2016, Sch 22 para 20(3)*].

During the passage of the 2007 Finance Bill through Parliament, the Government gave an undertaking that this penalty would be applied only where HMRC make an assessment in the absence of a return (Hansard Standing Committee Debate, 12th Sitting, 5 June 2007 (afternoon), Column 472).

Failure to keep and preserve records

[55.14] The maximum penalty for non-compliance with *TMA 1970, s 12B* (records to be kept and preserved for the purposes of self-assessment tax returns — see **64.5** RETURNS) in relation to any tax year is £3,000. [*TMA 1970, s 12B(5)–(5B)*].

A separate maximum £3,000 penalty applies in relation to records relating to a claim made otherwise than in a self-assessment tax return (see **16.3** CLAIMS). [*TMA 1970, Sch 1A para 2A(4)(5)*].

Simon's Taxes. See **A4.570, E1.205**.

Failure to comply with investigatory powers under *FA 2008, Sch 36*

[55.15] The penalties below apply to offences under the investigatory powers of *FA 2008, Sch 36*.

Failure to comply — fixed and daily penalties

Where a person fails to comply with an information notice within *FA 2008, Sch 36 Pt 1* (see **39.3** HMRC INVESTIGATORY POWERS) he is liable to a fixed penalty of £300 and, for each subsequent day of continuing failure, a further penalty not exceeding £60. If the failure continues for more than 30 days beginning with the date on which notice of an assessment to a daily penalty is given, an HMRC officer may make an application to the Appeal Tribunal for an increased daily penalty. Such an application can only be made if the person concerned has been told that it may be made. If the Tribunal decides to impose an increased daily penalty, that penalty replaces the maximum £60 daily penalty with effect for the day specified in HMRC's notification of the increased penalty and each subsequent day of continuing failure. The Tribunal, in determining the amount of the increased penalty, must have regard to the likely cost to the person of complying with the notice and any benefits of non-compliance, whether to that person or anyone else. The maximum increased penalty is £1,000 per day.

For this purpose, failing to comply with a notice includes concealing, destroying or otherwise disposing of, or arranging for the concealment, destruction or disposal of, a document in breach of *FA 2008, Sch 36 paras 42, 43* (see **39.6** HMRC INVESTIGATORY POWERS).

Where a person deliberately obstructs an HMRC officer in the course of an inspection of business premises under *FA 2008, Sch 36 Pt 2* (see **39.7**, **39.8** HMRC INVESTIGATORY POWERS) which has been approved by the Tribunal, he is liable to a fixed penalty of £300 and, for each subsequent day of continuing obstruction, a further penalty not exceeding £60.

No penalty is due where a person fails to do anything required to be done within a limited time period if he does it within such further time as an HMRC officer allows. A person is not liable to a penalty if he satisfies HMRC or (on appeal) the Tribunal that there is a reasonable excuse for the failure or obstruction. An insufficiency of funds is not a reasonable excuse for this purpose unless it is attributable to events outside the person's control. Where a person relies on another person to do anything, that is not a reasonable excuse unless the first person took reasonable care (see **55.6** above) to avoid the failure or obstruction. Where a person has a reasonable excuse which ceases, he is treated as continuing to have a reasonable excuse if the failure is remedied or the obstruction stops without unreasonable delay.

The Treasury can make regulations amending the maximum penalties.

[*FA 2008, s 113, Sch 36 paras 39–41, 44, 45, 49A, 49B*].

Failure to comply — tax-related penalty

A tax-related penalty may be imposed by the Upper Tribunal where a person's failure or obstruction continues after a fixed penalty has been imposed under the above provisions. An HMRC officer must have reason to believe that the amount of tax that the person has paid, or is likely to pay is significantly less than it would otherwise have been as a result of the failure or obstruction, and the officer must make an application to the Upper Tribunal before the end of the twelve months beginning with the 'relevant date'. In deciding the amount of the penalty (if any), the Upper Tribunal must have regard to the amount of tax which has not been, or is likely not to be, paid by the person.

The '*relevant date*' is the date on which the person became liable to the penalty. Where, however, the penalty is for a failure relating to an information notice against which a person can appeal, the relevant date is the later of the end of the period in which notice of such appeal could have been given and, where an appeal is made, the date on which the appeal is determined or withdrawn.

A tax-related penalty is in addition to the fixed penalty and any daily penalties under the above provisions. No account is taken of a tax-related penalty for the purposes of **55.17** below and no reduction in a penalty charged under *FA 2007, Sch 24* (see **55.6**, **55.13** above) or *FA 2008, Sch 41* (see **55.3** above) is to be made in respect of a penalty under these provisions.

[*FA 2008, Sch 36 para 50*].

The tax-related penalty is a penal provision reserved for serious cases of non-compliance, but it should not be used as a proxy for recovery of the unpaid tax. In reducing the near 100% penalties imposed by the UT, the CA declared it sufficient that the amount of tax unpaid, taken in conjunction with all the other relevant circumstances, inform the determination of quantum and produce a result proportionate to the scale and nature of the taxpayer's default. (*HMRC v Tager* CA, [2018] STC 1755).

Inaccurate information or documents

If, in complying with an information notice, a person provides inaccurate information or produces a document that contains an inaccuracy, he is liable to a penalty of up to £3,000 if:

- the inaccuracy is careless (i.e. due to a failure to take reasonable care) or deliberate; or
- the person knows of the inaccuracy at the time the information or document is provided but does not inform HMRC at that time; or
- the person subsequently discovers the inaccuracy but fails to take reasonable steps to inform HMRC.

If the information or document contains more than one inaccuracy, a penalty is payable for each inaccuracy.

The Treasury can make regulations amending the maximum penalty.

[*FA 2008, Sch 36 paras 40A, 41*].

A person is not liable to a penalty under any of the above provisions in respect of anything for which he has been convicted of an offence. [*FA 2008, Sch 36 para 52*].

Penalties in respect of data-gathering powers under *FA 2011, Sch 23*

[55.16] The penalties below apply to offences under the data-gathering powers of *FA 2011, Sch 23* (see **39.14** HMRC INVESTIGATORY POWERS).

Failure to comply

Where a person fails to comply with a data-holder notice, he is liable to a fixed penalty of £300. If the failure continues after the data-holder has been notified of the assessment of the penalty, he is liable, for each subsequent day of continuing failure, to a further penalty of up to £60 per day. If the failure continues for more than 30 days beginning with the date on which notice of an assessment to a daily penalty is given, an HMRC officer may make an application to the Appeal Tribunal for an increased daily penalty. Such an application can only be made if the data-holder has been told that it may be made. If the Tribunal decides to impose an increased daily penalty, that penalty replaces the maximum £60 daily penalty with effect for the day determined by the Tribunal and specified in HMRC's notification of the increased penalty and for each subsequent day of continuing failure. The Tribunal, in determining the amount of the increased penalty, must have regard to the likely cost to the person of complying with the notice and any benefits of non-compliance, whether to that person or anyone else. The maximum increased penalty is £1,000 per day.

Failure to comply with a notice specifically includes the concealment, destruction or disposal of a 'material document'. A document is a '*material document*' if a data-holder notice has been given in respect of it or of data contained in it or if an HMRC officer has informed the data-holder that such a notice will be or is likely to be given. If no such notice is given within six months after the data-holder was last so informed, the document ceases to be a material document. Once a data-holder notice has been given and complied with, a document is no longer a material document unless HMRC have notified the data-holder in writing that it must be preserved, in which case it continues to be a material document until that notification is withdrawn.

No penalty is due where a person fails to do anything required to be done within a limited time period if he does it within such further time as an HMRC officer allows. A person is not liable to a penalty if he satisfies HMRC or (on appeal) the Tribunal that there is a reasonable excuse for the failure. An insufficiency of funds is not a reasonable excuse for this purpose unless it is attributable to events outside the person's control. Where the data-holder relies on another person to do anything, that is not a reasonable excuse unless the data-holder took reasonable care to avoid the failure. Where a person had a reasonable excuse which has ceased, he is treated as continuing to have a reasonable excuse if the failure is remedied without unreasonable delay.

The Treasury can make regulations amending the maximum penalties.

[*FA 2011, Sch 23 paras 30, 31, 33, 34, 38, 39, 41, 65; FA 2016, s 177(2)(3)*].

Inaccurate data

If, in complying with a data-holder notice, a person provides inaccurate data, he is liable to a penalty of up to £3,000 if:

- the inaccuracy is careless (i.e. due to a failure to take reasonable care) or deliberate; or
- the person knows of the inaccuracy at the time the data is provided but does not inform HMRC at that time; or
- the person subsequently discovers the inaccuracy but fails to take reasonable steps to inform HMRC.

The Treasury can make regulations amending the maximum penalty.

[*FA 2011, Sch 23 paras 32, 41, 65*].

Double jeopardy

A person is not liable to a penalty under any of the above provisions in respect of anything for which he has been convicted of an offence. [*FA 2011, Sch 23 para 42*].

Two or more tax-related penalties in respect of the same tax

[55.17] Where two or more tax-related penalties are determined by reference to the same income tax, capital gains tax or corporation tax liability, the aggregate penalty is reduced to the greater or greatest of those separate penalties. The penalties at **55.6**, **55.11**, **55.13** and **55.15** above, **4.8** ANTI-AVOIDANCE (GAAR penalty), **4.48** ANTI-AVOIDANCE (follower notices), **4.52** ANTI-AVOIDANCE (accelerated payment notices) and **4.59** ANTI-AVOIDANCE (serial tax avoiders) are not taken into account for the purposes of this provision. A late payment penalty under **43.2** LATE PAYMENT INTEREST AND PENALTIES is not taken into account either. [*TMA 1970, s 97A; FA 2009, Sch 56 para 9A; FA 2013, Sch 43C para 8(4); FA 2014, ss 212(3), 226(7); FA 2016, s 158(3), Sch 18 para 40(3), Sch 22 para 21*]. See **55.23** below for mitigation of penalties.

Dishonest conduct by tax agents

[55.18] The following penalties apply to offences relating to HMRC's powers in relation to dishonest conduct by tax agents (see **39.10** HMRC INVESTIGATORY POWERS).

Penalties for dishonest conduct

An individual who engages in dishonest conduct (see **39.10** HMRC INVESTIGATORY POWERS) is liable to a penalty of no less than £500 and no more than £50,000. Such a penalty can be charged only if the individual has been given a conduct notice (see **39.10** HMRC INVESTIGATORY POWERS) and either the time allowed for appealing against the determination in the notice has expired without an appeal being made, any appeal which has been made has been withdrawn or the determination has been confirmed on appeal. For this purpose, a determination that is appealed is not considered to have been confirmed until the time allowed for any further appeal has expired or any further appeal has been withdrawn or determined.

In assessing the amount of the penalty regard must be had to whether the individual 'disclosed' the dishonest conduct, whether that disclosure was prompted or unprompted, the 'quality' of the disclosure and the quality of the individual's compliance with any file access notice (see **39.10** HMRC INVESTIGATORY POWERS) connected with the dishonest conduct. An individual '*discloses*' dishonest conduct by telling HMRC about it, giving them reasonable help in identifying the clients concerned and the amount of lost tax revenue and allowing HMRC access to records for the purpose of ensuring the recovery of that revenue. A disclosure is unprompted if made when the individual has no reason to think that HMRC have discovered or are about to discover the dishonest conduct; otherwise a disclosure is prompted. '*Quality*' in relation to disclosure or compliance includes timing, nature and extent.

If HMRC intend to assess a penalty of £5,000, they may, if they think it right to do so because of special circumstances, reduce the penalty below that amount (including to nil), stay the penalty or agree a compromise in relation to proceedings for the penalty. Such circumstances do not include ability to pay or the fact that a loss of tax revenue from a client is balanced by an overpayment by another person (whether or not a client).

[*FA 2012, s 223, Sch 38 paras 7(4), 26, 27, 29(2)(3)*].

Power to publish details of tax agents engaging in dishonest conduct

The Commissioners for HMRC may publish information about an individual who incurs a penalty under the above provisions — see **55.37** below.

Penalties for failure to comply with a file access notice

A person who fails to comply with a file access notice (see **39.10** HMRC INVESTIGATORY POWERS) is liable to a penalty of £300. If the failure continues after notification of the penalty, the person is liable to a further penalty of up to £60 for each subsequent day on which the failure continues. No penalty is due, however, if the file access notice is complied with within such further time as HMRC have allowed.

Failing to comply with a file access notice also includes concealing, destroying or otherwise disposing of (or arranging for the concealment etc. of) a 'required document'. A '*required document*' is a document that a person is required to provide by a file access notice where either the notice has not been complied with or, if it has been complied with, he has been notified in writing by HMRC that he must continue to preserve the document (and the notification has not been withdrawn). A document is also a required document if at the time the person conceals it etc. HMRC have informed him that he will, or is likely to, be required to provide the document by a file access notice and no more than six months have passed since he was, or was last, so informed.

Reasonable excuse

No penalty is due if the person otherwise liable to it satisfies HMRC (or, on appeal, the Appeal Tribunal) that there is a reasonable excuse for the failure to comply. An insufficiency of funds is not a reasonable excuse unless attributable to event's outside the person's control. If the person relies on another person to do anything, that is not a reasonable excuse unless the first person took reasonable care to avoid the failure to comply. If a person had a reasonable excuse which has ceased, he is treated as continuing to have the excuse if the failure is remedied without unreasonable delay after the excuse ceased.

[*FA 2012, Sch 38 paras 22–25*].

Double jeopardy

A person is not liable to a penalty under any of the above provisions in respect of anything for which he has been convicted of an offence or in respect of anything for which he is personally liable to a penalty under *FA 2007, Sch 24* (see **55.6**, **55.13** above), *FA 2008, Sch 41* (see **55.3** above) or *FA 2009, Sch 55* (see **55.5** above). [*FA 2012, Sch 38 paras 33, 34*].

Simon's Taxes. See A6.651.

Enabling offshore evasion

[55.19] With effect on and after **1 January 2017**, a penalty is payable by a person (P) who has 'enabled' another person (Q) to carry out offshore tax evasion or non-compliance if:

(a) P knew when his actions were carried out that they enabled, or were likely to enable, Q to carry out such evasion or non-compliance; and
(b) either:
  (i) Q has been convicted of one of the offences listed below and the conviction is final; or
  (ii) Q has been found to be liable to one of the penalties listed below and either the penalty is final or a contract settlement (see **6.9** ASSESSMENTS) with HMRC has been agreed under which HMRC undertake not to assess the penalty or to take proceedings to recover it.

For these purposes Q carries out offshore tax evasion or non-compliance by committing an offence within (1)–(3) below or engaging in conduct that makes him liable (if the applicable conditions are met) to a civil penalty within (A)–(D) below, where in either case the tax at stake is income tax, capital gains tax or inheritance tax. Nothing in (b) above affects the law of evidence as to the relevance of the conviction, penalty or contract settlement in proving that (a) above applies.

P has '*enabled*' Q to carry out offshore evasion or non-compliance if he has encouraged, assisted or otherwise facilitated such conduct. Where (b)(i) above applies, Q must have been convicted of the full offence and not, for example, an attempt. A conviction or a penalty becomes final when the time allowed for any appeal against it expires or, if later, when any appeal has been determined.

The offences referred to in (b)(i) above are:

(1) an offence of cheating the public revenue involving 'offshore activity';
(2) an offence under *TMA 1970, s 106A* (fraudulent evasion of income tax — see **55.33** below) involving offshore activity; and
(3) an offence under any of *TMA 1970, ss 106B–106D* (offences relating to offshore income, assets or activities — see **55.34**(a)–(c) below).

The penalties referred to in (b)(ii) above are:

(A) a penalty under *FA 2007, Sch 24* (errors in documents) involving an offshore matter or offshore transfer (see **55.8** above);
(B) a penalty for failure to notify chargeability where the failure involves offshore activity (see **55.4** above);
(C) the second tax-geared late filing penalty in **55.5** above where offshore activity is involved; and
(D) the offshore asset moves penalty at **55.10** above.

It is immaterial that any offence or penalty may also relate to conduct by Q other than offshore evasion or non-compliance. Conduct involves '*offshore activity*' if it involves an 'offshore matter', an 'offshore transfer' or an 'offshore asset move'. '*Offshore matter*' and '*offshore transfer*' are defined as in **55.8** above and '*offshore asset move*' has the same meaning as at **55.10** above. For the purposes of these provisions, '*conduct*' includes a failure to act.

A person is not liable to a penalty under these provisions in respect of conduct for which he has been convicted of an offence or has been assessed to a different civil penalty.

See HMRC factsheet CC/FS17a at www.gov.uk/government/publications/compliance-checks-penalties-for-enablers-of-offshore-tax-evasion-or-non-compliance-ccfs17a.

Amount of penalty

Except where (D) above applies, the amount of the penalty is the higher of 100% of the 'potential lost revenue' and £3,000.

Where (D) above applies, the amount of the penalty is the higher of 50% of the potential lost revenue in respect of the original tax non-compliance and £3,000. For this purpose, the potential lost revenue in respect of the original tax non-compliance is the potential lost revenue under *FA 2007, Sch 24* (see **55.8** above) or *FA 2008, Sch 41* (see **55.4** above) or the tax liability which would have been shown on the return (see **55.5** above) according to which provision the original penalty was incurred under.

Where (1), (2) or (3) above apply, the '*potential lost revenue*' is the same amount as the potential lost revenue applicable for the purposes of the corresponding civil penalty (determined as below). For offences within (1) or (2) above, the corresponding civil penalty is that to which Q is liable as a result of the offending conduct. For offences within (3) above, the corresponding civil penalty is *FA 2008, Sch 41* where the offence is under *TMA 1970, s 106B*; *FA 2009, Sch 55* where the offence is under *TMA 1970, s 106C*; and *FA 2007, Sch 24* where the offence is under *TMA 1970, s 106D*. The fact that Q has been prosecuted for the offending conduct is disregarded for this purpose.

Where (A) or (B) above apply, the '*potential lost revenue*' is the amount that is the potential lost revenue under *FA 2007, Sch 24* or *FA 2008, Sch 41*. Where (C) above applies, the '*potential lost revenue*' is the tax liability that would have been shown on the return.

Where any amount of potential lost revenue is only partly attributable to offshore evasion or non-compliance, a just and reasonable apportionment is made.

Reduction for disclosure

A reduction in the amount of a penalty will be given where P makes a disclosure to HMRC of a matter relating to an inaccuracy in a document, a supply of false information or a failure to disclose an under-assessment, a disclosure of P's enabling of Q's actions or a disclosure of any other information HMRC regard as assisting them in relation to the assessment of the penalty. A person is treated as making a disclosure of a matter for these purposes if he tells HMRC about it, gives them reasonable help in relation to it and allows them access to records for any reasonable purpose connected with resolving it.

A reduction will also be given if P assists HMRC in any investigation leading to Q being charged with an offence or found liable to a penalty. A person is treated as assisting HMRC for this purpose by assisting or encouraging Q to disclose all relevant facts to HMRC, allowing HMRC access to records or any other conduct which HMRC consider assists them in investigating Q.

The penalty will be reduced to an amount that reflects the quality of the disclosure or assistance (including its timing, nature and extent). The amount of the reduction will depend on whether the disclosure or assistance is 'prompted' or 'unprompted'. For unprompted disclosure or assistance, the penalty cannot be reduced below the higher of 10% of the potential lost revenue and £1,000. For prompted disclosure or assistance, it cannot be reduced below the higher of 30% of potential lost revenue and £3,000. Disclosure or assistance is '*unprompted*' if made at a time when P has no reason to believe that HMRC have discovered or are about to discover Q's offshore evasion or non-compliance. In all other cases, disclosure or assistance is '*prompted*'.

Reduction in special circumstances

HMRC can reduce, stay, or agree a compromise in relation to proceedings for, a penalty if they think it right to do so because of special circumstances. Ability to pay and the fact that a potential loss of revenue from one taxpayer is balanced by a potential overpayment by another are not special circumstances for this purpose.

[*FA 2016, s 162, Sch 20 paras 1–9, 15; SI 2016 No 1249*].

Information powers

The information and inspection powers of *FA 2008, Sch 36* (see **39.2** HMRC INVESTIGATORY POWERS) apply, with necessary modifications, for the purpose of checking the penalty position of a person who an HMRC officer has reason to suspect may have enabled offshore evasion or non-compliance. The modifications include, in particular, that the exclusions from information notices for auditors and tax advisers (see **39.4** HMRC INVESTIGATORY POWERS) do not apply and that there is no tax-related penalty for failure to comply (see **55.15** above). [*FA 2016, Sch 20 paras 18–21*].

Publishing details of enablers

The Commissioners for HMRC may publish information about a person who has been found to have incurred one or more penalties under these provisions (and has been assessed or has entered into a contract settlement) if the total potential lost revenue exceeds £25,000 or if that person has been found to have incurred five or more such penalties in any five-year period. Information cannot be published if the maximum reduction of the penalty has been given for disclosure or if the penalty has been reduced to nil, or stayed, as a result of special circumstances.

Before publishing any information HMRC must notify the person and give an opportunity to make representations. No information may be published before the day on which the penalty becomes final or, where there is more than one penalty, before the latest day on which any of them becomes final. Information may not be published for the first time more than one year after that day. For this purpose, a penalty becomes final when no further appeal can be made, any appeal is finally determined or when a contract settlement is made.

The information which can be published is the person's name (including trading name, previous name or pseudonym), address, the nature of the person's business. the amount of the penalties and the periods or times to which they relate and any other information HMRC consider appropriate to make the person's identity clear. HMRC may publish the information in any way they think appropriate.

[*FA 2016, Sch 20 paras 22, 23*].

Enabling defeated tax avoidance

[55.20] With effect for arrangements entered into on or after 16 November 2017, a penalty is payable by a person who has 'enabled' 'abusive tax arrangements' entered into by another person (T) that are 'defeated'. Any actions carried out by a person before that date are disregarded in determining whether that person enabled arrangements. The penalty applies to income tax in addition to a number of other taxes. For guidance, see www.gov.uk/government/publications/penalties-for-enablers-of-tax-avoidance-schemes-technical-guidance. See also HMRC factsheets CC/FS43 and CC/FS45 listed at **37.1** HMRC EXPLANATORY PUBLICATIONS.

Definitions

Arrangements (as widely defined) are '*tax arrangements*' if, taking into account all the circumstances, it would be reasonable to conclude that the obtaining of a tax advantage was a main purpose of the arrangements. Tax arrangements are '*abusive*' if entering into them or carrying them out cannot reasonably be regarded as a reasonable course of action in relation to the tax provisions in question, having regard to all the circumstances. Those circumstances include:

- whether the substantive results of the arrangements are consistent with any express or implied principles on which the provisions are based and their policy objectives;
- whether the means of achieving those results involves one or more contrived or abnormal steps; and
- whether the arrangements are intended to exploit any shortcomings in the tax provisions.

Where the tax arrangements form part of other arrangements, regard must be had to those other arrangements. The legislation gives the following non-exhaustive indicators that arrangements might be abusive:

- the arrangements result in taxable income, profits or gains significantly less than the economic amount; or
- they result in a tax deduction or loss significantly greater than the economic amount; or

- they result in a claim for repayment or crediting of tax (whether or not UK tax) that has not been, and is unlikely to be, paid,

and it is reasonable to assume that this was not the anticipated result when the tax provisions in question were enacted. If tax arrangements accord with established practice accepted by HMRC, this might indicate that the arrangements are *not* abusive.

A '*tax advantage*' includes relief or increased relief from tax, repayment or increased repayment of tax, receipt (or advanced receipt) of a tax credit, avoidance or reduction of a charge, assessment or liability, avoidance of a possible assessment, liability or obligation to deduct or account for tax, deferral of a payment of tax, and advancement of a repayment tax.

Defeat of arrangements

Arrangements are '*defeated*' if T incurs a defeat in respect of them. T incurs such a defeat if T (or anyone on T's behalf) has given HMRC a document on the basis that a tax advantage arose from the arrangements and the said tax advantage has been counteracted, with the counteraction having become final. The document must be of a kind listed in *FA 2007, Sch 24 para 1* (penalty for errors in documents — see **55.6** above) or a document amending such a document. A tax advantage is counteracted for this purpose if adjustments have been made to T's tax position (by assessment, modification of an assessment or return, amendment or disallowance of a claim, payment or entering into a contract settlement) on the basis that all or part of the tax advantage does not arise. Counteraction is final when the adjustments and any amounts arising from them can on longer be varied.

T also incurs a defeat in respect of arrangements if HMRC have made an assessment which counteracts (i.e. prevents T from obtaining all or part of) a tax advantage which it is reasonable to assume T expected to obtain from the arrangements and the counteraction is final. A counteraction is final for this purpose when either a contract settlement which prevents T from obtaining all or part of the tax advantage is made or the assessment and any amounts arising from it can no longer be varied.

Enabling of arrangements

A person has '*enabled*' arrangements if he falls within any of the following categories. In the case of (a)–(c) or (e) below, the person must be acting in the course of a business carried on by him. Note that it is possible for there to be more than one enabler of particular arrangements.

(a) **A designer of the arrangements.** A person who was to any extent responsible for the design of the arrangements or a proposal implemented by them. Providing advice which is taken account of in the design of the arrangements does not make a person a designer of the arrangements unless:
 (i) any of the advice suggested arrangements or an alteration of proposed arrangements (or a proposal for arrangements or an alteration of such a proposal) and it is reasonable to assume that

the suggestion was made with a view to arrangements being designed so that a tax advantage or greater tax advantage might be expected to arise from them; and

(ii) when the advice was given, the person providing it knew, or could reasonably be expected to know, that the advice would be taken account of in designing abusive tax arrangements or a proposal for such arrangements or that it was likely that the advice would be so taken account of.

In (i) above, advice does not suggest anything which was put forward for consideration if the advice can be reasonably read as advising against it. '*Advice*', for these purposes, includes giving an opinion.

(b) **A manager of the arrangements.** A person who was to any extent responsible for organising or managing the arrangements and who, when carrying out functions relating to such organising or managing, knew or could reasonably be expected to know that the arrangements were abusive tax arrangements. Facilitating T's withdrawal from the arrangements is not organising or managing the arrangements for this purpose if it is reasonable to assume that T's purpose in withdrawing is not to obtain a tax advantage.

(c) **A person who marketed the arrangements.** A person who made available for implementation by T a proposal subsequently implemented by the arrangements or who informed T or another person about a proposal subsequently implemented by the arrangements with a view to T entering into the arrangements or transactions forming part of them.

(d) **An enabling participant.** A person, other than T, who enters into the arrangements, or a transaction forming part of them, where, without that participation (or the participation of another person in the same capacity), the arrangements would not be expected to result in a tax advantage for T. The person must have known or have been reasonably expected to know, when entering into the arrangements or transaction, that what was being entered into were abusive tax arrangements or a transaction forming part of such arrangements.

(e) **A financial enabler.** A person who provided a financial product directly or indirectly to T or an enabling participant within (d) above where it is reasonable to assume that a purpose of T or the other participant in obtaining the product was to participate in the arrangements. The person must have known or have been reasonably expected to know, when providing the product, that a purpose of obtaining it was to participate in abusive tax arrangements. Financial products include loans, shares, derivative contracts, repos, stock lending arrangements, alternative finance arrangements and contracts which would be required to be treated under generally accepted accounting practice as a loan, deposit or other financial asset or obligation.

T (and, if T is a company, any member of the same group) cannot be treated as an enabler of the arrangements even if they fall within any of the above categories. Two companies are members of a group, for this purpose, if one is a 75% subsidiary of the other or both are 75% subsidiaries of a third company.

Amount of penalty

The amount of the penalty for each enabler of the arrangements is the total amount or value of the consideration received or receivable by that person for anything done by him which enabled the arrangements. Any consideration previously taken into account in calculating a penalty under these provisions is excluded, as is all VAT. Consideration paid (or payable), under arrangements with the enabler, to a person other than the enabler is treated for this purpose as paid (or payable) to the enabler. If consideration is attributable to more than one transaction it must be apportioned on a just and reasonable basis. Where consideration is given for what is in substance one bargain, the consideration must be treated as attributable to all elements of the bargain even if separate consideration is given for, or there are separate transactions in respect of, different elements.

Reduction and mitigation of penalty

HMRC have discretion to reduce a penalty, entirely remit a penalty or to stay or agree a compromise in relation to proceedings for the recovery of a penalty. The amount of the penalty is in any case reduced by the amount of any other penalty incurred by, and assessed on, the enabler in respect of the same conduct.

Assessment of penalty

For the general provisions relating to the assessment of a penalty under these provisions see **55.25** below. The decision to make an assessment must be taken by an HMRC officer designated by the Commissioners for HMRC for the purposes of these provisions (a '*designated HMRC officer*'). If HMRC do not have all the information needed to determine the amount of the consideration on which the penalty is based, they may make an assessment on the basis of a reasonable estimate, provided that they have taken all reasonable steps to obtain the information.

If a proposal for arrangements has been implemented more than once and all of the arrangements are substantially the same, HMRC cannot assess any penalty until more than 50% of the arrangements have incurred a defeat. Any person liable to a penalty may, however, request that an assessment be made sooner.

Notification of a penalty assessment must be accompanied by a report of the opinion of the GAAR Advisory Panel (see **4.2** ANTI-AVOIDANCE) on which HMRC relied in making the assessment (see below).

GAAR Advisory Panel opinion

A penalty assessment cannot be made unless either of the following applies.

(A) A 'GAAR final decision notice' has been given in relation to the arrangements or other 'equivalent' arrangements and a designated HMRC officer has considered the opinion of the GAAR Advisory Panel which was considered by HMRC in preparing that notice. If the GAAR final decision notice related to equivalent arrangements only, a designated HMRC officer must first give the person liable to the penalty a notice in writing explaining HMRC's view, specifying the arrangements concerned and describing the material characteristics of the equivalent arrangements. The notice must also include a report by HMRC of the opinion of the Panel and must explain the right of the person liable to the penalty to make representations. Representations as to why the arrangements under consideration are not equivalent to those considered by the Panel can be made in writing within 30 days beginning with the day the notice is given. HMRC may, on written request, extend the deadline (but are not required to do so). A penalty assessment cannot be made unless a notice has been given, the time allowed for representations has expired and the officer has considered any representations made.

A '*GAAR final decision notice*' is a notice of HMRC's final decision on whether arrangements are to be counteracted under the GAAR after considering the Panel's decision (see **4.3**(10) and **4.6** ANTI-AVOIDANCE). Arrangements are '*equivalent*' to one another if they are substantially the same with regard to their results or intended results, the means of achieving those results and the characteristics making them abusive tax arrangements.

(B) A designated HMRC officer has referred the arrangements to the GAAR Advisory Panel. An assessment cannot be made until the officer has considered the opinion of the Panel. See below for the procedure for referring arrangements. If the officer considers that a person is liable to a penalty in relation to particular arrangements on the basis that the opinion of the Panel 'applies' to the arrangements but that person was not notified of the referral to the Panel, then before making an assessment the officer must give that person a notice in writing explaining HMRC's view and specifying the arrangements concerned. The notice must also include a report by HMRC of the opinion of the Panel and must explain the right to make representations. Representations as to why the opinion does not apply to the arrangements in question can be made in writing within 30 days beginning with the day the notice is given. HMRC may, on written request, extend the deadline (but are not required to do so). A penalty assessment cannot be made unless a notice has been given, the time allowed for representations has expired and the officer has considered any representations made.

An opinion of the Panel '*applies*' to the arrangements in respect of which the referral was made and any equivalent arrangements.

Procedure

The procedure for referring arrangements to the GAAR Advisory Panel is as follows.

(1) The question to be referred by HMRC to the Panel is whether the entering into and carrying out of the tax arrangements described in the 'referral statement' is a reasonable course of action in relation to the tax provisions concerned. The '*referral statement*' must accompany the referral and is a general statement of the material characteristics of the arrangements including a factual description of them, HMRC's view as

to whether they accord with established practice, why HMRC consider that the tax advantage arises from abusive arrangements, any matters which may suggest that HMRC's view is not correct and any other matters which HMRC consider to be required for the purposes of the Panel's functions.

A designated HMRC officer may make such a referral if he considers that a person is liable to a penalty in respect of particular arrangements. A referral cannot be made if a GAAR final decision notice (see (A) above) has already been given in relation to the arrangements in question or equivalent arrangements. Before making a referral the officer must give a notice to each person who he then considers to be liable to a penalty in respect of the arrangements giving his view and explaining why he considers the arrangements to be abusive tax arrangements. The notice must also state that HMRC are considering making a referral and must explain the right to make representations. Representations can be made in writing within 45 days beginning with the day the notice is given. HMRC may, on written request, extend the deadline (but are not required to do so).

(2) Where a designated officer decides whether to make a referral he must, as soon as reasonably practicable, give written notice of that decision to each person to whom a notice within (1) above was given.

(3) A referral must be accompanied by the referral statement, a declaration that nothing material has been omitted from the statement, a copy of each notice within (1) above and (4) below and of any representations received, together with any comments on the representations.

(4) At the same time as the referral is made, a designated HMRC officer must give each person to whom a notice within (1) above was given a written notice confirming that the referral has been made and including a copy of the referral statement and of any comments on representations made by that person. It must also explain the right to make representations to the Panel and the requirement to send a copy of any representations to HMRC.

(5) A person who has received a notice under (4) above has 21 days beginning with the day on which the notice was given to send written representations to the GAAR Advisory Panel about the notice in (1) above or any comments made by HMRC on representations made by him in response to that notice. The Panel may, on written request, extend the deadline (but are not required to do so). A copy of the representations must be sent to HMRC. If no representations had been made in response to the notice in (1) above, HMRC may provide the Panel with comments on the representations now made, and must send a copy of any such comments to the person to whom the notice was given.

(6) The Chair of the GAAR Advisory Panel must arrange for a sub-panel of three members to consider the referral. The sub-panel may invite any person to whom a notice was given under (1) above or the designated HMRC officer (or both) to supply further information within a specified time. A copy of any information must be given to the designated officer or to each of the notice recipients.

(7) The sub-panel must produce an opinion notice stating their joint opinion as to whether or not the entering into and carrying out of the tax arrangements was a reasonable course of action in relation to the tax provisions concerned, having regard to the referral statement and the meaning of 'abusive'. An opinion notice may indicate that the sub-panel consider that it is not possible to reach a view on the information available. Alternatively, the sub-panel may produce two or three opinion notices which taken together state the opinions of all the members. An opinion notice must include the reasons for the opinion and is given to the designated HMRC officer.

In any court or Tribunal proceedings in connection with a penalty under these provisions, any question as to whether the arrangements were abusive must be determined taking account of the GAAR Advisory Panel's opinion on which HMRC relied in assessing the penalty. The court or Tribunal may also take into account any guidance, statements or other material (of HMRC, a Government minster or anyone else) in the public domain when the arrangements were entered into and any evidence of established practice at that time.

[*F(No 2)A 2017, Sch 16 paras 1–19, 21, 23–36, 53–56*].

Double jeopardy

A person is not liable to a penalty under these provisions in respect of conduct for which he has been convicted of an offence. [*F(No 2)A 2017, Sch 16 para 52*].

Information powers

The information and inspection powers of *FA 2008, Sch 36* (see **39.2** HMRC INVESTIGATORY POWERS) apply, with appropriate modifications, for the purposes of checking the position as regards liability for the above penalty of a person whom HMRC have reason to suspect may be liable to such a penalty. [*F(No 2)A 2017, Sch 16 paras 40–43*].

Privileged communications

Where a person cannot provide information to demonstrate that he is not liable to a penalty because communications by a lawyer are subject to legal professional privilege (or in Scotland, protected from disclosure in legal proceedings on grounds of confidentiality of communication), that lawyer or another lawyer can make a declaration that the person is not liable to the penalty. Such a declaration must be treated by HMRC, a court or tribunal as conclusive evidence of the things stated in it unless HMRC, the court or tribunal is satisfied that it contains incorrect information. The particulars and confirmations that must be contained in the declaration are set out in regulations. Lawyers, for this purpose, are barristers, advocates, solicitors and other legal representatives communications with whom may be subject to legal professional privilege (or Scottish equivalent). A penalty not exceeding £5,000 applies for carelessly or deliberately giving incorrect information in a declaration. A declaration can also be made, where relevant, in respect of such a penalty. An assessment to such a penalty must be made within the 12 months beginning with the date on which sufficient facts come to HMRC's knowledge to indicate that a penalty is due. Subject to this, the rules for making assessments and appeals are the same as for the main penalty under these provisions (see **55.25** and **55.26** below). [*F(No 2)A 2017, Sch 16 paras 44, 45; SI 2017 No 1245*].

Publishing details of enablers

HMRC may publish information about a person who has been found to have incurred one or more penalties under these provisions (and has been assessed or entered into a contract settlement) if the total amount of the penalty or penalties exceeds £25,000 or if that person has been found to be liable to 50 or more other such penalties. Penalties and their amounts are only aggregated for this purpose if the 'entry dates' of the penalties fall within a period of 12 months. For this purpose, the '*entry date*' of a penalty is the date (or latest date) on which the arrangements, or any agreement or transaction forming part of them, was entered into by the person whose defeat resulted in the penalty arising. Penalties which have been reduced to nil or stayed are disregarded as are penalties by reference to which information has already been published and penalties where the arrangements concerned are related to other arrangements in respect of which a penalty has been charged and information published. Penalties are also disregarded if the arrangements are related to other arrangements and it is not the case that HMRC reasonably believe that defeats have been incurred in all of the related arrangements and that each penalty in relation to those arrangements has become final. Arrangements are related to each other if they implement the same proposal for tax arrangements and are substantially the same.

Before publishing any information HMRC must notify the person and give an opportunity to make representations. No information may be published before the day on which the penalty becomes final or, where there is more than one penalty, before the latest day on which any of them becomes final. Information may not be published for the first time more than one year after that day. For this purpose, a penalty becomes final when no further appeal can be made, any appeal is finally determined or when a contract settlement is made. Information cannot be republished or continue to be published after the 12 months beginning with the date of first publication.

The information which can be published is the person's name (including trading name, previous name or pseudonym), address, the nature of the person's business, the number and amount of the penalties and any other information HMRC consider appropriate to make the person's identity clear. HMRC may publish the information in any way they think appropriate.

[*F(No 2)A 2017, Sch 16 paras 46–51*].

Interest on penalties

[55.21] Penalties chargeable under any of the provisions of *TMA 1970, ss 93–98B, 99A, 99B* carry interest under *TMA 1970, s 103A*, calculated from the due date (broadly, 30 days after issue of a notice of determination by an officer of HMRC — see **55.25** below, or immediately upon determination by the Appeal Tribunal — see **55.27**, **55.28** below) to the date of payment. [*TMA 1970, s 103A; SI 1998 No 311; SI 2019 No 918, Art 3*].

Where interest is not chargeable under *TMA 1970, s 103A* above, it will usually be chargeable under the harmonised interest regime at **43.2** LATE PAYMENT INTEREST AND PENALTIES. This regime applies to any penalties assessed in relation to any tax in relation to which, for any tax year, a tax return falls to be made or a discovery assessment is made. It is also applied specifically (as set out in **55.25** below) to the penalties at **55.10**, **55.11**, **55.12**, **55.19** and **55.20** above. Similarly, interest is payable by HMRC on repayment of any such penalties (see **62.2** REPAYMENT INTEREST).

Rates of interest on penalties are synonymous with those on late paid and overpaid tax — see **43.2** LATE PAYMENT INTEREST AND PENALTIES and **62.2** REPAYMENT INTEREST.

Special returns

[55.22] Failure to render any information or particulars or any return, certificate, statement or other document which is required, whether by notice or otherwise, under the provisions listed in *TMA 1970, s 98* is the subject of a maximum penalty of £300, plus £60 for each day the failure continues after that penalty is imposed (but not for any day for which such a daily penalty has already been imposed). The maximum penalty for an incorrect return etc. given fraudulently or negligently is £3,000. Penalties for failure to render information etc. required by notice cannot be imposed after the failure is rectified, and daily penalties can similarly not be imposed where the information etc. was required other than by notice. [*TMA 1970, s 98*].

Failure to allow access to computers renders a person liable to a maximum £300 penalty. [*FA 1988, s 127; FA 2008, s 114*].

See **52.30** PARTNERSHIPS as regards penalties under *TMA 1970, s 98B* in relation to European Economic Interest Groupings.

PAYE returns etc.

Special penalties are imposed for failure to make annual returns where these are required under PAYE (see **53.21**(a) PAY AS YOU EARN) or the construction industry scheme (see **20.11** CONSTRUCTION INDUSTRY SCHEME) by the statutory filing date, i.e. by 19 May following the end of the tax year for which the return is required. These are a penalty of £100 for each month or part month (up to twelve) during which the failure continues and for each 50 persons (or part where the total is not a multiple of 50) in respect of whom particulars should have been included in the return, and, if the failure continues beyond twelve months, an additional penalty of the amount payable for the tax year to which the return relates which remained unpaid at 19 April following that year. [*TMA 1970, s 98A; SI 2003 No 2682, Regs 73, 146*]. These penalties do not apply under Real Time Information (RTI), for which no annual returns are required, but see **53.24** PAY AS YOU EARN for late filing penalties for RTI.

The fact that *TMA 1970, s 98A* might produce a disproportionately harsh penalty for an employer with just one employee is of no consequence and is not in breach of *Human Rights Act 1998* (*Bysermaw Properties Ltd v HMRC* (Sp C 644), [2008] SSCD 322).

In a number of cases heard by the First-tier Tribunal, penalties were discharged on grounds of HMRC's alleged unfairness in delaying the issue of *TMA 1970, s 98A* penalty notices with the result that monthly penalties accumulated. In a test appeal (*HMRC v Hok Ltd* UT 2012, 81 TC 540) the Upper Tribunal ruled that the First-tier Tribunal had exceeded its jurisdiction in discharging penalties on the grounds that their imposition was unfair; ' . . . it does not matter whether the Tribunal purports to exercise a judicial review function or instead claims to be applying common law principles; neither course is within its jurisdiction'. A similar conclusion was reached in *HMRC v Bosher* UT, [2014] STC 617 where it was claimed that fixed monthly penalties charged were disproportionate and contrary to human rights law; the correct remedy is for the taxpayer to seek judicial review.

A genuine and reasonable belief that a return had been successfully filed online, when it had accidentally been submitted in test mode, amounted to a reasonable excuse (*Lifesmart Ltd v HMRC* FTT (TC 1832), [2012] UKFTT 137 (TC)).

See **53.24** PAY AS YOU EARN as regards penalties for late in-year payments of PAYE.

Simon's Taxes. See **A4.571.**

Mitigation of penalties

[55.23] The Commissioners for HMRC may mitigate penalties before or after judgment. [*TMA 1970, s 102*]. This rule does not apply to penalties under *FA 2007, Sch 24* (see **55.6**, **55.13** above), *FA 2008, Sch 36* (see **55.15** above), *FA 2008, Sch 41* (see **55.3** above), *FA 2009, Sch 55* (see **55.5** above), *FA 2009, Sch 56* (see **43.4** LATE PAYMENT INTEREST AND PENALTIES), *FA 2011, Sch 23* (see **55.16** above), *FA 2012, Sch 38* (see **55.18** above), *FA 2013, s 212A* (see **4.8** ANTI-AVOIDANCE), *FA 2014, s 208* (see **4.48** ANTI-AVOIDANCE), *FA 2014, s 226* (see **4.52** ANTI-AVOIDANCE), *FA 2016, Sch 18 Pt 5* (see **4.59** ANTI-AVOIDANCE), *FA 2016, Sch 22* (see **55.11** above), *F(No 2)A 2017, Sch 16* (see **55.20** above) and *F(No 2)A 2017, Sch 18* (see **55.12** above). [*TMA 1970, s 103ZA; FA 2016, s 158(10), Sch 18 para 59, Sch 22 para 20(1); F(No 2)A 2017, Sch 16 para 58, Sch 18 para 29(2)*]. A binding agreement by a taxpayer to pay an amount in composition cannot be repudiated afterwards by him or his executors (*A-G v Johnstone* KB 1926, 10 TC 758; *A-G v Midland Bank Trustee Co* KB 1934, 19 TC 136; *Richards* KB 1950, 33 TC 1).

Negotiated settlements

In the case of tax-based penalties (other than those under *FA 2008, Sch 41* at **55.3** above and those at **55.6**, **55.13** and **55.15** above) where a maximum penalty of 100% is in strict law exigible, HMRC will start with the figure of

100% and then take the following factors into account in arriving at the penalty element which he will expect to be included in any offer in settlement of liabilities.

(a) Disclosure. A reduction of up to 20% (or 30% where there has been full voluntary disclosure), depending on how much information was provided, how soon, and how that contributed to settling the enquiry.
(b) Co-operation. A reduction of up to 40%.
(c) Seriousness. A reduction of up to 40%, depending upon the nature of the offence, how long it continued and the amounts involved.

(HMRC Pamphlet IR 160). See, for example, *Caesar v Inspector of Taxes* (Sp C 142), [1998] SSCD 1.

For power of HMRC to enter into agreements in full settlement of liabilities in investigation cases, see **6.9** ASSESSMENTS.

See **55.3** and **55.7** above for the statutory reductions for disclosure in relation to penalties under *FA 2008, Sch 41* and *FA 2007, Sch 24* respectively.

See also **55.38** below as regards *TMA 1970, s 118(2)* (reasonable excuse for failure etc.).

For the validity of tax amnesties, see *R v CIR (ex p. National Federation of Self-Employed and Small Businesses Ltd)* HL 1981, 55 TC 133.

Certificates of full disclosure

Where it is established that tax has been lost due to a careless or deliberate inaccuracy (see **55.6** above — previously due to fraudulent or negligent conduct), HMRC may request that the taxpayer complete a 'certificate of full disclosure' stating that complete disclosure has been made of, inter alia, all banking, savings and loan accounts, deposit receipts, building society accounts, and accounts with other financial institutions; all investments including savings certificates and premium bonds and loans (whether interest-bearing or not); all other assets, including cash and life assurance policies, which the taxpayer now possesses, or has possessed, or in which he has or has had any interest or power to operate or control during the stated period; all gifts (in any form) by the taxpayer to his spouse, domestic partner, children or other persons during the stated period; all sources of income and all income derived therefrom; and all facts bearing on liability to income tax, capital gains tax and other duties for the stated period. Great care must be exercised before signing such a certificate, since subsequent discovery of an omission could lead to heavy penalties including, in serious cases, criminal prosecution.

Specific disclosure opportunities

[55.24] See **39.11** HMRC INVESTIGATORY POWERS for HMRC's contractual disclosure facility. HMRC also announce campaigns from time to time under which specified categories of taxpayer are given the opportunity to report previously undeclared income and make a payment comprising tax, interest and penalties; reduced penalties are usually offered as an incentive. Guidance for taxpayers who wish to make a disclosure but are not eligible for a current HMRC campaign is provided at www.gov.uk/government/publications/hmrc-your-guide-to-making-a-disclosure. See also HMRC's Worldwide Disclosure Facility, referred to in **55.12** above, at www.gov.uk/guidance/worldwide-disclosure-facility-make-a-disclosure.

Procedure and assessment

[55.25] *Except* in the case of:

(a) penalties under *FA 2007, Sch 24*, *FA 2008, Schs 36, 41*, *FA 2009, Sch 55*, *FA 2011, Sch 23*, *FA 2012, Sch 38*, *FA 2015, Sch 21*, *FA 2016, Sch 20*, *FA 2016, Sch 22*, *F(No 2)A 2017, Sch 16* and *F(No 2)A 2017, Sch 18* (see further below) and *FA 2009, Sch 56* (see **43.4** LATE PAYMENT INTEREST AND PENALTIES); or
(b) penalty proceedings instituted before the courts in cases of suspected fraud (see **55.28** below); or
(c) penalties under:
  (i) *TMA 1970, s 98(1)(i)* (£300 penalty for non-filing of returns etc. under the provisions listed in *TMA 1970, s 98* — see **55.22** above);
  (ii) *TMA 1970, s 98C(1)(a)* (penalty of up to £5,000 under **25.9** DISCLOSURE OF TAX AVOIDANCE SCHEMES);
(d) penalties in respect of which application to the Appeal Tribunal is specifically required;
(e) penalties under *FA 2013, s 212A* (the GAAR — see **4.8** ANTI-AVOIDANCE);
(f) penalties under *FA 2014, s 208* (follower notices — see **4.48** ANTI-AVOIDANCE) or *FA 2014, s 226* (accelerated payment notices — see **4.52** ANTI-AVOIDANCE);
(g) penalties under *FA 2014, Sch 35* (see **25.23** DISCLOSURE OF TAX AVOIDANCE SCHEMES) other than daily penalties of a maximum of £600; or
(h) penalties under *FA 2016, Sch 18 Pt 5* (serial avoiders regime — see **4.59** ANTI-AVOIDANCE),

an authorised officer of HMRC may make a determination imposing a penalty under any tax provision and setting it at such amount as, in his opinion, is correct or appropriate. The determination can be made using automated processes (see **35.6** HMRC — ADMINISTRATION).

The exception in (c)(i) above does not apply where the penalty relates to the non-filing of quarterly returns by agencies (see **53.10** PAY AS YOU EARN under Information powers).

The notice of determination must state the date of issue and the time within which an appeal can be made. It cannot be altered unless:

- there is an appeal (see **55.26** below); or
- an authorised officer of HMRC discovers that the penalty is or has become insufficient (in which case he may make a further determination).

A penalty under these provisions is due for payment 30 days after the issue of the notice of determination, and is treated as tax charged in an assessment which is due and payable.

[*TMA 1970, ss 100, 100A, 103ZA, Sch 35 para 10; FA 2016, s 158(10), Sch 18 para 59, Sch 22 para 20(1); F(No 2)A 2017, Sch 16 para 58, Sch 18 para 29(2)*].

For a penalty excepted by (c) or (g) above, an authorised officer of HMRC can commence proceedings before the First-tier Tribunal (see **55.27** below).

Penalties under *FA 2007, Sch 24* and *FA 2008, Sch 41*

Penalties under *FA 2007, Sch 24* (see **55.6** and **55.13** above) and *FA 2008, Sch 41* (see **55.3** above) are charged by HMRC assessment. The assessment is treated in the same way as an assessment to tax and can be enforced accordingly. It may also be combined with a tax assessment. The notice of assessment must state the tax year or the part of a tax year or the period in respect of which the penalty is assessed. Subject to the time limits below, HMRC can make a supplementary assessment if an earlier assessment operated by reference to an underestimate of the 'potential lost revenue' (see **55.3** and **55.7** above).

Penalties must be paid before the end of the period of 30 days beginning with the day on which the notification of the penalty is issued.

An assessment of a penalty within **55.3** above must be made before the end of the twelve months beginning with the end of the 'appeal period' for the assessment of tax unpaid by reason of the failure or, where there is no such assessment, the date on which the amount of tax unpaid by reason of the failure is ascertained. The '*appeal period*' is the period during which an appeal could be brought or during which an appeal that has been brought has not been determined or withdrawn.

An assessment of either of the penalties within **55.6** above must be made before the end of the twelve months beginning with the end of the 'appeal period' for the decision correcting the inaccuracy or, where there is no tax assessment correcting it, the date on which the inaccuracy is corrected.

An assessment of a penalty within **55.13** above must be made before the end of the twelve months beginning with the end of the appeal period for the tax assessment which corrected the understatement or, where there is no tax assessment correcting it, the date on which the understatement is corrected.

[*FA 2007, s 97, Sch 24 paras 13, 28; FA 2008, s 123, Sch 41 para 16*].

Penalties under *FA 2008, Sch 36*

Fixed and (in most cases) daily penalties for failure to comply or obstruction and penalties for inaccuracies (see **55.15** above) are charged by HMRC assessment. The penalty can be enforced as if it were income tax charged in an assessment. An assessment to a fixed or daily penalty must be made within twelve months of the date on which the liability arose. Where, however, the penalty is for a failure relating to an information notice against which a person can appeal, the assessment must be made within twelve months of the later of the end of the period in which notice of such appeal could have been given and, where an appeal is made, the date on which the appeal is determined or withdrawn. An assessment to a penalty for an inaccuracy must be made within twelve months of HMRC's first becoming aware of the inaccuracy and within six years of the person becoming liable to the penalty. The penalty must be paid within the 30-day period beginning with the date on which HMRC issue notification of the penalty assessment or, if an appeal against the penalty is made, within the 30-day period beginning with the date on which the appeal is determined or withdrawn.

A liability to an increased daily penalty imposed by the Tribunal or to a tax-related penalty is notified by HMRC to the person liable and may be enforced as if it were income tax charged in an assessment. It must be paid within the 30-day period beginning with the date on which the notification is issued.

[*FA 2008, Sch 36 paras 46, 49, 49B, 49C, 50(4), 51*].

Penalties under *FA 2009, Sch 55*

Penalties under *FA 2009, Sch 55* (late filing penalty — see **55.5** above) are charged by HMRC assessment. The assessment is treated in the same way as an assessment to tax and can be enforced accordingly. It may also be combined with a tax assessment. The notice of assessment must state the period in respect of which the penalty is charged. The penalty is then payable within 30 days beginning with the date of the assessment.

There is provision for a supplementary assessment to be raised if the earlier assessment was made by reference to an underestimate of the tax liability which would have been shown in the return. Similarly, an amended assessment may be raised if the earlier assessment was made by reference to an overestimate of the tax liability. An amendment to an assessment does not affect when the penalty must be paid.

The assessment of the penalty must be made on or before the later of:

(i) (except for RTI returns — see below) the last day of the period of two years beginning with the filing date; and
(ii) the last day of the period of twelve months beginning with:
- the end of the 'appeal period' for the assessment of the tax liability which would have been shown in the return; or
- if there is no such assessment, the date on which that liability is ascertained (or is ascertained to be nil).

The '*appeal period*' is the period during which an appeal could be brought or during which an appeal that has been brought is awaiting determination.

In the case of penalties for late filing of Real Time Information (RTI) returns (see **53.24** PAY AS YOU EARN), item (i) above must be read as follows:

- in the case of a normal penalty, the last day of the two-year period beginning with the end of the tax month in respect of which the penalty is payable; and
- in the case of a penalty for extended failure(s), the last day of the two-year period beginning with the filing date for the extended failure in question (or, if the penalty is payable in respect of more than one extended failure, the latest such filing date).

None of the above time limits apply to a re-assessment of a tax-geared penalty following the submission of the late tax return (see **55.5** above).

[*FA 2009, Sch 55 paras 18, 19, 27*].

Penalties under *FA 2011, Sch 23*

Fixed and daily penalties (other than an increased daily penalty imposed by the Tribunal before 15 September 2016) for failure to comply and penalties for inaccuracies (see **55.16** above) are charged by HMRC assessment. An increased daily penalty imposed by the Tribunal on or after 15 September 2016 is also charged by HMRC assessment, and HMRC must notify the data-holder of the increased daily amount and the date from which it applies. The penalty can be enforced as if it were income tax charged in an assessment. An assessment to a fixed or daily penalty for non-compliance must be made within twelve months of the date on which the liability to the penalty arose. Where, however, the penalty is for a failure relating to a data-holder notice against which a person can appeal, the assessment must be made within twelve months of the later of the end of the period in which notice of such appeal could have been given and, where an appeal is made, the date on which the appeal is determined or withdrawn. An assessment to a penalty for an inaccuracy must be made within twelve months of HMRC's first becoming aware of the inaccuracy and within six years of the person becoming liable to the penalty. The penalty must be paid within the 30-day period beginning with the date on which HMRC issue notification of the penalty assessment or, if an appeal against the penalty is made, within the 30-day period beginning with the date on which the appeal is determined or withdrawn.

A liability to an increased daily penalty imposed by the Tribunal before 15 September 2016 is notified by HMRC to the person liable and may be enforced as if it were income tax charged in an assessment. It must be paid within the 30-day period beginning with the date on which the notification is issued.

[*FA 2011, Sch 23 paras 35, 38–40; FA 2016, s 177(2)–(4)*].

Penalties under *FA 2012, Sch 38*

Fixed and daily penalties under the dishonest conduct provisions at **55.18** above are charged by HMRC assessment. The penalty can be enforced as if it were income tax charged in an assessment. An assessment to a fixed or daily penalty under *FA 2012, Sch 38 paras 22, 23* (failure to comply with file access notice) must be made within twelve months of the date on which the liability arose. An assessment to a penalty under *FA 2012, Sch 38 para 26* (dishonest conduct) must be made within twelve months of the later of the first day on which HMRC may assess the penalty and 'day X'. If there is no loss of tax revenue as a result of the dishonest conduct, '*day X*' is the day on which HMRC ascertain that no tax revenue has been lost. If there is a loss of tax revenue, '*day X*' is the day immediately following the end of the 'appeal period' for the assessment or determination of the tax revenue lost (or the last such day) or, if there is no such assessment or determination, the day on which the amount of lost revenue is ascertained. The '*appeal period*' is the period during which an appeal could be brought or during which an appeal that has been brought has not been withdrawn or determined.

The penalty must be paid within the 30-day period beginning with the date on which HMRC issue notification of the penalty assessment or, if an appeal against the penalty is made, within the 30-day period beginning with the date on which the appeal is determined or withdrawn.

[*FA 2012, Sch 38 paras 29(1)(4), 30, 32*].

Penalties under *FA 2015, Sch 21*

The offshore asset moves penalty at **55.10** above is charged by HMRC assessment. The penalty can be enforced as if it were income tax charged in an assessment. The time within which an assessment must be made is the same as that allowed for the assessment of the 'original penalty' (see **55.10**) to which the offshore asset moves penalty is linked. If, after an offshore asset moves penalty is assessed, the amount of the original penalty changes (because HMRC either amend the assessment of it or make a supplementary assessment), HMRC must similarly amend the offshore asset moves assessment, or make a supplementary assessment, to ensure that it is based on the correct amount of the original penalty. The offshore asset moves penalty must be paid within the 30-day period beginning with the date on which HMRC issue the notice of assessment. [*FA 2015, Sch 21 paras 7, 9*].

By virtue of *SI 2019 No 1238*, interest is chargeable by HMRC on late payment of an offshore asset moves penalty, and is payable by HMRC on repayment of an offshore asset moves penalty, under the harmonised regime at, respectively, **43.2** LATE PAYMENT INTEREST AND PENALTIES and **62.2** REPAYMENT INTEREST. This has effect where the late payment interest start date (normally the date on which the penalty becomes due and payable — see **43.2**) or, as the case may be, the repayment interest start date (normally the date on which the penalty is paid to HMRC — see **62.2**) falls on or after 6 September 2019.

Penalties under *FA 2016, Sch 20*

Penalties under *FA 2016, Sch 20* (enabling offshore evasion — see **55.19** above) are charged by HMRC assessment. The assessment is treated in the same way as an assessment to tax and can be enforced accordingly. The notice of assessment must state the tax year in respect of which the penalty is assessed. Subject to the time limit below, HMRC can make a supplementary assessment if an existing assessment operates by reference to an underestimate of the tax liability. If an assessment is based on a tax liability found by HMRC to have been excessive, HMRC may amend the assessment accordingly, and may do so after the normal time limit for making the assessment has expired, but the amendment does not affect when the penalty must be paid. An assessment must be made no more than two years after the fulfilment of the conditions at **55.19**(a) and (b) above first came to the attention of an HMRC officer. Penalties must be paid within the 30-day period beginning with the day on which the notice of assessment is issued. [*FA 2016, Sch 20 paras 10, 11*].

By virtue of *SI 2019 No 1238*, interest is chargeable by HMRC on late payment of an enabling offshore evasion penalty, and is payable by HMRC on repayment of an enabling offshore evasion penalty, under the harmonised regime at, respectively, **43.2** LATE PAYMENT INTEREST AND PENALTIES and **62.2**

REPAYMENT INTEREST. This has effect where the late payment interest start date (normally the date on which the penalty becomes due and payable — see **43.2**) or, as the case may be, the repayment interest start date (normally the date on which the penalty is paid to HMRC — see **62.2**) falls on or after 6 September 2019.

Penalties under *FA 2016, Sch 22*

Penalties under *FA 2016, Sch 22* (asset-based penalty for offshore inaccuracies and failures — see **55.11** above) are charged by HMRC assessment. The assessment is treated in the same way as (and can be combined with) an assessment to tax and can be enforced accordingly. The notice of assessment must state the tax year in respect of which the penalty is assessed and the investigation period (see **55.11**) in which that tax year falls. An assessment must be made within the period allowed for making an assessment of the offshore tax penalty to which the asset-based penalty relates (or, where the asset-based penalty relates to more than one offshore tax penalty, within the latest of those periods). Penalties must be paid within the 30-day period beginning with the day on which the notice of assessment is issued. [*FA 2016, Sch 22 para 15*].

By virtue of *SI 2019 No 1238*, interest is chargeable by HMRC on late payment of an asset-based penalty, and is payable by HMRC on repayment of an asset-based penalty, under the harmonised regime at, respectively, **43.2** LATE PAYMENT INTEREST AND PENALTIES and **62.2** REPAYMENT INTEREST. This has effect where the late payment interest start date (normally the date on which the penalty becomes due and payable — see **43.2**) or, as the case may be, the repayment interest start date (normally the date on which the penalty is paid to HMRC — see **62.2**) falls on or after 6 September 2019.

Penalties under *F(No 2)A 2017, Sch 16*

Penalties under *F(No 2)A 2017, Sch 16* (enabling defeated tax avoidance — see **55.20** above) are charged by HMRC assessment. The assessment is treated in the same way as an assessment to tax and can be enforced accordingly. Penalties must be paid within the 30-day period beginning with the day on which the notice of assessment is issued.

An assessment to a penalty may not be made after whichever of the following times applies:

(i) where a GAAR final decision notice has been given in relation to the arrangements in question (see **55.20**(A) above), the end of 12 months beginning with the date on which T incurs the defeat;

(ii) where a GAAR final decision notice has been given in relation to equivalent arrangements and HMRC have given a notice stating their view that it is relevant to the arrangements in question (see **55.20**(A) above), the end of 12 months beginning with the end of the time allowed for representations in respect of that notice;

(iii) where HMRC have made a referral to the GAAR Advisory Panel (see **55.20**(B) above) in respect of the arrangements in question and (iv) below does not apply, the end of 12 months beginning with the date on which the Panel's opinion is given;

(iv) where the taxpayer was not given a notice within **55.20**(1) above before the referral of arrangements to the GAAR Advisory Panel but HMRC have given a notice stating their view that its opinion applies to the arrangements in question (see **55.20**(B) above), the end of 12 months beginning with the end of the time allowed for representations in respect of that notice.

If HMRC cannot assess a penalty until more than 50% of arrangements which are substantially the same have incurred a defeat, the time limit is extended to the end of the 12 months beginning with the date on which the required percentage is reached. If, in such a case, a person requests assessment of the penalty before the percentage is reached, the assessment must be made before the end of the 12 months beginning with the date of the request. If a declaration that a person is not liable to a penalty has been made by a lawyer under the provisions for privileged communications and facts then come to HMRC's knowledge that in their opinion are sufficient to indicate that the declaration contained a material inaccuracy, the deadline for assessing the penalty is extended to the end of the 12 months beginning with the date on which the facts come to HMRC's knowledge.

[*F(No 2)A 2017, Sch 16 paras 19(1), 20, 22*].

On and after 1 June 2019, *interest* is chargeable on the penalty if paid later than the due date; the charge to interest is under the harmonised regime at **43.2** LATE PAYMENT INTEREST AND PENALTIES. Similarly, interest is payable by HMRC on the penalty if, and to the extent that, it falls to be repaid; the interest is payable under the harmonised regime at **62.2** REPAYMENT INTEREST. [*SI 2019 No 921*].

Penalties under *F(No 2)A 2017, Sch 18*

Penalties under *F(No 2)A 2017, Sch 18* (failure to correct offshore tax non-compliance — see **55.12** above) are charged by HMRC assessment. The assessment is treated in the same way as an assessment to tax (and may be combined with an assessment to tax) and can be enforced accordingly. The notice of assessment must state the uncorrected offshore tax non-compliance to which the penalty relates and the tax year to which that non-compliance relates. Subject to the time limit below, HMRC can make a supplementary assessment if an existing assessment operates by reference to an underestimate of the tax liability. If an assessment is based on a tax liability found by HMRC to have been excessive, HMRC may amend the assessment accordingly, and may do so after the normal time limit for making the assessment has expired, but the amendment does not affect when the penalty must be paid. Penalties must be paid within the 30-day period beginning with the day on which the notice of assessment is issued.

Where the non-compliance is the delivery of a tax document containing an inaccuracy, the assessment must be made before the end of the 12 months beginning with the end of the 'appeal period' for the decision correcting the inaccuracy or, if there is no assessment to tax, the date on which the inaccuracy is corrected. In other cases, the assessment must be made before the end of the 12 months beginning with the end of the appeal period for the assessment of tax unpaid by reason of the non-compliance or, where there is no such assessment, the date on which the amount of tax unpaid by reason of the non-compliance is ascertained. The '*appeal period*' is the period during which an appeal could be brought or during which an appeal that has been brought has not been determined or withdrawn.

[*F(No 2)A 2017, Sch 18 paras 18, 19*].

By virtue of *SI 2019 No 1238*, interest is chargeable by HMRC on late payment of a 'failure to correct offshore tax non-compliance' penalty, and is payable by HMRC on repayment of such a penalty, under the harmonised regime at, respectively, **43.2** LATE PAYMENT INTEREST AND PENALTIES and **62.2** REPAYMENT INTEREST. This has effect where the late payment interest start date (normally the date on which the penalty becomes due and payable — see **43.2**) or, as the case may be, the repayment interest start date (normally the date on which the penalty is paid to HMRC — see **62.2**) falls on or after 6 September 2019.

Simon's Taxes. See **A4.580–A4.583.**

Appeals

[55.26] Subject to the following points, the general APPEALS (5) provisions apply to an appeal against a determination of a penalty as in **55.25** above.

TMA 1970, s 50(6)–(8) (see **5.19** APPEALS) do not apply. Instead (subject to below), on appeal the First-tier Tribunal can:

- in the case of a penalty which is required to be of a particular amount, set the determination aside, confirm it, or alter it to the correct amount; and
- in any other case, set the determination aside, confirm it if it seems appropriate, or reduce it (including to nil) or increase it as seems appropriate (but not beyond the permitted maximum).

In addition to the right to appeal to the Upper Tribunal on a point of law, the taxpayer can so appeal (with permission) against the amount of a penalty determined by the First-tier Tribunal.

[*TMA 1970, ss 100B, 103ZA; FA 2016, s 158(10), Sch 18 para 59, Sch 22 para 20(1); F(No 2)A 2017, Sch 16 para 58, Sch 18 para 29(2)*].

In considering whether a penalty should be reduced, the Tribunal is not confined to a review of the arithmetic and the extent of any mitigation allowed by HMRC; it is entitled, and required, to consider all the material circumstances (such as unreasonable delay in proceedings) (*Khawaja v HMRC*, UT, [2013] UKUT 353 (TCC), [2014] STC 150).

COVID-19 (coronavirus) special measure

Individuals and businesses affected by the 2020 COVID-19 pandemic are given an extra three months to appeal any penalty dated February 2020 or later (www.gov.uk/tax-appeals/penalty).

Penalties under *FA 2007, Sch 24* and *FA 2008, Sch 41*

Assessments of penalties under *FA 2007, Sch 24* (see **55.6** and **55.13** above) and *FA 2008, Sch 41* (see **55.3** above) are subject to specific appeal provisions. An appeal can be made against an HMRC decision that a penalty is payable or against a decision as to the amount of a penalty. In relation to penalty within **55.6** above, an appeal can be brought against a decision not to suspend a penalty or against conditions of suspension. An appeal against a penalty is generally to be treated in the same way as an appeal against an income tax assessment, but not so as to require payment of the penalty before the appeal is determined.

The powers of the Appeal Tribunal are restricted in certain cases, to where it thinks that HMRC's decision was flawed when considered in the light of principles applicable in proceedings for judicial review. The decisions concerned are as follows:

- a decision as to the extent to which the provisions for reduction of a penalty in special circumstances apply;
- a decision not to suspend a penalty; and
- a decision as to the conditions of suspension.

Where the Tribunal orders HMRC to suspend a penalty, there is a further right of appeal against the provisions of HMRC's notice of suspension.

[*FA 2007, s 97, Sch 24 paras 15–17; FA 2008, s 123, Sch 41 paras 17–19*].

In a case in which the taxpayer had suffered understandable stress and in which HMRC did not appear to have even considered the possibility of special circumstances, their decision was held to have been flawed, and the Tribunal reduced the penalties by 50% (*Roche v HMRC* FTT (TC 2019), [2012] UKFTT 333 (TC)). In *White v HMRC* FTT (TC 2050), [2012] UKFTT 364 (TC), the HMRC officer failed to give any reason for his conclusion that there were no special circumstances, and his decision was held to have been flawed for that reason; the Tribunal interpreted 'special circumstances' as something out of the ordinary, something uncommon, and reduced the penalties by 60%.

Penalties under *FA 2008, Sch 36*

Appeals can be made against an HMRC decision that a fixed or daily penalty (see **55.15** above) is payable or against a decision as to the amount of such a penalty. Notice of appeal must be given in writing within the 30-day period beginning with the date on which HMRC notification of the penalty assessment is issued, and must state the grounds of appeal. Subject to this, the general APPEALS (**5**) provisions apply as they apply to income tax assessments. [*FA 2008, Sch 36 paras 47, 48*].

Penalties under *FA 2009, Sch 55*

An appeal may be brought against the imposition of a late filing penalty (see **55.5** above) or against its amount. An appeal is to be treated in the same way as an appeal against an assessment to income tax (see **5** APPEALS), but not so as to require the taxpayer to pay the penalty before the appeal against its assessment is determined. Thus, notice of appeal must normally be given within 30 days after the date of issue of the penalty assessment (see **5.4** APPEALS).

If the appeal is against the imposition of a penalty and it goes to the Tribunal, the Tribunal may affirm or cancel HMRC's decision to impose.

If the appeal is against the amount of a penalty and it goes to the Tribunal, the Tribunal may affirm the amount charged or substitute its own amount (but only an amount that HMRC could have chosen to charge). The Tribunal has power, similar but more limited, to that of HMRC to make a 'reduction in special circumstances' (see **55.5** above). It may rely on the power to reduce to the same extent as HMRC, which may mean applying the same percentage reduction as HMRC but to a different starting point. It may also rely on the power to a different extent to HMRC, but only if it thinks that HMRC's application of the power was 'flawed'. '*Flawed*' means flawed when considered in the light of the principles applicable in proceedings for judicial review.

In partnership cases, an appeal can be brought only by the partner required to make the return or his successor (although this conflicts with human rights law under which every person is entitled to a fair and public hearing — see *Dyson v HMRC* FTT (TC 4336), [2015] UKFTT 131 (TC), [2015] SFTD 529). Such an appeal is treated as an appeal against every penalty payable by partners in respect of the failure in question.

[*FA 2009, Sch 55 paras 20–22, 25(4)(5)*].

Penalties under *FA 2011, Sch 23*

An appeal may be brought against the imposition of a penalty within **55.16** above or against its amount. Notice of appeal must be given in writing to HMRC within the 30-day period beginning with the date on which HMRC notification of the penalty assessment is issued, and must state the grounds of appeal. No such appeal could be made against an increased daily penalty imposed by the Tribunal before 15 September 2016 (see **55.16** above); and no appeal can be made against the amount of such a penalty imposed on or after that date.

If the appeal is against the imposition of a penalty and it goes to the Tribunal, the Tribunal may affirm or cancel HMRC's decision to impose. If the appeal is against the amount of a penalty and it goes to the Tribunal, the Tribunal may affirm the amount charged or substitute its own amount (but only an amount that HMRC could have chosen to charge). Subject to this, the general APPEALS (5) provisions apply as they apply to income tax assessments.

[*FA 2011, Sch 23 paras 36, 37; FA 2016, s 177(5)*].

Penalties under *FA 2012, Sch 38*

Assessments of penalties under *FA 2012, Sch 38* (dishonest conduct by tax agents — see **55.18** above) are also subject to specific appeal provisions. An appeal can be made against the imposition of a penalty under *FA 2012, Sch 38 paras 22, 23* (failure to comply with file access notice) or against the amount of a penalty under *FA 2012, Sch 38 paras 22, 23* or *FA 2012, Sch 38 para 26* (dishonest conduct). Notice of appeal must be given in writing within the 30-day period beginning with the date on which HMRC notification of the penalty assessment is issued, and must state the grounds of appeal.

If the appeal is against the imposition of a penalty and it goes to the Tribunal, the Tribunal may affirm or cancel HMRC's decision to impose. If the appeal is against the amount of a penalty and it goes to the Tribunal, the Tribunal may affirm the amount charged or substitute its own amount (but only an amount that HMRC could have chosen to charge). Subject to this, the general APPEALS (5) provisions apply as they apply to income tax assessments.

The Tribunal has power, similar but more limited, to that of HMRC to make a 'reduction in special circumstances' (see **55.18** above). It may rely on the power to reduce to the same extent as HMRC, which may mean applying the same percentage reduction as HMRC but to a different starting point. It may also rely on the power to a different extent to HMRC, but only if it thinks that HMRC's application of the power was 'flawed'. '*Flawed*' means flawed when considered in the light of the principles applicable in proceedings for judicial review.

[*FA 2012, Sch 38 para 31*].

Penalties under *FA 2015, Sch 21*

An appeal may be made against a decision by HMRC to impose an offshore asset moves penalty (see **55.10** above). If the appeal goes to the Tribunal, the Tribunal may affirm or cancel HMRC's decision. Subject to this, the general APPEALS (5) provisions apply as they apply to income tax assessments. [*FA 2015, Sch 21 paras 8, 9*].

Penalties under *FA 2016, Sch 20*

An appeal can be made against the imposition of a penalty under *FA 2016, Sch 20* (enabling offshore evasion — see **55.19** above) or against the amount of such a penalty. An appeal is treated in the same way as an appeal against an assessment to the tax at stake but not so as to require payment before the appeal is determined. If the appeal is against the imposition of a penalty and it goes to the Tribunal, the Tribunal may affirm or cancel HMRC's decision to impose. If the appeal is against the amount of the penalty and it goes to the Tribunal, the Tribunal may affirm the amount charged or substitute its own amount (but only an amount that HMRC had the power to charge). The Tribunal has power to make a reduction for disclosure or assistance or for special circumstances to the same extent as HMRC, which may mean applying the same percentage reduction as HMRC but to a different starting point. It may make a reduction to a different extent to HMRC, but only if it thinks that HMRC's decision was flawed when considered in the light of the principles applicable in proceedings for judicial review. [*FA 2016, Sch 20 paras 12–14*].

Penalties under *FA 2016, Sch 22*

An appeal can be made against the imposition of a penalty under *FA 2016, Sch 22* (asset-based penalty for offshore inaccuracies and failures — see **55.11** above) or against the amount of such a penalty. An appeal is treated in the same way as an appeal against an assessment to the tax concerned but not so as to require payment before the appeal is determined. If the appeal is against the imposition of a penalty and it goes to the Tribunal, the Tribunal may affirm or cancel HMRC's decision to impose. If the appeal is against the amount of the penalty and it goes to the Tribunal, the Tribunal may affirm the amount charged or substitute its own amount (but only an amount that HMRC had the power to charge). The Tribunal has power to make a reduction for special circumstances to the same extent as HMRC, which may mean applying the same percentage reduction as HMRC but to a different starting point. It may make a reduction to a different extent to HMRC, but only if it thinks that HMRC's decision was flawed when considered in the light of the principles applicable in proceedings for judicial review. [*FA 2016, Sch 22 paras 16–18*].

Penalties under *F(No 2)A 2017, Sch 16*

An appeal can be made against the imposition of a penalty under *F(No 2)A 2017, Sch 16* (enabling defeated tax avoidance — see **55.20** above) or against the amount of such a penalty. An appeal is treated in the same way as an appeal against an assessment to the tax concerned but not so as to require payment before the appeal is determined. If the appeal is against the imposition of a penalty and it goes to the Tribunal, the Tribunal may affirm or cancel HMRC's decision to impose. If the appeal is against the amount of a penalty and it is heard by the Tribunal, the Tribunal may affirm the amount charged or substitute its own amount (but only an amount that HMRC could have chosen to charge). If the Tribunal substitutes its own amount, it must rely on the provision to mitigate the penalty to the same extent as HMRC, which may mean applying the same percentage reduction as HMRC but to a different starting point. It may make a reduction to a different extent to HMRC, but only if it thinks that HMRC's decision was flawed when considered in the light of the principles applicable in proceedings for judicial review. [*F(No 2)A 2017, Sch 16 paras 37–39*].

Penalties under *F(No 2)A 2017, Sch 18*

An appeal can be made against the imposition of a penalty under *F(No 2)A 2017, Sch 18* (failure to correct offshore tax non-compliance — see **55.12** above) or against the amount of such a penalty. An appeal is treated in the same way as an appeal against an assessment to the tax concerned but not so as to require payment before the appeal is determined. If the appeal is against the imposition of a penalty and it goes to the Tribunal, the Tribunal may affirm or cancel HMRC's decision to impose. If the appeal is against the amount of the penalty and it goes to the Tribunal, the Tribunal may affirm the amount charged or substitute its own amount (but only an amount that HMRC had the power to charge). The Tribunal has power to make a reduction for disclosure or special circumstances to the same extent as HMRC, which may mean applying the same percentage reduction as HMRC but to a different starting point. It may make a reduction to a different extent to HMRC, but only if it thinks that HMRC's decision was flawed when considered in the light of the principles applicable in proceedings for judicial review. [*F(No 2)A 2017, Sch 18 paras 20–22*].

Simon's Taxes. See **A4.585**.

Proceedings before Tribunal

[55.27] For a penalty within **55.25**(c) or (g) above, an authorised officer of HMRC can commence proceedings before the First-tier Tribunal. The tax-payer will be a party to the proceedings. In addition to the right to appeal to the Upper Tribunal on a point of law, the taxpayer can so appeal (with permission) against the amount of a penalty determined by the First-tier Tribunal. The Upper Tribunal can set the determination aside, confirm it if it seems appropriate, or reduce it (including to nil) or increase it as seems appropriate (but not beyond the permitted maximum). The penalty is treated as tax charged in an assessment and due and payable. [*TMA 1970, s 100C*].

These rules do not apply to penalties under *FA 2007, Sch 24* (see **55.6**, **55.13** above), *FA 2008, Sch 36* (see **55.15** above), *FA 2008, Sch 41* (see **55.3** above), *FA 2009, Sch 55* (see **55.5** above), *FA 2009, Sch 56* (see **43.4** LATE PAYMENT INTEREST AND PENALTIES), *FA 2011, Sch 23* (see **55.16** above), *FA 2012, Sch 38* (see **55.18** above), *FA 2014, s 208* (see **4.48** ANTI-AVOIDANCE), *FA 2014, s 226* (see **4.52** ANTI-AVOIDANCE), *FA 2016, Sch 18 Pt 5* (see **4.59** ANTI-AVOIDANCE, *FA 2016, Sch 22* (see **55.11** above), *F(No 2)A 2017, Sch 16* (see **55.20** above) and *F(No 2)A 2017, Sch 18* (see **55.12** above). [*TMA 1970, s 103ZA; FA 2016, s 158(10), Sch 18 para 59, Sch 22 para 20(1); F(No 2)A 2017, Sch 16 para 58, Sch 18 para 29(2)*].

Proceedings before court

[55.28] If the Commissioners for HMRC consider that liability for a penalty arises from fraud by any person, proceedings can be brought in the High Court (or Court of Session). If the court does not find fraud proved, it can nevertheless impose a penalty to which it considers the person liable. [*TMA 1970, s 100D*].

This rule does not apply to penalties under *FA 2007, Sch 24* (see **55.6**, **55.13** above), *FA 2008, Sch 36* (see **55.15** above), *FA 2008, Sch 41* (see **55.3** above), *FA 2009, Sch 55* (see **55.5** above), *FA 2009, Sch 56* (see **43.4** LATE PAYMENT INTEREST AND PENALTIES), *FA 2011, Sch 23* (see **55.16** above), *FA 2012, Sch 38* (see **55.18** above), *FA 2013, s 212A* (see **4.8** ANTI-AVOIDANCE), *FA 2014, s 208* (see **4.48** ANTI-AVOIDANCE), *FA 2014, s 226* (see **4.52** ANTI-AVOIDANCE), *FA 2016, Sch 18 Pt 5* (see **4.59** ANTI-AVOIDANCE, *FA 2016, Sch 22* (see **55.11** above), *F(No 2)A 2017, Sch 16* (see **55.20** above) and *F(No 2)A 2017, Sch 18* (see **55.12** above). [*TMA 1970, s 103ZA; FA 2016, s 158(10), Sch 18 para 59, Sch 22 para 20(1); F(No 2)A 2017, Sch 16 para 58, Sch 18 para 29(2)*].

General matters

[55.29] Non-receipt of notice of the hearing at which the Appeal Commissioners awarded penalties is not a ground of appeal to the courts (*Kenny v Wirral Commrs* Ch D 1974, 50 TC 405; *Campbell v Rochdale Commrs* Ch D 1975, 50 TC 411).

A mere denial of liability to penalties implies an intention by the taxpayer to set up a case in refutation, and details must be supplied (*CIR v Jackson* CA 1960, 39 TC 357).

For the validity of penalty proceedings while assessments remain open, see *A-G for Irish Free State v White* SC (RI) 1931, 38 TC 666 and *R v Havering Commrs (ex p. Knight)* CA 1973, 49 TC 161. For other procedural matters, see *Collins v Croydon Commrs* Ch D 1969, 45 TC 566; *Bales v Rochford Commrs* Ch D 1964, 42 TC 17; *Sparks v West Brixton Commrs* Ch D, [1977] STC 212; *Moschi v Kensington Commrs* Ch D 1979, 54 TC 403; and for other appeals against penalties for failure to make returns, see *Dunk v Havant Commrs* Ch D 1976, 51 TC 519; *Napier v Farnham Commrs* CA, [1978] TR 403; *Garnham v Haywards Heath Commrs* Ch D 1977, [1978] TR 303; *Cox v Poole Commrs and CIR (No 1)* Ch D 1987, 60 TC 445; *Montague v Hampstead Commrs & Others* Ch D 1989, 63 TC 145; *Cox v Poole Commrs (No 2)* Ch D 1989, 63 TC 277.

For variation etc. of penalties by the court, see *Dawes v Wallington Commrs* Ch D 1964, 42 TC 200; *Salmon v Havering Commrs* CA 1968, 45 TC 77; *Williams v Special Commrs* Ch D 1974, 49 TC 670; *Wells v Croydon Commrs* Ch D 1968, 47 ATC 356; *Taylor v Bethnal Green Commrs* Ch D 1976, [1977] STC 44; *Stableford v Liverpool Commrs* Ch D 1982, [1983] STC 162; *Sen v St. Anne, Westminster Commrs* Ch D, [1983] STC 415; *Jolley v Bolton Commrs* Ch D 1986, 65 TC 242; *Lear v Leek Commrs* Ch D 1986, 59 TC 247; *Walsh v Croydon Commrs* Ch D 1987, 60 TC 442; *Fox v Uxbridge Commrs & CIR* Ch D 2001, [2002] STC 455.

For the test used by the court in considering whether penalties are excessive, see *Brodt v Wells Commrs* Ch D 1987, 60 TC 436. Per Scott LJ, penalties awarded by different bodies of Commissioners 'should, in relation to similar cases, bear some resemblance to one another'.

In determining whether the taxpayer has been negligent, the civil standard of proof (of the balance of probabilities) should be applied and not the criminal standard of proof (of beyond reasonable doubt) (*Khawaja v HMRC*, UT, [2013] UKUT 353 (TCC), [2014] STC 150).

Statements made or documents produced by or on behalf of a taxpayer are admissible as evidence in proceedings against him notwithstanding that reliance on HMRC's practice in cases of full disclosure (see **39.11** HMRC INVESTIGATORY POWERS) or their policy on mitigating penalties (see **55.23** above) may have induced him to make or produce them. [*TMA 1970, s 105*].

Time limits for imposing penalties

[55.30] The time within which a penalty (other than those within **55.6** and **55.13**, for which see **55.25** above) can be determined, or proceedings can be commenced, depends on the penalty, as follows.

(a) If the penalty is ascertainable by reference to tax payable, the time is:
   - (i) six years after the date the penalty was incurred; or
   - (ii) (subject to below) a later time within three years after the final determination of the amount of tax.

(b) In any other case, the time is six years from the time when the penalty was, or began to be, incurred.

[*TMA 1970, s 103*].

These rules do not apply to penalties under *FA 2007, Sch 24* (see **55.6, 55.13** above), *FA 2008, Sch 36* (see **55.15** above), *FA 2008, Sch 41* (see **55.3** above), *FA 2009, Sch 55* (see **55.5** above), *FA 2009, Sch 56* (see **43.4** LATE PAYMENT INTEREST AND PENALTIES), *FA 2011, Sch 23* (see **55.16** above), *FA 2012, Sch 38* (see **55.18** above), *FA 2013, s 212A* (see **4.8** ANTI-AVOIDANCE), *FA 2014, s 208* (see **4.48** ANTI-AVOIDANCE), *FA 2014, s 226* (see **4.52** ANTI-AVOIDANCE), *FA 2016, Sch 18 Pt 5* (see **4.59** ANTI-AVOIDANCE, *FA 2016, Sch 22* (see **55.11** above), *F(No 2)A 2017, Sch 16* (see **55.20** above) and *F(No 2)A 2017, Sch 18* (see **55.12** above). [*TMA 1970, s 103ZA; FA 2016, Sch 18 para 59, Sch 22 para 20(1); F(No 2)A 2017, Sch 16 para 58, Sch 18 para 29(2)*].

Provisional agreement of the amount due subject to the HMRC officer being satisfied later with statements of assets etc. is not final determination of the amount of tax (*Carco Accessories Ltd v CIR* CS 1985, 59 TC 45).

Simon's Taxes. See **A4.594.**

Bankrupts

[55.31] Penalties awarded after a bankruptcy are provable debts, but in practice HMRC does not proceed for penalties during a bankruptcy where there are other creditors. The trustee may agree to compromise any penalties awarded but the compromise must also be agreed by the bankrupt (*Re Hurren* Ch D 1982, 56 TC 494).

Liability under criminal law

[55.32] 'False statements to the prejudice of the Crown and public revenue' are criminal offences (*R v Hudson* CCA 1956, 36 TC 561). False statements in income tax returns, or for obtaining any allowance, reduction or repayment may involve liability to imprisonment for up to two years, under *Perjury Act 1911, s 5*, for 'knowingly and wilfully' making materially false statements or returns for tax purposes. Also, in Scotland, summary proceedings may be taken under *TMA 1970, s 107*.

HMRC have an unrestricted power to conduct a prosecution in the Crown Court, there being no requirement for the consent of the Attorney-General (*R (oao Hunt) v Criminal Cases Review Commission DC*, [2000] STC 1110).

See **6.9** ASSESSMENTS as regards acceptance of money settlements instead of institution of criminal proceedings. See **39.11** HMRC INVESTIGATORY POWERS for HMRC's published criminal investigation/prosecution policy. See **35.4** HMRC — ADMINISTRATION as regards HMRC powers generally.

Penalties imposed for non-declaration of income and calculated as a percentage of the tax lost have been held to be criminal (rather than civil) penalties for the purposes of the *European Convention on Human Rights (King v United Kingdom (No 2)* ECHR, [2004] STC 911).

Simon's Taxes. See **A6.311, A6.11.**

Offence of fraudulent evasion of income tax

[55.33] A person who is knowingly concerned in the fraudulent evasion of income tax (by him or any other person) is liable, on summary conviction, to imprisonment for up to six months and/or a fine not exceeding the statutory maximum (£5,000), or on conviction on indictment, to imprisonment for up to seven years and/or an unlimited fine. [*TMA 1970, s 106A*].

For an article giving HMRC's views on conduct amounting to this offence, see Revenue Tax Bulletin October 2000 pp 782, 783.

Simon's Taxes. See **A6.1112**.

Offshore evasion

[55.34] For 2017/18 and subsequent years, a new criminal offence is introduced for failure to properly declare offshore income or chargeable gains as set out below. It applies only if a threshold limit is exceeded for any particular tax year. The threshold is £25,000. There is no requirement for the prosecution to prove intent to evade tax. The offence does not apply to failures and inaccuracies in respect of notices or returns relating to any tax year prior to 2017/18.

The offence covers the following:

(a) failure to give timely notification of chargeability to tax (as in **55.2** above), where the tax in question is chargeable (wholly or partly) on offshore income, assets or activities and the threshold limit is exceeded (by which is meant that the total income tax and CGT chargeable for the tax year on offshore income, assets or activities exceeds the threshold);

(b) failure to file a personal tax return before the end of period during which the notice under *TMA 1970, s 8* to file the return can be withdrawn (see **64.2** RETURNS), where an accurate return would have disclosed liability to income tax or CGT (or both) chargeable for the tax year on offshore income, assets or activities and the threshold limit is exceeded (as in (a) above); and

(c) an inaccuracy in a personal tax return required by notice under *TMA 1970, s 8*, where (i) the return contains the inaccuracy at the end of the 'amendment period'; (ii) its correction would result in an increase in the income tax or CGT (or both) chargeable for the tax year on offshore income, assets or activities; and (iii) the amount of that increase exceeds the threshold limit. The '*amendment period*' is the period during which the taxpayer can amend the return (see **64.4** RETURNS).

References to tax being chargeable on offshore income, assets or activities include tax being chargeable by reference to offshore income, assets or activities. The offence does not apply in relation to offshore income, assets or activities reportable to HMRC in accordance with the Common Reporting Standard (see **35.14** HMRC — ADMINISTRATION) or article 8 of Council Directive 2011/16/EU on administrative co-operation in the field of taxation (see **35.12** HMRC — ADMINISTRATION). Whether the threshold limit has been exceeded is determined by reference to *SI 2017 No 988, Regs 4–9*. With regard to (a) and (c) above, these regulations operate by reference to the potential lost revenue provisions at, respectively, 55.3 and 55.7 above.

A person guilty of an offence is liable, on summary conviction, to, in England and Wales, an unlimited fine and/or imprisonment for up to six months for offences committed before the coming into force of *Criminal Justice Act 2003, s 281(5)* and 51 weeks thereafter and, in Scotland and NI, a fine of up to level 5 on the standard scale and/or imprisonment for up to six months.

It is a defence for a person to prove that he had a reasonable excuse for failing to give the notice required in (a) or deliver the return in (b) or to prove that he took reasonable care to ensure that the return in (c) was accurate. Where a deadline is extended under *TMA 1970, s 118(2)* (see **55.38** below), the extension applies for the purposes of the deadlines relevant to (a)–(c) above. A person is not guilty of an offence if the capacity in which he is required to give the notice or file the return is as a relevant trustee of a settlement (see **67.11** SELF-ASSESSMENT) or as executor or administrator of a deceased person.

Offshore income, assets or activities means income arising from a source in, assets situated or held in, or activities carried on wholly or mainly in, a territory outside the UK. 'Assets' has the meaning given in *TCGA 1992, s 21(1)*, but also includes sterling.

[*TMA 1970, ss 106B–106H; FA 2016, s 166; SI 2017 Nos 970, 988*].

Publishing details of deliberate tax defaulters

[55.35] The Commissioners for HMRC can publish information about a person (including his name and address) if as a result of an investigation one or more specified penalties have been incurred by him and the total 'potential lost revenue' in respect of which the penalty or penalties were calculated is more than £25,000.

The information can only be first published in the period of one year beginning with the last day on which any of the penalties becomes final. It cannot continue to be published for more than one year.

Before publishing the information, the Commissioners must inform the taxpayer that they are doing so and provide a reasonable opportunity to make representations about whether it should be published. No information will be published if the penalty is reduced, by reason of disclosure, to the full extent possible.

The specified penalties are those under **55.6** above (errors in documents), **55.3** above (failure to notify chargeability) and certain VAT and duty penalties, where in each case the error, failure or other action was deliberate. See **55.3** and **55.7** for the meaning of '*potential lost revenue*' in each case.

On and after 1 April 2017, the above applies also where a body corporate, a partnership or one or more of the trustees of a settlement has incurred a penalty under **55.6** above in respect of a deliberate inaccuracy involving an offshore matter or an offshore transfer (for which see **55.8**) or a penalty under

55.3 above in respect of a deliberate failure which involves an offshore matter or an offshore transfer (for which see **55.4**). In this case the Commissioners may publish information in respect of any individual who controls the body corporate or partnership ('control' being construed as in *CTA 2010, s 1124*) or any individual who is a trustee of the settlement, where in either case the individual has obtained a tax advantage (as in *FA 2013, s 208* — see **4.2** ANTI-AVOIDANCE) as a result of the inaccuracy or failure. This applies regardless of the amount of potential lost revenue, and the let-out applies only if the penalty is reduced, by reason of *unprompted* disclosure, to the full extent permitted.

[*FA 2009, s 94; FA 2016, s 164; SI 2017 No 261*].

Simon's Taxes. See **A6.651.**

Publishing details of persons failing to correct

[55.36] The Commissioners for HMRC may publish information about a person (P) if in consequence of an investigation they consider that:

- P has been found to have incurred (and been assessed to or had included in a contract settlement) one or more penalties under **55.12** above (failure to correct offshore tax non-compliance) in relation to which the offshore potential lost revenue (offshore PLR) totals more than £25,000 in aggregate; or
- P has been found to have incurred five or more penalties under **55.12**.

Penalties relating to failure to correct offshore tax non-compliance existing at the end of 2016/17 of which P was aware at any time during the RTC period (see **55.12**) are taken into account for the above purposes only if P was aware at any time during the RTC period (see **55.12**) of the existence at the end of 2016/17 of the offshore tax non-compliance in question.

The Commissioners can publish P's name (including previous name or pseudonym), trading name, address, the nature of any business carried on, the amount of the penalties, the amount of the offshore PLR, the periods or times to which the uncorrected offshore tax non-compliance relates, and any other information which they consider appropriate in order to make P's identity clear. The information can only be first published in the period of one year beginning with the last day on which the penalty (or the latest day on which any of the penalties involved) becomes final. It cannot continue to be published for more than one year. No information can be published if the amount of the penalty is reduced for disclosure to no more than 100% of the offshore PLR or is reduced or stayed because of special circumstances (see **55.12**).

Before publishing any information, the Commissioners must inform P that they are considering doing so and afford P an opportunity to make representations about whether it should be published.

[*F(No 2)A 2017, Sch 18 paras 30, 31*].

Publishing details of dishonest tax agents

[55.37] The Commissioners for HMRC can publish certain information about any individual who incurs a penalty under *FA 2012, Sch 38 para 26* (penalty for dishonest conduct — see **55.18** above) if the penalty is more than £5,000.

The Commissioners can publish the individual's name (including previous name or pseudonym), trading name, address, the nature of any business carried on, the amount of the penalty, the periods or times to which the dishonest conduct relates, any other information which they consider appropriate in order to make the individual's identity clear, and the link (if any) between the dishonest conduct and any inaccuracy, failure or action as a result of which information is published under **55.35** above. The information can only be first published in the period of one year beginning with the last day on which the penalty becomes final. It cannot continue to be published for more than one year.

Before publishing the information, the Commissioners must inform the taxpayer that they are doing so and provide a reasonable opportunity to make representations about whether it should be published.

[*FA 2012, Sch 38 para 28*].

Simon's Taxes. See **A6.651**.

Reasonable excuse

[55.38] It is generally provided that a person is deemed not to have failed to do anything required to be done where there was a reasonable excuse for the failure and, if the excuse ceased, provided that the failure was remedied without unreasonable delay after the excuse had ceased. Similarly, a person is deemed not to have failed to do anything required to be done within a limited time if he did it within such further time as HMRC, or the Appeal Tribunal or officer concerned, may have allowed. [*TMA 1970, s 118(2)*].

The phrase 'reasonable excuse' cannot be extended to demanding that a taxpayer demonstrate that there were exceptional circumstances or some exceptional event beyond his control before a 'reasonable excuse' can be established (*HMD Response International v HMRC* FTT (TC 1322), [2011] SFTD 1017). In *Creedplan Ltd v Winter* (Sp C 54), [1995] SSCD 352, the Special Commissioner, in confirming a penalty under *TMA 1970, s 94(1)(a)*, considered that 'there is no reasonable excuse . . . for sending in a return which was less than was required' (but cf. *Akarimsons Ltd v Chapman* (Sp C 116), [1997] SSCD 140 in which a penalty under *TMA 1970, s 94(1)(b)* was quashed). A person can be taken to have a reasonable excuse on de minimis grounds if the amount of tax involved in the failure is insignificant (*Parkinson v HMRC* FTT (TC 4526), [2015] UKFTT 342 (TC)).

Reliance on a third party is capable of being a reasonable excuse for direct tax purposes, though in determining whether a person had a reasonable excuse for failing to perform a particular task it is proper to have regard to the nature of that task (*Research & Development Partnership Ltd v HMRC* FTT (TC 271), 2010 STI 382). See also *Huntley Solutions Ltd v HMRC* FTT (TC 272), 2010 STI 571. In *Leachman (trading as Whiteley and Leachman) v HMRC* FTT (TC 1125), 2011 STI 1909 the taxpayer believed his accountant would file a PAYE return (P35) whereas his accountant believed his client would personally attend to it; this was held to be a reasonable excuse and was distinguished from the situation where a taxpayer relied upon his agent to do a particular act but the agent neglected to do it. Reliance on an accountant's advice as to the correct operation of the Construction Industry Scheme (CIS) has also been held to be a reasonable excuse (*Laithwaite v HMRC* FTT (TC 3879), [2014] UKFTT 759 (TC)), as has the fact that a CIS contractor employed an accountant, who evidently held himself out as able to provide a comprehensive service for a small business, and provided all relevant documentation to that accountant (*Barrett v HMRC* FTT (TC 4514), [2015] UKFTT 329 (TC)).

There is nothing in *TMA 1970, s 118(2)* that gives a person the right to appeal against an HMRC refusal to allow a late claim (*HMRC v Raftopoulou* CA, [2018] STC 988; *Ames v HMRC* FTT (TC 4523), [2015] UKFTT 337 (TC)).

There are separate 'reasonable excuse' let-outs as regards penalties for late returns (see **55.5** above, and see below for HMRC's approach), late payment interest and penalties (see **43.2, 43.4** LATE PAYMENT INTEREST AND PENALTIES), penalties for failure to make an accelerated payment (see **4.52** ANTI-AVOIDANCE) and penalties for failure to comply with a duty under the special compliance regime for high-risk promoters (see **25.23** DISCLOSURE OF TAX AVOIDANCE SCHEMES).

Late filing of a return

For HMRC's approach to reasonable excuse for late filing of a return, see HMRC Self-Assessment Manual SAM10090 and www.gov.uk/tax-appeals/reasonable-excuses. Common examples which HMRC might regard as reasonable are where they are satisfied that the taxpayer did not receive the return; where HMRC Online Service fails to accept the return; where the taxpayer's computer or software failed just before or while he was preparing his online return; where the return was posted in good time but held up by an unforeseen disruption to the postal service; where the taxpayer's records were lost through fire, flood or theft and could not be replaced in time to meet the deadline; where serious illness immediately before the filing date made timeous submission impossible; or the death of a close relative or domestic partner shortly before the deadline (provided that all necessary steps to meet the deadline had been taken). Examples of excuses *not* considered reasonable by HMRC are claims that the return is too difficult to complete; pressure of work on the taxpayer or agent; failure by an agent; unavailability of information needed to complete the return; or the absence of a reminder that the return was overdue. It is, however, stressed that these are HMRC's views, and that it is for the Appeal Tribunal to adjudicate where the taxpayer takes a different view. A taxpayer's political beliefs do not amount to a 'reasonable excuse' (*Gladders v Prior* (Sp C 361), [2003] SSCD 245).

See also *Steeden v Carver* (Sp C 212), [1999] SSCD 283, in which reliance on HMRC's advice as to the practical extension of a deadline, unequivocally given, was held to be 'as reasonable an excuse as could be found'. Following the decision in this case, HMRC's practice as regards paper returns is as follows. They regard a return due on 31 October as delivered on time if found in a tax office post box when first opened on 1 November (or if delivered by hand before midnight on 31 October). They do not charge a late filing penalty for returns subsequently delivered to the post box no later than first opening on 2 November (or delivered any time on 1 November by other means); however, such returns are nevertheless late, and the enquiry window is automatically extended as in **64.6**(b) RETURNS.

In *Brennan v HMRC* FTT (TC 4497), [2015] UKFTT 313 (TC), an appellant against the initial £100 penalty who was fully aware that no tax was due because her income was more than covered by her personal allowance was considered to have a reasonable excuse for late filing, though it should be noted that the non-receipt by the appellant of relevant correspondence sent to her overseas by HMRC contributed to the decision in this case. In *Galbraith (trading as Galbraith Ceramics) v HMRC* FTT (TC 2639), [2013] UKFTT 225 (TC), HMRC's failure to provide an online filing facility for partnership returns was accepted as a reasonable excuse for late manual filing of the return.

In its judgment in *Perrin v HMRC* UT, [2018] STC 1302, the UT sets out how the FTT might usefully approach matters when considering a reasonable excuse defence.

COVID-19 (coronavirus) and reasonable excuse

In view of the 2020 pandemic, HMRC will consider COVID-19 as a reasonable excuse for missing some tax obligations (such as payments or filing dates). The taxpayer should explain in their appeal how they were affected by coronavirus, and should still make the return or payment as soon as they can. (www.gov.uk/tax-appeals/reasonable-excuses).

56

Pension Income

Simon's Taxes. See **E4.126, E4.127, E4.314–E4.321, E4.323.**

Introduction to pension income

[56.1] The pensions, annuities etc. listed in **56.2** below are chargeable to tax as pension income. *Except where otherwise stated* in **56.2**:

- the chargeable amount is the full amount accruing in the tax year (regardless of when paid); and
- the chargeable person is the person receiving or entitled to the income.

The chargeable amount is subject to any deductions due under the payroll giving scheme (see **14.18** CHARITIES AND CHARITABLE GIVING) and the 10% deduction mentioned in **56.2**(f) below.

A deduction is also allowed if the pension income accrues or arises out of rights which represent, or have arisen or derived (directly or indirectly) from, a sum of money or asset which was the subject of a relevant step within **26.7** DISGUISED REMUNERATION by reason of which a charge to tax arose under that chapter. The deduction is the amount which counted as employment income under those provisions. If the deductible amount exceeds the pension income from which it is deductible, the excess is carried forward and is deductible against such pension income in subsequent years until fully utilised. If the said rights represent etc. only part of the sum of money or asset which was the subject of the relevant step, only a corresponding proportion of the amount which counted as employment income is deductible.

[*ITEPA 2003, ss 565–567, 567A, 568*].

Except where otherwise stated in **56.2** below, and subject also to the exemptions in **56.5** below, the charge applies regardless of the residence status of the recipient. See **56.4, 56.5** below for exempt pension income generally.

Most taxable pension income is within the scope of PAY AS YOU EARN (**53**) (see the list at *ITEPA 2003, s 683(3)*). Certain annuities were brought within PAYE from 6 April 2007 — see **56.2**(e) below and **53.27** PAY AS YOU EARN.

See **56.8** below for the taxation of State pension lump sums.

A disability benefit paid to a redundant employee from the former employer company pension fund was held to be chargeable as a pension (*Johnson v Holleran* Ch D 1988, 61 TC 428; *Johnson v Farquhar* Ch D 1991, 64 TC 385).

Taxable pension income

[56.2] The chargeable pensions, annuities etc. referred to in **56.1** above are as listed below. These are subject to the exemptions in **56.4**, **56.5** below.

(a) **UK pensions**, i.e. any pension paid by or on behalf of a person within the UK and not within any of (c)–(h) below. These include voluntary pensions and pensions capable of being discontinued. [*ITEPA 2003, ss 569–572*].
See **56.3** below as to the effect of temporary non-UK residence in certain cases.

(b) **Foreign pensions**, i.e. any pension paid by or on behalf of a person outside the UK to a person resident in the UK and not within any of (c)–(h) below. These include voluntary pensions, and pensions capable of being discontinued, paid by former employers or their successors. They also include annuities and income withdrawal from drawdown funds (see **56.6** below) under overseas pension schemes. For 2016/17 and earlier years, the chargeable amount is 90% of the amount of income arising in the tax year, other than where the remittance basis applies (for which see **61** REMITTANCE BASIS). For **2017/18** onwards, the full amount of the pension is chargeable. Where the tax year is a split year (see **63.19** RESIDENCE AND DOMICILE), the chargeable amount is the amount of income (or, before 2017/18, 90% of the amount of income) arising in the UK part of the split year (other than where the remittance basis applies).
The income is relevant foreign income (see **32.2** FOREIGN INCOME) for the purposes of the remittance basis and **32.4** (deductions and reliefs). See **32.5** FOREIGN INCOME for reliefs potentially available for unremittable income.
See (l) below as regards certain post-5 April 2017 lump sums from foreign pension schemes. See **56.4**(c) below for exemptions for beneficiaries' income withdrawal and **56.4**(d) below as regards exemption for certain beneficiaries' annuities.
[*ITEPA 2003, ss 573–576; FA 2017, Sch 3 para 2(1)(4)(6)*].

(c) **UK social security pensions**, i.e. the State pension and similar benefits included in the list at **73.1** SOCIAL SECURITY AND NATIONAL INSURANCE, subject to the partial exemption at **56.4**(l) below for child dependency additions. [*ITEPA 2003, ss 577–579*].
It is possible to defer the State pension and take a lump sum as a reward for doing so. For more details and for special rules relating to the taxation of this lump sum, see **56.8** below.

(d) **Pensions** paid under a **registered pension scheme** (see **57.4** PENSION PROVISION). For this purpose, a 'pension' includes an annuity under, or purchased with assets held for or representing acquired rights under, a registered pension scheme. It also includes an income withdrawal from drawdown funds (see **56.6** below). See **56.4**(b) below as regards exemptions for beneficiaries' income withdrawal and **56.4**(d) below as regards exemption for certain beneficiaries' annuities. No charge applies to the extent, if any, that the payment of the pension attracts an unauthorised payments charge (see **57.26**(d) PENSION PROVISION). [*ITEPA 2003, ss 579A–579D*]. The following lump sum death benefits are brought into charge as pension income where paid under a registered pension scheme to an individual (other than one acting in a representative capacity, e.g. a trustee other than a bare trustee):

- a pension protection lump sum death benefit (within *FA 2004, Sch 29 para 14*) or annuity protection lump sum death benefit (within *FA 2004, Sch 29 para 16*) paid in respect of a scheme member who had reached the age of 75 at date of death;
- a defined benefits lump sum death benefit (within *FA 2004, Sch 29 para 13*), an uncrystallised funds lump sum death benefit (within *FA 2004, Sch 29 para 15*), a drawdown pension fund lump sum death benefit (within *FA 2004, Sch 29 para 17(1)*) or a flexi-access drawdown fund lump sum death benefit (within *FA 2004, Sch 29 para 17A(1)*), where the benefit in question is paid in respect of a member who had reached the age of 75 at date of death or is paid in respect of a younger member but not within the two-year period starting when the scheme administrator first knew, or (if earlier) could first reasonably have been expected to know, of the member's death;
- a drawdown pension fund lump sum death benefit (within *FA 2004, Sch 29 para 17(2)*) or a flexi-access drawdown fund lump sum death benefit (within *FA 2004, Sch 29 para 17A(2)*) where the benefit in question is paid on the death of a dependant of a deceased member where the dependant had reached the age of 75 at the date of the dependant's death or is paid on the death of a younger dependant but not within the two-year period starting when the scheme administrator first knew, or (if earlier) could first reasonably have been expected to know, of the dependant's death; and
- a flexi-access drawdown fund lump sum death benefit (within *FA 2004, Sch 29 para 17A(3)* or *(4)*) where the benefit is paid on the death of a nominee or successor of a deceased member where the nominee or successor ('the beneficiary') had reached the age of 75 at the date of the beneficiary's death or is paid on the death of a younger beneficiary but not within the two-year period starting when the scheme administrator first knew, or (if earlier) could first reasonably have been expected to know, of the beneficiary's death.

[*ITEPA 2003, ss 636A(4ZA), 636AA*].

A serious ill-health lump sum (within *FA 2004, Sch 29 para 4*) is brought into charge as pension income where paid under a registered pension scheme after 15 September 2016 to a member who has reached the age of 75.

(e) Other **employment-related annuities** (where not covered by (d) above but including annuities from a non-UK source if paid to a UK resident). These comprise annuities purchased by someone in recognition of another's services in an office or employment, annuities under an occupational pension scheme (within *FA 2004, s 150(5)*) that is not a registered pension scheme. If the annuity arises from a UK source, the chargeable amount is the full amount of the annuity arising in the tax year. If the annuity arises from a non-UK source, the chargeable amount is determined on the same basis as for foreign pensions in (b) above.
Included under this heading are annuities granted for consideration consisting (wholly or partly) of sums (other than national insurance contributions) paid (or deducted from earnings) to secure a deferred annuity for an individual's widowed spouse or civil partner or making provision for an individual's surviving children.
See **56.4**(d) below as regards exemption for certain beneficiaries' annuities;
[*ITEPA 2003, ss 609–614; FA 2017, Sch 3 para 2(2)(4)–(6)*].

(f) **Overseas government pensions** payable in the UK *to* a UK resident (or to his widow, widower, surviving civil partner, child, relative or dependant) in respect of overseas government service, and *by* (or on behalf of) the government of a British dominion or protectorate or a country mentioned in *British Nationality Act 1981, Sch 3* and otherwise than out of UK or NI public revenue. These include voluntary pensions and pensions capable of being discontinued. A **10%** deduction is allowed from the amount otherwise chargeable. [*ITEPA 2003, ss 615–618*]. In *Magraw v Lewis* KB 1933, 18 TC 222, the taxpayer was given no reduction for foreign exchange differences and no deduction for costs of unsuccessful litigation against the overseas government.

(g) Periodical payments out of the **House of Commons Members' Fund.** The chargeable amount is the total amount of payments made in the tax year. [*ITEPA 2003, ss 619–622*].

(h) **Pre-1973 pensions previously paid by Commonwealth governments** and for which, under *Overseas Pensions Act 1973*, the British Government took over responsibility for payment. (Any part of the pension representing statutory increases is excluded from this heading and instead falls within (a) above.) The chargeable amount is determined on the same basis as for foreign pensions in (b) above. [*ITEPA 2003, ss 629–632*]. See also **56.4**(j) below.

(i) **Annual payments** made **voluntarily,** or **capable of being discontinued,** by former employers or their successors (including payments from a non-UK source to a UK resident). If the payment is from a UK source, the chargeable amount is computed as in **56.1** above. If from a non-UK source, the chargeable amount is determined on the same basis as for foreign pensions in (b) above. [*ITEPA 2003, ss 633–636; FA 2017, Sch 3 para 2(3)–(6)*].

(j) **Trivial commutation and winding-up lump sums** paid under a **registered pension scheme** (see **57.4** PENSION PROVISION). If a trivial commutation lump sum (within *FA 2004, Sch 29 para 7*) or a winding-up lump sum (within *FA 2004, Sch 29 para 10*) is paid to a member of a registered pension scheme, it is taxable as pension income for the year of payment. But if, immediately before the lump sum is paid, the member has uncrystallised rights (within *FA 2004, s 212*) under any one or more arrangements under the scheme, a deduction is allowable from the amount otherwise chargeable. If all the member's rights are uncrystallised rights, the deduction is 25% of the lump sum; otherwise, the deduction is 25% of the value of any uncrystallised rights extinguished by the lump sum. [*ITEPA 2003, s 636B; FA 2016, Sch 5 paras 8, 9*]. (A trivial commutation lump sum can be paid only if the value of the member's pension rights does not exceed £30,000 and a winding-up lump sum cannot exceed £18,000.) See *FA 2004, Sch 36 para 35* for a transitional modification of the above rules, affecting only winding-up lump sums paid by certain pre-6 April 1980 superannuation funds to which no contributions had been made since that date but which became registered pension schemes on 6 April 2006 (see **57.8** PENSION PROVISION). See *SI 2006 No 572, Reg 37* for a further transitional modification concerning 'equivalent pension benefits commutation lump sums' as therein defined.

(k) **Trivial commutation lump sum death benefits** paid under a **registered pension scheme** (see **57.4** PENSION PROVISION). If a trivial commutation lump sum death benefit (within *FA 2004, Sch 29 para 20*) is paid to a person under a registered pension scheme, it is taxable on that person as pension income for the year of payment. [*ITEPA 2003, s 636C*]. A trivial commutation lump sum death benefit is not permitted to exceed £30,000.

(l) Certain **lump sums from foreign pension schemes** are brought into charge as pension income where paid on or after 6 April 2017. This applies where:
- a 'relevant lump sum' is paid by (or on behalf of) a person outside the UK to a non-UK resident;
- it is paid to that person under a pension scheme and in respect of a member of that scheme; and
- the member is UK resident (or if he has died, was UK resident at time of death).

A lump sum is a 'relevant lump sum' if the scheme is neither a registered pension scheme, a relevant non-UK scheme (see **56.7** below) nor an employer-financed retirement benefits scheme (see **57.34** PENSION PROVISION) established in the UK. A lump sum under a relevant non-UK scheme is, however, a relevant lump sum if the charges listed under 'Other tax charges' at **57.28** PENSION PROVISION could not apply in relation to it. A sum is not a relevant lump sum if its payment is a relevant step under the disguised remuneration rules (see **26.7** DISGUISED REMUNERATION).

The charge is for the tax year in which the lump sum is paid. The amount chargeable is the amount of the lump sum after allowing for deductions as follows.

(1) Deduct so much of the lump sum as is payable by reason of commutation of rights to receive pension income on which no liability to income tax would arise.

(i) Where (ii) below does not apply, deduct so much of the balance of the lump sum after (1) above as is paid in respect of the value immediately before 6 April 2017 of rights then accrued to receive benefits by way of lump sum payments.

(ii) Where the lump sum is paid under a pension scheme that was an employer-financed retirement benefits scheme immediately before 6 April 2017, first calculate the value immediately before 6 April 2017 of the rights then accrued to payment of so much of the 'relevant amount' as is paid in respect of pre-6 April 2017 service. The '*relevant amount*' is so much of the balance of the lump sum after (1) above as is paid in respect of rights to receive benefits by way of lump sum payments. Whether the value thus calculated is fully deductible, or only a proportion of it, is dependant on the level of pre-6 April 2017 foreign service (as defined). See *ITEPA 2003, s 574A(6)*.

(3) If the lump sum is paid under an overseas pension scheme, deduct so much of the lump sum remaining after (2) above as would not be liable to income tax if the scheme were a registered pension scheme and the member's lifetime allowance were fully available.

[*ITEPA 2003, ss 573(4), 574(1)(aa), 574A; FA 2017, Sch 3 paras 8–10*].

UK pensions — effect of temporary non-UK residence

[56.3] Where the 'year of departure' is 2013/14 or any subsequent year, certain UK pensions accruing in a period of 'temporary non-UK residence' are treated for the purposes of **56.2**(a) above as if they accrued in the 'period of return'. The effect is that the charge to tax applies for the tax year that consists of or includes the period of return. For what is meant by '*temporary non-UK residence*', the '*year of departure*' and the '*period of return*', see **63.29** RESIDENCE AND DOMICILE.

A pension is treated in this way if:

- it is within **56.2**(a);
- it is in the form of a lump sum;
- it accrued in the 'temporary period of non-UK residence' (see **63.29**(d) RESIDENCE AND DOMICILE); and
- it is not otherwise chargeable to tax but would have been chargeable under **56.2**(a) if it were not for a double tax treaty. This includes a case where a charge could be prevented by the making of a claim to double tax relief but no claim has yet been made.

Nothing in any double tax treaty is to be read as preventing the individual from being chargeable to income tax in respect of any pension treated as accrued in the period of return.

[*ITEPA 2003, s 572A*].

PAYE

Amounts *treated as* accruing for the year of return are not subject to PAYE. [*ITEPA 2003, s 683(3B)*].

Exempt pension income

[56.4] General exemptions from the charge to tax on pension income are as listed below. See **56.5** below for exemptions specific to non-UK residents.

(a) The following types of **lump sum** paid under a **registered pension scheme** (see **57.4** PENSION PROVISION):
- a pension commencement lump sum (within *FA 2004, Sch 29 para 1* (see also *SI 2006 No 135*) — broadly a lump sum to which a person becomes entitled in connection with his becoming entitled to a pension);
- a serious ill-health lump sum (within *FA 2004, Sch 29 para 4*) paid to a member who has not reached the age of 75;
- (on or before 15 September 2016) a serious ill-health lump sum (as above) where paid to a member who has reached the age of 75, but see below;
- an uncrystallised funds pension lump sum (within *FA 2004, Sch 29 para 4A*), but only 25% of the sum is exempt, the remainder being taxed as pension income within **56.2**(d) above; if the recipient is aged 75 or over, the exempt amount is restricted to 25% of his available lifetime allowance if lower;
- a short service refund lump sum (within *FA 2004, Sch 29 para 5*), but see below;
- a refund of excess contributions lump sum (within *FA 2004, Sch 29 para 6*);
- a lifetime allowance excess lump sum (within *FA 2004, Sch 29 para 11*), but see below;
- a defined benefits lump sum death benefit (within *FA 2004, Sch 29 para 13*), but see **56.2**(d) above and see also below;
- a pension protection lump sum death benefit (within *FA 2004, Sch 29 para 14*), but see **56.2**(d) above and see also below;
- an uncrystallised funds lump sum death benefit (within *FA 2004, Sch 29 para 15*), but see **56.2**(d) above and see also below;
- an annuity protection lump sum death benefit (within *FA 2004, Sch 29 para 16*), but see **56.2**(d) above and see also below;
- a drawdown pension fund lump sum death benefit (within *FA 2004, Sch 29 para 17*), but see **56.2**(d) above and see also below;
- a flexi-access drawdown fund lump sum death benefit (within *FA 2004, Sch 29 para 17A*), but see **56.2**(d) above and see also below;
- a life cover lump sum (within *FA 2004, Sch 29 para 21A*); and
- a transitional 2013/14 lump sum (within *FA 2004, Sch 29 para 11A*).

Lump sums may, however, give rise to a lifetime allowance charge (see **57.18** PENSION PROVISION). A pension commencement lump sum paid in excess of the permitted maximum (see *FA 2004, Sch 29 paras 2, 3* and, for transitional protection of lump sum rights accrued before 2006/07, *FA 2004, Sch 36 paras 25–34*) is liable to the unauthorised payments charge at **57.26**(d) PENSION PROVISION.

There is a separate tax charge on short service refund lump sums (see **57.26**(a) PENSION PROVISION). There is also a separate tax charge on a pension protection lump sum death benefit, an annuity protection lump sum death benefit, a drawdown pension fund lump sum death benefit, a flexi-access drawdown fund lump sum death benefit or, in limited circumstances, a defined benefits lump sum death benefit and an uncrystallised funds lump sum death benefit, but this does not apply to lump sums paid direct to an individual (see **57.26**(b) PENSION PROVISION). The types of lump sum that are brought into charge as pension income (see **56.2**(d) above) do continue to be exempt (subject to the charge at **57.26**(b)) where paid to a person who either is not an individual or is an individual acting in a representative capacity, e.g. a trustee other than a bare trustee. A serious ill-health lump sum paid on or before 15 September 2016 to a member who has reached the age of 75 is liable to the separate charge at **57.26**(h) PENSION PROVISION; any such lump sum paid after that date is taxable as in **56.2**(d) above.

[*ITEPA 2003, ss 636A, 636AA; FA 2016, Sch 5 para 2; SI 2006 No 572, Reg 7*].

See **56.2**(j)(k) above as regards the charge to tax on trivial commutation lump sums and winding-up lump sums.

See **56.8** below as regards lump sums taken in connection with the *State* pension, which *are* taxable.

(b) In relation to the charge at **56.2**(d) above (pensions from registered pension schemes):

   (i) dependants' income withdrawal (within *FA 2004, Sch 28 para 21*) or nominees' income withdrawal (within *FA 2004, Sch 28 para 27D*) if it is paid in respect of a deceased member who died below the age of 75 and from a dependant's drawdown pension fund, dependant's flexi-access drawdown fund or nominee's flexi-access drawdown fund in respect of a money purchase arrangement (but see below);

   (ii) successors' income withdrawal (within *FA 2004, Sch 28 para 27J*) if it is paid in respect of a deceased beneficiary (i.e. dependant, nominee or successor) of a deceased member where the beneficiary died below the age of 75 and from A successor's flexi-access drawdown fund in respect of a money purchase arrangement.

As regards (i) above, dependants' income withdrawal is not exempt if before 6 April 2015 there was any drawdown payment from the same fund (counting a flexi-access drawdown fund as the same as the drawdown pension fund from which it is derived) or any payment of a dependants' short-term annuity purchased from that fund. Dependants' income withdrawal or nominees' income withdrawal is not exempt if paid in respect of 'relevant unused uncrystallised funds' designated on or after 6 April 2015 as available for the payment of dependants' drawdown pension or nominees' drawdown pension but not so designated within two years beginning with the day the scheme manager first

knew of the individual's death (or, if earlier, the day on which he could first reasonably have been expected to have known of it). Sums or assets held after the death of a member are '*relevant unused uncrystallised funds*' if they are unused uncrystallised funds (within *FA 2004, Sch 28 para 27E(4)(5)*) and the member was under 75 when he died.
[*ITEPA 2003, ss 579CZA, 579D*].

(c) In relation to the charge at **56.2**(b) above (foreign pensions):
- (i) an amount paid under an overseas pension scheme or 'relevant non-UK scheme' (see **56.7** below), which if the scheme were a registered pension scheme would be dependants' income withdrawal (within *FA 2004, Sch 28 para 21*) or nominees' income withdrawal (within *FA 2004, Sch 28 para 27D*), if the pension is paid in respect of a deceased member who died below the age of 75 and no pension payments to the person entitled to the pension were made out of the fund before 6 April 2015 in respect of that deceased member (but see below);
- (ii) an amount paid under an overseas pension scheme or relevant non-UK scheme, which if the scheme were a registered pension scheme would be successors' income withdrawal (within *FA 2004, Sch 28 para 27J*), if the pension is paid in respect of a deceased individual who died below the age of 75.

As regards (i) above, an amount is not exempt if the pension is paid in respect of sums or assets designated on or after 6 April 2015 as available for the payment of dependants' drawdown pension or nominees' drawdown pension but not so designated within two years beginning with the day the scheme manager first knew of the member's death (or, if earlier, the day on which he could first reasonably have been expected to have known of it).
[*ITEPA 2003, ss 573(2A)–(2D), 574*].

(d) The following annuities:
- (i) A dependants' annuity or nominees' annuity paid in respect of a deceased member of a registered pension scheme who died under the age of 75 and on or after 3 December 2014, provided no payment of the annuity was made before 6 April 2015. The annuity must have been purchased from unused drawdown funds or unused uncrystallised funds (see *FA 2004, Sch 28 para 27E(3)–(5)*) or together with a lifetime annuity payable to the member. If the annuity was purchased using (whether or not exclusively) unused uncrystallised funds, the recipient must have become entitled to it before the end of the two-year period beginning on the date the scheme administrator first knew, or could first reasonably have been expected to know, of the member's death.
- (ii) a successor's annuity paid in respect of a deceased member of a registered pension scheme on the subsequent death of a beneficiary (i.e. a dependant, nominee or successor of the member) where the beneficiary died under the age of 75 and on or after 3 December 2014, provided no payment of the annuity was

made before 6 April 2015. The annuity must have been purchased from undrawn funds (see *FA 2004, Sch 28 para 27FA(2)*).

(iii) A lifetime annuity payable to a person under Pension rule 2 in *FA 2004, s 165(1)* where a member of a registered pension scheme was entitled to be paid the annuity immediately before his death and he died under the age of 75 and on or after 3 December 2014, provided no payment of the annuity was made before 6 April 2015 other than to the member.

(iv) A dependants' short-term annuity, nominees' short-term annuity, dependants' annuity or nominees' annuity paid in respect of a deceased member of a registered pension scheme who died under the age of 75 and on or after 3 December 2014. The annuity must have been purchased using sums or assets out of the recipient's dependant's drawdown pension fund, dependant's flexi-access drawdown fund or nominee's flexi-access drawdown fund. If, however, there was any income payment before 6 April 2015 to a dependant in connection with the dependant's drawdown pension fund, or dependant's flexi-access drawdown fund, under which the annuity was purchased, the exemption does not apply.

If 'relevant unused uncrystallised funds' are designated on or after 6 April 2015 as available for the payment of dependants' drawdown pension or nominees' drawdown pension but are not designated before the end of the 'relevant two-year period', there is no exemption for an annuity if any of the sums or assets used to purchase it represent the whole or any part of those relevant unused uncrystallised funds. The '*relevant two-year period*' is the two years beginning on the date the scheme administrator first knew, or could first reasonably have been expected to know, of the member's death, and funds are '*relevant unused uncrystallised funds*' if they are unused uncrystallised funds (within *FA 2004, Sch 28 para 27E(4)(5)*) and the member was under 75 when he died.

(v) A successors' short-term annuity or successors' annuity paid in respect of a deceased beneficiary of a deceased member of a registered pension scheme where the beneficiary died under the age of 75 and on or after 3 December 2014. The annuity must have been purchased using sums or assets out of the recipient's successor's flexi-access drawdown fund.

(vi) Annuities equivalent to those in any of (i)–(iii) above where the facts are similar but the pension scheme in question is not a registered pension scheme but an overseas pension scheme or 'relevant non-UK scheme' (see **56.7** below). The two-year rule in (i) above does not apply in this case.

(vii) Annuities equivalent to those in (iv) or (v) above where the facts are similar but the pension scheme in question is not a registered pension scheme but an overseas pension scheme or relevant non-UK scheme. The two-year rule in (iv) above does not apply in this case.

There is transitional provision to ensure that where a member purchased an annuity before 6 April 2006 (when registered pension schemes came into effect), and dies on or after 3 December 2014 and before age 75, any annuity payable to a beneficiary purchased together with the member's annuity is exempt, provided no payment of the beneficiary's annuity was made before 6 April 2015.

An index of definitions for the purposes of (i)–(vii) above is provided by *ITEPA 2003, s 646F.*

[*ITEPA 2003, ss 646B–646F; FA 2004, Sch 36 para 45A*].

(e) Pensions and annuities paid to holders of an '**award for bravery**' in respect of the award. For this purpose, an '*award for bravery*' means the Victoria Cross, George Cross, Albert Medal, Edward Medal, Military Cross, Distinguished Flying Cross, Distinguished Conduct Medal, Conspicuous Gallantry Medal, Distinguished Service Medal, Military Medal or Distinguished Flying Medal. [*ITEPA 2003, s 638*].

(f) Pensions in respect of **death due to military or war service**, comprising pensions or allowances payable by the UK Government in respect of death due to service in the armed forces (including peacetime service before the 1939–1945 war), wartime service in the merchant navy or war injuries, and comparable pensions etc. paid under foreign law. Where such a pension is abated because of entitlement to another pension, the exemption extends to so much of the other pension as is equal to the abatement. [*ITEPA 2003, ss 639, 640*].

(g) **Lump sums provided under an armed forces early departure scheme** established by *Armed Forces Early Departure Payments Scheme Order 2005 (SI 2005 No 437)* or *Armed Forces Early Departure Payments Scheme Regulations 2014 (SI 2014 No 2328)*. [*ITEPA 2003, s 640A*].

(h) Certain **wounds, disablement, disability** and **injury** pensions granted to members of the armed forces (including nurses) or payable under War Risks Compensation Schemes for the Mercantile marine or under certain War Compensation Acts and Armed Forces Pensions Acts, and **retired pay** granted to a disabled officer on account of service-related medical unfitness. Where a pension or retired pay is certified by the Secretary of State as only partly attributable to disablement etc., only the part attributable attracts the exemption. The exemption extends to certain illness or injury benefits payable by way of lump sum or following termination of service in the armed or reserve forces. [*ITEPA 2003, s 641*]. Otherwise, the whole of the disability pension or retired pay is exempt provided that the immediate occasion of retirement was service-related disability, notwithstanding that a 'long service' element enters into the computation of the award. Further, where a member of the armed forces is invalided out in circumstances which qualify him for both a service-related disability pension and a service pension, the combined pension is regarded as within the above exemption. (HMRC Assessment Procedures Manual AP844).

(i) Pensions and annuities payable under provision of German or Austrian law for **victims of Nazi persecution**. [*ITEPA 2003, s 642*].

(j) Certain **pre-1973** pensions paid in respect of **government service** in **Malawi, Trinidad and Tobago** and **Zambia**. [*ITEPA 2003, s 643*].

(k) Where a person has ceased to hold an employment or office because of **disablement**, such amount (if any) of any pension as exceeds what would have been payable if the disablement had not been attributable to the performance of the duties of the employment or office or to war injuries. But this exemption does not apply to a pension within **56.2**(d) above. [*ITEPA 2003, s 644*].

(l) So much of any **social security pension** (as in **56.2**(c) above or a foreign equivalent) as is attributable to an increase in respect of a child. [*ITEPA 2003, s 645*].

(m) **Coal or smokeless fuel** provided to former colliery workers and their widows, widowers or surviving civil partners for personal use (and allowances paid in lieu of such provision). [*ITEPA 2003, s 646*].

(n) **Lump sums** from a **superannuation fund** to which *ICTA 1988, s 615(3)* (see **57.40** PENSION PROVISION) applies. [*ITEPA 2003, s 414A*].

Where pensions are paid to or from overseas, relief from double taxation may be available under the specific terms of a double tax treaty with the country concerned or by means of unilateral relief granted in the UK (see **27** DOUBLE TAX RELIEF). There is anti-avoidance legislation to prevent double tax treaties being used to avoid taxation of overseas pensions where pension savings have been transferred from a UK pension scheme to a non-UK scheme (see **27.10**(k) DOUBLE TAX RELIEF).

Exempt pension income — non-UK residents

[56.5] The exemptions listed below apply only if HMRC are satisfied, on his making a claim to that effect, that the person to whom the pension is payable is not resident in the UK. For the purposes of these exemptions, 'pension' includes a gratuity or any sum payable on death and a return of contributions (including any interest or other addition included therein). [*ITEPA 2003, s 647*].

(a) Pensions paid from the **Central African Pension Fund**. [*ITEPA 2003, s 648*].

(b) Pensions paid out of a fund established in the UK by a **Commonwealth government** (as defined) for the sole purpose of providing pensions payable in respect of service under that government. [*ITEPA 2003, s 649*].

(c) Pensions paid under the **Oversea Superannuation Scheme**. [*ITEPA 2003, s 650; Overseas Superannuation Act 1991, s 2*].

(d) Pensions paid under ***Overseas Pensions Act 1973, s 1***, whether or not out of a fund established under a scheme made under that *section* but excluding certain statutory increases. [*ITEPA 2003, s 651*].

(e) Pensions paid under the authority of the ***Overseas Service Act 1958*** to the extent that the pension is certified by the Secretary of State as attributable to the employment of a person in the public services of an overseas territory. [*ITEPA 2003, s 652*].

(f) Pensions paid out of the **Overseas Service Pensions Fund**. For this purpose only, 'pension' also includes any sum payable in respect of ill-health. [*ITEPA 2003, s 653*].

(g) Pensions paid under the authority of the ***Pensions (India, Pakistan and Burma) Act 1955***, excluding certain statutory increases. [*ITEPA 2003, s 654*].

(h) **Lump sums** from an overseas employer-financed retirement benefits scheme where certain conditions as to the employee's 'foreign service' are met. Exemption may be total or partial depending on the length of foreign service. It is only for 2017/18 onwards that the exemption is restricted to cases where the recipient is non-UK resident in the tax year in which the lump sum is received. [*ITEPA 2003, ss 395B, 395C; FA 2017, Sch 3 paras 5, 6*].

See also **50.2** NON-RESIDENTS for availability of UK personal reliefs to British and certain other residents abroad and **50.3** NON-RESIDENTS for limitation on income tax liability of non-UK residents.

Taxation of drawdown pensions

[56.6] Individuals are able to leave their pension funds invested in a drawdown arrangement and to make withdrawals throughout their retirement. All withdrawals from drawdown funds (drawdown pensions) are taxable as pension income under **56.2**(d) above (pensions under registered pension schemes) or **56.2**(b) (foreign pensions), whichever is appropriate.

Before 6 April 2015, withdrawals were potentially subject to an annual cap. The maximum withdrawal of income that an individual could make from most drawdown funds on reaching minimum pension age was capped at 150% of the equivalent annuity that could have been bought with the fund value. Individuals able to demonstrate that they had a secure pension income for life of at least £12,000 a year could have full access to their drawdown funds without any cap. The annual cap was removed on and after 6 April 2015 in relation to income withdrawal from flexi-access drawdown funds (see **57.2** PENSION PROVISION), but continues to apply in relation to short-term annuities and to pre-6 April 2015 capped drawdown funds. An uncapped drawdown fund automatically became a flexi-access drawdown fund from 6 April 2015, and a capped drawdown fund may be converted into a flexi-access drawdown fund.

Temporary non-UK residence

[56.7] 'Relevant withdrawals' from a pension fund under a registered pension scheme or 'relevant non-UK scheme' while a person is temporarily non-UK resident are treated as if they arose after the person returns to the UK. The precise rules differ according to whether the 'year of departure' is 2013/14 onwards or an earlier year, as set out below. The charge applies only if the total relevant withdrawals for the same period of temporary non-residence exceed £100,000. Where this limit is exceeded, *all* the relevant withdrawals (not just the excess over £100,000) are brought into charge following return to the UK. For the purpose of testing the £100,000 limit, non-sterling withdrawals are converted to sterling using the average exchange rate for the 12 months to 31 March falling in the tax year in which the withdrawal was made.

A relevant withdrawal is within these rules if it is not otherwise chargeable to tax as pension income (or, where the year of departure was 2013/14 or later, would not be otherwise chargeable if a claim for double tax relief were made). '*Relevant withdrawals*' comprise income withdrawals from a members', dependants', nominees' or successors' flexi-access drawdown fund (see **57.2** PENSION PROVISION), short-term annuities purchased using sums or assets out any such fund, any uncrystallised funds pension lump sum to the extent that it is not exempt (see **56.4**(a) above), any uncapped income withdrawal or dependants' income withdrawal made from a drawdown pension fund before 6 April 2015 (see **56.6** above), and any of the lump sum death benefits listed at **56.2**(d) above and paid direct to an individual on or after 6 April 2016. Also included in the definition are certain lifetime annuities or dependants' annuities which could decrease in amount, and certain payments of scheme pension or dependants' scheme pension under a money purchase arrangement where, at the time the recipient first acquired an actual (rather than prospective) right to receive the scheme pension, fewer than 11 other individuals were entitled to the present payment of a scheme pension or dependants' scheme pension under the scheme. On and after 6 April 2017, the payment of a relevant lump sum (as in **56.2**(l) above) is also a relevant withdrawal.

A '*relevant non-UK scheme*' is a non-UK pension scheme meeting conditions (a) to (c) at **57.28** PENSION PROVISION. These provisions do not apply to withdrawals from a relevant non-UK scheme unless the withdrawal is referable to either the member's UK tax-relieved fund or his relevant transfer fund or ring-fenced transfer funds. A member's UK tax-relieved fund is created by the accumulation of pension rights supported by UK tax relief. A member's relevant transfer fund is created by the transfer to the relevant non-UK scheme from a registered pension scheme or from another relevant non-UK scheme.

Year of departure 2013/14 or later

The following applies where the 'year of departure' is 2013/14 or any subsequent year. For what is meant by the '*year of departure*' and the '*period of return*', see **63.29** RESIDENCE AND DOMICILE.

A relevant withdrawal in the 'temporary period of non-UK residence' (see **63.29**(d) RESIDENCE AND DOMICILE) is treated as pension income for the 'period of return'. Nothing in any double tax treaty is to be read as preventing the charge.

If, in the case of withdrawals from a relevant non-UK scheme, the remittance basis applies (see **61.2** REMITTANCE BASIS) to the person for the tax year that consists of or includes the period of return, any amounts of income withdrawn that were remitted to the UK during the temporary period of non-UK residence are treated as if they were remitted in the period of return.

[*ITEPA 2003, ss 576A, 579CA; FA 2017, Sch 3 para 11, Sch 4 para 9*].

Year of departure before 2013/14

The following applies where the 'year of departure' (as defined in **63.29** RESIDENCE AND DOMICILE) was 2012/13 or an earlier year.

A relevant withdrawal during a year of temporary non-UK residence is treated as pension income for the tax year in which the person returns to the UK. The charge applies if:

- the recipient satisfies the residence requirements for the tax year in which he returns to the UK (the '*year of return*');
- he did not satisfy those requirements for one or more tax years immediately before the year of return but did satisfy those requirements for an earlier tax year;
- there are fewer than five tax years between the year of return and the last such earlier year (the '*year of departure*'); and
- the person satisfied those requirements for at least four out of the seven tax years immediately before the year of departure.

A person satisfies the residence requirements for a tax year if he is resident in the UK during that year and is not 'treaty non-resident' at any time in that year. A person is '*treaty non-resident*' at any time if, at that time, he falls to be regarded as resident in a territory outside the UK for the purposes of a double tax treaty. Nothing in any double tax treaty is to be read as preventing the charge under these provisions in the year of return.

If, in the case of withdrawals from a relevant non-UK scheme:

- the remittance basis applies to the person for the year of return (see **61.2** REMITTANCE BASIS); and
- the person is non-UK domiciled or not ordinarily UK resident in that year,

any amounts of income withdrawn that were remitted to the UK during the period of non-residence are treated as if they were remitted in the year of return.

The question of whether a person is or is not resident in the UK for 2013/14 or any subsequent year is to be determined for the above purposes in accordance with the statutory residence test (see **63.4** RESIDENCE AND DOMICILE), but the effect of split year treatment (see **63.19** RESIDENCE AND DOMICILE) is to be ignored.

[*ITEPA 2003, ss 576A, 579CA; FA 2017, Sch 3 para 12, Sch 4 para 10*].

PAYE

Amounts thus *treated as* pension income for the period of return or the year of return are not subject to PAYE. [*ITEPA 2003, s 683(3B)*].

Miscellaneous

Where, as a result of the above provisions, a relevant withdrawal falls to be taxed under **56.2**(b) above (foreign pensions) following a person's return to the UK, the chargeable amount is 90% for relevant withdrawals paid in 2016/17 or an earlier year and 100% for relevant withdrawals paid in 2017/18 or a subsequent year. [*FA 2017, Sch 3 para 2(7)*].

Taxation of State pension lump sums

[56.8] It used to be possible to defer receipt of the State pension and, in consequence, eventually claim an increased pension or a one-off lump sum plus the normal pension. The lump sum was the total amount of weekly pension forgone plus compound interest. If a lump sum was chosen, it is normally receivable at the time that payment of the pension commences (subject to the right of election referred to below), and it is within the charge to income tax but subject to the special rules below.

For those reaching State pension age on or after 6 April 2016 it is still possible to suspend receipt of State pension, and claim an increased pension in due course, but the lump sum option is no longer available.

Deferred pensions are taxable in the same way as any State pension. For more on the subject of pension deferral, see guidance at www.gov.uk/deferring-state-pension.

A State pension lump sum, where available, counts as income for tax purposes but does not count towards total income. This means, in particular, that it does not affect the availability or calculation of the age-related personal allowance (when this was available) or the married couple's allowance (for which see **1.17, 1.19** ALLOWANCES AND TAX RATES) and it has no effect on the rates at which income tax is payable on other income. The charge to tax is on the person (P) entitled to the lump sum, regardless of his UK residence or domicile status. Income tax is chargeable on the lump sum at a single rate as follows.

(a) If P's taxable income is nil, no tax is due on the lump sum.
(b) If P's taxable income is greater than nil but does not exceed the basic rate limit, the whole of the lump sum is taxable at the basic rate (20%).
(c) If P's taxable income exceeds the basic rate limit but does not exceed the higher rate limit, the whole of the lump sum is taxable at the higher rate (40%).
(d) If P's taxable income exceeds the higher rate limit, the whole of the lump sum is taxable at the additional rate (45%).

For Scottish taxpayers (see **1.8** ALLOWANCES AND TAX RATES), (a)–(d) above apply for 2017/18 by reference to Scottish rates and thresholds. For 2018/19 onwards, following the introduction of the Scottish starter rate and intermediate rate, (b)–(d) do not apply. If P is a Scottish taxpayer and P's taxable income is greater than nil, the whole of the lump sum is taxable at the highest Scottish rate at which P's taxable income is chargeable. For Welsh taxpayers (see **1.9** ALLOWANCES AND TAX RATES), (a)–(d) above apply for 2019/20 onwards by reference to Welsh income tax rates.

The reference above to taxable income is to net income after carrying out Steps 2 and 3 in the calculation of income tax liability at **1.10** ALLOWANCES AND TAX RATES. It excludes the lump sum itself, the tax on which is added at Step 7 of that calculation. For the current basic rate limit, see **1.3** ALLOWANCES AND TAX RATES; for the basic rate limits for other years, see **1.4** ALLOWANCES AND TAX RATES.

The tax year in which the lump sum falls to be taxed is the tax year in which falls the first benefit payment day, i.e. the day on which the deferred pension actually becomes payable. This will normally also be the tax year in which the lump sum entitlement arises, but the actual date of payment of the lump sum plays no part in determining when it is taxed. If the taxpayer dies before the beginning of that tax year, the lump sum is instead taxable in the year of death; this appears to cover the situation where a person has claimed his pension, but with effect from a future date, and then dies before the period of deferral is due to end. (No lump sum entitlement arises where death occurs before the pension is claimed, though the entitlement may pass to a surviving spouse.) In a case where a surviving spouse inherits a person's lump sum entitlement on his or her death *and is already receiving State pension*, the first benefit payment day is deemed to be the date of death of the spouse whose deferral gave rise to the lump sum entitlement.

Under DWP *regulations*, a person is able to elect to delay his lump sum entitlement until the tax year following that in which payment of the State pension commences. A person might do this, for example, because he is still in employment for a part of the tax year in which the pension commences and is likely to be in a lower rate band in the following tax year when he no longer has any earnings. Where such an election is made, the tax year in which the lump sum falls to be taxed is the tax year following that in which falls the first benefit payment day. But if, having made the election, the taxpayer dies before the beginning of that following tax year, the lump sum is instead taxable in the year of death.

Provision is made by the PAYE regulations to enable the DWP to deduct tax at source when paying a lump sum. The recipient can make a self-declaration as to the likely rate of tax that will apply. In the absence of a declaration, tax will be deducted at 20%. Any tax under- or over-deducted will become payable or repayable once the true applicable tax rate has been determined. It could possibly be the case that a person who has claimed a lump sum has to file a tax return for the year for which the lump sum is taxable, but the DWP has not actually paid the lump sum by the filing date; HMRC will not seek any further tax that may be due in respect of the lump sum until the actual payment has been made by the DWP (Treasury Explanatory Notes to the 2005 Finance Bill).

In addition to a 'State pension lump sum', the above provisions apply to a 'shared additional pension lump sum' (i.e. where a pension-sharing order has been made following divorce) and a 'graduated retirement benefit lump sum'. These expressions are defined by *F(No 2)A 2005, s 9* by reference to various social security and national insurance enactments. As regards the State pension, lump sums are not available for Category D (non-contributory) pensions.

[*F(No 2)A 2005, ss 7–9; Pensions Act 2014, ss 16–18; SI 2006 No 243; SI 2003 No 2682, Regs 133A–133H; SI 2015 No 1810, Arts 1, 13; SI 2017 No 468, Regs 1, 9; SI 2018 No 267, Regs 1, 17–20; SI 2018 No 459, Arts 1, 5; SI 2019 No 201, Arts 1, 11*].

Simon's Taxes. See **E7.117A.**

57

Pension Provision

Simon's Taxes. See E7.2.

Introduction to pension provision

[57.1] With effect for 2006/07 and subsequent years, the various pre-existing pension scheme regimes (broadly, retirement schemes for employees, personal pension schemes and retirement annuities) were replaced by *FA 2004, ss 149–284, Schs 28–36* with a single universal regime for tax-privileged pension provision.

Main features are as follows.

- The pre-existing requirement for pension schemes to obtain HMRC approval was replaced by a requirement to register the scheme with HMRC. Pre-6 April 2006 approved schemes are automatically treated as registered schemes unless, before 6 April 2006, they gave notice to opt out of deemed registration. See **57.4–57.10**.
- A registered scheme is exempt from income tax on its investment income and from capital gains tax on disposals of investments. See **57.11**.
- Contributions to registered schemes are not limited by reference to a fraction of earnings and there is no earnings cap. An individual may make unlimited contributions and tax relief is available on contributions of up to the full amount of his relevant earnings or, provided the scheme operates tax relief at source, on contributions of up to £3,600 even if relevant earnings are lower than that. Subject to protection for certain pre-existing policies, *FA 2007* withdrew the availability of relief for contributions that are effectively life assurance premiums. See **57.12**.
- Employer contributions to registered schemes are generally deductible for tax purposes, with statutory provision for the spreading of abnormally large contributions over a period of up to four years, and do not generally count as taxable income of the employee. See **57.14–57.17**.
- Where a member of a registered pension scheme becomes entitled to a scheme pension from a defined benefits scheme, the maximum permissible 'tax-free' lump sum payment by the scheme to the member is broadly the lower of 25% of the value of the pension rights and 25% of the member's lifetime allowance (see below). Where a member becomes entitled to a scheme pension from a money purchase arrangement, the maximum is broadly the lower of one-third of the amount used to provide the pension and 25% of the lifetime allowance. There is an anti-avoidance rule to deter people from converting or transferring from money purchase to defined benefits arrangements for the sole or main purpose of increasing the tax-free entitlement. Where, instead of becoming entitled to a scheme pension, the member becomes entitled to

an income withdrawal or lifetime annuity, the maximum is broadly the lower of one-third of the amounts designated into a drawdown pension or of the amount paid to purchase the annuity and 25% of the lifetime allowance. [*FA 2004, Sch 29 paras 2, 3; FA 2016, Sch 4 para 28(1)(3)*]. All registered schemes are able to offer lump sums. There is transitional protection of lump sum rights accrued before 6 April 2006 (see *FA 2004, Sch 36 paras 24–35; FA 2016, Sch 4 para 28(2)(4)*). The tax exemption for lump sums received is covered at **56.4**(a) PENSION INCOME, *but* is subject to the lifetime allowance below. For the taxation of 'trivial commutation lump sums' and 'winding-up lump sums', see **56.2**(j)(k) PENSION INCOME. For the taxation of 'uncrystallised funds pension lump sums', see **56.4**(a) PENSION INCOME. See **57.26**(a), (b) and (h) for other lump sum tax charges.

- Each individual has a **lifetime allowance** (indexed in line with CPI for 2018/19 onwards from a starting point of £1 million). When benefits crystallise, most commonly when a pension begins to be paid, the amount crystallised is measured against the individual's lifetime allowance and any excess taxed at 55% if taken as a lump sum and 25% in other cases. Any tax due may be deducted by the administrator from the individual's benefits. See **57.18–57.22**.
- Each individual also has an **annual allowance** of £40,000. To the extent (if any) that the annual increase in an individual's rights under all registered schemes of which he is a member exceeds the annual allowance, the excess is chargeable to tax at a rate computed as if the excess formed the top slice of the individual's income. The individual is liable for the tax due. Unused annual allowance can be carried forward for up to three years. A reduced annual allowance for money purchase savings has effect where an individual has flexibly accessed his savings as in **57.2**. See **57.23**, **57.24**. The amount of the annual allowance is reduced (tapered) for individuals with 'adjusted income' in excess of a specified limit — see **57.25**.
- The minimum pension age is 55. [*FA 2004, s 279(1)*]. Other than on ill-health grounds, a pension cannot be paid before the minimum age is reached. [*FA 2004, s 165(1)*]. There is an exception where, as at 5 April 2006, an individual had a right to take pension benefits from an occupational pension scheme before age 55 under a scheme rule in force on 10 December 2003. An individual who was a member of the scheme on 10 December 2003 must have had the right to take benefits before age 55 on 10 December 2003 as well as on 5 April 2006. There is also an exception for individuals who, as at 5 April 2006, had a right to take pension benefits from a personal pension scheme or retirement annuity contract before age 50 and were in certain prescribed occupations. *SI 2005 No 3451, Sch 2* prescribes for this purpose various occupations (mainly sports persons). However, except in the case of certain prescribed professions, e.g. police and armed forces, a reduced lifetime allowance will apply in the case of early retirement before age 50. [*FA 2004, Sch 36 paras 19, 22, 23, 23A; SI 2006 No 498; SI 2007 No 838*].
- As stated above, some individuals who were members of pension schemes before 6 April 2006 have protected pension ages, meaning they are able to receive pension benefits at an age below current minimum

pension age. These include some police, fire fighters and other uniformed service personnel. A COVID-19 (coronavirus) special measure provides that, after becoming entitled to their pension benefits, individuals can be re-employed by their former employer (or a connected employer) without losing the benefit of their protected pension age. This is to encourage retired members of public service pension schemes to rejoin the workforce to aid in the pandemic. The re-employment must commence during the period 1 March 2020 to 1 November 2020 inclusive, and the sole or main reason for it must be to help the employer to respond to the public health, social, economic or other effects of COVID-19. The Treasury has the option to defer the 1 November 2020 date by regulations but not beyond 5 April 2021. [*FA 2004, Sch 36 para 22; FA 2020, s 108*].

- Benefits must normally be taken by the age of 75 at the latest.
- Greater flexibility was introduced for individuals in money purchase arrangement schemes from 6 April 2015 onwards in terms of how they can access their pension savings. See **57.2**.
- Individuals are able to leave their pension funds invested in a drawdown arrangement and to make withdrawals throughout their retirement. All withdrawals from drawdown funds (drawdown pensions) are taxable as pension income (see **56.6** PENSION INCOME. Before 6 April 2015, withdrawals were potentially subject to an annual cap. The maximum withdrawal of income that an individual could make from most drawdown funds on reaching minimum pension age was capped at 150% of the equivalent annuity that could have been bought with the fund value). Individuals able to demonstrate that they had a secure pension income for life of at least £12,000 a year could have full access to their drawdown funds without any annual cap (see also *SI 2011 Nos 1783, 1792* at **57.10**).

  The annual cap was removed on and after 6 April 2015 in relation to income withdrawal from flexi-access drawdown funds (see **57.2**), but continues to apply in relation to short-term annuities and to pre-6 April 2015 capped drawdown funds. An uncapped drawdown fund automatically becomes a flexi-access drawdown fund from 6 April 2015, and a capped drawdown fund may be converted into a flexi-access drawdown fund.
- It is not necessary for an employee to leave his employment before accessing his occupational pension. Members of occupational schemes may, where permitted by the scheme rules, continue to work for the same employer whilst drawing retirement benefits from the employer's scheme.
- A 25% tax charge arises on a transfer of UK tax-relieved pension savings to a qualifying recognised overseas pension scheme (QROPS) where the transfer is requested on or after 9 March 2017. This overseas transfer charge does not apply if both the individual and the QROPS are in the same country, if the individual is in the UK or EEA and the QROPS is in the EEA, or if the QROPS receiving the transfer is provided by the individual's employer. However, a change of circumstances before the end of the five full tax years following the transfer can trigger the charge. See **57.29**.

- There are rules designed to prevent *self-directed* registered pension schemes from gaining tax advantages where there is investment by the scheme in residential property and certain tangible moveable property such as fine wines, classic cars, art and antiques. A self-directed scheme is one where a scheme member can direct which investments the scheme makes. See **57.30–57.33**.
- Non-registered employer pension schemes (known as 'employer-financed retirement benefits schemes') are permitted to exist but without the tax advantages of registered schemes; they are treated like any other arrangement to provide employees with benefits. On the other hand, they are not subject to restrictions such as the lifetime and annual allowance. See **57.34–57.38**.

HMRC publish detailed guidance in the form of a Pensions Tax Manual. They also publish regular online-newsletters on the subject. For links to both the guidance and the newsletters, see www.gov.uk/topic/business-tax/pension-scheme-administration.

Enhanced pension flexibility

[57.2] Greater flexibility was introduced with effect on and after 6 April 2015 for individuals with money purchase arrangements in terms of how they can access their pension savings. For a summary of all the measures see www.gov.uk/government/uploads/system/uploads/attachment_data/file/385065/TIIN_8130_2140.pdf. Some amendments were made by *FA 2016, Sch 5* to ensure that the previously introduced pension flexibility changes operate as intended.

Flexible access

Everyone aged 55 or over with pension savings from a money purchase arrangement can access them as they wish. The tax exemption for pension commencement lump sums not exceeding a specified proportion (broadly the lower of one-third of the amount used to provide the pension and 25% of the lifetime allowance) remain as before. Apart from that, income may be taken from a 'flexi-access drawdown fund' (see *FA 2004, Sch 28 para 8A*) either through a short-term annuity or as income withdrawal of whatever amount the individual chooses; it could be a regular amount or a single lump sum or a series of lump sums. All withdrawals from flexi-access drawdown funds count as pension income and are thus chargeable to tax at the recipient's marginal income tax rate for the year of access.

A reduced annual allowance has effect where an individual has flexibly accessed his money purchase savings as above. See **57.23** below under Money purchase annual allowance.

Dependants and nominees

Individuals are also able to pass on their unused money purchase arrangement pension to a nominated beneficiary when they die. If the individual dies with a drawdown arrangement or uncrystallised pension funds, he can pass on his remaining money purchase arrangement pension free of tax if death occurs before the age of 75. Where the individual dies at age 75 or over, the nominated beneficiary is able to access the pension funds flexibly, at any age, and pay tax on it at his marginal income tax rate. There is also an option to receive the pension as a lump sum, subject to a tax charge of 45% (the special lump sum death benefits charge — see **57.26**(b) below).

Beneficiaries of individuals who die under the age of 75 with an annuity can receive future payments from such policies tax-free. The rules were also changed to allow annuities to be passed on to any beneficiary and not just a dependant.

For details of the exemptions from the charge to tax on pension income, see **56.4**(b)–(d) PENSION INCOME.

Types of pension arrangement

[57.3] A pension scheme will have an arrangement with the member which governs the provision of benefits under the scheme. These may be defined benefit, money purchase or cash balance arrangements. A '*money purchase arrangement*' is one where all the available benefits are money purchase benefits, that is to say benefits determined by the size of the member's pension fund. A '*cash balance arrangement*' is a type of money purchase arrangement but the size of the fund is not wholly dependent on the amount of contributions made plus any investment return; it may be that the scheme specifies an amount that will be available for each year of service, and it may guarantee the rate of return on that amount. A '*defined benefit arrangement*' is one where all available benefits are defined benefits. They are normally calculated by reference to final salary and length of service (a 'final salary scheme'). [*FA 2004, s 152*].

Registered pension schemes

[57.4] A '*pension scheme*' for these purposes is a scheme or other arrangements comprised in one or more instruments or agreements, having effect (or capable of having effect) so as to provide benefits to (or in respect of) persons on retirement, on death, on having reached a particular age, on the onset of serious ill-health or incapacity or in similar circumstances to these. [*FA 2004, s 150(1)*]. *FA 2004, s 151* defines a 'member' in relation to a pension scheme.

A scheme administrator may make application, containing specified information and declarations, to HMRC to register a pension scheme. HMRC can refuse to register the scheme in cases of material inaccuracy or false declaration. HMRC can also refuse to register the scheme (i) if the administrator has failed to comply with an information notice given in connection with the application (see **57.5** below) or has deliberately obstructed an HMRC officer in the course of an inspection in that connection, or (ii) if it appears to HMRC that it is not the main purpose of the scheme to provide pension benefits, or (iii) (on and after 6 April 2018, regardless of when the application was made) the pension scheme is an occupational pension scheme, and a sponsoring employer in relation to the scheme is a body corporate that has been dormant during a continuous period of one month that falls within the year ending with the day on which the decision is made, or (iv) that the scheme administrator is not a fit and proper person to fulfil that role. For guidance, see www.gov.uk/government/publications/pension-administrators-guidance-on-the-fit-and-proper-person-criteria. With effect on and after 1 October 2018, and regardless of when the application is made, HMRC can also refuse to register the scheme if it is an unauthorised Master Trust scheme (see **57.42** below).

The scheme must be an occupational pension scheme (as defined by *FA 2004, s 150(5)* — i.e. an employer scheme) or a public service pension scheme (as defined by *FA 2004, s 150(3)* — broadly a scheme established by government) or else must be a scheme established by a person with permission under *Financial Services and Markets Act 2000* to establish in the UK a personal pension scheme or stakeholder pension scheme. A deferred annuity contract (made with an insurance company) which will eventually provide the benefits due from a registered scheme is treated as having become a registered scheme on the day it was made. The same applies to an annuity contract made with an insurance company, and paid for with monies repatriated to a pension scheme, by order of the Pensions Regulator or the courts.

In *BAV-TMW-Globaler-Immobilien SpezialFonds v HMRC* FTT (TC 6995), [2019] SFTD 631, [2019] UKFTT 129 (TC), it was held that a non-UK resident pension scheme cannot be registered so as to obtain the tax exemption at **57.11** below but that this was contrary to EU law. With effect on and after 21 November 2019 it is now provided by UK law that a pension scheme established by or under any enactment of an overseas country (or any political sub-division of any such country) is a public service pension scheme within *FA 2004, s 150(3)* above and can therefore be a registered pension scheme.

HMRC must notify the scheme administrator of their decision whether or not to register the scheme. An appeal may be made, within 30 days of the notice, against a decision not to register. HMRC do not have to decide immediately whether or not to register the scheme, but if they do not decide within six months of receipt of the application, the scheme administrator may appeal to the Appeal Tribunal as if the application had been refused.

[*FA 2004, ss 153, 154, 156, 156A; FA 2018, Sch 3 paras 1(3), 2(1)(2)(5); SI 2018 No 965; SI 2019 No 1425*].

See **57.5** below as regards HMRC information powers in connection with applications for registration and penalties for failure to comply and for material inaccuracies in applications.

The registered pension schemes regime is administered by Pension Schemes Services, FitzRoy House, Castle Meadow Road, Nottingham, NG2 1BD. See **57.6** below as regards de-registration.

For notes on the role of a scheme administrator, see www.gov.uk/guidance/information-requirements-for-pension-schemes-the-basics.

There are rules restricting the type of investment that can be made by a *self-directed* registered pension scheme — see **57.30–57.33** below.

HMRC are empowered to make regulations (see *SI 2006 No 569*) to treat prescribed registered pension schemes as if they were a number of separate registered pension schemes, each with its own administrator; this is aimed at very large schemes, spread over a number of employers, particularly those in the public sector, whose administrative functions are generally devolved from the centre. [*FA 2004, s 274A; SI 2006 No 569; SI 2007 No 793*].

Non-UK registered schemes

FA 2017 introduces the concept of a '*non-UK registered scheme*', i.e. a registered pension scheme established in a country or territory outside the UK. For 2017/18 onwards (and so far as would not otherwise be the case), the *FA 2004* regime for tax-privileged pension provision:

- applies in relation to UK-relieved funds (as defined) of a non-UK registered scheme as it applies in relation to sums or assets held for the purposes of, or representing accrued rights under, a UK registered pension scheme (a '*UK scheme*');
- applies in relation to a non-UK registered scheme, so far as the scheme relates to the scheme's UK-relieved funds, as it applies in relation to a UK scheme;
- applies in relation to members of a non-UK registered scheme, so far as their rights under the scheme are represented by UK-relieved funds, as it applies in relation to members of a UK scheme; and
- applies to contributions to a non-UK registered scheme as it applies in relation to contributions to a UK scheme.

In applying **57.30** below (self-directed registered pension schemes — investment restrictions) to a non-UK registered scheme, property is taxable property if it would be taxable property in relation to the scheme if it were a UK scheme.

[*FA 2004, ss 242A–242E; FA 2017, Sch 3 para 1, Sch 4 para 14*].

Simon's Taxes. See E7.208.

HMRC information powers and penalties

[57.5] An HMRC officer may issue an information notice to the scheme administrator or any other person, requesting any information or document that is reasonably required by HMRC to make a decision on whether to register the scheme or not. Various provisions of *FA 2008, Sch 36* (see **39** HMRC INVESTIGATORY POWERS) are applied in relation to such information notices. Any person other than the scheme administrator who is given an information notice may appeal against it or against any requirement imposed by it.

With similar effect, where an application for registration is made, HMRC have powers to enter business premises of the scheme administrator or any other person and inspect documents if an HMRC officer reasonably requires to do so in connection with the application. An HMRC officer may ask the Appeal Tribunal to approve such an inspection. Again, various provisions of *FA 2008, Sch 36* are applied.

Penalties apply where a person other than the scheme administrator fails to comply with an information notice or deliberately obstructs an inspection approved by the Tribunal. These are fixed and daily penalties similar to those for failure to comply with investigatory powers under *FA 2008, Sch 36* for which see **55.15** PENALTIES. There is also a penalty for inaccurate information in an application for registration. This is chargeable on the scheme administrator (SA) and applies where the inaccuracy is material and either it is careless or deliberate or SA knew of it when the application is made but did not inform HMRC or SA discovered it some time later and failed to take reasonable steps to inform HMRC. The maximum penalty is £3,000. If the information contains more than one material inaccuracy, a penalty is chargeable for each. A similar penalty is chargeable on a person where, in complying with an information notice, that person provides materially inaccurate information or produces a document that contains a material inaccuracy. Any person making a false declaration in an application for registration and either doing so carelessly or deliberately or failing to inform HMRC is similarly liable to a maximum penalty of £3,000. Where the declaration contains more than one falsehood, a penalty is payable in relation to each.

[*FA 2004, ss 153A–153F*].

There are also information and inspection powers to assist HMRC in establishing whether the scheme administrator is a fit and proper person to fulfil that role, and penalties for failure to comply, or for providing inaccurate information in complying, with an information notice and for obstructing an inspection. These provisions mirror the above provisions relating to information notices in connection with applications for registration. [*FA 2004, ss 159A–159D*].

De-registration

[57.6] HMRC may by notice withdraw a pension scheme's registration on any one or more of a number of grounds specified by *FA 2004, s 158*. One of those grounds is that the scheme administrator is not a fit and proper person to fulfil that role. An appeal may be made, within 30 days of the notice, against a decision to de-register the scheme. With effect on and after 1 October 2018, HMRC can de-register a scheme that is an unauthorised Master Trust scheme (see **57.42** below). See **57.26**(g) below as regards the tax charge on de-registration. [*FA 2004, ss 157–159; FA 2018, Sch 3 paras 1(4), 2(1)(2); SI 2018 No 965*]. For guidance on the fit and proper person criteria, see www.gov.uk/government/publications/pension-administrators-guidance-on-the-fit-and-proper-person-criteria.

Simon's Taxes. See **E7.209**.

Authorised and unauthorised payments

[57.7] There are rules as to the payments a registered pension scheme is and is not permitted to make (authorised and unauthorised payments — see *FA 2004, ss 160–181, Schs 28–30* and *SI 2005 No 3449*, *SI 2006 Nos 133, 137, 209, 499, 571, 574, 614, 1465; SI 2007 No 3532; SI 2009 No 1171* at **57.10** below) and dealing with unauthorised borrowing by registered schemes (see *FA 2004, ss 163, 182–185*); registered schemes may borrow up to 50% of the value of total scheme assets. The rules relating to payment of pensions are in

FA 2004, s 165, Sch 28 Pt 1 (see also *SI 2006 Nos 129, 138, 499, 568; SI 2007 No 493* at **57.10** below), those relating to pension death benefits are in *FA 2004, s 167, Sch 28 Pt 2* (see also *SI 2006 Nos 129, 499, 568; SI 2007 No 493* at **57.10** below), those relating to payment of lump sums are in *FA 2004, s 166, Sch 29 Pt 1* (see also *SI 2006 No 135* at **57.10** below) and those relating to lump sum death benefits are in *FA 2004, s 168, Sch 29 Pt 2*. As regards maximum permissible lump sums, see the sixth bullet at **57.1** above. See **57.26**(d)(e) below for the tax charge on unauthorised payments by a registered scheme.

There is an anti-avoidance rule to deter recycling of a tax-free pension commencement lump sum (i.e. the lump sum generally available when an individual begins to be paid a pension). 'Recycling' occurs where the member takes a pension commencement lump sum from a registered scheme with the intention of using it to pay significantly greater contributions to the same scheme or to other registered schemes. There are *de minimis* limits within which the rule does not apply. The rule does not apply if the member is 75 or over when the greater contributions are made, provided they are not made by his employer. Otherwise, the scheme is regarded as making an unauthorised payment of a specified amount. [*FA 2004, Sch 29 para 3A*].

Simon's Taxes. See E7.225.

Transitional

[57.8] Subject to the opt-out below, a pension scheme which, immediately before 6 April 2006, fell into one of the following categories became automatically a registered scheme:

- a retirement benefits scheme approved for purposes of *ICTA 1988, Pt 14 Ch 1*;
- a superannuation fund approved as at 5 April 1980 for purposes of *ICTA 1970, s 208* which has not since been approved for purposes of *ICTA 1988, Pt 14 Ch 1* and to which no contribution has since been made;
- a relevant statutory scheme or a scheme treated as such by HMRC as at 6 April 2006;
- a deferred annuity contract providing for the eventual payment of benefits under any of the above-listed schemes;
- a scheme or fund within *ICTA 1988, s 613(4)(b)–(d)* (Parliamentary pension schemes or funds);
- a retirement annuity contract approved under *ICTA 1988, s 620* or *s 621* (or a substituted contract within *ICTA 1988, s 622(3)*);
- a personal pension scheme approved under *ICTA 1988, Pt 14 Ch 4* (which includes a stakeholder scheme).

Where only part of a retirement benefits scheme was approved, only that part became automatically a registered scheme. A retirement benefits scheme or personal pension scheme approved after 5 April 2006 with retrospective effect for a period ending with that date becomes automatically a registered scheme with effect from 6 April 2006.

A scheme was able to opt out of becoming automatically a registered pension scheme by giving HMRC notice to that effect before 6 April 2006. Except in the case of a Parliamentary scheme or fund, this action gave rise to an income tax charge at 40% on the aggregate of the sums held for the purposes of the scheme immediately before 6 April 2006 and the market value of the scheme assets at that time.

[*FA 2004, Sch 36 paras 1–6; FA 2018, Sch 3 paras 1(8), 2(4)*].

Simon's Taxes. See **E7.202**.

Compliance

[57.9] A compliance regime for registered pension schemes is set out at *FA 2004, ss 250–274*. This covers such matters as completion and filing of returns, the providing of information to HMRC outside of returns and accounting for income tax (see below). See also *SI 2005 No 3456; SI 2006 Nos 136, 567* at **57.10** below.

Inevitably, there is also an extensive penalty regime covering all aspects of non-compliance (see *FA 2004, ss 257–266*).

The scheme administrator must account on a quarterly basis, and without the need for a notice or an assessment, for income tax for which he, as administrator, is liable, i.e. tax arising from the lifetime allowance charge at **57.18** below and the charges at **57.26**(a)(b)(c)(g)(h) below. (The scheme sanction charge at **57.26**(f) below is outside these rules and can be made only by assessment.) Where such a charge arises in any quarter (ending on 31 March, 30 June, 30 September or 31 December), the scheme administrator must both make an accounting return and pay the tax within 45 days after the end of that quarter. Where the scheme administrator is liable to the annual allowance charge (see **57.23** below), he must normally account for it in the return for the quarter ending 31 December of the year following that in which ended the tax year in which the charge arose, e.g. the quarter ending 31 December 2019 where the charge arises in 2017/18. [*FA 2004, s 254*]. In the event of non-compliance, HMRC may raise an assessment to collect the tax. [*FA 2004, s 255; FA 2017, Sch 4 paras 16, 25*]. Penalties similar to those in **53.24** PAY AS YOU EARN apply to late payments. [*FA 2009, Sch 56; FA 2017, Sch 4 paras 20, 25; SI 2010 No 466*]. See also *SI 2005 No 3454* at **57.10** below.

See *SI 2006 No 570* as to returns and other information which *must* be delivered *electronically* and the information which *may* be so delivered. See HMRC Pensions Tax Simplification Newsletters No 27, 10 April 2007 and No 30, 12 October 2007 for details).

Regulations

[57.10] Except where otherwise stated, the following applicable regulations have effect from the commencement of the regime on 6 April 2006. Note that this is not intended as a comprehensive list of all statutory instruments concerned with registered pension schemes; other statutory instruments are cited elsewhere in this chapter where appropriate.

The Registered Pension Schemes (Prescribed Interest Rates For Authorised Employer Loans) Regulations 2005 (SI 2005 No 3449) prescribe the minimum rate of interest to be charged on a loan by a registered scheme to a sponsoring employer or former sponsoring employer (see also *FA 2004, s 179*).

The Registered Pension Schemes (Discharge Of Liabilities Under Sections 267 And 268 Of The Finance Act 2004) Regulations 2005 (SI 2005 No 3452) make supplementary provision in connection with applications by scheme administrators and other persons for relief from certain charges.

The Registered Pension Schemes (Accounting And Assessment) Regulations 2005 (SI 2005 No 3454) make provision in relation to the making of assessments, and related matters (including interest on tax), in respect of certain charges to tax arising under the regime.

The regulations are further amended by *FA 2017, Sch 4 paras 21, 25* in connection with the overseas transfer charge at **57.29** below.

The Registered Pension Schemes And Employer-Financed Retirement Benefits Schemes (Information) (Prescribed Descriptions Of Persons) Regulations 2005 (SI 2005 No 3455) describe the persons to whom an officer of HMRC may give a notice requiring the production of documents and information about pension schemes.

The Registered Pension Schemes (Audited Accounts) (Specified Persons) Regulations 2005 (SI 2005 No 3456) (as amended) prescribe the persons who may audit the accounts of a registered pension scheme.

The Registered Pension Schemes (Relevant Annuities) Regulations 2006 (SI 2006 No 129) define the terms 'relevant annuity' and 'annual amount' as required by *FA 2004, Sch 28 para 14*. These terms are relevant in computing the 'basis amount' in Pension rules 5 & 7 (see *FA 2004, s 165*) and Pensions death benefit rule 6 (see *FA 2004, s 167*).

The Registered Pension Schemes (Co-ownership of Living Accommodation) Regulations 2006 (SI 2006 No 133) apply where living accommodation is owned partly by a registered pension scheme and partly by other persons, and determines how an unauthorised payment (see **57.7** above) is computed where the accommodation is used to provide a benefit for scheme members.

The Registered Pension Schemes (Meaning of Pension Commencement Lump Sum) Regulations 2006 (SI 2006 No 135) prescribe circumstances in which a lump sum may be treated as a pension commencement lump sum even though it fails to satisfy certain conditions of *FA 2004, Sch 29 para 1*. The circumstances are that there has been an overpayment of tax on the lifetime allowance charge which is refunded to the scheme by HMRC, and the scheme administrator passes on the overpayment to the member.

The Pension Benefits (Insurance Company Liable as Scheme Administrator) Regulations 2006 (SI 2006 No 136) provide that where an insurance company pays certain lump sum death benefits, it is treated as a scheme administrator, with the attendant compliance obligations. See also **57.26**(b) below.

The Registered Pension Schemes (Authorised Member Payments) Regulations 2006 (SI 2006 No 137) prescribe as authorised payments (see **57.7** above) certain demutualisation payments made by insurance companies to scheme members; *the Registered Pension Schemes (Authorised Payments) Regulations 2006 (SI 2006 No 209)* prescribe as authorised payments certain lump sums and state scheme premiums paid by a registered scheme under specified pre-existing legislation; *the Registered Pension Schemes (Authorised Payments — Arrears of Pension) Regulations 2006 (SI 2006 No 614)* prescribe as an authorised payment a payment of arrears of pension to which the member is entitled when the pension begins to be paid and which is taxable pension income.

The Registered Pension Schemes (Reduction in Pension Rates) Regulations 2006 (SI 2006 No 138) supplement the pension payment rules in *FA 2004, Sch 28 para 2* by prescribing circumstances in which a pension may be stopped or reduced.

The Pensions (Transfer of Sums and Assets) Regulations 2006 (SI 2006 No 499) provide for the transfer of sums and assets between registered pension schemes and insurance companies where those sums and assets represent pensions already in payment. The sums and assets transferred must meet the rules set out in the regulations, which require that the recipient scheme (or insurance company) must provide the member with the same type of pension that was paid previously; otherwise, the transfer will be an unauthorised payment (see **57.7** above). The regulations also provide that the new pension will stand in the shoes of the old for certain purposes.

These regulations are amended by *FA 2017, Sch 4 paras 23, 25* in connection with the overseas transfer charge at **57.29** below.

The Registered Pension Schemes (Provision of Information) Regulations 2006 (SI 2006 No 567) prescribe information which a scheme administrator is required to provide to HMRC in the form of an annual event report and other information which is required to be given to HMRC, to members (or their personal representatives) and to other schemes in connection with the administration of a registered pension scheme. They also set requirements for the keeping of records. These regulations include the information that scheme administrators and insurance companies must provide to scheme members as to the percentage of lifetime allowance thus far used up by benefit crystallization events (see **57.18** below). An obligation is imposed on an employer company to notify HMRC (on or before 31 January following the tax year) of any unauthorised payments received from a scheme. A person who ceases to be a scheme administrator must notify HMRC of that fact within 30 days.

These regulations are amended by *FA 2017, Sch 4 paras 24, 25* in connection with the overseas transfer charge at **57.29** below. The regulations are amended by *SI 2018 No 5* (for 2017/18 onwards) to take account of the reduction in the money purchase annual allowance from £10,000 to £4,000 and (for 2018/19 onwards) to require HMRC to be notified when a scheme becomes, or ceases to be, a Master Trust scheme (within *Pension Schemes Act 2017, s 1*).

The Registered Pension Schemes (Prescribed Manner of Determining Amount of Annuities) Regulations 2006 (SI 2006 No 568) provide for the amount by which certain annuities may vary where the amount of the annuity is linked with changes in one of the factors set out in the regulations, such as changes in the retail prices index or in the market value of assets.

The Taxation of Pension Schemes (Transitional Provisions) Order 2006 (SI 2006 No 572) supplements *FA 2004, Sch 36* by making further transitional provisions consequent upon the introduction of the new regime on 6 April 2006.

The Pension Schemes (Transfers, Reorganisations and Winding Up) (Transitional Provisions) Order 2006 (SI 2006 No 573) preserves the protection of certain pre-6 April 2006 rights in the event of particular types of transfer from one pension scheme to another.

The Registered Pension Schemes (Authorised Surplus Payments) Regulations 2006 (SI 2006 No 574) enable surplus funds in a registered occupational pension scheme to be paid to a sponsoring employer and to count as authorised payments subject to specified conditions. Such payments will, however, be subject to the tax charge at **57.26**(c) below.

The Registered Pension Schemes (Authorised Reductions) Regulations 2006 (SI 2006 No 1465) prevent a potential unauthorised payments charge where an armed forces pension is stopped upon admission of the pensioner to the Royal Chelsea Hospital.

The Registered Pension Schemes (Authorised Member Payments) Regulations 2007 (SI 2007 No 3532) prescribe as authorised payments (see **57.7** above) certain payments made by a registered scheme to with-profits policy holders that do not reduce the total value of the sums and assets held for the purposes of the scheme.

The Registered Pension Schemes (Authorised Payments) Regulations 2009 (SI 2009 No 1171) prescribe as authorised payments (see **57.7** above) certain commutation payments that are not otherwise permitted by the rules in *FA 2004*. They also prescribe as authorised payments, with retrospective effect, pensions or lump sums paid or overpaid in error.

These regulations are amended by *SI 2017 No 397* to introduce a new authorised payment known as the *pension advice allowance payment*. This can be made on or after 6 April 2017 by a registered pension scheme directly to a regulated financial advisor, for either the member of the scheme or his beneficiary. It enables the individual to use part of his pension fund towards the cost of obtaining and/or implementing retirement financial advice. A pension advice allowance payment cannot exceed £500. No more than three such payments, and no more than one in any tax year, can be made in respect of the same person.

The Registered Pension Schemes (Relevant Income) Regulations 2011 (SI 2011 No 1783) set out payments which do not count as income for the purposes of meeting the minimum annual income required under the drawdown rules to avoid withdrawals being subjected to an annual cap (**57.1** above).

The Registered Pension Schemes (Modification of Scheme Rules) Regulations 2011 (SI 2011 No 1791) provides that where a scheme administrator meets an annual allowance charge on behalf of a member (**57.23** below), any rules of the pension scheme which prevent a corresponding adjustment to the member's pension benefits are modified to allow such adjustments.

The Registered Pension Schemes (Notice of Joint Liability for the Annual Allowance Charge) Regulations 2011 (SI 2011 No 1793) provide details of the information a member must give in a notice to the scheme administrator if he wishes the latter to meet an annual allowance charge on the member's behalf (**57.23** below).

The Registered Pension Schemes (Bridging Pensions) and Appointed Day Regulations 2016 (SI 2016 No 1005) seek to ensure that pre-existing circumstances when a bridging pension can be reduced without breaching the rules to be a scheme pension are maintained following the introduction of a single-tier State pension on 6 April 2016. The regulations have effect in relation to reductions in payments of scheme pensions made on or after that date. A bridging pension is a higher level of scheme pension that may be paid between retirement and attainment of State pension age.

The Relevant Overseas Schemes (Transfer of Sums and Assets) Regulations 2018 (SI 2018 No 372) came into force on 6 April 2018 and provide for the situation where sums or assets representing pensions already in payment that have previously been transferred from a registered pension scheme (the '*original scheme*') to a non-UK scheme are transferred to another such scheme or to a registered pension scheme (the '*new scheme*'); the new scheme will stand in the shoes of the original scheme.

Tax exemptions

[57.11] A registered pension scheme is exempt from income tax on income derived from investments (including futures contracts and option contracts) or deposits held for the purposes of the scheme. (The exemption does not apply in relation to investments or deposits held as a member of a property investment LLP — see **52.28** PARTNERSHIPS.) [*FA 2004, s 186*]. A gain accruing on a disposal of scheme investments is not a chargeable gain for capital gains tax purposes. [*TCGA 1992, s 271(1A)*]. See, however, **57.30–57.33** below as regards the separate charge to tax where income is derived from certain property held by self-directed schemes or where gains are realised from such property.

Simon's Taxes. See **C1.216, E7.241.**

Relief for contributions by individual members

[57.12] An individual aged under 75 is entitled to tax relief on the contributions he pays to a registered pension scheme during a tax year if he is a 'relevant UK individual' for that year. An individual is a '*relevant UK individual*' for a tax year if:

- he has 'relevant UK earnings' 'chargeable to income tax' for the year; or
- he is resident in the UK at some time during the year; or
- he was resident in the UK both at some time within the period of five years immediately preceding the tax year and at the time he became a member of the scheme; or

- he, or his spouse or civil partner, has general earnings for the tax year 'from overseas Crown employment subject to UK tax' (see **28.5** EMPLOYMENT INCOME).

'*Relevant UK earnings*' means:

- employment income;
- income from a trade, profession or vocation (whether carried on individually or in partnership) chargeable under *ITTOIA 2005, Pt 2*;
- income immediately derived from a UK furnished holiday lettings business (whether carried on individually or in partnership) (see **60.20** PROPERTY INCOME);
- income immediately derived from an EEA furnished holiday lettings business (whether carried on individually or in partnership) (see **60.20** PROPERTY INCOME); or
- patent income (i.e. royalties or other sums paid in respect of the use of a patent charged to tax under *ITTOIA 2005, s 579* (see **41.2** INTELLECTUAL PROPERTY), amounts on which tax is payable under *ITTOIA 2005, s 587* or *s 593* (sale of patent rights — see **41.6, 41.7** INTELLECTUAL PROPERTY) and any balancing charges under the capital allowances code for patent rights — see **9.26** CAPITAL ALLOWANCES) but only where the individual, either alone or jointly, devised the invention for which the patent in question was granted.

The individual is entitled to relief on contributions up to the total amount of his relevant UK earnings 'chargeable to income tax' for the year. Provided, however, the scheme operates tax relief at source (see below), contributions of up to £3,600 (gross) attract relief even if total relevant UK earnings are less than that amount or there are no such earnings. (The £3,600 minimum may be increased from time to time by Treasury order.)

Relevant UK earnings are treated as *not* being '*chargeable to income tax*' if, by virtue of a double tax treaty, they are not taxable in the UK.

In the case of an employer scheme, the relief may be given under the so-called net pay arrangements, whereby the contributions are deducted by the employer from salary before applying PAY AS YOU EARN (53) and the individual's employment income to be included in his total income for tax purposes is net of such contributions.

Otherwise, a registered pension scheme must normally operate relief at source arrangements, whereby tax relief at the basic rate is deducted from the amount of the contribution payable and the scheme administrator recovers the tax deducted from HMRC. If the individual is a higher rate taxpayer, he then claims relief for the excess of the higher rate over the basic rate in his self-assessment tax return. Such relief is achieved by increasing his basic rate limit for the year by the gross amount of the contribution. The increased basic rate limit applies for the purposes of both income tax and capital gains tax. For the purposes only of age-related personal and married couple's allowances (see **1.17, 1.19** ALLOWANCES AND TAX RATES), the gross amount of the contribution is treated as a deduction in arriving at net income. The individual retains the basic rate relief given at source even if his tax liability is insufficient to cover it. Any excess of contributions over an individual's relevant UK earnings (but within the £3,600 minimum referred to above) can *only* be relieved if the scheme operates relief at source (and cannot be relieved under net pay arrangements).

The basic rate band is similarly extended for Scottish taxpayers, as is any other Scottish rate threshold that is above the Scottish basic rate limit. The tax deductible at source is tax at the Scottish basic rate. For 2019/20 onwards, similar rules apply as regards Welsh taxpayers. *FA 2004, ss 192A, 192B* make provision for a possible situation in future in which the Scottish or Welsh basic rate differs from the UK basic rate. If, for 2018/19 onwards, a Scottish taxpayer is liable only at the Scottish starter rate of 19%, then under the above rules he retains the 1% excess tax deducted (www.gov.uk/government/publications/pension-schemes-relief-at-source-for-scottish-income-tax-newsletter-february-2018).

An individual liable at the additional rate (see **1.3** ALLOWANCES AND TAX RATES) is entitled to relief for his contributions at the excess of the additional rate over the basic rate. This is achieved by increasing the higher rate limit (as well as the basic rate limit) by the gross amount of the contributions. Scottish rate thresholds are similarly increased.

The Registered Pension Schemes (Relief at Source) Regulations 2005 (SI 2005 No 3448) prescribe conditions which must be satisfied in order for relief to be given at source, provide for claims by the scheme for payment by HMRC of tax withheld at source and for recovery by HMRC of tax wrongly claimed, provide for annual returns by scheme administrators and grant other information and inspection powers to HMRC.

The relief applies to 'contributions paid'; this expression is restricted to contributions of money and cannot cover a transfer of ordinary shares by the individual to the pension scheme (*HMRC v Sippchoice* UT, [2020] STC 1331, [2020] UKUT 149 (TCC)).

Contributions to pre-6 April 2006 retirement annuity contracts that have become registered pension schemes (see **57.8** above) are not required to be included in relief at source arrangements but can instead be relieved, on the making of a claim, by deduction in arriving at net income.

There are other limited circumstances in which relief can be given, on the making of a claim, by deduction in arriving at net income. These apply to contributions to public service pension schemes or marine pilots' benefits funds by individuals who are not employees in relation to the scheme or fund and third party contributions made on behalf of individuals who are within net pay arrangements.

There is provision for shares acquired under a tax-advantaged share incentive plan or SAYE option scheme (see, respectively, **71.25**, **71.53** SHARE-RELATED EMPLOYMENT INCOME AND EXEMPTIONS) to be transferred to a registered scheme and treated as contributions made. The amount of the contribution is the market value of the shares at the date of transfer, and the transfer must be made within, broadly, 90 days after the shares are acquired by the individual.

Contributions made on a scheme member's behalf under a court order made on or after 1 September 2014 under various provisions of *Pensions Act 2004* (or NI equivalent) do not attract tax relief to the extent that the contribution has enabled the member to claim relief under *FA 2004, s 266A* (see **57.26**(d) below) from the unauthorised payments tax charge.

Life assurance premium contributions

Generally, no relief is available under the above provisions for any contributions which are 'life assurance premium contributions'. Contributions are '*life assurance premium contributions*' if rights under a non-group life policy (as defined) are held (or later become held) for the purposes of the pension scheme and either the payment of the contributions constitutes the payment of premiums under the policy or the payer of the contributions intends them to be applied towards the payment of such premiums. This restriction does not apply if the policy in question is a '*protected policy*', broadly a pre-21 March 2007 policy in the case of an occupational pension scheme or a pre-6 December 2006 policy in the case of any other scheme. A policy ceases to be a protected policy if and when the benefits under the policy are increased or its duration extended.

[*FA 2004, ss 188–192, 192A, 192B, 193–195, 195A, Sch 36 paras 39, 40; ITTOIA 2005, ss 328, 328B; SI 2015 No 1810, Arts 1–4; SI 2017 No 468, Regs 1, 3; SI 2018 No 459, Arts 1, 3; SI 2019 No 201, Arts 1, 4–6*].

Refunds of excess contributions

A refund of excess contributions, i.e. any contributions paid in excess of the tax relief limit in any tax year, may be made by the registered pension scheme to the member within six years after the end of the tax year in question without adverse tax consequences. [*FA 2004, Sch 29 para 6*]. Such refunds are not compulsory in law, so it is possible, subject to the scheme rules, to make contributions which do not attract tax relief. However, the refunds facility, if offered by the scheme, does enable the making of contributions based on estimated relevant UK earnings; this is particularly relevant to the self-employed, who will not usually know their exact profits until after the end of the tax year.

Simon's Taxes. See **E7.221–E7.222.**

Examples

[57.13]

(i) Henry carries on a trade in the UK in which he makes an allowable loss of £1,000 for 2018/19 (for which he claims relief against 2017/18 income), a taxable profit of £18,500 for 2019/20 and a taxable profit of £48,000 for 2020/21. His only other income consists of building society interest and UK dividends. Building society interest amounted to £9,700 for 2018/19, 2019/20 and 2020/21. UK dividends amounted to £900 for each of those years. Henry makes net contributions to a registered pension scheme of £2,400 during the tax year 2018/19 and £4,000 during each of the years 2019/20 and 2020/21. Henry's liability to income tax is at the main UK rates. His liabilities are as follows.

2018/19

	£
Trading income	Nil
Untaxed interest	9,700
UK dividends	900
Total and net income	10,600
Less Personal Allowance (maximum £11,850)	10,600
Taxable Income	Nil

Note

Henry has made gross pension contributions of £3,000 (£2,400 × 100/80). As his gross contributions do not exceed £3,600, he is entitled to tax relief even though he has no relevant UK earnings for the year and notwithstanding his having no tax liability. He is not required to repay the basic rate tax of £600 withheld at source from the contributions.

2019/20

		£
Trading income		18,500
Untaxed interest		9,700
UK dividends		900
Total and net income		29,100
Less Personal Allowance		12,500
Taxable Income		£16,600
Tax Liability		
6,000	@ 20% (basic rate)	1,200.00
1,000	@ 0% (personal savings allowance)	—
8,700	@ 20% (basic rate on savings income)	1,740.00
900	@ 0% (dividend allowance)	—
£16,600		
		£2,940.00

Note

Henry has made gross pension contributions of £5,000 (£4,000 × 100/80). His relevant UK earnings are £18,500, which is more than sufficient to cover the gross contributions. He is entitled to full tax relief, which he has already obtained by deduction at source.

2020/21

	£
Trading income	48,000
Untaxed interest	9,700
UK dividends	900

Total and net income		58,600
Less Personal Allowance		12,500
Taxable Income		£46,100

Tax Liability

35,500	@ 20% (basic rate on earnings)	7,100.00
500	@ 0% (personal savings allowance)	—
6,500	@ 20% (basic rate on savings income)	1,300.00
2,700	@ 40% (higher rate on savings income)	1,080.00
900	@ 0% (dividend nil rate)	—
£46,100		
		£9,480.00

Note

Henry has made gross pension contributions of £5,000 (£4,000 × 100/80). His relevant UK earnings are £48,000, which is more than sufficient to cover the gross contributions. He has obtained basic rate tax relief at 20% by deduction at source. He obtains higher rate relief by extension of the basic rate band; the normal basic rate limit of £37,500 is increased by £5,000 to £42,500. Without that increase, an additional £5,000 of savings income would have fallen into the 40% rate band). (Above the normal basic rate limit, the rate at which the pension contributions save tax will depend on the mix of taxable income, i.e. the extent to which it is dividend income, savings income or other income; see the examples at **14.14** CHARITIES AND CHARITABLE GIVING.)

(ii) Celia is a self-employed professional with taxable profits of £250,000 for the year to 30 April 2020. She has bank deposit interest of £4,000 for 2020/21. She makes net contributions to a registered pension scheme of £16,000 during the tax year ending on 5 April 2021. Celia's liability to income tax is at the main UK rates. Her tax position is as follows.

2020/21

	£
Professional income	250,000
Untaxed interest	4,000
Total and net income	254,000
Less Personal Allowance (note (b))	—
Taxable Income	£254,000

Tax Liability

57,500	@ 20% (basic rate)	11,500.00
112,500	@ 40% (higher rate)	45,000.00
84,000	@ 45% (additional rate)	37,800.00
£254,000		
		£94,300.00

Notes

(a) Celia has made gross pension contributions of £20,000 (£16,000 × 100/80) and has obtained basic rate relief at source. She obtains additional rate relief by extension of the basic rate band; the normal basic rate limit of £37,500 is increased by £20,000 to £57,500. The higher rate limit of

£150,000 is increased by the same amount, so that the higher rate band remains at £112,500. Without these adjustments, an additional £20,000 of income would have been taxable at 45% instead of 20%.

(b) No personal allowance is due as income is too far in excess of the £100,000 limit (see **1.17** ALLOWANCES AND TAX RATES).

(c) No personal savings allowance is due as Celia is an additional rate taxpayer (see **1.7** ALLOWANCES AND TAX RATES).

(d) Celia's annual allowance will be tapered for 2020/21. See the continuation of this example at **57.25** below.

Employer contributions

[57.14] Contributions made by an employer to a registered pension scheme in respect of an individual are deductible in computing profits for the period of account in which they are made (subject to the spreading provisions below). The contributions must meet the normal conditions for expenditure deductible in computing trading profits, in particular the 'wholly and exclusively' rule (see **75.44** TRADING INCOME and see also **57.15** below), but it is specifically provided that they are not treated as capital expenditure even if they would fall to be so treated under general principles.

Certain payments an employer may make to discharge his statutory obligations in relation to an under-funded defined benefits scheme are treated as contributions to the scheme for the above purposes and, if made after cessation of the employer's business, are treated as if made immediately before cessation. Otherwise, no sums other than contributions are deductible in connection with the cost of providing benefits under the employer pension scheme; this overrides any contrary rule that might apply under generally accepted accounting practice.

The Commissioners for HMRC are empowered to make regulations (see *SI 2005 No 3458*) restricting the deductibility of contributions to a registered scheme in respect of an individual if the individual's benefits from the scheme are dependent on the non-payment of benefits from an employer pension scheme which is not a registered scheme or if the transfer value of the individual's rights under the registered scheme is reduced by virtue of benefits being payable out of the non-registered scheme.

[*FA 2004, ss 196, 196A, 199, 200*].

No tax charge on employee

An employee is not liable to income tax in respect of a contribution by his employer to a registered pension scheme, i.e. it is not treated as a benefit-in-kind. The exemption is limited to contributions made to the employee's own registered pension scheme, as opposed to, for example, those set up for members of his family. [*ITEPA 2003, s 308; FA 2004, s 201(2)*].

Simon's Taxes. See E7.224.

Applying the 'wholly and exclusively' rule

[57.15] HMRC have published guidance on the application of the 'wholly and exclusively' rule to employer contributions to registered pension schemes. A pension contribution to a registered scheme is part of the cost of employing staff and will be allowable unless, exceptionally, there is an identifiable non-business purpose for the employer's decision to make the contribution or for the size of the contribution. Where the facts show that a definite part or proportion of an expense is not wholly and exclusively laid out or expended for business purposes, only that part or proportion is disallowable.

One situation where all or part of a contribution *may* not have been paid wholly and exclusively for business purposes is where it is paid in respect of a director who is also a controlling shareholder or in respect of an employee who is a close relative (e.g. a spouse) or friend of the business proprietor or of a controlling director. This will depend on the facts in each case. If the pension contribution paid for such directors or employees is the same as that paid for a third-party employee in similar circumstances, HMRC accept that there is no non-business purpose and will allow a deduction for the full amount of the contribution. Otherwise, HMRC will consider the taxpayer's object in making the payment, which includes his subjective intentions in making the payment. If the contribution is part of a remuneration package paid wholly and exclusively for the purposes of the business, the contribution is an allowable expense. However, if the level of the remuneration package is excessive in relation to the value of the work undertaken by the employee, this might be seen as an indication that the whole amount of the remuneration package, not just the pension contribution, fails the 'wholly and exclusively' test.

A payment may be made exclusively for business purposes even though it also secures a benefit for someone other than the business. This will be the case if the securing of that benefit was not the object of the payment but merely a consequential and incidental effect of the payment. A contribution made as part of a salary sacrifice arrangement will also usually meet the 'wholly and exclusively' test.

The guidance also considers, *inter alia*, contributions made in connection with the purchase, sale or cessation of a business, industry-wide pension schemes and group schemes.

(HMRC Business Income Manual BIM46001–46085).

Spreading of abnormally large contributions

[57.16] Where the contributions paid (or treated as paid) by an employer in a period of account exceed 210% of the contributions paid in the previous period of account, relief for the excess contributions may fall to be spread over more than one period of account as follows. Firstly, identify the amount of current period contributions that exceeds 110% of previous period contributions (the '*relevant excess contributions*'). If this amount is less than £500,000, spreading does not apply. Otherwise, relief for the relevant excess contributions is spread over the current and following periods of account as follows.

Amount of relevant excess contributions	*Spread equally over*
£500,000 to £999,999 inclusive	2 periods of account
£1,000,000 to £1,999,999 inclusive	3 periods of account
£2,000,000 or more	4 periods of account

If the current and previous periods of account are unequal in length, the amount of the previous period contributions is adjusted proportionately in order to determine the excess (if any). Any contributions paid in the current period to fund cost of living increases in current pensions are disregarded in determining any excess, as are any contributions to fund a future service liability for employees joining the scheme in the current period. If the employer ceases business, such that some of the excess contributions would otherwise remain unrelieved, the otherwise unrelieved amount is relieved in the period of account which ends with the date of cessation or, at the employer's option, is apportioned on a daily basis over the whole of the spreading period up to the date of cessation.

There are provisions to ensure that the spreading rules cannot be circumvented by routing the contributions through a third party such as a new company.

[*FA 2004, ss 197, 198, 199A*].

Employer asset-backed contributions

[57.17] Legislation is included in *FA 2012, Sch 13* to ensure that the amount of tax relief given to employers using asset-backed contribution (ABC) arrangements to fund their registered pension schemes accurately reflects, but does not exceed, the total amount of payments the employer makes to the scheme. An ABC arrangement involves offsetting an employer's legal obligation to pay a pension contribution against the registered pension scheme's legal obligation to purchase an asset from the employer, directly or indirectly, using the contribution. There are also ABC arrangements that involve an upfront monetary contribution. Without the legislation it was possible for an employer to obtain both an upfront deduction for the pension contribution and another deduction for income payments derived from the asset.

It is understood that, due to the complexity and transaction costs involved, these arrangements tend to be used only by very large companies. The Government expected about a dozen large employers with (predominantly defined benefit) pension schemes to be affected by these provisions. The legislation is not intended to apply to any straightforward monetary sum that an employer pays to a registered pension scheme as a pension contribution or any transfer of an asset by an employer to a pension scheme which is unconditional or outright so that the scheme gains full and irrevocable ownership of the asset.

The types of arrangement within the ambit of the legislation enable an employer, or a person connected with him, to provide for payments over a period of time (an 'income stream') to the pension scheme. A more complex ABC arrangement typically involves a special purpose vehicle (for example, a partnership of which the employer is a member), in which case the employer provides the pension scheme with the income stream indirectly through the vehicle. The income stream is derived from assets of the employer or a connected party such as a partnership as mentioned above.

Under the legislation, a key factor in determining whether an employer can claim upfront relief for an ABC is whether the structured finance arrangement legislation would apply to the ABC arrangement. This legislation is covered at **4.39** ANTI-AVOIDANCE.

Lifetime allowance

[57.18] Each individual has a '*lifetime allowance*' for the purposes of these provisions. The amount of the lifetime allowance is as follows.

2020/21	£1,073,100
2019/20	£1,055,000
2018/19	£1,030,000
2016/17 and 2017/18	£1 million

Each reduction in the lifetime allowance has given rise to transitional protection, as did the initiation of the lifetime allowance in 2006/07. See **57.19–57.22** below. The lifetime allowance increases in line with the Consumer Prices Index for 2018/19 onwards.

Whenever a 'benefit crystallisation event' occurs in relation to an individual, the amount crystallised is measured against the individual's lifetime allowance (or so much of it, if any, as remains after previous benefit crystallisation events). Any excess is chargeable to tax (the '*lifetime allowance charge*').

On a second or subsequent benefit crystallisation event, the *proportion* of the lifetime allowance utilised in relation to previous events is taken into account in computing how much lifetime allowance remains. Thus, if an amount of £500,000 is crystallised in 2006/07, one-third of the 2006/07 lifetime allowance of £1.5 million is utilised against it (and no charge applies). If a further amount is crystallised in 2011/12, the lifetime allowance remaining to be utilised against it is £1.2 million, i.e. two-thirds of the 2011/12 figure.

The legislation (*FA 2004, s 216, Sch 32*) lists a number of different '*benefit crystallisation events*' and gives the amount crystallised in each case. These events cover:

(i) the commencement of the individual's entitlement to receive a pension (and the various different ways in which this can occur);
(ii) increases in an individual's pension (already being paid) by more than a defined annual rate and by more than a permitted margin (applied on a cumulative basis);
(iii) the attainment of age 75 by an individual in a defined benefits scheme without his having received a pension or lump sum;
(iv) the attainment of age 75 by an individual who has previously designated sums or assets held in a money purchase arrangement (see **57.3** above) as available for the payment of drawdown pension;
(v) the attainment of age 75 by an individual when there is a money purchase arrangement relating to him;

(vi) the designation, before the end of the 'relevant two-year period', of 'relevant unused uncrystallised funds' as available for the payment, to a dependant or nominee of an individual, of dependants' flexi-access drawdown pension or nominees' flexi-access drawdown pension;
(vii) a person's becoming entitled, before the end of the 'relevant two-year period', to a dependants' annuity or nominees' annuity in respect of the individual if the annuity is purchased using (whether or not exclusively) 'relevant unused uncrystallised funds';
(viii) an individual's becoming entitled to receive a lump sum;
(ix) the payment of certain lump sum death benefits; and
(x) the transfer of funds from registered schemes to certain overseas schemes.

The amount crystallised when an individual starts to receive a pension is generally the amount of pension that will be payable in the first 12 months, disregarding any actual increases during that period, multiplied by a factor of 20. If, however, the scheme is a money purchase arrangement and the pension is a drawdown pension or lifetime annuity, the amount crystallised is the total sum (including market value of any assets) designated for the payment of the drawdown pension or used to purchase the annuity (and any related dependants' annuity or nominees' annuity — see *FA 2004, Sch 29 para 3(4A)(4B)*). In the case of an event within (iv) above, the amount crystallised is the growth (if any) in the individual's drawdown pension fund since the designation (though there is transitional exemption for certain drawdown funds already in payment on 6 April 2006). In the case of an event within (v) above, the amount crystallised is the amount of any remaining unused funds. In the case of an event within (vi) above, the amount crystallised is the value (including market value of any assets) of the funds designated. In the case of an event within (vii) above, the amount crystallised is so much of the funds used to purchase the annuity as are 'relevant unused uncrystallised funds'. The '*relevant two-year period*' in (vi) and (vii) is the two years beginning on the date the scheme administrator first knew, or could first reasonably have been expected to know, of the individual's death, and funds are '*relevant unused uncrystallised funds*' if they are unused uncrystallised funds (within *FA 2004, Sch 28 para 27E(4)(5)*) and the individual was under 75 when he died. In the case of a lump sum payment, the amount crystallised is the amount of the lump sum received by the individual. Any abatement of a pension under a public service pension scheme is generally disregarded in determining the time that a benefit crystallisation event occurs and the amount crystallised.

Where a benefit crystallisation event within (vi) or (vii) above occurs, the event is tested against the lifetime allowance in force at the time of the member individual's death.

Where a benefit crystallisation event within (ix) above occurs on or after 6 April 2012 by reason of the payment of a lump sum death benefit in respect of the death of the individual before that date, the lifetime allowance at the time of the event is taken to be £1.8 million. Similarly, where an event within (ix) above occurs on or after 6 April 2014 by reason of the payment of a lump sum death benefit in respect of death in 2012/13 or 2013/14, the lifetime allowance at the time of the event is taken to be £1.5 million. Likewise, where an event within (ix) above occurs on or after 6 April 2016 by reason of the payment of a lump sum death benefit in respect of death in 2014/15 or 2015/16, the lifetime allowance at the time of the event is taken to be £1.25 million.

To the extent that the amount chargeable to tax is paid as a lump sum to the individual (or as a lump sum death benefit in respect of the individual), the tax charge is at **55%**. Otherwise it is at **25%**. The tax is the joint and several liability of the individual and the scheme administrator, except in the case of (vi) and (vii) above, where the tax is the liability of the dependant or nominee in question, and (ix) above, where the tax is the liability of the person to whom the lump sum death benefit is paid. The tax will normally be paid by the scheme administrator (see *FA 2004, s 254*). The charge is not dependent upon the residence or domicile status of any person. Although chargeable to income tax, the chargeable amount is not treated for any tax purposes as income, which means that, for example, losses, reliefs and allowances cannot be set against it and it does not count as income for the purposes of any double tax treaty.

The scheme administrator may meet the liability out of scheme funds or by deducting it from the individual's scheme benefits. If it is paid by the scheme administrator, the tax itself is added to the chargeable amount. If the tax paid is then netted off against a lump sum payment, the chargeable amount above is effectively the aggregate of the lump sum actually received by the individual and the tax paid by the scheme administrator. If the tax paid is set against the individual's scheme pension entitlement (other than where funds are designated to pay a drawdown pension or to purchase an annuity), the reduction is ignored in computing the amount crystallised in events (i) to (iii) above; but if, applying normal actuarial practice, the reduction in pension fully reflects the amount of tax paid, the tax is not then regarded as having been paid by the scheme administrator. The intention is that the amount tested against the lifetime allowance should be the gross amount of benefits crystallised and not the net amount after deducting tax funded by the scheme.

Enhancement

An individual's lifetime allowance is enhanced (in accordance with *FA 2004, ss 221–223*) if, at any time during his membership of a registered pension scheme (treated for this purpose as commencing no earlier than 6 April 2006), either (i) he is not a 'relevant UK individual' (see **57.12** above) or (ii) he is such an individual only because he was UK resident at some time in the previous five tax years *and* he is not employed by a person resident in the UK. This is to reflect the fact that his pension provision will not have entirely benefited from UK tax reliefs. An individual's lifetime allowance is also enhanced (in accordance with *FA 2004, ss 224–226*) if pension rights of his are transferred from a recognised overseas pension scheme into a UK registered scheme, again reflecting the fact that rights will have built up without the benefit of UK tax relief. An individual who intends to benefit from either of these enhancements must give notice of that intention to HMRC in accordance with regulations made by the Commissioners for HMRC (see *SI 2006 No 131* which, *inter alia*, prescribes rules to determine the closing date for such notifications — see *Regs 7, 8*).

Where an individual's lifetime allowance falls to be enhanced for 2012/13 or any subsequent year under any of *FA 2004, ss 222–224* and by reference to an event occurring before 6 April 2012, the amount of the enhancement is computed by applying the enhancement factor to a lifetime allowance of £1.8 million (as long as this remains greater than the actual lifetime allowance). Similarly, where a lifetime allowance falls to be enhanced for 2014/15 or any subsequent year under any of those *sections* and by reference to an event occurring in 2012/13 or 2013/14, the enhancement is computed by applying the enhancement factor to a lifetime allowance of £1.5 million (if greater than the actual lifetime allowance). The same applies where a lifetime allowance falls to be enhanced for 2016/17 or a later year and by reference to an event occurring in 2014/15 or 2015/16; in this case the enhancement is computed by applying the factor to a lifetime allowance of £1.25 million (if greater than the actual lifetime allowance). Where an individual has more than one lifetime allowance enhancement factor, the earlier rule takes precedence.

Where, exceptionally, an individual acquires a new or increased lifetime allowance enhancement factor between two benefit crystallisation events, there is provision for this to be taken into account in computing the proportion of the total lifetime allowance already utilised.

[*FA 2004, ss 214–226, Sch 32; FA 2016, s 19(1)–(5)(8)(9); FA 2017, Sch 4 paras 18, 25; SI 2006 Nos 131, 3261; SI 2007 No 494; SI 2010 No 651; SI 2018 No 206; SI 2019 No 29; SI 2020 No 342*].

Simon's Taxes. See **E7.216–E7.220.**

The transition to 2006/07

[57.19] In relation to the lifetime allowance, there are two kinds of protection available in relation to pension rights built up before 6 April 2006 — primary protection and enhanced protection.

Primary protection

Primary protection applies where an individual's 'relevant pre-commencement pension rights' exceed £1.5 million (the amount of the lifetime allowance for 2006/07). The individual's lifetime allowance for each tax year is enhanced by the proportion which the excess bears to £1.5 million; for example, an individual with relevant pre-commencement pension rights of £2 million will have his lifetime allowance increased by one-third. An individual's '*relevant pre-commencement pension rights*' is the aggregate of (i) the value of his uncrystallised pension rights under all schemes of the kind listed at **57.8** above, rights being 'uncrystallised' if at 5 April 2006 the individual has not become entitled to the present payment of benefits, and (ii) the value of his crystallised rights (if any) at 5 April 2006, calculated at 25 times the annual rate of pensions payable at that date. In the case of occupational schemes, the value of uncrystallised pension rights is limited by a ceiling of 20 times the maximum permitted pension (as defined). An individual who intends to benefit from this enhancement had to give notice of that intention to HMRC in accordance with regulations to be made by the Commissioners for HMRC (see *SI 2006 No 131* which, *inter alia*, prescribed 5 April 2009 as the closing date for such notifications and also enables an individual to notify HMRC that he no longer wishes to benefit — see *Reg 3*).

Where an individual's lifetime allowance falls to be enhanced as above for 2012/13 or any subsequent year, the amount of the enhancement is computed by applying the primary protection factor to a lifetime allowance of £1.8 million (as long as this remains greater than the actual lifetime allowance). Where an individual has primary protection, a special rule applies in calculating the availability of lifetime allowance if a benefit crystallisation event occurred before 6 April 2014 and a further such event occurs on or after that date (see *FA 2004, s 219(5A)*).

Primary protection is extended in certain circumstances where the entitlement to death benefits in relation to an individual (his 'pre-commencement rights to death benefits', as defined and assuming his hypothetical death on 5 April 2006) is greater than the amount of his relevant pre-commencement pension rights. In relation to benefit crystallisation events consisting of the payment of lump sum death benefits, the amount of the enhancement is computed as above but by reference to the greater amount. For this to apply, lump sum death benefits must actually become payable in respect of the individual, and notice of intention to benefit from this enhancement must be given to HMRC (in accordance with HMRC regulations) by the recipient of those benefits (see *SI 2006 No 131*, as amended by *SI 2006 No 3261*, which, *inter alia*, prescribes rules to determine the closing date for such notifications — see *Reg 3A*).

Enhanced protection

Enhanced protection exempts an individual from the lifetime allowance charge if he has ceased active membership of a pre-existing pension scheme that becomes a registered scheme on 6 April 2006 and continues for so long as he does not resume active membership or join any registered scheme. An individual is taken to have resumed active membership if, in the case of a money purchase arrangement, a contribution to the scheme is made by (or on behalf of) him or his employer or, in the case of a defined benefits scheme, crystallised benefits exceed the 'appropriate limit' set out in *FA 2004, Sch 36 para 15* (see also *SI 2006 No 130*) or if pensionable earnings exceed a permitted maximum set out at *FA 2004, Sch 36 paras 16, 17* (see also *SI 2006 No 130*). Contributions consisting of the payment of life assurance premiums on a pre-6 April 2006 policy (or in some cases a replacement policy) are disregarded in certain circumstances, as are certain employer contributions made solely to provide certain lump sum death benefits. Enhanced protection also ceases to be available if certain transfers are made into or out of the scheme. An individual who intended to benefit from enhanced protection had to give notice of that intention to HMRC on or before 5 April 2009. A consequence of claiming enhanced protection is that the individual cannot be paid a lifetime allowance excess lump sum (within *FA 2004, s 166, Sch 29 para 11*).

Enhanced protection is extended where certain lump sum death benefits become payable in respect of an individual. The enhancement operates by computing the 'appropriate limit' as set out in *FA 2004, Sch 36 para 15A*, i.e. by reference to the value of the individual's 'pre-commencement rights to death benefits' (as defined and assuming his hypothetical death on 5 April 2006) and comparing it to the original 'appropriate limit' referred to above. In relation to benefit crystallisation events consisting of the payment of such lump sum death benefits, the greater of the two limits is used. Notice of intention to benefit from this enhancement must be given to HMRC (in accordance with HMRC regulations) by the recipient of the lump sum death benefit (see *SI 2006 No 131*, as amended by *SI 2006 No 3261*, which, *inter alia*, prescribes rules to determine the closing date for such notifications — see *Reg 4A*).

[*FA 2004, Sch 36 paras 7–20; SI 2006 Nos 131, 211, 3261*].

The transition to 2012/13

[57.20] If an individual is a member of a registered pension scheme on 6 April 2012, has ceased accruing benefits in all registered pension schemes before that date and does not have protection under **57.19** above, he is entitled to protection (known as '*fixed protection 2012*') from the reduction in the lifetime allowance for 2012/13 onwards. His lifetime allowance is taken to be the greater of the actual lifetime allowance and £1.8 million. Notice of intention to benefit from this protection had to be given to HMRC before 6 April 2012. The protection is lost if, on or after 6 April 2012:

- there is a benefit accrual (as defined) under any registered pension scheme; or
- there is an impermissible transfer (as defined) into a scheme; or
- there is a transfer of sums and assets that is not a permitted transfer (as defined); or
- a new arrangement relating to the individual is made under a registered pension scheme otherwise than in permitted circumstances (as defined).

Fixed protection 2012 is extended in similar circumstances and with appropriate modifications to members of relieved non-UK pension schemes (broadly schemes to which **57.28**(i) or (ii) below applies).

[*FA 2011, Sch 18 paras 14–17*].

The transition to 2014/15

[57.21] Protection from the reduction in the lifetime allowance for 2014/15 onwards is available as follows.

Fixed protection 2014 (FP2014)

If an individual is a member of a registered pension scheme or a relieved non-UK pension scheme (broadly a scheme to which **57.28**(i) or (ii) below applies) on 6 April 2014, has ceased accruing benefits in all such schemes before that date and does not have protection under **57.19** or **57.20** above, he is entitled to protection (known as '*fixed protection 2014*'). His lifetime allowance is taken to be the greater of the actual lifetime allowance and £1.5 million. Notice of intention to benefit from this protection had to be given to HMRC before 6 April 2014. The protection is lost if, on or after 6 April 2014:

- there is a benefit accrual (as defined) under any such scheme; or
- there is an impermissible transfer (as defined) into a scheme; or

- there is a transfer of sums and assets that is not a permitted transfer (as defined); or
- a new arrangement relating to the individual is made under any such scheme otherwise than in permitted circumstances (as defined).

[*FA 2013, Sch 22 paras 1–4*].

Regulations set out the steps the individual and HMRC have to take to enable an individual to rely on this transitional protection, and what happens if the notice of intention is refused or the individual ceases to meet the conditions. [*SI 2013 No 1741*]. The penalty provisions of *TMA 1970, s 98* are applied to such notices of intention.

Individual protection 2014 (IP2014)

As an alternative to FP2014, there is also IP2014. Notice of intention to rely on IP2014 must be received by HMRC no later than 5 April 2017. Where an individual has given notice to rely on IP2014, his personalised lifetime allowance is the greater of the value of his pensions savings (subject to an overall limit of £1.5 million) and the standard lifetime allowance in **57.18** above. For this purpose, the value of an individual's pension savings is broadly the value of his pensions in payment plus his pension savings, not yet taken, that have benefited from UK tax relief. Individuals with IP2014 are able to carry on actively saving in a registered pension scheme if they wish but will be subject to the lifetime allowance charge on any excess savings over their personalised lifetime allowance when they take their benefits.

Individuals with primary protection as in **57.19** above are not entitled to IP2014. An individual with enhanced protection (**57.19** above), fixed protection 2012 (**57.20** above) or FP2014 may give notice of his intention to rely on IP2014 but as long as his pre-existing protection is valid it takes precedence over IP2014.

[*FA 2014, Sch 6 paras 1–9*].

See guidance at www.gov.uk/government/uploads/system/uploads/attachment_data/file/347961/140821_published_standalone_v4.pdf, and see HMRC Pensions Tax Manual PTM094000.

The transition to 2016/17

[57.22] Protection from the reduction in the lifetime allowance for 2016/17 onwards is available as follows.

Fixed protection 2016 (FP2016)

This works in much the same way as fixed protection 2014 in **57.21** above, reading references to 6 April 2014 as references to 6 April 2016. An individual's lifetime allowance is taken to be the greater of the actual lifetime allowance and £1.25 million. It is a condition that the individual does not have protection under **57.19**, **57.20** or **57.21** above. [*FA 2016, Sch 4 paras 1–8*].

An innovation since fixed protection 2014 is that HMRC will issue a reference number to anyone notifying intention to benefit from FP2016. A reference number will be proof of entitlement to the protection but may be withdrawn by HMRC in certain circumstances, including where an event occurs that would cause the protection entitlement to be lost. There is provision to appeal against the non-issue or withdrawal of a reference number. Individuals must notify HMRC if an event occurs that would occasion the withdrawal of a reference number; the penalty provisions of *TMA 1970, s 98* apply to any failure to comply. Personal representatives of a deceased individual may apply for a reference number on the deceased's behalf. [*FA 2016, Sch 4 paras 14–20*].

Individual protection 2016 (IP2016)

As an alternative to FP2016, there is also IP2016. Where an individual has given notice to rely on IP2016, his personalised lifetime allowance is the greater of the value of his pensions savings (subject to an overall limit of £1.25 million) and the standard lifetime allowance in **57.18** above. For this purpose, the value of an individual's pension savings is broadly the value of his pensions in payment plus his pension savings, not yet taken, that have benefited from UK tax relief. Individuals with IP2016 are able to carry on actively saving in a registered pension scheme if they wish but will be subject to the lifetime allowance charge on any excess savings over their personalised lifetime allowance when they take their benefits.

Individuals with primary protection as in **57.19** above are not entitled to IP2016. In the case of an individual with enhanced protection (**57.19** above), fixed protection 2012 (**57.20** above), FP2014 (**57.21** above) or FP2016 above, that pre-existing protection takes precedence over IP2016.

[*FA 2016, Sch 4 paras 9–13*].

The above reference number system that operates for FP2016 is equally relevant to IP2016. There is additional provision requiring an individual to retain pertinent records for the six years beginning with the date the application for the reference number is made. [*FA 2016, Sch 4 paras 14–21*].

Annual allowance

[57.23] In addition to the lifetime allowance at **57.18** above, each individual has an '*annual allowance*' for the purposes of these provisions. The amount of the annual allowance is **£40,000.** This amount is tapered down to a minimum of £4,000 (£10,000 for 2019/20 and earlier years) in the case of 'high income individuals' (see **57.25** below).

A reduced annual allowance has effect where an individual has flexibly accessed his money purchase savings as in **57.2** above. See below under Money purchase annual allowance.

How the annual allowance charge works

The annual increase in an individual's rights under all registered pension schemes of which he is a member (see below under Pension input amounts) is measured against his annual allowance, and any excess over the annual allowance is chargeable to tax (the '*annual allowance charge*'). The excess is charged at:

- the basic rate of tax in relation to so much (if any) of the excess as, when added to the individual's taxable income, does not exceed the basic rate limit;
- the higher rate of tax in relation to so much (if any) of the excess as, when so added, exceeds the basic rate limit but does not exceed the higher rate limit; and
- the additional rate of tax in relation to so much (if any) of the excess as, when so added, exceeds the higher rate limit.

For Scottish taxpayers (see **1.8** ALLOWANCES AND TAX RATES), the above applies for 2017/18 onwards by reference to Scottish rates and thresholds. For Welsh taxpayers (see **1.9** ALLOWANCES AND TAX RATES), it applies for 2019/20 onwards by reference to Welsh income tax rates.

The individual himself is liable to the tax. The charge is not dependent upon the residence or domicile status of the individual or the scheme administrator. Although chargeable to income tax, the chargeable amount is not treated for any tax purposes as income, which means that, for example, losses, reliefs and allowances cannot be set against it and it does not count as income for the purposes of any double tax treaty. HMRC provide an online calculator tool which can be used to work out total pension input amounts and unused annual allowances for certain types of pension savings — see www.hmrc.gov.uk/tools/pension-allowance/index.htm.

If an individual's tax liability on the annual allowance charge for a tax year exceeds £2,000, he may arrange for the tax to be paid from his pension benefits. He does this by giving notice to the scheme administrator of a registered pension scheme of which he is a member specifying that the individual and the scheme administrator are to be jointly and severally liable in respect of the annual allowance charge specified in the notice. The maximum that can be specified is the tax liability on the excess of pension input amounts for that scheme over the amount of the allowance. If that excess is less than the total amount chargeable to the annual allowance charge for the year, the maximum liability is computed as if the excess formed the top slice of the total chargeable amount. The notice must be given no later than the first anniversary of 31 July following the tax year in question, e.g. by 31 July 2020 for the year 2018/19. *SI 2011 No 1793* sets out the information and declarations to be included in the notice. A notice may be amended by the giving of a further notice no later than the fourth anniversary of 31 July following the tax year in question but it cannot be revoked. Any notice given in a year in which an individual becomes entitled to all the remaining benefits under the scheme, or a benefit crystallisation event occurs by reason of his reaching the age of 75, must be given before the date on which he becomes entitled to those benefits or, as the case may be, the crystallisation event occurs.

Where the scheme administrator satisfies a liability of the individual as above, consequential adjustment must be made to the entitlement of the individual to benefits under the pension scheme on a basis that is just and reasonable having regard to normal actuarial practice.

The scheme administrator is not jointly and severally liable in respect of the annual allowance charge if the scheme enters the assessment period for the Pension Protection Fund or if payment from pension benefits would result in a reduction to the individual's benefits below the amount of the statutory Guaranteed Minimum Pension. The scheme administrator may also apply to an officer of HMRC for the discharge of his liability on either of the following grounds:

- that paying the amount to which he is liable would be to the substantial detriment of the interests of the members of the pension scheme; or
- that in all the circumstances of the case it would not be just and reasonable for the scheme administrator to be liable to that amount.

Pension input periods and amounts

The annual increase in an individual's pension rights is computed in terms of his total '*pension input amount*' for the tax year. This is found by aggregating the pension input amounts for all registered schemes of which he is a member. There is no pension input amount in respect of a pension arrangement if, before the end of the tax year, the individual satisfies the 'severe ill health condition' or the individual dies. An individual satisfies the '*severe ill health condition*' if he:

- becomes entitled to all the benefits to which he is entitled under the pension arrangement in consequence of the scheme administrator having received medical evidence that the individual is unlikely to be able to work again (otherwise than to an insignificant extent) in any gainful capacity before reaching pensionable age; or
- becomes entitled to a serious ill-health lump sum under the pension arrangement; or
- is a member of the armed forces and becomes entitled to a benefit which is exempt under **56.4**(g) PENSION INCOME.

Otherwise, the calculation of the pension input amount depends on the type of scheme and on the 'pension input period' that ends in the tax year. For money purchase arrangements (other than cash balance arrangements — see **57.3** above), the pension input amount is broadly the amount of contributions paid by or on behalf of the individual (including contributions by his employer) in that pension input period. For defined benefits schemes and cash balance arrangements, it is the excess (if any) of the value of his pension rights at the end of that pension input period (closing value) over the value of his pension rights at the end of the previous pension input period (opening value). For this purpose, the value of an individual's pension rights at a particular time is:

(a) (in the case of a defined benefits scheme) the aggregate of any lump sum to which the individual would have been entitled (otherwise than by commutation of pension) if he had become entitled to payment of it at that time and 16 times the annual pension that would have been payable if the individual had become entitled to payment of it at that time;

(b) (in the case of a cash balance arrangements) the amount that would have been available for provision of benefits if the individual had become entitled to the benefits at that time.

In determining any amount to which an individual would have been entitled if he became entitled to it at a particular time, certain assumptions are made as set out in *FA 2004, s 277*.

All '*pension input periods*' are aligned with the tax year by law. The first pension input period begins on the day the pension rights begin to accrue or, in the case of a money purchase arrangements (other than cash balance arrangements) the day on which the first contribution to the scheme is made. It ends on the following 5 April. The final pension input period in relation to a scheme is that in which the individual becomes entitled to all the benefits to which he is entitled under the pension arrangement.

In ascertaining the pension input amount, the opening value of the pension rights is increased in line with the consumer prices index. There is also provision for the adjustment in certain circumstances of the closing value of the pension rights.

Both the opening and closing values are subject to adjustment in the case of a defined benefits scheme if, during the pension input period, the individual enters into a scheme (as widely defined) for making a 'post-entitlement enhancement' and a main purpose of his doing so is to avoid or reduce a liability to the annual allowance charge. A '*post-entitlement enhancement*' is an increase in the annual rate of a scheme pension at a time after the individual has become entitled to that pension.

Information requirements

The scheme administrator of a registered pension scheme must provide to a member whose pension input amounts exceed his annual allowance for a tax year a pension savings statement showing:

- the member's aggregate pension input amounts for the pension input period ending in the tax year;
- his annual allowance for the tax year;
- his aggregate pension input amounts for each of the pension input periods ending in the three tax years immediately preceding the tax year; and
- his annual allowance for each of the three preceding tax years.

The pension savings statement must normally be provided no later than 6 October following the tax year. Any member or former member of a registered pension scheme may also make a written request to the scheme administrator for any such information, in which case the information must be provided within three months of the request or, if later, by 6 October following the tax year. If the scheme administrator has not received the necessary information from a sponsoring employer of an occupational scheme as below, he is given until three months after receipt of that information to satisfy the member's request.

The scheme administrator must supply HMRC with information as to pension savings statements provided. The sponsoring employer of an occupational registered pension scheme must provide to the scheme administrator such information as will enable the latter to calculate the pension input amount for the pension input period (see above) ending in each tax year (such information to be provided no later than 6 July following the tax year in which the pension input period ends

Carry-forward of annual allowance

Any unused part of the annual allowance for a tax year can be carried forward for up to three tax years. The current year's annual allowance is deemed to be used first. If this is insufficient to avoid an annual allowance charge, any unused annual allowance from the three previous years can then be used; the earliest year's unused allowance is used first and so on. The carry-forward is automatic and does not have to be claimed.

Unused annual allowance arises for a year if the amount of the annual allowance exceeds the total pension input amount for that year. Carry-forward is available even if the pension input amount for the year is nil (in which case the whole of the allowance for that year can be carried forward). However, unused annual allowance is only available for carry-forward if it arises during a tax year in which the individual is a member of a registered pension scheme. Brought forward annual allowance is used up in a tax year to the extent (if any) that the total pension input amount exceeds the amount of the annual allowance for that year, such that the excess serves to reduce or eliminate the annual allowance charge for that year.

An individual cannot bring forward to any unused annual allowance from a tax year preceding 2015/16 during which he had access to uncapped drawdown pension (see **57.1** above).

See the example at **57.24** below.

Money purchase annual allowance

A reduced annual allowance has effect where an individual has flexibly accessed his money purchase savings as in **57.2** above. This is achieved by providing for an 'alternative chargeable amount' where money purchase savings exceed a '*money purchase annual allowance*' of £4,000 (£10,000 for 2016/17). (The straightforward excess of pension input amounts over the normal annual allowance becomes the '*default chargeable amount*'.) If, for any tax year in which or after which the individual first flexibly accesses pension rights (see *FA 2004, s 227G*), the alternative chargeable amount exceeds the default chargeable amount, the individual's annual allowance charge for the tax year is based on the former rather than the latter. The '*alternative chargeable amount*' is the total of the amount by which defined benefit pension input amounts (see *FA 2004, s 227B(3)–(5)*) exceed the 'alternative annual allowance' and the amount by which money purchase input amounts (see *FA 2004, s 227C–227F*) exceed £4,000 (previously £10,000). The '*alternative annual allowance*' is the normal annual allowance minus £4,000 (previously £10,000), e.g. it is £36,000 for 2019/20.

Unused money purchase annual allowance cannot be carried forward to subsequent tax years. Where the alternative chargeable amount applies to an individual for a tax year (instead of the default chargeable amount), the only amount capable of carry-forward from that year is the excess (if any) of the alternative annual allowance over defined benefit pension input amounts.

As regard's an individual's option to have his tax liability on the annual allowance charge paid from his pension benefits (see above), the amount of his liability is computed *for this purpose only* as if the default chargeable amount applied to him instead of the alternative chargeable amount (i.e. in a case where the latter does in fact apply to him).

For as to how the money purchase annual allowance interacts with the taper of the annual allowance, see **57.25** below.

[*FA 2004, ss 227, 227ZA, 227B–227G, 228, 228A, 229–236, 236A, 237, 237A–237F, 238, 238ZA, 238ZB, 238A; F(No 2)A 2017, s 7; SI 2006 No 567, Regs 3, 14A, 14B, 15A; SI 2007 No 494; SI 2011 No 1793; SI 2011 No 1797, Regs 8, 9; SI 2015 No 1810, Arts 1, 7; SI 2017 No 11, Regs 1, 4, 5; SI 2017 No 468, Regs 1, 4, 5; SI 2019 No 201, Arts 1, 7, 8*].

Simon's Taxes. See **E7.211–E7.215**.

Example

[57.24]

This example illustrates the carry-forward of the annual allowance. Lily is self-employed and joins a registered pension scheme for the first time on 10 March 2017. The scheme's annual pension input period coincides with the fiscal year. Lily has fluctuating business profits and makes contributions to the scheme under deduction of basic rate tax at source as follows.

2016/17	£1,600 net (£2,000 gross)
2017/18	£36,800 net (£46,000 gross)
2018/19	£16,000 net (£20,000 gross)
2019/20	£52,000 net (£65,000 gross)
2020/21	£68,800 net (£86,000 gross)

No-one else makes contributions to Lily's pension arrangement under the scheme. Lily's total pension input amount for each year will be equal to the gross amount of her contributions. For each year, she will receive higher and additional rate tax relief, where appropriate, on the gross amount of her contributions provided she has sufficient relevant UK earnings to cover that amount, which it is assumed she does. It is also assumed that Lily is not subject to the annual allowance taper at **57.25** below for any of the years featured.

For 2016/17, Lily has unused annual allowance of £38,000 (£40,000 – £2,000). If her total pension input had exceeded the annual allowance, there would have been no question of her bringing forward any unused annual allowance from earlier years as she was not a member of a registered pension scheme in those years.

For 2017/18, she has excess pension input amounts of £6,000 (£40,000 – £46,000). In the absence of a carry-forward facility, she would have been liable to an annual allowance charge on £6,000 at her marginal rate of tax for the year. However, £6,000 of her unused allowance for 2016/17 is brought forward to extinguish her liability. She still has £32,000 unused allowance remaining from 2016/17.

For 2018/19, she has unused annual allowance of £20,000 (£40,000 – £20,000).

For 2019/20, she has excess pension input amounts of £25,000 (£40,000 – £65,000). £25,000 of her unused allowance for 2016/17 is brought forward to extinguish her liability.

For 2020/21, Lily has excess pension input amounts of £46,000 (£40,000 – £86,000). Although £7,000 of her 2016/17 annual allowance remains unused, it cannot be carried forward more than three years. However, her unused allowance of £20,000 for 2018/19 is available in full. She is liable to an annual allowance charge on £26,000 at her marginal rate of tax for the year and has no more unused allowance to carry forward.

The position can be summarised as follows.

	Annual allowance	Pension input amounts	Unused allowance b/fwd	Chargeable amount	Unused allowance c/fwd	Cumulative unused allowance c/fwd
	£	£	£	£	£	£
2016/17	(40,000)	2,000		Nil	38,000	38,000
2017/18	(40,000)	46,000	(6,000)	Nil		32,000
2018/19	(40,000)	20,000		Nil	20,000	52,000
2019/20	(40,000)	65,000	(25,000)	Nil		27,000
					3 year drop-out	(7,000)
						20,000
2020/21	(40,000)	86,000	(20,000)	26,000		Nil

Annual allowance taper

[57.25] The annual allowance at **57.23** above is tapered for high income individuals, i.e. broadly those with an adjusted income of over £240,000 (£150,000 for 2019/20 and earlier years). The carry-forward of unused annual allowance continues to be available, but the amount available for carry-forward is the unused *tapered* annual allowance.

If an individual is a 'high-income individual' for a tax year, the annual allowance is reduced by £1 for every £2 by which the individual's adjusted income' exceeds £240,000 (previously £150,000), but cannot be reduced below £4,000 (£10,000 for 2019/20 and earlier years). The £4,000 minimum will thus take effect where adjusted income is £312,000 or more. For 2019/20 and earlier years the £10,000 minimum took effect where adjusted income was £210,000 or more. The reduction is rounded down to the nearest £1.

A '*high-income individual*' is one whose 'threshold income' is over £200,000 (£110,000 for 2019/20 and earlier years) and whose 'adjusted income' is over £240,000 (previously £150,000). The £200,000 threshold (previously £110,000) is intended to provide an income floor. In the simple case where (b) and (d) below are not in point, an individual with net income (after pension contributions) at or below the threshold will not be subject to the taper, and a computation of adjusted income is then unnecessary.

Adjusted income

An individual's '*adjusted income*' is computed as follows.

(1) Start with the individual's net income for the tax year (see Step 2 of the calculation of income tax liability at **1.10** ALLOWANCES AND TAX RATES).
(2) Add back any deductions made in arriving at either employment income or net income in respect of relief given under the so-called net pay arrangements for employer schemes (see **57.12** above), relief given under a claim where exceptionally it has not been given at source (see **57.12**) or relief given by virtue of *FA 2004, Sch 36 para 51* (migrant member relief — see **57.27** below).
(3) Add the pension input amount for the tax year (see **57.23** above) net of the amount of any contributions paid by or on behalf of the individual during the year under registered pension schemes. This effectively means adding any employer contributions.
(4) Deduct the amount of any lump sum death benefits taxable on the individual as pension income for the year and included in the list at **56.2**(d) PENSION INCOME.

Threshold income

An individual's '*threshold income*' is computed as follows.

(a) Start with the individual's net income for the tax year (as in (1) above).
(b) Add any amount which would have been included in employment income for the year were it not for 'relevant salary sacrifice arrangements' or 'relevant flexible remuneration arrangements' made on or after 9 July 2015.
(c) Deduct the gross equivalent of pension contributions for the year on which basic rate tax relief has been given at source (see **57.12** above).
(d) Deduct the amount of any lump sum death benefits taxable on the individual as in (4) above.

In (b) above, '*relevant salary sacrifice arrangements*' and '*flexible remuneration arrangements*' are, respectively, arrangements designed to sacrifice employment income for pension provision and those giving a choice of employment income or pension provision. It is irrelevant whether the arrangements are made before or after the start of the employment. 'Pension provision' in this context is widely defined, so as to include any payment of contributions to secure an increase in benefits (actual or prospective) for the individual, his dependants or persons connected with the individual (within **19** CONNECTED PERSONS).

Interaction with money purchase annual allowance

The money purchase annual allowance rules in **57.23** above effectively operate as if references to the normal annual allowance were to the tapered annual allowance. For example, where the maximum taper applies (i.e. on adjusted income of £312,000 or more for 2020/21 onwards) so that the tapered annual allowance becomes £4,000, the 'alternative annual allowance' in **57.23** is thereby reduced to nil (i.e. £4,000 minus £4,000). Equivalent figures for earlier years, in cases where the maximum taper applies, were £6,000 (£10,000 – £4,000) for 2017/18 to 2019/20 inclusive and nil (£10,000 – £10,000) for 2016/17.

Anti-avoidance

There is anti-avoidance provision in *FA 2004, s 228ZB* to deter people from entering into arrangements (including any agreement, understanding, scheme, transaction or series of transactions, whether or not legally enforceable) with a main purpose of mitigating the taper by reducing adjusted or threshold income in one year at the expense of increasing it in another. The taper is calculated as if the arrangements had not been made.

[*FA 2004, ss 228ZA, 228ZB; FA 2020, s 22*].

See HMRC Pensions Tax Manual PTM057000.

NHS staff

Pending the changes to the taper for 2020/21 onwards, both NHS England and NHS Scotland announced measures in late 2019 to compensate staff for the effect of the taper for 2019/20. See www.gov.uk/government/publications/statement-from-the-secretary-of-state-on-the-clinician-pension-tax-scheme/statement-from-the-secretary-of-state-on-the-clinician-pension-tax-scheme and https://news.gov.scot/news/changes-to-protect-nhs-staff.

Example

Celia, the additional rate taxpayer in example (ii) at **57.13** above, has threshold income of £234,000 (net income £254,000 less gross pension contributions of £20,000) for 2020/21. She has adjusted income of £254,000 (equal to net income in this case). As threshold income is over £200,000 and adjusted income is over £240,000, Celia is a high-income individual and her annual allowance is subject to the taper. Annual allowance of £40,000 is reduced by £7,000 (one-half of (254,000 – 240,000)) and is thus £33,000 (being above the £4,000 minimum). However, Celia's pension input amount (£20,000) is still covered by her reduced annual allowance (£33,000), so she is not subject to an annual allowance charge for 2020/21. Her unused annual allowance carried forward is £13,000 (33,000 – 20,000).

Other tax charges

[57.26] In addition to the lifetime allowance charge at **57.18** above and the annual allowance charge at **57.23** above, other income tax charges may arise in relation to registered schemes as listed below. These are in addition to the normal taxation under *ITEPA 2003* of individuals' pension income, which is covered in **56** PENSION INCOME. See **57.30–57.33** below as regards charges arising from investment restrictions applicable to self-directed registered schemes.

(a) **Short service refund lump sum charge.** This is a charge on the scheme administrator at **20%** or, to the extent that the lump sum exceeds £20,000, **50%**. A '*short service lump sum*' is defined by *FA 2004, Sch*

29 para 5 and is broadly a refund in specified circumstances of a member's contributions to an occupational pension scheme. The charge is not dependent upon the residence or domicile status of the scheme administrator or the person to whom the lump sum is paid. Although chargeable to income tax, a short service refund lump sum is not treated for any tax purposes as income. The tax may be deducted at source by the scheme administrator from the lump sum payment if the scheme rules so permit. [*FA 2004, s 205*].

(b) **Special lump sum death benefits charge.** This is a charge on the recipient at his marginal rate of income tax where any of the following is paid: a pension protection lump sum death benefit, an annuity protection lump sum death benefit, a drawdown pension fund lump sum death benefit or a flexi-access drawdown fund lump sum death benefit. These terms are defined by *FA 2004, Sch 29 paras 14, 16, 17, 17A*. The charge applies to these payments only if made in respect of a member who dies at age 75 or over.

The special lump sum death benefits charge also applies in the following circumstances.

- Where a defined benefits lump sum death benefit or an uncrystallised funds lump sum death benefit is paid in respect of a member who was aged 75 or more at the time of his death. These terms are defined by *FA 2004, Sch 29 paras 13, 15*.
- Where a flexi-access lump sum death benefit is paid from a dependant's, nominee's or successor's flexi-access drawdown fund, or where a drawdown pension fund lump sum death benefit is paid from a dependant's drawdown pension fund.
- If a member dies before age 75, and a drawdown pension fund lump sum death benefit, a flexi-access drawdown fund lump sum death benefit or an uncrystallised funds lump sum death benefit is paid outside a two-year period starting on the date the scheme administrator first knew, or could first reasonably have been expected to know, of the member's death.
- It applies if a dependant, nominee or successor dies before age 75 and prescribed lump sum death benefits are paid outside the two-year period above.
- It applies if a member dies before age 75, and a defined benefits lump sum death benefit is paid outside the two-year period above. For lump sums paid before that date, a benefit of this kind paid outside that period is taxable as an unauthorised payment.

The lump sum is taxable as pension income (see **56.2**(d) PENSION INCOME). For lump sums paid before 6 April 2016 the charge was at a flat rate of 45% on the scheme administrator; the same comments applied as in (a) above as regards residence status etc., non-treatment as income and deduction at source. This continues to apply to lump sums paid on or after 6 April 2016 to a person who is not an individual or is an individual acting in a representative capacity, e.g. a trustee other than a bare trustee. Where a lump sum death benefit to which the special lump sum death benefits charge applies is paid on or after 6 April 2016 to trustees and paid out by them to a beneficiary who is an individual, both the amount received by the beneficiary and the tax paid by the trustees is taxable income of the beneficiary. However, the beneficiary may make a claim to deduct that tax from the income tax charged on his total income for the tax year in which the payment is made to him. Regulations provide for the provision of necessary information by the scheme administrator to the trustees and by the trustees to the beneficiary.

[*FA 2004, s 206; SI 2006 No 567, Regs 10A, 10B; SI 2017 No 11, Regs 1, 3*].

HMRC are empowered to make regulations to the effect that an insurance company paying certain types of lump sum death benefit be treated as a scheme administrator for this purpose — see now *SI 2006 No 136*. [*FA 2004, s 273A*].

(c) **Authorised surplus payments charge.** This is a charge on the scheme administrator at **35%** where an authorised surplus payment (i.e. a return of surplus funds — see *SI 2006 No 574* at **57.7** above) is made to the employer by an occupational scheme. The charge is not dependent upon the residence or domicile status of the scheme administrator or the employer. Although chargeable to income tax, an authorised surplus payment is not treated for any tax purposes as income. If the employer is a charity or is otherwise exempt from tax, the charge does not apply. In a case where the surplus derives from a surrender of rights, the charge does not apply to the extent that the surrender was treated as an unauthorised payment under *FA 2004, s 172A*. [*FA 2004, s 207*].

(d) **Unauthorised payments charge.** Where an unauthorised payment is made, a charge at **40%** arises on the amount thereof (and see also (e) below). The person liable is the scheme member (or former member) to whom (or in respect of whom) the payment is made (or, if made after the member's or former member's death, the recipient) or, where applicable, the employer to whom (or in respect of whom) it is made. If more than one person is liable, liability is joint and several. The charge is not dependent upon the residence or domicile status of the scheme administrator or any person who is liable. Although chargeable to income tax, an unauthorised payment is not treated for any tax purposes as income.

[*FA 2004, s 208*].

See *FA 2004, ss 160–181* as regards authorised and unauthorised payments by registered schemes. These include circumstances in which an unauthorised payment is treated as having being made, even though the scheme makes no actual payment. Examples, subject to detailed rules and conditions, are the assignment or surrender of benefits by the member, the reallocation within the scheme of members' benefits or employer contributions, the providing of non-cash benefits to a member and the shifting of value between scheme assets and members' assets. See *FA 2004, ss 172, 172A, 172B, 172BA (now repealed), 172B, 172C, 172D, 173, 174, SI 2006 No 133* and **57.30** below. Certain of the pension rules and pension death benefit rules in *FA 2004, Sch 28* also treat an unauthorised payment as having being made; see, for example, *Sch 28 paras 2A, 16B(1), 16C(1)*. See also the anti-avoidance rule at

57.7 above on recycling of lump sums. In applying the rules on unauthorised payments, 'member' generally includes a former member. For relief from the unauthorised payments charge, and the surcharge at (e) below, in cases where monies are repatriated to the scheme by order of the Pensions Regulator or the courts, see *FA 2004, s 266A*.

(e) **Unauthorised payments surcharge.** This is payable at **15%**, in addition to the unauthorised payments charge at (d) above, in respect of:

- unauthorised payments to or for a member (or former member) where, broadly, such payments made over a 12-month period use up at least 25% of the value of that person's pension fund; and
- unauthorised payments to or for a scheme employer (or former scheme employer) where, broadly, such payments made over a 12-month period use up at least 25% of the aggregate value of sums and assets held for the purposes of the pension scheme.

The person liable can apply to HMRC for discharge of the liability on the grounds that in all the circumstances of the case it would not be just and reasonable for the person to be liable to the unauthorised payments surcharge in respect of the unauthorised payment in question.
[*FA 2004, ss 209–213, 268*].
The circumstances in which it would not be just and reasonable to impose an unauthorised payments surcharge are limited; it is not necessary for there to be any dishonesty or negligence for liability to arise, and the fact that the member has taken professional advice is not sufficient of itself to make it unjust or unreasonable to impose a surcharge (*McCormack v HMRC* FTT (TC 6443), [2018] SFTD 1066, [2018] UKFTT 200 (TC)).

(f) **Scheme sanction charge.** This is a charge on the scheme administrator at **40%** in respect of unauthorised payments made by the scheme (with certain specified exemptions) and payments which the scheme is treated as having made by virtue of *FA 2004, s 183* or *s 185* (unauthorised borrowing). The charge is not dependent upon the residence or domicile status of any person liable. If payments subjected to this charge are also charged under (d) above, credit is given for the tax *paid* (as opposed to the tax charged) under (d); however, the available credit is limited to 25% of the chargeable payment.
[*FA 2004, ss 239–241, 268; SI 2006 No 365*].
See **57.30** below for the application of this charge to income and gains arising from certain investments held by self-directed schemes. For relief from the scheme sanction charge in cases where monies are repatriated to the scheme by order of the Pensions Regulator or the courts, see *FA 2004, s 266B*.

(g) **De-registration charge.** This is a charge on the scheme administrator at **40%** of the aggregate value of sums and assets held for the purposes of the pension scheme immediately before the withdrawal by HMRC of the scheme's registration (see **57.6** above). It is not dependent upon the residence or domicile status of any person liable.
[*FA 2004, s 242*].

For capital gains tax purposes, the scheme assets are then deemed to have been acquired immediately before withdrawal of registration for the amount on which they are charged to tax under *FA 2004, s 242*. [*TCGA 1992, s 239A*].

(h) **Serious ill-health lump sum charge.** For lump sums paid after 15 September 2016, the lump sum is taxable as pension income (see **56.2**(d) PENSION INCOME). For lump sums paid on or before that date, the charge is on the scheme administrator at the rate of 45% on serious ill-health lump sums paid to members who have reached the age of 75; the same comments apply as in (a) above as regards residence status etc., non-treatment as income and deduction at source. Serious ill-health lump sums are defined in *FA 2004, Sch 29 para 4*. They are tax-free when paid to members under 75. [*FA 2004, s 205A; FA 2016, Sch 5 paras 1, 4*].

In *HMRC v Bella Figura Ltd* UT, [2020] STC 922, [2020] UKUT 120 (TCC), the UT considered a number of issues relating to the power to assess tax chargeable as a result of a loan made by a pension scheme; the charges in point included the unauthorised payments charge/surcharge and the scheme sanctions charge.

An independent trustee (P) appointed by, or otherwise pursuant to, an order made by the Pensions Regulator (or by a court on an application made by the Pensions Regulator) does not become liable for specified tax charges that predate his appointment. Where a scheme administrator (Q) is appointed with effect from a time when a pension scheme has one or more independent trustees, that administrator does not assume liability to specified tax charges. In both cases, the liability in question is generally retained or assumed by the person who was the scheme administrator immediately before the relevant day (unless that person has died or no longer exists). The '*relevant day*' is the day on which P's appointment as trustee takes effect or, in the case where liability would otherwise be assumed by Q, the first day on which the pension scheme has an independent trustee. [*FA 2004, ss 272A–272C; FA 2016, Sch 5 para 3*].

Simon's Taxes. See **E7.247**.

Overseas pension schemes — migrant member relief

[57.27] Where an individual comes to work in the UK and is already a member of an overseas pension scheme, UK tax relief may be available for his contributions to the scheme and on his employer contributions. This is known as '*migrant member relief*'. It replaces the pre-existing 'corresponding relief' in *ITEPA 2003, s 355* (see **28.12** EMPLOYMENT INCOME), although where an individual obtained relief under that *section* for contributions made in 2005/06, HMRC may in certain circumstances continue to allow relief for contributions made in subsequent years to the same scheme (see *FA 2004, Sch 36 para 51* and *SI 2006 No 572, Arts 15–17*).

Migrant member relief is available for contributions made by an individual:

- who is a 'relevant migrant member' of a 'qualifying overseas pension scheme';

- who has relevant UK earnings chargeable to income tax for the tax year in which the contributions are made (see **57.12** above); and
- who has notified the scheme manager of his intention to claim the relief.

Relief is given as in **57.12** above, but is so given by deduction from total income on the making of a claim rather than by deduction at source and extension of the basic rate band. Relief for employer contributions applies as in **57.14** above.

An individual is a '*relevant migrant member*' of an overseas pension scheme if he:

- was non-UK resident when he joined the scheme;
- was a member of the scheme at the beginning of the period of UK residence in which the contributions in question are made;
- was, either immediately before or at any time in the ten years before the start of that period of UK residence, entitled to tax relief on his contributions in the country in which he was then resident; and
- has been notified by the scheme manager that information on benefit crystallisation events (see **57.18** above) will be given to HMRC.

HMRC have power to modify the above definition by statutory instrument (see *SI 2006 No 1957*) so that, in prescribed circumstances, the first three bullet points apply equally by reference to any earlier overseas pension scheme of which the individual was a member.

A '*qualifying overseas pension scheme*' is an overseas pension scheme which has provided certain notifications, evidence and undertakings to HMRC, including an undertaking to comply with information requirements regarding benefit crystallisation events, and which has not been excluded by HMRC from being a qualifying overseas pension scheme by reason of previous significant failures to comply with such information requirements. A scheme manager has the right of appeal against a decision of HMRC to exclude the scheme from qualifying.

SI 2006 No 208 prescribes the information which a qualifying overseas pension scheme must undertake to provide to HMRC, and the time limits within which the information must be provided.

[*ITEPA 2003, s 308A; FA 2004, ss 150(7), 170, 243, Sch 33; FA 2017, Sch 4 paras 22, 25; SI 2006 Nos 206, 208, 212; SI 2007 No 1600; SI 2017 No 398; SI 2018 No 5, Reg 7*].

Simon's Taxes. See **E7.223**.

Overseas pension schemes — tax charges

Lifetime allowance charge

[57.28] The lifetime allowance charge at **57.18** above applies, with appropriate modifications, in relation to a member of a non-UK pension scheme if:

(i) UK tax relief has been given, on contributions to the scheme made by the member or on his behalf, either under the migrant member relief provisions at **57.27** above or under a double tax treaty; or

(ii) the member has been given exemption under *ITEPA 2003, s 307* (see **28.52**(iii) EMPLOYMENT INCOME) in respect of provision for retirement or death benefits made under the scheme at a time after 5 April 2006 when it was an overseas scheme.

[*FA 2004, s 244, Sch 34 paras 13–20*].

Annual allowance charge

The annual allowance charge at **57.23** above applies, with appropriate modifications, in relation to a member of a non-UK pension scheme for any tax year in respect of which:

- UK tax relief is obtained, on contributions to the scheme made by the member or on his behalf, either under the migrant member relief provisions at **57.27** above or under a double tax treaty; or
- the member is given exemption under *ITEPA 2003, s 307* (see **28.52**(iii) EMPLOYMENT INCOME) in respect of provision for retirement or death benefits made under the scheme while it is an overseas scheme.

The value of the pension input amounts tested against the annual allowance is proportionately reduced where some of the member's employment income for the year is not subject to UK tax. The carry-forward provisions in **57.23** above also apply, with appropriate modifications, to a member of a non-UK pension scheme. A member of a non-UK pension scheme satisfying the above conditions can bring forward unused annual allowance from any of the three preceding years for which he was a member of the scheme. A member of a registered pension scheme can bring forward unused annual allowance from any of the three preceding years for which he was a member of a non-UK pension scheme satisfying the above conditions. The money purchase annual allowance rules in **57.23** also apply, with appropriate modifications, to a member of a non-UK pension scheme.

[*FA 2004, s 244, Sch 34 paras 8, 9, 9ZA, 9ZB, 9A, 9B, 10-12, 20; FA 2017, Sch 4 paras 7, 8*].

Other tax charges

The charges at **57.26**(a)(b)(d)(e) and (h) above, those at **56.2**(j) and (k) PENSION INCOME, the charge on any of the lump sum death benefits listed at **56.2**(d) PENSION INCOME and paid direct to an individual, and the charge on 'uncrystallised funds pension lump sums' at **56.4**(a) PENSION INCOME apply, in certain circumstances and with appropriate modifications, in relation to payments made to or in respect of a member of a non-UK pension scheme at a time when he is UK resident, if:

(a) UK tax relief has been given, on contributions to the scheme made by the member or on his behalf, either under the migrant member relief provisions at **57.27** above or under a double tax treaty; or

(b) the member has been given exemption under *ITEPA 2003, s 307* (see **28.52**(iii) EMPLOYMENT INCOME) in respect of provision for retirement or death benefits made under the scheme at a time after 5 April 2006 when it was an overseas scheme; or

(c) the member's pension rights have been transferred from a registered pension scheme to the non-UK scheme at a time when it was a 'qualifying recognised overseas pension scheme' (QROPS) (see *FA 2004, ss 150(7)(8), 169* and *SI 2006 No 206*), HMRC Pensions Tax Manual PTM112000 and *Equity Trust Singapore Ltd v HMRC* CA, [2012] STC 998).

The charges listed above (known collectively as the '*member payment charges*') similarly apply in relation to payments made to or in respect of a member of a non-UK scheme at a time when he is non-UK resident if he has been UK resident at some time earlier in the tax year in which the payment is made or at some time in the ten preceding tax years. This ten-year period has effect in so far as the payment is referable to so much of the member's UK pension fund as represents tax-relieved contributions, or tax-exempt provision, made on or after 6 April 2017. In any other case, the above applies by reference to the tax year in which the payment is made and the *five* preceding tax years. For post-5 April 2017 pension savings, even if the member is not caught by the ten-year test, a payment will trigger the member payment charges if made within five years after the transfer to the non-UK scheme.

Where tax would be payable on one of the member payment charges were it not for a double tax treaty, the chargeable amount counts as a foreign pension within **56.2**(b) PENSION INCOME and as a 'relevant withdrawal' for the purpose of the temporary non-UK residence rules at **56.7** PENSION INCOME.

The above provisions do not have effect where the unauthorised payments charge at **57.26**(d) above applies by virtue of **57.30** below (self-directed schemes). However, HMRC have power to make regulations imposing that charge, insofar as it so applies, on a member who is within the scope of (c) above; see now *SI 2006 No 1960*.

SI 2006 No 208 prescribes the information which a QROPS must undertake to provide to HMRC, and the time limits within which the information must be provided.

See **57.29** below for the overseas transfer charge on and after 9 March 2017.

[*FA 2004, s 244, Sch 34 paras 1–4, 4A, 5, 5A, 6, 7, 7ZA, 7A, 20; FA 2016, Sch 5 para 3; FA 2017, Sch 4 paras 2–6, 8, 22, 25; SI 2006 Nos 207, 208; SI 2007 No 493, Reg 3; SI 2009 No 2047; SI 2018 No 5, Reg 7; SI 2018 No 373; SI 2019 No 689, Reg 27*].

Where a lump sum death benefit listed at **56.2**(d) PENSION INCOME, or an uncrystallised funds pension lump sum, is paid, and tax is chargeable as above, the payment is nevertheless outside the scope of the PAYE system. [*ITEPA 2003, s 683(3C)*].

Simon's Taxes. See E7.248.

Overseas transfer charge

[57.29] Subject to the exclusions listed below, a 25% tax charge (the '*overseas transfer charge*') arises on a transfer of UK-tax relieved pension savings to a qualifying recognised overseas pension scheme (QROPS) (see *FA*

2004, ss 150(7)(8), 169 and *SI 2006 No 206*) where the transfer is requested on or after **9 March 2017**. See also the official guidance at www.gov.uk/government/publications/qualifying-recognised-overseas-pension-schemes-charge-on-transfers.

The charge applies where a transfer is made to a QROPS or an 'onward transfer' is made during the 'relevant period' for the 'original transfer'. An '*onward transfer*' is a transfer from one QROPS (or former QROPS) to another QROPS. The '*relevant period*' is the period beginning with the date of the original transfer and ending on the fifth anniversary of the following 5 April; so if the original transfer is made on 15 July 2017, the relevant period runs from 15 July 2017 to 5 April 2023 inclusive. There is an exception for transfers made on 6 April, in that the relevant period then ends on the fourth anniversary of the following 5 April. The common factor is that the relevant period runs for at least five full tax years. The '*original transfer*' in relation to an onward transfer is the most recent transfer to the QROPS from a registered pension scheme or a transfer to the QROPS from a non-UK scheme which is a transfer of the whole or part of the scheme member's UK tax-relieved fund.

A transfer is taken to be requested if a member instructs the scheme administrator/manager of the transferor scheme to transfer a certain amount or percentage of his pension funds to a named overseas pension scheme. A casual enquiry is not a transfer request (see official guidance para 1.13). The term 'scheme administrator/manager' is used here and below to denote the scheme administrator of a registered pension scheme or the scheme manager of a QROPS.

Exclusions

The overseas transfer charge does not apply if one of conditions (a) to (e) below is met. However, as regards (a) and (b), see also below under Changes of circumstances.

(a) The member is resident in the same country in which the transferee QROPS is established.
(b) The member is resident in the UK or a European Economic Area (EEA) State and the transferee QROPS is established in an EEA state.
(c) The transferee QROPS is an occupational pension scheme, and the member is an employee of a sponsoring employer of the QROPS.
(d) The transferee QROPS is set up by an international organisation for the purpose of providing benefits for, or in respect of past service as, an employee of the organisation, and the member is an employee of that organisation. On and after 6 April 2017, the international organisation condition is satisfied if the scheme is established by the United Nations, the European Union, or any other organisation to which *International Organisations Act 1968, s 1* applies, for the purpose of providing benefits for service as an employee. Additional conditions applied before 6 April 2017 (see *SI 2006 No 206, Reg 2(4)* as originally enacted). A multinational company is not an international organisation for these purposes.

(e) The transferee QROPS is an 'overseas public service pension scheme' and the member is an employee of a participating employer. An '*overseas public service pension scheme*' is a scheme set up by law or with government approval, solely to provide benefits in respect of service rendered to the country in question or any political sub-division or local authority thereof.

Certain onward transfers are excluded from charge under rules intended to avoid a double charge on the same funds and under transitional rules on ring-fenced transfer funds (see official guidance paras 2.40, 2.41).

Changes of circumstances

With regard to (a) and (b) above, the overseas transfer charge is triggered if, within the relevant period (see above) following an excluded transfer, the member ceases to be:

- (in a case within (a)) resident in that country; or
- (in a case within (b)) resident in the UK or an EEA State.

The charge arises at the time of the change of circumstances. There is a requirement (under *SI 2006 No 567, Reg 11BB* for a registered scheme and *SI 2006 No 208, Reg 3AF* for a QROPS) for a member to inform the scheme administrator/manager of any such change.

The charge

The amount of the overseas transfer charge is broadly 25% of the total amount of the sums, and the value of the assets, transferred (see official guidance paras 5.1 to 5.13). Any lifetime allowance charge due on the transfer is deductible in arriving at transferred value. The member and the scheme administrator/manager of the transferor scheme are jointly and severally liable to the tax charged. The scheme administrator/manager must deduct the tax due from the member's funds before making the transfer, and must account for it to HMRC. If, however, the overseas transfer charge becomes due after the transfer, and within the relevant period, the persons jointly and severally liable to the tax are the member and the scheme manager of the QROPS (or former QROPS) currently holding the transferred funds. A person's liability does not depend on his being UK resident or domiciled. In certain circumstances, the scheme administrator/manager may apply to HMRC for discharge of liability (see official guidance paras 8.1 to 8.12).

Where the overseas transfer charge was paid on a transfer, a change in the member's circumstances within the relevant period may mean the tax can be reclaimed from HMRC. *SI 2019 No 774*, effective from 25 April 2019, sets out how the claim should be made, the information to be provided, the processing of the claim by HMRC, and to whom the repayment should be made, and also makes provision for appeals. It is supplemented by *SI 2006 No 208, Reg 3AL*, which provides the time limit for making a claim.

Information requirements

When a member requests a transfer to a QROPS, the member is statutorily required (by *SI 2006 No 567, Reg 11BA* for a registered scheme and *SI 2006 No 208, Reg 3AE* for a QROPS) to provide specified information to the scheme administrator/manager of the transferor scheme. If the member does not do so before the transfer is made, the transfer attracts the overseas transfer charge regardless of any applicable exclusions.

There are reporting requirements applicable to the transferor scheme or QROPS and the transferee QROPS. *SI 2006 No 567* prescribes the information which a registered pension scheme must provide. *SI 2006 No 208* prescribes the information which a QROPS must provide.

[*FA 2004, ss 244A–244N; FA 2017, Sch 4 paras 11, 22, 25; SI 2006 No 208; SI 2018 No 5, Reg 7; SI 2019 Nos 773, 774; SI 2019 No 689, Reg 12(2)*].

Self-directed registered pension schemes — investment restrictions

[57.30] There are provisions designed to prevent *self-directed* registered pension schemes from gaining tax advantages where there is investment by the scheme in residential property and certain tangible moveable property such as fine wines, classic cars, art and antiques (all collectively described below as 'taxable property' — see also **57.32** below). A self-directed scheme is broadly one where a scheme member can direct which investments the scheme makes, and is described below as an 'investment-regulated pension scheme' (see **57.31** below for the full definition). For transitional provisions, see **57.33** below.

See HMRC Pensions Tax Manual PTM125000.

Charges to tax

An 'investment-regulated pension scheme' (see **57.31** below) is treated as making an unauthorised payment to a member (thus subject to the tax charge at **57.26**(d) above, potentially the surcharge at **57.26**(e) above and the scheme sanction charge at **57.26**(f) above) if:

(a) the scheme acquires 'taxable property' which is held by it for the purposes of an arrangement relating to the member; or
(b) 'taxable property' that the scheme holds for such purposes is improved; or
(c) property that the scheme holds for such purposes is converted into, or adapted to become, 'residential property' (see **57.32** below).

References to acquiring or holding property are to acquiring or holding an interest in the property.

[*FA 2004, s 174A*].

There are extensive provisions for determining the timing and the amount of the unauthorised payment. In the simplest case within (a) above, the unauthorised payment is treated as made at the time of the acquisition and the taxable amount is the acquisition cost of the taxable property (including incidental costs of acquisition). However, this is subject to rules applying where the property is held only indirectly by the investment-regulated pension scheme and where property is acquired for less than market value.

In a case within (b) above, the unauthorised payment is treated as made whenever a payment is made in connection with the improvement works, and the taxable amount is equal to the amount of that payment.

In a case within (c) above, the unauthorised payment is treated as made when the conversion or adaptation works are substantially completed or, if earlier, when the property ceases to be held by the pension scheme after it has become residential property. However, if the property becomes residential property more than three years after the first payment in respect of the said works, the unauthorised payment is treated as made at the expiry of that three-year period. The taxable amount is broadly acquisition cost plus development costs if the works commenced within twelve months of the acquisition of the pension scheme's interest in the property or market value (as defined) plus development costs if the works commenced at a later date.

In all cases, there is provision for apportioning only a part of the taxable amount to the pension scheme where its interest in the property is less than 100%; the amount of the unauthorised payment is then the amount so apportioned. Where the taxable property is held by the pension scheme for the purposes of more than one arrangement, the amount of the unauthorised payment is apportioned between those arrangements on a just and reasonable basis; otherwise, the whole of the payment is treated as made to the member to which the arrangement relates.

[*FA 2004, s 174A, Sch 29A paras 31–45*].

The above rules are supplemented by Treasury regulations made by statutory instrument (see *SI 2006 No 1958, Regs 3–9*).

In addition to the above, for any tax year in which an 'investment-regulated pension scheme' (see **57.31** below) holds 'taxable property', the scheme sanction charge at **57.26**(f) above is imposed on the net income from the property or, if there is no such income or if actual net income is lower, on a notional amount of income. The notional income is computed in accordance with *FA 2004, ss 185A–185C*. In the most straightforward case where the scheme holds an interest in taxable property directly for the whole of the tax year, the notional income is equal to 10% of a deemed market value of the property. Where the scheme holds its interest in the property indirectly, there are rules as to what proportion of the otherwise chargeable amount should be charged on the scheme. Where the scheme holds its interest in the property indirectly and a person receives profits on which he has paid tax, there is provision for a similar proportion of the tax paid to be allowed as a credit against the tax liability resulting from the scheme sanction charge.

Gains on disposals of taxable property (net of any losses on such disposals) are also subject to the scheme sanction charge — in accordance with *FA 2004, ss 185F–185H*. A disposal is also deemed to arise for this purpose if the scheme ceases to hold all or part of an interest in a vehicle through which the scheme holds its interest in the property indirectly. There is provision for a proportion of any tax paid by another person in connection with a disposal to be allowed as a credit against the tax liability resulting from the scheme sanction charge.

[*FA 2004, ss 185A–185I; TCGA 1992, s 271(1B)*].

The Treasury has power to make regulations (see *SI 2006 No 1958, Reg 10*) imposing the scheme sanction charge where 'taxable property' situated outside the UK is held by a non-UK resident 'investment-regulated pension scheme'.

The regulations may, in particular, transfer liability to such a charge from the scheme administrator to the member(s) for the purposes of whose arrangement(s) the interest in the property is held. [*FA 2004, s 273ZA; SI 2006 No 1958, Reg 10*].

Definition of 'investment-regulated pension scheme'

[57.31] For the purposes of 57.30 above, a registered pension scheme that is *not* an occupational scheme is an '*investment-regulated pension scheme*' if one or more of its members (or persons 'related' to them) is (or has been) able (directly or indirectly) to direct, influence or advise on the manner of investment of any of the sums and assets held for the purposes of an arrangement under the pension scheme relating to the member.

A registered pension scheme that *is* an occupational scheme is an '*investment-regulated pension scheme*' if the scheme has 50 or fewer members and one or more of them (or persons 'related' to them) is (or has been) able (directly or indirectly) to direct, influence or advise on the manner of investment of any of the sums and assets held for the purposes of the scheme.

If an occupational scheme does not meet the above condition, it is nevertheless an '*investment-regulated pension scheme*' if one or more of its members (or persons 'related' to them) is (or has been) able (directly or indirectly) to direct, influence or advise on the manner of investment of any sums and assets that are held for the purposes of an arrangement under the pension scheme relating to the member (unless this is merely by reason of a just and reasonable apportionment of the sums and assets held for the purposes of the pension scheme). The Treasury has power to amend this rule by statutory instrument and to modify the investment-regulated pension scheme provisions insofar as they apply to such an arrangement.

For the above purposes, a person is '*related*' to a member of a pension scheme if he and the member are CONNECTED PERSONS (**19**) or if he acts on behalf of the member or a person connected with the member.

Where an investment-regulated pension scheme holds sums or assets otherwise than for the purposes of the administration or management of the scheme, then, to the extent that they do not otherwise fall to be treated as held for the purposes of arrangements relating to members, they are apportioned between all such arrangements according to the respective rights of the members and treated as held for the purposes of those arrangements.

[*FA 2004, Sch 29A paras 1–5*].

Taxable property

[57.32] For the purposes of 57.30 above, property is '*taxable property*' if it is residential property or tangible moveable property. 'Residential property' is defined for these purposes to include buildings used (or suitable for use) as dwellings and their gardens or grounds. It includes property located outside the UK. It does not include, for example, certain care homes, children's homes, hospices and students' halls of residence. The Treasury may include or exclude other types of building by means of statutory instrument. Residential property is not '*taxable property*' if it is:

(a) occupied by an employee as a condition of his employment; or
(b) used in connection with business premises held as an investment of the pension scheme,

provided that the occupant is neither a member of the pension scheme nor connected (within **19** CONNECTED PERSONS) with a member or, in the case of (a), with the employer.

'Tangible moveable property' has its general meaning and will include, for example, fine wines, classic and vintage cars, art, antiques, jewellery, boats, stamp collections and rare books. The Treasury may exclude particular items by statutory instrument; *SI 2006 No 1959* excludes gold bullion (as defined) and any items with a market value not exceeding £6,000 held by a vehicle solely for the purposes of its administration or management, being property in which the pension scheme does not hold an interest directly and which no member of the scheme (or connected person) occupies or uses (or has a right to do so). Printing presses have been held to be tangible moveable property (*Morgan Lloyd Trustees Ltd (as administrator of the Wren Press Pension Scheme) v HMRC* FTT (TC 5625), [2017] UKFTT 131 (TC)).

[*FA 2004, Sch 29A paras 6–11; SI 2006 No 1959*].

There are extensive provisions determining what is meant by an investment-regulated pension scheme acquiring or holding an interest in property, defining both direct and indirect holdings and, in both cases, providing exceptions. There are also rules whereby a scheme is deemed to have acquired property in particular circumstances. An indirect holding in property is broadly a holding by the pension scheme in a vehicle (such as a company, collective investment scheme or trust) that holds the property (whether directly or indirectly). [*FA 2004, Sch 29A paras 12–30*]. Generally, self-directed pension schemes are permitted to invest in genuinely diverse commercial vehicles that hold what would be otherwise be 'taxable property', but subject to rules preventing the use of such vehicles as a means to facilitate investment in prohibited assets where there remains scope for personal use of those assets (HMRC Technical Note, 5 December 2005).

Transitional

[57.33] Subject to below, the charges at **57.30** above do not apply if the pension scheme acquired the property in question before 6 April 2006 and it is property that the scheme was not prohibited from holding under the rules in force before that date (see, for example, *SI 1991 No 1614* and *SI 2001 No 117*), such that approval to the scheme could have been withdrawn. The same applies if the property is held directly by another person and the scheme was not prohibited from holding its interest in that other person. The exemption also applies where the acquisition occurs on or after 5 April 2006 under a pre-6 April 2006 contract.

References to acquiring or holding property are to acquiring or holding an interest in the property.

The above exemption ceases to apply in any of the following scenarios.

- There is a change in the occupation or use of the property that, had it occurred before 6 April 2006, would have prohibited the pension scheme from holding the property; in this case, the exemption ceases to apply on the date of change (or, if later, on the date the scheme acquires the property).
- The property was residential property as at 6 April 2006 and improvement works are begun on it on or after that date; the exemption ceases to apply on the date the works are substantially completed (or, if later, on the date the scheme acquires the property). There are provisions as to what is meant by 'improvement works' for this purpose and as to when such works are to be treated as having begun (see *FA 2004, Sch 36 para 37B(9)–(12)*).
- There is a change in the pension scheme's interest in any person who holds the property directly or any person who has contracted to acquire it, such that, had the change occurred before 6 April 2006, the scheme would have been prohibited from holding the interest in that person; the exemption ceases to apply on the date of change (or, if later, on the date the scheme acquires the property).

The pension scheme is treated for the purposes of **57.30** above as acquiring the property on the date the exemption ceases to apply. There are provisions to determine the taxable amount for the purposes of any unauthorised payments charge arising from that deemed acquisition (see *FA 2004, Sch 36 para 37B(7)*).

If the above exemption does not apply and this is due to the pension scheme being prohibited from holding the property (or from holding its interest in the person who holds the property directly) under the pre-6 April 2006 rules, the scheme is treated for the purposes of **57.30** above as acquiring the property on 6 April 2006. There are provisions to determine the taxable amount for the purposes of any unauthorised payments charge arising from that deemed acquisition (see *FA 2004, Sch 36 para 37C(4)*).

Where the exemption would otherwise apply, special rules apply if: (i) the pension scheme was, immediately before 6 April 2006, either a small self-administered scheme (SSAS) or a self-invested personal pension scheme (SIPP); (ii) the property was residential property on 6 April 2006; and (iii) improvement works are begun on it on or after 5 December 2005. If the scheme was a SASS, the special rules apply if it held the property directly on 6 April 2006 and acquired it before 5 August 1991 or if it held the property indirectly on 6 April 2006 (or, if later, the date of acquisition). If the scheme was a SIPP, the special rules apply if it held the property indirectly on 6 April 2006 (or, if later, the date of acquisition). The special rules are that:

- if the improvement works are completed on or after 6 April 2006, they are treated as having begun on or after that date, such that the exemption ceases to apply (see above); and
- if the improvement works are completed before 6 April 2006, the exemption does not apply and the scheme is treated as acquiring the property on 6 April 2006 (as above).

The exemption does not apply to an occupational pension scheme approved under *ICTA 1988, s 590* after 5 December 2005. Unless it is still to acquire the property on that date, the scheme is treated as acquiring the property on 6 April 2006 (as above).

[*FA 2004, Sch 36 paras 37A–37E*].

There is a separate exemption from the charges at **57.30** above in the following circumstances:

- the pension scheme acquires the property on or after 6 April 2006 but only because a person in whom the scheme holds an interest comes to hold the property directly;
- the pension scheme acquired its interest in that person before 6 April 2006 and was not prohibited from holding that interest under the rules then in force;
- at no time between 6 April 2006 and the acquisition of the property has the pension scheme's interest in that person been such as would have been prohibited under the pre-6 April 2006 rules;
- (in the case of tangible moveable property) the property is acquired by the person for use in its trade, profession or vocation or for the purposes of its administration or management; and
- (in the case of residential property) the property is acquired by the person for the purposes of its property rental business, and, after its acquisition, the property is not occupied or used by a member of the pension scheme or a person connected with such a member (within **19** CONNECTED PERSONS). It is a further condition that the property rental business was in operation (by the same person) immediately before 6 April 2006 and involved the direct holding of at least five assets consisting of interests in residential property.

Again, there are provisions whereby the exemption ceases in specified circumstances and for determining the taxable amount for the purposes of any unauthorised payments charge arising from the resulting deemed acquisition of the property by the pension scheme.

[*FA 2004, Sch 36 paras 37F–37I*].

Employer-financed retirement benefits schemes

[57.34] The term 'employer-financed retirement benefits scheme' is used after 5 April 2006 to describe, broadly, any UK occupational pension scheme that is not a registered pension scheme. Payments and other benefits from an employer-financed retirement benefits scheme are taxable on the employee on receipt. Employer contributions to the scheme are deductible against profits at the time when payments are made to, or benefits provided for, employees out of those contributions. Employees are not charged tax in respect of contributions made to the scheme by their employer on their behalf. Employer-financed retirement benefits schemes are not subject to the tax charges at **57.18–57.26** above (lifetime allowance charge etc.) For HMRC guidance on employer-financed retirement benefits schemes, see HMRC Employment Income Manual EIM15000–15429.

Subject to conditions, a charge to tax may arise under **26** DISGUISED REMUNERATION on the employee where an employer gives an undertaking to pay a contribution to an unregistered pension scheme (e.g. an employer-financed retirement benefits scheme) and subsequently assures that the contribution will be paid by either earmarking property for the purpose or otherwise providing security. See **26.12** for details. This is subject to the anti-forestalling provisions at **26.13**, which have effect on and after 9 December 2010.

Simon's Taxes. See E7.251–E7.255.

Definitions

[57.35] The statutory definition of '*employer-financed retirement benefits scheme*' is a 'scheme' for the provision of benefits consisting of, or including, 'relevant benefits' to, or in respect of, employees and former employees of an employer. Registered pension schemes (as in **57.4** above) are specifically excluded from the definition, as are superannuation funds within *ICTA 1988, s 615(3)* (superannuation funds for overseas employees — see **57.40** below). '*Scheme*' is very widely defined to include any deed, agreement, series of agreements or other arrangements. [*ITEPA 2003, s 393A; FA 2004, s 249(3)*].

Relevant benefits

For the above purposes, '*relevant benefits*' means any lump sum, gratuity or other benefit (including a non-cash benefit) provided (or to be provided) on (or in anticipation of) retirement or on death or in connection with any change in nature of service or, following retirement or death, in connection with past service. Benefits under a 'pension sharing order or provision' (as defined) are also included. But *excluded* from relevant benefits are any benefits charged to tax as PENSION INCOME (**56**) or which would be so charged were it not for specified exemptions and deductions, any benefits charged to tax under *FA 2004, Sch 34* (overseas pension schemes — see **57.28** above), benefits in respect of the death by accident, or the disablement or ill-health, of an employee during service, benefits under certain life policies and benefits excluded by statutory instrument (see below). Note also the **£100 exemption** referred to in **57.36** below.

HMRC may add to the list of *excluded benefits* by statutory instrument and may do so with retrospective effect. Consequently, the following are now on this list.

- A number of exclusions similar to those applicable to employee benefits (with necessary modifications to reflect the fact that the recipient is retired). These relate to continued provision of accommodation and related expenses (including removal expenses), welfare counselling, recreational benefits, annual parties and similar functions, continued provision of equipment for disabled former employees and yearly health screenings and medical check-ups.
- The provision of a service for the writing of wills where the cash equivalent of the benefit (see **28.54** EMPLOYMENT INCOME) does not exceed £150.
- Non-cash benefits provided in connection with the termination before 6 April 1998 of the employee's employment.

- Certain payments made by the Ministry of Defence to or for former members of the armed forces or where appropriate members of their family or their personal representatives. The payments are (i) the payment of tuition fees for further and higher education; (ii) payments under the resettlement commutation, resettlement grants and gratuity earnings schemes; and (iii) the provision of independent inquest advice in connection with death in service.
- Benefits from the Armed Forces Compensation Scheme.
- Non-accidental death lump sum benefits if provided for under the rules of a scheme on 6 April 2006.
- 'Trivial benefits' provided to the former employee or a member of his family or household. '*Trivial benefits*' are low value benefits that would have been trivial benefits within **28.51** EMPLOYMENT INCOME if they had been provided in the course of the employee's employment. If the former employer is a close company when the benefit is provided, and the former employee was a director or other office-holder at any time when the former employer was a close company (or is a member of the family or household of such a director etc.), the £300 annual cap in **28.51** applies.
- (For 2020/21 onwards) lump sum benefits paid pursuant to the National Health Service and Social Care Coronavirus Life Assurance (England) Scheme 2020 or Welsh equivalent. Under these schemes, NHS England and NHS Wales are paying a lump sum in respect of the deaths of NHS and social care staff which are caused by COVID-19.

[*ITEPA 2003, s 393B; FA 2004, s 249(3); FA 2017, Sch 3 para 13; SI 2005 No 3453; SI 2006 Nos 132, 210; SI 2007 No 3537; SI 2020 No 615*].

For official guidance, see HMRC Employment Income Manual EIM15000.

Relevant benefits provided during a tax year must be reported to HMRC by the 'responsible person' no later than 7 July following that year. Guidance on the reporting of non-cash benefits is included in HMRC Pensions Tax Simplification Newsletter No 28, 2 July 2007.

A one-off payment to a former employee for agreeing to leave the former employer company's healthcare scheme was held to be a relevant benefit (*Forsyth v HMRC* FTT (TC 4029), [2014] UKFTT 915 (TC)).

The 'responsible person'

The '*responsible person*' in relation to an employer-financed retirement benefits scheme is determined as follows.

(a) If there are one or more trustees of the scheme who are UK resident, the responsible person is that trustee or each of those trustees.
(b) If no-one qualifies under (a) above but there are one or more persons who control the management of the scheme, the responsible person is that person or each of those persons.
(c) If no-one qualifies under (a) or (b) above, the responsible person (if still alive or in existence) is the employer who established the scheme (or any such employers where more than one) or anyone who has succeeded that employer (or those employers) in relation to the provision of benefits under the scheme.

(d) If no-one qualifies under (a), (b) or (c) above, the responsible person is anyone who employs employees to whom benefits are provided under the scheme.

(e) If no-one qualifies under (a), (b), (c) or (d) above but there are one or more trustees of the scheme who are non-UK resident, the responsible person is that trustee or each of those trustees.

[*ITEPA 2003, s 399A; FA 2004, s 249(11)*].

Charge to tax on benefits

[57.36] *Pensions* from employer-financed retirement benefits schemes are charged to tax as in **56.2**(a) or **56.2**(e) PENSION INCOME.

If a *non-pension* relevant benefit under an employer-financed retirement benefits scheme is received by an individual, the amount of the benefit is charged to tax as employment income of the individual for the tax year of receipt. There is an exemption where all such benefits received by the individual in the tax year do not exceed £100. See **57.35** above for the meaning of 'relevant benefit' and for exclusions. If a relevant benefit is received by a person other than an individual, the 'responsible person' (see **57.35**) in relation to the scheme is charged income tax at 45% for the tax year of receipt. Where the relevant benefit is a *lump sum*, any contributions made by the employee towards its provision are deductible in arriving at the amount chargeable on the employee or, where applicable, the 'responsible person'. See also the transitional provisions at **57.38** below.

If the receipt of a non-pension relevant benefit gives rise to 'other relevant income' of the employee, or former employee, in question, the benefit is chargeable as above only to the extent that it exceeds the other relevant income. '*Other relevant income*' means:

(a) general earnings; or

(b) amounts within the charge to tax in **26** DISGUISED REMUNERATION; or

(c) amounts which would have fallen within (b) above but for the application of Rule 2 (overlap with earlier relevant step) in **26.4** DISGUISED REMUNERATION; or

(d) amounts which would have fallen into one of (a)–(c) above apart from the employee having been non-UK resident for any tax year or apart from any tax year having been a split year (see **63.19** RESIDENCE AND DOMICILE) as regards the employee.

[*ITEPA 2003, ss 394, 395; FA 2004, s 249(4)–(8)*].

Non-pension benefits from certain closed or frozen schemes that enjoyed approval under *ICTA 1970, s 222* immediately before 6 April 1980 are excluded from the charge above. [*ITEPA 2003, s 395A*].

Valuation of benefits

The amount of a cash benefit is the amount received. The amount of a non-cash benefit for these purposes is the greater of the 'cash equivalent of the benefit' and the amount chargeable under the normal employment income rules if the benefit were taxable as earnings. The '*cash equivalent of the benefit*' is determined under the benefits code rules (see **28.21** EMPLOYMENT INCOME), modified as appropriate in the case of living accommodation and cheap loan arrangements (with relief being potentially available in the latter case for the notional interest as it is under those rules — see **28.32** EMPLOYMENT INCOME). [*ITEPA 2003, ss 398, 399; FA 2004, s 249(9)(10)*].

Temporary non-UK residence

Where the 'year of departure' is 2013/14 or any subsequent year, certain lump sum benefits received by an individual during a 'temporary period of non-UK residence' that would otherwise have been chargeable to tax as above are treated as if they were received by him in the 'period of return'. For what is meant by '*temporary period of non-UK residence*', the '*year of departure*' and the '*period of return*', see **63.29** RESIDENCE AND DOMICILE.

The above applies to a benefit in the form of a lump sum which is not chargeable to tax for the year of receipt but which would have been so chargeable if it were not for a double tax treaty. This includes a case where a charge to tax for the year of receipt could be prevented by the making of a claim to double tax relief but no claim has yet been made. Nothing in any double tax treaty is to be read as preventing the individual from being chargeable to income tax in respect of any benefit treated as received in the period of return.

For the purpose only of applying the exemption where all benefits received by an individual in a tax year do not exceed £100, the lump sum benefit is still treated as having been received in the tax year in which it was actually received.

[*ITEPA 2003, s 394A*].

Benefits *treated as* chargeable for the year of return are not subject to PAYE. [*ITEPA 2003, s 683(3ZA)*].

Relief for employer contributions and other expenses

[57.37] Relief for employer contributions to an employer-financed retirement benefits scheme is given under the employee benefit contribution rules in *ITTOIA 2005, ss 38–44* (see **75.65** TRADING INCOME for details). Broadly, the employer is entitled to make a deduction for contributions in computing trading etc. profits for a period of account to the extent that, during that period or within nine months after the end of it, payments are made to or benefits provided to employees out of those contributions. Contributions made in one period of account may thus remain non-deductible until a later period of account.

The following applies to expenses incurred by an employer in providing benefits under an employer-financed retirement benefits scheme and shown in the employer's accounts in accordance with generally accepted accounting practice. If the recipient is chargeable to income tax on receipt of the benefits, then, provided they are deductible under general principles, the expenses are deductible in computing trading etc. profits for the period of account in which they are paid. Otherwise the expenses are not deductible at all. [*FA 2004, s 246*].

An employer's contributions and other expenses in providing 'relevant benefits' (see **57.35** above) to an employee are not, however, deductible where the provision of those benefits is linked to a reduction in the benefits payable to the same employee under a registered pension scheme. But if relief for contributions to the registered pension scheme has been restricted in accordance with *SI 2005 No 3458* (see **57.14** above), contributions and other expenses in providing the relevant benefits are not prevented from being deductible to an extent that is just and reasonable. [*FA 2004, s 246A*].

Transitional

[57.38] Under the pre-6 April 2006 regime for non-approved occupational pension schemes, payments by an employer towards the provision of benefits for employees were generally taxed on the employee as employment income for the year in which the payments were made. This treatment does not continue after 5 April 2006 for employer-financed retirement benefits schemes, and the relevant legislation (*ITEPA 2003, ss 386–392*) is repealed by *FA 2004, s 247*. Included in this legislation was a provision (*ITEPA 2003, s 392*) enabling the tax charge to be refunded, or otherwise relieved, where the employee (or his personal representative) proves to the satisfaction of HMRC that no benefit has yet been provided and that an event has occurred by reason of which no benefit will subsequently be provided (in both cases other than as a result of a pension sharing order or provision — as defined). The tax would be refunded or otherwise relieved on an application made within six years after the occurrence of the said event. In appropriate circumstances and on a just and reasonable basis, *partial* repayment could be made. Notwithstanding its repeal, *ITEPA 2003, s 392* continues to have effect after 5 April 2006 so as to give relief in a case where the tax charge was for 2005/06 or an earlier year but the said event occurs after 5 April 2006. [*FA 2004, Sch 36 para 52*].

Transitional relief is provided as in (a) and (b) below where a lump sum benefit is provided by an employer-financed retirement benefits scheme after 5 April 2006, such that the charge in *ITEPA 2003, ss 394, 395* at **57.36** above applies, and the employee was taxed for 2005/06 and/or earlier years under *ITEPA 2003, ss 386–392* (see above) or their predecessors.

(a) Where all of the scheme's income and gains are charged to tax or the scheme was in existence before 1 December 1993 and has not since been varied, no charge arises under **57.36** above if the employer has paid no sums to the scheme after 5 April 2006. If the employer has paid sums to the scheme since that date, the amount charged is restricted to any excess of: (i) the lump sum over; (ii) the employee's share of the market value of the scheme assets at 5 April 2006 as adjusted for inflation since that date. Post-5 April 2006 employee contributions are deductible from that excess.

(b) In any case not within (a) above, the amount charged is restricted to any excess of the lump sum over the amount taxed on the employee for 2005/06 and earlier years. Post-5 April 2006 employee contributions are deductible from that excess.

[*FA 2004, Sch 36 paras 53–55*].

Inducement payments

[57.39] Where an employer offers employees an inducement to agree to a reduction in their benefits from the employer scheme or to transfer from one kind of employer scheme to another, the tax treatment depends on the form of the inducement. Such inducements are most likely to be offered to members of a defined benefit arrangement and may involve a transfer from that scheme to a money purchase arrangement.

If, or to the extent that, the inducement payment takes the form of an enhancement to a transfer value of the pension fund, such that it is included in the funds transferred between schemes, it is treated like any other employer contribution to a scheme.

If, or to the extent that, the inducement payment takes the form of a direct payment to the scheme member, HMRC's view is that such inducement payments paid to encourage scheme members to give up future pension rights or to move from one pension scheme to another are subject to income tax (and NIC). The income tax liability arises under *ITEPA 2003, s 394* at **57.36** above (and this is the case regardless of the fact that the scheme in question and/or the scheme to which the fund is to be transferred is a registered pension scheme).

(HMRC Statement 24 January 2007; HMRC Employment Income Manual EIM15155).

Other pension funds

[57.40] The Trustees of the **House of Commons Members' Fund** are exempt from income tax on all income derived from that Fund and its investments. [*ICTA 1988, s 613(4)*].

Income from investments or deposits of any fund within **56.5**(a)–(d) PENSION INCOME (certain **overseas funds**) is exempt from tax. Any tax deducted from such income is repayable by HMRC to the recipient. [*ICTA 1988, s 614(3)*].

Judicial pension schemes are subject to their own legislation and are outside the registered pension schemes regime — see *SI 2006 No 497*.

Superannuation funds to which ICTA 1988, s 615(3) applies

Income from investments or other property of a superannuation fund to which *ICTA 1988, s 615(3)* applies is exempt to the like extent as if it were income of a person non-UK domiciled and non-UK resident. *ICTA 1988, s 615(3)* applies to a superannuation fund: (i) established under irrevocable trusts in connection with a trade carried on wholly or partly overseas; (ii) solely to provide **superannuation benefits to overseas employees** (incidental duties in UK being ignored); and (iii) recognised by both employer and employees. Annuities paid to non-UK residents from such a fund are payable gross, and trustees are not liable under *ITA 2007, Pt 15 Ch 6* (deduction of tax at source from annual payments etc.).

On and after **6 April 2017**, it is no longer possible to benefit from the above exemption by making further contributions to a fund to which *ICTA 1988, s 615(3)* applies. However, income arising, and annuities paid, on or after

6 April 2017 are still covered by the exemption insofar as they relate to contributions made to money purchase arrangements before that date or rights accrued in defined benefit arrangements before that date. The legislation achieves this by treating any post-5 April 2017 contributions as not made to, and any increases in rights as not arising under, the *section 615(3)* superannuation fund. Instead, contributions are treated as made to, and increases in rights as arising under, a separate superannuation fund (the 'shadow fund') to which *ICTA 1988, s 615(3)* does not apply. Increases in rights are disregarded to the extent that they arise from acceptable index-linking.

[*ICTA 1988, ss 614(5), 615(3)(6)(6A)–(6G)(7)(11)–(14); FA 2017, Sch 3 para 3*].

National Employment Savings Trust

[57.41] The National Employment Savings Trust (NEST) is a national workplace registered pension scheme designed to meet the needs of low-to-moderate earners and their employers. It is intended to be a low cost, easy to use, online pension scheme that is open to any employer and is run by a not-for-profit trustee corporation called NEST Corporation. *FA 2004, s 274B(1)* enables NEST to be treated as an occupational pension scheme. [*FA 2004, ss 150(5A), 274B(1); F(No 3)A 2010, s 30; FA 2018, Sch 3 paras 1(2)(5)(9), 2(3)*].

There is no tax charge on unauthorised borrowing where the borrowing is linked to the cost of establishing, managing or administering NEST. The Treasury has power to make regulations by statutory instrument to deal with any unintended tax consequences that may emerge as a result of the implementation of NEST (see *SI 2012 No 1258*).

Master Trust schemes

[57.42] A Master Trust scheme is a form of multi-employer money purchase occupational pension scheme which employers are able to select for their workers rather than needing to set up their own pension scheme. Master Trust schemes are regulated under *Pension Schemes Act 2017*. *FA 2004, s 274B(2)* enables Master Trust schemes to be treated as occupational pension schemes. A Master Trust scheme is an *unauthorised Master Trust scheme* for the purposes of this chapter if it is not authorised under *Pension Schemes Act 2017, Pt 1* (or corresponding NI legislation, and its operation would be unlawful under those provisions without such authorisation). [*FA 2004, ss 150(5A), 274B(2), 279(1B)–(1D); FA 2018, Sch 3 paras 1(2)(5)(6), 2(1)(3), 3, 4*].

Pension Protection Fund

[57.43] The Pension Protection Fund (PPF) was set up by *Pensions Act 2004*. Its purpose is to assume responsibility for final salary occupational pension schemes (and other pension schemes with defined benefit elements) whose sponsoring employers have become insolvent, leaving insufficient assets in the scheme. The PPF will pay compensation to pension scheme members in lieu of the benefits that would have been payable under the scheme. The Board of the PPF also took over responsibility for the fund previously held by the Pension Compensation Board (PCB), hold that fund as the Fraud Compensation Fund, and pay compensation to pension schemes in cases of fraud.

The PPF is a body corporate and is funded by statutory levies on eligible schemes, for which tax relief would not necessarily be given. As it is not itself a pension scheme, the PPF would not be able to pay tax-free lump sums. In order to remove these and other anomalies, the PPF is given broadly equivalent tax treatment to that of a registered pension scheme (as in **57.4** above). *FA 2005, s 102* gives the Treasury a wide-ranging power to make appropriate regulations giving effect to these matters. See *SI 2006 No 575* and *SI 2013 No 1117*, which provide that tax legislation applies in relation to the PPF in the same way as it applies in relation to a registered pension scheme, and modify that legislation where appropriate to ensure that the tax treatment of the PPF is equivalent to that of a registered scheme.

Payment of the PPF levy by an employer is part of the everyday cost of employing staff and will usually be an allowable deduction in computing the employer's trading profits for tax purposes (HMRC Business Income Manual BIM46090). A transfer of the property, rights and liabilities of a registered pension scheme to the PPF is an authorised payment (see **57.7** or **57.26**(d) above) by the scheme (*SI 2006 No 134*).

58

Personal Service Companies etc. (IR35)

Cross-reference. See **47** MANAGED SERVICE COMPANIES.

Simon's Taxes. See **E4.10**.

Introduction to personal service companies etc.

[58.1] There are provisions designed 'to remove opportunities for the avoidance of tax and Class 1 National Insurance contributions (NICs) by the use of intermediaries, such as [personal] service companies or partnerships, in circumstances where an individual worker would otherwise be an employee of the client or the income would be income from an office held by the worker'. (Annex to Revenue Press Release 23 September 1999). These are based on rules first published as Revenue Budget Press Release IR35 on 9 March 1999 (though highly significant changes have been made subsequently) and are commonly referred to as the 'IR35' rules.

The rules do not prevent an individual providing his services through an intermediary. Instead, **and subject to new rules effective for 2021/22 onwards** (see below), where the individual would otherwise have been categorised under pre-existing case law and practice as an employee in relation to a particular engagement, his income from that engagement is deemed to have been paid to him (if not *actually* paid to him) by the intermediary as earnings from an employment and is subject to PAY AS YOU EARN (**53**) and NICs. See **58.2–58.15**. This applies even if the income is, in fact, paid to the individual in some other way, for example in the form of dividends from a personal service company (but see **58.13**) or as a share of partnership profits, or is retained within the intermediary. Some allowance is made for deductible expenses (see **58.7**, **58.8**). Although proposed as an attack on avoidance, the provisions apply to any situation within their ambit (see **58.2**, **58.4**) and are not dependent on the taxpayer's motive.

The tax provisions are contained in *ITEPA 2003, ss 48–61* and are described in this chapter. For the NIC position, see *The Social Security Contributions (Intermediaries) Regulations 2000 (SI 2000 No 727)* (or, as regards Northern Ireland, *SI 2000 No 728*), and see Tolley's National Insurance Contributions.

The operation of *ITEPA 2003, ss 44–47* (workers supplied by agencies — see **28.96** EMPLOYMENT INCOME) is not affected by these provisions. Those *sections* apply only where the worker engaged through the agency is an individual. If a service company, for example, is engaged by a client via an independent agency, the provisions in this chapter may well apply but will not directly affect the agency. Nothing in these provisions applies to a payment or transfer subject to deduction of tax under *ITA 2007, s 966(3)* or *(4)* (payments to non-resident entertainers and sportsmen — see **50.11** NON-RESIDENTS). [*ITEPA 2003, s 48(2)*].

Separate legislation applies to 'managed service companies' (see **47** MANAGED SERVICE COMPANIES).

Public sector engagements

For 2017/18 onwards, where an intermediary provides the services of a worker to a public sector body, such as a Government department, NHS trust or local authority, the responsibility for determining whether or not the IR35 rules apply, operating those rules where they do apply, and accounting for tax and NICs, shifts from the intermediary to the public sector body (or, where applicable, the recruiting agency through which the public sector body engages). See **58.23–58.37**.

Private sector engagements for 2021/22 onwards

FA 2020, Sch 1 shifts responsibility for operating the rules, and deducting any tax and NICs due, from the individual to the organisation, agency or other third party paying the individual's personal service company. Thus, private sector engagements are brought into line with public sector engagements (see above). This has effect, subject to transitional provisions at **58.24**, where the deemed direct payment (as in **58.27**) falls to be treated as made on or after 6 April 2021. See **58.23–58.37**.

Where the client (i.e. the person for whom the services are performed) qualifies as small or does not have a UK connection, the new rules do *not* apply. The individual's personal service company or other intermediary will continue to be subject to the pre-existing IR35 rules at **58.2–58.15**.

Broadly, a company or limited liability partnership qualifies as '*small*' for this purpose if it meets two of the following three criteria: turnover no more than £10.2 million, balance sheet total no more than £5.1 million, and number of employees no more than 50. A non-corporate body qualifies as small if its turnover is no more than £10.2 million. There are specific rules for applying the tests to joint undertakings and members of a group of companies. There are also rules around connected persons. For the detailed rules as to whether a client is small, see **58.16–58.21**. As to whether a client has a UK connection, see **58.22**.

The client will be required to provide a statement of status determination to the worker (see **58.28**). Until it does so, the client, and not the person making the payment to the intermediary, will be responsible for the operation of PAYE. The statement must be to the effect that the client has reached a conclusion as to whether or not the worker would be regarded as an employee of the client if the services were provided under a contract directly between client and worker; it must state that conclusion and explain the reasons for it. The client must take reasonable care in making this status determination.

HMRC are to take a light-touch approach to penalties in the first twelve months, unless there is evidence of deliberate non-compliance. They also commit to not using information resulting from the extension of the rules to the private sector to open a new compliance check into an intermediary for tax years prior to 2021/22, unless there is reason to suspect fraud or criminal behaviour.

Travel expenses where services provided through intermediary

Relief is denied for home-to-work travel expenditure for engagements via personal service companies and other employment intermediaries. See **28.18** EMPLOYMENT INCOME.

Guidance

See generally the guidance at www.gov.uk/topic/business-tax/ir35 and HMRC Employment Status Manual ESM3000 *et seq.*

Services provided through an intermediary

[58.2] The IR35 rules at **58.4–58.15** below apply in relation to an engagement where the following conditions are all present:

(a) an individual (the worker) personally performs, or is under an obligation personally to perform, services for another person (the client);

(b) the client is not a public authority (as regards which see the special rules at **58.23–58.37** below);

(c) the services are provided not under a contract directly between worker and client but under arrangements involving a third party (the 'intermediary') to which these provisions apply (see **58.4** below); and

(d)

- if the services had been provided under a direct contract as mentioned in (c) above, the worker would have fallen to be categorised for income tax purposes as an employee of the client (see **58.3**, **58.38** below) or the holder of an office under the client; or
- the worker is an office holder who holds that office under the client, and the services relate to the office.

For **2021/22** onwards, the special rules referred to in (b) above will apply also to private sector engagements where the client is medium or large (i.e. does not qualify as small), unless the client does not have a UK connection. The long-standing IR35 rules at **58.4–58.15** below will thus apply *only* where the client qualifies as small for the tax year (see **58.16** below) or does not have a UK connection for the tax year (see **58.22** below).

The term '*intermediary*' in (c) above can refer to a company or to an individual. It is expressly provided that the term also refers to a partnership or unincorporated body of which the worker is a member. It is expressly provided for 2017/18 onwards that holding office as statutory auditor of the client does not count as holding office under the client for the purposes of (d) above.

[*ITEPA 2003, ss 48(1), 49, 61(1); FA 2017, Sch 1 paras 3, 11, 15; FA 2020, Sch 1 paras 3(2), 24*].

Whether or not employment?

[58.3] In applying the test at **58.2**(d) above, i.e. whether or not the worker would have been an employee if engaged directly, the circumstances to be taken into account include the terms on which the services are provided, having regard to the terms of contracts forming part of the arrangements (as in **58.2**(c) above) under which the services are provided. [*ITEPA 2003, s 49(4)*]. Otherwise, no statutory rules are provided, the test instead being based on pre-existing case law and practice as to the distinction between employment and self-employment — see **28.66** EMPLOYMENT INCOME,

Tolley's National Insurance Contributions. See also Revenue Tax Bulletin February 2000 pp 715–723 for a comprehensive article and practical illustrations devoted to the provisions in this chapter. The main text of this article is summarised at the end of this chapter — at **58.38** below. It is the reality of the working relationship that counts, irrespective of whether the parties have chosen to attach a different label to it (*Massey v Crown Life Insurance* Co CA 1977, [1978] 2 All ER 576).

Taxpayers may seek an opinion from HMRC as to whether or not a contract falls within the provisions in this chapter. The request, together with copies of contracts and any other relevant information, should be sent to IR35 Customer Services Unit, HMRC, Ground Floor North, Princess House, Cliftonville Road, Northampton, NN1 5AE (tel. 0300 200 3885, fax. 03000 527 450). Advice can be given on existing contracts only. See also HMRC Employment Status Manual ESM3280 *et seq*.

A number of cases have come before the Appeal Tribunals and the Courts on the question of whether an individual would have been an employee if engaged directly by the client rather than via a service company. Each case turns on its own facts. For summaries of these cases, see Tolley's Tax Cases under Employment Income — Personal service companies and managed service companies.

HMRC also identified a standard contract said to be common to service company workers engaged, through agencies, in the information technology industry. Such a contract requires the worker:

(a) to work where the client requests, for an agreed number of hours per week, and at an agreed hourly rate;
(b) to keep a timesheet for checking by the client;
(c) to be subject to the client's control; and
(d) not to sub-contract the work to anyone else.

Where a worker is engaged for a month or more on a contract of this type, and cannot demonstrate a recent history of work including engagements which have the characteristics of self-employment, HMRC will treat the engagement as being within the provisions in this chapter. (Note that whilst this may be a convenient rule of thumb, the taxpayer is not precluded from arguing for a different treatment.) Where the contract is for less than a month, HMRC will consider each case on its merits. (Revenue Press Release 7 February 2000 and Revenue Tax Bulletin February 2000 p 717).

The income tax legislation on personal service companies does not bite if the worker's only relationship with the client is as non-executive director of the client, as the wording in **58.2**(d) above refers to an 'employee' rather than an office-holder. (There is no such exemption for National Insurance purposes.) If, however, a non-executive director performs other services for the client through an intermediary, such that under a direct contract he would have been an employee as well as an office-holder, those services do fall within the legislation. (Revenue Internet Statement 29 April 2003).

Intermediaries to which these provisions apply

[58.4] The provisions apply only if the intermediary meets the relevant conditions below.

Companies

Where the intermediary is a company, the provisions apply in relation to an engagement if either:

(a) the worker has a 'material interest' (see below) in the intermediary; or
(b) the payment or benefit in **58.6**(ii) below is received or receivable by the worker directly from the intermediary and can reasonably be taken to represent remuneration for services provided by the worker to the client.

The provisions do not, however, apply if either of the above is satisfied but the intermediary is an associated company of the client by reason of both the intermediary and the client being under the control of the worker (or of the worker and other persons). See the examples at HMRC Employment Status Manual ESM3108.

For these purposes, the worker has a material interest if he, and/or certain 'associates' of his (within *ITEPA 2003, s 60* and with the extended meaning of 'husband and wife' at **58.5**(c) below), has a material interest in the company. A '*material interest*' in a company means:

(i) beneficial ownership or ability to control (directly or indirectly) more than 5% of the ordinary share capital; or
(ii) possession of, or entitlement to acquire, rights to more than 5% of any distributions that the company may make; or
(iii) (where the company is a close company) possession of, or entitlement to acquire, rights to more than 5% of the assets available for distribution among the participators (within *CTA 2010, s 454*) in a winding-up or in any other circumstances.

[*ITEPA 2003, ss 51, 61(1)*].

Providing (a) or (b) above is satisfied, the provisions apply equally to a 'composite service company' employing several workers as to a service company employing only one or two workers. (Revenue Tax Bulletin August 2002 pp 956, 957). For more on composite service companies and also on managed service companies (i.e. one-worker service companies set up and run by a promoter for an administration fee), see Revenue Tax Bulletin December 2004 pp 1165–1168; and see now **47** MANAGED SERVICE COMPANIES.

In both places in which it is mentioned above, '*control*' is as defined by *ITA 2007, s 995*. [*ITEPA 2003, s 719*].

Partnerships

Where the intermediary is a partnership, the provisions apply in relation to payments or benefits received or receivable by the worker as a member of the partnership if:

(A) the worker, *alone or with one or more 'relatives'*, is entitled to at least 60% of partnership profits; or

(B) most of the partnership profits derive from provision of services under engagements within **58.2** above or **58.25** below to a single client (or to a single client and his 'associates' — within *ITEPA 2003, s 60*); or

(C) the partnership profit sharing arrangements are such that the income of any of the partners is based on the income which that partner generates from engagements within **58.2** above or **58.25** below.

'*Relative*' is broadly defined to include a spouse or civil partner (or cohabitant treated as such — as in **58.5**(c) below), parent or child or remoter relation in the direct line, or brother or sister). Most family partnerships are thus potentially within these rules.

In addition, the provisions apply in relation to payments or benefits received or receivable by the worker directly from the partnership, but in a capacity other than as a member of the partnership, if they can reasonably be taken to represent remuneration for services provided by the worker to the client.

[*ITEPA 2003, s 52; FA 2017, Sch 1 paras 4, 15*].

Individuals

Where (exceptionally) the intermediary is an individual, the provisions apply in relation to a payment or benefit if it is received or receivable by the worker directly from the intermediary and can reasonably be taken to represent remuneration for services provided by the worker to the client. [*ITEPA 2003, s 53*].

Overseas intermediaries

There is no requirement that the intermediary be resident or incorporated in the UK. An offshore service company, for example, can fall within these provisions (and see **58.10** below as regards place of business). See also HMRC guidance — as in **58.1** above.

Supplementary

[58.5] For the purposes of the above (and of these provisions generally):

(a) whether a person is an '*associate*' of an individual is construed in accordance with *CTA 2010, s 448* (with the extended meaning of 'spouse or civil partner' at (c) below), except that special rules apply to determine whether an individual is an associate of an employee benefit trust of which he is a beneficiary;

(b) a payment or benefit receivable from a partnership or unincorporated association includes any such payment or benefit to which a person may be entitled in his capacity as a member of the partnership or association;

(c) a payment or benefit provided to a member of an individual's family or household (within *ITEPA 2003, s 721(4)(5)* but treating a cohabiting couple as if they were spouses or civil partners) is treated as provided to the individual; and

(d) anything done by an 'associate' (as defined) of an intermediary is treated as done by the intermediary.

[*ITEPA 2003, ss 60(1)(a) (2)–(6), 61(2)–(4), 721(4)(5); SI 2019 No 1458, Sch 3 para 25(2)*].

The 'deemed employment payment'

[58.6] If, as regards any engagement within **58.2** above, in any tax year:

(i) the intermediary is within these provisions by virtue of **58.4** above;
(ii) the worker (or an 'associate' of his) receives, is entitled to receive, or has rights entitling him to receive, from the intermediary (directly or indirectly) a payment or benefit that is not employment income; and
(iii) (for 2021/22 onwards) the client qualifies as small (see **58.16** below) or does not have a UK connection (see **58.22** below),

the intermediary is deemed to have made to the worker, normally on 5 April in that tax year (though see **58.14** below for exceptions), a payment (a '*deemed employment payment*') the amount of which is computed as in **58.7** below and which is treated as earnings from an employment. Where such payments would be treated as having been made in respect of multiple engagements, a single such payment is deemed to have been made. See **58.11** below as regards the application of PAYE.

The condition in (iii) above is to be ignored in cases where the client is an individual and the services provided are performed otherwise than for the purposes of the client's business. In such cases, therefore, only (i) and (ii) above need to be met for the provisions to apply. Also in (iii) the client is to be treated as not qualifying as small for the tax year if the client is treated as medium or large for that tax year by reason of **58.33** below).

[*ITEPA 2003, s 50; FA 2020, Sch 1 paras 4, 24*].

See **58.5** above for the meaning of 'associate' in relation to an individual and other supplementary provisions.

Computation of deemed employment payment

[58.7] The deemed payment in **58.6** above is computed as follows (and see the supplementary points at **58.8** below).

(1) Take the total of all 'payments' and 'benefits' (see **58.8** below) received by the intermediary in the tax year in respect of engagements falling within **58.6** above by reference to the worker (the '*relevant engagements*') and reduce it by **5%** (see **58.8** below).
Where a payment received by the intermediary has been subjected to deduction of tax at source under the CONSTRUCTION INDUSTRY SCHEME (**20**), it is the gross amount before tax that must be brought into account in arriving at this total.

(2) Add in any 'payments' and 'benefits' (see **58.8** below) received direct by the worker (and see **58.5**(c) above) in that tax year in respect of the relevant engagements, *from anyone other than the intermediary*, that are not chargeable as employment income but would have been if the worker had been employed by the client.

(3) Deduct:
   (a) any expenses met by the intermediary (see below) in that tax year which, if incurred by the worker as an employee of the client, would have been deductible under normal rules — see **28.16** EMPLOYMENT INCOME;
   (b) any capital allowances which on that basis could have been deducted by the worker from employment income under *CAA 2001, s 262* (plant and machinery allowances — see **10.5** CAPITAL ALLOWANCES ON PLANT AND MACHINERY); and
   (c) any contributions made to a registered pension scheme by the intermediary in that tax year for the benefit of the worker which, if made by an employer for the benefit of an employee, would not be regarded as the employee's income for tax purposes — see **57.14** PENSION PROVISION.

(4) Deduct:
   (a) any 'payments' and 'benefits' (see **58.8** below) received in that tax year by the worker from the intermediary and chargeable as employment income in his hands (but excluding anything already deducted under (3)(a) above); and
   (b) any employer's Class 1 and Class 1A NICs (on salary and benefits) payable by the intermediary for that tax year in respect of the worker.

If the result is a negative amount, or is nil, there is no deemed employment payment. In any other case, the deemed employment payment is the amount which, together with employer's NICs thereon, is equal to the result of applying steps (1)–(4) above. In other words, allowance is made at this point for the fact that employer's NICs are chargeable on the deemed payment itself (see Tolley's National Insurance Contributions).

[*ITEPA 2003, ss 54(1)(2), 61(1)*].

There is to be ignored, for the purposes of (1) above, any payment or benefit which is employment income of the worker by virtue of the anti-avoidance rule at **52.27** PARTNERSHIPS whereby the limited liability partnership (LLP) salaried member rules apply in the case of an individual who is not a member of an LLP. [*ITEPA 2003, s 54(1A)*].

For the purposes of (3)(a) above, an intermediary 'meets' an expense on the date it pays the bill. (HMRC guidance — as in **58.1** above). Expenses met by an intermediary include expenses met by the worker and reimbursed by the intermediary and also, in the case of a partnership intermediary of which the worker is a member, expenses met by the worker for and on behalf of the intermediary. In a situation where the intermediary provides a vehicle for the worker, expenses deductible under (3)(a) above include any 'mileage allowance relief' (see **28.91** EMPLOYMENT INCOME) that would have been due to the worker if he had been an employee of the client and had provided the vehicle himself.

This also applies, in the case of a partnership intermediary of which the worker is a member, in a situation where the worker provides the vehicle for the purposes of the partnership business. Any 'approved mileage allowance payments' or 'approved passenger payments' made by the intermediary to the worker and exempt from the charge to tax on EMPLOYMENT INCOME (**28.91**) are deductible under (4)(a) above (if not deductible under (3)(a) above), notwithstanding the said exemption. The duties performed under the relevant engagements are treated, for the purpose of determining the deductibility under (3)(a) above of any travelling expenses (see **28.11**, **28.17** EMPLOYMENT INCOME), as duties of a continuous employment with the intermediary. [*ITEPA 2003, s 54(3)–(7)*].

For notes on the deductibility of travel and subsistence expenses reimbursed to workers in a composite service company or managed service company, see Revenue Tax Bulletin December 2004 pp 1166–1168; and see **47** MANAGED SERVICE COMPANIES.

See the example at **58.9** below.

Supplementary

[58.8] For the purposes of computing the deemed employment payment as in **58.7** above, any amounts received by the intermediary that refer to more than one worker, or partly to a worker and partly to other matters, are to be apportioned on a just and reasonable basis. [*ITEPA 2003, s 54(8)*].

For the purposes of **58.7**(1), (2) and (4) above, a '*payment*' or '*benefit*' means anything that, if received by an employee for performing the duties of an employment, would be earnings from the employment. The amount of a payment or cash benefit is taken to be the amount received. The amount of a non-cash benefit is computed in the same way as if it were earnings of an employment, which means that it will normally, in practice, be computed under the employee benefit rules at **28.20** *et seq.* EMPLOYMENT INCOME. A payment or cash benefit is treated as received when payment is actually made (or a payment is made on account). A non-cash benefit calculated by reference to a period within the tax year is treated as received at the end of that period; otherwise the time of receipt is determined under normal rules (see **28.20** EMPLOYMENT INCOME). [*ITEPA 2003, s 55*].

Where the intermediary is VAT-registered, the amount to be brought into account at **58.7**(1) above is the VAT-exclusive amount, and this applies even where the optional flat-rate scheme is used (though in that case the VAT-exclusive amount is the amount inclusive of output VAT at the normal rate less the flat-rate VAT payable) (Revenue Tax Bulletin April 2003 p 1024).

The 5% deduction

The 5% deduction at **58.7**(1) above is a standard allowance intended to cover the intermediary's running costs. It is given regardless of the actual occurrence or amount of such running costs, and does not have to be justified or supported by records. The limited deductions at **58.7**(3) above, based on actual expenditure, are given in addition to the 5% deduction. The 5% deduction applies purely for the purpose of computing the deemed employment payment under these provisions, and is not deductible in computing the business profits of the intermediary (actual running costs being deductible or not, as the case may be, under normal rules — see **75** TRADING INCOME and see also **58.12** below as regards partnerships). See **58.12** below as regards deductibility of the deemed employment payment itself. Note that the 5% deduction does not apply to public sector engagements (see **58.29** below).

Example

[58.9]

Harry is a systems analyst trading through his own personal service company, ABC Ltd, in which he owns 99% of the ordinary shares. During 2020/21, he is engaged at different times by two independent companies, DEF Ltd and GHJ Ltd (the client companies), in each case under a contract between the client company and ABC Ltd. It is accepted that each engagement is in the nature of employment and is within the IR35 provisions. ABC Ltd is paid £40,000 by DEF Ltd and £20,000 by GHJ Ltd for the services provided by Harry.

For 2020/21, Harry draws a salary of £28,000 from ABC Ltd which is taxed under PAYE and on which employer's NICs of, say, £2,800 are due. He is also provided with a company car on which the taxable benefit is £4,000 and on which Class 1A NICs of, say, £550 are due. ABC Ltd makes pension contributions of £3,100 into a registered pension scheme on Harry's behalf and reimburses motor expenses of £1,500 which, if Harry had been employed directly by the client companies, would have been qualifying travelling expenses within **28.17** EMPLOYMENT INCOME and which do not cover any home-to-work travel (see **28.18** EMPLOYMENT INCOME). ABC Ltd pays a salary of £8,000 to Harry's wife who acts as company secretary and administrator.

The deemed employment payment for 2020/21 is computed, using steps numbered in accordance with **58.7** above, as follows.

		£	£	£
Step (1)	Total amount from relevant engagements			60,000
	Deduct 5%			3,000
				57,000
Step (2)	Not applicable			
Step (3)	*Deduct* (a) Expenses	1,500		
	(b) Not applicable	—		
	(c) Pension contributions	3,100	4,600	
Step (4)	*Deduct* Salary	28,000		
	Benefits	4,000		
	Employer's Class 1 NICs	2,800		
	Employer's Class 1A NICs	550	35,350	39,950
Total				£17,050

Deemed employment payment $£17{,}050 \times \frac{100}{113.8}$ 14,982

Employer's NICs due on deemed payment £14,982 @ 13.8%	2,068
Total as above	£17,050

Note

The salary paid by ABC Ltd to Harry's wife is not deductible in arriving at the deemed employment payment, except to the extent that it, and other expenses of the company, are covered by the 5% deduction at **58.7**(1) above. (The salary may of course be deductible under the normal TRADING INCOME (75) rules in computing ABC Ltd's taxable business profits.)

Tax treatment of deemed employment payment

[58.10] The deemed employment payment is generally treated in the same way as an actual payment of employment income, as if the worker were employed by the intermediary and as if the relevant engagements (see **58.7**(1) above) were undertaken by him in the course of performing the duties of that employment. The PAYE provisions are applied as in **58.11** below. Where:

- the worker is UK resident, and
- the services in question are provided in the UK,

the intermediary is treated as having a place of business in the UK (and is thus obliged to operate PAYE for example — see **53.43** PAY AS YOU EARN) even if this is not, in fact, the case.

To the extent that, by reason of any combination of:

- the worker being resident or domiciled outside the UK or meeting the section 26A test in **28.7** EMPLOYMENT INCOME;
- the client being resident outside the UK; and
- the services in question being provided outside the UK,

the worker would not be chargeable if employed directly by the client, he is not chargeable to tax in respect of the deemed employment payment. (See **28.5**, **28.8** EMPLOYMENT INCOME for the relevant charging provisions.)

In particular, the deemed employment payment counts:

- as taxable earnings for the purpose of deducting qualifying travelling expenses and other necessary expenses incurred by the worker (see **28.16–28.19** EMPLOYMENT INCOME) or mileage allowance relief (see **28.91** EMPLOYMENT INCOME); and
- as relevant UK earnings for registered pension scheme contributions purposes (see **57.12** PENSION PROVISION).

[*ITEPA 2003, ss 56, 218(1)(d)*].

Where the work is carried out outside the UK, and the worker is UK resident, a service company may suffer foreign tax. Where the company's tax liability is insufficient to give full effect to DOUBLE TAX RELIEF (27), HMRC suggest that the balance of foreign tax may be allowed against UK tax (but not NICs) on the deemed employment payment, but only where it is possible to directly link the work in the overseas country and the deemed payment. (HMRC guidance — as in **58.1** above).

For an article, including case studies, on the international issues surrounding the personal service company legislation, concentrating mainly on the National Insurance aspects, see Revenue Tax Bulletin April 2003 pp 1016–1020.

PAYE

[58.11] By virtue of **58.10** above, the intermediary must account for tax under PAY AS YOU EARN (**53**) as if the deemed employment payment to the worker were an actual payment of employment income. Where, as is normally the case, the employment payment is deemed to be made on 5 April in the tax year (see **58.6** above), then, strictly, the total tax, employee's NICs and employer's NICs due in respect of the deemed payment must be paid over to HMRC on or before 19 April following the tax year (as in **53.19** PAY AS YOU EARN), which may leave insufficient time for the amount of the deemed payment to be computed. In practice, HMRC will accept a provisional amount on account provided:

- a provisional calculation is reported on a Full Payment Submission (see **53.22** PAY AS YOU EARN) on or before 5 April;
- the appropriate payment of tax and NICs is made in relation to that Submission;
- the final return in the tax year clearly indicates that IR35 applies;
- the final figures for the deemed employment payment are reported on an Earlier Year Update (see **53.22** PAY AS YOU EARN) submitted on or before 31 January following the tax year; and
- any balance of tax and NICs based on the final figures is paid on or before 31 January in that year.

Interest will be due on the balancing payment but no late payment penalty will be due (www.gov.uk/guidance/ir35-find-out-if-it-applies) Before the introduction of Real Time Information for PAYE, a similar practice applied, but by reference to the Employer's Annual Return Form P35 (see **53.21** PAY AS YOU EARN) followed by a supplementary P35 (HMRC Employment Status Manual ESM3182).

See **58.15** below as regards joint and several liability of multiple intermediaries.

Interaction with construction industry scheme — concession

Where a deemed employment payment is based on amounts received by a company under deduction of tax under the CONSTRUCTION INDUSTRY SCHEME (**20**), the amounts deducted are treated as corporation tax paid in respect of company profits, and are therefore not available for offset against any liability in respect of the deemed employment payment. By concession, where, as a result of such deductions, a company is entitled to a corporation tax repayment for an accounting period which overlaps a tax year for which a deemed employment payment is treated as made, the company may claim to set off the corporation tax repayment against any outstanding tax and NICs due in respect of the deemed employment payment, using 19 April in the following tax year as the effective date of payment for the set-off. Provided that the claim is made by the following 31 January (and is accepted), no interest will be charged on the amount of any late-paid tax and NICs in respect of the deemed employment payment which is matched by the corporation tax repayment. (HMRC ESC C32). See also Revenue Tax Bulletin June 2001 p 861 and HMRC Employment Status Manual ESM3262, 3269–3271.

Computation of intermediary's business profits

[58.12] Subject to the special rules below for partnerships, a deemed employment payment (and related employer's NICs) is an allowable expense in computing the business profits (or losses) of the intermediary for the period of account in which the payment is treated as made (but for no other period of account). [*ITTOIA 2005, s 163; CTA 2009, s 139*].

Partnerships — special rules

The above applies equally where the intermediary is a partnership except that:

(a) the deduction for the deemed employment payment can reduce the partnership profits to nil for tax purposes but it cannot create a trading loss; and
(b) the expenses of the partnership in connection with the relevant engagements (see **58.7**(1) above) for the period of account are deductible only to the extent that they do not exceed the sum of:
  (i) the 5% deduction at **58.7**(1) above; and
  (ii) the deduction at **58.7**(3)(a) above.

[*ITTOIA 2005, s 164; CTA 2009, s 140*].

Cash basis for smaller businesses

Neither *ITTOIA 2005, s 163* nor *s 164* above apply in calculating profits on the cash basis (see **76.14** TRADING INCOME — CASH BASIS FOR SMALLER BUSINESSES).

Relief where dividends etc. paid by intermediary

[58.13] A relief from double taxation is available where a **company** intermediary is treated as making a deemed employment payment in any tax year and also pays a dividend (or otherwise makes a distribution) in that or a subsequent tax year. A claim for relief must be made in writing by the intermediary within five years after 31 January following the tax year in which the dividend is paid. Relief is given by reducing the dividend (not the deemed employment payment) but only if HMRC are satisfied that this is necessary to avoid a double charge to tax. The reduction is made, as far as practicable, by setting the amount of the deemed payment against:

- dividends etc. of the same tax year in priority to those of other years;
- dividends etc. received by the worker before those received by another person; and
- dividends etc. of earlier years before those of later years.

See **1.5** ALLOWANCES AND TAX RATES for taxation of dividends and other distributions generally.

[*ITEPA 2003, s 58; FA 2016, Sch 1 paras 61, 73*].

Earlier date of deemed employment payment in certain cases

[58.14] As stated in **58.6** above, the deemed employment payment is normally treated as made on 5 April in the relevant tax year. If, however, a 'relevant event' occurs in relation to the intermediary in that tax year and before that date, the deemed employment payment is treated as made immediately before that event, or, if there is more than one, immediately before the first of them. The fact that the deemed payment is treated as made before the end of the tax year does not affect the way in which it is computed and the receipts and other matters that are taken into account.

In relation to a **company** intermediary, any of the following is a '*relevant event*':

- where the worker is a member of the company (which normally means a shareholder), his ceasing to be a member;
- where the worker holds an office with the company (for example, as a director), his ceasing to hold that office;
- where the worker is an employee of the company, his ceasing to be an employee;
- the company ceasing to trade.

In relation to a **partnership** intermediary, any of the following is a '*relevant event*':

- the dissolution of the partnership or cessation of the partnership trade;
- a partner ceasing to act as such;
- where the worker is an employee of the partnership, his ceasing to be an employee.

Where the intermediary is an **individual** and the worker is employed by him, a '*relevant event*' occurs if the worker ceases to be so employed.

[*ITEPA 2003, s 57*].

Multiple intermediaries

[58.15] Where, in the case of an engagement within **58.2** above, the arrangements (as in **58.2**(c) above) involve one or more intermediaries within **58.4** above, then, except as below, these provisions apply separately in relation to each such intermediary.

Where a payment or other benefit has been made or provided, directly or indirectly, by one such intermediary to another in respect of the engagement, the amount taken into account at **58.7**(1) or (2) above (computation of deemed employment payment) in relation to any intermediary is to be reduced as necessary so as to avoid double-counting.

All such intermediaries are jointly and severally liable to account for PAY AS YOU EARN (53) on a deemed employment payment treated as made by any of them in respect of the engagement in question, or in respect of multiple engagements which include the engagement in question, except that an intermediary is excepted from such liability if has not received any payment or benefit in respect of the engagement(s).

[*ITEPA 2003, s 59*].

Meaning of 'small' for 2021/22 onwards

[58.16] The provisions at **58.17–58.19** apply for 2021/22 onwards, subject to a connected persons rule at **58.20** below, to determine if the client qualifies as 'small' for a tax year. If so, the engagement will potentially be within the long-standing IR35 provisions at **58.2–58.15** above. If not, the engagement will potentially be within the provisions at **58.23–58.37** below, unless the client does not have a UK connection (see **58.22** below).

Different types of client are considered at **58.17–58.19** as follows:

58.17 — Companies;
58.18 — LLPs and other undertakings;
58.19 — Other persons.

The client has a duty to state, on request, whether it qualifies as small for a tax year (see **58.21** below).

When a company qualifies as small

[58.17] A company qualifies as small for a tax year if either:

(a) the company's first financial year is not relevant to the tax year; or
(b) the 'small companies regime' applies to the company for its last financial year that is relevant to the tax year.

For these purposes, a financial year of a company is relevant to a tax year if the period for filing the company's accounts and reports for the financial year ends before the beginning of the tax year. The above conditions mean that a company is assumed to be small for its first financial year if the period for filing for that year does not end before the beginning of the tax year. It continues to qualify as small until such time as the accounts due before the start of the tax year in question relate to a financial year in which the small companies regime does not apply.

[*ITEPA 2003, s 60A; FA 2020, Sch 1 paras 5, 24*].

Small companies regime

Under company law (which is applied here), the '*small companies regime*' applies to a company for a financial year in relation to which the company qualifies as small under *Companies Act 2006, ss 382, 383* and is not excluded from the regime by *Companies Act 2006, s 384* (which relates mainly to financial and insurance companies but which also excludes *any* public company from the regime).

Single companies

For the purposes of the small companies regime, a company qualifies as small for a financial year if the qualifying conditions below are met in that year. A company also qualifies as small for a subsequent financial year if the qualifying conditions are met in that year. In relation to any financial year other than the first, where on its balance sheet date a company ceases to meet the qualifying conditions, its qualification as a small company is affected only if this occurs in two consecutive financial years; it then ceases to be small for the second of those years but not the first.

The qualifying conditions are met by a company in a year in which it satisfies two or more of the following requirements:

Turnover	Not more than £10.2 million
Balance Sheet Total	Not more than £5.1 million
Number of Employees	Not more than 50

The above turnover figure is proportionately adjusted for a financial year not equal to twelve months. The balance sheet total means the aggregate of the amounts shown as assets in the company's balance sheet. The number of employees means the average number of persons employed by the company in the year, determined by reference to monthly totals.

Parent companies

A *parent company* qualifies as a small company for a financial year only if the group headed by it qualifies as a small group. The qualification rules for a small group are similar to those for a small company, and apply by reference to financial years of the parent. The qualifying conditions are met by a group in a year in which it satisfies two or more of the following requirements:

Aggregate turnover	Not more than £10.2 million net (or £12.2 million gross)
Aggregate Balance Sheet Total	Not more than £5.1 million net (or £6.1 million gross)
Aggregate Number of Employees	Not more than 50

'Net' means after any set-offs and other adjustments made to eliminate group transactions. 'Gross' means without those set-offs and other adjustments. A company may satisfy any relevant requirement on the basis of either the net or the gross figure. The figures to be taken into account for each subsidiary are those included in its accounts for the relevant financial year. If the subsidiary's financial year ends with that of the parent company, that is the relevant financial year. If not, the relevant financial year is the financial year ending last before the end of the financial year of the parent. If the figures cannot be obtained on this basis without disproportionate expense or undue delay, the latest available figures are to be taken.

[*Companies Act 2006, ss 381–384*].

Joint ventures

The following applies in determining for the above purposes whether the small companies regime applies to a company for a financial year in a case where:

- at the end of the financial year the company is jointly controlled by two or more other persons; and
- one or more of those other persons are undertakings (the '*joint venturer undertakings*').

If the company is not a parent company, the company and the joint venturer undertakings are to be treated as constituting a group of which the company is the parent company. If the company is a parent company anyway, the joint venturer undertakings are to be treated as members of the group headed by the company. The expression 'jointly controlled' is to be construed in accordance with those provisions of international accounting standards which relate to joint ventures.

[*ITEPA 2003, s 60B; FA 2020, Sch 1 paras 5, 24*].

Subsidiaries

A company does not qualify as small for a tax year by reason of the condition at (b) above (that the small companies regime applies to the company) being met if:

(i) the company is a member of a group at the end of its last financial year that is relevant to the tax year;
(ii) the company is not the parent undertaking of that group at the end of that financial year; and
(iii) the undertaking that is the parent undertaking of that group at that time does not qualify as small in relation to its last financial year that is relevant to the tax year.

For these purposes, a financial year of a company is relevant to a tax year if the period for filing the company's accounts and reports for the financial year ends before the beginning of that tax year. A financial year of an undertaking that is not a company is relevant to a tax year if it ends at least nine months before the beginning of the tax year. Where the parent undertaking referred to in (iii) above is not a company, *Companies Act 2006, ss 382, 383* (see above) have effect with appropriate modifications for determining whether the parent undertaking qualifies as small.

[*ITEPA 2003, s 60C; FA 2020, Sch 1 paras 5, 24*].

When an LLP or other undertaking qualifies as small

[58.18] The rules at 58.17 above apply in relation to 'relevant undertakings' as they apply in relation to a company, subject to any necessary modifications. The term '*relevant undertakings*' comprises limited liability partnerships (LLPs), unregistered companies and overseas companies. [*ITEPA 2003, s 60D; FA 2020, Sch 1 paras 5, 24*].

An '*undertaking*' is defined by *Companies Act 2006, s 1161* as: (i) a body corporate or partnership; or (ii) an unincorporated association carrying on a trade or business with or without a view to profit. An undertaking that is neither a company nor a relevant undertaking (as above) qualifies as small for a tax year if either:

- the undertaking's first financial year is not relevant to the tax year; or
- the undertaking's turnover for its last financial year that is relevant to the tax year is not more than £10.2 million.

For these purposes a financial year of an undertaking is relevant to a tax year if it ends at least nine months before the beginning of the tax year. 'Turnover', in relation to an undertaking, means the amounts derived from the provision of goods or services after the deduction of trade discounts, VAT and any other taxes based on those amounts.

[*ITEPA 2003, s 60E; FA 2020, Sch 1 paras 5, 24*].

When other persons qualify as small

[58.19] A person who is not a company, relevant undertaking (as in **58.18** above) or other undertaking qualifies as small for a tax year if the person's turnover (defined as in **58.18**) for the last calendar year before the tax year is not more than £10.2 million. [*ITEPA 2003, s 60F; FA 2020, Sch 1 paras 5, 24*].

When a client qualifies as small — connected persons rule

[58.20] A special rule applies where it is necessary, in determining whether a person (P) qualifies as small for a tax year, to establish the amount of P's turnover for a financial year, and at the end of that financial year P is 'connected' with one or more other persons. Where, as in **58.19** above, a person is not a company, relevant undertaking or other undertaking, references to a financial year are to be taken as references to a calendar year.

Whether persons are '*connected*' is determined in accordance with **19 CONNECTED PERSONS**. However, where P is a company or relevant undertaking (see **58.18** above) and at the end of the financial year P is a member of a group, P is treated for these purposes as not being connected with any person that is a member of that group.

P's turnover for the financial year is to be taken to be the sum of P's own turnover for the financial year and the 'relevant turnover' of each of the persons connected with P. The '*relevant turnover*' of a connected person means:

- in a case where the connected person is a company, relevant undertaking or other undertaking (see **58.18** above), its turnover for its last financial year that is relevant to the tax year; and
- in a case where the connected person is not a company, relevant undertaking or other undertaking, the turnover of the connected person for the last calendar year ending before the tax year.

For these purposes, a financial year of a company or relevant undertaking is relevant to the tax year if the period for filing accounts and reports for the financial year ends before the beginning of the tax year. A financial year of any other undertaking is relevant to the tax year if it ends more than nine months before the beginning of the tax year.

'Turnover' is defined as in 58.18 above.

[*ITEPA 2003, s 60G; FA 2020, Sch 1 paras 5, 24*].

Client's duty to state whether it is small

[58.21] In the case of an engagement that meets conditions (a) to (c) at 58.2 above, the client may receive from its agent (ie a person with whom it entered into a contract as part of the arrangements mentioned in 58.2(c)) or from the worker (see 58.2(a)) a request to state whether, in the client's opinion, the client qualifies as small for a specified tax year. The client must provide a statement of its opinion to the person making the request. The client must provide this within 45 days of receiving the request or, if later, by the beginning of the 45 days immediately preceding the tax year specified in the request. If it fails to do so, the duty to provide the statement is enforceable by an injunction or, in Scotland, by an order for specific performance. [*ITEPA 2003, s 60H; FA 2020, Sch 1 paras 5, 24*].

Meaning of 'UK connection' for 2021/22 onwards

[58.22] For the purpose of determining whether the client has a UK connection for a tax year, a person has such a connection if (and only if) immediately before the beginning of the tax year the person either is resident in the UK or has a permanent establishment in the UK. The term 'permanent establishment' is to be read (by virtue of *ITA 2007, s 1007A*) in accordance with *CTA 2010, ss 1141–1153* (as if references to a company were references to the person in a case where the person is not a company). [*ITEPA 2003, s 60I; FA 2020, Sch 1 paras 5, 24*].

The broad rule, under *CTA 2010, s 1141*, is that a company has a permanent establishment in a territory if (and only if): (i) it has a fixed place of business there through which the business of the company is wholly or partly carried on; or (ii) an agent acting on behalf of the company has, and habitually exercises there, authority to do business on behalf of the company.

Services provided to public sector or to medium/large clients

[58.23] For 2017/18 onwards, the provisions at 58.25–58.37 below have effect, instead of those at 58.2–58.15 above, with respect to the provision of services through an intermediary to a public sector body such as a Government department, NHS trust or local authority. Broadly, the responsibility for determining whether or not the IR35 rules apply, and for operating those rules where they do apply, is shifted from the intermediary to the public sector body (or its agency). This includes making deductions for income tax and NICs and accounting for them to HMRC.

As is the case for the main IR35 rules (see **58.1** above), the operation of *ITEPA 2003, ss 44–47* (workers supplied by agencies — see **28.96** EMPLOYMENT INCOME) is not affected by these provisions, and nothing in these provisions applies to a payment or transfer subject to deduction of tax under *ITA 2007, s 966(3)* or *(4)* (payments to non-resident entertainers and sportsmen — see **50.11** NON-RESIDENTS).

[*ITEPA 2003, s 61K; FA 2017, Sch 1 paras 9, 16; FA 2020, Sch 1 paras 8, 9, 25*].

See the guidance signposted at www.gov.uk/topic/business-tax/ir35, and the detailed guidance at HMRC Employment Status Manual ESM10000.

Extension of provisions to private sector

In relation to deemed direct payments (see **58.27** below) treated as made on or after **6 April 2021**, these provisions and those at **58.25–58.37** below have effect also with respect to the provision of services through an intermediary to any person (not being a public sector body) who is medium or large (i.e. who does not qualify as small — see **58.16** above) and has a UK connection (see **58.22** above) for a tax year. See also the **transitional provisions** at **58.24** below.

HMRC have set out their compliance approach to the extension of the rules to private sector engagements (HMRC Employment Status Manual ESM10036 (draft)). They will take a light-touch approach to penalties; penalties will not be charged for inaccuracies in the first twelve months of the extended regime, unless there is evidence of deliberate non-compliance. HMRC also commit to not using information resulting from the extended provisions to open a new compliance check into an intermediary for tax years prior to 2021/22, unless there is reason to suspect fraud or criminal behaviour.

Public sector bodies

The legislation uses the term 'public authority' rather than 'public sector body', and this is defined mainly by reference to *Freedom of Information Act 2000* (and Scottish equivalent) but with the addition of the House of Commons, the House of Lords and the Welsh and Northern Irish Assemblies and with the specific exclusion of private sector retail businesses, such as high street pharmacies and opticians, who provide services on behalf of the National Health Service. Various bodies dealing with security matters are added to the definition in relation to deemed direct payments treated as made on or after 6 April 2021, as are companies connected to public authorities within the definition. [*ITEPA 2003, s 61L; FA 2017, Sch 1 paras 9, 16; FA 2020, Sch 1 paras 10, 25*]. In practice, the term embraces, for example, Government departments, NHS trusts and local authorities.

Simon's Taxes. See **E1.1040–E1.1045**.

Transition on extension of provisions to private sector

[58.24] There are transitional provisions as set out below in connection with the extension to the private sector of the provisions at **58.23** above and at **58.25–58.37** below. Broadly these transitional provisions remove services performed by the worker before 6 April 2021 from the extended rules.

For the purposes of (1) and (2) below the question of whether the client is a public authority is determined without regard to the amendments made to the definition of public authority with effect in relation to deemed direct payments treated as made on or after 6 April 2021 (see **58.23** above).

(1) Where the client is not a public authority and a chain payment (see **58.27** below) is made on or after 6 April 2021 that can reasonably be taken to be for services performed by the worker before 6 April 2021, the chain payment is to be disregarded in applying the extended rules. [*FA 2020, Sch 1 para 30*].

(2) Where the client is not a public authority and one or more 'qualifying chain payments' are made in 2021/22 or a subsequent tax year to the intermediary, the long-standing IR35 rules at **58.2–58.15** above (as well as the extended rules) apply to the engagement for the tax year in question, but as if:
   - no amendments had been made to those long-standing rules to allow for the extension of the public body rules to the private sector; and
   - the qualifying chain payments received by the intermediary in the tax year in question were the only payments and benefits received by the intermediary in that tax year in respect of the engagement.

   A chain payment (see **58.27** below) made to the intermediary is a '*qualifying chain payment*' if it can reasonably be taken to be for services performed by the worker before 6 April 2021.

   A chain payment made to the intermediary is also a '*qualifying chain payment*' if:
   - another chain payment (the '*earlier payment*') was made before 6 April 2021 to a person other than the intermediary;
   - the earlier payment can reasonably be taken to be for the same services as the chain payment now made to the intermediary; and
   - the person who made the earlier payment would, if the extended rules had then applied, have been treated under **58.27** below as making a deemed direct payment to the worker at the time of making the earlier payment.

   [*FA 2020, Sch 1 para 31*].

(3) Where a chain payment is made that can reasonably be taken to be for services of the worker performed during a period beginning before and ending on or after 6 April 2021, it is to be treated, in applying (1) and (2) above, as if it were two separate chain payments. The amount or value of the actual payment is apportioned on a just and reasonable basis for this purpose between services performed before 6 April 2021 and services performed on or after that date. [*FA 2020, Sch 1 para 32*].

Services provided through an intermediary

[58.25] The provisions referred to at **58.23** above apply in relation to an engagement where the following conditions are all present:

(a) an individual (the worker) personally performs, or is under an obligation personally to perform, services for another person (the client);

(b) the services are provided not under a contract directly between worker and client but under arrangements involving a third party (the '*intermediary*') to which these provisions apply (see **58.26** below);

(c) the client is a public authority or (in relation to deemed direct payments treated as made on or after 6 April 2021 — see **58.27** below) is a person who, for one or more tax years during which the arrangements mentioned in (b) above have effect, does not qualify as small (see **58.16** above) and has a UK connection (see **58.22** above); and

(d)
- if the services had been provided under a direct contract as mentioned in (b) above, the worker would have fallen to be categorised for income tax purposes as an employee of the client (see **58.3** above and **58.38** below) or the holder of an office under the client; or
- the worker is an office holder who holds that office under the client, and the services relate to the office.

However, notwithstanding anything above, the provisions referred to at **58.23** above do not apply if the client is an individual and the services are provided otherwise than for the purposes of the client's trade or business.

The term 'intermediary' in (b) above can refer to a company or an individual or to a partnership or unincorporated body of which the worker is a member. In applying the test at (d) above, i.e. whether or not the worker would have been an employee if engaged directly, the circumstances to be taken into account include the terms on which the services are provided, having regard to the terms of contracts forming part of the arrangements under which the services are provided. Holding office as statutory auditor of the client does not count as holding office under the client.

[*ITEPA 2003, s 61M; FA 2017, Sch 1 paras 9, 16; FA 2020, Sch 1 paras 11, 25*].

Intermediaries to which these provisions apply

[58.26] The provisions referred to at **58.23** above apply only if the intermediary meets the relevant conditions below.

Where the intermediary is a **company**, it meets the conditions if it is not an associated company of the client that is associated by reason of both the intermediary and the client being under the control (within *ITA 2007, s 995*) of the worker (or of the worker and other persons), and:

(a) (in relation to deemed direct payments, as in **58.27** below, treated as made before 6 April 2021) the worker has a 'material interest' (defined as in **58.4** above) in the intermediary; or

(b) (in relation to deemed direct payments treated as made on or after 6 April 2021) the worker either has a material interest in the intermediary, or has received a chain payment (see **58.27**) from the intermediary, or has rights which entitle (or which in any circumstances would entitle) the worker to receive such a chain payment.

[*ITEPA 2003, ss 61N(1)(9), 61O, 61X, 719; FA 2017, Sch 1 paras 9, 16; FA 2020, Sch 1 paras 14, 25*].

Where the intermediary is a **partnership**, it meets the conditions if:

- the worker is a member of the partnership;
- the provision of the services is by the worker as a member of the partnership; and
- the circumstances at **58.4**(A), (B) or (C) above apply in relation to the partnership.

[*ITEPA 2003, ss 61N(1)(10), 61P; FA 2017, Sch 1 paras 9, 16*].

The intermediary also meets the conditions if, exceptionally, it is an **individual**. [*ITEPA 2003, s 61N(1)(11); FA 2017, Sch 1 paras 9, 16*].

In certain cases where the worker fails to provide information, the relevant conditions are treated as being met whether or not they are, in fact, met. See **58.35** below.

The 'deemed direct payment'

[58.27] If, as regards any engagement within **58.25** above, a 'chain payment' is made, there is treated as having been made to the worker (and as having been received by him) a payment (the '*deemed direct payment*') which represents earnings from an employment. A '*chain payment*' is a payment of money, a transfer of money's worth, or the providing of a benefit, that can reasonably be taken to be for the worker's services to the client. Where a payment, money's worth or benefit can reasonably be taken to be for both the worker's services to the client and for something else, it must be apportioned on a just and reasonable basis, and only so much of it as is for the worker's services to the client is a chain payment.

In order to determine who has made the deemed direct payment, one must identify a chain of two or more persons. The highest person in the chain will be the client and the lowest is the intermediary. Where the client pays the intermediary direct, there will be no other person in the chain. In other cases, one must identify and include each person in the chain who makes a chain payment to the person immediately below them in the chain. This might, for example, include a recruiting agency through which the client engages. The person (the '*fee-payer*') treated as making the deemed direct payment to the worker is the lowest person in the chain other than the intermediary. The deemed direct payment is treated as made at the same time as the chain payment is made by the fee-payer. These provisions apply to deemed direct payments treated as made on or after 6 April 2017, and they do so apply even if the chain payment related to services provided by the worker before that date.

With effect in relation to deemed direct payments treated as made on or after 6 April 2021, and if the client is not a public authority, there is an overriding rule that a person is to be treated as making a deemed direct payment to the worker only if the chain payment made by that person is made in a tax year for which the client does not qualify as small (see **58.16** above) and has a UK connection (see **58.22** above).

Unless and until the client gives a 'status determination statement' (see **58.28** below) to the worker, with effect in relation to deemed direct payments treated as made on or after 6 April 2021, it is the client (and no-one else) who is treated as making the deemed direct payment, and that payment is treated as made at the same time as the chain payment is made by the client.

The following applies if:

- the client is not the fee-payer;
- the fee-payer is not a 'qualifying person'; and
- (with effect in relation to deemed direct payments treated as made on or after 6 April 2021) the client has given a status determination statement (see **58.28** below) to the worker.

If there is no qualifying person in the chain in between the client and the intermediary, it is the client who is treated as making the deemed direct payment. Otherwise, the lowest qualifying person in the chain in between the client and the intermediary is treated as making the deemed direct payment.

A '*qualifying person*' is a person:

(a) who is resident in the UK or has a place of business there;
(b) who is not a person who is controlled by (i) the worker, alone or with one or more associates (within *ITEPA 2003, s 60*), or (ii) an associate of the worker, with or without other associates;
(c) who, if a company, is not one in which a 'material interest' (defined as in **58.4** above) is held by (i) the worker, alone or with one or more associates, or (ii) an associate of the worker, with or without other associates; and
(d) (with effect in relation to deemed direct payments treated as made on or after 6 April 2021) who has been given by the person immediately above them in the chain the status determination statement (see **58.28** below) given by the client to the worker.

[*ITEPA 2003, ss 61N(1)–(8)(8A)(12), 61X; FA 2017, Sch 1 paras 9, 16; FA 2020, Sch 1 paras 12, 25*].

Fraudulent documents

If the worker provides any person with a fraudulent document intended to constitute evidence that an engagement is outside these provisions, liability to account for income tax and NICs on the deemed direct payment is transferred to the worker. This applies equally where the document is provided by a person connected with the worker (within **19** CONNECTED PERSONS) or, in a case where the intermediary is a company, an office holder in that company.

[*ITEPA 2003, s 61V; FA 2017, Sch 1 paras 9, 16*].

Status determination statements

[58.28] Status determination statements have effect as in **58.27** above in relation to deemed direct payments treated as made on or after **6 April 2021**. A '*status determination statement*' is a statement by the client to the effect that the client has concluded that the condition in **58.25**(d) (employment status of the worker) is met, or is not met. in the case of the engagement. The statement must explain the reasons for the conclusion. If the conclusion is that the condition is not met, the fact that this may be incorrect does not prevent the statement being a status determination statement. However, in all cases, a statement is not a status determination statement if the client fails to take reasonable care in coming to the conclusion stated. [*ITEPA 2003, s 61NA; FA 2017, Sch 1 paras 9, 16; FA 2020, Sch 1 paras 13, 25*].

In all the references in **58.27** above to the giving of status determination statements, it does not matter whether the statement is given before 6 April 2021 or on or after that date. [*FA 2020, Sch 1 para 33*].

Computation of deemed direct payment

[58.29] The deemed direct payment in **58.27** above is computed as follows.

(1) Identify the amount or value of the chain payment made by the person treated as making the deemed direct payment.

(2) Add back any tax deducted at source from the payment (as in **58.30** below).

(3) Deduct so much of the chain payment as represents either VAT or the direct cost to the intermediary of materials used (or to be used) in the performance of the services.

(4) Deduct, at the option of the person treated as making the deemed direct payment, so much of the amount in (1) above as represents expenses met by the intermediary that would have been deductible from taxable earnings if the worker had been employed by the client and the expenses had been met by the worker out of earnings. These may include expenses met by the worker and reimbursed by the intermediary. Where the intermediary is a partnership of which the worker is a member, they may include expenses met by the worker for and on behalf of the partnership. The fixed 5% deduction in **58.7**(1) above is *not* available.

If the resulting amount is negative, or is nil, there is no deemed direct payment. In any other case, the resulting amount is the amount of the deemed direct payment.

If the amount or value of the chain payment is increased because its recipient is to bear the cost of amounts due under PAYE or NICs regulations in respect of the deemed direct payment, the amount or value to be included in Step (1) above is whatever would be the amount or value of the chain payment if that cost were not being passed on to the recipient in this way.

There is to be ignored, for the purposes of (1) above, any part of the chain payment which is employment income of the worker by virtue of the anti-avoidance rule at **52.27** PARTNERSHIPS whereby the limited liability partnership (LLP) salaried member rules apply in the case of an individual who is not a member of an LLP.

[*ITEPA 2003, s 61Q; FA 2017, Sch 1 paras 9, 16*].

Tax treatment of deemed direct payment

[58.30] The deemed direct payment is generally treated in the same way for tax purposes (and, in particular, PAYE purposes) as an actual payment of employment income, as if the worker were employed by the person treated as making the deemed direct payment and as if the services in question were performed, or to be performed, by the worker in the course of performing the duties of the employment. Where the intermediary is a partnership or unincorporated association, the deemed direct payment is treated as received by the worker in his personal capacity and not as income of the partnership or association.

To the extent that, by reason of any combination of:

- the worker being resident or domiciled outside the UK or meeting the section 26A test in **28.7** EMPLOYMENT INCOME;
- the client being resident outside, or not resident in, the UK; and
- the services being provided outside the UK,

the worker would not be chargeable if employed directly by the client, he is not chargeable to tax in respect of the deemed direct payment. (See **28.5**, **28.8** EMPLOYMENT INCOME for the relevant charging provisions.) [*ITEPA 2003, s 61R; FA 2017, Sch 1 paras 9, 16; FA 2020, Sch 1 paras 15, 25*].

See **58.31** below as regards recovery by HMRC of outstanding PAYE debt.

In relation to deemed direct payments (see **58.27** above) treated as made before 6 April 2021, where:

- the client is the person treated as making the deemed direct payment;
- the worker is UK resident;
- the services in question are provided in the UK; and
- the client is neither UK resident nor has a place of business in the UK,

the client is treated as UK resident for the above purposes (so that it must operate PAYE).

Deduction of tax at source

Where, by virtue of the above, the person treated as making the deemed direct payment is required to account to HMRC for tax under PAYE, that person may deduct an equivalent amount from the chain payment in question. Where the chain payment is treated as increased because its recipient is to bear the cost of amounts due under PAYE or NICs regulations (see **58.29** above), the amount that may be deducted from it is limited to any excess of the amount due to HMRC over the amount of that increase.

Where a person in the chain other than the intermediary receives a chain payment from which an amount has been deducted as above, that person may deduct the same amount when making the equivalent payment to a person further down the chain.

[*ITEPA 2003, s 61S; FA 2017, Sch 1 paras 9, 16*].

On and after 11 May 2020, where a payment included in an RTI return (see **53.22** PAY AS YOU EARN) is a payment in respect of an engagement that meets the conditions in **58.25** above, the return must include an indicator of that fact. [*SI 2003 No 2682, Sch A1 para 22E; SI 2020 No 373*].

Recovery of PAYE

[58.31] The Commissioners for HMRC may by regulations make provision for the recovery of a 'deemed employer PAYE debt' from a 'relevant person'. A '*deemed employer PAYE debt*' is an amount:

- that a person (the '*deemed employer*' is liable to pay under PAYE in consequence of being treated under **58.27** above as having made a deemed direct payment to a worker; and
- that an HMRC officer considers there is no realistic prospect of recovering from the deemed employer within a reasonable period.

A '*relevant person*' is a person who is not the deemed employer and who is:

- the highest person in the chain identified in **58.27** above (the client) in determining that the deemed employer is to be treated as having made the deemed direct payment; or
- the second highest person in that chain (the '*first agency*') and is a qualifying person (as in **58.27**) at the time the deemed employer is treated as having made the deemed direct payment.

Late payment interest (see **43.2** LATE PAYMENT INTEREST AND PENALTIES) will apply on and after 6 April 2021 to amounts payable or paid to HMRC under the above-mentioned regulations.

[*ITEPA 2003, s 688AA; FA 2020, Sch 1 paras 19, 29*].

Further information on the forthcoming regulations is given in a letter from the Financial Secretary to the Treasury to the Public Bill Committee, regarding the 2020 Finance Bill clauses that introduce the power to make secondary legislation, at www.gov.uk/government/publications/finance-bill-2020-public-bill-committee. The regulations will allow for the recovery of unpaid PAYE debts from other persons within the labour supply chain. HMRC's intention is to first seek to recover any unpaid tax liabilities from the first agency where this agency is UK based. Where HMRC consider there is no realistic prospect of recovering the debt from the first agency, they will seek to recover it from the client.

The regulations will require HMRC to issue a recovery notice when seeking to recover the unpaid liability from the client or first agency. There are two sets of circumstances in which HMRC will issue a recovery notice. The first is where they have issued a determination under *SI 2003 No 2682, Reg 80* (see **53.19** PAY AS YOU EARN) to the deemed employer and the outstanding tax remains unpaid. The second is where HMRC would have issued such a determination, but are unable to do so because of the liquidation, dissolution or other incapacity of the deemed employer. The regulations will provide for appeal rights in relation to a recovery notice. However, clients and first agencies will not be able to appeal in relation to the existence of the underlying PAYE debt if that matter has previously been the subject of an appeal that has been determined.

Client-led status disagreement process after 5 April 2021

[58.32] The following rules apply in relation to deemed direct payments (see **58.27** above) treated as made on or after **6 April 2021**. See **58.34** below for earlier rules.

If, before the final chain payment (see **58.27** above) is made in the case of an engagement within these provisions (see **58.25**), the worker or the 'deemed employer' makes representations to the client that the conclusion contained in a status determination statement (see **58.28** above) is incorrect, the client must either:

- give a statement to the worker or (as the case may be) the deemed employer, stating that the client has considered the representations and has decided that the conclusion in the status determination statement is correct, and giving the reasons for that decision; or
- give a new status determination statement to the worker and the deemed employer, giving a different conclusion to the one in the previous status determination statement, stating the date from which the client considers that the new conclusion became correct, and stating that the previous status determination statement is withdrawn

The '*deemed employer*' is the person who, assuming the intermediary meets the relevant condition at **58.26** above, would be treated by virtue of **60.19** above as making a deemed direct payment to the worker on the making of a chain payment.

If the client fails to comply with the above duty before the end of the period of 45 days beginning with the date the client receives the representations, then, from the end of that period until the duty is complied with, the same consequences ensue as if the client had not yet given a status determination statement to the worker, i.e. it is the client who is treated as making the deemed direct payment, and that payment is treated as made at the same time as the chain payment is made by the client (see **58.27** above). If the representations to the client were made before 6 April 2021, the client has a period of 45 days beginning with 6 April 2021 in which to comply with the above duty; apart from that, it is of no consequence whether the representations were made before 6 April 2021 or on or after that date.

A new status determination statement given as above to the deemed employer is treated for the purposes of **58.27**(d) above as having been given to the deemed employer by the person immediately above the deemed employer in the chain.

[*ITEPA 2003, s 61T; FA 2017, Sch 1 paras 9, 16; FA 2020, Sch 1 paras 16, 25, 34*].

Client's duty to withdraw status determination statement

[58.33] The following rules apply in relation to deemed direct payments (see **58.27** above) treated as made on or after **6 April 2021**.

If the client (not being a public authority) has given a status determination statement to the worker, the 'client's agent' or both, and the client qualifies as small for a tax year beginning after the status determination statement is given, the client must give a statement to the effect that it qualifies as small for the tax year and that the status determination statement is withdrawn with effect from the beginning of the tax year. The statement must be given before the beginning of the tax year in question. It must be given to the worker if the status determination statement was given to the worker and/or to the 'deemed employer' (see **58.32** above) if the status determination statement was given to the client's agent. '*Client's agent*' means a person with whom the client entered into a contract as part of the arrangements mentioned in **58.25**(b) above.

If the client fails to comply with the above duty, the client is treated as medium or large for the tax year, and it is the client who is treated as making the deemed direct payment, and that payment is treated as made at the same time as the chain payment is made by the client (see **58.27** above).

[*ITEPA 2003, s 61TA; FA 2017, Sch 1 paras 9, 16; FA 2020, Sch 1 paras 16, 25*].

Information to be provided by client — position before 6 April 2021

[58.34] The rules set out below apply in relation to deemed direct payments (see **58.27** above) treated as made before 6 April 2021. In relation to deemed direct payments treated as made on or after 6 April 2021, those rules are replaced by status determination statements in **58.27** above and by the client-led status disagreement process at **58.32** above.

Where the conditions in **58.25**(a)–(c) above are met (i.e. an individual performs services for a client via an intermediary to which these provisions apply), and a person as part of the arrangements mentioned in **58.25**(b) enters into a contract with the client, the client must inform that person (either within the contract or otherwise) of its conclusion as to whether or not the condition in **58.25**(d) (employment status of the worker) is met. The client must provide the information on or before the time the contract is entered into or, if the services begin to be performed at a later time, before that later time. There is an exception for contracts entered into before 6 April 2017; in such a case the client must provide the information on or before the date of the first payment made under the contract on or after 6 April 2017.

Once the above information has been provided, the client must, on written request by the person in question, provide a written response to any questions raised by that person about the client's reasons for reaching its conclusion. The response must be provided within 30 days after the request is received.

If in the case of any contract the client:

- fails to provide the required information within the time allowed; or
- fails to provide a response to questions within the time allowed; or
- provides the information but has failed to take reasonable care in coming to its conclusion,

then, not withstanding the chain identified in **58.27** above, it is the client who is treated as making deemed direct payments to the worker.

[*ITEPA 2003, s 61T (as originally enacted); FA 2017, Sch 1 paras 9, 16; FA 2020, Sch 1 paras 16, 25*].

Information to be provided by worker

[58.35] In the case of an engagement potentially within 58.25 above, depending on whether or not the intermediary in the case is one to which these provisions apply (see 58.26 above), the worker must inform the 'potential deemed employer' whether or not the intermediary is such an intermediary. If he fails to do so, the intermediary is treated as one to which these provisions do apply, so that the engagement is brought within 58.25. The '*potential deemed employer*' is the person who would potentially be treated as making a deemed direct payment to the worker. [*ITEPA 2003, s 61U; FA 2017, Sch 1 paras 9, 16*].

Effect on payment by the intermediary to the worker

[58.36] Although the deemed direct payment is treated as made to, and received by, the worker, the chain payment giving rise to it will actually have been received by the intermediary. There is potential double taxation where:

- the worker receives any payment or benefit (the '*end-of-line remuneration*') from the intermediary which can reasonably be taken to represent remuneration for his services to another person ('*the client*');
- a deemed direct payment has been treated as made to the worker in respect of those same services; and
- the cost of the PAYE deductions on the deemed direct payment has been borne (by deduction at source or otherwise) by the recipient of the chain payment in question,

as the payment made by the intermediary to the worker is from income already subjected to PAYE. In such a case, the intermediary and the worker may treat the end-of-line remuneration as reduced (but not below nil) by the amount of the deemed direct payment (as computed in 58.29 above).

In addition, the intermediary and the worker may treat the end-of-line remuneration as reduced by:

- any plant or machinery capital allowances on expenditure incurred by the intermediary that would have been deductible from employment income if the worker had been employed by the client and had incurred the expenditure himself; and
- the amount of any excess contributions made, in the same tax year as the end-of-line remuneration, by the intermediary to a registered pension scheme for the benefit of the worker that if made by an employer for the benefit of an employee would not be chargeable to tax as the employee's income. Pension contributions are excess contributions if they cannot be deducted at Step 3(c) of 58.7 above (computation of deemed employment payment) because to do so would leave a negative amount (and for this purpose the deductions at Step 3(c) are made after those at Step 3(a) and (b)).

All the above reductions can be made regardless of whether the end-of-line remuneration is earnings of the worker or is a dividend or other distribution of the intermediary or takes some other form.

[*ITEPA 2003, s 61W; FA 2017, Sch 1 paras 9, 16; FA 2020, Sch 1 paras 17, 25*].

Computation of intermediary's business profits

[58.37] In computing the business profits of an intermediary in a case where a deemed direct payment has been treated as having been made to the worker, the chain payment received by the intermediary and giving rise to that deemed direct payment is not required to be brought into account as income. [*ITTOIA 2005, s 164B; CTA 2009, s 141A; FA 2017, Sch 1 paras 13–15, 17; FA 2020, Sch 1 para 22*].

Deciding employment status — summary of HMRC's views

[58.38] The following is a summary of HMRC's opinions on deciding employment status and, in particular, of the main text of the article in Revenue Tax Bulletin February 2000 pp 716–723 referred to at **58.3** above. The views expressed are those of HMRC, who emphasise that their role is 'to provide advice and guidance about the employment status resulting from a given set of circumstances, not to impose any particular status. The terms and conditions of any engagement are entirely a matter for the parties involved.' Those views are reproduced here for the sole purpose of providing some general guidance on what is itself a specialist topic, and readers are advised to seek an independent view also. See also **58.3** above as regards HMRC's identification of a 'standard contract' and their advice thereon (which is included in the said article but not covered again below). See also **28.66** EMPLOYMENT INCOME, particularly as regards relevant case law, and HMRC Employment Status Manual.

Although not covered by the article, it is accepted that, in order for a contract for service to exist, there must be an irreducible minimum of **mutual obligation**. That irreducible minimum is that the engager must be obliged to pay remuneration and that the worker must be obliged to provide his own work or skill (HMRC Employment Status Manual ESM8550). HMRC's approach, which some have suggested is flawed, is that mutuality of obligation is required for a contract to exist and must therefore already have been established before one considers whether it is one of employment or self-employment. See https://assets.publishing.service.gov.uk/government/uploads/system/uploads/attachment_data/file/722316/HMRC_paper_on_Mutuality_of_Obligation.pdf.

The summary of the article follows immediately below.

Whether a worker would have fallen to be treated as an employee of the client if engaged directly by the client rather than though an intermediary depends on a range of factors. However, it is not a mechanical exercise of running through a checklist with a view to adding up, and comparing, the number of factors pointing towards employment and self-employment respectively. The overall effect must be evaluated, which is not necessarily the same as the sum of the individual factors; the factors may not be of equal weight or importance in a given situation and may also vary in importance from one situation to another. See also *Hall v Lorimer* CA 1993, 66 TC 349. The intention of the parties may be conclusive if, but only if, the evidence is otherwise evenly balanced.

It is first necessary to establish the terms and conditions of the engagement, which is usually achieved mainly by considering the contract (whether written, oral or implied — or a mixture of those) between the client and the intermediary. Next, it is necessary to consider any relevant surrounding facts, for example whether the worker has other clients and a business organisation. In this context, other contracts under which the worker's services are supplied by the intermediary may be taken into account, as may any business organisation of the intermediary which is relevant to that supply.

Relevant factors in determining whether a contract is a 'contract of service' (i.e. employment) or a 'contract for services' (self-employment) are listed below.

- Does the client have the right to exercise **control** over the worker? This may be a right to control what work is done, where or when it is done and/or how it is done. A working relationship involving no control at all is unlikely to be employment. Where the client has the right to determine *how* the work is done or *what* work is carried out, this is, in either case, a strong pointer towards employment.
- Personal service is an essential element of a contract of employment. If the worker has the freedom to choose whether to do the job himself or hire a **substitute** to do it for him or a helper to provide substantial help, this points towards self-employment.
- The provision by the worker of significant **equipment** and/or materials which are fundamental to the engagement is a strong pointer towards self-employment. If the client provides the office space (where relevant) and equipment, this points towards employment. Note that in some trades it is not uncommon for *employees* to provide their own small tools.
- The taking on by the worker of **financial risk**, for example his buying significant assets and materials and/or quoting a fixed price for the job with the consequent risk of bearing the extra costs if it overruns, is a strong pointer towards self-employment.
- **Basis of payment.** Employees tend to be paid a fixed wage or salary, weekly or monthly, and possibly bonuses or overtime. A self-employed contractor tends to be paid a fixed sum for a particular job. (Piece work or payment by commission can be a feature of both employment and self-employment.)
- A person who may **profit from sound management**, i.e. his reward for the job varies according to his ability to organise the work effectively and reduce overheads, may well be self-employed. Though not mentioned in the Tax Bulletin text, an obligation to correct unsatisfactory work in the worker's own time and at his own expense suggests self-employment.
- A person who becomes **'part and parcel' of the client's organisation** may well be an employee.

- A **right of dismissal** is a common feature of employment. A contract for services, on the other hand, usually ends only when it is completed or is breached.
- The right to sick pay, holiday pay, pensions, expenses and/or other **employee benefits** points towards employment, though their absence does not necessarily indicate self-employment — especially where the engagement is short-term.
- **Length of engagement.** A long period working for one engager is typical of employment, but is not conclusive. Where a single engagement is covered by a series of short contracts, it is the length of the engagement that is relevant, and not the length of each contract.
- It may be appropriate to take into account factors which are personal to the worker and have little to do with the terms of the particular engagement. For example, if a skilled worker works for a number of clients and has a business-like approach to securing his engagements (perhaps involving expenditure on office accommodation, office equipment etc.), this points towards self-employment. Such **personal factors** carry less weight in the case of an unskilled worker, where factors like a high degree of control exercised by the client are more likely to be conclusive of employment.

59

Post-Cessation Receipts and Expenditure

Post-cessation receipts of trades etc.

Introduction

[59.1] Income tax is charged under *ITTOIA 2005, ss 241–257* on 'post-cessation receipts' (see **59.2** below) arising from a trade, profession or vocation to the extent that they have not been brought into account in computing trading profits for any period and that they are not otherwise chargeable to tax. The charge is not subject to the rules covering TRADING INCOME (75), but is made on the full amount of post-cessation receipts received in the tax year (subject to any allowable deductions at **59.3** below and any carry-back election at **59.4** below). The person liable is the person receiving, or entitled to, the post-cessation receipts.

In the rest of this chapter, the word 'trade' is used to denote a trade, a profession or a vocation.

A post-cessation receipt is not chargeable as above if:

(a) it represents income arising outside the UK and accruing to a non-UK resident; or

(b) it arises from a trade carried on wholly outside the UK (other than one of dealing in or developing UK land — see **78.2** TRANSACTIONS IN UK LAND); or

(c) (in the case of a member of a partnership) it represents partnership trading income arising outside the UK and the partner's share of such income falls to be taxed on the remittance basis (see **52.22** PARTNERSHIPS); or

(d) the person who would be liable to tax on the receipt was born before 6 April 1917 *and* the cessation occurred before 6 April 2000.

If an individual has permanently ceased to carry on a trade and his income from the trade was 'relevant UK earnings' (see **57.12** PENSION PROVISION), his post-cessation receipts are similarly relevant UK earnings.

If the tax year is a split year (see **63.19** RESIDENCE AND DOMICILE) as regards a UK resident individual, the above has effect as if, for the overseas part of the split year, the individual were non-UK resident.

[*ITTOIA 2005, ss 241–245, 256, Sch 2 paras 60, 61; FA 2016, s 78(4)*].

Simon's Taxes. See **B2.801–B2.808.**

Meaning of 'post-cessation receipt'

[59.2] For these purposes, a '*post-cessation receipt*' is a sum which is received after a person ceases to carry on a trade (including his leaving a partnership and thus ceasing his notional trade — see **52.4** PARTNERSHIPS) but which arises from the carrying on of the trade before cessation. Certain sums as below are specifically treated as being, or as not being (as the case may be), post-cessation receipts. Certain enactments listed at *ITTOIA 2005, s 247* also specifically treat certain amounts as being, or as not being, post-cessation receipts; these are referred to elsewhere in this work where relevant. If immediately before the cessation a cash basis election is in force (see **76** TRADING INCOME — CASH BASIS FOR SMALLER BUSINESSES), a sum is a post-cessation receipt only if it would have been brought into account in calculating profits on the cash basis had it been received immediately before cessation. [*ITTOIA 2005, ss 246, 247*].

Receipts within the legislation will include, *inter alia*, royalties and similar amounts which under decisions such as *Carson v Cheyney's Exor HL* 1958, 38 TC 240, prior to the original legislation being enacted, had been held not to be taxable.

See **59.5** below for circumstances in which amounts relieved as post-cessation expenditure may be clawed back as post-cessation receipts.

Debts

To the extent that a deduction has been made, in computing the profits of the trade, for a bad or doubtful debt (see **75.48** TRADING INCOME), any amount received after cessation in settlement of that debt is a post-cessation receipt. If an amount owed *by* the trader is released, in whole or in part, after cessation, the amount released is a post-cessation receipt; this applies only if a trading deduction was allowed for the expense giving rise to the debt and does not apply if the release of the debt is part of a statutory insolvency arrangement (as defined in **75.48**). [*ITTOIA 2005, ss 248, 249, 259*].

Transfers of rights

If the right to receive a post-cessation receipt is transferred for value to another person (other than one who succeeds to the trade), the transferor is treated as receiving at that point a post-cessation receipt equal to the consideration for the transfer or, if the transfer is not at arm's length, the value of the rights transferred. The post-cessation receipts themselves are not then charged when received by the transferee.

If, however, the right to receive any sums arising from the transferors trade are transferred to someone who does succeed to the trade, then, to the extent (if any) that they were not brought into account in computing the transferor's profits for any pre-cessation period, those sums are treated as trading receipts of the transferee as and when received. They are not post-cessation receipts. This rule was applied in *Rafferty v HMRC* (Sp C 475), [2005] SSCD 484.

[*ITTOIA 2005, ss 98, 251*].

Stock and work in progress

A sum realised by the transfer of trading stock or work in progress is not a post-cessation receipt provided that a valuation of the stock or work in progress at cessation has been properly brought into account under *ITTOIA 2005, s 173 et seq.* (see **75.117** TRADING INCOME). In the case of work in progress, this is subject to any election for valuation at cost on cessation (again see **75.117**). [*ITTOIA 2005, s 252*].

Lump sums paid to personal representatives for copyright etc.

A lump sum paid to the personal representatives of the deceased author of a literary, dramatic, musical or artistic work for the assignment by them, in whole or in part, of the copyright or public lending right in the work is not a post-cessation receipt. A similar rule applies in relation to personal representatives of the designer of a design in which a design right subsists. [*ITTOIA 2005, s 253*].

Allowable deductions

[59.3] A deduction from post-cessation receipts is allowed for any loss, expense or debit that would have been deductible if the trade had not ceased, has not been relieved in any other way and which does not arise directly or indirectly from the cessation itself. In the case of a loss, relief is given against the first available post-cessation receipts, i.e. receipts for an earlier year in priority to those for a later year, but not so as give relief for a loss against receipts charged for a tax year before that in which the loss is made.

If immediately before the cessation a cash basis election was in force (see **76** TRADING INCOME — CASH BASIS FOR SMALLER BUSINESSES), it is assumed for the above purpose that the election remains in force, so that a deduction is allowed only for any loss, expense or debit that would have been deductible on the cash basis.

If immediately before the cessation the fixed rate deduction scheme applied in relation to a vehicle (see **77.2** TRADING INCOME — FIXED RATE DEDUCTION SCHEME), the relief against post-cessation receipts for any post-cessation loss, expense or debit in relation to that vehicle is given in accordance with that scheme.

[*ITTOIA 2005, ss 254, 255(1)–(3)*].

Election to carry back

[59.4] If a post-cessation receipt is received in a tax year beginning no later than six years after the date of cessation, an election may be made (by the former trader or his personal representatives) to treat the receipt as having been received on the date of cessation. See **16.2** CLAIMS for the way in which effect is given to this election. The election must be made no later than the first anniversary of 31 January following the tax year of actual receipt. [*ITTOIA 2005, s 257*].

Post-cessation expenditure

[59.5] Relief against income (and capital gains, see below) is available (on a claim under *ITA 2007, s 96*) for certain payments made by a person in connection with a trade, profession or vocation which he has permanently ceased to carry on (including his leaving a partnership and thus ceasing his notional trade — see **52.4** PARTNERSHIPS). The relief applies where such payments are made within seven years after cessation. Relief is given for the year in which the payment is made and unused relief cannot be carried forward (but may qualify as a deduction from post-cessation receipts within **59.1** above). Relief is available (under *ITA 2007, s 125*) in relation to a UK property business (see **60.2** PROPERTY INCOME).The relief is given by deducting the payment in arriving at net income for the tax year in which it is made (see Step 2 at **1.10** ALLOWANCES AND TAX RATES).

There is a cap on the total amount of prescribed income tax reliefs that individuals can claim. See **1.11** ALLOWANCES AND TAX RATES. Post-cessation relief against income is one of the prescribed reliefs.

Payments qualifying for relief

Payments qualifying for this relief are those made wholly and exclusively:

(a) in remedying defective work done, goods supplied or services provided or by way of damages (awarded or agreed) in respect of defective work etc.;
(b) in meeting legal and professional fees in connection with a claim that work done etc. was defective;
(c) in insuring against such a claim or against the incurring of such legal etc. fees; or
(d) for the purpose of collecting a debt taken into account in computing profits of the former trade etc.

In addition, where, within seven years after cessation, an unpaid debt taken into account in computing profits of the former trade etc. proves to be bad or is wholly or partly released as part of a statutory insolvency arrangement (see **75.48** TRADING INCOME), then, to the extent that the former trader is entitled to the benefit of that debt, he is treated in the same way as if he had made a payment qualifying for relief under these provisions and equal to the amount lost or released. In the case of a debt proving to be bad, the claimant must specify the tax year for which relief is to be given, which may be the tax year in which the debt proves to be bad or any subsequent tax year throughout which it remains bad and which begins within the seven years after cessation. In the case of a debt released, relief is given for the year in which the release occurs. To the extent that relief has been given under these provisions, any subsequent recovery of the debt is taxed as a post-cessation receipt (see **59.1** above) with no deduction available against it under **59.3** above.

Where relief becomes available in respect of a payment within any of (a) to (d) above, the following are taxed as post-cessation receipts with no deduction available against them under **59.3** above: (i) in the case of (a) or (b), any insurance proceeds, or similar, to allow the payment to be made or to reimburse it, (ii) in the case of (c), any refund of the insurance premium, or similar receipt, and (iii) in the case of (d), any sum received to meet the costs of collecting the debt. Where the receipt occurs in an earlier tax year than the related payment, it is treated as instead having been received in the year of payment.

Set-off of unpaid expenses against relief

Where a deduction was made in computing profits or losses of the former trade etc. in respect of an expense not actually paid, relief otherwise due and claimed under these provisions is reduced by the amount of any such expenses remaining unpaid at the end of the year to which the claim relates (to the extent that those expenses have not so reduced relief for an earlier year). If an unpaid expense has reduced relief but is subsequently paid, wholly or partly, the amount paid (or, if less, the amount of the reduction) is treated as a payment qualifying for relief under these provisions for the year of payment.

Exclusion of double relief

Relief is not available in respect of an amount for which income tax relief is otherwise available. In determining whether an amount could otherwise be relieved under **59.3** above (allowable deductions from post-cessation receipts), amounts not available for relief under these provisions are assumed to be relieved under **59.3** above in priority to amounts that are so available.

Time limit

The relief must be claimed on or before the first anniversary of 31 January following the tax year for which relief is due.

Relief against capital gains

Where a claim is made as above and the claimant's total income for the year is insufficient to fully utilise the relief (or is nil), he may claim to have the excess relief treated as an allowable loss for that year for capital gains tax purposes. The allowable loss may not exceed the amount of the claimant's gains for the year *before* deducting any losses brought forward, the capital gains tax annual exemption and any relief due and claimed under **45.5** LOSSES for trading losses or under these provisions.

Anti-avoidance

Post-cessation relief (whether against income or capital gains) is not available to a person in respect of a payment (or an event) which is made (or occurs) in consequence of (or otherwise in connection with) arrangements (as widely defined) to which the person is a party and a main purpose of which is to obtain a reduction in tax liability as a result of the relief.

[*ITA 2007, ss 96–98, 98A, 99–101, 125, 126, Sch 2 para 26; TCGA 1992, ss 261D, 261E; ITTOIA 2005, ss 248(3)(4), 250, 255(4)*].

Simon's Taxes. See B2.809, B2.810.

Example

[59.6]

Simcock ceased trading in February 2020. In 2020/21, the following events occur in connection with his former trade.

(i) He pays a former customer £9,250 by way of damages for defective work carried out by him in the course of the trade.

(ii) He incurs legal fees of £800 in connection with (i) above.

(iii) He incurs debt collection fees of £200 in connection with trade debts outstanding at cessation and which were taken into account as receipts in computing profits.

(iv) He writes off a trade debt of £500, giving HMRC notice of his having done so.

(v) He incurs legal fees of £175 in relation to a debt of £1,000 owing by him to a supplier which, although disputed, was taken into account as an expense in computing his trading profits.

(vi) He eventually agrees to pay £500 in full settlement of his liability in respect of the debt in (v) above, paying £250 in March 2021 and the remaining £250 in May 2021.

In 2021/22, he receives £3,000 from his insurers in full settlement of their liability with regard to the expense incurred in (i) above.

For 2020/21, Simcock's total income before taking account of the above events is £9,000, and he also has capital gains of £13,400 (with £900 capital losses brought forward from 2019/20). His liability to income tax is at the main UK rates.

Simcock makes a claim under *ITA 2007, s 96* for 2020/21 and a simultaneous claim under *TCGA 1992, s 261D* to have any excess relief set against capital gains.

Simcock's tax position is as follows.

2020/21

		£	£
Income			
Total income before claim under *ITA 2007, s 96*			9,000
Deduct post-cessation expenditure —			
	(i)	9,250	
	(ii)	800	
	(iii)	200	
	(iv)	500	
	(v)	—	
	(vi) *less* expenses unpaid at 5.4.21 (£1,000 – £250)	(750)	
		10,000	
Restricted to total income		(9,000)	(9,000)
Excess relief		£1,000	
Capital gains			
Gains before losses brought forward and annual exempt amount			13,400

Deduct excess post-cessation expenditure (as above)		1,000
Net gains for the year		12,400
Losses brought forward	900	
Used 2020/21	100	100
Losses carried forward	£800	
Net gains (covered by annual exemption)		£12,300

2021/22

Simcock will have taxable post-cessation receipts of £3,000 arising from the insurance recovery. He will be able to offset expenses of £175 under (v) above which, whilst not within **59.5** above, should qualify as a deduction under **59.3** above. He will also have post-cessation expenditure of £250 in respect of the further payment in 2021/22 under (vi) above, the 2020/21 post-cessation expenditure having been restricted by at least that amount.

60

Property Income

Simon's Taxes. See **Part B6.**

Other sources. See HMRC Property Income Manual.

Introduction to property income

[60.1] Income tax is charged on rents etc. (see **60.2** below) less deductible expenses (see **60.10, 60.15** below). Certain lease premiums etc. are also taxable (see **60.26** below).

See **9.13** CAPITAL ALLOWANCES for flat conversion allowances.

Where this work refers simply to a '*property business*', then unless the context clearly suggests otherwise, it means either a UK property business or an overseas property business (see in both cases **60.2** below). Any reference to something being charged to tax as property income or within the charge to tax on property income is a reference to its having to be brought into account in computing the profits of a property business.

In this chapter, '*lease*' includes an agreement for a lease (insofar as the context permits) and any tenancy. '*Premises*' includes land. [*ITTOIA 2005, s 364*]. '*Land*' includes an estate or interest in land.

ITTOIA 2005, ss 4(1), 261, 262 set out certain priority rules where a receipt or other credit item could be dealt with either as trading income or as property income or either as property income within **60.33**, **60.34** below or as other property income. See **75.94** TRADING INCOME as regards the inclusion in trading profits of receipts from, and expenses of, the letting of **surplus business accommodation.** See **75.49** TRADING INCOME as regards the inclusion in trading profits of receipts and expenses in respect of **tied premises** which would otherwise be brought into account in calculating profits of a property business.

ITTOIA 2005, s 274 contains a rule intended to resolve any conflict between statutory rules prohibiting a deduction in computing property income and statutory rules permitting such a deduction. It does so by giving priority, with specified exceptions, to the rule permitting the deduction. In practice, such conflict will rarely occur. The order of priority is reversed in cases where a deduction would otherwise be given for an amount which arises directly or indirectly in consequence of, or in connection with, tax avoidance arrangements. [*ITTOIA 2005, s 274; F(No 2)A 2017, Sch 2 paras 20, 64(1)*].

A £1,000 property allowance is introduced for individuals for 2017/18 onwards. Gross receipts from property of £1,000 or less are exempt, though an election can be made to disapply the exemption. Where gross receipts exceed £1,000, an election can be made to be taxed on the excess. In either case no relief is then given for otherwise deductible expenses. See **60.11** below.

Before 2017/18, property income was calculated in accordance with generally accepted accounting practice (GAAP) (see **60.10** below). For 2017/18 onwards, a cash basis is introduced as the default basis where receipts do not exceed £150,000, with GAAP continuing to apply otherwise. An election can be made to disapply the cash basis, and the cash basis cannot in any case be used in certain cases. See **60.4** below.

UK and overseas property businesses

[60.2] Income tax is chargeable on the profits of a property business, whether it be a 'UK property business' or an 'overseas property business'. Profits of a UK property business are chargeable whether or not the business is carried on by a UK resident. Profits of an overseas property business are chargeable only if the business is carried on by a UK resident (and see below as regards split year treatment). The charge is on the full amount of profits arising in the tax year; there are no basis periods as there are for trading income. Normally, one would expect profits to be computed by reference to a 5 April accounting date, but see **60.10** below as regards apportionment of profits to a tax year where accounts are prepared to some other date. For more on overseas property income, including the remittance basis, see **60.3** below.

See **60.10** below as regards the computation of the profits of a property business. The person liable to tax is the person in receipt of, or entitled to, the profits.

For these purposes, a person's '*UK property business*' consists of every business which he carries on for 'generating income from land' (see below) in the UK and any other transaction which he enters into for that purpose. An '*overseas property business*' is similarly defined, but by reference to land outside the UK. Note that a person cannot have more than one UK property business or more than one overseas property business; a property business carried on by a partnership is separate from any property businesses carried on by its individual members.

See **60.10** below as regards the computation of the profits of a property business.

Where this work refers simply to a '*property business*', it means either a UK or an overseas property business (unless the context clearly suggests otherwise). Any reference to something being charged to tax as property income or within the charge to tax on property income is a reference to its having to be brought into account in computing the profits of a property business.

'*Generating income from land*' means exploiting an estate, interest or right in or over land as a source of rent or other receipts. Expenditure by a tenant on maintenance and repairs which the lease does not require him to carry out counts as rent in the landlord's hands. The reference above to 'any other transaction' brings into charge, for example, one-off or casual lettings. 'Other receipts' include:

- payments in respect of a licence to occupy or otherwise use land or in respect of the exercise of any other right over land; and
- rent charges and any other annual payments reserved in respect of, or charged on or issuing out of, land.

For the above purposes, the following activities are *not* treated as carried on for generating income from land:

- farming or market gardening in the UK, which is instead treated as a trade — see **75.77** TRADING INCOME;
- any other *occupation* of land, but commercial occupation of land is treated as a trade (with the exemption for woodlands) — see **75.1** TRADING INCOME; and
- activities for the purposes of a concern within *ITTOIA 2005, s 12* (mines, quarries etc.) — see **75.1** TRADING INCOME — but see also **60.34** below.

Split year treatment

Where the tax year is a split year (see **63.19** RESIDENCE AND DOMICILE), profits of an overseas property business are chargeable only to the extent that they arise in the UK part of the split year. To determine how much of the profits arise in the UK part of the split year, first apportion the profits before any capital allowances and balancing charges between the UK part and the overseas part on a just and reasonable basis; then adjust the portion of the profits arising in the UK part by deducting any capital allowances for the year and adding any balancing charges for the year.

[*ITTOIA 2005, ss 263–271, 859(2)(3)*].

Caravans, caravan sites and houseboats

Income from the letting of immobile caravans or permanently moored houseboats is specifically brought within the charge to income tax on property income. [*ITTOIA 2005, s 266(4)*]. See *ITTOIA 2005, s 875* for the meaning of 'caravan' and *ITTOIA 2005, s 878(1)* for the meaning of 'houseboat'.

Income from letting caravan pitches, i.e. site rents, is chargeable to income tax as property income to the extent that it arises from exploitation of land. However, if a person carries on material activities connected with the operation of a caravan site and those activities themselves constitute a trade or a part of a trade, the income and expenses of letting the caravans and/or pitches can be included in computing the profits of that trade instead of being treated as those of a property business. [*ITTOIA 2005, s 20*].

Miscellaneous

Receipts from sales of turf have been held to be within the charge to tax on property income although they may alternatively be taxed as trading income (*Lowe v J W Ashmore Ltd* Ch D 1970, 46 TC 597); but receipts from sale of colliery dross bings held to be capital (*Roberts v Lord Belhaven's Exors* CS 1925, 9 TC 501). Sums received for licence to tip soil on land held to be capital (*McClure v Petre* Ch D 1988, 61 TC 226). Note that these cases were decided under the pre-1995/96 property income regime, which differed in a number of material respects from the current rules.

Partnerships

Ancillary property income of a trading or professional partnership is taxable on an accounts year basis (see **52.5** PARTNERSHIPS). Joint ownership of property does not, of itself, create a partnership. Where the letting is not ancillary to a trade or profession, there will only be a partnership if, exceptionally, the exploitation of property constitutes the carrying on of a business (using that term without regard to the concept of a property business) jointly with a view to profit. See Revenue Tax Bulletin December 1995 pp 271, 272 and HMRC Property Income Manual PIM1030.

Mutual businesses

The normal exemption for mutual trading (see **75.38** TRADING INCOME does not extend to property businesses, the transactions and relationships involved in mutual business being instead treated as if they were between persons between whom no relationship of mutuality existed. The taxable person is the person who would be taxable if the business were not mutual business. (This does not affect the treatment of Co-operative Housing Associations — see Tolley's Corporation Tax.) [*ITTOIA 2005, s 321*].

Rules on commencements/cessations in particular cases

If a property business is being carried on by trustees of a trust or by personal representatives of a deceased person, a mere change of trustee etc. does not give rise to a cessation and re-commencement of the property business. [*ITTOIA 2005, s 361*].

Non-resident companies are within the charge to income tax (not corporation tax) in certain circumstances (see Tolley's Corporation Tax under Residence). Where a company starts or ceases to be within the charge to income tax in respect of a UK property business, it is treated as starting or permanently ceasing to carry on the business at that time. [*ITTOIA 2005, s 362*].

See generally HMRC Property Income Manual.

Simon's Taxes. See **B6.201, B6.202, B6.211.**

Overseas property income

[60.3] See **60.2** above as regards an overseas property business generally. As regards the application of the property income legislation to an overseas property business and to overseas land, domestic concepts of law are to be interpreted to produce the result most closely corresponding with that produced in relation to a UK property business or land in the UK. [*ITTOIA 2005, s 363*].

The REMITTANCE BASIS (**61**) can apply to overseas property income, due to profits of an overseas property business being classed as relevant foreign income (see **32.2** FOREIGN INCOME).

Under general principles, relief is available for travelling expenses incurred wholly and exclusively for the purposes of an overseas property business. Subject to **60.12** below, interest on a loan to purchase an overseas property is deductible as an expense to the extent that it is incurred wholly and exclusively for the purposes of the overseas property business, with the interest being apportioned accordingly where the owner occupies the property, or it is otherwise unavailable for letting, for part of the year or if only part of the property is used exclusively for letting. (Revenue booklet SAT 1(1995), paras 9.151–9.153). For the application of capital allowances to an overseas property business, see **10.4** CAPITAL ALLOWANCES ON PLANT AND MACHINERY. Although all overseas let properties are regarded as a single business (see **60.2** above), the income from each must be calculated separately for the purposes of computing DOUBLE TAX RELIEF (**27**) (SAT 1(1995), para 9.160).

Simon's Taxes. See **B6.214.**

Cash basis

[60.4] For **2017/18** onwards, the profits of a property business for a tax year must be calculated on the cash basis *unless* one of the following conditions is met:

(a) an election to disapply the cash basis is made by the person carrying on the property business;

(b) the business is carried on at any time in the tax year by a company, a limited liability partnership, a partnership in which one or more partners is not an individual, or the trustees of a trust;

(c) the cash basis receipts, i.e. the amount that would be brought into account as receipts if the cash basis applied, exceed **£150,000** (proportionately reduced if the property business is carried on for only part of the tax year);

- the property business is carried on by an individual and includes a share of 'joint property income'; and
- a share of that joint property income is included in a property business carried on by that individual's spouse or civil partner for the same tax year, the profits of which are *not* calculated on the cash basis; or

(e) business premises renovation allowances (see **9.3** CAPITAL ALLOWANCES) have been made to the property business at any time and, if profits were to be calculated in accordance with generally accepted accounting practice (GAAP), a balancing event would give rise to a balancing allowance or balancing charge for the tax year.

Where a person has a UK property business and an overseas property business, the conditions apply separately to each.

The election in (a) above must be made on or before the first anniversary of 31 January following the tax year in question. It has effect for that tax year only. It will be noted that, where none of the conditions are met, the cash basis is the default position. This is in contrast to the cash basis for trading income, where the taxpayer has to elect *into* the cash basis if eligible. In (d) above, '*joint property income*' is income to which the spouses or civil partners are treated for income tax purposes as beneficially entitled in equal shares under the jointly-held property rule in **48.7** MARRIED PERSONS AND CIVIL PARTNERS.

If any of conditions (a)–(e) above is met, the profits of the property business for a tax year must be calculated in accordance with GAAP, subject to any adjustment required or authorised by law in calculating profits for income tax purposes. See **60.10** below. This was the statutory position for *all* property businesses before 2017/18. In practice, a cash basis could be used before 2017/18, instead of the full earnings basis required by GAAP, but only where gross annual receipts did not exceed £15,000. The basis had to be used consistently and give a reasonable overall result not substantially different from that produced on an earnings basis. See HMRC Property Income Manual PIM1101. This is now superseded by the statutory cash basis.

[*ITTOIA 2005, ss 271A, 271C; F(No 2)A 2017, Sch 2 paras 13, 64(1)*].

See Tolley's Capital Gains Tax for an exemption for certain disposals of assets made while the cash basis is in use or after leaving the cash basis.

Cash basis — calculating profits

[60.5] In calculating profits of a property business on the cash basis for 2017/18 onwards, receipts are brought into account at the time they are received, and expenses are brought into account at the time they are paid. This is subject to any adjustment required or authorised by law, and certain special rules apply to the cash basis (see **60.6–60.9** below). Otherwise, the general rule applies that the profits of a property business are calculated in the same way as the profits of a trade. See also **60.10** below. The specific trading income provisions of *ITTOIA 2005* which apply to property businesses where profits are calculated on the cash basis are, however, limited to those listed at *ITTOIA 2005, s 272ZA(1)* and reproduced below. These include the fundamental rule that, subject to any specific rule to the contrary, expenditure is not deductible unless incurred wholly and exclusively for the purposes of the business. As stated at **60.2** above, the basis period rules for trades do not apply to property businesses. Although property income is computed similarly to trading income, it retains its nature as investment income as opposed to earnings and does not count as relevant earnings for pension contribution purposes (subject to the rules at **60.20** below for furnished holiday lettings).

If the calculation on the cash basis produces a loss, that loss *cannot* be set against general income (in a case where this would otherwise be possible — see **60.25** below).

See **60.11** below for relief for small amounts of income (the property allowance) for 2017/18 onwards.

The list of included trading income provisions is as follows.

ITTOIA 2005	**Brief description**	**See main coverage at**
s 26	losses computed on same basis as profits	**45.1** LOSSES
s 28A	money's worth	**75.42** TRADING INCOME
s 29	interest payable	**42.2** INTEREST PAYABLE
s 34	'wholly and exclusively' rule for expenditure	**75.44** TRADING INCOME
ss 38–42, 44	timing of deductions for employee benefit contributions	**75.65** TRADING INCOME
ss 45–47	expenditure on business entertainment and gifts	**75.76** TRADING INCOME
s 52	interest payable — exclusion of double relief	**42.13** INTEREST PAYABLE

ITTOIA 2005	**Brief description**	**See main coverage at**
s 53	employee and employer National Insurance contributions	**75.72** TRADING INCOME
s 54	interest, surcharges and penalties in relation to tax — non-deductible	**75.93, 75.129** TRADING INCOME
s 55	illegal payments non-deductible	**75.91** TRADING INCOME
s 55A	expenditure on integral features of buildings and structures	**75.110**(a) TRADING INCOME
s 57	pre-trading expenditure	**75.106** TRADING INCOME
ss 58, 59	incidental costs of obtaining finance	**75.97** TRADING INCOME
s 69	payments for restrictive undertakings	**75.75** TRADING INCOME
ss 70, 71	employees seconded to charities or educational bodies	**75.74** TRADING INCOME
s 72	payroll deduction schemes: contributions to agents' administrative costs	**14.18** CHARITIES AND CHARITABLE GIVING
s 73	counselling etc. services to employees	**75.70** TRADING INCOME
ss 74, 75	retraining employees	**75.73** TRADING INCOME
ss 76–80	redundancy payments etc.	**75.69** TRADING INCOME
s 81	expenditure on personal security	**75.114** TRADING INCOME
ss 82–86	subscriptions and contributions	**75.119** TRADING INCOME

ITTOIA 2005	**Brief description**	**See main coverage at**
ss 86A, 86B	contributions to flood and coastal erosion risk management projects	**75.119** TRADING INCOME
ss 87, 88	research and development and scientific research	**75.113** TRADING INCOME
ss 89, 90	expenditure on trademarks, designs and patents	**75.102, 75.103** TRADING INCOME
s 91	payments to Export Credits Guarantee Department	**75.102** TRADING INCOME
ss 94D–94G	(for 2017/18 onwards) fixed rate deduction scheme — expenditure on vehicles (and see below)	**77.2–77.4** TRADING INCOME — FIXED RATE DEDUCTION SCHEME
s 96	capital receipts excluded from profits	**75.105** TRADING INCOME
s 97	debts incurred and later released	**75.106** TRADING INCOME
s 104	distribution of assets of mutual concerns	**75.102** TRADING INCOME
s 105 (but not *s 105(2)(a)*)	industrial development grants	**75.120** TRADING INCOME
s 106	insurance recoveries	**75.92** TRADING INCOME
ss 106C –106E	amounts not reflecting commercial transactions (*s 106D* to be read with appropriate modifications)	**76.11** TRADING INCOME — CASH BASIS FOR SMALLER BUSINESSES
s 109	receipt by donor etc. of benefit attributable to certain gifts	**75.88** TRADING INCOME

As regards the inclusion in the above table of the fixed rate deduction scheme for expenditure on vehicles, a transitional rule enables the scheme to be used (for 2017/18 onwards) regardless of whether or not the person carrying on the property business claimed plant and machinery capital allowances on the vehicle in question for any of the years 2013/14 to 2016/17 inclusive. See also **10.26** CAPITAL ALLOWANCES ON PLANT AND MACHINERY. The rule at **77.1** TRADING INCOME — FIXED RATE DEDUCTION SCHEME whereby the fixed rate deduction scheme cannot be used by partnerships that include non-individuals applies equally for the purpose of calculating profits of a property business.

As regards allowable legal and professional costs, see HMRC Property Income Manual PIM2120. For guidance on deductibility of repairs in a property business see HMRC Business Income Manual BIM46900. See HMRC Property Income Manual generally.

The provisions at **60.29** below (deductions for tenants where landlord taxed on a lease premium) do not apply in calculating the profits of a property business on the cash basis.

[*ITTOIA 2005, ss 271D, 271E, 272ZA, 276A; F(No 2)A 2017, Sch 2 paras 13–15, 17, 22, 64(1); FA 2018, s 36(5)(8)(9)*].

Cash basis — capital expenditure

[60.6] On the cash basis, no deduction is allowed for expenditure of a capital nature incurred on, or in connection with:

(1) the acquisition or disposal of a business (or part of a business);
(2) education or training;
(3) the provision, alteration or disposal of land (other than certain fixtures);
(4) the provision, alteration or disposal of an asset for use in 'ordinary residential property' (but not so as to deny relief for replacement domestic items as in **60.14** below); or
(5) the provision, alteration or disposal of:
   (a) an asset that is not a 'depreciating asset';
   (b) an asset that was not acquired or created for use on a continuing basis in the property business;
   (c) a car (as defined by *CAA 2001, s 268A* — see **10.15** CAPITAL ALLOWANCES ON PLANT AND MACHINERY);
   (d) a 'non-qualifying' 'intangible asset'; or
   (e) a 'financial asset'.

References above to acquisition, provision, alteration or disposal include potential acquisition, provision, alteration or disposal. Reference to the provision of an asset includes its creation or construction as well as its acquisition.

As regards (3) above, a deduction can be made for expenditure incurred on the provision of a depreciating asset installed or otherwise fixed to 'qualifying land' so as to become, in law, part of it. Notwithstanding this, no deduction can be made for expenditure incurred on, or in connection with, the provision of a building or other fixed structure; a wall, floor, ceiling, door, gate, shutter or window or stairs; a waste disposal system; a sewerage or drainage system; or a lift or escalator shaft or similar. '*Qualifying land*' is land that is not part of ordinary residential property as defined below.

In (4) above, '*ordinary residential property*' means a dwelling-house (or part of a dwelling-house) in relation to which an 'ordinary property business' is carried on. An '*ordinary property business*' is so much of a property business as does not consist of furnished holiday lettings within **60.20** below. If an asset is provided partly for use in ordinary residential property and partly for other purposes, the expenditure is apportioned on a just and reasonable basis for the purposes of (4) above. Apportionments are similarly made if there is a letting of accommodation only part of which is furnished holiday accommodation.

In (5) above, the terms 'depreciating asset', 'non-qualifying', 'intangible asset' and 'financial asset' have similar meanings as in the equivalent rules covering the cash basis for trades (see **76.7** TRADING INCOME — CASH BASIS FOR SMALLER BUSINESSES).

[*ITTOIA 2005, s 307B; F(No 2)A 2017, Sch 2 paras 23, 64(1)*].

Cash basis — adjustments for capital allowances

[60.7] No capital allowances are available to a person carrying on a property business where profits are calculated on the cash basis, other than an allowance in respect of expenditure incurred on the provision of a car (as defined) (see **9.1** CAPITAL ALLOWANCES and **10.1** CAPITAL ALLOWANCES ON PLANT AND MACHINERY).

The provisions described below apply where a person enters the cash basis. A person carrying on a property business enters the cash basis for a tax year if profits are calculated on the cash basis for that tax year but were calculated in accordance with GAAP for the previous tax year. As regards persons *leaving* the cash basis, see **10.35** CAPITAL ALLOWANCES ON PLANT AND MACHINERY.

Unrelieved qualifying expenditure

When a person enters the cash basis for a tax year (Year Z), any qualifying expenditure on plant or machinery which is unrelieved at the end of the chargeable period which is the preceding tax year (Year Y) is allowable as a deduction on the cash basis in Year Z. The rule applies only to the extent that a deduction would have been allowable on the cash basis for the expenditure in Year Z if it had been paid in that year. Thus, it does not apply to cars, for example, and does not apply to any other asset to the extent (if any) that it is used for purposes other than those of the property business. The rule does not apply where the asset had not been fully paid for as at the end of Year Y. For what is meant by unrelieved qualifying expenditure, see **10.26** CAPITAL ALLOWANCES ON PLANT AND MACHINERY.

Assets not fully paid for

If a person enters the cash basis for a tax year (Year Z) and:

- at any time before the beginning of Year Z the person has obtained plant and machinery allowances on an item of 'relevant expenditure', but
- not all of the expenditure has actually been paid by the person,

an adjustment must be made in calculating profits on the cash basis for Year Z. If the amount of the expenditure in question that the person has actually paid exceeds the amount of capital allowances given in respect of it, the difference must be deducted in calculating profits. If the amount of the expenditure actually paid is less than the amount of capital allowances given, the difference must be treated as a receipt.

'*Relevant expenditure*' is expenditure on plant or machinery for which a deduction would have been allowed in calculating profits on the cash basis if it had been paid in Year Z. The extent (if any) to which expenditure was relevant expenditure, or to which a capital allowance was in respect of relevant expenditure, is to be determined on such basis as is just and reasonable in all the circumstances, for example where the expenditure was pooled.

If the amount of capital allowances given was reduced due to its having been incurred only partly for the purposes of the qualifying activity (see **10.15**, **10.19**, **10.32** CAPITAL ALLOWANCES ON PLANT AND MACHINERY), the amount of the expenditure that the person has actually paid is proportionately reduced for the above purposes.

Successions between connected persons

Where a person succeeds to a qualifying activity carried on by a person connected with him (as defined), the predecessor and successor can jointly elect for plant or machinery to be treated as sold by one to the other, when the succession takes place, at its written-down value for capital allowances purposes. For details, see **10.69** CAPITAL ALLOWANCES ON PLANT AND MACHINERY. If a person enters the cash basis for a tax year and plant or machinery is treated as sold to him during that tax year as a result of such an election, the cash basis rules apply as if everything done to or by the predecessor had been done to or by the successor. Where the election is made, any expenditure actually incurred by the successor on acquiring the plant or machinery is not deductible on the cash basis.

[*ITTOIA 2005, ss 334B–334E; F(No 2)A 2017, Sch 2 paras 29, 64(1)*].

Cash basis — capital receipts

[60.8] The 'proceeds' of an asset received by a person in a tax year for which the profits of the property business are calculated on the cash basis must be brought into account as a receipt in calculating profits if an amount of 'capital expenditure' relating to the asset:

(a) has been brought into account in calculating profits on the cash basis; or
   - (i) was incurred (or treated as incurred) by the person before he last entered the cash basis;
   - (ii) would have been deductible on the cash basis if incurred in the first tax year after he last entered the cash basis; and
   - (iii) was brought into account in calculating profits in accordance with GAAP, either:
     - by means of a deduction allowed under *ITTOIA 2005, ss 58, 59* (incidental costs of obtaining finance) (see **75.97** TRADING INCOME) as applied by **60.10** below; or

- by means of a deduction allowed under *ITTOIA 2005, s 311A* (replacement domestic items relief) (see **60.14** below); or
- for the purposes of plant and machinery capital allowances.

'*Capital expenditure*' means expenditure of a capital nature incurred (or treated as incurred) on, or in connection with, the provision, alteration or disposal of an asset or the potential provision, alteration or disposal of an asset. Reference to the provision of an asset includes its creation or construction as well as its acquisition. If only part of the capital expenditure relating to an asset is brought into account in calculating profits (whether on the cash basis or under GAAP), the proceeds to be brought into account are proportionately reduced. '*Proceeds*' means:

- any proceeds on the disposal (or part disposal) of the asset;
- any proceeds arising from the grant of any right in respect of, or any interest in, the asset;
- any damages, insurance proceeds or other compensation received in respect of the asset; and
- any amount that is (in substance) a refund of capital expenditure relating to the asset.

If the whole (or any part) of the proceeds that would fall to be brought into account is otherwise brought into account as a receipt, or as a disposal value for capital allowances, the proceeds (or that part) do not fall to be brought into account again under these rules.

A person carrying on a property business enters the cash basis for a tax year if profits are calculated on the cash basis for that tax year but were calculated in accordance with GAAP for the previous tax year.

Proceeds arising after leaving the cash basis

The proceeds of an asset arising to a person after he leaves the cash basis must be brought into account as a receipt in calculating profits if an amount of capital expenditure relating to the asset meets condition A or B below. For this purpose, a person carrying on a property business has left the cash basis if profits are calculated in accordance with GAAP when the proceeds arise but were calculated on the cash basis at some time previously.

Condition A is that an amount of capital expenditure relating to the asset:

- was paid in a tax year for which profits were calculated on the cash basis;
- was brought into account in calculating profits on the cash basis; and
- would not have been qualifying expenditure for the purposes of plant and machinery capital allowances if profits had not been calculated on the cash basis at the time the expenditure was paid.

Condition B is that an amount of capital expenditure relating to the asset was brought into account in calculating profits for a tax year in accordance with GAAP and that tax year preceded the person's last entry into the cash basis.

The reference here to expenditure being brought into account is to its being brought into account as in (b)(iii) above, except that it does not include its being brought into account for capital allowances purposes.

Deemed disposals

If at any time the person ceases to use the asset (or any part of it) for the purposes of the property business, but does not dispose of the asset (or that part of it) at that time, he is treated for the above purposes as disposing of the asset (or that part) at that time for its 'market value amount'. '*Market value amount*' is the amount that would be regarded as normal and reasonable in the market conditions then prevailing, and between persons dealing with each other on an arm's length basis in the open market.

If at any time there is a material increase in the person's non-business use of the asset (or any part of it), he is treated for the above purposes as disposing of the asset (or that part) at that time for an amount equal to the 'relevant proportion' of its market value amount. There is an increase in a person's non-business use of an asset (or part of an asset) only if the proportion of business use decreases *and* the proportion of use for other purposes increases. 'Material increase' is not defined. The '*relevant proportion*' is the difference between the proportion of non-business use before the increase and the proportion of non-business use after it.

If the property business in question is an overseas property business, there is a deemed disposal at market value amount (as above) if the person ceases to be UK resident. The deemed disposal occurs on the last day of the tax year for which he is UK resident. If, however, a tax year is a split year (see **63.19** RESIDENCE AND DOMICILE) as regards the person, and the overseas part of the split year is the later part, the deemed disposal occurs on the last day of the UK part of the split year.

[*ITTOIA 2005, ss 307E, 307F; F(No 2)A 2017, Sch 2 paras 23, 64(1)*].

Cash basis — costs of loans

[60.9] Where profits are calculated on the cash basis, any deduction for the cost of loans is restricted where the business proportion of the loans is greater than the value of the properties contained in the property business. Once the restriction has been made, the revised deductible amount is then subject to the provisions at **60.12** below (mortgage interest and other finance costs).

The restriction applies where an amount of the principal of one or more relevant loans is outstanding at the end of the tax year and the 'total outstanding amount of relevant loans' is greater than the sum of the values of all the properties involved in the property business at the end of the tax year ('*relevant properties*'). A property is involved in the property business if its exploitation forms the whole or part of the business. If there is only one loan (a '*relevant loan*'), the costs of which would be deductible in calculating property income for the tax year (or would be deductible but for **60.12** below), the '*total outstanding amount of relevant loans*' is the 'outstanding business amount' of that loan. If there are two or more relevant loans, the total outstanding amount is the aggregate outstanding business amount. The '*outstanding business amount*' of a relevant loan is:

$$\frac{X}{Y} \times A$$

where:

A	=	the amount of the principal of the loan which is outstanding at the end of the tax year;
X	=	the amount otherwise deductible (disregarding **60.12** below) for costs of the loan in calculating the profits of the property business for the tax year; and
Y	=	the amount that would be so deductible if one were also to disregard the rule that expenditure is deductible only if incurred wholly and exclusively for the purposes of the business.

If the person carrying on the business permanently ceases to carry it on at some time during the tax year, the outstanding loans and the values of properties involved in the business are measured as at the end of the date of cessation instead of at the end of the tax year. A property counts as a 'relevant property' even if it is not involved in the business at the end of the tax year (or, where appropriate, the date of cessation), provided it was last involved in the business at an earlier time in the tax year and continues to be held by the person carrying on the business throughout the period from that earlier time to the end of the tax year (or the cessation date). So those who cease to use a property in the business, but continue to hold the same interest in it up to the time the outstanding loans are measured, are not prevented from including that property in considering whether the restriction applies.

The costs of a loan comprise the interest on the loan (or any amount which is economically equivalent to interest) and the 'incidental costs of obtaining finance' (as defined at **75.97** TRADING INCOME) by means of the loan.

The value of a property for these purposes is its market value at the time that it is first involved in the property business plus any capital expenditure incurred by the landlord in respect of it that has not been brought into account in calculating the profits of the business for any tax year. A property's market value is the price it might reasonably be expected to fetch at arm's length in the open market in conditions then prevailing.

Once it is established that the restriction applies, the value of X above is multiplied by the relevant fraction to give the amount allowable as a deduction (subject to **60.12** below). The relevant fraction is:

$$\frac{V}{L}$$

where:

V	=	the sum of the values of all the relevant properties; and
L	=	the total outstanding amount of relevant loans.

[*ITTOIA 2005, ss 307C, 307D; F(No 2)A 2017, Sch 2 paras 23, 64(1)*].

Computing profits under GAAP

[60.10] Other than where the cash basis applies (see **60.4** above), the profits (or losses) of a property business must be computed in accordance with generally accepted accounting practice (GAAP) (for which see **75.21** TRADING INCOME), subject to any adjustment required or authorised by law in calculating profits for income tax purposes. The profits (or losses) are computed in the same way as those of a trade (see **75** TRADING INCOME). The specific trading income provisions of *ITTOIA 2005* which apply to property businesses are, however, limited to those listed at *ITTOIA 2005, s 272(2)* and reproduced below. These include the fundamental rules that capital receipts and expenditure be excluded and that, subject to any specific rule to the contrary, expenditure is not deductible unless incurred wholly and exclusively for the purposes of the business. As stated at **60.2** above, the basis period rules for trades do not apply to property businesses. Although property income is computed similarly to trading income, it retains its nature as investment income as opposed to earnings and does not count as relevant earnings for pension contribution purposes (subject to the rules at **60.20** below for furnished holiday lettings).

The above was the statutory position for *all* property businesses before the introduction of the cash basis for 2017/18 onwards. In practice, a cash basis could be used before 2017/18, instead of the full earnings basis required by GAAP, but only where gross annual receipts did not exceed £15,000. The basis had to be used consistently and give a reasonable overall result not substantially different from that produced on an earnings basis. See HMRC Property Income Manual PIM1101. This is now superseded by the statutory cash basis at **60.4** above.

See **60.11** below for relief for small amounts of income (the 'property allowance') for 2017/18 onwards.

The list of included trading income provisions is as follows.

ITTOIA 2005	**Brief description**	**See main coverage at**
s 26	losses computed on same basis as profits	**45.1** LOSSES
s 27	meaning of 'receipts' and 'expenses'	**75.21** TRADING INCOME
s 28A	money's worth	**75.42** TRADING INCOME

ITTOIA 2005	**Brief description**	**See main coverage at**
s 29	interest payable	**42.2** INTEREST PAYABLE
s 33	capital expenditure non-deductible	**75.43** TRADING INCOME
s 34	'wholly and exclusively' rule for expenditure	**75.44** TRADING INCOME
s 35	bad and doubtful debts	**75.48** TRADING INCOME
ss 36, 37	timing of deductions for remuneration	**75.64** TRADING INCOME
ss 38–44	timing of deductions for employee benefit contributions	**75.65** TRADING INCOME
ss 45–47	expenditure on business entertainment and gifts	**75.76** TRADING INCOME
ss 48–50B	car hire	**75.50** TRADING INCOME
s 52	interest payable — exclusion of double relief	**42.13** INTEREST PAYABLE
s 53	employee and employer National Insurance contributions	**75.72** TRADING INCOME
s 54	interest, surcharges and penalties in relation to tax — non-deductible	**75.93, 75.129** TRADING INCOME
s 55	illegal payments non-deductible	**75.91** TRADING INCOME
s 55A	expenditure on integral features of buildings and structures	**75.110** (a) TRADING INCOME
s 57	pre-trading expenditure	**75.106** TRADING INCOME
ss 58, 59	incidental costs of obtaining finance	**75.97** TRADING INCOME

ITTOIA 2005	Brief description	See main coverage at
s 69	payments for restrictive undertakings	**75.75** TRADING INCOME
ss 70, 71	employees seconded to charities or educational bodies	**75.74** TRADING INCOME
s 72	payroll deduction schemes: contributions to agents' administrative costs	**14.18** CHARITIES AND CHARITABLE GIVING
s 73	counselling etc. services to employees	**75.70** TRADING INCOME
ss 74, 75	retraining employees	**75.73** TRADING INCOME
ss 76–80	redundancy payments etc.	**75.69** TRADING INCOME
s 81	expenditure on personal security	**75.114** TRADING INCOME
ss 82–86	subscriptions and contributions	**75.119** TRADING INCOME
ss 86A, 86B	contributions to flood and coastal erosion risk management projects	**75.119** TRADING INCOME
ss 87, 88	research and development and scientific research	**75.113** TRADING INCOME
ss 89, 90	expenditure on trademarks, designs and patents	**75.102, 75.103** TRADING INCOME
s 91	payments to Export Credits Guarantee Department	**75.102** TRADING INCOME
s 94AA	deductions in relation to salaried members of limited liability partnerships	**52.27** PARTNERSHIPS

ITTOIA 2005	**Brief description**	**See main coverage at**
ss 94D–94G	(for 2017/18 onwards) fixed rate deduction scheme — expenditure on vehicles (and see below)	**77.2–77.4** TRADING INCOME — FIXED RATE DEDUCTION SCHEME
s 96	capital receipts excluded from profits	**75.105** TRADING INCOME
s 97	debts incurred and later released	**75.106** TRADING INCOME
s 104	distribution of assets of mutual concerns	**75.102** TRADING INCOME
s 105	industrial development grants	**75.120** TRADING INCOME
s 106	insurance recoveries	**75.92** TRADING INCOME
s 109	receipt by donor etc. of benefit attributable to certain gifts	**75.88** TRADING INCOME
ss 148A–148J	long funding leases of plant and machinery	**75.99, 75.100** TRADING INCOME
s 155	levies and repayments under *Financial Services and Markets Act 2000*	**75.115** TRADING INCOME
ss 188–191	unremittable amounts	**75.127** TRADING INCOME

As regards the inclusion in the above table of the fixed rate deduction scheme for expenditure on vehicles, a transitional rule enables the scheme to be used (for 2017/18 onwards) regardless of whether or not the person carrying on the property business has claimed plant and machinery capital allowances on the vehicle in question for any of the years 2013/14 to 2016/17 inclusive. See also **10.26** CAPITAL ALLOWANCES ON PLANT AND MACHINERY. The rule at **77.1** TRADING INCOME — FIXED RATE DEDUCTION SCHEME whereby the scheme cannot be used by partnerships that include non-individuals applies equally for the purpose of calculating profits of a property business.

[*ITTOIA 2005, ss 271B, 272; FA 2016, ss 71(3)(7), 72(2)(4)(5); F(No 2)A 2017, Sch 2 paras 13, 16, 64(1); FA 2018, s 36(4)(8)(9)*].

Profits or losses on contracts taken out to hedge interest payments deductible in computing profits or losses of the property business will normally be taxed or relieved as receipts or deductions of that business. Such profits or losses would generally be computed on an accruals basis in accordance with normal accountancy practice. Similarly deposits paid to landlords by tenants or licensees will ordinarily be receipts of the business, to be recognised in accordance with generally accepted accountancy practice, normally by being deferred and matched with the related costs. Excess deposits which are refunded should be excluded from the business receipts. (HMRC Property Income Manual PIM1051).

As regards allowable legal and professional costs, see HMRC Property Income Manual PIM22120. For guidance on deductibility of repairs in a property business see HMRC Business Income Manual BIM46900. See **60.12** below as regards restrictions to deductions of mortgage interest and other finance costs for 2017/18 onwards. See HMRC Property Income Manual generally.

Apportionment of profits to tax year

Where, exceptionally, a period of account of a property business does not coincide with a tax year, profits must be apportioned to tax years. This must normally be done by reference to the number of days in the periods concerned, but the taxpayer may choose any other method, e.g. months and part-months, if it is reasonable to do so and so long as the chosen method is applied consistently. [*ITTOIA 2005, s 275, Sch 2 para 62*].

Simon's Taxes. See **B6.202.**

Relief for small amounts of income (the property allowance)

[60.11] A £1,000 allowance (the '*property allowance*') is introduced for property income with effect for **2017/18** onwards. It does not apply to property businesses carried on in partnership or where rent-a-room relief is available (see **60.22** below), but otherwise it applies to both UK and overseas property income and to income from both furnished and unfurnished lettings. An entirely separate £1,000 allowance is introduced simultaneously for trading income and certain miscellaneous income (see **75.3** TRADING INCOME).

The allowance operates by reference to the gross receipts (i.e. before deducting expenses) brought into account in calculating the profits of an individual's 'relevant property businesses'. Rent-a-room receipts (**60.22** below) are excluded if the individual qualifies for rent-a-room relief for the tax year. Post-cessation receipts (**60.16** below) and adjustment income (**60.17** below) are effectively excluded from 'gross receipts' as they are subject to separate tax charges and not brought into account in computing profits. Balancing charges for capital allowances purposes are also excluded if they relate to a business or transaction which is carried on, or entered into, for the purpose of generating receipts which would themselves be excluded. See below for general exclusions.

Relevant property businesses

Any property business carried on by an individual is a '*relevant property business*' unless:

- the individual qualifies for rent-a-room relief, and the business is a rent-a-room property business, i.e. a property business all of whose receipts are rent-a-room receipts; or
- the business is a notional property business in receipt of distributions from a Real Estate Investment Trust (see **60.24** below) or a Property Authorised Investment Fund (see **80.4** UNIT TRUSTS ETC.).

A partnership property business is distinct from any business carried on by its individual members (see **60.2** above) and is thus automatically excluded.

Where an individual has both a UK and an overseas relevant property business, these are considered together for the purpose of the £1,000 allowance, i.e. it is not possible to have full or partial relief (see below) for one relevant property business but not the other. Under partial relief, it is for the individual to decide how the £1,000 allowance should be allocated between two relevant property businesses, except that it cannot be used to create a loss in any business.

Full relief

Where an individual's gross receipts (as above) for the tax year do not exceed the £1,000 property allowance, there is no charge to tax. This means that the receipts themselves are not brought into account as property income, and there is no tax relief for the expenses that would otherwise have been deductible from those receipts in computing property income. The individual can elect for full relief not to be given. The election must be made no later than the first anniversary of 31 January following the tax year in question, and has effect only for the tax year for which it is made.

Partial relief

Where gross receipts (as above) exceed the £1,000 allowance, the individual can elect to use an alternative method of calculating property income. Under this method the charge to tax is on the excess of gross receipts over £1,000. There is no tax relief for the expenses that would otherwise have been deductible from gross receipts in computing property income.

The election for partial relief must be made no later than the first anniversary of 31 January following the tax year in question, and has effect only for the tax year for which it is made.

Exclusions

Neither full nor partial relief is available for a tax year in any of the following circumstances.

- The individual receives a basic rate tax reduction for mortgage interest and/or other finance costs under **60.12** below.
- The individual is entitled to full rent-a-room relief in respect of a property business other than the relevant property business (see above) but elects to disapply the relief, or the individual would be entitled to partial rent-a-room relief (the alternative method of calculation) but no election is in force to apply it. The stated intention is to prevent individuals from using the property allowance if they have chosen to deduct actual expenses in calculating the profits of another property business for the same tax year.

- The individual's gross receipts (as above) include a payment made by (or on behalf of) a person at a time when the individual is an employee of that person or the spouse or civil partner of such an employee. This is to prevent employers reclassifying payments to employees etc. so as to bring those payments within the ambit of the property allowance.
- The individual's gross receipts include a payment made by (or on behalf of) a firm at a time when the individual is a partner in the firm or is connected with a partner in the firm.
- The individual's gross receipts include a payment made by (or on behalf of) a close company (broadly a company under the control of five or fewer participators) at a time when the individual is a participator in the close company or an associate (see *CTA 2010, s 448*) of a participator.

[*ITTOIA 2005, ss 307G, 783B–783BQ; F(No 2)A 2017, Sch 3 paras 1, 8, 13*].

For official guidance see HMRC Property Income Manual PIM4400.

Mortgage interest and other finance costs

[60.12] Deductions for 'finance costs' incurred on or after **6 April 2017** are restricted in computing residential property income (other than from furnished holiday lettings) for income tax purposes. Broadly, 'finance costs' include mortgage interest, interest on loans to buy furnishings, and fees incurred when taking out or repaying mortgages or loans (see further below). Only a percentage of otherwise allowable finance costs are deductible in computing property income. Subject to the further limitations below, the balance attracts relief at the basic rate only; the basic rate relief is given as a tax reduction at Step 6 of the calculation of income tax liability at **1.10** ALLOWANCES AND TAX RATES. For 2020/21 onwards, all finance costs will be relieved at basic rate only. In the meantime, the percentage of otherwise allowable costs given as a deduction in computing profits will be as follows.

2017/18	75%
2018/19	50%
2019/20	25%

The restriction applies equally to UK and overseas property businesses. For official guidance with examples see www.gov.uk/guidance/changes-to-tax-relief-for-residential-landlords-how-its-worked-out-including-case-studies. See also HMRC Property Income Manual PIM2054–2058. The restriction applies whether profits are calculated on the cash basis or in accordance with GAAP, but see **60.9** above as regards computation of loan costs on the cash basis before the above restriction is taken into account.

The basic rate reduction

The basic rate reduction is available to an individual who is liable to income tax on any of the profits of the property business. The reduction is limited to 20% of the lower of:

(a) the amount (the '*relievable amount*') that would have been deductible in computing profits had it not been for the above restriction (or, in the case of a partnership, the individual's share of that amount) plus any unrelieved amount brought forward from the previous year (see below);
(b) the taxable profits of the property business for the tax year (or, in the case of a partnership, the individual's share of them), net of any losses brought forward; and
(c) the individual's 'adjusted total income' for the year.

If the amount on which relief is available is less than the total in (a) above (i.e. because it is limited by (b) and/or (c) above), so much of that total as is unrelieved is carried forward and included in (a) in the following tax year.

Where there is more than one residential property business (e.g. a UK and overseas business), the actual amount on which the reduction is based is apportioned between the businesses by reference to the lower of (a) and (b) above for each business.

'*Adjusted total income*' in (c) above is found by taking the individual's net income for the year (see Step 2 of the calculation of income tax liability at **1.10** ALLOWANCES AND TAX RATES), subtracting so much of it as is savings income or dividend income, and then subtracting the personal allowance and, where applicable, the blind person's allowance.

The order in which tax reductions are given against an individual's tax liability is set out at **1.12** ALLOWANCES AND TAX RATES, which also makes clear that a tax reduction must be restricted to the extent (if any) that it would otherwise exceed an individual's remaining income tax liability after making all prior reductions.

Estate income

Where:

- an individual is liable to tax on estate income arising from an interest in a deceased person's estate (see **22** DECEASED ESTATES);
- the deceased's personal representatives are liable to tax on the profits of a residential property business; and
- the individual's estate income for the year consists of, or includes, a share of those profits,

the individual's share of the amount that would have been deductible in computing profits had it not been for the above restriction is included in (a) above. More than one such amount may fall to be included where an estate distribution includes amounts representing profits of more than one tax year.

Trusts with accumulated or discretionary income

To the extent that the income of a property business is accumulated or discretionary income of a trust (see **70.11** SETTLEMENTS), the basic rate reduction is available to the trustees in similar manner as to individuals but disregarding (c) above. (In the case of trust property income to which an individual is beneficially entitled, it will be the beneficiary who is eligible for the basic rate reduction as above.) For the order in which tax reductions are given to persons other than individuals, e.g. trusts, see **1.12** ALLOWANCES AND TAX RATES.

Finance costs

Finance costs within this restriction are those incurred in respect of a 'dwelling-related loan'. A '*dwelling-related loan*' is so much of any amount borrowed for property business purposes as is referable (on a just and reasonable apportionment) to so much of the business as is carried on for the purpose of generating income from land consisting of a dwelling-house or part of a dwelling-house (or from an estate, interest or right in or over such land). It would thus include a loan to buy furnishings. It also includes a loan for constructing a dwelling-house or adapting a property for use as a dwelling-house. A loan is not a dwelling-related loan so far as it is referable (on a just and reasonable apportionment) to so much (if any) of the business as consists of the commercial letting of furnished holiday accommodation within **60.20** below. A dwelling-house includes for these purposes any land occupied or enjoyed with it as garden or grounds.

'*Finance costs*' incurred in respect of a dwelling-related loan comprise:

- interest on the loan;
- any amount that is economically equivalent to interest from the point of view of the lender; and
- incidental costs of obtaining the finance represented by the loan. See **75.97** TRADING INCOME for what is meant by incidental costs of obtaining finance.

[*ITTOIA 2005, ss 272A, 272B, 274A, 274AA, 274B, 274C; FA 2016, s 26; F(No 2)A 2017, Sch 2 paras 19, 64(1)*].

Example

[60.13]

Jacob owns a property in Coventry which he acquired with the aid of a mortgage. Part of the building is rented out as office premises and part as residential accommodation. The latter is not furnished holiday accommodation. A comparison of the floor areas of the commercial and residential parts of the building shows that the latter comprise 64% of the total floor area of the building.

For 2020/21, the interest paid on the mortgage amounts to £5,600. The profits of Jacob's UK property business, before deducting any mortgage interest but otherwise as adjusted for tax purposes, amount to £32,000. There is an allowable loss of £3,200 brought forward from 2019/20 (see **60.25** below). Jacob has no overseas property business. He is a lecturer with taxable profits of £26,716 for the year to 30 June 2020 but has no other source of taxable income. His liability to income tax is at the main UK rates.

Jacob's property income for 2020/21 is calculated as follows.

		£	£
Profits before deducting mortgage interest			32,000
Deduct:	Mortgage interest:		
	commercial accommodation £5,600 @ 36%		2,016
	residential accommodation (£5,600 @ 64%) x 0%	—	
			(2,016)
			29,984
Deduct:	Loss brought forward		3,200
Taxable property income			£26,784

Jacob's income tax liability for 2020/21 is calculated as follows.

				£
Professional income				26,716
Property income as above				26,784
Total and net income				53,500
Deduct:	Personal allowance			12,500
Taxable income				£41,000
Tax payable:				
		37,500	@ 20%	7,500.00
		3,500	@ 40%	1,400.00
		£41,000		
				8,900.00
Less:	Basic rate reduction (see below): £3,584 @ 20%			716.80
Tax payable				£8,183.20

The basic rate reduction is based on the lowest of the following:

		£
(i)	interest otherwise unrelieved (£5,600 – 2,016)	3,584
(ii)	the taxable profits of the property business for the year, net of losses brought forward	26,784
(iii)	the individual's 'adjusted total income' for the year, i.e. net income, exclusive of any savings income or dividend income, minus the personal allowance (and any blind person's allowance)	41,000

Notes

(a) Where a property business consists of the letting of both residential and other accommodation, the restriction to basic rate applies only to the proportion of finance costs that relates to the residential letting. Any apportionment should be made on a just and reasonable basis. In this example, the mortgage interest has been apportioned by reference to floor space. One alternative would have been to apportion it by reference to the respective values of the different parts of the building. See HMRC Property Income Manual PIM2056.

(b) If the amount on which the basic rate deduction is based had been less than the figure given by option (i) (i.e. because option (ii) or (iii) gave a lower figure), the deficit would have been carried forward and added to the option (i) figure for the following tax year.

Replacement domestic items relief

[60.14] Replacement domestic items relief enables landlords of residential property to deduct capital expenditure on domestic items, e.g. furniture, furnishings, appliances (including white goods) and kitchenware, where the expenditure is on a replacement item provided for use in the property. The relief applies to both furnished and unfurnished lettings, but not to furnished holiday lettings (within **60.20** below) where the property constitutes some or all of the furnished holiday accommodation for the tax year. A fixture is not a domestic item for this purpose, and '*fixture*'is defined as plant or machinery that is so installed, or otherwise fixed in or to, a property as to become, in law, part of that property; the definition specifically includes any boiler or water-filled radiator installed as part of a space or water heating system.

The relief is available where all the following conditions are met:

- a person (P) carries on a property business in relation to land which consists of or includes a dwelling-house;
- P incurs expenditure on replacing a domestic item; the new item must be provided solely for the 'lessee' for use in the dwelling-house, and the old item must no longer be available for such use following its replacement; a '*lessee*' for this purpose is a person who is entitled upon payment to the use of the dwelling-house, whether or not a formal lease exists;
- the expenditure is incurred wholly and exclusively for the purposes of the business but is non-deductible due to its being of a capital nature; and
- no capital allowances are available on the expenditure.

The relief is available whether profits are calculated on the cash basis or in accordance with GAAP. It is not available where P has rent-a-room receipts for the tax year from the dwelling-house, unless no rent-a-room relief (see **60.22** below) is applied in respect of those receipts.

The deduction is made in computing the profits of the property business, and does not require the making of a claim. The amount of the deduction is the cost of the replacement item, but is limited to the cost of an equivalent item if the new item is not the same, or substantially the same, as the old. If P incurs incidental capital expenditure in connection with the disposal of the old item or the purchase of the new, the deduction is increased by the amount of that expenditure. If the old item is disposed of for consideration, the deduction is reduced by the amount or value (in money or money's worth) to which P, or a person connected with him (within **19** CONNECTED PERSONS), is thus entitled. If the disposal is in part-exchange for the new item, the part-exchange value is treated as expenditure incurred on the new item but the deduction is then reduced by the same amount.

[*ITTOIA 2005, s 311A; FA 2016, s 73(1)(8)(9); F(No 2)A 2017, Sch 2 paras 24, 64(1)*].

Miscellaneous deductions

[60.15] Special deductions may be available as follows.

(a) *Capital allowances on plant and machinery.* A property business is a qualifying activity for the purposes of such allowances under *CAA 2001, Pt 2* (see **10.4** CAPITAL ALLOWANCES ON PLANT AND MACHINERY). Allowances are thus given as expenses, and charges treated as receipts, of the business. Plant or machinery provided for use in a dwelling-house is excluded (with a just and reasonable apportionment of expenditure where such use is partial). [*CAA 2001, ss 15, 16, 35*].
For HMRC's definition of 'dwelling-house' in this respect, with particular reference to buildings in multiple occupation, see HMRC Capital Allowances Manual CA11520. In *Tevfik v HMRC* FTT (TC 7383), [2019] UKFTT 600 (TC), the FTT observed that the common parts of such a building such as the entrance lobby, corridors, stairs or lifts and those parts of the building which do not provide any living facilities would not comprise a dwelling-house, and neither would installations to the building such as mains, gas or electrical services, or security and communication systems.

(b) *Sea walls.* For allowances for expenditure on making sea walls, see *ITTOIA 2005, ss 315–318* and *Hesketh v Bray* CA 1888, 2 TC 380.

Simon's Taxes. See **B3.304, B6.208.**

Post-cessation receipts and expenditure

[60.16] Income tax is charged on any 'post-cessation receipts' of a UK property business by adopting the rules applicable to trades at **59.1–59.4** POST-CESSATION RECEIPTS AND EXPENDITURE in suitably modified form. A '*post-cessation receipt*' is a sum which is received after a person permanently ceases to carry on a UK property business and which arises from the carrying on of the business before cessation. If profits for the tax year of cessation are calculated on the cash basis (see **60.4** above), a sum is a post-cessation receipt only if it would have been brought into account in calculating profits on the cash basis had it been received immediately before cessation. The charge for any tax year is on the full amount of post-cessation receipts for that year. In contrast to the rules for trades, post-cessation receipts of a UK property business do not count as relevant earnings for the purposes of making pension contributions. As regards the making of allowable deductions from post-cessation receipts (as in **59.3** POST-CESSATION RECEIPTS AND EXPENDITURE), if profits for the tax year of cessation are calculated on the cash basis, it is assumed that this continues to be the case, so that a deduction is allowed only for any loss, expense or debit that would have been deductible on the cash basis. The charge on post-cessation receipts does not apply in relation to an overseas property business. [*ITTOIA 2005, ss 310, 349–356; F(No 2)A 2017, Sch 2 paras 30–32, 64(1)*].

Relief for post-cessation expenditure is available in relation to a UK property business in the same way as in relation to a trade, profession or vocation (see **59.5** POST-CESSATION RECEIPTS AND EXPENDITURE). The relief is not available to a person in respect of a payment (or an event) which is made (or occurs) in consequence of (or otherwise in connection with) arrangements (as widely defined) to which the person is a party and a main purpose of which is to obtain a reduction in tax liability as a result of the relief. [*ITA 2007, ss 125, 126*].

Simon's Taxes. See **B6.213**.

Adjustments on change of basis

[60.17] An adjustment similar to that described at **75.24** TRADING INCOME is required where:

- there is, from one period of account of a UK property business to the next, a 'change of basis' in computing taxable profits;
- the old basis accorded with the law or practice applicable in relation to the period of account before the change; and
- the new basis accords with the law and practice applicable in relation to the period of account following the change.

A '*change of basis*' for this purpose is either (i) a change of accounting principle or practice that, in accordance with generally accepted accounting practice (see **75.21** TRADING INCOME), gives rise to a prior period adjustment, or (ii) a change in the statutory tax adjustments applied (including a change resulting from a change of view as to application of the statute but excluding a change made to comply with an amendment to the statute which was not applicable to the earlier period of account).

The rules are based on those described at **75.24** TRADING INCOME, as suitably modified.

Tax is charged on the full amount of any adjustment income arising in a tax year. The adjustment income is charged separately from the profits of the UK property business. However, for loss relief purposes adjustment income is treated as profits of the UK property business for the tax year in which tax is charged on it.

These rules are of no application to an overseas property business.

Entering or leaving the cash basis

Where profits are calculated on the cash basis (see **60.4** above) for one tax year but not the next, or vice versa, this counts as a change of basis for the above purposes. Where profits were calculated on the cash basis for the preceding tax year but are calculated in accordance with GAAP for the current tax year, any resultant adjustment income is automatically spread over six years as set out in, and with a similar election available as in, **76.16** TRADING INCOME — CASH BASIS FOR SMALLER BUSINESSES.

[*ITTOIA 2005, ss 329, 329A, 330–334, 334A, 860, Sch 2 para 76; F(No 2)A 2017, Sch 2 paras 27–29, 34, 64(1)*].

Adoption of IFRS 16

There are rules enabling the resulting adjustment to be spread over a period for tax purposes in a case where a lessee treats a lease as giving rise to a right-of-use asset under International Financial Reporting Standard 16 (IFRS 16) and had not previously accounted for it as a finance lease. See **75.82** TRADING INCOME.

Simon's Taxes. See **B6.212.**

Three-line accounts

[60.18] Landlords whose total annual gross income from UK property is below the VAT registration threshold (currently £85,000), or the appropriate proportion of that amount where they have been receiving income from property for less than a full tax year, need only show rental income, total expenses and net profit or loss in their self-assessment tax returns. There is, of course, still a need to keep accurate records to ensure the correctness of the three-line accounts. (www.gov.uk/government/publications/self-assessment-the-three-line-account-what-you-need-to-know). See generally **64.2, 64.5** RETURNS.

Furnished lettings

[60.19] Furnished lettings are taxable as, or as part of, a property business (and the computational rules at **60.10** above thus apply). See **60.20, 60.22** below for, respectively, special rules for furnished holiday lettings and rent-a-room relief.

A furnished letting is a lease or other arrangement under which a sum is payable for the use of premises (which expression includes a caravan or houseboat, as in **60.2** above) and the person entitled to the use of the premises is also entitled to the use of furniture. Any consideration receivable for the use of furniture is chargeable as property income in the same way as rent (and expenditure incurred in providing furniture is treated accordingly). This does not apply to any amount taken into account in computing profits of a trade involving the making available of furniture for use in premises.

[*ITTOIA 2005, s 308; FA 2016, s 73(4)(8)(9)*].

Dependent on the nature of the lettings, including their frequency and the extent to which the landlord provides services, e.g. cleaning, laundry and meals, the letting may amount to a trade of providing serviced accommodation and be chargeable to tax as trading income rather than property income.

Alternatively, the provision of services may amount to a trade separate to the letting (cf. *Salisbury House Estate Ltd v Fry* HL1930, 15 TC 266). In *Gittos v Barclay* Ch D 1982, 55 TC 633, the letting of two villas in a holiday village was held not to amount to trading. A similar decision was reached in *Griffiths v Jackson*; *Griffiths v Pearman* Ch D 1982, 56 TC 583 in relation to the extensive letting of furnished rooms to students. Note that these cases were decided under the pre-1995/96 property income regime, which differed in a number of material respects from the current rules.

Prohibition of capital allowances

Capital allowances are not due on plant or machinery let for use in a dwelling-house (see **10.4** CAPITAL ALLOWANCES ON PLANT AND MACHINERY) (but see **60.20** below as regards furnished holiday lettings).

Simon's Taxes. See **B6.204**.

Furnished holiday lettings

[60.20] In so far as a property business consists in the 'commercial letting' of 'furnished holiday accommodation' (a 'furnished holiday lettings (FHL) business') for a tax year, it is treated for the following income tax purposes as a trade:

(i) carry-forward of losses against income of the same trade (see below);
(ii) disapplication of the 50:50 joint property rule for spouses and civil partners (see **48.7** MARRIED PERSONS AND CIVIL PARTNERS); and
(iii) relief for contributions to a registered pension scheme (see **57.12** PENSION PROVISION).

In addition, an FHL business is a qualifying activity for the purposes of capital allowances on plant and machinery (see **10.4** CAPITAL ALLOWANCES ON PLANT AND MACHINERY). In contrast to furnished lettings generally, plant or machinery provided for use in a dwelling-house is not precluded, but the replacement domestic items relief at **60.14** above is not available. Also, the restriction at **60.12** above for mortgage interest and other finance costs for 2017/18 onwards does not apply to an FHL business, and nor does the restriction at **42.10** INTEREST PAYABLE on relief for interest paid in 2017/18 onwards on a loan used to invest in a partnership. See Tolley's Capital Gains Tax as regards relief from capital gains tax in respect of furnished holiday lettings.

All commercial lettings of furnished holiday accommodation by a particular person (including a partnership) in the UK are treated as a single trade (or for capital allowances purposes as a single qualifying activity) separate from any genuine trade (or other qualifying activity) carried on by that person. The same applies (though separately) to all such lettings outside the UK but in the EEA (see below).

If a UK property business consists only partly of the commercial letting of furnished holiday accommodation, the profits and losses of the separate parts of the business must be separately calculated. If there is a letting of accommodation only part of which is holiday accommodation, such apportionments are to be made as are just and reasonable. The same rules apply to an overseas property business by reference to accommodation outside the UK but in the EEA (see below).

See also HMRC Helpsheet 253 at www.gov.uk/government/publications/furnished-holiday-lettings-hs253-self-assessment-helpsheet/cvgg.

Relief for losses

An FHL business is treated as a trade for the purpose of loss relief under **45.19** LOSSES (carry-forward of losses against income of the same trade in subsequent years). A UK business and an overseas business are treated separately for this purpose.

There is nothing to prevent losses of a UK property business (whether in the same year or brought forward from earlier years) from being set against profits of a UK FHL business as the latter is part of the UK property business. The same applies as regards losses of an overseas property business against profits of an EEA (excluding the UK) FHL business. However, losses of an FHL business are ring-fenced by *ITA 2007, s 127ZA* and cannot be set against profits of an ordinary rental business.

Property outside the UK

The special treatment of furnished holiday lettings described above applies also to the commercial letting of qualifying furnished holiday accommodation outside the UK but in the European Economic Area (EEA). It does not to apply to furnished holiday accommodation outside the EEA. Apart from the UK, the EEA consists of: Austria, Belgium, Bulgaria, Cyprus, Czech Republic, Denmark, Estonia, Finland, France, Germany, Gibraltar, Greece, Hungary, Iceland, Ireland, Italy, Latvia, Liechtenstein, Lithuania, Luxembourg, Malta, Netherlands, Norway, Poland, Portugal, Romania, Slovakia, Slovenia, Spain, Sweden and Switzerland.

Meaning of 'commercial letting'

'*Commercial letting*' is letting (whether or not under a lease) on a commercial basis and with a view to the realisation of profits. For a case in which the 'commercial letting' test was satisfied despite a significant excess of interest over letting income, see *Walls v Livesey* (Sp C 4), [1995] SSCD 12, but see also *Brown v Richardson* (Sp C 129), [1997] SSCD 233 in which the opposite conclusion was reached. See Revenue Tax Bulletin October 1997 pp 472, 473 for HMRC's view of the requirements in this respect.

Meaning of 'furnished holiday accommodation'

For any tax year, '*holiday accommodation*' is accommodation which:

(a) is available for commercial letting to the public generally as holiday accommodation for at least 210 days in the twelve-month period referred to below; and
(b) is so let for at least 105 such days (but see below as regards the possibility of averaging).

See also the 'period of grace' rule described below.

Any period of more than 31 consecutive days during which the accommodation is in the same occupation (otherwise than because of abnormal circumstances), does not count towards fulfilling the number of days required in (b) above. Any such period is known as a '*period of longer-term occupation*', and if, during the twelve-month period referred to below, more than 155 days fall during periods of longer-term occupation, the accommodation is *not* '*holiday accommodation*'. The words 'in the same occupation' refer to tenants and do not prevent relief being due where the owner himself occupies the property outside the holiday season (HMRC Property Income Manual PIM4110).

The twelve-month period referred to above is the tax year in question, unless:

(1) the accommodation was not let by the person concerned as furnished accommodation in the preceding tax year, in which case the twelve-month period runs from the date such letting commenced in the tax year in question; or
(2) the accommodation was let by the person concerned as furnished accommodation in the preceding tax year but is not so let in the succeeding tax year, in which case the twelve-month period is the twelve months ending with the date such letting ceased in the tax year in question.

Holiday accommodation is '*furnished holiday accommodation*' if the tenant is entitled to use of the furniture.

Averaging

In satisfying the test in (b) above, averaging may be applied to the number of let days of any or all of the accommodation let by the same person which either is holiday accommodation or would be holiday accommodation if it satisfied the test on its own. An election for averaging must be made no later than the first anniversary of 31 January following the tax year to which it is to apply. It must specify the accommodation to be included in the averaging calculation. Holiday accommodation cannot be included in more than one averaging election for a tax year. See below for an example of how averaging works.

An averaging election has to be made separately for properties in the UK and for properties in the EEA. A single election cannot cover both.

Period of grace

A period of grace is allowed if:

- during a tax year (Year 1), a person lets furnished holiday accommodation that qualifies for the special treatment (whether on its own or as a result of averaging but other than as a result of this 'period of grace' rule);
- he continues to let the accommodation during the following year (Year 2) or the following two years (Years 2 and 3);
- it does not qualify for the special treatment for Year 2 (or Years 2 and 3) purely because the letting condition in (b) above is not met; and
- there was a genuine intention to meet that letting condition for Year 2 (or for each of Years 2 and 3).

If the person so elects for either Year 2 or each of Years 2 and 3, the accommodation is treated as qualifying for the special treatment for the year or years in question. Holiday accommodation that qualifies for the special treatment by virtue only of this rule cannot be included in an averaging claim. If an election is not made for Year 2, no election can be made for Year 3. Any election must be made no later than the first anniversary of 31 January following the tax year to which it is to apply.

HMRC Helpsheet 253 includes a useful section on the interaction between averaging and the period of grace.

[*ITTOIA 2005, ss 322–326, 326A, 327, 328, 328A, 328B, Sch 2 paras 74, 75; CAA 2001, ss 13B, 15, 17, 17B; ITA 2007, ss 127, 127ZA; FA 2016, ss 73(5)(8)(9), 74(1)(2); F(No 2)A 2017, Sch 2 paras 26, 64(1); SI 2019 No 689, Reg 13(2)*].

Simon's Taxes. See **B6.4.**

Example

[60.21]

Mr B owns and lets out furnished holiday cottages. None is ever let to the same person for more than 31 consecutive days. Three cottages have been owned for many years but Rose Cottage was acquired on 1 June 2020 (and first let on that day) while Ivy Cottage was sold on 30 June 2020 (and last let on that day).

In 2020/21, days available for letting and days let are as follows.

	Days available	Days let
Honeysuckle Cottage	270	240
Primrose Cottage	195	150
Bluebell Cottage	225	90
Rose Cottage	225	90
Ivy Cottage	30	5

Additional information

Rose Cottage was let for 45 days between 6 April and 31 May 2021.

Ivy Cottage was let for 103 days in the period 1 July 2019 to 5 April 2020 and was available for letting for 180 days in that period.

Qualification as 'furnished holiday accommodation'

Honeysuckle Cottage qualifies as it meets both the 210-day availability test and the 105-day letting test.

Primrose Cottage does *not* qualify although it is let for more than 105 days as it fails to satisfy the 210-day test. Averaging (see below) is only possible where it is the 105-day test which is not satisfied.

Bluebell Cottage does not qualify by itself as it fails the 105-day test. However it may be included in an averaging election.

Rose Cottage qualifies as furnished holiday accommodation. It was acquired on 1 June 2020 so qualification for 2020/21 is determined by reference to the period of twelve months beginning on the day it was first let, in which it was let for a total of 135 days.

Ivy Cottage was sold on 30 June 2020 so qualification is determined by reference to the period from 1 July 2019 to 30 June 2020 (the last day of letting). It qualifies as it was available for letting for 210 days and let for 108 in this period.

Averaging election for 2020/21

	Days let
Honeysuckle Cottage	240
Bluebell Cottage	90
Rose Cottage	135
Ivy Cottage	108

$$\frac{240 + 90 + 135 + 108}{4} = 143.25 \quad \text{days} \quad \text{note (a)}$$

Notes

(a) All four cottages included in the averaging election now qualify as furnished holiday accommodation as each is deemed to have been let for 143.25 days in the year 2020/21.

(b) If Bluebell cottage had still not qualified as a result of averaging but qualified in 2019/20, it would have been possible to make a 'period of grace' election, provided there had been a genuine intention to meet the 105-day letting condition for 2020/21. The same applies if the cottage had qualified for 2018/19 and a period of grace election had been made in respect of it for 2019/20.

Rent-a-room relief

[60.22] The taking in of domestic lodgers may be treated as the carrying on of a trade, where services other than accommodation are provided, or as furnished lettings.

An individual qualifies for a special relief (rent-a-room relief) for a tax year if he has 'rent-a-room receipts' for that year and does not derive any taxable income other than rent-a-room receipts from any trade, letting or agreement from which the rent-a-room receipts are derived. Receipts are '*rent-a-room receipts*' if:

(a) they arise from the use of furnished accommodation in a 'residence' (see below) in the UK or from goods or services (e.g. meals, cleaning, laundry) supplied in connection with such use;

(b) they accrue to the individual during the 'income period' (see below);

(c) the residence in question is the individual's only or main residence for all or part of the income period; and

(d) the receipts would otherwise be brought into account in computing trading income or property income or be chargeable to income tax as miscellaneous income.

For these purposes, a '*residence*' is a building, or part of a building, occupied or intended to be occupied as a separate residence; a caravan or houseboat can also be a residence. If a building (or part) designed for permanent use as a single residence is *temporarily* divided into two or more separate residences, it is still treated as a single residence.

If the receipts would otherwise be brought into account in computing the profits of a trade, the '*income period*' is the basis period for that trade for the tax year in question; see **75.6** *et seq.* TRADING INCOME for basis periods generally. Otherwise, the '*income period*' is the tax year itself, but disregarding any part of the tax year before the letting in question commenced or after it ceased.

Where, in the case of a trade, a cash basis election is in force (see **76** TRADING INCOME — CASH BASIS FOR SMALLER BUSINESSES), the reference in (b) above to receipts accruing to an individual during a period should be read as receipts being received by him in that period. Any amounts brought into account under *ITTOIA 2005, s 96A* (capital receipts — see **76.9** TRADING INCOME — CASH BASIS FOR SMALLER BUSINESSES) as a receipt in computing trading income are treated as receipts within (a) above. Similar rules apply for 2017/18 onwards where the profits of a property business are calculated on the cash basis (see **60.4** above); in this case, any amounts brought into account under *ITTOIA 2005, s 307E* (capital receipts — see **60.8** above) as a receipt in computing property income are treated as receipts within (a) above.

Full rent-a-room relief

If an individual meets the 'exclusive receipts condition' and his total rent-a-room receipts for the tax year, *before* deducting any expenses or capital allowances but *after* adding any 'relevant balancing charges', are no greater than **£7,500**, the receipts are exempt from tax. This means that neither the receipts themselves nor any related expenses, relevant allowances or relevant balancing charges are included in computing any trading profits, letting income or miscellaneous taxable income. A '*relevant balancing charge*' or '*relevant allowance*' is a balancing charge or an allowance falling to be made under the plant and machinery capital allowances code in respect of any plant or machinery provided for the purposes of a trade or letting from which the rent-a-room receipts are derived. If an individual does not meet the 'exclusive receipts condition', the receipts limit is halved, i.e. it is £3,750.

An individual meets the '*exclusive receipts condition*' for a tax year if, for each residence of his from which he derives rent-a-room receipts, no receipts accrue to any other person during the 'relevant period', for the use of residential accommodation (furnished or not) in that residence or for goods or services supplied in connection with such use, at a time when the residence is the individual's only or main residence. The '*relevant period*' is normally the income period (see above) for the tax year, except that if the income period is less than 12 months, the relevant period is extended to the 12 months beginning or ending at the same time as the income period begins or ends.

An election can be made to disapply the relief, for example if the individual would otherwise make an allowable loss. The election is made under *ITTOIA 2005, s 799*. It must specify the tax year to which it applies and has effect for that year only. It must be made, and can be withdrawn, no later than the first anniversary of 31 January following the tax year to which it applies (or such later date as HMRC may, in a particular case, allow — see HMRC Property Income Manual PIM4050).

Alternative method of calculation

If an individual's total rent-a-room receipts for the tax year, *before* deducting any expenses or capital allowances but *after* adding any relevant balancing charges (as above), exceed the limit for full rent-a-room relief (whether it be the higher limit or half that amount), he may make an election to use an alternative method of calculating profits. Under this method, an individual's taxable rent-a-room receipts are restricted to the said excess. No deduction is given for any expenditure or capital allowances. If the individual's rent-a-room receipts are derived from different sources, e.g. a trade and a letting, there is provision for apportioning the limit between the sources for the purpose of applying this method.

The election is made under *ITTOIA 2005, s 800*. It must specify the tax year for which it is made, but has effect for that year and all subsequent years until withdrawn. It must be made no later than the first anniversary of 31 January following the year for which it first has effect (or such later date as HMRC may, in a particular case, allow — see HMRC Property Income Manual PIM4050). A similar time limit applies to a notice of withdrawal, by reference to the tax year for which the withdrawal is to first have effect. A notice of withdrawal is without prejudice to the right to make a fresh election for a subsequent year. Where an election would otherwise apply to a tax year for which the individual's total rent-a-room receipts do *not* exceed the limit, the individual is treating as having withdrawn the election with effect from that year (again without prejudicing the right to make a fresh election for a subsequent year).

Assessments

If an assessment is necessary to give effect to either of the above elections being made or withdrawn, the pre-2005/06 legislation specified that the assessment, if otherwise time-barred, could be made at any time no later than the first anniversary of 31 January following the tax year *in which* the election was made or withdrawn. *ITTOIA 2005* incorporates this rule but with the words 'for which' instead of 'in which'; this is thought to be a drafting error.

[*ITTOIA 2005, ss 784–802; F(No 2)A 2017, Sch 2 paras 10, 33, 64*].

Rent-a-room relief will not normally be available to taxpayers who are living abroad (or in job-related accommodation) and letting their home while they are away; this applies even in the years of departure and return since the property will not normally have been their residence at any time during the income periods for those years. If, however, the letting commences *before* departure and/or ceases *after* return, relief may then be due for the year of departure and/or return (HMRC Property Income Manual PIM4010, 4015).

HMRC consider that rent-a-room relief is inapplicable to the letting of a residence (or part) as an office or for other trade or business purposes (other than the business of providing furnished living accommodation) (Revenue Tax Bulletin August 1994 p 154).

Simon's Taxes. See **B6.6.**

Example

[60.23]

Emily and Charlotte are single persons sharing a house as their main residence. They have for some years taken in lodgers to supplement their income. As Emily contributed the greater part of the purchase price of the house, she and Charlotte have an agreement to share the rental income in the ratio 2:1, although expenses are shared equally.

Gross rents and allowable expenses are as set out below. In the year ended 5 April 2016, the pair faced a heavy repair bill after uninsured damage to one of the rooms.

	Gross rents	Allowable expenses
	£	£
Year ended 5 April 2015	5,700	1,100
Year ended 5 April 2016	3,600	4,400
Year ended 5 April 2017	11,400	4,000
Year ended 5 April 2018	10,500	4,400
Year ended 5 April 2019	10,500	4,400
Year ended 5 April 2020	13,500	8,000
Year ended 5 April 2021	12,000	1,000

For 2014/15, the position is as follows.

Normal computation of property income:

	Emily	Charlotte
	£	£
Gross rents (y/e 5.4.15)	3,800	1,900
Allowable expenses	550	550
Net rents	£3,250	£1,350

Charlotte's share of *gross* rents is less than £2,125, i.e. half of the £4,250 limit then in place. It is assumed that she would not make the election for full rent-a-room relief not to apply. Her share of net rents is thus treated as nil.

Emily's share of gross rents exceeds £2,125, so full rent-a-room relief cannot apply. She can, however, elect to apply the alternative method of calculation. Under that method, she is taxed on the excess of *gross* rents over £2,125. It is assumed that she will make the election as she will then be taxed on £1,675 rather than £3,250.

For 2015/16, the position is as follows.

Normal computation of property income:

	Emily	Charlotte
	£	£
Gross rents (y/e 5.4.16)	2,400	1,200

Allowable expenses	2,200	2,200
Net rents	£200	£(1,000)

Charlotte's share of gross rents continues to be less than £2,125. Under full rent-a-room relief, her share of net rents will be treated as nil. However, she will obtain no relief, by carry-forward or otherwise, for her loss. In order to preserve her loss, she could elect for full rent-a-room relief not to apply, the election having effect for 2015/16 only.

Emily's share of gross rents exceeds £2,125. Therefore, her previous election for the alternative method will not be automatically treated as withdrawn. She will be taxed under the alternative method on £275 (£2,400 – £2,125). However, this is greater than the amount taxable on the normal property income computation (£200), so it is assumed she would withdraw the election with effect for 2015/16 and subsequent years. The notice of withdrawal does not prejudice the making of a fresh election for 2016/17 or any subsequent year.

For 2016/17, the position is as follows.

Normal computation of property income:

	Emily	Charlotte
	£	£
Gross rents (y/e 5.4.17)	7,600	3,800
Allowable expenses	2,000	2,000
Net rents	£5,600	£1,800

Charlotte's share of gross rents now exceeds £3,750, i.e. half of the new £7,500 limit introduced for 2016/17 onwards, so full rent-a-room relief will not apply. She could elect for the alternative method to apply, and her chargeable income will then be reduced to £50 (£3,800 – £3,750). This is further reduced to nil by the bringing forward of her £1,000 loss for 2015/16. If Charlotte did not make the election, her chargeable income would be £800 with the whole of her 2015/16 loss having been utilised.

Emily can make a fresh election to apply the alternative method, with effect from 2016/17, and she will then be taxed on £3,850 (£7,600 – £3,750).

For 2017/18, the position is as follows.

Normal computation of property income:

	Emily	Charlotte
	£	£
Gross rents (y/e 5.4.18)	7,000	3,500
Allowable expenses	2,200	2,200
Net rents	£4,800	£1,300

Charlotte's share of gross rents is below £3,750, so that the election to apply the alternative method is treated as having been withdrawn, and full rent-a-room relief applies instead (assuming no election to disapply it). The balance of £950 of her 2015/16 loss is carried forward. Emily's election to apply the alternative method will continue to have effect (unless withdrawn), so that her chargeable property income will be £3,250 (£7,000 – £3,750).

For 2018/19, the position is as follows.

The normal computation of property income is as for 2017/18. Emily's election to apply the alternative method continues to have effect, so that her chargeable property income is again £3,250, and full rent-a-room relief continues to apply for Charlotte.

For 2019/20, the position is as follows.

Normal computation of property income

	Emily	Charlotte
	£	£
Gross rents (y/e 5.4.20)	9,000	4,500
Allowable expenses	4,000	4,000
Net rents	£5,000	£500

For both Emily and Charlotte, their share of gross rents now exceeds £3,750, so that full rent-a-room relief will not apply, and since their share of the expenses also exceeds £3,750, the election to apply the alternative method will be unfavourable. It is therefore assumed that Emily withdraws her election (by 31 January 2022). They are accordingly both charged to tax on the basis of the normal property income computation, with Charlotte's £950 loss brought forward being set against her share, the balance of £450 being carried forward to 2020/21.

For 2020/21, the position is as follows.

Normal computation of property income

	Emily	Charlotte
	£	£
Gross rents (y/e 5.4.21)	8,000	4,000
Allowable expenses	500	500
Net rents	£7,500	£3,500

For both Emily and Charlotte, their share of gross rents exceeds £3,750, so that full rent-a-room relief will not apply. Both could now elect to apply the alternative method of calculation (the election to be made by 31 January 2023). Emily's chargeable property income will be £4,250 (£8,000 – £3,750) and Charlotte's will be £250 (£4,000 – £3,750). Charlotte's is reduced to nil by offsetting £250 of her remaining 2015/16 loss (of which the balance of £200 is carried forward to 2021/22).

Property Income Distributions (PIDs) from Real Estate Investment Trusts (REITs)

[60.24] A distribution received from a Real Estate Investment Trust (REIT) (see below) by a shareholder within the charge to income tax is treated in the shareholder's hands as profits of a UK property business to the extent that it is paid out of the tax-exempt profits (including tax-exempt chargeable gains) of the REIT. Basic rate tax is deducted at source by the REIT; the shareholder remains liable for any excess liability, i.e. excess of the higher rate of tax over the basic rate. Manufactured dividends (see **4.13** ANTI-AVOIDANCE) that are representative of such dividends are treated similarly; however, where the payer is non-UK resident regulations may provide for the recipient to account for and pay the tax in respect of the manufactured dividend.

Distributions made by an REIT out of profits other than tax-exempt profits are taxed in the same way as any other distribution made by a UK resident company, for which see **65.10** *et seq.* SAVINGS AND INVESTMENT INCOME. A distribution made by a company that has ceased to be an REIT is subject to the special treatment to the extent that it is paid out of tax-exempt profits made while the company was an REIT.

Distributions within the special treatment (known as Property Income Dividends or PIDs) are treated in the shareholder's hands as profits of a single business, regardless of the fact that they may come from different REITs or be received by the shareholder in different capacities. The single business is separate from any property business carried on by the shareholder. These rules apply to an individual partner's share of any PIDs received by a partnership as if it were received by him as a direct shareholder.

If the shareholder is non-UK resident, a PID is again treated as profits of a UK property business, but this does not preclude its being dealt with under the relevant dividend article of a double tax agreement. PIDs are outside the non-resident landlords scheme at **60.31** below.

The special treatment does not apply to distributions falling to be taken into account in computing the recipient's trading profits (see **75.115** TRADING INCOME under Dealers in securities) or on shares held in a Lloyd's underwriter's premium trust fund or ancillary trust fund (see **79.3** UNDERWRITERS AT LLOYD'S).

See HMRC Investment Funds Manual IFM21000–30000.

Attribution rules

There are rules to determine the extent to which a distribution of an REIT is made out of its tax-exempt profits. It is one of the conditions of tax-exempt status that at least 90% of the profits of an REIT's property rental business is paid out as dividends within a specified time; distributions are thus attributed firstly to those profits (i.e. to tax-exempt profits) until the 90% condition is met. Once that condition is met with regard to an accounting period, the REIT may identify as much as it chooses of the balance (if any) of the distributions as being paid out of income (not gains) from activities of a kind in respect of which corporation tax is chargeable (i.e. out of profits other than tax-exempt profits). This apparently includes distributable profits of the tax-exempt business to the extent that such profits differ from the profits as computed for tax purposes, but any part of the distribution so attributed is nevertheless regarded as a distribution out of profits other than tax-exempt profits (Treasury Explanatory Notes to Finance Bill 2006). Any remaining balance of the distribution is next attributed to profits of the property rental business (i.e. to tax-exempt profits) to the extent that these have not yet been matched with distributions; these may include profits of an earlier accounting period. Next, the distribution is matched with any tax-exempt gains on disposals of assets used in the property rental business. Any part of the distribution still not attributed is regarded as a normal distribution out of profits other than tax-exempt profits. For worked examples on these attribution rules, see the Treasury Explanatory Notes to Finance Bill 2006.

Stock dividends

An REIT is able to offer investors a stock dividend instead of a cash dividend (or a combination of both) when making a distribution out of its tax-exempt profits. In these circumstances a stock dividend is subject to the same tax rules as a cash dividend, including the requirement that tax be deducted at source. The amount of a distribution, insofar as it consists of share capital issued in lieu of a cash dividend, is the cash equivalent of the share capital. That cash equivalent is computed as in **65.19** SAVINGS AND INVESTMENT INCOME, i.e. it is normally the amount of the cash dividend alternative but in certain cases it is the market value of the shares received by the investor.

[*CTA 2010, ss 548–550, 554A, 599A; ITA 2007, ss 576, 918, 973, 974; FA 2006, ss 121–123; FA 2016, Sch 1 paras 32, 73*].

Deduction of tax at source

The requirements concerning deduction of basic rate tax at source are set out in regulations (see *SI 2006 No 2867 as amended*). These *inter alia* specify classes of shareholder to whom PIDs can be made without deduction of tax (e.g. local authorities, health service bodies, public offices and Crown departments, charities, ISAs, Child Trust Funds, registered pension schemes). They also require REITs to provide shareholders with tax deduction certificates (e.g. to assist with preparation of self-assessment tax returns) and provide the framework for returns and payment to HMRC of the tax deducted by the REIT.

There is a tax charge on an REIT if it makes a distribution to a shareholder with a 10% interest or more in the company or its dividends. A distribution that is withheld in order to prevent or reduce such a charge is nevertheless treated as having been made for the purposes of the regulations dealing with deduction of basic rate tax at source. [*CTA 2010, ss 530(6), 551–554; ITA 2007, s 974(3); FA 2006, ss 107(9)(b), 114, 122(4)*].

General note on REITs

Any listed UK resident company may opt into REIT status. It then continues to have REIT status for subsequent accounting periods until it opts out or its status is withdrawn by HMRC or it ceases to meet fundamental conditions. The company must carry on a property rental business (as defined), and both the company and the business must satisfy a number of conditions. The property rental business may include overseas properties, but certain properties are excluded; it must account for at least 75% of the company's business. At least 90% of the profits of the property rental business must be distributed as dividends. For so long as a company has REIT status, the profits and gains of its property rental business are exempt from corporation tax. The regime extends, with the appropriate modifications, to groups of companies. The intention of the REIT regime is to provide a collective investment vehicle for property investment where the returns received by investors mirror the treatment of direct holding in property; the legislation effectively shifts the burden of taxation of property rental from a company to its investors. A company within the regime may elect to apply it to a joint venture carried on by a group of companies in which it has an interest. For detailed coverage of REITs themselves, the corporation tax exemption, the conditions that the companies and their businesses must satisfy and the consequences flowing from breaches of those conditions, see Tolley's Corporation Tax under Investment Trusts.

Property AIFs

On and after 6 April 2008, new *regulations* enable open-ended investment companies to become Property AIFs (Property Authorised Investment Funds). This is a separate regime for collective investment in real property and in REITs and foreign equivalents. The regime is similar to the REIT regime itself. For more details and, in particular, the treatment of distributions to individual investors, see **80.4** UNIT TRUSTS ETC.

Simon's Taxes. See **D7.11.**

Losses

Carry-forward

[60.25] Where a person carrying on a UK property business or an overseas property business (see **60.2** above) (alone or in partnership) makes a loss in that business for a tax year, the loss is automatically carried forward to subsequent tax years without time limit. The carried-forward loss is relieved by deduction in arriving at net income for subsequent tax years (see Step 2 at **1.10** ALLOWANCES AND TAX RATES). However, it can only be deducted from profits of the same property business. The deduction must be made from the first available profits (and then, if those profits are insufficient, from the next available, and so on until the loss is exhausted). The deduction is made in priority to deducting any other reliefs from available profits. A loss is not carried forward to the extent that it is set against general income under the provisions described below. [*ITA 2007, ss 118, 119*].

There is nothing to prevent losses of a UK property business (whether in the same year or brought forward from earlier years) from being set against profits of a UK furnished holiday lettings (FHL) business (see **60.20** above) as the latter is part of the UK property business. The same applies as regards losses of an overseas property business against profits of an EEA (excluding the UK) FHL business. However, losses of an FHL business are ring-fenced by *ITA 2007, s 127ZA* and cannot be set against profits of an ordinary rental business.

Limited set-off against general income

Where a person carrying on a UK property business or an overseas property business (see **60.2** above) (alone or in partnership) makes a loss in that business for a tax year (the year of loss) and as regards that year:

(a) there is a net amount of capital allowances, (i.e. capital allowances exceed any balancing charges); and/or
(b) the property business has been carried on in relation to land that consists of or includes an 'agricultural estate', and 'allowable agricultural expenses' (see below) deducted in computing the loss are attributable to that estate,

a claim may be made under *ITA 2007, s 120* to set the available loss relief against his general income for the year of loss or the following tax year. For 2017/18 onwards, relief against general income is possible only if the loss is calculated in accordance with GAAP and not where it is calculated on the cash basis (see **60.4** above). The structures and buildings allowance at **9.30** CAPITAL ALLOWANCES is ignored for the purposes of (a) above.

The available loss relief is the lower of the loss itself and either:

- the net capital allowances (where (a) above applies); or
- the allowable agricultural expenses (where (b) applies); or
- the sum of those two items (where both (a) and (b) apply).

There is a cap on the total amount of prescribed income tax reliefs that individuals can claim. See **1.11** ALLOWANCES AND TAX RATES. Relief for property business losses against general income is one of the prescribed reliefs.

A claim is given effect by deducting the loss in arriving at net income for the tax year in question (see Step 2 at **1.10** ALLOWANCES AND TAX RATES).

Relief cannot normally be claimed for both the year of loss and the following year in respect of the same loss, but where the whole of the available loss relief cannot be given in one year (i.e. due to an insufficiency of income), the balance may be separately claimed for the other year. Where, against income of the same year, claims are made both (i) in respect of the previous year's loss and (ii) in respect of the current year's loss, (i) takes precedence over (ii).

A claim must be made no later than the first anniversary of 31 January following *the year to which the claim relates* (i.e. the year for which relief is to be given). If the loss was previously being carried forward, the claim must be accompanied by any necessary amendments to the claimant's tax return for any year for which relief has been given on that basis and is now superseded by the claim.

In a case where (b) above would otherwise apply, relief against general income is denied to the extent (if any) that the loss is applicable to otherwise allowable agricultural expenses arising directly or indirectly in consequence of (or otherwise in connection with) arrangements (as widely defined) to which the person making the loss is a party and a main purpose of which is to obtain a reduction in tax liability as a result of the relief. For this purpose, the otherwise available loss is treated as attributable to any such expenses before anything else.

An '*agricultural estate*' (see (b) above) means any land (including any houses or other buildings) which is managed as one estate and which consists of or includes land occupied wholly or mainly for husbandry. '*Allowable agricultural expenses*' (see (b) above) are any deductible expenses attributable to the agricultural estate in respect of maintenance, repairs, insurance or estate management (but excluding loan interest). For these purposes, expenses are taken into account only if they are attributable to the parts of the estate used for husbandry, with those attributable to parts used *partly* for other purposes being proportionately reduced.

[*ITA 2007, ss 120–124, 127B, 127BA; F(No 2)A 2017, Sch 2 paras 62, 64(1); SI 2019 No 1087, Reg 6*].

Tax-generated losses attributable to annual investment allowance

An anti-avoidance rule applies if a loss arises directly or indirectly in consequence of, or otherwise in connection with, 'relevant tax avoidance arrangements' and (a) above applies. No property loss relief against general income may be given to the person making the loss for so much of the available loss relief as is attributable to an annual investment allowance (AIA) (see **10.13** CAPITAL ALLOWANCES ON PLANT AND MACHINERY). For this purpose, the available loss relief is treated as attributable to capital allowances before anything else and to an AIA before any other capital allowance.

'*Relevant tax avoidance arrangements*' are arrangements (as widely defined) to which the person making the loss is a party and a main purpose of which is to be in a position to make use of an AIA in reducing a tax liability by means of property loss relief against general income.

[*ITA 2007, s 127A*].

Mixed membership partnerships

Both the carry-forward of losses and the set-off of losses against general income are denied if the loss is sustained in a partnership and arrangements are in place to secure that losses are allocated to an individual, rather than to a non-individual. See **52.19** PARTNERSHIPS.

Simon's Taxes. See **B6.203**.

Lease premiums etc.

[60.26] If a premium is payable under a '*short-term lease*' (i.e. a lease whose effective duration, see below, is 50 years or less), or under the terms on which such a lease is granted, the person to whom it is due (whether or not the landlord) is treated as entering into a transaction for the purpose of generating income from land. An amount must be brought into account as a receipt in computing the profits of the property business which consists of or includes that transaction (see **60.2** above) for the tax year in which the lease is granted. The amount to be brought into account is:

$$P \times \frac{50 - Y}{50}$$

where:

P = the amount of the premium; and
Y = the number of *complete* periods of twelve months (*other than the first*) comprised in the effective duration of the lease.

Example

Tom grants a 14-year lease of premises for a premium of £50,000 in June 2020. The amount to be included as a receipt in computing the profits of his property business for 2020/21 is as follows:

$$£50{,}000 \times \frac{50 - 13}{50} = £37{,}000$$

Note that these provisions refer to leases granted and not to leases assigned. See *Banning v Wright* HL 1972, 48 TC 421. *ITTOIA 2005, ss 303, 304, Sch 2 paras 70, 71* contain rules for ascertaining the effective duration of a lease, which is not necessarily the same as its contractual duration; in particular, any rights the tenant has to extend the lease, or any entitlement of his to a further lease of the same premises, may possibly be taken into account.

If the terms on which a lease is granted oblige the tenant to carry out work on the premises (other than work such as normal repairs or maintenance which, if incurred by the landlord, would be deductible expenditure in computing the profits of his property business), the lease is treated as requiring the payment of a premium (or additional premium) to the landlord of the amount by which the value of the landlord's interest increases as a result of the obligation.

If the terms on which a lease is granted require the tenant to pay a sum in lieu of rent for a period, and that period is less than 50 years, the person to whom the sum is due (whether or not the landlord) is treated as if he were entitled to a premium equal to that sum. This applies irrespective of the duration of the lease itself, and in particular whether or not it is a short-term lease. The charge to tax is made for the tax year in which the sum becomes payable. The value of Y in the above formula is the number of complete periods of twelve months (other than the first) comprised in the period in relation to which the sum is payable (but excluding any part of that period falling after the expiry of the effective duration of the lease).

'Premium' is widely interpreted for the above purposes by *ITTOIA 2005, ss 306, 307* and, in particular, includes payments to a person connected with the landlord (as in **19** CONNECTED PERSONS).

See generally HMRC Property Income Manual PIM1200–1214.

Payment by instalments

Where any premium etc. is payable by instalments, the tax thereon may itself be paid by such instalments as HMRC may allow in the particular case; the tax instalment period cannot exceed eight years or, if less, the period during which the premium instalments are payable. See HMRC Property Income Manual PIM1220.

[*ITTOIA 2005, ss 276(6), 277–279, 299, 303–307, Sch 2 paras 63, 64, 70, 71*].

Determinations affecting liability of more than one person

Special rules apply where a determination is needed of an amount to be brought into account as a receipt under the lease premium rules and the determination could affect another person's tax liability. HMRC will issue a provisional determination to both the taxpayer and the other party, to which either (or both) may object (within 30 days). Where an objection is made, the said amount must be determined in the same way as an appeal. [*ITTOIA 2005, ss 302A–302C*].

Capital gains tax

See Tolley's Capital Gains Tax for the treatment of chargeable gains arising from disposal by way of a lease. Note particularly that the part of the premium chargeable to income tax is omitted from the computation of the chargeable gain.

Surrender under the terms of a lease

If, under the terms on which a short-term lease is granted, a sum becomes payable by the tenant as consideration for the surrender of the lease, consequences ensue as above as if that sum were a premium. See HMRC Property Income Manual PIM1214. [*ITTOIA 2005, s 280, Sch 2 para 65*].

Variation or waiver of terms of lease

If:

- a sum becomes payable by a tenant (otherwise than by way of rent) as consideration for the variation or waiver of the terms of a lease, and
- the sum is due to the landlord or to a person connected with the landlord, and
- the period for which the variation or waiver has effect is 50 years or less,

consequences ensue as above as if that sum were a premium. This applies irrespective of the duration of the lease itself, and in particular whether or not it is a short-term lease. The charge to tax is made for the tax year in which the contract for the variation or waiver is entered into. The value of Y in the above formula is the number of complete periods of twelve months (other than the first) comprised in the period for which the variation or waiver has effect (but excluding any part of that period falling after the expiry of the effective duration of the lease). See HMRC Property Income Manual PIM1216. [*ITTOIA 2005, s 281*].

Trustees

Chargeable lease premiums etc. arising to trustees of a settlement (including those deemed to arise under **60.27** below) are treated as being income chargeable at the trust rate. See **70.12** SETTLEMENTS.

Factoring of income receipts etc.

The lease premium rules at *ITTOIA 2005, ss 277–281* above are disapplied where the grant of the lease constitutes the disposal of an asset for the purposes of applying the income factoring provisions at **4.39** ANTI-AVOIDANCE. [*ITTOIA 2005, s 281A*].

Simon's Taxes. See **B6.301–B6.313**.

Anti-avoidance — leases granted at undervalue etc.

[60.27] If a short-term lease (as in **60.26** above) was granted at an undervalue and is assigned at a profit, similar consequences ensue as in **60.26** above as regards the assignor as if he had received a premium (except that the opportunity to pay the tax by instalments is not available). The charge to tax is made for the tax year in which the consideration for the assignment becomes payable. The value of P in the formula in **60.26** above is the lesser of the profit on the assignment and the amount of the undervalue (adjusted to take account of any profits on earlier assignments of the same lease). This does not apply in relation to a lease granted before 6 April 1963 or pursuant to a contract entered into before that date. [*ITTOIA 2005, ss 282, 283, Sch 2 para 66*].

If land is sold subject to terms requiring it to be reconveyed on a future date to the seller or a person connected with him (within **19** CONNECTED PERSONS) for a price lower than the sale price, similar consequences ensue as in **60.26** above as regards the assignor as if he had received a premium. This applies only if the period beginning with the sale and ending with the earliest date on which, under the said terms, the land could fall to be reconveyed is 50 years or less. The charge to tax is made for the tax year in which the sale occurs. The value of P in the formula in **60.26** above is the excess of the sale price over the price at which the land is to be reconveyed. The value of Y is the number of complete periods of twelve months (other than the first) comprised in the period of 50 years or less referred to above.

Similar provisions apply (with appropriate modifications) if, instead of being reconveyed, the land is to be leased back to the seller or to a person connected with him. (They do not, however, apply if the lease is granted and begins to run within one month after the sale.) In this case, the sale price is compared to the total of (i) any premium payable for the lease and (ii) the value on the date of sale of the right to lease back the land.

If the date for the reconveyance (or leaseback) is not fixed under the terms of the sale and the reconveyance price (or the total of (i) and (ii) above) varies dependent upon that date, the price (or total) is taken to be the lowest possible under the terms of the sale. There is provision for any overpaid tax to be repaid if the actual date of reconveyance (or of the grant of the lease) turns out to be different to the date by reference to which the tax charge was calculated. A claim for repayment must be made no later than four years after the reconveyance (or the grant of the lease).

[*ITTOIA 2005, ss 284–286, 301, 302; SI 2009 No 403*].

See HMRC Property Income Manual PIM1222, 1224, 1226. For the so-called 'treasury arrangement' to avoid a charge under these provisions where there is a genuine commercial reason for the owner of mineral-bearing land to sell with a right to repurchase, see HMRC Property Income Manual PIM1228. See **4.32** ANTI-AVOIDANCE for other provisions concerning the sale and leaseback of land.

Sub-leases etc.

[60.28] Relief is due if any of the charges at **60.26** above apply, or the charge on assignment (but not the other charges) at **60.27** above applies, and the grant of the lease in question is out of a 'taxed lease' or, as the case may be, the assignment in question is of a 'taxed lease'. A '*taxed lease*' is one in respect of which there has already been such a charge (or there would have been a charge but for the availability of this relief). Thus, in broad terms, the relief applies where the taxable person is himself a tenant and his own landlord has received a premium or other taxable sum in respect of the same property.

The amount given by the formula in **60.26** above is reduced by an amount found by the formula:

$$\frac{PC \times LRP}{TRP}$$

where:

PC	=	the amount given by the formula in **60.26** above in respect of the previous charge,
LRP	=	the 'receipt period' of the receipt under calculation, and
TRP	=	the 'receipt period' of the receipt by reference to which the previous charge was made.

The '*receipt period*' is:

- in the case of a premium (or similar sum) or a sum payable for the surrender of a lease, the effective duration of the lease (see **60.26** above);
- in the case of a sum payable in lieu of rent, the period for which it is payable;
- in the case of a sum payable for variation or waiver, the period for which the variation or waiver has effect; and
- in the case of an assignment, the effective duration of the lease remaining at the date of the assignment.

If the current charge is under **60.26** above and the sub-lease relates to only part of the premises subject to the head-lease, the relief is reduced proportionately on a just and reasonable basis.

Example

Tom grants a 14-year lease of premises to Jerry for a premium of £50,000 in June 2020. The amount to be included as a receipt in computing the profits of Tom's property business for 2020/21 is £37,000 as computed in the example in **60.26** above.

After 4 years, i.e. in June 2024, Jerry grants a ten-year sub-lease for which he receives a premium of £60,000. The amount to be included as a receipt in computing the profits of Jerry's property business for 2024/25 is as follows.

		£
Normal calculation	$£60{,}000 \times \frac{50-9}{50}$	49,200
Less relief as above	$\frac{£37{,}000 \times 10}{14}$	26,429
		£22,771

The relief is restricted to the 'unrelieved balance' of the value of PC in the above formula. The '*unrelieved balance*' is found by deducting the following from the value of PC:

- any relief previously given under these provisions;
- any deductions allowed under **60.29** below; and
- any deductions allowed under *ITTOIA 2005, ss 60–67* (deductions allowed where the land is used for the purposes of a trade etc. — see **75.108** TRADING INCOME),

so far as attributable to the charge to which PC relates.

If there is more than one previous charge in relation to which there is an unrelieved balance, an amount of relief is computed separately for each previous charge and then aggregated, but the total relief cannot exceed the total of the unrelieved balances.

For these purposes, in a case where the previous charge resulted from the tenant's obligation to carry out work on the premises (see **60.26** above), the value of PC in the above formula is recomputed as if that obligation had not included the carrying out of any work that results in expenditure qualifying for capital allowances.

If the relief would otherwise exceed the amount from which it is deductible, it is restricted to that amount.

[*ITTOIA 2005, ss 287–290, Sch 2 paras 67–69*].

Similar provisions apply for corporation tax. The income tax and corporation tax rules interact so that, for example, where the landlord is a company and the tenant is an individual, the tenant remains entitled to the above relief even though the previous charge, i.e. the charge on the landlord etc., is a charge to corporation tax rather than income tax.

See generally HMRC Property Income Manual PIM2300–2340.

Other deductions available to tenant

[60.29] A tenant is allowed a deduction, in computing the profits of a property business carried on by him, by reference to a premium etc. charged on the landlord. The deduction is available to a tenant under a 'taxed lease'. A '*taxed lease*' is a lease by reference to which any of the charges at **60.26** have arisen, or the charge on assignment (but not the other charges) at **60.27** above has arisen (or would have done so but for the availability of the relief at **60.28** above). The deduction is available for any 'qualifying day' on which the whole or part of the premises subject to the taxed lease is either occupied by the tenant for the purposes of carrying on his property business or sub-let. It is given by treating an amount calculated as below as a revenue expense of the tenant's property business, but *not* so as to override any statutory rule, e.g. the 'wholly and exclusively' rule, governing deductible expenditure generally (see **60.10** above). A '*qualifying day*' is a day that falls within the 'receipt period' (as defined in **60.28** above) of the receipt charged under **60.26** or **60.27** above).

The amount of the expense for *each* qualifying day is the amount given by the formula in **60.26** above in respect of the charge under **60.26** or **60.27** above divided by the number of days in its receipt period.

Example (i)

Tom grants a 14-year lease of premises to Jerry for a premium of £50,000 on 1 June 2020. The amount to be included as a receipt in computing the profits of Tom's property business for 2020/21 is £37,000 as computed in the example in **60.26** above. Jerry immediately sub-lets the premises but does not receive any premium.

The number of days in the 14-year receipt period is 5,113. The deduction due to Jerry in calculating the profits of his property business for any one qualifying day is £37,000 divided by 5,113 = £7.24. For a full tax year, Jerry is entitled to a deduction of £7.24 × 365 = £2,643. For the tax year 2020/21, the available deduction is £7.24 × 309 (1.6.20–5.4.21) = £2,237.

If, however, the tenant is also entitled to relief under **60.28** above, he is treated as incurring a revenue expense for a qualifying day only to the extent (if any) that the daily amount computed as above exceeds the daily amount of the relief under **60.28**.

Example (ii)

The sub-letting in *Example (i)* above ceases in 2022/23. On 6 April 2023, Jerry again grants a sub-lease of the premises but this time for a period of 11 years at a premium of £70,000. The amount to be included as a receipt in computing the profits of Jerry's property business for 2023/24 is as follows.

		£
Normal calculation as in **60.26**	$£70{,}000 \times \frac{50-10}{50}$	56,000

Less relief as in **60.28**	$\frac{£37,000 \times 11}{14}$	29,071
		£26,929

The number of days in the 11-year receipt period of the sub-lease is 4,017. The daily amount of the relief given is therefore £29,071 divided by 4,017 = £7.24. This equals the daily expense computed in *Example (i);* as there is no excess, Jerry is not entitled to any deduction for a revenue expense under these provisions for any of the 4,017 qualifying days covered by the sub-lease.

Supposing Jerry had been able to obtain a premium of only £30,000 for the 11-year sub-lease. The amount to be included as a receipt in computing the profits of Jerry's property business for 2023/24 would then be as follows.

		£
Normal calculation as in **60.26**	$£30,000 \times \frac{50-10}{50}$	24,000
Less $\frac{£37,000 \times 11}{14}$	= £29,071 but restricted to	24,000
		Nil

The daily amount of the relief given is now £24,000 divided by 4,017 = £5.97. This is less than the daily expense of £7.24 computed in *Example (i)*, the deficit being £1.27. Jerry would be entitled to a deduction of £1.27 as a revenue expense for each of the 4,017 qualifying days covered by the sub-lease.

If a sub-lease relates to only part of the premises covered by the main lease, the above rules are applied separately to the different parts of the premises, the premium under the main lease being apportioned between those parts on a just and reasonable basis.

With effect in relation to leases granted on or after 6 April 2013, the above deduction is not available to a tenant under a taxed lease if the lease is a taxed lease only because of Rule 1 in *ITTOIA 2005, s 303* (effective duration of leases — see **60.26** above) or its corporation tax equivalent. (Rule 1 treats a lease as ending on a date before the end of the term for which it was granted if it is unlikely that the lease will continue beyond that date and the premium is not substantially greater than if it had ended on that date; it can thus turn a lease of more than 50 years into a short-term lease.)

If the premises subject to the taxed lease are used for the purposes of a trade, profession or vocation instead of for those of a property business, very similar rules apply under *ITTOIA 2005, ss 60–67*, with the deduction being given as an expense in computing the profits of the trade etc. See **75.108** TRADING INCOME.

The total of the deductions allowed under these provisions, any deductions allowed under *ITTOIA 2005, ss 60–67* referred to above and any relief given under **60.28** above cannot exceed the amount charged under **60.26** or, where appropriate, **60.27** above.

[*ITTOIA 2005, ss 291–295, Sch 2 paras 67–69*].

The above deductions are not available when calculating the profits of a property business on the cash basis (see **60.5** above).

Similar provisions as above apply for corporation tax. The income tax and corporation tax rules interact so that, for example, where the landlord is a company and the tenant is an individual, the tenant is entitled to the above deduction even though the lease premium was charged to corporation tax rather than income tax.

See generally HMRC Property Income Manual PIM2300–2340.

Simon's Taxes. See **B6.310**.

Reverse premiums

[60.30] There are provisions to ensure that reverse premiums are taxable as revenue receipts. They apply in relation to any 'reverse premium' (as defined but broadly a payment made or benefit provided by a landlord to a prospective tenant as an inducement to enter into a lease). Other than in cases where the transaction is entered into for purposes of the recipient's trade, profession or vocation. (or prospective trade etc.), a reverse premium is to be treated as a receipt of a UK property business, or (as the case may be) an overseas property business, carried on by the recipient. Subject to a specific anti-avoidance rule where the transaction involves connected persons, it is understood that accountancy principles require the receipt to be brought into account by spreading over the period of the lease or, if shorter, the period to the first rent review. See **75.109** TRADING INCOME for the full provisions. [*ITTOIA 2005, s 311, Sch 2 para 72*].

Simon's Taxes. See **B6.205**.

Non-resident landlords scheme — collection from agents or tenants

[60.31] Where a landlord is non-resident (i.e. his usual place of abode is outside the UK), tax is to be deducted at source by the agent for the property or, where there is no agent, the tenant, with a final settling up with the non-resident landlord (the '*non-residents landlords scheme*'). [*ITA 2007, ss 971, 972*]. The regulations giving effect to these requirements provide broadly as follows.

(i) Letting agents who receive or have control over UK property income of a non-resident must operate the scheme.
(ii) Where there is no letting agent acting, tenants of a non-resident must operate the scheme.

(iii) Tenants who pay less than £100 per week do not have to operate the scheme unless asked to do so by HMRC.

(iv) Letting agents and tenants who have to operate the scheme must pay tax at the basic rate each quarter on the non-resident's UK property income less certain allowable expenses and deductions, and must give the non-resident an annual certificate showing details of tax deducted.

(v) Non-residents whose property income is subject to deduction of tax may set the tax deducted against their UK tax liability through their self-assessment.

(vi) Non-residents may apply to HMRC for approval to receive their UK property income without deduction of tax provided that:
  (a) their UK tax affairs are up to date; or
  (b) they have never had any obligations in relation to UK tax; or
  (c) they do not expect to be liable to UK income tax,

  and that they undertake to comply with all their UK tax obligations in the future. An appeal may be made against refusal or withdrawal of approval.

The regulations also make provision for interest on unpaid tax and for payments on account under self-assessment, and set out details of the annual information requirements on those operating the scheme, and of other information to be supplied on request. Penalties apply under *TMA 1970, s 98* for non-compliance with these return and information provisions.

[*ITA 2007, s 972, Sch 2 para 169; SI 1995 No 2902; SI 2020 No 151*].

For official guidance see www.gov.uk/government/publications/non-resident-landord-guidance-notes-for-letting-agents-and-tenants-non-resident-landlords-scheme-guidance-notes. For information bulletins for letting agents and tenants see www.gov.uk/government/collections/non-resident-landlord-nrl-scheme-information-bulletins.

On and after 6 April 2020, non-UK resident *company* landlords that carry on a UK property business, or have other UK property income, are chargeable to corporation tax on their property income, having previously been chargeable to income tax. For details of how the non-residents landlord scheme applies to non-resident company landlords from 6 April 2020, see www.gov.uk/government/publications/income-tax-changes-to-the-regulations-for-the-non-residents-landlord-scheme/guidance-note. See also Tolley's Corporation Tax under both Non-resident landlords scheme and Non-resident companies.

Simon's Taxes. See **B6.217**.

Items apportioned on sale of land

[60.32] If, on a sale of land, receipts and outgoings due to be received or paid by the buyer are apportioned to the seller, then, in computing the profits of the seller's property business, the part apportioned to him is treated as being of the same nature, i.e. revenue or capital, as the receipt or outgoing itself. [*ITTOIA 2005, s 320*]. So, for example, if rent is receivable in arrears and the sale price includes an adjustment for rent receivable up to date of sale, the amount of that adjustment is income in the hands of the seller and not capital.

Electric-line wayleaves

[60.33] Rent receivable for a UK electric-line wayleave is chargeable to income tax as property income. If a person carries on a UK property business in relation to some or all of the land to which the wayleave relates and the business has other receipts for the tax year in question, the rent receivable for the wayleave is brought into account in the property business. Otherwise, it is taxed as a separate item; the charge is on the full amount of profits arising in the tax year, and the person liable to tax is the person in receipt of, or entitled to, the rent.

Rent is receivable for a UK electric-line wayleave if it is receivable in respect of an easement, servitude or right, in or over land in the UK, enjoyed in connection with an electric, telegraph or telephone wire or cable, including supporting poles or pylons and related apparatus. All references above to 'rent' include any other receipt in the nature of rent and, in particular, the 'other receipts' referred to in **60.2** above.

If, however, a person carries on a trade, profession or vocation on some or all of the land to which the wayleave relates and, apart from rent receivable, or expenses incurred, in respect of the wayleave, no other receipts or expenses in respect of any of the land are included in computing the profits of any property business of the trader, rent receivable, or expenses incurred, in respect of the wayleave may be brought into account, at the trader's option, in computing the profits of the trade etc. instead of being charged as above. This treatment extends to certain wayleaves other than those described above and to wayleaves relating to land outside the UK which would otherwise be included in an overseas property business.

[*ITTOIA 2005, ss 22, 344–348*].

Simon's Taxes. See **B6.502**.

Mines, quarries etc.

[60.34] As stated at **75.1** TRADING INCOME, profits of mines, quarries, gravel pits, sand pits, brickfields, ironworks, gas works, canals, railways, rights of fishing, rights of markets, fairs and tolls and like concerns are computed and charged to income tax as if the concern were a trade carried on in the UK. The full list of the types of concern to which this applies is at *ITTOIA 2005, s 12(4)*, and such concerns are referred to elsewhere in *ITTOIA 2005* as '*UK section 12(4) concerns*'.

Where *rent* is receivable 'in connection with' (see *ITTOIA 2005, s 336*) a 'UK section 12(4) concern' it is chargeable to income tax as property income. The charge is on the full amount of profits arising in the tax year, and the person liable to tax is the person in receipt of, or entitled to, the rent. Where the letting is of a right to work minerals, a deduction is allowed for any sum paid wholly and exclusively as an expense of management or supervision of the minerals.

All references above to 'rent' include any other receipt in the nature of rent and, in particular, the 'other receipts' referred to in **60.2** above.

[*ITTOIA 2005, ss 335–339*].

Simon's Taxes. See **B6.501.**

61

Remittance Basis

Cross-references. See **63** RESIDENCE AND DOMICILE for the meaning of these terms, and **63.36** RESIDENCE AND DOMICILE as regards deemed UK domicile for 2017/18 onwards; **28.5** EMPLOYMENT INCOME for the charge to tax on the remittance basis on chargeable overseas earnings and foreign earnings; **30.36** EXEMPT INCOME for an exemption for low-income non-UK domiciled employees; **32.2** FOREIGN INCOME for the meaning of 'relevant foreign income'; **71.22–71.24** SHARE-RELATED EMPLOYMENT INCOME AND EXEMPTIONS for the charge to tax on the remittance basis on foreign securities income.

For guidance see HMRC Residence, Domicile and Remittance Basis Manual RDRM30000 *et seq*. and RDR1 (Guidance Note: Residence, Domicile and the Remittance Basis) at www.gov.uk/government/publications/residence-domicile-and-remittance-basis-rules-uk-tax-liability.

Simon's Taxes. See **E6.324–E6.332.**

Introduction to the remittance basis

[61.1] UK residents are normally liable to UK tax on the whole of their worldwide income and chargeable gains arising in a tax year (the arising basis). The remittance basis is available to UK resident individuals who are not domiciled in the UK. It provides for foreign source income (and, in the case of non-domiciled individuals only, foreign source chargeable gains) to be charged to tax by reference to the extent to which they are remitted to, or received in, the UK. The deemed domicile rule at **63.36** RESIDENCE AND DOMICILE applies for most purposes of the remittance basis for 2017/18 onwards (see **61.2** below).

The remittance basis applies to 'relevant foreign income' as defined at **32.2** FOREIGN INCOME, relevant foreign earnings (see **61.6** below) and, for non-domiciled individuals only, foreign chargeable gains. For aspects of the remittance basis that are specific to chargeable gains, see the corresponding chapter of Tolley's Capital Gains Tax.

Application of the remittance basis

[61.2] The remittance basis can only apply to an individual for a particular tax year if, for or in that tax year, the individual is resident in the UK, but not domiciled in the UK.

The deemed domicile rule at **63.36** RESIDENCE AND DOMICILE applies for the above purpose for 2017/18 onwards. Thus, an individual who is non-UK domiciled under general law cannot take advantage of the remittance basis if he is deemed to be domiciled in the UK for income tax and CGT purposes. See the exception to this in (2) below. (There is a further exception for the purposes of CGT following a period of temporary non-UK residence, for which see Tolley's Capital Gains Tax under Overseas Matters.)

The remittance basis does apply to an individual for a particular tax year if he makes a claim as in (1) below or if either (2) or (3) below apply to him.

(1) An individual who meets the residence and domicile condition above for a tax year can make a claim to be chargeable on the remittance basis for that year. No time limit is specified for making the claim, so the default deadline at **16.4** CLAIMS applies. An individual who claims the remittance basis loses entitlement to personal reliefs (see **61.8** below). An additional tax charge of £30,000, £60,000 or (for 2015/16 and 2016/17 only) £90,000 applies to a 'long-term UK resident' who makes a claim for the remittance basis to apply for a particular tax year (see **61.9** below).

(2) No claim is required if an individual meets the residence and domicile condition above but the total of his 'unremitted foreign income and gains' for the tax year amounts to less than **£2,000**. An individual's '*unremitted foreign income and gains*' is the total of his 'foreign income and gains' (see **61.3** below) for the tax year less the total amount of those income and gains that are remitted to the UK in that year. Where the £2,000 threshold condition is met, it is assumed that

the remittance basis applies unless the individual is not UK domiciled and meets the conditions for the exemption at **30.36** EXEMPT INCOME. If, however, the individual does not wish the remittance basis to apply for any year, he may give notice of that fact in a self-assessment tax return for the year.

The deemed domicile rule at **63.36** RESIDENCE AND DOMICILE does *not* apply for the purpose of the £2,000 threshold. An individual who meets the residence and domicile condition above, and is non-UK domiciled under general law, can still take advantage of this threshold even if he is deemed to be domiciled in the UK for other tax purposes.

Even if split year treatment applies upon an individual's becoming or ceasing to be UK resident (see **63.19**, **63.33** RESIDENCE AND DOMICILE), the level of unremitted foreign income and gains for the whole tax year is taken into account in considering whether or not the £2,000 threshold condition is met.

Where the £2,000 threshold condition is met and the individual's remittances for a tax year amount to less than £500 and are in cash, he is not required to complete a self-assessment tax return just for the sake of paying UK tax on the amount remitted. However where such an individual is required to complete a self-assessment tax return for any other reason, or if HMRC gives him notice to make a return, he will need to include those small remittances on the return and pay the tax due. (HMRC Brief 17/09, 25 March 2009).

(3) Additionally, no claim is required if an individual meets the residence and domicile condition above but also meets all the following conditions:

   (a) he has no 'UK income or gains' for the tax year other than taxed investment income of no more than £100 gross;
   (b) no 'relevant income' or 'gains' are remitted to the UK in the tax year; and
   (c) he is either under 18 or has been UK resident in no more than six of the nine immediately preceding tax years.

   If, however, the individual does not wish the remittance basis to apply for any year, he may give notice of that fact in a self-assessment tax return for the year.

For the purposes of (3)(a) above, an individual's '*UK income and gains*' means the total of his income and gains other than his 'foreign income and gains' (see **61.3** below). For the purposes of (3)(b) above, an individual's '*relevant income*' and '*gains*' comprise his foreign income and gains for the tax year in question, his foreign income and gains for every other tax year for which (1), (2) or (3) applies to him and his foreign income and gains for any tax year before 2008/09 in which he was UK resident and either not domiciled in the UK or not ordinarily resident in the UK (see **63.34** RESIDENCE AND DOMICILE). For this purpose, an individual's foreign income and gains for a year prior to 2008/09 include 'relevant foreign income' (as in **32.2** FOREIGN INCOME) only if the remittance basis applied to him for that year (whether as the result of a claim in the case of 2005/06 to 2007/08 inclusive or by default for years prior to 2005/06 — see **61.36** below). The point of (3) above is to ensure that an individual does not have to complete a tax return only for the purpose of claiming the remittance basis if he would have no tax to pay on that basis.

[*ITA 2007, ss 809A, 809B, 809D, 809E; FA 2008, Sch 7 para 85; F(No 2)A 2017, Sch 8 para 14(2)(4)(6)*].

Effect of the remittance basis applying

[61.3] Where any one of **61.2**(1)–(3) above applies to an individual for a tax year, the following income and gains of his for that year are chargeable to tax on the remittance basis (even if they are remitted in a tax year for which none of **61.2**(1)–(3) above apply):

(a) 'relevant foreign income' as in **32.2** FOREIGN INCOME (see **61.4** below);
(b) 'relevant foreign earnings' (see **61.6** below);
(c) 'foreign securities income' as in **71.22–71.24** SHARE-RELATED EMPLOYMENT INCOME AND EXEMPTIONS;
(d) amounts chargeable under **26.5** DISGUISED REMUNERATION; and
(e) foreign chargeable gains, but only if the individual is not domiciled in the UK in that tax year.

[*ITA 2007, s 809F; FA 2019, Sch 1 paras 102, 120*].

The items in (a)–(e) above together comprise an individual's '*foreign income and gains*' for a tax year. [*ITA 2007, s 809Z7(2)*].

For the purposes of applying the remittance basis, an individual's '*foreign specific employment income*' for a tax year is such of his specific employment income (see **28.1** EMPLOYMENT INCOME) for the year as is:

- foreign securities income as in (c) above; or
- any income (or any part of any income) of the individual as is within **26.5** DISGUISED REMUNERATION as in (d) above.

[*ITA 2007, s 809Z7(4)(4A)(4B)*].

Charge on relevant foreign income

[61.4] The charge on relevant foreign income for any tax year is on the full amount remitted to the UK (see **61.11** below) in that year. This applies to relevant foreign income for a year for which any one of **61.2**(1)–(3) above applies to the individual; it applies regardless of whether or not the source still exists when the income is remitted and regardless of whether or not any one of **61.2**(1)–(3) above applies to the individual for the year in which it is remitted. It does not apply if the individual is non-resident in the UK for the year in which the income is remitted, but see **61.5** below as regards temporary non-UK residence.

The only circumstance in which any deductions are allowed is where the income is from a trade, profession or vocation carried on outside the UK, in which case the same deductions are allowed as for trades etc. carried on in the UK.

In contrast to the position before 2008/09 (see **61.36** below), relevant foreign income arising in the Republic of Ireland is treated in the same way as relevant foreign income from any other non-UK source; the remittance basis thus applies to such income.

The above charge applies equally to relevant foreign income for 2007/08 and earlier years where it is remitted to the UK in 2008/09 or a later year, but only if the remittance basis applied to the individual for the year in which the income arose (whether as the result of a claim in the case of 2005/06 to 2007/08 inclusive or by default for years prior to 2005/06 — see **61.36** below). Income that arose in the Republic of Ireland is excluded.

Split year treatment

Where a tax year is a split year (see **63.19** RESIDENCE AND DOMICILE), the charge on relevant foreign income for that year is only on the amount remitted to the UK in the UK part of that year.

[*ITTOIA 2005, ss 832, 832B*].

Temporary non-UK residence

[61.5] Relevant foreign income (as in **32.2** FOREIGN INCOME) remitted to the UK while an individual is temporarily non-UK resident is treated as remitted after the individual returns to the UK. The provisions differ according to whether the 'year of departure' is 2013/14 onwards or an earlier year, as set out below.

Year of departure 2013/14 or later

The following applies where the 'year of departure' is 2013/14 or any subsequent year. For what is meant by the '*year of departure*' and the '*period of return*', see **63.29** RESIDENCE AND DOMICILE.

Relevant foreign income remitted to the UK in the 'temporary period of non-UK residence' (see **63.29**(d) RESIDENCE AND DOMICILE) may fall to be treated for income tax purposes as if it were remitted in the 'period of return'. This is the case if the income in question arose in the UK part of the year of departure or in an earlier tax year, where the year in which it arose was a year for which any one of **61.2**(1)–(3) above applied to the individual.

In determining the extent to which income arose in the UK part of the year of departure, any necessary apportionment is to be done on a just and reasonable basis. Nothing in any double tax treaty is to be read as preventing the individual from being chargeable to income tax in respect of any relevant foreign income treated as remitted in the period of return.

[*ITTOIA 2005, s 832A*].

Year of departure before 2013/14

The following applies where the 'year of departure' (as defined in **63.29** RESIDENCE AND DOMICILE) is 2012/13 or an earlier year. It applies where an individual has left the UK for a period of temporary residence outside the UK and:

- four out of the seven tax years immediately preceding the 'year of departure' (as defined below) were years for which the individual satisfied 'the residence requirements'; and
- there are fewer than five tax years (the '*intervening years*') falling between (and not including) the 'year of departure' and the 'year of return'.

In this case, the '*year of departure*' means the last tax year before the year of return for which the taxpayer satisfied the 'residence requirements'. The '*year of return*' is any tax year for which the individual satisfies the 'residence requirements' and which immediately follows one or more tax years for which he did not satisfy those requirements.

An individual satisfies the '*residence requirements*' for a tax year if during any part of the year he is resident in the UK and not 'treaty non-resident' or if for the year he is ordinarily resident in the UK (see **63.34** RESIDENCE AND DOMICILE) and not treaty non-resident.

An individual is '*treaty non-resident*' at any time if he falls at that time to be regarded for the purposes of double tax arrangements (see **27.2** DOUBLE TAX RELIEF) as resident in a territory outside the UK.

Where the above conditions are satisfied, relevant foreign income remitted during the intervening years (but not in a year preceding 2008/09) may fall to be treated for income tax purposes as if it were remitted in the year of return. This is the case if the income in question arose in the year of departure or in any earlier year, where the year in which it arose was a year for which any one of **61.2**(1)–(3) above applied to the individual.

The question of whether a person is or is not resident in the UK for 2013/14 or any subsequent year is to be determined for the above purposes in accordance with the statutory residence test (see **63.4** RESIDENCE AND DOMICILE), but the effect of split year treatment (see **63.19** RESIDENCE AND DOMICILE) is to be ignored.

[*ITTOIA 2005, s 832A*].

Relevant foreign earnings

[61.6] An individual's '*relevant foreign earnings*' for a tax year depend on whether or not he meets the section 26A test in **28.7** EMPLOYMENT INCOME. If the individual does not meet the section 26A test, his relevant foreign earnings are his 'chargeable overseas earnings' (see **28.6** EMPLOYMENT INCOME). See **28.6** EMPLOYMENT INCOME as regards earnings excluded from being chargeable overseas earnings where dual contract arrangements are in force and certain conditions met. If the individual meets the section 26A test, his relevant foreign earnings are his 'foreign earnings' (see **28.7** EMPLOYMENT INCOME). [*ITA 2007, s 809Z7(3)*].

Costs of claiming the remittance basis

[61.7] Where, for any tax year, an individual makes a claim as in **61.2**(1) above for the remittance basis to apply (but not where either **61.2**(2) or (3) above apply to an individual), he loses entitlement to personal reliefs (see **61.8** below) and, if he is a 'long-term UK resident', he is also liable to an additional tax charge of either £30,000, £60,000 or, for 2015/16 and 2016/17 only, £90,000 (see **61.9** below).

Loss of personal reliefs etc.

[61.8] An individual who claims the remittance basis for any tax year is not entitled to any personal reliefs for that tax year and is not entitled to the CGT annual exempt amount. Personal reliefs comprise the personal allowance, married couple's allowance, blind person's allowance and the miscellaneous reliefs at **44.2** LIFE ASSURANCE POLICIES. Such an individual also cannot benefit from the transfer of part of the personal allowance from a spouse or civil partner (see **1.18** ALLOWANCES AND TAX RATES.

[*ITA 2007, s 809G; FA 2019, Sch 1 paras 103, 120*].

It is possible under the terms of some double tax agreements for non-UK residents to claim the remittance basis and still obtain personal reliefs. This can occur where the individual is resident in both the UK and another territory and, under the provisions of the agreement with that territory, is treated as 'treaty resident' in the other territory. See HMRC Residence, Domicile and Remittance Basis Manual RDRM32050.

Additional tax charge

[61.9] An individual who claims the remittance basis for any tax year incurs an additional tax charge for that year if the following circumstances apply to him:

- he is 18 years of age or over in that tax year; and
- he meets:
  - the '7-year residence test' below (in which case the charge is £30,000); or
  - the '12-year residence test' below (in which case the charge is £60,000); or
  - with effect for 2015/16 and 2016/17 only, the '17-year residence test' below (in which case the charge is £90,000).

For 2015/16 and 2016/17, the charge is increased to £90,000 if the individual meets the 17-year test. The 17-year test must be applied before applying the 12-year and 7-year tests. The 17-year test is abolished for 2017/18 onwards as the deemed domicile rule at **63.36** RESIDENCE AND DOMICILE makes it impossible for someone meeting this test to claim the remittance basis.

The '7-*year residence test*' is met for a tax year if the individual does not meet the 12-year residence test but has been UK resident in at least 7 of the 9 tax years immediately preceding that year.

The '*12-year residence test*' is met for a tax year if the individual has been UK resident in at least 12 of the 14 tax years immediately preceding that year.

The '*17-year residence test*' (for 2015/16 and 2016/17) is met for a tax year if the individual has been UK resident in at least 17 of the 20 tax years immediately preceding that year.

The additional tax charge is made on income and gains not remitted to the UK and is thus in addition to the tax charge on remitted income and gains. The individual can nominate the income and/or gains on which this charge is to be levied, and the remittance basis does not then apply to the nominated amount. For example, a taxpayer liable to the £30,000 charge could nominate £75,000 of interest on an overseas bank deposit on which tax is chargeable at 40%, giving a liability of £30,000. Scottish income tax rates and thresholds are ignored for this purpose. The point of nominating is that the nominated income and/or gains are not then charged to tax again if they are remitted in a later year. The nomination is made in the individual's claim within **61.2**(1) above, and the nominated amount must be part (or all) of his 'foreign income and gains' for the year (see **61.3** above). If the nominated amount is insufficient to increase the taxpayer's total income tax and CGT liability by the amount of the additional tax charge (after taking into account all reliefs and deductions due), he is treated for this purpose only as if he had nominated sufficient additional *income* to bring the tax increase up to that amount; this remains the case even if in reality he has insufficient income to nominate. Income *treated as* nominated does not count as nominated income for the purpose of **61.10** below.

As the additional charge is a charge to tax (whether it be income tax or CGT), the normal self-assessment payment dates apply. It is also available to cover Gift Aid payments. The Treasury are of the view that it should be recognised as tax for the purposes of double tax agreements. If, however, insufficient income and gains are nominated, the income *treated as* nominated, and the tax on that income, does not qualify for double tax relief as it is not tax on specific income. (Treasury Explanatory Notes to the 2008 Finance Bill). The US Internal Revenue Service has ruled that the charge is a tax on income and that credit is allowed under US tax law (www.irs.gov/pub/irs-drop/rr-11-19.pdf).

[*ITA 2007, ss 809C, 809H; F(No 2)A 2017, Sch 8 para 14(3)(5)(6)*].

Direct payments to HMRC from untaxed foreign income or gains in settlement of the additional tax charge are not treated for tax purposes as remittances to the UK (see **61.20** below).

All years of actual residence in the UK count towards the residence tests, even if for some or all of those years the taxpayer was treated as 'treaty resident' in another territory under a double tax agreement. See HMRC Residence, Domicile and Remittance Basis Manual RDRM32250. If, for any tax year, split year treatment applies upon an individual's becoming or ceasing to be UK resident (see **63.19**, **63.33** RESIDENCE AND DOMICILE), that year still counts in full towards the years of residence tests.

Nominated income and gains subsequently remitted

[61.10] For the purpose of applying the exemption from charge of nominated income and gains if later remitted, nominated income and gains are treated as not remitted (even if, in fact, they have been) until all other previously unremitted foreign income and gains have been remitted. In considering the extent to which other previously unremitted foreign income and gains have been remitted, one takes into account income and gains arising in the tax year under review and all other years for 2008/09 onwards for which the remittance basis has applied to the individual (on a claim or otherwise).

'Nominated income and gains' means income and gains actually nominated and does not include income merely treated as nominated (see **61.9** above).

The above treatment is disapplied (and the steps below do not need to be taken) if the cumulative total of nominated income and gains from each year that have been remitted in years up to and including the current year does not exceed £10.

Where nominated income and gains are, in fact, remitted but are to be treated as above as having not been remitted, the following steps determine the income and gains that are to be treated as having been remitted instead.

(i) Find the amount of nominated income and gains remitted in the tax year (taking account of nominated income and gains for the tax year in question and all earlier tax years). Add this to the amount of other foreign income and gains remitted in the tax year that has arisen in any year for 2008/09 onwards for which the remittance basis has applied to the individual.

(ii) Next, find the amount (if any) of the individual's foreign income and gains for the year (other than nominated income and gains) that fall within each of the following categories:
- 'relevant foreign earnings' (see **61.6** above), other than those subject to a foreign tax;
- 'foreign specific employment income' (see **61.3** above, other than income subject to a foreign tax;
- 'relevant foreign income' (see **32.2** FOREIGN INCOME), other than income subject to a foreign tax;
- foreign chargeable gains, other than gains subject to a foreign tax;
- 'relevant foreign earnings' subject to a foreign tax;
- 'foreign specific employment income' subject to a foreign tax;
- 'relevant foreign income' subject to a foreign tax; and
- foreign chargeable gains subject to a foreign tax.

  If the tax year is one to which the remittance basis does not apply, ignore this step and step (iii) below.

(iii) Compare the total in step (i) to each of the amounts in step (ii) in the order in which those amounts are listed. If the first such amount does not exceed the total in step (i), regard the total in step (i) as containing the income and gains in that category. Reduce the total in step (i) by the amount of that income and gains and compare what remains with the next of the amounts in step (ii) and so on.

If the first such amount does exceed the total in step (i), regard the total in step (i) as containing the appropriate proportion of each kind of income and gains in that category; similarly if the amount in any subsequent category exceeds what remains of the amount in step (i).

(iv) If, after going through all the categories, the total in step (i) is still not fully matched, repeat the process by reference to income and gains of the 'appropriate tax year' that had not yet been remitted (or treated under these provisions as remitted) by the beginning of the tax year mentioned in (i). The '*appropriate tax year*' is the latest of the preceding years (ignoring years before 2008/09) for which the remittance basis applied.

If the tax year in (i) is one to which the remittance basis does not apply, carry out this step instead of steps (ii) and (iii).

(v) If the total in step (i) is still not fully matched, repeat steps (ii) and (iii) by reference to the next latest of the preceding years for which the remittance basis applied, and so on.

[*ITA 2007, ss 809I, 809J*].

Meaning of 'remitted to the UK'

[61.11] Subject to **61.19** below, an individual's income is, or his chargeable gains are, '*remitted to the UK*' in any of circumstances (a)–(c) below.

(a) Property (which may include money) is brought to, or received or used in, the UK by, or for the benefit of, a 'relevant person' (see **61.12** below) or a service is provided in the UK to, or for the benefit of, a relevant person, and:

  (i) the property, service or consideration for the service (as the case may be) is (wholly or in part) the income or gains; or

  (ii) the property, service or consideration derives from the income or gains and, in the case of property or consideration, is property of, or consideration given by, a relevant person; or

  (iii) the income or gains are used outside the UK (directly or indirectly) in respect of a 'relevant debt' (see **61.13** below); or

  (iv) anything deriving from the income or gains is used as mentioned in (iii) above.

  The references in (ii) and (iv) above to something 'deriving from the income or gains' are references to its so deriving wholly or in part and directly or indirectly.

(b) 'Qualifying property' of a 'gift recipient' (see in both cases **61.14** below):

  (i) is brought to, or received or used in, the UK, and is enjoyed by a relevant person; or

  (ii) is consideration for a service that is enjoyed in the UK by a relevant person; or

  (iii) is used outside the UK (directly or indirectly) in respect of a relevant debt.

(c) Property of a person other than a relevant person (apart from qualifying property of a gift recipient as in (b) above):

(i) is brought to, or received or used in, the UK, and is enjoyed by a relevant person; or

(ii) is consideration for a service that is enjoyed in the UK by a relevant person; or

(iii) is used outside the UK (directly or indirectly) in respect of a relevant debt,

in circumstances where there is a 'connected operation' (see **61.15** below).

In (a)(iii), (b)(iii) and (c)(iii) above, 'used . . . in respect of a relevant debt' includes repayment or partial repayment of a relevant debt, payment of interest on a relevant debt and use as collateral for a relevant debt. In a case where (b)(i) or (ii) or (c)(i) or (ii) above applies to the importation or use of property, the income or gains are taken to be remitted at the time the property or service is first enjoyed by a relevant person by virtue of that importation or use.

Enjoyment of property or a service by a relevant person is to be disregarded for the above purposes if it is minimal (i.e. the property or service is enjoyed virtually to the entire exclusion of all relevant persons); if the relevant person gives full consideration in money or money's worth for the enjoyment; or if the property or service is enjoyed by relevant persons in the same way (and on the same terms) that it may be enjoyed by the public (or a section of the public).

[*ITA 2007, ss 809L(1)–(6)(9)(10), 809N(9), 809O(6)*].

In determining whether a remittance has been made in the case of a foreign chargeable gain on a disposal at undervalue (and if so, how much), the amount of the gain is taken to be the gain that would have arisen if the disposal had been at least equal to market value. [*ITA 2007, s 809T*].

If income (or a gain) would otherwise be treated as remitted to the UK before the income arises (or the gain accrues), by virtue of anything done in relation to anything regarded as deriving from the income (or gain), the remittance is instead treated as made at the time the income arises (or the gain accrues). [*ITA 2007, s 809U*].

Transitional

In either of the following cases, an individual's relevant foreign income (as in **32.2** FOREIGN INCOME) is treated as not remitted to the UK on or after 6 April 2008 if it otherwise would be treated as so remitted:

- if, before 6 April 2008, property (including money) consisting of or deriving from the relevant foreign income was brought to, or received or used in, the UK by, or for the benefit of, a relevant person; and
- if, before 12 March 2008, property (other than money) consisting of or deriving from the relevant foreign income was acquired by a relevant person.

[*FA 2008, Sch 7 para 86(1)–(3)(5)*].

Relevant persons

[61.12] The persons listed at (a)–(i) below are '*relevant persons*' for the purposes of **61.11** above and these provisions generally:

(a)	The individual.
(b)	The spouse, civil partner or cohabiting partner of the individual.
(c)	A child or grandchild (under 18) of any person within (a) and (b) above.
(d)	A close company in which any other person within this definition is a participator.
(e)	A 51% subsidiary of a close company within (d) above.
(f)	A company in which any other person within this definition is a participator and which would be a close company if it were UK resident.
(g)	A 51% subsidiary of a company within (f) above.
(h)	The trustees of a settlement of which any other person within this definition is a beneficiary.
(i)	A body connected with a settlement within (h) above.

For the above purposes, a cohabiting couple are treated as if they were spouses or civil partners; a close company has the meaning given in *CTA 2010, Pt 10 Ch 2* (broadly a company with five or fewer participators); in relation to a settlement that would otherwise have no trustees, a 'trustee' means any person in whom the settled property or its management is for the time being vested; a body is 'connected with' a settlement if the body falls within any of **19.3**(c)–(f) CONNECTED PERSONS as regards the settlement.

The question of whether a person whose property is dealt with as in **61.11**(c) above is a relevant person is to be determined at the time the property is so dealt with.

[*ITA 2007, ss 809M, 809O(2); SI 2019 No 1458, Sch 3 para 29(4)*].

Transitional

In relation to an individual's income or chargeable gains for any year before 2008/09, only the individual himself is a relevant person for the purposes of the provisions in **61.11** above (other than the transitional provision). [*FA 2008, Sch 7 paras 86(4)(4A), 87, 88*].

Transitional trust income

For the purposes of applying **61.11** above in relation to 'transitional trust income', the trustees of the settlement in question are not 'relevant persons'. This exception was introduced in conjunction with the deemed domicile rule at **63.36** RESIDENCE AND DOMICILE'. '*Transitional trust income*' is income:

(i) that arises under a settlement in the period 2008/09 to 2016/17 inclusive (the '*protection period*');

(ii) that would be protected foreign-source income (see **70.27** SETTLEMENTS) under the following assumptions:
- that the rules in **70.27** had effect for the protection period; and
- that they had effect with the absence of the condition at **70.27**(f);

(iii) that prior to 6 April 2017 has neither been distributed by the trustees of the settlement nor treated as income of the settlor due to his retaining an interest in settlement property (see **70.29** SETTLEMENTS); and

(iv) that, for the tax year in which it arose under the settlement, would have been treated as the settlor's income (as mentioned in (iii) above) if the settlor had been UK domiciled for that year.

The rule at **70.28**(d) SETTLEMENTS, whereby relevant foreign income is treated as arising under a settlement only if and when it is remitted to the UK, does not apply for the purposes of (i) and (iv) above.

[*ITTOIA 2005, s 628C; F(No 2)A 2017, Sch 8 paras 22, 39*].

Relevant debts

[61.13] For the purposes of **61.11** above, a '*relevant debt*' is a debt that relates (wholly or in part, and directly or indirectly) to property within **61.11**(a); a service within **61.11**(a); property dealt with as in **61.11**(b)(i) or (c)(i); or a service falling within **61.11**(b)(ii) or (c)(ii).

[*ITA 2007, s 809L(7)(8)*].

Gift recipient and qualifying property

[61.14] For the purposes of **61.11**(b) above, a '*gift recipient*' is a person (other than a relevant person as in **61.12** above) to whom the individual makes a gift of money or property that is (or derives from) income or chargeable gains of the individual. The question of whether a person is a relevant person is determined by reference to the time of the gift; but if a person subsequently becomes a relevant person, he then ceases to be a gift recipient. A disposition of property at less than full consideration is a gift to the extent of the deficit. Property is considered to have been gifted even in a case where the disponor retains an interest in it or a right to benefit from it.

'*Qualifying property*' in **61.11**(b) above, in relation to a gift recipient, means the property gifted or anything that derives from it (as widely defined). It also means any other property if it is dealt with as in **61.11**(b)(i), (ii) or (iii) above by virtue of an operation effected with reference to, or to enable or facilitate, the gift of the property to the gift recipient.

[*ITA 2007, s 809N(1)–(8)(10)*].

Transitional

In relation to an individual's income or chargeable gains for any year before 2008/09, the initial reference above to a relevant person is to the individual, and the subsequent references are to be disregarded. [*FA 2008, Sch 7 para 87*].

Connected operations

[61.15] A '*connected operation*' in relation to property dealt with as mentioned in any of **61.11**(c)(i)–(iii) above is an operation which is effected with reference to, or to enable or facilitate, a 'qualifying disposition'. A '*qualifying disposition*' is a disposition made by a relevant person (as in **61.12** above) to or for the benefit of the person whose property is dealt with as in **61.11**(c) above, which is a disposition of money or other property that is, or derives from, income or chargeable gains of the individual. There is no qualifying disposition if the disposition represents, or is part of, the giving of full consideration for the fact that the property is so dealt with.

[*ITA 2007, s 809O(1)(3)–(5)(7)*].

Transitional

In relation to an individual's income or chargeable gains for any year before 2008/09, only the individual is a relevant person for the above purposes. [*FA 2008, Sch 7 para 88*].

Determining the amount remitted to the UK

[61.16] *ITA 2007, s 809P* provides rules to determine the amount remitted by reference to **61.11** above. In the most straightforward case, where the property, service or consideration for a service is the income or chargeable gains, or derives from them, the amount remitted is equal to the amount of the income or gains or (as the case may be) the amount of income or gains from which the property, service or consideration derives. If the income or gains, or anything deriving from them, are used outside the UK in respect of a relevant debt, the amount remitted is equal to the amount of income or gains used, or the amount from which what is used derives. In cases within **61.11**(b) and (c), the amount remitted is in each case equal to an amount of income or gains determined by reference to the definitions in **61.14** and **61.15** above.

In all cases involving a relevant debt, if the debt relates only partly to the property or service in question (see **61.13** above), the amount remitted is limited (if it would otherwise be greater) to the amount the debt would be if it related wholly to the property or service.

Where the property remitted is part of a set, the amount remitted is an appropriate proportion of the value of the whole set.

In all cases, where the amount remitted, together with amounts previously remitted, would otherwise exceed the amount of the income or gains, the amount remitted is limited to an amount equal to the amount of income or gains.

[*ITA 2007, s 809P*].

Mixed funds

[61.17] Where money or other property is brought to, or received or used in, the UK by, or for the benefit of, a relevant person or a service is provided in the UK to, or for the benefit of, a relevant person (i.e. the first leg of **61.11**(a) above), the property or the consideration for the service may be, or may derive from, a transfer from a 'mixed fund' (or part of it may), or a transfer from a mixed fund (or something deriving from such a transfer) may be used in respect of a relevant debt (as in **61.11**(a)(iii) above). in such cases, there are rules to determine if the second leg of **61.11**(a) above (i.e. any of **61.11**(a)(i)–(iv)) applies and, if so, to determine the amount remitted. See also **61.18** below (income from mixed employments).

A '*mixed fund*' is broadly a source that consists partly of amounts of taxable income or gains and partly of amounts that have already been taxed or are not taxable. Its statutory definition is money or other property containing (or deriving from) income or capital of more than one of the nine categories listed at (a)–(i) below, or income or capital for more than one tax year.

(a)	Employment income (other than income within (b) or (c) below or income subject to a foreign tax).
(b)	'Relevant foreign earnings' (see **61.6** above), other than those subject to a foreign tax.
(c)	'Foreign specific employment income' (see **61.3** above), other than income subject to a foreign tax.
(d)	'Relevant foreign income' (see **32.2** FOREIGN INCOME), other than income subject to a foreign tax.
(e)	Foreign chargeable gains, other than gains subject to a foreign tax.
(f)	Employment income subject to a foreign tax.
(g)	'Relevant foreign income' subject to a foreign tax.
(h)	Foreign chargeable gains subject to a foreign tax.
(i)	Any income or capital not within any of (a)–(h) above.

For each of categories (a)–(i), find the amount of income and capital for the 'relevant tax year' in the mixed fund immediately before the transfer in question. The '*relevant tax year*' is the tax year in which the transfer takes place. For the purpose of determining the composition of the mixed fund, treat property which derives wholly or in part (and directly or indirectly) from an individual's income or capital for a tax year as consisting of or containing that income or capital. If a debt relating (wholly or in part, and directly or indirectly) to property is at any time satisfied (wholly or in part) by an individual's income or capital for a tax year (or anything deriving from such income or capital), treat the property from that time as consisting of or containing the income or capital if, and to the extent that, it is just and reasonable to do so. If an 'offshore transfer' is made from a mixed fund, it is to be regarded as containing the same proportion of each kind of income or capital as was contained in the fund before the transfer. A transfer is an '*offshore transfer*' if these rules (i.e. the rules in *ITA 2007, s 809Q*) do not apply to it; a transfer is *treated as* an offshore transfer if, and to the extent that, these rules do not apply to it at the end of the tax year in which it is made and will not do so on the best estimate that can reasonably be made at that time. If these rules apply to part only of a transfer, apply the rules in relation to that part before applying the 'offshore transfer' rule to the remaining part.

If the amount in category (a) does not exceed the amount of the transfer in question, regard the transfer as containing the income and gains in that category for the relevant tax year. Reduce the amount of the transfer by the amount in (a) and compare what remains with the amount in category (b). Continue by reference to each category, in the order in which they are listed, until the amount of the transfer is reduced to nil.

If, after going through all the categories, the amount of the transfer is still not fully matched, repeat the process by reference to income and capital of the preceding tax year, and so on until the amount of the transfer is fully matched.

If the amount in category (a) does exceed the amount of the transfer, regard the transfer as containing the appropriate proportion of each kind of income and gains in that category for the relevant tax year; similarly if the amount in subsequent category exceeds what remains of the amount of the transfer.

For the purposes of these rules, nothing is to be regarded as deriving from income or capital within (i) above if it is itself (or if it derives from) income or gains within any of (a)–(h) above.

[*ITA 2007, ss 809Q, 809R*].

The above rules do not apply for the purposes of determining whether income or chargeable gains for any tax year before 2008/09 are remitted to the UK in 2008/09 or any subsequent year (or of determining the amount of any such income or chargeable gains so remitted). [*FA 2008, Sch 7 para 89*].

Anti-avoidance

If, by reason of an arrangement (as widely defined) a main purpose of which is to secure an income tax advantage or a CGT advantage (both as defined), a mixed fund would otherwise be regarded as containing income or capital within any of (f) to (i) above, the mixed fund should be treated as containing so much of such income or capital as is just and reasonable. [*ITA 2007, s 809S; FA 2016, Sch 1 paras 63(13), 73*].

The above rules do not apply for the purposes of determining whether income or chargeable gains for any tax year before 2008/09 are remitted to the UK in 2008/09 or any subsequent year (or of determining the amount of any such income or chargeable gains so remitted). [*FA 2008, Sch 7 para 89*].

Transitional — cleansing of mixed funds

In conjunction with the introduction of the deemed domicile rule at **63.36** RESIDENCE AND DOMICILE, there are transitional provisions that enable certain individuals who have been taxable on the remittance basis to transfer amounts between overseas mixed fund bank accounts during a limited period (consisting of the tax years 2017/18 and 2018/19) without being subject to the offshore transfer rules. This is to allow the different elements within the accounts to be separated, so that individuals will be able to move their clean capital, foreign income and foreign gains into separate accounts, and will then be able to remit from any of these accounts as they wish. For example, clean capital could be remitted in priority to income and gains, and gains could be remitted in priority to income. There is no requirement for individuals to make remittances from their newly segregated accounts in any particular order or within any particular time limit. The opportunity is not restricted to those who become UK domiciled under the deemed domicile rule.

These transitional provisions apply to any individual who was not born in the UK with a UK domicile of origin and who was taxable on the remittance basis for any tax year before 2017/18. They operate by disregarding the rule above that if an offshore transfer is made from a mixed fund, it is to be regarded as containing the same proportion of each kind of income or capital as was contained in the fund before the transfer. That rule is disregarded in respect of an offshore transfer of money made from a mixed fund account, e.g. an overseas bank account (account A) to another account (account B) in 2017/18 or 2018/19 which is nominated for this purpose by the individual. (There is no opportunity to cleanse mixed funds that are not accounts.) It is a condition that, at the time of the nomination, no other transfer from account A to account B has been similarly nominated. Such an offshore transfer is treated as containing such kinds, and such amounts, of income and capital as are specified in the nomination. The kinds of income and capital nominated must actually be in the mixed fund account immediately before the transfer, and an amount specified in the nomination may not exceed the amount of that kind which is in the mixed fund.

The above applies equally where the transfer of money is made from a mixed fund in 2017/18 or 2018/19 to another overseas account and account A contains pre-6 April 2008 income or chargeable gains, i.e. income and gains dating from before the current remittance basis regime came into effect but which have not yet been remitted. The nomination may also specify income or gains for a particular tax year. *F(No 2)A 2007, Sch 8 para 46* provides some rules required to determine what is in the mixed fund before the transfer. They apply where a transfer was made before 6 April 2008 from the mixed fund to another overseas account and/or vice versa, but apply for this purpose only and not, for example, to determine the make-up of remittances direct from the mixed fund.

[*F(No 2)A 2017, Sch 8 paras 44–46*].

Income from mixed employments

[61.18] The term '*mixed employment*' is used here to describe a single employment or office the general earnings from which for a tax year include general earnings from duties performed in the UK (chargeable under *ITEPA 2003, s 15(1)* (see **28.4** EMPLOYMENT INCOME)) and foreign earnings (see **28.7** EMPLOYMENT INCOME).

The following rules apply where an individual is in 'mixed employment' for a tax year and at least some of the earnings from UK duties and at least some of the foreign earnings (or, in each case, sums deriving from such earnings) are paid into a single account of the individual in that tax year at a time when that account is a 'qualifying account'.

The composition of each transfer made from the account in that tax year at a time when it is a 'qualifying account (a '*relevant time*') is determined by treating, for this purpose only, all the 'condition A transfers' made from the account at a relevant time as a single transfer made at the end of the tax year and treating all other transfers from the account at a relevant time as a single offshore transfer made at the end of the tax year but immediately after the afore-mentioned single transfer. The rules in **61.17** above are then used to determine: (i) the extent to which the first single transfer is of the individual's income or gains; and (ii) the content of the single offshore transfer. Each 'condition A transfer' made from the account in the tax year at a relevant time is then treated as containing the same proportion of each kind of income or capital as the first single transfer; and every other transfer made at a relevant time is treated as containing the same proportion of each kind of income or capital as the single offshore transfer.

A transfer from the account is a '*condition A transfer*' if and to the extent that:

- money or other property is brought to, or received or used in, the UK by, or for the benefit of, a relevant person or a service is provided in the UK to, or for the benefit of, a relevant person (i.e. the first leg of **61.11**(a) above); and
- either the property or the consideration for the service is (wholly or partly) (or derives (wholly or partly) from) the transfer, or the transfer (or anything deriving from it) is used outside the UK in respect of a relevant debt (i.e. as in **61.11**(c)(iii) above).

If and to the extent that, at the end of the tax year, it is not yet clear if a transfer is a condition A transfer, and the best estimate is that it will not become a condition A transfer, it cannot be treated as a condition A transfer.

If the tax year is the year in which the account becomes a qualifying account or ceases to be such an account (other than by breach of the deposit rule — see below), it is treated for these purposes only as split into two, with the above rules applying only to the appropriate part of the year.

Qualifying accounts

An individual may, by written notice to the Commissioners for HMRC, nominate an account of his to be a qualifying account. The notice must specify the 'qualifying date' for the account; the '*qualifying date*' is the first date on which there is credited to the account general earnings for a 'relevant tax year' (in relation to the employment) which (in total) are more than £10. A tax year is a '*relevant tax year*' (in relation to an employment) if the employment is a 'mixed employment' for that year (see above). The individual may withdraw his nomination by further written notice to the Commissioners, specifying the date with effect from which the nomination is withdrawn. A notice or further notice must include such information as the Commissioners may reasonably require. It must be given no later than 31 January in the tax year following the tax year in which falls, as the case may be, the qualifying date for the account or the date from which the nomination is withdrawn (or by such later date as the Commissioners may allow in a particular case).

Once an individual nominates an account, it is a '*qualifying account*' throughout the period beginning with the qualifying date and ending with the day before the earliest of the following dates:

(i) the date on which the account is closed or ceases to be an ordinary bank (current or savings) account held by and for the benefit of the individual (alone or jointly with others);
(ii) the date from which the nomination is withdrawn;
(iii) the qualifying date for another qualifying account of the individual;
(iv) 6 April in a tax year in which there is a breach of the deposit rule (see below) which is not, or cannot be, remedied (but not if the breach occurs on or after a date in any of (i)–(iii) above); and
(v) 6 April in a tax year for which the individual has no foreign earnings.

The account is not a qualifying account at all in either of the following circumstances:

- if at any time on the qualifying date, the account is not an ordinary bank (current or savings) account held by and for the benefit of the individual (alone or jointly with others) or if, immediately before the qualifying date, the account is more than £10 in credit; or
- if the qualifying date falls in a tax year for which the individual has no foreign earnings or in which there is a breach of the deposit rule (see below) which is not, or cannot be, remedied (but not if the breach occurs on or after a date in any of (i)–(iii) above).

If an account would otherwise be a qualifying account of two or more individuals at any time, it is not a qualifying account of either or any of them at any time.

Breaches of the deposit rule

There is a breach of the deposit rule if a 'prohibited sum' is paid into the account on or after the 'qualifying date' (see above). A breach is, however, remedied if, within 30 days beginning with the day on which the individual became or ought reasonably to have become aware of the payment of the prohibited sum, the 'required amount' is transferred out of the account by way of a single one-off transfer. The '*required amount*' is the amount of the prohibited sum plus any other prohibited sums paid into the account since that sum was paid in. If there are three breaches of the deposit rule in any twelve-month period, the third breach cannot be remedied. A '*prohibited sum*' is broadly any amount containing anything other than certain earnings from the individual's employment, consideration for the disposal of certain employment-related securities or securities options, and interest on the account (see *ITA 2007, s 809RC(6)–(10)*).

If a breach of the deposit rule is remedied, both the payment of the prohibited sum(s) into the account and the single one-off transfer out of the account are ignored for the purposes of applying the mixed fund rules. Each prohibited sum represented by the required amount is instead treated for those purposes as if it had been transferred directly (at the time it was paid into the qualifying account) into the account or other property into which the required amount was subsequently transferred.

[*ITA 2007, ss 809RA–809RD*].

Property treated as not remitted to the UK

[61.19] To the extent described at **61.20–61.26** below, money and other property brought into the UK are treated for tax purposes as not remitted to the UK. See also **61.35** below (offshore mortgages).

Payment of the additional tax charge

[61.20] Direct payments to HMRC from untaxed foreign income or gains in settlement of the additional tax charge in **61.9** above are not treated for tax purposes as remittances to the UK. This exemption applies only if the additional charge is paid in respect of the tax due for a tax year for which the remittance basis has been claimed and for which the charge applies. The exemption covers any number of direct payments up to the total of the additional charge. If any of the money is repaid by HMRC, for example because the taxpayer withdraws his claim, the exemption is to that extent deemed never to have applied. [*ITA 2007, s 809V*].

To qualify for this exemption, the money must be sent direct from an overseas bank account to HMRC by way of a cheque drawn on the overseas bank account or a form of electronic transfer, and not via a UK bank account (Treasury Explanatory Notes to the 2008 Finance Bill).

Repayment of self-assessment payments on account

Where an individual is liable to the additional tax charge for a tax year (year A), any self-assessment payments on account (see **67.5** SELF-ASSESSMENT) that are made for the following tax year (year B) will be at least partly based on that charge. If the individual does not claim the remittance basis for year B, and is thus not liable to the additional charge for that year, a repayment may be due from HMRC of all or part of the payments on account. If the payments on account were made out of untaxed foreign income or gains, that repayment constitutes a taxable remittance.

The 'relevant amount of income or gains' is treated as not remitted to the UK if money equal to that amount is taken offshore by 15 March in the tax year following year B or such later date as HMRC may allow on a claim by the individual. A claim may be made only if the individual has submitted a personal tax return for year B and reasonably expects to receive a tax repayment for that year; it must be made no later than 5 April in the tax year following year B.

The '*relevant amount of income or gains*' is the lower of:

- the amount brought to the UK by virtue of the making of the payments on account; and
- either £30,000, £60,000 or £90,000 depending on whether the individual met the 7-year test, the 12-year test or, where relevant, the 17-year test for year A (see **61.9** above).

See **61.23** below as to what is meant by taking money offshore. Money that is thus taken offshore is treated as having the same composition of kinds of income and capital as the money used to make the payments on account.

[*ITA 2007, ss 809UA, 809Z9*].

Property used to make qualifying investments

[61.21] Where a 'relevant event' occurs, and income or chargeable gains of an individual would otherwise be regarded as remitted to the UK by virtue of that event, the income or gains are treated as not remitted to the UK if the individual makes a claim under *ITA 2007, s 809VA* for the relief. A '*relevant event*' occurs if money or other property:

(a) is used by a relevant person (as in **61.12** above) to make a 'qualifying investment' (see **61.22** below); or
(b) is brought to or received in the UK in order to be used by a relevant person for the purpose of making such an investment (but see below for 45-day time limit).

The relief (known as **business investment relief**) is equally available where income or gains would otherwise be treated under **61.26** below as remitted to the UK by virtue of the relevant event, e.g. because exempt property is sold to raise the capital for the investment.

A claim for relief must be made no later than the first anniversary of 31 January following the tax year in which the income or gains would otherwise be regarded as remitted to the UK. No relief is available if the relevant event occurs, or the investment is made, as part of, or as a result of, a tax avoidance scheme or arrangement.

45-day rule

Relief by virtue of (b) above is available to the extent only that the investment is made within the period of 45 days beginning with the day on which the money etc. is brought to or received in the UK. If this requirement is only partly satisfied, the portion of the income or gains which attracts the relief is determined on a just and reasonable basis. Where money etc. is brought to the UK with the intention of making a qualifying investment but some or all of that money etc. is not invested within the 45-day limit, the income or gains thereby not qualifying for the relief are nevertheless treated as not remitted to the UK if and to the extent that the unused money etc. is taken offshore within the same 45-day period. Where only part of the unused amount is taken offshore within the time limit, the portion of the income or gains which attracts the relief is again determined on a just and reasonable basis.

[*ITA 2007, ss 809VA, 809VB, 809Z10*].

Investment funded by loan

HMRC has confirmed to the CIOT that foreign income or gains remitted to the UK to repay a loan used to fund a qualifying investment are, in principle, eligible for business investment relief; this is the case even where the remittance and repayment occur in a later tax year than that in which the investment is made (CIOT Press Release, 15 August 2012).

Qualifying investments

[61.22] For the purposes of **61.21** above, a person makes an investment if shares in, or securities of, a company are issued to him or acquired by him or if he makes a loan (whether secured or unsecured) to a company. Where the relevant event in **61.21** occurred before 6 April 2017, shares and securities acquired by an investor, but not issued to him, did not count as investments for this purpose. In order to be a '*qualifying investment*', the investment must satisfy both conditions A and B below at the time it is made.

Where a loan agreement authorises a company to draw down amounts of a loan over time, entry into that loan agreement is not treated as the making of a loan for these purposes. Instead, a separate loan is treated as being made each time an amount is drawn down; each drawdown will thus be a separate investment.

Condition A

The company in which the investment is made (the '*target company*') must be an 'eligible trading company', an 'eligible stakeholder company', an 'eligible holding company' or, where the relevant event occurs after 5 April 2017, an 'eligible hybrid company'.

A company is an '*eligible trading company*' if:

- it is a 'private limited company';
- it carries on one or more 'commercial trades' or is preparing to do so within the next five years (previously, where the relevant event occurred before 6 April 2017, two years); and
- carrying on commercial trades is all or substantially all of what it does (or of what it is expected to do when it begins trading).

A company is a '*private limited company*' if none of its shares are listed on a recognised stock exchange; limited liability partnerships are not private limited companies.

A company is an '*eligible stakeholder company*' if:

- it is a private limited company (as above);
- it exists wholly for the purpose of making investments (as defined above) in eligible trading companies (ignoring any minor or incidental purposes); and
- it holds one or more such investments or is preparing to do so within the next five years (previously, where the relevant event occurred before 6 April 2017, two years).

A company is an '*eligible holding company*' if:

- it is a member of an 'eligible trading group' or of an 'eligible group' that is reasonably expected to become an eligible trading group within the next five years (previously, where the relevant event occurred before 6 April 2017, two years); and
- an eligible trading company in the group is a 51% subsidiary of it. Where the eligible holding company owns the share capital of the eligible trading company indirectly, each intermediary company must also be a member of the group.

A company is an '*eligible hybrid company*' if:

- it is a private limited company (as above), and neither an eligible trading company nor an eligible stakeholder company;
- it carries on one or more 'commercial trades' or is preparing to do so within the next five years;
- it holds one or more investments in eligible trading companies or is preparing to do so within the next five years; and
- the carrying on of commercial trades and the making of investments in eligible trading companies are all (or substantially all) of what it does (or of what it is reasonably expected to do once it begins operating).

For the above purposes, a group means a parent company and its 51% subsidiaries. A group is an '*eligible group*' if the parent company and each of its 51% subsidiaries are private limited companies (as defined above). An eligible group is an '*eligible trading group*' if carrying on 'commercial trades' is all or substantially all of what the group does (taking the activities of its members as a whole).

A trade is a '*commercial trade*' if it is conducted on a commercial basis and with a view to the realisation of profits. For this purpose, a trade includes anything that is treated for corporation tax purposes as if it were a trade and also includes a business carried on for 'generating income from land' (as defined by *CTA 2009, s 207*). It includes the carrying on of research and development activities from which it is intended that a commercial trade will be derived or will benefit. A corporate partner in a partnership is not regarded for these purposes as carrying on a trade carried on by the partnership; this has statutory effect where the relevant event in **61.21** above occurs after 5 April 2017 but confirms a view previously applied in practice by HMRC.

Condition B

Condition B is that no relevant person (as in **61.12** above) has (directly or indirectly) obtained, or become entitled to obtain, any related benefit, and that no relevant person expects to obtain any such benefit. A benefit is related if it is directly or indirectly attributable to the making of the investment or if it is reasonable to assume that the benefit would not be available in the absence of the investment. A benefit includes the provision of anything which would not be provided to the relevant person in the ordinary course of business or would be provided on less favourable terms. It does not include the provision of anything to the relevant person in the normal course of business and on arm's length terms.

[*ITA 2007, ss 809VC–809VF, 809Z10; F(No 2)A 2017, s 15(2)–(4), (8)*].

HMRC can be asked for their view on whether a proposed investment will be a qualifying investment. See www.gov.uk/guidance/seeking-clearance-or-appro val-for-a-transaction under Business Investment Relief Provisions.

Potentially chargeable events

[61.23] Where relief has been given as in **61.21** above, the occurrence of a 'potentially chargeable event' (PCE) may result in the 'affected income or gains' being treated as having been remitted to the UK. This can be avoided if appropriate steps are taken in mitigation but each step must be taken within a specified period of grace allowed for that step. In the absence of one or more mitigation steps, the remittance is deemed to take place immediately after the end of the appropriate grace period. The '*affected income or gains*' means such portion of the income or gains relieved as in **61.21** above as reflects the portion of the qualifying investment affected by the PCE. This will usually be the whole of the qualifying investment, but where the event is a part disposal it is the portion disposed of. Where there is a second or subsequent PCE in relation to a single investment, the relieved income or gains that may then be treated as remitted do not include any amounts treated as remitted or used in mitigation as a result of a previous PCE.

Where an investment is made which consists partly of funds which qualify for relief under the qualifying investment provisions and partly of other funds, the investment is treated as two separate investments for these purposes.

Potentially chargeable events

Any of the following is a '*potentially chargeable event*':

- the target company (see **61.22** above) is for the first time neither an eligible trading company nor an eligible stakeholder company nor an eligible holding company nor, where the relevant event in **61.21** above occurs after 5 April 2017, an eligible hybrid company;
- the relevant person who made the investment disposes of all or part of it;
- the extraction of value rule is breached (see below); or
- the five-year start-up rule (previously, where the relevant event occurred before 6 April 2017, the two-year start-up rule) is breached (see below).

If consideration for a disposal is paid in instalments, the disposal is treated for these purposes as if it were separate disposals, one for each instalment and each giving rise to a separate PCE.

In *Allam v HMRC* FTT (TC 7702), [2020] UKFTT 216 (TC), the FTT held that certain payments made to the appellant by a company controlled by him represented the part disposal of a qualifying investment and thus a PCE. In this case, an unpaid dividend was treated as an investment as it could be inferred from the facts that it was the shareholder's intention to reinvest the dividend proceeds and put them at the disposal of the company.

If a PCE occurs because of an 'insolvency step' taken for genuine commercial reasons, it will not be treated as a PCE. However, this does not prevent the receipt of value as a result of the insolvency step from being a PCE. Broadly, an '*insolvency step*' is taken if a company enters into administration or receivership, or is wound up or dissolved (or the overseas equivalent in each case).

Extraction of value rule

Where the relevant event in **61.21** above occurs after 5 April 2017, the extraction of value rule is breached if the relevant person who made the investment or any other relevant person receives, or receives the benefit of, value in money or money's worth from any person in circumstances that are directly or indirectly attributable to the investment.

Where the relevant event occurs before 6 April 2017, the extraction of value rule is breached if the relevant person who made the investment or any other relevant person receives, or receives the benefit of, value in money or money's worth from either an 'involved company' or from anyone else in circumstances which are attributable to the investment or to any other investment made by a relevant person in an involved company. Any of the following is an '*involved company*': the target company; (if the target company is an eligible stakeholder company) any eligible trading company in which it has made or intends to make an investment; (if the target company is an eligible holding company) any eligible trading company that is a 51% subsidiary of it; and any company that is connected with any such company (within **19** CONNECTED PERSONS).

At all times, the extraction of value rule is not breached if the value is received as a result of a disposal that is itself a PCE. Also, the rule is not breached merely because a relevant person receives value which is treated as income for tax purposes (or would be if the relevant person were liable to income tax or corporation tax), provided the value is paid or provided on arm's length terms and in the ordinary course of business; an example of such value would be director's remuneration.

Five-year start-up rule

The five-year start-up rule is breached if:

- immediately after the end of the five years beginning with the day on which the investment was made, the target company is not operational; or
- at any time after the end of that period, the target company ceases to be operational.

Where the relevant event occurred before 6 April 2017, the above applied by reference to two years rather than five. In order to be operational, the target company must either be trading (i.e. carrying on a commercial trade as in **61.22** above), be a stakeholder in at least one eligible trading company which is trading, be a member of an eligible trading group and have at least one 51% subsidiary which is trading or, where the relevant event occurs after 5 April 2017, be an eligible hybrid company which is trading or is a stakeholder in at least one eligible trading company which is trading.

Mitigation steps and periods of grace

If the PCE is a disposal, the appropriate mitigation step is to take the proceeds offshore or use them to make another qualifying investment (whether in the same or a different company). If the proceeds are themselves a qualifying investment (for example on a share for share exchange), the appropriate step is regarded as having been taken. Otherwise, the period of grace allowed to take the step is the 45 days beginning with the day on which the disposal proceeds first become available for use by, or for the benefit of, the investor or any other relevant person. See below for the meaning of disposal proceeds and for what is meant by taking proceeds offshore.

If the PCE is anything other than a disposal, the appropriate mitigation step is twofold, as follows. Firstly, the investor must dispose of the entire investment (or so much of it as he still holds when the PCE occurs). Secondly, he must take the proceeds of that disposal offshore or use them to make another qualifying investment. The period of grace allowed for the first leg of this mitigation step is the 90 days beginning (if the PCE is a breach of the extraction of value rule) with the day on which value is received or (in any other case) with the day on which a relevant person first became aware, or ought reasonably to have become aware, of the PCE. The period of grace allowed for the second leg is the 45 days beginning with the day on which the disposal proceeds first become available for use by, or for the benefit of, the investor or any other relevant person. If the first leg is not carried out within the 90 days allowed, it is immediately after the end of those 90 days that the affected income or gains is deemed to have been remitted to the UK.

Where the relevant event occurs after 5 April 2017, the above does not apply if the PCE is a breach of the five-year start-up rule by virtue of the target company ceasing to be operational after the end of the five-year period. Instead, the total period of grace allowed for carrying out both legs of the mitigation step is the two years beginning with the day on which the investor or any other relevant person first became aware, or ought reasonably to have become aware, of the PCE.

Where a breach of the extraction of value rule takes place in connection with the winding-up or dissolution of the target company, there is no need to dispose of the holding, and references to the disposal proceeds in these provisions are to the value received.

Applicable proceeds

In any case where proceeds need to be taken offshore or reinvested, the amount of proceeds to which this applies is the total disposal proceeds or, if less, so much of those proceeds as equals the sum originally invested (as defined). For this purpose, the sum originally invested is deemed to be reduced by so much of it as has, on previous occasions involving the same investment:

- been taken into account in determining the amount of income and gains treated as remitted after a PCE; or
- been taken offshore or reinvested as an appropriate mitigation step; or
- been used to purchase a certificate of tax deposit (see below under Retention of funds to meet CGT liabilities).

For example, in Year 1 an individual invests £3 million of foreign income in an eligible trading company. In Year 5, he sells half the holding for £2 million. The appropriate mitigation step is to take £2 million offshore or reinvest it. In Year 6, he sells the remaining holding for £3.5 million. The appropriate mitigation step is to take £1 million (£3 million less £2 million) offshore or reinvest it. In all, he has invested £3 million and realised £5.5 million; the amount he has been required to take offshore or reinvest is limited to £3 million.

Extension of grace periods

An officer of HMRC may agree in a particular case to extend the grace period allowed for an appropriate mitigation step in exceptional circumstances (to be defined in HMRC published guidance). The Commissioners for HMRC may also make regulations permitting grace periods to be extended in specified circumstances where an investor may be temporarily prevented from disposing of shares. In either case, the extension may be for a length of time that is indefinite but is capable of becoming definite by means identified in advance, such as the satisfaction of conditions. *SI 2012 No 1898* permits the grace period to be extended at an officer's discretion where the investor is unable to dispose of his shares because of a lock-up agreement, a prohibition imposed by or under any enactment, or the terms of any court order.

Amounts reinvested

Where disposal proceeds are used to make another qualifying investment as part of appropriate mitigation steps, these provisions apply with the necessary modifications to the new investment as they applied to the original investment; for example, references to the sum originally invested are henceforth to the sum reinvested. Where the new investment is made in a greater sum than is required to satisfy the rules, it is treated as two separate investments, one of an amount equal to the minimum amount required to meet the rules and the other of an amount equal to the balance; the latter then falls outside these provisions.

A reinvestment of proceeds requires a further claim under *ITA 2007, s 809VA* (see **61.21** above). This must be made no later than the first anniversary of 31 January following the tax year in which the reinvestment is made. If the claim is not made, the appropriate mitigation steps will not be regarded as having been taken.

Retention of funds to meet CGT liabilities

The legislation recognises that the disposal proceeds of a qualifying investment may have to be retained in the UK to meet a CGT liability on that disposal. It deals with this by enabling the amount otherwise required to be taken offshore or reinvested to be reduced by a set amount, provided the amount is used to purchase a certificate of tax deposit (CTD) within the 45-day grace period allowed as above. It must be confirmed in writing to HMRC that the CTD purchased is intended to relate to *ITA 2007, s 809VK* and that the amount of the deposit is no greater than the 'shortfall'. The '*shortfall*' is the amount (if any) by which the actual disposal proceeds fall short of Amount Y, where Amount Y is the sum of the amount otherwise required to be taken offshore or reinvested and the amount resulting when the highest potential CGT rate is applied to the chargeable gain on the disposal. (The shortfall is calculated by reference to proceeds actually received even if the disposal was not made on arm's length terms.) The set amount can be anything up to the amount of the shortfall. See **13.1** CERTIFICATES OF TAX DEPOSIT for CTDs generally, and note there that CTDs can no longer be purchased on and after 23 November 2017. The legislation is to be amended at a future date to remove references to CTDs.

If the CTD is used to pay the individual's CGT liability for the tax year in which the disposal took place, this does not count as remitting to the UK the portion of the affected income or gains that is represented by the payment. If, however, any of the 'CTD conditions' is breached, the portion of the affected income or gains to the UK that is affected by the breach are treated as having been remitted to the UK immediately after the day on which the breach occurs. The '*CTD conditions*' are as follows.

- The CTD must not be used to pay any other tax liability.
- If any of the amount deposited is withdrawn by the depositor, the amount withdrawn must be taken offshore or invested in a qualifying company within the 45 days beginning on the date of withdrawal.
- Any part of the amount deposited that has been neither used to pay a tax liability nor withdrawn by the due date for payment of the said CGT liability must be withdrawn by the depositor and taken offshore or invested in a qualifying company within the 45 days beginning with that date.

Where an amount withdrawn is invested in a qualifying company, these provisions apply with the necessary modifications to the new investment as they applied to the original investment. Again, a further claim is required under *ITA 2007, s 809VA*.

Order of disposals

There are rules to determine the order in which disposals are treated as being made where there are multiple acquisitions and disposals in the same target company or group and also where both qualifying and non-qualifying investments have been made.

The first rule applies where income or gains of an individual are treated as not remitted to the UK as a result of more than one qualifying investment in either the same target company or the same eligible trading group or in both an eligible trading company and its eligible stakeholder company or, where the relevant event occurs after 5 April 2017, its eligible hybrid company. The investments are treated as a single investment for the purpose of applying the PCE rules. A disposal of all or part of that deemed single investment affects it in the order in which the qualifying investments were made, i.e. first in, first out. It does not matter whether the investments in question are held by the same relevant person (as in **61.12** above) or different ones.

The second rule applies where income or gains of an individual are treated as not remitted to the UK as a result of one or more qualifying investments and a relevant person holds at least one non-qualifying investment in the same target company, the same eligible trading group or a 'related eligible company'. The investments are treated as a single investment for the purpose of applying the PCE rules. A disposal of all or part of that deemed single investment is taken to be a disposal from a qualifying investment until all the qualifying investments have been disposed of. It does not matter whether the investments in question are held by the same relevant person or different ones. Two companies are '*related eligible companies*' if one is an eligible trading company and the other is its eligible stakeholder company or, where the relevant event occurs after 5 April 2017, its eligible hybrid company.

Meaning of disposal proceeds

For these purposes, in relation to a sale or any other disposal, the disposal proceeds are the amount of consideration for the disposal less any fees or other incidental costs deducted from the consideration before it is accounted for to the person making the disposal or to any relevant person (as in **61.12** above). If the consideration is provided in the form of property rather than money, the amount of the consideration is the market value of the property at the time of the disposal. If the disposal is not at arm's length, it is deemed to be made for a consideration equal to the market value of the thing being disposed of. A disposal made to another relevant person or to a person connected with a relevant person is always treated as made other than at arm's length.

Fees and other incidental costs are not deductible if payable by one relevant person to another except to the extent that they relate to a service actually provided by the recipient in connection with effecting the disposal and do not exceed what would normally be charged for that service on arm's length terms.

Taking proceeds etc. offshore or investing them

For the purposes of these provisions, things (e.g. disposal proceeds) are to be regarded as '*taken offshore*' if (and only if) they are taken outside the UK such that, on leaving the UK, they cease to be available to be used or enjoyed in the UK by, or for the benefit of, a relevant person (as in **61.12** above) or used or enjoyed in any other way that would count as remitting income or gains to the UK. If money needs to be taken offshore or invested in order to satisfy a statutory requirement, and it is paid temporarily into an account pending satisfaction of that requirement, the requirement is satisfied only if the money actually taken offshore or invested is taken from the same account. If the thing required to be taken offshore or invested is something in money's worth, the requirement can be satisfied either by taking the thing offshore or investing it or by taking offshore or investing money or other property of equivalent value. A requirement to take something offshore or invest it can be met by taking part of it offshore and investing the other part. If a disposal is deemed to be made at market value (see above under Meaning of disposal proceeds), the requirement can be satisfied by taking offshore or investing money or other property of a value equal to the amount of the deemed consideration less any deductible fees or other incidental costs.

Where, as above, a statutory requirement can be met by taking offshore or investing property of equivalent value, that property is treated as deriving from the thing required to be taken offshore or invested and as having the same composition of kinds of income and capital as that thing (see **61.16, 61.17** above). Such property must not be exempt property (as in **61.26** below) or consideration for a disposal of exempt property, and it must not be consideration for the disposal of all or part of a qualifying investment.

[*ITA 2007, ss 809VG–809VN, 809Z8, 809Z9, 809Z10; F(No 2)A 2017, s 15(5)–(8); FA 2019, Sch 1 paras 105, 120; SI 2012 No 1898*].

Investments made from mixed funds

[61.24] The following applies if, but for **61.21** above, income or gains would have been remitted to the UK by virtue of a relevant event and *ITA 2007, s 809Q* (transfers from mixed funds — see **61.17** above) would have applied in determining the amount that would have been so remitted. The relevant event (as in **61.21**) counts as an offshore transfer for the purposes of **61.17**. The investment holding is treated as containing a proportion of each of the kinds of income and capital in **61.17**(a)–(i) equal to the proportion of that kind of income or capital contained in the money or other property used to make the investment.

The following applies where, under the rules at **61.23** above, money or other property is treated as not remitted to the UK because an amount is taken offshore, reinvested or used to purchase a certificate of tax deposit. The amount in question is treated, immediately after the step is taken, as containing the same proportion of each kind of income and capital contained in the investment holding.

The following applies where income and gains are treated as remitted to the UK because the appropriate mitigation steps were not taken within the grace period (see **61.23** above). The mixed fund rules at **61.17** above do not apply to determine the amounts remitted. The affected income and gains (see **61.23**) are so much of the 'fixed amount' of each kind of income or gain that would have been remitted to the UK by virtue of the relevant event as reflects the portion of the investment affected by the potentially chargeable event. The '*fixed amount*' is the amount of that kind of income or gain that the investment holding is treated as containing (as above).

The anti-avoidance rule at *ITA 2007, s 809S* (see **61.17** above) applies equally in relation to the above.

[*ITA 2007, s 809VO*].

Consideration for certain services

[61.25] An exemption applies if:

- income or gains would otherwise be regarded as remitted to the UK because of **61.11**(a) above;
- the first leg of **61.11**(a) is met because a service is provided in the UK;
- the second leg of **61.11**(a) is met because **61.11**(a)(i) or (ii) applies to the consideration for that service; and
- both Conditions A and B below are met.

Where this exemption applies, income or gains are treated as not remitted to the UK.

Condition A is that the service provided relates wholly or mainly to property situated outside the UK.

Condition B is that the whole of the consideration for the service is given by way of payments to bank accounts held outside the UK by, or on behalf of, the person providing the service.

This exemption does not apply if the service relates (to any extent) to the provision in the UK of:

- a benefit treated as deriving from the income by virtue of *ITA 2007, s 735* (application of 'transfer of assets abroad' rules to non-UK domiciled individuals to whom the remittance basis applies — see **4.15** ANTI-AVOIDANCE); or
- a relevant benefit within *TCGA 1992, s 87B* that is treated by virtue of that section as deriving from the gains. (That section is concerned with the attribution of gains of non-UK resident settlements to non-UK domiciled individuals to whom the remittance basis applies — see Tolley's Capital Gains Tax under Offshore Settlements.)

[*ITA 2007, s 809W*].

Condition A would cover, for example, fees paid to a UK bank for managing an individual's overseas investments. It would also cover legal or brokerage fees in respect of offshore assets, such as legal fees on the sale of a foreign house. The term 'wholly or mainly' in Condition A is not statutorily defined, but will be taken to mean more than half (Treasury Explanatory Notes to the 2008 Finance Bill).

Exempt property

[61.26] 'Exempt property' which is brought to, or received or used in, the UK, such that the first leg of **61.11**(a) above applies, is treated as not remitted to the UK.

The following are '*exempt property*' for this purpose:

(a) property which meets the 'public access rule' (i.e. works of art etc. — see **61.30** below);
(b) clothing, footwear, jewellery and watches which meet the 'personal use rule' (see **61.31** below); and
(c) property of any kind if:
 (i) the 'notional remitted amount' (see **61.34** below) is less than £1,000; or
 (ii) the property meets the 'repair rule' (see **61.32** below); or
 (iii) the property meets the 'temporary importation rule' (see **61.33** below).

For these purposes, 'property' does not include money (or specified items equivalent to money). Subject to **61.27** and **61.28** below, if property ceases to be exempt property at any time after it is brought to, or received or used in, the UK, it is treated as remitted to the UK at that time. Subject to **61.28** below, property ceases to be exempt property if it (or part of it) is sold (or otherwise converted into money or specified items equivalent to money) whilst in the UK. Property which is exempt by virtue of one or more of the 'public access rule', the 'personal use rule', the 'temporary importation rule' and the 'repair rule' also ceases to be exempt property if it ceases to meet the rule(s) relied upon whilst in the UK, provided it does not meet any of the remaining rules. There is an exception if, by no later than the time when it ceases to meet the rules, the property has been donated as a qualifying gift to the nation as in **14.20** CHARITIES AND CHARITABLE GIVING; in such a case the property continues to be treated as not remitted to the UK.

[*ITA 2007, ss 809X, 809Y(1)–(4)(5), 809YE, 809Z6*].

See also **61.29** below (property lost, stolen or destroyed).

Property used to make qualifying investments

[61.27] With effect where property ceases to be exempt property and a claim for this relief is made, it is *not* treated as remitted to the UK at that time if the property is used by a relevant person (as in **61.12** above) to make a qualifying investment (as in **61.22** above) within the 45 days beginning with the day on which it ceased to be exempt property. The claim must be made (by the individual whose income or gains would otherwise be treated as remitted) no later than the first anniversary of 31 January following the tax year in which the property ceases to be exempt property. The relief also applies where the formerly exempt property is disposed of or otherwise converted into money and the disposal proceeds or the money are used to make the investment.

Where this relief has effect, the rules at **61.23** apply if there is subsequently a potentially chargeable event in relation to the qualifying investment. If the investment is made using more than just the formerly exempt property, only the part made using that property is treated as the qualifying investment for the purposes of applying those rules.

In applying the mixed fund rules, the formerly exempt property (or thing into which it was converted) used to make the investment is treated as containing (or deriving from) an amount of each kind of income and gain mentioned in **61.17**(a)–(h) above equal to the amount of that kind of income or gain contained in the property when it was brought to, or received or used in, the UK (as in **61.26** above).

[*ITA 2007, ss 809Y(6)–(10), 809Z10*].

Sales of exempt property

[61.28] If property ceases to be exempt property because the whole of it is sold whilst in the UK (see **61.26** above), it is *not* treated as remitted to the UK at that time if all the conditions listed at (a)–(f) below are met. This relief does not apply if the sale is made as part of, or as a result of, a tax avoidance scheme or arrangements.

(a) The sale is to a person other than a relevant person (as in **61.12** above).
(b) The sale is by way of a bargain made at arm's length.
(c) Once the sale is completed, no relevant person:
  - has any interest in the property;
  - is able or entitled to benefit from the property by virtue of any interest, right or arrangement; or
  - has any right to acquire any such interest, ability or entitlement.
(d) The whole of the disposal proceeds are 'released' (whether all at once or in instalments) on or before the first anniversary of 5 January following the tax year in which the property ceases to be exempt property.

(e) The whole of the disposal proceeds are taken offshore or used by a relevant person to make a qualifying investment (as in **61.22** above) within the 45 days beginning with the day on which the proceeds are 'released'. If the disposal proceeds are paid in instalments, the condition is that each instalment is taken offshore or used in that way within the 45 days beginning with the day on which the instalment is released. In both cases, there is an overriding deadline of the first anniversary of 5 January following the tax year in which the property ceases to be exempt property, if this falls within the 45 days normally permitted.

(f) If (e) above is satisfied wholly or partly by the making of a qualifying investment, a claim for relief must be made (by the individual whose income or gains would otherwise be treated as remitted) on or before the first anniversary of 31 January following the tax year in which the property is sold.

For the purposes of (d) and (e) above, proceeds or instalments are '*released*' on the day on which they first become available for use by or for the benefit of any relevant person. An officer of HMRC may (on the request of the individual whose income or gains would otherwise be treated as remitted) agree to extend any deadline within (e) above if circumstances are exceptional.

In applying the mixed fund rules, where this relief has effect, the disposal proceeds are treated as containing (or deriving from) an amount of each kind of income and gain mentioned in **61.17**(a)–(h) above equal to the amount of that kind of income or gain contained in the exempt property when it was brought to, or received or used in, the UK. Also where this relief has effect and (e) above was satisfied by the making of a qualifying investment, the rules at **61.23** apply if there is subsequently a potentially chargeable event in relation to the investment. If the investment is made using more than just the disposal proceeds, only the part made using those proceeds is treated as the qualifying investment for the purposes of applying those rules.

[*ITA 2007, ss 809YA–809YC, 809Z10*].

See the corresponding chapter of Tolley's Capital Gains Tax for the treatment of any chargeable gain that arises on the sale of the exempt property.

Property lost, stolen or destroyed

[61.29] In relation to property lost, stolen or destroyed whilst in the UK, the property cannot cease to be exempt property in the circumstances outlined in **61.26** above after it is lost, stolen and destroyed and (in the case of loss or theft followed by recovery) before it is 'recovered'. For this purpose, property is '*recovered*' on the day it becomes available to be used or enjoyed in the UK by or for the benefit of a relevant person (as in **61.12** above).

Compensation received

Property ceases to be exempt property where a payment of compensation (whether under an insurance policy or otherwise) is 'released' in respect of exempt property that has been lost, stolen or destroyed. A compensation payment is '*released*' on the day on which it first becomes available for use in the UK by or for the benefit of any relevant person (as in **61.12** above).

However, property is not treated as remitted to the UK by virtue of a release of compensation as above if the whole of the compensation payment is taken offshore or used by a relevant person to make a qualifying investment (as in **61.22** above) within the 45 days beginning with the day on which the payment is released. To the extent that this relief arises from the making of a qualifying investment, a claim for the relief must be made no later than the first anniversary of 31 January following the tax year in which the payment is released.

For the purposes of the mixed fund rules, the compensation payment is treated as containing (or deriving from) an amount of each kind of income and gain mentioned in **61.17**(a)–(h) above equal to the amount of that kind of income or gain contained in the exempt property when it was brought to, or received or used in, the UK (as in **61.26** above).

Where this relief has effect by virtue of the making of a qualifying investment, the rules at **61.23** above apply if there is subsequently a potentially chargeable event in relation to the investment. If the investment is made using more than just the compensation payment, only the part made using that payment is treated as the qualifying investment for the purposes of applying those rules.

See **61.23** above as to what is meant by taking money offshore.

[*ITA 2007, ss 809Y(4A)(4B), 809YF, 809Z6(5)–(8), 809Z9*].

Public access rule

[61.30] The '*public access rule*' in **61.26**(a) above allows certain property to be imported into the UK, without giving rise to a tax charge on the remittance basis, if all the conditions set out below are met.

(a) The property must be a work of art, a collectors' item or an antique, within the meaning of *Council Directive 2006/112/EC* (and, in particular, *Annex IX* to that *Directive*). This condition is abolished on and after 6 April 2013 or, in the case of property already in the UK on that date, from the time it ceases to be in the UK or is lost or stolen.

(b) The property must be available for public access (as defined) at an approved museum, gallery or similar establishment or in storage at, or in transit to or from, the establishment (or other commercial premises in the UK used by the establishment for storage) pending or following public access.

(c) During the 'relevant period', the property must meet condition (b) for no more than two years (or such longer period as HMRC may in a particular case allow). The '*relevant period*' is the period beginning with the importation of the property and ending when it next ceases to be in the UK, except that if the property is lost or stolen the relevant period is suspended.

(d) The property must attract a 'relevant VAT relief' (for which see *ITA 2007, s 809Z1*). This condition is abolished on and after 6 April 2013 or, in the case of property already in the UK on that date, from the time it ceases to be in the UK or is lost or stolen.

[*ITA 2007, ss 809Z, 809Z1, 809Z6(5)*].

Personal use rule

[61.31] The '*personal use rule*' in **61.26**(b) above is that the clothing, footwear, jewellery or watches are property of a relevant person (see **61.12** above) and are for the personal use of the individual with the income or gains, the spouse or civil partner (or co-habiting partner) of the individual, or a child or grandchild (under 18) of any of the aforementioned. [*ITA 2007, s 809Z2*].

Repair rule

[61.32] The '*repair rule*' in **61.26**(c)(ii) above is that the property must be under repair or restoration at premises in the UK, in storage at the restorers pending or following repair or restoration or in transit between there and a place outside the UK. This rule interacts with the public access rule at **61.30** above in that if these conditions are met for only part of the time the property is in the UK the repair rule is nevertheless treated as met provided the property meets the public access rule for the remainder of that time. [*ITA 2007, s 809Z3*].

Temporary importation rule

[61.33] The '*temporary importation rule*' in **61.26**(c)(iii) above is that the property is in the UK for no more than 275 'countable days' (approximately 9 months). The 275-day limit applies cumulatively to all periods of importation. A '*countable day*' is a day on which (or on part of which) the property is in the UK by virtue of its being brought to, or received or used in, the UK such that **61.11**(a) above applies. A day is not a countable day if on any part of that day the property meets the personal use rule or the repair rule or if the notional remitted amount (see **61.34** below) in relation to the property is less than £1,000.

With effect on and after 6 April 2013 (except in relation to property already in the UK on that date), a day is also not a countable day if on any part of that day the property meets the public access rule. For property already in the UK on 6 April 2013 this is the case only if other conditions are met. Broadly, the property must meet the public access rule during the whole of the period it is in the UK in which that day falls, or must meet the public access rule and the repair rule (and no other rule) during the whole of that period, or it must be imported under the temporary importation rule prior to a period of public access and then exported after the period of public access. If such property is lost or stolen, the current period of importation comes to an end.

In relation to property that is lost, stolen or destroyed whilst in the UK, a day is not a countable day if on any part of that day the property has been lost, stolen or destroyed, it has not been recovered (if lost or stolen) and no compensation payment has been released in respect of it (see **61.29** above). If property that has been lost or stolen is recovered and the first day after the day on which it is recovered is a countable day, the individual is effectively given an extra 45 days to take the property offshore before falling foul of the 275-day rule.

Finally, a day is not a countable day if on any part of that day all or any of the income or gains contained in the property (or from which the property derives) falls to be treated by virtue of **61.21, 61.27, 61.28** or **61.29** above as not remitted to the UK.

[*ITA 2007, ss 809Z4, 809Z6(5)–(8)*].

Notional remitted amount

[61.34] The '*notional remitted amount*' in **61.26**(c)(i) above is the amount that would be regarded as remitted to the UK if the exemption did not apply. [*ITA 2007, s 809Z5*].

Offshore mortgages

[61.35] In the circumstances set out below, relevant foreign income of an individual used outside the UK before 6 April 2028 to pay the interest on a debt is treated as not remitted to the UK.

The circumstances are that:

- before 12 March 2008, money was lent to the individual outside the UK for the sole purpose of his acquiring an interest in residential property in the UK; and
- before 6 April 2008, the money was received in the UK and used by the individual to acquire such an interest, and repayment of the debt (or of payments made under a guarantee of that repayment) is secured on the interest in property acquired.

If at any time on or after 12 March 2008, any term on which the loan was made (or any term of the guarantee) is varied or waived, or repayment of the debt (or of payments made under the guarantee) ceases to be secured on the interest in the property, or repayment of any other debt is secured on the same interest(or is guaranteed by the same guarantee), or the interest ceases to be owned by the individual, the exemption does not apply to any relevant foreign income used to pay the interest after that time.

For these purposes, a 'guarantee' includes an indemnity.

Remortgaging

A similar exemption applies to interest on a subsequent loan if:

- before 12 March 2008, money was lent to the individual outside the UK (the subsequent loan) for the sole purpose of his repaying the above-mentioned loan; and
- before 6 April 2008, the money was used by the individual to repay the above-mentioned loan, and repayment of the subsequent loan (or of payments made under a guarantee of that repayment) is secured on the same interest in property as above.

This can apply to a third loan taken out to repay the second loan, and so on, provided all the conditions are met in relation to the loan in question.

[*FA 2008, Sch 7 para 90*].

Remittance basis before 2008/09

[61.36] For years before 2008/09, the remittance basis could be claimed by certain UK residents (see (i) and (ii) below) in respect of 'relevant foreign income' (as in **32.2** FOREIGN INCOME).

A claim was required for the remittance basis to apply to a person's income for a tax year. For 2005/06 to 2007/08 inclusive, the claim had to be to an officer of HMRC and had to indicate that the person met either of the following conditions:

(i) he was not domiciled in the UK (see **63.35** RESIDENCE AND DOMICILE); or
(ii) he was not ordinarily resident in the UK (see **63.34** RESIDENCE AND DOMICILE).

No time limit was specified for making the claim, so by default the deadline is as stipulated in **16.4** CLAIMS.

The effect of a claim for a tax year was that income tax was charged on the full amount of the sums received in the UK in the tax year in respect of relevant foreign income. It did not matter whether the income arose in the year for which the claim was made or in an earlier year in which the person was UK resident. No charge arose if income for the tax year to which the claim related was remitted in a subsequent year for which no claim was made (but see **61.4** above where the income is remitted in 2008/09 or a subsequent year).

The charge was normally on the actual remittances in respect of the income in the tax year without any deduction (subject to the addition of any foreign tax for which credit is allowable — see **27.10**(a)(i) DOUBLE TAX RELIEF). However, where the income was from a trade, profession or vocation carried on outside the UK, the same deductions were allowed as for trades etc. carried on in the UK.

The remittance basis did not apply for any year before 2008/09 to relevant foreign income arising in the Republic of Ireland. See also **27.4** DOUBLE TAX RELIEF.

[*ITTOIA 2005, ss 831, 832, Sch 2 para 150; ITEPA 2003, ss 575, 613, 631, 635, 679* (as originally enacted)].

There were also rules governing constructive remittances; these are superseded for 2008/09 onwards by the rules at **61.11** above. There was a relief for delayed remittances, i.e. where income could not have been transferred to the UK any earlier because of the laws, or the executive action of the government, of the territory in which it arose or because of the impossibility of obtaining currency there that could be transferred to the UK.

Simon's Taxes. See **E1.603**.

Case law

[61.37] The following decisions pre-dated the fundamental legislative changes made to the remittance basis for 2008/09 onwards.

A remittance of capital is not taxable as such (unless within CGT — see Tolley's Capital Gains Tax) but a taxable remittance may include the proceeds of investments made abroad out of overseas income (*Scottish Provident*

Institution v Farmer CS 1912, 6 TC 34). Where the proceeds were of investments made before the taxpayer came to reside in the UK, there was no liability (*Kneen v Martin* CA 1934, 19 TC 33). Similarly, a remittance from a foreign bank into which overseas income had been paid may be assessable, dependent on the circumstances. For this see *Walsh v Randall* KB 1940, 23 TC 55 (sterling draft on foreign bank in favour of London hospital received by taxpayer before handing to hospital, held to be remittance) and *Thomson v Moyse* HL 1960, 39 TC 291 (dollar cheques on US bank sold to Bank of England held to be remitted) and compare *Carter v Sharon* KB 1936, 20 TC 229 (drafts on foreign bank posted abroad to taxpayer's daughter for maintenance, held not to be remittance as, under relevant foreign law, gift to daughter completed on posting of draft). See also *Fellowes-Gordon v CIR* CS 1935, 19 TC 683. In *Harmel v Wright* Ch D 1973, 49 TC 149 an amount received via two South African companies, ending as a loan from one of them, was held to be a remittance of South African emoluments within *Sch E, Case III*. Where, contrary to the customer's instructions, a bank erroneously remitted untaxed overseas income to him, it was held there was no liability (*Duke of Roxburghe's Exors v CIR* CS 1936, 20 TC 711). In *Grimm v Newman & another CA*, [2002] STC 1388 (a negligence case in which the Revenue were not a party), an absolute inter-spousal gift, perfected abroad, of overseas assets subsequently used to purchase a matrimonial home in the UK was held not to be a remittance.

62

Repayment Interest

Cross-reference. See also **53.23** PAY AS YOU EARN.

Simon's Taxes. See **A4.630**.

Introduction to repayment interest

[62.1] A harmonised regime for interest applies to all of the taxes and duties administered by HMRC. In relation to interest on income tax repaid by HMRC, the regime is described at **62.2** below.

Repayment interest

[62.2] A harmonised regime for interest applies to all of the taxes and duties administered by HMRC. To the extent that this regime is in force (see below) in relation to interest on income tax repaid by HMRC, it replaces the rules referred to at **62.3** below.

An amount carries interest only if it is payable by HMRC to any person under or by virtue of an enactment or if it is a repayment by HMRC of any sum that was paid in connection with any liability (including any purported or anticipated liability) to make a payment to HMRC under or by virtue of an enactment.

For the purposes of any 'self-assessment amount' payable by HMRC to any person, the regime has been in force since 31 October 2011. A '*self-assessment amount*' means:

- any tax or other amount in relation to which, for any tax year, a personal, trustees' or partnership tax return falls to be made or a discovery assessment is made; and
- any penalties assessed in relation to that tax or amount.

Interest added to a repayment of a self-assessment amount is known as '*repayment interest*'. Where interest was already accruing immediately prior to that date on a self-assessment amount, it accrues on and after that date under the current regime. No liability to income tax arises in respect of repayment interest.

Rates of repayment interest will be significantly lower than those by reference to which late payment interest is charged (see **43.2** LATE PAYMENT INTEREST AND PENALTIES). The rates are set by reference to the official bank rate set by the Bank of England Monetary Policy Committee; for details, see *SI 2011 No 2446, Reg 4*. There is a minimum rate of repayment interest of 0.5%, so that some interest will be due even when the official rate would otherwise be too low. Changes to the rate of repayment interest will be announced by HMRC News Release.

Rates of interest

0.5% p.a. from 31 October 2011

Period for which interest accrues

A repayment within these provisions carries interest at the repayment interest rate from the 'repayment interest start date' until the date on which the repayment is made. The '*repayment interest start date*' is arrived at as set out below. It matters not that the repayment interest start date might be a non-business day.

- Where the repayment is of an amount which has been paid to HMRC, the repayment interest start date is the *later* of date A and date B, where:
  date A = the date on which the amount was paid to HMRC; and
  date B = the date on which payment of the amount to HMRC became due and payable to HMRC (where the amount was paid in connection with a liability to make a payment to HMRC).
- Where the repayment is of an amount which has not been paid to HMRC but is payable by them by virtue of a return having been filed or a claim having been made, the repayment interest start date is the *later* of date C and date D, where:
  date C = the date (if any) on which the return was required to be filed or the claim was required to be made; and
  date D = the date on which the return was in fact filed or the claim was in fact made.
- Where the repayment is of an amount of income tax deducted at source for a tax year, the repayment interest start date is 31 January following that year. Income tax deducted at source for a tax year includes PAYE deductions except to the extent (if any) that these relate to tax due for previous years, i.e. where tax is being collected by coding adjustment.
- Where the repayment is the result of a loss relief or averaging claim affecting two or more years (see **16.2** CLAIMS), the repayment interest start date is 31 January following the *later* year in relation to the claim, i.e. on a claim to carry back a loss, the tax year in which the loss arises; on an averaging claim (for farmers or creative artists), the last of the tax years being averaged.
- Where the repayment is the result of a claim under *ITA 2007, s 496B* (relief for payments by discretionary trust taxable as employment income — see **70.15** SETTLEMENTS), the repayment interest start date is 31 January following the tax year to which the claim relates.

A repayment may take the form of a set-off against an amount owed to HMRC, in which case the date on which the repayment is made is the date from which the set-off takes effect.

As regards the date on which an amount is treated as paid to HMRC, see **54.2** PAYMENT OF TAX.

Repayments relating to claims under *ITA 1952, s 228* (income accumulated under trusts — see **70.24** SETTLEMENTS) are treated as repayments of tax paid for the tax year in which the contingency happened.

Attribution

The following rules apply for the purpose of determining how a repayment of income tax for a tax year is to be attributed to payments of income tax made.

- Firstly, the repayment is attributed to the final payment (if any) of income tax for the year (see **67.7** SELF-ASSESSMENT).
- Secondly, it is attributed in two equal parts to the interim payments (if any) for the year (see **67.5** SELF-ASSESSMENT).
- Finally, it is attributed to income tax deducted at source for the year.

Where an amount was paid in instalments, any repayment of that amount is attributed to later instalments before earlier ones.

Supplementary

Repayment interest is not payable on an amount payable in consequence of an order or judgment of a court having power to allow interest on the amount (for which see **54.6** PAYMENT OF TAX).

[*FA 2009, ss 102, 103, 104, Sch 54 paras 1–9, 9A, 13, 14; ITTOIA 2005, s 749; FA 2016, Sch 1 paras 66(6), 73; SI 2011 No 2446*].

Interest is similarly paid on repayments of Class 4 national insurance contributions (see **73.7** SOCIAL SECURITY AND NATIONAL INSURANCE).

Interest on overpaid tax (the old regime)

[62.3] For the purposes of income tax self-assessment, the old rules were superseded by those at **62.2** above on and after 31 October 2011. Where interest was already accruing immediately prior to 31 October 2011 on a 'self-assessment amount' (as defined in **62.2**), it accrues on and after that date under the regime at **62.2**.

Unauthorised demands for tax

[62.4] There is a general right to interest under *Supreme Court Act 1981, s 35A* in a case where a taxpayer submits to such an unauthorised demand, provided that the payment is not made voluntarily to close a transaction (*Woolwich Equitable Building Society v CIR* HL 1992, 65 TC 265). (*Note.* The substantive decision against the Inland Revenue which gave rise to the repayment was subsequently upheld in the HL. See *R v CIR (ex p Woolwich Equitable Building Society)* HL 1990, 63 TC 589.)

Over-repayments

[62.5] Where interest has been *overpaid* by HMRC it can be recovered by the making of an assessment — see **54.16** PAYMENT OF TAX.

63

Residence and Domicile

Cross-references. See **50** NON-RESIDENTS for situations in which the residence or domicile of an individual may be of relevance for income tax purposes; **61** REMITTANCE BASIS.

Simon's Taxes. See **E6.1, E6.300A–E6.311**.

Introduction to residence and domicile

[63.1] UK tax liability may depend on a person's **domicile** (the country or state which is his 'natural home' — see **63.35** below) and/or on whether or not he is **resident** in the UK for tax purposes in a particular tax year. Before 6 April 2013 it would also sometimes depend on whether a person was *ordinarily resident* in the UK (see **63.34** below).

EU law does not prevent a member State from imposing more onerous fiscal charges on nationals resident in another member State than those imposed on its own resident nationals (*Werner v Finanzamt Aachen-Innenstadt (Case C–112/91)* CJEC, [1996] STC 961).

For official guidance, see RDR1 (Guidance Note: Residence, Domicile and the Remittance Basis) at www.gov.uk/government/publications/residence-domicile-and-remittance-basis-rules-uk-tax-liability.

Statutory residence test

A statutory residence test has effect. See **63.4** below.

Residence for 2012/13 and earlier years

The statutory residence test did not apply before 2013/14. As regards residence for 2012/13 and earlier years, see **63.32** below, and see generally HMRC Leaflet HMRC6 (Residence, Domicile and the Remittance Basis) (available at www.gov.uk/government/uploads/system/uploads/attachment_data/fil e/430830/hmrc6.pdf), to which reference is made in this chapter where relevant. This replaced Leaflet IR20 with effect from 6 April 2009. See *R (oao Davies) v HMRC; R (oao Gaines-Cooper) v HMRC* at **63.32** below for an appeal to the Supreme Court involving *inter alia* the proper construction of IR20.

Deemed domicile for 2017/18 onwards

With effect on and after 6 April 2017, individuals resident but not domiciled in the UK in any tax year are deemed to be domiciled in the UK for income tax and capital gains tax purposes if they are UK born and have a UK domicile of origin or they have been UK resident for at least 15 of the 20 preceding tax years. See **63.36** below.

Self-assessment

Under self-assessment, individuals who regard themselves as not resident or not domiciled in the UK are required to self-certify their status in the self-assessment tax return and to complete the 'non-residence etc.' supplementary pages to the return. HMRC queries on residence status and domicile aspects may be made by way of, or as part of, an enquiry into the self-assessment return or into an initial claim made outside the return (see **64.6** RETURNS, **16.3** CLAIMS). See Revenue Tax Bulletin June 1997 pp 425–427.

UK residents

[63.2] A person who is resident in the UK is liable to UK tax on all his income and gains, whether from UK or overseas sources, subject to limited categories of EXEMPT INCOME (**30**).

In certain circumstances, the charge to UK tax is limited to remittances to the UK out of the income or gains. See **61** REMITTANCE BASIS.

Deductions are made from the amounts otherwise taxable as follows.

Seafarers

Employments wholly abroad where the employee is abroad for a qualifying period (as defined) of 365 days or more — a deduction of 100% is made (i.e. complete exemption) from taxable earnings if all relevant conditions are satisfied. See **28.10** EMPLOYMENT INCOME.

Overseas government pensions

A deduction of 10% may be made, as set out in **56.2**(f) PENSION INCOME.

Non-UK residents

[63.3] Non-UK residents are liable to UK tax on UK income, including income from property etc. in the UK, income from trades, professions etc. exercised in the UK and on employment income for duties performed in the UK.

See also **30.37** EXEMPT INCOME and **65.4** SAVINGS AND INVESTMENT INCOME for the special exemption to non-UK residents in respect of certain government stocks and **23.12** DEDUCTION OF TAX AT SOURCE for a similar relief in respect of the interest or dividends on certain foreign stocks and securities payable in the UK.

The appropriate double tax agreement should be examined for exemptions and for restrictions on the rates of tax to be borne. Otherwise non-UK residents are chargeable at the full rate and not entitled to personal or other reliefs. Thus a person carrying on a business in the UK but claiming to be non-resident may thereby have his tax allowances reduced or even refused. But see **50.2** NON-RESIDENTS for reliefs available to certain non-UK residents.

Non-UK residents have no UK income tax liability on overseas income.

See generally **50** NON-RESIDENTS.

Statutory residence test

[63.4] Statutory rules apply to determine whether an individual is resident or not resident in the UK. These rules are known collectively as the '*statutory residence test*'. [*FA 2013, s 218, Sch 45*]. References in the rules to an individual are to one acting in any capacity, including as trustee or personal representative. [*FA 2013, Sch 45 para 145*]. The rules do not apply to determine whether an individual is resident or not resident in England, Wales, Scotland or Northern Ireland specifically (rather than in the UK as a whole). [*FA 2013, Sch 45 para 1(3)*]. Any reference in any income tax enactment to an individual being resident (or not resident) in the UK is to be taken as a reference to his being resident (or not resident) in the UK in accordance with the statutory residence test. [*FA 2013, Sch 45 paras 2(1)(2), 145*].

Subject to the split year treatment at **63.19** below where there are certain changes of circumstances, an individual who, in accordance with the statutory residence test, is resident (or not resident) in the UK *for* a tax year is regarded as being UK resident (or not UK resident) at *all* times in that tax year. [*FA 2013, Sch 45 para 2(3)(4)*].

See **63.30** below for transitional provisions.

For HMRC guidance, with examples, on the statutory residence test see HMRC Residence, Domicile and Remittance Basis Manual RDRM11000.

HMRC stress the importance of individuals keeping records and documents to support statements made when considering the statutory residence test, and give some examples of the types of records required (see HMRC Residence, Domicile and Remittance Basis Manual RDRM12900).

COVID-19 (coronavirus) special measure

The statutory residence test is amended by *FA 2020, s 109* with the effect that days between 1 March 2020 and 1 June 2020 inclusive spent by individuals in the UK for specified reasons connected with the detection, treatment or prevention of COVID-19 (see **63.8** below) will not count towards the relevant tests. See also **63.5**(2), (3), **63.6**(3), **63.10**, **63.14**, **63.15**, **63.16**, **63.17** and **63.18** below. See also 'Technical Note: Modifications of the Statutory Residence Test in connection with coronavirus' at www.gov.uk/government/publications/finance-bill-2020-report-stage, which includes detailed practical examples.

This special measure applies for the purposes of determining:

- whether an individual was or was not resident in the UK for 2019/20; and
- if an individual was not resident in the UK for 2019/20 (including the case where the individual's non-resident status was as a result of the special measure), whether the individual is or is not resident in the UK for 2020/21.

[*FA 2020, s 109(1)*].

The basic rule

Under the statutory residence test an individual (P) is resident in the UK for a tax year if for that year:

- the 'automatic residence test' is met; or
- the 'sufficient ties test' (see **63.12** below) is met.

If neither of those tests is met, P is not resident in the UK for that year.

[*FA 2013, Sch 45 paras 3, 4*].

Automatic residence test

The '*automatic residence test*' is met for a year if P meets at least one of the 'automatic UK tests' (see **63.5** below) and none of the 'automatic overseas tests' (see **63.6** below). [*FA 2013, Sch 45 para 5*].

Simon's Taxes. See **E6.102A–E6.102L.**

The automatic UK tests

[63.5] There are four '*automatic UK tests*'. As stated in **63.4** above, an individual (P) need meet only one of them to pass the automatic residence test.

(1) The first UK test is that P spends at least 183 days in the UK in the tax year in question (year X). See **63.8** below as regards days spent in the UK.

(2) The second UK test is that:
   - P has a home (see **63.9** below) in the UK for at least part of year X;

- P is present at that home (while it is a home of his) for at least some of the time on at least 30 days (whether consecutive or intermittent) in year X;
- while it is a home of P's, there is at least one period of 91 consecutive days throughout which condition A or condition B (or a combination of those conditions) is met; and
- at least 30 days of that 91-day period fall within year X.

Condition A is that P has no home overseas. Condition B is that P does have one or more homes overseas but each of them is a home at which he is present for at least some of the time on fewer than 30 days (whether consecutive or intermittent) in year X.

If, in fact, P has more than one home in the UK, the test must be applied to each of those homes individually, but the test has to be met only in relation to at least one of them.

The COVID-19 (coronavirus) special measure at **63.4** above applies to this test, and does so for the purposes stated there. In this respect, the special measure is that a day does not count as a day when P is present at a home of P's in the UK if it is a day that would fall within the COVID-19 relaxation at **63.8** below if P were present in the UK at the end of it.

(3) The third UK test is that:

- P works 'sufficient hours in the UK' (see **63.10** below), as assessed over a period of 365 days;
- there are no 'significant breaks' from UK work within that period;
- at least part of that period falls within year X;
- of the total number of days in that period when P does more than three hours' work, more than 75% of them are days when he does more than three hours' work in the UK; and
- at least one day which falls in both that period and year X is a day on which P does more than 3 hours' work in the UK.

For these purposes there is a '*significant break*' from UK work if at least 31 days go by and not one of them is a day on which P does more than three hours' work in the UK (or would have done so but for being on annual leave, sick leave, parenting leave or emergency volunteering leave under *Coronavirus Act 2020, Sch 7*). The reference here to emergency volunteering leave is part of the COVID-19 (coronavirus) special measure at **63.4** above, and it applies for the purposes stated there.

See **63.10** below as regards work generally.

The third UK test does not apply to P if:

- at any time in year X he has a 'relevant job' on board a vehicle, aircraft or ship (see **63.11** below); and
- at least six of the trips that he makes in year X as part of that job are cross-border trips that begin or end in the UK (or both begin and end in the UK).

(4) The fourth UK test is that:

(a) P dies in year X;

(b) for each of the previous three tax years, P was resident in the UK by virtue of meeting the automatic residence test;

(c) the tax year preceding year X would not be a split year (see **63.20** below) as regards P, even if he is non-UK resident for year X;
(d) when P died, his home (see **63.9** below) (or at least one of his homes if more than one) was in the UK; and
(e) if P had a home overseas during all or part of year X, P did not spend a 'sufficient amount of time' there in year X.

In (b) above, the words 'by virtue of meeting the automatic residence test' do not apply where the previous year in question is 2012/13 or an earlier year, unless the election in **63.30** below is made in respect of that year.

For the purpose of (e) above, P spent a '*sufficient amount of time*' in a home overseas in year X if:

- there were at least 30 days (whether consecutive or intermittent) in year X when P was present there for at least some of the time; or
- P was present there for at least some of the time on each day of year X up to and including the day he died.

The reference to P being present at the home is to his being present there at a time when it was a home of his. If P had more than one home overseas, condition (e) must be applied to each of those homes individually and must be met in relation to each of them.

[*FA 2013, Sch 45 paras 6–10, 29(1), 145, 146, 154(5); FA 2020, s 109(3)(7)*].

The automatic overseas tests

[63.6] There are five '*automatic overseas tests*'. As stated in **63.4** above, the automatic residence test is failed if an individual (P) meets at least one of the automatic overseas tests.

(1) The first overseas test is that:
- P was resident in the UK for one or more of the three tax years preceding the tax year in question (year X);
- the number of days in year X that P spends in the UK is less than 16; and
- P does not die in year X.

(2) The second overseas test is that:
- P was resident in the UK for none of the three tax years preceding year X; and
- the number of days in year X that P spends in the UK is less than 46.

(3) The third overseas test is that:
- P works 'sufficient hours overseas' (see **63.10** below), as assessed over the course of year X;
- there are no 'significant breaks' from overseas work during year X;
- the number of days in year X on which P does more than three hours' work in the UK is less than 31; and

- the number of days spent by P in the UK in year X is less than 91 (disregarding any days *treated* as spent in the UK under the 'deeming rule' in **63.8** below).

For these purposes there is a '*significant break*' from overseas work if at least 31 days go by and not one of them is a day on which P does more than three hours' work overseas (or would have done so but for being on annual leave, sick leave, parenting leave or emergency volunteering leave under *Coronavirus Act 2020, Sch 7*). The reference here to emergency volunteering leave is part of the COVID-19 (coronavirus) special measure at **63.4** above, and it applies for the purposes stated there.

See **63.10** below as regards work generally.

The third overseas test does not apply to P if:

- at any time in year X he has a 'relevant job' on board a vehicle, aircraft or ship (see **63.11** below); and
- at least six of the trips that he makes in year X as part of that job are cross-border trips that begin or end in the UK (or both begin and end in the UK).

(4) The fourth overseas test is that:

(a) P dies in year X;

(b) P was resident in the UK for neither of the two tax years preceding year X; and

(c) the number of days that P spends in the UK in year X is less than 46.

P also meets the condition in (b) above if he was not resident in the UK for the tax year preceding year X but the year before that was a split year as regards P because the circumstances fell within Case 1, Case 2 or Case 3 at **63.21–63.23** below.

(5) The fifth overseas test is that:

(a) P dies in year X;

(b) P was resident in the UK for neither of the two tax years preceding year X because he met the third automatic overseas test for each of those years; and

(c) P would meet the third automatic overseas test for year X if that test were assessed by reference to the period from the start of year X up to (but not including) the date of death.

In (b) above, the words 'because he met the third automatic overseas test for each of those years' do not apply where the preceding year in question is 2012/13 or an earlier year, unless the election in **63.30** below is made in respect of that year.

P also meets the condition in (b) above if he was not resident in the UK for the tax year preceding year X because he met the third automatic overseas test for that year but the year before that was a split year as regards P because the circumstances fell within Case 1 at **63.21** below. If that preceding year is 2012/13, the words 'because he met the third automatic overseas test for that year' do not apply unless the election in **63.30** below is made in respect of that year.

[*FA 2013, Sch 45 paras 11–16, 29(2), 145, 146, 154(5); FA 2020, s 109(7)*].

See **63.8** below as regards days spent in the UK.

Automatic tests — supplementary

[63.7] The following paragraphs (**63.8–63.11**) supplement, and provide definitions for the purposes of, the automatic UK and overseas tests at **63.5** and **63.6** above and these provisions generally.

Days spent in the UK

[63.8] Generally, if an individual (P) is present in the UK at the end of a day, that day counts as a day spent by P in the UK for the purposes of the statutory residence test. If, however, P arrives in the UK on one day and departs on the next, he is not treated as spending a day in the UK (despite his presence at the end of the day of arrival) if between arrival and departure he does not engage in activities that are to a substantial extent unrelated to his passage through the UK, i.e. he is merely a passenger in transit. Note that this precludes not only his engaging in activities relating to business or employment but also in many activities of a non-business nature such as spending time with family.

A day at the end of which P is present in the UK due only to exceptional circumstances beyond P's control that prevent his leaving the UK does not count as a day spent by P in the UK. Exceptional circumstances include, for example, a sudden or life-threatening illness or injury and national or local emergencies such as war, civil unrest or natural disasters; in all cases it must be P's intention to leave the UK as soon as those circumstances permit. The maximum number of days in a tax year on which P can rely on this exclusion is limited to 60. Accordingly, once the number of days for which the exclusion applies reaches 60 (counting forward from the start of the tax year), any subsequent days, whether involving the same or different exceptional circumstances, will count as days spent by P in the UK.

For further information about how HMRC interpret the term 'exceptional circumstances' see HMRC Residence, Domicile and Remittance Basis Manual RDRM13240. See HMRC Residence, Domicile and Remittance Basis Manual RDRM11005 for circumstances resulting from the impact of COVID-19 (coronavirus) that are accepted by HMRC as being exceptional.

COVID-19 relaxation

A day at the end of which P is present in the UK due where the following circumstances are present does not count as a day spent by P in the UK:

- the day in question falls within the period 1 March 2020 to 1 June 2020 inclusive;
- on that day P is present in the UK for an 'applicable reason' related to COVID-19; and
- in the tax year under consideration (whether it be 2019/20 or 2020/21), P is resident in a territory outside the UK, i.e. P is considered for tax purposes to be a resident of that territory in accordance with that territory's laws.

The following are '*applicable reasons*':

- that P is in the UK as a medical or healthcare professional for purposes connected with the detection, treatment or prevention of COVID-19;

- that P is in the UK for purposes connected with the development or production of medicinal products (including vaccines), devices, equipment or facilities related to the detection, treatment or prevention of COVID-19.

The Treasury have power to make regulations to defer the 1 June 2020 date above (provided the revised date is no later than 5 April 2021) and/or to add one or more 'applicable reasons'.

This is the integral part of the COVID-19 (coronavirus) special measure at **63.4** above, and it applies for the purposes stated there.

The 'deeming rule'

If P is not present in the UK at the end of a day, that day does not count as a day spent by P in the UK, but this is subject to a rule known as the 'deeming rule'. The '*deeming rule*' applies if:

- P has at least three 'UK ties' (see **63.13** below) for a tax year (year X) (determined without reference to the deeming rule itself);
- P was resident in the UK for at least one of the three tax years preceding year X; and
- the number of days ('*visiting days*') in year X when P is present in the UK at some point in the day, but *not* at the end of it, is more than 30.

The deeming rule is that, once the number of visiting days in year X reaches 30 (counting forward from the start of the tax year), each subsequent visiting day in year X is treated as a day spent by P in the UK.

The COVID-19 (coronavirus) special measure at **63.4** above applies to the deeming rule, and does so for the purposes stated there. In this respect, the special measure is that a day does not count as a visiting day if it is a day that would fall within the COVID-19 relaxation above if P were present in the UK at the end of it.

[*FA 2013, Sch 45 paras 22–24; FA 2020, s 109(4)(5)*].

An individual's home

[63.9] For the purposes of the statutory residence test, an individual's home could be a building or part of a building or, for example, a vehicle, vessel or structure of any kind. Whether, for a given building etc., there is sufficient degree of permanence or stability about an individual's arrangements there for it to count as his home (or one of his homes) depends on all the circumstances of the case. A place that an individual uses periodically as nothing more than a holiday home or temporary retreat (or similar) does not count as a home of his. A place can count as an individual's home whether or not he holds any estate or interest in it; but the mere fact that he still holds an estate or interest does not continue to make a place an individual's home once he has moved out. [*FA 2013, Sch 45 para 25*].

For further information about how HMRC interpret the term 'home' in the context of applying the statutory residence test see HMRC Residence, Domicile and Remittance Basis Manual RDRM13020–13060.

Work

[63.10] For the purposes of the statutory residence test, an individual (P) is considered to be 'working' (or 'doing work') at any time when he is doing something either in performing the duties of an employment or in the course of a trade carried on by him (whether alone or in partnership). A voluntary post for which P has no contract of service does not count as an employment for these purposes. Throughout these provisions 'trade' includes a profession or vocation, anything treated as a trade for income tax purposes and the commercial occupation of woodlands. Whilst in most cases it will be obvious, *FA 2013, Sch 45 para 26(2), (3)* contain extra rules for determining whether something is being done in performing the duties of an employment or in the course of a trade etc.

Time spent *travelling* counts as time spent working:

- if the cost of the journey would, if incurred by P, be deductible in calculating his taxable earnings or, as the case may be, taxable profits (on the assumption that P is within the charge to income tax); or
- to the extent that P does something else during the journey that would itself count as work.

Time spent undertaking *training* counts as time spent working if:

- in the case of employment, the training is provided or paid for by the employer and is undertaken to help P in performing his duties; and
- in the case of a trade etc., the cost of the training is deductible in calculating taxable profits (on the assumption that P is within the charge to income tax).

[*FA 2013, Sch 45 para 26*].

Being on-call or stand-by may count as time spent working depending on the conditions of P's employment and the nature of P's duties (HMRC Residence, Domicile and Remittance Basis Manual RDRM11750).

Location of work

Work is regarded as done where it is actually done, regardless of where the employment is held or the trade is carried on. However, work done by way of, or in the course of, travelling to or from the UK by air, sea or tunnel is assumed to be done overseas even during the part of the journey in or over the UK. For this purpose, the travelling begins when P boards the aircraft, ship or train that will take him from another country to the UK or vice versa and ends when he disembarks.

In the case of people with relevant jobs on board vehicles, aircraft or ships (see **63.11** below), the above is subject to **63.16** below.

[*FA 2013, Sch 45 para 27*].

Working sufficient hours

For the purposes of the third automatic UK test at **63.5**(3) above, P works '*sufficient hours in the UK*' if his weekly 'net UK hours' are at least 35.

P's total '*net UK hours*' are determined by identifying, for any given period of 365 days and including all employments held and trades carried on by him, the total number of hours that P works in the UK during that period. However, any hours that he works in the UK on 'disregarded days' are not to be included in this total. A '*disregarded day*' is a day on which P does more than three hours' work overseas (even if he also does work in the UK on the same day).

Similarly, for the purposes of the third automatic overseas test at **63.6**(3) above, P works '*sufficient hours overseas*' if his weekly 'net overseas hours' are at least 35. P's total '*net overseas hours*' are determined by identifying, for year X and including all employments held and trades carried on by him, the total number of hours that P works overseas during that period. Any hours that he works overseas on 'disregarded days' are not to be included in the total. A '*disregarded day*' is a day on which P does more than three hours' work in the UK (even if he also does work overseas on the same day).

The reference period

P's weekly net UK hours is his total net UK hours divided by the number of weeks in the 'reference period'. The '*reference period*' is calculated by subtracting from 365 the total number of disregarded days as above and, if appropriate, reducing the total as described below. The number of weeks in the reference period is calculated by dividing the reference period by seven; the result is rounded down to the nearest whole number, unless it is less than one in which case it is rounded up to one.

P's weekly net overseas hours are computed in similar fashion, except that if year X is a leap year the starting point in calculating the reference period is 366. Where **63.6**(5)(c) is in point, the starting point is the number of days in the period from the start of year X up to (but not including) the date of P's death.

In all cases the reference period can be reduced to take account of:

(a) reasonable amounts of annual leave or parenting leave taken (having regard to, for example, the nature of the work and the country in which it is performed);
(b) reasonable sick leave taken;
(c) absences from work at times during the period specified in an emergency volunteering certificate issued to P under *Coronavirus Act 2020, Sch 7* (emergency volunteering leave); and
(d) any 'non-working days' 'embedded' within a block of leave for which a reduction is made under (a), (b) or (c).

No such reduction can be made in respect of a disregarded day. If the total days for which a reduction is available under (a) or (b) is not a whole number, the number is rounded down (but the rounding is ignored for the purposes of (d)). A '*non-working day*' is any day on which P is not normally expected to work (according to his contract of employment or usual pattern of work) and does not in fact work. Non-working days are '*embedded*' within a block of leave only if there are at least three consecutive days of leave taken both before and after the non-working day (or series of non-working days) in question.

If there is a change of employment during the reference period, with a gap in between the two jobs, the reference period is reduced by the number of days in the gap. The reduction for any one gap is limited to 15 days; if there is more than one such gap, the maximum reduction for all the gaps is limited to 30 days.

Item (c) above is part of the COVID-19 (coronavirus) special measure at **63.4** above, and it applies for the purposes stated there.

[*FA 2013, Sch 45 paras 9(2), 14(3), 16(3), 28, 145, 146; FA 2020, s 109(6)*].

Relevant job on board vehicle, aircraft or ship

[63.11] For the purposes of the statutory residence test, an individual (P) has a relevant job on board a vehicle, aircraft or ship if conditions A and B are both met. Condition A is that:

(a) P holds an employment, the duties of which consist of duties to be performed, or
(b) carries on a trade, the activities of which consist of work to be done or services to be provided,

on board a vehicle, aircraft or ship while it is travelling. The condition at (b) is met only if, in order to do the work or provide the services, P has to be present (in person) on board the vehicle etc. while it is travelling.

Condition B is that substantially all of the trips made in performing those duties or carrying on those activities are trips that involve crossing an international boundary ('*cross-border trips*').

In determining whether conditions A and B are met, duties or activities of a purely incidental nature are ignored.

[*FA 2013, Sch 45 para 30*].

See also **63.16** below.

The sufficient ties test

[63.12] As stated in **63.4** above, the sufficient ties test is an alternative to the automatic residence test. The '*sufficient ties test*' is met by an individual (P) for the year in question (year X) if P meets none of the automatic UK tests (**63.5** above) and none of the automatic overseas tests (**63.6** above), but P has sufficient 'UK ties' (see **63.13** below) for the year. Whether P has sufficient UK ties for year X depends upon whether he was resident in the UK for any of the previous three tax years and the number of days he spends in the UK in year X. See the tables below, and note the modifications where death occurs in year X. See **63.8** above as regards days spent in the UK.

Sufficient UK ties tables

Where P was UK resident for at least 1 of the 3 tax years preceding year X

Days spent by P in the UK in year X	*Number of UK ties that are sufficient*
More than 15 but not more than 45	At least 4
More than 45 but not more than 90	At least 3
More than 90 but not more than 120	At least 2
More than 120	At least 1

Where P was UK resident for none of the 3 tax years preceding year X

Days spent by P in the UK in year X	*Number of UK ties that are sufficient*
More than 45 but not more than 90	4
More than 90 but not more than 120	At least 3
More than 120	At least 2

Modification of tables on death in year X

If P dies in year X, the first modification is that in the first table the top row of the first column reads 'not more than 45' instead of 'more than 15 but not more than 45'.

The second and final modification is that if the death occurs before 1 March in year X, both tables have effect as if each number of days quoted in the first column were reduced by the 'appropriate number'. The '*appropriate number*' is found by multiplying the number of days quoted, in each case, by $^{A}/_{12}$, where A = the number of 'whole months' in year X after the month in which P dies. A '*whole month*' means an entire calendar month, e.g. the month of January. If the appropriate number is not a whole number it is rounded down if the first figure after the decimal point is less than 5; otherwise it is rounded up. If P dies on, say, 17 December in year X, the number of whole months is 3. So, for example, in the top row of the first column of the second table, the figure of 45 is reduced by 11 (45 x $^{3}/_{12}$) and the figure of 90 is reduced by 23. The top row then reads 'more than 34 but not more than 67', reflecting the fact that P is alive for approximately only three-quarters of the tax year.

[*FA 2013, Sch 45 paras 17–20, 145*].

UK ties

[63.13] If the individual (P) was resident in the UK for at least one of the three tax years preceding the tax year in question (year X), each of the following counts as a '*UK tie*' for the purposes of **63.12** above and these provisions in general:

(a) a 'family tie' (**63.14** below);
(b) an 'accommodation tie' (**63.15** below);
(c) a 'work tie' (**63.16** below);
(d) a '90-day tie' (**63.17** below); and

(e) a 'country tie' (63.18 below).

If P was resident in the UK for none of the three tax years preceding year X, each of the types of tie listed at (a)–(d) above, but not (e) above, counts as a UK tie.

In order to have the requisite number of UK ties for year X, each of P's ties has to be of a different type.

[*FA 2013, Sch 45 para 31*].

Family ties

[63.14] For the purposes of 63.13(a) above, P has a '*family tie*' for year X if:

(a) in year X, a 'relevant relationship' exists at any time between P and another person; and
(b) that other person is resident in the UK for year X (see further below).

A '*relevant relationship*' exists at any time between P and another person if at that time:

- they are husband and wife or civil partners and are not separated (whether by court order, deed of separation or in circumstances where the separation is likely to be permanent);
- they are living together as if they were spouses or civil partners; or
- the other person is a child of P's and is under 18.

P does not have a family tie by virtue of the last of these conditions if P sees the child in the UK on fewer than 61 days in total in year X (or, where relevant, in the part of year X before the child's 18th birthday); a day counts as a day on which P sees the child if he sees the child in person for all or part of the day. But a day does not count as a day on which P sees the child if the day on which P sees the child would be a day falling within the COVID-19 relaxation at 63.8 above if P were present in the UK at the end of it; this is part of the COVID-19 (coronavirus) special measure at 63.4 above, and it applies for the purposes stated there.

Whether 'other person' is UK resident

The following rules apply in determining whether a person is resident in the UK for year X for the purposes of (b) above (and only for those purposes).

A family tie based on the fact that a family member has, by the same token, a relevant relationship with P is to be disregarded in deciding whether that family member is someone who is resident in the UK for year X.

A family member who:

- is a child of P's under 18,
- is in full-time education in the UK at any time in year X, and
- is resident in the UK for year X but would not be so resident if time spent in full-time education in the UK were disregarded,

is treated as being not resident in the UK for year X if the number of days that he spends in the UK in the part of year X outside term-time is less than 21. Half-term breaks, and any other breaks when teaching is not provided during a term, are considered to form part of term-time for these purposes.

[*FA 2013, Sch 45 paras 32, 33; FA 2020, s 109(8); SI 2019 No 1458, Sch 3 para 36(2)*].

For further information about how HMRC interpret the term 'family tie', see HMRC Residence, Domicile and Remittance Basis Manual RDRM13300.

Accommodation ties

[63.15] For the purposes of **63.13**(b) above, P has an '*accommodation tie*' for year X if:

(a) P has a place to live in the UK;
(b) that place is available to P during year X for a continuous period of at least 91 days (but see below); and
(c) P spends at least one night at that place in that year (but see below).

For the purposes of (a) above, P is considered to have a place to live in the UK if:

- P's home or at least one of his homes (if more than one) is in the UK; or
- P has a holiday home or temporary retreat (or similar) in the UK; or
- accommodation is otherwise available to P where he can live when in the UK. Accommodation may be regarded as available to P even if he holds no estate or interest in it and even if he has no legal right to occupy it.

See **63.9** above for what is meant by an individual's home.

For the purposes of (b) above, if there is a gap of fewer than 16 days between periods in year X when a particular place is available to P, that place is treated as continuing to be available to P during the gap.

For the purposes of (c) above, if the accommodation is the home of a 'close relative' of P's, the condition is met only if P spends a total of at least 16 nights there in year X (as opposed to one night). For this purpose, a '*close relative*' means a parent or grandparent, a brother or sister, a child aged 18 or over or a grandchild aged 18 or over; it is irrelevant whether the relationship subsists by blood or half-blood or by virtue of marriage or civil partnership.

The COVID-19 (coronavirus) special measure at **63.4** above applies to the conditions at (a)–(c) above, and does so for the purposes stated there. In this respect, the special measure is that:

- if the place in (a) above is available to P on a day that would fall within the COVID-19 relaxation at **63.8** above if P were present in the UK at the end of it, that day is to be disregarded for the purposes of (b) above; and
- a night spent by P at the place immediately before or after a day that would fall within the COVID-19 relaxation is to be disregarded for the purposes of (c) above.

[*FA 2013, Sch 45 para 34; FA 2020, s 109(9)*].

For further information about what HMRC consider to be an accommodation tie, see HMRC Residence, Domicile and Remittance Basis Manual RDRM13070–13090.

Work ties

[63.16] For the purposes of **63.13**(c) above, P has a '*work tie*' for year X if he works in the UK for at least 40 days (whether continuously or intermittently) in year X. For these purposes, P works in the UK for a day if he does more than three hours' work in the UK on that day. See **63.10** above for what is meant by working.

The COVID-19 (coronavirus) special measure at **63.4** above applies to the above rule, and does so for the purposes stated there. In this respect, the special measure is that a day that would fall within the COVID-19 relaxation at **63.8** above, if P was present in the UK at the end of it, does not count as a day on which P works in the UK.

Relevant job on board vehicle, aircraft or ship

If P has a relevant job on board a vehicle, aircraft or ship (see **63.11** above), he is assumed for the above purposes to do more than three hours' work in the UK on any day on which he starts a cross-border trip (as part of that job) that begins in the UK. He is assumed to do fewer than three hours' work in the UK on any day on which he completes a cross-border trip (as part of that job) that ends in the UK. Any day on which P both starts and completes a cross-border trip is treated as one on which he does more than three hours' work in the UK. In the case of a cross-border trip to or from the UK that is undertaken in stages, the day on which the trip begins or, as the case may be, ends is the day on which the stage of the trip that involves crossing the UK border begins or ends. Any day on which a stage of the trip is undertaken by P solely within the UK is to be counted, if it lasts for more than three hours, as a day on which P does more than three hours' work in the UK.

[*FA 2013, Sch 45 paras 35, 36; FA 2020, s 109(10)*].

90-day ties

[63.17] For the purposes of **63.13**(d) above, P has a '*90-day tie*' for year X if P has spent more than 90 days in the UK in either or both of the two tax years preceding year X.

The COVID-19 (coronavirus) special measure at **63.4** above applies to the above rule, and does so for the purposes stated there. In this respect, the special measure is that a day that would fall within the COVID-19 relaxation at **63.8** above, if P were present in the UK at the end of it, does not count as a day P has spent in the UK in the tax year in question.

[*FA 2013, Sch 45 para 37; FA 2020, s 109(11)*].

Country ties

[63.18] For the purposes of **63.13**(e) above, P has a '*country tie*' for year X if the country in which P meets the 'midnight test' for the greatest number of days in year X is the UK. P meets the '*midnight test*' in a country for a day if he is present in that country at the end of that day. In the event that the greatest number of days is equal for two or more countries, P has a country tie for year X if one of those countries is the UK.

The COVID-19 (coronavirus) special measure at **63.4** above applies to the midnight test, and does so for the purposes stated there. In this respect, the special measure is that P is to be treated as not being present in the UK at the end of a day that would fall within the COVID-19 relaxation at **63.8** above.

[*FA 2013, Sch 45 para 38; FA 2020, s 109(12)*].

Split year treatment

[63.19] The effect of a tax year being a split year is to relax the general rule in **63.4** above that treats individuals who are UK resident (or not resident) *for* a tax year as being UK resident (or not resident) at all times in that tax year. A split year is divided into a UK part and an overseas part as set out in each of **63.21–63.28** below.

The effect of split year treatment on the various income tax charging rules is covered throughout this work where relevant: see in particular **26.4** DISGUISED REMUNERATION, **28.4**, **28.16** EMPLOYMENT INCOME, **44.3**, **44.11**, **44.23** LIFE ASSURANCE POLICIES, **49.2** MISCELLANEOUS INCOME, **52.22** PARTNERSHIPS, **56.2**(b) PENSION INCOME, **59.1** POST-CESSATION RECEIPTS AND EXPENDITURE, **60.2** PROPERTY INCOME, **61.4** REMITTANCE BASIS, **65.1** SAVINGS AND INVESTMENT INCOME, **71.4**, **71.10–71.13**, **71.16** SHARE-RELATED EMPLOYMENT INCOME AND EXEMPTIONS, and **75.1**, **75.16**, **75.19** TRADING INCOME.

See also the transitional provisions on split year treatment in **63.30** below.

Split year treatment does not apply to personal representatives, and applies to only a limited extent to trustees (see **70.5** SETTLEMENTS). The existence of special charging rules for cases involving split years is not intended to affect any question as to whether an individual would fall to be regarded under a double tax treaty as UK resident.

[*FA 2013, Sch 45 paras 39–42, 153(2)*].

Simon's Taxes. See **E6.124A–E6.124D.**

What is a split year?

[63.20] For the purposes of **63.19** above and the statutory residence test generally, a tax year (year X) is a '*split year*' as regards an individual (P) if he is resident in the UK for year X and the circumstances of the case fall within any of Cases 1–8 at **63.21–63.28** below. Cases 1–3 involve departure from the UK, and Cases 4–8 involve arrival in the UK. [*FA 2013, Sch 45 para 43*].

If P's circumstances fall within more than one Case, the overseas part of the split year is determined in accordance with the Case which has priority. Where the circumstances fall within two or all of Cases 1–3, Case 1 has priority over Case 2 and Case 3, and Case 2 has priority over Case 3. Where the circumstances fall within two or more of Cases 4–8, the following rules apply to determine priority.

(a) If Case 6 applies, then if Case 5 also applies and the 'split year date' in relation to Case 5 is earlier than the split year date in relation to Case 6, Case 5 has priority; if it is not earlier, Case 6 has priority.

(b) If Case 7 (but not Case 6) applies, then if Case 5 also applies and the split year date in relation to Case 5 is earlier than the split year date in relation to Case 7, Case 5 has priority; if it is not earlier, Case 7 has priority.
(c) If two or all of Cases 4, 5 and 8 apply (but neither Case 6 nor Case 7), the Case with the earliest split year date has priority.
(d) If, in a case within (c), two or all of the Cases which apply share the same split year date, and no Case which applies has an earlier split year date, the Cases with that split year date have priority.

For these purposes, the '*split year date*' is the final day of the overseas part of the split year as determined under the Case in question (see **63.21–63.28** below).

[*FA 2013, Sch 45 paras 53(1), 54, 55*].

Case 1

[63.21] The circumstances of a case fall within Case 1 if they are of the description below. The overseas part of the split year is the part beginning with the first day of the period mentioned in (2) below. If there is more than one such period, the overseas part of the split year is the part beginning with the first day of the longest of those periods. The UK part of the split year is the part that is not the overseas part.

(1) P was resident in the UK for the tax year preceding year X (whether or not that previous year was itself a split year).
(2) There is a period that:
   - begins with a day in year X on which P does more than three hours' work overseas;
   - ends with the last day of year X; and
   - satisfies the 'overseas work criteria'.

   There may be more than one such period.
(3) P is not resident in the UK for the tax year following year X, and this is because he meets the third automatic overseas test (see **63.6**(3) above) for that following year.

For the purposes of (2) above, a period satisfies the '*overseas work criteria*' if:

- P works 'sufficient hours overseas', as assessed over that period;
- there are no 'significant breaks' from overseas work during that period (see **63.6**(3) above);
- the number of days in that period on which P does more than three hours' work in the UK does not exceed the 'first permitted limit'; and
- the number of days in that period spent by P in the UK does not exceed the 'second permitted limit'. (Any days *treated* as spent in the UK under the 'deeming rule' in **63.8** above do not count for this purpose.)

The question of whether P works '*sufficient hours overseas*' is determined as in **63.10** above except that the starting point in calculating the reference period is the number of days in the period mentioned in (2) above. The maximum number of days by which the reference period may be reduced for multiple gaps between employments is equal to the 'first permitted limit' (instead of 30 as in **63.10**).

The '*first permitted limit*' is 30 minus the 'appropriate number'; the '*second permitted limit*' is 90 minus the 'appropriate number'. The '*appropriate number*' is the product of:

$$A \times \frac{B}{12}$$

A	=	either 30 or 90, depending on whether one is calculating the first or second permitted limit; and
B	=	the number of whole months in the part of year X before the day on which begins the period mentioned in (2) above. A '*whole month*' means an entire calendar month, e.g. the month of January; the period from 6 April to 30 April inclusive also counts as a whole month.

If the appropriate number is not a whole number it is rounded down if the first figure after the decimal point is less than 5; otherwise it is rounded up.

[*FA 2013, Sch 45 paras 29(2), 44, 52–56, 145; FA 2020, s 109(7)*].

Case 2

[63.22] The circumstances of a case fall within Case 2 if they are of the description below. The UK part of the split year is the part of the tax year ending immediately before the 'deemed departure day' in (4) below; the remainder of the tax year is the overseas part of the split year.

(1) P was resident in the UK for the tax year preceding year X (whether or not that previous year was itself a split year).

(2) P has a 'partner' whose circumstances fall within Case 1 at **63.21** above for year X or the previous tax year. '*Partner*' means a spouse or civil partner or a person with whom P is cohabiting as if they were a married couple or civil partners.

(3) On a day in year X, P moves overseas in order to continue living with the partner while the partner is working overseas.

(4) In the part of year X beginning with the 'deemed departure day':
- P either has no home (see **63.9** above) in the UK or has homes in both the UK and overseas but spends the greater part of the time living in the overseas home; and
- the number of days that P spends in the UK does not exceed the 'permitted limit'. (See **63.8** above as regards days spent in the UK.)

(5) P is not resident in the UK for the tax year following year X.

If (2) above applies by reference to year X itself, the '*deemed departure day*' is the later of the day mentioned in (3) above and the first day of what is, for P's partner, the overseas part of the year (see **63.21** above). If (2) above applies by reference to the previous tax year, the '*deemed departure day*' is the day mentioned in (3) above.

The '*permitted limit*' is 90 minus the 'appropriate number'. The '*appropriate number*' is the product of:

$$A \times \frac{B}{12}$$

A = 90; and

B = the number of whole months in the part of year X before the deemed departure day. A '*whole month*' means an entire calendar month, e.g. the month of January; the period from 6 April to 30 April inclusive also counts as a whole month.

If the appropriate number is not a whole number it is rounded down if the first figure after the decimal point is less than 5; otherwise it is rounded up.

[*FA 2013, Sch 45 paras 45, 52–56, 145; SI 2019 No 1458, Sch 3 para 36(3)*].

Case 3

[63.23] The circumstances of a case fall within Case 3 if they are of the description below. The UK part of the split year is the part of the tax year ending immediately before the day mentioned in (2)(a) below; the remainder of the tax year is the overseas part of the split year.

(1) P was resident in the UK for the tax year preceding year X (whether or not that previous year was itself a split year).

(2) At the start of year X, P had one or more homes (see **63.9** above) in the UK but:

- (a) there comes a day in year X when P ceases to have any home in the UK; and
- (b) from then on, P has no home in the UK for the rest of that tax year.

(3) In the part of year X beginning with the day mentioned in (2)(a) above, P spends fewer than 16 days in the UK. (See **63.8** above as regards days spent in the UK.)

(4) P is not resident in the UK for the tax year following year X.

(5) At the end of the period of six months beginning with the day mentioned in (2)(a) above, P has a 'sufficient link' with a country overseas.

For the purposes of (5) above, P has a '*sufficient link*' with a country overseas if (and only if):

- he is considered for tax purposes to be a resident of that country in accordance with its domestic laws; or
- he has been in that country at the end of each day of the six-month period mentioned in (5) above; or
- his only home is in that country or, if he has more than one home, they are all in that country.

[*FA 2013, Sch 45 paras 46, 52–56*].

Case 4

[63.24] The circumstances of a case fall within Case 4 if they are of the description below. The UK part of the split year is the part of the tax year beginning on the day mentioned in (2) below; the earlier part of the tax year is the overseas part of the split year.

(1) P was not resident in the UK for the tax year preceding year X.

(2) At the start of year X, P did not meet the 'only home test', but there comes a day in year X when he starts to meet that test and he then continues to meet it for the remainder of the tax year; or
the '*only home test*' is met if P has only one home (see **63.9** above) and it is in the UK or if P has more than one home and all of them are in the UK.

(3) For the part of year X before the day mentioned in (2) above, P does not have sufficient UK ties.

The sufficient ties test at **63.12** above applies for the purposes of (3) above, but with the following modifications:

- references to 'year X' are to be read as references to the part of year X in question (except that when applying the family ties test in **63.14** above, the residence of the 'other person' is still determined by reference to year X); and
- both tables have effect as if each number of days quoted in the first column were reduced by the 'appropriate number'.

For this purpose, the '*appropriate number*' is found by multiplying the number of days quoted, in each case, by $^{A}/_{12}$, where A = the number of 'whole months' in year X beginning with the day mentioned in (2) above. A '*whole month*' means an entire calendar month, e.g. the month of January. If the appropriate number is not a whole number it is rounded down if the first figure after the decimal point is less than 5; otherwise it is rounded up.

[*FA 2013, Sch 45 paras 47, 52–56, 145*].

Case 5

[63.25] The circumstances of a case fall within Case 5 if they are of the description below. The overseas part of the split year is the part before the period mentioned in (2) below begins. If there is more than one such period, the overseas part of the split year is the part before the first of those periods begins. The UK part of the split year is the part that is not the overseas part.

(1) P was not resident in the UK for the tax year preceding year X.

(2) There is at least one period of 365 days beginning in year X in respect of which all the following conditions are met:
   (a) the period begins with a day on which P does more than three hours' work in the UK;
   (b) in the part of year X before the period begins, P does not have sufficient UK ties;
   (c) P works 'sufficient hours in the UK' (see **63.10** above), as assessed over the period;

(d) there are no 'significant breaks' from UK work (see **63.5**(3) above) during that period; and
(e) of the total number of days in the period when P does more than three hours' work, at least 75% of them are days when he does more than three hours' work in the UK.

The sufficient ties test at **63.12** above applies for the purposes of (2)(b) above, but with the same modifications as in **63.24** above; the appropriate number is computed in the same way as in **63.24** but by reference to the number of whole months in year X beginning with the day on which the 365-day period in (2) begins.

[*FA 2013, Sch 45 paras 48, 52–56, 145*].

Case 6

[63.26] The circumstances of a case fall within Case 6 if they are of the description below. The overseas part of the split year is the part ending with the last day of the period in (2) below. If there is more than one such period, the overseas part of the split year is the part ending with the last day of the longest of those periods. The UK part of the split year is the part that is not the overseas part.

(1) P was not resident in the UK for the tax year before year X due to his meeting the third automatic overseas test (see **63.6**(3) above) for that tax year (year W), but was resident in the UK for one or more of the four tax years immediately preceding year W.
(2) There is a period that:
- begins with the first day of year X and ends in that year;
- ends with a day on which P does more than three hours' work overseas; and
- satisfies the 'overseas work criteria'.

There may be more than one such period.
(3) P is resident in the UK for the tax year following year X (whether or not that following year is itself a split year).

Where year W is 2012/13 and the election in **63.30** below is not made in respect of that year, (1) above should read as follows: P was not resident in the UK for the tax year before year X in circumstances where he was working full-time overseas for the whole of that tax year (year W), but was resident in the UK for one or more of the four tax years immediately preceding year W.

In (2) above, '*overseas work criteria*' has the same meaning as in Case 1 at **63.21** above, except that, in computing the 'appropriate number', B = the number of whole months in the part of year X after the period in (2) ends.

[*FA 2013, Sch 45 paras 49, 52–56, 145, 154(5)*].

Case 7

[63.27] The circumstances of a case fall within Case 7 if they are of the description below. The UK part of the split year is the part of the tax year beginning with the 'deemed arrival day' in (4) below; the earlier part of the tax year is the overseas part of the split year.

(1) P was not resident in the UK for the tax year preceding year X.
(2) P has a 'partner' whose circumstances fall within Case 6 at **63.26** above for year X or the previous tax year. '*Partner*' means a spouse or civil partner or a person with whom P is cohabiting as if they were a married couple or civil partners.
(3) On a day in year X, P moves to the UK in order to continue living with the partner on the partner's return or relocation to the UK.
(4) In the part of year X before the 'deemed arrival day':
   - P either has no home (see **63.9** above) in the UK or has homes in both the UK and overseas but spends the greater part of the time living in the overseas home; and
   - the number of days that P spends in the UK does not exceed the 'permitted limit'. (See **63.8** above as regards days spent in the UK.)
(5) P is resident in the UK for the tax year following year X (whether or not that following year is itself a split year).

If (2) above applies by reference to year X itself, the '*deemed arrival day*' is the later of the day mentioned in (3) above and the first day of what is, for P's partner, the UK part of the year (see **63.26** above). If (2) above applies by reference to the previous tax year, the '*deemed arrival day*' is the day mentioned in (3) above.

In (4) above, '*permitted limit*' is the same as in Case 2 at **63.22** above, except that, in computing the 'appropriate number', B = the number of whole months in the part of year X beginning with the deemed arrival day.

[*FA 2013, Sch 45 paras 50, 52–56, 145, 156; SI 2019 No 1458, Sch 3 para 36(3)*].

Case 8

[63.28] The circumstances of a case fall within Case 8 if they are of the description below. The UK part of the split year is the part of the tax year beginning on the day mentioned in (2)(a) below; the earlier part of the tax year is the overseas part of the split year.

(1) P was not resident in the UK for the tax year preceding year X.
(2) At the start of year X, P had no home (see **63.9** above) in the UK, but:
   (a) there comes a day when, for the first time in that year, P does have a home in the UK; and
   (b) from then on, he continues to have a home in the UK for the remainder of year X and for the whole of the following tax year.
(3) For the part of year X before the day mentioned in (2)(a) above, P does not have sufficient UK ties.
(4) P is resident in the UK for the tax year following year X, and that following year is not a split year as regards P.

The sufficient ties test at **63.12** above applies for the purposes of (3) above, but with the same modifications as in **63.24** above; the appropriate number is computed in the same way as in **63.24** but by reference to the number of whole months in the part of year X beginning with the day mentioned in (2)(a) above.

[*FA 2013, Sch 45 paras 51–56, 145*].

Temporary non-UK residence

[63.29] For the purposes of certain income tax charges, certain periods are regarded as being periods for which an individual is temporarily non-resident in the UK. The effect in broad terms is that certain income accruing, arising or remitted in a period of temporary non-UK residence is chargeable in the tax year in which the individual returns to the UK. The rules have effect where the 'year of departure' (see below) is 2013/14 or any subsequent year. [*FA 2013, Sch 45 para 153(3)*].

The precise effect of temporary non-UK residence on income tax charging rules is covered throughout this work where appropriate: see **26.4**, **26.5** DISGUISED REMUNERATION, **44.4** LIFE ASSURANCE POLICIES, **49.7** MISCELLANEOUS INCOME, **50.5** NON-RESIDENTS, **56.3**, **56.7** PENSION INCOME, **57.36** PENSION PROVISION, **61.5** REMITTANCE BASIS and **65.16**, **65.22**, **65.22**, **65.22** SAVINGS AND INVESTMENT INCOME.

See also the transitional provisions on temporary non-UK residence in **63.30** below.

What is meant by 'temporarily non-resident'?

An individual is regarded as '*temporarily non-resident*' in the UK if:

(a) he has 'sole UK residence' for a 'residence period' (period A);
(b) immediately following period A, one or more residence periods occur for which the individual does not have sole UK residence;
(c) at least four of the seven tax years immediately preceding the 'year of departure' were either:
- a tax year for which the individual had sole UK residence; or
- a split year that included a residence period for which the individual had sole UK residence; and

(d) the '*temporary period of non-UK residence*', i.e. the period between the end of period A and the start of the next residence period for which the individual has sole UK residence, is five years or less.

Meaning of 'residence period'

A '*residence period*' is normally a tax year. However, when a tax year is a split year (see **63.19** above), the UK part and overseas parts of the split year are separate residence periods.

Meaning of 'sole UK residence'

An individual has '*sole UK residence*' for a residence period consisting of an entire tax year if he is resident in the UK for that year and is not 'treaty non-resident' at any time in that year. An individual has '*sole UK residence*' for a residence period consisting of the UK part of a split year if he is not 'treaty non-resident' at any time in that part of the year.

An individual is '*treaty non-resident*' at any time if at the time he falls to be regarded under a double tax treaty as resident in a country outside the UK.

Year of departure and period of return

In (c) above, and in the various income tax charging provisions covering temporary non-UK residence, the '*year of departure*' is the tax year that consists of or includes period A. In those charging provisions, the '*period of return*' is the first residence period after period A for which the individual again has sole UK residence.

[*FA 2013, Sch 45 paras 109–115*].

Simon's Taxes. See **E6.137A–E6.137D.**

Transitional provisions

[63.30] There will be occasions where, in applying the statutory residence test for any of the years 2013/14 to 2017/18, it will be necessary to determine whether an individual was UK resident or non-UK resident for a tax year before 2013/14 (a '*pre-commencement year*'); for example, in ascertaining which of the sufficient ties tables at **63.12** above should be applied. Where this is the case, the question of residence for any pre-commencement year is to be determined in accordance with the rules in force before the statutory residence test was introduced, for which see **63.32** below. However, the individual can elect for the question to be determined in accordance with the statutory residence test instead. The election can be made in respect of any one or more pre-commencement years. (The making of an election does not alter an individual's actual residence status for the pre-commencement year or affect his tax liability for that year.) The election must be made by notice in writing to HMRC no later than the first anniversary of the end of year X (where year X is the year 2013/14, 2014/15, 2015/16, 2016/17 or 2017/18, whichever one is in point); the election is irrevocable. [*FA 2013, Sch 45 para 154(1)–(4)*].

Split year treatment

Where the year for which income tax liability is being calculated is 2013/14 or a subsequent year and it is necessary to determine whether a pre-commencement year was a split year (see **63.19** above), the determination is made in accordance with the non-statutory split year treatment at **63.33** below. [*FA 2013, Sch 45 para 155*].

Temporary non-UK residence

In determining whether an individual is temporarily non-resident in the UK for a pre-commencement year, the test at **63.29**(c) above is that at least four of the seven tax years immediately preceding the year of departure were tax years meeting the following conditions:

- the individual was resident in the UK for the year; and
- there was no time in the year when the individual was treaty non-resident (see **63.29** above).

Whether an individual was resident in the UK for a pre-commencement tax year is to be determined in accordance with the rules in force before the statutory residence test was introduced, for which see **63.32** below.

[*FA 2013, Sch 45 para 157*].

Simon's Taxes. See E6.102L.

Residence of personal representatives

[63.31] Where at least one of the personal representatives of a deceased person is non-UK resident and at least one is UK resident, then provided that the deceased was resident or domiciled in the UK at the time of his death, the non-UK resident personal representative(s) is (are) treated as UK resident for income tax purposes. Otherwise, the UK resident personal representative(s) is (are) treated as not resident in the UK. The deemed domicile rule at **63.36** below applies for the above purpose for 2017/18 onwards.

[*ITA 2007, s 834; F(No 2)A 2017, Sch 8 para 17*].

As regards the residence of **trustees**, see **70.5** SETTLEMENTS.

Residence before 6 April 2013

[63.32] Prior to the introduction of the statutory residence test at **63.4** above for 2013/14 onwards, there was relatively little statutory guidance on the determination of the 'residence' of an individual, despite its importance in determining the individual's tax liabilities (see **63.1–63.3** above). For practical purposes, HMRC's interpretation as set out in Leaflet HMRC6 and other sources referred to below was, subject to appeal, likely to determine the issue in any particular case. It was held by the courts that residence is a question of fact for the Appeal Tribunal to decide on the particular circumstances of each case, and there are a number of important decisions indicative of the courts' views (see below). See also **63.39** below regarding appeals. A person could be resident for a particular tax year in more than one country for tax purposes (or may even be resident in none).

These rules continue to be of some relevance on and after 6 April 2013 because of the application of the transitional rules at **63.30** above in applying the statutory residence test for the years 2013/14 to 2017/18.

There are three circumstances in which the residence status of an individual is subject to statutory provisions.

(a) An individual in the UK for some temporary purpose only, and not with the intention of establishing his residence here, is UK resident for any tax year in which he spends 183 days or more (in aggregate) in the UK, and is not resident for any tax year in which spends less than 183 days in the UK. In determining whether the individual is in the UK for some temporary purpose only and not with the intention of establishing his residence here one of the considerations is that an individual is regarded as resident if visits to the UK average 91 days or more per tax year, calculated over a maximum of four years (see Leaflet HMRC6, para 7.6 for method of averaging). Any days which are spent in the UK due to exceptional circumstances beyond the individual's control, for example illness, can be excluded from the calculation (HMRC SP 2/91). The question is determined without regard to any available accommodation in the UK.

Strictly, periods of time in terms of hours are relevant in determining a period of presence in the UK (see *Wilkie v CIR* Ch D 1951, 32 TC 495). However, an individual is treated as spending a day in the UK if (and only if) he is in the UK at the end of that day. If, however, an individual arrives in the UK on one day and departs on the next, he is not treated as spending a day in the UK (despite his presence at the end of the day of arrival) if between arrival and departure he does not engage in activities that are to a substantial extent unrelated to his passage through the UK, i.e. he is merely a passenger in transit. Note that this precludes not only his engaging in activities relating to business or employment but also in many activities of a non-business nature such as spending time with family; the Treasury Explanatory Notes to the 2008 Finance Bill gave a number of examples of how this passenger-in-transit test would be applied.

[*ITA 2007, ss 831, 832; SI 2006 No 1963, Reg 4*].

(b) An individual who is both resident and ordinarily resident (see **63.34** below) in the UK, and who leaves the UK for the purpose only of occasional residence abroad, continues to be UK resident. [*ITA 2007, s 829*]. 'Occasional residence' is not defined, but generally refers to short stays on holiday or business trips (and see *Reed v Clark* Ch D 1985, 58 TC 528).

(c) The residence of an individual working full time in a trade, profession or vocation no part of which is carried on in the UK, or in an office or employment all of the duties of which are performed outside the UK (other than any whose performance is merely incidental to the duties abroad), is determined without regard to any place of abode maintained for his use in the UK. [*ITA 2007, s 830*]. As to whether duties are incidental, see *Robson v Dixon* Ch D 1972, 48 TC 527 (airline pilot employed abroad but occasionally landing in UK where family home maintained, held UK duties more than incidental). See also Leaflet HMRC6, para 10.6. 'Full-time' employment, in an ordinary case involving a standard pattern of hours, requires an individual working hours clearly comparable with those in a typical UK working week. See Leaflet HMRC6, sidenote to para 8.5 for this and for HMRC's interpretation of the requirement in less straightforward cases.

Case law

Resident in Eire making monthly visits to UK as director of British company (having no UK residence, but a permanent one in Eire) held to be resident and ordinarily resident in UK (*Lysaght v CIR* HL 1928, 13 TC 511) (but cf. *CIR v Combe* CS 1932, 17 TC 405). Officer succeeding to Eire estate, intending to return there permanently but prevented by military duties in UK, held on facts to be resident in both countries (*Lord Inchiquin v CIR* CA 1948, 31 TC 125). In *CIR v Brown* KB 1926, 11 TC 292 and *CIR v Zorab* KB 1926, 11 TC 289, however, held that retired Indian civil servants making periodical visits to the UK, but having no business interests here, were not UK resident.

An American holding a lease of a shooting box in Scotland and spending two months there every year (*Cooper v Cadwalader* CES 1904, 5 TC 101), and a merchant usually resident and doing business in Italy but owning house in UK where he resided less than six months (*Lloyd v Sulley* CES 1884, 2 TC 37) were both held to be UK resident.

A Belgian who had at his disposal, for the visits he paid here, a house owned not by him but by a company which he controlled, so that it was in fact available whenever he chose to come, was held to be UK resident (*Loewenstein v De Salis* KB 1926, 10 TC 424). In *Withers v Wynyard* KB 1938, 21 TC 724, however, an actress (after 18 months abroad) performing in UK, and for $3^1/_2$ months in 1933/34 occupying a leasehold flat (unable to be disposed of and sublet when possible), was held to be non-resident for that year.

Where neither the individual nor spouse physically present in UK during tax year, although children here, the individual was non-resident (*Turnbull v Foster* CES 1904, 6 TC 206). See also *Reed v Clark* Ch D 1985, 58 TC 528, where individual held non-resident for tax year of absence from UK during which continuing trade carried on. If, however, either an individual or spouse, while they are still living together, has established a UK family home, any visit during a tax year, however short, to that home, may render the individual UK resident for that tax year (although cf. *Withers v Wynyard* above).

HMRC practice

Leaflet HMRC6 (to which paragraph numbers in the following text refer) considers the application of the above tests first generally, then in relation to those leaving the UK, then in relation to those coming to the UK.

General

The only occasion when the number of days that an individual is physically present in the UK will determine his UK residence status is when he is physically present in the UK for 183 days or more during a tax year (para 2.2).

Full personal allowances are available for the year UK residence begins or ends (subject, for 2008/09 onwards, to any claim for the REMITTANCE BASIS (**61**)) (para 6.7).

For detailed HMRC procedures in relation to matters concerned with residence, see HMRC Residence Guide Manual.

Leaving the UK

Short trips abroad, e.g. on holiday or business trips, do not alter the residence status of a person who usually lives in the UK (see (b) above) (para 8.2).

An individual (and accompanying spouse) leaving to work abroad 'full-time' (see (c) above) under a contract of employment is treated as non-UK resident provided that both the absence from the UK and the employment cover a complete tax year, and that any interim visits to the UK do not amount to either 183 days or more in any tax year or an average of 91 days or more per tax year (averaged over a maximum of four years (see para 8.5 for method of averaging), and ignoring days spent in the UK for exceptional circumstances beyond the person's control (for example own or family illness and see (a) above). Similar conditions apply to an individual leaving to work abroad full-time in a trade, profession or vocation. These conditions are applied separately in relation to the employee and the accompanying spouse, but must be satisfied by the employee for the concession to be available to the accompanying spouse. See also **63.34** below as regards ordinary residence of the accompanying spouse (paras 8.5–8.9). See *R (oao Davies and another) v HMRC; R (oao Gaines-Cooper) v HMRC* below for discussion of the operation of this rule.

In order to successfully cease UK residence (and ordinarily residence — see **63.34** below), it is necessary to make a distinct break from the UK, and any remaining ties with the UK should be consistent with not being resident there. HMRC may require evidence to show that an individual has left the UK permanently or indefinitely and that there has been a clear change in the pattern of his life. For example, they might expect the individual to show that he has acquired accommodation abroad to live in as a permanent home. If he still has property in the UK which remains available for his use, he may be required to explain how retaining that property is consistent with leaving the UK. If the individual can show that he has left the UK permanently or indefinitely, UK residence (and ordinary residence) will be treated as ceasing on the day after departure from the UK. If, however, the circumstances of the individual's life change only gradually, he will become non-UK resident only when he has sufficiently reduced his ties to the UK and is more than occasionally resident abroad (paras 8.1, 8.2.1). In *R (oao Davies and another) v HMRC; R (oao Gaines-Cooper) v HMRC* SC 2011, 81 TC 134, the taxpayers failed to establish non-UK residence under this rule as they had not established 'a distinct break' from their social and family ties in the UK. The Supreme Court in these cases rejected the appellants' contention that, on its proper construction, the guidance in Leaflet IR20 contained a more benevolent interpretation of the circumstances in which an individual became non-UK resident (and not ordinarily resident) than was reflected in ordinary law; IR20, taken as a whole, would have informed the ordinarily sophisticated taxpayer that he had to make a distinct break. The judgment did offer some benevolence to taxpayers in general by ruling that a distinct break encompasses a substantial loosening of social and family ties but not necessarily the severance of such ties. The 'distinct break' principle was also applied in HMRC's favour in *Glyn v HMRC (No 2)* FTT (TC 6452), [2018] UKFTT 219 (TC).

See *Barrett v HMRC* (Sp C 639), [2008] SSCD 268 in which the Sp C gave a list of reasons as to why the appellant had not, as he claimed, ceased to be UK resident.

Coming to the UK

UK residence (and ordinary residence, see **63.34** below) will commence on the date of arrival in the UK where an individual whose home has been abroad comes to the UK to live here permanently or intending to stay for three years or more (disregarding holidays or short business trips abroad) (para 7.2). Otherwise, short-term visitors will be treated as resident for a tax year in which they are in the UK for 183 days or more in the year (see (a) above), or from the fifth tax year where in the preceding four tax years regular visits have been made to the UK averaging 91 days or more per tax year (subject to exceptional circumstances, as above). If such visits are clearly intended on arrival in the UK, residence will commence with the first of those four years, and if the decision to make such visits is taken before the start of the fifth year, residence will commence with the year in which the decision was taken (para 7.5). Longer-term visitors are treated as resident throughout any period for which they come to the UK for a purpose (such as employment) that will mean remaining (apart from holidays or short business trips) for at least two years. This will also apply if accommodation is owned or is acquired or taken on a lease of three years or more in the year of arrival. Otherwise, such visitors will be treated as ordinarily resident from the beginning of the tax year in which such accommodation is acquired or leased (paras 7.7.1–7.7.4).

As regards visits for education, see **63.34** below.

91-day tests

Before 6 April 2008, in counting the days spent in the UK for the purposes of the 91-day tests referred to above (and in **63.34** below), HMRC normally disregarded days of arrival in and departure from the UK. It was suggested by some commentators that the Sp C decision in *Gaines-Cooper v HMRC* (Sp C 568), [2007] SSCD 23 superseded HMRC practice and changed the basis on which the 91-day test was applied. HMRC stated that this was incorrect and that the practice continued as before (HMRC Brief 01/07, 4 January 2007). However, for 2008/09 onwards, the same criteria is applied for the 91-day tests as for the 183-day test in (a) above, i.e. an individual is treated as spending a day in the UK if he is in the UK at the end of that day, but with the same exclusion as in (a) above for passengers in transit (Treasury Explanatory Notes to the 2008 Finance Bill).

Mobile workers

For how HMRC consider the residence and ordinary residence rules apply to individuals who usually live in the UK but make frequent and regular trips abroad in the course of their employment or business (e.g. lorry or coach drivers driving to and from the Continent and those working on cross-Channel transport), see the article in Revenue Tax Bulletin April 2001 pp 836–838. For this purpose individuals 'usually live' in the UK if their home and settled domestic life continue to be there, and trips abroad are 'frequent and regular' where they are made every two or three weeks or more often. Only in exceptional cases are HMRC likely to accept that such workers are other than resident and ordinarily resident in the UK.

Simon's Taxes. See **C4.104, E6.101–E6.114, E6.120–E6.124.**

Split year treatment by concession

[63.33] Strictly, residence status applies only by reference to whole tax years. By concession, however, an individual coming to the UK to take up permanent residence or to stay for at least two years, or leaving the UK to live abroad permanently (or for at least three years), is treated as UK resident only from the date of arrival or up to and including the date of departure, tax liabilities which are affected by residence status being calculated on the basis of the period of residence. In either case, HMRC must be satisfied that the person was not ordinarily resident in the UK (see **63.34** below) prior to arrival or on departure. Similarly, subject to the further conditions as described in **63.32** above in relation to leaving the UK, an individual (and accompanying spouse) going abroad under a contract of employment will be so treated only up to and including the date of departure and from the date of return to the UK. The provisions limiting the income chargeable on non-residents (see **50.3** NON-RESIDENTS) do not apply to the non-resident part of a split year. (Leaflet HMRC6, para 2.4; HMRC ESCs A11 and A78).

There was uncertainty in the past over whether HMRC regard ESC A11 as applying to income within *ITEPA 2003, Pt 7* (security-related employment income — see **71** SHARE-RELATED EMPLOYMENT INCOME AND EXEMPTIONS). In an online statement on 17 July 2008 (webarchive.nationalarchives.gov.uk/20140109143644/http://www.hmrc.gov.uk/esc/esc-a11.htm), HMRC announced that, whilst they had previously been of the view that the ESC does not apply to such income in the year of arrival in the UK, they would treat it as applying for open years and until further notice. With regard to the year of departure from the UK, ESC A11 has always been regarded as not applicable where the charge to tax is within **71.12** SHARE-RELATED EMPLOYMENT INCOME AND EXEMPTIONS (shares acquired for less than market value). As regards other chargeable income under *ITEPA 2003, Pt 7*, HMRC treat the concession as applying in the year of departure. As regards both the year of arrival and the year of departure, HMRC reserve the right to depart from their stated position in cases of tax avoidance. (In certain cases, a charge to tax can arise where securities are acquired by exercise of an option granted overseas and this remains the case, as explained in the HMRC statement.)

Earnings from overseas employment

If an individual leaves the UK and becomes non-UK resident from the day following departure, he is not charged UK tax on earnings from an employment carried on wholly abroad which arise after his departure. Similarly, if an individual comes to the UK and becomes UK-resident from the date of arrival, he is not charged UK tax on earnings from an employment carried on wholly abroad which arise before his arrival. If an individual is paid for a period of leave spent in the UK following work overseas, HMRC treat this as arising during the leave period to which it relates, even if the individual's entitlement to it was built up over a period of employment carried on wholly abroad. (Leaflet HMRC6, para **10.7**).

Overseas investment income

Applying ESC A11 above, liability for the year of departure is on untaxed overseas investment income arising (or, where applicable, remitted) up to the date of departure (Leaflet HMRC6, paras **10.14.2–10.14.4**), with comparable rules for the year of arrival (Leaflet HMRC6, para **10.14.1**).

Trading income etc.

For the effect of a change of residence on a trade, profession or vocation carried on by an individual wholly or partly outside the UK, see **75.19** TRADING INCOME.

Ordinary residence before 6 April 2013

[63.34] The concept of ordinary residence was abolished for income tax purposes with effect on and after 6 April 2013. It will still be of relevance where, for example, the tax system contains rules concerning *temporary non-UK residence* in cases where the year of departure from the UK was before 2013/14 (see, for instance, **61.5** REMITTANCE BASIS).

The term 'ordinary residence' is not defined in the *Taxes Acts*. See below for the case law on its interpretation. Broadly, it denotes greater permanence than the term 'residence' (see **63.32** above), and is equivalent to habitual residence; if an individual is resident year after year, he is ordinarily resident. An individual may be resident in the UK under the 183-day rule (see **63.32**(a) above) without becoming ordinarily resident. Equally, he may be ordinarily resident without being resident in a particular year, e.g. because he usually lives in the UK but is absent throughout a tax year. (Leaflet HMRC6, para 3.2).

An individual will be treated as ordinarily resident in the UK if he visits the UK regularly and his visits average 91 days or more per tax year, ignoring days spent in the UK for exceptional circumstances beyond his control (for example his own or family illness and see note at **63.32**(a) above). Ordinary residence will commence from 6 April in the tax year of first arrival if the intention to make such visits to the UK for at least four tax years is clear on that first visit, or from 6 April in the fifth tax year after four years of such visits (unless the decision to make regular visits was made in an earlier tax year, in which case it applies from 6 April in that earlier year). (Leaflet HMRC6 paras 3.2, 7.5).

Longer-term visitors — commencement of ordinary residence

If it is clear on arrival in the UK that the intention is to stay for at least three years (disregarding holidays and short business trips abroad), ordinary residence commences on arrival. An individual coming to the UK, but not intending to stay more than three years (and not buying or leasing for three years or more accommodation for use in the UK), is treated as ordinarily resident from the beginning of the tax year in which falls the third anniversary of arrival. (This is according to Leaflet HMRC6, but SP 17/91 says 'from the beginning of the tax year after the third anniversary of arrival'.) If, before the beginning of that tax year, either there is a change in the individuals' intention (i.e. to an intention to stay in the UK for three years or more in all) or accommodation for use in the UK is bought (or leased for three years or more), ordinary residence is treated as commencing at the beginning of the tax year in which either of those events happens. If an individual is treated as ordinarily resident solely because he has accommodation in the UK and he disposes of the accommodation and leaves the UK within three years of arrival, he will be treated as not ordinarily resident for the duration of his stay. (HMRC SP 17/91 and Leaflet HMRC6, paras 7.7–7.7.4).

Education

A student who comes to the UK for a period of study or education and will be in the UK for less than four years will be treated as not ordinarily resident providing (i) he does not own or buy (or lease for three years or more) accommodation in the UK, and (ii) he will not, following his departure from the UK, be returning regularly for visits averaging 91 days or more per tax year. (Leaflet HMRC6, para 7.3).

91-day tests

See **63.32** above.

Mobile workers

See **63.32** above.

Relevant case law

In *Reid v CIR* SC 1926, 10 TC 673, British subject was held '*ordinarily resident*' in the UK although no fixed residence either in the UK or abroad and regularly absent abroad 8½ months every year. But she had here an address, family ties, banking account and furniture stored.

Levene v CIR HL 1928, 13 TC 486 was decided similarly. (British subject abroad for health reasons since 1918, no fixed residence in the UK since (or abroad till 1925), but having ties with the UK and in the 'usual ordering of his life', making habitual visits to the UK 20 weeks yearly for definite purposes.) The judgments in this case interpreted the meaning of 'ordinarily resident' by the following phrases: 'habitually resident', 'residence in a place with some degree of continuity', and 'according to the way a man's life is usually ordered'. In *Peel v CIR* CS 1927, 13 TC 443, although appellant had his business and house in Egypt, he was held ordinarily resident in the UK because he also had a house there, and spent an average of 139 days of each year in the UK.

In *Kinloch v CIR* KB 1929, 14 TC 736, a widow living mostly abroad with a son at school in the UK, who had won an appeal in previous years but continued regular annual visits, was held to be resident and ordinarily resident.

In *Elmhirst v CIR* KB 1937, 21 TC 381 appellant held on facts to have been ordinarily resident although denying any intention at the time to become so. And see *Miesegaes v CIR* CA 1957, 37 TC 493 (minor at school in the UK for five years, spending the occasional vacation with his father in Switzerland, held ordinarily resident). See also cases under **63.32** above.

In *R v Barnet London Borough Council (ex p Nilish Shah)* HL 1982, [1983] 1 AER 226 (a non-tax case), the words 'ordinarily resident' were held to mean 'that the person must be habitually and normally resident here, apart from temporary or occasional absence of long or short duration'. However, ordinary residence does not require an intention to live in a place permanently or indefinitely (followed in *Tuczka v HMRC* UT, [2011] STC 1438).

In *Shepherd v HMRC*, Ch D 2006, 78 TC 389, an airline pilot born and domiciled in the UK, and previously habitually resident in the UK, had during 1999/2000 spent 80 days in the UK, 77 days in Cyprus, 180 days flying in the course of his employment, and 28 days holidaying elsewhere. Whilst in the UK, he had stayed in the house which he shared with his wife. The Sp C held that the appellant's absences from the UK were temporary absences. The appellant was held to be resident and ordinarily resident in the UK for 1999/2000.

In *HMRC v Grace* CA, [2009] STC 2707; *Grace v HMRC* FTT (TC 913), [2011] SFTD 669, a South Africa-born airline pilot (G) moved to the UK in 1986 and began to work for a British airline, purchasing a house near Gatwick Airport. In 1997 he bought a house in Cape Town. He continued to work for a British airline and to own the house near Gatwick, where he stayed for about two or three days before and after long-haul flights to and from the UK. The Inland Revenue issued a determination that he had continued to be resident and ordinarily resident in the UK from 1997/98 to 2002/03 inclusive. On appeal, the Sp C found that G was neither resident nor ordinarily resident in the UK during that period and visited the UK 'for temporary and occasional purposes only'. The decision was reversed on appeal. The recurring presence of G in the UK in order to fulfil duties under a permanent (or at least indefinite) contract of employment could not be described as casual or transitory and thus was not for a temporary purpose. It is difficult to show that UK residence has been relinquished unless a distinct break in a taxpayer's pattern of life can be shown to have occurred; G was held not to have demonstrated a sufficient break. On the facts the only possible conclusion was that G was resident in the UK.

In *Mackay v HMRC* UT, [2019] STC 83, [2018] UKUT 378 (TCC), the Tribunal observed that in determining what is ordinary, settled or regular, at any time in a tax year, the pattern of life or long-term intentions were not relevant, but what mattered were habits and purpose at that particular time. On this basis, it found that the individual, an Australian, had been ordinarily resident in the UK in the disputed years; in those years the ordinary course of his life was that he was resident in the UK, his base both for work and domestically. The fact that he may have intended to leave did not alter the analysis. The Tribunal added that the individual had been in the UK for a settled purpose, fulfilling the duties of his employment. This involved a sufficient degree of continuity, and the period for which he intended to stay in the UK (and actually stayed there), about three years, was long enough.

See also *R (oao Davies and another) v HMRC; R (oao Gaines-Cooper) v HMRC* at **63.32** above.

When assessing what a person's intention was at a particular point in time, one should not seek to evidence that intention by reference to subsequent events as they actually occurred and thus with the benefit of hindsight (*Carey v HMRC* FTT (TC 4634), [2015] UKFTT 466 (TC)).

Simon's Taxes. See **E6.103, E6.114, E6.122.**

Domicile

[63.35] It may be necessary to determine domicile in relation, *inter alia*, to the application of the REMITTANCE BASIS (**61**) to foreign income and chargeable gains. See also **30.36** EXEMPT INCOME for an exemption for 2008/09 onwards for low-income non-UK domiciled employees working in the UK.

A person may have only one place of domicile at any given time denoting the country or state considered his permanent home. He acquires a **domicile of origin** at birth (normally that of his father). It may be changed to a **domicile of choice** (to be proved by subsequent conduct). If a domicile of choice is established but later abandoned (by actual action, not by intention or declaration only — see *Faye v CIR* below) reversion to domicile of origin is automatic.

With effect on and after 6 April 2017, individuals resident but not domiciled in the UK in any tax year are **deemed** to be domiciled in the UK for tax purposes if certain conditions are met. See **63.36** below.

Domicile is a highly technical matter and does not necessarily correspond with either residence or nationality (see *Earl of Iveagh v Revenue Commissioners Supreme Court* (IFS) [1930] IR 431, *Fielden v CIR* Ch D 1965, 42 TC 501, and *CIR v Cohen* KB 1937, 21 TC 301). This last case shows how difficult it is to displace a domicile of origin by a domicile of choice, but contrast *In re Lawton* Ch D 1958, 37 ATC 216. A new domicile of choice may be acquired whilst continuing to be resident in the domicile of origin, but only if the residence in the domicile of choice is the 'chief residence' (*Plummer v CIR* Ch D 1987, 60 TC 452). See also *In re Wallach* HC 1949, 28 ATC 486, *Faye v CIR* Ch D 1961, 40 TC 103, *Buswell v CIR* CA 1974, 49 TC 334, *Steiner v CIR* CA 1973, 49 TC 13, *CIR v Bullock* CA 1976, 51 TC 522, *In re Furse decd., Furse v CIR* Ch D, [1980] STC 597, *Re Clore decd. (No 2)* Ch D, [1984] STC 609, *Anderson v CIR* (Sp C 147), [1998] SSCD 43, *Mrs F and S2 (personal representatives of F (dec'd)) v CIR* (Sp C 219), [2000] SSCD 1, *Civil Engineer v CIR* (Sp C 299), [2002] SSCD 72, *Moore's Executors v CIR* (Sp C 335), [2002] SSCD 463, *Surveyor v CIR* (Sp C 339), [2002] SSCD 501 and *Gaines-Cooper v HMRC* Ch D 2007, 81 TC 61.

In determining domicile for income tax purposes, no action taken at any time in relation to registration as an 'overseas elector', or in voting as such, is taken into account in determining domicile, unless the person whose liability is being determined (whether or not the person whose domicile is in question) wishes it to be taken into account (in which case the domicile determination applies only for the purpose of ascertaining the liability in question). An '*overseas elector*' is broadly a non-UK resident British citizen to whom the parliamentary franchise is extended under *Representation of the People Act 1985, s 1* or *s 3*. [*ITA 2007, s 835B*].

See Leaflet HMRC6, chapter 4 and, for more technical guidance, HMRC Residence, Domicile and Remittance Basis Manual RDRM20000.

Married women

Up to 31 December 1973, a woman automatically acquired the domicile of her husband on marriage. From 1 January 1974 onwards, the domicile of a married woman is to be ascertained 'by reference to the same factors as in the case of any other individual capable of having an independent domicile' except that a woman already married on that date will retain her husband's domicile until it is changed by acquisition or revival of another domicile. [*Domicile and Matrimonial Proceedings Act 1973, ss 1, 17(5)*]. But an American woman who married a husband with UK domicile before 1974 will be treated, for determining her domicile, as if the marriage had taken place in 1974. See Article 4(4) of the US/UK Double Tax Agreement. A **widow** retains her late husband's domicile unless she later acquires a domicile of choice (and see *CIR v Duchess of Portland* Ch D 1981, 54 TC 648).

Minors

The domicile of a minor normally follows that of the person on whom he is legally dependent. Under *Domicile and Matrimonial Proceedings Act 1973, s 3* (which does not extend to Scotland), a person first becomes capable of having an independent domicile when he attains 16 or marries under that age. Under *s 4* of that Act, where a child's father and mother are alive but living apart, his domicile is that of his mother if he has his home with her and has no home with his father.

Simon's Taxes. See **E6.301–E6.323.**

Deemed domicile

[63.36] With effect on and after **6 April 2017**, an individual not domiciled in the UK at a particular time in any tax year (the 'tax year in question') is deemed to be domiciled in the UK for income tax purposes at that time if either of the two conditions below is met. For the application of this deemed domicile rule to income tax see below. The rule applies also for CGT purposes, for which see Tolley's Capital Gains Tax.

The first of the two conditions, of which only one needs to be met, is that the individual:

- was born in the UK;
- has a UK domicile of origin (see **63.35** above); and
- is UK resident for the tax year in question.

Thus, an individual with a UK domicile at date of birth (i.e. a UK domicile of origin) who has subsequently moved abroad and acquired a domicile of choice overseas will not retain that domicile of choice for tax purposes upon returning to the UK. Irrespective of his intentions, such an individual will be deemed to be UK domiciled for tax purposes once he becomes UK resident. This affects any individual meeting the above condition at a time falling on or after 6 April 2017, including those who returned to the UK before that date.

The second condition (the '*15-year rule*') is that the individual has been UK resident for at least 15 of the 20 tax years immediately preceding the tax year in question. It is irrelevant that some or all of those years of UK residence will have fallen before 6 April 2017. However, the condition is *not* met if the individual is not UK resident for the tax year in question *and* has not been UK resident for any preceding tax year from 2017/18 onwards. Thus, the 15-year rule does not take effect for as long as an individual remains non-UK resident on and after 6 April 2017.

It follows that an individual who is deemed to be UK domiciled under the 15-year rule and who wishes to reset the clock will need to become non-UK resident for at least six complete tax years before becoming UK resident once more.

[*ITA 2007, s 835BA; F(No 2)A 2017, s 29*].

The fact that an individual is deemed to be domiciled in the UK for tax purposes does not affect his domicile status under general law (for which see **63.35** above), and nor does it affect the domicile status (for tax purposes or otherwise) of his children or other family members.

Application of the deemed domicile rule

The application of the deemed domicile rule to income tax is referenced throughout this work wherever relevant. See **4.14** ANTI-AVOIDANCE (transfer of assets abroad: meaning of 'person abroad'); **28.11** EMPLOYMENT INCOME (board and lodging expenses where employee performs overseas employment duties wholly outside UK); **28.12** EMPLOYMENT INCOME (travel costs and expenses of non-UK domiciled employees); **61.2** REMITTANCE BASIS (application of the remittance basis); **63.31** above (residence of personal representatives); and **70.5** SETTLEMENTS (residence of trustees).

Related provisions

For other amendments to income tax legislation made in conjunction with the introduction of the deemed domicile rule, see in particular **4.14–4.16** ANTI-AVOIDANCE (transfer of assets abroad); **61.17** REMITTANCE BASIS (cleansing of mixed funds); **70.27** settlements (charge on settlor: exclusion for protected foreign-source income); **70.34** (benefits provided out of protected foreign-source income); and **70.35** (onward gifts of benefits provided out of protected foreign-source income).

Members of Parliament

[63.37] A person who for any part of a tax year is a member of the House of Commons or, with certain exceptions, the House of Lords is treated for income tax purposes as resident and domiciled in the UK for the whole of that tax year. [*Constitutional Reform and Governance Act 2010, ss 41, 42*].

Visiting forces etc.

[63.38] If the following conditions are met by an individual throughout a period, the period is not treated for income tax purposes as a period of residence in the UK or as creating a change of the individual's residence or domicile. The conditions are that the individual:

- is either:
  - a member of a visiting force of a designated country or of a civilian component of such a force; or
  - is of a category for the time being agreed between the UK Government and the other members of the North Atlantic Council and is employed by a designated allied headquarters (as defined);
- is in the UK, but only by virtue of being a member of the force or civilian component or being employed by the allied headquarters (as the case may be); and

- is not a British citizen, a British overseas territories citizen, a British National (Overseas) or a British Overseas citizen.

The above privileges are extended to members of EU military forces and EU civilian staff (working alongside military forces) serving in the UK or attached to international military headquarters in the UK.

[*ITA 2007, s 833; SI 2012 Nos 3070, 3071*].

See also **30.50** EXEMPT INCOME.

Claims and appeals

[63.39] Claims for the special reliefs referred to at **63.3** above are made to the Commissioners for HMRC. If, on an appeal in connection with any claim, the issues arising include any question of residence or domicile, the normal time limit of 30 days in which to appeal is extended to three months. [*TMA 1970, Sch 1A para 9(2)(b)*]. Other disputes regarding residence are settled by way of appeal against the relevant assessment in the normal way.

64

Returns

Cross-reference. See **55.2–55.8** PENALTIES as regards duty to notify chargeability to tax and penalties for late or incorrect returns. See also generally **67** SELF-ASSESSMENT and **46** MAKING TAX DIGITAL.

Simon's Taxes. See **A4.1, A6.4, E1.202A–E1.214.**

Introduction to returns

[64.1] HMRC have considerable powers to obtain information and these are generally exercised initially by the requirement to complete and submit various returns, with PENALTIES (55) for non-compliance, omissions or incorrect statements. Explanatory notes are usually issued with the returns.

Annual returns of income and chargeable gains

[64.2] For the purposes of establishing a person's income, chargeable gains and net income tax liability, an officer of HMRC may by notice require that person to make a return. See **55.5** PENALTIES as regards failure to make the return on time. The return must contain such information and be accompanied by such accounts, statements, documents and other records as may reasonably be required. The return must include a declaration that, to the best of the knowledge of the person making it, it is complete and correct. The information, accounts and statements required by the notice may differ in relation to different periods, or different sources of income, or different descriptions of person.

The deadline for submitting the completed return is determined as follows.

- If the return is an online return, it must be submitted to HMRC on or before **31 January** following the tax year to which it relates or, if later, within three months beginning with the date of the notice.
- If the return is a manual return, it must be submitted to HMRC on or before **31 October** following the tax year to which it relates or, if later, within three months beginning with the date of the notice.

[*TMA 1970, ss 8, 12; FA 2016, Sch 1 paras 51(2), 73*].

Similar provisions apply in relation to returns by trustees, by reference to any 'relevant trustee' (see **67.11** SELF-ASSESSMENT). [*TMA 1970, ss 8A, 12; FA 2016, Sch 1 paras 51(3), 73*]. A notice to make a return cannot be given to the trustees of an interest in possession trust all of the income of which is mandated to the life tenant and which realises no chargeable gains (*Trustees of the Paul Hogarth Life Interest Trust 2008 v HMRC* FTT (TC 6757), [2019] SFTD 257, [2018] UKFTT 595 (TC)).

See **64.12–64.14** below as regards partnership returns.

HMRC will, on request, issue a return before the end of the tax year:

(a) in which the taxpayer dies (or administration of the estate is completed), to the personal representatives of the deceased; or
(b) in which a trust is wound up, to the trustees.

(Revenue Press Release 4 April 1996).

Under current criteria, fewer taxpayers (including higher rate taxpayers) whose affairs can be adequately dealt with using the PAYE system are asked to complete a return, though they may choose to do so if they wish. See the guidelines on who needs to complete a return at www.gov.uk/self-assessment-tax-returns/who-must-send-a-tax-return#5. There is also a Short Tax Return (STR) for those with relatively straightforward tax affairs which can be issued by HMRC as an alternative to the standard self-assessment return (see guidance at www.gov.uk/government/uploads/system/uploads/attachment_data/file/506435/sa211-2016.pdf).

Most individuals now file their returns online. For 2019/20 returns onwards, self-assessment taxpayers will no longer receive automatic paper returns. Taxpayers who have filed on paper in the past will receive a short notice to file. If they still wish to file on paper they can download a blank version of the return or call HMRC to request one. (HMRC News Release 16 March 2020 at www.gov.uk/government/news/hmrc-to-stop-automatically-sending-paper-self-assessment-returns).

Agents are authorised to file individual clients' personal tax returns online, subject to conditions as to authorisation of the agent by the client, authentication of the information by the client and use of HMRC-approved software

(Revenue Directions under *SI 2000 No 945, Reg 3*, 21 August 2001). For online filing and payment generally, see Revenue Tax Bulletin June 2000 pp 757, 758, and see www.gov.uk/log-in-register-hmrc-online-services.

The Upper Tribunal in *HMRC v Rogers* UT 2019, [2020] STC 220, [2019] UKUT 406 (TCC) found an automated notice to file to have been validly served. This reversed a decision of the First-tier Tribunal to the effect that a notice to file under *TMA 1970, s 8* could be served only by an individual officer and not by HMRC as a collective body. Legislation has since confirmed that notice to file can be given using automated processes (see **35.6** HMRC — ADMINISTRATION).

Unsolicited returns

If a person delivers a return *without* having been given a notice under *TMA 1970, s 8* or *s 8A* as above (i.e. an unsolicited or voluntary return) but which is treated by HMRC as a legitimate return (i.e. as if made and delivered in pursuance of such a notice), then a notice to make a return is treated as having been given to the person on the day the return was delivered. The return is consequently treated as having been made and delivered in pursuance of that notice, with all the consequences that attach, e.g. HMRC's right to enquire into the return. This rule applies to anything that is in a form, and is delivered in a way, in which a return could have been made and delivered had a notice been given and which purports to be a return of a kind that such a notice would have required. It does not affect the operation of any tax legislation that specifies the time frame in which an assessment or a self-assessment can or must be made.

The above rule was introduced by *FA 2019* but with effect as if it had always been in force. However, it does not apply in relation to a return delivered by a person if, before 29 October 2018, that person made an appeal under the Taxes Acts, or a claim for judicial review, on the grounds (or partly on the grounds) that the return was unsolicited. See **64.6** below (notice of enquiry) and **55.5** PENALTIES for Tribunal cases in which pre-29 October 2018 appeals succeeded on those grounds.

[*TMA 1970, s 12D; FA 2019, s 87(1)(3)–(8)*].

Withdrawal of notice to make a return

HMRC may withdraw a notice to an individual or trustee ('*the taxpayer*') to make a return (a '*notice to file*'). They may do so at their own volition or, if they agree, at the taxpayer's request. They must notify the taxpayer accordingly and specify the date on which notice to file is withdrawn. Notice to file may be withdrawn at any time within the two years following the tax year to which it relates or, in exceptional circumstances, within such extended period as HMRC may determine. Notice to file cannot be withdrawn if the taxpayer has already made the return for the year or if HMRC have made a determination under **64.11** below. The withdrawal of a notice to file does not prevent HMRC subsequently issuing a further notice to file for the same tax year. A notification of withdrawal may contain provision cancelling any penalty for failure to make the return (see **55.5** PENALTIES).

[*TMA 1970, s 8B; FA 2016, s 169(1)–(5)(7)*].

Provisional figures

A return containing a provisional figure will be accepted provided that the figure is reasonable, taking account of all available information, and is clearly identified as such. An explanation should be given as to why the final figure is not available, all reasonable steps having been taken to obtain it, and when it is expected to be available (at which time it should be notified without unreasonable delay). The absence of such explanation and expected date will influence HMRC in selecting returns for enquiry (see **64.6** below). Pressures of work and complexity of tax affairs are not regarded as acceptable explanations. If the final figure is not provided by the expected date HMRC will take appropriate action to obtain it, which may mean opening an enquiry. See HMRC Tax Return Guide, Revenue Tax Bulletins October 1998 pp 593–596, December 1999 p 705, June 2001 p 848 and February 2002 p 916, and Revenue 'Working Together' Bulletin July 2000 p 5. Note that a provisional figure is different in concept to an estimate that is not intended to be superseded by a more accurate figure.

Where the replacement of a provisional figure by a final figure leads to a *decrease* in the self-assessment, and the time limit for making amendments (see **64.9** below) has passed, the amendment may be made by way of claim for recovery of tax (see **16.7** CLAIMS). Where such replacement leads to an *increase* in the self-assessment, a discovery assessment (see **6.6** ASSESSMENTS) may be made to collect the additional tax due. (Revenue Tax Bulletin December 2000 p 817).

Accounts

Business accounts are not generally required with the return. Instead, the taxpayer must complete the self-employment supplementary pages to the return, of which there are now full and short versions (to be used according to various criteria such as turnover and complexity). See also **75.20** TRADING INCOME. See **6.6** ASSESSMENTS re the option of submitting accounts (in addition to completing the supplementary pages) to possibly reduce the risk of a discovery assessment. Accounts should otherwise be retained in case of enquiry (see **64.6** below). (Revenue Press Release 31 May 1996, Tax Bulletins June 1996 pp 313–315, June 1997 p 436 and HMRC Income Tax Self-Assessment: The Legal Framework Manual SALF203, paras 2.18, 2.19).

Signature of returns etc.

HMRC will accept returns signed by an attorney acting under a general or enduring power where the taxpayer is physically unable to sign (and not merely unavailable to do so). The attorney must have full knowledge of the taxpayer's affairs, and provide the original power or a certified copy when such a return is first made. In cases of mental incapacity, the signature of an attorney appointed under an enduring power registered with the Court of Protection (or of a receiver or committee appointed by that Court) will be accepted. Similar requirements apply to the signature of claims on behalf of physically or mentally incapacitated taxpayers, and to other documents. (HMRC SP A13 as revised and Revenue Tax Bulletin February 1993 p 51). Although this practice pre-dates self-assessment, the Inland Revenue published further information in their Tax Bulletin, which confirms that the only exceptions to the personal signature requirement are where, due to his age, physical infirmity or mental incapacity, the taxpayer is unable to cope adequately with the management of his affairs or where his general health might suffer if he were troubled for a personal signature. In all other cases, HMRC expect the return to be signed personally and will reject the return as unsatisfactory, and send it back to whoever submitted it (taxpayer or agent), if it is not. In the case of a return submitted online, the taxpayer's personal authentication (password and User ID) takes the place of his signature. (Revenue Tax Bulletin June 2001 pp 847, 848).

Substitute return forms

The Inland Revenue issued a Statement of Practice (HMRC SP 5/87, 15 June 1987) concerning the acceptability of facsimile and photocopied tax returns. Whenever such a substitute form is used, it is important to ensure that it bears the correct taxpayer's reference.

Facsimiles must satisfactorily present to the taxpayer the information which HMRC have determined shall be before him when he signs the declaration that the return is correct and complete to the best of his knowledge. They should be readily recognisable as a return when received by HMRC, and the entries of taxpayers' details should be distinguishable from the background text. Approval must be obtained from HMRC, Corporate Communications Office, Room 9/3A, 9th Floor, NW Wing, Bush House, London WC2B 4PP before a facsimile return is used, and the facsimile must bear an agreed unique imprint for identification purposes.

Photocopies must bear the actual, not photocopied, signature of the relevant person. They are acceptable provided that they are identical (except as regards use of colour) to the official form. Where double-sided copies are not available, it is sufficient that all pages are present and attached in the correct order. Although the copying of official forms is in strictness a breach of HMSO copyright, action will be taken only where forms are copied on a large scale for commercial gain.

Simon's Taxes. See **A4.105–A4.115, A4.165–A4.171, E1.210–E1.212.**

Self-assessments

[64.3] Every return under *TMA 1970, s 8* or *s 8A* (see **64.2** above) must include, subject to the exception below, an assessment (a self-assessment) of the amounts in which, based on the information in the return and taking into account any reliefs and allowances claimed therein, the person making the return is chargeable to income tax and capital gains tax for the tax year and of his net income tax liability for the year.

The tax to be self-assessed does not include any chargeable on the scheme administrator of a registered pension scheme (see **57.4** PENSION PROVISION), (for 2017/18 onwards) the scheme manager of a qualifying recognised overseas pension scheme or a former such scheme, or the responsible person in relation to an employer-financed retirement benefits scheme (see **57.35** PENSION PROVISION).

A person need not comply with this requirement if he makes and makes his return on or before 31 October following the tax year to which the return relates or, if later, within two months beginning with the date of the notice to make the return. This deadline is of no significance where returns are filed online (see **64.2** above) as the tax due is automatically computed during the filing process. In the event of a person making no self-assessment, an officer of HMRC *must* make the assessment on his behalf, based on the information in the return, and send the person a copy. Such assessments are treated as self-assessments by the person making the return and as included in the return.

[*TMA 1970, s 9(1)–(3A); FA 2016, Sch 1 paras 51(4), 73; FA 2017, Sch 4 paras 19, 25*].

HMRC need not give notice to make a return under **64.1** above, and thus a self-assessment will not be required, in cases where tax deducted under PAY AS YOU EARN (**53**) equates to the total tax liability for the year. See, however, **53.1** PAY AS YOU EARN for the taxpayer's right to request that a return be issued to him.

Taxpayers with employment income who wish to have a liability of less than £3,000 coded out through PAY AS YOU EARN (**53**) must file their return by an earlier date than the 31 January deadline at **64.2** RETURNS. That date is 31 October (following the tax year) if the return is filed manually and 30 December if it is filed online (see **64.2** RETURNS). [*SI 2003 No 2682, Reg 186; SI 2011 No 1584, Regs 1, 2*]. A 2018/19 underpayment, for example, will be coded out for 2020/21. (Revenue Tax Bulletin June 1996 p 315; Revenue 'Working Together' Bulletin February 2001 p 2; Revenue Press Release 23 September 2002; webarchive.nationalarchives.gov.uk/20140109143644/http://www.hmrc.gov.uk/thelibrary/collect-debts-paye.pdf). Coding out of an underpayment for a tax year has the consequential effect of reducing any payments on account (see **67.5** below) due for the following tax year.

Simon's Taxes. See **E1.204, E1.230.**

Amendments of returns other than where enquiries made

[64.4] At any time within twelve months after the 'filing date', a person may by notice to an officer of HMRC amend his return. It should, however, be noted that amendment of a return does not preclude penalties for inaccuracies brought about carelessly or deliberately (HMRC Self-Assessment Legal Framework Manual SALF206). For this purpose, and regardless of whether or not the return is filed online, the '*filing date*' is regarded as 31 January following the tax year to which the return relates, except that, if later, it is the last day of the period of three months beginning with the date of the notice requiring the return.

At any time within nine months after the submission of a person's return, an officer of HMRC may by notice to that person amend his return to correct obvious errors and omissions (whether of principle, arithmetical or otherwise).

An officer may also correct anything else in the return that he has reason to believe is incorrect in the light of information available to him. Where a correction is required in consequence of an amendment by the taxpayer as above, the nine-month period begins immediately after the date of the taxpayer's amendment. The taxpayer has the right to reject an officer's correction, by notice within 30 days beginning with the date of the notice of correction. In practice HMRC will reverse a correction regardless of this 30-day limit, unless they are no longer empowered to do so, i.e. if all deadlines for corrections and amendments (by HMRC or taxpayer) have passed and the HMRC enquiry window (see **64.6** below) has closed. (Revenue Tax Bulletin June 2001 pp 850, 851).

[*TMA 1970, ss 9(4)(6), 9ZA, 9ZB*].

Individuals whose tax office is served by a Contact Centre may notify certain amendments by telephone (HMRC SP 1/10). See also **16.5** CLAIMS. It is HMRC policy to itself make increasing use of the telephone to resolve minor queries arising in connection with completed returns (Revenue Tax Bulletin February 2004 p 1080).

Otherwise, amendments may be made in the form of a letter, an amended return form, an extra supplementary page or an amended supplementary page. HMRC will normally accept an amendment to a return or self-assessment whether notified by the taxpayer or by an agent authorised to act on the taxpayer's behalf, but it must be supplied in writing. (HMRC Working Together' Bulletin September 2007 p 4).

See **64.9** below for amendments to returns where HMRC make enquiries into the return.

Simon's Taxes. See **E1.213, E1.214.**

Record-keeping

[64.5] Any person who may be required to make a return under **64.1** above (personal and trustee's returns) or **64.12** below (partnership returns) for a tax year or other period is statutorily required to keep all necessary records and to preserve them until the end of the 'relevant day'. The '*relevant day*' is normally:

(a) in the case of a person carrying on a trade (including, for these purposes, any letting of property), profession or business alone or in partnership, the fifth anniversary of 31 January following the tax year or, for partnership returns, the sixth anniversary of the end of the period covered by the return; and
(b) otherwise, the first anniversary of 31 January following the tax year,

or, in either case, such earlier day as the Commissioners for HMRC may specify in writing.

Where, as is normal, notice to make the return is given before the day in whichever is the applicable of (a) or (b) above, the '*relevant day*' is the *later* of that day and whichever of the following applies:

(i) where HMRC enquiries are made into the return, the day on which the enquiries are fully completed (see **64.8** below);
(ii) where no such enquiries are made, the day on which HMRC no longer have power to enquire (see **64.6** below).

Where notice to make the return is given *after* the day in whichever is the applicable of (a) and (b) above, (i) and (ii) above still apply to determine the relevant day but only in relation to such records as the taxpayer has in his possession at the time the notice is given.

In the case of a person within (a) above, the records in question include records concerning business receipts and expenditure and, in the case of a trade involving dealing in goods, all sales and purchases of goods. All supporting documents (including accounts, books, deeds, contracts, vouchers and receipts) relating to such items must also be preserved.

Generally, copies of documents may be preserved instead of the originals. (For computer records in particular, see HMRC Compliance Handbook CH13400.) Exceptions to this are vouchers, certificates etc. which show deductions at source of UK or foreign tax, e.g. interest vouchers (including those issued by banks and building societies) and evidence of tax deducted from payments to sub-contractors under the CONSTRUCTION INDUSTRY SCHEME (**20**), which must be preserved in their original form.

The maximum penalty for non-compliance in relation to any tax year is £3,000. This penalty does not apply where the failure relates to records which might have been requisite only for the purposes of claims, elections or notices which are *not* included in the return (but see **16.3** CLAIMS for the requirement as regards records relating to such claims etc. and the penalty for non-compliance), or to vouchers, certificates etc. showing UK dividend tax credits or deductions at source (e.g. dividend vouchers and interest certificates) where an HMRC officer is satisfied that other documentary evidence supplied to him proves any facts he reasonably requires to be proved and which the voucher etc. would have proved.

[*TMA 1970, s 12B; FA 2016, Sch 1 paras 51(7), 73; F(No 2)A 2017, Sch 15 paras 9, 44*].

See HMRC Compliance Handbook at CH10000 *et seq.* (technical guidance: record-keeping).

Enquiries into returns

Notice of enquiry

[64.6] An officer of HMRC may enquire into a personal or trustees' return, and anything (including any claim or election) contained (or required to be contained) in it. He must give notice that he intends to do so (notice of enquiry) within whichever of the following periods is appropriate:

(a) in the case of a return submitted on or before the filing date (i.e. the date on or before which the return must be submitted — see **64.2** above), the twelve months after the day on which the return was submitted;

(b) in the case of a return submitted after the filing date, the period ending with the 'quarter day' next following the first anniversary of the date of submission;

(c) in the case of a return amended by the taxpayer under **64.4** above, the period ending with the 'quarter day' next following the first anniversary of the date of amendment.

For these purposes, the '*quarter days*' are 31 January, 30 April etc. A return cannot be enquired into more than once, except in consequence of an amendment (or further amendment). If notice under (c) above is given at a time when the deadline in (a) or (b) above, as the case may be, has expired or after an enquiry into the return has been fully completed, the enquiry is limited to matters affected by the amendment. The same applies if a partial closure notice has been issued (see **64.8** below) in relation to the matters to which the amendment relates.

[*TMA 1970, s 9A; F(No 2)A 2017, Sch 15 paras 2, 44*].

Whilst the form of a notice of enquiry is not prescribed by law, it has to be clear from the notice that HMRC intend to open a formal enquiry into the return (*Raftopoulou v HMRC* CA, [2018] STC 988; *Credit Suisse Securities (Europe) Ltd v HMRC* FTT (TC 6394–6397), [2020] UKFTT 86 (TC)).

It was held by a Special Commissioner that service of a notice is treated as effected at the time at which the letter would be submitted in the ordinary course of post, i.e. on the second working day after posting for first class mail or on the fourth working day after posting for second class mail (*Wing Hung Lai v Bale* (Sp C 203), [1999] SSCD 238). See also *Holly v Inspector of Taxes* (Sp C 225), [2000] SSCD 50. HMRC now accept that it is the time of receipt of the notice, rather than that of its issue, by reference to which the time limit applies (Revenue 'Working Together' Bulletin April 2000 p 8). Notice of enquiry given to the taxpayer's accountants, on reliance of form 64-8, does not constitute a valid notice of enquiry given to the taxpayer (*Tinkler v HMRC* CA, [2019] STC 1685).

Claims affecting more than one year

Where a claim affects more than one tax year, the above enquiry procedure applies to the return for the earlier year if the taxpayer has accounted for the claim in his self-assessment of the tax due for that earlier year. Otherwise, the correct procedure is an enquiry under *TMA 1970, Sch 1A* (as in **16.3** CLAIMS). See *HMRC v Cotter* SC, [2013] STC 2480; *R (oao Derry) v HMRC* SC, [2019] STC 926; *R (oao Rouse) v HMRC* UT 2013, [2014] STC 230.

In the above cases, the claims were for loss reliefs to be carried back (see **16.2** CLAIMS) from one year (Year 2) to another year (Year 1). In broadly similar cases, the courts made the important distinction that the year being enquired into was Year 2 and not, as in the above cases, Year 1 (*R (oao De Silva) v HMRC* SC, [2017] STC 2483; and see *Spring Salmon & Seafood Ltd v HMRC* UT, [2017] UKUT 205 (TCC)). For a useful discussion of the *De Silva* decision and its ramifications, see *Knibbs v HMRC; R (oao Astley) v HMRC* CA, [2019] STC 2262, in which the CA followed *De Silva*.

Other matters

Before *FA 2019*, an enquiry could not be made into an unsolicited (voluntary) return, i.e. in a case where notice to file a return had not been given or had been given but not properly served (but see now **64.2** above under Unsolicited returns) (*Revell v HMRC* FTT (TC 4887), [2016] SFTD 618, [2016] UKFTT 97 (TC); *Patel v HMRC* FTT (TC 6426), [2018] UKFTT 185 (TC), [2018] SFTD 1000).

An enquiry cannot subsequently be opened into a particular matter or point at issue that has been the subject of an agreement under *TMA 1970, s 54* to settle an appeal (see **5.9** APPEALS) (*Easinghall Ltd v HMRC* UT, [2016] STC 1476).

In the case of a return by the personal representatives of a deceased taxpayer (for the year of death or of completion of administration of the estate), HMRC will give early written confirmation if they do not intend to enquire into the return (although, in exceptional circumstances, an enquiry at a later date would not thereby be precluded if the return was discovered to be incomplete or incorrect). Such early confirmation will also be given to trustees in relation to the return for the year in which the trust is wound up. (Revenue Press Release 4 April 1996). See also **64.1** above as regards early issue of returns in such cases.

See **64.12** below as regards similar provisions as regards enquiries into partnership returns.

Simon's Taxes. See **A6.302A, A6.401–A6.406.**

Conduct of enquiry

[64.7] A Code of Practice (COP 11, or, in certain simple cases, a short, single-page version) is issued at the start of every such enquiry. This sets out the rules under which enquiries are made into income tax returns and explains how taxpayers can expect HMRC to conduct enquiries. It describes what HMRC do when they receive a return and how they select cases for enquiry, how they open and carry out enquiries, and what happens if they find something wrong.

Where an enquiry remains open after the time by which notice to enquire into the return had to be given solely because of an unagreed capital gains tax valuation, HMRC will not raise further enquiries into matters unrelated to that capital gains tax computation unless, had the enquiry already been completed, a discovery under *TMA 1970, s 29* (see **6.6** ASSESSMENTS) could have been made. (HMRC SP 1/99).

HMRC also publish an Enquiry Manual as part of their series of internal guidance manuals (see **35** HMRC — ADMINISTRATION) and, as an extended introduction to the material on operational aspects of the enquiry regime covered in the manual, a special edition of their Tax Bulletin (Special Edition 2, August 1997). The following points are selected from the Bulletin.

(i) Early submission of a tax return will not increase the likelihood of selection for enquiry.

(ii) HMRC do not have to give reasons for opening an enquiry — and they *will not do so.*

(iii) Enquiries may be full enquiries or 'aspect enquiries'. An aspect enquiry will fall short of an in-depth examination of the return (though it may develop into one), but will instead concentrate on one or more aspects of it.

(iv) Greater emphasis than before will be placed on examination of underlying records. HMRC will make an informal request for information before, if necessary, using their powers under **39.2–39.9** HMRC INVESTIGATORY POWERS.

(v) Where penalties are being sought, HMRC will aim to conclude the enquiry by means of a contract settlement (see **6.9** ASSESSMENTS) rather than by the issue of a final closure notice under *TMA 1970, s 28A* (see **64.8** below).

In March 2002, the Inland Revenue published a framework within which enquiries will be worked and to which professional advisers are encouraged to adhere. Particular topics covered are the opening enquiry letter, requests for and conduct of interviews and meetings, and requests for non-business bank and building society accounts (plus credit/charge/store card details). (Revenue 'Working Together' Bulletin March 2002 pp 1–6).

Where income is received from co-owned property where the letting activity does not amount to a partnership (see **60.2** PROPERTY INCOME), and the name and address of the managing co-owner is provided in co-owners' returns, HMRC will confine initial enquiries relating to that income to the managing co-owner's return. (Revenue Tax Bulletin October 1996 p 350).

For the allowability of additional accountancy expenses incurred in connection with self-assessment enquiries, see **75.96** TRADING INCOME and Revenue Tax Bulletin October 1998 p 596.

Completion or part completion of enquiry

[64.8] An enquiry is completed when an officer of HMRC gives the taxpayer notice (a final closure notice) that he has completed his enquiries. As regards enquiries commenced on or after 16 November 2017, or in progress on that date, an HMRC officer can issue a partial closure notice, which completes the enquiry insofar as it concerns the matters specified in the notice. The enquiry is not fully completed until a final closure notice has been issued to inform the taxpayer that the officer has completed his remaining enquiries. A partial or final closure notice takes effect when it is issued and must state the officer's conclusions and make the necessary amendments to the return to give effect to those conclusions or state that no amendment is required. An amendment made by a closure notice is in the nature of an assessment by HMRC (*R (oao Archer) v HMRC* QB, [2017] STC 1037).

During the course of an enquiry, the taxpayer may apply to the Appeal Tribunal for a direction requiring HMRC to issue a partial or final closure notice within a specified period, such application to be heard and determined in similar manner to an appeal. The Tribunal must give the direction unless satisfied that there are reasonable grounds for not issuing the partial or final closure notice within a specified period. In *Embiricos v HMRC* FTT (TC 7083), [2019] SFTD 795, [2019] UKFTT 236 (TC), HMRC were required to issue a partial closure notice notwithstanding that they could not yet quantify the tax due.

[*TMA 1970, s 28A; F(No 2)A 2017, Sch 15 paras 12, 44*].

Guidance is given to HMRC officers as to when they might agree to an application to issue a closure notice without the need for a Tribunal hearing (HMRC Enquiry Manual EM1976, 1980). HMRC will make use of partial closure notices where the taxpayer's affairs are complex or where there is tax avoidance or large amounts of tax at risk; HMRC officers may issue a partial closure notice at their own discretion by agreement with the taxpayer (www.gov.uk/government/publications/tax-enquiries-closure-rules).

In an application for closure as above, the Sp C considered that an investigation into the applicant's personal expenditure aimed at establishing the correct amount of tax due did not breach his rights under *Human Rights Act 1998, Sch 1, Art 8* (right to private life) (*Gould and another (t/a Garry's Private Hire) v HMRC* (Sp C 604), [2007] SSCD 502). In *Perfectos Printing Inks Co Ltd v HMRC* FTT (TC 7203), [2019] UKFTT 388 (TC), the Tribunal, in directing that an enquiry be closed within 30 days, agreed with counsel for the appellants that the dividing line as to what was reasonably required when it came to the provision of personal bank statements lay between those cases where the HMRC officer could show a reason to suspect under-assessment and those where the officer was simply on a 'fishing expedition'.

Similar provisions apply in the case of an enquiry into a partnership return. Where a partnership return is amended under these provisions, HMRC will, by notice, make any necessary consequential amendments to the partners' returns (including those of company partners). [*TMA 1970, s 28B; F(No 2)A 2017, Sch 15 paras 13, 44*].

See **5.3** APPEALS for right of appeal against any conclusion stated or amendment made by a partial or final closure notice.

Where a personal or partnership return is amended, the taxpayer is given the same rights to make, revise and withdraw claims, elections, applications and notices as he would have had if a 'discovery' assessment had been raised under *TMA 1970, s 29* (see **6.6** ASSESSMENTS). This is achieved by giving effect to *TMA 1970, ss 43A, 43B* (see **16.9** CLAIMS), to *TMA 1970, s 36(3)* (which enables the same reliefs and allowances to be given as if the necessary claims etc. had been made within the relevant time limits — see **6.3** ASSESSMENTS), and to *TMA 1970, s 43(2)* (extended time limit for claims — see **16.9** CLAIMS). These sections are given similar effect in relation to an amendment as they would have in relation to an assessment. Any late assessment required to give effect to such a claim etc., or as a result of allowing such a claim etc., can be made within a year after the claim etc. becomes final (i.e. becomes no longer capable of being varied, on appeal or otherwise). [*TMA 1970, s 43C*].

Amendment of returns where enquiries made

[64.9] If a return is amended by the taxpayer under **64.4** above or in accordance with the requirements of a follower notice (see **4.44** ANTI-AVOIDANCE) while an enquiry is in progress in relation to any matter affected by the amendment, the amendment does not restrict the scope of the enquiry but may itself be taken into account in the enquiry. The amendment does not take effect to alter the tax payable until a partial closure notice is issued in relation to the matters to which the amendment relates or, if no such notice is issued, a final closure notice is issued. See **64.8** above for partial and final closure notices. The amendment may then be taken into account separately or, if the officer so states in the closure notice, in arriving at the amendments contained in that notice. It does not take effect if the officer concludes in the closure notice that the amendment is incorrect.

The above has effect where the enquiry begins on or after 16 November 2017 or is in progress on that date, and allows for the fact that such an enquiry may be partly completed by the issue of a partial closure notice. Previously, if a return was amended by the taxpayer while an enquiry into it was in progress, the amendment did not restrict the scope of the enquiry but could itself be taken into account in the enquiry. The amendment did not take effect to alter the tax payable until the enquiry was completed.

[*TMA 1970, s 9B; F(No 2)A 2017, Sch 15 paras 3, 44*].

See **64.12** below as regards similar provisions for partnership returns. [*TMA 1970, s 9(5), s 12AB(3)*].

If in his opinion there is otherwise likely to be a loss of tax in relation to any matter, an officer may amend a self-assessment contained in the return while an enquiry is still in progress in relation to that matter. If the enquiry is itself limited to an amendment to the return (see **64.6** above), the officer's power in this respect is limited accordingly. [*TMA 1970, s 9C; F(No 2)A 2017, Sch 15 paras 4, 44*]. No similar power exists in the case of partnership returns.

Referral of questions during enquiry

[64.10] There is provision as below to enable specific contentious points to be litigated while an enquiry is still open, instead of waiting until it is completed. Enquiries into personal, trustees' and partnership returns are all included. Where the enquiry begins on or after 16 November 2017 or is in progress on that date, this applies while an enquiry is still open into any matter (allowing for the fact that such an enquiry may be partly completed by the issue of a partial closure notice as in **64.8** above).

At any time whilst the enquiry is in progress, any one or more questions arising out of it may be referred, jointly by the taxpayer and an officer of HMRC, to the Appeal Tribunal for their determination. More than one notice of referral may be given in relation to the enquiry. Either party may withdraw a notice of referral. Until the questions referred have been finally determined (or the referral withdrawn), no final closure notice may be given or applied for in relation to the enquiry, and no partial closure notice relating to the question referred may be given or applied for.

The determination of the question(s) by the Tribunal is binding on both parties in the same way, and to the same extent, as a decision on a preliminary issue in an appeal. HMRC must take account of it in concluding their enquiry. Following completion of the enquiry, the question concerned may not be reopened on appeal except to the extent (if any) that it could have been reopened had it been determined on appeal following the enquiry rather than on referral during the enquiry.

[*TMA 1970, ss 28ZA–28ZE; F(No 2)A 2017, Sch 15 paras 10, 11, 44*].

Determination of tax where no return submitted

[64.11] Where a notice has been given under *TMA 1970, s 8* or *s 8A* (notice requiring an individual or trustee to make a return — see **64.2** above) and the return is not submitted by the 'filing date', an officer of HMRC may make a determination of the amounts of taxable income, capital gains and income tax payable which, to the best of his information and belief, he estimates for the tax year. The officer must serve notice of the determination on the person concerned. Tax is payable as if the determination were a self-assessment, with no right of appeal. No determination may be made after the expiry of three years beginning with the filing date.

For these purposes, and regardless of whether or not the return is filed online, the '*filing date*' is regarded as 31 January following the tax year to which the return relates, except that, if later, it is the last day of the period of three months beginning with the date of the notice requiring the return.

A determination is automatically superseded by any self-assessment made (whether by the taxpayer or HMRC), based on information contained in a return. Such self-assessment must be made within the three years beginning with the filing date or, if later, within twelve months beginning with the date of the determination. Any tax payable or repayable as a result of the supersession is deemed to have fallen due for payment or repayment on the normal due date, usually 31 January following the tax year (see **67.7** SELF-ASSESSMENT).

Any recovery proceedings commenced before the making of such a self-assessment may be continued in respect of so much of the tax charged by the self-assessment as is due and payable and has not been paid.

See also **54.8** PAYMENT OF TAX for the continuation of action under the provisions for enforcement of tax debts by deduction from accounts where a determination is superseded by a self-assessment.

[*TMA 1970, ss 28C, 59B(5A)*].

Simon's Taxes. See **A6.304, E1.203.**

Partnership returns

[64.12] Any partner may be required by notice to make a return of the partnership profits (a 'partnership return') together with accounts, statements, documents and other records. The return must include information as to taxable partnership income, reliefs and allowances claimed, tax at source plus the names, residences and tax references of all persons (including companies) who were partners during the period specified in the notice and such other information as may reasonably be required by the notice, which may include information relating to disposals of partnership property. The general requirements are similar to those for personal returns under *TMA 1970, s 8* (see **64.2** above). See **64.13** below as to the *partnership statement* to be included with a partnership return.

The notice will specify the period (the relevant period) to be covered by the return and the date by which the return should be submitted (the filing date). For a partnership of individuals, the relevant period will be a tax year. For a partnership including one or more companies, the relevant period will usually be the partnership accounting period ending in the tax year; if there is no such accounting period or if the partnership does not carry on a trade or profession, the relevant period is the tax year.

As regards returns for a partnership including at least one individual, the filing date is determined as follows.

- If the return is an online return, it will be no earlier than **31 January** following the tax year to which the return relates.
- If the return is a manual return, it will be no earlier than **31 October** following the tax year to which the return relates.

As regards returns for a partnership including at least one company, the filing date is determined as follows.

- If the return is an online return, it will be no earlier than the first anniversary of the end of the relevant period.
- If the return is a manual return, it will be no earlier than the end of the period of nine months beginning at the end of the relevant period.

In all cases, the filing date will be deferred until, at the earliest, the last day of the three-month period beginning with the date of the notice, if this is a later date than that given above.

Where the partner responsible for dealing with the return ceases to be available, a successor may be nominated for this purpose by a majority of the persons (or their personal representatives) who were partners at any time in the period covered by the return. A nomination (or revocation of a nomination) does not have effect until notified to HMRC. Failing a nomination, a successor will be determined according to rules on the return form or will be nominated by HMRC.

In relation to returns for 2018/19 onwards, if the partnership making the return (ABC) has a partner which is itself a partnership, the return must cover ABC's 'indirect partners' (see **52.3** PARTNERSHIPS) as well as its actual partners.

[*TMA 1970, ss 12AA, 118(1); FA 2016, Sch 1 paras 51(5), 73; FA 2018, Sch 6 paras 3, 4(3), 6(2)(5)*].

Also in relation to returns for 2018/19 onwards, where a partner is acting as bare trustee for a beneficiary who is absolutely entitled to that partner's share of the partnership profits, and the beneficiary is chargeable to tax on those profits, the beneficiary is treated for income tax purposes as if he were a partner and is subject to the same rules for reporting as actual partners. [*ITTOIA 2005, s 848A; FA 2018, Sch 6 paras 1, 4(1)*].

See **55.5** PENALTIES as regards penalties for non-compliance.

It is not possible for individual partners to make, in their personal tax returns, supplementary claims for expenses incurred on the partnership's behalf or capital allowances on personal assets used in the partnership. If not included in the accounts, adjustments for such expenditure etc. must be included in the tax computation forming part of the partnership return. (Revenue booklet SAT 1(1995), para 5.17 and see Revenue Tax Bulletin August 1997 p 453).

It is not mandatory for the personal returns of the partners to be consistent with the partnership return (for example if partners believe the partnership return to be incorrect) (*King v HMRC* FTT (TC 5163), [2016] SFTD 1033, [2016] UKFTT 409 (TC)).

Provisions similar to those in **64.4** above apply as regards amendments and corrections to partnership returns. Where a return is so amended or corrected (and, in the case of an HMRC correction, it is not rejected by the taxpayer), the partners' returns will be amended by HMRC accordingly, by notice to each partner concerned. [*TMA 1970, ss 12ABA, 12ABB; FA 2018, Sch 6 paras 10(3), 14*].

Unsolicited returns

The rule in **64.2** above under unsolicited returns applies equally to partnership returns. In this case, the notice treated as given is one requiring the partner to deliver a return on or before the day on which it was, in fact, delivered by the partner or, if later, the earliest day that could be specified under *TMA 1970, s 12AA* above. [*TMA 1970, s 12D; FA 2019, s 87(1)(3)–(8)*].

Withdrawal of notice to make a return

A partner who has received a notice to make a partnership return may request HMRC to withdraw the notice. Such a request can be made within two years after the end of the tax year or relevant period to which the notice relates or, in exceptional circumstances, within such extended period as HMRC may agree. A partner cannot make such a request if he has already filed the return for the year.

HMRC may then agree to withdraw the notice by notifying the person accordingly and specifying the date on which the notice is withdrawn. The withdrawal does not prevent HMRC subsequently issuing a further notice for the same year or period.

A notification of withdrawal may also contain provision cancelling a penalty for failure to make a return (see **55.5** PENALTIES).

[*TMA 1970, s 12AAA*].

Enquiries into returns

Provisions similar to those in **64.6** above apply as regards enquiries into partnership returns. The notice of enquiry may be given to a successor (see above) of the person who made the return. The giving of such notice is deemed to include the giving of notice under *TMA 1970, s 9A* (or, where applicable, the equivalent corporation tax provision) to each partner affected. Similarly the rules in **64.8–64.10** above apply in relation to partnership returns, except that there is no provision equivalent to *TMA 1970, s 9C* for amendment of returns by HMRC while an enquiry remains in progress. There is also appropriate provision for HMRC by notice to each partner to consequentially amend the partner's own return; such notices do not operate to close an enquiry (*Reid v HMRC* UT, [2020] STC 622, [2020] UKUT 61 (TCC)).

If a dispute in relation to the return is referred to a Tribunal as in **64.14** below, the enquiry window for that return is extended to the 'quarter day' next following the first anniversary of the day on which HMRC received notification of the referral. For this purpose, the '*quarter days*' are 31 January, 30 April etc. If notice of enquiry is given as a result of the referral of any such dispute at a time when such notice could no longer have been given otherwise, or after an enquiry into the return has been fully completed, the enquiry is limited to matters to which the dispute relates or which are affected by it. The same applies if a partial closure notice has been issued in relation to the matters to which the dispute relates or which are affected by it. There is nothing to prevent a second enquiry being made into a partnership return where that return has been amended as a consequence of any such dispute. A referral of a dispute whilst an enquiry is in progress, in relation to any matter to which the dispute relates or which is affected by it, does not restrict the scope of the enquiry but may be taken into account in the enquiry.

[*TMA 1970, ss 12AC, 12AD, 28ZA–28ZE, 28B; F(No 2)A 2017, Sch 15 paras 7, 8, 10, 11, 13, 44; FA 2018, Sch 6 paras 10(4)–(6), 14*].

Overseas partners in investment partnerships

For returns made (for whatever period) on or after 15 March 2018, investment partnerships (those not carrying on a trade, profession or UK property business) are not required to include tax references of overseas partners (those outside the charge to UK income tax or corporation tax), provided the period covered by the return is one in respect of which the partnership is required to report details of the partner to HMRC under the FATCA agreement or the Common Reporting Standard (see **35.13, 35.14** HMRC — ADMINISTRATION). There is provision to require the partnership to subsequently provide the tax references in the event of the reporting requirement no being met. [*TMA 1970, s 12ABZA; FA 2018, Sch 6 para 8*].

Limited liability partnerships — anti-avoidance

FA 2020 includes provisions intended to make it clear that where a limited liability partnership (LLP) has delivered a return on the basis of operating with a view to profit (as required by *ITTOIA 2005, s 863* — see **52.25** PARTNERSHIPS) but has, in fact, been operating without a view to profit, HMRC can nevertheless amend the LLP's return (and the LLP members' returns) to give effect to the conclusions reached when an enquiry into the return has been completed. This is achieved by treating the LLP return in such circumstances as if it were a legitimate return. It applies not only for the purposes of enquiries into returns (see above) but for those of follower notices (see **4.44** ANTI-AVOIDANCE) and accelerated payment notices (see **4.49** ANTI-AVOIDANCE).

The above is treated as always having had effect, but it does not apply to any return where, before 11 March 2020, a court or tribunal determined, in proceedings to which an LLP was a party, that the 'return' was not a partnership return under *TMA 1970, s 12AA* (see above) and the determination had not (before that date) been set aside or overturned on appeal.

[*TMA 1970, s 12ABZAA; FA 2020, s 104(1)–(3)*].

The above legislation confirms the decision of the UT in *HMRC v Inverclyde Property Renovation LLP* UT, [2020] UKUT 161(TCC), after the decision had gone against HMRC before the First-tier Tribunal.

Simon's Taxes. See **A6.406, B7.130, B7.523, B7.524.**

Partnership statements

[64.13] Every partnership return as in **64.12** above must include a statement (a partnership statement) showing, in respect of the period covered by the return and each period of account ending within that period:

(a) the partnership income or loss from each source, after taking into account any relief or allowance due to the partnership and for which a claim is made under any of the provisions in *TMA 1970, s 42(7)* (see **16.1** CLAIMS);
(b) the amount of consideration for each disposal of partnership property; and
(c) the amounts of any tax deducted at source from partnership income,

and each partner's share of that income, loss, consideration, tax deduction or tax credit.

In the case of an individual carrying on a trade etc. in partnership, the personal tax return under *TMA 1970, s 8* (see **64.2** above) should include each amount which, according to any '*relevant partnership statement*' (i.e. one falling to be made, as respects the partnership, for a period which includes all or any part of the tax year or its basis period), is the individual's share of any income, loss, tax, credit or charge for the period covered by the statement. Where a partnership is dissolved before filing a return, this does not disqualify the partners from reporting their shares in their personal returns (*Shanks v HMRC* FTT (TC 7118), [2019] UKFTT 279 (TC)).

Where a partnership is itself a partner

In relation to returns for 2018/19 onwards, if the partnership making the return (DEF) is a partner in another partnership (ABC), and ABC carries on a trade, profession or business, the amounts in (a)–(c) above, to the extent that they arise from DEF's membership of ABC, must be shown separately in the partnership statement from amounts that do not so arise. (If DEF is a partner in more than one partnership, those amounts must be shown separately for each.) DEF must include in its partnership statement its share of all such amounts from any partnership statement made by ABC for all or any part of DEF's return period. DEF must also state which of the four assumptions made by ABC (see below) it has applied in arriving at the amounts so included.

If the partnership making the return (ABC) has a partner which is itself a partnership (DEF), ABC must compute, and include in its partnership statement, DEF's share of the income, loss, consideration, tax deduction or tax credit in (a)–(c) above on *each* of the following four assumptions about DEF: (i) that it is a UK resident individual; (ii) that it is a non-UK resident individual; (iii) that it is a UK resident company; and (iv) that it is a non-UK resident company. However, ABC may disregard any one or more of these assumptions if it is clear from information provided by ABC to HMRC that no 'indirect partner' (see **52.3** PARTNERSHIPS) in ABC is a person of a type described by the assumption in question. If this information is to be provided to HMRC, it must be included in the partnership return and must include the names of all indirect partners and information as to their status (i.e. whether an individual, company etc.) and their residence status for the period in question.

[*TMA 1970, ss 8(1B)(1C), 12AB; FA 2016, Sch 1 paras 51(6), 73; FA 2018, Sch 6 para 6(3)–(5)*].

Simon's Taxes. See B7.523.

Partnership return conclusive as to partnership shares

[64.14] In relation to returns for 2018/19 onwards, a partnership return as in **64.12** above (which includes the partnership statement in **64.13**) is conclusive for tax purposes as to whether a person has a share in the profits or losses of the partnership and what that person's share is. This applies regardless of whether the person is chargeable to tax on the partnership profits.

In light of the above, there is a procedure for dealing with disputes between partners over the allocation of profits or losses reported in the return. A party to the dispute may refer it to the Appeal Tribunal for determination. (A dispute over the amount (before sharing) of the partnership profits or losses is not within the scope of this procedure.) A referral must be made no later than the first anniversary of the date of delivery of the return or, if the dispute relates to an amendment to the return, the first anniversary of the date of the amendment. The party making the referral must simultaneously give notice of the referral to both HMRC and the reporting partner (i.e. the partner responsible for dealing with the return or that partner's successor). The reporting partner must in turn notify all the other partners and any other person who appears to be a party to the dispute.

If the Tribunal determines that the return was incorrect in regard to a person's share of the partnership profits or losses, it must state what the return should have contained instead. HMRC must then amend the return accordingly, and (so far as is necessary to effect the consequences) must also by notice to any party to the proceedings or any member of the partnership amend their personal, trustee or company tax return. If, before the Tribunal determines the dispute, the reporting partner gives HMRC notice that all the partners (whether or not party to the proceedings) have agreed in writing that the partnership return either is correct without variation or requires correcting in a particular manner, the like consequences shall ensue as would have ensued if the Tribunal had determined the dispute in like manner. within the period of 30 days beginning with the date of the agreement. A party to the written agreement may by notice to the other parties that the party repudiates or resiles from the agreement, but must do so within 30 days beginning with the date of the agreement. HMRC may by notice to the reporting partner object to the agreement, but must do so within 30 days beginning with the date on which they receive notice of the agreement. In either case, the said consequences do not then ensue.

A partnership return which has been the subject of a referral under this procedure cannot be the subject of another such referral, unless the new referral relates to a dispute arising in consequence of an amendment to the partnership return and is the first referral following that amendment.

[*TMA 1970, s 12ABZB; FA 2018, Sch 6 paras 10(2), 14*].

Simon's Taxes. See **B7.524**.

Pay as you earn

[64.15] See **53.21** PAY AS YOU EARN and **67.12** SELF-ASSESSMENT.

Trustees

[64.16] A return may be required from a trustee under *TMA 1970, s 8A* — see **64.2** above.

65

Savings and Investment Income

Cross-references. See **1.5** ALLOWANCES AND TAX RATES for the dividend allowance and rates of tax on dividend income; **1.6**, **1.7** ALLOWANCES AND TAX RATES for the personal savings allowance and rates of tax on savings income; **23** DEDUCTION OF TAX AT SOURCE; **29** ENTERPRISE INVESTMENT SCHEME; **30** EXEMPT INCOME; **44.3** *et seq.* LIFE ASSURANCE POLICIES for gains on such policies; **71** SHARE-RELATED EMPLOYMENT INCOME AND EXEMPTIONS; **75.59** TRADING INCOME re copyrights and royalties; **80** UNIT TRUSTS ETC.; **81** VENTURE CAPITAL TRUSTS.

Simon's Taxes. See **E1.4**.

Other sources. See HMRC Savings and Investment Manual.

Introduction to savings and investment income

[65.1] A list of the types of income included within the charge to tax on savings and investment income can be found at *ITTOIA 2005, s 365.*

The term 'savings and investment income' includes income arising to UK residents, whether or not the source is in the UK, and to non-UK residents to the extent that the income arises from a UK source. Where the tax year is a split year (see **63.19** RESIDENCE AND DOMICILE), income arising to a UK resident individual in the overseas part of the split year is treated for these purposes as arising to a non-UK resident. [*ITTOIA 2005, s 368*].

If an item of income is both a trade receipt and potentially within the charge to tax as savings and investment income (including dividend income), priority is given to the charge on trade profits. See **75.94** TRADING INCOME for circumstances in which investment income may be a trade receipt.

Similarly, where an item of income is employment, pension or social security income and also potentially savings and investment income, then priority is given to the charge to tax under *ITEPA 2003*, though this priority rule does not apply either to dividends from UK companies or to the charge at **65.21** below. [*ITTOIA 2005, s 366*]. However, in *HMRC v PA Holdings Ltd* CA 2011, 82 TC 1 in which bonuses were paid to employees in the form of dividends, the CA held that, notwithstanding any priority rule, once it was concluded that income was from employment it could not possibly be taxed as dividend income; one must consider the substance and purpose of the payments made and not the mere form in which they were received. This decision was subsequently applied in *Manthorpe Building Products Ltd v HMRC* FTT (TC 1778), [2012] UKFTT 82 (TC); 2012 STI 1207 and *James H Donald (Darvel) Ltd v HMRC* UT 2015, [2016] STC 616.

Interest

[65.2] Income tax is charged on the full amount of interest arising in the tax year, whether from a source within or outside the UK, (unless the REMITTANCE BASIS (**61**) applies). The person liable for any tax charged is the person receiving or entitled to the interest. [*ITTOIA 2005, ss 369(1), 370, 371*].

Interest on the proceeds of a life policy paid to the parents of a geologist missing in Angola was held not to be taxable as the parents were not the persons 'entitled' to it (*A & Mrs G Pope v HMRC*, UT, [2012] STC 2255).

Interest is receivable net of tax if tax is deductible at source under the provisions in **23** DEDUCTION OF TAX AT SOURCE or under paying and collecting agent arrangements. Otherwise, interest is receivable gross. See **1.6** ALLOWANCES AND TAX RATES as regards the rates of tax applicable to 'savings income'.

Any interest element included in a compensation package for the mis-selling of certain financial products, such as mortgage endowment policies or payment protection insurance, is normally taxable as savings income under general principles. If the package includes a payment for personal injury, interest on such payment is tax-exempt, as is interest on compensation for mis-sold pensions (see **30.15** EXEMPT INCOME). (Revenue Tax Bulletin August 2004 pp 1131, 1132).

The definition of interest is extended to include:

- building society dividends and other distributions;
- open-ended investment company interest distributions (see **80.3** UNIT TRUSTS ETC.);
- authorised unit trust interest distributions (see **80.2** UNIT TRUSTS ETC.);
- industrial and provident society payments;
- certain distributions of offshore funds (see **65.5** below);
- any dividend paid by an investment trust company which the company has opted to treat as an interest distribution (see **65.6** below);
- funding bonds (see **65.7** below);
- payments from the Financial Services Compensation Scheme (see below);
- discounts (see below); and
- (before 12 February 2019) payments (other than repayments of principal) in respect of '*regulatory capital securities*' (other than shares) as defined by *SI 2013 No 3209, Reg 2*, including Additional Tier 1 instruments and Tier 2 instruments issued in accordance with EU Regulations; for regulatory capital securities issued before 1 January 2019 this continues until 31 December 2023.

[*ITTOIA 2005, s 369(2); SI 2013 No 3209, Regs 1, 2, 5, 8; FA 2019, Sch 20 paras 1, 16*].

For details of certain types of interest which are exempt from tax, see **30.30, 30.34** EXEMPT INCOME.

Building society dividends and other distributions are charged to tax as interest and not as dividends. [*ITTOIA 2005, s 372*]. This does not apply to dividends etc. on 'core capital deferred shares', i.e. deferred shares that form part of the core tier one capital of a building society. [*SI 2013 No 460*].

Payments from the Financial Services Compensation Scheme ('FSCS') that are made on or after 6 October 2008 and which represent interest are treated as interest. A payment represents interest if it is calculated in the same way as interest which would have been paid to the recipient but for the circumstances giving rise to the making of payments under the FSCS, e.g. the failure of a bank or other financial institution. If the financial institution in default would have deducted tax from interest, the FSCS deducts an equivalent amount from the payment representing the interest; the payment is then treated in the hands of the recipient as an amount received net of basic rate tax. [*ITTOIA 2005, s 380A; ITA 2007, s 979A(1)–(4), (7)*].

The interest element of an Interest Rate Hedging Products redress payment from a bank is considered taxable and will have basic rate tax deducted at source (www.gov.uk/government/uploads/system/uploads/attachment_data/file/389395/irhpredress_PDF.pdf). See also **75.56**(e) TRADING INCOME.

Discounts are treated as interest for the purposes of the charge to tax. [*ITTOIA 2005, s 381*]. This is provided they represent income rather than capital. Where lending carries a reasonable commercial rate of interest and is either issued at a discount or repayable at a premium, it may normally be assumed that the discount or premium is not in the nature of income; the discount or premium may reflect factors other than the time value of money, such as market risk. See HMRC Savings and Investment Manual SAIM2220–2240. In *Healey v HMRC* UT, [2015] STC 1749, a case involving interest coupon stripping, the appellant was held to be within the charge to income tax on discounts. A similar conclusion was reached in *Savva v HMRC* UT, [2015] STC 1873. See now **65.8** below for the charge on 'disguised interest', and see **65.24–65.30** below for the separate charge to tax in relation to deeply discounted securities.

Premium bond prizes are free of income tax (and capital gains tax). For other National Savings products, see www.nsandi.com/savings.

Designated client account interest passed on to the client by a solicitor is within the definition of 'savings income' (see **1.6** ALLOWANCES AND TAX RATES) and payments made to clients in respect of money held in undesignated client accounts are similarly treated (Revenue Tax Bulletin February 1998 pp 512, 513).

Any dividend, bonus or other sum payable to a shareholder in either:

- a registered industrial and provident society; or
- a UK agricultural or fishing co-operative,

is treated as interest for income tax purposes if it is payable by reference to the amount of the shareholder's holding in its share capital. [*ITTOIA 2005, s 379*].

Dormant Bank and Building Society Accounts Act 2008 provides the framework for a scheme under which balances in dormant bank and building society accounts can be transferred to a reclaim fund to be used for social or environmental purposes. Any interest arising to a dormant account on transfer to the reclaim fund, and any interest arising on or after that date whilst the balance is held in the reclaim fund, is treated as if it arose at the time (if any) when the money is repaid to the depositor on a claim by him. [*FA 2008, s 39; SI 2011 No 22, Regs 1, 8*].

See **3.2, 3.7** ALTERNATIVE FINANCE ARRANGEMENTS for the treatment of alternative finance return and profit share return, both as therein defined, as if it were interest.

Simon's Taxes. See E1.404–E1.411.

Valuation of interest in kind

[65.3] There are rules as follows for placing a monetary value on interest paid in the form of goods or services or a 'voucher'.

- Where payment is in goods or services, the amount of the payment is to be taken to be equal to the market value, at the time the payment is made, of the goods or services.

- Where payment is in the form of a voucher, the amount of the payment is to be taken to be equal to whichever is the higher of:
  - the face value of the voucher;
  - the amount of money for which the voucher is capable of being exchanged; and
  - the market value, at the time the payment is made, of any goods or services for which it is capable of being exchanged.

For these purposes, a '*voucher*' means a voucher, stamp or similar document or token which is capable of being exchanged for money, goods or services.

[*ITTOIA 2005, s 370A*].

Simon's Taxes. See **E1.411A.**

Government stocks

[65.4] As regards deduction arrangements for UK public revenue dividends (other than gilt-edged securities), see **23.12** DEDUCTION OF TAX AT SOURCE.

Interest on gilt-edged securities is paid without deduction of tax. The option of deduction is, however, available (see **23.12** DEDUCTION OF TAX AT SOURCE). [*ITA 2007, s 893*].

Tax exemption for non-UK residents

The Treasury issues securities ('FOTRA securities') on terms that interest and gains arising from the securities are exempt from tax provided that they are beneficially owned by persons not resident in the UK. 'FOTRA' means 'Free of Tax to Residents Abroad'. See HMRC Savings and Investment Manual SAIM1180.

Provided that any conditions imposed are complied with, nothing in the *Tax Acts* overrides the above exemption, although this does not confer any exemption from charge where income is treated under anti-avoidance provisions as income of a UK resident etc. (see **70.29, 70.30** SETTLEMENTS, **4.14–4.18** ANTI-AVOIDANCE).

If interest forms part of the profits of a UK trade, exemption does not generally apply (depending on the Treasury conditions of issue) (see *Owen v Sassoon* Ch D 1950, 32 TC 101).

Interest from a FOTRA security held in trust is exempt (and therefore the beneficial ownership test is satisfied) where none of the beneficiaries of the trust is UK resident for the tax year in which the interest arises. Before 2013/14, this exemption applied where none of the beneficiaries of the trust was UK *ordinarily* resident at the time the interest arose; this continues to be the case in relation to FOTRA securities issued before 6 April 2013 and acquired by the trust before that date.

[*ITTOIA 2005, ss 713–716; F(No 2)A 1931, s 22*].

See **50.12** NON-RESIDENTS for the special position of *non-resident banks, insurance companies and dealers in securities* carrying on business in the UK.

For the exemption of non-residents from income tax on interest on local authority securities expressed in a foreign currency, see **23.12** DEDUCTION OF TAX AT SOURCE.

Simon's Taxes. See **E1.539–E1.542.**

Offshore fund distributions

[65.5] Certain dividends of 'offshore funds' are treated as interest for income tax purposes. This applies only where the offshore fund fails to meet the 'qualifying investments test' at any time in the 'relevant period'. For this purpose, a dividend includes any distribution that would otherwise be treated as a dividend for income tax purposes. Where the qualifying investments test is met throughout the relevant period, distributions continue to be taxed as dividends and not as interest.

For the meaning of '*offshore funds*', see **51.2** OFFSHORE FUNDS.

An offshore fund fails to meet the '*qualifying investments test*' if the market value of the fund's 'qualifying investments' exceeds 60% of the market value of all of the assets of the fund (excluding cash awaiting investment). The term 'qualifying investments' refers broadly to interest-bearing investments and to investments that are economically similar in substance to interest-bearing investments; for the full list, see *CTA 2009, s 494(1)*.

The '*relevant period*' is the last period of account of the offshore fund that ends before the dividend is paid, provided that the profits available for distribution at the end of that period (and not since used, by distribution or otherwise) equal at least the amount of the dividend (aggregated with any simultaneous distribution made by the offshore fund). In any other case, the relevant period is the period of account of the offshore fund in which the dividend is paid. In both cases, if the period of account in question is less than twelve months, the relevant period is taken to be the twelve months ending on the last day of the period of account in question.

[*ITTOIA 2005, s 378A*].

Simon's Taxes. See **E1.408A.**

Designated distributions from investment trust companies

[65.6] The Treasury have power to make regulations (see *SI 2009 No 2034*) enabling investment trust companies (within *CTA 2010, s 1158*) to designate specified dividends as payments of interest. The *regulations* set out the conditions under which an investment trust company may opt to designate a dividend (or part thereof) as an interest distribution. A recipient of such an interest distribution who is within the charge to income tax is treated for income tax purposes as if the interest distribution were a payment of yearly interest on the date it is made.

No tax is deductible at source from interest distributions made on or after **6 April 2017** (see **23.12**(g) DEDUCTION OF TAX AT SOURCE). For 2016/17 and earlier years, basic rate tax is deductible at source under *ITA 2007, s 874* from interest distributions unless:

- the recipient is either a company or the trustees of a unit trust scheme; or
- either the 'residence condition' or the 'reputable intermediary condition' is met with respect to the recipient on the date of the distribution.

The '*residence condition*' requires that any one of the following be met:

- the recipient has made a valid declaration that he is not resident in the UK; or
- the interest distribution is received by the personal representative of a deceased person in his capacity as such and the deceased had made a declaration, valid at the time of his death, that he was not resident in the UK; or
- the interest distribution is received by the personal representative of a deceased person in his capacity as such and the personal representative makes a valid declaration that the deceased, immediately before his death, was not resident in the UK; or
- the interest distribution is made to a trust under which the whole of the income is the income of a person other than the trustees and that person has made a valid declaration that he is not resident in the UK; or
- the interest distribution is made to a trust to which the above does not apply and the trustees have made a valid declaration that they are not resident in the UK and that each beneficiary is not resident in the UK.

Declarations as above must be made to the investment trust in prescribed form and must contain specified details and undertakings.

The '*reputable intermediary condition*' requires broadly that the interest distribution is paid on behalf of the recipient to a company which is subject to certain money laundering controls, and that the investment trust has reasonable grounds for believing that the recipient is not resident in the UK. If it subsequently transpires that the recipient was in fact resident (or, as the case may be, ordinarily resident), the tax which should have been deducted is payable to HMRC by the investment trust.

An investment trust must supply the recipient of any distribution with a certificate showing *inter alia* the date and amount of the distribution, the extent to which it is an interest distribution and the extent to which it is a dividend, and the amount of any tax deducted.

[*FA 2009, s 45; FA 2017, Sch 5 paras 2, 5; SI 2009 No 2034*].

Funding bonds

[65.7] Issues of 'funding bonds' to a creditor in respect of a liability to pay interest on a debt are charged to tax as interest. The issue is treated for income tax purposes as if it were a payment of interest equal to the market value of the bond at the date of issue. Charities are exempt from tax on all funding bond interest. '*Funding bonds*' includes bonds, stocks, shares, securities or certificates of indebtedness, whether issued by a government, a public institution, a public authority or a body corporate. Where the issue of funding bonds has been so treated, the redemption of the bonds is not treated as a payment of interest.

The person by or through whom the bonds are issued must retain bonds equal in value to income tax on the deemed interest at the basic rate in force for the year of issue of the bonds. The retained bonds can then be tendered to HMRC. Where this is impractical, information as to the recipients and the amount received must be supplied to HMRC.

HMRC can use the bonds tendered to it by the issuer to satisfy a tax repayment claim by the creditor.

In light of the rules at **65.3** above, it is made clear that a funding bond does not include any instrument providing for payment in the form of goods or services or a voucher.

[*ITTOIA 2005, ss 380, 754; ITA 2007, ss 939, 940, 940A*].

The reference above to interest on a debt includes a return under ALTERNATIVE FINANCE ARRANGEMENTS (3). [*ITA 2007, ss 564M(2), 564Q(4)*].

Simon's Taxes. See **E1.410.**

Disguised interest

[65.8] A charge to income tax applies where a person is party to an arrangement (as widely defined and whether or not legally enforceable) which produces for him a return, in relation to any amount, which is 'economically equivalent to interest'. The charge does not apply if the person became party to the arrangement before 6 April 2013, except where the transitional rules below have effect. The charge is on the full amount of the return arising in the tax year; the person liable is the person receiving or entitled to the return.

For these purposes a return in relation to any amount is '*economically equivalent to interest*' if (and only if):

- it is reasonable to assume that it is a return by reference to the time value of that amount of money;
- it is at a rate reasonably comparable to what is (in all the circumstances) a commercial rate of interest (see HMRC Savings and Investment Manual SAIM2730); and
- when the person becomes party to the arrangement or, if later, when the arrangement begins to produce a return for him, there is no practical likelihood (see HMRC Savings and Investment Manual SAIM2740) that the return will cease to be produced in accordance with the arrangement unless the person by whom it falls to be produced is prevented (e.g. by reason of insolvency) from producing it.

Avoidance of double taxation

Where a return is chargeable to income tax both as disguised interest under these provisions and under other legislation (or would be chargeable under the other legislation were it not for an available exemption), the other legislation takes priority. If at any time a tax other than income tax is charged in relation to a return on which income tax is charged under these provisions, the chargeable person can make a claim for one or more consequential adjustments to be made in respect of the other tax in order to avoid double taxation. An officer of HMRC must then make such of the consequential adjustments claimed (if any) as are just and reasonable. Consequential adjustments may be made for any period, by way of an assessment, modification of an assessment, amendment of a claim or otherwise, and regardless of any statutory time limit.

Exception for returns from certain shares

There is an exemption from the disguised interest provisions for arrangements that involve certain types of listed share. It applies where the arrangement involves only 'excluded shares' and no 'relevant arrangement' has been made (by any person) in relation to those shares. Shares are '*excluded shares*' if they are admitted to trading on a 'regulated market' (as defined by EU law) and:

- they were issued before 6 April 2013; or
- at the time of issue no arrangements involving only the shares would produce a return which is economically equivalent to interest.

An arrangement is a '*relevant arrangement*', in relation to excluded shares, where:

- the arrangement is made on or after 6 April 2013; and
- it is reasonable to assume that a main purpose of the arrangement is to secure that arrangements involving only the shares produce a return which is economically equivalent to interest (see HMRC Savings and Investment Manual SAIM2780).

Transitional

As a consequence of the introduction of the disguised interest rules above, a number of pre-existing anti-avoidance provisions were repealed. If any of those repealed provisions applied before 6 April 2013 in relation to an arrangement which produces for a person a return which is economically equivalent to interest, the disguised interest rules do apply for 2013/14 onwards in relation to that arrangement, notwithstanding that the person became party to the arrangement before 6 April 2013. The repealed provisions were: *ITTOIA 2005, ss 555–569* (disposals of futures and options involving guaranteed returns); *ITA 2007, ss 596–606* (deemed manufactured payments: stock lending arrangements); and *ITA 2007, ss 607–614* (price differences under repos).

[*ITTOIA 2005, ss 381A–381E; SI 2019 No 689, Reg 13(3)*].

Simon's Taxes. See **E1.405A.**

Peer-to-peer lending — bad debt relief

[65.9] Peer-to-peer (P2P) lending is an area of financial technology that enables lending and borrowing through the intermediary of a P2P website (a '*platform*'). P2P platforms connect investors with funds to lend with individuals or small businesses looking to borrow. The lender invests a lump sum using the platform which is then lent in small sub-loans to a number of borrowers. P2P lending is regulated by the Financial Conduct Authority, and the platforms are regulated under *Financial Services and Markets Act 2000, Pt 4A*.

Relief is available to enable P2P lenders to set any losses incurred, from loans which default, against interest they receive from other P2P loans. The loss (i.e. the irrecoverable amount of the loan) is set against interest received by the lender in that tax year from any other P2P loans made through the same P2P platform. The relief operates automatically without the need for a claim. It is given as a deduction in calculating net income for the year (see Step 2 in the calculation of income tax liability at **1.10** ALLOWANCES AND TAX RATES).

A bad debt arises when any outstanding amount of the principal of a P2P loan becomes irrecoverable, provided the lender has not assigned the right to recover that principal. For this purpose, 'irrecoverable' means irrecoverable other than by legal proceedings or by the exercise of any right granted by way of security for the loan.

In the event of an excess of bad debt relief over the interest against which it is set as above, the lender can claim under *ITA 2007, s 412B* to set the excess against interest received in the tax year from P2P loans made through other platforms. If there is still an excess the lender can claim under *ITA 2007, s 412C* to carry this forward against interest received from P2P loans (whether or not through the same platform) in the next four tax years, earliest year first.

If bad debt relief is given and some or all of the principal of the defaulted loan is subsequently recovered, the amount recovered is treated for income tax purposes as P2P interest received by the lender at the time of recovery. If a person assigns for consideration his right to recover any amount, he is treated as having recovered it at that time.

If a person (A) is assigned for consideration the right to recover the principal of a P2P loan, and the right is assigned through a P2P platform (P), then (provided A has not further assigned the right) the loan is treated for the purposes of bad debt relief as having been made by A and as having been made through P. The amount (if any) of the principal of the loan which can subsequently be treated as irrecoverable cannot exceed the consideration given by A.

Bad debt relief is restricted to P2P loans made on genuine commercial terms and not as part of arrangements a main purpose of which is to obtain a tax advantage. The lender must be a person who would be liable for income tax charged on the interest, and either the lender or the borrower (or both) must be (i) an individual; or (ii) a partnership of two or three persons; or (iii) an unincorporated body other than a partnership. In the case of (ii) or (iii) at least one of the members must not be a body corporate. If the lender is not within (i), (ii) or (iii), the loan must be a non-business loan or a loan not exceeding £25,000.

Generally, anything done by a nominee or bare trustee for a person is treated for these purposes as done by that person. In a case in which a person obtains any other income tax relief properly attributable to the loan, there is provision to prevent double relief.

[*ITA 2007, ss 412A–412J; FA 2016, s 32(1)(2)*].

Historically, a small number of P2P loans have been eligible for relief as a capital loss under CGT legislation. This has especially applied for lenders using P2P platforms specialising in loans to small businesses. *TCGA 1992, s 39* precludes expenditure deductible in computing income from being allowable expenditure for CGT, so irrecoverable loans are not eligible for capital loss relief.

Dividends and other distributions from UK-resident companies

[65.10] Dividends and other distributions of UK-resident companies are treated as income for income tax purposes (even if the distribution would otherwise be treated as capital) and charged to income tax.

The amount charged to tax in the year is the value of the dividend paid (or distribution made) in the year. The person liable for the charge is the one to whom the distribution is made (or treated as made) or the person receiving or entitled to the distribution.

Special rules apply to stock dividends (see **65.19** below).

Any income falling within both *ITEPA 2003* and *ITTOIA 2005* provisions is to be dealt with under the *ITTOIA 2005* provisions. There is an exception to this rule at **26.4** DISGUISED REMUNERATION.

[*ITTOIA 2005, s 383–385; ITEPA 2003, s 716A; FA 2016, Sch 1 paras 5, 73*].

See **1.5** ALLOWANCES AND TAX RATES for the rates of tax applicable to dividend income.

For the definition of a distribution, see *CTA 2010, s 1000*. A payment which is a repayment of share capital following a share capital or share premium reduction is not a distribution and is not chargeable to income tax. If, however, share capital or share premium is reduced and a reserve is created and treated as a realised profit, that treatment is applied for tax purposes also, with the result that any payment out of a reserve of this type is a distribution chargeable to income tax (see http://webarchive.nationalarchives.gov.uk/20140109143644/http://www.hmrc.gov.uk/specialist/draft-amended-indiv-guidance.pdf). In *Baker v HMRC* FTT (TC 2790), [2013] UKFTT 394 (TC), 2013 STI 3162, a case involving a purchase by a company of its own shares, it was held that there had been no distribution as the purchase was in breach of company law and therefore void.

HMRC may by notice require any person in whose name any shares or loan capital are registered to provide details as to the ownership of those investments. [*ITTOIA 2005, s 401B(1); FA 2016, Sch 1 paras 14, 73*].

Tax certificates

A company paying a dividend to a person must, within a reasonable period, send a 'tax certificate' to that person. Where it pays the dividend into the person's bank or building society account it may send the certificate to the bank or building society instead. A '*tax certificate*' is a written statement showing the amount of the dividend and the date of payment. [*CTA 2010, ss 1104–1106; FA 2016, Sch 1 paras 42, 73*]. The recipient of a distribution, or something treated as a distribution, can require the paying company to provide a written statement showing the amount or value of the distribution. [*CTA 2010, s 1100; FA 2016, Sch 1 paras 39, 73*].

Simon's Taxes. See E1.412.

Dividends etc. received by non-UK residents

[65.11] Where a non-UK resident's income for a tax year includes a distribution of a company, he is treated as having paid income tax at the dividend ordinary rate (see **1.5** ALLOWANCES AND TAX RATES) on the amount or value of the distribution. The tax treated as paid is not repayable. [*ITTOIA 2005, s 399; FA 2016, Sch 1 paras 11, 73*].

Simon's Taxes. See E1.415.

Choice of income or capital return

[65.12] Companies may use special purpose share schemes (often called 'B share schemes') to offer shareholders the option to receive, instead of a dividend, a similar amount via an issue of new shares. The shares issued are subsequently purchased by the company or are sold to a pre-arranged third party. Any amount thus received by a shareholder is chargeable to income tax as an 'alternative receipt'.

A shareholder receives an '*alternative receipt*' if:

- the company has given the shareholder the choice to receive either a dividend or something else;
- the shareholder has chosen to receive, from the company or a third party, something else (the alternative receipt) which is of the same or substantially the same value as the dividend; and
- that receipt would not otherwise be subject to income tax.

The receipt is treated as a distribution made to the shareholder by the company in the tax year in which it is received.

It does not matter if the choice given to the shareholder is subject to any conditions being met or to the exercise of any power. Where a person is offered one thing subject to a right to choose another thing instead, he is treated as making a choice if he fails to exercise the right. For example, where a shareholder will receive a bonus B share if he so elects and a bonus C share if he fails to elect, a failure to elect counts as a choice to receive the C share (Treasury Explanatory Notes to the first 2015 Finance Bill).

If at any time a tax other than income tax (e.g. capital gains tax) is charged in relation to the alternative receipt, then in order to avoid a double charge to tax, the recipient may make a claim for consequential adjustments to be made in respect of the other tax.

[*ITTOIA 2005, s 396A; FA 2016, Sch 1 paras 9, 73*].

Income treated as above as arising to trustees of a settlement is treated as being income chargeable at the dividend trust rate. See **70.12** SETTLEMENTS.

Distributions in a winding-up (anti-avoidance)

[65.13] A distribution made to an individual in respect of shares in the winding up of a UK resident company is a distribution within **65.10** above, and thus within the charge to income tax, if all the following conditions are met:

(a) immediately before the winding-up, the individual has at least a 5% interest in the company (by reference to either ordinary share capital or voting rights, and taking account of a proportionate value of any shares held jointly or in common with other persons);
(b) the company is a close company (broadly a company controlled by five or fewer participators — see Tolley's Corporation Tax under Close Companies) either when it is wound up or at any time in the two years preceding the winding-up;
(c) at any time within the two years following the distribution, the individual carries on a trade or activity similar to that previously carried on by the company or an effective 51% subsidiary of the company; and
(d) it is reasonable to assume, having regard to all the circumstances (especially the fact that (c) above is met), that the winding-up has as a main purpose the avoidance or reduction of a charge to income tax.

The condition at (c) above is met whether the individual carries on the trade as a sole trader, through a partnership in which he is a partner or through a company in which he (or a connected person) is a participator with at least a 5% interest. An individual who is involved with the carrying on of a trade or activity by a person connected with him is regarded as carrying it on for this purpose. *ITA 2007, s 993* applies to determine if persons are connected (as in **19** CONNECTED PERSONS).

None of the above applies to the extent that:

- the amount of the distribution does not exceed the amount that would result in no gain accruing for capital gains tax (CGT) purposes (generally the CGT base cost of the shares); or
- the distribution is a distribution of irredeemable shares.

Similar rules apply to distributions from non-UK resident companies. For purpose of (b) above, the company is treated as a close company if it would have been a close company had it been UK resident.

[*ITTOIA 2005, ss 396B, 404A; FA 2016, s 35*].

HMRC will not give clearances on the application of these rules. See HMRC Company Taxation Manual CTM36350 and, for general guidance on the rules, CTM36300.

Distribution repaying shares or security issued in earlier distribution

[65.14] The following applies where:

(a) a company makes a distribution which is a distribution only because it consists of redeemable share capital, or a security, issued by the company in respect of shares in, or securities of, the company and otherwise than for new consideration; and
(b) the company makes a subsequent distribution repaying the share capital or the principal of the security which constituted the distribution in (a) above.

Where a person is liable to income tax on the distribution in (a) above, his liability on the distribution in (b) above is reduced. The amount of the reduction is the lower of his liability on the distribution in (a) and his liability on the distribution in (b). In ascertaining those liabilities, the distribution in question is treated as the lowest part of the person's dividend income for the tax year in which it is made. If both distributions are made in the same tax year, the distribution in (b) is treated as the next lowest part of the person's dividend income for that year. The reduction is made at Step 6 of the calculation of income tax liability (see **1.10**, **1.12** ALLOWANCES AND TAX RATES).

[*ITTOIA 2005, s 401; FA 2016, Sch 1 paras 12, 73*].

Distributions from Real Estate Investment Trusts (REITs)

[65.15] A distribution received from a Real Estate Investment Trust (REIT) by a shareholder within the charge to income tax is treated in the shareholder's hands as profits of a UK property business to the extent that it is paid out of the tax-exempt profits of the REIT. Basic rate tax is deducted at source by the REIT. Distributions made by an REIT out of profits other than tax-exempt profits are taxed in the same way as any other distribution made by a UK resident company. See **60.24** PROPERTY INCOME for more details.

Close company distributions: temporary non-UK residence

[65.16] The following applies where an individual is 'temporarily non-UK resident', the 'year of departure' is 2013/14 or any subsequent year and the individual has income in the form of close company distributions. For what is meant by '*temporarily non-UK resident*', the '*year of departure*' and the '*period of return*', see **63.29** RESIDENCE AND DOMICILE.

The following consequences ensue where:

(a) a 'relevant distribution' is made or treated as made to the individual in the 'temporary period of non-UK residence' (**63.29**(d) RESIDENCE AND DOMICILE);
(b) the tax year in which it is made or treated as made (the '*distribution year*') is a tax year for which the individual is UK resident; and
(c) the income tax charged on the distribution is less than it would have been had it not been for the existence of a double tax treaty.

Where the distribution year in (b) above is not the tax year that consists of or includes the 'period of return' (year R), the individual's total income for income tax purposes for Year R is increased by an amount equal to that on which tax would have been charged on the distribution if the double tax treaty were disregarded. The 'notional UK tax' on the relevant distribution is allowed as a credit against the individual's liability to income tax for year R; the credit is given in the form of a reduction under Step 6 of the calculation of income tax liability at **1.10** ALLOWANCES AND TAX RATES. The '*notional UK tax*' on a relevant distribution is so much of the income tax paid by the individual for the distribution year as is attributable on a just and reasonable basis to the relevant distribution.

If the distribution year is the tax year that consists of or includes the 'period of return', the tax charged on the relevant distribution is charged and assessed without regard to the existence of the double tax treaty.

A dividend or other distribution is a '*relevant distribution*' if:

- it is a distribution of a close company (see Tolley's Corporation Tax under Close Companies); and
- it is made or treated as made to the individual because he was a 'material participator' (or an associate of a material participator) in the company at any time in the period consisting of the year of departure (or the UK part of the year of departure if it is a split year) and the three preceding tax years. A '*material participator*' is a participator who has a 'material interest' in the company (within *CTA 2010, s 457*). '*Participator*' and '*associate*' are as defined in *CTA 2010, Pt 10* (see Tolley's Corporation Tax under Close Companies).

However, a distribution in the form of a cash dividend is *not* a '*relevant distribution*' to the extent (if any) that it is paid in respect of 'post-departure trade profits'. The extent to which a distribution is paid in respect of such profits is to be determined on a just and reasonable basis. '*Post-departure trade profits*' are trading profits of the company arising in an accounting period beginning after the start of the temporary period of non-UK residence. They also include so much of any trading profits arising in an accounting period straddling the start of that temporary period as is attributable (on a just and reasonable basis) to a time after the start of that temporary period.

Nothing in any double tax treaty is to be read as preventing the individual from being chargeable to income tax under these provisions.

[*ITTOIA 2005, ss 368A, 401C*].

Simon's Taxes. See **E1.415A.**

Dividends from non-UK resident companies

[65.17] Income tax is also charged on dividends from companies not resident in the UK. The charge is on the amount of dividends arising in the tax year (though DOUBLE TAX RELIEF (**27**) may be available for any foreign tax suffered). Dividends of a capital nature are excluded from the charge. [*ITTOIA 2005, ss 402–404*].

Temporary non-UK residence

[65.18] Where the 'year of departure' is 2013/14 or any subsequent year, certain dividends receivable by an individual from non-UK resident companies during a period when the individual is 'temporarily non-UK resident' are treated as if they were receivable in the 'period of return'. This does not apply to the extent (if any) that a dividend is paid in respect of 'post-departure trade profits'. Otherwise, the effect is that the charge to tax applies for the tax year that consists of or includes the period of return.

For what is meant by '*temporarily non-UK resident*', the '*year of departure*' and the '*period of return*', see **63.29** RESIDENCE AND DOMICILE.

A dividend is treated in this way if:

(a) the individual receives or becomes entitled to it in a 'temporary period of non-UK residence' (see **63.29**(d) RESIDENCE AND DOMICILE);
(b) it is a dividend of a company that would be a close company (see Tolley's Corporation Tax under Close Companies) if it were UK resident;
(c) the individual receives or becomes entitled to it by virtue of his being a 'material participator' (or an associate of a material participator) in the company at any time in the period consisting of the year of departure (or the UK part of the year of departure if it is a split year) and the three preceding tax years; and
(d) the individual is not liable to tax under **65.17** above on the dividend but would have been if he had received or become entitled to it in the period of return. This includes a case where liability to tax could be avoided by the making of a claim to double tax relief, even if no such claim has yet been made.

In (c) above, a '*material participator*' is a participator who has a 'material interest' in the company (within *CTA 2010, s 457*). '*Participator*' and '*associate*' are as defined in *CTA 2010, Pt 10* (see Tolley's Corporation Tax under Close Companies).

As previously stated, the above does not apply to the extent (if any) that a dividend is paid in respect of 'post-departure trade profits' (as defined in **65.16** above and calculated as if the company were UK resident). The extent to which a dividend is paid in respect of such profits is to be determined on a just and reasonable basis.

Nothing in any double tax treaty is to be read as preventing the individual from being chargeable to income tax in respect of any dividend treated as receivable in the period of return.

Application of remittance basis

Where the remittance basis applies (see **61.2** REMITTANCE BASIS) to the individual for the tax year that consists of or includes the period of return, any dividend within the above description that was remitted to the UK in the temporary period of non-UK residence is to be treated as remitted to the UK in the period of return.

[*ITTOIA 2005, ss 368A, 408A*].

Stock dividends

[65.19] Shares issued by a UK company in lieu of a cash dividend are chargeable to income tax on the individual beneficial shareholder on an amount equal to the cash equivalent. Similarly chargeable are bonus shares issued in respect of shares held under terms which carry the right to the bonus.

The cash equivalent is normally the amount of the cash dividend alternative. If, however, the difference between the cash dividend alternative and the market value of the shares received is at least 15% of the market value of the shares received, the cash equivalent is taken to be that market value instead. If there is no cash dividend alternative, as in the case of bonus shares, the cash equivalent is the market value of the shares received. For listed shares, market value is determined as at the first day of dealing; for other shares, it is determined as at the earliest day on which the company was required to issue the shares.

The shareholder is treated as receiving the shares on the earliest date on which the company was required to issue the shares. Where more than one person is entitled to the shares issued, apportionment is made according to their respective interests.

If the shareholder is a settlement and a cash dividend would have been 'accumulated or discretionary income', the trustees are chargeable under these provisions (see also **70.11** SETTLEMENTS). '*Accumulated or discretionary income*' is as defined in **70.11** except that it does not include income arising under a charitable trust.

[*ITTOIA 2005, ss 409, 410, 410A, 411–413, 414, 414A, Sch 2 para 78A; FA 2016, Sch 1 paras 1, 17, 73*].

Stock dividends issued to personal representatives during the administration period are deemed to be part of the aggregate income of the estate (see **22** DECEASED ESTATES).

Temporary non-UK residence

Special rules apply where an individual is 'temporarily non-UK resident', the 'year of departure' is 2013/14 or any subsequent year and the individual has income in the form of close company stock dividends. These rules are similar to those for close company distributions at **65.16** above. For what is meant by '*temporarily non-UK resident*' and '*year of departure*', see **63.29** RESIDENCE AND DOMICILE. [*ITTOIA 2005, ss 368A, 413A*].

Capital gains tax

The issue of shares treated as income as in above does not constitute a reorganisation of share capital within *TCGA 1992, ss 126–128*. The person acquiring the shares is treated for capital gains tax purposes as having acquired them for whichever of the cash dividend alternative or the market value was used in determining the amount treated as income. [*TCGA 1992, s 142*].

Simon's Taxes. See **E1.420**.

Enhanced stock dividends received by trustees of interest in possession trusts

[65.20] Where the trustees of an interest in possession trust have concluded that either:

(a) an enhanced stock dividend belongs to the income beneficiary; or
(b) it forms part of the trust's capital; or
(c) while adding the enhanced stock dividend to capital, the trustees should compensate the income beneficiary for the loss of the cash dividend he would otherwise have received,

and the view they have taken of the trust law position is supportable on the facts, HMRC will not seek to challenge what the trustees have done. The income tax consequences of each of the views at (a)–(c) above are as follows.

(i) As in (a) above the beneficiary is beneficially entitled to the shares comprised in the dividend, the provisions described at **65.19** above apply.
(ii) As in (b) above the stock dividend is regarded as capital, there is no income tax liability.
(iii) The payment in (c) above to the beneficiary is an annual payment from which basic rate tax must be deducted.

For full details of this treatment and of the capital gains tax consequences, and for differences under Scottish law, see HMRC SP 4/94.

Release of loan to participator in close company

[65.21] Where a close company that is chargeable to tax under *CTA 2010, s 455* in respect of a loan or advance to a participator (or to an associate of a participator) (see Tolley's Corporation Tax under Close Companies), releases or writes off the debt, the amount released or written off is included in the taxable income of the borrower for the year in which the release or write-off occurs.

Generally the person liable to income tax is the person to whom the loan or advance was made. If, however, a loan or advance made to a partnership or LLP on or after 20 March 2013 is released or written off such as to be within these provisions, the person liable to income tax is any partner who is an individual; if there is more than one individual, the liability is apportioned between the partners who are individuals in a just and reasonable manner.

[*ITTOIA 2005, ss 415–420, 421, 421A; FA 2016, Sch 1 paras 1, 18, 19, 73*].

Where an amount released or written off is charged as above, that amount is not charged as taxable earnings under *ITEPA 2003, ss 188–190* — see **28.34** EMPLOYMENT INCOME.

Where sums owed by a director were released by a company by way of a bonus for his services to the company, the FTT decided that no release had taken place for the purposes of this legislation but that the loan had been repaid, which left the amount in question to be taxed as earnings as HMRC had contended (*Esprit Logistics Management Ltd v HMRC* FTT (TC 6517), [2018] SFTD 1318, [2018] UKFTT 287 (TC)).

Simon's Taxes. See **E1.424**.

Temporary non-UK residence

[65.22] Where the 'year of departure' is 2013/14 or any subsequent year, a debt released or written off during a period when the borrower (if an individual) is 'temporarily non-UK resident' is treated for the purposes of **65.21** above as if it were released or written off in the period of return. The effect is that the charge to tax applies for the tax year that consists of or includes the period of return. For what is meant by '*temporarily non-UK resident*', the '*year of departure*' and the '*period of return*', see **63.29** RESIDENCE AND DOMICILE.

The above applies to the extent that the debt is released or written off in the 'temporary period of non-UK residence' (see **63.29**(d) RESIDENCE AND DOMICILE) and the individual is not liable for tax under **65.21** above in respect of the release or write-off but would have been if it had taken place in the period of return. This includes a case where liability to tax could be avoided by the making of a claim to double tax relief, even if no such claim has yet been made.

Nothing in any double tax treaty is to be read as preventing the individual from being chargeable to income tax in respect of any debt treated as released or written off in the period of return.

[*ITTOIA 2005, ss 368A, 420A*].

Purchased life annuities

[65.23] The income element of a 'purchased life annuity' payment is regarded as income for income tax purposes from which tax is deducted under *ITA 2007, s 901* (see **23.7–23.10** DEDUCTION OF TAX AT SOURCE). Tax is charged on the full amount of the payment arising in the year, subject to the special rules for foreign income (see **32** FOREIGN INCOME) and a credit for the tax deducted at source. The capital element is not treated as income and is thus exempt from the charge to income tax (see **23.11** DEDUCTION OF TAX AT SOURCE).

HMRC operate special arrangements whereby the income element of a purchased life annuity payment may be paid gross if the annuitant is UK resident but unlikely to have any income tax liability for the tax year in question (HMRC Relief Instructions Manual RE1600, 1620). The annuitant must send completed HMRC form R89 to the payer of the annuity.

A '*purchased life annuity*' is one which is purchased for money or money's worth from a person whose business it is to grant annuities and which is payable for a term ascertainable only by reference to the end of a human life (notwithstanding that the annuity may in some circumstances end before or after the life).

[*ITTOIA 2005, ss 422–426*].

The charge to tax on the income element of a purchased life annuity is at the rate of tax applicable to savings income (see **1.6** ALLOWANCES AND TAX RATES). Tax is deductible at source at the basic rate.

A proportion of a purchased life annuity payment is regarded as capital, and therefore exempt from income tax, and is thus not within the above charge. The exemption does not apply to annuities purchased wholly or partly with sums satisfying the conditions for relief under *ICTA 1988, s 266* (life assurance premiums), annuities purchased following a direction in a will or annuities purchased to provide for an annuity payable as a result of a will or settlement out of income of property disposed of by the will or settlement. It also does not apply to annuities forming part of the income of a trade or to annuities chargeable as pension income under *ITEPA 2003* (due to the priority rules at **65.1** above).

If the amount of the annuity payments depends solely on the duration of a human life or lives, the same proportion of each payment is the exempt amount of that payment. The proportion is that which the purchase price bears to the actuarial value of the annuity payment, determined by reference to mortality tables or, failing that, by the Government Actuary. If the amount of the annuity payments depends on an additional contingency, each payment is regarded as exempt to the extent it does not exceed a fixed sum given by a formula in *ITTOIA 2005, s 721*. If a particular payment falls short of the fixed sum, the shortfall is added to the fixed sum for the next payment, and so on. If the term of the annuity does not depend solely on the duration of a human life or lives, the exempt proportion or the fixed sum is adjusted as is just and reasonable, having regard to the contingencies affecting the annuity. Consideration given partly for an annuity and partly for something else is apportioned on a just and reasonable basis in determining the purchase price of the annuity for these purposes.

[*ITTOIA 2005, ss 717–724, Sch 2 paras 143–145*].

Procedure

Under the current regulations, the annuity provider sends the annuitant a form on which he must enter or confirm certain basic information and make a declaration as to whether the annuity is a purchased life annuity which is eligible for the partial tax exemption. The annuitant must then return the form to the annuity provider. Until the annuitant returns the completed form, the annuity must be treated as one for which no part of the payments are eligible for the tax exemption. Upon receipt of the form, the annuity provider must calculate and enter the exempt capital element of the annuity, if any, in accordance with a prescribed mortality table. He must then return the form to the annuitant within 30 days of receipt or, if later, within 30 days of the date of the first payment under the annuity, and send a photocopy to HMRC within three months of the date of that first payment. If the annuitant fails to provide a completed form, the annuity provider must supply HMRC with the known details of the annuity within that three-month period.

If the annuity is purchased from a non-UK insurer, the latter must usually nominate a UK resident tax representative in accordance with set procedures. The representative will normally undertake the above compliance instead of the annuity provider.

[*FA 2007, s 46(5)–(7)(9); SI 2008 No 562; SI 2019 No 689, Reg 29*].

Simon's Taxes. See **E1.428–E1.430D.**

Deeply discounted securities

Charge to tax

[65.24] A profit on the disposal of a 'deeply discounted security' (as defined at 65.26 below) is treated as taxable income. Tax is charged on the full amount of such profits arising in the tax year. The person liable is the person making the disposal. The profit on disposal is the excess (if any) of the disposal proceeds over the acquisition cost and is taken to arise when the disposal occurs. See below for certain disposals treated as made at market value. No deduction is available for incidental costs of acquisition or disposal, except to the extent that any such costs were incurred before 27 March 2003 (and see also the special rules at **65.25** below for listed securities held since before 27 March 2003). No relief is available for a loss on disposal, again subject to the special rules at **65.25** below for listed securities held since before 27 March 2003.

If the securities are located outside the UK, the REMITTANCE BASIS (**61**) applies where appropriate.

See **65.27** below for special rules on strips of government securities and **65.28** below for special rules on corporate strips.

A disposal of a deeply discounted security occurs:

- when it is redeemed; or
- when it is transferred by sale, exchange, gift or otherwise; or
- when it is converted under its terms into shares in a company or other securities (including other deeply discounted securities).

A transfer or acquisition under an agreement is treated as taking place when the agreement is made if entitlement to the security passes at that time. A conditional agreement is treated as made when the condition is met.

Where a conversion into euros of deeply discounted securities from the currency of a State which has adopted the euro (a '*euroconversion*' — see *SI 1998 No 3177, Reg 3*) is effected solely by means of an exchange or conversion of those securities, the conversion is not treated as constituting either a transfer or a conversion. Provision is made for an adjustment to the acquisition cost in respect of any cash payment received as a result of the conversion.

Where the holder of a deeply discounted security dies, he is treated as having transferred the security immediately before his death to his personal representatives and thus as having made a disposal.

Market value disposals and acquisitions

The following transfers are treated for the above purposes as made at market value (determined as for capital gains tax purposes) at the time of the disposal:

(a) a transfer made otherwise than by way of bargain at arm's length;
(b) a transfer between CONNECTED PERSONS (**19**);
(c) a transfer for consideration not wholly in money or money's worth;
(d) a transfer treated as made on death (see above); and
(e) a transfer by personal representatives to a legatee (as defined by *ITTOIA 2005, s 440(6)(7)*).

In each case, the transferee is also treated as having acquired the security at market value.

Where a deeply discounted security is converted under its terms into shares in a company or other securities, such that a disposal is treated as occurring (see above), the proceeds of the disposal are the market value of the shares or other securities at the time of the conversion. Where the conversion is into securities which are themselves deeply discounted securities, the acquisition cost of those securities for the purposes of these provisions is their market value.

Where a security is issued to a person in accordance with the terms of a 'qualifying earn-out right', the amount paid for the acquisition is taken to be the sum of the market value, immediately before the issue, of the right to be issued with the security in accordance with those terms and any amount payable for the issue in accordance with those terms. A '*qualifying earn-out right*' is so much of any right conferred on a person as:

(i) constitutes the whole or any part of the consideration for the transfer by him of shares in or debentures of a company or for the transfer of the whole or part of a business or interest in a business carried on alone or in partnership;
(ii) consists in either a right to be issued with securities of another company or a right which is capable of being discharged in accordance with its terms by the issue of such securities; and
(iii) is such that the value of the consideration referred to in (i) above is unascertainable at the time when the right is conferred.

[*ITTOIA 2005, ss 427–429, 437–442, 460(1)(3), Sch 2 para 79*].

Simon's Taxes. See **D9.5**.

Listed securities held since before 27 March 2003

[65.25] Where a deeply discounted security has been held continuously since before 27 March 2003 by the person making the disposal *and* the security was listed on a recognised stock exchange (within *ITA 2007, s 1005*) at some time before that date, relief is available for losses and for incidental costs of acquisition and disposal as follows.

A loss on disposal, i.e. the excess (if any) of acquisition cost over disposal proceeds (together with any incidental costs of disposal and/or acquisition incurred before 6 April 2015), is allowed as a deduction in computing net income for the year of disposal (at Step 2 of the calculation of income tax liability at **1.10** ALLOWANCES AND TAX RATES). A claim for the relief must be made no later than the first anniversary of 31 January following the tax year in which the disposal occurs. See **65.29** below as regards trustees.

There is a cap on the total amount of prescribed income tax reliefs that individuals can claim. See **1.11** ALLOWANCES AND TAX RATES. The above relief for losses is one of the prescribed reliefs.

Where the loss is sustained by a charity or a pension scheme, such that a profit on the disposal would have been relieved from tax under any of the provisions listed at *ITTOIA 2005, Sch 2 paras 82, 83* (i.e. general tax reliefs for charities and pension funds), the loss can only be set off against profits from other disposals of deeply discounted securities in the tax year in which the loss is sustained.

A profit on disposal is reduced by any incidental costs of acquisition and/or disposal incurred before 6 April 2015.

See **65.27** below for special rules on strips of government securities.

Restriction of a loss: connected persons transactions

Notwithstanding the above, no loss relief is available to a person on the transfer of a deeply discounted security to a person connected with him (within **19** CONNECTED PERSONS), where:

- the transferor acquired the security on issue;
- the amount paid by transferor in respect of the acquisition exceeded the market value of the security at the time of issue; and
- either:
  - (a) the transferor was, at the time of issue, connected (as above) with the issuer; or
  - (b) the following conditions are met:
    - (i) the security was issued by a close company (as in *CTA 2010, Pt 10 Ch 2*, but without the exclusion of non-UK resident companies); and
    - (ii) the transferor controlled (within *CTA 2010, ss 450, 451*) that company at the time of issue together with other persons to whom securities of the same kind were also issued.

[*ITTOIA 2005, ss 453–456, Sch 2 paras 82, 83*].

Meaning of 'deeply discounted security'

[65.26] Subject to the exceptions below, a security is a '*deeply discounted security*' if, at the time it is issued, the amount payable on maturity or any other possible occasion of redemption exceeds (or may exceed) the issue price by more than:

$R \times 0.5\% \times Y$

Where:

R = the amount payable on maturity or any other possible occasion of redemption; and

Y = the number of years in the 'redemption period' up to a maximum of 30.

The '*redemption period*' is the period between the date of issue and the date of the occasion of redemption in question. So if a security is issued at £80 and is redeemable in 35 years' time at £100, the calculation is £100 × 0.5% × 30 = £15. As this is less than the £20 difference between issue price and maturity value, the security is a deeply discounted security. If, however, the issue price is £135 and the security is redeemable in 20 years' time at £150, the calculation is £150 × 0.5% × 20 = £15, and the security is not, therefore, a deeply discounted security.

If the redemption period is not a complete number of years but is less than 30 years, the value of Y in the above calculation is increased by a twelfth for each month or part month in excess of a whole number of years. Any interest payable on an occasion of redemption is disregarded in establishing the value of R (and see *Pike v HMRC* CA, [2014] STC 2549). Where a security is issued in accordance with the terms of a qualifying earn-out right, its issue price is taken to be the amount paid to acquire it, determined as in **65.24** above.

Notwithstanding the above, none of the following can be deeply discounted securities:

(a) shares in a company;
(b) gilt-edged securities (other than strips — see below);
(c) 'excluded indexed securities' (but see below);
(d) LIFE ASSURANCE POLICIES (**44**); and
(e) capital redemption policies.

Strips of government securities are always treated as being deeply discounted securities (see **65.27** below).

A possible occasion of redemption (other than maturity) is ignored for the purposes of the above calculation if either of the following two conditions is met. The first is that:

- the security may be redeemed on the occasion at the option of a person other than its holder;
- it is issued to a person not connected with the issuer; and
- the obtaining of a tax advantage (within *CTA 2010, s 1139*) by any person is not one of the main benefits that might have been expected to accrue from the provision for redemption on that occasion.

The second condition is that redemption on that occasion can be achieved only on the exercise of an option that is exercisable only on an event adversely affecting the holder (see *ITTOIA 2005, s 431(8)*) or the default of any person, but the condition is met only if exercise of the option on that occasion appears unlikely at the time of issue.

If a security was not a deeply discounted security only because the first of these conditions is met, but at some time after its issue it is acquired by, or its holder becomes, a person connected with the issuer, the security is treated as a deeply discounted security from that time onwards. Notwithstanding (c) above, an 'excluded indexed security' (see below) can be a deeply discounted security in these circumstances.

If a person (P) not connected with the issuer acquires a security issued to or held by a person connected with the issuer and treated as a deeply discounted security for that reason alone, the security ceases to be a deeply discounted security from the time of P's acquisition of it.

For the above purposes, the rules in **19** CONNECTED PERSONS apply to determine whether persons are connected, but without taking any account of the security under review or any security issued under the same prospectus.

Meaning of 'excluded indexed security'

For the above purposes, a security is an '*excluded indexed security*' if, broadly, its redemption value is found by indexing its issue price by reference to the value of chargeable assets of a particular description or by an index of the value of such assets (but not the retail prices index or similar price indices). See *ITTOIA 2005, s 433* for the full definition. If the terms of issue provide that the redemption value will be at least a specified percentage of the issue price regardless of movements in the index, the security cannot be an excluded indexed security if the specified percentage exceeds 10%.

Securities issued in separate tranches

The following special rules apply where securities are issued under the same prospectus but on separate occasions. If securities in any one of the separate issues are not deeply discounted securities, securities in the subsequent issues are not deeply discounted securities either, *unless* they fall to be treated as such only because of their being issued to, or coming to be held by, a person connected with the issuer (see the rules above).

If none of the securities in the first issue is a deeply discounted security, but at least some of the securities in one or more later issues are deeply discounted securities (or would be were it not for the foregoing rule), the rule below applies for any disposal or acquisition after the time when the following condition is first met. The condition is that the aggregate nominal value of the deeply discounted securities exceeds the aggregate nominal value of all other securities so far issued under the prospectus. The rule is that all securities issued under the prospectus at any time (including subsequent issues) are treated as being deeply discounted securities and as having been acquired as such. For the purpose only of applying this rule in the case of a person not connected with the issuer, securities falling to be treated as deeply discounted securities only because of their being issued to, or coming to be held by, a person connected with the issuer (see above) are treated as if they were not deeply discounted securities.

[*ITTOIA 2005, ss 430–436, 460(1)(2)*].

In determining whether a security is a 'deeply discounted security' it is necessary, on a purposive construction of the statutory definition, that there should be a real possibility of a deep gain occurring. In the instant case, terms of issue which were essential for the securities to qualify as deeply discounted securities had to some extent no practical reality and had therefore to be disregarded. (*Astall and another v HMRC* CA, 80 TC 22).

Strips of government securities

[65.27] Every strip is treated as a deeply discounted security, even it would not otherwise be so. This and the following rules were originally limited to strips of UK Government (i.e. gilt-edged) securities. In relation to securities acquired on or after 27 March 2003, strips of overseas government securities are also within the rules. However, for these purposes, strips do not include 'corporate strips', for which see **65.28** below. A strip, in relation to any stock or bond (the underlying security), is a security that meets the conditions in *ITTOIA 2005, s 444*.

For the purposes of applying the deeply discounted security provisions:

- on the exchange of a security for strips of that security, the acquisition cost of each strip is determined by apportioning the market value of the security *pro rata* to the market value of each strip;

- when a person consolidates strips into a single security by exchanging them for that security, each strip is treated as being redeemed at market value;
- any person holding a strip on 5 April in any tax year, and not disposing of it on that day, is treated as having transferred it at market value on that day and to have immediately re-acquired it at the same value (without incurring any incidental costs in connection with the notional transactions); and
- the Treasury has wide powers to modify by regulations the deeply discounted security provisions as they apply to strips.

Losses

A loss on disposal, i.e. the excess (if any) of acquisition cost over disposal proceeds (*disregarding* any incidental costs of disposal and/or acquisition), is allowed as a deduction in computing net income for the year of disposal (at Step 2 of the calculation of income tax liability at **1.10** ALLOWANCES AND TAX RATES). A claim for the relief must be made no later than the first anniversary of 31 January following the tax year in which the disposal occurs. But see the anti-avoidance rules below and see **65.29** below as regards trustees. For disposals before 27 March 2003, incidental costs could be taken into account in determining the amount of a loss; they may still be taken into account where the disposal falls within **65.25** above.

There is a cap on the total amount of prescribed income tax reliefs that individuals can claim. See **1.11** ALLOWANCES AND TAX RATES. Relief for losses on strips of government securities is one of the prescribed reliefs.

Special rules for determining market value

The market value of a strip or of any security exchanged for strips of that security is determined in accordance with regulations (see *SI 2015 No 616*). [*ITTOIA 2005, s 450*]. The regulations require calculations based on prices quoted in the London Stock Exchange Daily Official List or, for overseas strips or securities not included in that list, an equivalent foreign stock exchange list.

Anti-avoidance

The following anti-avoidance provisions apply.

(i) With effect in relation to any strip held on 15 January 2004 or subsequently acquired (disregarding any notional re-acquisition as above): where, as a result of a scheme or arrangement aimed at securing a tax advantage, a person acquires (or acquired) a strip at more than market value or transfers or redeems a strip at less than market value (disregarding any costs incurred in connection with any acquisition, transfer etc.), market value is substituted for the purpose of determining both profits and losses. Market value for these purposes is determined in accordance with the special rules above.

(ii) Where, as a result of a scheme or arrangement aimed at securing a tax advantage or producing an allowable loss for capital gains tax purposes, the circumstances are (or might have been) as in (i) above and a payment resulting in a capital loss falls to be made other than in respect of the acquisition or disposal of a strip, that loss is not allowable for capital gains tax purposes.

(iii) With effect in relation to any strip acquired on or after 15 January 2004 (disregarding any notional re-acquisition as above): a loss on the disposal of a strip is restricted for tax purposes *by* the amount (if any) by which proceeds are less than 'original acquisition cost'. A profit is restricted *to* the amount (if any) by which disposal proceeds exceed 'original acquisition cost'. These rules cannot reduce a loss or a profit to a negative amount, i.e. a profit cannot be converted into a loss or *vice versa*. '*Original acquisition cost*' is determined without taking account of any earlier notional transfers and re-acquisitions by the person concerned but otherwise takes account of any rule requiring market value to be substituted for actual cost.

[*ITTOIA 2005, ss 443–452, 460(2)(3), Sch 2 paras 80, 81; TCGA 1992, s 151C; FA 2007, Sch 26 para 5; SI 2015 No 616*].

In *Berry v HMRC* UT, [2011] STC 1057, a gilt strip planning scheme failed to produce an allowable loss. No amount was paid by the claimant for the gilt strips nor was there any transfer of the strips; the claimant suffered no economic loss. Similarly, in *Audley v HMRC* FTT (TC 1084), [2011] SFTD 597, it was held that no loss was sustained where the stated terms of a loan note had no commercial reality and were designed specifically to produce that loss.

Corporate strips

[65.28] Every 'corporate strip' is treated as a deeply discounted security, even it would not otherwise be so, in the hands of any person who acquires such a strip on or after 2 December 2004 and otherwise than in pursuance of an agreement entered into before that date. This is an anti-avoidance measure designed to thwart schemes that involve taking normal interest-bearing securities issued by companies and stripping the rights to some or all of the coupons away from the right to the repayment of the principal. The resultant rights have a value which is less than the amount which will eventually be paid by the issuer in respect of them, and thus produce the effect of discount. But, in the absence of this measure, the rights may not have been deeply discounted securities because the underlying security from which they derive was not issued at a discount.

For the purposes of these provisions, a person converts an 'interest-bearing corporate security' into corporate strips of the security if, as a result of any scheme or arrangements, he acquires, in place of the security, two or more separate assets each of which satisfies Condition A below and all of which (taken together) satisfy Condition B below. The rules equally apply where a corporate strip is itself stripped into separate assets.

Condition A is that the asset represents the right to, or secures, one or more 'stripped payments'. A '*stripped payment*' is a payment of (or corresponding to) the whole or a part of one or more payments (whether of interest or principal) remaining to be made under the security. Condition B is that the assets represent the right to, or secure, every payment so remaining to be made. Once a security has gone ex-dividend in respect of the next interest payment, that payment is no longer treated as one 'remaining to be made'.

A '*corporate strip*' is then defined as any asset which is, or has at any time been, one of the separate assets referred to above. However, an asset cannot be a corporate strip if it represents the right to, or secures, payments of (or corresponding to) a part of every payment remaining to be made under an 'interest-bearing corporate security' or a corporate strip. This is to ensure that a corporate strip is not created merely by the re-denomination of the principal into smaller amounts. Also, an asset cannot be a corporate strip in the case of any person if he acquired it, or entered into an agreement to acquire it, before 2 December 2004.

An '*interest-bearing corporate security*' is any interest-bearing security, including loan stock, other than one issued by a government (for which see **65.27** above) or a share in a company.

Where a person sells or transfers the right to one or more payments remaining to be made under a security, that is treated as a conversion into corporate strips followed by a sale of one or more of the assets created by that conversion.

The acquisition cost for income tax purposes of a corporate strip acquired by conversion is found by taking the cost of the original security (excluding any incidental costs of acquisition) and apportioning it between all the assets resulting from the conversion by reference to the proportion that the market value of each asset bears to the market value of all of them. If the converted security was itself a deeply discounted security, the conversion is treated as a transfer of that security, but for an amount equal to its acquisition cost. Where corporate strips are consolidated into a single security, they are treated as being thereby disposed of at their then market value.

There are anti-avoidance rules similar to those at **65.27**(i) above (disregarding the reference there to losses). For the purposes of those rules, market value is determined without regard to any increase or diminution in the value of a corporate strip as a result of the scheme or arrangement in question. Where, as a result of a scheme or arrangement aimed at securing a tax advantage or producing an allowable loss for capital gains tax purposes, the circumstances are (or might have been) as in **65.27**(i) above (as applied to corporate strips) and a payment resulting in a capital loss falls to be made other than in respect of the acquisition or disposal of a corporate strip, that loss is not allowable for capital gains tax purposes.

[*ITTOIA 2005, ss 452A–452G; TCGA 1992, s 151D*].

Trustees

[65.29] Profits chargeable under these provisions on the disposal of a deeply discounted security by trustees are treated for the purposes of *ITTOIA 2005, ss 619–648* (income treated as that of the settlor — see **70.25–70.35** SETTLEMENTS) as income arising under the settlement from the security, and for the purposes of **70.11** SETTLEMENTS as income arising to the trustees. To the extent that tax on such profits is chargeable on the trustees, it is chargeable at the trust rate (see **70.11** SETTLEMENTS).

In the case of trustees, relief for losses under **65.25** above can be set off only against profits from other disposals of deeply discounted securities in the tax year in which the loss is sustained.

See **65.27** above for special rules on strips of government securities. The above rule restricting the set-off of losses does *not* apply to a loss sustained by trustees on the disposal of a strip.

Non-resident trustees

Tax is not charged, and losses are not relieved, under the deeply discounted securities rules if the disposal is made by a settlement of which the trustees are non-UK resident.

[*ITTOIA 2005, ss 454(5), 457, 458*].

Miscellaneous

Accrued income scheme

[65.30] Deeply discounted securities within these provisions are outside the accrued income scheme, except where the person making the disposal has held the security continuously since before 27 March 2003 and the security was listed at some time before that date (see **2.2** ACCRUED INCOME SCHEME).

Transfer of assets abroad

Any profit realised by a person resident or domiciled outside the UK from a disposal within these provisions is treated as income becoming payable to that person under *ITA 2007, Pt 13 Ch 2* (see **4.14–4.18** ANTI-AVOIDANCE) in determining whether a UK resident individual has an income tax liability in respect of the profit or gain. [*ITTOIA 2005, s 459*].

Recovery of assets under Proceeds of Crime Act 2002, Pt 5

Where the transfer of a deeply discounted security is a *Pt 5* transfer under *Proceeds of Crime Act 2002* (as in **9.2**(x) CAPITAL ALLOWANCES) and no compensating payment is made to the transferor, it is not treated as a transfer for the purposes of these provisions. [*Proceeds of Crime Act 2002, Sch 10 paras 5, 10*].

66

Seed Enterprise Investment Scheme

Simon's Taxes. See E3.8.

Introduction to Seed Enterprise Investment Scheme

[66.1] The Seed Enterprise Investment Scheme (SEIS) is a tax-advantaged venture capital scheme similar to the ENTERPRISE INVESTMENT SCHEME (**29**) but focused on smaller, early stage companies. [*ITA 2007, s 257A*]. The main features of the SEIS are as follows.

- Income tax relief is available for investment in small companies (i.e. those with 25 or fewer employees and assets of up to £200,000) that are carrying on, or preparing to carry on, a new qualifying business.
- The relief is available on share subscriptions of up to £100,000 per individual. Relief can be carried back to the preceding year.
- The maximum relief is 50% of the amount subscribed.
- The shares must be retained for at least three years.
- The scheme incorporates many of the requirements of the Enterprise Investment Scheme (EIS), for example the requirement that the investor have no more than a 30% stake in the investee company.
- Any one company may raise investment of up to £150,000 under the SEIS in any three-year period.
- Chargeable gains on disposals of SEIS shares are exempt from CGT provided the shares are held for the requisite three-year period.
- Partial exemption applies to chargeable gains on disposals of assets if the proceeds are invested via the SEIS in the same tax year.

An investor is eligible for SEIS income tax relief in respect of an amount subscribed by him on his own behalf for an issue of shares in a company if:

- (with effect for shares issued on or after 15 March 2018) the risk-to-capital condition is met (see **66.20** below);
- the shares are issued to the investor;
- the general requirements at **66.21** below are met in respect of the shares;
- the investor is a 'qualifying investor' (see **66.28** below) in relation to the shares; and
- the company issuing the shares is a 'qualifying company' (see **66.34** below) in relation to the shares.

[*ITA 2007, s 257AA; FA 2018, s 14(2)(4)(5); SI 2018 No 931, Reg 2*].

This chapter concentrates on the income tax relief but a brief summary of the CGT reliefs is included at **66.17**, **66.18** below. For the form of the income tax relief see **66.3** below and for the restriction or withdrawal of relief in certain circumstances see **66.6** *et seq.* below.

For guidance on the SEIS, see www.gov.uk/topic/business-tax/investment-schemes and HMRC Venture Capital Schemes Manual VCM30000 *et seq.*

Advance assurance

A company may apply to HMRC for assurance, in advance of a share issue, that it will meet the qualifying conditions of the SEIS. Application should be made using form EIS/SEIS(AA) available at www.gov.uk/government/publications/enterprise-investment-scheme-advance-assurance-application-eisseisaa. On and after 4 December 2017 HMRC will not provide advance assurances for investments that, taking into account all the facts that HMRC have available, will fail, or appear likely to fail, the risk-to-capital condition at **66.20** below (HMRC Venture Capital Schemes Manual VCM8550).

Bare trustees and nominees

[66.2] SEIS relief is available where shares which satisfy the requirement at **66.22**(a) below are held on a bare trust for two or more beneficiaries as if each beneficiary had subscribed as an individual for all of those shares, and as if the amount subscribed by each was the total subscribed divided by the number of beneficiaries.

Shares subscribed for, issued to, held by or disposed of for an individual by a nominee are treated for the purposes of SEIS relief as subscribed for, issued to, held by or disposed of by the individual.

[*ITA 2007, s 257HE*].

SEIS income tax relief

[66.3] Subject to the carry-back facility described below, relief is given for the tax year in which the shares are issued. It is given by means of a reduction in what would otherwise be the individual's income tax liability (a '*tax reduction*') equal to tax at the SEIS rate for the year on the amount (or aggregate amounts) subscribed for shares in respect of which he is eligible for and claims SEIS relief. The SEIS rate is 50%. Investors can restrict their claim for SEIS relief to only some of the shares issued to them at any one time.

There is an upper limit of £100,000 on the amount of investment on which an individual may obtain relief in a tax year.

The tax reduction is given effect at Step 6 in the calculation of income tax liability at **1.10** ALLOWANCES AND TAX RATES. The order in which tax reductions are given against an individual's tax liability is set out at **1.12**, which also specifies that a tax reduction must be restricted to the extent (if any) that it would otherwise exceed the individual's remaining income tax liability after making all prior reductions.

Carry-back

Where shares in respect of which an individual is eligible for SEIS relief are issued at any time in any tax year, the individual may claim relief as if any number of shares up to the full number issued to him had been issued in the tax year preceding that in which they were actually issued. This carry-back is subject to the overriding rule that the total amount of investment on which relief can be obtained for any one year cannot exceed the annual maximum for that year. See **16.2** CLAIMS for general provisions regarding claims for payments made in one tax year to be carried back to an earlier year.

[*ITA 2007, s 257AB*].

Attribution of relief to shares

[66.4] Subject to any reduction or withdrawal of relief (see **66.6** *et seq.* below), where an individual's income tax liability is reduced for a tax year as in **66.3** above by reason of an issue or issues of shares made (or treated as made) in that year, the tax reduction is attributed to that issue or those issues (being apportioned in the latter case according to the amounts claimed for each issue). Issues of shares of the same class by a company to an individual on the same day are treated as a single issue for this purpose. A proportionate amount of the reduction attributed to an issue is attributed to each share in the issue in respect of which the claim was made and is adjusted correspondingly for any subsequent bonus issue of shares of the same class and carrying the same rights.

An issue to an individual part of which is treated as having been made in the preceding tax year (as in **66.3** above) is treated as two separate issues, one made on a day in the previous year.

Where relief attributable to an issue of shares falls to be withdrawn or reduced, the relief attributable to each of the shares in question is reduced to nil (if relief is withdrawn) or proportionately reduced (where relief is reduced).

[*ITA 2007, ss 257E, 257HI*].

Claims for relief

[66.5] A claim for SEIS income tax relief is valid only if it is made no later than the fifth anniversary of 31 January following the tax year in which the shares are issued.

The claimant must have received a compliance certificate from the issuing company before making the claim. The certificate must state that the requirements for relief, except in so far as they fall to be satisfied by the investor, are for the time being satisfied in relation to the shares in question.

A certificate cannot be issued without the authority of an HMRC officer. Where a notice under *ITA 2007, s 257GF* (see **66.19** below) has been given to HMRC, a compliance certificate must not be issued unless the authority is given or renewed after receipt of the notice. For appeal purposes, an officer's refusal to authorise a certificate is treated as a decision disallowing a claim by the company.

Before issuing such a certificate, the company must supply to HMRC a compliance statement (Form SEIS1) that the requirements for relief are satisfied for the time being and have been satisfied at all times since the shares were issued. The statement must contain such information and declarations as

HMRC may reasonably require, and a declaration that it is correct to the best of the company's knowledge and belief. A compliance statement cannot be supplied until at least one of the following conditions is met:

- at least 70% of the money raised by the share issue has been spent for the purposes of the qualifying business activity (see **66.47** below) for which it was raised;
- the 'new qualifying trade' (see **66.48** below) which constitutes the qualifying business activity (or to which that activity relates) has been carried on by the issuing company or a 'qualifying 90% subsidiary' (see **66.46** below) of that company for at least four months.

The compliance statement must state which of those conditions is met at the time the statement is made.

References above to requirements being satisfied for the time being are, in the case of requirements that cannot be satisfied until a future date, references to nothing having occurred to prevent their being satisfied.

If a certificate or statement is made fraudulently or negligently, or a certificate was issued when it should not have been, the issuing company is liable to a fine of up to £3,000.

No application for postponement of tax pending appeal can be made on the ground that relief is due under these provisions unless a claim has been duly submitted. No regard is to be had to SEIS relief for the purposes of PAY AS YOU EARN (**53**) unless a claim for relief has been made.

An issue to an individual part of which is treated as having been made in the preceding tax year (as in **66.3** above) is treated as two separate issues, one made on a day in the previous year.

[*ITA 2007, ss 257EA–257EG, 257HJ(8), 989*].

Reduction or withdrawal of relief

[66.6] The following provisions apply to reduce or withdraw SEIS income tax relief in certain circumstances. References to a reduction of relief include its reduction to nil, and references to the withdrawal of relief in respect of any shares are to the withdrawal of the relief attributable to those shares (see **66.4** above). Where no relief has yet been given, a reduction applies to reduce the amount which would otherwise be available for relief, and a withdrawal means the shares cease to be eligible for relief. [*ITA 2007, s 257HJ(4)*].

Disposal of shares

[66.7] Where, before the end of 'period B' below, the investor disposes of shares to which relief is attributable (see **66.4** above) or grants an option the exercise of which would bind him to sell the shares, then:

(a) if the disposal is at arm's length, relief attributable to those shares (see **66.4** above) is withdrawn or, if that relief is greater than an amount equal to tax at the SEIS rate (see **66.3** above) on the disposal consideration, is reduced by that amount; or

(b) if the disposal is not at arm's length, the relief is withdrawn.

Where the relief attributable to the shares is less than tax at the SEIS rate on the amount subscribed for the issue, the amount referred to in (a) above is correspondingly reduced. The calculation is similar to that used in connection with a reduction of EIS relief, for which see the example at **29.20** ENTERPRISE INVESTMENT SCHEME. An issue to an individual part of which is treated as having been made in the preceding tax year (as in **66.3** above) is treated as two separate issues, one made on a day in the previous year. Where the relief attributable to the shares has been reduced (otherwise than as a result of an issue of bonus shares — see **66.4** above) before the relief was obtained, then in calculating the amount referred to in (a) above the relief attributable to the shares before that reduction is used.

A share exchange within *TCGA 1992, s 136* is treated as a disposal of shares for these purposes, as is a disposal of an interest or right in or over shares. If, at any time in 'period A' below, a person grants the investor an option the exercise of which would bind the grantor to purchase any shares to which relief is attributable, the relief is withdrawn.

These provisions do not apply to a disposal of shares occurring as a result of the investor's death. See **66.15** below for transfers of shares between spouses or civil partners.

Periods A and B

'*Period A*' is the period beginning with the incorporation of the issuing company and ending immediately before the third anniversary of the issue of the shares.

'*Period B*' is the three-year period beginning with the issue of the shares.

Identification rules

For the above purposes, disposals are identified with shares of the same class issued on an earlier day before shares issued on a later day, i.e. first in/first out (FIFO). Where shares within two or more of the categories listed below were acquired on the same day, any of those shares disposed of (applying the FIFO basis) are treated as disposed of in the order in which they are listed, as follows:

- shares to which no SEIS income tax relief is attributable;
- shares to which SEIS income tax relief, but not SEIS reinvestment relief (see **66.18** below), is attributable;
- shares to which both SEIS income tax relief and SEIS reinvestment relief are attributable.

Shares transferred between spouses or civil partners living together are treated as if they were acquired by the transferee spouse or partner on the day they were issued (see also **66.15** below). Shares comprised in a 'new holding' following a reorganisation to which *TCGA 1992, s 127* applies (see Tolley's Capital Gains Tax under Shares and Securities) are treated as having been acquired when the original shares were acquired.

[*ITA 2007, ss 257AC, 257FA–257FD, 257HA, 257HH*].

Value received by investor

[66.8] If, at any time in period A (as in **66.7** above), the investor 'receives value' (other than 'insignificant value' — see below) from the issuing company, any relief attributable to those shares (see **66.4** above), and not previously reduced in respect of the value received, is withdrawn or, if that relief exceeds an amount equal to tax at the SEIS rate on the value received, is reduced by that amount. See **66.9** below for further computational provisions.

The provisions apply equally to value received from a person who is connected (within **19** CONNECTED PERSONS) with the issuing company at any time in period A, whether or not at the time the value is received.

An investor '*receives value*' from the issuing company if it:

(a) repays, redeems or repurchases any part of his holding of its share capital or securities, or makes any payment to him for giving up rights on its cancellation or extinguishment; or

(b) repays, in pursuance of any arrangements for or in connection with the acquisition of the shares in respect of which the relief is claimed, any debt owed to him other than one incurred by the company on or after the date of issue of those shares and otherwise than in consideration of the extinguishment of a debt incurred before that date; or

(c) pays him for the cancellation of any debt owed to him other than an '*ordinary trade debt*' (i.e. one incurred for normal trade supply of goods or services on normal trade credit terms (not in any event exceeding six months)) or one in respect of a payment falling within (i) or (vi) below; or

(d) releases or waives any liability of his to the company (which it is deemed to have done if discharge of the liability is twelve months or more overdue) or discharges or undertakes to discharge any liability of his to a third person; or

(e) makes a loan or advance to him (defined as including any debt either to the company (other than an 'ordinary trade debt' as above) or to a third party but assigned to the company) which has not been repaid in full before the issue of the shares; or

(f) provides a benefit or facility for him; or

(g) transfers an asset to him for no consideration or for consideration less than market value, or acquires an asset from him for consideration exceeding market value; or

(h) makes any other payment to him apart from an 'excluded payment' (see below) or a payment in discharge of an 'ordinary trade debt' as above; or

(i) is wound up or dissolved for genuine commercial reasons and not as part of a tax avoidance scheme, and he thereby receives any payment or asset in respect of ordinary shares held by him.

References to the investor include an 'associate' (see below) of the investor. All payments or transfers (direct or indirect) to, or to the order of, or for the benefit of, the investor or associate are brought within these provisions.

An investor does *not* receive value from a company by reason only of the payment to him (or an associate) of reasonable remuneration (including any benefit or facility) for services as a company director (and if the individual is an employee of the company as well as a director, for services as an employee).

If an individual to whom shares in a company have been issued entered into a convertible loan agreement with the company under the Future Fund on or after 20 May 2020, and subsequently receives value from the company under the terms of that agreement, the value received is ignored in relation to any SEIS relief attributable to shares issued before the individual entered into the agreement. This is to ensure that investors in a company who also support the company using a Future Fund convertible loan note will not lose relief on any previous SEIS investments when that loan is redeemed or converted into shares. The Future Fund was set up as part of Government support to companies impacted by the 2020 COVID-19 (coronavirus) pandemic (see www.gov.uk/guidance/future-fund).

Where value is received, the amount of that value is the amount paid to or received by the individual from the company; or the amount of the individual's liability extinguished or discharged; or the difference between the market value of the asset and the consideration (if any) given for it; or the net cost to the company of providing the benefit. In the case of value received within (a)–(c) above, the market value of the shares, securities or debt in question is substituted if greater than the amount receivable.

Additionally, the investor 'receives value' from the company if any person with a substantial interest in the company (see **66.30** below) or any director or employee of the company purchases any shares or securities of the company from him, or pays him for giving up any right in relation to such shares or securities. The value received is the amount received or, if greater, the market value of the shares etc.

Where relief is withdrawn or reduced by reason of a disposal (see **66.7** above), the investor is not treated as receiving value in respect of the disposal.

An individual who acquired shares by means of a transfer from a spouse or civil partner within **66.15** below is treated for these purposes as the investor.

Insignificant value

An amount of '*insignificant value*' is an amount of value which:

- does not exceed £1,000; or
- in any other case is insignificant in relation to the amount subscribed by the investor for the shares.

If, at any time in the period beginning one year before the issue of the shares and ending with the date of issue, there are in existence 'repayment arrangements', no amount of value received by the individual is treated as an amount of insignificant value. 'Repayment arrangements' are arrangements (as broadly defined) which provide for the investor to receive, or be entitled to receive, any value from the issuing company at any time in period A (see **66.7** above) relating to the shares. References to the investor include any person who is an associate of the investor at any time in period A. The reference to the issuing company include any person who is connected with the company at any time in period A.

There are provisions to aggregate a receipt of value, whether insignificant or not, with amounts of insignificant value received previously in period A, and treating that aggregate, if it is not itself an amount of insignificant value, as an amount of value received at the time of the latest actual receipt.

Excluded payments

Each of the following is an '*excluded payment*' for the purposes of (h) above:

- any payment or reimbursement of travelling or other expenses, exclusively and necessarily incurred by the investor or his associate in the performance of their duties as a director;
- any interest which represents no more than a reasonable commercial return on money lent to the issuing company (or any person connected with it);
- any dividend or other distribution which does not exceed a normal return on the investment;
- any payment for the supply of goods which does not exceed their market value;
- any payment of rent for any property occupied by the issuing company (or a person connected with it) which does not exceed a reasonable and commercial rent; and
- any necessary and reasonable remuneration which is paid for services rendered to the issuing company (or a person connected with it) in the course of a trade or profession and is taken into account in calculating taxable profits of that trade or profession. This exclusion does not cover secretarial or managerial services or services of a kind provided by the person to whom they are rendered.

Meaning of 'associate'

The SEIS provisions adopt the EIS definition of 'associate' in *ITA 2007, s 253*. An '*associate*' of any person is any 'relative' (i.e. spouse, civil partner, ancestor or linear descendant) of that person, the trustee(s) of any settlement in relation to which that person or any relative (living or dead) is or was a settlor and, where that person has an interest in any shares of obligations of a company which are subject to any trust or are part of a deceased estate, the trustee(s) of the settlement or the personal representatives of the deceased. For this purpose, 'settlor' is defined as in **70.3** SETTLEMENTS.

[*ITA 2007, ss 257FE–257FI, 257FM, 257HJ(1); FA 2020, s 110(1)(3)(5)*].

Reduction in relief — further computational provisions

[66.9] Adjustments are made in the amount by which relief is to be reduced in the following circumstances. Where more than one circumstance is relevant, the adjustments are made in the order in which they are set out below.

(a) Where two or more issues of shares have been made by the same company to the same investor, in relation to each of which income tax relief is claimed, and value is received during the applicable period A for more than one such issue, the value received is apportioned between them by reference to the amounts of relief obtained for each of those issues.
(b) Where any of the shares are treated as issued in the previous tax year by virtue of the carry-back provisions at **66.3** above, the value received is apportioned between the shares allocated to each year on the basis of the amount on which relief was obtained for each year. The normal provisions for reducing relief are then applied to each of the apportioned amounts as if there were separate issues of shares (taking (c) below into account where appropriate, but not (a) above) and the resulting amounts are added together.
(c) Where maximum relief is not obtained, the amount of value received is treated as reduced by multiplying that amount by the relief attributable to the shares divided by tax at the SEIS rate on the amount on which the investor claims relief in respect of the shares. For this purpose, where the relief attributable to the shares has been reduced (otherwise than as a result of an issue of bonus shares — see **66.4** above) before the relief was obtained, the relief attributable to the shares before that reduction is used in this calculation.

[*ITA 2007, ss 257FE(3), 257FJ–257FM*].

Replacement value

[66.10] The value received provisions in **66.8** above are disapplied if the person from whom the value was received (the '*original supplier*') receives, by way of a 'qualifying receipt', and whether before or after the original receipt of value, at least equivalent replacement value from the original recipient. A receipt is a '*qualifying receipt*' if it arises by reason of:

(a) any one, or any combination of, the following:
  (i) a payment by the original recipient to the original supplier other than a payment within (1) to (6) below or a payment covered by (c) below;
  (ii) the acquisition of an asset by the original recipient from the original supplier for consideration exceeding market value;
  (iii) the disposal of an asset by the original recipient to the original supplier for no consideration or for consideration less than market value; or
(b) (where the original receipt of value falls within **66.8**(d) above) an event having the effect of reversing the original event; or
(c) (where the original receipt of value arose from the purchase from the individual by certain persons of shares or securities of the company, or a payment by such a person to the individual for his giving up any right in relation to them) the repurchase by the original recipient of the shares or securities in question, or the reacquisition of the right in question, for consideration not less than the original value.

The amount of replacement value is:

- in a case within (a) above, the amount of any such payment plus the difference between the market value of any such asset and the consideration received;
- in a case within (b) above, the same as the amount of the original value; and
- in a case within (c) above, the consideration received by the original supplier.

The receipt of replacement value is disregarded if:

- it occurs before the start of period A (as in **66.7** above) relating to the shares in question; or
- there was an unreasonable delay in its occurrence; or
- it occurs more than 60 days after the relief falling to be withdrawn (or reduced) has been determined on appeal.

A receipt of replacement value is also disregarded if it has previously been set against a receipt of value to prevent any reduction or withdrawal of relief.

The following payments are excluded from (a)(i) above:

(1) a reasonable (in relation to their market value) payment for any goods, services or facilities provided (in the course of trade or otherwise) by the original supplier;
(2) a payment of interest at no more than a reasonable commercial rate on money lent to the original recipient;
(3) a payment not exceeding a reasonable and commercial rent for property occupied by the original recipient;
(4) a payment not exceeding market value for the acquisition of an asset;
(5) a payment in discharge of an 'ordinary trade debt' (as in **66.8**(c) above);
(6) a payment for any shares or securities in any company in circumstances not within (a)(ii) above.

Each reference in (1)–(3) above to the original supplier or recipient includes a reference to any person who at any time in period A is an 'associate' (see **66.8** above) of his or, in the case of the supplier, is connected with him (within **19** CONNECTED PERSONS).

Where:

- the receipt of replacement value is a qualifying receipt (as above);
- any receipts of value are consequently ignored in relation to the shares in question or any other shares subscribed for by the investor; and
- the event giving rise to the receipt is (or includes) a subscription for shares by the individual or by a person who is an associate of his at any time in period A,

the subscriber is not eligible for SEIS income tax relief in relation to those shares or any other shares in the same issue.

For the above purposes, any apportionment made of value received where there are two or more share issues (see **66.9**(a) above) is disregarded in determining the amount of the original receipt of value; and payments to a person include any made indirectly or to his order or for his benefit.

[*ITA 2007, ss 257FN, 257FO*].

Acquisition of trade or trading assets

[66.11] Relief attributable (see **66.4** above) to any shares in a company held by an individual is withdrawn if:

(a) at any time in period A (as in **66.7** above), the company or any 'qualifying subsidiary' (see **66.46** below):
- begins to carry on as its trade, business or profession (or as part of its trade etc.) a trade etc. previously carried on at any time in that period by someone other than the company or any qualifying subsidiary; or
- acquires the whole or the greater part of the assets used for the purposes of a trade etc. previously so carried on; and

(b) the individual is a person or one of a group of persons:
  (i) who owned at any time in period A more than a half share in the trade etc. previously carried on, and also own or owned at any such time such a share in the trade etc. carried on by the company; or
  (ii) control (within *CTA 2010, ss 450, 451*), or at any time in period A has controlled, the company, and also, at any such time, controlled another company which previously carried on the trade etc.

In determining, for the purposes of (b)(i) above, the ownership of a trade and, if appropriate, the shares owned by multiple owners, *CTA 2010, s 941(6)* and *s 942* apply. Interests, rights or powers of 'associates' (see **66.8** above) of a person are treated as those of that person.

[*ITA 2007, ss 257FP, 257HJ(3)*].

Acquisition of share capital

[66.12] Relief attributable (see **66.4** above) to any shares in a company held by an individual is withdrawn if:

- the company, at any time in period A (as in **66.7** above), comes to acquire all the issued share capital of another company, and
- the individual is a person, or one of a group of persons, who control (within *CTA 2010, ss 450, 451*) or has, at any time in period A, controlled the company and who also, at any such time, controlled the other company.

[*ITA 2007, ss 257FQ, 257HJ(3)*].

Relief subsequently found not to have been due

[66.13] Relief is withdrawn if it is subsequently found not to have been due. If relief is to be withdrawn on the ground that the issuing company is not a qualifying company (see **66.34** below) or that the purpose of the issue or spending of the money raised requirements at **66.23**, **66.24** are not met:

- the issuing company must have given notice under the provisions at **66.19** below; or
- an HMRC officer must have given notice to the issuing company of his opinion that the whole or part of the relief was not due because of the ground in question.

The issuing company may appeal against an HMRC notice as though it were refusal of a claim by the company.

[*ITA 2007, ss 257FR, 257GA*].

Procedure for withdrawing or reducing relief

[66.14] An assessment to income tax withdrawing or reducing SEIS relief is made for the tax year for which the relief was given.

Such an assessment may not be made, and any notice by an HMRC officer under the provisions at **66.13** above may not be given, more than six years after the end of the tax year in which period B ends (as in **66.7**) or the tax year in which the event giving rise to withdrawal or reduction occurs, whichever is the later. This restriction is without prejudice to the extension of time limits in cases of loss of income tax brought about deliberately (see **6.3** ASSESSMENTS). No assessment may be made by reason of any event occurring after the death of the individual to whom the shares were issued.

Where an individual has made an arm's length disposal (or disposals) of all the shares issued to him by a company in respect of which either relief is attributable or period A (as in **66.7** above) has not come to an end, no assessment may be made in respect of those shares by reason of any subsequent event unless at the time of that event the individual has a substantial interest in the company (see **66.30** below) or is a director or employee of the company.

The date from which interest accrues (as in **43.3** LATE PAYMENT INTEREST AND PENALTIES) is 31 January following the tax year in which the assessment is made.

[*ITA 2007, ss 257G, 257GB–GD*].

Married persons and civil partners

[66.15] The provisions for withdrawal of relief on the disposal of shares in respect of which relief has been given (see **66.7** above) do not apply to transfers between spouses or civil partners living together. On any subsequent disposal or other event, the spouse or partner to whom the shares were so transferred is treated as if:

- he or she were the person who subscribed for the shares;
- the amount he or she subscribed for the shares were the same amount as subscribed by the transferor spouse or partner;
- his or her liability to income tax had been reduced in respect of the shares by the same amount, and for the same tax year, as applied on the subscription by the transferor spouse or partner; and
- that amount of SEIS income tax relief had continued to be attributable to the shares despite the transfer.

Where the amount of SEIS relief attributable to the shares had been reduced before the relief was obtained by the transferor spouse or partner, the transferee is treated as if his or her relief had been correspondingly reduced before it was obtained (but this does not prevent the relief before reduction being used for the purposes of the calculations at **66.7** and **66.9**(c) above).

Any assessment for reducing or withdrawing relief is made on the transferee spouse or partner. The identification rules for disposals at **66.7** above apply to determine the extent (if any) to which shares to which relief is attributable are comprised in the transfer.

[*ITA 2007, ss 257FA(4), 257H, 257HA(1)*].

Issuing company acquired by new company

[66.16] Where a company (Company A) has issued shares under the SEIS (and has issued a compliance certificate — see **66.5** above) and subsequently, by means of an exchange of shares, all of its shares (the old shares) are acquired by a company (Company B) in which the only previously issued shares are subscriber shares, then, subject to the further conditions below being satisfied:

- the exchange is not regarded as involving a disposal of the old shares (and a consequent withdrawal of relief) and an acquisition of the Company B shares (the new shares); and
- SEIS relief attributable to the old shares is regarded as attributable instead to the new shares for which they are exchanged. For SEIS purposes generally, the new shares stand in the shoes of the old shares, e.g. as if they had been subscribed for and issued at the time the old shares were subscribed for and issued and as if anything done by or in relation to Company A had been done by or in relation to Company B.

The further conditions are as follows.

(a) The consideration for the old shares must consist entirely of the issue of the new shares.

(b) The consideration for old shares of each description must consist entirely of new shares of the 'corresponding description'.

(c) New shares of each description must be issued to holders of old shares of the 'corresponding description' in respect of and in proportion to their holdings.

(d) Before the issue of the new shares, on the written application (for which see **4.12** ANTI-AVOIDANCE) of either Company A or Company B, HMRC must have notified to that company their satisfaction that the exchange:
  - is for genuine commercial reasons; and
  - does not form part of a scheme or arrangements designed to avoid liability to corporation tax or capital gains tax.

  HMRC may, within 30 days of an application, request further particulars, which must then be supplied within 30 days of the request (or such longer period as they may allow in any particular case).

For the purposes of (b) and (c) above, old and new shares are of a '*corresponding description*' if, assuming they were shares in the same company, they would be of the same class and carry the same rights.

References above to 'shares' (other than those to 'shares issued under the SEIS' or 'subscriber shares') include references to securities.

An exchange within these provisions does not breach the control and independence requirement at **66.40** below.

[*ITA 2007, ss 257HB–257HD; TCGA 1992, s 138(2)*].

Capital gains tax

[66.17] In determining the gain or loss on a disposal of shares to which any SEIS income tax relief is attributable (see **66.4** above):

- if a loss would otherwise arise, the consideration the individual is treated as having given for the shares is treated as reduced by the amount of the relief;
- if the disposal is after the end of period A (as in **66.7** above) and a gain would otherwise arise, the gain is not a chargeable gain (although this does not prevent a loss arising in these circumstances from being an allowable loss). Where the reduction in liability in respect of the issue of the shares was less than the amount corresponding to income tax at the SEIS rate (see **66.3** above) on the amount subscribed for the shares (other than because there is insufficient income tax liability to make full use of the relief), there is a corresponding reduction in the amount of the gain which is not chargeable.

Where, because of the above exemption, a gain (or part of a gain) on a disposal is not a chargeable gain, but the income tax relief on the shares disposed of is reduced on account of value received from the company (see **66.8** above) before the disposal, then a corresponding proportion of the gain is brought back into charge.

The identification rules at **66.7** above apply for the above purposes.

[*TCGA 1992, ss 150E, 150F*].

For full coverage, see the corresponding chapter of Tolley's Capital Gains Tax.

SEIS reinvestment relief

[66.18] Reinvestment relief is available where:

- an individual realises a chargeable gain on a disposal; and
- he is eligible for, and claims, SEIS income tax relief for the year in which the gain accrues in respect of an amount subscribed for an issue of shares in a company made to him in that year.

On a claim by the individual, 50% of so much of the acquisition cost of the SEIS shares as is specified in the claim and does not exceed the amount of the chargeable gain is set against the gain.

If the issue of shares precedes the disposal, it is an additional condition that the individual continue to hold the SEIS shares at the time of the disposal. To the extent that an amount is set against the gain, the gain ceases to be a chargeable gain. The time limit for claims is the same as for SEIS income tax relief — see **66.5** above. More than one claim can be made in relation to a gain until it is exhausted. Similarly, more than one gain can be set against the acquisition cost of an issue of SEIS shares until the 50% limit is exhausted. The total amount that can be set against gains cannot exceed £100,000, i.e. the maximum amount on which SEIS income tax relief is available.

If SEIS income tax relief attributable to shares is withdrawn, any SEIS reinvestment relief attributable to those shares is also withdrawn. If SEIS income tax relief attributable to shares is reduced, any SEIS reinvestment relief attributable to those shares is reduced in the same proportion. In either case, a chargeable gain is then deemed to accrue to the individual in the year in which the shares were issued of an amount equal to the amount of reinvestment relief to be withdrawn or the amount by which reinvestment relief falls to be reduced.

[*TCGA 1992, s 150G, Sch 5BB*].

The above is intended as a summary only; for the detailed coverage, see the corresponding chapter of Tolley's Capital Gains Tax.

Notification requirements and information powers

[66.19] Certain events leading to withdrawal or reduction of SEIS income tax relief must be notified to HMRC, generally within 60 days, by either the individual who received the relief, the issuing company, or any person connected with the issuing company having knowledge of the matter. An HMRC officer may require such a notice and other relevant information where he has reason to believe it should have been made.

It should be noted that:

- the notification requirement extends to cases where income tax relief would have fallen to be withdrawn or reduced were it not for the replacement value rules at **66.10** above; and in all cases a notice under these provisions should include details of any such replacement value received (or expected to be received) where this is within the knowledge of the person giving the notice; and
- HMRC's powers extend to cases where notice would have been required were it not for value received being of an insignificant amount (see **66.8** above), and they may require notice and other information from persons giving or receiving such value.

The penalty provisions of *TMA 1970, s 98* apply for failure to comply with the notification requirements.

HMRC also have broad powers to require information in other cases where relief may be withdrawn, restricted or not due. The obligations of secrecy do not prevent HMRC disclosing to a company that relief has been given or claimed on certain of its shares.

[*ITA 2007, ss 257GE–257GI*].

The risk-to-capital condition

[66.20] The risk-to-capital condition mentioned at **66.1** above is an over-arching condition which is met if, having regard to all existing circumstances at the time of issue of the SEIS shares, it would be reasonable to conclude that:

- the issuing company has objectives to grow and develop its trade in the long term; and
- there is a significant risk of loss of capital of an amount greater than the net investment return, i.e. the net return to investors (whether by way of income or capital growth) taking into account the value of SEIS relief. The risk and the return is to be determined with reference to the investors in general, and a loss of capital means a loss of at least part of the amounts subscribed for the shares by the investors.

[*ITA 2007, s 257AAA; FA 2018, s 14(2); SI 2018 No 931, Reg* 2].

As stated at **29.1**, the risk-to-capital condition has effect for shares issued on or after 15 March 2018. The intention is to prevent tax-relieved investment in companies whose activities are geared towards preservation of investors' capital rather than the company's long-term growth and development. *ITA 2007, s 257AAA(3)* provides an illustrative, non-exhaustive list of the types of circumstance that may be taken into account in reaching any conclusion. For guidance on the condition, with examples, see HMRC Venture Capital Schemes Manual VCM8500–8560.

SEIS — general requirements

[66.21] The general requirements mentioned in **66.1** above are described at **66.22–66.27** below.

The shares requirement

[66.22] The shares must:

(a) be ordinary shares which do not, at any time during period B (as in **66.7** above), carry (subject to below) any present or future preferential right to dividends or to assets on a winding-up or any present or future right to be redeemed; and

(b) unless they are bonus shares, be subscribed for wholly in cash and be fully paid up at the time of issue.

Shares are, however, permitted to carry a preferential right to dividends provided the amount and timing of the dividends do not depend on a decision of the company, the shareholder or any other person and provided the dividends are not cumulative.

[*ITA 2007, ss 257CA, 257HJ(1)*].

The 'purpose of the issue' requirement

[66.23] The shares (other than any bonus shares) must be issued to raise money for the purposes of a 'qualifying business activity' (see **66.47** below) carried on, or to be carried on, by the issuing company or a 'qualifying 90% subsidiary' (see **66.46** below) of that company. [*ITA 2007, ss 257CB, 257HJ(1)*].

There is no statutory minimum as to the amount that has to be raised by a SEIS share issue, and HMRC cannot use *ITA 2007, s 257CB* as a means of creating one (*Oxbotica v HMRC* FTT (TC 6538), [2018] UKFTT 308 (TC)).

The 'spending of the money raised' requirement

[66.24] Before the end of period B (as in **66.7** above) all of the money raised by the issue of the shares (other than any of them which are bonus shares) must be spent for the purposes of the qualifying business activity (see **66.47** below) for which the money was raised. However, this requirement does not fail to be met merely because an amount of money which is not significant is spent for another purpose or remains unspent at the end of period B. The spending of money on the acquisition of shares or stock in a company does not of itself amount to spending it for the purposes of a qualifying business activity.

[*ITA 2007, ss 257CC, 257HJ(1)*].

The 'no pre-arranged exits' requirement

[66.25] The 'issuing arrangements' must not:

(a) provide for the eventual disposal by the investor of the shares in question or other shares or securities of the issuing company; or
(b) provide for the eventual cessation of a trade of the company or of a person connected with it; or
(c) provide for the eventual disposal of all, or a substantial amount (in terms of value) of, the assets of the company or of a person connected with it; or
(d) provide (by means of any insurance, indemnity, guarantee or otherwise) complete or partial protection for investors against what would otherwise be the risks attached to making the investment (disregarding any arrangements which merely protect the issuing company and/or its subsidiaries against normal business risks).

Arrangements with a view to the company becoming a wholly-owned subsidiary of a new holding company within the terms of *ITA 2007, s 257HB(1)* (see **66.16** above) are not caught by (a) above. In relation to shares issued on or after 5 December 2016, arrangements with a view to any shares in the company being exchanged for, or converted into, shares in that company of a different class are also not caught by (a) above. Arrangements applicable only on an unanticipated winding-up of a company for genuine commercial reasons are excluded from (b) and (c) above.

'*Issuing arrangements*' means the arrangements under which the shares are issued to the individual or any arrangements made, before the shares were issued, in relation to or in connection with the issue. If, before the shares were issued, information on pre-arranged exits, i.e. information indicating the possibility of making during period B (as in **66.7** above) arrangements of the kind described in any of (a)–(d) above, was made available to prospective subscribers, the term also includes any arrangements made during period B. The term 'arrangements' is broadly defined.

[*ITA 2007, ss 257CD, 257HJ(1); F(No 2)A 2017, s 11(3)(4)*].

The 'no tax avoidance' requirement

[66.26] The shares must be issued for genuine commercial reasons and not as part of a scheme or arrangement a main purpose of which is the avoidance of tax. [*ITA 2007, s 257CE*].

The 'no disqualifying arrangements' requirement

[66.27] The shares must not be issued, nor any money raised by the issue employed, in consequence or anticipation of, or otherwise in connection with, 'disqualifying arrangements'. Arrangements (as broadly defined) are '*disqualifying arrangements*' if a main purpose of them is to ensure that any of the 'relevant tax reliefs' are available in respect of the issuing company's business (or, where applicable, that of its qualifying 90% subsidiary) and either or both of conditions A and B below are met. It is immaterial whether the issuing company is a party to the arrangements.

Condition A is that, as a result of the money raised by the issue of the shares being spent as required by **66.24** above, an amount representing the whole or most of the amount raised is, in the course of the arrangements, paid to (or for the benefit of) one or more 'relevant persons'. Condition B is that, in the absence of the arrangements, it would have been reasonable to expect that the whole or greater part of the component activities (as defined) of the qualifying business activity for which the issue of the shares raised money would have been carried on as part of another business by one or more 'relevant persons'.

A '*relevant person*' is a person who is a party to the arrangements or a person connected with such a party (within **19** CONNECTED PERSONS).The '*relevant tax reliefs*' are those listed at **29.40** ENTERPRISE INVESTMENT SCHEME.

[*ITA 2007, ss 257CF, 257HJ(1); F(No 2)A 2017, Sch 1 paras 11(3), 16*].

Qualifying investor

[66.28] An individual is a '*qualifying investor*' in relation to shares if the requirements at **66.29–66.33** are met.

The 'no employee investors' requirement

[66.29] Neither the investor nor an associate (see **66.8** above) of the investor may at any time during period B (as in **66.7** above) be an employee of the issuing company or of any 'qualifying subsidiary' (see **66.46** below) of that company. However, for this purpose a person is not to be treated as an employee of the issuing company etc. at any time when he is a director of the company. [*ITA 2007, ss 257BA, 257HJ(1)*].

The 'no substantial interest in the issuing company' requirement

[66.30] The investor must not have a 'substantial interest' in the issuing company at any time during period A (as in **66.7** above).

An individual has a '*substantial interest*' in a company if:

(a) he directly or indirectly possesses, or is entitled to acquire, more than 30% of the ordinary or issued share capital of, or more than 30% of the voting power in, the company or any 'subsidiary'; or
(b) he directly or indirectly possesses, or is entitled to acquire, such rights as would entitle him to more than 30% of the assets of the company or a subsidiary that are available for distribution to equity holders in, for example, a winding-up; or
(c) he has control (within *ITA 2007, s 995*) of the company or any subsidiary.

For these purposes a company (Y) is a '*subsidiary*' of another (Z) if Y is a 51% subsidiary of Z at any time in period A. For the purposes of (b), *CTA 2010, Pt 5 Ch 6* has effect, with appropriate modifications, to determine the persons who are equity holders of a company and the percentage of assets to which an individual would be entitled.

An individual is treated as entitled to acquire anything which he is entitled to acquire at a future date or will at a future date be entitled to acquire. Rights or powers of associates (see **66.8** above) are attributed to the individual.

An individual does *not* have a substantial interest in a company merely because one or more shares in the company are held by him, or by his associate, at a time when the company has not issued any shares other than subscriber shares and has not begun to carry on, or make preparations for carrying on, a trade or business.

[*ITA 2007, ss 257BB, 257BF, 257HJ(1)*].

The 'no related investment arrangements' requirement

[66.31] The investor must not subscribe for the shares as part of an arrangement (as broadly defined) which provides for another person to subscribe for shares in another company in which the investor, or any other individual who is party to the arrangement, has a 'substantial interest' (see **66.30** above). [*ITA 2007, ss 257BC, 257HJ(1)*].

The 'no linked loans' requirement

[66.32] No loan may be made by any person to the investor or to an associate (see **66.8** above) at any time in period A (as in **66.7** above) if it would not have been made, or would not have been made on the same terms, if the investor had not subscribed, or had not been proposing to subscribe, for the shares. The giving of credit to, or the assignment of a debt due from, the investor or associate is counted as a loan for these purposes. [*ITA 2007, s 257BD*].

In their interpretation of the above, HMRC apply SP 6/98 (see **29.43** ENTERPRISE INVESTMENT SCHEME) (HMRC Venture Capital Trusts Manual VCM32050).

The 'no tax avoidance' requirement

[66.33] The shares must be subscribed for by the investor for genuine commercial reasons and not as part of a scheme or arrangement a main purpose of which is the avoidance of tax. [*ITA 2007, s 257BE*].

Qualifying company

[66.34] The issuing company is a '*qualifying company*' in relation to the shares if the requirements at **66.35–66.46** below are met.

The trading requirement

[66.35] The company must meet the 'trading requirement' throughout period B (as in **66.7** above). The '*trading requirement*' is that:

(a) the company exists wholly for the purpose of carrying on one or more new qualifying trades (see **66.48** below) (disregarding purposes having no significant effect on the extent of its activities); or
(b) the company is a '*parent company*' (i.e. a company with one or more 'qualifying subsidiaries' — see **66.46** below) and the business of the '*group*' (i.e. the company and its qualifying subsidiaries) does not consist wholly or as to a substantial part in the carrying on of 'non-qualifying activities'. HMRC generally take 'a substantial part' to mean more than 20% (HMRC Venture Capital Schemes Manual VCM3010).

If period B begins after the incorporation of the company, the requirement must have been complied with since incorporation, apart from any interval between incorporation and commencement of business.

Where the company intends that one or more other companies should become its qualifying subsidiaries with a view to their carrying on one or more new qualifying trades, then, until any time after which the intention is abandoned, the company is treated as a parent company and those other companies are included in the group for the purposes of (b) above.

For the purpose of (b) above, the business of the group means what would be the business of the group if the activities of the group companies taken together were regarded as one business. Activities are for this purpose disregarded to the extent that they consist in:

(i) holding shares in or securities of any of the company's qualifying subsidiaries;
(ii) making loans to another group company;

(iii) holding and managing property used by a group company for the purposes of one or more qualifying trades (see **66.48** below) carried on by a group company; or

(iv) holding and managing property used by a group company for the purposes of research and development from which it is intended either that a qualifying trade to be carried on by a group company will be derived or that a qualifying trade carried on or to be carried on by a group company will benefit.

References in (iv) above to a group company include references to any existing or future company which will be a group company at any future time.

Activities are similarly disregarded to the extent that they consist, in the case of a subsidiary whose main purpose is the carrying on of qualifying trade(s) and whose other purposes have no significant effect on the extent of its activities (other than in relation to incidental matters), in activities not in pursuance of its main purpose.

Non-qualifying activities

'*Non-qualifying activities*' are:

- excluded activities within **29.59** ENTERPRISE INVESTMENT SCHEME; and
- non-trading activities (not including research and development — see **66.47** below).

Winding-up etc.

A company is not regarded as ceasing to meet the trading requirement merely because of anything done in consequence of the company or any of its subsidiaries being in administration or receivership (both as defined by *ITA 2007, s 252*) or because the company or any of its subsidiaries is wound up or otherwise dissolved. The entry into administration or receivership, winding-up or dissolution, and anything done as a consequence of the company concerned being in administration or receivership, must be for genuine commercial reasons and not part of a tax avoidance scheme or arrangements.

[*ITA 2007, ss 257DA, 257DB, 257HJ(1)(2)*].

The 'issuing company to carry on the qualifying business activity' requirement

[66.36] At no time in period B (as in **66.7** above) must any of the following be carried on by a person other than the issuing company or a 'qualifying 90% subsidiary' (see **66.46** below) of that company:

- the '*relevant new qualifying trade*', i.e. the 'new qualifying trade' (see **66.48** below) which is the subject of the qualifying business activity referred to in **66.23** above;
- '*relevant preparation work*', i.e. preparations to carry on a new qualifying trade where such preparations are the subject of that qualifying business activity (see **66.47**(a) below);
- research and development which is the subject of that qualifying business activity (see **66.47**(b) below); and

- any other preparations for the carrying on of the new qualifying trade.

Where relevant preparation work is carried on by the issuing company or a qualifying 90% subsidiary, the carrying on of the relevant new qualifying trade by a company other than the issuing company or a qualifying 90% subsidiary is disregarded for these purposes if it occurs before the issuing company (or subsidiary) carries on that trade.

The requirement is not regarded as failing to be met if, by reason only of a company being wound up or dissolved or being in administration or receivership (both as defined by *ITA 2007, s 252*), the relevant new qualifying trade ceases to be carried on in period B by the issuing company or a qualifying 90% subsidiary and is subsequently carried on in that period by a person who is not connected (within **19** CONNECTED PERSONS) with the issuing company at any time in period A (as in **66.7** above). This let-out applies only if the winding-up, dissolution or entry into administration or receivership (and everything done as a consequence of the company concerned being in administration or receivership) is for genuine commercial reasons and not part of a tax avoidance scheme or arrangements.

[*ITA 2007, ss 257DC, 257HJ(2)*].

The UK permanent establishment requirement

[66.37] Although the issuing company need not be UK resident, it must have a permanent establishment in the UK. The company must meet this requirement throughout period B (as in **66.7** above).

In determining whether or not a company has a permanent establishment in the UK, the same rules apply as for the identical requirement under the EIS — see **29.47** ENTERPRISE INVESTMENT SCHEME.

[*ITA 2007, ss 257DD, 257HJ(1)*].

The financial health requirement

[66.38] This requirement must be met at the beginning of period B (as in **66.7** above). The requirement is that the issuing company is not 'in difficulty'. A company is '*in difficulty*' if it is reasonable to assume that it would be regarded as a firm in difficulty for the purposes of the *EU Guidelines on State Aid for Rescuing and Restructuring Firms in Difficulty (2004/C 244/02)*. [*ITA 2007, s 257DE*].

The 'unquoted status' requirement

[66.39] The issuing company must be 'unquoted' at the beginning of period B (as in **66.7** above), and no arrangements must then exist for it to cease to be unquoted. If, at the time of issue, arrangements exist for the company to become a wholly-owned subsidiary of a new holding company by means of a share exchange within **66.16** above, no arrangements must exist for the new company to cease to be unquoted. A company is '*unquoted*' if none of its shares etc. are listed on a recognised stock exchange or on a foreign exchange designated for the purpose, or dealt in outside the UK by such means as may be designated for the purpose.

[*ITA 2007, s 257DF*].

The control and independence requirement

[66.40] The issuing company must not at any time in period A (as in **66.7** above) either:

(a) control another company (other than a 'qualifying subsidiary' — see **66.46** below), 'control' being construed in accordance with *CTA 2010, ss 450, 451* and being considered with or without CONNECTED PERSONS (**19**); or

(b) (subject to **66.16** above) be under the control of another company, 'control' being construed in accordance with *ITA 2007, s 995* and again being considered with or without connected persons; or

(c) be capable of falling within (a) or (b) by virtue of any arrangements (as broadly defined).

Any 'on-the-shelf period' is ignored in determining whether the requirement in (b) above is met. An '*on-the-shelf period*' is a period during which the issuing company has not issued any shares other than subscriber shares or begun to carry on, or make preparations for carrying on, any trade or business.

[*ITA 2007, ss 257DG, 257HJ(3)*].

The 'no partnerships' requirement

[66.41] Neither the issuing company nor any 'qualifying 90% subsidiary' (see **66.46** below) of that company may, at any time during period A (as in **66.7** above), be a member of a partnership. This includes a limited liability partnership and a foreign entity of similar nature to a partnership. [*ITA 2007, s 257DH*].

The gross assets requirement

[66.42] The value of the issuing company's assets must not exceed £200,000 immediately before the issue of SEIS shares. If the issuing company is a parent company, the gross assets test applies by reference to the aggregate gross assets of the company and all its qualifying subsidiaries (disregarding certain assets held by any such company which correspond to liabilities of another). [*ITA 2007, ss 257DI, 257HJ(1)*].

In their approach to the gross assets requirement, HMRC apply SP 2/06 (see **29.53** ENTERPRISE INVESTMENT SCHEME) (HMRC Venture Capital Trusts Manual VCM34100).

The 'number of employees' requirement

[66.43] The issuing company must have fewer than the equivalent of 25 full-time employees when the SEIS shares are issued. If the company is a parent company, this rule applies by reference to the aggregate number of full-time employees of itself and its qualifying subsidiaries. To ascertain the equivalent number of full-time employees of a company, take the actual number of full-time employees and add to it a just and reasonable fraction for each employee who is not full-time. For this purpose, an 'employee' includes a director but does not include anyone on maternity, paternity, shared parental or parental bereavement leave or a student on vocational training. [*ITA 2007, ss 257DJ, 257HJ(1); Parental Bereavement (Leave and Pay) Act 2018, Sch para 52; SI 2020 No 45, Reg 2*].

The 'no previous other risk capital scheme investments' requirement

[66.44] This requirement is that:

- no EIS investment or VCT investment is or has been made in the issuing company on or before the day on which the SEIS shares are issued; and
- no EIS investment or VCT investment has been made on or before that day in a company which at the time the SEIS shares are issued is a 'qualifying subsidiary' (see **66.46** below) of the issuing company.

An EIS investment is made if the company issues shares (for which money has been subscribed) and provides a compliance statement (see **29.7** ENTERPRISE INVESTMENT SCHEME) in respect of the shares. The investment is made when the shares are issued. A VCT investment is made if an investment (of any kind) in the company is made by a VCT (see **81** VENTURE CAPITAL TRUSTS). [*ITA 2007, s 257DK*].

The 'amount raised through the SEIS' requirement

[66.45] The total amount of SEIS investments made in the issuing company, together with any other de minimis State aid received by the company, in the period of three years and one day ending on the date of the current issue must not exceed £150,000.

A SEIS investment is made if the company issues shares (for which money has been subscribed) and provides a compliance statement under **66.5** above in respect of them; the investment is made on the day the shares are issued. De minimis aid is defined by reference to Article 2 of Commission Regulation (EC) No 1998/2006; the amount of the aid is the amount of the grant or, if the aid is not in the form of a grant, the gross grant equivalent amount (within the meaning of that Regulation).

Where the current share issue would take the total amount of SEIS investments (plus de minimis aid) to more than £150,000, the requirement is treated as met in relation to an appropriate proportion of the shares in the issue (and in any other issue made on the same day). For example, if 200,000 shares are issued for £1 each and there has been no previous issue in the last three years (and no de minimis aid), 150,000 of the shares can be SEIS shares. Those shares and the remainder of the shares comprised in the issue are then treated as two separate issues for SEIS purposes.

[*ITA 2007, s 257DL*].

The subsidiaries requirements

[66.46] At all times in period B (as in **66.7** above), any subsidiary of the issuing company must be a 'qualifying subsidiary' (see below). [*ITA 2007, s 257DM*].

The company must not at any time in period B have a 'property managing subsidiary' which is not a 'qualifying 90% subsidiary' (see below) of the company. A '*property managing subsidiary*' is a subsidiary whose business consists wholly or mainly in the holding or managing of land or any 'property deriving its value from land'. For this purpose, '*property deriving its value from land*' includes any shareholding in a company, and any partnership interest or interest in settled property, which derives its value directly or indirectly from land and any option, consent or embargo affecting the disposition of land. [*ITA 2007, s 257DN*].

Qualifying subsidiary and qualifying 90% subsidiary

Both '*qualifying subsidiary*' and '*qualifying 90% subsidiary*' have the same meanings as they do for EIS purposes. See respectively **29.56** and **29.57** ENTERPRISE INVESTMENT SCHEME. [*ITA 2007, s 257HJ(1)*].

Qualifying business activity

[66.47] Either of the following is a '*qualifying business activity*' in relation to the issuing company:

(i) the carrying on of a 'new qualifying trade' (see **66.48** below) which, on the date of issue of the shares, the company or a 'qualifying 90% subsidiary' (see **66.46** above) is carrying on; or
(ii) the activity of preparing to carry on such a trade which, on the date of issue of the shares, is intended to be carried on by the company or any such subsidiary and which is eventually carried on by the company or any such subsidiary; or
(iii) the eventual carrying on of the trade mentioned in (ii) above; and

(b) the carrying on of 'research and development' which, on the date of issue of the shares, the company or a 'qualifying 90% subsidiary' is carrying on or which the company or any such subsidiary begins to carry on immediately afterwards, and from which it is intended on that date that a new qualifying trade which the company or any such subsidiary will carry on will be derived or will benefit.

For the purposes of (b) above, when research and development is begun to be carried on by a qualifying 90% subsidiary of the issuing company, any carrying on of the research and development by it before it became such a subsidiary is ignored. '*Research and development*' has the meaning given by *ITA 2007, s 1006* (see **75.113** TRADING INCOME). References in (a) and (b) above to a qualifying 90% subsidiary include, in cases where the new qualifying trade is not carried on at the time of issue of the shares, references to any existing or future company which will be such a subsidiary at any future time.

[*ITA 2007, ss 257HG, 257HJ(1)*].

New qualifying trade

[66.48] '*Qualifying trade*' is defined as for EIS purposes — see **29.59** ENTERPRISE INVESTMENT SCHEME. A qualifying trade carried on by the issuing company or a 'qualifying 90% subsidiary' (see **66.46** above) of that company is a '*new qualifying trade*' if (and only if):

- the trade does not begin to be carried on (whether by the company concerned or any other person) before the period of two years ending immediately before the day on which the shares are issued; and
- at no time before the company concerned begins to carry on the trade was any other trade being carried on by the issuing company or by any company that was a 51% subsidiary of the issuing company at the time in question.

[*ITA 2007, s 257HF*].

67

Self-Assessment

Cross-reference. See also 68 SELF-ASSESSMENT — KEY DATES.

Simon's Taxes. See E1.2.

See also HMRC Manual, 'Income Tax Self-Assessment: The Legal Framework'.

Introduction to self-assessment

[67.1] The term 'self-assessment' refers to a system whereby the annual tax return filed by individuals, partnerships and trustees should itself include an assessment of the taxpayer's liability to income tax and capital gains tax. Where returns are filed online, the self-assessment is generated automatically from the information entered in the return. Payment of tax is due automatically, based on the self-assessment, without the need for HMRC to issue its own tax assessments.

See 68 SELF-ASSESSMENT — KEY DATES for a calendar of key dates and events.

In 2015, the then Government announced an intention to abolish the tax return for millions of individuals through the phased introduction of digital tax accounts. This has yet to come to fruition. See 46 MAKING TAX DIGITAL.

Summary of the self-assessment system

[67.2] The tax return for individuals consists of a basic return to which will be attached any supplementary pages relevant to the individual concerned, forming a single 'customised' tax return. The supplementary pages cover employment, share schemes, self-employment, partnership income, land and property, foreign income, trust income, capital gains and non-UK residence etc. Each individual will also receive a tax return guide containing explanatory notes relevant to his circumstances. It is the individual's responsibility to obtain any supplementary pages he needs but has not received, which he may do by downloading from the HMRC website or telephoning an HMRC Orderline, by which means he may also obtain the relevant explanatory notes and/or 'helpsheets' on specific topics. Each return sent out will be accompanied by a tax calculation guide designed to assist the individual in calculating his tax liability if he chooses to do so. See generally **64.2** RETURNS. Partnership returns follow a similar pattern (see **64.12–64.14** RETURNS).

Most individuals now file online. For 2019/20 returns onwards, self-assessment taxpayers will no longer receive automatic paper returns. Taxpayers who have filed on paper in the past will receive a short notice to file. If they still wish to file on paper they can download a blank version of the return or call HMRC to request one. (HMRC News Release 16 March 2020 at www.gov.uk/government/news/hmrc-to-stop-automatically-sending-paper-self-assessment-returns.)

Returns must be filed on or before a specified date following the tax year (see **64.2** RETURNS). Different dates are specified for online filing and paper returns. Taxpayers who do not file online must file their return earlier than those who do (see **64.3** RETURNS). Taxpayers with employment income must also file their return by an earlier specified date if they wish to have a liability below a certain threshold coded out through PAY AS YOU EARN (**53**) (see **64.3** RETURNS). Penalties will be imposed for late submission of returns, subject to appeal on the grounds of reasonable excuse (see **55.5** PENALTIES). There are provisions for making amendments to returns (see **64.4** RETURNS). HMRC are given a window in which to give notice of their intention to enquire into the return (see **64.6** RETURNS). A formal procedure is laid down for such enquiries (see **64.6–64.10** RETURNS). If HMRC do not give such notice, the return becomes final and conclusive, subject to any overpayment claim by the taxpayer (see **16.7** CLAIMS) or 'discovery' assessment by HMRC (see **6.6** ASSESSMENTS). In the event of non-submission of a return, HMRC are able to make a determination of the tax liability; there is no right of appeal but the determination can be superseded upon submission of the return (see **64.11** RETURNS). Capital losses must be quantified if they are to be allowable losses (see Tolley's Capital Gains Tax).

A special return has to be filed by partnerships. This must include a statement of the allocation of partnership income between the partners. See **64.12–64.14** RETURNS.

Taxpayers (including higher rate taxpayers) whose affairs can be adequately dealt with using the PAYE system are not usually asked to complete a tax return, though they may choose to do so if they wish. For guidelines on who needs to complete a tax return, see www.gov.uk/self-assessment-tax-returns/who-must-send-a-tax-return#5. There is also a Short Tax Return (STR) for those with relatively straightforward tax affairs which can be issued by HMRC as an alternative to the standard self-assessment return (see guidance at www.gov.uk/government/uploads/system/uploads/attachment_data/file/506435/sa211-2016.pdf).

Payment of tax

Income tax (on all sources of taxable income) for a tax year is payable by means of two interim payments of equal amounts, based normally on the liability for the previous year and due on 31 January in the tax year and the following 31 July, and a final balancing payment due on the following 31 January (on which date any capital gains tax liability is also due for payment). Taxpayers have the right to reduce their interim payments if they believe their liability will be less than that for the previous year or to dispense with interim payments if they believe they will have no liability. Interim payments are not in any case required where substantially all of a taxpayer's liability is covered by deduction of tax at source, including PAYE, or where the amounts otherwise due are below *de minimis* limits prescribed by regulations. See **67.5–67.8** below.

Interest on late payments runs from the due date to the date of payment (see **43.2** LATE PAYMENT INTEREST AND PENALTIES). There is also a late payment penalty (see **43.4** LATE PAYMENT INTEREST AND PENALTIES). For interest on tax overpaid, see **62.2** REPAYMENT INTEREST.

Miscellaneous

There is a statutory requirement for taxpayers to keep records for the purpose of making returns and to preserve such records for specified periods (see **64.5** RETURNS). A formal procedure applies to the making of claims and elections and the giving of notices (see **16.1** CLAIMS).

Interpretation of references to assessments etc.

[67.3] References in the legislation to an individual (or trustee) being assessed to tax, or being charged to tax by an assessment, are to be construed as including a reference to his being so assessed, or being so charged, by a self-assessment under *TMA 1970, s 9* (see **67.4** below) or by a determination under *TMA 1970, s 28C* (see **64.11** RETURNS) which has not been superseded by a self-assessment. [*FA 1994, s 197*].

Self-assessments

[67.4] Every return under *TMA 1970, s 8* or *s 8A* (see **64.2** RETURNS) must include, subject to the exception below, an assessment (a self-assessment) of the amounts in which, based on the information in the return and taking into account any reliefs and allowances claimed therein, the person making the return is chargeable to income tax and capital gains tax for the tax year and of his net income tax liability for the year, taking into account tax deducted at source. In the event of non-compliance, an officer of HMRC *may* make the assessment on his behalf, based on the information in the return, and send the person a copy.

The tax to be self-assessed does not include any chargeable on the scheme administrator of a registered pension scheme (see **57.4** PENSION PROVISION), (for 2017/18 onwards) the scheme manager of a qualifying recognised overseas pension scheme or a former such scheme, or the responsible person in relation to an employer-financed retirement benefits scheme (see **57.35** PENSION PROVISION).

A person need not comply with this requirement if he makes and delivers his return on or before 31 October following the tax year to which the return relates or, if later, within two months beginning with the date of the notice to deliver the return. This deadline is of no significance where returns are filed online (see **64.2** above) as the tax due is automatically computed during the filing process. In the event of a person making no self-assessment under this option, an officer of HMRC *must* make the assessment on his behalf, based on the information in the return, and send the person a copy. Such assessments are treated as self-assessments by the person making the return and as included in the return.

[*TMA 1970, s 9(1)–(3A); FA 2016, Sch 1 paras 51(4), 73; FA 2017, Sch 4 paras 19, 25*].

Taxpayers with employment income who wish to have a liability of less than £3,000 coded out through PAY AS YOU EARN (**53**) must file their return by an earlier date than the 31 January deadline at **64.2** RETURNS. That date is 31 October (following the tax year) if the return is filed manually and 30 December if it is filed online (see **64.2** RETURNS). [*SI 2003 No 2682, Reg 186; SI 2011 No 1584, Regs 1, 2*]. A 2018/19 underpayment, for example, will be coded out for 2020/21. (Revenue Tax Bulletin June 1996 p 315; Revenue 'Working Together' Bulletin February 2001 p 2; Revenue Press Release 23 September 2002). Coding out of an underpayment for a tax year has the consequential effect of reducing any payments on account (see **67.5** below) due for the following tax year.

Time limits for self-assessments

The normal time limit for the making of an income tax assessment has no application to a self-assessment (see **6.2** ASSESSMENTS). A self-assessment contained in a personal or trust tax return must be delivered no later than four years after the end of the tax year to which it relates.

Notwithstanding the above, a person who within the said time limit receives a notice to submit a return including a self-assessment is always permitted three months in which to do so. The time limit also does not prevent a person in respect of whom a determination has been made (see **64.11** RETURNS) from making a self-assessment within the three years beginning with the filing date or, if later, within the 12 months beginning with the date of the determination.

[*TMA 1970, s 34A; FA 2016, s 168(3)*].

Simon's Taxes. See **E1.202A, E1.204.**

Payments of tax on account

[67.5] Where, as regards the year immediately preceding the tax year in question:

(a) a person is assessed to income tax under *TMA 1970, s 9* (self-assessment — see **64.3** RETURNS);
(b) the assessed amount exceeds any income tax deducted at source (including tax deducted under PAYE, taking in any deduction in respect of that year but to be made in a subsequent year but subtracting any amount paid in that year but in respect of a previous year, tax treated as deducted from, or as paid on, any income); and
(c) the said excess (the 'relevant amount') and the proportion which the relevant amount bears to the assessed amount are not less than, respectively, £1,000 and 20%,

the person must make two interim payments on account (POA) of his income tax liability for the tax year in question, each payment being equal to 50% of the relevant amount (see (c) above) and the payments being due on or before, respectively, 31 January in the tax year and the following 31 July. See below for the option to defer due to COVID-19 the payment otherwise due on 31 July 2020. If the preceding year's self-assessment is made late or is amended, the relevant amount is determined as if the liability as finally agreed had been shown in a timeous self-assessment, with further POA then being required where appropriate. If a discovery assessment (see **6.6** ASSESSMENTS) is made for the preceding year, each of the POA due is deemed always to have been 50% of the relevant amount plus 50% of the tax charged by the discovery assessment as finally determined.

At any time before 31 January following the tax year, the taxpayer may make a claim stating his belief that he will have no liability for the year or that his liability will be fully covered by tax deducted at source and his grounds for that belief, in which case each of the POA is not, and is deemed never to have been, required to be made. Within the same time limit, the taxpayer may make a claim stating his belief that his liability for the year after allowing for tax deducted at source will be a stated amount which is less than the relevant amount, and stating his grounds for that belief, in which case each of the POA required will be, and deemed always to have been, equal to 50% of the stated amount. Either claim should be made on form SA 303. The maximum penalty for an incorrect statement made fraudulently or negligently in connection with either claim is the amount or additional amount he would have paid on account if he had made a correct statement. Interim payments of tax are subject to the same recovery provisions as any other payments of tax.

An officer of HMRC may direct, at any time before 31 January following a tax year, that a person is not required to make POA for that year, such adjustments being made as necessary to give effect to the direction. For the circumstances in which such a direction will be made, see Revenue Tax Bulletin August 2001 p 875.

[*TMA 1970, s 59A; FA 2016, Sch 1 paras 51(8), 73; SI 1996 No 1654*].

For an article on HMRC practice on repayment, and allocations and reallocations of overpayments, see Revenue Tax Bulletin June 1999 pp 673, 674. For the interaction of loss relief claims and payments on account, see Revenue Tax Bulletin August 2001 pp 878, 879.

Interim payments made by an employer on an employee's behalf, as part of *tax equalisation* arrangements where full in-year gross up is used, should not figure in the employment pages of the employee's self-assessment tax return (see Revenue Tax Bulletin June 1998 p 551).

These provisions, and those described at **67.7** and **67.8** below, apply equally (with the necessary modifications) to Class 4 national insurance contributions. [*Social Security Contributions and Benefits Act 1992, s 16(1)(b)*].

COVID-19 (coronavirus) special measure

The Government announced in March 2020 that self-assessment taxpayers can choose to delay making their second payment on account for 2019/20, otherwise due on 31 July 2020, if they find it difficult to make the payment on time due to the impact of COVID-19. No claim is required. Those opting to delay will have until 31 January 2021 to make the payment. Whilst introduced principally to assist the self-employed, this measure applies to all self-assessment taxpayers. By virtue of the power available to HMRC at **43.5** LATE PAYMENT INTEREST AND PENALTIES, no late payment interest will be charged for the period 1 August 2020 to 31 January 2021 on the deferred payment (www.gov.uk/guidance/defer-your-self-assessment-payment-on-account-due-to-coronavirus-covid-19).

Simon's Taxes. See **E1.251**.

Example

[67.6]

Calculation of payments on account for 2020/21

For 2019/20, Kylie's self-assessment shows the following.

	£
Total income tax liability	8,164
Capital gains tax liability	2,122
Class 4 NIC liability	198
PAYE tax deducted (all relating to 2019/20)	3,740

The payments on account for 2020/21 (unless, on a claim, Kylie chooses to pay lesser amounts) are based on relevant amounts as follows.

	£
Income tax (£8,164 – £3,740 =)	4,424
Class 4 NIC	198

Half of the relevant amounts is due on each of 31 January 2021 and 31 July 2021. No payment on account is required in respect of capital gains tax liability.

Final payment (repayment) of tax

[67.7] A final payment (known as a '*balancing payment*') is due for a tax year if a person's combined income tax and capital gains tax liabilities contained in his self-assessment (see **64.3** RETURNS) exceed the aggregate of any payments on account (whether under *TMA 1970, s 59A*, see **67.5** above, or otherwise) and any income tax deducted at source. If the second total exceeds the first, a repayment will be made. Tax deducted at source has the same meaning as in **67.5**(b) above.

Subject to **67.8** below, the due date for payment (or repayment) is 31 January following the tax year. The one exception is where the person gave notice of chargeability under *TMA 1970, s 7* (see **55.2** PENALTIES) within six months after the end of the tax year, but was not given notice under *TMA 1970, s 8* or *s 8A* (see **64.2** RETURNS) until after 31 October following the tax year; in such case, the due date is the last day of the three months beginning with the date of the said notice.

In a case where HMRC have agreed to withdraw a notice to file a return (see **64.2** RETURNS), the references above to notices under *TMA 1970, ss 7, 8, 8A* are to notices given *before* such agreement and not to any notices given subsequently.

[*TMA 1970, s 59B(1)–(4)(4ZA)(4ZB)(7)(8); FA 2016, Sch 1 paras 51(9), 73*].

See **67.5** above as regards notifications to agents.

Simon's Taxes. See **E1.252.**

Due date — further provisions

[67.8] Where an amount of tax is payable (repayable) as a result of an amendment or correction to an individual's or trustees' self-assessment under any of (a)–(e) below, then, subject to the appeal and postponement provisions in **5.3** APPEALS and **54.5** PAYMENT OF TAX, the due date for payment (repayment) is as stated below (if this is later than the date given under the general rules in **67.7** above).

(a) Taxpayer amendment to return as in **64.4** RETURNS: 30 days after the date of the taxpayer's notice of amendment.

(b) HMRC correction to return as in **64.4** RETURNS: 30 days after the date of the officer's notice of correction.

(c) Taxpayer amendment to return whilst enquiry in progress as in **64.9** RETURNS, where accepted by HMRC: tax payable 30 days after the date of a final or partial closure notice; tax repayable 30 days after the date of a final closure notice, regardless of whether or not a partial closure notice was previously given (see **64.8** RETURNS, and see also **54.1** PAYMENT OF TAX).

(d) HMRC amendment to return where amendment made by a final or partial closure notice on completion or part completion of an enquiry (see **64.8** RETURNS): 30 days after the date of the closure notice.

(e) HMRC amendment of self-assessment to prevent potential loss of tax to the Crown (see **64.9** RETURNS): 30 days after the date of the notice of amendment.

As regards amendments and corrections to partnership returns, (e) above is not relevant, and the equivalent date in each of (a)–(d) above as regards each partner is 30 days after the date of the officer's notice of consequential amendment to the partner's own tax return. The same applies in the case of a consequential amendment by virtue of any of the following: an amendment of a partnership return on discovery (see **6.6** ASSESSMENTS); a reduction or increase in the partnership tax liability made by the Appeal Tribunal (see **5.3**, **5.19** APPEALS); or an amendment of a partnership return following the referral to the Tribunal of a dispute between partners over the allocation of profits or losses (see **64.14** PARTNERSHIPS).

[*TMA 1970, s 59B(5), Sch 3ZA; F(No 2)A 2017, Sch 15 paras 21, 44; FA 2018, Sch 6 paras 10(9)(10), 14*].

Where an officer of HMRC enquires into the return (see **64.6** RETURNS) and a repayment is otherwise due, the repayment is not required to be made until the enquiry is completed (see **64.8** RETURNS) although the officer may make a provisional repayment at his discretion.

For the due date for payment of tax charged by an assessment other than a self-assessment, see **54.1** PAYMENT OF TAX.

Appeals

[67.9] For appeals generally, see **5.1** *et seq.* APPEALS. For postponement of tax pending appeal and payment of tax on determination of the appeal, see respectively **54.5** and **54.6** PAYMENT OF TAX.

Claims etc.

[67.10] For full details as to the making of, and the ramifications of, claims and elections under self-assessment, see **16.1–16.4** CLAIMS.

Trusts

[67.11] Trustees of 'bare' (or 'simple') trusts treated as such for tax purposes (see **70.7** SETTLEMENTS) are not required to complete self-assessment returns or make payments on account, the beneficiaries under such trusts being liable to give details of the income and gains in their own tax returns. The trustees may, if they and the beneficiaries so wish, make returns of income (but *not* of capital gains or capital losses), accounting for tax at the basic rate or the dividend ordinary rate, as appropriate to the class of income, provided that they so notify the trust district and follow this course consistently from year to year. This does not, however, affect the liability of the beneficiaries to make the appropriate self-assessment returns of income and gains. (Revenue Tax Bulletin February 1997 p 395, December 1997 pp 486, 487).

A notice to file a self-assessment return cannot be given to the trustees of an interest in possession trust all of the income of which is mandated to the life tenant and which realises no chargeable gains (*Trustees of the Paul Hogarth Life Interest Trust 2008 v HMRC* FTT (TC 6757), [2019] SFTD 257, [2018] UKFTT 595 (TC)).

Trusts and estates allowance

HMRC do not require trustees and personal representatives to submit self-assessment returns where the only source of income of the trust or estate is savings interest and the tax liability is less than £100. This is an interim arrangement following the abolition of deduction at source from savings income for 2016/17 onwards. However, the arrangement will continue to apply at least up to and including 2020/21, and HMRC are keeping the matter under review for future years. (HMRC Trusts and Estates Newsletter, August 2019 at www.gov.uk/government/publications/hm-revenue-and-customs-trust s-and-estates-newsletters).

Liability of relevant trustees

In relation to income and chargeable gains, the '*relevant trustees*' of a settlement are the persons who are the trustees when the income arises or in the tax year in which the chargeable gain or life assurance policy gain accrues or arises and, in both cases, any persons who subsequently become trustees. Where the relevant trustees are liable to a penalty under the self-assessment regime, to interest on a penalty, to make interim and final payments of income tax and payments on an assessment to recover tax over-repaid, or to interest on late paid tax, the penalty etc. may be recovered (but only once) from any one or more of them. As regards penalties (and interest on penalties), the liability of any relevant trustee is, however, restricted to those incurred after the day that he became a relevant trustee (a daily penalty being regarded as incurred on a daily basis). [*TMA 1970, ss 7(9), 107A; FA 2016, Sch 22 para 20(2); F(No 2)A 2017, Sch 18 para 29(3)*].

Information to be provided to employees

[67.12] Various measures are included in the *Income Tax (Pay As You Earn) Regulations 2003 (SI 2003 No 2682)* to ensure that sufficient information is given to employees, and in good time, to enable them to complete their self-assessment tax returns. The measures are as follows.

(a) A time limit applies for providing an employee with form P60 (certificate of pay and tax deducted — see **53.18** PAY AS YOU EARN). It must be provided no later than 31 May following the tax year to which it relates. [*SI 2003 No 2682, Reg 67*].

(b) There is a requirement for the employer to provide each employee for whom form P11D (see **53.21** PAY AS YOU EARN) is relevant with particulars of the information stated therein. This must be provided no later than 6 July following the tax year. An employer is not obliged to provide the above particulars to an employee who left during the tax year in question unless requested to do so within three years after the end of that tax year; the information must then be provided within 30 days of receipt of the request if later than the normal 6 July deadline. [*SI 2003 No 2682, Regs 85(1), 94, Sch 1 para 16*].

(c) Where a third party makes payments or provides benefits which if done by arrangement with the employer would have fallen to be included on forms P11D and P9D (see **53.21** PAY AS YOU EARN), he must provide particulars, including cash equivalents, to the employee by 6 July following the tax year. [*SI 2003 No 2682, Reg 95*].

Penalties under *TMA 1970, s 98* for failure to provide information to HMRC (see **55.22** PENALTIES) apply equally to failure to comply with the above requirements for providing particulars to employees.

Taxation of non-UK residents

[67.13] Individuals who regard themselves as not resident or not domiciled in the UK are required to self-certify their status in the self-assessment tax return. See **63.1** RESIDENCE AND DOMICILE.

68

Self-Assessment — Key Dates

Cross-reference. See also **67** SELF-ASSESSMENT.

[68.1] The Table below sets out key dates and events in the operation of the self-assessment regime.

Date	*Event*
April 2020	HMRC issue majority of notices to file a 2019/20 self-assessment tax return (see **64.2** RETURNS).
1 May 2020	HMRC may impose a daily penalty where failure to make a 2018/19 tax return continues on or after this date (see **55.5** PENALTIES).
31 May 2020	Deadline for employers to provide employees with Form P60 for 2019/20 (see **67.12** SELF-ASSESSMENT).
6 July 2020	Deadline for employers to provide both HMRC and employees with P11D information etc. for 2019/20 (see **53.21** PAY AS YOU EARN and **67.12** SELF-ASSESSMENT).
31 July 2020	Second interim payment on account due for 2019/20, but due to COVID-19 (coronavirus) this payment can be deferred until any time up to 31 January 2021 (see **67.5** SELF-ASSESSMENT).
1 August 2020	First tax-geared penalty due where 2018/19 tax return not filed before this date (see **55.5** PENALTIES).
1 August 2020	If 2019/20 tax return issued after this date, normal 31 October deadline for manual filing is deferred until three months from date of issue (see **64.2** RETURNS).
2 August 2020	Second late payment penalty due of 5% of any 2018/19 income tax and capital gains tax due on 31 January 2020 and remaining unpaid on this date (see **43.4** LATE PAYMENT INTEREST AND PENALTIES).
5 October 2020	Chargeability to tax for 2019/20 to be notified to HMRC on or before this date if no tax return received (see **55.2** PENALTIES).
31 October 2020	2019/20 tax return to be filed on or before this date if not filed online (see **64.2** RETURNS).

Date	*Event*
1 November 2020	If 2019/20 tax return issued on or after this date, normal 31 January deadline for online filing is deferred until three months from date of issue (see **64.2** RETURNS) as is due date of balancing payment and payment of capital gains tax provided notice of chargeability given timeously (see above, and **67.7** SELF-ASSESSMENT).
30 December 2020	2019/20 tax return to be filed on or before this date if taxpayer filing online wishes 2019/20 tax underpayment of less than £3,000 to be collected by adjustment to 2021/22 PAYE code (see **67.4** SELF-ASSESSMENT).
31 January 2021	2019/20 tax return to be filed on or before this date if filed online (see **64.2** RETURNS).
31 January 2021	Balancing payment of income tax and payment of capital gains tax due for 2019/20 (see **67.7** SELF-ASSESSMENT).
31 January 2021	First interim payment on account due for 2020/21 (see **67.5** SELF-ASSESSMENT).
1 February 2021	Second tax-geared penalty due where 2018/19 tax return not filed before this date (see **55.5** PENALTIES).
2 February 2021	Third late payment penalty due of 5% of any 2018/19 income tax and capital gains tax due on 31 January 2020 and remaining unpaid on this date (see **43.4** LATE PAYMENT INTEREST AND PENALTIES).
February 2021	HMRC begin to issue initial fixed penalty notices for non-filing of 2019/20 tax returns (see **55.5** PENALTIES).
3 March 2021	Initial late payment penalty due of 5% of any 2019/20 income tax and capital gains tax due on 31 January 2021 and remaining unpaid on this date (see **43.4** LATE PAYMENT INTEREST AND PENALTIES).
April 2021	HMRC issue majority of notices to file a 2020/21 self-assessment tax return (see **64.2** RETURNS).
1 May 2021	HMRC may impose a daily penalty where failure to make a 2019/20 tax return continues on or after this date (see **55.5** PENALTIES).
31 May 2021	Deadline for employers to provide employees with Form P60 for 2020/21 (see **67.12** SELF-ASSESSMENT).

Date	*Event*
6 July 2021	Deadline for employers to provide both HMRC and employees with P11D information etc. for 2020/21 (see **53.21** PAY AS YOU EARN and **67.12** SELF-ASSESSMENT).
31 July 2021	Second interim payment on account due for 2020/21 (see **67.5** SELF-ASSESSMENT).

69

Self-Employment

Introduction to self-employment

[69.1] The individual in business, whether full-time or part-time, on his own or in partnership with others, is subject to particular tax legislation and practices. Such legislation etc. is covered in this work under various subject headings, and the following paragraphs indicate where the detailed provisions are to be found.

See the HMRC Guide 'Giving your business the best start with tax', available at www.gov.uk/government/uploads/system/uploads/attachment_data/file/377657/working-yourself.pdf.

See 28.66 EMPLOYMENT INCOME as regards the distinction between employment and self-employment.

See 58 PERSONAL SERVICE COMPANIES ETC. as regards individuals providing their services through an intermediary in circumstances such that they would fall to be categorised as employees if engaged directly.

Charge to income tax etc.

[69.2] Profits are chargeable to tax under the rules in 75 TRADING INCOME. Special provisions relate to the opening and closing years of a business. Particular items of expenditure or receipt may, or may not, be included in the computation of taxable profits. An optional fixed rate deduction scheme applies to certain types of expenditure; see 77 TRADING INCOME — FIXED RATE DEDUCTION SCHEME. Where a business is discontinued, see also 59 POST-CESSATION RECEIPTS AND EXPENDITURE. Partnership matters are dealt with under 52 PARTNERSHIPS. Farmers may elect for the HERD BASIS (34) to apply to their animals. Special provisions apply to UNDERWRITERS AT LLOYD'S (79).

Some transactions may result in a tax charge because they contravene legislation on ANTI-AVOIDANCE (4).

For general procedure, see SELF-ASSESSMENT (67). See also 6 ASSESSMENTS and 5 APPEALS.

Cash basis for smaller businesses

A smaller business (defined by reference to turnover) may opt to use a simplified cash basis in calculating taxable profits. See 76 TRADING INCOME — CASH BASIS FOR SMALLER BUSINESSES.

Property letting

See 60 PROPERTY INCOME.

Assets

The acquisition or ownership of business assets may give rise to capital allowances as the tax substitute for the disallowable depreciation charge (if any) in the accounts (see 9 CAPITAL ALLOWANCES and 10 CAPITAL ALLOWANCES ON PLANT AND MACHINERY). The disposal of assets may result in balancing adjustments for capital allowances purposes, and also to a charge to capital gains tax (see Tolley's Capital Gains Tax) unless certain exemptions and reliefs apply.

Overseas

Income from trades etc. carried on wholly abroad by a UK resident is within the charge to tax (see 75.1 TRADING INCOME). See 50.6 NON-RESIDENTS for non-residents trading in the UK.

Losses

If trading losses are incurred, relief may be obtained by various alternatives, see under 45 LOSSES.

Employees

[69.3] If staff are employed, then the regulations under the PAY AS YOU EARN (53) system must be complied with.

Payment of tax

[69.4] For due dates for payment, see under SELF-ASSESSMENT (67). See also 54 PAYMENT OF TAX and 43 LATE PAYMENT INTEREST AND PENALTIES. Special provisions apply to the construction industry, see CONSTRUCTION INDUSTRY SCHEME (20).

Provision for retirement

[69.5] Special legislation allows tax relief for payments made to secure a pension in retirement. See 57 PENSION PROVISION.

National insurance contributions

[69.6] Class 4 contributions are charged on business profits, see 73 SOCIAL SECURITY AND NATIONAL INSURANCE.

Value added tax

[69.7] The detailed provisions of VAT are outside the scope of this book but registration is generally required when the 'taxable turnover' of the business will exceed £85,000 in a year. See Tolley's Value Added Tax.

70

Settlements

Cross-references. See **4.14–4.18** ANTI-AVOIDANCE for transfer of assets abroad; **22** DECEASED ESTATES for the income of estates of deceased persons in course of administration; 23 DEDUCTION OF TAX AT SOURCE generally and at **23.7–23.10** for annuities etc. and **23.16** for tax-free annuities under wills etc.; **55.2** PENALTIES, **64.2** RETURNS, **67.11** SELF-ASSESSMENT for administrative provisions relating to trustees under self-assessment.

Simon's Taxes. See Part C4.

Introduction to settlements

[70.1] Trustees of settlements are taxed in their representative capacities (see **70.8** below). They are charged to income tax at the basic rate or the dividend ordinary rate (see **1.5** ALLOWANCES AND TAX RATES), as appropriate to the class of income, except in the case of discretionary and accumulation trusts (see **70.11** below). The latter are generally charged at the 'trust rate' or, in respect of dividend income, the 'dividend trust rate', with a standard rate band of £1,000. Certain narrow categories of income are charged at the trust rate or dividend trust rate regardless of the type of trust involved (see **70.12**(1)–(10) below).

The trustees of a settlement are together treated for income tax purposes as if they were a single person (distinct from the persons who are the actual trustees from time to time). Where part of the property comprised in a single settlement is vested in one trustee or body of trustees and part in another, those two trustees or bodies of trustees are together treated as constituting a single body of trustees. In a case where the trustees of a settlement carry on a trade, profession or vocation, the introduction of this rule or the definition of settled property at **70.2** below cannot in itself invoke the cessation and/or commencement rules for trades etc. [*ITA 2007, s 474*].

For residence of trustees, see **70.5** below. For guidance on non-UK resident trusts see HMRC Trusts, Settlements and Estates Manual TSEM10000.

Beneficiaries receive income from settlements which is treated as net of the tax accounted for by the trustees. The grossed-up amount of the income is treated as part of the total income of the beneficiary for tax purposes. If the total income of a beneficiary is high enough, he will suffer income tax at the excess of the higher rate or the dividend upper rate over the tax accounted for by the trustees on the grossed-up income from the trust. He may alternatively be entitled to a repayment of some or all of the tax suffered by the trustees where it exceeds his own liability. See also **70.15** below for tax repayments to non-residents.

The following should also be noted.

(a) **Trusts with vulnerable beneficiaries.** Special income tax and capital gains tax treatment is given if the trustees and the vulnerable beneficiary concerned opt for it to apply. The income tax liability is computed as if the beneficiary had received the income directly, i.e. applying his own tax rates and allowances. See **70.19** below.

(b) **Scottish trusts.** Provided that the trustees are UK resident, the rights of a beneficiary of a Scottish trust are treated for income tax purposes as including an equitable right in possession to any trust income to which such a right does not arise under the law of Scotland but would have arisen if the trust had effect under the law of England and Wales. [*ITA 2007, s 464*].

(c) **Demergers.** For the income and capital gains tax treatment of shares received by trustees as a result of exempt demergers (for which see Tolley's Corporation Tax under Groups of Companies), see HMRC Capital Gains Tax Manual CG33900 *et seq.*

(d) **Trustees are also liable to capital gains tax.** See the corresponding chapter of Tolley's Capital Gains Tax for full coverage.

(e) **Trusts must normally be registered online with HMRC.** For guidance on the registration process, including which trusts should register and which should not, and when to register, see www.gov.uk/guidance/register-your-clients-trust and www.gov.uk/guidance/register-a-trust-as-a-trustee.

Definition of settled property

[70.2] A statutory definition of 'settled property' is provided for income tax purposes as follows. It applies unless 'the context otherwise requires' and, in particular, does not alter the wide definition of 'settlement' given in **70.28** below for the purposes therein stated.

'*Settled property*' means any property held in trust other than:

(a) property held by a person as nominee for another; and
(b) property held by a person as trustee for another person who is absolutely entitled as against the trustee or who would be so entitled were he not an infant or otherwise lacking legal capacity; (any such trustee is generally referred to as a bare trustee).

Any reference in income tax legislation to 'property comprised in a settlement' has the same meaning as above.

For the purposes of (b) above, and for general income tax purposes, a person is absolutely entitled to property as against the trustee if he has the exclusive right to direct how the property is to be dealt with (subject only to the trustees' right to resort to the property for payment of duties, taxes, costs or other outgoings). Any reference in income tax legislation to a person being so entitled is to be taken as including a reference to two or more persons being so entitled.

[*ITA 2007, s 466*].

Definition of 'settlor'

[70.3] A statutory definition of 'settlor' is provided for income tax purposes as set out below. The definition applies 'except where the context otherwise requires', and it should be noted that a separate definition continues to have effect as in **70.28** below for the purposes therein stated.

'*Settlor*' in relation to a settlement means the person, or any of the persons, who has made, or is treated for income tax purposes as having made, the settlement. A person is treated as having made a settlement if:

- he has made or entered into the settlement, directly or indirectly; or
- the settlement arose on his death, whether by will, intestacy or otherwise, and the settled property (see **70.2** above), or property from which the settled property is derived (see below), is (or includes) property which he could have disposed of by will (if certain assumptions were made and powers ignored) or which represented his severable share in property as a joint tenant.

In particular, a person is treated as having made a settlement if he has provided property (directly or indirectly), or has undertaken to provide property (directly or indirectly), for the purposes of the settlement.

Where one person (A) makes or enters into a settlement in accordance with reciprocal arrangements with another person (B), B is treated as having made the settlement and A is not treated for that reason alone as having made it. 'Arrangements' is widely defined to include any scheme, agreement or understanding, whether or not legally enforceable.

A person ceases to be a settlor in relation to a settlement if:

- no property of which he is the settlor remains in the settlement;
- he has not undertaken to provide property (directly or indirectly), for the purposes of the settlement in the future; and
- he has not made reciprocal arrangements with another person for that other person to enter into the settlement in the future.

A person is a settlor of any property which is settled property by reason of his having made the settlement (or by reason of an event which causes him to be treated as having made the settlement) or which derives (see below) from such property.

For the above purposes, property is derived from other property if it derives (directly or indirectly and wholly or partly) from the other property or any part of it. In particular, property is derived from other property if it derives (as before) from *income* from the other property or any part of it.

[*ITA 2007, ss 465(7)(8), 467–469*].

Identification of settlor

[70.4] Rules apply for identifying the settlor of property that has been transferred between settlements otherwise than for full consideration and other than by way of arm's length bargain. The rules apply 'except where the context otherwise requires'. For these purposes, a transfer of property involves a disposal by the trustees of a settlement (Settlement 1) and an acquisition by the trustees of another settlement (Settlement 2) of either the property disposed of by Settlement 1 or property created by the disposal (an example of the latter being the grant by Settlement 1 of a leasehold interest out of a freehold interest in land). The '*transferred property*' (see below) is the property thus acquired by Settlement 2. The question of whether there is a disposal or an acquisition is determined as for CGT purposes.

Broadly, the settlor of the property disposed of by Settlement 1 is treated, from the time of the disposal, as having made Settlement 2. If there is more than one such settlor, all the settlors are treated as having made Settlement 2, and each of the settlors is treated in relation to Settlement 2 as the settlor of a proportionate part of the transferred property. The transferred property is treated, from the time of the disposal, as provided for the purposes of Settlement 2 (to the extent that the property disposed of was provided for the purposes of Settlement 1). The person who provided the property for the purposes of Settlement 1 (or property from which it was derived — see **70.3** above) is treated as having provided the transferred property. If there is more than one such person, each of them is treated as having provided a proportionate part of the transferred property.

These rules are disapplied in relation to a transfer of property:

(a) that occurs by reason only of the assignment, by a beneficiary of Settlement 1 to the trustees of Settlement 2, of an interest in Settlement 1;
(b) that occurs by reason only of the exercise of a general power of appointment; or
(c) in particular circumstances (as mentioned below) which involve the variation of a will or an intestacy.

[*ITA 2007, ss 470, 471*].

The following rules apply to identify the settlor in a case where a disposition of property (whether by will or intestacy) following a person's death is varied within two years after the death in a case where the instrument of variation requires that *TCGA 1992, s 62(6)* should apply. (*Section 62(6)* treats the variation as having effectively been made by the deceased and as not itself constituting a CGT disposal — see Tolley's Capital Gains Tax under Death.)

Where property becomes 'settled property' (see **70.2** above) by reason only of the variation, the person treated as having made the settlement and as having provided the property for the purposes of the settlement is the person who immediately before the variation was entitled to the property, or to property from which it derives (see **70.3** above), absolutely as legatee (which is given a broad meaning for this purpose). This rule is extended to include a person who would, but for the variation, have become so entitled and a person who would have fallen into either of these two categories but for his being an infant or otherwise lacking legal capacity.

Where property would have become comprised in a settlement that arose on or pre-dated the deceased person's death, but in consequence of the variation becomes comprised in another settlement, the deceased is treated as having made the other settlement.

Where, immediately before the variation, property is comprised in a settlement and is property of which the deceased is a settlor and, immediately after the variation, it becomes comprised in another settlement, the deceased is treated as having made the other settlement. These are the circumstances referred to at (c) above.

References in the two rules immediately above to the property becoming comprised in another settlement include references to property derived from that property (see above) becoming so comprised. In both rules, the time at which the deceased is treated as having made the other settlement is immediately before his death (other than where the other settlement actually arose on his death).

[*ITA 2007, ss 472, 473*].

Residence of trustees

[70.5] The rules set out below have effect for the purpose of determining the residence status of the trustees of a settlement.

As stated at **70.2** above, the trustees of a settlement are together treated for income tax purposes as if they were a single person (distinct from the persons who are the actual trustees from time to time). That notional single person is treated for income tax purposes as UK resident at any time when *either* of the following two conditions are satisfied. If neither condition is satisfied, the notional person is treated as non-UK resident.

Condition A is that all the trustees are UK resident.

Condition B is that at least one trustee is UK resident (with at least one trustee being non-UK resident) *and* that a settlor in relation to the settlement meets Condition C (see below).

If the settlement arose on the settlor's death and, immediately prior to death, the settlor was resident or domiciled in the UK, the settlor meets Condition C from the time of his death until such time as he ceases to be a settlor in relation to the settlement. If the settlement arose otherwise than on the settlor's death and the settlor made it (or is treated for income tax purposes as making it) at a time when he was resident or domiciled in the UK, the settlor meets Condition C from that time until such time as he ceases to be a settlor in relation to the settlement. The deemed domicile rule at **63.36** RESIDENCE AND DOMICILE applies in each case, and does so where the settlor dies, or (in the second alternative) the settlement is made, on or after 6 April 2017. Where the settlor died, or (as the case may be) the settlement was made, before 6 April 2013, Condition C has effect as if it continued to refer to the settlor's being ordinarily UK resident, as an alternative to his being UK resident or domiciled, in accordance with pre-6 April 2013 legislation.

Where there has been a transfer within *ITA 2007, ss 470, 471* between settlements (see **70.4** above), then Condition C is met by the person treated as having made Settlement 2 if it was met by him, immediately before the transfer, as a settlor in relation to Settlement 1.

Split year treatment

If:

- an individual becomes or ceases to be a trustee of a settlement during a tax year which is a split year (see **63.19** RESIDENCE AND DOMICILE) as regards that individual, and
- the only period in that year when the individual is a trustee of the settlement falls wholly within the overseas part of the split year,

the individual is to be treated for the purposes of Conditions A and B above as if he had been non-UK resident for the tax year (and hence for the period in that year when he was a trustee of the settlement).

Professional trustees

For the purposes of Conditions A and B above, a trustee who is non-UK resident is nevertheless treated as UK resident at any time when he is acting as trustee in the course of a business that he carries on in the UK through a branch, agency or permanent establishment there. This also takes precedence over the split year treatment above, so that an individual who is thereby treated as having been non-UK resident is, in spite of that, to be treated as UK resident whenever he acts as trustee in the course of a UK business.

See HMRC Trusts, Settlements and Estates Manual TSEM10005. See also, at www.step.org/sites/default/files/Policy/pdfs/trustee-residence-guide-2015.pdf, the joint guidance note originally published as TAXGUIDE 3/10 (Trustee Residence) by the ICAEW Tax Faculty, CIOT and STEP in August 2010, and updated as TAXGUIDE 06/15, in response to the HMRC guidance.

[*ITA 2007, ss 475, 476; FA 2013, Sch 46 para 57; F(No 2)A 2017, Sch 8 para 12*].

Simon's Taxes. See **C4.405**.

Sub-fund settlements

[70.6] Under *TCGA 1992, Sch 4ZA*, subject to conditions, the trustees of a settlement may make an irrevocable election ('a sub-fund election') to treat a fund or other specified portion of the settled property ('the sub-fund') as a separate settlement ('the sub-fund settlement') for CGT purposes. The election must specify the date on which it is to be treated as having taken effect, which can be earlier, but not later, than the date it is made. For the full rules, conditions, procedures and consequences, see the corresponding chapter of Tolley's Capital Gains Tax. See also HMRC Tax Bulletin August 2006 pp 1305, 1306.

Where a sub-fund election has been made, the following consequences ensue for income tax purposes.

- The sub-fund settlement is treated as a settlement, and as having been created on the 'effective date' (see below).
- Each trustee of the trusts on which the property comprised in the sub-fund settlement is held is treated as a trustee of the sub-fund settlement.
- Each trustee of the sub-fund settlement is treated from the 'effective date' as having ceased to be a trustee of the principal settlement unless he is also a trustee of trusts on which property comprised in the principal settlement is held.
- No trustee of the principal settlement is treated as a trustee of the sub-fund settlement unless he is also a trustee of trusts on which property comprised in the sub-fund settlement is held.

- The trustees of the sub-fund settlement are treated as having become absolutely entitled, from the 'effective date', to the property comprised in that settlement as against the trustees of the principal settlement.

References above to the '*effective date*' are to the date the sub-fund election is treated as having taken effect (see above). However, *TCGA 1992, Sch 4ZA para 2* contains rules as to exactly when on that date the election takes effect (see Tolley's Capital Gains Tax), and these apply equally for the above income tax purposes.

[*ITA 2007, s 477*].

Simon's Taxes. See **C4.6**.

Bare trusts

[70.7] Trustees of 'bare' (or 'simple') trusts treated as such for tax purposes are not required to deduct tax from payments to beneficiaries or to complete self-assessment returns or make payments on account. The beneficiaries under such trusts are liable to give details of the income and gains in their own tax returns. The trustees may, if they and the beneficiaries so wish, make returns of income (but *not* of capital gains or capital losses), accounting for tax at the basic rate or the dividend ordinary rate, as appropriate to the class of income, provided that they so notify the trust district and follow this course consistently from year to year. This does not, however, affect the liability of the beneficiaries to make the appropriate self-assessment returns of income and gains. (Revenue Tax Bulletin February 1997 p 395, December 1997 pp 486, 487). See **70.2**(b) above as regards what is meant by bare trusts, and see HMRC Trusts, Settlements and Estates Manual TSEM1563.

Where a chargeable event gain arises on a life policy held in a bare trust for a minor, HMRC regard the minor himself as the person chargeable. Where, however, either or both of the child's parents are the settlors of the bare trust, the children's settlements rules at **70.30** below apply so that the parent is potentially the person chargeable. (HMRC Brief 51/08, 8 October 2008).

A bare trust may exist in the absence of any documentation to that effect; its existence or otherwise may be supported by other evidence (*Tang v HMRC* FTT (TC 6965), [2019] UKFTT 81 (TC)).

Assessments on trust income

[70.8] Income may be assessed and charged on (and in the name of) any one or more of the persons who are trustees in the tax year in which the income arises or on any one or more subsequent trustees. [*TMA 1970, s 30AA*]. References here to assessment include self-assessment.

Untaxed income

The untaxed income of a trust may be assessed on the trustee as the person receiving it (see, for example, *ITTOIA 2005, s 271* and *Reid's Trustees v CIR* CS 1929, 14 TC 512). See *Williams v Singer* HL 1920, 7 TC 387 (trustees not assessable where overseas income paid direct to non-resident beneficiary) and compare *Kelly v Rogers* CA 1935, 19 TC 692 (UK trustee of foreign trust held assessable in respect of overseas income as there was no ascertainable non-resident beneficiary entitled to the income) and *Dawson v CIR* HL 1989, 62 TC 301 (sole UK resident trustee of foreign trust with three trustees held not assessable in respect of income not remitted). See, however, **70.5** above for current law on residence of trustees. Held in *Pakenham* HL 1928, 13 TC 573 that settlement trustees not assessable in respect of beneficiary's super-tax liability.

Expenses of administering the trust

Expenses of administering the trust are not deductible in the assessments on the trustee (*Aikin v Macdonald Trustees* CES 1894, 3 TC 306; *Inverclyde's Trustees v Millar* CS 1924, 9 TC 14) even though deductible in arriving at the beneficiaries' income as in **70.9** below. However, see **70.14** below for the effect of trust expenses on the rates of tax applicable to income otherwise chargeable at special rates.

Returns

Trustees are within the self-assessment regime (see **64.2** RETURNS, **67.4, 67.11** SELF-ASSESSMENT). Trustees cannot make separate returns for different funds into which the settlement may be split (unless a sub-fund election has been made as in **70.6** above) (HMRC Tax Bulletin August 2006 p 1305).

Simon's Taxes. See **C4.201–C4.208.**

Effect of trustees' expenses on beneficiaries' income

[70.9] Trustees' expenses (sometimes called 'management expenses') can be used to reduce the taxable income of the beneficiary as set out below. These rules apply only if, before being distributed, some or all of the income arising to the trustees in the tax year is the income of another person (i.e. the beneficiary). They thus apply to an interest in possession trust but not to a discretionary trust (for which see **70.14** below). The beneficiary is regarded as not entitled to the income used to pay the expenses; therefore, such income does not enter into any calculation of his income tax liability.

Expenses can be used in this way only if they are chargeable to income by the trustees either under a term of the settlement (subject to any overriding law) or, if the settlement deed contains no such term, under general trust law (subject to any overriding term of the settlement). The expenses to be considered are those incurred by the trustees in the current tax year or brought forward from an earlier tax year.

HMRC take the view that, except in 'rare circumstances where it can be demonstrated [that] the payments are solely for managing income, payments of trustees' remuneration are linked to the management of the trust as a whole and are therefore regarded as attributable to capital'. In other words, trustees' remuneration is not regarded as chargeable to income under general law. (HMRC Tax Bulletin August 2005 p 1228).

For HMRC guidance on trustees' expenses, see www.gov.uk/government/publications/trust-management-expenses-tmes-hs392-self-assessment-helpsheet/hs392-trust-management-expenses-tmes-2016 and HMRC Trusts, Settlements and Estates Manual TSEM8000.

In *HMRC v Trustees of the Peter Clay Discretionary Trust* CA 2008, 79 TC 473, it was held in the Ch D that trustees' remuneration fell to be regarded as incurred for the benefit of the whole estate and, therefore, to be treated as a capital expense; there had to be a heavy evidential burden upon those who asserted a contrary conclusion, and that burden was not satisfied in the instant case. However, whilst reasserting that it was generally only those expenses which had been incurred exclusively for the benefit of the income beneficiaries that might be charged against income, the CA nevertheless held that, on the particular facts of this case, a proportion of trustees' fees could be so charged. The CA also held that investment management fees had to be charged to capital; significantly the fees were incurred *after* the trustees had resolved to accumulate the trust income.

The order of set-off of expenses is determined by *ITA 2007, s 503*; firstly against dividend income (see **1.5** ALLOWANCES AND TAX RATES), then against savings income (see **1.6** ALLOWANCES AND TAX RATES) and finally against basic rate income. Expenses set against dividend income is set against UK dividend income in priority to dividends from non-UK resident companies. The beneficiary's taxable income is computed by subtracting from the amount of each of those three types of income the income tax payable on it by the trustees and the expenses set against it. The resulting net amount of each of type of income is then grossed up at the rate of tax applicable to that type of income to give the beneficiary's taxable income of that type from the trust.

See the examples at **70.10** below.

Where a beneficiary is not liable to income tax on part of his share of the trust income, by virtue wholly or partly of his being non-UK resident or being deemed under a double tax agreement to be resident in a territory outside the UK, the trustees' expenses otherwise available to reduce his income are reduced in the same proportion as that which such non-taxable income bears to his full share of income (using in each case the income net of UK and foreign tax). Where the beneficiary's income tax liability is limited under the provisions at **50.3** NON-RESIDENTS, excluded income (see **50.3**), other than that which has suffered deduction of UK income tax at source, must be included in non-taxable income for the purposes of this apportionment.

[*ITA 2007, ss 499–503; FA 2016, Sch 1 paras 63(8), 73*].

Simon's Taxes. See **C4.205**.

Example

[70.10]

A is sole life-tenant of a settlement which has income and expenses in the year 2020/21 as follows.

	£
Property income	500
Bank interest	1,500
Dividends	1,000
	£3,000
Expenses chargeable to income	£400

The tax payable by the trustees is as follows:

	£
Property income — £500 @ 20% (basic rate)	100.00
Bank interest — £1,500 @ 20% (basic rate)	300.00
Dividends — £1,000 @ 7.5% (dividend ordinary rate)	75.00
	£475.00

The expenses are not deductible in arriving at the tax payable by the trustees. The starting rate for savings, dividend allowance and personal savings allowance are not available to trustees.

A is sole life-tenant of the above settlement and as such is absolutely entitled to receive the whole settlement income.

A's income for 2020/21 will include the following.

		£	£	£
Trust dividend income		1,000		
Trust interest income			1,500	
Other trust income				500
Deduct: dividend ordinary rate tax (7.5%)		(75)		
basic rate tax (20%)			(300)	(100)
		925	1,200	400
Deduct expenses (note (b))		400		
Net income entitlement		£525	£1,200	£400
Grossed-up amounts:	£525 × 100/92.5	£567		
	£1,200 × 100/80		£1,500	
	£400 × 100/80			£500

Notes

(a) This income falls to be included in A's return even if it is not actually paid to him, as he is absolutely entitled to it. He will receive a tax certificate (form R185 (Trust Income)) from the trust agents, showing three figures for gross income (£567, £1,500 and £500), tax deducted (£42, £300 and £100) and net income (£525, £1,200 and £400).

(b) The trust expenses are deducted from dividend income in priority to other income (see **70.9** above).

(c) That part of A's trust income which is represented by dividend income (£567) is treated in A's hands as if it were dividend income received directly by A. A is entitled to a credit against his tax liability for the £42 dividend ordinary rate tax deducted by the trustees, and this is repayable to him if he has insufficient liability to cover it.

Similarly, that part of A's trust income which is represented by savings income (£1,500) is treated in A's hands as if it were such income received directly by A. It will thus qualify wholly or partly for the 0% starting rate for savings (see **1.6** ALLOWANCES AND TAX RATES) to the extent (if any) that A's other taxable income is less than the starting rate limit of £5,000, and for the personal savings allowance (see **1.7** ALLOWANCES AND TAX RATES) if A is not an additional rate taxpayer.

Special trust rates of tax

[70.11] 'Accumulated or discretionary income' arising to the trustees of a settlement (other than under a charitable trust) is taxed at either the 'trust rate' or the 'dividend trust rate' (rather than at the basic rate, higher or additional rate or the dividend ordinary, higher and additional rates). The '*trust rate*' and '*dividend trust rate*' are as follows:

		Trust rate	*Dividend Trust rate*
For	2016/17 onwards	45%	38.1%

The dividend trust rate applies if the income is 'dividend income' (as defined in **1.5** ALLOWANCES AND TAX RATES). See Revenue Tax Bulletin February 1999 pp 629, 630 for an illustrative interpretation of the application of the dividend trust rate. See *Howell & Morton (Robin Settlement Trustees) v Trippier* CA 2004, 76 TC 415 in which it was held that the dividend trust rate applies to stock dividends (see **65.19** SAVINGS AND INVESTMENT INCOME) received by discretionary trusts even if treated under the terms of the settlement as a capital receipt in the hands of the trustees.

Income is '*accumulated or discretionary income*' for the above purpose in so far as it must be accumulated or it is payable at the discretion of the trustees or any other person. However, income is excluded from being 'accumulated or discretionary income' in so far as:

(a) before being distributed, the income is the income of any person other than the trustees; or

(b) the income arises from property held for the purposes of an overseas employee superannuation fund to which *ICTA 1988, s 615(3)* applies (see **57.40** PENSION PROVISION) or certain pre-2006/07 retirement benefit or personal pension schemes; or

(c) the income is from 'service charges' which are paid in respect of UK dwellings and which are held on trust; (for this purpose, '*service charges*' has the meaning given by *Landlord and Tenant Act 1985, s 18* but as if that section also applied in relation to dwellings in Scotland and NI).

The exclusion at (b) above does not apply to property held as a member of a property investment LLP (see **52.28** PARTNERSHIPS). In a case in which the facts pre-dated (c) above, income arising from service charges held on trust was held to be liable at the trust rate (*Retirement Care Group Ltd (as trustees) v HMRC* (Sp C 607), [2007] SSCD 539).

The trust rate and dividend trust rate thus apply mainly to discretionary trusts and accumulation trusts, but see **70.12** below for items treated as income within these provisions when arising to the trustees of any settlement.

See **70.13** below for the standard rate band available to trustees liable at the trust rate and/or dividend trust rate. See **70.14** below for the treatment of trust expenses.

See **70.19** *et seq*. below as regards special treatment of trusts with vulnerable beneficiaries.

[*ITA 2007, ss 9, 479, 480; FA 2016, s 5(4)(10)*].

Any sum received by trustees of a settlement from personal representatives on or before completion of the administration of an estate that would be accumulated or discretionary income or income within **70.12** below if the personal representatives were trustees is regarded as income of the trustees and treated as having borne tax at the applicable rate (for which see **22.6** DECEASED ESTATES). [*ITA 2007, s 483*].

Simon's Taxes. See **C4.210.**

Other items chargeable at the special trust rates

[70.12] The items listed at (1)–(10) below are chargeable at the special rates in **70.11** above where they arise to the trustees of any settlement (and not just a discretionary trust or an accumulation trust). However, the following exclusions apply:

(a) income arising to a trust established for charitable purposes only;

(b) 'accumulated or discretionary income' (within **70.11** above);

(c) income that would be 'accumulated or discretionary income' were it not for the exclusions at **70.11**(a) or (c) above; and

(d) income from property held for the purposes of an overseas employee superannuation fund to which *ICTA 1988, s 615(3)* applies (see **57.40** PENSION PROVISION).

Items (1) and (10) below are chargeable at the dividend trust rate and items (2)–(9) at the trust rate.

(1) Payments receivable from a company for the purchase, redemption or repayment of its own shares or for the purchase of rights to acquire its own shares. The amount chargeable is restricted to the distribution element of the payment and excludes that part of the payment that represents the original subscription price received for the shares by the issuing company.
(2) Chargeable event gains on life policies other than where the settlement is a charitable trust (see **44.12** LIFE ASSURANCE POLICIES).
(3) Profits on disposals of deeply discounted securities unless the trustees are non-UK resident (see **65.29** SAVINGS AND INVESTMENT INCOME).
(4) Lease premiums etc. (see **60.26, 60.27** PROPERTY INCOME).
(5) Profits on disposals of CERTIFICATES OF DEPOSIT (**12**).
(6) Chargeable events occurring in relation to a qualifying employee share ownership trust (QUEST).
(7) Offshore income gains (see **51.3** OFFSHORE FUNDS).
(8) Profits and gains on disposals of land etc. that are brought within the charge to income tax by the provisions in, for disposals on or after 5 July 2016, **78.3–78.8** TRANSACTIONS IN UK LAND and, for disposals before that date, **4.30** ANTI-AVOIDANCE.
(9) Accrued income profits chargeable under **2.4** or **2.14** ACCRUED INCOME SCHEME.
(10) Income treated as arising to the trustees under *ITTOIA 2005, s 396A* (shareholders given choice of income or capital return — see **65.12** SAVINGS AND INVESTMENT INCOME).

[*ITA 2007, ss 481, 482; FA 2016, ss 79(3), 82(1), Sch 1 paras 63(5), 73*].

Standard rate band

[70.13] A standard rate band is available for any trust whose income for the tax year consists of or includes income otherwise chargeable at the special rates at **70.11** above, i.e. the trust rate or the dividend trust rate. The standard rate band is **£1,000**. So much of that income as does not exceed that amount is chargeable not at the said rates but at the basic rate or the dividend ordinary rate (see **1.3–1.5** ALLOWANCES AND TAX RATES) depending on the type of income. For the purpose of determining which income falls within the standard rate band (where the total income otherwise chargeable at the special rates exceeds that band), income normally chargeable on trustees at the basic rate is deemed to form the lowest part of that total income, and income normally chargeable on trustees at the dividend ordinary rate is deemed to form the highest part of that total income. For the purposes of applying the standard rate band, chargeable event gains on life policies count as savings income. See the examples at **70.16** below.

The £1,000 standard rate band is divided equally between all settlements made by any one settlor and in existence for any part of the tax year in question, subject to a minimum band of £200 for each such settlement. In the case of a settlement with more than one settlor, the band is determined by reference to the settlor with the greatest number of settlements.

[*ITA 2007, ss 463(2), 491, 492*].

Treatment of trustees' expenses

[70.14] The trustees may offset their expenses (sometimes referred to as management expenses) against trust income for the purpose of determining income chargeable at the special rates, i.e. the trust rate or the dividend trust rate, although income so relieved remains subject to basic rate or dividend ordinary rate tax, as the case may be. They must, however, be expenses properly chargeable to income (or which would be so chargeable but for any express terms of the settlement) (see *Carver v Duncan*; *Bosanquet v Allen* HL 1985, 59 TC 125). HMRC take the view that, except in 'rare circumstances where it can be demonstrated [that] the payments are solely for managing income, payments of trustees' remuneration are linked to the management of the trust as a whole and are therefore regarded as attributable to capital'. In other words, trustees' remuneration is not regarded as properly chargeable to income. (HMRC Tax Bulletin August 2005 p 1228). Generally, the expenses allowable are those incurred in exercising the trustees' powers and duties in so far as they relate to managing the trust assets to produce or maintain an income flow.

For HMRC guidance on trustees' expenses, see www.gov.uk/government/publications/trust-management-expenses-tmes-hs392-self-assessment-helpsheet/hs392-trust-management-expenses-tmes-2016 and HMRC Trusts, Settlements and Estates Manual TSEM8000.

In *HMRC v Trustees of the Peter Clay Discretionary Trust* CA 2008, 79 TC 473, it was held in the Ch D that trustees' remuneration fell to be regarded as incurred for the benefit of the whole estate and, therefore, to be treated as a capital expense; there had to be a heavy evidential burden upon those who asserted a contrary conclusion, and that burden was not satisfied in the instant case. However, whilst reasserting that it was generally only those expenses which had been incurred exclusively for the benefit of the income beneficiaries that might be charged against income, the CA nevertheless held that, on the particular facts of this case, a proportion of trustees' fees could be so charged. The CA also held that investment management fees had to be charged to capital; significantly the fees were incurred after the trustees had resolved to accumulate the trust income.

Expenses are to be taken into account when incurred. Expenses remaining unrelieved in a tax year, due to an insufficiency of income chargeable at the special rates, can be carried forward and treated as if incurred in a subsequent tax year.

As income properly covered by expenses is no longer income chargeable at the special rates, it is left out of account in applying the standard rate band at **70.13** above.

The order of set-off of expenses is determined by *ITA 2007, s 486*. First, reduce the expenses by any unallowable proportion computed as described below; then set them firstly against dividend income (see **1.5** ALLOWANCES AND TAX RATES), then against savings income (see **1.6** ALLOWANCES AND TAX RATES) and finally against basic rate income. The expenses set against each type of income must be grossed up by reference to the normal rate of tax applicable to that type of income, e.g. the amount set against dividend income should be such amount as, when grossed up by reference to the dividend ordinary rate, equals the dividend income or, if less, the total allowable expenses grossed up by reference to that rate. Expenses set against dividend income is set against UK dividend income in priority to dividends from non-UK resident companies (but are in either case grossed up by reference to the dividend ordinary rate). See the examples at **70.16** below.

Where the trust has income not chargeable to income tax, by virtue wholly or partly of the trustees being non-UK resident or being deemed under a double tax agreement to be resident in a territory outside the UK, the trustees' expenses otherwise available for offset are reduced in the same proportion as that which such non-taxable income bears to the total trust income for the year. Where the trustees' income tax liability is limited under the provisions at **50.3** NON-RESIDENTS, excluded income (see **50.3**), other than that which has suffered deduction of UK income tax at source, must be included in non-taxable income for the purposes of this apportionment.

[*ITA 2007, ss 484–487, Sch 2 para 102; FA 2016, Sch 1 paras 63(6), 73*].

Simon's Taxes. See **C4.205**.

Discretionary payments by trustees

[70.15] A discretionary payment is treated as a net amount corresponding to a gross amount from which the trustees have deducted income tax *at the trust rate*. That gross amount is chargeable to income tax on the beneficiary as an annual payment, and the beneficiary is treated as having paid the income tax deducted. This treatment applies only if the discretionary payment is income of the beneficiary for tax purposes by virtue of its having been paid to him or if the payment is made to the settlor's minor children (neither married nor in a civil partnership) such that the payment is treated under *ITTOIA 2005, s 629* as the settlor's income (see **70.30** below) (in which case it is the settlor who is treated as having paid the income tax). The treatment normally applies only if the trustees are UK resident for the tax year in which the payment is made. By concession and subject to conditions, tax paid by trustees of a *non-UK resident* trust may similarly be set against any liability of the settlor under *ITTOIA 2005, s 629* (HMRC ESC A93).

For whether a payment is received as income, see *Stevenson v Wishart and Others (Levy's Trustees)* CA 1987, 59 TC 740. A payment received as employment income is excluded from these provisions but see ESC A68 below. A payment in money's worth is potentially within the provisions as is a payment to a company (see Tolley's Corporation Tax for the treatment of discretionary payments in the company's hands).

Note that, in contrast to the position for interest in possession trusts in **70.9** above, no distinction is made between dividend income, savings income and other income in the hands of the beneficiary. Also, the beneficiary's position is unaffected by the availability of the standard rate band to the trustees. The full amount of the payment to him is treated having suffered tax at a single rate, i.e. the trust rate.

Trustees' tax pool

The total tax treated as deducted by the trustees from discretionary payments in the tax year is chargeable on the trustees but only if, and to the extent that, it exceeds the amount of the 'trustees' tax pool'. The trustees are liable for any tax chargeable. The '*trustees' tax pool*' is computed by taking the balance brought forward (if any) from the previous tax year (net of the tax treated as deducted from payments in that year) and adding the following items:

- in the case of income chargeable at the trust rate (other than chargeable event gains on life policies), tax suffered by the trustees at that rate;
- in the case of chargeable event gains on life policies, tax suffered by the trustees at the excess of the trust rate over the basic rate;
- in the case of income chargeable at the dividend trust rate, tax suffered by the trustees at that rate;
- tax suffered by the trustees at the basic rate or the dividend ordinary rate (due to the income in question falling within the standard rate band — see **70.13** above); and
- tax suffered by the trustees under the special tax treatment at **70.19** below for trusts with vulnerable beneficiaries.

None of the above items can be added to the pool for a year for which the trustees are non-UK resident.

Where, for 2017/18 onwards, trustees are entitled to a basic rate tax reduction in respect of mortgage interest and other finance costs in relation to residential property income (see **60.12** PROPERTY INCOME), logic suggests that the tax represented by the reduction should be excluded from the trustees' tax pool as it is not tax suffered by the trustees. In fact, the legislation does not appear to require this; the tax charged on the property income can be added to the pool without allowing for the reduction.

Also included in the trustees' tax pool where relevant (and on the making of a claim by the trustees) is tax treated as suffered on income available for distribution at the end of the 1972/73 tax year; for this purpose, the tax suffered is taken as two-thirds of the net amount of that available income.

See HMRC Trusts, Settlements and Estates Manual TSEM3020 et seq., and see the examples at **70.16** below.

Certificate of tax deducted

A person in receipt of a discretionary payment on which he is treated as having paid tax at source has power to require from the trustees a certificate of tax deducted. This power is extended to a settlor whom *ITTOIA 2005, s 629* treats as having received the income and paid the tax.

[*ITA 2007, ss 493–498, Sch 2 para 104; FA 2016, Sch 1 paras 63(7), 73*].

Double tax relief

Where 'taxed overseas income' arises to a settlement and the trustees make a discretionary payment out of such income, the trustees may certify:

- that the payment is one made out of income consisting of, or including, taxed overseas income of an amount, and from a source, stated in the certificate; and

- that the said amount of taxed overseas income arose to the trustees not earlier than tax years before the end of the tax year in which the discretionary payment is made.

The effect of certification is that the beneficiary to whom the payment is made may claim that the payment, up to the certified amount, is to be treated for the purposes of DOUBLE TAX RELIEF (27) as income received by him from the certified source and in the tax year in which the discretionary payment is made. '*Taxed overseas income*' means income in respect of which the trustees are entitled to relief by way of credit for tax under the law of a territory outside the UK. That entitlement is effectively transferred from the trustees to the beneficiary.

[*TIOPA 2010, s 111*].

Employee benefit settlements

Employee benefit settlements are able to reclaim from HMRC tax at the trust rate on discretionary payments to employee beneficiaries which are taxable earnings in the hands of the employees without credit being available for the tax deducted at source from the payments. The repayment is limited to the amount of the trustees' tax pool, which is then treated as reduced or extinguished by the amount of the repayment. [*ITA 2007, ss 496A, 496B, 497(1)*].

Payments to beneficiaries — reliefs given by concession

A non-resident beneficiary of a UK resident discretionary trust who receives income treated as net of tax may claim relief in respect of the tax exemption on 'FOTRA' securities (see **65.4** SAVINGS AND INVESTMENT INCOME) or under the terms of a double taxation agreement, where such relief would have been available had the beneficiary received the income directly instead of through the trustees. Repayment may similarly be claimed where the beneficiary would not have been chargeable to UK tax in those circumstances. Relief is granted provided that the payment is out of income which arose to the trustees not earlier than six years before the end of the tax year in which the payment was made to the beneficiary. The trustees must have submitted trust returns supported by tax certificates and relevant information. They must also have paid all tax, interest, surcharge and penalties and must keep available for inspection any relevant tax certificates, and the beneficiary must claim the relief or exemption within five years and ten months after the end of the tax year in which the payment was received from the trustees.

A similar concession applies where a beneficiary receives a discretionary payment from trustees which is not within the main provisions above (e.g. a payment from a non-resident trust). A non-resident beneficiary who, had he received the income out of which the payment was made, would have been liable to UK tax thereon may claim personal reliefs under **50.2** NON-RESIDENTS and may be treated as if he received the payment from a UK resident trust, but credit may be claimed only for UK tax actually paid by the trustees on the income out of which the payment was made. Exemption may also be claimed in respect of income arising from 'FOTRA' securities (as above). A UK resident beneficiary of a non-UK resident trust may similarly claim credit for tax actually paid by the trustees on the income out of which the payment was made as if the payment were from a UK resident trust. In all cases, the trustees must have submitted trust returns supported by tax certificates and relevant information. They must also have paid all tax due and any interest, surcharge and penalties, and must keep available for inspection any relevant tax certificates, and the beneficiary must claim the relief or exemption within five years and ten months after the end of the tax year in which the payment was received from the trustees. No credit is given for tax treated as paid on income received by the trustees which would not be available for set-off under the main provisions above if they applied, and that tax is not repayable and is not taken into account in calculating the beneficiary's gross income.

(HMRC ESC B18).

However, where the beneficiary is resident in a country with which the UK has a double taxation agreement, and the 'Other Income' Article in that agreement gives sole taxing rights in respect of such income to that country, the above concession does not apply, and the tax paid by the trustees will be repaid in full to the beneficiary, subject to the conditions in the Article being met (HMRC SP 3/86).

Simon's Taxes. See **C4.212, C4.507, C4.509.**

Examples

[70.16]

(i) Standard rate band

For 2020/21, a small discretionary trust has property income of £500, building society interest of £300 and UK dividends of £600. It has no other income or expenses. The settlor has made no other settlements.

The tax liability of the trust for 2020/21 is as follows.

	£
Standard rate band (£1,000)	
Property income — £500 @ 20% (basic rate)	100.00
Gross interest — £300 @ 20% (basic rate)	60.00
Dividends — £200 @ 7.5% (dividend ordinary rate)	15.00
	175.00
Income exceeding standard rate band	
Dividends — £400 @ 38.1% (dividend trust rate)	152.40
	£327.40

Notes

(a) The property income and building society interest form the lowest slice of the total income; thus, it all falls within the standard rate band and is charged at basic rate. £800 of the £1,000 standard rate band is now used up; thus, £200 of the dividend income falls within the standard rate band and is charged at the dividend ordinary rate. The remainder of the dividend income is charged at the dividend trust rate.

(b) Note that if the trustees were to distribute the whole of the net income of £1,072.60 (£500 + £300 + £600 – £327.40) to beneficiaries, they will have further tax to pay (assuming no balance, or insufficient balance, brought forward from earlier years in the trustees' tax pool). The total tax payable will be £877.58 (£1,072.60 × 45/55), from which can be deducted tax paid of £327.40, leaving a further £550.18 to pay (if no balance is brought forward in the pool). See also note (c) to *Example (ii)* below.

(c) See *Example (ii)* below for the position of a beneficiary to whom income is distributed by the trustees.

(ii) General

The XYZ trust, an accumulation and maintenance settlement set up by W for his grandchildren in 2001 now comprises quoted investments and an industrial property. The property is let to an engineering company. Charges for rates, electricity etc. are paid by the trust and recharged yearly in arrears to the tenant. As a result of the delay in recovering the service costs, the settlement incurs overdraft interest. There are no other settlements in existence in relation to which W is a settlor.

The relevant figures for the year ended 5 April 2021 are as follows.

	£
Property rents	40,500
Dividends	5,000
Bank interest	3,500
	£49,000
Trust administration expenses — proportion chargeable to income	1,350
Overdraft interest	1,050
	£2,400

The tax liability of the trust for 2020/21 is as follows.

	£	£
Property income — £1,000 @ 20%, £39,500 @ 45%		17,975
Bank interest — £3,500 @ 45%		1,575
Dividends	5,000	
Deduct Expenses (£2,400 grossed at 100/92.5)	(2,595)	
	£2,405	
Tax on £2,595 @ 7.5% (dividend ordinary rate)	194.63	
Tax on £2,405 @ 38.1% (dividend trust rate)	916.31	1,110.94
Tax payable		£20,660.94

Notes

(a) Expenses (including in this example the overdraft interest) are set firstly against the dividend income and then against non-dividend savings income and then non-savings income (see **70.14** above). The effect of the calculation is that the expenses, grossed-up at 7.5%, save tax at 30.6% (the difference between the 7.5% dividend ordinary rate and the 38.1% dividend trust rate).

(b) The net revenue available for distribution to the beneficiaries, at the trustees' discretion, will be £25,939.06 (£49,000 – £20,660.94 – £2,400), but see note (c).

(c) If the whole of the distributable income is in fact distributed, then unless there is sufficient balance brought forward from earlier years in the trustees' tax pool, there will be insufficient tax in the pool to frank the distribution (£25,939.06 × 45/55 = £21,222.97). The tax paid of £20,660.94 will partly cover this, but the trustees will have a further liability which they may not have the funds to settle.

(d) The property income and savings income form the lowest slice of the total income. Thus, the first £1,000 of such income falls within the standard rate band; as it is normally basic rate income, that £1,000 is chargeable at the basic rate of 20%.

M, the 17-year-old grandson of W, is one of the beneficiaries to whom the trustees of the XYZ trust can pay the settlement income. The trustees make a payment of £6,930 to M on 30 January 2021. He has no other income in the year 2020/21. His liability to income tax is at the main UK rates.

M's income from the trust is:

	£
Net income	6,930
Tax at 45/55	5,670
Gross income	£12,600

He can claim a tax repayment for 2019/20 as follows

	£
Total income	12,600
Deduct Personal allowance	12,500
	£100
Tax thereon at 20% (within basic rate band)	20.00
Tax accounted for by trustees	(5,670.00)
Repayment due	£(5,650.00)

Note

Unlike the position with interest in possession trusts (see **70.10** above), no distinction is made between dividend income, savings income and other income in the beneficiary's hands, the full amount of the payment to him having suffered tax at a single rate of 45% in the hands of the trustees. The beneficiary is not entitled to the dividend allowance (see **1.5** ALLOWANCES AND TAX RATES) the starting rate for savings (see **1.6** ALLOWANCES AND TAX RATES) nor the personal savings allowance (see **1.7** ALLOWANCES AND TAX RATES) as a payment from a discretionary trust is neither dividend income nor savings income in his hands.

Personal position of trustee

[70.17] Annual remuneration paid to a trustee under a will or settlement is an annual payment from which tax is deductible at source (*Baxendale v Murphy* KB 1924, 9 TC 76; *Hearn v Morgan* KB 1945, 26 TC 478 and cf. *Clapham's Trustees v Belton* Ch D 1956, 37 TC 26). Where a trustee is empowered to, and does, charge for his professional services, his fees are part of his receipts for the purposes of computing his professional profits (*Jones v Wright* KB 1927, 13 TC 221) even where he is also a beneficiary (*Watson & Everitt v Blunden* CA 1933, 18 TC 402).

Income of beneficiaries

[70.18] In the case of life-tenants and those with similar interests in trust income, the beneficiary's income for tax purposes is the grossed-up amount of the net income after deducting any trust outgoings payable out of the income (*Lord Hamilton of Dalzell* CS 1926, 10 TC 406; *Murray v CIR* CS 1926, 11 TC 133; *MacFarlane v CIR* CS 1929, 14 TC 532) — see **70.9** above re trust expenses generally. In other cases, the tax treatment of payments under a trust depends on the circumstances. Payments to a parent for the maintenance of children were held to be income of the children assessable on the parent in *Drummond v Collins* HL 1915, 6 TC 525 (remittances to mother as guardian of minors, all resident in UK, of income of American trust) and *Johnstone v Chamberlain* KB 1933, 17 TC 706. Payments for the rates etc. and the super-tax of a beneficiary and payments for the maintenance of beneficiaries were held to be income in their hands in *Lord Tollemache v CIR* KB 1926, 11 TC 277; *Shanks v CIR* CA 1928, 14 TC 249; *Waley Cohen v CIR* KB 1945, 26 TC 471. In a number of cases, the outgoings of a residence provided for the beneficiary, grossed-up, have been held to be income of the beneficiary (*Donaldson's Exors v CIR* CS 1927, 13 TC 461; *Sutton v CIR* CA 1929, 14 TC 662; *Lady Miller v CIR* HL 1930, 15 TC 25). Income applied in reducing charges on the trust fund was held not to be income of the life-tenant (*Wemyss* CS 1924, 8 TC 551). Shares allotted to trustees in consideration of arrears of dividends were held to be income and not capital of the trust fund (*In re MacIver's Settlement* Ch D 1935, 14 ATC 571).

Interest on money loaned interest-free, subject to conditions and repayable on demand, by the employer to a trust for the benefit of an employee held to be earnings within the charge to tax on employment income (*O'Leary v McKinlay* Ch D 1990, 63 TC 729).

The tax treatment of income accumulated (e.g. during the minority of a beneficiary) has arisen in a number of cases. The test is whether the beneficiary's interest under the trust is vested or contingent. If vested, the accumulated income is his income as it arises. (N.B. If the accumulated income is the beneficiary's, **70.11** above does not apply. If the interest was contingent, see **70.24** below). Decision involves the general law of trusts, outside the scope of this book. For tax cases in which the accumulated income has been treated as income of the beneficiary, see *Gascoigne v CIR* KB 1926, 13 TC 573; *Stern v CIR* HL 1930, 15 TC 148, and *Brotherton v CIR* CA 1978, 52 TC 137; for cases where the income was held not to be the beneficiary's, see *Stanley v CIR*

CA 1944, 26 TC 12 (where the position under the *Trustee Act 1925, s 31* was considered); *Cornwell v Barry* Ch D 1955, 36 TC 268, and *Kidston* CS 1936, 20 TC 603. For the release of accumulated income on the termination of a trust, see *Hamilton-Russell's Exors v CIR* CA 1943, 25 TC 200, and on termination of legally permissible period of accumulation, see *Duncan v CIR* CS 1931, 17 TC 1.

See also **22** DECEASED ESTATES.

Simon's Taxes. See **C4.501–C4.509.**

Trusts with vulnerable beneficiaries

[70.19] Special income tax and capital gains tax (CGT) treatment is given if the trustees and the vulnerable beneficiary concerned opt for it to apply. The income tax treatment is described below. For the CGT treatment, see the corresponding chapter of Tolley's Capital Gains Tax. For income tax purposes, the special treatment is most likely to be beneficial where the income would otherwise be chargeable at the trust rate or the dividend trust rate. For HMRC guidance on the special treatment (including CGT treatment), see www.gov.uk/trusts-taxes/trusts-for-vulnerable-people.

The special treatment applies to income arising to trustees from property held on 'qualifying trusts' (see **70.20** below) for a 'vulnerable person' and to chargeable gains accruing to trustees from the disposal of such property. '*Vulnerable person*' means a disabled person (see **70.20** below) or a person under 18 at least one of whose parents has died. The trustees can claim the special treatment for any tax year in which they hold such property and for all or part of which a 'vulnerable person election' is in force (see **70.21** below). But the special treatment does not apply if the property from which the income arises is property in which the settlor is regarded for the purposes of **70.29** below as having an interest.

The special treatment operates for income tax purposes by comparing:

(i) what would otherwise be the trustees' liability on the income in question (the '*qualifying trusts income*') (computed as below); and
(ii) what would be the beneficiary's liability on the qualifying trusts income if it were income arising to him directly (computed as below).

The excess (if any) of (i) over (ii) is then treated as a reduction in the trustees' income tax liability for the tax year. The reduction is given at Step 6 in the calculation of income tax liability and is given effect after any other tax reductions have been made (see **1.10, 1.12** ALLOWANCES AND TAX RATES).

In computing the amount in (i), any allowable trustees' expenses of the trust (within **70.14** above) are apportioned between the qualifying trusts income and other income (if any).

The amount in (ii) is the excess of:

(a) the beneficiary's income tax liability for the year if the qualifying trusts income were his own income over
(b) what would otherwise be his income tax liability for the year.

But in computing *both* (a) and (b), the following are ignored:

- any income distributed by the trustees to the beneficiary in the tax year (regardless of when that income arose); and
- any reliefs to which he is entitled which are given by way of a reduction of income tax liability (e.g. married couple's allowance).

Where the beneficiary is non-UK resident for the tax year, his income tax liability for the purposes of both (a) and (b) is computed as if he were resident in the UK for the year and domiciled in the UK throughout the year and on the assumption that the tax year is not a split year (see **63.19** RESIDENCE AND DOMICILE) as regards the beneficiary.

Where the vulnerable person election in **70.21** below is in force for part only of a tax year, the above applies only as respects qualifying trusts income arising in that part of the year, and any necessary apportionment of allowable trustees' expenses as above is made by reference to the income and expenses of that part of the year only.

The rule at **70.30** below, which treats income paid to an unmarried minor child of the settlor as the settlor's income, is disapplied for any tax year in respect of which the child in question is a vulnerable person, the income is qualifying trusts income and the trustees have successfully claimed the special income tax treatment above.

[*FA 2005, ss 23–29, 39, 41(1)(2)*].

These provisions, including those in **70.20**, **70.21** below, are appropriately modified in their application to Scotland by *FA 2005, s 42* so that they conform with Scottish trust law generally.

Simon's Taxes. See **C4.255–C4.260.**

Qualifying trusts

[70.20] Where property is held on trusts for the benefit of a 'disabled person', those trusts are '*qualifying trusts*' for the purposes of **70.19** above if they secure that the conditions below are met during the lifetime of the disabled person or until the termination of the trusts (if that precedes his death). The conditions are:

- that if any of the property is applied for the benefit of a beneficiary it is applied for the benefit of the disabled person; and
- either that the disabled person is entitled to all the income (if any) arising from any of the property or that if any such income is applied for the benefit of a beneficiary, it is applied for the benefit of the disabled person.

The trusts are not to be treated as failing to secure that the above conditions are met by reason only of:

(a) the trustees' having powers that enable them to apply in any tax year otherwise than for the benefit of the disabled person amounts (whether consisting of income or capital or both) not exceeding the 'annual limit'; or

(b) the trustees' having the powers conferred by *Trustee Act 1925, s 32* (powers of advancement) (or its NI equivalent); or
(c) the trustees' having those powers but free from, or subject to a less restrictive limitation than, the limitation imposed by *Trustee Act 1925, s 32(1)(a)* (or its NI equivalent); or
(d) the trustees' having powers to the like effect as the powers mentioned in (b) or (c).

The '*annual limit*' in (a) above is £3,000 or, if lower, 3% of the maximum value of the settled property during the tax year in question.

If the property is held on trusts of the kind described in *Trustee Act 1925, s 33* (protective trusts), the reference above to 'the lifetime of the disabled person' is to be interpreted as the period during which the property is held on trust for him.

Meaning of 'disabled person'

The meaning of '*disabled person*' is given by *FA 2005, Sch 1A*. It means either a person who by reason of mental disorder is incapable of administering his property or managing his affairs or a person in receipt of any one or more specified State benefits. A person is treated as being a disabled person for these purposes if he satisfies HMRC that he would be entitled to receive the State benefit in question were it not for his being resident outside the UK or in a care home, hospital or prison.

Trusts for the benefit of bereaved minors

Where property is held on trusts for the benefit of a minor at least one of whose parents have died, those trusts are '*qualifying trusts*' for the purposes of **70.19** above if they are:

- statutory trusts under *Administration of Estates Act 1925, ss 46, 47(1)* (rules relating to intestacy);
- trusts established under the will of a deceased parent which secure that the conditions set out below are met; or
- trusts established under the Criminal Injuries Compensation Scheme (as defined) which secure that the conditions set out below are met.

The said conditions are:

- that the minor will become entitled to the property, any income arising from it and any accumulated income on reaching the age of 18;
- that, in the meantime and for so long as the minor is living, if any of the property is applied for the benefit of a beneficiary it is applied for the benefit of the minor; and
- that, in the meantime and for so long as the minor is living, either the minor is entitled to all the income (if any) arising from any of the property or if any such income is applied for the benefit of a beneficiary, it is applied for the benefit of the minor.

But trusts are not to be regarded as failing to secure the meeting of these conditions by reason only of the trustees' having powers as in (a)–(d) above.

Parts of assets

For the purposes of these provisions, property held on trusts includes a part of an asset if that part (and any income arising from it) can be identified for the purpose of determining whether the trusts are qualifying trusts.

[*FA 2005, ss 34–36, 38, 39, Sch 1A*].

Vulnerable person election

[70.21] The '*vulnerable person election*' referred to at **70.19** above is an irrevocable election that may be made jointly in relation to qualifying trusts by the trustees and the vulnerable person. It must be made in such form as HMRC may require (form VPE 1), must specify the date on which it is to come into force (the 'start date') and must be made by notice to HMRC no later than the first anniversary of 31 January following the tax year in which the start date falls (or within such further time as the Commissioners of HMRC may allow in a particular case). It must contain certain specified information relating to the trusts, the trustees, the vulnerable person, the entitlement of the vulnerable person, and any other person connected with the trusts. It must also contain certain declarations including a declaration of its accuracy and the vulnerable person's authority for the trustees to claim the special tax treatment for any tax year for which they feel it is appropriate.

An election ceases to be in force when the vulnerable person ceases to be a vulnerable person, when the trusts cease to be qualifying trusts or when the trusts are terminated. If the trustees become aware that any such event has occurred, they must notify HMRC accordingly within 90 days of their becoming so aware.

Where the property held on qualifying trusts becomes treated as comprised in a sub-fund settlement (see **70.6** above), there is provision to treat a pre-existing vulnerable person election as made by the trustees of the sub-fund settlement (and the vulnerable person) from the date the sub-fund election is treated as having taken effect.

[*FA 2005, s 37*].

HMRC powers

Where a vulnerable person election has been made, HMRC are given powers to require information from the trustees and/or the vulnerable person. In appropriate circumstances, HMRC may give notice to the effect that the election is deemed never to have come into force or that it has ceased to be in force from a specified date. An aggrieved person has a right of appeal; the notice of appeal must be given to HMRC within 30 days. [*FA 2005, s 40*].

Penalties under *TMA 1970, s 98* (see **55.22** PENALTIES) apply for failure to comply with any of the information requirements referred to above. For penalty purposes, any information, statements or declarations given or made jointly by the trustees and the vulnerable person are treated as given or made by the trustees. [*FA 2005, s 43*].

Annuities and other annual payments

[70.22] Annuities and other annual payments under settlements or wills are subject to the normal rules for DEDUCTION OF TAX AT SOURCE (**23**). Annual remuneration to a trustee is an annual payment for this purpose (see **70.17** above). Where the annuity etc. is paid out of the capital of the trust fund, the tax deducted is assessed on the trustees. (Where tax is not deducted, the beneficiary may be assessed instead.) Payments out of capital may be directed or authorised by the settlor or testator, as where he directs a stipulated annual amount to be paid out of capital (*Jackson's Trustees v CIR* KB 1942, 25 TC 13; *Milne's Exors v CIR* Ch D 1956, 37 TC 10) or authorises the beneficiary's income to be augmented to a stipulated amount out of capital (*Brodie's Trustees v CIR* KB 1933, 17 TC 432; *Morant Settlement Trustees v CIR* CA 1948, 30 TC 147), or direct payments out of capital for the maintenance etc. of the recipient (*Lindus & Hortin v CIR* KB 1933, 17 TC 442; *Esdaile v CIR* CS 1936, 20 TC 700) even though discretionary (*Cunard's Trustees v CIR* CA 1945, 27 TC 122). For position if annuity exceeds income of fund on which charged, see *Lady Castlemaine* KB 1943, 25 TC 408. Annuities directed to be paid out of capital but paid out of accumulated income forming part of the capital were held to have been paid out of income (*Postlethwaite v CIR* Ch D 1963, 41 TC 244).

For 'free of tax' annuities, see **23.16** DEDUCTION OF TAX AT SOURCE.

Foreign trust income

[70.23] There are no special provisions for the income tax treatment of foreign trust income. For the liability of trustees within the jurisdiction as regards foreign trust income, see the case of *Williams v Singer, Dawson v CIR* and *Kelly v Rogers* at **70.8** above.

The income of a life-tenant of a foreign trust fund depends first on the nature of his interest under the relevant foreign law. See for this the cases of *Archer-Shee v Baker* HL 1927, 11 TC 749 and *Garland v Archer-Shee* HL 1930, 15 TC 693, dealing with the same life-tenancy. In the first, with no evidence as to the foreign law, the life-tenant was held to be assessable on the basis that the investments forming part of the fund were separate foreign possessions or securities. In the second case, relating to later years, it was held that having regard to evidence given as to the foreign law, she was assessable on the basis that the income was from a single foreign possession. (N.B. The decisions have lost some of their practical importance because of subsequent changes in the basis rules of Schedule D, Cases IV and V, but the principles established remain important.) See also *Nelson v Adamson* KB 1941, 24 TC 36 and *Inchyra v Jennings* Ch D 1965, 42 TC 388. Stock dividends received by trustees of an American trust fund were part of the trust income under the relevant American law but held not to be income of a UK life-tenant, as not of an income nature under UK principles (*Lawson v Rolfe* Ch D 1969, 46 TC 199).

Discretionary remittances from foreign trustees are assessable and become income when the discretion is exercised (*Drummond v Collins* HL 1915, 6 TC 525) but cf. *Lawson v Rolfe*.

See 32.5 FOREIGN INCOME for unremittable foreign income and 32.1 FOREIGN INCOME for overseas income generally.

Claims for personal allowances etc. on income up to 1968/69 — from specified 'contingent interests' on obtaining a specified age or marrying

[70.24] Under *ITA 1952, s 228*, where an individual has an interest under a will or settlement that is contingent on his or her attaining a specified age or marrying, and income is directed to be accumulated meantime, claims by that individual for personal allowances etc. may be made within six years after the end of the tax year in which the contingency happens, in respect of all income so compulsorily accumulated prior to 6 April 1969. [*ICTA 1970, Sch 14 para 1*]. Such claims cannot be made in respect of income which is deemed to be the income of the settlor as below. See 62.2 REPAYMENT INTEREST.

Where income is legally vested in beneficiaries, relief as above is refused; it is important, therefore, to ascertain whether income legally vested or contingent (*Roberts v Hanks* KB 1926, 10 TC 351; *Jones v Down* KB 1936, 20 TC 279), and when the 'contingency' happens (*Stonely v Ambrose* KB 1925, 9 TC 389, and *Lynch v Davies* Ch D 1962, 40 TC 511).

The section applies only when the contingency is the claimant's attainment of a specified age or marriage (*Bone* CS 1927, 13 TC 20 and *White v Whitcher* KB 1927, 13 TC 202). Claimant's right must depend solely on happening of one of these contingencies *and on nothing else*, and no claim can be made if right to receive income is wholly at trustee's discretion (*Dain v Miller* KB 1934, 18 TC 478, and see *Maude-Roxby* CS 1950, 31 TC 388). See also *Cusden v Eden* KB 1939, 22 TC 435 as to accumulations.

Tax on income accumulated but directed to be capitalised on happening of contingency may nevertheless be claimed under this section (*Dale v Mitcalfe* CA 1927, 13 TC 41).

The amount recovered belongs to the beneficiary (*Fulford v Hyslop* Ch D 1929, 8 ATC 588). In *Chamberlain v Haig Thomas* KB 1933, 17 TC 595 where accumulations directed (from 1913 onwards) for infant children subject to power of appointment (which not in fact exercised until 1922), section held to apply to income of intervening period.

Amounts treated as income of settlor or close family

[70.25] Where:

(a) the settlor retains an interest in a settlement (see 70.29 below);
(b) payments are made out of, or, in certain cases, income is accumulated in, a settlement to or for a minor child of the settlor who is neither married nor in a civil partnership (see 70.30 below);
(c) capital sums are paid to the settlor by the trustees of a settlement or by a body connected with a settlement (see 70.30 below);
(d) (for 2018/19 onwards) otherwise untaxed benefits are provided by the trustees to the settlor or a close family member out of protected foreign-source income (see 70.34 below); or

(e) (for 2018/19 onwards) onward gifts of benefits provided by the trustees out of protected foreign-source income are made to the settlor or a close family member (see **70.35** below),

an amount is treated as income of the settlor (or in some, but not all, cases within (d) and (e) the close family member), and income tax is charged accordingly.

See **70.29–70.35** below for the calculation of the amounts chargeable. As regards (a) and (b), see **70.26** below for the exclusion for income given to charity and **70.27** below for the exclusion for protected foreign-source income. See **70.28** below for definitions.

In calculating an amount chargeable on an individual, the same deductions and reliefs are allowed as if the income had actually been received by the individual. Where the charge is under (a) or (b), the income treated as the settlor's is charged in his hands at the rates that would have applied if the income had arisen to him directly.

Income treated under (a) or (b) as income of the settlor is deemed to be the top slice of his income, but before taking into account income chargeable under *ITEPA 2003, s 403* (payments on loss of office, see **18.4** COMPENSATION FOR LOSS OF EMPLOYMENT) or *ITTOIA 2005, s 465* (life assurance gains, see **44.3** LIFE ASSURANCE POLICIES) and subject to the rules at **1.5**, **1.6** ALLOWANCES AND TAX RATES.

[*ITTOIA 2005, ss 619, 619A, 621–623; FA 2018, Sch 10 paras 4–7, 21(1)*].

Adjustments between settlor and trustees etc.

The settlor is entitled to recover tax paid under (a) or (b) above from any trustee or any person to whom the income is payable under the settlement, and to that end can obtain from HMRC a certificate specifying the amount of income charged on him and the tax paid.

If a settlor chargeable under (a) or (b) above receives a tax repayment as a result of tax paid by any trustee or any other person to whom the income is payable under the settlement, he must pay it over to the trustee or that other person. If there are two or more persons (which may include the trustee), the amount must be apportioned among them as the case may require. This requirement applies if the tax repayment arises from the setting of an allowance or relief against the trust income, and also where, for example, the settlor is liable at a rate of income tax lower than that of the trustees. The settlor may to this end obtain from HMRC a certificate stating that he has received such a repayment and specifying the amount thereof. Subject to this, the Appeal Tribunal has the final decision on any question as to the amount to be paid over by the settlor and as to any apportionment required.

(Repayments of tax on trust income paid over by the settlor to the trustees under this statutory obligation are not treated as diminishing the value of the settlor's estate and so cannot be liable to inheritance tax if they otherwise might have been.)

Nothing in the settlement provisions precludes tax being charged on trustees as persons by whom any income is received.

[*ITTOIA 2005, s 646*].

Settlors have an obligation to notify their tax office of any liability under the provisions even if they do not normally receive a tax return. (Revenue Press Release 4 January 1995).

Relief for recipients of annual payments

Where a person receives a discretionary annual payment of income from a trust and a settlor is chargeable as above (whether in the same tax year or a previous year) on the trust income out of which the payment is made, the recipient is treated as having paid tax at the additional rate, the Welsh additional rate (in the case of a Welsh taxpayer) or the highest Scottish rate (in the case of a Scottish taxpayer) on the income. The income is then treated as the highest part of the recipient's total income apart from chargeable event gains on life policies etc. (see **44.3** LIFE ASSURANCE POLICIES). The notional additional rate tax credit is not repayable and cannot be used to reduce the tax chargeable on other income. If only a proportion of the total trust income is chargeable on the settlor, only a similar proportion of the annual payment carries the additional rate credit. If the recipient is himself a settlor in relation to the settlement, the foregoing does not apply but the payment is not treated as taxable income in his hands. The normal tax treatment of discretionary payments by trustees (see **70.15** above) is disapplied insofar as the payment falls within these provisions.

[*ITTOIA 2005, s 685A; SI 2015 No 1810, Arts 1, 11; SI 2017 No 468, Regs 1, 8; SI 2019 No 201, Arts 1, 10*].

Simon's Taxes. See **C4.320, C4.329, C4.353.**

Exclusion for income given to charity

[70.26] The charge to tax on the settlor under **70.25**(a) or (b) above does not apply to 'qualifying income' which arises to a 'UK settlement' and which either:

(a) is given by the trustees to a 'charity' in the tax year in which it arises; or
(b) is income to which a 'charity' is entitled under the terms of the settlement.

For these purposes, a '*UK settlement*' is a settlement the trustees of which are resident (previously resident and ordinarily resident) in the UK (see **70.5** above). '*Charity*' has the meaning in **14.2** CHARITIES AND CHARITABLE GIVING but also includes the Trustees of the National Heritage Memorial Fund and the Historic Buildings and Monuments Commission for England. '*Qualifying income*' is widely defined to cover the income of accumulation, discretionary and interest in possession trusts.

Where the qualifying income arises from different sources (e.g. interest, dividends etc.) and *part* of that income for any tax year is excluded as above, the remainder is rateably apportioned for tax purposes between the different sources. However, this rule is overridden by any requirement in the terms of the settlement that the whole or part of a *particular* source of income be given to charity. For the purposes of **70.9** and **70.14** above, trustees' expenses are rateably apportioned between income excluded as above, with the effect that relief is to that extent available for such expenses, and any remainder.

[*ITTOIA 2005, ss 628, 630, 646A*].

Exclusion for protected foreign-source income

[70.27] For 2017/18 onwards, the charge to tax on the settlor under **70.25**(a) or (b) above does not apply to income arising under a settlement if it is 'protected foreign-source income' for a tax year. This exclusion was introduced in conjunction with the deemed domicile rule at **63.36** RESIDENCE AND DOMICILE. Income arising under a settlement is '*protected foreign-source income*' if all of conditions (a)–(f) below are met. (The rule at **70.28**(d) below, whereby relevant foreign income is treated as arising under a settlement only if and when it is remitted to the UK, does not apply for this purpose.) The conditions are that:

(a) the income would be relevant foreign income (see **32.2** FOREIGN INCOME) if it were income of a UK resident individual;
(b) the income is from property originating from the settlor (see **70.29** below);
(c) when the settlement was created the settlor was not domiciled in the UK and, if it was created on or after 6 April 2017, the settlor was not deemed domiciled in the UK under the deemed domicile rule;
(d) there is no time in the tax year in question when the settlor is domiciled in the UK under general law or is deemed domiciled in the UK by virtue of the first of the two conditions at **63.36** RESIDENCE AND DOMICILE;
(e) the trustees of the settlement are not UK resident for the tax year in question (see **70.5** above as to residence of trustees); and
(f) subject to the exceptions below, no property or income is provided (directly or indirectly) for the purposes of the settlement by the settlor, or by the trustees of any other settlement of which the settlor is a beneficiary or settlor, at any time in the 'relevant period' when the settlor is domiciled or deemed domiciled in the UK. In this regard, the addition of value to property comprised in the settlement is treated as the direct provision of property for the purposes of the settlement. The '*relevant period*' is the period from 6 April 2017 (or from the creation of the settlement if later than that) to the end of the tax year in question.

Exceptions

In deciding whether property or income is provided as in (f) above, the following are ignored:

- property or income provided, other than by way of loan, on arm's length terms (see below);
- property or income provided, other than by way of loan, without intent to confer a gratuitous benefit;
- the principal of a loan made to the trustees of the trustees on arm's length terms;

- the repayment to the trustees of the principal of a loan made by them;
- the payment of interest to the trustees under a loan made by them on arm's length terms;
- property or income provided in pursuance of a liability incurred by any person before 6 April 2017; and
- any property or income provided to meet the excess, if any, of the settlement's administration expenses and tax liabilities for a tax year over its income (or over so much of its income as can be used to cover such expenses and liabilities).

Where a loan is made on arm's length terms to the trustees of the settlement by either the settlor or the trustees of a settlement connected with the settlor (see below), and a 'relevant event' then occurs, the principal of the loan is to be regarded as having been provided as in (f) above, at the time of that event, and the exceptions above do not apply. '*Relevant events*' are capitalisation of interest, failure to pay interest and variation of terms such that they cease to be arm's length terms.

In certain cases, the outstanding amount of a loan is regarded as property directly provided by the lender for the purposes of the settlement, and the exceptions to (f) above do not apply. This occurs where:

- the settlor becomes deemed domiciled in the UK on or after 6 April 2017 under the deemed domicile rule;
- before the date on which the settlor becomes deemed domiciled (the '*deemed domicile date*'), a loan has been made, other than on arm's length terms, to the trustees of the settlement by either the settlor or the trustees of a settlement connected with the settlor (see below); and
- any amount of the loan that is outstanding on the deemed domicile date is payable or repayable on demand on or after that date.

The outstanding amount is treated as provided for the purposes of the settlement on the deemed domicile date. If, however, the deemed domicile date is 6 April 2017, the outstanding amount is not treated as provided for the purposes of the settlement in either of the following circumstances:

- if the principal of the loan is repaid, and all interest payable under the loan is paid, before 6 April 2018; or
- if the loan becomes a loan on arm's length terms before 6 April 2018, interest is paid in respect of the tax year 2017/18 as if those arm's length terms had applied throughout that year, and interest continues to be payable from 6 April 2018 in accordance with those terms.

Definitions

For the above purposes:

- a loan made *to* the trustees of a settlement is on arm's length terms if interest on it is payable at least annually and at the official rate or more, and a loan made *by* the trustees of a settlement is on arm's length terms if any interest on it is payable at no more than the official rate; and
- a settlement is connected with a person if the person is the settlor or a beneficiary of it.

[*ITTOIA 2005, ss 628A, 628B, 630A; F(No 2)A 2017, Sch 8 paras 22, 23(2), 39*].

For technical guidance, see www.gov.uk/government/publications/trust-protections-and-capital-gains-tax-changes.

Definitions etc.

[70.28] The following apply for the purposes of **70.25** above and **70.29–70.35** below.

(a) '*Settlement*' includes any disposition, trust, covenant, agreement, arrangement or transfer of assets, wherever made. [*ITTOIA 2005, s 620(1)(4)*]. The latter includes a gift of shares (*Hood Barrs v CIR* CA 1946, 27 TC 385) or of National Savings Bank deposit (*Thomas v Marshall* HL 1953, 34 TC 178). For shares in new company issued at par, see *Butler v Wildin* Ch D 1988, [1989] STC 22. See also *Yates v Starkey* CA 1951, 32 TC 38 re Court Orders and *Harvey v Sivyer* Ch D 1985, 58 TC 569 re provision for children whether under compulsion or not.
The creation of a new class of preference shares in a company, and their allotment to the wives of the directors, who had previously also been the sole shareholders, was held to be a settlement by the directors (*Young v Pearce; Young v Scrutton* Ch D 1996, 70 TC 331).
Parent's release of expectant life interest is a settlement (*Buchanan* CA 1957, 37 TC 365) and see *D'Abreu v CIR* Ch D 1978, 52 TC 352.
A distinction can be made between arrangements which amount to a settlement and bona fide commercial transactions without any element of bounty which do not (*Copeman v Coleman* KB 1939, 22 TC 594; *Bulmer v CIR* Ch D 1966, 44 TC 1) and this notwithstanding that tax avoidance was a motive for the transactions (*CIR v Plummer* HL 1979, 54 TC 1). See also *CIR v Levy* Ch D 1982, 56 TC 67. For whether 'arrangements' are a settlement, see also *Prince-Smith KB 1943, 25 TC 84*; *Pay* Ch D 1955, 36 TC 109; *Crossland v Hawkins* CA 1961, 39 TC 493; *Leiner* Ch D 1964, 41 TC 589; *Wachtel* Ch D 1970, 46 TC 543; *Mills v CIR* HL 1974, 49 TC 367; *Chinn v Collins* HL 1980, 54 TC 311; *Butler v Wildin* Ch D 1988, 61 TC 666; *Bird v HMRC* (Sp C 720) at **70.30** below.
For 'property comprised in a settlement', see *Vestey v CIR* HL 1949, 31 TC 1. Where the settlement is of shares in a company controlled by the settlor, the assets of the company are not comprised in the settlement (*Chamberlain v CIR* HL 1943, 25 TC 317; *Langrange Trust v CIR* HL 1947, 28 TC 55).
Where the trust is imperfect, income not disposed of reverts to the settlor (*Hannay's Exors v CIR* CS 1956, 37 TC 217).
A foreign settlement of UK income by a non-resident was held to be within the ambit of the pre-*FA 1995* settlements legislation (*Kenmare* HL 1957, 37 TC 383).

A settlement does not include any arrangement consisting of a loan of money by an individual to a charity (as defined in **70.26** above) either for no consideration or for a consideration consisting only of interest. [*ITTOIA 2005, s 620(1)(5)*].

See also **70.31** below (settlements not involving trusts).

(b) '*Settlor*', in relation to a settlement, means any person by whom the settlement was made. A person is deemed to have made a settlement if he has made or entered into it directly or indirectly and/or has provided or undertaken to provide funds directly or indirectly for the purpose of the settlement or has made reciprocal arrangements for another person to make or enter into the settlement. [*ITTOIA 2005, s 620(1)–(3)*]. See *Crossland v Hawkins* CA 1961, 39 TC 493, *Leiner* Ch D 1964, 41 TC 589 and *Mills* HL 1974, 49 TC 367.

(c) If there is *more than one settlor*. Each is to be treated as the sole settlor, but only in respect of income or property he has himself provided, directly or indirectly. [*ITTOIA 2005, ss 644, 645*].

(d) '*Income arising under a settlement*' includes any income chargeable to income tax, by deduction or otherwise, or which would have been so chargeable if received in the UK by a person domiciled and resident in the UK. However, it does not include income for a tax year on which the settlor, if he were himself entitled to it, would not have been chargeable by reason of his being non-UK resident in the tax year.

If, for a tax year, the settlor is chargeable on the REMITTANCE BASIS (**61**), '*income arising under a settlement*' includes, in relation to any 'relevant foreign income' (see **32.2** FOREIGN INCOME) arising under the settlement in that tax year, only such of it as is remitted to the UK (whether in that tax year or any subsequent tax year) in circumstances such that, if the settlor had remitted it, the settlor would have been chargeable to income tax. The remitted income is then treated as arising under the settlement in the tax year in which it is remitted. (For the purpose only of applying the transitional rule at **61.12** REMITTANCE BASIS, the income is treated as arising in the tax year in which it did, in fact, arise to the settlement.)

[*ITTOIA 2005, s 648; FA 2008, Sch 7 para 86(4A)*].

(e) *Payment of inheritance tax by trustees on assets put into settlement by settlor*. Where the trustees have power to pay, or do in fact pay, inheritance tax on assets which the settlor puts into the settlement, HMRC will not argue that such a power renders that income the settlor's income for income tax purposes. This is because both the settlor and the trustees are liable for such inheritance tax (HMRC SP 1/82).

Settlor retaining an interest

[70.29] As indicated at 70.25 above, income arising under a settlement during the life of the settlor is treated for all income tax purposes as the income of the settlor (and not of any other person), *unless* the income arises from property in which the settlor has no interest (see below). See **70.26** above for the exclusion for income given to charity, **70.27** above for the exclusion for protected foreign-source income and **70.28** above for definitions. The rule applies even where the income in question consists of a payment made by the settlor to the trustees (*Rogge and others v HMRC* FTT (TC 1747), [2012] UKFTT 49 (TC)).

These provisions do not apply in respect of an outright gift between spouses or civil partners of property from which income arises (but a gift which does not carry a right to the whole of that income is not excluded, nor is a gift of a right to income).

A gift is not an outright gift if it is conditional or if the property or any 'related property' could in any circumstances become payable to the giver or be applied for his benefit. See also **70.31** below as regards the application of the above exception in cases involving income shifting.

The following income is excluded from these provisions:

(i) income arising under a marriage settlement (or civil partnership settlement) made between spouses (or civil partners) after separation, divorce or annulment, being income payable to or for the benefit of the spouse (or civil partner) being provided for;
(ii) annual payments by an individual for *bona fide* commercial reasons in connection with his trade, profession or vocation;
(iii) qualifying donations within **14.15** CHARITIES AND CHARITABLE GIVING (Gift Aid); and
(iv) benefits under a registered pension scheme or foreign government pension scheme or any such pension arrangements as may be specified in regulations under *Welfare Reform and Pensions Act 1999* (or NI equivalent).

A settlor has an *interest in property* if that property or any 'related property' could in any circumstances become payable to the settlor or the settlor's spouse or civil partner or be applied for the benefit of either. For this purpose, a spouse does not include a possible future spouse, a separated spouse or a widow/widower of the settlor; and similar exclusions apply in the case of a civil partner. A settlor does *not* have an interest in property if it could become so payable or be so applied only in the event of:

(A) the bankruptcy of a current or potential beneficiary;
(B) an assignment of, or charge on, the property or 'related property' being made or given by a current or potential beneficiary;
(C) in the case of a marriage settlement or civil partnership settlement, the death of both parties to the marriage or civil partnership and of all or any of the children of one or both parties;
(D) the death of a child of the settlor who has become beneficially entitled to the property etc. at an age not exceeding 25,

or if (and so long as) there is a beneficiary alive under the age of 25 during whose life the property etc. cannot become so payable etc. except in the event of the beneficiary becoming bankrupt or assigning or charging his interest.

'*Related property*', in relation to any property, means income from that property or any other property directly or indirectly representing proceeds of, or of income from, that property or income therefrom.

Where the settlement is a trust, expenses of the trustees do not reduce the income attributed to the settlor under these provisions.

The rule treating the settlement income as income of the settlor does not apply to settlement income originating from any settlor who is not an individual. For this purpose, income originates from a settlor if it is income from property originating from the settlor or it is income provided directly or indirectly by the settlor.

[*ITTOIA 2005, ss 624–627, 645, Sch 2 para 132; F(No 2)A 2017, Sch 8 paras 21, 26, 39*].

See also **49.8** and **49.11** MISCELLANEOUS INCOME for apportionment rules and relief for miscellaneous losses.

Simon's Taxes. See **C4.325–C4.329.**

Children's settlements

[70.30] As indicated at **70.25** above, income arising under a settlement which during the life of the settlor is paid (whether in money or money's worth) to or for the benefit of an unmarried minor child (i.e. a child under 18, including a stepchild or illegitimate child) of the settlor in any tax year is treated for all income tax purposes as income of the settlor (and not of any other person) for that year. A child is not regarded for this purpose as 'unmarried' if he is in a civil partnership. See **70.26** above for the exclusion for income given to charity, **70.27** above for the exclusion for protected foreign-source income and **70.28** above for definitions.

However, the above rule does *not* apply for any tax year if the aggregate amount that would otherwise be treated as the settlor's income for that year in relation to any particular child does not exceed £100. Nor does it apply if the income falls to be treated under **70.29** above as that of the settlor. The rule is also disapplied in the circumstances described in **70.19** above (trusts with vulnerable beneficiaries).

As regards income arising under a settlement made on or after 9 March 1999, and income arising directly or indirectly from funds added on or after that date to a pre-existing settlement (any necessary apportionment being made on a just and reasonable basis), the provisions are extended to apply the same treatment as above to undistributed income which would otherwise be treated as income of an 'unmarried' minor child of the settlor in any tax year. This is intended to catch income accumulated in a bare trust. The above-mentioned £100 limit applies, per parent per child, by reference to the aggregate of income paid out or accumulated.

Retained or accumulated income

Where the trustees retain or accumulate income, any payment made on or after 9 March 1999 under the settlement to or for the child is taken into account as above only to the extent that there is available retained or accumulated income, i.e. aggregate income arising since the settlement was made exceeds the aggregate amount of such income which has been:

(a) treated as income of the settlor;
(b) paid (as income or capital) to or for the benefit of, or otherwise treated as the income of, a beneficiary other than an 'unmarried' minor child of the settlor;
(c) treated as the income of an unmarried minor child of the settlor, and 'subject to income tax', in any of the years 1995/96, 1996/97 or 1997/98; or
(d) used to pay expenses of the trustees which were properly chargeable to income (or would have been so chargeable but for express terms of the settlement).

For the purposes of (c) above, the income so treated is '*subject to income tax*' to the extent that it does not exceed the child's taxable income (i.e. total income, inclusive of the settlement income, after allowances and deductions). For payments made before 9 March 1999, similar rules applied as above, the main difference being that any income treated as the income of an unmarried minor child, whether charged to tax or not, was deductible in arriving at available retained or accumulated income.

Where trustees hold assets for a person who would be absolutely entitled as against the trustees but for being a minor, any offshore income gains (see **51.3** OFFSHORE FUNDS) liable to income tax which accrue on the disposal of those assets are deemed to be paid to that person for the purposes of these provisions.

[*ITTOIA 2005, ss 629, 631, 632, Sch 2 para 133; F(No 2)A 2017, Sch 8 paras 23(1), 39; SI 2009 No 3001, Reg 128(3)*].

Any provision by a parent for his child may create a settlement, whether made under compulsion or merely under parental obligation (*Harvey v Sivyer* Ch D 1985, 58 TC 569), although in practice HMRC do not treat payments made under a Court Order as being under a settlement for this purpose. '*Stepchild*' includes a child of the wife by a previous marriage (*CIR v Russell* CS 1955, 36 TC 83). In *Bird v HMRC* (Sp C 720), the issue to children of shares in the family company was held to be a settlement within these provisions with the result that dividends were taxable as the parents' income, though the Sp C also found that there had been no negligent conduct on the part of the parents in failing to declare this dividend income in their tax returns.

Simon's Taxes. See **C4.330, C4.331.**

Settlements not involving trusts — income shifting

[70.31] In its 2008 Pre-Budget Report, the then Government stated that 'given the current economic challenges' they would *not* be bringing forward new legislation on the matters detailed below, but that the issue would be kept under review.

The history

In April 2003, the Inland Revenue (now HMRC) published guidance, including some examples, as to how they intend to apply the settlements legislation at **70.25** above in situations not involving trusts and especially in relation to businesses carried on by companies and partnerships, but see now the HL decision in the *Arctic Systems* case below. Subject to that HL judgment, situations in which the settlements legislation might be applied include: the issue or gifting of shares (to spouses or other relatives, for example) carrying no right (or a restricted right) to a share of the assets on a winding-up, and the payment of dividends on those shares; the issue or gifting to another person, typically a spouse, of shares in a company with minimal capital value that derives its income from the work of one person; the gifting, or transfer at undervalue, of a share of profits in a partnership; the waiving of dividends by one or more shareholders so that other shareholders can receive larger dividends; the payment of larger dividends than would otherwise be possible on one or more classes of shares but not on others; and the gifting to children of shares by a parent, or by someone other than a parent where the company's profits, and decisions on the level of dividends, are made by a parent. The guidance also includes examples of situations in which the settlements legislation would not be applied, mainly involving transactions in which there is no element of bounty and outright gifts between spouses which are not wholly or substantially a right to income (see **70.29** above). (Revenue Tax Bulletin April 2003 pp 1011–1016). References above to spouses must be taken to include civil partners.

A detailed joint response by seven professional bodies, including CIOT and ICAEW, was published on 11 September 2003 (and reproduced at *2003 STI 1605*). This reflected the bodies' concerns both as to HMRC's interpretation of the settlements legislation as summarised above, and as to the retrospective nature of that interpretation, and made clear that they do not accept a number of key technical issues that underpin the above guidance.

HMRC responded with a further article. It contained no relaxation of their views. The examples included in the original article were revisited purely for the purpose of setting out the entries required on self-assessment tax returns where the settlements legislation applies. A number of new examples were also included. (Revenue Tax Bulletin February 2004 pp 1085–1094).

The Arctic Systems case

HMRC initially won a case before the courts involving the issue of one of the two shares in an information technology personal service company to a spouse (in this case the wife), the payment of only a small salary to the husband and the subsequent payment of dividends, but subsequently *lost* the case on appeal to the HL. The HL decision meant that dividends paid on the wife's shareholding do *not* fall to be taxed as the income of the husband (*Jones v Garnett* HL 2007, 78 TC 597 known colloquially as the *Arctic Systems* case). The HL held that the arrangement did constitute a settlement but that it fell within the exception at **70.29** above (outright gifts between spouses which are not wholly or substantially a right to income). In their judgment, the arrangement had the necessary element of bounty to be a settlement; it was not an arrangement that the taxpayer would have entered into with someone with whom he was dealing at arm's length. It was the husband's consent to the issue of the ordinary share to the wife that gave the arrangement the element of bounty but the share was not wholly or even substantially a right to income. It was an ordinary share conferring a right to vote, to participate in the distribution of assets on a winding-up, to block a special resolution etc.; those were all rights over and above the right to income.

Most recent guidance

Following the HL decision in *Jones v Garnett*, HMRC published guidance on 30 July 2007 as to how they would approach open cases. They would consider each case on the basis of its own facts but, unless there are additional factors which might lead them to take a different view, they expect that most cases involving inter-spouse settlements where the settled property comprises ordinary shares in a company or a non-limited interest in a partnership will fall within the exemption at **70.29** above.

HMRC have now made available their detailed guidance on the settlements legislation following *Jones v Garnett*. See HMRC Trusts, Settlements and Estates Manual TSEM4000 *et seq*.

Other recent cases

HMRC were partly successful in *Patmore v HMRC* FTT (TC 619), [2010] SFTD 1124. The tribunal considered that a decision by the controlling shareholder (the husband) to pay dividends on one class of shares rather than another (in this case on B shares held by the wife in preference to A shares) could be an arrangement caught by **70.29** above. However, the settlements legislation applies only where the arrangement involves an element of bounty (see above). In this case, the arrangement was only partly bounteous; the purchase of the business had been a joint enterprise by husband and wife, with each having contributed half the purchase price. On the facts, the tribunal concluded that the dividends should be assessed on the wife to the extent only that they exceeded her dividend entitlement as beneficial owner of 42.5% of the A shares.

In *Donovan & McLaren v HMRC* FTT (TC 3188), [2014] UKFTT 048 (TC), dividend waivers had the effect of diverting income from the main shareholders to their spouses who were the minor shareholders. The arrangement was held to constitute a settlement. In contrast to *Jones v Garnett*, there was no outright gift between the spouses, and thus the exception at **70.29** above (outright gifts between spouses which are not wholly or substantially a right to income) did not apply here. It was held that the waivers would not have taken place at arm's length; the fact that there were insufficient distributable reserves to pay the dividends were it not for the waivers also supported HMRC's argument that there was an element of bounty. The dividend waivers were therefore ineffective for tax purposes. A similar decision had been reached in *Buck v HMRC* (Sp C 716), [2009] SSCD 6.

The future?

Following the HL decision in *Jones v Garnett*, there was the possibility of legislation being introduced to reverse the effect of that decision. The Government of the day eventually announced that they would not be bringing forward any such legislation, but that the issue would be kept under review (Pre-Budget Report Press Notice 03, 24 November 2008). No such legislation has been introduced to date.

Simon's Taxes. See D6.651.

Capital sums, loans and repayments of loans to settlor from settlement or connected body corporate

[70.32] As indicated at **70.25** above, where in any tax year the trustees of a settlement pay any 'capital sum' to the settlor or spouse or civil partner (or to the settlor (or spouse or civil partner) jointly with another person), such an amount (grossed up at the trust rate) is treated as income of the settlor to the extent that it falls within the amount of 'income available' in the settlement up to the end of that tax year or, to the extent that it does not fall within that amount, to the end of the next and subsequent years of assessment up to a maximum of ten years after the year of payment.

There is a corresponding reduction in the amount so treated as a settlor's income for any amount included in his income under *ITTOIA 2005, s 415* (see **65.21** SAVINGS AND INVESTMENT INCOME) in respect of a loan. See also **70.36** below.

The amount charged on the settlor is taxed as part of his total income but he receives credit for the grossing up. The notional tax credit can only be set against the tax charged on the amount treated as the settlor's income. The credit is restricted to, broadly, the tax actually paid by the trustees on the equivalent amount of income; though, for this purpose and for the purpose of the grossing up itself, there is disregarded the fact that dividend income is in reality charged at the dividend trust rate as opposed to the trust rate.

[*ITTOIA 2005, ss 633, 634(7), 639, 640*].

'*Income available*' in the settlement up to the end of any tax year is the aggregate amount of income arising under the settlement, for that and any previous year, which has not been distributed, less:

(a) any amount of that income which has already been 'matched' against a capital sum for assessment on the settlor (see above);
(b) any income taken into account under these provisions in relation to capital sums previously paid to the settlor;
(c) sums treated as income of the settlor under *ITTOIA 2005, s 624* or *s 629* or their predecessors (see **70.29**, **70.30** above); and
(d) the tax at the trust rate on the accumulated undistributed income less the amounts in (c) above.

See **70.28** above as to income arising under a settlement. With relevance for 2017/18 onwards, protected foreign-source income (see **70.27** above) is not counted as income for this purpose. The amount of income which has not been distributed is calculated according to rules in *ITTOIA 2005, ss 636, 637*.

[*ITTOIA 2005, ss 635–637; F(No 2)A 2017, Sch 8 paras 24, 25, 39; FA 2018, Sch 10 paras 8–10, 21(1)*].

In a case which involves one or more previous years earlier than 1995/96, the list at (a)–(d) above includes a number of additional items. See *ITTOIA 2005, Sch 2 para 134(1)–(3)*.

'*Capital sum*' includes a loan or loan repayment and any other sum (other than income) paid otherwise than for full consideration (but excluding sums which could not have become payable to the settlor except in one of the events mentioned in **70.29**(A)–(D) above (or on the death under the age of 25 of the person referred to in the paragraph following **70.29**(A)–(D) above) or under earlier legislation. As regards loans and repayment of loans, see *Potts' Exors v CIR* HL 1950, 32 TC 211; *De Vigier* HL 1964, 42 TC 24; *Bates v CIR* HL 1966, 44 TC 225; *McCrone v CIR* CS 1967, 44 TC 142; *Wachtel* Ch D 1970, 46 TC 543 and *Piratin v CIR* Ch D 1981, 54 TC 730.

There is also treated as a capital sum paid to the settlor any sum paid to a third party at the settlor's direction or by assignment of his right to receive it and any other sum otherwise paid or applied for the settlor's benefit.

[*ITTOIA 2005, s 634, Sch 2 para 134(4)(5)*].

Loan to settlor

Where the capital sum represents a loan to the settlor, there will be no tax charge on him for any tax year after the year in which the loan is repaid. If previous loans have been made and wholly repaid, any new loan will only be charged on its excess, if any, over so much of the earlier loans as have been treated as his income. [*ITTOIA 2005, s 638(1)–(3)*].

Repayment to settlor of loan

Where the capital sum is repayment of a loan by a settlor, a charge arises on him but will not apply for any year after the year in which he makes a further loan at least equal in amount to the loan repaid. [*ITTOIA 2005, s 638(4)(5)*].

Payment of IHT by trustees, see **70.28** above.

Connected companies

A capital sum (as above) paid to a settlor by a body corporate connected with the settlement (see **19.8** CONNECTED PERSONS) is treated as paid to him by the trustees of the settlement irrespective of whether or not the funds originated from that settlement if there has been an 'associated payment' (made directly or indirectly) to the body (or to another body corporate associated with that body under *CTA 2010, s 449* at that time) from the settlement. Such payments to the settlor in a tax year will be 'matched' with associated payments from the trustees to the body corporate up to the end of that year (less any amounts already 'matched') in order to determine the amount deemed paid to the settlor by the trustees in the year, any 'unmatched' balance being 'matched' with associated payments in subsequent years.

'*Associated payment*' is any capital sum paid, or any other sum paid or asset transferred for less than full consideration, to the body corporate by the trustees within five years before or after the capital sum paid to the settlor by the body corporate.

Loans

The above provisions do not apply to any payment to the settlor by way of loan or repayment of a loan if (i) the whole of the loan is repaid within twelve months and (ii) the total period during which loans are outstanding in any period of five years does not exceed twelve months.

[*ITTOIA 2005, ss 641–643, Sch 2 para 135*].

Simon's Taxes. See **C4.335–C4.340.**

Example

[70.33]

The trustees of a settlement with undistributed income of £1,340 at 5 April 2016 made a loan of £30,000 to B, the settlor, on 30 September 2016.

B repays the loan on 31 December 2020. Undistributed income of £3,500 arose in 2016/17, £6,490 in 2017/18, £4,510 in 2018/19, £10,450 in 2019/20 and £9,200 in 2020/21. The trustees duly settle all their liabilities to tax on trust income.

The following income amounts will be treated as part of B's total income.

		£
2016/17	£4,840 × 100/55	8,800
2017/18	£6,490 × 100/55	11,800
2018/19	£4,510 × 100/55	8,200
2019/20	£10,450 × 100/55	19,000
2020/21	£3,710 × 100/55 note (a)	6,745

The notional tax credits available to B are

		£
2016/17	£8,800 @ 45%	3,960.00
2017/18	£11,800 @ 45%	5,310.00
2018/19	£8,200 @ 45%	3,690.00
2019/20	£19,000 @ 45%	8,550.00
2020/21	£6,745 @ 45%	3,035.25

Note

(a) The amount treated as income in 2020/21 is limited to the amount of the loan less amounts previously treated as income (£30,000 – (£4,840 + £6,490 + £4,510 + £10,450)).

Benefits provided out of protected foreign-source income

[70.34] With effect for **2018/19** onwards, otherwise untaxed benefits provided by the trustees of a settlement to the settlor or a close family member out of protected foreign-source income are treated as income of the settlor or family member. The legislation applies if an individual has 'an untaxed benefits total' for a settlement for a tax year. The amount (the '*chargeable amount*') treated as income is so much of that total as does not exceed the settlement's 'available protected income' up to the end of the year.

If the individual is UK resident for the year (and is not chargeable on the REMITTANCE BASIS (**61**)), the chargeable amount is treated as taxable income of the individual for the year. If the individual is non-UK resident, the chargeable amount is treated as income, but not as *taxable* income, of that individual; but if that individual is *not* the settlor *and* certain conditions regarding the settlor are met, the chargeable amount is treated as taxable income of the *settlor* for the year. The same applies if the individual is UK resident but is chargeable on the remittance basis, but then only to the extent that the income representing the chargeable amount is not remitted to the UK in the tax year. The conditions regarding the settlor are that the settlor is UK resident for the year and that there is no time in the year when the settlor is either domiciled in the UK or deemed domiciled by virtue of the first of the two conditions at **63.36** RESIDENCE AND DOMICILE.

Where chargeability is effectively transferred as above to the settlor from another individual, the settlor is entitled to recover from the other individual the amount of tax paid. For this purpose, the settlor is entitled to require from an officer of HMRC a certificate specifying the amount of income in question and the amount of tax paid.

If there is a choice of individuals to whom income could be treated as arising (before considering any transfer of chargeability to the settlor as above), income is to be treated as arising to such one or more of them, and in such proportions, as appears to an officer of HMRC to be just and reasonable.

Untaxed benefits total

Whether an individual has an '*untaxed benefits total*' for a settlement for a tax year (Year Z), and if so the amount of it, is determined in accordance with the following steps.

(1) If the individual is the settlor, identify each benefit provided by the trustees to the individual in Year Z or earlier (but not in any year preceding 2018/19) and at a time when the individual is neither domiciled in the UK nor deemed domiciled by virtue of the first of the two conditions at **63.36** RESIDENCE AND DOMICILE. A benefit is provided if it is provided out of property comprised in, or income arising under, the settlement. If income, before being distributed, is the income of a person other than the trustees, it is treated for these purposes as provided by the trustees to that person at the time the income arises; the amount of the benefit is in this case subject to any reduction for trustees' expenses. If the individual is not the settlor, identify each benefit so provided in Year Z or earlier (but not in any year preceding 2018/19) and at a time when the individual is a 'close member of the settlor's family'.

(2) Quantify the aggregate of the amounts and values of the benefits identified in step (1). As regards the valuing of benefits, the valuation rules at **4.15** ANTI-AVOIDANCE apply for these purposes also.

(3) Deduct from that aggregate the following:

- any part of it on which the individual is liable to income tax otherwise than under these provisions;
- any income treated under these provisions or those at **70.35** below as arising to any person for a tax year preceding Year Z by reference to any of the benefits identified at step (1);
- the amount or value of so much (if any) of any identified benefit as is taken into account in charging income tax under the 'transfer of assets abroad rules at **4.14–4.18** ANTI-AVOIDANCE; and
- any chargeable gains treated by specified provisions of *TCGA 1992* (see *ITTOIA 2005, s 643D*) as accruing to a person in a tax year preceding Year Z by reference to the whole or part of the identified benefits.

The result given by step (3), if greater than nil, is the individual's untaxed benefits total for the settlement for Year Z.

Close family members

For these purposes and those of **70.35** below, the following persons are '*close members of the settlor's family*' at any time (provided the settlor is living at that time):

- the settlor's current spouse or civil partner; and
- any minor child of the settlor (or of the settlor's current spouse or civil partner).

Cohabiting couples are treated for the above purpose as if they were spouses or civil partners.

Available protected income

A settlement has '*available protected income*' up to the end of a tax year if the excess (if any) of PFSI over TOAA is greater than T1, where:

PFSI is the total amount of any 'protected foreign-source income' (see **70.27** above) arising under the settlement in Year Z or any earlier tax year (excluding years prior to 2018/19) that would be treated as income of the settlor under **70.25**(a) or (b) above if it were not for the protected foreign-source income exclusion at **70.27** and on which no income tax liability arises (ignoring the provisions currently under discussion). Where **70.25**(a) would be in point but for the said exclusion, income falls within PFSI only if it can be used directly or indirectly to provide benefits for the individual. The rule at **70.28**(d) above, whereby relevant foreign income is treated as arising under a settlement only if and when it is remitted to the UK, does not apply for these purposes, and is also ignored in deciding for these purposes if income would be treated as income of the settlor.
TOAA is so much of PFSI as is, in respect of benefits provided by the trustees in Year Z or an earlier tax year (including years prior to 2018/19), taken into account in charging income tax under the 'transfer of assets abroad' rules at **4.14–4.18** ANTI-AVOIDANCE for Year Z or an earlier year; and
TI is the total of:

- so much of PFSI as is, in respect of benefits provided by the trustees to the individual, treated under these provisions or those at **70.35** below as income for any year preceding Year Z (excluding years prior to 2018/19); and
- so much of PFSI as is, in respect of benefits provided by the trustees to other individuals, treated under these provisions or those at **70.35** as income for Year Z or any earlier year (again excluding years prior to 2018/19).

The amount of the available protected income is PFSI – TOAA – TI.

Application of remittance basis

Where taxable income (the '*deemed income*') is treated as arising to an individual under the above provisions for a tax year, and the individual is chargeable on the remittance basis for that year, the income is treated as relevant foreign income of the individual, with the consequences in **61.4 REMITTANCE BASIS** but ignoring the reference there to split year treatment. For the purpose of applying the remittance basis rules, treat a benefit, or any PFSI income, that 'relates' (see *ITTOIA 2005, s 643G*) to any part of the deemed income as deriving from that part of the deemed income.

[*ITTOIA 2005, ss 643A–643H; FA 2018, Sch 10 paras 11, 21(1)(2), 22; SI 2019 No 1458, Sch 3 para 27*].

Onward gifts of benefits provided out of protected foreign-source income

[70.35] It might have been possible to avoid the charge at **70.34** above by providing benefits to individuals outside the scope of those provisions, who would subsequently make an onward gift to the settlor or a close member of the settlor's family. The following provisions seek to prevent this by taxing onward gifts and have effect in relation to onward gifts made on or after **6 April 2018**.

The conditions

These provisions apply where:

(a) an amount is treated under **70.34** above as income of an individual (the '*original beneficiary*') for a tax year (Year Z) but is not taxed, either because the original beneficiary is non-UK resident or is chargeable on the remittance basis and does not remit the amount before the end of the charging year and in a tax year for which he is UK resident, or because the rules for transferring chargeability to the settlor do not apply or because those rules do apply but the settlor is chargeable on the remittance basis and does not remit the amount before the end of the charging year and in a tax year for which he is UK resident;
(b) under matching rules the amount is matched with a benefit provided in Year Z, or an earlier tax year, to the original beneficiary;
(c) at the time the benefit is provided, there are arrangements, or there is an intention, to pass on the benefit (or part of it) to another person who it is anticipated will be UK resident when the benefit is passed on;

(d) the original beneficiary makes a gift (the '*onward payment*') to a person (the '*subsequent recipient*') in anticipation of the benefit being provided or within the three years after it is provided;

(e) the gift is of, or includes, the whole or part of the benefit or anything deriving from it or the gift is of other property but the benefit is provided with a view to enabling or facilitating, or otherwise in connection with, the making of the gift; and

(f) the subsequent recipient is the settlor or, at the time the onward payment is made, is a 'close member of the settlor's family' (see **70.34** above).

The '*charging year*' (see (a) above) is the gift year or, if later, Year Z. The matching rules referred to in (b) above are in *ITTOIA 2005, s 643G* and broadly match income in the order it is treated as received with benefits in the order they are received. Where (d) and (e) above are met, it is to be presumed (unless shown to the contrary) that (c) is also met. If the onward payment is made in anticipation of the benefit being provided (see (d) above), it is treated for the purposes of these provisions as made immediately after, and in the tax year in which, the benefit is provided to the original beneficiary. The question of whether the subsequent recipient is a close member of the settlor's family is then judged by reference both to that time and the time the onward payment is actually made.

If the benefit mentioned in (b) above is one that is treated as provided by the rules below under Onward gift to settlor or close family member by other recipient, the conditions have effect with the omission of (c).

The charge

If the above conditions are met and the subsequent recipient is UK resident for the tax year in which the onward payment is made (the '*gift year*'), and also for Year Z if that is later than the gift year, an amount (Amount A) is treated as income of the subsequent recipient for the charging year. Amount A is equal to so much of the amount or value of the onward payment as falls within (e) above. If the subsequent recipient is chargeable on the remittance basis for the charging year, the amount treated as income is equal to so much (if any) of Amount A as is remitted to the UK in that year. In either case the amount treated as income is reduced by any part of it on which the subsequent recipient is liable to income tax otherwise than under this charge. If the amount to be treated as income (after any such reduction) would otherwise exceed the amount mentioned in (a) above, it is restricted to that amount.

If the subsequent recipient is non-UK resident for the gift year, or if Year Z is later than the gift year and the subsequent recipient is UK resident for the gift year but not for Year Z, it will be seen that the above charge cannot have effect. In such a case, the subsequent recipient is treated as if he were an individual within (a) above, with the result that the charge can apply in the event of a further onward payment, but only if it is made no later than three years after the providing of the original benefit. The amount of the income for the purpose of (a) above (Amount B) is so much of the amount or value of the onward payment as falls within (e) above and is not treated as arising to the settlor under the rules below under Transfer of chargeability to settlor. A similar rule applies if the subsequent recipient is UK resident for both the gift year and Year Z (if later than the gift year) and is chargeable on the remittance basis for the charging year, but there is at least a part of the onward payment that is not remitted to the UK in the charging year. In this case the amount of the income for the purpose of (a) is so much of Amount B as is not remitted. In either case, the amount of the income for the purpose of (a) is not to exceed the amount mentioned in (a) in the case of the original beneficiary. In applying the charge above in the event of a subsequent onward payment, the conditions at (a)–(f) above have effect with the following modifications: (b) and (c) are omitted; the reference in (d) to the benefit being provided is to the previous onward payment being made; and the reference in (e) to the benefit is a reference to so much of that onward payment as was on that previous occasion within (e).

Once the above charge has applied in relation to an amount of income, neither the original beneficiary nor the settlor is liable to tax for any subsequent tax year on that same income.

Transfer of chargeability to settlor

Where conditions (a)–(f) above are met, chargeability is transferred from the subsequent recipient to the settlor in the following circumstances:

- the subsequent recipient is a close member of the settlor's family when the onward payment is made and either is UK resident for the charging year and chargeable to tax on the remittance basis for that year or is non-UK resident for that year;
- (in a case where the subsequent recipient is UK resident and chargeable on the remittance basis) none, or part only, of the onward payment is remitted to the UK in the charging year;
- there is a time in the charging year when the settlor is UK resident; and
- there is no time in the charging year when the settlor is domiciled in the UK or is deemed domiciled by virtue of the first of the two conditions at **63.36** RESIDENCE AND DOMICILE.

An amount (Amount C) is treated as income of the settlor for the charging year. Amount C is equal to the amount or value of so much of the onward payment as falls within (e) above. In a case where part only of Amount C is remitted to the UK in the charging year, the amount treated as income is equal to so much of Amount C as is not remitted. In either case the amount treated as income is reduced by any part of it on which the settlor is liable to income tax otherwise than under this charge. If the amount to be treated as income (after any such reduction) would otherwise exceed the amount mentioned in (a) above, it is restricted to that amount.

Where chargeability is effectively transferred as above to the settlor from the subsequent recipient, the settlor is entitled to recover from the subsequent recipient the amount of tax paid. For this purpose, the settlor is entitled to require from an officer of HMRC a certificate specifying the amount of income in question and the amount of tax paid.

Once the above charge has applied to the settlor in relation to an amount of income, the original beneficiary is not liable to tax for any subsequent tax year on that amount of income.

Application of remittance basis

Where income is treated as arising to an individual under the above provisions for a tax year, and the individual is chargeable on the remittance basis for that year, the income is treated as relevant foreign income of the individual, with the consequences in **61.4** REMITTANCE BASIS but ignoring the reference there to split year treatment. For the purpose of applying the remittance basis rules, treat the onward payment, or (as the case may be) the part of it whose amount or value is equal to the amount of the income, as deriving from the income.

[*ITTOIA 2005, ss 643I–643L, 643M(6), 643N; FA 2018, Sch 10 paras 11, 21(3)*].

Onward gift to settlor or close family member by other recipient

Consequences also ensue in relation to onward payments made on or after 6 April 2018 (including where the onward payment is referable to a benefit received before that date) where the set of conditions at (a)–(f) above is not fully met but the following conditions are met:

(i) the trustees of a settlement provide a benefit (the '*original benefit*') to an individual (the '*original recipient*') who is neither the settlor nor, judged at the time the benefit is provided, a close member of the settlor's family;

(ii) the original recipient is not taxed on the original benefit (see below); and

(iii) conditions (c)–(f) above are met by reference to the original benefit and the original recipient.

So much of the onward payment as is within (e) above (as applied by (iii) above) is treated for the purposes of step (1) in **70.34** above as a benefit provided by the trustees to the subsequent recipient at the time the onward payment is made. If the onward payment is made in anticipation of the original benefit being provided (see (d) above as applied by (iii)), it is treated for these purposes as made immediately after, and in the tax year in which, the original benefit is provided to the original recipient. The question of whether the subsequent recipient is a close member of the settlor's family is then judged by reference both to that time and the time the onward payment is actually made.

For the purposes of (ii) above, the original recipient is taxed on the original benefit if he is liable to income tax or capital gains tax by reference to the amount or value of the original benefit. Where the original recipient is so liable by reference to the amount or value of part only of the original benefit, the rules apply as if the two parts of the original benefit were separate benefits.

Where there is a series of gifts. of which the first gift is made by the original recipient within the time frame in (d) above (as applied by (iii) above) and the last (but no earlier gift in the series) is made to the settlor or a close member of the settlor's family, then provided all of the gifts are within (e) above (as applied by (iii)) the last gift in the series is brought within these provisions as if its maker were the original recipient and not its actual maker.

[*ITTOIA 2005, s 643M; FA 2018, Sch 10 paras 11, 21(4)*].

Heritage maintenance settlements — tax exemptions for settlors etc.

[70.36] Where the Treasury has directed under *IHTA 1984, Sch 4 para 1* (a '*heritage direction*') that funds put into a settlement (a '*heritage maintenance settlement*') for the maintenance of, or for making provision of public access to, 'qualifying property' are exempt for inheritance tax purposes, the trustees may elect, in relation to any tax year, that:

(a) any income arising from the settlement property in respect of which the heritage direction has effect ('*heritage maintenance property*') which would otherwise be treated as income of the settlor (see **70.25–70.35** above) shall not be so treated; and

(b) any sum applied out of heritage maintenance property for the maintenance of, or for making provision of public access to, qualifying property shall not be treated as income of any person by virtue of his interest in, or occupation of, the property in question or by virtue of *ITTOIA 2005, s 633* — see **70.32** above).

The election must be made no later than the first anniversary of 31 January following the tax year to which it relates. There is provision for splitting the tax year if there is a change of circumstances, e.g. if a heritage direction takes effect, or ceases to have effect, during the year; an election can then be made for part of the year only.

If no election is made for a tax year and income arises from the heritage maintenance property which is treated as income of the settlor, the exemption at (b) above nevertheless applies to any excess of the sum applied as in (b) over that income.

'*Qualifying property*' is defined at *IHTA 1984, Sch 4 para 3(2)* and includes:

- land of outstanding scenic, historic or scientific interest;
- buildings of outstanding historical or architectural interest and land essential to protect the character and amenities of such buildings; and
- objects historically associated with such buildings.

If a settlement comprises both heritage maintenance property and other property, the heritage maintenance property and the other property are treated as comprised in separate settlements for a number of purposes now listed at *ITA 2007, s 507(3)*.

Prevention of double taxation — reimbursement of settlor

Where income arising from heritage maintenance property (i) is treated as income of the settlor by virtue of **70.25–70.35** above; (ii) the income is paid to the settlor to reimburse him for expenditure incurred by him on the maintenance of, or for making provision of public access to, qualifying property; *and* (iii) the expenditure is deductible in computing the profits of a trade or UK property business (see **60.2** PROPERTY INCOME) carried on by the settlor, the reimbursed amount does not count as a taxable receipt of the trade or business and is not regarded as income of the settlor otherwise than by virtue of **70.25–70.35** above.

Application of property for non-heritage purposes; charge to tax

An income tax charge potentially arises on the trustees of a heritage maintenance settlement in any of the circumstances below. The rate of tax applicable is equal to the excess of the additional rate of income tax over the trust rate; as these rates are, in fact, the same, no charge arises.

The circumstances are as follows:

- where any property comprised in the settlement (whether capital or income) is applied otherwise than for the maintenance of, or for making provision of public access to, qualifying property or, in the case of income not so applied and not accumulated, for the benefit of a '*heritage body*' (i.e. a body or charity of a kind mentioned in *IHTA 1984, Sch 4 para 3(1)(a)(ii)*);
- where any of that property, on ceasing to be comprised in the settlement, devolves otherwise than on a heritage body;
- where the heritage direction ceases to have effect in respect of the settlement; and
- where any of that property, on ceasing at any time to be comprised in the settlement, devolves on a heritage body and at or before that time an interest under the settlement is or has been acquired for money or money's worth by that or another such body (but any acquisition from another such body will be disregarded).

The charge is on all income which has arisen from the property comprised in the settlement since the last charge under this provision or, otherwise, since the creation of the settlement, and has not been applied for the maintenance of, or for making provision of public access to, qualifying property or for the benefit of a heritage body. The charge will not apply to income which is treated as income of the settlor under **70.25–70.35** above, and sums applied otherwise than for the above-mentioned purpose are treated as paid first out of income treated as the settlor's. There is no charge where the whole of the settlement property is transferred to another settlement by means of a '*tax-free transfer*', i.e. a transfer in respect of which *IHTA 1984, Sch 4 para 9* provides an exception from charge or a transfer where both immediately before and after the transfer the property is heritage maintenance property. Instead, the transferee settlement stands in the shoes of the transferor settlement.

[*ITA 2007, ss 507–517*].

Simon's Taxes. See **C4.355–C4.357.**

71

Share-Related Employment Income and Exemptions

For HMRC's own guidance on this subject, see www.gov.uk/topic/business-tax/employment-related-securities, HMRC Employee Tax Advantaged Share Scheme User Manual and HMRC Employment-Related Securities Manual.

Simon's Taxes. See E4.5.

Introduction to share-related employment income and exemptions

[71.1] For general tax liability in respect of shares given to directors or other employees as part of their employment income, see **28.76** EMPLOYMENT INCOME.

The expression 'shares' is used in this chapter in its broadest sense. For the application of the chapter to stocks and securities, as well as shares, see **71.3** below.

Legislation applies where there are arrangements to allow a person to acquire shares by reason of their (or in some cases another person's) employment, as follows.

(a) Restricted shares under *ITEPA 2003, ss 422–432* — see **71.4** below.

(b) Convertible shares under *ITEPA 2003, ss 435–444* — see **71.8** below.
(c) Shares with artificially depressed market value, under *ITEPA 2003, ss 446A–446J* — see **71.10** below.
(d) Shares with artificially enhanced market value, under *ITEPA 2003, ss 446K–446P* — see **71.11** below.
(e) Shares disposed of for more than market value, under *ITEPA 2003, ss 446X–446Z* — see **71.13** below.
(f) Post-acquisition benefits under *ITEPA 2003, ss 447–450* — see **71.14** below.
(g) Non-tax-advantaged share options under *ITEPA 2003, ss 471–484* — see **71.15** below.
(h) Share incentive plans under *ITEPA 2003, ss 488–515, Sch 2* — see **71.25** below.
(i) Enterprise management incentives under *ITEPA 2003, ss 527–541, Sch 5* — see **71.41** below.
(j) SAYE option schemes under *ITEPA 2003, ss 516–520, Sch 3* see **71.53** below.
(k) Company share option plan (CSOP) schemes under *ITEPA 2003, ss 521–526, Sch 4* — see **71.66** below.
(l) Priority share allocations under *ITEPA 2003, ss 542–548* — see **71.79** below.

See also the notional loan provisions of *ITEPA 2003, ss 446Q–446W* at **71.12** below for shares acquired partly-paid, and see **71.80** below as regards research institution spin-out companies. For reporting obligations, see **71.18–71.21** below.

For tax deductions (against trading profits etc.) available to employer companies in connection with employee share schemes, see Tolley's Corporation Tax.

Internationally mobile employees

There are no territorial limits to the application of (a) to (g) above; but if, under any of those provisions, something counts as employment income of an internationally mobile employee, there are rules (see **71.22–71.24** below) to determine the amount of that income which is taxable in the UK.

Employee shareholder shares

A new employment status, known as 'employee shareholder' status, was introduced in *Growth and Infrastructure Act 2013, s 31*. Employee shareholders will be issued or allotted at least £2,000 worth of shares in consideration of an employee shareholder agreement. For income tax purposes, subject to conditions, employee shareholders are deemed to have paid £2,000 for their employee shareholder shares. Subject to conditions, a monetary limit and a lifetime limit, employee shareholder shares are also exempt from capital gains tax when disposed of. These income tax and capital gains tax reliefs are **abolished** by *FA 2017* with effect where the employee shareholder agreement is entered into on or after, in most cases, **1 December 2016**. See **71.78** below.

Share-related employment income and exemptions — general matters

[71.2] The following miscellaneous items are dealt with in alphabetical order.

Armed Forces Reservists

By concession, a reservist called up for service under *Reserve Forces Act 1996* will have his consequent employment with the Ministry of Defence (MOD) treated as fulfilling the employment conditions for the tax-advantaged schemes at **71.25**, **71.53** and **71.66** below and for enterprise management incentives at **71.41** below. In addition, employers and scheme providers may take such action as is necessary to maintain the reservist's participation in the scheme for the period they are away serving with the MOD; provided the action does no more than that, it will not compromise the scheme's tax-advantaged status. (See HMRC ESC A103). Guidance notes for employers, setting out possible courses of action within the concession, are attached to the published concession.

Earn-outs

Where the consideration passing on the sale of a business includes an earn-out, typically a right to receive securities in the purchasing company after a certain period of time has elapsed and dependent on the performance of the newly taken-over business, any element of remuneration for services as an employee or prospective employee included in the earn-out may give rise to a tax charge under the provisions at **71.5** below (restricted shares), **71.9** below (convertible shares) or **71.15** below (share options), whichever is relevant, always bearing in mind the extended meaning of 'shares' at **71.3** below. Guidance has been issued as to how the rules will be applied and how to identify if an earn-out is 'remuneration' or further sale consideration or an element of both. See HMRC Employment-Related Securities Manual ERSM110900–110940.

HMRC Employment Related Securities Bulletin

HMRC publish an occasional Employment Related Securities Bulletin to provide information and updates on developments relating to employment-related shares. See www.gov.uk/government/publications/employment-related-securities-bulletin. Previously, they published a newsletter, Share Focus, with a similar remit.

Memoranda of Understanding

Two Memoranda of Understanding between the Inland Revenue (as it then was) and the British Venture Capital Association, covering certain matters arising from substantial changes made by *FA 2003* to the provisions at **71.3–71.16** below, were published on 25 July 2003 and are reproduced in the HMRC Employment-Related Securities Manual at ERSM30520 and 30530. As regards ratchet arrangements (commonly seen in management buy-outs), both within and without the relevant Memorandum, a change of opinion was published by HMRC on 21 August 2006 — see now ERSM90500.

Restricted Stock Units (RSUs)

RSUs are arrangements used particularly by US companies to incentivise employees, including internationally mobile employees, over the long term via reward linked to shares or securities. Any charge to UK income tax arises specifically under the share option rules in **71.15** and **71.16** below instead of the general rules charging income tax on earnings. [*ITEPA 2003, s 418(1)(1A); FA 2016, s 17(1)(2)(4)*]. For more on RSUs, see HMRC Employment Related Securities Manual ERSM20192–20194.

Transfer pricing

For HMRC guidance on the implications of transfer pricing (see **4.19** ANTI-AVOIDANCE) on employee share schemes operated by groups of companies, see HMRC International Manual INTM440210–440250.

Extended meaning of 'shares'

[71.3] For the purposes of **71.4–71.16** below, the meaning of 'shares' is extended to embrace a broader range of financial products, including, for example, government and local authority stocks. All of the following are now 'shares' for these purposes:

- shares (including stock) in any body corporate, wherever incorporated, or in any unincorporated body constituted under the law of a foreign country;
- debentures, debenture stock, loan stock, bonds, certificates of deposit and other instruments creating or acknowledging indebtedness (other than contracts of insurance);
- warrants and other instruments entitling the holders to subscribe for securities;
- certificates and other instruments conferring rights in respect of securities held by persons other than the persons on whom the rights are conferred and which may be transferred without the consent of those persons;
- units in a collective investment scheme (as defined by *ITEPA 2003, s 420(2)*);
- futures (as defined by *ITEPA 2003, s 420(3)*);
- rights under contracts for differences (or under similar contracts — as defined by *ITEPA 2003, s 420(4)*) (other than contracts of insurance);
- rights under contracts of insurance, whenever acquired, other than: (i) contracts for annuities which are, or will be, pension income; (ii) contracts of long-term insurance, other than annuity contracts, which do not have, and cannot acquire, a surrender value; and (iii) contracts of general insurance which would not fall to be accounted for under generally accepted accounting practice as financial assets or liabilities;
- options (but see below under Share options);
- arrangements falling within **3.5** ALTERNATIVE FINANCE ARRANGEMENTS (alternative finance investment bond arrangements).

However, none of the following are 'shares' for these purposes:

- cheques, bills of exchange, bankers' drafts and letters of credit (other than bills of exchange accepted by a banker);
- money and statements showing balances on a current, deposit or savings account;
- leases and other dispositions of property and heritable securities;
- 'share options' — see below.

The above lists can be amended by Treasury order.

Share options

In the list of exclusions above, '*share options*' are rights to acquire shares (with 'shares' having its extended meaning for this purpose). *However*, the term does not include a right to acquire shares that is itself acquired pursuant to a right or opportunity made available under arrangements having as a main purpose the avoidance of tax or national insurance contributions; such options are therefore omitted from the list of exclusions and do count as 'shares'. The effect of this is that such an option is a convertible share within **71.8** below (as it can be converted into 'shares' of a different description). In particular, it means that a tax charge may arise on acquisition of the option, and, for that purpose, the market value of the option may be determined on the basis that there is an immediate and unfettered right to convert (see **71.8** below). This contrasts with the normal treatment of share options at **71.15** below where there is usually no tax charge on the grant of the option. A share option that remains within the above list of exclusions (i.e. it is not acquired as part of avoidance arrangements) continues to be within **71.15** below rather than **71.8** below.

General

It is important to note that the above extended meaning of 'shares' does *not* apply for the purposes of the tax-advantaged schemes at **71.25** *et seq.* below. For the purposes of **71.41** *et seq.* below, 'shares' includes stock but not securities, and see also the specific rules at **71.35**, **71.47**, **71.61** and **71.73** below.

An '*interest in shares*', for the purposes of **71.4–71.16** below, means an interest which is less than full beneficial ownership. It includes an interest in their sale proceeds but not a right to acquire them.

[*ITEPA 2003, ss 420, 516(4), 521(4), 548(1), Sch 5 para 58; SI 2007 No 2130*].

Phantom share schemes

HMRC's view is that phantom share schemes (see **28.76** EMPLOYMENT INCOME) are simply arrangements for the payment of cash bonuses measured in a certain way and cannot constitute 'shares' or 'share options' (HMRC Employment-Related Securities Manual ERSM20196).

Simon's Taxes. See **E4.507A.**

Restricted shares

[71.4] These provisions apply to 'employment-related shares' if, at the time of acquisition, they are 'restricted shares' (or a 'restricted interest in shares'). For the extended meaning of 'shares', in relation to these provisions, see **71.3** above. See below for exclusions from the charge and **71.7** below for the possibility of electing to disapply or moderate these provisions. See **71.18–71.21** below for reporting obligations. See also the anti-avoidance provisions at **71.10**, **71.11** below.

'*Employment-related shares*' are shares (or an interest in shares) acquired by a person by virtue of a right or opportunity made available by reason of the employment (present, past or prospective) of that or any other person. For this purpose, shares are deemed to be acquired when the beneficial entitlement to them is acquired and not, if different, at the time of conveyance or transfer. Any right or opportunity made available by a person's employer, or by a person connected (within **19** CONNECTED PERSONS) with a person's employer, is treated as made available by reason of the employment of that person, other than in the case of an individual conferring a right or opportunity in the normal course of his domestic, family or personal relationships. There are rules dealing with company reorganisations (such as conversions, scrip issues and rights issues); these treat replacement shares or additional shares acquired on such a reorganisation as acquired by virtue of the same right or opportunity as the original interest and treat any consequent reduction in the market value of the original shares as consideration given for the replacement shares or additional shares.

For the circumstances in which HMRC will accept that shares or share options were acquired by an employee by virtue of a family or personal relationship and not by reason of the employment, see HMRC Employment-Related Securities Manual ERSM20220.

A right etc. is made available to the taxpayer even though he may himself have stipulated its being granted (*CIR v Herd* CS 1992, 66 TC 29).

An increase in a person's interest in shares is treated for the purposes of these provisions as a separate interest acquired by virtue of the same right or opportunity as the original interest. A decrease in a person's interest is treated as a disposal, otherwise than to an 'associated person', of a separate interest proportionate to the reduction.

For the purposes of these provisions, consideration given for the acquisition of employment-related shares includes consideration given by the employee or by the person who acquired the shares (if not the employee) and any consideration given for a *right* to acquire the shares. Any consideration given partly for one thing and partly for another is apportioned as is just and reasonable. Rules similar to those at **71.16** below (under Option exchanged for another) apply to determine the amount of consideration where a right to acquire the shares is assigned or released for consideration consisting of or including another right to acquire the shares.

In *Tower Radio Ltd v HMRC (and related appeal)* UT, [2015] UKUT 0060 (TCC), [2015] STC 1257, a company entered into a tax avoidance scheme involving the award of restricted shares in a subsidiary company to its managing director (MD), with the aim of paying him a substantial bonus without incurring any PAYE liability. The subsidiary was subsequently liquidated, and its assets were distributed to MD. The UT, reversing the First-tier Tribunal's decision, found for the appellants, deciding that MD had to be treated as having acquired shares rather than money.

Definition of restricted shares

Employment-related shares are '*restricted shares*' (or a '*restricted interest in shares*') if there is a contract, agreement, arrangement or condition that imposes any of the three types of restriction listed below *and* the market value of the shares or interest (determined as for capital gains purposes) is less than it otherwise would have been. The types of restriction covered are as follows:

(a) any provision for the transfer, reversion or forfeiture of the shares etc. if certain circumstances arise or do not arise, such that the holder will cease to be beneficially entitled to them and will not be entitled to receive an amount at least equal to their unfettered market value;
(b) any restriction (not within (a) above) on the freedom of the holder to dispose of the shares etc. (or to retain the proceeds if they are sold) or on his right to retain the shares or proceeds or on any right conferred by the shares themselves;
(c) any provision (not within (a) or (b) above) whereby the disposal or retention of the shares etc., or the exercise of a right conferred by them, may result in a disadvantage to the holder or (if different) the employee or a connected person (within **19** CONNECTED PERSONS) of either.

However, neither of the following is sufficient in itself to confer 'restricted shares' status on employment-related shares:

- (in the case of unpaid or partly paid shares) a provision for forfeiture in the event of non-payment of calls (provided the meeting of calls is not itself restricted);
- a requirement that the shares be offered for sale or transfer in the event of the employee's losing his employment by reason of misconduct.

These disregards are disapplied if the arrangements under which the right or opportunity to acquire the shares was made available have as a main purpose the avoidance of tax or national insurance contributions.

The reference above to the 'three types of restriction' at (a)–(c) is to be construed as being limited to provision having a business or commercial purpose, and not to commercially irrelevant conditions whose only purpose is the obtaining of the exemption on acquisition below and/or the exception from charge in **71.5** below (*UBS AG v HMRC; DB Group Services (UK) Ltd v HMRC* SC, [2016] UKSC 13; *Cyclops Electronics Ltd v HMRC* UT, [2018] STC 254, [2018] UKUT 7 (TCC)).

Exclusions

These provisions do not apply in relation to shares acquired under the terms of a public offer (including an 'employee offer' as in **71.79** below), unless a main purpose of the arrangements under which the shares are acquired, or for which the shares are held, is the avoidance of tax or national insurance contributions.

When provisions cease to apply

These provisions cease to apply to shares (or an interest in shares):

- following a disposal to a person other than an 'associated person'; or
- immediately before the death of the employee (so that no charge arises on death); or
- on the seventh anniversary of the first date on which the employee is employed neither by the employer who made available the right or opportunity to acquire the shares nor by the company that issued the shares (where applicable) nor by a connected person (within **19** CONNECTED PERSONS) of either that employer or that issuing company.

Associated persons

For the purposes of these provisions, any of the following are '*associated persons*' in relation to employment-related shares:

- the person who acquired them;
- (if different) the employee; and
- any 'relevant linked person'.

A '*relevant linked person*' is any person who is either connected (within **19** CONNECTED PERSONS) with, or is a member of the same household as, either the person who acquired the shares or the employee. The statutory definition also embrace past connections etc. so as to ensure the link cannot be broken. However, a *company* cannot be a relevant linked person if it is the employer or (if different) the person by whom the right or opportunity to acquire the shares was made available or the person from whom the shares were acquired or by whom they were issued.

Tax exemption in certain cases on acquisition

No liability to income tax arises on the *acquisition* of employment-related shares under the normal rules at **28.76** EMPLOYMENT INCOME if the shares are restricted under (a) above and will cease to be so within five years after the acquisition (whether or not they may remain restricted under either (b) or (c) above). However, the employer and employee may jointly and irrevocably elect to disapply this exemption. The point of an election would be to reduce the charge to tax on a future chargeable event (see **71.5** below). (See **71.7** below for the separate possibility of electing to disapply or moderate *all* these provisions.) The election is implemented by way of an agreement (between employer and employee), in a form approved by HMRC, that must be made no later than 14 days after the acquisition; there is no requirement for it to be submitted to HMRC. Prescribed forms of election are available on the HMRC website. Whether or not the election is made, and where relevant, income tax charges may arise on acquisition under **71.15** below (share options), **71.8** below (conversion) or **71.12** below (acquisition for less than market value).

The above election is available only if, at the time of acquisition, the earnings from the employment are (or would be if there were any) general earnings to which any of the charging provisions in **28.4–28.8** EMPLOYMENT INCOME apply. These charging provisions apply broadly where an employee is UK resident, or is non-UK resident but performs duties in the UK.

[*ITEPA 2003, ss 419, 421, 421A–421D, 421E(1)(1A)(1B)(3)–(5), 421F–421I, 422–425, 432, 718*].

Simon's Taxes. See **E4.507B–E4.507FA.**

The charge to tax

[71.5] If a chargeable event occurs in relation to restricted shares, there is a charge to tax on the employee for the tax year in which it occurs; the amount chargeable, computed as below, counts as employment income for tax purposes. This is subject to the exception from charge detailed below. Any of the following is a chargeable event:

(i) the employment-related shares ceasing to be restricted shares (or a restricted interest in shares) without their having been disposed of to a person who is not an 'associated person' (see **71.4** above);
(ii) the variation or removal of any restriction without the employment-related shares having been disposed of to a person who is not an associated person and without their ceasing to be restricted shares (or a restricted interest in shares);
(iii) the disposal for consideration of the employment-related shares (or any interest in them) by an 'associated person' otherwise than to another associated person at a time when they are still restricted shares (or a restricted interest in shares).

Computation of chargeable amount

The chargeable amount is found by applying a formula, UMV × (IUP – PCP – OP) – CE (see *ITEPA 2003, s 426*), where:

UMV	=	Unrestricted Market Value, i.e. what would be the market value of the employment-related shares immediately after the chargeable event but for any restrictions;
IUP	=	Initial Uncharged Proportion. This is that part, expressed as a proportion (e.g. 0.25), of the Initial Unrestricted Market Value (IUMV) in respect of which an income tax charge is still required. It is found by taking the difference between IUMV and any deductible amounts (see below) and dividing it by IUMV. IUMV is what would have been the market value of the shares at the time of acquisition but for any restrictions;
PCP	=	Previously Charged Proportion. This is the aggregate obtained by applying the formula, IUP – PCP – OP, on each previous chargeable event since acquisition. If there has not been a previous chargeable event, PCP is nil;
OP	=	Outstanding Proportion. This is the proportion of the share value that is still reduced by restrictions and is found by taking the difference between UMV and the actual market value of the shares immediately after the chargeable event and dividing it by UMV; and

CE	=	Consideration and Expenses. This consists of any consideration given by the shareholder for, and any expenses incurred by him in connection with, the lifting or variation of restrictions, plus (where relevant) any expenses incurred by him in connection with the disposal of the shares; and any amount charged under **25** DISGUISED REMUNERATION in relation to the shares where the relevant step (within **26.7**) was taken before the chargeable event occurred.

If the employment-related shares are convertible shares (see **71.8** below), or an interest in convertible shares, their market value is to be determined for the purposes of the above formula as if they were not. In arriving at the value of IUP, deductible amounts include any consideration given for the shares and amounts charged to income tax. See *ITEPA 2003, s 428(7)(7A)* for the full list of deductible amounts. These include any amount that was charged to 'non-UK income tax' in respect of the acquisition of the shares, but only insofar as this exceeds any amount charged to UK income tax in that respect. '*Non-UK income tax*' means a tax chargeable (whether nationally or locally) in an overseas territory that corresponds to UK income tax.

If the chargeable event is a disposal for less than actual market value, the chargeable amount as determined above is reduced in the proportion that the consideration given on the disposal bears to the market value of the shares. However, this reduction is unavailable if something that affects the shares has been done at or before the time of the chargeable event as part of arrangements which have as a main purpose the avoidance of tax or national insurance contributions.

The employer and employee may jointly and irrevocably elect to omit OP from the above formula. The effect is to preclude any further application of these provisions. The election is implemented by way of an agreement (between employer and employee), in a form approved by HMRC, that must be made no later than 14 days after the chargeable event; there is no requirement for it to be submitted to HMRC. Prescribed forms of election are available on the HMRC website. The election is available only if, at the time of the chargeable event, the earnings from the employment are (or would be if there were any) general earnings to which any of the charging provisions in **28.4–28.8** EMPLOYMENT INCOME apply. These charging provisions apply broadly where an employee is UK resident, or is non-UK resident but performs duties in the UK.

PAYE

For the requirement to operate PAYE on chargeable amounts, see **53.3**(g) PAY AS YOU EARN.

Relief for employer national insurance contributions

Where, under a voluntary agreement or a joint election under *Social Security Contributions and Benefits Act 1992, Sch 1 para 3A* or *para 3B* (or NI equivalent), whenever made, a liability to secondary Class 1 national insurance contributions (i.e. employer contributions) on an amount chargeable to tax under these provisions is borne by the employee, the amount so borne is deductible from the chargeable amount computed as above. In the case of a voluntary agreement, or an election to which HMRC approval is withdrawn, no such amount is deductible to the extent that it is borne by the employee later than 4 June following the tax year in which the chargeable event occurs.

Exception from charge

No charge to tax arises on the occurrence of a chargeable event if the restriction in question applies to all the company's shares of the same class, all the company's shares of that class are affected by an event similar to the chargeable event (disregarding the references in (i)–(iii) above to associated persons) and *either* of the conditions below is satisfied. (The extended meaning of shares in **71.3** above does not apply for this purpose.) This exception from charge does not apply if anything that affects the shares is done at or before the time of the chargeable event as part of arrangements which have as a main purpose the avoidance of tax or national insurance contributions.

The first of the conditions mentioned above is that, immediately before the event, the company is 'employee-controlled' (within *ITEPA 2003, s 421H*) by virtue of holdings of shares of the class in question. The second condition is that, immediately before the event, the majority of the company's shares of the class in question are not 'employment-related shares' (see **71.4** above).

[*ITEPA 2003, ss 426–430*].

Capital gains tax

For capital gains tax purposes, the consideration for the acquisition is taken as the aggregate of the actual amount or value given for the restricted shares (or restricted interest in shares), any amount charged to income tax as earnings in relation to the acquisition and any amount that counts as employment income on the occurrence of a chargeable event. (No account is taken of any relief given for employer national insurance contributions — see above.) If the shares are employee shareholder shares (see **71.78** below), the consideration for the acquisition is the same, except that no account is taken of any actual amount or value given for the shares. None of this affects the calculation of the consideration received by the person from whom the acquisition is made. If any amount that would otherwise have counted as employment income is unremitted or non-chargeable foreign securities income (see **71.22–71.24** below) it does not form part of the consideration given. However, in the case of any unremitted foreign securities income that would otherwise have been chargeable foreign securities income, the taxpayer may make a claim to adjust the consideration given if any amount is subsequently remitted. [*TCGA 1992, ss 119A, 119B, 149AA*]. See Tolley's Capital Gains Tax for full details.

Exchange for further restricted shares

[71.6] A form of rollover relief from income tax applies in certain cases in which restricted shares held by an employee are exchanged for other restricted shares. It applies where:

- an 'associated person' (see **71.4** above) disposes of the restricted shares (the '*old shares*') for consideration, otherwise than to another associated person;
- the consideration consists wholly or partly of other restricted shares (the '*new shares*') being acquired by an associated person;
- the 'value of the consideration' is no more than what would have been the market value of the old shares immediately before the disposal but for the restrictions; and
- the avoidance of tax or national insurance contributions is not a main purpose of the disposal.

For the above purposes, the '*value of the consideration*' is the sum of (i) what would have been the market value of the new shares immediately before the disposal but for the restrictions and (ii) the value of any consideration other than the new shares.

If the consideration consists wholly of the new shares, neither the disposal of the old shares, nor the acquisition of the new shares, gives rise to any income tax liability, and the disposal is not a chargeable event within **71.5**(iii) above. Subject to what is said below, the new shares stand in the shoes of the old for income tax purposes.

If the consideration consists only partly of the new shares, the disposal is treated as two separate disposals. One is a disposal of the 'appropriate amount' of the old shares for such of the consideration as does not consist of the new shares; this disposal is a chargeable event. The other is a disposal of the remaining old shares for consideration consisting wholly of the new shares; this disposal attracts the treatment above. The '*appropriate amount*' of the old shares is:

$$OS \times \frac{OC}{TC}$$

where

OS = the total number of the old shares;
OC = the value of such of the consideration as does not consist of the new shares; and
TC = the 'value of the consideration' as defined above.

The tax exemption on acquisition in **71.4** above and the elections at **71.7** below are of no application in relation to the new shares. If the chargeable event rules at **71.5** above do not apply to the old shares, e.g. because of an election, they do not apply to the new shares either.

If there is a chargeable event in relation to the new shares, the values of IUP and PCP in the formula in **71.5** above are modified (see *ITEPA 2003, s 430A(8)–(10)*). The following applies if no liability to income tax arose on the acquisition of the old shares (because of the exemption in **71.4** above) and at the time of the exchange, there is still a restriction such that the old shares are restricted shares within **71.4**(a) (provision for forfeiture etc.). The restricted shares legislation has effect in relation to any of the new shares that are not restricted shares within **71.4**(a) as if there were a restriction relating to them corresponding to the restriction relating to the old shares and as if that restriction were removed immediately after the acquisition of the new shares. If there is a restriction by virtue of which some or all of the new shares are, at the time of the exchange, restricted shares within **71.4**(a), that restriction is to be treated as being removed five years after the acquisition of the old shares (if it has not actually been removed by then). This rule applies again on any subsequent exchange within these rules, and so applies by reference to the original acquisition date.

[*ITEPA 2003, s 430A*].

Simon's Taxes. See **E4.507EA.**

Election to disapply or moderate the provisions

[71.7] The employer and employee may jointly and irrevocably elect to disapply the provisions at **71.4, 71.5** above in full and to disregard the restrictions attaching to the shares when computing their acquisition value for the purposes of any charge to tax on employment income (including the charge on conversion at **71.9**(a) below and the provisions at **71.12, 71.15** and **71.78** below). The election is implemented by way of an agreement (between employer and employee), in a form approved by HMRC, that must be made no later than 14 days after the acquisition; there is no requirement for it to be submitted to HMRC. Prescribed forms of election are available on the HMRC website.

Alternatively, an election may be made, in similar manner, to disregard one or more specified restrictions in applying the provisions at **71.4, 71.5** above and in computing acquisition value for the above-mentioned purposes.

The employer and the employee are deemed to have made the election to disapply the provisions in full if the shares in question are acquired under a tax-advantaged share incentive plan (as in **71.25** below), SAYE option scheme (as in **71.53** below) or CSOP scheme (as in **71.66** below) or by the exercise of an enterprise management incentive qualifying option (as in **71.41** below) in circumstances such that (in each case) no income tax liability arises on acquisition.

The above election is available only if, at the time of acquisition, the earnings from the employment are (or would be if there were any) general earnings to which any of the charging provisions in **28.4–28.8** EMPLOYMENT INCOME apply. These charging provisions apply broadly where an employee is UK resident, or is non-UK resident but performs duties in the UK.

The employer and the employee are deemed to have made the election to disapply the provisions in full if:

- the arrangements under which the right or opportunity to acquire the shares was made available have as a main purpose the avoidance of tax or national insurance contributions; and
- at the time of the acquisition, the earnings from the employment are (or would be if there were any) general earnings to which any of the charging provisions in **28.4–28.8** EMPLOYMENT INCOME apply.

[*ITEPA 2003, ss 431, 431A, 431B*].

Convertible shares

[71.8] These provisions apply to 'employment-related shares' if, at the time of acquisition, they are 'convertible shares' (or an interest in 'convertible shares'). For the extended meaning of 'shares', in relation to these provisions, see **71.3** above. See below for exclusions from the charge. See **71.18–71.21** below for reporting obligations. See also the provisions at **71.10** below.

'*Employment-related shares*' are defined as in **71.4** above. There are rules dealing with company reorganisations (such as conversions, scrip issues and rights issues); these treat replacement shares or additional shares acquired on such a reorganisation as acquired by virtue of the same right or opportunity as the original interest and treat any consequent reduction in the market value of the original shares as consideration given for the replacement shares or additional shares.

An increase in a person's interest in shares is treated for the purposes of these provisions as a separate interest acquired by virtue of the same right or opportunity as the original interest. A decrease in a person's interest is treated as a disposal, otherwise than to an 'associated person' (as defined in **71.4** above), of a separate interest proportionate to the reduction.

For the purposes of these provisions, consideration given for the acquisition of employment-related shares includes consideration given by the employee or by the person who acquired the shares (if not the employee) and any consideration given for a *right* to acquire the shares. Rules similar to those at **71.16** below (under Option exchanged for another) apply to determine the amount of consideration where a right to acquire the shares is assigned or released for consideration consisting of or including another right to acquire the shares.

Definition of convertible shares

Employment-related shares are '*convertible shares*' if:

- they confer on the holder an entitlement (whether immediate or deferred and whether conditional or unconditional) to convert them into shares of a different description; or
- a contract, agreement, arrangement or condition authorises or requires the grant of such an entitlement to the holder if certain circumstances arise, or do not arise (for example, where the shares can only be converted following a stipulated period after acquisition) or makes provision for the conversion of the shares (otherwise than by the holder) into shares of a different description.

Exclusions

The same exclusions from charge apply as in **71.4** above.

Tax relief on acquisition

For the purposes of any liability to tax in respect of the acquisition of shares (under the general charging rules at **28.76** EMPLOYMENT INCOME, under **71.15** below (share options), under **71.12** below (acquisition for less than market value), under **71.78** below (employee shareholder shares) or under **26** DISGUISED REMUNERATION), the market value of the employment-related shares is to be determined as if they were not convertible shares or an interest in convertible shares. Thus, if the market value per share is £1,100 with a conversion right and would be £1,000 without the conversion right, only £1,000 is taxed; previously, any tax charge on acquisition would have been calculated by reference to the full market value (£1,100). However, this rule is disapplied if the arrangements under which the right or opportunity to acquire the shares was made available have as a main purpose the avoidance of tax or national insurance contributions. Instead, market value is determined on the basis that there is an immediate and unfettered right to convert (even if this is not, in fact, the case). But if this would produce a lower market value than that produced by the main rule above (i.e. ignoring the right to convert), the main rule applies instead.

[*ITEPA 2003, ss 419, 421, 421A–421D, 421E(1)(3)–(5), 421F–421I, 435–437, 444*].

Simon's Taxes. See **E4.507G–E4.507L.**

The charge to tax

[71.9] If a chargeable event occurs in relation to convertible shares, there is a charge to tax on the employee for the tax year in which it occurs; the amount chargeable, computed as below, counts as employment income for tax purposes. This is subject to the exception from charge referred to below. Any of the following is a chargeable event:

(a) the conversion of the employment-related shares (or the shares in which they are an interest) into shares of a different description, where an 'associated person' (see **71.4** above) is beneficially entitled to the shares into which the employment-related shares are converted;
(b) the disposal for consideration of the employment-related shares (or any interest in them) by an associated person otherwise than to another associated person at a time when they are still convertible shares (or an interest in convertible shares);
(c) the release, for consideration, of the conversion right;
(d) the receipt by an associated person of a benefit in money or money's worth in connection with the conversion right; this could be, for example, compensation for loss of the conversion right but excludes any benefit received on account of disability (as defined) or anything within (a)–(c) above.

Computation of chargeable amount

The chargeable amount is found by computing the gain (if any) realised on the occurrence of the chargeable event (see below) and deducting from it any consideration given for the conversion right and any expenses incurred by the shareholder in connection with the conversion, disposal, release or receipt (whichever is applicable). For this purpose, consideration given for the conversion right is the excess (if any) of the consideration given for the acquisition of the shares (or interest in shares) over their market value, at the time of acquisition, determined as if they were not convertible shares (or an interest in convertible shares).

The gain realised on the chargeable event depends on the nature of the event, as follows:

(i) on an event within (a) above, it is the amount given by the formula, CMVCS – (CMVERS + CC), see below;
(ii) on an event within (b) above, it is the amount given by the formula, DC – CMVERS, see below;
(iii) on an event within (c) above, it is the amount of the consideration received by an associated person in respect of the release; and
(iv) on an event within (d) above, it is the amount or market value of the benefit.

For the purposes of (i) and (ii) above:

CMVCS	=	the market value, at the time of the event, of the shares acquired on conversion (determined, if those shares are themselves convertible shares, as if they were not); in the case of an interest in shares, a proportionate amount of the market value is taken instead;
CMVERS	=	the market value, at the time of the event, of the convertible shares (or the interest in them), again disregarding the effect on value of the conversion right;
CC	=	the amount of any consideration given for the conversion; and
DC	=	the amount of any consideration given on the disposal in (b) above.

If

- prior to the acquisition, the shares were the subject of a relevant step within **26.7** DISGUISED REMUNERATION by reason of which the charge to tax in that chapter applied in respect of the employment, and
- the amount that counted as employment income as a result exceeds the market value of the shares when the relevant step was taken, determined as if they were not convertible shares (or an interest in convertible shares),

the amount of the gain realised in (i) or (ii) above is reduced by the excess.

If, in computing the tax charge on acquisition, the market value of the shares was determined on the basis that there was an immediate and unfettered right to convert (see **71.8** above under Tax relief on acquisition), the chargeable amount (on the occurrence of the chargeable event) is reduced by the amount by which that value exceeded what would otherwise have been the market value (i.e. ignoring the right to convert).

For the purposes of these provisions generally, market value is determined as for capital gains tax purposes and *ITEPA 2003, ss 421(2), 421A* apply in determining the amount of any consideration given.

PAYE

For the requirement to operate PAYE on chargeable amounts, see **53.3**(g) PAY AS YOU EARN.

Relief for employer national insurance contributions

Where, under a voluntary agreement or a joint election under *Social Security Contributions and Benefits Act 1992, Sch 1 para 3A* or *para 3B* (or NI equivalent), whenever made, a liability to secondary Class 1 national insurance contributions (i.e. employer contributions) on an amount chargeable to tax under these provisions is borne by the employee, the amount so borne is deductible from the chargeable amount computed as above. In the case of a voluntary agreement, or an election to which HMRC approval is withdrawn, no such amount is deductible to the extent that it is borne by the employee later than 4 June following the tax year in which the chargeable event occurs.

Exception from charge

The exception from charge detailed at **71.5** above, in relation to chargeable events under the restricted shares provisions, applies equally, subject to the necessary modifications, in relation to chargeable events under these provisions.

[*ITEPA 2003, ss 438–443*].

Capital gains tax

For capital gains tax purposes, the consideration for the acquisition is taken as the aggregate of the actual amount or value given for the convertible shares (or interest in convertible shares), any amount charged to income tax as earnings in relation to the acquisition and any amount that counts as employment income on the occurrence of a chargeable event within (a) above. (No account is taken of any relief given for employer national insurance contributions — see above.) If the shares are employee shareholder shares (see **71.78** below), the consideration for the acquisition is the same, except that no account is taken of any actual amount or value given for the shares. None of this affects the calculation of the consideration received by the person from whom the acquisition is made. If any amount that would otherwise have counted as employment income is unremitted or non-chargeable foreign securities income (see **71.22–71.24** below) it does not form part of the consideration given. However, in the case of any unremitted foreign securities income that would otherwise have been chargeable foreign securities income, the taxpayer may make a claim to adjust the consideration given if any amount is subsequently remitted. [*TCGA 1992, ss 119A, 119B, 149AA*]. See Tolley's Capital Gains Tax for full details.

Shares with artificially depressed market value

[71.10] The following provisions are 'designed to ensure that if the value of employment-related securities is depressed by means of non-commercial transaction(s), then that reduction in value is taxed on the employee' (Treasury Explanatory Notes to Finance Bill 2003). They apply in certain cases where the market value of 'employment-related shares' (or, where relevant, other shares or interests in shares) is reduced by things done otherwise than for genuine commercial purposes; this specifically includes anything done as part of a scheme or arrangement a main purpose of which is to avoid tax *or national insurance contributions* and any transaction (other than a payment for corporation tax group relief) between members of a 51% group of companies otherwise than on arm's length terms. See **71.3** above for the extended meaning of 'shares', in relation to these provisions.

For these purposes, '*employment-related shares*' and 'consideration given for the acquisition of employment-related shares' are defined as in **71.4** above. Subject to the rules below requiring the importing of certain fictions into the determination of **market values**, such values are to be determined as for capital gains tax purposes.

See **71.22** below for the effect of the REMITTANCE BASIS (**61**) where applicable.

Charge on acquisition

If anything done otherwise than for genuine commercial purposes within the seven years ending with the acquisition reduces the market value of employment-related shares at acquisition by at least 10%, there is a charge to tax on the employee for the tax year in which the acquisition occurs; the amount chargeable (see below) counts as employment income for tax purposes. This does not apply in the case of *restricted shares* if the tax exemption on acquisition at **71.4** above applies. The charge does not displace other income tax charges that may arise on acquisition.

The chargeable amount is the amount by which market value has been reduced. If the consideration given for the shares is greater than actual market value, the chargeable amount is reduced by the excess. Where the shares are convertible shares as in **71.8** above (or an interest in convertible shares), the chargeable amount is determined as if they were not. Where the shares are restricted shares as in **71.4** above (or a restricted interest in shares), the chargeable amount is the excess of what would have been their market value, disregarding both the avoidance device and the effect of restrictions, over their actual market value taking account of restrictions; in such circumstances though, there is no charge under **71.5** above on any chargeable event.

If:

- prior to the acquisition, the shares were the subject of a relevant step within **26.7** DISGUISED REMUNERATION by reason of which the charge to tax in that chapter applied in respect of the employment, and
- the amount that counted as employment income as a result exceeds the market value of the shares at acquisition or, if greater, the consideration given for the shares,

the chargeable amount is reduced by the excess.

Other tax charges

Restricted shares

The consequences described below ensue where the market value of restricted shares (or a restricted interest in shares) as in **71.4** above is 'artificially low' at any of the following times:

(a) immediately after a chargeable event within **71.5**;
(b) immediately before the shares are disposed of (in circumstances not giving rise to a chargeable event within (a) above) or are cancelled without being disposed of; or
(c) on 5 April in any year.

For this purpose, market value is '*artificially low*' where it has been reduced by at least 10% as a result of anything done otherwise than for genuine commercial purposes within the 'relevant period'. The '*relevant period*' is normally the seven years ending with the event in question or, in the case of (c) above, with that 5 April. If, however, the tax exemption on acquisition at **71.4** applied in relation to the shares, the start of the relevant period is extended back to a point seven years before the acquisition.

The consequences are as follows.

- In a case within (b) above, a chargeable event within **71.5**(i) (lifting of restrictions) is deemed to occur on the date of disposal or cancellation. The reference to OP (Outstanding Proportion) in the formula in **71.5** (for charging tax on chargeable events) is deemed to be omitted (so that all remaining untaxed proportions are brought into charge).
- In a case within (c) above, a chargeable event within **71.5**(i) is deemed to occur on that 5 April.
- In *all* cases, the value of UMV (Unrestricted Market Value) in the formula in **71.5** (for charging tax on chargeable events) is suitably modified so as to disregard the things done otherwise than for commercial purposes and also, where (b) above applies, the fact that the shares are about to be disposed of or cancelled.
- In a case within (a) above, where the chargeable event concerned is a disposal for less than actual market value, the normal reduction in the chargeable amount determined by the formula in **71.5** is disapplied.

Convertible shares

As detailed in **71.9** above, any consideration given for the right to convert shares enters into the computation of the chargeable amount on a chargeable event. If anything done otherwise than for genuine commercial purposes within the seven years ending with the acquisition reduces the market value of the shares (or interest in shares) at acquisition by at least 10%, the market value of the shares at acquisition (determined as if they were not convertible shares or an interest in convertible shares) is taken as what would be their market value (as so determined) if it were not for the reduction. This has the effect of reducing the amount deductible in the said computation.

If, on a chargeable event within **71.9**(a) above (conversion of the shares), the market value, at the time of conversion, of the shares *into which* the shares are converted is reduced by 10% or more as a result of anything done otherwise than for genuine commercial purposes within the seven years ending with the event, the value of CMVCS in the formula at **71.9**(i) above is adjusted to what it would have been without the reduction.

Adjustments to consideration etc.

Where the consideration or benefit referred to in specific provisions contained in **71.4**, **71.8** above and **71.13**, **71.14** below (as listed at *ITEPA 2003, s 446I(1)*) consists wholly or partly of shares (or an interest in shares) whose market value at that time is reduced by 10% or more as a result of anything done otherwise than for genuine commercial purposes within the seven years ending with the receipt of the consideration or benefit, that market value is taken for the purpose of that provision to be what it would have been if it were not for the reduction. This rule also applies for the purpose of determining 'consideration given for the shares' under 'Charge on acquisition' above.

Exceptions from charge disapplied

The exception from charge in **71.5** above (restricted shares) and the similar exceptions in **71.9** above (convertible shares), **71.12** below (shares acquired for less than market value) and **71.14** below (post-acquisition benefits) do not apply if a charge or an adjustment to market value or consideration would otherwise arise under the above provisions.

[*ITEPA 2003, ss 419, 421, 421A–421D, 421E(2)(2A)(3)–(5), 421F–421I, 446A–446J*].

PAYE

For the requirement to operate PAYE on chargeable amounts, see **53.3**(g) PAY AS YOU EARN.

Simon's Taxes. See **E4.507M–E4.507QA.**

Shares with artificially enhanced market value

[71.11] The following provisions are 'designed to ensure that if the value of employment-related securities is enhanced by means of non-commercial transaction(s) during any tax year, then that appreciation in value is taxed on the employee at the earlier of the disposal of the employment-related securities or 5 April.' (Treasury Explanatory Notes to Finance Bill 2003). They apply in certain cases where the market value of 'employment-related shares' is increased by things done otherwise than for genuine commercial purposes (a '*non-commercial increase*'); this specifically includes anything done as part of a scheme or arrangement a main purpose of which is to avoid tax *or national insurance contributions* and any transaction (other than a payment for corporation tax group relief) between members of a 51% group of companies otherwise than on arm's length terms. See **71.3** above for the extended meaning of 'shares', in relation to these provisions. See **71.18–71.21** below for reporting obligations.

For these purposes, '*employment-related shares*' are defined as in **71.4** above. Subject to the rules below requiring the importing of certain fictions into the determination of **market values,** such values are to be determined as for capital gains tax purposes.

See **71.22** below for the effect of the REMITTANCE BASIS (**61**) where applicable.

Charge on non-commercial increases

Where, on the 'valuation date' for a 'relevant period', the market value of employment-related shares is at least 10% greater than it would be if any 'non-commercial increases' (see above) during the relevant period were disregarded, the whole of the excess is taxed as employment income of the employee for tax purposes for the tax year in which the valuation date falls. In determining both actual and notional market values for this purpose, one must ignore any restrictions (of the kind at **71.4**(a)–(c) above) having effect in relation to the shares on the valuation date and any non-commercial reductions (i.e. the opposite to non-commercial increases) during the relevant period. For these purposes:

- the '*valuation date*' is the last day of the 'relevant period'; and
- the '*relevant period*' means any tax year, except that the first such period runs from date of acquisition to the following 5 April and the last runs from 6 April to the date in the tax year on which the provisions cease to apply (see **71.4** above under Exclusions). If these provisions cease to apply to an interest in the shares, the relevant period ends at that time in relation to that interest, but these provisions apply separately to that interest and to what remains.

Special provision applies where on the valuation date the employment-related shares are restricted shares (as in **71.4** above) (or a restricted interest in shares) and no election has been made to wholly disapply the restricted shares provisions in full or to ignore outstanding restrictions (i.e. to omit OP from the formula) in relation to a chargeable event preceding the valuation date. See **71.5, 71.7** above for these elections. The chargeable amount determined above (i.e. the excess) is reduced by the proportion of the non-commercial increase that remains to be taxed when the restriction is eventually lifted. This is achieved by multiplying the otherwise chargeable amount by (1 – OP), where OP is determined in accordance with **71.5** above on the assumption that a chargeable event (resulting in no tax charge) occurs on the valuation date. This rule is suitably modified where an election has been made to disregard one or more specified restrictions in applying the restricted shares provisions.

Where the employment-related shares have been restricted shares (or a restricted interest in shares) at any time during the relevant period and there have been one or more chargeable events during that period, the otherwise chargeable amount under these provisions is reduced by the excess of chargeable amounts under **71.5** above over what they would have been if one were to disregard non-commercial increases during the relevant period (and before the chargeable event).

Exceptions from charge disapplied

The exception from charge in **71.5** above (restricted shares) and the similar exceptions in **71.9** above (convertible shares), **71.12** below (shares acquired for less than market value) and **71.14** below (post-acquisition benefits) do not apply if the market value of the shares in question at the time of acquisition has been increased by at least 10% by non-commercial increases in the seven years preceding acquisition. If the above charge on non-commercial increases applies in relation to any shares, the exception from charge in **71.5** above does not subsequently apply in relation to those shares.

[*ITEPA 2003, ss 419, 421, 421B–421D, 421E(2)(2A)(3)–(5), 421F–421H, 446K–446P*].

PAYE

For the requirement to operate PAYE on chargeable amounts, see **53.3**(g) PAY AS YOU EARN.

Simon's Taxes. See E4.507R–E4.507TA.

Shares acquired for less than market value

[71.12] The following provisions deal with the acquisition of 'employment-related shares' for less than their market value and do so by creating the fiction of a notional interest-free loan on the amount of the under-value. The provisions apply to all employees. The provisions are aimed principally at shares that are acquired partly-paid, such that the employee pays an amount for the shares (which may well be equal to their market value) but does so wholly or partly by instalments.

For these purposes, '*employment-related shares*' are defined as in **71.4** above. The rules therein dealing with company reorganisations treat any reduction in the market value of the original shares consequent to the reorganisation as a payment made for the acquisition of the shares at or before the time of the acquisition.

For the extended meaning of 'shares', see **71.3** above. See **71.22** below for the effect of the REMITTANCE BASIS (**61**) where applicable.

See **71.18–71.21** below for reporting obligations.

Exclusions

The same exclusions from charge apply as in **71.4** above.

Split year treatment

The same rule applies as in **71.10** above.

When the provisions apply

The provisions apply, subject to the exception referred to below, where, at the time of acquisition of employment-related shares, either no payment is (or has been) made for them or a payment is (or has been) made of an amount which is less than market value (determined as for capital gains tax purposes and as if, where it is not the case, the shares were fully paid up). For this purpose, any obligation to make further payment(s) after the time of acquisition is disregarded.

If the tax exemption at **71.4** above applies on an acquisition of restricted shares, the current provisions apply as if the acquisition took place at the first occurrence of a chargeable event within **71.5** above.

The application of these provisions does not displace the application of other tax charges arising in respect of the acquisition of employment-related shares under specified provisions at *ITEPA 2003, s 446V*.

Exception from charge

An exception similar to that applying on chargeable events in **71.5** above is imported into the current provisions; the provisions are disapplied if *all* the company's shares of the same class are acquired at an under-value and *either* of the conditions detailed at **71.5** above is satisfied. (The extended meaning of shares in **71.3** above does not apply for this purpose.) This exception from charge does not apply if anything that affects the shares is done at or before the time of the acquisition as part of arrangements which have as a main purpose the avoidance of tax or national insurance contributions.

Interest-free notional loan

Where these provisions do apply, an interest-free notional loan is deemed to have been made to the employee by the employer at the time the employment-related shares are acquired. For so long as the employment continues, the loan counts as an 'employment-related loan' for the purposes of applying *ITEPA 2003, s 175* (benefit of cheap loan arrangements) and related provisions (see **28.32** EMPLOYMENT INCOME). The initial amount of the loan is the market-value of the shares (or the interest in them) at the time of acquisition (determined as above) less any payment made at or before that time by the employee or (if different) the person who acquired the shares, any amount on which tax is charged as earnings by reason of the acquisition, any amounts on which tax is charged under specified other provisions relating to non-tax-advantaged share options, restricted shares, convertible shares and employee shareholder shares and any amounts charged under **26** DISGUISED REMUNERATION (see *ITEPA 2003, s 446T(3)(3A)*). The loan may be reduced subsequently by payments or further payments for the shares.

The notional loan is treated as discharged upon:

(a) the disposal, otherwise than to an 'associated person' (as defined at **71.4** above), of the shares (or the interest in shares), unless at the time the shares were acquired there was an actual or contingent liability to make one or more further payments for them equal to the initial amount of the loan (i.e. the shares were not fully paid up); or

(b) any outstanding or contingent liability to pay for the shares is released, extinguished, transferred or adjusted so as no longer to bind any associated person (other than in circumstances in which (e) below applies); or

(c) the doing of anything that affects the shares and is part of arrangements which have as a main purpose the avoidance of tax or national insurance contributions; or
(d) the making by associated persons of payments or further payments for the shares that are sufficient to clear the loan; or
(e) the disposal of the shares, together with the liability to make such payments as are mentioned in (d) above, otherwise than to an associated person and for consideration of an amount that reflects the transfer of the liability; or
(f) the death of the employee.

If the discharge of the loan is within (a), (b) or (c) above, the amount outstanding immediately before the discharge is taxed as employment income of the employee for the tax year of discharge, and this applies regardless of whether or not the employment has terminated.

[*ITEPA 2003, ss 192–197, 419, 421, 421B–421D, 421E(2)(2A)(3)–(5), 421F–421H, 446Q–446U, 446V, 446W, Sch 7 paras 28, 29*].

For *capital gains tax* purposes, any amount that counts as employment income on discharge of the notional loan normally counts as part of the acquisition cost of the shares. [*TCGA 1992, ss 119A, 119B, 120*]. See Tolley's Capital Gains Tax for full details.

PAYE

For the requirement to operate PAYE on the chargeable amount on discharge of the loan, see **53.3**(g) PAY AS YOU EARN.

Anti-avoidance

The notional loan rules above do not apply if the arrangements under which the right or opportunity to acquire the shares was made available had as a main purpose the avoidance of tax or national insurance contributions. Instead, an amount equal to what would have been the initial amount of the notional loan is taxed as employment income of the employee for the tax year in which he acquires the shares. [*ITEPA 2003, s 446UA*].

Simon's Taxes. See **E4.507U–E4.507W.**

Shares disposed of for more than market value

[71.13] The following provisions impose an income tax charge on the employee when an 'associated person' (as defined at **71.4** above) disposes of 'employment-related shares' for more than their market value. They apply to all employees.

For these purposes, '*employment-related shares*' are defined as in **71.4** above.

For the extended meaning of 'shares', see **71.3** above. See **71.22** below for the effect of the REMITTANCE BASIS (**61**) where applicable.

See **71.18–71.21** below for reporting obligations.

When a charge to tax arises

The charge to income tax arises where employment-related shares are disposed of by an associated person, such that no associated person is any longer beneficially entitled to them, for consideration which exceeds their market value (determined as for capital gains tax purposes) at the time of disposal. *ITEPA 2003, ss 421(2), 421A* apply in determining the amount of any consideration given.

The chargeable amount is the excess of the consideration given for the shares (or the interest in shares) over the market value of the shares (or interest). Any expenses incurred in connection with the disposal are also deductible in arriving at the chargeable amount. The chargeable amount is taxed as employment income of the employee for the tax year of disposal.

A *Pt 5* transfer of shares under *Proceeds of Crime Act 2002* (as in **9.2**(x) CAPITAL ALLOWANCES) does not give rise to an income tax charge under these provisions.

[*ITEPA 2003, ss 198–200, 419, 421, 421A–421D, 421E(2)(2A)(3)–(5), 421F–421H, 446X–446Z, Sch 7 paras 30, 31, 61A*].

The first appeal to reach the courts in relation to the above was decided in favour of HMRC (*Grays Timber Products Ltd v HMRC* **SC 2010, 81 TC 96**).

PAYE

For the requirement to operate PAYE on chargeable amounts, see **53.3**(g) PAY AS YOU EARN.

Simon's Taxes. See **E4.507X, E4.507Y.**

Post-acquisition benefits from shares

[71.14] For these purposes, '*employment-related shares*' are defined as in **71.4** above. See **71.18–71.21** below for reporting obligations. See **71.22** below for the effect of the REMITTANCE BASIS (**61**) where applicable.

The charge

These provisions apply if an 'associated person' (as defined at **71.4** above) receives a benefit in connection with 'employment-related shares'. The amount or market value (determined as for capital gains tax purposes) of the benefit is taxed as employment income of the employee for the tax year in which the benefit is received.

Exceptions

These provisions do not apply if the benefit is otherwise chargeable to income tax. However, this let-out is unavailable if something that affects the shares is done as part of arrangements which have as a main purpose the avoidance of tax or national insurance contributions. In addition, an exception similar to that applying on chargeable events in **71.5** above is imported into the current provisions; the provisions are disapplied if a similar benefit is received by the owners of *all* the company's shares of the same class and *either* of the conditions detailed at **71.5** above is satisfied. (The extended meaning of shares in **71.3** above does not apply for this purpose, though the term does include stock.) This exception from charge does not apply if anything that affects the shares is done as part of arrangements which have as a main purpose the avoidance of tax or national insurance contributions.

[*ITEPA 2003, ss 421, 421B–421D, 421E(1)(1A)(1B)(3)–(5), 421F–421H, 447–450, Sch 7 para 54*].

PAYE

For the requirement to operate PAYE on chargeable amounts, see **53.3**(g) PAY AS YOU EARN.

See generally HMRC Employment-Related Securities Manual ERSM90000 *et seq*.

Simon's Taxes. See **E4.507Z, E4.508A.**

Share options

[71.15] This section is essentially concerned with *non-tax-advantaged* share options. For EMI options, tax-advantaged SAYE option schemes and tax-advantaged CSOP schemes, see respectively **71.41**, **71.53** and **71.66** below. However, as noted in those sections where relevant, the breach of certain conditions under EMI options and tax-advantaged schemes can lead to a charge under the provisions at **71.16** below.

For reporting obligations, see **71.18–71.21** below. See 70.2 above as regards Restricted Stock Units (RSUs).

Meaning of 'share option'

A '*share option*' is a right to acquire 'shares'. '*Shares*' has the extended meaning in **71.3** above.

A share option is outside the above definition (and thus outside the rules below) if it is a right to acquire 'shares' that is itself acquired pursuant to a right or opportunity made available under arrangements having as a main purpose the avoidance of tax or national insurance contributions — see **71.3** above under Share options. [*ITEPA 2003, s 420(8)*].

Application of these provisions

These provisions apply to a share option (an '*employment-related share option*') acquired by a person where the right or opportunity to acquire it is available by reason of the employment (past, present or prospective) of that person or any other person. Any right or opportunity made available by a person's employer, or by a person connected (within **19** CONNECTED PERSONS) with a person's employer, is treated as made available by reason of the employment of that person, other than in the case of an individual conferring a right or opportunity in the normal course of his domestic, family or personal relationships.

A right to acquire a share option becoming available by reason of an existing holding of 'employment-related shares' (as defined at **71.4** above) is treated for these purposes as available by reason of the employment by reason of which the right or opportunity to acquire those shares was available.

For the circumstances in which HMRC will accept that shares or share options were acquired by an employee by virtue of a family or personal relationship and not by reason of the employment, see HMRC Employment-Related Securities Manual ERSM20220.

A gain realised following cessation of the employment on the exercise, assignment, release etc. of an employment-related share option falls within *these* provisions and not those at **18** COMPENSATION FOR LOSS OF EMPLOYMENT (AND DAMAGES) (*Bluck v Salton* (Sp C 378), [2003] SSCD 439).

Grant of option

If an employment-related share option is potentially within the charge to tax in **71.16** below on exercise, assignment, release etc., no income tax liability arises in respect of the receipt of the option.

Where the option is outside the charge to tax in **71.16** below on exercise, assignment, release etc. (because the earnings from the employment in question were within the relevant exceptions from charge), a charge to tax can arise on receipt of the option (regardless of when it is capable of being exercised) but not on its exercise etc. See also *Abbott v Philbin* HL 1960, 39 TC 82 and HMRC Employment-Related Securities Manual ERSM110100.

[*ITEPA 2003, ss 419, 421–421B, 421D, 471, 475, 484, 718*].

Simon's Taxes. See **E4.508H–E4.508O.**

Chargeable events

[71.16] Subject to the exceptions detailed below, the occurrence of a chargeable event in relation to an employment-related share option (as in **71.15** above) results in the chargeable amount (computed as below) being taxed as employment income of the employee for the tax year in which the event occurs. For these purposes, any of the following is a chargeable event:

(a) the acquisition of shares on the **exercise** of the option by an 'associated person' (see below);
(b) the **assignment** (for consideration) of the option by an associated person otherwise than to another associated person;
(c) the **release** (for consideration) of the option by an associated person;
(d) the receipt by an associated person of a benefit in connection with the option.

The reference in (a) above to the '*exercise*' of an option embraces any acquisition of shares in pursuance of a right to acquire them, which includes, for example, a right under a so-called long-term incentive plan to receive shares after a specified period of time without the need to exercise the right.

For the purposes of (a) above, shares are deemed to be acquired when the beneficial interest is acquired and not, if different, at the time of conveyance or transfer. Specifically included in (d) above is consideration received for omitting, or undertaking to omit, to exercise the option, or granting, or undertaking to grant, to another person a right to acquire the option shares (or an interest in them). Specifically excluded from (d) above is any benefit received on account of disability (as defined) and anything already covered by (a)–(c) above.

For the purposes of these provisions, any of the following are '*associated persons*' in relation to an employment-related share option:

- the person who acquired it;
- (if different) the employee; and
- any 'relevant linked person'.

A '*relevant linked person*' is any person who is either connected (within **19** CONNECTED PERSONS) with, or is a member of the same household as, either the person who acquired the option or the employee. The statutory definition also embraces past connections etc. so as to ensure the link cannot be broken. However, a *company* cannot be a relevant linked person if it is the employer or (if different) the person by whom the right or opportunity to acquire the option was made available or the person from whom the option was acquired.

The **chargeable amount** depends on the type of chargeable event. On an event within (a) above (exercise of option), it is the excess (if any) of:

- the market value, at time of acquisition, of the shares acquired, over
- the consideration given (if any) for the shares acquired.

If the shares are employee shareholder shares acquired under a pre-1 December 2016 agreement, the consideration given for the shares is the payment (if any) which the employee is treated as having made for them (see **71.78** below). If the chargeable event is within (b) or (c) above, the chargeable amount is the amount of consideration given for the assignment or release of the option. On an event within (d) above, it is the amount or market value of the benefit. However, if that consideration or that benefit consists wholly or partly of shares (or an interest in shares) the market value of which has been reduced by 10% or more as a result of things done otherwise than for genuine commercial purposes (see **71.10** above) within the preceding seven years, such reduction is added back.

For the purposes of these provisions generally, market value is determined as for capital gains tax purposes and *ITEPA 2003, ss 421(2), 421A* apply in determining the amount of any consideration given for anything.

Whatever the type of event, any consideration given for the option itself (on its original acquisition) is also deductible, as are any expenses incurred in connection with the exercise, assignment or release or the receipt of benefit. Where, in consequence of the acquisition of the option itself or the acquisition of shares under the option or any transaction of which either forms part, there is a reduction in the market value of any employment-related shares held by an associated person, the amount of that reduction is deductible as if it were consideration given for the option. Any amount charged on *grant* of the option is also deductible, as is any amount charged under **26** DISGUISED REMUNERATION in relation to the option or to any sum of money or asset held solely for the purposes of the option. See *ITEPA 2003, s 480(5)(5A)*. Where there is more than one chargeable event in relation to the same option, the same deductions cannot be made more than once.

The charge on exercise etc. is independent of any charge on grant of the option (see also above), and depends solely on the above conditions being satisfied (*Ball v Phillips* Ch D 1990, 63 TC 529). A special rule applies if an employee is divested of a share option by operation of law; in such case, there is an income tax charge on a chargeable event and it is on the person who exercises the option or receives the consideration or benefit (whichever is applicable).

See **71.22** below for the effect of the REMITTANCE BASIS (**61**) where applicable.

Death of employee

No charge arises on any event within (a)–(d) above if it occurs on or after the death of the employee.

Option exchanged for another

The following rules apply where an employee-related share option is assigned or released for consideration consisting of or including another share option. For the purpose of computing the chargeable amount (if any) on the assignment or release, the new option is not treated as consideration given for the old. For the purposes of computing the charge on any future chargeable event, the consideration (if any) given for the new option consists of any actual consideration given (apart from the old option) plus the excess (if any) of any consideration given for the old option over any consideration received (apart from the new option) for its assignment or release. There are provisions (see *ITEPA 2003, s 483(5)(6)*) which in specified circumstances treat for these purposes two or more transactions as a single transaction by which an option is assigned for consideration consisting of or including another share option.

Relief for employer national insurance contributions

Where, under a voluntary agreement or a joint election under *Social Security Contributions and Benefits Act 1992, Sch 1 para 3A* or *para 3B* (or NI equivalent), whenever made, a liability to secondary Class 1 national insurance contributions (i.e. employer contributions) on a share option gain chargeable to tax under these provisions is borne by the employee who realised the gain, the amount so borne is deductible in arriving at the amount on which the employee is chargeable to tax. In the case of a voluntary agreement, or an election to which HMRC approval is withdrawn, no such amount is deductible to the extent that it is borne by the employee later than 4 June following the tax year in which the chargeable event occurs. (Any deduction for national insurance contributions is disregarded in determining the allowable cost of the shares for capital gains tax purposes — see also below.)

[*ITEPA 2003, ss 472–474, 476–483, Sch 7 paras 63, 64, 65; FA 2017, s 12(3)(5)–(7)*].

PAYE

For the requirement to operate PAYE on chargeable events, see **53.3**(e)(f) PAY AS YOU EARN.

Capital gains tax

For capital gains tax purposes, when shares acquired on exercise of an employment-related share option are disposed of, any sum that counts as employment income is normally treated as part of the cost of acquiring the shares. Thus, the cost of acquisition for capital gains tax purposes normally comprises the actual consideration given for the shares, any consideration given for the option itself and any amount charged to income tax on the exercise. In computing the latter amount, for this purpose only, relief given for national insurance contributions (see above) is added back, as is any deduction made in respect of any tax charged on *grant* of the option (mainly relevant to long-term options under pre-*FA 2003* rules). For full details, see Tolley's Capital Gains Tax.

If any amount that would otherwise have counted as employment income is unremitted or non-chargeable foreign securities income (see **71.22–71.24** below) it does not form part of the consideration given. However, in the case of any unremitted foreign securities income that would otherwise have been chargeable foreign securities income, the taxpayer may make a claim to adjust the consideration given if any amount is subsequently remitted. A similar rule applies to income within **26.5** DISGUISED REMUNERATION to which the remittance basis applies.

[*TCGA 1992, ss 119A–119C, 120, 144ZA*].

Example

[71.17]

An employee is granted an option exercisable within five years to buy 1,000 shares at £5 each. The option costs 50p per share. He exercises the option in 2020/21 when the shares are worth £7.50. The option is not granted under a tax-advantaged scheme.

The amount taxable as employment income in 2020/21 is as follows:

		£	£
Open market value of shares 1,000 × £7.50			7,500
Price paid	1,000 × £5 — shares	5,000	
	1,000 × 50p — option	500	
			5,500
Amount taxable as employment income			£2,000

Notes

(a) The result would be the same if, instead of exercising the option, the employee transferred his option to a third party for £2,500.

(b) The capital gains tax cost of the shares is £7,500 (£5,000 + £500 + £2,000) — see **71.16** above.

Reportable events

[71.18] For the purposes generally of **71.4–71.16** above, there are extensive requirements (see **71.20**, **71.21** below) for employers and others ('responsible persons' — see **71.19** below) to provide HMRC with information concerning any of the following '*reportable events*':

- an acquisition (or event treated as such) of shares, an interest in shares or a share option pursuant to a right or opportunity available by reason of employment;
- chargeable events within either **71.5** above (restricted shares) or **71.9** above (convertible shares);
- the doing of anything that gives rise to an income tax charge under **71.11** above (shares with artificially enhanced market value);
- an event discharging a notional loan as in **71.12** above (shares acquired for less than market value);
- a disposal within **71.13** above (shares disposed of for more than market value);
- the receipt of a benefit within **71.14** above (post-acquisition benefits from shares);
- the assignment or release of a share option acquired pursuant to a right or opportunity available by reason of employment;
- the receipt of a benefit in money or money's worth received in connection with a share option (see **71.16**(d) above).

[*ITEPA 2003, s 421K*].

See **71.3** above for the extended meaning of 'shares' in these respects.

Simon's Taxes. See E4.508R–E4.508T.

Responsible persons

[71.19] Each of the following is a '*responsible person*' in relation to a 'reportable event' (see **71.18** above):

(a) the employer;
(b) the 'host employer' if any;
(c) if the employee in question is a continental shelf worker and the employer is outside the scope of PAYE, any person who is a 'relevant person' in relation to the employee (see **53.9** PAY AS YOU EARN);
(d) the person from whom the shares, interest or option was acquired; and
(e) unless the shares are excluded from these requirements (see below), the person by whom they were issued.

For the purposes of (b) above, a '*host employer*' is a person for whom the employee works at the time of the event and who would be treated as making payments of PAYE income if such payments were actually made by a non-UK employer (see **53.8** PAY AS YOU EARN under 'Non-UK employer'). For the purposes of (e) above, shares excluded from these requirements are, broadly, government and local authority stocks/bonds and quoted shares issued by a person who, at the time of the event, is not connected (within **19** CONNECTED PERSONS) with the employer.

[*ITEPA 2003, ss 421L, 718*].

See **71.3** above for the extended meaning of 'shares' in these respects.

Annual returns

[71.20] A person (P) who is (or has been) a 'responsible person' (see **71.19** above) in relation to reportable events (as in **71.18** above) must make a return for each tax year falling (wholly or partly) in P's 'reportable event period'. P's '*reportable event period*' is the period beginning when the first reportable event occurs in relation to which P is a responsible person and ending when P will no longer be a responsible person in relation to reportable events. The return for a tax year must contain such information as HMRC may require, and must be filed on or before 6 July in the following tax year. If P becomes aware of any error, omission or inaccuracy in a return, he must make an amended return without delay.

A return must be made, and any accompanying information must be given, electronically. However, if they consider it appropriate to do so, HMRC may allow a person to make a return or give any accompanying information in another way.

P's return for a tax year need not contain, or be accompanied by, 'duplicate information', and P is not required to make a return for a tax year if it would contain only, or be accompanied only by, such information. '*Duplicate information*' means information which is contained in or accompanies a return made by another person for the tax year under these provisions or a return made by any person for the tax year under any of the annual return provisions relating to tax-advantaged employee share schemes.

[*ITEPA 2003, ss 421JA, 421JB*].

Penalties

If P fails to make a return by the due date, he is liable for a penalty of £100. If the failure continues for more than three months beginning with the due date, P is liable for a further penalty of £300. If the failure continues for another three months, another £300 penalty is incurred. If it continues for nine months in all, HMRC may, upon giving notice, charge a daily penalty of £10. The notice must specify the period in respect of which the penalty is payable; this period may begin earlier than the date on which the notice is given but cannot begin until after the end of the said nine-month period or, if relevant, after the end of any period specified in any previous notice given by HMRC in relation to the same failure. Liability for a penalty does not arise if P satisfies HMRC (or, on appeal, the Tribunal) that there is a reasonable excuse. Reasonable excuse does not include insufficiency of funds (unless attributable to events outside P's control) or reliance on another person (unless P took reasonable care to avoid the failure); a failure must be remedied without unreasonable delay after a reasonable excuse ceases.

If a return contains a material inaccuracy which is either careless or deliberate or is not corrected by an amended return upon P's becoming aware of it, P is liable for a penalty of up to £5,000. The same applies if a return is not made electronically where required.

[*ITEPA 2003, ss 421JC, 421JD*].

For assessment of penalties, see *ITEPA 2003, s 421JE*. An appeal may be made against the imposition and/or the amount of penalties. Notice of appeal must be given to HMRC no later than 30 days after the date of the notice of assessment of the penalty. For these and other matters related to appeals, see *ITEPA 2003, s 421JF*.

Further HMRC information powers

[71.21] HMRC may give notice to any person, requiring him to provide written particulars of reportable events (as in **71.18** above) which take place during a period specified in the notice and in relation to which that person is a 'responsible person' (see **71.19** above) or to state that there are no such events. Such notice must specify a deadline for compliance, which must be at least 30 days after the notice is given. Penalties can be imposed under *TMA 1970, s 98* for non-compliance. [*ITEPA 2003, s 421J(4)–(6)(8)(10)*].

Internationally mobile employees

[71.22] If, under any of the provisions at **71.4–71.16** above (non-tax-advantaged employment-related shares and share options), something counts as employment income of an internationally mobile employee, there are rules as set out below to determine the amount of that income which is taxable in the UK.

The extended meaning of 'shares' at **71.3** above applies throughout, and 'share option' should be construed accordingly.

The rules apply if an amount counts under any of **71.4–71.16** above as employment income of an individual for a tax year (the '*securities income*') in respect of an employment and *at least one* of the 'international mobility conditions' is met. The '*international mobility conditions*' are:

- that any part of the 'relevant period' (see **71.23** below) is within a tax year for which the remittance basis applies to the individual by virtue of any one of **61.2**(1)–(3) REMITTANCE BASIS;
- that any part of the relevant period is within a tax year for which the individual is not UK resident;
- that any part of the relevant period is within the overseas part of a tax year that is a split year (see **63.19** RESIDENCE AND DOMICILE) as regards the individual.

There are two rules to ascertain the employee's taxable specific income from the employment in respect of the securities income. (See **28.1** EMPLOYMENT INCOME for the charge to tax on taxable specific income.) Rule 1 determines what is chargeable on the arising basis and Rule 2 determines what is chargeable on the remittance basis where applicable. Rule 1 is that an amount equal to the excess of the securities income over so much of that income as is 'foreign securities income' is taxable specific income for the tax year for which the securities income counts as employment income of the individual. '*Foreign securities income*' means the sum of any 'chargeable foreign securities income' and any 'non-chargeable foreign securities income' (for both of which see **71.24** below).

Rule 2 is that the full amount of any 'chargeable foreign securities income' (see **71.24** below) which is remitted to the UK in a tax year is an amount of taxable specific income from the employment for that tax year. (This applies whether or not the employment in question is still held when the remittance is made.) See **61** REMITTANCE BASIS for the meaning of 'remitted to the UK'. For the purpose of applying the provisions described in that chapter, generally treat the shares or the share option as deriving from the chargeable foreign securities income; but where the chargeable event is the disposal of the shares, or the assignment or release of the share option, in question for consideration of not less than market value, treat the consideration (and not the shares or the option) as deriving from the chargeable foreign securities income.

[*ITEPA 2003, s 41F*].

For official guidance, see HMRC Employment-Related Securities Manual ERSM162000–163200.

Simon's Taxes. See **E5.310**.

The relevant period

[71.23] The definition of the *'relevant period'* in **71.22** above depends on the charging provision under which an amount counts as employment income, as follows.

- If the charge is under **71.4** above (restricted shares) or **71.8** above (convertible shares), the relevant period is the period beginning with the day the shares are acquired and ending with the day on which the chargeable event occurs.
- If the charge is the charge on acquisition in **71.10** above (shares with artificially depressed market value), the relevant period is the tax year in which the acquisition occurs.
- If the charge arises by virtue of **71.10**(b) or (c) above (market value of restricted shares artificially low), the relevant period is the period beginning at the start of the tax year in which the chargeable event is deemed to occur and ending with the day on which that chargeable event is deemed to occur.
- If the charge is under **71.11** above (shares with artificially enhanced market value), the relevant period is the period beginning at the start of the tax year in which the valuation date falls and ending with the valuation date.
- If the charge arises from the discharge of the notional loan in **71.12** above (shares acquired for less than market value), or from the anti-avoidance rule in **71.12**, the relevant period is normally the tax year in which the notional loan is treated as made or, if the chargeable event occurs in that tax year, the period beginning at the start of that tax year and ending with the day on which the chargeable event occurs. If,

however, the shares are acquired by means of an option, the relevant period is the period beginning with the day the option is acquired and ending with the day on which the option 'vests'.

- If the charge is under **71.13** above (shares disposed of for more than market value) or **71.14** above (post-acquisition benefits), the relevant period is the tax year in which the chargeable event occurs.
- If the charge is under **71.16** above (unapproved share options), the relevant period begins with the day the option is acquired and ends with the day on which the chargeable event occurs or, if earlier, the day on which the option 'vests'.

For the above purposes, an option '*vests*' when it becomes exercisable or, if earlier, when it becomes exercisable subject only to a period of time expiring. If the relevant period determined as above would not, in all the circumstances, be just and reasonable, the relevant period is adjusted to such period as is just and reasonable.

[*ITEPA 2003, s 41G*].

Chargeable and non-chargeable foreign securities income

[71.24] The extent to which the securities income in **71.22** above is '*chargeable foreign securities income*' or '*non-chargeable foreign securities income*' is determined according to whichever of the rules below is applicable. If, however, these rules do not produce a split that is just and reasonable (having regard to all the circumstances), the amounts of the securities income that are chargeable foreign securities income and non-chargeable foreign securities income are to be adjusted to such amounts as are just and reasonable. See HMRC Employment-Related Securities Manual ERSM162700 for guidance. For the purposes of these rules, an equal amount of the securities income is treated as accruing on each day of the relevant period. See below as regards the location of employment duties for these purposes.

Rule 1 is that if any part of the 'relevant period' (see **71.23** above) is within a tax year for which all the conditions at (a)–(d) below are met, the securities income accruing in that part of the relevant period is chargeable foreign securities income. Those conditions are that:

(a) the remittance basis applies to the individual for that year by virtue of any one of **61.2**(1)–(3) REMITTANCE BASIS;
(b) the individual does not for that year meet the section 26A test at **28.7** EMPLOYMENT INCOME (which requires broadly a three-year period of non-UK residence);
(c) the employment in question is with a 'foreign employer' (see **28.6** EMPLOYMENT INCOME); and
(d) the duties of the employment are performed wholly outside the UK in that year.

See below for a limit on chargeable foreign securities income where the duties of an associated employment are performed in the UK. Also see below as regards dual contract arrangements.

Rule 2 is that if any part of the relevant period is within a tax year for which all the conditions at (i)–(iii) below are met, and the duties of the employment in question are performed wholly outside the UK, the securities income accruing in that part of the relevant period is chargeable foreign securities income. If any part of the relevant period is within a tax year for which all the conditions at (i)–(iii) below are met, and some but not all of the duties of the employment are performed outside the UK, the securities income accruing in that part of the relevant period must be apportioned on a just and reasonable basis between duties performed in and outside the UK; the income apportioned to duties performed outside the UK is chargeable foreign securities income. The conditions are that:

(i) the remittance basis applies to the individual for that year by virtue of any one of **61.2**(1)–(3) REMITTANCE BASIS;
(ii) the individual meets for that year the section 26A test at **28.7** EMPLOYMENT INCOME; and
(iii) at least some of the duties of the employment are performed outside the UK in that year.

Rule 3 is that if any part of the relevant period is within a tax year for which the individual is not UK resident, and the duties of the employment in question are performed wholly outside the UK in that year, the securities income accruing in that part of the relevant period is non-chargeable foreign securities income. If any part of the relevant period is within a tax year for which the individual is not UK resident, and some but not all of the duties of the employment are performed outside the UK in that year, the securities income accruing in that part of the relevant period must be apportioned on a just and reasonable basis between duties performed in and outside the UK; the income apportioned to duties performed outside the UK is non-chargeable foreign securities income.

Rule 4 is that if any part of the relevant period is within the overseas part of a tax year that is a split year (see **63.19** RESIDENCE AND DOMICILE) as regards the individual, and the duties of the employment in question are performed wholly outside the UK in that overseas part, the securities income accruing in that part of the relevant period is non-chargeable foreign securities income. If some but not all of those duties are performed outside the UK in that overseas part, an apportionment similar to that in Rule 3 above is carried out, and the income apportioned to duties performed outside the UK is non-chargeable foreign securities income.

Duties of associated employment performed in UK

There is a limit on the extent to which Rule 1 above applies in relation to a period when the individual holds 'associated employments' (see **28.6** EMPLOYMENT INCOME) in addition to the employment in question and the duties of the associated employments are not performed wholly outside the UK. The amount of the securities income for the period that would otherwise be chargeable foreign securities income is limited to such amount as is just and reasonable, having regard to:

- the employment income for the period from the employment in question and all the associated employments;

- the proportion of that income that consists of general earnings that are 'chargeable overseas earnings' (see **28.6** EMPLOYMENT INCOME);
- the nature of, and time devoted to, the duties performed outside the UK, and those performed in the UK, in the period; and
- all other relevant circumstances.

Dual contract arrangements

Rule 1 above does not apply to a tax year if the 'dual contract legislation' applies for that year in relation to the employment in question. The '*dual contract legislation*' means the provisions in **28.6** EMPLOYMENT INCOME that restrict the application of the remittance basis in cases involving dual contract arrangements. In such a case, it is to be assumed that it is just and reasonable for none of the securities income accruing in that tax year to be chargeable foreign securities income.

Location of employment duties

The rule at **28.3**(ii) EMPLOYMENT INCOME (incidental duties in the UK) applies for the purposes of these provisions, as do the rules for seafarers and aircraft crew at **28.3**(iii) EMPLOYMENT INCOME. In addition, the duties of an employment performed in the UK sector of the continental shelf (under *Continental Shelf Act 1964, s 1(7)*) in connection with exploration or exploitation activities are treated as being performed in the UK.

Securities income from overseas Crown employment

If securities income is 'from overseas Crown employment subject to UK tax' (see **28.7** EMPLOYMENT INCOME), then notwithstanding anything else in these rules it is *not* foreign securities income. If securities income is partly from overseas Crown employment subject to UK tax, a just and reasonable proportion of the income is taken to be from such employment.

[*ITEPA 2003, ss 41H–41L*].

Share Incentive Plans

[71.25] A share incentive plan ('SIP') is a tax-advantaged plan established by a company, providing for shares to be appropriated without payment to employees ('*free shares*' — see **71.27** below) and/or for shares to be acquired on employees' behalf from sums deducted from their salary ('*partnership shares*' — see **71.28** below). A plan providing for partnership shares may also provide for shares to be appropriated without payment to employees ('*matching shares*' — see **71.29** below) in proportion to the partnership shares acquired by them. See **71.31, 71.32** below for tax consequences in each case. See **71.30** below as to reinvestment of dividends on plan shares. Where a plan provides for more than one of the above kinds of shares, it may leave it to the company to decide when each such provision is to have effect. A plan established by a company which controls (within *ITA 2007, s 995*) other companies (a '*parent company*') may extend to one or more of those other companies, whereupon it is known as a '*group plan*'. Companies that for the time being are party to a group plan are known as '*constituent companies*'.

A SIP ceases to be a tax-advantaged plan if (and with effect from the time when) a disqualifying event occurs, where such event occurs on or after 15 September 2016 — see **71.39** below.

Companies must self-certify that a SIP meets the statutory requirements to be a tax-advantaged plan; HMRC have powers of enquiry (see **71.38** below).

[*ITEPA 2003, ss 488, 719, Sch 2 paras 1–4; FA 2016, Sch 3 para 2(2)(4)*].

See Tolley's Corporation Tax as regards deductions which the employer company may make for corporation tax purposes.

See generally HMRC Employee Tax Advantaged Share Scheme User Manual at ETASSUM20000 *et seq*.

Simon's Taxes. See **E4.528–E4.542**.

General requirements

[71.26] The purpose of the plan must be to provide, in accordance with *ITEPA 2003, Sch 2*, benefits to employees by way of shares which give them a continuing stake in a company. A plan must contain no features which are neither essential nor reasonably incidental to that purpose.

A plan must not provide benefits to employees otherwise than in accordance with *ITEPA 2003, Sch 2* and, in particular, must not provide cash to employees as an alternative to shares; this does not prohibit an employee receiving a benefit from a company as a result of any of that company's shares held on his behalf under a plan if he would have received the same benefit had he acquired the shares otherwise than by virtue of the plan.

The plan *must* provide that every employee who is eligible (as in **71.33** below) in relation to an award of shares under the plan, and who is a 'UK resident taxpayer', may participate in the award and be invited to do so, and it should not contain any features (other than those required or authorised under these provisions) to discourage participation. It *may* provide for an eligible employee to be invited to participate in an award even though he is not a 'UK resident taxpayer'. An individual who *must* be invited, or who under terms as above *may* be invited, to participate in an award is a '*qualifying employee*' in relation to that award.

For the above purposes, an employee is a '*UK resident taxpayer*' if his earnings, from the employment by reference to which he meets the employment requirement at **71.33** below, are (or would be if there were any) general earnings within **28.4** EMPLOYMENT INCOME (earnings for year when employee UK resident).

All employees invited to participate in an award must be invited to participate on the same terms, and those who do participate must actually do so on the same terms. Free shares may be awarded by reference to remuneration, length of service or hours worked, or (within confines) more than one of these factors, but not by reference to other factors. Free shares may, however, be allocated, in accordance with **71.34** below, by reference to performance. Subject to the above, no feature of the plan must have the likely effect of conferring benefits wholly or mainly on directors or on employees receiving higher levels of remuneration. In the case of a group, the identity of the company, or of the constituent companies in a group plan, must not be such as to have similar likely effect. No conditions may be imposed on an employee's participation in an award, except as required or permitted under these provisions. The arrangements (as broadly defined) for the plan must not provide for loans to employees of the company (or of constituent companies in a group plan), and neither those arrangements nor the operation of the plan must in any way be associated with any such loans.

[*ITEPA 2003, Sch 2 paras 6–12*].

Awards of shares

Shares are '*awarded*' under a plan on each occasion when, in accordance with the plan, free or matching shares are appropriated to employees or partnership shares are acquired on behalf of employees. Shares are awarded to a particular employee (a '*participant*') when free or matching shares are appropriated to him, or partnership shares are acquired on his behalf, as part of the global award. [*ITEPA 2003, Sch 2 para 5*].

Shares leaving the plan

Shares '*cease to be subject to the plan*' when:

(a) they are 'withdrawn from the plan'; or
(b) the participant ceases to be in '*relevant employment*' (which term comprises employment by the company and employment by any 'associated' company), in which case his shares cease to be subject to the plan on the date of leaving (but see below for exception); or
(c) the plan trustees dispose of the shares in order to meet PAYE obligations (see **71.31** below).

For the purpose of determining any charge to income tax, shares cease to be subject to the plan in the order in which they were awarded to the participant. Shares awarded on the same day cease to be subject to the plan in the order which results in the lowest income tax charge. (Dividend shares are treated as awarded when the trustees acquire them on behalf of, or appropriate them to, the participant.)

Shares are '*withdrawn from the plan*' (see (a) above) when, on the direction of the participant (or, after his death, of his personal representatives), the plan trustees either transfer them (whether to the participant etc. or to another person) or dispose of them and similarly account for the proceeds, or when the participant etc. assigns, charges or otherwise disposes of his beneficial interest in them.

For the purposes of (b) above and of these provisions generally (except where otherwise stated), two companies are '*associated*' if one controls the other or they are under common control, 'control' being interpreted in accordance with *CTA 2010, ss 450, 451*.

Where an individual ceases to be in relevant employment during the 'acquisition period' relating to an award of partnership shares, he is treated for the purposes of (b) above as ceasing to be in such employment immediately after the shares are awarded. The '*acquisition period*' begins with the deduction from salary and ends with the 'acquisition date' or, where relevant, begins with the end of the 'accumulation period' and ends immediately before the 'acquisition date' (see **71.28** below for meaning of terms used here).

[*ITEPA 2003, s 508, Sch 2 paras 94–97*].

Jointly owned companies

To enable a jointly owned company to take part in a group plan (though it cannot thereby take part in more than one), such a company, and any company under its control (within *ITA 2007, s 995*), is treated as being under the control of each of its two joint owners (though not for the purposes of **71.35**(ii) below). A company controlled *by* a jointly owned company may not take part in more than one group plan or in a different plan to that (if any) in which the jointly owned company (or any other company controlled by it) takes part. [*ITEPA 2003, s 719, Sch 2 para 91, Sch 7 para 70*].

In the case of a company registered outside the UK, **shares** include fractions of shares for the purposes of these provisions, where such fractions are recognised under local law. [*ITEPA 2003, Sch 2 para 99(2)*].

Free shares

[71.27] The 'initial market value' of free shares awarded (see **71.26** above) to a participant in any tax year under a plan providing for free shares (see **71.25** above) must not exceed **£3,600**. The '*initial market value*' of shares is their market value (determined as for capital gains tax purposes) on the date of the award. Where the market value of shares on any date falls to be determined, HMRC and the plan trustees may agree that it be determined by reference to a different date or a number of specified dates. In arriving at the market value of restricted shares as in **71.4** above, the restrictions (or risk of forfeiture) are disregarded. [*ITEPA 2003, Sch 2 paras 34, 35, 92(2), 99(4)*].

As regards each award of free shares, the plan must require the company to specify a period (the holding period) during which a participant is bound by contract, for so long as he remains in relevant employment (see **71.26** above), to permit his shares to remain in the hands of the trustees and not to assign, charge or otherwise dispose of his beneficial interest. The holding period must not be less than three years, nor more than five, beginning with the date the shares are awarded to the participant, and must be the same for all shares in the same award. See **71.31** below for income tax consequences of free shares leaving the plan. The plan *may* enable different holding periods to be specified from time to time, though not so as to increase the holding period for free shares already awarded. Notwithstanding the foregoing, the participant may direct the trustees to accept or agree to:

(a) an offer resulting in a new holding being equated with his original free shares for capital gains tax purposes (see Tolley's Capital Gains Tax under Shares and Securities); or
(b) an offer of cash and/or a qualifying corporate bond (see Tolley's Capital Gains Tax), with or without other assets, which is part of a general offer designed to give the person making it control of the company; or

(c) a transaction pursuant to a compromise, arrangement or scheme affecting all the shares or all the shares of the particular class concerned or all those held by a class of shareholders (identified otherwise than by reference to employment or participation in the plan).

For the purposes of (b) above, it does not matter if the general offer is made to different shareholders by different means.

If in the case of a takeover offer (as defined) there arises a right under *Companies Act 2006, s 983* to require the offeror to acquire the participant's free shares, or such of them as are of a particular class, the participant may direct the trustees to exercise that right.

[*ITEPA 2003, Sch 2 paras 36, 37*].

The holding period requirement is subject to the provisions for termination of plans (see **71.40** below) and those requiring the trustees to be enabled to meet certain PAYE obligations (see **71.31** below).

Partnership shares

[71.28] A plan providing for partnership shares (see **71.25** above) must provide for qualifying employees (see **71.26** below) to enter into agreements ('*partnership share agreements*') with the company whereby the employee authorises the employer company to make deductions from his salary for the purchase of partnership shares to be awarded to him under the plan. It must specify the amount or percentage to be deducted from salary and the intervals at which deductions are to be made, although the company and employee may agree to vary both of these. It must also contain a notice giving prescribed information in prescribed form (see *SI 2000 No 2090*) as to the possible effect of deductions on an employee's entitlement to social security benefits, statutory sick pay and statutory maternity pay.

The amount deducted from salary in any tax year must not exceed **£1,800.** Furthermore, the amount deducted must not exceed 10% of the employee's salary for the tax year. The plan may authorise the setting of maximum limits which are lower than the aforementioned; different limits may be set for different awards. A lower limit may be expressed in terms of a monetary amount, a percentage or a stipulation that earnings of a specified kind (e.g. overtime payments, bonuses etc.) be excluded from employees' salaries for these purposes. Any amount deducted from salary in excess of the applicable limits must be returned to the employee. The plan may also set a minimum amount that can be deducted on any occasion (previously in any month, regardless of actual pay intervals); the specified minimum must not exceed £10.

Subject to the above, for these purposes an employee's salary means the employee's earnings (from the employment in question) otherwise subject to PAYE, excluding any taxable benefits and expenses within the benefits code (see **28.21** EMPLOYMENT INCOME). HMRC take this to mean salary after deduction of allowable pension contributions and charitable donations made under payroll giving schemes (Revenue Share Focus Newsletter December

2003 p 8). The term is extended to include emoluments which are outside the scope of the charge to tax on employment income, excluding benefits etc., which would have been chargeable had the individual been within the scope of that charge. See **71.31** below as regards tax relief for amounts deducted.

The plan must provide that partnership shares are not to be subject to any provision for forfeiture. (This was always effectively the case because of what is said at **71.35** below about shares subject to restrictions.) It can nevertheless be provided that partnership shares acquired on behalf of an employee can be offered for sale, so long as the consideration at which they are required to be offered for sale is at least equal to the amount applied in acquiring the shares on the employee's behalf or, if lower, the market value of the shares at the time they are offered for sale.

[*ITEPA 2003, Sch 2 paras 43–48; SI 2000 No 2090; SI 2007 No 109*].

Amounts deducted from salary are to be paid over to the trustees and held by them (in a bank, building society etc.) on the employee's behalf until applied in acquiring partnership shares on his behalf (which includes their appropriating to him shares already held by them). If such monies are held in an interest-bearing account, the plan must require the trustees to account to the employee for the interest.

If the plan does not provide for an accumulation period (see below), it must provide for deductions from salary to be applied as above on the '*acquisition date*', which for *this* purpose is a date which is set by the trustees and is within 30 days after the date of the last salary deduction in relation to the partnership share award in question. Subject to any restriction imposed in accordance with the plan (see below), the number of shares awarded (see **71.26** above) to each employee is to be determined by reference to market value at the acquisition date.

Accumulation periods

A plan may provide for accumulation periods not exceeding twelve months. If it does so, the partnership share agreement must specify when each such period begins (which in the case of the first period must be no later than the date of the first salary deduction) and ends. The accumulation period for each award of shares must be same for all individuals entering into the partnership share agreements. Subject to this, the agreement may specify that an accumulation period shall end on the occurrence of a specified event, and may additionally provide that salary deductions be in such cases returned to participants. The plan may provide for continuity in the event of certain share exchanges. The plan must provide for deductions from salary to be applied by the trustees in acquiring, on the employee's behalf, partnership shares on the '*acquisition date*', which for *this* purpose is a date which is set by the trustees and is within 30 days after the end of the accumulation period applicable to the partnership share award in question.

Subject to any restriction imposed in accordance with the plan (see below), the number of shares awarded to each employee is to be determined in accordance with one of the following (and the partnership share agreement must specify which one of these is to apply):

(i) the market value of the shares at the beginning of the accumulation period;
(ii) the market value of the shares on the acquisition date; or
(iii) the lower of (i) and (ii).

If an employee ceases to be in relevant employment (see **71.26** above) during an accumulation period, salary deductions made must be paid over to him.

Any surplus monies held after acquiring shares as above may, with the employee's agreement, be carried forward to the next deduction or, where applicable, carried forward to the next accumulation period; otherwise they must be paid over to the employee.

[*ITEPA 2003, Sch 2 paras 43(3), 49–52*].

Restricting the award

The plan *may* authorise the company to restrict the number of shares to be included in a particular partnership share award to a specified maximum, subject to its giving employees advance notification. Where necessary, in such case, the number of shares in each individual award is to be scaled down.

Stopping, re-starting and withdrawal

An employee may, by written notice to the company, stop salary deductions under a partnership share agreement. He may similarly re-start deductions (though the plan *may* impose a limit of one re-start per accumulation period, where applicable) but is not permitted to make up deductions missed. The company must give effect to a notice to stop or re-start within 30 days of receiving it, unless the employee specifies a later date in the notice. An employee may also, again by written notice to the company, withdraw from a partnership share agreement, such notice to take effect within 30 days unless a later date is specified therein. Any monies deducted and still held on his behalf must then be paid over to him. On the withdrawal by HMRC of a plan's tax-advantaged status (see **71.38** below), or on the issue of a plan termination notice (see **71.40** below), any monies deducted and still held on an employee's behalf must be paid over to him as soon as practicable. [*ITEPA 2003, Sch 2 paras 53–56*].

Access to partnership shares

An employee may at any time withdraw from the plan any or all of the partnership shares awarded to him. See **71.31** below for income tax consequences of withdrawal. [*ITEPA 2003, Sch 2 para 57*].

COVID-19

HMRC have confirmed that CJRS (Coronavirus Job Retention Scheme) payments to employees furloughed during the 2020 COVID-19 (coronavirus) pandemic can constitute a salary and that SIP contributions can be deducted from CJRS payments. There remains the option to stop deductions as above, but participants will not be permitted to make up missed deductions even if they stop only because of COVID-19. (Employment Related Securities Bulletin No. 35, June 2020).

Matching shares

[71.29] In a plan providing for matching shares (see **71.25** above), the partnership share agreement (see **71.28** above) must specify the ratio of matching shares to partnership shares for the time being offered by the company and the circumstances and manner in which the ratio may be changed. The ratio must apply by reference to the *number* of shares and must not be greater than **two matching shares to each partnership share.** If the ratio changes before partnership shares are awarded under the agreement, employees must be notified accordingly. Matching shares must be of the same class and carry the same rights as the partnership shares to which they relate. They must be awarded (see **71.26** above) on the day the related partnership shares are awarded and must be awarded to all participants on exactly the same basis. See **71.35** below as to permitted provision for forfeiture. The provisions of *ITEPA 2003, Sch 2 paras 36, 37* (holding period and related matters — see **71.27** above) apply to matching shares as they apply to free shares. [*ITEPA 2003, Sch 2 paras 58–61*].

Dividend shares

[71.30] The plan *may* provide that, where the company so directs, some or all of the cash dividends on plan shares are to be reinvested in further shares ('*dividend shares*') on participants' behalf. Participants may be allowed to choose whether or not to reinvest. The company's direction must set out the amount of the cash dividends to be reinvested or how such an amount is to be determined. The company may modify or revoke a direction. To the extent that cash dividends are not required to be reinvested, they must be paid over to the participants. There is no limit on the amount of dividends that can be reinvested per participant per tax year.

Dividend shares must be of the same class and carry the same rights as the shares on which the dividend is paid and must not be subject to any provision for forfeiture. It can nevertheless be provided that dividend shares acquired on behalf of an employee can be offered for sale, so long as the consideration at which they are required to be offered for sale is at least equal to the amount applied in acquiring the shares on the employee's behalf or, if lower, the market value of the shares at the time they are offered for sale.

The trustees must acquire dividend shares on participants' behalf (which includes their appropriating to participants shares already held by them) on the '*acquisition date*', which for this purpose is a date which is set by the trustees and is within 30 days after they receive the dividend. The number of shares acquired on behalf of each participant is to be determined by reference to market value at the acquisition date. There are provisions for carrying forward for future reinvestment, as a separately identifiable amount, any remaining balance, and for such amounts to be paid over to the participant in certain circumstances.

The holding period, during which dividend shares must not leave the plan (other than on cessation of employment), must be three years. In other respects, the provisions of *ITEPA 2003, Sch 2 paras 36, 37* (holding period and related matters — see **71.27** above) apply to dividend shares as they apply to free shares.

[*ITEPA 2003, Sch 2 paras 62–69; ITTOIA 2005, s 397A(7); FA 2016, Sch 1 paras 1, 73*].

Income tax consequences for participants

[71.31] An award of shares (see **71.26** above) to an employee, or an acquisition of dividend shares (see **71.30** above) on his behalf, under a tax-advantaged SIP does not attract an income tax charge.

Neither the employer's nor the plan trustees' incidental expenses in running the plan can give rise to any income tax charge. This exemption is extended to cover any such incidental expenses of the company which established the plan (if different from the employer).

Neither the above exemption nor the income tax consequences below apply to an individual if, at the time of the award in question, his earnings (from the employment by reference to which he meets the employment requirement at **71.33** below) are not (or would not be if there were any) within the charge to UK tax on employment income.

The income tax exemptions do not apply if the shares are awarded or acquired under arrangements a main purpose of which is the avoidance of tax or national insurance contributions.

[*ITEPA 2003, ss 489–491, 494, 495, 499, 500*].

Capital receipts

Where a 'capital receipt' is received by a participant in respect of, or by reference to, free, matching or partnership shares awarded to him fewer than five years previously or dividend shares acquired on his behalf fewer than three years previously, the amount or value of that receipt is chargeable to tax as employment income of the participant for the tax year of receipt (see below as regards PAYE). For these purposes, a '*capital receipt*' means any money or money's worth except to the extent that:

- it constitutes taxable income of the recipient (or would do so but for the exemptions conferred by these provisions);
- it consists of the disposal proceeds of the shares;
- it consists of the proceeds of a part disposal by the trustees (at the direction of the participant) of rights under a rights issue where those proceeds are used to take up other such rights;
- it consists of 'new shares' following a company reconstruction (see **71.36** below); or
- it is received by the participant's personal representatives after his death.

[*ITEPA 2003, ss 501, 502, Sch 2 para 99*].

Free or matching shares leaving plan

If free shares (see **71.27** above) or matching shares (see **71.29** above) cease to be subject to the plan (see **71.26** above) within less than five years of their being awarded to him, an amount is chargeable to tax as employment income of the participant (subject to the exceptions at (a)–(c) below) for the tax year in which the shares cease to be subject to the plan. If the shares leave the plan in less than three years, the chargeable amount is their market value (determined as in **71.27** above) when they leave the plan. If they leave the plan after three years or more but less than five years, the chargeable amount is the lower of their market value when they leave the plan and their market value at the date they were awarded. If the latter, the tax is reduced by any tax paid on 'capital receipts' (see above) in respect of the shares.

Any tax due as above is reduced by any tax paid by virtue of **71.11** above (shares with artificially enhanced market value) in relation to the shares.

If, within the holding period (see **71.27**, **71.29** above) specified for the award of free or matching shares, the participant, in breach of his obligations under the plan, assigns, charges or otherwise disposes of his beneficial interest, then, instead of the above, the market value of the shares at the time they cease to be subject to the plan is chargeable to tax as employment income of the participant for the tax year in which that time falls.

There is no charge on free or matching shares leaving the plan after five years or more, nor is there any charge on the forfeiture of such shares.

[*ITEPA 2003, ss 497(1), 505, 507*].

There is no income tax charge on shares ceasing to be subject to the plan within five years by reason of the participant's ceasing to be in relevant employment (see **71.26** above) due to:

(a) injury, disability, redundancy (as defined), his employer company losing its 'associated company' status (see **71.26** above), or a transfer within the *Transfer of Undertakings (Protection of Employment) Regulations 2006 (SI 2006 No 246)*; or
(b) the participant's retirement; or
(c) the participant's death.

Cash takeovers

A participant is not liable to income tax charge on shares withdrawn from the plan on specified kinds of takeover of the company provided he receives cash (and no other assets) in exchange for his plan shares. (It does not matter if he receives other assets in exchange for shares other than the plan shares.) This exemption does not apply to the plan shares (or to a proportion of them) if:

- in connection with the takeover offer, a course of action was open to the participant which, had it been followed, would have resulted in other assets being received instead of cash in exchange for the plan shares (or the proportion of them); or
- it is reasonable to suppose that the plan shares (or the proportion of them) would not have been awarded had the cash takeover not been in place or under consideration.

[*ITEPA 2003, s 498, Sch 2 paras 98, 99*].

Partnership shares generally

Deductions from an employee's salary in accordance with a partnership share agreement (see **71.28** above) are allowable deductions for income tax purposes. [*ITEPA 2003, s 492*].

Any amount deducted from an individual's salary but subsequently returned to him under any of the relevant provisions in **71.28** above is chargeable to tax as employment income of the individual for the tax year in which the amount is paid over to him. Any money or money's worth received by an individual in respect of the cancellation of a partnership share agreement entered into by him is chargeable to tax as employment income of the individual for the tax year of receipt. [*ITEPA 2003, ss 503, 504*].

Partnership shares leaving plan

If partnership shares (see **71.28** above) cease to be subject to the plan (see **71.26** above) within less than five years of the 'acquisition date', an amount is chargeable to tax as employment income of the participant (subject to the same exceptions as for free and matching shares — see (a)–(c) above) for the tax year in which the shares cease to be subject to the plan. (The '*acquisition date*' depends on whether or not there is an accumulation period, and is separately defined in **71.28** above for each such possibility.) If the shares leave the plan in less than three years, the chargeable amount is normally their market value (determined as in **71.27** above) when they leave the plan. If they leave the plan after three years or more but less than five years, the chargeable amount is normally the lower of their market value when they leave the plan and the amount of salary deductions used to acquire them. If the latter, the tax is reduced by any tax paid on 'capital receipts' (see above) in respect of the shares. Any tax due is reduced by any tax paid by virtue of **71.11** above (shares with artificially enhanced market value) in relation to the shares. There is no charge on partnership shares leaving the plan after five years or more.

If partnership shares leave the plan by virtue of a provision to the effect that partnership shares can be offered for sale (see **71.28** above), the chargeable amount is the lower of the market value of the shares at the time they are offered for sale and the amount of salary deductions used to acquire them. Market value is determined as in **71.27** above, and in arriving at the market value of any restricted shares (as in **71.4** above) when offered for sale, the restriction is to be disregarded.

[*ITEPA 2003, ss 497(2), 506, Sch 2 para 92(2)*].

Dividend shares generally

The amount applied by the trustees in acquiring dividend shares (see **71.30** above) on behalf of a participant is not treated as his income for any tax purposes. Any balance carried forward as in **71.30** above is treated in the same way, but any amount eventually paid over to the participant is chargeable to income tax as if it were a dividend received by him in the tax year in which it is paid over (see **1.5** and **65.10** *et seq.* SAVINGS AND INVESTMENT INCOME for taxation of dividends generally). [*ITTOIA 2005, ss 393, 396, 401C(11), 405, 406, 408A(10), 770; ITEPA 2003, ss 493, 496, Sch 2 para 80(4); FA 2016, Sch 1 paras 6, 15, 73*].

Dividend shares leaving the plan

If dividend shares (see **71.30** above) cease to be subject to the plan (see **71.26** above) within less than three years after their acquisition on the participant's behalf, the participant is chargeable to income tax on a notional dividend (subject to the same exceptions as for free and matching shares — see (a)–(c) above). The notional dividend is normally equal to the amount of cash dividend applied to acquire the shares, and is chargeable to income tax as if it were a dividend received by the participant in the tax year in which the shares cease to be subject to the plan (see **1.5** ALLOWANCES AND TAX RATES and **65.10** *et seq.* SAVINGS AND INVESTMENT INCOME for taxation of dividends generally). The tax due is reduced by any tax paid on 'capital receipts' (see above) in respect of the shares. There is no charge on dividend shares leaving the plan after three years or more.

If dividend shares leave the plan by virtue of a provision to the effect that dividend shares can be offered for sale (see **71.30** above), the notional dividend is equal to the market value of the shares at the time they are offered for sale if that would give a lower amount than that given above. Market value is determined as in **71.27** above, and in arriving at the market value of any restricted shares (as in **71.4** above) when offered for sale, the restriction is to be disregarded.

[*ITTOIA 2005, ss 394–396, 397A(7), 407, 408, 408A(10); ITEPA 2003, s 497(3), Sch 2 para 80(4)(5); FA 2016, Sch 1 paras 1, 7, 8, 15, 16, 73*].

PAYE

Where a tax charge arises as above on any shares leaving the plan and those shares are 'readily convertible assets', PAYE must be applied by the 'employer company'. A '*readily convertible asset*' is as defined in *ITEPA 2003, s 702* (see **53.4** PAY AS YOU EARN) except that, in determining for these purposes whether or not shares fall within that definition, there is disregarded:

- any market for the shares which is created by virtue of the trustees acquiring shares for the plan and which exists solely for the purposes of the plan; and
- *ITEPA 2003, s 702(5A)–(5D)*, which in certain circumstances treat shares and securities as readily convertible assets even if they would otherwise not be (see **53.4** PAY AS YOU EARN).

The '*employer company*' is the company which employs the participant in 'relevant employment' (see **71.26** above) at the time the shares cease to be subject to the plan, or , if the participant is not employed in relevant employment at that time, the company which last so employed him. The plan may require the participant to pay to the employer company a sum sufficient to meet the PAYE liability. Otherwise, the trustees must make such payment to the employer company (see **71.37** below as regards the raising of the necessary funds). The company must account for PAYE and return any unused balance to the participant. If there is no employer company, or if HMRC consider that it is impracticable for the employer company to make a PAYE deduction and they so direct, the obligation to make the deduction falls on the trustees instead. *ITEPA 2003, s 689* (non-UK employers — see **53.8** PAY AS YOU EARN) is then disapplied.

[*ITEPA 2003, ss 509–512*].

Where the trustees receive a sum of money by way of a capital receipt chargeable to tax on receipt by the participant (see above), the trustees must pay to the 'employer company' (defined as above but by reference to the time of receipt by the trustees) the amount on which such tax is chargeable. The employer company must make a PAYE deduction and account to the participant for the net amount. The obligation to deduct PAYE and account for the net amount may be transferred to the trustees in similar circumstances to those described above. [*ITEPA 2003, ss 513, 514*].

Plan trustees

For the tax position of the trustees in respect of dividends on unappropriated shares, see **71.37** below.

Capital gains tax

[71.32] A participant is treated for capital gains tax purposes as absolutely entitled as against the plan trustees to any shares awarded to him under a tax-advantaged SIP. Shares ceasing to be subject to the plan (see **71.26** above) at any time are deemed to have been disposed of and immediately reacquired by the participant at their then market value, but no chargeable gain or allowable loss arises on the deemed disposal. If any of a participant's shares are forfeited (see **71.35** below as regards provision for forfeiture), they are deemed to have been disposed of by the participant and acquired by the plan trustees at their market value at the date of forfeiture, but again no chargeable gain or allowable loss arises. [*TCGA 1992, Sch 7D paras 1, 3, 5, 7*]. A form of rollover relief is available for shares transferred (other than by a company) to the trustees of a tax-advantaged SIP. [*TCGA 1992, s 236A, Sch 7C*].

For details, see Tolley's Capital Gains Tax under Employee Share Schemes.

Eligibility of employees

[71.33] A tax-advantaged SIP must provide that only an individual who is eligible may participate in an award of shares (see **71.26** above), such eligibility to be judged, in the case of free shares, at the time the award is made and, in the case of partnership shares (and related matching shares), at the time of the salary deduction relating to the award or, if there is an accumulation period (see **71.28** above), the first such salary deduction. An individual is eligible only if the requirements (as detailed below) are met as to employment and participation in other schemes. An individual who is not a 'UK resident taxpayer' (as defined in **71.26** above) must satisfy any further eligibility requirements set out in the plan. [*ITEPA 2003, Sch 2 para 14*].

Employment

The individual must be an employee of the company which established the plan or, in the case of a group plan, of a constituent company (see **71.25** above). The plan *may* provide for a qualifying period, in which case the individual is required to have been at all times during that period an employee of the company or of a company that is a constituent company at the end of that period. This condition can also be satisfied by reference to employment with an associated company (as in **71.26** above and judged as at the time of that employment) and, in the case of a group plan, with a company that was a constituent company at the time of that employment or with a then associated company of such a company. The qualifying period, if any, must be:

(i) (in the case of free shares) a period of not more than 18 months ending with the date of the award; and
(ii) (in the case of partnership shares and related matching shares) a period of not more than 18 months ending with the salary deduction related to the award, or, where relevant, a period of not more than six months ending with the start of the accumulation period (see **71.28** above) related to the award.

In relation to an award, the same qualifying period must apply in relation to all employees of the company or, where applicable, of the constituent companies. The plan may authorise the company to specify different qualifying periods in respect of different awards.

[*ITEPA 2003, Sch 2 paras 15–17*].

Participation in other schemes

An individual is not eligible to participate in an award of free, matching or partnership shares under a tax-advantaged SIP at the same time as participating in an award under another tax-advantaged SIP established by the same company or by a 'connected company' (simultaneous participation). It also used to be the case that an individual was also not eligible to participate in an award if he had in the same tax year participated in an award under another tax-advantaged SIP established by the same company or by a 'connected company' (successive participation). From 10 July 2003, successive participation *is* permitted but the limits on the number of free shares an individual can obtain, the amount of salary he can invest in partnership shares and the amount that can be reinvested on his behalf in dividend shares apply as if all such plans were a single plan. For these purposes, an individual is treated as having participated in an award of free shares under a SIP if he would have done so but for his failure to obtain a performance allowance (see **71.34** below).

For these purposes, a '*connected company*' is:

(I) a company which controls (within *ITA 2007, s 995*) the first company, or which is controlled by the first company, or which is controlled by a company which also controls the first company; or
(II) a company which is a member of a consortium owning the first company or which is owned in part by the first company as a member of a consortium.

[*ITEPA 2003, s 719, Sch 2 paras 18, 18A*].

Performance allowances

[71.34] If the plan provides for performance allowances, i.e. for the award of free shares, or the number or value of free shares awarded, to be conditional on performance targets being met, the company must use one of the two methods described below.

Under *Method 1*, in relation to a particular award of shares (see **71.26** above):

(a) at least 20% of the shares must be awarded other than by reference to performance; and
(b) the highest performance-related award (in terms of the number of shares) made to any individual must not exceed four times the highest non-performance-related award so made.

If different classes of share are awarded, the above applies separately in relation to each class. The overall requirement (at **71.26** above) to award free shares on similar terms to all participating employees is disapplied as regards the performance-related shares.

Under *Method 2*, in relation to a particular award of shares, some or all of the shares must be awarded by reference to performance, and the overall requirement to award free shares on similar terms to all participating employees is applied separately as regards each performance unit. The performance targets set must be consistent, which means they must be capable of being reasonably viewed as being comparable in terms of the likelihood of their being met by the performance units to which they apply.

Whichever method is used, performance allowances in relation to an award must be available to each qualifying employee. Performance targets must be set for performance units comprising one or more employees, and performance measures must be based on business results or other objective criteria and be fair and objective measures of the performance of the applicable units. An employee cannot belong to more than one performance unit for the purposes of a particular award of free shares. The plan must require:

(i) performance targets and measures to be notified to prospective participants; and
(ii) (in general terms and subject to reasonable considerations as to commercial confidentiality) performance measures to be notified to all qualifying employees (see **71.26** above) of the company (or of all constituent companies under a group plan),

such notifications to be given as soon as reasonably practicable.

[*ITEPA 2003, Sch 2 paras 34(4), 38–42*].

Requirements as to type of share used

[71.35] The requirements below must all be met with respect to any shares ('*eligible shares*') that may be awarded under a tax-advantaged SIP.

Eligible shares must form part of the ordinary share capital of:

(a) the company which established the plan;

(b) a company which has control (within *ITA 2007, s 995*) of the company in (a) above;

(c) a company which is a member of a consortium owning either the company in (a) above or a company within (b) above; or

(d) a company which has control of a company within (c) above.

Eligible shares must be:

(i) shares of a class listed on a recognised stock exchange;

(ii) shares in a company not under the control (within *ITA 2007, s 995*) of another company;

(iii) shares in a company which is subject to an employee-ownership trust; or

(iv) shares in a company under the control of a company (other than a close company) whose shares are listed on a recognised stock exchange. Reference here to a close company includes a company which would be a close company if it were UK resident, but a company is not a close company for these purposes if it is subject to an employee-ownership trust.

For the purposes of (iii) and (iv) above, a company (C) is subject to an employee-ownership trust if:

- C meets the 'trading requirement' in **28.57** EMPLOYMENT INCOME;
- C meets the 'indirect employee-ownership requirement' in **28.57** EMPLOYMENT INCOME (as suitably modified by *ITEPA 2003, Sch 2 para 27(5)*);
- neither C, nor any other company in the same group, is a 'service company' as in **28.56** EMPLOYMENT INCOME (as suitably modified by *ITEPA 2003, Sch 2 para 27(6)*); and
- C is not under the control of another company (ignoring any company acting in its capacity as the trustee of the settlement by virtue of which C meets the indirect employee-ownership requirement).

Eligible shares must be fully paid up and, except in relation to shares in certain co-operatives (as defined), not redeemable (or capable of becoming redeemable). Shares are not fully paid up for this purpose if there is any undertaking to pay cash to the company at a future date.

Eligible shares must not be shares in a '*service company*', i.e. a company whose business is substantially the provision of the services of its employees either to persons, including partnerships, who control the company or to associated companies (as specially defined for this purpose). The prohibition extends to shares in certain companies which have control of service companies. '*Control*' for these purposes is determined in accordance with *CTA 2010, ss 450, 451*.

[*ITEPA 2003, s 719, Sch 2 paras 2(2), 25–30*].

Voting rights

For the purposes of (C) above, eligible shares may be shares carrying no voting rights or limited voting rights.

Provision for forfeiture

Provision for forfeiture means provision to the effect that a participant shall cease to be beneficially entitled to the plan shares on the occurrence of certain events. For the purposes of (C) above, as regards free or matching shares (see **71.27**, **71.29** above), provision may be made for forfeiture if the participant:

(1) ceases to be in relevant employment (see **71.26** above); or
(2) withdraws the shares from the plan (see **71.26** above),

within the '*forfeiture period*', i.e. a period not exceeding three years as specified in the plan and beginning with the date on which the shares were awarded (see **71.26** above) to the participant. However, shares cannot be made subject to provision for forfeiture in the event of shares ceasing to be subject to the plan for any of the reasons at **71.31**(a)–(c) above. As regards matching shares only, provision may be made for forfeiture if the participant withdraws from the plan, within the said forfeiture period, the partnership shares in respect of which the matching shares were awarded to him. Forfeiture cannot be linked to performance, and the same provision for forfeiture, if any, must apply to all free or matching shares included in the same award.

Pre-emption conditions

For the purposes of (C) above, eligible shares may be made subject to provision requiring shares awarded to an employee and held by him (or by a permitted transferee under the company's articles) to be offered for sale on his ceasing to be in relevant employment (see **71.26** above). Such provision can be made only if, under the company's articles, the same provision applies to all employees, the shares must be offered for sale at a specified price, and anyone disposing of shares of the class in question (whether or not as an employee) is required to offer them for sale on no better terms.

[*ITEPA 2003, Sch 2 paras 31–33, 99(1)*].

Company reconstructions

[71.36] For the purposes of the SIP provisions (and subject to the rules below for rights issues):

(a) a company reconstruction (see below) is treated as not involving a disposal of shares comprised in the original holding;
(b) new shares (see below) are deemed to have been awarded to (or acquired on behalf of) a participant on the date the corresponding original shares were awarded or so acquired;
(c) the requirements at **71.35** above are treated as fulfilled with respect to new shares if they were fulfilled (or treated as fulfilled) with respect to the original shares;
(d) references throughout the provisions to a participant's plan shares are to be construed as including any new shares; and
(e) the tax provisions at **71.31, 71.32** above apply to new shares as they would have applied to the original shares.

If, as part of a company reconstruction, the trustees become entitled to a capital receipt, their entitlement is deemed to arise before the new holding comes into being.

For the above purposes, a '*company reconstruction*' is a transaction in relation to any of a participant's plan shares:

(i) which results in a new holding being equated with the original holding for capital gains tax purposes (see Tolley's Capital Gains Tax under Shares and Securities); or
(ii) which would do so but for the new holding consisting of or including a qualifying corporate bond (see Tolley's Capital Gains Tax under Qualifying Corporate Bonds),

and '*new shares*' means shares, securities and rights comprised in the new holding. Certain share issues treated as distributions chargeable to income tax are treated for the purposes of these provisions as *not* forming part of the new holding.

[*ITEPA 2003, Sch 2 paras 86, 87*].

Rights issues

Subject to the exceptions below, where the trustees take up rights under a rights issue in respect of a participant's plan shares, the resulting new shares or securities or rights are treated as synonymous with the original shares. This does not apply where:

(A) the funds used to acquire the new shares etc. are provided other than by the part disposal of rights in order to take up other rights under the issue; or
(B) the rights are not conferred in respect of all ordinary shares in the company.

Where the rule is disapplied, the new shares etc. are not plan shares and do not fall to be equated with the original shares for capital gains tax purposes.

[*ITEPA 2003, Sch 2 paras 88, 99(1)*].

The plan trustees

[71.37] A SIP must provide for the establishment of a trust, constituted under UK law and consisting of UK-resident trustees, the principal duties of the trustees being to acquire shares and appropriate them as free or matching shares to employees, and to acquire partnership and dividend shares on behalf of employees, in accordance with the plan. The trustees' other duties must include:

(a) giving an employee notice of shares awarded to him and of dividend shares acquired on his behalf, such notice to include specified information;
(b) maintaining such records as may be necessary for the purposes of their own, and the employer's, plan-related PAYE obligations (see **71.31** above);
(c) (where relevant) giving a participant notice of any foreign tax deducted at source from plan share dividends from a non-UK resident company;
(d) informing a participant of the facts relevant to determining any income tax liability which he incurs under these provisions; and

(e) maintaining records of individuals who have participated in other tax-advantaged SIPs established by the same company or a connected company (see **71.33** above).

The trust instrument must require the trustees to act only at the direction of a participant as regards disposing of his plan shares and dealing with rights issues, but, except in the case of partnership shares, must also prohibit them from disposing of shares (to the participant or otherwise), except in certain specified circumstances, within the holding period for those shares (see **71.27**, **71.29**, **71.30** above), unless the participant has ceased to be in relevant employment (see **71.26** above). The plan may provide for participants' directions to be given in general terms. Subject to the above, the trustees may partly dispose of rights under a rights issue in order to raise funds to take up other rights under the issue. With certain exceptions, the trust instrument must require the trustees to account to participants for any money or money's worth received by them in respect of or by reference to plan shares.

The plan must provide for the trustees to raise funds to meet PAYE obligations on shares leaving the plan (see **71.31** above), either by disposing of a participant's plan shares (including a disposal to themselves as trustees) or by obtaining the necessary amount from the participant.

The trust instrument must not contain any terms which are neither essential nor reasonably incidental to complying with the statutory requirements. If authorised by the trust instrument, the trustees may borrow to acquire shares and for other specified purposes. The trust instrument *may* contain provision for at least half of the non-professional trustees to be selected from the employees of participating companies.

[*ITEPA 2003, Sch 2 paras 70, 71, 71A, 72–80, 99(1)*].

Tax exemption for dividends on unappropriated shares

Tax is not chargeable at the dividend trust rate (see **70.11** SETTLEMENTS) in respect of dividends or other distributions on shares held by the trustees on their own account, provided that the shares satisfy the requirements at **71.35** above as to the type of share that may be used in the plan and are awarded (see **71.26** above) (or acquired as dividend shares) within a statutory period. The period within which shares must be awarded depends on whether or not any of the shares in the company in question are 'readily convertible assets' (see **71.31** above under PAYE) at the time of the acquisition of shares by the trustees. If they are, the period is the two years from acquisition. Otherwise, it is five years from acquisition, but if within those five years any of the shares in the company become readily convertible assets the period ends no later than two years after the date on which they did so. For these purposes:

(A) shares of a particular class are deemed to be awarded by the trustees on a first in/first out basis; and
(B) shares subject to provision for forfeiture (see **71.35** above) are deemed to be acquired by the trustees if and when forfeiture occurs.

The period within which shares must be awarded is extended to ten years from acquisition if the shares are part of a significant block of shares acquired by the trustees in relation to which the employer company has been given an up-front corporation tax deduction.

[*ITA 2007, ss 488–490*].

For *capital gains tax* matters relevant to the trustees, see Tolley's Capital Gains Tax under Employee Share Schemes.

Self-certification, returns and enquiries

[71.38] In order for a SIP to be a tax-advantaged SIP under *ITEPA 2003, Sch 2*, notice of the SIP (the '*self-certification notice*') must be given to HMRC. It must be given by the company and must contain such information as HMRC may require and a declaration (that the SIP meets the statutory requirements) by such persons as HMRC may require. Once the self-certification notice is given, the SIP is a tax-advantaged SIP at all times on and after the date on which the declaration is made or, if the declaration is made later than the first award of shares, on and after the date of that award. However, if the self-certification notice is given after the 'initial notification deadline', the SIP is a tax-advantaged SIP only from the beginning of the 'relevant tax year', unless the company can show that it had a reasonable excuse for missing the deadline. The company can appeal within 30 days against a decision of HMRC that it had no reasonable excuse; for more on 'reasonable excuse', see below under Annual returns.

The '*initial notification deadline*' is 6 July in the tax year following that in which the first award of shares is made. The '*relevant tax year*' is the tax year in which the self-certification notice is given or, if that notice is given on or before 6 July in that tax year, the previous tax year.

The self-certification notice, and any information accompanying it, must be given electronically but, if they consider it appropriate to do so, HMRC may allow the company to give the notice etc. in another way.

[*ITEPA 2003, Sch 2 paras 81A, 81D(1)(3)(4), 81K(A1)(6)(7)(10); FA 2016, Sch 3 para 3*].

Annual returns

The company must make a return for each tax year, starting with the year in which falls the date on which the plan becomes a tax-advantaged SIP. The return for a tax year must contain such information as HMRC may require, and must be filed on or before 6 July in the following tax year. If during a tax year an alteration is made in a 'key feature' of the SIP or the plan trust, the return for that year must contain a declaration, made by such persons as HMRC may require, that the alteration has not caused the statutory requirements to fail to be met in relation to the SIP. For this purpose a '*key feature*' is a provision of the SIP or plan trust which is necessary in order for those requirements to be met. If the company becomes aware of any error, omission or inaccuracy in a return, it must make an amended return without delay. A return is not required for any tax year following that in which the 'termination condition' is met; the '*termination condition*' is met when a plan termination notice (see **71.40** below) has been issued in relation to the SIP and the trustees have completed their resulting statutory obligations.

A return must be made, and any accompanying information must be given, electronically. However, if they consider it appropriate to do so, HMRC may allow a company to make a return or give any accompanying information in another way.

If a company fails to make a return by the due date, it is liable for a penalty of £100. If the failure continues for more than three months beginning with the due date, the company is liable for a further penalty of £300. If the failure continues for another three months, another £300 penalty is incurred. If it continues for nine months in all, HMRC may, upon giving notice, charge a daily penalty of £10. The notice must specify the period in respect of which the penalty is payable; this period may begin earlier than the date on which the notice is given but cannot begin until after the end of the said nine-month period or, if relevant, after the end of any period specified in any previous notice given by HMRC in relation to the same failure. Liability for a penalty does not arise if the company satisfies HMRC (or, on appeal, the Tribunal) that there is a reasonable excuse. Reasonable excuse does not include insufficiency of funds (unless attributable to events outside the company's control) or reliance on another person (unless the company took reasonable care to avoid the failure); a failure must be remedied without unreasonable delay after a reasonable excuse ceases.

If a return contains a material inaccuracy which is either careless or deliberate or is not corrected by an amended return upon the company's becoming aware of it, the company is liable for a penalty of up to £5,000. The same applies if a return is not made electronically where required.

[*ITEPA 2003, Sch 2 paras 81B, 81C, 81D(2)–(4), 81E*].

For assessment of penalties, see *ITEPA 2003, Sch 2 para 81J*. An appeal may be made against the imposition and/or the amount of penalties. Notice of appeal must be given to HMRC no later than 30 days after the date of the notice of assessment of the penalty. For these and other matters related to appeals, see *ITEPA 2003, Sch 2 para 81K*.

Enquiries

HMRC may open an enquiry into a tax-advantaged SIP. They must give the company notice of their intention to do so on or before 6 July following the tax year in which falls the 'initial notification deadline' (see above). This is with the exception that if the self-certification notice is given after the initial notification deadline, HMRC have until 6 July in the second tax year following the 'relevant tax year' (see above) to give the notice of enquiry. They may also enquire into the SIP if they give notice of intention to do so within twelve months after the date on which a declaration is given that an alteration made in a key feature has not caused the statutory requirements to fail to be met (see above under Annual returns).

Notwithstanding the above time limits, if at any time HMRC have reasonable grounds for believing that requirements of *ITEPA 2003, Sch 2* are not, or have not been, met in relation to the SIP, they can enquire into the SIP by giving notice of intention to do so.

The fact that the 'termination condition' may have been met in relation to the SIP (see above under Annual returns) does not prevent HMRC opening and conducting an enquiry.

An enquiry is completed when HMRC give the company a notice (a '*closure notice*') stating that they have completed the enquiry and giving the result of the enquiry. In the meantime, a company may apply to the Appeal Tribunal for a direction requiring a closure notice to be given within a specified period. The Tribunal must give a direction unless satisfied that HMRC have reasonable grounds for not giving the closure notice within the specified period.

The result of the enquiry will be either that, in HMRC's opinion, the requirements of *ITEPA 2003, Sch 2* are, and have been, met in relation to the SIP, in which case no further action is required, or that, in their opinion, those requirements are not, or have not been, met. In the latter case, HMRC will also decide how serious the situation is, based on two possible levels of seriousness (see HMRC Employee Tax Advantaged Share Scheme User Manual ETASSUM27150), and their decision must be stated in the closure notice. At the more serious level, the SIP is not to be a tax-advantaged SIP with effect from such past time as is specified in the closure notice or, if no such time is specified, from the time of the giving of the closure notice. This does not affect the operation of the SIP code in relation to shares appropriated to, or acquired on behalf of, an individual under the SIP before it ceases to be tax-advantaged. In particular, if the SIP was tax-advantaged when shares were appropriated to, or acquired on behalf of, an individual, it continues to be a tax-advantaged SIP in relation to those shares. The company will also be liable for a penalty of an amount decided by HMRC. This must not exceed an amount equal to twice HMRC's reasonable estimate of the income tax and national insurance contributions forgone due to the SIP having had tax-advantaged status whilst failing to meet the statutory requirements.

At the less serious level, the SIP retains its tax-advantaged status but the company is liable for a penalty of up to £5,000, and must, within 90 days after the 'relevant day', secure that the statutory requirements are met in relation to the SIP. The latter does not apply if the termination condition is met before the end of that 90-day period. The '*relevant day*' is the last day of the period in which notice of appeal may be given or, if notice of appeal is given, the day on which the appeal is determined or withdrawn. The period in which notice of appeal may be given is the 30 days following the closure notice. If the company then fails to secure that the statutory requirements are met, HMRC may give the company a default notice, in which case the same consequences ensue as if the company's original failure had been at the more serious level, but so ensue by reference to the default notice rather than the closure notice.

[*ITEPA 2003, Sch 2 paras 81F–81I, 81K(6)*].

For assessment of penalties, see *ITEPA 2003, Sch 2 para 81J*. An appeal may be made against the amount of any penalty. Notice of appeal must be given to HMRC no later than 30 days after the date of the notice of assessment of the penalty. Appeal may also be made against the result of the enquiry, a time specified in the closure notice or the absence of any such time, a decision to issue a default notice, and a time specified in the default notice or the absence of any such time. Notice of appeal must be given to HMRC within 30 days after the date of the closure notice or default notice. For these and other matters related to appeals, see *ITEPA 2003, Sch 2 para 81K*.

HMRC information powers

HMRC have wide-ranging powers to require any person to furnish them with such information as they reasonably require and as that person possesses or can reasonably obtain. The information must be supplied within a period specified in the notice, which must not be less than three months. Penalties under *TMA 1970, s 98* can be imposed for non-compliance. [*ITEPA 2003, Sch 2 para 93*].

Simon's Taxes. See **E4.542, E4.542A, E4.542B.**

Disqualifying events

[71.39] A SIP ceases to be a tax-advantaged plan if (and with effect from the time when) a 'disqualifying event' occurs, where such event occurs on or after 15 September 2016. A '*disqualifying event*' could be:

(a) an alteration in the share capital of a company any of whose shares are subject to the plan, or in the rights attaching to any shares of such a company, where the alteration materially affects the value of the shares subject to the plan; or
(b) any shares of a class subject to the plan receiving different treatment from the other shares of that class.

The different treatment referred to in (b) above could in particular be in respect of dividends payable, repayment or any offer of substituted or additional shares, securities or rights in respect of the shares; but (b) is not brought into play where the difference in treatment arises from a 'key feature' of the plan or from any of the participants' shares being subject to any restriction. For this purpose a '*key feature*' is a provision of the SIP which is necessary in order for the statutory requirements to be met. If newly-issued shares receive, in respect of dividends payable for a period beginning before the issue date, treatment less favourable than that accorded to pre-existing shares, this does not in itself cause a disqualifying event to occur.

The occurrence of a disqualifying event does not affect the operation of the SIP code in relation to shares awarded to participants before the event; the SIP continues to be a tax-advantaged plan in relation to those shares.

[*ITEPA 2003, Sch 2 para 85A; FA 2016, Sch 3 para 2(3)(4)*].

Termination of plan

[71.40] A SIP may provide for the company to terminate the plan in such circumstances as the plan may specify. This is accomplished by the issue of a plan termination notice, a copy of which must be given without delay to the plan trustees and each individual who has plan shares or has entered into a current partnership share agreement. Any money held on an individual's behalf by the plan trustees must be paid over to him as soon as practicable after the plan termination notice is issued. Plan shares must be removed from the plan as soon as practicable after the end of three months following the distribution of the plan termination notice or, if later, after the first date on which they may be removed without giving rise to an income tax charge (see **71.31** above). Shares may be removed earlier with the consent of the participant (or, after his death, his personal representatives). The trustees can remove shares from the plan either by transferring them to, or at the direction of, the participant (or his personal representatives) or by disposing of them and similarly accounting for the proceeds.

[*ITEPA 2003, Sch 2 paras 89, 90*].

Enterprise Management Incentives (EMI)

[71.41] 'Small higher risk' trading companies are able to grant options over shares worth (at time of grant) up to £250,000 to eligible employees without income tax consequences (except to the extent that the option is to acquire shares at less than their market value at time of grant). The total value of shares in respect of which unexercised options exist must not exceed £3 million. Any gain on the disposal of the shares by the employee is chargeable to capital gains tax; the gain may be eligible for capital gains tax business asset disposal relief (previously known as entrepreneurs' relief) (see **71.43** below).

The company may be quoted or unquoted but must be an independent company trading or preparing to trade whose gross assets do not exceed £30 million and which has less than 250 full-time employees. The company must have a permanent establishment in the UK. A company carrying on certain specified activities does not qualify (see **71.45**(a)–(m) below). Broadly, an employee is eligible if he is employed by the company for at least 25 hours per week or, if less, at least 75% of his total working time, and he controls no more than 30% of the company's ordinary share capital. Companies must give notice of the grant of an option to HMRC within 92 days after it is granted (see **71.49** below).

[*ITEPA 2003, ss 527–541, Sch 5*].

HMRC will on request give written advance assurance that a company will be a qualifying company for these purposes, though not about any other aspect of the scheme. Applications should be made in writing to Venture Capital Relief Team, HM Revenue and Customs, WMBC, BX9 1BN (email enterprise.centre@hmrc.gsi.gov.uk) and must be accompanied by all relevant information, including latest accounts, memorandum and articles, and details of trading activities, covering in each case the company and each of its subsidiaries.

EU State aid approval for the EMI scheme expired on 6 April 2018 but has subsequently been renewed (Employment Related Securities Bulletin No. 28, May 2018). HMRC will treat share options granted during the hiatus between 7 April and 15 May 2018 as qualifying under the scheme. HMRC will also waive the three-year limit under the maximum entitlement rules at **71.42** below if a company cancelled options granted during the hiatus and wishes to grant them again (Employment Related Securities Bulletin No. 30, October 2018).

See HMRC Employee Tax Advantaged Share Scheme User Manual at ETASSUM50000 *et seq.*

Providing of State aid information

A claim made on or after 11 July 2018 for exemptions and reliefs in connection with EMI share options must include any information required by HMRC for the purpose of complying with certain EU State aid obligations. This may include information about the claimant (or his activities), information about the subject-matter of the claim and other information relating to the grant of State aid through the provision of the exemptions and reliefs. See **36.5** HMRC — CONFIDENTIALITY OF INFORMATION as regards the publishing by HMRC of State aid information. [*FA 2016, s 180(1)–(4), Sch 24 Pt 1; SI 2018 No 737*].

Simon's Taxes. See **E4.543–E4.551.**

Qualifying options

[71.42] A qualifying option is an option (i.e. a right to acquire shares) in relation to which the general requirements below and the further requirements at **71.44–71.47** below are met at the time it is granted, and of which notice is given to HMRC as in **71.49** below. [*ITEPA 2003, s 527, Sch 5 para 1*].

The option must be granted for commercial reasons in order to recruit or retain an employee in a company, and not as part of a tax avoidance scheme or arrangement. It must be granted to the employee by reason of his employment with the '*relevant company*' (i.e. the company whose shares are the subject of the option) or, if the relevant company is a parent company, his employment with that company or another member of the group. See **71.44** below as to qualifying companies and **71.46** below as to eligible employees. See **71.47** below for requirements as to the terms of the option, including the type of share that may be acquired.

The total value (see below) of shares in the relevant company in respect of which unexercised qualifying options exist must not exceed £3 million. If the limit is already exceeded at the time an option is granted, that option is not a qualifying option. If the grant of an option causes the limit to be exceeded, that option is not a qualifying option so far as it relates to the excess. For this purpose, where more than one option is granted simultaneously, the excess is divided *pro rata* between them according to the value of shares which each represents.

Maximum entitlement

An employee cannot at any time hold unexercised qualifying options in respect of shares with a total value (see below) of more than **£250,000.** If the limit is already exceeded at the time an option is granted, that option is not a qualifying option. If the grant of an option causes the limit to be exceeded, that option is not a qualifying option so far as it relates to the excess. Where an employee has been granted qualifying options in respect of shares with a total value of £250,000, then, whether or not those options remain unexercised (and disregarding any release of options), no further *qualifying* option may be granted to him within three years after the date of grant of the last qualifying option. If, at the time an option is granted under these provisions, the employee holds unexercised options under a tax-advantaged CSOP scheme (as in **71.55** below), those options count towards the limit as if they were qualifying options.

The £250,000 limit is a global limit covering options granted by reason of employment with one company or with any number of companies in the same group. The legislation is framed to prevent the above provisions being circumvented if options are granted to an individual by reference to his employment with different companies within a group.

For the above purposes, the value of shares is the market value (determined as for capital gains tax purposes), *at the time the option is granted*, of shares of the same class, and an option is treated as granted in respect of the maximum number of shares that may be acquired under it. Where the market value of shares on any date falls to be determined for any purpose of these provisions, HMRC and the employer company may agree that it be determined by reference to a different date or a number of specified dates. If market value is not agreed between HMRC and the employer company, HMRC have power to determine it. The employer company may appeal within 30 days against a notice of determination (see also **71.52** below as regards compliance with time limits). Alternatively, the company may, by notice to HMRC before a notice of determination is given, refer the question of market value to the Appeal Tribunal, who must then determine it in like manner as on appeal. In arriving at the market value of restricted shares as in **71.4** above, the restrictions (or risk of forfeiture) are disregarded.

[*ITEPA 2003, Sch 5 paras 1(3)(d), 2–7, 54–57*].

A company can ask HMRC Shares and Assets Valuation to agree a valuation before an option is granted (HMRC Employee Tax Advantaged Share Scheme User Manual ETASSUM51040). Valuations are normally valid for 90 days from the date of the agreement, but see the COVID-19 special measure below. For detailed guidance on valuation for these purposes, see HMRC Shares and Assets Valuation Manual SVM110050.

COVID-19 special measure

The 2020 COVID-19 (coronavirus) pandemic may lead to delays in granting EMI options which then breach the above-mentioned 90-day period for which a valuation remains valid. Provided that there has been no change that may affect an appropriate value, any new EMI valuation agreement letter issued by HMRC on or after 1 March 2020 will be valid for 120 days. Any EMI valuation agreement letters already issued, where the 90-day period expires on or after 1 March 2020, can be automatically treated as being extended by 30 days. (Employment Related Securities Bulletin No. 35, June 2020).

See **71.49** below re possibility and consequences of HMRC enquiry into an option.

Tax consequences of qualifying option

[71.43] No income tax is chargeable on the *receipt* of a qualifying option. The *exercise* of a qualifying option attracts the following special treatment (but only if it occurs within ten years after the time of the grant). Subject to any disqualifying event (see below), no income tax charge arises under **71.16** above on the exercise of a qualifying option to acquire shares at not less than their market value at the time of the grant. On the exercise of a qualifying option to acquire shares at nil cost or otherwise at less than their market value at the time of the grant, an amount is chargeable under **71.16** above, but is limited (if it would otherwise be greater) to the excess of the 'chargeable market value' over the aggregate of any consideration given for the option itself and (if any) the amount for which the shares are acquired. If there is no such excess, no charge arises. The '*chargeable market value*' is the lower of:

(a) the market value of the shares at the time of grant; and
(b) the market value of the shares at the time the option is exercised.

If the shares are employee shareholder shares acquired under a pre-1 December 2016 agreement, the amount for which they are acquired is the payment (if any) which the employee is treated as having made for them (see **71.78** below).

[*ITEPA 2003, ss 419, 475, 528–531, 532(6); FA 2017, s 12(3)(5)–(7)*].

For guidance on the interaction between the above rules and the restricted shares rules at **71.4** above (where the shares acquired on exercise are restricted shares), see HMRC Employment-Related Securities Manual ERSM30470.

The notional loan provisions at **71.12** above in respect of shares acquired at less than market value do not apply in relation to shares acquired by the exercise of a qualifying option (whether or not at a discount). [*ITEPA 2003, s 540*].

Other than on *exercise* of the qualifying option, there is no exemption from the charge at **71.16** above (e.g. on release of the option). In addition, the provisions at **71.4–71.11**, **71.13** and **71.14** above all apply to shares acquired under a qualifying option as they would to other employment-related shares. However, amounts deductible in computing the chargeable amount under **71.5** above (restricted shares), i.e. in ascertaining the value of IUP in the given formula, include the amount (or additional amount) that would have been chargeable under **71.16** above on exercise if the shares had not been acquired under a qualifying option. [*ITEPA 2003, s 541*].

Disqualifying events

Where a 'disqualifying event' occurs in relation to a qualifying option before it is exercised, and the option is not exercised within 90 days after the date of that event, an amount is chargeable under **71.16** above on the eventual exercise of the option. The amount chargeable is:

- (where there would otherwise be no charge) the 'post-event gain' (if any) less any consideration given for the option itself; or
- the amount otherwise chargeable under *ITEPA 2003, s 531* (above) plus the 'post-event gain',

but not so as to substitute a greater chargeable amount than would be the case if these provisions (including *ITEPA 2003, ss 530, 531*) were disregarded. The '*post-event gain*' is the amount (if any) by which the market value of the shares on exercise exceeds their market value immediately before the disqualifying event.

Any of the following is a '*disqualifying event*' in relation to a qualifying option.

(i) The 'relevant company' (see **71.42** above) becomes a 51% subsidiary of another company or otherwise comes under the control of another company (with or without the aid of CONNECTED PERSONS (**19**)). In a case where a replacement option has been granted (see **71.48** below), such an event is not a disqualifying event in relation to the original option if it occurred during the period beginning at the same time as the period within which the replacement had to be granted and ending with the release of rights under the old option. Additionally, such an event is not a disqualifying event if the relevant company is subject to an employee-ownership trust (determined as in **71.35** above); this enables a company controlled by an employee-ownership trust to operate an EMI option scheme.

(ii) The relevant company ceases to meet the trading activities requirement (see **71.44** below).

(iii) The relevant company was a qualifying company by virtue only of its *preparing to carry on* a qualifying trade (see **71.44**, **71.45** below), and either the preparations cease or two years elapse from the date of grant without the relevant company or any company in its group commencing that trade.

(iv) The employee ceases to be an eligible employee in relation to the relevant company by reason of his ceasing to satisfy the requirements at **71.46**(a) or (b) below (and see also below as to actual working time).

(v) A variation is made of the terms of the option, the effect of which is to increase the market value of the option shares or that the statutory requirements would no longer be met in relation to the option.

(vi) An alteration of a specified kind (see *ITEPA 2003, s 537(2)*) is made to the share capital of the relevant company where the effect is either:
   - to increase the market value of the option shares, where the alteration is not made by the relevant company for commercial reasons or the said increase is one of its main purposes; or
   - that the statutory requirements would no longer be met in relation to the option.

(vii) Any of the shares to which the option relates are converted to shares of a different class. There is an exception, and subject to conditions, where all the shares of one class only are converted into shares of one other class only.

(viii) The employee is granted a CSOP option (i.e. an option under a tax-advantaged CSOP scheme — see **71.66** below) by reason of his employment with the same company or by a company in the same group as that company, *and* immediately afterwards holds unexercised 'employee options' in respect of shares with a total value of over

£250,000. For this purpose, '*employee options*' include the qualifying option in question and any other qualifying option or CSOP option granted by reason of employment with the same company or group.

In addition, a disqualifying event is treated as occurring in relation to a qualifying option *at the end of any tax year* if, during that year (disregarding any part of it before the option was granted), the average amount per week of the employee's 'reckonable time in relevant employment' was less than 25 hours or, if less, 75% of his 'working time' (as defined in **71.46**(b) below). An employee's '*reckonable time in relevant employment*' is the time he spent, as an employee in 'relevant employment' (as defined in **71.46**(b) below), on the business of the relevant company or, if it is a parent company, of its group (inclusive of any permissible periods of absence as in **71.46**(b) below).

[*ITEPA 2003, ss 419, 532–539, 718, Sch 5 paras 2, 54, Sch 7 para 78(2); FA 2016, Sch 3 para 1; FA 2017, s 12(3)(5)–(7)*].

The comments in **71.42** above regarding the market value of shares apply equally for the above purposes.

COVID-19 (coronavirus) special measure

For the purposes of determining whether a disqualifying event occurs, the various references above to **71.46**(b) (commitment of working time) are to be read, in relation to the period 19 March 2020 to 5 April 2021 inclusive, as if in **71.46**(b) any time during which, for reasons connected with COVID-19, the employee is not required to work were a permissible period of absence. The Treasury has the option to make regulations to defer the 5 April 2021 date by one year but has to exercise that option during 2020/21 if at all. [*FA 2020, s 107*]. This measure seeks to ensure that a disqualifying event does not occur purely as a result of an individual taking leave, being furloughed or working reduced hours because of the 2020 pandemic.

Capital gains tax

Any gain on the disposal by an individual of shares acquired under a qualifying option is chargeable to capital gains tax. The cost of acquisition of the shares is computed according to the rules at **71.16** above.

Chargeable gains realised on shares acquired by the exercise of qualifying options may be eligible for capital gains tax business asset disposal relief (previously known as entrepreneurs' relief). The twelve-month minimum holding period required for business asset disposal relief begins when the option is granted rather than when the shares are acquired. Throughout the twelve-month period the company must be a trading company or the holding company of a trading group and the individual must be an officer or employee. However, the normal requirement for business asset disposal relief that the individual must hold at least 5% of the company's ordinary share capital does not apply. [*TCGA 1992, s 169I(7A)–(7R)*].

For the detailed provisions, see Tolley's Capital Gains Tax.

Qualifying companies

[71.44] The company whose shares are the subject of the option must be a qualifying company. [*ITEPA 2003, Sch 5 para 1(3)(b)*]. To be a qualifying company, it must, at the time the option is granted, meet the requirements detailed below as to independence, qualifying subsidiaries, property managing subsidiaries, gross assets, number of employees, trading activities and UK permanent establishment. [*ITEPA 2003, Sch 5 paras 1(4), 8*]. The company may be quoted or unquoted, and there is no requirement that it be UK resident.

Independence

The company must not be a 51% subsidiary of another company or otherwise under the control (within *ITA 2007, s 995*) of another company, or of another company and persons connected with it (within **19** CONNECTED PERSONS). No arrangements must exist whereby the company could become such a subsidiary or fall under such control. 'Arrangements' is very broadly defined, but for this purpose any arrangements with a view to a 'qualifying exchange of shares' (see **71.48** below) are disregarded. The independence requirement is treated as met if the company is subject to an employee-ownership trust; the question of whether a company is subject to such a trust is determined as in **71.35** above. [*ITEPA 2003, ss 718, 719, Sch 5 paras 9, 58*].

Qualifying subsidiaries

If the company has subsidiaries, each 'subsidiary' must be a 'qualifying subsidiary'. A '*subsidiary*' is a company which the company controls (within *CTA 2010, ss 450, 451*), with or without the aid of CONNECTED PERSONS (**19**). A subsidiary is a '*qualifying subsidiary*' of a company (the holding company) if the following conditions are met.

The subsidiary must be a **51%** subsidiary (see *CTA 2010, Pt 24 Ch 3*) of the holding company and no person other than the holding company or another of its subsidiaries may have control (within *ITA 2007, s 995*) of the subsidiary. Furthermore, no arrangements (as very broadly defined) may exist by virtue of which either of these conditions would cease to be satisfied.

The above conditions are not regarded as ceasing to be met by reason only of the subsidiary or any other company being in the process of being wound up or by reason only of anything done as a consequence of its being in administration or receivership (both as defined by *ITA 2007, s 252*), provided the winding-up, entry into administration or receivership or anything done as a consequence of its being in administration or receivership is for commercial reasons and is not part of a tax avoidance scheme or arrangements.

The above conditions are not regarded as ceasing to be satisfied by reason only of arrangements being in existence for the disposal of the interest in the subsidiary held by the holding company (or, as the case may be, by another of its subsidiaries) if the disposal is to be for commercial reasons and is not to be part of a tax avoidance scheme or arrangements.

[*ITEPA 2003, ss 718, 719, Sch 5 paras 10, 11, 58; ITA 2007, s 989*].

Property managing subsidiaries

The company must not have a 'property managing subsidiary' which is not a 'qualifying 90% subsidiary' of the company. A '*property managing subsidiary*' is a qualifying subsidiary (see above) whose business consists wholly or mainly in the holding or managing of land or any 'property deriving its value from land' (as defined by *ITA 2007, s 188(3)* — see **4.30** ANTI-AVOIDANCE).

A company (the subsidiary) is a '*qualifying 90% subsidiary*' of another company (the holding company) if:

- the holding company possesses at least **90%** of both the issued share capital of, and the voting power in, the subsidiary;
- the holding company would be beneficially entitled to at least **90%** of the assets of the subsidiary available for distribution to shareholders on a winding-up or in any other circumstances;
- the holding company is beneficially entitled to at least **90%** of any profits of the subsidiary available for distribution to shareholders;
- no person other than the holding company has control (within *ITA 2007, s 995*) of the subsidiary; and
- no arrangements (as very broadly defined) exist by virtue of which any of the above conditions would cease to be met.

The above conditions are not regarded as ceasing to be met by reason only of the subsidiary or any other company being in the process of being wound up or by reason only of anything done as a consequence of its being in administration or receivership (both as defined by *ITA 2007, s 252*), provided the winding-up, entry into administration or receivership or anything done as a consequence of its being in administration or receivership is for commercial reasons and is not part of a tax avoidance scheme or arrangements. Nor are they regarded as ceasing to be met by reason only of arrangements being in existence for the disposal of the holding company's interest in the subsidiary if the disposal is to be for commercial reasons and is not to be part of a tax avoidance scheme or arrangements.

[*ITEPA 2003, s 719, Sch 5 paras 11A, 11B, 58*].

Gross assets

The value of the company's gross assets must not exceed £30 million. If the company is the parent company of a group, that limit applies by reference to the aggregate value of the gross assets of the group (disregarding certain assets held by any member of the group which correspond to liabilities of another member). [*ITEPA 2003, Sch 5 paras 12, 54; SI 2001 No 3799*].

See HMRC SP 2/06 (at **29.53** ENTERPRISE INVESTMENT SCHEME) for HMRC's approach to the gross assets requirement.

Number of employees

The company must have less than 250 full-time employees. If the company has qualifying subsidiaries, the company and its subsidiaries must have less than 250 full-time employees in aggregate. In applying this test, any employee who is not full-time is given such numerical value as is just and reasonable, so that, for example, two employees each working half the normal hours would count as one full-time employee. Directors are employees for these purposes; but employees on maternity, paternity, shared parental or parental bereavement leave are excluded, as are students on vocational training. [*ITEPA 2003, Sch 5 para 12A; Parental Bereavement (Leave and Pay) Act 2018, Sch para 48; SI 2020 No 45, Reg 2*].

Trading activities

If the company is a single company (i.e. not the parent company of a group), it must exist wholly for the purpose of carrying on one or more qualifying trades (see **71.45** below) and must actually be carrying on such a trade or preparing to do so. Purposes having no significant effect (other than in relation to incidental matters) on the extent of the company's activities are disregarded.

If the company is a parent company, the business of the group (treating the activities of the group companies, taken together, as a single business) must not consist wholly or as to a substantial part (i.e. broadly 20% — see HMRC guidance at webarchive.nationalarchives.gov.uk/20140109143644/http://www.hmrc.gov.uk/shareschemes/emi-new-guidance.htm) in the carrying on of 'non-qualifying activities', and at least one group company must satisfy the above trading activities requirement for a single company. '*Non-qualifying activities*' means 'excluded activities' (as in **71.45** below) and non-trading activities.

Purposes for which a company exists are disregarded to the extent that they consist of:

(i) (as regards a single company) the holding and managing of property used by the company for one or more qualifying trades carried on by it; or
(ii) (as regards a group company) any activities within (a)–(c) below.

For the purposes of determining the business of a group, activities of a group company are disregarded to the extent that they consist of:

(a) holding shares in or securities of, or making loans to, another group company;
(b) holding and managing property used by a group company for the purposes of one or more qualifying trades carried on by a group company; or
(c) incidental activities of a company which meets the above trading activities requirement for a single company.

[*ITEPA 2003, Sch 5 paras 13, 14, 58*].

UK permanent establishment

The company must have a 'permanent establishment' in the UK. If the company is the parent company of a group, the requirement is treated as met if any other member of the group meets the trading activities requirement above and has a permanent establishment in the UK. [*ITEPA 2003, Sch 5 para 14A*].

'*Permanent establishment*' has the same meaning as in *CTA 2010, ss 1141–1153*. [*ITA 2007, s 1007A*].

Informal clearance

Enquiries from companies as to whether they meet the conditions of the EMI scheme should be directed to Venture Capital Relief Team, HM Revenue and Customs, WMBC, BX9 1BN (email. enterprise.centre@hmrc.gsi.gov.uk).

Qualifying trades

[71.45] A trade is a qualifying trade (see the trading activities requirement at **71.44** above) if:

(i) it is conducted on a commercial basis and with a view to profit;
(ii) it does not consist wholly or as to a 'substantial' part in the carrying on of 'excluded activities' (see below).

'*Substantial*' in (ii) above is not defined, but in its application to similar legislation is taken by HMRC to mean 20% or more of total activities (see **29.59** ENTERPRISE INVESTMENT SCHEME).

Activities of 'research and development' from which it is intended that a 'connected qualifying trade' will be derived or will benefit are treated as a notional qualifying trade, but preparing to carry on such activities is not treated as preparing to carry on a qualifying trade. A '*connected qualifying trade*' is a qualifying trade carried on either by the company carrying out the research and development or, where applicable, by another member of the group. '*Research and development*' is as defined by *ITA 2007, s 1006* (see **75.113** TRADING INCOME).

'*Excluded activities*' are as follows:

(a) dealing in land, commodities or futures, or in shares, securities or other financial instruments;
(b) dealing in goods otherwise than in an ordinary trade of wholesale or retail distribution (see further below);
(c) banking, insurance, money-lending, debt-factoring, hire purchase financing or other financial activities;
(d) leasing (including letting ships on charter or other assets on hire) or receiving royalties or licence fees (see further below);
(e) providing legal or accountancy services;
(f) property development (see further below);
(g) farming or market gardening;
(h) holding, managing or occupying woodlands, any other forestry activities or timber production;
(i) shipbuilding (defined by reference to relevant EU State aid rules);
(j) producing coal or steel (both defined by reference to relevant EU State aid rules and including the extraction of coal);
(k) operating or managing hotels or comparable establishments (including guest houses, hostels and other establishments whose main purpose is to offer overnight accommodation with or without catering) or property used as such (see further below);

(l) operating or managing nursing homes or residential care homes (both as defined) or property used as such (see further below);

(m) providing services or facilities for any business consisting to a substantial extent of activities within (a)–(k) above and carried on by another person, where a person (other than a parent of the service provider company) has a controlling interest (see below) in both that business and the business of the service provider company.

The exclusions at (j) and (k) above apply only if the person carrying on the activity has an estate or interest (e.g. a lease) in the property concerned or occupies that property.

As regards the application of (d) above, a trade is not excluded from being a qualifying trade solely because it consists to a substantial extent in the receiving of royalties or licence fees substantially (in terms of value) attributable to the exploitation of 'relevant intangible assets'. An intangible asset is an asset falling to be treated as such under generally accepted accounting practice (see **75.21** TRADING INCOME). A '*relevant intangible asset*' is an intangible asset the whole or greater part of which (in terms of value) has been created by the 'relevant company' (see **71.42** above) or by a company which was a 'qualifying subsidiary' (within **71.44** above) of the relevant company throughout the period during which it created the whole or greater part of the asset. The definition also includes an intangible asset the whole or greater part of which was created by a company when it was not a qualifying subsidiary of the relevant company, provided it subsequently became a qualifying subsidiary under a particular type of company reconstruction. Where the asset is 'intellectual property', it is treated as created by a company only if the right to exploit it vests in that company (alone or with others). The term '*intellectual property*' incorporates patents, trade marks, copyrights, design rights etc. and foreign equivalents.

As regards (b), (d), (e), (f), (g) and (m) above, the additional comments in **29.59** ENTERPRISE INVESTMENT SCHEME, on the similar list of exclusions there, apply equally to the above provisions.

[*ITEPA 2003, Sch 5 paras 15–23, 58*].

Eligible employees

[71.46] The individual to whom the option is granted must be an eligible employee in relation to the 'relevant company' (see **71.42** above). An individual is an eligible employee in relation to the relevant company if he satisfies the following three requirements at the time the option is granted.

(a) **Employment.** He must be an employee of that company or, if it is a parent company, of that company or a qualifying subsidiary (see **71.44** above).

(b) **Commitment of working time.** The average amount per week of his 'committed time' must be at least 25 hours or, if less, 75% of his 'working time'. (See **71.45** above for disqualifying event where *actual* working time falls below this average.) His '*committed time*' is the time he is required, as an employee in 'relevant employment', to spend on the business of the relevant company or, if it is a parent company, of its group (inclusive of certain permissible periods of absence, for example through ill-health, pregnancy, childbirth, maternity or paternity leave, shared parental leave, parental bereavement leave or parental leave, reasonable holiday entitlement, gardening leave etc.) His '*working time*' is time spent on 'remunerative work' as an employee or self-employed person (including the same permissible periods of absence). '*Remunerative work*' means work undertaken to produce income taxable as employment income or trading income (or which would be so taxable if the employee were UK resident and the remittance basis did not apply). An employee is in '*relevant employment*' if he is employed by the relevant company or, if it is a parent company, by any company in its group.

See also the COVID-19 (coronavirus) special measure at **71.43** above.

(c) **Material interest test.** He must not have a 'material interest' in the company or, where applicable, in any of its subsidiaries. For these purposes, an individual has a '*material interest*' in a company if he, and/or certain 'associates' of his (within *ITEPA 2003, Sch 5 paras 31–33*):

   (i) beneficially owns or controls (directly or indirectly) more than 30% of ordinary share capital (as defined by *ITA 2007, s 989*); or

   (ii) (where the company is a close company, or would be but for its being non-UK resident or having a stock exchange quotation) possesses or is entitled to acquire rights to more than 30% of the assets available for distribution among the participators (within *CTA 2010, s 454*) in a winding-up or in any other circumstances.

   Rights to acquire shares must be taken into account (in accordance with *ITEPA 2003, Sch 5 para 30*, though see below as regards qualifying options). Shares or rights held by trustees of a tax-advantaged share incentive plan (see **71.25** above) and *not* appropriated to, or acquired on behalf of, any individual are disregarded.

   In applying the material interest test, no account is taken of shares that the individual may acquire under a qualifying option, although account *is* taken of shares already so acquired.

[*ITEPA 2003, Sch 5 para 1(3)(c), (4), paras 24–33, 59, Sch 7 para 87; Parental Bereavement (Leave and Pay) Act 2018, Sch para 48; SI 2020 No 45, Reg 2*].

Requirements as to terms of option etc.

[71.47] An option is not a qualifying option unless all the requirements set out below are met at the time of grant. [*ITEPA 2003, Sch 5 para 34*].

The *shares that can be acquired* under the option must be fully paid up shares forming part of the 'ordinary share capital' (within *ITA 2007, s 989* of the 'relevant company' (see **71.42** above), and must be neither redeemable nor capable of becoming redeemable. Shares are not fully paid up for this purpose if there is any undertaking to pay cash to the company at a future date. [*ITEPA 2003, Sch 5 paras 35, 59*].

The option must be *capable of being exercised within ten years* beginning with the date of grant. If the exercise of the option is dependent on conditions being fulfilled, it is treated as so capable if the conditions may be fulfilled within those ten years. [*ITEPA 2003, Sch 5 para 36*].

The option must take the form of a *written agreement* between the person granting the option and the employee, which states:

(a) the date on which the option is granted;
(b) that it is granted under *ITEPA 2003, Sch 5*;
(c) the number, or maximum number, of shares that may be acquired;
(d) the price (if any) for which the shares may be acquired, or the method by which that price is to be determined;
(e) when and how the option may be exercised;
(f) any conditions, e.g. performance conditions, affecting the employee's entitlement; and
(g) details of any restrictions attaching to the shares.

[*ITEPA 2003, Sch 5 para 37*].

Non-assignability of rights

The terms on which the option is granted must prohibit the grantee from transferring any of his rights under it. The terms *may* permit the option to be exercised within up to one year after the grantee's death. [*ITEPA 2003, Sch 5 para 38*].

Replacement options

[71.48] A company (the acquiring company) which obtains control (within *ITA 2007, s 995*) of a company whose shares are subject to an as yet unexercised qualifying option (as a result of a general offer to acquire the whole of its issued share capital or all the shares of the same class as those to which the option relates) may grant to the holder of a qualifying option (by agreement with him, and in consideration of his releasing his rights under the option) equivalent rights (a '*replacement option*') relating to shares in the acquiring company. It does not matter if the general offer is made to different shareholders by different means; also the reference to the whole of the issued share capital or all the shares of the same class is amended to specifically exclude any capital/shares already held by the offeror or a person connected with the offeror. The replacement option must be granted within six months after the acquiring company obtains control and any condition subject to which the offer is made is satisfied. The replacement is a qualifying option only if the requirements listed below are met.

The same applies where the acquiring company obtains such control in pursuance of a compromise or arrangement with creditors and members which is sanctioned by the court under *Companies Act 2006, s 899* (or earlier equivalent) (in which case the replacement option must be granted within six months after the acquiring company obtains control) or becomes bound or entitled to acquire shares (of the same class as those to which the option relates) under *Companies Act 2006, ss 979–982* or *ss 983–985* (in which case the replacement option must be granted within the period during which the acquiring company remains so bound or entitled). The added reference to *Companies Act 2006, ss 983–985* is intended to preserve the tax advantages of EMI options where minority shareholders exercise so-called tag-along rights i.e. rights in a takeover to have their share options acquired by the offeror company and exchanged for share options in that company.

The above also applies where the acquiring company obtains all the shares of the company (the old company) whose shares are subject to such an option as a result of a 'qualifying exchange of shares' (in which case the replacement option must be granted within six months after the acquiring company obtains control). A '*qualifying exchange of shares*' means arrangements whereby the old company becomes a wholly-owned subsidiary of a new holding company (the new company) by means of an exchange of shares. All the following conditions must be met (and for these purposes, references to 'shares', other than to 'subscriber shares', include references to securities).

(1) The consideration for the shares in the old company (the old shares) must consist wholly of the issue of shares (new shares) in the new company.
(2) The new shares must be issued only at times when the new company has no issued shares other than subscriber shares (and any new shares already issued in consideration of old shares).
(3) The consideration for new shares of each description must consist wholly of old shares of the corresponding description (i.e. shares of equivalent class and carrying equivalent rights).
(4) New shares of each description must be issued to holders of old shares of the corresponding description in respect of, and in proportion to, their holdings.
(5) The exchange of shares must not fall to be treated as a disposal and acquisition for capital gains tax purposes.

Requirements for replacement option to be a qualifying option

The replacement option is itself a qualifying option if it is granted to the holder of the old option by reason of his employment with the acquiring company or with a member of a group of which it is the parent company, and:

(a) at the time of the release of rights under the old option:
  - (i) the replacement option is granted for the reasons given in **71.42** above;
  - (ii) the limit on the total value of unexercised qualifying options (previously the limit of 15 on the number of employees holding qualifying options) (see **71.42** above) is met in relation to the replacement option;
  - (iii) the requirements in **71.44** above as to independence and trading activities are met in relation to the acquiring company;
  - (iv) the individual to whom the replacement option is granted is an eligible employee (see **71.46** above) in relation to the acquiring company; and
  - (v) the requirements at **71.47** above (terms of option etc.) are met in relation to the replacement option;

(b) the total market value, immediately before the release, of shares which were subject to the old option is equal to the total market value, immediately after the grant of the replacement option, of the shares in respect of which it is granted; and
(c) the total amount payable by the employee for shares under the option remains the same.

General

For the purposes of the EMI provisions, a replacement option which is a qualifying option is treated as if granted on the date the original option was granted. (This does not apply for the purposes of the 'notice of grant' provisions at **71.49** below — Revenue Share Focus Newsletter December 2003 pp 8, 9.) Such a replacement option may be replaced by a further replacement option if one of the above circumstances and the above qualifying requirements are again satisfied. For the purpose of applying the monetary tests at **71.42** above, the value of the shares in the acquiring company that are subject to a replacement option is taken to be equal to the value of the shares that were subject to the old option immediately before the release of rights under the old option (or the appropriate proportion of that value in a case where the replacement option has been partially exercised).

[*ITEPA 2003, s 719, Sch 5 paras 39–43; FA 2016, Sch 3 para 8*].

Notice of grant of option

[71.49] Notice of the grant of an option must be given to HMRC by the employer company within 92 days after the option is granted, failing which the option is not a qualifying option (see **71.42** above). The notice must contain, or be supported by, such information as HMRC may require for the purpose of determining whether the statutory requirements of *ITEPA 2003, Sch 5* are met. It must also contain a declaration by a director or the company secretary (of the employer company) that the statutory requirements are met in relation to the option and that the information provided is to the best of that person's knowledge correct and complete. That declaration must also state that the individual to whom the option has been granted has made and signed a written declaration that he meets the requirement at **71.46**(b) above as to commitment of working time, and must further state that the employee's declaration is held by the employer company. The employer company must give a copy of the employee's declaration to the employee within seven days after the employee has signed it, and must retain the original. It must, if requested to do so by an officer of HMRC, produce the original to such an officer within seven days after the request is made. A company may be liable for a penalty of £500 if it fails to comply with one or both of these requirements regarding the employee's declaration. For assessment of penalties, see *ITEPA 2003, Sch 5 para 57D*. For rights of appeal, and matters related to appeals, see *ITEPA 2003, Sch 5 para 57E*.

The notice, and any information supporting it, must be given electronically but, if they consider it appropriate to do so, HMRC may allow the employer company to give the notice etc. in another way. HMRC may correct obvious errors or omissions in the notice. They must give notice of such correction to the employer company within nine months after the notice of grant is given, and the company may give notice to HMRC rejecting the correction within three months from the date of issue of the notice of correction.

Enquiries

Where notice of grant of an option is given as above, HMRC may:

(a) enquire into the option, by giving the employer company notice of enquiry; and/or
(b) enquire into the employee's commitment of working time, in which case notice of enquiry must be given to the employee, with a copy to the employer company.

In either case, notice of enquiry must normally be given no later than twelve months after the end of the period within which notice of the grant of the option must be given (see above), but it may be given at any time if HMRC *discover* that any of the information provided was false or misleading in a material respect. In the absence of such discovery, no more than one enquiry can be made under either of (a) or (b) above.

While an enquiry under (a) above remains open, the employer company may apply to the Appeal Tribunal for a direction that it be closed within a specified period, such application to be heard and determined in the same way as an appeal. The Tribunal must give such a direction unless satisfied that HMRC have reasonable grounds for keeping the enquiry open. On completion of the enquiry, HMRC must issue a 'closure notice' informing the company that the enquiry is complete and stating their decision as to whether the statutory requirements are met in relation to the option. If that decision is negative, HMRC must also notify the employee. The employer company may appeal, within 30 days after a closure notice is given, against an HMRC decision that the statutory requirements have not been met or that notice of grant was not properly given. These provisions also apply, with appropriate modifications, to an enquiry under (b) above.

In the absence of an enquiry, the option can be taken to be a qualifying option. In the event of an enquiry, HMRC's decision, as stated in the closure notice, is conclusive, subject to any appeal and, where the option has been found to be a qualifying option, to any further enquiry as a result of an HMRC discovery (see above).

[*ITEPA 2003, Sch 5 paras 1(4), 44–50, 57A*].

See also **71.52** below as regards compliance with time limits.

Simon's Taxes. See E4.552.

Annual returns

[71.50] A company whose shares are (or have been) subject to qualifying options must make a return for each tax year falling (wholly or partly) in the company's 'qualifying option period'. The '*qualifying option period*' is the period beginning when the first qualifying option to which the company's shares are subject is granted and ending when the 'termination condition' is met. The '*termination condition*' is met when the company's shares are no longer subject to, and will no longer become subject to, qualifying options. The return for a tax year must contain, or be accompanied by, such information as HMRC may require, and must be made on or before 6 July in the following tax year. If the company becomes aware of any error, omission or inaccuracy in a return, it must make an amended return without delay.

A return must be made, and any accompanying information must be given, electronically. However, if they consider it appropriate to do so, HMRC may allow a company to make a return or give any accompanying information in another way.

Penalties

If a company fails to make a return by the due date, it is liable for a penalty of £100. If the failure continues for more than three months beginning with the due date, the company is liable for a further penalty of £300. If the failure continues for another three months, another £300 penalty is incurred. If it continues for nine months in all, HMRC may, upon giving notice, charge a daily penalty of £10. The notice must specify the period in respect of which the penalty is payable; this period may begin earlier than the date on which the notice is given but cannot begin until after the end of the said nine-month period or, if relevant, after the end of any period specified in any previous notice given by HMRC in relation to the same failure. Liability for a penalty does not arise if the company satisfies HMRC (or, on appeal, the Tribunal) that there is a reasonable excuse. Reasonable excuse does not include insufficiency of funds (unless attributable to events outside the company's control) or reliance on another person (unless the company took reasonable care to avoid the failure); a failure must be remedied without unreasonable delay after a reasonable excuse ceases.

If a return contains a material inaccuracy which is either careless or deliberate or is not corrected by an amended return upon the company's becoming aware of it, the company is liable for a penalty of up to £5,000. The same applies if a return is not made electronically where required.

For assessment of penalties, see *ITEPA 2003, Sch 5 para 57D*. An appeal may be made against the imposition and/or the amount of penalties. Notice of appeal must be given to HMRC no later than 30 days after the date of the notice of assessment of the penalty. For these and other matters related to appeals, see *ITEPA 2003, Sch 5 para 57E*.

[*ITEPA 2003, Sch 5 paras 52, 52A, 57B, 57C*].

See also **71.52** below as regards compliance with time limits.

Simon's Taxes. See E4.553.

HMRC information powers

[71.51] HMRC have wide-ranging powers to require any person to furnish them with such information as they reasonably require and as that person possesses or can reasonably obtain. The information must be supplied within a period specified in the notice, which must not be less than three months. Penalties can be imposed under *TMA 1970, s 98* for non-compliance. [*ITEPA 2003, Sch 5 para 51*]. See also **71.52** below as regards compliance with time limits.

Compliance with time limits

[71.52] For the purposes of **71.49–71.51** above and for determining market value as in **71.42** above, a person (P) is not taken to have failed to do anything within a time limit if he had a reasonable excuse and, if the excuse ceased, did it without unreasonable delay thereafter. In such circumstances, any further time limit expressed by reference to the original time limit operates by reference to the actual time of performance of the original task. It is specified that reasonable excuse does not include insufficiency of funds (unless attributable to events outside P's control) or reliance by P on another person (unless P took reasonable care to avoid the failure). [*ITEPA 2003, Sch 5 para 53*].

SAYE option schemes

[71.53] Tax-advantaged SAYE option schemes (also known as savings-related share option schemes) are covered in *ITEPA 2003, ss 516–520, Sch 3*. A company may establish a scheme for its directors and employees to obtain options to acquire shares in itself or another company without any charge to income tax on the receipt of the options and on any increase in value of the shares between the date of the option being granted and the date on which it is exercised. The shares must be paid for from the proceeds of an approved savings arrangement (see **71.57** below). Up to a limit (see **71.62**(a) below), the share option price may be set at a discount to the value of the shares at the time the option is granted, and such discount is also exempt from income tax.

Companies must self-certify that a SAYE option scheme meets the statutory requirements to be a tax-advantaged scheme; HMRC have powers of enquiry (see **71.65** below).

See Tolley's Corporation Tax as regards deductions available to the employer company for corporation tax purposes.

See generally HMRC Employee Tax Advantaged Share Scheme User Manual at ETASSUM30000 *et seq*.

Simon's Taxes. See **E4.570–E4.580**.

General

[71.54] To qualify for the favourable income tax treatment described at **71.55** below, the share option must be granted to an individual under a tax-advantaged SAYE option scheme (see **71.53** above) and by reason of his office or employment as a director or employee of a company (not necessarily the company whose shares are the subject of the option). [*ITEPA 2003, ss 516, 517*].

See **71.59** below for the statutory requirements that need to be met in order for a scheme to have tax-advantaged status. The taxation of *non-tax-advantaged* share options is covered at **71.15** above.

Income tax treatment

[71.55] No income tax liability arises in respect of the receipt of the option. [*ITEPA 2003, s 475*]. No income tax liability arises in respect of the exercise of the option if it is exercised in accordance with the scheme at a time when the scheme is a tax-advantaged scheme. The exemption on exercise does not, however, apply if the option is exercised before the third anniversary of the date of grant by virtue of the inclusion in the scheme of a non-compulsory provision within **71.62**(g) or **71.63**(b) below. The exemption on exercise does not apply if the option was granted, or is exercised, under arrangements a main purpose of which is the avoidance of tax or national insurance contributions. Where the exemption does not apply, **71.16** above (exercise of non-tax-advantaged share options) applies instead. [*ITEPA 2003, s 519(1)–(3)*].

Other than on *exercise* of the qualifying option, there is no exemption from the charge at **71.16** above (e.g. on release of the option).

Cash takeovers

No income tax liability arises in respect of the exercise of the option before the third anniversary of the date of grant on specified kinds of takeover of the company provided the individual receives cash (and no other assets) in exchange for the shares acquired by the exercise of the option. This exemption does not apply if:

- the cash takeover was in place or under consideration at the time it was decided to grant the option; or
- the avoidance of tax or national insurance contributions is a main purpose of any arrangements under which the option was granted or is exercised.

The exercise of the option must be by virtue of a provision included in the scheme under *ITEPA 2003, Sch 3 para 37* (see **71.63**(b) below). If the scheme includes a provision under *ITEPA 2003, Sch 3 para 38* (exchange of share options — see **71.64** below) in connection with the takeover, no course of action must have been open to the individual which, had it been followed, would have resulted in his making an agreement under that provision which would have prevented his acquiring the shares by the exercise of the option.

[*ITEPA 2003, s 519(3A)–(3J)*].

Capital gains tax treatment

[71.56] There is no special capital gains tax treatment on the disposal of shares acquired under a tax-advantaged SAYE option scheme and exempt from income tax on exercise of the option, except that *TCGA 1992, s 17(1)* (under which acquisitions are treated as made at their market value rather than their actual cost) is disapplied in relation to such acquisitions. [*TCGA 1992, Sch 7D paras 9, 10*]. The date of acquisition of the shares is the date the option is exercised. For details, see Tolley's Capital Gains Tax under Employee Share Schemes.

Approved savings arrangements

[71.57] In order to qualify for tax-advantaged status, a SAYE option scheme must provide for shares acquired on the exercise of options granted under the scheme to be paid for from the proceeds (including any interest or bonus added) of a 'certified SAYE savings arrangement' (within the meaning of *ITTOIA 2005, s 702* — see also **30.30**(iv) EXEMPT INCOME) which has been approved by HMRC for these purposes. The SAYE scheme must link the amount of a person's contributions under the approved savings arrangement to the total amount needed to acquire at the option price the number of shares in respect of which options are granted to him. The savings arrangement may provide for a bonus to be added in respect of a person's contributions; this is to be determined at the time the options are granted and is to be taken into account in the linking calculation.

The maximum total amount of contributions a person may make at any time to savings arrangements linked to tax-advantaged SAYE schemes cannot exceed **£500 per month**. A SAYE scheme may impose a minimum contribution, but this must not exceed £10 per month. Subject to any such minimum that may be imposed, monthly contributions of as low as £5 are permitted.

[*ITEPA 2003, Sch 3 paras 23–26*].

Interest and bonuses from the savings arrangement are exempt from income tax. [*ITTOIA 2005, s 702*]. Three- or five-year savings contracts are available. The Treasury may alter permitted levels of interest and bonuses, but not so as to affect pre-existing savings contracts.

An employee is permitted to delay the payment of up to 12 monthly contributions (and see the COVID-19 special measures below) without causing the savings arrangement to be voided. This temporary contributions holiday will put back the three or five-year maturity date of the savings contract, and the rights of option exercise linked to it, by up to 12 months. (HMRC Employee Tax Advantaged Share Scheme User Manual ETASSUM34140; Employment Related Securities Bulletin No. 29, June 2018).

COVID-19 special measures

CJRS (Coronavirus Job Retention Scheme) payments to employees furloughed during the 2020 COVID-19 (coronavirus) pandemic can constitute a salary, and SAYE contributions can be deducted from CJRS payments. For participants who find themselves unable to make monthly contributions from their salary, due to having to take unpaid leave during the pandemic, HMRC will permit payments to be made via standing order. Deductions from salary should recommence at the earliest opportunity.

Where participants are unable to contribute because they are furloughed or on unpaid leave during the pandemic, HMRC will extend the contributions holiday terms above. SAYE contracts beginning on or after 10 June 2020 will provide that monthly contributions can be postponed in excess of 12 months where the additional months are due to COVID-19. All employees with a savings contract in place on 10 June 2020 can similarly delay the payment of monthly contributions, without the need for a revised contract. All contributions holidays will delay the maturity date of the contract.

(Employment Related Securities Bulletin No. 35, June 2020).

Group schemes

[71.58] A SAYE option scheme established by a company that controls (within *ITA 2007, s 995*) one or more other companies may extend to all or any of those other companies. A scheme which so extends is a '*group scheme*' and each company to which it extends (including the parent) are '*constituent companies*'. [*ITEPA 2003, s 719, Sch 3 para 3*].

Jointly owned companies

To enable a jointly owned company to take part in a group scheme (though it cannot thereby take part in more than one), such a company, and any company under its control (within *ITA 2007, s 995*), is treated as being under the control of each of its two joint owners. A company controlled by a jointly owned company may not take part in more than one group scheme or in a different scheme to that (if any) in which the jointly owned company (or any other company controlled by it) takes part. [*ITEPA 2003, s 719, Sch 3 para 46*].

General requirements

[71.59] In order to qualify for tax-advantaged status, a SAYE option scheme must meet the statutory requirements of *ITEPA 2003, Sch 3* at **71.58, 71.58** above and **71.60–71.64** below. The purpose of the scheme must be to provide, in accordance with those statutory requirements, benefits for employees and directors in the form of share options. A scheme must not provide benefits to employees otherwise than in accordance with those statutory requirements and, in particular, must not provide cash to employees as an alternative to share options or the shares they cover. [*ITEPA 2003, Sch 3 paras 1, 4, 5*].

Eligibility of employees

[71.60] Eligible employees must include every person who:

(a) is an employee or a full-time director of the company which established the scheme or, in the case of a group scheme, a constituent company;
(b) has been such an employee or director at all times during a qualifying period, not exceeding five years; and
(c) whose earnings from the office or employment in question are (or would be if there were any) general earnings within **28.4** EMPLOYMENT INCOME (earnings for year when employee UK resident).

The scheme *must* ensure that, other than as required or authorised under the statutory provisions, no-one is eligible to participate in the scheme at a particular time unless he is at that time a director or employee of the company or, as regards a group scheme, a constituent company. It *may*, however, include part-time directors and any employees and directors whose earnings are not within (c) above and/or who do not meet the condition in (b) above.

The scheme must not contain any feature, other than as required or authorised under the statutory provisions, which is likely to discourage any description of persons within (a)–(d) above from participating. Every person within (a)–(d) above must be eligible to participate on similar terms, and those who participate must actually do so on similar terms. However, the rights of participants to obtain and exercise share options may vary according to such factors as remuneration levels and length of service. If the company which established the scheme is a member of a group (comprising for this purpose a company and any companies it controls) the scheme must not have the likely effect of conferring benefits wholly or mainly on directors or on the more highly-paid employees.

[*ITEPA 2003, Sch 3 para 2(2), paras 4–10*].

Scheme shares

[71.61] Scheme shares (i.e. the shares which may be acquired under the scheme) must be fully paid up and not redeemable and must:

(a) form part of the ordinary share capital of:
  - (i) the company which established the scheme; or
  - (ii) a company which has control (within *ITA 2007, s 995*) of that company; or
  - (iii) a member of a consortium which owns the company within (i) above or a company within (ii) above; or
  - (iv) a company which has control of a member of a consortium within (iii) above; and

(b) be either shares of a class listed on a recognised stock exchange, or shares in a company not under the control of another company, or shares in a company which is subject to an employee-ownership trust, or shares in a company under the control of a listed company (other than a company which is, or would be if UK resident, a close company). The question of whether a company is subject to an employee-ownership trust is determined as in **71.35** above. A company is not a close company for these purposes if it is subject to an employee-ownership trust.

Except where the scheme shares are in a company whose ordinary share capital consists of shares of one class only, the majority of the issued shares of the same class as the scheme shares must be either 'open market shares' or 'employee-control shares'. '*Open market shares*' are shares held by persons other than (i) persons who acquired them by virtue of their being directors or employees, or (ii) trustees for such persons, or (iii) (in the case of unlisted shares in a company under the control of a listed company — see (b) above) companies which control the company concerned or of which that company is an 'associated company' (within the meaning of *ITEPA 2003, Sch 3 para 47*). '*Employee-control shares*' are shares held by persons who are or have been directors or employees, and who are together able to control the company by virtue of their holdings.

[*ITEPA 2003, s 719, Sch 3 paras 2(2), 17–22, 48(2)*].

Share options

[71.62] A SAYE option scheme *must* meet all the following requirements.

(a) The price at which shares may be acquired under the scheme must be fixed and stated at the time the option is granted and must not be less than 80% of the market value of shares of the same class at that time or, with effect on and after 15 September 2016, at such earlier time as may be determined in accordance with guidance published by HMRC (or, with effect before that date, such earlier time as may be agreed in writing between the company and HMRC). The scheme *may* provide for (i) the stated price, or (ii) the number or description of shares that may be acquired, to be varied as necessary to take account of any variation in the share capital of which the scheme shares form part. Such variations must in particular secure that the total market value of the shares which can be acquired by the exercise of the option, and the total price at which those shares can be acquired, remain substantially the same.

It must be stated, at the time the option is granted, whether or not the shares which may be acquired by its exercise may be subject to any restriction. If so, details of the restriction must also be stated. The market value of shares subject to a restriction is to be determined as if they were not subject to the restriction.

(b) Options granted under the scheme must be non-transferable.

(c) Except as otherwise permitted under any of (d)–(g) below and **71.63** below, options granted under the scheme must not be capable of being exercised before the 'bonus date' or more than six months after it. The '*bonus date*' is the date on which the proceeds of the approved savings arrangement are due to be released to the participant; that date is taken to be, in a case where those proceeds will include the maximum bonus under the scheme, the earliest date on which that bonus is payable and, in any other case, the earliest date on which a bonus is payable.

(d) The scheme must provide that, if a participant dies before exercising his options, they can be exercised at any time on or after the date of death. However, in a case where the participant dies before the bonus date (defined as in (c) above), the options can be exercised only within the twelve months following the date of death; and in a case where the participant dies on or within six months after the bonus date, the options can be exercised only within the twelve months following that date.

(e) The scheme must provide that, if a participant 'ceases to hold scheme-related employment' (see below) because of injury, disability, redundancy or retirement, a relevant transfer within the meaning of the *Transfer of Undertakings (Protection of Employment) Regulations 2006* (*SI 2006 No 246*) or (on and after 17 July 2013 and in a case where the participant's employer company is an associated company of the scheme organiser) the company ceasing to be an associated company of the scheme organiser by reason of a change of control, the participant has six months (after so ceasing) in which to exercise his options. (This is subject to the overriding six-month rule at (c) above.)

(f) The scheme must provide that, if a participant 'ceases to hold scheme-related employment' (see below) for any reason other than those in (f) above, options granted more than three years previously either may not be exercised at all or may only be exercised within six months after so ceasing, whichever of those alternatives is specified in the scheme. (This is subject to the overriding six-month rule at (c) above.)

(g) The scheme must provide that, if a participant 'ceases to hold scheme-related employment' (see below) for any reason other than those in (f) above, options granted within the immediately preceding three years may not be exercised at all. The scheme *may*, however, permit such exercise where the scheme-related employment ceases only because it relates to a business (or part) which is transferred to a person other than an 'associated company' (within the meaning of *ITEPA 2003, Sch 3 para 47*), provided the transfer is not a relevant transfer within the meaning of the *Transfer of Undertakings (Protection of Employment) Regulations 2006*. If the scheme does permit such exercise, it must provide either that the options may be exercised within six months after the participant 'ceases to hold scheme-related employment' or that they may be exercised within six months after the participant subsequently leaves the employment for the reasons given in (f) above. (This is subject to the overriding six-month rule at (c) above.) Note that the income tax exemptions on exercise are forgone in these circumstances (see **71.55** above).

For the purposes of (e)–(g) above, a participant normally '*ceases to hold scheme-related employment*' on the date when he ceases (other than by reason of his death) to hold the office or employment by reference to which he is eligible for the scheme. If, however, he continues after that date to hold office or employment with the company that established the scheme or with any 'associated company' (within the meaning of *ITEPA 2003, Sch 3 para 35(4)*), he '*ceases to hold scheme-related employment*' not on that earlier date but on the date he ceases to hold office or employment with any company of such description.

[*ITEPA 2003, s 719, Sch 3 paras 2(2), 27–35, 48(3); FA 2016, Sch 3 para 6*].

Discretionary provisions

[71.63] A SAYE option scheme may make provision as follows.

(a) It may provide that options may be exercised within six months after the bonus date (defined as in **71.62**(c) above) if at that date the participant holds an office or employment in a company which is not a constituent company in a group scheme but which is an 'associated company' (within the meaning of *ITEPA 2003, Sch 3 para 47*) of the company that established the scheme.

(b) It may provide that options may be exercised in any of the following circumstances (in relation to the company whose shares may be obtained under the scheme) within six months after the 'relevant date'.

   (i) A person obtains control of the company as a result of making a general offer to acquire the whole of its issued share capital or of all the shares of the same class as the scheme shares. It does not matter if the general offer is made to different shareholders by different means; also the reference to the whole of the issued share capital or all the shares of the same class is amended to specifically exclude any capital/shares already held by the offeror or a person connected with the offeror (which had it been in force at the time would probably have led to a different finding in *Tailor v HMRC* FTT (TC 2614), [2013] UKFTT 199 (TC)). In this case, the '*relevant date*' is the date when the person obtains unconditional control. For this purpose, a person is treated as obtaining control of a company if he and others acting in concert obtain control of it (within *ITA 2007, s 995*).

(ii) A court sanctions, under *Companies Act 2006, s 899*, a compromise or arrangement. In this case, the '*relevant date*' is the date of the sanction.

(iii) The company passes a resolution for voluntary winding up. In this case, the '*relevant date*' is the date the resolution is passed.

(iv) There is a '*non-UK company reorganisation arrangement*', i.e. an arrangement made in relation to a company under the law of a territory outside the UK which gives effect to a reorganisation of the company's share capital by specified methods and which is approved by a resolution of the company's members. In this case, the '*relevant date*' is the date the arrangement becomes binding on the shareholders covered by it.

Heads (ii) and (iv) apply only if the compromise or arrangement affects all the ordinary share capital of the company or all the shares of the same class as the shares to which the option relates, or if it affects all the shares, or all the shares of that same class, which are held by a class of shareholders identified otherwise than by reference to their employments or directorships or their participation in a SAYE option scheme. The resolution mentioned in (iv) does not count for the purpose stated therein unless the members voting in favour represent more than 50% of the voting rights.

(c) It may provide that options may be exercised at any time when any person is bound or entitled to acquire shares in the company under *Companies Act 2006, ss 979–982* or *ss 983–985* (takeover offers: right of offeror to buy out minority shareholder etc.).

All of the above are subject to the overriding six-month rule at **71.62**(c) above. Note that the income tax exemptions on exercise are forgone in any of the above circumstances if the option is thus exercised within three years after it was granted (see **71.55** above).

Exercise within 20 days

If the scheme makes provision under (b) or (c) above it may also provide that if, in consequence of a 'relevant event', shares to which a share option relates no longer meet the requirements in **71.61** above (scheme shares), the share option may be exercised under the provision made under (b) or (c) (as the case may be) no later than 20 days after the day on which the relevant event occurs, notwithstanding that the shares no longer meet those requirements. Such provision cannot authorise the exercise of an option outside the six-month period mentioned in (b) or at a time not covered by (c). Either of the following is a '*relevant event*':

- a person obtaining control of the company as mentioned in (b)(i) above, or as a result of a compromise or arrangement within (b)(ii) or (iv); or
- a person who is bound or entitled to acquire shares in the company as mentioned in (c) above obtaining control of the company.

If the scheme makes provision under (b) or (c) above it may also provide that a share option relating to shares in a company which is exercised during the period of 20 days ending with the relevant date for the purposes of (b)(i), (ii) or (iv), or ending with the date on which any person becomes bound or entitled to acquire shares in the company as mentioned in (c), is to be treated as if it had been exercised in accordance with the provision made under (b) or (c). If the scheme makes that provision it must also provide that if an option is duly exercised in anticipation of an event occurring, but the event does not, in fact, occur during the 20 days beginning with the date of exercise, the exercise of the option is to be treated as having had no effect.

[*ITEPA 2003, s 719, Sch 3 paras 27, 36, 37, 47A*].

Exchange of share options

[71.64] A SAYE option scheme *may* provide that, if any other company (the 'acquiring company') obtains control of the company whose shares are scheme shares, or is bound or entitled to acquire shares in the company, in any of the circumstances described in **71.63**(b) above (disregarding (b)(iii)), a participant may agree with the acquiring company to release his options to acquire scheme shares in consideration of being granted options to acquire shares in the acquiring company (or in some other company falling within **71.61**(a)(ii)–(iv) above). The new share options must be equivalent to the options under the pre-existing scheme as regards their being subject to the provisions of the scheme, the manner in which they are exercisable, the total market value of shares to which they are subject and the total amount payable by the participant on exercise. The market value of shares for these purposes is to be determined using a methodology agreed by HMRC. The new options are then treated as having been granted at the time the original options were granted. The agreement must be made within six months of the acquiring company's obtaining unconditional control, or of the court's sanctioning the compromise or arrangement, or of the non-UK company reorganisation arrangement becoming binding on the shareholders covered by it, or within the period during which the acquiring company remains bound or entitled to acquire shares, whichever of these is applicable.

The market value of shares subject to a restriction is to be determined as if they were not subject to the restriction.

[*ITEPA 2003, Sch 3 paras 38, 39, 48(3)*].

Self-certification, returns and enquiries

[71.65] In order for a SAYE option scheme to be a tax-advantaged SAYE option scheme under *ITEPA 2003, Sch 3*, notice of the scheme (the '*self-certification notice*') must be given to HMRC. It must be given by the company and must contain such information as HMRC may require and a declaration (that the scheme meets the statutory requirements) by such persons as HMRC may require. Once the self-certification notice is given, the scheme is a tax-advantaged SAYE option scheme at all times on and after the date on which the declaration is made or, if the declaration is made later than the first date on which share options are granted under the scheme, on and after that date (the '*first grant date*'). However, if the self-certification notice is given after the 'initial notification deadline', the scheme is a tax-advantaged SAYE option scheme only from the beginning of the 'relevant tax year', unless the company can show that it had a reasonable excuse for missing the deadline. The company can appeal within 30 days against a decision of HMRC that it had no reasonable excuse; for more on 'reasonable excuse', see below under Annual returns.

The '*initial notification deadline*' is 6 July in the tax year following that in which the first grant date falls. The '*relevant tax year*' is the tax year in which the self-certification notice is given or, if that notice is given on or before 6 July in that tax year, the previous tax year.

The self-certification notice, and any information accompanying it, must be given electronically but, if they consider it appropriate to do so, HMRC may allow the company to give the notice etc. in another way.

[*ITEPA 2003, Sch 3 paras 2(2), 40A, 40D(1)(3)(4), 40K(A1)(5)(6)(9); FA 2016, Sch 3 para 4*].

Annual returns

The company must make a return for each tax year, starting with the year in which falls the date on which the plan becomes a tax-advantaged SAYE option scheme. The return for a tax year must contain such information as HMRC may require, and must be filed on or before 6 July in the following tax year. If during a tax year an alteration is made in a 'key feature' of the scheme, or variations are made to take account of a variation in any share capital (see **71.62**(a) above), the return for that year must contain a declaration, made by such persons as HMRC may require, that the alteration or variations have not caused the statutory requirements to fail to be met in relation to the scheme. For this purpose a '*key feature*' is a provision of the scheme which is necessary in order for those requirements to be met. If the company becomes aware of any error, omission or inaccuracy in a return, it must make an amended return without delay. A return is not required for any tax year following that in which the 'termination condition' is met; the '*termination condition*' is met when all share options granted under the scheme have been exercised, or are no longer capable of being exercised, and no more share options will be granted under the scheme.

A return must be made, and any accompanying information must be given, electronically. However, if they consider it appropriate to do so, HMRC may allow a company to make a return or give any accompanying information in another way.

If a company fails to make a return by the due date, it is liable for a penalty of £100. If the failure continues for more than three months beginning with the due date, the company is liable for a further penalty of £300. If the failure continues for another three months, another £300 penalty is incurred. If it continues for nine months in all, HMRC may, upon giving notice, charge a daily penalty of £10. The notice must specify the period in respect of which the penalty is payable; this period may begin earlier than the date on which the notice is given but cannot begin until after the end of the said nine-month period or, if relevant, after the end of any period specified in any previous notice given by HMRC in relation to the same failure. Liability for a penalty does not arise if the company satisfies HMRC (or, on appeal, the Tribunal) that there is a reasonable excuse. Reasonable excuse does not include insufficiency of funds (unless attributable to events outside the company's control) or reliance on another person (unless the company took reasonable care to avoid the failure); a failure must be remedied without unreasonable delay after a reasonable excuse ceases.

If a return contains a material inaccuracy which is either careless or deliberate or is not corrected by an amended return upon the company's becoming aware of it, the company is liable for a penalty of up to £5,000. The same applies if a return is not made electronically where required.

[*ITEPA 2003, Sch 3 paras 2(2), 40B, 40C, 40D(2)–(4), 40E*].

For assessment of penalties, see *ITEPA 2003, Sch 3 para 40J*. An appeal may be made against the imposition and/or the amount of penalties. Notice of appeal must be given to HMRC no later than 30 days after the date of the notice of assessment of the penalty. For these and other matters related to appeals, see *ITEPA 2003, Sch 3 para 40K*.

Enquiries

HMRC may open an enquiry into a tax-advantaged SAYE option scheme. They must give the company notice of their intention to do so on or before 6 July following the tax year in which falls the 'initial notification deadline' (see above). This is with the exception that if the self-certification notice is given after the initial notification deadline, HMRC have until 6 July in the second tax year following the 'relevant tax year' (see above) to give the notice of enquiry. They may also enquire into the scheme if they give notice of intention to do so within twelve months after the date on which a declaration is given that an alteration made in a key feature has not caused the statutory requirements to fail to be met (see above under Annual returns).

Notwithstanding the above time limits, if at any time HMRC have reasonable grounds for believing that requirements of *ITEPA 2003, Sch 3* are not, or have not been, met in relation to the scheme, they can enquire into the scheme by giving notice of intention to do so.

The fact that the 'termination condition' may have been met in relation to the scheme (see above under Annual returns) does not prevent HMRC opening and conducting an enquiry.

An enquiry is completed when HMRC give the company a notice (a '*closure notice*') stating that they have completed the enquiry and giving the result of the enquiry. In the meantime, a company may apply to the Appeal Tribunal for a direction requiring a closure notice to be given within a specified period. The tribunal must give a direction unless satisfied that HMRC have reasonable grounds for not giving the closure notice within the specified period.

The result of the enquiry will be either that, in HMRC's opinion, the requirements of *ITEPA 2003, Sch 3* are, and have been, met in relation to the SAYE option scheme, in which case no further action is required, or that, in their opinion, those requirements are not, or have not been, met. In the latter case, HMRC will also decide how serious the situation is, based on two possible levels of seriousness (see HMRC Employee Tax Advantaged Share Scheme User Manual ETASSUM37090), and their decision must be stated in the closure notice. At the more serious level, the scheme is not to be a tax-advantaged SAYE option scheme with effect from such past time as is specified in the closure notice or, if no such time is specified, from the time of the giving of the closure notice. If share options were granted under the scheme before the time it ceased to be tax-advantaged and are exercised at or after that time, the income tax exemption on exercise of the options (see **71.55** above) applies as if the scheme were still a tax-advantaged scheme. The company will also be liable for a penalty of an amount decided by HMRC. This must not exceed an amount equal to twice HMRC's reasonable estimate of the income tax and national insurance contributions forgone due to the scheme having had tax-advantaged status whilst failing to meet the statutory requirements.

At the less serious level, the scheme retains its tax-advantaged status but the company is liable for a penalty of up to £5,000, and must, within 90 days after the 'relevant day', secure that the statutory requirements are met in relation to the scheme. The latter does not apply if the termination condition is met before the end of that 90-day period. The '*relevant day*' is the last day of the period in which notice of appeal may be given or, if notice of appeal is given, the day on which the appeal is determined or withdrawn. The period in which notice of appeal may be given is the 30 days following the closure notice. If the company then fails to secure that the statutory requirements are met, HMRC may give the company a default notice, in which case the same consequences ensue as if the company's original failure had been at the more serious level, but so ensue by reference to the default notice rather than the closure notice.

[*ITEPA 2003, Sch 3 paras 2(2), 40F–40I, 40K(5)*].

For assessment of penalties, see *ITEPA 2003, Sch 3 para 40J*. An appeal may be made against the amount of any penalty. Notice of appeal must be given to HMRC no later than 30 days after the date of the notice of assessment of the penalty. Appeal may also be made against the result of the enquiry, a time specified in the closure notice or the absence of any such time, a decision to issue a default notice, and a time specified in the default notice or the absence of any such time. Notice of appeal must be given to HMRC within 30 days after the date of the closure notice or default notice. For these and other matters related to appeals, see *ITEPA 2003, Sch 2 para 40K*.

HMRC information powers

HMRC have wide-ranging powers to require any person to furnish them with such information as they reasonably require and as that person possesses or can reasonably obtain. The information must be supplied within a period specified in the notice, which must not be less than three months. Penalties under *TMA 1970, s 98* can be imposed for non-compliance. [*ITEPA 2003, Sch 3 para 45*].

Simon's Taxes. See E4.572, E4.572A, E4.572B.

Company Share Option Plan (CSOP) schemes

[71.66] Company share option plan (CSOP) schemes are tax-advantaged share option schemes and are covered in *ITEPA 2003, ss 521–526, Sch 4*. Unlike SAYE schemes above, CSOP schemes are discretionary schemes, in that there is no requirement to include all employees.

Companies must self-certify that a CSOP scheme meets the statutory requirements to be a tax-advantaged scheme; HMRC have powers of enquiry (see **71.77** below).

To qualify for the favourable income tax treatment on exercise described at **71.67** below, the share option must be granted to an individual under a tax-advantaged CSOP scheme and by reason of his office or employment as a director or employee of a company (not necessarily the company whose shares are the subject of the option). [*ITEPA 2003, ss 521, 522*]. The taxation of *non-tax-advantaged* share options is covered at **71.15** above.

See Tolley's Corporation Tax as regards deductions available to the employer company for corporation tax purposes.

See generally HMRC Employee Tax Advantaged Share Scheme User Manual at ETASSUM40000 *et seq*.

Simon's Taxes. See E4.581–E4.590.

Income tax treatment

[71.67] If, exceptionally, the aggregate of:

- the amount payable by the grantee, on exercise, in order to acquire the maximum number of shares that may be acquired under the option; and
- the amount or value of consideration given (if any) for the grant of the option,

is less than the market value, at the time the option is granted, of a similar quantity of issued shares of the class in question (in other words, if the option is granted at a discount), the difference is taxed as employment income of the grantee for the tax year in which the option is granted. Any amount thus taxed is deductible in computing any amount that subsequently falls to be taxed under **71.16** above (charge on exercise, assignment or release etc. of non-tax-advantaged share option), e.g. because the scheme has ceased to be tax-advantaged, or in determining the amount of any notional loan as in **71.12** above.

Except as above, no income tax liability arises in respect of the receipt of a CSOP option.

[*ITEPA 2003, ss 475, 526*].

No income tax liability arises in respect of the *exercise* of an option if it is exercised in accordance with a CSOP scheme at a time when the scheme is tax-advantaged, provided that the option is exercised no earlier than the third anniversary of the date it was granted and no later than the tenth anniversary of that date. There is an exception for options exercised within three years of grant but no later than six months after the individual ceases to be a full-time director or qualifying employee of the scheme organiser (or of a constituent company in a group scheme — see **71.69** below) because of injury, disability, redundancy or retirement (where the scheme rules allow such early exercise — see **71.75** below).

There is also an exception for options exercised within three years of grant but no later than six months after the individual ceases to be a full-time director or qualifying employee of the scheme organiser (or of a constituent company in a group scheme) because of a relevant transfer within the meaning of the *Transfer of Undertakings (Protection of Employment) Regulations 2006* (*SI 2006 No 246*) or (in the case of a group scheme where the employment in question is as a director or employee of a constituent company) because of that company ceasing to be controlled by the scheme organiser (but this does not cover a case where the constituent company was controlled by the scheme organiser by virtue of *ITEPA 2003, Sch 4 para 34* (jointly owned companies — see **71.69** below)).

The exemption on exercise does not apply if the option was granted, or is exercised, under arrangements a main purpose of which is the avoidance of tax or national insurance contributions.

Where the exemption does not apply, **71.16** above (exercise of non-tax-advantaged share options) applies instead.

[*ITEPA 2003, ss 524(1)–(2D), 525, Sch 4 para 35A*].

Other than on *exercise* of the qualifying option, there is no exemption from the charge at **71.16** above (e.g. on release of the option).

Cash takeovers

No income tax liability arises in respect of the exercise of the option before the third anniversary of the date of grant on specified kinds of takeover of the company provided the individual receives cash (and no other assets) in exchange for the shares acquired by the exercise of the option. This exemption does not apply if:

- the cash takeover was in place or under consideration at the time it was decided to grant the option; or
- the avoidance of tax or national insurance contributions is a main purpose of any arrangements under which the option was granted or is exercised.

The exercise of the option must be by virtue of a provision included in the scheme under *ITEPA 2003, Sch 4 para 25A* (see **71.75** below). If the scheme includes a provision under *ITEPA 2003, Sch 4 para 26* (exchange of share options — see **71.76** below) in connection with the takeover, no course of action must have been open to the individual which, had it been followed, would have resulted in his making an agreement under that provision which would have prevented his acquiring the shares by the exercise of the option.

[*ITEPA 2003, s 524(2E)–(2N)*].

Capital gains tax treatment

[71.68] There is no special capital gains tax treatment on the disposal of shares acquired under a tax-advantaged CSOP scheme and exempt from income tax on exercise of the option, except that:

- *TCGA 1992, s 17(1)* (under which acquisitions are treated as made at their market value rather than their actual cost) is disapplied in relation to such acquisitions; and
- where, exceptionally, an income tax charge arose on receipt of the option (see **71.67** above), the amount thus taxed forms part of the cost of acquisition of the shares for capital gains tax purposes; this applies equally if the scheme has ceased to be tax-advantaged at time of exercise or if the exercise is made otherwise than in accordance with the scheme and/or if the income tax charge arose under earlier legislation preceding **71.67** above.

[*TCGA 1992, Sch 7D paras 11–13*].

The date of acquisition of the shares is the date the option is exercised. For further detail, see Tolley's Capital Gains Tax under Employee Share Schemes.

Group schemes

[71.69] A CSOP scheme established by a company that controls (within *ITA 2007, s 995*) one or more other companies may extend to all or any of those other companies. A scheme which so extends is a '*group scheme*' and each company to which it extends (including the parent) are '*constituent companies*'. [*ITEPA 2003, s 719, Sch 4 para 3*].

Jointly owned companies

To enable a jointly owned company to take part in a group scheme (though it cannot thereby take part in more than one), such a company, and any company under its control (within *ITA 2007, s 995*), is treated as being under the control of each of its two joint owners. A company controlled by a jointly owned company may not take part in more than one group scheme or in a different scheme to that (if any) in which the jointly owned company (or any other company controlled by it) takes part. [*ITEPA 2003, s 719, Sch 4 para 34*].

General requirements

[71.70] In order to qualify for tax-advantaged status, a CSOP scheme must meet the statutory requirements of *ITEPA 2003, Sch 4* at **71.68, 71.68** above and **71.71–71.76** below. The purpose of the scheme must be to provide, in accordance with those statutory requirements, benefits for employees and directors in the form of share options. A scheme must not provide benefits to employees otherwise than in accordance with those statutory requirements and, in particular, must not provide cash to employees as an alternative to share options or the shares they cover. [*ITEPA 2003, Sch 4 paras 1, 4, 5*].

Limit on value of shares subject to options

[71.71] The scheme must provide that an individual cannot be granted options under it which would cause the value referred to below to exceed (or to further exceed) £30,000. The value in question is the aggregate market value (determined at time of grant or, where applicable, at the earlier time mentioned in **71.74** below) of the shares which the individual may acquire by exercising outstanding share options under the scheme or under any other tax-advantaged CSOP scheme established by the same company or by an 'associated company' (within the meaning of *ITEPA 2003, Sch 4 para 35*).

The market value of shares subject to a restriction is to be determined as if they were not subject to the restriction.

[*ITEPA 2003, Sch 4 paras 2(2), 6, 36(1)(3)*].

Where an option is granted that causes the £30,000 limit to be exceeded, the whole of that option (and not just the excess) becomes a non-tax-advantaged share option (Revenue Share Focus Newsletter December 2003 p 3).

Eligibility of employees

[71.72] The scheme *must* ensure that no-one is eligible to be granted share options under it at a particular time unless he is at that time a 'full-time' director or an employee (full-time or part-time) of the company or, as regards a group scheme, a constituent company. [*ITEPA 2003, Sch 4 paras 2(2), 7, 8*]. A director is treated as a 'full-time' director for these purposes if he works more than 25 hours per week for the company or, as regards a group plan, for constituent companies. See also **71.75** below.

No material interest

The scheme must ensure that an individual is not eligible to participate in the scheme if he has, or has had within the preceding twelve months, a 'material interest' in a 'close company':

- whose shares may be acquired under the scheme; or
- which has control (within *ITA 2007, s 995*) of a company whose shares may be acquired under the scheme; or
- is a member of a consortium which owns a company whose shares may be acquired under the scheme. (For this purpose, a company is a member of a consortium owning another company if it is one of a number of companies which between them beneficially own at least 75% of, and each of which beneficially owns at least 5% of, the other company's ordinary share capital.)

For these purposes, an individual has a '*material interest*' in a company if he, and/or certain associates of his (within *ITEPA 2003, Sch 4 paras 12–14*):

- beneficially owns or controls (directly or indirectly) more than 30% of ordinary share capital; or
- possesses or is entitled to acquire rights to more than 30% of the assets available for distribution among the participators (within *CTA 2010, s 454*) in a winding-up or in any other circumstances.

Rights (including CSOP options) to acquire shares must be taken into account (in accordance with *ITEPA 2003, Sch 4 para 11*). Shares or rights held by trustees of a tax-advantaged SIP (see **71.25** above) and not appropriated to, or acquired on behalf of, any individual are disregarded.

For these purposes, '*close company*' has the meaning given by *CTA 2010, Pt 10 Ch 2* but also includes a company which would be a close company but for its being a non-UK resident company or a quoted company.

[*ITEPA 2003, s 719, Sch 4 paras 9–14, 36(2)*].

Scheme shares

[71.73] CSOP scheme shares (i.e. the shares which may be acquired under the scheme) must satisfy broadly the same conditions as apply for SAYE option schemes, for which see **71.61** above. There is one notable exception in that CSOP scheme shares must not be shares in a company which is under the control of a listed company.

[*ITEPA 2003, Sch 4 paras 15–20*].

Share options

[71.74] The following terms of a share option which is granted under a CSOP scheme must be stated at the time the option is granted:

(a) the price at which shares may be acquired by the exercise of the option;
(b) the number and description of the shares which may be acquired by the exercise of the option;
(c) the restrictions (if any) to which those shares may be subject;
(d) the times at which the option may be exercised (in whole or in part); and
(e) the circumstances under which the option will lapse or be cancelled (in whole or in part), including any conditions to which the exercise of the option is subject (in whole or in part).

The terms in (a)–(e) above may be varied to the following extent after the grant of the option: (i) the price may be varied as set out below; (ii) the number and description of shares may be varied as set out below or by way of a mechanism which is stated at the time the option is granted; and (iii) anything else may be varied by way of such a mechanism. Any such mechanism must be applied in a way that is fair and reasonable. The terms and any varying mechanism must be notified to the participant as soon as practicable after the grant.

The price in (a) above must not be less than the market value of shares of the same class at the time the option is granted or, with effect on and after 15 September 2016, at such earlier time as may be determined in accordance with guidance published by HMRC (or, with effect before that date, such earlier time as may be agreed in writing between the company and HMRC). The scheme must ensure that share options granted are non-transferable. The market value of shares subject to a restriction is to be determined as if they were not subject to the restriction.

The scheme *may* provide for (i) the stated price, or (ii) the number or description of shares that may be acquired, to be varied as necessary to take account of any variation in the share capital of which the scheme shares form part. Such variations must in particular secure that the total market value of the shares which can be acquired by the exercise of the option, and the total price at which those shares can be acquired, remain substantially the same.

[*ITEPA 2003, Sch 4 paras 21, 21A, 22, 23; FA 2016, Sch 3 para 7*].

Discretionary provisions

[71.75] A CSOP scheme may make provision for share options to be exercised after a grantee has ceased to meet the requirement in **71.72** above to be a full-time director or an employee.

A CSOP scheme may also provide that a participant's options can be exercised after his death. Any such provision must permit the exercise of the options at any time on or after the date of death but not later than twelve months after that date.

[*ITEPA 2003, Sch 4 paras 24, 25*].

A CSOP scheme may also make provision as follows.

(a) It may provide that options may be exercised in either of the following circumstances (in relation to the company whose shares may be obtained under the scheme) within six months after the 'relevant date'.
  (i) A person obtains control of the company as a result of making a general offer to acquire the whole of its issued share capital or of all the shares of the same class as the scheme shares. It does not matter if the general offer is made to different shareholders by different means; also the reference to the whole of the issued share capital or all the shares of the same class specifically excludes any capital/shares already held by the offeror or a person connected with the offeror. In this case, the '*relevant date*' is the date when the person obtains unconditional control. For this purpose, a person is treated as obtaining control of a company if he and others acting in concert obtain control of it (within *ITA 2007, s 995*).
  (ii) A court sanctions, under *Companies Act 2006, s 899*, a compromise or arrangement. In this case, the '*relevant date*' is the date of the sanction.
  (iii) There is a '*non-UK company reorganisation arrangement*', i.e. an arrangement made in relation to a company under the law of a territory outside the UK which gives effect to a reorganisation of the company's share capital by specified methods and which is approved by a resolution of the company's members. In this case, the '*relevant date*' is the date the arrangement becomes binding on the shareholders covered by it.

  Heads (ii) and (iii) apply only if the compromise or arrangement affects all the ordinary share capital of the company or all the shares of the same class as the shares to which the option relates, or if it affects all the shares, or all the shares of that same class, which are held by a class of shareholders identified otherwise than by reference to their employments or directorships or their participation in a CSOP scheme. The resolution mentioned in (iii) does not count for the purpose stated therein unless the members voting in favour represent more than 50% of the voting rights.

(b) It may provide that options may be exercised at any time when any person is bound or entitled to acquire shares in the company under *Companies Act 2006, ss 979–982* or *ss 983–985* (takeover offers: right of offeror to buy out minority shareholder etc.).

Exercise within 20 days

If the scheme makes provision under (a) or (b) above it may also provide that if, in consequence of a 'relevant event', shares to which a share option relates no longer meet the requirements in **71.73** above (scheme shares), the share option may be exercised under the provision made under (a) or (b) (as the case may be) no later than 20 days after the day on which the relevant event occurs, notwithstanding that the shares no longer meet those requirements. Such provision cannot authorise the exercise of an option outside the six-month period mentioned in (a) or at a time not covered by (b). Either of the following is a '*relevant event*':

- a person obtaining control of the company as mentioned in (a)(i) above, or as a result of a compromise or arrangement within (a)(ii) or (iii); or
- a person who is bound or entitled to acquire shares in the company as mentioned in (b) above obtaining control of the company.

If the scheme makes provision under (a) or (b) above it may also provide that a share option relating to shares in a company which is exercised during the period of 20 days ending with the relevant date for the purposes of (a)(i), (ii) or (iii), or ending with the date on which any person becomes bound or entitled to acquire shares in the company as mentioned in (b), is to be treated as if it had been exercised in accordance with the provision made under (a) or (b). If the scheme makes that provision it must also provide that if an option is duly exercised in anticipation of an event occurring, but the event does not, in fact, occur during the 20 days beginning with the date of exercise, the exercise of the option is to be treated as having had no effect.

[*ITEPA 2003, Sch 4 paras 25A, 35ZA*].

Exchange of share options

[71.76] A CSOP scheme *may* make provision comparable to that for SAYE option schemes in **71.64** above to allow old options to be exchanged for new in the event of a company takeover etc. and for the new options to be treated as having been granted at the time the original options were granted. [*ITEPA 2003, Sch 4 paras 26, 27*].

Self-certification, returns and enquiries

[71.77] In order for a CSOP scheme to be a tax-advantaged CSOP scheme under *ITEPA 2003, Sch 4*, notice of the scheme (the '*self-certification notice*') must be given to HMRC. It must be given by the company and must contain such information as HMRC may require and a declaration (that the scheme meets the statutory requirements) by such persons as HMRC may require. Once the self-certification notice is given, the scheme is a tax-advantaged CSOP scheme at all times on and after the date on which the declaration is made or, if the declaration is made later than the first date on which share options are granted under the scheme, on and after that date (the '*first grant date*'). However, if the self-certification notice is given after the 'initial notification deadline', the scheme is a tax-advantaged CSOP scheme only from the beginning of the 'relevant tax year', unless the company can show that it had a reasonable excuse for missing the deadline. The company can appeal within 30 days against a decision of HMRC that it had no reasonable excuse; for more on 'reasonable excuse', see below under Annual returns.

The 'initial notification deadline' is 6 July in the tax year following that in which the first grant date falls. The 'relevant tax year' is the tax year in which the self-certification notice is given or, if that notice is given on or before 6 July in that tax year, the previous tax year.

The self-certification notice, and any information accompanying it, must be given electronically but, if they consider it appropriate to do so, HMRC may allow the company to give the notice etc. in another way.

[*ITEPA 2003, Sch 4 paras 2(2), 28A, 28D(1)(3)(4), 28K(A1)(5)(6)(9); FA 2016, Sch 3 para 5*].

Annual returns

The company must make a return for each tax year, starting with the year in which falls the date on which the plan becomes a tax-advantaged CSOP scheme. The return for a tax year must contain such information as HMRC may require, and must be filed on or before 6 July in the following tax year. If during a tax year an alteration is made in a 'key feature' of the scheme, or variations are made to take account of a variation in any share capital (see **71.74** above), the return for that year must contain a declaration, made by such persons as HMRC may require, that the alteration or variations have not caused the statutory requirements to fail to be met in relation to the scheme. For this purpose a '*key feature*' is a provision of the scheme which is necessary in order for those requirements to be met. If the company becomes aware of any error, omission or inaccuracy in a return, it must make an amended return without delay. A return is not required for any tax year following that in which the 'termination condition' is met; the '*termination condition*' is met when all share options granted under the scheme have been exercised, or are no longer capable of being exercised, and no more share options will be granted under the scheme.

A return must be made, and any accompanying information must be given, electronically. However, if they consider it appropriate to do so, HMRC may allow a company to make a return or give any accompanying information in another way.

If a company fails to make a return by the due date, it is liable for a penalty of £100. If the failure continues for more than three months beginning with the due date, the company is liable for a further penalty of £300. If the failure continues for another three months, another £300 penalty is incurred. If it continues for nine months in all, HMRC may, upon giving notice, charge a daily penalty of £10. The notice must specify the period in respect of which the penalty is payable; this period may begin earlier than the date on which the notice is given but cannot begin until after the end of the said nine-month period or, if relevant, after the end of any period specified in any previous notice given by HMRC in relation to the same failure. Liability for a penalty does not arise if the company satisfies HMRC (or, on appeal, the Tribunal) that there is a reasonable excuse. Reasonable excuse does not include insufficiency of funds (unless attributable to events outside the company's control) or reliance on another person (unless the company took reasonable care to avoid the failure); a failure must be remedied without unreasonable delay after a reasonable excuse ceases.

If a return contains a material inaccuracy which is either careless or deliberate or is not corrected by an amended return upon the company's becoming aware of it, the company is liable for a penalty of up to £5,000. The same applies if a return is not made electronically where required.

[*ITEPA 2003, Sch 4 paras 2(2), 28B, 28C, 28D(2)–(4), 28E*].

For assessment of penalties, see *ITEPA 2003, Sch 4 para 28J*. An appeal may be made against the imposition and/or the amount of penalties. Notice of appeal must be given to HMRC no later than 30 days after the date of the notice of assessment of the penalty. For these and other matters related to appeals, see *ITEPA 2003, Sch 3 para 28K*.

Enquiries

HMRC may open an enquiry into a tax-advantaged CSOP scheme. They must give the company notice of their intention to do so on or before 6 July following the tax year in which falls the 'initial notification deadline' (see above). This is with the exception that if the self-certification notice is given after the initial notification deadline, HMRC have until 6 July in the second tax year following the 'relevant tax year' (see above) to give the notice of enquiry. They may also enquire into the scheme if they give notice of intention to do so within twelve months after the date on which a declaration is given that an alteration made in a key feature has not caused the statutory requirements to fail to be met (see above under Annual returns).

Notwithstanding the above time limits, if at any time HMRC have reasonable grounds for believing that requirements of *ITEPA 2003, Sch 4* are not, or have not been, met in relation to the scheme, they can enquire into the scheme by giving notice of intention to do so.

The fact that the 'termination condition' may have been met in relation to the scheme (see above under Annual returns) does not prevent HMRC opening and conducting an enquiry.

An enquiry is completed when HMRC give the company a notice (a '*closure notice*') stating that they have completed the enquiry and giving the result of the enquiry. In the meantime, a company may apply to the Appeal Tribunal for a direction requiring a closure notice to be given within a specified period. The tribunal must give a direction unless satisfied that HMRC have reasonable grounds for not giving the closure notice within the specified period.

The result of the enquiry will be either that, in HMRC's opinion, the requirements of *ITEPA 2003, Sch 4* are, and have been, met in relation to the CSOP scheme, in which case no further action is required, or that, in their opinion, those requirements are not, or have not been, met. In the latter case, HMRC will also decide how serious the situation is, based on two possible levels of seriousness (see HMRC Employee Tax Advantaged Share Scheme User Manual ETASSUM46150), and their decision must be stated in the closure notice. At the more serious level, the scheme is not to be a tax-advantaged CSOP scheme with effect from such past time as is specified in the closure notice or, if no such time is specified, from the time of the giving of the closure notice. The company will also be liable for a penalty of an amount decided by HMRC. This must not exceed an amount equal to twice HMRC's reasonable estimate of the income tax and national insurance contributions forgone due to the scheme having had tax-advantaged status whilst failing to meet the statutory requirements.

At the less serious level, the scheme retains its tax-advantaged status but the company is liable for a penalty of up to £5,000, and must, within 90 days after the 'relevant day', secure that the statutory requirements are met in relation to the scheme. The latter does not apply if the termination condition is met before the end of that 90-day period. The '*relevant day*' is the last day of the period in which notice of appeal may be given or, if notice of appeal is given, the day on which the appeal is determined or withdrawn. The period in which notice of appeal may be given is the 30 days following the closure notice. If the company then fails to secure that the statutory requirements are met, HMRC may give the company a default notice, in which case the same consequences ensue as if the company's original failure had been at the more serious level, but so ensue by reference to the default notice rather than the closure notice.

[*ITEPA 2003, Sch 4 paras 2(2), 28F–28I, 28K(5)*].

For assessment of penalties, see *ITEPA 2003, Sch 4 para 28J*. An appeal may be made against the amount of any penalty. Notice of appeal must be given to HMRC no later than 30 days after the date of the notice of assessment of the penalty. Appeal may also be made against the result of the enquiry, a time specified in the closure notice or the absence of any such time, a decision to issue a default notice, and a time specified in the default notice or the absence of any such time. Notice of appeal must be given to HMRC within 30 days after the date of the closure notice or default notice. For these and other matters related to appeals, see *ITEPA 2003, Sch 2 para 28K*.

HMRC information powers

HMRC have wide-ranging powers to require any person to furnish them with such information as they reasonably require and as that person possesses or can reasonably obtain. The information must be supplied within a period specified in the notice, which must not be less than three months. Penalties under *TMA 1970, s 98* can be imposed for non-compliance. [*ITEPA 2003, Sch 4 para 33*].

Simon's Taxes. See **E4.583, E4.583A, E4.583B.**

Employee shareholder shares

[71.78] A new employment status, known as 'employee shareholder' status, was introduced by *Growth and Infrastructure Act 2013, s 31*. Employee shareholders can be issued or allotted at least £2,000 worth of shares in consideration of an employee shareholder agreement. Where the shares are acquired under pre-1 December 2016 agreements (see further below), and subject to conditions, employee shareholders are deemed for income tax purposes to have paid £2,000 for their employee shareholder shares, thus reducing the potential tax charge on acquisition. Subject to conditions, a monetary limit and a lifetime limit, employee shareholder shares acquired under such agreements are also exempt from capital gains tax (CGT) when disposed of. Businesses wishing to award shares under an employee shareholder agreement may propose a share valuation to HMRC's Shares and Assets Valuation team in advance of the award (HMRC Employment Related Securities Bulletin No. 10, September 2013). For official guidance on employee shareholder status see www.gov.uk/guidance/employee-shareholders.

These income tax and CGT reliefs are **abolished** with effect where the employee shareholder agreement is entered into on or after the relevant day. The relevant day is in most cases **1 December 2016**. The one exception is where independent advice on entering into the agreement was received before 1.30 pm on 23 November 2016. In this case the relevant day is 2 December 2016, and references below to 1 December 2016 should be read with this in mind.

The Government have announced their intention to close employee shareholder status to new users at the earliest opportunity (Autumn Statement, 23 November 2016 at www.gov.uk/government/publications/income-tax-and-capital-gains-tax-employee-shareholder-status).

Charge to income tax

When shares ('*employee shareholder shares*') with a market value of at least £2,000 are acquired by an employee in consideration of an 'employee shareholder agreement' entered into before 1 December 2016, an amount is treated as earnings from the employment, in respect of the acquisition of the shares, for the tax year in which they are acquired. The amount is found by applying a formula, MV – P where:

> MV = the market value of the shares (see below) on the day on which they are acquired; and
> P = the payment (if any) that the employee is treated as having made for the shares as set out below.

If P exceeds MV, the amount is nil.

Where the shares are acquired in consideration of an employee shareholder agreement entered into on or after 1 December 2016, the amount to be treated as earnings is the market value of the shares.

Where the above applies, no other sums can constitute earnings from the employment in respect of the acquisition of the employee shareholder shares.

The above does not apply where the employee shareholder shares are acquired pursuant to an employment-related share option (as defined in **71.15** above). Any payment that the employee is treated as having made for the shares under a pre-1 December 2016 agreement is taken into account when calculating any tax chargeable under the normal share option rules. See **71.16** above as regards non-tax-advantaged options and **71.43** above as regards EMI options.

Market value is determined as for CGT purposes. For the purposes only of determining if the shares acquired by an employee have a market value of at least £2,000, the following are to be ignored:

- any election under *ITEPA 2003, s 431* for market value of restricted shares to be calculated as if not restricted (see **71.7** above); and
- the provisions of *ITEPA 2003, s 437* (market value of convertible securities to be determined as if not convertible — see **71.8** above).

An '*employee shareholder agreement*' means an agreement by virtue of which an employee is an employee shareholder (see *Employment Rights Act 1996, s 205A(1)(a)–(d)*). Shares are acquired by an employee for these purposes if the employee becomes beneficially entitled to them; they are acquired at the time when the employee becomes so entitled.

Deemed payment for the shares

Provided that, as above, shares with a market value of at least £2,000 are acquired by an employee in consideration of a pre-1 December 2016 employee shareholder agreement, the employee is treated, for income tax purposes, as having made a payment for those shares as follows. Where all the shares acquired in consideration of the agreement are acquired on the same day, the employee is treated as having made on that day a payment of £2,000 for those shares. Where shares are acquired by the employee in consideration of the agreement on more than one day, with shares with a market value of at least £2,000 acquired on the first of those days, the employee is treated as having made, on the first of those days, a payment of £2,000 for the shares acquired on that day. Where shares with a value in excess of £2,000 are acquired, the payment which the employee is treated as having made for each share is determined on a pro rata basis.

Where the above applies, then except as provided above, the employee is to be treated for income tax purposes as having given no consideration for shares acquired in consideration of the employee shareholder agreement.

Associated agreements

An employee who is treated as having made a payment for shares acquired in consideration of an employee shareholder agreement (the '*relevant agreement*') is not to be treated at any time as having made a payment for any other 'qualifying shares'. '*Qualifying shares*' means employee shareholder shares in:

- the employer company in relation to the relevant agreement, or
- an associated company of the employer company,

which are acquired by the employee in consideration of either another employee shareholder agreement with the same employer company or an employee shareholder agreement with an associated company of that company.

For these purposes, a company is an associated company of another if one has control of the other or both are under the control of the same person(s). 'Control' is construed in accordance with *CTA 2010, ss 450, 451*. If a company controls another when an employee shareholder agreement is entered into with an employee, this is treated as continuing to be the case when any subsequent employee shareholder agreement is entered into with that same employee. However, this does not apply if:

- one of the two companies has been dissolved;
- two years have passed since the date of dissolution; and
- the employee has not, at any time in that two-year period, been engaged in any office or employment (including engagement under a contract for services) with any company which is an associated company of the dissolved company.

Exclusion of persons with material interests

No payment is treated as made as above in respect of any shares if:

- on the date on which the shares are acquired or at any time in the twelve months ending on that date, the employee has (or has had) a 'material interest' in the employer company or a parent undertaking (within *Companies Act 2006, s 1162*) of the employer company; or
- on the date on which the shares are acquired, the employee is connected (within **19** CONNECTED PERSONS) with an individual who has a material interest in the employer company or a parent undertaking or who has had such an interest at any time in the twelve months ending on that date.

For these purposes, an individual (A) has a '*material interest*' in a company if at least 25% of the voting rights are exercisable by A, or by persons connected with A, or by A and persons connected with A together. If the company is a close company, or would be but for being a non-UK resident company or a quoted company, A has a material interest in it if A, or persons connected with A, or A and persons connected with A together, are entitled to at least 25% of the assets available for distribution among the participators in a winding-up or in any other circumstances. A is *treated* as having a material interest in a company on the date on which the shares are acquired if A, or persons connected with A, or A and persons connected with A together, have an entitlement to acquire such rights as would (together with any existing rights) give A a material interest in the company. Any arrangements in place (as widely defined and to which the employer company or a parent undertaking is also party) to acquire such rights must also be taken into account.

[*ITEPA 2003, ss 226A–226D; FA 2017, s 12(1)(2)(5)–(7)*].

Advice relating to proposed employee shareholder agreements

Under *Growth and Infrastructure Act 2013, s 31*, an employee shareholder agreement is ineffective unless the employee first receives independent advice as to the terms and effect of the proposed agreement. Reasonable costs incurred by the employee in obtaining the advice (whether or not he does become an employee shareholder) must be met by the company. No income tax liability accrues to the employee by virtue of the provision of the advice or of the company's meeting those costs. This exemption continues notwithstanding the above-mentioned abolition of income tax and CGT reliefs relating to employee shareholder shares. See **28.52**(xxvii) EMPLOYMENT INCOME.

Capital gains tax

Where the shares were acquired in consideration of an employee shareholder agreement entered into before 1 December 2016, gains on disposals of 'exempt' employee shareholder shares by the person who acquired them under the agreement are not chargeable gains. An employee shareholder share acquired in consideration of an employee shareholder agreement is '*exempt*' if, immediately after its acquisition, the total value of employee shareholder shares, in the employer company or an associated company, which have been acquired by the employee does not exceed £50,000. For these purposes, the value of a share at any time is its unrestricted market value at the time when it was acquired by the employee. There are similar provisions to those above in that an employee shareholder share is not exempt if the employee or a person connected with him has, or has had, a material interest in the employer company or a parent undertaking. There is a cumulative limit of £100,000 on the amount of exempt gains that a person can make on the disposal of shares acquired under employee shareholder agreements entered into on or before 30 November 2016. [*TCGA 1992, ss 236B–236F; FA 2016, s 88(1)–(6)(10); FA 2017, s 13(4)(6)–(8)*]. See Tolley's Capital Gains Tax for the detailed provisions.

Purchase of shares by company

Where the shares were acquired in consideration of an employee shareholder agreement entered into before 1 December 2016, no income tax charge arises when exempt employee shareholder shares (see above under Capital gains tax) are sold back to the company by an individual who is no longer an employee of, or office-holder in, the employer company or an associated company. Where the agreement is entered into before 1 December 2016, the payment made by the company for the shares is potentially chargeable to income tax as a distribution. [*ITTOIA 2005, s 385A; FA 2017, s 14*].

Simon's Taxes. See E4.591–E4.593.

Priority share allocations

[71.79] Where a director or employee (or future or past director or employee and whether or not of the company in question) is entitled, as such, to priority allocation of shares in a genuine public offer at fixed price or by tender, no liability to income tax in respect of earnings arises by virtue of any benefit derived therefrom, provided that:

(a) the shares reserved for such priority allocation do not exceed:
   - 10% of the total shares subject to the offer; or
   - (if the offer is part of arrangements under which shares of the same class are offered to the public under more than one offer), either 40% of the total shares subject to the offer or 10% of all the shares of that class subject to any such offers;

(b) all persons entitled to priority allocation are so entitled on similar terms (which may, however, vary according to level of remuneration, length of service or similar factors); and

(c) the persons entitled to priority allocation are not restricted to directors or to those whose remuneration exceeds a particular level.

Paragraph (b) above is still satisfied where allocations to directors and employees of the company are greater than those to other persons, provided that:

- the aggregate value of priority allocations made under the offer and under other public offers made at the same time in respect of the shares of other companies to those persons; and
- the aggregate value of the shares allocated to comparable directors and employees of the company,

are, as nearly as reasonably practicable, the same.

The above exemption does not apply to the benefit of any discount given to the director or employee on the fixed price or lowest price successfully tendered. Any 'registrant discount' is disregarded for this purpose. Broadly, the '*registrant discount*' is any discount which, subject to any conditions imposed, may be available in respect of all or some part of the shares allocated to any person, whether a member of the public or an employee or director applying for shares as such. For the disregard to apply, at least 40% of the shares allocated to members of the public (other than employees or directors entitled, as such, to priority allocation) must be allocated to individuals entitled either to the discount or to some alternative benefit of similar value for which they may elect.

The above exemption is extended to cases where:

- there is a genuine offer to the public of a combination of shares in two or more companies at a fixed price or by tender (the '*public offer*'); and
- there is at the same time an offer (the '*employee offer*') of shares, or a combination of shares, in one or more but not all of those companies to directors or employees (with or without others) of any company; and
- any of those directors or employees is entitled, by reason of his office or employment, to an allocation of shares under the employee offer in priority to any allocation to members of the public under the public offer.

The conditions at (a)–(c) above apply in relation to this extended exemption, and, for each company included in the employee offer, the limits in (a) above must be satisfied by reference to both offers. Where the extended exemption applies, the denial of exemption on any director- or employee-discount on the offer price (see above) is imposed by reference to an '*appropriate notional price*' for shares in each company concerned, i.e. the fixed price at which the shares might reasonably have been expected to be offered in a separate offer to the public, proportionately varied where the sum of the notional prices for all the companies concerned would otherwise differ from the actual fixed price, or lowest successfully tendered price, for the combination of shares subject to the public offer.

The term '*director*' is widely defined for the purposes of these provisions (see *ITEPA 2003, s 548(1)(2)*) and includes, for example, any person in accordance with whose instructions (disregarding advice given in a professional capacity) the directors are accustomed to act.

[*ITEPA 2003, ss 542–548*].

For capital gains tax purposes, *TCGA 1992, s 17(1)* (under which acquisitions are treated as made at their market value rather than their actual cost) is disapplied in relation to acquisitions within the above exemption. [*TCGA 1992, s 149C*].

Simon's Taxes. See **E4.506**.

Research institution spin-out companies

[71.80] It is common for universities, public sector research establishments, entities such as NHS Trusts and some charities to own intellectual property (IP) created by their own employees. These institutions may have IP Sharing Policies (sometimes also called employee incentive or compensation schemes) to reward the employees (the researchers) who created the IP in the event of its being subsequently exploited. The reward may be in cash form, representing a share of royalties received by the university etc. from licensing or selling the IP, in which case normal income tax rules apply. But alternatively, it could be in the form of a transfer of value to researchers via their ownership of shares in a spin-out company set up to further develop the IP to the point where it can be exploited commercially. The value of the shares in the spin-out company held by the researcher will be affected by an agreement for the transfer of the IP into the spin-out or by the transfer of the IP pursuant to such an agreement. Consequently, a charge to tax can arise under the general earnings rules on the acquisition of the shares (see **28.76** EMPLOYMENT INCOME) or under the rules for non-tax-advantaged share schemes in this chapter, and the tax liability can arise before funds are available to meet it. The legislation summarised below seeks to address these and related issues.

The legislation applies where:

- an agreement (an IP agreement) is made for one or more transfers of IP from one or more research institutions (RIs) to a company (a 'spin-out company');
- a person (the researcher) acquires shares in the spin-out company either before the IP agreement is made or within 183 days after it is made;
- the right or opportunity to acquire the shares was available by reason of employment by the RI (or any of them) or by the spin-out company; and
- the person is involved in research in relation to any of the IP that is the subject of the IP agreement.

The legislation does not, however, apply where a main purpose of the arrangements under which the above right or opportunity is made available is the avoidance of tax or national insurance contributions.

References in this coverage to shares include an interest in shares. For these purposes, 'shares' includes stock but does not have the extended meaning in **71.3** above. '*Intellectual property*' is defined by *ITEPA 2003, s 456*, and the '*transfer*' of IP includes any of the following: a sale, the grant of a licence or other right in respect of it or the assignment of a licence etc. in respect of it.

'*Research institution*' includes a university or a similar publicly funded institution and any institution that carries out research activities other than for profit and that is neither controlled nor wholly or mainly funded by a person who carries on activities for profit. A person is '*involved in research in relation to IP*' if he has been actively engaged (as an employee or otherwise) for the RI (or any of them) in connection with research which is relevant to anything to which the IP relates. If an RI has control (within *CTA 2010, ss 450, 451*) of a company, a transfer of IP from the company is treated for the purposes of these provisions as a transfer from the RI (and similarly where two or more RIs together have control of a company).

Tax relief on acquisition

For the following purposes, the market value of the shares at time of acquisition by the researcher is to be calculated disregarding the effect on that value of the IP agreement and any transfer of IP under it:

- the determining of any amount that is to constitute earnings from the employment as a result of the acquisition;
- the determining of any amount that is to constitute earnings from the employment under **71.78** above (employee shareholder shares);
- the determining of the amount of any gain realised on the occurrence of a chargeable event within **71.9**(a) above (conversion of convertible shares);
- the operation of the provisions at **71.12** above (shares acquired for less than market value);
- the determining of any amount counting as employment income by virtue of **71.16** above (non-tax-advantaged share options); and
- the determining of any amount that counts as employment income under **26** DISGUISED REMUNERATION.

Post-acquisition benefits

If the shares are acquired before IP agreement is made, or before any transfer of any IP under it, and any benefit deriving from the agreement or any such transfer is received by the employee in connection with the shares, the taxable amount of the benefit for the purposes of **71.14** above (post-acquisition benefits) is treated as nil. (The receipt of the benefit continues to be a reportable event under **71.18** above.) But this is disapplied if something affecting the shares is done as part of an avoidance scheme at or before the time the IP agreement is made or the IP is transferred.

Restricted shares

If the shares are restricted shares (within **71.4** above), the employer and employee are treated as making the election referred to in **71.7** to fully disapply the restricted shares provisions. This means that on acquisition of the shares, relief can be given as above by reference to their unrestricted market value and that no later charges will arise under the restricted shares rules. As regards shares acquired before 2 December 2004, the notional election is treated as made on that date.

However, employer and employee may agree to disregard the foregoing. This course of action may be chosen if the unrestricted market value at acquisition reflects things other than the transfer of IP, so that bringing it into charge would result in a larger taxable amount. The agreement to disregard must be in a form approved by HMRC and must be made within 14 days after the acquisition.

For examples of both the notional election and the agreement to disregard, see the Treasury Explanatory Notes to the 2005 Finance (No 2) Bill.

If the agreement to disregard is made, then in determining the taxable amount on the occurrence of a chargeable event, the value of IUMV in **71.5** above is to be calculated disregarding the effect on that value of the IP agreement and any transfer of IP under it.

Shares with artificially enhanced market value

For the purposes of **71.11** above, neither the IP agreement nor any transfer of IP under it are things done otherwise than for genuine commercial purposes.

[*ITEPA 2003, ss 451–460*].

The above provisions cease to apply to shares in the same circumstances as those at **71.4** cease to apply to shares (disposal to a person other than an associated person etc.). [*FA 2005, s 20(3)*].

Capital gains tax

Consequential amendments are made to the CGT legislation with the aim of ensuring that the correct amount is charged to CGT on disposal of the shares after taking account of the changes to income tax liability brought about by the above provisions. See Tolley's Capital Gains Tax under Employee Share Schemes for details.

Guidance

See HMRC Employment-Related Securities Manual at ERSM100000 *et seq.*

Simon's Taxes. See **E4.508AA–E4.508AD.**

72

Social Investment Tax Relief

Simon's Taxes. See E3.9.

Introduction to social investment tax relief (SITR)

[72.1] Social investment tax relief (SITR) is an income tax relief available to individuals making an eligible investment in a 'social enterprise' (see **72.2** below). See **72.7** below as to eligibility. The measure of relief is 30% of the amount invested, and this is deducted from the individual's income tax liability for the tax year in which the investment is made. The investment may be a subscription for shares or a 'qualifying debt investment' (see **72.3** below). There is a £1 million limit on the annual amount of investment per investor that can qualify for SITR, but relief can be carried back to the previous tax year. There is also a maximum amount that a qualifying social enterprise can raise by such investment over a period of three years (see **72.35** below).

Chargeable gains attributable to an increase in the value of an eligible investment are not liable to capital gains tax (CGT) if the investment is held for a minimum period. CGT on chargeable gains on other assets can be deferred in certain circumstances where the individual liable to tax invests in a social enterprise. See **72.19**, **72.20** below.

Under current law, SITR will cease to be available for investments made after 5 April 2021. [*ITA 2007, s 257K(1)(5); F(No 2)A 2017, Sch 1 para 2*].

The relief is administered by HMRC's Venture Capital Relief Team. For guidance see www.gov.uk/business-tax/investment-schemes.

Meaning of Periods A and B

In these provisions, '*Period A*' is the period beginning with:

- the day on which the social enterprise is incorporated (if it is a body corporate) or established, or
- if later, the day which is one year before the date the investment is made,

and ending with the third anniversary of the date the investment is made.

'*Period B*' is the period beginning with the date the investment is made and ending with the third anniversary of that date.

[*ITA 2007, s 257KC*].

When is an investment made?

So far as the investment is in shares, the investment is made when the shares are issued to the investor by the social enterprise.

So far as it is in qualifying debt investments, the investment is made when the social enterprise issues the debenture or debentures to the investor; in a case where there is no such issuing, the investment is made when the debenture or debentures take effect between the social enterprise and the investor. If the investment is the second of multiple advances covered by the debenture(s) concerned, or a subsequent one of those advances, it is treated as made when the amount of that advance is fully advanced in cash, if that would give an earlier date than under the aforementioned rule.

[*ITA 2007, s 257KB*].

Confidentiality

HMRC's normal obligations of confidentiality neither prevent their disclosing to a social enterprise that relief has been given or claimed in respect of a particular number or proportion of any investments nor prevent disclosure, subject to safeguards, to the Regulator of Community Interest Companies for the purposes of the Regulator's functions. In the case of an accredited social impact contractor (see **72.2** below), those obligations do not prevent disclosure to a Minister of the Crown (or his delegate) for the purposes of his functions. [*ITA 2007, s 257SI*].

Social enterprises

[72.2] For the purposes of SITR, '*social enterprise*' means:

(a) a '*community interest company*' (within *Companies (Audit, Investigations and Community Enterprise) Act 2004, Pt 2*);
(b) a 'community benefit society' (see below) that is not a charity;
(c) a charity (as in **14.2** CHARITIES AND CHARITABLE GIVING);
(d) an 'accredited social impact contractor'; or
(e) any other body prescribed, or of a description prescribed, by Treasury order made by statutory instrument. There is provision to the effect that where a body is a social enterprise as a result of a Treasury order that has come into force, no subsequent Treasury order can undo that fact in respect of times before the subsequent order comes into force.

[*ITA 2007, s 257J(2)(3)*].

Community benefit societies

A '*community benefit society*' is a body that:

- is registered as a community benefit society under *Co-operative and Community Benefit Societies Act 2014*, or
- is a society that, immediately before 1 August 2014, is registered or treated as registered under *Industrial and Provident Societies Act 1965* (or NI equivalent) and whose business is being, or is intended to be, conducted for the benefit of the community,

and is of a kind prescribed by *Reg 5* of *Community Benefit Societies (Restriction on Use of Assets) Regulations 2006* (*SI 2006 No 264*) (or NI equivalent) and whose rules include a rule in the terms set out in *Sch 1* of those Regulations. [*ITA 2007, s 257JB*].

Accredited social impact contractors

An '*accredited social impact contractor*' is a company limited by shares that is accredited under these provisions as a social impact contractor. Applications for accreditation must be made to a Minister of the Crown in specified form and manner. A Minister is to accredit a company only if satisfied that (i) it has entered into a 'social impact contract'; (ii) it is established for the sole purpose of entering into and carrying out such a contract; and (iii) its activities in carrying out the contract will not consist wholly, or as to a substantial part, in 'excluded activities' (within **72.48** below, taking the 2017 changes to excluded activities as having come into force on 6 April 2017). If, subsequently, a Minister is satisfied that condition (ii) or (iii) has ceased to be met in relation to an accredited social impact contractor, he must withdraw the accreditation with effect from the time the condition ceased to be met or a later time. A '*social impact contract*' is a contract that meets criteria specified in Treasury regulations (see *SI 2014 No 3066, Reg 3*). The specified criteria may include, in particular, criteria as to a party to the contract other than the company seeking accreditation. An accreditation must be made in such a way as to be conditional on compliance with requirements imposed by Treasury regulations and any other requirements considered appropriate by the accrediting Minister. [*SI 2014 No 3066*].

An accreditation as a social impact contractor has effect for a period beginning with the day specified in the accreditation and of a length specified in, or determined in accordance with, the accreditation. The start date may be backdated.

[*ITA 2007, ss 257JD–257JH*].

Social impact contracts (known as social impact bonds) are awarded by public sector bodies for the delivery of social outcomes; payment is made according to outcomes agreed with the contractor and is dependent on the desired social outcomes being achieved. The accreditation process is administered by the Minister for the Cabinet Office. Guidance on accreditation, and application forms, are available at www.gov.uk/government/publications/social-investment-tax-relief-accreditation-for-sib-contractors.

Special meaning of 'company'

In these provisions (except in the above definition of 'accredited social impact contractor') any reference to a company includes a charity that is a trust. [*ITA 2007, s 257JC*].

Types of investment permitted

[72.3] At all times during Period B (see **72.1** above) the investment in the social enterprise must be in the form of:

- shares that meet conditions A and B below and are issued to the investor by the social enterprise in return for the amount invested; or
- 'qualifying debt investments' of which the investor is the holder in return for his advancing the amount invested to the social enterprise.

Condition A is that the shares must carry neither of the following:

- a right to a return which (or any part of which) is a fixed amount; or is at a fixed rate; or is otherwise fixed by reference to the amount invested; or is fixed by reference to some other factor that is not contingent on successful financial performance by the social enterprise; and
- a right to a return at a rate greater than a reasonable commercial rate.

Condition B is that, for the purpose of determining the amounts due to holders of the shares on a winding-up of the social enterprise:

- those amounts rank after all debts of the social enterprise except any due to holders of qualifying debt investments in their capacity as such; and
- the shares do not rank above any other shares in the social enterprise (ignoring any debts postponed by rules under *Insolvency Act 1986, s 411* or any other enactment).

Shares acquired from another investor do not qualify.

Qualifying debt investments

'*Qualifying debt investments*' are any debentures of the social enterprise in respect of which the following conditions are met:

- neither the principal of the debt, nor any return on that principal, is charged on any assets;
- the rate of return on the principal is no greater than a reasonable commercial rate of return; and
- in the event of a winding-up of the social enterprise and so far as the law allows, any sums due in respect of the debt (whether principal or return):
  - are subordinated to all other debts of the social enterprise (ignoring any debts postponed by rules under *Insolvency Act 1986, s 411* or any other enactment) except sums due in the case of other unsecured debentures which rank equally;
  - rank equally, if there are shares in the social enterprise and they all rank equally among themselves, with amounts due to shareholders; and
  - rank equally, if there are shares in the social enterprise and they do not all rank equally, with amounts due to the holders of the lowest ranking shares.

For these purposes, 'debenture' includes any instrument creating or acknowledging indebtedness.

[*ITA 2007, s 257L*].

Form of relief

[72.4] Where an individual who is eligible for SITR (see **72.7** below) makes a claim for relief, he is entitled to a reduction in his tax liability for the year in which the investment is made. The claim may be for all or part of the amount invested. The reduction is equal to 30% (the '*SI rate*') of the amount on which relief is claimed for the year, subject to a maximum relief for any year of 30% of £1 million.

The order in which tax reductions are given against an individual's tax liability is set out at **1.12** ALLOWANCES AND TAX RATES, which also makes clear that a tax reduction must be restricted to the extent (if any) that it would otherwise exceed the individual's remaining income tax liability after making all prior reductions.

As to *when* an investment is made, see **72.1** above.

Carry-back of relief

A claim for SITR may be made as if all or part of the amount eligible for relief had been invested in the tax year preceding that in which the investment was, in fact, made. This carry-back is subject to the overriding rule that the total amount of investment on which relief can be obtained for any one year cannot exceed the maximum referred to above.

[*ITA 2007, s 257JA*].

Attribution of relief to investments

[72.5] Subject to any withdrawal or reduction of relief (see **72.8** *et seq.* below), where an individual's income tax liability is reduced for a tax year as in **72.4** above by reason of one or more 'distinct investments' made (or treated as made) in that year, the tax reduction is attributed to that investment or those investments (being apportioned in the latter case according to the amounts claimed by the investor in respect of each of those investments). A '*distinct investment*' is an investment, made on a single day, in:

(a) a single share or a single 'qualifying debt investment' (see **72.3** above); or
(b) two or more shares, or two or more qualifying debt investments, where the shares or qualifying debt investments are in the same social enterprise and of the same class.

A proportionate amount of the tax reduction attributed to a distinct investment within (b) above is attributed to each of the shares, or qualifying debt investments, concerned. An investment of which part is treated as having been made in the preceding tax year (as in **72.4** above) is treated for these purposes as two separate investments, one made on a day in the preceding year. If bonus shares (in the same company, of the same class, and carrying the same rights) are issued to an investor in respect of any shares to which relief is attributed, the bonus shares are treated as if they had been issued to the investor on the same day as the original shares, and the tax reduction attributed to the original shares is then apportioned between the increased number of shares now held.

[*ITA 2007, s 257N*].

Claims to relief

[72.6] A claim for relief must be made not earlier than the end of the four-month minimum period at **72.45** below, and not later than the fifth anniversary of 31 January following the tax year in which the investment is made (or, in the case of a carry-back claim as in **72.4** above, in which it is *treated* as made). The four-month minimum does not apply where the social enterprise is an accredited social impact contractor (see **72.2** above).

The claimant must have received a compliance certificate from the social enterprise before making the claim. The certificate must state that the requirements for relief, except in so far as they fall to be satisfied by the investor, are for the time being fulfilled in relation to the investment. A certificate may not be issued without the authority of an HMRC officer. Where a notice under *ITA 2007, s 257SF* (see **72.21** below) has been given to HMRC, a compliance certificate must not be issued unless the authority is given or renewed after receipt of the notice. For appeal purposes, an HMRC officer's refusal to authorise a certificate is treated as a decision disallowing a claim by the social enterprise.

Before issuing such a certificate, the social enterprise must supply to HMRC a compliance statement that those requirements are fulfilled for the time being and have been fulfilled at all times since the investment was made. The statement must contain such information as HMRC may reasonably require, and a declaration that it is correct to the best of the social enterprise's knowledge and belief. The statement must be provided to HMRC within two years after the end of the tax year in which the investment was made (or, if the four-month minimum period at **72.45** below ends in a subsequent tax year, within two years after the end of that four-month period). The statement cannot be provided to HMRC before the four-month minimum period (where applicable) expires.

References above to requirements being fulfilled for the time being are, in the case of requirements that cannot be fulfilled until a future date, references to nothing having occurred to prevent their being fulfilled.

If a certificate or statement is made fraudulently or negligently, or a certificate is issued despite being prohibited (as above), the social enterprise is liable to a penalty of up to £3,000.

No application for postponement of tax pending appeal can be made on the ground that relief is due under these provisions unless a claim has been duly submitted. No regard is to be had to SITR for the purposes of PAY AS YOU EARN (**53**) unless a claim for relief has been made.

[*ITA 2007, ss 257P–257PE*].

Eligibility for SITR

[72.7] In order for an individual to be eligible for SITR on an investment in a social enterprise, a number of conditions must be met. See **72.3** above as to the types of investment permitted. See **72.22–72.32** below for other conditions relating to the investor and the investment and **72.33–72.47** below for conditions relating to the social enterprise.

An investor is not eligible for SITR on an amount invested if:

- the investor has obtained in respect of that amount, or any part of it, COMMUNITY INVESTMENT TAX RELIEF (**17**) or relief under the ENTERPRISE INVESTMENT SCHEME (**29**) or the SEED ENTERPRISE INVESTMENT SCHEME (**66**); or

- that amount, or any part of it, has been set against a chargeable gain under the capital gains deferral provisions at **29.24** ENTERPRISE INVESTMENT SCHEME.

Nominees

The investment in the social enterprise must be made by the investor on his own behalf. However, investments made by, subscribed for, issued to, held by or disposed of for an individual by a nominee are treated for these purposes as made by, subscribed for, issued to, held by or disposed of by the individual.

[*ITA 2007, s 257K(1)–(4)*].

Withdrawal or reduction of SITR

[72.8] The following provisions apply to withdraw or reduce SITR in certain circumstances. References to a reduction of relief include its reduction to nil, and references to the withdrawal of relief in respect of an investment are to the withdrawal of the relief attributable to that investment (see **72.5** above). Where no relief has yet been given, a reduction applies to reduce the amount which would otherwise be available for relief, and a withdrawal means the investment ceases to be eligible for relief.

Disposal of investment

[72.9] The rules below apply where the investor disposes of the whole or part of an investment to which social enterprise relief is attributable (see **72.5** above) before the end of Period B (see **72.1** above). Reference to a 'disposal', in relation to any shares or other investments, includes a disposal of an interest or right in or over them.

If the disposal is at arm's length, the relief attributable to the investment is normally withdrawn. However, if that relief exceeds an amount equal to tax at the SI rate (see **72.4** above), for the tax year for which the relief was obtained, on the disposal consideration, the relief is instead reduced by that amount. If the disposal is not at arm's length, the relief is always withdrawn.

Where the relief attributable to the investment is less than tax at the SI rate on the amount on which relief is claimed, the amount referred to in (a) above is correspondingly reduced. Where the relief attributable has been reduced (otherwise than as a result of an issue of bonus shares — see **72.5** above) before the relief was obtained, then in calculating the amount referred to in (a) above, the gross relief attributable to the investment before that reduction is used.

If the investor grants an option the exercise of which would bind him to sell the whole or part of the investment, the grant of the option is treated for the above purposes as a disposal. Relief is also withdrawn where, during Period A (see **72.1** above), an option is granted to the investor, the exercise of which would bind the grantor to purchase the whole or part of the investment; where applicable. there are rules for identifying the part of an investment to which an option relates.

These provisions do not apply to a disposal occurring as a result of the investor's death. See **72.18** below for transfers of shares between spouses or civil partners.

[*ITA 2007, ss 257R–257RC, 257TE*].

Identification rules

For the above purposes, disposals are identified with investments of the same class made on an earlier day before those made on a later day (i.e. first in/first out (FIFO)). Investments made on the same day are treated as disposed of in the following order:

(i) firstly, investments to which neither social investment income tax relief nor social investment capital gains deferral relief (see **72.20** below) is attributable;
(ii) next, those to which capital gains deferral relief, but not income tax relief, is attributable;
(iii) next, those to which income tax relief, but not capital gains deferral relief, is attributable; and
(iv) finally, any to which both income tax relief and capital gains deferral relief are attributable.

Any investment within (iii) or (iv) above which is treated as issued on an earlier day by virtue of the carry-back provisions at **72.4** above is to be treated as disposed of before any other investment within the same category. Investments transferred between spouses or civil partners living together are treated as if they were acquired by the transferee spouse or partner on the day they were made (see also **72.18** below). Shares comprised in a 'new holding' following a reorganisation to which *TCGA 1992, s 127* applies (see Tolley's Capital Gains Tax under Shares and Securities) are treated as having been acquired when the original shares were acquired.

[*ITA 2007, s 257TA*].

Value received by investor

[72.10] If the investor 'receives value' (other than an 'insignificant receipt' — see below) from the social enterprise at any time in Period A (see **72.1** above), any SITR given in respect of the investment is normally withdrawn. However, if that relief exceeds an amount equal to tax at the SI rate (see **72.4** above), for the tax year for which the relief was given, on the value received, the relief is instead reduced by that amount. See **72.11** below for further computational provisions.

All payments or transfers, direct or indirect, to, or to the order of, or for the benefit of, the investor are brought within these provisions. The provisions apply equally to value received from a person who is connected (within **19** CONNECTED PERSONS) with the social enterprise at any time in Period A, whether or not at the time value is received. Any reference to the investor includes a reference to an 'associate' of the investor (see **72.26** below).

These 'value received' provisions apply to all receipts, insignificant or otherwise, within Period A if, at any time on the date the investment is made or in the preceding twelve months, arrangements (as widely defined) are in existence providing for the investor to receive (or to be entitled to receive) value from the social enterprise at any time in Period A. For this purpose, 'the investor' includes any person who at any time in Period A is an associate of the investor, and 'the social enterprise' includes any person who at any time in Period A is connected with the social enterprise.

Meaning of 'receives value'

An investor '*receives value*' from the social enterprise if it:

(a) repays, redeems or repurchases any investments in the enterprise which belong to the investor, or makes any payment to him for giving up his rights to investments on their cancellation or extinguishment;

(b) repays, in pursuance of any arrangements for or in connection with the making of the investment on which the relief is claimed, any debt owed to him other than one incurred by the enterprise on or after the date the investment was made and otherwise than in consideration of the extinguishment of a debt incurred before that date;

(c) makes to the investor any payment for giving up on its extinguishment his right to any debt owed to him other than an '*ordinary trade debt*' (i.e. one incurred for normal trade supply of goods or services on normal trade credit terms not exceeding six months) or one in respect of a payment falling within **72.30**(i) or (vi) below;

(d) releases or waives any liability of his to the enterprise (which it is deemed to have done if discharge of the liability is twelve months or more overdue) or discharges or undertakes to discharge any liability of his to a third person;

(e) makes a loan or advance to him (defined as including any debt either to the enterprise (other than an 'ordinary trade debt' as in (c) above) or to a third party but assigned to the enterprise) which has not been repaid in full before the investment is made;

(f) provides a benefit or facility for the investor by providing, free of charge or at less than arm's-length price, goods or services which it normally provides at a charge;

(g) otherwise provides any benefit or facility for the investor;

(h) transfers an asset to him for no consideration or for consideration less than market value, or acquires an asset from him for consideration exceeding market value;

(i) makes any other payment to him except one that is either permissible under **72.30** below or is in discharge of an 'ordinary trade debt' (as in (c) above); or

(j) is wound up or dissolved (other than in circumstances that would cause the failure of the conditions at **72.33–72.47** below) and the investor consequently receives any payment or asset in respect of ordinary shares or qualifying debt investments held by him.

Additionally, the investor '*receives value*' from the social enterprise if:

- a person purchases any investments in the enterprise which belong to the investor or pays him for giving up any right in relation to any such investments; and

- that person is an individual in relation to whom not all of the requirements in **72.30** and **72.31** below would be met if references in those provisions to the investor were references to that person.

If the investor is a director of the social enterprise, the investor is *not* treated as receiving value from the enterprise merely because of the payment to him of reasonable remuneration (including any benefit or facility) for any services rendered to the enterprise as a director or employee.

Amount of value received

The amount of value received by the investor is, in a case within (a), (b) or (c) above, the amount received by the investor or, if greater, the market value of the investments or debt; in a case within (d) above, the amount of the liability; in a case within (e) above, the amount of the loan or advance, less any repayment made before the investment is made; in a case within (f) above, the arm's-length price of the goods or services, less any amount paid for them by the investor; in a case within (g) above, the cost to the enterprise of providing the benefit or facility, less any consideration given for it by the investor; in a case within (h) above, the difference between the market value of the asset and the consideration (if any) given for it; in a case within (i) above, the amount of the payment; or, in a case within (j) above, the amount of the payment or the market value of the asset.

In the additional case above (person purchasing investments etc.), the value received is the amount received by the investor or, if greater, the market value of the investments.

Miscellaneous

Value received is to be ignored for the above purposes insofar as relief attributable to the investment has already been withdrawn or reduced on account of that value. Where relief is withdrawn or reduced by reason of a disposal (see **72.9** above), the investor is not treated as receiving value in respect of the disposal.

An individual who acquired the investment by means of a transfer from a spouse or civil partner within **72.18** below is treated for these purposes as the investor.

Insignificant receipts

For the above purposes, an '*insignificant receipt*' is a receipt which:

- does not exceed £1,000; or
- does exceed £1,000 but is insignificant in relation to the amount invested.

The amount of the first receipt to which the above 'value received' provisions apply is treated as increased by the total amount of any earlier insignificant receipts. Once the 'value received' provisions have applied to a receipt, they apply also to all other receipts within Period A except any earlier insignificant receipts.

[*ITA 2007, ss 257Q, 257QA, 257QE–257QG, 257TE(1)*].

Reduction in relief — further computational provisions

[72.11] Adjustments are made in the amount by which relief is to be reduced in the following circumstances. Where more than one circumstance is relevant, the adjustments are made in the order in which they are set out below.

(a) Where two or more investments have been made in the same social enterprise by the same investor, in relation to each of which income tax relief was claimed, and the 'value received' provisions apply to more than one such investment, the value received is apportioned between them by reference to the amounts on which relief was obtained for each of those investments.

(b) Where any part of an investment is treated as issued in the previous tax year by virtue of the carry-back provisions at **72.4** above, the value received is apportioned between the parts of the investment allocated to each year on the basis of the amount on which relief was obtained for each year. The normal provisions for reducing relief are then applied to each of the apportioned amounts as if there were separate investments (taking (c) below into account where appropriate, but not (a) above) and the resulting amounts are added together.

(c) Where maximum relief was not obtained, the amount of value received is reduced by multiplying that amount by the relief attributable to the investment (see **72.5** above) divided by tax at the SI rate (see **72.4**), for the tax year for which relief was obtained, on the amount on which the investor claimed the relief. For this purpose, where the relief attributable to the investment has been reduced (otherwise than as a result of an issue of bonus shares — see **72.5**) before the relief was obtained, the gross relief attributable to the investment before that reduction is used in calculating the reduction in the value received.

[*ITA 2007, ss 257Q(4), 257QB–257QD*].

Replacement value

[72.12] The 'value received' provisions in **72.10** above (other than **72.10**(j)) are disapplied if the person from whom the value was received (the '*original supplier*') receives, by way of a 'qualifying receipt', and whether before or after the original receipt of value, at least equivalent replacement value from the original recipient. A receipt is a '*qualifying receipt*' if it arises by reason of:

(a) any one, or any combination of, the following:
    (i) a payment by the original recipient to the original supplier other than a payment within (i)–(vi) below or a payment covered by (c) below;
    (ii) the acquisition of an asset by the original recipient from the original supplier for consideration exceeding market value;
    (iii) the disposal of an asset by the original recipient to the original supplier for no consideration or for consideration less than market value; or

(b) (where the original receipt of value falls within **72.10**(d) above) an event having the effect of reversing the original event; or
(c) (where the original receipt of value arose from the purchase by a person from the investor for investments in the social enterprise or the payment to the investor for giving up rights in relation to such investments) the repurchase by the original recipient of the investments in question, or the reacquisition of the right in question, for consideration not less than the original value.

Any apportionment made of value received where there are two or more investments (see **72.11**(a) above) is disregarded in determining the amount of the original receipt of value. Payments to a person include any made indirectly or to his order or for his benefit.

The following payments are excluded from (a)(i) above:

(i) a reasonable (in relation to their market value) payment for any goods, services or facilities provided (in the course of trade or otherwise) by the original supplier;
(ii) a payment of interest at no more than a reasonable commercial rate on money lent to the original recipient;
(iii) a payment not exceeding a reasonable and commercial rent for property occupied by the original recipient;
(iv) a payment not exceeding market value for the acquisition of an asset;
(v) a payment in discharge of an 'ordinary trade debt' (as in **72.10**(c) above);
(vi) a payment for any shares in or securities of any company in circumstances not within (a)(ii) above.

Each reference in (i)–(iii) above to the original supplier or recipient includes a reference to any person who at any time in Period A is an 'associate' (as in **72.26** below) of his or, in the case of the supplier, is 'connected' with him (within **19** CONNECTED PERSONS).

Amount of replacement value

The amount of replacement value is, in a case within (a) above, the amount of any such payment plus the difference between the market value of any such asset and the consideration received; in a case within (b) above, the same as the amount of the original value; and, in a case within (c) above, the consideration received by the original supplier.

Disregard of replacement value

The receipt of replacement value is disregarded if:

- it occurs before the start of Period A (see **72.1** above); or
- there was an unreasonable delay in its occurrence; or
- it occurs more than 60 days after the relief falling to be withdrawn (or reduced) has been determined on appeal.

A receipt of replacement value is also disregarded if it has previously been set against a receipt of value to prevent any reduction or withdrawal of relief.

Supplementary

Where:

- the receipt of replacement value is a qualifying receipt (as above); and
- the event giving rise to the receipt is (or includes) the making of an investment by the investor or by a person who is an 'associate' of his (as in **72.26** below) at any time in Period A,

the person who makes the investment concerned is not eligible for social investment income tax relief in relation to the investment concerned or any other investment in the same issue.

[*ITA 2007, ss 257QH, 257QI*].

Repayments etc. of share capital to other persons

[72.13] If SITR is attributable (see **72.5** above) to the whole or any part of an investment and, at any time in Period A (see **72.1** above), the social enterprise or any 'subsidiary':

(a) repays, redeems or repurchases any of its share capital which belongs to any member other than:
   (i) the investor; or
   (ii) a person whose relief is thereby withdrawn or reduced by virtue of **72.9** or **72.10**(a) above; or

(b) makes any payment to any such member for giving up his right to any of the share capital of the social enterprise or subsidiary on its cancellation or extinguishment,

the relief is normally withdrawn. If, however, the relief exceeds an amount equal to tax at the SI rate (see **72.4** above), for the tax year for which the relief was obtained, on the sum received by the member, the relief is instead reduced by that amount. See below for an exception for insignificant payments.

A person also falls within (a)(ii) above if his relief would have been withdrawn or reduced by virtue of **72.10**(a) above were it not an 'insignificant receipt' (as in **72.10**).

A '*subsidiary*' of the social enterprise means a company which at any time in Period A, whether or not at the time of the repayment etc., is a 51% subsidiary of the social enterprise.

This restriction of relief does not apply to the redemption, within twelve months of issue, of any share capital of nominal value equal to the authorised minimum issued to comply with *Companies Act 2006, s 761*.

A repayment etc. is ignored for the above purposes to the extent that relief attributable to any shares has already been withdrawn or reduced on its account.

Insignificant payments

A repayment, redemption, repurchase or payment within (a) or (b) above is disregarded if both the amount received by the member in question and the market value of the shares to which it relates immediately before the event occurs are insignificant in relation to the market value of the remaining issued share capital of the social enterprise, or (as the case may be) the subsidiary, immediately after the event occurs. The assumption is made that the shares in question are cancelled at the time of the event. This let-out does not apply if, at any time in the period beginning twelve months before the investment is made and ending with the date the investment is made, there are in existence arrangements (as widely defined) providing for a payment within these provisions to be made, or entitlement to such a payment to come into being, at any time in Period A.

Further computational matters

Adjustments are made in the amount by which relief is to be reduced in the following circumstances. Where more than one circumstance is relevant, the adjustments are made in the order in which they are set out below.

(i) Where, in relation to the same repayment etc., relief attributable to two or more issues of shares falls to be reduced, the amount received by the member is apportioned between the issues by reference to the amounts of relief obtained for each of them.
(ii) Where, in relation to the same repayment etc., relief attributable to shares held by two or more individuals falls to be reduced, the amount received by the member is apportioned between the individuals by reference to the amounts of relief obtained by each.
(iii) Where any of the shares are treated as issued in the previous tax year by virtue of the carry-back provisions at **72.4** above, the amount received by the member is apportioned between the shares allocated to each year on the basis of the amount on which relief was obtained for each year. The normal provisions for reducing relief are then applied to each of the apportioned amounts as if there were separate issues of shares (taking (iv) below into account where appropriate, but not (i) or (ii) above) and the resulting amounts are added together.
(iv) Where maximum relief was not obtained, the amount received by the member is reduced by multiplying that amount by the relief attributable to the shares divided by tax at the SI rate, for the tax year for which relief was obtained, on the amount on which the investor claimed the relief. For this purpose, where the relief attributable to the shares has been reduced (otherwise than as a result of an issue of bonus shares — see **72.5** above) before the relief was obtained, the gross relief attributable to the shares before that reduction is used in calculating the reduction in the amount received by the member.

[*ITA 2007, ss 257QJ–257QP, 257TE(1)*].

Acquisition of trade or trading assets

[72.14] Social enterprise relief attributable to an investment (see **72.5** above) is withdrawn if, at any time in Period A (see **72.1** above), the social enterprise or any qualifying subsidiary (see **72.49** below), begins to carry on as its trade, business or profession (or part), a trade etc. (or part) previously carried on at any time in that period otherwise than by the social enterprise or a qualifying subsidiary, or acquires the whole or the greater part of the assets used for a trade etc. previously so carried on, and the investor is a person who, or one of a group of persons who together, either:

(a) owned at any time in Period A more than a half share in the trade etc. previously carried on, and also own or owned at any such time such a share in the trade etc. carried on by the social enterprise; or
(b) 'control' (see below), or at any time in Period A have controlled, the social enterprise, and also, at any such time, controlled another company which previously carried on the trade etc.

In determining, for the purposes of (a) above, the ownership of a trade and, if appropriate, the shares owned by multiple owners, *CTA 2010, s 941(6)* and *s 942* apply. For those purposes, interests etc. of 'associates' (see **72.26** below) are taken into account.

There are special rules relating to shares held by certain directors of, or of a partner of, the social enterprise or any subsidiary.

[*ITA 2007, s 257QQ*].

Meaning of 'control'

'*Control*' is to be construed in accordance with *CTA 2010, ss 450, 451* but as if references there to a company included a charity that is a trust. A charity that is a trust has control of another person if the trustees (in their capacity as such) have (or any of them has) control of the person. A trustee of a charity who, alone or together with other trustees who are connected with him (within **19 CONNECTED PERSONS**), can exercise some or all of the powers of the trustees, is regarded as controlling the charity. A person who either alone or with others has the power to appoint or remove trustees of a charity, or to approve or direct the trustees' functions, is also regarded as controlling the charity. A regulator is to be treated as not having control of any company regulated by him. [*ITA 2007, s 257TD*].

Acquisition of share capital

[72.15] Social enterprise relief attributable to an investment (see **72.5** above) is withdrawn if:

- the social enterprise, at any time in Period A (see **72.1** above), comes to acquire all the issued share capital of another company; and
- the investor is a person, or one of a group of persons, who control (see **72.14** above) or has, at any time in Period A, controlled the social enterprise and who also, at any such time, controlled the other company.

There are special rules relating to investments held by certain directors of, or of a partner of, the social enterprise or any subsidiary.

[*ITA 2007, s 257QR*].

Relief subsequently found not to have been due

[72.16] SITR is withdrawn if it is subsequently found not to have been due. Relief cannot be withdrawn on the ground that the conditions at **72.33–72.47** below relating to the social enterprise are not met unless:

(a) the social enterprise has given notice under the provisions at **72.21** below; or
(b) an HMRC officer has given notice to the social enterprise of his opinion that the whole or part of the relief was not due because of the ground in question.

The social enterprise may appeal against an HMRC notice as in (b) above as though it were the refusal of a claim.

[*ITA 2007, ss 257QS, 257SA*].

Procedure for withdrawing or reducing relief

[72.17] An assessment to income tax withdrawing or reducing SITR is made for the tax year for which the relief was given.

Such an assessment may not be made, and any notice by an HMRC officer under the provisions at **72.16** above may not be given, more than six years after the end of the tax year in which falls the end of the 28 months beginning with the date the investment was made or, if later, in which occurs the event giving rise to the withdrawal or reduction. This restriction is without prejudice to the extension of time limits in cases of loss of income tax brought about deliberately (see **6.3** ASSESSMENTS). No assessment may be made by reason of any event occurring after the investor's death.

Where an investor has made an arm's length disposal or disposals of all his investments in the social enterprise to which relief is attributable or which have not been held by him until the end of the third anniversary of the date on which they were made, no assessment (i.e. to recover any unrelieved balance) may be made in respect of those investments by reason of any subsequent event unless, at the time of that event, the investor fails the requirements of **72.30, 72.31** and **72.32** below by reference to any of those investments.

The relevant date for the purposes of **43.3** LATE PAYMENT INTEREST AND PENALTIES is 31 January following the tax year for which the assessment is made.

[*ITA 2007, ss 237S, 257SB–257SD*].

Married persons and civil partners

[72.18] The provisions for withdrawal of relief on the disposal of investments to which SITR is attributable (see **72.9** above) do not apply to transfers between spouses or civil partners living together. On any subsequent disposal or other event, the spouse or partner to whom the investment was transferred is treated as if:

- he or she were the person who made the investment;
- his or her liability to income tax had been reduced in respect of the investment by the same amount, and for the same tax year, as applied on the making of the investment by the transferor spouse or partner; and
- that amount of SITR had continued to be attributable to the investment despite the transfer.

Where the amount of relief attributable to the investment had been reduced before the relief was obtained by the transferor spouse or partner, the transferee is treated as if his or her relief had been correspondingly reduced before it was obtained (but this does not prevent the gross relief before reduction being used for the purposes of the calculations at **72.9**, **72.11**(c) and **72.13**(iv) above).

Any assessment for withdrawing or reducing relief is made on the transferee spouse or partner. The identification rules for disposals at **72.9** above apply to determine the extent (if any) to which investments to which relief is attributable are comprised in the transfer.

[*ITA 2007, ss 257R(1)(d), 257T, 257TA(1)*].

Capital gains tax

[72.19] In determining the gain or loss on a disposal of an asset to which any SITR is attributable (see **72.5** above):

(a) if a loss would otherwise arise, the consideration the individual is treated as having given for the asset is treated as reduced by the amount of the relief;

(b) if the disposal is after the end of the three years beginning with the day the individual acquired the asset, and a gain would otherwise arise, the gain is not a chargeable gain (although this does not prevent a loss arising in these circumstances from being an allowable loss).

Where SITR was not given on the full amount invested (other than by reason of the income tax liability being insufficient to support the relief), the capital gains tax exemption in (b) above is restricted to a proportion of the gain. This will usually be because the individual's social enterprise investments exceeded the annual maximum on which relief is available (see **72.4** above). The exempt gain is the proportion of the gain found by applying the multiple A/B where:

A = the income tax relief given; and
B = tax at the SI rate (see **72.4** above), for the tax year for which the relief was obtained, on the amount invested in the asset.

Where, because of (b) above, a gain (or part of a gain) on a disposal would not be a chargeable gain, but the income tax relief on the asset disposed of is reduced on account of value received from the company by the claimant or by other persons (see **72.10–72.13** above) before the disposal, then a corresponding proportion of the gain is chargeable.

[*TCGA 1992, ss 255B–255D*].

The identification rules at **72.9** above apply for the above purposes.

See *TCGA 1992, s 255E* as regards reorganisations of share capital involving shares to which social enterprise relief is attributable. For full coverage of all these matters, see Tolley's Capital Gains Tax.

Capital gains deferral relief

[72.20] If an amount equal to the amount of a chargeable gain is invested in a social enterprise within a specified time then the individual making the gain and the investment may claim for the gain be treated as accruing when the investment is disposed of and not at an earlier time.

This deferral relief applies where:

(a) a chargeable gain accrues to an individual on the disposal of any asset;
(b) the individual makes an investment on his own behalf in a social enterprise on which he is eligible for SITR;
(c) the gain accrues before 6 April 2021;
(d) the individual is UK resident both when the gain accrues and when he makes the investment; and
(e) the investment is made during the three years beginning with the day the gain accrues or during the twelve months immediately preceding that day.

The investor may make a claim for the chargeable gain to be reduced by the amount invested or by a smaller amount specified in the claim. The total of all such reductions claimed for any tax year cannot exceed £1 million. A chargeable gain equal to the amount of the reduction is treated as accruing when a chargeable event occurs in relation to the investment. If a chargeable event occurs in relation to part only of the investment, only an appropriate proportion of the gain is treated as accruing. A chargeable event occurs if the investment is disposed of or the asset representing it is cancelled, extinguished, redeemed or repaid or any of the eligibility conditions for social enterprise income tax relief (see **72.22–72.46** below) fails to be met. Nothing which occurs at or after the time of the investor's death is a chargeable event.

Deferral relief also applies if:

- a gain accrues as a result of a chargeable event as above (other than one involving the failure of eligibility conditions);
- the event is the disposal to a social enterprise of shares in or debentures of the enterprise or the cancellation, extinguishment, redemption or repayment by a social enterprise of its shares or debentures;
- as part of the chargeable event or in connection with it, and in place of the shares or debentures, the investor acquires one or more assets from the social enterprise, being shares in or debentures of the enterprise; and
- but for **72.23** below (consideration for acquisition to be wholly in cash and fully-paid) the investor would be eligible for SITR in respect of consideration given for the assets thus acquired.

Conditions (c) to (e) above apply equally here but by reference to the above-mentioned acquisition, and for this purpose 'debenture' includes any instrument creating or acknowledging indebtedness.

[*TCGA 1992, s 255A, Sch 8B; SI 2019 No 1237*].

The above is intended as a summary only. For full coverage, see Tolley's Capital Gains Tax.

Notification requirements and information powers

[72.21] Certain events leading to withdrawal or reduction of SITR must be notified to HMRC, generally within 60 days, by either the investor, the social enterprise, or any person connected with the social enterprise having knowledge of the matter. If the event results in the failure of the requirement at **72.34** below (the 'continuing to be a social enterprise' requirement), the duty to notify extends to the former social enterprise and to any body into which it has been converted. An HMRC officer may require such a notice and other relevant information where he has reason to believe it should have been made.

It should be noted that:

- the notification requirement extends to cases where income tax relief would have fallen to be withdrawn or reduced were it not for the 'replacement value' rules at **72.12** above; and in all cases a notice under these provisions should include details of any such replacement value received (or expected to be received) where this is within the knowledge of the person giving the notice; and
- HMRC's powers extend to cases where notice would have been required were it not for 'value received' being an insignificant receipt (see **72.10**), and they may require notice and other information from persons giving or receiving such value.

The penalty provisions of *TMA 1970, s 98* apply for failure to comply with the notification requirements.

HMRC also have broad powers to require information in other cases where relief may be withdrawn, restricted or not due.

[*ITA 2007, ss 257SE–257SH; F(No 2)A 2017, Sch 1 paras 5, 14(3)*].

Providing of State aid information

On and after 16 November 2017, where SITR has been given, or may in future be given, HMRC may give the social enterprise a notice requiring it to supply HMRC with specified information for the purpose of compliance with certain EU State aid obligations. This may include information about the enterprise, its activities and/or its investors, information about the SITR and information relating to the grant of State aid through the provision of the SITR. See **36.5** CONFIDENTIALITY OF INFORMATION as regards the publishing by HMRC of State aid information. [*FA 2016, s 180(5)–(9)(11), Sch 24 Pt 2; F(No 2)A 2017, Sch 1 para 13*].

Conditions relating to investor and investment

[72.22] The conditions mentioned at **72.7** above relating to the investor and the investment are described at **72.23–72.32** below. These are in addition to the condition at **72.3** above as to the types of investment permitted.

Condition that amount invested must be paid over

[72.23] So far as the investment is in shares, they must be subscribed for wholly in cash and fully paid-up at the time of issue. So far as the investment is in 'qualifying debt investments' (see **72.3** above), the full amount of the advance covered by the debenture(s) must have been advanced wholly in cash by the time the investment is made. There must be no undertaking to pay cash to any person at a future time in respect of the acquisition of the shares or qualifying debt investments. [*ITA 2007, s 257LA*].

The 'no pre-arranged exits' requirements

[72.24] There must not at any time in Period B (see **72.1** above) exist any arrangements (as widely defined) for the investment to be redeemed, repaid, repurchased, exchanged or otherwise disposed of in that period. Except where the social enterprise is an accredited social impact contractor (see **72.2** above), the 'issuing arrangements' for the investment must not include:

(a) arrangements for, or with a view to, the cessation of any trade which is being, or is to be or may be, carried on by the social enterprise or a person connected with it (within **19** CONNECTED PERSONS); or
(b) arrangements for the disposal of, or of a substantial amount (in terms of value) of, the assets of the social enterprise or of a person connected with it.

The '*issuing arrangements*' are the arrangements under which the investor makes the investment, but also include any arrangements made before, and in relation to or in connection with, the making of the investment by the investor. The arrangements referred to in (a) and (b) above do not include any arrangements applicable only on the winding-up of a company unless the issuing arrangements include arrangements for the company to be wound up or they are applicable otherwise than for genuine commercial reasons.

[*ITA 2007, ss 257LB, 257TE(1), 993*].

The 'no risk avoidance' requirement

[72.25] There must not at any time in Period B (see **72.1** above) exist any arrangements (as widely defined) a main purpose of which is (by means of any insurance, indemnity, guarantee, hedging of risk or otherwise) to provide partial or complete protection for the investor against what would otherwise be the risks attached to the investment. This does not include any arrangements which are confined to the provision for the social enterprise itself (and/or, where applicable, its subsidiaries) of any such protection against the risks arising in the ordinary course of carrying on business. [*ITA 2007, ss 257LC, 257TE(1)*].

The 'no linked loans' requirement

[72.26] No loan may be made to the investor or to an 'associate' at any time in Period A (see **72.1** above) if it would not have been made, or would not have been made on the same terms, if the investor had not made the investment or had not been proposing to do so. The giving of credit to, or the assignment of a debt due from, the investor or associate is counted as a loan. [*ITA 2007, s 257LD*]. It is anticipated that HMRC SP 6/98 (see **29.43** ENTERPRISE INVESTMENT SCHEME) will be applied for this purpose.

Meaning of 'associate'

An '*associate*' of any person is any 'relative' (i.e. spouse, civil partner, ancestor or linear descendant) or partner of that person, the trustee(s) of any settlement in relation to which that person or any relative (living or dead) is or was a settlor and, where that person has an interest in any shares or obligations of a company which are subject to any trust or are part of a deceased estate, the trustee(s) of the settlement or the personal representatives of the deceased. For this purpose, 'settlor' is defined as in **70.3** SETTLEMENTS. [*ITA 2007, s 257TC*].

The 'existing investments' requirement

[72.27] This requirement applies to investments made on or after 6 April 2017. If, immediately before the investment is made, the investor holds any shares in or debentures of the social enterprise, or a company which is at that time its qualifying subsidiary (see **72.49** below), those shares or debentures must be 'risk finance investments' or (in the case of shares) 'permitted subscriber shares'.

A share or debenture is a '*risk finance investment*' for these purposes if:

- it is a share issued to the investor, or a debenture of which the investor is the holder in return for advancing an amount; and
- at any time, an SITR compliance statement (see **72.6** above), an EIS compliance statement (see **29.7** ENTERPRISE INVESTMENT SCHEME) or an SEIS compliance statement (see **66.5** SEED ENTERPRISE INVESTMENT SCHEME) is provided in respect of it or of shares or investments including it.

Subscriber shares are '*permitted subscriber shares*' for these purposes if:

- they were issued to the investor and have been continuously held by him ever since; or
- they were acquired by the investor at a time when the issuing company had issued no shares other than subscriber shares and had not begun to carry on, or make preparations for carrying on, any trade or business.

For these purposes 'debenture' includes any instrument creating or acknowledging indebtedness.

[*ITA 2007, s 257LDA; F(No 2)A 2017, Sch 1 paras 3, 14(1)*].

The 'no tax avoidance' requirement

[72.28] The investment must be made for genuine commercial reasons and not as part of any arrangements (as widely defined) a main purpose of which is the avoidance of tax. [*ITA 2007, ss 257LE, 257TE(1)*].

The 'no disqualifying arrangements' requirement

[72.29] This requirement applies to investments made on or after 6 April 2017, but arrangements which include any transaction entered into before that date are excluded from being disqualifying arrangements. The investment must not be made, and money raised by the social enterprise from the making of the investment must not be employed, in consequence or anticipation of, or otherwise in connection with, 'disqualifying arrangements'. Arrangements are '*disqualifying arrangements*' if:

- a main purpose is to secure both that an activity is (or will be) carried on by the social enterprise (or its 90% social subsidiary — see **72.50** below) and that one or more of the 'relevant tax reliefs' are available in respect of the activity;
- the activity in question is the qualifying trade or activity in **72.44** below for the purposes of which the investment raised money; and
- one or both of Conditions A and B below are met. It is immaterial whether the social enterprise itself is a party to the arrangements.

Condition A is that, as a result of the money raised by the investment being employed as required by **72.45** below, an amount representing the whole or most of the amount raised is, in the course of the arrangements, paid to or for the benefit of one or more 'relevant persons'. Condition B is that, in the absence of the arrangements, it would have been reasonable to expect that the whole or greater part of the activities making up the qualifying trade or activity would have been carried on as part of another business by one or more 'relevant persons'.

A '*relevant person*' is one who is a party to the arrangements or a person connected with such a party (within **19** CONNECTED PERSONS). The '*relevant tax reliefs*' are those listed at **29.40** ENTERPRISE INVESTMENT SCHEME.

[*ITA 2007, s 257LEA; F(No 2)A 2017, Sch 1 paras 4, 14(3)(4)*].

Restrictions on being an employee, partner or paid director

[72.30] Neither the investor nor any individual who is an associate of his (see **72.26** above) can at any time in Period A (see **72.1** above) be:

(a) an employee of the social enterprise, or of a 'subsidiary' of the enterprise, or of a partner of the enterprise, or of a partner of a subsidiary of the enterprise;
(b) a partner of the enterprise or of a subsidiary of the enterprise;
(c) a trustee of the enterprise or of a subsidiary of the enterprise; or
(d) a 'remunerated' director of the enterprise or of a 'linked company'.

For these purposes, a '*subsidiary*' of the social enterprise means a company which at *any* time in Period A is a 51% subsidiary of the enterprise. In (d) above, 'director' does not include a trustee of a charity that is a trust. For the purposes of (d), a '*linked company*' means (i) a subsidiary of the enterprise or (ii) a company which is a partner of the enterprise or (iii) a company which is a partner of a subsidiary of the enterprise.

Meaning of 'remunerated'

For the purposes of (d) above, an individual who is a director of the social enterprise or of a linked company is '*remunerated*' if the individual (or a partnership of which he is a member):

- receives at any time in Period A a payment from a 'related person', or
- is entitled to receive a payment from a related person in respect of any time in Period A,

other than by way of:

(i) payment or reimbursement of travelling or other expenses wholly, exclusively and necessarily incurred by the individual in the performance of his duties as a director;
(ii) interest at no more than a commercial rate on money lent;
(iii) dividends etc. representing no more than a normal return on investment;
(iv) payment for supply of goods at no more than market value;
(v) rent at no more than a reasonable and commercial rent for property occupied by a related person; or
(vi) any necessary and reasonable remuneration for services rendered to a related person in the course of a trade or profession (other than secretarial or managerial services or of a kind provided by the person to whom they are rendered) which is taken into account in computing the profits of that trade or profession.

'*Related person*' means (i) the social enterprise, (ii) a person connected with the enterprise (within **19** CONNECTED PERSONS), (iii) a linked company (see above) of which the individual is a director, or (iv) a person connected with any such linked company.

If either of the following two conditions are met, there is also disregarded for the above purpose any other reasonable remuneration (including any benefit or facility) received by the individual, or to which he is entitled, for services rendered by him to the company (whether the social enterprise or a linked company) of which he is a director and rendered by him in his capacity as a director (or in his capacity as an employee where he is both director and employee). The first condition is that the investor made the investment, or previously made another investment meeting the requirements in **72.3** above, at a time (the '*qualifying time*') when:

- the above requirements and also those of **72.31** and **72.32** below would have been met even if each reference in those provisions to any time in Period A were a reference to any time before the qualifying time; and
- the investor had never been involved (whether on his own account or as a partner, director or employee) in carrying on the whole or any part of the trade, business or profession carried on by the social enterprise or by a subsidiary.

The second condition applies only where the first is not met and is that the investment is made before the third anniversary of the date when the investor last made an investment in the social enterprise which did meet the first condition.

Generally, an individual who is both a director and an employee of a company is treated for these purposes as a director and not an employee.

[*ITA 2007, ss 257LF, 993*].

The requirement not to be interested in capital etc.

[72.31] Neither the investor nor any individual who is an associate of his (see 72.26 above) must at any time in Period A (see **72.1** above):

- have control (see **72.14** above) of a 'related company'; or
- directly or indirectly possess or be entitled to acquire (whether he is so entitled at a future date or will at a future date be so entitled):
  - more than 30% of the ordinary share capital of a related company;
  - more than 30% of the loan capital of a related company; or
  - more than 30% of the voting power in a related company.

'*Related company*' means the social enterprise or any company which at *any* time in Period A is a 51% subsidiary of the enterprise.

There is to be disregarded any shares in a related company held by the individual, or by an associate of his, at a time when that company has not issued any shares other than subscriber shares and has not begun to carry on, or make preparations for carrying on, any trade or business. Loan capital includes any debt incurred by the company (i) for money borrowed, (ii) for capital assets acquired, (iii) for any right to income created in its favour, or (iv) for insufficient consideration, but it excludes any debt incurred for overdrawing a bank account in the ordinary course of the bank's business. Rights or powers of associates of an individual are attributed to the individual for the purposes of these provisions.

[*ITA 2007, s 257LG*].

The 'no collusion' requirement

[72.32] There must not at any time in Period A (see **72.1** above) be any arrangements (as widely defined):

(a) as part of which either the investor makes the investment or the investor (or an individual who is an associate of his — see **72.26** above) makes any other investment in the social enterprise;

(b) which provides for a person to make an investment in a company other than the social enterprise, where that person is not the individual who invests as in (a) above; and

(c) to which there is a party (whether or not the individual who invests as in (a) above) who is an individual in relation to whom not all of the requirements in **72.30** and **72.31** above would be met if (i) references in those provisions to the investor were references to that individual, and (ii) references in those provisions to the social enterprise were references to the company mentioned in (b) above.

[*ITA 2007, ss 257LH, 257TE(1)*].

Conditions relating to the social enterprise

[72.33] The conditions mentioned at **72.7** above relating to the social enterprise are described at **72.34–72.47** below.

The 'continuing to be a social enterprise' requirement

[72.34] The social enterprise must be a social enterprise throughout Period B (see **72.1** above). [*ITA 2007, s 257M*].

The 'maximum amount raised' requirement before 6 April 2017

[72.35] This requirement applies in relation to investments made before 6 April 2017. See the replacement rules at **72.47** below as regards investments made on or after that date.

A limit is set on the amount of tax-advantaged investment which a social enterprise may receive in a rolling three-year period. This limit is imposed by the need to comply with EC regulations on de minimis State aid, which restrict such aid to an amount not exceeding 200,000 euros in any three-year period. The total amount invested in the social enterprise must not be more than the amount given by:

$$\left(\frac{€200,000 - M}{RCG + RSI}\right) - T$$

where

T = the total in euros of any 'scheme investments' made in the 'aid period';
M = the total in euros of any de minimis State aid, other than scheme investments, that is granted during the aid period to the social enterprise or to a 'qualifying subsidiary' (see **72.49** below) at a time when it is such a subsidiary;
RCG = the highest rate at which capital gains tax is charged in the aid period; and
RSI = the highest SI rate (see **72.4** above) in the aid period.

The '*aid period*' is the three years ending with the day on which the investment is made. In the case of that day itself, the aid period includes only the part of the day before the investment is made. For these purposes, a '*scheme investment*' is an investment in respect of which the social enterprise (at any time) provides a compliance statement (see **72.6** above). The rules in **72.1** above on when an investment is made apply with appropriate modifications to determine when scheme investments are made.

If the investment or any scheme investments are made, or any aid is granted, in sterling or any other currency that is not the euro, its amount is to be converted into euros at an appropriate spot rate of exchange for the date on which the investment is made or the aid is paid.

[*ITA 2007, ss 257MA, 257MB; F(No 2)A 2017, Sch 1 paras 6(2), 14(1)*].

The gross assets requirement

[72.36] If the social enterprise is a single company, the value of its gross assets must not exceed £15 million immediately before the investment is made and must not exceed £16 million immediately afterwards. If the social enterprise is a parent company, the gross assets test applies by reference to the aggregate gross assets of all the group members (disregarding certain assets held by any group company which correspond to liabilities of another). [*ITA 2007, s 257MC*]. It is anticipated that HMRC SP 2/06 (see **29.53** ENTERPRISE INVESTMENT SCHEME) will be applied for this purpose.

The 'unquoted status' requirement

[72.37] At the beginning of Period B (see **72.1** above), the social enterprise must not be a quoted company, and no arrangements (as widely defined) must then exist for it to become a quoted company. Also, there must be no arrangements then in existence for the social enterprise to become a subsidiary of a company by virtue of a share exchange if arrangements have been made with a view to that company becoming a quoted company. A company is a quoted company if any of its shares etc. are listed on a recognised stock exchange or on a designated foreign exchange, or dealt in outside the UK by such means as may be designated. [*ITA 2007, ss 257MD, 257TE(1)*].

The control and independence requirement

[72.38] The social enterprise must not at any time in Period B (see **72.1** above) either:

(a) control (whether on its own or together with any person connected with it — within **19** CONNECTED PERSONS) another company other than a 'qualifying subsidiary' (see **72.49** below); or
(b) be a 51% subsidiary of another company or otherwise be under the control of a company or under the control of a company and a person connected with that company; or
(c) be capable of falling within (a) or (b) above by virtue of any arrangements (as widely defined).

'*Control*' is construed as in **72.14** above.

[*ITA 2007, ss 257ME, 257TD, 257TE(1)*].

The subsidiaries requirements

[72.39] At all times in Period B (see **72.1** above) any subsidiary of the social enterprise must be a 'qualifying subsidiary' (see **72.49** below). [*ITA 2007, s 257MF*].

The social enterprise must not at any time in Period B have a 'property managing subsidiary' which is not a '90% social subsidiary' (see **72.50** below) of the social enterprise. A '*property managing subsidiary*' is a subsidiary whose business consists wholly or mainly in the holding or managing of land or any property deriving its value (directly or indirectly) from land. [*ITA 2007, s 257MG*]. The legislation does not define what is meant by property deriving its value indirectly from land, but examples given by the explanatory notes are the enterprise having shareholdings in a company deriving its value from land, having any interest in settled property deriving its value from land, or having any option, consent or embargo affecting the disposition of land.

The 'number of employees' requirement

[72.40] If the social enterprise is a single company, it must have fewer than the equivalent of 250 full-time employees when the investment is made. In relation to investments made before 6 April 2017, this figure was 500. If the social enterprise is a parent company, this rule applies by reference to the aggregate number of full-time employees of itself and its 'qualifying subsidiaries' (see **72.49** below). To ascertain the equivalent number of full-time employees of a company, take the actual number of full-time employees and add to it a just and reasonable fraction for each employee who is not full-time. For this purpose, an 'employee' includes a director but does not include anyone on maternity, paternity or parental bereavement leave or a student on vocational training. [*ITA 2007, s 257MH; F(No 2)A 2017, Sch 1 paras 7, 14(1); Parental Bereavement (Leave and Pay) Act 2018, Sch para 53; SI 2020 No 45, Reg 2*].

The 'no partnerships' requirement

[72.41] At no time in Period B (see **72.1** above) can the social enterprise be a member of a partnership or can any '90% social subsidiary' (see **72.50** below) of the social enterprise be a member of a partnership. [*ITA 2007, s 257MI*].

The 'financial health' requirement

[72.42] This requirement applies in relation to investments made on or after 6 April 2017. The requirement must be met at the beginning of Period B (see **72.1** above) and is that the social enterprise is not 'in difficulty'. The social enterprise is '*in difficulty*' if it is reasonable to assume that it would be regarded as a firm in difficulty for the purposes of the *EU Guidelines on State Aid for Rescuing and Restructuring Firms in Difficulty (2004/C 244/02)*. [*ITA 2007, s 257MIA; F(No 2)A 2017, Sch 1 paras 8, 14(1)*].

The trading requirement

[72.43] Except where it is an accredited social impact contractor (see **72.2** above), the social enterprise must, throughout Period B (see **72.1** above), be:

(a) a charity; or
(b) a single company that is not a charity and whose business does not, if things done for incidental purposes are ignored, consist to any extent in the carrying-on of 'non-trade activities' and does not consist wholly, or as to a substantial part, in the carrying-on of 'excluded activities' (within **72.48** below); or
(c) a parent company that is not a charity, where the business of the group (i.e. the company and its qualifying subsidiaries) does not consist wholly, or as to a substantial part, in the carrying-on of 'non-qualifying activities'.

For the purposes of (b) above, '*non-trade activities*' are activities which are neither activities carried on in the course of a trade nor activities carried on in the course of preparing to carry on a trade. For the purposes of similar legislation elsewhere, a 'substantial part' (see (b) and (c) above) is generally taken to mean more than 20%.

If the social enterprise intends that one or more companies should become its qualifying subsidiaries with a view to their carrying on one or more qualifying trades, then, until any time after which the intention is abandoned, the social enterprise is treated as a parent company and those other companies are included in the group for the above purposes.

The business of the group means what would be the business of the group if the activities of the group companies taken together were regarded as one business. Activities are for this purpose disregarded to the extent that they consist in:

- holding shares in or securities of any of the parent company's subsidiaries;
- making loans to another group company; or
- holding and managing property used by a group company for the purposes of a qualifying trade or trades carried on by any group company.

Activities of a group company are also disregarded to the extent that they are activities carried on by a 'mainly trading subsidiary' otherwise than for its main purpose. A '*mainly trading subsidiary*' is a qualifying subsidiary which exists wholly for the purpose of carrying on one or more qualifying trades (disregarding purposes having no significant effect on the extent of its activities).

Non-qualifying activities

'*Non-qualifying activities*' are:

- excluded activities within **72.48** below; and
- activities, other than activities carried on by a charity, that are carried on otherwise than in the course of a trade.

[*ITA 2007, ss 257MJ, 257TE(1)*].

Administration or receivership etc.

The social enterprise is not regarded as ceasing to meet the trading requirement merely because of anything done in consequence of the enterprise or any of its subsidiaries being in administration or receivership (both as defined by *ITA 2007, s 257TB*). The entry into administration or receivership, and everything done as a result of the company concerned being in administration or receivership, must be for genuine commercial reasons and not part of arrangements (as widely defined) of which a main purpose is tax avoidance.

The social enterprise ceases to meet the trading requirement if before the end of Period B (see **72.1** above) a resolution is passed, or an order is made, for the winding-up of the social enterprise or any of its subsidiaries or in the event of a dissolution without winding-up, but this does not apply if the winding-up or dissolution is for genuine commercial reasons, and is not part of arrangements of which a main purpose is tax avoidance.

[*ITA 2007, ss 257MK, 257TE(1)*].

The 'purpose of the issue' requirement

[72.44] Except where it is an accredited social impact contractor (see **72.2** above), the social enterprise must be a party to the making of the investment (so far as not in bonus shares) in order to raise money for the carrying on (by the social enterprise or a '90% social subsidiary' — see **72.50** below) of:

- a 'qualifying trade' (see **72.48** below) which on the date the investment is made is carried on by the social enterprise or a 90% social subsidiary; or
- the activity of preparing to carry on a qualifying trade which is intended to be carried on by the social enterprise or a 90% social subsidiary and which is begun to be carried within two years after the date the investment is made. In determining when a qualifying trade is begun to be carried on by a 90% social subsidiary, any carrying on of the trade by it before it became such a subsidiary is disregarded.

[*ITA 2007, s 257ML*].

The 'minimum period' requirements

[72.45] Except where the social enterprise is an accredited social impact contractor (see **72.2** above), all of the money raised by the social enterprise from the making of the investment must, no later than the end of 28 months beginning with the date the investment is made, be employed wholly for the purpose for which it was raised (as to which see **72.44** above). Employing money on the acquisition of shares or stock in a body does not of itself amount to employing the money for such purpose. In relation to investments made on or after 6 April 2017, employing money on the repayment of a loan does not amount to employing the money for such purpose. The requirement does not fail to be met merely because an amount of money which is not significant is employed for other purposes.

The chosen trade must have been carried on for a period of at least four months ending at or after the time the investment is made. The trade must have been carried on for those months by no person other than the social enterprise or a '90% social subsidiary' (see **72.50** below) of the enterprise. A trading period shorter than four months is permitted if this is by reason only of the winding-up or dissolution of any company or anything done as a consequence of a company being in administration or receivership, provided the winding-up etc. is for genuine commercial reasons and not part of arrangements (as widely defined) of which a main purpose is tax avoidance.

Where the social enterprise is an accredited social impact contractor, all of the money raised by it from the making of the investment must, no later than the end of 24 months beginning with the date the investment is made, be employed wholly for the carrying out of the social impact contract in question. Again, insignificant employment of money for other purposes is ignored.

[*ITA 2007, ss 257MM, 257TE(1); F(No 2)A 2017, Sch 1 paras 9, 14(1)*].

The 'social enterprise to carry on the trade' requirement

[72.46] Except where the social enterprise is an accredited social impact contractor (see **72.2** above), there must not be a time in Period B (see **72.1** above) when the chosen trade (or the preparation activity for the chosen trade) is carried on by a person who is neither the social enterprise nor a '90% social subsidiary' (see **72.50** below) of the enterprise.

Where preparation work is carried on in Period B by the social enterprise or a 90% social subsidiary, the carrying on of the chosen trade in that period by any other person is disregarded for these purposes if it occurs before the enterprise or a 90% social subsidiary carries on that trade.

The requirement is not regarded as failing to be met if, as a consequence a company being wound up or dissolved or being in administration or receivership (both as defined by *ITA 2007, s 257TB*), the chosen trade ceases to be carried on in Period B by the social enterprise or a 90% social subsidiary and is subsequently carried on by a person who is not connected (within **19** CONNECTED PERSONS) with the enterprise at any time in Period A (see **72.1** above). This let-out applies only if the winding-up, dissolution or entry into administration or receivership (and everything done as a consequence of the company concerned being in administration or receivership) is for genuine commercial reasons and not part of arrangements (as widely defined) a main purpose of which is the avoidance of tax.

[*ITA 2007, ss 257MN, 257TE(1), 993*].

Limits on amounts that may be invested

[72.47] The following rules apply in relation to investments made on or after 6 April 2017 and supersede **72.35** above.

Where investment made in first seven years

Where either:

(a) the investment is made before the end of the seven years beginning with the 'relevant first commercial sale'; or
(b) the investment is made later than that but a 'relevant investment' had been made in the social enterprise before the end of that seven-year period and some or all of the money raised by that relevant investment was employed for the purposes of the same qualifying trade or activity (see **72.44** above) for which the money raised by the current investment is employed,

the total amount of relevant investments made in the social enterprise on or before the date the investment is made must not exceed £1.5 million. In determining whether or not this investment limit has been reached, certain investments made other than in the social enterprise itself are taken into account. These include investments in 51% subsidiaries of the social enterprise, investments in companies that were previously 51% subsidiaries of the social enterprise, and investments in a trade prior to that trade being acquired by the social enterprise or a subsidiary (see *ITA 2007, s 257MNB*).

'*Relevant investments*' have the same meaning as in **29.30** ENTERPRISE INVESTMENT SCHEME (reading references there to a company as including any social enterprise). '*First commercial sale*' has the same meaning as in the EC's Guidelines on State aid to promote risk finance investments. The '*relevant first commercial sale*' is defined in *ITA 2007, s 175A(6)* (as modified by *ITA 2007, s 257MNA(4)*) by reference to the earliest date of any commercial sale made by (broadly) the social enterprise or a 51% subsidiary or any other person who has carried on any trade which is carried on by the social enterprise or a subsidiary. Definitions are suitably modified (by *ITA 2007, s 257MNA(6)*) where the social enterprise is an accredited social impact contractor (as in **72.2** above).

Other cases

Where the investment is made after the end of the seven-year period in (a) above and the condition in (b) above is *not* met, the £1.5 million limit applies as above but with the additional proviso that the amount invested in the social enterprise must not be more than the amount given by:

$$\left(\frac{€200,000 - M}{RCG + RSI}\right) - T$$

where

T = the total in euros of any relevant investments made in social enterprise in the 'aid period';
M = the total in euros of any de minimis State aid, other than relevant investments, that is granted during the aid period to the social enterprise or to a 'qualifying subsidiary' (see **72.49** below) at a time when it is such a subsidiary;
RCG = the highest rate at which capital gains tax is charged in the aid period; and
RSI = the highest SI rate (see **72.4** above) in the aid period.

The '*aid period*' is the three years ending with the day on which the investment is made. In the case of that day itself, the aid period includes only the part of the day before the investment is made. If the investment or any scheme investments are made, or any aid is granted, in sterling or any other currency that is not the euro, its amount is to be converted into euros at an appropriate spot rate of exchange for the date on which the investment is made or the aid is paid.

[*ITA 2007, ss 257MNA–257MNE; F(No 2)A 2017, Sch 1 paras 6(3), 14(1)(2)*].

For the purposes of determining entitlement to social investment tax relief in respect of shares issued or investments made on or after 1 December 2017, investments are not prevented from constituting relevant investments by virtue only of their having been made before certain historical dates. Previously, under earlier transitional provisions, certain investments made before 6 April 2012 did not count as relevant investments. [*FA 2018, s 15*].

Qualifying trade

[72.48] A trade is a '*qualifying trade*' if it is conducted on a commercial basis with a view to the realisation of profits and it does not, at any time in Period B (see **72.1** above), consist to a substantial extent in the carrying on of 'excluded activities'. For these purposes, 'trade' does not include a venture in the nature of trade. HMRC will regard activities as not being 'substantial' if they are less than 20% of the whole (Notes for Social Investment Tax Relief compliance statement at www.gov.uk/government/publications/social-investment-tax-relief-compliance-statement-sitr2014).

'*Excluded activities*' are:

(a) dealing in land, commodities or futures, or in shares, securities or other financial instruments;
(b) banking, insurance, money lending, debt factoring, hire-purchase financing or other financial activities;
(c) (in relation to investments made on or after 6 April 2017) leasing (including letting ships on charter or other assets on hire);
(d) (in relation to investments made on or after 6 April 2017) receiving royalties or licence fees;
(e) (in relation to investments made on or after 6 April 2017) operating or managing nursing homes or residential care homes (both as defined) or managing property used as such;
(f) (in relation to investments made on or after 6 April 2017) generating electricity, exporting electricity or making electricity generating capacity available;
(g) (in relation to investments made on or after 6 April 2017) generating heat;
(h) (in relation to investments made on or after 6 April 2017) generating any form of energy not within (f) or (g);
(i) (in relation to investments made on or after 6 April 2017) producing gas or fuel;
(j) 'property development';
(k) fishery and aquaculture production activities (defined by reference to relevant EU State aid rules);
(l) primary production of agriculture products (which includes both livestock and crops and the production of alcohol from plants and fruit);
(m) (in relation to investments made before 6 April 2017) subsidised generation or export of electricity;
(n) road freight transport for hire or reward; and
(o) providing services or facilities for a business in (a)–(n) which is carried on by another person (other than a parent company), where one person has a 'controlling interest' in both businesses.

As regards (b) above, the activity of lending money to a social enterprise was not an excluded activity in relation to investments before 6 April 2017.

Exclusion (e) above applies only if the person carrying on the activity has an estate or interest (e.g. a lease) in the property concerned or occupies that property.

For the purposes of (f) and (m) above, electricity is exported if it is exported onto a distribution or transmission system.

'*Property development*' in (j) above means the development of land by a company, which has (or has had at any time) an 'interest in the land' (as defined), with the sole or main object of realising a gain from the disposal of an interest in the developed land.

The exclusion in (m) above referred to the generation or export of electricity in respect of which the company received a feed-in tariff under a UK Government scheme to encourage small-scale low-carbon generation of electricity or a financial incentive granted under a similar overseas scheme.

As regards (o) above, a person has a '*controlling interest*' in a business carried on by a company if (i) he 'controls' (see **72.14** above) the company; or (ii) the company is a close company and he or an 'associate' (see **72.26** above) is a director of the company and the owner of, or able to control, more than 30% of its ordinary share capital; or (iii) at least half the business could, under *CTA 2010, s 942*, be regarded as belonging to him for the purposes of *CTA 2010, s 941* (company reconstructions without change of ownership). In any other case a person has a controlling interest in a business if the person is entitled to at least half of the assets used for, or of the income arising from, the business. In any case, the rights and powers of a person's associates are attributed to him for these purposes.

[*ITA 2007, ss 257MP–257MQA, 257MR–257MT, 257MW; F(No 2)A 2017, Sch 1 paras 10, 12, 15*].

Qualifying subsidiaries

[72.49] In order to be a '*qualifying subsidiary*' a subsidiary must be a '51% subsidiary' (within *CTA 2010, Pt 24 Ch 3*) of the parent, and no person other than the parent or another of its subsidiaries may have 'control' (see **72.14** above) of the subsidiary. No arrangements (as widely defined) may exist by virtue of which either of these conditions would cease to be met.

The above conditions are not regarded as ceasing to be met by reason only of the subsidiary or any other company being wound up or dissolved or by reason only of anything done as a consequence of any such company being in administration or receivership (both as defined by *ITA 2007, s 257TB*), provided the winding-up, dissolution, entry into administration or receivership or anything done as a consequence of its being in administration or receivership is for genuine commercial reasons and is not part of arrangements a main purpose of which is the avoidance of tax. Also, the above conditions are not regarded as ceasing to be met by reason only of arrangements being in existence for the disposal of the interest in the subsidiary held by the parent (or, as the case may be, by another of its subsidiaries) if the disposal is to be for genuine commercial reasons and is not to be part of arrangements a main purpose of which is the avoidance of tax.

[*ITA 2007, ss 257MU, 257TE(1)*].

90% social subsidiaries

[72.50] A company ('*the subsidiary*') is a '*90% social subsidiary*' of another company ('*the parent*') if:

- the subsidiary is a social enterprise;
- the parent possesses at least 90% of both the issued share capital of, and the voting power in, the subsidiary;
- the parent would be beneficially entitled to at least 90% of the assets of the subsidiary available for distribution to equity holders on a winding-up or in any other circumstances;
- the parent is beneficially entitled to at least 90% of any profits of the subsidiary available for distribution to equity holders;
- no person other than the parent has control (see **72.14** above) of the subsidiary; and
- no arrangements (as widely defined) exist by virtue of which any of the above conditions would cease to be met.

For the above purposes, *CTA 2010, Pt 5 Ch 6* applies, with appropriate modifications, to determine the persons who are equity holders and the percentage of assets available to them. Similar let-outs apply as in **72.49** above where a company is wound up or dissolved or enters into administration or receivership or where arrangements exist for the disposal of the interest in the subsidiary.

A company ('company A') which is a subsidiary of another company ('company B') is a 90% social subsidiary of a third company ('company C') if:

- company A is a 90% social subsidiary of company B, and company B is a '100% social subsidiary' of company C; or
- company A is a 100% social subsidiary of company B, and company B is a 90% social subsidiary of company C.

For this purpose, no account is to be taken of any control company C may have of company A, and '*100% social subsidiary*' is defined similarly to '90% social subsidiary' but substituting '100%' for '90%'.

[*ITA 2007, s 257MV*].

73

Social Security and National Insurance

Cross-references. See Tolley's Social Security and State Benefit and Tolley's National Insurance Contributions.

Taxable social security benefits

[73.1] The provisions for the taxation of social security benefits are in *ITEPA 2003, Pt 10.*

Benefits taxable (as earned income) are as follows:

Bereavement allowance	Retirement pension
Carer's allowance	Retirement pension taken as lump sum (see **56.8** PENSION INCOME)
(On and after 12 February 2019) carer's allowance supplement (Scotland only)	Statutory adoption pay
Employment and support allowance (contributory)	Statutory maternity pay
Incapacity benefit (see below)	Statutory paternity pay
Income support when paid to strikers (see below)	Statutory sick pay
Industrial death benefit (if paid as pension)	Statutory shared parental pay
Invalidity allowance when paid with retirement pension	Statutory parental bereavement pay
Jobseeker's allowance (up to 'taxable maximum')	Widowed parent's allowance
Old persons' pension	

[*ITEPA 2003, ss 577–579, 658–662, 670–675; FA 2019, s 12(2)–(4); Parental Bereavement (Leave and Pay) Act 2018, Sch para 47; SI 2017 No 338, Regs 2, 5, 6, 12–14; SI 2020 No 45, Reg 2*].

See **30** EXEMPT INCOME for certain exemptions on war widow's pension and **30.47** for other exemptions. See inside back cover for **rates** of main taxable benefits.

For the application of PAYE to payments of contributory employment and support allowance, see *SI 2003 No 2682, Regs 184A–184S.*

Incapacity benefit

Incapacity benefit is taxable (and may be within PAYE) *except for* short-term benefit payable otherwise than at the higher rate, i.e. benefit payable for the first 28 weeks of incapacity (and except for any child addition). There is also an exclusion for certain payments where invalidity benefit was previously payable in respect of the same period of incapacity. [*ITEPA 2003, ss 663, 664*]. For the application of PAYE to taxable payments of incapacity benefit, see *SI 2003 No 2682, Regs 173–180.*

Income support

Income support is taxable only if the claimant is one of a couple (whether or not married and including a same-sex couple) and *Social Security Contributions and Benefits Act 1992, s 126* (or NI equivalent) (trade disputes) applies to the claimant but not to the other person (i.e. broadly if the claimant is on strike). There is a maximum amount in any period which is taxable, and this maximum applies to the sum of income support and jobseeker's allowance where both are in payment. There is provision for notification of, and objection to, determination of the taxable amount by the benefit officer. [*TMA 1970, ss 54A–54C; ITEPA 2003, ss 665–669; SI 2017 No 338, Regs 2, 7–11*]. See HMRC Employment Income Manual EIM76190.

See also **53.52** PAY AS YOU EARN regarding the withholding of tax refunds from the unemployed and strikers.

Statutory sick pay etc.

Statutory sick pay, statutory maternity pay, statutory paternity pay, statutory shared parental pay and statutory adoption pay paid by employers is taxable.

Supplementary welfare payments: Northern Ireland

Supplementary welfare payments made to individuals in NI are chargeable to income tax if they top up a taxable benefit and exempt from income tax if they top up a tax-exempt benefit. [*FA 2016, s 44; F(No 2)A 2017, s 70; SI 2017 No 338*].

Simon's Taxes. See **E1.590, E4.329.**

Non-taxable social security benefits

[73.2] Benefits not taxable are as follows:

Income-related benefits

Child tax credit (see **73.6** below)
Council tax benefit
(On and after 12 February 2019) council tax reduction scheme payment (England and Wales)
(On and after 12 February 2019) discretionary housing payment
(On and after 12 February 2019) discretionary support award (Northern Ireland)
Educational maintenance allowance
Hospital patients' travelling expenses
Housing benefit
Employment and support allowance (income-related)
Income support (if not taxable as in **73.1** above)
Social fund payments
State pension credit
Student grants
Universal credit
Working tax credit (see **73.6** below)

Industrial injury benefits

Industrial death benefit child allowance
Disablement benefit, including
Constant attendance allowance
Exceptionally severe disablement allowance
Reduced earnings allowance
Retirement allowance
Unemployability supplement

Short-term benefits

Incapacity benefit (not at the higher rate, see **73.1** above)
Maternity allowance

War disablement benefits

Disablement pension, including
Age allowance
Allowance for lowered standard of occupation
Clothing allowance
Comforts allowance
Constant attendance allowance
Dependant allowance
Education allowance
Exceptionally severe disablement allowance
Invalidity allowance
Medical treatment allowance
Mobility supplement
Severe disablement occupational allowance
Unemployability allowance

Benefits payable in Scotland
(On and after 12 February 2019) best start grant
(On and after 6 April 2020) disability assistance for children and young people
(On and after 12 February 2019) discretionary housing payment
(On and after 12 February 2019) funeral expense assistance
(On and after 6 April 2020) job start
(On and after 6 April 2020) Scottish child payment
(On and after 12 February 2019) young carer grant

Other benefits
Attendance allowance
Back to work bonus (paid by way of jobseeker's allowance or income support)
Bereavement payment
Child benefit (but see 73.4 below)
Child dependency additions *paid with* widowed mother's allowance, retirement pension, invalid care allowance or unemployment benefit
Child's special allowance
Christmas bonus for pensioners
Cold weather payments
Disability living allowance
Employment rehabilitation allowance
Employment training allowance
Fares to school
(On and after 12 February 2019) flexible support fund payment
Guardian's allowance
Health in pregnancy grant
Home renovation grants
Invalidity allowance when paid with invalidity pension
Invalidity pension
In-work credit
In-work emergency discretion fund payment
In-work emergency fund payment
Jobfinder's grant
Jobmatch payments and training vouchers
Jobseeker's allowance (in excess of 'taxable maximum')
Job search allowances
Personal independence payment
Return to work credit
Severe disablement allowance
Vaccine damage payment
War orphan's pension
War widow's pension
Winter fuel payments

Bereavement support payment, which will replace bereavement allowance, bereavement payment and widowed parent's allowance for deaths on or after a date to be appointed, will be exempt from income tax.

See also **56.4** PENSION INCOME for general exemptions from the charge to tax on such income and **73.1** above as regards supplementary welfare payments made to NI individuals.

[*ITEPA 2003, ss 641, 645, 656, 677, Sch 7 para 88, Sch 8; Health and Social Care Act 2008, s 138; FA 2019, s 12(5)–(7); FA 2020, s 12; SI 2017 No 338, Regs 2, 15*]. See also **73.1** above.

Childcare payments top-up scheme

Under *Childcare Payments Act 2014*, the Government make a top-up contribution towards an eligible person's childcare costs (see www.gov.uk/help-with-childcare-costs/tax-free-childcare). A Government top-up payment is not taxable income of the recipient. Tax due from a person cannot be collected by set-off under *FA 2008, s 130* (see **54.7** PAYMENT OF TAX) against any top-up payments due to that person. [*Childcare Payments Act 2014, ss 66, 67; SI 2017 No 578, Reg 3*].

New Deal 50 plus programme

In-work training grants are disregarded for income tax purposes. [*ITTOIA 2005, s 781*].

Employment Zones programme

Payments to a person as a participant in an Employment Zones programme are disregarded for income tax purposes. [*ITTOIA 2005, s 782*].

Foreign benefits

Foreign social security benefits substantially similar to UK taxable benefits are brought into charge by *ITEPA 2003, ss 678–680*, the taxable amount being the full amount arising in the tax year. The income is relevant foreign income (see **32.2** FOREIGN INCOME) for the purposes of **32.4** FOREIGN INCOME (deductions and reliefs) and **61** REMITTANCE BASIS. See also **32.5** FOREIGN INCOME for relief for unremittable income. There is an exemption if the corresponding UK benefit is exempt. [*ITEPA 2003, s 681*].

Simon's Taxes. See E4.328.

Benefits under Government pilot schemes

[73.3] The question as to whether or not, or to what extent, any benefit under a Government pilot scheme is to be within the charge to income tax is to be determined by Treasury Order. The Treasury may also by order provide for any such benefit to be wholly or partly left out of account in determining whether expenditure otherwise qualifying for capital allowances has been met by the Crown etc. (see **9.2**(vi) CAPITAL ALLOWANCES). For these purposes, a

Government pilot scheme means, broadly, any arrangements made for a trial period by the Government which provide for new social security benefits or benefits under work incentive schemes. [*FA 1996, s 151*]. No new Treasury Order has been made under these provisions since 2008/09.

High income child benefit charge

[73.4] An income tax charge (the '*high income child benefit charge*') is imposed on an individual whose adjusted net income exceeds £50,000 in a tax year and who is, or whose partner is, in receipt of child benefit. In the event that both partners have an adjusted net income that exceeds £50,000, the charge applies only to the partner with the highest income. The amount of the charge is 1% of the amount of the child benefit for every £100 of income above £50,000. If the individual's adjusted net income exceeds £60,000, the charge is on the full amount of the child benefit. Child benefit itself remains non-taxable but the high income child benefit charge effectively claws back the benefit from high income taxpayers.

Meaning of 'adjusted net income'

See **1.17** ALLOWANCES AND TAX RATES for the full meaning of 'adjusted net income'. It is broadly taxable income before deducting personal reliefs but adjusted by deducting the gross equivalent of any Gift Aid donations or any pension contributions paid net of basic rate tax.

Meaning of 'partner'

For the purposes of these provisions, two people are '*partners*' if:

- they are married or in a civil partnership and are neither separated under a court order nor separated in circumstances in which the separation is likely to be permanent; or
- they are not married to each other or in a civil partnership but are living together as if they were a married couple or civil partners.

The charge to tax

A person (P) is liable to the high income child benefit charge for a tax year if P is entitled to an amount of child benefit for a 'week' in the tax year and P's adjusted net income for the year exceeds £50,000. If P has a partner (Q) throughout that week and Q's adjusted net income for the year exceeds £50,000 but P's does not, the charge falls on Q. If both partners have adjusted net incomes of more than £50,000, the charge falls on whichever has the higher adjusted net income; if they have identical adjusted net incomes, the charge falls on P.

Where the charge falls on the partner not in receipt of child benefit, it applies by reference only to child benefit entitlement in those weeks of the tax year throughout which the partnership exists. So, for example, If the couple break up during the year, that partner will be liable only for the period from 6 April (or, if later, the first full week in which the couple are partners as defined above) up to and including the last full week in which they are partners.

For the purposes of these provisions, a '*week*' is a period of seven days beginning on a Monday. A week falls within a tax year if (and only if) the Monday on which it begins is part of the tax year.

There is nothing in the legislation which deems the person liable to be in receipt of an amount of taxable income in connection with the charge. For this very reason, a discovery assessment was quashed in *Wilkes v HMRC* FTT (TC 7740), [2020] UKFTT 0256 (TC). The tax payable is brought into account at Step 7 of the calculation of income tax liability at **1.10** ALLOWANCES AND TAX RATES. It is collectible via PAYE wherever possible (unless the taxpayer objects) and otherwise via the normal self-assessment system.

Any entitlement to child benefit after the death of the child is ignored for the purposes of these provisions.

A number of cases have been heard by the First-tier and Upper Tribunals on failure to notify chargeability to tax (see **55.2** PENALTIES where such chargeability has arisen from the incidence of the high income child benefit charge, with the decisions favouring HMRC. See, for example, *HMRC v Robertson* UT, [2019] STC 1602, [2019] UKUT 202 (TCC); *Lau v HMRC* FTT (TC 6463), [2018] UKFTT 230 (TC); *Nonyane v HMRC* FTT (TC 5577), [2017] UKFTT 11 (TC).

Computing the charge

The amount of the charge is 1% of the amount of 'child benefit entitlement' for every £100 of the chargeable person's adjusted net income above £50,000. For example, if total child benefit is £1,820 and adjusted net income is £54,000, the tax charge will be £728.00 (£18.20 × 40). The maximum charge is an amount equal to the full amount of child benefit entitlement and applies where the chargeable person's adjusted net income is £60,000 or more. The '*child benefit entitlement*' is for this purpose the amount of child benefit to which the chargeable person or his partner was entitled for the total number of weeks for which the charge applies, determined as above (and see the example at **73.5** below).

Both the child benefit entitlement a the amount of the charge itself are rounded down to the nearest whole number. Adjusted net income is rounded down to the nearest multiple of £100 so that the percentage to be applied will always be a whole number.

Child not living with claimant

There will be cases where a person (R) claims child benefit on the grounds that, although the child is question is not living with R, R is contributing to the child's upkeep. (Under child benefit rules, the amount contributed must be at least equal to the amount of child benefit claimed.) Where:

(a) R is entitled to an amount of child benefit for a child for a week in a tax year;
(b) neither R, nor any person who is a partner of R throughout that week, is liable for the high income child benefit charge in respect of that amount; and

(c) there is another person (S) who has the child living with them in that week,

the high income child benefit charge applies as if S were entitled to the amount of child benefit in (a). If there is more than one person to whom (c) applies in relation to an amount of child benefit for a week, then this treatment applies only to the one with the highest adjusted net income for the tax year, i.e. that person is S.

There is an exception to the above. This is where R had previously claimed child benefit on the basis that R was living with the child and, after a temporary period of no more than 52 weeks, resumes the claim on the same basis and for the same child. An example of such an occurrence is where a parent moves away temporarily for work purposes and leaves the child with a family member until the parent's return. R's entitlement to child benefit for any week within that temporary period is deemed not to fall within (a) above.

Polygamous relationships

In a case where there are more than two persons in a relationship, for example a polygamous marriage entered into outside the UK, such that more than one person is a partner of P or S above at the same time, only the person with the highest adjusted net income for the year can be liable to the charge.

Election not to receive child benefit

A person (P) who is entitled to child benefit for one or more children can elect not to receive that benefit. An election may be made only if P reasonably expects that, in the absence of an election, P or another person would be liable to a high income child benefit charge in respect of child benefit payments made for weeks beginning after the making of the election and in the first tax year in which it has effect. For the purposes of the high income child benefit charge provisions, there is then deemed to be no entitlement to child benefit during the currency of the election. It should be noted that only the person entitled to the benefit can make an election, even if it is that person's partner who would be liable to the tax charge. HMRC have power to make directions setting out how an election should be made.

An election has effect in relation to child benefit payments for weeks beginning after it is made. If, however, entitlement to child benefit is backdated, an election may have effect in relation to payments for weeks beginning in the three months ending immediately before the child benefit claim was made. An election may be revoked, and the election then ceases to have effect in relation to payments for weeks beginning after the revocation is made. However, if P made an election on an incorrect assumption that P or another would be liable to the high income child benefit charge for a tax year, P has two years from the end of the tax year to revoke the election retrospectively so that it is treated as never having been in force during that tax year.

[*ITEPA 2003, ss 681B–681H, 684(2); Social Security Administration Act 1992, s 13A; Social Security Administration (Northern Ireland) Act 1992, s 11A; SI 2003 No 2682, Reg 14B; SI 2019 No 1458, Sch 3 para 25(5)*].

See www.gov.uk/child-benefit-tax-charge, which includes links to online forms for making and revoking an election not to receive child benefit.

Simon's Taxes. See **E1.102B**.

Example

[73.5]

Jill is a single parent of one child and is entitled to child benefit of £20.70 per week throughout 2019/20 and £21.05 per week throughout 2020/21. Her adjusted net income is less than £50,000 for both those tax years. On 14 May 2020 she moves in with her boyfriend Jack, who has an adjusted net income of £56,344 for 2020/21. They continue to live together beyond 5 April 2021.

Jill has no liability to the high income child benefit charge for either year as her adjusted net income does not exceed £50,000. Jack is liable to the charge in respect of Jill's child benefit entitlement for the week beginning Monday 18 May 2020 and the subsequent 46 weeks falling in the tax year 2020/21.

The amount of the charge on Jack is computed as follows. Child benefit entitlement for the 47 weeks beginning Monday 18 May 2020 is £21.05 × 47 = £989.35 which is rounded down to £989. Adjusted net income is rounded down to £56,300. Therefore, the tax charge is:

£989 × 1% × 6,300/100 = £623.07

This is rounded down to £623, which is added to Jack's income tax liability for the year.

Child tax credit and working tax credit

[73.6] Both child tax credit ('CTC') and working tax credit ('WTC') are administered by HMRC through their Tax Credit Office, are awarded in respect of a tax year and are computed initially on the claimant's income of the preceding tax year (see further below). They are non-taxable and are neither related to nor deducted from the claimant's income tax liability. Thus, they are not 'tax credits' in the conventional sense, but social security benefits. The main provisions are in *Tax Credits Act 2002*, but most of the detail is provided by regulations made by statutory instrument.

Same-sex couples, who are living together as partners (whether or not they have formed a civil partnership), are treated the same way for tax credits purposes as opposite-sex couples.

The detailed tax credit rules are beyond the scope of this work. The following brief summary is intended to serve as an initial reference.

Child tax credit

Subject to the tapering rules below, child tax credit is payable to UK resident single parents and couples, married or otherwise, who are responsible for a child aged under 16 (tax credits will continue to be paid until 1 September following their 16th birthday) or a young person (generally a person aged over 16 and under 19 in full-time, non-advanced, education or on approved training (other than where provided by virtue of employment) or who is enrolled or has been accepted to undertake such training). It includes: a family element for all who qualify for CTC (£545 for 2019/20 and 2020/21) and a child element for each child or young person (£2,780 for 2019/20 and £2,830 for 2020/21), increased if the child or young person is disabled (to £6,135 for 2019/20 and £6,245 for 2020/21) and further increased where the child or young person is severely disabled (to £7,495 for 2019/20 and £7,630 for 2020/21).

Working tax credit

Subject to the tapering rules below, working tax credit is payable to UK residents who are at least 16 years old and who work (or in the case of a couple, one of whom works) at least a set number of hours a week. Additionally, the claimant (or one of the claimants in the case of a couple) must either:

(a) have dependent children, or a mental or physical disability which puts them at a disadvantage in getting a job and have been previously in receipt of some form of disability benefit; or
(b) be at least 25 years old.

A person within (a) above must generally work at least 16 hours a week. However, for couples with at least one child the rule is that, if both partners work, their joint weekly hours must be at least 24 with one of them working at least 16 or, if only one works, his or her weekly hours must be at least 24. A limit of 16 hours per week applies if the person working is over 60 or qualifies for the disability element of WTC or if the other person is on certain ill-health benefits, hospitalised or in prison. A person within (b) above must work at least 30 hours a week. Any person over 50 (or his or her partner) must work at least 30 hours a week, reduced to 16 if the person is over 60 or qualifies for the disability element. If responsible for children, such a person need only work 16 hours a week if single or otherwise meet the above rule for couples with children.

WTC may consist of:

- a basic element which is paid to all who qualify for WTC (£1,960 2019/20 and £1,995 for 2020/21);
- a second adult element in the case of a cohabiting couple or a lone parent element where the claimant has a dependent child (£2,010 for 2019/20 and £2,045 for 2020/21);
- a 30 hour element where the claimant works (or, in the case of a couple, one of whom works) at least 30 hours a week or where the couple have a dependent child or young person and one of the couple works at least 16 hours a week and in aggregate they work at least 30 hours a week (£810 for 2019/20 and £825 for 2020/21);
- a disability element where the claimant satisfies (or, in the case of a couple, one of whom satisfy) one of a wide range of disability conditions (£3,165 for 2019/20 and £3,220 for 2020/21);

- a severe disability element where the claimant receives (or, in the case of a couple, one of whom receives) either higher rate attendance allowance or the higher rate care component of the disability living allowance (or would do so if not in hospital) (£1,365 for 2019/20 and £1,390 for 2020/21); and
- a childcare element equal to 70% of eligible childcare costs up to a maximum of £175 a week for one child or £300 a week for two or more children.

Tapering rules

The tax credits are subject to tapering if relevant gross annual income, or (in the case of a couple) aggregate joint income, exceeds specified thresholds. For claimants entitled to only WTC or to both CTC and WTC, the maximum credits, apart from the family element of CTC, are withdrawn at the rate of 41p for each £1 of the excess of relevant income (see below) over (£6,420 for 2019/20 and £6,530 for 2020/21). For claimants entitled only to CTC the maximum credits are withdrawn at the rate of 41p for each £1 of the excess of relevant income over (£16,105 for 2019/20 and £16,385 for 2020/21). The taper is applied first to the non-childcare elements of WTC, then to the childcare element of WTC, then to the child element of CTC and finally to the family element of CTC. Where tax credits are awarded at different rates within the same tax year, the figures are calculated for each relevant period (in which the rates remain the same) on a daily basis and the amounts for each period then aggregated.

Relevant income

The income taken into account is the annual gross income of the claimant or, in the case of a cohabiting couple, the aggregate gross annual income of the couple. Claims are based on income for the preceding tax year. These awards are provisional only and will be altered retrospectively to the extent that income in the year in which tax credits are received (the current year) increases by more than £2,500 from that in the year on which the award is based. Any resulting underpayment will be paid to the claimant and any overpayment collected from him (see further below). Awards are also altered if income decreases, but a decrease of up to £2,500 is disregarded.

Gross annual income includes the aggregate amount (if it exceeds £300) of pension income, investment income, property income, foreign income and notional income (as defined in *SI 2002 No 2006, Regs 5, 10–17*). It also includes taxable income from employment (including most taxable benefits-in-kind), trading income, social security benefits (with some specific exclusions), student grants (other than for dependent children, travel, books or equipment) and other taxable income not covered above by the regulations. Certain types of income are specifically excluded such as maintenance payments and student loans, and certain deductions are allowed such as trading losses, charitable donations and pension contributions.

Claims

Claims for CTC and WTC can be made on form TC600 or online (www.gov.uk/government/organisations/hm-revenue-customs). Couples must make a joint claim. Claims can be backdated by up to one month provided the claimant met all the entitlement conditions at the earlier date. Claims have to be renewed annually, normally by 31 July.

Payment by HMRC

CTC and WTC are paid by HMRC, at weekly or four-weekly intervals, to the main carer, normally through a bank account. In the case of a joint claim, the couple may jointly nominate the main carer, otherwise HMRC will decide who is the main carer (normally the mother or the person who receives child benefit).

Notifiable changes in circumstances

Certain in-year changes of circumstances must be notified to HMRC, normally within one month of the change, if tax credit entitlement will fall to be reduced as a result. Notifiable changes include, *inter alia*, marriage, start of cohabitation, separation, leaving the UK, and decreases in average weekly childcare charges where the childcare element of WTC is claimed.

Underpayments and overpayments

After the year-end, once entitlement to tax credits for the tax year has been determined, any underpayment will be paid by HMRC in a lump sum to the designated claimant. Overpayments are recovered by deduction from tax credit entitlement in the following year, or through the PAYE system, or by assessment as if they were unpaid tax. HMRC must serve notice on the claimants of the overpayment to be recovered specifying how it is to be recovered. Liability for the overpayment in the case of a couple is joint and several.

See HMRC Code of Practice COP 26 'What Happens if We've Paid You Too Much Tax Credits'.

Interest and penalties

If a person fraudulently or negligently makes an incorrect statement or declaration in connection with a claim for CTC or WTC or incorrectly notifies a change of circumstances or provides incorrect information or evidence, a penalty may be imposed up to a maximum of £3,000. A penalty up to £3,000 may also be imposed on the other claimant in a joint claim (but not exceeding £3,000 in aggregate for both claimants) unless the other claimant was not, and could not reasonably have been expected to have been, aware of the fraud or neglect. Interest may also be charged on overpayments arising through fraud or neglect of the claimant(s). If a person fails to provide any information or evidence which is required in connection with the claim or fails to notify in-year changes of circumstances (where these must be notified), a penalty may be imposed of up to £300. If the failure persists, an additional penalty of up to £60 a day can be imposed for each day the failure continues after the initial penalty has been imposed.

See also HMRC leaflets WTC1 and WCT2.

Simon's Taxes. See Part E2.

National insurance contributions

[73.7] National insurance contributions for **2020/21** (and for 2019/20 in brackets where different) are as set out below. See Tolley's National Insurance Contributions for more details.

Class 1 (earnings-related)

Not contracted out

The employee contribution is **12%** of earnings between **£183** p.w. (£166 p.w.) and **£962** p.w. and **2%** of all earnings above **£962** p.w.

The employer contribution is **13.8%** of all earnings in excess of the first **£169** p.w. (£166 p.w.). The contribution is reduced to **0%** of earnings between **£169** p.w. (£166 p.w.) and **£962** p.w. if the employee is aged under 21; see *SSCBA 1992, ss 9(1A), 9A*. The contribution is similarly reduced for certain apprentices below the age of 25; see *SSCBA 1992, ss 9(1A), 9B*.

Notional Class 1 contributions are deemed to have been paid on the band of earnings from **£120** p.w. (£118 p.w.) to **£183** p.w. (£166 p.w.) to protect contributory benefit entitlement.

Employers can claim an '**employment allowance**' to offset against their liability for employer Class 1 contributions. The allowance is **£4,000** annually (£3,000 for 2019/20 and earlier years), but it is not available to companies with a single employee who is also a director of the company. For 2020/21 onwards, entitlement to the employment allowance is further restricted to employers with an employer national insurance contribution liability of less than £100,000 for the previous tax year. Where employer companies or charities are connected, this threshold applies to their aggregate liability. [*National Insurance Contributions Act 2014, ss 1–8, Sch 1; SI 2020 Nos 218, 273*].

For 2021/22 onwards, it was announced at Spring Budget 2020 that an employer will not be liable to pay employer contributions on the salary of a veteran up to the upper earnings limit (the 2021/22 equivalent of the £962 p.w. limit) in the veteran's first year of civilian employment (see Overview of Tax Legislation and Rates at www.gov.uk/government/publications/budget-2020-overview-of-tax-legislation-and-rates-ootlar at para 2.13).

Married women

The reduced employee rate for certain married women and widows with a certificate of election is **5.85%** of earnings between **£183** p.w. (£166 p.w.) and **£962** p.w. and **2%** of all earnings above **£962** p.w..

Class 1A (cars and car fuel and other benefits)

Employer contributions at **13.8%** are required on the benefit of cars and fuel made available to employees for private use and on most other employment-related benefits.

Class 1B (PAYE settlement agreements)

Employer contributions at **13.8%** are required on the value of all items included in a PAYE settlement agreement and the tax paid under the agreement (see **53.25** PAY AS YOU EARN).

Class 2 (self-employed, flat rate)

The flat weekly rate of contribution is **£3.05** (£3.00). The annual limit of net earnings for exception from Class 2 liability is **£6,475** (£6,365). Special rates apply for share fishermen and for volunteer development workers.

Class 3 (voluntary contributions)

The flat weekly rate of contribution is **£15.30** (£15.00).

Class 4 (self-employed, profit-related)

The 2020/21 contribution rate is **9%** on the band of profits between **£9,500** and **£50,000** and **2%** on all profits above **£50,000**.

The Class 4 rates and bands for earlier years are as follows.

	Rate	**Band**
2019/20	9% + 2%	£8,632 – £50,000
2018/19	9% + 2%	£8,424 – £46,350
2017/18	9% + 2%	£8,164 – £45,000
2016/17	9% + 2%	£8,060 – £43,000

Class 4 contributions are levied, generally, on the profits of any trade, profession or vocation (not carried on wholly outside the UK) which are chargeable to income tax under *ITTOIA 2005, Pt 2*. Class 4 contributions are dealt with separately in the self-assessment tax return (or notice of assessment where applicable) and are payable at the same time as the income tax on the profits (see **67.5–67.8** SELF-ASSESSMENT). Profits for this purpose are after capital allowances, loss reliefs and certain interest and annual payments for trade purposes. [*Social Security Contributions and Benefits Act 1992, Sch 2 paras 2, 3(1)(5)*]. Trading losses set against other income may, *for Class 4 purposes*, be carried forward and set against the first available profits. [*SSCBA 1992, Sch 2 para 3(4)*].

Contributions to registered pension schemes do not reduce profits for Class 4 purposes as they are not deductible from any particular type of income (see **57.12** PENSION PROVISION).

There are various exceptions from Class 4 liability, including persons over State pensionable age, divers etc. within the charge to tax on trading income (see **75.29** TRADING INCOME) and, on application, those under 16 at the beginning of the tax year. [*SI 1979 No 591, Regs 58–60*]. Non-UK residents and sleeping partners are not within the scope of Class 4.

Interest is chargeable on late payment of Class 4 contributions in the same way as for late payment of income tax (see **43.2** LATE PAYMENT INTEREST AND PENALTIES), and interest on repayments (see **62.2** REPAYMENT INTEREST) is similarly available. [*SSCBA 1992, Sch 2 para 6; SI 1993 No 1025; SI 2011 No 701, Art 9*].

National Insurance contributions made by employees or by the self-employed are not allowable for tax purposes. An employer is allowed its contributions for employees as an expense or deduction. [*ITEPA 2003, s 360A; ITTOIA 2005, ss 53, 272, 868*]. See **75.72** TRADING INCOME.

Simon's Taxes. See Part **E8**.

[illegible]

74

Time Limits

Introduction to time limits

[74.1] The first part of this chapter (**74.2–74.5**) lists fixed date time limits falling in the year to 30 June 2021.

Certain time limits that operate by reference to variable dates are set out in the second part of the chapter (**74.6** and **74.7**).

There are a few time limits that HMRC have discretion to extend in individual cases; this is mentioned in the main coverage in this work where relevant.

See also **26.8** DISGUISED REMUNERATION and **75.40** TRADING INCOME for duty to provide information before 1 October 2020 regarding loans and quasi-loans outstanding on 5 April 2019; **53.21** PAY AS YOU EARN for PAYE returns; **67.5–67.8** SELF-ASSESSMENT as regards payment of tax; **67.12** SELF-ASSESSMENT for information to be provided by employers to employees; and **68** SELF-ASSESSMENT — KEY DATES. Note that this chapter does not list the time limits in operation under the rules for DISCLOSURE OF TAX AVOIDANCE SCHEMES (**25**); these are noted in that chapter wherever appropriate.

Fixed date time limits of one year or less

[74.2] The following are miscellaneous short time limits.

(a) **6 July 2020** for action in respect of 2019/20.

- (i) *Making good of benefits-in-kind.* Employees need to make good any part of the cost of a benefit on or before this date if a deduction is to be allowed for the amount made good. See **28.54**, **28.24**, **28.26**, **28.27**, **28.36**, **28.41**, **28.47** and **28.49** EMPLOYMENT INCOME.
- (ii) *Election for treatment as a single loan of beneficial loans to director* by close company lender. [*ITEPA 2003, s 187*]. See **28.32** EMPLOYMENT INCOME.

- (iii) *Employment-related shares (outside tax-advantaged employee share schemes).* Annual return relating to 'reportable events' to be filed by employer company or other 'responsible person'. See **71.20** SHARE-RELATED EMPLOYMENT INCOME AND EXEMPTIONS.
- (iv) *Share incentive plans, enterprise management incentives, SAYE option schemes and company share option plans.* Annual return to be filed by employer company. See **71.38, 71.50, 71.65** and **71.77** SHARE-RELATED EMPLOYMENT INCOME AND EXEMPTIONS.

(b) **5 October 2020** for action in respect of 2019/20.
Notification of chargeability. Any person who is chargeable to tax for a tax year must give notice to HMRC that he is so chargeable, unless his income comes solely from certain sources (e.g. income dealt with under PAYE or dividend income chargeable at the dividend ordinary rate) and he has no chargeable gains. [*TMA 1970, s 7*]. See **55.2** PENALTIES.

(c) **31 October 2020** for action in respect of 2019/20.
Returns under self-assessment for 2019/20 when required by notice given before 2 August 2020 and filed manually. See **64.2** RETURNS.

(d) **31 January 2021** for action in respect of 2019/20 or 2020/21 (whichever is stated below).

- (i) *Returns under self-assessment* for 2019/20 when required by notice given before 2 November 2020 and filed online. See **64.2** RETURNS.
- (ii) *Gift Aid donations to charity by individuals.* Election for qualifying donation(s) made in 2020/21 to be relieved as if made in 2019/20; election must be made no later than the date the 2019/20 self-assessment tax return is filed. See **14.13** CHARITIES AND CHARITABLE GIVING.
- (iii) *Change of accounting date.* Notice of change to be given (in a return) where it affects basis period for 2019/20. See **75.10** TRADING INCOME.
- (iv) *Charge on benefits from pre-owned assets.* Election to disapply the charging provisions for 2018/19 and subsequent years where 2019/20 is the first tax year for which a charge under those provisions would otherwise arise by reference to enjoyment of the property in question (or any substituted property). See **4.43** ANTI-AVOIDANCE.

(e) **5 April 2021** — advance time limits for action in respect of 2021/22.

- (i) *Transfer of married couple's allowance (where available) and blind person's allowance.* Election by non-claimant spouse to receive one-half of the married couple's allowance, or by spouses jointly for non-claimant spouse to receive the whole of the allowance, or by claimant spouse to receive one-half where a joint election has been made for non-claimant spouse to receive the whole of the allowance, must be made before the start of the first tax year to which the election is to apply (subject to a 30-day extension where notice of intention to elect was given to HMRC before the start of that year). Withdrawals of such elections similarly do not have effect until the tax year after that in which notice of withdrawal was given. Similar rules apply to transfers between spouses of blind person's allowance and to transfers between civil partners of married couple's allowance and/or blind person's allowance. See **48.3** MARRIED PERSONS AND CIVIL PARTNERS.

(ii) *Election by couple married before 5 December 2005 to opt into the married couple's allowance rules for couples marrying on or after that date.* The election must be made before the start of the first tax year for which it is to have effect but then continues to have effect for all succeeding tax years and is irrevocable. See **1.19** ALLOWANCES AND TAX RATES.

(f) **5 April 2021** for action in respect of 2019/20.

(i) *Claims following late assessments.* A claim (including a supplementary claim) which could not have been allowed but for the making of an assessment to income tax or capital gains tax after the tax year to which it relates may be made before the end of the tax year following that in which the assessment was made. This applies in relation to an HMRC amendment to a self-assessment personal or partnership tax return as it does in relation to an assessment. See **16.9** CLAIMS, **64.8** RETURNS.

Fixed date time limits of one to two years

[74.3] 31 January 2021 for action in respect of 2018/19.

(i) *Plant and machinery capital allowances.* The following time limits apply.

(A) *Ships.* Notice requiring the postponement of first-year allowances, see **10.19** CAPITAL ALLOWANCES ON PLANT AND MACHINERY. Also notice requiring postponement of writing-down allowances, and disapplying the 'single ship pool' provisions, see **10.31** CAPITAL ALLOWANCES ON PLANT AND MACHINERY. Also claim for deferment of balancing charge, see **10.31** CAPITAL ALLOWANCES ON PLANT AND MACHINERY.

(B) *Short-life assets.* Election for certain expenditure to be treated as on short-life assets. See **10.33** CAPITAL ALLOWANCES ON PLANT AND MACHINERY.

(C) *Equipment leasing.* Election for fixtures to be treated as belonging to the lessor and not the lessee. See **10.39** CAPITAL ALLOWANCES ON PLANT AND MACHINERY.

(D) *Long funding leasing.* Election by lessor for all his plant and machinery leases finalised on or after a date of his choosing to be treated in his hands as long funding leases if they would not otherwise be so treated. See **10.51** CAPITAL ALLOWANCES ON PLANT AND MACHINERY.

(ii) *Cheap loan arrangements.* Election (or requirement by HMRC officer) for alternative method of calculating benefit. See **28.32** EMPLOYMENT INCOME.

(iii) *Unremittable overseas income.* Claim for relief from assessment. See **32.5** FOREIGN INCOME.

(iv) *Foster care and other qualifying care.* Election for alternative method of calculating profit. See **33.4** FOSTER CARE ETC.

(v) *Herd basis.* Election where 2018/19 was either the first tax year (after that in which trading commenced) during whose basis period a herd was kept, or the first tax year in the basis period for which compensation was received for compulsory slaughter. See **34.3, 34.7** HERD BASIS.

(vi) *Sale of patent rights.* Election to disapply or apply spreading provisions (depending on whether UK resident or non-UK resident). See **41.7** INTELLECTUAL PROPERTY.

(vii) *Sale of patent rights by a partnership followed by cessation of trade.* Election by partner to reduce amount chargeable in tax year of cessation. Time limit operates by reference to tax year of cessation. See **41.7** INTELLECTUAL PROPERTY.

(viii) *Claim for loss in trade etc.* to be set off against general income (see **45.2** LOSSES) or capital gains (see **45.5** LOSSES) or to be carried back (see **45.7** LOSSES).

(ix) *Claim for share loss relief.* See **45.23** LOSSES.

(x) *Claim for loss in employment* to be set off against general income. See **45.31** LOSSES.

(xi) *Post-cessation receipts.* Election for such receipts to be treated as received on date of cessation. See **59.4** POST-CESSATION RECEIPTS AND EXPENDITURE.

(xii) *Post-cessation expenditure.* Claim for relief against total income. See **59.5** POST-CESSATION RECEIPTS AND EXPENDITURE.

(xiii) *Cash basis for property income.* Election to disapply the cash basis where it would otherwise apply. See **60.4** PROPERTY INCOME.

(xiv) *Property allowance.* Election for full relief not to be given or for partial relief to be given. See **60.11** PROPERTY INCOME.

(xv) *Furnished holiday lettings (1).* Election for averaging treatment. Separate elections required for UK and EEA properties. See **60.20** PROPERTY INCOME.

(xvi) *Furnished holiday lettings (2).* Election for 'period of grace' rule to apply where 2018/19 is the first year or second successive year for which accommodation does not otherwise qualify for special treatment due to insufficient number of days let. See **60.20** PROPERTY INCOME.

(xvii) *Rent-a-room relief.* Election (or withdrawal of election) for relief not to apply, or for profits to be treated as equal to excess of gross rents over relief limit. See **60.22** PROPERTY INCOME.

(xviii) *Property losses.* Claim for relief, against general income, for certain capital allowances and agricultural expenses. See **60.25** PROPERTY INCOME.

(xix) *Remittance basis.* Claim for income or gains to be treated as not remitted to the UK in 2018/19 if used to make a qualifying investment. See **61.21** REMITTANCE BASIS. For similar types of claim, see **61.23, 61.27, 61.28, 61.29** REMITTANCE BASIS.

(xx) *Amendment of self-assessment tax return.* Amendments by taxpayer to return must be made within 12 months after the filing date (itself normally 31 January following the tax year). See **64.4** RETURNS.

(xxi) *Deeply discounted securities*. Claim for relief for loss on disposal where security has been held continuously since before 27 March 2003 by the person making the disposal *and* the security was listed on a recognised stock exchange at some time before that date. See **65.25** SAVINGS AND INVESTMENT INCOME. Claim for relief for loss on disposal of a strip of a government security. See **65.27** SAVINGS AND INVESTMENT INCOME.

(xxii) *Vulnerable person election*. Election must be made jointly in relation to qualifying trusts by the trustees and the vulnerable person by the first anniversary of 31 January following the tax year for which it is first to apply. See **70.21** SETTLEMENTS.

(xxiii) *Heritage maintenance settlements*. Election for tax exemption on income. See **70.36**.

(xxiv) *Trading allowance*. Election for full relief not to be given or for partial relief to be given. See **75.3** TRADING INCOME.

(xxv) *Opening years of a business*. Election for accounts prepared to 31 March or on any of the first four days in April *not* to be treated as if prepared to 5 April. See **75.7** TRADING INCOME.

(xxvi) *Accounts prepared to a variable date*. Election to treat such accounts as if prepared to a fixed date so that change of accounting date rules are not triggered by slight variations. See **75.10** TRADING INCOME.

(xxvii) *Change from realisation basis of computing profits to a mark to market basis*. Election for adjustment income to be spread equally over six periods of account beginning with the first period to which the new basis applies. See **75.24** TRADING INCOME.

(xxviii) *Change of basis in computing barrister's or advocate's profits*. Election for increased adjustment charge to be made for 2018/19 under the spreading provisions. See **75.25** TRADING INCOME.

(xxix) *Creative artists*. Claim to average profits of 2017/18 and 2018/19, see **75.60** TRADING INCOME.

(xxx) *Farming: compensation for compulsory slaughter*. Claim for spreading relief where compensation received for compulsory slaughter of animals to which herd basis does not (and could not) apply. See 75.77(b) TRADING INCOME.

(xxxi) *Farming: two-year averaging*. Claim to average profits of 2017/18 and 2018/19, see **75.78** TRADING INCOME.

(xxxii) *Farming: five-year averaging*. Claim to average profits of the five years 2014/15 to 2018/19, see **75.78** TRADING INCOME.

(xxxiii) *Appropriations to and from trading stock*. Election for market value to be adjusted in certain cases where a chargeable gain or allowable loss would otherwise arise. See **75.118** TRADING INCOME.

(xxxiv) *Leaving the cash basis*. Election for increased adjustment charge to be made for 2018/19 under the spreading provisions. See **76.16** TRADING INCOME — CASH BASIS FOR SMALLER BUSINESSES.

(xxxv) *Valuation of trading stock on cessation*. Election for transfers between connected persons to be reduced below arm's length value in certain cases. See **75.117** TRADING INCOME.

(xxxvi) *Work in progress on cessation*. Election for work in progress to be taken at cost on cessation in 2017/18. See **75.117** TRADING INCOME.

Fixed date time limits of three to four years

[74.4] 31 October 2020 for action in respect of 2016/17.

- PAYE taxpayer to request that a tax return be issued to him. See **53.1** PAY AS YOU EARN.

31 January 2021 for action in respect of 2016/17.

- Claim for adjustment of assessments where administration of estate was completed in 2016/17. See **22.13** DECEASED ESTATES.

Fixed date time limits of four years or more

[74.5] Claims by 31 January 2021 in respect of 2014/15.

- Claim for income tax relief in respect of enterprise investment scheme shares issued in 2014/15. See **29.7** ENTERPRISE INVESTMENT SCHEME.
- Claim for income tax relief in respect of seed enterprise investment scheme shares issued in 2014/15. See **66.5** SEED ENTERPRISE INVESTMENT SCHEME.
- Claim for social investment tax relief where the investment was made in 2014/15. See **72.6** SOCIAL INVESTMENT TAX RELIEF.

Claims by 5 April 2021 in respect of 2016/17. Except where other time limits are prescribed, claims must be made within four years after the end of the tax year to which they relate (see **16.4** CLAIMS).

(a) *Transferable tax allowance (aka marriage allowance).* Election to transfer part of personal allowance to spouse or civil partner (see **1.18** ALLOWANCES AND TAX RATES).
(b) *Overpayment relief.* See **16.7** CLAIMS.
(c) *Claim against double assessment* where the same person has been assessed 'for the same cause' in the same year. [*TMA 1970, s 32*].
(d) COMMUNITY INVESTMENT TAX RELIEF (**17**).
(e) DOUBLE TAX RELIEF (**27**).
(f) INTEREST PAYABLE (**42**).
(g) *Claim for loss in trade etc.* for 2016/17 to be carried forward against future profits of the same trade (see **45.19** LOSSES).
(h) *Claim for terminal loss relief* in relation to a trade etc. that ceased in 2016/17 (see **45.20** LOSSES).
(i) *Claim for remittance basis* to apply. See **61.2** REMITTANCE BASIS.
(j) *Post-employment deductions* (for employee liabilities and indemnity insurance) to be relieved against total income of former employee. See **28.65** EMPLOYMENT INCOME.
(k) VENTURE CAPITAL TRUSTS at **81.3**. Claim for income tax relief in respect of investments.
(l) Any other matter not specified in this chapter for which relief from income tax is claimed.

Variable time limits of one year or less

[74.6] The following are miscellaneous short time limits.

(a) **14 days**
Various elections to disapply or moderate the restricted shares provisions at **71.4** SHARE-RELATED EMPLOYMENT INCOME AND EXEMPTIONS. Such elections are implemented by way of agreement between employer and employee to be made no later than 14 days after acquisition or after a chargeable event (whichever is applicable); there is no requirement for elections to be submitted to HMRC.

(b) **30 days**
  (i) Rejection of HMRC corrections to self-assessment tax return or partnership return. See **64.4, 64.12** RETURNS.
  (ii) Appeals against assessments, amendments to self-assessment return or partnership return or claim made outside return, and HMRC conclusions on completion of enquiry. Lodging of notice of appeal. See **5** APPEALS, **16.3** CLAIMS.
  (iii) There are many instances in which HMRC information powers and clearance procedures require a response within 30 days, see, for example, **4.11, 4.12** ANTI-AVOIDANCE.

(c) **45 days**
Various actions need to be taken within 45 days to avoid a charge under the remittance basis where a qualifying investment is made or where exempt property is sold whilst in the UK. See **61.21, 61.27, 61.28, 61.29** and **61.33** REMITTANCE BASIS.

(d) **60 days**
  (i) A 'simple assessment' can be queried within 60 days after the date the assessment is issued. See **6.5** ASSESSMENTS.
  (ii) There are a number of circumstances in which information is required to be provided within 60 days. See, for example, **29.25** ENTERPRISE INVESTMENT SCHEME.
  (iii) Notice of declaration by husband and wife (or civil partners) of their beneficial interests in jointly-held property, and income arising from it, where these are not equal. See **48.7** MARRIED PERSONS AND CIVIL PARTNERS.

(e) **90 days**
  (i) Qualifying option under Enterprise Management Incentives scheme to be exercised within 90 days after a disqualifying event if adverse tax consequences would otherwise ensue. See **71.43** SHARE-RELATED EMPLOYMENT INCOME AND EXEMPTIONS.
  (ii) Various actions need to be taken within 90 days where HMRC have issued to a person a follower notice (see **4.44–4.48** ANTI-AVOIDANCE) or an accelerated payment notice (see **4.49–4.52** ANTI-AVOIDANCE).

(f) **Three months**
  (i) Returns of income, partnership returns etc., following notice requiring delivery (if this gives a date later than the normal filing date for the year for which return required). See **64.2, 64.12** RETURNS.

(ii) Appeals relating to questions of (i) personal reliefs for non-residents, (ii) residence or domicile, (iii) pension funds for service abroad. [*TMA 1970, Sch 1A para 9*].

(iii) Application for judicial review must be made within three months of the date when the grounds for application arose. See **5.34** APPEALS.

(iv) There are instances in which HMRC information powers require a response within three months. See e.g. **71.38, 71.51, 71.65, 71.77** SHARE-RELATED EMPLOYMENT INCOME AND EXEMPTIONS.

(g) **92 days**
Notice of grant of option under Enterprise Management Incentives scheme to be given to HMRC within 92 days after option granted. See **71.49** SHARE-RELATED EMPLOYMENT INCOME AND EXEMPTIONS.

(h) **12 months**
Double tax relief. Notice must be given to HMRC within one year of a foreign tax credit becoming excessive. See **27.9** DOUBLE TAX RELIEF.

Variable two-year time limits

[74.7] The following have a deadline of two years after a specific event.

(a) *Sales without change of control.* Election for transfer of assets at tax written-down value. See **9.20, 9.28** CAPITAL ALLOWANCES.

(b) *Short-life assets.* Election for certain transfers between connected persons to be treated as at tax written-down value. See **10.33** CAPITAL ALLOWANCES ON PLANT AND MACHINERY.

(c) *Expenditure incurred on fixtures by incoming lessee.* Election for certain fixtures on which expenditure incurred by incoming lessee to be treated as belonging to lessee within two years of date of lease taking effect. See **10.41** CAPITAL ALLOWANCES ON PLANT AND MACHINERY.

(d) *Changes in ownership of fixtures.* Joint election by seller and purchaser (or, where applicable, lessor and lessee) of land and buildings to fix the price at which fixtures are transferred. Election to be made within two years after the sale (or granting of the lease). See **10.44** CAPITAL ALLOWANCES ON PLANT AND MACHINERY.

(e) *Long funding leasing.* Joint election by seller (or assignor) and lessor within two years of sale etc. to prevent a finance lease that is part of sale and finance leaseback arrangements from losing 'short lease' status. See **10.50**(1)(A) CAPITAL ALLOWANCES ON PLANT AND MACHINERY.

(f) *Successions.* Election for transfers between 'connected persons' to be at tax written-down value. See **10.69** CAPITAL ALLOWANCES ON PLANT AND MACHINERY.

(g) *Know-how disposal.* Joint election by vendor and purchaser within two years of disposal for the consideration not to be treated as a payment for goodwill. See **75.95** TRADING INCOME.

75

Trading Income

Cross-references. See subjects dealt with separately under 4 ANTI-AVOIDANCE; 9 CAPITAL ALLOWANCES; 10 CAPITAL ALLOWANCES ON PLANT AND MACHINERY; 27 DOUBLE TAX RELIEF; 34 HERD BASIS; 42 INTEREST PAYABLE; 45 LOSSES; 50 NON-RESIDENTS; 52 PARTNERSHIPS; 54 PAYMENT OF TAX; 58 PERSONAL SERVICE COMPANIES ETC.; 59 POST-CESSATION RECEIPTS AND EXPENDITURE; 67 SELF-ASSESSMENT; 76 TRADING INCOME — CASH BASIS FOR SMALLER BUSINESSES; 77 TRADING INCOME — FIXED RATE DEDUCTION SCHEME; and 78 TRANSACTIONS IN UK LAND.

Introduction to trading income

[75.1] For 'Basis Periods', see 75.6–75.15; for 'Whether a Trade Carried On', see 75.27–75.37; and for 'Chargeable Income and Allowable Deductions', see 75.42–75.130. See also the full contents list above.

The law relating to the taxation of 'trading income' was consolidated in *Income Tax (Trading and Other Income) Act 2005* (*ITTOIA 2005*) as part of the Tax Law Rewrite programme. *ITTOIA 2005* has effect for 2005/06 onwards. [*ITTOIA 2005, s 883(1)*]. See HMRC Tax Bulletin June 2005 pp 1210, 1211 for a note on the purposes, nature and structure of *ITTOIA 2005*.

'*Trading income*' comprises profits from a trade, profession or vocation. Income tax is charged for any tax year on the full amount of the profits of the basis period for that tax year. For basis periods, see **75.6–75.13**. The person liable for the tax is the person receiving or entitled to the profits.

The charge extends to profits arising to a non-UK resident from a trade etc. carried on wholly in the UK or, where a trade etc. is carried on partly in the UK and partly elsewhere, from that part of the trade etc. carried on in the UK. If the tax year is a split year (see **63.19** RESIDENCE AND DOMICILE) as regards a UK resident individual, then for the purpose of determining whether or not he is within the charge to tax on trading income the individual is treated as if, for the overseas part of the split year, he were non-UK resident. In relation to disposals on or after 5 July 2016, profits of a trade of dealing in or developing UK land arising to a non-UK resident are chargeable to tax wherever the trade is carried on (see **78.2** TRANSACTIONS IN **UK** LAND. See **50.6** NON-RESIDENTS as regards non-UK residents trading via a UK branch or agency.

Before 2005/06, the charge was made under *Sch D, Case I* (for trades), *Sch D, Case II* (for professions and vocations) or *Sch D, Case V* (for trades, professions and vocations carried on wholly abroad by a UK resident — see **75.16**), but these labels were removed by *ITTOIA 2005*.

[*ITTOIA 2005, ss 5, 6, 7(1)(2), 8; FA 2016, ss 78, 82*].

Trade 'includes every venture in the nature of trade' [*ITA 2007, s 989*]. For what is a trade, see generally **75.27–75.37** and in particular, in relation to isolated or speculative transactions, **75.33**. For a discussion on the *scope* of a trade, see HMRC Business Income Manual BIM21000–21040.

There is no statutory definition of 'profession or vocation'. There are certain provisions applicable only to trades and others applicable only to professions or vocations but the distinction between the two is of limited practical importance. There is no reported case in which it was necessary to decide between the two for income tax purposes, but in a Hong Kong case it was held that stockbrokers were carrying on a trade, not a profession or business (*Kowloon Stock Exchange Ltd v Commr of Inland Revenue* PC, [1984] STC 602). There are a number of cases turning on whether a business was an exempt profession as specially defined for the purposes of (now defunct) excess profits duty and similar taxes. For these see Tolley's Tax Cases. For professions or vocations (e.g. actor) which necessarily involve carrying out numerous engagements see **75.47** and **28.66** EMPLOYMENT INCOME.

In the rest of this chapter, 'trade' includes 'profession or vocation' unless otherwise stated or the context indicates otherwise.

For whether income is liable to tax as trading income or as employment income, see **28.66** EMPLOYMENT INCOME. See also **75.29** for special treatment of certain divers and diving supervisors. Legislation introduced in 2017 seeks to nullify the use of disguised remuneration schemes by the self-employed by imposing a charge to income tax on trading profits disguised as something else. It has effect mainly in relation to payments and other benefits arising on or after 6 April 2017, but applies also to pre-6 April 2017 loans and quasi-loans that are outstanding on 5 April 2019. See **75.39, 75.40.**

Income from land

Rents and other income derived from the exploitation of proprietary interests in land are charged to income tax as PROPERTY INCOME (**59**) and not as income derived from a trade. [*ITTOIA 2005, s 4(1)*]. The leading case is *Salisbury House Estate Ltd v Fry* HL 1930, 15 TC 266, and see also *Sywell Aerodrome Ltd v Croft* CA 1941, 24 TC 126; *Webb v Conelee Properties Ltd* Ch D 1982, 56 TC 149. For relaxations to this rule, see **75.49** (tied premises), **75.94** (surplus business accommodation), **60.2** PROPERTY INCOME (caravan sites) and **60.33** PROPERTY INCOME (electric-line wayleaves). The commercial *occupation* of UK land with a view to realisation of profits is treated as the carrying on of a trade (though this does not apply to woodlands, for which see also **30.53** EXEMPT INCOME or if the land in question is being prepared for forestry purposes). [*ITTOIA 2005, ss 10, 11*]. See **75.77** as regards farming and market gardening.

It is possible for a person to have a separate trade of providing services in conjunction with a letting activity but the services provided must go well beyond those normally provided by a landlord. Even then, the provision of those services does not make the letting activity a trade.

Profits of mines, quarries, gravel pits, sand pits, brickfields, ironworks, gas works, canals, railways, rights of fishing, rights of markets, fairs and tolls and like concerns are computed and charged to income tax *as if* the concern were a trade carried on in the UK, with corresponding treatment for losses. This applies only where the concern is not, in fact, a trade on first principles and is not treated as such under the commercial occupation rule above. It does not impose a charge to tax on a non-UK resident in respect of a non-UK concern. [*ITTOIA 2005, s 12*]. As regards rent received in connection with such concerns, see **60.34** PROPERTY INCOME.

Oil-related activities

The carrying on of oil-related activities (i.e. oil extraction activities within *ITTOIA 2005, s 225A* and any activities consisting of the acquisition, enjoyment or exploitation of oil rights) as part of a trade is treated for income tax purposes as a separate trade in itself. [*ITTOIA 2005, s 16*].

Periods of account

A '*period of account*' in relation to a trade, profession, vocation or other business means a period for which accounts are drawn up. [*ITA 2007, s 989*].

Trading allowance

A £1,000 allowance was introduced for individuals for 2017/18 onwards. Gross trading receipts of £1,000 or less are exempt, though an election can be made to disapply the exemption. Where gross receipts exceed £1,000, an election can be made to be taxed on the excess. In either case no relief is then given for otherwise deductible expenses. See **75.3**.

Gig economy

The fast expanding gig economy might be described as the modern online equivalent of cards placed in shop windows offering services. It will in most cases give rise to trading income. The Low Incomes Tax Reform Group have published a useful factsheet 'Tax if you work in the gig economy' at www.litrg.org.uk/sites/default/files/Gig%20economy%20factsheet%20FINAL.pdf.

Simon's Taxes. See **B1.1**, **B1.2**.

Simpler income tax for businesses

[75.2] Two measures were introduced in 2013 to simplify the calculation of taxable income for unincorporated businesses. The first measure allows smaller businesses to calculate taxable income on a cash basis — see **76** TRADING INCOME — CASH BASIS FOR SMALLER BUSINESSES. The second allows *all* unincorporated businesses to use flat rate expenses for particular items of business expenditure — see **77** TRADING INCOME — FIXED RATE DEDUCTION SCHEME.

Relief for small amounts of income (the trading allowance)

[75.3] A £1,000 allowance (the '*trading allowance*') is introduced for trading income with effect for **2017/18** onwards. It applies equally to professions and vocations, but not to businesses carried on in partnership. The allowance also covers certain miscellaneous income. An entirely separate £1,000 allowance is introduced simultaneously for property income (see **60.11** PROPERTY INCOME). For official guidance, see HMRC Business Income Manual BIM86000.

Relevant income

The allowance operates by reference to an individual's '*relevant income*'. This is the sum of:

(a) the gross receipts (i.e. before deducting expenses) brought into account in calculating the profits of the individual's 'relevant trades' for the tax year (which means for any period that is a basis period for the tax year); and

(b) any income for the tax year (before any deduction for expenses or any other matter) which is miscellaneous income within the residual charge to tax at **49.7** MISCELLANEOUS INCOME.

In (a) above a '*relevant trade*' is a trade, profession or vocation carried on otherwise than in partnership. Post-cessation receipts (see **59.1** POST-CESSATION RECEIPTS AND EXPENDITURE) and adjustment income (see **75.24** below) are effectively excluded from (a) above as they are subject to separate tax charges and not brought into account in computing profits. If the individual qualifies for rent-a-room relief for the tax year (see **60.22** PROPERTY INCOME), a trade is not a relevant trade if there are rent-a-room receipts which would be brought into account in calculating the trading profits. Rent-a-room receipts cannot be included in (b) above either. See below for further exclusions.

Full relief

Where an individual's relevant income (as above) for the tax year does not exceed the £1,000 trading allowance, there is no charge to tax. This means that the receipts themselves are not brought into account as trading or miscellaneous income, and there is no tax relief for the expenses that would otherwise have been deductible from those receipts in computing the trading or miscellaneous income. Thus, the profits or losses of each relevant trade are treated as nil. The individual can elect for full relief not to be given. The election must be made no later than the first anniversary of 31 January following the tax year in question, and has effect only for the tax year for which it is made.

If the individual's relevant income exceeds the trading allowance, such that full relief is not available, and no cash basis election has effect (see **76.2** TRADING INCOME — CASH BASIS FOR SMALLER BUSINESSES), it is assumed that a cash basis election does have effect if full relief would be available on that assumption. Such an assumption can be made only if the individual would be eligible to make a cash basis election for the tax year *and* either the cash basis had effect for the preceding tax year or the individual was eligible to make a cash basis election for that year. The making of this assumption is not the same as treating the individual as having made a cash basis election, which might then continue to have effect for subsequent years, except that he is so treated for the purpose of adjustments on a change of basis (see **76.16** TRADING INCOME — CASH BASIS FOR SMALLER BUSINESSES). The assumption cannot be made if an election for partial relief (see below) is made for the year.

It would appear that the giving of full relief precludes the deduction of any overlap relief (see **75.14** below) that may otherwise be due for the tax year. This may be disadvantageous as overlap relief can create an allowable trading loss.

Partial relief

Where relevant income (as above) exceeds the £1,000 allowance, the individual can elect to use an alternative method of calculating income. Under this method the charge to tax is on the excess of relevant income over £1,000. Where an individual's relevant income comes from more than one 'relevant trade' (as above) or is partly income from a relevant trade and partly miscellaneous income, it is for the individual to decide how much of the trading allowance to allocate to each source, except that the deduction of the trading allowance cannot create a loss. In computing the profits of any relevant trade of the individual, or in computing miscellaneous income within (b) above, where partial relief is given, there is no tax relief for the expenses that would otherwise have been deductible from the relevant income. The election for partial relief must be made no later than the first anniversary of 31 January following the tax year in question, and has effect only for the tax year for which it is made.

In the case of a relevant trade for which overlap relief (see **75.14** below) is due for the tax year, the deduction of the trading allowance (or part of it) does not preclude the deduction of overlap relief but precedes it. This should be to the taxpayer's advantage as overlap relief can create an allowable trading loss whereas the trading allowance cannot.

Further exclusions

Neither full nor partial relief is available for a tax year in any of the following circumstances.

- The individual is entitled to full rent-a-room relief in respect of rent-a-room receipts (other than those accruing to any property business of his) but elects to disapply the relief, or the individual would be entitled to partial rent-a-room relief (the alternative method of calculation) in respect of any such rent-a-room receipts but no election is in force to apply it. The intention is to prevent individuals from using the trading allowance if they have chosen to deduct actual expenses in calculating the profits of another trade for the same tax year or in computing miscellaneous income.
- The individual's relevant income (as above) includes a payment made by (or on behalf of) a person at a time when the individual is an employee of that person or the spouse or civil partner of such an employee. This is to prevent employers reclassifying payments to employees etc. so as to bring those payments within the ambit of the trading allowance.
- The individual's relevant income includes a payment made by (or on behalf of) a firm at a time when the individual is a partner in the firm or is connected with a partner in the firm.
- The individual's relevant income includes a payment made by (or on behalf of) a close company (broadly a company under the control of five or fewer participators) at a time when the individual is a participator in the close company or an associate (see *CTA 2010, s 448*) of a participator.

[*ITTOIA 2005, ss 22A, 783A–783AR; F(No 2)A 2017, Sch 3 paras 1, 4, 13*].

Effect of trading allowance on calculation of overlap profit

In the case of a relevant trade (as above), the calculation of overlap profit at **75.14** below is modified as follows where an overlap period falls within the basis period of the trade for two tax years (year A and year B) and relief for the trading allowance is given for at least one of those years. References below to the '*standard overlap profit*' are to what would have been the overlap profit for the overlap period in the absence of the trading allowance.

- If full relief (as above) is given for at least one of years A and B, the overlap profit arising by reference to the overlap period is treated as nil.
- If, in relation to year A or year B (or both), partial relief (as above) is given, and the amount of trading allowance deducted in relation to the trade equals or exceeds the standard overlap profit, the overlap profit arising by reference to the overlap period is treated as nil.

- Where (i) partial relief is given in one year, (ii) neither full nor partial relief is given in the other year, and (iii) the amount of trading allowance deducted is less than the standard overlap profit, the overlap profit arising by reference to the overlap period is the standard overlap profit less that amount of trading allowance.
- Where partial relief is given in both years, and the amount of trading allowance deducted is less than the standard overlap profit, the overlap profit arising by reference to the overlap period is the standard overlap profit less the higher of (i) the amount of trading allowance deducted for year A and (ii) the equivalent amount for year B.

[*ITTOIA 2005, s 204A; F(No 2)A 2017, Sch 3 paras 5, 13*].

Example

[75.4]

Jennifer is in employment earning £25,000 per annum but for the last few years has been earning extra money by buying and selling rare DVDs online. After taking advice she accepts that her online activities amount to the carrying on of a trade, and she calculates profits to 5 April each year on the cash basis. For the year ended 5 April 2021, she has online sales of £2,100. Her purchases amount to £500 and she has allowable expenses of £100.

Jennifer's taxable profits for the year to 5 April 2021 are as follows.

		£	£
Sales (i.e. gross receipts)			2,100
Deduct:	Purchases	500	
	Expenses	100	
			600
Taxable profit			£1,500

Jennifer elects to use the trading allowance and is instead taxed as follows.

		£
Gross receipts		2,100
Deduct:	Trading allowance	1,000
Taxable profit for 2020/21		£1,100

Companies

[75.5] Companies (and other bodies corporate, unincorporated associations and authorised unit trusts — but not partnerships, local authorities or local authority associations) are chargeable to corporation tax on their trading income. Many of the provisions below from **75.27** onwards (relating to chargeable income, allowable deductions and other trading income matters) apply in similar fashion to companies, but from the mid-1990s the move has been towards a separate computational regime for corporation tax, with special rules on, for example, interest (the 'loan relationships' rules), intangible assets and research and development. Due to this divergence, and the fact that the income tax rules are in *ITTOIA 2005* and the corporation tax rules are in *CTA 2009*, it cannot be assumed that the coverage in this chapter of any particular type of trading receipt or deduction etc. applies equally for corporation tax purposes. Instead, see Tolley's Corporation Tax. The basis period rules at 75.6 *et seq*. below do not apply to companies, which are instead charged to tax by reference to accounting periods (as defined). See **75.17** below for 'notional' commencements or cessations by companies.

Basis periods

[75.6] The basis period for a tax year is the period by reference to which the profits of a business are taxed for that year. The basis period rules are set out in detail in 75.7–**75.14** below. In summary the basis periods are generally as follows (subject to any change of accounting date — see 75.**10** below).

Opening years of the business (see 75.7 below)

Year 1	Actual
Year 2	Twelve months ending with the accounting date in the year or, if the period from commencement to the accounting date in the year is less than twelve months, the first twelve months or, if there is no accounting date in the second year, actual

See 75.**14** below for relief (overlap relief) where the above rules have the effect of the same profits being taxed in each of two successive tax years.

Intermediate years (see 75.9 below)

The assessment is based on the profits shown by the annual accounts ended within the current tax year.

Closing year (see 75.12 below)

Period from the end of the basis period in the penultimate year to the date of cessation in the year (which may exceed twelve months).

Accounting date

For the purposes of computing basis periods, an 'accounting date' is the date in the tax year to which accounts are drawn up or, if there are two or more such dates, the latest of them. [*ITTOIA 2005, s 197*].

Apportionment of profits to basis periods

Power is given to apportion profits or losses, on a time basis in proportion to the number of days in the respective periods, if required for the purposes of arriving at the profits or losses of a basis period that does not coincide with a period of account. But any reasonable time-based method of apportionment may be used, at the taxpayer's discretion, instead of days, provided it is used consistently for the particular trade; the worked examples in this chapter use months for instance. [*ITTOIA 2005, s 203*]. This applies only where such time apportionment is necessary (see *Marshall Hus & Partners Ltd v Bolton* Ch D 1980, 55 TC 539) and only to the *extent* that it is necessary (see *Lyons v Kelly* (Sp C 334), [2002] SSCD 455).

Simon's Taxes. See **B4.101–B4.106.**

Opening years

[75.7] On the commencement of a business by an individual (which includes his commencing to carry on an existing business in partnership), the following rules apply. As to what constitutes a commencement etc. see **75.17** below.

First tax year

The assessment will be on the profits (as adjusted for tax purposes) from the commencement date to the following 5 April. [*ITTOIA 2005, s 199*].

Second tax year

If there is an accounting date in the year, the assessment is based on the twelve months to that date. If the period from commencement to the accounting date in the second year is less than twelve months, the assessment is based on the profits for the first twelve months of the business. If there is no accounting date in the second year, the second year's assessment will be on the actual profits for the year, i.e. 6 April to 5 April. [*ITTOIA 2005, s 200*].

See **75.14** below for relief (overlap relief) where the above rules have the effect of the same profits being taxed in each of two successive tax years.

Accounts prepared to 31 March etc. treated as prepared to 5 April

Where the first accounting date (or the first intended accounting date) of the business falls on 31 March or on any of the first four days in April, and that first accounting date falls in the tax year of commencement or either of the next two tax years, the accounts are treated as if prepared to 5 April. (If the business commences after 31 March, profits and losses are treated as nil for that tax year and the actual profits or losses for the short period to 5 April are treated as arising in the basis period for the following tax year.) This treatment avoids creating very short overlaps of basis periods and therefore small amounts of overlap profit. The taxpayer may elect for it *not* to have effect in relation to any tax year. The election must be made on or before the first anniversary of 31 January following the tax year to which it relates. [*ITTOIA 2005, ss 208–210*].

Simon's Taxes. See **B4.102, B4.103, B4.108.**

Example

[75.8]

Quentin commences trade on 1 September 2019 and prepares accounts to 30 April, starting with an eight-month period of account to 30 April 2020. His profits (as adjusted for tax purposes) for the first three periods of account are as follows.

	£
Eight months to 30 April 2020	24,000
Year to 30 April 2021	39,000
Year to 30 April 2022	40,000

His taxable profits for the first four tax years are as follows.

	Basis period		£	£
2019/20	1.9.19 – 5.4.20	£24,000 × 7/8		21,000
2020/21	1.9.19 – 31.8.20:			
	1.9.19 – 30.4.20		24,000	
	1.5.20 – 31.8.20	£39,000 × 4/12	13,000	
				37,000
2021/22	Y/e 30.4.21			39,000
2022/23	Y/e 30.4.22			40,000

	£
Overlap relief accrued:	
1.9.19 – 5.4.20 — 7 months	21,000
1.5.20 – 31.8.20 — 4 months	13,000
Total overlap relief accrued (see 75.14 below)	£34,000

Intermediate years

[75.9] (Intermediate years are tax years for which the special rules for Opening Years, as in 75.7 above, or for the Closing Year, see 75.12 below, do not apply).

The general rule is that the basis period for a tax year is the period of twelve months ending with the accounting date falling in that tax year. This is subject to any change of accounting date, for which see 75.10 below. If, in a case where neither the opening years rules nor the change of accounting date rules apply (e.g. the next but one tax year after the year of commencement), there is no accounting date in the tax year, the basis period for that tax year is the twelve months immediately following the end of the basis period for the previous tax year. [*ITTOIA 2005, ss 198, 201*].

Simon's Taxes. See **B4.104**.

Change of accounting date

[75.10] Where a change from one accounting date (the old date) to another (the new date) is made in a tax year, the conditions below must be satisfied if the change of accounting date is to result in a change of basis period. (This does not apply if the year is the second or third tax year of the business.) A change of accounting date is made in a tax year if accounts are not made up to the old date in that year or are made up to the new date in that year. The conditions, *all of which must be satisfied*, are as follows.

(1) The period of account ending with the new date does not exceed 18 months. (This condition must be met by the accounts in existence when the tax return is submitted and not by accounts drawn up retrospectively (*Grint v HMRC* UT, [2019] STC 439, [2019] UKUT 28 (TCC)).)

(2) Notice of the change is given to HMRC in a personal (or, where appropriate, a partnership or trust) tax return on or before the day on which that return is required to be delivered (see **64.2, 64.12** RETURNS).

(3) Either:

 (i) no change of accounting date resulting in a change of basis period has been made in any of the previous five tax years;

 or

 (ii) the change is made for commercial reasons (which does not include the obtaining of a tax advantage). If this condition is relied upon, the notice in (2) above must set out the reasons for the change and HMRC then have 60 days, beginning with receipt of the notice, in which to give notice to the trader, if they wish, that they are *not* satisfied that the change is made for commercial reasons. (An appeal may be made against such an HMRC notice, within 30 days beginning with the date of issue, and the Appeal Tribunal may either confirm the notice or set it aside.)

Where all the conditions are satisfied, or the change of accounting date is made in the second or third tax year of the business, the basis period for the tax year is as follows.

(a) If the year is the second tax year of the business, the basis period is the twelve months ending with the new date in the year (unless the period from commencement of the business to the new date in the second year is less than twelve months, in which case the basis period is the first twelve months of the business).

(b) If the 'relevant period' is a period of less than twelve months, the basis period is the twelve months ending with the new date in the year.

(c) If the 'relevant period' is a period of more than twelve months, the basis period consists of the relevant period.

The '*relevant period*' is the period beginning immediately after the end of the basis period for the preceding year and ending with the new date in the year.

It will be seen that a basis period can be of more than twelve months' duration but cannot be less than twelve months. If not all of the above conditions are satisfied (and the year is not the second or third tax year of the business), the basis period for the year is the twelve months beginning immediately after the end of the basis period for the preceding year. However, the change of accounting date is then treated as made in the following tax year and can thus result in a change of basis period for that following year if all the above conditions are satisfied as regards that year. A change of accounting date can continue to be 'carried forward' in this way until such time, if any, as a change of basis period results or the old accounting date is reverted to.

[*ITTOIA 2005, ss 214–219*].

See **75.14** below for relief (overlap relief) where the rules in (a) or (b) above have the effect of the same profits being taxed in each of two successive tax years, and for the use of overlap relief brought forward in computing profits in a situation within (c) above.

For partnership trades, notice in (2) above and an appeal within (3)(ii) above must be given or brought by such one of the partners as is nominated by them for the purpose (any resulting change of basis period affecting the notional trades of individual partners — see **52.4** PARTNERSHIPS). [*ITTOIA 2005, s 853(3)*].

Accounts prepared to a variable date

Sometimes accounts are prepared to a particular day in the year (e.g. the last Friday in September) rather than a particular date. Provided that day can fall on one of only seven consecutive dates (or eight where 29 February is involved), there are provisions enabling the fourth of those seven or eight dates (the '*middle date*') to be treated, for these purposes only, as the normal accounting date, so that the change of accounting date rules above are not triggered by these minor changes from one year to the next. These provisions apply in relation to any particular tax year only if the taxpayer makes an election to that effect. The election must be made on or before the first anniversary of 31 January following the tax year to which it relates, and must specify both the actual accounting date for that tax year and the middle date. A change from an accounting date determined under these rules to an actual accounting date is, however, treated as a change of accounting date, even if those two dates happen to be the same. On cessation or a change of accounting date, basis periods are determined as if the basis period for the previous tax year had ended on the actual accounting date in that year and not on the middle date. [*ITTOIA 2005, ss 211–213, 214(2)*].

Simon's Taxes. See **B4.109**, **B4.110**.

Examples

[75.11]

(i) Change to a date earlier in the tax year

Miranda commenced trade on 1 September 2017, preparing accounts to 31 August. In 2020, she changed her accounting date to 31 May, preparing accounts for the nine months to 31 May 2020. The conditions in **75.10**(1)–(3) above are satisfied in relation to the change. Her profits (as adjusted for tax purposes) are as follows.

	£
Year ended 31 August 2018	18,000

Year ended 31 August 2019	21,500
Nine months to 31 May 2020	17,000
Year ended 31 May 2021	23,000

Taxable profits for the first five tax years are as follows.

	Basis period		£	£
2017/18	1.9.17 – 5.4.18	£18,000 × 7/12		10,500
2018/19	Y/e 31.8.18			18,000
2019/20	Y/e 31.8.19			21,500
2020/21	1.6.19 – 31.5.20:			
	1.6.19 – 31.8.19	£21,500 × 3/12	5,375	
	1.9.19 – 31.5.20		17,000	
				22,375
2021/22	Y/e 31.5.21			23,000

Overlap relief accrued (see **75.14** below)

1.9.17 – 5.4.18 — 7 months	10,500
1.6.19 – 31.8.19 — 3 months	5,375
Total overlap relief accrued	£15,875

Note

(a) In this example, the 'relevant period' is that from 1 September 2019 (the day following the end of the basis period for 2019/20) to 31 May 2020 (the new accounting date in the year 2020/21 — the year of change). As the relevant period is less than twelve months, the basis period for 2020/21 is the twelve months ending on the new accounting date.

(ii) Change to a date later in the tax year

Dennis starts a business on 1 July 2017, preparing accounts to 30 June. In 2020, he changes his accounting date to 31 December, preparing accounts for the six months to 31 December 2020. The conditions in **75.10**(1)–(3) above are satisfied in relation to the change. His profits (as adjusted for tax purposes) are as follows.

	£
Year ended 30 June 2018	18,000
Year ended 30 June 2019	21,500
Year ended 30 June 2020	23,000
Six months to 31 December 2020	12,000
Year ended 31 December 2021	27,000

Taxable profits for the first five years are as follows.

	Basis period		£	£
2017/18	1.7.17 – 5.4.18	£18,000 × 9/12		13,500
2018/19	Y/e 30.6.18			18,000
2019/20	Y/e 30.6.19			21,500

	Basis period		£	£
2020/21	1.7.19 – 31.12.20:			
	1.7.19 – 30.6.20		23,000	
	1.7.20 – 31.12.20		12,000	
			35,000	
	Deduct	Overlap relief	9,000	
				26,000
2021/22	Y/e 31.12.21			27,000

Overlap relief accrued:

1.7.17 – 5.4.18 — 9 months	£13,500
Less utilised in 2020/21	£9,000
Carried forward	£4,500

Utilisation of overlap relief in 2020/21

$$\text{Apply the formula: } A \times \frac{B - C}{D}$$

(see **75.14** below)

where:

A = aggregate overlap relief accrued (£13,500);
B = length of basis period for 2020/21 (18 months);
C = 12 months; and
D = the length of the overlap period(s) by reference to which the aggregate overlap profits accrued (9 months).

Thus, the deduction to be given in computing profits for 2020/21 is:

$$£13{,}500 \times \frac{18 - 12}{9} = £9{,}000$$

Notes

(a) In this example, the 'relevant period' is that from 1 July 2019 (the day following the end of the basis period for 2019/20) to 31 December 2020 (the new accounting date in the year 2020/21 — the year of change). As the relevant period is more than twelve months, the basis period for 2020/21 is equal to the relevant period. Note that a basis period of 18 months results in this case, even though accounts were prepared for a period of only six months to the new date.

(b) The overlap relief accrued (by reference to an overlap period of nine months) is given on cessation or, as in this example, on a change of accounting date resulting in a basis period exceeding twelve months (the relief given depending on the extent of the excess). The balance of overlap relief (£4,500) is carried forward for future relief on the happening of such an event. See **75.14** below. If Dennis had changed his accounting date to, say, 31 March or 5 April (instead of 31 December), the use of the formula in 75.14 below would have resulted in overlap relief of £13,500 being given in full in 2020/21.

Closing year

[75.12] On cessation of a business carried on by an individual (which includes his leaving a continuing partnership and his transferring the ownership of a business, e.g. on sale, incorporation or death), the following rule applies. As to what constitutes a cessation, see **75.17** below.

The basis period for the **final tax year**, i.e. that in which cessation occurs, is the period beginning immediately after the end of the basis period for the penultimate year and ending with the date of cessation. (If a business starts and ceases in the same tax year, the basis period is the actual period of trading.) [*ITTOIA 2005, s 202*].

The basis period may thus exceed twelve months, but see **75.14** below as regards the use of overlap relief brought forward in computing profits for the final year.

See **45.20** LOSSES for terminal losses and **45.19** LOSSES for the carry-forward of certain losses where a private business is converted into a company.

Simon's Taxes. See **B4.105**.

Example

[75.13]

Robin commenced to trade on 1 May 2016, preparing accounts to 30 April. He permanently ceases to trade on 30 June 2020, preparing accounts for the two months to that date. His profits (as adjusted for tax purposes) are as follows.

	£
Year ended 30 April 2017	24,000
Year ended 30 April 2018	48,000
Year ended 30 April 2019	96,000
Year ended 30 April 2020	36,000
Two months ended 30 June 2020	5,000
	£209,000

Taxable profits for the five tax years of trading are as follows.

	Basis period		£	£
2016/17	1.5.16 – 5.4.17	£24,000 × $^{11}/_{12}$		22,000
2017/18	Y/e 30.4.17			24,000
2018/19	Y/e 30.4.18			48,000
2019/20	Y/e 30.4.19			96,000
2020/21	1.5.19 – 30.6.20:			
	1.5.19 – 30.4.20		36,000	
	1.5.20 – 30.6.20		5,000	

	41,000	
Deduct Overlap relief	22,000	
		19,000
		£209,000

Overlap relief accrued (see **75.14** below):

1.5.16 – 5.4.17 — 11 months	22,000
Utilised in 2020/21	(22,000)

Overlap relief

[75.14] An **'overlap profit'** is an amount of profits which, by virtue of the basis period rules above, is included in the computations for two successive tax years. It may arise as a result of the opening year rules in **75.7** above or on a change of basis period within **75.10**(a) or (b) above (i.e. resulting from a change of accounting date). An **'overlap period'** in relation to an overlap profit is the number of days in the period for which the overlap profit arose. For example (working in terms of months for simplicity), if a business commences on 1 May 2019 and prepares its first accounts for the year to 30 April 2020 showing tax-adjusted profits of £24,000, the 2019/20 assessment is based on the period 1 May 2019 to 5 April 2020 (£24,000 × $^{11}/_{12}$ = £22,000) and the 2020/21 assessment is based on the year ended 30 April 2020 (£24,000). The overlap profit is £22,000 by reference to an overlap period of 11 months.

Relief for an overlap profit is given, by way of a deduction in computing profits, on a change of accounting date resulting in a basis period of more than twelve months (see **75.10**(c) above) and/or in the final tax year of the business (see **75.12** above).

Change of accounting date

On the first such change of accounting date, if any, the deduction is:

$$A \times \frac{B - C}{D}$$

where:

A	=	the aggregate of any overlap profits;
B	=	the number of days in the basis period (i.e. more than 365 or 366);
C	=	the number of days in the tax year (365 or 366); and
D	=	the aggregate of the overlap periods by reference to which the overlap profits in A are calculated.

For example (working in terms of months for simplicity), if the overlap profit brought forward is £22,000 by reference to an overlap period of 11 months, and the basis period for a tax year is 15 months, the overlap relief deductible in computing profits for that year is £22,000 × $^{3}/_{11}$ = £6,000, leaving an overlap profit of £16,000, by reference to an overlap period of eight months, to be carried forward. On subsequent applications of this formula, A and D are reduced by, respectively, the overlap profit previously relieved and the number of days referable to the previous relief.

At the taxpayer's discretion, a change of accounting date to 31 March or to any of the first four days in April can be treated for overlap relief purposes as if it were a change to 5 April, thus enabling all outstanding overlap relief to be deducted.

In the above formula, any reasonable measure may be used at the taxpayer's discretion instead of days, provided that measure is used consistently for the particular trade, so that, over the lifetime of the business, the taxable profit charged equals the taxable profit made (see also **75.6** above under Apportionment of profits to basis periods). (The worked examples in this chapter use months for instance.)

If days are used in the formula and the change is to 5 April (or is treated as such, as above), the occurrence of 29 February can be ignored in making the calculation if the overlap relief would not otherwise be relieved in full.

Cessation

On cessation, the deduction in computing profits for the final tax year is equal to the total overlap profits previously unrelieved.

Effect of overlap relief on losses

Relief for an overlap profit is not restricted to the amount of profits available, and may convert a taxable trading profit into an allowable trading loss, or increase an allowable trading loss, which may be relieved in the same way as any other trading loss (see **45** LOSSES). Where it creates or augments a terminal loss claim (see **45.20** LOSSES), the full amount of the overlap profit is included, without any apportionment.

[*ITTOIA 2005, ss 204, 205, 220*].

See **75.15** below for overlap profits arising under transitional rules for businesses commenced before 6 April 1994.

Overlap losses

Where an amount of loss would otherwise fall to be included in the computations for two successive tax years, that amount (the '*overlap loss*') is not to be so included for the second of those years. [*ITTOIA 2005, s 206*].

Trading allowance

See **75.3** above for the interaction between overlap relief and the trading allowance available for 2017/18 onwards, and also for modifications to the calculation of overlap profit where relief for the trading allowance is given for at least one of the two tax years in which the overlap period falls.

Simon's Taxes. See B4.107.

Transitional rules for businesses commenced before 6 April 1994

[75.15] A business commenced before 6 April 1994 is treated as having a transitional overlap profit for 1997/98. This is equal to the amount of profits taxable for 1997/98, but before deduction/addition of capital allowances/balancing charges (except in the case of a partnership with a corporate partner), which arises after the end of the basis period for 1996/97 and before 6 April 1997. For example, if accounts are regularly made up to 30 June and those for the year to 30 June 1997 showed tax-adjusted profits of £20,000 before capital allowances, the 1997/98 assessment would have been £20,000 *less* capital allowances and there will be a transitional overlap profit of £15,000 by reference to a transitional overlap period of nine months, 1 July 1996 to 5 April 1997 (working in terms of months rather than days, for simplicity). The transitional overlap profit is carried forward indefinitely in the same way as other overlap profits until fully relieved (see **75.14** above). [*FA 1994, Sch 20 para 2(4)–(4B)*].

Trades carried on abroad

[75.16] Trading profits arising to a UK resident are chargeable to income tax wherever the trade is carried on. This encompasses trades, professions and vocations carried on either wholly or partly abroad. If the tax year is a split year (see **63.19** RESIDENCE AND DOMICILE) as regards a UK resident individual, this rule has effect as if, for the overseas part of the split year, the individual were non-UK resident. [*ITTOIA 2005, s 6(1)(2A)(3)*].

A non-UK resident is chargeable to income tax to the extent that he carries on a trade etc. in the UK (see **75.1** above and **50.6** NON-RESIDENTS).

Where a business is 'carried on' for these purposes depends on from where it is managed and controlled, irrespective of where the day-to-day business activities are conducted. See for this *Trustees of Ferguson, decd v Donovan Supreme Court* (IFS) 1927, 1 ITC 214 (trustees delegated control of Australian business to Australian company and did not interfere in any way; held not within Case I) and contrast *Ogilvie v Kitton* CES 1908, 5 TC 338 (Canadian business managed by Canadians but 'head and brains' in UK where owners resided; Case I applied) and *Spiers v Mackinnon* KB 1929, 14 TC 386.

See **75.19** below for provisions applying where an individual carrying on a business wholly or partly outside the UK becomes or ceases to be UK resident.

For special considerations concerning partnership trades carried on wholly or partly outside the UK, see **52.22** PARTNERSHIPS.

Trades carried on wholly abroad — remittance basis

For trades carried on wholly outside the UK (see *ITTOIA 2005, s 7(5)*), the remittance basis may apply to individuals who are either not domiciled or not ordinarily resident in the UK. See **60** REMITTANCE BASIS.

Trades carried on wholly abroad — loss reliefs

Where the trade is carried on wholly outside the UK, loss reliefs under **45.2**, **45.7**, **45.19** and **45.20** LOSSES are available only against the profits of trades carried on wholly abroad, chargeable overseas earnings (see **28.5** EMPLOYMENT INCOME), overseas government pensions (as in **56.2**(f) PENSION INCOME) and certain other foreign pensions (see **56.2**(b)(e)(h)(i) PENSION INCOME), but excluding any 'relevant foreign income' (see **32.2** FOREIGN INCOME) charged on the REMITTANCE BASIS (**61**). Relief under **45.5** LOSSES (set-off against chargeable gains) is not available at all. [*ITA 2007, s 95*].

Trades carried on wholly abroad — travelling etc. expenses

If, either alone or in partnership, an individual carries on a trade wholly outside the UK (a 'foreign trade'), a deduction is available for certain expenditure on travel, board and lodging which is incurred in connection with that trade and which would not otherwise be allowable due to its failing to meet the 'wholly and exclusively' rule at **75.44** below. The deduction is given in computing profits of the foreign trade, but is not available where such profits are charged on the remittance basis. It is given only where the trader's absence from the UK is wholly and exclusively for the purpose of carrying on either the foreign trade or that trade and one or more other trades (be they foreign trades or not).

The deductible expenses are as follows.

(a) Expenses incurred by the trader in travelling between a UK location and the location of the foreign trade.

(b) Expenses incurred by the trader on board and lodging at the location of the foreign trade.

(c) Expenses incurred by the trader in travelling between the location of the foreign trade and the non-UK location of any other trade carried on by him wholly or partly outside the UK.

(d) If the trader's continuous absence from the UK lasts 60 days or more, expenses of a journey made by his spouse (or civil partner) or by any child of his between a UK location and the location of any of the trades in question where that journey is made in order to accompany the trader at the beginning of his period of absence or to visit him during that period or is a return journey in connection with a journey of either of those kinds. The deduction is limited to the expenses of two such outward journeys and two return journeys per person per tax year. 'Child' includes a stepchild or an illegitimate child but does not include a person aged 18 or over at the start of the outward journey.

Where more than one foreign trade is carried on at the overseas location, expenses within (a) and (b) above are allocated between the trades on a just and reasonable basis. Where the trader's absence is for the purpose of carrying on more than one foreign trade, expenses within (d) above are likewise allocated on a just and reasonable basis. Expenses within (c) above are allocated to the trade carried on at the journey's destination if that is a foreign trade; otherwise they are allocated to the foreign trade carried on at the place of departure. If more than one foreign trade is carried on at the place of destination or at the place of departure, as the case may be, the expenses are again allocated between the foreign trades on a just and reasonable basis.

[*ITTOIA 2005, ss 92–94*].

Simon's Taxes. See **B1.207, B2.440, E1.1025.**

Whether or not there has been a commencement or cessation

[75.17] The rules at **75.7** and **75.12** above for the opening and closing years apply (i) on the commencement of a new business or the permanent cessation of a business by an individual (including a transfer of the ownership of a business, e.g. when it is sold or incorporated or it passes on death) and (ii) on an individual becoming or ceasing to be a member of a partnership (*but not so as to affect the continuing partners*) — see **52.4** PARTNERSHIPS.

See **52.9** PARTNERSHIPS as regards partnership mergers and demergers.

If a trade is being carried on by trustees of a trust or by personal representatives of a deceased person, a mere change of trustee etc. does not give rise to a cessation and re-commencement of the trade. [*ITTOIA 2005, s 258*].

Non-resident companies are within the charge to income tax (not corporation tax) in certain circumstances (see Tolley's Corporation Tax under Residence). Where a company starts or ceases to be within the charge to income tax in respect of a trade, it is treated as notionally starting or permanently ceasing to carry on the trade at that time. [*ITTOIA 2005, s 18*]. For a short article on the distinction between succession to a trade, extension of an existing trade and commencement of a new trade, see Revenue Tax Bulletin February 1996 pp 285, 286. For an in-depth discussion, see HMRC Business Income Manual BIM80500–80690.

Simon's Taxes. See **B1.6.**

Case law

[75.18] Whether or not a person has commenced/ceased trading and, if so, the date, are questions of fact. Preliminary activities in setting up a business do not amount to trading (*Birmingham & District Cattle By-Products Co Ltd v CIR* KB 1919, 12 TC 92). Negotiations to enter into the initial contracts are part of setting up the trade and do not mean trading has commenced (*Mansell v HMRC* (Sp C 551), [2006] SSCD 605). For pre-trading expenditure, see **75.106** below. For whether the sale of a business can be effective for tax purposes before the vending agreement, see *Todd v Jones Bros Ltd* KB 1930, 15 TC 396 and contrast *Angel v Hollingworth & Co* Ch D 1958, 37 TC 714. 'Permanent discontinuance' does not mean a discontinuance which is everlasting (see *Ingram v Callaghan* CA 1968, 45 TC 151) but a trade may continue notwithstanding a lengthy break in active trading (*Kirk & Randall Ltd v Dunn* KB 1924, 8 TC 663 but contrast *Goff v Osborne & Co (Sheffield) Ltd* Ch D 1953, 34 TC 441). An intensification by a freelance television producer of his freelance activities could not effect a discontinuance and commencement of a new business (*Edmunds v Coleman* Ch D 1997, 70 TC 322).

In *Mansell v HMRC* above, the Special Commissioner observed that a trade commences when the trader, having a specific idea in mind of his intended profit-making activities, and having set up his business, begins operational activities; 'operational activities' means dealings with third parties immediately and directly related to the supplies to be made which it is hoped will give rise to the expected profits, and which involve the trader putting money at risk. This dictum was followed in *Hunt v HMRC* FTT (TC 7311), [2019] UKFTT 515 (TC).

In a case where the global business of a company was run on the basis of divisions operating autonomously with their own operational management and reporting lines, supply chain, products, manufacturing, premises, sales organisation, notepaper, invoicing and accounting, the closure of two out of six UK divisions, all concerned with electronics products, did not amount to cessation for purposes of terminal loss relief; the company was held to be carrying on a single trade (*Electronics Ltd v HM Inspector of Taxes* (Sp C 476), [2005] SSCD 512).

A company which used to deal in computers and computer software and subsequently went on to provide IT consultancy services instead was held for loss relief purposes to have carried on two different trades at different times; it was inappropriate to regard both activities as part of a single trade carrying the general description of IT-related activities (*Kawthar Consulting Ltd v HMRC* (Sp C 477), [2005] SSCD 524). An optician was denied the carry-forward of loss relief on the grounds that his current profession as a freelance locum dispensing optician was different from his previous trade as a franchisee dispensing optician (*Amah v HMRC (No 2)* FTT (TC 4173), [2014] UKFTT 1084 (TC). Expenditure incurred by a suspended medical practitioner with zero turnover was held to have been incurred not for the purpose of preserving a trade from destruction but with the aim of re-establishing a trade that had ceased to exist (and was therefore not trading expenditure) (*Admirals Locums and Bhadra v HMRC* FTT (TC 1416), [2011] UKFTT 573 (TC)).

The trade was held to have been continuous when the owner of a drifter continued to manage it after its war-time requisition (*Sutherland v CIR* CS 1918, 12 TC 63); when a merchant sold stock on hand after announcing retirement (*J & R O'Kane v CIR* HL 1922, 12 TC 303); when a flour miller and baker gave up a mill (*Bolands Ltd v Davis* KB(IFS) 1925, 4 ATC 532); when a barrister took silk (*Seldon v Croom-Johnson* KB 1932, 16 TC 740); when a partnership was dissolved but completed open forward contracts (*Hillerns & Fowler v Murray* CA 1932, 17 TC 77); when a building partnership transferred construction activities to a company but retained building land and continued to sell land with houses built thereon by the company (*Watts v Hart* Ch D 1984, 58 TC 209). A new trade was held to have commenced when the vendor of a business retained the benefit of outstanding hire-purchase agreements (*Parker v Batty* KB 1941, 23 TC 739) and when the vendor of a business got commission on open contracts completed by the purchaser (*Southern v Cohen's Exors* KB 1940, 23 TC 566).

It is similarly a question of fact whether a trader expanding by taking over an existing business and operating it as a branch has succeeded to the trade. See e.g. *Bell v National Provincial Bank of England Ltd* CA 1903, 5 TC 1 (bank succeeded to trade of single-branch bank taken over); *Laycock v Freeman Hardy & Willis Ltd* CA 1938, 22 TC 288 (shoe retailer did not succeed to trade of manufacturing subsidiaries taken over); *Briton Ferry Steel Co Ltd v Barry* CA 1939, 23 TC 414 (steel manufacturer succeeded to trade of tinplate manufacturing subsidiaries taken over); and *Maidment v Kibby* Ch D 1993, 66 TC 137 (fish and chip shop proprietor did not succeed to trade of existing business taken over). See also *H & G Kinemas Ltd* KB 1933, 18 TC 116 (cinema company disposed of existing cinemas and opened new one, held to commence new trade).

Because farming is statutorily treated as trading (see **75.77** below), activities that in other trades might be seen as merely preparations for trading may be indications that trading has commenced (*Howes v HMRC* (FTT (TC 1874), [2012] UKFTT 179 (TC)).

Change of residence

[75.19] A special rule applies where a sole trader becomes or ceases to be resident in the UK. The trade is deemed to have been permanently discontinued at the time of the change of residence and, in so far as the individual continues to carry on the actual trade, a new trade is deemed to have been set up immediately afterwards. This applies equally for the purposes of loss reliefs except that it does not prevent a loss incurred in the 'old' trade from being carried forward under *ITA 2007, s 83* (see **45.19** LOSSES) and set against profits of the 'new' trade.

The rule also applies where a tax year is a split year (see **63.19** RESIDENCE AND DOMICILE). In this case the change of residence is treated as occurring at the start of whichever of the UK part or the overseas part of the split year is the later part.

[*ITTOIA 2005, s 17*].

Similar rules apply to individuals trading in partnership (see **52.22** PARTNERSHIPS).

Accounts and accounts information

[75.20] Under self-assessment, it is not a requirement that accounts should accompany tax returns. Instead (except in cases where the annual turnover is less than the VAT registration threshold — see below), accounts information has to be provided on the self-employment supplementary pages to the return. There are full and short versions of these supplementary pages; the version to be used depends on various criteria such as turnover and complexity (see HMRC's Notes on Self-Employment — SA103F for the criteria).

Three-line accounts

Where turnover is less than the VAT registration threshold (currently £85,000), or the appropriate proportion of that amount where the period of account is less than a year, only turnover, total expenses and profit or loss need be shown in a tax return.

See **75.96** below for deductibility of accountancy fees.

Rounding of tax computations

To reduce the compliance burden on large businesses whose statutory accounts are produced in round thousands, HMRC are generally prepared to accept profit returns for tax purposes in figures rounded to the nearest £1,000 from single businesses with an annual turnover of at least £5 million (including investment and estate income) in the accounts in question or in the preceding year, where rounding at least to that extent has been used in preparing the accounts. Such returns must be accompanied by a certificate by the person preparing the computations stating the basis of rounding, and confirming that it is unbiased, has been applied consistently and produces a fair result for tax purposes (and stating the program or software used where relevant), or, if there have been no changes from the previous year in these respects, confirming the unchanged basis. The rounding may not extend to the tax payable or other relevant figures of tax. Rounding is not acceptable where it would impede the application of the legislation, or where recourse to the underlying records would normally be necessary to do the computation. Thus it is not acceptable e.g. in computations of chargeable gains (except in relation to the incidental costs of acquisition and disposal), in accrued income scheme computations (see **2** ACCRUED INCOME SCHEME), in computations of tax credit relief or in certain capital allowance computations. HMRC officers may exceptionally insist that rounding is not used in other circumstances. (HMRC SP 15/93).

Examination of accounts information by HMRC

For HMRC's enquiry powers under self-assessment, see **64.6** *et seq.* RETURNS. An enquiry into a tax return may well include an examination of the accounts information included in the return and/or the underlying accounts themselves. See generally HMRC Pamphlet COP 11. See also **55.6, 55.23** PENALTIES.

Understated profits

The measure of understated profits is calculated from the available data, but if this is unsatisfactory, on the increase of capital from year to year, with adjustments for cost of living etc. See for this, *Deacon v Roper* Ch D 1952, 33 TC 66; *Horowitz v Farrand* Ch D 1952, 33 TC 221; *Moschi v Kelly* CA 1952, 33 TC 442; *Kilburn v Bedford* Ch D 1955, 36 TC 262; *Roberts v McGregor* Ch D 1959, 38 TC 610; *Chuwen v Sabine* Ch D 1959, 39 TC 1; *Erddig Motors Ltd v McGregor* Ch D 1961, 40 TC 95; *Hellier v O'Hare* Ch D 1964, 42 TC 155; *Hurley v Young* Ch D 1966, 45 ATC 316; *Hope v Damerel* Ch D 1969, 48 ATC 461; *Driver v CIR* CS 1977, 52 TC 153; *Kovak v Morris* CA 1985, 58 TC 493 and cf. *Rose v Humbles* CA 1971, 48 TC 103. For a case in which similar principles were applied in determining directors' true remuneration, see *Billows v Robinson* Ch D 1989, 64 TC 17.

HMRC officers will not automatically insist on annual capital statements (see above) where understated profits can be measured satisfactorily in other ways, such as by use of expected rates of gross trading profits (Revenue Press Release 1 August 1977).

Adherence to GAAP

[75.21] The profits of a trade, profession or vocation must be computed in accordance with '*generally accepted accounting practice*' (GAAP) (see also 75.22 below), which is defined (by *ITA 2007, s 997*) by reference to the practice adopted in UK company accounts that are drawn up to give a true and fair view. Despite this reference to 'company accounts', it must be emphasised that the requirement applies for income tax as well as corporation tax purposes. The requirement is, however, subject to any adjustment required or authorised by law; see, for example, the prohibition at 75.43 below on deducting capital expenditure. GAAP also incorporates international accounting standards in cases where accounts are prepared in accordance with such standards; in all other cases, the expression is restricted to UK GAAP.

The above requirement imposes a general requirement to apply an earnings basis (see below) for tax purposes, whilst at the same time importing the accountancy concept of 'materiality', allowing a practical view to be taken of the time at which immaterial amounts are recognised. It requires neither the auditing of accounts, nor additional disclosure, nor the preparation of a balance sheet. Neither does it require accounts to be drawn up on any particular basis (provided the necessary adjustments are made in the tax computation). For HMRC's view of what is meant by 'true and fair view', see Revenue Tax Bulletin December 1998 pp 606–615. See HMRC Business Income Manual BIM31045, 31047 as regards the concept of materiality. See also 75.22 below.

The special computational rules for UNDERWRITERS AT LLOYD'S (79) are not affected by the above requirement.

[*ITTOIA 2005, s 25; ITA 2007, s 997*].

The earnings basis

Prior to the introduction of the above requirement, case law had previously established that the legal basis for computation of profits was the earnings basis with provision for debtors, creditors, accruals and stock and work in progress (cf. *CIR v Gardner Mountain & D'Ambrumenil Ltd* HL 1947, 29 TC 69). Hence profits and losses which have not accrued cannot be anticipated (cf. *Willingale v International Commercial Bank Ltd* HL 1977, 52 TC 242) nor can future expenses. Conversely an expense actually incurred may be allowable in full even though the benefit from it will not accrue until later years (*Vallambrosa Rubber Co Ltd v Farmer* CES 1910, 5 TC 529; *Duple Motor Bodies Ltd v Ostime* HL 1961, 39 TC 537).

See 75.57 below as regards future and contingent liabilities generally.

Meaning of 'receipts' and 'expenses'

Wherever they appear in income tax legislation in the context of computing trading profits, the words 'receipts' and 'expenses' refer generally to items brought into account as credits or debits in computing those profits, and contain no implication that an amount has been actually received or paid. [*ITTOIA 2005, s 27*]. This is of no application where an election under *ITTOIA 2005, s 25A* below (cash basis for smaller businesses) has effect. [*ITTOIA 2005, s 25A(4)*].

Cash basis for smaller businesses

A person carrying on a trade with turnover not exceeding a specified limit (e.g. £150,000 for 2017/18 onwards and £83,000 for 2016/17) can elect for the profits of the trade to be calculated on the cash basis (instead of in accordance with GAAP). For claimants of Universal credit, this turnover limit is doubled. [*ITTOIA 2005, s 25A(1)–(3)*]. See **76** TRADING INCOME — CASH BASIS FOR SMALLER BUSINESSES.

Simon's Taxes. See **B2.102.**

Application of accountancy principles

[75.22] See 75.21 above as regards the requirement that generally accepted accounting practice (GAAP) be adhered to in the computation of taxable profits. Even prior to the introduction of this requirement, it had long since been the case that, since the starting figure in computing profits was that brought out by the accounts of the business, accountancy principles were of the greatest importance. They could not, however, override established income tax principles (*Heather v P-E Consulting Group Ltd* CA 1972, 48 TC 293; *Willingale v International Commercial Bank Ltd* HL 1977, 52 TC 242; but see *Threlfall v Jones* CA 1993, 66 TC 77; *Johnston v Britannia Airways Ltd* Ch D 1994, 67 TC 99). See also *RTZ Oil & Gas Ltd v Elliss* Ch D 1987, 61 TC 132. A 'provision for a future operating loss', whose inclusion could not be said to have 'violated existing accounting principles', was disallowed in *Meat Traders Ltd v Cushing* (Sp C 131), [1997] SSCD 245. See *Robertson v CIR* (Sp C 137), [1997] SSCD 282 as regards timing of inclusion of insurance agents' advance commission. See also *Herbert Smith v Honour* Ch D 1999, 72 TC 130 for the timing of deductions in respect of future rents under leases of premises ceasing to be used for business purposes, and Revenue Press Release 20 July 1999 for Inland Revenue practice following that decision.

Per Sir Thomas Bingham MR in *Threlfall v Jones*: ' . . . I find it hard to understand how any judge-made rule could override the application of a generally accepted rule of commercial accountancy which (a) applied to the situation in question, (b) was not one of two or more rules applicable to the situation in question and (c) was not shown to be inconsistent with the true facts or otherwise inapt to determine the true profits or losses of the business'. FRS 18 now requires companies to choose accounting policies that are most appropriate to their particular circumstances (see Revenue Tax Bulletin April 2002 p 924).

For HMRC's view on the relationship between accounting profits and taxable profits, see HMRC Business Income Manual BIM31000–31115. For generally accepted accounting practice and accounting standards, see BIM31020–31065. For the timing of deductions where an expense is taken to the balance sheet rather than charged immediately against profits, i.e. *deferred revenue expenditure*, see HMRC Business Income Manual BIM42215. For *provisions*, see HMRC Business Income Manual BIM46500–46565.

Financial Reporting Standards (FRS) 101, 102 and 105

Entities which apply UK GAAP are likely to be using FRS 101, FRS 102 or, for eligible micro entities, FRS 105. FRS 105 is based on the recognition and measurement requirements of FRS 102, but with some accounting simplifications and reduced disclosure requirements. HMRC will generally accept calculations of profit for unincorporated businesses prepared under FRS 105 if the business meets the size criteria for that Standard. HMRC publish three overview papers at www.gov.uk/government/publications/accounting-standards-the-uk-tax-implications-of-new-uk-gaap. Their purpose is to assist companies applying FRS 101, FRS 102 or FRS 105. They concentrate on the corporation tax position, but may also assist individuals (and other entities within the charge to income tax) as many of the accounting and tax issues will be similar.

International Financial Reporting Standard 16 (IFRS 16)

This new international accounting standard significantly alters the treatment of leases for accounting purposes, mainly for the lessee. It becomes effective for accounting periods beginning on or after 1 January 2019, although earlier adoption is possible. Lessees using IFRS 16 are not required to distinguish between finance leases and operating leases. The distinction is, however, retained by statute for tax purposes (see **75.82** below).

Simon's Taxes. See **B2.104**, **B2.501**.

Barristers and advocates

[75.23] Barristers and advocates in independent practice were exempt from the above requirement for periods of account ending not more than seven years after they first held themselves out as available for fee-earning work. They could instead compute their profits either on a cash basis or by reference to fees earned whose amount had been agreed or in respect of which a fee note had been delivered. The basis adopted must be applied consistently. Under the cash basis, profits are measured by excess of cash receipts over cash outlay, ignoring debtors and creditors, accruals, unbilled or uncompleted work. Once an accounting basis complying with *ITTOIA 2005, s 25* (as above) is adopted for any period of account, the exemption ceases and that *section* applies for all subsequent periods of account.

The above was repealed for 2013/14 onwards in light of the introduction of the cash basis for smaller businesses. By way of transition, where the profits of a barrister or advocate for a period of account ending in the tax year 2012/13 were calculated on the basis above, they may continue to use that basis for any subsequent period of account for which it would have been available if it were not for the repeal, i.e. any periods within the seven years mentioned above, assuming they do not choose to adopt an earnings basis before the end of those seven years.

[*ITTOIA 2005, s 160; FA 2013, Sch 4 para 57(1)*].

If a change of accounting basis arises on a barrister or advocate ceasing to take advantage of the above exemption or on its ceasing to be available, any resulting adjustment income is automatically spread over ten years. This includes a case in which they continue to take advantage of the exemption under the transitional rule above. See 75.25 below.

Adjustments on a change of basis

[75.24] The adjustment described below is required where:

- there is, from one period of account of a trade, profession or vocation to the next, a 'change of basis' in computing taxable profits;
- the old basis accorded with the law or practice applicable in relation to the period of account before the change; and
- the new basis accords with the law and practice applicable in relation to the period of account following the change.

A '*change of basis*' for this purpose is:

- a change of accounting policy; or
- a change in the statutory tax adjustments applied (including a change resulting from a change of view as to application of the statute but excluding a change made to comply with an amendment to the statute which was not applicable to the earlier period of account).

A change of accounting policy can include, but is not limited to, a change from using UK GAAP (see **75.21** above) to using international accounting standards and vice versa.

Tax treatment of adjustment

Subject to the exceptions at (i)–(iv) below, an adjustment of a positive amount ('adjustment income') is treated for income tax purposes as income arising on the last day of the first period of account for which the new basis is adopted. Tax is charged on the full amount of any adjustment income arising in a tax year. The adjustment income is charged separately from the trading profits. However, for loss relief purposes it is treated as profits of the trade etc. for the tax year in which tax is charged on it. In the case of an individual for whom the income from the trade etc. is 'relevant UK earnings' (see **57.12** PENSION PROVISION) the adjustment income is similarly relevant UK earnings. An adjustment of a negative amount (an 'adjustment expense') is treated as an expense of the trade arising on the last day of the first period of account for which the new basis is adopted.

Calculation of adjustment

Subject to the exceptions at (i)–(iv) below, the calculation of the required adjustment can be summarised as follows.

(a) Taxable receipts and allowable expenses of the trade etc. for periods of account before the change are determined and compared on both the old and new bases to give a net understatement (or overstatement) of profits or losses on the old basis (when compared with the new). See *ITTOIA 2005, s 231, Step 1 (Items 1 & 2) and Step 2 (Items 1 & 2)*.

(b) That figure is then adjusted for any difference between the closing stock or work in progress for the last period of account before the change and the opening stock or work in progress for the first period of account after the change, also taking account of any change in the basis of calculating those amounts. See *ITTOIA 2005, s 231, Step 1 (Item 3) and Step 2 (Item 3)*.

(c) Finally an adjustment is made for depreciation to the extent that it was not the subject of an adjustment for tax purposes in the last period of account before the change but would be the subject of such an adjustment on the new basis. See *ITTOIA 2005, s 231, Step 1 (Item 4)*.

The resultant figure, be it positive or negative, is accorded the tax treatment described above. Amounts deducted in making the calculation cannot again be deducted in computing the profits of any period of account.

Exceptions

Exceptions to the above are as follows.

(i) **Expenses spread over more than one period of account after the change** on the new basis which were brought into account before the change on the old basis are excluded from the calculation at (a) above, but may not be deducted for any period of account after the change.

(ii) **Adjustment not required until asset realised or written off.** Where the change of basis results from a tax adjustment affecting the calculation of amounts within (b) or (c) above, the adjustment required by (b) or (c) is brought into account only when the asset concerned is realised or written off.

(iii) **Change from realisation basis to mark to market,** i.e. from recognition of a profit or loss on an asset only when it is realised to bringing assets into account in each period of account at fair value. Any adjustment required by (a) above for an understatement of profit (or overstatement of loss) in relation to an asset that is trading stock within *ITTOIA 2005, s 174* is not given effect until the period of account in which the value of the asset is realised. An election may, however, be made for the adjustment income to be spread equally over six periods of account beginning with the first period to which the new basis applies. The election must be made on or before the first anniversary of 31 January following the tax year in which the change of basis occurs. If the person permanently ceases to carry on the trade before the whole of the adjustment income has been brought into charge, the uncharged balance is charged as if it arose immediately before cessation.

(iv) **Barristers and advocates.** See **75.25** below.

Partnerships

In the case of trades, professions or vocations carried on in partnership, the adjustment (as above) is calculated as if the partnership were an individual resident in the UK. Each partner's share of any adjustment income is determined according to the profit-sharing arrangements for the twelve months immediately before the first day of the first period of account for which the new basis was adopted, and an election for spreading of an adjustment under (iii) above must be made jointly by all persons who were partners in that twelve-month period.

Death

In the case of the death of an individual otherwise chargeable to tax on adjustment income, his personal representatives assume the outstanding liabilities and may make any election under these provisions that the deceased might have made.

[*ITTOIA 2005, ss 226, 227, 228–237, 240, 860, Sch 2 paras 56, 57*].

Cash basis for smaller businesses

The system described above for dealing with adjustments on a change of basis applies equally where a person carrying on a trade, profession or vocation enters or leaves the cash basis. In the case of a person leaving the cash basis, there is provision for spreading the adjustment income. See **76.16** TRADING INCOME — CASH BASIS FOR SMALLER BUSINESSES.

Adoption of IFRS 16

There are rules enabling the resulting adjustment to be spread over a period for tax purposes in a case where a lessee treats a lease as giving rise to a right-of-use asset under International Financial Reporting Standard 16 (IFRS 16) and had not previously accounted for it as a finance lease. See **75.82** TRADING INCOME.

Simon's Taxes. See **B4.2**.

Barristers and advocates

[75.25] If a change of basis arises on a barrister or advocate ceasing to take advantage of the exemption at *ITTOIA 2005, s 160* (now repealed — see **75.23** above) or on its ceasing to be available, any resulting adjustment income is automatically spread over ten years, as follows. In each of the nine tax years beginning with that in which the full adjustment income would otherwise be charged to tax, the amount charged is instead 10% of the full amount or, if less, 10% of taxable profits *before* capital allowances or balancing charges. In the tenth tax year, the outstanding balance is brought into charge. If, within the ten years, the individual permanently ceases to carry on the profession, the annual charge continues to be made as before but without the '10% of taxable profits' alternative. An individual may elect for an additional amount of his own choosing to be added to the amount otherwise chargeable for a particular tax year. The election must be made on or before the first anniversary of 31 January following the tax year concerned, and must specify the additional amount. The maximum charge for each remaining year is then reduced proportionately. An election may be made more than once during the ten-year period. These spreading rules were repealed for 2013/14 onwards but the repeal does not apply in a case where advantage was taken of the exemption under *ITTOIA 2005, s 160* for any period(s) of account ending in or before the tax year 2012/13.

[*ITTOIA 2005, ss 238, 239, Sch 2 para 58; FA 2013, Sch 4 para 57(2)*].

See HMRC Business Income Manual BIM70075–70100.

Whether a trade carried on

[75.26] See also **75.38** below (mutual trading) and see generally **75.1** above.

Simon's Taxes. See **B1.4.**

Avoidance schemes

[75.27] A line is drawn between transactions of a trading nature which remain trading even though entered into to secure tax advantages and transactions so remote from ordinary trading as to be explicable only as fiscal devices and hence not trading.

In *Ransom v Higgs and Kilmorie (Aldridge) Ltd v Dickinson etc.* HL 1974, 50 TC 1 the taxpayers entered into complex arrangements to siphon development profits into the hands of trustees. They succeeded, the Crown failing to establish that, looked at as a whole, the arrangements constituted trading. In *Johnson v Jewitt* CA 1961, 40 TC 231 an elaborate and artificial device to manufacture trading losses was held not to amount to trading, but see *Ensign Tankers (Leasing) Ltd v Stokes* HL 1992, 64 TC 617, where the company's investment in two film production partnerships was entered into with a view to obtaining first-year capital allowances. In *Degorce v HMRC* CA, [2017] STC 2226, a case involving the purchase and sale of film distribution rights, the Appeal Tribunal agreed with HMRC that even if the transaction could be said to have the character of trading, it was so affected/inspired by fiscal considerations that it was no longer a trading transaction; the UT noted that the case was distinguishable from *Ensign Tankers* above in which the taxpayer had contributed to the financing of the production of the films. See also *Samarkand Film Partnership No 3 v HMRC* CA, [2017] STC 926; *Hardy and Moxon v HMRC* FTT (TC 6165), [2017] UKFTT 754 (TC); *Black Nominees Ltd v Nicol* Ch D 1975, 50 TC 229; *Newstead v Frost* HL 1980, 53 TC 525 and *Flanagan v HMRC* FTT (TC 3314), 82 TC 392, [2014] SFTD 881. See generally ANTI-AVOIDANCE (4).

Betting

[75.28] Betting by professional bookmakers is assessable (*Partridge v Mallandaine* QB 1886, 2 TC 179) even if carried on in an unlawful way (*Southern v A B* KB 1933, 18 TC 59) but not private betting however habitual (*Graham v Green* KB 1925, 9 TC 309). Also exempt from CGT. [*TCGA 1992, s 51(1)*]. Receipts from newspaper articles based on betting system held assessable in *Graham v Arnott* KB 1941, 24 TC 157.

Lotteries and football pools promotion constitutes trading, but where a pool or small lottery is run by a supporters club or other society on terms that a specified part of the cost of the ticket is to be donated to a club or body within the purposes in *Lotteries and Amusements Act 1976, s 5(1)*, the donation element is not treated as a trading receipt (HMRC SP C1).

Activities that are pure speculation, without the application of a profit-making system, may not amount to the carrying on of a trade (*Sherrington v HMRC* FTT (TC 7629), [2020] UKFTT 128 (TC)); this case involved claims for trading loss relief.

See HMRC Business Income Manual BIM61600–61615. See **14.7** CHARITIES AND CHARITABLE GIVING as regards charitable lotteries.

Divers and diving supervisors

[75.29] The performance of his duties by a person employed in the UK (including a designated area under *Continental Shelf Act 1964, s 1(7)*, see **32.3** FOREIGN INCOME) as a diver in operations to exploit the sea-bed, or as a supervisor in relation to such operations, is treated for income tax purposes as the carrying on of a trade and not as an employment. [*ITTOIA 2005, s 15*]. This treatment does not extend to the question of which article of a double tax treaty (in this case the employment income article or the business profits article) applies to these activities (*HMRC v Fowler* SC, [2020] UKSC 22). The legislation treats only the income of an individual employee as trading income; it does not allow a partnership (in these cases a husband/wife partnership) in which one partner is employed as a diver or diving supervisor to be treated as carrying on a trade (*Puttnam v HMRC* FTT (TC 7204), [2019] UKFTT 0389 (TC); *Green v HMRC* FTT (TC 7205), [2019] UKFTT 0390 (TC)).

Futures, options and swap contracts

[75.30] Any gain arising in the course of dealing, other than in the course of trade, in commodity or financial futures or in traded or financial options on a recognised exchange is dealt with under the chargeable gains rules and is not chargeable to tax as trading income. [*ITTOIA 2005, s 779; SI 2006 No 959, Reg 3(2)*]. See Tolley's Capital Gains Tax under Disposal.

Where dealing is in the course of a trade, any profit or loss is chargeable as trading income or deductible as a trading loss. In general, relatively infrequent transactions, and transactions to hedge specific investments, would not be regarded as trading, nor would purely speculative transactions. For HMRC's view on what constitutes trading in this context, see HMRC SP 3/02.

Special rules are applied (by regulation) to the market formed by the merger of the London International Financial Futures Exchange (LIFFE) and the London Traded Options Market (LTOM), which operates outside the Stock Exchange. These relate to bond-washing and to stamp duty and stamp duty reserve tax. See *SI 1992 Nos 568, 570*.

Pension schemes etc.

For the purposes of approved retirement benefit schemes, futures and options contracts are treated as investments (and thus as attracting tax exemption for income and capital gains). Any income derived from transactions relating to such a contract is regarded as arising from the contract, and a contract is not excluded from these provisions by the fact that any party is, or may be, entitled to receive and/or liable to make only a payment of a sum in full settlement of all obligations, as opposed to a transfer of assets other than money. This continues to apply after 5 April 2006 for the purposes of funds within *ICTA 1988, s 613(4)* and *s 614(3)* at **57.40** PENSION PROVISION. [*ICTA 1988, s 659A; TCGA 1992, s 271(10)(11)*].

Swaps

The word 'swap' is not defined for tax purposes but is taken to mean any financial arrangement that would be regarded by the financial markets as a swap. Profits or losses on a swap are chargeable as trading income if on trading account and are otherwise chargeable as miscellaneous income (if not of a capital nature). When considering whether or not a swap transaction constitutes trading, HMRC apply the general principles set out in SP 3/02 referred to above, and for an overview see also Revenue Tax Bulletin August 2003 pp 1054, 1055.

Pension schemes etc.

ICTA 1988, s 659A referred to above has no bearing on the tax status of swaps. Where a swap transaction by an approved scheme falls close to the trading/investment borderline, HMRC judge the case on its merits. Where an approved scheme uses interest rate swaps, currency swaps, equity swaps, credit derivatives or similar instruments to hedge risks inherent in, or as part of a strategy to enhance the return from, its existing investment portfolio or (in line with its normal policies of investing directly in such investments) to create a synthetic exposure to investments of a particular type or in a particular market, HMRC normally regard such swaps as investments (and thus as attracting tax exemptions for income and capital gains). (Revenue Tax Bulletin August 2003 pp 1055, 1056).

Simon's Taxes. See **B1.447**.

Horse racing etc.

[75.31] 'Private' horse racing and training is not normally trading (cf. *Sharkey v Wernher* HL 1955, 36 TC 275). But racing and selling the progeny of a brood mare held to constitute trading in *Dawson v Counsell* CA 1938, 22 TC 149 and in *Norman v Evans* Ch D 1964, 42 TC 188 share of prize monies for letting racehorses held within *Sch D, Case VI* (now miscellaneous income). Profits from stallion fees are assessable and assessments under both *Sch D, Case I* (trading income) and *Case VI* have been upheld (*Malcolm v Lockhart* HL 1919, 7 TC 99; *McLaughlin v Bailey* CA (I) 1920, 7 TC 508; *Jersey's Exors v Bassom* KB 1926, 10 TC 357; *Wernher v CIR* KB 1942, 29 TC 20; *Benson v Counsell* KB 1942, 24 TC 178) but wear and tear allowances (the forerunner of modern capital allowances on plant etc.) for stallions refused in *Derby v Aylmer* KB 1915, 6 TC 665. Profits from greyhound breeding held trading in *Hawes v Gardiner* Ch D 1957, 37 TC 671.

Illegal trading

[75.32] Crime, e.g. burglary, is not trading but the profits of a commercial business are assessable notwithstanding the business may be carried on in an unlawful way, e.g. 'bootlegging' (*Canadian Minister of Finance v Smith* PC

1926, 5 ATC 621 and cf. *Lindsay Woodward & Hiscox v CIR* CS 1932, 18 TC 43), operating 'fruit machines' illegal at the time (*Mann v Nash* KB 1932, 16 TC 523), street bookmaking illegal at the time (*Southern v A B* KB 1933, 18 TC 59) and prostitution (*CIR v Aken* CA 1990, 63 TC 395). But penalties for trading contrary to war-time regulations held not deductible (*CIR v E C Warnes & Co* KB 1919, 12 TC 227; *CIR v Alexander von Glehn & Co* CA 1920, 12 TC 232). See also **75.28** above.

See **75.91** below as regards prohibition on deduction of expenditure involving crime.

Simon's Taxes. See **B1.420**.

Isolated or speculative transactions

[75.33] For futures, property transactions and share dealing see **75.30, 75.36** and **75.37** respectively.

Whether the surplus on the acquisition and sale of assets, otherwise than in the course of an established commercial enterprise, is derived from an 'adventure or concern in the nature of trade' (see **75.1** above) depends on the facts. Para 116 of the Final Report of the Royal Commission on the Taxation of Profits and Income (1955 HMSO Cmd. 9474) lists six 'badges of trade': (i) the subject matter of the sale; (ii) length of period of ownership; (iii) frequency or number of similar transactions; (iv) supplementary work on assets sold; (v) reason for sale; (vi) motive. Other relevant factors may be the degree of organisation, whether the taxpayer is or has been associated with a recognised business dealing in similar assets, how the assets were acquired and, if purchased, how the purchase was financed. For a recent review of the factors to be considered, see *Marson v Morton* Ch D 1986, 59 TC 381.

Although in disputed cases the Inland Revenue could make alternative *Sch D, Case I* and *Sch D, Case VI* assessments, it would seem from *Pearn v Miller* KB 1927, 11 TC 610 and *Leeming v Jones* HL 1930, 15 TC 333 (see **75.36** below) that as regards isolated transactions the income tax liability, if any, was under Case I. As regards commodity futures, see **75.30** above.

Case I assessments were upheld on a purchase and resale of war surplus linen (*Martin v Lowry* HL 1926, 11 TC 297 — a leading case); a purchase, conversion and resale of a ship (*CIR v Livingston* CS 1926, 11 TC 538); transactions in brandy (*Cape Brandy Syndicate v CIR* CA 1921, 12 TC 358), whisky (*Lindsay Woodward* at **75.32** above), whisky in bond (*P J McCall decd v CIR* KB(IFS) 1923, 4 ATC 522; *CIR v Fraser* CS 1942, 24 TC 498); 'turning over' cotton mills (*Pickford v Quirke* CA 1927, 13 TC 251); purchase and resale of cotton spinning plant (*Edwards v Bairstow & Harrison* HL 1955, 36 TC 207); and purchase and resale of toilet rolls (*Rutledge v CIR* CS 1929, 14 TC 490). But in *Jenkinson v Freedland* CA 1961, 39 TC 636 the Commissioners' finding that a profit on the purchase, repair and sale (to associated companies) of stills was not assessable, was upheld, and in *Kirkham v Williams* CA 1991, 64 TC 253, the Commissioners' decision that the sale of a dwelling house built on land partly acquired for storage etc. was an adventure in the nature of trade was reversed in the CA.

Case I and *Case VI* do not apply for income tax purposes for 2005/06 onwards; the alternatives are now a charge to tax on trading income or a charge to tax on miscellaneous income.

Simon's Taxes. See **B1.401, B1.405.**

Liquidators etc. and personal representatives

[75.34] Whether a liquidator or receiver is continuing the company's trade or merely realising its assets as best he can, is a question of fact and similarly for the personal representatives of a deceased trader. For liquidators or receivers see *Armitage v Moore* QB 1900, 4 TC 199; *CIR v 'Old Bushmills' Distillery* KB(NI) 1927, 12 TC 1148; *CIR v Thompson* KB 1936, 20 TC 422; *Wilson Box v Brice* CA 1936, 20 TC 736; *Baker v Cook* KB 1937, 21 TC 337.

Personal representatives were held to be trading while winding up the deceased's business in *Weisberg's Executrices v CIR* KB 1933, 17 TC 696; *Wood v Black's Exor* HC 1952, 33 TC 172; *Pattullo's Trustees v CIR* CS 1955, 36 TC 87 but not in *Cohan's Exors v CIR* CA 1924, 12 TC 602 (completion of ship under construction at death) and *CIR v Donaldson's Trustees* CS 1963, 41 TC 161 (sale of pedigree herd). For property sales after death of partner in property dealing firm, see *Marshall's Exors v Joly* KB 1936, 20 TC 256 and contrast *Newbarns Syndicate v Hay* CA 1939, 22 TC 461.

Miscellaneous

[75.35] Assessments under *Sch D, Case I* (trading income) were upheld on a committee operating golf links owned by a Town Council (*Carnoustie Golf Course Committee v CIR* CS 1929, 14 TC 498); trustees under a private Act managing a recreation ground (*CIR v Stonehaven Recreation Ground Trustees* CS 1929, 15 TC 419); temporary joint coal merchanting (*Gardner and Bowring Hardy & Co v CIR* CS 1930, 15 TC 602); promotion of mining companies to exploit mines (*Murphy v Australian Machinery etc. Co Ltd* CA 1948, 30 TC 244 and cf. *Rhodesia Metals v Commr of Taxes* PC 1940, 19 ATC 472); purchase and resale of amusement equipment (*Crole v Lloyd* HC 1950, 31 TC 338).

A company which made loans to another company to finance a trading venture was held not to be trading itself (*Stone & Temple Ltd v Waters; Astrawall (UK) Ltd v Waters* Ch D 1995, 67 TC 145).

The activities of the British Olympic Association (which included the raising of funds through commercial sponsorship and the exploitation of its logo, but many of which were non-commercial) were held as a whole to be uncommercial and not to constitute a trade (*British Olympic Association v Winter* (Sp C 28), [1995] SSCD 85).

For whether or not an *athlete* is within the charge to tax on trading income, see HMRC Business Income Manual BIM50605; for the treatment of Lottery Sports Fund Athlete Personal Awards, see BIM50650–50675.

For whether *ostrich farming* (i.e. the ownership of ostriches which are looked after on the owner's behalf by others) amounts to trading, and for the consequences of such trading, see Revenue Tax Bulletin June 1996 pp 318, 319.

See also *Smith Barry v Cordy* CA 1946, 28 TC 250 in which a taxpayer was held liable on his surplus from the sale or maturing of endowment policies he had purchased, *J Bolson & Son Ltd v Farrelly* CA 1953, 34 TC 161 (deals in vessels by company operating boat services held a separate adventure) and *Torbell Investments Ltd v Williams* Ch D 1986, 59 TC 357 (dormant company revived for purpose of acquiring certain loans held to have acquired them as trading stock). But a company formed to administer a holidays with pay scheme for the building etc. industry was held not trading (*Building & Civil Engineering etc. Ltd v Clark* Ch D 1960, 39 TC 12). Assessments on profits from promoting a series of driving schools were upheld in *Leach v Pogson* Ch D 1962, 40 TC 585; in concluding that the profit from *first* sale was assessable, Commissioners were entitled to take into account the subsequent transactions.

In *Daarasp LLP and Betex LLP v HMRC* FTT (TC 6718), [2018] UKFTT 548 (TC), the Tribunal found that two limited liability partnerships (LLPs) were not entitled to capital allowances as they were not trading. Exploitation of the software licences the LLPs had purchased had been minimal as the LLPs did not have the necessary framework, resources or know-how to support significant trading activities. The availability of capital allowances had also been a major factor in deciding to purchase the licences.

For circumstances in which the profits of a trade may not accrue to the proprietor, see *Alongi v CIR* CS 1991, 64 TC 304.

Property transactions

[75.36] This paragraph relates to transactions in land and buildings otherwise than in the course of an established business of property development, building etc. For HMRC's view, see HMRC Business Income Manual BIM60000–60165. For other sales of property see **75.107** below.

A line is drawn between realisations of property held as an investment or as a residence and transactions amounting to an adventure or concern in the nature of trade. The principles at **75.33** above apply suitably adapted.

In *Leeming v Jones* HL 1930, 15 TC 333 an assessment on the acquisitions and disposal of options over rubber estates was confirmed by Commissioners. The Crown had defended the assessment under both *Sch D, Case I* (trading income) and *Sch D, Case VI* (miscellaneous income). In a Supplementary Case the Commissioners found there had been no concern in the nature of the trade. The Court held there was no liability. Per Lawrence LJ 'in the case of an isolated transaction . . . there is really no middle course open. It is either an adventure in the nature of trade, or else it is simply a case of sale and resale of property.' See also *Pearn v Miller* KB 1927, 11 TC 610 and *Williams v Davies* below.

Property transactions by companies were held to be trading in *Californian Copper Syndicate v Harris* CES 1904, 5 TC 159 (purchase of copper bearing land shortly afterwards resold); *Thew v South West Africa Co* CA

1924, 9 TC 141 (numerous sales of land acquired by concession for exploitation); *Cayzer, Irvine & Co v CIR* CS 1942, 24 TC 491 (exploitation of landed estate acquired by shipping company); *Emro Investments v Aller* and *Lance Webb Estates v Aller* Ch D 1954, 35 TC 305 (profits carried to capital reserve on numerous purchases and sales); *Orchard Parks v Pogson* Ch D 1964, 42 TC 442 (land compulsorily purchased after development plan dropped); *Parkstone Estates v Blair* Ch D 1966, 43 TC 246 (industrial estate developed—land disposed of by sub-leases for premiums); *Eames v Stepnell Properties Ltd* CA 1966, 43 TC 678 (sale of land acquired from associated company while resale being negotiated). See also *Bath & West Counties Property Trust Ltd v Thomas* Ch D 1977, 52 TC 20. Realisations were held to be capital in *Hudson's Bay v Stevens* CA 1909, 5 TC 424 (numerous sales of land acquired under Royal Charter — contrast *South West Africa Co* above); *Tebrau (Johore) Rubber Syndicate v Farmer* CES 1910, 5 TC 658 (purchase and resale of rubber estates — contrast *Californian Copper* above).

In *Rand v Alberni Land Co Ltd* KB 1920, 7 TC 629 sales of land held in trust were held not trading but contrast *Alabama Coal Iron Land v Mylam* KB 1926, 11 TC 232; *Balgownie Land Trust v CIR* CS 1929, 14 TC 684; *St Aubyn Estates v Strick* KB 1932, 17 TC 412; *Tempest Estates v Walmsley* Ch D 1975, 51 TC 305. Sales of property after a period of letting held realisations of investments or not trading in *CIR v Hyndland Investment Co Ltd* CS 1929, 14 TC 694; *Glasgow Heritable Trust v CIR* CS 1954, 35 TC 196; *Lucy & Sunderland Ltd v Hunt* Ch D 1961, 40 TC 132 but held trading in *Rellim Ltd v Vise* CA 1951, 32 TC 254 (notwithstanding that company previously admitted as investment company); *CIR v Toll Property Co* CS 1952, 34 TC 13; *Forest Side Properties (Chingford) v Pearce* CA 1961, 39 TC 665. But sales by liquidator of property owned by companies following abandonment of plan for their public flotation held not trading in *Simmons v CIR* HL 1980, 53 TC 461 (reversing Commissioners' decision). In *Rosemoor Investments v Inspector of Taxes* (Sp C 320), [2002] SSCD 325, it was not open to the Commissioners to recharacterise as trading a complex transaction routed via an investment company subsidiary and structured to produce capital.

Property transactions by individuals and partnerships were held to be trading in *Reynold's Exors v Bennett* KB 1943, 25 TC 401; *Broadbridge v Beattie* KB 1944, 26 TC 63; *Gray & Gillitt v Tiley* KB 1944, 26 TC 80; *Laver v Wilkinson* KB 1944, 26 TC 105; *Foulds v Clayton* Ch D 1953, 34 TC 382 and *Kirkby v Hughes* Ch D 1992, 65 TC 352; in all of which the taxpayers were or had been associated with building or estate development, and contrast *Williams v Davies* KB 1945, 26 TC 371 in which the taxpayers were closely associated with land development but a profit on transactions in undeveloped land in the names of their wives held not assessable. The acquisition and resale of land for which planning permission had been or was obtained held trading in *Cooke v Haddock* Ch D 1960, 39 TC 64; *Turner v Last* Ch D 1965, 42 TC 517 and *Pilkington v Randall* CA 1966, 42 TC 662 (and cf. *Iswera v Ceylon Commr* PC 1965, 44 ATC 157), but contrast *Taylor v Good* CA 1974, 49 TC 277 in which a house bought as a residence was found unsuitable and resold to a developer after obtaining planning permission and held not an adventure. In *Burrell v Davis* Ch D 1948, 38 TC 307; *Johnston v Heath* Ch D 1970, 46 TC 463; *Reeves v Evans, Boyce & Northcott* Ch D 1971, 48 TC 495 and *Clark v Follett* Ch D 1973, 48 TC 677 the short period of ownership or other evidence showed an intention to purchase for resale at a profit and not for investment, but contrast *CIR v Reinhold* CS 1953, 34 TC 389, *Marson v Morton* Ch D 1986, 59 TC 381 and *Taylor v Good* above. For other cases in which profits were held to be taxable as trading income see *Hudson v Wrightson* KB 1934, 26 TC 55; *MacMahon v CIR* CS 1951, 32 TC 311 and *Hartland v HMRC* FTT (TC 4187), [2014] UKFTT 1099 (TC).

For sales after a period of letting see *Mitchell Bros v Tomlinson* CA 1957, 37 TC 224 and *Cooksey & Bibby v Rednall* KB 1949, 30 TC 514.

For sale of houses built by taxpayer and used as residences see *Page v Pogson* Ch D 1954, 35 TC 545 and *Kirkham v Williams* CA 1991, 64 TC 253.

For sales after death of partner in property dealing transactions, see cases at **75.34** above. See also re partnership sales *CIR v Dean Property Co* CS 1939, 22 TC 706 and *Dodd and Tanfield v Haddock* Ch D 1964, 42 TC 229.

Simon's Taxes. See **B5.2**.

Share dealing

[75.37] Share dealing with the public is strictly controlled by the *Financial Services and Markets Act 2000*. This paragraph is concerned with share transactions entered into (generally through the Stock Exchange) by persons not authorised to deal under that Act and the question arises whether they amount to an adventure or concern in the nature of trade. The principles of **75.33** above apply suitably adapted. The prudent management of an investment portfolio may necessitate changes in the holdings but this is not normally trading. Stock Exchange speculation, particularly by individuals, may be quasi-gambling and not trading — see Pennycuick J in *Lewis Emanuel & Son Ltd v White* Ch D 1965, 42 TC 369 in which, reversing the Commissioners' finding, he held that the Stock Exchange losses of a fruit etc. merchanting company were from a separate trade of share dealing but observed that gambling by the company would at that time have been *ultra vires*. In *Cooper v C & J Clark Ltd* Ch D 1982, 54 TC 670, the losses of a manufacturing company on its sale of gilts, in which it had invested temporarily surplus cash, were allowed as a set-off against its general trading profits. An individual speculating in stocks and shares and commodity futures was held to be trading in *Wannell v Rothwell* Ch D 1996, 68 TC 719 (although loss relief was refused on the grounds that the trading was 'uncommercial', see **45.11** LOSSES), but the opposite conclusion was reached in *Salt v Chamberlain* Ch D 1979, 53 TC 143 and *Manzur v HMRC* FTT (TC 830), [2010] UKFTT 580 (TC).

For share dealing by investment companies see *Scottish Investment Trust Co v Forbes* CES 1893, 3 TC 231 and *Halefield Securities Ltd v Thorpe* Ch D 1967, 44 TC 154. For trading in secured loans, see *Torbell Investments Ltd v Williams* Ch D 1986, 59 TC 357.

For share sales connected with an existing business see **75.115** below.

Mutual trading

[75.38] A person cannot derive a taxable profit from trading with himself except in certain cases of self-supply by a trader of trading stock, see *Sharkey v Wernher* HL 1955, 36 TC 275 and **75.118** below. This extends to a group of persons engaged in mutual activities of a trading nature if there is an identifiable 'fund' for the common purpose with complete identity between contributors to, and participators in, the fund (the *mutuality principle*). A body not liable as regards transactions with members may nevertheless be within the charge to tax on trading transactions with non-members and is liable in the ordinary way on investment income.

Whether the mutuality principle applies depends on the facts. For mutual insurance, see *Styles v New York Life Insce Co* HL 1889, 2 TC 460 (an early leading case on the mutuality principle but there are now special provisions for life insurance companies); *Jones v South-West Lancs Coal Owners' Assn* HL 1927, 11 TC 790; *Cornish Mutual Assce Co Ltd* HL 1926, 12 TC 841; *Municipal Mutual Insce Ltd v Hills* HL 1932, 16 TC 430; *Faulconbridge v National Employers' Mutual General Insce Assn Ltd* Ch D 1952, 33 TC 103; *Medical Defence Union Ltd v HMRC* FTT (TC 7713), [2020] UKFTT 0227 (TC).

For other cases see *Liverpool Corn Trade Assn Ltd v Monks* KB 1926, 10 TC 442 (trade association providing corn exchange etc. held to be trading and not 'mutual' — but see **75.119** below for special arrangement available for trade associations); *English & Scottish CWS Ltd v Assam Agricultural IT Commr* PC 1948, 27 ATC 332 (wholesale co-operative with two members held to be trading and not mutual — there was no 'common fund'). Similarly a members' club is not trading and is not liable on its surplus from the provision of its facilities for members (*Eccentric Club Ltd* CA 1923, 12 TC 657) but liable on the surplus attributable to non-members (*Carlisle and Silloth Golf Club v Smith* CA 1913, 6 TC 48; *NALGO v Watkins* KB 1934, 18 TC 499; *Doctor's Cave Bathing Beach (Fletcher) v Jamaica IT Commr* PC 1971, 50 ATC 368).

For a detailed discussion of mutual trading, see HMRC Business Income Manual BIM24000–24995.

For distribution of assets by a mutual concern to a trader, see **75.102** below.

Simon's Taxes. See **B1.436** *et seq.*

Trading income provided through third parties

[75.39] Legislation was introduced by *F(No 2)A 2017* to nullify the use of disguised remuneration schemes by the self-employed. It has effect in relation to 'relevant benefits' arising on or after 6 April 2017, but see **75.40** as regards its application to pre-6 April 2017 loans and quasi-loans outstanding on 5 April 2019. The legislation applies to sole traders and to individuals in partnership, and applies to professions/vocations as it does to trades.

'*Relevant benefit*' means any payment (including a payment by way of a loan), a transfer of money's worth or any other benefit. 'Loan' includes any form of credit and any payment purported to be made by way of a loan. The assumption of a liability of one person (P) by another person is treated as the provision of a relevant benefit to P. The assumption, by a person other than P, of a liability of a person (Q) who is or has been connected with P, is treated as the provision of a relevant benefit to Q. The question of whether persons are connected is determined for the purposes of these provisions in accordance with **19** CONNECTED PERSONS, but disregarding **19.4** (partners in partnerships).

The provisions apply where a person (T) carries on a trade and:

(a) there is an arrangement (as widely defined) in connection with the trade, and either T is a party to the arrangement or it otherwise relates to or affects T;
(b) it is reasonable to suppose (taking all relevant circumstances into account) that, the arrangement (or the arrangement insofar as it relates to or effects T) is at least partly a means of providing, or is otherwise concerned with the provision of, relevant benefits;
(c) either:
    (i) a relevant benefit thereby arises to T or a person who is, or has been, connected with T; or
    (ii) a relevant benefit thereby arises to another person and any of the 'enjoyment conditions' below are met in relation to the relevant benefit;
(d) it is reasonable to suppose that the relevant benefit (directly or indirectly) represents, or has arisen or derives from, or is otherwise connected with, the whole or part of a 'qualifying third party payment'; and
(e) it is reasonable to suppose that a tax advantage (as widely defined) would be obtained by T, or a person who is, or has been, connected with T, as a result of the arrangement.

Where the provisions apply, the amount of the relevant benefit is treated as profits of the trade for the tax year in which the relevant benefit arises. If T has ceased to carry on the trade in an earlier tax year the relevant benefit is treated as profits for that earlier year. If the relevant benefit is a payment other than by way of a loan, its amount is the amount paid. If it is a payment by way of a loan, its amount is the principal amount lent. If it is not a payment, its amount is its market value when it arises or, if higher, the cost of providing it.

Any arrangements a main purpose of which is to secure that the above does not apply are to be disregarded. If an effect of any such arrangements is that a relevant benefit (or any part of it) would arise before 6 April 2017 rather than on or after that date, the benefit (or part) is treated as arising on the day it would have arisen without the arrangements.

Where any amount brought into charge under these provisions is also charged to tax of any kind under any other provision, the individual subject to charge under these provisions can make a claim for adjustments to be made in respect of that other charge so as to prevent double taxation. On a claim being made, an HMRC officer must make any such adjustments claimed as are just and reasonable. Adjustments can be made in respect of any period, despite any statutory time limit, and by any method. The value of the adjustments cannot exceed the tax doubly charged.

Qualifying third party payments

For the purposes of (d) above, any 'third party payment' is a '*qualifying third party payment*' if either the 'deduction condition' or the 'trade connection condition' is met in relation to the payment. A payment is a '*third party payment*' if it is made (by T or another person) to any person other than T or to T acting as a trustee.

The '*deduction condition*' is that a deduction for the payment is made in calculating the profits of the trade or, where the trade is a partnership trade, in calculating T's share of the profits. The 'trade connection condition' is that it is reasonable to suppose, taking all relevant circumstances into account, that the payment is by way of consideration for goods or services provided in the course of the trade, or there is some other connection between the payment and any such provision of goods or services.

Enjoyment conditions

The '*enjoyment conditions*' referred to in (c)(ii) above are:

- that the relevant benefit, or part of it, is in fact so dealt with by any person as to be calculated at some time to enure for the benefit of T;
- that the arising of the relevant benefit operates to increase the value to T of any assets held by him or for his benefit;
- that T receives (or is entitled to receive) at any time any benefit provided out of, or deriving from, the relevant benefit (or part of it);
- where the relevant benefit is the payment of a sum of money (including a payment by way of loan):
  - that T may become entitled to the beneficial enjoyment of the sum (or part of it) if one or more powers are exercised or successively exercised; or
  - that T is able in any manner to control the application of the sum (or part of it).

References throughout this list to T include references to a person who is, or has been, connected with T. In determining whether any of the enjoyment conditions is met, regard must be had to the substantial result and effect of all the relevant circumstances. Where an enjoyment condition is met in relation to part only of a relevant benefit, that part is treated as a separate benefit.

[*ITTOIA 2005, ss 23A–23H; F(No 2)A 2017, s 35(2)(4)*].

Pre-6 April 2017 loans and quasi-loans (the 'loan charge')

[75.40] Where a loan or 'quasi-loan' was made before 6 April 2017 (and on or after 9 December 2010), and any part of it is outstanding immediately before the end of 5 April 2019, the loan or quasi-loan is treated as a relevant benefit for the purposes of 75.39 above. The amount of the relevant benefit is the amount of the loan or quasi-loan outstanding at that time, and is treated as profits of the trade for 2018/19. If the trader ceases to carry on the trade in an earlier tax year, the amount of the relevant benefit is treated as a post-cessation receipt (see 59 POST-CESSATION RECEIPTS AND EXPENDITURE).

The loan charge was originally to apply to loans made on or after 6 April 1999 (and before 6 April 2017). Loans made before 9 December 2010 were removed from charge by *FA 2020, s 15*. See www.gov.uk/guidance/find-out-how-the-changes-to-the-loan-charge-affect-you.

For those who earned less than £50,000 in the tax year 2017/18 and have no other source of wealth, HMRC will agree a payment plan spread over a minimum of five years. For those who earned less than £30,000, they will agree a payment plan of at least seven years. Other payment plans might be agreed based on individual circumstances. See www.gov.uk/guidance/find-out-how-the-changes-to-the-loan-charge-affect-you. Interest will be charged from 1 October 2020 (see below under Relief from late paid interest).

See also www.gov.uk/guidance/report-and-account-for-your-disguised-remuneration-loan-charge.

Election to spread charge over three years

T can make an irrevocable election (under *F(No 2)A 2017, Sch 12 para 1(3A)*) for the chargeable amount to be split into three equal parts. Any election should be made via HMRC's loan charge reporting form (see www.gov.uk/guidance/find-out-how-the-changes-to-the-loan-charge-affect-you). Only the first part of the chargeable amount is then chargeable for 2018/19. The second part is chargeable for 2019/20 and the third for 2020/21 (treated as post-cessation receipts if and where necessary). The election must be made before 1 October 2020, unless an HMRC officer allows a later election in a particular case. The Commissioners for HMRC may by regulations apply a later time limit to any class of persons specified in the regulations. Any person who has made the similar election at **26.8** DISGUISED REMUNERATION is treated as having made this election also (and vice versa). The election cannot be made until the requirement to provide information to HMRC (see below), or where applicable the equivalent requirement under the disguised remuneration rules, has been complied with.

Loans and quasi-loans

A 'loan' includes any form of credit and any payment purported to be made by way of a loan. A '*quasi-loan*' is made by a person (P) to another person (T) if (and when) P acquires a right to a payment or a transfer of assets and a connection exists between the acquisition of the right and a payment made (by way of a loan or otherwise) to T or a transfer of assets to T. Where loans or quasi-loans are replaced by other loans or quasi-loans, the replacement loans or quasi-loans are within the scope of these provisions. In these provisions, T is the same person as in **75.39** above, i.e. the person carrying on the trade, and references to T include references to any person who is, or has been, connected (defined as in **75.39**) with T.

Loans and quasi-loans: amounts outstanding

The question of whether and to what extent a loan or quasi-loan is outstanding at a particular time is determined in accordance with the following, and does not depend on the loan or quasi-loan subsisting at that time.

An amount of a loan is outstanding if the principal lent exceeds the amount repaid. The principal lent is exclusive of any capitalised interest. The amount repaid for this purpose is the amount of principal that was repaid on or before 4 December 2016 plus payments in money made by T after that date by way of repayment of principal. However, no such post-4 December 2016 payment can be included in the amount repaid if there is any connection between the payment and an arrangement which has a tax avoidance purpose (other than the arrangement in pursuance of which the loan was made), and this applies even if T is unaware of the avoidance arrangement.

An amount of a quasi-loan is outstanding if the 'initial debt amount' exceeds the amount repaid. The '*initial debt amount*' is the value of the right acquired by P (at the time it was acquired) plus the value of any additional debt that occurs on the acquisition of further rights by P (to a payment or a transfer of assets) in connection with the original payment or transfer of assets made to T. Where the right is to a payment, its value is the amount payable. However, where a further right acquired is a right to a payment, and the additional debt accrues to P by means of the capitalisation of interest, the value of that further right is nil. Where the right is to a transfer of assets, its value is the market value of the assets at the time the right is acquired (or, if the assets are non-fungible and not then in existence, the value of the right at that time) or, if higher, the cost of the assets at that time.

The amount repaid in the case of a quasi-loan is the amount (if any) by which the initial debt amount has been reduced (by way of repayment) on or before 4 December 2016 plus any payments in money made by T after that date by way of repayment of the initial debt amount. If the debt is a right to a transfer of assets, and the assets have been transferred, an amount equal to the market value of the assets at the time of transfer also constitutes an amount repaid. However, no post-4 December 2016 payment, and no transfer of assets at any time, can be included in the amount repaid if there is any connection between the payment or transfer and an arrangement which has a tax avoidance purpose (other than the arrangement in pursuance of which the quasi-loan was made).

There are special rules to determine whether and to what extent a loan or quasi-loan is outstanding at a particular time where the loan or quasi-loan is made in a foreign currency or is repayable in a currency other than that in which it was made or is made in a currency expected to depreciate against sterling. For these rules, see *F(No 2)A 2017, Sch 12 paras 4–8, 10–14*.

Reduction of loan charge where reasonable disclosure made

Where a loan or quasi-loan falls to be treated as a relevant benefit as above, the chargeable amount will be reduced where:

- a reasonable case could have been made that, for any tax year earlier than 2016/17, T was chargeable to income tax on an amount referable to the loan or quasi-loan;

- at a time when HMRC still had power to recover (from T or any other person) income tax for the year in question in respect of that amount, a 'qualifying tax return' (or two or more qualifying tax returns taken together) contained a reasonable disclosure of the loan or quasi-loan; and
- as at 6 April 2019 HMRC had not taken steps to recover that tax.

The reduction does not apply if a reasonable case could be made that T was liable to tax on all or part of the loan amount identified above (or an amount representing that loan amount) in an alternative tax year, and either the alternative year is a later year than 2015/16 or HMRC took steps before 6 April 2019 to recover the tax for the alternative year. Where the reduction does apply, the amount of the loan or quasi-loan that is outstanding immediately before the end of 5 April 2019 is reduced by the amount identified above.

For this purpose a '*qualifying tax return*' is a self-assessment tax return made by T for 2015/16 or any earlier year, and any accompanying accounts, statements or documents. In order to have contained a reasonable disclosure of the loan or quasi-loan, the qualifying tax return(s) must have identified the loan or quasi-loan, identified the person to whom it was made (if other than T), identified the arrangements in pursuance of which, or in connection with which, it was made, and provided such other information sufficient for it to be apparent that a reasonable case could be made that for the year in question T was chargeable to income tax on an amount referable to the loan or quasi-loan.

See also www.gov.uk/guidance/find-out-how-the-changes-to-the-loan-charge-affect-you.

Repayment or waiver of voluntary restitution

The Government has agreed that HMRC should repay voluntary restitution that has been paid by individuals and employers under settlement agreements, entered into since the loan charge was announced in March 2016 in cases where the loan charge would have applied but for the removal from charge of loans made before 9 December 2010 (see above) and cases involving loans made on or after the date where reasonable disclosure was made.

The Commissioners for HMRC are thus legally obliged to establish a scheme under which they may, on an application made to them before 1 October 2021, repay an amount paid (or treated as paid) to them under a 'qualifying agreement' or waive the payment of certain amounts payable to them under such an agreement. Amounts can be repaid or waived in whole or in part. A '*qualifying agreement*' is an agreement made with the Commissioners for HMRC on or after 16 March 2016 and before 11 March 2020 which imposes an obligation on any party thereto to pay an amount of income tax that is referable to any such loan or quasi-loan.

The scheme applies to any amount referable (directly or indirectly) to a loan or quasi-loan made on or after 6 April 1999 and before 6 April 2016, provided the amount is one that HMRC had no power to recover at the time the agreement was made. An amount referable to a loan or quasi-loan made on or after 9 December 2010 is within the scope of the scheme only if, at a time when HMRC had power to recover the amount, a tax return (or two or more tax returns taken together), and any accompanying accounts, statements or documents, contained a reasonable disclosure of the loan or quasi-loan. What constitutes reasonable disclosure is defined similarly as above under Reduction of loan charge where reasonable disclosure made.

An amount paid, treated as paid or due to be paid under a qualifying agreement is also within the scope of the scheme if it is interest on another amount paid, treated as paid or due to be paid under that agreement and within the scope of the scheme.

HMRC have published a draft scheme at www.gov.uk/government/publications/implementation-of-changes-to-the-loan-charge.

Relief from late paid interest

Where a person is chargeable to income tax on any amount by reason of the loan charge, relief from late payment interest (see **43.2** LATE PAYMENT INTEREST AND PENALTIES) has effect provided:

- the person files a self-assessment return for 2018/19 before 1 October 2020;
- at the beginning of 1 October 2020 the self-assessment included in that return is complete and accurate.

The relief applies equally to cases where income tax would be chargeable but for the removal from charge of loans made before 9 December 2010 or the reduction of the loan charge where reasonable disclosure was made (see above in each case).

The relief takes the following form. If before 1 October 2020, the person discharges their liability to income tax and CGT for 2018/19:

(a) any amount paid in discharging that liability (other than a self-assessment payment on account) is to be taken as not carrying interest;

(b) any self-assessment payment on account made for 2019/20 is to be taken as not carrying interest.

The reliefs in (a) and (b) above also apply if before 1 October 2020 the person enters into an agreement with HMRC as to the discharge of their liability to income tax and capital gains tax for 2018/19. In this case, the relief in (a) applies only to amounts paid before 1 October 2020 (other than a self-assessment payment on account). In addition, the late payment interest start date, in respect of any amount *subsequently* paid under the agreement, is deferred to 1 October 2020.

The relief in (b) above does not apply if by the end of January 2021 the person has neither discharged their liability to income tax and CGT for 2019/20 nor entered into an agreement with HMRC as to its discharge.

The Commissioners for HMRC may by regulations provide that the above applies to any class of persons specified in those regulations as if the references to 1 October 2020 were to a later date.

Interaction with accelerated payments rules

A special rule applies where an accelerated payment notice (or partner payment notice) has been given by HMRC in relation to a charge under these provisions, and an accelerated payment is made by T on or before 5 April 2019 in respect of the understated or disputed tax to which the notice relates. The special rule applies only if the amount of the accelerated payment is at least equal to the outstanding amount of the loan or quasi-loan at the end of 5 April 2019. See **4.50** ANTI-AVOIDANCE as regards the giving of an accelerated payment notice (or partner payment notice).

T may make an application to the Commissioners for HMRC to be treated as if the relevant benefit arises only if any part of the accelerated payment is repaid, whether on withdrawal of the notice or the determination of an appeal. If HMRC grant the application, and a repayment is subsequently made, the relevant benefit arises immediately before the end of the 30 days beginning with the date of repayment. The application had to be made in 2018, unless an HMRC officer considers it reasonable for it to be made at a later date in any particular case.

Requirement to provide information to HMRC

Certain information must be provided to the Commissioners for HMRC where a loan or quasi-loan is treated as a relevant benefit as above and falls to be treated as profits of a trade. The information requirement applies equally if a successful application is made in response to an accelerated payment notice as above. The information is to be provided by T (i.e. the person carrying on the trade), or T's personal representatives, after 5 April 2019 and before 1 October 2020, and must be provided in such form and manner as may be specified by HMRC. HMRC have specified that their loan charge reporting form should be used (see www.gov.uk/guidance/find-out-how-the-changes-to-the-loan-charge-affect-you). The requirement does not apply if, before 1 October 2019, terms were agreed with HMRC for the discharge of all liability for income tax arising on the relevant benefit.

The information to be provided is listed in *F(No 2)A 2017, Sch 12 para 23* and includes information about T and, if different, the person(s) providing the information; specified information on the loan or quasi-loan itself; the name of the arrangement mentioned in 75.39(a) above and any reference number allocated to it by HMRC; and information identifying any terms agreed with HMRC for partial discharge of liability for income tax arising.

Failure to comply with the duty to provide information results in a fixed penalty of £300, plus a penalty of up to £60 for each day, up to a maximum of 90, on which the failure continues after the fixed penalty is imposed. Liability to these penalties is cancelled if the person satisfies HMRC, or the Tribunal on appeal, that there is a reasonable excuse for the failure. Reasonable excuse does not include insufficiency of funds (unless attributable to events outside the person's control) or reliance on another person (unless the first person took reasonable care to avoid the failure). A reasonable excuse is treated as continuing if the failure is remedied without unreasonable delay after the excuse ceased.

If a person provides *inaccurate* information, that person is liable to a penalty of up to £3,000 if:

- the inaccuracy is either careless (i.e. due to a failure to take reasonable care) or deliberate; or
- the person knows of the inaccuracy at the time the information is provided but does not inform HMRC at that time; or
- the person discovers the inaccuracy some time later but fails to take reasonable steps to inform HMRC.

Where the information contains more than one inaccuracy, there is a separate penalty for each one.

All of the above penalties are chargeable by HMRC assessment. Neither a fixed nor a daily penalty can be assessed any later than 30 September 2021. No penalty for inaccuracy can be assessed after 30 September 2023. There is a right of appeal against the imposition or the amount of any of these penalties, the appeal to be made in writing to HMRC, stating grounds of appeal, within 30 days of the issue of the notice of assessment. On an appeal against imposition of the penalty that is notified to the Appeal Tribunal, the Tribunal may confirm or cancel the imposition. If the appeal is against the amount of the penalty, the Tribunal may confirm the amount assessed or substitute any different amount that HMRC had the power to assess.

A penalty must be paid within 30 days of its being assessed, and may be enforced as if it were income tax charged in an assessment and due and payable. If appealed against, the penalty is instead payable within 30 days of the appeal being determined or withdrawn.

[*F(No 2)A 2017, Sch 12; FA 2018, Sch 2; FA 2020, ss 15(2), 16(4)(5), 17(2), 18, 19(4), 20, 21, Sch 2 paras 17–22*].

Profit fragmentation arrangements

[75.41] Anti-avoidance rules have been introduced to counter arrangements ('*profit fragmentation arrangements*') under which UK businesses seek to divert some or all of their profits to an offshore entity which pays significantly lower tax than would be payable in the UK. The UK trader may purport that business receipts have been earned by the offshore entity, even though that entity does not have the substance to earn those receipts, or the arrangements may involve the payment of fees and expenses to the offshore entity that are much higher than is justified by the work done by that entity. The entity might, for example, be an offshore company owned by an offshore trust. The UK trader would not necessarily be a settlor or trustee of that trust and may even be excluded from benefitting from the trust assets but there will be some means by which amounts can accrue to him or to persons linked to him. The anti-avoidance rules operate by applying tests which consider whether profits have been fragmented and diverted so as to obtain tax advantages. They then counteract those advantages by requiring just and reasonable adjustments to be made to the expenses, income, profits or losses of the UK business. They apply to value transferred (as in (b) below) on or after **6 April 2019**.

For official guidance, see HMRC International Manual INTM610000.

Meaning of 'profit fragmentation arrangements'

Arrangements are '*profit fragmentation arrangements*' if:

(a) they involve a UK resident person (R) and an 'overseas person or entity' who is non-UK resident (NR);
(b) they give rise to a transfer of value from R to NR, and the value derives from the profits of a business (meaning a trade, profession or vocation) chargeable to UK income tax or corporation tax;
(c) the value transferred is greater than it would have been if the transfer had been between independent parties acting at arm's length;
(d) either there is a 'tax mismatch' or it is reasonable to conclude that a main purpose for which the arrangements were entered into was to obtain a tax advantage (as widely defined); and
(e) any of the 'enjoyment conditions' is met in relation to an individual who is either R himself or a member of a partnership of which R is also a member or, if R is a company, a participator in that company.

In (a) above, an '*overseas person or entity*' is either a person abroad (within *ITA 2007, s 718* — see **4.14** ANTI-AVOIDANCE) or a company, partnership, trust or other entity or arrangement established outside the UK or having effect under the law of a country outside the UK.

As regards (b) above, a typical means of transferring value is for trading receipts to be attributed to and paid to NR or for expenses to be paid to NR. The legislation requires account to be taken of any method, however indirect, by which any property or right is transferred or transmitted or the value of any property or right is enhanced or diminished, and gives some examples (see *FA 2019, Sch 4 para 3*).

Tax mismatch

For the purposes of (d) above, a '*tax mismatch*' arises where the following conditions are met for the tax year. Firstly, there must be an increase in the expenses for which R obtains a deduction and/or a reduction in the income brought into account by R in computing his tax liability. Secondly, it must be reasonable to conclude that the resulting reduction in UK tax payable by R exceeds the increase in tax payable by NR for the corresponding period. If these conditions are met entirely because of certain specified matters, e.g. payments of pension contributions or to a charity (see *FA 2019, Sch 4 para 5(5)*), they are treated as if not met. If the increase in tax payable by NR is at least 80% of the reduction in tax payable by R, no tax mismatch is regarded as having occurred.

The reduction in R's tax liability is computed by subjecting the amount of the reduction in R's profits (Amount A) to the highest rate at which tax would be chargeable on that amount if it were added to R's total income. The increase in tax payable by NR is the tax that would be payable by NR on income equal to Amount A, on the assumption that account is taken of available deductions and reliefs and that all reasonable steps, e.g. the claiming of reliefs and making of elections, are taken to minimise the amount of tax that NR would have to pay. However, any loss reliefs available to NR against profits are not brought into account here, and nor is any deduction for expenditure incurred by NR that does not arise directly from the arrangements and is of a kind for which R would have obtained a deduction of at least an equivalent amount if R had incurred the expenditure. Any non-refunded withholding tax suffered on payments made to NR is treated as tax payable by NR and not the person making the payment.

It may be that some or all of NR's income falls to be treated for the purposes of overseas tax as the income of a person or persons other than NR. This would apply, for example, where NR is an overseas partnership that is treated as a transparent or hybrid entity. In such cases, tax payable by those persons on that income are treated for these purposes as if they were tax payable by NR.

Enjoyment conditions

The '*enjoyment conditions*' consider whether any individual in (e) above, or anyone connected with such an individual, is able to enjoy the amounts arising from the value transferred from R to NR. The legislation sets out the various ways in which an individual may be able to enjoy such amounts (see *FA 2019, Sch 4 para 4*). All benefits which may at any time accrue to a person as a result of the value being transferred must be taken into account, irrespective of their nature or form or whether the person has any legal or equitable rights in respect of them. If it is reasonable to conclude that an individual within (e) above (acting alone or otherwise) procured the transfer of value from R to NR in such a way as to avoid the enjoyment conditions being met, those conditions are treated as if they nevertheless had been met.

Counteraction of profit fragmentation arrangements

The tax advantages that would otherwise arise to R as a result of the profit fragmentation arrangements are to be counteracted by the making of such adjustments as are just and reasonable. The adjustments must relate to the expenses, income, profits or losses of R for the tax year in which the value is transferred, and must be based on what the value transferred would have been if the transfer had been between independent parties acting at arm's length. The net adjustment will effectively be an increase in R's taxable profits.

Taxpayers are required to determine whether the profit fragmentation rules apply to them and make any necessary counteracting adjustments. See HMRC International Manual INTM610280 for individuals and INTM610290 for partnerships, which give details of how to make the adjustments.

Where profit fragmentation arrangements are counteracted, relief is available where R or another person pays any UK tax at any time such that there is a double payment of tax calculated by reference to the same income or profits. The relief must be claimed by R.

Application to partners

These provisions apply to a member of a partnership by reference to his share of any expenses, income, profits or losses. A member's share, for this purpose, is determined by apportioning the amount in question between the members on a just and reasonable basis.

[*FA 2019, Sch 4*].

Chargeable income and allowable deductions

[75.42] Apart from 75.43 below (capital expenditure and receipts) and 75.44 below (the 'wholly and exclusively' rule), which are arguably the most fundamental rules on the calculation of taxable business profits, the remainder of this chapter is arranged in alphabetical order — with a general example at the end. See the contents list at the head of the chapter.

See **75.21** above for the requirement to adhere to generally accepted accounting practice (GAAP), **75.22** above re the application of accountancy principles generally and **75.24** above re adjustments required on a change of basis. See also **9** CAPITAL ALLOWANCES and **10** CAPITAL ALLOWANCES ON PLANT AND MACHINERY.

See HMRC Business Income Manual BIM50000 et seq. for HMRC guidance on measuring the profits of a wide range of particular trades.

Priority of statutory rules

ITTOIA 2005, s 31 contains a rule intended to resolve any conflict between statutory rules prohibiting a deduction in computing trading profits and statutory rules permitting such a deduction. It does so by giving priority, with specified exceptions, to the rule permitting the deduction. In practice, such conflict will rarely occur. The order of priority is reversed in cases where a deduction would otherwise be given for an amount which arises directly or indirectly in consequence of, or in connection with, tax avoidance arrangements. [*ITTOIA 2005, s 31*].

Money's worth

It was established in *Gold Coast Selection Trust v Humphrey* HL 1948, 30 TC 209 that where a trader in the course of his trade receives a new and valuable asset, not being money, as the result of sale or exchange, that asset, for the purpose of computing the trading profits, should be valued as at the end of the period of account in which it was received, even though it be neither realised nor realisable till later. The legislation now puts beyond doubt that where a transaction involving money's worth is entered into in the course of a trade, and an amount would have been brought into account as a receipt if the transaction had involved money, then an amount equal to the value of the money's worth must similarly be brought into account. Where another statutory rule expressly provides for the bringing into account of an amount in respect of money's worth as a receipt in calculating trading profits, priority is given to that other rule. [*ITTOIA 2005, s 28A; FA 2016, s 71(2)(7)*].

Capital expenditure and receipts

[75.43] In computing trading profits, no deduction is allowed for items of a capital nature. [*ITTOIA 2005, s 33*]. By the same token, capital receipts are not brought into account. [*ITTOIA 2005, s 96*].

As to the distinction between capital and revenue expenditure and between capital and income receipts, 'no part of our law of taxation presents such almost insoluble conundrums as the decision whether a receipt or outgoing is capital or income for tax purposes' (Lord Upjohn in *Strick v Regent Oil Co Ltd* HL 1965, 43 TC 1 q.v. for a comprehensive review of the law). A widely used test is the 'enduring benefit' one given by Viscount Cave in *Atherton v British Insulated & Helsby Cables Ltd* HL 1925, 10 TC 155. For recent reviews of the cases, see *Lawson v Johnson Matthey plc* HL 1992, 65 TC 39 and *Halifax plc v Davidson* (Sp C 239), [2000] SSCD 251. In the latter case, costs incurred by a building society on conversion to a public limited company were disallowed as capital expenditure to the extent that they related to payment of statutory cash bonuses to non-voting members of the society, but otherwise allowed.

It is by virtue of the rule in *ITTOIA 2005, s 33* above that depreciation of fixed assets is not allowable in computing profits (see **9.1** CAPITAL ALLOWANCES) (*In re Robert Addie & Sons* CES 1875, 1 TC 1). Where the depreciation charge in the accounts is reduced by capitalising part of it and including that part in the balance sheet value of stock (i.e. as an overhead cost), only the net depreciation (i.e. the amount after reduction) falls to be added back to trading profits in order to arrive at taxable profits (*HMRC v William Grant & Sons Distillers Ltd; Small v Mars UK Ltd* HL 2007, 78 TC 442). See HMRC Business Income Manual BIM33190.

A gain or loss on the sale of a capital asset not included in trading profits is dealt with according to the provisions relating to capital gains tax. A sale of a fixed asset on which capital allowances have been claimed may result in a balancing charge or allowance, see **9** CAPITAL ALLOWANCES and **10** CAPITAL ALLOWANCES ON PLANT AND MACHINERY.

The revenue or capital nature of a payment is fixed at the time of its receipt (*Tapemaze Ltd v Melluish* Ch D 2000, 73 TC 167, following *Morley v Tattersall* CA 1938, 40 TC 671). The nature of a payment is determined by reference to the taxpayer's trade and does not require a consideration of how the money has been ultimately dealt with by the recipient (*Icebreaker 1 LLP v HMRC* UT, [2011] STC 1078).

A sum paid for, in effect, the acquisition of a business was held to be capital in *Triage Services Ltd v HMRC* (Sp C 519) [2006] SSCD 85. Transactions involving the acquisition of partnership interests and the making of capital contributions were held to be revenue in nature because they were short-term, recurrent transactions that had the character of trading transactions (*HMRC v Investec Asset Finance plc* UT, [2018] STC 874). Where a lump sum payment is made to extinguish an obligation to make payments of capital expenditure (in this case an obligation to pay an annuity assumed as part of the consideration for the acquisition of a business), it is a capital payment (*Parnalls Solicitors Ltd v HMRC* FTT (TC 261), [2010] SFTD 284).

In *Acornwood LLP v HMRC* UT, [2016] STC 2317, sums paid to a company to exploit intellectual property rights acquired by the taxpayer were held to be payments for a guaranteed income stream and capital in nature.

A property acquired by a company for the purpose of remunerating a director was adjudged to have been acquired, and to have been held, on capital account (*Lion Co v HMRC* FTT (TC 295), [2010] SFTD 454).

The receipt of a lump sum in return for entering into an exclusivity agreement was held to be an income receipt in *Countrywide Estate Agents FS Ltd v HMRC* UT 2011, [2012] STC 511; the sum was income earned by the taxpayer from the use of its goodwill, not a capital sum received by it in return for giving up a part of its goodwill.

The acquisition of rights to the receipt of future income was held to be capital expenditure; the period over which the rights were to play a part in the business was the factor weighing most heavily in reaching that conclusion despite the fact that the rights were ordinary commercial contracts and were the source of income rather than the setting in which it was generated (*Ingenious Games LLP v HMRC* UT, [2019] UKUT 226 (TCC)).

For a brief note on HMRC's approach to challenging schemes or arrangements designed to turn income into capital (or capital expenditure into a revenue deduction), see Revenue Tax Bulletin June 1997 p 438.

For the HMRC's own guidance on capital *v* income, see HMRC Business Income Manual BIM35000–35910. See also HMRC toolkit 'Capital v Revenue Expenditure' at www.gov.uk/government/uploads/system/uploads/attachment_data/file/553553/2015-16_Capital_vs_Revenue_toolkit_-_MT_amendments_v2.pdf.

Simon's Taxes. See **B2.202–B2.204, B2.304–B2.309.**

The 'wholly and exclusively' rule

[75.44] For an expense to be deductible, it must, *inter alia*, have been incurred 'wholly and exclusively for the purposes of the trade'. It is specifically provided that if an expense is incurred for a *dual purpose*, this rule does not prohibit a deduction for any *identifiable* part or *identifiable* proportion of the expense which is incurred wholly and exclusively for the purposes of the trade; but this simply reflects a long-established principle (see below). [*ITTOIA 2005, s 34*].

For a review of the leading cases on the 'wholly and exclusively' rule, see *Harrods (Buenos Aires) Ltd v Taylor-Gooby* CA 1964, 41 TC 450 and for a frequently quoted analysis of the words see *Bentleys, Stokes & Lowless v Beeson* CA 1952, 33 TC 491. Following that case the dual purpose rule now in *ITTOIA 2005, s 34* has figured prominently in Court decisions. If an expense is for a material private or non-business purpose, the whole is strictly disallowable as it is thereby not wholly and exclusively for business purposes. For examples of its application see **75.104** and **75.125** below. 'Dual expenditure is expenditure that is incurred for more than one reason. If one of the reasons is not for business purposes, the expenditure fails the statutory test and there is no provision that allows a "business" proportion' (HMRC Business Income Manual BIM37007). *However*, where an *identifiable* part or proportion of an expense has been laid out wholly and exclusively for the purposes of the trade, HMRC do not disallow that part or proportion on the grounds that the expense is not *as a whole* laid out wholly and exclusively for the purposes of the trade (BIM37007). For rent etc. of premises used both for business and as residence, see **75.108** below.

See *Mallalieu v Drummond* (**75.104** below) for an important HL discussion of the 'wholly and exclusively' rule, in which it was held that ascertaining the purposes of the relevant expenditure involved looking into the taxpayer's mind at the time of the expenditure, later events being irrelevant except as a reflection of that state of mind. However, the taxpayer's conscious motive at the time was not conclusive; an object, not a conscious motive (in this case the human requirement for clothing), could be taken into account.

A purely incidental consequence of a business expense does not, however, preclude its being wholly and exclusively for business purposes (HMRC Business Income Manual BIM37007, 37400). See, for example, *Robinson v Scott Bader Ltd*, **75.63** below and *McKnight v Sheppard* HL 1999, 71 TC 419, **75.96**, **75.104** below. In *Duckmanton v HMRC* UT, [2013] STC 2379, [2013] UKUT 305 (TCC)) (see also **75.96** below) the preservation of the taxpayer's liberty and personal reputation was not merely a secondary purpose of his incurring legal fees to successfully defend a gross negligence manslaughter charge; the fees breached the 'wholly and exclusively' rule. A similar decision was reached in *Raynor v HMRC* FTT (TC 1649), [2011] UKFTT 813 (TC) where a haulage contractor had been convicted of river pollution. *Mallalieu v Drummond* was applied in *Watkis v Ashford, Sparkes and Harward* Ch D 1985, 58 TC 468, where expenditure on meals supplied at regular partners' lunchtime meetings was disallowed, overruling the Commissioner's finding that the expenditure was exclusively for business purposes. Expenditure on accommodation, food and drink at the firm's annual weekend conference was, however, allowed as a deduction. For deduction of payments by partnerships to individual partners generally, see *MacKinlay v Arthur Young McClelland Moores & Co* HL 1989, 62 TC 704. Salaries paid to partners are not deductible as trading expenses (*PDC Copyprint (South) v George* (Sp C 141), [1997] SSCD 326).

See also **75.104** below as regards personal and domestic expenses.

The question of whether or not a payment satisfies the 'wholly and exclusively' rule is determined by reference to the taxpayer's trade and does not require a consideration of how the money has been ultimately dealt with by the recipient (*Icebreaker 1 LLP v HMRC* UT, [2011] STC 1078). It should be borne in mind that the trade for whose purposes the expenditure is incurred must be that in which the expense arose; for a successful appeal against a decision in favour of the Inland Revenue on this point, see *Vodafone Cellular Ltd v Shaw* CA 1997, 69 TC 376.

For HMRC's own guidance on the 'wholly and exclusively' rule, see HMRC Business Income Manual BIM37000–38600.

Simon's Taxes. See **B2.315–B2.323.**

Advertising

[75.45] Expenditure generally is allowable (but not capital outlay such as fixed signs (but see *Leeds Permanent Building Society v Proctor* Ch D 1982, 56 TC 293), nor initial costs etc. of new business). Contribution to campaign for

Sunday opening held allowable (*Rhymney Breweries* Ch D 1965, 42 TC 509). As to political campaign see *Tate & Lyle* HL 1954, 35 TC 367, contrasted with *Boarland v Kramat Pulai* Ch D 1953, 35 TC 1. See HMRC Business Income Manual BIM42550–42565.

In *McQueen v HMRC* (Sp C 601), [2007] SSCD 457 the Sp C found on the evidence that expenditure on motor rallying and capital allowances on rally cars were deductible trading expenses and that any private benefit to the taxpayer was a merely incidental effect of the expenditure rather than its purpose; in this case the taxpayer, a keen rally driver, owned a minibus business and used motor rallying as a means of advertising that business.

In *Interfish Ltd v HMRC* CA 2014, [2015] STC 55, expenditure on sponsorship of the local rugby club was held to be for a dual purpose; the immediate purpose was that of promoting the trade of someone other than the taxpayer, i.e. the club, which could not be considered an incidental effect of the expenditure, and it was immaterial that the business purpose was the predominant purpose intended to be served; the expenditure was disallowed.

Simon's Taxes. See **B2.402**.

Application of profits

[75.46] A requirement that a trading surplus is to be applied in a particular way does not remove the trade from the charge to tax on trading income (*Mersey Docks and Harbour Board v Lucas* HL 1883, 2 TC 25) and applications of the profits under the requirement are not allowable deductions (*City of Dublin Steam Packet Co v O'Brien* KB(I) 1912, 6 TC 101; *Hutchinson & Co v Turner* HC 1950, 31 TC 495; *Young v Racecourse Betting Control Board* HL 1959, 38 TC 426 and cf. *Pondicherry Rly Co* PC 1931, 10 ATC 365; *Tata Hydro-Electric Agencies* PC 1937, 16 ATC 54; *India Radio & Cable Communication Co* PC 1937, 16 ATC 333).

For circumstances in which the profits of a trade may not accrue to the proprietor, see *Alongi v CIR* CS 1991, 64 TC 304.

Simon's Taxes. See **B2.324**.

Artistes

[75.47] For creative artists, see **75.59** below.

An actress based in the UK but with engagements abroad was held to be carrying on a single profession. Hence receipts from her overseas engagements fell to be included in her *Sch D, Case II* (professional income) assessment (*Davies v Braithwaite* KB 1933, 18 TC 198 and compare *Withers v Wynyard* KB 1938, 21 TC 724).

An artiste engaged by a theatre under a standard contract was held to be within the charge to tax on employment income (*Fall v Hitchen* Ch D 1972, 49 TC 433), but see now **28.66** EMPLOYMENT INCOME as regards application of trading income rules to artistes generally.

A sum received by a company, formed to exploit the services of an actor, on cancellation of an agreement giving another his exclusive services was held a trading receipt (*John Mills Productions Ltd v Mathias* Ch D 1967, 44 TC 441). Payment to actor for entering into restrictive covenant held not assessable (*Higgs v Olivier* CA 1952, 33 TC 136).

For deductibility of expenses of actors and other entertainers, including clothing, costume and cosmetic surgery, see HMRC Business Income Manual BIM50160.

See **4.29** ANTI-AVOIDANCE for the treatment as income of certain capital sums received in lieu of earnings and **50.11** NON-RESIDENTS as regards certain non-resident entertainers and sportsmen.

Simon's Taxes. See **B5.602**.

Bad and doubtful debts

[75.48] See generally HMRC Business Income Manual BIM42700–42750.

Bad debts, and doubtful debts to the extent they are estimated to be bad, are deductible. Where the debtor is bankrupt or insolvent, the debt is deductible except to the extent that any amount may reasonably be expected to be received on it.

A debt is also deductible to the extent that it is released wholly and exclusively for the purposes of the trade as part of a statutory insolvency arrangement, i.e. either:

(i) a voluntary arrangement under, or by virtue of, *Insolvency Act 1986* (or Scottish or NI equivalents); or

(ii) a compromise or arrangement under *Companies Act 2006, Pt 26* (or earlier equivalent); or

(iii) any foreign law equivalents of (i) or (ii).

Where a trade is treated as notionally discontinued (see **52.7** PARTNERSHIPS and **75.17** above), the relief applies to debts taken over by the successor.

[*ITTOIA 2005, ss 35, 259*].

The above does not apply in calculating profits on the cash basis (see **76.14** TRADING INCOME — CASH BASIS FOR SMALLER BUSINESSES).

If a debt owed *by* a trader is released (otherwise than as part of a statutory insolvency arrangement — see above), and the expense giving rise to the debt has been allowed as a deduction for tax purposes, the amount released counts for tax purposes as a trading receipt arising on the date of release. [*ITTOIA 2005, ss 97, 259*]. As regards trade debts *not* released but nevertheless written back, HMRC take the view that the requirement that GAAP be adhered to in computing taxable profits (see **75.21** above) requires such write-backs to be taxed, subject only to the exception provided by *ITTOIA 2005, s 97* for releases under statutory insolvency arrangements (HMRC Business Income Manual BIM40265). See generally Business Income Manual BIM40200–40265.

For debt recoveries and releases after the cessation of a trade, see 59 POST-CESSATION RECEIPTS AND EXPENDITURE. For VAT on bad debts, see 75.129 below.

A *provision* for bad debts can be deducted if based on a separate valuation of each debt. A general reserve, for example one calculated as a percentage of total debts or of total sales, is not deductible if made without regard to the circumstances of the particular debtors (HMRC Business Income Manual BIM42701). No provision for the estimated cost of collecting future debt instalments is permissible (*Monthly Salaries Loan Co Ltd v Furlong* Ch D 1962, 40 TC 313).

The provision for a bad or doubtful debt for a period of account may reflect events after the balance sheet date insofar as they furnish additional evidence of conditions that existed at the balance sheet date. See HMRC Business Income Manual BIM42705. It is not possible to employ hindsight to revisit a past computation of taxable profit so as to provide for a debt in a period of account in which there was no evidence that it would eventually prove to be bad (*Thompson v CIR* (Sp C 458), [2005] SSCD 320).

Where an asset accepted in satisfaction of a trading debt is of market value (as at the date of acceptance) less than the outstanding debt, the deficit may be allowed as a deduction, provided the trader agrees that, on a disposal of the asset, any excess of disposal proceeds over that value (up to the amount by which the debt exceeds that value) will be brought in as a trading receipt (such receipt being excluded from any chargeable gain computation on the disposal) (HMRC Business Income Manual BIM42735).

An allowance agreed under conditions of full disclosure cannot be withdrawn because of a subsequent change in the circumstances (*Anderton & Halstead Ltd v Birrell* KB 1931, 16 TC 200) but an allowance for year 1 may be revised, upwards or downwards, in the year 2 computation by reference to the circumstances for year 2 and similarly for later years. The amount of the allowance depends on the likelihood of recovery. This is a question of fact but the fact that the debtor is still in business is not itself a reason for refusing an allowance (*Dinshaw v Bombay IT Commr* PC 1934, 13 ATC 284). See also *Lock v Jones* KB 1941, 23 TC 749.

Where a builder sold houses leaving part of the sale proceeds with building societies as collateral security for mortgages by the purchasers, held the amounts should be brought in at valuation when houses sold and if practicable and otherwise when released by Building Society (*John Cronk & Sons Ltd v Harrison* HL 1936, 20 TC 612 and cf. *Chibbett v Harold Brookfield & Son Ltd* CA 1952, 33 TC 467). A similar decision was reached in *Absalom v Talbot* HL 1944, 26 TC 166 where amounts were left on loan to the purchasers. See also *Lock v Jones* above. The HL judgments in *Absalom v Talbot* are an important review of the treatment of trading debts.

The normal debt considered for allowance under *ITTOIA 2005, s 35* is a debt for goods or services supplied or a debt in a business, such as banking or money-lending, which consists of advancing money (see e.g. *AB Bank v Inspector of Taxes* (Sp C 237), [2000] SSCD 229). Losses on advances by a brewery company to its customers were allowed as on the evidence it habitually acted as banker for them in the course of its brewing business (*Reid's Brewery v Male* QB 1891, 3 TC 279). But losses on advances to clients by solicitors were refused as there was no evidence that they were money-lenders (*CIR v Hagart & Burn-Murdoch* HL 1929, 14 TC 433; *Rutherford v CIR* CS 1939, 23 TC 8. See also *Bury & Walkers v Phillips* HC 1951, 32 TC 198 and contrast *Jennings v Barfield* Ch D 1962, 40 TC 365). An allowance was refused for an irrecoverable balance due from the managing director of a company as outside the company's trade (*Curtis v J & G Oldfield Ltd* KB 1925, 9 TC 319). See also *Roebank Printing Co Ltd v CIR* CS 1928, 13 TC 864.

Advances to finance or recoup the losses of subsidiary or associated companies are capital. Allowances were refused in *English Crown Spelter v Baker* KB 1908, 5 TC 327 and *Charles Marsden & Sons v CIR* KB 1919, 12 TC 217 for losses on advances to facilitate the supply of materials for the trade of the lender as were losses on an advance to a company under the same control (*Baker v Mabie Todd & Co Ltd* KB 1927, 13 TC 235), amounts written off in respect of the losses of a subsidiary (*Odhams Press Ltd v Cook* HL 1940, 23 TC 233) and payments to meet the operating losses of a subsidiary (*Marshall Richards Machine Co Ltd v Jewitt* Ch D 1956, 36 TC 511). See also *CIR v Huntley & Palmers Ltd* KB 1928, 12 TC 1209; *Henderson v Meade-King Robinson & Co Ltd* KB 1938, 22 TC 97; and *Stone & Temple Ltd v Waters; Astrawall (UK) Ltd v Waters* Ch D 1995, 67 TC 145. The writing off of rent arrears of a company under common ownership was held to be predominantly to benefit the debtor at the expense of the taxpayer, and relief was refused (*Sere Properties v HMRC* FTT (TC 2429), [2013] UKFTT 006 (TC)).

Losses relating to trade debts with a subsidiary were, however, held allowable in *Sycamore plc and Maple Ltd v Fir* (Sp C 104), [1997] SSCD 1.

Payments by the purchaser to discharge the unpaid liabilities of the vendor to preserve goodwill etc. allowed in *Cooke v Quick Shoe Repair Service* KB 1949, 30 TC 460.

See **75.127** below for relief for certain unremittable overseas debts of trades carried on at least partly in the UK.

For losses under guarantees see **75.89** below.

Simon's Taxes. See **B2.206, B2.410.**

Breweries, distilleries, licensed premises

[75.49] See 75.123 below for rules on 'tied premises'. Those rules are of general application, although of most common application in the licensed trade.

Repairs, rates, insurance premiums paid on behalf of tied tenants allowable (*Usher's Wiltshire Brewery v Bruce* HL 1914, 6 TC 399) but not extra expenditure incurred to keep licensed houses open while undergoing rehabilitation (*Mann Crossman & Paulin Ltd v Compton* KB 1947, 28 TC 410) or compensation to a tenant displaced on a licence transfer (*Morse v Stedeford* KB 1934, 18 TC 457). For compensation paid on the termination of tenancies of tied houses, see *Watneys (London) Ltd v Pike* Ch D 1982, 57 TC 372. Losses on advances to 'customers and connections' held allowable (*Reid's Brewery v Male* QB 1891, 3 TC 279).

The expenses of an unsuccessful application for licences were held not allowable (*Southwell v Savill Bros* KB 1901, 4 TC 430 — it was conceded that expenses of successful applications are capital) nor expenses of applying for licence transfers (*Morse v Stedeford* above; *Pendleton v Mitchells & Butlers* Ch D 1968, 45 TC 341). Contributions by a brewer to a trade association to promote Sunday opening in Wales allowed in *Cooper v Rhymney Breweries* Ch D 1965, 42 TC 509. Compensation Fund levies deductible (*Smith v Lion Brewery* HL 1910, 5 TC 568) but not monopoly value payments (*Kneeshaw v Albertolli* KB 1940, 23 TC 462; *Henriksen v Grafton Hotels Ltd* CA 1942, 24 TC 453).

Damages paid to hotel guest injured by falling chimney held not allowable — see *Strong & Co v Woodifield* at **75.55** below. For accrued whisky storage rents see *Dailuaine-Talisker Distilleries v CIR* CS 1930, 15 TC 613; *CIR v Oban Distillery Co* CS 1932, 18 TC 33 and *CIR v Arthur Bell & Sons* CS 1932, 22 TC 315.

Where a brewery company ceased brewing but continued to sell beer brewed for it by another company it was held to have discontinued its old trade and commenced a new one (*Gordon & Blair Ltd v CIR* CS 1962, 40 TC 358).

Simon's Taxes. See **B5.611–B5.614.**

Car and motor cycle hire

[75.50] The deduction allowed for the expenditure incurred in hiring a 'car' for the purposes of a trade falls to be restricted if it is not one of the following:

- a car with 'low CO_2 emissions';
- an electrically-propelled car (as defined by *CAA 2001, s 268B*);
- a 'qualifying hire car'; or
- a car first registered before 1 March 2001.

The deduction which would otherwise be due is reduced by 15%. See below for exceptions in cases of short-term hire or long-term sub-hire. No restriction applies if the car falls into one of the above categories.

Where the restriction has applied, any subsequent rental rebate (or debt release other than as part of a statutory insolvency arrangement — see **75.48** above) is also reduced for tax purposes by 15%. This treatment extends to amounts brought in as post-cessation receipts (see **59.1** POST-CESSATION RECEIPTS AND EXPENDITURE) after the trade has ceased.

For this purpose, a '*car*' is a mechanically propelled road vehicle which is neither:

(1) of a construction primarily suited for the conveyance of goods or burden of any description; nor
(2) of a type not commonly used as a private vehicle and unsuitable for such use; nor

(3) a motor cycle.

As regards (2), see the case law referred to at **10.15**(ii) CAPITAL ALLOWANCES ON PLANT AND MACHINERY.

A car has '*low CO_2 emissions*' if its CO_2 emissions (see *CAA 2001, s 268C*) do not exceed 110g/km or if, when first registered, it was registered on the basis of a qualifying emissions certificate (as defined by *CAA 2001, s 268C*). The figure was 130g/km before 1 April 2018; the reduction to 110g/km does not apply to car hire expenditure incurred under a contract entered into before 6 April 2018 for a period of hire commencing before that date.

A car is a '*qualifying hire car*' if:

- it is hired under a hire-purchase agreement (as defined by *ITA 2007, s 998A*) under which there is no option to purchase or an option to purchase that is exercisable on payment of a sum of not more than 1% of the retail price when new; or
- it is leased under a long funding lease (for which see **10.50**(1) CAPITAL ALLOWANCES ON PLANT AND MACHINERY).

Expenditure is *excepted* from these provisions if either Condition A or Condition B is satisfied. Condition A is that the hire period is no more than 45 consecutive days. Condition B is that the expenditure relates to a period (the '*sub-hire period*') throughout which the taxpayer makes the car available to another person and the sub-hire period is more than 45 consecutive days.

For the purpose of applying Condition B, the expenditure on hiring the car is apportioned on a time basis between the hire period and the sub-hire period. For the purpose of applying either condition, where arrangements for the hiring of a car include arrangements for the provision of a replacement car in the event that the first car is not available, the first car and any replacement car are to be treated as if they were the same car.

For the purposes of both conditions, two or more hire periods of the same car are aggregated in determining the number of consecutive days if those periods are no more than 14 days apart.

Neither condition is met if the car is hired under tax avoidance arrangements. Condition B is not met if the sub-lessee is an employee of the taxpayer or of a person connected with the taxpayer (within **19** CONNECTED PERSONS) or if, during any part of the period in question, the sub-lessee himself makes any car available to an employee of the taxpayer (under arrangements with the taxpayer) or of a person connected with the taxpayer.

Where there is a chain of leases involving CONNECTED PERSONS (**19**), the 15% restriction applies only to expenditure incurred by a '*commercial lessee*' or, where there is more than one, by the first 'commercial lessee' in the chain. A '*commercial lessee*' is someone who incurs the expenditure under commercial arrangements, i.e. arrangements the terms of which are such as would reasonably have been expected if the parties thereto had been dealing at arm's length. If one or more persons in the chain is a company, the similar restriction that applies for corporation tax purposes is taken into account also, so that only one restriction applies overall.

[*ITTOIA 2005, ss 48, 49, 50A, 50B; SI 2016 No 984, Arts 5, 7; SI 2017 No 740*].

The above does not apply in calculating profits on the cash basis (see **76.14** TRADING INCOME — CASH BASIS FOR SMALLER BUSINESSES).

See HMRC Business Income Manual BIM47714–47775.

See also the optional fixed rate deduction scheme for expenditure on vehicles at **77.2** TRADING INCOME — FIXED RATE DEDUCTION SCHEME.

Future development

With effect on and after 1 April 2021, the above CO_2 emissions threshold is to be reduced from 110g/km to 50g/km. See www.gov.uk/government/publications/capital-allowance-carbon-dioxide-emissions-thresholds-for-business-cars-goods-vehicles-and-equipment-for-gas-refuelling-stations-from-april-2021.

Previous regime

A different set of rules applied where a car was hired under an agreement under which the hire period began before 6 April 2009. For details, see HMRC Business Income Manual BIM47775–47785.

Simon's Taxes. See **B2.413**.

Cemeteries and crematoria

[75.51] In computing profits of a trade consisting of, or including, the carrying on of a cemetery or the carrying on of a crematorium (and, in connection therewith, the maintenance of memorial garden plots), a deduction as a trading expense for any period of account is allowed for:

- the capital cost of purchasing and preparing land (including cost of levelling, draining or otherwise making suitable) sold for interments or memorial garden plots *in that period*; and
- a *proportion* (based on the ratio of number of grave-spaces/garden plots sold in the period to that number plus those still available — see the example below) of 'residual capital expenditure'.

'*Residual capital expenditure*' is the total 'ancillary capital expenditure' incurred before the end of the period of account in question after subtracting:

(i) amounts previously deducted under these provisions;
(ii) any sale, insurance or compensation receipts for assets representing ancillary capital expenditure and sold or destroyed; and
(iii) certain expenditure before the basis period for 1954/55.

'*Ancillary capital expenditure*' is capital expenditure incurred on any building or structure (other than a dwelling-house), or on the purchase or preparation of other land not suitable or adaptable for interments or garden plots, which is in the cemetery or memorial garden and is likely to have little or no value when the cemetery or garden is full; it also includes capital expenditure on the purchase or preparation of land taken up by said buildings and structures.

For these purposes, sales of land in a cemetery include sales of interment rights, and sales of land in a memorial garden include appropriations of part of the garden in return for dedication fees etc. Expenditure met by subsidies cannot be deducted as above (the detailed rules being similar to those at **9.2**(vi) CAPITAL ALLOWANCES).

Any change in the persons carrying on the trade is ignored; allowances continue as they would to the original trader, disregarding any purchase price paid in connection with the change itself.

[*ITTOIA 2005, ss 169–172*].

Where, in the case of a crematorium, the trade includes the sale of niches or memorials and/or the making of inscriptions, certain deductions are available. For niches, two-thirds of both revenue and capital costs are allowable. For memorials and inscriptions, the whole of the revenue costs and two-thirds of the capital costs are allowable. Capital costs are an appropriate proportion of the associated building costs or, for inscriptions, the associated framework costs. [*ITTOIA 2005, ss 172ZA–172ZE*]. See HMRC Business Income Manual BIM52520–52530.

None of the above applies in calculating profits on the cash basis (see **76.14** TRADING INCOME — CASH BASIS FOR SMALLER BUSINESSES).

As regards crematoria, see also *Bourne v Norwich Crematorium* Ch D 1967, 44 TC 164.

Simon's Taxes. See B5.620.

Example

[75.52]

GR, who operates a funeral service, owns a cemetery for which accounts to 31 December are prepared. The accounts to 31.12.20 reveal the following:

(i)	Cost of land representing 110 grave spaces sold in period	£3,400
(ii)	Number of grave spaces remaining	275
(iii)	Residual capital expenditure on buildings and other land unsuitable for interments	£18,250

The allowances available are

		£
(a)	Item (i)	3,400
(b)	$\frac{110}{110+275} \times £18,250$	5,214
		£8,614

Note

£8,614 will be allowed as a deduction in computing GR's trading profits for the period of account ending on 31 December 2020.

Clergymen

[75.53] The following apply for the purpose of computing the profits of the profession or vocation of a minister of religious denomination. See **28.62** EMPLOYMENT INCOME as regards clergymen in employment.

If the minister pays rent for a dwelling-house any part of which is used mainly and substantially for the purposes of his duty, a deduction is allowed for such part of the rent as on a just and reasonable apportionment is attributable to that part, subject to a maximum deduction of one-quarter of the rent.

If a charity or ecclesiastical corporation owns an interest in the premises in which the minister resides and from which he performs his duty, one-quarter of any expenses he incurs on the maintenance, repair, insurance or management of the premises is deductible even if it would not be so under general principles, e.g. the 'wholly and exclusively' rule at **75.44** above. The deduction may exceed one-quarter to the extent that it is allowable under general principles.

[*ITTOIA 2005, s 159, Sch 2 para 43*].

The above does not apply in calculating profits on the cash basis (see **76.14** TRADING INCOME — CASH BASIS FOR SMALLER BUSINESSES).

Simon's Taxes. See B5.665.

Commission, cashbacks and discounts

[75.54] HMRC Statement of Practice SP 4/97 sets out HMRC's views on the tax treatment of commissions, cashbacks and discounts. The types of payment with which the Statement is concerned are as follows.

- **Commissions.** Sums paid by the providers of goods, investments or services to agents or intermediaries as reward for the introduction of business, or in some cases paid directly by the provider to the customer. Sums paid to an agent or intermediary may be passed on to the customer or to some other person.
- **Cashbacks.** Lump sums received by a customer as an inducement for entering into a transaction for the purchase of goods, investments or services and received as a direct consequence of having entered into that transaction. The payer may be either the provider or another party with an interest in ensuring that the transaction takes place.
- **Discounts**, i.e. where the purchaser's obligation to pay for goods, investments or services is less than the full purchase price, other than as a result of commissions or cashbacks.

The Statement also deals with commissions or cashbacks which are netted off, or invested or otherwise applied for the benefit of the purchaser, or where extra value is added to the goods, investments or services supplied (e.g. the allocation of bonus units in an investment) (although in the case of the addition of value to investments this may represent a return on the investment, which is outside the scope of the Statement).

The Statement provides detailed guidance on the circumstances in which liability may arise, either as trading income or as miscellaneous income, on receipts of commission etc. It also considers deductibility of commission etc. passed on to customers. It also considers possible liabilities to tax on employment income or to capital gains tax, and the effect of commissions etc. on life insurance policies.

Generally, ordinary retail arm's length customers will not be liable to income tax or capital gains tax. The Statement outlines the circumstances in which receipts are treated as tax-free, or payments qualify for tax relief, and contains an element of concession for those who, in the ordinary course of their business, earn commission relating to their own transactions. It contains a warning that the principles outlined may not be followed where tax avoidance schemes are involved, or where the arrangements for the commission etc. include an increase in the purchase price of the goods etc. involved. The tax treatment of the payer and the recipient are in all cases considered independently of one another.

For an article explaining the legal basis of this approach, see Revenue Tax Bulletin February 1998 pp 505–509.

Compensation, damages, fines etc. — payments

[75.55] For compensation and redundancy payments to directors or employees see **75.69** below. An important case is *Anglo-Persian Oil Co Ltd v Dale* CA 1931, 16 TC 253 in which a substantial payment by a company for the cancellation of its principal agency, with ten years to run, was held to be allowable. It was not for a capital asset nor to get rid of an onerous contract (cf. *Mallett v Staveley Coal* CA 1928, 13 TC 772) but to enable it to rationalise its working arrangements. The decision was applied in *Croydon Hotel & Leisure Co Ltd v Bowen* (Sp C 101), [1996] SSCD 466, in which a payment for the termination of a hotel management agreement was held to be allowable. See also *Vodafone Cellular Ltd v Shaw* CA 1997, 69 TC 376 (payment for release from onerous agreement), in which the principle underlying the decision in *Van den Berghs Ltd v Clark* (see **75.56**(b) below) was applied, but cf. *Tucker v Granada Motorway Services Ltd* HL 1979, 53 TC 92, where a payment to modify the method of calculating the rent was held to be capital, and *Whitehead v Tubbs (Elastics) Ltd* CA 1983, 57 TC 472, where a payment to alter the terms of a capital loan by removing borrowing restrictions on the borrower was held to be capital.

A payment by a shipping company for cancelling an order it had placed for a ship was held capital (*'Countess Warwick' SS Co Ltd v Ogg* KB 1924, 8 TC 652 and contrast *Devon Mutual Steamship Insce v Ogg* KB 1927, 13 TC 184). A payment to an associated company in return for its temporarily ceasing production held allowable (*Commr of Taxes v Nchanga Consolidated Copper Mines* PC 1964, 43 ATC 20) as were statutory levies on a brewery for a Compensation Fund where a licence is not renewed (*Smith v Lion Brewery Co Ltd* HL 1910, 5 TC 568) and a payment to secure the closure of a rival concern (*Walker v The Joint Credit Card Co Ltd* Ch D 1982, 55 TC 617). Payments by a steel company to secure the closure of railway steel works were held capital (*United Steels v Cullington (No 1)* CA 1939, 23 TC 71) as were payments to safeguard against subsidence on a factory site (*Bradbury v United Glass Bottle Mfrs* CA 1959, 38 TC 369; compare *Glenboig Union Fireclay* at **75.56**(c) below) and a payment for cancelling electricity agreement on closure of a quarry (*CIR v Wm Sharp & Son* CS 1959, 38 TC 341). For compensation paid on the termination of tied houses of breweries, see *Watneys (London) Ltd v Pike* Ch D 1982, 57 TC 372.

Where damages awarded by a Court against a solicitor were later compounded, the compounded amount (accepted as allowable) was held to be an expense of the year in which the Court award was made (*Simpson v Jones* Ch D 1968, 44 TC 599). See also *CIR v Hugh T Barrie Ltd* CA(NI) 1928, 12 TC 1223.

Damages paid by a brewery to a hotel guest injured by a falling chimney were held to have been incurred by it *qua* property owner and not *qua* trader and not deductible (*Strong & Co of Romsey Ltd v Woodifield* HL 1906, 5 TC 215). Penalties for breach of war-time regulations and defence costs not allowed (*CIR v Warnes & Co* KB 1919, 12 TC 227; *CIR v Alexander von Glehn & Co Ltd* CA 1920, 12 TC 232), nor fines imposed by professional regulatory body (*McKnight v Sheppard* Ch D 1996, 71 TC 419), nor damages for breach of American 'anti-trust' law (*Cattermole v Borax & Chemicals Ltd* KB 1949, 31 TC 202). In *HMRC v McLaren Racing Ltd* UT 2014, 82 TC 345, it was held by the FTT that a substantial fine imposed by the FIA, the governing body for Formula 1 motor racing, for a serious breach of rules was deductible; this was overturned by the UT: the activities which gave rise to the fine were not carried out in the course of the taxpayer's trade, and the fine was non-deductible in any case as it was a punishment. See also *G Scammell & Nephew v Rowles* CA 1939, 22 TC 479; *Fairrie v Hall* KB 1947, 28 TC 200; *Golder v Great Boulder Proprietary* HC 1952, 33 TC 75; *Knight v Parry* Ch D 1972, 48 TC 580; *Hammond Engineering v CIR* Ch D 1975, 50 TC 313.

Simon's Taxes. See **B2.417**.

Compensation, damages etc. — receipts

[75.56] Where, pursuant to a legal right, a trader receives from another person compensation for the trader's failure to receive a sum of money which, if it had been received, would have been credited to the amount of profits (if any) arising in any year from the trade carried on by him at the time when the compensation is so received, the compensation is to be treated for income tax purposes in the same way as that sum of money would have been treated if it had been received instead of the compensation (*London & Thames Haven v Attwooll* CA 1966, 43 TC 491; *Gadhavi v HMRC* FTT (TC 6762), [2018] UKFTT 600 (TC)).

The following matters are also relevant.

(a) **Capital sums** (i.e. sums not taken into account in computing income) received as compensation for damage, injury, destruction or depreciation of assets are subject to capital gains tax [*TCGA 1992, s 22(1)*] (or corporation tax in the case of a company), but this does not apply to compensation or damages to an individual for wrong or injury to his person or in his profession or vocation. [*TCGA 1992, s 51(2)*]. See Tolley's Capital Gains Tax.

(b) **Cancellation or variation of trading contracts and arrangements.** An important case is *Van den Berghs Ltd v Clark* HL 1935, 19 TC 390 in which a receipt on the termination of a profit-sharing arrangement was held to be capital. The arrangement related to the whole structure of the recipient's trade, forming the fixed framework within which its circulating capital operated. Compensation etc. receipts were also held to be capital in *Sabine v Lookers Ltd* CA 1958, 38 TC 120 (varying car distributor's agreement); *British-Borneo Petroleum v Cropper* Ch D 1968, 45 TC 201 (cancelling a royalty agreement); *Barr Crombie & Co Ltd v CIR* CS 1945, 26 TC 406 (terminating agreement as ship-managers); but the opposite conclusion was reached in *Consultant v Inspector of Taxes* (Sp C 180), [1999] SSCD 63 (termination of profit participation agreement). A payment by the liquidator of a shipping company to its managers as authorised by the shareholders held not assessable (*Chibbett v Robinson & Sons* KB 1924, 9 TC 48).

Compensation etc. receipts on the cancellation of contracts receipts from which, if completed, would have been trading receipts are normally themselves trading receipts, to be credited in the computations for the period in which cancelled. See *Short Bros Ltd v CIR* and *Sunderland Shipbuilding Co Ltd v CIR* CA 1927, 12 TC 955 (cancellation of order for ships); *CIR v Northfleet Coal Co* KB 1927, 12 TC 1102; *Jesse Robinson & Sons v CIR* KB 1929, 12 TC 1241 (cancellation of contracts for sale of goods etc.); *Greyhound Racing Assn v Cooper* KB 1936, 20 TC 373 (cancellation of agreement to hire greyhound track); *Shove v Dura Mfg Co Ltd* KB 1941, 23 TC 779 (cancellation of commission agreement). Similarly compensation to a merchanting company on cancellation of a contract to supply goods to it was held a trading receipt (*Bush, Beach & Gent Ltd v Road* KB 1939, 22 TC 519). See also *United Steel v Cullington (No 1)* CA 1939, 23 TC 71; *Shadbolt v Salmon Estates* KB 1943, 25 TC 52; *Sommerfelds Ltd v Freeman* Ch D 1966, 44 TC 43; *Creed v H & M Levinson Ltd* Ch D 1981, 54 TC 477.

Compensation received on the termination of agencies is a trading receipt unless the agency, by reason of its relative size etc., is part of the 'fixed framework' (see *Van den Berghs* above) of the agent's business. See *Kelsall Parsons* CS 1938, 21 TC 608; *CIR v Fleming & Co* CS 1951, 33 TC 57; *CIR v David MacDonald & Co* CS 1955, 36 TC 388; *Wiseburgh v Domville* CA 1956, 36 TC 527; *Fleming v Bellow Machine Co* Ch D 1965, 42 TC 308; *Elson v James G Johnston Ltd* Ch D 1965, 42 TC 545 (in all of which the compensation etc. was held to be a trading receipt). See also *Anglo-French Exploration Co Ltd v Clayson* CA 1956, 36 TC 545.

For payments received on termination of building society agencies, see HMRC Capital Gains Tax Manual CG13050 *et seq.*

The treatment of compensation on the termination of posts held in the course of a business (particularly a profession), the yearly remuneration having been included in the business receipts (see **28.66** EMPLOYMENT INCOME), has arisen in a number of cases. In *Blackburn v Close Bros Ltd* Ch D 1960, 39 TC 164, compensation on the cancellation of an agreement by a merchant banker to provide secretarial services was held to be a trading receipt but in *Ellis v Lucas* Ch D 1966, 43 TC 276 compensation on the termination of an auditorship was held to be within the ambit of the special provisions on termination payments (see **18.3** COMPENSATION FOR LOSS OF EMPLOYMENT) and hence could not be included in the profits for *Sch D, Case II* (professional income) purposes (except a small part of the payment held to be compensation for the loss of general accountancy work). Similar decisions were reached in *Walker v Carnaby Harrower, Barham & Pykett* Ch D 1969, 46 TC 561 (loss of auditorship by firm of accountants) and *CIR v Brander & Cruickshank* HL 1970, 46 TC 574 (loss of company secretaryships by firm of Scottish advocates) and in *Carnaby Harrower* the payment was also held not to be a professional receipt because of its *ex gratia* nature. For *ex gratia* payments, see also (f) below. For compensation on cancellation of contracts of actors, authors etc. see **75.47** above, **75.59** below.

(c) **Compensation etc. relating to capital assets.** Compensation to a company making fireclay goods for refraining from working a fireclay bed under a railway line was held to be capital (*Glenboig Union Fireclay Co Ltd v CIR* HL 1922, 12 TC 427 and cf. *Thomas McGhie & Sons v BTC* QB 1962, 41 ATC 144 and *Bradbury v United Glass Bottle* CA 1959, 38 TC 369), but compensation to a colliery from the Government for requisition of part of its mining area was held to be a trading receipt (*Waterloo Main Colliery v CIR (No 1)* KB 1947, 29 TC 235). Compensation to a shipping company for delay in the overhaul of a ship was held to be a trading receipt (*Burmah Steam Ship Co v CIR* CS 1930, 16 TC 67) as was compensation to a jetty owner for loss of its use after damage by a ship (*London & Thames Haven v Attwooll* CA 1966, 43 TC 491) and compensation for the detention of a ship (*Ensign Shipping Co v CIR* CA 1928, 12 TC 1169 but contrast *CIR v Francis West* CS 1950, 31 TC 402). Compensation for what turned out to be only a temporary loss of the use of land was held to be a trading receipt (*Able (UK) Ltd v HMRC* CA 2007, 78 TC 790). A settlement to cover the dilapidated state of let property where the tenant was responsible for upkeep was held to be compensation for the fall in capital value of the property, and not for a loss of rental income, and was thus a capital receipt (*Thornton v HMRC* FTT (TC 5494), [2016] UKFTT 767 (TC)).

For insurance recoveries see **75.92** below.

(d) **Compensation on compulsory acquisition etc.** Where compensation is paid for the acquisition of business property by an authority possessing powers of compulsory acquisition, any amounts included as compensation for temporary loss of profits or losses on trading stock or to reimburse revenue expenditure, such as removal expenses and interest, are treated as trading receipts. (See HMRC SP 8/79. This Statement of Practice was originally issued as consequence of *Stoke-on-Trent City Council v Wood Mitchell & Co Ltd* CA 1978, [1979] STC 197.)

(e) **Interest Rate Hedging Products redress payments.** These redress payments may be received from banks in 2014 onwards because of previous mis-selling by some banks of Interest Rate Hedging Products (IRHP) to businesses taking out business loans, such products being intended to offer protection against rising interest rates. Any such redress payment can be made up of three elements: basic redress (the difference between the actual payments made by the business based on the mis-sold product and the payments that would have been made otherwise); compensatory interest (for loss of use of the money in the meantime); and consequential losses (for losses suffered due to loss of use of the money). The full redress payment is generally considered taxable as income; this is based on the assumption that tax relief will have been claimed on the payments under the IRHP as an allowable business deduction. The redress payment will have basic rate tax deducted at source. It should be accounted for in the period of account, or in the case of compensatory interest the tax year, in which received. If received in instalments, each instalment should be so accounted for. (www.gov.uk/government/publications/tax-interest-rate-hedging-products-irhp).

The above treatment was confirmed in *Gadhavi v HMRC* FTT (TC 6762), [2018] UKFTT 600 (TC).

(f) **Other compensation etc. receipts.** Voluntary payments to an insurance broker on the loss of an important client company (made by its parent company) were held, approving *Chibbett v Robinson* and *Carnaby Harrower* (see (b) above), not to be assessable (*Simpson v John Reynolds & Co* CA 1975, 49 TC 693) and similarly for voluntary payments from a brewer to a firm of caterers for the surrender of the leases of tied premises (*Murray v Goodhews* CA 1977, 52 TC 86) but *ex gratia* payments to an estate agent who had not been given an agency he expected were held, on the facts, to be additional remuneration for work already done and assessable. (*McGowan v Brown & Cousins (Stuart Edwards)* Ch D 1977, 52 TC 8). A payment to a diamond broker under informal and non-binding arbitration as damages for the loss of a prospective client was held assessable (*Rolfe v Nagel* CA 1981, 55 TC 585). Compensation for 'loss of profits' following the destruction of the premises of a business not recommenced was held to be of a revenue nature in *Lang v Rice* CA (NI) 1983, 57 TC 80. For compensation receipts relating to the terms on which business premises are tenanted, see **75.108** below.

For the treatment of compensation received by businesses as customers of e.g. utility companies for interruptions and other service deficiencies, see Revenue Tax Bulletin December 1997 pp 490, 491.

Where a payment (sometimes called a financial loss allowance) is made by a relevant authority (defined as in **30.51** EXEMPT INCOME) to a person (P) holding a voluntary office with the authority where P carries out duties of that office in a period in which P is also self-employed, and the payment is made solely to compensate P for lost profits, the payment is chargeable as a receipt of P's trade, profession or vocation. [*ITTOIA 2005, s 16A; SI 2018 No 282, Arts 1, 3(3)*]. This applies by statute for 2018/19 onwards but was previously the case in practice (see HMRC Business Income Manual BIM40475). In the absence of any exemption, an identical rule applies where P does not hold an office with the relevant authority but performs services (e.g. jury service) for it for no financial benefit in a period in which P is also self-employed. See **30.51** EXEMPT INCOME for the contrasting position where the person concerned is employed rather than self-employed and the payment is to compensate for lost employment income.

Damages awarded to a theatrical company for breach of a licence it had, were held to be assessable (*Vaughan v Parnell & Zeitlin* KB 1940, 23 TC 505) as was compensation received by a development company under legislation for restricting development (*Johnson v W S Try Ltd* CA 1946, 27 TC 167). A retrospective award for a war-time requisition of trading stock was held to be a trading receipt of the year of requisition (*CIR v Newcastle Breweries Ltd* HL 1927, 12 TC 927).

Contingent and future liabilities

[75.57] For forward contracts see **75.58** below.

Where a company is required under overseas legislation to make leaving payments to its employees, a provision in its accounts for its prospective liability is permissible if capable of sufficiently accurate calculation (*Owen v Southern Railway of Peru* HL 1956, 36 TC 602). The allowance each year is the actual payments as adjusted for any variation between the opening and closing provisions but the deductible provision for the year in which the legislation was enacted may include an amount in respect of previous services of the employees (*CIR v Titaghur Jute Factory Ltd* CS 1978, 53 TC 675).

No deduction is normally permissible for future repairs or renewals (*Clayton v Newcastle-under-Lyme Corpn* QB 1888, 2 TC 416; *Naval Colliery Co Ltd v CIR* HL 1928, 12 TC 1017; *Peter Merchant Ltd v Stedeford* CA 1948, 30 TC 496). However, this rule is now subject to Financial Reporting Standard FRS 12 (see **75.111** below). No deduction is permissible for the future cost of collecting debts (*Monthly Salaries Loan Co v Furlong* Ch D 1962, 40 TC 313) or for future payments of damages in respect of accidents to employees unless liability has been admitted or established (*James Spencer & Co v CIR* CS 1950, 32 TC 111). See also *Albion Rovers Football Club v CIR* HL 1952, 33 TC 331 (wages deductible when paid). A provision for regular major overhaul work accrued due on aircraft engines was allowed in *Johnston v Britannia Airways Ltd* Ch D 1994, 67 TC 99 (but see now Revenue Tax Bulletin February 1999 p 624 and further below as regards changes in accounting practice superseding this decision).

For provisions by insurance companies for unexpired risks etc., see *Sun Insurance Office v Clark* HL 1912, 6 TC 59. For the liability of cemetery companies in receipt of lump sums for the future maintenance of graves, see *Paisley Cemetery Co v Reith* CES 1898, 4 TC 1 and *London Cemetery Co v Barnes* KB 1917, 7 TC 92.

A provision by a company engaged in the exploitation of a North Sea oil field, for anticipated future expenditure on the completion of the exploitation, in dismantling installations used and (as required under its licence) in 'cleaning up' the sea bed, was disallowed as capital when incurred in *RTZ Oil & Gas Ltd v Elliss* Ch D 1987, 61 TC 132.

See generally HMRC Business Income Manual BIM42201, 46500–46565.

Simon's Taxes. See **B2.504**.

Contracts

[75.58] For compensation etc. on the cancellation or variation of contracts see **75.55** and **75.56** above. For work in progress under contracts see **75.116** below.

Where a taxpayer took over a coal merchanting business on the death of his father, an amount paid for the benefit of contracts between his father and suppliers was held capital (*John Smith & Son v Moore* HL 1921, 12 TC 266 and see *City of London Contract Corpn v Styles* CA 1887, 2 TC 239). The completion of outstanding contracts following a partnership dissolution (*Hillerns & Fowler v Murray* CA 1932, 17 TC 77) and on a company going into liquidation (*Baker v Cook* KB 1937, 21 TC 337) held to be trading.

Where under a long-term contract goods were invoiced as delivered, the sale proceeds are receipts of the year of delivery (*J P Hall & Co Ltd v CIR* CA 1921, 12 TC 382). If contract prices are varied retrospectively the resultant further sums are assessable or deductible for the years applicable to the sums at the original prices (*Frodingham Ironstone Mines Ltd v Stewart* KB 1932, 16 TC 728; *New Conveyor Co Ltd v Dodd* KB 1945, 27 TC 11). Compare *English Dairies Ltd v Phillips* KB 1927, 11 TC 597; *Isaac Holden & Sons Ltd v CIR* KB 1924, 12 TC 768 and contrast *Rownson Drew & Clydesdale Ltd v CIR* KB 1931, 16 TC 595.

Losses because of a fall in prices fixed under forward contracts etc. cannot be anticipated (*Edward Collins & Sons Ltd v CIR* CS 1924, 12 TC 773; *Whimster & Co v CIR* CS 1925, 12 TC 813) and cf. *Wright Sutcliffe Ltd v CIR* KB 1929, 8 ATC 168; *J H Young & Co v CIR* CS 1924, 12 TC 817; *CIR v Hugh T Barrie Ltd* CA(NI) 1928, 12 TC 1223.

Creative artists

[75.59] A taxpayer who, after writing plays in his spare time which were not sold, wrote a successful play was held to be carrying on the vocation of dramatist (*Billam v Griffith* KB 1941, 23 TC 757). Receipts from the occasional writing of articles are normally chargeable as miscellaneous income but *Sch D, Case II* (i.e. professional income) assessments on a regular newspaper contributor were upheld in *Graham v Arnott* KB 1941, 24 TC 157. Receipts from the sale of an author's notebooks and memorabilia were held to be taxable as part of the fruits of his profession (*Wain v Cameron* Ch D 1995, 67 TC 324).

A sum received by an author on cancellation of his contract as script writer was held a revenue receipt (*Household v Grimshaw* Ch D 1953, 34 TC 366). Film writer's loss under guarantee of indebtedness of film company held allowable (*Lunt v Wellesley* KB 1945, 27 TC 78).

Whether a literary prize or award is a receipt of the author's profession depends on the precise facts — see HMRC Business Income Manual BIM50710.

See **75.60** below for averaging of profits. See **75.47** above for the taxation of *artistes*. See **4.29** ANTI-AVOIDANCE for the treatment as income of certain capital sums received in lieu of earnings.

Copyright and royalties

Amounts held to be assessable include advance payments of gramophone royalties to a singer (*Taylor v Dawson* KB 1938, 22 TC 189); commutations of future royalties paid to an authoress (*Glasson v Rougier* KB 1944, 26 TC 86); receipts from sale of film rights in books (*Howson v Monsell* HC 1950, 31 TC 529); sales of copyright in novels written when the author was non-resident (with no deduction for his expenses then incurred — *Mackenzie v Arnold* CA 1952, 33 TC 363). But contrast *Mitchell v Rosay* CA 1954, 35 TC 496. *Sharkey v Wernher* (see **75.118** below) does not apply to a gift of copyright (*Mason v Innes* CA 1967, 44 TC 326). Royalties etc. arising after an author etc. dies or otherwise ceases to carry on his profession or vocation may be chargeable as POST-CESSATION RECEIPTS AND EXPENDITURE (59).

Simon's Taxes. See **B5.603, B5.626.**

Creative artists — averaging of profits

[75.60] The averaging provisions below apply in respect of profits of a 'qualifying trade, profession or vocation', i.e. one whose profits derive wholly or mainly from 'creative works'. '*Creative works*' means literary, dramatic, musical or artistic works, or designs, created by the individual personally or, in the case of a partnership, by one or more of the partners personally. The potential for averaging is extended to profits of a qualifying trade, profession or vocation carried on wholly outside the UK by a UK resident.

Where, in relation to two consecutive tax years, the profits for one year are less than 75% of the profits for the other (or the profits for one year, but not both, are nil, e.g. where a loss is incurred), a two-year averaging claim can be made, with the following results.

Where the second of the two years in question is 2016/17 or a subsequent year, the profits for each year are adjusted to the average of the two years.

Where the second of the two years is 2015/16 or an earlier year and the profits for either year do not exceed 70% of the profits for the other (or are nil), the profits for each year are adjusted to the average of the two years.

Where the second of the two years is 2015/16 or an earlier year and either year's profits exceed 70% of the other's, but are less than 75%, the profits are adjusted by adding to the lower and subtracting from the higher the amount obtained by first multiplying the difference by three and then deducting 75% of the higher figure. (Thus, if the profits are £29,200 and £40,000, the averaged profits would be £31,600 and £37,600.)

'*Profits*' for this purpose are those before any deduction for losses. An averaging claim does not prevent a claim for loss relief. (Thus, if there were a loss of £10,000 for one tax year and a profit of £30,000 for the other, the first-mentioned year is taken to be a year of nil profit and the averaged profits for each year are £15,000; the loss of £10,000 remains eligible for loss relief in the normal way.)

If an averaging claim is made for a pair of tax years, Years X and Y, a claim is also permitted for Years Y and Z, the profits for Year Y being taken as those adjusted on the first claim, and so on for subsequent years. However, no averaging claim is subsequently permissible involving any year prior to Year X. No averaging claim can be made for the tax year in which the taxpayer starts, or permanently ceases, to carry on the trade. This includes the tax years in which an individual joins and leaves a partnership. Neither can a claim be made involving any tax year in which the business begins, or ceases, to be a 'qualifying trade, profession or vocation' (see above).

An averaging claim must be made on or before the first anniversary of 31 January following the later of the two tax years to which it relates. An averaging claim can be made only by an individual. In the case of a partnership, an individual partner may make his own claim, based on his own profit shares, irrespective of whether or not other partners make claims.

If, after a claim, the profits of either or both years are adjusted for some other reason, the claim lapses but a new one may then be made, in respect of the adjusted profits, on or before the first anniversary of 31 January following the tax year in which the adjustment is made.

See **16.2** CLAIMS for the method of giving effect to an averaging claim.

A claim for relief under any other provision of the *Income Tax Acts* for a tax year included in an averaging claim can be made, amended or revoked at any time on or before the latest possible date on which the averaging claim itself could have been made. See **16.2** CLAIMS for the method of giving effect to such a claim, amendment or revocation that would otherwise be out of time.

[*ITTOIA 2005, ss 221, 222, 223–225; FA 2016, s 25(2)(4)–(7)(12)*].

Averaging does not apply in calculating profits on the cash basis (see **76.14** TRADING INCOME — CASH BASIS FOR SMALLER BUSINESSES).

Simon's Taxes. See **B5.326–B5.328.**

Example

[75.61]

Richard is an established author by profession and has the following profits/losses as adjusted for income tax purposes (including a deduction for capital allowances) for the six years mentioned.

Year ended	Tax-adjusted profit/loss
	£
31.12.15	35,000
31.12.16	30,000
31.12.17	6,000
31.12.18	25,000
31.12.19	13,000
31.12.20	(2,000)

Averaged profits for all years would be:

		No averaging claims	Averaging claims for all possible years
		£	£
2015/16	note (i)	35,000	35,000
2016/17	note (ii)	30,000	18,000
2017/18	note (iii)	6,000	21,500
2018/19	note (iv)	25,000	17,250
2019/20	note (v)	13,000	8,625
2020/21	note (v)	Nil	8,625
		£109,000	£109,000

Notes

(i)	2015/16	35,000	
	2016/17	30,000	
		£65,000	

As £30,000 is not less than 75% of £35,000, no averaging claim is possible.

(ii)	2016/17	30,000	
	2017/18	6,000	
		£36,000	÷ 2 = £18,000

As £6,000 is less than 75% of £30,000, averaging applies. No claim can now be made to average 2016/17 (as adjusted) with 2015/16, even though this would now be possible purely on the figures.

(iii)	2017/18	18,000	
	2018/19	25,000	
		£43,000	÷ 2 = £21,500

As £18,000 is less than 75% of £25,000, averaging applies.

(iv)	2018/19	21,500	
	2019/20	13,000	
		34,500	÷ 2 = £17,250

As £13,000 is less than 75% of £21,500, averaging applies.

(v)	2019/20	17,250	
	2020/21	Nil	
		17,250	÷ 2 = £8,625

The loss of £2,000 for 2020/21 does not enter into the averaging claim, but is available to reduce either the 2019/20 or 2020/21 averaged profits on a claim under *ITA 2007, s 64* (see **45.2** LOSSES).

The 2020/21 averaged profits of £8,625 may themselves be averaged with 2021/22 profits if the 75% rule is satisfied. Any loss claim against income of 2020/21 is disregarded for this purpose.

Embezzlement etc.

[75.62] Losses from embezzlement are allowed as deductions, but misappropriations by a partner or director are not deductible. See *Bamford v ATA Advertising* Ch D 1972, 48 TC 359 and cf. *Curtis v J & G Oldfield Ltd* KB 1925, 9 TC 319. Where defalcations were made good by the auditor who admitted negligence, refund held to be a trading receipt for the year in which made (*Gray v Penrhyn* KB 1937, 21 TC 252).

See **75.91** below as regards prohibition on deduction of expenditure involving crime.

Employees (and directors)

[75.63] *Bona fide* remuneration is deductible including bonuses, commissions, tax deducted under PAYE and the cost of board, lodging, uniforms and benefits provided. The deduction is for the remuneration etc. payable; future payments cannot be anticipated (*Albion Rovers Football Club v CIR* HL 1952, 33 TC 331). The remuneration etc. must be shown to be wholly and exclusively for the purposes of the trade. In *Stott & Ingham v Trehearne* KB 1924, 9 TC 69 an increase in the rate of commission payable to the trader's sons was disallowed as not on a commercial footing. See also *Johnson Bros & Co v CIR* KB 1919, 12 TC 147, *Copeman v Wm Flood & Sons Ltd* KB 1940, 24 TC 53 and *Earlspring Properties Ltd v Guest* CA 1995, 67 TC 259. Payments by a farming couple to their young children for help on the farm were disallowed in *Dollar v Lyon* Ch D 1981, 54 TC 459. For excessive payments to 'service company' see *Payne, Stone Fraser* at **52.4** PARTNERSHIPS. For wife's wages see *Thompson v Bruce* KB 1927, 11 TC 607; *Moschi v Kelly*

CA 1952, 33 TC 442. The salary etc. of an employee for service in an overseas subsidiary was allowed in computing the profits of the parent in *Robinson v Scott Bader & Co Ltd* CA 1981, 54 TC 757. The secondment was wholly and exclusively for the purposes of the parent's business, notwithstanding the benefit to the subsidiary's business.

For **payroll giving schemes,** see **14.18** CHARITIES AND CHARITABLE GIVING.

Simon's Taxes. See **B2.421**.

Timing of deductions

[75.64] In calculating trading profits for a period of account, no deduction is allowed for an amount charged in the accounts in respect of employees' remuneration unless it is paid no later than nine months after the end of the period of account. Remuneration paid at a later time (and otherwise deductible) is deductible for the period of account *in which* it is paid. For these purposes, 'remuneration' includes any amount which is, or falls to be treated as, earnings for income tax purposes, and includes remuneration of office holders as well as other employees. Remuneration is treated as paid when it falls to be treated for tax purposes as received by the employee (see **28.9** EMPLOYMENT INCOME). These provisions apply whether the amount charged is in respect of particular employments or employments generally and apply equally to remuneration for which provision is made in the accounts with a view to its becoming employees' remuneration. Computations prepared before the end of the said nine-month period must be prepared on the basis that any still unpaid remuneration will not be paid before the expiry of that nine-month period and thus will not be deductible for the period of account in question. If, in fact, such remuneration *is* paid by the end of the nine-month period, then the matter may be dealt with by way of amendment to the self-assessment tax return (see **64.4** RETURNS).

These provisions apply to non-trade businesses as they do to trades, professions and vocations.

[*ITTOIA 2005, ss 36, 37, 865, Sch 2 para 12*].

The above does not apply in calculating profits on the cash basis (see **76.14** TRADING INCOME — CASH BASIS FOR SMALLER BUSINESSES).

Payments to an employee benefit trust were held to fall within these restrictions (as originally enacted) in *Macdonald v Dextra Accessories Ltd and Others* HL 2005, 77 TC 146, in *Sempra Metals Ltd v HMRC* (Sp C 698), [2008] SSCD 1062 and in *JT Dove Limited v HMRC* FTT (TC 893), [2011] SFTD 348. But see now **75.65** below.

Simon's Taxes. See **B2.422**.

Employee benefit contributions: timing of deductions

[75.65] There are statutory rules for the timing of deductions for 'employee benefit contributions' (EBCs). They apply instead of the more general rules at **75.64** above. For these purposes, an '*employee benefit contribution*' was originally defined as a payment of money, or the transfer of an asset, by the employer to a scheme manager (e.g. the trustees of an employee benefit trust) who is entitled or required, under the terms of an employee benefit scheme, to hold or use the money or asset to provide benefits to employees (including former employees). This definition is extended so as also to include any other act (for example, a declaration of trust), or any omission, which results in property being held, or becoming capable of being used, under such a scheme or which increases the total net value of property already so held or capable. The definition of an employee benefit scheme is extended to include a trust, scheme or other arrangement for the benefit of persons who are, or include, persons linked with present or former employees of the employer. The question of whether a person is linked with another is determined as in **26.2** DISGUISED REMUNERATION under Persons 'linked with A'. The definition is further extended to also include, insofar as it would not otherwise come within the definition, a relevant arrangement within **26.2**(c) or, in relation to EBCs made on or after 6 April 2018, **26.3**(b), and any other arrangement connected (directly or indirectly) with that relevant arrangement.

A deduction is allowed only to the extent that, during the period in question or within nine months after the end of it, 'qualifying benefits' are provided, or 'qualifying expenses' are paid, out of the contributions. (If the employer's contribution is itself a qualifying benefit, it is sufficient that the contribution be made during the period or within those ensuing nine months.) Subject to what is said below, any amount thus disallowed remains available for deduction in any subsequent period during which it is used to provide qualifying benefits. For these purposes, qualifying benefits are treated as provided, and expenses are treated as paid, as far as possible out of EBCs, with no account being taken of any other receipts or expenses of the scheme manager.

Computations prepared before the end of the said nine-month period must be prepared by reference to the facts at the time of computation. If any contributions are used for qualifying purposes after that time, but within the nine months, the computation may be adjusted accordingly (subject to the normal time limits for amending self-assessment tax returns). This does not apply in calculating profits on the cash basis (see **76.14** TRADING INCOME — CASH BASIS FOR SMALLER BUSINESSES).

In relation to EBCs made on or after **6 April 2017**, the above is subject to an overriding rule preventing any deduction of EBCs for a period of account beginning more than five years after the end of the period of account in which the contributions were made. Also in relation to EBCs made on or after that date, where the provision of qualifying benefits out of (or by way of) the contributions gives rise to both a charge to tax on employment income and a charge to NICs, a deduction is denied for the EBCs, for any period of account for which it would otherwise be available, unless the tax and NICs are paid no later than 12 months after the end of that period of account. It is also specified that where a deduction would otherwise be allowable for an amount of employees' remuneration paid on or after 6 April 2017 in respect of which EBCs are made (or are to be made), the deduction is to be treated as a deduction in respect of EBCs and not as a deduction in respect of remuneration, thus bringing it within the restrictions.

These restrictions do not apply to disallow deductions for consideration given for goods or services provided in the course of a trade or profession or for contributions to a registered pension scheme (see **57.4** PENSION PROVISION), qualifying overseas pension scheme (if the employee is a relevant migrant member — see **57.27** PENSION PROVISION) or accident benefit scheme (as defined).

Qualifying benefits and expenses

A '*qualifying benefit*' is a payment of money or transfer of assets (other than by way of loan) that:

(a) gives rise to *both* a charge to tax on employment income and a charge to NICs (or would do so but for available exemptions for duties performed outside the UK); or
(b) is made in connection with termination of employment; or
(c) is made under an employer-financed retirement benefits scheme (see **57.34** PENSION PROVISION).

However, a payment or transfer within (c) above is a qualifying benefit only if it gives rise to a tax charge under **57.35** PENSION PROVISION or as PENSION INCOME (**56**) or is an excluded benefit (see **57.35**).

A 'chargeable relevant step' is also the provision of a qualifying benefit. A '*chargeable relevant step*' is a relevant step within **26.7** DISGUISED REMUNERATION which gives rise to a charge under that chapter.

'*Qualifying expenses*' are those expenses (if any) of the scheme manager in operating the scheme that would have been deductible in computing profits if incurred by the employer.

Money benefits are treated for the above purposes as provided at the time the money is treated as received (applying the rules at **28.9** EMPLOYMENT INCOME).

To the extent that the provision of a qualifying benefit is a chargeable relevant step (see above), the benefit is treated as provided when the relevant step is taken or, if later, when A begins his employment with B (where A and B are the persons mentioned in **26.2** or **26.3** DISGUISED REMUNERATION).

Where a qualifying benefit takes the form of the transfer of an asset which meets a condition at (a) to (c) above, the amount provided is the aggregate of:

(i) the amount that would otherwise be deductible by the employer (in a case where the scheme manager acquired the asset from the employer);
(ii) the amount expended on the asset by the scheme manager; and
(iii) (in a case where the transfer is a chargeable relevant step and so far as not already taken into account under (i) or (ii)) the cost of the relevant step; this is determined as in **26.4** DISGUISED REMUNERATION.

If, however, the amount charged to tax under *ITEPA 2003* (or which would be so charged if the duties of employment were performed in the UK) is lower than that aggregate, any amount deductible under these provisions at any time is limited to that lower amount; this rule is aimed at a situation where the asset falls in value after its acquisition by the scheme manager but before its transfer to the employee (Treasury Explanatory Notes to the 2003 Finance Bill).

If the provision of a qualifying benefit is a chargeable relevant step which is not covered by the above and does not involve a sum of money, the amount provided is the cost of the relevant step. However, the amount provided cannot exceed the amount that is charged to tax under *ITEPA 2003* in relation to the relevant step or would be so charged if A (the person in **26.2** or **26.3** DISGUISED REMUNERATION) had not been non-UK resident in any tax year. This limit applies equally if the chargeable relevant step does involve a sum of money.

[*ITTOIA 2005, ss 38–44, 866, Sch 2 paras 13–15; F(No 2)A 2017, s 36, Sch 2 paras 35, 64(1); FA 2018, Sch 1 paras 6, 15*].

Case law

Payments to a trust the beneficiaries of which were members of employees' families were held to fall within these restrictions in *Sempra Metals Ltd v HMRC* (Sp C 698), [2008] SSCD 1062. If a contrived scheme is effected to achieve the opposite result to that intended by Parliament, it fails if only because for that very reason the contributions then have a duality of purpose (see **75.44** above) that itself undermines a deduction (*Scotts Atlantic Management Ltd v HMRC* UT, [2015] STC 1321), and see also *Alway Sheet Metal Ltd v HMRC* FTT (TC 5686), [2017] SFTD 719, [2017] UKFTT 198 (TC).

Simon's Taxes. See **B2.422**.

Employees' council tax

[75.66] An employer who pays the council tax for an employee will normally be able to claim a deduction for it. If such payments are also made on behalf of members of the employee's family, they too are deductible if they are part of the employee's remuneration package (which would normally mean they were paid under the contract of employment). (Revenue Press Release 16 March 1993).

Employment income

[75.67] Employment income received by a trader should in law be excluded from his trading income but in practice the strict position is modified in certain circumstances. See HMRC Employment Income Manual EIM 03002. See *Walker v Carnaby Harrower* Ch D 1969, 46 TC 561 and *CIR v Brander & Cruickshank* HL 1970, 46 TC 574 for the inclusion in professional profits of remuneration as auditor etc. For the tax treatment of directors' fees received by partnerships and other companies and the distinction between employment income and trading income, see **28.3**(vi) and **28.66** EMPLOYMENT INCOME. See **28.71** EMPLOYMENT INCOME as regards certain payments to redundant steel workers.

Retirement and benevolent provisions for employees

[75.68] See **57.14** PENSION PROVISION for the deductibility of payments by the employer under registered pension schemes. *Bona fide* voluntary pensions and retirement gratuities, including pensions to widows, are deductible (*Smith* *v Incorporated Council of Law Reporting* KB 1914, 6 TC 477). The cost of an annuity to replace a pension is deductible but not the cost of a policy to secure payment *to the employer* of an annuity equal to pensions payable by him (*Hancock v General Reversionary & Investment Co Ltd* KB 1918, 7 TC 358; *Morgan Crucible Co Ltd v CIR* KB 1932, 17 TC 311). For provisions for directors of 'family companies' see *Samuel Dracup & Sons Ltd v Dakin* Ch D 1957, 37 TC 377.

Payments directly or indirectly for the benefit of employees are generally allowed as deductions, including donations to hospitals and charities, unless capital or abnormal (*Rowntree & Co v Curtis* CA 1924, 8 TC 678; *Bourne & Hollingsworth v Ogden* KB 1929, 14 TC 349). See also *Hutchinson & Co v Turner* HC 1950, 31 TC 495 and **75.88** below. Subscriptions to BUPA and similar group schemes for employees are deductible (see **28.77** EMPLOYMENT INCOME for position regarding the employees).

See also **75.65** above (employee benefit contributions).

Redundancy payments

[75.69] Redundancy payments, or other employer's payments, under *Employment Rights Act 1996* (or NI equivalent) are allowable. Rebates recoverable are trading receipts. [*ITTOIA 2005, ss 76–78, 80; ITEPA 2003, s 309*].

Non-statutory redundancy and similar payments are normally deductible unless made on the cessation of trading (but now see following paragraphs) (*CIR v Anglo-Brewing Co Ltd* KB 1925, 12 TC 803; *Godden v Wilson's Stores* CA 1962, 40 TC 161; *Geo Peters & Co v Smith* Ch D 1963, 41 TC 264) or as part of the bargain for the sale of shares of the company carrying on the business (*Bassett Enterprise Ltd v Petty* KB 1938, 21 TC 730; *James Snook & Co Ltd v Blasdale* CA 1952, 33 TC 244). See also *Overy v Ashford Dunn & Co* KB 1933, 17 TC 497 and contrast *CIR v Patrick Thomson Ltd* CS 1956, 37 TC 145. A payment to secure the resignation of a life-director who had fallen out with his co-directors was allowed in *Mitchell v B W Noble Ltd* CA 1927, 11 TC 372. See also *O'Keeffe v Southport Printers Ltd* Ch D 1984, 58 TC 88. For provisions for future leaving payments see **75.57** above.

Payments made, to employees taken on for trade purposes, under a pre-existing contractual or statutory obligation which was a consequence of their being so taken on are not disallowed by virtue of the 'wholly and exclusively' rule at **75.44** above merely because it is the cessation of the trade that crystallises the liability to pay (Revenue Tax Bulletin February 1999 pp 630, 631).

Payments in addition to the statutory payment made on cessation of trading are allowable deductions if they would have been allowable had there been no cessation. Allowance is up to three times the statutory payment. On a change in the persons carrying on the trade, the trade is treated as ceasing only if no person who carried on the trade before the change does so after the change. [*ITTOIA 2005, ss 79, 79A*]. Relief is similarly given under these provisions for such payments made on cessation of *part* of a trade.

A gratuitous payment made on partial cessation of a company's trade to a managing director who nevertheless continued thereafter to be a director was held non-deductible in *Relkobrook Ltd v Mapstone* (Sp C 452), [2005] SSCD 272.

Relief under *ITTOIA 2005, ss 76–80* above is given for the period of account in which the payment is made (or, if paid after cessation, for the period of account in which falls the last day on which the trade is carried on). Where, instead, relief is due under general principles, a provision for future payments may be allowed as a deduction for a period of account provided that:

- it appears in the commercial accounts in accordance with generally accepted accounting principles;
- it was accurately calculated (normally requiring the identification of the individual employees affected) using the degree of hindsight permitted by SSAP 17;
- a definite decision to proceed with the redundancies was taken during the period; and
- payment was made within nine months of the end of the period.

(Revenue Tax Bulletin February 1995 p 195).

See generally HMRC Business Income Manual BIM47200–47215.

Simon's Taxes. See B2.426.

Counselling services etc.

[75.70] Expenditure on counselling and other outplacement services which falls within the earnings exemption of *ITEPA 2003, s 310* (see **28.63** EMPLOYMENT INCOME) is deductible in computing the profits of the employer's trade. [*ITTOIA 2005, s 73*].

Simon's Taxes. See B2.428.

Key employee insurance

[75.71] Premiums on policies in favour of the employer insuring against death or critical illness of key employees are generally allowable, and the proceeds of any such policies trading receipts. However, in *Beauty Consultants Ltd v Inspector of Taxes* (Sp C 321), [2002] SSCD 352, premiums on a policy insuring a company against the death of either of its controlling shareholder-directors were disallowed; the 'dual purpose rule' at **75.44** above applied, in that the premiums benefited the shareholders personally by improving the value of their shares. In *Greycon Ltd v Klaentschi* (Sp C 372), [2003] SSCD 370, it was held that the company's sole purpose in taking out key man policies was to meet a requirement of an agreement under which funding and other benefits were obtained from another company, that the policies had a capital purpose and that, consequently, the proceeds of those policies were not trading receipts. See generally HMRC Business Income Manual BIM45525, 45530.

Simon's Taxes. See B2.425.

National insurance contributions (NICs)

[75.72] Secondary (i.e. employers') Class 1 NICs are deductible in computing profits. Relief is similarly available for Class 1A NICs (payable by an employer where benefits-in-kind are provided to employees) and for Class 1B NICs (payable in respect of PAYE settlement agreements — see **53.25** PAY AS YOU EARN). (But no deduction is allowed for any NICs paid for the benefit of the trader himself, e.g. Class 2 or Class 4 contributions.) [*ITTOIA 2005, ss 53, 272, 868; F(No 2)A 2017, Sch 2 paras 37, 64(1)*].

Simon's Taxes. See B2.425.

Training costs

[75.73] Costs incurred by an employer in respect of employee training are generally allowable as a trading expense. For HMRC's view of the circumstances in which such relief may be prohibited by the 'wholly and exclusively' rule at **75.44** above, see Revenue Tax Bulletin February 1997 pp 400, 401 (which also indicates that it is extremely unlikely that such expenditure would be disallowed as a deduction on the grounds that it was of a capital nature).

Retraining course expenses paid or reimbursed by an employer and satisfying the conditions of the earnings exemption in *ITEPA 2003, s 311* (see **28.83** EMPLOYMENT INCOME) are deductible in computing the profits of the employer's trade. Similar provisions relating to recovery of tax, information and penalties as apply in relation to the earnings exemption apply in relation to this deduction. [*ITTOIA 2005, ss 74, 75, Sch 2 paras 22, 23; SI 2009 No 2035, Sch para 42*]. See **75.119** below as regards contributions to training and enterprise councils.

Simon's Taxes. See B2.428.

Employees seconded to charities or educational bodies

[75.74] If an employer seconds an employee temporarily to a charity (as defined at **14.2** CHARITIES AND CHARITABLE GIVING), any expenditure of the employer which is attributable to the employment is deductible in computing the employer's profits. This relief is extended to secondments to educational establishments (as defined and including education authorities, educational institutions maintained by such authorities, and certain other educational bodies). [*ITTOIA 2005, ss 70, 71*].

Simon's Taxes. See B2.430.

Payments for restrictive undertakings

[75.75] Payments to employees for restrictive undertakings, falling to be treated as earnings of the employee under *ITEPA 2003, s 225* (see **28.73** EMPLOYMENT INCOME), are deductible in computing profits. [*ITTOIA 2005, s 69*].

Entertainment and gifts

[75.76] Subject to the exceptions below, no deduction is allowed in computing profits for expenses incurred in providing entertainment or gifts. This includes sums paid to or on behalf of an employee (including a director), or put at his disposal, *exclusively* for meeting expenses incurred, or to be incurred, by the employee in providing the entertainment or gift. See **28.19** EMPLOYMENT INCOME for the employee position. It also includes expenses incidental to providing entertainment or gifts.

Entertainment expenditure is not within the above prohibition if:

- the entertainment is of a kind which it is the trader's trade to provide and it is provided in the ordinary course of that trade either for payment or free of charge for advertising purposes; or
- the entertainment is provided for the trader's employees (except where such entertainment is incidental to the entertainment of non-employees).

Gifts are not within the above prohibition if:

- they are of an item which it is the trader's trade to provide and are made for advertising purposes; or
- they incorporate a conspicuous advertisement for the trader *and* do not consist of food, drink, tobacco or a token or voucher exchangeable for goods *and* the cost to the trader of all such gifts to the same person in the same basis period does not exceed £50; or
- they are provided for the trader's employees (except where such gifts are incidental to the providing of gifts for non-employees); or
- they are made to a charity (i.e. a body of persons or trust established for charitable purposes only) or to either of the similar organisations specified in *ITTOIA 2005, s 47(5)*.

[*ITTOIA 2005, ss 45–47, 867; ITA 2007, s 989; F(No 2)A 2017, Sch 2 paras 36, 64(1)*].

In *Bourne & Hollingsworth v Ogden* KB 1929, 14 TC 349 an abnormally large donation was disallowed. See also **75.88** below. For donations of part of cost of ticket in football pools and lotteries, see **75.28** above.

The cost of hiring a room for a function to which potential customers were invited was held to be deductible (although the catering costs of the function were disallowed as being expenditure on business entertainment); as far as the room-hire was concerned, it was held to be for the purposes of attracting business; the entertainment was incidental to that purpose (*Netlogic Consulting Ltd v HMRC* (Sp C 477), [2005] SSCD 524).

Deductions were allowed for items provided in the ordinary course of a trade of providing entertainment in *Fleming v Associated Newspapers Ltd* HL 1972, 48 TC 382. See also the VAT cases of *C & E Commissioners v Shaklee International and Another* CA, [1981] STC 776 and *Celtic Football and Athletic Co Ltd v C & E Commissioners* CS, [1983] STC 470.

There is also a restriction on capital allowances where plant or machinery is used to provide entertainment, with similar exceptions as above where relevant (see **10.4** CAPITAL ALLOWANCES ON PLANT AND MACHINERY).

For an article on the scope and application of these rules, see Revenue Tax Bulletin August 1999 pp 679–682 as supplemented by Revenue Tax Bulletin February 2000 p 729. For further comprehensive guidance on business entertainment, see HMRC Business Income Manual BIM45000–45090.

Simon's Taxes. See **B2.432, B2.441.**

Farming and market gardening

[75.77] Farming or market gardening in the UK is treated for income tax purposes as trading. All the UK farming carried on by a particular person (other than as part of a different trade) is treated as a single trade. Farming carried on by a partnership is, however, separate from any farming carried on by individual partners. [*ITTOIA 2005, ss 9, 859(1); ITA 2007, s 996*]. See *Bispham v Eardiston Farming Co* Ch D 1962, 40 TC 322 and *Sargent v Eayrs* Ch D 1972, 48 TC 573. The matters listed below are of particular application to farming or (where relevant) market gardening.

(a) **Averaging of profits.** See **75.78** below.

(b) **Compensation for compulsory slaughter.** Where compensation is received for compulsory slaughter of animals to which the HERD BASIS (**34**) does not and could not apply, any excess of the amount received over the book value or cost of those animals may be excluded from the year of slaughter and treated, by equal instalments, as profits of the next three years. The profit on an animal born in the year of slaughter is deemed to be 25% of the compensation received. The relief must be claimed no later than the first anniversary of 31 January following the tax year for which the year of slaughter is the basis period. [*ITTOIA 2005, ss 225ZA–225ZG*]. For a worked example, see HMRC Business Income Manual BIM55185.

The above does not apply in calculating profits on the cash basis (see **76.14** TRADING INCOME — CASH BASIS FOR SMALLER BUSINESSES).

Compensation paid under the BSE Suspects Scheme and the BSE Selective Cull (where the animal was born after 14 October 1990) is for compulsory slaughter, and for these purposes includes Selective Cull 'top-up' payments. Payments under the Calf Processing Scheme, the Over Thirty Month Scheme and the BSE Selective Cull where the animal was born before 15 October 1990 are *not* for compulsory slaughter. (Revenue Tax Bulletin February 1997 pp 396, 397).

(c) **Drainage.** Where land is made re-available for cultivation by the restoration of drainage or by re-draining, the net expenditure incurred (after crediting any grants receivable) will be allowed as revenue expenditure in farm accounts provided it excludes (i) any substantial element of improvement (e.g. the substitution of tile drainage for mole drainage) and (ii) the capital element in cases in which the present owner is known to have acquired the land at a depressed price because of its swampy condition (HMRC SP 5/81).

(d) **Farmhouses.** The apportionment of the running costs of a farmhouse between business and private use should be based on the facts of the case for the year of account in question (Revenue Tax Bulletin February 1993 p 54).

(e) **Gangmasters.** A special unit within HMRC, the Agricultural Compliance Unit (based within Special Compliance Office in Sheffield) monitors compliance by agricultural gangmasters in relation to PAYE and National Insurance in respect of their workers and their own returns. (Revenue Press Release 2 September 1988). For whether a worker also responsible for selection of other workers acts as gangmaster, see *Andrews v King* Ch D 1991, 64 TC 332.

(f) **Grants and subsidies.** See generally 75.120 below. As regards the time at which a receipt should be brought in for tax purposes, a distinction should be drawn between grants to meet particular costs and those subsidising the sale proceeds of a specific crop. The former should reduce the costs in question (and if those costs are included in the closing stock valuation, the net cost should be used), whereas the latter should be recognised as income of the year in which the crop is sold. (Revenue Tax Bulletin February 1993 p 53). A grant subsidising trading income generally is a trading receipt of the period when the entitlement to the grant was established, provided that it can be quantified with reasonable accuracy. As regards instalments of grant, the tax treatment should follow accounting practice, which provides that information available before accounts are completed and signed should be taken into account as regards those to which entitlement arose in the period of account. (Revenue Tax Bulletin February 1994 p 108).

As regards animal grants and subsidies, these are generally recognised either at the end of the retention period or on receipt. Either of these bases will be accepted for tax purposes provided that it is consistently applied, as will any other basis which reflects generally accepted accounting practice provided that it does not conflict with tax law. A change of basis should be made only where the need for change outweighs the requirement for accounts to be prepared on a consistent basis. (Revenue Tax Bulletin December 1994 p 182).

The following relate to specific types of farm support payment.

(i) *Advances under British Sugar Industry (Assistance) Act 1931*, linked with sugar production and prices, were held to be assessable as trading receipts (*Smart v Lincolnshire Sugar Co Ltd* HL 1937, 20 TC 643).

(ii) *Dairy herd conversion scheme*. Grants for changing from dairying to meat production were held to be assessable as trading receipts (*White v G & M Davis* Ch D 1979, 52 TC 597; *CIR v Biggar* CS 1982, 56 TC 254).

(iii) *Flood rehabilitation grants* in excess of rehabilitation costs (admitted to be capital) were held to be capital receipts (*Watson v Samson Bros* Ch D 1959, 38 TC 346).

(iv) *Oilseed support scheme*. Payments of aid under the 1992 scheme are a subsidy towards the selling price, and as such should be recognised as income at the time of sale. If the final amount is not known when the accounts are prepared, but it is reasonably certain that a further payment will be received, the tax computations should be kept open to admit the final figure. If a reasonable estimate is included in the accounts and the difference when the final amount is known has only a small effect on the overall tax liability, the inspector may agree to recognise the difference in arriving at profits of the following year. (Revenue Tax Bulletin February 1993 p 53).

(v) *Ploughing subsidies* were held to be assessable as trading receipts (*Higgs v Wrightson* KB 1944, 26 TC 73).

(g) **EU Common Agricultural Policy Basic Payment Scheme.** The assumption is that the taxation treatment of Basic Payment follows that of the earlier Single Payment Scheme. The income tax treatment of Single Payment was that, broadly, all Single Payments were chargeable to tax, whether as trading receipts or, depending on the circumstances, as miscellaneous income. For the Basic Payment Scheme generally see www.gov.uk/government/collections/basic-payment-scheme. For further discussion on eligibility and taxation issues see **Simon's Taxes** B5.120–B5.124.

(h) **Milk.** *SLOM compensation*. HMRC's view is that such compensation is on revenue account, and should be recognised for income tax purposes in one sum in the accounting period in which legal entitlement to it arises and the amount can be quantified with reasonable certainty using information available at the time of preparation of the accounts. Additions for interest to the date of payment should be dealt with under the normal Sch D, Case III (now savings income) rules. (Revenue Tax Bulletin May 1994 p 127).

Superlevy. HMRC's view is that superlevy is an allowable trading deduction, but that the purchase of additional quota to avoid superlevy does not give rise to a deduction for either the superlevy thus avoided or the sum which would have been paid to lease rather than purchase the additional quota (Revenue Tax Bulletin August 1994 p 151). A deduction for the cost of milk quota purchased to avoid superlevy was refused, on grounds of its being capital expenditure, in *Terry and Terry (t/a C & J Terry & Sons) v HMRC* (Sp C 482), [2005] SSCD 629.

Residuary Milk Marketing Board receipts. B Reserve Fund distributions and sums repaid to producers under the Rolling Fund arrangements on the flotation of Dairy Crest (in the latter case whether taken in cash or in shares) are income receipts of the trade. Any element of a B Reserve Fund payment described as interest may also be treated as a trade receipt. Post-cessation treatment (see **59.1** POST-CESSATION RECEIPTS AND EXPENDITURE) will apply where appropriate. (Revenue Tax Bulletin August 1997 p 461).

(i) **Pig industry — plant and machinery capital allowances.** HMRC have published guidance illustrating the range of assets on which the pig industry might claim plant and machinery capital allowances (HMRC Brief 03/10, February 2010).

(j) **Share farming.** HMRC consider that both parties to a share farming agreement based on the Country Landowners Association model may be considered to be carrying on a farming trade for tax purposes. In the case of the landowner, he must take an active part in the share farming venture, at least to the extent of concerning himself with details of farming policy and exercising his right to enter onto his land for some material purpose, even if only for the purposes of inspection and policy-making. (Country Landowners Association Press Release 19 December 1991).

(k) **Short rotation coppice.** The cultivation of 'short rotation coppice' (i.e. a perennial crop of tree species planted at high density, the stems of which are harvested above ground level at intervals of less than ten years) is treated for tax purposes as farming and not as forestry, so that UK land under such cultivation is farm or agricultural land and not woodlands. [*ITA 2007, s 996(4)(6); ITTOIA 2005, s 876(3)(4)(6)*]. For HMRC's view of the taxation implications of short rotation coppice, see Revenue Tax Bulletin October 1995 p 252.

(l) **Stock valuations.** See HMRC Business Income Manual BIM55400–55460. See also **34** HERD BASIS and, for trading stock generally, **75.116** below. In general, livestock is treated as trading stock unless the herd basis applies, and home-bred animals may be valued, if there is no adequate record of cost, at 75% for sheep and pigs (60% for cattle) of open market value. Deadstock may be taken at 75% of market value.

Where an animal grant or subsidy for which application has been made has not been taken into account for a particular period but has been applied for, and that application materially affects the value of the animal, the grant or subsidy should be taken into account as a supplement to the market value when deemed cost is computed. Grants or subsidies applied for but not recognised as income in the period concerned should also be taken into account in arriving at net realisable value for stock valuation purposes. (Revenue Tax Bulletin December 1994 p 182).

(m) **Subscriptions** to the **National Farmers Union** are allowable in full.

(n) **Sugar beet outgoers scheme.** Receipts and payments derived from the disposal of contract tonneage entitlement under contracts between farmers and British Sugar are to be dealt with on revenue and not capital account, i.e. as taxable receipts and allowable deductions in computing profits. Payments for entitlement which are amortised in the accounts over the period for which the entitlement may reasonably be expected to be of value to the business are similarly allowed for tax purposes. (Revenue Tax Bulletin October 2001 pp 891, 892).

(o) **Trading profits.** Proceeds from the sale of trees (mostly willows planted by the taxpayer) were held to be farming receipts (*Elmes v Trembath* KB 1934, 19 TC 72), but no part of the cost of an orchard with nearly ripe fruit purchased by a fruit grower was an allowable deduction in computing his profits, which included receipts from the sale of the fruit (*CIR v Pilcher* CA 1949, 31 TC 314). Proceeds from sales of turf were held to be trading receipts from farming (*Lowe v J W Ashmore Ltd* Ch D 1970, 46 TC 597).

(p) **Woodlands grants.** The Forestry Commission's Woodland Grant Scheme (WGS) provides grants for the establishment and maintenance of woodlands. These grants are not taxable. Where the woodland concerned is being established on agricultural land, WGS participants can also apply to join the Farm Woodland Premium Scheme (FWPS). This is administered by the Department for Environment, Food and

Rural Affairs (Defra)and provides annual payments of up to £300 per hectare for up to 15 years to the farmer to compensate for lost farming income as a result of converting the land to woodland. Because the annual payments are made in lieu of farming income, they must be included in trading profits and are chargeable to income tax. It matters not that the woodlands are likely to be commercial woodlands and thus outside the charge to income tax. (Sources: Defra and HMRC Business Income Manual BIM55165). For the general tax exemption for woodlands, see **30.53** EXEMPT INCOME.

For these and other aspects of farming taxation, see HMRC Business Income Manual BIM55000–55730, 84000–84185 and 85600–85650.

Simon's Taxes. See **B1.502–B1.505, B5.1.**

Farming and market gardening — averaging of profits

[75.78] Where for two consecutive tax years the profits of an individual from a trade of farming or market gardening in the UK for one year are less than 75% of the profits for the other (or the profits for one year, but not both, are nil, e.g. where a loss is incurred), a two-year averaging claim may be made under *ITTOIA 2005, s 222* as described below.

Alternatively, in the case of any such individual, where in relation to five consecutive tax years:

- either A or B is less than 75% of the other (where A is the average of the profits of the first four years and B is the profits of the fifth year); or
- the profits for one or more years, but not all five years, are nil,

a five-year averaging claim may be made under *ITTOIA 2005, s 222A* as described below. This has effect where the last of the five years is 2016/17 or a subsequent year; for example, a five-year averaging claim could be made with 2016/17 as the final year, which would involve averaging the profits of the years 2012/13 to 2016/17 inclusive.

The potential for two-year or five-year averaging is extended to the intensive rearing of livestock or fish on a commercial basis for the production of food for human consumption. Both two-year and five-year averaging apply also to partnerships, but a partnership cannot make a claim. An individual partner must make his own claim, based on his share of the profits, and can do so regardless of whether or not the other partners make claims. Averaging does not apply in calculating profits on the cash basis (see **76.14** TRADING INCOME — CASH BASIS FOR SMALLER BUSINESSES).

For an article on five-year averaging and the circumstances in which it may be beneficial see Taxation Magazine, 12 May 2016, p 12.

Effect of averaging

In the case of a two-year averaging claim where the second of the two years in question is 2016/17 or a subsequent year, the profits for each of the two years are adjusted to the average of the two years.

In the case of a two-year averaging claim where the second of the two years in question is 2015/16 or an earlier year and the profits for either year do not exceed 70% of the profits for the other (or are nil), the profits for each year are adjusted to the average of the two years.

In the case of a two-year averaging claim where the second of the two years in question is 2015/16 or an earlier year and either year's profits exceed 70% of the other's, but are less than 75%, the profits are adjusted by adding to the lower and subtracting from the higher the amount obtained by first multiplying the difference by three and then deducting 75% of the higher figure. (Thus, if the profits are £21,900 and £30,000, the averaged profits would be £23,700 and £28,200.)

In the case of a five-year averaging claim, the profits for each of the five years are adjusted to the average of the five years.

'*Profits*' for this purpose are those before any deduction for losses but after any spreading relief in 75.77(b) above (compensation for compulsory slaughter of animals). The averaging adjustments are effective for all income tax purposes but do not prevent a claim for loss relief. For example, in the case of a two-year averaging claim, if there was a loss of £5,000 in the basis period for one year and a profit of £15,000 in the basis period for the other, the first-mentioned year is taken to be a year of nil profit and the profits chargeable for each year become £7,500; the loss of £5,000 remains eligible for loss relief in the normal way.

Claims

A two-year averaging claim must be made on or before the first anniversary of 31 January following the *second* year. The earlier of the two years to which the averaging claim relates (Year X) may be a tax year in relation to which a two-year or five-year averaging claim has already been made. For example, the 2018/19 profits may be averaged with those of 2019/20, and the 2019/20 profits may then be averaged with those of 2020/21. In any such case, the profits of Year X (2019/20 in this example) to be used in the later claim are the profits as averaged as a result of the earlier claim. However, a tax year cannot be included in a two-year averaging claim if a later tax year has already been included in either a two-year or a five-year averaging claim. So once the 2019/20 and 2020/21 profits have been averaged, a claim cannot then be made in hindsight to average the profits for 2018/19 and 2019/20.

A five-year averaging claim must be made on or before the first anniversary of 31 January following the fifth year. Any of the first four tax years to which the averaging claim relates may be a tax year in relation to which a two-year or five-year averaging claim has already been made. For example, the profits of the five years up to and including 2019/20 may be averaged, and the profits of the last four of those years (as adjusted for the averaging claim) may then be averaged with the profits of 2020/21. However, a tax year cannot be included in a five-year averaging claim if a two-year or five-year averaging claim has already been made in relation to a tax year which is later than the last of the tax years to which the new claim relates. So if, for example, the 2019/20 and 2020/21 profits have been averaged, a claim cannot then be made to average the profits for the five years up to and including 2019/20.

See **16.2** CLAIMS for the method of giving effect to an averaging claim.

No averaging claim is available for the tax year in which the taxpayer starts, or permanently ceases, to carry on the trade. This includes the tax years in which an individual joins and leaves a partnership.

If, after an averaging claim, the profits of any of the years in question are adjusted for some other reason, the claim lapses. This does not prevent the making of a new averaging claim, provided the new claim is made on or before the first anniversary of 31 January following the tax year in which the said adjustment is made.

A claim or election for other relief for any of the years affected by an averaging claim can be made, amended or revoked at any time on or before the latest possible date on which the averaging claim itself could have been made. See also **16.2** CLAIMS for the way in which claims for other relief are given effect.

[*ITTOIA 2005, ss 221, 222, 222A, 223–225; FA 2016, s 25(2)–(7)(12)*].

See HMRC Business Income Manual BIM84000–84185.

Simon's Taxes. See **B5.170–B5.172.**

Examples

[75.79]

(i) *Example with five-year averaging.* Boycie has been carrying on a farming trade for ten years. In December 2019, the farm suffered heavy flooding. The farm initially had taxable profits as follows for the six years to 30 June 2020.

Year ended	£
30.6.15	34,000
30.6.16	52,000
30.6.17	44,000
30.6.18	50,000
30.6.19	47,000
30.6.20	26,000

Boycie made an averaging claim for the two years 2015/16 and 2016/17. The profits for one of those years are less than 75% of the profits of the other, meaning that a claim was possible. The taxable profit of each of those two years was adjusted to £43,000.

For 2019/20 and 2020/21, a two-year averaging claim is possible, the profits of one year being less than 75% of the profits of the other. If such a claim was made, the taxable profit of each of those two years would be adjusted to £36,500.

As an alternative, after taking into account his other income and his tax rates and allowances for each year, Boycie decides to make a five-year averaging claim for the years 2016/17 to 2020/21 inclusive. The average of the profits of the first four years is £(43,000 + 44,000 + 50,000 + 47,000) divided by 4 = £46,000. (The 2016/17 profit is taken to be £43,000, i.e. the averaged profit resulting from the earlier claim.) The profits of the fifth year are less than 75% of £46,000, so five-year averaging is possible. Following the claim, the taxable profit of each of the five years is now £(43,000 + 44,000 + 50,000 + 47,000 + 26,000) divided by 5 = £42,000.

(ii) *General example.* Giles, who has been farming for many years, has the following profits as adjusted for income tax purposes.

Year ended	Tax-adjusted profit/ (loss)
	£
30.9.13	8,500
30.9.14	12,000
30.9.15	15,000
30.9.16	10,000
30.9.17	4,000
30.9.18	(1,000)
30.9.19	(10,000)
30.9.20	1,600

Two-year averaged profits for all years would be:

		No averaging claims	Averaging claims for all years
		£	£
2013/14	note (i)	8,500	10,000
2014/15	notes (i)(ii)	12,000	12,750
2015/16	note (ii)(iii)	15,000	12,750
2016/17	notes (iii)(iv)	10,000	7,000
2017/18	notes (iv)(v)	4,000	3,500
2018/19	notes (v)(vi)	Nil	1,750
2019/20	notes (vii)(viii)	Nil	1,750
2020/21	note (ix)	1,600	1,600
		£51,100	£51,100

Notes

(i)	2013/14	8,500
	2014/15	12,000
		£20,500

As £8,500 exceeds 70% of £12,000 but is less than 75%, the adjustment is computed as follows.

Difference £3,500 × 3	10,500	
Deduct ¾ × £12,000	9,000	
Adjustment	1,500	(1,500)
Existing 2013/14	8,500	
Existing 2014/15		12,000
Revised averaged profits 2013/14 and 2014/15	£10,000	£10,500

Note that this methodology is no longer valid where the second of the two years in question is 2016/17 or a later year. Straightforward averaging applies instead.

(ii)	2014/15	10,500

	2015/16	15,000	
		£25,500	÷ 2 = £12,750

As £10,500 does not exceed 70% of £15,000, the straight average applies.

(iii)	2015/16	12,750	
	2016/17	10,000	
		£22,750	

As £10,000 is not less than 75% of £12,750, no averaging is permitted.

(iv)	2016/17	10,000	
	2017/18	4,000	
		£14,000	÷ 2 = £7,000

As £4,000 is less than 75% of £10,000, averaging applies.

(v)	2017/18	7,000	
	2018/19	Nil	
		£7,000	÷ 2 = £3,500

(vi) The loss for the year to 30 September 2018 is not taken into account for averaging, but would be available to reduce the averaged profits for 2018/19 on a claim under *ITA 2007, s 64* (see **45.2** LOSSES).

(vii)	2018/19	3,500	
	2019/20	Nil	
		£3,500	÷ 2 = £1,750

(viii) The loss for the year to 30 September 2019 is not taken into account for averaging, but would be available to set off against the balance of the averaged profits for 2018/19 and against the averaged profits for 2019/20 on a claim under *ITA 2007, s 64* (see **45.2** LOSSES).

(ix)	2019/20	1,750	
	2020/21	1,600	
		£3,350	

As £1,600 is not less than 75% of £1,750, a two-year averaging claim is not possible. See Example (i) above as regards five-year averaging.

Films and sound recordings

[75.80] The current film reliefs regime replaced the earlier income tax rules in *ITTOIA 2005*. The relief is available only to corporate filmmakers. The current regime applies to films beginning principal photography on or after 1 January 2007 and to certain films started before that date but which were not completed before that date. As the regime has no application for income tax, please see Tolley's Corporation Tax instead.

ITTOIA 2005, s 134 and *s 135* below (and relevant definitions) *continue to apply* for income tax purposes in relation to *sound recordings* only. These provisions are described below insofar as they do relate to sound recordings. They do not apply in calculating profits on the cash basis (see **76.14** TRADING INCOME — CASH BASIS FOR SMALLER BUSINESSES).

Treatment of expenditure as revenue

If there were no legislation to the contrary, expenditure on the production or acquisition of sound recording would generally be capital expenditure (and may qualify for plant and machinery capital allowances under general principles — see **10** CAPITAL ALLOWANCES ON PLANT AND MACHINERY). Instead, 'production expenditure' or 'acquisition expenditure' (see (a) and (b) below) incurred by a person carrying on a trade is treated for income tax purposes as revenue expenditure. Where expenditure is treated as revenue, any receipts from the disposal of any interest or right in or over the 'original master version' and any insurance, compensation etc. derived from it are treated as revenue receipts.

[*ITTOIA 2005, s 134, Sch 2 paras 31, 32; SI 2006 No 3265; SI 2007 No 1050, Reg 7*].

Definitions

Definitions for the purposes of the provisions both above and below insofar as they relate to sound recordings.

(a) '*Production expenditure*' is expenditure incurred on the production of the 'original master version' of a sound recording. It does not include interest or incidental costs of obtaining finance (the normal rules for deducting such expenditure applying instead).
(b) '*Acquisition expenditure*' is expenditure incurred on the acquisition of the 'original master version' of a sound recording. Again, it does not include interest or incidental costs of obtaining finance (see (a) above).
(c) The '*original master version*' means, in relation to a sound recording, the original master audio tape or disc. The expression includes any rights in the original master version that are held or acquired with it.

[*ITTOIA 2005, ss 130–132, Sch 2 para 31; SI 2007 No 1050, Reg 12*].

Allocation of expenditure to periods of account

In a trade consisting of or including the exploitation of the original master versions (see (c) above) of sound recordings, production or acquisition expenditure (see (a) and (b) above) otherwise deductible is allocated to periods of account on a just and reasonable basis. In so allocating expenditure to any period of account, regard must be had to the expenditure unallocated at the beginning of the period, the expenditure incurred in the period, the proportion which the estimated value of the original master version realised in the period (whether by way of income or otherwise) bears to the sum of the value so realised and the estimated remaining value at the end of the period, and the need to bring the whole expenditure into account over the time during which the value of the original master version is expected to be realised (known as the 'income matching' method of allocation). The amount thus allocated to the period can then be increased up to an amount equal to the value of the original master version realised in the period (whether by way of income or otherwise) (known as the 'cost recovery' method).

These provisions do not apply if the original master version in question constitutes trading stock under *ITTOIA 2005, s 174* (see **75.117** below).

Expenditure cannot be allocated to a period of account under the above rules if it is allocated to any period under any other of these sound recording provisions. If any expenditure in respect of an original master version is allocated to a period of account under those other provisions, no other production or acquisition expenditure in respect of that original master version can be allocated to that period under the above rules.

[*ITTOIA 2005, s 135, Sch 2 para 32; SI 2006 No 3265; SI 2007 No 1050, Reg 7*].

If, exceptionally, no accounts are drawn up, any reference above to a period of account is to be taken as a reference to the basis period for the tax year. [*ITTOIA 2005, s 133*].

Anti-avoidance

For deferred income agreements in relation to films, see **75.81** below. For claw-back in certain circumstances of reliefs for trading losses derived from income tax film reliefs, see **45.15** LOSSES. For restrictions on relief for partnership losses derived from certain expenditure in a trade involving the exploitation of films, see **52.17** PARTNERSHIPS. For restriction of relief for interest on a loan used to buy into a film partnership in certain circumstances, see **42.10** INTEREST PAYABLE. For modification of the long funding leasing rules where the subject of the lease is a film, see **75.99** below.

Leasing

See **75.83** below as regards restrictions on relief under the above provisions where finance leasing arrangements are involved.

Simon's Taxes. See **B5.501**, **B5.502**.

Film reliefs — deferred income agreements

[75.81] The following provisions are designed to counter tax avoidance by persons who benefited from income tax film tax reliefs and deferred income from the film for more than 15 years; they have effect where any deferred income agreements are entered into on or after 2 December 2004. There are two sets of provisions, depending on whether the deferred income agreement was already in existence when the relief was given or was entered into after that time.

For these purposes, a person is not to be regarded as entering into an agreement on or after 2 December 2004 if he did so in pursuance of an obligation of his which immediately before that date was an unconditional obligation; and an obligation is not to be regarded as conditional if it depended on a condition the fulfilment of which was outside that person's control.

The first set of provisions applies where:

- a deduction is made by a person (P) under any of the now defunct *ITTOIA 2005, ss 138–140* (production and acquisition expenditure on certified films, whether or not limited-budget films), for expenditure relating to a film; and
- there are in existence at that time one or more 'deferred income agreements' in respect of the film, being agreements to which P is or has been a party and which he entered into on or after 2 December 2004.

An amount of excess relief, computed as below, is brought into account as a receipt in computing P's trading profits for the period of account for which the deduction was made. If, however, immediately after the end of the '15-year period', P is still carrying on the trade, he is treated as incurring at that time production or acquisition expenditure of an amount equal to the excess relief, but this notional expenditure can be allocated to periods of account only under the normal allocation rules of *ITTOIA 2005, s 135* in **75.80** above. The excess relief for these purposes is:

$$D \times \left(1 - \frac{T1}{T2}\right)$$

where:

D	=	the deduction made;
T1	=	the number of days in the '15-year period'; and
T2	=	the number of days from the 'operative date' to the 'final deferral date' inclusive.

The '*15-year period*' is the 15 years beginning with the 'operative date'. The '*operative date*' is the date of acquisition where the expenditure deducted is acquisition expenditure; in any other case, it is the date the film is completed (see **75.80**(d) above). The '*final deferral date*' is the 'last date of deferral' in relation to the deferred income agreement or, where there is more than one such agreement, the latest of those dates. The '*last date of deferral*' is the last date on which an amount of guaranteed income will or may arise under the 'deferred income agreement. A '*deferred income agreement*' is an agreement which:

- (whether or not it supplements or varies another agreement) guarantees an amount of income arising from exploitation of the film and has the effect that the 'last date of deferral' (as above) falls after the end of the 15-year period referred to above; or
- supplements or varies an earlier agreement which guarantees an amount of income arising from exploitation of the film and has the effect that the 'last date of deferral' (as above) falls after the end of the 15-year period and after the last date of deferral (if any) in relation to the earlier agreement.

The fact that any earlier agreement may have existed before 2 December 2004 does not prevent the deferred income agreement in question from falling within these provisions if it is entered into on or after that date, and 'agreement' includes a series of agreements. An agreement guarantees income for these purposes if it sets out to achieve the receipt of at least that amount.

The second set of provisions is similar, but applies where the deduction had already been made before the deferred income agreement is entered into. This time, the excess relief is brought into account as a receipt in computing P's trading profits for the period of account in which he enters into the agreement and is reduced by any amounts already recovered under these provisions, including any amounts recovered by virtue of P's entering into any previous deferred income agreements in respect of the film concerned after the deduction or claim was made.

[*ITTOIA 2005, ss 142A–142E*].

For a successful attempt by HMRC to apply this legislation in a particular case, see *HMRC v Micro Fusion 2004-1 LLP* CA, [2010] STC 1541.

Simon's Taxes. See **B5.508**.

Finance leasing etc.

[75.82] The rules on leasing of *plant or machinery* under long funding leases are described at **10.48–10.54** CAPITAL ALLOWANCES ON PLANT AND MACHINERY and **75.98–75.100** below. The Statement of Practice on finance lease rentals described below has no application to any such long funding lease. The *ITA 2007, Pt 11A* anti-avoidance provisions at **75.83, 75.84** below are specifically disapplied in relation to such leases.

Finance lease rentals payable — Statement of Practice

HMRC's practice described below applies to rentals payable by a lessee under a finance lease, i.e. a lease which transfers substantially all the risks and rewards of ownership of an asset to the lessee while maintaining the lessor's legal ownership of the asset. The treatment of such rentals depends upon whether or not SSAP 21 has been applied. This practice has no implications for the tax treatment of rentals receivable by the lessor, nor for the availability of capital allowances to the lessor. (HMRC SP 3/91 and Revenue Press Release 11 April 1991).

Finance lease rentals are revenue payments for the use of the asset, and, both under normal accounting principles and for tax purposes, should be allocated to the periods of account for which the asset is leased in accordance with the accruals concept. Where there is an option for the lessee to continue to lease the asset after expiry of the primary period under the lease, regard should be had, in allocating rentals to periods of account, to the economic life of the asset and its likely period of use by the lessee, as well as to the primary period.

Under SSAP 21, the lessee is required to treat a finance lease as the acquisition of an asset subject to a loan, to be depreciated over its useful life, with rentals apportioned between a finance charge and a capital repayment element. This treatment does not, however, affect the tax treatment, which remains as described above.

Where SSAP 21 has not been applied, the lessee's accounting treatment of rental payments is normally accepted for tax purposes, provided that it is consistent with the principles described above. If not, computational adjustments are made to secure the proper spreading of the rental payments.

Where SSAP 21 has been applied, the finance charge element of the rental payments for a period of account is normally accepted as a revenue deduction for that period. In determining the appropriate proportion of the capital repayment element to be deducted for tax purposes, a properly computed commercial depreciation charge to profit and loss account will normally be accepted. Where, however, the depreciation charge is not so computed, the appropriate proportion for tax purposes will be determined in accordance with the principles described above.

For comment on the principles set out in SP 3/91, and on their application to particular arrangements, see Revenue Tax Bulletin February 1995 pp 189–193. This considers in particular: sums paid before the asset comes into use; depreciation of leased assets (and the interaction with SSAP 21); long-life assets; termination adjustments; fixtures leases; and the interaction of SP 3/91 with statutory restrictions on relief for rental payments.

See generally HMRC Business Leasing Manual.

Changes to GAAP before 1 January 2019

For periods of account beginning before 1 January 2019, any business that accounts for lease transactions (whether as lessor or lessee) using a 'leasing accounting standard' (as defined) that changes on or after 1 January 2011 had to compute taxable profits as if the change had not taken place. Any such change was to be ignored when considering whether accounts are prepared in accordance with generally accepted accounting practice (GAAP) (see **75.21** above). This had effect in relation to any period of account in respect of which a change to a leasing accounting standard which occurred on or after 1 January 2011 could or had to be adopted by any person for accounting purposes. The rule did not apply to a change in a leasing accounting standard if it was a change to UK GAAP that permitted or required businesses to account for a lease (or a transaction accounted for as a lease) in a manner equivalent to that provided for by the International Financial Reporting Standard for Small and Medium-sized Entities issued by the International Accounting Standards Board (but ignoring any change made to the leasing section of that Standard).

FA 2011, s 53 was repealed by *FA 2019* as it is considered no longer necessary in view of the legislation introduced in consequence of IFRS 16 (see below).

[*FA 2011, s 53; FA 2019, Sch 14 para 11*]

International Financial Reporting Standard 16 (IFRS 16)

FA 2019 introduced provisions to deal with the tax implications for periods of account beginning on or after 1 January 2019 of the adoption of IFRS 16. Persons who apply FRS 101 or international financial reporting standards are required to adopt IFRS 16 for such periods of account, though earlier adoption was also possible. IFRS 16 removes the pre-existing distinction between finance leases and operating leases for lessees (but not for lessors) on which a number of tax rules depend. Under IFRS 16, a lessee recognises all leases on the balance sheet, other than certain exempted leases which are short term or of low value. The statutory provisions preserve the distinction for tax purposes and ensure that the taxation of leases is broadly consistent regardless of which accounting standard is adopted; for example, where FRS 102 is applied, the distinction between operating and finance leases continues in any case. Leases dealt with under IFRS 16 are referred to for tax purposes as 'right-of-use leases' — for the full definition see **10.50**(5) CAPITAL ALLOWANCES ON PLANT AND MACHINERY. Broadly, in relation to a lessee, a right-to-use lease is treated for tax purposes as a finance lease if it would have been accounted for as a finance lease had the lessee been required by GAAP to determine whether or not it was a finance lease.

Transition to IFRS 16

Transitional rules apply where a lessee treats a lease as a right-of-use asset under IFRS 16 and had not previously accounted for the lease as a finance lease. These modify the effect of *ITTOIA 2005, ss 226–240* (adjustments on change of basis — see **75.24** above) and the similar rules under *ITTOIA 2005, ss 329–334* for property businesses (see **60.17** PROPERTY INCOME).

If the first period of account for which the right-of-use asset falls to be recognised begins on or after 1 January 2019, any adjustments under the change of basis rules are spread across the average length of the leases giving rise to them (by applying the steps in *FA 2019, Sch 14 para 13*). If the lessee adopted IFRS 16 early, so that the right-of-use asset fell to be recognised in an earlier period of account, the change of basis is nevertheless treated for this purpose as occurring in the first period of account beginning on or after 1 January 2019. If a lease is transferred to a connected party during the period over which the adjustments are spread, the remaining adjustment amounts are treated as arising to the transferee and are spread over the remaining spreading period. Any apportionments needed for this purpose must be made on a just and reasonable basis. This rule does not apply if it is reasonable to suppose that the transfer, or arrangements of which it is part, are designed to avoid tax. If the lessee permanently ceases to carry on activities within the charge to income tax before the end of the spreading period (and the remaining adjustment amounts are not treated as arising to a transferee), the remaining amounts are treated as arising to the lessee immediately before the cessation. If the lessee prepares accounts by reference to a portfolio of leases, these provisions apply to the portfolio as they apply to individual leases, subject to any necessary modifications.

[*FA 2019, Sch 14 paras 12–17; FA 2020, s 35*].

General

See **10.26, 10.58, 10.60** CAPITAL ALLOWANCES ON PLANT AND MACHINERY for other finance lease capital allowance restrictions. It was held in *Caledonian Paper plc v CIR* (Sp C 159), [1998] SSCD 129 that annual or semi-annual payments of commitment fees, guarantee fees and agency fees relating to guarantees required in relation to finance leasing arrangements were deductible in computing profits, but that a one-off management fee was not.

Finance leases — return in capital form

[75.83] *ITA 2007, Pt 11A Ch 2 (ss 614B–614BY* apply in relation to asset leasing arrangements which fall to be treated under generally accepted accounting practice (GAAP) (see **75.21** above) as finance leases or loans, and whose effect is that some or all of the investment return is or may be in the form of a sum that is not rent and would not, apart from these provisions, be wholly taxed as lease rental. The principal purposes of the Chapter 2 provisions are to charge any person entitled to the lessor's interest to income tax by reference to the income return for accounting purposes (taking into account the substance of the matter as a whole, e.g. as regards connected persons or groups of companies); and to recover reliefs for capital and other expenditure as appropriate by reference to sums received which fall within the provisions.

The Chapter 2 provisions apply where an asset lease (as widely defined) is or has at any time been granted in the case of which the conditions at (a)–(e) below are or have been met at some time (the '*relevant time*') in a period of account of the current lessor. Where the conditions have been met at a relevant time, they are treated as continuing to be met unless and until the asset ceases to be leased under the lease or the lessor's interest is assigned to a person not connected with any of the following: (i) the assignor, (ii) any other person who was the lessor at some time before the assignment, and (iii) any person who at some time after the assignment becomes the lessor under arrangements made by a person who was the lessor (or was connected with the lessor) at some time before the assignment. A lease to which the Chapter 2 provisions cease to apply can come within those provisions again if the conditions for their application are again met.

For the purposes of these provisions generally, and those at **75.84** below, **18** CONNECTED PERSONS applies initially to determine if persons are connected. But persons who are thus connected at any time in the 'relevant period' are then treated as being connected throughout that period. The '*relevant period*' runs from the earliest time at which any of the leasing arrangements were made to the time when the current lessor finally ceases to have an interest in the asset or any arrangements relating to it.

The Chapter 2 provisions do *not* apply if (or to the extent that), as regards the current lessor, the lease falls to be regarded as a long funding lease (within **10.50** CAPITAL ALLOWANCES ON PLANT AND MACHINERY) of plant or machinery.

The conditions referred to above are as follows.

(a) At the 'relevant time' (see above), and in accordance with GAAP, the leasing arrangements fall to be treated as a finance lease or loan, and either:
   (i) the lessor (or a connected person) is the finance lessor in relation to the finance lease or loan; or

(ii) the lessor is a member of a group of companies for the purposes of whose consolidated accounts the finance lease or loan is treated as subsisting.

(b) under the leasing arrangements, there is or may be payable to the lessor (or to a connected person), a sum (a '*major lump sum*') that is not rent but falls to be treated, in accordance with GAAP, partly as a repayment of some or all of the investment in respect of the finance lease or loan and partly as a return on that investment.

(c) Not all of the part of the major lump sum which is treated as a return on the investment (as in (b) above) would, apart from these provisions, be brought into account for income tax purposes, as 'normal rent' (see below) from the lease for periods of account of the lessor, in tax years ending with the 'relevant tax year'. The '*relevant tax year*' is the tax year (or latest tax year) consisting of or including all or part of the period of account in which the major lump sum is or may be payable under the arrangements.

(d) The period of account of the lessor in which the relevant time falls (or an earlier period during which he was the lessor) is one for which the 'accountancy rental earnings' in respect of the lease exceed the normal rent. The normal rent is determined by treating rent as accruing and falling due evenly over the period to which it relates (unless a payment falls due more than twelve months after any of the rent to which it relates is so treated as accruing).

(e) At the relevant time, either:

(i) arrangements exist under which the lessee (or a person connected with the lessee) may directly or indirectly acquire the leased asset (or an asset representing it — see *ITA 2007, s 614DD*) from the lessor (or a person connected with the lessor), and in connection with that acquisition the lessor (or connected person) may directly or indirectly receive a 'qualifying lump sum' from the lessee (or connected person); or

(ii) in the absence of such arrangements, it is in any event more likely that the acquisition and receipt described in (i) above will take place than that, before any such acquisition, the leased asset (or the asset representing it) will have been acquired in an open market sale by a person who is neither the lessor nor the lessee nor a person connected with either of them.

In (i) above, a '*qualifying lump sum*' is a sum which is not rent but at least part of which would be treated under GAAP as a return on investment in respect of a finance lease or loan.

For the purposes of the Chapter 2 provisions (and also the provisions at **75.84** below):

- a '*normal rent*' for a period of account of a lessor is the amount which (apart from these provisions) the lessor would bring in for income tax purposes in the period as rent arising from the lease;
- '*rental earnings*' for any period is the amount that falls for accounting purposes to be treated, in accordance with GAAP, as the gross return for that period on investment in respect of a finance lease or loan in respect of the leasing arrangements; and

- the '*accountancy rental earnings*' in respect of a lease for a period of account of the lessor is the greatest of the following amounts of rental earnings for that period in respect of the lease:
  (i) the rental earnings of the lessor;
  (ii) the rental earnings of any person connected with the lessor;
  (iii) the rental earnings for the purposes of consolidated group accounts of a group of which the lessor is a member.

  Where (ii) or (iii) applies and the lessor's period of account does not coincide with that of the connected person or the consolidated group accounts, amounts in the periods of account of the latter are apportioned as necessary by reference to the number of days in the common periods.

Current lessor to be taxed by reference to accountancy rental earnings. If for any period of account of the current lessor (L):

- the Chapter 2 provisions apply to the lease, and
- the accountancy rental earnings exceed the normal rent,

L is treated for income tax purposes as if in that period of account L had been entitled to, and there had arisen to L, rent from the lease of an amount equal to those accountancy rental earnings (instead of the normal rent). That rent is deemed to have accrued at an even rate throughout the period of account (or so much of the it as corresponds to the period for which the asset is leased).

Reduction of taxable rent by cumulative rental excesses

If a period of account of the current lessor is one in which the normal rent in respect of the lease exceeds the accountancy rental earnings, and there is a 'cumulative accountancy rental excess', the rent otherwise taxable for the period (the '*taxable rent*') is reduced by setting that excess against it. It cannot be reduced to less than the accountancy rental earnings.

There is an '*accountancy rental excess*' for a period if the period is one in which the current lessor is taxed by reference to accountancy rental earnings as above; it is the excess of the accountancy rental earnings over the normal rent. If, however, the taxable rent for that period is reduced by a 'cumulative normal rental excess' (see below), the accountancy rental excess for the period is limited to the excess (if any) of the accountancy rental earnings, reduced by the same amount as the taxable rent, over the normal rent. A '*cumulative accountancy rental excess*' is so much of the aggregate of accountancy rental excesses of previous periods of account as has not already been used, whether under these rules, the bad debt rules below or the rules below on disposals.

If a period of account of the current lessor is one in which the current lessor is taxed by reference to accountancy rental earnings, and there is a 'cumulative normal rental excess', the taxable rent is reduced by setting that excess against it. It cannot be reduced to less than the normal rent.

The '*normal rental excess*' for a period of account is the excess (if any) of normal rent over accountancy rental earnings. If, however, the taxable rent for that period is reduced by a cumulative accountancy rental excess (as above), the normal rental excess for the period is limited to the excess (if any) of the normal rent, reduced by the same amount as the taxable rent, over accountancy rental earnings. A '*cumulative normal rental excess*' is so much of the aggregate of normal rental excesses of previous periods of account as has not already been used, whether under these rules or the bad debt rules below.

Bad debts

Where accountancy rental earnings for a period of account are substituted for normal rent for income tax purposes (as above), and a 'bad debt deduction' in excess of the accountancy rental earnings falls to be made for the period, any cumulative accountancy rental excess for the period is reduced (but not below nil) by that excess. If the accountancy rental earnings do not exceed the normal rent, any bad debt deduction acts to reduce the amount of the normal rent against which a cumulative accountancy rental excess may be set, and the cumulative accountancy rental excess is reduced (but not below nil) by any excess of the bad debt deduction over the normal rent. There is provision for such reductions in the cumulative accountancy rental excess to be reversed in the event of subsequent bad debt recoveries or reinstatements. A '*bad debt deduction*', in relation to a period of account of the lessor, means the total of any sums falling within *ITTOIA 2005, s 35* (see **75.48** above), in respect of rents from the lease of the asset, which are deductible as expenses for that period.

There are similar provisions relating to the effect of bad debt deductions on cumulative normal rental excesses.

Effect of disposals

If the current lessor (or a connected person) disposes of its interest under the lease or the leased asset or an asset representing the leased asset (see *ITA 2007, s 614DD*), the Chapter 2 provisions have effect as if immediately before the disposal (or simultaneous such disposals) a period of account of the current lessor ended and another began.

In determining the amount of any chargeable gain on the disposal, the disposal consideration is reduced by setting against it any cumulative accountancy rental excess (as above) for the period of account in which the disposal occurs. *TCGA 1992, s 37* does not exclude any money or money's worth from the disposal consideration so far as it is represented by any cumulative accountancy rental excess set off under this rule (whether on the current disposal or previously). On a part disposal, the cumulative accountancy rental excess is apportioned in the same manner as the associated acquisition costs. Where there are simultaneous disposals, the cumulative accountancy rental excess is apportioned between them on a just and reasonable basis.

On an assignment of the current lessor's interest under the lease treated under *TCGA 1992* as a no gain/no loss disposal (see *TCGA 1992, s 288(3A)*), a period of account of the assignor is treated as ending, and a period of account of the assignee as beginning, with the assignment. Any unused cumulative accountancy rental excess or cumulative normal rental excess at the time of the assignment is transferred to the assignee.

Capital allowances etc.

Where an occasion occurs on which a major lump sum (as in (b) above) falls to be paid, there are provisions (see *ITA 2007, ss 614BR–614BW*) for the withdrawal of earlier reliefs for expenditure incurred by the current lessor in respect of the leased asset. This applies to capital allowances and to reliefs for capital expenditure under **75.51** above (cemeteries and crematoria) and **75.130** below (waste disposal). Deductions allowed under any of the now mostly defunct *ITTOIA 2005, ss 135, 138, 138A, 139, 140* (films and sound recordings) are similarly withdrawn. The earlier reliefs are withdrawn either by the bringing in of a disposal value or by the imposition of a balancing charge or, in the case of expenditure allowed in respect of cemeteries etc., waste disposal or films etc., by the bringing in of a countervailing receipt. These provisions apply equally to capital allowances for contributors to capital expenditure under *CAA 2001, ss 537–542*.

Schemes previously within Chapter 3 provisions

If the Chapter 2 provisions come to apply to a lease to which the Chapter 3 provisions at **75.84** below applied immediately beforehand, the cumulative accountancy rental excess and the cumulative normal rental excess are determined as if the Chapter 2 provisions had applied throughout the period for which the Chapter 3 conditions in fact applied.

[*ITA 2007, ss 614A, 614AA–614AC, 614B–614BY, 614D–614DG; TCGA 1992, s 37A*].

For HMRC's views on various points of interpretation regarding the Chapter 2 provisions, see HMRC Business Leasing Manual BLM70005 *et seq.*

Simon's Taxes. See **B3.340E, B5.416.**

Finance leases not within the above provisions

[75.84] *ITA 2007, Pt 11A Ch 3* (*ss 614C–614CD*) (the Chapter 3 provisions) apply to arrangements, not within the Chapter 2 provisions at **75.83** above, which involve the lease of an asset and would fall to be treated under generally accepted accounting practice (GAAP) as finance leases or loans. The main purpose of the Chapter 3 provisions is to charge any person entitled to the lessor's interest to income tax on amounts falling to be treated under GAAP as the income return on investment in respect of the finance lease or loan (taking into account the substance of the matter as a whole, e.g. as regards connected persons or groups of companies). The Chapter 3 provisions accordingly apply where:

- a lease of an asset is granted on which forms part of a scheme;
- condition (a) at **75.83** above (or its corporation tax equivalent) is met at some time in a period of account of the current lessor; and
- the Chapter 2 provisions described at **75.83** above do not apply because not all of conditions (b)–(e) at **75.83** above (or their corporation tax equivalents) have been met at that time.

Where condition (a) at **75.83** above is met, it is treated as continuing to be met until either the asset ceases to be leased under the lease or the lessor's interest is assigned to a person not connected with any of the following: (i) the assignor,

(ii) any other person who was the lessor at some time before the assignment, and (iii) any person who at some time after the assignment becomes the lessor under arrangements made by a person who was the lessor (or was connected with the lessor) at some time before the assignment. A lease to which the Chapter 3 provisions cease to apply can come within those provisions again if the conditions for their application are again met.

If for any period of account of the current lessor (L):

- the Chapter 3 provisions apply to the lease; and
- the 'accountancy rental earnings' (**75.83** above) exceed the 'normal rent' (**75.83** above),

L is treated for income tax purposes as if in that period of account L had been entitled to, and there had arisen to L, rent from the lease of an amount equal to those accountancy rental earnings (instead of the normal rent). That rent is deemed to have accrued at an even rate throughout the period of account (or so much of the it as corresponds to the period for which the asset is leased).

The provisions at **75.83** above relating to reduction of taxable rent by cumulative rental excesses, bad debt relief and the effect of disposals apply equally for the purposes of the Chapter 3 provisions.

The Chapter 3 provisions do *not* apply if (or to the extent that), as regards the current lessor, the lease falls to be regarded as a long funding lease (within **10.50** CAPITAL ALLOWANCES ON PLANT AND MACHINERY) of plant or machinery.

[*ITA 2007, ss 614C–614CD, 614D–614DG*].

For HMRC's views on various points of interpretation regarding the Chapter 3 provisions, see HMRC Business Leasing Manual BLM74600 *et seq.*

Simon's Taxes. See **B3.340E, B5.416.**

Foreign exchange gains and losses

[75.85] In general, for income tax purposes, foreign exchange differences are taken into account in computing trading profits if they relate to the circulating capital of the business but not otherwise. In *Overseas Containers (Finance) Ltd v Stoker* CA 1989, 61 TC 473, exchange losses arising on loans transferred to a finance subsidiary set up to convert the losses to trading account were held not to arise from trading transactions.

In *Davies v The Shell Co of China Ltd* CA 1951, 32 TC 133, a petrol marketing company operating in China required agents to deposit Chinese dollars with it, repayable on the ending of the agency. Exchange profits it made on repaying the deposits were held to be capital. In *Firestone Tyre & Rubber Co Ltd v Evans* Ch D 1976, 51 TC 615, a company repaid in 1965 a dollar balance due to its US parent, the greater part of which represented advances in 1922–1931 to finance the company when it started. The Commissioners' finding that 90% of the resultant large exchange loss was capital and not allowable, was upheld. A profit by an agent on advances to the principal to finance purchases by the agent on behalf of the principal, was held to be a trading receipt (*Landes Bros v Simpson* KB 1934, 19 TC 62) as was a profit by a tobacco company on dollars accumulated to finance its future purchases (*Imperial Tobacco Co v Kelly* CA 1943, 25 TC 292). See also *McKinlay v H T Jenkins & Son* KB 1926, 10 TC 372; *Ward v Anglo-American Oil* KB 1934, 19 TC 94; *Beauchamp v F W Woolworth plc* HL 1989, 61 TC 542; and contrast *Radio Pictures Ltd v CIR* CA 1938, 22 TC 106. Where a bank operated in foreign currencies and aimed at, and generally succeeded in, matching its monetary assets and liabilities in each currency, it was held that there could be no profit or loss from matched transactions where there were no relevant currency conversions (*Pattison v Marine Midland Ltd* HL 1983, 57 TC 219). In *Whittles v Uniholdings Ltd (No 3)* CA 1996, 68 TC 528 it was held that a dollar loan and a simultaneous forward contract with the same bank for dollars sufficient to repay the loan had to be treated, for tax purposes, as separate transactions, each giving rise to its own tax consequences.

Following the *Marine Midland Ltd* case (above) the Inland Revenue issued a Statement of Practice setting out their views on the general treatment of exchange differences for tax purposes. The principles outlined in this Statement, as subsequently revised, are broadly summarised below. These extend to trades, professions and property businesses.

In accordance with the rule that generally accepted accounting practice (GAAP) be adhered to in computing taxable profits (see **75.21** above), tax computations should follow the accounting treatment where the latter is based on GAAP (and, in particular, on SSAP 20). Where, for example, under SSAP 20, gains and losses on monetary assets and liabilities are taken to reserve rather than profit and loss account, then, even if they are not capital items, they should not be recognised for tax purposes. Previously, the nature of the assets and liabilities had to be considered to determine whether or not a tax adjustment was required.

Where currency assets are matched by currency liabilities in a particular currency, so that a translation adjustment on one would be cancelled out by a translation adjustment on the other, no adjustment is required for tax purposes.

Where currency assets are not matched, or are incompletely matched, with currency liabilities in a particular currency, the adjustment required to the net exchange difference debited or credited in the profit and loss account is determined along the following lines:

(i) the aggregate exchange differences, positive and negative, on capital assets and liabilities in the profit and loss account figure are ascertained;
(ii) if there are no differences as at (i), no adjustment is required;
(iii) if the net exchange difference as at (i) is a loss, and the net exchange difference in the profit and loss account is also a loss, the smaller of the two losses is the amount disallowed for tax purposes as relating to capital transactions;
(iv) if the net exchange difference as at (i) is a profit, and the net exchange difference in the profit and loss account is also a profit, the smaller of the two profits is allowed as a deduction for tax purposes;
(v) if the net exchange difference as at (i) is a loss, and the net exchange difference in the profit and loss account is a profit, or *vice versa*, no adjustment is required for tax purposes.

In considering whether a trader is matched in a particular foreign currency, *forward exchange contracts* and *currency futures* entered into for hedging purposes may be taken into account, provided the hedging is reflected in the accounts on a consistent basis from year to year and in accordance with accepted accounting practice. *Currency swap agreements* are treated as converting the liability in the original currency into a liability in the swap currency for the duration of the swap. Hedging through *currency options* does not result in any matching.

Where the profits on disposal of assets held by a financial concern other than as trading stock fall to be treated as trading receipts and the concern does not account for those assets on a mark to market basis, such profits are taxable only on disposal (the 'realisation basis'). It may, however, be the practice to revalue the assets in the accounts to reflect exchange rate fluctuations. Where the resulting exchange differences are taken to profit and loss account or set against exchange differences on liabilities, the accounts treatment *must* be followed for tax purposes.

Where an *overseas trade*, or an *overseas branch* of a trade, is carried on primarily in a non-sterling economic environment, accounts are usually drawn up in the local currency and translated into sterling using the 'closing rate/net investment' method (SSAP 20 paras 25, 46). Under the revised Statement of Practice, tax computations *must* now be based on those translated accounts. (Under the original Statement of Practice, other specified methods of preparing computations were allowed if applied consistently.) The principles outlined in the Statement of Practice should be applied in considering any adjustment necessary in respect of exchange differences in the foreign currency accounts.

(HMRC SP 2/02).

For further discussion, see HMRC Business Income Manual BIM39500–39580.

If not taken into account in computing trading profits, a profit/loss on the sale of currency is within the ambit of CGT unless exempted by *TCGA 1992, s 269* as currency required for an individual's (or his dependant's) personal expenditure abroad (including provision or maintenance of a residence abroad).

Simon's Taxes. See **B2.433, B2.704–B2.707.**

Franchising

[75.86] Under a business system franchising agreement (i.e. an agreement under which the franchisor grants to the franchisee the right to distribute products or perform services using that system), there is generally an initial fee (payable in one sum or in instalments) and continuing, usually annual, fees.

The capital or revenue treatment of the initial fee depends on what it is for. To the extent that it is paid wholly or mainly for substantial rights of an enduring nature, to initiate or substantially extend a business, it is a capital payment (as are any related professional fees). (See **75.43** above for general principles.) It is immaterial that the expenditure may prove abortive, and the treatment of the payment in the hands of the franchisor is irrelevant. However, where goods or services of a revenue nature are supplied at the outset (e.g. trading stock or staff training), HMRC will accept that an appropriate part of the initial fee is a revenue payment, provided that the sum claimed fairly represents such items, and that it is clear that the items are not separately charged for in the continuing fees. The costs of the franchisee's own initial training are not normally allowable.

The continuing fee payable by the franchisee is generally a revenue expense.

(Revenue Tax Bulletin June 1995 p 224).

See generally HMRC Business Income Manual BIM57600–57620.

Gifts and other non-contractual receipts and payments

[75.87] See also 75.76 above (entertainment and gifts).

The fact that a receipt is gratuitous is not in itself a reason for its not being a trading receipt. See *Severne v Dadswell* Ch D 1954, 35 TC 649 (payments under war-time arrangements held trading receipts although *ex gratia*); *CIR v Falkirk Ice Rink* CS 1975, 51 TC 42 (donation to ice rink from associated curling club held taxable); *Wing v O'Connell Supreme Court* (IFS) 1926, [1927] IR 84 (gift to professional jockey on winning race taxable).

In relation to *ex gratia* payments on the termination of long-standing business arrangements, a distinction is drawn between parting gifts as personal testimonials (not taxable as business receipts) and payments which, on the facts, can be seen as additional rewards for services already rendered or compensation for a loss of future profits (taxable). For cases see **75.56**(f) above and compare the position for employees, see **28.68** EMPLOYMENT INCOME.

Cremation fees (often known as 'ash cash') assigned in advance, and paid directly, to a medical charity may escape liability to tax on miscellaneous income where the doctor entitled to them is not chargeable to tax on trading income, but liability to tax on trading income is not affected by such assignment. See HMRC Business Income Manual BIM54015.

Simon's Taxes. See **B2.320.**

Gifts to charities and educational establishments

[75.88] A relief is available for certain gifts by traders for the purposes of a charity (within **14.2** CHARITIES AND CHARITABLE GIVING), any of the similar bodies listed in *ITTOIA 2005, s 108(4)*, a 'designated educational establishment' or a registered community amateur sports club (see Tolley's Corporation Tax under Voluntary Associations).

Where the gift is of an article manufactured by the trader, or of a type sold by him, in his trade, the trader is not required to bring in any amount as a trading receipt in respect of the disposal of the article.

Where the gift is of an item of plant or machinery used in the course of the donor's trade, its disposal value for capital allowances purposes (see **10.27** CAPITAL ALLOWANCES ON PLANT AND MACHINERY) is nil.

The value of any benefit received by the donor or by a person connected with him (see **19** CONNECTED PERSONS), which is in any way attributable to the making of a gift for which relief has been given as above, must be brought into account as a trading receipt arising on the date of receipt of the benefit or, if the trade has ceased, as a post-cessation receipt within **59.1** POST-CESSATION RECEIPTS AND EXPENDITURE.

'*Designated educational establishment*' means any educational establishment designated (or of a category designated) in regulations, broadly all UK universities, public or private schools and further and higher educational institutions (see *SI 1992 No 42*).

The relief is subject to the tainted donations rules at **14.21** CHARITIES AND CHARITABLE GIVING.

[*ITTOIA 2005, ss 107–110; CAA 2001, s 63(2)–(4)*].

Where the above relief does not apply, donations of trading stock to charities are dealt with on normal trading income principles; see Revenue Tax Bulletin June 1996 p 319 for HMRC's view of the application of those principles.

An ordinary annual subscription by a trader to a charity, made for the benefit of his employees, may be allowed as a trade expense where the availability of the charity to the employees can reasonably be regarded as a direct and valuable advantage to the employer's business and the amount is not unreasonably high (see *Bourne & Hollingsworth v Ogden* KB 1929, 14 TC 349). This would include reasonable annual subscriptions made by a trader to, for example, a general hospital in the locality of his place of business, or to a trade charity maintained primarily for the benefit of employees in the type of trade in question. It can also include subscriptions made to charities of benefit to a specific category of the employees.

A deduction for a contribution made to a charity in response to a special appeal may be allowed if an annual subscription would be allowed as above, provided that the employer has been or has become an annual subscriber, the proceeds of the appeal are to be used to meet revenue as opposed to capital expenditure, and the amount is reasonable.

For annual subscriptions to charities see HMRC Business Income Manual BIM47410.

Simon's Taxes. See **B2.442.**

Guarantees

[75.89] Losses under guarantees of the indebtedness of another are analogous to bad debt losses (see **75.48** above) and similar principles apply. Losses allowed as a deduction to a solicitor under the guarantee of a client's overdraft (*Jennings v Barfield* Ch D 1962, 40 TC 365) and to a film-writer under guarantee of loans to a film company with which he was associated (*Lunt v Wellesley* KB 1945, 27 TC 78) but refused to a company under a guarantee of loans to an associated company with which it had close trading connections

(*Milnes v J Beam Group Ltd* Ch D 1975, 50 TC 675) and a guarantee of loans to a subsidiary (*Redkite Ltd v Inspector of Taxes* [1996] SSCD 501). See also *Bolton v Halpern & Woolf* CA 1980, 53 TC 445 and *Garforth v Tankard Carpets Ltd* Ch D 1980, 53 TC 342.

A loss by an asphalt contractor under a guarantee to an exhibition (for which he hoped but, in the event, failed to work) allowed (*Morley v Lawford & Co* CA 1928, 14 TC 229). For commission paid to guarantors see *Ascot Gas Water Heaters Ltd* at **75.93** below.

Payments under guarantees made to a trader for the setting up or the purposes of his trade and irrecoverable are in certain circumstances allowable as a loss for capital gains tax. See Tolley's Capital Gains Tax.

Hire-purchase

[75.90] Where assets are purchased under hire-purchase agreements, the charges (the excess of the hire-purchase price over the cash price, sometimes referred to as interest) are, appropriately spread, allowable deductions (*Darngavil Coal Co Ltd v Francis* CS 1913, 7 TC 1). See **75.48** above for the bad debt etc. provisions of hire-purchase traders. For relief on capital element, see **10.58** CAPITAL ALLOWANCES ON PLANT AND MACHINERY.

For whether goods sold under hire-purchase are trading stock, see *Lions Ltd v Gosford Furnishing Co Ltd & CIR* CS 1961, 40 TC 256 and cf. *Drages Ltd v CIR* KB 1927, 46 TC 389.

See generally HMRC Business Income Manual BIM40550–40555 (hire-purchase receipts) and BIM45350–45365 (hire-purchase payments).

Illegal payments etc.

[75.91] In computing profits, no deduction may be made in respect of expenditure incurred:

- in making a payment the making of which constitutes a criminal offence; or
- in making a payment outside the UK where the making of a corresponding payment in any part of the UK would constitute a criminal offence there.

A deduction is similarly denied for any payment induced by a demand constituting blackmail or extortion.

[*ITTOIA 2005, ss 55, 870; F(No 2)A 2017, Sch 2 paras 39, 64(1)*].

For a discussion of the circumstances in which the above may apply, see HMRC Business Income Manual BIM43100–43185.

Simon's Taxes. See **B2.420**.

Insurance

[75.92] Premiums for business purposes are normally allowable including insurance of assets, insurance against accidents to employees, insurance against loss of profits and premiums under mutual insurance schemes (cf. *Thomas v Richard Evans & Co* HL 1927, 11 TC 790; for trade associations, see **75.119** below).

Any corresponding recoveries are trading receipts (or set off against trading expenses) or capital, according to the nature of the policy. Where a deduction was allowed for a loss or expense and the trader recovers a capital sum under an insurance policy or contract of indemnity in respect of that loss or expense, the sum must be brought into account, up to the amount of the deduction, as a trading receipt. [*ITTOIA 2005, s 106*]. Otherwise, if capital, the recovery may be taken into account, where appropriate, for the purposes of capital allowances or capital gains tax.

The whole of a recovery in respect of the destruction of trading stock was held to be a trading receipt of the year of destruction, notwithstanding that it exceeded the market value of the stock lost or not all the stock was replaced (*Green v J Gliksten & Son Ltd* HL 1929, 14 TC 364; *Rownson Drew & Clydesdale Ltd v CIR* KB 1931, 16 TC 595). The total recovery under a loss of profits was held a trading receipt although in excess of the loss suffered (*R v British Columbia Fir & Cedar* PC 1932, 15 ATC 624). See also *Mallandain Investments Ltd v Shadbolt* KB 1940, 23 TC 367. For recoveries under accidents to employees see *Gray & Co v Murphy* KB 1940, 23 TC 225; *Keir & Cawder Ltd v CIR* CS 1958, 38 TC 23. Where a shipping company insured against late delivery of ships being built for it, both premiums and recoveries held capital (*Crabb v Blue Star Line Ltd* Ch D 1961, 39 TC 482).

Premiums on policies in favour of the employer insuring against death or critical illness of key employees are generally allowable, and the proceeds of any such policies trading receipts. However, in *Beauty Consultants Ltd v Inspector of Taxes* (Sp C 321), [2002] SSCD 352, premiums on a policy insuring a company against the death of either of its controlling shareholder-directors were not allowed as deductions; the 'dual purpose rule' at **75.44** above applied, in that the premiums benefited the shareholders personally by improving the value of their shares. In *Greycon Ltd v Klaentschi* (Sp C 372), [2003] SSCD 370, it was held that the company's sole purpose in taking out key man policies was to meet a requirement of an agreement under which funding and other benefits were obtained from another company, that the policies had a capital purpose and that, consequently, the proceeds were not trading receipts.

Accountancy fee protection insurance

See **75.96** below.

Health insurance

See **30.29** EXEMPT INCOME.

Locum and fixed practice expenses insurance

HMRC take the view that premiums for such policies are deductible, and benefits taxable, under the trading income rules, whether the professional person is obliged to insure (e.g. under NHS regulations) or does so as a matter of commercial prudence. This view relates to premiums paid by professional people such as doctors and dentists to meet locum and/or fixed overhead costs. It does not apply to any part of a premium relating to other, non-business, risks such as the cost of medical treatment for accident or sickness. (Revenue Press Release 30 April 1996).

Professional indemnity insurance

Professional indemnity insurance premiums are normally allowable on general principles, and HMRC will not seek to disallow a premium paid prior to cessation of trading on the grounds that the cover extends to claims lodged after cessation. (Premiums paid after cessation will generally be relievable as post-cessation expenditure, see **59.5** POST-CESSATION RECEIPTS AND EXPENDITURE.) (Revenue Tax Bulletin October 1995 p 257).

Commissions

HMRC Statement of Practice SP 4/97 (see **75.54** above) deals widely with commissions, cashbacks and discounts.

See also *Robertson v CIR* (Sp C 137), [1997] SSCD 282 as regards timing of inclusion of insurance agents' advance commission.

Simon's Taxes. See **B2.445**.

Interest and other payments for loans

[75.93] Interest paid for business purposes, if not claimed as a relief under *ITA 2007, s 383*, is deductible, subject to certain restrictions, as described at **42.2** INTEREST PAYABLE. For hire-purchase charges, see **75.90** above.

See **76.10** TRADING INCOME — CASH BASIS FOR SMALLER BUSINESSES for the position where a cash basis election is in force.

Premium on repayment of mortgage (*Arizona Copper Co v Smiles* CES 1891, 3 TC 149) and on repayment of loan to finance estate development (*Bridgwater v King* KB 1943, 25 TC 385) held not allowable, as were exchange losses attendant on foreign borrowings by a company to finance its purchase of a controlling interest in another company (*Ward v Anglo-American Oil Co Ltd* KB 1934, 19 TC 94). A share of profits paid as partial consideration for a loan was held to be distribution of profits and not allowed in *Walker & Co v CIR* KB 1920, 12 TC 297.

Late payment interest, penalties and surcharges (see **43** LATE PAYMENT INTEREST AND PENALTIES) are not allowable deductions in computing profits. This applies equally to interest (and certain penalties and surcharges) in respect of unpaid or under-declared value added tax, insurance premium tax, landfill tax, climate change levy, aggregates levy, stamp duty land tax, excise duties and customs, excise or import duties. It also applies to penalties under *FA 2007, Sch 24* and *FA 2008, Sch 41*. For a list of the specific charges to which this prohibition applies, see *ITTOIA 2005, s 54*. [*ITTOIA 2005, ss 54, 869; F(No 2)A 2017, Sch 2 paras 38, 64(1), Sch 16 paras 59, 62(1)*].

For the treatment of the incidental costs of obtaining loan finance, see **75.97** below.

Simon's Taxes. See **B2.446**.

Investment income (including letting income)

[75.94] Investment income may be treated as a trading receipt where it is the fruit derived from a fund employed and risked in the business (see *Liverpool and London and Globe Insurance Co v Bennett* HL 1913, 6 TC 327). This treatment is not confined to financial trades, but the making and holding of investments at interest must be an integral part of the trade. See *Nuclear Electric plc v Bradley* HL 1996, 68 TC 670, in which (in refusing the company's claim) the crucial test was considered to be whether the investments were employed in the business (of producing electricity) in the tax year in question. The Court of Appeal, whose judgment was approved, considered decisive the facts that the liabilities against which the investments were provided were liabilities to third parties, not to customers, and that, in view of the long-term nature of the liabilities, the business could be carried on for a long period without maintaining any fund of investments at all. See also *Bank Line Ltd v CIR* (above).

See **44** LOSSES for treatment of certain investment income as trading profits for loss relief purposes.

Payments received in lieu of dividends in contango operations held trading receipts (*Multipar Syndicate Ltd v Devitt* KB 1945, 26 TC 359); also co-operative society 'dividends' on trading purchases (*Pope v Beaumont* KB 1941, 24 TC 78) and interest earned by solicitors on short-term funds on clients' account where it was understood between solicitor and client that the interest would form part of the solicitor's total fee for conveyancing (*Barnetts (a firm) v HMRC* FTT (TC 575), [2010] SFTD 1074). For interest received by underwriters on securities deposited with Lloyd's see *Owen v Sassoon* HC 1950, 32 TC 101 and for discount receivable on bills see *Willingale v International Commercial Bank Ltd* HL 1978, 52 TC 242.

In certain cases pre-dating *ITTOIA 2005* (which abolished all the remaining labels under which income was charged to tax, e.g. *Sch D*), income received under deduction of tax was unable to be included in a *Sch D, Case I* or *II* assessment (cf. *F S Securities Ltd v CIR* HL 1964, 41 TC 666; *Bucks v Bowers* Ch D 1969, 46 TC 267; *Bank Line Ltd v CIR* CS 1974, 49 TC 307), and nor, subject to the Crown option between Cases (see **6.1** ASSESSMENTS), could income received gross from sources within *Sch D, Cases III, IV* or *V* (cf. *Northend v White & Leonard & Corbin Greener* Ch D 1975, 50 TC 121) and also from sources *explicitly* within *Sch D, Case VI*.

Letting income

Rents receivable and other letting income are within the charge to tax on property income as opposed to trading income (see **75.1** above).

Letting of surplus business accommodation

If, however, a trader lets surplus business accommodation and the conditions below are satisfied, he may choose to include the receipts and expenses of the letting in computing his trading profits instead of treating them as receipts and expenses of a property business. The conditions are that the let accommodation must be 'temporarily surplus to requirements', it must not be part of trading stock, it must be part of a building of which another part is used to carry on the trade, and the letting receipts must be relatively small. For these purposes, 'letting' includes a licence to occupy. Once the receipts and expenses of a letting are included in trading profits, all subsequent receipts and expenses of the letting must similarly be so included. For accommodation to be '*temporarily surplus to requirements*', it must have been used for trading within the last three years or acquired within that period; the trader must intend to use it for trading in future; and the letting itself must be for a term of no more than three years. The position is judged as at the beginning of a period of account. [*ITTOIA 2005, s 21*].

See **60.2** PROPERTY INCOME for a further relaxation of the main rule above, this time in relation to caravan site operators.

Simon's Taxes. See **B2.218**.

Know-how

[75.95] '*Know-how*' is any industrial information and techniques likely to assist in (a) manufacturing or processing goods or materials, (b) working, or searching for etc., mineral deposits, or (c) agricultural, forestry or fishing operations. For capital allowances on purchases of know-how, see **9.14** CAPITAL ALLOWANCES.

Where know-how used in the vendor's trade is disposed of, with the trade thereafter continuing, the consideration received is treated as a trading receipt, except to the extent that it is brought into account as a disposal value for capital allowances purposes (see **9.14** CAPITAL ALLOWANCES). This does not apply to a sale between bodies of persons (which includes partnerships) under the same control.

If the know-how is disposed of as part of the disposal of all or part of the trade, both vendor and purchaser are treated for income tax purposes as if the consideration for the know-how were a capital payment for goodwill (in which case capital gains tax may apply). They may, however, jointly elect to disapply this treatment (within two years of the disposal, and provided they are not bodies under common control), and it is disapplied in any event in relation to the purchaser if, prior to his acquiring it, the trade was carried on wholly outside the UK. In either case, the purchaser may then claim capital allowances on his expenditure (see **9.14**(iii) CAPITAL ALLOWANCES).

Any consideration received for a restrictive covenant in connection with a disposal of know-how is treated as consideration received for the disposal of the know-how. An exchange of know-how is treated as a sale of know-how.

[*ITTOIA 2005, ss 192–195*].

The above does not apply in calculating profits on the cash basis (see **76.14** TRADING INCOME — CASH BASIS FOR SMALLER BUSINESSES).

For disposals of know-how by non-traders, see **41.5** INTELLECTUAL PROPERTY.

In *Delage v Nugget Polish Co Ltd* KB 1905, 21 TLR 454, payments for the use of a secret process, payable for 40 years and based on receipts, were held to be annual payments subject to deduction of tax at source. See also *Paterson Engineering v Duff* KB 1943, 25 TC 43.

For patents, see **75.103** below.

Simon's Taxes. See **B5.343–B5.346.**

Legal and professional expenses

[75.96] The expenses of a company incorporated by charter in obtaining a variation of its charter etc. were allowed (*CIR v Carron Co* HL 1968, 45 TC 18). See also *McGarry v Limerick Gas* HC(IFS) [1932] IR 125 and contrast *A & G Moore & Co v Hare* CS 1914, 6 TC 572.

In general, the costs of maintaining existing trading rights and assets are revenue expenses (*Southern v Borax Consolidated* KB 1940, 23 TC 597; *Bihar etc. IT Commr v Maharaja of Dharbanga* PC 1941, 20 ATC 337 and compare *Morgan v Tate & Lyle Ltd* HL 1954, 35 TC 367). But the incidental costs of acquiring new assets etc. are part of their capital cost. The expenses of obtaining or renewing a lease of business premises are strictly capital but, in practice, the expenses of renewing leases under 50 years are generally deductible (although a proportionate disallowance may apply where a lease premium is involved — see HMRC Business Income Manual BIM46420). The cost of an unsuccessful application to vary a carrier's licence was disallowed (*Pyrah v Annis & Co* CA 1956, 37 TC 163) as was the cost of an unsuccessful application for planning permission (*ECC Quarries Ltd v Watkis* Ch D 1975, 51 TC 153. For excise licences, see **75.49** above.

Legal expenses in defending charges brought by a professional regulatory body were allowed as deductions on the grounds that they were incurred to prevent suspension or expulsion and thus to protect the taxpayer's business (applying *Tate & Lyle Ltd* (above)), although the fines imposed were disallowed (see **75.55** above) (*McKnight v Sheppard* HL 1999, 71 TC 419). In *Key IP Ltd v HMRC* FTT (TC 1552), [2012] SFTD 305, the legal costs of bringing defamation proceedings were allowed in full on the grounds that, on the facts of the case, the sole purpose of the proceedings was to protect the business reputation of the appellant company and not to benefit its sole shareholder and director. However, legal fees incurred by the owner of a car transporter business in successfully defending a gross negligence manslaughter charge were fully disallowed, notwithstanding that one reason for defending the charge was to enable him to retain his operator's licence (*Duckmanton v HMRC* UT, [2013] STC 2379, [2013] UKUT 305 (TCC)). Fees incurred by a haulage contractor convicted of river pollution were similarly disallowed due to their having been incurred for personal as well as business purposes (*Raynor v HMRC* FTT (TC 1649), [2011] UKFTT 813 (TC)).

Costs incurred by a partner in connection with the dissolution of the partnership were disallowed in *C Connelly & Co v Wilbey Ch D 1992, 65 TC 208.*

The cost of tax appeals, even if successful, is not deductible (*Allen v Farquharson Bros & Co* KB 1932, 17 TC 59; *Smith's Potato Estates v Bolland* HL 1948, 30 TC 267; *Rushden Heel Co v Keene* HL 1948, 30 TC 298). Where an accountant etc. agrees the tax liabilities based on the accounts he prepares, normal annual fees are allowed as a deduction but not fees for a special review of settled years (*Worsley Brewery Co v CIR* CA 1932, 17 TC 349).

Additional accountancy expenses incurred as a result of an investigation by HMRC of a particular year's accounts (see **75.20** above) will normally be allowed as a deduction if the investigation does not result in an adjustment to the profits of any earlier year or in the imposition of interest or interest and penalties in relation to the current year. Where the investigation reveals discrepancies and additional liabilities for earlier years, or results in a settlement for the current year including interest (with or without penalties), the expenses will be disallowed. Where, however, the investigation results in no addition to profits, or an adjustment to profits for the year of review only without a charge to interest or to interest and penalties, the additional accountancy expenses will normally be allowed. (HMRC SP 16/91).

It is HMRC's view that premiums for a fee protection insurance policy, which entitles the policy holder to claim for the cost of accountancy fees incurred in negotiating additional tax liabilities resulting from negligent or fraudulent conduct, are not allowable. Even if the policy covers other risks as well, the premiums cannot be apportioned between allowable and non-allowable elements. (Revenue Tax Bulletin June 2003 p 1036).

Simon's Taxes. See **B2.449**.

Loan finance incidental costs

[75.97] In computing profits, a deduction is allowed for 'incidental costs of obtaining finance' by means of a loan (or the issue of loan stock) the interest on which would be deductible in computing profits (see **75.93** above and **42.2** INTEREST PAYABLE) and which does not carry a right, exercisable within three years, of conversion into, or to the acquisition of, shares or other (non-qualifying) securities. The said restriction does not apply if the right is not wholly exercised within the three-year period; in such a case, incidental costs incurred within the three-year period are treated as incurred immediately after that period. Where part only of the loan or loan stock is so converted, only the corresponding proportion of the incidental costs is disallowed.

'*Incidental costs of obtaining finance*' are expenses incurred on fees, commissions, advertising, printing and other incidental matters which are incurred wholly and exclusively for the purpose of (i) obtaining the loan finance or (ii) providing security for it or (iii) repaying it. Expenses within (i) and (ii) are deductible under these provisions even if the loan finance is not in fact obtained. But incidental costs of obtaining finance do not include stamp duty, sums paid because of foreign exchange losses (or sums paid for protection against them) or the cost of repaying the loan or loan stock so far as attributable to its being repayable at a premium or its having been obtained at a discount.

[*ITTOIA 2005, ss 58, 59*].

Where a cash basis election is in force, a limit is imposed on the above deduction (see **76.10** TRADING INCOME — CASH BASIS FOR SMALLER BUSINESSES).

See also **3.2**, **3.7** ALTERNATIVE FINANCE ARRANGEMENTS.

Costs incidental to the taking out of a life insurance policy as a condition of obtaining the loan finance are deductible, but not premiums payable on such a policy (Revenue Tax Bulletin February 1992 p 13). Costs of a flotation the proceeds of which were used to repay loan finance were held not allowable as the motive of the company in arranging for the flotation was not wholly and exclusively to repay the debt (*Focus Dynamics plc v Turner* (Sp C 182), [1999] SSCD 71).

It was held in *Cadbury Schweppes plc v Williams* (Sp C 302), [2002] SSCD 115 that the period for which the relief is available is that in which the finance is obtained, rather than that in which the facility is used, notwithstanding the accountancy treatment. See, however, Revenue Tax Bulletin April 1996 p 306 for HMRC's view that the timing of the deduction must be in accordance with normal principles (i.e. it follows the accounting treatment, provided that the accounts are correctly drawn up in accordance with applicable UK accounting standards).

In *Kato Kagaku Co Ltd v HMRC* (Sp C 598) [2007] SSCD 412, it was held that part of an indemnity payment was deductible as an incidental cost of obtaining finance. The appellant had repaid a bank loan before the scheduled repayment date, and became liable to pay the bank approximately £21 million under an indemnity agreement. The Sp C disallowed all but about £3 million of this on the grounds that, on the facts of the case, the disallowed amount was a payment made in consequence of foreign exchange losses.

Simon's Taxes. See **B2.437**.

Long funding leases of plant or machinery

[75.98] The rules on leasing of plant and machinery were reformed by *FA 2006, s 81, Sch 8* with effect from, broadly, 1 April 2006. For 'long funding leases', the new regime grants entitlement to capital allowances to the lessee rather than to the lessor as previously (see **10.48 –10.54**CAPITAL ALLOWANCES ON PLANT AND MACHINERY). There were corresponding changes to the tax treatment of lease rentals, to ensure that the lessor is no longer taxed on, and the lessee does not obtain a deduction for, the capital element of rentals (see below). The current regime applies only to leases which are essentially financing transactions, known as '*funding leases*', comprising mainly finance leases but also some operating leases. Leases of no more than five years' duration are excluded from the regime, as are pre-1 April 2006 leases. There are transitional rules to enable leases finalised on or after 1 April 2006 to remain within the pre-existing regime in appropriate circumstances. See **10.54** CAPITAL ALLOWANCES ON PLANT AND MACHINERY. The coverage below considers firstly the lessor's position (**75.99**) and then the lessee's (**75.100**). Neither **75.99** nor **75.100** applies in calculating profits on the cash basis (see **76.14** TRADING INCOME — CASH BASIS FOR SMALLER BUSINESSES).

For an HMRC Technical Note published on 1 August 2006 on the long funding leasing rules, see webarchive.nationalarchives.gov.uk/20140109143644/http://www.hmrc.gov.uk/leasing/tech-note.pdf. See also HMRC Business Leasing Manual BLM 40000 *et seq*.

As regards finance leases that fall outside the definition of a long funding lease or preceded the introduction of those rules, see **75.82–75.84** above.

Simon's Taxes. See **B5.405A–B5.409A.**

Long funding leases — lessors

[75.99] The treatment depends on whether the lease is a long funding operating lease or a long funding finance lease.

For any period of account for the whole or any part of which the trader is the lessor of plant or machinery under a 'long funding operating lease' (see **10.50**(3) CAPITAL ALLOWANCES ON PLANT AND MACHINERY), he is entitled to a deduction as follows in computing his profits (so as to compensate him for non-entitlement to capital allowances). Firstly, determine the 'starting value' in accordance with *ITTOIA 2005, ss 148DA, 148DB*. This varies depending on whether or not there has been any previous use of the plant or machinery by the lessor and on the nature of any such previous use. In the most straightforward case where the sole use has been leasing under the long funding operating lease, the starting value is equal to cost. Secondly, deduct from the starting value the amount that is expected (at the commencement of the term of the lease — see *CAA 2001, s 70YI(1)*) to be the 'residual value' of the plant or machinery (i.e. its estimated market value assuming a disposal at the end of the term of the lease, less the estimated costs of that disposal). This gives the expected gross reduction in value over the term of the lease. Next, time-apportion that figure between all periods of account that coincide wholly or partly with the term of the lease. The resulting figure for each period of account is the amount deductible for that period.

Where the lessor (as above) incurs additional capital expenditure on the plant or machinery that is not reflected in its market value at the commencement of the term of the lease, an additional deduction is due as follows. Determine the amount which, at the time the additional expenditure is incurred, is expected to be the residual value of the plant or machinery. Deduct the amount previously expected to be the residual value. If this produces a positive amount, determine how much of that amount is attributable to the additional expenditure. Next, deduct the attributable amount from the amount of the additional expenditure. This gives the expected reduction in value of the additional expenditure over the remainder of the term of the lease. Time-apportion that figure between all periods of account that coincide wholly or partly with the term of the lease and which end after the additional expenditure is incurred. The resulting figure for each such period of account is the additional amount deductible for that period.

In the period of account in which a long funding operating lease *terminates*, any profit arising to the lessor from the termination must be brought into account as trading income and any loss so arising must be brought into account as a revenue expense. The profit or loss is computed as follows.

(1) Determine the 'termination amount' (for which see **10.51** CAPITAL ALLOWANCES ON PLANT AND MACHINERY) and subtract from it any sums paid to the lessee that are calculated by reference to the 'termination value' (as defined by *CAA 2001, s 70YH*), e.g. lease rental refunds.
(2) Determine the 'starting value' as above and subtract from it all deductions (other than additional deductions) allowable as above to that same lessor up to the date of termination.
(3) If any additional capital expenditure has been incurred as above, determine the total amount thereof and subtract from it all additional deductions allowable as above to that same lessor up to the date of termination.
(4) If the total in (1) above exceeds the aggregate of the totals in (2) and (3), a profit arises equal to the excess.
(5) If the total in (1) above falls short of the aggregate of the totals in (2) and (3), a loss arises equal to the deficit.

In computing the lessor's profits for the period of account in which termination occurs, no trading deduction is allowed for any sums paid to the lessee that are calculated by reference to the 'termination value' (as these are brought into account in (1) above).

[*ITTOIA 2005, ss 148D, 148DA, 148DB, 148E, 148EA, 148EB, 148F, 148J(2)(4)*].

Long funding finance leases

For any period of account in which the trader is the lessor of plant or machinery under a 'long funding finance lease' (see **10.50**(4) CAPITAL ALLOWANCES ON PLANT AND MACHINERY), the amount to be brought into account as his taxable income from the lease is the amount of the 'rental earnings' in respect of the lease. The '*rental earnings*' for any period is the amount that, in accordance with generally accepted accounting practice (GAAP), falls to be treated as the gross return on investment for that period in respect of the lease. If, in accordance with GAAP, the lease falls to be treated as a loan in the accounts in question, so much of the lease rentals as fall to be treated as interest are treated for these purposes as rental earnings. There is also provision for exceptional profits or losses (including capital items) arising from the lease to be brought into account for tax purposes, as trading income or as revenue expenditure, if they fall to be brought into account under GAAP in the period of account in question but otherwise than as part of the profits calculation.

Where the lease *terminates* and any sum calculated by reference to 'termination value' (as defined by *CAA 2001, s 70YH*) is paid to the lessee, e.g. lease rental refunds, no deduction is allowed for that sum in computing the lessor's trading profits, except to the extent (if any) that it is brought into account in determining rental earnings.

[*ITTOIA 2005, ss 148A–148C, 148J(4)*].

ITTOIA 2005, ss 148A–148F above are disapplied where:

(a) expenditure incurred on the leased plant or machinery is (apart from anything in *ITTOIA 2005, ss 148A–148F*) allowable as a deduction in computing the lessor's trading profits because the plant or machinery is held, or comes to be held, as trading stock; or
(b) the long funding lease is part of an arrangement, including one or more other transactions, entered into by the lessor a main purpose of which is to secure that, over the term of the lease, there is a substantial difference between the amounts brought into account under GAAP and the amounts brought into account in computing taxable profits, such difference being at least partly attributable to the application of any of *ITTOIA 2005, ss 148A–148F*.

There are also provisions to counter an avoidance scheme involving a mismatch in the treatment of lease rentals under a head lease and a sub-lease of the same plant or machinery. Under a typical scheme, the head lease from A to B will not be a long funding lease from B's (the lessee's) point of view but the sub-lease from B to C will be a long funding lease from B's (the lessor's) point of view. The result is that B would be entitled to tax relief on the full amount of the lease rentals under the head lease (i.e. including the capital element) but would not be chargeable to tax on the capital element of the sub-lease rentals. The legislation seeks to ensure that B is taxed on the full amount of the sub-lease rentals by disapplying *ITTOIA 2005, ss 148A–148F* above in these circumstances in relation to the sub-lease.

[*ITTOIA 2005, ss 148FA–148FC*].

Film lessors

ITTOIA 2005, ss 148A–148F above are disapplied where the subject of the long funding lease is a film. This has effect where the 'inception' (see *CAA 2001, s 70YI(1)*) of the lease is after 12 November 2008. Where the inception of the lease was on or before 12 November 2008 and rentals are due after that date and relate to a time falling after that date, the lessor is taxed on both the finance charge element of the rentals and so much of the capital element of the rentals as relates to the time falling after 12 November 2008. [*ITTOIA 2005, s 148FD*].

Long funding leases — lessees

[75.100] The treatment depends on whether the lease is a long funding operating lease or a long funding finance lease.

Long funding operating leases

In computing the profits of a trader for any period of account in which he is the lessee of plant or machinery under a 'long funding operating lease' (see **10.50**(3) CAPITAL ALLOWANCES ON PLANT AND MACHINERY), the otherwise allowable deductions in respect of amounts payable under the lease must be reduced as follows. Firstly, determine the 'relevant value' in accordance with *ITTOIA 2005, s 148I(4)(5)*. In the straightforward case where the sole use of the plant or machinery has been in a qualifying activity (within **10.4** CAPITAL ALLOWANCES ON PLANT AND MACHINERY) carried on by the lessee, the relevant value is equal to the market value of the plant or machinery at the commencement (see *CAA 2001, s 70YI(1)*) of the term of the lease. Secondly, deduct from the relevant value the amount that is expected (at the commencement of the term of the lease) to be the market value of the plant or machinery at the end of the term of the lease. This gives the expected gross reduction over the term of the lease. Next, time-apportion that figure between all periods of account that coincide wholly or partly with the term of the lease. The resulting figure for each period of account is the amount of the reduction for that period.

[*ITTOIA 2005, ss 148I, 148J*].

Long funding finance leases

In computing the profits of a trader for any period of account in which he is the lessee of plant or machinery under a 'long funding finance lease' (see **10.50**(4) CAPITAL ALLOWANCES ON PLANT AND MACHINERY), the amount deducted in respect of amounts payable under the lease must not exceed the amount that, in accordance with GAAP, falls to be shown in the lessee's accounts as finance charges or interest expenses in respect of the lease. If, in accordance with GAAP, the lease falls to be accounted for as a loan, it is for this purpose treated as if it fell to be accounted for as a finance lease.

Where the lease *terminates* and a sum calculated by reference to 'termination value' (as defined by *CAA 2001, s 70YH*) is paid to the lessee, e.g. lease rental refunds, that sum is not brought into account in computing the lessee's trading profits for any period. (It is, however, brought into account in calculating the disposal value of the plant or machinery for capital allowances purposes — see **10.49** CAPITAL ALLOWANCES ON PLANT AND MACHINERY).

[*ITTOIA 2005, ss 148G, 148H, 148J(4); FA 2019, Sch 14 paras 2(2), 6(1)*].

Right-to-use leases

Where a trader is, for any part of a period of account beginning on or after 1 January 2019, the lessee of plant or machinery under a 'right-to-use lease' (where the lessee applies IFRS 16 — see **10.50**(5) CAPITAL ALLOWANCES ON PLANT AND MACHINERY and **75.82** above) which is a long funding finance lease, the following applies if there is a change in the amounts payable under the lease as a result of which (and in accordance with GAAP) either a remeasurement of the lease liability is shown in the trader's accounts or a deduction is shown in the accounts (other than an interest expense or depreciation or impairment of the right-of-use asset arising from the lease). In computing the profits for the period, the deduction in respect of amounts payable under the lease is, after taking account of any limitation under the above provisions, increased or decreased to take account of the remeasurement or deduction resulting from the change. This does not apply if the remeasurement or deduction results in the lessee being treated as incurring further capital expenditure on plant or machinery under *CAA 2001, s 70D* (see **10.49** CAPITAL ALLOWANCES ON PLANT AND MACHINERY). [*ITTOIA 2005, s 148GA; FA 2019, Sch 14 paras 2(3), 6(1)*].

Mines, quarries etc.

[75.101] See 9.15 *et seq.* CAPITAL ALLOWANCES for mining etc. expenditure so allowable. The relevant legislation originated in 1945 and may therefore affect any pre-1945 decisions below.

The cost of sinking (*Coltness Iron Co v Black* HL 1881, 1 TC 287), deepening (*Bonner v Basset Mines* KB 1912, 6 TC 146) or 'de-watering' (*United Collieries v CIR* CS 1929, 12 TC 1248) a pit is capital. Provision for the future costs of abandoning an oil field and of restoring hired equipment used therein to its original state held capital (*RTZ Oil and Gas Ltd v Elliss* Ch D 1987, 61 TC 132). For shortworkings, see *Broughton & Plas Power v Kirkpatrick* QB 1884, 2 TC 69; *CIR v Cranford Ironstone* KB 1942, 29 TC 113.

For HMRC's view of the treatment of payments by mining concerns to landowners for restoration for surface damage, see HMRC Business Income Manual BIM62025. In particular, a payment of compensation for ascertained past damage is allowable, as is a provision for such expenditure where made in accordance with generally accepted accounting practice and accurately quantified.

Purchase of unworked deposits by sand and gravel merchant held capital (*Stow Bardolph Gravel Co Ltd v Poole* CA 1954, 35 TC 459) as was purchase of land with nitrate deposits by chemical manufacturer (*Alianza Co v Bell* HL 1905, 5 TC 172) and payment by oil company for unwon oil in wells it took over (*Hughes v British Burmah Petroleum* KB 1932, 17 TC 286). See also *Golden Horse Shoe v Thurgood* CA 1933, 18 TC 280 (purchase of tailings for gold extraction, allowable) and *CIR v Broomhouse Brick* CS 1952, 34 TC 1 (purchase of blaes for brick manufacture, allowable).

See generally HMRC Business Income Manual BIM62000–62085.

Production wells etc.

The costs of drilling the second and subsequent production wells in an area are not generally allowable. [*ITTOIA 2005, s 161*]. Although not specifically stated in the statute, this prohibition applies particularly to intangible drilling costs. For a discussion of this, see HMRC Oil Taxation Manual OT26237. Such costs may attract mineral extraction capital allowances (see **9.15** *et seq.* CAPITAL ALLOWANCES).

Simon's Taxes. See **B5.652, B5.653.**

Miscellaneous expenses and receipts

[75.102] The items below are arranged in alphabetical order. See also *Thompson v Magnesium Elektron* CA 1943, 26 TC 1 (payments based on purchases, held trading receipts); *British Commonwealth International Newsfilm v Mahany* HL 1962, 40 TC 550 (payments to meet operating expenses, trading receipts); *CIR v Pattison* CS 1959, 38 TC 617 (weekly instalments for business, capital).

Bitcoin and other cryptoassets

The profits and losses of a business on bitcoin transactions must be reflected in the business accounts, and are taxable under normal income tax rules (HMRC Brief 09/14, 3 March 2014).

HMRC does not consider cryptoassets to be currency or money. They have identified three types of cryptoasset: exchange tokens (like bitcoin), utility tokens and security tokens. The tax treatment of all types of tokens is dependent on the nature and use of the token and not the definition of the token. Only in exceptional circumstances would HMRC expect individuals to buy and sell cryptoassets with such frequency, level of organisation and sophistication that the activity amounts to a financial trade in itself. See HMRC policy paper 'Cryptoassets: tax for individuals' at www.gov.uk/government/publications/tax-on-cryptoassets. HMRC have published a separate policy paper 'Cryptoassets: tax for businesses', also at www.gov.uk/government/publications/tax-on-cryptoassets. This includes additional guidance that whether the buying and selling of exchange tokens amounts to a trade depends on a range of factors including degree and frequency of activity, level of organisation, and intention (including risk and commerciality).

Card winnings

Card winnings of club proprietor were held to be trading receipts (*Burdge v Pyne* Ch D 1968, 45 TC 320). For lotteries and football pools, see **75.28** above.

Carers

Any profits arising from payments by local authorities for taking the elderly or infirm into the home as family are chargeable as trading income (although the availability of 'rent-a-room' exemption (see **60.22** PROPERTY INCOME) will often obviate the need for further enquiry). See also **33** FOSTER CARE ETC and HMRC Business Income Manual BIM52750–52815.

Computer software

HMRC's views on the treatment of expenditure on computer software are summarised as follows.

Software acquired under licence

Regular payments akin to a rental are allowable revenue expenditure, the timing of deductions being governed by correct accountancy practice (see **75.21** above). A lump sum payment is capital if the licence is of a sufficiently enduring nature to be considered a capital asset in the context of the licencee's trade (see **75.43** above), e.g. where it may be expected to function as a tool of the trade for several years. Equally the benefit may be transitory (and the expenditure revenue) even though the licence is for an indefinite period. Inspectors will in any event accept that expenditure is on revenue account where the software has a useful economic life of less than two years. Timing of the deduction in these circumstances will again depend on correct accountancy practice.

Where the licence is a capital asset, capital allowances are available (see **10.10** CAPITAL ALLOWANCES ON PLANT AND MACHINERY).

Expenditure on a package containing both hardware and a licence to use software must be apportioned before the above principles are applied.

Software owned outright

The treatment of expenditure on such software (including any in-house costs) follows the same principles as are described above in relation to licensed software.

(Revenue Tax Bulletin November 1993 p 99 reproduced at HMRC Business Income Manual BIM35805).

See HMRC Business Income Manual BIM35800–35865 for a detailed analysis of HMRC's views generally.

DVD/video rental etc.

Relief for the cost of acquiring video tapes for hire may be obtained by way of either:

(i) capital allowances (provided the useful economic life is at least two years);
(ii) valuation basis (where the useful economic life is two years or less); or
(iii) renewals basis.

The tax treatment of DVDs and similar items (e.g. blu-ray discs and computer/console games) follows the same lines. See HMRC Business Income Manual BIM67200–67220.

Export Credits Guarantee Department

A deduction is allowed for amounts payable by a trader to that Department under an agreement entered into by virtue of arrangements made under *Export and Investment Guarantees Act 1991, s 2* or with a view to entering into such an agreement. [*ITTOIA 2005, s 91*].

Mutual concerns, distribution of assets from

If a deduction has been allowed (in computing trading profits) for a payment to a corporate mutual concern for the purposes of its mutual business and the trader receives a distribution in money or money's worth upon the winding-up or dissolution of the mutual concern, the amount or value received is a trading receipt. This applies only if the assets being distributed represent profits of the mutual concern. It does not apply to distributions of chargeable gains. If the trade has ceased by the time of the distribution, the amount or value received is a post-cessation receipt (within **59.1** POST-CESSATION RECEIPTS AND EXPENDITURE). [*ITTOIA 2005, s 104*]. For mutual trading generally, see **75.38** above.

Overpayments

Overpayments received, due to errors by customers or their banks which the taxpayer neither caused nor facilitated, were held not to be trading receipts (*Anise Ltd and others v Hammond* (Sp C 364), [2003] SSCD 258). But this decision was disapproved by the Tribunal in *Pertemps Recruitment Partnership Ltd v HMRC* UT, [2011] STC 1346 in which overpayments were held to have the same characteristics in the hands of the recipient trader as payments not made in error and thus to be trading receipts. The Tribunal distinguished this case from *Morley v Tattersall* and *Jay's, the Jewellers v CIR* at **75.126** below; in those cases the taxpayer held the funds in question in a fiduciary capacity and not as beneficial owner.

Purchases/sales of assets

See *T Beynon & Co v Ogg* KB 1918, 7 TC 125 (profits of colliery agent from deals in wagons held trading receipts); *Gloucester Railway Carriage v CIR* HL 1925, 12 TC 720 (sale by wagon manufacturer of wagons previously let, held trading receipts); *Bonner v Frood* KB 1934, 18 TC 488 (sale of rounds by credit trader, held trading receipts).

Reimbursements of capital expenditure

Reimbursements of capital expenditure spread over 30 years held capital as regards both payer and recipient (*Boyce v Whitwick Colliery* CA 1934, 18 TC 655). For allowances from railway in respect of traffic on sidings paid for by trader see *Westcombe v Hadnock Quarries* KB 1931, 16 TC 137; *Legge v Flettons Ltd* KB 1939, 22 TC 455.

Rental rebates

There is a restriction on the amount of the trading deduction allowable to a lessor of plant or machinery where he makes a rental rebate to the lessee. A rental rebate means any sum payable to the lessee that is calculated by reference to the value of the plant or machinery at or about the time when the lease terminates. The deduction is limited to the aggregate of all the amounts receivable in connection with the lease that have been brought into account in computing the lessor's taxable income. In calculating this aggregate, however, one excludes any amount brought into account as a disposal value as in **10.27** CAPITAL ALLOWANCES ON PLANT AND MACHINERY and any amounts that represent charges for services or 'taxes' to be paid by the lessor. ('*Taxes*' means UK or foreign taxes or duties, but not income tax, corporation tax or foreign equivalents.) In the case of a finance lease, one also excludes the finance charge element of the rentals (as defined). The limit does not apply where the lease is a long funding finance lease as in **75.99** above.

Where the whole or part of a rental rebate is disallowed as above as a deduction in computing trading profits, an amount may be treated as an allowable loss for capital gains tax purposes accruing to the lessor on the termination of the lease. The amount which may be so treated is the lower of the amount disallowed and the amount by which the rental rebate exceeds the lessor's capital expenditure. The loss is deductible only from chargeable gains accruing to the lessor on the disposal of the plant or machinery.

[*ITTOIA 2005, s 55B*].

The legislation is aimed at identified tax avoidance schemes. In circumstances not involving tax avoidance, the rebate would not normally exceed the taxable income from the lease and the restriction would not be relevant.

Solicitor's fees as trustee

Solicitor's fees as trustee were held to be professional receipts (*Jones v Wright* KB 1927, 13 TC 221) even if the solicitor is also a beneficiary (*Watson & Everitt v Blunden* CA 1933, 18 TC 402).

Sub-postmasters

Introductory fees paid by sub-postmasters were held not to be allowable (*Dhendsa v Richardson* (Sp C 134), [1997] SSCD 265).

Timber purchases and sales

For purchases and sales of standing timber by timber merchants see *Murray v CIR* CS 1951, 32 TC 238; *McLellan, Rawson & Co v Newall* Ch D 1955, 36 TC 117; *Hood Barrs v CIR (No 2)* HL 1957, 37 TC 188; *Hopwood v C N Spencer Ltd* Ch D 1964, 42 TC 169; *Russell v Hird and Mercer* Ch D 1983, 57 TC 127. For sales of trees by farmer see *Elmes v Trembath* KB 1934, 19 TC 72.

Trade marks or designs

Expenses are deductible if incurred in obtaining, for the purposes of a trade (not a profession or vocation), the registration of a trade mark or design, the renewal of registration of a trade mark or the extension of the period for which the right in a registered design subsists. [*ITTOIA 2005, s 90*].

Websites

The cost of setting up a website is likely to be capital expenditure; the regular update costs are likely to be revenue expenses (see HMRC Business Income Manual BIM35815).

Patents

[75.103] Expenses (agent's charges, patent office fees etc.) are deductible if incurred in obtaining, for the purposes of a trade (not a profession or vocation), the grant of a patent or the extension of its term or in connection with a rejected or abandoned application for a patent made for the purposes of the trade. [*ITTOIA 2005, s 89*].

For capital expenditure on the purchase of patent rights see **9.26** CAPITAL ALLOWANCES.

Sums received on the sale of patent rights may, dependent on the facts, be trading receipts (*Rees Roturbo Development v Ducker* HL 1928, 13 TC 366; *Brandwood v Banker* KB 1928, 14 TC 44; *CIR v Rustproof Metal Window* CA 1947, 29 TC 243 and cf. *Harry Ferguson (Motors) v CIR* CA(NI) 1951, 33 TC 15). Other sums are taxable under *ITTOIA 2005, ss 587–599*, see **41.6**, **41.7** INTELLECTUAL PROPERTY.

Where a company held a patent for renovating car tyres, lump sums received by it under arrangements for giving the payer a *de facto* franchise in his area, were held to be capital receipts (*Margerison v Tyresoles Ltd* KB 1942, 25 TC 59).

For spreading of patent royalties received, see **41.4** INTELLECTUAL PROPERTY and for DTR treatment of royalties from abroad, see **27.10**(h) DOUBLE TAX RELIEF.

For copyright, know-how and trade marks, see **75.59**, **75.95** and **75.102** respectively.

Simon's Taxes. See B5.331.

Personal and domestic expenses

[75.104] Expenditure incurred for domestic and private purposes is by its very nature incurred otherwise than wholly and exclusively for business purposes and is thus disallowable by virtue of *ITTOIA 2005, s 34* at **75.44** above.

The 'dual purpose rule' at **75.44** above is relevant here. Hence the cost of treatment at a nursing home was disallowed even though motivated by need for room from which to conduct business (*Murgatroyd v Evans-Jackson* Ch D 1966, 43 TC 581) as was the cost of a minor finger operation to enable a professional guitarist to continue playing as, on the evidence, he also played the guitar as a hobby (*Prince v Mapp* Ch D 1969, 46 TC 169) and expenditure on child care by a graphic designer working from home (*Carney v Nathan* (Sp C 347), [2003] SSCD 28). Medical expenses where illness said to be due to working conditions were not allowed in *Norman v Golder* CA 1944, 26 TC 293, but were allowed in *Parsons v HMRC* FTT (TC 421), [2010] UKFTT 110 (TC) where the taxpayer's profession was that of a film and television stuntman such that injuries were an inherent part of his work.

Expenditure on ordinary clothing is not normally allowable, the leading case here being *Mallalieu v Drummond* HL 1983, 57 TC 330, in which, reversing the decisions in the lower Courts, it was held that the cost of sober clothing worn by a lady barrister to comply with Bar Council guidelines was for the dual purpose of her profession and her requirements as a human being, and not allowable. See also **75.44** above and the 'clothing' cases at **28.19** EMPLOYMENT INCOME. In *Daniels v HMRC*, FTT (TC 6640), [2018] UKFTT 462 (TC), expenditure on clothing by an exotic dancer was allowed; the clothing consisted of dresses, lingerie, stockings, shoes etc. that were unsuitable for use outside the nightclub where she performed and were akin to a costume purchased by a self-employed actor for use in a performance.

In *Watkis v Ashford, Sparkes and Harward* Ch D 1985, 58 TC 468, expenditure on meals at regular partners' lunchtime meetings was disallowed, whilst expenditure on accommodation, food and drink at the firm's annual weekend conference was allowed.

In *McKnight v Sheppard* HL 1999, 71 TC 419, legal expenses in defending charges brought by a professional regulatory body were allowed despite the fact that the taxpayer's 'personal reputation was inevitably involved'. In *Key IP Ltd v HMRC* FTT (TC 1552), [2012] SFTD 305, the legal costs of bringing defamation proceedings were allowed in full on the grounds that, on the facts of the case, the sole purpose of the proceedings was to protect the business reputation of the appellant company and not to benefit its sole shareholder and director. But see also *Duckmanton v HMRC* UT, [2013] STC 2379, [2013] UKUT 305 (TCC) and *Raynor v HMRC* FTT (TC 1649), [2011] UKFTT 813 (TC) at **75.96** above and *Vaines v HMRC* CA, [2018] STC 297. In *MacKinlay v Arthur Young McClelland Moores & Co* HL 1989, 62 TC 704, contributions towards the removal expenses of a partner moved in the interests of the firm were not allowed. For rent etc. of premises used both as residence and for business see **75.108** below and for travelling and subsistence expenses see **75.125** below. See also *Mason v Tyson* Ch D 1980, 53 TC 333 (expenses of occasional use of flat) and *McLaren v Mumford* Ch D 1996, 69 TC 173 (expenses of residential accommodation required to be occupied with licensed premises).

The personal costs (e.g. accommodation, food and drink) of a UK resident individual of living abroad on business are not disallowed under *ITTOIA 2005, s 34* (HMRC Business Income Manual BIM47710 and HMRC SP A16).

For the 'dual purpose rule' in relation to expenditure with an intrinsic duality of purpose, e.g. food, warmth, health and shelter, see also HMRC Business Income Manual BIM37900–37970.

Simon's Taxes. See **B2.318**, **B2.458**.

Pooling of profits

[75.105] Where traders pool profits or act together in consortia but so as not to form PARTNERSHIPS (**52**) or trade jointly (cf. *Gardner and Bowring Hardy v CIR* CS 1930, 15 TC 602; *Geo Hall & Son v Platt* Ch D 1954, 35 TC 440) each trader's share of the pooled profits will normally be treated as a receipt of his main trade and any payment under the arrangement by one trader to another will be deductible in computing his profits (*Moore v Stewarts & Lloyds Ltd* CS 1905, 6 TC 501 and cf. *United Steel v Cullington (No 1)* CA 1939, 23 TC 71). In *Utol Ltd v CIR* KB 1943, 25 TC 517 payments by one company to another under a profit sharing arrangement were held to be dividends payable less tax under the law then in force. For compensation received on the termination of a profit sharing arrangement see *Van den Berghs* at **75.56**(b) above.

Pre-trading expenditure

[75.106] The general principle is that trading expenditure is deductible when incurred and hence is not allowable if incurred before trading commenced (cf. *Birmingham & District Cattle By-Products Ltd v CIR* KB 1919, 12 TC 92). The rule is modified for certain pre-trading capital expenditure, including scientific research expenditure and abortive exploration expenditure by mining concerns (see **9** CAPITAL ALLOWANCES).

However, there is a statutory relief for expenditure incurred by a person within the seven years before he commences to carry on a trade which, had it been incurred on the first day of trading, would have been deductible in computing the profits. The expenditure is treated as if it was incurred on the on the first day of trading and is thus deductible. Expenditure otherwise deductible, e.g. pre-trading purchases of stock or advance payments of rent, is not within this special relief. [*ITTOIA 2005, s 57*].

Simon's Taxes. See **B2.460.**

Property sales and other property receipts

[75.107] As to whether a trade of property dealing carried on, see **75.36** above; for rents receivable, see **75.94** above. For builders and property developers generally, see HMRC Business Income Manual BIM51500–51665.

Sales of property by builders in special circumstances have been considered in a number of cases. Profits held trading receipts in *Spiers & Son v Ogden* KB 1932, 17 TC 117 (building activities extended); *Sharpless v Rees* KB 1940, 23 TC 361 (sale of land acquired for hobby abandoned for health reasons); *Shadford v H Fairweather & Co* Ch D 1966, 43 TC 291 (sale of site after development plan dropped); *Snell v Rosser, Thomas & Co* Ch D 1967, 44 TC 343 (sale of land surplus to requirements); *Bowie v Reg Dunn (Builders)* Ch D 1974, 49 TC 469 (sale of land acquired with business); *Smart v Lowndes* Ch D 1978, 52 TC 436 (sale of land in wife's name). Sales of property built but let meanwhile held trading in *J & C Oliver v Farnsworth* Ch D 1956, 37 TC 51; *James Hobson & Sons v Newall* Ch D 1957, 37 TC 609; *W M Robb Ltd v Page* Ch D 1971, 47 TC 465 and this notwithstanding active building given up (*Speck v Morton* Ch D 1972, 48 TC 476; *Granville Building Co v Oxby* Ch D 1954, 35 TC 245). But in *Harvey v Caulcott* HC 1952, 33 TC 159 the sales were held realisations of investments and in *West v Phillips* Ch D 1958, 38 TC 203 some houses were treated as investments and others as trading stock. See also *Andrew v Taylor* CA 1965, 42 TC 557. Sales of houses retained after business *transferred* held sales of investments in *Bradshaw v Blunden (No 1)* Ch D 1956, 36 TC 397; *Seaward v Varty* CA 1962, 40 TC 523. See also *Hesketh Estates v Craddock* KB 1942, 25 TC 1 (profit on sale of brine baths held trading receipt of mixed business including land development).

For house sales subject to ground rents etc., see *CIR v John Emery & Sons* HL 1936, 20 TC 213; *B G Utting & Co Ltd v Hughes* HL 1940, 23 TC 174; *McMillan v CIR* CS 1942, 24 TC 417; *Heather v Redfern & Sons* KB 1944, 26 TC 119. For ground rents (England) and feu duties (Scotland) there should be credited the lower of their market value and cost, the cost being taken as the proportion of the cost of the land and building in the ratio of the market value to the sum of the market value and the sale price. For ground annuals (Scotland) which are perpetual the realisable value is brought in. The right to receive the rent then becomes part of the fixed capital of the trade, whose subsequent sale is not taken into account for income tax purposes. Any premiums on the grant of leases are part of the sale proceeds.

Turf sales by a farmer were held to be farming receipts in *Lowe v J W Ashmore Ltd* Ch D 1970, 46 TC 597. For timber sales see **75.102** above and for woodlands managed on a commercial basis see **30.53** EXEMPT INCOME.

A lump sum received by a property investment company in return for the assignment for a five-year term of a stream of rental income was held to be a capital receipt for part disposal of the company's interest (*CIR v John Lewis Properties plc* CA, [2003] STC 117), but see now Tolley's Corporation Tax under Property Income as regards special rent factoring provisions.

Any excess of allowable deductions over rent received by a builder from property held as trading stock may be allowed as a trading expense (HMRC Business Income Manual BIM51555).

See also **4.30** ANTI-AVOIDANCE for provisions affecting land or land development.

Simon's Taxes. See **B2.216–B2.219, B5.2.**

Rents, premiums etc. for business premises

[75.108] Rents paid for business premises are deductible in computing profits. For repairs see **75.110** below. As regards rents receivable, see **75.94** above.

For allowance for use of home for business, see *Thomas v Ingram* Ch D 1979, 52 TC 428. See also *Mason v Tyson* Ch D 1980, 53 TC 333 (expenses of flat used occasionally to enable professional man to work late not allowed as a deduction). In *Healy v HMRC* FTT (TC 4425), [2015] UKFTT 233 (TC), the rent of a London flat by an actor appearing in a West End play was held non-deductible. The expenditure had the dual purpose of enabling the appellant to perform his duties under his performer's contract and enabling him to receive visitors in London, the latter being a non-business purpose; the FTT found it unnecessary to reach a view on whether the expenditure had a further non-business purpose of meeting the appellant's ordinary needs for warmth and shelter.

Where premises became redundant or were closed down, continuing rents (less sub-letting receipts) were allowed as a deduction (*CIR v Falkirk Iron* CS 1933, 17 TC 625; *Hyett v Lennard* KB 1940, 23 TC 346) but not payments to secure the cancellation of leases no longer required (*Mallett v Staveley Coal & Iron* CA 1928, 13 TC 772 (the leading case here); *Cowcher v Richard Mills & Co* KB 1927, 13 TC 216; *Union Cold Storage v Ellerker* KB 1939, 22 TC 547; *Dain v Auto Speedways* Ch D 1959, 38 TC 525; *Bullrun Inc v Inspector of Taxes* (Sp C 248), [2000] SSCD 384). See also *West African Drug Co v Lilley* KB 1947, 28 TC 140. Where the rent of a motorway service station was calculated by reference to takings, a lump sum payment for the exclusion of tobacco duty from takings was held capital (*Tucker v Granada Motorway Services* HL 1979, 53 TC 92), but, distinguishing *Granada Motorways*, an amount received by a company in respect of its agent's negligent failure to serve its landlord with counter-notice of a notice of an increase in its rent, was held to be a trading receipt in *Donald Fisher (Ealing) Ltd v Spencer* CA 1989, 63 TC 168. Rent for a building not required for occupation for business purposes but to control access to the lessee's works was held deductible (less sub-let rents) in *Allied Newspapers v Hindsley* CA 1937, 21 TC 422.

For allowance of a provision in respect of future rents under leases of premises ceasing to be used for business purposes, see *Herbert Smith v Honour* Ch D 1999, 72 TC 130. Following that decision, HMRC changed their opinion and accepted that there is no tax rule denying provisions for anticipated loses or expenses (see Revenue Press Release 20 July 1999).

Additional rent liability incurred to obtain the freehold reversion to premises already rented held capital (*Littlewoods Mail Order v McGregor* CA 1969, 45 TC 519 following *CIR v Land Securities* HL 1969, 45 TC 495), as were periodical payments to reimburse capital expenditure incurred by landlord (*Ainley v Edens* KB 1935, 19 TC 303) and payments based on production for grant of sisal estates (*Ralli Estates v East Africa IT Commr* PC 1961, 40 ATC 9). But payments for the use of a totalisator calculated by reference to its cost were allowed (*Racecourse Betting Control Board v Wild* KB 1938, 22 TC 182) as were rents subject to abatement dependent on profits (*Union Cold Storage v Adamson* HL 1931, 16 TC 293). For Scottish duplicands see *Dow v Merchiston Castle School* CS 1921, 8 TC 149. Rent paid by partnership to partner owning business premises allowed (*Heastie v Veitch & Co* CA 1933, 18 TC 305). For excessive payments to professional 'service company' see *Payne, Stone Fraser* at **52.4** PARTNERSHIPS.

Rates and council tax

Business rates are deductible in the same way as rent. Council tax may similarly be deducted where it is attributable to premises (or part) used for trade purposes. (Revenue Press Release 16 March 1993).

Premiums

Certain lease premiums etc. in relation to leases not exceeding 50 years are chargeable on the landlord to an extent which varies with the length of the lease (see **60.26** PROPERTY INCOME). For any part of the 'receipt period' (as defined in *ITTOIA 2005, s 288(6)* — generally the duration of the lease) during which the lessee occupies the premises for the purposes of a trade or (with certain limitations) deals with his interest therein as property employed for the purposes of a trade, he is treated as incurring expenditure of a revenue nature. This is deductible in computing his trading profits, subject to any rule that might prohibit such deduction in a particular case (e.g. the 'wholly and exclusively' rule). For each day of the receipt period on which the above conditions are satisfied, the amount of revenue expenditure treated as incurred is the 'taxed receipt' (as defined in *ITTOIA 2005, s 287(4)* — broadly the amount which falls to be included in computing the landlord's property income) divided by the total number of days in the receipt period. If only part of the leased land is used for trading purposes, the amount is proportionately reduced. The amount is also proportionately reduced to the extent, if any, to which the lessee is entitled to an allowance under *CAA 2001, s 403* (mineral asset expenditure — see **9.16**(b) CAPITAL ALLOWANCES).

If the lessee himself grants a sublease out of the leased property at a taxable premium, he is treated as incurring revenue expenditure only to the extent, if any, that the daily amount computed above exceeds the daily reduction in his own taxable premium. For more detail of how this rule operates, see **60.29** PROPERTY INCOME. If the sublease relates to only part of the premises covered by the main lease, the above rules are applied separately to the different parts of the premises, the premium under the main lease being apportioned between those parts on a just and reasonable basis.

The above rules apply whether the premium is chargeable to income tax or corporation tax in the hands of the landlord. They also apply in relation to leases of property *outside* the UK where the landlord's property business is an overseas property business.

[*ITTOIA 2005, ss 60–67*].

ITTOIA 2005, ss 60–67 do not apply in calculating profits on the cash basis (see **76.14** TRADING INCOME — CASH BASIS FOR SMALLER BUSINESSES).

Otherwise, lease premiums are not deductible in computing trading profits (cf. *MacTaggart v Strump* CS 1925, 10 TC 17).

In the case of a person dealing in land, there is provision to prevent a lease premium or similar sum being taxed as both (i) a trading receipt and (ii) a receipt of a property business (as in **60.26** *et seq.* PROPERTY INCOME). This is achieved by reducing the amount at (i) by the amount at (ii). [*ITTOIA 2005, s 158*]. This does not apply in calculating profits on the cash basis (see **76.14** TRADING INCOME — CASH BASIS FOR SMALLER BUSINESSES).

See **75.109** below as regards *reverse* premiums.

General

See **4.31** ANTI-AVOIDANCE regarding restrictions where there is a lease-back at a non-commercial rent and **4.32** ANTI-AVOIDANCE for taxation of capital sums received on certain lease-backs.

Simon's Taxes. See **B2.411, B2.447, B2.448, B2.465.**

Reverse premiums

[75.109] In *New Zealand Commissioner of Inland Revenue v Wattie and another* PC 1998, 72 TC 639, it was held that a lump sum paid by a landlord to a prospective tenant as an inducement to enter into a lease at an above-market rental (generally known as a reverse premium) was a receipt of a capital nature. Legislation was introduced in the UK to counter this decision. For the purposes of the legislation, a '*reverse premium*' is a payment or other benefit received by way of inducement in connection with a transaction (the '*property transaction*') entered into by the recipient or a person 'connected' with him (see below), where:

(a) the property transaction is one under which the recipient or connected person becomes entitled to an estate or interest in, or a right in or over, land; and
(b) the payment (or other benefit) is made (or provided) by:
  (i) the person (the '*grantor*') by whom that estate, interest or right is granted, or was granted at an earlier time; or
  (ii) a person 'connected' with the grantor; or
  (iii) a nominee of (or a person acting on the directions of) the grantor or a person connected with the grantor.

As regards (b)(i) above, the use of the word 'grantor' means that the provisions do not apply when a freehold is conveyed. The most common occasion on which the provisions will apply will be a payment by a landlord as an inducement to a tenant to take a new lease, but they may apply where an existing tenant pays a new tenant an inducement to take over the remaining term of a lease if (and only if) (b)(ii) or (iii) applies to the existing tenant (Revenue Tax Bulletin December 1999 pp 711–713).

For the purposes of these provisions, persons are '*connected*' with each other if they are connected within **19** CONNECTED PERSONS at any time during the period when the 'property arrangements' are entered into. The '*property arrangements*' comprise the property transaction and any arrangements entered into in connection with it (whether earlier, simultaneously or later).

A reverse premium is treated for income tax purposes as a receipt of a revenue nature. Where the property transaction is entered into by the recipient of the reverse premium for the purposes of a trade carried on (or to be carried on) by him, the reverse premium must be taken into account in computing the trading profits. In any other case, the reverse premium is to be treated as a receipt of a UK property business, or (as the case may be) an overseas property business (see **60** PROPERTY INCOME), carried on by the recipient.

It is understood that accountancy principles require the receipt to be brought into account by spreading over the period of the lease or, if shorter, to the first rent review. This treatment must normally be followed for tax purposes (see **75.21** above) but, as an anti-avoidance measure, is overridden where:

(A) two or more parties to the property arrangements (see above) are connected persons (see above); and
(B) the terms of the those arrangements differ significantly from those which, at that time and under prevailing market conditions, would be regarded as reasonable and normal between persons dealing at arm's length in the open market.

In such case, the full amount or value of the reverse premium must be brought into account in the period of account in which the property transaction (see above) is entered into or, where applicable, the first period of account of the trade which the recipient subsequently begins to carry on.

None of these provisions apply where the recipient is an individual and the property in question is, or will be, occupied by him as his only or main residence. Nor do they apply to the extent that the payment or benefit is consideration for the first leg of a sale and leaseback arrangement within **4.31** or 4.32 ANTI-AVOIDANCE or is taken into account under *CAA 2001, s 532* (contributions to expenditure) to reduce the recipient's expenditure qualifying for capital allowances (see 9.2(vi) CAPITAL ALLOWANCES).

[*ITTOIA 2005, ss 99–103*].

It will be seen that a reverse premium within the above provisions is not confined to a lump sum payment and that 'other benefit' may include, for example, a contribution to the tenant's costs or an assumption of the recipient's liabilities under an existing lease. 'Other benefit' must, however, represent money or something capable of being turned into money. It does not include a sum foregone or deferred by the provider, rather than actually expended, such as a rent free period. See the article in the Revenue Tax Bulletin December 1999 pp 711–713, in particular in relation to the meeting of the tenant's costs.

Payment of reverse premium

The payment of a reverse premium by a company to achieve the assignment of a lease which had become disadvantageous (due to the company's failure to meet its obligations under a repairing covenant) was held to be on capital account (*Southern Counties Agricultural Trading Society Ltd v Blackler* (Sp C 198), [1999] SSCD 200). HMRC take the view that where a reverse premium is paid by a developer trading in property, it is deductible in computing his trading profits (Revenue Press Release 9 March 1999).

For HMRC's approach to these rules, see HMRC Business Income Manual BIM41050–41140.

Simon's Taxes. See **B2.208**.

Repairs and renewals

[75.110] Any allowable expenditure is deductible in the period when incurred and not when the repairs etc. accrued (*Naval Colliery Co Ltd v CIR* HL 1928, 12 TC 1017). Provisions for future repairs and renewals were held not allowable in *Clayton v Newcastle-under-Lyme Corpn* QB 1888, 2 TC 416 and *Peter Merchant Ltd v Stedeford* CA 1948, 30 TC 496, but see now **75.21** above, and HMRC Business Income Manual BIM46515, 46901, for the wider current acceptance of the application of normal accountancy principles in this context. Hence a provision for regular major overhaul work accrued due on aircraft engines was allowed as a deduction in *Johnston v Britannia Airways Ltd* Ch D 1994, 67 TC 99 (but see now Revenue Tax Bulletin February 1999 p 624 as regards changes in accounting practice superseding this decision). See also **75.111** below.

No deduction is available for expenditure on providing or replacing an integral feature of a building or structure if the expenditure is qualifying expenditure for plant and machinery capital allowances purposes. [*ITTOIA 2005, s 55A(1)*]. See **10.11** CAPITAL ALLOWANCES ON PLANT AND MACHINERY.

See generally HMRC Business Income Manual BIM46900–46990.

Simon's Taxes. See **B2.409, B2.411, B2.466.**

Business premises

[75.111] The general rule is that expenditure on additions, alterations, expansions or improvements is capital but the cost of repairs, i.e. restoring a building to its original condition, is allowable. However, the use of modern materials in repairing an old building does not make the expenditure capital (*Conn v Robins Bros Ltd* Ch D 1966, 43 TC 266), and HMRC now consider that this applies to the replacement of single-glazed windows by double-glazed equivalents (see Revenue Tax Bulletin June 2002 p 936). If the expenditure is capital, the estimated cost of 'notional repairs' obviated by the work is not allowable (see *Wm P Lawrie* and *Thomas Wilson (Keighley)* below). In *Hopegar Properties Limited v HMRC* FTT (TC 2734), [2013] UKFTT 331 (TC), work on an industrial estate, which involved repairing and widening the main entrance road, constructing a temporary road, re-laying fibre optic cables, re-siting, enlarging and repairing a car park and reinstating footpaths was all held to be in the nature of repairs and allowable.

Where on taking a lease of dilapidated property the dilapidations were made good under a covenant in the lease, the cost was held disallowable as attributable to the previous use of the premises (*Jackson v Laskers Home Furnishers* Ch D 1956, 37 TC 69) but when cinemas were acquired in a state of disrepair (but still fit for public showings) because of war-time restrictions on building work, the cost of the repairs was allowed (*Odeon Associated Theatres Ltd v Jones* CA 1971, 48 TC 257). See also **75.112** below. Expenditure on repairing newly acquired premises is allowable unless it is effectively part of the cost of acquiring the asset; whether the cost of the repairs is part of the cost of the asset is a question of fact in each case (HMRC Business Income Manual BIM46935).

A renewal of a building, i.e. a complete re-construction, is capital (*Fitzgerald v CIR Supreme Court* (IFS) 1925, 5 ATC 414; *Wm P Lawrie v CIR* CS 1952, 34 TC 20). The cost of rebuilding a factory chimney was held capital in *O'Grady v Bullcroft Main Collieries* KB 1932, 17 TC 93 but allowed in *Samuel Jones & Co v CIR* CS 1951, 32 TC 513 where the chimney was an integral part of the building. For roof replacements see *Wm P Lawrie* (above) and *Thos Wilson (Keighley) v Emmerson* Ch D 1960, 39 TC 360. The replacement of the ring in a cattle auction mart and of a stand in a football ground were held not to be repairs in *Wynne-Jones v Bedale Auction Ltd* Ch D 1976, 51 TC 426 and *Brown v Burnley Football Co Ltd* Ch D 1980, 53 TC 357 respectively in which the problem is reviewed.

Cost of barrier against coastal erosion held to be capital (*Avon Beach & Cafe v Stewart* HC 1950, 31 TC 487); also replacing a canal embankment (*Phillips v Whieldon Sanitary Potteries* HC 1952, 33 TC 213) and building new access road (*Pitt v Castle Hill Warehousing* Ch D 1974, 49 TC 638).

For a modern case (involving the insertion of plastic pipes within dilapidated metal ones over substantial lengths of a gas pipe network, held to be capital), see *Auckland Gas Co Ltd v CIR* PC, [2000] STC 527. *Auckland Gas* was considered but distinguished in *Transco plc v Dyall* (Sp C 310), [2002] SSCD 199, in which the insertion of plastic pipes in cast iron ones was on a selective basis and had not changed the character of the pipeline system as a whole.

Dilapidations of a repair nature on the termination of a lease are generally deductible.

For repairs to tied premises see **75.49** above.

Provisions for future expenditure

An Inland Revenue contention to the effect that no deduction was available for such provisions was rejected by the Special Commissioners in *Jenners Princes Street Edinburgh Ltd v CIR* (Sp C 166), [1998] SSCD 196. HMRC now accept that a provision for future repairs correctly made in accordance with generally accepted accounting practice (GAAP) and estimated with sufficient accuracy is an allowable expense except where there are specific tax rules to the contrary (e.g. that capital expenditure is non-deductible) (HMRC Business Income Manual BIM46905, 46510).

UK GAAP defines provisions as being 'liabilities of uncertain timing or amount'. It requires provisions to satisfy the definition of a liability: 'a present obligation arising from past events, the settlement of which is expected to result in an outflow of resources embodying economic benefits'. Mere anticipation of future expenditure, however probable and no matter how detailed the estimate, is not enough in the absence of an obligation at the accounting date. See generally BIM46500–46565.

Plant and other business assets

[75.112] The general rules at **75.111** above apply also to plant. Under what is known as the **valuation basis**, a class of assets, for example spare parts for plant and machinery, are dealt with in a similar way to trading stock, involving opening and closing valuations. For further detail, and for change from capital allowances to valuation basis, see HMRC Business Income Manual BIM46970, 46975.

For repairs soon after the acquisition of an asset see *Law Shipping v CIR* CS 1923, 12 TC 621 and *CIR v Granite City SS Co* CS 1927, 13 TC 1 in which the cost of repairs to ships attributable to their use before acquisition, was held capital. But see *Odeon Associated Theatres* at **75.111** above in which *Law Shipping* was distinguished. See also *Bidwell v Gardiner* Ch D 1960, 39 TC 31 in which the replacement of the furnishings of a newly acquired hotel was held capital.

Expenditure on renewal of railway tracks was allowed in *Rhodesia Railways v Bechuanaland Collector* PC 1933, 12 ATC 223, distinguishing *Highland Railway v Balderston* CES 1889, 2 TC 485 in which held capital. Abnormal expenditure on dredging a channel to a shipyard was held capital in *Ounsworth v Vickers Ltd* KB 1915, 6 TC 671 but the cost to a Harbour Board of removing a wreck (*Whelan v Dover Harbour Board* CA 1934, 18 TC 555) and of renewing moorings (*In re King's Lynn Harbour* CES 1875, 1 TC 23) was allowed. For shop fittings see *Eastmans Ltd v Shaw* HL 1928, 14 TC 218; *Hyam v CIR* CS 1929, 14 TC 479. See also *Lothian Chemical v Rogers* CS 1926, 11 TC 508.

Assets held under an operating lease

A deduction may be allowed for a provision to cover future repairs of assets held under an operating lease which contains a repairing obligation (for example, tenants' repairing leases of property). The lessee has a legal obligation to repair the asset and so it would be appropriate to include a provision for the expected cost of undertaking any necessary repairs at the accounting date. (HMRC Business Income Manual BIM46535).

Research and development and scientific research

[75.113] Revenue expenditure incurred by a trader on 'research and development' related to his trade, whether undertaken directly or on his behalf, is allowable as a deduction in computing profits. Expenditure incurred in the acquisition of rights in, or arising out of, the research and development is excluded, but the allowable expenditure otherwise includes all expenditure incurred in, or providing facilities for, carrying it out. Research and development 'related' to a trade includes any which may lead to or facilitate an extension of the trade, or which is of a medical nature and has a special relation to the welfare of workers employed in the trade. These provisions apply equally to expenditure on oil and gas exploration and appraisal (within *ITA 2007, s 1003*).

A deduction is similarly allowed for any sum paid to an approved scientific research association having as its object 'scientific research' related (with the extended meaning given above) to the class of trade concerned, and for any sum paid to an approved university, college research institute etc. to be used for such research. '*Scientific research*' means any activities in the fields of natural or applied science for the extension of knowledge. Any question as to what constitutes scientific research is to be referred by HMRC to the Secretary of State, whose decision is final. In relation to sums paid to a scientific research association in an accounting period of the association beginning on or after 1 January 2008 (see *SI 2007 No 3424*), these provisions, insofar as they apply to sums paid to such associations, are amended in line with amendments made to the tax legislation granting exemption to scientific research associations (see Tolley's Corporation Tax under Exempt Organisations). The scientific research association to which the sum is paid no longer has to be approved, but it does have to be potentially within the exemption for such associations at *CTA 2010, s 469*; and it must have as its object the undertaking of 'research and development' which may lead to or facilitate an extension of the class of trade to which the payer's trade belongs.

The above reliefs are *not* available to professions or vocations.

[*ITTOIA 2005, ss 87, 88*].

'*Research and development*' means activities that fall to be treated as such in accordance with generally accepted accounting practice (see **75.21** above). However, this is subject to Treasury regulations which narrow the definition by reference to published Government guidelines. [*ITA 2007, s 1006*]. The latest regulations refer to Government guidelines issued on 5 March 2004 (for which see www.gov.uk/government/publications/guidelines-on-the-meaning-of-research-and-development-for-tax-purposes). [*SI 2004 No 712*].

For *capital expenditure* on research and development, see **9.28** CAPITAL ALLOWANCES.

Simon's Taxes. See B2.467.

Security (personal)

[75.114] If an individual carries on a trade (either alone or as a member of a partnership of individuals) and there is a special threat to his personal physical security arising wholly or mainly because of the trade, expenditure incurred in connection with his use, or the provision for him, of a service or asset to meet that threat is not subject to the 'wholly and exclusively' rule at **75.44** above (and may therefore be deductible in computing profits), subject to the following conditions.

- In the case of a service, the benefit to the trader must consist wholly or mainly of an improvement to his personal physical security.
- In the case of an asset, the person incurring the expenditure must intend the asset to be used to improve personal physical security. If he intends it to be solely used for that purpose, any incidental use of the asset may be disregarded. If he intends it to be only partly used for that purpose, the potential deduction is restricted to the appropriate proportion of the expenditure.

The fact that a member of the trader's family or household also benefits from improved personal physical security does not preclude the potential deduction.

An 'asset' for these purposes includes equipment and a structure (e.g. a wall), but does not include a car, ship or aircraft. It is immaterial whether or not the asset becomes fixed to land and whether or not the trader acquires the property in the asset or (in the case of a fixture) an estate or interest in the land. But the provision or use of a dwelling or grounds appurtenant to a dwelling are excluded from the relief.

[*ITTOIA 2005, s 81*].

See also **10.9** CAPITAL ALLOWANCES ON PLANT AND MACHINERY, **28.75** EMPLOYMENT INCOME.

Simon's Taxes. See B2.471.

Shares and securities

[75.115] For whether a trade of 'share dealing' carried on see **75.37** above.

Profits and losses on realisations of investments by a bank in the course of its business enter into its *Sch D, Case I* profits (*Punjab Co-operative Bank v Lahore IT Commr* PC 1940, 19 ATC 533 and see *Frasers (Glasgow) Bank v CIR* HL 1963, 40 TC 698) and similarly for insurance companies (*Northern Assce Co v Russell CES 1889, 2 TC 551*; *General Reinsurance Co v Tomlinson* Ch D 1970, 48 TC 81 and contrast *CIR v Scottish Automobile* CS 1931, 16 TC 381). Profits/losses held capital in *Stott v Hoddinott* KB 1916, 7 TC 85 (investments acquired by architect to secure contracts); *Jacobs Young & Co v*

Harris KB 1926, 11 TC 221 (shares held by merchanting company in subsidiary wound up); *Alliance & Dublin Consumers' Gas Co v Davis* HC(IFS) 1926, 5 ATC 717 (investments of gas company earmarked for reserve fund). A profit by a property dealing company on the sale of shares acquired in connection with a property transaction was held a trading receipt (*Associated London Properties v Henriksen* CA 1944, 26 TC 46) but contrast *Fundfarms Developments v Parsons* Ch D 1969, 45 TC 707 and see now **4** ANTI-AVOIDANCE.

Shares allotted for mining concessions granted by company dealing in concessions held trading receipts at market value (*Gold Coast Selection Trust v Humphrey* HL 1948, 30 TC 209). See also *Murphy v Australian Machinery & Investment Co* CA 1948, 30 TC 244 and *Scottish & Canadian Investment Co v Easson* CS 1922, 8 TC 265.

For options, see *Varty v British South Africa Co* HL 1965, 42 TC 406 (no profits or loss until shares sold). See also *Walker v Cater Securities* Ch D 1974, 49 TC 625.

Conversion etc. of shares and securities held as circulating capital

Where a new holding of shares or securities (as defined) is issued in exchange for an original holding a profit on sale of which would fall to be treated as part of trading profits, the transaction is treated as not involving any disposal of the original holding, the new holding being treated as the same asset as the original holding. This applies only to transactions which result in the new holding being equated with the original holding under *TCGA 1992, ss 132–136* (capital gains rollover in cases of conversion etc.) or *TCGA 1992, s 134* (compensation stock). The above rule does not apply to shares or securities for which unrealised profits or losses (computed on a mark to market basis by reference to fair value) are brought into account in the period of account in which the transaction takes place. Where consideration is receivable in addition to the new holding, the above rule applies only to a proportion of the original holding, computed by reference to the market value of the new holding and the other consideration received. [*ITTOIA 2005, s 150; SI 2017 No 1204, Regs 1, 11*].

Gilt-edged securities — stripping and consolidation

Where the profit on the sale of a gilt-edged security (as defined) or strips (as defined) of a gilt-edged security would fall to be brought into account in computing the profits of a trade, there are special provisions dealing with the exchange of such a security for strips of the security and *vice versa*. On an exchange for strips, the security is treated as having been redeemed at its market value, and the strips as having been acquired at that market value apportioned *pro rata* to their market value at the time of the exchange. Similarly on a consolidation, each strip is treated as having been redeemed at its market value, and the security as having been acquired at the aggregate market value of the strips. The Treasury may make regulations for determining market value for these purposes.

The above rules on conversion etc. of securities held as circulating capital do not apply where these provisions apply. These provisions have the opposite effect as they effectively require a profit on the exchange to be brought into account for tax purposes.

[*ITTOIA 2005, ss 151–154*].

Stock lending fees

Such fees relating to investments eligible for relief under *FA 2004, s 186* (pension scheme funds — see **57.11, 57.40** PENSION PROVISION) are themselves eligible for relief under that *section*. [*ICTA 1988, s 129B*].

Dealers in securities

Any distribution by a UK resident company (or payment representative of such a distribution) *received by* a dealer in securities is taken into account in computing the dealer's trading profits. This takes precedence over the normal charge on dividends at **65.10** SAVINGS AND INVESTMENT INCOME. Any payment *made by* a dealer which is representative of a UK company distribution is similarly brought into the computation of trading profits. [*ITTOIA 2005, ss 366(1), 398(2); FA 2016, Sch 1 paras 1, 73*].

In cases where, in accordance with generally accepted accounting practice (see **75.21** above), profits and losses on the sale of securities are calculated by reference to the fair value of the securities and taken to reserves rather than profit or loss account, they are nevertheless brought into account in computing trading profits. [*ITTOIA 2005, s 149; SI 2017 No 1204, Regs 1, 11*].

Cash basis

None of *ITTOIA 2005, ss 149–154* above apply in calculating profits on the cash basis (see **76.14** TRADING INCOME — CASH BASIS FOR SMALLER BUSINESSES).

FISMA levies

A deduction is available for certain levies payable under *Financial Services and Markets Act 2000* ('FISMA') where, exceptionally, such levies would not otherwise be deductible. A deduction is also available for payments made as a result of an award of costs under costs rules (as defined). Certain repayments under FISMA must be brought into account as a trading receipt. [*ITTOIA 2005, s 155*].

Extra return on new issues of securities

Where:

(a) securities of a particular kind are issued (being the original issue of securities of that kind);
(b) new securities of the same kind are issued subsequently;
(c) a sum (the 'extra return') is payable by the issuer in respect of the new securities, to reflect the fact that interest is accruing on the old securities and calculated accordingly; and

(d) the issue price of the new securities includes an element (separately identified or not) representing payment for the extra return,

the extra return is treated for income tax purposes as a payment of interest (so far as it would not otherwise be treated as such), but the issuer is not entitled to tax relief, either as a deduction in computing profits or otherwise as a deduction or set-off, for the payment. [*ITA 2007, ss 845, 846*].

General

See also **4.9–4.12** ANTI-AVOIDANCE (transactions in securities to obtain tax advantage).

Simon's Taxes. See **B5.628**.

Stock and work in progress

[75.116] See generally HMRC Business Income Manual BIM33000–33630. Following the adoption of the rule that GAAP be adhered to in computing taxable profits (see **75.21** above), HMRC Statement of Practice SP 3/90 (to which references are made below) was generally superseded and was accordingly withdrawn. However, the principles drawn from that Statement continue to be relevant for subsequent accounting periods (except as referred to below).

Basis of valuation

The general rule has long been that stock is to be valued at the lower of cost and market value. Leading cases are *Minister of National Revenue v Anaconda American Brass Co* PC 1955, 34 ATC 330 and *BSC Footwear v Ridgway* HL 1971, 47 TC 495. Market value held to be replacement price for a merchant (*Brigg Neumann & Co v CIR* KB 1928, 12 TC 1191) and retail price for a retailer in *BSC Footwear* above (Inland Revenue prepared to take price net of any selling commission). Stock may be valued partly at cost and partly at market value where lower (*CIR v Cock Russell & Co* KB 1949, 29 TC 387). The base stock method is not permissible (*Patrick v Broadstone Mills* CA 1953, 35 TC 44) nor is 'LIFO' (*Anaconda American Brass* above). See also *Ryan v Asia Mill* HL 1951, 32 TC 275. The cost should include as a minimum the cost of materials and direct labour but the accounts treatment of overheads is normally accepted (*Duple Motor Bodies v Ostime* HL 1961, 39 TC 537).

However, HMRC now take the view that any valuation of stock included in financial statements prepared in accordance with generally accepted accounting practice (GAAP) (see **75.21** above) should be accepted provided that:

- it reflects the correct application of GAAP;
- the method pays sufficient regard to the facts; and
- the basis does not violate the taxing statutes as interpreted by the courts.

(HMRC Business Income Manual BIM33115).

A mark to market basis of valuation, used mainly by financial institutions and commodity dealers and under which stock is valued at market value, may also be acceptable (HMRC Business Income Manual BIM33160).

The principal accounting standard governing stock is SSAP 9.

For the use of formulae in computing stock provisions and write-downs, see Revenue Tax Bulletin December 1994 p 184. Broadly, HMRC will accept formulae which reflect a realistic appraisal of future income from the particular category of stock and which result in the stock being included at a reasonable estimate of net realisable value. Where computations are accepted without enquiry, it is on the assumption that profits are arrived at in accordance with such principles.

For the treatment of depreciation taken into account in arriving at stock valuations, see Revenue Tax Bulletin June 2002 pp 936, 937.

For motor dealer stock valuations, see Revenue Tax Bulletin August 1994 p 156.

As regards valuation of professional work in progress, uncompleted contracts for services should be valued in accordance with GAAP. Briefly, this means that revenue for service contracts are to be accounted for under what is known as the 'percentage of completion' method. In very simple terms, this means that if a contract is in progress at the year end, the supplier of services would include the proportion undertaken to that date in its accounts as revenue (HMRC Business Income Manual BIM33165). See also below under UITF Abstract 40.

For a discussion on the application of GAAP to the valuation of the work in progress of a contractor in the construction industry, see *Smith v HMRC* UT, [2011] STC 1724.

UITF Abstract 40

In 2005, UITF (Urgent Issues Task Force) Abstract 40 changed the way that all service providers (not just those providing professional services) must account for uncompleted (and unbilled) work at the year end. Firms must recognise turnover in respect of ongoing work by reference to the proportion of the work completed, rather than only when the contract is completed. This may require, for example, the bringing into account of a sole proprietor's (or partner's) own time (at its charge-out value) as well as that of his staff.

Changes in basis of valuation

Where the stock was found to be grossly undervalued it was held that an assessment to rectify the closing undervaluation must be reduced by the opening undervaluation to bring out the true profits (*Bombay IT Commr v Ahmedabad New Cotton Mills Co* PC 1929, 9 ATC 574). But where a company altered its method of dealing with accrued profits on long-term contracts and the closing work in progress in the year 1 accounts on the old basis was substantially below the opening figure in the year 2 accounts on the new basis, held, distinguishing *Ahmedabad*, the difference must be included in the year 2 profits (*Pearce v Woodall-Duckham Ltd* CA 1978, 51 TC 271). See also HMRC SP 3/90.

Where there is a change in the basis of valuation, the following practice is applied for tax purposes. If the bases of valuation both before and after the change are valid bases, an adjustment may be required under the change of basis rules at **75.24** above. If the change is from an invalid basis to a valid one, both the opening stock valuation and the closing stock valuation for the period of change must be computed on the new valid basis, and liabilities for earlier years will be reviewed where it is possible to do so (HMRC Business Income Manual BIM33199). See, however, *Woodall-Duckham Ltd* (above) as regards long-term contracts.

Valuation of stock and work in progress on cessation of trade

See **75.117** below.

Long-term contracts

HMRC accept that accurate provisions for foreseen losses on long-term contracts (e.g. in the construction industry) made in accordance with GAAP are tax deductible (HMRC Business Income Manual BIM33025).

In *Symons v Weeks and Others* Ch D 1982, 56 TC 630, it was held that progress payments under the long-term contracts of a firm of architects did not fall to be brought into account for tax before the relevant contract was completed, notwithstanding that they exceeded the figure brought in for work in progress, calculated on the correct principles of commercial accounting.

See above for changes of basis.

What constitutes stock

The provisions in *ITTOIA 2005, ss 172A–172F* have their own definition of stock (see **75.118** below). For other purposes, case law applies as follows. Greyhounds kept by greyhound racing company not trading stock (*Abbot v Albion Greyhounds (Salford)* KB 1945, 26 TC 390). Payments by cigarette manufacturer for cropping trees (not owned by it) for leaves used in manufacture, held to be for materials (*Mohanlal Hargovind of Jubbulpore v IT Commr* PC 1949, 28 ATC 287). For payments for unworked minerals, sand and gravel etc., (including tailings etc.) by mines, quarries etc. see **75.101** above. For payments for oil by oil companies, see *Hughes v British Burmah Petroleum KB 1932, 17 TC 286*; *New Zealand Commr v Europa Oil (NZ)* PC 1970, 49 ATC 282; *Europa Oil (NZ) v New Zealand Commr* PC, [1976] STC 37. For timber see **75.102** above and *Coates v Holker Estates Co Ch D 1961, 40 TC 75*.

Trading stock acquired or disposed of other than in the course of trade

See **75.118** below.

Goods sold subject to reservation of title etc.

Where the supplier of goods reserves the title in them, for example until they are paid for, the accountancy treatment will follow the substance of the transaction and not the legal form. A sale will be regarded as taking place at the point when the risks and rewards of the ownership of the asset are substantially transferred, even though legal title may not pass until later.. The treatment adopted, so long as it is in accordance with GAAP, should normally be followed in computing taxable profits. (HMRC Business Income Manual BIM33375).

Goods on consignment stock are normally treated as stock in the hands of the supplier until disposed of by the consignee (e.g. sale or return) (HMRC SP B6).

For **forward contracts**, see **75.58** above.

Insurance recoveries

See **75.92** above.

Recovery of assets under Proceeds of Crime Act

Where the transfer of trading stock is a *Pt 5* transfer under *Proceeds of Crime Act 2002* (as in **9.2**(x) CAPITAL ALLOWANCES) and the stock is to be treated, as a result of the transfer, as if sold in the course of the trade, it is treated, for the purpose of computing taxable profits and notwithstanding *ITTOIA 2005, s 173* at **75.117** below (if applicable), as sold at cost price. [*Proceeds of Crime Act 2002, Sch 10 para 11*].

Simon's Taxes. See **B2.6.**

Valuation of stock and work in progress on cessation of trade

[75.117] If a person permanently ceases to carry on a trade, any 'trading stock' at cessation must be valued as set out in (a) and (b) below in computing taxable profits. This does not apply on the death of a sole trader (see also below for HMRC practice where the trade continues); neither does it apply on a change in the persons carrying on the trade which does not fall to be treated as a cessation (see **52.7** PARTNERSHIPS). '*Trading stock*' is widely defined for these purposes by *ITTOIA 2005, s 174* and includes any work in progress of a trade (though not of a profession or vocation, for which see below).

(a) If the trading stock at cessation is sold to a person carrying on (or intending to carry on) a trade, profession or vocation in the UK who can deduct the cost as an expense for income tax or corporation tax purposes, the stock is valued at the amount realised on the sale. If, however, the two parties to the sale are connected persons (defined more broadly than in **19** CONNECTED PERSONS — see *ITTOIA 2005, s 179*), arm's length value is to be taken instead. (Neither rule applies to a transfer of farm animals where the anti-avoidance rules at **34.8** HERD BASIS apply.) If the stock is sold with other assets, the amount realised is arrived at on a just and reasonable apportionment. For the purposes of these rules, a 'sale' includes a transfer for valuable consideration, with related expressions then being defined accordingly. Where arm's length value exceeds both (i) actual sale price and (ii) acquisition value (broadly, the amount that would have been deductible in respect of the stock had it been sold in the course of trade immediately before cessation), connected persons may jointly elect to substitute the greater of (i) and (ii) for the arm's length value. The election must be made no later than the first anniversary of 31 January following the tax year in which the cessation occurred.
The cost of the trading stock to the buyer is taken to be the value determined under the above rules (or the corresponding corporation tax rules) in relation to the seller.

Any question as to the application of these rules is to be determined in the same way as an appeal.

These rules are not applicable to woodlands managed on a commercial basis (*Coates v Holker Estates* above). For their application to 'hire-purchase debts' see *Lions Ltd v Gosford Furnishing Co Ltd & CIR* CS 1961, 40 TC 256. A contention by the Inland Revenue that the rules did not apply to a transfer of closing stock simultaneous to a cessation was rejected in *Moore v Mackenzie* Ch D 1971, 48 TC 196.

(b) In all cases not within (a) above, trading stock is to be valued at the price it would have realised if sold in the open market at the time of the cessation.

In a case where a transfer pricing adjustment (see **4.19** *et seq.* ANTI-AVOIDANCE) falls to be made in connection with any provision made or imposed in relation to any trading stock and having effect in connection with the cessation, the above provisions and the transfer pricing rules both effectively apply, so as to bring into overall charge an amount not less than the amount calculated under (a) or (b) above.

Similar rules as in (a) and (b) above apply in relation to '*work in progress*' (as defined by *ITTOIA 2005, s 183*) on cessation of a profession or vocation, except that there is no special rule for a transfer of work in progress to a connected person. Additionally, an election is available to the effect that, in computing profits to the date of cessation, closing work in progress is valued at cost and any realised excess over cost is then treated as a post-cessation receipt (see **59.1** POST-CESSATION RECEIPTS AND EXPENDITURE); the election must be made no later than the first anniversary of 31 January following the tax year in which the cessation occurred. Again, the rules do not apply either on the death of a sole practitioner etc. or on a change in the persons carrying on a profession which does not fall to be treated as a cessation.

[*ITTOIA 2005, ss 173–186*].

Where a sole trader dies, the closing value of stock or work in progress is the lower of cost or net realisable value. If, following the death, the executors continue trading, their opening stock *must* be brought in at market value even though valued differently on death. Where the business passes direct to a beneficiary, the opening stock in his hands *may* be brought in at market value. (HMRC Business Income Manual BIM33520).

Simon's Taxes. See **B2.617**.

Trading stock acquired or disposed of other than in the course of trade

[75.118] The tax treatment of changes in trading stock on or after 12 March 2008 are placed on a statutory footing. (See below for the case law that previously established the correct tax treatment.) These provisions cover:

(i) trading stock appropriated by the trader for another purpose (e.g. for his own consumption), in which case market value is brought into account as a receipt on the date of appropriation and any actual consideration received is left out of account;

(ii) items owned by the trader otherwise than as trading stock being appropriated to trading stock, in which case the cost for tax purposes (treated as incurred at the time it became trading stock) is the market value of the item on the date it became trading stock, with any actual value given for it being left out of account;

(iii) trading stock disposed of otherwise than in the course of a trade where (i) above does not apply, in which case market value is brought into account as a receipt on the date of disposal and any actual consideration is left out of account;

(iv) trading stock acquired other than in the course of a trade where (ii) above does not apply, in which case the cost for tax purposes (treated as incurred at time of acquisition) is the market value of the item at time of acquisition, with any actual value given for it being left out of account.

Where the transfer pricing rules at **4.19** *et seq.* ANTI-AVOIDANCE have effect, the rules at (iii) and (iv) above apply together with the transfer pricing rules, so as to bring into overall charge an amount not less than the market value of the stock.

For these purposes only, trading stock is defined as stock held for sale in the course of a trade, or partially completed or immature items which are intended for sale when complete or mature. It does not include materials used for manufacture etc., services carried out in the course of a trade or materials used in the performance of these services.

[*ITTOIA 2005, ss 172A–172F*].

The above does not apply in calculating profits on the cash basis (see **76.14** TRADING INCOME — CASH BASIS FOR SMALLER BUSINESSES).

Case law

Where trading stock is disposed of otherwise than by way of trade, the realisable value is to be credited for tax purposes. This was established by *Sharkey v Wernher* HL 1955, 36 TC 275 approving *Watson Bros v Hornby* KB 1942, 24 TC 506. It applies, *inter alia*, to goods taken out of stock by a retailer for his own use (see below). It was applied in *Petrotim Securities Ltd v Ayres* CA 1963, 41 TC 389 to a disposal of shares at gross under-value as part of a tax avoidance scheme, but in *Ridge Securities Ltd v CIR* Ch D 1963, 44 TC 373, dealing with the other end of the same scheme, it was held that the same principle applied to acquisitions of trading stock otherwise than by way of trade, market price being substituted for the actual purchase price. But the principle is not applicable to sales or purchases by way of trade notwithstanding not at arm's length. Hence when a share dealing company acquired shares at substantial overvalue from an associated company, the claim by the Inland Revenue for market value failed (*Craddock v Zevo Finance Co* HL 1946, 27 TC 267), and when a property dealing company acquired property from its controlling shareholder at substantial undervalue, its claim to substitute market value failed (*Jacgilden (Weston Hall) v Castle* Ch D 1969, 45 TC 685). See also *Skinner v Berry Head Lands* Ch D 1970, 46 TC 377 and *Kilmorie (Aldridge) v Dickinson* HL 1974, 50 TC 1.

The leading case of *Sharkey v Wernher* above established the principle that stock taken for own use or disposed of otherwise than by sale in the normal course of trade should be treated as if it were a sale at market value. HMRC officers have been authorised to take a reasonably broad view in applying this principle. The case is not considered to apply to:

(a) services rendered to the trader personally or to his household the cost of which should be disallowed under the 'wholly and exclusively' rule at **75.44** above;
(b) the value of meals provided for proprietors of hotels, boarding houses, restaurants etc. and members of their families, the cost of which should be disallowed as in (a) above;
(c) expenditure incurred by a trader on the construction of an asset which is to be used as a fixed asset in the trade.

(HMRC SP A32).

General

For HMRC's view of the application of normal trading income principles to donations of trading stock to charities, see Revenue Tax Bulletin June 1996 p 319.

Where a chargeable gain or allowable loss would otherwise arise for capital gains tax purposes under *TCGA 1992, s 161(1)* on the appropriation to trading stock of an asset held in another capacity, the trader may elect for the market value of the asset to be reduced for income tax purposes by the amount of the chargeable gain (or, before 8 March 2017, increased by the amount of the allowable loss), the trading profits being computed accordingly and the appropriation being disregarded for capital gains tax purposes. The election must be made within twelve months after 31 January following the tax year in which ends the period of account in which the asset is appropriated. With effect for appropriations of assets to trading stock made on or after 8 March 2017, the election is permitted only where appropriation at market value would give rise to a chargeable gain and not where it would give rise to an allowable loss. [*TCGA 1992, s 161(3)(3A); F(No 2)A 2017, s 26*].

Simon's Taxes. See **B2.205**.

Subscriptions and contributions

[75.119] The following are relevant.

Flood or coastal erosion risk management projects

Expenses incurred by a person carrying on a trade in making a 'qualifying contribution' to a qualifying 'flood or coastal erosion risk management project' are deductible in computing profits. A contribution can be a sum of money paid or services provided. A contribution is a '*qualifying contribution*' if it is made for the purposes of the project and under an agreement between the person making it and either the applicant authority or the Environment Agency, whichever is carrying out the project (or between those two parties and other persons). A '*flood or coastal erosion risk management project*' is to be interpreted in accordance with *Flood and Water Management Act 2010, ss 1–3*. Such a project is a qualifying project if an English risk management authority (within *Flood and Water Management Act 2010, s 6(14)*) has applied to the Environment Agency for a grant under *Flood and Water Management Act 2010, s 16* in order to fund the project, or the Environment Agency has determined that it will itself carry out the project, and the Environment Agency has allocated funding by way of grant-in-aid to the project.

No such deduction is allowed if, in connection with the making of the contribution, the contributor or a person connected with him (see **19** CONNECTED PERSONS) receives (or is entitled to receive) a 'disqualifying benefit', whether from the carrying out of the project or from any person. A '*disqualifying benefit*' is any benefit consisting of money or other property, but structures to be used for the purposes of flood or coastal erosion risk management, and put in place in carrying out the project, are excluded from being disqualifying benefits. Land, plant or machinery to be used, in the realisation of the project, for the purposes of flood or coastal erosion risk management are similarly excluded. Refunds of money contributions, and compensation for contributions consisting of services, are not disqualifying benefits. However, where a deduction has been made and the contributor or a connected person receives any such refund or compensation (whether in money or money's worth), the amount or value received must be brought into account as a trading receipt arising on the date on which the refund or compensation is received. If the trade has ceased before that date, the refund or compensation is instead treated as a post-cessation receipt (within **59.1** POST-CESSATION RECEIPTS AND EXPENDITURE).

The above rules apply where, disregarding any available capital allowances, a deduction would not otherwise be allowable for the expenses incurred.

[*ITTOIA 2005, ss 86A, 86B*].

Local organisations

Ordinary annual subscriptions to local associations, including Chambers of Commerce, are normally allowed as deductions in computing profits. Subscriptions to larger associations are deductible, and receipts therefrom chargeable, if the association has entered into an arrangement with HMRC under which it is assessed on any surplus of receipts over allowable expenditure (the association should be asked). Most associations enter into the arrangement but if not the deduction is restricted to the proportion applied by the association for purposes such that it would have been deductible if so applied by the subscriber (*Lochgelly Iron & Coal Co Ltd v Crawford* CS 1913, 6 TC 267). For other cases see Tolley's Tax Cases. Subscriptions to the Economic League are not deductible (*Joseph L Thompson & Sons Ltd v Chamberlain* Ch D 1962, 40 TC 657).

The payment of an ordinary annual subscription to a local trade association by a non-member is normally deductible as expenditure incurred for the purposes of the subscriber's trade with members of the association (HMRC Business Income Manual BIM47430).

Contributions to mutual insurance associations are deductible even though used to create a reserve fund (*Thomas v Richard Evans & Co Ltd HL 1927, 11 TC 790*).

Local enterprise organisations

Expenditure incurred in making any contribution (whether in cash or kind) to a 'local enterprise organisation' is specifically allowed as deduction in computing profits if it would not otherwise be deductible. If, however, in connection with the making of the contribution, the trader or a person connected with him (see **19** CONNECTED PERSONS) receives (or is entitled to receive) a 'disqualifying benefit' of any kind, whether or not from the organisation itself, the value of the benefit is subtracted from the deduction otherwise available. Any such benefit received after such a deduction has been given is recovered by treating its value as a trading receipt for the period of account in which it is received. If received after the trade has permanently ceased, it is treated as a post-cessation receipt (within **59.1** POST-CESSATION RECEIPTS AND EXPENDITURE). A '*disqualifying benefit*' is a benefit the expenses of obtaining which would not be deductible if incurred directly by the trader in an arm's length transaction.

For these purposes, a '*local enterprise organisation*' means any of the following.

- A local enterprise agency, i.e. a body for the time being approved as such by the relevant national authority (e.g. for England and NI, by the Secretary of State). Various conditions are prescribed for approval. In particular, the body's sole aim must be the promotion or encouragement of industrial and commercial activity or enterprise in a particular area of the UK, with particular reference to small businesses. If that is only one of its main aims, it must maintain a separate fund for the sole purpose of pursuing that aim and the above relief applies only to contributions to that fund. Also, the body must be precluded from transferring its income or profits to its members or its managers, other than as a reasonable return for goods, labour or services provided, money lent or premises occupied. Approval may be conditional and may be withdrawn retrospectively.
- A training and enterprise council, i.e. a body which has an agreement with the Secretary of State to act as such.
- A Scottish local enterprise company, i.e. a company which has an agreement with Scottish Enterprise or Highlands and Islands Enterprise to act as such.
- A business link organisation, i.e. a person authorised by the Secretary of State to use a trade mark designated for these purposes.

[*ITTOIA 2005, ss 82–85*].

Urban regeneration companies

Identical provisions to those described above in relation to local enterprise organisations apply to a contribution made to an urban regeneration company designated as such by Treasury order. A body may be so designated only if its sole or main function is to co-ordinate the regeneration of a specific urban area in the UK in association with public and local authorities. Designation orders may be backdated by up to three months. [*ITTOIA 2005, ss 82, 86; SI 2004 No 439*].

Subsidies, grants etc.

[75.120] The following items are dealt with in alphabetical order. See **9.2**(vi) CAPITAL ALLOWANCES for effect of grants and subsidies on capital allowances.

Farming support payments

See 75.77 above.

Fishing grants

For the tax treatment of decommissioning grants, laying-up grants, exploratory voyage grants and joint venture grants under *SI 1983 No 1883*, see HMRC Business Income Manual BIM57001.

Industrial development grants

Grants to a trader under *Industrial Development Act 1982, s 7 or s 8* (or corresponding NI legislation) are trading receipts, unless the grant is designated as made towards the cost of specified capital expenditure or as compensation for loss of capital assets or, exceptionally, is made towards the meeting of a corporation tax liability. This is of no application to professions or vocations. [*ITTOIA 2005, s 105(1)(2)(3)*].

An earlier interest relief grant under *Industry Act 1972* was held to be assessable in *Burman v Thorn Domestic Appliances (Electrical) Ltd* Ch D 1981, 55 TC 493, as was a similar grant undifferentiated between revenue and capital in *Ryan v Crabtree Denims Ltd* Ch D 1987, 60 TC 183, applying *Gayjon Processes Ltd* (below) and distinguishing *Seaham Harbour* (below).

New Enterprise Allowance

The New Enterprise Allowance was introduced as part of a Government plan to help people to move from benefits to work. If an individual's business plan is accepted, he is entitled to a weekly grant for six months. The grant payments are exempt from income tax and should therefore be excluded from the calculation of trading profits. (HMRC Business Income Manual BIM40401).

Research grants

A research grant by trading company to a medical practitioner was held to be taxable (*Duff v Williamson* Ch D 1973, 49 TC 1). For research grants and fellowships generally, see HMRC Business Income Manual BIM65150.

Temporary employment subsidy

Temporary employment subsidy was paid under *Employment and Training Act 1973, s 5* (as amended by *Employment Protection Act 1975, Sch 14 para* 2) as a flat-rate weekly payment or (in the textile, clothing and footwear industries) by way of reimbursement of payments made to workers on short time.

Such payments were held to be taxable as trading receipts in *Poulter v Gayjon Processes Ltd* Ch D 1985, 58 TC 350, distinguishing the grants made by the Unemployment Grants Committee in *Seaham Harbour* (below).

Unemployment grants

Subsidy to dock company (from Unemployment Grants Committee) for extension work to keep men in employment held, although grant made in terms of interest, not a 'trade receipt' for tax purposes (*Seaham Harbour v Crook* HL 1931, 16 TC 333).

Taxation

[75.121] Income tax liabilities are not deductible in computing profits (cf. *Allen v Farquharson Bros & Co* KB 1932, 17 TC 59). Overseas taxes may be subject to DOUBLE TAX RELIEF (**27**) but any such tax not relieved by credit on overseas income included in the profits may generally be deducted [*TIOPA 2010, s 112*] but not on UK income, e.g. profits of UK branches (*CIR v Dowdall O'Mahoney & Co Ltd* HL 1952, 33 TC 259).

In *Harrods (Buenos Aires) v Taylor-Gooby* CA 1964, 41 TC 450 an annual capital tax imposed by the Argentine on foreign companies trading there was not a tax on the profits and was allowable.

As regards relief for national insurance contributions by employers in respect of employees, see **75.72** above.

For taxation appeals, see **75.96** above. For VAT, see **75.129** below.

Simon's Taxes. See B2.472.

Telecommunications rights

[75.122] Special rules apply in relation to licences granted under *Wireless Telegraphy Act 1949, s 1* as a result of bidding for such licences under *Wireless Telegraphy Act 1998, s 3* regulations, and to rights derived directly or indirectly therefrom. This would include, for example, the licences granted in response to the Government auction of third generation mobile phone licences in April 2000. The rules also apply to an indefeasible right to use a telecommunications cable system, and to rights derived from such a licence or indefeasible right.

Acquisition costs and disposal proceeds in respect of such rights which, in accordance with generally accepted accounting practice (see **75.21** above), are taken into account in determining accounting profit or loss are treated as being of a revenue nature in computing profits chargeable to income tax. This applies equally to costs of extension of attached rights or of cancellation or restriction of rights attached to derivative rights, and to receipts from cancellation or restriction of attached rights or from granting derivative rights or extensions of rights attached to derivative rights.

If, in accordance with generally accepted accounting practice, an amount in respect of the revaluation of such rights is recognised in the accounts (whether or not in determining accounting profit or loss), that amount is also treated for income tax purposes as being of a revenue nature. In computing profits for those purposes, it is brought into account for the period of account in which it is so recognised.

[*ITTOIA 2005, ss 145–148*].

The above does not apply in calculating profits on the cash basis (see **76.14** TRADING INCOME — CASH BASIS FOR SMALLER BUSINESSES).

For articles giving the HMRC's view on the interpretation of the above legislation, see Revenue Tax Bulletins December 2000 pp 815–817, February 2004 p 1094.

Tied premises

[75.123] Receipts and expenses in respect of 'tied premises' which would otherwise be brought into account in calculating profits of a property business (see **60.2** PROPERTY INCOME) are instead brought into account as trading receipts or expenses. Any necessary apportionment (e.g. where rents etc. relate only in part to the tied premises or where only part of the premises qualifies) is on a just and reasonable basis. '*Tied premises*' are premises through which goods supplied by a trader are sold or used by another person, where the trader has an estate or interest in the premises which he treats as property employed for trade purposes. [*ITTOIA 2005, s 19*].

These rules are of general application, although of most common application in the licensed trade. As regards the licensed trade generally, see **75.49** above.

'Exclusivity payments' by petrol company to retailers undertaking to sell only its goods were allowed in computing its profits in *Bolam v Regent Oil Co Ltd* Ch D 1956, 37 TC 56 (payments for repairs carried out by retailer), *BP Australia Ltd* PC 1965, 44 ATC 312 (lump sums paid for sales promotion) and *Mobil Oil Australia Ltd* PC 1965, 44 ATC 323, but held capital in *Strick v Regent Oil* HL 1965, 43 TC 1 where the payment took the form of a premium to the retailer for a lease of his premises (immediately sub-let to him).

In the hands of the retailer, exclusivity payments were held capital when for capital expenditure incurred by him (*CIR v Coia* CS 1959, 38 TC 334; *McLaren v Needham* Ch D 1960, 39 TC 37; *Walter W Saunders Ltd v Dixon* Ch D 1962, 40 TC 329; *McClymont and Another v Jarman* (Sp C 387) 2003, [2004] SSCD 54) but revenue when for repairs etc. (*McLaren v Needham* above) or sales promotion (*Evans v Wheatley* Ch D 1958, 38 TC 216) or where petrol sales were a relatively small part (some 30%) of the company's turnover (*Tanfield Ltd v Carr* (Sp C 200), [1999] SSCD 213]).

For a summary of HMRC's view of such arrangements, see Revenue Tax Bulletin August 1993 p 88.

Simon's Taxes. See **B2.216.**

Training costs

[75.124] Costs incurred by an employer in respect of employee training are generally allowable as a trade expense. See **75.73** above for this and as regards certain other allowable employee training costs, and **75.119** above as regards contributions to training and enterprise councils.

In general, the expenses of a training course undertaken by a self-employed person are allowed as a trade deduction under general principles only where the training is undertaken for the purposes of the trade and relates to the updating of existing expertise rather than the acquisition of new skills. See HMRC Business Income Manual BIM35660. This principle was confirmed in *Dass v Special Commissioner and others* Ch D 2006, [2007] STC 187.

Travelling and subsistence expenses

[75.125] The cost of travelling in the course of the business activities is allowable but not that of travelling between home and the place at or from which the business is conducted. For this see *Newsom v Robertson* CA 1952, 33 TC 452 in which the expenses of a barrister between his home and his chambers were refused and contrast *Horton v Young* CA 1971, 47 TC 60 in which a 'self-employed' bricklayer was allowed his expenses between his home and the sites at which he worked as, on the evidence, his business was conducted from his home. *Horton v Young* was distinguished in *Samadian v HMRC* UT 2014, 82 TC 252, involving a consultant geriatrician who worked for the NHS but also maintained a private practice; the Tribunal characterised the consulting rooms hired by him at two private hospitals as places of business and held that travel between his home and these hospitals had a dual purpose and was non-deductible. A similar decision was reached in a case not dissimilar but involving a flying instructor operating from two airports (*White v HMRC* FTT (TC 3354), [2014] UKFTT 214 (TC)). In *Jackman v Powell* Ch D, 76 TC 87, a milkman was not allowed the costs of travelling between his home and the dairy-owned depot from which he collected his supplies and to which his milk round was adjacent. Any expenses of an employment ancillary to a profession that are not allowable against employment income may not be deducted in computing the profits of the profession (*Mitchell & Edon v Ross* HL 1961, 40 TC 11).

The 'dual purpose rule' (see **75.44** above) entails the disallowance of *all* travelling expenses with a material private purpose, i.e. the part attributable to business purposes is not allowable. Thus the expenses of a solicitor in travelling abroad partly for a holiday and partly to attend professional conferences were disallowed in *Bowden v Russell & Russell* Ch D 1965, 42 TC 301 (but the expenses of an accountant to attend a professional conference abroad were allowed in *Edwards v Warmsley, Henshall & Co* Ch D 1967, 44 TC 431). Similarly the expenses of a dentist in travelling between his home and surgery were disallowed even though he collected dentures from a laboratory on the way (*Sargent v Barnes* Ch D 1978, 52 TC 335). The expenses of a farmer in visiting Australia with a view to farming there were held inadmissible (*Sargent v Eayrs* Ch D 1972, 48 TC 573). Car expenses are normally apportioned if the car is used partly for private purposes.

Parking and other motoring fines are normally disallowed in their entirety either under the 'dual purpose rule' (see **75.44** above) or under the general principles applicable to allowable trading deductions (see *CIR v Alexander von Glehn & Co Ltd* CA 1920, 12 TC 232). They are statutory fines imposed for breaking the law and are not incurred solely for the purposes of a trade (*G4S Cash Solutions (UK) Ltd v HMRC* FTT (TC 5015), [2016] UKFTT 239 (TC)) Reimbursement of employees' fines is normally deductible, but see **28.13** EMPLOYMENT INCOME as regards the employee's liability.

The 'dual purpose rule' also requires the disallowance of costs of food, drink and accommodation. The extra cost of lunching away from home was disallowed in *Caillebotte v Quinn* Ch D 1975, 50 TC 222. However, a deduction is allowed for any reasonable expenses incurred on food or drink for consumption by the trader at a place to which he travels in the course of carrying on the trade, or while travelling to a place in the course of carrying on the trade, but only if conditions A and B below are met.

- Condition A is that a deduction is available for the associated travelling costs (or, in a case where such costs are not incurred by the trader, a deduction would be available if they were so incurred).
- Condition B is that either:
  - (i) at the time the expenses on food and drink are incurred, the trade is by its nature itinerant (for example a commercial traveller); or
  - (ii) the trader does not visit the place more than occasionally in the course of the trade and the travel is undertaken otherwise than as part of a normal pattern of travel in the course of the trade.

[*ITTOIA 2005, s 57A; SI 2009 No 730, Art 3*].

The above legislation deals only with food and drink and not with overnight accommodation. However, in practice, where a business trip necessitates one or more nights away from home (and away from the business base), the hotel accommodation is deductible (HMRC Business Income Manual BIM47705).

Where a UK resident individual trader spends time outside the UK on business, his personal living expenses are not disallowed if the absence abroad is for the purpose of the trade. Living expenses include for these purposes the cost of accommodation, food and drink attributable to the individual. If he is accompanied by his family or other dependants, the costs attributable to them are non-deductible. (HMRC SP A16).

Motoring expenses

See the optional fixed rate deduction scheme for expenditure on vehicles at **77.2** TRADING INCOME — FIXED RATE DEDUCTION SCHEME. See **75.16** above for extended relief for travelling expenses in overseas trade. For car hire, see **75.50** above. For travelling and subsistence generally, see HMRC Business Income Manual BIM47700–47714. For the 'dual purpose rule' in relation to travel and subsistence costs, see BIM37600–37635, 37660.

Simon's Taxes. See **B2.318, B2.476.**

Unclaimed balances

[75.126] Unclaimed balances for which a firm was liable to account were held not assessable despite their being distributed to partners (*Morley v Tattersall* CA 1938, 22 TC 51). Such balances held by a pawnbroker are, however, assessable when claimants' rights expire (*Jay's, the Jewellers v CIR* KB 1947, 29 TC 274). Deposits on garments not collected were held to be trade receipts assessable when received (*Elson v Prices Tailors* Ch D 1962, 40 TC 671); the same applied to refundable deposits in respect of returnable containers in which goods were supplied to customers (*Gower Chemicals Ltd v HMRC* (Sp C 713), [2008] SSCD 1242). The fact that trading receipts were subsequently, and correctly, treated for accountancy purposes as an element in a sale of fixed assets did not alter their nature for tax purposes (*Tapemaze Ltd v Melluish* Ch D 2000, 73 TC 167). See **75.48** above for releases of debts owing.

Unremittable amounts

[75.127] Where a trade is carried on at least partly in the UK, so that liability to UK income tax arises on the profits, amounts received or receivable overseas (e.g. from export sales) which cannot be brought to the UK because of foreign exchange restrictions would nevertheless fall to be included in computing profits, with no relief being available under *ITTOIA 2005, ss 841–845* (unremittable overseas income — see **32.5** FOREIGN INCOME), i.e. because the overall profits of the trade do not arise outside the UK, or under *ITTOIA 2005, s 35* (bad and doubtful debts — see **75.48** above), i.e. because a debt is not bad merely because it is unremittable. The provisions described below are designed to give relief in such circumstances.

The relief applies where an amount received by, or owed to, a trader is brought into account as a receipt in computing his profits, it is paid or owed in a territory outside the UK, and some or all of it is 'unremittable'. For these purposes, an amount is '*unremittable*' if:

- it is received but cannot be transferred to the UK because, and only because, of 'foreign exchange restrictions'; or
- it is owed but temporarily cannot be paid in the overseas territory, due only to such restrictions; or
- it is owed and can be paid in the overseas territory but the amount paid there would not be transferable to the UK, due only to such restrictions.

'*Foreign exchange restrictions*' are restrictions imposed by the law of the overseas territory, by any executive action of its government or by the impossibility of obtaining there currency which is transferable to the UK.

Relief is given for the amount in question by deducting it from profits but not so as to create a trading loss. Any excess of unremittable amounts over profits for any period of account is carried forward to the next period of account, aggregated with any unremittable amounts for that period and used to reduce or extinguish profits for that period, and so on *ad infinitum*. If no profit has been made for a period of account, any unremittable amounts are similarly carried forward.

However, no such deduction is allowed to the extent that:

- the amount in question is used to finance expenditure or investment outside the UK or is otherwise applied outside the UK; or
- a deduction is allowed for it under *ITTOIA 2005, s 35* (see **75.48** above) because it represents a bad or doubtful debt; or
- it is an amount owed and an insurance recovery is received in respect of it,

and no deduction is allowed if relief under *ITTOIA 2005, s 842* (see **32.5** FOREIGN INCOME) could be claimed instead.

Relief given for an unremittable amount or any part of it is withdrawn if, subsequently, the amount (or part) ceases to be unremittable or is exchanged for (or discharged by) a remittable amount, or is used to finance overseas expenditure etc., or is deducted as a bad or doubtful debt or, in the case of an amount owed, is the subject of an insurance recovery. The amount (or part) is treated as a trading receipt for the period of account in which the said event occurs.

[*ITTOIA 2005, ss 187–191*].

The above does not apply in calculating profits on the cash basis (see **76.14** TRADING INCOME — CASH BASIS FOR SMALLER BUSINESSES).

Use of home for business purposes

[75.128] If part of a trader's home is for any period used solely for business purposes, he may be able to deduct part of the household expenses in computing his trading profit for tax purposes. The deductible expenditure will represent the costs incurred on that part of the home for that period. As it is unlikely that such costs will be separately billed, this means apportioning household bills. The factors to be taken into account when apportioning an expense include the following.

- Area: what proportion in terms of area of the home is used for business purposes?
- Usage: how much is consumed? This is appropriate where there is a metered or measurable supply such as electricity, gas or water.
- Time: how long is that part used for business purposes as compared to its total use?

At Business Income Manual BIM47820, HMRC provide a (non-exhaustive) list of, and commentary on, the types of expenditure that may be allowable, split between fixed costs and running costs. The types of expenditure considered are rent, mortgage interest, council tax, heat, light and power, telephone, internet connection charges, water rates, repairs and maintenance, cleaning and insurance.

If there is only minor use of the home, for example writing up the business records at home, HMRC officers will usually accept a reasonable estimate. The examples in HMRC's own manual suggest that £2 per week might be accepted as a reasonable estimate, but this is not to say that a higher figure would not be accepted.

(HMRC Business Income Manual BIM47800–47825).

Where private use of telephone/internet costs is insignificant in proportion to total use, HMRC will accept that the full amount of expenditure can be claimed (HMRC Brief 14/13, 2 July 2013).

See also the optional fixed rate deduction scheme for use of home for business at **77.5** TRADING INCOME — FIXED RATE DEDUCTION SCHEME. See also mixed use premises at **77.6** TRADING INCOME — FIXED RATE DEDUCTION SCHEME.

Value added tax

[75.129] For treatment in computing business profits see HMRC SP B1.

In general, if the trader is not a 'taxable person' for VAT his expenditure *inclusive* of any VAT on it, is treated in the ordinary way.

If he is a taxable person, the receipts and expenses (including capital items) to be taken into account will generally be exclusive of VAT but if he suffers VAT on any expenditure which does not rank as 'input tax' (e.g. entertaining expenses and certain expenditure relating to motor cars) that expenditure inclusive of VAT will be taken into account for income tax etc. purposes (although any such inclusive sum in respect of entertaining expenses may also be disallowed for income tax purposes). Any allowance for bad debts (see **75.48** above) is inclusive of any VAT not recovered but accounted for to Customs and Excise. (*VATA 1994, s 36* and regulations made thereunder now provide for VAT on bad debts to be refunded in certain cases.)

VAT interest, penalties and surcharge are not allowed as a deduction for income tax purposes (see **75.93** above). Repayment supplement is disregarded for income tax purposes (see **30.42** EXEMPT INCOME).

Where the trader uses the optional *flat-rate scheme* for smaller businesses, receipts and expenses to be taken into account will generally be *inclusive* of normal output and input VAT, but the flat-rate VAT itself can either be deducted from turnover or treated as a separate expense and in either case is an allowable deduction for income tax purposes. Any irrecoverable VAT on capital items will form part of their cost for the purposes of capital allowances. (Revenue Tax Bulletin April 2003 pp 1023, 1024).

VAT refunds

See Revenue Tax Bulletin October 1995 pp 255, 256 for the timing of the recognition, for the purposes of computing trading profits, of certain VAT refunds (specifically, of refunds to opticians following acceptance by Customs and Excise that they had incorrectly required VAT to be charged on certain outputs).

See HMRC Business Income Manual BIM31500–31625, and see generally Tolley's Value Added Tax.

Simon's Taxes. See **B2.477**.

Waste disposal

[75.130] Expenditure on purchase and reclamation of tipping sites by a company carrying on a waste disposal business was held to be capital in *Rolfe v Wimpey Waste Management Ltd* CA 1989, 62 TC 399, as were instalment payments for the right to deposit waste material in *CIR v Adam* CS 1928, 14 TC 34. See also *McClure v Petre* Ch D 1988, 61 TC 226, where the receipt of sum for licence to tip soil was also held to be capital.

Site preparation and restoration expenditure

A deduction is allowed as below in computing profits where a person incurs, in the course of a trade, 'site preparation expenditure' in relation to a 'waste disposal site', and, at the time when he first deposits waste materials on the site in question, he holds a current 'waste disposal licence'. Expenditure incurred for trade purposes by a person about to carry on the trade is for this purpose treated as incurred on the first day of trading. The deduction is not available where the person incurring the expenditure recharges it to another person who holds the licence when first depositing waste (see Revenue Tax Bulletin April 1998 p 533). No claim is required but any supporting documentation should still be retained in case of an HMRC enquiry into a return.

A '*waste disposal site*' is a site used (or to be used) for the disposal of waste materials by their deposit on the site, and in relation to such a site, '*site preparation expenditure*' is expenditure on preparing the site for the deposit of waste materials. This includes expenditure incurred before the waste disposal licence is granted, and in particular expenses associated with obtaining the licence itself (Revenue Tax Bulletin November 1992 p 45). For preparation expenditure generally, see also Revenue Tax Bulletin April 1998 p 533, February 2001 p 828. A '*waste disposal licence*' is a disposal licence under *Control of Pollution Act 1974, Pt 1* (or NI equivalent), a waste management licence under *Environmental Protection Act 1990, Pt 2* (or NI equivalent), a permit under regulations under *Pollution Prevention and Control Act 1999, s 2* (or NI equivalent), an authorisation for the disposal of radioactive waste, or a nuclear site licence.

The deductible amount of site preparation expenditure for a period of account is the amount allocated to that period, which itself is given by the formula:

$$RE \times \frac{WD}{SV + WD}$$

where:

RE	=	residual expenditure (see below);
WD	=	volume of waste materials deposited on the site during the period; and
SV	=	volume of the site not used up for the deposit of waste materials at the end of the period.

The residual expenditure for a period of account is the site preparation expenditure incurred by the trader at any time before and up to the end of that period, less any expenditure which either has been allowed as a trading deduction for a prior period or is capital expenditure qualifying for capital allowances. If the trade commenced before 6 April 1989, a proportion of the expenditure incurred before that date (OE) is excluded, such proportion being calculated by reference to the volume of materials deposited before that date (OWD) and the unused volume of the site immediately before that date (OSV). The reduction is the amount given by the formula:

$$OE \times \frac{OWD}{OSV + OWD}$$

Any site preparation expenditure incurred by a predecessor of the current trader is brought into account above as if it had been incurred by the trader. For this purpose, a predecessor of the trader is a person who, on or after that date, has ceased to carry on the trade carried on by the trader or has ceased to carry on a trade so far as relating to the site in question and who, in either case, has transferred the whole of the site to the trader (though not necessarily the same estate or interest in the site).

Site restoration payments

A person making a 'site restoration payment', in the course of carrying on a trade, may (subject to below) deduct the payment in computing profits for the period of account in which the payment is made. A payment cannot, however, be deducted to the extent that it represents either expenditure allowed as a trading deduction for prior periods or capital expenditure qualifying for capital allowances. A provision made in the accounts for future site restoration payments is not deductible (*Dispit Ltd v HMRC* (Sp C 579), [2007] SSCD 194).

If the site restoration payment is made, whether directly or indirectly, to a connected person (within **19** CONNECTED PERSONS), the deduction is permitted only for the period of account in which that part of the restoration work to which the payment relates is completed. No deduction can be made for any site restoration payment, no matter whom the recipient, if the payment arises from arrangements (as widely defined) to which the person carrying on the trade is a party and a main purpose of which is to obtain a deduction.

A '*site restoration payment*' is a payment made:

- in connection with the restoration of a site (or part thereof); and
- in order to comply with (i) any condition of a waste disposal licence (as defined above), or (ii) any condition imposed on the grant of planning permission to use the site for the carrying out of 'waste disposal activities', or (iii) a 'relevant planning obligation'.

'*Waste disposal activities*' means the collection, treatment, conversion and final depositing of waste materials, or any one or more of those activities.

A 'relevant planning obligation' is defined by *ITTOIA 2005, s 168(6)* by reference to *Town and Country Planning Act 1990* and Scottish and NI equivalents.

[*ITTOIA 2005, ss 165–168, Sch 2 paras 44–46; SI 2000 No 1973*].

None of the above applies in calculating profits on the cash basis (see **76.14** TRADING INCOME — CASH BASIS FOR SMALLER BUSINESSES).

See generally HMRC Business Income Manual BIM67400–67550.

Leasing

See 75.83 above as regards restrictions on relief under the above provisions where finance leasing arrangements are involved.

Simon's Taxes. See **B2.478.**

Landfill tax

HMRC's views on the deductibility of landfill tax in computing trading income are as follows.

Site operators

Treatment of landfill tax charged on to customers will follow the generally accepted accounting practice. As regards self-generated waste, landfill tax (net of any credit following a contribution to an environmental trust) will be allowed as a deduction so long as the other costs incurred in disposing of the waste are deductible.

Customers of site operators

The landfill tax element of the global charge does not need to be separately invoiced, and deductibility of the landfill tax element will follow that of the non-landfill tax element of the charge.

Environmental trust contributions

Site operators may obtain relief from landfill tax by making such contributions, the deductibility of which is to be determined in the circumstances of each particular case under the normal test of whether the expenditure is incurred wholly and exclusively for trade purposes. In the case of an unconnected trust engaged in projects of possible use to the operator, the payment would *prima facie* be deductible. If the operator has some degree of control over the trust, or the income of the trust is ultimately received by a person connected with the operator, it might be less clear that the payment was for the purposes of the operator's own trade. Similarly if the trust's objects were insufficiently related to the operator's trade, it might be considered that contributions were for a general philanthropic, and hence non-trade, purpose.

(Revenue Tax Bulletin June 1996 pp 317, 318).

Simon's Taxes. See **B2.478.**

General example on trading income

[75.131]

A UK trader commences trading on 1 October 2019. His profit and loss account for the year to 30 September 2020 is as set out below. He does not elect to use the cash basis.

		£	£
Sales			110,000
Deduct Purchases		75,000	
Less	Trading stock at 30.9.20	15,000	
			60,000
Gross profit			50,000
Deduct			
Salaries (all paid by 30.6.21)		15,600	
Rent and rates		2,400	
Telephone		500	
Heat and light		650	
Depreciation		1,000	
Motor expenses		2,700	
Entertainment		600	
Bank interest		900	
Hire-purchase interest		250	
Repairs and renewals		1,000	
Accountant's fee		500	
Bad debts		200	
Sundries		700	
			27,000
Net profit			23,000
Gain on sale of fixed asset			300
Rent received			500
Bank interest received			150
Profit			£23,950

Further Information

- Rent and rates. £200 of the rates bill relates to the period from 1.6.19 to 30.9.19.
- Telephone. Telephone bills for the trader's private telephone amount to £150. It is estimated that 40% of these calls are for business purposes.
- Motor expenses. All the motor expenses are in respect of the proprietor's car. 40% of the annual mileage relates to private use and home to business use.

		£
• Entertainment	Staff	100
	UK customers	450
	Overseas customers	50
		£600

- Hire-purchase interest. This is in respect of the owner's car.
- Repairs and renewals. There is an improvement element of 20% included.
- Bad debts. This is a specific write-off.
- Sundries. Included is £250 being the cost of obtaining a bank loan to finance business expenditure, £200 for agent's fees in obtaining a patent for trading purposes and a £50 inducement to a local official.
- Other. The proprietor obtained goods for his own use from the business costing £400 (resale value £500) without payment.
- Capital allowances for the year to 30 September 2020 amount to £1,520.

Computation of taxable trading income — Year to 30.9.20

		£	£
Profit per the accounts			23,950
Add			
Repairs — improvement element			200
Hire-purchase interest (40% private)			100
Entertainment	note (e)		500
Motor expenses (40% private)			1,080
Depreciation			1,000
Telephone (60% × £150)			90
Goods for own use	note (f)		500
Illegal payment	note (g)		50
			27,470
Deduct			
Bank interest received (savings income)		150	
Rent received (property income)		500	
Gain on sale of fixed asset		300	
			950
			26,520
*Less*Capital allowances			1,520
Chargeable trading income			£25,000

Notes

(a) Costs of obtaining loan finance are specifically allowable (see **75.97** above).

(b) Capital allowances are deductible as a trading expense (see **9.1** CAPITAL ALLOWANCES, **10.1** CAPITAL ALLOWANCES ON PLANT AND MACHINERY).

(c) The adjusted profit of £25,000 would be subject to the commencement provisions for assessment purposes (see **75.7** above).

(d) Pre-trading expenses are treated as incurred on the day on which trade is commenced if they are incurred within seven years of the commencement and would have been allowable if incurred after commencement. See **75.106** above.

(e) All entertainment expenses, other than staff entertaining, are non-deductible (see **75.76** above).

(f) Trading stock appropriated for personal use must be accounted for at market value (see **75.118** above).

(g) Expenditure incurred in making a payment which itself constitutes the commission of a criminal offence is specifically disallowed as a deduction. This includes payments which are contrary to the Prevention of Corruption Acts. See **75.91** above.

76

Trading Income — Cash Basis for Smaller Businesses

Cross-references. See **75** TRADING INCOME; **77** TRADING INCOME — FIXED RATE DEDUCTION SCHEME.

Simon's Taxes. See **B2.101B.**

Other sources. See also HMRC Business Income Manual BIM70000–70073.

Introduction to cash basis for smaller businesses

[76.1] The cash basis is optional, and is available to unincorporated trades, professions and vocations (including those carried on in partnership) with an annual turnover not exceeding the turnover limit. For 2017/18 onwards, the turnover limit is £150,000; previously it was equal to the VAT registration threshold. For recipients of Universal credit, the turnover limit is doubled. See **76.2** below. Certain types of business are excluded from using the cash basis (see **76.3**). Businesses must leave the cash basis the year after their receipts exceed £300,000 (previously twice the VAT registration threshold) (see **76.4** below). In practice, elections to adopt the cash basis will be made via the tax return by ticking a box. If more than one business is carried on by the same person, the combined receipts must be taken into account when applying the turnover test.

There are no special rules as to the date to which accounts may be prepared.

Businesses using the cash basis calculate their taxable income by deducting business expenses paid in a year from business receipts for the year (see **76.5**). They do not have to compute figures of debtors, creditors and stock. Receipts must include all amounts received in connection with the business including those from the disposal of certain assets (see below). Allowable expenses are those paid wholly and exclusively for the purposes of the trade, including payments for certain assets (see below). Interest payments are allowed up to a limit of £500; it is not a condition of this deduction that the interest be paid wholly and exclusively for business purposes. Adjustments are required for certain non-commercial transactions (see **76.11**).

Expenditure on acquiring plant and machinery used in the business is allowable on the cash basis, obviating the need to routinely distinguish between revenue and capital items or to calculate and claim capital allowances. Expenditure on acquiring cars is excluded, though this is provided for in the mileage rates available under the optional fixed rate scheme (see **77.2–77.4** TRADING INCOME — FIXED RATE DEDUCTION SCHEME). To the extent that a payment for acquiring an asset was deductible, any receipt on its disposal must be brought into account (see **76.9**).

Trading losses on the cash basis can be carried forward to set against profits of future years but cannot be carried back or set off against other income.

Adjustments are necessary when entering and leaving the cash basis to ensure that receipts are taxed, and payments are deducted, once and once only. This is achieved by applying the change of basis rules at **75.24** TRADING INCOME. When leaving the cash basis any adjustment income under those rules will be spread over six years, though the taxpayer can accelerate the charge if he wishes. See **76.16**. Adjustments are also necessary for plant and machinery capital allowances (see **76.8**).

Certain tax legislation does not apply to a business for which a cash basis election is in force (see **76.14**). Certain other legislation is modified (see **76.15**). The normal rules for calculating trading profits apply equally to the cash basis (see **76.5**), except to the extent that they are specifically disapplied or modified.

See Tolley's Capital Gains Tax for an exemption for certain disposals of assets made while the cash basis is in use or after leaving the cash basis. For the calculation of *property income* on the cash basis for 2017/18 onwards, see the separate provisions at **60.4–60.9** PROPERTY INCOME.

Eligibility for cash basis

[76.2] A person is eligible to make an election (under *ITTOIA 2005, s 25A*) to adopt the cash basis (a '*cash basis election*') for a tax year if his 'cash basis receipts' do not exceed the 'turnover limit' (see below). An 'excluded person' (see **76.3** below) cannot make a cash basis election. See **76.4** below as to the effects of a cash basis election. The legislation provides no time limit for making a cash basis election, but in practice an election is made by ticking a box in the tax return for the year in question (HMRC Technical Note,

28 March 2013, Chapter 2 para 4). The cash basis is an alternative to preparing accounts for tax purposes on an earnings basis and in accordance with generally accepted accounting practice (GAAP) (see **75.21** TRADING INCOME).

If the person carries on more than one trade, profession or vocation during the tax year, an election is possible only if the aggregate cash basis receipts from all such activities do not exceed the turnover limit. If the person is either an individual who controls a partnership or a partnership that is controlled by an individual, the cash basis election must be made by both the individual and the partnership if it is to be made at all, and the aggregate cash basis receipts of trades etc. carried on by both the individual and the partnership must be taken into account. '*Control*' means the right to a share of more than half the assets, or of more than half the income, of the partnership.

The '*cash basis receipts*' of a trade, profession or vocation, in relation to a tax year, are the receipts that are received during the 'basis period' for the tax year and which would fall to be brought into account in calculating the profits of the trade etc. for that tax year on the cash basis.

There are no special rules as to the date to which accounts may be prepared. The rules determining the '*basis period*' for a tax year are the same as those at **75.6–75.14** TRADING INCOME.

[*ITTOIA 2005, ss 31A, 858(6); ITA 2007, s 995(3)*].

The turnover limit

For 2017/18 onwards, the '*turnover limit*' is **£150,000**. For earlier years it was an amount equal to the VAT registration threshold for the tax year (£83,000 for 2016/17). If, however, the person is a 'universal credit claimant' in the tax year, the '*turnover limit*' is doubled, e.g. it is £300,000 for 2017/18 onwards. A '*universal credit claimant*' is an individual who is entitled to the State benefit known as Universal credit for an assessment period (within the meaning of *Welfare Reform Act 2012, Pt 1* or NI equivalent) that falls within the basis period for the tax year in question.

If the basis period for the tax year is less than twelve months, the turnover limit is proportionately reduced. So if, for example, the basis period for 2017/18 or a subsequent year is three months, the turnover limit is £37,500 or, if the person is a universal credit claimant, £75,000.

[*ITTOIA 2005, s 31B(1)(2)(5)–(9); SI 2017 No 293*].

Excluded persons

[76.3] A person is an '*excluded person*' in relation to a tax year, and thus cannot make a cash basis election for that year, if he meets any of the following conditions:

- the person is a partnership and one or more of the persons who were partners at any time in the basis period for the tax year was not an individual;

- the person was a limited liability partnership at any time during the basis period for the tax year;
- the person is an individual who was a Lloyd's underwriter at any time during the basis period for the tax year;
- the person has made an election for the HERD BASIS (**34**) that has effect in relation to the tax year;
- the person has made an averaging claim in relation to the tax year (see **75.60** and **75.78** TRADING INCOME respectively as regards creative artists and farmers);
- at any time within the period of seven years ending immediately before the basis period for the tax year, the person obtained a business premises renovation allowance (see **9.3** CAPITAL ALLOWANCES);
- the person carried on a mineral extraction trade (as in **9.15** CAPITAL ALLOWANCES) at any time during the basis period for the tax year; or
- at any time before the beginning of the basis period for the tax year the person obtained a research and development allowance (see **9.28** CAPITAL ALLOWANCES) in respect of qualifying expenditure incurred by him and he owns an asset representing that expenditure.

[*ITTOIA 2005, s 31C; FA 2016, s 25(8)(12)*].

Rules concerning the tax treatment of some specific trades are also disapplied on the cash basis (see **76.14** below).

Effects of a cash basis election

[76.4] A cash basis election has effect for the tax year for which it is made and, subject to the exceptions below, for every subsequent tax year (regardless of the turnover limit in **76.2** above). A cash basis election that has effect for a tax year has effect in relation to every trade, profession or vocation carried on during the tax year by the person who made the election.

A cash basis election made by a person ceases to have effect for a subsequent tax year (Year S) if:

(a) the aggregate cash basis receipts of all trades, professions or vocations carried on by the person during the tax year (Year R) immediately preceding Year S is greater than £300,000 *and* the aggregate cash basis receipts exceed the turnover limit for Year S (see further below);
(b) the person is an excluded person (as in **76.3** above) in relation to Year S;
(c) the control rule in **76.2** above (i.e. that if the person is an individual who controls a partnership or a partnership that is controlled by an individual, the cash basis election must be made by both) ceases to be satisfied for Year S; or
(d) there is a change of circumstances relating to any trade, profession or vocation carried on by the person which makes it more appropriate for its profits for Year S to be calculated on an earnings basis and in accordance with generally accepted accounting practice (as in **75.21** TRADING INCOME) and the person duly elects to calculate those profits in that way.

The effect of (a) above is that any person whose cash basis receipts exceed £300,000 for Year R must continue to use the cash basis for Year R (unless (b), (c) or (d) apply to Year R) but must cease to use the cash basis for Year S, *unless* cash basis receipts fall in Year S so that the turnover limit is met for that year.

If the basis period for the tax year in question is less than 12 months, the above figure of £300,000 is proportionately reduced for these purposes.

Where Year S was 2016/17 or an earlier year, an amount equal to twice the VAT registration threshold had effect instead of the figure of £300,000 above. The VAT registration threshold was proportionately reduced for these purposes if the basis period for the year in question was less than 12 months.

As regards (d) above, examples given by HMRC of changes of circumstances include a business that is expanding and wishes to claim more than £500 in interest deductions (contrary to **76.10** below) and a business that wishes to claim loss relief against general income or chargeable gains (contrary to **76.6** below) (HMRC Technical Note, 28 March 2013, Chapter 2 para 10).

In all cases, there is nothing to prevent the person making a further cash basis election for any future tax year for which he is eligible to adopt the cash basis as in **76.2** above.

[*ITTOIA 2005, ss 31B(3)(4)(7)–(9), 31D; SI 2017 No 293*].

Capital allowances

Capital allowances are not available (and balancing charges do not apply) to a person in calculating the profits of a trade, profession or vocation in relation to which a cash basis election has effect. There is an exception for cars (as defined). See **9.1** CAPITAL ALLOWANCES and **10.1** CAPITAL ALLOWANCES ON PLANT AND MACHINERY.

National insurance contributions

Where a cash basis election is in force, profits calculated on the cash basis are used for the purposes of Class 2 and Class 4 national insurance contributions (HMRC Technical Note, 28 March 2013, Chapter 2 para 17).

Calculation of profits and losses

[76.5] The profits of a trade, profession or vocation for a tax year on the cash basis are determined by taking the total amount of receipts of the trade etc. received during the basis period for the tax year and deducting the total amount of expenses of the trade etc. paid during that basis period. This is subject to any adjustments required or authorised by law. [*ITTOIA 2005, s 31E*].

Adjustments required or authorised by law include, for instance, the special rules set out in this chapter. The normal rules for calculating trading profits apply equally to the cash basis, except to the extent that they are specifically disapplied (see **76.14** below) or modified (see **76.15** below). For example, the rule in *ITTOIA 2005, s 33* that no deduction is allowed for items of a capital nature (see **75.43** TRADING INCOME) is disapplied (though see **76.7** below). However, the rule in *ITTOIA 2005, s 34* that expenses, in order to be deductible, must be incurred wholly and exclusively for the purposes of the trade etc. (see **75.44** TRADING INCOME) is neither disapplied nor modified; that rule therefore applies to the cash basis as it does to the normal earnings basis.

By virtue of *ITTOIA 2005, s 26*, the same rules apply in calculating losses of a trade etc. as apply in calculating profits.

Receipts

Key principles are that:

- receipts include all amounts received in connection with the trade, profession or vocation, when they are received;
- amounts received include those from the disposal of assets that would give rise to an allowable deduction on the cash basis when acquired; and
- receipts include all forms of payment whether it be in cash, card, cheques and payments in kind.

(HMRC Technical Note, 28 March 2013, Chapter 2 para 20).

See also **76.9** below (capital receipts).

Expenses

Key principles are that expenses are allowable:

- only when they are paid; and
- only if incurred wholly and exclusively for the purposes of the trade, profession or vocation.

(HMRC Technical Note, 28 March 2013, Chapter 2 para 20).

Within reason, expenses can be treated as paid at the date of the trader's choosing, but the treatment must be consistent. For example, an expense may be paid when a card payment is made, or on the date that a payment appears on the bank statement (HMRC Business Income Manual BIM70005).

See also **76.7** below (capital expenditure) and **76.10** below (interest paid on loans).

Motor vehicles

Capital expenditure on a car (as defined by *CAA 2001, s 268A* — see **10.15**(ii) CAPITAL ALLOWANCES ON PLANT AND MACHINERY) cannot be deducted as an expense on the cash basis, but can qualify for capital allowances. Revenue expenditure relating to a car is deductible as an expense subject to the key principles above for expenses generally. Alternatively, the fixed rate deduction scheme at **77.2** TRADING INCOME — FIXED RATE DEDUCTION SCHEME can be used for a particular vehicle; this is intended to give relief for both capital and revenue expenditure.

As regards motor cycles and goods vehicles, both capital and revenue expenditure can be deducted as an expense on the cash basis subject to the key principles above for expenses generally; capital allowances are not available. The fixed rate deduction scheme can be used instead as regards any particular vehicle.

VAT

The cash basis does not change the way a business accounts for VAT. If a person is registered for VAT, he can compute his profits on the cash basis either by including receipts and expenses net of VAT or inclusive of VAT. If he chooses the latter course, he must also include any payments of VAT to HMRC as an expense and any VAT repayments from HMRC as a receipt. (HMRC Technical Note, 28 March 2013, Chapter 2 para 16).

Restrictions on loss relief

[76.6] Where a person makes a loss in any trade, profession or vocation in a tax year and a cash basis election is in force for that year, relief is not available for the loss against general income or chargeable gains. There is nothing to prevent the loss from being carried forward against profits of the same trade, profession or vocation. See **45.10** LOSSES.

Capital expenditure

[76.7] For 2016/17 and earlier years, in calculating the profits of a trade, profession or vocation on the cash basis, a deduction was allowed for expenditure (other than on the provision of a car) that would otherwise be qualifying expenditure for the purposes of capital allowances on plant and machinery. No deduction was allowed for other items of a capital nature. See **76.5** above for further information as regards cars and other vehicles.

For **2017/18** onwards, there is a new, more detailed, rule as to which types of capital expenditure cannot be deducted on the cash basis. However, for 2017/18, if a deduction would have been allowed under the old rule above but is not allowed under the new rule, the old rule will still apply for that one year only so that the deduction *is* allowed. The new rule is that no deduction is allowed for expenditure of a capital nature incurred on, or in connection with:

(1) the acquisition or disposal of a business (or part of a business);
(2) education or training; or
(3) the provision, alteration or disposal of:
  (a) an asset that is not a 'depreciating asset';
  (b) an asset that was not acquired or created for use on a continuing basis in the trade;
  (c) a car (as defined by *CAA 2001, s 268A* — see **10.15**(ii) CAPITAL ALLOWANCES ON PLANT AND MACHINERY);
  (d) land (other than certain fixtures);
  (e) a 'non-qualifying' 'intangible asset'; or
  (f) a 'financial asset'.

The reference in (3) above to provision, alteration or disposal includes *potential* provision, alteration or disposal. Reference to the provision of an asset includes its creation or construction as well as its acquisition.

In (3)(a) above, an asset is a '*depreciating asset*' if, based on a reasonable expectation at the time the capital expenditure is incurred, the asset either has a useful life of less than 20 years or will decline in value by at least 90% in that time. For this purpose, the useful life of an asset ends when it is no longer of use to any person as an asset of a business.

In (3)(c) above, the non-deductibility of capital expenditure on the *provision* of a car is unchanged from before 2017/18. See **76.5** above for further information as regards cars and other vehicles.

As regards (3)(d) above, a deduction can be made for expenditure incurred on the provision of a depreciating asset installed or otherwise fixed to land so as to become, in law, part of it. Notwithstanding this, no deduction can be made for expenditure incurred on, or in connection with, the provision of a building or other fixed structure; a wall, floor, ceiling, door, gate, shutter or window or stairs; a waste disposal system; a sewerage or drainage system; or a lift or escalator shaft or similar.

In (3)(e) above, '*intangible asset*' is defined by reference to Financial Reporting Standard (FRS) 105. In particular, it includes an internally-generated intangible asset and intellectual property (as defined). An intangible asset is '*non-qualifying*' unless it has a fixed maximum duration and must thereby cease to exist within 20 years from the time the capital expenditure is incurred. A right to obtain an intangible asset is itself non-qualifying if this would otherwise circumvent the 20-year rule. An intangible asset (asset A) is also non-qualifying if it consists of a licence or other right granted to the taxpayer in respect of another intangible asset (asset B) in respect of which the taxpayer grants a licence etc. to someone else.

In 3(f) above, a '*financial asset*' means any right under, or in connection with, either a 'financial instrument' or an arrangement capable of producing an economically equivalent return to that produced under any financial instrument. '*Financial instrument*' is defined by reference to FRS 105.

[*ITTOIA 2005, s 33A; F(No 2)A 2017, Sch 2 paras 2, 64*].

Adjustments for capital allowances

[76.8] No capital allowances are available to a person carrying on a trade, profession or vocation in relation to which a cash basis election is in force, other than an allowance in respect of expenditure incurred on the provision of a car (as defined) (see **9.1** CAPITAL ALLOWANCES and **10.1** CAPITAL ALLOWANCES ON PLANT AND MACHINERY).

The provisions described below apply where a person enters the cash basis. A person carrying on a trade enters the cash basis for a tax year if a cash basis election is in force in relation to the trade for that tax year but no such election was in force immediately before the beginning of the basis period for that tax year. As regards persons *leaving* the cash basis, see **10.35** CAPITAL ALLOWANCES ON PLANT AND MACHINERY.

Unrelieved qualifying expenditure

When a person enters the cash basis for a tax year (Year Z), any qualifying expenditure on plant or machinery which is unrelieved at the end of the basis period for the preceding tax year (Year Y) is allowable as a deduction on the cash basis in Year Z. The rule applies only to the extent that a deduction would have been allowable on the cash basis for the expenditure in Year Z if it had been paid in the basis period for that year. Thus, it does not apply to cars, for example, and does not apply to any other asset to the extent (if any) that it is used for purposes other than those of the trade etc. The rule does not apply where the asset had not been fully paid for as at the end of the basis period for Year Y.

For 2017/18 onwards, it is specified that the above applies also to any unrelieved qualifying expenditure on know-how or patent rights; this was previously by no means clear. The above is also applied for 2017/18 onwards to unrelieved qualifying expenditure for mineral extraction allowances even though mineral extraction trades are currently excluded trades for cash basis purposes (see **76.3** above). For what is meant by unrelieved qualifying expenditure, see **9.14**, **9.19** and **9.26** CAPITAL ALLOWANCES (for know-how, mineral extraction and patent rights respectively) and **10.26** CAPITAL ALLOWANCES ON PLANT AND MACHINERY.

Assets not fully paid for

If a person enters the cash basis for a tax year (Year Z) and:

- at any time before the beginning of the basis period for Year Z the person has obtained 'capital allowances' on an item of 'relevant expenditure', but
- not all of the expenditure has actually been paid by the person,

an adjustment must be made in calculating profits on the cash basis for Year Z. If the amount of the expenditure in question that the person has actually paid exceeds the amount of capital allowances given in respect of it, the difference must be deducted in calculating profits. If the amount of the expenditure actually paid is less than the amount of capital allowances given, the difference must be treated as a receipt in calculating profits.

For 2017/18 onwards, '*relevant expenditure*' is expenditure for which a deduction would have been allowed in calculating profits on the cash basis if it had been paid in Year Z, and '*capital allowances*' means capital allowances on plant or machinery, mineral extraction, research and development, patent rights or know-how. For 2016/17 and earlier years, '*relevant expenditure*' was expenditure on plant or machinery (other than a car), and '*capital allowances*' thus referred to plant and machinery allowances only. The extent (if any) to which expenditure was relevant expenditure, or to which a capital allowance was in respect of relevant expenditure, is to be determined on such basis as is just and reasonable in all the circumstances, for example where the expenditure was pooled.

If the relevant expenditure was on plant or machinery, and the amount of capital allowances given was reduced due to its having been incurred only partly for the purposes of the trade etc. (see **10.15**, **10.19**, **10.32** CAPITAL ALLOWANCES ON PLANT AND MACHINERY), the amount of the expenditure that the person has actually paid is proportionately reduced for the above purposes.

Successions between connected persons

Where a person succeeds to a trade, profession or vocation carried on by a person connected with him (as defined), the predecessor and successor can jointly elect for plant or machinery to be treated as sold by one to the other, when the succession takes place, at its written-down value for capital allowances purposes. For details, see **10.69** CAPITAL ALLOWANCES ON PLANT AND MACHINERY. If a person enters the cash basis for a tax year and plant or machinery is treated as sold to him during the basis period for that tax year as a result of such an election, the cash basis rules apply as if everything done to or by the predecessor had been done to or by the successor. Where the election is made, any expenditure actually incurred by the successor on acquiring the plant or machinery is not deductible on the cash basis.

[*ITTOIA 2005, ss 240A–240CA, 240D, 240E; F(No 2)A 2017, Sch 2 paras 7–9, 64*].

Capital receipts

[76.9] For 2017/18 onwards, 'proceeds' of an asset received by a person when a cash basis election has effect must be brought into account as a trading receipt in calculating profits on the cash basis if an amount of 'capital expenditure' relating to the asset:

(a) has been brought into account in calculating profits on the cash basis; or

(b)
- was incurred (or treated as incurred) by the person before he last entered the cash basis;
- would have been deductible on the cash basis if incurred in the first tax year after he last entered the cash basis; and
- was brought into account in calculating profits for a tax year for which no cash basis election had effect. This includes its being brought into account for capital allowances purposes (except for the purposes of the structures and buildings allowance at **9.30** CAPITAL ALLOWANCES).

'*Capital expenditure*' means expenditure of a capital nature incurred (or treated as incurred) on, or in connection with, the provision, alteration or disposal of an asset or the potential provision, alteration or disposal of an asset. Reference to the provision of an asset includes its creation or construction as well as its acquisition. If only part of the capital expenditure relating to an asset is brought into account in calculating profits (whether or not on the cash basis), the proceeds to be brought into account are proportionately reduced. '*Proceeds*' means:

- any proceeds on the disposal (or part disposal) of the asset;
- any proceeds arising from the grant of any right in respect of, or any interest in, the asset;
- any damages, insurance proceeds or other compensation received in respect of the asset; and
- any amount that is (in substance) a refund of capital expenditure relating to the asset.

If the whole (or any part) of the proceeds that would fall to be brought into account is otherwise brought into account as a trading receipt, or as a disposal value for capital allowances, the proceeds (or that part) do not fall to be brought into account again under these rules.

Proceeds arising after leaving the cash basis

Also for 2017/18 onwards, proceeds of an asset arising to a person after a cash basis election has ceased to have effect must be brought into account as a trading receipt in calculating profits if an amount of capital expenditure relating to the asset meets condition A or B below.

Condition A is that an amount of capital expenditure relating to the asset:

- was paid at a time when a cash basis election had effect;
- was brought into account in calculating profits on the cash basis; and
- would not have been qualifying expenditure for capital allowances purposes (other than the purposes of the structures and buildings allowances) if no cash basis election had been in force.

Condition B is that is that an amount of capital expenditure relating to the asset was brought into account in calculating profits for a tax year for which no cash basis election had effect and which preceded the person's last entry into the cash basis. This does not include its being brought into account for capital allowances purposes.

Deemed disposals

If at any time the person ceases to use the asset (or any part of it) for the purposes of the trade, profession or vocation, but does not dispose of the asset (or that part of it) at that time, he is treated for the above purposes as disposing of the asset (or that part) at that time for its 'market value amount'. '*Market value amount*' is the amount that would be regarded as normal and reasonable in the market conditions then prevailing, and between persons dealing with each other on an arm's length basis in the open market.

If at any time there is a material increase in the person's non-business use of the asset (or any part of it), he is treated for the above purposes as disposing of the asset (or that part) at that time for an amount equal to the 'relevant proportion' of its market value amount. There is an increase in a person's non-business use of an asset (or part of an asset) only if the proportion of business use decreases *and* the proportion of use for other purposes increases. 'Material increase' is not defined. The '*relevant proportion*' is the difference between the proportion of non-business use before the increase and the proportion of non-business use after it.

2016/17 and earlier years

For 2016/17 and earlier years, if the whole or part of any expenditure incurred in acquiring, creating or improving an asset was brought into account in calculating profits on the cash basis (or would have been so brought into account if a cash basis election had been in force at the time the expenditure was paid), any 'proceeds' relating to the asset had to be brought into account as a receipt in calculating profits on the cash basis. '*Proceeds*' were defined as above, except that they did not include refunds of capital expenditure. If only part of the expenditure incurred in acquiring, creating or improving the asset was (or would have been) so brought into account, the capital receipt to be brought into account was proportionately reduced. There were rules identical to those described above under Deemed disposals. There were no rules covering proceeds (or deemed disposal proceeds) arising after a person leaves the cash basis.

[*ITTOIA 2005, ss 96A, 96B; F(No 2)A 2017, Sch 2 paras 4, 5, 64; SI 2019 No 1087, Reg 5*].

Interest paid on loans

[76.10] In calculating the profits of a trade, profession or vocation on the cash basis, a deduction is allowed for interest paid on a loan regardless of whether or not the interest was paid wholly and exclusively for the purposes of the trade etc. However, the maximum aggregate amount that may be deducted in any period of account for interest paid and incidental costs of obtaining finance (under *ITTOIA 2005, s 58* — see **75.97** TRADING INCOME) is £500. [*ITTOIA 2005, ss 51A, 57B*].

It should be noted that the above restriction does not apply to interest paid other than on a loan. For example, interest paid to suppliers of goods on credit, hire-purchase interest, leasing interest and credit card interest on purchases are allowable without restriction (provided the underlying expenditure is for business purposes) (HMRC Business Income Manual BIM70040).

Amounts not reflecting commercial transactions

[76.11] Where a person carries on a trade, profession or vocation for which a cash basis election is in force, adjustments must be made in respect of any non-commercial transactions. An adjustment applies where:

(a) a person does anything in relation to the trade etc.;
(b) there is a difference between:
  (i) the amount (if any) that would otherwise as a result be brought into account in calculating profits; and
  (ii) the '*arm's length amount*', i.e. the amount (if any) that would have been brought into account in calculating profits if the thing done had consisted of a transaction between persons dealing with each other at arm's length in the open market; and
(c) the profits are less than they would have been if the arm's length amount had been so brought into account.

Instead of the amount in (b)(i) above, the amount to be brought into account in calculating profits is such amount as is just and reasonable in all the circumstances.

No such adjustment applies where:

- as a result of the thing done the person is treated as disposing of an asset (or part of an asset) under the capital receipts rules in **76.9** above; or
- any of the provisions of *ITTOIA 2005, ss 107–110* (gifts to charities and educational establishments — see **75.88** TRADING INCOME) applies in relation to the thing done.

[*ITTOIA 2005, ss 106A–106E; F(No 2)A 2017, Sch 2 paras 6, 64*].

Stock and work in progress

[76.12] The rules at **75.118** TRADING INCOME (trading stock acquired or disposed of other than in the course of trade) do not apply in calculating profits on the cash basis. [*ITTOIA 2005, s 172AA*]. This means, for example, that no adjustment at market value need be made when the trader takes goods out of stock for his own use. However, an adjustment under **76.11** above (non-commercial transactions) will be required; HMRC will accept an adjustment at the cost price of the stock to the trader, thus removing it from the calculation of taxable profit (HMRC Business Income Manual BIM70015).

When a person permanently ceases to carry on a trade in a tax year for which a cash basis election is in force, the value of any trading stock at cessation must be brought into account as a receipt in calculating profits for the year. The same applies, in the case of a profession or vocation, to work in progress. The value of stock or work in progress is to be determined on a basis that is just and reasonable in all the circumstances. If there is a change in the persons carrying on a trade or profession, no such receipt need be brought into account if a person carrying on the trade or profession immediately before the change continues to carry it on after the change, e.g. on a change in the members of a partnership where at least one partner continues. [*ITTOIA 2005, ss 97A, 97B*].

Post-cessation receipts

[76.13] If, immediately before a person permanently ceases to carry on a trade, profession or vocation, a cash basis election is in force, a sum is to be treated as a post-cessation receipt only if it would have been brought into account in calculating profits on the cash basis had it been received immediately before cessation (see **59.2** POST-CESSATION RECEIPTS AND EXPENDITURE).

As regards deductions from post-cessation receipts where a cash basis election was in force immediately before the cessation, see **59.3** POST-CESSATION RECEIPTS AND EXPENDITURE.

Tax rules disapplied for cash basis

[76.14] The provisions of *ITTOIA 2005* listed below do not apply to a trade, profession or vocation in relation to which a cash basis election is in force. The provisions are listed in the order in which they appear in the legislation.

Provisions disapplied *ITTOIA 2005:*	Brief description	Disapplied by ITTOIA 2005:	Main coverage at:
s 33	capital expenditure non-deductible (but see 76.7 above)	*s 32A*	75.43 TRADING INCOME
s 35	bad and doubtful debts	*s 32A*	75.48 TRADING INCOME
ss 36, 37	timing of deductions for remuneration	*s 32A*	75.64 TRADING INCOME
s 43	timing of deductions for employee benefit contributions — profits computed within nine months	*s 32A*	75.65 TRADING INCOME
ss 48–50B	car hire	*s 32A*	75.50 TRADING INCOME
ss 60–67	tenants under a lease subject to a premium	*s 56A*	75.108 TRADING INCOME
ss 111–129	herd basis	*s 111A*	34 HERD BASIS
ss 130–135	sound recordings	*s 130A*	75.80 TRADING INCOME
ss 145–148	telecommunication rights	*s 144A*	75.122 TRADING INCOME
ss 148A–148J	long funding leases of plant and machinery	*s 148ZA*	75.98 TRADING INCOME
ss 149–154A	various provisions on dealing in securities	*s 148K*	75.115 TRADING INCOME, 50.12 NON-RESIDENTS
s 158	dealers in land — reduction of lease premiums etc.	*s 148K*	75.108 TRADING INCOME
s 159	clergymen	*s 148K*	75.53 TRADING INCOME
s 161	mineral exploration and access	*s 148K*	75.101 TRADING INCOME

Provisions disapplied *ITTOIA 2005:*	Brief description	Disapplied by ITTOIA 2005:	Main coverage at:
ss 163, 164	computation of intermediary's business profits	*s 148K*	58.12 PERSONAL SERVICE COMPANIES ETC.
s 164A	computation of managed service company's business profits	*s 148K*	47.8 MANAGED SERVICE COMPANIES
ss 165–168	waste disposal	*s 148K*	75.130 TRADING INCOME
ss 169–172ZE	cemeteries and crematoria	*s 148K*	75.51 TRADING INCOME
ss 172A–172F	trading stock (see 76.12 above)	*s 172AA*	75.118 TRADING INCOME
ss 187–191	unremittable amounts	*s 188A*	75.127 TRADING INCOME
ss 192–195	disposal and acquisition of know-how	*s 191A*	75.95, 75.78 TRADING INCOME
ss 221–225	averaging profits of creative artists and farmers	*s 221A*	75.60 TRADING INCOME
ss 225ZA–225ZG	compensation for compulsory slaughter	*s 225ZAA*	75.77(b) TRADING INCOME

Tax rules modified for cash basis

[76.15] In those provisions of *ITTOIA 2005* that do apply calculating the profits of a trade, profession or vocation on the cash basis, any reference to the incurring of expenses should generally be read as a reference to the paying of expenses. In addition, certain provisions are modified as set out below in relation to a trade etc. in relation to which a cash basis election is in force.

Qualifying care relief

See **33.2** FOSTER CARE ETC.

Rent-a-room relief

See **60.22** PROPERTY INCOME.

Integral features of buildings and structures

ITTOIA 2005, s 55A provides that no deduction is available for expenditure on providing or replacing an integral feature of a building or structure if the expenditure is qualifying expenditure for plant and machinery capital allowances purposes. See **75.110** TRADING INCOME. This does not apply in calculating profits on the cash basis. [*ITTOIA 2005, s 55A(2)*]. See **10.11** CAPITAL ALLOWANCES ON PLANT AND MACHINERY as regards integral features.

Employee benefit contributions

By virtue of *ITTOIA 2005, s 38*, a deduction for employee benefit contributions is allowed only to the extent that, during the period of account in question or within nine months after the end of it, qualifying benefits are provided, or qualifying expenses are paid, out of the contributions. See **75.65** TRADING INCOME. This is suitably modified to allow for the fact that on the cash basis no deduction could be made in any case for contributions paid after the period of account has ended. [*ITTOIA 2005, s 38(2A)*].

Industrial development grants

Except in specified circumstances, industrial development grants to a trader are trading receipts. One of the excepted circumstances is where the grant is designated as made towards the cost of specified capital expenditure. See **75.120** TRADING INCOME. This exception is disapplied on the cash basis, so that grants are trading receipts in these circumstances. [*ITTOIA 2005, s 105(2)(2A)*].

Adjustments on change of basis

[76.16] Where a cash basis election is in force in relation to a trade, profession or vocation for one tax year but not the next, or vice versa, the provisions at **75.24** TRADING INCOME (adjustments on change of basis) have effect. This is to ensure that no receipt is taxed twice and no allowable payment is deducted twice, and similarly that neither receipts nor payments fall out of tax. This includes the situation where a person enters the cash basis for the first time but does not apply to income charged on the REMITTANCE BASIS (**61**). [*ITTOIA 2005, s 227A; F(No 2)A 2017, Sch 3 paras 6, 13*].

See also HMRC Business Income Manual BIM70060–70073.

Example

Keith has been running a business for a number of years, preparing accounts to 30 September. For the year ended 30 September 2020, his turnover is £140,000, and he elects for his trading profits to be calculated on the cash basis for 2020/21 onwards. His accounts for the year ended 30 September 2019 showed closing stock of £12,600, trade and other creditors of £4,800 and trade debtors of £600.

Without an adjustment, the value of £12,600 placed on the previous year's closing stock would be taxed twice, once in the previous year and again when the stock is sold. The £600 brought forward as trade debts would also be taxed twice, once in the previous year and again when the debts are settled. Similarly, the £4,800 brought forward as trade and other creditors would be relieved twice.

The adjustment expense is: £(12,600 + 600) – £4,800 = £8,400.

This is treated as an expense of the trade arising on the last day of the year ending 30 September 2020, i.e. the first period of account for which the new basis is adopted.

Spreading on leaving cash basis

Where a cash basis election is in force for one tax year but not the next, any resultant adjustment income arising as in **75.24** TRADING INCOME is automatically spread over six years, as follows. In each of the six tax years beginning with that in which the full adjustment income would otherwise be chargeable to tax, the amount charged is instead one-sixth of the full amount. An individual may elect for an additional amount of his own choosing to be added to the amount otherwise chargeable for a particular tax year. The election must be made on or before the first anniversary of 31 January following the tax year concerned, and must specify the additional amount. The maximum charge for each remaining year is then reduced proportionately. An election may be made more than once during the six-year period. [*ITTOIA 2005, ss 239A, 239B*].

Interaction with the trading allowance

In certain circumstances where no cash basis election has effect it is assumed that such an election does have effect if full relief for the trading allowance would be available on that assumption. See **75.3** TRADING INCOME. Where that assumption is made, the individual is treated for the purposes of the adjustment provisions as entering the cash basis. In such a case the rules at **75.24** TRADING INCOME are modified with the effect that the adjustment is made in the first subsequent tax year for which full relief for the trading allowance is not given. If there is no such tax year, no adjustment is made. Where an individual enters the cash basis solely by virtue of this rule, spreading does not apply to any adjustment income arising if and when he subsequently leaves the cash basis. [*ITTOIA 2005, ss 227B, 227C; F(No 2)A 2017, Sch 3 paras 7, 13*].

77

Trading Income — Fixed Rate Deduction Scheme

Cross-reference. See 75 TRADING INCOME.

Simon's Taxes. See **B2.439A**.

Other sources. See also HMRC Business Income Manual BIM75000–75015.

Introduction to fixed rate deduction scheme

[77.1] All unincorporated businesses can deduct certain types of expenditure on a simplified flat rate basis in computing their taxable trading income (the '*fixed rate deduction scheme*'). The types of expenditure covered by the fixed rate deduction scheme are expenditure on vehicles (**77.2** below), on use of home for business purposes (**77.5** below), and on premises used both as a home and as business premises (**77.6** below). The fixed rate deduction scheme is entirely optional.

The fixed rate deduction scheme applies to professions and vocations as well as to trades. It applies equally to partnerships provided all the partners are individuals. [*ITTOIA 2005, ss 94B, 94C*].

For 2017/18 onwards insofar as it relates to expenditure on vehicles, the fixed rate deduction scheme can also be used by property businesses (see **60.5**, **60.10** PROPERTY INCOME).

In the rest of this chapter, 'trade' includes 'profession or vocation'.

Expenditure on vehicles

[77.2] If, in computing the profits of a trade for a period of account, a deduction would otherwise be allowable in respect of 'qualifying expenditure' incurred in relation to a 'relevant vehicle' (see **77.3** below), a fixed rate deduction is allowed for the period in respect of the qualifying expenditure. This applies equally if a deduction would be so allowable but for the fact that the qualifying expenditure is capital expenditure, e.g. expenditure on the acquisition of the vehicle. The amount of the deduction is the 'appropriate mileage amount' (see **77.4** below) for the relevant vehicle for the period. Use of a fixed rate deduction is optional.

'Qualifying expenditure', in relation to a vehicle, means expenditure incurred in respect of the acquisition, ownership, hire, leasing or use of the vehicle, other than incidental expenses incurred in connection with a particular journey.

If a fixed rate deduction is made for a period of account in respect of qualifying expenditure incurred in relation to a vehicle, no other deduction is allowed (for that or any other period) in respect of the qualifying expenditure. As regards subsequent periods of account, the fixed rate deduction scheme is then compulsory for that vehicle for every period for which it is used for the purposes of the trade. No capital allowances can be claimed on the vehicle once the fixed rate deduction is made — see **10.3, 10.26** CAPITAL ALLOWANCES ON PLANT AND MACHINERY.

[*ITTOIA 2005, s 94D*].

Vehicles included in the scheme

[77.3] A '*relevant vehicle*' in **77.2** above means a 'car', motor cycle or 'goods vehicle' that is used for the purposes of the trade and is not an 'excluded vehicle'.

For these purposes, a '*car*' is any mechanically propelled road vehicle other than a motor cycle, goods vehicle, invalid carriage or vehicle of a type not commonly used as a private vehicle and unsuitable to be so used. A '*goods vehicle*' is any mechanically propelled road vehicle, other than a motor cycle, which is of a construction primarily suited for the conveyance of goods or burden of any description.

A vehicle is an '*excluded vehicle*' if:

- the person (P) carrying on the trade has at any time claimed plant and machinery capital allowances on any expenditure incurred on the provision of the vehicle; or
- the vehicle is a goods vehicle or motor cycle and any expenditure incurred on its acquisition has been deducted in calculating the profits of any 'relevant trade or business' for any period on the cash basis (see **76** TRADING INCOME — CASH BASIS FOR SMALLER BUSINESSES and **60.4** PROPERTY INCOME). A '*relevant trade or business*' is any trade or property business carried on by P. For 2017/18 and earlier years, the second limb of this condition was that any expenditure incurred on acquisition had been deducted in calculating the profits of the trade in question for any period on the cash basis.

[*ITTOIA 2005, ss 94D(2), 94E, 94G; FA 2018, s 36(2)(3)(7)*].

Appropriate mileage amount

[77.4] The '*appropriate mileage amount*' (see **77.2** above) for the relevant vehicle for the period of account is:

$$M \times R$$

where M is the number of miles of 'business journeys' made by a person (other than as a passenger) using the vehicle in the period; and

R is the rate applicable for that kind of vehicle. The rates are as follows.

	Per each of the first 10,000 miles	*Per each mile over 10,000*
Cars and goods vehicles	45p	25p
Motor cycles	24p	24p

For these purposes a '*business journey*' is any journey, or any identifiable part or proportion of a journey, that is made wholly and exclusively for the purposes of the trade. Where the total number of miles of 'relevant business journeys' made in the period is greater than 10,000, the rate of 45p per mile is available only in relation to 10,000 of those miles; a '*relevant business journey*' is any business journey made in the period by *any* car or goods vehicle which is used for the trade and in relation to which a fixed rate deduction is made for the period; in other words the business mileage of all such vehicles is considered in aggregate.

[*ITTOIA 2005, s 94F*].

Use of home for business

[77.5] If, in computing the profits of a trade for a period of account, a deduction would otherwise be allowable for the use of the trader's home for the purposes of the trade (see **75.128** TRADING INCOME), a fixed rate deduction can be made instead. Use of a fixed rate deduction is optional.

The amount of the fixed rate deduction for the period is the sum of the 'applicable amounts' for each month, or part of a month, falling within the period. The '*applicable amount*' for any month (or part of a month) is based on the number of hours worked as set out below. For these purposes the number of hours worked in a month (or part of a month) is the number of hours spent wholly and exclusively on work done by the trader, or any employee of the trader, in the trader's home, being work that is done wholly and exclusively for the purposes of the trade. If the trader has more than one home, these rules have effect as if all his homes were a single home.

Number of hours worked	*Applicable amount*
25 or more	£10.00
51 or more	£18.00
101 or more	£26.00

The fixed rate deduction is available for use of a partner's home for work done by the partner, or by any employee of the firm, in that home. Where more than one person does work in the same home at the same time, any hour spent on that work can be taken into account only once in calculating the deduction. Where a firm makes a fixed rate deduction under *ITTOIA 2005, s 94H* for a period of account in respect of the use of a partner's home, the only deduction which the firm may make for that period for the use of any other partner's home is a deduction under that same *section*.

[*ITTOIA 2005, s 94H; FA 2016, s 24(3)–(7)(11)*].

HMRC regard the 'number of hours worked' as relating to hours worked wholly and exclusively for the purposes of the trade by the trader, or an employee, on the following core business activities: providing goods and/or services; maintaining business records; and marketing/obtaining new business. The fixed rate deduction covers heat, light, power, telephone and internet connection. A separate deduction can still be claimed for fixed costs, such as council tax (or domestic rates in NI), insurance and mortgage interest, if an identifiable proportion can be attributed to business use. (HMRC Business Income Manual BIM75010).

Mixed use premises

[77.6] A fixed rate deduction can be made in relation to expenses incurred in relation to premises if:

- a person carries on a trade at the premises;
- the premises are used mainly for the purposes of carrying on the trade, but are also used by the person as a home;
- the expenses are incurred mainly (but not wholly and exclusively) for the purposes of the trade; and
- a deduction would otherwise be allowable for the period of account in respect of a part or proportion of the expenses in accordance with the dual purpose rule in **75.44** TRADING INCOME (deduction available for any *identifiable* part or proportion of an expense which is incurred wholly and exclusively for the business purposes).

Use of a fixed rate deduction is optional. The amount of the fixed rate deduction for the period is the amount of expenses incurred less an amount representing non-business use. The restriction for non-business use is the sum of the 'disallowable amounts' for each month, or part of a month, falling within the period. The '*disallowable amount*' for any month (or part of a month) is based on the number of 'relevant occupants' as set out below. A '*relevant occupant*', in relation to a month (or part of a month), means an individual who, at any time during that month (or that part of a month), either occupies the premises as a home or stays at the premises otherwise than in the course of the trade.

Number of relevant occupants	*Disallowable amount*
1	£350.00
2	£500.00
3 or more	£650.00

The fixed rate deduction applies to premises used mainly for carrying on the business but also by a partner as a home. Once a deduction under *ITTOIA 2005, s 94I* is made by a partnership for a period of account in respect of particular premises, the only deduction which the partnership may make for that period for the use of any other premises used both for home and business is a deduction under that same section. This also applies where the person making the deductions is an individual with more than one home.

[*ITTOIA 2005, s 94I; FA 2016, s 24(8)–(11)*].

78

Transactions in UK Land

Introduction to transactions in UK land

[78.1] There are statutory provisions that seek to ensure that tax is charged on the full amount of profits from dealing in or developing land in the UK, regardless of whether the taxpayer is resident or non-resident in the UK. They generally have effect in relation to disposals on or after 5 July 2016. In order to prevent forestalling, there is a targeted anti-avoidance rule (see **78.9** below) that applies in relation to disposals on or after 16 March 2016, the day the measures were first announced.

The provisions in **78.2** below override the general territorial rule for trading income whereby the charge on profits arising to a non-UK resident normally depends on the extent to which the trade is carried on in the UK (see **75.1** TRADING INCOME).

The provisions in **78.3–78.8** below introduce a specific income tax charge on profits from dealing in or developing UK land. The charge applies in specified circumstances to profits arising when land is disposed of, and also to disposals of assets deriving their value from land in the UK. There is provision to ensure that the charge applies only to profits not otherwise chargeable to UK tax as income.

Some changes were necessary to the UK's double tax treaties. Whilst the majority of these treaties attribute full taxing rights to the UK over profits from land in the UK, some of the older treaties did not. This meant that the charge would not be fully effective, as businesses resident in affected jurisdictions could claim relief from UK tax under the treaty. In this connection, the UK's treaties with Guernsey, Jersey and the Isle of Man were amended with backdated effect from 16 March 2016 (see the list at **27.2** DOUBLE TAX RELIEF).

For the purposes of these provisions, where any property is disposed of under a contract, the time at which the disposal is made is the time the contract is made and not, if different, the time at which the property is conveyed or transferred. [*FA 2016, s 82(9)*]. This effectively meant that the provisions did not have effect in relation to disposals made on or after 5 July 2016 under a pre-5 July 2016 contract. However, *F(No 2)A 2017* provides that all profits recognised in accounts drawn up (in accordance with generally accepted accounting practice) for a period of account beginning on or after 8 March 2017 are to be brought into charge regardless of when the contract was entered into. This also applies for periods of account straddling 8 March 2017, but only by reference to profits that would be so recognised if the period of account began on that date. [*F(No 2)A 2017, s 39*].

See generally the HMRC Technical Note at www.gov.uk/government/publications/profits-from-trading-in-and-developing-uk-land and the guidance at www.gov.uk/government/publications/profits-from-a-trade-of-dealing-in-or-developing-uk-land-guidance.

Non-resident dealing in or developing UK land

[78.2] In relation to disposals on or after 5 July 2016, profits of a 'trade of dealing in or developing UK land' arising to a non-UK resident are chargeable to UK tax wherever the trade is carried on.

A non-UK resident's '*trade of dealing in or developing UK land*' consists of any of the following activities: dealing in UK land; developing UK land for the purpose of disposing of it; and any activities the profits from which are treated under **78.3**–**78.8** below as profits of the person's trade of dealing in or developing UK land. 'Land' includes buildings and structures, any estate, interest or right in or over land, and land under water; 'UK land' means land in the UK. For the meaning of 'disposal', see **78.8** below, which applies for this purpose also.

Anti-avoidance

Where a person has entered into an arrangement on or after 16 March 2016 of which a main purpose is to obtain a tax advantage in relation to income tax to which the person is chargeable (or would otherwise be chargeable) by virtue of the above rule, the tax advantage is to be counteracted by means of adjustments. Such adjustments may be made (whether by an officer of HMRC or by the taxpayer) by way of assessment, the modification of an assessment, the amendment or disallowance of a claim, or otherwise. The expressions 'arrangement' and 'tax advantage' are both widely defined for this purpose. If the tax advantage arises by virtue of any provisions of a double tax treaty between the UK and an overseas territory, adjustments fall to be made only if the tax advantage is contrary to the object and purpose of the provisions of the treaty.

See also the targeted rule at **78.9** below as regards disposals on or after 16 March 2016 and before 5 July 2016.

[*ITTOIA 2005, ss 6(1A), 6A, 6B; FA 2016, ss 78(1)(2), 82(1)(2)*].

Disposals of UK land

[78.3] Subject to the conditions below, a profit from the disposal on or after 5 July 2016 of land in the UK is treated for income tax purposes as profits of a trade. This applies where the person who realises the profit is:

(a) the person acquiring, holding or developing the land; or
(b) a person who is 'associated' with the person in (a) at a 'relevant time'; or
(c) a person who is a party to, or concerned in, an arrangement which is effected with respect to all or part of the land and enables a profit to be realised by any indirect method or any series of transactions,

and any of the following conditions are met in relation to the land:

(i) a main purpose of acquiring the land was to realise a profit from its disposal;
(ii) a main purpose of acquiring any property deriving its value from the land was to realise a profit from the disposal of the land;
(iii) the land is held as trading stock; or
(iv) in a case where the land has been developed, a main purpose of developing it was to realise a profit from the disposal of the land when developed.

All references to a profit include references to a gain (including a gain which is capital in nature), and see **78.8** below for the meaning of 'disposal'. For the purposes of (b) above, a person (A) is '*associated*' with another person (B) if A and B are related parties (within *ITA 2007, s 517U* — see **78.8** below) or if A is connected with B (within any of **19.2–19.4** CONNECTED PERSONS). A '*relevant time*' is any time in the period beginning when the activities of the 'project' begin and ending six months after the disposal in question. The '*project*' means all activities carried out for any of the purposes of dealing in or developing the land and any other purposes mentioned in (i)–(iv) above.

For the purposes of (c) above and these provisions generally, 'arrangement' is widely defined, and any number of transactions can be regarded as constituting a single arrangement if a common purpose can be discerned in them or there is other sufficient evidence of a common purpose.

The charge to tax

The profit is treated as profits of a trade carried on by the 'chargeable person' (see below), but only to the extent that it would not otherwise fall to be brought into account as income in calculating profits of any person for UK income tax or corporation tax purposes. The profits are treated as arising in the tax year in which the profit on the disposal is realised. If the chargeable person is non-UK resident, the trade in question is the person's trade of dealing in or developing UK land, the profits of which are chargeable to UK tax wherever the trade is carried on (see **78.2** above).

See also the targeted anti-avoidance rule at **78.9** below as regards disposals on or after 16 March 2016 and before 5 July 2016.

The chargeable person

In most cases the '*chargeable person*' is the person (P) who realises the profit, but this is subject to the following special rules. If all or any part of the profit accruing to P is derived from value provided (directly or indirectly) by another person (B), whether or not the value is put at P's disposal, B is the chargeable person. If this is not the case but all or any part of the profit accruing to P is derived from an opportunity of realising a profit provided (directly or indirectly) by another person (D), D is the chargeable person. See also **78.6** below (fragmented activities), which overrides these special rules.

In interpreting the phrase 'another person' in the special rules above:

- a partnership or members of a partnership may be regarded as a person or persons distinct from the individuals or other persons who are for the time being partners;
- the trustees of settled property may be regarded as persons distinct from the individuals or other persons who are for the time being trustees; and
- personal representatives may be regarded as persons distinct from the individuals or other persons who are for the time being personal representatives.

[*ITA 2007, ss 517B, 517C, 517F, 517G, 517P, 517Q; FA 2016, ss 79(1), 82(1)*].

Disposals of property deriving its value from UK land

[78.4] A profit from the disposal on or after 5 July 2016 of property deriving its value from land in the UK is treated for income tax purposes as profits of a trade. The charge applies where:

- a person realises a profit from a disposal of any property which (at the time of disposal) derives at least 50% of its value from land in the UK;
- the person is a party to, or concerned in, an arrangement concerning some or all of that land (the '*project land*'); and
- a main purpose of the arrangement is to deal in or develop the project land and realise a profit from a disposal of property deriving the whole or part of its value from that land.

All references to a profit include references to a gain (including a gain which is capital in nature), and see **78.8** below for the meaning of 'disposal'. 'Arrangement' is widely defined, and any number of transactions can be regarded as constituting a single arrangement if a common purpose can be discerned in them or there is other sufficient evidence of a common purpose.

The charge to tax

So much of the profit as is attributable, on a just and reasonable apportionment, to the 'relevant UK assets' is treated as profits of a trade carried on by the 'chargeable person' (defined as in **78.3** above), but only to the extent that it would not otherwise fall to be brought into account as income in calculating profits of any person for UK income tax or corporation tax purposes. The '*relevant UK assets*' means any land in the UK from which the property disposed of derives any of its value at the time of disposal. The profits are treated as arising in the tax year in which the profit on the disposal is realised. If the chargeable person is non-UK resident, the trade in question is the person's trade of dealing in or developing UK land, the profits of which are chargeable to UK tax wherever the trade is carried on (see 78.2 above).

See also the targeted anti-avoidance rule at 78.9 below as regards disposals on or after 16 March 2016 and before 5 July 2016.

[*ITA 2007, ss 517D–517G, 517Q; FA 2016, ss 79(1), 82(1)*].

Exemption for period before intention to develop formed

[78.5] If, in a case in which 78.3(iv) above (developed land) applies, part of the profit on disposal is fairly attributable to a period before the intention to develop was formed, that part of the profit is exempt from the charge to tax under these provisions. Similarly, in a case in which 78.4 above applies, if part of the profit on disposal is fairly attributable to a period before the person realising the profit was a party to, or concerned in, the arrangement in question, that part of the profit is exempt from the charge under these provisions. [*ITA 2007, s 517L; FA 2016, ss 79(1), 82(1)*].

Fragmented activities

[78.6] The following is intended to prevent profits being fragmented between associated parties with the aim of placing those profits outside the charge to income tax, for example by moving some or all of the profit to a person not carrying on a trade of dealing in or developing land in the UK. It applies where a person (P) disposes of UK land in relation to which any of conditions (i)–(iv) in 78.3 above are met, and a person (R) who is 'associated' with P at a 'relevant time' has made a 'relevant contribution' to the development of the land and/or any other activities aimed at realising a profit from its disposal. In any such case any profit realised by P from the disposal is taken to be what it would be if R were not a distinct person from P and, accordingly, as if everything done by or in relation to R had been done by or in relation to P.

If R makes any payment to P for the purpose of meeting or reimbursing the income tax which P is liable to pay as a result of the above rule, the payment is not to be taken into account in calculating profits or losses of either R or P for income tax or corporation tax purposes. Where R is a company the payment is not treated as a company distribution.

For the above purposes, a '*relevant time*' is any time in the period beginning when the activities of the 'project' began and ending six months after the disposal. The '*project*' means all activities carried out for any of the purposes of dealing in or developing the land and any other purposes mentioned in 78.3(i)–(iv) above. Any 'contribution' made by R is a '*relevant contribution*' unless R's profit in respect of the contribution is insignificant having regard to the size of the project. '*Contribution*' means any kind of contribution, including, for example, a financial contribution, the assumption of a financial risk, and the providing of professional or other services. R is '*associated*' with P if R and P are related parties (within *ITA 2007, s 517U* — see **78.8** below) or if R is connected with P (within any of **19.2–19.4** CONNECTED PERSONS).

[*ITA 2007, s 517H; FA 2016, ss 79(1), 82(1)*].

Arrangements for avoiding tax

[78.7] Where a person has entered into an arrangement on or after 16 March 2016 of which a main purpose is to obtain a 'relevant tax advantage', the tax advantage is to be counteracted by means of adjustments. Such adjustments may be made (whether by an officer of HMRC or by the taxpayer) by way of assessment, the modification of an assessment, the amendment or disallowance of a claim, or otherwise. See **78.3** above as to the meaning of 'arrangement'. A '*relevant tax advantage*' is an advantage (as widely defined) in relation to income tax chargeable (or otherwise chargeable) in respect of amounts treated as profits of a trade by virtue of **78.3** or **78.4** above. If the relevant tax advantage arises by virtue of any provisions of a double tax treaty between the UK and an overseas territory, adjustments fall to be made only if the relevant tax advantage is contrary to the object and purpose of the provisions of the treaty. [*ITA 2007, s 517K; FA 2016, ss 79(1), 82(1)(3)*].

Supplementary rules and definitions

[78.8] The following apply for the purposes of **78.3–78.7** above.

Computing a profit

Subject to any modifications that may be appropriate, the profit (if any) on a disposal of any property must be computed in accordance with the principles applicable to the computation of trading profits. The same principles apply in computing losses as apply in computing profits. [*ITA 2007, s 517I; FA 2016, ss 79(1), 82(1)*].

Realising a profit for another person

It does not matter whether the person realising the profit in **78.3** or **78.4** realises it for himself or for another person. If, for example by a premature sale, a person (A) directly or indirectly transmits the opportunity of realising a profit to another person (B), A realises B's profit for B. [*ITA 2007, s 517T; FA 2016, ss 79(1), 82(1)*].

Exception for main residence

No liability arises under these provisions in respect of a gain accruing to an individual if it is exempt from capital gains tax (CGT) due to the CGT exemption covering an individual's only or main residence, or if it would have qualified for that exemption were it not that the residence was acquired wholly or partly for the purpose of realising a gain. [*ITA 2007, s 517M; FA 2016, ss 79(1), 82(1)*].

Meaning of disposal

References to a disposal of any property include any case in which the property is effectively disposed of by one or more transactions or by any arrangement. References to a disposal of land or any other property include a part disposal. Where, on a a disposal of an asset, any form of property derived from the asset remains undisposed of (including where an interest or right in or over the asset is created by the disposal as well as where it subsisted before the disposal), the disposal counts as a part disposal. [*ITA 2007, s 517R; FA 2016, ss 79(1), 82(1)*].

Meaning of 'land' etc.

'Land' includes buildings and structures, any estate, interest or right in or over land, and land under water. References to property deriving its value from land include any shareholding in a company, partnership interest or interest in settled property deriving its value (directly or indirectly) from land, and also include any option, consent or embargo affecting the disposition of land. [*ITA 2007, s 517S; FA 2016, ss 79(1), 82(1)*].

Related parties

Two persons (A and B) are related parties on any particular day if, within the six months beginning with that day, one of the parties directly or indirectly participates in the management, control or capital of the other, or the same person or persons directly or indirectly participate in the management, control or capital of each of A and B. See *ITA 2007, s 517U(7)* as to interpretation of the reference to direct and indirect participation. A and B are also related parties if one has a 25% investment in the other, or a third person has a 25% investment in each of A and B. The question of whether there is a 25% investment is determined in accordance with *TIOPA 2010, s 259NC*.

[*ITA 2007, s 517U; FA 2016, ss 79(1), 82(1)*].

Value tracing and indirect methods

Where it is necessary to determine the extent to which the value of any property or right is derived from any other property or right, value may be traced through any number of companies, partnerships, trusts and other entities or arrangements, at each stage attributing property held by the company etc. to its shareholders etc. in such manner as is appropriate in the circumstances. In determining whether the charge to tax in **78.3** or **78.4** applies, account may be taken of any method, however indirect, to transfer any property or right, or enhance or diminish its value, e.g. by sales at less, or more, than full consideration, assigning share capital or rights in a company or partnership or an interest in settled property, disposal on the winding-up of any company, partnership or trust etc. Any such transfer or enhancement may give rise to the charge to tax. [*ITA 2007, ss 517N, 517O; FA 2016, ss 79(1), 82(1)*].

Apportionments

Any apportionment (whether of expenditure, consideration or any other amount) that is required for the purposes of these provisions is to be made on a just and reasonable basis. [*ITA 2007, s 517J; FA 2016, ss 79(1), 82(1)*].

Targeted anti-avoidance rule

[78.9] If, on or after 16 March 2016 and before 5 July 2016, a person disposes of land to a person who is 'associated' with him at the 'relevant time', and any person obtains a 'relevant tax advantage' as a result, the tax advantage is to be counteracted by means of adjustments. Such adjustments may be made (whether by an officer of HMRC or by the taxpayer) by way of assessment, the modification of an assessment, the amendment or disallowance of a claim, or otherwise. For these purposes, property disposed of under a contract (whether or not a conditional contract) is disposed of at the time the contract is made (and not, if different, the time at which the property is conveyed or transferred). 'Land' includes property deriving the whole or part of its value from land. For the meaning of 'disposal', see **78.8** above, which applies for these purposes also.

A '*relevant tax advantage*' is a tax advantage in relation to tax to which the person in question is charged or chargeable (or would otherwise be charged or chargeable) either:

(a) by virtue of the rule in **78.2** above; or
(b) in respect of amounts treated as profits of a trade by virtue of **78.3–78.8** above.

A person (A) is '*associated*' with another person (B) for these purposes if A and B are related parties (within *ITA 2007, s 517U* — see **78.8** above) or if A is connected with B (within any of **19.2–19.4** CONNECTED PERSONS). The '*relevant time*' means, where (a) above applies, the time when the disposal was made and, where (b) above applies, any time in the period which ends six months after the disposal in **78.3** or the disposal in **78.4** above and which began when the activities of the project in **78.3** began or, as the case may be, the dealing in or developing activities in **78.4** began.

'Tax advantage' is widely defined for these purposes. If the tax advantage arises by virtue of any provisions of a double tax treaty between the UK and an overseas territory, adjustments fall to be made only if the tax advantage is contrary to the object and purpose of the provisions of the treaty.

[*FA 2016, s 82(4)–(15)*].

79

Underwriters at Lloyd's

Simon's Taxes. See E5.6.

Introduction to Underwriters at Lloyd's

[79.1] Special tax provisions for Lloyd's underwriters are contained in *FA 1993, ss 171–184, Schs 19, 20.*

As regards underwriters who are Scottish limited partnerships or limited liability partnerships, see *SI 1997 No 2681.*

See also HMRC Lloyd's Manual.

Basis of assessment

[79.2] The profits or losses in a tax year are those declared in the underwriting year ending in the tax year, i.e. profits of underwriting year 2017 are generally declared in 2020 and assessed for 2020/21. [*FA 1993, s 172(1)*].

On cessation (on death or otherwise), the final tax year is that which corresponds to the underwriting year in which the underwriter's Lloyd's deposit is paid over to him or his personal representatives or assigns. Any underwriting profits or losses which do not fall to be taken as profits or losses of an earlier tax year are taken to be profits or losses of the final tax year. [*FA 1993, s 179*]. Where a member dies:

- he is treated for these purposes as having died on 5 April in the underwriting year in which he actually died; and
- the business is treated as continuing until the member's deposit is paid over to his personal representatives, whose carrying on of the business is not treated as a change in the persons so engaged.

[*FA 1993, s 179A*].

An underwriting year '*corresponds*' to the tax year in which it ends and *vice versa*, i.e. the 2017 underwriting year ends on 31 December 2017 and thus corresponds to the tax year 2017/18. [*FA 1993, s 184(2)*].

If underwriting commenced before 2 January 1971 and a cessation occurs, a claim may be made for assessments:

- for the final tax year for which underwriting profits or losses fall to be included (being profits or losses declared in the underwriting year following the closing year) to be based on the actual profits from 6 April to 31 December in that underwriting year, and
- for the preceding year to be reduced by the lesser of the whole of the profits of that year and the underwriting profits for the underwriting year 1972.

[*SI 1995 No 351, Reg 13*].

For double tax relief arrangements, see *SI 1997 No 405*.

Underwriting profits

[79.3] The aggregate of a member's underwriting profits is chargeable to tax as the profits of a trade carried on in the UK. Underwriting profits include income from premium trust fund assets and income from 'ancillary trust fund' assets. An '*ancillary trust fund*' does not include a premium trust fund or special reserve fund but otherwise means any trust fund required or authorised by Lloyd's rules or required by an underwriter's member's agent. [*FA 1993, ss 171(1)(2)(4), 184(2)(b)*].

Annual appreciation in value of and profits on disposal of premium trust fund assets are included in underwriting profits for income tax purposes and annual depreciation in value and losses on disposal are deducted in arriving at such profits. [*FA 1993, ss 174, 184(2)*]. Gains and losses on ancillary trust fund assets are subject to the capital gains tax regime. [*FA 1993, s 176(2)*].

Underwriting profits are treated as derived from the carrying on of a business and thus count as relevant UK earnings for pension purposes (see **57.12** PENSION PROVISION). [*FA 1993, s 180*].

Stop-loss premiums

Stop-loss insurance premiums are allowable as an expense in computing underwriting profits, and insurance money received in respect of a loss is a trading receipt of the tax year corresponding to the underwriting year in which the loss was declared. This treatment is extended to payments into and receipts out of the High Level Stop Loss Fund, i.e. the fund of that name established under Lloyd's rules. A repayment of insurance money received etc. is likewise allowed as an expense, as is any amount payable under a quota share contract, i.e. a contract made in accordance with Lloyd's rules and practice between the underwriter and another person which provides for that other person to take over any rights and liabilities of the underwriter under any of his syndicates.

As regards quota share contracts, the deduction may be limited by reference to certain prior 'transferred losses', and if such losses exceed the amount payable under the contract, a trading receipt will arise. Amounts paid in respect of conditional contracts which do not come into effect are, however, allowed in full, and certain cash calls in respect of undeclared transferred losses are treated as payments under the contract. The treatment of insurance receipts etc. is modified where the inspector is not notified of the receipt in time to raise the necessary assessment for the year corresponding to that in which the loss arose; in such a case, the trading receipt is treated as arising in the tax year corresponding to the underwriting year in which the payment of insurance money etc. was made to the underwriter. [*FA 1993, ss 178, 184(1)*].

Reinsurance premiums

A restriction is placed on relief for such premiums payable in respect of liabilities outstanding at the end of an underwriting year for the purpose of closing the accounts for the underwriting year, where the member by whom the premium is payable is also a member of the syndicate as a member of which the reinsurer is entitled to receive it. Relief is restricted to an amount which must not exceed an assessment, arrived at with a view to producing neither profit nor loss to the member to whom it is payable, of the value of the liabilities in respect of which it is payable, and a corresponding reduction is made in his profits or gains as a member of the reinsurer syndicate. [*FA 1993, s 177*].

See Revenue Tax Bulletin October 1998 p 599 as regards the proportion of such premiums generally allowable for tax purposes.

General insurance reserves

There are provisions for bringing in as a trading receipt or expense an amount representing interest on any allowance in respect of technical provisions to the extent that it subsequently becomes apparent that it was excessive or insufficient. [*FA 2000, s 107; SI 2001 No 1757*].

Miscellaneous deductions

It is understood that subscriptions to the **Association of Lloyd's members** are allowable, as is the cost of League Tables and Syndicate Results. Two-thirds of the cost of prospective names seminars, and one-half of the cost of most other conferences and meetings, is also allowable, with proportionate allowance of travelling expenses other than to or from London (the place of business).

Bank guarantee fees paid initially to secure membership as a Lloyd's underwriter are not deductible, but annual payments for the maintenance of such facilities are deductible.

Personal accountancy fees are allowed on the usual 'wholly and exclusively' basis applicable to traders generally, by reference to the amount paid in the year of account.

Compensation payments from managing or members' agents are likely to be treated as trading receipts of the underwriting year in which the entitlement to compensation arises, and thus as not being chargeable to capital gains tax. Any legal fees incurred, together with any payments out of the compensation to stop-loss insurers, are deductible for tax purposes. (Revenue Tax Bulletin May 1992 p 17). For confirmation that such compensation payments are taxable, see *Deeny and others v Gooda Walker Ltd* HL 1996, 68 TC 458.

Members' agent pooling arrangements (MAPAs)

For the tax treatment of individuals' shares of the various syndicate membership rights held through each MAPA, see Tolley's Capital Gains Tax under Underwriters at Lloyd's. [*FA 1999, ss 82–84*].

Underwriting losses

[79.4] An underwriting loss can be **carried forward** for relief against underwriting profits in subsequent tax years (under the normal provisions for carry-forward of losses under *ITA 2007, s 83*).

An underwriting loss for a tax year can also be **offset against other income** of the underwriter under the normal provisions of *ITA 2007, s 64.*

An underwriting loss in the early years of the business may be carried back and offset against other income under *ITA 2007, s 72.*

See **45** LOSSES.

An *anticipated* underwriting loss may not be taken into account in a PAYE coding until title to it has been established, i.e. until it has actually been sustained (*Blackburn v Keeling* CA, 75 TC 608).

Carry-forward of losses against income from successor company or partnership

[79.5] Where, under a conversion arrangement made under the rules or practice of Lloyd's (conversion to limited liability underwriting), a member transfers the whole of his outstanding syndicate capacity to a company (the successor company) for a consideration consisting entirely of shares in the company, any income which he derives from the company (e.g. earnings or dividends) is treated for the purposes of carry-forward of losses under *ITA 2007, s 83* as if it were profits of the member's former underwriting business, thus enabling any unrelieved losses brought forward to be set against it. The successor company must be one which the member controls (within the meaning of *CTA 2010, ss 450, 451*) and of which he owns more than 50% of the ordinary share capital and, for the relief to apply in respect of income of a particular tax year, these conditions must continue to be satisfied from the time of transfer until the end of that tax year.

The transfer of syndicate capacity must take effect from the beginning of the underwriting year immediately following the member's final underwriting year, and the successor company must commence underwriting in that following year. The member must also have given notice of resignation to Lloyd's and must not undertake any new insurance business at Lloyd's after the end of his final underwriting year. If the member withdraws his resignation after claiming relief under these provisions, the relief fails; the member must give HMRC written notice of the withdrawal within six months after it occurs.

A similar relief applies if a member transfers the whole of his outstanding syndicate capacity to a Scottish limited partnership, provided he is the only person who disposes of syndicate capacity under a conversion arrangement to that partnership. The income to which the relief applies is the profits of the successor partnership's underwriting business to which the member is beneficially entitled and, for the relief to apply in respect of income of a particular tax year, the member must be beneficially entitled to more than 50% of such profits throughout the period from the time of transfer to the end of that tax year. The relief is extended to cover a transfer to a UK limited liability partnership.

[*FA 1993, s 179B, Sch 20A paras 1, 2, 5–11*].

Syndicate managing agents — tax obligations

[79.6] The administrative machinery under which syndicate managing agents must operate with regard to their tax obligations is set out in regulations (*SI 2005 No 3338*). These provide for the determination of the syndicate profit/loss and its apportionment between the members, the filing of returns and HMRC's powers to determine syndicate profits in certain cases. For the purpose of determining the liability to tax of each member of the syndicate, a determination of a syndicate's profit or loss for an underwriting year and its apportionment between members is conclusive against that member. For the purpose of the extended time limits at **6.3**, **6.4** ASSESSMENTS, anything done or omitted to be done by a syndicate's managing agent is deemed to have been done or omitted to be done by each member of the syndicate.

The regulations also provide for the managing agent to claim from HMRC the repayment of tax suffered by way of deduction on the syndicate's investment income, to apportion the amount repaid between the members of the syndicate and (except in so far as it is required to meet a share of a loss of the syndicate) pay the amount so apportioned to each member, within 90 days of the repayment, to the members' agent of that member. Such repayment does not carry interest.

[*SI 2005 No 3338*].

Special reserve fund

[79.7] An underwriter may set up a Special Reserve Fund into which he may make payments (eligible for tax relief — see **79.9** below) for the purpose of meeting future losses.

A special reserve fund may be set up in relation to each underwriter under arrangements complying with the requirements of *FA 1993, Sch 20 Pt I* and approved by HMRC (who may consent to any variation of the arrangements). The fund must be vested in trustees who have control over it, and there must be appointed a fund manager, authorised under Lloyd's rules and who may be the trustees or one or more of them, to invest the capital and vary the investments. Payments into and out of the fund (which, unless a contrary intention appears in the legislation, must be in money) must be allowed only where required or permitted (expressly or by necessary implication) by the provisions of *Sch 20*. Otherwise, the income arising from the fund must be added to capital and retained in the fund. The underwriter is absolutely entitled as against the trustees to the fund assets, but subject to the rules of cessation (see **79.11** below) and without affecting the operation of capital gains tax on a disposal of an asset by the underwriter to the trustees. The fund manager must value the fund in a manner prescribed by regulations (see *SI 1995 No 353*) as at the end of each underwriting year, and must report the value (and such other matters as may be prescribed by regulations) to the underwriter. [*FA 1993, s 175(1)(2), Sch 20 paras 1(1), 2, 6(1), 8*].

Payments into and out of the special reserve fund are, respectively, deductions and additions in arriving at the underwriter's profit. [*FA 1993, Sch 19 para 10(2)(a)(3)(a), Sch 20 para 10*].

Where a member dies and his personal representatives carry on his underwriting business after his death, the special reserve fund provisions are modified to apply to the personal representatives. [*SI 1995 No 353, Regs 7, 7A*].

Tax exemption

[79.8] Profits arising from special reserve fund assets are exempt from both income tax and capital gains tax, and losses are not allowable. The fund manager may, at any time after the end of an underwriting year, claim repayment of income tax deducted from such profits for that year. [*FA 1993, Sch 20 para 9*].

Payments into the fund out of syndicate profits

[79.9] For the purposes of the provisions described below, an underwriter's '*syndicate profit*' for an underwriting year is the excess of his aggregate profits over his aggregate losses, profits or losses being those shown in syndicate accounts as arising to him and disregarding payments into or out of the special reserve fund. Profits of a run-off underwriting year are attributable to the last underwriting year but one preceding the run-off year. An underwriter's '*syndicate loss*' is to be construed accordingly. [*FA 1993, Sch 20 para 1; SI 1995 No 353*].

If an underwriter has made a syndicate profit for an underwriting year, he may pay into his special reserve fund, before the end of a period prescribed by regulations (see *SI 1995 No 353*), the lesser of:

(i) 50% of that profit; and
(ii) the excess, if any, of an amount equal to 50% of the underwriter's 'overall premium limit' for the closing year (i.e. the year next but one following the underwriting year) over the value of the fund at the end of that year.

An underwriter's '*overall premium limit*' for an underwriting year means the maximum amount which, under Lloyd's rules, he may accept by way of premiums in that year. If the underwriter did not accept premiums in the closing year, the reference in (ii) above to the closing year is to be taken as a reference to the latest underwriting year in which he did so. The above provisions are not to apply, in the case of any underwriter, to any tax year after a tax year in which HMRC cancel their approval of the arrangements referred to in **79.7** above, having first given notice to Lloyd's of their intention to do so.

The payment into the fund in respect of an underwriting year is deductible as an expense in arriving at underwriting profits. It is made for the tax year next but two after the tax year to which the underwriting year corresponds (i.e. a payment made in underwriting year 2017 is deducted in 2020/21).

[*FA 1993, s 175(3), Sch 20 paras 1(1), 3, 10(1)*].

Payments out of the special reserve fund

[79.10] Payments *must* be made out of the fund in the following circumstances.

(i) To cover 'cash calls'. A '*cash call*' means a request for funds made to the underwriter by an agent of a syndicate of which he is a member, being made in pursuance of a contract made in accordance with Lloyd's rules and practices. If a cash call is made in respect of an underwriting year, there must be paid out of the underwriter's special reserve fund into a premium trust fund of his an amount equal to the amount of the call (or, if less, the amount of the special reserve fund). There are provisions for a payment to be made back into the special reserve fund if a stop-loss payment (i.e. a payment of insurance money under a stop-loss insurance or a payment out of the High Level Stop Loss Fund — see **79.3** above) is made to the underwriter, and for a further payment out of the fund if a stop-loss payment is wholly or partly repaid. [*FA 1993, Sch 20 para 4; SI 1995 No 353*].

(ii) To cover syndicate losses. If an underwriter sustains a syndicate loss for an underwriting year, there must be paid out of his special reserve fund into a premium trust fund of his an amount equal to the 'net amount of the loss' (or, if less, the amount of the special reserve fund). The '*net amount of the loss*' is the amount of the syndicate loss as reduced by any payment made out of the special reserve fund for the year to cover a cash call (see (i) above). As in (i) above, there are provisions for payments into and out of the special reserve fund in the event of stop-loss payments and repayments of stop-loss payments. If a stop-loss payment is made in respect of the loss before any payment out of the special reserve fund in respect of the loss, no payment is required into the fund but the said payment out of the fund is determined as if the net amount of the loss were reduced by the amount of the stop-loss payment. [*FA 1993, Sch 20 para 5*].

(iii) To eliminate excess amounts. If on the valuation (see **79.7** above) of the special reserve fund at the end of the underwriting year, it is found that the value of the fund exceeds 50% of the higher of the underwriter's overall premium limit (see **79.9** above) for that year and the corresponding figure for the previous year (or 50% of his overall premium limit for the last year in which he accepted premiums), the excess must be paid to the underwriter (or to his personal representatives or assigns). [*FA 1993, Sch 20 para 6(2)*].

(iv) On cessation. On a person ceasing to be an underwriter (on death or otherwise), the amount of his special reserve fund (net of any amount required to be paid out to cover cash calls or syndicate losses) must be paid over to the underwriter (or to his personal representatives or assigns), the payment to be in money or in assets forming part of the fund, as the recipient may direct. [*FA 1993, Sch 20 para 7*].

Any payments required to be made out of or into the fund under (i)–(iii) above must be made before the end of a period to be prescribed in each case by regulations (see *SI 1995 No 353*). [*FA 1993, Sch 20 paras 4(8), 5(10), 6(3)*].

In computing underwriting profits for a tax year, payments into the special reserve fund under (i) and (ii) above in respect of the 'relevant' underwriting year are deductible as expenses, and the following are treated as trading receipts:

- payments out of the fund in respect of the 'relevant' underwriting year to cover cash calls and losses;
- payments out of the fund as a result of the repayment of stop-loss payments (see (i) and (ii) above) in the 'relevant' underwriting year; and
- any payment out of the fund under (iii) above in respect of the 'relevant' underwriting year's closing year (i.e. the underwriting year next but one following the 'relevant' underwriting year).

The '*relevant*' underwriting year for this purpose is the underwriting year next but two before the corresponding underwriting year, i.e. for 2020/21, for which the corresponding underwriting year is 2020, the relevant underwriting year is 2017.

[*FA 1993, Sch 20 para 10(2)–(4)*].

Cessation

[79.11] The aggregate of any payments made out of the special reserve fund under **79.10**(iv) above is treated, in computing underwriting profits for the 'relevant tax year', as made immediately after the end of the 'relevant underwriting year' and as being a trading receipt. The amount of the trading receipt is the value of the fund at the end of the 'penultimate underwriting year' as reduced by subsequent payments out (other than under **79.10**(iii) or (iv) above) and as increased by:

- subsequent payments in;
- subsequent repayments of tax in respect of fund income;
- the amount of any subsequent profits, net of any losses, arising to the trustees from assets (any net deficit being deducted), leaving aside any gain or loss on an asset transferred to the member etc. and treated as an acquisition by him for capital gains tax purposes (see below); and
- any payments made before the end of the penultimate underwriting year by the trustees to the member etc., whether under **79.10**(iv) above or otherwise than out of the special reserve fund, including the market value of any asset transferred by way of such payment.

On the transfer of an asset by the trustees to the member, his personal representatives or assigns, whether under **79.10**(iv) above or otherwise, there are rules to determine for capital gains tax purposes both the date and cost of acquisition by the member etc., for which see the corresponding chapter of Tolley's Capital Gains Tax.

The '*relevant tax year*' is the final tax year except that, where a member dies before the occurrence of certain events, it is the tax year at the end of which he is treated as having died (see **79.2** above). The events in question are where the member's deposit is paid over to any person (or a substituted arrangement ceases) or the last open year of account of any syndicate of which he was a member is closed or is regarded as having closed. The '*relevant underwriting year*' is the underwriting year corresponding to the tax year immediately preceding the final tax year except that, where the member dies before the occurrence of certain events (as above), it is the underwriting year immediately preceding that corresponding to the relevant tax year (as above). The '*penultimate underwriting year*' is the underwriting year corresponding to the tax year immediately preceding the final tax year.

[*FA 1993, Sch 20 para 11*].

80

Unit Trusts etc.

Simon's Taxes. See **D8.1**.

Introduction to unit trusts etc.

[80.1] This chapter (at **80.2–80.7** below) covers authorised investment funds (AIFs) (see below), principally from the point of view of an investor within the charge to income tax. From a similar viewpoint the chapter also covers unauthorised unit trusts (**80.8** below) and court common investment funds (**80.11** below). See also **80.10** below as regards pension fund pooling vehicles. For the corporation tax provisions applicable to AIFs and the treatment of distributions in the hands of corporate participants in AIFs, see Tolley's Corporation Tax under Investment Funds. See **51** OFFSHORE FUNDS for unit trusts which are offshore funds.

For official guidance on unit trusts and other collective investment schemes, see HMRC Investment Funds Manual IFM02000–11000.

An AIF may be either an authorised unit trust (see **80.2** below), an open-ended investment company (see **80.3** below) or a qualified investor scheme (see **80.5** below where a condition is met as to diversity of ownership — otherwise see **80.2** or **80.3** below, whichever is appropriate). A UK AIF that meets certain conditions may elect to be treated as a tax elected fund (see **80.6** below). A special regime is available for AIFs which invest in non-reporting offshore funds (see **80.7** below).

An AIF which is authorised or registered, or has its registered office, in a foreign territory and is a body corporate which would otherwise be treated as UK resident for the purposes of UK taxation of income and gains, i.e. because it is managed from the UK, is treated as if it were not UK resident. The following are, however, excluded from this rule: unit trust schemes the trustees of which are UK resident, companies incorporated in the UK, investment trusts and Real Estate Investment Trusts. [*TIOPA 2010, s 363A; SI 2017 No 1204, Regs 1, 14*].

Authorised unit trusts (AUTs)

[80.2] An '*authorised unit trust*' (AUT) is a 'unit trust scheme' which is the subject of an order under *Financial Services and Markets Act 2000, s 243* for the whole or part of an accounting period. A '*unit trust scheme*' is defined by *Financial Services and Markets Act 2000, s 237* as a collective investment scheme under which the property is held on trust for the participants. A unit holder is a person entitled to a share of the investments subject to the trusts of the scheme. The *Tax Acts* have effect as if the trustees were a company resident in the UK, and the rights of unit holders were shares in the company (but without prejudice to the making of 'interest distributions' (see below)). [*CTA 2010, s 617(1); ITA 2007, s 1007; SI 2006 No 964, Reg 88*].

For capital gains tax (CGT) purposes, any unit trust scheme is treated as if the scheme were a company and the rights of the unit holders were shares in the company, and, in the case of an AUT, as if the company were UK resident. Different rules apply on and after 1 January 2018 in the case of offshore 'transparent funds' (within **51.4** OFFSHORE FUNDS). [*TCGA 1992, s 99(1)(1A); SI 2017 No 1204, Regs 1, 3*]. See Tolley's Capital Gains Tax.

A special rate of corporation tax applies to the trustees of an AUT, equivalent to the basic rate of income tax for the tax year beginning in the financial year concerned. [*CTA 2010, s 618*].

'*Umbrella schemes*' (i.e. schemes which provide separate pools of contributions between which participants may switch) which are AUTs are treated as if each of the separate pools were an AUT. [*CTA 2010, s 619*].

For guidance on the tax treatment of income from AUTs, see HMRC Investment Funds Manual IFM03000.

Distributions

The rules on distributions are largely contained in the *Authorised Investment Funds (Tax) Regulations 2006 (SI 2006 No 964)*. See also *ITTOIA 2005, ss 376–378, 389–391*.

The total amount available for distribution to unit holders is to be allocated either for distribution as dividends or for distribution as yearly interest. This and the other distribution rules below do not apply to an AUT that is a registered pension scheme (see **57.4** PENSION PROVISION).

A '*distribution period*' of an AUT is the period by reference to which the amount available for distribution is ascertained. The '*distribution date*' for a distribution period is the date specified for that purpose under the terms of the trust or instrument of incorporation or, if there is no such date specified, the last day of the distribution period.

Where the total amount available is allocated for distribution as dividends, it is treated for tax purposes as if it were dividends on shares paid on the distribution date to the unit holders in proportion to their holdings. Where the total amount available is allocated for distribution as yearly interest, it is treated for tax purposes as if it were yearly interest paid on the distribution date to the unit holders in proportion to their holdings. See **1.5–1.7** ALLOWANCES AND TAX RATES as regards taxation of dividends and savings income (including interest) generally.

The retention and reinvestment by an AUT of an otherwise distributable amount in respect of a unit holder's accumulation units counts as a distribution.

There is a *de minimis* provision whereby an authorised investment trust may choose to waive a distribution if, in accordance with rules made by the Financial Services Authority (now the Financial Conduct Authority), the trust has an agreed *de minimis* limit and the total amount available to be allocated for distribution is below that limit. The amount available must then be carried forward to the next distribution period as income available for distribution for that period. It is a condition that none of the units of the fund in issue on the distribution date are in bearer form. Where these conditions are satisfied, the amount carried forward is treated as not having been distributed.

No amount may be allocated for distribution as yearly interest unless the AUT satisfies the qualifying investments test throughout the distribution period, which it does if, at all times in that period, the market value of 'qualifying investments' exceeds 60% of the market value of all the investments of the trust (disregarding cash awaiting investment). '*Qualifying investments*' are any of the following:

(a) money placed at interest;
(b) building society shares;
(c) securities (other than company shares);
(d) units in another AUT or in an open-ended investment company, provided that, throughout the distribution period in question, more than 60% of the market value of the other unit trust's or the open-ended investment company's investments is represented by investments falling within (a)–(c) above and (f)–(i) below;
(e) units in an offshore fund, provided that, throughout the distribution period in question, more than 60% of the market value of the offshore fund's investments is represented by investments falling within (a)–(c) above and (f)–(i) below;
(f) derivative contracts whose underlying subject matter consists wholly of any one or more of (a)–(e) above and currency;
(g) contracts for differences (within *CTA 2009, s 582*) whose underlying subject matter consists wholly of any one or more of interest rates, creditworthiness or currency;
(h) derivative contracts (not within (f) or (g) above) where there is a hedging relationship between the derivative contract and an asset within (a)–(e) above; and
(i) alternative finance arrangements (see **3** ALTERNATIVE FINANCE ARRANGEMENTS).

Tax deductible at source from interest distributions before 2017/18

Tax is not deductible at source from interest distributions made on or after **6 April 2017** (see **23.12**(h) DEDUCTION OF TAX AT SOURCE). For 2016/17 and earlier years, basic rate tax is deductible at source under *ITA 2007, s 874* from interest distributions unless:

- the unit holder to whom the payment is made is either a company or the trustees of a unit trust scheme; or
- either the 'residence condition' or the 'reputable intermediary condition' is met with respect to the unit holder on the distribution date; or
- the 'offshore marketing condition' is met with respect to the class of units in relation to which the distribution is made.

The '*residence condition*' requires that any one of the following be met:

- the unit holder has made a valid declaration that he is not resident in the UK; or
- the units are held by the personal representative of a deceased person in his capacity as such and the deceased had made a declaration, valid at the time of his death, that he is not resident in the UK; or
- the units are held by the personal representative of a deceased person in his capacity as such and the personal representative makes a valid declaration that the deceased, immediately before his death, was not resident in the UK; or
- the distribution is made to a trust under which the whole of the income is the income of a person other than the trustees and that person has made a valid declaration that he is not resident in the UK; or
- the distribution is made to a trust to which the above does not apply and the trustees have made a valid declaration that they are not resident in the UK and that each beneficiary is not resident in the UK.

Declarations as above must be made to the trustees of the AUT in prescribed form and must contain specified details and undertakings.

The '*reputable intermediary condition*' requires broadly that the interest distribution is paid on behalf of the unit holder to a company which is subject to certain money laundering controls, and that the trustees of the AUT have reasonable grounds for believing the unit holder to be not resident in the UK. If it subsequently transpires that the unit holder was in fact UK resident, the tax which should have been deducted is payable to HMRC by the trustees of the AUT. See *TMA 1970, s 98(4E)* (as amended) for penalty provisions.

The '*offshore marketing condition*' is met with respect to a class of units if:

- marketing of units of that class is not directed to investors resident in the UK; and
- before units of that class are acquired, information in relation to them is available to investors to the effect that no income tax will be deducted at source from interest distributions but that an investor must notify HMRC of any distribution to which he is entitled in relation to such units if he is chargeable to income tax for the tax year in which the distribution date falls.

The trustees of an AUT were required to notify HMRC about distributions made without deduction of tax, within a specified time and subject to penalties for non-compliance. HMRC have power to require information about such distributions and to inspect records (see *SI 2006 No 964, Regs 71–75*).

[*ITTOIA 2005, ss 376–378, 389–391; F(No 2)A 2005, ss 17–19; SI 2006 No 964, Regs 8, 15–33A, 70–75*].

Rebates of annual management charges etc.

See HMRC Brief 04/13, 25 March 2013 at **49.5** MISCELLANEOUS INCOME.

Simon's Taxes. See **D8.110–D8.122, E1.408, E1.413.**

Open-ended investment companies (OEICs)

[80.3] The rules on distributions are largely contained in the *Authorised Investment Funds (Tax) Regulations 2006 (SI 2006 No 964)*. Those rules are the same as those described at **80.2** above, subject only to a few minor necessary modifications. See also *ITTOIA 2005, ss 373–375, 386–388*, which mirror the equivalent provisions for authorised unit trusts.

For official guidance on the tax treatment of income from OEICs, see HMRC Investment Funds Manual IFM03000.

Property AIFs

[80.4] OEICs (see **80.3** above) may opt into the Property AIF (Property Authorised Investment Fund) regime. This is similar to the Real Estate Investment Trust (REIT) regime (see **60.24** PROPERTY INCOME). An OEIC carrying on a property investment business (as defined) and meeting the other required conditions can elect for the Property AIF regime to have effect. Its property-related income is then exempt from tax in the OEIC's hands. A distribution received from a Property AIF by an individual investor is treated in his hands as profits of a UK property business to the extent that it is paid out of the tax-exempt profits of the AIF. Basic rate tax is deducted at source by the Property AIF; the shareholder remains liable for any excess liability, i.e. excess of the higher rate of tax over the basic rate. A distribution of taxable income (not including dividends) is treated as interest in the hands of the investor and is also subject to deduction of basic rate tax at source. A distribution out of UK dividend income is treated as a dividend in the hands of the investor. [*SI 2006 No 964, Pt 4A*].

For official guidance on Property AIFs, see HMRC Investment Funds Manual IFM04000.

Simon's Taxes. See **D8.130–D8.133.**

Qualified Investor Schemes

[80.5] A Qualified Investor Scheme (QIS) is a type of (non-retail) authorised investment fund (either an open-ended investment company or a unit trust) authorised by the Financial Services Authority (now the Financial Conduct

Authority) and aimed at sophisticated and institutional investors. The instrument constituting the scheme must contain a statement that the scheme is a QIS. The taxation of investors in a QIS is determined in accordance with the *Authorised Investment Funds (Tax) Regulations 2006* (*SI 2006 No 964*).

A QIS is treated for tax purposes in the same way as any other open-ended investment company or authorised unit trust provided that it meets a 'genuine diversity of ownership condition'. Where the genuine diversity of ownership condition is not satisfied for an accounting period of the scheme, the QIS is treated for tax purposes as if it were a close investment holding company within *CTA 2010, s 34* (see Tolley's Corporation Tax).

[*SI 2006 No 964, Reg 14B*].

A QIS meets the '*genuine diversity of ownership condition*' for an accounting period if:

(a) the scheme documents contain a statement that units in the scheme will be widely available and must specify the intended categories of investor and that the scheme manager must market and make available the units in accordance with (c) below;

(b) neither the specification of intended investor categories nor any other terms or conditions of investing in the scheme have the effect of either restricting investors to a limited number of specified persons or specified groups of connected persons (within *ITA 2007, s 993*) or of deterring any reasonable investor within the intended categories from investing in the scheme;

(c) units in the scheme are marketed and made available sufficiently widely to reach the intended categories of investor and in a way appropriate to attract those categories; and

(d) any person within one of the specified categories of intended investor can, on request to the scheme manager, obtain information about the scheme and acquire units in it.

Conditions (c) and (d) above are treated as met even where the scheme has no current capacity to receive additional investments, unless the capacity to receive investments is fixed and a pre-determined number of specified persons (or groups of connected persons) make investments which collectively exhaust all, or substantially all, of that capacity.

A QIS also meets the genuine diversity of ownership condition if an investor in the fund is a feeder fund, i.e. a unit trust, offshore fund or other authorised investment fund, and the conditions at (a)–(d) above are met after taking into account investors in the feeder fund. Both the QIS and the feeder fund must have the same manager (or proposed manager).

[*SI 2006 No 964, Regs 9A, 14C*].

There are procedures under which a QIS may obtain clearance from HMRC that it satisfies the genuine diversity of ownership condition. See *SI 2006 No 964, Regs 9B, 14D*.

For CGT aspects of holding and disposing of units in a QIS, see the corresponding chapter of Tolley's Capital Gains Tax.

For official guidance on Qualified Investor Schemes, see HMRC Investment Funds Manual IFM02300.

Simon's Taxes. See **D8.125, D8.126.**

Tax elected funds

[80.6] A UK authorised investment fund (AIF) that meets certain conditions may elect to be treated as a tax elected fund (TEF). The effect is to move the point of taxation from the AIF to the investor, so that investors are taxed as though they had invested in the underlying assets directly. TEFs are required to make two types of distribution of the income they receive — a dividend distribution and a non-dividend (interest) distribution. For all income that is distributed as interest, the TEF obtains a corresponding tax deduction.

Of the total amount shown in the distribution accounts of a TEF as available for distribution to participants, dividends, property investment income and property business income must be attributed to dividend distributions, and all other income must be attributed to interest distributions. If an amount distributed by the TEF includes sums attributed to dividend distributions, the same tax consequences ensue as if those sums were dividends on shares paid on the distribution date by the fund to the participants in proportion to their rights. If an amount distributed by the TEF includes sums attributed to interest distributions, the same tax consequences ensue as if those sums were payments of yearly interest made on the distribution date by the fund to the participants in proportion to their rights. As regards the deduction of basic rate tax at source from interest distributions, the same rules and exceptions apply as in **80.2** above.

An TEF may elect out of the regime or have its TEF status terminated by HMRC.

[*SI 2006 No 964, Pt 4B*].

For official guidance on TEFs, see HMRC Investment Funds Manual IFM06000.

Simon's Taxes. See **D8.140–D8.143.**

Funds investing in non-reporting offshore funds (FINROFs)

[80.7] A special regime is available for authorised investment funds (AIFs) which invest in 'non-reporting offshore funds' (as in **51.3** OFFSHORE FUNDS). Such AIFs are known as 'FINROFs'. The regime moves the point of taxation from the AIF to the investor in the AIF.

The regime applies to:

(a) an AIF which meets the 'investment condition' below;
(b) an AIF which has elected into the regime;
(c) a participant in an AIF in (a) or (b) above; and

(d) a participant in an AIF which has left the FINROF regime, where the participant has not made the 'deemed disposal election' outlined below.

The '*investment condition*' in (a) above is that the total amount invested by the AIF in non-reporting offshore funds or other FINROFs is more than 50% of the gross asset value of the fund. For this purpose, gross asset value does not include cash awaiting investment. The election in (b) above must be made in writing by the fund manager and must specify the date from which the fund is to enter the FINROF regime. That date cannot be more than three months before the date of the election.

An AIF enters the regime from the date that the investment condition is first met or, if earlier, the date specified in an election. The AIF must notify its participants within three months that the fund has entered the FINROF regime and inform them that any gains made on the disposal of units in the fund shall be treated as income gains (see below) rather than as capital gains. If an AIF inadvertently and temporarily meets the investment condition, there is provision for it to be treated as if it had never met that condition.

Holdings by AIFs in non-reporting offshore funds are in specified circumstances (see *SI 2006 No 964, Reg 14ZA*) treated as if they were holdings in reporting funds. In addition, AIFs that have an investment strategy that requires tracking a market equity index do not incur a charge to tax on an offshore income gain in respect of the disposal of an interest in a non-reporting fund where this has been held as part of the index tracking strategy.

A participant in an AIF that enters the FINROF regime may elect to be treated for CGT purposes as having disposed of and immediately reacquired his fund units at market value on the date the AIF enters the regime. If the participant is chargeable to income tax, the election can be made only by being included in his tax return for the year which includes that date.

Where an AIF ceases to meet the investment condition, the fund manager may, subject to certain conditions, elect for the fund to cease to be a FINROF. The AIF must notify its participants within three months that the fund has left the FINROF regime. The regime nevertheless continues to apply to the participants. However, a participant may elect to be treated as having disposed of and immediately reacquired his fund units at market value on the date the AIF leaves the regime (the '*deemed disposal election*' referred to at (d) above), in which case the regime ceases to apply to him. If the participant is chargeable to income tax, the election can be made only by being included in his tax return for the year which includes that date. The election can be made only if the deemed disposal produces a gain (which will then be charged to tax as income as below).

The charge to tax

Where a participant in an AIF is within (c) or (d) above, a gain on a disposal of his units is charged to tax as income and is referred to as an '*income gain*'. The income gain is treated for tax purposes as miscellaneous income which arises at the time of the disposal to the person making the disposal. The tax is charged on that person. An income gain is computed in the same way as a chargeable gain would be computed under CGT legislation. If such a computation would produce a loss, the income gain is taken to be nil. In a computation of a gain arising on the disposal for CGT purposes, a sum equal to the income gain is deductible from the consideration for the disposal. The detailed rules are not dissimilar to the rules for offshore income gains at **51.3–51.7, 51.9** OFFSHORE FUNDS.

[*SI 2006 No 964, Regs 14ZA–14ZD, Pt 6A; SI 2019 No 689, Reg 28*].

For official guidance on the tax treatment of investors in funds Investing in FINROFs, see HMRC Investment Funds Manual IFM03520.

Simon's Taxes. See **D8.150–154.**

Unauthorised unit trusts

[80.8] The Treasury has power to introduce regulations (see *SI 2013 No 2819*) governing the tax treatment of the trustees and unit holders of UUTs. (The pre-existing rules were at *ITA 2007, ss 504, 504A, 505*.) The regulations enable an eligible UUT to apply to HMRC for approval as an 'exempt UUT', and provide for the taxation of exempt UUTs, non-exempt UUTs and, in each case, their investors.

A UUT is an '*exempt UUT*' for a period of account if (i) its trustees are UK resident, (ii) all of its unit holders are 'eligible investors', (iii) it is approved by HMRC, and (iv) it is not treated by regulations as not being a unit trust scheme for the purposes of the definition of 'unauthorised unit trust' in *ITA 2007, s 989*. Otherwise any UUT not within (iv) is a '*non-exempt UUT*'. A unit holder is an '*eligible investor*' if any gain on a disposal of its units would be wholly exempt from CGT or corporation tax (otherwise than by reason of residence).

Non-exempt UUTs are within the charge to corporation tax, unless they are 'mixed UUTs'. A UUT is a '*mixed UUT*' if at all times in the period beginning with 24 May 2012 and ending with 5 April 2014 it had at least one unit holder which was, and at least one unit holder which was not, an eligible investor. The pre-existing rules continue to apply to a mixed UUT until such time, if any, as it no longer has any eligible investors or until appropriate tax reliefs are introduced to enable mixed UUTs to restructure in a way that prevents exempt investors being adversely affected.

The provisions at **60.12** PROPERTY INCOME restricting deductions for finance costs in computing residential property income do not apply to trustees of UUTs.

Income tax charge on investors

Exempt UUTs

Tax is charged on income treated as received by a unit holder from an exempt UUT in a tax year. The charge is on the unit holder, and unit holders are not treated as having received such income net of income tax. Income is treated as received by unit holders if an amount is shown in the UUT's accounts for a period of account as income available for payment to them or for investment.

The income is treated as received by a unit holder for a 'distribution period', and the income for a distribution period is treated as received on the date (or the latest date) provided by the terms of the trust for any distribution for the period. If there is no such date, or if that date is more than 12 months after the distribution period ends, the income for the period is treated as received on the last day of the period. A unit holder has the right to request from the UUT a voucher showing the amount of income treated as received by him for a distribution period.

The amount of income treated as received by a unit holder for a distribution period is given by the formula:

$$TAI \times \frac{R}{TR}$$

where

TAI = the total amount shown in the trust's accounts as income available for payment to unit holders or for investment;
R = the unit holder's rights; and
TR = the rights of all the unit holders.

If the terms of the trust provide for a period over which income from the trust investments is aggregated to ascertain the amount available for distribution, the '*distribution period*' is that period. If, however, that period is longer than 12 months, each period of 12 months from the beginning of that period is a distribution period, as is any balance of less than 12 months. In any other case, the '*distribution period*' is each successive period of 12 months beginning with the day on which the trust was established.

If any income would fall to be taxed as trading profits or as profits of a UK property business, those tax charges take priority of the above charge.

Non-exempt UUTs

A non-exempt UUT is treated as if the trustees were a UK resident company and the rights of the unit holders were shares in the company. The unit holder is not *deemed* to receive distributions of income. Actual distributions are treated in the recipient's hands in the same way as company dividends.

[*FA 2013, s 217; SI 2013 No 2819, Regs 1–9, 15–17, 26–28, 30–32*].

For official guidance, see www.gov.uk/government/collections/unauthorised-unit-trusts and HMRC Investment Funds Manual IFM10000, IFM11000.

Authorised contractual schemes

[80.9] An '*authorised contractual scheme*' is a type of collective investment scheme authorised by the Financial Conduct Authority. It may take the form of either a co-ownership scheme or a partnership scheme (as defined). [*Financial Services and Markets Act 2000, s 235A*]. Such schemes are broadly transparent for tax purposes, i.e. the scheme itself incurs no tax liability. This means that its investors are treated as if they had invested directly in the underlying assets of the scheme and are subject to personal taxation accordingly.

For scheme accounting periods beginning on or after 1 April 2017, an operator of a CoACS carrying on a qualifying activity can elect to compute plant and machinery capital allowances and allocate them to investors (see **10.70** CAPITAL ALLOWANCES ON PLANT AND MACHINERY). This now applies equally to structures and buildings allowances (see **9.34** CAPITAL ALLOWANCES).

Regulations impose requirements on the operator of a co-ownership authorised contractual scheme (CoACS) in relation to the provision of information to participants in the scheme, to enable them to meet their tax obligations, and to HMRC. These regulations have effect for scheme accounting periods beginning on or after 1 April 2017. The information must be provided no later than the '*information reporting date*', i.e. the date falling six months after the end of the scheme accounting period. There are penalties, chargeable on the operator, for non-compliance. [*F(No 2)A 2017, s 41; SI 2017 No 1209, Regs 1–9*].

Regulations also provide for how participants in a CoACS are to be treated for income tax purposes in relation to scheme investments in an offshore fund. These regulations have effect for scheme accounting periods beginning on or after 27 December 2017. They require a CoACS to treat income accumulated in the offshore fund as additional income of the participants. The income must be notified to participants on or before the information reporting date (see above) for the scheme accounting period in which the income accrues to the CoACS, and is deemed to arise to the participants on that date. [*F(No 2)A 2017, s 42; SI 2017 No 1209, Regs 1, 2, 10–13*].

See the HMRC technical note at www.gov.uk/government/publications/technical-note-co-ownership-authorised-contractual-schemes. See also HMRC Investment Funds Manual IFM08000.

Pension fund pooling vehicles

[80.10] Regulations make special provision to ensure that certain international pooled pension funds (registered as 'pension fund pooling vehicles') are transparent for UK tax purposes. Participants in such schemes must be approved by HMRC, and are treated for income tax, capital allowances and CGT purposes as though they themselves owned directly a share of each of the trust assets. There is also relief from stamp duty (or stamp duty reserve tax) on transfers of assets (other than land or buildings) by participants into the scheme. Participation in pension fund pooling vehicles is restricted to registered pension schemes, UK-based superannuation funds used primarily by companies employing British expatriates working overseas, and recognised overseas pension schemes within *FA 2004, s 150(8)*. [*SI 1996 Nos 1583, 1584, 1585*]. See generally HMRC Savings and Investment Manual SAIM6200–6220. The position in the country in which any overseas participator is based will of course be crucial to the operation of such schemes.

Court common investment funds

[80.11] Court common investment funds (CCIFs) are a form of unit trust set up by the Lord Chancellor under *Administration of Justice Act 1982, s 42(1)*. They are available only for individuals whose money is under control of certain Courts, e.g. road accident victims and the mentally incapacitated. CCIFs are treated for tax purposes as authorised unit trusts within **80.2** above. The investment manager is treated as the trustee, and the persons with qualifying interests are treated as the unit holders. For the above purposes, the persons with qualifying interests are, in relation to shares in the fund held by the Accountant General (or other person authorised by the Lord Chancellor), the persons whose interests entitle them, as against him, to share in the fund's investments. They also include any persons authorised by the Lord Chancellor to hold shares in the fund on their own behalf. [*CTA 2010, s 620*].

81

Venture Capital Trusts

Simon's Taxes. See D8.2, E3.2.

Introduction to venture capital trusts

[81.1] The venture capital trust (VCT) scheme described at **81.2** *et seq*. below was introduced to encourage individuals to invest in unquoted trading companies through such trusts. It sets out to achieve this by a combination of income tax and capital gains tax reliefs.

Requirements as to returns, records and providing of information by VCTs are contained in Treasury regulations. [*ITA 2007, ss 272, 284; SI 1995 No 1979; SI 2016 No 1192*].

See generally HMRC Venture Capital Schemes Manual VCM50000 *et seq.*.

Income tax reliefs for investments in VCTs

[81.2] Relief from income tax is granted in respect of both investments in VCTs and dividends from VCTs.

Investment relief

[81.3] Subject to the conditions described below, an individual may claim relief ('investment relief') for a tax year for the amount (or aggregate amounts) subscribed by him on his own behalf for 'eligible shares' issued to him in the tax year by a VCT (or VCTs) for raising money. There is a limit of **£200,000** on the amount in respect of which relief can be claimed for any one tax year.

For this purpose, '*eligible shares*' are ordinary shares in a VCT which, throughout the five years following issue, carry no present or future preferential right to dividends or to assets on a winding up and no present or future right to redemption.

Relief is given by a reduction (a '*tax reduction*') in what would otherwise be the individual's income tax liability for the tax year by **30%** of the amount eligible for relief.

Investors may restrict a claim to relief in respect of a tax year to only some of the shares issued to them. The order in which tax reductions are given against an individual's tax liability is set out at **1.12** ALLOWANCES AND TAX RATES, which also makes clear that a tax reduction must be restricted to the extent (if any) that it would otherwise exceed the individual's remaining income tax liability after making all prior reductions.

An individual is **not** entitled to relief where:

(a) he was under 18 years of age at the time of issue of the shares;
(b) circumstances have arisen which, had the relief already been given, would have resulted in the withdrawal or reduction of the relief (see **81.5** below);
(c) the shares were issued or subscribed for other than for genuine commercial purposes or as part of a scheme or arrangement a main purpose of which was the avoidance of tax; or

(d) a loan is made to the individual (or to an 'associate') by any person at any time in the period beginning with the incorporation of the VCT (or, if later, two years before the date of issue of the shares) and ending five years after the date of issue of the shares, and the loan would not have been made, or would not have been made on the same terms, if he had not subscribed, or had not been proposing to subscribe, for the shares. The granting of credit to, or the assignment of a debt due from, the individual or associate is counted as a loan for these purposes.

For the purposes of (d) above, an '*associate*' of any person is any 'relative' (i.e. spouse, civil partner, ancestor or linear descendant) of that person, the trustee(s) of any settlement in relation to which that person or any relative (living or dead) is or was a settler and, where that person has an interest in any shares of obligations of a company which are subject to any trust or are part of a deceased estate, the trustee(s) of the settlement or the personal representatives of the deceased. For this purpose, 'settlor' is defined as in *Income Tax Act 2007 (ITA 2007), ss 467–473.*

An individual is *not* eligible for relief by reference to any shares *treated as* issued to him by virtue of *FA 2003, s 195(8)*, which provides for a disposal to a person by a company of its own shares (so-called 'treasury shares') to be treated as a new issue of shares and for the recipient to be treated as having subscribed for them. In such a case, the VCT must, at the time the shares are issued, give the individual a notice stating that he is not eligible for relief, and must copy that notice to HMRC within three months after the issue.

Investment relief applies to shares issued before 6 April 2025 but this date may be amended by the Treasury via statutory instrument.

[*ITA 2007, ss 261–264, 265, 271(4), 273, 332, Sch 2 paras 59–61, 63; SI 2003 No 3077*].

As regards (d) above, for this restriction to apply, the test is whether the lender makes the loan on terms which are connected with the fact that the borrower (or an associate) is subscribing for eligible shares. The prime concern is why the lender made the loan rather than why the borrower applied for it. Relief would not be disallowed, for example, in the case of a bank loan if the bank would have made a loan on the same terms to a similar borrower for a different purpose. But if, for example, a loan is made specifically on a security consisting of or including the eligible shares (other than as part of a broad range of assets to which the lender has recourse), relief would be denied. Relevant features of the loan terms would be the qualifying conditions to be satisfied by the borrower, any incentives or benefits offered to the borrower, the time allowed for repayment, the amount of repayments and interest charged, the timing of interest payments, and the nature of the security. (HMRC SP 6/98).

An individual subscribing for eligible shares may obtain from the VCT a certificate giving details of the subscription and certifying that certain conditions for relief are satisfied. [*SI 1995 No 1979, Reg 9*].

Relief for a year can only be claimed after the end of the year, and any in-year claims for relief by repayment through self-assessment will be rejected. This does not affect the right to claim a reduction in payments on account (see **67.5** SELF-ASSESSMENT), and relief may still be given through a PAYE coding. (Revenue Tax Bulletin April 2002 p 924).

Linked sales

Investment relief is restricted if an individual subscribes for shares in a VCT and makes at least one 'linked' sale of other shares. The amount the individual subscribes is treated as reduced by the total consideration given for the linked sales. If a sale is linked in relation to more than one subscription, the consideration for it is applied to reduce subscriptions in the order in which they are made. A sale of shares is '*linked*' if:

(i) the shares sold are in the VCT or (but only where Condition X below applies) in a company which is (or later becomes) a successor or predecessor of the VCT as a result of a merger or restructuring; and

(ii) either

- the circumstances are such that the purchase of the shares from the individual is conditional upon his making the subscription or *vice versa*; or
- the subscription and the sale occur within six months of each other (regardless of which occurs first).

The above does not apply if, or to the extent that, the subscription is the result of the individual's electing to reinvest dividends on his VCT shares in acquiring further shares in the VCT. Condition X in (i) above was introduced by *FA 2018* but with backdated effect in relation to claims for relief by reference to shares issued on or after 6 April 2014. The condition is that the date of the merger or restructuring is no later than two years after the individual subscribes for the VCT shares and either the individual could reasonably be expected to know when subscribing that the merger or restructuring would take place or a main purpose of the merger or restructuring is to enable individuals to obtain a tax advantage in connection with VCT relief. For this purpose the date of the merger or restructuring is generally the date of the issue of shares by means of which it is effected.

[*ITA 2007, s 264A; FA 2018, Sch 5 paras 1, 12*].

Nominees

Shares subscribed for, issued to, held by or disposed of for an individual by a nominee are treated as subscribed for, issued to, held by or disposed of by the individual. [*ITA 2007, s 330A*].

Providing of State aid information

On and after 15 September 2016, where VCT investment relief has been given (whether before, on or after that date) or may in future be given, HMRC may give the VCT a notice requiring it to supply HMRC with specified information for the purpose of compliance with certain EU State aid obligations. This may include information about the VCT, its activities and/or its investors, information about the investment relief and information relating to the grant of State aid through the provision of the relief. See **36.5** HMRC — CONFIDENTIALITY OF INFORMATION as regards the publishing by HMRC of State aid information. [*FA 2016, s 180(5)–(9)(11), Sch 24 Pt 2*].

Simon's Taxes. See **E3.211**.

Example

[81.4]

On 1 May 2020, Kay, who has annual earnings of £81,000, subscribes for 100,000 eligible £1 shares issued at par to raise money by VCT plc, an approved venture capital trust. On 1 September 2020 she purchases a further 225,000 £1 shares in VCT plc for £175,000 on the open market. The VCT makes no distribution in 2020/21. Kay's other income for 2020/21 consists of dividends of £18,000. PAYE tax deducted is £19,900.00. Kay's liability to income tax is at the main UK rates.

Kay's tax computation for 2020/21 is as follows.

	£
Employment income	81,000
Dividends	18,000
Total and net income	99,000
Deduct Personal allowance	12,500
Taxable income	£86,500
Tax payable:	
37,500 @ 20%	7,500.00
31,000 @ 40%	12,400.00
2,000 @ 0% (dividend nil rate)	—
16,000 @ 32.5% (dividend upper rate)	5,200.00
	25,100.00
Deduct Relief for investment in VCT plc: 30% of £100,000 subscribed = £30,000 but restricted to	25,100.00
Net tax payable	—

PAYE tax of £19,900.00 is repayable.

Withdrawal of investment relief

[81.5] Where an individual disposes of eligible shares, in respect of which relief has been claimed as under **81.3** above, within five years of their issue and other than to a spouse or civil partner when they are living together (see below), then:

(a) if the disposal is otherwise than at arm's length, relief given by reference to those shares is withdrawn;
(b) if the disposal is at arm's length, the relief given by reference to those shares is reduced by 30% of the consideration received for the disposal and is withdrawn entirely if thereby reduced to nil.

For the above purposes, disposals of eligible shares in a VCT are identified with those acquired earlier rather than later. As between eligible shares acquired on the same day, shares by reference to which relief has been given are treated as disposed of after any other eligible shares.

Relief is *not* reduced or withdrawn where the disposal is by one spouse or civil partner to the other at a time when they are living together. However, on any subsequent disposal the spouse or civil partner to whom the shares were transferred is treated as if he or she were the person who subscribed for the shares, as if the shares had been issued to him or her at the time they were issued to the transferor spouse or civil partner, and as if his or her liability to income tax had been reduced by reference to those shares by the same amount, and for the same tax year, as applied on the subscription by the transferor spouse or civil partner. Any assessment for reducing or withdrawing relief is made on the transferee spouse or civil partner.

[*ITA 2007, ss 266, 267, Sch 2 para 62*].

Withdrawal of approval

Where approval of a company as a VCT is withdrawn (but not treated as never having been given) (see **81.14** above), relief given by reference to eligible shares in the VCT is withdrawn as if on a non-arm's length disposal immediately before the withdrawal of approval. [*ITA 2007, s 268*].

Relief subsequently found not to have been due

Relief which is subsequently found not to have been due is withdrawn. [*ITA 2007, s 269*].

Assessments withdrawing or reducing relief

Such assessments are made for the tax year for which the relief was given. Any such assessment may be made within six years after the end of the tax year concerned. No such assessment is, however, to be made by reason of an event occurring after the death of the person to whom the shares were issued. [*ITA 2007, s 270*].

Information

Particulars of all events leading to the reduction or withdrawal of relief must be notified to HMRC by the person to whom the relief was given within 60 days of his coming to know of the event. The requirements of secrecy do not prevent HMRC disclosing to a VCT that relief has been given or claimed by reference to a particular number or proportion of its shares. [*ITA 2007, s 271(1)–(3)(5)*].

Simon's Taxes. See **E3.212**.

Example

[81.6]

On 1 May 2022, Kay in the example at **81.4** above, who has since 2020/21 neither acquired nor disposed of any further shares in VCT plc, gives 62,500 shares to her son. On 1 January 2023, she disposes of the remaining 262,500 shares for £212,500. The relief given as in **81.4** above is withdrawn as follows.

Disposal on 1 May 2022

	£
The shares disposed of are identified, on a first in/first out basis, with 62,500 of those subscribed for, and, since the disposal was not at arm's length, the relief given on those shares is withdrawn.	
Relief withdrawn $\frac{62,500}{100,000} \times 25,100 =$	15,687.50

Disposal on 1 January 2023

The balance of £9,412.50 of the relief originally given was in respect of 37,500 of the shares disposed of. The disposal consideration for those 37,500 shares is

$$212,500 \times \frac{37,500}{262,500} = £30,357$$

The relief withdrawn is the lesser of the relief originally given (£9,412.50) and 30% of the consideration received, i.e.
30% of £30,357 = £9,107.10

Relief withdrawn is therefore	9,107.10
The 2020/21 assessment to withdraw relief is therefore	£24,794.60

Dividend relief

[81.7] No liability to income tax arises in respect of a 'VCT dividend' to which a 'qualifying investor' is beneficially entitled.

A '*qualifying investor*' is an individual aged 18 or over who is beneficially entitled to the distribution either as the holder of the shares or through a nominee (including the trustees of a bare trust).

A '*VCT dividend*' is a dividend paid in respect of ordinary shares:

- in a company which is a VCT;
- which were acquired by the recipient of the dividend at a time when the company was a VCT;
- which were acquired for genuine commercial reasons and not as part of a tax avoidance scheme or arrangements; and
- which are *not* shares acquired in excess of the 'permitted maximum' for the year of acquisition.

A 'VCT dividend' does not include any dividend paid in respect of profits or gains of any accounting period ending when the company was not a VCT.

Shares are acquired in excess of the '*permitted maximum*' for a year where the aggregate value of ordinary shares acquired in VCTs by the individual or his nominee(s) in that year exceeds **£200,000,** disregarding shares acquired other than for genuine commercial reasons or as part of a scheme or arrangement a main purpose of which is the avoidance of tax. Shares acquired later in the year are identified as representing the excess before those acquired earlier. In relation to same-day acquisition of different shares, a proportionate part of each description of share is treated as representing any excess arising on that day. Shares acquired at a time when a company was not a VCT are for these purposes treated as disposed of before other shares in the VCT. Otherwise, disposals are identified with earlier acquisitions before later ones, except that as between shares acquired on the same day, shares acquired in excess of the permitted maximum are treated as disposed of before any other shares. There are provisions for effectively disregarding acquisitions arising out of share exchanges where, for capital gains purposes, the new shares are treated as the same assets as the old.

[*ITTOIA 2005, ss 709–712*].

Simon's Taxes. See **E3.213.**

Example

[81.8]

All the facts are as in the example at **81.4** above, except that all events in that example occurred one year earlier. In 2020/21, Kay, whose circumstances are otherwise unchanged, then receives a dividend from VCT plc of 9p per share.

The shares in VCT plc were acquired for £275,000, so that dividends in respect of shares representing the £75,000 excess over the permitted maximum of £200,000 are not exempt. The 100,000 shares first acquired for £100,000 are first identified, so that the shares representing the excess are three-sevenths (75,000/175,000) of the 225,000 shares subsequently acquired for £175,000, i.e. 96,429 of those shares.

Kay's tax computation for 2020/21 is as follows.

	£	£
Employment income		81,000
Dividends (other than VCT plc)		18,000
VCT plc distribution in respect of 96,429 shares		8,679
Total and net income		107,679

Deduct Personal allowance	12,500	
Restricted by excess of income over £100,000: (£7,679 × ½)	3,839	8,661
Taxable income		£99,018
Tax payable:		
37,500 @ 20%		7,500.00
34,839 @ 40%		13,935.60
2,000 @ 0% (dividend nil rate)		—
24,679 @ 32.5% (dividend upper rate)		8,020.67
Net tax liability (subject to PAYE)		£29,456.27

Capital gains tax reliefs for investments in VCTs

[81.9] The capital gains of a VCT are not chargeable gains. [*TCGA 1992, s 100(1)*].

In addition, individual investors in VCTs are entitled to exemption on the disposal of VCT shares (see **81.10** below).

Withdrawal of approval

Where approval of a company as a VCT is withdrawn (but not treated as never having been given) (see **81.14** above), shares which (apart from the withdrawal) would be eligible for the relief on disposal (see **81.10** below) are treated as disposed of at their market value at the time of the withdrawal. For the purposes of the relief on disposal, the disposal is treated as taking place while the company is still a VCT, but the re-acquisition is treated as taking place immediately after it ceases to be so. [*TCGA 1992, s 151B(6)(7)*].

Exemption on disposal

[81.10] A gain or loss accruing to an individual on a 'qualifying disposal' of ordinary shares in a company which was a VCT throughout his period of ownership is not a chargeable gain or an allowable loss. A disposal is a '*qualifying disposal*' if:

(a) the individual is 18 years of age or more at the time of the disposal;
(b) the shares were not acquired in excess of the 'permitted maximum' for any tax year; and
(c) the shares were acquired for genuine commercial purposes and not as part of a scheme or arrangement a main purpose of which was the avoidance of tax.

The identification of those shares which were acquired in excess of the '*permitted maximum*' is as under **81.7** above (in relation to dividend relief — broadly those in excess of an annual limit of £200,000), and the identification of disposals with acquisitions for this purpose is similarly as under **81.7** above.

[*TCGA 1992, ss 151A, 151B*].

See **81.9** above as regards relief on withdrawal of approval of the VCT.

Simon's Taxes. See **C3.1103**.

Example

[81.11]

On the disposals in the example at **81.6** above, a chargeable gain or allowable loss arises only on the disposal of the shares acquired in excess of the permitted maximum for 2020/21. As in the example at **81.8** above, these are 96,429 of the shares acquired for £175,000 on 1 September 2020. The disposal identified with those shares is a corresponding proportion of the 262,500 shares disposed of for a consideration of £212,500 on 1 January 2023.

Kay's capital gains tax computation for 2022/23 is therefore as follows.

		£
Disposal consideration for 96,429 shares —		
	$212,500 \times \frac{96,429}{262,500} =$	78,061
Deduct Cost —		
	$175,000 \times \frac{96,429}{225,000} =$	75,000
Chargeable gain		£3,061

Conditions for approval of a VCT

[81.12] A '*venture capital trust*' ('VCT') is a company approved for this purpose by HMRC, close companies being excluded. The time from which an approval takes effect is specified in the approval, and may not be earlier than the time the application for approval was made. [*ITA 2007, ss 259, 283*].

Approval may not be given unless HMRC are satisfied that the following conditions are met in relation to the most recent complete accounting period of the company and will be met in relation to the accounting period current at the time of the application for approval. [*ITA 2007, s 274(1)*].

Where any of the conditions are not met, approval may nevertheless be given where HMRC are satisfied as to the meeting of those conditions (and in some cases other conditions imposed by regulations) in future accounting periods. [*ITA 2007, s 275; FA 2018, Sch 5 paras 3, 13, 14; SI 2018 No 931, Reg 4*].

See below as to the meaning of 'securities', **81.14** below as regards withdrawal of approval, **81.15** below for special rules where two or more VCTs merge and **81.16** below for special rules where a VCT is wound up.

The listing condition

The company's ordinary shares (or each class thereof) must be admitted to trading on a regulated market (defined by reference to EU law) throughout those periods.[*ITA 2007, s 274(2), (4); SI 2019 No 689, Reg 15(2)*].

The nature of income condition

The company's income (as defined) must be derived wholly or mainly from shares or securities. [*ITA 2007, ss 274, 276, 285*].

The income retention condition

An amount greater than 15% of its income (as defined) from shares and securities must not be retained by the company.

This condition does not apply for an accounting period if the amount the company would be required to distribute is less than £10,000 (proportionately reduced for periods of less than 12 months), or if the company is required by law to retain income in excess of the 15% limit. The latter exclusion only applies, however, if the aggregate of the excess of retentions over those required by law and any distribution is less than £10,000 (proportionately reduced for periods of less then 12 months). [*ITA 2007, ss 274, 276*].

The 15% holding limit condition

No 'holding' in any company other than a VCT (or a company which could be a VCT but for the listing condition above) may represent more than 15% of the value of the company's investments at any time in those periods.

For this purpose, and that of the 80% qualifying holdings condition below, the meaning of 'the company's investments' is extended to include (if it would not otherwise include) money in the company's possession and any sum owed to the company over which the company has 'account-holder's rights', i.e. the right to require payment either to the company or at its direction. Anything to which the company is not beneficially entitled is excluded (though, for this purpose, a company *is* beneficially entitled to sums subscribed for shares issued by it and anything representing such sums).

If this condition was met when a holding in a company was acquired, it is treated as continuing to be met until any more shares or securities of the company are acquired (otherwise than for no consideration).

'*Holding*' means the shares or securities of whatever class or classes held in any one company. Where, in connection with a 'scheme of reconstruction' (within *TCGA 1992, s 136*), a company issues shares or securities to persons holding shares or securities in another in respect of, and in proportion to (or as nearly as may be in proportion to) such holdings, without the recipients' becoming liable for any consideration, the old and the new holdings are treated as the same. Holdings in companies which are members of a group (i.e. a company and its 51% subsidiaries), whether or not including the company whose holdings they are ('company A'), are treated as holdings in a single company if they are not excluded from the 15% holding limit condition. If company A is a member of a group, money owed to it by another group member is treated as a security and, as such, as part of its holding in that other group member.

See **81.13** below for the value of the company's investments.

[*ITA 2007, ss 274, 277, 285, Sch 2 para 64*].

The 80% qualifying holdings condition

Throughout the accounting periods at least 80% by value of the company's investments must be represented by shares or securities in 'qualifying holdings' (see **81.17** below). In relation to accounting periods beginning before 6 April 2019, the specified minimum is 70%; all subsequent references to the '80% qualifying holdings condition' should be read accordingly.

Where this limit is breached inadvertently, and the position is corrected without delay after discovery, approval will in practice not be withdrawn on this account. Full details of any such inadvertent breach should be disclosed to HMRC as soon as it is discovered. (Revenue Press Release 14 September 1995).

On a second and subsequent issue of shares by an approved VCT, this condition and the 70% eligible shares condition below do not have to be met, in relation to the money raised by the further issue, in the accounting period of the further issue or any later accounting period ending no more than three years after the making of the further issue. *SI 2004 No 2199, Reg 14* limits the operation of this rule by stipulating that the money raised by the further issue must be for the purposes of acquiring additional investments which do fulfil the conditions. Where any of that money (or assets derived therefrom) is used for another purpose, then from a time immediately before that use the whole of the money raised by the issue is deemed to be included in the company's investments in applying the percentage tests in the two conditions. If any of the money is used by the VCT to buy back its own shares, this stipulation is treated, in particular, as not fulfilled if HMRC regard the purchase as not insignificant in relation to the issued ordinary share capital of the VCT or if it is made as a result of a general offer to members. If the money is raised by a successor VCT (in a merger) and used to buy shares in the merging companies, the stipulation is treated, in particular, as not fulfilled if the money so used exceeds the least of three specified limits.

Where a VCT disposes of a holding that was comprised in its qualifying holdings throughout the six months ending immediately before the disposal, both the fact of the disposal and any monetary consideration for it are disregarded for a period of 12 months beginning with the disposal in determining whether or not the 80% qualifying holdings condition is met. This does not apply if the holding was acquired with money raised by a second or subsequent issue of shares such that the 80% qualifying holdings condition does not for the time being have to be met in relation to that money (see above). It also does not apply if the consideration for the disposal consists entirely of new qualifying holdings. If the consideration for the disposal consists partly of new qualifying holdings, the above treatment applies only to an appropriate proportion of the holding disposed of. The treatment does not apply at all to disposals between companies that are merging. In relation to disposals made before 6 April 2019, the period of disregard is six months.

See the 15% holding limit condition above for the meaning of 'the company's investments' and see **81.13** below for the value of investments.

[*ITA 2007, ss 274, 280, 280A, 285, 989, Sch 2 para 66; FA 2018, Sch 5 paras 2, 4, 13, 14; SI 2004 No 2199, Reg 14; SI 2018 No 931, Reg 4*].

The 70% eligible shares condition

At least 70% of the company's qualifying holdings (by value) must be represented throughout the accounting periods by holdings of 'eligible shares'. For this purpose, '*eligible shares*' are ordinary shares carrying no present or future preferential right to assets on a winding-up and no present or future right to redemption; the shares are permitted to carry a present or future preferential right to dividends except in circumstances specified at *ITA 2007, s 285(3B)*.

See the 80% qualifying holdings condition above where a VCT makes a second or subsequent issue of shares and see **81.13** below for the value of investments.

[*ITA 2007, ss 274, 280, 285, Sch 2 para 66; SI 2004 No 2199, Reg 14*].

The non-qualifying investments condition

This condition is that the company has not made and will not make, in the accounting periods, an investment which does not form part of its qualifying holdings and does not come under any of the following descriptions:

(a) shares or units in an alternative investment fund which may be repurchased or redeemed on no more than seven days' notice given by the investor; or
(b) shares or units in a UCITS (an undertaking for collective investment in transferable securities) which may be repurchased or redeemed on no more than seven days' notice given by the investor; or
(c) ordinary shares or securities which are acquired by the investor on a regulated market (defined by reference to EU law); or
(d) money in the investor's possession; or
(e) a sum owed to the investor over which the investor has the right to require payment, either to the investor or at the investor's direction, on no more than seven days' notice given by the investor.

[*ITA 2007, ss 274, 285; FA 2016, s 31; SI 2019 No 689, Reg 15(2)*].

The investment limits condition

This condition is that the company has not made, and will not make, in the accounting periods, an investment which breaches the permitted investment limits.

An investment breaches the permitted investment limits if:

(i) the 'total annual investment' in the investee company exceeds £5 million; or
(ii) the 'total investment' in the investee company at the date the current investment is made (the '*investment date*' exceeds £12 million or, if the company is a 'knowledge-intensive company' (see **81.30** below) at the investment date, £20 million; or
(iii) the total investment in the investee company at any time during the five-year post-investment period exceeds the limits in (ii) above *and* the company effectively acquires a company or trade after it receives the

investment in question. This mirrors the requirement at **81.31** below, which is described there in more detail, and the 'five-year post-investment period' is defined in similar manner.

In (i) above, the '*total annual investment*' in the investee company comprises the investment under review (the '*current investment*') and the total amount of other relevant investments made in the investee company by all investors in the 12 months ending with the day on which the current investment was made. The following also count towards the total annual investment:

- any investment in the said 12-month period in a 51% subsidiary (within *CTA 2010, Pt 24 Ch 3*) of the investee company (including any made before it became a 51% subsidiary but not any made after it last ceased to be one);
- any investment made in any company to the extent that the money raised by the investment has been employed for the purposes of a trade (as widely defined) carried on by another company that has at any time in the said 12-month period been a 51% subsidiary of the investee company (disregarding any money so employed after it last ceased to be such a subsidiary); and
- any other investment made in any company to the extent that the money raised has been employed for the purposes of a trade (as widely defined), and within that 12-month period, but after the investment was made, the trade (or a part of it) was transferred to the investee company, a 51% subsidiary or a partnership of which the investee company or a 51% subsidiary is a member.

In (ii) above, the '*total investment*' in the investee company is defined similarly to 'total annual investment' but disregarding references to a 12-month period and instead taking into account all times before the investment date. In (iii) above, 'total investment' also has a similar meaning but taking into account all times before the time in the five-year post-investment period when (iii) above is being tested.

For the purpose of the conditions for approval of a VCT, a '*relevant investment*' is made in a company if and when:

- an investment (of any kind) in the company is made by a VCT; or
- the company issues shares (for which money has been subscribed) in respect of which it provides a compliance statement under **29.7** ENTERPRISE INVESTMENT SCHEME or **66.5** SEED ENTERPRISE INVESTMENT SCHEME; or
- an investment is made in the company and (at any time) the company provides a compliance statement under **72.6** SOCIAL INVESTMENT TAX RELIEF in respect of it; *ITA 2007, s 257KB* (see **72.1** SOCIAL INVESTMENT TAX RELIEF) applies in determining when such an investment is made; or
- any other investment is made in the company which is aid received by it pursuant to a measure approved by the EC as compatible with Article 107 of the Treaty on the Functioning of the European Union in accordance with the principles laid down in the EC's Guidelines on State aid to promote risk finance investment (previously the Community Guidelines on Risk Capital Investments in Small and Medium-sized Enterprises).

Investments listed above under the non-qualifying investments condition are disregarded for the purpose of the investment limits condition.

[*ITA 2007, ss 274, 280B, 285*].

For the purposes of determining entitlement to VCT income tax relief in respect of investments made on or after 1 December 2017, investments are not prevented from constituting relevant investments by virtue only of their having been made before certain historical dates. Previously, under earlier transitional provisions, certain investments made before 6 April 2012 did not count as relevant investments. [*FA 2018, s 15*].

The minimum investment on further issue condition

This condition has effect in relation to money raised by a further issue that is made in an accounting period beginning on or after 6 April 2018. It must not be breached by the company at any time in the accounting periods. A company breaches the minimum investment on further issue condition where:

- there has been an issue of ordinary share capital of the company;
- the company has been approved as a VCT with effect on or before the date of that issue;
- a further issue of ordinary share capital of the company has since been made; and
- the company does not, on or before the 'relevant deadline', invest at least 30% of the money raised by that further issue in shares or securities which are then comprised in the company's qualifying holdings. The '*relevant deadline*' is the last day of the 12 months immediately following the end of the accounting period in which the further issue is made.

[*ITA 2007, ss 274, 280BA, 285, 989; FA 2018, Sch 5 paras 5, 6, 13, 14; SI 2018 No 931, Reg 4*].

The permitted maximum age condition

This condition is that the company has not made and will not make an investment, in the accounting periods, in a company which breaches the permitted maximum age limit. An investment breaches the limit if it is made after the 'initial investing period' and none of the conditions set out below is met. The '*initial investing period*' is the seven years beginning with the 'relevant first commercial sale' (ten years where the investee company is a 'knowledge-intensive company' (see **81.30** below) when the current investment is made).The conditions are that:

- a 'relevant investment' (as under the investment limits condition above) was made in the investee company before the end of the initial investing period, and some or all of the money raised by that investment was employed for the purposes of the same activities as the money raised by the current investment; or
- the amount of the current investment plus the total amount of any other relevant investments made in the investee company in a period of 30 consecutive days which includes the date of the current investment date

is at least 50% of the annual turnover of the investee company averaged over five years (see *ITA 2007, s 280C(8)–(9)*), and the money raised by those investments is employed for the purpose of 'entering a new product or geographical market' (as defined in the General Block Exemption Regulation (Commission Regulation (EU) No 651/2014); or

- the condition immediately above or the equivalent condition for EIS investments (see **29.36**(b) ENTERPRISE INVESTMENT SCHEME) was previously met in relation to one or more relevant investments in the investee company, and some or all of the money raised by those investments was employed for the purposes of the same activities as the money raised by the current investment.

'*First commercial sale*' has the same meaning as in the EC's Guidelines on State aid to promote risk finance investments. The '*relevant first commercial sale*' is defined in *ITA 2007, s 280C(7)* by reference to the earliest date of any commercial sale made by (broadly) the investee company or a 51% subsidiary or any other person who has carried on any trade which is carried on by the company or a subsidiary.

With effect for investments made on or after 6 April 2018, an investee company which is a knowledge-intensive company may elect to alter its initial investing period by substituting, for the date of the relevant first commercial sale, the date by reference to which it is treated as reaching an annual turnover of £200,000. That date is normally the last day of the accounting period in which annual turnover first reaches £200,000 or more (with modifications for accounting periods exceeding 12 months). Turnover of other companies in the group (where relevant) must also be taken into account. Any necessary apportionments must be made on a time basis, i.e. in the case of short or long accounting periods or companies joining or leaving the group part way through an accounting period.

Investments listed above under the non-qualifying investments condition are disregarded for the purpose of the permitted maximum age condition. See **81.42** below as regards modification of the permitted maximum age condition on and after 6 April 2017 in the event of certain company restructuring.

[*ITA 2007, ss 274, 280C, 285; FA 2016, ss 29(3)(6), 30, 31; FA 2018, Sch 4 paras 7, 10; SI 2018 No 931, Reg 3*].

The no business acquisition condition

This condition is that the company has not made and will not make an investment, in the accounting periods, in a company which breaches the prohibition on business acquisitions. An investment breaches the prohibition if any of the money raised by it is employed (whether on its own or with other money) on the acquisition (directly or indirectly) of: an interest in another company such that a company becomes a 51% subsidiary of the investee company; a further interest in a 51% subsidiary of the investee company; a trade (as widely defined); or goodwill or other intangible assets employed for the purposes of a trade.

Investments listed above under the non-qualifying investments condition are disregarded for the purpose of the no business acquisition condition.

[*ITA 2007, ss 274, 280D, 285; FA 2016, s 31*].

Meaning of 'securities'

'*Securities*' for the purposes of the VCT provisions include liabilities in respect of certain loans to the company not repayable within five years, and any stocks or securities relating to which are not re-purchasable or redeemable within five years of issue. Provided that the loan is made on normal commercial terms, HMRC will not regard a standard event of default clause in the loan agreement as disqualifying a loan from being a security for this purpose. If, however, the clause entitled the lender (or a third party) to exercise any action which would cause the borrower to default, the clause would not be regarded as 'standard'. (HMRC SP 8/95).

With effect for loans made on or after 15 March 2018, there is to be excluded from 'securities' any liability in respect of a loan to the company which either carries a return exceeding a commercial rate or is made on terms enabling a person to acquire any security or preferential rights in relation to assets of the company or the ability to control the company. For this purpose, a loan is regarded as made on the day on which the amount lent, or (as the case may be) the first day on which any part of the amount lent, is paid or made available to the company. The return on a loan is not to be treated as representing more than a commercial rate if it meets conditions set out in *ITA 2007, s 285(2B)*. Where the return over the term of the loan cannot be determined in advance, best estimates are to be used initially, subject to subsequent adjustment when actual figures are known.

[*ITA 2007, s 285(2)(2A)–(2E); FA 2018, Sch 5 paras 7, 13, 14; SI 2018 No 931, Regs 4, 5*].

Simon's Taxes. See **D8.205–D8.212.**

Value of investments

[81.13] The value of any investment for the purposes of the 15% holding limit condition, the 80% qualifying holdings condition and the 70% eligible shares condition in **81.12** above, is the value when the investment was acquired, except that where it is added to by a further holding of an investment of the same description (otherwise than for no consideration), or a payment is made in discharge of any obligation attached to it which increases its value, it is the value immediately after the most recent such addition or payment.

For this purpose, where, in connection with a 'scheme of reconstruction' (within *TCGA 1992, s 136*; previously a 'scheme of reconstruction or amalgamation'), a company issues shares or securities to persons holding shares or securities in another in respect of, and in proportion to (or as nearly as may be in proportion to) such holdings, without the recipients' becoming liable for any consideration, the old and the new holdings are treated as the same.

Where:

- shares or securities in a company are exchanged for corresponding shares and securities in a new holding company; or

- a VCT exercises conversion rights in respect of certain convertible shares and securities,

then, subject to detailed conditions (see *ITA 2007, ss 326–329*), the value of the new shares is taken to be the same as the value of the old shares when they were last valued for these purposes.

Where, under a company reorganisation or other arrangement:

- a VCT exchanges a qualifying holding for other shares or securities (with or without other consideration); and
- the exchange is for genuine commercial reasons and not part of a tax avoidance scheme or arrangements,

regulations provide a formula which values the new shares or securities by reference to the proportion of the value of the old shares or securities that the market value of the new shares or securities bears to the total consideration receivable. If no other consideration is receivable, the value of the new is identical to that of the old. The provisions extend to new shares or securities received in pursuance of an earn-out right (see Tolley's Capital Gains Tax under Shares and Securities) conferred in exchange for a qualifying holding, in which case an election is available (under *SI 2002 No 2661, Reg 10*) to modify the formula by effectively disregarding the earn-out right itself.

[*ITA 2007, ss 278, 279, Sch 2 para 65; FA 2018, Sch 5 paras 3, 13, 14; SI 2002 No 2661; SI 2018 No 931, Reg 4*].

Simon's Taxes. See **D8.210**.

Withdrawal of approval

[81.14] Approval may be withdrawn where there are reasonable grounds for believing that:

- the conditions for approval were not satisfied at the time the approval was given; or
- a condition that HMRC were satisfied would be met has not been or will not be met; or
- in either the most recent complete accounting period or the current accounting period, one of the conditions in **81.12** above has failed or will fail to be met (unless the failure was allowed for); or
- where, in relation to a second or further issue by an approved VCT, the 80% qualifying holdings condition and the 70% eligible shares condition do not have to be met in the period of issue or certain following accounting periods (see **81.12** above), one of the conditions in **81.12** above will fail to be met in the first period for which those two conditions must be met; or
- any other conditions prescribed by regulations have not been met in relation to, or to part of, an accounting period for which the 80% qualifying holdings condition and the 70% eligible shares condition in **81.12** above do not have to be met; or
- the VCT has issued shares and, before the end of the three years beginning at the end of its accounting period in which the shares were issued, it has:

- made a payment to all or any of its shareholders of an amount representing a repayment of its share capital, whether that payment was made out of a reserve arising from a reduction of share capital or otherwise, or
- (where the shares were issued at a premium) made a payment to all or any of its shareholders of an amount representing that premium or any part of it, whether that payment was made out of a share premium reserve or otherwise, or
- used an amount which represents its share capital or an amount by which that share capital has been diminished, or (where the shares were issued at a premium) that premium (or any part of it), to pay up new shares to be allotted to all or any of its shareholders,

and has done so other than for the purpose of redeeming or repurchasing any of the issued shares. A distribution of assets counts as a payment unless it is made in connection with the winding-up of the VCT. References above to 'share capital' do not include so much (if any) of the VCT's share capital as consists of shares issued before 6 April 2014.

The withdrawal is effective from the time the company is notified of it, except that:

- where approval is given on HMRC's being satisfied as to the meeting of the relevant conditions in future accounting periods, and is withdrawn before all the conditions in **81.12** above have been satisfied in relation to either a complete twelve-month accounting period or successive complete accounting periods constituting a continuous period of twelve months or more, the approval is deemed never to have been given; and
- for the purposes of relief for capital gains accruing to a VCT under *TCGA 1992, s 100* (see **81.9** above), withdrawal may be effective from an earlier date, but not before the start of the accounting period in which the failure occurred (or is expected to occur).

An assessment consequent on the withdrawal of approval may, where otherwise out of time, be made within three years from the time notice of the withdrawal was given.

For the detailed requirements as regards granting, refusal and withdrawal of approval, and appeals procedures, see *SI 1995 No 1979, Pt II.*

The Treasury have power to make regulations setting out circumstances in which HMRC will not withdraw approval from VCTs that breach the conditions for approval. See now *SI 1995 No 1979, Regs 8–8J* which enable HMRC to determine that they will not withdraw their approval in a particular case provided that:

- the circumstances in which the VCT breached the conditions are outside its control;
- the VCT took all reasonable measures to continue to meet the conditions; and
- the breach is rectified by the VCT as soon as is reasonably possible or, in a case in which no measures could be taken by the VCT to rectify it, is nevertheless rectified in the course of events.

[*ITA 2007, ss 281, 282, 284*].

Simon's Taxes. See **D8.209**.

Mergers

[81.15] For mergers (as defined) of two or more VCTs, Treasury regulations (*SI 2004 No 2199, Regs 9–13*) enable the merging VCTs to retain VCT status and provide for investors in the merged VCTs who continue as investors in the successor company (as defined) to retain their tax reliefs. Broadly, the shares issued to effect the merger stand in the place of the shares for which they are exchanged or in respect of which they are issued. But these rules apply only where HMRC have notified their approval to the merger in advance of its taking place. The regulations lay down the detailed conditions for approval and the procedure for obtaining approval (including right of appeal against non-approval); approval will not be granted to mergers carried out other than for genuine commercial reasons or as part of tax avoidance arrangements. [*ITA 2007, ss 321–325; SI 2004 No 2199*].

Simon's Taxes. See **D8.211**.

Winding-up

[81.16] Treasury regulations (*SI 2004 No 2199, Regs 3–7*) enable a VCT to retain its status as a VCT for a maximum of three years from the commencement of the winding-up. To qualify for this extension, the VCT must normally have been approved for at least three years prior to commencement of winding-up. The intention is to provide a period of grace during which investors' reliefs can continue; the grace period does not, however, prevent a withdrawal of income tax investment relief (see **81.5** above) where the minimum holding period is not otherwise met (Treasury Explanatory Notes to Finance Bill 2002).

Regulations (*SI 2004 No 2199, Reg 8*) also permit a VCT commencing winding-up to transfer investments to another VCT and for such investments to be treated as meeting the requirements of a qualifying holding (see **81.17** below) in the hands of the recipient VCT to the same extent as they did in the hands of the first VCT. The transfer must be by way of arm's length bargain or for consideration not below market value, and it must occur within the period of grace referred to above and after all other reasonable endeavours to sell the investments at or near to market value have failed. No more than 7.5% of the value of investments at the commencement of winding-up can be transferred in this way.

In all cases, the winding-up must be for genuine commercial reasons and not part of tax avoidance arrangements.

[*ITA 2007, ss 314–320, 324, 325; SI 2004 No 2199*].

Simon's Taxes. See **D8.212**.

Qualifying holdings of a VCT

[81.17] A VCT's holding of shares or securities in a company is comprised in its '*qualifying holdings*' at any time if:

- the requirements at **81.18–81.41** below are satisfied at that time in relation to the company and the shares or securities;
- the shares or securities were first issued to the VCT, and have been held by it ever since; and
- the shares or securities were first issued by the company in order to raise money for the purposes of promoting the growth and development of the company or, where the company is a parent company, the group.

See also the supplementary provisions at **81.42** below.

Where any of the 'maximum qualifying investment' requirement (**81.21**), 'use of money raised' requirement (**81.32**) or 'relevant company to carry on the relevant qualifying activity' requirement (**81.33**) would be met as to only part of the money raised by the issue, and the holding is not otherwise capable of being treated as separate holdings, it is treated as two separate holdings, one from which that part of the money was raised, the other from which the rest was raised, with the value being apportioned accordingly to each holding. In the case of the use of money raised requirement, this does not require an insignificant amount applied for non-trade purposes to be treated as a separate holding.

[*ITA 2007, ss 286, 293(7); FA 2018, s 14(3)–(5); SI 2018 No 931, Reg 2*].

Advance assurances

A potential investee company may seek advance assurance from HMRC that meets the conditions for investment in it by a VCT (HMRC Venture Capital Schemes Manual VCM55360–55410). On and after 4 December 2017, HMRC will not provide advance assurances for investments that, taking into account all the facts that HMRC have available, will fail, or appear likely to fail, the risk-to-capital requirement at **81.18** below (HMRC Venture Capital Schemes Manual VCM8550).

Simon's Taxes. See **D8.220–D8.234.**

The risk-to-capital requirement

[81.18] This requirement has effect for shares or securities issued on or after 15 March 2018. The requirement is that, having regard to all existing circumstances at the time of issue to the VCT of the holding in question, it would be reasonable to conclude that:

- the issuing company has objectives to grow and develop its trade in the long term; and
- there is a significant risk that the investing VCT will suffer a loss of capital of an amount greater than its net investment return, i.e. its net return irrespective of whether it takes the form of income, capital growth, fees or other payments or anything else. A loss of capital means a loss of at least part of the amount given by the VCT in consideration for the holding in question.

[*ITA 2007, s 286ZA; FA 2018, s 14(3); SI 2018 No 931, Reg 2*].

The intention is to prevent tax-relieved investment in companies whose activities are geared towards preservation of investors' capital rather than the company's long-term growth and development. *ITA 2007, s s 286ZA(3)* provides an illustrative, non-exhaustive list of the types of circumstance that may be taken into account in reaching any conclusion. For guidance on the requirement, with examples, see HMRC Venture Capital Schemes Manual VCM8500–8560.

The UK permanent establishment requirement

[81.19] The requirement is that the company has a 'permanent establishment' in the UK. The company must have met this requirement at all times from the time of issue to the VCT of the holding in question.

For the above purpose, a company has a '*permanent establishment*' in the UK if (and only if):

- it has a fixed place of business in the UK through which the business of the company is wholly or partly carried on; or
- an agent acting on behalf of the company has the authority to enter into contracts on behalf of the company and habitually exercises that authority in the UK.

The activities carried on at the fixed place of business or carried on in the UK by the agent must, in relation to the company's business as a whole, be more than simply activities of a preparatory or auxiliary character. Examples of such preparatory/auxiliary activities are given at *ITA 2007, s 302A(6)* and include storage.

A company is not regarded as having a permanent establishment in the UK simply because:

- it carries on business in the UK through an independent agent (including a broker or a general commission agent) acting in the ordinary course of his business; or
- it controls a UK resident company or a company carrying on business in the UK (whether or not through a permanent establishment).

[*ITA 2007, ss 286A, 302A*].

The financial health requirement

[81.20] This requirement must have been met at the time of issue to the VCT of the holding in question. The requirement is that the issuing company is not 'in difficulty'. A company is '*in difficulty*' if it is reasonable to assume that it would be regarded as a firm in difficulty for the purposes of the *EU Guidelines on State Aid for Rescuing and Restructuring Firms in Difficulty (2004/C 244/02)*. [*ITA 2007, s 286B*].

The 'maximum qualifying investment' requirement

[81.21] This requirement applies if:

(a) at the time of issue the company or any of its qualifying subsidiaries (see **81.40** below) was a member of a partnership or a party to a joint venture;

(b) the qualifying trade in **81.26** below was at that time being carried on, or to be carried on, by that partnership or joint venture; and
(c) the other partners or parties to the joint venture include at least one other company.

The requirement is that the holding in question must not, when it was issued, have represented an investment in excess of the 'maximum qualifying investment' for the period from six months before the issue in question (or, if earlier, the beginning of the tax year of the issue) to the time of the issue. For this purpose, the maximum qualifying investment for a period is exceeded so far as the aggregate amount of money raised in that period by the issue to the VCT during that period of shares or securities of the company exceeds £1 million. Where this limit is exceeded, the shares or securities which represent the excess are treated as not being part of the holding concerned (so that £1 million can be included as a qualifying holding) and the money raised by those shares or securities is ignored for the purpose of any subsequent application of this requirement. Disposals are treated as far as possible as eliminating any such excess.

Where the conditions at (a)–(c) above are met, the £1 million limit is reduced by dividing it by the number of companies (including the company in question) which are members of the partnership or joint venture.

[*ITA 2007, s 287, Sch 2 para 68*].

The 'no guaranteed loan' requirement

[81.22] The holding in question must not include any securities (as defined in **81.12** above) relating to a guaranteed loan. A security relates to a guaranteed loan if there are arrangements entitling the VCT to receive anything (directly or indirectly) from a 'third party' in the event of a failure by any person to comply with the terms of the security or the loan to which it relates. It is immaterial whether or not the arrangements apply in all such cases. '*Third party*' means any person other than the investee company itself and, if it is a parent company that meets the trading requirement at **81.24** below, its subsidiaries. [*ITA 2007, s 288, Sch 2 para 69; FA 2018, Sch 5 paras 8, 13, 14; SI 2018 No 931, Reg 4*].

The 'proportion of eligible shares' requirement

[81.23] At least 10% (by value) of the VCT's *total* holding of shares in and securities of the company must consist of 'eligible shares' (as defined for the purposes of the 70% eligible shares condition at **81.12** above — broadly, ordinary, non-preferential, shares). For this purpose, the value of shares etc. at any time is taken to be their value immediately after the most recent of the events listed below, except that it cannot thereby be taken to be less than the amount of consideration given by the VCT for the shares etc. The said events are as follows.

- The acquisition of the shares etc. by the VCT.
- The acquisition by the VCT (other than for no consideration) of any other shares etc. in the same company which are of the same description as those already held.

- The making of any payment in discharge (or part discharge) of any obligation attached to the shares etc. in a case where such discharge increases the value of the shares etc.

[*ITA 2007, s 289, Sch 2 para 70; FA 2018, Sch 5 paras 8, 13, 14; SI 2018 No 931, Reg 4*].

The trading requirement

[81.24] The company must either:

(a) exist wholly for the purpose of carrying on one or more 'qualifying trades' (see **81.25** below), disregarding any purpose having no significant effect on the extent of its activities; or

(b) be a '*parent company*' (i.e. a company that has one or more 'qualifying subsidiaries' — see the subsidiaries requirements at **81.40** below) and the business of the '*group*' (i.e. the company and its qualifying subsidiaries) must not consist wholly or as to a substantial part (i.e. broadly 20% — see HMRC Venture Capital Schemes Manual VCM55090) in the carrying on of 'non-qualifying activities'.

Where the company intends that one or more other companies should become its qualifying subsidiaries with a view to their carrying on one or more qualifying trades, then, until any time after which the intention is abandoned, the company is treated as a parent company and those other companies are included in the group for the purposes of (b) above.

For the purpose of (b) above, the business of the group means what would be the business of the group if the activities of the group companies taken together were regarded as one business. Activities are for this purpose disregarded to the extent that they consist in:

(i) holding shares in or securities of any of the company's subsidiaries;

(ii) making loans to another group company;

(iii) holding and managing property used by a group company for the purposes of a qualifying trade or trades carried on by any group company; or

(iv) holding and managing property used by a group company for the purposes of research and development from which it is intended either that a qualifying trade to be carried on by a group company will be derived or a qualifying trade carried on or to be carried on by a group company will benefit.

References in (iv) above to a group company include references to any existing or future company which will be a group company at any future time.

Activities are similarly disregarded to the extent that they consist, in the case of a subsidiary whose main purpose is the carrying on of qualifying trade(s) and whose other purposes have no significant effect on the extent of its activities (other than in relation to incidental matters), in activities not in pursuance of its main purpose.

'*Non-qualifying activities*' are excluded activities within **81.25** below and non-trading activities.

[*ITA 2007, ss 290, 332, Sch 2 para 71*].

A company does not cease to meet this requirement by reason only of anything done as a consequence of its being in administration or receivership (both as defined — see *ITA 2007, s 331*), provided everything so done and the making of the relevant order are for genuine commercial (and not tax avoidance) reasons. [*ITA 2007, s 292, Sch 2 para 73*].

Qualifying trades

[81.25] A trade is a '*qualifying trade*' if it is conducted on a commercial basis with a view to the realisation of profits and it does not, at any time in the period since the issue of the shares to the VCT consist to a substantial extent in the carrying on of 'excluded activities'. For these purposes, 'trade' (except in relation to the trade mentioned in (q) below) does not include a venture in the nature of trade. '*Excluded activities*' are:

(a) dealing in land, commodities or futures, or in shares, securities or other financial instruments;
(b) dealing in goods otherwise than in an ordinary trade of wholesale or retail distribution (see below);
(c) banking, insurance or any other financial activities;
(d) leasing or letting or receiving royalties or licence fees;
(e) providing legal or accountancy services;
(f) 'property development';
(g) farming or market gardening;
(h) holding, managing or occupying woodlands, any other forestry activities or timber production;
(i) shipbuilding (defined by reference to relevant EU State aid rules);
(j) producing coal or steel (both defined by reference to relevant EU State aid rules and including the extraction of coal);
(k) operating or managing hotels or comparable establishments (i.e. guest houses, hostels and other establishments whose main purpose is to offer overnight accommodation with or without catering) or property used as such;
(l) operating or managing nursing homes or residential care homes (both as defined) or property used as such;
(m) generating or exporting electricity or making electricity generating capacity available;
(n) generating heat;
(o) generating any form of energy not within (m) or (n);
(p) producing gas or fuel;
(q) providing services or facilities for any business consisting of activities within any of (a) to (p) and carried on by another person (other than a parent company), where one person has a 'controlling interest' in both that business and the business carried on by the provider.

HMRC regard as 'substantial' for the above purposes a part of a trade which consists of 20% or more of total activities, judged by any reasonable measure (normally turnover or capital employed) (HMRC Venture Capital Schemes Manual VCM3010). As regards (a) above, dealing in land includes cases where steps are taken, before selling the land, to make it more attractive to a purchaser; such steps might include the refurbishment of existing buildings (HMRC Venture Capital Schemes Manual VCM3020).

As regards (b), (d)–(g), (k) and (l) above, see the comments in **29.59** ENTERPRISE INVESTMENT SCHEME on the corresponding exclusions there. As regards (q) above, the question of whether a person has a '*controlling interest*' in a business is determined in a similar manner as in **29.59**; for this purpose, '*control*' is determined in accordance with *CTA 2010, ss 450, 451* but with the same modifications as in **81.36** below.

[*ITA 2007, ss 300(1)(4), 303–307, 307A–307C, 308, 309, 309A, 309B, 310, 313(4)–(7), Sch 2 paras 81–85; FA 2016, s 28(2)(4)(6); FA 2018, Sch 5 paras 8, 13, 14; SI 2018 No 931, Reg 4*].

Research and development

'Research and development' from which it is intended that a qualifying trade either will be derived or will benefit is treated as the carrying on of a qualifying trade. Preparing to carry on such research and development does not, however, count as preparing to carry on a trade. '*Research and development*' has the meaning given by *ITA 2007, s 1006* — see **75.113** TRADING INCOME.

[*ITA 2007, s 300(2)(3), Sch 2 para 78*].

The 'carrying on of a qualifying activity' requirement

[81.26] A 'qualifying company' (whether or not the same such company at all times) must, when the shares were issued to the VCT and at all times since, have been carrying on one of the following two '*qualifying activities*':

(a) carrying on a 'qualifying trade' (see **81.25** above); or
(b) preparing to carry on a qualifying trade which, at the time the shares were issued, was intended to be carried on by a qualifying company.

The second of these conditions is, however, relevant only for a period of two years after the issue of the shares, by which time the intended trade must have been commenced by a 'qualifying company', and ceases to be relevant at any time within those two years after the intention is abandoned.

For these purposes, '*qualifying company*' means the issuing company itself or any 'qualifying 90% subsidiary' of that company. (In determining the time at which a qualifying trade begins to be carried on by a 'qualifying 90% subsidiary', any carrying on of the trade by it before it became such a subsidiary is disregarded.) For the purposes of (b) above only, a qualifying 90% subsidiary includes any existing or future company which will be a qualifying 90% subsidiary at any future time.

A company (the subsidiary) is a '*qualifying 90% subsidiary*' of the issuing company at any time when:

- the issuing company possesses at least 90% of both the issued share capital of, and the voting power in, the subsidiary;
- the issuing company would be beneficially entitled to at least 90% of the assets of the subsidiary available for distribution to equity holders on a winding-up or in any other circumstances;

- the issuing company is beneficially entitled to at least 90% of any profits of the subsidiary available for distribution to equity holders;
- no person other than the issuing company has control (within *ITA 2007, s 995*) of the subsidiary; and
- no arrangements exist by virtue of which any of the above conditions would cease to be met.

For the above purposes, *CTA 2010, Pt 5 Ch 6* applies, with appropriate modifications, to determine the persons who are equity holders and the percentage of assets available to them. A subsidiary does not cease to be a qualifying 90% subsidiary by reason only of it or any other company having commenced winding up or by reason only of anything done as a consequence of any such company being in administration or receivership, provided the winding-up, entry into administration or receivership (both as defined) or anything done as a consequence of its being in administration or receivership is for genuine commercial reasons and is not part of a tax avoidance scheme or arrangements. Also, the listed conditions are not regarded as ceasing to be satisfied by reason only of arrangements being in existence for the disposal of the issuing company's interest in the subsidiary if the disposal is to be for genuine commercial reasons and is not to be part of a tax avoidance scheme or arrangements.

A company ('company A') which is a subsidiary of company B (a company that is not the issuing company) is a qualifying 90% subsidiary of the issuing company if:

- company A would be a qualifying 90% subsidiary of company B (if company B were the issuing company), and company B is a 'qualifying 100% subsidiary' of the issuing company; or
- company A is a 'qualifying 100% subsidiary' of company B, and company B is a qualifying 90% subsidiary of the issuing company.

For this purpose, no account is to be taken of any control the issuing company may have of company A, and '*qualifying 100% subsidiary*' is defined similarly to 'qualifying 90% subsidiary' above but substituting '100%' for '90%'.

[*ITA 2007, ss 291, 301, Sch 2 paras 72, 79*].

A company does not cease to meet this requirement by reason only of anything done as a consequence of its being in administration or receivership (both as defined), provided everything so done and the making of the relevant order are for genuine commercial (and not tax avoidance) reasons. [*ITA 2007, s 292, Sch 2 para 73*].

The 'maximum amount raised annually through risk finance investments' requirement

[81.27] With effect for investments made on or after 6 April 2018, the total amount of 'relevant investments' (see **81.28** below) made in the issuing company in the 12 months ending with the date of issue to the VCT must not exceed:

(i) if the company is a knowledge-intensive company at that date, £10 million; and

(ii) in any other case, £5 million.

See **81.30** below for meaning of knowledge-intensive company, and note the special rule there for companies that have traded for less than three years before issuing the EIS shares.

Prior to the above taking effect the limit is £5 million in all cases.

The following also count towards the above limit:

(a) any relevant investment in a 51% subsidiary (within *CTA 2010, Pt 24 Ch 3*) of the issuing company (including any made before it became a 51% subsidiary but not any made after it last ceased to be one);
(b) any relevant investment made in any company to the extent that the money raised by the investment has been employed for the purposes of a trade (as widely defined) carried on by another company that has at any time in the said 12-month period been a 51% subsidiary of the issuing company (disregarding any money so employed after it last ceased to be such a subsidiary); and
(c) any other relevant investment made in any company to the extent that the money raised has been employed for the purposes of a trade (as widely defined), and within that 12-month period, but after the investment was made, the trade (or a part of it) was transferred to the issuing company, a 51% subsidiary or a partnership of which the issuing company or a 51% subsidiary is a member (but disregarding trades transferred after a 51% subsidiary in question last ceased to be such a subsidiary).

[*ITA 2007, s 292A(1)–(2B)(7); FA 2018, Sch 4 paras 3(2), 10; SI 2018 No 931, Reg 3*].

Relevant investments

[81.28] For the purposes of the VCT qualifying holding requirements, '*relevant investments*' comprise:

(a) investments (of any kind) made by a VCT;
(b) money subscribed for shares issued by the investee company under the ENTERPRISE INVESTMENT SCHEME (EIS) (**29**) or the SEED ENTERPRISE INVESTMENT SCHEME (SEIS) (**66**);
(c) investments made under the SOCIAL INVESTMENT TAX RELIEF (**72**) scheme; and
(d) any other investment made in the company which is aid received by it pursuant to a measure approved by the EC as compatible with Article 107 of the Treaty on the Functioning of the European Union in accordance with the principles laid down in the EC's Guidelines on State aid to promote risk finance investment (previously the Community Guidelines on Risk Capital Investments in Small and Medium-sized Enterprises).

As regards (b) above, shares are treated as having been issued under the EIS or SEIS if at any time the investee company provides an EIS compliance statement (see **29.7** ENTERPRISE INVESTMENT SCHEME) or SEIS equivalent (see **66.5** SEED ENTERPRISE INVESTMENT SCHEME) in respect of those shares; an investment is regarded as made when the shares are issued. As regards (c) above, an investment is treated as made under the social investment relief scheme if at any time the investee company provides a compliance statement as in **72.6** SOCIAL INVESTMENT TAX RELIEF; *ITA 2007, s 257KB* (see **72.1** SOCIAL INVESTMENT TAX RELIEF) applies in determining when such an investment is made. If the provision of a compliance statement causes this requirement not to be met, the requirement is treated as having been met from the time the shares in question were issued to the VCT to the time the compliance statement was provided.

[*ITA 2007, s 292A(3)–(6)*].

For the purposes of determining entitlement to VCT income tax relief in respect of investments made on or after 1 December 2017, investments are not prevented from constituting relevant investments by virtue only of their having been made before certain historical dates. Previously, under earlier transitional provisions, certain investments made before 6 April 2012 did not count as relevant investments. [*FA 2018, s 15*].

The 'maximum risk finance investments when holding is issued' requirement

[81.29] The total amount of 'relevant investments' (see **81.28** above) made in the issuing company on or before investment date (i.e. the date the holding in question is issued) must not exceed £12 million or, if the company is a 'knowledge-intensive company' (see **81.30** below) at the investment date, £20 million. Relevant investments of the kind in **81.27**(a)–(c) above also count towards these limits, but disregarding references there to a 12-month period and instead taking into account all times before the investment date. If at any time the company provides a compliance statement under **29.7** ENTERPRISE INVESTMENT SCHEME, **66.5** SEED ENTERPRISE INVESTMENT SCHEME or **72.6** SOCIAL INVESTMENT TAX RELIEF and this requirement ceases to be met as a result, it is nevertheless treated as having been met throughout the period from the investment date until the provision of the compliance statement. [*ITA 2007, s 292AA*].

Knowledge-intensive companies

[81.30] A '*knowledge-intensive company*' is broadly a company whose costs of research and development or innovation are at least 15% of its operating costs in at least one of the years comprising the 'relevant three-year period' or at least 10% of its operating costs in each of those years, and which meets at least one of the two conditions below. The '*relevant three-year period*' is normally the three years ending immediately before the beginning of the last accounts filing period. However, if the last accounts filing period ends more than 12 months before the applicable time, the relevant three-year period is the three years ending 12 months before the applicable time. The applicable time is the date on which the matter of whether a company is a knowledge-intensive company falls to be judged. A company's operating costs are defined by reference to the items recognised as expenses in its profit and loss account. The conditions to be met are that:

- the company has created, is creating or is intending to create, intellectual property (the '*innovation condition*'); or

- the company's full-time employees with a relevant Masters or higher degree who are engaged in research and development or innovation comprise at least 20% of the total of its full-time employees (the '*skilled employee condition*').

In order to meet the innovation condition, the company must be engaged in intellectual property creation at the applicable time, and it must be reasonable to assume that, within ten years after that time, the exploitation of its intellectual property, or business which results from new or improved products, processes or services utilising its intellectual property, will form the greater part of its business. A company is engaged in intellectual property creation if intellectual property is being created by the company, or has been created by it within the previous three years; or the company is taking (or preparing to take) steps in order that intellectual property will be created by it; or the company demonstrates via an independent expert's report that it is reasonable to assume it will create intellectual property in the foreseeable future. Intellectual property is taken into account only if the whole or greater part (in terms of value) of it is created by the company and it is created in circumstances in which the right to exploit it vests in the company (whether alone or jointly with others).

If the company is a parent company, the above rules are appropriately modified to also take account of its 'qualifying subsidiaries' (see **81.40** below).

[*ITA 2007, ss 313(5), 331A; FA 2016, ss 29(5)(6), 30*].

Companies that have traded for less than three years

If the company commenced trading less than three years before the date the holding in question is issued, the above definition is modified for the purposes of **81.27**(i) and (ii) above ('maximum amount raised annually through risk finance investments' requirement). The '*relevant three-year period*' is for those purposes the three years *beginning* on the date of issue of the holding. If the company is a parent company, operating costs of a qualifying subsidiary (at time of issue) are not taken into account for any of those three years during any part of which it is not a qualifying subsidiary. [*ITA 2007, s 292A(6A); FA 2018, Sch 4 paras 3(3), 10; SI 2018 No 931, Reg 3*].

The 'maximum risk finance investments in five-year post-investment period' requirement

[81.31] This is a requirement which is tested only during a '*five-year post-investment period*', i.e. the period of five years beginning the day after the date the holding in question is issued (the '*investment date*'), and only if the company effectively acquires a company or trade after it receives the investment in question. The requirement is that at any time in the five-year post-investment period the total of the relevant investments (see **81.28** above) so far made must not exceed £12 million or, if the company is a 'knowledge-intensive company' (see **81.30** above) at the investment date, £20 million. Without this requirement, the investment limits in **81.29** above could be sidestepped where the acquired company or trade had already benefited from earlier relevant investments. Relevant investments of the kind in **81.27**(a)–(c) above also count towards these limits, but disregarding references there to a 12-month period and instead taking into account all times before the time in the five-year post-investment period when the requirement is being tested. The requirement applies where:

- a company becomes a 51% subsidiary of the issuing company at a time during the five-year post-investment period;
- all or part of the money raised by the issue of the holding in question is employed for the purposes of a relevant qualifying activity consisting (wholly or partly) of a trade (as widely defined) carried on by that company; and
- the trade (or a part of it) was carried on by that company before that time.

The requirement also applies where all or part of the money raised by the issue of the holding in question is employed for the purposes of a relevant qualifying activity consisting (wholly or partly) of a trade (as widely defined) which, during the five-year post-investment period, is transferred as in **81.27**(c) above.

Similar provision applies as in **81.29** above if at any time the company provides a compliance statement under one of the other venture capital schemes or the social investment relief scheme and this requirement ceases to be met as a result. It is nevertheless treated as having been met throughout the period from the investment date until the provision of the compliance statement.

[*ITA 2007, s 292AB*].

The 'use of the money raised' requirement

[81.32] The money raised by the issue of shares to the VCT must be employed *wholly* (disregarding insignificant amounts) for the purposes of the 'relevant qualifying activity'. This condition does not have to be met in the first two years after the issue (or in the two years after the commencement of the qualifying trade where this was later than the date of issue).

For these purposes, a qualifying activity is a '*relevant qualifying activity*' if it was a qualifying activity at the time the shares were issued or if it is a qualifying trade and preparing to carry it on was a qualifying activity at that time.

Employing money on the acquisition of shares in a company does not of itself amount to employing it for the purposes of a relevant qualifying activity. Additionally, employing money on the acquisition of any of the following does not amount to employing it for the purposes of a relevant qualifying activity: an interest in another company such that a company becomes a 51% subsidiary of the issuing company; a further interest in a 51% subsidiary of the issuing company; a trade (as widely defined); and goodwill or other intangible assets employed for the purposes of a trade.

[*ITA 2007, s 293, Sch 2 para 74*].

In relation to buy-outs (and in particular management buy-outs), HMRC will usually accept that where a company is formed to acquire a trade, and the funds raised from the VCT are applied to that purchase, the requirement that the funds be employed for the purposes of the trade is satisfied. Where the company is formed to acquire another company and its trade, or a holding company and its trading subsidiaries, this represents an investment rather than employment for the purposes of the trade. However, HMRC will usually accept that the requirement is satisfied if the trade of the company, or all the activities of the holding company and its subsidiaries, are hived up to the acquiring company as soon as possible after the acquisition. In the case of a holding company and its subsidiaries, to the extent that the trades are not hived up, the holding cannot be a qualifying holding. (Revenue Tax Bulletin August 1995 pp 243, 244).

The 'relevant company to carry on the relevant qualifying activity' requirement

[81.33] At all times after the issue of the holding, the relevant qualifying activity by reference to which the use of money raised requirement is satisfied must not be carried on by any person other than the issuing company or a 'qualifying 90% subsidiary' (see **81.26** above) of that company.

This requirement is not treated as not met merely because the trade in question is carried on by a person other than the issuing company or a qualifying subsidiary at any time after the issue of the shares and before the issuing company or a qualifying 90% subsidiary carries on the trade. The carrying on of the trade by a partnership of which the issuing company or a qualifying 90% subsidiary is a member, or by a joint venture to which any such company is a party, is permitted.

The requirement is also not regarded as failing to be met if, by reason only of a company being wound up or dissolved or being in administration or receivership (both as defined), the qualifying trade ceases to be carried on by the issuing company' or a qualifying 90% subsidiary and is subsequently carried on by a person who has not been connected (within **19** CONNECTED PERSONS — but with the modifications to the meaning of 'control' that apply for the purposes of the control and independence requirement at **81.36** below) with the issuing company at any time in the period beginning one year before the shares were issued. This let-out applies only if the winding-up, dissolution or entry into administration or receivership (and everything done as a consequence of the company being in administration or receivership) is for genuine commercial reasons and not part of a tax avoidance scheme or arrangements.

[*ITA 2007, s 294, Sch 2 para 75; SI 2007 No 1820, Reg 4*].

The 'permitted company age' requirement

[81.34] If the holding in question is issued after the 'initial investing period', one of three conditions must be met. These are that:

(a) a 'relevant investment' (see **81.28** above) was made in the issuing company before the end of the initial investing period, and some or all of the money raised by that investment was employed for the purposes of the same qualifying activity as that for which the money raised by the current issue is employed; or

(b) the total amount of relevant investments made in the issuing company in a period of 30 consecutive days which includes the date of issue of the holding in question is at least 50% of the annual turnover of the company averaged over five years (see *ITA 2007, s 294A(7)–(8)*), and the money raised by those investments is employed for the purpose of 'entering a new product or geographical market' (as defined in the General Block Exemption Regulation (Commission Regulation (EU) No 651/2014); or

(c) the condition in (b) or the equivalent condition for EIS investments (see **29.36**(b) ENTERPRISE INVESTMENT SCHEME) was previously met in relation to one or more relevant investments in the issuing company, and some or all of the money raised by those investments was employed for the purposes of the same qualifying activity as that for which the money raised by the current issue is employed.

The '*initial investing period*' is the seven years beginning with the 'relevant first commercial sale' (ten years where the issuing company is a 'knowledge-intensive company' (see **81.30** above) when the holding in question is issued). '*First commercial sale*' has the same meaning as in the EC's Guidelines on State aid to promote risk finance investments. The '*relevant first commercial sale*' is defined in *ITA 2007, s 294A(6)* by reference to the earliest date of any commercial sale made by (broadly) the company or a 51% subsidiary or any other person who has carried on any trade which is carried on by the company or a subsidiary.

With effect for investments made on or after 6 April 2018, a company which is a knowledge-intensive company may elect to alter its initial investing period by substituting, for the date of the relevant first commercial sale, the date by reference to which it is treated as reaching an annual turnover of £200,000. That date is normally the last day of the accounting period in which annual turnover first reaches £200,000 or more (with modifications for accounting periods exceeding 12 months). Turnover of other companies in the group (where relevant) must also be taken into account. Any necessary apportionments must be made on a time basis, i.e. in the case of short or long accounting periods or companies joining or leaving the group part way through an accounting period.

[*ITA 2007, ss 294A, 331B; FA 2016, ss 29(4)(6), 30; FA 2018, Sch 4 paras 8, 9, 10; SI 2018 No 931, Reg 3*].

See **81.42** below as regards modification of the permitted company age requirement on and after 6 April 2017 in the event of certain company restructuring.

The unquoted status requirement

[81.35] The issuing company must be an '*unquoted company*' (whether or not UK resident), i.e. none of its shares, stocks, debentures or other securities must be:

- listed on a recognised stock exchange, or a designated exchange outside the UK; or

- dealt in outside the UK by such means as may be designated for the purpose by order.

The Alternative Investment Market (AIM) and the PLUS Markets (with the exception of PLUS-listed) are not considered to be recognised exchanges for these purposes (HMRC Venture Capital Schemes Manual VCM55180).

If the company ceases to be an unquoted company at a time when its shares are comprised in the qualifying holdings of the VCT, this requirement is treated as continuing to be met, in relation to shares or securities acquired before that time, for the following five years.

[*ITA 2007, ss 295, 989, 1005*].

The control and independence requirement

[81.36] The company must not 'control' (with or without 'connected persons') any company other than a 'qualifying subsidiary' (see the subsidiaries requirements at **81.40** below), nor must another company (or another company and a person connected with it) control it. Neither must arrangements be in existence by virtue of which such control could arise. For these purposes, '*control*' is as under *CTA 2010, ss 450, 451*, except that the following are disregarded:

- possession of, or entitlement to acquire, fixed-rate preference shares (as defined) of the company which do not, for the time being, carry voting rights;
- possession of, or entitlement to acquire, rights as a loan creditor of the company;
- any right to dividends carried by shares in the company where the shares are eligible shares (as in **81.12** above) and are held by the VCT.

'*Connected persons*' are as under *ITA 2007, s 993* (see **19** CONNECTED PERSONS) except that the definition of 'control' therein is similarly modified.

[*ITA 2007, ss 296, 313(4)–(7)*].

For the application of the control and independence requirement to co-investors in a company, and in particular the question of whether co-investors are connected by virtue of their acting together to secure or exercise control of the company, see Revenue Tax Bulletin October 1997 pp 471, 472.

The gross assets requirement

[81.37] The value of the company's gross assets or, where the company is a parent company, the value of the 'group assets', must not have exceeded £15 million immediately before the issue or £16 million immediately thereafter.

'*Group assets*' are the gross assets of each of the members of the group, disregarding assets consisting in rights against, or shares in or securities of, another member of the group.

[*ITA 2007, s 297, Sch 2 para 76*].

The general approach of HMRC is that the value of a company's gross assets is the sum of the value of all the balance sheet assets. Where accounts are actually drawn up to a date immediately before or after the issue, the balance sheet values are taken provided that they reflect usual accounting standards and the company's normal accounting practice, consistently applied. Where accounts are not drawn up to such a date, such values will be taken from the most recent balance sheet, updated as precisely as practicable on the basis of all the relevant information available to the company. Values so arrived at may need to be reviewed in the light of information contained in the accounts for the period in which the issue was made, and, if they were not available at the time of the issue, those for the preceding period, when they become available. The company's assets immediately before the issue do not include any advance payment received in respect of the issue. Where shares are issued partly paid, the right to the balance is an asset, and, notwithstanding the above, will be taken into account in valuing the assets immediately after the issue regardless of whether it is stated in the balance sheet. (HMRC SP 2/06).

The 'number of employees' requirement

[81.38] The company must have fewer than the equivalent of 250 full-time employees when the shares or securities are issued. The limit is doubled to 500 if the company is a 'knowledge-intensive company' (see **81.30** above) at the time the holding in question is issued. If the company is a parent company (see **81.24**(b) above), the 'number of employees' requirement applies by reference to the aggregate number of full-time employees of the company and its qualifying subsidiaries (see **81.40** below). To ascertain the equivalent number of full-time employees of a company, take the actual number of full-time employees and add to it a just and reasonable fraction for each employee who is not full-time. For this purpose, an 'employee' includes a director but does not include anyone on maternity, paternity, shared parental or parental bereavement leave or a student on vocational training. [*ITA 2007, s 297A; Parental Bereavement (Leave and Pay) Act 2018, Sch para 54; SI 2020 No 45, Reg 2*].

The 'proportion of skilled employees' requirement

[81.39] There is a requirement, where the conditions below are met, that at all times in the period of three years beginning with the issue of the holding in question the company's full-time employees with a relevant Masters or higher degree who are engaged in research and development or innovation must comprise at least 20% of the total of its full-time employees. The conditions are that:

- one or more of the requirements in **81.27** ('maximum amount raised annually through risk finance investments' requirement), **81.29** ('maximum risk finance investments when holding is issued' requirement), **81.34** ('permitted company age' requirement) and **81.38** above ('number of employees' requirement) is or are met only by reason of the company being a knowledge-intensive company at the time the holding in question was issued; and

- the innovation condition in the definition of 'knowledge-intensive company' at **81.30** above was not met by the company at that time.

If the company is a parent company, the above is appropriately modified to also take account of the company's 'qualifying subsidiaries' (see **81.40** below). The requirement is not treated as failing to be met at a time when the company, by virtue of *ITA 2007, s 292* (companies in administration or receivership — see **81.24** above), is not regarded as having ceased to meet the trading requirement.

[*ITA 2007, s 297B; FA 2018, Sch 4 paras 4, 10; SI 2018 No 931, Reg 3*].

The subsidiaries requirements

Qualifying subsidiaries

[81.40] Any subsidiary that the issuing company has must be a 'qualifying subsidiary'.

A subsidiary is a '*qualifying subsidiary*' of the issuing company if the following conditions are satisfied in relation to that subsidiary and every other subsidiary of the issuing company.

The subsidiary must be a **51%** subsidiary (see *CTA 2010, Pt 24 Ch 3*) of the issuing company and no person other than the issuing company or another of its subsidiaries may have control (within *ITA 2007, s 995*) of the subsidiary. Furthermore, no arrangements may exist by virtue of which either of these conditions would cease to be satisfied.

The conditions are not regarded as ceasing to be satisfied by reason only of the subsidiary or any other company being in the process of being wound up or by reason only of anything done as a consequence of its being in administration or receivership, provided the winding-up, entry into administration or receivership or anything done as a consequence of its being in administration or receivership is for genuine commercial reasons and is not part of a tax avoidance scheme or arrangements.

The conditions above are not regarded as ceasing to be satisfied by reason only of arrangements being in existence for the disposal of the interest in the subsidiary held by the issuing company (or, as the case may be, by another of its subsidiaries) if the disposal is to be for genuine commercial reasons and is not to be part of a tax avoidance scheme or arrangements.

[*ITA 2007, ss 298, 302, 989, Sch 2 para 80*].

Property managing subsidiaries

The company must not have a 'property managing subsidiary' which is not a 'qualifying 90% subsidiary' (see **81.26** above) of the company. A '*property managing subsidiary*' is a subsidiary whose business consists wholly or mainly in the holding or managing of 'land' or any 'property deriving its value from land' (as defined). [*ITA 2007, s 299, Sch 2 para 77*].

The 'no disqualifying arrangements' requirement

[81.41] The holding in question must not have been issued, nor any money raised by the issue employed, in consequence or anticipation of, or otherwise in connection with, 'disqualifying arrangements'. Arrangements (as broadly defined) are '*disqualifying arrangements*' if a main purpose of them is to ensure that any of the 'relevant tax reliefs' are available in respect of the issuing company's business and either or both of conditions A and B below are met. It is immaterial whether the issuing company is a party to the arrangements.

Condition A is that, as a result of the money raised by the issue of the shares to the VCT being employed as required by **81.32** above, an amount representing the whole or most of the amount raised is, in the course of the arrangements, paid to (or for the benefit of) one or more 'relevant persons'. Condition B is that, in the absence of the arrangements, it would have been reasonable to expect that the whole or greater part of the component activities (as defined) of the relevant qualifying activity in **81.32** would have been carried on as part of another business by one or more 'relevant persons'.

A '*relevant person*' is a person who is a party to the arrangements or a person connected with such a party (within **19** CONNECTED PERSONS). The '*relevant tax reliefs*' are those listed at **29.40** ENTERPRISE INVESTMENT SCHEME. The addition of SOCIAL INVESTMENT TAX RELIEF (**72**) to that list has effect for the purpose of determining whether shares or securities issued on or after 6 April 2017 are to be regarded as comprised in a VCT's qualifying holdings, but not so as to apply to arrangements involving transactions entered into before that date.

[*ITA 2007, ss 299A, 313(5); F(No 2)A 2017, Sch 1 paras 11(4), 16*].

Information powers

If an officer of HMRC has reason to believe that shares or securities have been issued to a VCT in consequence of, or otherwise in connection with, disqualifying arrangements, he may by notice require persons concerned to supply information within a specified time (at least 60 days). The penalty provisions of *TMA 1970, s 98* apply for failure to comply. [*ITA 2007, s 312A*].

Supplementary provisions

[81.42] The following supplementary provisions apply.

Winding-up of the issuing company

Where the company is being wound up, none of the requirements listed at **81.19–81.41** above are regarded on that account as not being satisfied provided that those conditions would be met apart from the winding-up, and that the winding-up is for genuine commercial reasons and is not part of a scheme or arrangement a main purpose of which is the avoidance of tax. [*ITA 2007, s 312, Sch 2 para 86*].

Restructuring

Where shares or securities in a company are exchanged for corresponding shares and securities in a new parent company, then subject to detailed conditions, including HMRC approval, to the extent that any of the conditions, and (at any time) any of the requirements, mentioned below was satisfied in relation to the old shares, it will generally be taken to be satisfied in relation to the new shares. The consideration for the old shares must consist wholly of the issue of shares in the new company. Certain deemed securities (see **81.12** above) which are not thus acquired by the new company may be disregarded where these provisions would otherwise be prevented from applying.

The said conditions are the investment limits condition, the permitted maximum age condition and the no business acquisition condition at **81.12** above. The said requirements are those at **81.21**, **81.23**, **81.24**, **81.26**, **81.27**, **81.29**, **81.31–81.34** and **81.36–81.39** above.

Legislation introduced in 2017 enables a new parent company (as above) which has acquired a company that has previously received funding from a VCT to use the funding history of the acquired company when considering if follow-on funding is admissible to fund the continuing activities of that acquired company. The legislation achieves this by effectively treating relevant investments made in the acquired company before the restructuring, and before the end of the initial investing period, as having been made in the new company. This is relevant to the permitted maximum age condition at **81.12** above, in which case it has effect in relation to investments made on or after 6 April 2017, and the permitted company age requirement at **81.34** above, in which case it has effect in relation to shares or securities issued to a VCT on or after that date.

[*ITA 2007, ss 326, 326A, 327, 327A, 328, Sch 2 para 87; F(No 2)A 2017, s 12*].

Conversion of shares

Where a VCT exercises conversion rights in respect of certain convertible shares and securities, then subject to detailed conditions, for the purposes of the following requirements, the conversion is treated as an exchange of new shares for old shares to which the restructuring provisions above apply: **81.21**, **81.23**, **81.26**, **81.32**, **81.33** and **81.37** above. [*ITA 2007, s 329, Sch 2 para 87*].

Reorganisations etc.

Where, under a company reorganisation or other arrangement:

(a) a VCT exchanges a qualifying holding for other shares or securities (with or without other consideration); and
(b) the exchange is for genuine commercial reasons and not part of a tax avoidance scheme or arrangements,

the new shares or securities may be treated as being qualifying holdings for a specified period even if some or all of the requirements at **81.19–81.41** above are not otherwise satisfied. Regulations specify the circumstances in which, and conditions subject to which, they apply and which requirements are to be treated as met. Where the new shares or securities are those of a different company than before and they do not meet any one or more of the above requirements (disregarding the maximum qualifying investment requirement and the use of the money raised requirement), those requirements are treated as met for, broadly, three years in the case of shares or five years in the case of securities, reduced in either case to, broadly, two years where the company is not, or ceases to be, an unquoted company as in the unquoted status requirement. A formula is provided for valuing the new shares or securities for the purposes of the proportion of eligible shares requirement. The provisions extend to new shares or securities received in pursuance of an earn-out right (see Tolley's Capital Gains Tax under Shares and Securities) conferred in exchange for a qualifying holding, in which case an election is available (under *Reg 10*) to modify the said valuation formula by effectively disregarding the earn-out right itself. [*ITA 2007, s 330, Sch 2 para 88; SI 2002 No 2661*].

F(No 2)A 2017 gives the Treasury power to make regulations covering cases where, on an exchange of *non-qualifying* shares or securities that otherwise meets the condition in (b) above, a VCT receives other non-qualifying shares or securities. For context, see the non-qualifying investments condition in **81.12** above. The regulations may, inter alia, make provision as to when the new shares or securities are to be regarded as having been acquired. [*ITA 2007, s 330; F(No 2)A 2017, s 13*].

Simon's Taxes. See **D8.235, D8.240–D8.242.**

82

Finance Act 2020 — Summary of Income Tax Provisions

[82.1] (Royal Assent: 22 July 2020)

s 1	**Income tax charge for 2020/21.** The annual charge to income tax is renewed.
s 2	**Income tax main rates for 2020/21.** The basis, higher and additional rates remain at 20%, 40% and 45% respectively. See **1.3** ALLOWANCES AND TAX RATES.
s 3	**Income tax savings rates for 2020/21.** The rates of tax on savings income remain the same as for 2019/20, i.e. 20%, 40% and 45%. See **1.6** ALLOWANCES AND TAX RATES.
s 4	**Starting rate limit for savings for 2020/21.** The starting rate limit remains at £5,000. See **1.6** ALLOWANCES AND TAX RATES.
s 7, Sch 1	**Workers' services provided through intermediaries.** Where services are provided through an intermediary, e.g. a personal service company, a separate tax regime already applies where the client is a public sector body. That regime is now extended to the private sector, broadly for 2021/22 onwards, except where the client qualifies as small or does not have a UK connection. Where the regime does not apply, the long-standing IR35 rules continue to apply instead. See **58** PERSONAL SERVICE COMPANIES ETC..
s 8	**Determining the appropriate percentage for a company car.** The WLTP (worldwide harmonised light vehicles test procedures), a new regime for calculating a car's CO_2 emissions figure, applies to cars first registered on or after 6 April 2020. The previous regime still applies to cars first registered between 1 October 1999 and 5 April 2020 inclusive. See **28.24** EMPLOYMENT INCOME.
s 9	**Determining the appropriate percentage for a company car: 2020/21 only.** This sets out the appropriate percentages for 2020/21 for cars whose CO_2 emissions fall to be measured under WLTP, and also makes an amendment to the appropriate percentages for other cars. See **28.24** EMPLOYMENT INCOME.

s 10 **Determining the appropriate percentage for a company car: 2021/22 only.** This sets out the appropriate percentages for 2021/22 for cars whose CO_2 emissions fall to be measured under WLTP, and also makes an amendment to the appropriate percentages for other cars. See **28.24** EMPLOYMENT INCOME.

s 11 **Apprenticeship bursaries paid to care leavers.** For 2020/21 onwards, one-off bursaries paid out of the public revenue to young people leaving local authority care to take up apprenticeships are exempt from income tax. See **30.4** EXEMPT INCOME.

s 12 **Exemption of Scottish social security benefits.** Three new social security benefits paid by the Scottish Government are exempted from income tax for 2020/21 onwards. See **73.2** SOCIAL SECURITY AND NATIONAL INSURANCE.

s 14 **Voluntary office-holders: payments for expenses.** No liability to income tax arises on a payment to a person holding a voluntary office if the payment is in respect of reasonable expenses incurred in carrying out the duties of that office. This applies for 2020/21 onwards but gives statutory footing to a long-standing practice. See **30.51** EXEMPT INCOME.

s 15, Sch 2 Pt 1 **The loan charge: removal of loans made before 9 December 2010.** This removes loans and quasi-loans made before 9 December 2010 from the scope of the loan charge. See **26.8** DISGUISED REMUNERATION and **75.40** TRADING INCOME.

s 16, Sch 2 Pt 2 **The loan charge: election for charge to be split over three tax years.** This enables an election to be made (before 1 October 2020) to split the chargeable amount equally over the three tax years 2018/19 to 2020/21. See **26.8** DISGUISED REMUNERATION and **75.40** TRADING INCOME.

s 17 **The loan charge: reduction of charge where reasonable disclosure made.** This provides for a reduction in the amount chargeable where a loan was made before 2016/17, a reasonable disclosure of the loan was made and HMRC did not take steps prior to 6 April 2019 to recover the tax. See **26.8** DISGUISED REMUNERATION and **75.40** TRADING INCOME.

s 18 **The loan charge: relief from interest on late paid tax.** This provides for no interest to be charged on persons subject to the loan charge on any tax liability due for 2018/19 and outstanding between 1 February 2020 and 30 September 2020. A complete and accurate self-assessment for 2018/19 must be made on or before 30 September 2020. See **26.8** DISGUISED REMUNERATION and **75.40** TRADING INCOME.

s 19 **The loan charge: miscellaneous amendments.** The significant amendment is that the date by which information must be provided to HMRC regarding a loan is put back from 30 September 2019 to 30 September 2020. See **26.8** DISGUISED REMUNERATION and **75.40** TRADING INCOME.

s 20 **The loan charge: repayment or waiver of voluntary restitution.** This requires HMRC to set up a scheme whereby they may repay amounts paid, or waive amounts due, where voluntary restitution was payable to HMRC under a settlement agreement made between 16 March 2016 and 10 March 2020 inclusive, but an amount would no longer be due because of the changes made by *section 14* and/or *section 16* above. See **26.8** DISGUISED REMUNERATION and **75.40** TRADING INCOME.

s 21 **The loan charge: disguised remuneration repayment scheme 2020.** This gives the detail of what may be provided by the scheme referred to in *section 19* above. See **26.8** DISGUISED REMUNERATION and **75.40** TRADING INCOME.

s 22 **Pensions annual allowance.** For the purpose of applying the annual allowance taper for 2020/21 onwards, adjusted income is increased from £150,000 to £240,000, and threshold income from £110,000 to £200,000. The minimum annual allowance is reduced from £10,000 to £4,000. See **57.25** PENSION PROVISION.

s 29 **Structures and buildings allowance (SBA): rate of allowance.** The rate of the SBA is increased from 2% to 3% with effect on and after 6 April 2020, and the writing-down period reduced from 50 to 33⅓ years. See **9.30** CAPITAL ALLOWANCES.

s 30, Sch 5 **Structures and buildings allowance (SBA): miscellaneous amendments.** Miscellaneous amendments are made to ensure various rules operate as intended. Many of these are treated as having always had effect. Changes to the rules for contribution allowances and to the interaction of SBAs with research and development capital allowances take effect on 11 March 2020. See **9.2**(vii), **9.30**, **9.31**, **9.34** CAPITAL ALLOWANCES.

s 35 **Changes to accounting standards affecting leases.** Amendments are made to the transitional rules applicable where a lessee treats a lease as a right-of-use asset under IFRS 16 and had not previously accounted for the lease as a finance lease. The amendments simply remove ambiguities and are treated as always having had effect. See **75.82** TRADING INCOME.

s 36 **Enterprise investment scheme (EIS): approved knowledge-intensive funds.** The EIS approved fund rules are amended to focus investment on knowledge-intensive companies. The amendments also give approved funds a longer period over which to invest fund capital They have effect on and after 6 April 2020 in relation to funds which, on or after that date, close for the acceptance of further investments. See **29.2** ENTERPRISE INVESTMENT SCHEME.

s 37 **Life assurance chargeable event gains: top slicing relief.** With effect in relation to chargeable event gains occurring on or after 11 March 2020, the personal allowance to be included in the computation of tax payable on the annual equivalent is determined as if the chargeable event gain is limited to the annual equivalent. With similar effect, in each of the computations made for the purpose of top slicing relief, deductible reliefs and allowances can be set against the chargeable event gain or annual equivalent only to the extent that they cannot be set against other income. In practice and by concession, HMRC will apply the first of these changes to all gains arising in 2019/20 onwards. See **44.9** LIFE ASSURANCE POLICIES.

s 38 **Share loss relief: abolition of UK business requirement.** In relation to disposals made on or after 24 January 2019, the requirement that the shares be in a company carrying on its business wholly or mainly in the UK is abolished, thus complying with EU treaty rules and widening the availability of relief. See **45.26, 45.28** LOSSES.

s 101, Sch 14 **Operation of the General Anti-abuse Rule (GAAR).** This makes procedural and technical amendments to the GAAR with effect broadly from the date of Royal Assent (see above). The primary change is the replacement of provisional counteraction notices with protective GAAR notices, which is intended to both simplify procedures and deter abuse. See, in particular, **4.2, 4.4** ANTI-AVOIDANCE.

s 102, Sch 15 **Windrush Compensation Scheme and Troubles Permanent Disablement Payment Scheme.** An exemption from income tax is introduced for payments from these schemes, effective in each case from the date of launch of the scheme. See **30.49, 30.52** EXEMPT INCOME.

s 103 **HMRC automated processes.** Following judicial challenges to HMRC's ability to automate certain functions, this section puts beyond doubt that functions given to an officer may be carried out by HMRC using automated processes or other means. It is treated as always having been in force, but not so as to interfere with any court or tribunal decision made before 11 March 2020. See **35.6** HMRC — ADMINISTRATION.

s 104 **Partnership tax return by LLPs not carrying on business with view to profit.** This is an anti-avoidance measure enabling HMRC to deal as necessary with returns where a limited liability partnership (LLP) has delivered a return on the basis that it carried on business with a view to profit but did not, in fact, do so. The measure is treated as always having had effect, but does not apply to any return where, before 11 March 2020, a court or tribunal decided in the LLP's favour on the point. See **64.12** RETURNS.

s 105 **Late payment interest: national disasters and emergencies.** This gives the Treasury power to specify liabilities that will not accrue late payment interest if payment is deferred. An example of its use is in relation to the deferral of the second self-assessment payment on account for 2019/20 otherwise due on 31 July 2020 (see **67.5** SELF-ASSESSMENT). See **43.5** LATE PAYMENT INTEREST AND PENALTIES.

s 106, Sch 16 **Taxation of coronavirus support payments.** This confirms that coronavirus support payments made to businesses are within the scope of tax as income, and sets out the rules for applying this. It also imposes a charge to income tax on a recipient of certain coronavirus support payments who was not entitled to the payment in accordance with the scheme under which it was made, which includes the case where a payment under the Coronavirus Job Retention Scheme is not used for the purposes for which it was made. See **21.2–21.10** CORONAVIRUS (COVID-**19**).

s 107 **Enterprise management incentives: disqualifying events.** This is a COVID-19 (coronavirus) special measure. It seeks to ensure that a disqualifying event does not occur purely as a result of an individual taking leave, being furloughed or working reduced hours because of COVID-19. It has effect in relation to the period 19 March 2020 to 5 April 2021 inclusive. See **71.43** SHARE-RELATED EMPLOYMENT INCOME AND EXEMPTIONS.

s 108 **Pension provision: protected pension age.** This is a COVID-19 (coronavirus) special measure. It provides that retired individuals can be re-employed by their former employer (or a connected employer) without losing the benefit of a protected pension age. This is to encourage certain retired members of public service pension schemes, such as police, fire fighters and other uniformed service personnel, to rejoin the workforce to aid in the 2020 pandemic. Re-employment must commence during the period 1 March 2020 to 1 November 2020 inclusive. See **57.1** PENSION PROVISION.

s 109 **Statutory residence test.** This is a COVID-19 (coronavirus) special measure. It has effect for the purposes of determining whether an individual was UK resident for 2019/20 and, if an individual was not UK resident for 2019/20, whether that individual is UK resident for 2020/21. It provides relaxations to the rules where days were spent in the UK within the period 1 March 2020 to 1 June 2020 inclusive on certain activities related to the detection, treatment or prevention of COVID-19. See **63.4** RESIDENCE AND DOMICILE.

s 110 **Enterprise Investment Scheme (EIS) and Seed Enterprise Investment Scheme (SEIS): value received by investor.** This is to prevent EIS or SEIS relief being reduced or withdrawn in a case where, on or after 20 May 2020, an EIS or SEIS shareholder enters into a convertible loan agreement under the Future Fund with a company and subsequently receives value from the company under the agreement. See **29.12** ENTERPRISE INVESTMENT SCHEME and **66.8** SEED ENTERPRISE INVESTMENT SCHEME.

83 Table of Statutes

The list below is in chronological order.

84 Table of Statutory Instruments

Note. The double tax agreements listed at 26.2 DOUBLE TAX RELIEF are not listed again below.

The list below is in chronological order.

85 Table of Leading Cases

This Table lists those of the 2,000 or so cases referred to in this book which are considered to be of most general application and interest. For fuller details of these cases, and of all other tax cases relevant to current or recent legislation, see Tolley's Tax Cases.

A

B

C

D

E

F

G

I

J

K

L

M

N

O

P

Q

R

CA 2019, [2019] EWCA Civ 51.
R (oao Prudential plc and another) *v* Special Commr of Income Tax and another 39.4
SC 2013, 82 TC 64; [2013] UKSC 1; [2013] STC 376.
R (oao Rouse) *v* HMRC 16.3; 64.6
UT 2013, [2014] STC 230; [2013] UKUT 0615 (TCC).
R (oao Rowe) *v* HMRC 4.50
CA 2017, [2018] STC 462; [2017] EWCA Civ 2105.
R (oao De Silva) *v* HMRC 16.2, 16.3; 64.6
SC 2017, [2017] STC 2483.
R (on the application of Aozora GMAC Investment Ltd) *v* Revenue and Customs Comrs 37.2
[2019] EWCA Civ 1643, [2020] 1 All ER 803, [2019] STC 2486, 22 ITLR 191, [2019] SWTI 1683, [2019] All ER (D) 87 (Oct).
R (on the application of Astley) *v* Revenue and Customs Comrs 16.2, 16.3; 64.6
[2019] EWCA Civ 1719, [2020] 3 All ER 116, [2020] 1 WLR 731, [2019] STC 2262, 169 NLJ 7863, [2019] SWTI 1723, [2019] All ER (D) 154 (Oct).
R (on the application of Locke) *v* Revenue and Customs Comrs 4.44
[2019] EWCA Civ 1909, [2020] 1 All ER 459, [2019] STC 2543, 169 NLJ 7865, [2019] SWTI 1805, [2019] All ER (D) 82 (Nov).
Raftopoulou, HMRC *v* 16.4; 55.38; 64.6
CA 2018, [2018] STC 988; [2018] All ER (D) 15 (May).
Ramsay, CIR *v* 23.7
CA 1935, 20 TC 79.
Ramsay (W T) Ltd *v* CIR 4.1
HL 1981, 54 TC 101; [1981] STC 174; [1981] 2 WLR 449; [1981] 1 All ER 865.
Ransom *v* Higgs (and associated appeals) 75.27
HL 1974, 50 TC 1; [1974] STC 539; [1974] 1 WLR 1594; [1974] 3 All ER 949.
Re an Application by HMRC to give an information notice under Para 3 of Sch 36 to the Finance Act 2008 ..... 39.4
FTT (TC 6710), [2019] SFTD 117, [2018] UKFTT 541 (TC)).
Reed *v* Clark 63.32
Ch D 1985, 58 TC 528; [1985] STC 323; [1985] 3 WLR 142; [1986] Ch 1.
Reed *v* Seymour 28.68; 28.79
HL 1927, 11 TC 625; [1927] AC 554.
Reed *v* Young 52.24
HL 1986, 59 TC 196; [1986] STC 285; [1986] 1 WLR 649.
Reed Employment plc *v* HMRC 28.17
CA 2015, [2015] STC 2516; [2015] All ER (D) 322 (Jul).
Regent Oil Co Ltd, Strick *v* 75.43; 75.123
HL 1965, 43 TC 1; [1966] AC 295; [1965] 3 All ER 174.
Reid *v* Revenue and Customs Comrs 64.12
[2020] UKUT 61 (TCC), [2020] STC 622.
Reid's Brewery Co Ltd *v* Male 75.48; 75.49
QB 1891, 3 TC 279; [1891] 2 QB 1.
Reid's Trustees *v* CIR 22.3; 70.8
CS 1929, 14 TC 512.
Rendell *v* Went 28.50; 28.70
HL 1964, 41 TC 641; [1964] 1 WLR 650; [1964] 2 All ER 464.
Reynolds (John) (Insurances) Ltd, Simpson *v* ..... 75.56(f)
CA 1975, 49 TC 693; [1975] STC 271; [1975] 1 WLR 617; [1975] 2 All ER 88.
RFC 2012 plc (in liquidation) (formerly The Rangers Football Club plc) *v* Advocate General for Scotland 26.1
SC 2017, [2017] STC 1556; [2017] UKSC 45; [2017] All ER (D) 19 (Jul).
Richards, Gurney *v* 10.15; 28.23
Ch D 1989, 62 TC 287; [1989] STC 682.
Richards and another *v* HMRC 29.35
UT 2011, [2012] STC 174.
Richardson & Bottoms Ltd, Slater *v* 5.19
Ch D 1979, 53 TC 155; [1979] STC 630; [1980] 1 WLR 563; [1979] 3 All ER 439.
Ricketts *v* Colquhoun 28.84
HL 1925, 10 TC 118; [1926] AC 1.

T

U

V

W

Y

B

C

E

G

H

J

K

L

M

N

O

S

T

W

Y

Z